ENGLISH-CHINESE DICTIONARY OF LAW

英汉法律词典

【第五版】

FIFTH EDITION

夏登峻 主编

北京大学出版社
PEKING UNIVERSITY PRESS

图书在版编目(CIP)数据

英汉法律词典：第五版/夏登峻主编. —北京：北京大学出版社，2021.12
ISBN 978-7-301-32435-6

Ⅰ. ①英… Ⅱ. ①夏… Ⅲ. ①法律—词典—英、汉 Ⅳ. ①D9-61

中国版本图书馆 CIP 数据核字(2021)第 176794 号

书　　　名	英汉法律词典（第五版） YINGHAN FALÜ CIDIAN（DI-WU BAN）
著作责任者	夏登峻　主编
责 任 编 辑	焦春玲　方尔埼
标 准 书 号	ISBN 978-7-301-32435-6
出 版 发 行	北京大学出版社
地　　　址	北京市海淀区成府路 205 号　100871
网　　　址	http://www.pup.cn　http://www.yandayuanzhao.com
电 子 信 箱	yandayuanzhao@163.com
新 浪 微 博	@北京大学出版社　@北大出版社燕大元照法律图书
电　　　话	邮购部 010-62752015　发行部 010-62750672 编辑部 010-62117788
印 　刷 　者	南京爱德印刷有限公司
经 销 者	新华书店
	880 毫米×1230 毫米　A5　48.875 印张　2730 千字 2021 年 12 月第 1 版　2021 年 12 月第 1 次印刷
定　　　价	288.00 元

未经许可，不得以任何方式复制或抄袭本书之部分或全部内容。
版权所有，侵权必究
举报电话：010-62752024　电子信箱：fd@pup.pku.edu.cn
图书如有印装质量问题，请与出版部联系，电话：010-62756370

第五版修订序

今年是 2021 年,《英汉法律词典》1985 年 11 月首版问世至今已有三十年以上了。三十余年间,共修订过四次:

第一次修订(第二版)1998 年;

第二次修订(第三版)2008 年;

第三次修订(第四版)2012 年;

第四次修订(第五版)2021 年。

一、第五版修订的旨意

修订的旨意不外乎两条:一条是我们自己的;另一条是"外为中用"的。

二、第五版修订的准则

1. 不断改进,日臻完善,与时俱进,保持其实用性、专业性、科学性和时代性。让读者喜欢它,信赖它,使用它,在实践中得益于它。

2. "整理法律词条达到最可能完善的内容,并给予它们确切的定义。此外,还继续伴随第七版起始的努力:追求在选择主标题和运用词义表达定义上要坚持词典学的原则,通过严格研究和精心再评估达到易读和提高学术水平之目的。"(Bryan A. Garner, ed., Black's Law Dictionary, 8th ed., 2004, p. ix.)

如果以后继续修订也必须按此两项准则进行。本版(第五版)因某些原因在时间上拉得较长,所以将原准备的第六版内容也并入第五版,以弥补时间的蹉跎。这样,第五版的修订就成为以前各版修订中内容最丰富、最新鲜的一版。

三、第五版修订的几点说明

1. 词条后的年代,即《布莱克法律词典》(第九版)的"词典指南"(Guide of Dictionary)中的 4"Date"(时期或年代)解说:"在许多释义之前用括号括入的时期表明该英语字或词条短语(word or phrase)所知道在最早使用的时间。有些字仅为世纪(如 14C)但大多数新近出现的词汇(vocabulary)都提供有确切的年代……"[参见夏登峻:《法律英语英汉翻译技巧》(第二版),法律出版社 2014 年版,第 54 页。]

2. 为使词条"达到最可能完善的内容,并给予它们确切的定义"而参考《布莱克法律词典》第九版、第八版,以及《韦氏新世界法律词典》《元照英美法词典》等更换或完善词条四百五十个以上。如 accusation、descent、domestic、integration、mortmain、*pactum*、reversal、reverse consensus、statute、stipulation、surrender……

3. "税收"是美国政府重要的财源,税目繁杂,减免情况多样。美国人的纳税意识强并非其先天自觉性,而实属政府政策和法律制度长期使然。税法为美国法的重要组成部分,故增加了"美国税务"方面的词条四十多个,以强化本词典的薄弱部分。

4. 为了 up-to-date,增加新词八十余个。如 online sale、remote online sale、digital cultural goods、Carbon Sink、forest carbon sink、overvote、e-mail listserves 等。

5. 在实践中增加词条 ——个人翻译美国法律作品和为研究生校改译文时感到一些词条有必要收入词典。如 no-action letters、front page、profile、ethics opinion 等。

6. 增加拉丁语法律格言约六十五个,另还增加民法、刑法、诉讼法、法理、金融、信息、网络、知识产权、专利、家庭法等词条三百余个;缩略语,包括援引的缩略增加了约二百一十个。通过增加、更换、充实、修订,第五版的内容基本达到修订目的和旨意,使本词典朝着完善、全面、实用、与时俱进、符合时代和客观要求迈上一大步,总增字数约四十万字。

7. 全部增加、修订的内容,包括改换的词条,均来自两个方面:(1)《布莱克法律词典》第八版、第九版、第十版和《布维尔法律词典》(2015)、《韦氏法律词典》《牛律现代法律用语词典》,并经过翻译、整合、审定。(2)国内外的核心法律期刊和《元照英美法词典》《新英汉词典》等。

在修订过程中,西南政法大学文兰兰、梅凌云、孙一丹、邹云、汤伟佳、曾秀丽、刘春梅、刘舒、刘铃悦等同学为修订稿的电脑输入、打印、校改做了大量工作,特别是邹云、曾秀丽同学以及西南政法大学外语学院研究生张恒、文银、曹蕊、黎雨萱、李静、胡春艳、冉明祥、姜婕、郭海霞同学在牛奔林老师的指导下,最后统一排序,统一再次校订,工作十分认真细致。对于他们的辛勤表示最衷心的感谢。对于李雨峰、邓宏光、王衡、郑达轩、吕垚瑶等老师给予的关注和大力支持表示谢意并致以崇高敬意。

　　水平有限,学习不断。欢迎读者对本词典提出批评、指正和建议。谢谢。

夏登峻　重庆歌乐山下西南政法大学
2021 年 6 月

第四版修订序

《英汉法律词典》于 1985 年 11 月出版第一版,1998 年 12 月第一次修订(即第二版),2008 年 1 月第二次修订(即第三版)。在此期间,承蒙广大读者的厚爱,不少同行、同志、朋友们给予了大量关怀和支持,并提出一些意见和宝贵建议,特此深表感谢。现在为第三次修订(即第四版),将于 2012 年问世。二十七年中修订了三次,其目的只有一个:不断改进,日臻完善,与时俱进,保持其实用性、专业性、科学性、时代性;希望读者喜欢它、信赖它、使用它,在实践中解决实际问题,有所收益。

1998 年第二版修订序中曾说:"一部完美的词典,经过一次修订绝不可能成功,需要经几次甚至几代人的努力才行。"目前全球最权威的英美法律词典公认为《布莱克法律词典》(Black's Law Dictionary),其第一版于 1891 年问世,至今已一百二十年,按西方的"代"(generation)计算,已有四代了,共修订九次。它的第八版(2004 年)和第九版(2009 年)只相隔五年,第七版(1999 年)与第八版也相隔五年。而第五版(1979 年)与第七版相隔二十年。不管相隔多久,如何修订,每次修订都追随 1891 年亨利·坎贝尔·布莱克(Henry Campbell Black)一开始编此巨著的旨意:"整理法律词条达到最可能完善的内容,并给予它们确切的定义。此外,还继续伴随第七版起始的努力,追求在选择主标题和运用词语表达定义上要坚持词典学的原则。通过严格研究和精心再评估达到易读和提高学术水平目的。"("to marshall legal terms to the fullest possible extent and to define them accurately. But more than that, it continues the effort begun with the seventh edition: to follow established lexicographic principles in selecting headwords and in phrasing definitions, to provide easy-to-follow pronunciations, and to raise the level of scholarship through serious research and careful reassessment.")(Bryan A. Garner, ed., Black's Law Dictionary, 8th ed., 2004, p. ix.)。同样,我们也是沿着这样一个旨意进行修订,在这次修订中,结合本词典的读者和实际情况,增加了民法、刑法、诉讼法、商法、宪政、国际法和法理、知识产权等方面内容约七百五十个词条,另还增加智力障碍方面词条一百三十多个,因原词条解释不够确切,内容不充分而进行更换或补充的有二百五十余个,同时增加拉丁语法律格言近二百个,拉丁语及外来法律用语一百一十个,这样,充实并大大改进了本词典内容,使其更趋于全面、适用、与时俱进,并在一定程度上提高了学术水平。

在第四版的修订中,西南政法大学民商法硕士研究生李媛、徐志超和刑侦硕士生王宏以及刑法硕士研究生陈书敏,对修改稿的电脑输录、打印、校改等工作付出了汗水,在此表示深深感谢。特别是陈书敏同学,她全程输录、排序、打印、校改,做了大量工作,还提供一些适用的词条,对她的认真、细致和努力再次表示诚挚谢意。

编者

2011年10月于歌乐山下西南政法大学

第三版修订序

中国有句古话:"工欲善其事,必先利其器。"意思是工匠要做好活,必先把工具搞好。这是千真万确的常理。

《英汉法律词典》自1985年问世以来已是二十二个春秋。1998年第一次修订至今也有九个年头,该修订版第一次印刷6000册,现已是第四次印刷,增印三次9000册,仍然不能满足客观形势之需要。其因专业性、科学性、实用性、时代性以及便携性而深受读者欢迎。

当然,一部工具书要达到至善至美,还须不断修订,正如1998年第二版修订序中所说:"一部完美的词典,经过一次修订绝不可能成功,需要经几次甚至几代人的努力才行。我们愿在有生之年,在这方面略尽绵力。"正是本着这一意愿和充实、提高并保持其特点的指导思想,进行了第二次修订(即第三版),希望它逐步达到日臻完善、与时俱进的目的。

尽量突出实用性和现代性是这次修订的核心。从1998年修订后起,即从翻译实践中累积增加近万词条,其中多侧重于本词典欠缺的法理、美国民事诉讼法、知识产权法、国际经济法、国际贸易和法经济学等方面;同时也增加百余条拉丁语术语以及英美法常用的和判例汇编的缩略语。

在这次修订过程中,承蒙法律出版社和西南政法大学美国法与政治研究中心的大力支持,郭诚、张莹、陈佳佳三位硕士研究生为电脑输录及反复修正所做的大量工作,陈龙环、郑达轩、邓宏光、郭东四位博士研究生的支持及提供的部分词条。在这里一并表示衷心的感谢。

由于本人水平和实践经验有限,本词典中难免有缺点和错误,请读者提出宝贵意见(E-mail:Xiadengjun26@yahoo.com.cn),以便今后再次修改、订正。

夏登峻
2007年8月

第二版修订序

自本词典问世以来,已经历了十三个春秋。在这期间,承蒙广大读者厚爱以及不少同行的关怀和支持,有的还提出了许多宝贵的意见。我们谨借此机会,在这里表示衷心的感谢。

随着我国改革开放的逐步深入,国民经济的持续发展,法制建设日臻完善,对外交往日益广泛和扩大,与此同时,在当前国际形势和科技文化发展日新月异的新情况下,本词典已愈来愈显得不能适应客观形势发展的需要。现趁法律出版社再版之际,我们做了一次全面的修订和增补,以飨读者。

本着充实、提高,融专业性、科学性、实用性、现代性于一体的指导方针,我们这次修订在收录上力求正确,编排上力求合理,并突出它的实用价值。经这次修改、节删、增补后,正文增加一万五千余词条;另外在附录中增加缩略语一千多条,并删去了原有的汉英对照部分。无疑,通过修订将使本词典有较大的充实和提高。但仍会有错漏和不足之处,敬请读者和同行们不吝批评和指正。一部完美的词典,经过一次修订绝不可能成功,需要经几次甚至几代人的努力才行。我们愿在有生之年,在这方面略尽绵力。

这次修订过程中,西南政法大学卢东凌、重庆工业管理学院李迎兰同志为电脑输录、编排、校对做了大量工作,其中李迎兰同志还提供了部分词条,特此衷心致以谢意。

夏登峻　何联昇

1998 年 12 月

出版前言

本词典是我国第一部收入英美法系和大陆法系以及我国法律的法律用语最多的中型专业词典,包括法理、法史、宪法、行政法、民法、民事诉讼法、刑法、刑事诉讼法、经济法、国际公法、国际私法、国际经济法等各个法律学科的英语词条以及英美法律书刊中常用的拉丁语、法语词条,有四万余条;另有常见缩略语近三千条,以及西方主要国家的法院组织系统表,作为附录。它是在党的实行对外开放、对内搞活经济和加强法制建设的方针指引下,为了满足广大法律工作者、经济工作者和外事工作者以及有关的大专院校师生在阅读和翻译英语法律书刊方面的迫切需要而编写、出版的。

由于各国的法律及制度是在本国特定的经济基础和其他条件下产生和发展的,因而一部分法律用语有各自特定的解释,加之长期以来我国翻译界在翻译英美法和大陆法时缺乏规范的标准,往往一个用语存在多种译法,这就难免使读者在理解西方国家的法律时产生词义上甚至理论上的混淆。为了逐步实现译法规范化,本词典除尽可能做出必要的简释外,在译法上还采取兼收并蓄的原则,收入了我国常见的多种译法(包括台湾、香港地区出版物中的译法),有些提出了我们倾向的译法。譬如 chairman 和 president 两个词,一般前者译"主席",后者译"总统",但 chairman 一词原意是指集体机构如会议或委员会的首席职位,而 president 则是指独任职位,因此,除保留这两个词的一般译法外,在涉及我国的法律制度时,chairman 译为"(中)委员长",president 译为"(中)(国家)主席"。又譬如,adhesion contract,国内现有译法达五六种之多,我们根据兼顾原词词义和法律释义的原则,倾向于译为"附意合同"(即一方当事人在订约权利上受到一定限制,需要附和另一方当事人意思表示的合同),而在"附意合同"后加括号说明旧译"定式合同""附合合同"等。法律用语要实现译法规范化,这不是一件容易的事,更不是由译者或出版社说了算的事,我们希望经过广大读者和译者阅读和翻译的实践,逐步地达到"约定俗成"。此外,我们对许多词条虽然采取一词多译,但仍难以完全准确译出,读者使用本词典时仍须注意各个国家、各个时期对同一法律用语的不同解释,做出选择或调整译法。

本词典系在西南政法学院、中山大学法律系、广州外语学院、上海财经学院等单位的大力支持下,经本社组织集体编写的。参加编写的有张仲绛、夏登峻、朱建成、何联昇、杨世宏、夏斗寅、温光均等同志。李昌道、肖明松两位同志提供了部分词条;曾享瑞、宋海军两位同志参加了汉英词条对照的选编。负责审核定稿的有夏登峻、何联昇、张仲绛同志。我社负责本词典的责任编辑安日华同志也提供了部分词条、法律习语和谚语,并参加了全书审核定稿工作。在此谨向给予大力支持的上述单位表示谢意。

由于缺乏编写词典的经验,加之对西方法律研究不够,编写时间又比较仓促,词典中肯定存在不少缺点和错误,谨以试用本先行出版以应读者需要,我们恳切希望广大读者提出宝贵意见,以便进一步修改、订正和补充。

1985 年 11 月

目 录
Contents

体例和使用说明 ………………………………………………… （1）
Style and Instruction of Use

词典正文 ………………………………………………………… （1）
Main Body of the Dictionary

附录一：常用缩略语 …………………………………………… （1399）
Appendix I: Abbreviations Used in Common

附录二：西方主要国家的法院组织系统 ……………………… （1509）
Appendix II: Judicial System of Western Major Countries

附录三：美国全国判例汇编系统 ……………………………… （1533）
Appendix III: U. S. National Reporter System

附录四：英国国王即位纪元表 ………………………………… （1537）
Appendix IV: Table of British Regnal Years

附录五：美国联邦（司法）巡回区图 …………………………… （1539）
Appendix V: United States Federal Circuits Map

附录六 …………………………………………………………… （1540）
Appendix VI

附录七：参考书目 ……………………………………………… （1542）
Appendix VII: References

目 录

体例和使用说明
Style and Instruction of Use

1. 词目:全部词目均按字母顺序编排;其中词组首先按第一个单词的字母顺序,以此类推。括号内的词(或字母)不参加排列顺序。单词后带有省略号(')或两词之间有连接符(-)的,则可先比词根或单词,然后是单词后的所有格省略号('),再接着是词根或单词间用连接符(-)组成的组合词,例如:

court

court closed

court sentence

court's place

court's stance

court-martial

court-packing plan

courtesy

courtesy of England

外来语,主要是拉丁语和一部分法语,亦按上述顺序排入,改用斜体字以示区别。凡成句的法律习语和谚语,均在词条前加* 号表示。

2. 译法:凡一词多译的均依英、美法律词典的释义参照我国用法,采取多种译法,其中仅适用于某一国家或地区的译法,在译名前用括号注明,如(中)、(英)、(美)、(苏格兰)……分别代表中国、英国、美国、苏格兰等的用法。同一词条在国内有多种译法的,为了逐步实现译名统一,除列出拟采取的译名外,并接着在括号内列出"又译""港译""旧译"等译名,以供参考;其中"港译"系指我国香港特别行政区依当地方言的译法,"旧译"多指旧时和我国台湾地区现时的译法。

3. 释义:有两种。一种是译名前、译名中或译名后所加的简要词语,借以帮助了解该译名的词义和用法的；另一种是在译名后所加的注释，两种释义，均加括号，以免与译名混同。

4. **词义和词类**：凡英语独立的单词和作中心词或词组开头词用的单词，均在词条后分别注明 n.（名词）、v.（动词）、a.（形容词）、ad.（副词）或 prep.（介词），并分别列出不同词类所取的词义。每一词条多种译法，如词义相近的，均用逗号隔开；词义不大相近的，均用分号隔开；词义相差较远的，用 1. 2. 3. ……隔开。同一词条在词义上单数、复数用法相同的，在词条后加（s）；单数、复数用法不同的，只在复数用法前加（复）。同一词条在词义上大写、小写用法不同的，只在大写用法前加（大写）。

5. **常用缩略语**：由于大、小写和缩略符号以及缩略繁简因作者使用习惯往往不同，本词典不便一一加以区别。如 A.A.A.亦可看做 AAA，C. Cr. Pr. 亦可看做 CCRPR，查阅时主要应看全称是否符合要查找的内容。此外，缩略语前后有数字的，如 1917A. C.，W2d 等，数字均不参与字母排序。

A

A and B, lists 甲表和乙表(指在不列颠公司法上,公司解散时对负连带偿还责任者所作出的目录。甲表包括解散时持有股份的人;乙表包括原先是但现在不是公司成员的人)

a bit of 一点儿⟨give sb. a bit of one's mind⟩(对某人直言不讳),⟨know a bit of Spanish⟩(懂点西班牙语)

à bon droit 以正当理由;合法地,公正地

*** A change in forum only means a change in courtroom, not a change of law.** 法院的变化仅仅意味着法庭的变化,而不是法律的变化。

*** A case which is ommitted is proposely ommitted.** "省略规定之事项,应认为有意省略"(法律谚语)

a cause de cy For this reason 因此原因,因此理由

a code state 一个采用法典诉辩的州

a coelo usque ad centrum 土地所有者的权利范围(原意为从土地之上,上至天,下至地球中心,此原则已废),财产所有人的权利范围

a contrario sensu 从另一方面来说;相反,反之

a court *a quo* 转移案件的法庭

a court *ad quem* 受理案件的法庭

à dessein 故意

*** A digniori fieri debet denominatio et resotio.** The title and exposition of a thing ought to be derived from, or given, or made with reference to, the more worthy degree, quality, or species of it. 一物的名称和说明应当参照与该物更相当的等级、质量或品种加以确定。

*** A dwarf is as much a man as a giant; a small republic is no less a sovereign state than the most powerful kingdom.** 侏儒与巨人都是人,小国和强国均为主权国家[埃麦里克·德·瓦特尔的一句名言。(Emeric de Vattel, 1714—1766)]

a fortiori 更不用说;更不容置疑地,更有充分理由;更加,何况

a gratia 恩赐;赦免;仁慈

a great deal of overlap 大量重叠(常指普通法院与衡平法院的事件)

a latere 附属的,旁系的;旁系亲属

a least fault 错误较少的一方(见 comparative rectitude)

a limited amount of discretion 有限范围的酌处权,有限程度的酌处权

*** A l'impossible nul n'est tenu.** No one is bound to do what is impossible. 没有人有义务做不可能的事情。

*** A little breath would be enough to kindle a flame.** 星星之火,可以燎原(一丝气息会燃起火焰)。

a mensa et thoro (夫妻)分居(原意为不共寝食。见 divorce *a mensa et thoro*)

a mere scientilla 仅一点,微弱的

a mini hearing 小型听证

a natural growing or common nucleus of operative facts 产生法律效果的事实的自然群体或共同内核

A New Deal for Victims & Witnesses (英)《证人和受害人的新规定》

*** A person who is aboveboard does nothing underhand.** 明人不做暗事(光明磊落的人绝不搞阴谋诡计)。

a posteriori 推溯的;后天的;归纳的;自果至因的,由果溯因的;逆推的;经验的;归纳推理的,由事实推论出原理的

a priori 公理的;自明的;推理的;先天的;演绎的;自因至果的;先验的;演绎推理的

a priori limitation 预定限制

a priori theories of law and justice 法律与

正义先验论
* **A privilege avails not against public good or against the interests of the public. A privilege avails not against the state.** 特权不得用来反对国家;损害国家之利益特权无效。(根据这一原则,妻子在丈夫胁迫下犯叛国罪仍因该罪行受惩罚。)
a retro(或 *aretro*) 迟延;拖欠;过期;向后
a rule of thumb 一条经验
A shares(或 **stock**) A 类股票(甲级股票)
a statement cause 诉因陈述
a tooth for a tooth 以牙还牙(报复)
a trial within a trial 审理中的审理
a small think tank 小型智囊机构
* ***A verbis legis non est recendendum*** From the words of the law there must be no departure./A court is not at liberty to disregard the letter of a statute, in favor of a supposed intention./You must not vary the words of a statute./The words of a statute must not be departed from. 法律的文字不容背离(指法院不得支持假定的意图而任意置法律文字于不顾)
a vinculo matrimonii 完全解除婚姻的约束,离婚(见 divorce *a vinculo matrimonii*)
a verdict for plaintiffs 有利于原告判决
a white elephant (喻)沉重的负担
a year and a day 满一年,一整年(见 year-and-a-day rule)
A-G for Northern Ireland v. Gallagher 北爱尔兰总检察长诉加拉赫(指"荷兰式勇气"规则形成的案例,即该案中被告人决定杀死其妻,于是买酒,并饮酒陷入醉态后杀死他的妻子,他被控犯有谋杀罪,而他则提出了醉态辩护以及精神病辩护。法院判定谋杀罪的控告成立。丹宁法官对该案形成的规则曾作出精辟解释:"如果一个人在精神正常和头脑清醒的时候形成一种杀人的意图,并为此作了准备。由于他知道自己要做的事情是错误的,因此他自己先喝醉以便给予自己做这一事情的荷兰式勇气;当他醉醺醺地实施自己的意图时,他就不能以自我引起的醉酒来为谋杀罪的指控作辩护,也不能以此将谋

杀罪减轻为非预谋杀人罪。他也不能说,他使自己陷入这样愚蠢境地以致不能形成杀人的故意。")
AAA 最高债券
ab 自,从
* ***Ab abusu ad usum non valet consequentia.*** From the abuse of a thing can draw no conclusion as to its legitimate use. 对某物的滥用不能被推导为对此物的合法利用
ab agendo 无行为能力的;无处理事务能力的
ab ante 以前
ab antiquo 自过去,往昔;昔日的,旧时的
* ***Ab assuetis non fit injuria.*** From things to which we are accustomed no wrong can arise. 过错不可能来自我们习惯了的事情
ab extra 从外部,外来
ab inconveniente 出于不便
ab initio 自始,发端;从头开始
ab intestato (大陆法)来自无遗嘱的继承;在无遗嘱死亡情况下
ab intra 从内部
ab irato 盛怒之下,一时气愤
ab origine 从起源,从最初起,一开始
ab origines law 土著法
ab ovo 从开始起,自始
ABA Model Code of Judicial Conduct(**2011 Edition**) (美国律师协会)《司法行为示范守则》(2011 年版)[该守则中明确规定"在所有活动中,法官都必须避免不适当的言行和不适当的表现",还明确规定,法官必须维护并弘扬独立、正直和司法的公正无私(impartiality of judiciary)。该守则和 2000 年 9 月美国联邦最高法院司法会议修订的《合众国法官行为准则》(其中也有与该守则类似的规定,如法官应避免公开评论"悬案 'pending' 和紧迫案或即将审理 'impending' "的案件,直至上诉程序完成)在司法政策中作为指南]
abacinare 酷刑(指遮蒙眼睛将烧红的铁块烫伤面部的一种肉刑)
abacter(=abactor) n. 一次盗窃一群家畜者
abaction n. 盗窃家畜
abalienate v. 让渡(产权、财产等);转移,出让,转让

abalienatio （罗马法）让渡（指财产从一个罗马公民转移给另一个罗马公民）
abalienatio mentis 精神错乱
abalienation n. （大陆法）让渡,转让
abandon v. 委付;弃船;抛弃;放弃,遗弃,废弃;弃权;叛离
abandon a patent 放弃专利权
abandon jurisdiction 自动弃权,放弃管辖权
abandoned a. 被遗弃的,被抛弃的,被废弃的,被取消的;荒废的;无主的;无约束的,自我放任的
abandoned infant 弃婴,被遗弃的婴儿
abandoned land 熟荒地,撂荒地
abandoned motion 已取消的申请,被取消的动议
abandoned property 被抛弃的财产;无主财产
abandoned ship（或 **vessel**） 被委付船只;被弃船只
abandoned wife 被遗弃的妻子
abandoned woman 被遗弃的妇女;妓女;坏女人
abandonee n. 1.被遗弃者 2.(受领或主张有权受领被遗弃财物的)弃物受领人(指打捞到的货物的接受人) 3.(海上保险中的)受委付人(指由投保人委以海损财物全部权利的承保人)
abandonment n. 1.委付(指海运中遇有风险,投保货主放弃原货而要求取得保险赔偿的行为) 2.放弃,遗弃 3.撤销 4.放任,放纵
abandonment of action 放弃诉讼
abandonment of appeal 放弃上诉;撤销上诉
abandonment of children 遗弃子女
abandonment of claim 放弃索赔,放弃请求权
abandonment of contract 撤销合同(契约);不承认(或否认)合同(契约)
abandonment of domicile 放弃户籍;废弃住所
abandonment of husband 遗弃丈夫;弃夫
abandonment of right 放弃权利;弃权
abandonment of ship 委付船只;弃船
abandonment of the voyage 放弃航次
abandonment of wife 遗弃妻子;弃妻
abandonor n. 遗弃者,放弃者
abandum（= abandonum） 没收物,扣押物,遗弃物(有排除法律保障之意)
abatable nuisance 可减轻的妨害行为(指此种妨害行为易于停止或变成无损害之行为)
abate v. 中止,停止;减免,减轻;降(价);成为无效;废除,撤销,排除(骚扰、妨碍等)
abate a cause of action 中止诉讼原因
abate a debt 减免债务
abatement n. 放弃;减(税),免(税);取消(部分或全部)索赔;扣减权,减轻(指债权人准许债务人少还债款;海关准许损坏的货物减少税额等);折扣,降(价);撤销(法令等);中断(或终止)诉讼(程序)
abatement and exemption from penalty 减免刑罚
abatement clause 撤销条款(指使土地保有人在遇到不可抗力或其他特殊原因失去占有时从承租义务中解脱的条款)
abatement from（或 **of**）**penalty** 减刑
abatement of action 撤销诉讼;诉讼中断(指从前英国法院因缺少必要的诉讼当事人,或因法院传讯令有缺点,致使诉讼程序搁置中止,现已废)
abatement of debts 废(免)除债务;减轻债务(指债务人资不抵债时,按比例减少其对各项债务的偿付)
abatement of fire hazard 消除火患;减轻火灾危害
abatement of freehold (英史)(侵占继承的)土地完全保有权的排除
abatement of illegal activity 停止非法活动,停止侵害
abatement of legacies (英)减少遗赠(指遗赠产中的资金依遗嘱不足以支付所有各项遗赠时,应按规定的次序和比例减少遗赠的支付)
abatement of nuisance 减轻损害;排除妨害(或滋扰)
abatement of purchase money 压低买价

abatement of tax(es) 减税
abatement order 废除令,撤销令
abatementum 强夺财产
abater (=abator) n. 撤销者;(英)(不动产法上)强占(继承的完全土地保有权人的)地产者;(侵权法上)排除滋扰者;非法妨害人;起诉不当答辩人
abating rents 减少租额
abattis of procedural obstacles 程序上的种种障碍
Abbreviatio Placitorum (英)《普拉西特判例辑略》(指根据查理一世到爱德华二世期间国王法庭、御前会议、议会和普通法法院的诉讼案卷选编成的汇编,后来加上伊丽莎白一世和詹姆斯一世时期的,因这是对国王法庭工作和对普通法的最早描述,很有参考价值)
abbreviation n. 缩写,缩略
abbreviature(或 **abbreviation**)**of adjudication** 判决令的摘要(或要点)
abbro(a)chment n. 垄断投机(指批发式地购进货物,垄断供应并以高价卖出),对市场的垄断
ABC analysis approach 分类重点管理法,重点管理法
ABC test (1962年)ABC测定规则[指一项法规规定,如果:A.雇员未受雇主的控制("A"= alone,意为独立工作而不受雇主控制),B.在雇主经营的地方之外进行工作("B"= business,意为独立创业保持自己的地位),C.从事某一独立完整的业务("C"= control,意为由自己控制规划和运作方法),则该雇员无权主张失业保险金。因这种排除失业保险金的方法是用ABC表示的,故而得名]
abdicate v. 放弃(职位、权力等);废嫡;(国王)让(退)位
abdication n. 自动放弃(职位、权力等);废嫡;(国王)自动让(退)位
abdicator n. 放弃者;弃权者;退(让)位者
abduct v. 诱拐;胁持,劫持(见 hijack)
abducting of individuals 拐卖人口
abduction n. 诱拐(罪);胁持,劫持(罪)(见 hijack);绑架(尤指对妇女或小孩)
abduction of woman 勾引妇女,诱拐妇女(罪)
abductor n. 诱拐者(旧译拐子),绑架者,胁持者,劫持者
abearance n. 所作所为,行为
aberrant behavio(u)r 不正常的行为;反常行为
aberrant personality 变态心理
aberration n. 脱离常规;过失;反常行为;心理失常;畸变
abesse v. (大陆法)失踪;不出庭;缺席,不在
abet v. 教唆,唆使;煽动;怂恿;支持,帮助(见 aid and abet)
abet (sb.) in a crime 教唆(某人)犯罪
abetment n. 教唆,唆使;教唆犯罪
abetter (=abettor) n. 教唆者;唆使者;煽动者;(英)帮助犯(指在他人犯罪时在法律上明知和自愿予以协助的人,为共犯的一种)
abeyance n. 1.中止,停止;暂搁,缓议,缓办 2.(英)(所有权等的)权利未定
abeyance of seizin 中止地产占有
abeyant a. 中止的;未定的;有人未定的
abeyant verdict 异常裁判,非公裁决
abhorrent a. 可恶的;令人憎恶的;相反的
abidance n. 遵守;履行;持续;居住
abidance by law 遵守法律,守法
abidance by the rules 遵守规则,照章办事
abide v. (12世纪前)1.容忍,忍受;抵挡,反抗,顶得住(withstand)〈the widow found it difficult to abide the pain of losing her husband〉(该寡妇感到很难忍受失去丈夫的痛苦)2.服从,遵从,遵守(with by);行为,与……相一致〈try to abide the doctor's order to quit smoking〉(遵照医生之令远离吸烟),〈abide by the rules〉(遵守规则)3.期待,等候〈the death-row prisoners abide execution〉(死囚区罪犯等待死刑执行)4.履行或执行(命令或判决)〈the trial court abided the appellate court's orders〉(审理法庭执行上诉法庭的命令)5.停留,住;住,留住,居住〈the right to abide in any of 50 states〉(在50个州中的任何一州均有居住权)
abide by agreement(或 **contract**) 遵守合

同,遵守合约
abiding a. 持久的,永久的
abiding place 住所,寓所;居住地
ability n. 能力,才能,才智,(复)技能
ability of persons to enjoy rights and to exercise them 人享有权利和行使权利的能力
ability to cooperate 合作能力
ability to defend oneself against sexual abuse 性自卫能力(指被害人对两性行为的社会意义、性质及其后果的理解能力)
ability to inherit 继承能力
ability to pay 支付能力
ability to repay in foreign exchange 外汇偿付能力
ability to securities cash flows 证券现金(流量)的能力
ability to stand trial 接受审判的能力(见 competency)
Abingdon law 阿宾顿法则(用于即决审判的一个术语)
abiogenous a. 自然发生的
abject a. 卑鄙的,卑下的;可怜的;难堪的
abject (或 **absolute**) **poverty** 赤贫
abjudicate v. 判为不法
abjuration n. 宣誓断绝(或撤回);公开放弃
abjuration of the realm (古英国法)(重罪犯人的)弃国宣誓,出逃(或逃亡)宣誓
abjure v. 宣誓断绝(或撤回),弃绝;公开放弃(意见等)
able a. 能;有才能的;有(法定)资格的;有权的
able-bodied a. (经检查)身心健康的
able-bodied citizen 有劳动能力的公民,(能服役的)强壮的公民
able-bodied seaman 合格水手;(英)二等水兵;一等水手
able lawyers 有法定资格的律师们,有才干的律师们
abnegation n. 否认,拒绝,放弃(权利等)
abnormal a. 反常的,变态的;不规则的
abnormal baseline 不正常基线
abnormally dangerous activities 高度危险活动(责任)(指《欧洲侵权法原则》第五章"危险责任"中规定的"高度危险活动责任"),异常危险之活动[指即使在尽了合理的小心义务或注意义务(reasonable care)的情况下,仍必然与重大危险的严重伤害相联系的一项赔偿承诺或保证(an undertaking),因为当事人进行这项活动本身必面临着产生伤害的严格责任(strict liability),特别是一项如爆炸性(dynamiting)活动,对此行为人负严格法律责任(strictly liable)。因为这项活动①涉及对人或对财产产生严重伤害之危险;②这个活动不可能无危险地去履行而不顾及已提出的预警;③社区之内一般不会出现这种情况。根据《侵权法重述》(Restatement of Torts),决定一项活动是否是异常危险的,包括分析是否有一个高等级的伤害风险(high degree of risk of harm)、所产生的伤害是否都是实质性的、是否尽了合理的注意义务就可免除这种风险、这项活动是否是普通习惯(common usage)的事情,这一活动发生问题的地点是否合适。以前此词条称为 abnormally hazardous activity;extrahazardous activity]
abnormal dangerousness allocation 异常危险性配置
abnormal person 变态的人
abnormal phenomenon 反常现象
abnormal psychology 变态心理学,病态心理学
abnormal risk 异常危(风)险
abnormal sexuality 变态性欲
abnormality n. 失常,反常;变态,畸形;不规则
abnormality of mind 精神失常
ABO 人类血型体系
aboard commercial aircraft 在商业飞机上
abode n. (13世纪)1.住所,常住地;(较久的)居住所 2.abide的过去式和过去分词(见 domicile;place of abode)
abolish v. 废止,废除(法律、习惯等);取消,撤销
abolishable a. 可废止的,可废除的,可取消的,可撤销的
abolished by clear expression 已明文废止

（或撤销）的
abolisher n. 废除者；撤销者
abolishment n. 废止，废除（法律、习惯等），取消，撤销
abolishment of law 法律的废止（废除）
abolition n. （法律、习惯等的）废除，取消；（美）废除黑奴制度
Abolition Acts （英）废除奴隶法（指1807—1838年间颁布的一系列废除奴隶制度的法令）
abolition of the monarchy 废除君主制
abominable a. 可恶的，可恨的，恶劣的
abominable crime 可鄙的罪行（对鸡奸或兽奸罪的婉称）
abominable offence 可憎的罪行，可鄙的罪行；兽奸罪
aboriginal n. 土著居民
abort v. 流产，早产，（计划等）失败，夭折，使流产，使计划夭折
aborted a. 流产的，失败的，发育不健康的
aborticide n. 堕胎（罪）；堕胎药
abortifacient n. 堕胎药物
abortion n. 堕胎、流产；（计划等）失败、夭折[19世纪后半叶，美国对堕胎施以刑事制裁较为普遍。20世纪后半叶，性自主是宪法权利的观念才在公众脑海中出现，这才决定堕胎最终成为司法问题。美国早期历史上，堕胎被认为其本身就危及生命，立法者认为无必要把堕胎规定为犯罪。19世纪当医学进步使堕胎安全以后，一些禁止堕胎主要为了保护孕妇，反堕胎的立法通常被称为"小康斯托克法"（Little Comstock Laws），它是州淫秽物品立法（Obsceneity Statutes）的组成部分。20世纪初，玛格南特·圣格（Margnant Sanger）等改革派提倡控制生育。1960年全美国有46个州使生育控制合法化。生育控制的非犯罪化增进了妇女对其生殖力的控制，强化了个人权利。但避孕（contraception）并不能确保妇女在生育上的自决。由于妇女遭遇不情愿的怀孕，所以堕胎就成为必要。而堕胎一直是比避孕更为有争议的问题。到20世纪60年代，除了为拯救母亲的生命，堕胎在全美各处仍为非法。1965年美国联邦最高法院裁定使用避孕药品的权利处于权利法案（Bill of Rights）中的几个条款的"延伸"所保护的"隐私权领域"之内，同时在格里斯沃尔德诉康涅狄格州（Griswold v. Conneticut）（1965年）一案中废除了一部有效的反对生育控制的法律。1973年，联邦最高法院把隐私权延伸至堕胎的选择权。罗诉韦德（Roe v. Wade）案一直是美国联邦最高法院历史上最富争议的判决之一。提倡生育自由的人对该案表示欢迎。但该案也导致"生命权"运动的形成，人们提出一项宪法修正案界定"人"包括未出生之胎儿。1986年当伦奎斯特（Rehnquist）取代沃伦·伯格（Warran Burger）成为联邦最高法院首席大法官后，法官们将妇女选择堕胎权设置障碍和拒绝促进堕胎进行了区分，前者宣布大多数无效，后者效力得到维持。见Roe v. Wade。但罗诉韦德案又作了重新的肯定，大法官苏特和奥康纳（O'connor）、肯尼迪以多数意见再次肯定该案的中心观点；在生命存在之前有权堕胎，州有权在生命存在之后限制堕胎，州的立法利益修着重于整个怀孕期间母亲健康和胎儿的生命上，联邦最高法院首次承认阻止堕胎权是一个有效的州的利益]
abortion law 堕胎法
abortion on demand （美）有求必应的堕胎
abortion right 堕胎权
abortionist n. 为人堕胎者
abortive child （大陆法系）流产的孩子，流产婴儿（指流产的婴儿或过早生产以致不能存活24小时的婴儿）
abortive trial 流产审讯，毫无结果的审讯
abortus n. 堕胎胎儿；（不能存活的）早产儿；流产儿
abound v. 充满，多产，富于（in, with）
about to 即将，马上
about to abandon 即将放弃
above ad. 在上面，以上；上述；在上游；超出
above all 首先，首要
above par 超出票面价值
above reproach 无可指责
above suspicion 无可置疑，不足怀疑
above-cited a. 前面已述的；前面所引的

above-mentioned a. 上述的
above-the-line expenditure （经常）预算支出
abrasion n. 皮外损伤,擦伤;表皮剥(脱)落
abrasive a. 损伤性的,有损害的,有损伤的
abridge v. 剥夺(权利、自由等);节略
abridge sb. of his rights 剥夺某人的权利
abridged copy 节本
Abridgement of All Sea Laws 《海上法纲要》(1613年 William Welwood 著)
Abridgement of the Book of Assises （英）《判例大全节本》(指16世纪出版的,将从年鉴中选出的案件编成的一部节本,其中约有1/4来自《判例大全》)
Abridgements of the Statutes （英）制定法节略(指中世纪对议会通过的大量制定法出版的各种节略本)
Abridgements of the Year Books （英）法律年鉴节略(指自制定法节略问世后出现的一批年鉴节略);法律年鉴概览
abridging the freedom of speech 剥夺言论自由
abridg(e)ment n. 节本,摘要;法律年报摘要;(权利、自由等的)剥夺
abridg(e)ment of rights 剥夺权利
abroad ad. 在国外,在海外,到国外;广泛,到处
abrogate v. 撤销,废除(法令、条约、习惯等)
abrogation n. 取消,撤销,废除
abrogation of damages 取消损害赔偿
abrogation of judg(e)ment 撤销判决
abrogation of the treaty 废除条约
abscond v. （为躲避罪责、债务等）潜逃,逃亡
abscond to avoid punishment 畏罪潜逃;逃避惩罚
abscond with the money 卷款潜逃
abscondence n. 潜逃;逃亡
absconder n. 潜逃者;逃亡者
absconding n. 潜逃
absconding by person released on bail 被保释犯人潜逃(罪)
absconding defendant 在逃被告

absence n. 缺席;不到庭;不在,失踪;缺乏
absence *cum dolo et culpa* 自愿不出庭
absence of consideration （英美法）缺乏对价
absence of discernment 无意识
absence of fault 无过失,无错误
absence of jurisdiction 没有管辖权
absence of probable cause 缺乏可信诉因
absence of proof 缺乏证据
absence of right 缺少权利
absence of the accused 被告未到庭
absence on leave 因假缺席
absence without leave 擅离职守
absent a. 缺席的,不在的,缺席人的;缺乏的;不在场的;不存在的
absent class member 缺席集团成员
absent defendant's property rights incident to a marriage 缺席被告与婚姻有关的财产权
absent domiciliary 住所地主人不在,主人不在住所地
absent fraud 缺席欺诈
absent from work without reason 无故旷工
absent parties 缺席当事人
absent showing of extraordinary 在无异常的情况下,未显示特殊情况下
absent voting 缺席投票
absent voting laws 缺席投票法,通信投票法
absente reo 在被告缺席的情况下
absentee n. 不在住所的人;缺席者;居住国外者;外住者;失踪人;缺席诉讼者
absentee ballot 缺席选举人的投票(指缺席者预先交给选举机构的投票)
absentee landlord 不在地主,不在房东(主)
absentee owner 未在场(的)物主,不在地主
absentee ownership 不在地主所有权(指土地所有人不在该土地上居住,也不亲自耕种却享有土地收益)
absentee voting 缺席投票(即使不能亲自到指定的选举地点也能进行投票的一种选举手续)

absenteeism n. 旷课,旷工(行为);有计划的旷工(工人斗争方式之一);不在地主身份

* *Absentem accipere debemus eum qui non est eo loci in quo petitur.* We must consider absent he who is not in that place in which he is demanded (or sought). 未在指定地点出现者应视为缺席;未在被寻找之地点出现者,应视为失踪。

* *Absoluta sententia expositore non indiget.*
An absolute sentence or proposition (one that is plain without any scruple or absolute without any saving) needs not an expositor. 绝对的句子或命题(字义明白而无疑义,或绝对而无保留的)不需要解释。

absolute a. 绝对的;完全的;纯粹的;专制的;独裁的;无条件的;确实的

absolute acceptance 绝对(无条件)承诺;绝对(无条件)承兑;绝对(无条件)接受

absolute assignment 绝对(无条件)转让

absolute bill 绝对诉状;绝对票据

absolute bill of sale 绝对(无条件)卖契

absolute body of doctrine 绝对的原则体系,不受限制的原理系统(或主要内容)

absolute conditions of an action 绝对诉讼条件

absolute contraband 绝对禁制品(禁运品,违禁品)

absolute covenant 绝对合同条款(指不受任何条件限制的合同条款)

absolute conveyance 绝对(无条件)转让

absolute (full) cover 绝对(全部)保险;绝对(全部)保证金

absolute decree 最后判决,最终裁定,绝对裁判

absolute deed 无限制契据,绝对契据(指无限制条件的契据,相对于抵押契据"mortgage deed"而言)

absolute defence 绝对抗辩(见 absolute plea)

absolute delivery 绝对让渡,绝对给付

absolute disability 完全无行为能力

absolute discharge 1.绝对(无条件)释放,绝对(无条件)免于刑事处分 2.完全清偿

absolute documentary conveyance 无条件书面财产转让

absolute duties 绝对义务;绝对责任

absolute embargo 绝对禁运物品

absolute estate 不附条件的产权,绝对产权(指产权所有人对其不动产拥有完全的、无条件的占有、支配、管理以及处分的权利。"absolute"是 pure"纯粹"和 simple"简明"的同义词,也表明这种地产权不会因某种事件而终止其所有人的拥有,或给予任何附加条件。在此产权所有人去世后,该不动产由其继承人继承)

absolute fact 确凿事实

absolute governments 专制政府

absolute guaranty 绝对(无条件)担保

absolute immunity 绝对豁免权

absolute immunity of the state 国家的绝对豁免权

absolute impossibility 绝对不可能(之事)

absolute inheritance 绝对继承权

absolute interest 绝对利益

absolute invalidity 绝对无效

absolute law 绝对法(指假定的自然法,原则上是不变的,但因情况不同在方式上有所变化)

absolute legacy 绝对遗赠(指无条件给予的遗产,而且有意立即赠与。见 vested legacy)

absolute liability 绝对责任;绝对赔偿责任(见 strict liability)

absolute literal compliance 绝对的字面相符

absolute majority 绝对多数

absolute mechanical social laws 绝对的机械社会法则

absolute monarchy 绝对君主政体;君主专制制度

absolute net loss 绝对净损

absolute novelty 绝对新颖性(专利)[此为大多数国家之规则,但在美国并非如此,而是该项发明通常在公开使用,投入销售或被披露之前必须进行专利申请。根据美国法律,专利发明人被给予1年的宽限期"grace period"(开始于任何公开使用、销售、买卖报价的日期或由发明人或其代理人公布的日期)在此宽限期间提出

专利申请(patent application)。在此期间之后,此专利申请即被停止。加拿大、墨西哥也给予第一发明人(first inventor)或发明人的受让人(inventor's assignee)1年的宽限期以便提出专利申请。如果该项发明被独立开发并由某人也在此期限披露,则它们会对此第一发明人停止其专利申请。此词条亦称为absolute novelty requirement。见 bar date]

absolute nuisance 绝对妨害(指并非由于过失或疏忽而造成的妨害)

absolute nullity 绝对无效

absolute nullity of marriage 绝对无效的婚姻

absolute offence 绝对罪行

absolute order 绝对指令,绝对命令

absolute owner 绝对所有人(指不可转移的所有权持有者)

absolute ownership 绝对所有权

absolute payment 全部支付

absolute personal rulers 个人专制者,个人统治者

absolute plea (=absolute defense) 绝对抗辩(又称对物抗辩或客观抗辩)

absolute poverty 绝对性贫穷

absolute predictability 绝对可预见性

absolute presumption 绝对性推定

absolute privilege 绝对特权(指行为免予起诉的一种特权)

absolute prohibition 绝对禁制(令)

absolute proof of guilt 有罪的绝对证明(据)

absolute property 绝对财产权;绝对财产

absolute real right 绝对物权

absolute responsibility 绝对责任

absolute right 绝对权利[指任何人均应享有的权利,如人身自由权(right of personal liberty);自然权(natural right)]

absolute rules 绝对规则

absolute scale 绝对尺度

absolute sovereignty 绝对主权

absolute territorial sovereignty 绝对领土主权

absolute theories 绝对理论,终极概念

absolute theory of law 法律的绝对理论

absolute title 绝对所有权,绝对产权

absolute total loss 绝对全损

absolute universal jurisdiction 绝对的普遍管辖原则[广义的普遍管辖原则的又一称谓,也称纯粹的普遍原则(pure universal jurisdiction)或被告人缺席的普遍管辖原则(universal jurisdiction in absentia)它是指:当一个国家既不是犯罪地国,也不是行为人和被害人的国籍国,犯罪行为也未损害到该国的公共利益,甚至行为人也未在该国被拘捕或出现在该国,这个国家仍可以对该人犯下的国际罪行进行管辖,该国在行为人不在该国境内时,开展调查,签署逮捕令,甚至起诉该人]

absolute veto 绝对否决权;绝对的否决

absolute voidness 绝对无效

absolute warrandice (苏格兰)绝对保证书;绝对保证

absolute wrong 绝对过失(错)

absolutely fatal wound 绝对致命伤

absolutely incapacitated person 完全无行为能力人,绝对无行为能力人

absolutely void 根本无效,绝对无效

absolutio n. (罗马法)开释(指宣告被告人或受到指控当事方无罪或不承担法律责任)

absolution n. 免罚;赦免;免除(责任等);(宗教上的)赦免罪过;免予起诉,驳回起诉,(法)无罪判决(大陆法)

absolutism n. 专制主义,专制政体;专制政府;(美)绝对原则,绝对论(美国联邦宪法中"absolutism"是指美国联邦宪法第一修正案绝对禁止政府干预公民的言论和出版,即任何人不得因其所说或其出版物而受到起诉或指控,这是一种理论,而非专制主义)

absolutist n. 专制主义者,绝对论者

absolutory a. 给予赦免的,可免除的

absolvable a. 可赦免的,(责任等)可解除的

absolve v. 宣告无罪;解除,赦免,宽恕;免除,开脱

absolve sb. from an obligation 免除某人的一项债务

absolve sb. from sin (宗教上)赦免某人

的罪
absolvent n./a. 赦免者/赦免的
absolver n. 免罪,赦免
absolvitor n. 赦免;(苏格兰)解除(被告)责任令(见 assoilzie)
absorb v. 吸收;吸引(注意);并入
absorbed tax 吸收税(指合同中不确指的各种因素组成的复合价格税,又作为整个税的不可分割部分而未单列一项,这种税叫吸收税)
absorption n. 包含,吸收;(国际法)通过自愿或征服的(合并);(劳工法)优势条款;(不动产)租赁(或出售)比率;(商法)运费免收(指在向卖方报价之前,由制造商支付卖方的运输费用的销售方法)
absorption of alcohol 酒精(在体内的)吸收
absorptive capacity 吸收能力
absorptive consolidation (企业的)吸并(又译合并,指将一企业并入另一企业,以及两个或两个以上的企业合并成一新企业)
absquatulate v. 潜逃,逃走;拐逃;(俚)开小差
absquatulated with funds 拐款潜逃
absque prep. 没有,无
absque hoc 无此事;没有
absque hoc of denials 无此事的否认
absque hoc of traverses 无此事的反驳
abstain v. 1.弃权,停止(from);避免(指自愿停止做某事,如在审议会进行表决)2.联邦法院对某一事件停止行使管辖权
abstain from an act 不作为
abstain from pleading 放弃申辩权
abstain from replying 不答辩,放弃答辩
abstain or disclose theory 拒绝交易或披露信息说(一些公司任职人员在因职务原因而获悉公司机密的情况下,在进行证券交易时应遵守"拒绝交易或披露信息"的原则)
abstention n. 弃权,戒除;避免,避开;规避行为
abstention doctrine (美)回避原则,规避原则,避让原则[指联邦最高法院在涉及州法律或州政策的案件时所采取的一种政策,亦称普尔曼(Pullman)规避原则。

因在得克萨斯铁路委员会诉普尔曼公司(Railroad Commission of Texas v. Pullman co.)(1941)一案中所采纳的,故名。为了避免与各州对本州事务的管理发生不必要的冲突,联邦法院可自主决定放弃对该案行使管辖权,而由州法院或其他州机构处理,实际的基本点即除非绝对必要,联邦法院不得干预各州事务]
abstention from voting 放弃投票
abstinence approach 回避法(防范滥用税收协定的措施之一)
abstinence of drug 戒(除)毒(癖)
abstinence syndrome 戒酒、戒毒所引起的心理和生理反应
abstract n./a. 摘要;概括;简介;抽象(观念或物)/抽象的;纯粹的;难解的,深奥的;理论上的;无因的
abstract action 无因行为
abstract contract 无因合同(契约)
abstract crime 抽象犯罪
abstract free man of full age 成年的抽象自由人
abstract formal right 抽象的形式权利
abstract harmonizing of human wills 抽象的人类意志和谐
abstract individual free self-assertion 坚持抽象的自由,不可抗拒的抽象自由
abstract individual man 抽象的个人
abstract jurisprudence 纯粹法理学
abstract juristic act 无因法律行为
abstract justice of abstract rules 抽象规则的抽象公正
abstract labor 抽象劳动(指物品生产为了交换时,涉及的具体劳动目的是可交换的产品,这些劳动价值的实现是它们再生产的内在部分,但作为商品的生产者也创造了抽象的价值量,即为抽象劳动)
abstract method 抽象方法
abstract of a fine 见 note of a fine
abstract of record 记录提要;案卷摘录(指案卷中记下诉讼活动全部过程的摘要)
abstract (或 epitome) of title 产权书的摘要
abstract right 抽象法(指黑格尔提出的概念,认为抽象法是自在的法,是人们自然

享有的普遍权利,而实在法是被国家以法律形式加以确定的法律权利;实在法必须反映和符合抽象法,抽象法可以通过国家的介入转化为实在法)
abstraction n.　窃取;提取;抽取
abstraction of electricity　盗用电力,偷电
abstracto n.　抽象(方法)
absurdity n.　荒谬,谬论,荒唐行为
Abu Nidal Organization　阿布·尼达尔组织(1974年从巴勒斯坦解放组织分离出来的恐怖组织,总部设在利比亚)
Abu Sayyaf Group　阿布·萨亚夫集团(1991年从摩洛哥民族解放战线分离出来的以色列极端组织,主要在菲律宾南部活动)
abuse n./v.　1.滥用(远离法律和理性),妄用;辱骂,虐待;弊端,陋习 2.虐待,摧残(身体上、精神上的虐待,通常造成精神上、感情上、性方面和身体上的伤害。亦称cruel and abuse treatment)(见cruelty)/1.滥用损坏一件事物(thing) 2.虐待(对待人或事物不讲理智与法律) 3.伤害他人(指在身体上、精神上伤害他人) 4.用虐待手段伤害儿童身心,剥夺他们的幸福(美国大多数州已有相应规定,造成或威胁致使儿童持久伤害的虐待行为普遍受到限制或禁止)
abuse a privilege　滥用特权
abuse *du droit*　权利的滥用
abuse of authority　滥用职权
abuse of civil liberties　滥用公民自由权
abuse of civil proceedings　滥用民事诉讼
abuse of discretion　滥用自由裁量权;滥用酌处权
abuse of distress　滥用扣押权
abuse of dominant position　滥用支配地位
abuse of economic power　滥用经济权力
abuse of franchise　滥用选举权,滥用特许权
abuse of judicial discretion　滥用司法自由裁量权
abuse of law　滥用法律
abuse of police authorities　滥用警察权力
abuse of power　滥用权力
abuse of process　滥用诉讼程序
abuse of rights　滥用权利
abuse of sentencing power　量刑的滥用
abuse of tax treaty　滥用税收协定
abuse of the aged　虐待老者
abuse of the elective franchise　妨碍选举罪;妨碍投票罪
abuse of the power of agency　滥用代理权
abuse one's official powers　滥用职权
abused child　受虐待的儿童(指曾遭受身体上或精神上的忽视或伤害的儿童。见child abuse)
abuser n.　虐待者,滥用者[指①虐待他人或滥用某些事物者;②致使损害(to damage)者]
abusing children　虐待儿童(见child abuse)
abusive exercise of right(s)　滥用权力,滥用权利
abusive statement　侮辱性陈述
abusus n.　(罗马法)处理个人财产权(见dismemberment of ownership)
abut v.　邻接,毗连,紧靠
abuttals (复) n.　地界
abutter n.　邻近住户;相邻房地产业主
abutting owner　毗邻房地产所有者
abutting property　毗邻房地产所有者,毗邻财产所有人
abyssal a.　海底深处的;深渊的
abyssal benthic zone　深渊底(栖)带
abyssal floor　深海底;深渊底
abyssal plain　深海平原,海盆
abyssal region　深海区
ac etiam　同样
***ac etiam* clause**　同样条款(以"同样"一词开头引出的、用来陈述诉讼真实理由的一项条款)
academic a.　专科院校的,研究院的;学术的;学会的
academic body　学术团体
academic career　学术生涯
academic circles　学术界
academic degrees regulations　学位条例
academic discussion　学术讨论
academic freedom　学术自由(特别指大学教师)(指关于政治上或意识形态上的问

题的言论权利,不怕因此而丢失地位或遭到报复)
academic interpretation (法律上的)学理解释
academic jurists 书斋法学家
academic lawyers 学术律师,法学研究工作者,法律工作者
academic qualification 学历
academic rank 学衔(等级)
academic records 学历
academic setting 学术环境,学术背景
academic staff 科研人员
academic status 学籍
academic title 学衔(称号)
academy of law 法律研究学院,法学研究所
academy training (刑事审判人员应该接受的)正规业务训练
accedas ad curiam You are to go to the court 你必须去法庭[这是一个原始令状,指从两个采邑法庭(即采邑民事法庭或百户邑法庭)中的任一法庭将追回原物诉讼转移至王室法院]
accede v. 加入(to);同意,答应(to);就任(to)
acceding state 参加国
Accelerate Cost Recovery System (ACRS) (美)加速成本回收制(该制度规定固定资产不同折旧年限以及每年可摊销的百分比,目的在于鼓励企业投资)
accelerated judicial proceedings 速决的司法程序
acceleration n. 提前;提前收益;加速,促进;(英)爵位承袭状
acceleration clause 提前条款(指贷款合同中规定,在某种情况下可要求提前偿还的条款)
acceleration proceedings 速决程序
accept v. 承认,认可,承兑;接受;认领;认付;同意;受理
accept a complaint 受理控诉
accept a draft 承兑汇票
accept and hear a case 受理案件
accept bail 准许保释
accept bribe 受贿

accept insurance (保险的)承保
accept sb.'s bid 接受某人投标
acceptable a. 可接受的,合意的,受到欢迎的
acceptance n. 承诺;承认,认可;认付,承兑;接受,受领;受理;验收
acceptance bill 承兑票据,承兑汇票
acceptance by intervention 参加承兑
acceptance by part of the drawees 部分付款人的承兑
acceptance commission 承兑手续费
acceptance fee 承兑费用
acceptance for hono(u)r 参加承兑[见 accepter for hono(u)r]
acceptance house 承兑商行
acceptance in blank 空白承兑,不记名承兑
acceptance in default 受领迟延
acceptance invoice 承兑交单
acceptance letter of credit 承兑信用证(状)
acceptance market 证券市场
acceptance of a judg(e)ment 服从判决,接受判决
acceptance of a rule 接受规则(是哈特的法学理论中至关重要的法律观念。在哈特看来,社会规则与纯粹的习惯的区别在于,行为人"接受"规则作为准则,据以证明自己行为的正当性并批评违反规则之行为。哈特认为规则的存在等同于规则被一些人接受为行为的准则)
acceptance of abandonment 接受委付
acceptance of appointment 应聘;应聘书
acceptance of bill (of exchange) 承兑汇票,票据承兑
acceptance of bribes 受贿(罪)
acceptance of delivery 接受转让;受领给付
acceptance of estate 接受遗产,受领遗产
acceptance of goods 货物的受领
acceptance of object 标的之受领
acceptance of offer 承诺;接受捐赠
acceptance of partial performance 部分履行之受领
acceptance of persons 不公正,偏袒

acceptance of protest 接受抗议书；受理抗诉

acceptance of punishment 接受处罚；服罪

acceptance of risk 承担风险

acceptance of service 接受送达（指律师代表当事人接受传票）

acceptance of succession 接受继承

acceptance of *victime* 被害人承诺

acceptance payable 应付承兑票据

acceptance payment credit 承兑信用证

acceptance receivable 应收（受）承兑票据

acceptance register 承兑票据登记册；验收登记册

acceptance test 验收试验

accepted a. 已承兑的，已保付的；已接受的；公认的；已承诺的，已受领的

accepted bill 已承兑汇票，已承兑票据

accepted cheque 保付支票

accepted draft 已承兑汇票

acceptee n. 被接受人；被承兑人；受承诺人，被受领人

accepter (= acceptor) n. 承兑人；接受人；领受人；承诺人

accepter for hono(u)r 参加承兑人（指汇票付款人拒绝付款后，第三者为维持出票人信誉而出面承兑）

accepter supra protest 参加承兑人[见 accepter for hono(u)r]

acceptilatio v. （大陆法和苏格兰法）免除（债务）

acceptilatio verbis （大陆法和苏格兰法）1.口头免除（债务）2.口头承担合同（契约）（指名义上受领债务）

acceptilation n. 减免债务

accepting bank 承兑银行

accepting house 承兑商行

accepting service (= acceptance of service)

acceptor of a bill 汇票的承兑人

access n. （14世纪）1.一种权利，机会，进入能力，方法，往复，交流（communicate with）〈access to the courts〉（与法院交往）2.（家庭法）探视权（指具有合法权利，可利用适当时间看望子女、犯人等。见 visitation 1）3.（家庭法）性交（具有可实行的机会，即性交机会）4.（专利的商标）享用权

[指获得有关审视、复制美国专利商标注册局(U. S. Patent and Trademark Office)的专利文档、专利申请、商标申请以及当事双方的诉讼进程或程序的信息] 5.(版权法) 查看或复制版权作品的机会[指在指控侵权发生之前，一个侵权被告有查看、听证或复制版权作品(copyrighted work)的机会]〈the duplication of the error proved that the defendant had access to the works〉（重复的错误已证明被告具有查看或复制作品的机会）。这个机会的证据是要求证明版权侵权，除非这两种作品惊人地相似

access clerk 贵重物品保管处的保管员

access order 见 visitation order

access to court 向法院申诉的权利

access to justice 接近正义；司法救助；向法院申诉的权利

access to market 进入市场

access to the sea 通往海洋，出入海洋

access to trials （美）媒体旁听审判[指在里士满报业公司诉弗吉尼亚州(Richmond Newspapers, Inc. v. Virginia, 448 U.S.555)(1980)一案中联邦最高法院根据美国联邦宪法第一修正案宣判公众和新闻媒体有参与刑事审判的权利。另在纽约时报公司诉合众国(New York Times Co. v. United States)(1971)一案中也根据第一修正案承认新闻媒体享有报道他们所拥有任何信息(无论信息是机密的和以非公开方式获得的)的权利。但有些案件如环球报业公司诉高级别法院(Globe Newspaper Co. v. Superior Court)(1982)一案中联邦最高法院认定马萨诸塞州的一部法律违宪，该法律要求在强奸犯罪受害人为未成年人的案件中，受害人作证陈述时不公开审理。代表多数意见的布伦南大法官强调只有特定类型案件的审理方可不公开，因对这类未成年人的伤害有单独的法律规定和合理考虑，所以该法律并不属于特定类型的案件中]

accessibility to justice 司法的可接近性

accessible branch of the federal government 联邦政府的群访机构

accessio v. （罗马法）加入；添附；增加

accessio cedit principali 从物属于主物的

所有人
accession n. 1.添附（指财产自然增益）2.加入（指未签署国在条约生效前，表示完全接受而参加该条约）3.到达，接近 4.增加 5.继承 6.就职，就任
accession council （联合王国君主去世后召开的）继位会议
accession declaration （联合王国新任君主的）登基宣言
accession of property 财产的继承；财产的增加
accession of sovereign 王位的继承
accession of territory 领土（版图）的扩张
accession of wealth 财富的增加
accession to a treaty 加入条约；加入同盟
accession to an estate 继承产业
accession to sovereignty 成为主权国家
* *Accessorium non ducit, sed sequitur, suum principale.* That which is the accessory or incident does not lead, but follows, its principal. 从物不吸收主物而从属于主物。
accessorium sequitur principale 从物随主物原则
* *Accessorius sequitur naturam sui principalis.* An accessory follows the nature of his principal, thus, an accessory can not be found guilty of a greater crime than his principal. 从犯随主犯行事，因而对从犯的定罪不得重于主犯。
accessory （英国常用 **accessary**） n./a. 1.附属物，附件，从物 2.同谋，帮凶，从犯/附属的，从属的，附加的；同谋的
accessory act 从犯行为，从犯行为
accessory after the fact 事后从犯
accessory before the fact 事前从犯
accessory character 从属性质；从属人物
accessory charges 额外费用；附加指控
accessory claim 附属要求；附加请求权；附加诉讼请求
accessory contract 从合同（契约），附加合同（契约）
accessory debtor 从债务人
accessory during the fact 作案时的从犯，在场从犯

accessory law 辅助性的法律
accessory obligation 从属义务；从债
accessory offender 从犯
accessory punishment 从刑，附加刑
accessory real rights 从物权
accessory right 从属权利，从权利
accessory risk （保险）附加险
accessory things 从物
accessory to a crime 帮凶，从犯，同谋犯
accessory to adultery 唆使（自己）配偶一方（夫或妻）通奸者
accessory trust 从属信托
accident n. 事故；意外事件；偶然事故，保险事故，意外事故；交通事故
accident and health insurance 意外及健康保险（亦称 sickness and health insurance。见 health insurance）
accident at sea 海上事故，海难
accident boat 救生艇
accident case 事故案件
accident collision 意外碰撞
accident compensation 事故损失赔偿
accident cost 意外事故损失费用
accident damage 意外事故损害
accident death 意外事故死亡
accident due to（或 **out of**）**negligence** 过失责任事故
accident enquiry（或 **inquiry**） 事故调查
accident frequency 事故发生率；意外事故频率
accident insurance 事故保险，意外保险
accident involving civil liability 民事责任事故
accident involving criminal liability 刑事责任事故
accident involving serious bodily injuries 重伤事故
accident leave 工伤假，意外事故假
accident medical reimbursement insurance 意外事故医疗费保险
accident policy 意外保险（单）[指一种商业型或人身型的意外保险，它对于因意外事故直接造成的人身伤害或损失在保险期间（policy term）给予保险]
accident records 事故记录，事故档案

accident report　事故报告书;海事报告
accident secenario　事故情况说明
accidental n./a.　1.偶然事故 2.非本质的属性;附属物 3.杂形(指)纹(指与箕、弧以及其他类型相似,但均不能归入这些类型的指纹)/意外的;偶然的;附属的
accidental criminal　非故意作案的刑事罪犯
accidental death　意外事故死亡
accidental destruction　意外毁损,事故毁损
accidental force　不可抗力
accidental harm　意外的伤害(指①非有意行为造成的伤害;②非侵犯行为造成的伤害)
accidental homicide　意外杀人,非故意杀人
accidental injury (to third person)　(对第三者的)意外伤害(或误伤)
accidental killing　意外杀人,非故意杀人
accidental obstacle　意外障碍
accidental omission　偶然疏忽;意外遗漏
accidental poisoning　意外中毒
accidental slip　偶然过错
accidental trauma　意外伤
accidental whorl　杂形斗形纹
accidental work injury　工伤事故
accidental wound　意外伤
accidentia　偶然因素
accidents at work　工伤事故
* *Accipere quid ut justitiam facias, non est tam accipere quam extorquere.*　To accept anything as a reward for doing justice is rather extorting than accepting.　因主持公道而接受任何报酬,与其说是接受,不如说是勒索。
accommodate v.　调停(争端);变通,通融优惠于;供应;使适应;提供(贷款或住宿)
accommodated party　借款当事人
accommodation n.　(争端等的)和解;变通,通融;优惠;贷款;供应;适应;(复)招待设备,膳宿供应
accommodation allowance　住房津贴
accommodation arrest　(警方与被捕者事先有默契的)假捕
accommodation bill　通融票据,通融汇票;

欠单;空头票据
accommodation note　通融票据
accommodation paper　优惠证,优惠单
accommodation party　调解当事人;汇票代发人(旧译:担当关系人)
accommodation surety　调解担保人
accommodation tax　住宿税
accommodation works　便利工程(指铁路或运河工程的建设单位为方便毗连的土地所有人或占有人而修建的工程设施)
accommodator n.　贷款人;调解人;(帮佣的)替工
accomplice n.　共犯,同谋,帮凶;从犯
accomplice as witness　作为证人的共犯
accomplice under duress　胁从(犯)
accomplished a.　完成的;既成的
accomplished fact　既成事实
accomplished offence　既遂罪
accomplished offender　既遂犯
accord n./v.　一致,调和,符合;赞成(国家之间的)协议;协定/和解,调停;同意,赞同,达成协议
accord and satisfaction　和解和清偿,解除债务的一种方法;和解和清偿协议(指在违反合同或非法侵犯的纠纷中,受害一方和损害他人一方达成的和解,并要使受害一方得到赔偿)
accordingly ad.　相应地,因此,从而
accord priority　给予优先权
accost v.　(妓女等)勾引,引诱
account n.　1.原因,理由 2.叙述,详细报告 3.账,账目,账户;算账 4.重要性;价值;考虑 5.利润,利益
account balance　账户结余
account balanced　结平的账户
account book　账册,账本
account day　结算日
account for the year　年度结算
account note　账单
account of executors　遗产清册
account of profit　利润数额(指在认定侵犯版权后,计算对被侵权人的赔偿额)
account on the spot　现场报告
account payable　应付账款,应付而未付账款

account payee （在支票上标明的）收款人账户
account payee only 只付给收款人本人
account receivable 应收账款,应收而未收账款
Account Registered Law 《注册会计师法》
account rendered 结欠清单;借贷细账
account settled 决算账
account stated 1.(债务人认为无误的)确认欠账清单 2.账目陈述(单据)(指能用作表面证据表明债务人承认欠账的两种单据形式,一种为债务人经过亲笔写上"我欠你""IOU"的签名账单;另一种为经过债务人承认的账目结算单)
account transfer check 转账支票
account transfer voucher 转账传票
account verification 会计鉴定,账目鉴定
accountability n. 责任;有义务,有责任
accountable a. 有说明义务的;负有责任的;可说明的;可解释的;有待支付的
accountable receipt 负有解释义务的收据
accountable to the people 对人民承担责任
accountable warrant 支付书,支付令
accountant n. 会计(师)
accountant general 总会计师,会计主任;（英）（最高法院的）总会计官
accountant in bankruptcy 破产核算员
accountant of court 法院会计官
Accountant Registration Law 《注册会计师法》
accountant to the Crown （英）政府会计官
accountant-client privilege 会计师拒绝泄露内情权(指保护由会计师准备好的或呈交的提供给客户而未经批准的证券信息资料)
accounting n. 借贷对照表;核算,清算账目;会计;会计学
accounting circular 会计通告
accounting control system 核算管理制度
accounting document（或 voucher） 会计凭证
accounting identity 会计方程式,会计恒等式
Accounting Law 会计法
accounting officer 会计人员
accounting policy 会计政策,会计原则
Accounting Practice Committee 审计实务委员会
accounting procedure 会计程序,会计处理程序
accounting records 负债和资产的详细记录
accounting reference period 账目查询期
accounting report 会计报告(书)
accounting rule 会计规则
accounting unit 核算单位;会计单位
accredit v. 委任,任命(大使等);归咎于;认可;相信;承认资格;鉴定合格
accreditation n. 立案,备案;任命;鉴定
accredited a. 委任的,任命的,授权的;公认的;特派的;经备案的;鉴定合格的
accredited bodies 委托机关（见 Central Authorities）
accredited journalist 特派新闻记者
accredited law school 备(立)案的法学院（见 approved law school）
accredited representative 被委任的代表;认可代理人
accretion n. （大陆法）添附(指财产的自然增值);增加物;积成物;（国际法）自然添附(指国家取得领土主权的一种方式)
accrual a. （权利）增积的
accrual basis 权责发生制
accrue v. （利息等的）自然增长,增加
accrued a. 累积的,累计的;自然增长的
accrued assets 增值资产;流动资产
accrued capital 累计资本
accrued charges 积欠费用;应付费用
accrued duties and tax 应缴的捐税
accrued expenditure 应付开支;累计开支
accrued expenses 应付费用
accrued interest 应计利息
accrued interest on mortgage 应计的抵押利息
accrued leave 积存假期
accrued liabilities 应付而未付的债务
accrued profits 应计利润
accrued rental 累计租金总额
accrued tax (1872年)应计税款,应付税

款(指在一定的会计期间内应该支付的税款但尚未支付)
accruing costs 自然增加的讼费
accruing right 自然扩大的权利
accumulated a. 累积的,累加的
accumulated case 积案
accumulated earnings tax (1957年)累积盈余税,累积收益税(指为了尽力防止以公司盈利形式逃避股东个人所得税,而在公司所得之外又课以一种税,以免公司保留过多的留存收益。亦称为 undistributed-earning tax)
accumulated legacy 尚未给予遗产承受人(legatee)的遗产
accumulated loss 累积损失
accumulated profit 累积利润
accumulated proprietorship 累积所有权
accumulated surplus 累积盈余
accumulation n. (资金)积累,聚积,堆积物,积聚物
accumulation account 积累账户
accumulation of funds 资金积累
accumulations, rule against (1924年)限制累集规则[指一项对来自财产引入监督(direction)的规则,即迟于受益人所分配到的收入,也就是超出财产永久权限内的收入,是无效的。见 rule against perpetuities]
accumulative a. 积累的;累进的;堆积的;贪得的
accumulative evidence 复证,累积证据
accumulative legacy 见 additional legacy
accumulative offence 累犯,累次犯罪
accumulative penalty 累积刑罚;(对罪犯的)加重处罚
accumulative sentence 与前刑合并的判决;(连续服刑的)累计判决;累积服刑判决
accumulative sinking fund 累积偿债基金
accumulative trust 累积信托
accuracy n. 准确(性);精确(度)
accurate a. 准确的;精确的
accusa publica (罗马法中的)人民控告(制度)(又称公诉,是允许任何公民就犯罪提出控诉的制度)

accusable a. 可指控的,可指责的
accusant n. 原告,控告人;指责者
* *Accusare nemo se debet (or sccusare nemo se debet); nisi coram Deo.* No one is bound to accuse himself except to God. 任何人无指控自己的义务,但面对上帝时不在此限。
accusation n. (14世纪)1.正式刑事犯罪,指控[这种刑事控告通常提交法院或有管辖权去审查所指称罪行的司法官员(magistrate)]2.进行对非法或不道德行为人的陈述
accusation evidence 检举材料,检举证据
accusation of crime 被指控犯罪
accusatorial procedure 发现和提出证据的程序
accusatorial procedure system (英)控告式诉讼制度
accusatorial process of proof 控告举证程序;控告证明程序
accusatory a. 控诉的,起诉(式)的,告发的;非难的,指责的
accusatory instruments 刑事起诉(文)书
accusatory pleading (1908年)刑事起诉书[指国家依据大陪审团起诉书(indictment)、检察官起诉书(information)、犯罪控告书(complaint)而开始提起刑事检控或刑事起诉(criminal prosecution)的文书]
accusatory procedure 控诉式诉讼程序(又译控诉式审判程序。指双方当事人及其辩护人应向法庭提交他所认为需要的和充分的证据,而法官不对事实进行调查的一种审判制度)
accusatory system 控诉式(审判)制度;起诉式(诉讼)制度
accusatory witnesses 指控性证人
accuse v. 1.控诉,控告 2.指责,谴责
accuse falsely 诬告
accused poacher 被指控的侵害人,被告侵害人
accuse sb. of a crime 控告某人有罪
accused n. 被告,刑事被告(人)
accused as witness 作为证人的被告
accused person 被检控人,被控告人;刑事被告(人)

accuser n. 原告,指控人,控告者;起诉者(人)
accusing party 控诉方,控方当事人
achieve v. 完成,达到,得到(胜利)
achieve the equal protection of the law 使达到法律平等保护的目的,达到法律平等保护
achieve vertical uniformity 追求纵向一致性,达到纵向的一致性
achieved status (经过努力而)获得的地位、成就
achievement test 成就测验(指测验各人现时已经获得的知识与技能)
acid n. (美俚)麻醉毒品,麻醉药物
acknowledge v. 公认;承认;表示谢意;告知收到;确认
acknowledged obligation 承认的债务
acknowledg(e)ment n. (私生子的)认领;承认;承认书;确认;收讫;表示感谢
acknowledg(e)ment of a child 认领子女(指生父对非婚生子女的认领行为)
acknowledg(e)ment of certificate 对证书的确认(或认可)
acknowledg(e)ment of claim 承认请求权,请求权的确认
acknowledg(e)ment of debt 承认负债,确认债务
acknowledg(e)ment of deeds 契据的认可
acknowledg(e)ment of guilt 认罪
acknowledg(e)ment of natural child 非婚生(私生)子女的认领
acknowledg(e)ment of right to production of documents 承认提供文据的权利;对出示文据权利的认可
acknowledg(e)ment of will 签认遗嘱;遗嘱的认可
acknowledg(e)ment of wrongdoing 承认犯罪,承认犯有不法行为
ACPO Good Practice Guide for Digital Evidence 英国高级警察协会(制定的)《数据证据良好操作指南》(该指南由英国高级警察协会编制,其内容涉及颇多数据证据问题。如该指南指出:"数据设备的不断增容以及数据交流的不断发展意味着现在数据证据存在于或可能存在于几乎每一起犯罪之中……操作系统和其他程序频繁地变动,增加和删除电子存储信息的内容。这一现象可能是自动发生的,使用者可能根本没有意识到数据已经被改变了……"正因如此,电子数据的证明力长期以来一直受到质疑。美国法院对电子数据的真实性提出很高要求。不过,20世纪80年代以来,随着电子数据在法庭上越来越多地出现,法院对电子数据采取与其他证据一视同仁的态度)
acqietandis pleyiis (英)免责令状(指主债务清偿后,担保人可据以迫使债权人免其责任令状)
acquest n. 新获得的财产,购得产;非继承所得的财产
acquiesce v. 默许,默认
acquiescence n. 默许,默认,消极承诺
acquiescence in custom 对惯例默认(指使某一惯例对合同当事人具有合同约束力的本质要件)
acquiescent a. 默许的,默认的
acquire v. 获得,取得
acquire by fraud 诈骗取得
acquired company 被接收的公司
acquired freedom 后天的自由(指与智慧和美德相联系的自由,只有在其个人发展过程中已经获得了一定程度的美德和智慧的人才拥有的这种自由)
acquired property 夫妻(婚姻关系持续期间的)取得财产
acquired right 既得权利,得来权(指非由所有物本身而获得的物权,而是由所有物以外获得的特许权等)
acquired territory 取得的领土
acquirement n. 取得,获得;学得,学到
acquirement of nationality 国籍的取得
acquirenda n. (苏格兰)后得财产(指破产人破产后或已婚女婚后所取得的财产)
acquirer n. 获得者,取得人,受让人
acquiring company 接收公司
acquiring party 取得方,受让方
acquiring state (领土)取得国,受让国
acquisition n. 取得,获得;获得物;收购;财产取得
acquisition agreement 收购协议
acquisition and merger 收购与合并

acquisition by cession 转让取得
acquisition by occupancy 占有取得
acquisition cost 购置成本
acquisition of a patent 专利权的取得
acquisition of nationality 国籍的取得
acquisition of ownership（或 title） 所有权的取得
acquisition of property (right) 取得财产(权)
acquisition of territory 领土的取得
acquisition of the right to a mark 取得商标权
acquisition without consideration 无偿取得
acquisitive a. 取得的,获得的;能够获得的;(对财富、知识等)渴望得到的
acquisitive competitive self assertion 渴望取得竞争的自我坚持的权利(或要求)
acquisitive prescription 取得时效(见 positive prescription)
acquit v. 宣判无罪,开释,释放,免(罪);履行,尽责;偿还;(债务的)清偿
acquit sb. of a crime 宣判某人无罪
acquit the innocent 释放无罪者
acquittal n. 1.宣告无罪;开释(凡被判无罪释放或申请赦免获准释放者,或者在同一案件以前曾被判开释,或以前曾被定罪而又由法庭释放者,都称为开释。被开释的人均可免除因原先案件而再次受到检控) 2.清偿(债务) 3.履行(职责)
acquittal by a jury 陪审团判决无罪
acquittal by reason of the unwritten law 根据不成文法作出的无罪判决
acquittal in fact 依事实宣告无罪
acquittal in law 依法宣告无罪
acquittance n. 免除;(债务的)清偿;偿债收据;解除债务证书;释放
acquittance of a debt 免除债务,清偿债务
acquittance register 偿债登记册
acquitted a. 被宣告无罪的
acquitted of a charge 无罪释放
acreage n. 土地面积,英亩数
acrimonious debates 严厉的争辩
across groups of cases 适用各类案件
across judges within a federal court district in the US. 横贯美国境内联邦地区法院法官

across state lines 跨州
across system lines 跨系统
across types of case 跨各类案件
across-the-board a. 全部的,一致的,包括一切的
across-the-board tax-cut 全面减税
act n./v. 行动,作为,行为;法,法令(港译:法例)条例,决议,决议书,(国际组织的)总文件/代理(for);作为,行动,做,假装,演出,起作用;担当(as)
act against 违反
act against duty 违反义务行为
act and deed 有约束力的契约
act and warrant （苏格兰）保管授权令
act as agent 作为代理人,代理
act as an assessor 陪审,作陪审员
act as bail (for sb.) 作(某人的)保释人
act contrary to moral 违反道德的行为
act contrary to offending against and punishable by law 违背,触犯法律并应受法律惩罚的行为
act damage to a third party 损害第三人的行为
act for 代理
Act for the Prevention of Frauds and Perjuries （美）《预防诈欺和伪证法》
act formerly done 在先行为(指要约、代理授权、遗嘱等)
act in collusion 勾结(行为);串通(行为)
act in collusion to make each other's confession tally 相互串供行为
act in concert （美）协同行为(直至 20 世纪初期,美国连带责任仅适用于"协同行为",即基于共同故意而实施的加害行为。大陆法系、传统民法无不坚持以共同加害行为为共同侵权的构造模式)
act in excess of authority 越权行为
act in law 法律上的行为;法律行为(见 act in the law)
act in *pais* 法院外行为;和解行为
act in the law （1829 年）法律行为[指当事人意图创设、转让或消灭某一法律上的权利并使其产生法律上的效果,为此而实施法律上的权力（legal power）订立合同、签订遗嘱以及转让财产等都是法律行为,

其构成所需要的法律要素包括行为人预期法律后果的法律权力,行为人的意图、目的以及为此所作的表示,在某些情况下还有诸如不得违法、违俗等消极因素。法律行为可是单方的,也可是双方的。亦称 juristic act; act of the party; legal act]

act in violation of regulations　违章行为
act *inter vives*　生前行为
act *jure gestionis*　管理权行为
act *jure imperii*　统治权行为
act *mortis causa*　死因行为(见 *mortis causa*)
act of accepting bribe　受贿行为
act of adjournal　(苏格兰)休庭法
act of attainder　褫夺公权法令(指含有褫夺公权内容的、关于处死刑或放逐刑等的法令)
act of authorization　授权行为
act of bankruptcy　破产行为
act of clemency　宽恕行为
act of commission　委任行为,委托行为;作为
act of concealment　隐匿事实,隐匿行为
Act of Congress　(美)国会立法,(美)国会(制定的)法令(指经国会依法定程序通过后,并按规定颁布的法令)
act of connivance　纵容行为,默许行为
act of consideration　有偿行为
act of court　(有关案件性质的)法庭备忘录;法庭行为
act of defence　防御行为,防卫行为;辩护行为,抗辩行为
act of disposition　处分行为;处置行为
act of embezzlement　侵吞行为,挪用行为;贪污行为
act of execution　执行行为
act of force　武力行为,暴力
act of foreign states　非本国行为,外国行为
act of God　自然灾害;不可抗力
act of government　政府行为;政府法令
act of grace　宽恕行为,恩赦行为;大赦法,特赦法;(大写)(英)大赦令
act of indecency　猥亵行为
act of indemnity　特赦行为;赔偿法;赦免法

act of infringing the exclusive right to use　(专利、商标等)侵犯专有权的行为
act of insolvency　(银行)破产法
act of law　1.见 act of the law 2.见 legal act
act of legislation　立法条例,立法法案,立法行为
act of life-time　生前行为
act of nonperformance　不履行(债务)行为
act of notary public　公证行为
act of omission　(不履行法律责任的)懈怠行为,消极行为,不作为
act of parliament　(英)议会(制定的)法令(指法案经议会通过后颁布施行的法令)
act of party　当事人的行为(见 act of the party)
act of passion　冲动行为
act of piracy　海盗行为;侵犯版权(或专利权)行为
act of private right　私权行为
act of procedure　诉讼行为
act of public enemy　公敌行为
act of rape　强奸行为
act of ratification and acknowledg(e)ment　承认和批准书
act of sederunt　(苏格兰)开庭规则(指苏格兰最高民事法院的法官们制定的诉讼程序规程)
act of self-defence　自卫行为,正当防卫行为
act of self-help　自助行为
Act of Settlement　(英)《王位继承法》[指威廉三世第 12、13 执政年颁布的《1701 年英格兰法》(第 2 号法令)。该法规定在威廉三世和他的妻妹安妮公主无后嗣去世后应由汉诺威的女候选索菲娅(伊丽莎白之女,波希米亚女王,英格兰国王詹姆斯一世及苏格兰国王詹姆斯六世的孙女)及其亲生子女继承,并要求必须是新教徒。这是 1688 年"光荣革命"之后的基本法律规定。《1707 年合并条约》规定对大不列颠的王位继承,应依照《王位继承法》的规定进行]
act of state　国家行为,治理行为
act of supremacy　(英)君主最高权力

法令
act of swindling 诈骗行为
act of terrorism 恐怖行为
act of the law （17世纪）法律（本身）的实施（指因法律本身的实施所引起的权利的产生、转让和消灭与相关当事人的意图或同意无任何关系。亦称 legal act; act of law）
act of the party 见 act in the law
act of theft 盗窃行为
act of tort 侵权行为
act of undermining the state financial system （中）破坏国家财政制度的行为
act of unfair competition 不正当竞争行为
Act of Uniformity （英）（宗教）《统一礼仪（信仰）法》（港译：划一法例）
Act of Union of 1707 1707年联盟法案（指苏格兰和威尔士的合并法案，或译"合并法案"）
act of unlawful interference 不法干扰行为
act of usury 暴利行为，高利盘剥行为
act of violence 暴力行为
act of war 战争行为
act on （或 upon） 对……起作用；按照……行动〈act on sb.'s advice〉（听从或按照某人的劝告）
Act on Boycott 《联合抵制法》（旧译：《杯葛法》）（见 Boycott）
act one's age 从事适龄行为（意为其行为与年龄相称）
act or omission 作为或不作为
act recklessly 轻率行事
act to rescue 救援行为；紧急避险（行为）（旧译：紧急避难）；越狱行为
act *ultra vires* 滥用权力行为；作出违法的决定
act under coercion 强制执行，强迫（的）行为
act up to 遵照（原则等）办事；做（与自己声望相称的）事
act which is in fraud of the law 避法行为（指为了规避法律禁止的行为，而以其他的"合法行为"达到法律所禁止所做之事）
act with a commercial appearance 表见

商行为
act without compensation 无补偿行为
act without consideration 无偿行为；（英美法）无对价的行为
act without its material cause （大陆法）不要因行为
act without responsibility 无责任行为
act-of-state 国家行为（指一个国家行使主权的行为）
act-of-state doctrine （act of state doctrine） 国家行为理论，国家行为原则（指排除一个法院对已获承认之主权国家在其自己领域内作出国家行为的合法性进行审查的权力）
acta n. （罗马皇帝所制定的）法令（总称）；（古罗马）通报，公报（指公务记录及政治和社会事件的公报）
Acta Apostolicae sedis 《罗马教廷法集》（1909年开始发布）
Acta Diurna （或 *Acta Populi*; *Acta Publica*; *Simply Acta*） （罗马帝国的）《每日公告》（指将法院、人民议会、元老院每日进行的议事录、公众登记以及每日法令和大事等刊入的一种公告）
* *Acta exteriora indicant interiora secreta.* External acts indicate undisclosed thoughts. 人之外部行为反映其内心秘密。
acta publica 众所周知之事
acta senatus （=*commentarrii senatus*） （罗马帝国的）元老院议事录
acting a. 代理的，临时的
acting agent 临时代理人
acting as a guardian while not qualified 未取得监护人资格而行使监护人权利
acting complainant 原告代理人，代行告诉人
acting consul 代理领事
acting contrary to declaration 违反明文规定（或声明）的行为
acting crowd （具有敌意的）行动集结，结伙
acting in a certain way 以一定方式行事
acting in good faith 依诚信行事，依诚意行事

acting more out of conviction than principle 更多地超出原则判罪

acting prosecutor 代理检察官(员)

acting pursuant to statute 依法规行事

actio n. (罗马法)(大陆法)1.诉讼,诉权;权利或权利请求 2.(历史)普通法上的诉讼,复数为 actiones,事实上指某人在取得权利发生争议时,有权依据法律按诉讼程序提起诉讼,维护个人权利

actio ad exhibendum (罗马法)提呈财产诉讼,出示物品之诉[指要求或迫使被告向法庭出示某一财产以确定处于被告占有之诉讼。通常在原告提起返还所有物(rei vindicatio)之前进行]

actio ad supplendam legitimam 继承份补充的诉讼

actio arbitraria (罗马法)仲裁诉讼

actio bonae fidei 诚信诉讼

actio commodati contraria 借用人的诉权

actio commodati directa 出借人的诉权

actio confessoria 地役权保全的诉讼

actio contraria (罗马法)反诉(见 actio directa)

actio de dffuses et deiectis 倒泼与投掷之诉(指罗马法中因从建筑物中落下或投掷物品在公众场所造成对人损害而引起的诉讼)

actio de effusis vel de juctus 因自屋内向外投弃物件致人损害而引起的诉讼

actio de pauperie 因动物致人损害而引起的诉讼

actio de sepulchro violato 侵犯坟墓之诉[指经历史发展,该罗马法中的这一诉权后来针对故意侵犯坟墓(包括盗墓行为,在墓中居住、建造房屋等方式侵犯坟墓之人)]

actio depositis vel suspensi 因悬挂物件在街上致人损害而引起的诉讼

actio directa (罗马法)直接诉讼(与 actio contraria 相对而言)

actio doli (罗马法)欺诈之诉

actio empti 买物之诉,买主诉权

actio ex contratu 由合同(契约)所引起的诉讼

actio exercitoria 对船舶所有人的诉讼

actio furti (向盗窃者)追偿罚款的诉讼

actio hypothecaria (或 quasiserviana) 抵押诉权

actio in personam (1800年)(罗马法)1.对人诉讼、债权诉讼[指对人诉讼而非对物诉讼,因个人权利受到侵犯而要求获得补偿之诉,对人(债务人)判决具有约束力,即对其财产具有强制执行力,使债务人之财产偿还债务人所欠债务] 2.对自然人或法人提起的诉讼(该诉讼的被告为自然人或法人)。亦称 personal action (在罗马法与大陆法中); actio in personam; action personlis。复数为 actiones in personam; actiones personales

actio iniuria 不法之诉(指罗马法中的不法之诉,它和阿奎利亚法"Lex Aquilia"构成侵权法成为民法体系变化的一个阶段的代表,也是当今欧洲大陆法系侵权法两个最重要的来源)

actio injuriarum (罗马法)伤害诉讼;侵害诉讼;妨害权利诉讼(见 injuria)

actio legis Aquilliae (罗马法)阿奎利亚法诉讼(指对任何非法损害财产寻求补救的措施)

actio mandati 委托合同(契约)之诉

actio mixta 混合诉讼(指兼具物权和债权性质的诉讼)

actio negatoria (=negativa) 排除妨害所有权的诉讼;拒绝地役权的诉讼

Actio non facit reum, nisi mens sit rea. An act does not make one guilty, unless the intention is bad. 人的行为除非具有犯意,否则便不构成犯罪。

Actio paenalis in haeredem non datur, nisi forte ex damno. A penal action is not given against an heir, unless, indeed, such heir is benefited by the wrong. 违法行为不能用来追究违法人的继承人,除非其继承人确实是从该项违法行为中获取利益的。

actio per quod servitium amisit (英普通法)请求赔偿服务损失之诉

actio perpetua (罗马法)永久诉讼(指市民法上不受时间限制的诉讼)

Actio personalis moritur cum persona. A

personal right of action dies with the person. 对人身权之诉与当事人共存亡。
actio popularis 民众诉权(指我们把保护人民自己法的诉权叫作民众诉权)(*Eam Popularem actionem dicimus, quae ius populi tuetur*)
actio praejudicialis (*or praeiudicialis*) (罗马法)预备诉讼(指为主诉讼而进行的准备诉讼,主要用来审查是否具备主诉讼所要求的条件、身份或情形,如某人是否具有自由人的身份,诉讼所涉及的财产数量等,在经过预备诉讼对特定情况核实后,再提起主诉讼。复数为 *actiones praejudiciales*)
actio praescripits verbis 根据前书进行的诉讼;基于不成文法的诉讼(指基于习惯或法学家解答提起的诉讼);口头合同(契约)之诉(指根据口头合约所提起的诉讼)
actio pro socio 合伙案件之诉(指合伙之一方当事人为强制其合伙人执行合伙协议条款而提起的诉讼)
actio publiciana 因时效取得财产而提起的诉讼
* ***Actio quaelibet in sua via.*** Every action proceeds in its own course. 每宗诉讼都按其自身的程序进行。
actio quanti minoris (罗马法)(因标的物有瑕疵)减少价款之诉,轻度瑕疵索赔之诉
actio quod metus causa. 基于胁迫行为的诉讼
actio redhibiotoria 合同解除之诉
actio sacramento (古老的罗马法上的)誓金诉讼
actio spolii (寺院法)收回恃强占有物诉讼,索回非法取走财物之诉
actio stricti iuris 严法诉讼;(罗马法)法官重视严格法律规则的诉讼(与 *actio bonae fidei* 相对而言)
actio utilis (罗马法)授权诉讼,扩用诉讼
actio venditi (罗马法)基于销售(合同)的诉讼(指卖者通过诉讼可以获得对价和买卖合同中义务的履行)
actio vi bonorum raptorum (罗马法)返还被抢劫财产并要求惩罚之诉。成功的原告还可获得被抢劫财产三倍价值之罚金

action n. 诉讼,起诉权;行为,作为,行动,活动;作用(现今多指民事)诉讼
action against tortfeasors 对侵权者的诉讼
action agency 诉讼代办(所),经办诉讼(处)
action *arbitraria* (罗马法)公断诉讼、仲裁诉讼[指法官(index=judex)在诉讼中发布一项中间裁决令(interlocutory order)要求被告做某些事情(诸如归还财产给原告,被告如果违反则需向原告赔偿罚金),之所以叫公断诉讼,是因为法官在被告不履行中间裁决令的情况下可以确定(损害)赔偿的最高数额。复数为 *actiones; arbitrariae*]
action arising under the laws of the United States 根据美国法律提起的诉讼
action at common law 按普通法(审理)之诉(指按普通法而不以制定法、衡平法上的救济或大陆法为基础的诉讼)
action at law 普通法上的诉讼,法律诉讼[指起始于法定诉因(legal cause of action)的民事诉讼,并只是寻求法律救济(legal remedy)。见 suit at law 和 suit in equity]
Action *auten nihil laiud est, guam ius persequendi judicio quod sibi debetur*. 向法院主张自己应得之物的权利。
action based on contract 依合同(契约)之诉
action between husband and wife 夫妻之间的诉讼
action between parent and child 父母和子女之间的诉讼
action brought against the estate of a deceased owner 对于死者遗产的诉讼
action by infants for torts 未成年人所提出的侵权行为的诉讼
action by parent for abducting, enticing, or harboring child 父母对诱拐、不法诱惑或藏匿子女所起诉的诉讼
action by parent for injuries to child 父母对子女受伤害所起诉的诉讼
action by parent for seduction or debauching of daughter 父母对女儿被奸污或诱奸所起诉的诉讼
action *de in rem verso* 既得利益的诉权

action decided against sb. （判决）某人败诉
action decided in favo(u)r of sb. （判决）某人胜诉
action *depositi* （罗马法）（寄托人提起的）保管之诉（保管人须承担赔偿责任）
action en declaration de simulated （美）（路易斯安那州法律）无效合同诉讼（见 simulated contract）
action en rescission 撤销之诉
action *ex contractu* （美）（大陆法和普通法）依合同（契约）之诉，根据合同（契约）所提起的诉讼
action *ex delicto* 依侵权行为（或损害赔偿）之诉，根据侵权行为提起的诉讼
action *ex stipulatu* 强制执行要式口约的诉讼（见 stipulation 3）
action for（或 of）account 请求清算账目之诉
action for a declaratory judg(e)ment 确认之诉
action for alienation of affections 对（第三者）破坏夫妻关系所提起的诉讼
action for annulment of contract 申请宣告合同（契约）无效之诉
action for annulment of patent 撤销专利之诉
action for avoidance 撤销（案件）的诉讼
action for bad faith breach of contract 恶意违约之诉
action for breach of contract 违约之诉
action for cattle trespass 家畜侵扰土地之诉
action for collision 为（船舶）碰撞所提起的诉讼
action for consortium 主张配偶权利之诉
action for conversion 侵占动产之诉
action for criminal conversation 因通奸所提起的诉讼
action for damages 损害赔偿诉讼
action for debt 债务诉讼
action for deceit 因欺诈所提起的诉讼
action for declaratory judg(e)ment 确权之诉，确认判决之诉
action for dissolution of the partnership 解除合伙关系之诉
action for divorce 请求离婚之诉
action for exemption of property from attachment 请求免除财产扣押之诉
action for indemnity 请求损害赔偿之诉，要求赔款（尤指战败国的战争赔款）的诉讼
action for infringement of a patent 因侵犯专利权所提起的诉讼
action for libel 因诽谤所提起的诉讼
action for *mesne* profits 要求收回中间收益（指非法占有土地期间的收益）之诉
action for money had and received 返还已支付款项之诉，返还金钱之利之诉[指在普通法上，原告可以通过诉讼复得已支付给被告的款项，可以收回此款的两种原因为：此款因错误或因强迫而被支付或对价（consideration）是不充分的（insufficient）]
action for money paid 要求偿还已付款之诉[普通法上指原告要求被告偿付其为被告获得益处（defendant had benefited）已付出之款项的诉讼。要求偿还已付款之诉实际为挪用之诉（appropriate action），原告所主张的是已付之款不是给予被告人的而是给予第三人的，可被告从中已经受益。原告已表明由这笔款项支付是应被告之要求为他人之利益而支付的，所以"原告为了被告之受益并应其请求而已付出之款"要求偿还]
action for negligence 因过失所提起的诉讼
action for nuisance 因妨害所提起的诉讼，因公害所提起的诉讼
action for passing-off 假冒商品之诉；"仿冒"之诉
action for poinding 请求扣押之诉[指债权人要求扣押债务人的地租（land rents）和物品以清偿债务或执行财物扣押之诉]
action for re-trial 要求再审之诉
action for recourse 主张追索权之诉
action for reimbursement 申请赔偿之诉
action for restitution 请求返还原物之诉；请求恢复原状之诉
action for support 扶养之诉
action for the restitution of the conjugal

community 要求恢复夫妻同居之诉
action for trespass 因侵犯(土地等)行为所提起的诉讼(见 trespass)
action for unfair competition 不正当竞争之诉
action for wrongful arrest 因非法逮捕所提起的诉讼
action founded on torts 依侵权行为之诉
action in bankruptcy 破产诉讼
action in chief 主诉,本诉
action in equity (18世纪)衡平法上的诉讼[指为寻求衡平法上的救济,如禁制令、特定履行(special performance)而提起的诉讼,不同于普通法上的损害赔偿诉讼,现此种方式诉讼已不复存在。见 suit in equity]
action in *factum* (罗马法)事实诉讼(指当裁判官无标准适用时,所采取依据事实制定程序的诉讼。英美法与之相当的是 action on the case 或 trespass on the case)
action in *forma pauperis* 穷困者取得法律援助的诉讼
action in question 有争议的诉讼
action in *rem* (罗马法)对物诉讼,物诉讼(指当事人确定某项财产的所有权和当事人对该财产之权的一项诉讼。不仅对当事人有效,而且在任何时候对该财产的权益主张人有效。美国路易斯安那州法,指主张收回不动产的被占有的诉讼。另亦为保护物权的占有人,所有人或其他的在不动产中物权所有人而提起的诉讼。亦称 *actio in rem*, *actio realis*)
action in tort 侵权之诉(指因侵权行为而提起的诉讼)
action of account 账目诉讼
action of accounting 账目核查之诉
action of assumpsit 要求赔偿违约所造成损失之诉(旧译:担当之诉),违约诉讼
action of conversion (英国法)侵占之诉(指拍卖人的拍卖物品被同行夺去拍卖,拍卖人虽无所有权,只有暂时的占用权,但可对同行的侵占行为提起诉讼,追索此项物品)
action of covenant 违反合同(契约)之诉
action of damages arising from ship 船舶碰撞所致损害赔偿之诉
action of debt 见 *condictio*
action of detinue (要求)收回被非法占用动产之诉
action of ejectment (要求)收回不动产之诉
action of (the) first impression 新诉(指无先例的诉讼)
action of malicious prosecution 诬告的行为;对诬告所提起的诉讼
action of *mandamus* 请求法院命令被告履行义务之诉;请求法院发给强制执行令
action of nullity 要求宣告(合同或婚姻)无效之诉
action of passing off 假冒之诉(指任何人以不实之事实,使公众误信其营业或商品而为他人营业或商品的行为时,他人有权提起之诉)
action of performance (要求)履行的诉讼,给付之诉
action of prestation 给付之诉
action of re-exchange (执票人因汇票在国外被拒绝承兑而遭受损失向发票人、背书人提出的)请求赔偿之诉
action of real right 产权诉讼,物权诉讼
action of recourse 行使追索权之诉
action of reduction 减除之诉
action of subrogation 主张代位权之诉(指第三人取代债权人的地位向债务人提起的诉讼)
action of trespass 非法侵入之诉
action of (或 in, 或 for) trover (要求)追索侵占物之诉,请求追索非法占用之诉
action on a contract 因合同引起的诉讼
action on an oral contract 口头合同诉讼,口头合同之诉(=parol contract, verbal contract)
action on decision (AOD) 有关判决的法律备忘录[指一个法律备忘录(legal memorandum)是来自美国国内税务署(Internal Revenue Service)民事诉讼部(Litigation division)的首席法律顾问(chief counsel),内容涵盖咨询建议有关税务署是否应保持默许、上诉或采取其他行为来对待不利于税务署的法院判决]

action on the case （英）类案诉讼，案情写在令状上之诉，依既定判例之诉，依照先例的诉讼

action orientation （美）诉讼导向（纽约州常用的一种方法，让法庭在整体上将诉讼定性为具有"普通法"或"衡平法"性质进而又在此基础上判定该诉讼是否可获得陪审团审判的权利）

action *publiciana* （罗马法）因时效取得财产而提起的诉讼，返还丢失物之诉，普布利奇安诉权（指某人因诚信取得对一物的占有，在取得时效进行但未完成的期间第三人攫取了对此物之占有，使"某人"的取得时效不能完成，从而使第三人的取得时效开始，其结果当然对诚信占有人不公，因为他拥有对标的物的准所有权或形成中的所有权，保护他的此项权利有利于维护和平的诚信。于是普布利奇安裁判官发布告示，授予诚信占有人恢复占有的诉权，此等诉权亦称为 actio publiciana）

action *rem* 1.见 action in rem 2.见 real action

action to abate an interference with the right of ownership 排除所有权上的权利侵犯之诉

action to enforce judg(e)ments 申请强制执行判决的诉讼

action to quiet title 判决产权归属之诉（不同于 suit to remove a cloud）确权之诉；确认地产权诉讼

*****(The) action will not lie.** 此项起诉不能成立。

actionable a. 可予以起诉的，可引起控诉的(指可就某种行为提起诉讼)

actionable claim 可起诉的请求权，可予起诉的索赔

actionable fraud 可起诉的欺诈(行为)

actionable libel 可起诉的诽谤(行为)

actionable negligence 可起诉的过失(行为)

actionable nuisance 可起诉的妨害(行为)，可起诉的公害(行为)

actionable *per se* （属诽谤词语）自身可诉，行为"自身可诉"（英美侵权法中别具特色的术语。行为自身可诉侵权系指原告或受害人只须向法院证明被告实施了相关侵权行为，而无须进一步证明自己因被告行为所遭受的损害，即可要求被告承担侵权责任的侵权行为类型。此词属内在的中伤和本质性的侮辱。不同于语言诽谤，可起诉的当然诽谤无须证明遭受特殊损害作为构成诽谤的要件。见 *per se*）

actionable torts 可予起诉的侵权行为

actionable words 可起诉的言论(罪)

actionable wrongdoing 可起诉的损害行为，可起诉的违法行为

actiones 诉讼(法)

actiones adjuctici qualitatis 附带债务之诉

actiones commodati 借贷之诉

actiones commodati directa 直接借贷诉讼

actiones legis （罗马法）合法行为；法律诉讼；法律行为

actions civil 民事诉讼

actions of legislation majorities 立法多数派的行为

actions penal 刑事诉讼

actions real 物权诉讼，对物诉讼

active a. 现行的，现役的；实际的；主动的；积极的；活动的；自动的；有意的

active agency 自动代理

active assets 流动资产

active balance 顺差

active breach of contract （大陆法）积极违约，积极违反合同[指对合同债务，就合同术语之外的行动意义(point of acting)讲，完全疏忽履行(negligent performance)。依据1984年以前美国路易斯安那州法，积极违约与消极违约(passive breach of contract)形成对比，它指不履行依照合同产生的义务。与消极违约不同，积极违约可以引起根据合同的请求权(claim in contract)，但二者的区别已于1984年被摒弃。见 passive breach of contract]

active capital 流动资本

active citizens 积极公民

active concealment 故意隐匿，故意隐瞒

active contact 主动联系

active counter revolutionary （中）现行反革命分子

active credit 流动债权

active crime 现行犯罪；主要罪行

active debt 有息债款;流动债务
active duty 现役
active express trust 积极的(或自动的)明示信托
active military service 现役
active misrepresentation 有意的虚伪陈述
active negligence 有意的过失,(狭义)故意过失
active participant 积极参与者
active partner 执行业务的合伙人
active right 积极权利
active sabotage 现行破坏活动
active service 现役
active supervision (反垄断法)实际监督,积极监督[指根据私方实体可以权利请求州的行为(state action)以获得反垄断法的豁免准则。见 Midcal test]
active tortfeasor 故意的(民事)侵害人
active trust 自动信托
active trustee 自动信托受托人
active waste 人为的毁损(见 waste)
activism n. 激进主义,能动主义,(主张为政治目的采取有力行动)行动主义;活跃,积极
activities *jure imperii* 争(统治)权活动
activities of production 生产活动
activities relating to civil law 民事活动
activity n. (16 世纪)1.活动,作业,集体作业行为(指二人以上或更多人从事共同事业的集体行为或集体活动)2.作业,能动性,活跃 3.市场证券或股票交易量(见 market volume)
activity in investment 积极投资
activity in market 市场活动
activity in production 生产活动
activity level 作业水平,活动水平
activity list 工作表
actor n. 1.原告 2.行为者(人)3.演员,艺人
Actor(或 Act)and Part (苏格兰刑法)同谋犯和参与犯

* *Actor sequitur forum rei.* The plaintiff follows the forum of the property in suit, or the forum of the defendant's residence. 原告应向系争财产所在地或被告住所地的管辖法院提起诉讼。

* *Actore non probante reus absolvitur.* When the plaintiff does not prove his case the defendant is acquitted (or absolved). 只要原告对其诉案不举证,被告即可获得宣判无罪(或开脱)。

* *Actori incumbit onus probandi.* The burden of proof rests on the plaintiff (or on the party who advances a proposition affirmatively). 举证的责任归原告(或归肯定地提出事实主张的一方当事人)。

actrix n. 女性原告
Acts of state-sponsored terrorism 国家支持的恐怖主义行为
act-SW framework 行动—相对处境的框架
actual a. 实际的,现实的,事实上的
actual authority 1.(18 世纪)实际代理权,事实上的授权 2.实际权力[指被代理人(principal)有意授予代理人的权力,或代理人有理由相信其已具有与被代理人交易的成果。这种实际权力既可明示亦可默示授予代理人。亦称 real authority]
actual bias 实质偏见
actual bodily harm 实际身体伤害
actual budget 决算
actual business practice 商业现实
actual capacity to repay 实际偿还能力
actual capital 实际资本
actual carrier 实际承运人
actual case 具体案件
actual cash value 实际现金价值;现值
actual causes 实际诉案
actual change of possession 占有(权)事实上的改变
actual compensation 实际损失的完全赔偿(full compensation)
actual conditions 实际情况,具体条件
actual consent 实际同意
actual content of the law 法律的具体内容,该法的实际内容
actual contractor 实际立约人,实际合同(契约)签订人
actual costs 实际成本
actual court practices 实际法院的常规(或惯例)

actual damage　实际损害
actual damages　应予的赔偿损失(与 compensatory damages 同)
actual danger　实际危险
actual debts　实际债务
actual delivery　实际让渡,实际交付
actual discharge　实际清偿;实际负担
actual dishono(u)r　实际拒付,实际拒绝承兑
actual effect in the forum　在法院地产生实际效果原则
actual entry　(对房屋、土地的)实际侵入
actual escape　见 escape ②
actual existence of the right　权利确实存在;现有权利
actual fault　实际过失
actual fraud　实际欺诈,直接欺诈
actual harm　实际伤害
actual holder　实际占有人;事实上的占有人
actual intent　直接故意
actual judg(e)ment　实质性判决(指对争议事实所作的判决)
actual knowledge　(16世纪)实际知道 [①指直接、清楚知道某件事的事实状况,与推定知道(constructive knowledge)相对〈the employee, having witnessed the accident, had actual knowledge of the worker's injury〉(因为这个职工目睹意外车祸的发生,他已知道工人受了伤害),亦称 express actual knowledge。②知晓(某种)信息,指这种信息和情况会导致一个理智的人(reasonable person)对事实作进一步的探究〈under the discovery rule, the limitations period begins to run once the plaintiff has actual knowledge of the injury〉(根据开示规则,时效期限开始适用于原告已知伤害的情况)。在②的意义上,亦称 implied actual knowledge。③帮助侵权人实际认识到直接侵权行为的发生,且这种直接侵权行为是特定和具体的]
actual law　实在法
actual liability　实际负债;现时义务
actual loss　实际损失
actual malice　实际恶意(指有外来证据证明有实施伤害的故意。由对诽谤和失实起诉的公职人员或公共人物承担的一种证明责任。要求他们以明确令人信服的证明行为证明被告虚假或无视事实真相而发表诽谤性言论。要证实实际恶意,需要证明一系列相关因素,包括依据来源的可靠,在有怀疑其准确性的实质理由时未查明事实真相等。又称 express malice, malice in fact)
actual military service　服现役
actual navigable water　现实可航行水域,实际可航行水域
actual neutrality　实际中立
actual notice　现实通告,实际通知
actual occupation　事实上占有,实际占有
actual occupier　实际占有人
actual parties　实际当事人
actual performance　实际履行
actual population　实际人口
actual possession　实际占有,事实上的占有
actual prejudice　实际损害(或侵害);实际偏见
actual presence　实际在场
actual protection　实际保护
actual refreshment of memory　记忆实际上的恢复
actual reliance　实际信赖
actual requirement　实际需要,现实要求
actual residence　目前住所;实际住所;居所
actual seizin　实际上的(土地)占有
actual service　实际送达;直接送达
actual significance　重大意义
actual taking　事实上的取得
actual total lose　实际全损
actual total loss　(海上保险的)实际全损
actual transfer of possession　实际移转占有(权)
actual user　实际使用者
actual value　实际价值,实际价格
actual violence　实际暴力,确实的暴行
actuality n.　现实性,(复)现状
actually behave in a certain way　实际上以某种方式行为
actuarial a.　保险统计的;由保险统计员计

算出来的
actuarial cost 精算费用;保险成本
actuarial evidence 保险证明
actuarial method 保险计算方法
actuarial report 保险率计算报告
actuarial science 保险计算学
actuarial value 保险统计价值
actuary n. (保险)统计师,(保险)统计员,精算员,保险费审计师;保险清算所
actus n. (大陆法)诉讼,行为;(英史)法案;兽车通行权

Actus curiae (or legis) neminem gravabit.
An act of the court shall prejudice no man. An act of the court shall hurt no man. 法院的行为不得损害任何人。

Actus dei neminem gravabit (or nemini nocet). An act of God prejudice no man. The Law holds no man responsible for the act of God. 不可抗力不损害任何人(指任何人本身无过错而可归因于不可抗力的意外事件不承担任何责任或因此受损)。

Actus inceptus, cujus perfectio pendet ex voluntate partium, revocari potest; si autem pendet ex voluntate tertiae personae, vel ex contingenti, revocari non potest.
An act already begun, the completion of which depends on the will of the parties, may be revoked; but if it depend on the will of a third person, or on a contingency, it cannot be revoked. 依双方当事人的意图所实施的(法律)行为,虽然已开始,还可撤回;而依第三者意图或依某意外事件而实施的(法律)行为则不能撤回。

actus injuria 侵害行为,不法行为,侵权行为

Actus judiciarius coram non judice irritus habetur, de ministeriali autem a quocunque provenit ratum esto. A judicial act by a judge without jurisdiction is void; but a ministerial act, from whomsoever proceeding, may be ratified. 一项由无司法管辖权的法官所做的司法行为是无效的;但一项行政行为,不管是由谁进行的,都是可予认可的。

actus legitimus 合法行为

Actus me invito factus non est meus actus.
An act done by me, against my will, is not my act. 本人所做的行为,如果违反本人的意愿,就不是本人的行为。

Actus non facit reum, nisi mens sit rea.
An act does not make (the doer of it) guilty; unless the mind be guilty; unless the intention be criminal. 没有犯罪意图或犯意的行为就不能(使行为人)构成犯罪。

actus reus 犯意,具有犯罪意图的行为;被告的行为

acuerdo n. (西班牙)法院判决;委员会的决定

Acuerdo de Cartagena Countries 西班牙港市卡塔赫纳地区法院判决

acute a. 尖锐的,敏锐的,急性的
acute poisoning 急性中毒
acute stress disorder 急性应激障碍[以急剧、严重的精神打击作为直接原因,受刺激后立即(1小时内)发病,表现为强烈恐惧体验的精神性兴奋,行为有一定的盲目性,或为精神性运动抑制,如应激源被消除,症状往往历时短暂,即可缓解。这类障碍中的急性应激反应在民事索赔类案件中常见。从伤害程度看多为轻微伤害,结合责任方和受害方过错大小可获得抚慰性的精神损害赔偿]

ad v. 到,达;根据
ad abundantiorem cautelam 为了给予特别注意,为了更加谨慎
ad aemulationem 斗争行为,争斗行为
ad arbitrium 随意地,独断地,任意,随心所欲
ad audiendum et determinandum 听审后判决,听而后决
ad colligenda bona 收集财产(或货物)
ad colligendum bona defuncti 收集死者的财物(遗产)
ad damnum 赔偿损失(诉状中原告提出的金钱损失和请求的损害赔偿的用语)
ad diem 在指定日期

Ad ea quae frequentius accidunt jura ad aptantur. Laws are adapted to those cases which most commonly occur. 法律应适应那些最常出现的情况。

ad factum praestandum　（苏格兰）义务履行,实际履行

ad finem ad.　到最后、在最后、最后、最终,这也是指引符号,缩略为 *ad fin*,以前只是表示关系到某节的第一页,但现在则通常告知读者处于最近页次的状态(to a stated span of pages)

ad hoc　特别,特定;临时;特设;由于,考虑到

ad hoc appointment　临时任命,特别任命

ad hoc arbitration　特别仲裁,专项仲裁

ad hoc assignment　临时任务,特别任务,专门委派,临时委派

ad hoc committee　特别(设)委员会,专门委员会;临时委员会

Ad hoc Committee of Jurists　法学家特别委员会

ad hoc court　特别法庭,专门法庭

ad hoc diplomacy　特别外交

ad hoc election　特别选举

ad hoc judge　专案法官;特设法官,临时法官

ad hoc judgment　临时或特定的判决

Ad hoc Political Committee　（联合国）特别政治委员会

ad hoc public officials　特殊(目的之)公务人员;临时公务员

ad hoc representative　临时代表,特别代表

ad hoc request　特别要求

ad hoc rule　特别规则

ad hoc task　特殊任务

ad hoc tribunals　特别(临时)审判庭

ad hoc trust for sale　特别买卖信托

ad hominem　仅从个人偏见出发,以偏见代替说理

Ad idem(at the same point)　意见一致(经常用于表示谈判双方已达成协议,彼此间已确立具有约束力的契约关系的一个短语)

ad infinitum　无限,永远

ad instantian partis　经一方要求

ad interim　临时的,暂时的,过渡的

ad libitum　随意,任意

ad litem　诉讼的,为了诉讼(目的),诉讼进行中;特定诉讼建议

ad medium filum viae（或 *aquae*）　道路(或河流)的中间线(指对道路或河流划界时,通常以道路或河流的中心线作为分界线)

ad melius inquirendum　复验尸体令

* *Ad officium justiciariorum spectat, unicuique coram eis placitanti justitiam exhibere.*　It is the duty of justices to administer justice to every one pleading before them. 为每一个前来诉讼的人主持公道(执法)是法官的职责。

ad opus　工作权,用益权,作用权

* *Ad quaestionem facti non respondent judices; ad quaestionem juris non respondent juratores.*　Judges do not answer questions of fact; juries do not answer questions of law. 法官不负责事实问题;陪审员不负责法律问题。

ad quod damnum　关于什么样的损失(英国的衡平法院在令状中指令司法行政官查询有什么样的损失的用语)

ad rectum　被控诉,应诉;作法律要求的答辩

ad referendum　尚待核准,待进一步审议

ad referendum contract　草约,草签合同(契约)

ad rem　中肯、贴切;得要领;适宜地

ad respondendum　答辩;辩诉

ad sectam　由于……诉讼,在……诉案中

ad sectam Jones　琼斯为原告

ad summam　总括来说,总之

ad testificandum　作证,提供证言

ad tune et ibidem　Then and there being found　(此术语常用于公诉书),当时当场(发现)(诉状中一项陈述诉由条款之名称)

ad unum　直到最后一个

ad usum　按照习惯,依照惯例

ad valorem　从价,照价;按值

ad valorem bill of lading　货值提单

ad valorem deposit　按值交保证金

ad valorem duty　按值征税;从价税

ad valorem freight　从价运费

ad valorem import duty　从价进口税

ad valorem method　从价(方)法

ad valorem property taxes　从价财产税(指依价值征收的财产税)

ad valorem tax　（1810 年）（美）从价税[指一些应税财产,尤其是不动产的估定价值,按一定比例所课之税,与从税量(on

its quantity)或某种其他估量相对]
ad valorem taxation 从价征税
ad verbum 逐字地
ad vitam aut culpam 只要一息尚存;只要不犯错误
adamant a. 坚硬的,坚强不屈的
adapt v. 使适应,使适合;适应(to);改编,改写
adaptability n. 适应性
adaptation n. 适合,适应;修改;改制物,改编本;调整
adaptation of a program 程序的改编(或改写)
adaptation of a work 作品的改编
adaption of laws 法律的适应性
adaptive efficient 适应性效率
adarism n. 裸体主义;裸体者
Adat law 亚达德法[亦译作传统法。指马来西亚和印度尼西亚土著居民中的习惯法,后含有早期伊斯兰教法的主要部分]
add v. 增加,添加
added damages 附加损失赔偿(指以示惩戒的损失赔偿);惩罚性损害赔偿(有时亦称 smart money 赔偿金)
added substance 添加物质,添加成分;添加剂
added value 增值
addendum n. 补遗,附件,附录;附加物
addict n./v. 吸毒成瘾者/使吸毒成瘾,使有嗜好
addicted a. 有嗜好的,使成瘾的,上瘾的;惯于的
addicted to drugs 吸毒成癖
addicted to wine 嗜好喝酒
addictio in diem 日后准予解除合同(契约)的附约
addiction n. 吸毒成瘾;沉溺
addiction to drugs 毒瘾
addictiveness n. 沉溺;使成瘾;上瘾
adding mortgage 增加抵押
additament n. 附加物
addition n. 1.增加,追加;附加(物) 2.(加在姓名后的)头衔,称号 3.附录,增补,补充,附件
additional activity 进一步活动

addition of actions 追加诉讼
addition to budget 追加预算
additional a. 附加的,追加的;另外的,补充的
additional allegation 额外主张
additional arbitrator 补充仲裁人;追加仲裁人
additional articles 附加条款,增订条款
additional assessment 追加课税(额)
additional ballot 再决投票
additional brief 追加的诉讼要点
additional budget 追加预算
additional budget allocation for education 教育事业的追加预算
additional cargo 加载货
additional charge 附加费用
additional claim(s) 增加的诉讼请求,增加的请求;补赔,追加索赔
additional condition(s) 附加条件
additional consideration 补偿,额外报酬
additional cost 额外费用
additional discovery 补充披露,补充出示
additional district court 区附属法院,区法院分院
additional duty 附加税,追加关税
additional duty allowance 附加工作津贴
additional insurance 补充保险,加保
additional insured (保单中指名的)附加被保险人
additional interpretation problems 额外的解释问题
additional investment 追加投资,额外投资
additional judge 增补法官
additional judg(e)ment 追加判决;附加判决
additional juror 额外(或补充)陪审员
additional laws 补充法规
additional legacy 附加遗赠,追加遗赠[指按同一遗嘱给予遗产继承人第二次遗赠(a second legacy)或根据同一遗嘱的附加修改书"*codicil*"追加的遗赠。附加遗赠或追加遗赠是对上一遗赠的补充,而非同一遗赠的重复表示。亦称 accumulative legacy; cumulative legacy]
additional litigation 额外诉讼,增加的

诉讼
additional part of a bill 期票附件
additional party 追加当事人,附加当事人,额外当事人
additional payment 额外付款
additional pleading 追加性诉辩
additional premium 附加保险费,增加保险费
additional privilege 附加特权
additional protocol 附加议定书
additional provision(s) 附加条款
additional provisions on export subsidies 对出口补贴的附加规定
additional remedial problems 额外的补偿问题
additional rent 额外租金
additional requirement established by state law (美)州法所规定的另外要求
additional right 额外权利
additional savings (美)救助方式(指民事诉讼中由于裁决被上诉或被推翻而发生的救助方式)
additional sentence of preventive detention 预防性拘留的附加判决
additional statement of reasoning 追加理由书
additional tax 附加税
additur n. (审理法院)确定损害赔偿金(或增加因陪审团所作不适当裁决的金额)的权利;增加损害赔偿金(指美初审法院经被告同意签发的一种命令,以免赔偿不足而重新审判)
addled parliament 腐败议会(指英国由詹姆斯一世于1614年4月5日召开的旨在集款的议会)
address n./v. 1.地址 2.演说,讲话 3.谈话,风度 4.(大写)(英)(议会两院对女王开幕词的)致答词 5.委托 6.质问/提出(理由、请愿、抗议等)(to)
address commission 租船、代理佣金,委托佣金
address for service (令状,传票的)送达地址
address in mitigation 请求减刑
address to Parliament 致议会的请愿书

addressee n. 收件人;收信人
addressing inquiries 质询,质问
addressor n. 发件人;发信人;发言人;署名人
adduce v. 援引,引证;提出(理由、证据等);引出
adduce evidence 提出(提供)证据;引用证言
adducible a. 可援引的,可引证的
adduction n. 援引,引证
adduction of new facts or proof 提出新事实或新证据
adeem v. 收回遗赠;废止,撤销
adeem a bequest 撤销遗赠
ademption n. 收回遗赠(指通过遗嘱人生前行为收回一部或全部遗赠),废止,撤销遗赠;取走
ademption by extinction 废除遗赠(或赠与),遗赠(或赠与)的收回
ademption of a devise 收回(不动产)遗赠(见devise)
ademption of a gift 收回赠与
ademption of a legacy (或bequest) 收回(动产)遗赠
adequate a. 胜任的;适当的;充分的,足够的
adequate care 充分注意(见reasonable care)
adequate cause 充分理由
adequate consideration (英美法)适当的对价;适当补偿
adequate measure(s) 适当措施
adequate notice 充分的通知,适当的通知(亦称due notice)
adequate provocation 过分激怒(常用于杀人及伤害案件之辩护理由,意在说明杀害动机)
adequate reason 适当理由
adequate remedy 足够补偿,足额补偿;适当的法律救济
adequate state court case reporting systems 适当的州法院判例汇编制度,适当州法院判例报告制
adessee v. 出庭(与 abesse 相对)
adeu ad. 不定期,无限期(休会等)
adhere v. 依附,追随(to),坚持(to)

(to) adhere to principle 坚持原则
adherence n. 1.依附,追随 2.坚持,忠于,信守 3.同意加入条约(指经原来条约各方同意接受第三国加入条约) 4.(苏格兰)配偶相互忠诚的义务
adherence to a contract 信守合同(契约)
adherence to the principle of the constitution 忠于宪法的原则;坚持宪法的原则
adherent n./a. 追随者,信徒;拥护者/附着的,追随的
adhering motion 附议
adhesion n. 1.参加,加附 2.支持 3.(国际法)部分参加(指条约国仅加入条约的某一部分或某项原则)
adhesion contract 附意合同(契约)(旧译:定式合同,附和合同等;又称"订不订由你的合同"。见 take-it-or-leave-it 和 contract of adhesion,指一方须依附对方意思表示的合同)
adipocere formation 尸蜡,尸蜡的形成
adipocere wax 尸蜡
aditio hereditatis (罗马法)接受遗产
adjacent n./a. 助手;附属品(to)/邻接的,相邻的,毗连的
adjacent area 邻接区,毗连区
adjacent sea 毗连海,邻海;边缘海
adjacent states 毗邻国家
adjacent waters 毗连水域
adjective a. 有关程序的;从属的;辅助的
adjective law 程序法(与 subject law 相对而言。边沁创造的类名词,表示不同于实体法。程序法的对象不是人们的权利和义务,而是用来申明、证实或强制实现这些权利义务的手段或保证它们遭到侵害时能得到补偿。程序法的内容包括各法院管辖范围、审判程序、诉讼的提起和审理、证据、上诉、判决的执行代替和法律援助、诉讼费用、文件的交付登记以及行政请求的程序等原则和制度)(亦称 adjectival law)
adjectus solutionis gratia 破产债务分配受领人
adjoining landowner 毗连土地所有人
adjoining owner 相邻(土地、房屋的)所有者(人);相邻业主
adjoining tenement 相邻住宅;相邻地产
adjourn v. 中止;休会;休庭;延期(审讯)
adjourn a case 延期审理案件
adjourn for a session of the court 延缓开庭
adjourn *sine die* 无限期休庭;不定期休庭
adjourn the court 休庭
adjourn the trial of the case 延期审理案件
adjourned a. 延期的
adjourned hearing 延期的审讯
adjourned session 延期的开庭
adjourned summons 延期(发出的)传票
adjournment n. 休庭;休会;延期;押后(指法庭暂时停止听审,同时可以指定或不指定下次审讯日期)
adjournment day 休庭日
adjournment day in error 复审休庭日
adjournment in eyre 巡回法庭休庭
adjournment motion (议会)休会动议
adjournment of hearing 审讯延期
adjournment of inquiry 讯问押后
adjournment of trial 审判延期
adjournment *sine die* 无限期休庭;不定期休庭
adjudge v. 宣判;依法判处,(对有争议的问题在法庭上作出)裁决;判给
adjudge sb. (to be) guilty 裁决某人有罪
adjudge sb. to death 判处某人死刑
adjudged a. 判决的,裁决的
adjudged bankrupt 被判决的破产人
adjudgement n. 依法判决,裁决,判定,定罪
adjudicate v. 判决,宣判;裁决,宣判,审断
adjudicate according to law 依法裁决
adjudicate in a case 判决案件,断案
adjudicate on a matter 判定某事件(实);审断案件
adjudicate sb. guilty 宣布裁决某人有罪
adjudicated in one's favo(u)r 宣判某人胜诉
adjudicated lunatic 因精神病而被宣告为无行为能力的人(旧译:禁治产者)
adjudicating officer 裁判官
adjudicatio n. 分割共有物裁判

adjudication n. 1.宣布裁决(或法令),审断裁决(指由法庭作出或宣告一个判决或命令,也指判决本身)2.判决,判案,裁定 3.破产宣告,宣告
adjudication division 宣判庭,审判庭
adjudication fee 法庭费用
adjudication in the inquisition of lunacy 对精神错乱(心神丧失)的事实审问的裁定
adjudication of bankruptcy 宣告破产
adjudication of death 宣告死亡
adjudication of disappearance 宣告失踪
adjudication of justice 依法裁决
adjudication of parameters of the constitution division 宪法的分权参项裁定
adjudication order 裁决令,判决令
adjudication rule 审判规则
adjudication supervision 审判监督
adjudication under law 依法裁决
adjudicative a. 判决的;审判的;裁决的
adjudicative facts 裁决的事实
adjudicative principle 裁判原则
adjudicator n. 审判者,判决者,裁决者;公断人,仲裁人
adjudicatory authority 审判权
adjudicatory procedure 裁决性程序
adjunct medical examiner 兼职法医
adjunct professor (美)副教授
adjuration n. 誓约;宣誓,立誓;恳求,祈求
adjust v. 整顿,调整;调节;适用于(to);(保险业中)评定(赔偿要求);(海损)理算;核准,校正(误差等)
adjusted basis (1932年)调整后的基准(是美国联邦所得税使用的计税基准,即对纳税人财产投资的价值予以调整,按其改良增值或折旧减值之后的数额作为基准)
adjusted figures 调整后数字
adjusted gross income 调整后的总收入
adjuster n. 调停人;调解处理人;评定人;(海损)理算人
adjustment n. 1.调整,理算,海损理算 2.调处;调解 3.配合,适应
adjustment of average 海损理算
adjustment of loss 海损损失理算
adjustment of pleading 诉辩调整
adjustment of property relationships 调整财产关系
adjustment of purchase price 调整卖价;降低卖价
adjustment securities 调节证券(指一个公司重新改组时所发行的股票和其他证券)
adjustment tax 调节税
admeasure v. 分配,赋予;测量,量度
Adminalty and Maritine law 海事与海商法[美国联邦宪法第3条(the Article Ⅲ)第2款赋予联邦法院审理"一切有关海事法和海商管辖权的案件"。之所以如此,是因为国际和州际航运对美国至关重要。有序地解决航运方面的国家利益都超过地方利益]
adminicle n. (大陆法)副证;补充性证明(或证据);辅助,辅助物
adminicular evidence 副证,补充证据;辅助证据
adminiculate v. 以副证支持
administer (= administrate) v. 1.管理,掌管,管制,支配 2.执行,施行,实施 3.管理遗产 4.提出,使(某)人宣誓 5.给予
administer an oath to sb. 使某人宣誓
administer justice 执法;主持公道;行使审判权;行使审判职能
administer the law 执法
administer the rules of the combat 提出辩论的规则
administer upon an estate 管理遗产
administered prices 有管理的价格(指公营或私营大小企业在自由市场上按自身意志在他们自己所确定的时间内定出的价格。此价格一经确定,在"短期"内不随供需而波动)
administering n. 管理;执行;实施
administering authority 管理当局,行政主管机关
administering justice 司法
administering legal rules 实施法律规则
administering of property (受托的)财产管理(旧译:治产)
administering the judicial business 管理司法业务

administers of an estate 遗产管理人

administration n. 管理,经营,遗产管理;(美)政府;行政,行政管理,行政机关,局,署,处;执行,(大写)实施总统制国家的政府;行政官员或机关的任期;给予;(药的)服法,用途

administration act 遗产管理法

administration action 遗产管理诉讼,产业诉讼

administration bill 政府议(法)案,行政性议案

administration bond 遗产管理人的管理保证书;财产管理保证金

administration budget 行政预算

administration de bonis non 后任遗产管理(指对前任遗产执行人或遗产管理人尚未管理之遗产进行管理)(亦称 de bonis non administratis)

Administration Management Society 行政管理学会

administration matter 遗产管理诉讼案件;遗产管理事项

administration of assets 财产管理

administration of civil justice 民事司法行政,民事司法审判

administration of court 法院的司法行政,法院的执法

administration of estate 遗产管理,财产管理

Administration of Estates Act (英)《管理遗产法》

administration of evidence 审查证据

administration of federal courts 联邦法院的管理[19世纪的联邦最高法院通过其规则制定权和联邦最高法院大法官对地方法院的巡视对泛司法系统的行政管理进行监督。对于分散的、实际处于自治状态的各个联邦法院的集中监督则由国会授权财政、内政、司法等部来行使。1922年在塔夫特(Taft, William Howard)出任首席大法官期间,泛司法系统的管理则由国会授权设立资深巡回法官会议(the Conference Senior Circuit Judges,即美国司法会议 Judicial Conference of the United States)承担。1939年,一部设立由该会议资助并监督的美国行政管理办公室的法律在很大程度上妨碍并阻断了联邦最高法院和司法部门对低级别法院的直接行政管理。20世纪80—90年代美国法院行政管理办公室对低级别法院管理具有集中化的功能,而司法会议为适应行政管理和治理职能而进行重组。1939年的法律还创建了巡回委员会(Circuit Council),并赋予其发布改进地区行政管理的命令权。1990年以后,它还可对法官的不当行为进行先期调查,进行约束,或在严重情况下,提交司法会议,以便对其采取行动,甚至建议众议院对其进行弹劾。美国联邦最高法院在整个历史上对于管理联邦法院系统起到了重要作用。这一角色使联邦最高法院在立法、裁判和行政管理方面发挥重要作用]

administration of foreign affairs 外交事务行政

administration of internal affairs 国内事务管理(旧译:内务行政,但与我国内务或民政管理有别)

administration of justice 执法,司法,司法行政(机关和部门),执法机关;处罚,处刑,法律裁判;维护正义,司法审判

administration of justice act 司法工作条例;司法行政法

administration of law 司法,执法;法律的实施

administration of own finance 自有财务管理

administration of punitive justice 实施因果报应

Administration on Aging (美)老年管理局(指美国卫生健康及公共服务部的一个机构,通常与政府机构合作改善老年人的幸福生活,为老年人提供各种服务和关怀)

administration position on secession (美)脱离母国的行政职务(美国在反殖民统治后的统一阶段时专设的职务,主管那些想要脱离统一政策的州势力),分管脱离母国的行政职务

administration of quantitative restrictions 实施数量限制

Administration of State-owned Assets 国有资产管理局

administration of territory 领土管理
administration of trade regulations 贸易规定的实施
administration of trademark 商标管理
administration of wife's estate 妻子财产的管理
administration order 行政命令;遗产管理令
administration reconsideration 行政复议
administration suit 遗产管理诉讼(案)
administration with the will annexed 依遗嘱的遗产管理
administrative a. 行政的;管理的;遗产管理的
administrative absolutism 行政专制主义
administrative act 管理行为;执行行为
administrative action 行政诉讼;行政行为(活动)
administrative activities 行政活动,行政职能
administrative adjudication 行政裁决
administrative affairs 行政事务
administrative agency (美)指行政单位,行政部门[其一切活动必须遵照法规,其所签订的合同、誓约要受到司法审查(judicial review)]
administrative and procedural rules 管理规则和程序规则
administrative appeal 行政申诉
administrative area 行政区域
administrative assistant to chief justice (美)首席大法官的行政助理(联邦最高法院于1972年增设的行政官,主要协助办理首席大法官的非司法行政事务,该官职由国会授权任命)
administrative attachment 行政拘留
administrative audit 行政审核(计)
administrative authority 行政管理部门,管理机关
administrative authority for industry and commerce 工商行政管理部门
administrative authority for patent affairs 专利(事务)管理机关
administrative authorization 行政机关的许可(授权)
administrative autonomy 行政上的自主权
administrative board 行政委员会;理事会

administrative budget 行政预算
Administrative Bureau for Industry and Commerce (中)工商行政管理局
administrative business 行政事务(与contentious business 相对而言)
administrative capacity 行政管理资格;管理能力
administrative case 行政事件,行政案件
administrative chamber 行政庭
administrative chores 行政的零星工作,行政琐事
Administrative Code 《行政法典》
administrative committee 行政委员会;管理委员会
Administrative Conference of the United States 美国行政会议(根据1964年的行政会议法案而设立的一个常设独立机构)
administrative contract 行政性合同(契约)
administrative council 行政管理委员会
administrative county (英)行政郡
administrative court 行政法庭(院)
administrative court of first instance 初级(审)行政法院
administrative court system 行政法院体制
administrative decentralization 行政上的分权制,分散管理(原则)
administrative decision and ruling 行政判决和裁定
Administrative Decision Judicial Review Act (1997) (澳大利亚)《行政决定(司法审查法)》(1997年)
administrative decree 行政法令
administrative demand 行政请求,行政诉愿
administrative detainees 行政犯(以色列人对阿拉伯政治犯的委婉称呼)
administrative detention 行政拘留
administrative directions 行政管理细则,管理条例
administrative disciplinary measure 行政纪律处分
administrative discretion 行政自由裁量权
administrative dispute 行政争议
Administrative Dispute Resolution Act

(1990年美国国会通过的)《行政争议解决法》(其目的是"授权并鼓励联邦行政机构适用调解、协商、仲裁或其他正式程序,对行政争议迅速处理")
administrative district 行政管理区
administrative division 行政区划;(法院的)行政(分)庭
administrative duty 行政职责
administrative expenditure 行政管理开支,行政管理费
administrative expense 行政费用
administrative fee 行政费;管理费
administrative feedback 行政反馈(指在行政进程中由行政措施所引起的反应,依正确目标予以适当改正)
administrative function 行政职务;行政职能
administrative generalist 行政工作的行家,行政通才
administrative head 行政首长(脑);(中)县长,(自治州)州长,(自治区)主席
administrative hearing 行政听证
administrative high court 高级行政法院
administrative interference 行政干预
administrative judge 见 examiner; hearing officer
administrative judg(e)ment 行政裁决
administrative judiciary 行政法院系统;行政法院体制
administrative jurisdiction 行政管辖权;行政管辖范围;行政裁决权(见 quasi-judicial jurisdiction)
administrative jurisprudence 行政法(理)学
administrative jurist 行政法学家
administrative justice 行政司法
administrative law 行政法
administrative law judge (美)行政法法官[主持行政司法听审,有权掌管宣誓、取证、规定有关证据的问题和使确定的事实有力,以前称为听审官(hearing officer)或听审考官(hearing examiner)]
Administrative Law Treatise (美)《行政法论文集》(肯尼思·C. 戴维斯著,K. C. 戴维斯出版公司1978年出版第2版。该书是一部多卷本论文,包括本领域内有关实体的和程序的各个方面的内容)
administrative laws(或 **rules**) **and regulations** 行政法规
administrative legislation 行政立法
administrative license revocation hearing 行政许可证撤销听证程序
administrative litigation 行政诉讼
administrative litigation act 行政诉讼法;行政诉讼行为
administrative machinery 行政机构
administrative matter 行政事件,行政案件;行政事项
administrative measure 行政措施
administrative offenses 行政罪行
Administrative Office of the U. S. Courts 美国法院行政管理局
Administrative Office of U. S. Courts (美)联邦最高法院行政管理办公室(见 administration of federal courts)
administrative officer(s) 行政官员,行政人员
administrative order 行政命令
Administrative Order Review Act (美)《司法审查法》(1956)
administrative organ 行政机关;管理机构
administrative organ abolished 已撤销的行政机关
administrative organ for reconsideration (中)行政复议机关
Administrative Penalties Law (中)《行政处罚法》
administrative penalty 行政处罚,行政罚款
administrative personnel (总称)行政人员,行政班底
administrative petition 行政请愿,行政诉愿,行政申请(诉)
administrative police 行政警察
administrative powers 行政权;管理权
administrative practice 行政程序
administrative problem 行政问题,管理问题
administrative procedure 行政诉讼程序(手续)
Administrative Procedure Act 《行政诉讼法》,《联邦行政程序法》(1964)(简称 APA)

administrative proceedings 行政诉讼
administrative punishment 行政处罚
administrative question 行政性争议
administrative receivership 破产管理人之一种
administrative reconsideration 行政复议
administrative reform 行政改革
administrative region 行政区
administrative regulation(s) 行政规章,行政管理条例
administrative remedy 行政救济方法;行政补救
administrative reorganization 行政改组
administrative responsibility system （中）行政责任制
administrative review 行政复议
administrative review tribunal 行政复议裁判庭
administrative rule （1856年）行政规则［指官方颁布的具有法律效力的行政规章（regulation），典型地详尽说明法律的要求和政策,亦即行政机关解释法律或政策,或者规定行政机关的要求,这些都具有广泛的适用性］
administrative sanction 行政处分;行政制裁;行政处罚
Administrative State 行政国家（指美国联邦宪法将政府权力划分为:立法权授予参众两院组成的国会行使;行政权授予总统;司法权授予联邦最高法院和国会选择设立的其他联邦低级别法院行使）;（小写）行政州
administrative statute 行政法规,管理法规
administrative supervision 行政监督(察)
administrative system 行政管理体制;行政制度;行政系统
administrative tribunal 行政裁判庭
administrative unit 行政单位
administratively advantageous 行政上的优点,操作上的优势,行政上的优势
administrator n. 1.管理人 2.行政长官,行政人员 3.(港务)监督员 4.遗产管理人(指由法院指定的遗产管理人。死者生前亦可指定遗产管理人,这类管理人通常作 executor)
administrator *ad colligenda bona* 收集财产执行官
administrator in law （苏格兰）（幼年人的）法定监管人
administrator of oath 监誓人
administrator of property 财产管理人
administrator with the will annexed 依遗嘱（而由法院认可的）指定的遗产管理人
administrator with will 遗嘱指定的遗产管理人
administrator's deed 遗产管理人的证明（书）（指死后无遗嘱时,遗产管理人处理有关财产让与的证明）
administratrix n. 女管理人;女遗产管理人
admiralty n. 1.海军上将的职位 2.(大写)(英)海军部 3.海事法;海事法庭
admiralty action 海事诉讼
admiralty advocate 海事高级律师
admiralty bond （英）海事债券（指为取得被扣押船舶开释出具的债券）
admiralty cause 海事诉讼
admiralty court 海事法院;(大写)(英)海事分庭(高等法院王座法庭的一个分庭,始建于1970年)
admiralty dispute 海事纠纷,海事争议
admiralty division 海事分庭
admiralty droits 海军权利（见 *droit* of admiralty)
admiralty （或 maritime） jurisdiction 海事管辖(权);海事裁判权;海事管辖范围
admiralty law 海事法
admiralty lien 船舶留置权,海事留置权
admiralty proceedings 海事诉讼
admiralty remedy 海事救济方法
admiralty short cause 海事简易诉讼
admissibility n. 可采纳(性),(证据)可接受(性);有资格加入
admissible evidence （18世纪）可接受的证据,可采信的证据,可采纳的证据。亦称 competent evidence; proper evidence; original evidence(见 best evidence)
admissibility of confession 供词的可接受性
admissibility of documents 文件的可采性;文件形式,书证形式(见 documentary evidence)

admissibility of hearsay evidence 传闻证据的可采性
admissible a. 可(获得法庭)接受的;(证据)可接受的,可采纳的;有资格加入的,有权进入(某一位置、行业等)的;具有可采纳性的(证据)(在美国联邦民事或刑事案件中,用来描述能被陪审团听审和考虑的证据的术语)
admissible assets 可(纳)税资产
admissible document 可作证据的文件
admissible evidence 可接受的证据,可采信的证据,可采纳的证据
admissible plea 可受理的抗辩
admissible rules 行政规定
admissible witness (法庭)允许(作证)的证人
admission n. 1.承认;招认;供认 2.允许进入,入场(许可),入境(许可)
admission against interest 不利于己的供认
admission in pleading (或 evidence) (在辩论中)承认对方所提的事实(这种事实的法律效力一般很少需要证据再加以证明)
admission of a debt 承认债务
admission of fact 自白(交代);承认事实,事实的招认
admission of foreign investment 外资准入阶段[在外资立法上,通常把外国投资活动划分为外资建立之前和外资建立之后两大阶段及外资准入阶段和外资经营阶段(operation of foreign investment)];外资准入
admission of guilt 承认有罪,认罪
admission of liability 承认负有责任;认债
admission of new states (美)接纳新州
admission tax 入场税,通行税[指对一种特殊活动(比赛、影院、娱乐场所等)准入的价格部分所征的一个税种]
admission to a crime 承认犯罪,认罪
admission to practice 准予开业
admission to the bar 进入司法界;进入律师界
admit v. 承认;允许;接纳,招收;让进入;让享用

admit of sth. 容许某事物;对某事物留有余地
admit (sb.) to bail 允许(某人)保释
admittable a. 可承认的,可允许的;可接纳的
admittable to bail 可以保释的
admittance n. (英)准许保有土地
admitted to the bar 准许当律师
admonition n. 警告,申诫,劝告;斥责
admonition with deferment of sentence 延期判刑警告(联邦德国处理轻罪时的一种惩罚)
admonitory a. 告诫的;劝告的;责备的
admonitory tort 责备性侵权(一种有意侵权,惩罚侵权者比补偿受伤害者更为重要)
adnotationes n. (罗马皇帝的)签名诏书;签名文件
adolescence (=adolescency) n. (罗马法)青春期(指男14岁、女12岁至18岁)
adolescent n./a. 青年,青少年/青春期的
adolescent age 青年期(指发育期与成年期之间的中间阶段)
adolescent offender 青少年犯
adopt v. 收养;正式通过;采用,采取,采纳
adopt a pseudonym 用化名,用笔名
adopted a. 被收养的;被采纳的
adopted child (或 children) 养子,养女(或养子女)
adopted children register 收养子女登记册
adopted law 继受法
adopted son 养子,义子(旧译:嗣子)
adoptee n. 被收养者(旧译:被立嗣者)
adopter n. 收养人
adopter person 被收养人
adopting husband 有收养孩子的丈夫
adopting parents 养父母
adopting wife 有收养孩子的妻子
adoptio v. (罗马法)他权人收养;收养
adoptio minus plena 不完全收养(又称简单收养或限制收养)
adoptio plena 完全收养
adoption n. (14世纪)1.(家庭法)收养[根据司法指示说明,通常在没有什么关系的当事双方之间创建父母和孩子的亲

属关系。这种父母和孩子的关系是法律在非真实的父母和孩子之间创建的。这种亲属关系通过法院裁定不仅会导致孩子是孤儿或被遗弃状态的终结,而且使父母的亲权(parent's parental right)结束。收养确立了被收养的子女和收养的父母之间的亲属关系,这种关系也带来各种权利、特权和由此而产生的责任。即使可能有约定的例外(agreed exception),收养和婚生(legitimati)是有区别的。另外,收养与非亲抚养(fostering)也不同。收养通常是一些无血亲关系人之间的行为,而婚生则是有血亲关系人之间的行为。总之,收养裁决令(decree of adoption)授予被收养的孩子合法的身份。见 adopted child; foster child; foster care〕2.(罗马法)认领〔指与一位仍在另一父权(power of another father)之下的年轻人创建父子关系的法律程序(legal process)。该被收养人(adopted person)即成为新的男性家长的同族家庭(paterfamilias's agnostic family)中的组成成员,并且有如同其子女(或孙子、孙女)完全相同的血亲身份。这是后来查士丁尼时期修订明确的〕3.(契约)承担、接受(指某人同意承担或接受以前所订契约上对另一人的权益。如同一个新成立的公司承认以前公司的合同)4.(商标)智力行为必须获得在商标上的法定权力(legal right)。这包括知识和在与产品和商业服务相关联中的商标意图使用 5.(议会法)认可,批准〔指对一个动议或报告经表决获得审议会(a deliberative assembly)批准或认可〕。亦称 acceptance; consent〕

Adoption and Safe Families Act (美)《收养和安全家庭法》[指 1997 年的联邦法,该法要求各州提供安全、永久性的家(或住宅)以应对(或防止)比以前州法和联邦法所要求更短的时期内虐待儿童问题。主要的问题是儿童的安全与幸福。与以前父母的首要权利(paramount rights of the parent)形成鲜明对比。自 1980 年的《收养协助和儿童福利法》以来,《收养和安全家庭法》在已控制的儿童保护进程宗旨上暗示着引人注目的转变。缩略 ASFA。见 Adoption Assistance and Child Welfare Act]

Adoption Assistance and Child Welfare Act《收养协助和儿童福利法》[指 1980 年的联邦制定法,其旨意在于强化各州运用合理的努力(reasonable efforts):①避免将孩子从家中迁离;②在孩子被迁出后受虐待时再重新与家庭团聚;③重新团聚不成,结束亲权(parental rights),然后将孩子们送到永久性的家(permanent home),参见《美国注释法典》第 42 标题卷第 620 节以及下列等等(42 USCA § § 620 et seq)。该法提供基金进行照顾安排、儿童保护服务、家庭维护和重新团聚,以及各州要遵守该法改善对儿童的照料。其目的在于防止将孩子从家中迁出,后又匆匆返回他们自己的家进行照管。现该法从宗旨(in philosophy)上已被 1997 年制定的《收养和安全家庭法》所推翻。见 Adoption and Safe Families Act]

adoption agency　收养办事处
adoption by close relative　近亲收养
adoption by consensus　协商一致收养
adoption by estoppel　不容后悔的收养,不容否认的收养〔指①一个衡平法上的子女收养,即由一个人作出收养的承诺或行为后,就不得拒绝给予被收养人以养子女的身份。②必须完成衡平法上的收养法令,处理好应该处理的事,在最终收养法令(final decree of adoption)没有到达之时,此法令即已开始。即使当事人已经作为,好像收养已经成功。申请人必需出示一个收养合同,孩子的亲生父母放弃亲权,由养父母承担父母的责任。并且在整个孩子实质成长期间成为事实上的父母与子女的关系。当养父母无遗嘱死亡时,权利主张即会发生,孩子即被指定为一名继承人。在美国少数州,不容否认的收养成为一个允准孩子参与非正常死亡诉讼(wrongful-death action)的依据。亦称 equitable adoption, virtual adoption。见 de facto adoption]
adoption by femme sole　独身妇女收养
adoption contract　收养合同(契约)
adoption convention　收养协议(约)
adoption de facto　事实上的收养
adoption doctrine　(国际法上的)采纳说

adoption of black market babies 黑市婴儿的收养
adoption of children 子女的收养
Adoption of Children Act （英）《收养子女法》
adoption of report 报告的通过
adoption order （英）收养令
adoption petition 收养申请(书)
adoption posthumous 遗腹子的领养(指父亲死后出生子女的领养)
adoption proceedings 收养程序；收养诉讼
adoption society 收养协会
adoption warranty 收养担保(书)
adoption-registry statute （美）收养注册法[指规定发表收养信息的法律，如果生身父母、养父母和被收养者(他或她)达到一定的法定规定的年龄之后)均可读到所有他们想要的正式记录。亦称 voluntary-registry law]
adoptive a. 收养的；采用的
adoptive act 收养法；(复)采纳性法令(指只有在采纳该法令的地方政权管辖范围内才能适用的法令)
adoptive children 养子女，义子女
adoptive descent 养子女
adoptive father 养父
adoptive filiation 收养关系
adoptive parents 养父母
adoptive relationship 收养关系
adoptor n. 收养者；采纳者
adprehensio n. 主权者占有的假定
adpromissio 见 *adpromission*
adpromission n. （罗马法）1.担保性质的契约[契约中担保人承诺仅对债务人所欠之债承担偿还责任。罗马法上曾有三种形式的担保：要式口头合同(*sponsion*)、诚意允诺担保(*fidepromission*)和诚意负责担保(*fidejussion*)。此外，可以通过担保方式间接使用(无偿)委任和履行债务简约(*mandatum and pactum de constitutio*)] 2.担保关系(亦称 *adpromissio*)
adpromissiones n. 保证合同(契约)
adpromissor n. （罗马法）根据契约条款中实质性允诺，为债务人作的担保或担保人(见 adpromission)

adquisitiones n. 取得方法
adquisitiones civiles （罗马法）市民法的取得方法
adquisitiones praetorium （罗马法）裁判官法的取得方法
adropatio n. （罗马法）自权人收养[指某一家父收养另一家父的行为，被收养的家父必然会将自己的家子以及财产带入新的家庭，使之转归收养人所有。这种收养也被称为生者间继承(*successio tra vivi*)。在早期实践中，自权人收养必须在由大祭司主持的民众会议前进行，大祭司在听取有关当事人的意见后向会议征询同意，要求批准收养关系成立，再由民众会议表决；在收养建议被批准后，被收养人应当宣布放弃自己原来的家宗教信仰。最初的自权人收养不适用于妇女和未适婚人(见 *impuber*)；这一限制在帝国时期被放宽，即实行有条件自权人收养，不再使收养人继承收养人之财产，但对此财产享有用益权和经营权]
adscripti (= adscriptitii glebae) n. （罗马法）(附属于土)地(上的)奴(隶)
adstioulator 债权代理人
adult n./a. 成年人/成年人的，已成人的
adult education 成人教育
adult family member 成年家属
adult offender 成年犯
adult population 成年人口
Adult Protective Services （1973年）成人保护局(署)(指美国的一个政府机构，负责调查成人受到虐待的肯定性陈述，并采取相应措施。在美国，每个州都有这类机构。缩略为 APS。见 Child Protective Services)
adulterate v. 掺假；掺杂；假冒
adulterate wine with water 酒中掺水
adulterated goods 伪劣产品
adulteration n. 伪造；掺假；劣等货；掺假货
adulterator n. 造假(货)者，掺假者；伪造者
adulterer n. 奸夫
adulteress n. 奸妇
adulterine a./n. 通奸的，私生的，非法的，涉及通奸的，伪造的，掺杂的/非婚生子女
adulterine guild(s) 无特许商会[指旧时

一团体(或组)生意人以法人名义行事,但无特许状,而且每年缴纳一笔罚金来获得行使法人特权的许可]
adulterous a. 通奸的
adulterous bastard 奸生子
adulterous children 奸生子女
adultery n. 通奸
adultery by consent 和奸
advance n./v. 前进,进行;(常用复)建议,提议;预付,预付款,贷款;(价格、工资等)增长,增高/预付,预支,垫付,推进,进展,促进;提出(建议等),提前,提高,提升,上涨,增高
advance by overdraft 透支
advance charge 预付款
advance copy 预发件,预发本;(售前)新书样本
advance deposit 预付租金
advance freight 预付运费
Advance Informed Agreement "提前知情同意"程序[简称 AIA,关于(生物多样性公约)的《卡塔赫纳生物安全协定书》将事先知情同意程序的适用范围扩展至改性活生物体(即转基因生物体)的越境转移领域。根据该公约第 19 条第 3 款的授权,特别设立了"提前知情同意"程序,适用于直接引入进口国环境的改性活生物体首次越移的情况]
advance interest computed on a debt 债中计算贴息
advance money on security 预付保证金,垫付保证金
advance note 预付票据
advance notice 预先通知,预告
advance of fund 预支金
advance of sea 海进,海侵
advance payment 预付,预先付款
advance payment of income tax 预缴所得税
advance remittance 预付汇款
advance sheet 印刷(案例判决)样品;(大写)(复)(美)先行本(最高法院判决和许多其他法院判例汇编的每本判例汇编都要出版一种初印本,包括最高法院以临时形式发行的一些新近的判决,这些小册子称为"先行本")
advanced a. 预付的,预支的,垫付的;先进的,高级的
advanced bill of lading 预借提单
advanced charge 预付费用
Advanced conventional arms 已发展的常规武器
advanced country 已发展的国家;先进国家,发达国家
advanced economics 发达的经济
advanced payment 预付定金
advancement n. 1.促进,进步,发达 2.预付,垫付;(父母生前给予子女财产的)预赠,预先遗赠
advancement of justice 促进正义
advantage n. 优点,好处,优势;有利条件;利益
adventitious property 非直接继承所得的财产
adventure n. 投机活动;冒险活动;冒险性
adventurer n. 投机者;冒险家
adventuress n. 女投机者;女冒险家
adversarial court proceeding 对抗式法庭审判程序
adversarial courtroom 对抗式的法庭
adversary n. 对方当事人;对造;对手,敌手;(英美法)对抗制,辩论式
adversary evidence 对抗性证据(指原不可采纳的证据,但由于对方当事人提出相关或类似证据,从而允许一方当事人提出此证据)
adversary opinion (法官之间)相对抗的意见
adversary proceedings (或 **procedure**) 辩论式的诉讼程序(与 accusatory procedure 相对而言);(英美法)对抗制的诉讼程序(见 adversary system)
adversary quotient 应付逆境处理能力
adversary right theory 诉讼防御权理论
adversary Supreme Court decisions (美)联邦最高法院有争议的判决
adversary system 对抗制(又译:当事人主义的或辩论式的诉讼制度,英美法中的一种诉讼制度。这种制度允许双方当事人为了获得有利于自己的判决而进行辩论,

法官只能就辩论范围以第三者姿态加以决断。区别于大陆法国家纠问式的诉讼制度)
adversary's position 对抗性立场
adverse a. 相反的,敌对的;逆的;有害的,不利的;非法的
adverse arbitration award 不利之仲裁决定
adverse effect 不利影响,不利效果
adverse enjoyment 非法享用
adverse-inference rule 见 adverse-interest rule
adverse-interest rule 相反利益原则(根据此项原则,如果当事人未能提供对其有利的重要证言和有力的证人出庭作证,且未能说出未能出庭的正当理由,则法官可指示陪审团推断该证人到庭作证将会作出不利于该当事人的证言。亦称 empty-chair doctrine; adverse-inference rule)
adverse judg(e)ment 不利判决
adverse judgment on the merits 不利的实体判决
adverse occupation of residential premises 非法占用(他人)住宅
adverse party 他方当事人(旧译:他造)
adverse possession 对立占有,时效占有,(英)相反占有权(取得不动产所有权的一种方法。凡无法律根据而占有不动产,根据时效在一定条件下依法可取得此项不动产的所有权,在发生纠纷时,对此项占有权称为相反占有权);因非法占有取得时效;事实上占有
adverse ruling(s) 相反的裁定;不利的裁决
adverse selecting 逆向选择,他方选择(见 asymmetric information; asymmetry of information)
adverse suit (美)对方所有权之诉,对方的权利请求之诉
adverse title 对方所有权
adverse trade balance 贸易逆差
adverse use 未经许可的使用(权);时效使用[指未经土地所有人许可,持续公开独占、为众人所知地公开使用土地,同时主张与土地所有人对抗的权利,这一状态持续至法定时效取得时限(prescriptive period)届满时,可导致地役权的产生]
adverse verdict (对某方)不利的裁决

adverse witness 相反证人(指偏袒一方当事人的证人),敌对证人
adversity requirement (美)敌对性要求(指在确定竞合权利诉讼中,争议财物保管人必须能够证明这些确定竞合权利诉讼的请求人彼此之间是"敌对"的,敌对性在确定竞合权利诉讼制度法中有明确要求)
adversus v. 相反,反对;(英美法)(某某)诉(某某)案
advert n. 1.(事件、时间等的)出现,到来 2.基督降临节(the Second Advert)耶稣降临,降临节 3.(英)(普通法、教会法)[自 11 月 30 日至圣安德鲁日(St. Andrew's Day)或自最接近该节日的星期日始直至圣诞节的一段时期。古时,在此段时间内停止一切法律诉讼,但爱德华一世(Edward I)时的一项法令允准进行一些诉讼]
advertent negligence 注意的过失
(an) advertent state of mind 注意之思想状态
advertise v. 告知,做广告;大肆宣扬
advertisement (=advertizement) n. 广告;公告;告示,通知
advertisement for creditor 债权人通知
advertisement offering a reward 悬赏广告,悬赏通告
advertisement (或 **advertising**) **publisher** 广告发布者
advertisement reward 悬赏
advertiser (=advertizer) n. 登广告者(人)
advertising (=advertizing) n. (总称)广告;广告业;刊登广告
advertising agency 广告公司;广告经营者
advertising agents 广告经营者
advertising expenses (或 **fee**) 广告费
advertising relating to consumer credit 与消费信用有关的广告业
advertising sign 广告标志
advertising supervision and control organ 广告监督管理机关
advertorial 软文[指广告行业的一个流行术语,即以报道形式发布广告主所需要的信息,其意义与近年来英语的拼接相似

(advertorial: advertisement + editorial),可译为"付费文章"。但"软文"掩盖其付费服务性质,混淆广告和新闻报道之间的界限,以达到使读者将付费服务误以为是客观报道的目的]
advice n. 通知;消息;(复)报道;劝告;意见;咨询
advice and consent 咨询和同意
advice for(或 **of**)**collection** 托收委托书
advice note 通知书
advice of audit 审核(计)通知书
advice of(或 **for**)**drawing** 汇票通知书,提款通知
advice of payment 付款通知
advice on evidence 证据指导(指律师在法庭传唤证人和提出文据作证时,对当事人应如何准备加以指导)
advise v. 1.劝告;通知,告知 2.提出意见,做顾问;商量;建议(不同于"persuade"及"instruct"。对被建议者来说,是否按照建议行事有自由裁量权或选择权)
advised a. 经过考虑的;得到消息的
advisement n. 深思熟虑,提供劝告,提出意见
adviser(=advisor)n. 顾问;劝告者
adviser on legal affairs 法律顾问
advising bank 通知银行
advising on law 法律问题思考
advisory a. 劝告的,忠告的;咨询的,顾问的
advisory arbitration 建议性仲裁
advisory board 顾问委员会,咨询委员会
advisory body 咨询机构,咨询团体,顾问团体
advisory committee 顾问委员会,咨询委员会
Advisory Committee on Civil Rules (美)民事规则顾问委员会
Advisory Committee on Restrictive Practice and Dominant Positions in Maritime Transport (欧盟)"海运限制竞争和优势地位咨询委员会"
Advisory Conciliation and Arbitration Services (简称 ACAS)咨询、调解、仲裁服务局(1975 年,英国政府设立的独立劳动争议调解机构)
Advisory Jurisdiction of International Court 国际法院的咨询管辖
advisory jury (美)咨询陪审团(在联邦法院,法庭在不实行陪审团审判时可召集一个咨询陪审团帮助审理案子,但此陪审团的裁断对法庭无约束力)
advisory machinery (总称)顾问机构,咨询机构
advisory opinion (1837 年)1.咨询意见(指法院如果应利害关系之一方或政府之要求,就某一事项提交诉讼,将提供如何解决的意见,它是对法律的解释,无法律拘束力。通常联邦法院因宪法规定其管辖权仅仅限于审判案件和争议,而不得提供咨询意见,只有有些司法区可以就某些争点提供咨询意见)2.国际法院应联合国或其专门授权机构的请求,就某一事项或问题提供的意见,但此项意见无法律拘束力 3.(美)上级法院的意见(指美国上级法院对下级法院就某法律观点提供的意见)4.(雇员福利计划管理人的)书面声明[指由受雇人福利计划行政管理人发表的书面声明,用以解释"受雇人退休收入保障法"(Employee Retirement Income Security Act,ERISA)和适用该法的具体实际情况或条件,只有命名的当事人对此声明提出要求时方可依据此声明意见,而且它的可靠性取决于所有重要事实的确切性和全面性]
advisory service 咨询服务
advisory verdict 建议性裁决
advocacy n. 辩护;支持;拥护;提倡;辩护术
advocate n./v. 律师(法国律师的统称),(出庭)辩护人;(法国,苏格兰等地的)律师;咨询人;鼓吹者,提倡者;拥护者/拥护;提倡;辩护
advocate-general 1.(英女王的)法律总顾问 2.(欧洲共同体法院的)法律顾问;总检察长(大写)
advocates-depute (苏格兰)总检察长助理
advocati n. (罗马法)赞助人;辩护人;说话人

advocatus n. (单数为 *advocati*)"advocate" 1.(罗马法)法律顾问或帮助当事人在司法法庭上办案者,即诉讼代理人(见 *causidicus*) 2.具有圣职推荐权的人(*patron*),亦称 *advowee*(见 advowson) 3.(古)保证代诉人具有从业资格的人

advocatus futuri 隔代利益代表制度

advowee n. 圣职推荐权人,亦拼写成"*avowee*"(见 *advocatus* 2)

advowson n. (宗教法)牧师推荐权,圣俸授予权[享有这种权利的人被称为圣职荐人"patron"(*patronus*) of the church, 以前被称为"*advocatus*", advocate or defender 或英语中称为 the *advowee*。圣职推荐人将被提名的候选人(nominee)推荐给主教(bishop)或有时介绍给教会职位高的人(church dignitary)。如果没有圣职推荐人,或者圣职推荐人在6个月内疏忽履行其推荐权,则此权利失效(lapses), 此项资格常恢复到主教手中,然后由他任命1名教士或牧师掌握此推荐权。见 presentation 2; institution 5]

advowtry (=advoutry) n. (古英国法)姘居

*****Aedificare in tuo proprio solo non licet quod alteri noceat.** It is not lawful to build upon one's own land what may injure another. 在自己的土地上进行有损于他人的建筑是不合法的。

*****Aedificatum solo solo cedit.** What is built upon land belongs to or goes with land. 凡建筑于土地上的均属土地的一部分。

aedile (古罗马)民政官

aedilitium edictum (见 *edictum aedilicium*)

aegis n. 庇护,保护;主办,赞助,领导

aequitas n. (罗马法上的)衡平

*****Aequitas agit in personam.** Equity acts upon the person. 衡平法是对个别的人讲公平的。

*****Aequitas aquit in personam.** Equity acts in person. Equity acts on the person. Equity operates upon the conscience. 衡平法对人行事(衡平法的基本原则之一)。(指衡平法以人作出判决的方式提供救济,通常只是对人判决而及于对物、对事之处理。判决金钱损害赔偿等方式进行救济)

*****Aequitas est quasi aequalitas.** Equity is as it were equality (Equity is a species of equality or equalization). 衡平法可以说就是平等(衡平法是平等或实现平等的一种形式)。

*****Aequitas factum habet quod fieri oportuit.** Equity considers that to have done which ought to have been done. 衡平法将本应成就者视为已经就。

*****Aequitas ignorantiae opitulatur, oscitantiae non item.** Equity assists ignorance, but not carelessness. 衡平法帮助不知情(无辜)者,但不帮助粗心大意者。

*****Aequitas non facit jus, sed juri auxiliatur.** Equity does not make law, but assists law. 衡平法并不造法,但对法律起辅助作用。

*****Aequitas nunquam contravenit legis.** Equity never counteracts the laws. 衡平法绝不与法律背道而驰。

*****Aequitas sequitur legem.** Equity follows the law. 衡平法依从法律。

*****Aequitas supervacua odit.** Equity abhors superfluous thing. 衡平法对多余的东西深恶痛绝。

aerarium n. 宝库,国库

aerial a. 空气的,大气的;航空的;由空中经过的;无形的,空想中的

aerial blockade 空中封锁

aerial cabotage 国内两地间空运

aerial domain 领空

aerial espionage 空中间谍活动

aerial hijacking 空中劫持

aerial liner 定期民航班机

aerial navigation 航空,空中航行

aerial port 空运港,空运站

aerial warfare 空战

aero a. 飞机的;飞船的;航空的,飞行的

aero boat 水上飞机

aerocraft (=aircraft) n. 飞机,飞行器

aerofoil n. 气翼;机翼

aeroso irritant projectors (警察执行任务时使用的)刺激喷雾器

aes et libra (早期罗马法)铜衡方式(一种通过铜板和衡器达成交易的方式)

A

aesthetic(al) experience 美感（见 practial reasonableness）
aestimatum n. 可退货的销售合同
aetas infantiae proxima （罗马法）童年时代的前半期［幼年时期（出生至 7 岁）与青春期之间（12 岁至 14 岁）的儿童时期为前半期，特别是男孩 7 岁至 10 岁半之间的时期。见 aetas pubertati proxima］
aetas pubertati proxima （罗马法）接近青春期的年龄［童年时代的第二半期，即童年时代的后半期，男孩指 10 岁半至 14 岁之间的时期。在此期间，视行为人有无犯罪能力（doli capax）来确定其是否应承担刑事责任，但对其处罚上有减缓之处］
aetiology of crime 犯罪推理学；犯罪成因
affair n. 事件，事情；（复）事务；事态；私通事件
affair of hono(u)r 决斗
affairs in order 事态井然有序
Affd.（Aff'd）Affirmed 确认，维持（原判），证实
Aff'd sub nom affirmed under the name 根据名称确认
affect v. 影响；假装；倾向于；变化（使扩大，削弱，常用于对人或物的伤害影响）
affect approach 影响方法（指被告通过互联网所从事的行为在法院地产生的实际影响作为法院确定管辖权的标准）
affected estate 附有抵押权的财（地）产
affected laws 受影响的法律，已改变的法律
affected multipolar interests 多种相关利益
affected persons 受影响的人
affected riparian owners 受到影响的河岸土地所有人
affectio manitalis （罗马法）婚意
affective disorders 情感性障碍（见 mood disorders）
affective insanity 影响言行的精神错乱
affiance n. 信用，信托；信约；婚约
affiant n. 宣誓人；宣誓作证者；立誓词者
affiant's personal knowledge 宣誓作证人的亲自知悉（或亲身所知）
affidavit n. 口供（宣誓）书；宣誓作证书；正式书面陈述；（作证）保证书
affidavit by process-server 送达人的笔录
affidavit evidence 誓证；宣誓证据
affidavit of consent 同意证明书
affidavit of defense 辩护宣誓书
affidavit of document 文件证明书
affidavit of finding 遗嘱寻回证明书
affidavit of increase 额外费用证明书
affidavit of means 有能力（偿债）的证明书
affidavit of merits 有根据的书面陈述；（美）陈述真实事实宣誓书
affidavit of plight and condition 遗嘱完整证明书
affidavit of reserve capital 备用资本证明书
affidavit of script （以遗嘱手稿作为）副本证明书（如果遗嘱毁损或丢失，遗嘱承受人拥有遗嘱手稿的证明书）
affidavit of service （按规定日期）送达证明书、传票、令状等
affidavit with vouchers 附有账务单据的书面陈述
affiliate n./v. 1.附属公司，分支机构 2.联号 3.关联公司（指根据美国《投资公司法》，两家公司之间直接或间接拥有 5 名或更多有投票权股东的公司即为关联公司）4.（美）会员/1.使加入 2.收为养子 3.追溯来源 4.交往 5.对（私生子女等的）生身父亲的确认
affiliated a. 附属的，分支的
affiliated agency 分支机构；附属机构
affiliated association 隶（下）属社团，分会，分社
affiliated company 附属公司，联络公司（又译关联公司，指持有某公司股份并与之发生联系的公司）
affiliated corporation （美）关联公司，附属公司，联营公司［指两个或两个以上的公司因商业共同目的而联合经营，由一个公司控制大部分股份，但总的是不符合《所得税法》（Income Tax Law）意义下的公司］
affiliated group 联营公司，连锁集团，联营集团［指可选择提交统一纳税申报表（consolidated return）的联营公司，因为

两个公司至少有80%被其他公司控股]
affiliated interests 附属权益,附属股权
affiliated trademark 联合商标
affiliating circumstances 密切联系情况(没有借以使自己获诉讼地州法律权力和利益的密切联系情况,则法院对其管辖不能成立)
affiliation n. (18世纪)1.加入,加盟 2.立嗣,私生子女,认领诉讼;对私生子女父亲的鉴定、亲子关系确认 3.与政治、宗教等相关联的人或事;附属公司、子公司
affiliation and aliment 私生子确认和扶养之诉
affiliation order (英)私生子女生父确认令(亦称亲子认定令,指由法院根据证据判定一个人为非婚生子女之生身父亲的令状,被确认的父亲应付出一定数额的抚养费、教育费)
affiliation proceedings 对私生子女生父的鉴定(确认)程序(又译亲子认定程序)
affined a. 有义务约束的;有密切关系的
affines n. (大陆法)姻族
* *Affinis mei affinis non est mihi affinis.*
One who is related by marriage to a person who is related to me by marriage has no affinity to me. 凡与我的姻亲有姻亲关系的人则与我无姻亲关系。
affinity n. 姻亲关系;姻族、亲戚;密切关系;吸引;有吸引力的人
affirm v. 证实(指立契约人将可取消的契约当作有效契约来遵守);批准;断言;追认,确认;声明;判决确认,维持原则(指上级法院维持下级法院的判决);(不经宣誓)提供正式证词
affirm the original judg(e)ment 维持原判
affirmance n. 证实;断言,确认;声明;判决确认
affirmance by acquiescence 用默认作肯定声明
affirmance in general 一般的肯定声明
affirmant n. 誓言者;事实陈述人
Affirmanti non neganti incumbit probation.
The proof is incumbent on the one who affirms, not on the one who denies. The one who affirms, not the one who denies, should provide evidence. 举证责任应为肯定事实者,而非由否定事实者。
* *Affirmantis est probare.* He who is affirming must prove. 要确认事实就须提出证据。
affirmation n. 1.证实;批准;追认,确认;断言,声明 2.誓言,事实的陈述 3.(不经宣誓而作的)正式证词 4.判决确认
affirmative a. 确认的,证实的;肯定的,赞成的
affirmative act 确认行为
affirmative action (1961年)纠偏行动[指一系列行为旨在消灭现存的和事实的(种族)歧视,补救过去歧视造成的拖延的影响,同时创立一种制度和程序以防止未来的歧视。见 reverse discrimination]
affirmative allegations 积极答辩,积极主张
affirmative countervailing consideration at work here 对审理本案的积极补偿考虑,对审理本案肯定的补偿考虑
affirmative countervailing considerations 肯定性补偿考虑
affirmative covenant 肯定性协议,肯定性合同[指要求一方当事人从事某些行为以偿还受合同约束的债务的合同或协议,尤其是不动产将以某种方式经营并有收益(use)的协议。肯定性协议在使用或运作(use)财产时更具有约束力]
affirmative defense (美)积极答辩,肯定性答辩,积极抗辩(被告对原告答辩的一部分,即原告虽提出新的事实和论据,能够驳倒被告否认的事实和论据并可能胜诉,即使这些事实和证据被认定为真实,被告对此仍可继续采取积极的答辩)
affirmative duty 肯定性责任,肯定性现象,积极性义务
affirmative easement 积极地役权(指使用非己有土地的权利,如在他人土地上的通行权等类似权利)
affirmative matter 确认的事项,重申的事项
affirmative plea 重申某一事实的答辩
affirmative proof 确认的证据
affirmative relief 肯定性救济

affirmative resolution of both Houses 两院均持赞同意见的决议
affirmative side 积极的一面(政府政策的制定和执行代表个人和社会利益并能增进这些利益)
affirmative steps 积极步骤,有效步骤
affirmative vote 赞成票
affirmative warranty 积极担保,肯定担保
affirmed without opinion 维持原判而未发表判决意见书
affix v. 1.签署;盖(印章)2.贴上,粘上3.加添(附言)
affix one's private mark (由某人)画押
affix the process to the door 把传票贴在门上
affixing of seal 盖印
afflictive punishment 酷刑
afford v. 提供,给予;担负得起(费用、损失、后果等);(常用于 can, be able to 之后)
afford proof 提供证据
affray n. 吵嘴,打架,闹事,在公共场所互殴;(英)斗殴罪
affreight v. 租船;雇船
affreighter n. 租船者
affreightment n. 租船运货;租船合同(契约)
affront n. 当众侮辱;有意冒犯
Afonsine **Ordinance** (葡萄牙法)《阿方索法令集》(由国王阿方索五世摄政于1446年编成的葡萄牙法令汇编)
aforementioned a. 前面提到过的,前述
aforesaid a. 如上所述的,上文提到的
aforesaid right 此项权利,上述权利
aforethought a. 预谋的,故意的
aforethought malice 蓄意;预谋(犯罪或害人)
afoul ad. 碰撞;缠住;冲突
African Charter on Human and People's Rights 《非洲人权和人民权利宪章》(1981年,冈比亚首都班珠尔)
African traditional court 非洲传统法院
after ad. 在……之后
after acquired property 1.(债务人在抵押成交)后取得的财产 2.(美)(根据美国《统一商法典》第9.204款,也可指立遗嘱人在执行遗嘱)后获得的财产

after colonialism 后殖民主义(时代)
after consent 事后承诺
after date 出票后
after exhaustion of administrative remedies 用尽行政救济方法以后
after sight 见票后(即付)
after the fact (犯罪)事后(见 accessory after the fact)
after-acquired community property 婚后取得的共同财产
after-acquired property clause 后取得财产条款
after-acquired title 后取契据原则(指让与人在转让土地所有权给受让人后获得所有权凭证的原则)
after-arrival-of-goods-draft n. 货到后见票即付汇票
after born child (18世纪)遗腹子[指父亲死后,在执行遗嘱以后或在概括赠与(class gift)结束时间之后出生的孩子,亦可写成 after-born child。见 posthumous child(父亲订立遗嘱后,孩子出生不影响该遗嘱的效力)]
after-effect 后效作用,后效,后果
afterbirth n. 遗腹子;胎盘
aftercare n. (罪犯释放后的)安置
afterclap n. 节外生枝的事件
aftermath n. 事件的余波,后果
against prep. 1.违反,反对,逆着 2.对……发生法律关系,(狭义)对抗 3.与……对比(对照),与……抵触(冲突),与……不符(不一致)4.防备;以……为背景;迎着(困难等)5.凭……
against all the world 对抗全世界
against persons generally 对抗一般人
against persons only 对抗特定人
against public interest 与公共利益相抵触
against the form of the statute 违反制定法形式,与制定法体制不符
age n. 1.年龄;寿命;成年;老年 2.时代,时期 3.陈旧程度
age at entry into employment 就业年龄
age at (或 of) retirement 退休年龄
age at withdrawal 退休年龄
age discrimination 年龄歧视

Age Discrimination in Employment Act of 1967 (ADEA) （美）《1967年防止就业年龄歧视法》(《1978年防止就业年龄歧视法》将年龄上限提高到70岁，并将执行权由劳动部移转给平等就业委员会)
age discrimination suit arising out of single reduction in work force 产生于单一劳力总数削减的年龄歧视诉讼
age distribution 年龄结构
age for making a valid will 订立有效遗嘱的年龄
age for（或 of）marriage 结婚年龄
age of blood stain 血痕陈旧度
age of consent 同意年龄；（结婚等的）合法年龄；和奸年龄
age of criminal responsibility 刑事责任年龄（一般指有辨认是非能力而应负刑事责任的年龄）
age of digital media 数字化媒体时代
age of discretion （解事）责任年龄（指有辨别是非能力的年龄，英国法律规定为满14岁）
age of legislative quiescence 立法停滞时期
age of (legal) majority 成年；法定的成年年龄
age of migration 移民时代
age of reason 理性年龄（指儿童开始能思考、选择、表达愿望并为自己行为负责的年龄段）
age of responsibility 责任年龄
age of vessel 船龄
age set 年龄群
ageism (=agism) n. 年龄歧视；对老年人的歧视
agency n. 1.代理（权）；代理关系 2.机构；经销处；代理处；代理机构 3.媒介；经办 4.力量；（能动）作用；（政府或国际组织的）专业行政部门；行政机关（亦称 government agency, Administrative agency, public agency, regulatory agency）
agency action 行政行为；机关行为
agency agreement 代理协定，代理关系协议
agency by agreement 协议代理，委托代理
agency by commission 委托性代理

agency by estoppel(s) 不可否认的代理（指被代理人以行为表示授权给代理人的表意代理权，如果第三人据此与代理人订立合同而造成损害时，被代理人不得否认此项表意代理权），表见代表，表意代理
agency by mandate 委任代理
agency by operation of law 法律行为构成的代理（与 agency by estopel; apparent agency 同）
agency by ratification 经追认后的代理
agency by representation 代表性代理
agency commission 代理手续费
agency consideration 代理补偿
agency contract 委任合同（契约）；代理合同（契约）
agency costs 代理成本（经济分析中的一个术语，是在相对复杂的商业投机中追求利润最大化带来的。代理"成本"包括那些委托方监督他们的代理方的成本，以及代理方让他们的委托方确信他们事实上忠实地代表委托方的利益。代理成本问题常被称为"委托代替问题"）
agency coupled with an interest （1844年）附有利益的代理，连带利益的代理［指代理人得到授权，不仅具有代理被代理人的权利，而且还有涉及动产或不动产的相关法定利益（legal interest）。这种形式的代理并不因利益终止而废止，除非双方在创造新的权益时同意以另外的形式合作。即使被代理人精神错乱甚至死亡，这种代理关系仍不能终止。见 power coupled with an interest］
agency decisions 机关决议
Agency Doctrine 代理说（指美国法院适用揭开公司面纱时的四种学说之一，另三种为：Enterprise Entity Doctrine 企业整体说；Instrumentality Doctrine 工具说；Alter Ego Doctrine 另一自我说）代理说认为公司的设立、存续和经营完全依附于控股股东的指令，该公司只是以控股代理人身份存在。其背后的控股股东才是"未披露身份的本人"）
agency endorsement 代理背书
agency fee 代理费
agency in fact 事实上的代理

agency of justice 正义的力量
agency of progress 进步的力量
agency of necessity 紧急处分的代理
agency on long-term basis 长期代理关系
agency on trip basis 航次代理关系
agency relation 代理关系
Agency Security （美）固定收益证券（由国有公司或政府担保的公司发行的一种证券，但不属于政府债券，有人称之为"Agency Security"）
agency record 行政机构记录（指根据信息自由法"Freedom of information Act"，政府所制定或获得的文件，均由政府管理控制，只有在信息要求时才制定这种文件记录）
agency shop agreement 工会代理制企业的集体协议
agency unnamed principal 不指明委托人的代理
agenda n. 1.议事日程；会议事项；备忘录 2.行动计划；蓝图；一览表；记事册
agenda building 议题构建
agenda items 议事项目
agenda-setting 议事日程调整，议事日程安排
agenesis n. 生殖不能，无生殖能力，发育不全
agent n. 行为者，动作者；代理人；代理商；力量；原因，动因；总办，总管；间谍，特务；行动者
agent acting without authority 无因管理，未授权管理
agent ad litem 诉讼代理人，委托代理人
agent caretaker 代理管理
agent cost 代理成本
agent de change 证券交易经纪人
agent for collection 托收代理人
agent middleman 代理中间人
agent of a company 公司代理人
agent of necessity 紧急处分的代理人；必要的代理人
agent of overseas principal 海外代表
agent of the commission agent 行纪的代理人
agent of the merchant 商业代理人

agent provocateur 密探，间谍；罪行的诱饵（指引诱他人做一种明显违法的行为，如果不是他的引诱，这个行为则不会发生）
Agent Technology 兴趣跟踪软件（亦称 Push Technology）
agent to accept process 接受传票的代理人
agent's lien 代理人留置权
agent's remuneration 代理人的酬金
agent's tort 代理人的侵权行为
agents of change 变革代理人
agents-consular 领事代表
ager n. 原野，田地；（一块确定了地界的）土地
ager privatus 私地
ager publicus 公地
ager vectigalis 纳税地
agglomeration economics 聚集经济
aggravate v. 加剧，恶化，更加严重；加重（病情，负担，罪行等）
aggravated a. 严重的；加重的
aggravated assault 严重暴行，加重暴行，严重侵犯他人身体
aggravated burglary 严重入屋行窃罪，严重盗窃罪
aggravated criminal responsibility 加重罪责
aggravated damages 严重损害（他人）财产（罪）；严重损害
aggravated larceny 严重盗窃（罪）
aggravated libel 加重的诽谤（罪）
aggravated misconduct 严重的不法行为
aggravated misdemeanor 见 serious misdemeanor
aggravated negligence 严重过失
aggravated punishment 加重的处罚
aggravated theft 有加重情节的盗窃罪
aggravating circumstances 从重处罚情节，加重处罚情节
aggravation n. 加重；严重
aggravation from repetition 因再犯而加重刑罚
aggravation of penalty 刑罚的加重；加重处罚

aggravation of the crime 加重情节的犯罪
aggravation of the situation 事态的恶化；事态严重
aggregate n./a. 1.集合，集体 2.聚集 3.总数，合计/合计的；聚集的
aggregate accountability 聚合责任（指有关行政合法性的问题，越来越多的私人主体因承担政府经营职能而涉及私人主体者与公共治理的问题，在公私合作和协商背景下产生此聚合责任）
aggregate cost of coverage 承保总值
aggregate demand 1.总要求，总需求，总需求量（指在特定时期，节约措施上所耗尽的商品和服务）2.总需求（指在特定时期，对公司产品和服务的总需求）
aggregate fund in flow and out flow 资金流入与流出累积总额
aggregate income (1926年)(美)总收入，累计收入[指夫妻双方合并的收入，夫妻应提交个人所得税合并申报表(joint tax return)]
aggregate interest bill 集体有息票据
aggregate losses 累计损失
aggregate of operative facts 产生法律效果的总体事实
aggregated rebate cartel 统一回扣卡特尔（同行联盟）
aggregatio mentium (合同当事人)意思表示一致
aggregation n. (专利)互不起作用的组合，聚集物，聚集体；显而易见的组合[指①一套在结构上或功能上相互不合作的配件，因此不能授予其作为一项发明的专利，它与"联合体"或"结合体"(combination)含义相反；②历史上看，专利审查人对于主张发明专利的标记(label)可能或不能授予专利的结合体，而其权利主张不能清楚表明这些配件如何协作或互起作用而产生新的或不可预期的成果。在《1952年专利法》(the Patent Act of 1952)第103节中，作为聚集物(aggregation)的这个用语失去了实用性(usefulness)，而由法定测试(statutory test)所替代。亦可称为juxtaposition。见combination ④]
aggress v. 侵略；侵犯，挑衅，攻击

aggress against 挑衅；攻击；侵略
aggression n. 侵略；攻击；侵略行为；侵犯行为
aggressive a. 侵略的；爱寻衅的；行为过火的，放肆的，敢作敢为的
aggressive bloc 侵略集团
aggressive collection (通过拘留、传第三债务人出庭令、执行令)收取债款
aggressive conduct 寻衅行为，攻击行为，侵犯行为
aggressive policy 侵略政策
aggressive practice 侵犯性商业行为(欧共体条约指令的第8条对侵犯性商业行为作出了界定；如果通过骚扰，对身体实施暴力威胁而强迫或施加不适当影响，显著地损害了"一般消费者"对产品的自由选择，并导致消费者作出在正常情况下不会作出的交易决定，这种商业行为就被认定为侵犯性商业行为)
aggressive unilateralism 挑衅性单边主义
aggressive war 侵略战争
aggressive wars flow from imperialism system 帝国主义制度产生的侵略战争
aggressor n. 侵略者，攻击者
aggressor country 侵略国
aggressor troop 侵略军
aggrieve v. 侵害；使悲痛，使委屈
aggrieved n./a. 受害者，受委屈者/受害的；悲痛的；受委屈的
aggrieved alien 受害外籍人
aggrieved party 受害人(方)，被害人(方)
aggrieved person 被害人；受委屈者
aggrieved state 受害国
agio n. 贴水，折扣；汇水；银行手续费
agiotage n. 汇兑业务；股票经纪人的业务；股票投机；套利差额
agistment (=agist; agister) n. (收费为他人)放牧牛马合同(契约)
agitate v. 骚动；煽动，鼓动；激烈辩论(讨论)
agitation n. 骚动；煽动，鼓动；焦虑；激烈辩论(讨论)
agitator n. 煽动者，鼓动者；骚动者
agitator of armed fighting 武斗煽动者，械斗煽动者

agitator of rebellion 叛乱煽动者
agitator of unlawful strike 非法罢工煽动者
agnate n. （罗马法）男系亲属,父系亲属,男系卑亲属;同族,同种
agnatic a. 男系亲属的,男方的;同族的
agnatio n. （罗马法）父系的亲属关系,宗族,宗亲[不涉及血缘关系,特别是官员或年长者的家父权家中任何性别的自由人（free persons）的从属关系,男系亲属关系可以通过收养（adoption）或通过血缘关系（blood relationship）,由男方家庭追溯来建立]
agnation n. 宗亲关系;父系亲属关系
agnatus （罗马法）父（男）系关系者,同宗,同宗族（见 *cognatus*）
agoing ad. 在进行中
agonal stage 濒死状态
agonal trauma 濒死伤
agony n. 濒死;痛苦的挣扎;强烈的爆发
agoranomi n. （雅典）民政官
agraphia n. 书写不能,失写症
agrarian a. 土地的;土地所有制的;农民的;促进农民利益的
agrarian economy 土地经济
agrarian laws （古罗马）公地法律
agrarian reform 土地改革
agrarian reform law 土地改革法
agreamentum n. （古英国法）同意,一致;一个合同（契约）,一个协定
agree v. 同意,赞成;应允;约定;一致;认为无误
agree in *absentia* 缺席同意
agree on something 同意某事（指往往在强调经过了讨论或争论后才同意的或者不得不同意）
agree to differ 各自保留不同意见（不再说服对方）
agreed a. 同意的;赞成的;双方协议的;约定的
agreed and declared 一致同意并宣称的
agreed case （双方当事人）无异议的案件
agreed date 约定的日期
agreed formula 一致同意的办法,商定的方案
agreed minutes 商定的记录;协定记录
agreed period 商定的期限,约定期限
agreed (upon) price 商定的价格,约定价格
agreed quantity of trade 议定的贸易量,约定贸易量
agreed reduction 议定的裁减,约定裁减
agreed rent 议定的租金;约定租金
agreed statement of facts （双方当事人）一致赞成的事实陈述
agreed submission of a case 一致同意的案件移交
agreed text 协议文本;（双方）一致同意的文本
agreed upon remedies 补救协议
agreed value 商定的价值,约定价值
agreed-upon levels 商定的水准
agreement n. 1.协同行为 2.协定,协议 3.合议,合约;（双方）意思表示一致 4.合同（契约）5.同意
agreement concerning aid 援助协定
agreement concerning general contract terms 合同（契约）的一般条件协议
agreement concerning price discounts 价格折扣协议
agreement fixing prices 确定价格协议
agreement for bilateral legislation 双边司法协定
agreement in restraint of trade 限制贸易协议
agreement in undue restraint of trade 不正当限制贸易协议
agreement mistake 协议错误
agreement not of alienate territory 不割让领土的协定
agreement of alliance 联盟协定,联姻协议
agreement of election of forum （国际私法）协议管辖
agreement of mandate 委任合同（契约）
agreement of separation 夫妻分（别）居的协议
Agreement of the People （英）《人民公约》
agreement officer 签约聘任的官员
Agreement on an international Energy Program IEP 《国际能源纲领协议》

agreement on labo(u)r protection 劳动保护协议

Agreement on Trade—Related Aspects of Intellectual Property Rights (TRIPs) 与贸易有关的知识产权协议

agreement regulating output 控制产量协议

agreement takes effect as of June 5 协定从六月五日起生效

agreement to differ （英国责任制内阁曾在极短一段时间内实行过的）允许分歧原则

Agreement to Establish the South Center 建立南方中心协定（南方中心是指一个政府的组织，主要在加强南方各国的团结，针对发展中国家所面临的问题，特别在经济全球化加快发展新形势下面临的多种问题，以及它们在国际舞台上应有的共同政策取向和集体联合行动方针，加强研究，提出建议供77国集团及其他发展中国家决策当局采用）

agreement to sell 销售协议（指货物转移在将来完成或受一些条件制约的货物销售协议）

agreement to transfer 转让合同（契约）；转让协议

agreement year 协议年度

agreement-as-written 书面协议

agreement-in-fact 事实上的协议

agrement n. （驻在国对派遣外交使节的）同意

agribusiness n. 农业综合企业（指美国垄断资本家拥有的大型农场，包括农业机械经营项目、农产品加工及分配等）

agricultural a. 农业的，耕作的；农艺的，农学的

Agricultural Adjustment Act of 1933 （美）《1933年农业调整法》（指代表主要"新政"成果，通过限制生产改善农业萧条和提高土地价值的法规）

agricultural bank 农业银行

agricultural code 农业法典

agricultural commodity 农产商品

agricultural credit act 农业信贷法

agricultural gain tax 农业收益税

agricultural holding 农业占有地

agricultural land 农业用地，农用土地

agricultural lands tribunal 农用土地裁判庭

agricultural law 农业法

agricultural leases tribunal 农业租赁法庭

agricultural lien 农业留置权

agricultural population 农业人口

agricultural pricing policy 农业价格政策

agricultural producers' cooperative （中）农业生产合作社

agricultural production mutual-aid team （中）农业生产互助组

agricultural production responsibility system （中）农业生产责任制

agricultural raw material 农业原料

agricultural surplus 剩余农产品

agricultural tax 农业税

Agriculture Adjustment Act 农业调整法

agriculture sector 农业部门

agro-economic zone 农业经济区

agro-industrial complex 农工联合企业

agro-pastoral economy 农牧经济

agro-technician n. 农业技术人员，农艺师

agro-town n. 建在农业地区的城镇

aground n. (go, run) 搁浅，触礁

aguna n. （犹太教正统派和保守派名词）（自称丧夫但未经证实的）无夫之妻（指按教规不得另嫁的妇人）；（自称丧夫的）未亡人（按规定丈夫之死未经证实不得再嫁）

ahimsa n. （佛教的）不杀生

ahl al-kitāb （伊斯兰教法）掌经人（指分别享有律法书、福音书和《波斯古经》的犹太教徒、基督教徒和琐罗亚斯德教徒）

AIBD (= Association of International Bond Dealers) 国际债券交易协会

aid n. 帮助，援助，救护；助手，辅助物；补助税（指中世纪欧洲由个人或团体向某个当权者交纳的一种捐税）

aid agreement 援助协定

aid and abet 教唆，帮凶；帮凶；伙同作案，同谋

aid and comfort （美）支持和援助，鼓励[主要指行为人给予美国的敌人以援助和支持，而且大量援助以叛国方式进行，实

为叛国罪构成要件之一。这个词语是从法语"aide et confort"翻译过来的。早在15世纪法语翻译的《圣经》中就出现过。第一次使用这个词语的英语是《格拉夫顿编年史》(1568年)(Grafton's chronicles of 1568)中]

aid and comfort the enemy 叛逆,通敌

Aid for Family with Dependent Children 单亲家庭育儿津贴(简写 AFDC)

aid for lawsuit 求助于诉讼

aid prayer 救济请求(指依普通法提起的不动产诉讼中的一种请求)

Aid to Family with Dependent Children Program 未成年子女家庭协助规定

aid-giving nation 援助国

aide-mémoire (外交)备忘录

aided person 受援者

aider n. 助手,帮手;辅助人

aider and abettor 共犯,帮凶;(英)帮助和教唆犯

aider by verdict 通过裁决的帮助(美民事诉讼程序中通过提交证据的方式对有缺陷的诉辩文书进行矫正的称谓)

aiding and abetting 帮助(犯)和教唆(犯)

aiel (=aile;ayle;ayel) n. 祖父令状(收回土地时适用的一种不动产诉讼形式)

ailing enterprises 有问题的企业

air v. 发表,播送〈air one's opinion〉(发表意见),〈air one's grievance〉(申诉冤情),〈clear the air〉(①让空气流通;②澄清真相;③清除误会)

air charter movement 包机空运

Air Code 《航空法典》

air control 空中管制,制空权

air crash 飞机失事

Air Defence Identification Zone 防空识别区["防空识别区"是国家在实践中出现的一个特殊区域。通常是指一些国家基于防空安全原因所设置的、超出本国领海以外的空间区域,对进入该区域的航空器要立即予以识别、定位和控制。其宽度不定,有的国家规定宽度超过本国领海以外300英里。防空识别区一般是沿海国面向海洋方向上空在领空之外划设的区域,通常情况下以该国的战略预警机和预警雷达所能覆盖的最远端作为界限,要大于专属经济区的范围。防空识别区最初在第二次世界大战后由美军太平洋司令部设定,用于规范美国及其盟国之间的对空防御作战。20世纪50年代以来,包括一些大国和中国周边部分国家在内的20多个国家和地区先后设立了防空识别区。中国政府设立了东海防空识别区,符合《联合国宪章》等国际法和国际惯例的规定。由于国际法上对该制度并无明确规定,因此各国对该区域的范围和进入该范围的航空器应履行何种手续,以及违反其规定的航空器给予何种处理,规定并不一致。依照国际法,各国航空器在其他国家领空以外的飞行是自由的,国家不能把公海上空据为己有。天空是自由的(*caelim liberum*)。众所周知,美国是世界上最早设置防空识别区的国家,早在20世纪50年代便以国防安全为由设了数个不同的防空识别区。缩略为 ADIZ]

air domain 领空

air dunnage bag (集装箱运输)空气(隔离)囊

Air Force Act (英)《空军法》

air freight 空中货运;空中货运费

air freight container 空运集装箱

air harbo(u)r 航空港

air hijacking 空中劫持

air law 航空法,大气空间法

air line 1.航空系统;航空公司 2.航线

air liner 客机;班机

air mass 气团

air medical quarantine station 航空卫生检疫所(站)

Air Navigation Act 《空中导航法》

air piracy 空中劫持,劫机

air pirate 空中劫持者;劫机者

air pollutant 污染空气的物质

air pollution 大(空)气污染

Air Pollution Control Commission (美)大气污染控制委员会

air pollution index 大(空)气污染指数

air pollution surveillance system 大(空)气污染监测系统

air port 航空港,机场

air purifier 空气净化器,空气净化物
Air Quality Act （美）《大(空)气质量法》(1967年立法)
air quality and emission standard 大气质量和排放标准
air recording 对广播信号的录音(指直接将广播节目录制下来,如果该录制不是为个人使用,又不属于法定许可范围,将会构成侵犯版权或邻接权)
air right 空间所有权
air risks 空运险
air space 空气空间,大气空间;空域;领空(法律上指领土的上空)
air space above sea 海上空间,海面上空
air space law 空气空间法
air supremacy 制空权
Air Traffic and General Operating Rules （美）《空中飞行和一般操作规则》[美国于1950年设立了防空识别区,后来射程远、速度快导弹的出现已使这种防空识别区对怀有敌意航空器的识别失去战略意义。但美国仍保持了下来,并不断改进。2003年美国制定了关于防空识别区的联邦法规,即《空中飞行和一般操作规则》。详情可参见《美国联邦法规汇编》(2003年)第14标题卷本]
air traffic control 航空管制
air transportation insurance 空运保险
air violation 侵犯领空
air warfare 空战
air-borne trade 空运贸易
air-mail n. 航空邮件,航空邮政,航空邮票
air-shed n. 大(空)气域(环境)
airborne a. 1.空降的 2.空运的,机载的 3.飞机在飞行中的 4.(飞机)离开地面的 5.通过无线电播送的,通过电视播送的
airborne lead contaminant from (cities) industry 导致来自城市工业的污染物散发在空气之中
airborne pollutant 空气传播的污染物
aircraft n. 飞机,航空器
aircraft accident 飞机失事,空中失事
aircraft all risks 飞机一切险
aircraft lien 航空器优先权(指英美法上设定在航空器上的法定非移转占有型

担保)
aircraft noise 飞行器噪声
aircraft papers 飞行证件
airlift n. 空运,空中桥梁
airline regs 航空区
Airplane Law （美）《航空(班机)法》
airplane product liability 飞机产品责任
airport n.（=air port） 机场
airport concession 机场特许权
airport noise 机场噪声
airport owner's and operator's liability insurance 机场责任保险
airway bill (of lading) 空运单,航空货运单
airways act 航空法
airways corporation 航空公司
aisne (或 eigne) n. （古英国法）长子,最先出生者
ajustment disorder 适应障碍(因长期存在应激源或困难处境,加之病人有一定人格缺陷,以烦恼、抑郁等情感障碍为主,同时有适应不良的行为障碍或出现功能障碍,并使社会功能受损。随着事过境迁,刺激消除经调整形成新的适应,精神障碍随之缓解)
akin a. 同族的,有血缘关系的;同类的,相近似的(to)
al-Qaida "基地"组织
Alamannic Code （德史）《阿拉曼尼法典》(公元600—718年间德国南部的苏阿比亚领土上阿拉曼尼人辑成的一部民间法典,涉及宗教法、公法和私法)
AL QAEDA 基地
alarm n./v. 警报;惊恐/使惊恐,使警觉,报警,向……报警
albeit conj. 尽管,虽然
album n. （古罗马）布告栏;法院的书面记录
Albus Liber 白皮书(英国的古法律书,包括伦敦市法律和习惯的汇编,依照案卷掌管主事法官的命令,已经重印)
alcalde n. （西班牙等）城镇长官(兼有司法职能)
alcohol control 酒精控制
alcohol consumption 酗酒

alcoholic a. 酒精的,酒精性的
alcoholic drinks 含酒精的饮料
alcoholic paranoia 酒毒性妄想狂
alcoholic psychosis 酒精性精神病
alcoholism n. 酒精中毒
alcohometer n. 见 breathalyzer
Alcoran n. （古）（伊斯兰教法）《古兰经》
alderman n. （英）（市、郡一级的）高级市政官（又译：市府参事，其地位仅次于市长）；市参议员（指自治市议会的成员）
aleator n. 侥幸者,赌博者
aleatory a. 以侥幸为目的的,赌博的
aleatory contract 赌博合同（契约）（旧译：射幸合同）
alegal a. （1991年）（美）准法律的,法律边缘的[指法律范畴之外,但又不可归类为法定的、合法的或非法的、违法的。如法律通常处理非婚同居许诺（the promise of unmarried cohabitants）作为合同用语（contractual words）而不是作为一个准法律的承诺用语（alegal words of commitment）]
alert n./v. 警报；警戒状态,警戒期间/使警觉,使处于待命状态
Alex Boncayao Brigade 阿历克斯·邦卡尧队伍（20世纪80年代成立的在马尼拉活动的恐怖组织）
Alford plea （1972年）奥尔福德答辩,认罪答辩[指认罪答辩（guilty plea）已加入了辩诉交易（plea bargain）的部分,即由刑事被告否认有罪行或者事实上承认犯有罪行。联邦法院可以采纳这种答辩,直到有证据证明刑事被告犯有罪行。此词条来源于北卡罗来纳州诉阿尔福德案（North Carolina v. Alford, 400 US, 25, 91 S. Ct 260, 1970）。认罪答辩是指刑事被告进入辩诉交易但不承认犯有罪行。在有些情况下类似于"不辩护也不认罪的答辩"（nolo-contendere）,这种答辩符合美国联邦宪法第五修正案,如果此答辩表示自愿、故意和适当的智力选择〈the defendant-realizing the strength of the prosecution-evidence and no wanting to risk the death penalty-entered an Alford plea〉（认清指控证据的强度而不愿承担死刑风险的被告参加奥尔福德答辩）]

algorithms n. 算法,规则系统
alguazil n. （西班牙）警官
alia n. 其他事物或其他人
alia enormia 其他严重错误或不法行为（other serious wrong）[指在普通法上侵害之诉（a trespass action）中原告在总的事实陈述中列举不法行为或一些伤害的宣告后的结束语]
alias dictus 1.别名,化名；绰号 2.第二（或三）令状（或传票）
alias execution 第二次执行令状
alias summons （原传票由于形式或传送错误而未起到作用时）再次发出的传票
alias writ （因第一次令状未能送达而发出的）第二次令状（或进一步令状）
alibi n. 不在犯罪现场（指以不在犯罪现场为理由的申辩）；托词,借口
alien n./v./a. 外国国籍者,外国人,外侨/转让,让渡（所有权）/外国的,异己的；相异的
alien act 1.外侨法,外籍人法 2.（英）外国人法（1705年）；（美）移民法（1798年）
alien ami 友国人
Alien and Sedition Acts （美）《外侨和煽动叛乱（治罪）法》（1978年的联邦法规,惩处指责或诽谤政府的人,此法规授予总统权力,以驱逐不受欢迎的外侨和延长其取得公民资格的居住时间要求等）
alien characters 异质,外来的特点
alien class element （中）阶级异己分子
alien conception 外来概念,舶来概念
alien corporation 外国公司
alien crop 引进作物
alien enemies act 敌侨法
alien enemy 敌侨,敌对的外国人
alien firm 外国商行
alien friend 友侨
alien law 移民法,外籍人法,外国人法
Alien Order （英）《外国人法令》（1920年）
alien property 外国人的财产
Alien Registration Act (**Smith Act**)（美）《外侨登记法》（又称史密斯法,1940年的联邦立法）
alien species 外来物种
alien tax 外国人入境税

alien's ownership 外国人所有权
* *Aliena negotia exacto officio geruntur.*
The business of another is to be carried out with particular care. 对他人的事务应当特别认真地办理。
alienability n. 可让渡性,可转让性
alienable a. 可让渡的,可转让的
alienage n. 外侨的法律地位;外国人的地位
alienage jurisdiction 侨民管辖权,外国人管辖权
alienate v. 转让,让渡(所有权);使疏远
* *Alienatio rei praefertur juri accrescendi.*
Alienation is favored by the law rather than accumulation. 法律更有利于财产转让,而不是财产积累。
alienation n. 转让,让渡;疏远;离间
alienation clause (财产的)让渡条款
alienation in mortmain 死后土地转让(旧译:死手土地转让,指将土地转让给任何世俗的或教会的社团)
alienation mutual affection 夫妻感情的破裂
alienation of affection (第三者)离间夫妻感情,破坏他人夫妻感情
alienation of chattel personal 属人动产的转让
alienation of pledge 转让抵押品
alienation of property 财产的转让
alienator n. 让渡人,转让人
alienee n. 受让人
alieni juris (罗马法)他权人(指在他人权力之下的人,如服从家长或监护人权力的未成年人);受监护人;受权力支配者(与 *sui juris* 相对)
alienism n. 1.外侨身份 2.精神错乱;精神病学
alieno nomine possidere 代理人为本人(被代理人)管理占有物,代理人为本人(被代理人)取得占有物
aliens checkpost 外国人检查站
aliens holding diplomatic (或 service) **passports** 持有外交(公务)护照的外国人
align v. 使成一线,使成一行,使结盟,使密切合作

alignment n. 结盟,联合,组合;一直线,列队
alignment of the boundary line 边界走向
aliment n. (苏格兰法)财经上的支持[指穷人或贫困者(indigent)才有资格接受这样的财经支持。它可以来自配偶一方;如果未婚,可来自一位亲戚或法定命令中的亲戚。首先关注的是这个人的孩子,亦称(英国法) alimony]
alimentary a. 有营养的
alimentary allowance 膳食津贴
alimentation n. 供给食物;营养;抚养
alimony n. 1.法院命令的抚养费(allowance),(离婚后或诉讼期间)一方给另一方的生活费、抚养费[抚养费(alimony)与(夫妻)财产协议(property settlement)有明显区别。抚养支付(alimony payment)是应交纳税收的所得,用它给予接受的夫或妻一方,而且是从支付方扣除;财产协议中的支付则完全不同。美国联邦最高法院认为制定法规定只安排丈夫支付抚养费是违宪的。亦称 spousal support; maintenance。见 child support;] 2.(英国法) aliment
alimony judg(e)ment 关于扶养费的裁决
alimony *pendente lite* 诉讼期间的抚养(生活)费
alimony pending suit 诉讼期间的抚养(生活)费
alio intuitu 别有用心;阴谋;持不同意见
* *Aliquis non debet esse judex in propria causa, quia non potest esse judex et pars.*
A person ought not to be judge in his own cause, because he can not act as judge and party. 任何人不得在自己的案件中担任法官,因为他不能同时既是法官,又是当事人。
aliquot n. 部分,按比例的部分
* *Aliud est celare, aliud tacere.* To conceal is one thing; to be silent is another. 隐瞒(匿)是一回事,保持沉默是另一回事。
* *Aliud est distinctio, aliud separation.*
Distinction is one thing; separation is another. 区别是一回事,分类是另一回事。
* *Aliud est vendere, aliud vendenti consen-*

tire. To sell is one thing, to consent to a sale (sellor) is another. 销售是一回事,(销售者)同意销售是另一回事。
Aliunde a. 出于别处的,来自外面的
alive (to) 注意到,意识到
Alkali Court (伊斯兰教法)阿卡里法院(一种处理穆斯林事务的法院)
all against one 集体对抗单一
all but 几乎,差一点
* **All citizens of the People's Republic of China are equal before the law.** 中华人民共和国公民在法律面前一律平等。
all deliberate speed (美)十分审慎的速度(1955 年联邦最高法院命令各地教育委员会以"十分审慎速度"尽早消除公立学校中的种族隔离制度。见 deliberate speed)
all doubt 一切怀疑(区别于 reasonable doubt 合理怀疑。见该条)
all else equal 其他情况(条件)都相同(时)
All England Law Reports (英)《全英法律判例汇编》[由巴特沃思公司出版,包括 1936 年至今的判例汇编。比《法律判例汇编》有更多的判例,但并不都附有全文。还有一个补充的追溯成套本《(1558—1935 年)全英法律判例汇编再版》(1957—1968 年),增加约 5000 个早期的案例]
all fours 完全类似(指两个案件或判例完全一致,不管在法律上或事实上大体一致)
All is permissible unless prohibited 无法禁止即自由,无法禁止即可为[指古希腊的政治准则,与"法无授权即禁止"或"法无授权不可为"(All is prohibited unless permissible)有着相辅相成的关系,体现了"规范公权、保障私权"的现代法治理念,这也就是职权法定的内涵。职权法定的逻辑结果是,政府的权力是有限的,因为法律授予它的权力是特定的,政府只能做法律授权它做的事,而不能做它想做的一切事]
all jurisdictional exercises 所有管辖的行使
all loss risks 不论原因一切险,不论原因的全险

* **All men are created equal (All men are equally free-willing beings).** 所有人生来就是平等的。
* **All men are equal before the law.** 法律面前人人平等。
* **All nationalities in the People's Republic of China are equal.** 中华人民共和国各民族一律平等。
all necessary means 一切必要方法
all orders of society 社会各阶层
all other perils 一切其他风险
all peoples 所有民族
* **All power belongs to the people.** 一切权力属于人民。
* **All proceedings are really against persons.** 所有的程序都是针对人的。
all records 所有记录,所有信息
all rights reserved 版权所有;保留一切权利
all risks 一切险,综合险
all risks clause 综合险条款,一切险条款
* **All the countries of the world, big or small, should be equal and none should impose its own will on others.** (中)世界上所有的国家,不管是大国或小国,都应该平等,谁也不应当把自己的意志强加给别国。
all the relevant circumstances 一切相关情况
all the way 1.从远道〈he comes all the way from America〉(他远从美国来)2.从头至尾,自始至终〈Hein Online has full coverage with searchable PDFs of U. S. Reports all the way from volume one to the most recent slip opinions〉(Hein Online 具有全文概要,还附有可检索从第 1 卷本至最新判决原文单行本的《美国判例汇编》的 PDF 版本)3.一路上
all things considered 周全考虑
all walks of life 各行各业
all working time saved both ends 在装、卸港口节省的全部工作时间
all-encompassing Internet 无所不至的因特网
all-encompassing pleadings 无所不包的诉

辩文书
all-inclusive 无所不包
all-male federal jury 全部男性联邦陪审团
all-risk insurance 综合保险,一切险(指覆盖各种类别的可保险的损失,特殊情况不在此限)
allay v. 减轻(病痛等)
*Allegans contraria non est audiendus. He is not to be heard who alleges things contradictary to each other. 自相矛盾的陈述将不被采信(前言不对后语充耳不闻)。
*Allegans suum trpitudinem non est audiendus. He is not to be heard who alleges his own turpitude or infamy. 任何人因有丑行而不得主张权利(援引衡平法的人自己必须清白)。
allegata et probata 有证据可资证明之陈述;有证据之主张(指诉讼当事人提出主张,并以证据支持其主张)
*Allegatio contra factum non est admittenda. An allegation contrary to the deed is not admissible. 违背契据(或事实)的主张(或辩解)是不可接受的。
allegation n. (15世纪)1.主张,断言,宣称(指当事方在诉状中所陈述的某些事情是属实的)2.宣称的某事[指实际上所宣称或所主张的某事,特别是在法定答辩诉讼文件(legal pleading)中的某事;一方当事人对真实事实的正式陈述,因为它是真实的,是可以证明的,所以无须再对它进行证实。allege v.]
allegation falsi 虚假托词,虚假断言,虚假事实辩护
allegation for wrongful termination of an exclusive agency agreement 对一项独家代理协议的不当终止的指控
allegation of brutality 声称被虐待
allegation of fact 事实陈述,事实主张
allegation of faculties (妻子为了获取离婚扶养费而对丈夫的)支付能力(所作)的书面陈述
allegation of fraud 声称被欺诈
allegation of invalidity 声称无效;主张无效

allegation of malice 声称被恶意中伤
allegation of rape 声称被强奸
allege v. 1.断言,指称(尤其在提不出证明的情况下);指证;声称;主张;引例证明 2.(作为事实、理由、借口、辩解)提出
allege sth. as a reason 提出某事作为理由
alleged a. 提出而尚未证实的;声称的,宣称的;被指称的;被说成的(allegedly ad.)
alleged agent 自命代理人
alleged cause 陈述的理由,引证的理由
alleged claim 所主张的请求权
alleged confession (尚未证实的)认供
alleged corrupt 所指称的贪污
alleged criminal 被指控的刑事犯
alleged debt (已经提出但)未经证实的债务
alleged evidence 所供述的证据
alleged loss 所声称的损失,所主张的损失
alleged offence 被指称的罪行
alleged offender 被指称的罪犯
alleged stolen property 声称被盗窃的财产
alleged tort 被指称的侵权行为
allegiance n. (对国家、政府、事业、个人等的)忠诚;效忠
alleviate v. 减轻,缓和
alliance n. 1.同盟,联盟,联合 2.联姻
alliance of industrial and agricultural workers (中)工农联盟
alliance of workers and peasants (中)工农联盟
alliance pact 盟约
alliances of enterprises 联合企业
allied a. 联合的,同盟;联姻的;同源的;(大写)(第一次世界大战中的)协约国的,(第二次世界大战中的)同盟国的
allied company 联合公司;联号
allied powers 联盟国;(大写)(第一次世界大战中的)协约国;(第二次世界大战中的)同盟国
allocate v. 分配,配给;拨款;分派;划归
allocation n. 分配,配置
allocating the parties litigation costs 分配当事人诉讼成本
allocation n. 拨款;分配,配给;分派;配

给物
allocation functions between judge and jury 法官和陪审团之间的分工职能,法官与陪审团之间的分工
allocation of materials 物资分配;配给物
allocation of power 权力分配
allocation of property rights 财产权的配置
allocation of risks 风险分担
allocation of special drawing rights 特别提款权分配
allocation of various function 各种职能的分权,不同职责的分配
allocation to the lowest tenderer 减价投标
allocation warrant 分配令,分配通知书
allocative efficiency 配置效率
allocatur n. 诉讼费评定证明书;税额评定证明书;公文有效证明书
allocution n. (法院审查犯人是否具有)不服判罪的任何合法理由的手续;训谕(尤指罗马教皇的)
allocutus n. (法院审查犯人是否具有)不服判罪的任何合法理由的手续;训谕(尤指罗马教皇的)
allodial land 自由私有土地
allodium n. (土地的)绝对所有权;(封建时代的)自主地产;自由地
allographa 他人代书
allonge n. 票据背书的附单,票据的粘单
allonym n. (作者的)假名,别名
allorney work-product 见 work product
allot v. 配合,拨给;规定,派定
allotment n. 分配,配给;拨给;派定;拨款
allotment certificate 分配证书
allotment issued 已拨款项
allotment letter 股票(红利)分配通知书
allotment note 分配通知书(指海员在签订服务合约的时候,指定将其薪金的一部分交给他的近亲属,如父母、妻子、子女等收受。这种分配合约称为分配通知书。)
allotment of shares 股份的分配
allotment system 分配制,配给制
allottee n. 领受人;接受分配者;接受拨给物资的人员(或机构)
allow v. 准许,容许;允给;承认,认为;酌加(减);考虑到;计划,打算
allowable a. 可允许的,可以承认的;正当的
allowable in general average 可作为共同海损获取补偿
allowance n. 1.允许,准许;被允许的限期(限额) 2.津贴;折让;减免;免税额;补助 3.抚养费 4.手续费
allowance for a person bring up children 抚育子女者的补助
allowance for damage 货损折扣
allowance in kind 实物津贴
allowance in respect of a dependent spouse 扶养配偶的津贴
allowance of an application 批准申请;申请免税额
allowance of holidays 假日津贴
allowance system 津贴制度
allowance to parent out of children's estate 从子女的财产中给予父母的补贴
allowed by law 法律允许的
allowed into evidence 可接受作为证据
allure n./v. 引诱力,吸引力/引诱,诱惑
alluvion n. 冲积层;涨滩;沙洲;洪水
ally n. 1.伙伴,助手 2.同盟者 3.(大写)(第一次世界大战时的)协约国,(第二次世界大战时的)同盟国
almanc n. 1.历书 2.年鉴
Almanac of Federal judiciary 联邦司法机构年鉴(指美国司法机构中有关联邦法官的传记信息,值得关注的裁决、概要,媒体报道范畴以及律师对法官能力和气质的评估等资料。它是活页两卷本出版的参考书)
almoner n. 施赈官,救济品分发人员;寺院的施赈人员;(英)医院的社会服务员
almonry n. 施赈所,救济品分发处
alms n. 施舍物,救济金
alms man 领救济金者,受施舍者
along with 与……一起,和……一道〈a variety of other documents are printed in the Federal Register along with executive orders and proclamations〉(各种不同的文件均与行政令和宣言一起在《联邦公报》中出版)
alongside the state courts 与州法院并行

already existing provisions 原有规定
alta proditio (古英国法)重大叛逆罪
alta via (古英国法)公路,大路
alter v. 改变,改动,阉割;变样,变作
alter ego 1.代办人,知己,心腹;私人交易的工具 2.(美)(公司法)代办人原则(指允许法庭不顾公司"揭穿法人面纱"并坚持个人对以公司名义所做的有意行为负责。见 piercing the corporate veil)
Alter Ego Doctrine 另一自我说[美国布拉姆伯格(Blumberg)教授提出,该说认为两个关联公司在所有利益方面如此一致,以致失去相互独立性,或者一公司(子公司)完全为另一公司(母公司)的利益而存在,则该公司的存在被认为是另一公司的另一个自我,Agency Doctrine]
alteration n. 更正,修改;变动,改变;修订;订正
alteration of a crossed cheque 更改划线支票
alteration of article 物品加工;修改条文
alteration of instrument 法律文书的订正
alteration of law 法律的修改
alteration of original judg(e)ment 变更原判
alteration of private right 民事权利的变更,私权的变更
alteration of share capital 股份资本的变更
alterative a. 引起改变的,改变的
alterative mandamus 引起改变的训令
alterative pleading 引起旁议的抗辩
altercation n. 争辩,争吵
alteri stipulari nemo potest 不得为他人缔约
altering the pay of members of congress 改变国会议员的薪金(支付)
alternate a./n. 转换的;交替的;预备的,候补的/代理人,代表人;比较方案
alternate deputy 候补代表,候补众议员
alternate legacy 可选择的遗赠[指遗赠人(testator)允准遗赠受人(legatee)在两个或两个以上遗赠项目中选择一项]
alternate judge (美)代理推事,代理法官
alternate juror 候补陪审团员,预备陪审员
alternate member 候补会员,候补委员,候补议员,候补社员
alternate possibilities(或 alternative possibilities) 可供取舍可能性原则(指哲学界自由意志讨论中认为只有当一个人本来能够做其他行为时,他才对他所做的行动负有道德责任,这一原则起统辖性作用)
alternate senator 候补参议员
alternating insanity 躁狂抑郁交替型精神病
alternating presidentialism 交替式总统制
alternation of works 作品的修改(一般修改不产生新作,不产生新的版权,只有修改量大,引起质变,增加了修改者创造性劳动成果,才构成"改编")
alternative a./v. 在两者中任择其一的,选择性的,交替的,替代的/取舍,抉择,双者挑一
alternative amalgamation 选择合并
alternative assumptions 替代假设
alternative choice of law 替代法律选择
alternative claim 替代的索赔;选择性的请求权
alternative condition 选择条件
alternative counts (检控)交替的罪项(指一宗案件涉及若干罪行,可同时分开若干罪名来检控)
alternative danger 选择性危险(指危急中力求脱险的选择行为)
alternative delegate 替换的代表
Alternative Dispute Resolution(s) [ADR(s)] 替代解决争议方法,解决争议的替代方法[指非司法或非诉讼的争议解决方式,如在美国,包括调解—仲裁(Mediation-Arbitration)、无约束力的仲裁(non-binding Arbitration)、借用法官(Rent Judge)、小型审判(Mini-trial)仲裁等];选择性争端解决方式(相对于传统的法院解决民事或商业争端诉讼方式的多样性选择方式;也称解决纠纷的另类选择,英、美、澳大利亚、加拿大等国把调解视为"解决纠纷的另类选择","ADR"之一。与诉讼相比,调解较为省钱、省时,还能保持当事人之间的关

系,其至最终达到和解)
alternative dispute resolution techniques 可选择性争议解决技巧
alternative form 代替方式
alternative insemination 另类受精
alternative joinder 选择性合并
alternative joinder of plaintiff (defendants) 对原告(被告)的选择性合并
alternative jurisdiction 选择管辖
alternative legacy 未确定具体项目的遗赠
alternative minimum tax (1972年)最低替代税(指针对公司和高收入的个人所课的一种统一收费的税种,以保证那些纳税人面对全部应纳所课税的责任采用合法的免交、扣减或赊欠等方法而使其不致过多逃税。亦称 minimum tax)
alternative model 替代模式(刑事和解模式之一,这种模式通常由司法官员在量刑和执行中适用,替代监禁刑。该模式法律依据是各国的刑法、刑事诉讼法、少年法、被害人保护法、被害人赔偿法等。目前德国已明文规定刑事和解制,瑞士、奥地利、法国等亦已采用。见 community model)
alternative obligation 选择之债
alternative offence 交替罪
alternative price 可供选择的价格
alternative proposition 选择性主张,交替的建议
alternative punishment 替代刑罚
alternative relief 选择性救济,择一补救[指与另一种司法救济形式相互排斥的司法救济,在诉讼程序中,由于存在寻求特定履行(special performance)和特定履行可能被阻止时的损害赔偿两个方面,所以当事方可以选择救济。见 election of remedies]
alternative remainders 选择性的剩余财产
alternative remedy 替代补偿;选择性补偿;替代的法律救济方法
alternative settlement patterns 可供选择的定居方式
alternative system 选择(投票)制
alternative texts 可供选择的条文,备选条文
alternative to imprisonment (=alternative to prison) 监禁替代措施
alternative use 交替使用,选择使用
alternative writ 示出案由令状
alterum non laedere 不损及他人
altius non tollendi (罗马法和苏格兰的)采光权
altruistic a. 利他的,无利
altruistic steak 利他主义的特点
altum mare (古英国法)公海
Alumni Lectureship 校友讲座
alveus n. 河床
Am. Jur. 2d. American Jurisprudence, Second Edition 《美国法理学大全》第二版[《布莱克法律词典》第九版、第十版缩略语第1763页,第1862页〈Dictionary of Legal Abbreviations used in American Law Books〉(Doris M. Bieber)(William S.Herin. & Co.) 1979 P.12〉]
Am. Jur. 2d American Jurisprudence Second Series 《美国法理学大全》(第二套系列丛书)[《美国法理学大全》(第二套系列丛书)和《美国法律百科》(第二版)这两部国家百科全书旨在提供关于州和联邦的法律原理的综合性纲要,以前二者曾是竞争性著作,但当今这两部著作均由汤姆逊·路透(Thomas Reuters)正式出版。《美国法理学大全》(第二套系列丛书)和《美国法律百科》(第二版)都在140卷本以上,并附有相关广泛法律论题400篇以上的论文。有些论文,诸如"墓地""死尸",这些狭窄含义的论题文章估计不到12页;相反,那些广泛含义的标题论文,如"公司,企业"或"证据"可能占据好几卷本。每篇文章按节分开编号,并附有其内容的逐节提要起始,然后扩大范围。两部著作十分相似,但亦有不同之处。《美国法律百科》(第二版)开始的每一节或附小节均有简要"黑体字"表述一般法律原则,而且一般来说还有比《美国法理学大全》(第二套系列丛书)更多的脚注。在《美国法理学大全》(第二套系列丛书)中的论述趋向于聚焦联邦法,而《美国法律百科》(第二版)寻求提供全面综合的州法,而且通常援引比《美国法理学大全》(第二套系列丛书)更多的州的判例。两

部著作中的正文对法院判决、联邦的制定法和统一法规的特殊案例参考均附有丰富的脚注。在明显研讨州的制定法条文时，两部著作均援引州的制定法，脚注也涉及援引这些制定法的判例。当搜索判例参考时，常常核查一下这两部著作是值得的。它们覆盖相同的争点(issue)问题而不会重叠援引的判例]

Am. Jur. Legal Forms 2d （美）《美国法理学法律格式第二套丛书》(亦译为《美国法律百科全书法律格式第二套丛书》，指由律师合作出版公司出版的一套有关文据、契约、遗嘱等格式的丛书)

Am. Jur. Pleading and Practice Forms （美）《美国法理学诉讼程序和实践格式丛书》(亦译作《美国法律百科全书诉讼程序和实践格式丛书》，与 Am. Jur. Legal Forms 2d 具有同等作用，但着重于法院和行政机构的诉讼和其他法院的诉讼时间。见 Am. Jur. legal Forms 2d)

amalgamated a. 合并的，混合的，联合的，合成一体的
amalgamated action 合并诉讼
amalgamated consolidation 联合(合并)组建，合并设置(旧译：创立合并，设立合并)
amalgamated jurisdiction 合并管辖
amalgamation n. 合并，混合，联合；联合(合并)组建，合并设置；混合物
amalgamation of actions 诉之合并
amalgamation of company 公司的合并
amateur n. (泛指)非专业人员；业余活动者；业余爱好者
ambassador n. 大使；使节
ambassador at-large 巡回大使，无任所大使
ambassador extraordinary and plenipotentiary 特命全权大使
ambassador plenipotentiary 全权大使
ambassador without destination 无任所大使
ambassadorial a. 大使的，大使一级的
ambassadorial privilege 大使特权
ambassadorial talks 大使级会谈
ambassadorial-level diplomatic relations 大使级外交关系

ambassadress n. 女大使，大使夫人
ambidexter n. 两面受贿(常指陪审员收受原告和被告两方面的贿赂)；诡诈者；两面讨好者
ambient a. 周围的，环境(四周)的
ambient air 环境空气
ambient humidity 环境温度
ambient light 环境光照度
ambient noise 环境噪声
* *Ambigua responsio contra proferentem est accipienda.* An ambiguous answer is to be taken against him who offers it. 模棱两可的答辩得用来反驳提出此种答辩的人。
* *Ambiguitas verborum latens verificatione suppletur; nam quod ex facto oritur ambiguum verificatione facti tollitur.* A latent verbal ambiguity may be removed by evidence; for whatever ambiguity arises from an extrinsic fact may be explained by extrinsic evidence. 用语上隐含的模棱两可可以通过证据加以清除，因为任何从非本质的事实中所产生的模棱两可都可以用非本质的证据来解释。
* *Ambiguitas verborum patens nulla verificatione excluditur.* A patent ambiguity in the words of a written instrument can not be cleared up by extrinsic evidence to the instrument. A patent ambiguity is not removed by extrinsic evidence(or is never helped by averment). 法律文件上的文字显然含糊不能用验证来解决，用语意义不明之处不能通过验证解决
ambiguity n. 意思含糊；模棱两可的话；可作两种(或多种)解释
ambiguity of the main facts 主要事实不清
ambiguity upon the factum 事实不明确，事实含糊不清
ambiguous a. 意思含糊的，模棱两可的
ambiguous language 含糊不清的语言
ambiguous statement 含糊不清的陈述
ambit n. 界限，边缘线；范围
* **Ambition must be made to counteract ambition.** 野心必须用野心来对抗。
ambivalence n. (对一个人、物的爱与恨的)矛盾心理

ambulance n. 救护车;救护船;救护飞机
ambulance chaser （美俗）专办交通案件的律师;鼓励受害者起诉的律师
ambulance man 救护人员
* *Ambulatoria est voluntas defuncti usque ad vitae supremum exitum.* The will of a deceased person is ambulatory until the latest moment of life. 立遗嘱人直至临终前仍可变更其遗嘱。
ambulatory a. 流动的;可变更的
ambulatory chattel 动产
ambulatory deed 可变更的契据
ambulatory disposition 可变更的或可撤销的裁判(指①依照修订或撤销的裁判或判决;②依据变更的遗嘱条文,因立遗嘱人仍然在世,且有能力制定新的遗嘱。②的意见符合①中的 disposition 含义。见 ambulatory)
ambulatory will 可变更(撤销)的遗言(嘱)
ambustion n. 烧伤,烫伤
AmE (American English) 美国英语
amelioration n. 改善,改进,改良
amelioration of soils 土壤改良
amenability n. 顺从性;管辖;对……负有义务
amenability n. [=legal answerability, liability to being brought to judgment (amenability to the jurisdiction of foreign forum)] 法律上的义务性,有责任被提交判决(服从外州法院管辖)
amenability question 受管辖问题;顺从问题;负有……义务的问题
amenability to suit 诉讼的服理性,诉讼的顺从性,顺从管辖
amenable a. 服从(法律)的,有责任的,有服从义务的;可依照的;经得起检验(或查考)的
amenable to law 服从法律
amenable to process 依照传票,按程序
amenable to process absent consent 依照传票而不存在同意
amend v. 1.改正,(正式)修改(提案、议案等);修订,修订 2.改过;改进,改善
amend a judg(e)ment 改判
amend pleading 修改答辩状,修改诉状

amendatory a. （1895年）修订的,改正的
〈An amendatory rider to an insurance policy〉（保险单上一项更正的附加条款）
amendé v. （法）赔（罚）款;赔偿;道歉
amendé honorable 公开谢罪;正式赔偿;公开道歉与赔偿
amended a. 修正的,修改过的;改善的
amended bill 修正案
amended complaint （美）修改的起诉状[依据《联邦民事诉讼规则》第15(a)条](指通过增加相关事实修改或替代原来的民事起诉状,或对原起诉状中的错误或遗漏进行修改、变更或补充诉讼的权利主张等,以便案件在真实的事实基础上得到处理。在有些情况下,当事人必须获得法院的允准方可修改其起诉状。亦可称为 substituted complaint)
amended ordinance 修正的条例
amended pleading （1809年）修改过的诉状(指经修改而代替以前的诉状,此诉状包括以前不知道或遗漏的一些事实。见 supplemental pleading)
amended return （1861年）修订税单,修正的纳税申报表(指原来的申报表经修正其错误后重新申报的纳税单)
amended valuation 重新估计
amended writ 修正的令状
amending n. 修正,修改
amending clause 修正条款
amending statute 修改成文法规
amendment 修订,修改,修正,变更,改善[指①对制定法、宪法、诉讼文本(pleading)命令或其他法律文件(instrument)的正式修订、修改或建议的增加,特别是增、减、改正等的变动,还有词字的选择和推敲。(大写)修正案(特别指宪法修正案,如 Fifth Amendment"第五修正案")。②构成这种修改的过程。③(议会法)更改动议(指对一个动议的词句,通过删除、插入、增添文本,或替换文本来变更动议)]
amendment advice 修改通知书
amendment by adding （议会法）以添加修订[指在动议的末了或某个段落放些新的词句或将可分开的部分放入动议内。某些权威对待以添加修订作为一种嵌入

或插入的修订形式(form of amendment)。见 amendment by inserting]

amendment by inserting (议会法)以插入或嵌入修订(指在动议的现行措辞内或围绕这些措辞置入一些新的词语进行修订。某些权威认为以添加修订是在现行措辞末了添加新词以此区别以嵌入修订)

amendment in a statute 法规中的修订(条文)

amendment of constitution 宪法的修改

amendment of indictment 诉状的修改,修改诉状

amendment of pleading 诉状修正本,修正答辩状

amendment of treaty 条约修正案

amendment of writ 令状的修正

amendment to a will 修改遗嘱

amendment to draft law 修正法律草案

amendment to the press law 新闻法修正案

Amendment to U. S. Constitution 美国联邦宪法修正案

amends (复) n. 赔偿;赔罪

amenity n. (环境、建筑物等依法规定的)舒适、方便、雅洁

amentia n. 智力缺陷,精神错乱

amerce v. 罚款;罚金;惩罚

amerciable a. 应罚款的

amerciament (或 **amercement**) n. 金钱处罚;罚款;罚金;惩罚

American a./n. 美国的,美洲的/美洲人,美国人;美国英语

American 99ers' Union 美国 99 周失业者联盟(见 99er)

American Academy of Forensic Sciences 美国法庭(应用)科学学会

American Arbitration Association 美国仲裁协会

American Association for the Comparative Study of Law 美国法律比较研究协会

American Association for Legal and Political Philosophy 美国法律和政治哲学协会

American Association of Criminology 美国犯罪学协会

American Association of Law Libraries 美国法律图书馆协会

American Bar Association 美国律师协会

American Bar Association Model Rules of Professional conduct 《美国律师协会模范职业行为规则》

American Business Law 美国商务法

American Chamber of Commerce 美国商会

American citizenship 美国公民权

American Civil Liberties Union 美国民权自由联盟(ACLU)

American College of Trial Lawyers 美国出庭律师学会

American common law 美国普通法(指①采用英国法体系作为美国殖民时期的法律,地方制定法和判决作为补充;②在美国殖民时期以后特别是独立运动之后,法官造法体系得以发展。见 common law)

American Correction Association 美国改造协会

American Council of Learned Societies 美国人文学会理事会

American depository receipt 美国存托凭证(证券)

American depository share 美国保管人股份

American Digest System 美国判决摘要汇编系统(包括全国判例汇编系统中各种联邦判例和所有出版公司出版的个别州的判例汇编中出现的判例,并在收集每个判例的概述、眉标的同时,按主题类别进行编排)

American Enterprise Institute 美国企业研究所

American Export Definition 美国出口用语定义

American federal prosecutors (美)美国联邦检察官

American Federation of Labor-Congress of Industrial Organization 美国劳工联合会—产业工会联合会(劳联—产联)

American for Constitutional Action 美国人维护宪法行动党

American gloss 美国的解释

American Indian Law 见 Native American Law
American Indians 美洲印第安人
American International Law 美洲国际法
American Jurisprudence 《美国法理学》（亦译作《美国法律百科全书》，是一本具有广泛意义的法律丛书，包括对法律的注释，共有 426 个条目）
American Jurisprudence 2d（Am. Jur 2d）[或 Corpus Iuris Secumdum（C. I. S.）]《美国法理大全全书》（第二套丛书）、《美国法律百科》（第二套）或《美国法律释义百科》（第二版）。[《美国法理大全》（第二套丛书）是律师合作出版公司（简称律师版）出版。《美国法律释义百科（第二版）》为西方出版公司出版。前者通常称为（并缩写）Am. Jur. 2d, 为较全面的法律百科全书。它代替了《美国法理全书》（American Jurisprudence）（60 卷, 1936 年至 1960 年）。而"全书"又依次替代它的前者《首要判例法》（Ruling case law）（38 卷, 1914 年至 1931 年）。《美国法理大全全书》（第二套丛书）在几个方面不同于《美国法律释义百科》（第二版），它包括有编号的 82 卷、118 本书，而"释义百科" 150 多卷本。在规模上的不同之处：Am. Jur. 2d 在脚注中有西方版判例汇编中精选的重要案例；而 C. I. S.则力求援引所有相关案例。另外 Am. Jur. 2d 每年均有袋装部分对其内容有新的补充，并每 30 年进行一次全面修订。这两套百科都有其他案例查阅的资料参考，另还提供钥匙号（key number）、分类，便于在西方版《判例摘要汇编》（West Digest）中查阅判例。至于"2d" 实际为 second series, 系第二套丛书, 出于出版商的需要每套丛书为 100 卷本, 而不是第二次修订版或第二版]
American law 美国法
American Law Institute 美国法学会（指一个由律师、法官、学者组成的国家组织，其目的在于通过一些研究项目, 诸如法律重述,《示范刑法典》以及其他法学专著, 来促进法律法规的一致性、明确性和简易性）
American Law Institute Model Code 《美国法学会示范法典》

American Law Journal 《美国法律杂志》（最早的一本美国法律期刊, 由马里兰大学教授约翰·艾里胡·赫尔于 1806 年创办）
American Law Reports （美）《美国法律判例汇编》（从重大的判例中选择一小部分进行注释的一套丛书, 包括经过仔细选择的州法院每年约 250 个判决的全文, 其中每个判例均根据法律方面的讨论加以注释。1969 年以前, 该汇编还收集一些附有注释的联邦判例, 但自 1969 年起, 这些判例被分别出版, 取名为《美国法律判例汇编——联邦本》, 该版本每年编入约 150 个判例。其中包括下列丛书：第一套丛书：1918—1974 年；第二套丛书：1948—1965 年；第三套丛书：1965—1980 年；第四套丛书：1980 年至今）
American Law Review 《美国法律评论》（由约翰·奇普曼·格雷和约翰·古德曼罗普斯于 1866 年创办）
American Lawyer 《美国律师》（1978 年由国家创办的双周期刊）
American legal profession 美国的法律职业（由律师、法官、检察官和法学教师组成, 这几种都可能称为"lawyer", 而且都可以参加律师协会。美国法律职业的划分并不像世界大部分国家和中国那样严格）
American legal realism 美国法律实在论
American Online (AOL) 美国在线（一家在网络开发利用方面称雄的美国公司, 在交互式服务、网络技术和电子商务等方面处于世界领先地位, 为美国杰出企业。成立于 1985 年, 是全球最大的因特网接入服务供应商, 目前拥有客户超过 2200 万户。其电子商务网络技术与 SUN 等公司联盟以对抗微软）
American Revolution 美国独立战争（1775—1783 年）
American Rules 美国的规则（指在诉讼中, 胜诉当事人不能从败诉当事人那里获得请律师的费用, 除非法规授权或败诉方有欺诈、缠讼、放肆行为, 或因其他重大理由）
American scheme of justice 美国司法体制
American Skeptics 美国怀疑论者（他们认

为,美国是一个普通国家,因此应像普通国家一样行事,不要以为美国的想法也必须是世界其他国家的想法)

American Society for Judicial Settlement of International Dispute 美国司法调解国际争端协会 [为当代最重要的国际机构之一,讨论国际争议的司法决定,(相对于仲裁调解)它强调倾向司法调解意识,并相信设立长久的由职业法官组成的法庭,而不是临时指定的法官组成的法庭]

American Society for Public Administration 美国行政学会

American Want to Work Act 美国人想工作法案(见 99er)

American with Disabilities Act 美国残疾人法案

American's youth 美国建国初期

Americanisation n. 美国化

Americanism n. 美国用词(或词意),美国发音,美国习俗,美国方式;对美国习俗的效仿

Americanization n. 美国化

amiable a. 亲切的,和蔼可亲的

amiable compositeur 和解者

amicable a. 友好的,和睦的;温和的,和平的

amicable action 协议诉讼,合意诉讼(指双方当事人通过商定,为了取得法院对法律问题的裁决而进行的诉讼,对于事实问题通常由双方协议解决)

amicable adjustment 友好方式解决,和解

amicable allowance 友好让价

amicable lawsuit 合意诉讼(见 amicable action)

amicable litigant 参与合意诉讼者

amicable settlement 和平解决,友好方式解决

Amicus Brief 友好意见书,友好诉讼要点书

amicus briefs (美)友人诉讼状 [法庭之友的诉讼状是由某位非案件当事人呈交的,但他对其中要涉及的法律原理十分感兴趣。因为此法理与他们偏爱的政策或以后的立法均有关联,所以法庭之友(*amicus curiae*)总是不可避免地使他们自己与一当事人密切合作,成为其主要朋友,而不顾"法庭之友"的牌子。友人诉讼状具有潜在重要性,因为它们把当事人的化名在不同方面的观点和法律辩证带给法庭,引起法官注意。这种诉讼状帮助大法官指明如何作暗中裁定的努力。"法庭之友"通常是一个组织,虽然它也可能是个人]

amicus curiae 法庭之友[从字面看是友谊法庭(a friend of court),并非提起诉讼的当事人,而是向法院呈交一份法律简要诉状,或诉讼要点的人,因人与案件标的有重大利害关系。通常缩写为 *amicus*,即 "法庭之友" 之意,复数形式为 *amici curiae*。实际上,就是法院的"法律顾问",对案中疑难法律问题提出意见,协助法庭解决问题]

amidar n. (印度本地的)税收员

Amir(或 **Ameer**;**Emir**) n. 埃米尔(伊斯兰教国家统治者,王族;穆罕默德后裔的尊称。现中亚的一些国家统治者的称号)

Amir immovable 统治者的土地(埃米尔土地)

amittere curiam 丧失到庭权利

amittere legem terrae 丧失土地法所给予的保护

amity n. 和好,和睦(尤指国与国之间)

ammunition n. 弹药

amnesia n. 健忘(症),记忆丧失

amnesty n./v. 赦免,大赦/赦免,实行大赦

amnesty law 大赦法案

among political powers 政治国家之间

amoral a. 非道德性的,不属道德范围的

amorphous law 无定性的法律

amortization n. (1851 年)1.摊提(固定资产等),有时亦称 amortizement(见 depreciation);分期(偿付);偿还 2.转让(尤指让不动产)3.分期注销费用

amortization payment 摊还付款

amortize v. (1867 年)1.逐渐清偿债务,通常用清偿基金(sinking fund)2.安排以逐渐增加的方式清偿债务 3.(历史上)把财产、地产让与社会团体(corporation)永久营业(in mortmain)。亦拼写为 amortise。见 mortmain(法语"死手")

amortizement 见 amortization

amount n./v. 金额;数额/合计,等于,相当于(to)
amount assessed 分摊额
amount ceded （保险上的）分出金额
amount due 债务,债项;欠款
amount in controversy 争议金额
amount in controversy for diversity jurisdiction 为异籍管辖权而设定的争议标的额
amount in dispute 有争议的金额
amount in money of claim 索赔金额
amount insured 保险额
amount of currency in circulation 货币发行量,货币流通量
amount of debt 债务额
amount of evaded customs duty 逃漏关税额
amount of loss 损失额
amount of obligation 负债额
amount of paper money in circulation 纸币发行量,纸币流通量
amount of proof 证据分量
amount of share 股本额
amount of tax exemption 免税额
amount of the claim 诉讼请求额,索赔额
amount of the original contribution 最初出资数额
amount of value 价格,价值数额
amount unjustly accepted 不当的受领额,不当得利额
amount-in-controversy 诉讼请求的数额,争诉额
amour n. 奸情;不正当的男女关系
amoveas manus （要求处于王室占有下的）财产归还令状
amparo n. （西班牙—美洲法用语）1.颁发给要求土地保护者的文件,直至命令勘查并由指定的地方官员发给土地拥有证明（地契）2.宪法权利保护令
ample a. 丰富的,详细的,相当的
ample safeguards 充分的保护措施,充分的保证条款,充分的防护设施
ampliatio n. （罗马法）判决延期
ampliation n. 推迟期限,延期;（大陆法）延期判决（直至下次审理）

amplification n. 扩大,加强;扩充,详述
amplified a. 扩大的,放大的
amplified interpretation 扩大解释,引申解释（又译扩张解释）
amplify v. 详述,阐述;引申;增强,详述
amuck a. 有杀人狂的
amusement n. 娱乐,娱乐活动,乐趣
amusement tax 娱乐税（指对于音乐会、运动会或类似活动的门票所征收的税。这种税通常按门票价格的百分比明示）
an able court 资深法官,一名资深的法官
an act for to aside fraudulent conveyance 请求撤销一项欺诈性转让之诉
* An analogues problem arises in the context of quasi in rem jurisdiction in which property, if not attached before the action is commenced, may be removed, destroying the court's jurisdiction. 在准对物管辖的语境中也引起类似的问题,如果起诉前对财产采取扣押措施,财产可能被转移,法院的管辖也落空。
an attempt at conciliation 实行调解
* An easygoing attitude toward right and justice bodes as ill for law as an easygoing attitude toward policies bodes ill for government and administration. 对于权利和正义的不严肃态度对法律来说正是凶兆,就如同不严肃对待政治,对于政府和行政管理来说也是凶兆一样。
an eye for an eye 以眼还眼（报复）
an indispensable party 一个必不可少的当事人
an interest in a condominium unit 共有寓单元的权益
an interest in a cooperative unit （对）合作制单位的权益
an interest in a trust 信托受益权
anabaptism n. 再浸礼论,再洗礼论,再洗（浸）礼运动;再洗（浸）礼
Anabaptist(s) n. 再洗礼教徒,再浸礼教徒;再浸(洗)礼
anachronism n. 时代错误（指与时代不合而引起的错误）;弄错年代;与时代不合的人（或事）
anachronisms of the older common law

rules 较古老普通法规则的时代错误
anachronistic a. 与时代不符的,时代错误的,不合时宜的
anacrisis (罗马法)审问;调查(指为了了解事实真相或获取证据所进行的调查、审问,亦指刑讯逼供的审问调查)
anaesthesia sexualis 性欲缺失症
anaesthetic n. 麻醉药物(剂)
analects (=analecta) (复) n. 论文集,文选
analogical extension 类推延伸
analogical reasoning 类比推理[指法律推理中的一种推理形式。其基本构成如下:如两个东西或情境在某些方面相似,那它们在其他方面也应视为相似,事实上这种推理充其量是概率性的,明显不及演绎推理和归纳推理。但类比推理在日常实践推理中发挥了至关重要作用。没有理由认为它是无效的不正当的法律推理(或司法推理)]
analogical thinking 类推思维
analogies to precedents 对先例的类推
analogism n. 类比推理,类推
analogize v. 作类似推理,用类似法说明,适用类推
analogous art (专利法)类推技术,类似技术[指由于发明而提出解决合理的相关问题的技术、产品、申请、机器或方法,而这些都是发明者较为熟悉的。这些类似技术是显而易见(obviousness)的,因此不应授予专利,此词亦称为 pertinent art。见 nonobviousness]
analogous crime 类似的犯罪
analogous law 比附援引法则,类推法
analogy n. 类比
analogy explanation 类推解释
analogy in criminal law 刑法类推,刑事类推
analogy of law 法律的推理
analogy of legal principle 法律原则类推
analogy of statute 法规类推
analogy procedure 类推方法,类推程序
analytical jurisprudence 分析法理学,分析法学(指其研究重点在于对法律原则及规则进行分类,对法制中的概念如法律、义务、权利和财产、责任等的分析。与一般性"分析哲学"有密切联系。该学派主要由边沁与奥斯汀创立)
analytical jurists 分析法学家
analyse v. 分析,解析,分解
analysis n. 分析,化验
analysis certificate 化验证明书
analysis of legal problems 法律问题的分析
analysis of the crime scene 现场分析
analysis of variance 方差分析
analysis report 化验报告
analyst n. 化验师,分析师
analytic(al) a. 分析的;解析的
analytic(al) jurisprudence 分析法(理)学
analytic(al) positivism 分析实证主义
analytic(al) school (of law) 分析法学派(该法学派创始人英国法学家奥斯丁,是边沁的功利主义学说的信徒,认为法学任务是从逻辑上分析各种成熟的实在法制度的共同原则、概念和特征。这种法学以实证主义哲学作为思想基础,故又称为分析实证主义法学)
analytical exposition 分析法学派阐述
anarchic(al) a. 不守法的;无政府主义的
anarchism n. 无政府主义
anarchist n. 无政府主义者
anarcho-liberal n. 无政府自由主义者
anarchy n. 混乱,无秩序;无政府(自由主义)状态
anathema n. 革出教门;强烈的谴责;被诅咒的人;被诅咒的物
anatomical gift (1971年)人体器官捐献、遗体捐献[指按遗嘱进行的遗体或器官捐献,用于移植或医学研究。在美国,进行遗体捐献的法律是《统一器官捐献法》(Uniform Anatomical Gift Act),其规定死后可以捐献部分器官或全部遗体。该法已为大部分州所采纳]
ancester (=ancestor) n. 祖先;直系亲属;(英)(1926年前的不动产法上的)被继承人
ancestor-wisdom on the field of the law 法律领域里祖先的智慧
ancestral a. 祖先的,祖传的
ancestral home 原籍,祖籍

ancestral property 祖传财产
ancestress n. 女性被继承人;女性祖先
ancestry n. (总称)祖先,列祖;家世,家系;名门出身
anchorage n. 停泊税;停泊地,抛锚(地)
anchorage dues 停泊税
ancienne coutume de Normandie 诺曼底古代习惯法
ancient a. 古老的;古代的,老(旧)的;老式的
ancient city-state 古(罗马)城邦
ancient demesne (英)旧有土地保有制
ancient document (真实的)旧文据(见 ancient writings)
ancient Egyptian law 埃及古代法
ancient Greek law 希腊古代法
ancient house (历史上)在英国古代,房子如果占据的地方足够长,可获得相邻的土地和建筑的地役权(easement)
ancient law 古代法
ancient lights 老窗户的采光权
ancient messuages 旧宅院
ancient monuments 历史纪念物
ancient ordeals 古代神明裁判[指英古法中包括探火神判(烧伤后用布包裹伤口三天后伤口不愈便判有罪)、热水神判(与探火神判相似)、冰水神判(把被告投入水中,浮便有罪)即 *Judicium Dei*, judgment of God,其方式: fire ordeal, cold water ordeal, hot water ordeal;还有一种决斗(compfight)。在英国于 1883 年被废除]
ancillary attachment 附带扣押,附属扣押(指从原告的诉讼请求待决时,对被告财产的占有和没收导致的扣押,以便提起诉讼的顺利进行。亦称 attachment on mersne process)
Ancient Regime 旧制时代
Angevin Reform (亨利二世及其进行的)金雀花改革(1154—1189 年)
ancient serjeant (英史)年长(王室)高级律师
ancient writings (真实的)旧文据(一种来自官方经保管 20 年或 30 年的文据)
ancients n. 元老(四大律师学院及大法官法院的某些成员)

ancillary a. 辅助的,附属的;附加的
ancillary acts 从行为
ancillary administration 附加遗产管理权
ancillary agreement 附属协定
ancillary attachment 附属于诉讼上的财产扣押
ancillary bill 附加起诉状
ancillary contract 从合同(契约);附加合同(契约)
ancillary credit 从属信用(证),辅助信用(证)
ancillary credit business 附属信用业
ancillary document 辅助文据
ancillary instrument 附属文件
ancillary investment 辅助投资
ancillary judicial personnel in court 法院的司法辅助人员
ancillary jurisdiction 附属管辖权;附带管辖
ancillary laws(或 **statute**) 附属法规,辅助法规,补充法规
ancillary obligation 从属债,从债
ancillary power 附属权(力)
ancillary probate 附加的遗嘱检验(认证)
ancillary proceedings 附加程序
ancillary provision 附则
ancillary relief 附加救济金;附加补偿
ancillary right 附属权利
ancipitis usus (国际法)用途不明
and the like 诸如此类,等等
Andean Pact 《安第斯条约》(为确定玻利维亚、哥伦比亚、智利、厄瓜多尔及秘鲁等五国地区经济一体化而签订的条约)
Andes region (南美)安第斯山脉地区
Andeutungstheorie 暗示说(指只有那些在要式的意思表示中有所暗示的东西才能在解释时加以考虑,此说在德、英、加等国法律上长期居于通说地位)
andromania n. 慕男狂
androphany n. 女子男化
androphobia n. 恐男症
androphonomania n. 杀人狂,杀人癖
anew ad. 更新审理(如案经审理,因法官之更换,须重新讯问);重新,再
angary n. 非常征用权,战时船舶征用权

（指战时交战国可征用或破坏中立国的财产或船舶,留待以后予以赔偿的权利）
Anglia England 的拉丁名
Anglo-America law（或 **legal**）**system** 英美法系;英美法律制度
Anglo-American common law 英美普通法
Anglo-American Law 英美法(系)
Anglo-American trial jury 英美小陪审团（由 12 人组成的陪审团）
Anglo-Indian Codes 《英属印度法典》
Anglophonic African countries 英属非洲国家
Anglo-Saxon law 盎格鲁-撒克逊法
animal are not thing 动物不是物
animal cruelty 虐畜罪
animal right "动物权力论"[指美国学者 P.Singer 作为其代表人物,他撰写《动物的解放》一书提出"人的生命,或者只有人的生命是神圣不可侵犯的信念,是物种歧视(speciesism)的形态之一",他还认为"所有的动物都是平等的"]
animal rights 动物权利(指动物或某类动物是否能够拥有权利这个抽象问题。往往与人类应当怎样对待动物的道德问题交织在一起。有人根据一种不同概念和道德伦理提出一种主张:虽然动物是一类能够拥有权利的存在体,但事实上并不拥有任何权利。或者说在相关的环境中人类持有的权利压倒了动物拥有的权利)
Animals-Patentability 动物专利性
animistic character 泛灵论的特征
animosity n. 仇恨,憎恶,敌意
animus n. 意愿,意图;心素
animus cancellandi 意图删除
animus deserendi 意图遗弃
animus domini 意图(像所有者那样)拥有;意图盗窃
animus donandi 有赠与意图
animus et factum 思想和行为,意向和行为(指一个人意向在一个给定的国家长期或是不定期居住)
animus furandi (= *furandi animus*) 盗窃犯罪意图
animus gerondi 意图作为继承人
animus indorsendi 背书意图,背书意向,签署意向[给支票背书(animo indorsandi)者对这一数额负责,否则会遭到拒付]
animus injuriandi 损害意向,冒犯意图
animus immiscendi et adenundi hereditatem 意图干预并接受继承权
animus lucrandi 图利
animus manendi 意在留下,意在居住,意图确定一个永久住所,亦称 *animus remanendi*
animus morandi 意图停留,意在等候,意在留住(虽然 *animus morandi* 从广义上与 *animus manendi* 为同义词,但 *morandi* 暗含长久不变之意)
animus nocendi 意图伤害,意图危害,有危害意向
animus novandi 意图更改
animus obligandi 意图签订合同
animus occidendi 意图杀害
animus occupandi 意图占领
animus possidendi 占有(人)的意图,拥有(人)的意图
animus recipiendi 意图接受
animus recuperandi 收回债权意向,意图收回(债权)
animus remanendi 见 *animus manendi*
animus revocandi 放弃的意图,撤销的意图;解职的意图
animus testandi 书立遗嘱的意图
animus stijaulandi 达成要式口约的意图
annals n. (复)编年史;历史记载;学会(或学科等)年刊;年鉴
Annals of Congress 《国会编年史》(指 1789 年至 1824 年,在国会发表或陈述的非正式记录)
annats (= Annates) 见 first fruits
annex n./v. 附录,附件;附属建筑物,附加物/1.添加,附加,合并 2.并吞,霸占(领土),侵占 3.盖(印)
annexation n. (领土的)兼并;(财产的)侵吞;附加物
annexation of property 侵吞财产
annexed a. 附加的,附属的
annexed document 附件
anni nubiles 可嫁之年(英国在以前规定女子在 12 岁为可结婚年龄。现依《婚姻

annotate

法》,男女任何一方需在 16 岁以上结婚方为有效),女子法定结婚年龄
annotate v. 1.摘要 2.作注释,给……作注释,评注
annotated a. 注解的,注释的
annotated bibliography 附说明的资料目录
annotated code 注释法典
Annotated Law Reports (美)《注释法律判例汇编》
annotated list of items 附说明的项目表
annotated preliminary list 附说明的暂定项目表
Annotated Statutes (美)《注释法规汇编》(指《美国法典》注释版和各州的法规汇编注释版)
annotation n. 1.判例摘要(指对案件事实和判决的简要陈述,特别是涉及成文法规解释的摘要) 2.评注,注释(指对法律依据,尤其是案件的法律依据的解释或评注),比如注释出现于《美国注释法典》(United States Code Annotated, USCA) 3.包含这类注释、评注的注释卷本 4. 见 rescript 3(见 note 2)
annotation of statute 法规的注释
annotative a. 注释的,评注的
annotator n. 注释者,解释者
announce v. 宣布,宣告,发表
announce amnesty 宣布赦免
announcement n. 公告,宣告,通告,告示,预告
announcement by court 法院公告
annoyance n. 使人烦恼的事物,麻烦事,讨厌事
* *Annua nec debitum judex non separat ipsum.* A judge does not divide annuities nor debt. 法官既不分配年金,也不分割债务。
annual a. 年度的,每年的
annual accounts 年度结算;年度账目
annual allowance 年度免税额
annual balance 年终结存
annual balance sheet 年度决算表
annual budget speech (英)(财政大臣向国会的)年度预算报告
annual expenditure 岁出,年度支出

Annual Finance Act (英)年度财政法令
Annual Finance Bill (英)年度财政法案
annual income tax return 年度所得税申报表
annual interest 年利
annual leave 年度假
annual licence 一年期执照
annual meeting 年会
annual output 年产量
annual quota 年度定额
annual recurrent direct cost 年度经常费用
Annual Register (英)《年刊》(1758 年创办)
annual rent 年租
annual rental 年租额
annual report 年度报告;年报
annual returns 年度统计表;年度利润率
annual revenue 岁入,年度收入
annual review 年度审查
annual surplus 岁计盈余,年度盈余
annual value (财产的净)年值
annual vote (公司等的)年度表决
Annuals of Congress (英)《国会年录》(指公元 1238—1824 年国会中发言和陈述的非官方记录)
annuitant n. 领取年金者,年金享受权人
annuities without compensation 无偿年金
annuity n. 年金;养老金,年金享受权
annuity beneficiary 年金受益人
annuity certain 可靠的年金(指超过规定期限,不管年金享受者是否过世均应支付的年金,亦称 term annuity)
annuity due 预期年金,约定年金(指在每次支付期开始时给予支付的年金。见 ordinary annuity)
annuity policy 年金政策(指向被保险人提供每月支付或定期支付款项的保险政策。这种支付款可以从一开始在固定日期给予或给予被保险人终生支付款)
annul v. 废止,废除,取消;宣告无效
annulment n. 废止,废除,取消;无效;取消法律关系
annulment decree 判决无效令
annulment of law 法律的废除
annulment of marriage (宣告)婚姻无效
annulment of order 命令的废止

annulment suit 无效诉讼
annunciation n. 通告,公布
annus n. (大陆法和古英国法)一年
annus et dies 整一年(即一年零一天)
annus luctus 悲伤周年(罗马法规定丈夫死后的一个年头内,寡妇不准再嫁,称为悲伤周年)
anomalous a. 例外的,异常的;破格的;不规则的
anomalous event 异常事件
anomalous plea 半真半假的答辩
anomalous pleading (1845年)反常诉答[指在其主张(allegations)中,部分诉答为肯定的,部分为否定的。衡平法上部分肯定、部分否定的答辩(anomalous plea)]
anomalous situs statute 异常的所在地法规
anomaly n. 异常,反常,破格
anomic(或 anomy) n. 社会的反常状态;社会道德的颓废
anonym n. 化名者;假名,化名;作者不明的出版物
anonymity n. 匿名(者),无名(者);作者不明
anonymous a. 匿名的,无名的,不具名的
anonymous informer 匿名告发人
anonymous letter 匿名信
anonymous letter of accusation 匿名控告信
anonymous partnership 隐名合伙
anonymous works 匿名作品(《保护文学作品伯尔尼公约》第15条第1—4款中提出的概念)
anorthosis n. (阴茎)勃起不能
answer n./v. 1.回答,答案,答复 2.答辩,抗辩;答辩状 3.补偿;报复/1.回答,答复 2.答辩 3.符合 4.负责,抵偿
answer a debt 偿债,付债款
answer brief 答辩状
answer by word of mouth 口头答辩
answer for a crime 负有罪责,受刑罚
answer for a debt of other 对他人债务负责,担保他人债务
answer in writing 文字答辩,书面答辩
answer the charge 答辩

answer with cross claim 交叉请求答辩状
answerable a. 应负责任的,有义务的
answerer n. 回答者;答辩者
answering evidence 申辩材料
antagonism n. 对抗,对抗性;敌对;对抗作用
antagonist n. 对抗者,对手,敌手
antagonistic goals 对立的目标
antagonistic(al) a. 对抗(性)的,敌对(性)的;有反作用的
antagonistic(al) contradictions 对抗性矛盾
antagonize v. 对……起反作用,中和,抵消;无意识地引起对抗,反抗
Antarctic Treaty 《南极条约》(1959年)
ante n. 赌注,预付的一笔款
ante ad. 在……以前
ante litem motam 诉讼开始前
ante mortem(或 *antemortem*) 死前
ante natus(=*antenati*) 先于(某一特定事件或他人)出生(或发生)
antebellum period (美)南北战争以前的时期
antecedent n./a. 1.前事,前例;前提 2.(复)经历,出身;履(学)历;祖先/事前的,先前的,前提的
antecedent intent 事前故意
antecedent right 先行权,优先权
antecedent trial 预审
antecedents to the Court 联邦最高法院之前身[英国人对北美实行殖民统治时存在三种普通法法院:1.高等民事法院(common pleas)行使一般民事管辖权;2.王座法院(King's Bench),刑事审判法院;对民事诉讼具有一定的上诉管辖权;3.财税法院(Exchequer)最初只是个财政税收机构。后对王室作为一方当事人的争议作出裁断。此外还有第4种法院即高等衡平法院(High Court of Chancery)它对因严格普通法规则而不能获得保护的当事人提供衡平法救济机制。这四种法院构成殖民地法院体系的基础。1686年之后,一些殖民地采用艾德蒙·安德鲁斯(Edmund Andros)为新英格兰(美国东北部地区)确立的管辖模式:即将高等民事法院、王座法院和财税法院的管辖权交由单一的普通

法院——通常称最高法院(Supreme Court of Judicature)行使。英国的法院体制给北美殖民地时期的法律制度的管辖权观念奠定了基础。美国联邦最高法院既使普通法管辖权又行使衡平法管辖权。代表美国这一趋势的延续。总之,美国联邦最高法院的制度最早可追溯到英美普通法。其功能与早期的英格兰司法机关,大英帝国的司法机关和早期殖民地以及各州的司法机关和《邦联条例》所规定的司法机关相类似。同时,联邦最高法院的前身显示,它正是美国在特定的州和殖民地,以及在与英帝国更大范围关系中的历史经验的产物]

antecessor n. 1.地产的故主,祖先 2.发起人 3.先驱者

antedate v. 倒填日期;先于;使提前发生

antedate bill of exchange 倒填日期的汇票

antedate bill of lading 倒签提单

antemortem a. 死前的

antemortem **injury** 死前伤

antemortem **inspection** 死前检查

antenatal a. 胎儿的,出生前的;产前的

antenatus n. 婚前所生子女

antenuptial a. 婚前的

antenuptial(或 **marriage**) **settlement** 婚前授产协议

antenuptial contract 婚前契约,亦称 antenuptial agreement(见 prenuptial agreement)

antenuptial gift 见 prenuptial gift

antenuptial gift 婚前赠与

antenuptial surname 婚前固有姓氏

anteroom n. 接待室

anthrax n. 炭疽病

anthrax bacillus 炭疽杆菌(一种化学武器)

anthropology n. 人类学

anthropology of law 法律人类学[指倾向于关注作为社会秩序渊源的法律。法律人类学的名著:《原始人的法》(1954年) E. Adamson Hoebel (E. 亚当森·霍贝尔)、《原始社会的犯罪与习俗》(1926年) Bronislaw Malinoaski (布罗尼斯拉夫·马林诺斯基)、《北罗得西亚的巴罗策的司法过程》(1967年) Max Gluckman (马克斯·格卢克曼)。这些著作展示了不同的社群指引行为和解决纠纷的种种方式。人类学应用于法律的重要在于:展示了其他社会组织的法律在形式上的特点和多样性,法律的人类学研究影响社会学探究:以一种允许更丰富的比较和分析的普遍方法界定"法律"。此外,人类学研究被用来支持和反对"历史法学"派有关社会发展、法制和法律规范之间关联的各种观点]

anti-bucketshop 禁止地下期货

anti-circumvention 反规避[指避开进口国采取批销措施行为,问题源于 20 世纪 80 年代末的一桩著名案件——改锥(Sreewdriver)案]

anti-colonialism n. 反殖民主义

anti-competitive practices(＝antitrust legislation) 反竞争措施(反垄断立法);(美)通谋限制贸易

anti-coste rationale 反等级理论

anti-court campaign (美)反对最高法院运动(指美总统与联邦最高法院的权力扩张而引起的宪政冲突和宪政危机在美国现代宪政史上屡见不鲜。从老罗斯福执政时起,亦即从由老 La Follelte 领导的进步党所展开的反对最高法院运动时起,此类冲突构成美国当代政论史中的持续性特征)

anti-delegation principle 反授权原则

anti-dumping code 反倾销法

anti-fascist a. 反法西斯主义的

Anti-Fascist People's Freedom League 反法西斯人民自由联盟

anti-feudal a. 反封建主义的

anti-imperialism n. 反帝国主义,反帝

anti-manipulation 反操纵

anti-okie Law (美)反对流动农业工人法(尤指美国 20 世纪 30 年代因干旱使俄克拉何马农业工人移落别处);(加利福尼亚州法律,禁止任何人对非本州居民的穷人给予帮助,因该法对州际贸易施压而被认为违宪)

anti-party a. 反党的

anti-party clique 反党集团

anti-prejudice 反对偏见,克服不利

anti-racketeering law 反诈骗法

anti-rebate legislation 反回诉立法
Anti-Secession Law （中）《反分裂国家法》
anti-Semitism 反犹太主义
anti-sex n. 反对性行为
Anti-smuggling Act （美）(1935年美国会通过的)《反走私法》
anti-social exercise of incidents of ownership 反社会行使所有权的附属权利
anti-subrogation rule （保险法）反对代理规则,反代位行使准则[指保险承运人没有代位行使的权力,也就是无权代理投保人(the insure)主张权利申请或保单获取的支付,反对其自身投保由保单所涵盖的风险准则。见 subrogation]
antidotal a. 解毒的,有解毒功效的
antidote n. 解毒药(for, against, to) 矫正方法,除害物
antisocial personality disorder 反社会性人格障碍(指人格障碍类型中的一种,他们好像对任何人或事既不爱也不忠实。很明显他们从不懊悔,亦不内疚,反而易冲动,甚至什么都干,由于这些特点,反社会性人格障碍患者常和朋友、家庭,甚至法律发生冲突。总之,这类人道德严重缺失,又称悖德狂。见 paranoid personality disorder)
antitrust a./n. 反托拉斯的/反托拉斯法(指是由制定法、司法判决和强行措施组成的法律整体,目的在于制约威胁自由市场竞争的商业活动) (又称 antitrust act 或 laws 反托拉斯法)
Antitrust Guideline for the Licensing of Intellectual Property （美司法部和联邦贸易委员会1995年4月6日联合发布的）《知识产权许可的反垄断指南》
antiabortionist n. 反对堕胎者
antiauthoritarianism n. 反权力主义,反独裁主义
Antiballistic Missile Treaty 《反弹道导弹条约》(1972年)
antibribery n. 反贿赂
antibureaucratism n. 反官僚主义
antichresis tacita （大陆法）取得孳息的暗约
anticipate v. 1.期望 2.抢先,(采取措施来)防止 3.使提前发生

anticipated a. 预期的;预支的;先期的
anticipated net profit 预期纯利
anticipated revenue 预期收入
anticipation n. 事前行为;(信托金的)预先分派,预支;预期,预料,预知;占先
anticipation of litigation 诉讼前
anticipatory a. 期待着的;提早发生的;预期的;先发制人的
anticipatory breach (= anticipatory repudiation) (1989年) 预期违约[指由于当事方预期拒绝履行合同(anticipatory repuliation)而造成的违约,就是说,毫无疑问地指明当事方在履行到期之时仍无意履行。依据这些情况,未违约的当事方(nonbreach party)可以决定以现时违约(immediate breach)对待预期违约并提起损害赔偿之诉。亦称 breach by anticipatory repudiation; constructive breach。见 anticipatory repudiation; breach of contract]
anticipatory breach of contract 预期违约
anticipatory letter of credit 预支信用证
anticipatory prior act （专利）预期的现在技术
anticipatory prior art （专利）预期的现在技术
anticipatory repudiation (1913年) 预期违约[指在履行期限到来之前,合约义务的拒绝履行会使受损害方因全面违约而具有要求损害赔偿的现时权利(immediate right to damages)以及免除受害方履行全面的义务(remaining duties)。当履行义务到来期间,允诺人(promisor)毫无疑问地表示拒绝履行的意图随即产生这种拒绝履行合同的类型。一旦这种拒绝履行(repudiation)发生,非履行当事方(nonrepudiation party)有三个选择:①将拒绝履约当成要求损害赔偿而进行起诉的现时权利(immediate right to damages)。②不管它,但加紧督促拒绝履行者(repudiator)履行合同义务,等待特定的履行时间(specific time of performance)。如果拒绝履行当事方仍不履行则对其行为进行起诉。③终止或废弃合同。亦称 renunciation。见 anticipatory breach]
anticontraband personnel (总称)缉私人员

anticorruption 反贪污
anticrime a. 反对犯罪的;预防犯罪的
anticulated pleading (1953年)逐项陈述[指在分别已编号的请愿书、起诉状、答辩状的每一段的内容中陈述各个主张(allegation)]
antidraft n. 反征兵,抗拒征兵
antidumping (= anti-dumping) a. 反倾销(政策)的
Antidumping Code 反倾销守则
antiespionage n. 反间谍
antiestablishment n. 反正统派;反政府(体制)
antiestablishmentarian n. 反政府(体制)者
antiforeign a. 排外的
antifraud rules 反欺诈条款
antigovernment n. 反政府
antigraphy n. 契据副本
antigun a. 军火管制的
antihijacking n. 防止劫机的
antiinflationary measures 反通货膨胀措施
antikidnapping a. 防止绑架的
antilabo(u)r law 反劳工法
antilapse statute 反遗赠失效法规[该法规规定当受遗赠人(beneficiary)先于遗赠人死亡时,遗赠并不失效,受遗赠人的代理人仍可获得遗赠(gift)。这视为受遗赠人在遗赠人死亡之后立即死亡,从而向其继承人作出遗赠。除非遗嘱中有相反之意思表示。依据普通法和各州之法规,受遗赠人或遗嘱受益人必须比遗赠人活的时间长,遗赠才不致失效。虽然多数州均制定反遗赠失效法规,但各州的条文均有差异,亦称 lapse statute; non lapse statute]
antilogy n. 自相矛盾(之词),前后矛盾
antiman n. 反人类
antimissile system 反导弹系统
Antimonopoly Party 反垄断党
antimonopoly provisions 反垄断条款
antimonopoly law 反垄断法
antinarcotic raid 扫毒突击搜捕
antinomy n. 矛盾;两种法律间的矛盾;法律上的自相矛盾;自相矛盾的话
antiobscenity n. 反猥亵品,反诲淫

antipathy n. 不相容,反感,厌恶
antipersecution n. 反迫害
antipiracy a./n. (版权和商标)反侵权版权的[指属于或有关具有的版权或商标的非法复制、供销或使用进行斗争并防止此种行为而达到预期效果〈an antipiracy group〉(一个反侵犯版权的团体)]/反侵犯版权
antipode n. 绝对差异;正相反;相互矛盾;正相反的事物
antipolitical a. 反政治的
antipollutant n. 抗污染物质(或手段)
antipollution n. 反污染,抗污染
antipopular a. 反人民的,反大众的
antiqua statuta 见 *vetera statuta*
antiquarian a. 研究文物的,收藏古物的
antiquary n. 文物工作者,古物收藏者,古董商
antiquated consideration 变得过时的对价
antiracism n. 反种族歧视;反种族主义
antiracist n. 反种族主义者
antirevolution n. 反革命
antislavery a. 反奴隶制度的
antislavery publicists 反奴隶制的公法
antismuggling a. 反走私的
antismuggling partol boat 缉私船
antismuggling raid 反走私突击搜捕
antismut a. 查禁淫秽书报的
antisocial behavio(u)r 反社会行为
antisocialist a. 反社会主义的
antisocialist element 反社会主义分子
antisuit injunction 反诉禁令
Antiterrorism and Effective Death Penalty Act 《反恐和死刑绩效法》(美国克林顿上任总统时通过的)
antiterrorism laws 反恐怖法
antitreason pact 防奸公约
antitrust a. 反托拉斯的
antitrust act(或 **laws**) 反托拉斯法
antitrust liability 反托拉斯责任
antitrust legislation 反托拉斯立法
antiwar a. 反战的
antiwar pact 反战公约
anything... but 除……绝不
anything under the sun made by men 在阳

光下由人类制成的物品(皆可受到保护)
ap(p)anage n. 属地;附属财产;(封建制度下)王子的封地(或封禄等)
apartheid n. 种族隔离(制);种族隔离法(尤指南非)
apart from this consideration 除非考虑这一点
apart from 除非,撇开;离开,离去
apartment n. 1.房间 2.(复)(英)一套房间(尤指备有家具供短期出租的);(美)一套公寓房间
apartment property 公寓式财产权,公寓式所有权
apartment warning 警告设备
apella n. 公民议会(古代斯巴达的国民大会)
apex(复 **apices**, **apexes**)n. 顶点,顶
aphonia n. 失音症(见 mutism)
aphorism n. 格言,警句
apnea n. 窒息,呼吸暂停
apocrypha n./a. (宗)伪造书,不足凭信(或作者不明的书籍或奏章等)/伪的,不足凭信的〈apocryphal materials〉(伪造的材料)
apolitical a. 不关心政治的;无政治意义的
apologetic a. 辩护的,辩解的;道歉的,认错的
apologia n. 自辩书;辩解
apology n. 道歉,谢罪;辩解
apology of the Commons 下院的声辩
apologist n. 辩护者,辩解者;辩护士(尤指卫护基督教义的辩护者)
apophthegm (=apothegm) n. 格言,箴言;警语
apostasy n. 叛教,背教;脱党;变节
apostate n. 背教者,变节者;脱党者
apostille (=apostil) 1.眉批,注 2.(国际法)附注或注意(observation),特别是根据《海牙公约》(Hague Convention)为在外国使用的认证文件(authentication documents)提供的标准证明(standard certification)。亦可拼写成 apostil(见 certificate of authority)
Apostolic Constitutions 《使徒法令》(早期基督教徒留下最庞大的一部基督教宗教

法大全,为后来寺院法的渊源)
apostolic nuncio 教廷大使
Apostolic See 罗马教会(Church of Rome 之别称)
apostolic signatura 罗马教会最高裁判庭
apothecary n. 药剂师;药商
appall v. 使沮丧,使吃惊
appall at 被……吓坏
appalling accident 骇人听闻的意外事故
apparatus n. 机构,器官,仪器,设备
apparatus of game theory 博弈论之谜
apparent a. 明显的,显而易见的;外表上的;表面上的
apparent agency 表见代理[英美法系也称不容否认的代理制度,或禁止反言的代理(agency by estopel),即基于本人的行为使第三人合理地认为代理关系存在并根据法律规定所产生之代理。通常是由于本人疏于监督,使代理人实施未经授权之行为,并使第三人信任代理人有代理权的情况,亦称 agency by operation of law, ostensible agency。见 Restatement of Agency]
apparent and reality 表面和实际
apparent authority (1808 年)表见代理权,表见授权[指第三人基于其与被代理人(principal)的交易关系,甚至在被代理人并未授予或意图授予此代理权的情况下,有理由相信代理人所享有的授权。即使在没有实际代理权(actual authority)授予的情况下,也可由法律创设表见授权,亦称为 ostensible authority; authority by estoppel]
apparent availability 市场供应量
apparent condition 明显的条件;已明确的条件
apparent danger 迫在眉睫的危险
apparent death 假死
apparent defect (商品等的)明显的缺陷;表面瑕疵
apparent easement 明显地役权
apparent heir 当然继承人
apparent marriage 表见婚姻(一种无效的婚姻)
apparent necessity 明显的必要性

apparent right 表见权利
apparent trial 徒有形式的审判
apparent validity 明显的效力
apparently infirm person 明显的心神耗弱者
appeal n./v. 1.上诉状;上诉;申诉 2.要求,呼吁;号召力,感染力/上诉;诉诸,请求,求助;呼吁;有吸引力
appeal 28 USC 158 根据《美国法典》第28标题卷第158节提出的上诉(见withdrawal 28 USC 157)
appeal against 不服……上诉
appeal against a charge 罪名不当的上诉,不服指控的上诉
appeal against a decision 不服判决的上诉
appeal against a sentence 不服判刑的上诉
appeal against conviction 不服定罪的上诉
appeal against finding 不服裁决的上诉
appeal against punishment 不服刑罚的上诉
appeal against valuation 不服估价的上诉
Appeal arbitrator 上诉仲裁人(指劳伊兹委员会指定的上诉仲裁人)
appeal board 上诉委员会,上诉局
appeal bond 上诉保证书
appeal by order of *certiorari* (英)依提卷复查令状的上诉
appeal by stated case (英)基于决定性要点陈述的上诉
appeal by way of prerogative (英)通过特权令状方式的上诉
appeal by writ of error (英)依调卷复审令状的上诉
appeal cases 上诉案件
appeal committee 上诉委员会,(大写)(英)原上诉委员会
appeal court 上诉法院
appeal disallowed 驳回的上诉
appeal dismissed 驳回上诉
appeal extraordinary 非常上诉
appeal file 上诉案卷
appeal for compensation 诉请赔偿
appeal for mercy 请求从宽(处理),诉请从宽处刑
appeal for retrial 再审申请
appeal for review 复审申请
appeal from a decision 对判决(不服)提出上诉;对决定不服提出申诉
appeal from a judg(e)ment 不服判决而上诉
appeal from philip drunk to philip sober 请求复телей审(指因初审在某种情况下不够郑重,故请求复审)
appeal in civil case 民事案件中的上诉
appeal in criminal case 刑事案件中的上诉
appeal in *forma pauperis* 以贫民起诉人的身份上诉
appeal jurisdiction 上诉管辖权;上诉审判权;上诉审管辖范围
appeal made against part of a judg(e)ment 部分上诉(指对判决的一部分不服而上诉)
appeal of fee determination under Equal Access to Justice 根据平等获得公正法就费用确定提出上诉
appeal of inapplicability of the law 适用法律不当的上诉
appeal of larceny 非法侵占他人财产的上诉;(英)窃案上诉
appeal on a question of fact 有关事实争议的上诉
appeal on a question of law 有关法律争议的上诉
appeal on points of law 就法律要点的上诉,就法律问题的上诉
appeal on points of the fact 就事实要点的上诉,就事实问题的上诉
appeal on questions of fact and law 有关事实和法律问题的上诉
appeal procedure 上诉程序
appeal to 呼吁,要求;求助于;诉诸,上诉
appeal to arms 诉诸武力
appeal to crown court (英)(被告不服判决)向刑事法庭上诉
appeal to district judge from magistrate judgment 针对治安法官的判决向地区法院上诉
appeal to force 诉诸暴力

appeal to reason 用理性,讲道理
appeal to the country （英）（解散国会后）诉诸国民公断,诉诸舆论
appeal tribunal 上诉法庭,诉愿裁判所
appealability n. 可上诉性
appealable a. 可上诉的
appealable judg(e)ment 可上诉的判决
appealed decision 被上诉的判决
appear v. （由本人或律师）代理出庭,到案;出现,显露;出版,发表;似乎（后跟不定式）
appear against sb. 出庭控告某人
appear and stand 到庭候审
appear at the proceeding 参与全部诉讼程序,出庭参与全部诉讼程序
appear before the court 出庭,到庭
appear for sb. 为某人出庭,代表某人出庭
appear to stand trial 出庭受审
appearance n. 1.外表,面貌 2.出庭,到案（指作为当事方或相关人员或代替利益相关人的律师出席法庭,特别是参与诉讼的被告出庭、提交书面答辩或采取审后步骤在审判庭或上诉法院提出上诉而出庭）3.出版,发表 4.出现,露面
appearance before the court 出庭
appearance before the meeting 出席会议
appearance bond 出庭保证金
appearance by attorney 由代理人出庭,由律师出庭
appearance by guardian 由监护人代理出庭
appearance day 出庭日
appearance docket 出庭顺序表（指由法庭书记官掌握的一种备审案件目录,按此目录顺序出庭）
appearance of bias 表面偏见
appearance of environment of city 市容市貌
appearance of justice 看得见的公正;显然的公正（指中立的裁判者主持程序和作出决定,可以使程序表现出一种看得见的公正,对于正义的实现而言,那种被人们感受到的正义才是真正的正义,而且使人们相信它的存在）

appearance of ownership 表见所有权
appearance order 出庭令
appearance to defend 到庭应诉（on merits）到庭辩护,到庭根据事件实质作辩护
appeasable order 可上诉的裁决［指可受到上诉审查的终局裁或指令、裁定、中间裁决（interlocutory order）,对后者通常要到案件经过庭审并作出判决后才可提出上诉］
appease v. 使和缓;使满足;姑息;安抚
appeasement n. 缓和,绥靖;安抚,平息
appeasement policy 绥靖政策;姑息主义
appellant n./a. 上诉人/上诉的,有关上诉的
appellant matter 有关上诉事宜
appellant pending appeal 等候上诉者
appellate a. 受理上诉的;上诉的,投诉的
appellate brief 上诉事实摘要;辩护状
appellate business 上诉审判业务
appellate civil jurisdiction 上诉审民事管辖权
Appellate Committee of the House of Lords （英）上议院上诉委员会
appellate court 上诉（审）法院;受理上诉的法院
appellate criminal jurisdiction 上诉审刑事管辖权
appellate decision 上诉审判决
appellate division （法院的）上诉庭
appellate hierarchy 上诉等级制
appellate judge 受理上诉的法官
Appellate Jurisdiction Act （英）《上诉管辖权法》（最早颁布于1876年,随后又于1887年、1913年、1929年和1947年颁布此法,规定上议院作为终审的上诉法院）
appellate jurisdiction 上诉管辖权［指美国联邦宪法和联邦制定法将联邦最高法院的管辖分为两大类:初审管辖（original jurisdiction）和上诉管辖,审理从低级别联邦法院或州法院上诉的案件的权力］;上诉审判权,上诉审管辖范围
appellate litigation 受理上诉的诉讼
appellate procedure 上诉程序;（检察官提出的）抗诉程序
appellate review 受理上诉的复审,上诉

复审
appellatio n. （罗马法上的）上诉
appellatio tertii 第三人上诉制度
appellation n. 称呼;名称;名目
appellation of origin （产品）原产地名称
appellee n. 被申诉者;被上诉人
appellor n. 申诉人;上诉人
append v. 放进注释;盖章,签名
appendage n. 附属物,附属品
appendant (=appendent) n./a. 附属物;附属遗产;附属权利/附属的,附加的
appendant and appurtenant 附属遗产和附属物
appendant power of appointment 附属指定权;附属委任状
appendix n. 附录,补遗;附属物;附件（在英国指:①按惯例,上诉到枢密院和上议院的上诉书所附的重要文件,如证据、法院判词等,统称附件;②指一般附在主件中的附属文件）
appendix of forms 格式附录
applicability n. （可）适用性,（可）适应性
applicability of bankruptcy 破产适用性
applicable a. （可）适用的,（能）适应（当）的,适合的
applicable criteria 可适（应）用的标准
applicable exclusion amount 税法(tax)可适用的免除额（指遗产的美元价值可从联邦遗产和赠与税中豁免。见 unified estate-and-gift tax credit）
applicable exclusion credit 见 unified estate-and-gift tax credit
applicable law 可适用的法律;（国际私法）准据法,法律适用法
applicable law for adoption 收养的准据法
applicable law for capacity for rights of natural persons 自然人权利能力准据法
applicable law for contracts 合同（契约）准据法
applicable law for contracts of international maritime transport of goods 国际海上货物运输合同（契约）准据法
applicable law for disposing capacity of natural persons 自然人行为能力准据法
applicable law for divorce 离婚准据法
applicable law for extinctive prescription 消灭时效准据法
applicable law for guardianship 监护准据法
applicable law for inheritance 继承准据法
applicable law for marriage 结婚准据法;婚姻准据法
applicable law for matrimonial regime 婚姻财产制准据法（又译夫妻财产制准据法）
applicable law for quasi-contracts 准合同（契约）准据法
applicable law for real rights 物权的准据法
applicable law for the form of juristic act 法律行为的形式准据法
applicable law for the legal capacity of juridical persons 法人的权利能力和行为能力（法律上的能力）准据法
applicable law for torts 侵权行为准据法
applicable law rules 可适用的法律规则（范）
applicant n. （保险）投保人;申请人,（信用证开证）申请人;请求者;候补人
applicant contracting party 申请缔结方
applicant creditor 请求还款的债权人
applicant for insurance 要保人,投保人
applicant for registration 申请登记人;注册申请人
application n. 1.应用,适用,运用 2.请求,申请 3.申请书 4.诉请书（在国际审判法庭前提起诉讼的形式之一）
application and interpretation of law 法律的适用和解释
application by analogy 类推适用
application fee 申请费
application for a change of venue 申请改变审判地点
application for a stay of execution 延期执行的请求
application for adjournment 申请延期
application for admission 请求批准;请求允许进(加)入
application for bail 请求保释;请求担保;保释申请书

application for business 营业申请(书)
application for grant of a patent 申请授予专利权
application for leave to appeal (1882年)请求准予上诉[指在当事方无权上诉或其有权上诉但时限已过时,要求上诉法院听审当事方对一项判决上诉的动议,并允准或拒绝这样的动议,复审法院(reviewing court)对此具有酌处权(discretion)]
application for letter of credit 信用证申请书;申请信用证
application for measures of attachment on property prior to litigation 诉前财产保全申请书
application for naturalization 申请入籍
application for payment 申请付款,请求付款
application for reconsideration 申请复议
application for registration 申请登记,申请注册
application for retiring bill 赎票(单)申请书
application for review 请求复审
application for shares 认股书
application for the protection of an invention 申请保护发明权
application for the reissue of a patent 申请重新颁发专利证书
application for the renewal of a patent 申请续展专利权
application for transfer 申请转移(书),申请转移法院(书)[指在有些管辖区,可以在中级上诉法院要求州最高法院(state's highest court)听审一个上诉案件。此上诉案件似乎原曾在最高法院上诉过,该法院可以不顾中级法院的判决,而且还可认为未曾在中级法院提起诉讼是个错误]
application form 空白申请书;投保单
application instituting proceedings 起诉书(书);起诉书
Application of English Law Ordinance《英国法适用范围条例》
application of foreign laws 外国法的适用
application of foreign public law 外国公法的适用
application of law 法的适用(又译法律的适用);法律的运用
application of long-arm statute to activities on the internet 长臂法适用于因特网上的活动
application of punishment 刑罚的适用
application of the *renvoi* (国际私法)反致原则的适用
application right (for shares) 认购(股份)权
application to the court 向法院申请
applied a. 应用的,实用的
applied art 实用艺术
applied economics 应用经济学
apply v. 提出正式申请(或要求等);申请,运用,实施,适用;指定……用于
apply by letter 书面申请
apply for acquisition of a nationality 申请取得国籍
apply in person 亲自申请
apply the law 实施法律,运用法律
apply to debts contracted in another state 适用在另一州内合同所引起的债务
appoint v. 1.派,委任,任命 2.指定,约定 3.命令 4.处置财产
appoint an expert 指定(委派)鉴定人
appoint under a will 依遗嘱指定
appointed a. 委任的,任命的;指定的
appointed arbitrator 指定仲裁人,委任公断人
appointed day 指定的日期,(法案生效的)规定日期
appointed notaries 委托公证人
appointed officer 任命的官员
appointee n. 被指定人,被委任者
appointing authority 委任机关,任命机关
appointing country 派遣国(对外交人员等)
appointing members of the government 任命政府官(成)员
appointing officer (负责)任命的官员
appointive a. 委任的(指非选举的),任命的
appointment n. 1.(15世纪)任命,委托,选派[指对某人任命一项职务,特别是任命1

名非选举的公职(public office)〈Article Ⅱ of the U.S.Constitution grants the President the power of appointment for principal federal officers, subject to senatorial consent.〉(美国联邦宪法第 2 条授予总统任命权以任命联邦官员,任命后需获得参议院的同意。)] 2.职位[指已被任命之人所居(联邦政府的高级任命)之职位] 3.(议会法)任命[指任命 1 名官员、委员会的委员(members of committee)或一个组织的其他头衔持有人(holder),而不是由组织选举的] 4. 财产的分配行为,分配权[指为达到"土地保有人对土地的分配"(the tenant's appointment of lands)的目的而行使被授予的权利。见 power of appointment; appoint; appointor]

appointment and dismissal 任免
appointments clause (1976年)(美)任命条款[指美国联邦宪法给予总统提名任命联邦法官和各类其他官员权利的条款(美国联邦宪法第 2 条第 2 款)]
appointment of a receiver 指定财产接管人
appointment of an agent 代理人的指定(或选派)
appointment of an adjuster 理算人的指定(或选派)
appointment of an arbitrator 仲裁人的任命
appointment of a counsel (美)辩护人的指定(或选派)
appointment of a curator 保佐人的选任;临时监护人的选任
appointment of a guardian 监护人的选任
appointment of judges 法官的任命
appointment of trustee 受托人的指定
appointment on agreement 订约聘用
appointment on probation 试用
appointment on secondment (短期)调用,借用,借调(见 secondment)
appointment on transfer 调任职位
appointment power 任命权
appointor n. 指定人,任命人
apportion v. 分派,分摊,分配;按比例(或计划)分配
apportioned cost 分派费用
apportionment n. (16世纪)分摊,分配[指①股票分配的部分,尤指两人或两人以上的多数人或单位之间的权利分配或责任分摊(或分担)。②(税务)按既定方式(in a given way)分摊或归属款项或消费的行为。比如纳税人将部分盈利所得交付特别完税年度(particular tax year)或部分个人使用资产投入生意。③议席之分配(指立法机构之席位"legislative seats"),在有代表权的地区分配,特别指根据美国联邦宪法第十四修正案的规定所要求的以人口为基准在各州之间对国会众议员席位的分配。州拒绝其公民因分配不当而作的事实陈述代表权(right of representation)的权利主张而应用司法裁决的争点(justiciable issue)。亦称 legislative apportionment。见 apportionment。④遗产税分摊[指依据"制定法的规定或遗嘱人的指示",在遗产享有利益的人之间承担并分摊遗产税之责任(estate-tax liability)](apportion v.)

Apportionment Act (美)众议院名额分配法
appointment and removal power 任免权(指美国联邦宪法第 2 条 2 款规定,总统"经参议院建议和同意,任命联邦最高法院法官",第 3 条第 1 款规定:"最高法院和低级别法院的法官如忠于职守,得终身任职。"这是司法独立部分决定了对上述条款中包含对行政权的限度)(普通行政的)任命权与免职权
apportionment of damages 损害赔偿的分摊
apportionment of liability 责任分担
apportionment of profit 盈余(利)分配
apportionment of shares 股票分配
appose v. 核查(书面记录持有人的)记录
apposer n. (英)(检查县司法行政官员账目的)财政税务部官员
appraisal n. 评сто,估价;估计的价值
appraisal company 估价公司
appraisal meeting 评议会,评估会议
appraisal of damage 估损;损害估价
appraisal remedy 评价救济
appraisal right 评估权(指美国州公司法中为少数股东提供的法定补偿。公司的重大决策通常由股东大会决定,决策程序

采取民主模式。若少数股东坚决反对公司的某项重大举措,但却无力加以阻拦,则他们可以行使评估权要求公司回购其拥有的公司股票,价格相当于公司"重大行为"发生之前的股票市场价,"重大行为"视个案具体情况而定,但通常涉及公司合并或兼并)
appraisal right of dissenters 持异议股东的股份收买请求权
appraise v. 估价;评价;议价,定价;鉴定
appraise by expert 专家鉴定,鉴定人的鉴定
appraised a. 估价的;评价的;议价的;鉴定的
appraised price 估定价格,议价
appraised value 鉴定价值
appraisement n. 估价;议价,评价;鉴定
appraiser n. 估价人,评价人;议价人;鉴定人
appreciation n. 感谢,赞赏
appreciation on investments 投资增值
apprehend v. 1.理解,领悟,认识 2.逮捕,拘押;扣押 3.料想;了解;忧虑
apprehend danger 觉察危险
apprehended distress (英)已扣押的扣押品
apprehensio n. 逮捕,拘押,扣押
apprehension n. 1.逮捕,拘押;捉拿归案 2.担心,忧虑;恐惧 3.理解
apprehension of battery 殴打之虑
apprehension of danger 危险之虑
apprehension of injury 伤害之虑
apprehension of violence 暴力之虑
apprentice n. 学徒,艺徒,生手
apprentice *en la ley* (古称)学法律的学生
apprentice worker 学徒工
apprenticeship and employee training 学徒和雇员培训
apprenticeship system 学徒制
apprenticius ad legem 见习律师;学法律的学生;(低于 serjeant 高级撰状律师的)律师(见 apprentice *en la ley*)
apprise (=apprize) v. 通知,报告(~sb. of sth.)

approach v./n. 靠近;与……打交道;提议;处理,看待,探讨(to);(美)企图贿赂/方法,态度
approach a problem 研究一个问题
approach a ship 检查船只(指港口当局检查船舶的国籍、货载等事项)
approach a subject 1.靠岸,登陆 2.讨论一个问题,涉及一个问题
approach to constitutional meaning 对宪法意义的入门
approach to this subject 对此问题的探讨(研究)
approachable a. 可接近的,可进入的;可亲近的
approbate v. 依法认可;核准;通过;感觉满意
approbate and reprobate (苏格兰)或接受或拒绝(指当事人对同一契据不得只取其有利部分,而拒绝其不利部分)
approbate the act 通过议案
approbation n. 认可,批准,核准;感觉满意
appropriate v./a. 侵吞;盗用;挪用;侵占;占用;拨款;拨归……之用;分配;圣俸转让;占用拨款/适当的,恰如其分的
appropriate body 有关机关,主管机构
appropriate for a (forums) 适当的审判地,正当的审判地
appropriate grounds 适当证据(根据)
appropriate heir 合格继承人,合法继承人
appropriate interpretative guide 适当的解释指南
appropriate investment 被划拨的投资,适当的投资
appropriate level of details 适当的细化程序
appropriate method of service 适当的送达方式
appropriate performance 适当履行
appropriate persons 适格的人
appropriate punishment 适当刑罚
appropriate retained earning 划拨留存盈余
appropriate sentence 适当判决,适当刑罚
appropriate substitute 适当的代理人
appropriate tribunal 管辖法庭

appropriated profit 划拨利润
appropriateness texts 适当性测试["适当性测试"要求投资公司根据客户或潜在客户是否拥有投资领域或相关产品或服务的必要知识和经验,评估投资服务或交易对客户来说是否适当,而不同于"适宜性测试"(suitability texts)适宜性测试。要求投资公司不只基于请求而从客户或潜在客户获得必要信息,以便其能够了解有关客户的重要事实,而该事实可以表明其所提供服务的性质和范围,使其有合理的根据相信,所推荐或在投资组合管理过程中进行的特定交易足以满足以下条件:①符合客户的投资目的;②客户在资金上可承受任何投资的相关风险;③客户具有了解风险所需要的经验和知识]
appropriation n. 1.侵吞;盗用;挪用,侵占;占用 2.拨款;拨归……之用;分配 3.圣俸转让
appropriation bill 岁出预算法案
appropriation budget 岁出预算;拨款预算
appropriation committee (美)拨款委员会(美国众议院审计预算的机构。美国总统每年一月间国会开会后第一周,即将联邦政府总预算案提交国会审议,其审议程序先由国会各立法委员会审议认可,但仅有提议认许之权而无拨款之权,所以必须再经拨款委员会审议和众议院大会通过)
appropriation of land 侵占土地
appropriation of money 拨出款项
appropriation of payment 挪用支付款项
appropriation of property 侵占他人财产
appropriation resolution 拨款决议(案)
appropriations reserve 经费准备金
Appropriations Subcommittees (美)(参众两院)拨款委员会分会
appropriative a. 拨出(款项等)的;占用的,盗用的,挪用的
appropriator n. 1.盗用者;侵吞者;挪用者 2.拨给者 3.拥有转让圣俸的宗教团体
approvable a. 可批准的,可赞成的,可同意的
approval n. 认可,赞同;核准,批准;许可
approval authority 核准权,批准权;批准机关

approval by the procuratorate 经检察官(或检察院)批准
approval jurisdiction 批准权限
approval of arrest 批准逮捕
approval of the court 法院批准,法院核准
approval of the legislature 立法机关批准
approval procedure 批准程序,审核手续
approve v. 批准;核准;许可,赞成,同意
approve estimates 核定概算
approved a. 批准的,通过的,赞成的
approved agenda 通过的议程
approved association 已被批准的社团
approved budget 已核定的预算
approved by 经……批准
approved law school (亦称 accredited law school)(美)(美国或州协会)认可的法学院(如未经认可者,其毕业生不准当律师)
approved program 已核定的计划
approved school (英)少年罪犯教养院
approved tenderer 指定投标人
approvement of waste (古英国法)圈占荒地权
approver n. 1.批准者,赞同者 2.(英)告密者 3.共同正犯,共犯;(英)自首给发共犯者
approving authority 核准机关;军法审核权;有权核准军事法院判决的机关
approximation of laws 法律接近(欧洲共同体的条约用语)
appurtenance n. 从属权利,附加(附带)权利;从属物,附属物
appurtenance to realty 不动产的附属物
appurtenant n./a. 附属物/附属的,从属的;恰当的,贴切的
appurtenant right 从属权利
appurtenant to land 附属于土地
apriorism n. 先验论;演绎的推论
apt example 适例,贴切的例子,适当的例子
apt out 宣布放弃选择(权),退出
aqua cedit solo water passes with the soil (A grant of the land includes the water on it) 水随土地而转移(土地的转让包括地上的水)
aquaeductus (=aquae ductus) 引水权

aquaehaustus (= *aquae haustus*) 抽水权
aquatic ecosystem 水域生态系统
aquatic products 水产品
Aquinas Thomas 托马斯·阿奎那(1224—1274),中世纪最重要的哲学家和神学家。他的著作《神学大全》试图表明教会信条与亚里士多德教条相一致,信仰与理性相一致。他还认为自然法与实在法之间的联系有时为直接派生,有时则为归属的问题。有一个框架内可供挑选的、平等的立法方案进行选择
Arabian law 阿拉伯法(系)
arbiter n. 仲裁人,公断人;独断者,主宰者
arbitrage n. 1.套利,套汇;套汇买卖,投机买卖,套购 2.仲裁,公断
arbitrage in commodities 套购商品
arbitrage in foreign exchange 套购外汇
arbitrage in securities 套购证券
arbitrage of exchange 套汇
arbitrage of price 价格套利
arbitrage transaction 套汇交易
arbitrager n. 套汇人,套汇人
arbitral a. 可仲裁的;仲裁的,公断的;仲裁人的,公断人的
arbitral adjustment 仲裁,调解;仲裁调停
arbitral award 仲裁裁决(书);裁决书
arbitral award for which no reason are given 未说明理由的仲裁裁决
arbitral body 仲裁机构,公断机构
arbitral clause 仲裁条款
arbitral decision 仲裁裁决
arbitral procedure 仲裁程序,公断程序
arbitral proceeding(s) 仲裁程序,公断程序
arbitral settlement 仲裁解决,公断解决
arbitral tribunal 仲裁庭,公断庭
arbitrament n. (英)少年罪犯教养院,感化院;仲裁,公断,仲裁人(或公断人)所作出的决定;裁判权
arbitrament and award 裁决,判断;仲裁人(或公断人)所作出的决定
arbitrariness n. 专横,手段
arbitrary a. 擅自的,任意的;武断的,专制的,专横的
arbitrary act 武断行为,任意行为
arbitrary arrest 擅自逮捕,乱捕
arbitrary assertion 武断,任意断定
arbitrary confiscation 任意征用,没收
arbitrary, capricious and abuse of discretion 专横,任性,滥用自由酌处权
arbitrary decision 武断的决定,专断;(婚姻)包办
arbitrary deportation 任意放逐(犯人)
arbitrary detention 擅自拘留,任意扣押(或羁押)
arbitrary discretion 任意酌处权
arbitrary exercise of the power of state 滥用国家权力
arbitrary interpretation 任意解释
arbitrary judg(e)ment 任意的判决;武断的判决
arbitrary mark 任意商标(指使用与所表述的商品或服务没有特别联系的单词所作的商标。如"苹果"电脑、"骆驼"香烟等)
arbitrary monetary requirement 仲裁金额标准(要求)
arbitrary power 专制的权力,专权
arbitrary punishment 任意处罚
arbitrary sentence 任意判刑,不合道理的判决
arbitrary standards 任意标准
arbitrary taxation 任意征税,擅自征税
arbitrary value 武断价格
arbitrary verdict 任意裁决
arbitrate v. 仲裁,公断;交付仲裁,使听任公断
arbitrate between two parties in a dispute 仲裁双方间的纠纷
arbitration n. 1.仲裁,公断 2.(通过第三方约束)解决争端,(通过第三方按照法律规定)解决争端
arbitration act 仲裁法,公断法
arbitration agency 仲裁机构,公断机构
arbitration agreement 仲裁协定,公断(或仲裁)合同(契约)
arbitration award 仲裁裁决,仲裁裁决书,公断书
arbitration bond 仲裁书面文件(指争议双方同意仲裁的书面文件)
arbitration by equity 依衡平法的仲裁

arbitration by law 依法仲裁,依普通法的仲裁(与 arbitration by equity 相对而言)
arbitration by summary procedure 简易仲裁
arbitration chamber 仲裁庭
arbitration clause 仲裁条款(指对因条约或合同的适用和解释而引起的争端,在条约或合同中规定通过仲裁解决的条款),公断条款
arbitration commission 仲裁委员会,公断委员会
arbitration convention award 仲裁公约判定书
arbitration court 仲裁法庭,公断法庭
arbitration forum 仲裁庭
arbitration in civil matter 民事仲裁
arbitration in commercial matter 商事仲裁
arbitration in equity 按公平合理准则仲裁
arbitration in law 依法仲裁
arbitration judge 仲裁法官,公断法官
Arbitration Institution of Stockholm Chamber of Commence 斯德哥尔摩商会仲裁院
arbitration meeting 仲裁会议,公断会议
arbitration notice 仲裁通知书,公断通知书
arbitration of contract dispute 合同纠纷仲裁
arbitration office 仲裁机关,公断机关
arbitration order 仲裁令,公断令
Arbitration Ordinance 仲裁条例
arbitration pending trail 仲裁未决审理,仲裁期待审理
arbitration procedural rules 仲裁程序规则
arbitration process 仲裁手续
arbitration provision 仲裁条文;仲裁规定
arbitration treaty 仲裁条约
arbitration tribunal 仲裁庭,公断庭
arbitrational a. 有关仲裁(或公断)的;由于仲裁(或公断)的
arbitrative a. 有权仲裁(或公断)的;由仲裁(或公断)决定的
arbitrator n. 仲裁人,公断人
arbitrator de jure 依法仲裁人,依法公断人
* *Arbitrium est judicium boni viri, secundum aequum et bonum.* An award is the judgement of a good man, according to justice. 仲裁裁决是德高望重的人根据公平与正义所作的判决。
arcane legal terminology 神秘的法律术语
arch a. 为首的;主要的,总的
arch-criminal n. 首恶
Archaic institution of status 古代身份制度
Archaeonomia 《盎格鲁-撒克逊法汇编》(1568年出版的一部拉丁文汇编)
archaic legal systems 古代法制
archaism of the statute 法规的陈旧部分,法规的不合时宜部分
archbishop n. 大主教[指宗教省内有权处理全部教务的教会官员,在英国的教会坎特伯雷大主教是最高级别的,但并不管辖约克大主教,约克则是约克教省的最高权力主管,他们二人均由英国君主政体(England's monarch),犹如英国教会首领(head of the church of England)任命终身职务。但这需征求首相和全体上议院议员之意见]
archetypation n. 诉诸范型
archidiaconal court (英)副主教法庭(已于1963年废除)
Archie 阿奇(工具)(因特网上的一种自动搜索服务工具,用以查找其标题满足特定条件的全部文档)
archipelagic state 群岛国
architect n. 建筑师,设计师,(喻)缔造者
architectural malpractice 建筑上的玩忽职守
architecture n. 建筑风格;建筑样式
archive n. 公文档案,案卷;(常用复)档案馆,档案室
archives and documentation services 档案文献馆
archives of procedures 诉讼案卷
archivist n. 档案保管人(员)
Archivist of United States 美国档案官员(指负责国家档案、记录、案卷管理工作的联邦官员)
archon n. (古希腊、雅典)执政官;主要

官员

Arctic Northwest passage 北极地区之西北通道

area n. 地区,区域;范围,领域;地面,空地;面积

area assessment 分区评定;地区评税

area bargaining 见 area wide agreement

area committee 地区委员会

area court 区域法院

area of computer vulnerability 计算机易受侵袭的范围

area variance 区域变更

area wide agreement (美)地区范围联合协议(在同一地理区域内某一工会与许多雇主订立的集体劳务合同,亦称"area bargaining")

area within (或 under) **the jurisdiction of** 在……管辖(权限)范围内,在……管辖的地区

arenas n. 竞技场,活动场所,竞争场地

Areopagite n. (古代雅典司法机关阿雷古斯的)法官

Areopagus n. 阿雷古斯(古代雅典最早的司法机关,在阿雷古斯山上开庭)

argle-bargle n. (英口)讨价还价;争论,辩论

arguable a. 可争辩的;可论证的

arguable claim 可以论证的请求权,可争辩的索赔

arguably ad. 可以论证地,可争辩地;可以推断地

arguably procedural ergo constitutional test (美)论证程序性的因而也是宪法性的标准

argue v. 争辩,辩论,争论;表明,证明,主张;说服

argue a matter out 把事务争个水落石出

argue one's case 为自己意见作解释

arguendo 缘于辩论;在辩论过程中

arguer n. 争辩者,辩论人

argufy v. 争辩,辩论,争论不休,(以论证)说服

argument n. 争论,辩论;理由;论证;论据;论点

argument at the bar 法庭辩论

argument concluded 辩论终结

argument from disappearing beneficiaries "不存在受惠者"的争论(环境法上的代际公平理论,持这种观点的人认为,由于后代人是不确定的,那么本代人给自己设定义务时的权利享有主体并不确定,即受惠者并不确定,则代际公平问题便无从论起。见 argument from temporal location)

argument from ignorance "不知情"的争论(环境法上的代际公平理论,持此观点的支持者认为,未来的人究竟是谁以及他们的权利和需求等都是本代人无法确知的,因此本代人与未来的后代人之间的公平也就无从论起。见 argument from temporal location)

argument from temporal location "时间定位"的争论(持此观点者认为,本代人无法确定资源枯竭的问题和环境破坏的问题到底影响到未来哪个时间上、哪一代人,所以也无法讨论代际公平的问题。见 argument from ignorance; argument from disappearing beneficiaries)

argumentation n. 争辩,辩论;推论,论证;辩论文,辩论性的演说

argumentative a. 争辩的,辩论的;有争议的

argumentative affidavit 有争议的供词

argumentative denial 有争论的否定

argumentative plea 有争论的答辩;重要事实的答辩

argumentative pleading 1.可争论的答辩(状),争议的辩护[指一种陈述主张(allegations)而非事实(facts)的答辩。因而,法院推论,寻求的约束力只是支持或证实的事实。在法院文件(court papers)中,推断性陈述(conclusory statements)都以可争论答辩的形式作出(即非以作出直接或肯定的陈述形式来提出其主张的答辩)。亦称 inferential pleading]2.有争议的答辩状,争议的辩护[指陈述的多为辩解而非事实的答辩,这迫使法庭或法官去推断或寻求事实。这种事实的推断而未表事实依据的陈述(conclusory statement)在法院文件中都是有争议的辩护状的形式,亦称 inferential pleading]

argumentum 论证
argumentum a contrario 反面的论证
argumentum a fortiori 顺理成章的论证
* *Argumentum ab auctoritate est fortissimum in lege.* An argument drawn from authority is the strongest in the law. 出自权威的论证是法律上最有力的论证。
* *Argumentum ab impossibilii valet in lege.* The argument from impossibility is of great force in law. 从事情的不可能性上所作的论据在法律上具有极大的说服力。
argumentum ab inconvenienti 选择性的论证
* *Argumentum ab inconvenienti est validum in lege; quia lex non permittit aliquod inconveniens.* An argument from that which is inconvenient is good in law; because the law will not permit an inconvenience. 针对歧义的证论在法律上有效;因为法律不允许有任何歧义。
* *Argumentum ab inconvenienti plurimum valet in lege.* An argument drawn from inconvenience is forcible in law. An argument based on inconvience is of great weight in the law. 选择性论证在法律上是有说服力的(不仅考虑事情的合法,也要考虑它的合理可行)。
argumentum ad baculum 恫吓性的论证
argumentum ad captandum 迎合听者偏见或利益的论证
argumentum ad hominem 攻击性论证(指攻击对方人格品德、癖好的论证)
argumentum ad ignorandiam 迎合无知听众的论证
argumentum ad misericordiam 争取同情的论证
argumentum ad populum 争取信任的论证
argumentum ad rem 中肯的论证
argumentum ad verecundiam 奉承性的论证
argy-bargy n. (口)争辩,讨价还价
aright ad. (不可用于动词之前)对;正确
arise v. 出现,呈现,由……引起(from)
arising under requirement 因要求而产生
aristocracy n. 贵族政治,贵族统治;贵族政体,贵族政治制度
aristocratic a. 贵族的,主张贵族政治的;贵族式的
aristocratic government 贵族政府
aristocratic stock 贵族世系
Aristotle 亚里士多德(公元前384—322)(希腊哲学家,与其老师柏拉图一起为西方哲学的开山鼻祖之一。其理论的主要领域:正义;自然法理论;法律中修辞的运用)
arm n. 1.权力,效力 2.(复)武器,兵器,凶器;军备,军火;(英)纹章
arm of the law 法律的权力(效力)
arm's length principle 公平交易原则,独立竞争原则(指强调关联企业之间业务往来应当如同"陌生社会"的"陌生企业"一样,任何一方都不受对方控制或影响的正常业务交往。这样形成的市场才符合市场经济原则的正常交易,这样也才为税法和其他相关法律所认可)
arm's length relationship 保持距离关系(指政府与经济人在法治的基础上建立的一种关系。政府在法治下应是有限的和有效的政府。这是好的市场经济建立和得以维系的关系)
arm's-length test 公平价值交易标准
arm's length transaction 公平交易
* *Arma in armatos sumere jura sinunt.* The law permit the taking up of arms against armed person. 法律允许拿起武器来对付持有武器的人。
armament n. 军队;武装;备战;军械,武器;(复)武装力量
armament factory 军火工厂
armament supervision 军械监督
armchair principle 订立遗嘱的推定原则(即"扶手椅主义")
armed a. 武装的,持械的,携带武(凶)器的
armed attack 持械袭击;武装进攻
armed bands 武装匪帮
armed burglary 持械盗窃
armed clash 武装冲突
armed confrontation 武装对抗
armed *coup d'état* 武装政变
armed element 武装人员
armed felony 持械的重罪犯人

armed fighting 械斗,武斗
armed force committee （国会）军事委员会
armed forces 武装力量,武装部队
armed guards 武装警卫(人员)
armed hold up of vehicles 武装拦车,武装拦劫汽车
armed hostilities 武装敌对行动
armed intervention（或 interference） 武装干涉
Armed Islamic Group 武装伊斯兰集团（指1992年初成立的伊斯兰极端主义组织,目的在于推翻世俗的阿尔及利亚王国,建立伊斯兰国家）
armed neutrality 武装中立
armed police 武装警察
armed provocation 武装挑衅
armed rape 持械强奸
armed rebellion 武装叛乱
armed resistance to arrest 持械拒捕
armed retaliation 持械报复
armed rioting 武装暴乱
armed riots 武装暴动
armed robber 持械抢劫犯
armed robbery 持械抢劫
armed self-defence 武装自卫
armed ship 武装船只
armed subversion 武装颠覆
armistice n. 休战,停战
armistice agreement 停战协定
armistice pact 停战公约
arms certificate 枪械证书;持枪证
arms control 军备控制
arms dealer（或 merchant） 军火商
arm's length n. 正常交易关系
arm's length deal 正常商业交易
arm's length pricing 公平定价,合理定价;公平市价
Arm's Length Principle 独立竞争原则（强调关联企业之间的业务往来,应当像"陌生社会"的"陌生企业"所形成的外部市场一样,这样的经济交往才符合市场经济原则的正常交易,这样才为税法和其他相关法律所认可）
arms race 军备竞赛

army n. 军队;陆军;兵团;大军
Army Act （英）《军队条例》
Army Discipline and Regulation Act （英）《军纪法规》
army vote 通过的军事拨款
army-civilian a. 军民(联合)的
army-civilian defence 军民联防
arra（=arrha; arrhoe; arrhae） （大陆法）定金,保证金
arraign v. 传讯,提审;控告;指责,责难
arraigner n. 传讯人,提审人,审问人
arraignment n. 1.提审,传问,审问,传讯,到庭答复指控罪行(英美刑事诉讼中的一种正式程序,即把犯人带到法官面前唱名之后,庭吏宣读犯人被控罪状,然后问犯人是否承认被检控的罪名。犯人可承认控罪或不作回答)2.弹劾;控告;指责 3.起诉书
arraignment of defendant 传讯被告,提审被告
arraignment of government officials 弹劾政府官员
arrange v. 调解,调停;安排,整理;筹备;商定
arrange bail 安排保释
arranged a. 计划的,安排好的;约定的
arranged (and forced) marriage （中）包办（强迫）婚姻
arranged standard 约定标准
arranged tax rate 约定税率
arrangement n. 调解,调停;和解;协议;整理,安排;商定
arrangement of clause 条款的议定
Arrangement on Guideline for Officially Supported Export Credit ［1978年2月经合组织(OECD)成员国之间达成的］《关于官方支持的出口信贷指导规则的安排》(此规则明确了出口信贷国际政策的一般原则,规定各参加国提供偿还期为2年或2年以上的官方支持的出口信贷时,所能给予的最优惠条件)
arrangement proceedings 调解程序
arrangement with creditors （破产法）与债权人和解(settlement)并就债务的清偿(satisfaction)或延期支付(extension of

time for payment)达成协议(见 Bankruptcy Plan)
arranger for disposal (美)(环保法)处理人处理(危险物)责任[指一个拥有危险物品(hazardous substance)的单位不论是处理好它们,还是有义务控制好它们,必须作出安排。作出安排的处理人根据《全面环境反应赔偿和责任法》为了环保有责任解决所需费用问题]
arrant a. 彻头彻尾的,臭名昭著的
arrant knave 大坏蛋
arrant nonsense 彻头彻尾的谬论
array n./v. 候选(出庭)陪审员名单;大量,一批;列陈/排列陪审员名单,列阵,打叠
array of online 在线陈列资源(指美国法律文献检索中的一个电子检索术语)
arrearage n. 债,欠款;拖延,到期未付的款项;(古)储备物
arrears n. 1.欠款;2.余债;尾数 2.拖延;落后
arrears in contribution 拖欠会费,拖欠款项
arrears in taxes 拖欠税款
arrears of rent 欠债,欠租
arrect v. (美)控诉,指责,起诉
arrêr v. 1.(法院的)判决 2.逮捕,拘押 3.官方命令
arrest n./v. 1.逮捕,拘留,拘押,扣留 2.阻止,抑制;中止/1.逮捕,拘留,扣押,扣留 2.阻止,抑制;中止
arrest a judg(e)ment 中止判决,延缓判决
arrest according to law 依法逮捕
arrest and deal with according to law 逮捕法办
arrest and detaining for questioning 为讯问而进行的逮捕和拘留
arrest and detention 逮捕与拘留
arrest by mistake 错捕
arrest of a criminal 捕捉罪犯,逮捕罪犯
arrest of a person accused 对被告的拘捕(或拘押)
arrest of inquest 中止审讯,中止讯问
arrest of judg(e)ment 阻止判决;中止判决
arrest of ships before suit 诉讼前扣押船只

arrest on final process 凭(执行判决的)最后传票逮捕
arrest ordinance 逮捕条例(令)
arrest procedure 逮捕程序
arrest sb. on a charge of 以……罪逮捕某人
arrest warrant 逮捕证,拘留状
arrest without a warrant 无证逮捕;擅自逮捕
arrest without a warrant of flagrant delictor 对现场作案者的无证逮捕
arrestable a. 应(可)予逮捕的
arrestable offence 应受逮捕的罪行;构成逮捕的罪行,(英)可逮捕罪
arrestable offender 应予逮捕的罪犯
arrested a. 被捕的[指刑事被告(of an accused)被带至法官面前并被指控犯有罪行]
arrested development of mind 无独立思考能力
arrested gambler 被捕赌犯
arrested property 被扣押财产
arrestee n. 被逮捕者,被拘押者
arrester (=arrestor) n. 逮捕人;拘押人
arresting officer 负责逮捕(犯人)的警官;有逮捕权的官员
arrestment n. 逮捕,拘留;扣押,扣留;阻止,中止;(苏格兰)(对处于第三人手中的债务人财产的)诉讼保全
arrestment ad fundandam 扣押财产
arrestment in execution 1.审前对刑事被告拘留 2.对民事被告未办理保释的拘留 3.(苏格兰法)对案外债务人财产扣押 4.审前拘押以保护财产便于执行判决
arrestum jurisdictionis fundandae causa 1.(罗马法)为行使司法管辖之目的而拘押 2.(苏格兰法)根据苏格兰法院管辖权可逮捕外籍人,这种类型之拘押源于荷兰法(Dutch Law)
arret de règlement (大陆法)规章之判决(指由议会颁布的判决以确立民法或习惯法的诉讼程序之规则)
arretes n. (政府机关的)决议,决定
arrha poenalis 罚扣定金(指违约定金不退还)

arrhae n. (大陆法)定金;订婚时的赠与物(见 arra)

arrha sponsalitia (罗马法)订婚时的保证金,订婚的礼金

arriage and carriage 不确定的义务(指古时英格兰和苏格兰领主对佃户的非分或不合理要求,18世纪已有法规明文禁止)

arrière ban 国王征召令(指①国王命令其臣属、奴仆等加入军队服兵役,违者则被没收产业;②被征召或传唤来的臣属组成的军队)

arrival n. 到达,来到;出现;到达者,到达物

arrival at a conclusion 得出结论

arrival card 入境证

arrivé n. 暴发户;新贵

arrogance n. 骄傲自大,傲慢

arrogate v. 冒称具有;僭取,侵占

arrogate to 没有来由地把……归于

arrogation n. 冒称(权利等);僭取,侵占

arrondissement n. (法)专区、省以下最大的行政区;大城市中的区

Arrow's Debren Model of General Equilibrium 阿罗-德布鲁的一般均衡模型

Arrow's theorem 阿罗定理(亦称"阿罗悖论"或"不可能性理论"。它是社会选择理论的一项基本原则。即经常表明没有理性的手段能把个人偏好聚合成一个社会选择)

Arrowsmith principle (美)阿罗史密斯原则

arsenic n./a. 砷,砒霜/砷的,含砷的

arsenical poison 砒毒

arser inle main burning in the hand (18世纪)手上烧烙印[指对非神职人员的刑事犯在左手大拇指上烧烙印的惩罚。这类刑事犯声称或冒充具有神职特权并获准享有神职人员(clergy)的特权。烧烙印后以便在其第二次声称神职人员时可供鉴别,以避免其再次享有神职人员不受普通法上酷刑的特权。该特权由1827年《刑法法》(Criminal Law Act)废止]

arson n. (17世纪)1.(普通法)纵火罪,放火罪(指恶意焚烧他人住所或宅基地内的附属建筑。如果该住宅或附属建筑属于自己所有,则不构成纵火罪,但若造成比邻安全之虞则构成烧房罪(house-burning) 2.(制定法)放火罪,纵火罪[根据现代制定法,恶意或不法行为烧毁他人财产(如烧毁建筑物)或自己的财产(如骗取财产保险金),实施点火或引起爆炸的,则构成二级重罪。参见《示范刑法典》第220.1(1)节。亦称 crimen incendii(在2的意义上) statutory arson。见 criminal damage to property]

arson suspect 纵火嫌疑犯

arsonist n. 纵火犯,放火犯

arsura n. (历史)检验钱币(①铸币后用火烧加热来检验钱币;②检验过程中钱币要失去一些分量)

art n. (13世纪)艺术,美术[指①创作性的表示或创作表示的产品。②需要技能的行业,一种工艺技巧(craft)。③(专利)有效努力的领域(field of useful endeavor);创立新事物中在方法上运用知识和技巧。在专利法上,技术(art)与 technology 同义,常用于现有技术(prior art)、相关技术(relevant art)。美国联邦宪法的专利与版权条款中亦以该词表示"技术",与"科学"(science)相对]

art and part (苏格兰)教唆及参与犯罪,策划并参与,同案犯

artfully pleaded 技术性方法起诉

art of arguing orally in the court 法庭上的口头辩论技巧

article n./v. 1.文章;(常用大写,法律条款的)条 2.物件,物品,商品 3.(复)章程,法(规);条款(有时指法律文书、合同等);规章;条例/订条款(或合同);约束;分条(解释);列举(罪状等),控告,订约……收徒弟

Article I Court (1955年)1.见 Legislative Courts 2.联邦立法法院的一种类型,不受美国联邦宪法第3条第2款(U.S. Cons. art. Ⅲ.§2)的约束,其法官也不享有终身职位和薪金保障之特权,其履行之职能与行政机构之职能相似,诸如发表一些咨询意见(issuing advisory opinions),参见美国联邦宪法第1条第8款(U.S. Const. art 1.§8.)(见 Article Ⅲ Court)

Article I Judge (1958年)第一条法官 [指①依据美国联邦宪法第1条,由国会授权的美国破产法官、治安法官以及任命的定期的行政法法官(administrative-law judge, appointed for a term of years),参见《美国注释法典》第28标题卷第151节及以下第631条及以下(28 USCA §§151 et seq. 631 et esg.)。②美国总统事先不经参议院批准即可临时任命联邦法官(federal judge)。这种任命权(appointment power)来自休会期任命条款(recess-appointment clause),该条款允准总统于国会非会议期间临时任命政府官员。参见美国联邦宪法第2条第2款(U. S. Const. §2 cl.)。③见 recess appointment,在 appointment 1 中]

Article III Court (1949年)第三条法院 [源于美国联邦宪法第3条第2款之管辖权(U. S. Const. art. III. §2),即联邦法院可以听审因宪法、合众国法律(laws)以及条约以美国为当事一方所引起的案件,州际之间以及公民与不同州之间所产生的案件。亦称 Constitutional Court。见 Article I Court]

Article III Judge (1937年)第三条法官 [指根据美国联邦宪法第3条任命联邦最高法院、上诉法院或地区法院的法官为终身法官]

articled clerk 见习律师;见习职员
articles free 无税商品
articles in a statute 法规条文
articles of agreement 同意条款,协议条款
articles of apprenticeship 学徒章程,学徒合同(契约)
articles of association 法人社团章程;公司章程;组织规章
Articles of Association of the Bank of China 《中国银行章程》
Articles of Association of the China International Trust and Investment Corporation 《中国国际信托投资公司章程》
Articles of Confederation (美)《邦联条例》(美国1781—1789年的第一部宪法)
Articles of Confederation and Perpetual Union (美)联邦条例(1777年美国联邦会议通过,这是美国最早的宪法文件)
articles of co-partnership 合伙合同(契约)
articles of crime 犯罪物品
articles of impeachment (美)弹劾状,弹劾条款(对高级公务官员免职的第一个步骤,如众议院可拟定控诉状,称为对总统的弹劾条款,经表决通过,则可将此弹劾条款呈交参议院以便审理)
articles of incorporation 公司(或团体)的组织章程
Articles of Incorporation and Bylaws 《公司组织章程和内部规章(细则)》
articles of law 法律条文
articles of organization 公司章程,组织章程
articles of partnership 合伙条款;组合规约
articles of peace 安全保障条款;(请求保护人身及财产)安全的诉状
articles of personal consumption 个人消费品
articles of pupilage 从师规约
Articles of Religion (英)宗教信纲(基督教圣公会最主要和最基本的教义纲要)
articles of roup (苏格兰法)拍卖(土地或建筑物的条件的)说明书
articles of the eyre (历史)总巡回审问条目[指巡回法庭不在时发生了什么违法事情。总巡回审法官团(community)成员面前都有一系列问题需要审问发现。这种调查询问可使法官对犯罪行为处以罚金并通过财产扣押或提交罚金为皇家增加财政收入。亦称 *capitula itineris*]
articles of war 战争法规;军法条例;(英)《军法条例》
articulate v./a. 连接,结合;使连接,使结合;(论据等)表达清楚有力/表达清楚有力的,表达力强的
articuli cleri 教士条例
artifact (=artefact) 人为的,人工的,人为的组织机构,人工制品,制造物
artificial a. 人工的,人造的;人为的;假的
artificial accretion 人工添附
artificial argument 诡辩,强词夺理
artificial boundary 人为边界

artificial capacity 人为权能
artificial contaminant 人工沾染物
artificial effect 拟制的效果
artificial idea 人为的意念,人为的理念
artificial insemination （家庭法）人工受孕；人工授精[指不通过性交方式而以注射之类的方法将男性的精子注入女性子宫内使其受孕。如果人工授精时该妇女已婚,并且孩子出生,同时其丈夫已同意人工授精,且由特许医生实施,则该丈夫被认为是孩子的父亲。如果该妇女在人工授精时未结婚,关于未决精卵赠与人（donor）是否为孩子的父亲,各个司法管辖区根据几个要素进行不同对待。见 in vitro fertilization; gamete intrafallopian transfer; Zygote Intrafallopian Transfer]
artificial law 立法,人造法
artificial person 法人；拟制的人
artificial presumption 人造推定[指人造推定属于未知事实的认识活动,这种认识不完全依赖于自身的形式和效能,而是掺杂了人的技术性加工。其结论取决于设立推定规则者的主观信念和价值取向。因此,有人称之为 decision rule presumption（裁决规则推定）]
artificial reason 人为理性
artificial refreshment of memory 诱导记忆的恢复
artificial succession 法人（或法人团体）的继承
artificial watercourse 人造水道
artificial year 法定年
artisan（=artizan）n. 手工业工人,工匠,技工
artistic work 艺术作品（有些国家版权法中艺术作品与美术作品"works of fine art"相同,而另一些国家艺术作品则将美术作品除外,但还包括外观设计及实用艺术作品）
as a consequence 结果,因此,从而
as a result (of) 作为……结果
as agreed upon 根据协议,根据合约
as appropriate 视情况而定,酌情
as by law enacted 按制定（颁布）的法律
as defined in article… 按第……条所规定

as evidence of 作为……依据,作为……根据
as is ad./a. 照现在的样子（不再做修理或改进）〈the customer bought the car as is〉（顾客照现在的样子购买了汽车）。根据美国《统一商法典》第 2-316 节（3）（2），销售方可以通过陈述货物"照现在的样子"（as is）售出,或以"不保证商品没有瑕疵"（with all faults）的方式拒绝所有的默示担保（all implied warranties）。总之,"照现在的样子"的财物（property）销售意思是财物的销售按现有情况（existing condition）,因此使用"as is"短语是在减轻销售方在那种"现有情况"下对瑕疵所承担的责任。亦称 with all faults/照现在的样子的或者按照现在样子的
as long as 1.达……之久 2.= so long as 只要
as of 在……时候；到……时为止,从……起
as of course 事实上,依法有权取得的,必需法院的干预
as of right 依法当然取得的
as opposed to 与……相对（比）
"as other nations do the same" 如其他国家采取同样行动
as the law stands 法律如此规定
as things are（或 go） 照目前情况看；依目前形势
as set out here 正如此处所表明（宣布）的
as sober as a judge 像法官一样严肃认真
as the case may be 看情况,根据具体情况
*As the debate progressed it became clearer and clearer which side was right.（中）是非愈辩愈明。
as though（=as if） 似乎,仿佛
as yet 到目前为止
as-if rights 虚假的权利
asbestos personal injury 石棉人身伤害
ASC（Australia Securities Council） 澳大利亚证券委员会
ascendant（=ascendent）n. 尊亲属；优势
ascending line 直系尊亲
ascension n. 升高,上升
ascent v. （17 世纪）上至尊亲属下至卑亲属的继承人的遗产继承,尊亲属对卑亲属的遗产继承（见 descent）

ascertain v. 查明,弄清;确定
ascertained by law 经法律确认
ascertained case 已查明的案件
ascertained goods 已查明的财产
ascertainment n. 查明;调查确实
ascertainment of foreign law 外国法的确定
ascertainment of loan 贷款审查
ascertainment of relevant truth 相关性真实情况的确认
ascertainment of the facts of particular controversies 确定特定争议的事实,特定争议事实的确认
ascribe v. 归咎于
ascribe a motive 归咎于动机
ashes n. 遗体,骨灰
Ashta pradhan 八头会议(印度马拉塔人领袖神西瓦台创立的行政和咨询会议)
Asian Legal Consultative Committee 亚洲法律协调委员会
Asian-African Legal Consultative Committee 亚非法律协调委员会
Asian-American Legal Defense and Education Fund (美)亚裔美国人法律辩护与教育基金会
aside from 除……外
ask v. 询问;要求,请求;讨(价还价);邀请;需要
ask the banns 预告婚事(问人有无异议)
asleep fall 玩忽职守,懈怠
asperse v. 诽谤,中伤;破坏(名誉等)
aspersion n. 中伤,诽谤
asphalt jungle (美)都市中犯罪猖獗的地区
asphyxia n. 窒息
aspiration n. 志气,渴望
asportation n. 窃走,窃取他人动产
asportavit n. 窃走
Assaciation de Malfaiteurs (法)犯罪团伙
assail v. 攻击,袭击;着手解决
assailant n. 攻击者;行凶者
assart (或 essart) n. 垦荒;垦荒地
assassin n. 暗杀者;行刺者(尤指政治性的)
assassinate v. 暗杀,行刺;中伤
assassination n. 暗杀,行刺

assassination syndrome 暗杀狂并发症
assassinator n. 暗杀者,行刺者;刺客
assault n./v. 1.侮辱,凌辱 2.侵犯他人身体(罪)(依习惯法,对他人身体使用武力或暴力,意图伤害,即构成侵犯他人身体罪) 3.殴打(罪) 4.威胁,袭击,突击 5.强奸(委婉语)/殴打,行凶;人身攻击;动武;袭击
assault and battery 殴打和侵犯人身罪,袭击和伤害罪(行为)
assault occasioning actual bodily harm 殴打引起的实际身体伤害
assault with a dangerous (deadly) weapon 用武(凶)器伤害罪;用凶器殴打
assault with intent to commit murder 意图谋杀而行凶
assault with intent to rape 因蓄意强奸而行凶伤害
assaulter n. 犯伤害罪者,侵犯者;殴人者;胁迫他人者
assaulting and battering 暴力殴击罪;侵犯人身罪;殴打罪;袭击和暴力伤害罪(行为)
assay n. 化验;分析;检定;质量检查;被化验(分析)物;化验报告
assayer n. 化验人;分析人,检定人;尝试者
assemblage n. 配合,集合;集合物;一群人,会众;装配
assemble v. 配合,集合;调集;汇编;装配
assembly n. (14世纪)1.集合,集会(指有组织的一些人集合一起并为共同目的联合在一起的集会) 2.在美国的许多州,指立法机构的下议院或众议院 3.(议会法)协议;大会议会(大写) 4.(专利)专利的权利主张;供以构成一个构造物(structure)的集中的部件(parts),组装
assembly of creditors 债权人大会
Assembly of Elders 长老议会
assembly of freemen 自由民大会,公民会议
Assembly of Notables (英)贵族议会
assembly of stockholders 股东大会
assemblyman n. 1.议员 2.(美国某些州的)州议会众议员
assent n. 同意,赞成;附和;认可

assent and consent 一致通过；无异议
assent to bills by commission （英）授权同意提案
assenting-silence doctrine （1976年）赞成沉默原则，同意沉默原则[指如果控告是在可能被认为是一种协议的境况下构成的，作为真实陈述而提起的控告（accusation）无须顾及刑事被告的沉默的一种原则。这个原则在衡量刑事被告的罪行时通常是无效的]
assentor n. 同意者，赞成者
assert v. 宣称，断言；维护；坚持；主张
assert a claim 主张债权，提出要求（主张）
assert a maritime claim 提出海商法上的债权主张（要求）
assert a set-off 提出抵消债权的主张
assert that 宣称，断言
assertion n. 宣称，断言；维护；坚持；主张
assertion of personal jurisdiction 对人管辖权的行使，主张（维护）对人管辖权，行使对人管辖权
assertion of rights 维护权利
assertive evidence 本证，有力证据
assertor （=asserter）n. 辩护人，律师；胜诉者；断言者；维护者
assertory covenant 确认条款[指针对特定事实予以确认，对盖印的允诺亦予以认定]
assess v. 1.确定（税款、罚款）的金额 2.对（财产等）进行估价；审估 3.征收（税款、罚款）4.评估
assess the damages 确定损害赔偿（额）
assess the evidence 审查证据，评定证据
assessable a. 可估价的，可估计的；可评定的；可征税的
assessable income 应课税的收入
assessable profit 应课税的盈利
assessed a. 已估价的；摊派的；征收的
assessed budget 摊派的预算
assessed contribution 分摊的会费
assessed program cost 摊派的计划费用
assessed valuation formula 课税评价公式
assessee n. 财产价值（或收入金额）已被估定的人
assessing and collecting of tax 评税和征税工作
assessment n. 1.估价，评价；评定 2.估价法；估计数；应缴额 3.确定数额；课税评定 4.征税
assessment connected with the leased property 与租赁财产相关的估价义务
assessment district 征税区
assessment lien 征收留置权
assessment of compensation for compulsory purchase 为强制购买补偿的估价
assessment of damages 评定损失赔偿额
assessment of hereditament 可继承财产的估价
assessment of property 征收财产税
assessment of results 成果评定
assessment of tax 征税
assessment rolls 应征税人和财产名册
assessor n. 1.确定罚款的人；财产估价人；税额审查员 2.（法官或官方委员会）顾问；助理；技术顾问；陪审员；顾问律师 3.保险财产估价人
assessor system 陪审制
assessor system of the people （中）人民陪审员制度
asset n. 财产，遗产；财富；（复）资产
asset for feiture laws 资产没收法规
Asset Management Corporation (AMC) 资产管理公司
asset mark 财产标志
asset securitization 资产证券化
asset-based board and open-ended definition of investment 以资产为基础、广义的、开放式的投资概念[指MAI草案（Multilateral Investment Agreement）多边投资协议所界定的投资的一种概念，将所有形成的间接投资都涵盖在内，包括各种形式的间接投资、知识产权、特许协议、公共债务、不动产等]
assets and liabilities 资产和负债
assets betterment 资产增值
assets in hand 现有资产
assets of a business 企业的资产
assets of trust corpus 信托集合资产
assets-backed securities (ABS) 资产证券
asseveration n. 声明，断言
assign v. 让与，转让，财产转让；过户；指

派,指定;委派;分配
assign a mark 转让商标
assign a patent 转让专利
assign in blank 不记名转让
assignable a. 可转让的,可过户的;可指派的,可分配的
assignable contract 可转让的合同(契约)
assignable credit 可转让的信用证
assignable instrument 可过户的证券
assignable interest 可转让的权益
assignation n. 转让,让与;分配,分派;指定,指派
assignation house 见 disorderly house
* *Assignatus utitur jure auctoris.* An assignee is clothed with the right (or has rights) of his principal. 代理人拥有其被代理人的权利。
assigned a. 转让的;指定的;指派的
assigned account 可由银行接收的账户担保(或作为贷款抵押品的代管人)
assigned agent 指定的代理人
assigned claim 转让的债权
assigned counsel (英美法)指定辩护人(经政府指定为贫困被告提供免费或低费法律帮助的律师)
assigned risk 强制接受的保险业务,分派风险
assignee n. 财产受让人;财产管理人;受托人;代理人;被指定人
assignee in insolvency 破产清算人
assignee of the claim 请求权的受让人,债权受让人
* **(the) assignee stands in the shoes of the assignor** "受让人承受了让与人的法律状况"
assigner (=assignor) n. 让与人,转让人;委派者,委托人,分配者
assigning responsibility 转让责任(转让财产承担责任性)
assignment n. 1.(权利、财产)转让,让与;分配;转让证书 2.委派,委托 3.指定,指派;指明 4.(理由、动机等的)陈述,说明
assignment allowance 委任津贴
assignment by operation of law 依法转让
assignment for the benefit of creditor 对债权人有利的转让
assignment of choses in action 无形财产的转让
assignment of claim 请求权的让与,债权转让
assignment of contract 合同(契约)转让
assignment of contractual right 合同(契约)权利的转让
assignment of copyright 版权转让
assignment of counsel 辩护人的指定(见 assigned counsel)
assignment of credit 债权转让
assignment of debts 转让债务,债务让与
assignment of dower 寡妇(扶养费)的分配(数)
assignment of error 原审错误陈述书(见 proposition of law)
assignment of lease 租赁权的转让
assignment of negotiable securities 有价证券的转让
assignment of obligation 债的转让,债的移转
assignment of office 公职的委派
assignment of patent 专利权的转让
assignment of policy 保险单的转让
assignment of privilege 特权转让
assignment of rights 权利转让
assignment of the floor (议会法)议长通过程序允准某人具有发言资格
assignment of the power of attorney 委任状的转手授予
assignment of wages (美)(为了抵债而)转让工资(给债权人)
assignment with preference 有优先权的转让
assignor n. 转让者,转让人;委托者,委派者
assigns n. 财产受让人,受让人
assimilated to a ship without nationality 视同无国籍船舶
assimilated to warship 视同军舰
assimilation n. 同化;吸收(作用)
assimilation clauses 同化条款
(the) assimilative capacity approach (环境)消解能力方法

assisa cadere 诉讼驳回

assise 见 *assize*

assiser n. 陪审员;估税员;鉴定人

assisors（复）n. （苏格兰）（总称）陪审员

assist v. 支持;援助,帮助;出席,参加

assist as one of the judges 作陪审法官,作陪审推事

assistance n. 援助,协助,帮助

assistance and salvage at sea 海上救助

assistance contribution 援助捐款

assistance of counsel 辩护人（对被告的）有效援助

assistant n. 助理,助手;辅助物;（复）总督助理,助理人员

assistant *ad litem* 诉讼辅助人

assistant attorney 助理检察官

assistant attorney general 司法部部长助理

assistant clerk 助理书记官

assistant collector 助理收税员

assistant judge 助理审判员,法官助手

assistant minister 助理部长,部长助理

assistant procurator general 总检察长助理;助理检察长

assistant prosecuting attorneys （美）助理检察官

assistant prosecutor 助理检察官（员）

assistant state attorney 州助理检察官

assistant supervisor 助理监察员

assistant whip （英）议会政党组织秘书助理

assisted a. 受援助的,受协助的

assisted country 受援国

assisted person 受（法律）援助的人;受援者

assisting n. 协助罪（属于妨碍司法执行罪之一）

assisting deserter 协助逃亡者

assisting offender 从犯,协助犯

Assiza de Ponderibus et Mensuris （英）《度量衡法令》

assiza de utrum（=assize of utrum） （英）土地归属令状,地产性质诉讼令状;创设地产性质令状,决定地产性质的陪审团

assize n. （14 世纪）1.法院或咨议的会议或开会期 2.有关制定度量、重量、价格和衡量等标准的法规 3.为制定法令或法规（enactment）做准备的程序 4.听审涉及程序案件的法庭 5.陪审团,咨审团 6.陪审团审议 7.陪审团裁决 8.令状（writ）["assize"源于拉丁文 "assideo" 意为 "sit together"（坐在一起）;后来的陪审即可能源于此]

assize（或 assise）court （英）巡回法庭;（法）重罪法庭

assize（或 assise）of *mort d'ancestor* 收回被占的继承土地的诉讼（古时英国收回土地的一种手续,原告因有继承权而就其父母、兄弟、姊妹、亲戚等的自由保有土地被侵占而提起的诉讼）

assize（或 assise）of nuisance 排除妨害的（巡回法庭）令状

assize（或 assise）rents 法定租金

Assize of Clarendon （英）《克拉伦法》（1166 年所确定的有关新近强占之诉的立法）

assize of darrein presentment 巡回审判中的最终推荐程序

assize of fresh force （英）返还近期占有土地令状

Assize of Northampton （英）《北安普敦法》（1176 年此法确认了这一令状,该令状规定:亨利二世将英格兰分为六个巡回审判区,每个巡回区指派三名巡回法官,该令还创设收回继承地之诉）

assize of novel disseisin （英）新近强占之诉（指收回新近被强夺或被侵占土地的诉讼）

associate n. 法庭记录官（英国普通法法庭的官员,坐在法官下面,记录法官命令及其他事项）;合伙人,同事;非正式会员;相关物;（复）诉讼记录;事件录

associate judge （美）（联邦法院或州法院的）首席法官和主审法官以外的法官（与 associate justice、puisne judge 相同）

associated a. 合伙的,联合的;有联系的,有关的;副（职）的

associated agency 委托机构;联合机构;联合代理（处）

associated company 联合公司,联营公司;联号

associated employers 联合雇主

associated form 协作方式
associated liability 连带责任
associated trade mark 联合商标
association n. 协会;合伙;交际;联盟;联想;社团(法人);联合体
association agreements (由欧共体和非成员国达成的)联合协定(议)
association clause 公司组合条款
Association de Droit International et de Relations Internationals 国际法及国际关系协会
Association *di tipio Mafiopso* (意)黑手党
association for making profits 营利社团
association for maximizing sell-interests 自我利益最大化的联盟
association in participation 隐名合伙
Association Internationale pour Protection de Propriete Industrielle (法)国际工业产权保护协会
association of a nonprofit-making nature 非营利性社团
Association of American Law Schools 美国法学院协会
association of consumers 消费者协会
association of hooligans 流氓团伙
association register 社团登记簿
associational a. 协会的,社团的;联想的
associative a. (倾向于)联合的,引起联合的,联想的
assoil v. 赦免;宽恕,释放;补偿,赎(罪)
assoilzie n. (苏格兰)解除被告责任令(指法院裁决被告人没有责任)
assorted rights 种种权利,各式各样的权利
assumable a. 可假定的,可设想的;可采取的;可假装的
assume v. 1.假定,假设 2.担任,承担,接受 3.采取,呈现(某种形式或面貌),带有
assume a statement to be correct 假设一种说法是正确的
assume jurisdiction over the case 对案件自行管辖
assume obligation 担负义务
assume office 就职
assume ownership 行使所有者的权利
assume responsibility 承担责任
assume the reins of government 开始执政
assumed a. 设想的,假定的;承担的;僭越的;虚构的
assumed bonds 承担公司债券(指一公司发行由另一公司承担责任的债券)
assumed intention 假定意图
assumed liability 担负的责任;代人承担的债务
assumed name 假名
assumed obligation 承担的义务,假设的债
assumed risk 承担的风险
assuming that… 假定……
assumpsit n. (普通法)要求赔偿违约所造成损失的诉讼;(承担向他人付款或做某事的口头或书面的)承诺(或约定)
assumption n. 假设,假定;臆断,担任,承担;采取,僭越,继承(他人的债务)
assumption of a succession (插手)干涉继承
assumption of debts 承担债务
assumption of duty 就职,任职
assumption of mortgage 承担抵押
assumption of obligation 债的承担
assumption of risk 冒风险,负担危险;承担风险,自担风险,又称"*velenti non fit injueria*"
assumption of the law 法律推定(如无罪推定),法律上的假定
assumptions of rationality 理性假定
assurance n. 1.担保,保证;保障 2.(英)保险(尤指人寿保险)3.财产转让(书)(指物业的让与、转让或物业转让、让与的契据) 4.自信,信念;狂妄自大
assurance of human rights 保障人权
assure v. 确信,保证,保障,担保;保险(主要用于人寿保险)
assured n./a. (保险合同中指定的)受益人;被保险人,要保人;被保证人(与insurer相对而言)/确定的,有保证的;自信的;感到放心的
(the) assured cannot sue himself 被保险人不能自己起诉自己
assured income 有保证的收入
assurer n. 保险人,保险商,承保人;保证人

Assyrian n./a. 亚述人/亚述人的
Assyrian law 亚述法
astitution n. 控告,起诉;传讯,审讯(见 arraignment)
astray ad. 误入歧途地;离开正道地,犯错误地
astreinte n. (法)执行程序,强制执行程序
astrict n. 束缚,限制;(在道德上和法律上的)约束
astronaut n. 宇宙航行员
astronavigation n. 宇宙航行,天文导航
astropolicy n. 宇宙保险单
asylum n. 庇护(权);避难,政治避难(权);收容所,避难所,庇护所;精神病院
asylum case 避难案,庇护案
asylum for lepers 麻风病院
asylum granted to aliens 给予外侨的庇护
asylum in the premises of a diplomatic mission 外交使团驻地内的庇护权
asylum of the aged (中)敬老院,养老院
asymmetric information 信息不对称(指西方经济学中的一个概念,日本学者称其为"信息偏在",亦称 asymmetric information。根据信息经济学理论,不对称信息在交易发生前后分别导致逆向选择和道德风险)
asymmetric information (AI) theory 不对称信息理论
asymmetric stakes 不对称预期
asymetric warfare 非对称战争
Asymmetrical Conception of Racial Equality "不相称的种族平等"的概念
asymmetry n. 不对称性,非对称性
asymmetry of information 信息不对称[西方经济学中的一个概念,日本的植草益、宫泽健一称它为"信息偏在"。两个概念的内涵外延均为一致,亦称 asymmetric information,即非对称信息或不对称信息,指阿罗—德布勒(Arrow-Debreu)模型,用以表达两个古典福利经济学定理的基本模型。根据信息经济学理论,不对称信息在交易发生前后分别导致逆向选择和道德风险]
asynodia n. 阳痿
at a determinable future time 在可确定的未来日期
at a price 以较市价高的价钱,高于市场价
at a single sitting 一次开庭
at all (用于否定或条件句中)根本,丝毫,(用于肯定句)全然,完全
at all event(s) 不管如何,总之,无论如何
at all times 任何时候,一直,随时,无论如何,始终
at any stage up to final appeal 直至终审上诉为止的任何阶段
at arm's length 疏远,在不利条件下,无关联(指甲、乙双方互不受到控制与支配,两无关联)
at bar 在审讯中,在法庭下
at best 以最佳汇率(或价格)
at call 通知
at (the) discretion 随意,任意;酌处
at expense of 以……为代价(靠牺牲)
at full length 详尽地,仔细地
at ground level 在基层一级
at hand 即将到来,在身边,在附近
at issue 在争论中,系争点(当事人对一案件进行辩论时所产生的一方肯定而另一方否定的论点)
at large (罪犯)未被捕获的,自由的,未受控制的;充分的,详尽的,(美)全州选举的;任意的,概括的
at large election 大区选举(见 election at large)
at law 依法,根据法律;在法律上
at no time 任何时候都不,决不〈at no time will China be the first to use nuclear weapon〉(中国在任何时候决不首先使用核武器)
at odds 有空,临时
at one time 同时;从前有个时期;曾经
at one's discretion 自行裁量,自行酌处
at one's disposal 自由处置,自行处分
at one's own risk 自己负责,自担风险
at or upon 在指定日期的特定时刻(根据上下文确定具体时刻)
at par 与票面价值相等;依照票面价格(值)
at pleasure appointment 见 pleasure appointment
at public expense 用公费

at random 任意地,随意地
at regular intervals 定期;每隔一定距离,每隔一定时间
at revised rate 按订正费率计算
at short interval 常常
at sight 见票即付
at stake 危若累卵,在危险中,生死攸关
at stake amount 受牵连额
at term 如期,在期限内
at the dock 码头交货;码头交货价
at the expense of 归……付费(或负担);在损害……的情况下;以……为牺牲
at the foot of the ladder 在基层方面
at the inception 一开始
at the instance of 根据要求,经……提议,应(经)……请求
at the local level 在地方一级
at the mercy of 在…支配中;任凭…摆布
at the national level 在国家一级,在国家范围内
at the outset 首先
at the outset of a lawsuit 诉讼之初,诉讼开始之时
at the point 那时
at the point of 靠近……接近……
at the same time 同时;但,然而
at the scene capture 现场查获,在现场捉拿归案
at the scene investigation 现场勘验
at times 有时,不时
at will (英)任意期(指合伙、土地保有或其他关系的持续期限)
at work 在工作,在运车手,从事于,在忙于
at-once-payment n. 立即偿付
at-railhead n. 铁路终点交货
Athenian polis 雅典的城邦制
athopia n. 精神衰弱
atia n. 恶意
atimia n. (古希腊)公民权利的剥夺
Atlantic Charter 《大西洋宪章》
Atlantic Pact 《太平洋公约》
Atlantic Reporter (美)大西洋区判例汇编
Atlantic Reporter Second Series (美)大西洋区判例汇编第二套丛书
atlas of the living resources of the sea 海洋生物资源分布图
atler ego of a joint venture 合营企业的代表机构(或代办处)
atmosphere n. 大气层;空气,大气;环境
atmospheric a. 大气的;空气的
atmospheric monitoring system 大气监测系统
atmospheric pollution 大气污染
atomania n. 原子弹狂
Atomic Energy Law 原子能法
atomic weapons 原子武器
atonable a. 可赎回的;可赎罪的;可补偿的
atone v. 赔偿,补偿,偿还;赎罪
atone one's crime by good deeds 戴罪立功
atonement n. 补偿;赎回;赎罪
atrocious cases 残暴案件,恶性案件
atrocity n. 暴行;残酷,残忍,凶恶
attach v. 扣押;逮捕;拘押;查封;附加,隶属;任命;缚系,贴
attach political conditions 附加政治条件
attachable a. 可拘留的,可逮捕的;可查封的,可扣押的;可附加的
attaché n. 使馆馆员;外交使节随员;专员
attaché of an embassy 使馆参赞
attached a. 附加的,隶属的;查封的,扣押的
attached clause 附加条款
attached condition 附加条件
attached property 查封的财产
attaching n. 扣押,查封;逮捕
attachment (14世纪)1.扣押[指扣押一个人的财产以提供判决的保证(secure a judgment)或出售该财产以保证判决,亦称(在民法上)临时扣押(provisional seizure)。见garnishment; sequestration 1] 2. 逮捕,拘禁(指或因藐视法庭或为保证判决的支付得以执行,对某人进行拘禁以逮捕)3.扣押令,拘禁令。亦称writ of attachment[指命令依法扣押财产(特别是满足债权人的权利主张)或拘禁人身的令状] 4. 担保权益的产生(creation of a security interest)[指根据《统一商法典》第9-203条(UCC§9-203),债权人同意担保,接受被担保方的代价(value),取得在担保物上的权利,即在该财产上产生了担保权益

(见 perfection)] 5.附加行为(act of affixing)或联系行为(act of connecting)
attachment and sequestration proceedings 查封与扣押程序
attachment bond 扣押担保(指①原告请求扣押被告的财产而提供的担保,以保证如果原告败诉可以赔偿因扣押而给被告造成的损失;②被告提供的保证自己可以履行判决的担保,从而可解除其被扣押的财产)
attachment execution 扣押财产以执行判决的传票
attachment in the hand of a third party 将第三人掌握的(债务人)财产进行扣押
attachment jurisdiction 扣押管辖;扣押管辖权(指采用准对物管辖,即原告寻求法院管辖被告在本州的财产,以替代法院对被告本人行使对人管辖权,因为往往非本州居民不在管辖地)
attachment of contractual obligation 扣押合同之债
attachment of debt 债款扣押(指由于债使第三债务人所受的法律约束)
attachment of earnings 扣发工资,扣发工薪(见 attachment of wages)
attachment of privilege 为逮捕享有特权的(某)人所发出的令状
attachment of property 扣押财产
attachment of real property 不动产的扣押
attachment of wages 工薪扣押,扣押工薪[指雇主扣押雇员所赚得的工薪。在有些管辖区,工薪扣押的指令则要求被告雇员的雇主扣除限定的数额(specified sum)或被告雇员工薪的多少百分比,并将扣押款交付给法庭,然后由法庭将款项送给原告雇主。联邦法规定(对债务人)扣发部分工资的扣押令的制定法必须满足对子女的抚养费和生活费的判决。根据这一规定,如果工薪赚得者只有一个家庭,则可扣押其可支配收入的50%。如果他还有另一个须扶养的家庭,则扣押其收入的60%。如果债务人(obligor)超过3个月的拖延期,则在原扣押的百分比基础上增加5%,直至完全支付,参见《美国注释法典》第15标题卷第1671(b)(2)节,亦称

attachment of earnings; wage-withholding; automatic wage-withholding; wage assignment。见 garnishment]
attachment on mersne process 诉讼中间阶段的扣押(见 ancillary attachment)
attachment order 查封令,扣押令;拘捕令
attack n./v. 攻击,袭击,打击,抨击,非难/攻击,非难,抨击;投入,着手;提出异议
attack and retaliation (中)打击报复
attacking party 提出异议的当事人
attainder n. 褫夺公权(指被判处死刑等罪犯的公民权利);剥夺公权
attaint n./v. 公民权或财产的剥夺;(英)陪审员公民权的剥夺/宣告褫夺公权;剥夺公民的公民权和财产;凌辱,玷污,损害(名誉)
attempt n./v. 着手犯罪,未遂罪;未遂行为;企图,试图/意图,企图,试图
attempt at an offence 未遂罪
attempt at conciliation (或 reconciliation)试图调解
attempt to commit a crime 犯罪企图
attempted a. 意图的,企图的,未遂的
attempted burglary 未遂盗窃(罪)
attempted contravention 违反的企图;意图触犯(法律等)
attempted crime 未遂罪
attempted escape 逃脱未遂
attempted homicide against the partner in marriage 企图杀害配偶罪
attempted injury 侵害未遂;意图伤害
attempted murder 谋杀未遂;意图谋杀
attempted rape 强奸未遂
attempted robbery 抢劫未遂
attempted suicide 自杀未遂
attempted theft 盗窃未遂
attempting for compromise 试图和解
attempts to alarm or injury the King (英)企图威吓或伤害国王罪
attend v. 出席,出庭,参加;照顾,护理;陪伴;专心,注意
attend court 出庭
attendance n. (对房地产的)照管;照料,资助;出庭,出席;出席人数
attendance allowance (残疾人)照料补助金;房产管理津贴

attendance centre （青少年罪犯）管教中心
attendance in chamber 在内庭出庭
attendance of trail 受审出庭
attendance officer 托管官员（见 truancy officer）
attendance of witness 证人出庭
attendance order 出庭（席）令
attendance rate 出勤率
attendant n./a. 对他人负有义务者；服务员；随从；出席者，出庭者/伴随的，附随的；在场的
attendant rights under the Fourteenth Amendment 根据第十四修正案伴随的权利
attendant term （1983年）长期伴有的地产权[指为了保护抵押人继承人（mortgagor's heirs）的权益而创设的一种特定时限的地产抵押权，其时限可长达1000年（固定时限，term of years），即使在清偿债务之后也不收回地产所有权，而是将它交给某一受托人（trustee），为抵押人及其继承人的利益而持有。这种安排予抵押人继承人另一种财产所有权，即使他们在继承的权益被证明存在某种瑕疵的情况下也不会受到影响。这些类型限期的地产权已大部被废除。见 tenancy attendant on the inheritance]
attending entering appearance 办理呈送到案状
attentat n. 企图
attermining n. 获准延期
attest v. 作证，证实，证明；使宣誓，表明；作为……证明
attest to its accuracy 就其准确性作出证明
attestation n. 证实，证明；证词，证据；宣誓
attestation clause 见证条款；（遗嘱或契据的）证明条款
attestation of a deed 契据的证明
attestation of a will 遗嘱的证明
attestation of hono(u)r 人格保证，人格担保
attested a. 证实的，证明的，作证的

attested copy 证件副本（旧译：检正本）
attesting n. 证明，证实，作证
attesting witness 文书见证人
attestment n. 证词，证据
attestor n. 证人，证明者
Att-Gen ex rel X v. Y 总检察长根据控告提起的X诉Y(案)
Attic a. 古希腊雅典城邦的，雅典的，雅典式的
Attic Code (of Solon) 《亚狄克法典》（希腊的第一部编纂法典，对罗马法的发展很有影响，公元前5世纪由梭伦起草）
attitude n. 态度，看法，姿态
attitude of absolute denial 完全抵赖的态度
attitude of service 服务态度
attitude toward admission of guilt 认罪态度
attitude toward repentance 悔改态度
attorn v. 让与，转让；(佃户)承认新地主，继续做新地主的佃户
* Attornatus fere in omnibus personam domini representat. An attorney represents the person of his master in almost all respects. 代理人几乎在所有方面都代表其委托人。
attorney n. 1.受托人，代办人，代理人，受权人 2.(美)律师 3.检察官，代诉人
attorney ad litem 特定诉讼代理人，诉讼期间代理人[指在法律诉讼过程中，法庭指定或任命一名律师在如离婚终止婚姻或虐待儿童的案件中代理儿童进行诉讼。这个代理人应对该儿童有踏实的职责，有可依赖的品质(confidentiality)，方为合格的代表(competent representation)。至于在青少年诉讼程序中一个儿童的法定代位继承(legal representation)权是在有关 Gault——《联邦最高法院判例汇编》第387卷第1页(387 U.S.1)或《最高法院判例汇编》第87卷第1428页(87 S.CT.1428)(1967年)——判例所要求的。一名特定诉讼代理人在特定诉讼(specific lawsuit)中是被限制只能1名。亦称 child's attorney；attorney for the child。见 guardian ad litem]
attorney fees 律师费，诉讼代理人费

attorney filing a case 提交案件的律师
attorney general 1.首席检察官,检察长 2.(大写)(美)司法部长;(英)检察总长
Attorney General's bill (英)(经法院同意直接)呈交给大陪审团的诉状
Attorney General's Chambers 总检察长议事室,总检察长接待室
Attorney General's Opinion (= Opinion of the Attorney general) 检察长意见(指①总检察长应总统和其他联邦政府行政官员的要求就有关法律问题提供意见;②州检察长应政府部分首长的要求就有关其职责的法律问题提供书面意见并解释法律条文)
attorney in practice 开业律师
attorney of record 在案律师
attorney of the day 值班律师(就业机会均等委员会机构中的法律顾问名称,负责解答案件方面的问题)
attorney work-product privilege 见 work-product rule
attorney's fees (attorney-fees) 给律师的酬金(指按照律师执业为客户服务履行职责,客户承担给律师的报酬。该酬金可包括胜诉费、每小时的费用、自付的补偿或有些混杂的费用)
attorney's lien 代理人的留置权;律师的留置权
attorney-at-law n. (美)律师
attorney-client privilege 律师—客户间守密之特权(指客户有拒绝披露并阻止他人披露其与律师间为获得法律咨询或帮助而进行的秘密交流之权利。但此种权利并不被广泛认可,亦称 lawyer-client privilege; client's privilege)
attorney-in-fact n. 代理人(指在法庭外受委托的代理人),事实代理人,私人代理人
attorneyship n. 代理权;代理人的职务(或身份)
attornment n. 转让,让与;土地转让合同(契约);承认新所有人
attract v. 吸引,引起(注意、兴趣、赞赏等);诱惑
attracting risk 吸收风险
attractive a. 有吸引力的;有迷惑力的;引起注意的
attractive nuisance 对儿童有诱惑力的危险物品(美国有些州规定,持有诱惑力的危险物品的人对其物品造成儿童伤害应负法律责任)
attributable a. 可归属于的,可归因的(be attributable to)(可归因于……)
attributable to the act or fault of the third party 可归责于第三人的行为或过错
attribute v./n. 1.把……归因于,把……归咎于 2.认为……为某人所有;认为……是某人创造(attribute an invention to sb.)(认为……是某人的发明)/属性,品质,特征,(人物)(职务等的)标志,特征,(语)定语
Attribute its properity to mild laws and to the spirit of the pioneer. 它的繁荣得益于温和的法律和拓荒的精神。
attribution n. 1.美国国内税收法则(IRD)中提示的程序[按此程序个人或单位的股权(stock ownership)可以被转让给相关的家庭或纳税部门,亦称 stock attribution] 2.归罪,归属;属性,归属物
attribution right (版权)归属权[指一个人作为一个作品的作者应具有在相关作品上署名或禁止未参与创作该作品的人署名的权利。归属权首先在大陆法系国家(civil-law countries)被承认为一种道德或精神方面的权利。根据1990年《美国形象化艺术家权利法》(Visual Artists Rights Act of 1990),受限制等级作品(a very limited class of works)亦被称为观赏艺术(visual art)作品,其作者具有一定的法定归属权(statutory attribution right),参见《美国注释法典》第17标题卷第106A节。依照《伯尔尼公约实施法》(提供给外国版权拥有人的归属权在美国可以是强制性的(enforcement)。亦称为 rights of attribution; paternity; maternity。见 integrity right; moral rights]
atypical a. 非典型的,不定型的,不规则的,不正常的
atypical contract 非典型合同(契约),不定型的合同(契约)
atypical facts 非常的事实
Auburn system 奥本监狱制度(19世纪20

年代起采用的一种管理犯人的方法,规定犯人白天劳动,晚上单独监禁并保持一直安静,禁止作声)
auction n. 拍卖,竞卖
auction by government 由政府拍卖
auction of ship 船舶拍卖
auction price 拍卖价格
auctioneer n. 拍卖商,拍卖人;拍卖行
auctor n. 卖主,拍卖人
auctorial a. 作者的,著作人的
auctorial comment 作者的说明
audi alteram parterm Hear the other side. No one should be condemned unheard. 听双方之词,且任何人不得下令不听取证词(见 *audiature et altera pars*)(应听取双方当事人的陈词,在未听取另一方意见之前不得对其实施惩罚)
audi alreem partem 应听取双方当事人的意见
audiature et altera pars 听取他方陈述
* *audiature et altera pars, audi alteram parterm* An injunction which means that no man should be condemned unheard or without having had an opportunity of being heard. 听取另一方之词(指应听取另一方的证词,而不得不经审讯即行判罪,含有兼听则明之意)
Audience Court (英)亲审法院[指坎特伯雷教省大主教亲自开庭主审的法院,与拱顶法院(court of arches)有相同权力]
audience n. 听讼;观众,听众;会见,谒见(指主权介入审理的权力,现今指国王与大臣与提交国书之大使等之间的会见。这一术语也用于教皇之会见);召见;陈述意见(或申诉)的机会;听证;立法质询
audience of solicitor 律师出庭
audiencia n. 检审法院(中世纪末期西班牙诸王国中为掌管王国司法所设立的法院)
Audio Home Recording Act (AHRA) (版权)《音频图像记录法》[指 1992 年联邦法,旨在防止基于制造、输入、发行或销售数字音频技术(digital-audio technology)等诸多面的版权侵权诉讼。数字设备的制造商必须在销售设备时支付版税(royalties)给相关媒体,同时还建立对每一设备

的保证机制(security mechanism),以此机制允许数字记录设备的拥有人可以先前的手段而不是用复制品进行复制,参见《美国注释法典》第 17 卷本第 1001—1010 节]
audio or visual 音频的或视频的
audio-video materials of criminal evidence 刑事证据的视听资料
audio-visual works 视听作品,音像作品[美国《版权法》中关于"视听作品"的独创要求很低,美国国会在关于 1976 年《版权法》的报告中明确指出:"当 4 台摄像机(从不同角度)拍摄一场足球赛时,导播要对 4 名摄影师发出指令,并选择要将哪些电子影像以怎样的顺序向公众播放。无疑,摄影师和导播的工作构成了创作"]
audiovisuals n. 视听资料
audit n./v. 审计,查账;清算;决算/审计,审核;查账;(美)大学生旁听
audit and control system 审核管理制度
audit coverage 审计承保范围
Audit Ordinance 《审计条例》
audit report 会计检查报告,审计报告,查账报告
audit system 审计制度
audit the books 查账
audit trail 审计追踪
audita querela (英)被告人补救令
audited financial information 已审财务信息
audited financial statement 已审财务报表
auditing body 审计机构
auditing law 审计法
auditor n. 审计员,审核人,查账人;听者,听众之一;(美)大学旁听生;(英)约克郡大法官法庭法官;天主教最高法院法官
auditor-general n. 审计长,总审计师
auditoriums n. 听众席,观众席
augmentative denials 可争议的否认
augmented physical quality of life index 物质生活水平增长指数
Augustan a./n. 1.(古罗马皇帝)奥古斯都的,奥古斯都时期的 2.古典的,典雅的/奥古斯都的全盛时期,文学全盛时期的作家
aula regia (或 *regis*) 王室法庭
Aulic Council Reichshofrat (神圣罗马帝国的)枢密院

austerity measures 紧缩措施
Australian ballot （美）秘密投票（因南澳大利亚州于 1858 年第一个实行秘密投票,而由此命名）
Australian law 澳大利亚法
Australian Intergovernmental Agreement on the Environment of 1992 《1992 年澳大利亚政府环境协定》（承认环境资源的代际公平享用,该协定申明:"当代人应该保证为后代人的利益维护或改善环境的健康、多样化或生产力。"）
Australian Patent Office 澳大利亚专利局
Austrian law 奥地利法
aut dedere aut punier 或引渡或起诉
autarchy (=autarky) n. 绝对主权
authentic a. 认证了的,确认的;正式的;可信的;有根据的;真的;有权威性的
authentic act 公证书,公证行为
authentic interpretation 可信解释,权威解释
authentic writing 正本,确认的文书
authenticate v. （17 世纪）1.认证、证明、鉴定（指对有些事物的证明,比如一个文件其主要含义是什么）,特别是有的项目经证实后在审理或听审时作为证据被采纳,例如希望将一封信作为证据的当事人可能询问这是否可作为证据,的确,他收到的这封信,如果是手写的,可以作为证据）2.对于一个标记的信件,如一个签名（署名）或一张邮票,在一个文件上表明这是可信的、有效的或无效的 3.使证实（指经过证实的或鉴定的,即通过证据或法律程序证明真实性的）;证明或采纳（指证明或采纳一件书面文件作为个人的文件）
authenticating document 认证文件,鉴定文件
authentication n. （18 世纪）证实,认证,鉴定（指①对法律文件如记录、书面文件等的认证行为,以鉴别其真实性或权威性,从而使其在真实的情况下可以作为证据被采纳;②认可,可采纳）
authentication of document 文件的认证
authenticator n. 确定者;证明人;确认者
authenticity n. 可靠性,确实性,真实性
Authenticum 《查士丁尼法规汇编》（制作于 6 世纪包括公元 535—556 年之间的 134 部查士丁尼法规的法规汇编）
author n./v. 作者,著作人;本人;创始人;发起人/著作,创始,写作
Author's moral rights 作者精神权利
author of derivative work 衍生或继有作品的作者
author of the injury 加害人
authoriantarianism n. 独裁主义;权力主义
authorised to intervene and participate in civil actions 授权（检察官）干预和参与民事诉讼
authorising paternity 确认亲子关系;确认生父
authoritarian n./a. 权力主义者;独裁主义者/权力主义的,独裁主义的
authoritarian country 专制国家
authoritarian government 专制政府
authoritarian regime 独裁政体,独裁制度
authoritarianism n. 权力主义;独裁主义
authoritative a. 官方的,当局的;权威的;命令式的;可信的;倚仗权势的
authoritative interpretation 有权威的解释,有权解释
authoritative power 当局的权力,有权威的权力
authoritative precedent 权威性判例
authoritative source of knowledge of international trade usage 国际商业惯例权威知识来源
authoritative sources of law 法的权威性渊源,权威性法律渊源
authoritative stamp of the compilation 汇编的权威性特征
authoritative statements of rule of law 法规的权威性论述;法律规范的权威性论述
authoritative techniques 特有技术
authoritative text 权威的教科书（教本）;权威性文本
authority （13 世纪）1.权力;授权;批准,代理权[指某人授予另一人从事某种行为的权力或权限。这也符合另一个人的同意,其所代理的权力或权限是主管人赋予代理人（agent）的〈authority to sign the contract〉（签署合同的代理权）,亦称 power o-

ver other person]2.权力,管辖权[指政府的权力或管辖权〈within the court's authority〉(在法院的管辖范围内)]3.政府的代理机构或管理公益事业的法人〈transit authority〉(货运机构),亦称 public authority 4. 规则;作为权威性和决定性的法律文书(legal writing);特别是援引作为先例的司法判决或行政判决〈that case if good authority in Massachusetts〉(那个判例在马萨诸塞州有很强的效果和很高的权威)(这个术语不仅包括法院的判决,还包括制定法、条例以及行政规定)5.渊源,法律根据[诸如制定法、判例、论文、法律辩护(legal argument)报告〈the brief's of table of authorities〉(判例汇编的判例摘要表)] 6.权威(指某些人对某个问题的知识和意见受到尊重,其原因是实践中证明他们是大学者或专家)

authority by sufferance 默认的代理权
authority byestoppel 见 apparent authority
authority conferred by law 法律赋予的权力
authority for civil cover sheet 填写民事(案件)登记表的授权
authority of agency 代理权
authority of approval 核定权,审批权
authority of arbitration 仲裁的权威性;仲裁的权限
authority of cases 案件的法律根据
authority of customary law 习惯法的权威性
authority of husband 夫权
authority of law 法律依据,法律的权威性
authority to draw 授权开立汇票
authority to exercise important or unusual powers 行使重要或特殊权力的授权
authority to grant 准许的权力
authority to order 授权命令
authority to pay 受权付款
authority to purchase 委托购买证
authority vested in the people 属于人民的权力
authority with responsibility 有权有责
authorizable a. 可授权的;可批准的;可认定的

authorization (= authorisation) n. 诉讼委托;委任,授权;认可;批准(书)
authorization of agent 授权书
authorize (= authorise) v. 授权;委托;认可;委任;批准;指定;审定
authorized a. 委任的;核准的,许可的;公认的;指定的;审定的
authorized agency 有权代理;批准的代理机构
authorized agent 指定的代理人,正式授权的代理人
authorized appropriation 核定的拨付;授权分配
authorized bank 指定的银行
authorized bond 核准发行的债券
authorized buyer 认可的买主
authorized by law 经法律许可
authorized capital 核定的资本,法定资本;(英美法)授权资本
authorized capital stock 核定的股本,法定股本;(英美法)授权股本
authorized capital system 授权资本制(英美设立公司的一种制度,即在设立公司时,资本额在基本章程中规定后,只要有一定数量的发起人各自认定并缴足资本总额的小部分,公司即可成立,其余未认定的部分,则授权董事会处理)
authorized cemetery 公墓,公设坟场,特许坟场
authorized delegate 授权委任
authorized infringement (vicarious infringement) 授权侵权
authorized investment 授权投资;核准的投资
authorized mortgage bonds 核定抵押债券
authorized officer 授权的官员
authorized personnel 编制人员
authorized representative 授权的代表
authorized security 公认证券;核准的证券
authorized shares 认可的股份
authorized translation (经原作者)同意的译本
authorized version 审定的译本
authorizing six-person federal civil juries

审定的六人联邦民事陪审团
authorship n. 著作人,原作者,作者身份;作品创作人之地位
Auto Cite (美)自动援引(利用计算机检索援引查对的服务系统,自动援引适用于 LEXIS)
auto liability insurance policy 汽车责任保(险)单
auto-da-fé (= auto-de-fé) (西班牙、葡萄牙用语)宗教公判大会(大约于 1481—1850 年进行过的、在宗教公开审判终结后举行的公开宣判仪式);对异教徒所处的火刑(或异端著作的焚毁)
auto-limitation clause 自行限制条款
autochthon n. 本地人,原居民,土著
autocide n. 撞车自杀;自我毁灭
autocracy n. 独裁政治,专制政治;独裁政府;独裁权;独裁统治的国家
autocratic(al) a. 独裁的,专制的;独断独行的(人)
autograph n. 亲笔签署,亲笔;手稿
autograph letter 亲笔信
autograph writings 亲笔文据
automated legal research 自动化(法律文献)检索
automatic a. 自动的;无意识的,机械的
automatic approval system 自行核定制
automatic effect 直接生效,自动生效;直接实施;直接影响
automatic exception 自行抗告(议)
automatic import quota system 自行进口配额制
automatic licence 自动许可证
Automatic Program control 自动程序控制
automatic protection 自动保护(原则)(伯尔尼公约三项重要原则之一)
automatic renewal 自动更新
automatic supermarket 自动化超级市场
automatic wage-withholding 见 attachment of wages
automatically ad. 自动地
automatically renewable loan 可自动展期的贷款
automatism n. 自动症(指患者在意识模糊情况下作出一些目的不明确的活动或

行为,且与当时的处境不相适应,此自动症有两种特殊发作形式:①fugue 神游症 ②somnambulism 梦游症,梦行症)
automaton n. 自动监控器,自动装置;自动开关,(复)automata
automobile n. 汽车,机动车
automobile accident 车祸,车辆事故
automobile insurance 车辆保险
automobile tort 机动车侵权行为
automotive a. 自动的,机动的;汽车的,机动车的
autonomist n. 自治制主张者;自治论者;自主论者
autonomous a. 自治的,自治权的;自主的
autonomous authority 自主权
autonomous body 自治机构
autonomous county (中)自治县
autonomous enterprise 自主企业
autonomous entity 自治实体,自治单位
autonomous institution 自治(组织)机构
autonomous jurisdiction 自治权限;自主管辖权(美国有 56 个自主的司法管辖区)
autonomous legislation 自主立法权
autonomous municipality (中)自治市
autonomous neutralization 自动中立化(即单方面宣布的永久中立)
autonomous organization 自治组织,自治团体
autonomous power 自主权
autonomous prefecture (中)自治州
autonomous public institution 自主的公共机构
autonomous region (中)自治区
autonomous region of the national minorities (中)少数民族自治地区
autonomous right 自主权;自治权
autonomous state 自主性国家
autonomous tariff 自主关税;国定关税(制)
autonomy n. 自治,自治权;自主权;人身自由;自治团体;有自主权的国家
autonomy doctrine 意志自由说
autonomy of enterprise 企业自治权;企业自主权
autonomy of law 法律的自主性(指一系列相互关联又相互区别的主张:法律推理

和法律裁判不同于其他形式的推理与裁判。它是自足的,不需借助其他方法)
autonomy of nationality 民族自治权
autonomy of private law 私法自主
autonomy of will 意志自主(原则)
autopalm printer outfit 自动手掌捺印器(机)
autopoiesis 自我再制
autopsy n. 1.尸体解剖,尸体解剖检验 2.亲自勘查,实地观察 3.(对意见等的)分析
autoptic(al) a. 尸体剖验的;以实地观察为根据的
autoptic(al) evidence (陪审团)亲眼所见的证据
autotype n. 复印品,复制品;(一种)单色照相版
autre action pendant 未结案的除外
autre or auter 他人
autre vie 他人的生命(见 *pur autre vie*)
autrefois acquit (普通法)(同一案件)前经开释(又译:原已开释,指犯人的抗辩,说明在本案中对他所指控的罪行,系从前曾被控诉过的罪行,并被法庭判决,结果获得法庭开释。此抗辩是否有效,要看该同一案件受审时是否按刑事程序受审,以及是否因证据不足而获得开释,如果是即可不再受审)
autrefois attaint (因已犯叛国罪或重罪被宣告)公民权已被剥夺(古英国法阻止起诉的抗辩用语,现已废除)
autrefois convict (普通法)(同一案件)前经定罪(又译:原已定罪,指犯人的抗辩,说明在本案中对他所指控的罪行,系从前已被检控过的罪行,并被法庭定过罪的,如这抗辩属实,即可不再受审)(见 double jeopardy)
auxiliary a. 附加的;附属的;从属的,辅助的,补助的
auxiliary body 附属机构
auxiliary coin 辅币
auxiliary facilities 辅助设备
auxiliary function 辅助职能
auxiliary jurisdiction 辅助管辖权,辅助审判权,辅助管辖范围
auxiliary labo(u)rer 辅助工
auxiliary law 辅助法,补充法

auxiliary means 辅助工具,辅助手段
auxiliary organ 辅助机构,辅助部门
auxiliary penal measure 辅助惩罚措施
auxiliary staff 辅助人员
avail n./v. 效用;帮助;利益,受益/有利于,有益于,有助于
avail of marriage (英史)(领主对被保护人的)婚姻收益(权)
availability n. 效力,有效性;可用性;可得性;可得到的东西(或人员)
availability of a limited appearance 有限出庭的有效性
availability register 签到簿,来宾签到册,(港译:主管人员留踪册)
available a. 1.可用的,合用的;可得到的;可达到的 2.通用的,有效的 3.(因政治背景等原因)有当选希望的;愿意接受(或参加)选举的
available act of bankruptcy 可宣告破产的行为
available coverage 保险承保的范围
aval v. 担保付款;担保,保证
aver v. 立证,证明,确证;断言;主张
aver and averment 立证和立证证明
average n./a. 海损;平均数;平均标准/平均的;中等的;正常的,通常的;按海损估价的
average adjuster(或 **adjustor**) 海损理算人
average adjustment 海损理算(书)
average agent 理赔代理人
average annual rate of growth 年平均增长率
average bond(或 **agreement**) 共同海损协议书
average citizen 一般公民
average clause 海损条款
average consumer 一般消费者(指受到良好通告,能够理性观察和小心谨慎的消费者),普通消费者
average contribution 共同海损分担
average demurrage agreement 海损滞期费协议书
average disbursements clause 共同海损费用条款
average layday 平均装卸货时间

average person(或 man) 正常人,普通人
average premium 平均保险费
average quality 中等品质
average rate of tax 平均税率
average statement 海损理算书
average tare 平均皮重
average tax rate (= average rate of tax)
（1895年）平均税率(指由应所得的总额分配的纳税人的纳税义务或纳税数额)
averment n. 证明,确认;确证;断言,主张;对事实的申述;(复)(英)立证证明
aversion n. 厌恶,对……反感(to)
avert v. 转移,防止
averting inflationary pressures 防止通货膨胀压力
aviatic a. 航空的,飞行的
aviation v. 航空;飞机制造业;航空学
aviation insurance 航空保险
aviation law n. 航空法
avizandum n. (苏格兰)法庭私下考虑
avocat n. (法)律师,辩护人
avocat general 代理检察官
avocation n. 法院之间诉讼的转移;副业,业余爱好;(罕)本职
avoid v. 1.避免,回避,躲开 2.使无效,废止,撤销
avoid a contract 废止合同(契约)
avoid undue delays in trials 免受不当的拖延审判
avoidable a. 可作为无效的;可回避的;可避免的
avoidable accident 可避免的事故
avoidable consequence 可避免的后果
avoidance n. 1.避免,回避 2.无效,废止;撤销;无效的主张 3.(职位等的)空缺
avoidance of a contract 可撤销合同,合同(契约)的撤销
avoidance of contractual liability 逃避合同(契约)责任
avoidance of double taxation 避免双重征税
avoidance of doubt 避免引起怀疑,免除怀疑
avoidance of fraudulent transfer 虚假转移的无效

avoidance of office 职位的空缺
avoidance of responsibility 逃避责任
avoidance of tax 逃税
avoiding service 回避送达
avoirdupois n. (英)常衡(以16盎司为1磅,1盎司为16打兰);重量;体重
avoirdupois weight 常衡制(英美用以称贵金属、珠宝及药物以外物品的制度)
avouch v. 保证,担保;断言,公开承认,主张
avouchment n. 保证,担保;断言,公开承认,主张
avoué n. (法)出庭律师,诉讼代理人
avow v. 宣称,声明;供认,坦白承认,招认
avow one's guilt 认罪
avowable a. 可直认的,可明言的,可公开宣布的
avowal n. 声明;公开宣布;供认,公开承认
avowant n. 供认者,承认者;申报者
avowed a. 公开承认的;公开宣布的
avowry n. 承认并声明正当性答辩[普通法上动产占有回复诉讼(action of replevin)中被告所作的答辩,即被告承认自己占有争诉的动产,并声明自己有为合法、合理的理由]
avowtry n. 通奸
avulsion n. (因洪水等引起的)土地的突然转位或断离的部分(其所有权仍归所有人)(港译:崩附地)
avus n. (大陆法)祖父
await v. 等候,期待;(事件等的)等待
await trial 候审
awake to one's errors 悔悟;认识错误
award n./v. 仲裁,判决,判定,仲裁书,公断书;裁定额,损害赔偿裁定额,核定损失赔偿金的陪审团的裁决;奖励,奖金,奖品,成绩优秀/判给,判断,判决;裁断,授予,给予
award and punishment 奖惩
award containing reasons 注明理由的仲裁裁决
award enforceable at law 可依法强制执行的仲裁裁决
award fund 奖励基金
award having the authority of *res judicata*

产生既判效力的仲裁裁决
award made *ex aequo et bono* 依据公平合理原则作出的仲裁裁决
award made in writing 书面的仲裁裁决
award of exemplary damages （英）（惩罚性）超过实际损失的（法院裁定的）损害赔偿额
award of punitive damages （英）惩罚性的损害赔偿（法院）裁定额
award on agreed terms 和解裁决
award punishment 判刑,判处罚刑
award rendered in the absence of the respondent 在被告缺席情况下作出的仲裁裁决
awarded by court 经法院判定
awardee n. 受奖者
awareness n. 意识,认知
away from engine room （或 below water line） 怕热货（或怕水货）
away from smelling cargo 怕染味货
away-going crop 已种庄稼收获权（佃农所种之农作物,在其成熟时土地租约已期满,但法律上规定仍归佃农收割的一种权利。亦作 waygoing crop）
ax(e) n. （经费、人员等的）削减
ax(e) to non-productive expenditures 削减非生产人员

axiom n. 公理,原理,原则;规律;格言
axiomatic(al) a. 公理的,自明的,格言的
axiomatic approach 公理化方式（见 cooperative bargaining,也称合理化方法）
axiomatic method 公理法[指包括公理化方法和公理体系,公理化方法是从初始概念和初始命题（公理）出发;按一定逻辑规则,推演出其他有关命题（定理）的一种方法。而公理体系则是由初始概念、公理、定义、推理规则和定理等构成的演绎体系。公理化方法是公理法的第一组成部分,公理体系是公理法的第二组成部分。公理体系是由公理化方法得到的理论体系,所以公理体系是建立在公理化方法的基础之上]
axioms of juristic thought 法律思想原则;法理思潮的格言
axiomatic theory 公理化理论
axioms n. 公理
Axis of Evil 邪恶轴心（美国总统布什称伊拉克、朝鲜、伊朗等为邪恶轴心的国家）
axones n. （雅典市政厅内一根垂直轴上的）轴法[刻有德拉古和梭伦制定的法律]
ay(e) n. 赞成（票）,投赞成票者
ayres n. （苏格兰）巡回法庭
azonic a. 非局部地区的,非本地的

B

B. R. （缩略语）1.破产判例汇编（Bankruptcy Reporter）2.王座法庭（Bancus Regis = King's Bench）（这一缩略语已被英国最早的 K. B.和 Q. B.两个法庭所替代）
baby n. 婴儿
baby act 诉讼时效抗辩,未成年（法律）行为的抗辩
baby farm 育婴院
Baby Jessica （美）婴儿杰西卡（20 世纪 90 年代轰动全美的一个案件,案中,虽养父母已经抚养女杰西卡达 3 年之久,且与该女相处融洽,有着深厚感情,但法院考量杰西卡生父对子女出生之忽视与是否给予生父机会与其子女建立亲子关系之判断中,仍判生父有权将子女带回,而无视养父母与子女建立之深厚感情）
baby market 婴儿市场（美国的黑市场,在市场上可将婴儿卖给养父母）
baby-snatching 见 child-kidnapping
Babylonian n./a. 巴比伦人/巴比伦的,巴比伦王国的
Babylonian law 巴比伦法
baccara(t) n. （欧洲赌场流行的）一种纸牌赌博

bachelor n.　学士;单身汉,未婚男子
bachelor of laws　法学士
back n./v./a.　支持(论点、行动、企业等);撑腰;背书(指在票据背面签字作担保);背;反面;后面/签字批准;担保;背签,(在票据背面)背书;支持;倒退;坐落/后面的;拖欠的,应付的;追溯的,偏僻的
back bencher　后座议员(英国议会议员,因他们未同时担任其他政府部门职务而仅有资格坐于上院的后排座位)
back benches　后座议员席
back cargo　(船只等载运的)回程货物
back door　后门,非法途径;秘密手段
back down　原先主张(原先态度)的转变
back freight　退货运费;额外运费
back order　延期交货的订货单(指现货售完,来日交货的订货单)
back order memo　延期订货通知单
back out(或 **of**)　收回(诺言、承担的责任等),不再承担,不承认
back pay　欠薪
back relation　追溯效力
back rent　欠租
back slums　贫民窟
back tax　以前的税,过去的税(指前一年或前几年已经核定但仍未交付的税款)
back to back escrow　背对背契据
back tracked　开了倒车
back wage　欠款
back-bond(或 **back-letter**) n.　保证给予担保人赔偿的证书;限制财产处理权证书;(苏格兰法)土地担保债券
back-order v.　订(期货)
back-stair intrigue　密谋
back-stopping cost　支助(援)费用
back-to-back (letter of) credit　背对背信用证,对开信用证
back-tracing guns used in crime　跟踪犯罪用枪
back-up remedy　预备救济
back-yardism n.　(美)排外主义
backbone n.　支柱,骨干,主要成分;骨气;坚定的品质
backbone element　骨干分子
backbone of agriculture　主要农产品

backdown n.　原先态度(或主张等)的改变
backdrop (= **backcloth**)　背景幕布
backdrop of global power politics　世界强权政治背景
backed for bail　批准可予保释的
backer n.　赞助人,支持者
backfire n./v　迎火,逆火,回火/迎火,逆火;发生意外,产生了事与愿违的恶果
backfired good intentions　产生了相悖于良好意愿的恶果,产生了事与善意相违的后果
backing n.　(行政官或法官)对令状的签署认可;背书
backing a warrant　背书逮捕证
backlash　(在政治和社会上)强烈不利的反应
backlog n.　(英)积压而未交付的订货,积压的工作;(美)紧急时可依靠的东西;储备
backlog of cases　积压案件
backpay　复职前工资,欠薪赔偿;拖欠的工资
backward-looking value line　向后价值线
backwardation n.　(英)(证券的)交割延期(费);现货升水(溢价)
backwardness n.　落后,向后,缓慢
backwardness of law with respect to social problems　法律对于社会问题滞后解决
backwoods n.　落后的边远地区;边远的森林地带
backwoods country towns　落后的边远地区的乡镇,落后的边远乡镇
backyard n.　后院,后花园
bacteriological warfare　细菌战
baculine a.　答刑的;棒的
bad a.　1.坏的;恶的,不道德的 2.无效的;证据不足的,法律上有漏洞的(或有错误的,或不成立的,或徒具虚名的) 3.(能力)拙劣的,(质量、价值)低劣的 4.不利的,有害的
bad character　歹徒,恶棍;不良品德
bad check(或 **cheque**)　空头支票(指户账上没有存款或存款不足的无信誉支票,亦称 hot check; worthless check; rubber check; bounced check; cold check; bogus

check; false check; dry check)
bad debt 坏账;呆账,倒账
bad decision 不良决策
bad element (中)坏分子
bad faith 不诚信,失信(good faith,诚信);欺骗,恶意[指故意不遵守明确的法律责任或合同义务,实际就是在行为上和交易中"不诚实"。"不诚信"在侵权法中的对应词为"恶意"(malice),亦即对信任或目的的不忠实,甚至欺诈,律师可以就常诈提起诉讼(file pleading),亦称为 *mala fides*]
bad guys 坏蛋,歹徒
bad law 徒具虚名的法律,法律上的例外
bad man (美)(带手枪的)暴徒,歹徒;(旧时美国西部)受人雇用的刺客;偷牲口的贼
bad order 暂时无法满足的订货;外观不良,包装不良
bad paper 不良票据,空头票据
bad plea 理由不足的答辩;无针对性的答辩
bad risk 风险率高的保险
bad steering 不良驾驶
bad stowage 堆装不良
bad tendency rule "不良倾向"原则
bad tendency test (美)不良倾向标准(一种分析英格兰普通法诽谤罪的言论自由问题的标准。美国革命前由布莱克斯通(Blackstone)综合而成。这种标准通过语言引起非法行为的倾向来衡量言论的合法性。亦称不良倾向测试)
bad title 失效产权,无效所有权
bad-neighbo(u)r policy 恶邻政策
badge n. 证章;标志;象征
badge of fraud 诈欺的标记(指诈骗的重大可疑点)
badger game 美人计(指诱人"下水",而后进行勒索)
badword n. 坏字眼
baggage n. 行李;精神包袱;过时货
baggage check 行李检查
baggage declaration 行李呈报
baggage office 行李房
bagman n. 贿赂事件的中间人;推销员,行商,小贩

bagnio n. (东方的)牢狱;妓院
bail n./v. 1.保释;保释人;保释金 2.寄托;(货物的)委托 3.服从(法院的)保证要求(指民事诉讼当事人对有关的财产扣押的担保,应服从法院的要求,才能免除扣押)/准许保释;为……作保释人;将(财货)委托于人;帮助摆脱困境
bail act 保释法(案)
bail bargaining 保释条件协商
bail bond (被告人交保签名保证出庭受审)保释保证书;保释保证金;保释协议,保释协定
bail court 保释法庭(指英国从前后座法院附设的法庭,专门办理保释事务和决定该法院的诉状和诉讼程序特别要点,因此亦叫诉讼程序法庭)
bail dock (英国伦敦中央刑事法院的一个)犯人受审的房间
bail hostel 保释犯人的招待所
bail in criminal proceedings 刑事诉讼中的保释
bail in error 复审保释金(被告为了要求颁发复审令状并中止其执行而交纳的保释金)
bail jumper 在保释中逃跑者
bail official 法庭的准执达官;法庭的警官;法庭法警
bail on security 委托财产
bail out 保释(被告);委托(货物);委托财产摆脱困境,调动头寸解决困难;抽资
bail piece 保释证明书,保释誓约
Bail Reform Act of (美)1966 年和 1984 年的《保释改革法》
bail with sureties 有担保的保释
bailable a. 保释的,允许保释的,可保释的
bailable action 允许保释的诉案
bailable offense 可保释的罪行
bailable process 保释程序
bailee n. 受寄托人,(财物的)受委托人
bailee for hire 租借受寄托人
bailee of goods 财物受寄托人
bailee policy 受托人(占有财物的)浮动保险单
bailer (=bailor) n. 寄托人
bailie n. (苏格兰)高级市政官(仅次于

市长)
bailiff n. 执达官;法警,法庭监守官;管理或监督财产者;(英)区镇的地方长官;地主代理人,地主管家
bailiff's follower 执达官的随从
bailiff-errant n. 助理执达官
bailiwick n. 执达官(或法警)的职业;执达官(或法警)的管辖范围(或职权范围)
bailment n./v. 保释;寄托/1.寄托[指一个人将个人财产交付给另一个人保管,按明示或事实上默示合同以达到某种目的。这不同于个人财产之买卖或赠与,寄托是变换持有位置而非改变权利根据(见 pawn)]2.寄托人(bailor)将个人财产交付给受寄托人(bailee)3.寄托合同(指合同或构成这种交付寄托的法律关系)4.保释[指为刑事被告交付保释金(bail)的保释行为]5.保释证明文件(指为刑事被告邮寄为保释提供的证明文件)
bailsman n. 保释人
bairns' part (苏格兰继承法) 年幼儿(继承)份额
bait and switch 诱购(指为某项目做广告,使人们去商店并促使他们买不同东西,如果这些东西不适宜做广告,则此行为为违法)
baiting n. 欺负;诱惑
baker n. 面包师
balance n./v. (收支)平衡;(收支)差额;结存,结欠;均势;余额;尾数,找头;天平/权衡,斟酌,对比,比较;使平衡,使均势;结算,清账;抵消,与……相抵,与……相等;平衡;(用天平)称
balance account 决算账户,(收支)差额账
balance affidavit 结存证明书,结算证明书
balance at bank 银行结存
balance book 分类账;余额簿
balance date 结算日期
balance due 结欠金额;不足额
balance of births and deaths 出生数与死亡数的差额
balance of contract 合同(契约)的限额(条款);现有合同(契约)限额
balance of evidence (对双方)证据的权衡、对照

balance of factors test 要素权衡标准
balance of financial revenue and expenditure 财政收支平衡
balance of forces 均势
balance of interest 利益均衡,利益衡量
balance of interests 利益均衡
balance of payments 收支平衡;收支差额
balance of payments deficit (国际)收支逆差(赤字)
balance of payments discipline (国际)收支纪律
balance of payments surplus (国际)收支顺差
balance of power 力量均势
balance of probabilities 可能差额
balance of probability 可能性更大(指加拿大的保释程序中证明标准是"可能性更大",即优势证据的标准)
balance of the account 对账,账户余额
balance of trade 贸易平衡;贸易差额
balance off (=balance-off) a./ad. 不平衡的(地)
balance on basis of official reserve transactions 按官方储备结算的国际收支差额
balance on liquidity basis 按清偿基础结算的国际收支差额
balance order 结欠通知单
balance outstanding 余额,余数
balance sheet 资产负债表,资金平衡表,借贷对照表
balance sheet test 资产负债表测试
balance to your credit 你方受益金额
balance to your debit 你方结欠金额
balanced budget 平衡预算
Balanced Budget and Emergency Deficit Control Act of 1985 (美)《1985年平衡预算和紧急情况亏损控制法》
Balanced Budget and Emergency Deficit Control Reaffirmation Act of 1987 (美)《1987年平衡预算与紧急赤字控制确认法》
balanced constitution 平衡宪法
balanced justice 平衡司法
balanced international trade account 平衡国际贸易收支
balanced view 均衡观点

balancing doctrine 平衡论
balancing of interests （美）（宪法上的）权益平衡论
balancing social and individual right 平衡社会利益和个人利益
balancing test （美）平衡原则（法院在权衡个人权利和政府权力或州权和联邦最高权之间相关权益时所使用的司法原则，尤其涉及宪法，则要决定哪种权占优势）；平衡的标准，衡平的标准，衡量的标准
balancing test of Byrd （美）伯德案判决的衡平标准［指伯德诉蓝岭农村电力合作社案（Byrd v. Blue Ridge Rural Electric Cooperative, Incy）的判决。见 judge-jury issue 和 balancing test］
ballistic verification of judicature 司法弹道检验
ballistics n. 弹道学
ballium n. 堡垒，要塞
balloon payment（或 loan） 分期付款中最后一笔大数目的本金贷款
ballot n./v. 选票；无记名投票用的选票；投票，投票权；投票总数；候选人名单；抽签/投票选举（某人），无记名投票，抽签，拉票
ballot box 投票箱
ballot paper 选票
ballot paper account 投票计算
ballot paper null and void 无效选票
ballot ticket 选票
ballotage n. 决选投票（指在各候选人得票均未能达到决定多数时，对其中得票最多的候选人再次进行投票选举）
balloting committee （投票）选举委员会
balnearii n. （罗马法）偷窃公共浴场洗澡人衣服者
ban n./v. 禁令；（大陆法）公告；查禁；舆论谴责；（封建时代）召集令；革除教门/禁止，取缔，诅咒
ban on handgun 手枪管制
banc（=banco）n. 法官席；（法官中的）专席；法庭
banc le roy （英）王座法院（见 King's Bench）
banci narratores （高级）律师
Bancroft Treaties 班克罗夫特协定［指 1867 年美国 19 世纪最大的历史学家之一班克罗夫特（George Bancroft）出任驻北德联邦大使后，开始通过双边协定协调双重国籍问题。美国先后与巴登大公国（The Grand Duchy of Baden）、巴伐利亚（Bavaria）、符腾堡王国（Kingdom of Wurtemburg）、黑森大公国（The Grand Duche of Hesse）、英国、奥匈帝国（Austria-Hungry）、比利时、丹麦、挪威和瑞典等国家签订类似协定，约 26 个国家之多，历史上称之为"班克罗夫特协定"］
bancus n. 法院；法官席
bancus publicus （英）公共法庭（摄政时期王座法院的称谓，亦称 bancus superior）
Bancus Reginae （英）后座法院（见 Queen's Bench）
Bancus Regis （英）王座法院（见 King's Bench）
Bancus Superior （英）上座法院（见 Upper Bench）
(a) band of gangsters （一帮）匪徒
bandit n. 土匪，盗匪；抢劫犯；歹徒
bandit with long records 惯匪；惯犯
banditry n. 有组织的抢劫；盗匪活动；盗窃罪
bane n./v. 毒物；祸根；犯罪分子；毁灭，克星/毒害，中毒
bane of jurisprudence 法理学的隐患，法理学的祸根，法理学的消亡
bane of punitive justice 因果报应祸根（或根源）
banish v. 驱逐，流放（旧译：充军）；清除，排除
banishment n. 驱逐出境；放逐；流放刑
bank n. 银行；（血）库；赌场主；（赌博的）庄家；法官席，审判席；法院；全体法官庭；法院全体法官会议；土埂，浅滩；堤
bank acceptance 银行承兑
bank account 银行账户，银行存款
Bank Account Settlements 银行账户结算
bank and banking 银行和银行业务
bank annuity （英）公债
bank bill （英）银行汇票；（美）钞票
bank book 银行存折
bank cable transfer 银行电汇

bank charge　银行收费
bank charter　(美)(允许社团开办)银行业务的文件
bank check account　银行支票户头
bank clearing　银行票据交换
bank credit　银行借贷
bank deposit　银行存款
bank deposit certificate　银行存款凭证
bank deposits and collections　银行押金和托收
bank discount　银行贴现
bank draft　银行汇票
Bank for International Settlement　国际清算银行
bank guarantee　银行担保
bank holding company　银行控股公司
bank holiday　(美)星期日以外的银行假日;(英)银行公假日
bank(或business) hours　银行营业时间
bank investment　银行投资
bank law　银行法
bank loan　银行借贷,银行贷款
bank money　(总称)银行票据(指支票、汇票等)
bank note　钞票
bank of issue　发行银行
bank operating　开业银行
bank order　银行汇票
bank overdraft　银行透支(额)
bank paper　(总称)(流通的)钞票;银行承兑的票据
bank post remittance　银行邮汇
bank rate　银行利率;银行贴现率
bank reconciliation statement　银行对账单
bank reference　银行征信
bank return　银行收益
bank robber　抢劫银行犯
bank robber fugitive　银行抢劫逃犯
bank stock　银行股本
bank supervision　银行监督
bank transfer　银行转账
bank's buying rate　银行买进行市
bank's orders (或 cashers' orders)　本票
bankable a.　(证券等)银行可承兑的;银行肯担保的;银行可贴现的

bankable bill　银行可贴现票据
bankable project　银行愿担保的项目
banker n.　银行家,银行业者;赌场中的管账(人),(赌博的)庄家
banker's acceptance　银行承兑
banker's acceptance bill　银行承兑的汇票
banker's bill　银行(对外国银行)开出的汇票;银行票据
banker's books　银行簿据(指可作表面证据的一种簿据。按英国1879年《银行簿据证据法》的规定,银行簿据账目副本,经过核对证实无误,即可成为表面证据)
banker's check　银行支票
banker's draft　银行汇票,银行票据
Banker's Evidence Act　(英)《银行簿据证据法》
banker's lien　银行留置权;银行对押品的扣押权
banker's reimbursement credit　银行偿付信用证
bankerout a.　(英)破产的;无力偿债的,无力支付的
banking n.　金融;银行业,银行业务;银行学
banking account　银行账户
banking agency　银行经纪业
banking business　金融业务,银行业务
banking capital　银行资本,金融资本
banking company　金融公司
banking contract　银行往来合同(契约);金融合同(契约)
banking group　银行集团
banking guarantee　银行担保
banking hours　银行营业时间
banking house　银行
banking institution　金融机构
banking law　银行法;金融法
banking(或money) market　金融市场
banking operation　金融行为;金融业务,银行业务
banking power　银行投资能力
banking reform　金融改革,银行改革
banking transaction　金融行为,金融业务,银行业务
bankroll n.　资金

bankroller n. 提供资金者,资助者
bankrupt n./v./a. 破产者;无力还债者;丧失了(名誉,智力等)的人/使破产/破产的;无力还债的;垮了的
bankrupt director 破产董事长
bankrupt landlord 破产地主,没落地主
bankrupt member 破产的议员
bankruptcy n. 无偿付能力,破产[破产是一个法定程序(statutory procedure),通过此项程序债人可以得到财产的救济(financial relief)和经受司法上的监督重组或债务人资产的清理以利于债权人之要求。也可指依破产法宣告破产的事实,或依该法宣告破产当事人的地位。根据美国联邦法(Federal Law)有不同类型的破产,亦称 bankruptcy proceeding, bankruptcy case]
bankruptcy act 破产法(案);破产行为
bankruptcy administrator (或 assignee) 破产财产管理人
bankruptcy and liquidation law 破产和清偿法
bankruptcy bill 破产票据
Bankruptcy Code (美)《破产法典》[指《1978 年破产改革法》(the Bankruptcy Reform Act of 1998),如《美国注释法典》第 11 标题卷的编纂和修订。1979 年 10 月 1 日以后向法院提起的破产案件均适用此法;即债务人无力或不愿偿还债务时,对债权人和债务人利益的保护及给予救济的联邦法规(11 USCA)]
bankruptcy court 破产法院
bankruptcy creditor 破产债权人
bankruptcy discharge 破产债务解除
bankruptcy estates account 破产财产账
bankruptcy judge (美)处理破产案件的法官[指由美国上诉法院任命的司法官主持审理根据《破产法典》(Bankruptcy Code)和相关破产案件的程序由美国地区法院提上来的案件。处理破产案件的法官通常有 14 年的任期参见《美国注释法典》第 28 标题卷第 151 节]
bankruptcy jurisdiction 破产管辖权
bankruptcy law 破产法
bankruptcy notice 破产通知书;催还债款通知

bankruptcy official 破产财产管理官员
Bankruptcy Plan (1944 年)破产计划[指由债务人或其债务人制订详细行为规划(program of action)来恢复权利,即整顿债务人的财产状况,使债务人可继续作为一个经济实体而存在,继续经营,清偿债务,债权人从其收益中得到清偿。在此计划实施之前必须经破产法庭批准。通常都要缩短此计划。亦称 plan of reorganization; plan of rehabilitation。见 arrangement with creditors]
bankruptcy petition 破产申请;破产诉状
bankruptcy proceeding 破产程序[1.明确"破产"含义。见 bankruptcy 词条 2.破产程序指任何涉及破产的司法诉讼或程序上的行为(procedural action)如听审等。破产诉讼可分别由债务人或债权人提起,前者可称为自愿破产,后者称为非自愿破产。破产开始后,破产法院可对债务人的剩余资产组织人员进行清算,并可分配给债权人,从而彻底免除债务人的债务,或者组织债务人与债权人协商制定破产计划和详细行为规划的协议来恢复权利,亦即重新整顿债务人的财产状况,使其继续经营并作为一个实体继续存在同时清偿债务,使债权人从其营业的收益中得到清偿。见 Bankruptcy Plan。另外法院亦可根据破产申请发出接管令(receiving order),将债务人的财产置于接管人(official receiver)控管之下。然后由接管人召集债权人会议,要求债务人提交财务状况报告(statement of affairs)。就债务人资不抵债进行调查。法院发布破产令,接管人即成为破产管理人(trustee in bankruptcy),债权人应就其的债权向破产财产管理人提供证明。最后,破产财产管理人按法定顺序将财产分配给提供证明的债权人。见 bankruptcy]
Bankruptcy Reform Act of 1978 (美)《1978 年破产改革法》
bankruptcy relief 破产救济
bankruptcy remote 破产隔离
bankruptcy rule 破产原则
bankruptcy trustee 破产受托人(=trustee in bankruptcy),破产财产管理人

Bankruptcy-remote entity （美）破产隔离实体（指由于 SPV "特种工具" 经营活动的单一性,除了证券持有人,即投资者外,没有其他主要债权人。因此 SPV 出现破产可能性不大。为此 SPV 也通常被称为 "破产隔离实体"）

banleuca (=*banlieue*) n. 城边地

banner n. 标帜,旗帜;（中国少数民族地区相当于县的）旗;（美）报纸的头号标题

banner ads 横额广告（指常见于网上的广告形式,在网页的上方出现）

banni muptiarum (=banns of matrimony)

banning n. 宣布为非法

bannitus (=*banni*) （古法）流放犯;被驱逐出境者;不法之徒

banns n. （英）结婚预告 (=banns of matrimony)

banns of matrimony 结婚预告（英国在 12 世纪末,在教堂结婚须于事前连续三周内公布三次的一种结婚预告,目的是了解他人有无提出异议）

banns publication （公布）结婚预告,结婚预告周知

bannum (=ban) 禁令;查禁

bar n./v. 1.（法庭、议院等内的）围栏（指律师席,审判席,被告席）;法庭 2.（大写）律师业;律师界;司法界 3.停止诉讼（或权利要求）的申请 4.阻碍,阻止 5.（喻）审判台;制裁,谴责 6.栅栏,障碍物/禁止,（用法律手段）阻止（诉讼等）;取消,免除;妨害,排斥

bar a debt by the statute of limitations 按有关时效的法规被免除债务

bar act （美）律师法

bar advertising 律师广告,律师做广告

bar date （美）（专利）停止权利申请日期（指美国专利申请必须呈请备案的日期,以避免丧失接受一项专利的权利。在美国,专利申请截止的日期为一项发明之后一年之内,即该项发明在公告披露之后或在其他国家取得专利,或在美国已公开投入使用、销售或报价买卖已过了一年,如该项发明在国内买卖于 2000 年 1 月 1 日报价,那在美国的专利申请截止日期则为 2001 年 1 月 1 日。见 absolute novelty）

bar （或 **break**) **an entail** 废除产业限定继承权

bar association 律师协会

bar at large 概括性答辩

bar council 司法委员会;律师委员会

bar examination （美）律师（资格）考试（为取得律师资格而必须通过的一种书面法律实务考试）

bar examiners 律师主考官（被任命测试一些考生并决定他们是否有资格执法的考官）

bar of an indictment 公诉庭

bar of public opinion 舆论制裁,舆论谴责

bar of the court 法院审判台

bar of the House of Commons （英）下议院审判场所（法庭）

bar of the House of Lords （英）上议院审判场所（法庭）

bar sb. from station a trial 阻止某人起诉

bar to divorce 受理离婚案件的法庭

bar-sponsored fee schedules 律师协会提出的费用一览表

barbarian laws 蛮族法（日耳曼部落法的早期称谓）

Barbarian Laws of Lower Germany 低地（下）日耳曼蛮族法典（指盎格鲁-撒克逊时期著名的撒克逊法、弗利然群岛法和邑林吉亚法）

barbarity n. 残暴,暴行

barbarous doctrines of the common laws 普通法的原始理论,普通法的不规范理论

barbarous government 残暴的政府

barbarus n. （罗马法）野蛮人（指无市民权者）

Barcelona Traction Case ［国际法院于 1970 年判的巴塞罗那牵引公司案,该案判决中首次提到 "普遍义务" (obligation *erga omnes*）,明确区分于其他义务］（见 obligation *erga omnes*）

bare a. 无附带物的;单纯的;无担保的;光秃的,无遮蔽的;缺少的,微小的

bare authority 单纯代理权,单纯授权

bare charter 光租船

bare concealment 公开隐瞒（事实真相）

bare contract（或 **agreement**) 无担保合同

(契约),无条件合同(契约);无约因合同(契约)
bare custody 单纯保管
bare handed ad./a. 赤手空拳的(地),手无寸铁的(地),(美口)确实有罪的(地)
bare licensee 领有单纯许可证的人;领有单纯执照的人
bare majority 单纯的多数
bare necessities 最低限度的必需品
bare ownership 虚有权
bare possession 单纯占有
bare promise 无偿的诺言
bare trust 无担保信托
bare trustee 被动受托人(只握有还款的财产,但不享有受托财产利益的义务受托人,或只在受益业主转让时,才得依受益业主的命令去办理受托事宜的人)
bareboat charter 光船租赁
Barebones' Parliament (英)贝尔明议会(又名小议会或提名人议会,是克伦威尔于1653年召开被提名者举行的大会,因一名虔诚的清教徒贝尔明而得名,该会采用共和政体时期国会称号,因其愚蠢的改革而受嘲讽)
bargain n./v. 买卖合同(契约),成交条件;(讨价还价达成的)协议;交易;经讨价还价成交的商品;廉价货/提出条件;议价;商定;订约;谈判,讨价还价
bargain and sale (英格兰)秘密土地买卖合同(契约)(旧时逃避公众注意,根据衡平法原则转让土地的一种方式)
bargain between trustee and beneficiary 受托人和受益人之间的讨价还价协议
bargain money 定金,定银(见 earnest money)
bargain's a bargain 达成的协议绝不可撕毁
bargain theory of consideration 交易约因论[指契约的成立当事人之间的交换关系为基础,允诺人只有从他的允诺中有"法律获益"(legal benefit),受诺人必须受"法律损失"(legal detriment),也就是付出某种东西作为该允诺的"约因"时,该允诺才有法律的强制力]
bargained-for exchange (合同)已谈判的

交易,交易谈判[指当事双方对于合同的获益或受损均同意执行的价格(price of performance)。美国《合同法重述》(第二次)(The Restatement of Contracts, Second)专门根据谈判为"对价"(consideration)作了界定,但它并未提及获益与受损(benefit or detriment)]
bargainee n. 买受人,买主
bargainer (= bargainor) n. 出卖人,卖主,议价者,讨价还价者
bargaining a. 讨价还价的,议价的
bargaining agent 议价代理人,谈判代理人;集体谈判代表人,谈判代表
bargaining(s) impasse 协商僵局
bargaining position 谈判地位(合同的谈判中处于优势或劣势的状态)
bargaining power 讨价还价能力,议价能力;谈判能力
bargaining problem 谈判问题
bargaining tariff 协议税则,互惠协定关税
barge n. 驳船,大型游艇
barge carrier 载驳母船
baron n. 男爵,贵族;(美)巨商
baron and feme 夫妇(妻)
baron court 庄园仲裁法庭;领地法庭
Baron of Exchequer (英)(历史上)理财法院的6名法官[1873年之后,法院的管辖(court's jurisdiction)转移到高等法院(High Court of Justice),原来的法官(judges)就成为高等法院大法官(justice),亦称 *barones scaccarii*。见 Court of Exchequer]
barones scaccarii 见 Baron of Exchequer
barracoon n. 奴隶(或罪犯等)集中场所
barrator (=barrater) n. 1.挑讼者(又译诉讼唆犯,指教唆、挑拨、资助他人诉讼者)2.(因疏忽或欺骗而)使船主蒙受损失的船长或船员 3.受贿的法官(推事)4.圣职(或官职)的买卖者
barratrous a. 欺诈的,为非作歹的;教唆诉讼的;受贿的;买卖圣职(或官职)的
barratry n. 1.诉讼教唆,挑拨诉讼,资助他人诉讼,无根据诉讼 2.船长或海员的非法行为 3.推事的受贿罪 4.圣职(官职)买卖行为

barratry of the master 船长的不法行为
barred claim 失去时效的债权(或请求权)
barren money 无息债款
barrenness n. 不育,不孕
barrier n. 障碍,阻碍;海关卡关;障碍物
barriere douaniere (法)关税壁垒
barriere juridigue (法)法律壁垒
barring prep. 除外,排除,在外
barrister (= barrister-at-law) n. 大律师(英国有资格出席高等法庭的律师);辩护律师
barrister called to the bar 已通过律师资格考试的大律师
barrister called within the bar 被聘为皇家法律顾问的大律师
barrister counsel 律师,辩护律师
barrister organization 见 Inns of Court
barrister's duty to the court 大律师对法庭负责
barrister's professional obligation 大律师的专业职责
barter n. 互易,物物交换;互易商品;(战时交战国间所订立的关于交换战俘的)军事协定
barter contract 互易合同(契约),易货合同(契约)
barter trade 易货贸易
Bartolus de Saxoferrato (*Bartolo di Sasso*) (*Bartolus*) 巴托鲁斯[指中世纪意大利最负盛名的评论法学家、注释法学家(1313—1357),在意大利裴洛基和波伦亚研究法律,他密切关注当时意大利各城邦法则间的相互冲突,亦即如何解决各城邦法则相互冲突问题,他与先哲们一样,力图从《国法大全》中找到法律冲突解决的一般原则。他在总结前人理论成果的基础上,构建了冲突法早期的完整理论体系,成为欧洲中世纪冲突法理论的集大成者。该理论体系被后人称为法则学说(statutes theories)。他的主要著作有:Commentarius in Tria Digesta; Commentarius in libros IX Codicis priores; Loctura Super Authenticis; Commentarius Super Libris III posteriortbus codicis 等]

base n./a./v. 基层,底部;根据;根据地;基地;基准/低级的,初级的;劣等的;卑鄙的/基于,建立在,以……为基层
base coin 劣等硬币;(含有贱金属的)硬币(指铜、镍币)
base court (古英国法)初级法院
base fee (继承人身份有待裁决的)世袭地产(有时称: conditional fee, determinable fee 或 qualified fee)
base of operation (战争)根据地
base of valuation 估价基准
base offense level 基础罪行的等级,基本罪行程度,犯罪的基础水平程度
base on fact and take law as the criterion 以事实为根据,以法律为准绳
base period 基期,基准期间
base port 基本港口
base (或 **basic**) **price** 基价
base (或 **basic**) **salary** 基本薪金,底薪
base tenure 下等阶层的土地保有(指奴隶或其他仆人享有的土地保有)
base year 基准年
based on 以……为基础;在……基础上;以……为依据
based on custom 以习惯为依据
based on fact 以事实为依据
based on the alliance of workers and peasants (中)以工农联盟为基础
baseline n. (国际法)基线(沿海国海岸线图上的线,据此测算领海、划定内水或国家水域范围)
baseline problem 起点问题(这一术语起源于如何选定分析事态标准的困难。"起点问题"与判断什么是正常的,或什么是不正常的有明显的关联。"起点"作为一般语境会影响到我们对某些问题的判断:比如政府行为是否中立? 是否平等对待不同的人或群体;或一个选择是否自愿,或经过同意以及一切期待或判断是否合理)
basic n./a. 基础;根据;基本/基本的;根本的;基础的;首要的
basic accounting unit (中)基本核算单位
basic administrative unit 基本行政单位
basic codes 基本法典

Basic Collection of Six Codes　（日）《六法要览》（日本岩波书店出版）
basic contention　基本论点
basic contradiction　基本矛盾
basic core of managerial prerogative　基本核心经营权论
basic court　基层法院
basic credit line　（美）贷款限额
basic evidence　基本证据
basic exemption　基本免税额
basic facts（＝core facts）　基本事实
basic food ration　（中）基本粮食定量
basic for identification　认定同一的根据
basic form of business　商业基本形式
basic forms of denials　否认的基本形式
basic freight rate　基本运费率
basic function　基本职能
basic goods　基本的善 [指英国法学家约翰·菲尼斯（1940—）在《自然法与自然权利》（Natural Law and Natural Rights, 1980）中列举的七种基本的善：生命、知识、游戏、审美体验、社交（友谊）、实践合理性和"宗教"。这是人类基本幸福生活不可缺少的基本条件。基本的善在菲尼斯的道德思想体系中起到了一个基础作用]
basic human needs　人类基本需要；生活必需品
basic human rights　基本人权
basic institutional regimes　基础制度体系
basic judicial-territorial unit　司法辖区基本单位
basic law　基本法；（大写）（德）《宪法》（1949年）
basic law courses　基本法律课程
Basic Law of the Hongkong Special Administrative Region of the People's Republic of China　《中华人民共和国香港特别行政区基本法》
basic legal conception and assumption　基本司法概念和假设
basic legal myth　基本的法律神话
basic legal principle　基本法律原则；基本司法原则
basic legal resources　基本法律原始资料
basic level court　基层法院
basic level economic organization　基层经济组织
basic level election　基层选举
basic level political organization　基层政权组织
basic level unit　基层单位
basic maxim　基本准则
basic militia　（中）基干民兵
basic norm (of law)　基本（法律）规范
basic normative rule　基本的规范性准则
basic norm　基本规范 [这术语最初以德语"*Grundnorm*"著称。为汉斯·凯尔森（Hans Kelsen, 1881—1973）法律分析的核心要素之一。他认为必定有一条这样的规范：它的有效性是被确定的，而不是来源于其他的规范，他把分析法律体系当作规范的体系，且把此体系基础规范视为"基本规范"]
basic policies　基本方针
basic precepts of Islam　伊斯兰教的基本教规
basic premium　基础保险费
basic presumption　基本推定，基本事实推定
basic principle　基本原则
basic procedure　基本程序
basic provisions　基本条款
basic rationale　基本原理
basic rights and duties　基本权利和义务
basic self-dealing　自我交易
basic source of law　法的基本渊源，基本的法律渊源
basic statistics　基本统计数字
basic tariff　基本关税率
basic unit of state power　基层政权单位
basic wages　基本工资
basic working day　（中）基本劳动日，基本工作日
basic-form policy　（1997年）基本型保险 [指提供有限承保范围（limited coverage）损失的保险。这种基本型保险一般覆盖火灾、风暴、爆炸、骚乱、飞行器和机动车失事、盗窃以及故意破坏（vandalism）等造成的损害赔偿。亦称 limited policy；specific policy]

basic-level market 初级市场
basic-level people's court （中）基层人民法院，初级人民法院
Basilica 《巴西尔法典》（由巴西尔皇帝一世倡议编撰的一部查士丁尼时代和中世纪期间最重要的法律汇编）
basis n. 基础；准则；根本，根据；主要成分；基准数（指所得税法中的术语，即以一定日期的财产价值或财产投资为基数来计算折旧）
basis for an action 诉讼根据
basis in custom 习惯根据
basis of allotment 摊派标准；分配标准
basis of an argument 论据
basis of assessment 课税标准
basis of jurisdiction 管辖根据；管辖基础
basket of securities 一揽子证券
basket purchase 一揽子购买，整批购买
bastard n. 非婚生子（指父母合法婚姻之前所生之子）；假冒品；劣货；杂种
bastard *ainé* 非婚生长子
bastard *eigné* （古英国法）非婚生长子（指男女二人在婚前生了儿子，结婚后又生了儿子，婚前所生之子，即非婚生长子，婚后所生的儿子叫合法次子 "*mulier puisné*"）
bastard elder 私生长子（见 bastard *eigné*）
bastarda n. 非婚生女
bastardization n. 非婚生子（或私生子）的判定
bastardize v. 判定……为非婚生，证明……为私生
bastardy n. 私生子（或非婚生子）身份
bastardy action 非婚生子女（身份）的诉讼（指确认生父之诉讼）
bastardy complaint 非婚生子身份案的申诉
bastardy statute （旧规）非婚生子抚养法（指惩罚非婚生子女的父亲不抚养其子女的刑事法规。这些法规已被认定为违宪。因为它们不公平地对待父亲，却不惩罚非婚生子女的母亲，所以这些法规不得强制执行）
bastardy proceedings 非婚生子身份案的诉讼
Bastille 巴士底狱［指法国巴士底国家监狱，原系查理五世（1338—1380）的城堡，路易十一世（1423—1483）将其作为囚禁犯人的监狱。1789 年法国大革命时群众奋起将它捣毁后即以"巴士底狱"喻指禁锢］
bastinado n. 击足心刑，打脚掌刑；棍，杖
batch processing 成批处理
baton n. 警棍；官杖；(乐队）指挥棒；棍
baton charge 警察的干涉
baton gun 防暴枪
battered child 被殴打的孩子（指经常在身体上受到亲戚、监护者或亲近家庭的朋友殴打和性侵犯的儿童。见 child abuse；domestic violence；battered child syndrome）
battered child syndrome （美）（家庭法）受虐待儿童综合征［指苦于连续受到伤害的儿童在医疗上和心理上聚集的体现（constellation）。这不是偶然的，而是推定为该儿童受到某人残酷的伤害，通常为其监管人（caregiver），如从 X 光照射诊断结果发现骨骼明显伤损和有意伤害造成的连绵的组织损伤，比如用暴力所造成的扭曲和打击。综合征这一术语由亨利·肯普博士医士（Dr. Henry Kempe）和他的同仁在 1962 年以"受虐待儿童综合征"为题的文章中最先使用。该文在《美国医疗协会刊物》（the Journal of American Medical Association）刊出。美国健康、教育福利部儿童署（the Child's Bureau of the United States Department of Health, Education and Welfare）起草了一份现代法规，要求医生报告疑有被虐待儿童的严重情况，作为一项有关虐待儿童综合征的研究成果。见 child-abuse and neglect reporting statute］
battered wife 被殴打的妻子
battery n. 殴打（港译：打斗），殴打罪
battle of the sexes 两性战争
battue n. 用驱赶方法猎获的猎物；大量捕杀
batture 河床加高
Bauffremont's Divorce Case 鲍富莱蒙王妃离婚案（自 1878 年法国最高法院对鲍富莱蒙王妃离婚案做出判决后，法律规避问题便引起国际司法界的广泛注意与研究，而此案亦成为有关法律规避的最有

名、最典型的案例)

Baumes Law (美)《鲍姆斯法》[指对四次判罚的重罪犯及一定的轻罪规定进行严格的刑事检控,其刑罚可处以终身监禁。1926年纽约州立法机构通过的《鲍姆斯法》因纽约州参议员卡利伯·H.鲍姆斯(Caleb H. Baumes)首次提出而命名。见Three Strikes Law]

bawd n. 妓院女老板;淫秽下流的言语;淫乱

bawdy-house n. 妓院

bay (国际法)海湾(指海的入口,沿海岸国家在此海湾领域行使管辖权,执行环保、移民和海关等)

bay delta 海湾三角洲

bay mouth 湾口

Bayes' Theorem 贝叶斯法则[现代经济法学中的一项法则,侵权的不确定性是当事人事前对侵权案件法官法适用结果预期的不确定性。贝叶斯法则就是用于解决观察者(比如侵权案件中的当事人)不能直接观察事物本质(如某行为是否"真正"构成侵权)所导致的不确定性问题。因此结合与本质具有相关性的因素进行分析,来考察观察者对事物本质准确观察的可能性。这种方法的运用是关于制度和信息的不确定性问题的研究,其意义在于把侵权法律制度的实现过程看作一个信息不充分的互动过程,进而从当事人事前判断的准确率来分析侵权问题]

Bayh-Dole Act (专利法)《贝赫-多尔法》[指一项联邦制定法,该法允许美国政府有资格(take title)向小企业或非营利组织的非官方发明发放许可证,只要参加联邦的基金项目(federally funded programs)。根据该法,由联邦政府融资的部门必须及时揭示联邦基金项目进程中的任何发明,该部门可选择保留专利名称(to contain title)并提出对发明专利申请投保(covering the invention)。如果该部门保留对发明的专利名称,则政府仍可(march in)强制该部门在适当情况下允准排他性或非排他性许可(exclusive or nonexclusive licenses)。此法已被编入《美国注释法典》第35标题卷第200—212节(35 USCA §§200-212)。此法亦称 Patent and Trademark Law Amendments Act。见 March-in Rights]

baymouth bar 湾口沙洲,湾口坝

baza(a)r n. (东方国家的)集市,市场;(英美等国的)廉价商店,商店,商场,商业中心,义卖市场

be about to 即将

be admitted to the bar 取得律师资格

be affronted in public 受到公开侮辱

be art and part in 策划并参与;同谋

be attached to 依附于,附属于;喜爱;推崇,爱慕

be aware of 意识到,知道

be better off 境况(尤指经济)较好

be called to (或 to come; go to) **the bar** 取得律师资格

be called to the stand (witness) 被传到庭(作证)

be cast in (或 for) **damages** 被判赔偿诉讼费用

be cast in lawsuit 败诉

be caught (或 take) **red handed** 当场被捕

be charged with 负……责任;受……指控

be covered by us 由我方负担

be conceived in plains words 用简明文字表达出来

(be) congenial to (or with) the Germanic spirit in Heberaism 与希伯来教义中的日耳曼精神相融合之处

be different (same) in essence 实质上不同(相同)

be discharged from prison 出狱,释放

be entitled to 有权做某事,得到

be entitled to file (one's) pleading (某人)有权利提出辩护

be fatal to… 对……致命的,对……致命伤

be given an audience 得到发表意见的机会

be guilty of a crime 承认犯了罪

be held for murder 因谋杀被捕

be held in restraint 受监禁

be implicative of each other (彼此)相互

牵连
be in a sad（或 sorry）plight 处于困境
be in clink （英）在牢房,在狱中
be in drink（或 the worse for drink；under the influence of drink） 酒醉
be in pledge 在抵押中,典当中
be in the box 出庭
be in the dock 在受审中
be in the minority 少数
be in the panel （苏格兰）在受审中
be incapacitated from voting 被剥夺选举权
be indicted on a charge of 因犯……罪而被起诉
be inside 在监狱中
be learned in the law 精通法学
be master of 掌握,控制
be no judge of 不能判（鉴）定
be note for 以……著称
be nothing to... 对……来说无足轻重；不能与……相比
be on intimate terms with 与……关系密切；有不正当性关系；熟悉……
be on the bench 当法官
be onto sb. (sth. ...) 充分了解某人(某事)
be out on bail 在保释中
be party in a suit 与诉案有关
be pushed for 被迫,迫使
be responsible for 对……负责
be shorn of one's right 被剥夺的权利
be summoned as a witness 被传唤作证
be sworn 宣誓,发誓
be that as it may 尽管如此
be under a pledge of secrecy 作了誓不泄密的保证
be under compulsion to 被迫……
be under house arrest 被软禁
be within（或 outside）the law 合（或不合）法
beach mark 基线（认定有倾销存在作比较时的基线,基线算得越高,越容易认定有倾销）
beadle n. 牧师助理；小官吏；法院差役
beadsman n. 被收容者
beagle n. 密探,间谍；执行官；警察

beak n. （英俗）治安法官,治安推事；教师
beakie n. （美俚）暗中监视工会会员的警察
bear n./v. 卖空,空头（卖空的证券交易投机商）；笨拙的人/1.负担；承担；忍受 2.支持；提供 3.负有,持有,享有；怀有 4.开动,压迫
bear a child 怀孕,怀有小孩
bear a grudge 含怨
(to) bear a hand 帮助,出一把力；参加(in)
bear a loss 负担损失
bear away 夺走,抢去
bear due liabilities 承担适当责任
bear（或 give）false as witness 作假见证
bear financial responsibility 承担经济责任
bear fruit 结果,产生果实
bear interest 有收益,产生利息
bear legal liability 承担法律责任
bear malice to（或 towards）sb. 对某人怀有恶意
bear market 空头市场
bear on（或 upon） 1.卡（人）,施加压力 2.有关系,有影响
bear out 1.证明,证实；辩护 2.支持,声援
bear testimony (to) 提供证据,（为）……作证
bear the record 向……作证
bear the responsibility 承担责任
bear upon（或 on） 施加影响,对……施加压力
bear witness 作证；证明
bearer n. 持有人；持票人；带信人
bearer bond 无记名债券
bearer certificate 无记名证券
bearer check（或 cheque） 无记名支票
bearer debenture 公司债券持有人
bearer draft 无记名汇票
bearer instrument 无记名票据
bearer of dispatches 信差,送信人,邮递员
bearer of the policy 保险单持有人
bearer paper 无记名票据
bearer policy 无记名保险单
bearer share（或 stock） 无记名股票
bearing n. 忍受,忍耐；关系,联系；方面

bearing in mind that... 应该记住……
bearing the crime 抵罪
beast of the chase 可猎兽
beat n./v. 1.(警察)巡逻地段 2.鞭打 3.骗子;食客/设法逃过;绕过;打败,胜过;(殴)打;诈骗
beat about 搜索
beat duty 分段巡逻
beat frequency 经常巡逻的路线
beat the rap 逃罪(指逃避法律制裁)
beat up (美)殴打;虐待;杀
beating n. 对他人施用暴力,笞打
beating, smashing and looting (中)打、砸、抢
beaupleader n. 公平答辩人;对公平答辩人不得处以罚金的禁令
becameralism n. 两院制主义
becameralist n. 主张两院制的人
Beccaria Cesare Bonesana 塞拉雷·伯尼萨那·贝卡利亚(1738—1794)[指一位意大利米兰理论家。他的著作涉猎广泛,从货币政策到认识论无所不包。《论犯罪与惩罚》(1764年)为其最重要的著作,他提出最有启蒙色彩的刑罚研究课题,并结合报应论、后果论因素提出:罪刑法定,罪责刑相适应和不使用酷刑]
become v. 成为,变得
become law 成为法律
become operative 生效
becoming of age 达到法定年龄
bed and board (夫妻)共同生活;同居
bedchamber question (英)王室内侍不得介入内阁事务原则
Beddoe order (允许受托人为取得补偿而起诉的)贝多法院
bedead v. 麻醉
bedel n. (英)(法庭的)传呼员;(法庭的)送信人;(教区的)下级工作人员
bedelary n. 法庭传呼人(或送信人)的管辖范围
bederepe n. 劳役;杂役
bedeweri n. 罪犯,歹徒
bedevil v. 使着魔;弄坏,弄糟;纠缠,折磨;使混乱;使迷惑,使烦恼
bedlam n. 精神病院;喧哗(声)

bedlamite n. 精神病院的人,疯子;狂人
bedrock n. (理论等根据的)基本事实(或原则);基本原则;最低点;最少量
beef n. (美俗)报告警察局,密告,告发
beef-squad n. (美俗)大力士打手队
befit v. 适合,适宜;为……所应做的
before the court 出庭,到案;在法庭上
before the fact 作案前,事前作案
before the tribunal of conscience 受良心的裁判
before the tribunal of public opinion 受舆论裁判
beget a child 生(子女)为……
beggar n. 乞丐;穷人;募捐者
beggary n. 赤贫;乞丐生涯;(总称)乞丐
begging n. 行乞
begin v. 开始;着手;创建
begin legal proceedings against... 对……起诉
begotten before marriage 婚前受孕的
begriffs jurisprudence 概念法学
behavio(u)r n. 行为,品行;举止,态度
behavio(u)r pattern 行为模式
behavioral economics 行为经济学
Behavioral Law and Economics 行为法经济学
behavioral marketing 行为关联营销(指不是根据用户所浏览的页面内容,而是根据用户网上搜索、浏览和点击行为来锁定用户,可大大提高广告效率)
behavioral regularity 行为规律性
behavio(u)ral method in public administration 行政行为研究法
behavio(u)ral sciences 行为科学
beheading n. 斩首(刑)
behest n. (书面用语)命令,训示;紧急指示
behind bars 在狱中;在押
behind bolt and bar 被关在监牢里
behind the Chinese Wall 隐藏在中国墙背后(美国法律界一般把决定者说成是"隐藏在中国墙背后",这是对用屏障进行隔离的一种易于描述的方式。法官、准法官、陪审团、专家咨询团等均被"隐藏在墙后边"。这种禁止规则旨在防止决定者在作出其决定时流于偏见,保持决定者的公

正性)
behind the scenes 秘密地;暗中;幕后
behoof n. 利益,利润;用途
being a member of bar 身为律师界的成员
being calculated to deceive 有意欺骗
belabo(u)r n. 重打,鞭打(刑);痛斥
belated a. 过了期的,落后了的;延误了的
belated claim 延误了的索赔款
belated opposition 过时异议(专利法中的用语)
Belgian law 比利时法
belie v. 给人以……假象,使被误解
belief n. 相信,信心,信念;信仰,信条
belief change theory 信念改变理论(见belief revision theory)
belief dynamics 信念动力学[指信念修正理论"belief revision theory"的又一称谓,又称认知动力学(epistemic dynamics)和信念改变理论(belief change theory),可见该词条]
belief revision theory 信念修正理论[此理论为模糊理论应用到证据学的又一分支领域,着重研究信息的引入对裁判的影响,在接受新信息后对已有的裁判观念或信念进行修正是所有动态审判所必须具备的素质。最早由威廉·哈珀(William Harper)和艾萨克·莱维(Isaac Levi)在1977年提出,又称信念动力学 belief dynamics]
believe v. 1.相信[①对于真实性感觉是肯定的,对于真实给予肯定;认为真实(见suspect);②充分理由相信(根据环境或情况,一个理智的人会相信特定的事实或一连串的事实)] 2.考虑或推理(to think or suppose)
belisha beacon (英)(城市中标明行人横道的)交通指示柱
bellicism n. 好战性;好战倾向;好斗性
bellicose a. 好战的,好斗的
bellicose element 好战分子
bellicosity n. 好战,好斗(性)
belligerency n. 交战,交战状态;交战国的地位;好战性
belligerent n./a. 交战一方(指国家、集团或个人),交战国,交战集团,交战人员;(复)交战双方/挑起战争的;交战中的,好战的;交战国的
belligerent community 交战团体
belligerent party 交战一方
belligerent power 交战国
belligerent state (或 country) 交战国
bellum internecinum 毁灭性战争
bellum justum 正义战争
belong by right to sb. 属某人的权限内,归某人管辖
belonger n. 居民
belonging n. 财产,所有物(着重说明所有权);行李;(复)附属物,亲属;(团体成员间的)亲密忠诚关系
below a. 下级的(指下一级法院或管辖)
below court (=court below) 下级法院
below par 低于票面价格
bench n. 1.法庭;(总称)法官;法官席,法官职;(特定法庭的)全体法官 2.(英)(议院的)议席;长凳
bench and bar 法官和律师
bench blotter (警察所作的关于)逮捕人犯等事项的记录(簿)
bench conference (美)法庭会议(法官与律师于审判前、审理中或审理后在法庭召开的讨论与该诉讼有关事项的会议)
bench mark 水准基准,基本标准
bench memo 法官备忘录(通常根据审判法官的请求,由律师对他在案件中所持的主张所提出的一种法律性的备忘录)
bench of bishops (英)主教法官
bench of lay justice 由非专业法官组成的法庭
bench parole 见 bench probation
bench probation (美)法庭缓刑(指罪犯同意在一定的环境或某些限制下并只对判刑法官而不向缓刑监督官汇报的一种缓刑,亦称 bench parole; court probation)
bench trial 法官审判(在美国指无陪审团的审判,法律与事实皆由法官决定)
bench warrant (=bench-warrant) 法院拘票,法院(对某人发出的)拘留(或逮捕)状
bench-bar-media 法官—律师—新闻界
bencher n. (英)律师学院主管人员,(英)

四法学会协会的老资格会员;下议院议员
bend v. (使)弯曲;(使)屈从;集中全力
bend the law 枉法
bene n. 正当,形式适当,合法,合适,充分
beneath notice 不值得注意
beneath prep. 在……下方(或底下),低于;有失……的身份,有损于……(尊严等);不值得
benefaction n. 善行,善举;捐助物,捐款
benefactor n. 捐赠(助)人;保护人;恩人
benefactress n. 女捐赠(助)人,女保护人,女恩人
benefice n. 恩惠佃田(18世纪法兰克王国实行的一种租佃制中的术语);封地;(英格兰教会)有俸圣职
benefice's patron 圣职推荐人(见 de clerico admittendo)
benefice's profits (宗)圣职的收益
beneficial complicity 受益同谋(指跨国公司从政府代理人实施人权滥用中受益时为受益同谋)
beneficial corporate complicity (从侵犯人权行为中)获益的公司同谋,又称间接同谋(见 corporate complicity)
beneficial interest 受益人利益(指实质上享有或从情理上享有的利益。如甲把自己的物品托给乙保管,甲就享有受益人利益,而乙只有法律上的利益,后者是名义上的利益并非实质利益)
(a) beneficial or ownership interest 受益权或所有权
bénéfice de discussion 要求先向主债务人追索债务的权利(见 benefit of discussion)
beneficent (=benefic) a. 慈善的,行善的
beneficial a. 有使用权的;有权益的;可受益的;有利益的,有益的
beneficial association 互助互益保险会
beneficial enjoyment (财产)收益使用权,财产享用权
beneficial interest 可享有的利益;受益人的权益;实际受益
beneficial owner (18世纪)受益所有人,受益所有权人[指①对信托或信托财产享有衡平法上所有权的信托受益人,亦称 equitable owner;②有权买卖股票的公司股东,但他在公司的注册本(corporation's books)上未以所有人名义注册;③(知识产权)即使法定所有权(legal title)已授权他人,仍有资格享有专利权、商标权或版权的个人或部门。受益所有人有资格对侵权(infringement)行为提起诉讼。公司是象征性的(typically)受益所有人,如果公司具有转让专利的签约权利(contracty of right),拥有专利的雇员(employee)则不可转让(assign)它。同样专利或版权的所有人,只要拥有转让资格(transferred title),就有资格对侵权行为起诉]
beneficial ownership 受益所有人,受益所有权[原本为英美法系国家衡平法中的概念用语。在这些国家,为了纠正普通法中财产所有权不可分的缺陷,衡平法承认任何财产所有权可分为法律上的所有权(legal ownership)和受益所有权(beneficial ownership)两类,并且这两种所有权既可归属于同一个人,亦可分别属于不同的人。在后一情况下,某种特定财产的所有权人也就存在法律上的所有人和受益所有人的区分。在双边税收协定中,最早采用受益所有人这一概念用语的见于1966年美英两国签订的关于避免对所得和财产重复征税的协定书中。现今各国相互间签订双边税收协定时普遍采用这一用语]
beneficial power 受益权
beneficial result 效益
beneficial title 受益所有权
beneficial use 使用收益权
beneficiary n. (遗嘱、信托、保险等的)受益人;受惠国;(国际汇兑的)收款人;(封建社会的)封臣,受俸牧师
beneficiary country 受惠国
beneficiary of a life estate 终生遗产的受益人
beneficiary of protection 受保护人,保护受益人,保护版权人
beneficiary of remittance 汇款收款人
beneficiary under testamentary disposition 依遗嘱处分的受益人
beneficium 恩赐
beneficium abstinendi (罗马法)拒绝继承

的权利
beneficium cedendarum actionum （罗马法）代位债权
beneficium competentiae （大陆法）破产债务人保留生活必需物的正当权利
beneficium divisionis （共同保证人的）分别利益或分摊利益
beneficium excussionis 财产检索的权利（见 *beneficium ordinis*）
beneficium inventarili 遗产清单特典（罗马法规定，继承人得知被指定为继承人后，应于60日内调查遗产，编制财产与负债目录，而被继承人所负一切债务仅以遗产为限。此目录称为遗产清单特典）
* *Beneficium invito non datur.* A privilege or benefit is not granted against one's will. 授予一项特权或恩惠不得违反受惠人的意志。
* *Beneficium non datur nisi officii causa.* A benefice is not granted except on account or in consideration of duty. 非因职责不得给予薪俸。
beneficium of priority 优先权益
beneficium of survivorship （财产共有中的）生存者取得的权益
beneficium ordinis （保证人的）后诉之权利（罗马法上又称财产检索的权利，指债权人不诉主债务人，而先诉诸保证人时，保证人具有要求债权人用尽办法先诉主债务人的抗辩权利）
benefit n. （14世纪）1.优点；利益，收益；好处，救济金，补偿；特权，特惠；特殊优惠〈the benefit of owing car〉（拥有汽车的特殊优惠）2.盈利，利润，特别是对价（consideration）转移给受允诺人（move to promisee）〈benefit received from the sale〉（从销售方得到盈利）。亦称 legal benefit；legal value（见 detriment）
benefit (from) 受益于，有益于
benefit already acquired 既得利益
benefit costs 福利补贴费用
benefit of argument 辩论权；举证权
benefit of cession （财产）让与权
benefit of clergy 1.牧师的特权（指在旧英格兰时期，牧师享有不受非宗教法庭审理

或免处死刑的权利）2.同居（指男女未婚同居）
benefit of customary law 习惯法上的权益
benefit of discussion 要求先向主债务人追索债务的权利（指保证人受到债权人追偿保证责任时，有权要求债权人用尽一切办法先向主债务人追索债务）
benefit of division （共同担保人的）分摊权（益）（见 *beneficium divisionis*）
benefit of inventory 遗产清单的特典（见 *beneficium inventarili*）
benefit of prescription 时效产生的权益
benefit of the bargain rule "交易盈利"规则
benefit of the doubt 无罪推定（见 give sb. the benefit of the doubt）
benefit payable 应付抚恤金，应付救济金
benefit value 受益值
benefit-cost analyze 成本—效益分析
Benelux n. 比、荷、卢三国；比荷卢关税同盟
Benelux Customs Union 比荷卢关税同盟
Benelux Economic Union 比荷卢经济联盟
Benelux Uniform Statute of 1962 《1962年比荷卢统一法规》
benevolence n. 捐助物，捐款；善举，仁慈；（英）强制捐助（指未经议会同意国王向臣民勒索的款项，已为《权利法案》宣布为非法）
benevolent association 慈善协会（指未授予法人资格的非营利组织，具有慈善、宽厚之目的。亦称 beneficial association；benefit association；benevolent society；fraternal society；friendly society）
benevolent dictator 乐善好施的口述者，乐善好施者
benevolent society 救济会，(大写) 共济会
* *Benignior sententia in verbis generalibus seu dubiis, est praeferenda.* The more favorable construction is to be placed on general or doubtful expressions. 较好的解释应是对笼统的或有疑惑的表述所作的解释。
* *Benignius leges interpretandae sunt quo*

voluntas earum conservetur. Laws are to be liberally construed, in order that their intent may be preserved. 为了保持法规的原意,应不拘泥于对其进行字面解释。

benign offices of wife & mother 妻子和母亲的慈祥职责

Benjamin order (受益人下落不明时,法庭处理其财产的)本杰明法令

bent n./a. 爱好,癖好;(bend 的过去式及过去分词)/决心的,一心的

Bentham, Jeremy 杰里米·边沁(1748—1832)[英国的法学家和政治家,哲学家,他的著作以多种不同方式影响了法律哲学,他是功利主义的奠基人并以此著称于世。他在1871年取得律师资格。在1776年他发表的《政府片论》(Fragment on Government, or a Comment on the Commentaries)中总结了功利主义:"最大多数人的最大幸福就是判断是非的标准。"(此短评世界闻名,实际虽不完美,但其理论概括引起人们对功利主义的一些误解)边沁试图将道德分析与政治分析化约为无争议之命题。边沁是一个比奥斯丁(Austin John)更为出色的思想者,但奥斯丁对法律实证主义和分析法系的发展发挥了更大的作用并具有深刻影响]

bequeath n. 动产遗赠,遗赠;按遗嘱(把动产)给予……(与 device 有区别。device 为遗赠不动产,而 bequeath 为遗赠动产)

bequeathal n. 1.(按遗嘱的)遗赠 2.遗产,遗物

bequeathal personal property 遗赠的动产;遗赠的个人财产

bequeathal real property 遗赠的不动产

bequeathment n. 遗赠

bequest n. (按遗嘱的)遗赠,(动产的)遗赠;遗产,遗物

bereave v. (bereaved or bereft) 丧失,使丧失

bereaved daughter-in-law 丧偶的儿媳

bereaved family 已故者的家属,遗族

bereaved husband 丧失妻子的人,鳏夫

bereaved son-in-law 丧偶的女婿

bereaved wife 丧失丈夫的人,寡妇

bereft a. 被剥夺的;被夺去的;失去的

beresy 崇拜异教

Bern(e) Convention 《伯尔尼(版权)公约》(1886年签订)

Bern(e) Union 伯尔尼联盟(版权,伯尔尼公约会员国条约联盟)

(the) Berne Convention Implementation Act (版权)《伯尔尼公约实施法》[指1988年的联邦法,使美国成为《伯尔尼公约》(Berne Convention)的签约国(signatory)。缩略为 BCIA]

berth n. 1.停泊地,锚位 2.住所 3.职业;地位

berth cargo rate 停埠船运费率(停泊在码头船只的剩余船位的运费率)

berth charter 泊位装货租船合同(契约);舱位包租

berth clause 泊位条款

berth note 订船单,订舱单

berth occupancy 泊位利用率

berthage n. 停泊费;停泊处;泊位

Bertillion measurement 贝尔蒂永验身法(见 Bertillion system)

Bertillion system 贝尔蒂永(1883年推行的)成年人人体稳定数据测量体系

besaiel n. (古英国法)恢复地产权请求(书)

besetting a./n. 不断侵扰的,老是困扰的/(英)侵扰行为(罪)

besides an eldest son 除长子之外

bespoke a. (英)定做的,专做订货的;(习语)已订婚的

best a. 最好的;最有利的;最合适的;最大的;大半的

best bids and offers 有利的报价和要约

best evidence (17世纪)最有力证据,主证据,最佳证据[指从案件实质来衡量是最高质量、最可靠的证据,而不是一般事物的证据。这一术语通常适用于书面形式或录音录像的内容,如果原始的可以适用,则必须提供而不得使用复制的或口头解说(oral rendition)。参见《联邦证据规则》第1002条(Fed. R. Evid. 1002)。亦称 primary evidence; original evidence。见 best evidence rule; secondary evidence]

best evidence rule (1894年)最佳证据规

则[该证据规则规定:为证明书面文件(或录音录像、照片)中的内容,当事方必须提供原始书面文件(或技工的及电子的及其他普通复制品照片的拷贝),只有在原件不合适或不存在的情况下,方可使用次级证据(secondary evidence),亦即起草人的或读过该文件者的证言。参见《联邦证据规则》第1001—1004条。亦称 documentary-originals rule; original writing rule; original-document rule]

Best information available 最佳可获得信息(指WTO的《反倾销协定》第6.8款)

best interest of society 社会最佳利益

(the) best justification 最佳正当化[指被赋予的目的或价值能够以最佳方式将实践展示出来。见 like cases treated alike]

best notice practicable 最佳切实可行通知

best possible intelligent 最可靠情报

best practices (or code of conducts) 行为规范

best prevailing local condition 当地一般最佳条件

best prevailing tariff rate 最好的通行税率

best scientific evidence available to the state concerned 有关国家可得到的最可靠科学证据

best use 最佳用途(如果将一笔财产以有偿方式使用,则此财产具有有用的价值)

bestiality n. 兽奸(罪);兽性,兽行(参阅 crime against nature)

bestow v. 把……赠与,把……给予;使用,花费;放置,安置;贮藏

bestowal n. 赠品;赠与;贮藏,收藏

bet n. 赌注,打赌;打赌的钱(或物);被打赌的对象

beth-din (=bet-din) 犹太教法庭

Bethlem (英)贝瑟姆精神病院[即麦克·纳顿最后被送至的医院,在此治疗,后又转至布罗德莫尔(Broadmoor)精神病院,并在杀害德拉蒙德20年后死在此院](见 M'Naghten Rules)

betray v. 出卖,背叛;辜负;暴露,泄露(机密);诱奸(妇女)

betray a secret 泄露秘密

betray oneself 自我暴露;原形毕露

betrayal n. 背叛;通敌;背信;告密;诱惑

betrayal of (state) secrets 泄露(国家)机密(罪)

betrayer n. 背信者,背叛者,叛逆者,叛徒;告密者;诱惑者

betrayer of the nation 叛国者

betroth v. 订婚,许配

betrothal n. 婚约,订婚

betrothed n./a. 订婚者,未婚妻(此术语常与 intended wife 同义)/已订婚的;未婚的

betrothed husband 未婚夫

betrothment n. 订婚

better equity 更有利的衡平法权利

better half (谑语)妻子

better law 较好法说

better off 境况(尤指经济性)较好的

better right (title) 更充分的权利(所有权)

betterment n. 改良,改善;地产增值,不动产增值;(复)修缮经费;房产的改善(指房屋租用人对房屋所作的修缮,以后依法可请求补偿)

betterment levy 地产增值税

betterment order 修缮房屋令;添购自用资产通知单

betterment tax 改良税

betting n. (英)打赌(指对当时未定的事物、未来可能发生的结果,用金钱或有价值的东西进行打赌,如对赛马、球赛的打赌,依英国《博彩法》,赌输的金钱或东西,不能取回);赌博,博彩

betting duty 博彩税

betting house 赌场

betting office (英)博彩公司(经政府许可经营博彩的机构,它要受有关的法律管制)

bettor n. 赌徒;打赌者

between meetings of the parliament 议会休会期间

Bevans' Treaties and Other International Agreements of United States of America 贝文斯编的《1776—1949年美国条约和其他国际协定集》(美国政府印刷局1968—1975年刊印的一套具有权威性的追溯汇编,包括1776—1949年美国参加的条约和

其他国际协定)
beyond(或 past) 不可挽回、不可恢复
beyond (all) question 毫无疑问
beyond all reason 毫无道理
beyond bounds 越界
beyond contemplation 预料不到,预料之外
beyond control 无法控制
beyond controversy 无可争议(辩)
beyond count 不计其数,数不尽
beyond dispute 不可争辩(议)
beyond doubt 不容置疑(毋庸置疑)
beyond economic theory 超越经济理论 [指美国芝加哥学派万达·简·罗杰斯 (Wanda Jane Rogers)《超越经济理论》一书中提出的一种理论,该理论指出:在独家交易的违法性认定中,法官应当结合案情具体问题具体分析,运用法律方法采信经济数据,不能机械地"从模型到模型"]
beyond expectation 出乎预料,意外
beyond national jurisdiction 国家管辖范围以外
beyond reason 不合理
beyong reasonable doubt 排除合理怀疑 (见 reasonable doubt)
beyond seas 在海外,在国外
beyond the mark 超过界限
beyond the reach of legislation 超出立法所及的范围;法规力所不能及的
beyond the shadow of doubt 无疑
bias n. 偏见;不公正;先入之见,倾向性
bias against sb. 对某人持有的偏见
bias for sb. 偏袒某人
biases and hostilities 偏见和敌意
Bible n. 《圣经》(指犹太教和基督教的经籍)
Biblical codes 圣经法典(指《旧约》,古代希伯来的一些法律汇编)
bibliographic(al) data 编目资料
bibliography n. 书目提要;文献目录学;目录学,文献学
bibliotics (复) n. 笔迹鉴定学,文件(真伪)鉴定学
bibliotist n. 笔迹(文件)鉴定专家
bicameral a. 两院制的
Bicameral Campaign Reform Act (美)

(2002 年制定的)《两院竞选活动改革法》[简称 BCRA,该法有两项重要规定:控制"软钱"和管制"问题宣传"。在 20 世纪,企业资助全国性竞选受到管制,第二次世界大战后团体捐助也受到控制。美国联邦最高法院首席大法官赞成控制捐助,但同时根据"美国联邦宪法第一修正案的相关规定,取消了候选人和个人支出的限制。"联邦最高法院认为 BCRA 第一部分旨在把全国性政党从"软钱"(soft money)事务中隔离开。联邦最高法院认为:①捐献限制对自由言论和结社仅有边缘性的约束;②对于选举程序依据 BCRA 而进行的管制审查,并不适用严格审查标准,而仅仅适用不甚严格的"紧密拉近"(closely drawn)标准。对于联邦最高法院的大多数而言,国会所作的证明金钱交易在立法进程安排、被选官员接触以及社会性立法不能通过严格审查标准影响的证据,而是符合"紧密拉近"标准要求。但美国联邦最高法院在 2010 年的公民诉联邦选举委员会(Citizens United v. Federal Election Commission)中,以 5 比 4 的极大争议判处该法案违宪,在美国就该案判决引起巨大争议]
bicameral legislature 两院制的立法机构
bicameral parliament 两院制议会
bicameral system 两院制
bicameralist n. 两院制主张者
bid n./v. (拍卖中的)出价;喊价;投标;出价(或投标)的机会,出价(或投标)的数目;企图/(拍卖中的)出价;投标
bid (performancy) bond 履行合约保证书;押标金
bid price 投标价(递价)
bid sheet 投标人名单
bid up 哄抬(价钱)
bidder n. (拍卖时的)竞投人,投标人;出价人
bidding n. (拍卖时的)出价,竞投,投标
bidding contract 投标合同(契约)
bien-fond' e apparent de l'actio' n publique 公诉的明显理由
biennial budget cycle 两年预算周期
biennial programming 制定两年期的计划
biens 财产

biens immeubles 不动产
biens meubles 动产
bifurcated jurisdiction standard 分立的管辖标准,分别的管辖标准,分开的管辖标准
bifurcated trial 分别审理,分开审理(对同一案件中的不同争点分别听审以便定罪判刑)
bifurcation n. 分开,分别(进行审理)
big a. 大的,巨大的,重要的,重大的
big bang policy (美)"大爆炸"政策(1975年美国通过的一项证券政策,它促进了竞争性佣金率,导致证券经纪业爆发业务重组)
Big Board 纽约证券交易所
Big Four 四巨头[四家最大的英国银行:巴克利银行(Bacelays Bank)(1896年创立)、劳埃德银行(Lloyds Bank)(1865年以泰勒与劳埃德名字建立,1889年改为现名)、中州银行(Midland Bank)(1836年创立,当时叫伯明翰与中州银行)、国立西敏斯特银行(National Westminster Bank)现名英格兰威尔士银行]
Big House (=the big house) 监狱,(美)州监狱,联邦监狱
big power politics 大国强权政治
big problem all along 自始至终的大问题
big shot 大人物,有权势的人
big stick policy 大棒政策,武力政策
Big-Brother "专制者"[《关于网络犯罪公约》(见 Convention on Cyber crime)赋予国家执法机关相当权力以有效打击网络犯罪的同时,应规定采取措施防止有权机关滥用被赋予的权力,阻止在自由国家出现"专制者",从而实现对个人通信自由和个人数据的充分保护]
big-city delinquency problems 大都(城)市的犯罪问题
big-nation(ality) chauvinism 大国沙文主义,大民族主义
bigamic a. 重婚的
bigamic marriage 重婚
bigamist n. (犯)重婚(罪)的人
bigamous a. (犯)重婚(罪)的
bigamus n. (大陆法)重婚者

bigamy n. 重婚;重婚罪
bigamy is prohibited 禁止重婚
bigotry n. 顽固,偏执,偏执的行为;歧视
bilan n. 资产负债对照表,资产负债表
bilateral a. 双务的;双方间的,双边的,互惠的
bilateral action 双方诉讼,两造诉讼
bilateral agency 双边代理
bilateral agreement 双边协定,互惠协定
bilateral agreement for protection of investment 保护投资的双边协定
bilateral assistance 双边援助
bilateral clearing 双边清算
bilateral conflict rules 双边冲突规范
bilateral contract 双务合同(契约)
bilateral convention 双边公约,双边协约,双边专约
bilateral discharge 双边履行;双方履行
bilateral juristic acts 双方法律行为
bilateral legal transaction 双方法律行为
bilateral monopoly 双边垄断(集体协商代表着一种双边垄断。见 industrial actions)
bilateral payment 双边支付,双方给付
bilateral preliminary agreement 双边预约
bilateral provisions 双边条款,互惠条款
bilateral trade 双边贸易,互惠贸易
bilateral trade and payment agreement 双边贸易和支付协定
bilateral treaty 双边条约,互惠条约
bilateralis n. 两面亲(罗马法上指同父同母者)
bilateralism n. (国际贸易)互惠主义
bilingual legislation 双语立法
bilingualism n. 使用两种语言
bilinguist n. 通(讲)两国语言的人
bill n./v. 1.法案,议案(在英国,指议会惯例中的法律草案,如果上下两院通过并获国王批准,一项议案便成为法律。在美国,指国会议员提交国会的一项建议立法的草案,让国会考虑和立法的可能) 2.诉状,起诉书(指刑事、民事诉讼中向法院提交的请求进行某种特定行为的正式诉状) 3.衡平法的起诉状(bill in equity) 4.(美)纸币,钞票 5.票据,汇票,本票 6.单据,发

票,证明书;账单,账款 7.广告,张贴/开账单;通告;宣告将……列成表

bill at sight 即期票据

bill broker 票据经纪人

bill chamber (苏格兰)诉状法庭(成立于1532年在最高民事法院休庭期间工作的法庭,1933年已取消)

bill de bene esse 临时诉状

bill discounted 票据贴现

bill discounted with collateral securities 附有担保品的贴现票据

bill for a new trial 再审申请书

bill for a term 兑换期票

bill for collection 托收汇票

bill for discovery 要求出示证据的诉状

bill for foreclosure 出卖抵押品申请书

bill ignored (陪审团)拒绝受理的诉状

bill in a set 联票

bill in aid of execution 要求(排除障碍)确保执行判决的诉状

bill in equity (或 **chancery**) 按衡平法提交的诉状(或向衡平法院提交的诉状)

bill in eyre (英史)巡回法庭诉状(1230—1330年实行过)

bill in nature of a bill of review 复审类的诉状,恢复诉讼的诉状性质的诉状

bill in nature of a bill of revivor (诉讼中止后恢复诉讼的)续审类的诉状

bill in nature of a supplemental bill 补充性的诉状

bill makers n. 广告制造厂,广告制造者

bill obligatory 保兑合同(契约),保兑期票

bill of a legal character 法律性质的议案

bill of adventure 货主承担风险的运单

bill of amendment 修正案

Bill of attainder 褫夺公民权法案(英国16—17世纪,指被认定犯有煽动性罪行如企图推翻政府的人则按英国议会褫夺公民权法案的法律,处以死刑,还伴随着"血统玷污"。即被褫夺公权者的财产不得交由继承人继承。如果适用的法律不是死刑,而是放逐,没收货物,褫夺选举权等。则被称为处以超出普通法范围的刑罚的法案。美国独立战争时期对于不忠于美国革命罪行的人,很多州议会亦采取同一褫夺公民权处以超过普通法范围的刑罚的法案。褫夺公民权法案和处以超过普通法范围的刑罚的法案都是不经审判即处以刑罚的立法法令。无论该法令是死刑或轻于死刑的刑罚,这类立法均违反了宪法的原则。美国联邦宪法第1条第9款第3项禁止联邦政府通过褫夺公民权法案,第1条第10款第1项对州施加同样的禁令)

bill of budget 预算案

bill of certiorari 要求(上级法院向下级法院)调取案卷复审的诉状(见 writ of certiorari)

bill of charges 费用清单

bill of clearance 结关证书;出口报告书,出港呈报表

bill of compliant 控诉书,控诉状

bill of conformity (遗嘱执行人)要求清理遗产的诉状

bill of costs 诉讼费用清单(指律师开给诉讼委托人的账单,账单上写明一切诉讼费用);账单

bill of credit 信用证取款凭单;付款通知书(美国发行的信用券)

bill of defense 答辩状

bill of discovery 要求告知的诉状(见 discovery);(美)请求披露诉状(衡平法诉讼中一方当事人要求对方披露其所知事实、契据、文书等而提出的诉状,现在美国民事诉讼规则已有有关规则)

bill of dishono(u)r 拒付票据

bill of divorcement 离婚证书

bill of document 单据

bill of entry 进口报关单;报税通知书

bill of estimate 估价单

bill of exceptions (诉讼进行中的)抗辩诉状

bill of exchange 汇票

Bill of Exchange Act (英)《汇票法》(1882年)

bill of exchange payable on a certain day 定日支付的汇票

bill of exchange payable on presentation 见票即付的汇票

bill of exchange payable within a certain period after a date 定期支付的汇票

bill of goods　货品清单
bill of goods adventure　（海商法）借贷抵押证书
bill of health　健康证明书；（船舶的）免疫证书
bill of impeachment　弹劾法案
bill of indictment　刑事起诉书，公诉书；控告状
bill of information　（英）公诉书
bill of interpleader　确定竞合权利诉状（衡平法上的一种起始诉讼，当有两个或两个以上的人对一方当事人提出相同权利或主张，履行相同义务时，该当事人可提出此诉状）
bill of lading　提(货)单
bill of law　法案
bill of Middlesex　（英史）米德尔塞克斯式诉状（指王座法院为夺取高等民事法院诉讼事务而采取的一种拟制式诉讼）
bill of mortality　死亡统计表
bill of oblivion　大赦令
bill of pains and penalties　（英）剥夺公权（或给予超过普通法范围的刑罚的）法案
bill of parcels　包裹单，发货单，发票
bill of particulars　详情诉状（美民事诉讼中指原告应被告请求详细列明其诉讼请求及有关解释或说明，目的在于向被告提供有关原诉因的信息，以帮助被告提供答辩给庭审作准备）
bill of peace　息诉状，要求禁止再行诉讼的诉讼，防止滥诉状（一种起源于17世纪英国衡平法上的一种诉状，当原告就同一权利与不同的人在不同的时间以不同的诉讼发生争议时，可提出此诉状请求法院一劳永逸地裁决此问题，以此禁止他人就同一请求再行起诉）
bill of *pratique*　无疫证书
bill of privilege　保护特权申请书
bill of prosecution　控诉状，公诉书
bill of quality　品质证明书
bill of review　复审状
bill of revivor　续审状（见 bill in nature of a bill of revivor）
bill of revivor and supplement　续审并补充事实的诉状

Bill of Rights　1.（英）《权利宣言》（旧译《民权法典》，1689年颁布的英国资产阶级确立君主立宪制的宪法性文件之一）2.（美）《权利宣言》（美国联邦宪法的前十个修正案作为一个整体称"人权法案"，亦称"权利宣言"；1789年由国会通过，1791年由11个州批准生效）
bill of sale　（16世纪）卖据，卖契［指财产所有权或动产以担保（security）方式转让给他人的一种契据（见 deed）。在实践中最常见的是将动产（如设备、马匹、商品等）的卖据进行抵押以作为债的担保。当债务清偿后，受让人按照约定将卖据返还于让与人，与质押或典当有所区别。动产的占有并不转让到让与人手中（见英国的 Bill of Sale Act）］
Bill of Sale Act　英国1878年《卖据法》（该法规定卖据成立后7日内向伦敦高等法院的中心办公室提交卖据和保证可以执行卖据的宣誓书，以防止让与人的秘密卖据对受让人进行欺诈。1882年《卖据法》则强调对卖据让与人的保护。现代商业中亦称卖据为发货单、销货证）
bill of sight　报关单，报税单；临时起岸报单
bill of store　船上用品免税单；再输入免税单；储存单
bill of sufferance　免税单
bill of suspension　（苏格兰）中止诉讼状（以缺乏管辖、不合程序等理由对轻罪法庭提出抗辩的方式）
bill payable at sight　见票即付票据
bill payable renewed　延期应付票据
bill payable retired　撤回的应付票据
bill payable to bearer　不记名应付汇票
bill *quia timet*　（要求衡平法院）保护产权诉状
bill receivable　应收票据
bill rediscounted　票据再贴现
bill relation　（总称）票据关系
bill sent for collection　托收票据
bill short　短期票据
bill to carry a decree into execution　申请执行判决的诉状
bill to establish will　确认遗嘱诉状

bill to fall due 票据到期,汇票到期
bill to mature 票据到期,汇票到期
bill to order 经签字盖章照付的票据,凭指定票据
bill to perpetuate testimony （为另案）保存证据诉状
bill to quiet possession and title 确保产权（免遭危害）诉状
bill to suspend a decree 暂时取消判决的诉状
bill with collateral securities 有担保品的票据
bill's language 法案用语
billa n. 起诉状;法案;票据,汇票
billa cassetur （或 cassetur billa） 使诉状得以取消,撤销诉状
billa excambii 汇票
billa exonerationis 提单,提货单
billa vera 正式的起诉书（见 true bill）
Billeting Act 《驻兵条例》（英国军队驻殖民地可占用私房屋,北美殖民地人民应为驻军提供膳食和居住条件）
billing rate 开单率
bills committee 法案委员会
bimetallic monetary system （金银）复本位货币制度
bimetallic standard （金银）复本位制
bimetallism n. （金银）复本位制
binary n. 二元,二进制
binary code of legal/illegal 合法/不合法二元准则
binary one 二进制的"1"
binary preference relation of DM (Decision Maker) 决策者的二元选择关系
bind v. 1.捆、绑 2.使受（法律、合同的）约束;使协议确定不变 3.具有约(拘)束力
binding effect rule 约束力规则
bind oneself to (do) sth. 立约做某事
bind sb. over 责令（某人）守法;使（某人）具结保证
(to) bind sb. (criminal suspect) over for trial 羁押某人（犯罪嫌疑人）交付审判
bind sb. over to appear at the assizes 责令（某人）在大审（巡回审判）期间出庭
bind sb. to fulfil(l) a contract 责令某人

保证履行合同（契约）
binder 1.临时定金合同（指不动产买卖双方就转让所有权订立的文据,通常附有买者的起始支付款）2.购买不动产临时定金（买者购买不动产的起始支付款项。见 earnest money）3.临时保险单[指在适用保险政策的进程中或正式的政策准备中,承保人将备忘录提供给被保险人（the insured）的临时保险单（temporary coverage）。亦称 blinding receipt; binding slip]
binding n./a. 约(拘)束力;承担义务/附有义务的;有效的;有约(拘)束力的
binding authority （美）有约(拘)束力的权威性根据（判案法官必须认真考虑的法律渊源,如应考虑本州的制定法或高级法院的判例）;强制权力;有约(拘)束力的授权
binding character 约(拘)束性
binding contract 附有义务的合同（契约）;有约(拘)束力的合同（契约）
binding distribution plans 有约束力的分配计划
binding effect 约(拘)束效能;约(拘)束力
binding effect of usage 约(拘)束性的惯例,习惯的约(拘)束力
binding enforceable contract 有约(拘)束力并可强制执行的合同（契约）
binding engagement 有约束力的约定
binding force 约(拘)束力
binding force of the precedent 判例的约(拘)束力
binding in all aspects 全面拘束力
binding instruction （法官给予陪审团的）有约(拘)束力的指示
binding interpretation （对法律）有约(拘)束力的解释
binding nature 约(拘)束性
binding nature of the award 仲裁裁决的约(拘)束力
binding obligation 有约(拘)束力的债
binding on all parties 对全体当事人均有约(拘)束力
binding over 强令,责令,使有约束;裁定（将犯罪人）交付审判;具结候讯,具保候传（亦称 to bind over,指保证开庭时到庭）

binding over to keep the peace （英）责令维持治安(治安官法院的一项职权)
binding personal judgment 有约束力的对人判决
binding precedent 有约(拘)束力的判例；有约(拘)束力的先例
binding receipt 承保收据
binding slip 见 binder
bio-parent n. 亲生父亲(或母亲)
biodegradation n. 生物降解(作用)
biodegradation of pollutants 污染物的生物降解作用
biodiversity n. 生物多样化,生物的变化
biodiversity and ecosystem management 生物多样化和生态系统管理
bioethics n. 医学和生物发展的伦理含义上的研究
biogeochemical a. 生物地理化学的
biogeochemical cycling 生物地理化学循环
biography n. 个人经历,传记
biologic control 生物防治
biologic damage 生物上的损害
biological a. 生物学(上)的,生态学的
biological balance 生态平衡
biological carrying capacity 生态承载能力
biological diversity 生态的多样化,生态的差异
biological father 生身父亲(指一个男人的精子使母亲受孕而成为小孩子的生身父亲,亦称 birth father, genetic father)
biological parents 生身父母
biological resources 生物资源
biological weapons 生物武器
biometrics n. 二元矩阵
bionomic n. 个体生态学；(复)生态学
biopsy n. 活(体)组织检验法
Biosafety in Microbiological and Biomedical Laboratory (BMBL) 《病原微生物实验室生物安全管理条例》(又称实验室生物安全的圣经)
bioscopy n. 生死检定法
biosecurity n. 生物安保
biotechnology n. 生物科技
bioteroism threat 生物恐怖威胁

bipartisan（或 **bipartizan**）a. 由两党成员组成的,代表两党的,由两党支持的
bipartisanship n. 两党制,两党关系(尤指两大政党在对外政策上达成的协议)
bipartite a. 1.由两部分构成的 2.(条约等)双方之间的
(a) bipartite contract 一式两份的合同(契约)
bipartite trust receipt 双方的信托收据
bipartite wagering 双方赌博合同(契约)
Birmingham School 伯明翰学派(托马斯·阿特伍德是该派的领导者,他提倡由通货膨胀维持的高价格)
birretum n. （英）高级律师资格(原意为高级律师所戴的白帽)
birth n. 出生,分娩；出身；血统；诞生；起源
birth and death records 出生与死亡档案
birth certificate 出生证明书(指一份记有一个人的出生日、出生地点及父母身份的正式文件。美国的 50 个州中,一个被收养的子女必须具有第二份出生证明书反映出他或她的养父母身份。在这种情况下,最早的出生证明书通常加以密封,只有按法院令方可打开。有些州允许有限制的接近,则取决于被收养者出生的年限,和有时依据亲生父母的同意。当今趋向于打开记录必要条件是：①子女和生身父母都同意,比如通过收养注册登记处打开；②子女要求并依据公告生身父母并未否决这一要求。俄勒冈州第一个制定法规根据被收养子女的单方要求。一旦子女达到成年即可参阅出生记录。见 adoption registry statute)
birth control 节育；控制生育
birth injury（或 **trauma**）分娩创伤
birth interval（或 **spacing**）生育间隔
birth mark 胎记,胎痣；人的特征
birth order 出生顺序
birth pill 避孕药丸
birth rank 出生排行
birth rate 出生率
birth registration 出生登记
birth report 出生报告书
birth right 长子继承权；生来就有的权利

births and deaths registration 出生与死亡登记(册)

bishop (基督教)主教[指教区最高级别的神职人员。主教直属一个省的大主教(archbishop)]

bitcoin 比特币[指一种为进行互联网交易而创造的电子货币。其中,bit(比特)是计算机的最小信息单位。2008年年末,署名"中本聪"(Satoshi Nakamoto)的神秘人物宣布开发出"比特币"开源P2P(指数据传输不再通过服务器,而是在网络用户之间直接传递)电子货币系统。一枚比特币实际是一个64位的数字符号。创造比特币的唯一方法是验证每个64位数的排列是否符合固定的密码算法。这一过程称作"挖矿"。人们也可使用主权货币购买比特币并存入网络数字钱包。比特币从痴迷计算机技术的极客手中的玩物摇身一变首次用来购买实物是在2010年5月。美国佛罗里达州程序员拉斯洛·豪涅茨用1万枚比特币(当时约合25美元)购买到两块比萨饼。此后,全世界数百个互联网企业相继接受比特币支付。加拿大安装了世界上首台比特币ATM机。]

biting injury 咬伤

bitter with the sweet (美)甜加苦的理论[联邦最高法院大法官伦奎斯特(Rehnquist)在1974年的阿内特诉肯尼迪(Arnett v. Kennedy)一案中提出的一种新理论。该理论认为既然政府有充分的自由裁量权来决定是否给予相对一方的某种福利,它自然也有充分的自由裁量权来决定福利的范围和授予或终止该福利的程序]

bis de eadem re ne sit action 同一案件无二次诉权

bit n. 拘束物,控制物

Bivens Actions (1972年)比文斯诉讼[寻求补偿联邦官员违反宪法性权利的诉讼。比文斯诉六个不知名的联邦毒品调查局的代理人案(Bivens v. Six Unknown name Agents of Federal Bureau of Narcotics),参见《美国联邦最高法院判例汇编》第403卷第388页、第91卷第1999页(1971年)。比文斯诉讼类似于《美国注释法典》第42标题卷第1983节(42 USCA §1983)中所阐明的根据州法的表面权利(under color of state law)。在州政府官员违反个人宪法权利的情况下,允准对联邦官员提起诉讼。如果没有同等有效的救济方法可用,立法机关未明确宣布禁止恢复该权利,另外又无特别因素推迟对该权利之维护,即可进行此类诉讼。见Federal Tort Claims Act]

.biz. (商标)国际管理域名的机构所指定的一个顶级域名(a top-level domain name),旨在商业上使用以区别于单独的、个人的或非商业上的使用(见domain name; Internet Corporation for Assigned Names and Numbers)

black a. 1.黑的;黑市的;非法交易的 2.黑人的 3.邪恶的,不吉利的 4.(英)(被罢工工人)抵制装卸的

Black Act (英)《取缔游民条例》

black and white 白纸黑字

black art 妖术;巫术

black book 黑名单

black cap (英)(宣判死刑时法官所戴的)黑色方帽

black coat workers (英)职员阶层

Black Code (美)《黑人法典》;(法)《黑人法令》

black constituents 黑人选民(指可参加选举参议员的选民)

black federal judge (美)联邦黑人法官[指1910年由第27任美国总统塔夫脱任命的哥伦比亚特区市法院的法官罗伯特·H. 特雷尔(Robert H. Terrel);另一位为1967年由第36任美国总统约翰逊任命的联邦最高法院大法官瑟古德·马歇尔(Thurgood Marshall),他们都是最早被任命的联邦黑人法官]

black flag (升在监狱外宣告执行死刑的)黑旗

Black Hand (美)黑手党(20世纪初,纽约的一个由意大利移民组织的诈骗集团);从事诈骗的秘密团体

black ink 顺差,余额

black law 关于黑人的法律

Black Lawyer (美)黑人律师

black letter law (美)黑体字法律(指通常

blockade *de facto* 事实(上的)封锁
blockade runner 封锁破坏者
blockaded a. 被封锁的
blockaded port 被封锁的港口
blockaded state 被封锁的国家
blockader n. 封锁者;执行封锁船
blockaderunner n. 偷越封锁线者(人或船)
blockage n. 封锁(状态),障碍
blocked a. 冻结的;阻塞的;不能兑换的
blocked account 冻结账目
blocked currency 不能兑换外汇的货币,使用范围受限制的货币;冻结货币(亦译作封锁货币)
blocked deposit 冻结存款
blocked fund 冻结资金
blogs (美)法律博客(law blogs),有时亦称"blawgs"[指及时传播新闻和判决意见书(opinion)的主要传媒。法律博客的书面形式关系到广泛的标题范畴,有时还会变成最新信息的主要原始资源。SCOTUSblog 网站(www.scotusblog.com)如同通常具有美国联邦最高法院特大新闻的首先报道者]
blood n. 血;血统;血亲;家族,门第;流血,杀人
blood alcohol content (1926 年)血液中酒精含量[指一个人血液中酒精的集中含量,通常以百分比表示。血液中酒精含量通常根据醉酒驾车法规用来决定一个人是符法定的饮酒量。在美国许多州,血液中酒精浓度在 0.08%即足以构成犯罪,缩写为 BAC。亦称 blood alcohol count; blood alcohol concentration。见 driving under the influence; driving while intoxicated]
blood brother 同胞兄弟
blood border (美)(俗语)血的边沿,血液边界[指邻近州之间不同的最低饮酒年龄(minimum drinking ages)的分界线。这个术语来源于这样的事实,即来自较高的最低年龄(higher minimum age)的州的少年开车到较低的最低年龄(lower minimum age)的州购买并消费含酒精的饮料,同时醉酒开车回家]
blood debt 血债(指使许多人致死的严重犯罪)

blood feud 血亲复仇(早期的一种习惯)
blood groups 血型
blood lineage 血统
blood money apply 偿付受害人家属赎罪金
blood relation(ship) 血缘(亲)关系;血亲(指有血缘关系的亲属)
blood revenge 血仇的报复
blood sample 血样
blood stain 血迹,血痕,血斑
blood stem cells 血干细胞(见 unbilical cord blood stem cells)
blood test 验血
blood ties 血亲关系
blood type 血型
blood-feud n. 械斗(指家族之间的仇杀)
blood-grouping test (1930 年)血型检验[指在父亲与非婚生(子女)发生争议的案件中用此测验来确定该特定人是否为某个孩子的亲生父亲,就是应用遗传标记测试(genetic-marker test)和人体白细胞抗原测试(human-leukocyte antigen test)的样本(examples)。这种测试结果并不能确定某人的父亲身份,但是它可以排除那些不可能是孩子父亲的人。见 paternity test; genetic-marker test; human-leukocyte antigen test]
blood-relative n. 血亲
blood-type verification 血型验定
bloodbath n. 血洗,大屠杀
bloodguilt n. 杀人;杀人罪
bloodguilty a. 杀过人的,犯杀人罪的
bloodhound n. 1.(嗅觉灵敏的)血提犬(警犬的一种)2.侦探;机警又勇猛的追捕者
bloodmoney n. (偿付给被害者家属的)赎罪金;血腥钱(如受雇杀人者所得的钱或损人、害人所获取的利益)
bloodstained a. 犯杀人罪的;沾染着血的
bloodthirstiness n. 杀人狂;残忍嗜杀人;凶恶
Bloody Assizes (英史)血腥审判(指 1685 年蒙茅斯公爵起义失败后,对参加起义者在英格兰西部进行的一次血腥审判)
blot n. 污点;污名;污渍;瑕疵
blot on one's escutcheon 名誉上的污点
blot on title 所有权的缺陷,所有权的瑕疵

blotter n. (记入正式档案前的)临时记录册;(警察分局)被捕人犯记录簿;吸墨纸,吸墨用具

blow up 爆炸

bludgeon n. 棍;棍打(刑)

blue a. 蓝色的;下流的,淫秽的,色情的

blue book 蓝皮书(英美等国政府就某一专题发表的,封皮为蓝色的正式报告书或外交文件);(复)(美)蓝皮书(指有关州立法机构及其成员、职员、委员会或组织的一种指导性资料。通常每一两年出版一次的官方的州手册)

blue box 蓝箱[指 WTO 的一种"蓝箱"规则,即 1995 年乌拉圭回合达成的 WTO《农业协定》,以"政府执行的国内农业政策是否对农业生产和贸易产生扭曲作用"为标准,将成员方现有的各种农业国内支持措施分为"要求削减承诺"与"免于削减承诺"两类。为了认识和理解上的方便,人们习惯用于"绿箱"(green box)、"黄箱"(amber box)与"蓝箱"(blue box)三种交通信号的颜色对其进行形象化的描述与区分。其中,"绿箱"属于免于削减承诺的国内支持措施,如政府一般服务、粮食安全储备补贴、自然灾害救济以及区域援助补贴等。"黄箱"指政府通过货币或特定产品形式给予农产品生产者的直接支持,如价格补贴、营销贷款、按产品种植面积或牲畜数量给予补贴以及种子、肥料、灌溉投入补贴等。"绿箱"是通过政府的服务计划提供,不构成对生产者的直接支付,对生产和贸易没有影响或只有最小扭曲作用,故免于被削减。"黄箱"的支持会刺激农民的生产积极性并降低农产品的生产成本,会给农业生产和贸易带来扭曲作用和影响,故属于被要求削减承诺的范畴。"蓝箱"则指那些本应削减,但因限产而无须削减的直接支付措施。按《农业协定》之界定,这些直接支付包括按固定面积和产量的补贴,按基期生产水平的 85%以下的补贴及按牲畜头数给予的补贴三种(《农业协定》第 6 条第 e 款)]

blue chip 热门股票;信誉可靠的股票

blue collar 蓝领阶级的,工人阶级的

blue collar workers 蓝领工人,体力劳动者

Blue Helmets 蓝色部队

Blue law (美)蓝色法规,清教徒法规,由于书写于蓝纸上,故以"蓝色法规"谓之。美国独立以后,此法规已经被人忘却。到二十世纪初,美国国会颁布禁酒法后,Blue law 又复苏了,有些州不准商店、戏院在星期日开业,此类法规也被称为 Blue law。1980 年代,当时许多法院认为该法规源于宗教而无效,现在如果这种法规是为非宗教目的而制定的,则要经过合宪性的审查。亦称 Sunday law(星期日法),Sunday closing law(星期日歇业法),Sabbath Law(安息日法)或 Lord's Day Act(Sabbath law 主日法)

blue movie 色情电影

blue peter 蓝旗(指船舶离埠时所挂的蓝底白方块旗)

blue print 蓝图

blue ribbon jury (美)蓝绶带陪审团(又译特别陪审团,指在十分重要和复杂的案件中,经任何一方当事人的动议,法庭便可命令组织此陪审团)

blue ribbon law schools (美)国立法学院

Blueprint for a Modernized Financial Regulatory Structure 《现代化金融监管架构蓝图》(简称《架构蓝图》)[指美国财政部在 2008 年 3 月发布的"架构蓝图",该蓝图提出应该建立基于目标监管的"监管构架",将金融消费者保护作为金融监管的三大种类与目标之一。其监管的三大目标为:①市场稳定性监管,用以解决可能影响实体经济的总体金融市场稳定状况的问题;②审慎金融监管,用以解决由于政府担保所导致的市场纪律受限的问题;③商业行为监管(与消费者保护监管相关),用以解决商业行为标准的问题]

blue sky laws (美)蓝天法(各州对投资公司、经营公司的债券买卖进行监督和保护投资者免遭诈欺的《公司证券欺诈防治法》之俗称)

blue-blue-ribbon jury 双蓝带陪审团,最优秀陪审团,精英陪审团(见 blue-ribbon jury)

blue-coat n. 穿蓝制服的人;警察

blue-collarite n. 蓝领工人,体力劳动者
blue-ribbon a. 头等的,第一流的;(陪审团等)特选的
blue-ribbon jury (1940年)蓝带陪审团,特别陪审团[指由具有特别资格且经过选择的人组成的陪审团,他们受过高等教育和特殊训练,该陪审团通常用来审理复杂的民事案件(按当事方的诉讼协议)。有时亦指大陪审团(尤其是指调查政府腐败行为的大陪审团)。蓝带陪审团不得审理刑事案件,因为它违反被告由与其同等地位的人组成的陪审团(jury of peers)审理的权利。一个更为优秀的、技术领域专家组成的陪审员小组被称为 blue-blue-ribbon jury]
blue-sky a. (股票等)不可靠的;财务不健全的
bluff n. 哄骗;吓唬;欺诈
blunt force injury 钝器伤
blunt language 坦率的语言
blurring n. 弱化[指商标淡化表现的两种形式:弱化和丑化;冲淡和污损(tarnishment)]
BNA computer system (美)国家事务管理局计算机系统
board n. (14世纪)1.董事会,委员会(指具有管理、监督或顾问权利的人员组成)〈board of directors〉(董事会), 或(议会法)审议委员会[board 是审议会的一种形式,并区别于委员会(board committee),该委员会通常附属于审议委员会(board)或其他审议会(deliberative assembly),board 具有较大自治和法律权威(autonomy and authority)] 2.在旅馆中供应宾客的餐饮,提供住房、寄存甚至娱乐(room and board)
Board of Admiralty 海事委员会
board of arbitration 仲裁委员会
board of auditors 审计委员会,审计局,审计院
board of child protection 儿童保护委员会
Board of Commissioner of Agriculture and Foresty (美)农林专员委员会
Board of Customs and Excise (英)关税和消费税局
board of directors 董事会,理事会
Board of Equalization 同 Equalization Board
board of governors 校董会;理事会,(大写)(美国律师协会的)董事会
Board of Governors of the State Bar (美)州律师协会主管委员会
Board of Immigration Appeals (美)移民上诉委员会(相当于最高移民上诉法院)
Board of Inland Revenue (英)国内税务局
board of inquiry 调查委员会
Board of Lords Commissioners of Her(或His)Majesty's Treasury (英)皇家财政委员会(英国财务行政的最高组织)
board of managers 理事会;董事会
board of ministers 大臣会议
Board of Patent Appeals (美)专利上诉委员会
Board of Prison Terms (美)假释审查委员会
board of public prosecutions 公诉委员会
board of referees 仲裁委员会
board of reference 咨询委员会
board of review 上诉委员会;审核委员会
board of supervisors 监察委员会;监事会
Board of tax Appeal (美)税务上诉委员会
board of trade (美)商会;(大写)(英)商务部;贸易局
board of trustees 信托委员会;监理委员会
board of visitors (英)(青少年感化院制度中的)视察者委员会(指对青少年感化院进行视察的机构)
board of workers (企业中的)工人委员会
boarding-house n. 供膳寄宿处(与客栈不同,无接待任何人的义务)
bobby-soxer (=bobby-socker) n. 少女,十多岁的女孩
bocland (=bookland) (益格鲁-撒克逊法)典籍(官册)土地保有制(根据特许状、典籍或其他契据享有的一种具有特权的土地保有制形式)
bode v. 预兆,预示
bode well(ill) 主吉(凶)
bodement n. 预兆,凶兆;预言,预示
bodies politic 政治团体

bodily a. 身体的,肉体的
bodily appropriation 全部侵占(指美国将"全部侵占"界定为"复制或擅自使用整个物品的实质部分",采用的标准来平衡反向假冒背后的竞争政策)
bodily harm (16世纪)身体上的伤害,疾病;身体健康的损害
bodily injury (或 **harm**) 人体伤害
bodily maltreatment 人身虐待
bodily pain 体罚
Bodily presence 人身保护状
bodily punishment 体罚,肉刑
body n. 1.人,身体;尸体 2.身份;本体 3.团体,机关 4.主体;本文,正文 5.(一)群,(一)批,(一)堆
body corporate (= corporate body) (美)法人(包括公法人与私法人)
body execution (依法院对未清偿判决金额的民事被告发出拘捕令并实行)对被告拘捕
body guard 警卫员,保镖
body of a claim (美)(专利)申请书的主体,申请书的主文[指专利申请书的一个部分必须明确表示发明的要件和步骤(elements and steps)。申请书的主文必须随着序文和过渡词语。在归扑申请书内容时,其主文要阐明可以取得专利的联合体(patentable combination)的要件或零件。见 preamble]
body of a county (美)作为一个整体的县,全县
(a) **body of case law** 判例法体系
body of civil or criminal law 民法、刑法的体系
body of constitutional law 宪法文本
body of convention 协约文本
body of deed 契据本文(指契据里详细陈述如何履行该契据的部分)
body of economic analyze of law 法律的经济分析体系
body of evidence 一堆证据
body of government 政府机关
body of laws 法的体系(又译法律体系),法规汇编
body of persons 社团;一群人
body of rules 法规体系,规范体系,规则体系
body of sea water 海水水域
body of the crime (或 **offense**) 罪体,犯罪遗体(见 *corpus delicti*)
body persecution 人身迫害;人身虐待
body politic 国家,政治团体(指政府、公民政治集团等)
body snatcher 盗尸人
body-snatching n. 掘尸
bogus a. (美)伪造的,虚假的
bogus certificate 伪造证件
bogus check 伪造的支票,空头支票(同 bad check)
bogus dividend 假红利
bogus government 伪政府
bogus money (= counterfeit notes) 伪币,伪造货币
boiler n. 锅炉
boiling to death (史)煮死刑
bold a. 大胆的,鲁莽的;无耻的;勇敢的;冒失的
bolster v. 支撑,垫
bolter n. (美)拒绝支持自己党派的政策(或提名)的人,退出党派(或团体)的人
bolts (=boltings)(复) n. 案例讨论(指四大律师学院为教学目的组织的案件辩论)
bomb n. 炸弹
bomb hoax 炸弹恐吓(行为)
bon pere de famille 善良管理人,善良家父[指以一个人格化的形象作为参照来评判个案当事人。这在法律实践中具有悠久历史,远在罗马法时代,便存在善良家父标准,未尽到一个善良家父之注意者具有抽象轻过失。在合同和准合同关系中,罗马法可运用善良家父标准来作出判断。契约法中善良家父的谨慎注意,由善意履行、履行能力和胜任程度三个因素构成,违反该谨慎注意标准而构成的过失属于过失过错,不同于契约外过错。英美法系判例法传统中,担当人格化判断标准的是理性人(Reasonable Man),最初被运用于过失侵权领域,以理性人的形象为参照来判断行为人过失之有无,后该标准不断扩张其适用范围,其间因女性主义者质疑其

中的男性色彩而逐渐演变为 Reasonable Person 标准,间或也会根据个案情况使用理性妇女(Reasonable Woman)标准。另有学者针对一些案型提出理性受害人(Reasonable Victim)标准]

bona a. 善良,真诚
bona fide 善意,真诚;信誉;正当[1.诚信(good faith)2.真挚,诚实坦率 3.如果一个人诚实行事,即不知也无理由相信其主张没有根据,一个善意的占有者(bona fide owner)具有一项他认为诚实的完好所有权,当其主张缺乏法律依据时则不存在"善意"]
bona fide approach 善意法(防范滥用税收协定的措施之一)
bona fide claim 善意要求;真诚要求
bona fide defence 正当辩护
bona fide holder 诚实持票人;善意执票人
bona fide intention 善意的意图
bona fide judicia 善意诉讼
bona fide motive 真诚动机;善意动机
bona fide possession (罗马法)善意占有
bona fide possessor (罗马法)善意占有人
bona fide purchaser 善意买主,善意买受人
bona fide residence 具有居住意思的居所,实际上在此生活的家
bona fides 善意;真诚,信誉;正当
* *Bona fides exigit ut quod convenit fiat.* Good faith demands that what is agreed upon shall be done. 信誉要求:达成协议者均应履行。
bona fides third party 善意第三人
bona gestura 善意行为
bona gratia (罗马法)两相情愿,自愿的(自愿离婚或解除婚约的用语)
bona paraphernalia 妻之特有产(指已婚妇女除妆奁以外拥有的财物,如首饰衣着等)
bona vacantia 无人继承的财产;无主物;政府接管物
bona waviata 弃赃(盗贼被追捕时遗弃的东西)
* *Bonae fidei non congruit de apicibus juris disputare.* It is incompatible with good faith to insist on the extreme subtleties of the law. 太强调法律的细枝末节则不利于诚信。强调法律的细节不利于诚信。
* *Bonae fidei possessor in id tantum quod sese pervenerit tenetur.* A possessor in good faith is liable only for that which he himself has obtained (or that which has come to him). 善意财产占有人只对本人业已获得(或到手)的财产承担责任。
bond n./v. 1.合同(契约);合同(契约)所规定的义务 2.同盟;盟约 3.公债,债券,证券 4.(付款)保证书;保证人;保证金;保单 5.保税仓库(旧译关栈)保存 6.(复)镣、铐;监禁,约束/作保释人,提供保释人;抵押;把(进口货物)存入保税仓库;使成为用债券保证的债
bond and disposition in security (苏格兰)债券与土地担保处分书
bond by writing under seal 书面并加盖印章的契据
bond certificate 债券
bond creditor 契据债权人,证券债权人
bond dividends 债券股利,公司债股利
bond for cash credit 现金信贷债券
bond indentures 债券信托合同(契约)
bond instrument 债券契据
bond interest 债券利息
bond investment 债券投资
bond notes 债券式票据;保税仓库证明书
bond of bottomry 押船借贷合同(契约)的担保
bond of respondentia 船货抵押借款的担保
bond premium 债券溢价
bond servant 被奴役的人,奴隶
bond service 奴役
bond-coupons n. 债券息票
bondage n. 束缚;监禁;奴役
bondage to creditor 债役(指因欠债而为债主服劳役)
bonded a. 保税的;有担保的;受债券保证的
bonded debts 债券债务;公债借款
bonded goods 保税货物;保税仓库货物
bonded price 保税价格

bonded rationality 有限理性论(指那种把决策者在认识方面的局限性考虑在内的合理选择——包括知识和计算能力两方面的局限性)
bonded warehouse 保税仓库(旧译关栈)
bondholder n. 公债券持有人,债券持有人
bonding 结合,黏合
bonding company 保税公司,担保公司
bonding insurance 保税保险,保税仓库保险
bonds authorized 额定公债,法定公债
bondsman n. 受合同(契约)约束的人,保证人,担保人;奴隶
bondswoman n. 女奴隶,女农奴;女保证人
bone of contention 争端的原因;争点
Bonham's case(1610) (英)博纳姆案(指由柯克报道的一个判例。其表明应坚持英格兰普通法的至高无上性,并有权控制违反公共利益和理性的议会之法案,同时亦可判议会法案无效。但这一原则,后来并未获得确认,反而长期确定了制定法优于普通法的至高无上原则)
* **Boni judicis est ampliare jurisdictionem.** It is the part of a good judge to enlarge (or use liberally) his remedial authority or jurisdiction. 扩大(或自由行使)自己的司法救济权或审判权是每一个好法官的本分。
* **Boni judicis est ampliare justitiam.** It is the duty of a good judge to make precedents which amplify justice. 作出表明公正审判的判例是每一个好法官的职责。
* **Boni judicis est judicium sine dilatione mandare executioni.** It is the duty of a good judge to issue judg(e)ments without delay. 及时作出判决是每一个好法官的职责。
bonis cedere 移转财产(指债务人将财产转移给债权人以抵偿债务)
bonitary a. 无所有权而有使用权的
bonorum cessio 财产转让
bonorum emptio 见 bonorum venditio
bonorum emptor (罗马法)财产买受人[指在财产拍卖中买下破产债务人全部财产的人。按裁判官法,他接替了债务人的法律地位,一方面成为债务人全部财产的权利人,另一方面他接受了债务人的全部债务;按诉讼中的裁决程式(condemnatio),财产买受人代替债务人接受清偿债务的判决,因此财产买受人对债务人财产的概括继承被看作依据裁判官法进行生者间继承。见 successio tra vivi]
bonorum possessio 物品占有,财产占有(权)
bonorum separatio 财产分离权
bonorum venditio (罗马法)拍卖财产(指为了清偿债务,以强制执行方式变卖债务人的财产,将资不抵债的债务人财产卖出以充分满足债权人要求的行为。同 bonorum emptio)
bonorum distractio (罗马法)财产零卖制 [由奥古斯都时期一项元老院决议(senatus-consultum de distractio bonorum)确定。它不要求拍卖涉案人的全部财产,而只拍卖其中可满足债权的一部分。这样,债务人的总体财产没有丧失,人格得以保留。财产零卖制意味一项特权,适用于元老阶级成员和未成年人,尊者和未成年人从而得到保护]
* **Bonum defendentis ex integra causa; malum ex quolibet defectu.** The success of a defendant depends on a perfect case; his loss arises from some defect. 被告的胜诉有赖于无懈可击的证据和争辩,某些缺陷往往会使其败诉。
* **Bonum necessarium extra terminos necessitatis non est bonum.** A good thing required by necessity is not good beyond the limits of such necessity. 按需要来说是好的东西,若超过这种需要的限度那未必就是好的。(基于需要而有效的,若超过需要的限度则未必有效。)
bonum publicum 公益
bonus n. 红利;奖金;花红;额外津贴
bonus and welfare fund 奖励及福利基金
bonus dividend 红利股,赢利股
bonus pater families (罗马法)善良家父;善良家父义务
bonus scheme 奖金制度
bonus share (或 **stock**) 红利股,赢利股
bonus system 分红制;奖金制度

bonus-penalty contract 奖惩合同(契约)
boodle n. 1.伪钞;贿赂品,赃物;不法利益 2.一堆;一群;一伙;一捆
boodler n. (美)(政治上)受贿者
book n. 书籍;支票(簿);账簿;登记册(簿);卷,篇
book account 往来账户(指无书面证据的交易事项的明细账簿)
book balance 账面余额
book cases 判例汇辑;判例汇编
book debt 账面负债
book hand 抄录手稿体
book loss 账面损失
Book of Assizes (=Liber Assisarum) (英)《判例大全》(指 1516 年起刊印的包括 1327—1377 年期间一些王座法庭和大法官法庭审理的案件的年鉴本)
book of births 出生登记簿
book of causes 诉讼登记本;被告出庭备忘录
book of criminal laws 刑法典
Book of Entries (英)《判例选编》(中世纪后期用拉丁文编成的一些判例集);《枢密院议事录》(亨利七世的枢密院法律事务工作的登记簿)
Book of the Consulate of the Sea (或 *Consolato del Mare*)《地中海海事法典》(亦译作《地中海领事全书》,1494 年出版的一部著名的有关地中海上惯例和法令的汇编)
Book of the Council (英格兰)《枢密院录》(从 1421—1435 年起,经 1540 年迄今)
Book of the Covenant (=Covenant Code)《圣约册》(根据圣经《出埃及记》中的有关记载所编成的一部古代法律汇编)
book rate 账面折合率,账面利率
book surplus 账面盈余
book value 账面价值
book value and intrinsic value 账面价值与固有价值(账面价值要算上公司现有全部资产,而净面价值要扣除负债;固有价值指某公司购买公司时愿支付的价值。此价值往往大于账面价值)
bookable a. (英)可预购的,可预约的

bookclub n. 图书合作社;读书俱乐部
booking n. 1.订票,售票;订舱;(演讲,演出等)预约;记账 2.核查(将被逮捕人员送至警察分局之后对其应采取的措施,涉及查对警察逮捕人员记录簿上的一些事实情况,如指纹等)
booking agent (代订机票、戏票等的)代订人;(演员等的)经纪人
booking container summary (集装箱)订舱汇总清单
booking list 订舱清单,货物订舱表
booking note 货物订舱单
booking office 订舱处;售票处
booking period 订载期限
bookkeeper n. 簿记员,记账人
bookkeeping n. 簿记
bookkeeping evidence 记账凭证
booklets popularizing of the law 普法读物
bookmaker n. 以赌为业者;博彩经纪;编书谋利者
bookmaking n. 博彩(赛马等赌博的)登记簿;编书,著作
books of account 账簿
books of authority 法学经典,法学权威著作
books of forms and precedents 有关契据格式和令状程式的书籍(提供各类契据和令状格式的书籍,专供起草法律契据时作为依据)
books registration 书刊登记,书报注册
books registration certificate 书刊登记证
boom v./n. 突然增加,迅速发展,兴旺;出名;支持,吹捧/景气,繁荣,激increment,(政治形势)突然好转
boon n. 恩惠;福利;裨益;方便
boon-day n. (领主要求佃户提供的)劳务日
boost v./n. 1.升,提,推 2.提高,促进,支持〈to boost your confidence〉(提高你的信心) 3.(用广告等)吹捧 4. 升压,助爆/1.升,提高;增加 2.帮助 3.宣传,吹捧
boot n. 1.(税务)应税差额[指在其他的一项免税交易(tax-free exchange)中补充的款项或财产主体税(property subject to tax)] 2.(公司,企业法)附加利益,附属财

产(指在公司重组时,从被控制公司取得的证券和股票之外所接收的任何财产)3.(商法)补价,补贴差额(指为平衡一项其他非公平交易所使用的对价或现金,如以价值500美元的机器与价值1000美元的机器交换,需进行500美元补贴)4.(古)采木权(estovers)5.(古英格兰)补偿;允准伐木 6.筒状刑具(夹足,腿用)

(the) boot is on other leg 1.事实正与此相反(原意:这个靴子应是另一只脚的)2.应由其他方面负责

boot-legging n. 走私漏税;违禁卖酒

booth n. 1.(选举的临时)投票站(同 voting booth 或 polling booth)2.电话亭;岗亭 3.(带篷)货摊

bootleg v./a. 违法制造;偷运贩卖(私酒等)/违法制造的,偷运的,违法的,秘密的

bootless a. 无益的,无用的

bootless crimes 不能以金钱抵偿的犯罪(指早期日耳曼社会中只能由国家惩罚的犯罪)

booty n. 赃物;劫掠物;战利品

booty of war 战利品

border n. 边界,边境;国界,国境,边境地区,边沿

border check point (或 **border checkpoint**) 边卡;边防检查站

border clash 边境冲突

border crossing agreement 边境通过协定

border crossing card 边境证

border defense authority 边防机关

border demarcation commission 划(分)边界委员会

border dispute 边界争端

border incidents 边界事件

border land 边疆,分界线,国界

border line 边界线

border region 边境地区

border tax 国境税,边境税

border tax adjustment 边境税的调整

border trade agreement 边界贸易协定

border warrant 边境搜捕令

border-guard forces 边防军

borderguard n. 边防战士,边防警卫

borderline personality disorder 边缘型人格障碍(人格障碍类型中的一种,在我国精神疾病分类标准中不存在。美国等英美法系有此类型,其特征有四个核心要素:1.建立稳定的自我形象困难 2.缺乏信任,依赖他人的同时又怀疑别人,总觉得他人会抛弃自己而成为他人的受害者 3.冲动和自我的破坏行为,且难于预测,如吸毒,乱开车,乱拉男女关系,以自杀威胁等 4.难于控制愤怒和其他情绪。见 paranoid personality disorder)

born a. 出生于……的,天生的,生来的

born during coverture 在父母结婚后出生的

born in (lawful) wedlock 婚生的

born out of wedlock 非婚生的

borne out by ironclad evidence 铁证如山

borough n. 1.(英)(享有特权的)自治(城)市;有议员选举权的(城)市 2.(美)纽约市行政区;自治村镇

borough council 自治市议会

borough court 自治市法院

borough policemen (英)区警;自治市警察

borough sessions (英)自治市法院开庭期

borough-English n. (英)幼子继承制(亦译作英区继承制,指英格兰普通法上全部不动产由幼子继承的制度,1925年的《土地经营法》将其废止)

borrow n./v. 借,借用(东西);担保物;抵押;十家互保制/借入;借用

borrow trouble 自找麻烦

borrowed capital 借入资本

borrower n. 借款人,借用人;剽窃者

borrowing of securities 担保品的借用

borrowing plan 贷款计划

borrowing venture 借款企业

Borstal (英)青少年感化院,教养院

Borstal boy 在感化院受感化的少年

Borstal institution (英)少年拘留感化院(16岁以上至21岁以下少年犯被拘留的地方,拘留期间,犯人要接受训练和改造);青少年(罪犯)管教所;青少年犯感化制度

Borstal system (英)博斯托尔青少年感化制度(始于1902年,旨在将未成年犯同成

年罪犯隔离开来,实行惩罚与矫正相结合,并进行职业训练的一种制度。见 Borstal institution)
Borstal training 青少年犯感化训练
Borstal treatment 青少年犯感化教育
boss n. 老板,党魁,(政治机构中的)首领,上司,头子;领班,工头
Boston Massacre 波士顿屠杀案(1770年3月5日波士顿人民与英军发生冲突,用雪球投掷英国士兵泄愤,英军向群众开枪,造成血案)
bote (=bot) n. (古英国法)赔偿,补偿
both pron. 两者;两人,双方
both litigants jointly 诉讼双方当事人,两造当事人
both parties 双方当事人,两造
both parties in a lawsuit 诉案中的双方当事人
both religious and temporal power 僧俗的双重统治权
both to blame collision clause 双方有责的碰撞条款
bottle club (不受法律管束的)饮酒俱乐部
bottle-neck n. (交通易堵塞的)狭窄地带(港译:樽颈地带),隧道;妨碍生产流程的一环
bottom price 最低价,最低限价;底价
bottom relief map 海底地形图
bottom-to-top 上下贯通(指新法律现实主义中深入理解法律过程 Legal process 中的一个用词)
bottomry n. 押船借贷合同(契约)(亦称冒险借贷,指船主或其代理人向他人借款,而用船舶作抵押的一种合同。借款的目的是使船舶能继续航行。如该船舶失去,借款也就跟着失去,借款人不得追讨,如船舶平安回来,借款人则可收回借款的优厚的利息)
bottomry and respondentia bonds 海损规则
bottomry bond 押船借贷合同(契约)(见 bottomry)
bottomry bond holder 船舶抵押合同(契约)持有人
bottomry bonds and respondential loans 船舶与船上货物抵押借款

bought and sold notes 代买代卖账单
Boule n. (现代希腊)议会,下议院;(大写)(古希腊)五百人会议(立法会议)
bounced check (被拒付而退还给开票人的)支票(见 bad check)
bound 1.bind 的过去式和过去分词 2.被约束的 3.密切关联的⟨be bound up with⟩与……有密切关系 4.一定的、必定的⟨just wars are bound to triumph over wars of aggression⟩(正义的战争必将战胜侵略战争),⟨I will be bound⟩(我敢肯定)5.装订的,合订的⟨a bound volume of law review⟩(合订本的法律评论)6.be bound up in 热心于,忙于
bound a./n. 负有责任的,有义务的;(道德上,法律上)受约束的,有约束的;一定的,必定的/范围,边界,界限
bound by law 受法律约束
bound by precedent 受先例约束
bound labo(u)r 合同(契约)工
bound volume 合订本⟨the book cover of a bound volume⟩(合订本的封面)
boundary n. 疆界,边界;分界线
boundary commission 边界委员会
boundary delimitation commission 边境划界委员会
boundary dispute 边界争端
boundary line 疆界线,边界线
boundary of state territory 国家领土的疆界
boundary pillar 界桩,界标
boundary river 疆界河流,边界河流
boundary tablet 界碑
boundary treaty 边界条约
boundary water 边界水域
boundary water course 界河水道
boundary-line n. 边界线
bounded rationality 束缚的合理性
bounded system 有界限的系统
boundedness n. 界限性
bounden a. 有责任的,必须负担的
bounden and solemn duty 必须承担的唯一责任;受法律约束的唯一责任
bounty n. 奖金;补助金;赠物,赠礼;恩惠;救济金,基金会

Bounty Hunter 奖金猎手(指鼓励律师主动对他认为有利可图的欺诈行为提起诉讼,而不是被动等待受害投资者"登门造访",律师即成为"奖金猎手")
bounty system 津贴制度
bouquet of arrangement(或 **treaties**) 一揽子合同(契约)
bourgeois n./a. (中世纪城镇dm)自由民;店主;商人;资产阶级分子;具有资产阶级观点的人/资产阶级的;中产阶级的
bourgeois democracy 资产阶级民主
bourgeois dictatorship 资产阶级专政
bourgeois jurisprudence 资产阶级法学
bourgeois jurist 资产阶级法学家
bourgeois law 资产阶级法律
bourgeois liberalization 资产阶级自由化
bourgeois right 资产阶级权利
bourgeoisie n. 资产阶级;中产阶级
bourse n. 交易所,证券交易所
bout n. 一回,一场,一阵;一个来回
bout of sentencing 审判时期
boutique law firms 作坊式律师事务所
bowdy house 见 disorderly house
bowing to the inevitable 迫于形势
box n./v. 1.法庭专席,陪审席;证人席 2.票房 3.箱,保险箱/1.拳击 2.装于箱中
box top license 盒顶许可证(美国等发达国家销售软件包时附在商品中的一种合同,与 tear open license 启封许可证同)
boxed in a paradox 处于自相矛盾的境地
boxed passage 专题文章段
boy n. 男孩;少年;儿子;练习生;男仆,服务员,勤杂工
Boycott 杯葛,联合抵制,抵制[1880年爱尔兰佃户为反对英国地主代理人杯葛(音译)Charles Cunringham Boycott,1832-1897)的虐待,同他断绝关系。以后成为政治和斗争的一种形式,即个人、团体或国家断绝全部或部分关系]
boycott plea 联合抵制诉辩(旧译:杯葛诉辩)
boycotting n. 结伙妨碍他人行动(罪)
Boyd-Weeks 博伊德-威克斯证据排除规则(指非法证据排除规则最早可追溯到美国1886年的 Boyd v. United States 判例。

此案只涉及关税案件,涉及刑事诉讼方面的相关判例是1914年的 Weeks v. United States 案。因此,非法证据排除规则就被称为 Boyd-Weeks 规则)
bracery n. (历史上)防止冒称有权利[指以冒称具有权利或土地所有权而进行买卖的犯罪行为。这种行为在英王亨利八世第32个执政年第9个制定法第2节贿赂陪审员行为(32)(Hen. 8. ch 9. 2. Embracery)中被宣布为非法行为]
Brachylogus 《市民法大纲》
Brachylogus Juris Civilis(或 **Summa Novellarum**,或 **Corpus, Legum**) 《市民法大纲》(12世纪初出现于法国的一部罗马法教学的学术指南)
bracket n. (金额收入的)等级;税收率(见 tax rate)
bracket creep 税收率晋升(指通货膨胀或增加收入的过程推进个人进入较高税率等级)
bracketed pointers 括号内的指示标记
Brady Act (美)《布雷迪法》[指建立全国体系的一个联邦法规,以便尽快核查未来的或预期的手枪买卖者的背景。该法的正式名称是《布雷迪手枪暴力预防法》(The Brady Handgun Violence Prevention Act)。美国联邦最高法院认定该法违宪;该法内条文规定要求首席州执法官员(chief state law-enforcement officers),通常为司法行政官(vsu. sheriffs),进行背景审核(background checks),甚至全国体系相应进行。该法因詹姆斯·布雷迪(James Brady)而命名,他是总统罗纳德·里根的参谋人员之一。在1981年一次试图谋杀总统事件中受到枪伤(《美国注释法典》第18标题卷第921—930节)(18 USCA §§921-930)。(非正式)亦称 Brady Bill)
Brady bill 见 Brady Act
Brady material (1972年)(刑诉)布雷迪证据(资料)[指有利于刑事被告的案件信息或证据,检控方(prosecution)有义务或责任披露(disclose)。检控方对这类信息的拒绝(withholding)违反刑事被告的正当程序权利(due process rights)。布雷迪诉马里兰州案(Brady v. Manyland),参见

《美国联邦最高法院判例汇编》第 33 卷第 83 页。见 exculpatory evidence; Jencks material]
brain n. 脑;(复)脑力,智能,智囊
brain child 脑力劳动产物
brain drain 智能(囊)流失;人才流失
brain fingerprinting (或称 **lie detection technique**) 测谎技术
brain trust (美)智囊团,专家顾问团
brain truster 智囊团成员,参谋
brainman n. 谋士,参谋
branch n. 分行;分庭;分支机构;部门
branch courts (法院的)分院;分庭
branch division 分庭;分部
branch division of a court 法院的分庭
branch division of district courts 地方法院分庭
branch of insurance 保险类别
branch of legislature 立法机构
branch of civil service 文职机构
branch of economy 经济部门
branch of law 法律部门
branch-office n. 分支机构;分局;分店
brand n. 1.商标(图记),牌子,所有权标记 2.(古时烙在犯人身上的)印记,犯罪(或耻辱的)标记
brand name 商标名称
brand name capital 商标名称资金
brand of Cain 杀人罪(见 Cain)
brand reputation 商标信誉
Brandeis Brief (美)布兰代斯辩护状[大法官布兰代斯·路易斯·登比兹(Brandeis Louis Dembitz)当律师时,在穆勒诉俄勒冈州(Muller v. Oregon)案中为俄州妇女10小时工作规定写的辩护状中,支持俄勒冈州限制妇女每日工作时间的法规合宪性,110页的辩护中提供大量证据说明妇女过度劳动对健康、安全、道德和福利的有害影响。见 brief]
branding n. 烙印(寺院法上的一种刑罚)也指古希腊人和罗马人在奴隶身上所烙上的烙印,以防止逃亡)
branks (=scoiding bridle)(复)n. 口钳(以前不列颠用于惩罚爱骂人的妇女的一种刑具)

brawler n. 争吵者;喧闹者
brawling n. 吵架,喧闹;(英)(寺院法)(在祭献神圣场所的)吵闹罪
BrE (Britain English) 英国英语
breach n./v. 破坏,违反,侵害,不履行,违犯[该词根据上下文而有不同含义,可指违反法律、侵害他人权利,不履行个人义务和职责,现多指合同一方当事人未履行合同条款、允诺、条件等。即为违约(breach of contract)、缺口、破裂、不和/破坏、违反、不履行;突破,使有缺口,攻破]
breach as to an instal(l)ment delivery or payment 违反分批交货(或分期付款)的义务
breach before performance in due (合同履行期)到期前违约
breach of agreement 违反协定,违反协议
breach of arrest 越押罪,脱逃罪
breach of arrestment (苏格兰法)擅自处理已查封的财产
breach of bail 破坏保释;弃保逃跑
breach of blockade 破坏封锁
breach of close 侵入私有地,非法侵入(他人)地界
breach of condition 违反(合同)要件
breach of contract (17世纪)违约,违反合同[指通过拒绝履行合同(repudiating)或干扰阻碍一方当事人的履行,不履行个人的承诺而违反合同义务。"这种违约可以采取不曾履行、拒绝履行或两者都有,但每种违约行为都会导致损害赔偿的权利主张,还会造成其他救济(remedies)。即便受损害方未蒙受特有的损失(peculiary loss)或不可能以足够的确定性(certainty)来表明这种损失,但他至少具有权利主张名义上的损害赔偿(nominal damages)。如果法院选择不顾这一微不足道的越轨诉讼行为(trifling departure),结果就不存在违约或权利主张的问题了。"]
breach of constitution 违宪
breach of contract 违约,违反合同(契约)
breach of deportation order 违背递解令
breach of discipline 破坏纪律;违反军纪
breach of duty 失职;不负责任;不履行义务

breach of engagement   违约,毁约
breach of faith   失信;出卖行为
breach of international law   违反国际法
breach of law   违法,不法行为
breach of morality   破坏道德,伤风败俗
breach of parole   违背誓言
breach of police regulations 违反警规
breach of prison   越狱(罪)
breach of privilege   侵犯特权
breach of promise   违约;违背允诺;违背婚约;食言
breach of recognizance   违背具结或保证
breach of regulations   违例,违章
breach of statutory duty   违反法定职责(义务)
breach of the peace   扰乱治安,破坏安宁(社会秩序)
breach of trading warranty   违反贸易保证
breach of trust   违反信托义务;违背诚实信用,背信
breach of warranty   违反担保义务
breach-of-promise suit   毁约诉讼,赖婚诉讼
breacher n.   违约人,违约方
bread n./v.   品种,种类;近亲结婚(bread in and in)/生产,孕育;繁殖,滋生;产生
breadth of territorial sea   领海宽度
break v.   1.违背,违犯;未遵守 2.打破,越出,毁坏 3.使中断;停止 4. 降职,降级;免职 5.破案,破获 6.闯入(房屋);证明(辩解的)虚假 7.使破产;使(证券等)的价格急剧下降 8.决裂,放弃(习惯)9.通过法律手续使(遗嘱)失效
break a case   破案
break a marriage   离婚;婚姻破裂
break a promise   违反诺言,负约
break a will   取消(或废除)一个遗嘱
break bulk   开舱起货;整批货物拆卸
break down the old loyal codes   破除旧法规
break in   1.训练,使训练〈break a horse in〉(训练一匹马)2.使新物件逐渐合用〈break in a new pair of shoes〉(使一双新鞋合脚)3.破门而入;闯入 4. 打断〈when the professor is telling the story, don't break in〉(教授正讲故事时,不要打断他)5.开始工作〈he broke in with us last year〉(他去年开始与我们一起工作)
break into   破门而入
break off   停止,折断,断绝
break one's oath   (或 oath-breaking)   违背誓言
break prohibition   违禁
break the chain of causation   因果关系中断
break the law   犯法;违反,违章
break up n.   分裂,解体,崩溃,停止,完结
break with   与……绝交;破除,结束,革除
break with a bad habit   去掉坏习惯
break-bulk container ship   杂货集装箱船
break-bulk form   杂货形式
break-promiser n.   违约者,食言者;不守信用的人
break-up value   破产者财产的清理价值
breakage n.   1.破损,毁损 2.破损险 3.(复)损耗赔款,损耗量
breakdown n.   1.损坏;故障;倒塌 2.分析;分类;分类明细账
breakdown clause   机器故障条款
breakdown of a family   家庭破裂,家庭崩溃
breakdown of a marriage   婚姻破裂
breakdown of the negotiation   谈判破裂
breaking n.   掠取、掠夺(指用暴力或某种不正当手段或破坏手段来取得财产)
breaking a case   分析案情(判决前法官之间对案内疑点予以澄清或对承审案件交换意见)
breaking a promise   违反诺言
breaking and entering   见 burglary 2
breaking bulk   (英)(普通法上的)整批货物拆卸(须以非法侵占货物的裁定为前提)
breaking into   破门而入
breaking point   临界点
breaking the law   违法
breakout n.   强行越狱
breakout of prison   越狱
breakthrough innovations   突破性创新
breath test   呼吸测试

breathalyzer (=breathalyser) n. 呼吸分析仪(用来测量驾驶员的呼吸从而确定其酒精含量的仪器)
breathing space 休息机会,考虑时间,喘气机会
bredwite n. (历史上)(英格兰古法)因面包不够分量而作的惩罚
breed n. 品种,种类
breed in and in 同种繁殖,近亲结婚生育
Brehon Law(s) (历史上)布莱恩法(指亨利二世征服爱尔兰时期的古代法律制度。此法律体制于1366年被正式废弃。有时可拼写为 Brehon Law)
brethren (=brothers) (复) n. 同行业(教会、社团)的人
breve n. 令状,(教皇)谕示;特许状
breve de recto 收回(土地实际占有或土地占有的)权利令状(被逐出者可凭此提起恢复产权之诉)
* *Breve ita dicitur, quia rem de qua agitur, et intentionem petentis, paucis verbis breviter enarrat.* A writ is so called because it briefly states, in few words, the matter in dispute, and the object of the party seeking relief. 所谓令状就是因为它用少量文字简要说明争讼事项和当事人寻求法律救济的标的。
* *Breve judiciale debet sequi suum originale, et accessorium suum principale.* A judicial writ ought to follow its original, and an accessory its principal. 法院令状应依据其原件,而附件应依据其主件。
* *Breve judiciale non cadit pro defectu formae.* A judicial writ fails not through defect of form. 法院令状不因格式上的缺陷而失去效力。
brevet d'introduction 专利权;引进专利
brevia magistralia 权威特许令状(处置紧急状况的一种令状)
Brevia Placitata (英)《诉状格式简编》(大约于1260年用法律语言写成的包括各种诉状格式和诉状上的注释和判例的著作)
breviary n. 1.摘要;缩略 2.(天主教)每日祈祷书
breviate n. 摘记,节略;法案提要;法案备忘录
brib(e)able a. 可收买的,可贿赂的
bribability n. 受贿的可能性;被收买的可能性
bribe n./v. 贿赂;贿赂物,诱饵/行贿,收买
bribee n. 受贿者
briber n. 行贿者
bribery n. 行贿,受贿,贿赂,利诱
bribery and corruption 贪污受贿
bribery at election 选举中(对选民)的行贿(罪)
bribery crime 贿赂罪
bribery fund 贿赂金
bribery-pander n. 串通贿赂
bribing witness 贿赂证人(罪)
BRICs 巴俄印中四国(崛起) [这是美国高盛集团经济学家吉姆·奥尼尔报告中首次提出的概念(即巴西、俄罗斯、印度、中国四国英文简称),他预测在40年左右时间内,这四国经济总量将超过目前的G6(G7除去加拿大),全球经济重心将向这些国家转移,并将对整个世界经济政治格局产生深远影响]
bridal n. 婚宴;结婚仪式
bride-price (=bride-wealth) n. (婚前男方给女方的)聘金,聘礼
bridewell n. 感化院;拘留所;(泛指)监狱,监牢
bridgebuilder n. 斡旋者,调解人
bridging loan 临时贷款
brief n./v./a. 摘要,训令;(律师)辩护状;答辩摘要,诉讼要点(指在上诉程序中一方当事人提出的对事实背景和法律争点的书面陈述。要求清楚、诚实、均衡、论据有力、有说服力的陈述,律师主要通过书面诉讼要点来说服上诉审法院);案情摘要;(英)(向辩护律师所作的)指示要点/摘要,(律师或法院)提供案情摘要;委托辩护;聘请(律师)/短暂的,简洁的
brief a barrister 聘请出庭律师
brief facts 案情概要
brief of service 简历
brief of title 所有权证摘要
brief on appeal 上诉摘要(见 proposition of law)

brief tenure 短暂的任职
brief-bag n. 律师文件包
briefing n. 简报,简令;情况的简要介绍(汇报);介绍情况会,汇报会
briefing and debriefing 介绍情况与听取汇报
briefing attorney 专项代理人,专项律师[指①只专门书写简要诉状,特别上诉的要点上诉状(appellate brief)和法律备忘录(legal memoranda)的代替人或律师;②法官助理(指帮助法官在研究、书写及案件管理等方面工作的人,亦称 brief attorney; staff attorney; research attorney)]
briefless a. (律师)无人委聘的;没生意的
briefless lawyer 生意冷淡的律师
brieves (复) n. (英)简令(中世纪由大法官法庭直接向司法行政官、法官或其他人发布的令状)
brigade n. 团体;队;(中)生产大队
brigand n. 绑匪;土匪,强盗
brigandism n. 掠夺;土匪行为
bright line rule 明线规则;判决的法定规则
bright-line rule 明确的法规
Brighton Co-operator Association 布莱顿合作社("合作社之父"英国人威廉·金于1827年创办的合作社)
bring v. 1.产生,引起,导致 2.提出(论据等),提起(诉讼);(货物)卖得(多少钱) 3.使处于某种状态,促使 4. 带来,拿来
bring (或 **lay**, 或 **proffer**) **an indictment** 提起控诉,提起公诉
bring a case before (或 **to**) **the court** 将案件提交法院审理,起诉;告状
bring a case to book 破案
bring a charge against sb. 控告某人;指控某人
bring a dispute before a court 把(案件)争讼提交法院
bring a fraud home to sb. 确实证明某人犯诈骗罪
bring a pressure to bear on (或 **upon**) 对……施加压力
bring a suit against sb. 控告某人
bring about 带来,造成;使船掉头

bring an action against sb. 对某人起诉,对某人提起控诉
bring forth an amendment 提出修正(案)
bring home to sb. 使人深切地感到或清楚地认识到;确实证明(罪行)为某人所犯
bring impeachment proceedings against Federalist judge 对联邦党法官提起弹劾诉讼程序
bring in a finding for (或 **against**) **sb.** 作出对某人有利(或不利)的裁决
bring in a finding of non liquet (法院)作出拒绝受理的裁决
bring in a verdict (of guilty) (陪审团)作出裁决宣判(有罪)
bring in an accusation against (sb.) 告发(某人);对(某人)起诉
bring into force 实施(法律等);使生效
bring into hotchpot(ch) 将财产混同起来
bring out 使显出,使明白表示出来;摆出(事实);出版,生产;使初次参加社交;说出,表达出
bring out the facts and reasons things out 摆事实,讲道理;出版,产生;说出
bring sb. before the court 提审某人
bring sb. in guilty 宣判某人有罪
bring sb. to book 要求某人解释自己的行为;谴责某人
bring sb. to justice 将某人捉拿归案,将某人绳之以法
bring sb. to light 揭发某人
bring sb. to trial 审问(或审讯)某人
bring suit (或 **action**) 开始诉讼,起诉
bring suit challenging the ordinance 提起反对法令的诉讼
bring the measure into compliance 使该项措施符合……
bring under subjection 使屈从于,使隶属于
bring up 教育,培养;使成长;提出(问题供讨论或考虑);使车辆(船舶等)突然停下;(船舶等)到终点;把(某人)带上法庭,并对他进行控告
bring up for trial 使经过审讯
bring up sb. before the court 传某人出庭
bringing of successive actions 连续起诉
bringing-up n. (儿童的)养育,抚养;教养

brings federal and state law claims 提起联邦和州法上的诉讼请求
brinkmanship n. 外交冒险政策,(战争)边缘政策
brink-of-war policy 战争边缘政策
British a. 不列颠的,英国的,英国人的
British civil police 英国民事警察
British Commonwealth (of Nations) 英联邦(由英国和已经独立的前英国殖民地或附属国组成的联合体,原称"英帝国"或"不列颠帝国",第一次世界大战后根据1931年《威斯敏斯特法》改用现名)
British Copyright Council 英国版权委员会(一个向英国版权人提供法律咨询、样本合同和协助版权人维护版权的民间机构)
British Crown Colony 英国直辖殖民地
British Crown Proceedings Act (英)《政府诉讼法》(1947年)
British Digest of International Law 《英国国际法判决摘要汇编》
British nationality 英国国籍
British parliamentary model 英国议会模式
British preferential tariff 英国特惠关税
British protectorate 英国保护的领地
British subject 英籍人(又译英国臣民,按《英国国籍法》规定,具备下列任何一项条件者,均可获得英籍人的公民身份:①出生于英国境内者;②有英籍人的血统者;③登记入籍;④归化入籍;⑤领土归并)
broad a. 宽阔的,广大的,辽阔的;广泛的,非限制的,明显的,主要的
broad arrow (英)(政府财产及囚犯制服上的)镞形记号(宽箭头的箭)
broad latitude 广泛的自由(指言论、行为等)
broad ocean 外洋,公海
broad powers 广泛的权力
broad reach of state judicial power 州司法权的广泛范围
broad reading of the clause 对条款的广义解释
broad restrictions 主要的限制
broad seal 国玺,中央政府的印章
broad spectrum of interests 广泛的利益范畴
broad understanding 广泛的理解,广泛的定义
Broadcast Receiving License 收听、收看广播电视节目许可证(在一些发达国家,收听收看广播电视节目需向政府缴纳一定的收看费用,才可取得许可证;否则,一经发现将处以罚款)
broadcasting n. 广播;播音
broadcasting corporation act 广播公司法
Broadly ad. 广义地说
brocage (=brokage) n. 经纪业;经纪费,佣金
brocard n. (古英国法)法律格言,法律原理
Brocardica Juris 《法律格言》(1805年巴黎出版)
broke a. 破产的
brokee n. (美)破产者
broken a. 破碎的;零碎的;被破坏的
broken and damaged cargo list 货物残损单
broken belt 冰带(海水与冰的过渡带)
broken home 破裂的家庭
broken lot 散批货物;零星股份
broken promises 失信
broken space (=broken stowage) 空舱位;亏舱位
"Broken Windows" theory "破窗"理论(指1982年3月,威尔逊和凯林在美国《大西洋月刊》发表《破窗——警察与邻居安全》一文。以"破窗"为喻,形象说明无序的环境与某些犯罪之间的关系,其理论核心即某些犯罪与具有诱发性的外部环境有相关性),犯罪的"破窗理论"(指不符合道德规范的行为,轻微犯罪与重大犯罪一样都会造成社会大众对受到犯罪侵害的恐惧感)
broker n. 经纪人,中间人,掮客;代理人;(英)对债务人财产的估价(或出售)人;(英)旧货商
broker market 经纪人市场
broker's cover note 保险经纪人暂保单
broker-agent n. 经纪人兼代理人
broker-dealers 经纪商

brokerage (=brocage, brokage) n. 经纪业,居间业;经纪费,佣金,回扣
brokerage business 居间业,经纪业,中间人业务
brokerage charge (或 fee) 经纪费,佣金,手续费
brokerage contract 居间合同,中介合同,经纪合同[指一项代理合同,雇用一位经纪人以委托人的名义或代替委托人(principal)订立合同或从事其他行为。经纪人从中获取约定的佣金(commission)]
brokerage expenses 佣金费,经纪费
brokerage operation 居间业务,经纪业务
broking n. 经纪业;经纪
bromatotoxismus n. 食物中毒
bromatoxism n. 食物中毒
Brookings Seminars (美)布鲁金斯研究班(法学)
brothel n. 妓院
brother n. 兄弟,同胞;同事;(美)律师伙计(旧习语);(复)同行业的人(常用 brethren)
brother in law 姐夫,妹夫;内兄,内弟;大伯,小叔
brothers-german n. 嫡亲弟兄
bruising n. 擦伤,瘀伤
brutal act 残酷行为,野蛮行为
brutality n. 残暴,残酷
brute force 暴力
bubble n. 妄想;骗局
Bubble Act (英)《取缔投机行业或诈骗团体法》
bubble company 泡沫公司(为行骗而虚设的公司)
bubble economy 泡沫经济(资产价格背离经济基础条件的虚假经济现象)
buck-passer n. 推卸责任者,诿过于人者
buck-passing n. 推卸责任
bucket shop (美)(利用顾客资金进行卖空买空的)非法证券经纪行
Bucketshop n. 地下期货业者,利用顾客资金买空卖空
Buddhist law 佛教徒法
budget n. 预算;预算案;预算书
budget (或 budgetary) year 预算年度

budget act 预算法
budget allocations 预算拨款
budget and accounting act 预算及会计法
budget appropriation 预算拨款
budget base 预算基数
budget classification 预算分类
budget committee 预算委员会
budget constraint 预算约束
budget control 预算管制
budget cuts 预算削减
budget debate 预算案辩论
budget deficit 预算赤字
budget estimates (或 estimation) 概算
budget for expenditures 支出预算
budget law 预算法
budget layout 预算编排
budget marking 预算编制
budget message (美)预算咨文
budget practice 预算办法
budget process 预算程序
budget proposal 概算
budget resolution 预算决议
budget sluiced 预算补贴
budget statement 预算表,预算书
budget subsidy 预算补贴
budget summary 预算简表
budget system 预算制度
budget warning system 预算告警制度
budgetary a. 预算上的
budgetary and proprietary accounts 预算账目与财务账目
budgetary biennium 预算两年期
budgetary outlays 财政预算
budgetary performance 预算执行情况
budgetary procedure 预算编制程序
budgetary requirement 所需预算经费,预算需要
budgetary resources 预算经费
budgetary saving 预算节余
budgetary support 预算资(援)助
budgetary surplus 预算结余
budgetary technique 预算编制方法
budgete(e)r n. 预算编制人
buffer n. 缓冲;水手长的副手;缓冲地带
buffer country (或 state) 缓冲国

Bureau International des Droits d'Auteur 国际版权局
bureau of Assembly 议会的执行委员会
Bureau of Arms Control （美）武器控制局[指美国国务院的一个单位,负责指导美国参与的多边武器、控制谈判和参与禁止化学武器的组织(Organization for the Prohibition of Chemical Weapons)。它也引领有关武器、兵器、化武等的控制和发展]
bureau of census 户口普查局
Bureau of Consular Affairs （美）领事务局[指美国国务院的一个单位,负责保护美国公民和海外利益。每年通过它的护照服务处(Office of Passport Service)发出700多万份护照]
Bureau of Customs （美）海关署(负有为政府缴收进口税责任的联邦机构)
Bureau of Democracy, Human Rights and Labor （美）民主、人权和劳工局[指美国国务院的一个单位,负责开展就人权和自由方面的政策,并准备年度"国家关于人权实践报告"(Country Report on Human Rights Practices)。缩略为DRL]
Bureau of Diplomatic Security （美）外事安全局[指美国国务院的一个单位,负责为美国的外交官和世界范围的美国利益开展安全规划(program)。它也开展"外交信使服务"(Diplomatic Courier Service)并监督各类文件和资料的运送。缩略为D. S.]
bureau of drug abuse control 吸毒管制局
Bureau of Economic Analysis （美）经济分析署(或所)(指美国商业部的一个单位,负责综合、分析有关美国经济的数据。它也是经济和统计行政部门的一个组成部分。缩写为BEA)
Bureau of Economic and Business Affairs （美）经济和商业事务局[指美国国务院的一个单位,负责相关食品、交通、能源、空运以及海事等方面国际问题的相关政策。缩略为EB]
Bureau of Engraving and Printing （美）照相制版(或用镌刻版)和印制局[指美国财政部的一个部门,负责设计和印制国家纸币(纸币货币)、邮票、财政债券(Treasury Securities)以及其他文件。缩略为BEP]
Bureau of Export Administration （美）出口行政管理局[指美国商业部下一个局以前的名称,该单位发放出口特许证并执行出口控制法规。该单位名称于2002年改为"工业与安全局"(Bureau of Industry and Security)。缩略为BXA]
bureau of foreign affairs 外事局,外事处
bureau of harbo(u)r administration 港务管理局
Bureau of Indian Affairs （美）印第安人事务局[指美国内政部的一个单位,负责帮助印第安和阿拉斯加州的土著居民按照与美国委托的关系管理他们的事务,并为他们的福利增加和改进作出规划。1824年,原来创设时是作战部(Department of War)的一部分,这个局在1849年转交给内政部。缩略为BIA]
Bureau of Industry and Security （美）工业与安全局[指美国商业部的一个单位,负责发放出口特许证并执行出口控制法规。该局还承担进一步的美国国家安全对外政策的责任。在美国出口不断增加时,还负责考量美国的经济利益。它曾经名为出口行政管理局(Bureau of Export Administration)。现此局缩略为BIS]
bureau of information 情报局
Bureau of Intelligence and Research （美）情报研究局[指美国国务院的一个单位,负责协调美国情报机构的活动以保证与美国对外政策的一致性。该局也引领公共舆论与媒体舆论。缩略为INR]
Bureau of International Labor Affairs （美）国际劳工事务局[指美国劳工部的一个单位,负责就有关美国工人的国际问题帮助制定政策。比如该局汇编并出版有关儿童劳工实践(child-labor practices)和对外劳工市场和规划(foreign labor markets and programs)在世界范畴的数据资料。它还研究移民建议和立法对于劳工的重要性]
Bureau of International Narcotic's and Law Enforcement （美）国际吸毒者和法律执行局[指美国国务院的一个单位,负责协调吸毒人员和该院的反对帮助活动,并负责向总统、国务卿以及其他方面就国际麻

醉剂情况提供咨询。缩略为 INL]
Bureau of International Organization Affairs （美）国际组织事务部[指美国国务院的一个单位，负责协调联合国的美国外事参与和其他国际组织以及各种会议。缩略为 IO]
bureau of justice 司法局，审判局
Bureau of Justice Statistics （美）联邦司法调查统计局
bureau of labo(u)r insurance 劳工保险局
Bureau of Labor Statistics （美）劳工统计局[指美国劳工部的一个独立机构，负责汇编并分析统计有关就业和经济方面的资料(information)。此局就就业、失业、消费品价格、制造者价格、消费者支出情况、进出口价格、工资、受雇者的福利、生产能力和技术更新、就业预测(employment projections)以及职业病(occupational illness)和伤害等情况提供报告。缩写为 BLS]
Bureau of Land Management （美）土地管理局[指美国内务部的一个单位，负责管理国家的土地资源（约有 4.5 亿英亩；1 英亩=6.01 亩）和它们的物力财力(resources)，还负责管理与已获取的土地相关的矿产资源、大陆架以外被淹没的土地。该局是土地总局（General Land Office, 1812 年设立）与牧草地服务局（Grazing Service, 1934 年设立）合并后于 1946 年 7 月 16 日设立的，参见《美国注释法典》第 35 标题卷第 1731 节及以下（35 USCA §§ 1731 et seq.）]
bureau of legislation 立法局，法制局
bureau of legislative affairs （中）（国务院）法制局
Bureau of National Affairs （美）国家事务管理局（主要是活页服务的出版单位。现该单位拥有有关劳务法、知识产权法等法规的计算机数据库，可提供法规和司法、行政两方面的判决资料）
Bureau of Nonproliferation （美）不扩散局[指美国国务院的一个局，负责引导、努力阻止大规模杀伤性武器（weapon of mass destruction）的扩散、转让体制和已发展的常规武器（advanced conventional arms）的扩散等。亦称 Nonproliferation Bureau]
Bureau of Oceans and International Environment and Scientific Affairs （美）海洋和国际环保、科学事务部[指美国国务院的一个单位，负责协调美国海洋、环保及健康政策。缩略为 OES]
Bureau of Political-Military Affairs （美）政治军事事务局[指美国国务院的一个部门，负责分析国际相关的政策问题、管理安全协助基金(security-assistance funds)，以及协调维护和平和人道主义运作的一致性。缩略为 PM，亦称 Political-Military Affairs Bureau]
Bureau of Population, Refugees, and Migration （美）人口、难民和移民局[指美国国务院的一个单位，负责制定相关政策和行政管理，执行美国对于难民和其他人员的帮助、准入规划。缩略为 PRM]
Bureau of Prisons （美）监狱局[指美国司法部的一个部门，负责联邦监狱体系的管理运作。它监督所有联邦刑罚和矫治设施，支持州和地方政府改善它们的惩治设施，并发布释放罪犯的通知（《美国注释法典》第 18 标题卷第 4041 节及以下）(18 USCA § § 4041 et seq.)。缩略为 BOP。见 National Institute of Corrections]
bureau of public security 公安局
Bureau of Reclamation （美）开拓局[指美国内务部的一个单位，它在 17 个州内修建水坝(dam)，现在它负责销售这些水坝水力发电的电力(hydroelectric power)和水库的水。所建的 600 个水坝中有胡佛大坝(Hoover Dam)和大河谷水坝(Grand Coulee Dam)]
Bureau of the Budget 见 Office of Management and Budget
Bureau of the Census （美）人口调查局[指美国商业部的一个部门，负责进行宪法所要求的每 10 年调查并公布一次的人口数额。该局自 1902 年建立，它还进行其他的人口调查并按法律要求进行评估。它是美国商业部经济和统计局（Economics and Statistics Administration）的一个部分。亦称为 Census Bureau]
Bureau of the Council of Ministers 部长

会议执行局
Bureau of the Mint　见 United States Mint
Bureau of the Public Debt　（美）公债局，国家债务局［指美国财政部的一个单位，负责发行、赎回短期国库券（treasury bills）、中期国库券（treasury notes）和长期国库券（treasury bonds），并负责管理美国储备金长期国库券项目规划（U.S.Saving Bond Program）］
Bureau of Transportation Statistics　（美）运输统计局［指美国交通运输部的一个单位，负责汇编出版交通运输统计。缩写为 BTS］
bureau of vital statistics　人事统计局
Bureau Veritas　见 Veritas
bureaucracy n.　官僚主义，官僚政治，官僚机构；官僚统治，行政统治
bureaucrat n.　官僚，官僚派头的人
bureaucrat capital　官僚资本
bureaucratic a.　官僚主义的；官僚政治的
bureaucratic bourgeoisie　官僚资产阶级
bureaucratic capital　官僚资本
bureaucratic capitalism　官僚资本主义
bureaucratic capitalist　官僚资本家
bureaucratic government　官僚政府，行政机构
bureaucratic process　繁文缛节的手续
bureaucratic rationality　行政机关理性化
bureaucratism n.　官僚主义
bureaucratist n.　官僚主义者
bureaucratization n.　官僚主义化
bureaucratization of charisma　魅力领袖官僚化
Bureaux Internationaux Reunis pour la Protection de laPropriété Intellectuelle　见 International Bureau for the protection of Intellectual Property
burgage n.　（英史）1.自治市农役土地保有权利形式之一，佃户每年向自治市镇领主交租。见 socage 2.（苏格兰法）通过农役土地保有权的形式自治市镇掌握其皇family的土地，于看守和保护时期进行服务（见 watch and ward；亦称 burgage tenure）
burgage boroughs　（英史）市镇土地保有制选区

burgage tenure　（英史）市镇土地保有权
burgeoning areas of the law　法律新开展的领域
Burger Court　（美）伯格法院（最高法院，因其首席法官为沃伦·耶尔·伯格，故而得名；同时又因另外三名高级法官均为尼克松总统提名，所以又称尼克松法院）
burgess n.　自治市公民，自由民，（英）自治市议员，（罕）地方行政长官
burgh n.　自治市（尤指苏格兰）
burgh Engloys　见 borough-English
burghal area　自治市地区
burgher n.　自治市的自由民
burglar n.　夜盗者；窃贼，盗窃者；入屋行窃者
burglar alarm　防盗警报器
burglarious a.　夜盗的，犯夜盗罪的
burglarious entry　夜盗侵入住宅（罪）
burglarious intent　夜盗意图，行窃意图
burglarize v.　进行夜盗；入屋行窃
burglarizing ring　盗窃集团
burglary n.　1.（普通法上的）侵入住宅罪［指夜间破门侵入他人住宅并有实施重罪（felony）之故意］2.现代成文法规定的破门侵入住宅的罪行［不一定是寓所和住处（dwelling），也不一定是夜间，但有实施重罪（felony）之故意。有些成文法规采取以轻罪（petit larceny）替代重罪以达到证实行窃意图的目的。亦称 breaking and entering；statutory burglary。见 robbery］
burglary attempt　蓄意盗窃；盗窃未遂
burglary insurance　盗窃保险
burglary tool　盗窃工具（指旨在帮助一个人行窃的用具。在许多管辖区，如果占有人意图以此行窃，这些用具被认为是非法占有）
burgle v.　夜盗，入屋行窃
burgundy n.　一种烈性酒，红（或白）色葡萄酒
burial n.　埋葬，葬
burial case　棺材
burke v.　1.扣压（议案等）；秘密取消（查讯等）；秘密禁止（书刊等）2.把人勒死以出卖尸体（供解剖用）；压制，避免（争端等）
burkism n.　杀人售尸罪［杀人后出售尸体

供尸体解剖用。源自 1829 年犯此种罪行之罪犯——威廉·伯克(William Burke),故名]
burning money 烧钱,耗钱(见 start-up)
burning to death 焚死(刑)
burying alive 活埋(旧时的一种酷刑)
bus n. 公共汽车,汽车
Bush administration 布什执政,布什政府
bushrangers n. 丛林土匪(18 世纪末和 19 世纪在澳大利亚丛林和内地骚扰居民的土匪)
business n. (18 世纪)1.商业,营业(指商业经营以求盈利)职责(指为生活的常规职业,赚钱谋生)2.商业交易(commercial transaction)〈the company has never done business in Louisiana〉(公司从不在路易斯安那州做交易) 3.商业企业(commercial enterprises)〈business and academic often have congruent aims〉[商业(企业)和学术界通常具有一致的目的] 4.(扩大含义)非商业性的交易或事项〈the courts' criminal business occasionally overshadows its civil business〉(法院的刑事业有时夺去了民事业的光彩) 5.(议会法)审议事项[指审议会(deliberative assembly)上的一些事宜,对这些事宜的考虑、对策以及未来可能采取一些措施的信息] 6.业务〈business of the Court〉(联邦最高法院的业务),联邦最高法院的业务不是静态的,相反,它要记载广泛的社会经济和政治变化。联邦最高法院的业务在量和质上的重大变化同样会推进辖区的改革和制度的变迁
business ability 营业能力
business acumen 商业锐觉,商业技能;商业敏锐
business administration 商业行政;商业管理
business advice 业务咨询
business affair 商业事务,商务
business agent 商业代理
business assets 经营资产
business association 商业性社团
business behavio(u)r 企业行为,营业行为
business capital 营业资本
business contract 商业合同
business corporation 商法人;营利法人;商业(贸易)公司
Business Corporation Act 《公司法》
business credit 商业信贷;延期付款
business custom 商习惯
business day (= business hours) 营业日
business deals 商业交易,商行为
business designation 商业标志
business duties 商业责任(或税)
business efficiency 商业功效
business enterprise 工商企业
business entertainment expense 交际应酬费
business entity 商行,商业实体,企业
Business Environment Risk Intelligence 商业环境风险情报机构
business ethics 商业道德
business failure 企业倒闭,企业破产
business finance 企业财务
business firm 商行,贸易公司
business goodwill 商业信誉
business guild (或 **association**) 同业公会,商业行会
business identifies 商业标识
business institution 企业机构
business intercourse 商务往来;民事流转
business is business 公事公办
Business Judgment Rules 商业判断规则;"业务"或"事业"判断规则(指用于追究董事、经理的责任时,称为"商业判断规则";用于在问责制下追究官员的责任则不妨称为"业务"或"事业"判断规则,官员必须对其职责范围内的事宜全面负责);经营判断原则[指即使董事的经营判断从结果上看给公司造成了损失,但只要能在一定程度上确保该经营判断的诚实性和合理性,而且该经营判断是在满足一定的要件下做出的,那么法院就不应当就其妥当性通过事后介入的方式,以该董事违反注意义务为由直接追究其责任的法理。该原则起源于 19 世纪在美国产生、发展起来的一个判例——珀西诉米劳顿(Percy v. Millaudon, 1829)——法理]
business law 营业法,商业法
business lawyer's effort 商务律师的成就

business letter （贸易）业务函件
business liability 职业责任;经营责任
business licence 营业执照
business loan 商业借款
business management 商业管理
business methods patent 商业方式专利,商业方法专利[指美国的一种专利,须描述并权利申请等一系列程序、步骤。作为一个整体构成一项正在进行的商业活动(doing business)方式/1998年以前这种进行商业活动方式尚未明确构成授予专利权的条件,正是当年,联邦上诉巡回法庭在1998年审理美国道富银行诉签名金融集团案(State Street Bank & Trust Co. v. Signature Fin Group. Inc., 140 F3d 1368, Fed Cir. 1998)后,这一商业方式即依据相同法定要求达到专利性(palentability)犹如其他方式。此词亦称cyber patent]
business name 商号（又译商业名称或企业名称）,业务用名
business of broker 经纪业务
business of collecting bill for customers 为客户办理托收票据业务
business of court 法庭业务
business of distributor 推销（员）业务
business of paying money on account of cheques 办理支票付款业务
business of underwriter 承销证券业务
business operations 经营（业务）
business partnership 商业合伙
business permit 营业许可证,营业执照
business picture 经济情况,商业情况
business practice 商业惯例,商业习惯,商业措施
business press 商业舆论
business principles 经营原则
business record 业务记录;商业记录
business record exception 商业记录例外原则（传闻作证的一项例外规则,即对于原有的和常规的记录,不管是否是商业的一部分,即使它们是传闻,也可允准其作为证据使用）
business reference 商业咨询
business registration 商业登记;商业注册
business reputation 商业信誉

business risk 商业风险
business scope 经营范围
business secret 商业秘密
business strife 竞业
business tax 营业税,销售税
business tenancy 商业租赁
business tradition 商业传统
business transaction 商业交易;商行为
business travel 公务旅行
business trust 商业信托
business unit 商行,商业单位,企业
business vouchers 商业证券
business year 营业年度
businesslike a. 有条理的,事务式的
businesslike raise 务实地提出
bust v. （俚）拘捕,搜捕;突然搜查（尤指警察的突然搜查或搜捕）;失败;破产;殴打;降级
Bustamante Code 《布斯塔曼特法典》（1928年订立的《国际私法典》）
busted a. 被逮捕的;破产的;被降级的
but see 见 sed vide
"but for" test "除非因为"判断标准（用于决定侵权责任的因果关系的一种判断标准,即通过采用"除非、因为"被告做了什么或未做什么,否则就不会导致原告受到伤害的问答方式来确定侵权责任的因果关系,常在有限的情况下使用）
butcher n. 残杀者,屠杀者,刽子手;（英）屠夫;（美）小贩
butchery n. 残杀,屠杀,惨杀;屠宰业;屠宰场
butt n. 目的,目标,靶;（复）射击场
Butterworth's Annotated Legislation Service （英）《巴特沃思注释法规选编》（巴特沃思公司出版的1939年至今的一种选择性的注释法规汇编）
buttress v. 加固,支持,支撑（论据等）
butts and bounds 地界（地权状上的用语。见 metes and bounds）
buy v. 买;（用贿赂等）收买;行贿;（以一定代价）获得;交易,买卖
Buy American Act （美）《购买美国货法》（美国政府要求其政府机构尽可能购买美国货的规定）

buy and sell agreement (= buy-sell agreement) 买卖协议(所有权人或合伙人之间的协议:如果一个人去世或歇业,其股份将由其他人获取,或按事先安排的计划处理)
buy insurance 投保,买保险
buy jawbone 赊购,赊买
buy on credit 赊,赊欠
buy or sell without authorization 私自买卖
buy over 收买,贿赂
buy peace 买静求安
buy-back n. 产品返销;回购
buy-back price 回购价,返销价
buy-out agreement (股权)承买协议
buyer n. 买受人,买方,买主;认购者
buyer's credit 买方信用
buyers in the ordinary course of business (美)依商业常规交易中的购买人(美国动产担保交易法所称的,即该购买人不受追及规则)
buyer's market 买方市场(指对买方有利的市场)
buyer's price 买价,买盘
buying agent 买入代理人,进货经纪人
buying drive 大量买进
buying in 购入,买进
buying off 1.出钱使摆脱服役(或勒索)等 2.收买
buying out 买下全部产权;用金钱诱使他人放弃产权(或地位)
buying over 收买
buying price 买价
buying rate 买价;买入汇率,银行买价
buyout n. 全部购买;控股购买(指购买一个企业的全部资产、股份或按控股比例购买全部产权或股份。见 merger 8)
Buzzo act 巴佐条例(1959年美国加利福尼亚机动车辆法规,该法对在公路上扔香烟、火柴或其他易燃物做了规定,其发起人叫保罗·巴佐,因而得名)
by prep. 根据,依据;由于;通过;在……旁;在……情况下;到……时(为止);经,由;用……方法(手段);靠近
by a preponderance of evidence in civil cases 民事案件中"占有优势证据"的法则

by administrative order 依行政程序,(复)依行政命令
by analogy 以此类推
by and large 1.总的来说,大体上,基本上〈the quality is good by and large〉(质量基本上是好的) 2.无论吃风不吃风(帆船照样能行驶)
by applying *mutatis mutandis* 比照……的规定
by authority of law 据法院命令
by birth 在血统上,生来,天生地
by blood 按照血统来说
by conforming to the statutory conditions 符合法定条件者
by contract 依合同(契约);根据承包
by convention 按照惯例;依照惯例,依照公约
by courtesy 为表示礼貌起见;承蒙好意
by deception 用欺骗手段
by duly approved charter 依经正当程序核准的章程
by error 错误地
by evidence of good character 根据品格良好的证据
by far (修饰比较级、最高级、强调数量、程序等)……得多;最……〈by far the most customary forms in both Houses〉[在两院中最惯有的形(格)式]
by force 凭借暴力,强制地
by force of 由于,通过;用……的手段
by force of law 用法律的手段,依靠法律的
by force, stealth or permission 用暴力、隐秘或得到许可(英美法官对时效的占有没有善意要求,对所有类型的时效占有的要求只规定不应使用暴力、隐秘或得到许可。见 *nec vi, nec clam, nec precario*)实施
by freight car 用普通货车运送
by hinting 根据暗示
by inference 根据推理,以推理
by instinct 出于本能
by means of 依靠;借用
by might of one's arms 运用某人武力手段,通过某人的强制手段
by mutual consent 经双方同意
by no mean a panacea 绝不是治百病灵药

by no means 绝不,绝不是
by operation of law 依法
by (或 at the) order of 奉……之命
by procuration 代理,代表(签名)
by product 副产品
by reason of (= because of) 因为,由于,凭借……
by refusing to compromise, poor countries have come away with nothing "由于拒绝让步,穷国空手而归"
by regulation 根据规章
by resolution 依决议
by right of 根据……的权利;由于……的理由
by right of blood 根据血统
by share 按份额
by statute 依照法规
by strong arm (或 hand) 强制地;用武力;用强制手段
by tender 拍卖,招标
by the law of the land (= by due process of law) 依法律的正当程序;依正当程序审判
by the same token 由于同样原因
by these presents 根据本文件,据此而言
by (或 in) virtue of 凭借,依靠,由于……
by way of 路经,途经,作为,当作,意在
by way of exception 作为例外
by-bidder n. 虚假竞买人,抬高竞价者(指无意购买,而在拍卖进行中出高价,使卖价抬高者,此种抬高卖价行为称 by-bidding)
by-bidding 抬价出卖
by(e)-blow n. 私生子;无意(或间接)的一击
by-election (= bye-election) 特别指进行补充空缺席位(vacant post)的一种选举
by(e)-laws n. 细则;(地方或社团所订的)章程,规章;附则
by-census n. 概括性人口调查
by-effect n. 副作用
by-line n. 副业;(每篇报刊文章题目下)作者的署名
by-name n. 假名,化名,别名;绰号
by-pass v./n. 规避,绕道,越过/旁道,环绕的旁路
by-product n. 副产品
Byrd's balancing test (美)伯德案判决提出的衡平标准
bystander n. 候补陪审员;旁观者
bystander in a court 法庭旁听者
Byzantine idea of sovereignty 拜占庭主权(或统治权)观念
Byzantine law 拜占庭法(东罗马帝国的法律,主要适用于拜占庭或君士坦丁堡地区的法律)
Byzantine lines 拜占庭沿袭的多位皇帝(时期)
Byzantine princeps 拜占庭君主,拜占庭皇帝
Byzantine sovereignty 拜占庭式主权

C

C & M Framework (美)卡-梅框架[卡拉布雷西(Guido Calabresi)和梅拉米德(Douglas Melamed)][指伴随法经济学的全面发展,卡、梅两位法经济学研究者在1972年提出的规则框架,对法学研究和法制改革的影响长盛不衰,而且成为主导范式。他们提出的"财产规则"(Property Rules)、责任规则(Liability Rules)和禁易规则(Inalienability)等类型划分,被学界称为卡—梅框架。这一框架是从法律后果的角度对法律规则作出的一种逻辑分类。我们知道法律逻辑结构包括假设条件、行为模式和法律后果三个要素。其中"法律后果"中的"违法后果"在中国常被称为"法律责任",在法经济学上则往往称为"法律救济"。一般而言,法律规则的效果模式就是违反这一规则所需承担的法律责任,亦即基于此项规则所能寻求的法律救济。卡—梅框架的独特性在于其规则分

类的着眼点不是传统上的行为模式(如公法,私法,民法或物权,债权),而是效果模式,是公民的"合法权益"受到侵犯时所能得到的不同法律救济。亦即侵犯公民合法权益可能产生不同的法律责任的保护力度。从法经济学的角度看,只有对于满足假设条件的行为模式给出了明确效果模式(法律救济或法律责任),一个规则才能构成一种科斯所谓的法律立场(legal position),清晰界定一项权益的法律边界(legal delimitation)。卡—梅框架就是从法益(legal entitlement)保护的效果模式出发,提供了用以理解整个法律体系的"一个统一视角"。卡—梅框架很多年来成为美国法学,特别是法经济学研究的一个基本框架]

C corporation (美)C公司[指该公司的所得非通过公司本身而是由其股东本人纳税。美国《国内税收法》(IRC)规定,任何因违约(by default)而未被选定享有S公司税收身份(S corporation tax statue)的公司即为C公司。亦称Subchapter C corporation。见S corporation]

cabal n./v. 阴谋集团;政治阴谋/参与阴谋集团活动;结党,阴谋

caballaria n. (英)骑士(土地保有)制度(战时适当准备提供给骑士的封建土地保有权的一种制度)

caballer n. 阴谋集团成员;阴谋家

cabinet n. (通常大写)(17世纪)内阁[指行政官员,特别是总统的咨询委员会(advisory council)的行政官员。总统的内阁(president's cabinet)是习惯和传统的创举,从乔治·华盛顿(George Washington)任总统时期就有了。美国联邦宪法提出一批总统的顾问(advisers)——"总统得令各行政部门主管长官,以书面发表关于其职务任何事项的意见"(第3条第1款第2节)(art. Ⅱ,§ 2, cl. 1)。但cabinet这个词没有特别值得提醒的。当今内阁包括15个行政部门的主管首脑;国务卿(the Secretary of State)、财政部长(the Secretary of the Treasury)、国防部长(the Secretary of Defense)、司法部长(总检察长)(the Attorney General)、内政部长(the Secretary of the Interior)、农业部长(the Secretary of Agriculture)、商务部长(the Secretary of Commerce)、劳工部长(the Secretary of Labor)、健康和人民医疗服务部长(the Secretary of Health and Human Service)、住房和城市发展部长(the Secretary of Housing and Urban Development)、运输部长(the Secretary of Transportation)、能源部长(the Secretary of Energy)、教育部长(the Secretary of Education)、退任军人事务部长(the Secretary of Veterans Affairs)以及国家安全部长(the Secretary of Homeland Security)。其他官员如美国驻外联合大使(the U. S. Ambassador to the United Nations)和管理与预算局局长(the Director of the Office of Management and the Budget)也已被列入内阁行列]

cabinet council 内阁会议
cabinet crisis 内阁危机
cabinet government (= ministerial government) 内阁制政府
cabinet in office 执政内阁
cabinet members 内阁阁员
cabinet minister 内阁部长(大臣)
cabinet official 内阁官员
cabinet reshuffle 改组内阁,改组政府
cabinet secretariat (英)内阁秘书处
cabinet system (of government) 责任内阁制;内阁制
cable car 缆车
cabotage n. 沿海贸易(权),沿海航行(权);国内交通运输(权)
cabotage right 沿海航行权,沿海贸易权;国内交通运输权
cacique n. (中南美等的)印第安人的酋长;(菲律宾的)大地主;(西班牙、拉美等地的)地方政治头子
caciquismo n. 酋长统治(指拉丁美洲和西班牙地方酋长的统治)
cadastral a. 地籍的
cadastral matters 地籍事项;地籍案件
cadastral surveying 地籍测量
cadaver n. 尸体
cadaver exhumation 尸体发掘
cadaveric a. 尸体的
cadaveric ecchymoses 尸斑

cadaveric rigidity 尸僵
cadaveric spasm 尸体痉挛
cadere v. 终止,停止;失败
cadere ab actione 败诉
cadet n. 军校学生;练习生;少子,幼子
cadet police 预备警察
cadi 卡迪
cadit quaestio 辩论终结
cadre n. 干部;骨干,基干
caduca n. (罗马法)绝产充公;无人继承之遗产
caduciary n. (英)绝产充公(又译无人继承的归公财产,指遗产因权利消灭或无人继承而归国王)
caelum liberum 天空是自由的
caesaropapism n. 政教合一(国家元首兼任教会首脑,有权裁断教会事务的一种政治制度)
caeteris paribus 在其他条件相同的情况下
caeteris tacentibus 余皆持沉默(指合议审理案件判决时,参与审判之陪审法官均不表意见,持沉默态度)
cahiers de doléances (法史)改良请愿书(指1789年前三级会议呈递给法兰西国王带有申述冤苦和改良要求的信函)
Cain 凯因[①基督教《圣经》中亚当的长子,曾杀害他的弟弟Abel;②(喻)杀害兄弟者,杀人者]
Cairo Declaration 《开罗宣言》(1944年发表)
cajole v. 哄骗;引诱,勾引
cajolement n. 哄骗;引诱
cajoler n. 骗子
cajolery n. 哄骗;引诱
calaboose n. (美)监狱,牢狱;拘留所
calamity n. 不幸事件;灾难,灾患
calculated a. 计划中的;有意图谋的,故意作出的,有目的的;推测的;很有可能的;适当的;专为自己打算的
calculated crime 故意犯罪,预谋犯罪
calculated homicide 谋杀
calculated injury 故意伤害
calculated insult 有意的侮辱
calculated risk 预期风险
calculated to deceive 蓄意诈欺,意图欺骗

calculation n. 计算;考虑;推定
calculation method in canon law 寺院法上的计算法
calefaction (=thermal pollution) n. 热污染
calendar n. 1.历法;历书 2.日程表,一览表;候审人名单及被控罪目录;案件日程表 3.(复)(英)记录大全(指由政府档案局出版的概括其所保存的不同种类文件的各种汇编本)
calendar of cases marked for hearing 审理案件日期单
calendar of prisoners 囚犯名单
calendar of sentence 判决记录
calendar or legal year 民用年或法定年
California Code of Civil Procedure (美)《加州民事诉讼程序法典》
California Safe Drinking Water and Toxic Enforcement Act of 1986 (美)《1986年加州安全饮用水和中毒执行法》
California substantive law controlled (美)适用加州实体法
California-Rhode Island type of Statute (美)加州—罗得岛法规模式
caliph n. 哈里发(伊斯兰国家执掌政教大权的领袖,原意为继承人)
caliphate n. 哈里发的职位(或统治区)(见 caliph)
call n./v. 1.召集(开);征召;传唤 2.号召,要求,请求;付款要求(或通知) 3.律师资格的准给 4. 催交股款 5.访问,通话,呼叫 6.按一定价格在一定时间内买进一定数量的股票(或粮食等)的权利/召集(开),征召,传唤;请求,要求;要求偿还,收兑;招聘,任命;停靠(泊),访问,打电话给;称呼;认为
call a prisoner to the bar of court 传唤犯人到法庭
call capital 未付股款
call credit 取回信贷(款)
call day (英)准许执行律师业务典礼日
call for 要求,需要,提倡,呼救,拿取,邀约
call for the order of the day 宣布本日议程
call forth 唤起,激起,引起,振作起,鼓起(精神、勇气等)
call heaven to witness 指天发誓,对天发誓

call in arrears 催收欠款,催到期未收之债
call in testimony 传唤出庭作证
call loan 通知贷款(见 call money);(银行业)同业拆借
call market (银行业)同业拆借市场,短期国际拆借市场
call money 通知贷款(旧译拆款,货币市场术语,指对证券经纪人或代理人以短期库券或债券作担保的短期借款,一般不超过24小时,基本上是向经纪人在票据过户时提供的);(银行业)同行拆款
call my witness face to face 传唤证人(面对面)对质
call night (英)唱名之夜(又译"呼入晚",用于取得大律师资格的一种手续)
call of the House 立法机关的唱名表决;(英)下院召集令(当必须听取整个下议院意见时所发出的传唤所有下议院议员的召集令)
call option (在合同期限内)按议定价购买股份权;购买选择权(在合同规定的期限内有决定提出是否要求交货的选择权)
call on(或 **upon**) 请求,恳求,邀约,邀请
call sb.(或 **sth.**) **in question** 对某人(或某案)提出异议(或怀疑)
call sb. in evidence 传唤某人出庭作证
call sb. to account 向某人问罪,谴责某人
call sb. to order 请某人守秩序
call the banns 预告婚事(问人有无异议)
call the jury 抽签决定陪审(团)员,选出陪审(团)员
call to task 找麻烦,责备
call to the bar 1.(英)(律师院学生被)接纳为律师的仪式(由此取得外席律师资格)2.(英)作为外席律师出庭
call witness to 请作证
Call-A-Mart 电脑化超级市场,电子计算机化超级市场
call-back service 回复(呼)服务
call-up n. (服兵役的)征集令,征召令
call-up age (服兵役的)征集年龄
call-up capital 已缴资本,已缴股本
callable a. 可缴纳的,应缴付的
callable bonds 可提前兑付债券,可通知偿还的债券,可通知赎回的债券,可提前偿还的债券,可收回的债券
called a. 被传唤的;召集的;受聘的;被称为……的
called meeting 特别会议
called out 奉令服役
called to testify 被传作证
called to the Bar 被接纳为大律师并准予开业
called within the Bar 受聘为御用大律师,被任为皇家法律顾问
calligraphy n. 笔迹;书法
calling n. 传唤,召集;职业,行业;停靠;名称
calling the docket 宣布审理案件名单,公布审理案件表
calling the jury 选出陪审团;宣布陪审团名单
calling the plaintiff 传唤原告到庭
calling the prisoner 法官询问罪犯是否有不服判罪理由陈述
calling upon a prisoner 传讯罪犯
cally n. (美)警察局
CALPERS California Public Employees' Retirement System (美)加利福尼亚州公务员退休基金
calumniae jusjurandum 防止诬告之陈述(美国有些州为防止恶意控告规定原告人于起诉时需附有陈述真实事实之宣誓书)
calumnia (大陆法)诬告
calumniate v. 诬告;诽谤,中伤
calumniation n. 诬告,诽谤,中伤
calumniator n. 诬告者;诽谤者,中伤者
calumniatory a. 诬告的,诽谤的,中伤的
calumny n. 诬告,诽谤,中伤
Calvin's Genera 加尔文教派
Calvo Clause 卡尔沃条款(拉丁美洲国家根据阿根廷国际法学家卡尔沃提出的"卡尔沃主义"形成的,主张在同外国人订立契约时附加一条由外国人声明在一切契约执行问题上放弃其本国政府外交保护的条款)
cambiale jus 交易法
cambist n. 熟悉汇兑的人,汇(兑)商;汇兑业务专家;货币比较表;各国货币和度量衡比值手册

cambium 汇兑,兑换;交换,交易
cambium reale 土地交换,不动产所有权之交换
cambricon n. 芯体,芯片
Cambridge 剑桥城[指美国哈佛大学的所在地(马萨诸塞州剑桥城,而非英国 University of Cambridge)]
camera n. 1.照相机,摄影机 2.法官私室(指在法庭后面的法官私室),审判员密议室 3.罗马教廷的财政部
camera regis 1.(古英国法)国王议事厅 2.(英)(尤指着眼于商业观点)拥有专有特权的地区 3.伦敦城的称谓
Camera Stellata 星室法院(亦称为星座法院。见 Star-Chamber)
camouflage(d) export 伪装输出
camouflaged protection 伪装的保护(打着反倾销旗号做幌子,行保护本国企业之实)
campaign n./v. 竞选;运动,活动;战役/1.竞选 2.参加运动,搞运动 3.出征,作战
campaign against bribery, tax evasion and smuggling, theft of state property, cheating on workmanship and materials, and theft of state economic information (中)反贿赂、反偷税漏税、反盗窃国家资财、反偷工减料、反盗窃国家经济情报的"五反"运动
campaign document (美)竞选文件
campaign finance (美)竞选资金[指在麦康奈尔诉联邦选举委员会(Mc connell v. Federal Election Commission. S40 U.S.93, 2003)一案判决意见中反映出许多方面存在不同意见。但判决支持了2002年制定的《两院竞选活动改革法》(Bicameral Campaign Reform Act,简称 BCRA)中的两项重要规定:控制"软钱"和"管制"问题的宣传。美国联邦最高法院审查了1974年美国联邦选举活动法修正案,特别是涉及政治活动委员会现金流向的部分,首席大法官赞成控制捐助,但同时根据"美国联邦宪法第一修正案的相关规定,取消了对候选人和个人支出的限制"。联邦最高法院认为 BCRA 的第一部分旨在把全国性政党从"软钱"事务中隔离开来。为了驳回上诉人关于第一修正案、联邦主义和平等保护目标的诉求,联邦最高法院得出两个重要结论:①捐献限制对自由言论和结社权有边缘性的约束;②对于选举程序依据 BCRA 而进行的管制审查,并不适用严格审查标准,而仅适用于不甚严格的"紧密拉近"(closely drawn)标准。总的来说,联邦最高法院支持并赞成在费用和宣传时间上对选举联络进行限制。但认为 BCRA 有谬误。国会无必要哀叹高额的竞选费用。2000年大选中以硬金(hard money)和软金形式花费的金钱为2000亿美元,但与美国人花费在电影上的78亿美元和用于化妆品及香水上的188亿美元相比,这个数字显得苍白多了。大法官斯卡利亚说:"如果我们的民主因太高的花费而淹死的话,那是因为它不会游泳",所以 BCRA 不会是有关全国性选举活动的最后一项法律]
campaign legislation 竞选运动立法
campaign strategy 竞选战略
campaigner n. 竞选人,参加运动的人,参加多次战役的军人
Campbell's Act, Lord (9&10 Vict. c. 93) 坎贝尔法(维多利亚第9个和第10个执法年通过的第93个法),坎贝尔勋爵法[①指著名的1846年《死亡事故法》(Fatal Accident Act)。坎贝尔勋爵为此法出了大力,因而此法以勋爵之名命名。后将1959年《死亡事故法》及历次修订合并为1976年《死亡事故法》。该法规定,死者家属可以获得损害赔偿。如果死者生前未进行死亡保险,其家属仍然有权获得损害赔偿。一般由死者的遗产管理人或遗嘱执行人为了死者配偶、父母、子女的利益而向有过错的一方当事人提起诉讼。②指《坎贝尔(勋爵)诽谤法》,即1843年和1845年的《诽谤法》(Libel Acts)]
Canadian law 加拿大法
canal n. 运河,水道
canal dues 运河通行费
canal tolls 运河通行税(费)
cancel v. 取消,把……作废,撤销,抵消;解除;注销,盖销,删去;省略
cancellaria curia 衡平法院

cancellation n. 退保注销;取消,抵消,盖销;作废,废除,解除;删去;省略
cancelling clause 撤销条款;解除合同(契约)条款
cancellation charge 注销费
cancellation of adoption 撤销收养
cancellation of contract 取消合同(契约),解除合同(契约)
cancellation of document 撤销证书,注销(废除)文件
cancellation of franchise 撤销特许权;取消专利权;取消选举
cancellation of household registration 注销户口
cancellation of insurance 退保注销
cancellation of licence 吊销执照
cancellation of registration 注销登记;撤销登记
cancellation of shares 注销股份
cancellation of the legacy 撤销遗赠
cancellation of will 撤销遗嘱
cancellation with a reopening of the case 撤销原判并重新审理案件
cancelled a. 取消的;废除的,解除的
cancelled ballot ticket (选票)废票
(a) cancellis curiae expodi to be expelled from the bar of the court 从审判台被赶出
candid a. 公正的,正直的,坦率的,无偏见的
candidacy (=candidature) n. 候选人的身份(或资格)
candidate n. 候选人,候补人;投考者
candidate for election 选举候选人
candor (=candour) n. 坦率,正直,公正;白色;光明;表白
cang(ue) n. 枷(中国与某些东方国家旧时的刑具)
canine jurisprudence 犬科法理学
caning n. 鞭笞,笞刑
cannabis n. 印度大麻
canon n. 1.法律,法规,判断标准;准则,标准,原则 2.教规,寺院法规,英国国教规则,解释规则,继承规则 3.牧师
canon law 寺院法,教会法规
Canon Law Code 《寺院法典》(又译教会法典,一部五册法典,有2414条教规,全为拉丁文写的,成为罗马天主教准则)
canon of inheritance (财产等的)继承归属原则
canon of professional ethics 职业道德准则
canonical a. 教规的,规范的,典范的
canonical case 典型案例
canonist n. 寺院法学家;宗教法规学者;(复)教会法学派,寺院法学派
canons of construction 解释原则(对书面文件注释或解释以决定法律效力的原则)
canons of interpretation 解释规则
canons of judicial ethics (美)司法(人员)道德准则
cant n. (总称)假话;行话,行业术语,切口,黑话
canton n. (瑞士等国的)州,(法)县(或乡)
cantonal judge 县(或州)法官
cantonal tribunal 县(或州)法庭
canvass v. 1.详细检查,细看〈that issue has been repeatedly canvassed by our state's courts〉(案件争议的问题已经由我们州的一些法院反复进行过检查)2.计算选票,计票,检票(指正式计算选票并报告结果)〈canvass the votes〉(统计选票)。"所有选票均被集中,包括主持人、秘书长,以及点票员等的选票均由这些点票员统计选票。详细检查票数意味更为准确的统计,这包括对识别出的无效票、空白选票、填写非法被提名人、字迹不清的弃权票等的评估,计算选票并向主持人报告总计结果以便主持人宣布选举结果。"Ray. E. Keesey 著《现代议会程序》(Modern Parliamentary Procedure)第113页(1994年)3.拉票(指诱惑选票人或选区在政治上的支持以估量公众舆论)〈the candidate is actively canvassing the Western States〉(候选人正积极统计西方一些州的选票)
canvass (或 **canvas**) **a district for votes** 为争取选票而在选举区进行游说
canvasser n. 检票员,推销员,游说(拉票)者
cap n./v. (1947年)限额(指如因侵权行为的追索损失赔偿的限额或银行可承担的利息的限额等)/限制

capable a. 有才能的,有能力的,有资格的;有技能的
capable of proof 可接受的举证,有资格的证明
capable person 有行为能力人
Capability n. 1.能力,才能 2.性能,容量,接受力 3.(复)潜在能力〈West Law has PACER dockets and updating capability〉[西方法律出版公司具有公开进入法院电子诉讼记录(public access to court electronic records)的档案摘要和跟进时代的潜在能力]
capacitate v. 使在法律上合格;使具有资格;给予能力
capacities of parties other than mental 意识能力以外的双方行为能力
capacity n. 权能;权利能力,行为能力;资格,职位,身份;能力,才能;容量,容积
capacity as a subject of law 法律主体资格
capacity for (或 of) rights 权利能力
capacity for duties (承担)义务的能力,责任能力
capacity for legal transactions 法律行为能力
capacity for private rights 私权能力,民事权利能力
capacity for public rights 公权能力
capacity for responsibility 责任能力
capacity for responsibility of juristic person 法人的责任能力
capacity for right of the natural person 自然人的权利能力
capacity for rights of thing 物权能力
capacity of acceptance 受领能力;承诺能力;承兑能力
capacity of child in criminal law 刑法上幼年人的行为能力;幼年人刑事(责任)能力
capacity of concluding contract (=capacity contracting) 缔约能力
capacity of discernment 识别能力
capacity of having private obligations 承担民事义务的能力
capacity of having private right 享有民事权利的能力,享受私权的能力

capacity of legacy 遗产继承资格;受遗赠能力
capacity of legal adviser 法律顾问的资格
capacity of management 管理能力,管理才能
capacity of marriage 结婚资格;结婚能力
capacity of party 当事人身份;当事人能力;当事人资格
capacity of self-government 自治能力
capacity of testator to devise 遗嘱人立遗嘱能力,遗嘱人遗赠(不动产)资格
capacity of will 自主能力,意识能力
capacity to act 行为能力
capacity to action 诉讼能力,诉讼资格
capacity to be a party 当事人能力,当事人资格
capacity to bear loss 承担损失的能力
capacity to benefit from legal rights 权利能力
capacity to carry out commercial act 办理商行为的能力
capacity to conclude treaties 缔结条约能力
capacity to contract 订立合同(契约)能力,订约资格
capacity to enjoy rights and assuming obligations 享受权利及承担义务的能力
capacity to enter into legal transactions 法律行为能力
capacity to hold office 担任职务的能力(或资格)
capacity to make will 立遗嘱的能力(或资格)
capacity to marriage (或 marry) 结婚能力
capacity to pay 支付能力
capacity to perform legal transactions 办理法律行为的能力
capacity to sue and defend 起诉和辩护的能力
capacity to sue and to be sued 诉讼能力
capacity tonnage 载重量,吨位
capax doli 犯罪能力
capax negotii 处理事务的能力;经营能力
caper n. 1.(俚)犯罪或非法行为(如盗窃、

抢劫等)2.戏弄;(媒体)玩弄手段
capias n. 拘票,拘捕令;(英)"卡皮欧"令状(以前英格兰法上的几种令状,发送给郡长由他来逮捕被指名的人)
capias ad audiendum judicium 令刑事被告出庭候审所发出的令状
capias ad computandum 命被告亲自到查账人处查清账目令(指清查账目诉讼中,向未按判决到查账人处查清账目的被告所发出的令状)
capias ad respondendum 拘捕轻罪案被告以便提讯令
capias ad satisfaciendum (命执达官)拘留(未依判决清偿债务或付清赔偿金的)民事被告到庭受审令(或拘票)
capias extendi facias 拘拿欠政府债务的债务人并扣押其财产令
capias pro fine 追缴罚金的令状
capiases ad addendums 令刑事被告出庭审所发出的令状,拘传被告人到庭听候有罪判决的令状
capita n. 见 per capita
capital n./a. 1.资方;资本;股本;资金,本金 2.首都,省会/1.资本的 2.首位的;基本的 3.可处死刑的;致死的
capital account (固定)资本账户
capital account balance sheet 资产负债表
Capital Adequacy Directive (CAD) 资本充足率指令(1993年欧盟通过的指令,1996年生效)
capital adequacy standard 资金充足标准
capital as a social relation 作为一种社会联系的资本
capital as factor of production 作为一种生产要素的资本
capital asset 固定资产,资本资产(指固定资产和专利权等)
Capital Asset Pricing Model (CAPM) 固定资产定价模式
capital association 资本社团
capital budgeting 资本预算
capital case 死刑案件
capital construction 基本建设
capital contribution 出资额
capital cost 资本费用
capital credit certificate 资本信用证明书
capital crime 死(刑)罪
capital deficit 资本亏损
capital duty 资本税
capital expenditure 基本建设费用
capital export 资本输出
capital felony 重罪,死罪
capital flight 资金外逃(流);抽逃资本
capital formation 资本形成
capital fund 资本基金
capital gain(s) 资本收益,资本获利[指在资产(capital assert)出售或交易时所获取的利润。见 ordinary gain]
capital gains and losses 资本的收益与亏损
capital gains distribution 资本利润分红(见 capital-gain dividend)
capital gains tax 资本收益税;资本利得税
capital goods 资本货物;生产资料;实物
capital goods investment contract 生产资料投资合同(契约)
capital in cash 资本金,现金资本
capital in general 一般资本
capital income 资本所得,资本收益
capital injection 注入资金,增资
capital input 资本投入,资本输入
capital intensity 资本密集(程)度
capital intensive 资本密集的,使用大量资本的
capital intensive industry 资本密集工业,使用大量资本的工业
capital investment 资本投资
capital issue 发行股票
capital levy 资本税(一种财产税,它是根据资本额,而非根据资本收益征收的税)
capital loan 资本信贷
capital market 资本市场
capital money 资本货币
capital murder 因罪杀人(指因在实施谋杀、盗窃、逃脱、拒捕等罪时杀死他人)
capital of circulation 流通资本
capital offence 可处死刑的罪行,死罪
capital outflow 资金外流
capital outlay 资本支出,耗资
capital prisoner 死刑囚犯

capital punishment （英）绞刑（1965 年的《谋杀法》虽把死刑废除，但叛逆罪、暴力海盗罪和放火焚烧皇家舰艇罪仍可处绞刑）；（美）死刑（尽管死刑在某些州已被宣布为不合法，但直到 2003 年仍有 38 个州、联邦政府以及联邦军队里死刑为合法）
capital receipts 资本收入
capital recipient country 资本接受国
capital redemption reserve fund 偿还资本债务储备金
capital reorganization 资本结构组
capital repairs 重要修缮，（船、机等的）主件（或重大）修理
capital revenue 资本收益
capital stock 股本，资本总额；股份总额
capital stock authorized 额定股本
capital stock certificate (=certificate of stock) 股票
capital stock outstanding 已公开发行股本
capital stock preferred 优先股
capital stock tax 股本税（指①对持股人可控的股本所课之税；②以公司形式经营商业的州税，特别指对具有在本州经营特权的州外公司所课之税，该税通常是按同等价值或公司股本价值的百分比所稽征之税）
capital subscription 认购股本
capital surplus 资本过剩
capital territory 首都辖区
capital transfer 资本转移
capital transfer tax 资本转让税，资本转移税
capital value 资本价值
capital-gain distribution 见 capital-gain dividend
capital-gain dividend 资本收益红利，资本收益股息[指将应纳税支付给互助基金持股人(mutual fund shareholder)。这一支付是股票持有人的比例股份(proportional share)，它来自互助基金投资组合(mutual fund's portfolio)中证券买卖的实际净资本盈利所得。亦可称 capital-gain distribution]
capital-gain divident 资本收益红利，资本收益股利(指给予互助基金股票持有人应纳税的付款。这项付款是股票持有人的

净资本收益。是来自互助基金有价证券的证券销售实现的。亦称为 capital-gain distribution)
capital-gain tax （1930 年）资本收益税，资本利得税[指来自资产出售的所得税。联邦所得税关于资本收益已有象征性的优惠税率，如个人的优惠 20% 和企业或公司的则优惠 34%，另外适用正常收入(ordinary income)的税率。见 capital gain]
capitalist n./a. 资本家；资本集中论者/资本主义的；有资本的；资本家的
capitalist law 资本主义法
capitalist legal system 资本主义法制
capitalist ownership 资本主义所有制
capitalist system 资本主义制度
capitalization (=capitalisation) n. 规定资本额；拨兑资本；投资，资本估价使转作资本使用
capitalization issue 红利股发行额
capitalization of interests 利息转充资金，滚利作本
capitalization of profits 利润转作资本
capitalization of reserves 储备金转作为发行资本
capitalization operation 投资业务
capitalize (=capitalise) v. 使转作为资本（使用），投资于；计算（某一时期内收益等的）现存价值；提供资金给；利用(on, upon)
capitally ad. 以死刑，按死刑程序
capitation n. （美）人头税，健康保持治疗费[指①人头税（见 poll tax）；②根据"健康福利计划"(health benefit plan) 中成员的数目，给健康（治疗或）关怀提供者(healthcare provider) 支付报酬的一种方法，而提供者承包了这项治疗。这一"健康福利计划"的赞助人同意按每一时期、每个人支付一个固定的报酬，而不管提供何种服务]
capitation grant 按人计算的补助费
capitation tax 见 poll tax
capitis n. （罗马法）人格
capitis deminutio （罗马法）人格减等（指社会地位的降低等级）
capitis deminutio maxima （罗马法）人格大减等（指丧失自由和沦为奴隶）

capitis deminutio media （罗马法）人格中（或次）减等(指丧失公民身份)
capitis deminutio minima （罗马法）人格小减等(指改变家庭地位,包括断绝父亲亲属关系,但不影响公民身份)
Capitol n. 美国国会大厦
Capitol Hill 美国国会
capitula n. 条款
***capitula* itineris** chapters of the eyre 见 articles of the eyre
Capitulare Italicum 《意大利法律汇编》(1090年编制的一部汇编)
Capitulary n. （常用复）(法史)《加洛林王朝法规汇编》(8—10世纪加洛林王朝各君主所颁布的通常已划好条目的法令的汇编本,其中有处理行政、王室领地、公共秩序和司法等各种问题的法令,也有处理宗教问题的法令)
capitulate v. (有条件地)投降,停止抵抗
capitulation n. 1.领事裁判权(条约);外侨权利(指奥斯曼苏丹给予友好的非伊斯兰国家臣民的各种经济特权,包括设立外国商人区,在该区内领事有解决争端的裁判权等)2.投降规约,投降书;(复)(投降条约的)全部条款 3.(有条件的)投降 4.(文件、声明等的)摘要
capitulationism n. 投降主义
capper n. (美)假买手(指拍卖场雇用来抬高价格的人);勾引者,引诱者
Caprice n. 反复无常,任性;突变
capricious a. 反复无常的,无定见的,任性的;不以事实、法律和正当理由为依据的
capricious power 反复无常的权力,无效的权力
captain n. 1.长,首领;船长,舰长;领班 2.(陆军)上尉;(海、空、军)上校
captain's mast （军事法)(美)海军上校的桅杆[指由军事指挥官对应征人员的非司法惩罚(nonjudicial punishment),这种类型的惩处通常是由于轻罪(minor offense)而惩处。见 non-judicial punishment]
caption n. 1.标题;解说词 2.(起诉书上的)案件说明（附在诉讼等文件上的说明部分,开头写明双方当事人的姓名,受理法院名称和案件的编号等部分),司法文书首部;法律书籍的标题(或引言)3.(苏格兰)羁押令
captive n./a. 被拿捕者;战俘,俘虏;被监禁者/被俘房的;被监禁的;为另一企业所控制并为其需要而经营的
captive market 供货者垄断市场
captive nation 被奴役国家
captive soldier 战俘
captivity n. 囚禁;被俘,俘虏;束缚
captor n. 捕获者;夺得者,攻夺者;捕捉船
capture n. 捕获(指交战国在战争期间对敌国船舶之拿捕),战利品
capture at sea 海上捕获
captured personnel 被俘人员
captured ship 被捕获船舶
capturer n. 捕获者,俘获者
caput n. 人格人(见 homo)
car n. 车,车辆,汽车,车厢,电梯;(美)(复)列车
car accident 汽车失事,车辆事故
car insurance 车辆保险
Carbon Capture and Storage 二氧化碳捕捉与封存技术(指将化石燃料中的碳以二氧化碳的形式从工业或相关能源的排放源中分离出来,输送到封存地点,并使之长期与大气隔离的技术。缩略为 CCS)
car licence 汽车执照
carbon copy (复写的)复本
carbon credits 碳权
carbon finance 碳金融[指在地球气候变化背景下,限制温室气体排放和发展低碳经济已成为全球性共识。碳金融是环境金融的一部分,已成为金融体系应对气候变化的重要创新机制。它的研究内容包括所有与温室气体减排有关的金融市场、金融机构、金融产品以及金融服务等要素,而其基础则是碳排放权的可交易性(简称"碳交易"),系因《京都议定书》创建的三大合作机制而逐步在全球范围内得以实现,从而推动碳金融在全球的发展。见 environmental finance]
carbon money (碳交易市场上每单位碳信用价值的)碳币(见 carbon finance)
Carbon Sink 碳汇[《京都议定书》对"碳汇""林业碳汇"进行了明确界定:"碳汇"

是指土地利用与土地利用变化活动(LU-LUCF),如造林及农业土壤等对大气中二氧化碳的吸收、固定、存储作用]

Carcer ad hominess custodiendos, non ad puniendos, dari debet. A prison should be used for the custody not the punishment of persons. 监狱应用来关押人而非惩罚人的。

cardiac a. 心脏的,心脏病的
cardiac arrest 心脏停止
cardiac concussion 心脏震荡
cardiac death 心脏死
cardiac shock 心休克
cardiogenic shock 心源性休克,心脏性休克
care n. 谨慎,小心;照顾,照料,看护;管理,监督;忧虑,担心
care of real estate 对不动产的照管
care of the reasonable man 有理智人应有的注意
care proceedings 关于青少年犯罪的诉讼
career n. 1.职业,专业 2.履历,经历 3.发展
career civil service 职业行政部门
career consular officer 职业领事官员
career criminals 职业罪犯
career deputies (美)职业助理执法官(见 Marshals of the Court)
career diplomat 职业外交官
career in law (美)律师业;法律生涯
career judiciary 职业性法官
career service 职业性工作人员;长期服务
career training 专业训练,职业训练
careerist n. 追求地位者,野心家
careful a. 小心的,仔细的,细致的,精心的
carefully crafted legislation 精心(或精致)立法
caregiver n. (家庭法)看管者,监护者,关怀提供者[通常指儿童或少年或残疾人负有监护责任者(并非父母),亦称为 caretaker; custodian。见 residential responsibility]
careless a. (12世纪之前)1.缺乏合理注意的(reasonable care);有过失的,不谨慎的 2.进行缺乏理性注意行为的;从事不谨慎行为的

careless and inadvertent negligence 疏忽大意的过失
careless and inconsiderate driving 粗心莽撞驾车(罪)
careless driving (英)不小心驾驶车辆(根据道路交通法,在路上驾驶汽车时,没有应有的小心和注意或没有考虑到其他使用道路的注意事项)
carelessness n. (12世纪之前)1.缺少适当或理性的注意(指事实、情况或实例,即一个人做了不该做的事或没有做应该做的事。不注意,漫不经心,疏忽) 2.漫不经心的气质(作风),大大咧咧(指一个人随之便之,不做他该做的事)
caretaker n. 见 caregiver
caretaker government (或 cabinet) 看守政府(或内阁)
caretaker president 看守总统
caretaking expenditure 付出小心程度,持有小心程度
caretaking function (家庭法)照顾职能,给予关怀照顾(指父母的或照管人的任务关系到与孩子的相互关系,或指导他们照顾孩子。有的照顾职能还包括喂养孩子、给孩子洗澡、指导孩子的语言以及驾驶汽车技术的开发;对生病孩子的护理;培养孩子遵纪守法;还有对孩子的教育开发,以及道德教育;等等。见 parenting function)
cargo n. 货物;船货
cargo afloat 船货,业经装船之货,可运送之货物
cargo capacity 载货能力,载货容积
cargo claims 货物理赔
cargo consolidation scheme 货运统筹计划
cargo consolidator 货物集运人
cargo damage prevention 货物损坏预防
cargo handling 货物装卸
cargo in bulk 散装物(指外运货物不加包装,散装于船舶或专门放入舱中,而且形态上不能成件数者,亦称 bulk cargo)
cargo inspection 货运查验,货物检查
cargo insurance 货物保险
cargo insurer 货物承保人
cargo marine insurance 海上货物运输

保险
cargo navicert 货物航运执照
cargo plan (=stowage plan) 货物积载图
cargo (insurance) policy 货物保险单
cargo premium 货物保险费
cargo receipt 交货收据
cargo reservation 货运保留,预定仓位
cargo safety insurance 货物安全险
cargo sharing 货载分担
cargo supervision and control 货运监管
cargo surveyor 商检人员
cargo sweat 货物潮湿
cargo underwriter 货物保险人
cargo worthiness n. 船舶之载货能力
carload n. 车辆装载量;整车(货物)
carnage n. 大屠杀,残杀;成堆尸体
carnal a. 肉体的;物质的;肉欲的;淫乱的,好色的,世俗的
carnal abuse 猥亵行为,猥亵幼童;强奸(指奸淫幼女)
carnal books 黄色书籍,色情书籍
carnal intercourse 奸淫罪
carnal knowledge (15世纪)(古)性交[特别是与未成年的女性。现今,与尚未达到法定承诺年龄(age of consent)的幼女性交即构成法定强奸罪(statutory rape),有时缩略为 knowledge]
carnality n. 肉欲,好色;淫荡
carnalize v. 淫淫;耽于肉欲
carnapper n. 偷窃汽车者
carnet n. 海关文件(指①入境时应出示的关于车辆所有权及已保险的"证明文件",允准该车辆可以从一国出口至另一国家;②笔记本,支票本)
carriage n. 运送业,运输,运送,载运;费;四轮马车;(议会中提案的)通过
carriage and insurance paid to 货运与保险支付[商业合同术语,指分担货物的卖家与买家就有关发货、支付、损失险(risk of loss)的权利与义务。因此,卖家必须办理货物结关手续(clear the goods)以便出口(for export),努力取得货运时期买家的损失险(buyer's risk of damage)保险支付、发货给买家已选定的承运人以及承运货运至指定目的地的费用(进口税除外)。

当货物已被发送至承运人之手,则卖家的发运工作已经完成,损失险则传给买家。货物可以采用各种运输模式。缩略为 CIP]
carriage by air 空运
carriage by sea 海运
carriage contract 运送合同(契约),运输合同(契约)
carriage forward 运费由收货人支付;运费未付
carriage free 运费免付
carriage of contraband 载运违禁品;载运走私货
carriage of dangerous goods 危险品运输
carriage of goods by air 航空货物运输
carriage of goods by land 陆地货物运输
carriage of goods by sea 海上货物运输
Carriage of Goods by Sea Act (美)《海上货物运输法》(海商法)[指1936年的联邦法规,规定承运人对于海洋货物运输的损失或损害赔偿,以及延期根据提单(bill of lading)而承担的责任(《美国注释法典》第46标题卷第1300-15节)(46 US-CA §§ 1300-15)。该法界定了海洋货运提单的签发人(issuer)和持有人之间的许多权利与责任。缩略为 COGSA]
carriage of passengers 旅客运输
carriage of passengers by air 航空旅客运输
carriage of passengers by rail 铁路旅客运输
carriage of passengers by road 公路旅客运输
carriage of passengers by sea 海上旅客运输
carriage paid 运费已付
carriageway n. 行车道(路);马路
carrier n. 承运人;从事运输行业的人(或公司),搬运工人,搬运工具;递送人,(美)邮递员
carrier haulage 承运人拖运,运送人拖运
carrier manifest 承运人舱单,载货清单
carrier MTO 联运承运人
carrier's agent 承运人的代理人
carrier's allowance 承运人津贴
carrier's immunities 承运人免责
carrier's liability insurance 承运人责任保险
carrier's lien 承运人留置权

carrier's note 提单,取货证
carrier's risk 商业过失,承运人风险
carrot n. 胡萝卜;政治诱骗,不能兑现的允诺
carrot and a stick policy "大棒加胡萝卜"政策
carry v. 贯彻,执行;运送;移转,传送(播);刊登;携带,持有,具有,包含;获得赞同(或通过);出产,生产,供养;攻克
carry a contract 履行合同(契约)
carry an election 竞选获胜
carry back (over) (允许个人或公司利用经营纯损失抵减在损失前后几年纳税额的)税务规则
carry forward 推进,发扬;结转,将(账目)转入次栏(或页,册)
carry into effect (或 execution)实行,实施,实现,开始生效
carry off 1.夺去……生命;2.获得(奖品等)3.(成功地)对付;若其事地应付;4. 使成为过得去或可以接受
carry out 贯彻,执行,实施,进行(到底),实现;落实,展开
carry out the law 执法
carry over 1.贮存(货物)2.将账目结转次页 3.延期 4.(英)(交易所中)转期交割
carry the cause 胜诉;在争论中获胜
carry-in 转入库存
carry-over rate 转期利率
carry-over stock 结转库存量
carrying n. 运载,携带
carrying arms 携带武器(罪)
carrying capacity 载货量;载重能力
carrying capacity of the environment 环境的负担能力,环境负荷量
carrying charges 流动费用,流动支出;持有(或租用)财产所带来的费用(如税款);(分期付款购货的)附加价格;财产维持费,存量资产费用;持有债务费用;迟延提货费用,维修成本;贮囤费用
carrying cost 保藏费;财产维持费;存储成本;流动成本;(复)准获诉讼裁决(指法官给予一方当事人享有要求对方支付诉讼费权利的附带裁决)
carrying (carry) down 结转,转下页

carrying offensive weapon 持有攻击型武器
carrying on business 营业
carrying trade 运输业
carrying vessel 承运船只
carrying weapons illegally 非法携带武器(罪)
Carta Mercatoria (英)(1303年发给某些外国商人的)商业特许状
cartage n. 货运费
carte blanche 全权委托(书);自由处理权;签好名的空白纸
cartel n. 交战国间进行某些非敌对活动的协定;决斗书,挑战书;卡特尔;为采取共同行动所结成的政治联盟
cartel register 卡特尔登记册(簿)
cartel ship 战时交换战俘用的运输船
carting a jury (英)马车上的陪审团(指巡回审判中的一种古老的习惯)
carting London whores (英)驱逐妓女出城(传说中的伦敦习惯说法)
cartridge n. 子弹;(美)胶卷
cartulary n. 契据登记簿,契据集
carunculae hymenales (或 carunculae myrtiformes) 处女膜痕
cas fortuity 偶然情况
cas royaux (法)侵犯国王罪(包括不敬罪、煽动叛逆罪和伪造玉玺罪等)
case n. 情况,状况;事例,事实,实情;案情,案件,诉讼(包括民事和刑事),判例;供词,证据和争论,诉讼当事人向法庭提出的证据和辩论;(英)事实陈述
case agreed on 双方(两造)均无异议的案件
case at bar 正在审讯中的案件,在审案件
case at hand 手边的案件
case at law 法律案件
case attrition (美)案件损耗[指犯罪嫌疑人被捕之后基于各种原因在正式审判前被过滤。就是说特定比例的案件在刑事诉讼运行过程中被"损耗"掉了。现在研究表明,刑事诉讼运行过程中有些案件损耗不可避免,但有些"损耗"却是不必要的(unnecessary)]
case based on excess of power 有关越权案件

case brief 案情摘要
case by case 逐案的,个案的
case citators 判例援引集
case concerning illegal official conduct 公务上的不法行为案件
case decision 判例
case file 立案〈supreme court case files are often quiet voluminous〉(最高法院立案通常是大量的)
case finder 判例查找工具,判例检索工具
case flow management (德)(法官对)案件的管理
case for Crown (英)刑事案件
case for decision 待决案件
case for the defendant 有利于被告的案情
case having a federal element (美)涉及联邦性的案件
case headnotes 判例眉标,判例眉批
case in a cassation-revisional procedure 上诉程序中的诉讼案件
case in chief 庭审中负证明责任一方先举证的阶段;主要案件(指一方当事人证人的证词和伴随其证词提出的任何文件或其他证物)
case in point 判例,先例,对口判例
case in question 有争议的判例;正讨论的判例
case involving a claim for alimony 请求扶养费的案件
case involving alien 涉及外国人的案件
case involving foundation 涉及基金的案件
case involving motor 有关机动车辆案件
case involving public security 公共安全案件;治安案件
case involving the swindling of state property 骗取国家财产案
case involving the violation of regulations 违章案件
case law 判例法(亦称法官制定法),案例法
case law study 判例教学法(19世纪后期美国法学家兰达尔执教于哈佛大学创立的判例教学法)
case load (法庭等的)承办案件数

case method (或 system) 判例方法(制度),判例教学法(指通过历史上的重要判例并从中提出普遍法律原则进行法律教学)
case name 判例名称,案件名称
case of abandonment 遗弃案
case of assault 行凶案,暴行案
case of concealed homicide 隐瞒不报的杀人案
case of contravention 违法行为案件(没有犯罪但有违法行为的案件)
case of counterrevolution (中)反革命案件
case of criminally caused explosion 爆炸案
case of defacing public property 毁坏公共财产案
case of deliberate humiliation 公然侮辱案
case of dyke-breaching 决水案,决堤案
case of extorting confessions by torture 刑讯逼供案
case of first impression "无先例的"案件,初见案件(见 primae impressionis)
case of first instance 第一审案件
case of forgery of national currency 伪造国家货币案
case of fornication 私通案件(亦称:和奸案)
Case of Gibbens v. Ogden (美)吉本斯诉奥格登案(该案确立联邦商事法规优于该竞争州的法规原则,吉本斯胜诉获得纽约州水域航行权)
case of harbo(u)ring criminals 窝藏罪犯案
case of indictable offences 可指控犯罪的案件
case of injustice 冤案
case of intentional harm 故意伤害案件
case of interference with the freedom of marriage 干涉婚姻自由案
case of libel 诽谤案
case of murder 谋杀案
case of negligence 过失案件
case of participation in dangerous sports 参与危险体育项目案件

case of private prosecution （刑事）自诉案件
case of robbery 抢劫案
case of second instance 第二审案件
case of treason 叛国案
case of undermining solidarity of the nationalities （中）破坏各民族团结案
case of victimization 欺（诈）骗案
case on appeal 上诉案件
case on constitutional guarantees 有关宪法保障案件
case records 判例记录
case screening （美）案件过滤[指具有案件过滤权的主体，基于特定目标，对刑事案件进行评估和审查后，将部分刑事案件过滤在刑事诉讼之外的职权行为，其本质上是对案件进行的评估与控制（evaluation and control），如撤销案件、不予起诉和宣判无罪等。普遍认为美国刑事案件过滤制至少产生两大正面影响：其一，将不应追诉的案件（如无罪之人）及时过滤到刑事诉讼之外，减少错误追诉；其二，将不必追诉之案件（如情节轻微）及时过滤到刑事诉讼之外，降低案件负担，提升司法效率]
case stated （=stated case） 判案要点陈述（指当事人不满法庭的判决而向法庭所作的书面陈述，目的在于要求将判案要点交高等法院决断）
case study 案例研究，专题研究
case study method 案例研究法
case title 判例标题，判例名称，案件名称
case to counsel 案件提交给律师（法院将案件的事实陈述提交给律师征求其意见）
case to move for new trial 转移到其他法院重新审讯的案件
case under dispute 有争议案件
case went against him 此案判决他败诉
case without any clue 无头案件
case-book n. 判例汇编；判例集
case-by-case 逐案
case-filing n. 立案
case-finding n. 判例查找
case-in-chief n. 主要证据（诉讼中一方所提供的主要证据，不包含反对另一方案件审理部分的证据）
case-in-point n. 对口判例（指同一法庭或较高一级法庭所判决的类似的判例，亦指手头的案件与所找的判例情节甚为吻合）
case-lawyer n. 精通判例的律师
case-oriented a. 以案例为中心的，以案例为导向的
case-system n. 以实际判例为基础的法律教学法
caseload n. 工作量；（法庭等的）承办案件数，案件负担
casenote n. 案例摘要
cases and controversies 案件和辩论（指在诉讼中进行的真实的而不是假想的或伪装的争辩，美国联邦宪法允许法院只判决这些真实的辩论）
cases of appeal against the judg(e)ment and rulings of higher courts 不服高等（级）法院判决和裁定的上诉案件
cases with national implications 全国有重大影响的案件
cash n./v. 现金；现款/兑现
cash account 现金账户；现金账
cash against （或 on） delivery 交货付款，付现交货
cash against document 凭单据付现，交单付款
cash allowance 现金补贴
cash and delivery 付款交货，货到付款
cash assets 现金资产
cash at bank 银行现金
cash balance 现款结存；现金余额
cash basis 现金收付制，收付实现制，现金基础
cash before delivery 现金交易，付款后交货
cash bonus 现金红利
cash budget 现金预算
cash compensation 现金赔偿
cash control 现金管理
cash credit 现金信贷，现金信用，现金支付；活期信用放款，保证放款
cash crop 经济作物
cash deposit （银行）现金存款
cash discount 现金折扣，贴现

cash dividend 现金股息(红利)
cash down 即付现款,即期付款
cash flow 现金流量
cash in order 订货付现
cash letter of credit 现金信用证
cash liquidity 现金流动情况
cash loan 现金贷款
cash loan contract 现金贷款合同(契约)
cash losses 现金赔偿
cash market 现金交易,现货市场,付现市场
cash nexus 现金交易关系
cash offer 实物提供,付现供货
cash on (或 in) hand 库存现金;现有金额;手头的现金
cash on arrival 货到付款(现金)
cash on sale 一手钱一手货,钱货两清;现金买卖
cash on the line 付现金
cash payment 现付,现金支付
cash pledge 押金
cash price 现货价格,现金付款的最低价
cash register 现金出纳机(用于记录销售交易的机器)
cash refund annuity 现金偿还年金,现金归还年金(指在年金享有权人去世后,按整个应接受的数额与支付价格之差,提供一次支付的年金)
cash remittance note 解款单
cash sales 现销,现金买卖
cash settlement 现金结算
cash surrender value 退保现金解约价值,(人寿保险单的)退保价值
cash tender offer 现金投标价
cash transaction 现金交易,现金买卖
cash value 市场价值,现值,市面价值
cash wage system 货币工资制
cash without discount 付现无折扣
cash working capital 流(活)动现金资本
cash-and-carry a. 仓库交付现(金)价的,现金购物自行运送的
cash-book n. 现金簿,现金账
cash-in n. 公债等的兑现
cashier n./v. 出纳员/撤职,革除,解雇,拒用;废除,抛弃

cashier's check (=bank check) 本票;银行开出的支票;银行内部支票,(美)银行本票
cashing check 兑现支票
cassation n. (案件、判决、选举等的)取消,(大陆法)撤销原判(一种审查司法判决的方式),废除;翻案
cassation appeal 撤销上诉
cassation of a judg(e)ment of court 推翻法院判决
cassation proceeding 废弃判决程序,撤销原判程序;最高上诉程序
cast v. 1.抛,扔,投(票)2.使败诉,驳回(上诉人之上诉)3.解雇,辞退 4.图谋,筹划,打算;计算 5.铸(造)
cast ballot (或 vote)投票
cast doubt upon (on) 引起对……怀疑
cast in a lawsuit 败诉
cast in damages 被判决赔偿损失
cast opposing votes 投反对票
cast out 逐出,驱逐
cast out sth. behind one's back 把某事置之脑后
cast subjects in broad terms to do more than present the law 取材广泛,不就法论法
cast the blame on a person 加罪于人,嫁祸于人
cast the lone dissenting rate 只投反对票,投单一的异议票
caste n. 1.社会等级,(印)种姓 2.特权阶级 3.等级制度
caste privileges 等级特权制度
caste system 种姓制度(印度的一种等级制度,包括四种等级:婆罗门、刹帝利、吠舍、首陀罗)
castigate v. 惩罚,鞭打;申斥,严厉批评,修订(书等)
castigator n. 鞭打者,申斥者,修订者
casting method (用)铸模方法(提取指印)
casting vote 决定性一票(议会表决提案时,如赞成和反对双方的票数相等,则主持会议的主席可投决定性的一票)
casting voter 决定性投票人

castration n.(中史)宫刑;阉割;删除
casual n./a. 临时工;(英)不定期接受救济金的人/偶然的;不定期的,临时的;不明确的;非正式的;随便的
casual condition 偶然条件,偶成条件
casual delegation 临时代表团
casual ejector 假定的被告;名义被告
casual evidence 偶然得到的证据
casual labo(u)r 临时工
casual offender 偶犯
casual use 偶然消费
casual vacancy 临时空缺,(复)由于种种原因的(职位)空缺
casual worker 临时工
casualty n. 意外;严重伤亡事故,事故中伤亡的人员(或损害的物品);受害者,横祸
casualty accident 伤亡事故
casualty account investigation report 事故伤亡调查报告书
casualty insurance (美)意外事故保险;灾害保险
casualty loss 事故损失,灾害损失
casuistic a. 诡辩的,决疑的
casus n. 案例;原因;事故;机会
casus belli 宣战原因;宣战理由
casus foederis 依条约或合同(契约)所规定的
casus fortuitus 偶然事件(故)
* Casus fortuitus non est sperandus, et nemo tenetur devinare. A fortuitous event is not to be foreseen and no one is bound to expect it. 偶然事故是不可预见的,任何人对没有料到的事均不承担责任。
* Casus fortuitus non est supponendus. A fortuitous event is not to be presumed. 意外事件不得擅自推断。
casus major (大陆法)严重事故,重大事故
casus omissus (法律)无明文规定者
cat burglar 从屋顶(或破窗)而入的窃贼
cataclysm n. 洪水;(政治和社会的)大变动
catalla (古英国法)动产
* Catalla juste possessa amitti non possunt. Chattels justly possessed cannot be lost.

合法(或正当)占有的动产不容剥夺。
* Catalla reputantur inter minima in lege. Chattels are considered in law among the least (or minor) things. 动产在法律上视为不重要(或次要)的财产之一。
catalog(ue) n. (图书或商品的)目录;(美)学校章程;货物价目表
catalog(ue) price 商品目录价格
catastrophe bonds 灾难证券(为发生地震、飓风或其他自然灾害而发行的证券)
catastrophes n. 大灾难,大灾祸,大败,大变动
catastrophic defeat 灾难性挫败
catch v. 1.抓住,逮住,捕获;截住 2.听到,理解,领会 3.赶上,引起(注意);突然制住
catch all in a dragnet 一网打尽
catch at shadow 捕风捉影
catch on 理解,变得流行,明白,投人所好
catch the Speaker's eye (英)获得议会发言权
catch with the goods 1.追回被窃物 2.行窃时捕获
catch-all exceptions "一揽子"免责
catch-all provision 包罗条款(指英美法上关于扩大文书和法律适用范围的条款)
catch-words n. 眉标,标语;引导词
catchall 表示反对的嘘声,嘲笑
catchcolt n. (美)私生子
catching bargain 期待物权合同(契约),与期待权人达成的显失公平的合同(契约)
catchpoll n. 法警,法庭执达员
catchword n. 标语
categorical a. 无条件的,绝对的;明白的,明确的,断言的;范畴的
categorical assistance 无条件的帮助
categorical rule 绝对的规则,绝对的原则
categorical schemes 范畴规划,范畴设计
categories of indeterminate reference (用以作判决的)不确定的参照标准
categories of law 法律范畴
categorization approach 归类方法
cater v. 迎合,投合(for/to),为……供应餐饮
catholic a./n. 一般的,普遍的,广泛的;(大

写)天主教的/天主教徒
catholicity n. 普遍性,广泛性的,天主教主义,宽容,大量"C"(大)天主教之教父(=catholicism)
catholicity of science 科学的广泛性
Catholic Emancipation Act《天主教解禁法》(英议会 1829 年制定的法案,准许天主教徒任职于议会及从事其他以前被禁止的公务活动)
catomite n. 鸡奸幼童
cats and dogs 可疑证券,投机性股票(或证券);(美)低价股票,劣质股票
cattle n. 家畜,牲畜
cattle contract 放牧合同(契约)
cattle epidemic insurance 家畜疾病保险
cattle lifter 偷家畜贼
cattle stealing 盗窃牲畜
cattle trespass (英)家畜侵地(诉讼)
cattle-raising 畜牧业
caucus n./v. (英)(政党的)决策委员会;(美)(政党选举候选人或决定政策的)秘密会议;干部(或核心小组)会议/(英)召开决策委员会会议;(美)召开秘密会议;召开干部(或核心小组)会议
caught in the act 当场被逮
caught with the fang 当场捕获
caupones n. (罗马法)旅店主
causa n. 理由,原因;条件;起因,动机
causa acguirendi 取得原因
causa causans 近因,直接原因
∗ *Causa causae est causa causati.* The cause of a cause is the cause of the effect. 诉讼的原因就是被诉事件的原因。
∗ *causa causantis, causa est causati.* The cause of the thing causing is the cause of the effect. 被诉事件的原因就是产生诉讼的原因。
causa credendi 信用原因
causa cognita 调查以后,业经查明的(事实)原因
causa data de non secuta 约定之条件未成,因约定条件未成而返还已为给付之诉
causa donandi 赠与原因
causa impulsendi 驱动原因
causa justa (罗马法)正当法的理由、原因、动机或根据;作为决定性证据的事实
∗ *Causa sine qua non.* A necessary cause; The cause without which the thing cannot be or the event would not have occurred. 不可缺少的原因,必需的原因。
causa solvendi 清偿原因
causae obligationum 债因
∗ *Causa et origo est materia negotii.* The cause and origin is the substance of the thing, the cause and origin of a thing are a material part of it. 起因和缘由是事物的实质,一事物的起因和缘由是该事物的主要部分(意指法律总是认真对待起始的行为)。
causa mortis 考虑死因
causa patet 理由明显,原因清楚
causa potestatis ex causa lucrative (历史上)出于有利可图的缘由;自愿地,免费地
causa proxima 近因,直接原因
∗ *Causa proxima non remota spectatur.* The immediate (or direct), not the remote, cause, is looked at, or considered. 应追究近因而非远因。
causa rei (大陆法)附属物
causa remota 远因
causa sine qua non 不可缺少的原因,不可缺少的条件
causa turpis (大陆法)卑鄙的(不道德或非法的)约因;卑鄙的原因
∗ *Causa vaga et incerta non est causa rationabilis.* A vague and uncertain cause is not a reasonable cause. 含糊不清的和不确定的理由不是合理的理由。
causal a. 由某种原因引起的,要因的,构成原因的;因果关系的
causal analysis 因果分析
causal juristic act 要因的法律行为
causal relationship 因果关系
causal responsibility 因果责任
causal sequence 因果顺序
causality n. 原因;因果律;因果关系;原因作用;诱发性;(刑法)犯罪的因果关系
causality of crime 犯罪的因果关系
causation n. 因果关系(过失或刑法领域间的重要原理),因果律;原因;(某种原因)引起,导致

causation in fact 事实上的因果关系(见 causation in law)
causation in law 法律上的因果关系(英国法区分事实上的因果关系与法律上的因果关系,前者运用"put for test",关注的是作为事实,被告的过失是否是原告损失的原因;后者涉及"remoteness"的判断,关注的是,作为法律,被告是否应对其事实上造成的损害承担责任)
causation within the meaning of criminal law 刑法意义上的因果关系
causation-in-fact approach 实际诱因计算法(见 out-of-pocket-measure)
causationism 因果论
causationist 因果论者
causative a. 成为原因的,引起的,要因的
causative action 要因行为
causative contract 要因合同(契约)
causative juristic act 要因的法律行为
cause n./v. 1.诉因,案件,诉讼 2.原因,起因,理由,缘故 3.事业,目标/造成,引起,导致,促使,使遭受
cause and effect 因果,因果关系
cause book 诉讼登记册,被告出庭备忘录
cause célèbre 著名案件;轰动一时的大案;(复)(法)《著名案件汇编》
cause considerable loss 造成相当损失
cause in fact 事实上的原因
cause in law 法律原因,法律上的原因
cause lawlessness 目无法纪
cause list 最高法院讼案排列表;诉讼案件表(逐日安排民事诉讼案件开庭审讯的时间次序表)
cause of action 1.诉因[指给诉讼提供一个或一个以上依据的一系列有效事实(operative facts),这一事实情况使得一个人有资格从另一个人身上获得救济。(见 claim)〈after the crash, Aronson had a cause of action〉(在飞机失事后,阿隆森上有了诉因)] 2.诉讼的法理(legal theory of a law suit)〈a malpractice cause of action〉(不当行为作为提起诉讼的法理)(见 right of action)。[在1和2的意义上亦称 ground of action] 3.(宽松地说)诉讼,提起诉讼,起诉〈there are four defendants in the pending cause of action〉(待决诉讼中有4名被告)
cause of action alleged 所指称的诉因,诉称的诉因,所主张的诉因
cause of action "arise out of" 诉因产生于,诉讼原因产生于
cause of action estoppel 见 collateral estoppel
cause of bankruptcy 破产原因
cause of criminality 犯罪原因
cause of death 死因
cause of invalidity 无效原因
(The) cause of the thing causing is the cause of the effect. 案件诉讼的原因就是被诉事件的原因,诉讼事件的原因即是实施法律效果之原因。
cause solventi 清偿原因
cause trouble 肇事
cause trouble by spreading rumors 造谣生事
Cause-and-prejudice rule (1977)(刑法)诉因和不利规则[该规则是指申请在合宪性异议(constitutional challenge)基础上的联邦人身保护令(federal habit of habeas corpus)的罪犯首先必须表明其权利主张(claim)依赖宪法的一项新规定(a new rule of constitutional law)(如该案在州法院听审,则不得采用这一条新规定)或依赖于虽竭尽努力亦不能可较早披露的事实,通过明显且有力的证据表明如果未出现宪法上的错误。该罪犯不得被判有罪。参见《美国注释法典》第28卷第2254节第(e)(2)款。这是"程序上未履行原则"(the procedural default doctrine)的一个例外。1996年以前诉因和不利规则允准联邦法院在合宪性异议基础上给予救济。如果该罪犯已表现出正当诉因(good cause)而未构成在审判上的对立(challenge),同时还表明审理法庭的错误实际上造成对罪犯不利的影响,则此救济并非提供给审判庭审。见 constitutional challenge]
cause-of-action estoppel 见 collateral estoppel
causer n. 惹起者;原因物;根由
causidicus n. (大陆法)职业辩护人,律师
causing a riot 聚众骚乱
**Causing tortuous injure in this state by an

act or omission outside the state. 在外州的行为或不作为导致侵权损害(或伤害)发生于本州之内。
caustic dissent 苛求的异议,讽刺的异议
cauterization n. 卡特尔主义
cautio n. 担保,保证;保释金;保证人
cautio indicatum solvi (罗马法)偿付判决额的担保(指破产人不得担任自治市的官员,他还要提供偿付判决额的担保,承诺在所有以他为被告的诉讼中偿付判决额)
cautio pro expensis 费用担保
caution n./v. 1.小心,谨慎 2.警官对被怀疑的犯罪人发出的警告(即他所述的一切将都被记录下来作为受审时的证据提交,如果未发出此种警告,法院对任何陈述可认为不能接受) 3.(一种存放在土地登记处的)正式宣言 4.(教会法上一种对履行义务的)保证 5.(苏格兰)(要求财产管理人或遗嘱执行人等为自己经管财产提供的)保证/警告,告诫
caution against 警告
caution money 见 earnest money
cautionary a. 告诫的,警告的;注意的
cautioned statement (英)告诫后录得的陈述书(在某项犯罪案件发生之后,警察对怀疑与此案有关系的人,在询问前经告诫手续,使其知道他依法没有回答询问的义务,如自愿回答,则所说的情况,就要记录下来,作为告诫后录得的陈述书,经签名后送交法院作为证据)
cautioner n. 警告者;保证人
cautious a. 细心的,谨慎的
cavalier parliament (英史)骑士国会(查理二世的第二届长期国会)
caveat 当心;中止诉讼程序的申请;遗产有争议时中止发给管理证书的申请;停止支付通知,(要求停止某些行为的)警告;(美)保护发明专利权的申请书;防止误解的说明;告诫某人当心,异议通知,暂停程序;(为防误解作的)解释;(海商法)免除扣押通知;(土地法)登记申请
Caveat emptor: qui ignorare non debuit quod jus alienum emit let a purchaser beware; who ought not to be ignorant that he purchasing the rights of another. 买主自慎之,不要误买到他人的权利;货物出门概不退换,买主需当心(买的货物是否有瑕疵)
caveat actor 行为者当心
caveat against arrest 中止财产扣押的申请
caveat against release and payment 中止解除财产的扣押及发给售卖财产所得款项的申请
Caveat emptor 货物出门概不退换,买主需当心
caveat subscriptor 签名者当心
caveat venditor 卖者当心
caveat viator 行路者当心,旅客当心
caveatee n. 受到告诫(或警告)者
caveator n. 申请中止诉讼者;提出告诫(或警告)的人
cavil n. 吹毛求疵
cavortings (复) n. 下流不端行为
CD-ROM 只读光盘
cease n./v. 停止,中止/停止;结束
cease being guarantor 退保,不做保证人
cease to have effect 停止生效
cease-and-desist order (美)禁止令[指法院或行政机关禁止个人(或企业)继续某种特定行为的命令](见 injunction; restraining order)
cease-fire n. 停火,停火命令
cease-fire order 停战令
cede v. 割让,让与;放弃;让步
cede insurance 分保险,分保保险
ceded territory 割让的领土,割让地
Cedel Bank 希德尔银行(见 Depository Trust Company)
ceding state 割让国
Ceiling n. 上升限度
ceiling and flour 上下限
celation n. 隐瞒怀孕;隐瞒分娩
celebration of marriage 结婚仪式
celestial a./n. 天的,天空的,天上的/天上的人,神仙,(大写)天朝的人
celestial body 天体
celibacy n. 独身状态,独身生活,独身
cell n. 小室,密室;(监狱中的)单人囚房
cellular licenses 泡沫特许
Celtic law 凯尔特法(公元前10世纪到1世纪出现于中欧并向西扩展的凯尔特人

的法律)
cemetery n. 公墓,墓地
censor n. 保密检查官(员);新闻出版审查官(员);户口调查员;(古罗马)监察官
censor of film 电影审查官(员)
censorial a. (古罗马的)监察官(员)的;检查官(员)的;审查官(员)的;非难的
censorious a. 吹毛求疵的,爱挑剔的
censorship n. 审查(制度)(美国联邦最高法院认定审查制度是对言论自由的一种特别不能容忍的限制),(书刊)检查(制度);检查官(或审查员)的职位,(古罗马)监察官的职位
censorship commission 书刊审查委员会
Censorship Laws 检查法(英国一种保障其君主政体的法律)
censorship of book 书刊审查(制度)
censorship of film 电影审查(制度)
censorship of press 出版物的审查(制度),新闻检查(制度)
censurable a. 该受指责的
censure n./v. 批评;谴责,指责;非难/指责,非难,苛评
censure motion 不信任动议;弹劾案
censure vote 不信任票
census n. 人口调查,人口普查;(调查获得的)统计数字
census act 人口调查法
Census Bureau 见 Bureau of the Census
census data 人口调查资料
census of housing 住房统计字数
census of population 人口统计字数
census officer 人口调查员
census paper 人口(或户口)调查表
census police 户籍警
census register 户籍登记簿
census registration 人口普查登记
census taker 户口调查员
census tract 户口片区
center (= centre) n./v. 中心,中心区;中央;中枢,核心;(议会等的)中间派;中心站(或场,所)/集中,把……聚集在(on)
center chair 中心坐席(指美国联邦首席大法官)
Centers for Disease Control and Provention

(CDC) (美)疾病控制和预防中心(指美国卫生和人类服务部的一个机构。负责进行医疗研究,促进疾病和伤害的预防以及应对公共卫生的紧急情况。这个机构是在美国卫生和人类服务部重组时建立的,前身是 1964 年设立的传染疾病中心)
Center for International Environmental Law 国际环境法中心(非政府组织之一)
Center for Law and Education (美)法律和教育中心(由法律服务公司创立、支持全美国地方法律服务机构的中心,该中心特别强调学生的权利)
Center for Law and Social Policy (美)法律和社会政策中心(美国的一种公共福利机构)
Center for Marine Conservation 保护海洋中心(非政府组织之一)
Center for Public Resources (美)公共援助中心
center for women policy studies 妇女政策研究中心
Center of Asian Studies 亚洲研究中心
center of discipline 管教所
center of gravity doctrine 最密切联系原则;法律关系重心原则(指在解决法律冲突时,适用与争议事项或争议当事方有最密切联系的地方法律原则。见 most significant theory)
Centers for Disease Control and Prevention (美)疾病控制和预防中心
central a. 中心的,中央的,中枢的,主要的
central administration 中央行政管理,中央政府
central administrative body 中央行政管理机关
Central Arbitration Committee (英)中央仲裁委员会
Central Authorities 中央机关[国际私法与行政合作机制的基本模式是通过在缔约国设立中央机关的方式来进行的除中央机关外还有主管机关(Competent Authorities)与委托机关(Accredited Bodies)的合作模式]
central authority 中央政权(政府)

central bank credit control 中央银行的信用统制
central court of general jurisdiction at law 具有一般管辖权的中级法院
Central Criminal Court (英)中央刑事法院[设在伦敦,取代了长期以来设在老贝利(Old Bailey)的法庭,其刑事审判权除伦敦外遍及米度息斯郡的若干郊区地方。该法院的审判仅根据指控进行,并不存在上诉审。该法院法官由高等法院的法官和伦敦的司法官等组成]
central committee 中央委员会
central competence 中央权限
Central Controlling Personnel Office (美)中央人事管理局(根据1883年的文官法,设立中央人事管理局作为联邦政府的人事统制机构,现改名为美国文官委员会)
central determinant 决定因素,核心因素
central executive 中央行政机关
central executive committee 中央执行委员会
central government 中央政府
centralized investigation 集中型侦查
Central Intelligence Agency (美)中央情报局
Central Military Commission (中)中央军事委员会
central monarchy 中央集权君主制
Central Moot 中央议会(国民咨询会)
Central Office (英)中央办公室,中心办公室[指大多数英国法院的首要办公室。该办公室于1879年建立,旨在加强普通法法院的主事官和助理或记录官,以及后座法庭分庭(Queen's Bench Division)的刑事部(Crown Office)办公室工作的功能(Clerical function)和大法官法庭(Chancery Division)的判例汇编、注册办公室、其他一些办事处的工作功能]
Central Office Review Committee (CORC) (美)中央审查委员会(由最高层监狱官及行刑局局长组成,拥有行刑局内部的最终决定权)
Central People's Government (中)中央人民政府
central tax 国税

centralism n. 中央集权制;集中制
centralist a./n. 拥护集中制的,集中制的/集中制的拥护者
centrality n. 中心地位,居于中心地位
centrality theory 主要证据理论
centralization n. 中央集权;集权;集中
centralization of authority 中央集权
centralization of power 集权
centralized a. 集中的;中央集权的
centralized government 集权政府;中央集权制政府
centralized licensing 中心许可证贸易(集体许可证合同的一种)
centralized management 集中管理(指美国公司治理较全面、完善的模式;即构建公司股东、董事和经理内部关系的一种权威的、标准的公司治理结构)
centralized planning 集中规划
centrally planned economy (country) 中央计划经济(国家)
centrism n. 温和主义,中间主义
centrist n. (某些欧洲国家议会里的)中间派议员,(不持极端观点的)温和派
Centumviri n. (复)(罗马法)百官法庭(指公元前150年设立的具有105名法官的法庭,具有审理重大案件的管辖权,特别是涉及继承和遗嘱纠纷的案件。法官来自35个部落,每一部落有3名)
Century Digest (美)百年判决摘要汇编(美国判决摘要汇编系统的第一个汇集。由西方出版公司出版,自1658年至1896年的判决摘要汇编。见American Digest System)
ceorl n. (英史)(盎格鲁-撒克逊社会)最下层的自由民
cepi v. 已拘捕
cepi corpus 已拘捕(扣押)
* **Cepi corpus et bail.** I have arrested and then released the defendant on bail bond. 我已拘捕被告并将其具保在外候审。
* **Cepi corpus et committitur.** I have arrested and committed the defendant to prison. 我已将被告拘押并将其送入监狱。
* **Cepi corpus et est languidus.** I have arrested the defendant and he is sick. 我已将

被告人拘捕,但其病情严重(在行政司法官的送达回证中指明该被告人病情十分严重而不能从拘捕之处安全转移)。
Cepi corpus et paratum habeo. I have made an arrest and am ready to produce the defendant. 我已将被告人拘捕并将其羁押听候发落。
cerebral a. 脑的,大脑的
cerebral concussion 脑震荡
ceremonial marriage 有仪礼的婚姻,举行仪式的结婚,按法律规定的结婚
ceremonial usage 礼仪上的惯例
ceremonialism n. (过分)讲究礼节,拘泥于仪式
ceremony n. 典礼,仪式;礼节,礼仪,客气
Cerofa 《行政官法》(见 *Leges Henrici Primi*)
cert denied (Den.) 调卷令(certiorari)被拒绝
cert pool (美)文书组(1922 年成立起初为 6 人至 1980 年代增至 8 人。其机制是明确的。联邦最高法院的一组书记员,审阅调卷令的申请,并为大法官写出事实和争点的摘要记录,同时提出调卷令是否可得以保证允准的建议);调卷复审申请库
certain a. 确凿的,无疑的;可靠的;确信的,必然的,一定的,某种
certain claim 必然要求,确实要求
certain game pairwise 特定双方都明智的博弈
certain part of the difference 差额的一定比例数
certain presumption 必然的推定
certain special case 特定情况
certainty n. 确定,确定性,肯定,必然的事,毫无疑问的事
certainty of allegation 主张的确定性
certainty of detection and conviction 破案和定罪的正确性
certainty of law 法律的确定性
certifiable a. 可证明的
certificate n./v. 证明文件,执照,证明书[指①其中事实已被证实的文件〈death certificate〉(死亡证明书)(见 stock certificate);②身份证明,指证明持有人的执照或批准从事一个特定行业的工作〈nursing certificate〉(护理证明书);③公告或通知,指一个法院通知另一个受理案件的法院〈when issuing its opinion, the Seventh Circuit sent a certificate to the Illinois Supreme Court〉(在发布判决意见书时,第七巡回法庭已送通知或公告给伊利诺伊州最高法院)]/批准,发证书给……用证书证明;认证
certificate for export 出口检验证
certificate for fire extinguishing and detecting apparatus 消防设备证书
certificate for passage 通行证(书)
certificate for refrigerating appliance 冷藏设备证书
certificate lands (美)凭证购买的土地
certificate of (ship) nationality (船舶)国籍证书
certificate of addition of improvement 专利改进附加证书
certificate of analysis 分析(鉴定)证书
certificate of appointment 委任证书
certificate of approval of the marking 载重线标志(批准)证书
certificate of assize (对巡回法庭处理过的事)重新审理核准令
certificate of auditing 审计证明书
certificate of authority (美)授权证书,权威性证明书[指①即将送往另一管辖的认证过的公证文件。此证明书确保州外或境外的受领人相信公证人(notary public)具有有效的授权(valid commission)。亦称 certificate of capacity; certificate of character; certificate of authentication; certificate of prothonotary; certificate of magistracy; a-postille; verification。②由国家机关(通常为国务卿)发布文件允准境外的企业在本国做生意]
certificate of bad faith 恶意证明或欺诈证明书[指一位当事人已被允准以贫民诉讼资格(in forma pauperis)在美国地区法院起诉,该法院发布一纸文件证明该当事人的上诉是轻浮的,所以除非交付正常的呈交诉状费,不准以此资格诉讼,参见《美国注释法典》第 28 标题卷第 1915 节。见

certificate of good faith]
certificate of breakage 货物损毁证明书
certificate of cause of death 死因证明书
certificate of citizenship 公民身份证明
certificate of clearance 结关单；手续完备证书
certificate of competency 合格证书
certificate of competency as master 合格船长执照
certificate of competency in first aid 急救合格执照，救伤执照
certificate of condition 品质检验证明书
certificate of conference （美）协议证明书 [指呈交法院的答辩状或动议的一部分，通常包括呈请答辩状或动议的当事方单独在文件末了向法院证明当事各方具有解决问题的意图，但需要一个司法判决，因为协议(agreement) 不能达到目的。法院要求某种动议附有协议证明书，这就迫使当事各方试图解决他们自己的问题，如无必要，就无须法院承担此项责任。参见《联邦民事诉讼规则》第 26 章]
certificate of coroner 死因裁判人员证书，验尸官证书
certificate of correction 补正证书
certificate of death 死亡证明书
certificate of delivery 送达证明
certificate of departure from port 离港证明书
certificate of deposit 存单，押金证书，存款证明书
certificate of diagnosis 诊断证明书
certificate of election 当选证明(书) [指由州长、地方长官、选举委员会或其他主管当局(competant authority) 发出的文件证明被提名的人(named person)已经当选]
certificate of entrustment 委托书
certificate of fitness 健康证明书
certificate of foreign insurance 外地保险证书
certificate of freeboard 干舷(高度)证书
certificate of good conduct 优良品行奖状
certificate of good faith 诚信证明书，善意证明书 [指一位当事人已被允许以贫困诉讼资格在美国地区法院进行起诉，该法院发布一纸文件证明该当事人上诉并非轻浮(frivolous)，故该当事人无须支付费用或保证金。地区法官有时发布一个善意证书，即使这些证书绝无要求；除非法院发布欺诈证明，否则该当事人允准以贫困诉讼资格(in forma pauperis)。参见《美国注释法典》第 28 标题卷第 1915 节。见 certificate of bad faith]
certificate of guarantee 保单；保证书
certificate of holder of attached property 扣押财产持有人证书
certificate of hono(u)r 荣誉证书
certificate of identification 身份证
certificate of identity 身份证明书
certificate of import licence 进口许可证
certificate of incorporation 公司注册证书，社团成立证书
certificate of indebtedness 债券，借据；负债证书
certificate of inspection 检验证明书
certificate of insurance 保险证书；保险凭证(亦称小保单，与保单有同样作用)
certificate of invention 发明证书
certificate of marriage 结婚证书
certificate of master 主事官证明书
certificate of merit 功过证明，法律依据证明(书) [指经过原告的代理人或律师签名的证明，并交予民事诉讼中的检举人(complaint)。此证明中断言，原告代理人至少已与一位有权威的专家协商过并在此后得出结论认为该项诉讼请求是有法律依据的。许多州有法令要求某些类型案件中需有法律依据证明，比如专业上的渎职(professional malpractice)。法律的目的是尽早去除缺少法律依据的权利请求(frivolous claims)，在这些州中，如果这一证明未交予检举人，则此项诉讼通常会被撤销。根据宣誓或对伪证罪的惩罚(penalty of perjury)，任何时候法律都会要求签署，有时它就被称为 affidavit of merit]
certificate of naturalization 入籍证明书
certificate of non-appearance 不到庭证明书
certificate of occupancy 占有证书
certificate of origin 原产地证明书

certificate of ownership 所有权状
certificate of ownership of land 土地所有权证
certificate of particulars of motor vehicle 机动车记录证明书
certificate of possession of land 土地占有权状
certificate of posting 投寄证明
certificate of *pratique* (发给船只的)无疫证书
certificate of protest 票据的拒付证书;船长证明书(证明船舶的损坏系由灾难造成)
certificate of purchase 购买证
certificate of quality 货物品质(质量)证书
certificate of quantity 货物数量证书
certificate of re-export 转口证明书
certificate of registration 登记证书,注册证书[指①(版权)美国版权局核准一项版权申请并说明核准著作的注册日记和版权登记号的证明文件;②(商标)确认美国专利和商标局已经核准并登记了商标和使用标记(service mark)的文件。该证书验证的内容包括已注册的商标、首次使用日期、产品的类型或正式申请的使用标记、注册号和登记日期、注册的期限、最早申请日期及注册的条件和有效期(condition and limitation)]
certificate of registry (海商法)注册或商船登记证明(书)(指证明该船已按法律要求进行登记的文件。见 registry)
certificate of rehabilitation 名誉恢复证明(书)[指①有些州由法院或其他授权的政府机关,如假释委员会(parole board),发布一个文件(document)作为一项证据证明一个已判罪的罪犯有资格至少重新获得一些公民身份的权利。州之间一般广泛使用名誉恢复证明这一术语,有些州,比如纽约州,则基于判罪的类型和数目发布不同种类的恢复名誉证明。②对一座具有历史意义的建筑物的整修、恢复、维护以及名声的恢复,通常由地方政府发布证明的文件。这类证明通常使财产所有人有资格享受优惠税收待遇。③证明低于标准规格的住房经过满意的整修已符合住房法规(housing-code)标准的文件]

certificate of satisfaction 清偿证书
certificate of seaworthiness 适航证书
certificate of security 担保证书;保证单
certificate of service 送达证明[指呈交法院的辩护或动议的一部分,通常单独地放在最后一页,其中提起诉讼的当事方(filing party)向法院证明复本已寄交或以其他方法送交所有当事方。送达证明通常不包括起始诉讼时原告呈交的辩诉状(pleading),因为该辩诉通常在送达之前就已呈交,即使原告被要求呈交送达证明。至于其他正式书面答辩状或申述以及动议,一般均要求送达证明。参见《联邦民事诉讼规则》第 5(d)条。亦称为 proof of service]
certificate of share (或 stock) 股票
certificate of shipment (装运)出口证明书,出口许可证
certificate of soundness 合格证书
certificate of stowage 装载证书
certificate of the only child (中)独生子女证书
certificate of title (土地)所有权证书(旧译地契)
certificate of title to share 股票所有权证书
certificate of utility (专利)利用证书
certificate of utility model 实用新型证书;实用型式证明
certificate of vaccination 防疫注射证书(检疫)
certificate of validity 有效证明书
certificate of weight 重量证明书
certificate to commence business 营业(贸易)证明书,开业证明书
certificate to practise 执业证书
certificate trial 证据审判
certificates of ownership 所有权证书
certification n. 保证;证明,证明书;确认,检定;(美)意见确认(指美国上诉法院以及联邦索赔法院通过一定程序可提交给联邦最高法院要求就案件中有争议的法律问题作出有关约束力的指示)
certification by a notary 公证证明
certification fee 认证费

certification hypothesis　背书理论
certification letter　证明信件
certification mark　证明标记,检测标记(系由一个组织,而不是厂家或销售商贴在货物上的证明标记,以表明这些货物质量符合标准要求)
certification of authorization of manufacture　生产许可证,批准生产的证明文件
certification of bond　债券确认证明
certification of cheque (或 check)　支票的保付
certification of question (of law)　(美)将法律问题提出审查(指下级法院可将案件涉及的特定法律问题移送上级法院裁决;最初是从联邦法院发展起来的一种程序,现已形成惯例)
certification of record on appeal　(审判法官签署的有关)上诉复审问题案卷的签认书
certification of the returns　选举结果报告
certification of transfer　让与证明书(股票)过户确认
certification order　认证命令
certification proceeding　(美)证明程序(国家劳资关系委员会弄清公司的雇员所要求的特定工会是否能代表他们的一种程序)
certification process　认证过程
certified a.　被证明了的;有保证的
certified check (或 cheque)　保付支票,由银行担保支付的支票
certified copy　经验证的副本,签证副本,证明文件
certified correct　证明无误,经验证无误
certified invoice　签证发票,证明发票
certified lunatic　已证明的精神病患者
certified mail　带有回执的邮件(只保证递送,而不负责赔偿的一类邮件)
certified public accountant　(美)持有执照的正式会计师,公证会计师
Certified Public Accountant Law of the People's Republic of China　《中华人民共和国注册会计师法》
certified question of law　法律认证问题
certified signature　经验证的签名

certified true copy　经验证无误的副本
certified under the hand of (sb.)　经由(某人)签名证明
certifier n.　证明者
certify v.　用书面形式证明,证明;(美)担保付款(指出银行担保票据的可靠性)
certifying bank　付款保证银行
certifying officer　核证人
certiorari　(上级法院向下级法院)调取案卷复审的令状(见 writ of *certiorari*)
certiorari petition　调取案卷,复审令状申请书
certans de captando　以获利为目的,为利益而奋斗;企图得到一种优势(诉讼中原告未获利而继续诉讼)
Certum est quod certum reddi potest.　That is certain which can be rendered certain.　可以使之确定的便是实在的。凡能使之确定者,即是确定。
cess n.　(英)税,捐;税额
* *Cessa regnare, si non vis judicare.*　Cease to reign, if you don't wish to adjudicate.　不愿断案就别把着案子不放(喻"不要身在其位,不谋其事")
* *Cessante causa, cessat effectus.*　The cause ceasing, the effect ceases.　原因消失,则其后果也就消失。
* *Cessante ratione legis, cessat et ipsa lex.*　The reason of the law ceasing, the law itself also ceases.　法律的立法理由消失,则法律本身也就不复存在。
cessation n.　中止,中断,休止,停止
cessation of arms　休战
cessation of business　暂停营业
cessation of hostilities　停止敌对行动
cessation of work　停工
cesse n.　税,税额
cesser n.　期限、责任等的中止,终结;疏忽;权利终止期
cesser and lien clause　责任终止与留置权条款
cesser clause　责任中止条款;债务中止条款
cesset executio　停止执行(令)
cesset processus　使诉讼中止;正式中止诉

讼令
cessio bonorum (罗马法)交出财产(指以货抵债);财产的让与
cessio in jure (罗马法)交出物权(指采取拟诉方式转让财产)
cessio legis 法定让与
cession n. (权利、财产等的)转让;(债权)让与;割让(指国家的一部分被割让给他国或为他国所吞并),割让的领土;放弃
Cession des biens 财产转让;以物抵债
cession legis 法定地转移给保证人
cession of property 财产转让
cession of territory 领土割让
cessionary n./a. (财产、权利等的)受让人/割让的,让与的;转让财产的
cestui que trust 信托受益人
cestui que use 有用益权的(人),有土地使用权的(人)
cestui que vie 以生存期作为他人(享有)的权利期限(指租期长短以人的寿命来计算)
ceteris paribus 假使其余情况均相同,假使其余情况保持不变
CFR Hamburg not later than CFR (按货运成本价规则)汉堡不迟于……
chaffer n. 1.讲价钱,讨价还价 2.开玩笑者
chafferer n. 议价人
chaffwax n. (英)(旧大法官法院的)封蜡事务官
chain n. 1.束缚;监禁 2.(复)联营公司;镣铐,囚禁;枷锁;一系列,连锁,一连串 3.(一个公司下属的)联号
chain referral 连销安排(见 pyramid sales scheme)
chains gang (美)用铁链锁在一起被罚做苦工的囚犯队
chains of causation 因果连锁
chain of custody (1947 年)物证连续保管,证据保管链[指①从获取证据时起到将证据提交法庭为止,关于实物证据(real evidence)的流转和安置的基本状况,以及保管证据的人员的历史情况。"证据保管链要求每一位证据持有人提供证言证明对证据保管的连续性。同时还要求每个人员提供证言证明其在保管期间,证

据实质上保持相同状态。所有更改、替代、变更状态的可能性均不得排除。比如,一般情况下,放在保险箱中的一个证据实物不止一个人接触过,那么其中没有一个人可以出示证据。但是,认证证据的真实性问题越重要,就越需要否定修改、更替的可能性。"引自 Michael H. Graham:《联邦证据法规》(系列丛书)(Federal Rules of Evidence,in a Natshell,1992 年第三版)第 402 页。②动产占有的历史,亦称 chain of possession]
chains of debt 连锁债务
chain of possession 见 chain of custody ②
chains of representation 继承的连续性
chains of title 所有权的连续性
chains store (美)联营商店(旧译联号,指具有统一管理和存储中心的两个以上的零售单位的联合)
chair n./v. 1.座位;议长;会长;主席 2.(美)证人席 3.(美)电椅/主持会议;任(会议)主席
chairman n. 主席,主任(指集体机构首脑),议长,会长
chairman of board of directors 董事长
Chairman of the Standing Committee of the National People's Congress (中)全国人民代表大会常务委员会委员长
chairman of ways and means (英)赋税委员会主席
chairwoman n. 女主席,女议长,女会长,(中)女委员长
challenge n./v. 1.挑战,正式提出反对 2.(对某一表决或某人投票资格表示的)质问;怀疑 3.回避(指要求陪审员回避)/挑战;反对;宣布反对;拒绝,回避
challenge a result 对表决结果提出质疑
challenge for cause 有因回避(美国民诉案件中律师作出的,旨在阻止准陪审员加入陪审团的努力。因依律师之见,该陪审员对预先审核问题的回答显示出她或他不能公正对待此案。如果法官赞同律师之意见,则以此理由取消该陪审员资格。见 peremptory challenge)
challenge for favo(u)r 因偏袒的回避(因存在有利或偏袒一方当事人的情况所提

出的回避)
challenge of juror 要求(某个)陪审员回避
challenge system 回避制度
challenge the constitutionality of a law 对一项法律的合法性(合宪性)提出质问
challenge the law personally 以身试法
challenge to fight 挑起决斗(指用书面或口头来挑动与他人打斗,依普通法为轻罪)
challenge to jury array 对陪审团人选提出的回避(因安排陪审团的司法行政官有差错对陪审团名单提出的,也可对回到陪审席上的所有陪审员提出)
challenge to panel 反对陪审团出庭;要求陪审团回避
challenge to the polls (= peremptory challenge) 无因回避(亦称为绝对回避,指由一方无需理由逐个对陪审员提出的绝对回避,仅适用于刑事审判,通常回避人数不得超过7人)
challenge to the ruling 对裁决提出异议
challenge witness 回避证人
challengeable a. 应回避的,可拒绝的
challenged sentence 受到异议的判决,被非难的判决
challenger n. 使回避者,行使拒绝权利的人;挑战者;反对者
chamber n./a. (13世纪)1.室或房间〈gas chamber〉(毒气室)2.立法或司法机构或其他审议会(deliberative assemble)〈chamber of commence〉(商会)3.(立法机构的)议事厅〈the senate chamber〉(参议院议事厅)/(议会)一院(参议院或众议院的)
chamber barrister 法庭顾问律师
chamber counsel 不出庭的律师;私人法律顾问;(律师的)私人意见,鉴定
chamber of accounts (法)理财法院财会庭,审计庭
chamber of agriculture 农会
chamber of cassation 最高上诉(法)庭
chamber of commerce 商会
chamber of commerce and industry 工商会
Chambers of Congress 国会两院;国会参众两院
(Both) Chambers of Congress (美)国会

的参众议院
chamber of deputies (法国等的)下议院,众议院;代表院
chamber of industrial commerce 工商业协会
Chamber of Peers (葡)参议院,贵族院
chamber of shipping 航运公会
chamber's clerk (英)大律师的文书
chamberlain n. 管家;国王侍从;收款员,财务主管人,会计员
chamberlain's court (英)(伦敦城的)管理大臣法庭
chambers of the King 英王专属海湾管辖区
chambers of trade 贸易协会
chambre ardente (法史)火刑法庭(一种调查审判异教徒的特别法庭)
chambre des comptes (法史)审计法庭(1320年从国王法庭分离出来处理国家财政问题的一个高等法庭,1807年为审计法院取代)
chambre des Enquêtes (法史)调查法庭(大革命前巴黎议会的一个法庭);侦查院(大革命前属于大理院,负责侦查审理刑事案件)
chambre des Requêtes (法史)申诉法庭(大革命前大理院的一个院,负责审理当事人向大理院提交的诉状)
champertor n. 帮诉者;包揽诉讼人;助讼者
champertous contracts 帮诉合同(契约)(约定出钱出力帮人诉讼,胜诉后分得利益的一种合同)
champerty (=champarty) n. 助讼行为,帮讼(出钱或出力帮人诉讼,胜诉后分得利益),助讼图利(罪)
champion n. 1.(决斗裁判中代表他人参加决斗的)角斗士 2.(英)世袭的英王加冕典礼护卫官
chance n. 1.偶发事件 2.机会 3.(复)或然性 4.偶然性,运气
chance about 见异思迁,变节
chance of election 当选机会
chance verdict (未经陪审团同意的以抽签决定的)碰运气的裁决(现被认为是非

法的)
chance-medley n. 1.非有意伤害或杀人，(受攻击者为减轻进一步打击而)自卫杀人,过失伤害或杀人 2.偶然的行为,偶然性
chancellor n. (英)大臣,司法官;(美)衡平法院大法官;法院的首席法官;大法官;(德奥)总理;(大使馆等的)参事官,一等秘书;(美)(某些大学)校长;(英)国王的法律顾问官;教区大法官
chancellery (=chancellory) n. 大臣(大法官或总理的)官职;大法官法庭,大臣官邸,总理官署;大使馆的办事处;大使馆(或领事馆的)全体工作人员
chancellor n. (英)大臣,司法官;(美)衡平法院大法官;法院的首席法官;大法官;(德)总理;(大使馆等的)参事官,一等秘书;(美)(某些大学)校长
chancellor democracy 总理制的民主政体
chancellor of the diocese (英)主教管区司法官
Chancellor of the Exchequer (英)财政大臣(从前的衡平法院法官,现为管理财政的大臣,亦是内阁部长)
chancellor's court (英国设立于剑桥大学和牛津大学的)大学校长法庭
chancellor's foot (英)大法官的步码(指对衡平法上衡平的衡量标准)
chancellorship n. 大法官(大臣,总理等)的职位
chancery n. (英)大法官法庭(今属高等法院的一部);(美)(处理普通法不能解决的案件的)衡平法院,衡平法院的法律和律师事务;(英)档案府;档案馆;文秘署;大臣(总理、大使等的)办事处;枢密院
Chancery Court of York (宗教法)约克郡教区法院[指约克省教区法院(The ecclesiastical Court of the province of York),受理来自省的各教区法院(provincial diocesan courts)的上诉案件。该约克郡教区法院相当于坎特伯雷省的拱顶法院(Court of Arches),即坎特伯雷大主教教务总长法院(Court of the Official Principal of the Archbishop of Canterbury)的通称。见 Court of Arches]

Chancery Division (美)衡平法庭;(英)大法官法庭
chancery guardians 衡平法上的监护人
chancery master (美)衡平法院院长,(英)大法官法院庭长,衡平法院存卷主事官
chancery order 衡平法院诉讼规程
chancery practice 衡平法院的诉讼程序
chancery registrar 衡平法院注册官
chancery reports (英)衡平法院判例汇编(集)
change n./v. 改变,变更,转变,更改;兑换,更换;找头,零钱;交易所/改变,更改,变更
change front 改变态度(或看法)
change hands 财产易主(手)
change in address 住址变更
change in the mode of transport 改变运输方式
change of circumstances 环境变迁
change of constitution 宪法的变更(指美国在保留原有的宪法形式条件下,不断改变其宪法,有三种手段:①宪法修正案;②最高法院解释;③宪法惯例)
change of name 姓名的变更,更换姓名
change of nationality 国籍的变更,改变国籍
change of ownership 所有权(财产)的转让(或让与)
change of residence 住所的变更
change of venue 变更审判地点,转移管辖
change of voyage 航道变更
change one condition 结婚
change one's condition 结婚
change one's mind 改变主意,改变计划
change residence 迁居,迁徙
change the cause of action 变更诉因
change the original sentence 改判,更改原判
change the venue 改变审判地点,转移管辖
changing body of price law 可变的价格法体系
changing fund 转变基金(特别是信托基金定期转变它的形式而作为投资或再投资)

channel n. 方法,路线,途径;航道;海峡;河床
channel approach 渠道方法(防范滥用税收协定的措施之一)
channel of communication 联络途径
channeling conduct (对行为)进行引导
chantage n. 敲诈,勒索
chaos n. 混乱,骚乱,无秩序
chaotic a. 混乱的,骚乱的,无秩序的
chaotic processes 混沌过程(在金融经济学中汇率变化是一个混沌过程)
chapter n. (法律条文的)章节;分社,分会
chapter Ⅱ (1970年)第十一章 1.美国破产法允准一个破产商业单位或具有破产风险的部门,在法院监督下(并得到债权人同意)重组其资本结构,而进行正常营业。虽然美国破产法允准个别的非商业债务人(non-business debtor)运用第十一章,但是大量的第十一章案件都涉及商业债务人(business debtor) 2.根据本章可引导商业重组(business reorganization)(见 reorganization)
chapters of the eyre (巡回法庭法官将案件提交陪审团前制作的)巡回案件清单
character n./v. 名声,声望;人格;身份,资格,品德评语,品德证明书,性格,特性,特征,性质;人物,角色/特点,(成立公司)发执照,租,包(船,飞机等)
character and habit 品德,品质,(一个人习惯行为中所体现的)品德,品质表现
character assassination 诽谤人格,诽谤名誉
character defamation 诽谤名誉的侵权行为,侵害名誉
character disorder 长期的社会失调
character evidence 品格证据
character information 品格信息(其可以带来不利影响,需特别对待)
character loan 信用借贷
character reference 身份证明书
character witness 对诉讼一方的人格、名誉等作证的证人
characterisation (= characterization)(国际私法)识别,定性;特性;描绘(他人)性格;毁损(他人)人格

characteristic n. 特性,特征,特色
characteristic features 显著特征
characteristic of a criminal 罪犯的特征
characteristic performance 特种履行
characterization n. 性格描述
characterize v. 刻画出……性格,描绘出……
charge n./v. (13世纪) 1.对犯罪的正式控告,作为刑事指控(或提起公诉)的第一步〈murder charge〉(谋杀罪的指控),〈criminal charge〉(刑事指控) 2.训导,训导〈a mother's charge to her son〉(母亲对儿子的训诫) 3.法官对陪审团的指示〈review the charge for appealable error〉(审查法官因可上诉错误的指示) 4.指示的义务(任务,责任)〈the manager's charge to open and close the office〉(管理人承担开、关办公室的责任) 5.财产负担,土地负担,抵押,留置,权利要求〈a charge on property〉(财产上的负担) 6.委托管理,托管(将人或物委托他人照管)〈a charge of estate〉(遗产委托管理,委托管理的遗产) 7.价值,价格,费用或消费〈free of charge〉(免费的)/1.指控,控告(一个人)(犯有罪行)〈police charged him with murder〉(警察控告他犯谋杀罪) 2.托办,任命,指示,使……承担任务(或义务、职责等)〈the dean charged the students to act ethically〉(院长要求学生进行有道德的活动) 3.(向陪审团)作出指示,作出法律上问题(matter of law)的指示〈the judge charged the jury on self-defense〉(法官就自身防卫问题指示陪审团)[联邦民事诉讼法规,钥匙号2173.1(1)];训导,训诫;归咎 4.使……承担经济负担,使……承担付款责任,使……承担留置权或债权;使……负债〈charge the land with a tax lien〉(让该土地作为税收抵押) 5.将责任或义务委托给某人,委托〈charge the guardian with ward's care〉(将监护的关照委托给监护人) 6.收费,要价,征税,开账单〈the clerk charged a small filing fee〉[书记员要收取少量的(诉状)申请费]
charge (或 **instruction**)(**to**) **the jury** 对陪审团(员)的指示
charge a crime upon sb. 归罪于某人;控

告某人
charge account（或 credit account） 赊购账；商店户头（指顾客在商店记账购物，定时付款的户头）
charge by way of legal mortgage 作为合法抵押的负担（担保）责任
charge certificate 收款证明书
charge conference 职责协商，诉讼案件协商[指审理法官和当事方律师之间就发挥陪审团作用(to develop a jury)进行协商]
charge d'affaires 代办
charge d'affaires ad hoc 常驻代办
charge d'affaires ad interim 临时代办
charge for remittance 汇费（旧译汇水）
charge in an indictment 罪状，罪名
charge of murder 谋杀罪名，控以谋杀罪
charge on land （设定于）土地（上的）负担，土地担保
charge on revenue 用税收作抵押
charge upon 作抵押
charge with 指控为；委以
charge with murder 控告（某人）犯谋杀罪
charge-sheet n. 警察局拘留人犯名册（或案件记录）
chargeable a. 可被指控的；应由某人负责的；应课税的，应收费的；可以记在某项账上的
charged crime 指控的罪行
charged extra 额外征收
charged party 被告，被告方
charged with administration of the new law 委于执行新法的任务
charger n. 控告者；委托人；诉讼当事人
charges of willfulness 故意的责任
charging document 起诉文书（包括状、告发状和陪审团提起的诉状）
charging instrument 指控文件
charging lien 先取留置权
charging order （债权人向法院申请的）动产扣押令；担保（责任）令
Charisma 卡里斯玛（对一位具有超人性质人物的称谓。此词原用来形容早期基督教神的启示所行神迹）；神授的能力，（迷信者所说的）领袖人物感人的超凡

魅力
charitable a. 慈善的；慷慨的；宽厚的
charitable bequest 慈善馈赠
charitable foundation 慈善基金会
charitable gift 慈善性赠与
charitable group 慈善团体
charitable institution 慈善机构
Charitable Irish Society 爱尔兰慈善会
charitable organization 慈善组织
charitable trusts 公益信托，慈善信托
charitable uses and trust（英） 慈善性受益和信托
charity n. 博爱，宽大，宽恕；慈善事业，慈善机构，养育院；救济物，施舍物；慈善捐款
charity commission 慈善事务署
charlatan n. 庸医，假充内行的人，骗子
Charming Betsy Doctrine 查明·贝特西原则（美）[来源于 Murray v. Schooner Charming Betsy 6 U. S.(2 Cranch)64, 118 (1804)判例，曾由美国联邦最高法院确定"在其他可能的法律解释存在的情况下，对国会通过的法律解释不应违反国际法"。该原则在美国又被称为 Charming Betsy Doctrine]
charred body 炭化尸体
chart n. 图，图表；海图，航（线）图；曲线（标绘）图
charter n./v. 契据，证书，执照；（英）（宪章）（国王的）特许状，（地方政府的）规章，（法人的）章程，国际组织宪章；特许，特权，豁免权；组织法；基本法；租船合同（契约），契约书；租船，包租/特许（发给公司执照等），包，租
charter contract 租船合同（契约）
charter for carriage of goods 载运货物的包船
charter freight 租船运价
charter hire 租金
charter land 特许土地证
charter law on the judiciary 司法机关组织法
charter member （社团，公司等的）创始成员，创办人
charter of concession 特许证

charter of liberties　（英史）自由权特许状
Charter of Liberties and Privileges　（英史）《自由和特权宪章》
charter of pardon　特赦证明书
Charter of Rights and Freedoms　权利与自由宪章
charter of the corporate body　法人章程
Charter of the Nuremberg Tribunal　《纽伦堡军事法庭规则》
Charter of the Organization of African Unity　《非洲统一组织宪章》(1963年在亚的斯亚贝巴通过)
Charter of the Organization of American States　《美洲国家组织宪章》(1948年在波哥大通过,通称《波哥大宪章》,Charter of Bogota)
Charter of the United Nations　《联合国宪章》
charter party　(=contract of affreightment)租船合同(契约);租船运货合同(契约);载船合同(契约)
charter party bill of lading　包租船提单
charter party by demise　光船租赁合同(契约)(指带船员或不带船员将船只交给承租人使用所订立的合同)
Charter Rolls　（英）特许状卷宗
charter under flag of convenience　悬挂方便旗(他国国旗)的租船
chartered a.　特许的;包租的
chartered accountant　（英）特许会计师
chartered bank　特许银行
chartered body　（英）特许团体,特许机构
chartered company　特许公司
chartered corporation　特许法人(社团)
chartered plane　包机
chartered right　特许权
charterer n.　船舶承租人,租船人;租用者
charterer's agent　租船（公司）代理人
chartering n.　包租(机、船)
chartering agent　承租人的代理人;租船代理人
chartering broker　租船经纪人
chartering space　订租舱位
charterparty n.　（租用船舶、飞机、车辆等的）租约
chartism n.　（英）宪章运动(1837—1848年);宪章主义
chartist n.　（复)宪章运动者;宪章派
Chartist Movement　（英）宪章运动[指1837年爆发的各类群众性、政治性的无产阶级革命运动,伦敦工人协会拟定了一个争取优先权的文件"人民宪章"(The People's Charter),以争取实现宪章内容而发动的运动称"宪章运动"]
chartulary (=cartulary) n.　契据原本登记簿;(复)特许状登记簿
chase n.　（英）狩猎地;(允许在一定地区打猎或饲养猎物的)狩猎权;追赶,追求,追击,追猎
chastise v.　责罚;惩办;处置;严惩;责打
chastisement n.　父母、师长等对少年儿童之体罚（权）
chastiser n.　惩罚者,责打者
chastity n.　贞操,贞洁;守节
chattel n.　物,(一件)动产,有形财产（又译:有体财产）;奴隶
chattel corporeal　有形动产
chattel incorporeal　无形动产
chattel interest in real property　不动产(实产)中的动产权益
chattel lien　动产留置权
chattel loan　以动产为担保的借贷
chattel mortgage　动产抵押（权）(指用动产作为借贷的担保,而债务人仍保持对该动产的占有)
chattel paper　动产(证明)文据(用以证明金钱债务、担保利益以及财产租赁等文件的总称)
chattel personal　动产,属人动产(指动产或无形权利,如专利。亦称personal chattel)
chattel real　属地动产[指一种不亚于完全保有地产或可继承地产（freehold or fee)的不动产权益,如租赁保有产(leasehold estate)。最重要的属地动产是一项土地的定期地产权(estate for years)]
chaud-medley　激愤杀人（与chance-medley相区别）
chauvinism n.　沙文主义;本民族（或性别）第一主义
cheap a.　便宜的,廉价的;低劣的,贬值的;（英）特别减价的

cheap talk　廉价磋商
cheat n./v.　欺骗行为;欺诈;骗子/哄骗,欺诈,诈取;逃脱(法网)
cheat in business　行骗
cheat the gallows　逃脱死罪
cheater n.　骗子
cheating n.　欺骗;欺诈;(考试)作弊
cheating at common law　普通法上的欺诈(罪)
cheating at gaming　赌博行为
cheating by false pretenses　(美)欺诈罪(英用 pretences)
cheating on government contract　偷工减料
cheating on workmanship and materials　(中)偷工减料
check n./v.　1.(美)支票(英用 cheque);账单 2.检查,检验,核对无误 3.寄存物的凭证,行李票,号牌 4.控制,制止/核对,检查;制止;(美)签发支票
check alteration　涂改的支票
check and balance　牵制与平衡(指国家机关之间的相互制衡),分权与制衡
check book　(美)支票簿(英用 cheque book)
check drawer　支票持有人,支票签票人
check holder　支票持有人
check in　登记,报到
check kiting(=kiting check)　用空头支票骗取钱财
check list　1.(核对用的)清单 2.(美)选举人名单
check off　核对无误后盖章(或做记号)查讫
check off funds　查讫(验讫)的基金
check on household occupants　查户口
check only for account　转账支票
check out　被认为无误;(购货时的)结账;(旅馆规定旅客结账后)必须离去的时间
check point　(边境上的)关卡;(过路车辆的)检查站
check post　检查哨所
check price　最低价格,限制价格
check residence cards　核对户口,查对户口
check to bearer　不记名支票,来人支票

check to order　记名支票;指定人支票
check up　检查,核对,检验;(美)体格检查
check-flashing　见 check-kiting
check-in counter　入口检查处;报到处
check-kitting　开出空头支票(指向银行账户开出一张支票,但该账户存款不足以支付支票上的款额。实际为一种非法之举。出票人之目的是希望银行将未兑现支票款项记入总额内之前,会有资金存入其账户。亦称 check-flashing)
check-off system　(雇主直接从雇员薪金中扣除工会费并转交工会的)扣除制
checked by (sb.)　由(某人)复核
checker n.　稽核(查)员;阻止者
checking n.　核实证词,经核实的证词
checking account　(美)活期存款
checking deposit　支票存款(指以支票提取的存款)
checklist n.　1.核对清单 2.(美)选举人名单
chemical a.　化学的,化学上用的,用化学方法得到的
chemical analysis　化学分析;化学鉴定
chemical examination of judicature　司法化学检验
chemical lesion　化学性损伤
chemical pollution　化学污染
chemical warfare　化学战争
chemical weapon　化学武器
chemist n.　化学家,化学师;(英)药剂师,药品商
chemosterilant n.　避孕剂,化学绝育剂
cheque n.　(英)支票(见 check)
cheque(或 check) crossed generally　普通划线支票
cheque(或 check) crossed specially　特别划线支票
cheque(或 check) only for account　转账支票
cheque(或 check) payable to order　记名支票
cheque(或 check) rate　支票利率
cheque(或 check) to be credited to payee's account　转账支票
cheques act(或 law)　支票法
cherish v.　爱护,热爱;抚育;怀有

Chernobyl explosion 切尔诺贝利爆炸(指 1986 年在乌克兰的切尔诺贝利核电站发生爆炸后,约 9.3 万人死于辐射引起的癌症)
Chicago Mercantile Exchange (美)芝加哥商品交易所
Chicago School 芝加哥学派(20 世纪 30 年代到 1985 年,该学派一直以芝加哥大学经济学系为中心,包括商业研究院的一大批经济学家和法学院的经济学家以及法学—经济学家团体)
chicanery n. 诡计,诈骗,诡辩
chicken game 斗鸡博弈(一种有多个纳什均衡的博弈)
chief n./a. 领袖,首领,首长,长官;头子;酋长;主任;重要部分/主要的,首要的,第一位的;首席的;主任的
chief accountant 会计主任
chief administrative device 主要行政手段
chief administrative patent judge (专利)美国专利和商标局(US Patent and Trademark Office)行政专利法官的督察(缩写为 CAP)
chief arbitrator 首席仲裁员,首席仲裁官,仲裁长;公断长
chief argument 主要凭证;主要理由
chief auditor 审计长
chief bailiff (英)法警警长;总执达吏,首席执达吏
chief baron (英)财务大臣;法院或理财法院的首席法官[1880 年首席法官凯利(Kelley)去世后,该职务即已废弃,依照 1925 年《司法法》(Judicature Act of 1925),英国高等法院院长成为首席法官。见 Baron of the Exchequer]
chief clerk 书记长(官)(衡平法院主事官的前身,只协助法官办理审讯传票、调查案件的审理经过等一些次要的事项)
chief constable (英)警察局长,警察总长
chief court 总法院
chief culprit 主犯,祸首
chief delegate 首席代表
Chief Deputy Clerk (美)联邦最高法院副总书记官
chief executive 行政首脑,(行政部门)主管人,(中)(香港特别行政区)行政长官,(美)行政首长(指总统、州长、市长等);(大写)(美)总统
chief executive officer (CEO) 董事长,总裁;首席执行官,总裁执行官
chief executor 总执行员(官)
Chief Grand Procurators (中)检察长
chief inspector 首席审查官;首席监察官
chief instigator 主谋
chief judge (美)(指巡回法庭、国际贸易法庭、巡回区的地区法院等的)首席法官,审判长,庭长,法院院长
chief judge in bankruptcy (英)首席破产法官(1881 年前旧称)
chief justice 1.首席法官,审判长 2.庭长,法院院长 3.(大写)(美)首席大法官,最高法院院长
chief justice of England 英国首席法官(旧时高等法院王座法庭的首席法官;在高等法院大法官缺席时主持高等法院;同时也是上诉法院的任职法官;现已由主持王座法庭的英国皇家首席法官代替)
Chief Justice of Common Pleas (英)(历史上)民事法院院长,民事诉讼法庭主审法官,美国有些州的中级法院院长[指以前,民事法院主持法官或民事诉讼法院院长。1875 年《司法法》(Judicial Act of 1875)将民事诉讼法院降低为民事诉讼分庭(Common Pleas Division)。1881 年,最后一任民事诉讼法院首席大法官科尔里奇勋爵(Lord Coleridge)被任命为英国首席法官勋爵(Lord Chief Justice of England),并将民事诉讼分庭与后座分庭(Queen's Bench Division)合并。现在英国首席法官行使以前的民事诉讼法院首席大法官所行使的权力。见 Lord Chief Justice of England]
chief justice of the King's Bench (英)王座法庭庭长
Chief Justice of the United States 美国首席大法官(指官员的正式头衔是美国联邦最高法院首席大法官。通常缩略为 the Chief Justice)
chief justiciar 首席法官(见 justiciar)
chief *kadi* (或 **Qādi**) 首席卡迪(又译首席

教法官)
chief law officer 主要司法官员,主要执法官员
chief legal adviser of the federal government (美)联邦政府首席法律顾问(实际上指司法部长,他是美国首席检察官,又是联邦政府首席法律顾问)
chief legislator 主要立法者
chief magistrate 1.首席司法行政官(又译首席地方法官)2.(英)首席治安官 3.政府首脑,(行政部门)主管人(=chief executive)
chief(或 **first**) **mate** 大副
chief minister 首席部长;(英)首席大臣
chief of a tribe 部落酋长
Chief of Protocol (美)外交礼宾事宜首长[指美国国务院的一名官员,负责管理礼宾司(Office of Protocol),并为总统、副总统、国务卿(Secretary of State)和其他美国官员就法律规定的外交程序(diplomatic procedure)以及国际惯例(international custom and practice)提供咨询或充当顾问]
chief of state 国家元首
chief of the special court 专门法庭庭长
chief officer of a corporation or business 公司或商行的主要管理人
chief officer of police 警察总长,警察局(局)长
chief operational officer 执行主管;经营总裁
chief pleas (海峡群岛的)萨克岛的地方议会
chief procurator 首席检察官,检察长
chief procurator general 总检察长
Chief Procurator of Supreme People's Procuratorate (中)最高人民检察院检察长
chief public procurator(或 **prosecutor**) 首席检察官,检察长;(美)首席检察官(实际上指美国司法部长)
chief registrar 首席登记官
chief rent (英)古采邑自由封地的年租(亦称免役地租)
chief representative 首席代表

chief secretary 首席次官
chief state's attorney 首席检察官
chief supervisor 首席监事
chief supporter 主要支持者
chief's court 酋长法院
chief-prosecutor n. 首席检察官,检察长
chiefdom n. 酋长领地,首领地位;酋长领地的居民
chiefly a. 首领的,首领般的
child n. 子女,幼年人,儿童,婴儿,小孩
child abuse 虐待儿童[指①故意伤害儿童或对儿童身体上、感情上的忽视,包括性骚扰、性摧残(sexual molestation),特别是父母或监护人的行为或不作为使儿童受剥削、身体和精神受到严重伤害,受到虐待甚至死亡;②因为一种行为或不作为而导致出现的对儿童急迫的严重伤害险情。虐待儿童有故意的,亦有疏忽的,前者曾于1894年在纽约市受到控告,一名叫玛丽•艾伦(Mary Ellen)的女孩被发现受到严重的虐待,她的虐待者受到指控,当时没有保护儿童的现行法律,只能依据《预防残忍对待动物法》(Law for Prevention Cruelty to Animals)。虐待儿童作为医疗关护(medical concern)第一次受到承认是在1962年,当时 C.亨利•肯普博士(Dr. C. Henry Kempe)列入了对受殴打虐待儿童的综合病的医疗关护概念,此词亦称 cruelty to a child; cruelty to children; child maltreatment。见 abused child; battered child; battered child syndrome; secondary abuse]
Child Abuse Prevention and Treatment Act (美)(家庭法)《儿童虐待预防及处理法》[指一项联邦制定法,规定提供有限基金给予各州,用以预防、鉴别、处理虐待儿童的问题。1974年制定颁布该法,1996年修订该法加强并强调保护儿童的安全。该法要求在卫生与人类服务部(Department of Health and Human Services)下设全国有关虐待儿童问题中心,来研究并了解虐待的原因,并授权该机构进行研究、预防和处理受虐待的儿童。参见《美国注释法典》第42标题卷第5101—5157节。见 child-abuse and-neglect reporting statute。缩略为 CAPTA]

child allowance 子女免税额,子女津贴
child benefit 儿童补助金(扶养未成年人的现金补贴)
child betrothal 童养媳(制)
child born in (lawful) wedlock 婚生子(女)
child born out of wedlock 非婚生子(女)
child bride 童养媳
child by another venter 异母所生子(女)
child care 儿童保育(见 child care rules)
child care rules (美)(家庭法)关照儿童规则(指美国的州对于孤儿或不良少年等关照的行政规定,大多数州均设有社会服务部门并强制执行以上这类儿童的福利规定,个别州决定专门创设管理照顾这类儿童的机构)
child criminal 少年罪犯
child custody 子女监护
child destruction (英)堕胎罪
Child Divorce Law 《儿童脱离关系法》(1979年瑞典儿童委员会的建议法规,规定儿童可以与父母脱离法律关系)
child en ventre sa mere 胎儿
child in the womb 胎儿
child endangerment (1981年)儿童处于危险处境(将儿童置于危及其生命及健康的场所或处境。亦称 endangering the welfare of a child)
child in need of supervision 必须监管的孩子,需要监督的少年儿童(指犯有过错的儿童或少年,这类少年儿童诸如十分任性、不听父母之言、擅自离家、违反宵禁、习惯逃学、违反年龄限制购买酒类和香烟等。亦称 person in need of supervision; minor in need of supervision)
child in tutelage 受监护的儿童
child in ward 被监护的儿童
child labor 童工[指雇用成年(18岁以上)以下的孩子做工。这一术语的焦点在于虐待儿童的实际,诸如剥削在工厂工作的童工;奴役;买卖、拿儿童做肮脏交易;把孩子当债奴(debt bondage)或农奴一样强迫劳动;用孩子作娼妓,色情描绘;毒品运输或从事危害他们身心健康、安全的一些其他事。一些记者根据国际劳工组织(ILO)的最低年龄协议,要求限制或禁止上述虐待童工的行为。参见《国际劳工组织》最低年龄协议第138章(1973年)(ILO Minimum Age Convention ch.138)(1973)]
Child Labor Law (1904年)(美)童工法(指州和联邦制定法,旨在规定必要工作条件和工作场所、工作时间等来保护儿童)
Child Labor Tax Law (1919年)(美)《童工税务法》[指1918年第一个联邦童工法遭到意外失效后,国会寻求另一方法保护非独立生活的人和在工作场所受剥削的儿童,两会一致通过了《童工税务法》,并于1919年正式颁布,该法是以当代先例为依据,尤其是依据首席大法官爱德华·D.怀特(Edward D. White)在麦克雷诉合众国案(McCray v. United States)(1904年)中的意思而制定。怀特支持通过罚没性课税来制止类似的违法行为]
child maltreatment 见 child abuse
child marriage 童婚
child neglect (1930年)对儿童的弃置不顾[指未尽应为对未成年人承担的在精神上和身体上必须关照的责任。这实际是一种虐待少年的形式,地方儿童福利部门对于儿童的弃置不顾作了专门调查报告,严重的情况可以提爬刑事报告,指控弃置不顾儿童的嫌疑人(person suspected of child neglect; suspect person of child neglect)]
child of divorce 离婚夫妇的子女
child of illegitimate birth 非婚生子女
child of nobody (美)私生子
child of tender age 幼(育)龄儿童
Child Online Protection Act 《儿童在线保护法》[指1998年的一项联邦制定法规,旨在通过禁止互联网上"伤害未成年人"的交流(speech)来控制儿童网上色情。不像《交流礼仪法》(Communication Decency Act),《儿童在线保护法》并不适用于电子邮件或"聊天室"(chat-room)交流。而在其他方面,对于显露出描绘未成年人性方面的清晰资料,甚至18岁以上人的性资料或电脑形成的图片,该保护法可以适用,以保护青少年不受伤害。缩略为 COPA]

child out of wedlock 见 illegitimate child

child pornography 儿童色情作品

Child Protective Services (美)儿童保护局(或署)(指负责调查对虐待儿童的状况陈述的政府机构,并对受虐待儿童的监护人、父母提供家庭服务,还对孤儿、不良少年等作出可执行的关照规划。缩略为CPS,有些州称为 Department of Social Services。在密歇根州则称"family independence agency"。见 Adult Protective Services)

child support (美)(家庭法)儿童抚养培育费[指①父母对于子女的经济抚养和教育尽力的法定义务(legal obligation),直至孩子达到成年(年龄),达到自立或完成中等教育为止。这种义务不管从民事上或刑事上说,都是强制性的[案例儿童抚养、培育费钥匙号 22(🖉22)];②在监护权和离婚诉讼中,父母一方欠另一方的法定款项中给予婚生子女的培养费用必须支付。这个对子女的抚养培育费的权利是孩子的权利,不得废弃,而且任一离婚条例均规定:废弃子女抚养培育费是无效的。见 alimony]

child welfare 儿童福利

child with disabilities 无行为能力的儿童,残疾儿童[指一个孩子只要具有下列情况:①智力障碍;②听力、语言、视力受到伤害;③严重的情感低沉、精神恍惚;④其他方面健康受损或无能力正常学习,即可适用具有《残疾教育法》(Disabilities Education Act)中的个人情况需要特殊教育或相关教育服务。见 Individuals with Disabilities Education Act]

child work (少年)儿童工作[指少年的有益职业,特别是在家庭中工作。这个词语有时与少年劳工(child labor)相对。其含义以家庭为单位的儿童工作是一种积极的历练,有的学者和法院注意到儿童或少年工作便于促进就业技术和社会适应,并且被看成家庭团结、共同担当责任的体现]

child's income tax (美)儿童所得税(见 kiddie tax)

child's part (美)一笔遗产;子女的部分[指根据有些州的法规,一个寡妇可以请求获得亡夫遗产或按其丈夫遗嘱得到这笔遗产。此笔遗产需经过计算,该寡妇如同死者子女一样享有与其他子女一样多的产权资格,参见《法律汇编判例大全》"继承与分配"篇第 60—67 节(C. J. S. Descent and Distribution §§ 60-67)]

child-abuse and-neglect reporting statute (家庭法)虐待及疏于照管儿童的纪录报告制定法[指州的法规要求一些人,其中包括保育员(healthcare providers)、老师(teachers)和儿童管理工作者(childcare workers),报告涉嫌虐待儿童之行为(者)。1967年以来,美国每个州均已采取某种形式的记录报告法规。在《预防虐待儿童和处理法》(《美国注释法典》第 42 标题卷第 5101—5157 节)(42 USCA §§ 5101-5157)中,国会提供联邦基金为美国各州按照各州的记录法规和界定的"粗暴对待儿童"(child maltreatment)广泛含义来实施联邦标准。见 Child Abuse Prevention and Treatment Act]

child-and dependent-care tax credit (2001年)子女及受抚养人关照的税收减免[指对于全日制的受雇人员,要维持家庭、生活、抚养幼小子女或无能力的妻子(或丈夫),或受抚养人,适合减免税款]

child-bearing n. 怀胎(指生育全过程)

child-birth n. 分娩,生产

child-care centre 儿童保育中心

child-care expense 子女扶养费用

child-care rules 儿童关照规则,儿童看管规则[指美国州对抚养儿童(foster children)的看管行政规则。在大多数州,有关社会服务部门均制定并执行一些治理关于养育儿童福利的规则。少数州已经创立专门机构为儿童事业献身服务]

child-destruction n. (人工)流产,堕胎(罪)

child-kidnapping 诱拐儿童[指通常不用暴力或欺诈的手段诱拐儿童(如有的人走路就把另一个人的小孩带走了)。亦称 child-stealing; baby-snatching; childnapping]

child-murder n. 杀(害)婴(儿)罪

child-rearing (childrearing) (家庭法)1.孩子的培养,孩子的教养(指无论是特别的家庭或社会在培养孩子的过程中都要

遵循的实践和习俗)2.养育子女,抚养子女(指按照实践和习惯养育孩子)
child-saving judges (美)"挽救儿童"的法官(指未成年人法院的法官)
Child-sexual Abuse Syndrome 见 child-sexual-abuse accommodation syndrome
child-sexual-abuse accommodation syndrome (CSAAS) (美)儿童性侵犯融通综合(病)征(指通常由于亲戚或家族友人使儿童屡次受到性侵犯而遭受痛苦所设想的医疗上和心理上的处境。至于"综合征"一词已由科学部门否定,因此它不具有法律效力,也不是虐待与非虐待之间的歧视字眼。亦称 Child-sexual Abuse Syndrome)
child-stealing 见 child-kidnapping
child-support guideline (美)(家庭法)子女抚养培育费准则[指负责任的父母(obligator parent)应支付的儿童抚养培育费款项总额的管理法律规定。子女抚养培育费准则已在各州发展并得到响应而创设"临时帮助贫困家庭规划"(Temporary Assistance to Needy Families Program)。参见《美国注释法典》第42标题卷第601—603(a)节]
Child-Support Recovery Act of 1994 (美)《1994年儿童抚养培育费追索法》[指对因故意不交纳过去拖欠的儿童抚养培育费者(尽管该儿童在另一州)制定的联邦罪行(federal offense)法规。此法规已由《拖欠的父母惩罚法》(Deadbeat Parents Punishment Act)所替代。参见《美国注释法典》第42标题卷第228节(42 USCA§228)。见 Deadbeat Parents Punishment Act]
child-support-enforcement agency (美)(家庭法)儿童抚养培育费强制执行机构[指帮助有监护权的父母收集儿童抚养培育费的政府机构。社会保障法(Social Security Act)标题Ⅳ(D),参见《美国注释法典》第42标题卷第654节(42 USCA§654),要求各州设立"儿童抚养培育费强制执行机构"为权利人父母(obligee parents)收集抚育费。尽管该机构按照一套联邦标准治理,但每个州均有自己的中心注册处。儿童抚养培育费强制执行机构可以通过"人类服务部"(Department of Human Service)、州司法部、税务机构或州的检察长办公室(Attorney-General's Office)进行操作。这个执行机构可以找到失踪父母的地点,并确定父系根源(paternity)。该机构可制定抚育费命令并严格执行这些命令。缩略为 CSE agency。亦称Ⅳ-D agency]
childless a. 无子女的
childnapping 见 child-kidnapping
childrearing 见 child-rearing
children for adoption and forester placement 供收养和寄养的儿童
children of the same venter 同母所生子女
children of the settlor (英)财产授予者的子女
children's court 少年法庭
children's right to know parents' identity (收养)子女有知晓其亲生父母身份的权利
(to) chill the assertion of constitutional right 打消行使宪法权利的念头,阻碍行使宪法权利
chilot n. (伊斯兰教法)齐洛法庭(一种由皇帝亲自主持的法庭)
chimerica 中美国,中美国共同体[指2007年3月4日哈佛大学学院教授尼尔·弗格森(Niall Ferguson)在英国《星期日电讯报》发表的《不是两个国家而是一个:中美国(chimerica)》一文,以强调中美经济关系密切]
China Council for the Promotion of International Trade 中国国际贸易促进委员会
China Council of Certified Public Accountants 中国注册会计师协会
China International Trust and Investment Corporation 中国国际信托投资公司
China's insurance clause 中国保险条款
China's Spring (Autumn) Export Commodities Fair 中国春季(秋季)出口商品交易会
China-ASEAN Free Trade Area 中国—东盟自由贸易区
Chinese customary mortgage 依中国习惯的抵押

Chinese joint venturer 中国合营者
Chinese law 中国法(总称)
Chinese Law (或 Legal) Family 中华法系
Chinese legal history 中国法制史
Chinese legal system 中华法系;中国法制
Chinese national residing abroad 华侨
Chinese nationality 中国国籍
Chinese Patent Office 中国专利局
Chinese patent right 中国专利权
Chinese People's Political Consultative Conference 中国人民政治协商会议
Chinese Wall 中国墙(英美等国证券制度中的一个特定术语,指多功能服务证券商 Multiservice Securities Firm 将其内部可能发生利益冲突的各职能相互隔开以防止敏感信息在这些职能部门之间相互流动)
Chinese-foreign joint venture 中外合资经营企业
chip v./n. 削,铲;破裂/赌注,赌钱
chip in 提供资助,捐助,集资
chirografi v. 亲笔示据
chirograph n. 正式签字的文件(如亲笔字据,手书契据,骑缝契据等);教皇亲笔特许证书;书法,笔迹
* *Chirographum apud debitorem repertum praesumitur solutum.* An evidence of debt found in the debtor's possession is presumed to be paid. 债务人手中保存的债据应推定为已付清的债。
* *Chirographum non extans praesumitur solutum.* An evidence of debt not existing is presumed to have been discharged. 已不存在的债据应推定为债已清偿。
chit (=chitty) n. 推荐信,短信;(小额债务的)单据,便条
chit-fund n. 银会
chit-fund company 银会公司
chit-system n. 单据支付制(用单据代替现金付款的制度)
chivalry n. (中世纪的)骑士制度;骑士团
chloroform n. 三氯甲烷,氯仿(旧译哥罗方);麻醉剂,迷药
choice n. 选择;被选的人(或物);选择的机会与权利;入选者
choice of behavior theory of motivation 激励的行为选择理论
choice of forum 协议选择管辖
choice of jurisdiction (国际私法)管辖权的选择
choice of law(s) (国际私法)法律的选择
choice of law clause 选择法律条款
choice of law rules 选择法律的规则
choice of substitute 代理人的选任
choice theory 选择论(亦称意志论)
Choice-Theoretic Approach 以选择理论为基础的分析方法(研究消费者行为的一种重要方法)
choke n./v. 窒息;噎/掐死,闷死;阻塞,抑制,阻止,扑灭
Choose (=chuse) v. 选择,挑选;预示,选择;决定;喜欢
chop n./v. 官印,戳记;护照,许可证;商标货物的品质/砍,斩
chop wound 砍伤
chopping block (一种刑具)斩砧板
chose n. 所有物;动产,物
chose in action 权利动产[指权利可作为一项权利动产,其权利人可以转让、设定担保,也可对他人许可使用(license)];诉讼上的财产(权);权利上的财产(指可依法在诉讼中赢得占有而实际尚未占有的财产)
chose in possession 占有物;实际上占有的财产(权)
chose jugee 既决事件,无需讨论之事
chose local 土地附有物
chose transitory 动产
chosen domicile 选定的住所,选择的户籍,临时住所
chosen-expert n. 选任的鉴定人
Christian dogma 基督教教义
Christian marriage 基督教式婚姻
Christian name 教名
Christianity n. 基督教;(总称)基督教徒;基督教徒的身份
Christopher Columbus Langdell (美)兰德尔教授(美国案例分析教学法的首创人)
chronic a. 长期的,慢性的;经常的,惯常的
chronic inflation 长期通货膨胀

chronic poisoning 慢性中毒
chronic schizophrenia like psychosis 慢性精神分裂症样精神病(癫痫人群的精神分裂症病患率在3%—7%,而癫痫性精神分裂症样精神病发作与首次癫痫发作之间有10—14年的间隔,其发作形式较重,常涉多种发作类型,年龄多在34—37岁。与精神分裂症极为相似。主要依靠病史、CT、MRI和脑电图检查鉴别。见 epileptic personality change)
chronic shortage 长期短缺
chronic unemployment 长期性失业
chronicle n. 记事,编年史,历史
Chronological Table (英)《制定法年代表》(1870年开始出版,汇录了从1235年《王国制定法》上登载的每一个法律以及从1797年起至今的大不列颠和联合王国通过的每件普遍适用的制定法)
chronologically published cases 按年代顺序出版的判例
chronologize v. 按年代排列
chronology n. (法令等)按年月次序编排;年表;年代学
chu rule 逐出条规(指纽约最高法院在一个案件中的裁决,要求被判有重罪的律师自动退出法律界);取消(律师)资格的规定
church law 教会法,寺院法
church polity 宗教的组织,宗教的政体
churchwarden n. 教会执事(指教区职员和监护人,负责管理该教区的产业)
churl (=ceorl) n. (盎格鲁-撒克逊法)普通自由民
cinematographic work 电影作品(伯尔尼公约和多数英语国家采用这一术语,但美国版权法使用 motion picture,亦有少数国家使用 film)
circuit n. 巡回审判,巡回律师令;巡回审判区;巡回法庭;巡回区[英国从12世纪始,英格兰高等法院法官被定期派往各郡审理案件。《1873年司法制度法》把全国分成7个区,各巡回区又叫巡回法庭,各有一名巡回法官主管。1971年后经过重组分成6个区:①中部加牛津区(伯明翰);②东北区(黑兹);③北区(曼彻斯特);④东南区(伦敦);⑤威尔士和切斯特区(加的夫);⑥西区(布里斯托尔)。美国以前划分若干个司法区(judicial division),法官经常到不同的地点巡回开庭听审案件。现在美国共13个司法巡回区,其中包括哥伦比亚特区(District of Columbia)的一个单独巡回区和一个联邦巡回区(Federal Circuit)。每一巡回区设一联邦上诉法院,受理上诉案件。参见《美国注释法典》第28标题卷第41节]
Circuit Council (美)巡回法庭议事会[美国第一个制定判决意见的实体单位,其成员包括上诉法院和地区法院法官,该会对联邦巡回院(判决)行使广泛分类系统化的权力,必要时可向司法大会提出建议]
Circuit Court of Appeals Act of 1891 (美)《1891年巡回上诉法法》
circuit riding 巡回办案
circuit (trial) system 巡回(审判)制度
circuit administrator 巡回法庭财产管理人,巡回审判区法庭主管
circuit and on-spot trial (中)巡回审判(即就地办案,中国民事诉讼法原则之一)
circuit attorney (美)地方检察官;巡回检察官
circuit branch division 巡回分庭
circuit breaker rules 断路器规则(指两种对卖空进行限制的方法:一是在市场范围和长期基础上,对卖空适用价格测试;二是在市场下滑特别严重的市场中,对特定证券施加的限制措施即断路器规则)
circuit court 巡回法院,巡回法庭
circuit court of appeals 巡回上诉法庭
circuit judge 巡回审判的法官,巡回区的法官
circuit justice 巡回法官;巡回审判
Circuit riding 巡回办案[(美)指按《1789年司法法》联邦最高法院法官也要担任巡回法院的法官。每年两次巡回办案。国会为了提高效率而于1801年取消巡回办案。但一年后新的杰斐逊共和党人以多数票使该做法恢复,并强令每个法官需和一名地区法院法官一起主持巡回审判。以后随着国家发展,国会于《1869年司法

法》中建立了单独的巡回法院司法系统,直到《1891 年上诉巡回法院法》(Circuit Court of Appeals Act of 1891)的出台,国会于1911 年正式结束了此项制度;(英国)指法官在法定的巡回区内不同时间在各个地点巡回听审案件。在美国这种巡回审判也是基于英国巡回法庭体制上在各县之间巡回办案。见Circuit-riding justice]

circuit session 巡回开审;巡回法院开庭期;(复)巡回法庭;环行,范围;同业性的联合组织

circuit tribunal 巡回法庭

Circuit-riding justice 巡回办案法官,巡回审判法官[指美国联邦最高法院法官,根据《1789 年司法法》(the Judiciary Act of 1789)被要求在巡回审判区内主持审判或办案。在三个巡回审判区中的任何一个巡回区均有两名大法官和一名联邦地区法院法官共同开庭。见 circuit riding]

Circuity of action 迂回诉讼,巡回诉讼,经诉或滥诉[指一种允许的复杂的诉讼程序,导致不必要的诉讼拖延和烦琐诉讼(indirect litigation),如被告原本未提出反诉,后来又单独起诉,请求裁决原可在本诉讼中一并解决的问题。现在依据诉讼规则已废止了许多与迂回诉讼相关的问题]

circular n. 通知,通告;传单

circular letter 通知书,传阅文件(旧译:通函)

circular letter of credit 流通信用证

circular notes 旅游信用证;旅行支票

circulating a. 流通的;通用的;流传的;循环的,流动的

circulating assets 流动资产

circulating capital 流动资本

circulating capital fund 流动资本资金

circulating note 流通货币

circulating pledge 流动抵押(品)(旧译:流动质押)

circulation n. 循环;运行;流通(额),传播;发行(额),销路;通货,货币

circulation of currency 货币流通

Circumlocution Office 办事拖拉的官僚机关

circumscribe v. 限制,约束,立界限于,给⋯⋯下定义

circumscribing the court's power 限制法院的权力,限制法院滥用权力

circumscription n. 界限,限制;区域,范围;定义

circumspect a. 慎重的,谨慎小心的

circumspecte agatis (英史)行为谨慎法(1285 年的一个文件名称)

circumstance n. 事实,事件,事项;详细情节;(复)情况,环境,境遇,仪式

circumstance of a crime 犯罪情节

circumstance of aggravation 情节严重;加重的情节

circumstance of case 案情

circumstance of tenancy 租赁情况

circumstantial evidence 情节证据(案件发生时周围事物所构成的证据,又称情况证据,环境证据,旁证,间接证据)

circumstantial freedom 环境自由

Circumstantial Guarantee of Trustworthiness 特别可信任的情况保障

circumstantial letter 海军军事法庭诉状

circumstantiate v. 证实,提供证据来证明

circumvent v. 围绕,包围,用计取胜,智取,防止⋯⋯发生,陷害

circumvent a law, rule, problem, difficulty 规避一个法规、规则、问题、困难

Circumvention n. 规避(版权法)[指 1.绕过,逃避,转移法或使其无效,或削弱技术手段或损害一项受美国版权法保护并控制接近的一项发明。依据美国版权法所保护的作品有效地控制对其查看的技术性规避(circumvention of technology),根据《美国注释法典》第 17 标题卷第 1201 节是被禁止的。参见钥匙号 67.3 判例;版权与知识产权。2.(苏格兰法)诈欺(指有意诱使他人进行自愿超出反对自己利益的影响范围的行为,如果实施了这种行为由此产生的交易或合同等均为无效。亦称 facility and circumvention,有时亦缩称 facility)]

citable a. 可引证的,可引用的,可援引的

citation n. 1.传讯(唤);传票;传讯(双方当事人以外的人)参加诉讼 2.引证,引用,

引文;援引判例[指引证有权威的判例或言论来支持争辩;在援引判例时要写明该判例的名称和出处。如 72 stat., 962, 即《美国制定法大全》(United Statutes at Large/Stat.)第 72 卷第 962 页;18 U.S.C.A. §1201(1934)指在 1934 年版《美国注释法典》第 18 标题卷第 1201 节]

citation for contempt 因藐视法庭引起的传讯

citation of act 法令的引用,援引法规

citation of hono(u)r (授予)荣誉奖章(状),传令嘉奖

citation of merit 记功

citation of statute 法规的引用,援引法规

citators(复)n. 援引集,援引汇编

cite v. (15 世纪)1.传唤(指传唤到法庭、传唤出庭)〈the witness was cited for the contempt〉[证人因藐视(罪)被传唤出庭〉2.援引、引用(指提交或引用先例或法律权威)〈counsel, then cited the appropriate statutory provision〉(法律咨询,然后援引适当的制定法条款)3.表扬、嘉奖、赞扬〈the solider was cited for bravery〉(战士因其英勇而受到嘉奖)

cited material 被援引的资料

citer(=citor)n. 传讯者,引证者,引用者,表扬者

citing and quoting 援引和引用

citing material 援引资料

citizen n. 公民;国民,市民,居民;(美)平民

citizen of the world 世界公民

citizen standing 公民诉讼资格

citizen suit (美)(环境法上的)公民诉讼

Citizen's Advocate Centre (美)公民的法律顾问中心(指一种监督组织,用以监督政府有关贫民福利事业的执行情况)

citizen's arrest (美)公民(自行对罪犯)的逮捕(指公民按惯例在一定情况下对于一个犯有重罪的罪犯的自行逮捕。但如果被捕的不构成犯罪,则应负有赔偿损失的责任)

citizen's property 公民财产

citizen's right 公民权

Citizen's rights of interstate movement (美)州际运动的公民权利

citizenhood n. 公民身份;公民权;国籍

citizenize v. (美)赋予公民权;使成为公民;(军职)转为文职

Citizenry n. 公民(总称)

Citizenship n. 公民资格,公民身份;国籍,公民权(在美国取得公民身份:依据美国联邦宪法第十四修正案第一款:"在合众国出生或归化合众国并受合众国管辖者均为合众国和他所居住州的公民。"另外,虽在外国出生但其父母为美国人,仍为美国公民,至于在合众国出生,则包括在合众国领地出生,同样是美国公民)

citizenship act 公民身份法,国籍法

citizenship by birth 根据出生地取得的国籍(或公民身份)

citizenship by descent 根据血统取得的国籍(或公民身份)

citizenship by incorporation of territory 因领土的合并而取得的国籍(或公民身份)

citizenship by nation 根据民族取得的国籍(或公民身份)

citizenship by naturalization 因入籍而取得的国籍(或公民身份)

citizenship jurisdiction 公民资格诉讼管辖权

citizenship of principal parties 主要当事人的州籍

citizenship of the corporation 法人的公民权,法人的公民权利义务

citizenship paper (美)公民证书(指签给取得美国公民权者的证书)

city n. 都市,城市;全市居民

city assembly 市民大会

city council 市议会;市参议会

city council(1)or 市参议会成员,市议员

city court (城)市法院

city father 市政府的主要成员(如市参议员等)

city hall 市政厅,市政府大厦;市政府

city man (英)金融家,实业家

city manager 市行政长官,市长

city not divided into districts (中)不设区的市

City of London Court （英）伦敦市法院（具有伦敦本市审判权的法院，实际是个郡级法院）
City of London Solicitor Company （英）伦敦市状师公司（又译：伦敦市事务律师公司）
city of patriarchal households 族长统治下的城邦
city real estate 市有财产
city-manager plan （美）市长制
city-state n. （古希腊的）城邦（国家）
civic a. （1656年）1.公民的，公民资格的〈civic responsibilities〉（公民的责任）2.城市的，市民的〈civic center〉（城市中心）
civic centre 市中心
civic vertue 公民道德体系
civic duty 公民义务
civic right 公民权利
civics （复）n. 公民学
civie n. （美）便衣警察
civil a. 1.公民的，国民的，市民的，民用的 2.国内的，民间的 3.民事的，根据民法的，法律规定的 4.文职的，文官的；非宗教的，世俗的 5.文明的，有礼貌的
civil action 民事诉讼
civil adjudication tribunal 民事审判庭
civil administration 民政；民政管理
civil administration department 民政部门
civil administrator 文职行政官员
(the) Civil Aeronautic Act of 1938 （美）《1938年民用航空法》（1950年修订了《1938年民用航空法》，授权美国总统制定与民用航空器相关的安全规定，无论何时，只要总统认为出于国家安全需要，即可采取相关行动，设立空中识别区。美国1950年就开始设置防空识别区，现已有20多个国家或地区设置了该区域。美国最为典型，已设了毗邻美国国防空识别区、阿拉斯加防空识别区、关岛防空识别区和夏威夷防空识别区四个识别区。在美国，总统依照其权限作出决定后，由商务部长享有执行权，只要商务部长认为出于国家安全利益需要，就有权在空域地区、美国领土或者其控制地带设置此类防空识别区，可以通过适用这些区域的法规、命令禁止或限制其所不能有效确认身份、位置和无法有效以现有设施予以控制的航空器的航行）
civil aeronautics 民用航空，民航
civil affair 民政事务；民事
civil affairs mediation law 民事调解法
civil and commercial code 民事和商事法典
civil appeal 民事上诉
civil arbitration 民事仲裁
civil arrest 民事拘禁，民事拘留（民诉中人为使当事人到案做答辩而采取的措施），诉讼中对船（或货物）的扣留
civil assault 民事侵犯［指被认为是侵权而不是犯罪的侵犯，虽是同样侵权行为，可以既是侵权，又是犯罪。这个词不同于引起民事责任的法律要素（legal elements）］
civil aviation 民航
civil bail 民事保释
civil bankruptcy 民事破产，个人破产
civil body 民间团体
civil branch （或 chamber） 民庭；民事法庭
civil capacity 民事行为能力（指民事主体据以独立参加民事法律关系，以自己的民事法律行为取得民事权利或承担民事义务的法律资格）
civil case 民事案件；民事诉讼；（复）民事案例（汇编）
civil case against minor 侵害未成年人的民事案件
civil case processing 民事案件流程
civil ceremony 世俗结婚仪式；民事结婚仪式
civil charge 民事指控
civil claim 民事权利请求
civil code 民法典
civil code system 民法体系
civil commitment 民事犯罪，民事拘押（指非刑事程序地拘禁在精神病院、戒毒中心等地）
civil commotion 民众骚乱
civil companies 民事社团，民事公司
civil compensation 民事赔偿
civil complaint 民事（原告的）投诉，民事案件的起诉

civil condition 民法上的条件
civil consequence 民事后果
civil conspiracy 民事方面的共谋(指两人或两人以上的共同行为,此种行为是以合法手段来达到非法的目的,或以非法手段来达到合法的目的)
civil contempt 民事上的藐视法庭罪(如故意不执行判决)
civil contempt proceedings 民事藐视法庭程序
civil contract 民事合同(契约)
civil court 民事法院,民事法庭(简称民庭)
civil cover sheet (美)民事案件登记表,备审案件登记表(指每起民事案件需填表格,内容有管辖权的根据、诉讼性质及案件发生所在的州等。书记员使用这些表格标注本案所属系统内的全部案件)
Civil Cover Sheet Form JS-44 (美)民事(案件)登记表 JS-44
civil damages 民事损害赔偿
civil death 剥夺政治权利终身(旧译:褫夺公权终身),(英)民事死亡(指从前一个人犯重罪、叛逆罪等被驱出国境,因被剥夺法律上的权益而失去法律保障,故名)
civil debt 民事债务
civil defendant 民事被告
civil defense 民防(系统)
civil disability 无民事行为能力
civil disobedience 温和抵抗,非暴反抗;不合作主义;民众扰乱,群众骚动,公民不服从
civil disorder 市民骚乱;民事骚乱
civil dispute 民事纠纷
civil division 民事法庭,民事庭(简称民庭);(大写)(英)(上诉法院的)民事上诉庭;(大写)民事局(见 Claims Division)
civil division of a people's court (中)人民法院民事庭
civil docket 民事卷(见 judgment roll)
civil docket sheet (美)民事案卷
civil domicile 公民住所,公民户籍
civil duties 民事义务
civil embargo 对本国船只或货物的扣留(或实行封港)

civil employees 文职雇员,文职人员
Civil Enforcement Act (加)(艾伯塔省)《民事执行法令》
civil evidence 民事案件的证据
Civil Evidence Act (美)(1968—1972年)《民事证据法》[其中有规定传闻证据在符合特定程序要求情况下具有可采用性,美《联邦证据规则》(Federal Rules of Evidence)的第 803—804 条明确列举 20 多种传闻证据例外]
Civil filings 民事文件归档,民事案件
civil forfeitures 民事上的罚款,民事上的没收
civil fruits 合法财产收益
civil government 国民政府
civil guard (西班牙)公民警卫队(指一种准军事性质的国家警察部队)
civil injury 民事损害
civil inquest (陪审团参加的)民事调查
civil interests (英国应征或志愿服兵役的人享有的)民事权益
civil judges 民事法官
civil judg(e)ment 民事判决
civil jurisdiction 民事管辖(权),民事审判(权);民事管辖范围
civil jurist 民法学家,民法学者
civil juristic act 民事法律行为
civil jury 民事陪审团
civil justice 民事司法
Civil Justice Reform Act of 1990 《1990美国民事司法改革法》
civil law (大陆法系)民法(这个词用于不同的上下文有其不同的概念,有些与大陆法系完全无关。在罗马法中,由于罗马天主教教规法的发展,此词系指一个国家的世俗法以区别于教会法。在国际法方面此词用来说明别的国家的国内法,以区别于称为国际公法的万国法。在普通法国家里,此词系指调整个人和私人实体之间关系的法律,以区别于刑法和行政法。在大陆法系国家里,此词也用来说明适用于公民私人之间普通民事之间的法律,以区别于控制贸易和其他商业活动的商法。在普通法和大陆法这两个法系中,此词说明民、刑等法规的

集合体,以区别于军事法规。在比较法中,"civil law"所涉及的则是惯例);(大写)罗马法;大陆法;大陆法系(或罗马法系)国家的法律制度
civil law countries 民法法系国家(又译:罗马法系国家,大陆法系国家)
civil law family (或 system) 民法法系;罗马法系,大陆法系
civil law in America 美国的大陆法
civil law in substantial sense 实质意义之民法
civil law policies 民法政策
civil law tradition 民法法系传统
civil lawsuit 民事诉讼,民事诉讼案件
civil legal relationship 民事法律关系
civil legislation 民事立法
civil liability 民事责任
civil liability insurance 民事责任保险
civil libel 民事诽谤(罪)
civil libertarians 公民自由意志论者
civil liberties 1.公民自由(指美国对公民自由、特权和豁免权的简称)2.公民自由权;(法律范围内的)个人自由
civil liberties guarantees 公民自由保证
civil list (英)王室费(又译:王室岁入规定);(美)文官薪俸表,文官薪俸(总额);(大写)(英)公务员职称表
civil marriage 民事婚姻(又译:世俗婚姻。指不采用宗教仪式,依照民法规定举行结婚仪式结成的婚姻)
civil matter 民事案(事)件
civil mediation 民事调解
civil motor accident case 民事车祸案件
civil negligence 民事过失
civil object 民事客体
civil obligation 公民义务;民事债务;法庭债务
civil offence 民法上的违法行为
civil panel (法院)民事合议庭
civil penalty 民事罚款
civil penalties 民事处罚[指当事人因违反制定法或法规的具体行为而受罚款的处罚〈the EPA levied a civil penalty of $10000 on the manufacturer for exceeding its pollution limits〉(环保局对制造厂家超过污染限度而将民事处罚提高至 10000 美元)。又如《反托拉斯法》或《证券法》。民事处罚通常是罚款或其他形式的经济赔偿]
civil personality 公民的人格
civil plaintiff 民事原告
civil policy 民事政策
civil possession 民法上的占有
civil posts 文职人员
civil power 维持治安的力量
civil practice law 民事诉讼程序法
civil prescription 民事时效
civil prisoner 普通犯(与政治犯、国事犯、军事犯、战犯等对称时用)
civil procedure at first instance 民事第一审程序
civil procedure at second instance 民事第二审程序
civil procedure at third instance 民事第三审程序
civil procedure convention 民事诉讼惯例
civil procedure law (或 act) 民事诉讼法
Civil Procedure Law of the People's Republic of China 《中华人民共和国民事诉讼法》
civil proceedings 民事诉讼程序,民事诉讼
civil process 民事传票,民事令状
civil process in rem 对物民事诉讼
civil registrar 民事书记官;民事登记员
civil registry office 民事登记处
civil relation 民事关系
civil relation containing foreign element 涉外民事关系
civil remedy 民事救济,民事补偿。(指实施一项权利或防止、纠正错误的一种手段,即通过诉讼或请求途径来解决私权的保护。使用法律上或衡平上的救济,即remedy,亦称 civil remedy)
civil responsibility 公民责任
civil right 民事权利;公民权利
Civil Right Acts 《民权法》(联邦法规总称,该法最重要的两条规定,即第 2、7 条,分别规定了在公共膳宿和就业问题上对种族和其他群体性的歧视所应给予的联邦行政补偿和司法赔偿。联邦最高法院参考该法广泛而深远的目的对其进行解

释,运用扩大给予少数的保护范围的方法以解决并适用该法引起的具体问题和赔偿问题)

civil right amendments （美）公民权利修正案(指美国联邦宪法第十三、十四、十五修正案所涉及的奴隶、种族歧视和选举权等的条款规定)

Civil Right Cases （美）民权法案(指美联邦宪法第十四修正案的规定)

Civil Rights Act of 1964 （美）《1964民权法》(指目的在于消除美国社会长期存在的少数反种族歧视的法案;同时贯彻实施美国联邦宪法赋予任何人不得被剥夺正当程序和法律平等保护的规定,即由国会通过有关法律的总称)

Civil Rights Act of 1991 （美）《1991民权法》[指美国国会为推翻联邦最高法院1988—1990年庭审期间的几则特别不利于妇女及少数族裔就业歧视判决而制定,它除减轻就业歧视案件原告(被害人)的举证责任,延长对歧视性年资制提起诉讼的时效期限,以及确定某些公平就业法律在境外适用(extraterritorial application)的原则外,并对1964年民权法所规定之补偿制度大幅度加以修正]

Civil Rights Attorney's Fee Award Act of 1976 《1976公民权利律师费仲裁法》

Civil Rights Law （美）民权法;公民权条例(指废除奴隶制的条例)

civil rights legislation 公民(自由)权利的立法

Civil Rights Movement （美）民权运动[指美国人为种族平等而斗争。很难清楚地划出它的时间界限。显然它包括弗雷德里克·道格拉斯(Frederick Douglass)的光辉作品、哈瑞特·塔普曼(Harriet Tubman)的勇气、索杰纳·特鲁斯(Sojourner Truth)的激昂热情的演说、亚伯拉罕·林肯(Abraham Lincoln)的解放黑奴宣言、W. E. B. Dubois的支持辩护、杰基·罗宾森(Jackie Robinson)的沉静精神,以及"二战"后瑟古德·马歇尔(Thurgood Marshall)的诉讼努力。此后,在马丁·路德金的语言中,独立宣言已经常代表了一种"意义的而非真实的宣言"(a declaration of intent rather than reality)]

civil salvage 海难救助;民事船舶救助
civil sanction 民事处分;民事制裁
civil servant 文职人员,公务员
civil service 1.文职(指非军职或立法、司法的公职) 2.文官制,文官考试任用制 3.文职人员(美国指被政府雇来办理公务领政府薪金的公务员,不包括政治、司法官员);公务员

Civil Service Commission （美）文官委员会[指以前的独立联邦机构,负责监督政府的人事制度(personal system)。该委员会于1883年创立,并因1978年的重组计划2号(Reorganization Plan No. 2)而撤销。其功能或任务全部转交给了功绩制度保护委员会(MSPB.)和人事管理局(the Office of Personal Management)。见U. S. Merit System Protection Board]

Civil Service Department （英）文官部
civil service directorate 文官指导处(指法国于第二次世界大战后所设立的人事机构)

civil service entrance examination （美）文官录用考试(旧译:文官入仕考试)
civil service official 文职官员
Civil Service Selection Board 文官考选委员会(指1945年英国在原临时考选委员会基础上改组的一个文官考选机构,主管公务人员的考试和选用)

civil (court of) sessions 民事法庭
civil (或 standard) time 法定时间,标准时间
civil society 文明社会;世俗社会,市民社会
civil society as social contract 作为社会契约的市民社会
civil state 全体国民
civil status 民事法律地位
civil status of aliens 外国人的民事法律地位
civil strife 内乱;内部纷争
civil subject 民事主体
civil suit 民事诉讼
civil trespass 民事侵权行为(见trespass)
civil trial 民事审判

civil war [大写](美)南北战争(1861—1865年);(英)查理一世与议会的战争(1642—1649年)
Civil War Income Tax Act (美)《内战所得税法》
civil wedding ceremony 民事结婚仪式,世俗结婚仪式
civil wrong 民事不法行为;民事过错行为
civil-law a. 民法的
civilian n./a. 公民,平民;文官;文职人员,民法(或大陆法、罗马法)学者(专家)/ 公民的,平民的;民政的;民间的,民用的
civilian authority 民政当局(机关)
civilian conservation corps (美)公共资源保护队
civilian internee (战时)被拘留的敌侨
civilian legal culture 市民法文化
civilian population 平民,老百姓
civilian staff 文职人员
civilian supplies 民用补给品
civilian worker 民工
civilis a. 民事的
civilis actio in factum 事实上的民事诉讼
civilis possessio 法定占有
civilization n. 文明;文化;(总称)文明国家;文明世界
civilized men 文明人
civilly ad. 民法上,法律上,根据民法;从公民权利角度来说
civilly actionable harm 可引起民事诉讼的伤害
civis romanus 罗马公民
civitas n. (古罗马)公民权
civitas maxima 超国家的最广泛文明体[现在此术语被包括中国学者在内的许多学者翻译为"超国家"(以此表示一个更高级别的政治实体)]
civitas gentium maxima 世界国家
Claflin-trust principle (美)克拉夫林信托原则,永久性信托原则[指如果信托设立人设立信托的主要目的(material purposes)之一受到挫折而终止,甚至全部受益人都寻求终止该信托,但受益人不得使该信托终止的原则。克拉夫林信托原则来源于克拉夫林诉克拉夫林案(Claflin v. Claflin),参见《东北区判例汇编》第20卷第454页(马萨诸塞州1889年)。该原则常被援引作为"永久营业财产限(控)制"(deadhand control)的例证,其中,信托设立人的愿望优于活着的受益人的愿望和需求,如果信托设立人仍然活着并同意改变或终止信托,那么通常信托可被终止,除非它是不可改变的。在克拉夫林类的信托中,信托属于挥霍者信托(spendthrift trust)、扶养信托(support),受托人在此类信托中具有酌处决定对受益人作出支付(make distributions)而且受益人有资格获得这一收入,直至一定年龄。对此,受益人将接受克拉夫林信托原则]
claim n./v. (13世纪)1.真实的声明,实情报告书(指一些事情被证实为真实的陈述或声明)〈claims of torture〉(酷刑的陈述、刑讯的真实情报)2.权利主张(指总体的有效事实导致由法院可以强制执行的权利)〈the plaintiff's short plain statement about the crash established the claim〉(原告就有关失事的简要陈述确定了权利主张)[亦即存在一个权利宣告或主张,或者一项请求支付的权利,或衡平法上的救济(equitable remedy)即使是期待性或临时性的],〈the spouse's claims to half of lottery winnings〉(配偶的权利主张赢得了博彩的一半)3.请求权,索赔[指对财产、金钱提出要求,或一个人主张法律上补偿的权利;特别是民事诉讼中控告的当事方指明原告请求的救济(relief),亦称claim for relief(1808年)] 4. 法定的权益[指法律上认可或承认的利益或补救(interest or remedy);意指通过此权益,某人可以获得特惠(privilege),占有或享有一项权利、一件物品(见cause of action 1)〈claim against the employer for wrongful termination〉(对雇主的错误终止合同提出权益主张)]
5.(破产法)(1842年)获得支付的权利(指因违背合同、不履行合同义务而引起的支付权利,即另一方应获得违约者支付的权利或衡平法上的救济。无论判决是否减轻,无论清算的或未清算的,确定的或不确定的,到期的或未到期的,有争议的或无争议的,保险的或未保险的,都不

存在关联)6.(专利法)专利授予请求(指专利申请人在专利申请书中声明其中申请专利的技术符合专利条件,要求授予专利的陈述)7.(采矿法)(立桩或以法定要求设立标记)主张产权,产权主张的地块(或一块面积的矿山土地)8.声索(国际法)[英国广播公司写道:"Brunnei does not claim any of the disputed islands, but Malaysia claims a small number of islands in the spratlys(文莱并没有对任何争议岛屿提出声索,而马来西亚对南沙群岛少数几个岛屿提出声索)."参见美国《华尔街日报》(2015.12.19)。〈a senior U.S.defense official said that bad weather had contributed to the pilot flying off course and into the area claimed by China〉(美国国防部1名高官称,恶劣天气造成飞行员偏离航向,进入中国声索主张的区域)。"claim"译成"声索"显得简练,同时也符合其原义〈to asset and demand the recognition of a right title possession, etc.〉(对权利,头衔,财产等提出要求),〈asset one's right to〉(声称享有权利的含义)]/要求,请求;索取;声称;主张;认领

claim adjuster (保险)索赔理算人
claim against carrier 向承运人索赔
claim against the United States 对美国政府的金钱请求权
claim and delivery 追回非法扣押财产的诉讼
claim board 索赔委员会
claim concerning movable(或**immovable**)**property** 涉及动产(或不动产)的诉讼请求
claim credit right 要求申报债权
claim detinue 收回不法占有动产请求权;要求返还扣留财产的诉讼请求
claim for compensation 求偿权,赔偿诉讼请求;索赔
claim for compensation for bodily injuries and death 人身伤害与死亡补助金的请求权
claim for damages 损害赔偿请求权;损害赔偿诉讼请求
claim for damages caused by animals 因动物所造成损害的赔偿请求权
claim for damages caused by children 因儿童造成损害的赔偿请求权
claim for damages caused by criminal act 因犯罪行为所造成损害的赔偿请求权
claim for general average 分担共同海损的请求权
claim for indemnification 赔偿请求权
claim for liability 有关民事责任请求权
claim for performance of an obligation 履行债的请求权
claim for possession of rented property 租赁财产占有请求权,租赁财产占有诉讼请求
claim for recovery 追索财产的请求权,返还原物的请求权
claim for relief 见 claim 1
claim for restitution 返回原物的请求权
claim for set-off 作为抵销的债权,作为抵销的请求权
claim in contract 根据合同(契约)的请求权
claim in equity 采用简易程序的诉讼请求,(英)平衡法上的诉讼请求
claim in personam 对人请求权
claim in tort 因侵权行为产生的请求权
claim indemnity 索赔
claim joinder 诉讼请求合并
claim of damage for personal injury 人身伤害请求权,人身伤害诉讼请求
claim of damages for loss of bargain 买卖合同(契约)损失的赔偿请求权
claim of everyday life 日常生活中的请求权
claim of liberties 自由(或特许)状的请求
claim of ownership 所有权之诉
claim of privilege 特权的请求,特权的权力请求,特权的权力主张
claim of unconstitutionality 确定违宪的诉讼
claim on defective packing 因包装低劣而要求索赔
claim on quality 因品质低劣而要求索赔
claim on shortage 因缺斤少两而要求索赔
claim preclusion 排除请求效力(见 res ju-

dicata)
claim right 主张权利
claim salvage 要求支付救助费用请求权
claim statement (或 bill) 索赔清单
claim the floor (1840年)(议会法)要求授予资格(指向议长提出请求以获得承认具有资格发言的目的)
claim the protection of the law 要求法律保护
claim to correctness 正确性要求
claim to exemption 请求免除
claim to family maintenance 家庭扶养(赡养)费请求权
claim to immunity 豁免请求权
claim to order 记名债券
claim to the counter-performance 对待给付请求权
claim-jumper n. (美)非法夺取权益者(指非法夺取他人采矿权或土地所有权者)
claim-made basis 索赔基础制
claim-splitting 请求权分离
claimable a. 可要求的;可认领的
claimant (=claimer) n. 原告;索赔人;认领人;(根据权利)提出要求者;请求人;债权人
claimant adjuster (权利要求请求人的)调解处理人(指为请求人从保险公司得到或向该公司坚持某项权利或请求的调解处理人)
claimed invention 对发明提出权利要求,主张发明的权利
claims agent 索赔代理人
claims commission 索赔委员会;求偿审查委员会
claims department 理赔部
Claims Division 索赔局(指美司法部内主管权利要求的一个部门,现在改为民事局——Civil Division)
claims document 索赔证件(单据)
claims enjoy priority in satisfaction before the claims of the mortgage 享有先于抵押人(物)的优先受偿权
claims expenses 理赔费用
claims for collection of rent 请求交付租金的权利

claims of patent application 专利申请权,专利申请书
claims inextricably intertwined with an earlier state-court judgment 不可能解决的、又与一项早期州法院的判决缠结在一起的权利请求
claims of several 分别权利,分别请求权
claims of sovereignty 主权主张
claims on account of defects 对瑕疵索赔的请求
claims paid 赔偿付讫,已支付赔款
claims payable abroad 国外领取的赔款
claims rejected 拒赔
claims setting agent 理赔代理人,清理赔偿代理人
claimsman n. 意外险赔偿额估算者
clan n. 1.氏族,宗族,部族 2.宗派,小集团
clan armed fighting 宗族械斗
clan authority 族权
clan chiefs' court 部落酋长法院
clan culture 家族文化
clan dispute 宗族纠纷
clan system 宗族制度
clandestine a. 秘密的,暗中的
clandestine immigration 秘密入境
clandestine marriage 秘密婚姻[指①仅建立当事双方合意的婚姻;②一种秘密方式的婚姻,并以非正式仪式进行,而欠缺各种要求的条件(formalities)]
clandestine operation 秘密活动
Clandestine Outlawries Bill 克兰德斯丁法定程序外议案(指每届议会开始之际,大会辩论前在下议院的一种一读议案,而以后不再继续进行下去的议案)
clandestine possession 隐蔽占有
clandestine sale 秘密交易,秘密销售
clannish a. 氏族的,宗族的;宗派的,小集团的
clansmen n. 同宗,族人;氏族(或部落)的人
clarification n. 阐明,澄清
clarify v. 阐明,澄清;变得易懂
clarify one's stand 表明个人立场
clarion call 响亮的号角声
clarity n. 透明,明晰

clash n. 1.冲突;抵触,对抗 2.不一致,不调和
clash of arms 武装冲突
clash with riot policeman (抗议者)与防暴警察发生冲突
class (17世纪)1.阶级,阶层;同类[指具有共同特性或共同属性的人群、集体,或同一品质事物的集合体〈a class of common stock shares〉(同一类的股票〉,〈the upper-middle class〉(上中等阶层)]。受保护的阶层(protected class)(指这一阶层的人民受益于制定法,如《1964年民权法第七权利条款》,该条禁止基于种族、性别、民族血统或宗教而进行歧视]2.顺序,等级[借此可对群众或事物作安排〈she flew first class to Chicago〉(她乘头等舱飞至芝加哥)]3.未定数额的群体〈a class of beneficiaries〉(受益人的集体或一群受益人)4.民事诉讼,集体诉讼,群体诉讼[指具有共同法律地位(legal position)的群体。他们的权利主张可在单一诉讼程序(single proceeding)中得到裁判〈a class of asbestos plaintiffs〉(受石灰伤害的原告群体)]
class 1 cover 第一类保险
class action (=representative action) 集团诉讼,代表诉讼(指20世纪发展起来的一种处理复杂、涉及众多当事人诉讼的方法或手段。即某一事情上有共同利益的人众多,他们可由其代表代为起诉或应诉,而无须集团所有人参与诉讼。集团诉讼的条件包括:①组成集团的人员众多,无法全体参与诉讼;②指定的集团代表能公平地代表集团全体成员;③集团明确;④集团或成员就所涉及的法律问题和事实问题有明确界定的共同利益;⑤审判法院必须将诉讼确定为集团诉讼。1966年的美国《联邦民事诉讼法规》修订后的第23条规则对此作了相应规定)
class action judgment 集团诉讼判决
class alignment 阶级阵线
class analysis 阶级分析
class attitude 阶级立场
class character 阶级本性
class claim (=class action) 集团诉讼,团体诉讼(指由个人或其他实体组成的一个大的群体或"集团"中,由其中一名或多名代表整个集团以"当事人代表"名义所提起的诉讼),群体诉讼
class contradiction 阶级矛盾
class damage remedy 集团损害赔偿救济
class exploitation 阶级剥削
class gift (1949年)概括赠与(指一种给予的赠与,赠与时人数不确定,但到将来人数被确定时,所有受赠人均可依特定比例或均等地分享赠与)
class legislation 同属性的立法,专属立法(同 local and special legislation)(这里的 class 不是阶级,也不是集团,而是指具有共同特性或属性的人、物等。class legislation 是指某些立法把人们或立法对象加以分类,在授予权利或设定负担上,根据专断的不公正的划分畛域而不公平的原则,则属于"违宪",即违反美国联邦宪法第十四修正案关于平等保护的保证条款)
class of appeals 上诉种类
class of habitual defendants 惯常的群体被告,传统的群体被告
class of habitual plaintiffs' lawyer 传统原告律师群
class of pollution 污染等级
class of practitioners 执业阶层
class of vehicle 车辆类别
class or representative action 集团或代表诉讼(见 class action)
class origin 阶级出身
class right 阶级权利
class status 阶级成分,阶级地位
class struggle 阶级斗争
class suit 集团诉讼
class viewpoint 阶级观点
class vote system 等级投票制度
class voting (1941年)类别表决,集体投票[指类别表决权(class voting right)即类别股东在普通股东大会之外分类召开的类别股股东会上的表决权。类别股股东对变更其在公司参与权的有关公司议案作出赞成、反对或弃权的意思表示,从而形成类别股股东团体的意思。类别表决权性质与普通表决权不同,公司规章可以规定类别表决权,而普通表决权源自法

律规定,是股东固有权,公司章程和决议不能剥夺和限制这种权利。亦称 voting by class; voting by voting group]
classic a. 古典的,古典派的;传统的;最优秀的,不朽的,典型的,著名的
classic book 经典著作
classic legal pluralism 经典的法律多元主义[指西方著名学者莎莉·恩格尔·玛丽(Sally Engle Marry)在文化多元是法律多元现象产生原因及法律多元现象研究视野扩大到西方社会的基础上区分了"经典的法律多元主义"和"新法律多元主义"(New Legal Pluralism)]
classical a. 经典的,第一流的;古典(派)的,古典作家的,传统的,权威的;文科的
classical common law 古典普通法
classical era of Roman law 罗马法的权威年代;罗马法的传统年代
classical institutions 传统制度
classical jurist 第一流的法学家
classical law of nature school (= classical nature law school) 古典自然法学派(指17—18世纪法学世界观的学说理论,是新兴资产阶级用以反对封建压迫、民族压迫和教会神学的法律思想,它的主要代表人物有荷兰的格劳秀斯,英国的霍布斯、洛克,法国的孟德斯鸠、卢梭,德国的普芬道夫和意大利的贝卡利亚等)
classical legal writers 古典法学家
classical liberalism 古典自由主义
classifiable fingerprints 可分类的指印
classification n. 类别;分类法;船级;类型;等级;规范分类;分类监䝞
classification certificate 船级证书
classification clause (航运)船级条款;分类条款
classification of crimes 罪行分类;犯罪类型
classification of evidence 证据分类
classification of expenditures 支出分类
classification of goods 商品分类(表)
classification of law 法的分类
classification of obligations 债之分类
classification of penalty 刑罚种类;刑罚类别

classification of risks 危险分级,危险类别
classification of states 国家的分类
classification of torts 侵权行为的类别
classification of vessel 船级
classification of writs (英)令状的分类[指对所诉讼程序的分类,同时也是对当时实质法律原则(substantive principle)和普通法(common law)的分类。见 original writ]
classification society 船级协会
classification survey 船级检验
classification system for fingerprints 指纹分类系统,指印分类系统
classified a.分类的;被归入一类的;机密的,保密的
classified advertisement 分类广告
classified document 保密文件
classified information 保密资料;机密情报
clausal a. 条款的,款项的
clause n. 条款(向议会提交法案时称为条款,经讨论通过后则为正式条文 provision);项目;款项
clause in a policy 保险单条款
clause of constitution 宪法条款
clause of contract 合同(契约)条款
clause of ratification 批准条款
clause of regulations 规章条款
clause of statute 法规条款;制定法条款
clause of the constitution 宪法条款
clause of treaty 条约条款
clause paramount 首要条款(指规定租船合同不得与"海牙规则"相抵触的合同条款)
clause *penale* 违约金条款
clause rider 追加条款
claused reasons 理由条款[指"保密理由"(confidential reasons)的又一称谓]
Clauses Acts (美)合同条款法(指1845年至1847年公布的大部分法规的统称)
clausula (或 clause) *rebus sic stantibus* 情势变迁条款(国际法上的一种理论)
* *Clausula generalis non refertur ad expressa.* A general clause does not refer to things expressed. 一般条款不涉及业已明示的事物。

* ***Clausula inconsuetae semper inducunt suspicionem.*** Unusual clauses (in an instrument) always induce suspicion. (法律文书中)少用的条款常会发生疑义。
* ***Clausula quae abrogationem excludit ab initio non valet.*** A clause which precludes repeal is void from the beginning. (法令、判决上)排除废止或撤销的条款是自始无效的。
clausum fregit 非法侵入(他人的)土地
clausum mare 领海
claw v. (美俗)逮捕,抓住;搜刮(钱财等)
claw-back provision (美)薪酬追回条款[指2002年《公众公司会计改革和投资者保护法案》(又称《萨班斯法案》)中第304节的"薪酬追回条款"规定,即若发行证券公司因为不当引起的原始材料与任何证券法之规定不符而被要求重编会计报表,则公司首席执行官(CEO)与首席财务主管(CFO)应偿还发行证券公司在特定时期内从公司收到的所有资金、红利或其他奖金性或权益性酬金,以及通过买卖该公司证券而实现的收益]
Clayton (Anti-trust) Act 《克莱顿(反托拉斯)法》(指美国1914年国会通过的补充《谢尔曼法》的法案,旨在禁止劳动力供应的垄断)
clean a. 干净的;健康的;健全的;无瑕疵的;清白的,正直的;端正的,彻底的,光洁的
clean acceptance 无条件承诺(指不附保留条件的承诺);无条件承兑
Clean Air Act (美国1970年的)《空气清洁法》(该法赋予公民借助联邦法院督促执法的权力,以确保该法的立法目标得以实现)
clean and convincing 无疑使人确信
clean bill 光票(指不附保留条件的票据)
clean bill of health (船舶的)无疫证明书;检疫证书;(合格)健康证明书
clean bill of lading 清洁提单(指不附带任何条件的提货单)
clean B/L 清单提单
clean collection 光票托收
clean credit 纯信(用)贷(款);光票信用证,

无跟单信用证,(对比 documentary credit)
clean development mechanism (CDM) 清洁发展机制[《京都议定书》创制的清洁发展机制,指发达国家通过提供资金和技术的方式与发展中国家开展项目合作,将项目可实现的"经核证的减排量"(CERs)用于发达国家缔约方完成在该议定书第3条下关于减少本国温室气体排放指标。发达国家和发展中国家之间借助 CDM 构建碳信用交易市场,通过林业碳汇项目的实施,实现森林生态效益价值补偿的市场化,使得具有很强外部性特征的森林生态效益在发达国家和发展中国家之间通过交易手段实现效益内部化。联合国《京都议定书》的清洁发展机制允许发达国家到发展中国家购买经核证的减排量,用来完成自己的减排任务,使发达国家能以较低成本履行减排任务,发展中国家则能借此从发达国家获得资金和技术以促进本国的可持续发展,企业则可以通过出售减排量获得额外收益]
clean draft 光票,清洁汇票(指不附单据的汇票)
clean government 廉洁政治(府)
clean handed 清白的,未做过坏事的
clean letter of credit 清洁信用证
clean loan 无抵押借款
clean payment credit 光票付款信用证
clean slate principle (国际法)白纸主义(又译:白板原则,指不受义务、口约等所拘束的主张)
clean out 1.结关后离港 2.离开,逃走 3.把……清出(出空);使人将钱用光
clean, unequivocal and convincing 确凿及毋庸置疑
clean up 1.整理,收拾 2.清除,消除,解除(误会,疑虑等)3.(天气)放晴
Clean Water Act (美)《清洁水法》;《净化水法》
clean-hands doctrine 净手原则[衡平法上的原则,即如果一方当事人的行为违背了衡平法上的原则,如善意或诚信原则(good faith),则该当事人不得在衡平法上寻求救济或作为主观辩护理由。需要求得衡平法上救济的当事人,自己必须清白

无瑕]
cleaning up of trouble cases 解决麻烦事件（trouble cases 指不满、纠纷或冒犯行为）
clear a./v. 无罪的；清白的；纯粹的；无疑的,确实的；明确的,明显的；畅通的/1.弄明白,澄清,宣布无辜；宣布无罪；开释2.付清,清偿；清理3.驱逐,赶走4.办好出港手续；(船)预备出港5.交换(票据)6.(文件)送交审批7.卸货8.(议案)通过,准许,批准
clear a port 出港,结关
clear and convincing evidence (或 proof) 明确而令人信服的证据(指较通常民事案件所要求的"有充分根据的证据"更有证据力,但还未达到刑事案件所要求的"无合理怀疑的证据"的程度)
Clear and present danger (美)清晰而现实的危险[指不管议论或演说是否应该受到限制或惩罚,只要它会立即引导暴行或产生严重威胁有碍国家安全这个标准,则可以受到惩罚。第一次使用该偶然术语的是大法官奥利弗·温德尔·霍姆斯(Oliver Wendell Holmes),将此作为一个重要标准来决定这种言论是否受美国联邦宪法第一修正案的保护,在申克诉合众国案(Sehenck v. U. S.)中,霍姆斯即引用此标准。见 seditious libel]
clear area 畅通区
Clear Command of the Seventh Amendment (美国联邦)宪法第七修正案的明确命令
clear days 十足日数(指采取去头、尾日来计算天数。亦叫日数),净日数
clear declaration 明示
clear evidence 明显的证据
clear expression 明白表示,明示
clear hold 空货舱
clear in 办理海关进口手续
clear income 纯收入
clear majority 绝对半数,过半数
clear of suspicion 消除嫌疑
clear off 清偿(债务)
clear proof 确证
clear the court 清理法庭；禁止旁听
clear the docket 清理积案,结束所有案件的审理
clear-cut a. 清晰的,明确的,轮廓清楚的
clear-cut majority 明显的过半数
clear-cut rule 明智的规则
clearance n. 1.结关,(船舶的)出(入)港证(=clearance papers)2.票据交换3.清理,清除,出清(空)4.了结；辞职照准；批准
clearance certificate 放行证书；结关单
clearance depot 结关货物
clearance fee 出(入)港手续费
clearance notice 出(入)港通知
clearance of debt 清理债务
clearance order (英)拆除令(指地方政府征得卫生部长的同意颁布拆除不适合居住的房屋的命令)
clearance papers 出(入)港单(证明出港结关手续已清)
clearance permit 出(入)港许可证
clearance sale 清货贱卖
cleared and settled in a single day 一天内清算和交割
clearing n./a. 1.表白,昭雪(冤屈)2.清算账目；结账,结算,划汇结算；(复)划汇结算款项的总金额；票据交换3.出海/结关的,清算的
clearing account 结算账户,记账
clearing agent 清算代理人
clearing agreement 清算协议
clearing bank 清算银行,(票据)交换银行
clearing day 结算日；票据交换日
clearing house 票据交换所,(技术情报)交流中心
Clearing House Interbank Payments System (CHIPS) 美国银行间支付清算系统
clearing label 出海证
clearing price of exchange 结汇价格
clearing-house for trade information 贸易情报交换所,贸易票据交换所
clearing-house service (技术)情报交换业务
clearly erroneous 明显错误
clearly inappropriate forum 明显不合适法院
clearly unjust 显失公平,明显不公平
clear-view doctrine 见 plain view doctrine

clemency n. 仁慈,宽厚;宽大(指对罪犯减轻惩罚或从宽处理)

clergy n. 1.神职人员,基督教的神职和教会人员的总称 2.基督教的牧师(宗教改革前,有 regular clerge"修道士",priors"修道院长,小隐修院院长";还有不受修道院誓约束缚的修道院神职人员 secular clergy,如主教、教长、堂区牧师。英国的神职人员可担任地方行政官,并有义务负责担任陪审团成员。美国不承认神职人员的特权)

clergy reserves (19世纪加拿大的)教会保留地

cleric n./a. 牧师,教士/牧师的,教士的

clerical a. 书写的,书记的;办公室工作的;教士的,牧师的

clerical error 书写错误,笔误

clerical officer 书记官

clerical staff 全体办事人员

clerical work 办公室工作(指誊抄、归档等工作)

clericalism n. 教权主义

clerk n./v. 书记官(指由国会任命的联邦最高法院的书记官。他负责履行最高法院的全部行政职责,并具有一定的独立性。第一任书记官1790年由国会任命),秘书,书记员(官);职员,办事员;(美)店员;执事;牧师,教士(见 secretary)/任(办事员,书记员,店员)的职务

clerk at the table 现场书记

clerk of arraigns (英)巡回法庭助理书记官

clerk of assize (英)巡回法庭书记官

clerk of court (英)(高等法院)书记官,法庭书记员

clerk of enrollments (英)(历史)注册处主管[指以前的注册登记处的主管,英国议会(British Parliament)于1879年将此机构废除,并将其任务指定给中央办公室(Central Office)承担。见 enrollment office; Central Office]

clerk of records and writs (英)高等法院主事官

clerk of the corporation 公司的秘书,公司主事秘书(见 secretary ②)

Clerk of the Council in Ordinary (英)枢密院常任书记官(主事官)

Clerk of the Crown in Chancery (英)大法官法庭国玺部掌礼官、保管官

Clerk of the Hanaper (或 Hamper) (英)(大法官法院的)大篮子令状保管官(指负责令状盖章装入袋中的普通法事务官员)

Clerk of the House of Commons (英)下议院主事官

Clerk of the Parliament (英)上议院主事官

clerk of the peace 治安书记官

Clerk of the Petty Bag 衡平法院主事官

clerk to the justices (由律师兼任的)法官秘书

clerk's office 书记员处

clerk's office assignment duties 书记员处的安排职责

clerk's office employees 书记处工作人员

Clerks of the Court (美)联邦最高法院书记员(指联邦最高法院法定的5名书记官员,他们负责日常法院需要审理案件的日常安排。此职位是按照1790年2月2日联邦最高法院第一个正式规定而设立的。只有19人已作为这一官员在联邦最高法院任职过)

Clerks of the justice (美)大法官秘书,大法官的书记员(大法官书记员或秘书制度开始于1882年,属大法官私人助理性质。曾聘请当时哈佛大学法学院一名毕业生,薪金由大法官自己支付,以后情况有所变。第二次世界大战后因联邦最高法院承担的案件大幅度增加,因此配给大法官的法律书记员亦从2名增至4名,主要任务是甄别案件)

Click Stream Data 浏览网站记录软件(或数据)

click-wrap contact 点击合同

clickprint 点击痕迹[可数名词,意指能够用来独特地辨认出某个互联网用户身份的有规律的上网模式。点击痕迹涵盖多种数据,其中包括互联网用户经常光顾哪些网页、浏览每个网页所用的时间、每周在哪些特定时段上网、每访问一个网站时所打开的网页数量以及点击网页上不同

区域的先后顺序。美国宾夕法尼亚大学沃顿商学院信息管理学教授巴拉吉·帕德马纳班和加州大学戴维斯分校管理学院教授杨颖慧(音)在 2006 年 9 月 18 日发表的研究论文中创造了该词。Clickprinting(监护用户的独特上网模式)的做法亦可追踪和收集点击痕迹所获得的 clickstream(点击流,即对用户上网点击的一系列网页的记录),可以帮助互联网企业为满足用户需求而特别定制网站内容或发布广告]
clickstream 点击流(见 clickprint)
client n. (律师的)当事人(旧译:事主);(诉讼)委托人;(古罗马)贵族保护下的平民;顾客
client account 诉讼委托人在银行的账户
client concerned 当事人
client department 主管部门
client state 附庸国;附庸政府
client's privilege (见 attorney-client privilege)
client-security fund 客户安全基金(这种基金的建立通常是由于客户的代理人盗用资金或其他不当行为,使客户因损失而受到痛苦。建立此基金是通过州或国家律师协会赔偿受损失的客户)
client-side geolication 客户端定位[指国家在控制和监督互联网方面具有能力时,可通过客户端定位或服务器端定位(server-side geolication)辨别出个人所处的地理位置。本质上,网络空间中已存在电子边界]
clientage n. 委托关系,保护关系;诉讼委托人的地位
clientele n. (律师等的)委托人,受保护者;门徒,追随者
clientelism n. 侍从主义
clients' money (律师等的)委托费
clientship n. 保护关系(指古罗马的权贵作为保护人和被保护人的关系)
climacteric insanity 绝经期精神病
climate refugee 气候难民(见 Global Weirding)
climate of opinion 意见气候,意见气氛
clinch v. 钉住,确定,决定(证据、交易等)
clinch an argument 使论据确定无疑

cling v. 依附(to)依靠(to),坚持,墨守(to)
cling to one's own views 坚持己见
clink n. (俚)监狱,牢房
clip wound 剪创(伤)
clique n. 小集团,朋党,派系,帮(派)
cliquism n. 排他主义,小集团主义
cloak v./n. 覆盖,包藏,掩盖;以……为借口/借口,伪装,覆盖物
clockless worker 不分昼夜工作的雇佣工
clog n. 阻碍,障碍
clog on equity of redemption (英)妨碍衡平法上的赎回权
Clonaid n. 克隆人协会(1997 年创立,设于美国内华达州拉斯维加斯)
clone n./v. 克隆(指无性繁殖)
clone sheep 克隆绵羊(指英国科学家以从绵羊身上抽取的乳腺细胞,成功克隆出另一只绵羊,英国、西班牙、丹麦、法国、澳大利亚等均有法例阻止以此无性繁殖人类的克隆)
close n./v./a. 1.终结,终止,了结;诉讼的结束 2.界内,境内;关闭,封锁(地方);有建筑物围绕的土地/1.终结,结束,结(案),结清(账目);商定(交易)2.缔结,订,定 3.靠近,(船)靠岸 4. 关,闭,封闭/亲近的,密切的;严格的;秘密的;关闭的,封闭的,有限制的;势均力敌的
close a bargain 成交;达成协议
close a case 销案,结案
close arrest 严格规定的逮捕;秘密逮捕
close confinement 严格限制(活动范围等)
close connection of criminal law with politics 与政治相关联的刑法,与政治紧密相关的刑法,触及政治的刑法
close corporation (= closely held corporation) 封闭公司[相对"公众公司"(public company)、(股份)上市公司而言,其股票,至少说有持票权的股份,掌握在某一股东或关系密切的一批股东之手,此类公司一般无公众投资者,股东积极参与公司的管理。实际上,封闭公司是家族成员持有大部分股份的"家族公司"(family corporation)的另一称呼。美国的法律用语中

通常使用 close corporation, 而在英国则称为 closed corporation]; 有限公司
close corporation laws（或 acts） 内部持股公司法, 不公开招股公司法
close family 近亲属
close down the enterprise 关闭企业
close imprisonment 秘密监禁
close interpretation 严格的解释
close of a bankruptcy 破产程序的终结
close of a business year 年度决算
close of argument at the first trial 一审辩论的终结
close of pleadings 书面事实陈述结束（接着开始书面辩论阶段）
close out 抛售; 停卖
close prisoner 秘密人犯
close proximity to provisions 与条款非常相近
close rank 紧密团结
close relative 近亲属
close rolls and close writs （英）密封（敕令）宗卷
close seasons （英）禁猎期
close supervision 严格监督
close the books 结账
close the polls 终止投票
close up shops 罢市
close with an offer 接受减价
close-out netting 终止净额结算 [指双方之间存在尚未履行完毕的双务合同, 根据约定及法律规定, 先终止合同, 然后抵销每一合同中的得与失, 最后再结算应当作出的相互履行。分两步走; 第一步, 解除尚未履行的合同（从破产中的待履行合同制度的原理看, 法律禁止破产债务人的相对人破产时解除合同, 因此除非有法律特殊规定, 终止净额结算条款在破产中是无效的); 第二步为计算得失, 并于之后进行抵销]
close-to-nature forestry 近自然林业
closed a. 关闭的, 封闭的, 闭合的; 排外的; 闭关自守的; 保密的
closed area 封闭区域; 禁区
closed auction 非公开拍卖
closed bid 秘密出价投标

closed career system 封闭式职业制（指英国的文官制, 考入政府服务后, 从最低级做起, 最后以年资、能力、考绩依次晋升, 在此制度下, 高级人员均是由低层升上来的, 外面的人是插不进去的, 与美国的 open career system 相对立）
closed case 已结案件
closed company 封闭型公司, 不公开招股的公司
closed corporation 见 close corporation
closed court 闭庭; （英）封闭型法院 [有时指英格兰皇家民事法院（Common Pleas Court of England)]
closed district 封锁区
closed economics 闭关自守的经济
(a) closed hard and fast system 紧密顽固封闭的体制（系）
closed issue 已决议的事项
closed order 限定订货
closed primary 闭锁式初选（制）; 排他性预选（指仅由某一政党成员参加的预选）
closed registry 封闭登记（国际海事上的用语）
closed rule 定案规则（指议会就某一议案不再考虑新的修正意见的规定）
closed sea 封（闭）海
closed season （美）禁猎期
closed session 禁止旁听的开庭
closed shop 封闭工厂; 只雇用某一工会会员的商店（或制度）
closed treaty 不开放条约
closed union 少数人拥有股, 不吸收新会员的工会
closed-door policy 闭关自守政策, 锁国政策
closed-end mortgage 闭锁式抵押（亦称限额型抵押、闭口抵押。指在抵押期间, 不论是抵押财产或抵押借款数额均不得变更的一种抵押）
close-ended claim 封闭式请求
closely held corporation 少数人拥有的公司（封闭式公司）; 股东人数有限的公司, 处于控制下的公司
closely-held corporations 封闭性公司（通常以股东性协议或其他方式改变法定的基本公司治理模式。见 public corporation

开放性公司)
closet n. 私室,小房间;密室
closet consultation 秘密会议
closet-homosexual 秘密同性恋者
close-to-nature forestry 近自然林业
close-up bullet wound 近射枪弹创(伤)
closing n. 终止,结尾;封闭,封锁;结账;进行最后的辩论;证据概述,总结;完成交易,交割(原指房地产交易中各方的最后成交仪式,各方在最后文件上签字、盖章、付款,房契交付对方或第三人保管等。现在亦指其他交易的最后成交,类似于外交上的文本签字和文本交换仪式。交割一般在银行或律师事务所举行,由合同方、律师以及有利害关系当事人共同参加)
closing n. 终止,结尾;封闭,闭锁;结账;决算
closing account 结账,决算
closing agreement (美)(所得税)结案书
closing argument 辩论终结,终止辩论
closing arguments 辩论终结,最后辩论(指美国民事诉讼所有的证据在审理中均被出示之后,律师利用证据说服陪审团作出对其委托人有利结论的陈述;与最初陈述一样,最后辩论自身亦非证据)
closing ceremony 闭幕典礼
closing cost 地产成交价
closing date 截止(收受)日期
closing day 停业日
closing of the country 闭关自守
closing of the court (法庭)闭庭
closing order 封闭令,封屋令
closing price (或 rate) 收盘价(格)
closing rate 收盘价
closing slip 承保单
closing statement 最后陈述;结案陈词;最后声明
closing the book 结账
closure n. 1.关闭,封闭,停止 2.终止辩论,付诸表决(指英国议会通过对议案的一种表决方法。要要缩短时间讨论议案,便将议案交议员即席表决,如赞成人数超过100人就算通过);限期结束辩论(=cloture)
closure insurance 关闭保险
closure of border 封锁边界

closure of debate 辩论终结
closure of liquidation 清算完结
closure of port 封(闭)港
closure order 终结令,封闭令
closure rule 终结规则(新分析实证主义法学代表英国牛津大学研究员拉兹认为:法院通过三种办法可改变现行法律。终结规则为其中一种,即根据英美法,在缺乏相应法律解决办法的情况下,法院可运用辩论终结规则使这一案件不再依靠先例制,另两种为识别和推翻)
clothe v. 为……提供衣服;覆盖,蒙蔽,使披上;表达,赋予,使具有权力(或特性)
clothed with an exequatur (美)附有认可的证书(指地方法院认可并使其有效且可在外国执行)
cloture n. 见 closure
cloud n. 阴影,模糊,缺点,缺陷;污点;招致暗晦(麻烦、疑虑、耻辱)的事物
cloud on title 所有权的缺陷(或瑕疵)
club n. 俱乐部,夜总会;会社;会所
club law 暴力统治(指由大棒或暴力统治,使用非法暴力代替法律进行国家统治)
club loan 国际银团贷款
clue n. 线索;暗示;端倪
clue to solving a case 破案线索
clutch n./v. (常用复)爪手;毒手;掌握,控制/抓住,攥住
clutter up 充斥,杂乱无章堆放
CMI Guidelines on Oil Pollution Damage 国际海事委员会通过的《油污损害指南》(1994年10月)
co-acceptor n. 共同承兑人
co-accused n. (刑事上的)同案犯(被告)(见 co-defendant)
co-adjutor n. 助手
co-administration n. 共同管理
co-belligerency n. 共同交战状态,共同作战地位
co-defendant (=codefendant) n. 共同被告(人)(可用于民事或刑事案件);同案犯
co-drawer n. 共同发票人
co-equal a. (程度、等级、价值等方面的)相互平等的
co-existence model 共存模式(指欧盟协调

利息税的共存模式)
co-felon n. 共同重罪犯
co-heir (=coheir) n. 共同继承人
co-obligor n. 共同债务人
co-operative company 合作公司
co-opt v. 指派,指定……为代表;(原有成员对新成员的)增选;接收,占有;同化,吸收
co-optative (=co-optive) a.增选的,由增选产生的
co-ordination of behaviour 行为的协调(指相当部分法学家的观念;认为法律本质上或主要是对个体行为的协调。有些法学家认为协调、权威和遵守法律的义务之间存在联系)
co-owner n. (财产)共同所有人;共有人
co-owner of a ship 船舶共有人
co-ownership n. 财产共同所有权;共有权
co-respondent n. 共同被告;离婚诉讼中的通奸者;(民事诉讼的)共同答辩人
co-responsibility n. 共同责任
co-tenancy (=cotenancy) 共有[指两人或两人以上共同享有同一财产的所有权和占有权,包括共同共有(joint tenancy),普通共有(tenancy in common)与夫妻共有(tenancy by the entirety)]
co-worker n. 共同工作的人,同事,合作者
coaching n. 告诉证人如何提供证据的律师(有时这是不适当的,甚至是违法的)
coaction n. 1.共同行动,协力 2.强制力,强迫
coalition n. 联合、(政党,个人或国家间临时性的)联盟;结合体
coalition builder 联盟的构造者
coalition cabinet 联合内阁
Coalition Government 联合政府
coalitionist n. 参加联盟者,(政治上的)联合论者
Coase theorem 科斯定理(法学和经济学的相互作用形成了一个重要的新的经济体系,这就是科斯定理,即"法定权利的最初分配从效率角度上看是无关紧要的,只要交换的成本为零"。换句话说,由法律所规定的法定权利分配不当,会在市场上通过自由交换得以校正)

Coasean bargain 科斯(原理)的磋商
Coasean World 科斯的范畴(学派)
coast n. 海岸,海滨地区;(The Coast)(美)太平洋沿岸,西海岸
coast zone 海岸带
coastal a. 海岸的,沿海的
coastal defense 海防,沿海防务
coastal jurisdiction 沿海管辖权
coastal shipping 沿海航运
coastal state 沿海国
coastal waters 沿海水域
coaster n. 沿海航行者,沿海贸易者,沿海航船
coastguard (=coast guard) n. 1.(总称)海岸警卫队,海上缉私队,海上救生队 2.警卫队员,缉私队员,救生队员
coasting trade 海岸贸易;沿海贸易
coastline n. 海岸线
coastwaiter n. (英)(监督沿海货运的)海关官员
coax v. 哄骗,诱骗
cobdenism n. 自由贸易主义
cobelligerent n. 共同参战(友)国
coborrower n. 共同借款人
cobuyer n. 共同买受人
cochair (=cochairman) n. 联合主席(指会议两主席中的一个),副主席
cocaine n. 可卡因
cocker v. 娇养,溺爱,放纵(up)
coconspirator n. 共谋者
coconspirators rule 共同共谋者规则(指共谋成员所作的声明或陈述,均为反对其他共谋者的有效证据)
cocontractor n. 共同承揽人,共同承包商
code n. 1.法典,法规,法 2.准则,标准 3.电码,密码,代号
code book 电码本
Code Civil 《拿破仑民法典》(即1804年颁布的法国民法典)
Code Coran (阿拉伯)《可兰法典》
Code de Commerce (法)《商法典》(1807年颁布,作为民法典的补充)
Code Europeen des Contracts 《欧洲合同法》,简称CEC
code flag 信号旗

code form 密语
code formulation 法典模式
code formulation for pleading a cause of action 诉因诉辩的法典程式
Code Justinian 《查士丁尼法典》(指东罗马皇帝查士丁尼一世下令编纂的法典,该法典分为自然法、万民法和民法三个部分)
Code Louis (法)《路易法典》(指路易十四制定的一部法令汇编)
Code Napoleon 《拿破仑法典》(见 Code Civil)
Code Noir (法)《黑色法典》(指 1685 年路易十四颁布的一个法典)
Code of Banking Practice 银行惯例守则
Code of Canon Law 《寺院法法典》(指现代对罗马天主教会的教规进行修订后编制的法典,1917 年颁布,1918 年生效)
code of civil and commercial procedure 民事和商事诉讼法典
code of civil procedure 民事诉讼法典,民事诉讼法
Code of Communal Administration (法)《市镇行政管理法典》
code of conducts 行为准则,行为规范(与 best practices 同)
code of conduct for responsible fisheries 责任渔业行为规约
code of ethics 道德准则,道德规范
Code of Fair Competition 市场公平竞争法规
Code of Federal Regulations (CFR) (美)《联邦法规汇典》(1937 年由国会创办。该"汇典"中的法规均收集自《联邦日志》,或《联邦注册》,并按包括 50 个标题的主题表编排,其中多数为《美国法典》的标题及其有关名称。见 Federal Register Act)
Code of Frederick the Great 《腓特烈大帝法典》(即 1751 年普鲁士法典)
Code of Hammurabi 《汉谟拉比法典》(指 4000 年前巴比伦第一个王朝的君主汉谟拉比在位时发展起来,一直到他在位末期所收集的他在法律方面的决定,篆刻在石柱上,共 282 条,包括经济条款、家庭法和民法,为现存最全面最完整的巴比伦法律

汇编)
code of hono(u)r 社交礼法
Code of Huesca 《韦斯卡法典》(中世纪阿拉贡最重要的法典)
code of industrial property 工业产权法典
code of international conduct 国际行为准则,国际行为规范
Code of Judicial Conduct (美)《司法行为法规》(指由美国律师协会和许多州所采纳使用的对法官行为的整套法规。见 Judge's Code of Judicial Conduct)
Code of Judicial Ethics (美)法官道德手册,法官道德准则
Code of Justinian 见 Justinian Code
code of labo(u)r law(on land) (陆上)劳工法典
Code of Law on Marriage, Family, and Guardianship 《婚姻、家庭及监护法典》
code of maritime commerce 海商法典
Code of Menes 《美尼斯法典》(公元前 3000 年制定的一部埃及法典,它规定了金银货币制度)
code of military justice 军法典,军事审判法典
code of pleading 诉讼请求和答辩法规(指以标准方式替代普通法和衡平法上的诉讼请求和答辩)
code of practice 惯例法;行规;工作守则;业务守则
Code of procedure 《程序法典》(依据 1848 年宪法而构成的三项改革:以"民事诉讼"代替各种形式的衡平法上的、普通法上的诉讼;简化普通法涉及当事人、诉辩文书以及最终判决的技术性规则;最后将普通法和衡平法融合)
code of professional ethics 职业道德准则(或规范)
code of professional responsibility 职业(道德)责任法规(指一整套管理律师行业的规定,包括一般道德上的准则和禁止作某些可能导致受到惩罚的特别规定)
code of rates 运费标准
code of signals 信号编码
Code of State Property 《国家财产法典》
Code of Tang (中)《唐律》

Code of the Great Ming Empire （中）《大明律》
code of warfare 战争法典
code of written law 成文法典
Code pleading （美）诉答程序准则，法典诉讼程序（指依照法典的诉讼规则，始于1848年）
code pleading requirement 法典诉辩要求
code pleading jurisdiction （美）法典诉辩管辖（指按法典进行诉讼辩、答的管辖区）
code state （1867年）（历史上）普通法与衡平法融合的州，非普通法州[指在一定时间段，这个州已按程序将普通法与衡平法合并。所以衡平法不再作为一个单独体制实施。在此州内只有一种民事诉讼（civil action）形式。此词早在20世纪中期就已流行。见 Noncode state]
code states 普通法和衡平法融合的一些州
Code Thora （希伯来）《多拉法典》
code word 约定言辞；暗语
codebtor n. 共同债务人
coded a. 译成电码的
codefendant n. 共同被告人
coder n. 编译员；译码器
codex n. （罗马帝国）古法典抄本；卷，卷本，卷宗
Codex Alimentarius 《食品规则》（指联合国自20世纪70年代开始编纂的国际食品标准）
Codex Eurici （或 *Euricianus*） 《尤里西法典》（指公元4世纪国王尤里西组织编写的西哥特部落的法律汇编）
Codex Gregorianus （罗马法）《格列高里法典》[指由罗马法学家格列高里（Gregorius）汇编的帝国法规汇编，并于公元291年出版。亦可称为 Gregorian Code]
Codex Hermogenianus （罗马法）《海默根尼法典》[指由罗马法学家海默根尼（Hermogenianus）编纂的帝国法汇编并于公元295年出版。《海默根尼法典》为《格列高里法典》的补篇或续编。亦可称为 Hermogenian Code]
Codex Iustinianus Repetitae Praelectionis 见 Justinian Code
Codex Juris Canonici 《天主教教会法典》（指1917年为使用拉丁礼仪的天主教会颁布的教会法典汇编）
Codex Justinianeus 《查士丁尼法典》（见 Code Justinian）
Codex Repetitae Praelectionis 《新查士丁尼法典》（即《修正法典》，是《查士丁尼法典》的修订版，公元534年颁布，为现存版本。见 Justinian Code）
Codex Theodosianus 《狄奥多西法典》（指一部由狄奥多西二世于429年编纂的一部正式法律汇编）
Codex Vetus （"Old Code"）旧法典[指《查士丁尼法典》的第一版，即公元529年的《查士丁尼法典》，现已散失。见 Justinian Code]
codicil （=codicille） n. 遗嘱修改附录，遗嘱追加书，遗嘱变更附件
codicillary a. 遗嘱附录的，遗嘱附件的
codicillus n. （罗马法）小文件，遗嘱相关文件[指1.一种非正式法律文件，指示继承人去实现某项履行义务（certain performance）。通常是支付款项或转移财产给第三者（third person）在奥古斯都统治时期（公元前27年至公元14年），这种包含在补充遗嘱中的指令（信托赠予"*fideicommissa*"）已具有合法的约束力。见 *fideicommissum* 2.一项最高权力（或皇家的）允准的任命或特权（special privilege）]
codification n. 法律编纂，法律集成，编纂成法典
codification conference 法律编纂会议
codification of international law 国际法编纂
codification of laws and regulations 法规编纂
codification of natural right 天赋权利法典化
codified law 成文法律
codifier n. 法律编纂者
codify v. 使成文法化；把（法律）编成法典，编纂；整理
codifying acts 法典编纂性法令
codifying statute 法典编纂性法（规）
Código Bustamante （或 **Bustamante Code**）《布斯塔曼特法典》（指1928年2月第

六届泛美会议通过的一部国际私法典)
Código de las siete partidas （中世纪西班牙的）《七章法典》
coefficient n. 系数;折算率;程度
coefficient of loading 载货容积系数
coemptio n. （罗马法）拟制买卖婚姻［指民俗婚姻(civil marriage)的一种形式,以这种形式,男方(丈夫)从女方父亲那里买到女子,即拟制买卖(fictitious sale),以后丈夫对该女子行使夫权(manus)。父亲将其女儿通过要式转移物(resmancipi)的严格法律程序的买卖将其女儿转让给她的丈夫。这种想象的买卖是在5个成年罗马公民和1个司称员或中证人(libripens)面前进行。丈夫或拟制的购买人(fictitious purchaser)被称为 *coemptionator* 或 *coemptioner*。随着共和政体时期的终止,这种拟制买卖婚姻作为民俗婚姻方式也消失了。复数为 co-emptiones。见 *confarreatio*; *usus* 3］
coemption (＝co-emption) n. 囤积居奇,独占,收购
coequal a. （地位、权力等）相互平等的
coerce v. 强制,强迫,胁迫,迫使
coerced accomplice 胁从(犯)
coerced confession (to the insanity defense) 胁迫患精神病的被告自白,胁迫供认
coerced confessions 被迫认罪［指以胁迫和暴力手段获得供认,犯罪嫌疑人被迫认罪在法院审判中一般被视为不可采纳的证据。美国联邦宪法第五修正案(the Fifth Amendment)规定犯罪嫌疑人有反对强迫自证其罪(self-incrimination)的特权］
coerced offender 胁从犯
coerced settlement 强制和解;胁迫和解
coercion n. 胁迫,强迫,强制,高压统治;压制;压迫,威逼
coercion act 高压统治法(案),强制行为
coercion action 强制行动
coercion in fact 事实上的胁迫
coercion of witness 对证人施加压力,威胁证人
coercion policy 强制政策;高压政策
coercion n. 1.威胁,胁迫［指以暴力胁迫或以暴力威胁。如签署一纸遗嘱必须是一个自愿行为,如果在胁迫影响下完成的签署,则无法律效力。因为有效婚姻是要求双方自愿同意,如以威胁或强制为基础或依据则失去婚姻法律效力。刑事威胁(criminal coercion),意图通过以下方式限制他人行为自由(freedom of action)：A.威胁或胁迫对人实施犯罪行为;B.强制去指控他人具有犯罪行为;C.胁迫揭露秘密使受害人遭受憎恨、藐视、讽刺或使受害人损害信誉和商誉或;D.采取或制止公务行为(official action)或促进一名公务员采取或制止这种公务行为。默示或暗示威胁(implied coercion)见不正当影响(undue influence)。道德胁迫 moral coercion 见不正当影响(undue influence)］2.不正当使用经济优势(economic power)胁迫他人屈服于控制经济优势者的愿望所构成的行为,亦称为经济胁迫(economic coercion)3.丈夫实际的或想象的影响于其妻子的行为［根据普通法胁迫原理(common-law doctrine of coercion),妻子实施犯罪于丈夫在现场时可被推定受丈夫之胁迫,因此妻子具有完整辩护(complete defense),法庭已废弃这一理论。亦称 doctrine of coercion］
coercive a. 强制的,强迫的,强行的
coercive acts 强制性法令(指美国历史上,1774年由英国议会颁布的针对殖民地人民反抗行为所采取的反击措施统称,亦称 intolerable acts)
coercive force of the state 国家强制力
coercive measure 强制手段,强制措施
coercive measure in civil suits 民事强制措施
coercive method 强制办法,强制手段
coercive nature 强制性
coercive power 强制权力
coercive powers of organized political society 有组织的政治社会强制权
coercive procedure 强制程序
coercive remoulding 强制(迫)改造
coersion error 强制错误(指侦查人员对犯罪嫌疑人进行有罪推定的控告式讯问,甚至对其进行刑讯、威胁,使其认罪)
coeval a. 同时代的,同年代的,同时期的,同龄的
coexecutor (＝co-executor) n. （遗嘱）共同执行人(的一方);共同受托人(的一

方)(见 joint executors)
coexecutrix n. 女(遗嘱)共同执行人(的一方),女共同受托人(的一方)
coexist v. 共存,共处;和平共处
coexistence n. 共存,共处;和平共处
coffer n. 保险箱,(复)资产,财源,国库,金库
cogency n. 说服力;(复)令人信服的说法
cogent a. 有说服力的,无法反驳的
cogent reason 正当理由
* *Cogitationis poenam nemo patitur.* No one is punished for his thoughts. 任何人都不得因其思想而受到惩治。
cognate n./a. 1.母系亲属,外戚 2.同源物;同性质的东西/同宗的,同族的;同种的,同类的
cognate forms 同词源的形式
cognate offense (1866年)同性质的罪行,同类罪行[指较重罪行中构成几个要素中一个与之相关的较轻罪行,并且与较重罪行为同一等级或同一类别。比如,入店行窃(shoplifting)与盗窃罪(larceny)为同一性质罪行。因为两种犯罪均要求有意窃取财产(taking property)的要素而剥夺该财产合法拥有人的占有。见 lesser included offense]
cognatio (大陆法)女性同系亲属,同族,同宗
cognation n. 1.血缘关系而非家庭关系 2.(大陆法)血缘关系,家庭关系,或二者兼有的亲属关系;民事上的血缘关系(civil cognation)指法律上的亲属关系如收养;混合亲属关系(mixed cognation)则指血缘关系,家庭关系二者兼有的亲属关系;自然亲属关系(natural cognation)通常指基于非法性关系(illicit connection)的血缘亲属关系 3.相似或相同性质的人或物之间的人际或事物关系
cognatus n./a. (罗马法)同宗,同一宗族者/同宗的(亦称 cognate。见 agnatus)
cognitio 1.(古)承认罚金或这类承认书(罗马法) 2.(罗马法)司法审讯,审理案件;诉讼制度;案件审判权,司法管辖权;非常诉讼程序(见 cognitio extraordinaria)
cognitio extraordinaria (古罗马)非常诉讼制度(指由官方任命的官员来裁决案件

的一种诉讼程序)
cognition n. 认知能力;认识,被认识的事物
cognitionis causa tantum (苏格兰法)查清债务(为了查明确实针对地产的债务的目的)[针对已去世债务人(deceased debtor)的遗产,债权人提起诉讼以确定债务总额]
cognitionibus mittendis (英)一个令状命令皇家民事法庭(common pleas)的法官证明一项已征收而未确认的罚金(现已废止)
cognitive test (刑法)认知测试,认知标准[指对被告了解某些事物能力的测试,特别了解他或她的行为的性质以及其行为是正确还是错误。这种测试通常用于评定被告是否精神错乱(insanity defense)]
collaborative consumption 协同消费(指消费者利用网络工具进行合作或互利消费的一种经济模式,包括在拥有、租赁、使用或互相交换物品与服务等方面的合作。协同消费这种经济模式还有一个名称叫 Zip Car capitalism,可译"同车资本主义")
cognitor n. (罗马法)诉讼代理人[指被正式任命在民事审判(civil trial)中代理的人。见 procuratoril]
cognizable a. (17世纪)1.可认识的,可承认的⟨for purposes of establishing standing, a plaintiff must allege a judicially cognizable injury⟩(为了设立起诉权,原告必须主张司法上承认的伤害) 2.可识别的,可鉴别的(指因具有相同特征或利益而可被作为一个群体来认识的,这个群体不能由他人来代表)⟨American Indians quality as a cognizable group for jury-selection purposes⟩(美籍印第安人被认可为陪审团选择的群体)
cognizable suspect 可审问的嫌疑(犯)
cognizance (= cognisance, conusance) n. 1.认识,认识范围;审判常识(指法官凭自己对某些事物所掌握的知识就能用以执行审判任务,而不需用证据加以证明者,如对国家颁布的法律、法令、条例以及本国历史等常识。亦作 judicial notice) 2.审理(权),审判管辖权;职权范围
cognizance of the court 法院审理权
cognizance proceeding 审判程序
cognizant a. 审理的;审理权的;有权审理

的;认识的
cognizee n. 被罚款者,被征收罚款的当事人
cognizer (=cognizor) n. 具保人,罚款者
cognomen n. (古罗马的)姓,名字,别名,绰号
cognosce n. (苏格兰)了解案情;进行预审
cognovit (被告承认原告诉讼为正当时所具结的)被告承认书,具结
cognovit actionem 被告已供认不讳,坦白书
cognovit clause 认债条款
cognovit of judgment 见 confession of judgment
cognovit note 判决认诺指示书(指令代理人认诺判决的书面授权)
cognovits 认债条款
coguarantor n. 共同担保人
coguitio extraordinaria (罗马法)非常诉讼制度[指帝政初期兴起的一种法律诉讼程序。按此程序,政府官员自始至终控制审理过程,因为反对以前的程式诉讼制度(formulary system),这种制度是由司法官将诉讼的系争点具体化,然后再分别由非专业法官进行事实审和法律审。非常诉讼制则将事实审和法律审合二为一,简化审理程序。亦称 *cognitio extra ordinem*]
cohabit v. 同居;姘居
cohabitant n. 同居者;姘居者
cohabitation n. 同居;姘居
cohabitation agreement 同居协议(指同居的男女双方对其财产和资金收入有共同安排的协议,亦称 living-together agreement。见 prenuptial agreement)
cohabitation contract 同居合同(契约)
cohabitation with habit and repute 经常性和众所周知的同居
Cohan doctrine (或 **rule**)(美)(税法的)科汉规则(指纳税人具有充分记录或理由而提出在商务旅游等方面减税要求,可依据的一种减税规则)
coheir n. 共同继承人之一(指两个或两个以上合法继承人之一)
coheiress n. 共同女继承人
Cohen doctrine (美)科恩学说[Cohens v. Virginia,(1821)6 Wheaton 264]
coherence n. 紧凑,连贯
coherency n. 黏结性,一致性
coherent a. 连贯的,系列的,相干的
coherent overviews 一系列的看法
coherent system 相干系统
coheres (罗马法)共同继承人之一(复数为 coheredes)
cohesiveness n. 连贯性,结合度,黏度度
coif n. 高级律师的职位(或资格);(在英国皇家法庭有特权的)高级律师所戴的白巾(原意为白丝头巾。以前具有高级律师头衔的人都在其假发上加上一块白丝巾,故名)
coin n./v. 硬币,货币,钱/铸币;(英)造假钞;创造 杜撰(新闻,新语)
coin money 获暴利,暴发
coinage n. 造币,铸币,造币权;货币
coinage offence 制造伪币罪
coinage system 货币制度,币制
coincide v. 相一致,相合,恰好相合;符合
coincident (with) 与……符合,一致的
coiner n. 造币者;(英)制造伪币者
coinheritance n. 共同继承
coinheritor n. 共同继承人
coining n. 制造货币;(英)制造伪币
coinstigator n. 共同教唆犯
coinsurance (=co-insurance) n. 共同保险,共同担保
coinsurance clause 共同保险条款
coinsure v. 共同保险;共同担保
coition (或 **coitus**) n. 性交;交媾
coitophobia n. 性交恐怖
cojuror n. 发誓证明(他人言论为确实)者
Coke, Sir Edward 爱德华·柯克爵士(1552—1634)(曾任律师、首席法官、检察总长等职,他在确定英国法律形式和发展现代英国法律方面有重大影响)
Coke's Institutes 科克的《法理概要》
cold a. 冷的;冷淡的,不热情的;使人寒心的,无情的
cold bench (美)(受理上诉的法院的)冷庭(见 hot bench)
cold blood (常用作表示)故意、蓄意和预谋杀人

cold check 见 bad check
cold turkey 必败无疑,必然的牺牲品;直截了当,如实
cold war 冷战
cold war law （美）冷战法(指预防和管制间谍的联邦法律)
cold warrior 冷战分子,冷战政治家
cold-blooded a. 冷血的,残忍的;无情的
cold-blooded murder 残忍的谋杀
coldcock v. 把……打昏
coleasee n. 共同承租人
colitigant n. 共同诉讼人
colitigation (=co-litigation) n. 共同诉讼
collaborate v. 1.合作,协作 2.勾结,通敌,资敌
collaboration n. 1.合作,协作 2.勾结,通敌,资敌
collaborationist n. 通敌者;共牟私利者;奸细
collaborator n. 合作者;协作者;勾结者
collapse v./n. 倒塌;崩溃,瓦解;(价格等的)暴跌;衰退/倒塌,崩溃,暴跌
collapse of the Soviet Union 苏联解体
collar of SS （英格兰首席法官佩戴的）双S护肩
collateral n./a. 1.旁系亲属 2.抵押品[指抵押的财产作为担保,这笔财产必须以担保利益(security interest)或农业留置权(agriculture lien)为条件]/旁系的;附加的;间接的;附属担保的;从属的;第二位的;并列的
collateral act 担保行为;(用票据、保证金等为担保的)履约行为
collateral advantages 担保优势
collateral ancestors 旁系尊血亲,旁系血亲尊亲属
collateral assignment 附属担保物的转让
collateral attack 附诉(指依照特别程序对法院的一种异议,有点类似上诉,但发生在附带程序之中,附诉在程序上为单独诉讼,一般在另一法院进行);间接攻击,附带攻击[指通过在不同法院的程序采取行动达到规避法院判决效力的意图,与其相对的是直接攻击(direct attack);其目的在于对某一判决提出攻击,意在撤销或否认该判决的效力]
collateral claim 从权利
collateral consanguinity 旁系亲属
collateral contract 附属合同(契约);从合同(契约)
collateral covenant 附带条款,附加协议(指不依附转让证书或盖印文件的条款,即不涉及被转让财产的条款。见 inherent covenant)
collateral damage 间接损害,附带损害
collateral estoppel 间接再诉禁止;间接禁止翻供的事实;间接再诉否认(指在同一当事人之间对于诉讼的事实和争点已经由法院做出具有约束力的判决,则禁止当事人以另一不同诉因作为依据再次争诉。亦称 issue preclusion; issue estoppel; direct estoppel; estoppel by judgment; estoppel by verdict; cause of action estoppel; estoppel by record; estoppel per rem judicatam。见 res judicata)
collateral estoppels 间接禁止翻供的事实;(英美法在法院上将此称作)排出争点效力,间接再诉禁止,间接再诉否认
collateral evidence 旁证,间接证据,情况证据
collateral fact 间接事实
collateral guaranty 间接担保;从担保
collateral heir 旁系继承人
collateral impeachment 间接弹劾
collateral-inheritance tax （美）旁系亲属继承税[指根据遗嘱或无遗嘱继承(intestate succession)的财产转让所课之税。此遗产转让给除夫妻、父母、死者的子孙(descendant of the decedent)之外的亲属。见 legacy tax]
collateral issue 附带问题;附带系争点;附带诉讼
collateral kin 旁系亲
collateral kinsmen to the sixth degree inclusive 包括六亲等在内的旁系亲属
collateral law 抵押(担保)法规
collateral limitation 附带性有效期,附带性时效
collateral line 旁系
collateral line of descent 旁系亲属

collateral loan 抵押贷款
collateral measure 并行措施
collateral mortgage 从抵押,附带抵押
collateral negligence 间接过失
collateral office 兼职,兼任差事
collateral order doctrine （美）附带裁决原则[依此原则,如果中间裁决(interlocutory order)确定性解决了与诉讼是非曲直(merit of action)完全无关问题,且以后又对终局判决所提起的上诉不能对该中间裁决有效审理,则允许对该中间裁决提起上诉,此原则亦称(Cohen doctrine)];并行命令原则(指该原则发端于联邦最高法院在 Cohen v. Beneficial Industrial Loan Corporation 一案中所作的判决。其关键在于初审法院判决必须就构成诉讼的基础权利的并行事项,以及那些十分重要而不能拒绝给予复审的事项作出决定)
collateral proceedings 间接诉讼程序
collateral relationship 旁系亲族关系
collateral relative 旁系亲属
collateral relatives by blood 旁系血亲
collateral relatives by marriage 旁系姻亲
collateral security 质押品,附加担保物;副担保,从保证
collateral source rule 间接来源规则,附加来源规则(指如果受伤害人接受为其伤害补偿的来源是与侵害人无关,则损害赔偿的补偿不得因此减少,且侵权人必须支付的规则)
collateral surety 副担保人,从保证人
collateral term 附属条款
collateral trust bonds 附属担保信托债券
collateral warranty 从担保;副担保
collatio bonorum 财产聚合(将按父母预先给予某个子女的钱财与其他财产混同在一起,使属人财产能在各子女间平均分配)
Collatio Legum Mosaicarum et Romanorum 《摩西罗马法汇编》(约公元400年的著作)
collation n. 勘技(指用副本与正本作对比,来确定真伪);核对;圣职委任仪式
collative advowson 主教继承者的推荐权
colleague n. 同僚,同事
collect v. 收集,采集;收(税、租、账等);领取;募捐(款);推断出,认定
collect evidence 取证
collect on delivery 货到付款(现)
collectable a. 可征收的,可收集的,可采集的
collecting bills, cheques and similar documents 托收汇票、支票及其他类似票据
collecting debts 收集债务
collecting society （向投保人收取保险费的）收款协会
Collectio Anselmo Dedicata 《寺院法汇编》(指10世纪编纂的一部宗教法资料汇编)
collection n. （票据的）托收,收集;征收;募捐;收藏物;捐（来的）款;（常用复）汇编
collection agency 代理收款机构(亦称债务调查机构)
collection agent 收款人
collection commission 托收手续费
collection demand draft 托收汇票
Collection of Atto 《阿托寺院法汇编》(指约于1075年编纂的一部寺院法概要和简编)
collection of commercial paper 商业票据托收
collection of documentary draft 跟单汇票收款;跟单托收
collection of revenue 收集岁入
collection of tax 征税
collection on bill 票据托收
collection on clean bill 光票托收
collection on documents 跟单托收
collection order 托收委托书
collection proceedings 托收诉讼,托收程序
collections of decisions 判决汇编
collections of laws 法规汇编
collections of text 法律文件汇编
collective a. 集体的,共同的;集团的;集体主义的
collective (bargaining) agreement 集体谈判协议(指经过劳资集体谈判结果而形成的合同)
collective association 集体社团
collective bargain 集体协商(指美国劳资集体协商政策。见 Industrial Democracy)

collective bargaining （雇佣者和被雇佣者的集体代表就工资、工时和雇用条件所进行的）集体谈判
collective bargaining act 集体谈判协议法
collective bargaining contract （劳资）集体谈判协议（简称集体协议）
collective bargaining process （劳资）集体谈判机制，劳资谈判制度
collective bargaining unit 集体谈判单位（指如非只选出一些雇员组成特定单位或部门可作为代表，否则一个公司的一个部门或一个公司类型的全体雇员均可作为代表）
collective body 集合体，集体单位
collective case study （=multiple case study）多个案研究
collective contract 集体合同（契约），集体协议
collective contract of employment 集体雇佣合同（契约）
collective defense 集体防卫
collective denationalization 集体剥夺国籍
collective dispute （劳工案件）集体争议
collective donation 集体捐助
collective ecological security 集体生态安全
collective economy 集体经济
collective enforcement 共同执行
collective enterprise 集体企业
collective execution proceedings 集体执行诉讼（程序）（指破产的和解）
collective exploitation of property 财产的集体使用
collective firm 结合性企业
collective insurance 集体保险
collective interest 集体权益，集体利益
collective interest 集合性利益（指超越个人并且不可分的利益，它属于先前在相互之间就有特定法律关系的特殊团体）
collective intervention 集体干预，共同干涉
collective land 集体土地
collective leadership 集体领导
collective licensing 集体许可证贸易
collective marketing 集体销售
collective mediation 集体调解
collective migration 集体移民
collective naturalization 集体入籍
collective output 合计产量
collective ownership 集体所有制
collective ownership by the working people 劳动群众集体所有制
collective panel 联合的合议庭，联合的审判小组；联合的专门小组
collective procedure 集体诉讼程序
collective property 集体财产
collective responsibility 集体责任（制）
collective security 集体安全
collective security system 集体安全体系
collective self-defense 集体自卫
collective theft 共同盗窃，集体盗窃
collective thievery 共同盗窃罪，集体盗窃罪
collective title （法令的）集合标题
collective trademark 集体商标
collective treaty 集体条约，共同条约
collective use 集体使用，共同使用
collective vote 集体投票
collective welfare 集体福利
collective work 集体作品
collectivism n. 集体主义（制度）
collectivist n./a. 集体主义者/集体主义的（制度等）
collectivization n. 集团化
collector n. 收款人，收税员；募捐人；收集者，收藏家
collector of customs 海关官员
college certificate 大学证书；学院证书
College of Arms （英）纹章院（见 Herald's College）
college of justice （苏格兰）高等民事法院法官
Cleveland crime survey （美）克利夫兰犯罪调查
collegial （=collegiate）a./n. 集体组织的，合议的；大学的；社团的/（美）联合教会，联合教会组成的单位
collegialiter 有法人资格；作为法人
collegiality n. 权利共享（指美国合议机构诸如联邦最高法院合议庭的唯一结构特征就是其成员的正式权力的平等性。因这里存在合议结构的个人责任和集体判

决需合作之间的冲突）
collegiate (=collegial) a. 集体组织的, 合议的；大学的；社团的
collegiate bench (或 panal) 合议庭
collegiate bench meeting 合议庭会议
collegiate bench of judges and people's assessors （中）审判员及人民陪审员组成的合议庭
collegiate body of judges 合议庭
collegiate court system 合议庭制度
collegiate notaries 合议公证
collegiate system 合议制
collegiate tribunal 合议审判庭
collegium 官方团体；委员会；学院；公司，法人
collide v. （车船等）碰撞,冲突；抵触(with)
collision n. 冲突；相撞；碰撞；撞伤；撞机；撞车
collision at sea 海上（船舶）碰撞
collision avoidance system （美）避免（飞机）碰撞制度（指美国联邦航空管理局创制的减少飞机碰撞的规定）
collision clause （船舶）碰撞处理条款
collision convention （船舶）碰撞公约
collision damages 碰撞损害赔偿
collision due to vis major 不可抗力的碰撞
collision liability 碰撞责任
collision liability of the ship at fault 船舶碰撞过失责任
collision on land 陆上碰撞
collocutor n. 对话者
colloquium n. （学术）讨论会,（学术讨论会上的）报告
colloquy n. （正式）谈话,会谈；会议（指通常在审理案件中律师和法官之间的私下会议）；采取以对话形式的著作
collude v. 共谋；串骗；勾结
collusion n. 通谋，勾结，串通舞弊；串骗
collusive a. 通谋的；勾结的，串通的；欺诈的
collusive action 共谋行动；共谋诉讼
collusive case 欺诈案件
collusive conduct 串谋行为
collusive suits (or action) 共谋诉讼，串通诉讼［指诉讼双方当事人之间并不存在实际争议,而是为了获得法院对某一法律问题的裁决之目的而提起诉讼。美国联邦宪法第 3 条 (Article Ⅲ) 限制了联邦法院对案件与争议 (cases and controversies) 的管辖权。同时联邦法院往往十分谨慎地对诉讼当事人的诉权进行复审］
colograph (=holograph) n. 亲笔证书,亲笔,手书；亲笔遗嘱
colonial n./a. 殖民地居民/殖民的,殖民地的,拥有殖民地的,由殖民地构成的
colonial aggrandizement 殖民扩张
colonial America 受殖民统治的美国
colonial charter 殖民地宪章
colonial domination 殖民统治
Colonial Judicial Service （英）殖民地司法服务团（指英国在英格兰、苏格兰和爱尔兰招募法律界人士分派到亚非两洲、加勒比海、太平洋岛诸殖民地任职）
colonial law 殖民地法；(复)(美国独立前的)殖民地法
Colonial Laws Validity Act （英）《殖民地法效力令》(1865 年)
colonial lawyers 殖民地律师
Colonial Legal Service （英）殖民地法律服务团（与 Colonial Judicial Service 同类型，只是法律服务团在殖民地政府法律界服务）
colonial nation 殖民国家
Colonial Office （英）殖民部(旧译：理藩院。1966 年 8 月与联邦关系部合并成联邦部, 1968 年 10 月联邦部又与外交部合并)
colonial policy 殖民政策
colonial power 殖民国家,殖民主义国家
colonial protectorate 被保护殖民地, 殖民保护国
colonial regime 殖民政权,殖民制度
Colonial Regulation （英）《殖民地规则》
colonial rule 殖民统治
colonial status 殖民地位
colonial system 殖民体系；殖民制度
colonial territory 殖民地(领土)
colonialism n. 殖民主义；殖民政策；殖民地的地位（或特征）
colonialist n./a. 殖民主义者/殖民主义的

colonialist regime 殖民主义政权,殖民主义制度
colonize v. 开拓殖民地于(某地区),移(民)于殖民地;移居于殖民地,派人打入(部门等)
colonizer n. 殖民地开拓者,殖民者
colonus 农奴,农民;移居者,殖民者
colo(u)r n. 颜色;肤色;表面(权利)
colo(u)r bar 肤色障碍(指对有色人种的种族歧视或隔离)
colo(u)r blind 色盲
color conscious law 生动有意识的法规
color depletion 颜色耗尽(指与color scarcity 颜色匮乏和 shade confusion 色差混淆三个要素构成否定商标注册的依据。这是美国颜色商标可注册的理论)
colo(u)r line (种族歧视制度下的)种族分界线
colo(u)r of office 权限假托;利用职权
colo(u)r of title 冒名;假托
(the) color *per se* **rule** (美)颜色本身原则(见 mere-color rule)
colo(u)r question 种族问题
colo(u)rable a. 虚伪的,假的,表面的;具有欺骗性的;似是而非的
colo(u)rable imitation 1.(商标)假冒(指任何商标,不管其是否因有意去欺骗而创设,只要与已注册的商标极为相似,其很可能造成混淆或误导大众。见 similarity) 2.伪造,假造
colo(u)rablelegal argument 似是而非的法律论据
colo(u)rable possession 假占有
colo(u)rable pretext 似是而非的借口
colo(u)rable title 表面所有权,非真实的产权
colo(u)red a. 有色人种的,黑人的;混血种的(尤指非纯白色人种)
colo(u)red-blind a. 无肤色障碍的,无种族歧视的
colony n. 殖民地,移居团,侨居地
colors or combination of colors 颜色或颜色的结合
columbarium n. 骨灰安置所,放骨灰盒的壁龛

coma n. 昏迷;麻木
comaker n. 共同签署票据人,共同签据人(指在票据如支票等上签署的第二人或第三人)
comb v./n. 梳;彻底搜查;扫荡⟨comb operation⟩(扫荡行动);卷起⟨comb out⟩(在……中去除不需要的人或物;彻底查出;搜罗)/篦子;蜂房;山顶;浪峰
comb out a department 在一个部门裁减人员
comb out traitors and spies 清除奸细
combat n./v. 战斗,格斗;竞争,争论;反对;与……作斗争;跟……战斗;战斗(with, against)
combat troops 战斗部队
combatant n. 战斗员,参赛者,格斗者
combination n. 结合,联合,联合体,结合体[指①两人以上或两个以上企业为了一个共同的目的(通常为经济上的)联合在一起工作的结合体。②阴谋集团(conspiracy)。③跨期买卖(straddle)。④(专利)在一项发明中由若干新旧零件组成的专利品,这个词不仅包含机械零件的组合,也包括一些实体(substances)在权利主张中的组合(in composition claim)或在程序权利主张中一些措施(steps in a process claim)的组合(见 aggregation②)。⑤(专利)一项发明:用两个或两个以上已成为专利的发明构成的一个独特的、有用的第三种产品的一项发明。在过去,寻求组合专利(combination patent)的发明者已经出示过"协助作用"(synergism),从结合体上获得了惊人的成果,但是美国联邦巡回上诉法院(the U. S. Court of Appeals for the Federal Circuit)规定"结合体"(combination)这个词没有法律效力(legal effect),因为绝大多数发明均是依靠现有技术来联合和创立的,现今对于"结合专利"(combination patent)没有专门规定。⑥(专利)若干零件的结合构成的一项发明,这是共同合作实现有效的作用,与互不作用的组合(aggregation)相反。见 aggregation]
combination carrier 联合货船;联合运输行

combination of actions 行动组合
combination of democracy with dictatorship （中）民主和专政相结合
combination of legislative and executive powers 议行合一制（指一种国家机关重要工作的决议和执行统一进行的制度，它是与三权分立制度相对立的）
combination of leniency with punishment （中）宽大与惩办相结合
combination of punishment and education （中）惩治和教育相结合
combination of the work of specialized organs with mass line （中）专门机关的工作和群众路线相结合
combination to a safe 保险箱的暗码
combinatus 联合制，康平纳
combine n./v. （为某种目的联合的）集团；（以操纵物价为目的的）联合企业；联合收割机/结合，联合，兼有，兼备
combine access 联合通讯，联合检索〈combine access to primary source with commentary and current information〉（联合检索评述和最新信息的首要原始资源）
combined a. 联合的，集团的
combined bill of lading 联运提单
combined city 群集城市，联合城市
combined offer 联合发价
combined transport 联运，联合运输
combined transport document 联运单据
combined transport operator 联合运输营业人
combing operation 扫荡（战）
combustibles （复）n. 易燃物品
combustio domorum 见 houseburning
come v. 导致，引起；发生；形成；遭遇；发现；来，来到
come after 跟在……后面
come forward with one's evidence 提出某人之证据
Come Home Americans 注重国内派（相信强大的防御作用，在某种情况下，如珍珠港事件或 9·11 事件，则需要采取积极的作用，但不能以牺牲满足国内紧迫需要为代价）
come in 1.进来 2.（潮水）升涨 3.（火车）到达 4.到成熟季节，当今 5.流行起来 6.（比赛时）获得……名〈come in second〉（在比赛时获得第二名）7.当选就任；（党派等）上台 8.钱到手，得到收入 9.用来〈This dictionary may come in handy now and then〉（这本字典可能随时用得上）10.起作用；有份儿〈where do I come in?〉（我该做什么?）
come in for vigorous invective 受到有力抨击
come in for 接受（遗产、赠礼等）
come in handy 迟早有用〈these may come in handy if a reference found in an older case or an index can no longer be found〉（即便某一参考在较老的案例或索引里不能再被查到，这些迟早也会有用）
come into 继承（遗产）；得到，进入
come into effect 生效
come into force 开始实行
come into one's own 得到自己名下应得的东西；继承（财产等）
come into operation （开始）实施
come into play 开始运行，开始动作，开始起作用
come into possession of sth. 占有（或获得）某物
come into power （开始）执政，当权，上台
come of age 成年，达到法定年龄
come on bid 带有津贴性质的递价（旨在招揽生意）
come out in defense 辩护
come over 过来，从远处来
come through 经历，脱险，获得成功，（消息）传出；（美俚）出力，资助；招认，提供
come to a consensus 达成共识，达到共认
come to a decision 作出决定
come to an agreement 达成协议
come to an understanding 达成谅解
come to little 没有什么结果
come to pass 实现，产生，出现
come to sb. (from sb.) 作为遗产送给或留给某人
come to see 终于明白……
come to terms 达成协议，谈判成功，商妥
come to understanding 达成谅解，取得谅

解,理解

come up 走进,上来,提出来,登上,流行起来

come within the provisions of the law 落入法网

come-back laws 对累犯的法律规定(指对累犯加重惩罚的规定)

comfort v. 安抚,安慰;舒适

comfort and compensate 抚恤

comitas gentium 国际礼让(说)

comitia (古罗马)民众大会(民会)

comitia centuriata (古罗马)兵员大会

comitia curiata (通常大写)库里亚大会,贵族人大会[指最早由贵族组成的大会,其主要功能是授权给予公民的私法令(private acts),比如宣布遗嘱和收养。这个议事大会实际是进行小范畴的立法活动。这是罗马人四种大会中的最古老的一种,即库里亚议事大会或库里亚民众会议。在帝国时期,这种大会是由30个库里亚——按照传统,罗莫洛将罗马人划分为三个部落,每个部落由10个库里亚(curia)组成,库里亚也被用来指毗邻的氏族或家族举行会议的地点——或(家族"family groups")罗马民众组成。这个大会只是按君主的召唤(summons)召开,只表示接受或拒绝君主提出的动议,而无权讨论或修订,没有元老院(senate)的授权也不能作出有效的决议(decision)。在共和国时期,这种会议很快进入幕后状态(fell into background),直到帝国时代。虽已有由30名侍从官(thirty lictors)代表陈述的正式议事会,但对于私法(private law),其重要性保持在议事会之中。在大祭司的管辖下,处理宗教上有重大意义的事项,比如自权人收养(adrogations)和遗嘱(wills)。参见《罗马法导论》(1934年第九版)(FH. Lawson ed.) pp.15-16(William A. Hunter)]

comitia (populi) tributa (古罗马)民团大会,平民大会

comity n. 礼让,司法管辖区的礼让或承认(指美国一个管辖区通过执行另一个管辖区的法律和承认司法判决,这是给对方的尊重,而不是出于义务)

comity of nations 国际礼让;国际间的相互尊重(指在不违反本国法律的基本原则及不损害本国国家和社会利益的前提下,承认并执行另一国的法律。这是国际刑法的基础)

command n./v. 统帅(地位),指挥(权),控制(权),掌握;命令;司令部,指挥部,部队/指挥,命令,控制,对……有支配权

command a ready sale 博得畅销

command control 命令控制

command economies 指令经济

command economy 中央管制经济(指企业的生命期和行为,对其失去调整及对企业间的协调,不由市场机制进行,而由行政手段、命令、指令和法令进行控制)

command of the air 制空权

command of the sea 制海权

command of the Seventh Amendment 宪法第七修正案的命令

command papers (英)《政府文件》[亦译做《钦命文件》],指根据女王命令由王室大臣向议会递送的文件。从1833年开始印出,分为五个系列:①No.1—4222(1833—1868—1869年);② C.1—9550(1870—1899年);③ Cd.1—9239(1900—1918年);④Cmd.1—9889(1919—1956年);⑤ Cmnd.1—(1956年至今)]

Command Software System Co. 命令软件系统公司

command system 中央管制系统

commandeer v. 强迫服役;征用(财产等)

commander n. 司令官,司令员,指挥官,指挥员

commander of the faithful 宗教领袖(尤指伊斯兰教的)

commander-in-chief 总司令

commander-in-chief of armed force 武装部队的总司令

commanditaires (或 *commandité*) (法)特别合伙人;有限责任合伙人;(两合公司的)无限责任股东

commanditores (法)出资人

commandment n. 戒律,诫,圣训

commence v. 开始;(英)得到学位

commencement n. 开始(实施);起始;开

端;授予学位典礼(日)
commencement of action 诉讼开始,起诉
commencement of risk 保险责任的开始
commencement of statute 法规开始实施
commencement of term 期限起算点
commend v. 表扬,嘉奖,推荐,把……托交给(to)
commend good people and good deeds 表扬好人好事
commenda 康美达合同(契约)(指具有信用和委托含义的一种合同。此词最初只用于海外贸易,资本家常以商品及金钱委托航海之人代为营业,如获盈余则投资者可得3/4,航海者得1/4,久后才形成此种习惯性制度)
commendable a. 值得表扬的,值得称赞的
commendation n. 1.称赞,表扬;推荐 2.(英)(封建时代)领主附庸
comment v. 评论;注释
comment on appeal 答辩状
comment on the evidence 对证据的评价(或评述)[指①由法官或辩护律师就某一证据的证明力或证据价值向陪审团所做的评述《联邦证据规则》第105条,Fed. R. Evid. 105)。②律师们在结束辩论时象征性做出这类评述,法官在联邦法院也可做这样评述,但大多数州法院法官在审查证人、指示陪审团……时不允许做这类评述。此词条有时称为 an impermissible comment on the evidence]
comment period 见 notice-and-comment period
commentarii 记事录,备忘录
commentarii senatus 《元老院议事录》(见 acta senatus)
commentary n. 注释(本),评注,解说词;评论
commentator n. 注释者,评论者;时事评论员,实况广播员;(复)评注法学派(亦称后注释法学派)
commerce n. 1.商业,贸易 2.社交,交流 3.性交
commerce clause (美)商业条款(指美国宪法第1条第8款第3项对国会管理合众国与外国、州际及与印第安部族间贸易的授权)
commerce exchange 商业汇兑价
commerce power (美)商业权,商业管理权(指由于许多州为保护本州商业企业而纷纷设立州际贸易壁垒而使得这个国家开始变得混乱。为此1787年召开的制宪会议的强大动力就是由联邦来控制整个国家商业。根据美国联邦宪法第1条第8款第3项之授权国会"规范各州中涉与外国的商业,以及规范涉及印第安部落的商业"。这一条款一直是并继续是一种维持州权力与构成联邦体系的全国性权力有效平衡的重要宪法工具)
commercia belli 交战者间的协定
commercial a. 商业的;商务的;商事的,商品化的,以营利为目的的;由广告商付费的
commercial accounts 商业账簿
commercial act 商法;商行为
commercial act in an objective sense 客观意义上的商行为
commercial action 商事诉讼
commercial activity 商务活动
commercial administration law 商业管理法
commercial advertisement 商业广告
commercial affair 商事,商业事务
commercial agent 商务代表;商务官员;代办商
commercial agreement 商业合约
Commercial and Financial Chamber (法)(最高上诉法院的)商事和财政法庭
commercial arbitration 商事仲裁,商业仲裁
commercial *attaché* 商务专员;商务参赞
commercial bankruptcy 商业破产
commercial bill 商业汇票
commercial blockade 商业封锁(又译:商务封锁,贸易封锁)
commercial broker 商业经纪人,商业掮客
commercial business and industrial enterprises 工商业企业
commercial case 商事案件;(复)商事案例(汇编)
commercial causes 商事诉讼
commercial chamber 商事法庭
commercial claims 商业上的债权

commercial code 商法典
commercial contract 商业合同(契约);商事合同(契约)
commercial contract of services 服务性的商业合同(契约)
commercial control system 商业管理体制
commercial corporation 商业公司
commercial counsel(l)or 商务参赞
commercial court 商事法庭(院)
commercial credit 商业信用;商业信贷
commercial credit agreement 信用证约定书
commercial crime 商业上的犯罪
commercial custom 商习惯,商业惯例
commercial customary law 商习惯法
commercial dispute 商业纠纷,商事纠纷(争议)
commercial distribution area 商业销售中心
commercial domicile 商业住所
commercial draft 商业汇票
commercial embargo 商业禁运,贸易禁运
commercial employee 商业雇员
commercial enterprise 商业性企业,商事企业
commercial exchange 商业汇兑
commercial exploitation 商业利用
commercial firm 商行
commercial flag 商旗
commercial general-liability policy 商业综合责任保单,商业概括责任保单[指综合性保单,它覆盖大部分商业风险、责任和事业损失。这种类型的保单包括两个方面:商业损失以及因一种环境影响而造成的人身伤害和财产损失会受到第三方的惩罚。这种保单首先出现于1986年,此种保单大部分已代替了综合性一般责任保单 (comprehensive general-liability polices),缩略为 CGL policy。见 comprehensive general-liability policy]
commercial goodwill 商业信誉
commercial instrument 商业票据
commercial integrity 商业道德,商业信用
commercial invoice 商业发票
commercial law 商法;商业法
commercial lease 商业租赁
commercial letter of credit 商业信用证
commercial leverage 商业上的调节手段
commercial liability 商务责任,商业责任
commercial list 商事案件目录
commercial loan 商业性借贷
commercial mandate 商业委托
commercial maritime code 海商法规,海商法典
commercial matter 商事案件
commercial middleman 商业经纪人,商业中介人
commercial order paper 商业指示证券
commercial paper 商业票据
commercial pledge 商业质权
commercial power of attorney 商业代理权
commercial practice 商业惯例,商业措施,商业做法;商习惯
commercial presence 面向商业(这是服务贸易的基本概念之一,面向商业是服务贸易活动中最主要的形式。指允许外国企业和经济实体到本国来开饭店,建零售商店和办律师事务所)
commercial procedure 商事诉讼程序
commercial register 商业登记册(簿)
commercial registration 商业登记
Commercial Regulation on Jurisdiction and the Recognition and Enforcement of Judgement in Civil and Commercial Matters 2000年12月22日欧盟通过的《民商事案件管辖权和判决执行的条例》(2002年3月1日生效)
commercial relation 商务关系,商业关系
commercial representative 商务代表
commercial reputation 商业信誉
commercial restriction 贸易限制,商业限制
commercial sale 商业性买卖
commercial sector 商业部门
commercial shipping 通商航运
commercial speech 商业言论
commercial standing 商业信用
commercial structure 商业结构
commercial supervision 商业监督
commercial things 商业物主
commercial transaction 商行为;商业交易,商务交往(业务)
commercial travel(l)er 商业推销员

commercial treaty 商务条约,商约
commercial us(e)ability 商业上的可适用性,合乎商业用途
commercial usage 商习惯,商业惯例
commercial value 商业价值
commercial warrant 商业栈单
commercial-litigation panel 商事诉讼审判组(指联邦德国由1名专职法官和2名具有商业经验的非专职法官组成审理商事争议的小组)
commercialism n. 商业主义,利润第一主义,商业精神,商业用语,商习惯
commercialist n. 商业主义者,商业家,营利主义者
commerciality n. 商业性
commercium 财产权,贸易,商业,交易权
commingle v. 混合,掺和,混杂
commingled investment account 联合投资账户
commingling n. 混合,合并,混合存款,联合存款(如将两个人的钱放到一个银行的账上)
commissaires du gouvernement (法)政府专员(指从参政院中任命的提供有关行政事务意见的官员)
commissaires-enqueteurs 询问证人的专员
commissary n. 委托人;代表;委员
commission n./v. (14世纪)1.委员会[根据法律授权履行某种公务的行政机关](certain public service)〈the Federal communication commission〉(联邦通讯或交流委员会)] 2.委托状,任职令(书)[指由政府、政府部门或法院授权某人从事特定行为或执行公务的令状(execute official act)〈the student received this commission to U. S. Navy after graduation〉(大学生接受毕业后去海军工作的任职令)] 3.授权,委托(指一个人为他人进行商业交易所根据的授权或委托)〈the client gave the attorney express commission to sign the contract〉(客户明确委托其代理人代为签订合同) 4.手续费,报酬;酬劳/授权;委任;任命
commission agency 行纪,代办处;经纪业
commission agency contract 行纪合同(契约)

commission agent 代理人,代理商,经纪人,代办人
commission broker 经纪人,居间人(旧译:掮客)
commission charges 手续费,回扣,佣金
commission day (英)大审开审日(又译委任开庭日,指巡回法庭开庭的日子。因为开始时,法官先将他的委任书拿出来宣读,故名)
commission *del credere* 支付能力保证(费),支付能力保证人(见 *del credere*)
commission fees 佣金,行纪报酬,手续费
commission for acceptance 承兑佣金,承兑手续费
commission for compilation of the laws and regulations 法规汇编委员会
commission for racial equality 种族平等委员会
commission house 经纪行,委托行
commission merchant 代销商(旧译:掮客)
commission of a crime 犯罪
commission of a tortuous act 实施侵权行为
commission of anticipation (英史)预征授权(指国玺大臣作出的提前征税或补助金的授权)
commission of appraisement (海事诉讼中对扣押财产的)估价委员会,估价代理
commission of appraisement and sale (海事诉讼中对扣押财产的)估价与出售委员会;估价与出售代理权
commission of assize (英)巡回审判(法官的或状师的)委任令(指委任法官或御用状师,授权他们在巡回法庭中审理民事案件);巡回审判委员会
commission of authority 授权书
commission of charitable uses (古英国法)查究纠正土地慈善用益权委任令
commission of conciliation 调解委员会
commission of crime 犯罪行为
commission of enquiry (或 inquiry) 调查团,调查委员会
commission of eyre 巡回(法官)委托状
Commission of First Instance for Disputes on Social Security (法)社会保险争议

初审委员会
commission of further offence 重新犯罪
commission of gaol delivery 提审囚犯委任令
commission of general gaol delivery 提审囚犯的一般委任令
commission of jurists 法学家委员会;法律工作者委员会;律师会
commission of legal(或 **legislative**)**affairs** 法制委员会
commission of lunacy 精神病的鉴定
commission of *nisi prius* 事实审委任令
commission of offence 犯罪行为
commission of oyer and terminer 1.(英)就地听审裁判委任令(即指示巡回法庭法官开庭审判刑事案件的令状) 2.(美)听审裁判委任令(指可向某些具有刑事管辖权的州法院发出的这种令状)
commission of rebellion (英)拘票(指以前由大法官法庭发出的一种逮捕令状,1841年已废)
Commission of the European Communities 欧洲共同体委员会
commission of (justice of) the peace (英)治安官的委任令(英国各地区内的治安官,均由一个专门委员会来委任的一人或多人担任);治安官裁判权
commission of trailbaston (英史)指挥(对扰乱治安、司法秩序或帮助犯罪者进行)调查委任令
commission on civil defense 民防委员会
Commission on Human Rights (联合国)人权委员会
commission on Interactional cooperation 国际种族合作委员会
Commission on New Technological Use of Copyright Works (CONTU) (美)版权作品的新技术使用委员会(指美国国会设置的专门研究新技术使用对版权影响的机构)
commission plan 委员市政制(指一种以委员五六人组成的委员会统一行使市的立法和行政事务以替代市长和市参议会制的计划)
commission principal 委托人

commission review (英)(宗教法)复查委员会;复审委员会
commission(或 **board**)**system** 委员会制
commission to examine witness 审问证人委托书
commission to seize escheated and forfeited land 没收无人继承土地和没收土地委任令
commission to serve as notary public 充当公证人的委任状
commission to take deposition 录取证言委托书
commission-general of prisoner 罪犯的总委托人
commissioned a. 经授权的;受委任的,受任命的;现役的
commissioned judge (经)授权的法官;任命的法官
commissioner n. 委员;政府的特派员;地方长官(专员,厅长,局长,处长,署长等);受委任的人
commissioner for oaths 宣誓公证人;监督官,监督委员
commissioner of customs 关税专员,海关税务司长
commissioner of state (中)国务委员
commissioner to take affidavits 录取证供的官员
commissioners in bankruptcy (英)破产行政官(指以前由司法长官颁布任命行使对破产者和破产的不动产的管辖权的行政长官)
commissioning 委托(指版权意义上的委托)
commissioning administrative organ (授权)委托的行政机关,任命的行政机关
commissioning party 委托方(当事人)
Commissions of Inquiry Ordinance 《调查委员会条例》
commissions with loosely defined power 未加严格界定的委员会
commissoria lex (罗马法)有关合同(契约)罚款的原则
commit v. 1.犯(错误,罪),干(坏事、傻事) 2.把……交托给,把……提交给 3.把……(下牢)押交,把……判处,提

审;关押;收容 4. 使承担义务,使作出保证 5. 调配……供用于,指定用于 6. 约束,连累
commit a prisoner for trial 把犯人交付审判
commit acts of violence (= to resort to violence) 诉诸武力
commit an offence 作案,犯罪
commit an outrage 使用暴力,犯下暴行
commit arson 纵火
commit bribery 行贿
commit manslaughter 误杀,过失杀人
commit murder 谋杀,凶杀
commit oneself 承担义务,做出承诺(要求等)说出肯定的意见
commit perjury 犯伪证罪
commit physical assault 行凶
commit suicide 自杀
commit suicide to escape punishment 畏罪自杀
commit to writing 记载,记入,记录
commitment (=committal) n. 行为,犯罪;委任;委托;押交,(候审)羁押;监禁,拘押,禁闭;入狱执行书;约束,约定,许诺,承担义务;信奉(to),赞成,赞助
commitment fee 贷款承诺费
commitment in default of sufficient distress 因扣押财物不足而被拘押
Commitment to the common law 信奉普通法,献身(或致力)于普通法;对普通法的承诺,担保,或承担义务
commitment to the right to civil jury in American system 授权美国体制中获得民事陪审团审判的权利
committable a. (罪犯或罪行)可以拘押的,可以判处的,可能犯的
committal 见 commitment
committal charge 起诉罪名;委托任务
committal for contempt 因藐视罪拘押
committal for disobedience to judg(e)ment 因不遵从判决而被监禁
committal for trial 交付审判;押交法院受审令
committal in civil proceedings 民事诉讼中的拘押

committal order 拘留令
committal warrant 拘押令
committed for trial 羁押候审
committed to prison 被判入狱,收监
committee n. 委员会;监护人;受托人
Committee for Democratic Election laws (美)争取民主选举法委员会
Committee for Environmental Conservation (美)环境保护委员会
committee for people's mediation (中)人民调解委员会(由居民委员会或村民委员会设立)
committee for privileges (英)(上议院)特权委员会
committee for public health (中)公共卫生委员会(由居民委员会或村民委员会设立)
committee for public security (中)治安保卫委员会(由居民委员会或村民委员会设立)
committee for qualification of membership 委(议)员资格审查委员会
Committee of Australian Law Deans 澳大利亚法学院长委员会
committee of discipline investigation (中)纪律检查委员会
committee of estimation 概算委员会
Committee of Experts of the Progressive Codification of International Law (1924年由国联行政院设立的)逐步编纂国际法专家委员会
(the) Committee of Experts on Access to Justice 司法救助专家委员会
committee of foreign affairs 外交事务委员会
committee of inspection (破产)监督委员会;检查委员会
Committee of Political and Legal Affairs (中)政法委员会
committee of property assessment 财产估算委员会
committee of selection (或 **committee on committees**) (议会内的)议员指派委员会
Committee of States (美)各州委员会(根

据美国1977年联邦条款规定,议会于每年休会期间得组织一委员会以处理全国性事务,称为各州委员会,由每州各派一名代表组成)
committee of supply (英)(下议院的)预算委员会
Committee of the American Bar Association on Improvements in the Law of Evidence 美国律师协会证据法改进委员会
committee of the whole (House) 议会全体委员会(指议会议决某些特殊事项所采用的由全体议员参加的一种议事方式)
committee of ways and means (英)(下议院)审议(税收)办法和措施委员会
Committee on Appeal of the Privy Council (英)枢密院上诉委员会(指审理殖民地司法上诉案件的机构)
committee on credentials 见 credentials committee
Committee on Criminal Abortion (美)堕胎刑事责任委员会
Committee on International Investment and Multinational Enterprises (CIME) 国际投资和多国企业委员会
Committee on Scholarly Communication with China 美中学术交流委员会
Committee on the Peaceful Uses of Outer Space (联合国)(1958年12月建立的)和平利用外层空间委员会
Committee on Unamerican Activities (美)非美活动调查委员会
Committee on Uniform State Laws (美)统一(各)州法律委员会
Committee Print of Bill 议案印刷委员会
committeeman n. 委员会成员,委员;选区的政党头子
committeewoman n. 女委员
commodatum 无偿使用合同(契约)(指无偿临时借用物品的合同)
commodities fair 商品展览会,商品交易会
commodity n. 商品,货物;日用品,农产品,矿产品
commodity arbitrage 套购商品,商品套利
commodity capital 商品资本

commodity composition 商品结构
commodity coverage 商品范围
commodity economy 商品经济
commodity entry 商品列名
Commodity Exchange (美)商品交易所
Commodity Exchange Act (美)《商品交易法》
commodity exchange tax 商品流通税
Commodity Futures Modernization Act (美)《商品期货现代化法案》(2000年10月19日众议院已通过该法案,待参议院通过后,两院进行立法协商,即可通过立法)
Commodity Futures Trading Commission (CFTC) 商品期货交易委员会
commodity inspection 商(品)检(验)
commodity inspection and testing bureau 商品检验局
commodity inspection certificate 商品检验证明书
commodity market 商品市场
commodity marketing board 商品销售局
commodity price control 物价管理
commodity rate 商品运价,特种商品运费率
commodity tax 货物税,商品税
commodity-based form 产品形式
commodity-by-commodity approach 逐项商品处理办法
commodore n. 船长,商船队队长
common n./a. 公地;公地使用权;对别人土地的使用权;共用权;普通股;(复)(总称)平民;(英)下议院(常作 Commons)/普通的;一般的;共同的;公共的;共有的,共用的
common action 普通诉讼
common ancestor 共同祖先,两个或两个以上的同一祖先
common aspiration 共同愿望
common assault 普通侵犯他人身体(指不严重地侵犯他人身体),普通企图伤害(罪)
common authority 公共权威
common barratry 煽动诉讼(罪),挑拨兴讼(罪)
Common bench (英)普通法院,(旧称)高等民事法庭

common benefit 共同利益,共同福利

common carrier 公共承运人,公共运输行;公共运输商(指接受雇代人搬运货物的商人)

common civil 共同关切事项(指当国际环境法逐渐发展成一门独立科学后,学界对"全球公域"又有新的诠释,即为"共同关切事项")

Common concern 公意

common consent 共同同意,公认

common council 市(或镇)议会,市(镇)立法机构

common counts 一般诉因,一般诉讼理由

common court 普通法院(庭)

common crime 普通犯罪

common criminal 普通刑事犯

common custom (英)普遍的习惯,普通习俗(指通行于整个王国具有普遍效力的规则,严格意义上说他们构成了普遍法)

common debts 共同债务

common defense 共同防卫;共同辩护;共同辩护之理由(指两名或两名以上被告合并审理时,所有被告共同主张的答辩理由);共同过失,互有过失[过失诉讼中的共同辩护实际是混合过失或互有过失(contributory negligence),美国许多州将共同过失或互有过失认为是具有行使完全的辩护的权力(complete defense)。最近几年,这种互有过失原理(the doctrine of contributory negligence)受到批评。因为它是一种全部或没有(an all-or nothing)的方法。比如,如果一件偶然事故当事一方为主要过错,而另一方只是轻微过错,而后者无需接受任何责任和损害赔偿,那么它的这个共同过失对于通过诉讼判决获得任何损害赔偿(recovery)都是一种完全的阻拦]

common diligence 一般勤勉;一般留意

common disaster 共同灾难(指两人或两人以上在同一事故中死亡,而无法断定谁先死的情况)

common domicile 共同住所

common employment 共同雇佣;共同作业(按英国普通法规定,雇主对他的雇员在共同作业时,因另一雇员的疏忽所致的伤害,不负责任。此原则已废)

Common External Tariff 欧洲共同市场对外统一关税

common fishery 公海捕鱼权

common form 普通格式(证明书)

common good "共同的善"(指古代国家崇尚的善)

common ground 共同点,一致点

common guideline 共同方针,共同准则

common heritage 共同继承的财产

common heritage of humankind 人类共同遗产

common heritage of mankind 人类共同遗产

common in soil 矿藏共用权

common income 共同收入

Common Informer Act (英)《一般起诉人法》(指 1951 年指定此法,而废止由一般起诉人提起诉讼的做法)

common informer 1.一般起诉人(指①为获得对罪犯判处的罚金在法律规定许可下任何对罪犯提起的诉讼者;②在美国有些管辖区,这类诉讼可由一般代理人代表州提起诉讼或由一般起诉人提起诉讼) 2.以告密为业的人;公众告发人;告发者,告密者(=professional informer)

common interest 共同利害关系,共同利益

common interests in international community 国际社会的共同利益

common interest privilege 见 newsman's privilege

common jail(或 gaol) 国家监狱

common judge 公共裁判,共同裁判

common juror 普通陪审员

common jury 普通陪审团(指由拥有一般人能拥有的财产的人作为陪审员所组成的陪审团。见 special jury)

common knowledge 普通知识(指广为人知的事实,法院可以接受而无需举证)

common land 公地

common law (英美法)普通法(又译:习惯法、不成文法、常法、判例法。指只是以年代久远的习惯和惯例或法院判决和裁定作为其先例和法律渊源的一种法律)[它是实施于英国皇家法院的判例法体系。普通法在美国殖民地被接受并在州

和联邦的宪法革命之后被采纳为美国法律体系之基础。联邦最高法院是普通法法院在美国司法实践中,作为联邦与州关系的最后公断人。普通法是两大法律体系之一(另一为衡平法),现在它已被联邦在内的所有管辖区采纳并已成为美国法律秩序之基础]

common law action　普通法诉讼
common law bond　普通法上的保函;普通法上的约束
Common law confers a right, it gives also a remedy or right of action for interference with or infringement of that right.　普通法赋予一项权利,同时亦赋予因干预或侵犯该项权利所提起的法律救济方法或诉权。
common law copyright　普通法版权[指依据普通法(即判例法)享有的版权。此版权在英美法系国家较为普遍。但1911年后,英国不再承认这种版权,而美国至今仍承认这类版权]
Common Law country with Federal system　联邦制普通法国家
common law court　普通法法院(指美国依据普通法,即中立立法机关而由法院和法官造法的法律体系进行审理案件的法院。尽管缺少联邦普通法,联邦宪在在解释宪法时依据的仍是普通法。先例引导法院,如前后案件事实完全相同,必须按以前案例判决,即遵循先例原则,但后来的判决也可改变先例所确立的法律。如新的案例事实不同,那么新的规则即会诞生。联邦最高法院是一个在只包括有很少联邦普通法 Federal common law 的体系中运作的普通法法院);(英)普通法法院(依普通法审理的法院)
common law heritage　普通法继承
common law jealousy of arbitrary executive action　普通法对专横行政诉讼的限制
common law legal family　普通法法系
common law lien　普通法留置权
common law marriage (= common-law marriage)　(英美法)普通法上的婚姻(指未举行任何仪式而自愿结合的婚姻,在美国有些州为合法婚姻)
common law negligence actions　(英美

法)普通法上的过失诉讼
common law of Continental Europe　欧洲大陆的普通法
common law of responsible superior　关于长官负责制的普通法
Common Law or case law contract　判例法合约
common law pedigree　普通法世系
common law polity　普通法国家,普通法政体,普通法体制
common law postulates　普通法所规定的,普通法的先决条件
Common Law Procedure Act of 1852, 1854 and 1860　《普通法程序法》(1852年,1854年和1860年)[该法将合并予以扩张,并将普通法和衡平法融合为1873年,1875年司法组织法(Judicature Act)]
common law reasoning　普通法推理
common law rule　普通法规则
common law tradition　普通法传统
common lawyers　普通法律师
(a) common legal science　普世意义的法学理论
common license (= licence)　普通许可证
Common Market　(欧洲)共同市场(即欧洲经济共同体的俗称)
Common Market Law　《共同市场法》(指参与共同市场的国家的法律总和)
common national language　民族共同语言
common name　普遍名义,普通名义
common nuisance　普通滋扰罪,普通妨害罪
common obligation　共同之债
common occurrence　共同事件的发生
common of pasture　共同放牧权
common of piscary　共渔权
common of turbary　炭泥共用权
common owner　共有人,共同所有人
common ownership　共同所有权
common place (或 commonplace) n./a.　老生常谈,平凡的事物,普通职务/平凡的
common pleas　普通诉讼,民事诉讼;(英)(大写)高等民事法院;(美)(某些州的)中级法院
common pleas court　见 Court of Common Pleas

common police 普通警察

common pool resources 1.公共水池资源[指公共水池所产生的资源单位是有限的,因此一个人使用公共水池会减少其他人对它的享用,由奥斯特罗姆(Ostrom)、加德纳(Gardnar)和瓦尔克(Walker)于1994年提出。大多数公共水池的数量是充足的,多种因素可以同时利用该项资源系统,而试图排除潜在受益者的代价是巨大的。公共水池资源包括人工共有资源和天然共有资源,包括地下水流域、灌溉系统、森林草场、计算机主机、政府公司财产以及互联网。共有资源的下属资源单位包括水、木材、草料、计算机处理系统、信息资料和预算分配。公共水池资源理论在过去半世纪中取得了长足进步,但这一领域仍有许多问题悬而未决] 2.共有资源(库)

common pool resources in the laboratory 共有实验资源(库)

common power 公共权力

common principles of international law 国际法的通用原则

common probate business 普通遗嘱检验业务

Common Professional Examination (英)共同职业考试(指在英国从事法律职业必须经过两个阶段。第一阶段为学术培养阶段。此阶段通过两个途径完成:一是取得合格的法律本科学位,但该资质只在申请律师资格前七年内有效,如果错过这一期间,就必须提交可靠的证据以证明其能力或参加基础知识考试——共同职业考试。另外,还需提供具备欧盟法知识的证据等。二是先修读一个其他专业的学士学位,再用一年时间修读"转化课程",即"共同职业考试"或"法律研究生证书"。但这种考试和学历,最多只能参加三次,三次通不过就不得再考,并且其成绩也同样只在申请资格前7年内有效)

common program(me) 共同纲领

Common property 公共财产[自然法学理论中,存在着"全球公域"的概念。最初关于"全球公域"的理解,是古典学派所主张的"共同财产",其范围包括公海及其资源、太空等。随着国际法的发展,"全球公域"的内涵发生了变化。变化之一是古典理论修正主义提出的"共同遗产"(Common heritage),包括公海海底资源和月球等天体上的矿产资源]

common property of mankind 人类共同财产

common proprietor 共有人,共同财产所有人

common purpose 共同目的

common question class action 共同问题集团诉讼

common question of law 共同法律问题

common recovery (历史上)废除限嗣设定合意诉讼,阻却限嗣继承的拟制诉讼[指一种完全的法律拟制(legal fiction)程序。借此程序,限嗣继承土地保有人(tenant in tail)解除限嗣继承的产权(fee-tail estate)。此诉讼有利于土地转让,即通过受法律禁止接受土地的可能受让人(potential transferee)对土地实际拥有人(actual owner)提起诉讼以"重新获得"(recovery)土地。早在19世纪已经废除的阻却限嗣继承的拟制诉讼原来是由神职人员或教会(clergy)作为一种避免由"永久管业法"(mortmain acts)所强制设立的土地转让的限制的方法。亦称feigned recovery。见 mortmain statute; cessio in jure]

common requisites 共同要件

common requisites in constitution of crime 犯罪构成的共同要件

common right 普通法上的权利(指源于普通法的权利);相对权利[即相对于绝对权利而言;相对权利(qualified right)只是在情理许可情况下方可行使的权利,而不考虑其动机及由此产生的损害]

common scheme (或 **plan**, **design**) 共同策划,共同谋划,共同筹谋(指涉及两个或两个以上的共同计划犯罪,或者两个或两个以上的人计划同一罪行,或者指将一片土地分成许多小块以便对土地使用进行相同限制)

common seal 公章;契据印章

common sense 常识,明明白白

common serjeant 1.(英)(伦敦市)司法行

政官(又译:伦敦法务官,指伦敦中央刑事法院的法官)2.公设律师
common serjeant-at-law (=common serjeant)
common share (或 stock) 普通股(份)
common shares 普通股
common sovereignty 共同主权
common theory of law 法律的命令理论(指把法律等同于主权者发布的命令。其优点是该理论把握了法律的强制方面和国家权力的重要性。其弱点在于试图把法律实践的多样性化约为一个范畴。命令理论很难解释授予权力的规则和法律体系自身的基本结构——在法律中扮演了重要角色的规则,规则体系制度化以及法律体系的连续性)
common thief 惯盗
common to our free institution 普遍适用于我们的自由制度
Common Trade Policy (欧盟)共同政策
common traverse 简单抗辩(指对诉方之主要事实陈述以直率方式加以简单否认);一般否认答辩
common trust fund 普通信托基金,共同信托基金
common trust fund proceedings 普通信托基金诉讼程序
common usage 共同习惯
common wall 共有的墙,界墙(见 *communis paries*)
Common Wealth Fund Committee (美)国家基金委员会
common will 共同意志
common woman 私娼
common-interest exception 见 newsman's privilege
common-law a. 根据普通法的;普通法上的;习惯法上的
common-law assignment 普通法上的转让,习惯法上的转让
common-law cheat 普通法上的欺诈,习惯法上的欺诈
common-law contempt 见 criminal contempt
common-law crime 普通法上的罪行,习惯法上的罪行
common-law criminal prosecution 普通法的检控机制
common-law dedication (1858年)普通法上的奉献行为[指土地拥有人为了公共利益和公共使用献出土地或土地的地役权(easement),由公众或以公众名义接受,并没有法规规定,常缩略为 dedication]
common-law exchange 普通法上的兑换,习惯法上的兑换
common-law jurisdiction 普通法上的管辖权;普通法上的审判权;普通法上的管辖范围
common-law lawyer 普通法上的律师,习惯法上的律师
common-law lien 普通法上的留置权,习惯法上的留置权
common-law mortgage 普通法上的抵押,习惯法上的抵押
common-law negligence 普通法上的过失,习惯法上的过失
common-law power of arrest 普通法上的拘捕权,习惯法上的拘捕权
common-law remedy 普通(习惯)法上的补偿,依普通(习惯)法的救济办法
common-law right 依普通法获得的权利,依习惯法获得的权利
common-law right of property 普通法上的财产权,习惯法上的财产权
common-law spouse 依普通(习惯)法结婚的配偶
common-law state (普通法州)1.见 Noncode state 2.未采取夫妻共同财产制(community property regime)的州(当今,有夫妻共同财产制的州与普通法的州之间的主要不同在于:在普通法州,夫妻一方持有财产上的权益只有在满足已提起离婚诉讼和夫妻另一方已死亡两个条件的情况下方能由另一方授予。见 common-property state)
common-law theory 普通法理论
common-law trust 商业信托,企业经营信托
common-property state 采取夫妻共同财产制的州[指该州要求婚姻期间夫妻持有所共有财产,不同于遗赠或单独赠与(inheritance or individual gift)被视为共同财产。见 com-

munity property; common-law state]
common-sense judgment 明确判决,常识判决
commonable a. 公用的;共有的;可在公地上放牧的,公地的
commonage n. 公地,(土地的)公有;共用权;(总称)老百姓
commonalty n. 社团法人;平民,(总称)百姓
commoner n. 平民;(英)下议院议员;对他人土地拥有使用权的人
commonweal n. 公益,公共福利
commonwealth n. 公益,公共福利;肯塔基、马萨诸塞、宾夕法尼亚和弗吉尼亚四州的称呼;政治实体;(全体)国民,国家,共和国,(英史)共和政体(指1649年查理一世至1660年王朝复辟这一期间的共和政体),联邦;(大写)(英)英联邦
Commonwealth citizenship 英联邦国家(共同的)公民资格
Commonwealth Court (美)州法院(指在宾夕法尼亚州,州法院具有全部民事诉讼或诉讼程序以抵制英联邦及其官员的起始管辖权、人身保护令状或不附属于其受理上诉管辖的判罪后的补救,而国家对一切产业的征用权不在此限)
Commonwealth Preference Certificate (英)联邦特惠关税证
commorancy n. (英)习惯住地;(美)临时住地
commorientes n. 推定为同时死亡者
commotio 震荡,震伤,震伤休克
commotion n. 骚动;混乱;动乱
communal a. 公共的;公有的;自治体的;公社的,公社制的;(大写)巴黎公社的
communal estate 共有财产
communal justice 公共正义
communal land 公地
communal marriage 杂婚,共同婚,群交
communal right 公共权利,共同权利
communal security 公安
communal tenure 共有权;共同所有权;(土地的)共同使用权
communalism n. 地方自治主义,公社制社会结构

Communard n. 巴黎公社社员,巴黎公社支持者
commune n. 1.公社;(大写)(法史)巴黎公社 2.(法国等国家的)最小行政区,乡 3.(英)(嬉皮士的)群居村
communicable disease 传染病
communicate v. 传达,传送;通讯;传染(疾病)
communication n. 1.通信,通讯;传达 2.交换,交流,交往;交通,交通工具;(疾病的)传染
communication agency 与委托人通讯(的保密)(指律师与当事人、医生与病人有关委托事务上的通讯秘密受到法律上的保护。见 confidential communication)
communication agreement 通讯协议
communication between husband and wife 夫妻间通讯(的保密)(指夫妻间有关私下言谈的通讯秘密受到法律保护,不得传讯出庭作证,公开其内容)
communication by implication 默示表达;默示的意思表示
communication media 交流媒介,交通工具
communication of the offer 要约的通知
communication of works 作品传播(指在版权领域中一般将使用作品称为"作品的传播",如出版、广播、表演等均系作品的传播)
communication police 交通警察
communication privilege 交流特权(指保护属于特殊关系的个人之间的谈话,如涉及律师与委托人、丈夫与妻子等)
communication theory 沟通论
Communications Act of 1934 (美)《1934年电信法》
communicative evidence 证人证言(区别于书证,物证)(同 testimonial evidence, oral evidence)
communicative processes 交流过程
communings (苏格兰法)要约,签约前谈判
communio 共有
communio bonorum (罗马法)货物之共有;夫妻共有之财产(复数形式 *communiones bonorum*)

communique n. 公函;官方公报
* ***Communis error facit jus.*** Common error, repeated many times makes law. 共同错误反复多次出现,就会制定规约。
communis juris 共同法权
communis militia 共同恶意
communis omnium 公有物
communis opinio 共同意见,(同行业的)普遍意见
communis opinion 共同意见[从法律观点上被普遍接受的确信,如在法律上毫无异议的一致认识,这种共同确信(common belief)在罗马法上具有很大的权威]
communis paries (罗马法)共有的墙(指两个分界连接的墙,分别由两个不同的所有人拥有的建筑物或土地之间的界墙。亦称 common wall)
communis stipes 同血统,共同祖先
communism n. 共产主义
communist a. 共产主义的;共产党的;共产主义者的
communist morality 共产主义道德
communist system 共产主义制度
communitarianism n. 社群主义(亦译:社区主义;共同体主义;公共社团主义;合作主义等)(指研究正义、道德和社会秩序方法途径,强调社群对个体认同,个体实现和社会福利的重要性)
communitarigation n. 共同体化
community n. 1.公社,团体,(政治)共同体 2.同一地区的全体居民;公众 3.共有,共同性,一致 4.居民区,聚居区,社区,镇,乡
Community Act 《共同体法》
Community Action for Legal Service (美)社区诉讼法律服务处(设立在纽约,收费较低,有法律援助性质)
community centre 社区中心;公共食堂
community chest 募集的救济基金
community control (美)社区控制(指针对在社区的罪犯的刑事判决,其判决条件包括加强和严格监督。按照限制罪犯的动向和活动,并实施电子监控,对于违反判决所包括的任何条件,必须进行严格惩处)
community correction (美)社区矫正(指美国 20 世纪 60、70 年代针对监狱犯人爆满的情况,采取非监禁化的途径,主要表现在社区矫正上)
community debt (夫妻)共同债务
community groups 社区团体
community home 公共教养所
community justice 社区司法
Community Law (欧洲经济)《共同体法》,(欧洲)《区域法》
community mediation 社区调解(西方国家尤其美国、加拿大的一种纠纷解决样式,常指适用于当事人不能自行解决的争议和双方都存在过错的案件,特别发生在邻里之间、家庭内部、学校管理过程和日常生活的其他方面)
community model 社区调停模式(20 世纪 70 年代西方国家的监狱矫正实务被认为是失败的,因此提出刑事和解理论和思想并在司法实践中适用,和对刑事法律进行相应改革,这是实践中的刑事和解模式之一。这种模式是在犯罪之后,犯罪人逮捕前,由社区进行调解。在英美法系国家仅适用于非可逮捕罪,在大陆法系适用于少年犯罪。另外,还有 diversion model "转处模式", alternative model "替代模式"和 justice model "司法模式")
community obligation 共同体义务
community of goods 财物的共有
community of nations 国际社会
community of property regime 夫妻共同财产制(亦译:婚姻共同财产制)
community of states (许多国家组合的)共同体
Community organization 社会组织
community property 夫妻共同财产,婚姻共同财产(指夫妇共同拥有的资产,婚姻期间已共同获得的成果,而不是遗产或赠与给一方配偶,此项财产夫妻一般均各持有一半的权益。在美国,只有亚利桑那、加利福尼亚、爱达荷、路易斯安那、内华达、新墨西哥、得克萨斯、华盛顿和威斯康星等九个州具有夫妻共同财产制度。见 marital property, title division)
community property states (夫妻)共同财产状况(指结婚时所获得的大部分财产

属双方所有,不管其财产的名义属谁)
community property system 社区财产体系
Community Reinvestment Act 《共同体再投资法》
community responsibility 社会责任
community sentence 社区刑罚,社区量刑
community service 社会服务
community soft law instruments 欧盟软法工具(指雷内·西尔顿和弗里茨·斯特因克在其合编的《欧盟及其成员国和美国的行政法——比较分析》一书中将软法视为欧盟治理的一种手段或工具)
community ties 社会关系
Community Trade Mark 共同体贸易商标
communize v. 使成为公有财产,使公有化
commutable a. 可减轻的(刑罚);可以抵偿的,可以变换的
commutation n. 1.交换,转换;代偿 2.减刑(指可以变换的;可以抵偿的;由高一等的刑罚改变为低一等的刑罚的一种刑罚变更,如死刑改为终身监禁)
commutation of fines in lieu of imprisonment 易科罚金
commutation of penalty 减轻刑罚
commutation of punishment 减刑,减轻惩罚
commutation of sentence 减刑
commutation pardon 减刑特赦
commutation tax 减税,替代税[指①可以由其他科税替代的一个或一个以上的结合的税,诸如申请其他税种或履行个人专属服务(personal services),比如营业税(excise tax)或特许权税(franchise tax)可以与地方税(local tax)合并替代所有其他相关税种。②历史上,对船东们所科的税,要求他们提交一份保证书(bond)或免去每一境外旅客的支付款项。在19世纪,税收常用来劝阻移民并提高税收去补偿维持那些已在美国的贫困移民的生活费用。③历史上,1784年的一项税种,意图减少茶叶走私,并通过削减茶叶税和提高要橱窗税来增加税收,为了免交橱窗税,许多人用木板堵住橱窗]
commutation ticket (在一定时间内,固定路线上使用的铁路)长期车票

commutative a. 交换的,代替的,可交换的
commutative justice 交换正义,(常于合同法中,目的在使每个人获得在交易中的平等的比例,不得因为他人的损失而获益,达到交换正义)
commute v. 1.用……交换;兑换;补偿 2.减刑 3.改变付款方式;经常来往于(某两地间)
commute a sentence 减刑
commuter time 上下班时间
commuterization n. 往返市区及郊区住所的生活方式
compact n./a. 合约,合同(契约),协定/紧凑的,简洁的,严密的
Compact theory 契约理论(指美国早期的一种关于联邦与州关系的政治理论。由杰弗里·麦迪逊1798年在《弗吉尼亚——肯塔基决议案》中提出,宣称联邦不过是各主权州的一种契约关系,各州有权决定何时终止这一关系。杰和麦提出这个观点,其目的是反对约翰·亚当斯利用联邦权力以政治高压反民主行为,但后来这一理论为州权主义者利用,并成为该理论的基础)
companion n. 1.伙伴;同事;同优乐者 2.检索,参考书;成套书〈the companion volume〉(成套书的一卷)3.指南,参考书,成套书
companion bill (1887年)伴随议案,相伴议案(指一项议案以相同的形式提到国会两院制立法机构的另一议院);同一形式议案(指两院制立法机构之外的另一院以实质相同形式推荐的一项议案)
companionate marriage 伴婚,试婚(指一种非法婚姻关系,一种婚前安排可能随时终止的婚姻)
company n. 公司,商行;同伴,交往,交际
company act 公司法;公司条例
company credit 公司信贷
Company Directors Disqualification Act 1986 (英)《1986年公司董事取消法》
company incorporation laws 公司合并法
company law 公司法
company limited by guarantee 担保有限责任公司

company limited by shares 股份有限公司
company liquidation account 公司清理账户
company man 忠于公司的雇员,公司资方的雇员
company of limited liability 有限责任公司
company of unlimited liability 无限责任公司
company promoter 公司发起人
company property 公司财产
company representative 公司代表
company stooges 工贼(指受雇于公司老板的暗探)
company union 公司工会(指一种由资本家控制的御用工会)
company's business 公司经营
company's register 公司注册(登记)簿
comparable a. 可比较的(with);类似的,比得上的(to)
comparable case 可比的案件,类似的案件
comparable index value line 可比指数值线
Comparably high level of ambition and NAMA "对于农产品市场准入和非农产品市场准入的开放幅度应当相称"(此种幅度应按特殊与差别待遇原则予以平衡和构成比例)
comparative a. 比较的;对比的;相对的
comparative advantage 比较优势
comparative advantages 相对有利条件,比较条件,比较利益
comparative advantages theory (国际贸易上的)相对比较利益论
comparative analysis 对比分析
comparative costs 比较成本
comparative impairment 比较损害说(指美国巴克斯特的比较损害说)
comparative interpretation 比较(性)解释
comparative jurisprudence 比较法理学
comparative jurist 比较法学家
comparative law 比较法
comparative legal history 比较法制史
comparative legal research 比较法学研究
comparative negligence 比较疏忽
comparative negligence case 比较过失或疏忽的案件
comparative penal law 比较刑法

comparative private international law school 比较国际私法学派
comparative rectitude (美)比较正直(原则)(指离婚诉讼中,当双方均具有离婚理由时,补救将给予过错少的一方的原则,亦称"a least fault"。见 divorce)
comparative reference group 比较参照群体
comparative study of jurisprudence 法学的比较研究
comparatively competence 相对管辖权
comparatively relation 相容关系
compare v. 比较,对照;对比;比喻
comparing the end points 两端比较法(指在选取了具体的调查年份以后,将调查初期的进口量与调查末期的进口量对比,从而考察是否满足进口增加要件的方法)
comparison of handwritings 笔迹比较
compartment n. (英)(议会中在政府规定的期限内讨论的)特殊协议事项
compass n. 范围;界限;指南针
compass of competency 管辖范围;管辖区域
compassing n. 预谋;设想,图谋
compassion n. 可怜,怜悯,同情
compatibility n. 相容性,一致性
compatibility of goals 目标的一致性
compatible computer 兼容机,兼容型电脑(指不同型号计算机均可运行同样软件,但应注意发展兼容机时可能侵犯软件版权问题)
compearance 被告出席,(苏格兰)出庭
compel v. 1.强迫,强逼屈从 2.强制获得(反应,同意,服从)
compellability of witness 对证人强制作证的能力
compellable witness 被强制作证的证人
compelled assumption 强制假定
compelling abortion 强制堕胎
compelling reason 有说服力的理由
compelling state interest 强制服从国家利益(指国家法律、法规、政策或行为均有足够力量来限定个人在宪法上的权利)
compendium n. 概要,纲要;简编
compensability n. 可补偿性

compensable a. 依法补偿的;可赔偿的
compensate v. 赔偿,补偿;酬报
compensating balance 抵偿结存
compensating expense 赔偿费(用)
compensatio 抵消,抵债(指二人间相互消灭债权、债务之谓);补偿
compensatio criminis 罪行相抵(如离婚赔偿案内原被告均有罪行,可相互抵消)
compensatio culpae 过失相抵(如离婚案中原被告均有过错)
compensatio lucri cum damno 损益相抵(指损害赔偿诉讼中如原告一方面受损,一方面又受益则可两相抵消再作赔偿之决定)
compensation n. 补偿,赔偿;补偿物,赔偿金,(债等的)抵消
compensation and damages 补偿和损害赔偿(金)
compensation claim 索赔诉讼请求
compensation for all damages 赔偿所受的一切损害
compensation for cancellation of contracts 解约金(指解除合同或契约的补偿金)
compensation for condemned property 被没收财产的补偿
compensation for damages (或 loss) 损害(损失)赔偿金
compensation for death injury or illness attributable to service 因公死亡、受伤或患病的补偿
compensation for non-performance 不履行债的赔偿
compensation for price of land 地价补偿
compensation for victims of violence 对受暴力行为的受害人的补偿
compensation money 赔偿金
compensation of guardian 监护人的报酬
compensation order 补偿令
compensation payment 补偿报酬,补偿金,赔偿金的支付
compensation period 补偿时期,补偿期限(指由失业法或工人补偿法规定的期限。在此时间的失业者或受伤的工人有资格得到补偿)
compensation system (进出口差损)补偿制度;赔偿制
compensation trade 补偿贸易
compensation tribunal 犯罪赔偿裁判庭
compensation undercontract 约定赔偿(金),按约赔偿(金)
compensative a. 赔偿的,补偿的;报酬的
compensative suretyship 赔偿保证
compensator n. 赔偿人;补偿人;赔偿物
compensatory a. 赔偿的;补偿的,报酬的
Compensatory Adjustment 补偿性调整
compensatory approach 补偿办法
compensatory damages 应予以赔偿的损害,赔偿金
compensatory financing 补偿贷款;(商品贸易)补偿性资金供应
compensatory financing facility 补偿贷款办法,补偿性资金供应办法
compensatory leave 补假
compensatory payment 补偿金,赔偿金,补偿报酬
compensatory relief 补偿救济
compensatory trade 补偿贸易
compete v. 参与竞争(with);对抗,竞争
compete on a fair playing (field) 正当竞争
competence n. (17世纪)1.作证资格,作证能力(指做某事的基本资格和最低限度的能力,特别是证明)⟨competence of witness⟩(证人的作证能力)2.权限,管辖权(指官方机关做某事的能力)⟨the court's competence to enter a valid judgment⟩(法庭具有作出有效判决的权力)3.可靠性,真实性,确实性(authenticity)⟨the documents were supported by a business records affidavit, leaving their competence as evidence beyond doubt⟩(这些文件受到商业记录宣誓书的支持,留下它们的真实性作为有力证据)(见 competency;competent)
competence of evidence 可受理的证据;证据的必要分量
competence of judge 法官的品质,法官的能力
competence of the legislature 立法机关的权限
competence of witness 证人的作证资格;

证人能力
competence to stand trial 受审能力(指刑事被告人参加庭审,接受审判的能力。具体指刑事被告人理解自己在诉讼中所处的地位和自己行为在诉讼中的意义,能行使诉讼权利,并能与辩护人合作为自己进行辩护的能力)
competency n. (=competence)(16世纪) 1.资格,能力(指理解问题和作出决定的智力能力)2.刑事被告接受审判的能力(ability to stand trial)(通过了解诉讼程序的能力,有目的地向法律顾问咨询,以及对答辩上的帮助等进考量。亦称 competency to stand trial)
competency of locality 土地管辖(权)
competency of mandate 委任权限
competency proceeding 承受能力的测定(指通过庭审来决定一个人是否应经过民事拘押或预审来确定其是否在刑事案件中有承受通常审判的精神能力。亦即指进行人的心理能力的听审)
competency to serve a sentence 服刑能力(指经过判决被定罪的罪犯或服刑人员,能承受法院对其剥夺部分权益的刑罚并能清楚理解自己犯罪性质、危害程度、危害后果,也能理解刑罚的性质、目的、意义以及能否有效接受劳动改造的生理和心理条件。亦称"刑罚承受能力")
competent a. 1.有权能的,有法定资格的,主管的2.有能力的,能胜任的3.被许可的,应该做的
competent administrative organ 主管行政机关
Competent Authorities 主管机关(见 Central Authorities)
competent authority 主管当局;主管机关;主管权限
competent court 管辖法院;主管法院
competent department 主管部门
competent evidence 有法律效力的证据,可接受的证据,可采纳的证据
competent jurisdiction 合法管辖权(见 jurisdiction 2)
competent knowledge 足够的知识
competent law 应适用的法律

competent organization 主管机构(组织),主管单位
competent person 合格人员,主管人员
competent public officer 有法定资格的公职官员
competent teaching 能胜任的讲授,有权威的讲学;主要讲学
competing 竞争的买价
competing analogy 竞争的类推
competing bases of representation 竞争代表的基础
competing demands 竞争性需求
competing legal Forman's 为法的部分构成而竞争
competing practice 竞争的诉讼程序
competition n. 竞争;角逐,比赛;竞争者
competition for prizes 捕获物分配的竞争
competitive a. 竞争的,比赛的
competitive bidding 公开招标,竞争性投标
competitive commodities 竞争性商品
competitive currency depreciation 竞争性货币贬值
competitive entry 竞争报单
competitive examination 甄选考核
competitive harm 见 competitive injury
competitive injury 竞争性损害[指由于商业竞争造成的非法经济损害,比如因不公平竞争而造成买卖损失,原告的劣势是在与被告竞争中由被告的不公平竞争造成的。多数法院要求原告陈述竞争性损害作为侵占行为(misappropriation action)的要件(element),或必须坚持依据《美国注释法典》第15标题卷第1125(a)(1)(B)节"15 USCA §1125(a)(1)(B)"提起虚假广告诉讼(false advertising action)。亦称为 competitive harm]
competitive practices 竞争行为
competitive price 竞争价格
competitive relationship 竞争关系
competitive tender 公开投标,竞投
competitiveneutrality 竞争中立(政策)(该政策原则强调国有企业应当和私有企业处于同样的外部环境,以保证它们在同等市场条件下公平竞争。表面上看,该原则只是要求公平待遇,但实质上是意图在

国际社会中约束甚至围堵国有企业)
competitor n. 竞争者;角逐者;对手;争霸者
competition advocacy 竞争倡导,竞争推进(指竞争主管机构实施的除执法以外所有改善竞争环境的行为)
compilation n. (15世纪)1.(版权)汇编,汇集[指以独创方法整理编排文学作品汇集;特别是收集、汇集原作的资料或经过挑选的资料,经过编排形成一个具有创作人身份(authorship)的新作品。创作汇编的作者拥有汇集作品的版权,但是没有组成部分(component parts)的版权。参见《美国注释法典》第17标题卷,第101节(17 USCA § 101)。见 collective work; derivative work]2.法规汇编(指现行的、编辑好的便于使用的法规汇集,亦称 compiled statutes)3.财务报告(指财务的汇集报告,但不保证符合一般可接受的会计原则。在准备汇编时,会计并不收集证据或鉴别客户所提供信息的准确性,而是审查汇编报告,以保证它们是适当的形式,并免于各种明显错误)(compile v.)
compilation decrees 汇编法令,法令汇编
compilation of statistics 编制统计资料
compile v. 编辑,编制(书籍,索引),搜集,汇编(资料)
compile statistics on matters affecting the courts' resources 编制对法院资源产生影响的事项统计数
complain v. 申诉,控诉,控告,叫屈,诉苦,抗议
complain and call for redress 鸣冤叫屈
complaint n. (14世纪)1.抱怨,叫屈 2.起诉(用于民事诉讼方面的词语。如向裁判法院提交诉状,申请强制对方付款。起诉不同于告发,告发是用在刑事方面的词语)3.(美)控告(常用于民事诉讼中原告方面的控诉方面的控诉);申诉;抗告 4.(民事诉讼中原告的)诉状或起诉书[指开始民事诉讼的起始诉讼状(initial pleading),向法院陈述司法管辖和权利请求的根据。在美国的有些州,这种诉状亦称为 petition(申诉书)]5.原告,起诉人,控告人 6.刑事控告书[指依据《联邦刑事诉讼规则》(Fed. R. Crim. P P. 3.),由受害人、警察、地区检察官或其他利害关系人向有管辖权的联邦司法官"Magistrate"提出某一犯罪行为已经发生和构成其指控罪行的重要事实的控告文书。但在诉讼中正式提起诉讼的,应由大陪审团提出起诉书(indictment)或由检察官提出起诉书(information)]
complainant n. 1.原告;投诉人;控诉人(=plaintiff)2.抗议者,抱怨者
complained of brief 对诉讼要点不满、叫屈
complaining party 申诉方
complaining state 起诉国
complaint n. 1.抱怨,叫屈 2.起诉(用于民事诉讼方面的词语。如向裁判法院投诉状,申请强制对方付款。起诉不同于告发,告发是用在刑事方面的词语)3.(美)控告(常用于民事诉讼中原告方面的控诉);(民事诉讼中原告的)诉状或起诉书;申诉;抗告
complaint and claim 投诉与索赔
complaint committees concerning consumer transactions 消费者交易投诉委员会
complaint defective 起诉状欠缺法律要件
complaint from private sources (私人提出的)起诉,自诉
complaint in nonproperty case 因非财产关系起诉的案件
complaint of wrongs (提出)损害赔偿(要求的)诉讼案件
complaint procedure 申诉程序
complement n./v. 补充物;补足物;余额;船上的定员/补充,补足
complementarity n. 互补性,并协性
complementary a. 补充的;补足的;互相信赖的
complementary convention 附约
complementary effects 互相制约的影响
complementary issue 互相制约的争点(或问题)
complementary laws 补充性法规
complementary provision 补充条款规定
complete v./a. 完成,结束;履行,执行;使完满/完全的;完成的;充实的,充分供应的、充满的、能满的〈law review are usually

complete with footnotes connecting to primary source〉(法律评论中通常满是链接原始文献的脚注)
complete action 法律上完全生效的行为
complete and perfect information 完全且完善的信息
complete but imperfect information 完全但不完美的信息
Complete Collection of Laws and Ordinance (日)《法例总览》
complete decision 全部判决,完整判决
complete defence 完整的辩护
complete defense 完整的辩护,具有行使完全的辩护权,完整的抗辩(指庇护被告而不承担任何责任并阻止通过原告提起诉讼经判决获得任何损害赔偿。所以实际是一种积极抗辩或不承担任何责任的完整辩护。见 common defense)
complete determinist 彻底决定论者
complete disarmament 全面裁军
complete grant of power 完全授权
complete immunity 完全豁免权
complete legislative provision 完全的立法条文,完美的立法规定
complete no-fault liability 完全的无过错责任
complete operation rule (保险)全程操作原则,完整操作规定[指对货物在运输过程中包括装卸货物承保风险起讫时间、地点的一项原则规定。在有些情况下,此规定还被延伸到在货物运输过程中发生对人伤害(personal injuries)的问题。见 warehouse-to-warehouse cover]
complete pardon 完全赦免,彻底赦免
complete payment (按合同)最后的支付
complete record of the case 案件的全部卷宗
complete willingness 完全的意愿
complete willingness of the two parties 双方当事人完全自愿
complete-preemption doctrine (美)完全优先原则[指一个联邦法规优先效力的规定,此规定如此特殊和无所不至,可使一项州普通法的诉讼转换为一项陈述联邦的权利主张以达到合理答辩的民事诉讼(well-pleaded complaint)的目的的一种规则。见 well-pleaded complaint]
completed a. 完成的,结束的
completed offense 既遂罪
completed offense of intentional homicide 故意杀人既遂罪
completed product 成品
completely without capacity to act 完全无行为能力
completion n. 实现;(土地买卖合同上的)最后交割完毕;完成,完成交易;结束
completion guarantee 完工担保
completion of purchase 买卖完成,成交
completion of the liquidation 清算完结;清理结束
completion of the term of imprisonment 刑期届满
complex a./n. 综合的,合成的,复杂的,复式的/复杂,合成物,综合企业
complex and time consuming cases 复杂而又费时的案件
complex crimes 复合犯罪
complex interdependence 错综复杂互赖关系论
complex tariff 复式税则
compliance n. 依从,顺从(指不违反一项法律或一个协定)
compliance auditing 符合审计,依法审计
compliance certificate 补偿信用证
compliance check 依法检查
compliance guidance (企业)合规指引(指反垄断主管机构,引领企业构建合规制度的行为。企业合规制度主要是通过培训、审计等方式告知员工可被竞争法接受的行为范围,发现违法行为为应如何处理,反竞争行为可能导致的处罚等,以最大限度确保公司商业行为符合竞争法)
complicate v. 使麻烦,使复杂,使陷入
complication n. 复杂,混乱纠纷;并发症
Complication of the Laws of Indies 《印度群岛法律汇编》
complice n. 共犯;从犯;共同犯罪人;帮凶;共谋
complicity n. 同谋,共谋,串谋,共犯关系,同谋关系

complicity in crime 共同犯罪关系人
complisult 明褒实贬 [此词是由 compliment(赞扬,称赞)和 insult(侮辱,冒犯)组合而成的名词,意指隐含贬损意味、带有言外之意的恭维。"城市词典"(Urban Dictionary)2004 年首次对该词进行解释,称它用于描述称赞某人的同时又有意或无意冒犯此人的做法]
comply v. 遵守,遵照(with)照做
comply in public but oppose in private 阳奉阴违
comply with its own constitution 遵照其自己的宪法
component n. 组成部分;成分,部分
component part 组成部分
comport v. (举动,行为等)一致(with),适合
compartment n. 举动,行为
compos mentis 心智健全,心神健全
composite a. 合成的;复合的;混合的
composite hybrid approach (美)复合式混合法[指诱陷抗辩(entrapment defense)的成立必须同时满足主、客观两种标准。对于证明犯罪意图的具体指标要素,美国法上没有统一标准,部分法院总结的判断因素包括刑事被告对引诱的回应是否积极、引诱前刑事被告的主观心态、刑事被告先前的类似犯罪活动、刑事被告是否对被引诱的犯罪已经有犯罪计划、刑事被告的声誉、与引诱人协商时刑事被告的行为、刑事被告是否表示过拒绝引诱的意思、被指控的犯罪性质、警方引诱时是否使用到了胁迫以及引诱的方式与性质。法官应在综合考量这些因素的基础上判断有无犯罪倾向。英国上议院 2001 年在卢塞利(Looseley)案判决中对诱惑侦查合法性判断标准进行集中全面梳理,作出标尺性判例,确立了偏重客观标准的检验方法,即更加注意执法人员引诱行为的恰当性,对被引诱人主观方面因素关注不多。其判断标准可要概括为三大要素:是否具有合理怀疑、是否遵循相应的授权和监督程序、引诱手段是否提供正常的犯罪机会。申言之,政府的引诱与手法必须与被引诱人在其他情况下可能遇到的引诱相当或相当普通;如果引诱提供的犯罪机会属于其他人在同类犯罪场景中难以遇见的特殊犯罪机会,则表明犯罪引诱已超过合法界限,而演变为过度引诱]
composite international person 复合国际人格者
composite mark 见 composite trademark
composite organ 复合机关
composite portrait 综合画像(指根据见证人描述的罪犯身体特征所绘出的画像)
composite states 复合国(在原则上一律平等,而具有共同国际机构的数国家结合称为复合国,复合国的各分子国在对内对外方面须保留一部分主权,否则为单一国)
composite trademark 综合商标,服务商标(由好几个词构成的商标或标识,以与一个整体的相区别。即使每个词都是很普通,提供某种为广告服务而采用的标记,可用单词、名称、符号、图案的组合以区别于为他人的服务标识。服务商标由某人使用或以某人的善意目的用于商业活动,并向商标法主管部门申请登记,才能确立个人拥有此项服务标识。亦称 servicemark; Hybrid mark; composite mark; Hybrid trademark)
composite treaty 复合条约
composite vessel 综合货船;混装货船
composition n. 1.和解协议(指债权人与债务人之间通过协商,达成少还或缓还的协议,一般需经签订契据,依法登记或经法院批准) 2.构成,组成;成分 3.(日耳曼法)和解金
composition and schemes of arrangement 了结债务的调解计划
composition deed 和解(了结债务)契据
composition of jury 陪审团的构成
composition of the court 法院的组成
composition with creditors (债务人)与债权人和解(了结债务)
compound v./a. 1.组成,构成 2.(由互让而)解决(争端、债务等);和解;妥协 3.一次付清(预约款等);以复利计算/复合的;合成的;混合的
compound discount 复贴现

compound interest 复利,复利息

compound larceny 复合盗窃罪[指有威胁性地从被盗人身上或其住宅直接窃取财产的一种盗窃罪。这种犯罪既盗窃财产又妨害人身或侵犯住宅,故名。亦称混合盗窃罪(mixed larceny),以区别于单纯盗窃罪(simple larceny)]

compound or aggravated larceny 复合或加重盗窃罪(= compound larceny)

compound penalty 复合刑

compound settlement 综合解决办法;土地协议文书

compound with creditors (债务人)与(多数)债权人和解(了结债务)

compounding n. 1.混合,配合 2.私下和解,私了(案件)3.一次付清,只偿还一部分(债款)

compounding a debt 一次付清债务

compounding a felony 私了重罪(见 compounding crime)

compounding crime 私下和解罪(亦称私了案件罪。指接受财物或其他报酬不去告发罪犯而私下了结案件的一种罪行)

comprador(e) n. 买办

comprador(e)-feudal a. 封建买办的

comprehension evidence regulations (美)综合证据规定[指加利福尼亚、堪萨斯、新泽西等州遵循 1953 年《统一证据规定》(Uniform Rules of Evidence),同时很早就采用综合证据规定]

comprehensive a. 包含的;包括的;综合(性)的;有理解力的

comprehensive agreement 综合性协定

Comprehensive Anti Apartheid Act of 1986 《1986 年全面反种族隔离法》

comprehensive approach 综合法(指要求投资公司拥有的资本相当于其固定比例的长期证券价值加上一定比例的短期证券价值)

comprehensive audit 综合审计,全面审计

comprehensive auditing 综合审计,全面审计

comprehensive balancing 综合平衡

comprehensive case 综合性判例

comprehensive co-operation 全面合作

comprehensive code 综合性的法典

comprehensive codification 综合法规编纂,综合法规汇典

Comprehensive Convention on International Terrorism 《关于国际恐怖主义的全面公约》(1999 年底联合国大会通过第 54/110 号决议,决定开始制定一部全面公约,简称"全面公约")

Comprehensive Crime Control Act (美)《综合犯罪控制法》(美国会 1984 年通过。该法规定:从 1992 年 12 月始废除对联邦犯人的假释,甚至美国很多州也取消了假释)

Comprehensive Drug Abuse Prevention and Control Act (美)《综合预防和控制滥用毒品法》

Comprehensive Environmental Response Compensation and Liability Act (CERCLA)《全面环境反应、赔偿和责任法(案)》

comprehensive faculty 理解力

comprehensive general-liability policy (1943 年)综合性一般责任保单(指一种广泛的覆盖商业保险单,包括各种一般风险。特别是给第三方造成人身伤害和财产损失的,保险公司要承担责任。这种保单最早出现于 1940 年,它现在大部分已由商业概括责任保单 commercial general-liability policy 所替代。亦称 CGL policy; general-liability policy。见 commercial general-liability policy)

comprehensive insurance 综合保险

comprehensive mandatory sanction 全面的强制性制裁

comprehensive method of protection 综合防护法

comprehensive of rights 全面的权利

comprehensive overall view 综合全面观点

comprehensive planning 全面规(计)划

comprehensive rationality 全盘理性

comprehensive report 综合性报告

Comprehensive review 全面审查

comprehensive sanction 综合制裁,综合裁判

comprise v. 包含,包括;构成;由……组成

compromis d'arbitrage 仲裁协定

compromise n./v. 1.妥协,折中,和解,相互了结案件(指诉讼开始前后,双方当事人自愿让步,解决纠纷或调整争议数额,放弃诉讼)2.公断条约;仲裁协定 3.和解协议,折中办法,妥协方案 4.遭到损害/1.妥协,让步,和解,互让了结,私下了结 2.连累,危害,损坏(名誉等);使受嫌疑 3.放弃(诉讼、原则等),泄露(秘密)

compromise and settlement 和解协议;争议和解;协议了结争议

compromise annulment 协议废除(债等);和解废除(债务)

compromise clause 仲裁条款

compromise of action 诉讼上的和解(或让步)

compromise of lawsuit 诉讼上的和解

compromise of one's good name 好名声受到损害

compromise offer 和解提议

Compromise Theory of Punishment 刑罚折衷论

compromise verdict 和解裁决;折中裁决,折中裁判

compromised total loss 约定全损

compter(或 **counter**) n. (英史)债务人监狱(指附属于自治市的市长法庭或司法行政官的债务人监狱)

comptroller n. 审计官,主计官;会计检查员(指代人管理和查核账务的人)

Comptroller General 总会计师,主计长,总审计长,总审查长

comptroller of the pipe (英)卷筒卷宗保管官

Comptroller-General of Patents, Designs and Trade Marks (英)专利、外观设计和商标(总局局长)主管、主计长

compulsa (一个经过公证的)契据证明副本

compulsion n. 强迫,强制;冲动

compulsive a. 强迫的;有强制力的;禁不住的

compulsive behaviou(u)r 失控行为

compulsive injunction 强制性禁令

compulsive means 强制手段

compulsive settlement 强制解决

compulsory a. 强制的;强迫的;义务的

compulsory acquisition(或 **purchase**) 强制获得(或通称为强制购买)

compulsory acquisition of land 强征土地,强制征用土地

compulsory administrative measure 行政强制措施

compulsory arbitration 强制(性)仲裁(或公断)

compulsory attendance 有法定义务的出席(或参加)

compulsory auction 强制拍卖

compulsory case law 强制性判例法

compulsory conciliation 强制和解

compulsory contribution 强迫捐献;强制摊派

compulsory counter claim 强制性反请求,强制性反诉

compulsory divorce 强制离婚

compulsory education 义务教育

compulsory enforcement 强制执行

compulsory execution 强制执行

compulsory expropriation 强制性征用

compulsory heir 强制性继承人

compulsory in nature 强制型

compulsory insurance 强制保险

compulsory joinder 强制合并(指美国《联邦民事诉讼规则》第9条)

compulsory judicial settlement 强制司法解决

compulsory jurisdiction 强制管辖权

compulsory license (专利)强制许可证

compulsory marriage on account of an arrangement (中)强迫包办婚姻

compulsory nonsuit 强制中止诉讼

compulsory party joinder 强制性当事人合并

compulsory payment 强制支付,有义务支付

compulsory portion 遗留份,应得份;特留份

compulsory power 强制权

compulsory process 强制性程序,强制到庭程序,强制性传票(指根据普通法,进行诉讼的当事人和了解案件信息的其他人,在被命令其提供证明时,有义务提出并与法院合作。法院通常以传票方法迫使其

compulsory production of records 强制生产记录

compulsory purchase 强制购买;征购

compulsory purchase order 强制征购令

compulsory rate 强制费率

compulsory registration 强制登记

compulsory retirement 强迫退休(或退职)

compulsory sale 强制出售

compulsory sanction 强制制裁

compulsory school age 强制入学年龄

compulsory sea peril insurance 强制海事事故保险

compulsory self-incrimination 强迫认罪(指用非法的高压手段来迫使犯人承认被指控的罪行)

compulsory service 强迫服役,义务服役

compulsory service system 义务兵役制

compulsory serviceman 义务兵

compulsory settlement of international disputes 国际争端的强制解决

compulsory share 特留份

compulsory submission to conciliation procedures 强制调解程序

compulsory trust 义务信托

compulsory voting 强迫投票;强制投票

compulsory winding up 强制结束营业;强制(公司)解散

compulsory winding up by the court 由法院裁决的强制(公司)解散

compurgation n. 依据宣誓断案,依据他人证词宣誓证明被告无罪的程序(见 compurgator)

compurgation of law (英)宣誓断讼程序(见 compurgation)

compurgator n. (依据他人证词)宣誓证明被告无罪者(英国古时的法庭,对准刑事或民事案件的被控人,可用宣誓来证明他是清白无辜的,但应按规定邀请一定数量的人,一般为 12 人,同来法庭宣誓,证明他所说的是真实的,这些人就称 com-

purgators);被控犯罪的人邻居(见 compurgation,wager of law)

computation n. 计算;估计;计算法;计算结果

computation of duration of punishment 计算刑期

computation of time 计算时间

computed price 推算价

computed tare 约定皮重,推定皮重

computer n. 电子计算机,计算机,计算器;计算者

computer access to civil law 计算机对大陆法的检索

Computer Aided Instructions 计算机辅助教学软件

Computer Aided Traffic Control 计算机交通管制系统

Computer Bureaux 计算机服务公司(指发达国家中为用户提供数据和数据处理等服务的公司)

computer capers 计算机的鬼把戏(指利用计算机进行非法活动的花招或手段)

computer centre 电脑中心

computer code 计算机代码

computer crime 计算机犯罪

computer criminology 计算机犯罪学

computer data banks 电脑数据库

computer data compilations 计算机数据编辑物(指编辑物与其他电子数据记录一样受到同等对待)

computer evidence 计算机证据(主要基于数字电子技术产生的,以数字形式表现出来的能作为证据使用的材料。有些学者把它叫作数字证据 digital evidence)

computer hardware 计算机硬件

computer instruction 计算机指令

Computer Matching and Privacy Protection Act (美)(1988 年制定的)《电脑匹配和隐私保护法》

computer network 计算机网络,电脑网络

computer network attack 计算机网络攻击(指有关网络使用者利用一方网络存在的既定漏洞和安全缺陷,对其网络系统和资源进行的入侵和破坏等行为。网络攻击的发生并不一定意味着会发生网络战)

computer operated management　计算机操作管理
computer operator　计算机操作员
computer program　电脑程序,计算机程序
computer programming　计算机编制程序
(the) Computer Protection Act of 1989　(美)国会通过的《1989年计算机保护法案》
computer related crime（或 computer-related crime）　与计算机有关的犯罪,计算机犯罪
computer rip-offs　计算机窃贼
computer software　计算机软件
computer software copyright　电脑软件版权,计算机软件版权
computer software programs　计算机软件
computer thief　计算机盗窃犯
computer thinking　计算机思维
computer virus　计算机病毒(计算机犯罪手段之一,隐藏在可执行程序或数据文件中,在计算机内部的一种干扰程序)
computer-connected antisocial behavio(u)r　与计算机相关的反社会行为
computer-on-a-chip　微型电子计算机
computer-processing system　计算机处理系统
computer-stored records　计算机存储记录,计算机贮存记录[美国司法界达成共识的观点;计算机证据可分为计算机存储记录, 计算机生成记录 (computer-generated records)和计算机衍生记录 (computer derived evidence)或计算机衍生证据]
computerization n.　计算机化,电脑化
computerization of criminal justice data　刑事司法资料电子计算机化
computerize v.　给……装备电子计算机;使电子计算机化;用电子计算机计算
computerized data file　计算机处理的数据文件,计算机数据文件
computerized legal information service　计算机法律情报服务机构
computerized research services　计算机检索服务
computerized search systems　计算机检索系统
computerman n.　电脑学家,电脑技师
computernik n.　电脑人员;电脑迷
computing network　计算机网络
Comstock Law　(1878年)《康斯托克法》[指一个1873年的联邦制定法,该法禁止邮寄"淫秽"书籍、图片以及"避孕和有助流产的用品"。因为该制定法的偏执,产生一个相当于"过于拘谨"(prudery)的英文词——Comstock,亦称 Comstock Law]
con n./a.　反对的论点,反对者,投反对票者/骗取信任的
con game（或 job）　骗局
conamen n.　自杀,自杀行为
conation n.　意向,意图
conceal v.　隐瞒;隐匿;保守秘密
conceal a deserter　包庇逃亡者,藏匿逃亡者
concealed a.　隐藏的,隐蔽的
concealed and unreported　隐瞒不报
concealed counter-revolutionaries　暗藏的反革命分子
concealed damage　隐蔽的损坏
concealed defect　隐藏的缺陷(瑕疵)
concealed weapon　有意隐藏的凶器
concealer n.　包庇者,隐藏者
concealment n.　隐匿,隐瞒;隐藏,隐蔽;隐蔽处,隐蔽物
concealment and nondisclosure　隐匿事实,隐瞒事实
concealment of birth　隐瞒婴儿出生(罪);隐瞒婴尸罪
concealment of known defect　隐瞒(财产的)已知缺陷(瑕疵)
concede v.　承认,给予,让步,对某人让步(to sb.)
concede sth. to sb.　将某物让出给某人,允许他人得到某物
conceivable a.　相信的,想得到的,可想象的
conceive v.　孕育,怀孕;构想,设想,想象(of)
conceive a prejudice　抱有偏见
conceiving that...　可以设想
concentrate v.　全神贯注于,集中全力于 (on/upon)

concentrated expression 集中表现
concentration of powers 中央集权
concept n. 概念,观念;思想
concept of crime 犯罪的概念
concept of criminal law 刑法的概念
concept of legal entities 法人概念
concept of ordered liberty 有秩序的自由概念
conception n. 概念,观念,想法;概念的形成,思想构成;胎儿,开始怀孕
conception of a sovereign 主权观念(指拜占庭时期,有组织政治社会的全部立法权和强制权均被含蓄在权力概念之中)
conception of good 善的感知
Conception of invention 发明的构想或设想(指发明者脑中的完整设想,并可能在以后实现,法院在确定发明优先权时对此有所考虑)
conception of justice 公正原则观念
conceptual a. 概念的
conceptual framework 概念的框架
conceptual jurisprudence 概念法理学(19世纪末20世纪初在美国占有主导地位)
conceptual knowledge 理性认识
conceptual model 概念模式(型)
conceptual model of natural law theory 自然法理论的概念模型
conceptualism n. 概念论;概念主义
concern n./v. [与德文 konzern(康采恩)同];商行,企业,公司;(利害)关系,关心的事/ 涉及,使关心,使担心,对……有关系
concerning prep. 关于
concerning encumbrances on the alienated property 有关让与财产所负担的抵押权(或留置权)
Concert of Europe 欧洲协调制度
concerted a. 一致的,协调的;共同的;商定的
concerted action 一致行动,协同行动
concerted declaration 意见一致的宣言(声明)
concerted effort 一致努力;协同努力
concessi 我已授予(特指不动产租赁权的转让,但这不成为有产权根据之理由,这只不过是创设一个定期租赁的合约。)
concessimus 我们已经授予[指不动产租赁权的转让术语。这个词创设一个数名授予人或让与人(grantors)的联合合约(joint convenant)]
concession n. 特许,特许权;租让;租界;让与,让步
concession agreement 租让条约(协定);特许协议
concession for the exploitation of natural resources 开发自然资源特许权
Concession Law 《特许法》(指1995年,巴西通过的第9074号法)
concession territory 租让地,租让领土;租界
concession theory (法人成立的)特许说
concessionaire (= concessioner) n. 受让人;特许权所有人
concessional a. 让步的;特许的;优惠的
concessional disposal 廉价处理
concessional loan 优惠贷款
concessional rate 优惠价,让价
concessional sale 优惠销售
concessional terms 特惠条件
concessionary a. 许可的;让与的,特许的
concessionary and contracting companies 特许承包公司
concessionary right 租让权利,特许权利
concessioner 见 concessionaire
concessionism n. 调和主义
concessit solvere 同意支付[指有关简易合同的债务诉讼的一种形式,原告声称被告已答应支付欠款,但都不履行,被告回复"从未欠债""plea of *nunquam indebitatus*" (never indebted)](见 *indebitatus assumpsit*, common count)
conciliar a. 政务会(或理事会,地方自治会,地方议会等)的;由政务会发表的
conciliate v. 调解;安抚,抚慰,赢得
conciliation n. 1.(争端的)和解,调解(指在愉快情况下解决了争端)2.调解进程 [指由中间人(neutral person)会同争端的当事双方探讨如何解决争端。有的管辖地区如加利福尼亚州就有家庭调解法庭(Family Conciliation Courts)去帮助解决家

庭内部纠纷。亦称为 facilitation; conciliation procedure] (见 mediation; arbitration) (conciliate v.; conciliative a.; conciliatory a.; conciliator n.)
conciliation and arbitration council 调解和仲裁委员会
conciliation and arbitration court 调解和仲裁法庭
Conciliation Boards 调解委员会
conciliation court 见 small-claim(s) court
conciliation committee (或 board) 调解委员会
conciliation court 调解法庭
Conciliation Model Rules 调解示范规则
conciliation out of court 院外调解,法庭外的调解
conciliation procedure 见 conciliation
conciliation proceedings 调解程序
conciliation statement 调解声明书
conciliator n. 和解者;调解者;安抚者
conciliatory body 协调机构
conciliatory policy 调和政策,调解政策
concilium plebis (古罗马)平民议会
concious negligence 认识过失
conclude v. 结束;终结;推断,断定,作结论;缔结,订立
conclude a peace treaty 订立和约
conclude a treaty with 与……订立条约
concluded cases 已结案件
conclusion n. 1.缔结,议定 2.结论;推论 3.完成,结束,终了;结案;辩论终结 4.(古老的普通法上的)抗辩部分;(古老的海事实践中的)否定性抗辩 5.传票上的救济请求
conclusion of an expert witness 鉴定人的鉴定结论
conclusion of contract 合同的订立
conclusion of fact 从事实所得的推论,事实结论;以事实为理由,以事实为依据
conclusion of law 以法律为依据;法律结论
conclusion of marriage 成婚,完婚,缔结婚姻
conclusion of peace 媾和
conclusion of the auction 拍定(成交)
conclusion of the hearing of evidence (英)听证终结
conclusion of treaty 缔结条约
conclusion of trial 审判结束;审判终结
conclusion to the country (古代)申诉的结尾部分,请求陪审团审理诉讼的系争点(见 going to the country)
conclusive a. 决定性的;不容置疑的;确定的,最后的,结论性的;确定性的
conclusive authority 结论性意见,结论性依据
conclusive evidence (或 proof) 结论性证据;确凿证据
conclusive judg(e)ment 最后判决
conclusive opening order (诉讼上的)结论性的开始程序(指开庭程序)
conclusive presumption 结论性推定,绝对推定
conclusory a. 推断性的(表明对事实的推断而未说明所依据的事实,也称 conclusional 或 conclusionary)
conclusory labeling of statute of limitation 推断性的时效性标签
concoct v./n. 调和,调制;混合,编造(借口,谎言)/调和,混合,编造,策划
concomitant a. 相伴的,伴随的
concomitant action 共同(提起的)诉讼(指为要求某些救济而一起提起的诉讼)
concomitant circumstances 伴随的情况
concomitant evidence 当时证据,伴随证据
concord n. 1.(对非侵害产生的诉讼权利作让步的)协议 2.土地罚金协议 3.(国际间的)协议,协定 4. 和谐,一致,(国际间的)和平友好
concordare leges legibus est optimus interpretandi modus 使法律之间相协调是最好的解释方法
concordat n. 合同(契约);教廷条约(指罗马教堂与一国君主或政府间就宗教事务签订的条约);协定;协约
concordatory a. (法国政府与教会间)协议的
concordatory marriage 教廷协定的婚姻
Concordia de Singulis Causis (或 *Capitula Legis Regum Langobardorum*) 《伦巴第法汇编》(指从公元 830 年起按时间程序

concrete a. 具体的,有形的
concrete analysis 具体分析
concrete crime 具体的罪行
concrete details 具体细节,具体情节
concubinage n. 纳妾;妾制;(罗马法)为妾,妾的身份;非法同居(与 *connubium* 相对);姘居
concubinatus 纳妾;蓄妾(在罗马法中指男方与女方永久同居,而男方对女方所生子女没有主权的关系)
concubine n. 妾,姘妇,情妇
concubine's child 庶子,庶女
concubine-mother n. 庶母
concubitor n. 娶妾者
concupiscent a. 欲望强烈的;色欲强的,好色的
concur v. 1.同时发生,俱发,并发 2.同意,一致,赞成
concurator n. (罗马法)共同监护人,共同管理人(同 cocurator)
concurrence n. 1.一致意见;赞成 2.法官投票表决[根据判决意见(opinion)中所表示的意见或解释判决(judgment)的意见,由法官(投票)表示支持此项判决]3.对此表决分别写出书面判决理由(opinion),亦称 concurrening opinion"并存意见"(即3的含义)4. 接受修订[指在两院制的立法机构(bicameral legislature)中,另一院已通过一项修正案,该院即接受或认可(acceptance)]
concurrence of crimes(或 **offences**) 数罪并发,数罪俱发
concurrent n./a. 并发事件;并发物/兼任的;同时的;有同等裁判权的;共存的
concurrent actions 并存诉讼
concurrent conditions 同时履行的条件
concurrent estate (18 世纪)(财产)共有权[在美国指基于契约或遗嘱而产生的若干主体对同一块土地所共同享有的所有权,共有权分为按份共有和共同共有,共同占有的财产(指两人或多人占有的财产)。亦称 concurrent interest]
concurrent finding (由两个不同的法院对一个特别系争事实所作的)同一认定,或一致的裁决
concurrent jurisdiction 共同管辖权
concurrent lease 同时(进行的)租借
concurrent negligence 共同过失
concurrent offense 俱发罪
concurrent opinion 并存意见(指由同意案件的结果或判决但不同意该判决的逻辑或推理的法官写的意见。简言之,持并存意见的法官接受判决结果,但对结果的解释则有不同于作出判决书的独立意见。并存意见可以澄清案件结果并为判决结果提供更多理由,同时它还阐述个别法官或几个法官的推论)
concurrent power 共同权力,并存权力[指美国联邦主义(federalism)是解决整个国家政府和国家与部分政府之间分权问题的独特方法。这一制度核心是将联邦最高法院作为联邦与州关系的最后公断人。美国国会和各州议会可以就某些事项共同或单独有制定法律的权力。联邦政府和州政府可以共同或单独行使的权力]
concurrent powers 共同权力,一致的权力
concurrent punishment 并合处罚
concurrent punishment for several crimes 数罪并罚
concurrent remedies 多种救济,并存救济方式
concurrent resolution (17 世纪)共同决议[指国会参众两院中的一院通过,另一院表示同意。它表明立法机构在某一特定问题上的共同意见,它必须经两院通过,但无须总统签署。它不同于联合决议(joint resolution),后者需要总统批准 后才有法律效力]
concurrent sentence 合并服刑;累积服刑;累计判决
concurrent summons 同时发出的传票
concurrent writ (由法院发出的)正、副本并存的令状,并存的法庭命令
concurring a. 赞同的,赞成的;并发的
concurring opinion (判决中的)并存意见,同意意见(指一个或少数法官所提出的意见,它赞同法庭的判决,但有自己的不同于法庭多数成员对判决所持的理由)

concussion n. 脑震荡(指轻度脑颅损伤)
condemn v. 1.宣告有罪,定罪[司法上宣布(某人)有罪]2.没收或征用财产(指没定并宣告财产归公使用。见 eminent domain)3.裁定建筑物(依法裁定一幢建筑物不适宜居住)4.裁定饮食[依法裁定食品或饮料(food or drink)不适于人们消费]5.(海商法)宣布一只船没有归属政府作为捕获品或不适于服务
condemnable a. 可定罪的;该受责备的
condemnatio n. (罗马法)判决程式,判罚[指程式诉讼(formula)的四大部分之一,即授权审判员根据当事人提出的事实是否真实而定判罚或开释(见 *absolutio*),所有诉讼均应经历判决程式,但预备诉讼(*actio praeiudicialis*)除外。比较常见的判罚程式表现为要求败诉方向胜诉方支付一笔款项]
condemnation n. 1.定罪,谴责;宣告有罪 2.征收(指政府给予适当奖金或赔偿费不经过征求私有主的同意将他的不动产收归公用)3.(判处)捕获船舶的裁定 4.(由法院)判付之款
condemnation action 征用之诉(指因国家征用财产而要求合理补偿所引起的诉讼)
condemnation suit 见 condemnation action
condemnation money (由法院)判付之款
condemnation proceedings 定罪程序
condemnator 控告人,检控人
condemnatory a. 定罪的,判罪的;(表示)谴责的
condemnee n. 财产被征用人(指其财产被征收公用或被公用工程项目使用的人)
condemned a. 已被判罪的;用于被判罪者的;被没收的;被认为不当的;被认为不适用的
condemned building 被宣布为危险的建筑;封闭楼宇
condemned cell (或 ward) 死囚牢房
condemned criminal 已决犯,死刑犯
condemned prisoner 死刑犯,死囚
condemned property 被没收财产
condemner (=condemnor) n. 1.宣判者;定罪者 2.财产征用人,征用财产的部门或单位(指征用财产公用的人或部门)

condensed balance sheet 简明资产负债表
condescend v. 1.俯就,屈尊 2.堕落;丢丑 3.(苏格兰)对……详细说明(upon)
condescend to take bribes 堕落到受贿
condescend upon particulars (苏格兰)对诉状详加说明
condescendence n. (苏格兰)原告人的详细陈诉书
condescendence in numbered paragraphs of the fact 对事实的分段详细说明
condictio indebiti 返还请求权,错债索回之诉,对抗债索回之诉
condictio (罗马法,大陆法)索回,追回;对人诉讼的术语:诉,诉求;请求返还之诉[指要求返还金钱对人之诉讼,为返还债务之诉。这里含义是指欠债(debt)必须从广义理解,不仅是契约性的抵偿,也是准契约性或侵权的权利主张(quasi-contractual or tort claims)。*condictio* 这个词常基于应有给付债务(obligation)或作为的义务。在英语中被称为 condiction; action of debt。复数为 condictiones; condictious, condictitious a.]
condictio causa data causa non secuta. An action for recovery of money paid when the consideration for the payment has not been furnished. (罗马法,大陆法)因对价落空,要求返还财产之诉
condictio ex lege (诉讼形式不当而)法律上可给予救济的诉讼
condictio indebitati (原告)要求(被告)返还错误给付的诉讼
condictio ob turpem causam 追偿支付用于非法或不道德目的的金钱之诉
condictio rei furtivae 追还被盗财物的诉讼
condictio sine causa 追偿无对价的给付物之诉
conditio 条件
Conditio illicita habetur pro non adjecta. An unlawful condition is deemed as not annexed. 附加非法的条件等于没有附加。
conditio impossibilis 不能实现的条件
conditio necessaria 必要条件
condition n./v. (14世纪) 1.条件[指未来发生的和不确定的事实或行为,据此条件

才导致权利和义务的依存。一种不确定的事实和行为,要根据产生条件的实现与否才可以使其权利义务存在、中止和终止。比如,Jones 允诺支付给 Smith 500 美元修理汽车,Smith 未修理汽车(一个默示或推定条件)致使 Jones 免除对 Smith 支付的允诺] 2.合同遗嘱或其他文据中的条件、条款或先决条件,可构成文件中的重要事项。如果法院解认定合同某一条款属于"条件",则它的不真实或违反将使得义务当事方有资格免除全部合同责任 3.(广义)合同中的条款、规定条文或条项 4. 附属于转让财产的合格证,它规定不管特殊情况发生与否,这一地产将会存在、扩大、被废弃或被转让 5.存在的状态、关键品质和法律地位。"condition"这个词在财产法中使用,也在合同中使用。有时它的意思很灵活,可以与"term""provision"或"clause"成为同义词/ 1.决定,规定,为……的条件;制约⟨he never conditioned his going upon the weather⟩(他从不因天气不好而不去) 2.使处于正常(或良好)状态⟨condition the air in the workshop⟩(调节车间空气) 3.使适应,使习惯于环境 4. 检验 5.(美)要求学生补考 6.引起(人或动物的)条件反射

condition for validity 有效条件
condition implied by law 见 constructive condition
condition implied-in-law 见 constructive condition
condition of affairs 事态
condition of alien 外国人身份
condition of appeal 上诉条件
condition of crime 犯罪条件
condition of grant 让与条件
condition of insurance 保险条件
condition of lawsuit 诉讼条件
condition of punishment 处罚条件
condition of recognition 承认条件
condition of recognizance 保释(具结)条件
condition of sale 销售条件,拍卖条件
condition of servitude 奴隶身份
condition of the injury 伤势
condition of validity 有效条件

condition pbturpem vel iniustam causam 因受讹诈的要求返还之诉
condition precedent 先决条件(亦称停止条件)
condition resolutive (=condition subsequent) 解除条件
condition resolutoire 解除条件
condition sine qua non (简称 C. S. Q. N. 公式)"如无前者即无后者"的关系
condition subsequent 后决条件(亦称解除条件)
conditional a. 有条件的;有限制的;受条件限制的;附条件的
conditional acceptance 有条件的承兑(港译:附条件认付)
conditional admissibility 有限制的接受(证据)
conditional agreement 有条件的协定;附条件的协议
conditional appearance 有条件的出庭
conditional bill 有条件的票据
conditional bill of sale 有条件的卖契
conditional bond 附条件的债券
conditional condemnation 缓刑
conditional contraband 附有条件的禁制品
conditional delivery 有条件的交付,附条件的交货
conditional discharge (英)附条件释放(令),有条件撤销
conditional divorce 见 conversion divorce
conditional endorsement 附条件的背书
conditional estate 有限制的不动产权(见 estate on condition)
conditional fee 有条件的世袭地产(见 base fee)
conditional gift 附条件的赠与
conditional guaranty 有条件的担保
conditional intent 间接故意
conditional legacy 附条件遗赠,有条件遗赠[指可能是有效的遗赠或因为一个事件(an event)的发生或未发生而成为无效的遗赠]
conditional limitation 有限制的时效;有条件的期限
conditional liquidity 有条件的(财产)流

动能力

conditional new trial 附条件的重新审理

conditional non prosecution 有条件不起诉(指联邦德国自1975年起实行检察官对罪行轻微或轻微财产罪的嫌疑人可取得他的同意,以强征一笔罚金为条件,决定不予起诉,但不得对此项决定进行上诉)

conditional obligation 附条件的债务,附条件之债

conditional on overall plan 决定于总的计划

conditional order 附条件的命令

conditional order for a won trial 附条件的重审令

conditional owner 有条件的所有人

conditional pardon 有条件的赦免

conditional payment 有条件的支付

conditional presumption 条件性推定

conditional privilege 有限制的特权

conditional promise 有条件的允诺

conditional proof 有条件的证据(指只要没有其他事实反驳,这个事实就是证据)

conditional ratification 条件性修正,有条件的修正

conditional recognition 附条件的承认

conditional release (或 **provisional release**) 假释;有条件的释放

conditional right 附有条件的权利

conditional sale 有条件的出售,附条件的销售

conditional universal jurisdiction 有限普遍管辖(原则)[普遍管辖原则有广义与狭义之分。狭义的管辖原则又称有限普遍管辖原则,也即行为人所在地国的管辖原则(*forum deprehensionis*)或控制地国管辖原则(jurisdiction of custodial state)。狭义管辖原则是指一个和犯罪没有任何具体连接点或联系因素的国家如果要对犯有国际罪行的罪犯进行调查、起诉和审判,只有当该人出现在该国或在该国被捕或控制起来后,该国才可起诉他。被告在该国领域内是行使普遍管辖权的先决条件]

conditional will 附条件的遗嘱

conditionality n. 渐进性;有条件性,条件限制,制约性,条件性

conditionally capable of acting 有条件的

行为能力

conditions and warranties 主要条款与从属条款(指各种版权合同中常使用的术语,违反了主要条款则构成违约;而违反从属条款,则不一定构成违约)

conditions for loans 贷款条件

conditions of an action 诉讼条件

conditions of an action in the private prosecution 自诉的诉讼条件

conditions of an action in the public prosecution 公诉的诉讼条件

conditions of labo(u)r 劳动条件

conditions of the contract 合同(契约)条件;招标细则

conditions unchangeable clause 情势不变条款

condominia (大陆法)共有权,有限制的所有权

condominium (由两个政府共同行使政府职能的)共管;共管下的政府(或领土);(多人合住的建筑物里的)单独住房的个人所有权与建筑物共同使用部分的共有权相结合的所有权;公寓

condonable a. 可宽恕的,可赦免的

condonation n. 宽恕(尤指夫妻间,一方犯了婚姻罪行,受害一方宽恕对方),不咎(罪过)

condone v. 宽恕,不咎(罪过);(行为等)抵消(过失)

Condorcet jury theorem 孔多塞陪审团定理[法国哲学家孔多塞(Condorcet, 1743—1794)证明的一种理论:如果单个投票者的正确率超过5%,那么投票者数量越大,集体(大多数)决定的正确率就越高。这条不仅适用陪审团,也适用于民主理论。]

Condorcet's voting paradox 孔多塞投票悖论[法国哲学家孔多塞(1743—1794)发现的悖论:大多数人的投票可引导不确定群体或"骑墙"派的偏好。投票者1偏好:A>B>C;投票者2偏好:B>C>A;投票者3偏好:C>A>B;给定的偏好如此,但大多数人的偏好是 A>B,且 B>C,但 C>A。同样是阿罗定理和社会选择理论的核心。他的含有此悖论的著作未引起人们的重视,直到邓肯·布莱克(Duncan Black)的

著作中才被融入公共选择理论]
conduce v. 导致(to),有助于(to)
conducing conduct 扶助行为
conducive a. 有助于……的,有益于……的,助长的(to)
conduct n./v. 实施;处理;经营,进行;行为,举动;品格,操行;指导,带领/实施;处理;指挥;引导;经营;进行
conduct an investigation 进行调查
conduct in question 有问题的行为
conduct in violation of security administration 违反治安管理的行为
conduct money 证人补助费(指补助证人在出庭作证时,来往法庭的交通费用)
conduct of business 事务处理,商业经营
conduct of bussiness in the House 议院的议事行为
conduct of government 政府工作,政府行为
conduct of proceedings 诉讼行为
conducting another's affair without his request 未经请求处理他人事务
conducting jury of non-jury trials 实施陪审团或非陪审团的审理
conducting prosecution 提起诉讼,提起公诉
conductor n. 1.指挥者,向导,管理人 2.(乐队)指挥;导体 3.售票员,(美)列车员 4.雇主;租借者
conduit taxation 见 pass-through taxation
confabulate v. 讨论,会谈,谈心(with)
confarreatio 共食婚(指罗马法中一种宗教上需经繁冗的结婚仪式的婚姻)
confederacy n. 1.共谋,违法的结社 2.联盟,同盟,联邦 3.(the Confederacy)(美史)美国南部邦联(1860—1861 年间由南部 11 个州组成的)
confederate n./a. 1.同犯,共犯;同谋者,党羽 2.同盟者;联盟者,同盟国/同盟的,联合的;(大写)(美史)南部联邦的
confederate government 邦联政府
Confederate States of America 美国南部各州联盟(指美国南部南卡罗来、佐治亚、佛罗里达、阿拉巴马、密西西比、路易斯安那、得克萨斯、北卡罗来、田纳西和阿肯色州等 11 个州于 1861 年组成联盟,并发动美国的南北战争)

confederation n. 邦联,同盟,(大写)(美史)(1781—1789 年间 13 个州的)邦联
confederaton of states 国家联盟(指存在一个中央政府联盟,行使一定权力的联盟,但并不控制成员国的所有对外关系,不是一个国家而是几个国家的存在才符合国际目的)
confer v. 授予(称号,学位等);交换意见,协商,比较,见
conference n. 讨论,会谈;讨论会;(正式)会议;协商会;(美)联合会;(律师间对案件的)讨论会;(各国行驶同一航线的)船舶公司公会
conference agenda 会议议程
conference freight rate 协议运费率
conference lines 班轮公会
conference of rulers (马来西亚)统治者会议
conference on judicial work 司法工作会议
Conference on Security and Cooperation in Europe 欧洲安全与合作会议(1973—1975 年,在芬兰赫尔辛基召开)
conference tariff 班轮公会运价表
conferment n. 授予,颁给
conferrable a. 能授予的
conferrer n. 授予人
confess v. 供认,坦白,认罪,承认,交代;忏悔;表明信仰
confess after torture 屈打成招
confess (oneself) to be guilty 服罪
confess without being pressed 不打自招
confessed a. 坦白的;认罪的,自己承认的;肯定的,毫无疑问的,众所周知的
confesser (=confessor) n. 1.认罪者,自首者,供认不讳者 2.(在受迫害时)声明坚持信仰的教徒 3.听取忏悔的神甫
confession n. 供认,坦白,交代,招供,自认有罪(尤指被控犯罪的人自认有罪,如果认罪确属自愿,法庭可接受它作为证据);供状,自白书;(表明信仰等的)声明
confession admitting guilt 认罪的自白
confession and avoidance (17 世纪)承认但无效答辩[一种答辩,指被告承认原告所提出的事实,但同时提出另外的事实(additional facts)以否定承认原告所申诉事实的法律效

果。比如本身占有过失(contributory negligence)在比较过失到来之前(before the advert of comparative negligence)的答辩就是承认但无效答辩(confession and avoidance),亦称 avoidance；plea in confession and avoidance；plea of confession and avoidance。见 affirmative defense；defense 1]

confession and defence of the accused 被告人的供述和辩护

confession in a public court 在公开庭审中认罪

confession of defence 辩护(供)状词

Confession of Faith (对长老制教义之一种阐述的)信纲声明

confession of judgment 判决的接受,判决的认诺(=*cognovit* of judgment)

confession of judgment provision 判决认诺规定,判决接受规定

confession of ville(i)nage (中世纪在法庭上的)农奴身份的承认

confessional a. 坦白的；供认的；忏悔的；公开声明的

confidence n. 1.确定的期盼,信任；坚定的信托,依赖；忠实⟨the partner has confidence in associate's work⟩(合伙人在合伙工作中有信心)2.信赖(依赖或信赖他人的酌处能力)；一种信托关系⟨she took her coworker into her confidence⟩(她把同事变成知己)3.信托构成的保密关系(commnicate)或信托关系,旨在不得公开披露,特别是受到律师、当事人保护的保密关系或类似的保密特权(similar privilege)⟨the confidence of lawyer and client⟩(律师和当事人之间的信赖关系或保密关系)[按照美国律师协会(ABA)的职业责任法规(Code of Professional Responsability),律师不得披露当事人的信赖秘密(confidence),除非充分披露得到当事人的同意。参见《惩戒性规则》第4—101条(DR. 4-101)(注:《示范职业责任法规》中的一部)。见 secret ②]

confidence game 骗局

confidence man (诈骗钱财的)骗子

confidence relationship 保密关系(英美法系中的概念,又称信任关系。指当创意人

与含意接受人之间存在事实上的保密关系,如创意人在保密状态下将其创意提供给了接受人,或后者在保密状态下获悉了相关创意,创意人即可依据保密关系要求未经允可擅自披露或使用其创意的接受人给予赔偿,而不论二者之间是否形成有书面的保密协议。)

confidential a. 机密的,秘密的；参与机密的；取得信任的,心腹的,极受信任的,易于信任他人的

confidential agent 密使

confidential clerk 机要秘书

confidential communication 通讯秘密的特权(指诉讼当事人和律师之间凡与诉讼进行有关的书面或口头的通讯,有特权不在法庭上作披露；对夫妻之间通讯亦然,均可拒绝提供作证)

confidential creditor 优先债权人

confidential debt 应优先偿还的债务

confidential document 机密文件；机密证件

confidential employee 机要人员

confidential information 机密情报

confidential inquiry 秘密调查

confidential paper 机密文件

confidential police information 机密的警方情报(或信息)

confidential relation 密切的关系,受信任之关系(指一个人有权期望从另一个人那里得到正常的关照和实在的彼此关系,如客户和律师、孩子和父母,如果存在很重大的义务或责任,即成为一种信托关系——fiduciary relationship)

confidential report 机密报告

confidential war 机密情报战

confidentiality n. 机密性,秘密性(指①对律师或为律师工作的任何人所要求的；不透露来自客户那里的情况,只有在律师听到其客户可能犯罪的情况例外；②对其他某些人如牧师、医生、丈夫和妻子等要求的不泄露在某些情况下所获得的情况。这也称为特许的通讯——privileged communication)

configuration n. 结构；形状,外形

confine n./v. (常用复)界限；范围,区域/禁闭；限制,控制

confined a. 有限的；狭窄的

confined by self-imposed limitation 自律约束,自我强制约束
confined explosion 局部爆炸
confined waters 限定的海域
confinement n. 禁闭;限制;拘留
confines a ballot 确认投票有效
confines a vote 确认表决有效
confirm v. 1.使(权力)巩固,使坚定 2.使有效,批准,进一步认可;确认……有效 3.确实,进一步证实
confirmable a. 可进一步确定的;能证实的;可批准的
* *Confirmare nemo potest prius quam jus ei acciderit.* No one can confirm before the right accrues to him. 任何人在权利生效之前都不得行使该项权利。
* *Confirmat usum qui tollit abusum.* He confirms a use who removes an abuse. 要防止滥用(权力或权利)就得确定(权力或权利)行使范围。
confirmation n. 确认,证实;证据;认可,批准
confirmation bill 确定的法案
confirmation commission 保兑手续费
confirmation of order 订货承诺书,订单确认书
confirmative a. 确实的,证实的;批准的
confirmatory sample (商品订货的)确认样本,确认样品
confirmed a. 被证实的;已认可的;顽固的,根深蒂固的;成习惯的
confirmed (letter of) credit 保兑信用证
confirmed criminal 惯犯
confirmed evidence 证实了的证据
confirmed habit 积习
confirmed invoice 保兑发货票
confirmed thief 惯偷惯窃者,惯窃
confirming bank 保兑银行,确认银行
confirming house 保付公司;保付商行
confirming judg(e)ment 确认判决
confirming order 保证书,确认书,保付书
confiscable a. 可没收的;可充公的
confiscate v./a. 没收,查抄;征用;充公/被没收的;被查抄的;被充公的;被征用的
confiscated goods 没收的货物

confiscation n. 没收,查抄;征用,充公
confiscation of land 征用土地,没收土地
confiscation of property 没收财产
confiscation of the driving licence 吊销驾驶执照
confiscation order 没收令
confiscation voucher 没收凭证;扣留凭单
confiscator n. 没收人,查抄人
confiscatory a. 没收的;征用的;充公的
confiscatory decree 没收令
confiscatory taxation 充公赋税
confisk v. (古)= confiscate
conflagration n. 大火灾;烧死;焚烧;(战争等)爆发
conflict n. 冲突;抵触,争论,斗争,战斗,倾轧
conflict justice 冲突法上的公正
conflict mobile 可变冲突
conflict of authority 权威冲突[指两个或两个法院之间(常为同级终审法院)关于法律原则或适用上有严重分歧;学者们之间或学者论著的不同观点]
conflict of interest 利益冲突(指损害他人利益方可获得私利或执行公务者利用执行公务而获取私利的情况);(美)违背公众利益的行为
Conflict of Jurisdiction Model Act 《管辖权冲突示范性》
conflict of jurisdictions (法院)管辖权的冲突(见 conflict of laws)
conflict of law and equity (英美法)普通法与衡平法的冲突
conflict of law rule 冲突法规则
conflict of laws 法律上的冲突(统称冲突法,又译国际私法,这是因为冲突法主要是解决对私人之间关系的不同国家的不同法律规定的冲突,包括管辖权的冲突)
conflict of marriage laws (不同国家的)婚姻法的冲突
conflict of nationalities 国籍冲突
conflict of opinions 意见冲突,意见分歧
conflict (of) rules (解决国际法上法律冲突的)冲突法规;冲突规范
conflict out v. (1981年)取消资格,使法官、律师失去资格,回避[指法官或代理

人、律师因涉及与一方当事人的利害关系而应回避〈the judge was conflicted out of the case by his earlier representation of one of the litigants〉(该法官因其早先代理过一方当事人而应回避此案)]

conflicting a. 冲突的,抵触的

conflicting presumption 冲突性推定

conflicting publication 冲突出版(指同一作者以完全相同素材在不同出版社投的不同书稿。西方的大出版公司的格式合同中,往往要求作者承担义务,不使冲突出版情况发生)

conflicting rights 冲突性权利(指两个或两个以上的独立权利人分别就同一权利自认为所有人)

conflicts of laws (1827年)1.法律冲突,法律抵触[指一个案件中的和解协议或意外事件或其案情均涉及两个或两个以上管辖区,或其当事方或其中一方的权利、义务、诉讼标的或多或少发生在另一国家、另一地区或另一州,而两国或两地区(州)处理该案件的法律规定不同,存在法律的冲突或抵触。缩略为 conflicts。见 choice of law(s)]2.冲突法,国际私法[指调整这类法律差异或冲突以及决定在民事关系中适用何种法律的一个部门法或一个法律体系(body of juris prudence),亦称 private international law]

conflicts resolutions 冲突解决

conflicts-mandatory rules 冲突法强制性规范

conform v. 1.(使)一致,(使)符合 2.(使)遵照,(使)遵奉;(英法)遵奉国教

conform to proof 与证据相一致

conform to rules 遵守规则

conform to (或 with) the interests of the people 符合人民的利益

conformable a. 相似的,一致的,适合的,符合的;顺从的

conformance (=conformity) 一致

conformation n. 一致,符合;构造,形态

conformed copy 相吻合的复制品(指带有书面解释,签署的文件真实的复制品)

conforming goods 同种类物

conformity n. 依照,遵照,遵奉;适合,和……一致

Conformity Act of 1872 (美)《1872年一致法》(指1872年制定的一项联邦法,规定联邦地区法院的诉讼程序,除衡平和海事外应尽量与当地州法院处理类似案件的诉讼程序相一致,1938年《联邦民事诉讼规则》失效后,该法废止。有时亦称 Conformity Statute)

conformity and comity 遵照与礼让

conformity hearing 核实是否一致的听审(听证)(指核实法庭指定的听证是否与胜诉方草拟判决与法院决定一致)

conformity use (美)符合(规定的)使用(指符合城市区划和土地使用计划法规允准的建筑物的使用)

confraternity n. (宗教或慈善团体的)社团,协会,公会,团体

confront v. 对证,使对质;使对面,正视,对抗;对照;面对

confront the accused with the accuser 使被告与原告对质

confrontation n. 对抗;对证;对质

confrontation clause (美)对质条款(指美国联邦宪法第六修正案,"在一切刑事诉讼中,被告应享有下列权利:……获知控告的性质和原因;同原告证人对质;以强制程序取得有利于自己的证据……"保障刑事被告人有权直接与控方证人对质。并向该证人进行交叉询问。如果证人十分脆弱,特别像一个未成年人被指称为性虐待的受害者,则此项权利会被撤销)

confrontation of both sides 互相对质,双方对质

confrontation of witnesses 证人对质

confrontation of witness 对质,对证,与证人对质(指美国联邦宪法第六修正案在刑事诉讼中得到了强化,规定中说:"被告享有同原告证人对质权利",这一规定使被告人面对证人能对其证词提出反对意见,或使证人能辨别被告人。对质权的实质不在于使被告人能见到证人,而是保障被告人有质问对方证人的宪法权利。作为一个现实问题,法院在没有其他机会的情况下已经允许使用一些证据如采用垂死的人的陈述和在以前审判中已作证的已

故证人的言词证据)
Confucian n. 儒学
Confucianism n. 儒教
confusable a. 可能被混淆的,可能被弄糊涂的
confuse v. 混淆;混同,弄错
confuse black and white 颠倒黑白(混淆是非)
confuse right and wrong 混淆是非
confuse the public 混淆视听
confusio 混合;混杂;(罗马法)(财产的)混同
confusion n. 1.货物的混合,混同,混淆,(财产的)混同 2.相当于普通法上的"merger"(指许多物混合在一起难以区分,或所有权分属多人的物混在一起无法识别。见 merger 9) 3.(商标)消费者对货物和服务(services)的起源产生错误的相信(见 likelihood-of-confusion test)
confusion issues 系争点的混淆
confusion of debts 见 merger 9
confusion of goods 同样物件的混淆,货物的混同
confusion of rights 见 merger 9
confusion of titles (大陆法系)两个相同土地所有权合并同一个名下(见 merger 9)
confute v. 证明……为错误;驳倒(某人论据等)
congeneric a. 同种的,同性质的,同源的,同属的
congenial a. 同类的,相适应的
congested district 交通拥挤地区
congestion n. 拥挤,拥塞;充满
conglomerate n. 密集体(如人群、房屋等);(跨行业、企业的)联合大企业(或公司)
conglomeration n. 混合体,凝聚体
congregation n. 集会;人群;(天主教的)红衣主教会议;大学教职员工全体会议
congregational missionary parents 基督教公理会传教士父母
congress n. 代表大会,大会;议会;委员会;(大写)(美)国会;(国会或议会)会议(期);聚会,社交
congress of workers and staff members (中)职工代表大会

Congress Party (印度)国大党
congress silence 国会的沉默
congressional a. 代表大会的,大会的,议会的,委员会的,(美)国会的
congressional action 国会议案,国会法案
congressional bills (美)国会议案
Congressional Budget Office (美)国会预算局[指美国联邦政府立法部门的一个机构,负责预测经济趋向、制定费用评估、对有关预算领域进行特别研究,发布有关研讨联邦消费和收入水平以及基金配置的年度报告。该预算局是根据《1974年国会预算和扣押控制法》(Congressional Budget and Impoundment Control Act of 1974)设立的。缩略为 CBO]
congressional clerk (美)国会书记员
Congressional committee (1855年)国会委员会(指众议院委员会、参议院委员会或两院联合委员会)
congressional debate 大会辩论
congressional district (美)众议员选区(指每个州按地理位置划分若干个区,每个区选一个众议院的议员)
Congressional Globe (美)《国会世界》[指由私人发行的国会听证议事录,该记录是唯一记载自1833年起在国会发表的演讲和陈述的。直到1873年,公开出版的《国会议事录》(Congressional Record)取代了《国会世界》。它涵盖了美国国会第23届至第42届辩论的内容。见 Congressional Record]
Congressional Information Service (美)国会情报服务处
congressional investigatory power 国会调查权
congressional legislation 国会立法
congressional opponents 国会里的反对派
Congressional Quarterly (美)《国会季刊》(指着重介绍国会活动,也包括一些条约的有用资料的国会出版物)
Congressional Quarterly Almanac (美)《国会季度会议年鉴》(指一届国会的立法概要,每年出版的国会活动的背景材料)
Congressional Record (美)(每日发布的)《国会议事录》(指美国参众两院议员代表在听证会上处理事务的官方记录,在印制之前

国会议员经允准对他们的发言进行编写作为内容插入,但绝不允许在未经相应议院同意的情况下对这些内容扩充或修订。见 Congressional Globe)
congressional regulatory statute 国会立法
congressional report (美)国会报告
Congressional Research Service (美)国会研究所[指美国国会图书馆内一个非党派机构,它为国内委员会及其会员研究分析立法问题。美国国会创立此机构于1914年,命名为立法参考所(Legislative Reference Service),再次命名于1970年,缩略为 CRS]
congressional statute 国会法规
congressional subpoena (美)国会传证令
congressional system 国会体制系统
congressman n. (美)国会议员(尤指美众议院议员)
congressmember n. 国会议员
congressus 性交
congresswoman n. (美)国会女议员(尤指美国女众议员)
congruence (congruency) n. 适合,一致,和谐
congruent generalisation (generalization) 协调的一般化
conjecture n./v. 推测,设想,假设,推测得出的结论
conjoint a. 结合的,联合的
conjoint robbery 共同抢劫
conjoint sovereignty 联合主权
conjugal a. 婚姻的,夫妇的,夫妇间的
conjugal family 无子女的家庭
conjugal offence 婚姻上的违法(犯罪)行为
conjugal relation 夫妻关系
conjugal right 夫妻同居权
conjugal rights 配偶权利,婚姻权利,两个间彼此的权利和特权(指夫妻间有相伴、同居以及性交的权利,但双方均不得强制实现这些权利。亦称 alienation of affections consortium)
conjugal union 夫妻结合关系
conjugal visit 夫妻间造访(指由合法的夫妻的一方来看望另一方,可获准同居、性生活等)

conjugium 结婚
conjunct a. 结合的,联合的,连接的
conjunction n. 同时发生;同处发生;结合,联合,并合;关联一连串事件(或情况)的结合
conjunction denials 联合否认[指高强度技术性诉辩时期的三种类型的否认,另两种为蕴涵肯定之否认(negative pregnant)和可争议的否认(argumentative denials)]
conjunctly (或 **jointly**) **and severally** 有连带责任地
conjuration n. 1.符咒,魔法 2.祈求,祈祷 3.(古英国法)犯罪企图,(经宣誓合伙进行危害公众的)同谋,阴谋
conjurator n. 同谋者;阴谋者
conman n. 骗子
connected a. 有关联的,相关的;联结的;连贯的
connected transaction 关联事件;关联交易
connecting affiliates 企业联营,企业联号
connecting factor 相互关联的因素;(复)(国际法)连结因素(旧译:系属)
connecting ground (国际私法)连结根据
connecting-up doctrine 相关原则、关联原则(指庭审时允许证据被采纳的规则。提供证据的当事人后来提出其他证据与早先证据相关联,该证据即可被法庭采纳)
connection (=connexion) n. 关系;联系;连接关系;上下文关系,方面;(通信等)联系手段,(车船等)联运;(贸易上的)往来关系;(电话等的)通信线路;(复)亲戚(尤指姻亲);(总称)顾客;(政治、宗教等)团体,教派;性交
connectors n. 联系者,联结物
Connelly Amendment 康诺利修正案(指1946年美国依照国际法院规定第36条第2项,接受国际法院管辖声明中附有"由美国所认定在本质上属于美国之内管辖的一切争执事件"不受国际法院管辖的保留条件,被称为"康诺利修正案")
connexio 附合
connexion n. 贸易上的往来关系;派系,宗派;政治关系;性交(=connection)
connexion ticket 联运票
connivance n. 纵容,默许(指丈夫默许或

纵容妻子犯通奸罪来获得离婚,该纵容或默许如被证实,则丈夫不能获得离婚的判决)
connive v. 默许,纵容;共谋;取得默契(with)
connoissement (法)(由船长或其代理人签署的)运货单
connotation n. 内涵,含蓄
connubiality n. 婚姻,有关婚姻生活中应有之事
connubium 婚姻;(罗马法)合法婚姻(与concubinage相对)
conociamento (西班牙法)具结,保证
conquest n. 1.征服,赢得,获得 2.(英)(继承法)获得产 3.(采邑法)购买 4.掠取物,掠取(土)地
Conquest n. (英史)征服(指1066年威廉征服英国,常作Norman Conquest)
consanguine a. (=consanguineous,亦作consanguined)
consanguineous a. 同血缘的,同宗的,近亲的
consanguineous marriage 近亲结婚
consanguineus 血亲
consanguineus frater 同父异母兄弟
consanguini 同父异母血亲
consanguinity n. 同宗,同血缘,血亲,亲属关系(见collateral consanguinity, lineal consanguinity), 亲密关系
conscience n. 良心,道德感,正义感
conscience clause 良心条款(指出于良心关系而不能遵守某一规定时,可不受处分的规定)
conscience of the court 法院的良知(指审理法院以衡平法上的权力根据公平、公正以及合理的理念作出裁判,解决争端)
conscience-money n. (为求得)心安(而付的)钱(如补交所逃避的税款等),补缴款项;悔罪金
conscientious a. 凭良心做的,有道德感的;认真的,诚心诚意的
conscientious conduct 正当行为,光明的行为
conscientious objection 出于良心上的反对(服兵役或参加战争)

conscientious objector 出于良心而拒绝(服兵役或参加战争)者
conscientious scruple 良心上的顾忌(指出于良心或道德而不是出于理性的原因,拒绝参加死刑案陪审团、服兵役或参加战争等)
conscious a. 有意识的,自觉的,意识到的
conscious activity 能动性,自觉行动
conscious application of laws 自觉适用法律
conscious uncoupling 理性分手[指一对夫妻或情侣为了以友好、温和的方式离婚或分手而进行的仪式程序(动词形式为consciously uncouple),并声明表示共同抚养孩子]
consciousness n. 意识,觉悟
conscript father 参议员,立法委员;(古罗马的)元老院议事官
conscription n. 征兵;征集,征募
conscription age 兵役年龄,应征年龄
conscription law 征兵法,兵役法
conscription of wealth (未应征人交纳的)兵役税;(战时向富人征收的)财产税
conscription system 兵役制度
consecrate v. 奉献,贡献
consecutive a. 继续的,连续的;依次的
consecutive confession 连续自白
consecutive days 连续日
consecutive hours 连续时
consecutive sentence 连续判决[指在一个处以监禁的判决后,紧接着作出另一判决,后一判决对前一判决必须有连续性。此类判决可适用于缓刑判决。亦称前后连续判决(from and after sentence)]
consecutive term 连任(职务)
consecutive voyages charter 连续航次租船
conseil d'administration 董事会
Conseil d'Etat (法)行政法院,(法)参政院(又译:最高行政法院。见Council of State)
conseil de surveillance 监督委员会,监事会
consensu 一致同意;意思表示一致;合意
consensual a. 两愿的;经双方同意而产生的

consensual contract 诺成合同(契约)(指经缔约双方同意而成立者)
consensual contract *bonae fidei* 善意诺成合同(契约)
consensual creditor 合意的贷款人,合意的债权人
consensual homosexual sodomy 合意的同性男奸行为
consensual marriage (仅由当事人)双方同意的婚姻(见 common law marriage)
consensual nature 合意性质
consensual obligation 合意之债;诺成之债
consensual process 一致程序,合意程序
consensual union 同居,(罗马法)姘居
consensual verdict 合意裁决
consensualism n. (合同的)合意主义
consensus n. 协议;共同意见;共识;意思表示一致;舆论
consensus ad idem (双方就同一事物)达成的协议,意思表示一致,合意
* *Consensus facit legem.* Consent makes the law. 协议产生法律效力。
consensus tollit errorem. The acquiescence of a party in an error obviates its effect. Consent removes an error. A person cannot object to something he has consented. 合意可排除错误。如已经同意不得有反悔。
consent n. (14世纪)1.合意赞成,认可,知情同意(见 informed consent),允诺[指一个有法定资格的人(competent person),尤其自愿地对某种行为或目的给予的表示。这是合法的有法律效力的同意。"consent"是"积极答辩"(affirmative defense)。对于凌辱、殴打、相关侵权以及诸如此类的侵权,如诽谤、干预私事、侵占他人财产和侵犯均可作积极答辩。consent 也可以是对"犯罪"(crime)或罪行的辩护。即如果受害者具有辩护(consent)能力,而且此辩护(consent)或否定犯罪要素,或挫败法律寻求阻止的伤害。参见《示范刑法典》第2.11节(Model Penal Code § 2.11)] 2.(议会法)采纳,采用;正式通过(见 adoption 5)
consent decree (衡平法诉讼中)双方(两造)同意的判决;协议裁决
consent in writing 书面同意
consent judg(e)ment (两造)同意的判决,同意(和解)的判决;合意判决(指美国民诉中,法院依据与诉讼人的合意协议作出的判决)
consent order 同意令(指法院给被告的一种指令,禁止其继续进行某行为,被告只需同意接受此令,至于该行为是否确实,是否违法,法院不予追查)
consentaneous a. 一致的,同意的,适合的;经一致同意的
consenting suspect 认定的嫌疑犯
consequence n. 1.结果,后果 2.推断,论断 3.重要(性),重大,举足轻重,自高自大
consequence of infraction of the criminal law 违反刑法的法律后果
consequence of the court's reasoning 联邦最高法院推论的结果
consequences of violation 违反的后果
consequent a. 由某事物引起的,随之发生的
consequent ideal law 由此(以上事物)而引起的理想的法律
consequential a. 作为结果的,相应而生的;接着发生的;推论(断)的;间接的;引起重要结果的,重大的,自大的;重要的
consequential amendment 相应修正案;相应的修正
consequential crime 间接犯罪
consequential damages 结果损害赔偿
consequential injury 间接伤害;继起的伤害;事后产生的损害
consequential loss 从属损失,间接损失
consequential man 重要人物
consequential provision 继起性的法律规定(指一法律制定后,随之所需制定的另一些法律规定)
consequential rights 继起权
consequentialism n. 结果论
consequently ad. 因而,所以
conservancy n. 1.(自然资源等的)保护,管理;资源保护区 2.(英)(河道、港口等的)管理局
conservation n. 保存;(自然资源的)保护;资源保护区;管理

conservation area （或 zone）（文物、自然）保护区

conservation easement 保存地役权[亦有译为"保育地役权"，在农田保护与自然、文化遗产保护领域的运用为其典型：①农业保存地役权，美国从20世纪50年代开始农地保护探索，其方法与经验对于面临城市化加速挑战的中国农地保护有借鉴意义。美国的这种制度创新被引介至其他国家和地区。②遗产保存地役权，它是指土地或历史建筑的拥有人、供役者(donor)和特定保护组织或政府机构(受役者donee; grantee)为实现遗产保护达成法定协议，供役者永久地出让部分权益，亦由此而受到物业使用的限制，这种遗产保护领域的地役权制度在美国从20世纪70年代起得到广泛应用，并催生出一系列相关政策]

conservation laws （英）自然资源保护法
conservation of energy 能量守恒
conservation of (natural) resources 自然资源保护
conservation of ocean 海洋保护
conservation of water and soil 水土保持
conservatism n. 保守主义，（英）保守党的主张和政策
conservative ideological direction 保守意识的形态导向
Conservative Party （英）保守党（其前身为托利党，1833年改称保守党）
conservative restraintist 保守的限制主义者
conservative supreme court justices 保守的联邦最高法院大法官
conservatives n. 保守主义者；（大写）保守党员
conservator n. （法定）保护人；监护人；（英）（河流、港口等的）管理人；（公共福利的）监督官
conservator of the peace （英）治安官，（郡、县）司法行政长官
conservatory measures in litigation 诉讼保全
conserved resource 保有资金
consider v. 考虑；认为；照顾，体谅
consider and decide 裁断

considerable a. 值得考虑的，值得重视的；重要的，相当大(多)的
considerable degree of control over jury behavior 对陪审团行为进行相当程度的控制
consideration n. 考虑，思考；报酬，补偿；约因；(英美法)对价；审议；体谅，关心，尊敬(复)
consideration of marriage （英美法）婚姻的对价
* *Consideratum est per curiam.* It is considered by the court. 业经法庭考虑。（判决开始时的套话）
considered repealed 实际上失效
consientia remordens rei alieni 干扰他人之物的意识
consign v. 移交，交付；委托，托付；寄存，寄售；托运，发货
consignation n. 交付；委托，寄存，寄售
consignatory n. 共同署名者
consigned goods 委托物，寄销品
consignee n. 收货人；受托人；承销人，受货人
consigner (consignor) n. 发货人，委托人，寄售人，托运人
consignment n. 寄售，委托；发货，托运货物；托付
consignment agent 寄售代理人
consignment business 寄售业务，委托买卖
consignment note 托运通知书,发货通知书
consignment of goods 货物托运，发货
consignment sale 寄售
consignment sale export insurance 寄售出口保险，寄售输出保险
consignment stock insurance 寄销货物保险
consignment tax 寄销税
consignment-in (=inward) n. 承销，承销品
consignment-out (=outward) 寄销，寄销品
* *Consilia multorum quaeruntur in magnis.* The advice of many are required in affairs of magnitude. 遇大事应当大家商量。
consilium principis （古罗马）（地方行政长官召集的）大顾问团
consist v. 由……组成，由……构成；在于，并存，一致
Consistency n. 一致性，连贯性，稠密度，

言行一致
consistency (of resources) (资源的)稠密度
consistency of decision 判决的一致性
consistency of state's action with the federal constitution 州的行为与联邦宪法的一致性
consistent a. 坚固的,坚实的;一致的,连贯的,始终如一的
consistent application of local substantive law 一致适用地方实体法;一致适用当地的实体法
consistent interpretation 一致的解释,统一的解释,一贯的解释
consistent policy 一贯的政策(方针)
consistent principles 协调一致的准(原)则
consistory n. 宗教法庭;(天主教)宗教会议上院;(庄严的)集会
consistory court 宗教法庭;主教法庭(指在主教管区内主管教士的纪律法庭)
consolation n. 安慰,慰问
Consolato del mare (1200—1400 A. D.) 康索拉多海法,又译《海事习惯法汇编》(指阿拉贡王国和地中海沿岸各城市商业法官所采用的欧洲海事习惯法和条例的汇编)
consolation money 抚慰金
Consolato del Mare (14世纪地中海的)《海事法典》(见 Book of The Consulate of Sea)
consolidate v. 1.巩固,加强;联合,合并 2.并案办理,同时审判
consolidate at every step 步步为营
consolidate the worker-peasant alliance (中)巩固工农联盟
consolidated a. 巩固的;合并的,综合的
consolidated action 合并诉讼
consolidated annuities (英)(1751年政府开始发行的)统一公债
consolidated balance sheet 综合资产负债(对照)表
consolidated cargo 混装货物
consolidated debt 固定债务
consolidated fund 统一公债;统一基金
consolidated net profit 综合纯利
consolidated profit and loss account 综合损益计算表
consolidated prosecution 合并论罪
consolidated return 统一纳税申报表,合并(所得税)申报表[指反映联营公司集团的联合财务信息(combined financial information)的(纳税)申报表。实际即为母公司为其全部所属公司出具的(纳税)申报表,以代替所有各分公司单独出具的申报表]
consolidated returns 合并收益
consolidated statute 统一法规
Consolidated Treaty Series 《联合条约丛书》(指大洋出版社1969年至1981年出版,由克莱夫·帕里编辑的包括各民族国家之间1648—1918年的全部条约的汇编)
consolidating acts 综合性法令
consolidation n. 1.合并程序或合并行为;合并 2.(立法)合而为一(指将过去分散的各个立法机构的不同法规合并为单一法规)3.(民事诉讼)合并诉讼并统一审理[指法院命令将两个或两个以上所涉及同一当事方和同一系争点的诉讼合并为单一诉讼,并统一审理,作出单一判决,但有时亦保留其特性而分别判决。参见《联邦民事诉讼规则》第42(a)条,亦称 consolidation of actions。见 joinder; severance 2] 4.重组合并成立新公司或组织[指联合两个或两个以上的公司或组织,通过解散现在的这些公司或组织重新创立一个新的公司或组织,亦称(关于公司)consolidation of corporation。见 merger 8] 5.公司(旧时)合并[指两个或两个以上公司的股权(stock)、财产或专营权联合,借此,经营业务即为长期的。无论它们之间的协议是租赁合同、买卖合同或其他形式的合同,无论其合并采取解散一个或两个公司,但都是在统一管理之下经营](consolidate v.)
consolidation and merger 合并与合营
consolidation by lease 租赁合并
consolidation by purchase 购买合并
consolidation of action 诉讼合并
consolidation of debt 债务的合并
consolidation of fragmented holdings 合并零星土地

consolidation of mortgage 抵押合并
consolidation of provisions 条款合并
consols(复) n. 英国政府公债,英国统一公债
consonant with 与一致,相符合
consort n. 配偶(尤指帝王的夫或妻);伙伴,协力,联合
consortia banks 国际银团,国际财团,联营银行
* *Consortio malorum me quoque malum facit.* The company of wicked men makes me also wicked. 以坏人为伴亦会使自己变坏(即近墨者黑之意)。
consortium n. 配偶的权利(指夫妻有相伴、相爱、相助,性交等权利,称配偶权利);国际财团;合作,合股,合伙;(银行、企业等的)国际性协议;联合企业,财团,联营集团
conspicuous a. 明显的,显著的,惹人注目的,触目的
conspicuous conception 清楚的概念,明确的概念
conspicuous terms 醒目条款,清晰条款
conspiracy n. 阴谋,通谋,共谋,同谋;阴谋集团;结伙阴谋罪
conspiracy at common law 普通法上的同谋罪
conspiracy in restraint of trade (美)通(合)谋限制贸易(反托拉斯法的术语,参见《谢尔曼法》第1条)
conspiracy of silence (在诉讼中)保持缄默的密约
conspiracy to commit crime 密谋犯罪
conspiracy to obstruct public justice 共谋妨碍司法执行
conspirator n. 共谋者,阴谋家
conspiratorial 阴谋的;共谋的;爱搞阴谋的;阴谋家的
conspiratorial clique 阴谋集团
conspiratorial means 阴谋手段
conspire v. 共谋,密谋策划;图谋;协力促成
conspire with sb. 与某人共谋
constable n. 1.(英)警察,警官,巡警(指古代低级治安官员,其任务是将破坏治安的人拿去治罪,并且送达传票,执行逮捕令等)2.(中古的)高级官员
constable police 警察
constable wick 警察管辖区
constabulary n. (总称)警察,保安队;军事警察
constant a. 经常的,不变的;坚定的,不断的
constant capital 不变资本
constant price 不变价格
constant return 经常的收益
"constant ribbon" method (美)真实价值恒定法(见"constant true value" method)
Constantine the Great 康斯坦丁大帝(约280—337)(指306—337年在位的罗马皇帝,312年他皈依基督教,所以成为第一个基督徒皇帝,324年重建拜占庭古城,更名为君士坦丁堡,决意使其成为新的罗马城和他的永久首都。330年设立元老院,命名为罗马第二。他颁许多与基督教相关的法律,废除十字架死刑,建立基督教帝国的统治阶级)
"constant true value" method (美)恒查法[指美国按照证券真实价值与买卖证券交易价格之间差额来确定原告的损失。在建立计算模式时选定的一种(某一基准日中)最高价与最低价的平均值作为证券的真实价值]
constantly functioning body 处理日常工作的机构
constituency n. 选区;全体选民;选区的选民
constituent n./a. 1.委托人(指委托并授权他人为自己的代理人)2.选民,选举人(指在自己所在选区选出代表该选区并在公共事务中关注他们利益的议员的选民)3.(形成或组成的)部分,成分,因素/1.组成的,构成的〈constituent element of criminal offense〉(刑事犯罪构成的要素)2.有权制宪或修宪的〈constituent council〉(立宪会议)
constituent assembly 立宪会议,制宪会议,国民代表大会;大会
constituent corporation (组成母公司的)子公司

constituent elements 构成要件,构成要素(指刑、民事构成犯罪、侵权或其诉因的要素)
constituent facts 构成事实
constituent instrument 组织法,基本约章
constituent power 制宪权
constituent units 构成(立法)单位
constituents of adequate notice 充分通知的构成要件,适当通知的构成要件(adequate notice 亦称 due notice)
constituere 任命,委任(某人)[此词主要用于委托书或授权书(power of attorney)中。现常为 constitute 所替代]
constitute v. 组成,构成;任命,选定;制定(法律等);设立;使(文件等)通过法律手续
constituted a. 设立的,制定的;设定的,创设的
constituted acquisition 创设取得
constituted annuity (路易斯安那州法律)设立的年金,创设的年金[指具有最长 10 年持续时间的年金,而且在有些情况下,在所定期限到期之前仍可重新获得此项年金。参见《路易斯安那州民法典》(La. Civ. Code)第 2796 条]
constituted authorities 合法当局;通过合法手续设立的机关
constituted succession 设定继承
constituting formalities (法人)成立手续
Constitutio Criminalis Carolina 《加洛林纳刑法典》(指 1532 年神圣罗马皇帝制定的一部法典)
constitution n. 1.组成,构成 2.设立,建立,制定,任命 3.政体,性格,素质 4. 章程,法规,宪法[美国联邦宪法的制定,最早于 1777 年,美国联邦议会通过了《联邦条例》(Articles of Confederation and Perpetual Union),这是最早的美国宪法性文件。1789 年美国立法机构大陆会议又通过了一部新的宪法性文件,也即联邦宪法,这部宪法至今仍是美国的最高法律。美国联邦宪法一共只有 7 条,以后又增加了一系列修正案(Amendments)(目前为止共 27 个修正案),前 10 个修正案作为一个整体称为"人权法案"(Bill of Rights),于 1789 年经国会通过,1791 年由 11 个州批准生效。由于美国联邦宪法内容简洁扼要,富有灵活性,又以修正案的方式不断完善,成为世界上公认的最完美的"长命宪法"。美国各州又有自己的宪法,但当州宪法或者由州立机关或美国国会通过的法律被发现与联邦宪法相抵触时,那些法则一律无效]
constitution act 宪法(性)法令;宪法法
constitution amendment act 宪法修正法令
Constitution for Oceans(in UN, The Law of the Sea) 《联合国海洋法公约》(以"约"为当代国际社会关系海洋权益和海洋秩序的基本文件,它确立了人类利用海洋和管理海洋的基本法律框架,标志着新的海洋国际秩序的建立,被誉为"海洋宪章")
constitution granted by the sovereign 钦定宪法
constitution made by the people 民定宪法
constitution made by the sovereign and people 协定宪法
constitution measuring rod 宪法上测量的尺标(rod 又称 perch,长度单位=5.5 码)
constitution of a committee 委员会的组织;委员会的组织章程
Constitution of Clarendon (英)《克拉伦敦宪章》[1164 年,亨利二世对其外祖父亨利一世作为国王享有哪些权利作了调查,其结果是《克拉伦敦宪章》的颁布,采取的方式是召集所有贵族、骑士等经宣誓后证实老国王曾享有"宪章"中列举的权利,旨在限制教会特权和宗教法庭的权力。亦称《克莱伦敦政令》(1164 年)]
constitution of court act 法院组织法
constitution of crime 犯罪构成
constitution of five powers 五权宪法
constitution of liberty 保障自由的宪法
constitution of real rights 物权的设定
Constitution of the People's Republic of China 《中华人民共和国宪法》
Constitution of the United States 《美国合众国宪法》《美国宪法》[1787 年 2 月 21 日邦联国会邀请各州代表在费城召开会议,着手修改《联邦条例》,实际上出席代

表(除罗德岛外)(12个州)共55名,先是提出改革建议,建立有效的国家政府。会议实质为制宪会议。经过激烈争议,最后终于在1787年9月15日通过协议后并经各州批准,于1789年3月4日世界政治史上一部了不起的文件《美国宪法》诞生了。《美国宪法》由序言和文本7条组成,修正案现已有27个。联邦立法权属国会参、众两院。行政权属国家元首——美利坚合众国总统。联邦最高司法机关即联邦最高法院]

constitution of three powers 三权宪法
constitution's text 宪法文本
constitutional a. 1.符合宪法的,符合规章的;合宪性的 2.宪法所规定的,宪法的 3.拥护宪法的 4.体质上的,气质上的
constitutional adjudication 合宪的裁定
constitutional amendment 宪法修正(案)
constitutional amendments 宪法修正案(指已成为国家法律的27个修正案都已被国会参众两院2/3多数提议和州3/4多数批准。这些修正案成了反映宪法系统内社会、经济和政治变化的指示器)
constitutional and unconstitutional 合宪的和违宪的
constitutional apportioning policy 合宪的按比例分配政策(指议员名额分配)
constitutional arrangement 合宪的安排,宪法安排
constitutional assembly 制宪会议;(大写)法国革命时期的制宪会议
constitutional authority 宪政机关
constitutional barriers 合宪的障碍
constitutional case 合宪性争议案件
constitutional challenge (美)合宪性异议(指主张某一法律或政府行为是违反宪法的诉讼)
constitutional chamber (法院的)宪法庭
constitutional civil rights 宪法私权利
constitutional committee (或 council) 宪法委员会
constitutional competence 宪法能力
constitutional complaint 宪法性申诉(指联邦德国宪法法院所独有的一种审查方式,即任何公民都可以根据基本法所保障的基本权利或其他权利受到侵犯为理由,对某一项法律、法令向宪法法院提起申诉)
constitutional controversy(或 issue) 宪法性争议,合宪性争议
constitutional convention 制宪会议,修改宪法会议
constitutional court (根据宪法设立的)宪法法院
Constitutional Criminal Procedure (美)宪法刑事诉讼程序(指美国的一些法学院开设的刑事诉讼法课程)
constitutional crisis 宪政危机
constitutional culture 宪政文化
constitutional declaration 宪政宣言
constitutional development 宪法的演进
constitutional document 宪法性文件
constitutional domestication 宪法归化
constitutional engineering 宪政工程
constitutional exegesis 合宪解释,宪法解释,宪法注释
constitutional freedom 宪法上(规定)的(公民)自由
constitutional frenzy 宪法狂飙
constitutional government 宪政,立宪政体
constitutional grounds 合宪性的根据
constitutional history 制宪史;宪法史
constitutional independence 宪法独立
constitutional infirmity 违宪之处
constitutional initiative 宪法创制权,制宪权
constitutional interpretation 宪法解释(宪法解释既是指确定美国宪法含义的程序,又是研究美国宪法的技艺,前者为政府官员私人律师以及普通公民每天都实践着的艺术,后者主要为学术活动。宪法解释就是确定宪法含义的过程)
constitutional judiciary 宪法法院系统,宪法法院体系
constitutional jurisdiction 合宪性(案件)审查权;违宪(案件)管辖权
constitutional law 1.宪法性法律 2.符合宪法的法律,宪政法规,(英)宪法规范(指英国法中一切规范,无论是直接或间接对君主的权力的实施和应用产生效能的都叫宪法规范,如关于立法、行政、司法等的法

律,均属宪法规范)
constitutional legitimacy 合宪的合法性
constitutional legitimacy of attachment jurisdiction 扣押管辖的合宪性
constitutional limitations on legislative act 制定法的合宪范围
constitutional location of actors 行为人的合宪身份
constitutional mandate 宪法上的指令,宪法上的要求
constitutional matter 合宪性案件
constitutional meaning of minimum contacts and fair play 宪法上的最低联系和公平对待的含义,最低联系和公平对待在宪法上的含义
constitutional monarchy 君主立宪制(度)
constitutional muster 合宪性的检验
constitutional norm 宪法规范
constitutional obligation (美)宪法上的义务(指提供给被告适当通知和受听审的机会,是正当程序对法院行使管辖予以限制的一个补充方面)
constitutional organ 宪政机关
constitutional police powers 合宪的治安权
constitutional position 宪法地位
constitutional practice 宪法(性)惯例
constitutional process 宪法程序
constitutional question 合宪性争议;宪法上的问题
constitutional regime 立宪政体
constitutional republic 宪政共和体
constitutional requirement 宪法规定的必要条件
constitutional review 合宪性审查,违宪审查
constitutional revolution 制宪革命,宪法革命
constitutional right 宪法权利(指宪法上规定的公民权利)
constitutional rules 宪法;宪法规范
constitutional scrutiny 合宪法的调查,合宪的研究调查
constitutional status 宪法性地位
constitutional statutes 宪法性法规
constitutional system 宪政制度,宪法体系
constitutional taking 见 taking 2

constitutional tenet 合宪的信条(或宗旨、原则)
constitutional terms 宪法条款
constitutional test for speech 合宪的言论标准
constitutional text 宪法文本
constitutional treaty 宪法性条约(指欧盟宪法的修改稿,经 27 个国家代表讨论新宪法草案,由它们达成的框架条约签约)
constitutional underpinning 宪法上的依据,宪法上的基础;宪法上的理论基础
constitutional violations 违宪
constitutional words 宪法的词句,宪法的言词
constitutionalism n. 立宪制度;立宪主义;宪法论;宪政的维护
constitutionalist n. 立宪主义者,拥护宪政者
constitutionality n. 符合宪法;合宪性;立宪;法治
constitutionality of state statutes (美)州立法的合宪性
constitutionality of the statute (或 laws) 法规的合宪性
constitutionalization of charisma 魅力领袖宪法化
constitutionalize v. 使具有宪法,使宪法化
constitutionally ad. 按宪法,合乎宪法地;在气质上,在本质上;在构造上
constitutiones 颁布的法令;(罗马)皇帝敕令(有 *edicta*;*decreta*;*rescripta* 或 *epistolae* 三类)
constitutiones principum (罗马皇帝颁布的)主要敕令(其中有 *Codex Gregorianus*,*Codex Hermogenianus*,*Codex Theodosianus*,*Codex Justinianius*)
* *Constitutiones tempore posteriores potiores sunt his quae ipsas praecesserunt.* Later laws prevail over those which preceded them. 后来的法规优于(更有效力于)其先前的法规。
Constitutuions of Clarendon (英)克拉伦登宪章(1164 年由克拉伦登在大谘议会中提出,经亨利二世国王批准,旨在限制教会特权和宗教法庭权力的法律)
Constitutions of Melfi 梅尔菲宪章(指 1217

年由弗里德里克二世皇帝颁布的中世纪西欧地区第一部法律,试图将西西里王国的拜占庭和伊斯兰的封建惯例编入成为法典)

Constitutions of The Countries of The World 《世界各国宪法汇编》(指 1971 年由美国大洋出版社出版共 17 卷本,收集 160 多个国家宪法及其有关资料,并按国家英文名称的字母顺序编排的各国宪法汇编)

constitutive a. 有设立权的,有制定权的;组成的,基本的,构成的;创设的;"工具说"和"构成说"(指从法的作用或功能上看法的概念有此两说之区分。工具说在法律规范和社会活动之间作严格区别,然后提示前者对后者的影响。与之相比,构成说主张社会生活离不开法律。法律对社会的影响是通过提出一些重要概念以达到自然常规、连续和凝聚状态)

constitutive acquisition 创设取得

constitutive elements of a crime 犯罪构成

constitutive law 组织法

constitutive theory of recognition 承认的构成说

constitutum 裁判官认定的保证;支付未规定日期的既存债务协议

constitutum debiti 在规定日期支付既存债务的协议

constitutum possessorium (转移所有权时,转移人与取得所有权人订立的)转移人仍继续使用转移物的协议

constrain v. 强使,迫使,抑制,使作出

constraint n. 强迫,强制;拘束,拘禁;拘束或限制的事物;强制力,紧张状态

constraints on the exercise of state jurisdiction in constitutional clause 宪法上的条款约束州法院行使管辖

construct v. 组成;构造;建筑;设计;创立(学说)

constructed price 构成价格

constructed value 推定价值

construction n. 1.建筑,建设;建筑物 2.结构,构成 3.意义,解释;解释过程;法律释义

construction area 建筑区域,建筑范围

construction contract 建设合同(契约)

construction lien(或 **mechanic lien**) 建筑工程上的优先权(指设在建筑工程上的法定非移转占有型担保)

construction of law 法律的解释,政策的解释

construction of policy 保险单的解释

construction of references 权限的解释

construction(或 **home**)**owner's warranty** 兴建产权所有人的担保(指建筑法中所允诺的建筑房屋权)

construction work at heights 在高度的建筑工程

constructionist n. (美)对宪法等成文法作解释的人

constructive a. 推定的;解释的;积极的,建设性的

constructive abandonment 推定遗弃,推定抛弃

constructive assent 推定的同意

constructive authority 推定权限

constructive breaking 推定侵入

constructive breaking into a house 见 constructive housebreaking

constructive condition (1837 年)推定条件 [虽然协议当事双方未有作为,即未有明示或默示内涵,但条件所包括的重要条款,即法院已提供合理的境况,同时法律也已设定公正保证等推定条件。当事双方对于合同的合作视为一种推定条件,亦称为 implied-in law condition; condition implied by law; condition implied-in-law (见 implied-in-fact condition)。"推定条件是由法律设定而公正处理……是明示条件的分界线。推定条件通常是十分模糊的。然而,清晰往往是极为重要的。支配明示条件的总规则必须严格得到履行,至于推定条件的总规则就是实质上的遵行足矣。"参见《合同法》第 11.8 节第 402 页(第四版)(1998 年),著者 John D. Calamari & Joseph M.Perillo]

constructive contempt of court 推定藐视法庭罪

constructive contract 准契约,准合同

constructive conversion 推定侵占(罪)

constructive crime 推定的犯罪

constructive delivery 推定的交付,推定

交货

constructive desertion 构成遗弃[指配偶一方的错误行为迫使另一方配偶离开婚姻居所,违法的配偶一方的行为亦需达到足够的严重程度以致配偶另一方被迫从家中发现婚姻继续不可容忍或十分危险以致他(或她)的安全和幸福受到威胁,因此必须寻求婚姻居所以外的住处]

constructive dismissal 推定驳回;推定解雇

constructive domicile 拟制住所

constructive fraud 推定诈欺(某种行为不一定属于诈欺,但产生诈欺的后果,法律上应以诈欺论)

constructive housebreaking 推定为破门行窃[该术语出自法律上的解释:即一个窃贼(burglar)使用威胁或欺诈手段入宅。亦称 constructive breaking into a house]

constructive intent 推定故意(指法律上可拟定有犯罪故意的)

constructive interpretation "建构性解释活动"(指德沃金认为理论性争论所从事的活动,从而法律也被认为是一种解释性概念),推定解释

constructive knowledge (或 notice) 视同告知,(法律)推定通知(指根据通告的明显和众所周知的性质,法律可以推定有关人已知悉通知);推定知情

constructive larceny 推定盗窃罪

constructive malice 推定的恶意

constructive malice aforethought 推定的恶意预谋

constructive notice 推定告知,推定知道(指法律上在对某一事由已给予足够关注,可取代事实上的告知,即视同已经告知)

constructive possession 法律确认的占有,推定占有

constructive seizin 推定(土地)占有

constructive service 推定送达(见 service of process ②)

constructive suggestion 建设性的建议

constructive taking 推定取得,推定占有(指一个不等于实际占有物品的行为,但其行为本身已表示出有占有物品之意图。正如受托保管商品的人着手使用这些东西则违反了拥有人的托管旨意)

constructive total loss 推定全损

constructive transfer of possession 推定移转占有权

constructive treason 推定叛逆(罪)

constructive trust 推定信托,推断托管,法定信托(指由法律产生的信托,所针对的对象以实际或推断欺诈、胁迫、滥用信托、侵权行为、不道德行为或其他任何产生疑问的手段获得财产所有权,而根据衡平法或良知,他不应拥有和使用这一财产。实际上,推断信托是指,拥有财产所有权者以不当手段得到并持有的财产必须物归原主)

constructive vote of no-confidence 积极的不信任投票

construe v. 1.分析;解释;推断;视为 2.逐字译出

consuetude n. (有法律效力的)习惯,惯例

***Consuetude vel lex Mercatoria* (the Ancient Law Merchant)** 《古代商法》(指 1622 年英格兰的第一部商法著作,作者杰勒德·马利内斯)

consuetudinary a. 习惯上的,惯例上的

consuetudinary law 习惯法,不成文法

* ***Consuetudo contra rationem introducta potius usurpatio quam consuetudo appellari debet.*** A custom introduced against reason ought rather to be called a "usurpation" than a "custom". 违反理性而作出的惯例,与其叫"惯例"不如叫"篡夺"。

* ***Consuetudo debet esse certa*; *nam incerta pro nulla habetur.*** A custom should be certain; for an uncertain custom is considered null. 惯例应当是确定的,因为不确定的惯例是视为无效的。

* ***Consuetudo est optimus interpres legum.*** Custom is the best expounder of the laws. 惯例是法律法规最好的解释者。

* ***Consuetudo et communis assuetudo vincit legem non scriptam, si sit specialis; et interpretatur legem scriptam, si lex sit generalis.*** Custom and common usage overcomes the unwritten law, if it be special; and interprets the written law, if the law be general. 就特殊的法律规范而言,惯例和普

遍性的习惯优于不成文法;就一般的法律规范看,惯例和普遍性的习惯解释成文法。
* *Consuetudo licet sit magnae auctoritatis nunquam tamen, praejudicat manifestae veritati.* A custom though it be of great authority, should never prejudice manifest truth. 即使是具有极大权威的惯例也决不应当有损于明显的真理。
* *Consuetudo semel reprobata non potest amplius induci.* A custom once disallowed cannot be again brought forward (or relied on). 惯例一旦遭到否决就再也不能加以援引。
* *Consuetudo volentes ducit, lex nolentes trahit.* Custom leads the willing, law compels (drags) the unwilling. 惯例使人们心服,法律则强制人们服从。
consul n. 1.领事 2.(古罗马)执政官 3.(1799—1804 年,法国)三执政官之一 4.执政官
Consul d'Etat (法)行政法院(指 1799 年法国建立的世界上第一个行政法院)
consul de carriere 职业领事
consul electi 选任领事
consul mussi 派任领事
consul-general n. 总领事
consulage n. (检验出口商品的)领事签证费
consular a. 领事(馆)的,领事职权的
consular agency 领事机构;领事代理处
consular agent 领事代办,领事人员
consular agreement 领事协定
consular authority 领事权
consular commission 领事任命书
consular court 领事法庭
consular decision 领事裁决
consular district 领事管辖区,领事辖区
consular fee (=consulage) 领事签证费
consular function 领事职能
consular immunity 领事豁免权
consular institution 领事机关
consular invoice 领事签证的发票(或货单)(亦称领事发票)
consular jurisdiction 领事裁判权
consular marriage 使领婚姻(指在国外按规定在大使或领事馆举行仪式的结婚)
consular officer 领事官员,领事人员
consular privileges 领事特权
consular relations 领事关系
consular representative 领事代表
consular service 领事馆;领事人员;领事业务
consular staff 领事馆工作人员
consular treaty 领事条约
consular visa 领事签证
consulat 执政之职务
consulate n. 领事馆;领事的职位(或任期);(the Consulate)(1799—1804 年法国的)执政府
consulate general 总领事馆
consulship n. 领事的职位(或任期)
consult v. 商量,磋商,协商;咨询(尤指向律师请教等);法院(对于特殊案件)的见解或主张,查阅(书籍);考虑
consult with the members of administration 与行政机构的成员商量
consultant n. 顾问;商议者;咨询者;查阅者,请教者
consultant papers 咨询文件
consultant service 咨询服务
consultary response 法院的见解;(在某种特殊情况下)法院的主张
consultation n. (将案件由普通法庭移交教会的法庭)裁定书;咨询;协商,磋商,评议会,(专家等的)会议
consultation (或 consultative) machinery 协商机构
consultative a. 咨询的;商议的;协议的
consultative assembly 咨询议会(指欧洲理事会的一个机构)
consultative body 咨询(顾问)机构,咨询团体
consultative committee 协商会议,咨询(顾问)委员会
consultative council 咨询议会,咨询议会,协商委员会,(日)审议会
consulting service 咨询服务
consumable a. 可消费的,能消耗尽的
consumable thing 消费物
consumable thing and nonconsumable thing

消费物与非消费物
consumables (复) n.(总称)消费商品
consume v. 消费,消耗;浪费;消灭,毁灭
consumer n. 用户;消费者
consumer class actions 消费者集团诉讼
consumer contract 消费合同
consumer(或 **consumption**) **credit** 消费信贷(用);消费者的赊欠;分期付款的销售(方法)
Consumer Credit Act 《消费者借贷法》
consumer credit agreement 分期付款销售协议
consumer credit business 分期付款销售业务
Consumer Credit Protection Act (美)《消费者信贷保护法》
Consumer Financial Protection Bureau (美)消费者金融保护局[独立的联邦机构,旨在调整消费者金融产品和服务。该保护局通过以下两项措施保护消费者:严禁不公平和欺诈业务、维护消费者申诉并强制执行联邦消费者金融保护法。2010年,此机构根据Dadd-Frank Act设立,并于2011年开始运作]
consumer goods 消费物资,消费品,生活资料
consumer internal market 消费者内部市场
consumer price index 消费品价格指数
consumer protection 消费者利益保护
consumer protection law 消费者保护法
Consumer Protection Statutes 消费者保护法规
consumer society 消费合作社,消费者协会
consumer strike 消费者罢购(以抗议物价上涨)
consumer-city n. 消费城市
consumerism n. (美)保护用户利益主义,用户第一主义(指关心和保护消费者利益,并建立组织介绍产品情况,促使工业提供优质产品和服务)
consumers' cooperative 消费合作社
consummate a./v. 完美无缺的,完满的;极为精通的;尽善尽美,无比的/完成,使完善,使(愉快等)达到顶点

consummated a. 完成的
consummated crime 既遂罪
consummated offender 既遂犯
consummation n. 1.完成;结果;完善 2.完婚 3.既遂
consummation of fornication 奸淫既遂
consummation of fraud 欺诈既遂
consummation of marriage (英)圆房(根据英国《婚姻诉讼法》,婚姻以圆房,即男女双方完成性交才成立,如任何一方拒绝圆房,可使婚姻失效),完婚
consumption n. 消费,消耗
consumption abroad 境外消费(服务贸易的基本概念之一。指一国消费者到另一国接受服务提供者提供的服务,例如,本国病人到外国就医,外国人到本国旅游,本国学生到外国留学等)
consumption credit 消费信用(贷)
consumption tax 消费税
contact n./v. 接触,联系,联络;交往,交际;门路
contain v. 包括,包含,等于,相当于;控制,遏制,抑制
container n. 集装箱(港译:货柜);容器
container bill of lading 集装箱提单
container consortium 集装箱联合企业
container depot 集装箱装卸站
container freight station 集装箱货运站
container hire 集装箱租金
container load plan 集装箱的装箱单
container loader 集装箱装箱机
container operator 集装箱营运人
container pool 集装箱堆放场
container rehandling report 集装箱翻舱报告,集装箱再次搬运报告
container ship 集装箱船
container standards 集装箱标准规格
container terminal 集装箱码头(港译:货柜码头)
container unit train 集装箱专用列车
container yard 集装箱堆场
container-carrying vessel 集装箱船
containerizable cargo flow 可集装箱化的货流
containerization n. 集装箱化;(港译:货柜

化);集装箱化运输
containized trade 集装箱化运输业
containment n. 抑制,牵制,遏制
containment policy 遏制政策
contaminant n. 沾染物;食品污染物
contaminant-free community gardens 无污染社区菜园
contaminated needles 有传染的针头
contaminated zone 沾染区,污染区
contamination n. (货物运输过程中的)沾染,污染(物)
contamination error 污染错误(指在犯罪嫌疑人认罪之后,讯问人员通过诱供或指供,让犯罪嫌疑人提供与警方已经收集到的证据相符的关于犯罪过程的详细描述)
contamination situation 污染环境
contaminator n. 污染者
contango n. 1.[伦敦股票交易所]交易延期费;延期日息 2.远期溢价(升水),期货溢价(升水)
contango day (= continuation day) 交割限期日,延期决算日
contemner n. 犯藐视法庭罪者;藐视者
contemplate v. 注视,期待,仔细考虑;意图;打算;沉思
contemplated future consequence 预期发生的后果(见 two-step "minimum contact" analysis)
contemplation n. 注视,打算,意图;期待;沉思,仔细考虑
contemplation of bankruptcy 破产意图
contemplation of death 对(他人)死亡的期待
contemporanea expositio 按当时情况解释
contemporaneous documents 当时(的)文件(英国证据法中的概念,指在出于争议事故前或当场或随后各当事人记忆犹新时所制作的文件)
contemporary international law 当代国际法
Contemporary Newspaper Accounts 当代新闻报道
contempt n. 藐视;侮辱;轻视;轻蔑;受辱,不顾
contempt conviction 藐视定罪

contempt in procedure 违背命令(指当事人和证人等不遵行法官的判决、命令或其他指示,违者要被拘留直至服从或到一定期限)
contempt of Congress (美)藐视国会罪
contempt of court 藐视法庭;对法院的藐视罪(指以妨碍、阻止或干扰法庭执行司法职务或有损法庭权威或尊严为目的的一切行为,藐视法庭分为两类:直接的和间接的,直接藐视法庭是在开庭时直接所为的行为,间接藐视法庭主要作为一个术语来应用的,即指不执行或拒绝服从合法的裁决)
contempt of legislature 藐视立法机关(罪)
contempt of Parliament (英)藐视议会(罪)
contempt power 惩罚藐视法庭的权力
contempt power of Congress (美)惩罚藐视国会行为的权力[指藐视国会涉及对一个不尊重、违抗或妨碍立法程序的行为予以惩罚的权力。虽然国会从1795年开始行使此项权力,但宪法上并无明确授权。只是在涉及试图贿赂国会成员的Anderson v. Durm(1821年)一案中联邦最高法院认为,立法机关处罚藐视行为的权力是"一个以人民的尊严名义专门组织的大会"固有的,从1857年国会即制定有关藐视国会的法律]
Contempt Power of the Courts 惩罚藐视法院行为的权力[在法院内或法院外,藐视法院是对法院命令不服从或不尊重法院权威,尽管美国宪法在此问题上保持沉默,但它起源于普通法(common law)的固有的惩处藐视的权力对于确保联邦法院能强制执行其判决和命令已被认为必要。《1789年司法法》(Judicial Act of 1789)授予了联邦法院以惩罚藐视行为的权力,而且现今还通过制定法和法规保留此种权力]
contempt proceedings 藐视法庭程序,藐视法庭罪的诉讼程序
contemptuous damage 歧视性损害(指法院和陪审员不支持胜诉原告人的行为,因为这种行为依法固当,依情不合)
contend v. 与……作斗争,坚决主张,竞争,争论,争夺

content n. 内容,要旨;容量;(复)(书刊等的)目录
content of evidence 证据内容
content review 内容审查(指对录音、录像的内容审查)
content specific 满足具体的,满足特定的
content with 满足于
contention n. 斗争;争论点,争执点;争论
contentions in writing (诉讼中的)书面答辩
contentious a. 诉讼的;争执的;引起争议的;好争论的
contentious administrative appeal 行政争议申诉
contentious administrative tribunal 行政法院的诉讼
contentious business 有争议的事项,诉讼事务
contentious case 诉讼案件;抗议事件
contentious clause (条约等中的)有争议条款
contentious clause in a treaty 条约中引起争议的条款
contentious jurisdiction 诉讼(案件)管辖权,诉讼审判权
contentious possession 有争议的占有(权)
contentious probate business 诉讼双方争执不决的遗嘱检验事件
contentious procedure 诉讼程序
contentious proceedings 引起争执的诉讼(程序)
conterminous (=conterminal) a. 有共同边界的,相邻的,相连的;在共同边界内的
contest n./v. 争辩,比赛,争夺/辩驳,争讼,争论,比赛,争夺,并议,争辩
contestable clause 可抗辩的条款
contestant n. 争辩者;竞争者
* *Contestatio litis eget terminos contradictarios.* An issue requires terms of contradiction. (To constitute an issue, there must be an affirmative on one side and a negative on the other.) 争议须有相互对立的说法。(或译:构成争议必须有肯定的一方和否定的另一方)
contested divorce 有争议的离婚[指①夫妻一方在法庭表示反对离婚。②夫妻双方提起诉讼的离婚。从这个意义上讲,虽然夫妻双方均想离婚,但他们不同意离婚令(divorce decree)的条件(terms)。见 uncontested divorce]
contested election 竞选
contestee n. (美)受(其他竞选人)挑战的候选人
contesting a. 争执中的
contesting party 诉讼当事人
contesting the merits 就实体问题答辩,对是非曲直进行争议
context n. 前后关系,上下文,(事物等出现的)来龙去脉,境况,情况,前后文;语境
context of bargain 交易的前后情况,合同的前后文;磋商的来龙去脉
context of treaty 条约上下文,条约条文的前后关系
contextual illustrations of headword 标题字的文字说明
contextual marketing 关联营销(指基于用户当前行为来识别广告对象,并在消费者需要时发送广告信息。见 behavioral marketing)
contiguity n. 毗连,邻接
contiguous right 相邻权
contiguous zone 毗邻区
continental a. 大陆的,大陆性的
continental block 大陆块
continental borderland 大陆边缘地
continental codes 大陆法典
Continental Congress (美)大陆会议[指经弗吉尼亚议会倡议,殖民地代表于1774年9月5日在费城召开了由殖民地代表参加的第一次大陆会议(the First Continental Congress)。除佐治亚州外,12个殖民地55名代表参加,通过"权利宣言",要求殖民地内部自治,取消对商业的限制,废除法制法令等。1775年5月10日在费城召开第二次大陆会议,资产阶级民主派托马斯·杰斐逊、本杰明·富兰克林、帕特里克·亨利等都参加了会议,会议采取坚定立场,对英宣战,把民兵编为"大陆军",任命乔治·华盛顿为总司令。经过长时间争论,1776年7月4日通过杰斐逊等人起草的"独立宣言"

(Declaration of Independence)后,这一天为美国的国庆日]

continental island 大陆性岛,附属于大陆的岛

continental land mass 大陆块,大陆地块

Continental Law Legal system（或 **Family**）大陆法系(又称罗马法系)

Continental Law System 大陆法系(有时称 Civil Law System)[亦称罗马法系。法系的理论最早是由日本学者穗积陈重(1855—1926)提出的。1881 年,穗积陈重从英、德留学回到日本,担任东京帝国大学法学部教授,在创设法理课(Jurisprudence)的同时,提出了"五大法律家族",将世界各国的法律制度划分为五大法族(Legal Family),其中,罗马法族就是大陆法系]

continental legal culture 大陆法文化

continental margin 大陆边缘

continental platform 大陆台(即"大陆架")

Continental publicists 欧洲大陆的公法学家

continental rise 大陆隆起(又译大陆隆堆,大陆基)

continental shelf 大陆架(又译:大陆台,大陆棚,大陆礁层)

continental slope 大陆(架)坡

continental-law countries 大陆法系国家

contingency n. 意外事故;未来事件;临时费用;偶然性;可能性

contingency allocations 意外开支拨款

contingency fee 胜诉酬金

contingency reserve 应急储备金(见 contingent fund ②)

contingent a. 可能有的;偶然的,意外的,不确定的;应急的,备用的

contingent annuity 不确定的年金,临时年金,应急年金(指①在某个未来事故发生时,如一个人而非年金享用人去世了,开始给予支付的年金;②依据未来事件的结果而给予不确定数额支付的年金)

contingent beneficiary 第二受益人,临时受益人

contingent claim 期待性请求权,不确定请求权

contingent debt 不确定债务,或然债务(指目前尚不确定,要待以后某些未定事件发生方能确定的债务)

contingent estate （17 世纪)意外的财产(指将来的情况发生时而取得财产的所有权或使用权)

contingent event 意外事件

contingent fee 成功酬金(如胜诉后付给律师的酬金);意外费用,或有费用

contingent fund 备用金,应急费用[指①通过市政当局(municipality)创立的基金,以备当这笔基金不能适当归入特定征税名目的税务年度时引起的急需。②从商业上分开的一笔资金作为将来无名的费用(unknown costs),亦称为 contingency reserve]

contingent gain 意外收益,有利可得

contingent governance 相机治理(机制);视情况治理(指确保企业支配权的有序顺利让渡的一套制度)

contingent legacy 意外遗赠(指依靠一项不确定的或意外事件的遗赠,所以这项遗赠未赠与。例如,一笔遗赠要赠给某人的孙女,但要其孙女达到 21 岁)

contingent liabilities 不确定的债务,或有债务

contingent on 视……而定,决定于

contingent pricing 或有定价,意外定价

contingent remainder 或然剩余地产;不确定的剩余地产(指一旦特定剩余地产权宣告终止,由于继承人尚未确定或者此项产权赖以成立的事件尚未发生,还没有人立即实际占有的地产)

contingent remainders 不确定的剩余地产权,期待性剩余地产权(指该地产权取决于地产接受人或导致在先地产权终止的事件而不确定,这只能是不确定的或期待的剩余地产权)

contingent right 偶然权利

contingent trust 临时信托,有条件的信托

continuance n. 继续,延续;持续时间,逗留;诉讼延期

continuance of tenancy 租借权的延续

continuando 连续侵犯

continuation n. 决算延期;继续;连续;持续;增加物,扩建物

continuation clause （保单）延续有效条款（指海上保险的保险单上有继续保留的条款，表明被保的船不能在保险期内完成航程的，保险单可延续到被保船到达另一港口，或在若干时日内继续有效）

continuation day (=contango day)

continuation of tenancies 延续租约，租约的延续

continue v. 1.继续，延续，延伸 2.使延续；使延长；使继续 3.留下 4.使(诉讼)延期

continued applicability of the Federal Rules (美)《联邦规则》的持续适用性

continued validity 继续效力

continuing a. 继续的，连续的，持续的

continuing an expiring tax 延续期限届满的捐税

continuing annuity 持续年金享受权（见 survivorship annuity）

continuing contract 连续(履行)合同(契约)(指要求在一定时间内分期履行的协议)

continuing damages 分阶段支付的损害赔偿(金)

continuing director 留任董事

continuing education （美）进修教育

continuing guaranty 连续担保

continuing legal education （美）连续法律教育，在职法学教育，法律进修(指在美国往往由律师公会与大学法学院协作，每年举办法律进修班，以跟上法律发展的形势)

continuing loan agreement 连续贷款协议

continuing offence 继续犯罪；连续犯，持续犯

continuing partner 继续合伙人

continuing trespass 连续侵犯行为

continuing trustee 连任受托人

continuing warranty 连续担保；不间断的担保

continuity of dealing and activity (美)"经营和活动的连续性"(指即使诉因与公司在当地从事的商业活动无关，公司也可在当地被诉)

continuity of statehood (国际法)国家地位的连续性

continuity of the state 国家的连续性

continuous a. 继续的；连续的；延长的

continuous bail 继续保释；(出庭)保证书

continuous crime 连续犯罪

continuous easement 连续地役权

continuous employment 连续雇用

continuous offence 连续犯罪，持续罪

continuous possession 继续占有

continuous voyage 连续航行(指战时运输违禁品有关的一项原则)

continuous working years 连续工龄

continuum n. [(复) continua] 连续统一体；连续区域

contours n. 轮廓，外形，概貌

contours of the action 诉讼的轮廓

contra n. 相反，相对；反对；相反的事物

contra account 对销账户，抵消账户

contra bonos mores 违反善良道德风尚的；有伤风化的

contra legem 背离法律，背离成文法的规定

* ***Contra non valentem agere nulla currit praescriptio.*** No prescription runs against a person unable to bring an action. 任何时效不受无权提起诉讼的人的影响。

contra pacem 扰乱治安

contra proferentem 不利(于文件草拟人和提出人的)解释(原则)

* ***Contra veritatem lex nunquam aliquid permittit.*** The law never suffers anything contrary to truth. 法律决不容忍违背任何真理的事情。

contraband n./a. 1.禁制品，违禁品，禁运品，走私货 2.非法买卖，非法运输 3.(美南北战争时)逃入或被带入北方的黑人/违禁的，违禁品买卖的

contraband goods 违禁品，禁运品，走私货

contraband of war 战时禁运品；战时禁制品

contraband vessel 禁运船舶

contrabandist n. 走私者；违禁品买卖者

contraception n. 避孕

contraceptive n./a. 避孕药物；避孕用具；避孕/避孕的，避孕用的

contraceptive device 避孕器，避孕工具

contraceptive drugs 避孕药

contract n./v. 合同(契约);承包合同(契约);契据;合同(契约)法;承揽;承包;承办/订约;立约;承办;承建,承包;承揽;收缩
contract administration 行政契约
contract at discretion 任意合同(契约)
contract based on bare consent 无担保承诺合同(契约);无约因的允诺合同(契约)
contract based upon the utmost good faith 最大诚意合同(契约)
contract by competition 竞争合同(契约)
contract by deed 契据;(必须使用)契据形式的合同(契约)
contract by post (使用)通讯订立的合同(契约)
contract by stipulation 通过约定成立的合同(契约)
contract by wife as husband's agent 妻为夫的代理人所缔结的合同(契约)
* contract can not be used as an engine of oppression "合同不能作为压迫的机器"(指在担保交易中,对担保的利用必须以债权为基础,债权的全部清偿是债权人能利用担保的最大限度,超出这个限度,债权人对担保的利用就不具有正当性,就不应获得法律保护)
contract clause (美)契约(合同)条款(指美国联邦宪法第1条中的条款,任何州不得通过废弃合同或否定其法律效力的法规,损害合同义务)
contract compliance 合同顺从(指政府利用其拥有的市场力量,在采购活动中的优越地位来支持社会的、政治的或环境的目标,这种对合同的利用有时被称作"合同顺从")
contract debt 合同(契约)债务
contract defective in some respect 在某些方面有瑕疵的合同(契约)
contract depending on chances 赌博合同(旧译:射幸合同)
contract discipline 合同(契约)纪律
contract disputes 合同纠纷,合同争议
contract for broadcasting 广播合同(契约)
contract for carriage of goods 货物运送合同(契约)
contract for carriage of passengers 旅客运送合同(契约)
contract for civil company 个人合伙合同(契约),民事公司合同(契约)
contract for deed 地契合同(即土地销售合同"a land sales contract")
contract for delivery 供应合同(契约);货到付款合同(契约)
contract for filming 电影摄制合同(契约)
contract for fixed output 包产合同(契约)
contract for forwarding 转运合同(契约)
contract for insurance 保险合同(契约)
contract for processing work 加工合同(契约)
contract for public performance 演出合同(契约)
contract for publication 出版合同(契约)
contract for purchase and sale 买卖合同(契约)
contract for services 劳务合同(契约)
contract for the benefit of third party (或 persons) 为第三人利益订立的合同(契约)
contract for the holding of matrimonial property (夫妻)保有结婚财产合同(契约)
contract for the supply of necessary goods 供应必需品合同(契约)
contract for work 承揽合同(契约)
contract formation 合同的成立
contract goods 合同所列货物
contract granting city lots for building construction 关于拨给城市地段,供建筑用的合同(契约)
contract implied by (或 in) law 准合同(契约),法律推定的合同(契约)
contract implied in fact 事实推定的合同(契约)
contract in 保证承担义务
contract in personal 个人契约
contract in prospect of death 死因合同(契约)
contract in restraint of trade 限制营业合同(契约)(指合同当事人一方对他方表示不经营同一商业的合同)
contract in writing 书面合同(契约)
contract intensive money 契约密集型货币

contract involving gratuitous transfer of property 无偿让与财产合同(契约)
contract labo(u)r 合同(契约)劳工,(中)合同工
contract labo(u)r agreement 包工合同(契约);包工协议
contract law 合同法,契约法
contract leasing governmental or municipal enterprise 出租国有或市有企业合同(契约)
contract market 契约(或合同)市场
contract month 到期月份,交货月份
contract not mutually enforceable 当事人双方均无执行效力的合同(契约)
contract notes 合同(契约)票据
contract novation 合同(契约)更新
contract of adhesion 附意合同(见 adhesion contract)
contract of affreightment 租船合同(契约)
contract of annuity 年金合同(契约)
contract of apprenticeship 学徒合同(契约),师徒合同(契约)
contract of arbitration 公断合同(契约),仲裁合同(契约)
contract of association 协作合同(契约),联营合同(契约)
contract of barter 互易合同(契约)
contract of bill 票据合同(契约)
contract of brokerage 居间合同(契约),佣金合同(契约)
contract of building tenancy 建筑权合同(契约),建筑物租赁合同(契约)
contract of carriage 运输合同(契约),运货合同(契约)
contract of carriage of goods by sea 海上货物运输合同
contract of carrier 运货人合同(契约)
contract of commission agency 行纪合同(契约)
contract of *commodatum* (罗马法)使用借贷(契约)
contract of copartnery 合伙合同(契约)
contract of deposit 保管合同(契约)
contract of *depositum* (罗马法)寄托合同(契约)
contract of dormant partnership 隐名合伙合同(契约)
contract of employment 雇佣合同(契约);聘约
contract of family arrangement 家财处分合同(契约)
contract of gift 赠与合同(契约)
contract of guarantee 担保合同(契约)
contract of indemnity 损失赔偿合同(契约)
contract of inheritance 继承合同(契约)
contract of insurance against loss 损失保险合同(契约)
contract of insurance system 国家强制保险合同(契约)制度
contract of labo(u)r 劳动合同(契约);劳工合同(契约);雇佣合同
contract of lease of property 财产租赁合同(契约)
contract of life insurance 人身保险合同(契约);人寿保险合同(契约)
contract of life interest 终身权益合同(契约)
contract of limited commitment 承担有限义务合同(契约)
contract of loan 借贷合同(契约)
contract of loan for consumption 消费借贷合同(契约)
contract of loan for use 使用借贷合同(契约)
contract of loss and compensation 损失补偿合同(契约)
contract of mandate 委任合同(契约)
contract of marriage 婚姻合同(契约),婚约
contract of master and servant 雇主和雇工合同(契约)
contract of *mutuum* (罗马法)消费借贷合同(契约)
contract of on-carriage (集装箱运输)续运合同(契约)
contract of ocean carriage 海运合同(契约)
contract of ordering agricultural products (中)农产品预购合同(契约)
contract of partnership 合伙合同(契约)
contract of *pignus* (罗马法)质押合同(契约)

contract of processing and assembling with foreign enterprises 对外加工装配合同(契约)
contract of property insurance 财产保险合同(契约)
contract of publication 出版合同
contract of purchase stock 买进股票合同(契约)
contract of record 记录合同(契约)(指在记录法院登记注册的交易)
contract of repayment 还款合同(契约)
contract of sale 买卖合同(契约)
contract of sale for cash 现金买卖合同(契约)
contract of sale of a building 建筑物买卖合同(契约)
contract of sale of goods 货物销售合同(契约);货物买卖合同(契约)
contract of sale of goods for export 出口货物销售买卖合同(契约)
contract of sale stock 卖出股票合同(契约)
contract of scientific and technical cooperation 科技协作合同(契约)
contract of service 劳务合同(契约);服务合同(契约);雇佣合同(契约)
contract of submission (或 adhesion contract) 附意合同(契约)
contract of supply 供应合同(契约)
contract of suretyship 保证合同(契约)
contract of tenancy 租赁合同(契约)
contract of the assumption of debts 承担债务合同(契约)
contract of transport by air 空运合同(契约)
contract of transportation 运输合同(契约)
contract officer 订约聘用的职员
contract on tenancy 合同的租赁期
contract out 保证不承担义务;(英)退出合约;(将工程)承包出去
contract partners 合同合伙人
contract period 合同(契约)期限
contract price 承揽价格
contract product liability 产品责任合同
contract provisions 合同(契约)规定
contract regulating the succession 规定继承的合同(契约)
contract ship 承揽船舶,承包船舶
contract sued on 在诉合同
contract supervision 合同(契约)监督
contract system 承包制
contract terms 合同(契约)条款
contract theory of the state 国家契约说
contract to be performed by third party 由第三方(人)履行(给付)的合同(契约)
contract to be performed to third party 向第三方(人)履行(给付)的合同(契约)
contract to marry at some future time 订婚合同(契约)
contract *uberrimae fidei* 诚实信用合同(契约)
contract under seal 盖印合同
contract voyage 合同规定的航次
contract with an absent party 非对话要约(订立的)合同(契约)
contract with consideration 有偿合同(契约);(英美法)有对价的合同(契约)
contract with deferred execution 延期履行的合同(契约)
contract without compensation 无偿合同(契约)
contract without consideration (英美法)无对价的合同(契约)
contract-intensive money ratio 通货紧缩(比)率
contractarian n. 契约主义派
contracted a. 已订约的,已订婚的,缩小的
contracted export price 推定的出口价
contracted property rule 约定财产法则
contracting a. 缔约的;承包的
contracting carrier 承运人
contracting countries 缔约国
contracting judges 联络法官(指国际上的联络法官制中的联络法官)
contracting out system 承包制
contracting party 立约当事人;缔约国;承办人
contracting power (或 state) 缔约国
contracting 承揽,承包
contracting-in (英)支付政治派款
contracting-out (英)拒绝支付政治派款;立约斥除(某些法定权益的可能)

contraction convergence 共同减排并趋同(模式)[指西方学者提出的温室气体排放标准的两种模式之一。另一种为 Common but differentiated Convergence(共同但有区别的趋同)。"人均平等排放权"作为远期温室气体排放额度的一个标准]
contractor n. 订约人,承揽人,承包人;承包商;包工头
contractor unit 承包单位,承揽单位
contractor's agreement 承揽合同(契约)
contracts *inter absentes* 当事人不在场的合同
contracts *inter presentes* 当事人在场的合同
contracts to carry products 运送产品合同
contracts-mandatory rules 合同法强制性规范
contractual a. 合同(契约)上的,合同(契约)性的,约定的,承办的
contractual acceptance 合同(契约)承诺
contractual acknowledgement 合同(契约)上的认可
contractual arrangements 合同(契约)安排
contractual capacity 缔约能力;立约资格
contractual clause of non-competition 非竞争性的合同(契约)条款
contractual damages 由合同(契约)引起的损害赔偿
contractual fines 合同(契约)上的罚金,违约罚金
contractual forum 合同(契约)规定的管辖法院
contractual forum-selection 合同约定法院选择条款
Contractual Freedom in Corporate Law 公司法中的合同自由(1988年12月9日至10日美哥伦比亚大学法学院法律经济研究中心举行此项主题的研讨会。Robert C. Clark, Frank H. Easterbrook, Daniel R. Fishel, Jeffery N. Gorden, John C. Coffee 等在公司法学界有影响的人物均参加此会并展开针锋相对的论战)
contractual forum-selection clause 合同对管辖法院的约定条款
contractual hypothec (罗马法)合同(契约)上的不转移财产占有权的担保
contractual investment 合同(契约)性投资
contractual issue 合同(契约)上的系争点
contractual joint venture 契约式合资企业
contractual joint venture law 契约或合资企业经营法,中外合作企业经营法
contractual liability 合同(契约)责任;合同(契约)规定的义务
contractual limits of time 合同规定的时间限制
contractual norms 合同的规范(或标准)
contractual obligation 合同(契约)之债,约定义务
contractual personnel 订约承办人员
contractual practice 合同(契约)惯例
contractual provisions 合同(契约)条款;合同(契约)规定
contractual regime 约定财产制
contractual relation (或 **relationship**) 合同(契约)关系
contractual rights 合同(契约)权利,约定权利
contractual route 合同(契约)规定的航线
contractual specifications 合同(契约)的专门规定
contractual theories of agency 委托契约的理论
contractual treaty 合同(契约)式的条约
contractual usage 合同(契约)惯例
contractus (罗马法)合同,契约(双方或多方当事人之间的协定,对当事人之间均有约束力。见 contrahere)
contractus bonae fidei 善意合同(契约)
contractus consensu 合意合同(契约)
* *Contractus ex turpi causa, vel contra bonos mores nullus est.* A contract founded on an evil consideration, or against good morals, is void. 基于含有邪恶的对价或违反善良风俗的合同(契约)无效。
contractus juris gentium (罗马法)万民法合同(契约)
* *Contractus legem ex conventione accipiunt.* Contracts take their law from the agreement of the parties. 合同(契约)要通过双方当事人的意思表示一致才能取得

法律效力。
contractus literis 书面合同(契约)
contractus re (罗马法)实践合同(契约);要物合同(契约)
contractus reinnominati (罗马法)无名合同(契约)
contractus verbis 口头合同(契约),言辞合同(契约)
contradict v. 反驳,抗辩;否认;同……相抵触
contradict the defendant's witness 反驳被告的证言(证据)
contradiction n. 矛盾;否认;反驳,反证
contradiction in terms 语词自相矛盾的说法
contradictions among the people (中)人民内部矛盾
contradictions between enemies and the people (中)敌我矛盾
contradictory a. 矛盾的,对立的;相反的
contradictory concept 矛盾观念;相反观念
contradictory decisions 相互对立的判决
contradictory principle (诉讼)对抗原则(大体同于 adversary system)
contradictory procedure 抗辩程序
contradictory testimony 互相矛盾的口供,有矛盾的证据
contrahere (罗马法)拉丁文原意;使团结一致;缔结[①通过协议建立或缔结(订立)正式关系:如夫妻之间的关系,债权人与债务人之间的关系;②犯罪;③接受一笔遗产;④一般来说,履行任何一项法律上有重大意义的行为。见 contractus]
contrariety n. 对立性,(复)对立因素,对立的事物
contrary a. 相反的;相违背的,矛盾的;相应的;对抗的
contrary evidence 反证
contrary holding 相反的裁定
contrary intention 反意,相反的动机
contrary result 相反结果,相反原则
contrary state procedure 相反的州诉讼程序
contrary to law 违法;违反法律
contrary to orders 违反命令
contrary to public order or good morals 违反公序良俗
contrary to public policy 违反公共秩序
contrary to the constitution 违反宪法,抵触宪法
contrast n./v. 对比,对照;大不相同,使对比,使对照(with),形成对比
contrastive terms 形成对比的词条或术语
contravene v. 触犯(法律等);违反;否认;反驳;破坏;侵犯
contravene a law 犯法
contravention n. 违反;触犯;抵触,否定;违法行为,轻罪(指没有犯意,但违反法律者)
contravention of a statutory instrument 触犯法律文件
contravention of criminal law 触犯刑法
contravention of statute 违反制定法
contravvenizioni 违誓罪
contribute v. 作贡献,起作用(to),出了一份力(to)
contributing authors 特约作者
contributing editor 特约编辑,特约撰稿者
contributing factor 起作用的一个因素
contributing to the delinquency (of a minor) (1913 年)促成未成年人犯罪,促成少年犯罪,促成青少年犯罪(指一个成年人以其行为导引青少年犯罪,或在青少年出现时导致青少年的犯罪行为。例如,包括怂恿、鼓励青少年入店扒窃、使其低龄饮酒或诱其进行性行为赚钱。通常缩略为 contributing to delinquency。见 impairing the morals of a minor)
contribution n. (14 世纪)1.分摊(额),分配(额)[指数人负有责任清偿共同债务(common debt)时,其中一人为了大家的利益清偿了债务,则他有权分摊债务,按比例向其他人追偿;对于第三人的损害负有连带责任(jointly responsible)的一些人也被要求对赔偿额进行分摊。此词亦称为 right of contribution]2.分配额[共同侵权人(joint tortfeasor)之间,每个侵权行为人均应分别承担侵权行为而给他人造成的损害赔偿。如果一个侵权行为人已支付给受害当事方多于他或她的比例份额,这个多给的比例份额又是偶然的错误(causal fault),

该行为人有权从共同行为人之间分摊补还的份额]3.共同侵权人按比例份额(proportionate share)应付的实际支付(actual payment)(见 indemnity)4.(海商法)因船上货物的舍弃而造成的损失,应由财产未受损失的各当事方分摊支付给财产受损失的当事方 5.占领军税(war contribution)
contribution clause 责任分担条款
contribution in general average 共同海损分摊
contribution of each party (夫妻)双方各自带来的财产
contribution value 分摊值
contributor n. 捐助人,捐赠人;投稿人
contributory n./a. 1.贡献者,捐助者 2.(企业倒闭时)负连带偿还责任的人 3.起作用的因素/有连带责任的;捐助的;分担的;有助于……的;促成……的
contributory cause 附带原因,连带原因
contributory infringement 共同侵权,参与侵害,协助侵害(主要用于专利法中)
contributory infringer 共同侵权人
contributory mortgage 共同议定的抵押,分担抵押
contributory negligence 被害人占有过失,被害人本身的过失;(车祸等案中)受伤一方自己的粗心;混合过失,混合过错,互有过失;共同过失(指被害人的人身或其财产的损害是被害人和加害人的共同过失所致);负有连带责任的过失
contributory negligence defense 分担过失辩护
contributory pension (英)(1925 年实施过的)共醵年金
contributory profits (对老、弱、病残者等的)捐助救济
contributory reinsurance 分摊再保险
contributory value 共同海损分摊价值
contrive v. 策划,设计,制造;想尽办法去做,筹划,发明;竟然弄到……的地步;图谋;设法对付过去
control n./v. 支配,控制;管制;管理,管辖,监督;调节/控制;抑制,克制;管制,监督;支配
control *de facto* 事实上的管制

control of document 文件管理
control of economic legality 经济合法性的监督
control of expenditure 经费开支控制
control of foreign affair 掌管外交事务
control of foreign trade 外贸管制,外贸管理
control of guns and ammunitions 枪支弹药管制
control of matter concerning civil servant 掌管有关文官事宜
control of poisonous materials 毒品管制
control power 控制权;监察权
control price 管制的物价,官价
control program 控制程序(即系统程序)
Control through a legal device without majority ownership 通过法律方式的控制(指经营者虽不拥有过半数股权,但通过某种法律方式的设计来控制过半数的表决权,从而控制公司的经营。见 Control through almost complete ownership)
Control through almost complete ownership 全部控制(指美国学者 Berle 和 Means 于 1932 年在《现代公司和私有财产》一书中讲公司的控制形态、概略分为五类;①全部控制:即经营者拥有公司全部或几乎全部的股份;②多数控制 Majority ownership;③通过法律方式的控制 Control through a legal device without majority ownership;④少数控制 Minority control;⑤经营者控制 Management control)
controlled a. 受管制的;受控制的;受管辖的
controlled airspace 所属领空,控制领空
controlled company 受控制的公司,受股权控制的公司
controlled mortgage 受控制的抵押
controlled procurement and distribution (中)统购统销
controlled substance 控制物品(或实体)(指任何类型毒品的拥有和使用均受法律管制,包括麻醉性的或吸毒成瘾的、兴奋刺激的或引起幻觉的药品或毒品)
controlled tenancy 受管制的租借
controlled trust 受控制的信托

Controlled-substance Act (美)《控制物品法》或《控制实体法》[指联邦或州的制定法,旨在控制某些药品或毒品的使用、销售的配给物或供销量、类别。大多数州均已制定这类法律法规,这些法规通常作为《统一控制实体法》(the Uniform Controlled Substance Act)的模式]

controller n. 主管人;监察人;审计师;管理人;主计员

Controller General 总审计长,主计长

controller of ballot 监票员

controlling a. 控制的,管制的

Controlling factor 决定性因素,关键的因素,支配的因素

controlling facts 支配性事实,控制的事实

controlling force 统治力量,控制力

controlling infectious diseases 可控制的传染性疾病

controlling interest (in the share capital) 控制股权

controlling law 应适用之法律

controlling question of laws 支配性的法律问题

controlling traffic 控(管)制交通

controversial a. 引起争论的,受争论的

controversial source of powers 引起权利之争之源

controversy n. 论战,争论,争吵,争议,纠纷

controversy between employees and management 劳资关系的争议

controversy between the parties 双方(当事人)的争议,当事人之间的争讼

controversy legal issue 法律问题的争议

controversy on the merits 实体性的实体问题的纠纷

controvert v. 辩驳,反驳(论点,等);争论;否认,反证;讨论

controvertible a. 可争论的,可辩驳的

contubernium (罗马法)奴隶之间的婚姻;奴隶婚姻,被允许的同居

contumacious a. 反抗法院命令的;不听命令的

contumacy n. 不听法院命令;藐视法庭;拒不服从

contumax n. 藐视法庭者,不受法律保护者

contumax nonappellat 缺一方不得上诉

contumely n. 傲慢无礼;谩骂,侮辱;傲慢无礼之语言和行为

contused wound 挫伤,挫创

contusion n. 挫伤

conundrum n. 难答的问题,谜,猜不透的问题

conurbation n. 集合城市(指拥有卫星城市的大都市)

conusance (=cognizance)

conusance of pleas 司法管辖

conusor n. (=cogniser)

convenance (法)(复)惯例,习俗;方便,适合

convenant of good faith and fair dealing (美)公平诚信原则约定(劳资双方成立的雇佣关系中,双方形成了默示性契约关系,雇主不得基于恶意任意解雇其员工。美国法院以违反公平诚信原则为理由,对雇主依据任意雇用原则任意解雇员工的权力加以限制,形成了任意雇用原则的公平诚信原则约定)

convene v. 召集;召开;传唤(被告等)

convenience n. 便利,适当的机会,便利设施

convenient a. 适当的,合理而可行的,方便的

convenient port 近便港

convenient power 实用主义的权力

convening authority 传唤(某人出庭受审)权

convenor n. (会议)召集人

conventicle n. 集会(尤指非法集会);集会场所

conventio 协议;合约

* *Conventio facit legem.* The agreement creates the law. (i.e. the parities to a binding contract must keep their promises.) 协议产生法律效力(受合同约束的双方当事人必须遵守其诺言)

* *Conventio privatorum non potest publico juri derogare.* The agreement of private persons cannot derogat from public right.(i.e.

cannot prevent the application of general rules of law, or render valid any contravention of law.) 私人间的协议不得有损于公共的权利(即不得有碍于适用一般法规或不得使任何违法行为合法化)。
* **Conventio vincit legem.** The express agreement of parties overcomes (prevails against) the law. 双方当事人明示的协议胜过法律。

convention n. 1.公约,协约,协定,宪章 2.惯例;常规 3.(全国性的)大会,会议;国际会议 4.召集,集会 5.惯例,常规,习俗

convention court 公约法院(指依照一定的国际公约而成立的具有跨国管辖权的机构,它不一定是传统意义上的"法院",如欧洲经济共同体的欧洲法院,法语非洲国家知识产权组织的"雅温得总部"均属公约法院性质)

convention double 两重公约[指多数国家适用不方便法院(forum non convenience),目的是要避免过分管辖权原则对案件审理带来的不便,海牙特别委员会已决定制定一个"二重公约";公约草案列出将管辖依据和禁止使用的"坏"管辖依据(即过分管辖原则)]

Convention for the Pacific Settlement of International Disputes 《和平解决国际争端公约》(1889年第一次海牙会议通过)

Convention for the Prevention and Punishment of Terrorism 《预防和惩治恐怖主义公约》(指1937年11月16日在国际联盟的主持下,27个国家的代表在日内瓦举行了旨在更有效地防止和惩治具有国际性质的恐怖主义的正式外交会议上签订的公约)

Convention for the Protection of Migratory Birds, 1916 1916年《保护候鸟公约》

Convention for the Regulation of Aerial Navigation 《关于航空管理公约》(1915年在巴黎签订,1922年生效,通称为《巴黎航空公约》)

Convention for the Suppression of Unlawful Acts Against the Safety of Civil Aviation 《关于制止危害民用航空安全的非法行为的公约》

Convention for the Suppression of Unlawful Seizure of Aircraft 《关于制止非法劫持航空器的公约》(1970年在海牙通过)

Convention of Constantinople 《君士坦丁堡公约》(1888年德、法、意、西、荷、俄、奥匈帝国等和奥斯曼帝国签订的关于苏伊士运河自由通航的国际条约)

convention of delegates 代表大会

Convention of Fishing and Conservation of the Living Resources of High Sea 《捕鱼与养护公海生物资源公约》

convention of the constitution 宪法惯例

Convention on Certain Conventional Weapons 《特定常规武器公约》

Convention on Cluster Munitions 《集束弹药公约》(指2008年5月19—28日,在爱尔兰首都都柏林举行的禁止集束弹药国际会议上,来自100多个国家的代表经过10天激烈争论,终于通过了一份关于全面禁止集束弹药使用、生产、转移和贮存的《集束弹药公约》并于2008年12月3日起在挪威首都奥斯陆向各国开放签署)

convention on consular relation 领事关系公约

Convention on Cybercrime 《关于网络犯罪的公约》(指2001年11月23日欧洲理事会在布达佩斯召开的网络犯罪大会上,举行《关于网络犯罪公约》开放签署仪式,26个与会国签署了该公约。加拿大、日本、南非、美国作为4个参与帮助起草的国家也参加了大会并签署了公约)

convention on diplomatic relations 外交关系公约

convention on genocide 禁止大规模屠杀公约

Convention on International Civil Aviation 《国际民用航空公约》(1944年在芝加哥通过)

Convention on International Interests in Mobile Equipment 《移动设备国际利益公约》(见 Protocol there on Matters Specific to Aircraft Equipment)

Convention on International Multimodal Transport of Goods 《国际货物多式联运公约》(1980年)

Convention on International Trade in Endangered Species of Wild Fauna and Flora, 1973 《濒危野生动植物种国际贸易公约》(1973 年)
convention on nationality 国籍公约
Convention on Offenses and Certain Other Acts Committed on Board Aircraft 《关于在航空器内的犯罪和某些其它行为的公约》(1963 年,亦称《东京条约》)
Convention on Recognition and Enforcement of Foreign Arbitral Awards 《承认及执行外国仲裁裁决公约》(即 1958 年纽约公约)
Convention on the Conservation and Management of Hake Resources in the Central Bering Strait 《中白令海峡鳕鱼资源养护与管理公约》
Convention on the Continental Shelf 《大陆架公约》(1958 年在日内瓦第一届海洋法会议上通过)
Convention on the European Patent for the Common Market 《欧洲共同体专利公约》
Convention on the High Seas 《公海公约》(1958 年 4 月 29 日在日内瓦签订)
Convention on the Immunity of State-Owned Vessel 《国有船舶豁免权公约》
Convention on the Law Applicable to Agency 《代理法律适用公约》
Convention on the Law Applicable to Products Liability 《产品责任法律适用公约》
Convention on the Limitation Period in the International Sale of Goods 《国际货物买卖时效期限公约》
Convention on the Prevention and Punishment of the Crime of Genocide 《防止及惩治灭绝种族罪公约》
Convention on the Privileges and Immunities of the United Nations 《联合国外交特权及豁免公约》
Convention on the Service Abroad of Judicial and Extrajudicial Documents in Civil or Commercial Matters 《关于向国外送达民事或商事司法文书和司法外文书公约》
Convention on the Territorial Sea and the Contiguous Zone 《领海及毗连区公约》(1958 年通过)
convention parliament (英)非常议会
conventional a. 惯例的,常规的;传统的;协定的,约定的;形式上的
conventional assumption 特定假设
conventional community 合同(契约)上的财产共有
conventional custom 约定的习惯(指当事人在协议中明示或默示具有拘束力的习惯)
conventional duty 协定关税
conventional (或 traditional) economics 传统经济学
conventional estates 各方协商的财产(权)
conventional forces 常规部队
conventional hypothec 约定不转移财产占有权的担保
conventional international law 协定国际法
conventional jurisdiction 约定管辖
conventional law 惯例法,协约法
conventional law of nations 条约国际法
conventional legislation 常规立法
conventional management 传统管理
conventional mortgage 约定抵押(权)
conventional neutrality 协定中立
conventional sequestration 常规保管(指在诉讼过程中,有争执的双方自愿地将有争执的财产提供保存)
conventional servitudes 条约地役(权)
conventional tariff 协定税则,协定税率
conventional theory 传统理论
conventional transcription 惯用译名(指地名);约定誊本
conventional trustee 约定受托人
conventional war 常规战争
conventional weapons 常规武器
conventionalism n. 惯例主义,依从习俗
conventionalist n. 依从俗习的人,因袭主义者
conventionalize v. 依照惯例,使习俗化
conventions of the constitution 宪法惯例
converge v. 为共同利益而聚合一起,集

中;合聚,使集中于一点
convergence n. 交汇点,会聚,集中
convergence of corporate governance 公司治理融合理论[指近二十年来,西方法学界围绕不同法域公司治理模式中法律规则与制度的差异在全球化背景下的发展方向及公司治理融合理论,展开一系列讨论:随着经济全球化的过程,国与国之间的贸易壁垒逐渐消除,公司间的竞争不仅体现在它们所能向市场提供的产品上,也体现在它们的治理结构上。在此背景下,为了提升本国公司在国际市场中的竞争力,公司法学者必须担负起本国公司探求最有效的公司治理法律规范进化到一个最有效率的模式。2001年美国哈佛大学教授哈斯曼(Hansmann)和耶鲁大学教授卡曼(Kraakman)在《公司法的历史已经终结》的论文中提出公司法"形式融合"(formal convergence)的理论,并宣称美国式的以股东权利为导向的公司治理模式将成为不同法域公司治理模式的范式。他们认为,市场自身的逻辑、竞争与利益集团的压力会使不同的法域选择相似的规则或制度去解决类似的公司治理问题,同时他们还认为在竞争激烈的市场环境中,对"经济效益"的追求是最为重要的。这种追求会使不同的公司治理模式向着一个单一的最有效率的模式演进,作为该项研究的延续,希门斯(Siems)教授对6个不同法域的与股东保护相关法律的研究中提出了"一致造就融合"(convergence though congruence)的观点,认为不同法域在文化和经济方面的不断趋同致使法律本身也必须去适应环境的变化,进而向一种相似的模式发展与融合。另外,不少学者持相反看法,认为没有一个完美的公司治理范式能适应所有国家的情况。法律和制度不仅要对"经济效益"作出回应,还受制于一国的政治制度、文化传承等因素,所以贝博查克(Bebchuck)和罗伊(Roe)运用"路径依赖理论"(path-dependence theory)得出了不同法域间公司治理模式的差异会继续存续的理论。他们认为,在小股东保护较弱的法域,控股股东可通过寻租行为攫取额外收益,这构成他

们保持这一制度的根本性改革。在经济全球化的压力之下,形势融合也会遭到既得利益群体的阻挠。与此相比,功能融合(functional convergence)则是改革更为可能采取的方式。依此观点,在全球化的竞争压力之下,当不同法域的公司治理模式面临一系列政治、经济、文化的制约因素时,它们会不断地巩固它们之间固有的制度差异,而非进入一种在制度模式上逐步趋同的发展路径。不同法域会通过制定、实行差异化的法律规则来达成在功能上相似的公司治理模式]
conversant a. 熟悉的,精通的(with)
conversation n. 交谈;社交;性交;非正式会谈
conversion n. 非法占有他人财产(在英联邦国家版法中,这个词可能具有非法占有侵权复制品、对非法占有侵权复制品提起之诉、将非法占有复制品移交被侵权人的司法救济三个含义)
conversion by detention 扣留他人之物的侵占行为
conversion by taking 转移他人之物的侵占行为
conversion by wrongful delivery 非法交付的侵占行为
conversion by wrongful destruction 非法毁损的侵占行为
conversion by wrongful disposition 非法处分的侵占行为
conversion divorce 有条件的离婚[指在允准的已进行的法定分居或当事双方已签订一项分居协议(Separation Agreement)之后,当事双方已分居生活了一个法定期间。亦称convertible divorce;conditional divorce]
conversion of cheques 侵占支票的行为
conversion of property 侵占财产
conversion of public money to one's own use 占用公款,挪用公款
conversion of the void act 无效法律行为的侵占行为
conversion rate 汇价,换算率,折算率
conversion with the co-efficient 按折算率换算
convert v. 占用,侵占;变换;转换;结汇,

兑换;使皈依宗教;使改变(宗教、党派、信仰等)
convert foreign exchange 结汇
converted a. 被强占的,已变换的
converted into money 折成现金
converted merchantman 改装商船
converter n. 使转换的人,使改变信仰的人
convertible a. 可兑换的;可转化的;可改变的
convertible bond 可兑现债券,可兑换证券
convertible currency 可自由兑换的货币
convertible debenture (1908年)持有人可兑换证券或股票的债券
convertible divorce 见 conversion divorce
convertible foreign exchange 可兑换的外汇(指国际上的硬通货,如美元、英镑、日元等。伯尔尼公约和世界版权公约在允许采用强制许可时,要求被允许一方向版权人支付"可兑换的外汇"),自由外汇
convertible notes 可兑换的货币
convertible preferred shares 转换优先股
convertible stock 可换股份
convertible subordinated debenture 可兑换的附属债券[指此种债券附属在其他债务(debt)之上,可兑换不同的证券(security)]
convey v. 让与;转让(财产等);传达,通知;转运,运输;搬运
conveyable a. 可转让的;可传达的;可转运的
conveyance n. 财产转让;让与,交付;交付文据,财产转让证书;运输工具;运送,搬运
conveyance of land 土地转让;土地转让证书
conveyance of leasehold 租赁权的转让
conveyance of property 财产转让;转让证书
conveyance of title 财产转让证书,所有权转让证书
conveyance on sale 卖据
conveyancer n. 撰写转让契据的律师
conveyancing n. 财产转让事务;转让证书制作业
conveyancing costs 转让证书制作费
conveyancing counsel 拟制转让证书的律师
conveyancing intermediaries 转让中介人
conveyancing precedents 财产转让惯例
conveyer (=conveyor) n. 财产转让人;交付人;传达者,搬运者;输送设备
convict n./v. 罪犯,(服刑中的)囚犯,已决犯,被判罪者/定罪;证明有罪;宣判有罪;使知罪
convict establishment 囚犯工场;罪犯自新劳动场,劳改场所
convict goods 囚犯生产的产品
convict hulk 犯人船,囚船
convict in prison 囚犯
convict prison 囚犯监狱
convict system 徒刑制度
convicted a. 已判过罪的;有罪的
convicted person 已决犯;已定过罪的人,已判过罪的人
convicted prisoner 既决罪犯,已决犯
convicted sex offenders 已判罪的性罪犯
convicting magistrate 判决(罪行的)裁判官
conviction n. 1.定罪,证明有罪,判罪(指犯人经法庭审讯后,判定有罪)2.深信,确信 3.服罪
conviction of crime 定罪
conviction on indictment 经公诉程序的判决;依诉状定罪
conviction rate 判罪率
convictive a. 定罪的
convince v. 1.使确信,使信服 2.使认识错误(或罪行)
convincing argument 有说服力的论据
convincing force 使人信服的力量
convocation n. 召集,集会;(英)评议会
convocation of parliament 召开议会
convoy n./v. 护航(队)(指战争时,军舰为商船护航或护卫商船的舰队)/替……护航,护送
cookies n. 跟踪软件
cool blood 精神冷静状态(在刑法上的杀人罪中指具有充分理智和思维能力,在激烈的、不可控制感情的精神状态)
cooler n. 冰箱;冷饮品;(俚)监狱(尤指单人牢房)
Cooley Doctrine (美)库利原则[指航运

垄断案后的半个多世纪里,几乎所有需要涉及贸易条款的诉讼中,考虑的都是州法律的合宪性问题。在"宾州领港调控案"(Cooley v. Board of Wardens of Port of Philadelphia)后将这一原则予以明确化,形成库利原则,即"贸易"权内的任何问题,只要性为全国性的,只允许一种统一制度或管理计划。即由原来禁止任何州际贸易障碍转为根据特定情况,给法院留下衡平空间]

cooling time 息怒时间(指刑法上的杀人罪中在受到激烈刺激或盛怒情况下恢复控制自己感情和意志的时间)
cooling-off period (劳资纠纷中的)冷却时间;(分期付款租购中的)试用期间,等待期
coop n. 禁闭地区;(俚)监狱;(关家禽的)笼;家禽饲养场
cooperate v. 合作,协作;配合
cooperation n. 合作;协作;合作化
cooperation among nations 国际合作
cooperation between judicial organs and masses (中)司法机关同群众相结合(原则)
cooperation in production 生产协作(合作)
cooperative n./a. 合作社;合作团体/合作的,协作的;合作化的
cooperative association 合作协会
cooperative bank 合作银行
cooperative bargaining 合作讨价还价[这一方法亦称合理化方法,它就理性参与人之间的协议应具有的特征提出一系列公理,并考察这样的协议可能存在所需的条件,以及这一结果是否是唯一的。纳什程序是将合作讨价还价的原理与非合作讨价还价原理联系起来的一种努力]
cooperative business operation 合作经营
cooperative counsel 合作律师
cooperative development 协(合)作发展,合(协)作开发
cooperative enterprise 合作企业
cooperative farm 合作农场
cooperative federalism 合作联邦主义,联邦合作制度[是一个未定型的宪法概念,它在"新政"(New Deal)时期首次被用于由国会提供资金、由各州实施旨在建立全国统一调控制度的联邦援助计划,为了替换竞争的联邦分权制度的概念。合作联邦主义的提法就成为对在制定政策中以各州权利和自制程度的减少为代价从而增加联邦政府权利的中央集权制的一种委婉提法]

cooperative law 合作社法
cooperative medical service 合作医疗(制度)
cooperative ownership system 合作社所有制
cooperative property 合作社财产
cooperative society 合作(会)社
cooperator n. (产销)合作社社员,合作者
cooptation n. (原有成员对新成员的)增选
coordinate n./a./v. 同等的人(或事物)/同等的,并列的;协调的/使协调,使同等
coordinate branch 同等分庭,并列分庭
coordinate jurisdiction (同等法院的)同等审判权
coordinated policy 协调的政策
coordinating body 协调机构
coordination n. 同等,调整,配合,协作,协调
coordination committee 协调委员会
coordination taxes 调整税
coordinator n. 协调人
Coordinator for International Intellectual Property Enforcement (美)国际知识产权执法协调员(指2005年国会通过立法,设立"国际知识产权执法协调员",其职责是协调联邦政府的资源,在美国国内外加强知识产权保护。其具体工作有:与相关联邦机构进行协调、担任美国知识产权执法协调委员会主席、制定政策解决国际知识产权侵权问题、执行知识产权法律和在海外实施保护美国知识产权战略)
cop v. 1.逮住;抓住 2.偷;获得;取得 3.(美)警察(作名词用)
cop a plea 避重就轻的认罪(企图达到减刑)
cop out 1.(美)被逮住(尤指正在作案时被捕)2.避重就轻地认罪;自首并告密 3.失

败,死 4. 放弃,投降,避开;逃避;逃避者;自首
coparcenary n./a. 共同继承;共同所有/共同继承的,共同所有的;共同继承土地
coparcener n. 共同继承人(之一),共同所有人(之一),土地的共同所有人(之一)
coparty n. 共同当事人
copartner n. 合股人;合伙人
copartnership n. 合伙
copartnery n. 合伙关系
cope v. (机会均等地)竞争,对付,克服;妥善处理(with)
copier n. 模仿者,抄写员
Copilacion de Canella (或 ***Huesca***)《西班牙法律汇编》(1245年出版)
copious footnotes 大量的脚注,丰富的脚注
coplaintiff n. 共同起诉人,共同原告
copula 性交
copulation n. 性交
copy n. 复制品;抄本,副本;范本;(电影)拷贝
copy fee 稿费,版费
copy of appeal 上诉版副本
copy of panel 陪审员名单副本
copy of the file 案卷的副本
copy of the writ 令状副本
copyhold n. (英)依官册(典籍)享有的土地保有权;经官册(典籍)登记的保有土地
copyhold freehold tenure (英)依官册(典籍)享有的自由(完全)土地保有权;经官册(典籍)登记的自由(完全)保有地
copyholder n. (英)依官册(典籍)享有的土地保有人
copyright n./v. 版权,著作权/取得版权,保护……的版权,版权法
Copyright Act (英)《版权法》(1710年);(美)《版权法》(1976年)
copyright action 版权诉讼,著作权诉讼
copyright case 版权案件;著作权案件
copyright clearance 版权许可,版权批准
copyright in information 信息版权
copyright infringement 侵犯版权;侵犯著作权
copyright infringement suit 侵犯版权诉讼;侵犯著作权诉讼
copyright law 版权法;著作权法
copyright licensing agency 版权许可证贸易代理公司
copyright mark 版权标记
copyright notice 版权声明,版权通知,版权标记
copyright office (美)版权办公室(指1897年建立于美国国会图书馆内,每年有40万版权注册登记)
copyright owner 版权拥有者,版权所有人
copyright proprietors (owner) 版权所有人
copyright registration 版权登记
copyright reserved 版权所有(不准翻印)
copyright royalty 版税
copyright royalty tribunal 版税法庭
copyright work 有版权的作品
copyrightability n. 可享有版权性[指在大多数国家中为独创性(原创性);在有些国家还包括已登记或已固定含义等]
copyrightable a. 可申请取得版权的
copyrighted work 版权所有的作品
copyrighter n. 版权所有人
coram 在(某人)面前
coram judice 1.在法官面前(意指在法院管辖范围内) 2.管辖权(jurisdiction)
coram nobi 在我们自己面前
coram nobis 错误提示状,本法院纠错令状(该词本意为"在我们自己面前"。在英格兰古法中,指在王座法庭纠正已判决案件存在事实上错误的令状)
coram non judice 在无审判权的法庭上;不是在法官面前
coram populo 在公众面前
coram rege (英史)御前法庭(指亨利二世时国王法庭派生出来的一个分庭)
Corbin on Contracts (美)《科尔宾论契约》(指由著名的耶鲁大学法学教授林顿·科尔宾著的优秀法学名著,是一种多卷本专门领域的有相当深度的法学学术概论)(已译有中文本)
cordictio indebiti 对抗债索回之诉
cordon n. 警戒线;封锁线
core n. 1.核心;中心花纹 2.箕形,箕斗

core facts (=basic facts) 基本事实(见 ultimate facts)
Core Labor Standards 核心劳工标准
core meaning 核心意义
core of meaning 中心意思(指语言的外延具有明确的中心区域,在此区域内人们不会产生争议,这与司法证明语言的模糊性有关)
core problem 关键问题,核心问题
core proceedings 核心诉讼
core theorem 核心定理
corelation (=co-relation) n. 相互关系
Corfu Channel Case (1949年)科孚海峡案(该判决中,国际法院指出,阿尔巴尼亚知道在其领水中存在雷阵却没有通告英国政府,违反了通告的国际义务)
corn-laws (复) n. (英史)(限制谷物进口的)谷物法(1846年已废除)
corn-rent n. (英)以谷物(或按谷价折合)缴纳的地租
corner v./n. 垄断(市场),囤积奇/角,地区;困境,囤积,垄断
corner the market 垄断市场,囤积奇
cornerstone n. 基础,基石;要件
corollary n. 必然结果,推论;系定理,定理
coronation n. 加冕典礼
coronation oath 加冕宣誓
coroner n. 验尸官(港译:死因裁判官);法医
coroner's court 验尸官法庭;死因调查法庭;(验尸官进行死因调查的)记录法庭
coroner's inquest 死因调查;验尸
coroner's jury 验尸陪审团
corporal a. 肉体的,身体的,有形的
corporal imbecility 无性交能力
corporal oath 手摸着圣经宣誓
corporal punishment 体罚,肉刑,肉体刑罚
corporal wound by mistake 过失伤害
corporales n. 有体物
corporate a. 社团的,法人组织的;公司的,团体的;共同的,全体的
corporate arrangement and reorganization 公司重整
corporate body (=body corporate) 法人,法人组织

corporate bonds 公司债券
corporate bonds and debentures 公司债券
corporate capacity 法人资格
corporate capacity question 法人能力问题
corporate charter 法人章程,公司章程(美国称 articles of incorporation,英国称 memoradum of association);(英)公司特许状
corporate community 公司财团,企业财团
corporate complicity 公司同谋[国际人权领域没有一个确定的公司同谋定义,有学者将公司同谋分为直接同谋、间接同谋和保持沉默的同谋。直接同谋指公司明知他人正在实施侵犯人权的行为却予以协助或鼓励。公司明知一国政府正在从事违反《世界人权宣言》所包含的习惯国际法原则的行为却对该国予以帮助,就构成直接同谋。间接同谋又称从侵犯人权行为中获益的同谋(beneficial corporate complicity),是指公司从他人所实施的侵犯人权行为中获取利益,尽管该侵犯人权的行为并非公司授权、指挥,或公司预先知悉该侵权行为,公司明知正在发生侵犯人权的行为却从该侵犯人权行为中获取直接的经济利益,并继续维持与东道国政府的伙伴关系,即构成间接同谋。例如一个公司容忍其商业伙伴在推进双方共同的商业目标过程中实施的侵权行为或故意对该侵犯人权的行为视而不见,该公司即构成从侵犯人权行为中获益的同谋。保持沉默的同谋(silent complicity)是指跨国公司对东道国政府侵犯人权行为保持沉默或不作为。保持沉默的同谋的概念反映了人们对公司的期盼,即公司应提请权力当局关注系统的或持续的侵犯人权行为。正如大赦国际(英国)商业协会主席 Geoffrey Chandler 先生所说的"沉默或不为将被看成对专制政府的安慰,将可能被判定为共谋……沉默并非中立,不作为不是一种选择"。根据国际法,如果个人所处的位置和道德权威对侵犯人权的行为形成鼓励,那么该个人可以仅仅因为其存在(presence)而被认为构成侵犯人权的同谋。因此,跨国公司仅仅因在发生严重侵犯人权国家的商业存在(commercial presence)构成保持沉默的同谋]

corporate consent theory 公司同意原理(指公司明示或暗示愿接受某州法院的管辖)
corporate counsel (=house counsel)
corporate court 市民事法院(在英国指市或享有特权的自治市的法院,具有民事管辖权,而在美国则指某些州的市民事法院,仍可听审刑事案件)
corporate document 法人文件
corporate excise tax 公司执照税
corporate failure 公司破产,公司失败
corporate finance 企业财务
corporate franchise 法人(公司)营业权
corporate governance 公司治理结构
corporate indemnification 公司补偿制度
Corporate Law Reform Act 《公司改革法》(指1992年澳大利亚的公司改革法)
corporate limits 公共领域,公共范围,公共区域;企业限额;公共界限范围
corporate merger 见 merger 8
corporate name 公司名称;商号
corporate officer 见 officer 1
corporate opportunity rule 公司机会规则(在英联邦国家,公司机会规则源自衡平法的受托人的信义义务规则,产生于1726年Keech v. Sandford一案,该案确立了"除非委托人明示同意,受托人不得利用其他地位谋利"的规则。在美国,一般认为关于公司机会规则的最早判例是1900年的Lagarde v. Anniston Lime & Stone Co.案。董事不得篡夺公司拥有利益之机会这一基本规则在该案得以确立,随后禁止篡夺公司商业机会规则成为英美公司法的一项重要规则。该规则被简称为公司机会规则)
corporate organization 法人组织
corporate performance 公司业绩,公司成效
corporate personality 法人人格
corporate philanthropy 法人的慈善事业;公司的慈善性捐赠
corporate power 法人权限,公司权力
corporate presence (美)公司在场,公司所在(指公司所在地管辖领域)
corporate presence theory 公司在场理论

corporate property 公司财产,法人财产
corporate responsibility 共同责任
corporate rip-offs 企业被盗
corporate seal 法人印章,公司印章
corporate securities 公司证券
corporate social responsibility 企业的社会责任[指企业不能仅以最大限度地为股东赢利或赚钱作为己任,还应最大限度地增进股东利益以外的其他所有社会利益,包括雇员(职工)利益,消费者和债权人、中小竞争者的利益,以及当地社区、环境、社会弱者等利益和整个社会公共利益。]
corporate spying 商业间谍活动
corporate state 社团国家(指不是个人,而是由经济和职业团体组成并管理的社会的国家)
corporate veil 法人借口,法人托辞(指一种法律上的假设,法人所提起的诉讼的这种法律上的假设,并不是对其所有权者的诉讼,而且这些所有权者通常并不对法人诉讼承担责任)
corporation n. 1.法人,社团 2.公司,企业,(美)有限公司
corporation activities 公司活动
corporation aggregate 社团法人;集体法人;合作法人
corporation boroughs (英史)自治市
corporation by estoppel 不容否认的公司(指一家商业公司从法律上看即为一个法人,因为第三方对待它犹如对待法人,这样可防止第三方持有该公司特有责任的股东或高管职位)
corporation by prescription 时效法人
corporation by-laws 公司章程
corporation created for the public benefit 公益社团,公益法人
corporation crime 法人犯罪
corporation de facto 事实上的公司,事实上的法人团体
corporation dependent 法人被告
corporation doctrine 合并原理
corporation duty 公司税;法人义务
corporation having the aim of public benefit 以公益为目的的社团(法人)
corporation income tax 公司所得税

corporation law 公司法
corporation lawyer 公司法律顾问,公司律师
corporation muscle 公司"肌肉"组织
corporation nerve center 公司神经中枢(指美国联邦法院认定公司主营业务地的三个标准,以确定该公司的州籍,以便解决其诉讼的管辖问题,另一个标准为 corporation muscle 和 corporation activities)
corporation of learning 学术机构
Corporation of the City of London (英)伦敦城自治会
corporation reorganization 公司重整,公司重组
(the) 2003 Corporate Responsibility Bill (英国)《2003 年公司责任法案》(指其透明的规则,并规定要求公司对利益相关者负责)
corporation securities 公司债券
corporation sole 单独法人,独体法人,单一法人
corporation tax 公司税
corporation ultra vires 越权的法人
corporation's creditor 公司的债权人
corporations incorporated in the state 在本州成立的公司
corporatism n. 位组主义;各阶级合作主义
corporatist approach of the NRA 国家恢复法的各阶级合作组织的方法
corporative state 合作国家(传统意义上的国家法律和非政府内部规则相互结合,政府和非政府组织的相互结合,形成了所谓的"合作国家"。政府不再是人民利益的唯一代表,也不再对所有的社会问题负责)
corporatization of state enterprises 国企公司化
corporator n. 公司成员;社团成员(或发起人);公司股票持有者
corpore 标的物
corporeal a. 有形的(指动产);有体的;具体的;物质的;肉体的
corporeal chattel 有形动产
corporeal hereditaments 有形的可继承的财产(指不动产)

corporeal property 有形财产,动产
corporeal thing 有形物,有形财产
(a) corporeal thing external to me 外在于我的有体物(见 external objects)
corps (复) n. 军团;部队;团体;兵种
corps diplomatique 外交使团
corpse n. 尸体
corpse dissection 尸体解剖
corpse ticket (战死后便于识别的)士兵身份牌
corpus 1.体,身体(尤指尸体)2.(文献、法典等的)全集;汇编 3.(事物的)主体 4.(基金的)本金,财产和投资的总额(以区别于利息或收益)5.(罗马法)实际支配的事实
corpus delicti 犯罪事实之物证(如被害者的尸体或焚烧房屋所留下的残余物)
corpus juris 法典,法令大全;(大写斜体)美国法律百科全书(此套丛书囊括好几部法律汇集,其中两部最主要的汇集是:《国法大全》或《民法大全》和《教会法》,也是美国法规原理百科全书式阐述的名称,即《法律百科全书》或《法律判例汇编大全》)
corpus juris canonici 教会法,(大写)《寺院法大全》(又译《天主教教会法典大全》,指中世纪天主教教会的法律汇编,共6卷)
Corpus Juris Civilis 《国法大全》,《民法大全》[指在罗马皇帝查士丁尼(Justinian)的指导下于公元 528—556 年间编纂汇典而成的《民法大全》。该汇集大全包括四大全书:《法学纲要》(Institutes)、《学说汇纂》或《潘德克特法学》、《法典》(Code)和《新律》(Novels)。《民法大全》较早时也受"Corpus Juris Canonict"(教会法)或《寺院法大全》影响。16 世纪或晚些时间正式签订出版包括这四大全书原文的罗马法大全书。见 Roman Law; Justinian Code]
corpus juris secundum 法律判例汇编大全,(大写)(美)《法律判例汇编大全》(此套丛书为西方出版公司出版的最全面、完整、有权威的成文法律百科全书,它是以 1658 年至今全部汇编过的判例为基础而重述美国法律汇编的最详尽、完整的百科全书式的重述)

corpus of a crime (一项)罪行的全部事实
corpus of civil law 民法典
corpus of the laws and regulations 法规汇编
corpus separatum 单独实体
corpus vilis 无用物
correct v./a. 纠正,改正;修改,校正;惩罚;制止,责备/正确的;改正的;适当的;符合一般准则的
correct conduct 端正行为
correct handling of contradictions among the people (中)正确处理人民内部矛盾
correction n. 1.改正,纠正;修改,校正 2.(对罪犯的)教养 3.责备,惩罚 4.制止 5.(价格上涨后的)回落
correction of deviation 纠正偏差
correction of the defect 修补瑕疵,弥补缺陷
correctional n./a. 教养院/教养的;纠正的,修正的;惩治的
correctional process 惩治改造程序
correctitude n. (行为)端正,正派
corrective a. 改正的,纠正的,矫正的,惩治的,抑制的
corrective justice (美)少年法庭的教养法官;矫正正义(亦称"rectificatory justice"),是指当某人以某种方式伤害了其他人时要求对这种情况给予矫正。矫正正义因而成为现代合同法,侵权法制度,赔偿和刑事司法的基础)
corrective training (对少年犯等的)教养处分,矫正处分
corrector n. 校正者,校对员,纠正者;处罚者,责备者
corregidor 1.(西班牙城镇的)警察长 2.(西班牙)民事司法行政官 3.(南美的)小行政区长
correlate v./n. 使相互关联(with to)/相互关联的事物
correlative a./n. 相关的,关联的/对应物,相关物;关联词
correlative duty 对应的义务
correlative liability 对应的责任
correlativity n. 相关(或依赖)性,相关(或依赖)程度

correspond v. 符合,一致;相当,相应,适应;通信
correspondence n. 信件;通信;相当,相应,一致
correspondence education 函授教育
correspondence school 函授学校
correspondence theory of causal relationship 相当因果关系说
correspondent n. 1.记者,通讯员;2.客户,商业代表
corresponding a. 相应的,对应的;一致的;通讯的
corresponding duty 相应的义务
corresponding meaning 相应含义
corresponding member (英)通信会员;(美)(参加议事而不参加票决的)准会员
corresponding reasons 相应的理由,相一致的理由
corrigendum 应更正处;应改正的错误;勘误表
corroborant n. 证实的事实
corroborate v. 证实;确定;(提供附加证据来)证实
corroborating evidence 确证的证据,认证证据(又译加强证据。指一种附加证据,这种证据使已经提供的证据更为有力、肯定)
corroboration n. 加强证据;独立证据,(以进一步的证据)确证
corroboration of witnesses 证据的确(证)认
corroborative a. 确证的,确定的
corroborative evidence 助证
corroborator n. 助证者,确证者;确证物
corrupt v./a. 使腐化;贿赂;收买/贪污的;腐化的
Corrupt and Illegal Practices Ordinances 《舞弊和非法行为条例》
corrupt element 贪污分子;腐化分子
corrupt practice 贪污行为;(选举中的)舞弊行为,行贿行为
Corrupt Practices Act (美)《腐败行为防止法》(指既是调节政治活动的州法规,也是调节国际法人金融活动的联邦法规)
corrupting n. 见 impairing the morals of

council of military court 陆军军法会议
council of ministers 部长会议;大臣会议;内阁会议
Council of Ministers of the European Communities 欧洲共同体部长理事会
Council of National Education (法)国家教育委员会
council of province 省政委员会
Council of Revision (美)法案修正委员会
council of state 国务院,国务会议;国务委员会;(大写)(法国等的)参政院(又译最高行政法院,指具有咨询机构和行政法院两重职能的高级机构)
council of state government (美)州政府委员会
council of the cabinet 内阁会议
council of the republic 共和国委员会
council of war (战地的)军事会议,(英美以外的)军事参议院
Council on Environmental Quality 环境质量委员会
Council on Legal Education Opportunities (美)法律教育机会委员会
council on tribunal 裁判庭审判委员会;(英)法庭评议会
Council Regulation (EC) No 1346/2000 of 29 May 2000 on Insolvency Proceedings (欧盟)《关于破产程序的条例》
council-manager plan (美)由市议会推选市长的市政制度
council-system in administration 行政合议制
councilman n. (地方议会)议员;(美)市议员[英国通常用council(l)or]
council(l)or n. (地方议会)议员;评议员;参赞,顾问;(日)参议员
council(l)orship n. (地方议会)议员(或顾问等)的身份(或职位)
councilor court(或 prerogative court) 政务会议法庭(或特有法庭)
councilwoman n. (地方)女议员
counsel n. 辩护人,法律顾问,律师;(就法律问题提出的)劝告,建议,意见
counsel and procure 劝诱和唆使(他人犯罪)

counsel fee 律师费
counsel for the defence 辩护律师;被告律师
counsel in chambers 顾问律师
counsel of record 记录律师,记录人(指专门案件的正式记录人或律师,其姓名在法院的记录簿中如同在案例中的律师一样)
counsel on both sides 双方当事人的共同律师,双边的共同律师
counsel's seat 律师席
counsel(l)ing n. 评议;商议;指导、咨询意见
counsel(l)or n. 律师;法律顾问;顾问;(使馆)参赞
counsel(l)or of state 国务顾问
counsellor-at-law [=counsel(l)or at law] n. 律师;法律工作者(与lawyer, attorney-at-law, counsellor同义,词义上没什么区别)
count v./n. 数,点,算入;认为,信为;看做;共计/(程序)1.一条罪状(指控告嫌疑犯明显犯罪的刑事起诉书中列举的罪项的一部分);一个理由,一个问题,争点问题 2.申诉状[在起诉状或类似诉答状(pleading)中显见的权利主张的陈述(见declaration 7)。count 这个词在旧法律书籍中与declaration 同义,但在诉讼中包括两个或两个以上诉因(causes of action)。每个诉因程序进程均要求各自不同的陈述或当原告要提供两个或两个以上的不同陈述。每一各自陈述均可称为court,而且所有陈述集中一起就构成declaration(原告的申诉)]3.计算选票(见canvass 2)4. 原告的申诉或物权诉讼(real action)中起始的诉状(见declaration 7)5.(专利)界定优势中的标的(指专利申请书的组成部分,它在两个及两个以上的申请之间或一个或两个申请和一个或更多的专利之间界定标的所处的优势。见interference 3)(控告的一条)罪告,理由;争点,问题;合计
count in indictment 起诉书中列举的罪项
count of declaration 宣言中的条项
count of law suit 诉讼事项,诉讼理由
count of pleading 答辩事项
count on (upon) 指望,依靠,期待
count out (美)因故意少计票数而使某人

落选;(英下议院)因法定人数不足而宣布休会;把……不计在内,把(某人)作不参加论

count out of the House (英)下议院因法定人数不足而宣告延会

count palatine (神圣罗马帝国的)大法官;(在领地内)享有王权的伯爵

count sb. to a guilt 认为某人有罪

counter n./a./v. 计算者,计算器,伪造的硬币;柜台;反对;反对物;(讨价还价的)本钱,有利条件;(大写)(英)债务人监狱(指伦敦的 Poultry Counter 和 Wood Street Counter 两监狱名称,后合并为一个专作对债务人和破坏治安者的惩罚的场所)/相反的,相应的,替代的,副的,对立的,反对的,敌意的;收回成命的/反对,反击;引证,辩驳,防御

counter cheque 银行取款单

counter claim 反请求,反诉(指被告为了回答原告的原诉提出的请求。提起反诉的被告是该案中的反诉原告,而原告则为反诉被告)

counter claimants n. 反请求人,反诉请求人

counter letter (大陆法)相反证书[指一件书证(document),其中当事方模拟合同(to a simulated contract)记录他们的真实意图。如登记的物权所有人可以在相反证书中确认另一人实际拥有该财产权。当此财产在一个时期以后被回复转让(reconveyed)时,则可使用此相反证书。针对依诚信行事的第三方,此相反证书则必然失效,产权仍归受让人。见 simulated contract]

counter measure 反措施
counter order 收回成命的命令
counter tariff 对抗关税,抵制关税
counter-argument 驳论
counter-benefaction 反补偿
counter-bond 反担保书
counter-case 辩诉状,反诉案件
counter-complaint 反民事诉讼(针对原告,被告呈上起诉书称原告已有违约行为,并应对被告承担损害赔偿责任)
counter-evidence 相反证据

counter-intervention n. 反干涉
counter-Reformation 反对宗教改革,与宗教改革相对立
counteraccusation n. 反控告;反诉
counteract v. 抵抗,抵制;阻碍;抵消
counteradvice n. 反对意见
counteraffidavit n. 反宣誓书
counterappeal n. 抗诉;抗告
counterargument n. 抗辩
counterattack n. 反击;反攻
counterbalance n. 平衡;平衡力;抗衡
countercase n. 反诉案件
countercharge n./v. 反诉;反控,反攻
countercheck n. 复查,对抗(手段)
counterclaim n./v. 反请求;反诉;反索赔
counterdeed n. 相反契据;反证证书
counterdemand 反请求(见 set-off; cross-demand)
counterespionage n. 反间谍
counterevidence n. 反证;对抗证据
counterfeit n./v./a. 假冒品;冒牌品;伪造品/伪造,仿造/假冒的,冒牌的,伪造的,仿造的,虚假的

(The) Counterfeit Access Device and Computer and Abuse Act (美国1984年11月12日经国会通过的)《虚伪进入的方法与计算机欺诈和计算机滥用法》

counterfeit coin 伪造的硬币,假硬币
counterfeit goods 伪造商品
counterfeit money 伪币,伪钞
counterfeit note 伪钞
counterfeit trademark 假冒商标
counterfeiter n. 伪造者;伪造货币者
counterfeiting n. 伪造罪;伪造货币罪
counterfeiting coinage 伪造货币罪,伪造铸币罪
counterfeiting money or securities of a foreign nation 伪造外国货币或证券罪
counterfeiting of (national) currency 伪造(国家)货币罪
counterfeiting of current money 伪造通货罪
counterfeiting of valuable securities 伪造有价证券罪
counterfeiting the King's seal (英)伪造

国玺罪
counterfoil n. (英)支票存根;(收据、汇票等)存根(美国亦作 stub)
counterfoil receipt 存根收据
counterintelligence n. 反情报
countermand v. 取消,撤回;召回
countermark n. (金银制品上保证可靠性的)戳记,附加记号;(共有货物上的)副号,副标
countermeasure n. 对策;反对手段,抵制措施
countermemorials n. (国际法院的)辩诉状
countermove n. 对抗手段,报复手段,反向运动
counternotice n. 取消通知
counteroffer n. 还价,还发价;反要约(指受要约人在承诺中对要约的条款作了扩大、限制或变动并以此作为承诺的条件)
counterpart n. 1.副本;复本 2.补足物 3.相对应的物(或人),对手方 4.极相似的东西 5.(英美法)相对给付(指具有 consideration 的含义)
counterperformance n. 对等物,对偿;对待给付
counterplea n. 反驳;抗辩
counterplead v. 反驳;抗辩
counterproposal n. 反建议;反提案
counterquestion n. 反诘,反问
counterrevolution n. 反革命
counterrevolutionary n./a. 反革命分子/反革命的
counterrevolutionary behavio(u)r 反革命行为
counterrevolutionary case 反革命案件
counterrevolutionary clique 反革命集团
counterrevolutionary conduct 反革命行为
counterrevolutionary criminal 反革命罪犯
counterrevolutionary criminal act 处置反革命罪犯条例
counterrevolutionary gang 反革命集团
counterrevolutionary league 反革命同盟
counterrevolutionary murder 反革命杀人(罪)

counterrevolutionary offence 反革命罪
counterrevolutionary organization 反革命组织
counterrevolutionary sabotage 反革命破坏活动
counterrevolutionary saboteur 反革命破坏分子
counterrevolutionary suspect 反革命嫌疑犯,反革命嫌疑分子
counterrevolutionist n. 反革命分子
countersecurity n. 副保证
countersign v. 副署,连署,会签;(文件等)确认
countersignature n. 副署,连署,会签
counterspy n. 反间谍
counterstatement n. 反陈述;反声明;抗辩书;反诉状
counterstrike n. 反击
countersuit n. 反诉
counterterror n. 反恐怖
countertrade n. 对销贸易,补偿贸易
countervail v. 对抗,抵消,补偿
countervail livery 抵消交付,抵消让渡
countervailing consideration 补偿考虑
countervailing duty 抵消关税;反补贴税,(为了保护本国产品,对有出口津贴的进口货物所征收的)反倾销税
countervailing effects 不利影响
countervailing equity 对等股权,抵消股权
countervailing evidence 对抗性证据
countervailing federal interests 补偿联邦利益
countervailing power 对抗力量
counterview n. 对质;(古)相反的意见
counting n. 计算;开票
counting method of the degree of relationship 亲等计算法
counting of ballot 点票;检票
counting overseer (或 **witness**) (开票)监票人
Countors (或 **Contors**) n. (英)(皇家法院的)高级律师;(出庭)辩护人
country n. 1.国家,国土;祖国;国籍所属国;故乡 2.地区,城区;农村,乡下;土地 3.(从被告的邻居或从本国人选出的)陪

审团 4.(总称)国民,选民
country note 地方银行发行的纸币
country of dependency 附属国
country of immigration 移民输入国
country of internment (战俘、敌侨、军事犯等的)拘留国(家)
country of multinationalities 多民族国家
country of origins 原产国,出产国;起源国,原籍国
country of refuge 避难国
country of registration 船舶注册国,船籍国
country of residence 居住国;驻在国
county officer (美)县政官员,县官员(指县官员的权力和管辖权均受县政范围的限制。他们仅能在任职县的范围行使其权力和管辖权)
country party 农民党(代表农民利益的政党)
Country Practice of the Law 国家执业律师业务;区域执业律师业务;区域律师执业
country profile 国家概况
country without internal and external debts 既无内债又无外债的国家
country's independence 国家独立
country-level n. 国家一级
countryside commissions (英)乡村委员会
countrywide a. 全国性的,全国范围的
county n. (英)郡(旧译:州);(美、中)县
County and Borough Police Act (英)《郡和自治市警察法》
county attorney 郡(县)检察官;镇(城市)检察官
county borough (英)郡(州)级自治市
county clerk (美)县法院书记官[殖民地时期的民事法院(court of common pleas)被称为县法院(county court),其书记官因此被称为"县书记官"]
county corporate (英)特别市(指国王命令特许设立的、享有特权的城市)
county council (英)郡(州)议会
county court (英)郡(州)法院;(中)县法院;地方法院
county head (中)县长

county of residence of first listed plaintiff 第一原告住所地所在县
county palatine (英)特权领,享有王权的伯爵的领地
county people's congress (中)县人民代表大会
county people's court (中)县人民法院
county people's government (中)县人民政府
county people's procuratorate (中)县人民检察院
county (或 district) prosecutor (美)县(或区)检察官
county seat 县府所在地
county sessions (英)郡(州)高等法庭开庭期(指在州或郡里按季开审的高等法庭开审期);县法院开庭期
county town (英)郡的首府
coup 突然袭击;(军事)政变
coup de grace 致命一击(原指犯人受刑时所受最后致死的一击,以免其多受痛苦)
coup de main 突击,奇袭
coup d'ètat 政变,(突然的)武力夺取政权
coupist n. 企图军事政变者,支持(军事)政变者
couple n. 一对,一双;配偶,夫妇;情侣,未婚夫妻
coupon n. 联(券)票;(公债、债券等)息票;(附在商品上的)赠券
coupon bond 附息票的债券;附息公债;固定收入证券
coupon clipper (专以剪兑公债的利息为生的)食利人
Cour d'Appel 上诉法院
Cour d'Assises (法)重罪法院,刑事法庭,刑事审判
Cour de Cassation (法国、比利时等国的)最高(上诉)法院
courier n. 送急件的人,信使(尤指外交信使、秘密情报递送者等)
course n. 1.过程,程序;经过;行动方向;路线;河流;航线 2.课程 3.(复)行为,做法
course of business 商业(公司)的正常经营,公司的正常运转
course of common law of contract 合同法

的普通法发展方向

course of dealing (16世纪)交易惯例,交易过程[指一系列交易中当事双方之间的固定行为模式(比如超过好几年的多方货物销售)。如果引起纠纷,当事双方的交易过程通常作为证据证明他们是如何有意实现这样的交易。见 course of performance; trade usage]

course of employment 就业过程(指在工作时间或工作地点与工作的直接关系)

course of legal development 法律发展的进程

course of litigation 诉讼过程;诉讼程序

course of litigation in administrative jurisdiction 行政管辖范围的诉讼程序

course of nature 自然的趋势,因果的过程

course of performance (18世纪)履约过程[指在合同涉及反复履行时机,而且当事双方均知道履行的性质并有机会反对时,合同生效后任何一方的先前履行行为即为履行过程。履行协约的过程应用于确定双方协议的意义,它与交易惯例(course of dealing)不同,后者还涉及双方当事人在本合同之前其他合同中的行为。见 course of dealing]

course of play 预测博弈可能的过程

course of things 事态;趋势

course of trade 见 trade usage

courses of conduct 行为,指导行为

court n. 法庭,法院,审判庭(court 一字和 judge 或 judges 在制定法中作同义词,特别是在由法庭或法官制定或作出命令时)

court above 上级法院

court adjourned 休庭;退庭

Court Administer 法庭管理员(指在美国负责法庭的行政管理和案件管理等事务者)

court administrator (主管法庭事务和记录等的)法庭主管人

court administrative orders 法院行政管理令

court administrator act 司法行政管理法

court attendant 法警

court bail 法庭保释(指被检控人在法官面前可提出保释的请求,只要控方不反对,法官就有权批准的一种保释)

Court Baron (英史)贵族私人法院(亦译:采邑民事法庭。指中世纪贵族用来审理佃户和解决佃户问题纠纷的法院)

court battles 法庭竞争

court below 下级法院

court calendars 法院审理案件日程表

court case 诉讼案件

court Christian 基督教法庭

court circular (英)(报纸上逐日发表的)宫廷活动录

court clerk 法庭书记员(官),法院办事员,法院文书

court closed 闭庭

court costs 诉讼费用,辩护、审理费用

court day 开庭日,审判日

court debate 法庭辩论

court decision 法院判决;法院裁定;(复)法院判例(汇编)

court docket 1.法院判决摘要书 2.法庭备审案件目录

court document 诉讼记录;法院公文,法院文书

court exhibit 开庭时出示的证物

court expert (或 **expert-witness**) 法庭上的鉴定人

court fee 法院费用

Court for Consideration of Crown Cases Reserved (英)审议被保留刑事案件法院(建于1848年,后移交给刑事上诉法院)

court for divorce and matrimonial causes 离婚及婚姻事务法庭(创建于1857年,1873年转入高等法院)

court for serious penal offenses 重罪法院

court hand 法庭手迹

court having jurisdiction 有管辖权的法院

court hearing 庭审,法庭认定

court holding 法院判决意见

court holds that 法庭确定……,法庭认定……

court house 法院(指法院所在地),法庭;法院大楼

court in bank 全席审判

court in session 开庭,在开庭中

court injunction　法院禁令
court jurisdiction　法院管辖权,管辖权
court law　法院法
court leet　(英)采邑(领地)刑事法庭(指诺尔曼王朝时代的刑事法庭,用来审理领地里租户所犯的轻罪)
court manager　法庭管理者
court martial reports　(美)军事法院判例汇编
court not of record　非存卷法院,非记录法院
court notice　法院通知书
court of a sovereign people　最高人民法庭(院)
court of accounts　账务纠纷法院
court of administrative litigation　行政诉讼审判庭
court of admiralty　海事法院;(英)海事法庭
court of ancient demesne　(英)旧领地法院
court of annulment　撤销判决法院
court of appeal　上诉法院
Court of Appeal for Federal Circuit　(美)联邦巡回上诉法院
court of appeal in chancery　(英)大法官法院上诉庭(创建于1851年,1857年同新设上诉法院合并)
court of appeals in cases of capture　(美)捕获案件上诉法院
court of arbitration　仲裁院(庭)
Court of Arbitration of the International Chamber of Commerce　国际商会的仲裁庭
Court of Arches　(英)拱顶法院,坎特伯雷大主教法庭[指坎特伯雷大主教的官方代表法庭以及大主教辖区法庭。其正式代表法庭和主教法庭世俗分庭都设在圣玛丽—勒—鲍(Mary)教堂,该教堂被建成拱形。这两个法庭于1875年合并,一切宗教案件的一审均由它受理。其管辖权是通过侵占主教区的管辖权取得的,它同时也是辖区内主教法庭的上诉法庭。1963年起该法庭已成为坎特伯雷大主教辖区法庭,对来自坎特伯雷省内的教区法院(consistory courts)的判决均有上诉管辖权]

Court of (the) Arches　(英)坎特伯雷大主教法庭(又译:大主教亲审法庭)
court of assizes　巡回法院
court of augmentations　(英史)增收法院(1535年成立,1554年解散)
court of bankruptcy　破产法庭(院)
court of borough　自治市法庭
Court of Budgetary and Financial Discipline　预算和财政纪律庭
court of cassation　撤销判决的法院,废弃原判的法院;(法国、比利时等国家的)最高(上诉)法院
Court of Chancery　(英)衡平法院,大法官法庭
court of chivalry　(英史)骑士法庭(指一种处理军队争端和纹章法律问题的司法机构)
court of civil appeals　民事上诉法院(庭)
court of civil jurisdiction　民事审判庭,民庭
court of claims　索赔(求偿)法院,(美)权利申诉法院;(美国华盛顿)行政法院
court of (the) clerk of the markets　(中世纪后期的)市场法庭,市场主事官法庭
court of common law　普通法(法)庭(亦称:习惯法法庭)
Court of Common Pleas　(英)三个皇家法院之一,高等民事法院,公诉院(参看Court of Kings Bench);(美国某些州的)中级民事及刑事法庭;普通法院(对民、刑等具有一般管辖权)
court of conciliation　调解法庭
court of conflicts in jurisdictional matter　处理管辖权冲突案件的法院
Court of Conflicts of Jurisdiction　(处理)管辖权冲突法院
court of conscience　(英史)良心裁判法庭(亦称court of request,1517年成立,1847年取消)
court of criminal appeal　刑事上诉法院
court of criminal equity　刑事衡平法院
court of criminal jurisdiction　刑事裁判庭,刑庭
court of customs and patent appeals　海关和专利上诉法院

court of delegates (英史)钦命法庭(指由国王通过特别授权任命的委员会,建于1533年,于1832年撤销)
court of divorce and matrimonial causes (英)离婚和婚姻诉讼法庭
court of domestic relation (美)家庭关系法院
court of ecclesiastical causes reserved (英)保留宗教案件法庭(建于1963年)
court of equity 衡平法院
court of equivalent standing 同级法院
court of error 复审法庭,上诉法庭
court of errors and appeals 复审上诉法院
Court of Exchequer (英)理财法院(又译:财务大臣法院。原系审理有关税收方面案件的法院,现已并入高等法院财务组)
Court of Exchequer Chamber (英)(三个皇家法院之一)理财法院上诉法院(亦译:财务大臣上诉法院)
court of faculties (英)主教授权法庭
court of fairs 定期集市法庭
court of final instance 终审法院(庭)
court of final jurisdiction 终审法院(庭)
court of final resort (美)终审(管辖)法院
court of final trial 终审法院
court of first degree 初级法院
court of first fruits (英)初贡法院(1540年成立,1554年撤销)
court of first instance 初审法院(庭);第一审法院
court of first resort 初审法院
court of forest 森林法庭
court of general jurisdiction (美)一般管辖法院;普通管辖法院
court of general sessions (美)地方刑事法庭
court of general surveyors of the King's lands (英)国王土地总监法庭
court of great sessions (威尔士)高等民事法院
court of *habeas corpus* 人身保护状法庭
court of high commission 高级专员公署法院;特设高等法院(伊丽莎白女王时代的宗教法院)

court of hono(u)r (英)名誉法庭(指审理有关私人名誉、纹章、勋章等案件的法庭);荣誉法庭(指骑士法庭)
court of human rights 人权法庭
Court of Hustings (英)哈斯汀斯法院[指伦敦市约克郡等地最古老的、最高一级的法院的旧称。具有对不动产权益诉讼(real action)、混合诉讼(mixed action)和占有回复之诉(act of replevin)的管辖权。在伦敦市政大厅(Guildhall)由记录法官(Recorder)、市长(Lord Mayor)、郡长(sheriff)(后两者充任荣誉法官)(honorary judge)主持审理。随着不动产权益诉讼和驱逐之诉(ejectment)外的混合诉讼的废除,哈斯汀斯法院的管辖权也相对被废弃。这种法院起始于威廉征服英国(Conquest)(1066年)之前。在美国,以前在弗吉尼亚州某地曾有过这样的地方法院(local court),亦称为 *curia burgi*]
court of inferior jurisdiction 低一级的法院
court of inferior rank 下级法院
court of inquiry (军事)调查法庭;预审(法)庭
court of insurance 保险法庭
court of intermediate appeal (美)中级上诉法院(指设立在一些州的一种上诉法院,用以减轻最高法院的负担,但最后复审权仍在最高法院)
Court of International Trade (美)国际贸易法院
court of jail delivery (美)监狱释放(犯人)法庭
court of judicature 法院,法庭
court of justice 法院,法庭
Court of Justice of the European Communities 欧洲共同体法院
Court of King's (或 Queen's) bench (英)(三个皇家法院之一)王(后)座法院(庭)(意译为国王或女王的御席法院或法庭,译为王座或后座法院或法庭,在我国已约定俗成。原系英国一个独立的法院,1873年并入高等法院作为其组成部分,现常译为高等法院)
court of last instance 终审法院

court of last resort 终审法院,最高上诉法院,最高审级法院(该法院有权处理经审的上诉案件,如美国联邦最高法院)

court of law 法庭,法院,(英美法)普通法法院(指与 court of equity 相对而言)

court of limited jurisdiction (=special jurisdiction) (美)有限管辖法院(指只对有限的几种类型案件或有限的争议数额有行使司法权的联邦或州的一种法院,如遗嘱检验等法院)

court of magistrates of judicial police (马耳他岛)治安司法警察法庭

court of marches (英)(英格兰和苏格兰的)边区法院

court of maritime prizes 海上捕获法庭

Court of (the) Marshalsea (英)皇家法院;宫廷侍臣法庭[指以皇室为中心转移的法庭,对皇室 12 英里内所发生的案件具有管辖权(众所周知的王室司法管辖"verge"范围)。王室总管(steward)和宫廷侍臣(mashal)作为法官主持法庭,可以听审刑事案件和债务合约以及某种侵害(tresspasses)的民事诉讼。另外,该法庭还审理王室内的债务案件、合同和盖印合同案件、查理一世创设的宫廷法庭的新法庭,由王室管家、宫内司法官和法庭总管及其助理主持,对于居住在白厅宫 12 英里内的各类案件行使管辖权。该法庭每周都要与古老的马歇尔西法庭一起开庭审案。法庭的流动性质造成诉讼的不便,于 1849 年被取消。此词条亦称 Court of the Steward and Marshal。见 Palace Court]

court of military appeals 军事上诉法院

court of motion against rulings 抗告法院

court of ordinary jurisdiction 拥有普通管辖权的法院

court of original jurisdiction 原审法院,初审法院

court of orphans 孤儿法庭

Court of Oyer and Terminer (英)重罪巡回审理法庭[指 17 世纪由国王授权设立的巡回法庭每年进行两次或两次以上巡回各郡听审重罪和叛国罪案件。法官根据一些委托状(several commissions)开庭。每一委任状都严格说明理由,要求组成独立的法庭。比如,具有就地听审裁判委任令的一名法官只允准听审重罪案件和叛国罪案件,他不得审理其他刑事犯罪的被告人。但是,如果法官负有提审在押未决犯之职责,他即可审理所有任何刑事罪行的在押未决犯,这样,大多重罪巡回审理法庭就集中了全部刑事管辖权。这种巡回法庭的管辖权于 1971 年已被刑事法院(Crown Court)所取代(巡回法庭已遭废弃)];(美)州刑事法庭或州高院的刑庭(审理重罪的法庭)

Court of Oyer and Terminer and General Goal Delivery (美)1.(宾夕法尼亚州)具有刑事管辖权原法庭,刑事法庭 2.具有提审在押未决犯任务之法庭

Court of Passage (英)利物浦市法院(指利物浦市内的低级法院,已废)

court of patent appeal 专利权上诉法院

Court of Peculiars (英)(宗教法)特殊教区法院[指具有管辖坎特伯雷省教区的坎特伯雷大主教法庭(Court of Arches)的分支法院。它不受主教辖区的主教(diocesan bishop)的管辖,而只专属于大主教,坎特伯雷省教区法院及其上诉法院。该特殊教区法院于 19 世纪已被废止]

court of pie poudre (亦作 Piepowder, Piepoudre, Pipowder, Pie Powder, Py-powder 等) (英)市墟法院(又译泥足法庭。亦称"赶集"法院,指英国 13 世纪在集市上定期或不定期举行的按商业习惯处理商人案件的一种法院)

court of policies of insurance 保险单争议法庭

court of private land claims 私人土地申诉院

court of probate (英)遗嘱检验法院(1875 年成为高等法院的遗嘱检验,离婚和海事法庭,现为该院的家事法庭的组成部分),遗嘱认证法院

court of probate and divorce 遗嘱检验和离婚法院

court of protection (英)保护法庭(指高等法院的一个部门。原名为精神病主事官办事处和经营管理部,1959 年改为此名)

court of public audit 国家审计院,(法院)

国家审计法庭
court of quarter sessions 季审法庭(指按季开审的法庭)
court of record 记录法院(指将诉讼活动记录并永久保存下来的一种法院。保管诉讼记录法院。这类法院有权对藐视法院者实行罚款或监禁,以区别无上述权利的非记录法院)
court of referees (英)(下议院的)鉴定人法庭
court of regard (英)森林保护法院
court of request (英)小额债权法院;债权法院;(英)(都铎时期的)权利请求法院
court of review 复审法庭,上诉法院
court of revision 更改原判的法院
court of rota 见 rota court
court of second degree 第二审级法院
court of second hearing (或 instance) 第二审法庭
court of session (苏格兰)最高民事法院(庭)
court of sewers (英)污水排放专员处
court of special jurisdiction 专门管辖法院(庭),专案裁判庭;特别裁判庭
court of special sessions (美)地方刑事法庭
court of special statutory jurisdiction 特种司法权的法院
court of St. James(') 圣·詹姆士的后庭(即指英政府),英国宫廷
court of (the) staple (英)(中世纪的)贸易中心城镇法庭
Court of (the) Star-Chamber (英)星室法院(因在威斯敏斯宫的星室开庭而得名。早期作为英王咨询会在此处理政务。亨利七世、八世授予司法管辖权,并重组这个机构。在其审理案件时不采用陪审团;其司法管辖的原则与程序均与衡平法庭类似;主要处理普通法院无法审理的刑事案件和特殊性质的案件。它还具有民事管辖可审理英格兰人与外国人的纠纷,捕获案件,海商案件,公司间诉讼以及遗嘱案件等。以后除刑事管辖外,其他均转移至普通法院。实际是一个"刑事衡

平"法庭,它以快捷有效的审理活动增强了王权。但在斯图亚特王朝时期,星室法院被用作镇压清教徒的工具,因其独断专行,非法扩大并滥用权力于 1641 年被撤销。以后星室法庭成为司法专断的同义语。见 Star-Chamber)
court of state security 国家安全法院
court of summary jurisdiction 简易审判庭(即决裁判庭)
court of survey 验船上诉法庭,船舶检查法庭(指船舶被当局指定为不安全而被扣留时,如船长或船主不服可向此法庭上诉)
court of teinds (英史)什一税法庭
Court of the Constable and Marshal 高级警官和纹章院院长法庭
court of the coroner 死因调查法庭
Court of the District of the Columbia (美)哥伦比亚特区法院
court of the Kādis (或 Qādi) 卡迪法院(亦译教法官法院。教法官指根据伊斯兰教法进行宗教审判的法官,所在国各级政府任命,除办案外还负责管理宗教基金、孤儿财产,为无依靠的妇女草拟婚约和主持婚丧仪式等)
Court of the Lord High Steward (英)上议院贵族审判庭
Court of the Lord Justices (英)高等上诉法庭(大法官法院中的上诉法庭)
Court of the Lord Steward of the Queen's Household (英史)皇家刑事审判法院(此种审判权 1828 年被取消)
Court of the Lord Warden of the Cinque Ports (英)五港监督法院(见 warden of cinque ports)
court of the same rank 同级法院
Court of the Steward and Marshal 见 Court of (the) Marshalsea
court of the union 联合法院(指美国提案法院,由 50 个州的高级法院的首席法官组成,该法院唯一职能是:对联邦最高法院的决议,不管是否特别决议,只要具有违宪性即可裁决)
court of third instance 第三审法院
court of trial 审判庭

Court of Tynwald （英）马恩岛议会（指马恩岛的总督、立法理事会和立法大会,泰恩沃尔德曾是议会的会址;从前在这里公布过马恩岛人的立法）
Court of Wards and Liveries （英）监护和财产让渡法庭（1540年设立,1660年被废除）
court on judiciary 司法法院（指一个专门执行司法纪律的法院）
Court Order Enforcement Act （加）（不列颠哥伦比亚省）《法院裁判执行法令》
Court Order Enforcement Exemption Regulation （加）《法院裁决执行豁免条例》
court order 法庭秩序;法院命令
court organization 法院组织
court papers 法院公报;法院文件;(案件审判始末的)法院公报
court party 在朝党,执政党
court policeman 法警,庭警
court practice 法院实务
court precedent 审判程序惯例
court probation 法庭缓刑（见 bench probation）
court procedure 法院诉讼程序
court proceedings 审判程序
court record 法院记录,法庭记录
court registrar 法院注册官;法庭登记员
court registry 法院登记处
court reporter 判决（或诉讼）发布人;法院书记官,法院证言速记员;法庭记录员（指在美国负责法官主持的所有正式程序的文字记录工作者）
court resolution 法院判决;法庭裁决
court roll （英）法庭中的租佃登记册
court rules （美）法院规则[指各种具有法律效力、治理实务以及诉讼程序的规则,如《联邦民事诉讼规则》《联邦刑事诉讼规则》《美国联邦最高法院规则》《联邦证据规则》以及法院颁布的地方规则（local rules that a court promulgates）。亦称 rules of court]
court seat 法庭席
Court Secretary 法庭秘书（指在美国负责法庭的档案管理和起草日常命令、信件等的工作者）

court seized of the case 受理案件的法院
court sentence 法庭判决;法院判决
court session （或 term） 开庭期
court structure 法院组织机构,法院系统
court summons 法院传票
court system 法院体制,法院系统
court trust 法庭信托
court warrant 法庭令状
court with exclusive jurisdiction 有专属管辖权的法院
court with jurisdiction in cases of unsound mind 管辖精神失常案件的法院
court with ordinary jurisdiction 有普通管辖权的法院
court writ 法院令状
court's calendar for arraignment 法院的提审日程表
court's inquiry 法庭调查
Court's place （美）联邦最高法院的场所
Court's stance on the Takings Clause of Constitution （美）联邦最高法院在《宪法》的"征用"条款上的态度
court's stance on the Takings 法院对征用或没收的态度
court's subject-matter jurisdiction 法庭的标的管辖
court's syllabus 法院的判决理由概要
Court-Annex Early Neutral Evaluation 法院附属者的早期中立评估（该方法指当事人可在法院门口寻找专家、律师或心理专家对争议进行分析评价、就地解决争议,而不诉诸法庭）
court-annexed arbitration 法院附属仲裁
Court-granted (freedom of a rich candidate to spend millions) 联邦最高法院准予
court-martial n./v. 军事法庭;军（事）法（庭）审判/由军事法庭审判,进行军法审判
court-martial appeal court 军事法庭上诉庭
court-martial jurisdiction 军事法院管辖权,军事法院司法权;军事法院管辖范围
court-packing plan （或 list） （美）法院重组计划[指1937年总统富兰克林·D.罗斯福将联邦司法机关组成更换的名单交

给国会,这个"法院重组名单"(court-packing bill)(好似刚刚被授予的)是罗斯福总统意图扩大联邦最高法院的成员,希望提名任命能支持新政立法合宪性的一些大法官]

court-parking incident of 1937 (美)1937年法院重组事件(指罗斯福总统拟将最高法院那些不同意他的社会哲学观点的人更换重组)

courtesy (=curtesy) n. 优待,谦恭,礼貌;恩惠,允许

courtesy card 特别优待券

courtroom n. 审判庭(指法院或法院大楼的一部分,审判或听审案件所在地。见 judge's chamber)

courts of criminal equity 刑事衡平法院

courts of justice 普通法院

courts of ordinary (in Georgia) (美)(佐治亚州)拥有普通管辖权的法院(这类法院以前拥有专门的对遗嘱检验管辖权,可批准遗嘱执行授权以及这方面的管理和撤销权;还有对死者、精神病患者等不动产的管理、处分和分配以及其他类似或相关事项的权力。现在该法院仍有这些事务的管辖权)

cousin n. 同辈表亲或堂亲(指堂兄、堂弟、堂姐、堂妹、表兄、表弟、表姐、表妹之一);亲戚,远亲;同民族而国籍不同的人;(国王对贵族的尊称)卿

cousin seven times removed 隔了好几代的远亲

cousin-german (或 first cousin, full cousin) n. 嫡堂(或表)兄(或弟、姐、妹)

coutume (或 *coustom*) (法)习惯法;习惯

coutumiers (或 *coustoumier*, *custumier*)(法)习惯法汇编(指对13—14世纪在法国北部特定地区问世的各种习惯法汇编的通称)

covenant n./v. 1.盟约,专约合同(契约) 2.合同(契约)条款(尤指合同或契约里大家同意的条款);违反合同(契约)的诉讼/用合同(契约)保证;订立合同(契约);缔结盟约

Covenant Code 《圣约书》(见 Book of the Covenant)

covenant for further assurance 再担保合同(契约)

covenant for quiet enjoyment 平静受益权保证合同(契约)(指合同的卖方担保土地所有权无瑕疵或买主不受其原先所有人或其他人对权利提出权利请求之诉干扰)

covenant for title 所有权合同(契约)

covenant in deed 明示合同条款(同 express covenant;见 implied covenant)

covenant not to sue 不起诉合约

covenant of salt 不可背弃的盟约

Covenant of the League of Nations 《国际联盟盟约》

covenant of warranty 担保合同(契约);保证书

covenant running with land 随土地(所有权)转移的合同(契约)(指规定任何承受地产者须承担与地产不可分的债务,并享有其权益的合同)

covenanted a. 立过合同(契约)的;有合同(契约)义务的

covenantee n. 合同(契约)受约人

covenanter n. 誓约者,订立盟约者,订立合同(契约)人

cover n./v. 庇护;(信函等)封袋;包(装)皮,封皮;隐匿(处);(支票的)保证金/ 1.盖,覆盖;封入(信封等) 2.包庇,掩饰,隐匿 3.供给,抵偿 4.负担支付(开支等);弥补(损失等),补进(卖完的货物);给(货物等)保险,投保 5.包括,适合于

cover dividend 储备股息

cover note 承保通知书,临时保单

cover the deficit 弥补赤字,弥补亏损,弥补欠款

cover torn (商品)包(装)皮破裂

coverage n. 1.保险险别;保险范围;保险总额;赔偿债务的准备金总额;保证金 2.有效范围,影响范围

coverage of criminal events 犯罪新闻

coverage ratio 偿债能力系数

covered agreement(s) 适用协定;涵盖协议

covered short sale 有交收保障的卖空(指有学者根据卖空方是否对证券交收作出安排,认为卖空可分:有交收保障的卖空和无交

收保障的卖空。见 naked short sale)
covering a. 附加说明的,随函所附的;掩护的
covering deed 承保说明书
covering every cases 普遍适用
covering letter (出票人致付款人的一种)通知书;(对函内附件的)说明书
covering license 综合输入许可证
covering memorandum 随函备忘录
covering note (= cover note) 承保条(不同于保险公司所发的暂保单)
covering report 总结报告书
covert a. 受保护的;受丈夫保护的;不公开的;隐藏的,暗地里的
covert wrecker 暗藏的破坏分子
covert-baron n. 有夫之妇;(受丈夫保护的)妻子
coverture n. 对已婚妇女在法律上无民事能力的简称;(英)妻的地位(指有夫之妇的法律身份);受夫监护;覆盖(物);掩护(物);隐匿;掩饰已婚妇女的法律身份
covetous a. 贪婪的,妄想占有的(of)
covetousness n. 贪婪;妄想占有者
covin n. 共谋;欺诈,密约
cozen v. 欺骗,哄骗;干欺骗的勾当
crack v./n. 裂开;打破;砸开;打,击;揭开(秘密);解开(难题);宣布(价格);破门而入(出);闯进,毁损,撞毁/破裂,弱点,夜盗行为
crack a criminal case 破案
crack-down n. 制裁,镇压
cracksman n. 夜贼,盗保险箱的贼
craft n./v. 工艺,手艺,行业;行会,同行;职业;技巧/精工制作
craft brother 同行
craft guild (手工业)行会
craft union 同业工会,行业工会
craftsman n. 手艺人,工匠,名匠
cramped reading 难于理解的解释,难懂的解释
cranage n. (货物装卸时的)起重机使用费,起重机的使用
crash n. 冲撞,碰撞;(飞机等的)坠毁;失事;市场总崩溃,大跌;失败,垮台
crash of cases 案件急剧增多

crate n. 条板箱,格子箱(用于货物包装)
craven n. 懦夫,胆小鬼(一种侮辱性的称呼)
crazy guilt without rational basis 没有理性基础狂热的犯罪
create v. 创立,建立;创造;创作;产生,引起,造成,封授(爵位);评定,授予
create a monopoly 垄断,专卖
creating litter 弃置废物
creation n. 封,授予;设置;创造,创作;作品;创造物;任命;产生
creation by the Federal court of common law rights 联邦法院对普通法权利的创立,创立联邦法院普通法权利
creation of company 公司的设立,公司的成立
creation of law (创)造法(律)
creation of leasehold 租赁权的设定
creation of mortgage 抵押权的设定
creation of obligation 债的发生;债权的设定
creation of ownership 所有权的设定;所有权的发生
creation of partnership 合伙的设定;建立合伙关系
creation of peerage for life (英)加封为终身贵族
creation of pledge 质权的设定
creation of rights 创设的权利
creation of superficy 地上权的设定
creation of trust 信托的设定
creative a. 创造性的,有创造力的,创作的;产生的,引起的
Creative Common License (CCL) 知识共享协议(指美国斯坦福大学 Lorry Lessig 教授2001年发起的这项协议,与 GPL 类似的网络著作权许可协议。它提供三类可选条件;是否要求署名;是否允许商业性使用;是否允许修改。)
creative group 创作小组
creative law 制造的法律,创制的法律
creative power 创造力
creative problem solving 创造性的解决问题
creativity (版权法)创造性,创作性[指一

个作品展示想象力的程度超出具有普通天资的人可以创作的程度。辛劳和费用不是创造性的要素,因此它们不受版权保护。菲斯特出版公司诉农村电话服务案(Feist Pubs. Inc. v. Rural Tel. Serv. Co.),参见《美国联邦最高法院判例汇编》第499卷第340页。见 originality; sweat-of-the brow doctrine。创造性(creativity)关系到作品本身的性质,独创性(originality)是有关作者对作品贡献的性质。美国学者贾斯汀休斯认为知识产权中存在三个相互分离的人格利益,除创作性外,还有目的性(creativity intentionality)和来源性(sourcehood)〕

creator n. (专利和外观设计等的)设计人;创立人,创设人;创作者;造物主
creator of the power 权力设定人
creator of trust 信托设定人,创立信托人
creatress n. 女创造人,女创作人,女设计人
credence n. 信任,信用;凭证,证件
credence goods 信赖商品
credential n. 凭证,(复)信任状;(大使等的)国书,证书
credentials committee (或 **committee on credentials**) 资格审查委员会;证件审核委员会
credibility n. 证据能力;可信程度,确实性;可靠性
credibility gap 信用差距
credibility of witnesses 证人的可靠性
credible a. 有公信力的
credible evidence 可靠的证据
credible intelligence 可靠情报
credible witness 可信证人;可靠证人
credit n./v. (16世纪)1.相信,信托(belief trust)〈the jury gave credit to Benson's version〉(陪审团对于本森的解释给予信任)2.信任,信用[指人具有借款能力,在此能力(ability)之中存在偿款的信用或信任(faith)]3.缓付款的期限(卖者给予买者缓付到期款项的期限)4.(银行)存款有效性[指基金既有来自金融机关的又有源自信用证(a letter of credit)的有效性]〈a bank extended a line of credit to custom-er〉(银行扩大对用户的信用额度)5.信用证〈the bank issued a credit in favor of exporter〉(银行发行信用证有利于出口商)6.信贷[指应还债务中的扣除金额,记账项目(accounting entry)反映了净值(net worth)收入的增加]〈confirm that the credit was properly applied to my account〉(确认此信贷恰好适用我的账目)。见 debit] 7.税务抵免(tax credit)〈the $500 credit reduced their income-tax liability by $500〉(500美元税务抵免减去了他们500美元所得税义务)8.相信/(17世纪)1.相信〈the jury did not credit this testmony〉(陪审团不相信此口供证明)2.抵免(税等)3.把……归于;入账;把账目……记入贷方〈the account was credited with $500〉(该账目已被记入贷方500美元)
credit account (客户购货的)赊购账
credit agency 信用调查机构
credit balance 贷方余额,贷方余款,结欠
credit base 信用基础
credit based on real property 不动产信用
credit bill 信用汇票
credit brokerage 信贷经纪业
Credit Bureau 征信所(又译商业资信处,指给商人提供有关顾客咨询情况的机构);(加)信用管理局
credit card 信用卡,赊购证,记账卡
credit certificate 信用证明书
credit checking 征信(见 credit investigation)
credit committee 信用委员会
Credit Control Act 《信贷管制法》
credit cooperation 信用合作
credit cooperative 信用合作社,信用社
credit defraud swap (CDS) 信用违约互换(以信用衍生产品为常见类型,指保值卖方同意预先支付一笔费用或连续的费用,以便在约定的信用事件发生时付款给买方。"信用事件"也由双方在合同中予以约定,常见的信用事件有债券级别下降、公司重组、交叉违约以及破产等)
credit document 信用票据(支票等)
credit freeze 冻结借贷时期[指1922年美国政府限制银行借贷(bank-lending)的

时期]
credit fund 信用贷款基金
credit guaranty 信用担保,信贷担保
credit inquiry (对商行的)信用调查
credit institution 信贷机构;金融机关
credit instrument 信用状,信用票证(证券等)
credit insurance 信用保险
credit investigation(或 **credit checking**)征信(之所以译"征信"是因《左传》有"君子之言,信而有征"的说法。征信机构是指依法设立的专门从事征信业务,即收集和提供信用信息服务的机构)
credit limit 信贷限额,信用期限
credit line (对客户的)放款最高限额;信贷业务;信贷额度;(电影、电讯等)注明制片人(记者,作者等)姓名的字行;授权字行
credit loan 信用借款
credit market 信用市场
credit memo (= credit note)贷记(项)凭单
credit note 信用证
credit of bankrupt 破产债权,破产信贷
credit operation 信贷业务
credit package 一揽子贷款
credit policy 信贷政策
credit rating (对公司或个人的)信用估计,客户信贷分类
credit reference agency 信贷消息查问机构;信誉查询机构
credit regulation 信贷调整
credit relation 信贷关系,信用关系
credit repayment 偿还贷款
credit restriction 信贷限制
credit sale 信用买卖,赊销
credit sale agreement 信用销售协议,赊售协议,信用买卖合同(契约)(指按分期付款买卖法,卖主准许买货的人把货款分五期或六期以上交付的合同)
credit side 贷方
credit society 信用合作社,信用社
credit squeeze 信贷紧缩,银根紧缩
credit terms 信用证条件;信贷条件
credit token 信用标记;信用表示物

credit transaction 信用交易
credit union 存款互助会;(美国、加拿大)信用合作组织(社)(指一种非营利性的信用合作协会)
credit with interest 有利息信贷
credit-debit voucher 收支凭证
credit-ticket system 赊单制
creditability n. 可信性,可信的事物,可接受性
creditable a. 可信的,值得给予贷款的,值得赞扬的
creditor n. 债权人,债主;贷方,贷项
creditor beneficiary 债权受益人
creditor committee (破产)债权人委员会
creditor country (或 **nation**) 债权国
creditor in a bankrupt estate 破产债权人
creditor of a third party 第三方债权人
creditor of bankruptcy 破产户的债权人
creditor of company 公司的债权人
creditor sale (美)破产者所有股票的拍卖
creditor's assets 债权资产
creditor's bill 债权人的请求状;债权人开出汇票
creditor's claim 债权人的请求权
creditor's creditor 债权人的债权人
creditor's equity 债权人产权,债权人权益,行使扣押权的债权人
creditor's preferential claim 债权人的优先求偿权
creditor-investor n. 债权投资人
creditors of bankrupt estate 破产债权人
* *Creditorum appellatione non hi tantum accipiuntur qui pecuniam crediderunt, sed omnes quibus ex qualibet causa debetur.* Under the head of "creditors" are included, not alone those who have lent money, but all to whom from any cause a debt is owing. 冠以"诸债权人"称谓者不只是包括对其提供借贷的人,也包括所有不论什么原因而应从其某项债(务)获得偿还的人。
creditworthy n./a. 资信可靠,信用声誉好/资信可靠的
credulity n. 轻信,易骗
creeds n. 信仰,多种信仰;信念,信条,

纲领
cremation n. 焚化,火葬
cremen incendii 见 arson
crew n. 全体船员,水手;空(地勤)人员
crib n. (学员在)法庭观摩席
crier n. (法庭上的)传呼员;法警;(巡行街道)大声宣读告示的人(=town crier)
crime n./v. 犯罪;罪(行),罪恶,憾事,耻辱事/(英)指控……违反军纪;宣告……犯违反军纪罪
crime act 犯罪法
crime against flag 侮辱国旗罪
crime against humanity 危害人类罪,违反人道罪
crime against international morality 违反国际道德罪
crime against international public order 破坏国际公共秩序罪
crime against law of nations 违反国际法罪
crime against military duty 违反军职罪
crime against nature 鸡奸罪;兽奸罪;(任何)违反自然的性关系(或行为)
crime against peace 破坏和平罪
crime against prisoners of war 虐待、杀害战俘罪
crime against the environment 危害环境罪(见 environmental crime)
crime against the sick and wounded 虐待战争伤病员罪
crime against the state 危害国家罪;国事罪
crime control and due process model 犯罪控制和正当程序模式
crime control of model 犯罪控制模式
crime motive 犯罪动机
crime of (misdemeanour) indecent act 猥亵罪
crime of abandonment 遗弃罪
crime of abortion 堕胎罪
crime of abuse of authority 滥用职权罪
crime of adultery 通奸罪
crime of affray 聚众斗殴罪,互殴罪
crime of aggression 侵略罪
crime of aggressive war （发动）侵略战争罪
crime of blackmail in general 一般敲诈罪
crime of children 少年犯罪
crime of conspiracy 阴谋罪,密谋罪
crime of corruption 贪污罪,腐化罪
crime of corruption and nonfeasance 贪污渎职罪
crime of counterrevolutionary homicide 反革命杀人罪
crime of counterrevolutionary propaganda and inflammatory delusion 反革命宣传煽动罪
crime of counterrevolutionary rumormongering 反革命造谣罪
crime of counterrevolutionary sabotage 反革命破坏罪
crime of counterrevolutionary subversion 反革命颠覆罪
crime of defamation 诽谤罪
crime of defrauding a citizen's property 诈骗公民财产罪
crime of destroying evidence 销毁证据罪
crime of disturbing the administrative order of society 妨害社会管理秩序罪
crime of disturbing the economic order 妨害经济秩序罪
crime of embezzlement of state property 侵吞国家财产罪
crime of endangering peace 危害(或妨害)治安罪
crime of endangering public affairs 妨害公务罪
crime of endangering public security 危害公共安全罪
crime of escape 脱逃罪
crime of escaping from custody 越狱(逃脱)罪
crime of espionage and sedition (美)危害国家安全罪
crime of false charge 诬告罪
crime of false pretenses 冒充罪,欺诈罪
crime of forcible entry 闯入罪(指闯入他人的房屋或土地)
crime of forgery 伪造罪
crime of forgery of documents and seals

伪造文书印章罪

crime of forgery of trade marks and trade names 伪造商标商号罪

crime of fornication with an underage girl 奸淫少女罪

crime of fraud 诈欺罪,诈骗罪

crime of fraudulent use of public seals 盗用公章罪

crime of gambling 赌博罪

crime of genocide 灭绝种族罪

crime of habitual theft 惯窃罪

crime of hooliganism 流氓罪

crime of impairing water conservancy 破坏水利罪

crime of inciting armed rebellion 煽动武装叛乱罪

crime of inflicting serious bodily injury 致人重伤罪

crime of instigation 煽惑罪,教唆罪

crime of insurrection 内乱罪,叛乱罪

crime of interference with marriage and the family 妨害婚姻、家庭罪

crime of interfering with election 妨害选举罪

crime of kidnapping for ransom 绑架勒索罪

crime of misconduct in office 渎职罪

crime of negligent homicide 过失杀人罪

crime of omission 不作为罪(指因不执行职责等构成的犯罪,与 commission 相对而言)

crime of perjury 伪证罪

crime of pillage 掠夺罪,抢劫罪

crime of piracy 海盗罪

crime of rescue 劫狱罪;非法劫走人犯罪;非法劫夺罪

crime of robbery 强盗罪

crime of sabotaging communications 破坏交通罪

crime of setting on fire 放火罪,纵火罪

crime of theft 盗窃罪

crime of torture 酷刑罪(《酷刑宣言》和《酷刑公约》基本上对酷刑罪概念作出了明确解释:指政府官员,或在怂恿下对一个人故意施加使之在肉体或精神上受到极度痛苦与苦难的行为,以谋求从他或第三者口中取得情报或供状或者对做过的或涉嫌做过的事加以处罚;或对他或别人施加恐吓的行为)

crime of treason 叛国罪;叛逆罪,卖国罪

crime of undermining the national currency and valuable securities 破坏国家货币及有价证券罪

crime of undermining the state financial system 破坏国家财政制度罪

crime of undermining valuable cultural relics 破坏珍贵文物罪

crime of unlawful assembly 非法集会罪

crime of violating government laws and decrees 违反政府法令罪

crime of violating the citizens' right of the person 侵犯公民人身权利罪

crime of violence 使用暴力罪

crime on cyber-space 网络空间犯罪

crime *passion(n)el* 因情欲妒忌而造成的犯罪;色情谋杀罪

crime prevention 犯罪预防

crime problem 犯罪问题

crime rate 犯罪率

crime reporter 罪案报道人

crime ridden 罪大恶极

crime scene 犯罪现场

crime scene investigation 犯罪现场勘查

crime scene procedure 犯罪现场勘查(程序)

crime sheet 处罚记载

crime syndicate 犯罪辛迪加(亦称犯罪集团,指美国对进行集团犯罪的诈骗组织的俗称)

crime termination 犯罪中止

Crime Victimes' Rights Act. 2004 (美)(2004年通过的)《犯罪受害人权利法》[该法标志着美国犯罪受害人保护立法达到了顶峰,被称为美国历史上对犯罪被害人保护最彻底的联邦法律。该法旨在赋予犯罪受害人权利,扩大犯罪受害人在刑事诉讼中的作用,并明确其在法庭审判中的地位。《犯罪受害人权利法》将犯罪受害人定义为"直接或间接遭受犯罪行为侵犯的个人"。该法赋予犯罪受害人8项权

利:①免受刑事被告伤害,得到合理保护权利;②任何与犯罪有关或与刑事被告释放、逃跑相关的公开审判程序和假释程序,受害人都有得到合理、准确、及时通知的权利;③不排除在任何公开法庭程序之外的权利,除非法院有明确会令人信服的证据表明该证据中的其他证词会使犯罪受害人的证词发生重大改变;④合理听取区法院所有公开审判,包括释放、答辩、量刑或被假释的权利;⑤与检察官进行合理协商的权利;⑥依法充分并及时获得赔偿的权利;⑦使诉讼程序不受任何不合理拖延的权利;⑧受到公平对待以及尊严和隐私受到尊重的权利。如果犯罪被害人依据该法寻求救济遭到区法院的拒绝,则其有权向上级法院申请强制纠正令,并要求受理该申请的上级法院在接到申请书的72小时内进行处理并作出决定。参见《美国法典》第18标题卷第3771节《犯罪被害人权利法》(18 USC §3771, The Crime Victims' Rights Act)]

crime-ridden a. 充满(犯)罪行(为)的,罪大恶极的

crimeless a. 无罪的

crimen 犯罪,对犯罪的指控

crimen expilatae hereditatis (罗马法)虚假认领人对一项遗产的有意掠夺

crimen falsi (the crime of falsifying) 伪证罪,伪造或虚假陈述罪[《联邦证据规则》第609(a)(2)条]

crimen feloniae imposuit 控告犯有重罪

crimen laesae majestatis 见 *crimen majestatis*

* *Crimen laesae majestatis omnia alia crimina excedit quoad paenam.* The crime of treason exceeds all other crimes in its punishment. 叛国罪在其判刑上应重于所有其他犯罪。

crimen majestatis 重大叛国罪(根据罗马法,这种罪行特指由罗马公民或其他人专门从事于推翻罗马共和国和皇帝的任何活动或罪行,亦称 *crimen laesae majestatis*。见 *lese majesty; perduellio*)

crimes against marriage and family 妨害婚姻家庭罪

crimes against property 侵犯财产罪

crimes against public security 危害公共安全罪

crimes against social administration 妨害社会管理秩序罪

crimes against socialist economic order (中)破坏社会主义经济罪

crimes against the person 侵犯人身罪

crimes against the right of person and the democratic rights of citizens (中)侵犯公民人身权、民主权利罪

crimes against the state, the government and the community, the administration of justice and public order 反对国家、政府和社会、反对司法执法和公共秩序的犯罪

crimes defined in terms of a failure to act 纯正不作为犯(罪)

crimes in respect of property 财产方面的犯罪

crimes of commission by omission 不纯正不作为犯(罪)

crimes of counterrevolution (中)反革命罪

crimes ordinance 刑事罪条例

criminal n./a. 罪犯,犯人/犯罪的,犯罪的;非法的;刑事(上)的;应受谴责的,可耻的

criminal abortion 非法堕胎

criminal account 非法账目

criminal act 犯罪行为;罪行

criminal action (或 **suit**) 刑事诉讼

criminal activities 犯罪活动

criminal adjudication tribunal 刑事审判庭

criminal affair 刑事

criminal analogues to T and P 对于盗窃的刑事类推(T&P=theft & pilferage)

criminal anatomy 刑事解剖学

criminal anthropology 刑事人类学

criminal appeal 刑事上诉

Criminal Appeal Reports (美)《刑事上诉判例汇编》

criminal arrest (美)刑事上的对自由的限制(有三种方式:限制人身自由;警方用武器限制其自由;官方声明限制其自由)

criminal assault 刑法上的伤害罪;暴力殴

打;强奸(指兼施暴行者,被认为是犯罪而不是侵权的一种侵犯)
criminal at large   在逃犯
criminal attempt   犯罪未遂,未遂罪
criminal bankruptcy   (英)刑事破产(指1972年开始在英国实行的一种破产形式)
criminal behavio(u)r   犯罪行为
criminal border-line   犯罪边缘
criminal capacity   刑事(责任)能力
criminal case   刑事案件;刑事诉讼
Criminal Cases Review Commssion   (英)英国刑事案件审查委员会[1997年成立,主要复审怀疑误判的刑事案件的独立机构。它不代表控方、辩方、法院或刑事司法系统的任何一方。该委员会的职责并非鉴定"有罪""无罪"或重新进行审判,而是决定是否将案件提交上诉法院再受审理。该委员会地位完全独立,其委员由女王任命,主要职责是对可疑的刑事案件进行复查,在认为存在错误并存在被推翻的可能性时,将案件提交上诉法院再审。该委员会的财政预算是400—500万英镑。该委员会虽从内政部获取资金,但对议会负责,不过议会并不干预其工作。相对丰厚的资金和人员任免上的不受控制都保证了其独立性。20世纪90年代后期,英国有大量刑事错案被披露,其中包括吉尔福德四人案(The Fuildford Four)、伯明翰六人案(Birmingham Six)和朱迪斯·华德(Judich Ward)案。这些案件的曝光在英国产生巨大影响,催生了英国刑事案件审查委员会的设立]
criminal character   犯罪性质
criminal charge   刑事控告,刑事罪
criminal code   刑法;(大写)《刑法典》
criminal coercive measures   刑事强制措施
criminal compensation   刑事赔偿
criminal complaint   (美)刑事控告书[指由受害人、警察、地区检察官或其他利害关系人向有管辖权的联邦司法官(magistrate)提出说明某一犯罪行为已经发生的文书,其中要阐明其所指控的犯罪事实。这个起诉文书必须给大陪审团指控犯罪的起诉书(indictment)或由检察官提起的公诉书(information)。此起诉书中(probable cause)表明指控某人实施该罪可成立的理由,即可依此而对该罪犯签发拘捕令]
criminal complicity   刑事共犯、刑事共同犯罪
criminal connexion   (男女间的)私通
criminal contempt   (1841年)刑事藐视,藐视法庭罪(指妨碍正义或攻击法庭的尊严,刑事藐视行为本身的性质是受惩罚性的,设立此罪之目的在于维护法庭的尊严和权威,并且惩罚不遵守法令的行为。比如法官开庭审理案件时,一个当事方喊叫侮辱法官,此行为即构成藐视法庭罪,通常要受到罚金或一定期限的监禁,亦称common law contempt)
criminal contempt fine   刑事藐视罚金
criminal contempt proceedings   刑事藐视诉讼程序
criminal contempts   藐视法庭罪;严重藐视法律的行为
criminal conversation   (英)通奸之诉(指和他人妻子或丈夫通奸或同居,英国1965年的《婚姻诉讼法》规定,受害丈夫可因妻子通奸而控告奸夫,索取赔偿)
criminal conviction   刑事定罪
criminal court   刑事法院(庭)
criminal damage   刑事损害
criminal damage to property   (1946年)刑事损害法,对财产的刑事损害[指①侵害,损害,毁坏。未获得财产拥有者的同意而对财产的使用受到实质上的损坏(而非火烧或爆炸)。②对财产使用的损害、毁坏或实质上损害,(非火烧或爆炸)有意损害或欺骗承保人或留置权持有人。见arson]
criminal defendant   刑事被告
criminal demography   刑事人口统计学
criminal desertion   刑事遗弃(指配偶一方无正当理由对处于疾病和紧急情况的配偶不给予关心、保护和生活资助)
criminal disability   无犯罪能力
criminal disposal(或 **disposition**)   刑事处分
criminal division   刑事庭,刑庭;(大写)(英)(上诉法院)刑事庭

criminal docket 刑事卷(见 judgment roll)
criminal element 刑事犯罪分子,刑事犯罪要素,犯罪原理
criminal evidence 刑事(案件的)证据
criminal execution 罪犯的处决
criminal fine 刑事罚金
criminal for trial 候审犯人
criminal gang 犯罪集团
criminal history category 刑事历史类别
criminal homicide 谋杀,刑事上的杀人
criminal identification 刑事鉴定
criminal in custody 在押犯
criminal information (刑事)控告;告发;检举;(检察官的)检控
criminal injuries compensation 刑事伤害赔偿
Criminal Injuries Compensation Board (英)刑事损害赔偿委员会
criminal instince 犯罪本性
criminal intent 犯意,犯罪动机,犯罪意图,犯罪目的
criminal interrogation 刑事讯问
criminal investigation 刑事侦查(学)
criminal investigator 刑事侦查员
criminal judg(e)ment 刑事判决
criminal jurisdiction 刑事管辖(权),刑事审判(权);刑法效力范围
criminal jurisprudence 刑法学
criminal jurist 刑法学家
Criminal Justice Act (英)1987年《刑事审判法》
criminal justice 刑事审判
Criminal Justice Agency (美)刑事司法(事务)代行机构(在美国只有较大的城市如纽约等地才设立这样的机构,它的主要工作是在被告被逮捕后和正式提审前,对被告进行讯问,然后根据情况向有关部门提出保释或释放推荐书)
* Criminal justice is justice for criminal. (美国法律格言)刑事公正就是对罪犯的公正。
criminal justice professional 刑事审判人员
criminal justice research 刑事审判研究
criminal justice revolution 刑事司法革命

criminal knowledge 犯罪意识
criminal landed in jail 罪犯被捕入狱
criminal law 刑法
criminal law expert 刑法学者(专家)
criminal lawyer 刑事诉讼律师
criminal liability 刑事责任
criminal libels on private persons (私人方面的)诽谤罪
criminal litigation procedures 刑事诉讼程序
criminal lunatic 精神病犯
criminal matter 刑事事件,刑事案件
criminal memorial (国际法院)刑事诉状
criminal miscarriage 见 abortion
criminal motive 犯罪动机
criminal negligence 刑法上之过失,过失犯罪,严重过失
criminal object 犯罪客体;(复)犯罪物件
criminal of war 战犯
criminal offence 刑事罪;刑事犯
criminal offender 犯罪分子,罪犯,刑事犯
criminal offender on a medical parole 保外就医的刑事犯
criminal offender serving his sentence on probation 缓期执行的刑事犯,保外执行的刑事犯
criminal omission 不作为犯罪,刑事上的懈怠
criminal operation 堕胎罪(指非法以人工手术堕胎)
criminal organization 犯罪组织;犯罪团体
criminal penalty 刑罚;刑事处罚
criminal physiology 犯罪生理学;刑事生理学
criminal police 刑警
criminal policy 刑事政策
criminal presentment (英)(陪审团的)刑事直接控诉书
criminal prisoner 刑事犯,在押犯,未决犯
criminal procedure 刑事诉讼程序
criminal procedure at first instance 刑事诉讼第一审程序
criminal procedure code 刑事诉讼法典
criminal procedure ordinance 刑事诉讼程

序条例
criminal proceedings 刑事诉讼
criminal profile 犯罪轮廓
criminal prosecution 刑事检控,刑事诉讼
criminal psychology 犯罪心理学
criminal punishment 刑事处罚
criminal purpose 犯罪目的
criminal record 前科,犯罪记录
criminal registration 刑事登记
criminal regulation 刑事规章
criminal responsibility 刑事责任
criminal ruling 刑事裁定
criminal sanction 刑事处分;刑事制裁
criminal science 犯罪科学,刑事科学[指以发现犯罪原因的观点对犯罪进行研究的一门科学,设计最有效的降低犯罪的方法和以完善的手段对付已实施犯罪的行为人。刑事科学的三大主要分支是犯罪学、犯罪对策(criminal policy)和刑法学]
criminal sentences 刑事判决,刑事判(量)刑
criminal sexual conduct in the third degree (美)第三等级的刑事的性行为(亦可称third degree criminal sexual conduct)
criminal side 刑事方面
criminal sociology 刑事社会学,犯罪社会学
criminal somatology 刑事人体学
criminal statute 刑事法规
criminal suspect 犯罪嫌疑,嫌疑犯
criminal syndicalism laws (美)犯罪集团法;工团主义犯罪法(指以教唆、鼓动破坏、暴力、恐怖等性质的犯罪达到工业产权或管理权的变更,或影响政治变化的目的)
criminal technique 刑事技术(又称犯罪侦查技术)
criminal trespass 非法侵入他人土地或房屋罪
criminal trial 刑事审判
criminal tribunal 刑事裁判庭
criminal twist 犯罪倾向
criminal type 犯罪类型
criminal wave 犯罪的浪潮
criminal with previous convictions 前科犯
criminal wrong 刑事过错行为;刑事犯罪行为
criminalistics n. 犯罪侦查学,刑事学;物证技术学
criminality n. 有罪;犯罪行为;犯罪性,犯罪因素
criminalization n. 定罪;宣布犯有罪行
criminalization of international law 国际法刑事化(现象)
criminalize v. 使有罪;定罪
criminalizing 犯罪化(指把某种行为当做犯罪来处理。犯罪化的显著特点就是扩大定罪处刑范围,即扩大犯罪圈)
criminally ad. 刑法上,犯罪上
criminaloid n. 有犯罪本性者,本性有犯罪倾向的人
criminate v. 1.告发,控告;归罪,定罪,证明有罪 2.指控的犯罪;陷人于罪;牵累(连)3.责备(行为等)
criminate oneself 自首;自陷法网
crimination n. 控告;定罪,证明有罪;控告;责备
crimination and recrimination 互相指控;互相嫁罪
criminative a. 定罪的,控告的
criminative man 控告犯罪的人
criminological a. 刑事学的,犯罪学的
criminological facts and figures 刑事犯罪的事实和数字(或数据)
criminologist n. 刑事学家,犯罪学家
criminology n. 犯罪学,刑事学
criminous a. 犯了罪的,犯罪的
crimp v. 诱迫
crimp into crime 诱骗(或迫使)犯罪
crippling disorder 伤残无序
crisis n. 危机,决定性时刻,转折点
crisis in governance 治理危机
crisis in sale 销售危机
crisis-ridden industries 危险深重的工业
crit. (1985年)批判法学派(critical legal studies)的思想追随者
criteria (=criterion) 标准,准则
criteria for statehood 国家地位的标准
criterion n. (判断)标准,准则,要求,依据
criterion for imposing penalty 量刑标准
criterion of efficiency 效率准则

criterion of family and marriage relationship 家庭婚姻关系的准则

criterion of liability 归罪原则,(民、刑事)责任准则

criterion of localisation 地方分权准则,地方化准则

critic n. 批评家,评论家

critical a. 紧急的,关键性的;批评的,批判的

critical cases 关键性案件

critical date 关键日(指在版权领域中,若外国作品首先在中国出版方享有版权。"首次出版日"即为关键日;另版权产生于作品创作完成之日,所以"完成之日"亦称关键日);关键时期(指对评价事实具有重要意义的日期)

critical election 关键性选举

critical evidence (18 世纪)足够强有力的证据,关键性的证据(指此证据出现将使陪审团员倾向于对认定有罪产生合理怀疑)

Critical Feminist Jurisprudence 女权主义法学

critical information 关键信息,重要信息

critical international legal studies 批判的国际法律研究方法

critical legal studies (1978 年)1.批判法学派[指一种思想学派,它推进一种思想观点(idea),即法律体系(legal system)依据经济学、种族、性别通过适应的观念(manipulable concepts)和创设想象的经法律调整的社会和谐领域保持永久的现状(status quo)。这一学派的马克思主义支流(Maxist wing)聚焦于社会经济学问题(socioeconomic issues)。女性主义追随者(Fem-crits)强调性别等级制(gender hierarchy),属于批判种族理论家(critical race theorists),集中注意于种族的附属关系(racial subordination)。见 Fem-crit;Critical Race Theory]2.此学派追随者所创作的作品(缩略为 CLS)

critical legal studies (= manipulable concepts) 适应的观念,运用的观念

Critical Legal Studies Movement (CLS) (美)批判法律研究运动

Critical Race Theory (1989 年)1.批判种族理论,改革运动[指法学界内部改革运动(reform movement),特别是在学术界(academia)内部,它的追随者相信法制已经剥夺了对于少数民族(racial minorities)的授权。这个术语第一次出现在 1989 年,批判种族理念观察到:即使法律隐含在中立语言之中,法律也不可能是中立的,因为使法律适应社会的这些人已有他们自己的观点,一旦这些观点深深藏在法律之中,则损害少数民族的利益,甚至会长期产生种族主义]2.追随者对于这种理论所创作的作品(缩略为 CRT)

critical scrutiny 严格审查;批判审查;严格的选票复查

critical steps 评论机制,评判步骤

criticism n. 批判,批评;评论

criticism and education 批评教育

criticism meeting 批判会,批评会

critics of first state 基本的(最先的)危险状态

critique n. 批评,批判,评论;短评,评论文;批判术,批判

cronyism (1950 年)变更限制(derogatory),任人唯亲(指将一个有权势的最佳位置给予亲戚和朋友。这是一种偏袒、偏爱,而不顾那些品质高尚、有德有才的人。见 nepotism, discrimination 2)

crop compensation 农作物补偿

cropper n. 种植者;(美)分益佃农,分成制农民

crosier n. 权杖

cross a. 相反的;相互的,交叉的;交替的;反对的;互相矛盾的;用不正当手段得来的

cross action 反诉,反控(指甲因一宗交易控告乙,乙用同一交易控告甲);反诉行为

cross appeal (当事人双方)交互上诉,反上诉(指胜诉方在败诉方上诉后提起上诉,即上诉时由被上诉方提出的反诉,与上诉方的上诉同时接受法院审理)

cross bill (= cross-bill) 反诉状;交叉汇票(见 cross-complaint)

cross claim 交叉请求[指在不止一个被告的案件中,由其中一个被告("交叉请求中的原告")向其他被告(交叉请求中的被

告)提出的请求,即共同原告相互之间或共同被告相互之间提出的请求。在交叉请求中可以主张对原告造成的损害是由交叉请求中的被告引起的,他应对原告有权获得的损害赔偿支付金钱,以及(或)主张交叉请求中的被告对交叉请求中的原告造成了有关联的损害]

cross demand 反要求
cross easement 交互地役权
cross entry 抵消记入
cross examination 见 cross-examination
cross licensing agreement 交叉许可证协议;相互许可证协议(见 cross-licence)
cross rate of exchange 套汇汇率,交叉汇率
cross reference 交叉参阅系统
cross section (有代表性的)典型,横截面
cross voting 投反对自己所属政党的票
cross-bill 反诉讼,反诉状(见 cross-complaint)
Cross-Border Insolvency Concordat 《跨国破产协定》
cross-border supply 边境交付(这是服务性贸易的基本概念之一。指一国向另一国提供的服务,没有人员和资金的流动,而通过电讯、邮电、计算机网络实现,如视听和金融)
cross-check n./v. (从不同角度或根据不同材料)反复核对
cross-claim n. 扣除金额;相互主张权利,相互提出诉讼请求;交叉债权,交叉请求
cross-claimants n. 交叉请求人
cross-complaint n. 反诉讼(指本诉被告向本诉原告提出反诉的诉状);交叉诉状(指本诉被告向本诉当事人以外的第三人就本诉有关事项提起诉讼的诉状)
cross-debt n. (彼此可以)相互抵消的债务
cross-demand n. (18 世纪)交互请求(指一方对另一方提出请求,后者又对前者提出请求,这种相互对立请求称为交叉请求)
cross-examination (=cross question) n. 盘问,反询问;反问,诘问(指由一方当事人或其诉讼代理人向另一方当事人所提供的证人提出的诘问,一般是在提供证人的一方向自己的证人提问后进行的)

cross-examine (=cross-query) v. 盘问,反诘问(指当事人或其诉讼代理人,对于双方证人经直接诘问提供的证言,为了发现矛盾以便推翻此证词所作的提问。见 direct examination)
cross-examining attorney 盘问的律师,诘问的律师
cross-exchange n. 交叉汇兑,套汇
cross-index v. (给词典、条目等)设互见索引
cross-interrogatory n. 盘问,反复交叉讯问(指对一个已作了审问的诉讼当事人可由其他所有的当事人对其进行反复交叉的追问)
cross-liability n. 交叉责任,交互债务
cross-licence n. 相互特许(指持有专利权者之间交换使用对方产品的特许权利)
cross-petition n. 相互请愿;反诉;反控
cross-reference n./v. 互参,相互参考(指在相同的或紧密相关文件中的一种对相关规定的明确援引。特别在专利申请中从连续专利申请直到所有相互关联的申请中的准确援引,可参考原始档案);交互参考。
cross-remainder n. (美)相互继承剩余遗产继承权(指几个人作为一个小团体继承的财产,在每一人去世时,其余的人则分享其应得份额)
cross-section n. 横断面,剖面;典型人物,样品(有代表性的)剖面,典型
cross-trade n. 买空卖空,套购套售交易
crossbench (英)中立议员席(指下院两大政党以外的中立政党议员的席位)
crosscutting incentives 相互削减动机,相互削减激励
crossed a. 交叉的,相交的,十字形的,划掉的,划线的,勾销的;遭反对的,受挫折的
crossed check 划线支票
crosswalk n. 人行横道
crousdfunded project/enterprise 众筹资金项目/企业
crowdfunding n. 众筹[指筹资人通过众筹平台发布资金需求信息,吸引众多个体投资人进行集合投资,从而为特定目标或企

业经营发展寻求资金支持的一种直接融资模式。根据融资标的不同,众筹可分为捐赠众筹(donate crowdfunding)、回报众筹(reward crowdfunding)、借贷众筹(lending crowdfunding)和股权众筹(equity crowdfunding)。在互联网时代,众筹让每个人都可以成为"天使投资人"。一边是天马行空的创意项目,一边是大批公众投资人,网站搭建了连接两者的平台,让有创造力的人获得他们所需的资金,帮助他们完成自己的梦想。这种模式的兴起还打破了传统的融资模式,融资的来源不再局限于风险投资,而可以来自大众,为创意项目和大众投资人牵线搭桥的典型网站是Kickstarter.com]

crowded court docket　塞满的待审案件目录

Crowdfunding Act　(美)《众筹法案》[指2013年《初创期企业推动法案》(Jumpstart Our Business Start-ups Act),简称"JOBS法案",其第Ⅲ章即《众筹法案》)。立法者不仅对众筹平台的一般经营行为设置了相关规则,还特别创建了集资门户(funding portal)这一全新的众筹平台类型,以期通过相对宽松的设立标准和规范化的经营规则,鼓励市场主体更多设立和经营众筹平台,带动股权众筹产业的发展]

crowdfunding platforms　(美)众筹平台

crown n. 皇冠,王位;君权;(大写)英王,英王室

Crown advocate　(英)海事高级律师

Crown agent　(大写)王室代理人;(复)英联邦(殖民地或保护国的)商务代理人

Crown Appointment Commission　(英)国王钦定委员会

Crown case　(英)刑事案件

crown case reserved　(巡回审判中发生的)留待刑事上诉法院解决的法律问题

Crown Copyright　皇家版权,国家版权,政府版权(多指英国及英联邦国家的版权法用语)

Crown copyrights　(英)王室版权,政府版权

Crown council　王室委员会

Crown counsel　(英)检察官

Crown Court　(英)刑事法院(1966年建立,并成为最高法院的组成部分)

Crown Courts of Liverpool and Manchester　(英)利物浦和曼彻斯特国家法庭(指根据1956年的《刑事审判法》规定而设立的,作为这两个地区的巡回法庭和季审法庭,专门审理初审和上诉审的刑事案件)

Crown debt　(英)国债,公债

Crown land　(英)政府土地,王室土地

Crown law　(英)刑法

Crown Law Office　(新西兰)法务局

Crown lawyer　(英)王室的律师;刑事律师

Crown lease　(英)政府租地契据,官契

Crown Office　(英)(高等法院)刑事部(最初是王座法院的一个部门,1879年成为最高法院中央部的一个部门,专门处理法院中的刑罚事务),公诉署,(英)(大法官法庭)国玺处

Crown Office in Chancery　(英)大法官法庭刑事部

Crown paper　(英)刑事案录

Crown private estate　国王私人财产

Crown privilege　(英)王室特权;政府特权(指政府有绝对权力可以违反公共利益为理由拒绝把文件提交法庭查阅)

Crown Proceeding Act, 1947　(英)《王权诉讼法》(1947年)

Crown proceedings　(英)政府诉讼程序(指1947年的《政府诉讼程序法》规定,政府在犯过失罪或违背合同时,可被指控及赔偿受害人的损失)

Crown Prosecution Service (CPS)　(苏格兰)检察署

Crown rent　(英)政府地税

Crown rent roll　(英)政府租金册

Crown servant　(英)王室官员;公务人员

Crown Side　(英)公诉部(该部为从前王座法院的一个部门,专门审理刑事案件,现已合并于高等法院中央办公室)

Crown solicitor　(英)御用大律师,政府律师(指以前财政部的律师,负责代表政府检控犯人,常由状师或律师担任)

Crown witness　(英)刑事诉讼中(原告方面)的证人

crowning a. (构成)顶部的,登峰造极的,至

高无上的
crowning glory 至高无上的光荣
CRS Reports (Congressional Research Service Reports) 美国国会研究所报告
crucial a. 决定性的,紧要关头的,严酷的,困难的
crucial and unusual punishment 残酷和独特的刑罚,酷刑(为美国联邦宪法第八修正案和第十四修正案所禁止)
crucial evidence 见 critical evidence
crucial moment 关键时刻,紧要关头
crucial problem 决定性问题
crucial role 关键作用,决定性作用
crucial swing vote 关键转变的一票
crucifixion n. 酷刑,折磨;苦难;钉在十字架上的酷刑
crude a. 天然的,未加工的,原始的,赤裸裸的,不成熟的
crude conception of primitive law 原始法的最初概念
crude facts 原始事实,赤裸裸的事实
crude ideas 不成熟的意见
crude offense 赤裸裸的罪行,粗野的罪行
crude statistics 未经整理的分类统计数字
crudities in judicial organization and procedure 在司法机构和程序中的简单粗糙做法(或落后做法)
cruel a. 残忍的,残酷的,令人痛苦的
cruel and abuse treatment 见 abuse 2
cruel and unusual (或 excessive) punishment 酷刑惩罚(指对犯人实行凌辱和残酷不人道的刑罚)
cruel beat 残酷鞭笞
cruel excess 过于残酷
cruel punishment 酷刑
cruelty n. 残酷,残忍,虐待[美国离婚法中夫妻一方对另一方有虐待行为可作为离婚依据。各州对此概念不同,有的要求必须极端虐待(extreme cruelty),有的则要求故意虐待(willful cruelty)和不可忍受的严酷程度(intolerable severity),方可作为离婚依据];虐待罪;(复)残酷行为
cruelty against human life 残害人命(罪)
cruelty to animal 虐待牲畜(罪)
cruelty to a child 见 child abuse

cruelty to children 虐待儿童(罪)
cruise car 警察巡逻车
cruise squad 警察巡逻缉捕队
crush of cases 案件急剧增多
crush trauma 挤压伤
crushing a. 压倒的,决定性的
crushing retort 使对方无话可说的反驳
cry n. 叫喊;要求,舆论;呼吁,传说;口号;哭泣
cry de pais (或 cri de pais) (古时)(刑事案件发生而警察不在场时)人们追捕罪犯的呼唤
cryptic(ally) a. 秘密的,隐蔽的;含义模糊的;使用密码的
cryptic colouring 保护色,隐蔽色
cryptic remark 含义隐晦的话
crypto n. (政党,社团的)秘密成员,秘密支持者
crypto-censorship n. 保密审查
crypto-opponent n. 隐蔽的对手
cryptonym n. 匿名
crystallisation n. 具体化,透明化,朗化;裹上的一层物体
Crystallization n. 结晶;担保具体化
crystallize v. 成形,使明朗,使具体
Cuban missile crisis 古巴导弹危机
cucking stool 浸水刑凳(英国古时用以惩罚泼妇的刑具,使泼妇坐在凳上,浸入水中以示惩罚。又名 ducking-stool, 或 castigatory, trebucket, tumbrel)
cuckold n. 奸妇的丈夫
cuckoldry n. (与有夫之妇的)私通,通奸
cudgel n./v. 棒;棍;棒打
cuff n. 1.袖口;(复)手铐 2.掌击,一巴掌
cuffing n. 打耳光;殴斗
cui bono 为了谁的好处? 为了谁的用益(或受益)权? (常用此语来衡量一切协议);(从谁从中得利来看这事)可能是谁干的?
* Cuicunque aliquis quid concedit, concedere videtur et id, sine quo res ipsa esse non potuit (or percipi non debet). Whoever grants a thing to any person is supposed tacitly to grant that also without which the grant itself would be of no effect. (The grantor of

anything to another grants that also without which the thing granted would useless.) 赠与某物者,为不使该物丧失效用,视为同时赠与该物所必需之物。
* ***Cujus est dare est disponere.*** Whose it is to give, his it is to dispose. The person who has a right to give has the right of disposition. 赠与人有权处理赠与物,(在合法情况下)有权赠与物的人有权处理赠与物。
* ***Cujus est solum, ejus est usque ad coelum.*** (= *cujus est solum, ejus est summits usque.*) The person who owns the soil owns up to the sky. 谁拥有土地,谁就拥有土地上方的天空; One who owns the surface of the ground owns, or has an exclusive right to everything that is on or above it to an indefinite height. 谁拥有土地表面,谁就对土地上空无限高空拥有一切事物的专有权。
culminate v. 达到顶点,告终(in)
culminate in bankruptcy 终致破产
culmination n. 达到顶点,达到极点;顶点,极点,最高潮
culpa (民事上的)过失,疏忽,过错(大陆法一般分三个等级:①*lata culpa*, gross fault, 大错;②*levis culpa*, ordinary fault, 一般错;③*levissima culpa*,slight fault 小错)
culpa & dolus 疏忽和有犯罪意图;过失与故意
culpa in abstracto 抽象的过失
culpa in concreto 具体的过失
culpa in contrahendo 缔约过失,契约中的过失;合同上的过失(违约责任用语,指合同双方当事人缔约时默示同意不损害对方利益,若一方当事人欺诈引发合同无效,显然违背承诺;被欺诈人可依缔约过失责任之规定,请求损害赔偿。亦即单方合同的要约人在被要约人已开始履行合同之后违约,且这种单方合同中接受要约的履行行为在完成之前被要约人予以终止)
culpa lata (= *lata culpa*) 重大过失,大错
* ***Culpa lata dolo aequiparatur.*** Gross negligence is held equivalent to intentional wrong. 重大过失应被视为相当于故意的

违法或犯罪。
culpa levis (= *levis culpa*) 轻微过失,普通过失,一般错
culpa levissima (= *levissima culpa*) 最轻过失,小错
culpability n. 应受指责,应受处罚;有罪(行为)
culpable a. 有罪的;应受惩罚的;可归咎的
culpable act 有罪行为
culpable causation 负有罪责的因果关系
culpable homicide 有罪杀人,刑事杀人
culpable neglect 负有罪责的过失,应受惩罚的过失
culpable negligence 重大过失;应受惩罚的过失,负有罪责的过失
culpable of punishment 罪有应得,应受惩罚
culprit n. 1.犯罪者,犯人,罪犯 2.(英)刑事被告,未决犯;嫌疑犯
culprit of murder 谋杀嫌疑犯
cult of personality 个人崇拜
cultural a. 文化的,文化上的;教养的,修养的
cultural amusement tax 文化娱乐税
cultural and linguistic diversity 文化和语言方面的独特性和多样性
cultural association 文化协会
cultural body 文化团体
cultural defense (美)文化辩护[指直到20世纪20年代,美国法院才开始采纳基于文化差异的辩护。美国之所以从否定到承认文化差异对刑事案件有影响,因为移民越来越多,文化相对主义(cultural relativism)的理念、文化多元化(cultural pluralism)表现日益突出。这种文化差异导致文化接受的群众行为心理上的不同,反映到刑事案件中文化冲突日益凸显。据统计,20世纪80年代的法律案件中有2%的案件在处理中存在文化冲突的事实,文化差异所导致的刑事案件在处理上的困难越来越受到法学界的关注。1985年的一个亚洲移民的刑事案件,即木村案(People v. Kimura, No. A 09113 Super. Ct. L. A. County Nov. 21. 1985),检察官使用了称为"文化辩护"(cultual defense)的新理论。

1986 年发表在美国《哈佛大学法学评论》上的一篇文章造出了"文化辩护"这个新词汇。自此,实务人与理论学者对此辩护的优缺点进行了长时期的辩论,有学者认为"文化辩护"这一概念本身就容易被误解;但有部分学者尝试对其进行界定,认为:"文化辩护,一种运用于移民的刑事被告解释自己的行为不构成犯罪,或主张减轻处罚的法律策略。"还有学者认为:"文化辩护是指任何在刑事案件中运用文化证据证明刑事被告行为的正当,其行为不具有刑事可罚性,或主张减轻刑事被告的刑事责任。"亦有学者认为:"文化辩护是指刑事被告可以提出文化证据以表明他在行为实施时的心理状态或意图。"从以上不同的界定中可以看出并应考虑以下各点:首先,"文化辩护"基于文化因素而提出,它将两个独立的概念——文化和法律的重要方面联系在一起;其次,文化是人内在的道德标准也是非尺度,甚至最不依习俗的人的行为都无法逃避他们文化的影响;再次,一个在本国法律文化中遵守法律的刑事被告在其他法律文化下可能会实施犯罪行为,因为他的价值观迫使他这么做;最后,当法律背后的道德价值内化为个人行为准则时,法律更为有效。一个正当的法律制度应考虑各个刑事被告的道德维度,人类行为特征在某种程度上由其社会和文化背景决定]

cultural goods 文化商品(见 culture industries)

cultural heritage 文化遗产

cultural organization 文化团体

cultural products 文化产品(见 culture industries)

cultural property 文物

cultural relics protection unit 文物保护单位

culture n. 文化,精神文明,教养,栽培

culture economy 文化经济(指在数字技术推动下,全球文化产业发展热潮一浪高过一浪,文化经济作为一种新的经济形态出现并正处于崛起阶段)

culture industries 文化产业[近年来,文化已不再单纯表现为一种价值符号,已经成为一种生产要素。联合国教科文组织于 1986 年提出了文化产业概念,认为文化产业是以艺术创造表达形式、遗产古迹为基础而引起的各种活动和产出,包括文化遗产、出版印刷业的著作文献、音乐、表演艺术、视觉艺术、音乐媒体、视听媒体、社会文化活动、体育和游戏、环境和自然等十大类。简言之,文化产业是制造和提供文化产品(cultural products)的产业。从宏观角度界定,文化产业包括文化商品(cultural goods)与文化服务(cultural service)]

culture system 定植制度(指印度尼西亚过去的一种税收制度);爪哇殖民地开拓法

cum communi pastura (古)共同牧场[此术语为授权牧场的地役权,而非财产上的共同所有权(right of common)]

cum fossa et furca (with pit and gallows) (授予封建领主设立)地牢和绞架(的授权条款)[指古代特许状中,此词语为授予封臣法庭(Baron court)具有审判死罪和处以死刑的权力]

cum laude 以优等学业成绩

cum libera et plena administratione (法律拉丁语)(苏格兰法)充分行政自由权[此术语表示一个人可以授予其代理人(attorneys)相关的权力]

cum maritagio (苏格兰法)附带嫁妆,带有嫁妆[根据长者对婚姻的监护,此词语出现适用于对长者的要求偿付(required payment)]

cum rights 附带权利

cum testamento annexo 遗嘱附件,带有附件的遗嘱

cum-copula 同房,性交

cumulatio criminum 罪行的累积(刑事起诉书被控一项以上罪行)

cumulation n. 堆集,累积

cumulation of crimes 罪行累积

cumulative a. 累积的;累加的;(证据、遗产、罪行等)与同一事实相重的,加重的;逐渐增加的

cumulative distribution function 累计分布函数

cumulative dividend 累加红利

cumulative error 累积错误

cumulative evidence 复证,重复以前的证词;累积证据(指补充或增强前一证据力的证据,或者各部分彼此加强可靠性的证据)

Cumulative Index of Congressional Committee Hearings (美)《国会委员会听证资料集汇索引》[由美国参议院图书馆出版,共若干卷,包括从第41届国会(1869年)至第95届国会(1977年)]

cumulative indirect taxes 累计间接税

cumulative interest 复利,累加利息(指逾时不付所追加的利息)

cumulative judgment 累积判决(指第一次判决期满后生效的第二次判决)

cumulative legacy 附加遗赠(见 additional legacy)

cumulative liabilities 累积责任;累积负债

cumulative offence 累犯,累罪

cumulative penalty (对累犯)加重判刑,加重处罚

cumulative poison 渐增的毒性

cumulative preference share (或 **stock**) 累积优先股

cumulative punishment 累加刑罚;数罪并罚

cumulative remedy 累积补救

cumulative sentence 累积判决(指对被控犯有数罪的犯人,根据其不同罪项,分别予以判刑并合并执行所作的一种判决。亦称"from and after" sentence, accumulative sentencing 或 consecutive sentencing)

cumulative stock (或 **share**) 累积股(指因股利逐年累积而其票面价值随之增高的股票)

cumulative voting 累积投票(制)(指选民所领选票数与候选人数相同的选举制,而选民可采取将所有选票权给予一人或分投数人的投票方法)

cumulatively punished with a fine 并科罚金

cuneiform law 楔形文字法(指3000年前美索不达米亚各奴隶国家用楔形文字镌刻的法律)

cunning a. 狡猾的,狡诈的;熟练的,巧妙的

cura (到达青春期少年人的)保佐(至25岁为止)

cura furiosi vel prodigi 精神病和挥霍者的保佐

cura minorum 未成年人的保佐

curare n. 箭毒

curatio 保佐,临时监护

curator n. (美)大事管理官(指联邦最高法院于1974年增设的一名官员,主要掌管值得纪念的历史大事和人员的一些大事);保佐人;临时监护人;馆长;管理者,掌管者;监护人身份

curator ad hoc 特别保佐人(指由法院指定其对某一事务或交易承担管理责任的人)

curator *ad litem* 诉讼保佐人

curator *furiosi* 精神病患者的保佐人

curator *minorum* 适婚而未成年人的保佐人

curator's office of U. S Supreme Court 美国最高法院资料办公室主管

curatorship n. 保佐,临时监护;馆长的职位(或身份)

curb n./v. (美)(证券股票的)场外市场;抑制,控制/约束,控制,抑制

curbs market (美)场外证券市场,场外交易的市场

curbs on prayer in public school 约束在公共学校祈祷

cure v./n. 治愈;矫正,消除(弊病等);纠正(指审判过程中,如果裁定或判决是有利于错误的控诉一方,此审理过程的错误可以纠正)

curfew n. 宵禁,宵禁令

curfew order 宵禁令

curia n. 1.(古罗马的)政治区划之一;古罗马的元老院 2.(中世纪的)法庭 3.元老院大厦

curia advisari vult 延期判决(原意为"法庭拟考虑",用作案件判决事项的开头语,表示暂不作判决,留待考虑后再判)

curia burgi 见 Court of Hustings

curia domini 领主宅院(指领主居住地或大厅,开庭时佃农聚集此处)

curia jus novit 法庭执行现行法
curia magna 大庭(英国议会的古老名称之一)
curia palatii (英古法)王宫法庭(已废)
curia regis 国王法庭,君主法庭;御前委员会(法庭)
curia Romana 罗马教廷
curiam decision 法院判决;法庭意见
curiam opinion 法庭意见
currency n. 通货,货币;通用,流通;流传,传播
currency bond 以通货偿付的债券
currency circulation 货币流通
currency control 货币管制
currency devaluation 货币贬值
currency in vogue 通用货币
currency note 流通券,钞票
currency parity 货币平价
currency realignment 币值调整
currency reserves 货币储备
currency restriction 货币限制
currency system 币制,货币体系
currency unit 货币单位
currency-transaction report 现金交易报告,通货交易报告(指在银行账户上存款10000美元或1万美元以上的存款人必须签署的存款报告单。此报告单为蓝色纸质凭证,很像卡通漫画中角色 smurfs 的皮肤颜色,所以亦称为 smurfs)
current a. 流通的,通用的;流行的,现行的,当前的,草写的
current account 往来账户,活期存款;交互计算
current annual revenue 本年度收入
current assets 流动资产
current coin 通行硬币,(硬)通货
current decrees 现行法令
current deposit 活期存款
current event 时事(指依照伯尔尼公约,成员国可将纯时事报道排除在版权保护之外)
current expenditure 经常开支,流动开支
current funds 流动基金
current hand-writing 草书,草体
current interest 现行利息,通行利息

Current Law Reporting 《现行法律判例汇编》
Current Law Statutes Annotated (英)《现行注释法规》(指 1948 年至今商业性年度会议按年代顺序并附有注释的法律汇编)
current laws 现行法律(规)
current liabilities 短期负债,流动负债
current market-value 时时市场价格,现价
current money unit 通用货币单位
current price 时价,现行价格,市价
current price undercutting method 当前削价法[指非损害价格(non-injurious price)根据国内同类产品的当前价格计算。这种方法适用于倾销进口产品以低于国内产品的价格销售并获得部分市场份额,但基本上未影响到国内产品价格水平]
current repairs 普通修缮
current taxes and delinquent taxes 当期赋税与过期赋税
current use 现行习惯,现行惯例
current value 现值,现行价值
current-cost accounting (1938 年)现行成本会计[指根据重置成本(replacement cost)计算资产的一种方法]
currente termino During the currency of the term (苏格兰法)通货流通期间(此术语常用于租约)
curriculum 过程;课程
curriculum vitae 简历,履历表
cursitor n. (衡平法院的)书记官,记录员;诉讼档案保管员
cursitor Baron (英)理财法院书记员
curtail v. 缩短,省略;剥夺(特权或官衔等);削减(经费等)
curtailment n. 缩短,裁断,减,剥夺
curtesy 见 courtesy
curtesy of England (英)亡妻财产收益享有权(又译鳏夫产。按英国习惯,鳏夫可享有对亡妻的遗产受益权,但必须有与亡妻生前共生的子女。1925 年已废除)
curtilage n. 庭园;宅基地
custodia 看管;拘押
custodia legis 合法拘押

custodial a. 看守的,监视的;监督人的,保管人的,管教的

custodial interference (家庭法)监管的干预,监护人的干预[指①诱惑儿童或诱拐少年儿童离开父母合法的监护而不再回到父母合法监护当中。②任何阻碍父母接近孩子的正当权利,以上情况均受法律干预。1977年美国《侵权法重述》(第二次)第700节规定:以有资格具有监护权的父母名义未经孩子父母同意将孩子带走或威胁、诱拐孩子离开其父母且不回到父母身边接受父母具有资格的合法监护,属于侵权行为。亦可称为custody interference]

custodial lgis 见in custodia legis
custodial officer 典狱官;(中)管教(人员)
custodial right 监管权,管理权
custodial sentence (判处)监禁刑罚,(处以)监禁的判决
custodial training 拘留感化,在押犯的感化教养
custodialegis 见in custodia legis
custodialresponsibility (家庭法)监护责任[指对孩子身体上的监护、照管(包括夜晚)承担责任,父母对孩子更具有监护责任,而不管对孩子用多少时间,都应尽责]
custodian n. 监护人,看管人,监督人;公共机构[指①承担监护、看管(儿童、财产、票据或其他有价值的东西)责任的人或公共机构。关于儿童的监护人,他应当对儿童身体进行监护,也具有法律上的监护权(见caregiver)。②(破产法)破产财产者代理人,为债权人的利益而负责管理债务人资产的预先申请追偿债务代理人(prepetition agent)。参见《美国注释法典》第11标题卷第101(11)节。custodianship]
custodian trustee 保管受托人
custodianship n. 监护人(保管人等)的身份(或地位)
custody n. (15世纪)监护,监管,保管(指①对人或物进行直接的监护和控制或保护,使其安全;②羁押,拘留,拘禁或监视,除对某人的实际关押监狱之外,对具结悔过释放的人亦进行监视或监管)
custody agreement (存托银行和托管人之间签订)托管协议(指托管人负责通知存托人有关分红和行使其他有关权利的信息,如果可行,按存托人的指示在股东大会上行使投票权)

custody disputes 监护人与第三者之间的诉讼
custody for trial 羁押候审
custody in the international clearing 国际清算系统中的保管人
custody interference 见custodial interference
custody of children 对儿童的监护
custody of exhibits 保管证物
custody standard 监护标准
custody-education n. 羁押教育
custom n. 1.风俗习惯;惯例(又译习惯。但有法律拘束力,与usage有别);惯例法(又译习惯法);常规 2.(复)关税,进口税;(the)海关 3.(总称)顾客;(对商店的)惠顾
custom and usage 惯例
custom based on tradition 传统习惯
custom declaration for imports and exports 进出口货物报关单
custom house 海关
custom made 定做,定制
custom of people 人民的习惯(法)(指盎格鲁—撒克逊王室时期不是国王的法律或领主的法律)
custom of (the) port 港口惯例
custom of judge of courts 法院的审判惯例
custom of merchant 习惯商法,商业惯例
custom of particular trade 特定的贸易惯例
custom of trade 贸易常规
custom software 用户软件,专用软件(在许多国家受到版权法的保护和商业秘密法的保护)
customs n. 海关,进出口税(关税)
customable a. (美)可征关税的
customary a. 依习惯的;惯有的;惯例法的(又译习惯法的)
customary common law 共同习惯法
customary court 习惯法法院
customary court baron (英)贵族习惯法法庭
customary formalities 习惯上的手续

customary freehold (英)习惯法上的完全土地保有
customary freehold tenure (英)依习惯享有的自由(完全)土地保有权
customary heir 惯例法上的继承人(又译习惯法上的继承人)
customary international law 国际惯例法(又译惯国际法,国际习惯法)
customary law 惯例法(又译习惯法)
customary law of indigenous Africans 非洲本土的习惯法
customary marriage 习惯式婚姻;(中)旧式婚姻
customary matter 习惯法案件
customary notice by publication 传统的公告通知
customary practice 惯例
customary procedure 惯例(法)程序
customary profession 惯常的职业
customary right 习俗权,惯有权利
customary rule 惯例(法)规则,惯例
customary stipulations 惯例条款
customary succession 惯例继承
customary tribunal 习惯法法庭
customer n. 主顾,顾客;用户
customer challenge 消费者异议
customized software 定做软件
customs act 关税法
customs administration zone 海关管理区
customs and excise 关税与国内税
Customs and Excise Act (英)《关税和消费税法》
customs bond 海关保税,保证货物(纳税)书,海关罚责
customs bonding 海关保税
customs classification procedure 结关手续
customs clearance 结关;出港许可证;海关放行;出口结关
customs confiscation 海关没收
customs court 海关法庭,关税法庭
customs declaration 报单单;海关申报单
customs declaration for imports and exports 进出口货物报关单
customs declaration made at the time of entry 入境申报单
customs detention 海关扣留
customs duty 关税
customs entry 海关进口(手续);进口报关单,海关登记
customs examiner 海关检查员
customs formality 海关手续
customs head office 海关总署
customs inspection 验关;海关检查
customs inspection post 海关检查站
customs law (或 code) 海关法(典)
customs lawyer 海关律师
customs nomenclature 海关税则明细表,海关税则目录
customs of business turnover 商业周转业的惯例
customs of the sea 海事惯例
customs of trader 商人习惯;商习惯
customs officer on duty 海关值勤官员,值勤关员
customs pass 海关通行证,关卡
customs police 海关警察
customs police station 海关派出所
customs preventive officer 海关缉私官员
customs regulations 海关章程
customs seal 海关封志
customs statute 海关法规
customs supervision and control 海关监督控制
customs supervision zone 海关监督区
customs tariff 海关税则,海关税率
customs territory 关税领土
customs treaty 关税条约
Customs Unions 关税同盟
customs unions and trade agreements 关税同盟与贸易协定
customs valuation 海关估价
custos 监护人;保管人,管理人,司法行政官(又译治安官)
custos rotulorum (英)首席司法行政官(又译首席治安官)
custumals (复) n. 习俗志(指古代采邑的习惯记录)
cut back 截短,缩减,中止,急转方向
cut down 1.砍倒,砍伤,砍死 2.(疾病等)夺去生命,夺去……生命;损害……健康

3.胜过;使逊色 4. 削减,缩短;改小;删节〈cut down on smoking〉(减少抽烟)
cut off 切掉,割下;删去;中止,断绝;剥夺……继承权
cut off clause 中断条款
cut off condition 关机条件
cut off date 截止日期;期限
cut off for liability 不负责任
cut off sb. with a shilling 给某人一先令象征以剥夺其实际继承权
cut short 使停止,打断;缩减,截短
cut-off date 截止日期
cut-off period 不得超过的期限
cut-purse n. 小偷,扒手
cut-rate a. 减价的,次等的,有减价货出售的
cut-throat n. 凶手,谋杀者;刺客
cutchery (=cutcherry) n. (印度的)法院,行政机关
cutting off the feet 砍足刑,剕足,(中史)刖刑
cutting off the nose 割鼻刑,(中史)劓刑
Cy pres doctrine 遵循本意原则
Cy pres recovery 近似补偿
cy-doctrine 力求实现遗嘱愿望原则
cy-pres 尽可能地,力求近似;近似原则(指力求解释符合遗嘱愿望的原则)
cyber law 网络法[指涉及互联网领域的法律。包括判例、制定法、法规和处理影响人们与商业通过电脑在互相行为产生的争议;网络法可以适用解决在线(on-line)言论和商业由于媒介性质包括知识产权、自由言论、隐私、电子商务和安全设施以及管辖问题所引起的争议,亦可称为 cyber space law]
cyber payment 网上支付[指通过互联网转付款项,通常通过支付服务(a payment service),亦称 internet payment]
cyber terrorism 网上的恐怖主义(指运用计算机进行非法攻击,并以攻击计算机、网络、电子储存的信息相威胁,实际上造成恐怖之目标和感受伤害)
cyber warfare 网络战(指敌对双方针对战争可利用的信息和网络环境,围绕信息权的争夺,通过计算机网络在保证己方信息和网络系统安全的同时,扰乱、破坏与威胁对方的信息和网络系统。从本质上讲,网络战是信息战的一种特殊形式,是在网络空间进行的一种作战行动)
cyberattack (cyber attacks) v./n. 网络攻击(一般指一种受国内管辖的普通刑事犯罪行为。实际上,网络中大部分攻击行为属于犯罪或间谍行为,除非这种网络攻击能构成国际法的"武力攻击")/网络攻击
cybercrime n. 网络犯罪
cyberfraud n. 网络诈骗
cyberlaw n. 网络法(指涉及计算机及互联网运用以及通信、信息领域方面的法律,其中还包括知识产权、言论自由以及公众检索信息等有关问题)(同 cyber law)
cybermetics 控制论(指对网络远程控制的研究)
Cybernetic(s) a./n. 控制论的/控制论
cyberpatent 见 internet patent
cyberpiracy (商标)网络侵犯商标权[指①注册或登记一个著名品牌或商标(或类似混淆的名称或商标)作为一个网址的域名(website's domain name),通常是为达到派生收益的目的;②指在互联网上盗窃域名的一种形式,另一种是使用类似名称或商标误导消费者。比如一个叫奈克·康姆 Nikee com.的地址,销售 Nikee 牌运动鞋和运动商品的这个域址就拉开消费者与名牌耐克(Nike)的距离。见 cybersquatting]
cybersecurity n. 网络安全[与 cyber insecurity(网络不安全、不可靠)相对]
cyberspace (=cyber-space) n. 电脑空间(指其不应视为地理上界的领土);网络空间
cyberspace law 见 cyber law
cyberspace as a means of communication 网络空间如同一个通信方式(见 cyberspace as a place)
cyberspace as a place 网络空间如同一个区域(网络争议中学者的看法,主要由对网络性质和空间的争论造成。目前主要有两种观点,一为网络空间如同一个区域,另一为网络空间如同一个通信方式)
cyberspace as a technological state of mind 网络空间如同人们思维的一种技术状态。(指对如何解决网络争议的另一部分学者的

看法)(见 cyberspace as a place 和 cyberspace as a means of communication)

cybersquatting n. 保持(互联网上的)域名权(指互联网上保持域名的行为,特别是与一个公司商标相关联的名称,然后通过销售和给公司特许名称而寻求盈利。因此该公司在与商标名称经鉴别相一致情况下获得利益。但这种情况是被1999年联邦法所禁止的);域名侵占,抢注域名(指互联网的域名注册,希望出售,或特许该域名而本人从中获利或使愿使用的单位获利。如果该域名相同于该人或单位使用的商标或与其商标产生混淆,则商标的持有人有理由对仍持有此域名的注册者提起诉讼)

cyberstalking v. 1.电子邮件干扰(指通常在系统基础上发送重复或多种邮件制造烦恼、干扰、恐吓、威胁使得受件人害怕其本人或家庭成员、家长受到伤害。亦称 e-mail harassment) 2.刑事受害(指运用互联网,通过聊天室和电子邮件寻找、鉴别或安排会见一个在刑事上致他人成为受害者的人) 3.网上侵扰行为(指通过多种电子邮件而进行的一种威胁、骚扰、令人烦恼的行为。如运用互联网,特别是具有使接受者处于恐怖境况之意图,使接受者或其家人、家属将会遭受一种非法行为侵扰或一种伤害)

cybersuicide n. 网络自杀

cybertheft n. 网上窃取,网上盗窃(指使用在线电脑服务的行为,比如在互联网上一个人盗窃他人财产或干预他人使用或享用的财产;网上盗窃的一些实例:侵入一个银行电脑的记录完全错误地将一个人的账户记入贷方并将他人记入借方,甚至通过互联网错误地寄出受保护的资料而侵犯了版权)

cyclic(al) inflation 周期性通货膨胀
cyclopedia n. 百科全书
cyclothymia n. 循环性精神病,更替性精神病
cypher (=cipher) n. 密码;花押
cyrographrius (古代英国普通民事法庭的)法官

D

dacoit n. (印度或缅甸的)土匪
dacoity n. 土匪抢劫
dactylogram n. 指纹
dactylography n. 指纹学;指纹法
dactyloscopy n. 指纹鉴定法;以指纹认明罪犯
Daesh n. "达伊什"组织(指"伊拉克和沙姆伊斯兰国",与 ISIS 或 IS 是同一组织);极端恐怖主义组织
dagger n. 匕首,短剑;短刀
Dane-Law (Danelage)丹麦法[指8世纪末9世纪初丹麦人入侵英格兰时占领英格兰中部和东部的一些郡,丹麦法就在这些地区推行。从埃德加国王统治时期直到埃德华国王时期,丹麦法成为英格兰盛行的三大法系之一,另两种法系为 Mercenlage 和 West-Sexon Law。9世纪、10世纪丹麦听取忏悔的神甫(confessor),将包括丹麦法在内的法规汇编成统一法律,在英格兰中部和东部各个郡中强制实施。此法亦称 lex Danorum;denelage]

danger of confusion (商品)混淆的危险
dagger-money n. (英)匕首钱(指詹姆斯一世时期的货币,值20先令)
dahir (摩洛哥)诏令
Dail Eireann 爱尔兰众议院
daily a. 每日的,按日的,日常的
daily cause list 每日审案一览表
Daily Digest (美)《每日文摘》(指记载议案通过各项程序后制成公法过程的文件,而在每届会期结束时被汇集成单独的《记录》合订卷本)
daily duty sheet 每日值勤表
daily premium 每日保费,每日贴水,每日升水
dak n. (印度)驿站;邮政

damage n. 1.损害,损失;破坏,毁坏 2.(复)损害赔偿,损害赔偿金(额);费用;(合同预定的)违约金
damage feasant(或 **faisant**) (英)牲畜闯入他人土地(使庄稼或树木)所致的损害(见 distress of damage-feasant)
damage in law 法定损害
damage of a non-economic character 非经济性质的损害
damage of a pecuniary character 金钱性质的损害
damage survey 损失调查
damaged cargo report 货物残损报告单
damaged party 受害一方
damages awards 损害赔偿仲裁书
damages by children 未成年人所造成的损害赔偿
damages caused by a domestic animal 因家畜所致的损害赔偿
damages caused by aircraft 飞机(或航空器)所致的损害赔偿
damages caused by default 因迟延所致的损害赔偿
damages caused by inherently dangerous activities 因固有危险活动所造成的损害赔偿
damages caused by the buyer's fault 因买受人过错所致(违约)的损害赔偿
damages caused by the fall of a building 因建筑物坍塌所致的损害赔偿
damages caused by the seller's fault 因出卖人过错所致(违约)的损害赔偿
damages claim 损害赔偿请求权
damages for (**delay**) **detention** 延误引起的损害赔偿损失费
damages for adultery 因通奸引起的损害赔偿
damages for enticement 引诱他人配偶的损害赔偿
damages for libel 因诽谤所致的损害赔偿
damages for loss of consortium 丧失配偶权利的损害赔偿
damages for prospective loss 丧失预期利益的损害赔偿
damages for trespass 侵害行为的损害赔偿
damages in compensation for the breach of contract 用违约金的损害赔偿
damages in substitution 用替代物的损害赔偿
damages resulting from 由于……而引起的损害赔偿
damages suit 损害赔偿诉讼
damasking n. (英)饰废玺花纹(指废弃旧玺)
damnification n. 损伤;损害,伤害
damnify v. 损伤;损害,伤害;伤,害
damning a. 导致定罪的;认定……有罪的;诅咒的
damning evidence 有罪的证据;有罪确证
damnosa haereditas (罗马法)有负担的继承(指得不到利益的继承)
damnum absque injuria 在法律意义上未构成侵权的损害[见 *damnum sine*(或 *absque*)*injuria*]
damnum emergens 偶发性利益的损失
damnum fatale 不可避免的意外损害;非人力所能预料(或防止)的损害
damnum infectum (罗马法)尚未发生(但近在眼前或有威胁)的损害
damnum injuria datum (罗马法)非法损害他人财物
damnum sine(或 *absque*)*injuria* 无侵权行为的损害(指法律上无过错行为所造成的损害);不能依法得到补救的损害
* *Damnum sine injuriá esse potest.* There may be damage or injury inflicted without any act of injustice. 也可能会出现有无任何非法行为所致的损害情况。
Danes 丹麦法(12世纪初全英格兰岛仍然使用至少有三种不同的传统习惯法:West Saxons, Mercians, Danes)
danger n. 危险;危险物;危机;威胁
danger area 危险区
danger line 危险界限
danger money 危险工作津贴
danger of repeating offences 重新犯罪的危险
danger signal 危险信号
danger zone 危险地带,危险区

dangerous a. 危险的;危害的
dangerous act 危害行为
dangerous and reckless driving 危险和鲁莽开车,开"飞"车
dangerous animal 危害性的兽畜
dangerous articles 危险(物)品
dangerous consequences of a crime 犯罪的危害后果
dangerous driving 危险驾驶
dangerous drugs 危险药品
dangerous goods 危险(物)品;危险货物
dangerous goods code 危险品符号;危险品规则
dangerous label 危险货物标签
dangerous mark 危险品标志
dangerous premises 危险屋宇,危楼,危房
dangerous things 有害物品,危险(物)品
dangerous weapon 危险性武器,凶器
Daniel n. 正直的法官,有非常智慧的人;(圣经中的)希伯来预言家
Danish Icelandic Union 丹麦冰岛联合国
Danish law 丹麦法
dare 给予之债,转让财产;使遭受危险
dark exchange 外汇黑市,黑市外汇
dark horse (在提名总统候选人中的)"黑马"(指实力难测的竞选者)
dark horse candidate "黑马"候选人
darrein (法)最终的,最后的
darrein presentment (或 last presentment) 最终圣职推荐权令状,最终推荐权(之诉)(指为解决圣职推荐权"advowson"的争端而向郡长"sheriff"签发的令状,要求郡长组成陪审团来最后确定真正的圣职推荐权人"patron"。斯蒂芬和亨利二世统治前,有关圣职推荐权的纠纷多在教会法庭解决。1179年第三次拉特兰宗教公会议规定,在圣职空缺三月后,主教将获得圣职推荐权)
data n. 资料,材料;作为论据的事实,理论数据
data base (或 bank) 数据库
data base access 数据库进入(方法),数据库检索方法
data communications 数据通信(指数据的传递、接收和确认)

data compilation 资料汇编;数据汇编
data deceiving 数据欺骗(计算机犯罪手段之一,指非法篡改输入、输出数据或输入假数据,如伪造或冒充输入文件,用事先准备好的替换内容更换正常的输入内容)
data encryption standards (美)数据加密标准
data matching program 数据匹配程序
data message 数据讯息
data of experience 经验的材料,经验的数据
data processing 资料处理,数据处理
data processing operation 数据处理程序
data protection 数据保护
data sources (计算机)数据资料
data-handling n. 数据处理
data-set-information v. 数据集信息
data-signaling-system n. 数据通信系统
datal n. 按日计算工资
dataller (=day-taler) n. 计日工
date n./v. 日期,时期,年代 date n.日期;约会(男女间);约会对象/注明日期;确定年代
date and time of sailing 开航时间(及日期)
date draft 定期汇票
date of acceptance 承付日期,承兑日期
date of application 申请日期
date of approval by senate (美)参院批准日期(指参院对条约"同意"的日期,即参院出席2/3议员投票通过之日)
date of arrival 抵港日期,到达日期
date of birth 出生时间,出生日期
date of chart corrections 海图改正日期
date of completion of discharge 卸讫日期
date of decision 判决日期
date of delivery 交货日期
date of departure 离港日期;开航日期
date of disbursement 支出日期,支付日期
date of draft 汇票日期,出票日
date of expiration (或 expiry) 期满日;截止日期
date of filing 申请日
date of hearing 讯问日期,听审日期
date of issue 签发日期

date of launch （船舶）下水日期
date of loading 装货日期
date of maturity 到期日
date of presentation 提出日期,送呈日期,颁发日期,出示日期
date of proclamation 宣告日期,公告日期
date of ratification by the president （美）总统批准日期
date of registration 登记日期
date of service 送达日期
date of settlement 决算日,决算日期
date of severance 退伙日
date of signing 签字日期(常指一国代表和另一国代表在条约上签字之日期,通常可在援引时用)
date of term 日期条款
date of the filing of the suit 起诉日期
date of value 起息日,起算利息日期
dated a. 注明日期的,过时的
dateless a. 无日期的,无期限的;远古的,经时间考验的
datio in solutum 代物清偿
dative a. 可随意赠与（或处分）的;（官员）可指派（或免职）的
dative executor 法院指派的遗嘱执行人
datum n. 作为论据的事实;理论数据;资料;材料
daughter n. 女儿
dawdler n. 二流子;懒汉
dawk n. （非鹰非鸽派的）中间派
day n. 日,日子;时代;白天;工作日,节日,限期,全盛日期;（复）寿命
day bill 定期票据
day by day 逐日、天天地(指逐渐转变)
day certain 特定的未来日子(期)
day fines 日罚金(按日来计算)
day in court 开庭审讯日;开庭日,出庭日
day in question 有关的那一天,事发的那一天
day of hearing 审讯日,审理日
day of remuneration 支薪日
day of the injury 损害发生日
day room （=dayroom） 日间拘留所;娱乐室,休息室
day to day 天天,从一天到另一天(通常指逐渐转变,不固定)
day-book n. 日记账,日记簿
day-to-day loan 逐日放款
day-to-day operation of business 企业的日常经营,商业的日常运营
daylight robbery 侵害采光权
days dismissed from criminal service 刑事免役日
days of grace （保险,票据等的）宽限日期,优惠日期
daysman n. 公断人,仲裁人;选定的法官
de 从,关于
de acquirendo rerum dominio 获得物权,（关于）得到物的所有权
de assisa continuanda （英）延审令状(指主要事实得不到证明时发给巡回法官用以延审的令状)
de bonis asportatis 取走财物
de bonis non administratis 遗产管理人的后继人(指遗产管理人死了,被指定来继续完成管理该遗产的人)
de bonis propriis 遗产管理人自己的财产
de cartis reddendis 返还契据,返还文据（指命令恢复或返还契据,或文据的令状,请求返还扣押物的诉讼令状）
de clerico admittendo （英）圣职授予令状[指命令主教接受安排有空缺圣职(vacant benefice)的执行令状,圣职的推荐权人(benefice's patron)在高等民事法院通过妨碍圣职推荐之诉(quare impedit)能有权强制执行填补这一空缺]
de cujus 通过谁,根据何人的权利主张;来自某人,通过某人[指①依靠某人,通过某人来主张权利;②在争议中(in issue)的某人的法律地位(legal position)]
de curia claudenda （历史上）强制修建围栏或围墙令(该令状要求某人环绕自己居住房屋修筑围墙或围栏以避免干扰邻居)
de cursu 当然的,正规的,通常的[此术语通常关系到正规的、正式的程序,区别于附带的简易诉讼(summary proceedings)]
de dato 即日起
de debito 债务令状（同 *debito*-缩写形式）
de debitore in partes secando （罗马法）将债务人切成碎片[十二铜表法中的一个题

目(title)意指债权人有权分割债务人的财产]

de die in diem 逐日,一天天

de facto 事实上,实际上

de facto adoption 事实收养[指在美国的个别州如果缺少必法定的条件则收养不能成功。当法定程序已经完成或法院裁定不容否认的收养条件已经成熟。收养协议(成熟)即可转入法律收养(de jure adoption)。当法定程序已经完成或法院裁定不容否认的收养条件已经成熟]

de facto bond 事实上受约束,事实上的盟约,(男女的)事实上的结合

de facto companies 事实上的伴侣(夫妻)

de facto corporation (或 **company**) 事实上的公司

de facto decriminalisation 事实上的非犯罪化(见 *de jure decriminalisation*)

de facto families 事实上的家庭(指未婚同居所建立的家庭)

de facto government 事实上(承认)的政府

de facto king 事实上的国王(指篡夺王位者)

de facto introduction 事实上的介入,事实上的使用

de facto marital relation 事实婚姻关系,事实婚姻

de facto marriage of free unions 自由结合的事实婚

de facto monopoly 事实上的独占权,事实上的垄断

de facto parent or parent by estoppel 事实上的父母或禁止否认之父母

de facto possession 事实上的占有

de facto protection 事实上的保护

de facto recognition 事实上的承认

de facto segregation (美)事实上的隔离,实质上的隔离(指事实上的存在,既非法律上的创设,亦非由法律或司法判决所实施的种族隔离,但实际具有隔离的效果。见 housing discrimination)

de facto servant 事实上的受雇人

de facto sovereignty 事实上的主权

de facto spouse 事实上的丈夫(或妻子),(复)事实上的配偶

de facto subjectee 事实上的国民

de facto tort 事实上的侵权行为

de facto union 事实上的结合(指非婚同居)

de fide 该信条遵守的,信仰上的

De fide et officio judicis non recipitur quaestio; sed de scienta, sive sit error juris sive facti. The good faith and honesty of a judge cannot be questioned; but otherwise concerning his knowledge, whether he be mistaken as to the law or as to the fact, i. e. his decision may be impugned for error either of law or of fact. 法官的正直和诚信毋庸置疑。而对其判决,不管是法律上或事实上均可表示质疑而不服。

de heretico comburendo (普通法上的)镇压异教徒令状

de homine replegiando (古代)保释令

de integro 重新,另行

de jure 法律上,按照法律的,合法的

De Jure Belli [詹蒂利斯(Gentilis)1598年著的]《战争法》

De Jure Belli ac Pacis (格劳秀斯著的)《战争与和平法》

de jure corporation (或 **company**) 法律上的公司,依法设立的公司

de jure decriminalisation 法律上的非犯罪化[指基于刑事政策的立法论与解释论的双重机能,现代刑事政策强调,对特定行为的非犯罪化的路径包括法律上的非犯罪化与事实上的非犯罪化(de facto decriminalisation),前者为立法者通过的正式立法程序,将迄今为止作为犯罪予以处罚的行为从法律上正式予以废除的立法过程;后者是立法者通过司法权的运用,特别是通过刑法适用解释、缩减、变更、搁置刑法的适用使特定犯罪在特定情况下不被作为犯罪予以处理的司法过程]

de jure domestic government 合法的本国政府

de jure examination 法律审查

de jure functional 法律上的功能性

de jure government 法律上(承认)的政府

*****De jure judices, de facto juratores respondent.*** The judges find the law, the jury recognises the facts. 法官裁决法律问

题,陪审团认定事实。
***de jure* ownership**   法律上的所有权
***de jure* population**   常住人口
***de jure* possession**   法律上的占有,合法占有
De Jure Praedae   (格劳秀斯 1605 年著的)《捕获法》
***de jure* recognition**   法律上的承认
***de jure* referenda**   根据应该适用的法律
De Jure Rerum et Juris in re Speciebus   《论物权与特殊物权》(指哈恩于 1639 年在荷尔姆斯泰大学答辩的博士论文;提出五大类别:所有权,质押权,地役权,占有权和继承权)
***de jure* segregation**   (美)理论上的隔离(指法律规定的种族隔离被称为"理论上的隔离")
***de jure* sovereignty**   合法主权,法律上的主权
De l'Esprit des Lois   《论法的精神》(法国孟德斯鸠的名著,于 1748 年出版)
de lege lata   实在法
de magna assisa eligenda   选择并召集大陪审团令状
*****Demajori et minori non variant jura.*** Concerning greater and less laws do not vary. 法规在涉及或大或小的问题上,不会有所不同。
*****Deminimis non curat lex. (*lex non curat de minimis*).** The law does not care for, or take notice of, very small or trifling matters. 法律不计较琐事。
de mininis non curat praetor   裁判不能偏离主要争端,裁判官不干预琐事
*****De morte hominis nulla est cunctatio longa.*** When the death of a human being is concerned, no delay is long. 事关人的死亡时刻不得拖延;人的生命攸关时,不得延误。
de nativo habendo   (英国中世纪的)逃奴拘捕令
*****de non apparentibus, et non existentibus, eadem est ratio.*** As to things not apparent, and those not existing, the rule is the same. 对未被证明的事实,如同不存在的事实

适用同一规则。
de novo   1.(案件的)重新审理 2. 重新,第二次
***de novo* hearing**   (或 **trial**)   再次听审,重新听审
***de novo* law**   重新修订的法律
***de novo* review**   重新审查
de odio et atia   (或 ***breve de bono et malo***)   谋杀调查令状(指命令司法行政官调查被捕的在押杀人嫌疑犯是否有充分嫌疑的令状)
De Officio Regis   《皇家官职》[英国法律思想和宗教思想的第一位改革者约翰·威克利夫(John Wycliffe)的著名短文。文中抨击官方和教会权威以及罗马教会敕令集];君王官职,皇家官职
de praesenti   现在的
de régle   依法;按规则
de salva gardia   安全保护令状(指发布的令状保护外籍人在英国诉求其合法权利时免受伤害)
de son tort   过失属他自己的
de son tort demesne   自己导致的侵权责任,咎由自取
***de ventre inspiciendo* jury**   寡妇妊娠查讯陪审团
de-bene esse   有条件的;临时的;先行录取证供;暂先处理
de-legitimation   去合法化
deacon n./v.   执事/以次货冒充上等货;欺骗
dead a.   尸体的,死的;(法律等)名存实亡的,已废的;无讯号的;(美)改邪归正的
dead account   死账,呆账
dead ahead   正前方
dead astern   正后方
dead bargain   卖价极便宜的交易
dead body   死尸
dead broke   完全破产
dead calm   风平浪静
dead capital   不生产资本,死资本
dead drop   情报秘密传递点
dead freight   空舱费(或译亏舱费。指租船未装货,未装满而应付的空舱费)
dead hand   永远管业(指永远占有权,但不

dead hand control 永远管业限制(指所有的财产,尤指不动产,不能变卖或转售的限制规定)

dead horse 预付工资,旧债

dead letter 徒具空文的文件;无法投递函;形同虚设的规定,无效力的信件

dead letter laws 徒具空文的法律,(法律上)已废弃的条文

dead list 死案名单(见 discuss list)

dead load 底载;静负载

dead loan 呆账,倒账

dead man's acts (或 **statute**) 死亡者的法规;死者生前口头承诺法(指死者生前承诺不得作为对死者财产提出权利主张者的证据的制定法)

dead men tell no tales 死人不会告密

dead man's part (英)死者部分(指无遗嘱死亡者的动产中除其妻子和子女有权取得的财产外剩余的财产);死亡人名下的财产份额;死者应有份额

dead mortgage 固定抵押品,名存实亡的抵押

dead rent 付空租(指租地开矿,矿厂停工,也要支付租金)

dead security 固定抵押品,固定担保物

dead stock 滞销货,滞销品,呆滞资金;农具,农业机械(与 live stock 相对)

dead stop 完全停止

dead use 未来使用权

dead-pledge (或 **dead pledge**) n. 死典权(见 *mortuum vadium*),死抵押(权)

deadbed declaration 见 dying declaration

deadbeat dad (美俚)拖欠的爸爸(指没有支付或迟于支付子女抚养培育费的父亲)

deadbeat mom (美俚)拖欠的妈妈[指①没有支付或迟于支付子女抚养培育费的母亲,这个术语较 deadbeat dad(拖欠的爸爸)和 deadbeat parent(拖欠的双亲)而言远远用之较少,或者由于离婚后男人差不多 10 倍于女人不支付其子女的抚养培育费(或接到命令才交付)。②身心健康的母亲的收入来自福利收入而非盈利的职业]

Deadbeat Parents Punishment Act (美)《拖欠的父母惩罚法》[指 1998 年制定的属轻罪的联邦法规,对于不支付儿童抚养培育费的父母,如果承担责任者(obligator)已跨过州界企图逃避支付这项费用,则可受到 2 年监禁的惩处。此法规定以下情况按轻罪惩处:①越过州界企图逃避支付儿童抚养培育费,且该费用在 5000 美元以上,已有 1 年以上未交者;②身居另外的州,故意不交儿童抚养培育费,且欠费超过 10000 美元,2 年以上未交者。此法替代《1994 年儿童抚养培育费追索法》,其最大的变化是关于承担债务责任人越过州界竭力逃避这项债务的规定。参见《美国注释法典》第 42 标题卷第 228 节。缩写为 DPPA。见 Child-Support Recovery Act of 1994]

deadborn n. 见 still-born

deadline n. 最后期限;监狱周围的死亡线(指囚犯如果逾越即可格杀勿论的警戒线)

deadline for demanding compensation 索赔期限

deadline for performance 履行期限

deadlock n. 僵局;纠纷;停止,阻止

deadlocked bill 僵持的议案

deadly force 致命力量,致命暴力、击中要害之力

deadlocked (dead-locked) jury 陷入僵局的陪审团[指陪审团不能达成一致意见的裁决,或叫悬而未决(hung)的裁决]

deadly weapon 致命的凶器(或武器)

deadweight n. (船舶)载重量;载重吨位,固定负载

deadweight charter 满载租船合同(契约)

deadweight loss 无谓损失(竞争市场变成垄断势必产生无谓损失,并且由于法律限制所致,还会产生"寻租"问题)

deaf-mute n. 聋哑人

deal n./v. 1.部分,量,交易,买卖 2.(美)密约,秘密妥协(尤指经济上的特殊政策)3.待遇/交易;待遇;处分;分配,处理,应付

deal in 经营,做买卖

deal in stolen goods 经营盗窃物资

deal with 1.对付;来往;打交道;交易;经

营 2.处理;考虑;对待;惩处 3.讨论,论及
deal with sb. according to… 根据……处理某人
dealer n. 商人,生意人,经销人;坦率无诈的人
dealer agreement 交易商协议
dealer in inflammable material 贩卖易燃物品的商人
dealer's license 经销商执照
dealership n. 商品经销特许权,代理商
dealing n. 1.待遇;处置;(对人的)行为 2.(复)来往;交易,交际 3.分配,分给
dealing in future 期货交易
dealing in securities 证券交易
dean n. 外交团长,使节团长;学院院长,教务长,系主任;前辈
Dean of Arches 主教法庭世俗法官
Dean of (the) Arches (英)主教法院法官,拱顶法院法官[指坎特伯雷大主教法庭(Court of Arches)的主审法官(presiding judge)。最初指的是坎特伯雷教省十三个不由其教区主教管辖的"特殊"分区行使管辖权的教会官员,后因其填补了教务总长(Official principal)的职务空缺,从而两者合并为一,习惯称之为拱形法院法官,实际正式名称为教务总长。1784年以来,这一职务必须是具有10年以上实践经验的出庭律师或曾担任过最高法院(supreme court)的法官,并且是英格兰国教会成员。该法官由两位大主教任命,经女王批准,同时担任约克教省法院法官(auditor)和拱顶法院大主教特许法院的主事官(Master of the Faculties)]
Dean of Faculty (苏格兰)律师学院院长
Dean of Guild Court 行会法庭庭长
death n. 死亡,死亡的原因;剥夺政治权利;灭亡
death annuity 死亡抚恤年金
death benefits 死亡抚恤金,丧葬福利金;人身保险金;死亡救济金
death blow 致命打击
death by a thousand cuts 千刀万剐
death by accident 事故死亡,意外死亡
death by hanging 绞死,绞刑
death by lightning 雷击死

death by misadventure 意外致死
death by suffocation 窒息死亡
death cell 死囚牢房
death certificate 死亡证明书
death chair (罪犯被处死的)电椅
death chamber 监狱中的行刑室,罪犯处决室
death duty 1.见 duty 2.见 estate tax
death grant 死亡补助金
death house 死囚行刑前的牢房
death in line of duty 因公殉职,因公死亡
death inquiry 死因调查
death knell 丧钟原则(见 inverse death knell doctrine)
death penalty (1948年)1.死刑,极刑 2.剥夺所有的权利能力[指一个人或一个实体无法定资格去参加过去他(它)曾参加过的活动]3.强制惩处(指因为有些严重渎职类型,所以强制惩处。见 death penalty sanction)
death penalty case 死刑案件
death Penalty Information Center (美)死刑信息中心(指一民间组织,设立于华盛顿,具有一套独立发现错案机制。该组织统计1973年至2010年2月美国共有139人从死囚牢中获得释放,恢复了法律上的清白之身)
death penalty sanction (1991年)(民事诉讼法)剥夺权利能力的惩处[指由于一方当事人过度滥用调查取证程序(discovery),故法院出示驳回诉讼令;由于当事一方的作为或不作为均显示其不愿参与此项诉讼,故法院作出进入不应诉判决令(default judgment)。这种惩处罕为作出,而且通常在此之前并有未遵守的较轻惩处(lesser sanction)或对于问题无法补救的安排。缩略为 death penalty]
death rate 死亡率
death row 死刑区(指被判死刑的囚犯被监禁的地区)
death roll 死亡人名册
death row (监狱中的一排)死囚牢房(指等待受死刑惩处的囚犯室)
death sentence 死刑判决
death sentence with reprieve 死刑缓刑判

决,判处死刑缓期执行
death tax 1.见 estate tax 2.见 inheritance tax
death warrant 死刑执行令
death with dignity 有尊严地死亡
death-bed a. 临终的,临终时做的……
death-bed declaration 临终供述;临终陈述
death-bed will 临终的遗嘱;临死愿望
death-blow n. 致命的一击;致命的事物
death-penalty n. 死刑
death-qualified jury (刑法)死刑案件合格陪审团(指适合裁断死刑案件的陪审团,因为这些陪审团绝对毫无意识上的偏见去反对死刑。见 life-qualified jury)
death-watch (或 **death watch**) n. 守尸;死囚(行刑前夜的)看守人;临终看护
debag v. 剥开裤子抽打
debar v. 阻止;排除;禁止
debasement n. 贬值
debatable a. 可争辩的,可争论的,会产生争论的;未决定的,争议中的
debate v./n. 1.(口头上的)争论,(与……)辩论;讨论⟨to debate the tax issue on television⟩(在电视上讨论税务问题) 2.思考,慎重考虑(指在作出决定之前仔细慎重考虑以调解争端,或掂量抉择)⟨to debate a matter in one's mind⟩(心中盘算着一件事),⟨to debate what course to take⟩(慎重考虑采取什么程序) 3.说服、辩论(指公开说服或参加争辩)⟨to debate about relationship between poverty and crime⟩(辩论贫穷与犯罪之间的关系) 4.深思、掂量(用自己的脑子深入考虑)赞成和反对的情况⟨to debate about the advantages and disadvantages of making telephone call⟩(深入考虑打电话的利弊)/辩论,争论⟨truth develops through debate between different views⟩(不同观点的辩论才能使真理得以发展),⟨debate with sb.⟩(与某人的一场辩论)
debate in court 法庭辩论
debate on the Address (英)(对女王在每届议会开幕式上的致辞所作的)致答辞的辩论
debauchery n. 奸污;放荡,纵欲

debauchery of youth 青年的纵欲行为,放荡青年
debenture (15世纪) 1.非(或无)担保之欠债[指无担保的欠债,只以依靠收入能力(earning power),而不是靠特定持有资产作抵押的债务。最早,这是契据的第一个诺言,根据细目承认所欠之债]2.无担保的欠债字据(承认欠债之文据)3.公司债券(bond)(此债券已由一般信用和公司发行人的财政信誉担保,而不是靠公司资产)4.(英国法)公司的有价证券(security)来担保金融贷款。这种有价证券通常建立一个偿还债的义务项目(change)作为公司股份或财产 5.(海关)退税凭单(或证书)[指海关的证书,证明提供了有关进口物资(goods)的偿付关税单据]
debenture bonds 信用债券,公司债券
debenture certificate 债券
debenture holder 债券持有人
debenture stock 附有利息而还本无定期的债券;公司债券
debenture to bearer 无记名债券
* *Debetquis juri subjacere ubi delinquit.* One (everyone) ought to be subject to the law (of the place) where he offends. 每个人均应受其犯罪地法的管辖。
* *Debet sua cuique domus esse perfugium tutissimum.* Every man's house should be a perfectly safe refuge. 任何人的住宅都应成为毋庸置疑的庇护所。
* *Debile fundamentum fallit opus.* A weak foundation frustrates (or renders vain) the work (built upon it). 不牢固的地基会使建筑其上的建筑物倒塌,软弱无力的根据会使事情徒劳。
debit n./v. (15世纪) 1.应承担的借款或欠款数额,借方金额 2.记入借方的款项[在簿计中,在分类账目或总账目的左边(left side)做账目,表明资产的增加或债务的减少] 3.账户结余(account balance)[表明一些项目应有结余(remains due)留给账户持有人。见 credit 6]/将……记入借方⟨credit sb. with $5⟩(把一笔5英镑的账记入某人的借方)
debit adjusting 债务调整

debit balance 借方差额,借差
debit card 借贷卡[指从买方银行账户以电子转账方式(electronic transfer)支付给买方使用的卡]
debit instrument 欠据,欠单
debit interest 欠息
debita fundi 土地担保义务
* *Debita sequuntur personam debitoris.* Debts follow the person of the debtor (i.e. they have no locality, and may be collected wherever the debtor can be found). 债务人跑到哪里,债就跟到哪里(即债是无处躲藏的,不论在什么地方,只要找到债务人就可以索债)。
debiti et crediti contribution (大陆法)借贷平衡(A balancing of debit and credit) (此术语与 set off 相关,set off 或 set-off 为抵销、债务抵销)
debilitation n. 衰弱,虚弱,落空
debilitation to the federal rights creation by the FELA 由联邦雇主责任法创的联邦权利落空
* *Debitorum pactionibus creditorum petitio nec tolli nec minui potest.* The rights of creditors can neither be taken away nor diminished by agreements among (or of) the debtors. 债权人的权益既不能由债务人间的协议而取消,也不能由债务人间的协议而缩减。
debitrix 女债务人
debitum 债务
debitum connexum 债务引起的留置权
debitum in praesenti solvendum in futuro 现今的债款(或债 obligation)将来偿还;已订约履行的借款(或债)则不能要求在某个未来时日之前履行
debt n. 债,债务;欠款;罪,罪过;(英)债务诉讼
debt adjustment 见 debt pooling
debt at call 即期债务
debt bondage 债奴
debt cancellation 取消债务
debt ceiling 债务限额
debt claim 债的请求权,债的诉讼请求
debt collection 收回债款

debt collector 收债人,讨债人
debt consolidation 见 debt pooling
debt contract 债务合同
debt court 债务法院
debt instrument 债务证书;欠据
debt limit (发行公债券的)债款限额
debt management (政府的)债务管理(指选择对现有国债构成和性质有影响的政策活动)
debt note 借款通知单
debt obligation 债务
debt of hono(u)r (法律上不能追索的)信誉贷款,信用贷款,信用借款;赌债
debt of record (英)法院记录(可证明的)债务
debt on bond 借据
debt on the date 到期的债务
debt paying ability 偿债能力
debt pooling 债务分享,债务共享(指将一个人的债务进行合并作出一种安排,而债权人也同意并接受较低的付款或提取较少现款项。亦称 debt consolidation, debt adjustment)
debt redemption 偿债
debt relief 免除债务
debt rescheduling 重定还债期限
debt retirement (公债券的)债务偿还
debt securities 债务证券,债权证券[指公司通过发行证券来获得运作的资金,是进行融资的一种手段。反映在公司账目上为债务的任何形式的公司证券,如债券、票据等。如果钱款是从个人或机构筹借则应由公司发给出借人借据(债权证券的一种形式)。公司可以向公众发行和出售债权证券额的方式向公众借款,即债券或债单,这些证券一般以每张 1000 美元面值发行。债券售出价高于面值称为溢价发行;如果低于面值则称为贴现发行]
debt service 债息
debt subject to statutory limit 法定限额的债务
debt-ridden a. 负债累累的
debtee n. 债权人,债主
debtor n. 负债者,债务人,借方
debtor act 债务人法

debtor acting in bad faith 有恶意行为的债务人
debtor and creditor agreement 债务人及债权人的协议
debtor attached 被扣押的债务人
debtor estate 债务人财产
debtor nation 债务国
debtor *paravail* 附属债务人
debtor summons 债务人传票
debtor's examination (破产法)债务人的审查[指债务人与债权人之间的一种会议,在此期间债权人要求债务人旨在不公开债务人的资产的地点、内容和债务清偿的可行性的有关信息的一些问题。]这种审查可以根据《联邦破产程序法规》(the Federal Rules of Bankruptcy Procedure)第2004条的规定或《破产法典》(the Bankruptcy Code)的第343节进行,破产财产管理人或委托人(bankruptcy trustee)可以参加或主持最初的审查。这个审查在提出破产之后持续时间很短,但当事方(常常是债权人)要求按第2004条规定方式主持会议,此会随时可以举行。参见《美国注释法典》第11卷第343节]
debtor's performance 债务人的给付,债务人的履行
debtor's petition 债务人的诉状
debtor-prisoners 债务囚犯,债务罪犯
debts exceeding assets 资不抵债
debts of equal degree 同等级的债权
decade of lawsuits 十年期的诉讼
decadence n. 堕落,颓废,衰微,衰败
decadence in the law of equity 衡平法的衰落
decamp v. 撤退;逃走,逃亡
decapitate v. 斩首,杀头;(美)解雇,(因政治原因)立即免职
decapitation n. 斩首(旧译:大辟刑);(美)解雇;立即免职
decapitator n. 刽子手;解雇者;免(别人)职的人
decease n. 死,死亡
deceased n./a. 死者;被继承人/已死的,已故的

deceased heir 已死亡的继承人
deceased person 死者
deceased victim 已死受害人
decedent n. (美)死者;死亡人
decedent estate 死者(死亡时所)遗留的财产,死者的遗产
deception n. 欺骗,诡计,诈欺,蒙骗(按英国1968年的《盗窃法》,指不管在语言上或行为上是否出于故意的欺骗)(同 fraud)
deceptive marks 欺骗性的标记
deceit n. 欺骗,欺诈行为;虚伪;虚假
deceitful a. 欺诈的,骗人的,不老实的
deceitful plea 欺骗性的答辩(或抗辩)
deceitful selling of a thing 欺诈性的销售物品
deceive v. 欺骗,欺诈;行骗
deceive sb. into doing sth. 骗某人去做某事
decemvir n. (古罗马的)十执政官之一;十人执政团中的一人
decemvirate n. (古罗马的)十执政官的职位(或任期);十人执政团
decemviri (古罗马)十人团(指由十人组成的一个委员会)
decemviri legibus scribundis (古罗马)法律起草十人团
decemviri stlitibus judicandis (古罗马)审案十人团
decency n. 正当,正派;合乎礼仪;(复)正当行为
Decennial Digest (美)《十年的判决摘要汇编》(见 American Digest System)
decentralism n. 地方分权
decentralization n. 分权制;地方分权(政策);分散
decentralize v. 分散行政权,撤销集中点
(to) decentralize the administration of justice 司法权下放
decentralized investigation 分散型侦查
decentralized management 分权管理(指统一领导,分权管理)
decentralized political system 分权的政治体制
deception n. 欺骗,诡计,诈欺,蒙骗(按英国1968年的《盗窃法》,指不管在语言上

或行为上是否出于故意的欺骗)
Deceptis non decipientibus, jura subveniunt. The laws help persons who are deceived, not those deceiving. 法律帮助受欺骗的人,而不帮助行骗的人。
decern v. (苏格兰)判决
decertify v. 收回……的证件,取消……执照
decessit sine prole 死后无子女
decessit sine prole legitima 死后无婚生子女
decessit sine prole mascula 死后无子
decessit sine prole mascula superstite 死后无活着的儿子
decessit sine prole superstite 死后无活着的子女
decessit sine prole virile 死后无子
decessus (古英国)死;离开
decide v. 1.决心,决意,决定 2.解决,判决,裁决 3.使下决心,使决断
decide against sb. 判决某人败诉
decide in favo(u)r of sb. 判决某人胜诉
decide on a verdict 定案
decide the case 办案,判案
decide the issues of fact 判定事实争议
decide the particular cause 判决一个特殊诉讼,审判一个特定诉案
decided case 已决案件
decider n. 决定人,裁决人
deciding controversies 裁决争议
deciding factor 决定因素
deciding vote 裁定票,决定票
decimalize v. 使成为十进位制的
decimalized currency 十进位制货币
decimate v. 选来……的十分之一;大批杀死;对……征什一税,取……的十分之一
decipher v./n. 译解(密码等);解释;辨认(字迹等)/译密电文;译解〈a researcher must be able to decipher 551 P.2d 334 (Cal. 1976)〉[检索人员必须能译解 551 P.2d 334 (Cal.1976)援引代码];解释(古文字等);密电或密函的译文(decipherment);译文〈you may not need to decipher the abbreviation in order to retrieve a case〉(你可不必缩略以便检索判例)
Decipi quam fallere est tutius. It is safer to be deceived than to deceive. 受骗要比行骗安全。
decision n. (法院的)决定;决议;判决;决断,裁定;坚定,果断,结果(见 judgment;verdict)
Decision Act (美)裁判法
decision by majority 多数议决,过半数的表决
decision in a case 定案,案件判决
decision in favo(u)r of the defendant 有利于被告的判决,被告胜诉的判决
decision in favo(u)r of the plaintiff 有利于原告的判决,原告胜诉的判决
decision making 作出决定,作出判决
decision of bankruptcy 破产裁定
decision of the court 法院判决
decision on appeal 上诉审法院的判决
decision on "general" matters 一般问题的判决
decision on guilt or innocence (或 not guilty) 有罪或无罪的裁定
decision on the merits 根据是非曲直的判决
decision reversed 撤销判决,废弃判决
decision rule presumption 裁决规则推定(见 artificial presumption)
decision standard 决策基准,决策准则
decision theory 决策理论
decision to prosecute 提起公诉的决定
decision-maker(decisionmaker) n. 决策者,判决者,裁判者
decision-making (decisionmaking) 制定判决意见,作出判决
decision-making and administrative organization 决策与行政组织
decision-making body 决策机构
Decision-making Dynamics 作出判决的动力学
decision-making power (中)(国营企业及集体经济组织在经营管理方面的)自主权
decision-making power of enterprises (中)企业自主权
decision-making processes 决策程序
decisive a. 决定性的;明确的,果断的

decisive evidence 确证
decisive factor 决定性因素
decisive issue 决定性的系争点
decisive oath 决定性的宣誓
decisive vote 决定性投票
deck n. 甲板,舱面;(美)盛海洛因等毒品的袋子
deck cargo 舱面货物
deck clause 舱面条款
deck risk 舱面险
declamation n. 正式演说,雄辩,雄辩术
declarable a. 须报关纳税的;可申报的
declarant n. 申诉人;供述人,原告,陈述者;宣誓者;(订立合同的)意思表示者
declarare voluntatem (declaratio voluntaris) 意愿表示
declaratio voluntatis 意思表示
declaration n. 1.正式陈述,正式声明,宣告,声明;特别包含着一项指示(instrument)(见 affidavit) 2.(国际法)款项(指按照条约的一些规定,签约的当事方均同意它们的行为。见 treaty) 3.(国际法)单方面的宣告(或声明)(指影响其他国家的权利和义务的单方宣告) 4. 管理某种类型物权的法定权利声明书,诸如共管的建筑物(condominium)或住房的附属部分 5.货物或商品传单[指一个人意图带入美国的商品清单(listing),此清单是在入美国国境时提供给海关上税用的] 6.(证据)对于争辩的事件,知道有关实情的某人所作未经宣誓的陈述 7.(纳税的)申报单;(缔约当事人的)意思表示 8.(证人的)陈述;供述 9.(英)(common-law-pleading)普通法上的民事诉讼[指民事诉讼中原告最先的起诉书,它是一件起始令状(original writ)的扩大或更改,据此再加上伤害地点、时间的情况,诉讼才有依据。物权诉讼中,declaration 亦被称为 court。当今,英国法中相当的术语是"权利主张的陈述"(statement of claim);在绝大部分美国司法管辖区,它被称为上诉状(petition)或起诉书(complaint),亦称 narratio。"declaration 是构成原告以条理清楚、法定形式的诉因的全部重要事实的陈述,它包括以下几个部分:①法院名称的说明;②管辖内审判地(venue)的陈述;③起始(时间);④正文,诉因陈述;⑤结尾或结论。"见 Benjamin J. Shipman 著《普通法诉讼手册》(Book of Common-Law Pleading)第192页第76节(Henry Winthrop Balantine ed., 3rd Ed., 1923年)]

declaration against interest 不利的供述
declaration by debtor of inability to pay his debts 负债人无力清偿债款声明
declaration concerning pedigree 关于家系的声明
declaration concerning rights 关于权利的声明
Déclaration des droits de l'homme (法)《人权宣言》(指法国资产阶级革命时期制宪会议于1789年8月26日通过的《人权与公民权宣言》)
declaration of alienage 放弃一个国籍声明(双重国籍的人拟定的声明);取得他国国籍声明
declaration of default 未履行债务的声明,未履行债务的通知(指债权人给予债务人告知其未履行债务的通知,即要求支付款项还清债务)
declaration of legitimacy 婚生声明(指孩子为合法的婚生子女的正式声明)
declaration of right 权利宣告[指英国在《王权诉讼法》(Crown Proceedings Act, 1947)实施之前,申诉人向英王要求主张契约上的权利时,需先提出权利请求书(petition of right),法院可凭借此书作出一个宣告,英王可批准予以补偿。在美国则指州宪法的一部分,即列举州公民享有的州政府应予尊重的各项权利]
Declaration of rights 《权利宣言》[指美国1774年10月在费城举行的第一届大陆会议(First Continental Congress)通过的体现各殖民地代表的意见的决议,宣称殖民地人民享有生存、自由、财产等权利。英殖民统治并未接受此决议,继续野蛮统治,最终导致1776年独立战争爆发。1776年第二届大陆会议通过了"独立宣言"(Declaration of Independence)。《权利宣言》的部分内容也规定在其中。在英国则指1689年2月13日议会通过的《权利宣言》,对

王权进行限制和规定议会所享有的一切权利。《权利宣言》被规定在后来通过的《权利法案》(Bill of Rights)之中〕

Declaration of Taking Act （美）《征用法》〔指依据国家征用权(eminent domain)(40 USCA §3114)调整政府征用私人财产为公共目的使用的联邦法律;对于征用的私人财产,必须公正补偿〕

Declaration of the Rights of Man and of the Citizen (法)《人权与公民权宣言》(又译《民权宣言》,1789年颁布)

declaration of the will of the parties 当事人意愿的表示

declaration form 申报表,报关单

declaration in course of 履行……职责的申述

declaration of acceptance of office 就职宣言

declaration of adjudication 判决公告

declaration of alienage 放弃国籍声明;取得他国国籍声明

declaration of association 宣告联合,联合宣言;宣告结社,结社宣言

declaration of avoidance 宣告无效

declaration of bankruptcy 宣告破产

declaration of births 申报出生

declaration of blockade 封锁宣告

declaration of ceased payment 停止支付宣告

declaration of deadweight tonnage of cargo 重载通知书

declaration of death 死亡宣告,宣告死亡

declaration of disappearance 失踪声明,宣告失踪

declaration of dividends 通知分红,分红通知

declaration of forfeiture 没收公告

Declaration of Human Rights (=Declaration of the Rights of Man) 《人权宣言》

Declaration of Independence (美国1776年7月4日颁布之)《独立宣言》

Declaration of Indulgence 《信教自由令》(指由查理二世所颁布)

declaration of insolvency 无偿付能力的声明

declaration of intent 意思表示

declaration of intent obtained by fraud or duress(e) 因被欺诈或胁迫所作的意思表示

declaration of intention (加入国籍的)动机宣告

declaration of interdiction 无行为能力的宣告(旧译:宣告禁治产)

declaration of neutrality 宣告中立;中立声明

declaration of ownership 所有权申报

Declaration of Paris 《巴黎宣言》

declaration of rights 权利宣告;(大写)《民权宣言》

declaration of secrecy 保密宣言

declaration of server 送达人声明

declaration of service 送达声明

declaration of solvency 有清偿能力的声明

declaration of third party joining the suit with independent claims 参加诉讼而有独立请求权的第三人的申诉

declaration of truce 宣告停战(或休战);宣告停止(休止或中止)

declaration of trust 信托宣言

declaration of use 宣告取得用益权;取得用益权声明

declaration of war 宣战

Declaration on the Elimination of Discrimination against Women (1967年联合国大会通过的)《消除对妇女歧视宣言》

declarative(declaratory) a. 宣言的,公告的,声明的,陈述的

declarative remedies 确权性救济(指衡平法上的一种救济方式,目的在于宣告并确认原告的权利、财产等是否合法,或在衡平法上是否有效);确认性补救

declaratory a. 解释性的、说明性的;肯定的,确认的,宣告的,宣言的,公告的;陈述的

Declaratory Act (英)《公告法》(指英《1719年公告法》,系议会制定的法律,确认其对爱尔兰的立法权的一项法律,把爱尔兰议会视为附属机构;亦指《1766年公告法》,该法坚持无论在何种情况下均有

权制定约束北美殖民地法律)
declaratory act（或 statute） 解释性法规
declaratory action 确权诉讼(指原告对自己的合法权利存有疑问,要求法院予以确认而提起的诉讼),确认性诉讼,宣告性诉讼
declaratory doctrine of recognition (国家)承认宣告说
declaratory judg(e)ment 确认判决,宣告式判决(亦称布告式判决或确认法律关系的判决。指法院宣告确认当事人某项权利或对有关的一个法律问题表明法院的意见,并不作出其他任何裁决性的一种判决)
Declaratory Judg(e)ment Act (美)《确认判决法》[指1934年制定的一部联邦法律,该法明确规定在实际争议(actual controversy)案件中,双方当事人请求确认各自权利和其他法律关系,法院有权利作出相应判决,而不论当事人请求给予进一步救济措施,法院所作此种判决为终局判决,并对诉讼双方现在、将来有约束力,大多数州有类似的立法]
declaratory judgement action 确认判决之诉
declaratory judg(e)ment procedure 宣告性判决的上诉程序
declaratory part of a law 法律的确认性部分(指法律中明确规定有权行使的权利和应当避免的违法行为等)
declaratory relief 宣告性(或确认法律关系)的法律救济方法
Declaratory Theory of the Common Law 普通法的宣告论
declare v. 宣布,宣告,声明,宣称,断言
declare contract avoided 宣告合同(契约)无效
declare in default 诉讼当事人的缺席宣告
declare neutrality 宣告中立
declare off 宣告作罢(作废),取消(约定等)
declare sb. a lunatic 宣告某人为精神病患者
declare sb. guilty 宣告某人有罪,定罪
declare sth. null 宣告(某事)无效
declare the ballot closed 宣布投票结束
declare vote closed 宣告表决结束
declared a. 公然宣称的,公然承认的,(纳税)申报的
declared legally incompetent 宣告为无行为能力的
declared value 申报价值
declass v. 使失去社会地位,使降低社会地位
declassify v. 使降低保密等级,使不再列入保密范围
declatory relief 确认性救济(见 declaratory judgment, declarative remedies)
declinature n. (法官的)回避
decline n./v. 下降,下垂;衰退;谢绝,拒绝/下降,下倾,衰退,衰落
decline to answer question 拒绝回答问题
decline to excise jurisdiction 拒绝行使管辖
declined jurisdiction 拒绝管辖
decollate v. 杀……的头,将……斩首
decolonization n. 脱离殖民地的地位;允许(殖民地)独立,非殖民化
decommission（或 **demobilization**）**pay** 复员费
decomposed body 腐败尸体
decomposition n. 腐败,分解
deconcentration n. 分治制,分散权力(指行政权)
decontrol n./v. 解除管制/解除对……管制
decorative design 装潢设计
decorum n. 正派;(复)礼节,礼仪
decoy v. 用欺骗手段引诱,勾引,诱惑
decoy letter 诱使他人上钩的信件
decrease n. 减少,减小;减少额,减少量
decrease of purchase price 减少购买的价金(格)
decreasing a. 减少的,渐减的
decreasing term insurance (受益)逐渐减少的定期保险
decree n./v. 1.判决;裁判;裁决;裁定 2.法令;政令;命令;布告/判决,裁决;颁布(法令、政令等);规定,注定
decree *a mensa et thoro* 判决分居令
decree a punishment 判刑

decree absolute (英)绝对判决(亦称最后判决。指英国解除婚姻或婚姻无效案件中的最终判决。见 decree nisi);最后确定批准令

decree an amnesty 颁布大赦

decree depriving parents of their parental right 剥夺父母亲权的判决

decree for pardon 大赦令,赦书

decree in effect 现行法令

decree nisi (英)非绝对判决(亦称离婚诉讼中的中期判决。这种判决,虽判决离婚,但附有一定期限,原规定为6个月,如无异议,离婚才生效;现规定为3个月,过此期限无异议便成为绝对判决)

decree nisi of divorce 离婚诉讼的中期判决(见 decree nisi)

decree of court 法院的判决

decree of dissolution (英)婚姻解除令

decree of foreclosure absolute 绝对禁止回赎的判决

decree of insolvency 财产不足支付(债务)的判决

decree of judicial separation (英)司法分居令

decree of nullity of marriage 宣告婚姻无效的判决

decree of restitution of conjugal right (英)恢复夫妻同居权令

decree of separation 判决分居

decree of special pardon 特赦令

decree of specific performance 强制履行令,特定履行令

Decree on Purge and Consolidation of Companies 1989年关于净化和公司合并的命令

Decree pro confesso 原告胜诉的判决(指衡平法诉讼中,被告未及时对原告起诉状做答辩时,则被视为承认原告主张,法庭从而判决原告胜诉)

decree-law n. (法)政府法令(指政府经议会授权颁布的法令)

Decree-Law (No. 9461 of 15, July 1946) 法令(1946年7月15日第9461号法令)

decrement n. 减小,缩减;消耗

decrement of debts 减少债务(指债务人资不抵债时,按比例减少其各项债务的偿付)

décret (法)政令

décret-loi (法)政府法令

decreta (罗马法)(皇帝作为最高法官所作的)裁决

decretal n./a. 法令;教令(指罗马教皇对有关教规问题的答复);(复)(罗马教皇的)教令集/法令的

decretal order 告示令

decretalist n. 教令法学家

decretists n. 教令法学派

decretive a. 法令的,命令的;有法令效力的

decretory a. 有法令效力的

decretum 教令集(指几部非常重要的寺院法汇编的名称)

Decretum Gratiani 《格拉奇教令集》(指天主教会法,系12世纪波伦僧侣格拉奇编纂而成,故名)

decrial n. 诽谤,诋毁;大声反对

decriminalise (=decriminalize) v. 使(原属非法的东西)合法化

decriminalization n. 非刑事化,非罪行化;合法化

decry v. (17世纪)大声诋毁,轻蔑,贬低(货币)价值

decrypt 解密

decurio (罗马法)1.元老(指罗马帝国时期行省大城市的长官或元老,负责管理行政内部事务)2.什长(古罗马时期管理10个士兵的队长或什长)3.代表(古罗马时期的10个士兵组成的队伍或代表)

dedi 我已经给了(指转让文据用语,亦即一种权利凭证。见 concessi)

dedication n. (1809年)(财产)为公共利益或公共使用奉献(私人拥有的)土地或土地的地役权(easement);捐献行为

dedication of way 公共通行权的设定

dedimus potestatem 权力已经授予

dedititii (罗马法)降服人(指奴隶犯重罪者,解放以后其地位与降服人相同,较第一级、第二级之解放自由人更劣,且不许在罗马百里以内居住,有犯者复捕为奴隶)

dedition n. 放弃,遗弃;让与,让渡
deduce v. 推断,推出;演绎
deduce a conclusion from premises 从前提推出结论
deduce from... 从……推断(推出)……
deduct v. 扣除,减去;演算
deductible a. 减除的,扣除的,(保险)免赔的
deductible clause (保险单上的)自负责任条款,免赔条款
deductible franchise (保险)免赔款
deductibility n. 可扣除性,可减免性
deduction n. (15世纪)1.扣除;拿去 2.(税务)扣除总额[指在计算可调整的总收入时,从总收入中扣除的总额或在计算应纳税所得额(taxable income)时从可调整的总收入中扣除的总额。亦称 tax deduction(见 exemption 3; tax credit)]3.(罗马法)先取份额,先取的部分(指某一继承人在分割遗产前,有权从遗产中先获得的份额)4. 推断,推论;由演绎得出的结论;演绎法 5.(保险)免赔
deduction from investigation 侦查推理
deduction of debts 扣除债务
deductive a. 推定的,推断的;演绎的
deductive inference 演绎推理;推断的结果
deductive reasoning 演绎推理
deed n./v. 文据;契据;证书;行为;事业/立据出让(财产)
deed book 文契汇编,文契集
deed indented 缺边契据(亦称多边契据,这是由多方当事人签订的契据,它的一边剪成锯齿形状,使契据分开,交双方收执,而合起来就成一张完整的契据,故名)
deed of accession 同意证书(指通常破产人的债权人同意债务人代表全体债权人设定信托保证的契据)
deed of appointment 任命证书
deed of appropriation 使用权证书
deed of arrangement (债务人和债权人的)和解契据;债务和解方案协议书
deed of association 合伙契据
deed of cession 转让契据
deed of constitution 宪法文献;立宪文献;组织文献
deed of covenant 契据,约据,条款契据
deed of gift 赠与证书,赠与契据
deed of grant 财产转让(授予)契据
deed of indemnity 赔偿契据
deed of mortgage 抵押契据
deed of release 转让证书;放弃权利契据
deed of sale 销售凭证,销售文据
deed of security 保证书,担保书
deed of separation 分居证书;分居协议
deed of settlement 协议契据;财产授予契据
deed of transfer 转让契据
deed of trust 信托契据,信托证书
deed poll 平边契据(亦称单边契据,这是由单方当事人签订的契据,如签发给代理人的授权契据,此种契据则不需用剪缺边办法来合契。与 deed indented 相对)
deed registration 契据登记
deed simple 单纯契据
deed-box n. 文件箱,契据箱
deem v. 认为,相信
deemed a crime 被视为犯罪
deemed acts 被视为作为;准作为
deemed spouse (美)(享有社会安全救济金权利的)推定的配偶
deemed to be 视为
deeming n. 法定拟制;推断
deemster n. (英国马恩岛的)法官,推事
deep pocket (美)深衣袋(雇主)(指拥有无限财源来打官司的雇主,不管胜诉、败诉,律师都有利可图)
deepen-seated forces 根深蒂固的力量,由来已久的力量
Deeping Tom (18世纪)窥视者汤姆[指通过窗户偷看他人以获得性快感的人(voyeur),亦称 peeping,实际为英国传说中的人物,因偷看戈黛娃夫人(lady Godiva)裸背骑马过市被打瞎双眼,现通常指那些为追求性满足而爬窗偷看他人裸体或性行为,侵犯他人隐私权的人]
deepwater harbo(u)rs 深水港
deface v. 毁伤外貌;破坏外观,涂污;销毁
defaced licence 已涂毁的执照
defacement n. 损毁;涂污;损毁物

defalcate v. 盗用公款,侵吞公款;亏空
defalcating motorists 不负责任的驾车人,随意的驾车人,歹意行为驾车人
defalcation n. 盗用公款;监守自盗;亏空额;亏空委托金
defalcator n. 盗用公款者,监守自盗者;委托金亏空人
defamation n. 破坏名誉;中伤,诽谤
defamation action 破坏名誉的诉讼
defamation of character 毁损名誉,中伤
defamation of personality 毁损人格
defamatory a. 破坏名誉的;诽谤的,中伤的
defamatory libel 诽谤名誉
defamatory matter 诽谤事件;诽谤案件
defame v. 诽谤,中伤,诋毁名誉
defamer n. 诋毁(他人)名誉者
default n./v. 缺席,不到案;不出庭;不参加;不履行(义务),拖欠,违约;玩忽,怠职/缺席,不到案;不参加,处以缺席裁判;不履行,拖欠,怠职,玩忽职守
default fine 违约罚金
default judg(e)ment (美)1. 缺席判决;不应诉判决;懈怠判决[美国法院对于当事人拖延诉讼的,可以以当事人懈怠诉讼为由作出懈怠判决,以使当事人承担因自己的迟延诉讼行为而造成的不利诉讼后果。对于懈怠判决,当事人可以懈怠是因错误造成为由,请求法院救济。或指不利于被告人的、满足原告在起诉状中要求的救济的判决。传票中必须告诉被告人不及时出席审判并对诉讼提出抗辩将要导致法院作出不应诉判决]2. 不履行判决(指当事人不服从法庭命令,尤其是要求其披露的命令,作为惩罚,法庭作出不利于其的判决)
default notice 不履行通知书
default of appearance 不出庭,不到案
default of creditor 债权人违约;债权人迟延(受偿)
default of debtor 债务人违约;债务人迟延(履行)
default of defence 无答辩
default of heirs 无人继承
default of the consignor 发运人违约;托运人违约
default (contract) remedy 违约(合同)救济方法
default rule of specific performance 实际履行的违约规则
default summons 传呼不出庭者传票;(英)(依简易诉讼程序发出的)收回拖欠债务的令状
defaulter n. 不出庭者;违约者;亏空公款者;拖欠债务者;犯军规者
defaulter of tax 欠税人
defaulting buyer 违约买主
defaulting nonresident defendant 缺席的非本州居民被告
defaulting party 不应诉当事人,缺席当事人
defeasance n. 废除,宣布(合同)无效;废约条件,撤销条件;无效条件;毁约证书
defeasance clause (美)撤销条款,解除合同(契约)条款(亦译导致合同无效条款)抵押合同的一种条款,意指抵押借款一旦全部偿清,则抵押终止,合同亦随之解除)
defeasibility n. 可废除性,可撤销性
defeasible a. 可作废的,可取消的;可撤销的
defeasible fee (英)可废除的世袭地产权
defeasible fees (美)附条件的完全所有权(见 fee simple absolute);(英)可废除的世袭地产权
defeasible interest 可取消的权益;可撤销的权益
defeasible title 可废除的土地财产所有权,可取消的土地财产所有权;可撤销的土地财产所有权
defeat n./v. 战胜,击败;败诉;废弃,无效/战胜,击败,使失败,使无效,废弃
defeated at the polls 落选,无效的选举投票
defeat in war 战败
defeated party 败诉方当事人,败诉方
defeated state 战败国
defeated suit 败诉,败诉案件
defeated suitor 败诉人
defeating justice 使司法执行无法实施

defeatism n. 失败主义

defect n./v. 缺陷,瑕疵,缺点;短处,不足;过失/开小差,逃跑;背叛,变节

defect in design or manufacture 设计或制造上的瑕疵

defect in title 所有权(上存在有的)缺陷(瑕疵)

defect of cattle 牲畜的瑕疵,牲畜的缺陷

defect of form (法律文件等的)形式不完善(或手续不全)

defect of possessor's right 占有人的权利存在瑕疵

defect of quality 质量上的瑕疵,质量上的缺陷

defect of substance 实质上的缺陷(瑕疵)

defection n. 缺点,过失;背信,背叛,变节;不履行(义务等)

defective a./n. 有缺陷的,有缺点的,有瑕疵的/身体或精神有缺陷的人

defective complaint(或 pleading) 有缺陷的起诉状

defective good 有瑕疵的商品

defective incorporation 公司设立瑕疵

defective judgment 有缺陷的判决

defective product 有缺陷的产品,有瑕疵的产品

defective service 有瑕疵的送达

defective title (美)有缺陷(瑕疵)的所有权(指不符合法律规定或用非法手段而取得的所有权)

defector n. 变节分子,背叛者;开小差者,逃兵

defectus sanguinis 无子女,无后嗣

defence (= defense) n. 1.辩护,答辩;抗辩,被告方(包括被告及辩护律师) 2.防御,防护,防御物

defence attorney 被告辩护人(指律师)

defence case 辩护方(被告)的证据和争论

defence certificate 辩护证书

defence costs 辩护费用

defence counsel 辩护律师

defence in lawsuit 诉讼答辩

defence of *alibi* 不在犯罪现场的辩护

defence of consent (原告)同意的答辩

defence of habitation 对(个人)住所的防卫(权)

defence of incrimination 受案件牵连的辩护

defence of insanity at the time of the crime 犯罪时精神错乱的辩护

defence of privilege 关于特权的答辩;维护特权

defence of property 对(个人)财产的(正当)防卫(权)

defence of self 自我辩护

defence of self-defence 属正当防卫的辩护

defence of tender before action 诉讼前已提出要求清偿的答辩

Defence Secretary 国防(部)部长,国防大臣

defence section 保卫科

defence to a tort action 侵权诉讼的答辩

defence to civil charge 民事指控的答辩

defence to criminal charge 刑事检控的答辩

defence witness 辩护方证人,被告证人

defence wound 防御伤,抵抗伤

defenceless a. 无防御的,无助的,无保护的,无防备的

defend v. 作……的辩护律师;辩护;为……答辩;防御,保卫

defend a case in court 出庭辩护

defend oneself 答辩,自行辩护

defendant n./a. 被告/处于被告的地位的

defendant in error 被上诉人(指上诉案件中下级法院判决中的胜诉方),复审案件的被告

defendant not physically present in case 在该州内身不在场的被告

defendant seat 被告席

defendant state 被告国

defendant's agent 被告代理人;被告辩护人

defendant's due process right 被告依正当程序享有的权利

defendant's identity and address 被告身份和地址

defendant's name or whereabouts 被告姓名或下落

defendant's right of contribution 被告的

分摊权
defended place 防卫地区
defender n. 辩护人;保护人
Defender of the Faith 护教者(指英国君主的称号)
defending a suit 被控告
defense n. 1.(=defence) 2.(大写)(美)国防部
defense of laches 迟误的辩护
defense of non-joinder 未合并抗辩
defense of the suit 诉讼的辩护应诉
defense's case-in-chief 辩护方主张
defensible a. 可辩护的;能防御的
defensive a. 自卫的,防御的;防护用的,防御用的
defensive enforcement 防御性执行(见 offensive enforcement)
defensive in nature 防御型
defensive interpleader 防御性确定竞合权利诉讼
defensive trademark 防护性商标
defensive war 防御战,自卫战争
defer v. 延缓,展期,推迟;遵从;听从
defer a ballot 推迟投票
defer a vote 推迟表决
defer to the opinion of justice 听从法官的判决意见
deference n. 遵从,尊重(to),表示敬意(to)
deference to the executives 尊重执行机关的意见
deferment n. 近期,推迟;(按军事法)缓役;暂缓服刑(指按军事法庭决定暂缓羁押直至判刑令到达执行);传唤(某人出庭受审)权允准推迟
deferment of increment 延迟加薪
deferment of leave 延期休假
deferrable a. 能延期的;(美)能缓刑的
deferral n. 延期,迟延;缓役;(deferrable a.)
deferred a. 迟延的,延期的
deferred assets 递延资产,滚存资金
deferred charges 递延费用,滚存费用
deferred execution 延期履行
deferred liabilities 递延的债务,延期的债务
deferred payments 迟付,延期付款

deferred retirement benefit 延迟退休金
deferred shares 红利后取股
deferred sight 迟延照票,过期照票
deferred sight credit 迟付即期信用证,迟延照票信用证
deferring of sentence 延期判决
defiance n. 挑衅,藐视,违抗
defiance of law 藐视法律
deficiency n. (17世纪)1.缺乏,短缺,不足;不完备;亏空 2.应纳税额中的不足(即应纳税财产的总数额超出纳税人在其申报表中所示出的总额,亦可称为 tax deficiency; income-tax deficiency; deficiency in tax)3.在财产抵押而无赎回权的贷款中,变卖抵押财产之后仍不清偿债务的部分(见 deficiency judgment)
deficiency in tax 见 deficiency 2
deficiency account 不敷账目,清算损失表
deficiency judg(e)ment (清偿)不足额判决(指在法院拍卖财产金额不敷负债时所作出的有利于一个债权以满足其偿债请求的判决)
deficiency payment 差价补贴
deficient performance of a contract 不完全履行合同(契约)
deficiente uno sanguine, non potest esse haeres. For lack of one blood, he cannot be hair. 缺乏完整的血缘不得为继承人;半血缘者不能成为继承人。柯克解释说:"父母的血是唯一可继承的血。而且两者的血是生育继承人必需的(血)。"
deficit n. 亏损;逆差;赤字,亏空额,不足额
deficit financing 赤字财政(指政府支出超过岁入以举债弥补赤字)
deficit spending 赤字开支
defile v. 弄脏,污损;亵渎;败坏
defilement n. 污辱,玷污;污损
defilement of girl 污辱少女
define v. 给……下定义,解释;规定,明确表示,限定,使清楚,界定
defined aims 规定的目标,有明确规定的目标
defined terms of the contract 合同(契约)规定的条款

defined-benefit plan 规定的福利计划[指由雇主设立和保持的计划,即由雇主最初有计划地提供给超过多年时间,通常为终身的、退休后的雇员一笔按规定确定的支付。任何的养老金计划(pension plan)都不是规定的分配计划。根据规定的福利计划,退休福利通常是以包括服务年限和补偿等要素为基础的。如果为以此计划投资的信托(trust)缺少足够资产去支付承诺的福利,则《埃里萨雇员退休收入保障法》(ERISA)要求雇主弥补这短缺部分。参见《美国注释法典》第29标题卷第1002节。见 defined-contribution plan]

defined-contribution pension plan 见 defined-benefit plan;defined-contribution plan

defined-contribution plan 规定的分配计划,限定的分配计划[指根据《埃里萨雇员退休收入保障法》(ERISA),在雇员的退休计划中,每个参与者有一个单独账户(separate account),是由雇主的分配支付建立的,这项雇员的分配通常是在预调账户(preset account)中。这项雇员的分配和每个参与者的福利都仅以已积累的福利为基础建立参与者账户。参见《美国注释法典》第29标题卷第1002节。此术语亦称为 defined-contribution pension plan; individual account plan。见 defined-benefit plan]

definite a. 明确的,确切的;一定的;限定的,特定的
definite intent 特定故意
definite intervals 定期
definite limitation of time 特定时效;特定期限
definite register of writs (英)严格的令状登记制度
definite sentence 见 determinate sentence
definite term 特定期限
definite thing 特定物
definite undertaking 明确承诺
definition n. 定义,说明;限定,定界,明确性
definition of aggression 侵略定义
definition of terms (条约等)条文的阐释
definitive a. 决定的;最后的;确定的;限制的,限定的,权威性的

definitive decision 结局性判决
definitive guideline 决定性的指导方针
definitive sentence (=determinate sentence) 最后判决,(服刑期)特定的判决
deflation n. 通货紧缩
deflationary measures 紧缩通货措施
defloration n. 奸污处女,破坏童贞
deforce v. 霸占,强占;强行剥夺
deforcement n. 抗拒法令;对抗执法;非法占有,强占;霸占土地
deforciant n. 侵权者,侵占者
deforestation n. 砍伐森林
deformation n. 残疾,畸形,毁坏
deformity n. 残疾,智力缺陷,畸形
deformity asylum 残疾收容所
defraud v. 骗取,诈取,欺骗(指故意做虚假陈述,明知此陈述与事实不符,或根本不顾事实真相,以骗取他人的钱财、权益或任何权利)
defraud money and property 诈取财物
defraudation n. 骗取钱财
defrauder n. 诈骗者,骗子
defray v. 补偿,支付
defrayal n. 支出,支付
defunct a./n. 死的,已亡故的;已倒闭的,非现存的/死人,死者
defunct journal 停刊的杂志,已停的期刊
defy v. 违抗,公然反抗,不服从
defy all precepts of scientific fact finding 无视科学事实认定的所有规则
defy laws, human and divine 无法无天
degenerate element 蜕化变质分子
degeneration n. 腐化,堕落;退化,变质
degradation n. 降级;贬黜,诋毁,堕落
degradation of the dignity of man 诋毁人格(罪)
degrading a. 品质低劣的;卑劣的;退化的,可耻的,堕落的
degrading punishment 羞辱刑
degrading treatment 有辱人格的待遇
degree n. 亲等(按有些国家版权法规定,只有三等亲之内亲属有权继承版权,三等亲之内如果无人,版权则归国家所有,或进入公有领域),程度;(罪行的)轻重;地位,身份;学位,学衔

degree and character of offence　犯罪程度和性质
degree in course　正式学位
degree of care required　必须照管的程度
degree of control　管制程度
degree of kinship　亲等
degree of latitude　活动范围
degree of legality　合法性的程度
degree of participation　参与程度
degree of prevalence of offence　犯罪率
degree of secrecy　机密程度,机密等级
degrees of criminality　犯罪的等差(轻重等级)
degrees of murder　谋杀罪的等级
degrees of relationship　亲等;亲等制
degrees of succession　继承亲等
degressive a.　(税率)递减的
dehors prep.　在外,在……以外
dehors the declaration　供述以外
deil n.　歹徒
del credere　(对买方)支付能力的保证(此词来源于意大利语,意思是"保证","担保";常用于卖方的代理人对买方的支付能力或履约能力向卖方所作的担保)
del credere agency　保证买方支付能力的代理
del credere agent　担保买方支付能力的代理人
del credere agreement　担保买方支付能力的协议
del credere commission　见 commission del credere
del credere contract　保付货价代理合同(契约)
delagata potestas non potest delegari.　A delegated power cannot be delegated.　不能将他人委托的权力再委托给第三人(在委托权力涉及自由裁量权适用此规则,无论行为人是谁,代理人均应向本人负责)。
delaney clause　禁止致癌条款(指美国政府法律规定禁止在食品中使用致癌的添加剂的条款)
delate v.　告发;弹劾;控诉,公开罪行;宣布
delation n.　告发;弹劾;控诉;宣布
delator n.　告密者;控告者

delay n.　拖延,延误,耽搁,延期;迟延
Delay defeats equities.　迟延使衡平法无效。
delay in (或 of) payment　延期支付,迟延给付,缓付
delay in performance　给付迟延,迟延履行
delay in the execution of the judg(e)ment　判决迟延执行
delay of justice　延期审判
delayed delivery　迟延交付(给付)
delayed payment　延迟付款
delayed performance of a contract　迟延履行合同(契约)
delaying power　(议会通过法案的)拖延权
delaying tactic　(拖延诉讼程序进行时所采取的)拖延战术
delectus personae　对人选择权(指在合伙关系中当事人个人品质是十分重要的,因此合伙人都享有未经全体合伙人同意不得变更合伙人的权利)
delegable a.　可委托的
delegacy n.　代表,代表权;代表制度;代表团
delegalize v.　使失去法律效力
delegant n.　(将他人欠自己的债作为偿还债权人之用的)债务人
delegate n./v.　(15世纪)1.代表,代理人(指某人代表或代理另一个人或团体,特别是某人被选择或被选举为代表发言,投票表决或作为团体作出决定)2.(议会法)立法(或特别)会议(convention)的表决成员,作为备选的或被任命的代表,不管以何名义投票表决(1 的意义上);被提升为候补或依职权(ex officio)被选举或被委托参加特别会议的众议院议员/(16世纪)1.授权[指权力委托给他人代表其本人行使〈to delegate Jones to represent the board before the commission〉(在委员会之前授权 Jones 代表董事会)] 2.部分授权(指将一个人的部分权力或职务授予下级代表,与 relegate 之意相同,relegate 指将权力委托给下级行使或将事务交其决定或执行);行使或执行〈delegate legislative function〉(获得授权具有立法功能)3.委托[指选择某人完成某项特定任务(job)或

为一个团体或一个组织的代表]〈she was delegated to organize the conference〉(她被委托组织这次的大会) 4.(大陆法)债务人的替代(指把自己的债务人转给自己的债权人)〈because Smith owed Johnson money and Johnson owed Luna the same account. Johnson delegated Smith to stand in his stead on the Luna debt〉(因为史密斯欠约翰逊款,而约翰逊又欠卢娜相同数额的款项,约翰逊让史密斯代替自己向卢娜清偿债务)

delegate function 代表职能
delegated a. 委托的,委任的,授权的
delegated authority 代理权限,授权
delegated laws 授权性法规
delegated legislation 授权立法(制)
delegated legislative capacity 授权立法的权能
delegated legislative power 授权立法权,委托立法权
delegated power 委托(的)权,授予的权力,授权(范围)
delegated theory 委托说[议会制下的代表与选民关系学说约有三种,委托说为其中之一,法国人称为"命令式委托说",认为代表机关的每名代表都是各自选区选民的代表,接受其选民的委托,代表他们行使主权。另两种为代表说(representative theory)和国家机关说(theory of state organ)]
delegatee n. 代债权人向第三者还债的债务人
delegation n. 代表团;使节;(代表的)委派,授权
delegation of duties (美)义务代行,代位履行
delegation of power (或 authority) 行政授权
delegation order 授权令
delegation under a statute 根据一项法律的授权
＊*Delegatus non potest delegare.* A delegate cannot delegate (unless he be expressly authorized so to do). 代理人不得再委托他人代理(除非被代理人明示授权他这样做)。A delegate (or deputy) cannot appoint another "被授权人不可转授权他人""代理人不得任命他人代理"
delegitimmized (= delegitimated) 不合法的,不合理的
delentio 握有
delete v. 删除,擦掉(字迹)
deleterious effect(s) (对身心的)负面影响,有害的后果
deleterious liquors 有害酒类,有毒酒类
deletion n. 删除(事项),删除部分
deliberate a. 蓄意的,故意的,审慎的,仔细考虑,预先计划,有预谋的,从容的
deliberate deception 蓄意行骗
deliberate deviation 蓄意曲解
deliberate falseness 蓄意欺骗
deliberate intent 故意
deliberate libel 蓄意诽谤
deliberate maiming 蓄意伤害他人身体
deliberate murder 谋杀
deliberate speed (美)审慎速度[在 Plessy v. Ferguson(1896)一案中,美国联邦最高法院认为两个种族成员如果被提供同等便利设施,则种族隔离不会构成歧视,这就是"隔离但平等"(Separate but equal)原则。1954 年在 Brown v. Board of Education 一案中推翻了上述判决,并裁定"隔离但平等"措辞矛盾。所以 1955 年联邦最高法院命令各地教委以"十分审慎的速度"尽早消除公立学校中的种族隔离制度]
deliberate state policy 审慎的州政策
deliberate violation 故意违犯,故意违反,蓄意违背
deliberately break the law 知法犯法
deliberating jurists 冷静而审慎的法学家
deliberation n. 慎重考虑,商讨,审议,商议
deliberative assembly (议会法)审议机构[指根据议会法(parliamentary law)处理事务的部门。该审议机构具有几个典型的显著特点:①它是人民的团体(group of people),他们聚在一起提议、讨论并以团体名义就一些活动进程中的问题进行表决;②参与人均可自由地运用他们自己的

判断能力(judgment);③相当多的人参与审议程序,其特定规格的程度是符合要求的;④每个参与人均有一票表决并可表示异议而无须担心被除名(expulsion);⑤当有些成员缺席时,实际上出席的成员有权代理整个团体(遵从法定人数和其他要求)(subject to quorum and other requirements)。参见 Henry M. Robert, Robert's Rules of Order Newly Revised §1 at 2 (10th ed. 2000)]

deliberative body 审议机构

deliberative democracy 审议民主[指在公共政治论坛上践行的"审议民主"应秉承公共理性(public reason)原则,即公共证实的内容应由一系列自由主义的"政治正义观念"给定,而不能直接来源于某种宗派性的善观念。与公共理性观相适应的民主观是一种罗尔斯意义上的审议民主观。见 public reason]

deliberative organ 审议机关,议事机构
deliberative power 审议权
deliberative vote 商讨性投票
delicate a. 微妙的;经慎重处理的
delict n. 轻罪;不法行为;违警罪;违法行为;侵权行为
delictual a. 犯法的,不法的;侵权的
delictual liability 不法行为的责任;侵权责任
delictum 不法行为,侵权行为,过错;(私法上的)犯罪
delimit v. 定……的界
delimit a frontier 划定边界
delimitation of boundaries 疆界划定
delineate v. 描绘,叙述,画出……的轮廓
delinquency n. 1.犯罪行为 2.失职,过失 3.少年犯罪 4.无法如期付出应付的款项;拖欠债务
delinquent n./a. 罪犯(尤指青少年犯罪);违法者;过失者/有过失的,违法的;过期未付的;怠职的,失职的,拖欠的
delinquent account 呆账,过期客账
delinquent child (1902年)犯罪少年(儿童)(尤指欧洲特别是意大利12—18岁的少年罪犯)[指犯有过错或罪行的少年,如为成年人所为则为罪行(crime)。如果此孩子在法定年龄(statutory age)以下,则可不受少年法庭管辖。见 child in need of supervision; juvenile delinquent]

delinquent conduct 不良行为
delinquent element 不良分子
delinquent juvenile 犯罪少年,少年犯
delinquent minor 见 juvenile delinquent
delinquent party 违约当事人
delinquent tax 过期未缴的税款
delirium 精神错乱;谵妄(伴有短暂幻觉的精神障碍)
délit (法)轻罪
delitescency movement 潜伏活动
delito 犯罪
delitti 重罪
deliver v. 1.释放,放;解救 2.移交,引渡;交付 3.投递,传送 4.提供,供给 5.发表,陈述 6.拉(票);给予(打击)
deliver a goal (或 **jail**) 把监狱中犯人全部提审
deliver an ultimatum 送达(或发出)最后通牒
deliver goods against surrender of the document 见单交货
deliver oneself to the police 向警察局自首
deliver oneself up 自首
deliver over 引渡,交出
deliver up 让与
deliverable state 可交付状态
deliverance n. 交保;判决;正式意见;解救,释放;(英)裁断
Deliverbot 送货机器人[该词由 delivery(投递、送交)的前半部分和 robot(机器人)的后半部分组成,也可写作 deliverbot。加拿大计算机软件设计师、企业家布拉德·坦普尔顿2008年6月23日为其个人网站撰文时最早使用这一表达方式。他写道:"送货机器人是由 robocar(无人驾驶汽车)演变而来的……送货机器人可能是手提箱大小、很小很轻的机器人,也可能是可移动沉重货物的全尺寸卡车。"它们可以按照客户需求和时间安排,把物品送到指定的住宅、办公室或停车场等任何地点。它们用充气的流线型衬垫加以包裹,即使碰上人或物体也不会造成损

害。送货机器人不仅可在地面上一显身手,在空中也能有所作为。亚马逊公司使用无人机完成物流配送。拥有无人机系统的小型八旋翼直升机可在用户下订单后30分钟内直接从亚马逊物流中心提货,然后送到用户的家门口。然而,从航空运输安全、国土安全再到个人隐私安全,亚马逊公司的快递计划面临不少风险]

delivered a. 交付的,交货的;含交货费用在内的

delivered price 到货价,(包括交货费用在内的)交货价

delivered terms 交货条件

delivered weight 交货重量

deliverer n. 引渡人;交保者;交付人;救助者;递送者

delivery n. 1.转让,让渡;给付;交付,交货;投递,传送 2.引渡;释放;解救 3.分娩 4.一次交付(或投递)的货物(或邮件),财产等的正式移交 5.陈述,讲演

delivery book 送货簿

delivery by attornment 承认(转让土地的)新所有人的交付

delivery by instal(l)ment 分期交货,分期给付

delivery by means of a sign 示意式交付方式

delivery by means of declaration 宣告式交付方式

delivery contract 产品交付合同(契约)

delivery date 交货期

delivery of a deed 交付契据;让渡证券

delivery of articles of proper quality 给付相当品质的物品

delivery of conforming good 交付同种类物

delivery of offender 交出罪犯;引渡罪犯

delivery of the goods 交货

delivery of the object 标的物的交付

delivery of the property 交付财产

delivery of thing 物的交付

delivery on spot 现场交货,即期交货

delivery on term 定期交货

delivery order 1.提货单;出货单,交货单;

栈单,仓单 2.引渡令

delivery port 交货港

delivery price 交货价格

delivery receipt 送货回单;送达回条,交接单

delivery room 1.交付(或交纳)地方 2.医院的分娩室,产房

delivery term 交货条件;交货期限

delivery-up (of copy) 送交(样书)(有的国家——作为一种制度——要求新出版的书须向国家主管部门或指定图书馆交送样书,否则即丧失版权或在诉讼中不能证明自己为版权人)

delivery-verse-payment (DVP) 款到交货

delusion n. 妄想(指一种思维内容障碍,妄想是一种在病理基础上产生的歪曲信念,病态推理和判断。处于妄想状态的病人没有受审能力,须经治疗。在美国约70%～80%的病人经治疗后可恢复受审能力。思维内容障碍共有11类:①delusion of persecution 被害妄想;②delusion of reference 关系妄想;③delusion of physical influence 物理影响妄想;④grandiose delusion 夸大妄想;⑤delusion of guilt 罪恶妄想;⑥hypochondriacal delusion 疑病妄想;⑦delusion of love 钟情妄想;⑧delusion of jealousy 嫉妒妄想;⑨delusion of remission 赦免妄想;⑩pregnant delusion 妊娠妄想;⑪delusion memory 妄想性记忆)

delusion clause 弱化条款

delusion memory 妄想性记忆(思维内容障碍之一种:对过去所经历过的某些事情,病人病后赋予某种妄想性的解释,即为妄想性记忆。见 delusion)

delusion of guilt 罪恶妄想(思想内容障碍的一种:抑郁症病人可能产生罪恶妄想,无缘无故地夸大自己过去所犯的一些小错,认为自己罪大恶极,死有余辜,并把这种犯罪感表露在遗书上,让人容易误会为"畏罪自杀"。见 delusion)

delusion of jealousy 嫉妒妄想(思想内容障碍的一种:指病人依据大量荒谬的"理由"推知配偶或恋人背叛了爱情,为此十分苦恼。不愿爱人与异性来往,不少男病人怀疑亲生子女非己出。其配偶或恋人最易

成为其攻击对象,其次为其"情敌"。这类患者亦会导致作案可能。见 delusion)

delusion of love 钟情妄想(思想内容障碍的一种;荒唐地认为某一各方面条件远胜于己的异性迷恋上了自己,而自己也深爱对方,对于对方所露出的反感不以为然,以为是考验自己对爱情是否忠贞不渝。有的病人开始发病表现的就是妄想,自然"孤恋"会以失败告终。可周围的人却误以为是失恋导致的精神失常,也会因此而产生违法,甚至轻罪的情况。见 delusion)

delusion of persecution 被害妄想(妄想类型中最多见的一种作案原因。病人坚信有人要害他,害他者可能局限于特定人身上,也可能难以计数,受其影响可能逃避,如自杀、搬家等,也可能发起攻击。不管突然行凶或事先有谋,周围人和受害者往往猝不及防。病人对别人"害"他的想法由来已久,但不轻易透露,所以被害人也常搞不懂为何对自己下此毒手。而病人事后交代,自己已忍耐很久,自己走投无路,在忍无可忍的情况下才动手的)

delusion of physical influence 物理影响妄想(指思维内容障碍的一种;患者坚信自己心身受到某种物理性的外力操纵与控制,如某种仪器、电波、激光、超声波等。这类病人具有现代科技知识,故带有现代科技气息的精神症状,可能诊断为精神分裂症。见 delusion of persecution)

delusion of reference 关系妄想[思维内容障碍之一,与被害妄想(delusion of persecution)合并存在。病人坚信周围无关紧要的事物都与自己有密切利害关系,认为他人的一举一动都是跟自己过不去。因而对周围人的举动敏感多疑,并怀有敌对情绪而不轻易流露出来。见 delusion of persecution]

delusion of remission 赦免妄想(思想内容障碍之一种;无根据或依据荒唐的"理由"坚信自己的罪行已经得到法律赦免,在拘禁中的犯罪嫌疑人或服刑中的囚犯,尤其重罪犯更易出现这一症状。他们不愿再接受服刑改造,强烈要求释放。有此赦免妄想后经常与狱管人员大吵大闹,冲撞狱门等情况发生。见 delusion)

delve (into) v. 探索,钻研
demagog(ue) n. 煽动者,蛊惑人心者,煽动政治家;(古代)民众领袖
demagogism n. 煽动主义,煽动
demagogy n. 蛊惑人心,煽动;恶意宣传;一群煽动者
demand n./v. (13世纪)1.主张合法的或程序上的权利 2.(议会法)请求,要求[通常关系到一项必须得到允准的议员动议(member's motion)的权利。见 request] 3.请求支付债务或支付一笔应付的总额 4.在经济学上,买主在有效性方面的压力强度和商品费用(cost of a commodity)或服务(service)的压力强度/(14世纪)1.要求,请求[指作为一个人应得权益的权利主张,要求,寻求救济(seek relief),寻求免责;寻求法律补救] 2.传讯,传唤;传唤出庭
demand bill 即期汇票,见票即付票据
demand clause (1919年)(票据中的)支付条款[指如果出票人(maker)对分期付款的每一期均未按时支付,该条款允准持票人强制出票人全部支付。见 acceleration clause]
demand deposit 活期存款
demand draft 即期汇票
demand for payment 催缴(通知)
demand for reimbursement 索赔,索偿
demand for restitution 要求赔偿,要求恢复原状
demand instrument (1924年)要求见票即付的票据(指要求见票即刻付款的票据,与确定未来日期支付票据相反。亦称 demand note)
demand letter (1911年)要求证书[指一纸证书,借此当事一方表明其在争端中的法律地位(legal position),并要求接受者(recipient)提起诉讼(如返还所欠之款)或其他可诉之险(risk)。根据有些制定法(特别见消费者保护法),这种要求证书是提起诉讼的先决条件]
demand loan 活期贷款,活期放款
demand note 1.见 note 1 2.见 demand instrument
demand of view (被告)要求查验
demand performance 催告履行义务

demand possession 要求(给予)引渡;要求占有

demand schedule 需求表(表明一种商品在不同价格时需求数量的表格)

demand with menaces 勒索,敲诈;威胁索财

demandable a. 可要求的

demandant n. 1.原告;提出物权诉讼的当事人,提出要求者 2.要挟性的要求

demandant of extradition 引渡请求书

demander n. 要求者

demanding with menaces 勒索,强取

demands for discovery 披露要求,出示需求

demands for wages 要求获得工资

demarcated national boundary lines 业已划定的国境线

demarcation n. 划分;分界;界限;定界线

demarcation between the enemy and ourselves 敌我界限

demarcation claim 界线纷争

demarcation line in policy 政策界线

démarche 手段,步骤,措施;(外交)新方针,方针的改变

dematerialization n. 非物质化(指目前西方生态理论中出现频率非常高的"非物质化"概念。实际指的是提高能源使用效率,减少向环境倾倒废料的数量,减少"每单位货币 GDP 增长对环境的影响")

demean v. 行为,举止,表现

demeano(u)r n. 行为,举止,品行,态度(指从证人态度、表现、语气、手势来推断证人的可信程度)

demeano(u)r evidence 行为证据,态度证据(亦译举止行为证据。指以证人或利害关系人在作证或陈述时的举止态度等表现,来作为推断其可信程度而提出来的证据)

demease n. (古英国法)死亡

demembration n. (古苏格兰法)断肢罪

démenti (外交上的)正式辟谣;(谣言等)正式否认

demerit n. 过;过失,缺点

demesne n. 1.领地 2.(英)领主(不出租的)自留土地 3.(土地)占有 4.领域,范围

demesne lands (庄园主的)自留土地

demilitarize (= demilitarise) v. 解除对……军事管制,使非军事化

demilitarized zone border 非军事区边界

deminutio capitis (罗马法)民事能力的丧失(罗马法上将其分为三类:①*maxima* 沦为奴隶丧失自由;②*media* 或 *minor*,因失去公民身份而失去与贵族的联系;③*minima* 男性公民失去家庭成员身份)

demisable a. 可让渡的;可遗赠的

demise n./v. 1.让与,让渡;过户 2.遗赠;(帝王)死亡,传位,逊位,禅让;终止 3.(英)地产授予/转让;遗赠;出租;让与;传(位),逊位;转移(君权)

demise charter party 转让租船合同(契约),光船租赁合同(契约),空船租赁合同(契约)

demise clause 卖船租船条款,光船租赁款,租船转让条款

demise land 让与的土地

demise messuage 出租的住宅

demise of the Crown 君权继承,传位,逊位

demise premises 遗赠房产

demission n. (古)辞职,退职

demobilization n. 复员;遣散

demobilized soldier 转业军人;退伍军人,复员军人

democracy n. 民主;民主主义;民主政治;民主政体;民主制;民主国家;民主精神;民众;(大写)民主党(美国)

6**democracy and efficiency** 民主和效率(的关系)

democracy in the widest sense 最广泛的民主

democrat n. 民主主义者,(中)民主人士;(大写)(美)民主党党员

democrat without party affiliation (中)无党派民主人士

democratic a. 民主的,民主政体的;平民的;(大写)(美)民主党的

democratic centralism 民主集中制

democratic centralization 民主集权制

democratic constitutionalism 民主宪政

democratic consultation 民主协商

democratic convention 民主党会议
democratic deficit 民主不足
democratic dictatorship 民主专政
democratic election 民主选举
democratic election of one-man-one-vote 一人一票的民主选举(制)
democratic government 民主政府
democratic law 民主法律
democratic management 民主管理
democratic party (中)民主党派;(大写)(美)民主党
democratic personage (中)民主人士
democratic personnel system 民主的人事制度
democratic recall 民主的罢免
democratic rights 民主权利
democratic state 民主国家
democratic system 民主制度
democratic united front 民主统一战线
democratic-egalitarian value 民主平等主义价值
democratism n. 民主主义
democratization n. 民主化
democratize v. (使)民主化
democrats with no party affiliation (中)无党派民主人士
demographic a. 人口统计的;人口学的
demographic date 人口统计日期
demography n. 人口统计学;人口学
demolish v. 破坏(组织),推翻(计划,制度等),拆毁(建筑物);毁损
demolition n. 废止,取消;拆毁(建筑物);破坏,毁损
demolition cost 拆除费
demolition of property 毁坏财产(罪)
demolition order (英)拆毁令(1957年的《住房法》授权地方政府对任何房屋只要认为不适合人们居住时,就可发出拆毁令或封闭令)
demonopolize v. 取消对……的专卖权
demonstrable a. 可证论的,可表明的
demonstrant n. 示威者
demonstrate v. 论证,证实,说明;表示,表明,示范;作示威运动
demonstratio n. (罗马法)1.描述,描写;在文据中对人或事物的虚伪描述(false demonstratio)〈falsa demonstratio non nocet〉(虚伪描述不能影响文件效力)2.根据程式程序(formulary procedure)以程式进行诉讼的事实陈述构成权利主张的基础(复数为 demonstrationes;见 formula 1)
demonstration n. 示威;示威游行;实证,确证;(商品的)宣传;示范
demonstrationist n. 示威运动参加者
demonstrative evidence 确证(指一目了然的物证);(17世纪)示意性证据,实物证据,展示证据[指可以看见并可审视的物证(physical evidence),如有解释的辅助物;图表、地图和计算机模拟图]
demonstrative legacy 指明数额的遗赠,明确的遗赠[指如果资源具有足够金额,遗赠则从特定的款项支付。如果资源不足,遗赠的总额则不从资源中支付,而从遗产的总资产(estate's general assets)中支付]
demonstrative speech 指明的(实际的)言论
demonstrator n. 示威者;示范员;证明者;(用来向顾客作示范的)表演产品
demoralization n. 道德沦丧,风俗败坏;士气低落,令人沮丧
demoralization cost 情感成本
demos n. (总称)(古希腊城邦的)平民,民众
demotion n. 降级
demotivate staff 降低职员的积极性
demur n./v. 抗辩(书);抗议;异议,迟疑,犹豫/抗辩,表示异议,反对;犹豫,迟疑
demur the instance 对诉讼程序提出抗辩
demurrable a. 可抗辩的
demurrage n. 滞期费,滞留停泊费;超过停泊期;(英)金银块兑换费
demurrage charge 滞留期停泊费
demurrage lien 滞期留置权
demurrant n. 抗辩者;表示异议者
demurrer n. 诉求不充分的抗辩,法律抗辩,异议;抗诉;有责任答辩,抗辩者,抗议者;(英)接受事实的抗辩
demurrer book 法律抗辩争点的文件记录,法律争点(记录)文件(指法律抗辩中争论点的记录,包括诉状副本,供法庭和

demurrer to evidence 对证据提出异议
demurrer to interrogatories 对讯问的抗辩;拒绝答辩
den n. 匪巢;贼窝
denamite n./a. 具有爆炸性的事(或物),(用炸药)炸毁;爆炸物;甘油炸药/充满爆炸性的
denationalization n. 非国家化
denationalize v. 剥夺国籍;剥夺……公民权利;使非国有化
denaturalization n. 剥夺国籍;剥夺公民权利;非国有化,失去独立民族资格
denelage 见 Dane-Law; Danelage
denaturalize v. 剥夺国籍;剥夺公民权利;使非国有化(恢复私营);使失去独立民族资格
deniable a. 可否认的,可否定的,可拒绝的
denial n. 否定,否认;拒绝接受;拒绝给予
denial of facts 否认事实,抵赖
denial of justice 拒绝司法
denier n. 拒绝者,否认者
denization n. (=denizen)
denizen n./v. 居民,公民;(享有部分或全部公民权的)外籍居民;归化者/给予永久居住权;使归化,使入籍
denizenship n. 永住权;公民权,市民权
denominate v. 给……命名,称呼为……
denomination n. 1.货币面额 2.宗派,派别;种类 3.名称,命名
denomination value 票面价值
denominator n. 命名者;共同特性;分母;标准,一般水准
denounce v. 1.谴责,斥责;告发 2.通告废除(条约、协定等)
denounce sb. to the authorities 向当局告发某人
denouncement n. 1.告发;谴责 2.通告废除
denouncer n. 谴责者,告发者
density n. 密度
density of traffic 交通密度
dental jurisprudence 牙医法学
denturist law (装、售)假牙法规(美国1978年通过、1980年7月生效的法规,该法规使俄勒冈州成为第一个准许非正式牙医给病人直接装、售假牙的州)
denunciation n. 谴责,斥责;告发;宣告(条约等)无效;合同(契约)废止;(古)恐吓,警告
denunciation of house-breach 不准侵入住宅
denunciative (=denunciatory) a. 指责的,谴责的;恐吓的
deny v. 否认,否定;拒绝;拒绝相信,拒绝给予;克制
deny oneself 节制,摒弃,戒绝
denying jurisdiction in large measure 很大程度上否定了管辖,基本上拒绝了管辖
deo dandum (=deodand)
deo volente 若顺天意,一切顺利
deoccupy v. 解除对……的占领
deodand n. (英)杀生性敬神物(指直接引起生灵死亡的属人有形财产,按普通法应没收用作敬神)
departing partner 退伙合伙人
department n. 部门;部,司,局;活动范围;(学院等的)系,研究室;(工厂的)车间;(法)省,郡
department in charge 主管部门
department in charge of confidential or important work 机要部门
Department of Agriculture (美)农业部
Department of Commerce (美)商业部
Department of Constitutional Affairs (英)宪法事务部(指 2003 年 6 月 12 日英国首相布莱尔对内阁进行重大改组,包括撤销了大法官等 3 个内阁大臣的建制,新设立了一个宪法事务部,调整议院下院领袖的部分重要内阁成员职位)
department of corrections 劳教部门;(大写)(美)教养院
Department of Defense (美)国防部(简称 Defense)
Department of Education (美)教育部
Department of Education and Science 教育和科学部
Department of Energy (美)能源部
Department of Foreign Affairs 外交部
Department of Health, Education and Welfare (美)卫生、教育和福利部

Department of Health and Human Service (美)健康与人类服务部,卫生与公共服务部,卫生部[指美国联邦政府内阁级(cabinet level)的一个部,负责健康、福利和收入保障(income security)事宜。最早,它是根据1953年1号"重组计划"(Reorganization Plan)以卫生、教育和福利部(Department of Health and Human, Education and Welfare)的名义设立的。缩略为 HHS]

Department of Health and Social Security 卫生与社会安全部

Department of Homeland Security (美)国家安全部、祖国安全部(指美国联邦政府内阁一级的一个部,负责美国境内和领土主权及领地、陆地的安全;该部有五个主要部门,分别是边境和交通安全局、紧急事务管理局、科技局、信息分析和基建结构局以及管理局。该部建于2002年,于2003年正式开始工作。缩略为 DHS)

Department of Housing and Urban Development (美)住宅及城市发展部

Department of Justice (美)司法部;(日)法务省

Department of Labo(u)r (美)劳工部

department of law 法律系

department of public safety(或 **security**) 公安局,公安机关

department of social security 社会保障机关

Department of Social Service 见 Child Protective Service

Department of State(或 **State Department**) (英)政府部门(指英中央政府的分支机构);(美)国务院(主管外交的部门,负责人为国务卿)

department of state(亦作 **state department**) 1.政府部门 2.(大写)(美)国务院

Department of State Bulletin (美)《国务院公报》(指报道有关条约的一种官方月刊,刊有条约原文,同时也报道官方谈判、国会活动等其他情况)

Department of State Press Releases (美)《国务院新闻发布》(指刊载美国签订的条约和大多数行政协定的首次出版物)

Department of the Environment 环境事务部

Department of the Interior (美)内政部

Department of the Treasury (美)财政部

Department of Transportation (美)交通部

departmental commission 省委员会

departmental committee (英)部委员会(指部长设立的就某一事进行调查和报告的委员会)

departmental discipline action 内部纪律处分

departmental executive authority 省行政机关

departmental government 省政府,郡政府

departmentalism n. 部门主义,分散主义,本位主义;官僚作风,分科制

departure n. 1.越轨诉讼行为(指诉讼辩论中一方所说事实或答辩理由与诉讼中的事实和理由前后矛盾,此行为违反正常诉讼规则,为法庭所不允许的);违背;背离(from) 2.出发;离开

departure card 离境证

departure from star decisis 背离遵照先例原则

depauperize (=depauperise) v. (美)使贫穷;(英)使脱离贫穷

depend v. 依靠,信赖;依……而定(on);悬而未决

dependant n. 受赡(扶、抚)养人;(复)家庭负担

dependant child 受抚养的孩子

dependant's final argument 被告的最后辩论

dependence n. 未决;从属,隶属;依赖;信任,相依性

dependency n. 附属国;属地;从属物;从属,依赖

dependency allowance 扶(抚)养津贴

dependency benefit 家庭扶(抚)养补助金

dependency exemption (1920年)扶养免税额[指个体纳税人因被扶养人(dependent)而总收入均低于免税额(exemption amout)以及因其子女未满19岁,如果是大学生(student)则未满24岁的情况,所

被允准的扶养免税额]
dependency school 依附学派
dependent n./a. 受赠(扶、抚)养人;家属;依靠者;从属物/受赠(扶、抚)养的;从属的;依靠的
dependent benefit 眷属补助金,扶(抚)养补助金
dependent child 无谋生能力的子女,受抚养的子女[指已丧失父母抚养费和父母关照的贫困儿童,因其父母及对其承担责任者均已过世,无家可归,身体上和精神上均无行为能力(或有的情况下),无职业。上述的界定在"帮助受抚养儿童家庭"(Aid to Families with Development Children,AFDC)中可以见到,参见《美国注释法典》第42标题卷第606节,此补助计划(program)已由"暂助贫困家庭"(Temporary Assistance to Needy Families,TANF)所替代。尽管可参考 TANF,《美国注释法典》第42标题卷第672节,但该界定已经被取消]
dependent children 无谋生能力的子女,受抚养子女
dependent contract 附属合同(契约);从合同(契约)
dependent event 相依事件,从属事件
dependent maintenance 家属扶(抚)养费
dependent of a revolutionary martyr (中)革命烈士家属
dependent of dead military heroes (中)烈军属
dependent of martyrs 烈属,烈士家属
dependent parent 受赡养的父亲或母亲
dependent person 受扶养者
dependent regulation 附属规章
dependent relative revocation (美)从属相对的撤销(原则)(指某些州的一种法律原则。依此原则,某人如拟废除一个遗嘱则可作出一新遗嘱来撤销之)
dependent spouse 受扶养配偶
dependent state 附属国[主要包括附庸国(vassal state)和被保护国(protected state)]
dependent territory 附属地,属地,附属领土,附属领地
dependent variable 从属变量,因变量

dependent's opening statement 被告开场陈述
dependent's presentation of direct evidence 被告出示直接证据
dependent's presentation of rebuttal evidence 被告出示反证
depersonalization n. 非人性化,非个性化
depersonalization of trade 贸易的(非人性化)一体化
depersonalize v. 使失去个性
depict v. 描写,描述,雕出
depletion n. 弄空,竭尽,耗尽,(资源)耗减
depletion allowance 税额扣减(指石油矿产和其他资源因其被使用率增高而扣减开采者的税率)
depletion amortization (of a natural resource) 自然资源耗竭
deployment n. 部署,展开,调度
depoliticize v. 使非政治化
depone v. 宣誓证实,宣誓作证
deponent n. 宣誓证人,证明人;提供书面证词者
deport v. 放逐(犯人);驱逐(出境),递解(出境),流放
deportatio in insulum 终身放逐
deportation n. 驱逐出境,递解出境,放逐,流放
deportation and expulsion 驱逐出境
deportation order 驱逐令,递解令
deportation ordinance 驱逐出境令
deportee n. 被驱逐出境者;被判处流放者
deposable a. 可免职的,可废黜的
deposal n. 免职,罢官;废黜(王位)
depose v. 提供书面证明,作证,作证人;宣誓作证;免……的职,废黜(王位),罢官
deposed from office 开除公职,免职
deposit n./v. (储蓄)存款;存放,寄存;委托款项;押金,保证金,(订立买卖合同用的)定金;公积金;寄存物;寄存处,仓库;(罗马法)无偿保管货物的寄托/交付;存放;寄存,储蓄;付(保证金)
deposit account 存款账户
deposit agreement 存托协议(指发行公司和存托银行签订存托协议,通常在其中规定发行的条件、条款和发行的结构,并且

规定存托人是以投资者的信托人或代理人的身份持有这些基础证券的)
deposit and return system 保证金和收回制度
deposit at bank 银行存款
deposit at notice 通知存款,即期存款
deposit bank 储蓄银行
deposit certificate 存款单;存放证明书
deposit in foreign currency 外币存款
deposit in security 保证金,押金
deposit in trust 信托存款
deposit insurance 存款保险,存储保险
deposit interest 存款利息
deposit money 押租,押金;存款
deposit of goods 货物的保管
deposit of instruments and cash 证券和现金的存放
deposit of key money 押租
deposit of negotiable instrument and other valuables 流通票据和其他有价物的保管
deposit of security 交存诉讼保证金
deposit of title deeds 房地契抵押;不动产所有权契据抵押
deposit premium 预付保险费
deposit rate 存款利率,贴现率,折扣率
deposit receipt 存单(存款收据)
deposit security for an action 诉讼保全
deposit with consideration 有偿寄托
deposit without consideration 无偿寄托
depositary (=depository)
deposition n. 1.书面证词 2.委托,寄存,存放,委托物 3.证据保全 4.向证人取证[指美国民事诉讼中在法院正式审理案件之前,双方律师先行取证。法律上称 discovery(发现),而发现的重要内容之一就是向证人取证]5.询问[指由律师询问对方要出庭的证人,在询问证人过程中将证人的证词逐字记录。如果证人亡故或失踪,此记录可作为证据向法庭出示(discovery)。此外,证人出庭作证时,律师亦可逐字记录揭示证人前后矛盾之处]6.罢官,免职;废黜(王位)
deposition by witnesses 证据保全
deposition on written questions 关于书面问题的证词
deposition procedure 证据保全程序
depositor n. 存款人,储户,寄托人
depository (=depositary) n. 存托人,受托人;保管人;寄存处,储蓄所,存放处,仓库;(美)(保存档案的)州立图书馆
depository libraries (美)指定出借政府出版物的图书馆
depository receipts (DR) 存托凭证(又称存股证,指在一国证券市场上流通的代表投资者对境外证券所有权的可转让凭证。它是一种在公司融资业务中使用的金融衍生工具)
depository rights 存货权
Depository Trust Company 存托人信托公司[美国经营股票市场清算系统的一种存托人信托公司。欧洲市场上,主要的结算系统是在布鲁塞尔运作的欧洲清算(Euroclear)和在卢森堡运作的欧洲债务交割清算中心塞德尔银行(Cedel Bank)]
depository-transfer check 托收转账支票[指一种未签名的不可流通的支票(non-negotiable check),用来从其支行将资金转到托收行(collection bank)]
depositum (罗马法)(无偿保管货物的)寄托
depositum irregule 变相寄托(亦称变例寄托,指罗马法中的灾害寄托、金钱寄托。这种寄托可返还同种类、同品种、同数量的物而免除交还寄托原物的义务)
deprave v. 堕落,腐化,败坏
depravity n. 堕落,腐化,败坏,腐化堕落行为
deprecate v. 对……表示不赞成;反对;(古)祈求免去
depreciate v. 1.贬低,使(货币)贬值,折旧,降低……价格 2.跌价
depreciated value 折旧价值
depreciation n. 贬值,跌价;折旧
depreciation allowance 折旧费
depreciation fund 折旧基金
depreciation insurance 折旧保险
depreciation of money 货币贬值
depreciation of plant 厂房折旧
depreciation of the currency 通货贬值

depreciation on franchises 专利折旧
depreciation rate 折旧率
depredate v. 劫掠,掠夺
depredator n. 掠夺者
depression n. 经济萧条期,不景气(见 recession)
depression economics 萎缩经济学
depressive insanity 抑郁性精神病
deprivable a. 可剥夺的,可褫夺的
deprival n. 剥夺,褫夺
deprival of civil right 剥夺公民权,褫夺公权
deprival of political right 剥夺政治权利,褫夺公权
deprivation n. 剥夺;丧失,免职(尤指圣职),宗教上的剥夺(指宗教处罚的一种)
deprivation of civil right 褫夺公权,剥夺公民权
deprivation of civil right for a term 有期褫夺公权
deprivation of civil right for life 褫夺公权终身
deprivation of freedom 剥夺自由
deprivation of liberty 剥夺自由权
deprivation of nationality 丧失国籍
deprivation of parental rights 剥夺亲权
deprivation of personal liberty 剥夺人身自由
deprivation of political rights 剥夺政治权利
deprive v. 剥夺,褫夺;夺去;使丧失;免职(尤指圣职)
deprived child 丧失良好教育的儿童[指①缺乏特有或适当的父母的关怀、管理、生活安排,教育或其他有关身心健康方面的关怀管理的儿童;②已被置于违法收养或关照的地方的孩子;③已被遗弃的儿童;④已是无父母、监护人或合法看护人(legal custodian)的儿童。见 neglected child]
deprived private rights 已丧失的民事权利,被剥夺的私权
depublished opinion (1983 年)不刊印的判决意见书(指中级上诉法院的判决意见书已被高一级的法院从官方的判例汇编中删去,而不能正式刊出)

deputation n. 委派;委任代理;委任代表,代表团
depute v. 授权;委任代理
depute one's authority to a substitute 授权给代理人
deputize (=deputise) v. 委为……代表,授权……为代理人;担任代表(for)
deputy n./a. 代表,代理人;(众议院的)议员/代理的;副的,助理的
deputy assistant secretary 助理部长帮办,(大写)(美)助理国务卿帮助;(英)小客栈经理
Deputy Assisted Secretary 副助理部长
Deputy Attorney General (美)助理司法部长
deputy chairman 副主席;(中)(人大常委会)副委员长;副议长;代理主席,代理议长
deputy chief judge 副庭长
deputy chief procurator 副检察长
deputy clerk 助理书记员
deputy consul 副领事;代理领事
deputy delegate 副代表
deputy grand *kādi* 副大卡迪,副首席卡迪(见 *kādi*)
deputy head (中)副职(副县长、副区长、副乡长、副镇长等)
deputy judge 助理法官,(英)代理推事(美 alternate judge),(中)助理审判员;(国际常设法庭的)备补法官
deputy mayor 副市长
deputy president 副总统;(中)(国家)副主席;副总裁,副大臣;副会长;(参议院的)副议长;(法院)副院长,副庭长;(银行的)副行长,副总裁;(大学的)副校长;副董事长;副经理;副社长
deputy procurator 助理检察官,(中)助理检察员
deputy procurator-general (中)(最高人民检察院)副检察长
deputy provincial governor 副省长
deputy registrar 副注册主任
deputy sheriff 副警长,副司法行政官
deputy Speaker (英下议院或美众议院)副议长

deputy to the people's congress (中)人民代表大会代表

deraign v. 以决斗来裁判;(对他人的请求控告)表示异议

derailment n. 出轨

derange v. 扰乱(秩序等),打乱(计划等);使神经错乱

derate v. 取消(或减低)对……征的税

deration v. 取消(对粮食等的)定额分配

derecognition n. 不承认,不同意,撤销承认

derecognize v. 撤销承认

deregister v. 撤销……的登记

deregistration n. 撤销登记

deregulate v. 解除管制

deregulation n. 撤销管制;放松管理;减少政府对商业的控制,允许市场竞争自由;规制缓和(此词原为经济学与公共政策学的术语,早在20世纪70、80年代,以哈克为代表的新自由主义经济完成对凯恩斯革命的反革命,哈克认为即使国家只对市场稍加干涉,也不可避免地引起新的强硬措施,逐渐导致计划经济和专政。当政府借着不同的和不可调和的原则来处处抑制自由竞争时,许多利于自由竞争而建立的基本社会架构无法完成。有鉴于此,欧美国家为推动金融、航空、电力、电话、燃气等网络产业的自由化,实现经济活性化,致力于压缩政府对上述产业的规制,以建立市场主导型的产业结构,促进市场自由竞争。这便是"规制缓和"的理念)

deregulation-oriented 非规则导向

derelict n. 遗弃物,无主物;无主(弃)船;被社会抛弃的人,(美)失职的人

derelict party 放弃主权的一方当事人

dereliction n. 1.抛弃,遗弃,放弃 2.玩忽职守;缺点,错误 3.新陆地

dereliction of duty 玩忽职守,渎职

dereliction of territory 领土的放弃

derequisition n. 退还被征收的财产

derestrict v. 取消对……限制

deride v. 嘲笑,嘲弄

derivation action (suit) 派生诉讼

derivativa potestas non potest esse major primitiva. The derivative power cannot be greater than the primitive. Derived power cannot be greater than that from which it is derived. 受托人的权力不能大于委托人的权力。

derivative a./n. (版权法)派生的,演绎的[指关系到或组编的一个作品,它是以某些方法从原先的作品中进一步开发,如翻译、演绎或改编而成的。版权保护包括这种派生作品的版权(exclusive right),比如根据一本书改编的电影剧本或不同的改编乐曲(musical arrangement)]/1.衍生物,派生物[指金融(或财经)上的单据,其价值取决于次级来源(secondary source)的履行状况,比如一个优先债券(underlying bond)、通货或商品。亦称 derivative instrument] 2.见 derivative work

derivative acquisition (所有权的)传来取得,继承取得;派生取得

derivative action (与 derivative suit 同义)

derivative evidence 派生证据

derivative income 派生收入

derivative landlord 转接地主

derivative liability 派生的责任(有两种:原告侵害造成他人损害的要求赔偿;原告对自己造成损害的要求赔偿,而该侵害是他人的不法行为作为近因而造成的)

derivative nationality 继受国籍

derivative securities 派生证券

derivative settlements (英)派生性共享救济金

derivative suit (美)股东代位诉讼,(股东向董事提起的);派生诉讼(对公司董事提起的诉讼为原始诉讼。但股东只能以公司名义单事提起的原始诉讼为根据才能代表公司对董事起诉,后一诉讼由前一诉讼"派生",故名"派生诉讼",亦作 representative suit)

derivative title 衍生的所有权,派生权利

derivative trust 次信托,从属信托

derivative work (1965年)派生作品,演绎作品(按版权法)[指根据原有作品(preexisting product)而产生的作品,如翻译、编曲(musical arrangement)、改编、电影译本、缩略或对原作的其他任何摘要、改

写等形式的作品。唯有版权持有人在原作形式的基础上才可以产生或允许他人产生演绎作品,参见《美国注释法典》第 17 标题卷第 101 节,有时缩略为 derivative。见 compilation 1]

derive v. 得到,取得;派生出,导出;推知;引申出

derived liability 分赔责任

derived right 派生的权利

derived source of law 派生的法的渊源(又译"派生的法律渊源");派生法源

derogate v. 取消(义务);限制(权利);废除;毁损,减损,贬低,抑损

derogation n. 减损,贬低,毁伤;(法律、合同、条约等)部分废除(of, to),取消

derogation of a preceding estate 前产权的消失

derogatory a. 毁损的;减损的,废除的

derogatory clause 自我限制条款;失效条款,废除条款;抑损条款(抑立遗嘱人在遗嘱中插入只有他自己才谙悉的密语,以此保护其遗嘱而不受伪造之损害)

Descartes, Rene 笛卡儿

descend v. 把财产传给,将(死亡者的财产)经过无遗嘱继承(by intestate succession)传下去;遗传;下降,降低身份(人格)

descendant (=descendent) n. 子孙,后裔,卑亲属

descending order 递降次序

descent n./v. (15 世纪)1.按法律取得,依法占有(指依法律获得不动产或产权),如根据继承,将无遗嘱继承的不动产分给继承人(见 succession 2;distribution 1;purchase 2)。共同祖先(common descestor)的渊源或依据共同祖先而形成的亲属关系体系(见 ascent; descend)/把财产传给;遗传;降低身份,降低

descent and distribution 继承与分配 1.见 intestate succession, succession 2 2.广义地说,无论有无遗嘱,其(死者)遗产必须传下去,这是规则、原则(见 distribution 1)

describe v. 1.描写,描绘,叙述;形容;把……说成(as)2.画(图形),制(图)

description n. 描写,叙述;详情;(商品性质或特征等)说明

description of goods 货物说明摘要
description of person 人物描述
description of property 财物描述
description of the land 土地标示

descriptive mark 描述性商标(指用来描述"商品用途、大小、供应者、性质、使用者类别,一个令人满意的特征或使用者的最终效果"的商标。美国联邦最高法院解释是:"仅仅描述产品的商标不具有内在的显著性。用它们描述产品时,它们本质上不能标识特写的来源,因此不能获得保护。然而,描述性商标可以获得显著性,这使它们能够根据法律获得保护")

descriptive statements 描述性陈述

descriptive term 描述名称(指商标法上术语)

descriptive word index (美)描述词索引(指辞典形式的一大套丛书,用来以标题查找判例的工具书。见 descriptive word method)

descriptive word method 描述词方法(指在判决摘要汇编中,依靠使用来自分析有争议的问题所得出特定事实的引导词来检索判例的一种最有效方法)

desecrate v. 亵渎;污辱

desecrate the U. S. flag 污辱美国国旗

desegregation (=integration) n. 消除种族隔离,取消种族隔离

desegregation orders 取消种族隔离命令

desert n./v. 功过(罪),(复)应得的赏罚/抛弃,遗弃;逃跑;擅离(职守等)

deserted a. 被遗弃的;无人(居住)的,放弃的,荒废的

deserted children 被遗弃的子女
deserted spouse 被遗弃的配偶
deserted wife 被遗弃的妻子

deserter n. 逃犯;逃亡者,逃兵,背弃者;擅离职守者

deserter from armed forces 军队逃兵

desertion n 擅离职守(指自愿、不正当地抛开一个人的职责和义务,特别是从军队开小差,遗弃配偶或家庭),遗弃配偶[指家庭法中,遗弃配偶有五大要素:①中止同居;②法定期间终止或权利失效;③一种遗弃意向(或故意);④遗弃一方未能同

意;⑤没有可以正当遗弃的配偶一方的不当行为,亦称 gros neglect of duty。见 abandonment 2]

deserve v. 1.应受,值得 2.应受报答,值得受赏

deserve punishment 受到惩罚

deservedness and dangerousness 该当性与危险性(指美国的一种量刑原则)

deserving n. 功过,赏罚

desiccation n. 干燥(现象)

desiccation of the body 尸体干燥(现象)

design v./n. 1.计划,谋划[design doing (to do) sth.] 2.设计〈design an engine〉(设计一台发动机) 3.预定,指定〈design sth. for some purpose〉(指定某物做某种用途),〈design sb. for some profession〉(某人打算从事某种职业)/1.计划、谋划 2.意图、目的、图谋 3.(专利)(美)外观设计[指对于一项原有作品计划进行新颖的外观、样式、模式设计。主要是装饰性外观设计,为了一个新的式样、新的模型、新的外形(novel pattern; model; shape)而或构图或描绘或结构,但都是装饰性的。被授予独占性的外观设计(design patent)具有排他性,并受到专利法的保护] 4.计划,设计,图样

design act 外观设计法

design effort 设计工作

design patent 外观设计专利

designate v. 委任,选派;指定;指明,指出,称作

designated a. 委任的,指定的,选派的

designated guardian 指定的监护人

designated heir 指定继承人

designated jurisdiction 指定管辖(权)

designated recipient 指定受益人

designated successor 指定的遗产继承人

* *Designatio unius est exclusio alterius, et expressum facit cessare tacitum.* The designation of one is the exclusion of the other and that which is expressed prevails over that which is implied. 指定一个便排除其他,而明示的,则胜过默示的。

designation n. 选任,任命,指明,指定;名称,牌号

designation of origin 原产地名称

designer n. 伪钞制造犯;谋划者;设计者,制图人

desirability n. 合乎需要性,合意性

desirable a. 称心的,合乎需要的,理想的

desire n./v. 愿望,欲望,情欲/要求,请求;期望,希望

desist v. 停止;离开

desolation n. 荒芜,颓败,废墟,凄凉

despatch n. 见 dispatch

despatch money 提前履约金

desperado n. 亡命之徒,暴徒

desperate a. 危急的,令人绝望的;不顾一切的;极端的,险恶的;极度渴望的

desperate remedy 孤注一掷的措施

despise v. 鄙视,藐视,看不起

despoil v. 抢夺,掠夺,剥夺

despoliation n. 掠夺,抢劫,夺取

despot n. 暴君;专制君主

despotic a. 专制的,专横的

despotic landlord (中)恶霸地主

despotic rule 专制统治

despotic state 专制国家

despotism (或 **absolute monarchy**) n. 专制政体(或绝对的君主政体),专制政治;专制主义

dessaisine-saisine 领主将土地授予受让人(新佃农)的占有

destination n. 目的(地);预定;目标

destination contracts 目的地合同(契约)(美国商业律师常用术语,此类协议或合同要求售货人有责任将所售货物装运到特定的地点)

destiny n. 命运;(复)(希腊神话)命运三女神

destitute a. 赤贫的,没有的,缺乏的

destitute of qualification 缺乏资格

destitute person 无资力者

destitution n. 赤贫

destroy v. 1.破坏,摧毁,毁坏 2.打破(计划,希望) 3.消灭,歼灭

destroy incriminating evidence 销毁罪证

destroy the material evidence 毁灭物证

destroyer n. 消灭者,破坏者

destroying of evidence 毁灭证据

destruction n. 破坏,毁坏,消灭
destruction certificate 毁坏证明书
destruction list 销毁清册
destruction of evidence 毁灭证据
destruction of human civilization 破坏人类文明罪
destruction of subject matter 标的物的灭失(或毁掉)
destruction-of-prior-judgement test 优先判决准则的灭失
destructive activity 破坏活动
destructive testing 毁灭性的测试
desuetude n. 废止,废绝;法律的失效
detached a. 分遣的,派遣的;分离的,独立的;超然的,公正的
detached defense 分离的防卫(或防御)
detached office 派出机构
detached tribunal 派出法庭
detached view 不偏不倚的见解
detachment n. 分遣队;派遣;分离;超脱;解开;支队;分遣的舰队;独立,不偏不倚
detail n./v. 细目,细则,详情;枝节/详述,细说
detailed a. 详细的,详尽的
detailed account 详细报表;详细账目
detailed circumstances 详细情节,详细情况
detailed consideration 细节审议
detailed implementation 实施细则
detailed packing list 详细装箱单
detailed procedures 详细手续
detailed provisions 详细条款规定
detailed regulations 规章细则
detailed regulations on rewards and penalties 奖惩细则
detailed rules 细则
details of a case 案情
details of contract 合同(契约)细节
detain n./v. 1.拘留,扣押 2.留住,阻止/扣押,扣留,羁押,拘留;留住,阻止
detained a. 扣押的,扣留的,拘留的
detained for further review 扣押审查;拘留审查
detained goods 被拘留(押)的货物
detained person 被拘留者,被扣押者
detained provisionally 暂行扣留,暂行拘留

detainee n. 被扣押者,被拘留者
detainer n. (对财产的)扣留,扣押,占有(非法占有);拘留,羁押;续行拘留令状;指控服刑犯的通知;即将释放服刑犯的通知;继续拘留状
detaining and delaying mail 扣押和延误邮件(罪)
detaining by police for questioning 被警方扣押审问
detainment n. 监禁,拘留;扣留(海事险承保范围术语);扣押;阻止
detect v. 发现,查明;探测;侦查
detect crime 侦查犯罪行为
detect in the act 现场侦查
detection n. 侦查;查明,发觉,侦破
detection rate 破案率
detective n./a. 侦探;(复)侦缉队/侦探的;侦探用的
detective constable 侦探,探员
detective police 侦探(警察)
detective section 侦探科
detemark n. 日戳
détente (法)(国际关系上的)缓和;和好
detention n. 非法保留他人财产(与conversion有近似的含义,不过它仅指暂时保留,而conversion系长期占有);指诉讼中因他人非法保留自己的财产而引起的诉讼;司法救济中,指对侵权物暂时扣押;刑法中指拘留,羁押,扣留,阻止,滞留
detention act 拘留条例
detention arrest procedure 捕押手续,捕押程序
detention barrack 军中拘留所
detention centre 拘留中心;集中营;感化中心;拘留所,收容所
detention during Her Majesty's pleasure 恢复神志期间的拘押(指英国对不满18岁的人在成年人要被判处终身监禁情况下所科刑罚,或者精神病患者的罪犯神智期恢复期的拘押)
detention evidence 拘留证据(材料)
detention for questioning 拘留查讯,拘留审问
detention hearing (美)拘留听审(指对拘留的少年犯的听审,按美国法律拘留后必

须在 24 小时内听审) 的)终止
detention home 少年感化院,青少年罪犯临时拘留所
detention house 拘留所
detention of good 扣押货物
detention of ship 扣留船舶
detention of women in a brothel 将妇女扣押在妓院
detention on remand 还押、在押
detention on suspicion 因受嫌疑而被拘留
detention order 扣押令
detention request 拘留请求书,羁押申请书
detention warrant 羁押令
detention with postponement 监候
detention without trial 未经审讯而监禁
détenu (法)被拘留者,被监禁者
deter v. 威慑,使不敢,阻止,阻拦;胁阻
detering others from offending in a similar way 威慑其他人以相同方式犯罪
detering the offender from offending again 威慑罪犯重新犯罪
deteriorate v. 使恶化,使变坏,使退化;恶化,变质,堕落
deteriorating condition 堕落环境,腐化环境
deterioration n. (货物)变质,退化,堕落
deterioration of cargo 货物变质
determinable a. 可裁决的;可终止的;可决定的,可确定的;有限期的
determinable estate 可终止的财产权
determinable fee 可终止的地产权;有限制继承的地产(见 base fee)
determinable freeholds (英)限制自由土地保有权
determinable interest 可终止的权益
determinacy n. 确定性,确切性;坚定性
determinate a. 决定性的,限定性的;有限的
determinate guidance 确定的指引作用
determinate sentence (服刑期)特定的判决(见 indeterminate sentence)
determination n.(美)(法院的)判决,裁判(可指终局性的判决,对初审法院作出的此种判决可以上诉);(行政机关的)裁决,决定;(地产权,财产利益,权力,权利等

determination of action 诉讼终结
determination of boundary 确定地界,划定边界
determination of crime 犯罪的认定
determination of crimes and punishment 定罪和量刑
determination of jurisdiction 限(指)定管辖(权)
determination of lease 租借期终止
determination of semen 精液鉴定
determination of the appropriate penalty 确定适当的刑罚
determine v. 1.决定,确定,测定;决心 2.使终止,终止,终结
determine controversies 解决争端(争吵,争论)
determine particular cases according to law 依法断案
determine the nature of an offence 确定犯罪性质
determined a. 已决定的,有决心的
determinism n. 决定论,宿命论,定数论
deterrence n. 威慑力量,制止物,阻碍物,威慑物;制止因素,威慑因素
deterrence theory (刑罚的)威慑说
deterrent n. 制止物,妨碍物,威慑物,制止因素,威慑因素
deterrent measures 警戒措施
deterrent penalty 恐吓性惩罚
deterrent threat 制止性威胁
dethrone v. 废黜(王位);使下台(指从重要岗位上撤下)
detinue n. 请求返还扣留物的诉讼(指一方因其动产、契据或文件为他方非法扣留所提起请求返还的一种诉讼);对他人动产的非法扣留
detinue *sur bailment* 请求返还扣留寄托物的诉讼
detinue *sur trouver* 请求返还扣留遗失物的诉讼
detio ob rem 特定目的的给予
detio ob rem honestam 诚信的给予
detonation n. 爆炸
detournement de pouvoir (法)权力滥用

detoxification (=detoxication) n. 解毒
detractor n. 损毁者,贬低者
detracts v. 毁损,贬低;减损(from),转移
detriment n. (15世纪)1.损害,损失;损伤,伤害(指人身或财产受到的伤害或损失)2.(合同法)放弃法定权利(指放弃某种法定权利,即允诺有资格者行使法定权利而放弃或暂缓行使其本可行使的某些法定权利,亦称legal detriment。见 benefit 2)
detriment of public 损害公众
detriment to competition 损害竞争[指反垄断法中的一个禁止标准,"损害竞争"是美国的审查标准。即美国认为在一些有竞争的市场,即使某项并购并不产生某一垄断者,但却明显削弱了竞争强度,仍应受到禁止或限制;另外,即使某一项并购产生或加强了垄断地位,但可能效率上受益更大,也不一定加以禁止。美国标准在掌握上有相当大的弹性。而"取得或加强了主导地位"(obtain or strengthen dominant status)为欧洲的限制或禁止的审查标准。与美国相比,欧洲标准可能会放过一些不会形成垄断地位的并购。美国标准反映了芝加哥学派主张,而欧洲标准更符合哈佛学派观点]
detriment to investment 有损投资
detrimental reliance 受损的依赖(指受约人依赖要约人的允诺而受到的损失或伤害)
detrimental testimony 不利的证据,受损的证明
Deus 天主,万物主宰
deuterogamy n. 再婚,再嫁,再娶
Deuteronomic Code 《申命法典》(指记载在《申命纪》第12—16卷中的古希伯来法的一个文本)
Deuteronomy n. 《申命纪》(指《圣经旧约》的第5卷,重申在何烈山颁布的律法)
devaluation n. (货币)贬值,平价
devastate v. 使荒废,毁灭;掠夺,蹂躏
devastator n. 劫掠者,破坏者,蹂躏者
devastavit 怠忽管理遗产的责任;遗产毁损、浪费
develop n. 展开(情节等),发展,发挥,发扬;开发,开辟,使发达(成长)

develop alternative non-polluting or non-burdensome technology 发展出替代性无污染或无损害之技术
developed contracting party 发达缔约方
developed country 发达国家
developed country member 发达国家成员
developed system of law 成熟的法律制度,发达的法律制度
developer n. 开发者;(土地)开发商;发展者;显像剂
developing country 发展中国家
developing country member 发展中国家成员
developing proposals 提出议案,提出建议
development n. 开展,发展;开辟,开发;新事物;成长,发达,进化
development agency 开发机构
development area (英)政府鼓励工业投资区;失业严重区
development bank 开发银行
development company (或 corporation)开发公司
Development Loan Fund (美)开发贷款基金
development plan 开发计划,开发规划
development risk 发展风险(又称开发风险、发展缺陷,是产品责任中广泛争议问题。争论焦点在于,日趋严格化的产品责任应否更进一步要求制造商对不能为当时科技水平发现的缺陷承担责任)
development tax 发展税,开发税
developmental programme 开发计划
developmentalists n. 发展主义学派
devest v. 剥夺,褫夺
deviance n. 越轨行为
deviant n./a. 不正常的人(或物),异常的人(或物)/不正常的,异常的
deviant behavio(u)r 越轨举止,异常行为
deviation n. 越轨;背离,偏差;偏离航道,航道变更
device n. 手段;设计,计策;计划,方法,方式;(复)意志;(特定用途的)器械,设备,仪表
device bomb 设备炸弹(指一种计算机程序,由于某特定的设备,如COM端口、磁

盘驱动器 D 等的出现而运行并伴随破坏性行为）

device of the plebiscite 公民投票的方法，公民投票的策（谋）略；（古罗马）公民表决的方法

devil n. 人面兽心者，恶人，恶棍，魔鬼；（律师的）助手

devilling n. 大律师代理出庭（或代撰诉状）；（律师之间）案件的移交；介绍案情

devil's advocate 诡辩者，诡辩律师

Devil's Island 魔岛（指法国的海外流放地）

devisable a. 可遗赠的；可设计的，可发明的

devise n./v. 遗赠，不动产遗赠（从广泛含义上讲包括动产和不动产的遗赠。但在英国制定法中，此词仅表示不动产遗赠）；遗赠财产的遗嘱（条款）/立遗嘱让与（不动产）；计划；图谋；设法；设计，想出

devise and bequeath 遗赠动产和不动产

devise land 立遗嘱给予的土地，遗赠的土地

devisee n. 接受遗赠不动产者，受遗赠人

deviser n. 设计者，发明者，计划者

devising rule 计划的规则；设想的规则

devisor n. 遗赠人

Devitt Committee Report （美）戴维特委员会报告[指由美国首席法官沃伦·伯格（Warren Burger）于1978年根据美国司法会议决议任命的24名有名望的法官、律师和教授组成的一个委员会，以考虑统一审批在联邦法院实习者的资格证书，该委员会以法官戴维特为首提出了一个十点建议的报告，因而得名]

devo max 最大分权[这是"maximum"（最大的）和"devolution"（权力下放）两个词的缩写，指的是苏格兰在经济上完全独立于联合王国，但是在外交政策和防务等领域仍是联合王国的一部分。2013年，苏格兰首席部长亚历克斯·萨蒙德和他的苏格兰民族党政府宣布，将在2014年秋天举行历史性的全民公决，决定苏格兰的独立方向。苏格兰民族党政府设计的公决问题是："你是否赞成苏格兰成为一个独立的国家？"当时苏格兰民族党还在考虑是否在公决中包括第二个问题，这个问题的具体措施尚未确定,但它所表达的是一种相对缓和的举措,即在不完全独立的情况下获得更大的自治权,这个方案被称为"devo max"。"devo max"常常被称为"devolution max"或"maximum devolution"。"devo max"仅次于实际上的独立,有时被称为"independence lite"（简化独立）。另一种表达方式是"independence minus"（次独立）]

devoid of criticism 缺少批判

devoir （法）义务，责任

devolution n. 1.（责任,权利等）的转移,授权代理；移交,家产转移 2.中央对地方的权力下放 3.移审 4. 相传

devolution agreement 案件移交协定

devolution of authority 权力移交

devolution of intestacy 无遗嘱的财产继承

devolution title 产权继承

devolve v. 移交,转移；转让,委任

devolved legislative power 委任立法权

devoted a. 忠诚的,献身的

devotion n. 献身,忠诚,忠实,专心；热爱

dewan n. （印度）政府官员（尤指财政官员），邦政府的首席部长

dey n. （土耳其）奥斯曼帝国驻北非的官员

Dharmasastra n. 《法论》（指年代早于罗马法的一本古印度法学文本）

diacetylmorphine 海洛因,吗啡

diagnosis n. 诊断；审查,细心研究；慎辨,查究真相；审查后所作之决定或判断

dialectic a. 辩证的,辩证法的；方言的

dialectical reasoning 辩论推理

diarchy (=dyarchy)

dicast n. （古希腊）陪审官（兼有法官的职能）；（古代雅典）（有资格参加抽签而充任法官的）市民

dicastery n. 陪审官审判,（大写）迪卡斯特里法庭（又译陪审官法庭,指古代雅典的一种司法机构,根据条件和重要程度可由1—500名陪审官参加审判,后为赫利亚法院的一部分）

dichotomous nature of sovereignty 主权概念的双重本质

dichotomous variable 对生变量

dichotomy n. 二分法
dicker n. 物物交换,小交易;(美)妥协(政治用语)
dictograph n. 窃听器
dicta dictum 的复数(见 dictum)
dictaphone n. 录话机
dictate v./n. 口述;口授;命令;支配/命令,支配
dictate of right reason 真理的命令,正当理由的授命
dictated a. 口述的,口授的
dictated contract 指令合同(契约)
dictated testament (或 will) 代笔遗嘱,口述遗嘱
dictates of nature 自然地命令,自然地使命,自然地支配
dictating prices 操纵物价
dictator n. 1.独裁者,专政者 2.独裁官(指罗马共和国握有非常权力的官吏)3.口授者,口授者
dictatorial (=dictatory) a. 独裁的,专政的,专横傲慢的
dictatorial system 专制制度
dictatorship n. 专政;独裁权
dictatorship apparatus 专政机关
dictatorship of bourgeoisie 资产阶级专政
dictatorship of proletariat 无产阶级专政
dictatress n. 女专政者,女独裁者;女口述者,女口授者
dictionary rule 字典规则
dictum n. 格言,名言;宣言,声明;(复 dicta,或作 obiter dicta) 法官(附带的)意见;(美)法官判决的附带意见(指此种意见对该案判决无直接关系,并无判例效力);有权威的意见
didactic education 说服教育
die v. 死;枯萎;灭亡,平息,消失
die by one's own hand 自杀
die by violence 横死
die by visitation God 突然死亡
die from (或 of) 由于……而死,死于
die from a wound 因伤而死
die hard 1.难断气 2.顽固得很,根深蒂固
die intestate 无遗嘱死亡
die of old age 年老而死,老死
die testate 留有遗嘱的死亡
die will-less 未留有遗嘱的死亡
die with one's shoes on (或 die in one's shoes) 不死在床上,横死,暴死
die without issue 身故无后,死后无后嗣
diehard n./a. 顽固分子,顽固派(the),死不屈从者,死硬分子,顽强的,顽固不化的,顽抗到底的;顽固的
diei dictio (罗马法)1.审判告示(行政执行官的告示传唤刑事被告于确定日期出庭受审)2.送达传票(有时亦写成 diei dictitio 或 diem dicere)
diem clausit extremum 通知(县、郡)行政官扣押已死的王室债务人的财产令
dies 期日,期限
dies a quo 起算日,开始生效日期
dies ad quem 截止日,停止生效日期
dies cedit 权利义务成立期,债权发生日期
dies communes in banco 规定出庭的日子(或日期)
dies fasti (罗马法)执政官出庭
dies gratiae 宽限日期
dies juridicus 开庭日,法定日期
dies nefasti (罗马法)执政官公休日
dies non (juridicus) 非庭讯日,法庭休庭日;不开庭日,法定假日
dies venit 债务履行日期,义务履行期
diet n. (欧洲史上的)议会,会议;(日本两院制的)国会;(神圣罗马帝国)议会
differ v. 1.不同,相异(from)2.意见不同,意见不一致〈we differ from him on/about/upon that question/agree to differ〉(各自保留不同意见)
difference n. 不和,争议,差异,差别;差额,余额;重要改变
difference contract 差额合同(契约)(指美国地下期货业者接受客户委托后未将委托单下至交易所,结果变成客户与客户间或客户与业者之间相互对赌。像这类以期货交易为名所进行的交易,交易人的真正本意是暂时以约定的商品履约价与市价间的差额决定输赢,加赔钱的一方支付金钱给另一方,美国法院称之为差额契约)
differences in opinion 意见分歧

different a. 不同的,差异的,各种,个别
different modes of ownership 各种所有权
different state theories about the proper situs of corporate stock 不同州的有关公司股份的适当所在地理论
different ways of acquiring ownership 取得所有权的各种方法
different-statute approach "不同制定法"方法
differential association 差异交往说(指犯罪行为说的一种理论)
differential distinctiveness (商标的)差异显著性(见 source distinctiveness)
differential measure 区别对待措施
differential minimum contacts threshold 不同的最低联系起点
differential voting 差别选举制,差别投票制
differentiate v. 区分,区别;使区分,使变异;使分化
difficult case 疑难案件
diffuse interest 扩散性利益(指事先没有任何关系而只是基于特写的事实原因才产生联系人共同拥有的一种超越个人的不可分的利益)
digamist n. 再婚者
digamous a. 再婚的
digamy n. 再婚
digest n. 1.文摘,摘要 2.(大写)《学说汇纂》(指公元 6 世纪东罗马皇帝查士丁尼下令汇编的法学家学说摘录,共 50 卷);《判例摘要》(指英美国家里一种判例摘要汇编);《法规教科书》(指现代法中出现的一种以法律原则和制度为内容的教科书)
digest of cases 案例摘要;判决要旨
Digest of Criminal Law (美)《刑法典》
Digest of International Law (美)《国际法判决摘要汇编》(指一种百科全书式的《国际法判决摘要汇编》,包括条约资料、司法解释、分析和历史注释以及其他学术上的评述)
Digest of Opinions of the Attorneys General (美)《检察长意见摘要》(指由州政府委员会出版的一种法律资料,但 1969 年该摘要停止出版,并无其他资料代替)

digging grave 挖掘坟墓
digital access 数字进入,网络查询
Digital Access Index 数字接入指数
digital agenda 数字议事日程,数字备忘录[指由世界知识产权组(WIPO)1999 年宣布的一系列 10 点建议对版权法的修改,旨在改进电子商务(e-commerce)时保护互联网(internet)上的知识产权。]
digital archives 数字档案库(指以数字信息的形式存在的档案库,但这些数字文件有诸多的局限性)
digital cash 见 e-money
digital certificate 数字证书[指公开使用于以记录为基础的电脑来认识颁发证明的当局和为电子传送文件(electronically transmitted documents)签发数字签名(digital signature)的签名人。同时也提供给使用人以公用秘诀(public key)来解密数字签名,签名人带有认证当局登记可以得到数字签名。一些证书可包括增加的信息,扩大发行,以及有效日期和凭借证书交易的建议的信赖规定范围(reliance limit)。当重点放在由发送人发送的电子文件时,此证书可作为电子公证证实的作用。]
Digital Crowding 数字拥挤[指无法控制或难以避免的过度在线社交往来。轰动全球的好莱坞女星"艳照门"事件凸显出互联网个人空间正不断遭到侵扰,数字拥挤现象的产生对人们的隐私已构成严重威胁。英国西英格兰大学行为变化学教师亚当·N.乔因森等人 2010 年 10 月 15 日发表的论文《数字拥挤:隐私、自我披露和科技》最先使用了该说法。该文称:"正如过度的身体接触会引起拥挤感一样,我们认为过度的数字式社会交往或许会产生'数字拥挤'现象。"这篇论文后来被收录《在线隐私》一书。论文称,通过社交网站过度地进行在线接触或分享会对人们的隐私和关系质量造成危害]
digital cultural goods 数字文化商品,又称数字商品(digital goods)[指是以数字技术构建或表达的,是可以脱离存储的介质和载体实现在线传递的唯一商品。它既不是物,也非知识财产。德国法学家施密特(Andreas U. Schmidt)认为对数字产品

的准确界定方式应是:先论其本身是否有形(tangible or not),只要产品本身能够透过数字形式(in a digital way)表现即可]
digital evidence 数字证据(见 computer evidence)
digital furrow 指纹
digital language 数字语言
Digital Millennium Copyright Act (美)《数字千年版权法》(1998年)[指1998年的联邦法,协调美国版权保护与国际法的关系,限定网络服务提供者(Internet service provider)承担版权责任的范畴,并且扩大软件所有者对复制项目的能力。在许多其他规定条文中,该法规扩大了对电脑程序(computer program)、电影和其他世界范围的视听资料的版权保护,试图调整网络空间(Cyberspace),禁止目的在于规避数字反侵犯版权工具(digital antipiracy tools)的一些设施,阻止假的版权管理信息(falsified copyright-management information)的产生和配置。缩写为 DMCA]
Digital Opportunity Index 数字机会指数(具有综合性特点)
digital right 数字化权
digital signatures 数字签名(指嵌入个人计算机的一种简单的加密数码)
digital watermaking 数字水印
digital wildfire 数字野火[意指非常迅速地在互联网上传播的虚假敏感信息。世界经济论坛发布的《2013年全球风险报告》以"高度紧密连接的世界中的数字野火"为题描述了这一现象造成的危害。《社交时报》网站撰文指出,"世界经济论坛把'数字野火'视为威胁全球稳定的一种风险……世界各国的政治和经济专家都认为社交网络上传播的错误或虚假信息可能会引发政治经济动荡"。2012年,1名用户在推特网站上注册了 fakester(冒充名人等含有虚假或误导信息的社交网络账户),谎称自己是俄罗斯内政部长,透露说叙利亚总统巴沙尔已经"受伤或被杀害",导致原油价格大幅上涨。等到石油交易商认清真相时为时已晚]
dignitary n. 职位高的人(尤指宗教方面的)
dignitary value 尊严价值

dignity n. 尊严;高贵;(属于无体财产权的一种)爵位,显职,显贵
dignity of courtroom 法庭尊严
dignity of human personality 人格尊严
dignity of individual 个人尊严
dignity of state 国家的尊严
dijudication 司法判决,法律判决;法律决定
diktat n. (强加于战败国等的)单方的苛刻解决条件
dilapidation n. 倒塌;毁坏;挥霍;(复)(租借期满时)对房屋修缮的程度
dilapidator n. 毁损者,挥霍浪费者
dilatory a. 延期的,拖延的;拖拉的,慢的
dilatory defense 延诉答辩,延诉抗辩[指当事人所作的旨在暂时或推迟的诉讼而不提供实质性证据的答辩。如错误的共同诉讼(misjoinder)、未使应参加诉讼的当事人参加诉讼(nonjoinder)、既决事项、一事不再理(res judicata)、名称错误(misnomer)、缺少提起诉讼能力(lack of capacity to sue)、其他未决诉讼(action pending)、诉讼时效法(statute of limitations)等]
dilatory evidence 延迟提出的证据
dilatory machinery of a common law prosecution 普通法控诉的拖延机制
dilatory motion 延期审理动议;延搁提案动议
dilatory plea 延诉的抗辩
dilecto et fideli 给他所爱的和忠实的,此术语常用于各种不同的令状(writs)之中,缩略为 di et fi
dilemma n. 1.两难推理 2.窘境,困境〈be in a dilemma〉(进退两难), dilemmatic a.
diligence n. 强制,强迫,勤奋;专心,小心;谨慎性
diligentia 注意,当心
dilute v. 冲淡,稀释
dilution n. 淡化,稀释[指减少某一事物的力量或价值的行为或情形。此词含义广泛:①在公司法中指由于公司发行新的股票而导致公司发行在外的股票价值减低,稀释了投票权的力量。如果新股不按有股东的持股比例配股,不按现有持股比例发行,而且新股发行价低于新股发行前的在外股票的市价或账面价格,则稀释

可能导致股票价值降低。②在商标法上则指他人使用某一强势商标,虽未导致相同或类似商品混淆,但对该商标的显著性造成伤害或使其产生令人厌恶感,因而对该商标的形象造成损害,这种商标淡化是对强势商标的一种侵权行为。③在宪法上指重新分配议会的(或国会)的席位或不正当划分选区的手段限制某一特定团体选票的效力。这种做法称为选票稀释(vote dilution)]

dilution claims 淡化诉讼

dim v. 使暗淡,使失辉(dimension, diminuendo, diminutive 三词的缩写)

dimension to interpretation 解释的层面

diminished capacity defense 限制能力的辩护规则(指美国加州最高法院在 1940 年代即开始使用减轻能力辩护,最初旨在减少麦克·纳顿条例的刚性。接着在 70 年代后延伸至意志和认识能力的减弱)

dimension n./v. 范围,尺度;(复)面积,容积;范围,方面/使方形成需要的尺寸;在……上标出尺寸

diminished responsibility 减轻的责任(指免除患精神病或精神不健全的被告应负的部分罪责)

diminution n. 缩减,减少,减小

diminution of crime 罪案的减少

diocese n. 主教管区

Diocletian n. 戴克里先(245—313 年,于 284—305 年为罗马皇帝)(指 Gaius Aurelivs Valerivs Dioletianus 盖乌斯·奥列利乌斯·瓦列里乌斯·戴克里先,著名的罗马帝国皇帝。他在执政的 20 年内实行一系列改革措施,使面临崩溃边缘的奴隶制帝国暂时得以稳定下来)

diota (大陆法)1.文盲,头脑简单的人 2.无职务的人

diploma n. 特许证;执照;学位证书;(学校毕业的)文凭;公文,文书

diplomacy n. 外交;外交手腕,权谋;外交使团(节)

diplomacy of equidistance 等距离外交

diplomacy-oriented approach 外交导向派(或称实用派 Pragmatic approach)[该派认为赋予私人直接诉讼权是有悖于传统国际法理论,并将成为政府间贸易争端解决的绊脚石。见 rule-oriented approach]

diplomaed (= diploma'd) a. 持有执照的,持有文凭的

diplomat n. 外交家,外交官;有权谋的人

diplomate n. 学位证书持有者,(大学)毕业文凭持有者;获有官方证明文件的专科医生

diplomatic a. 外交(上)的;文献上的,有外交手腕的;外交工作的

diplomatic act 外交行为

diplomatic agent 外交代表

diplomatic asylum 外交庇护

diplomatic bag 外交邮袋

diplomatic body 外交使团,外交机构

diplomatic channel 外交途径,外交渠道

diplomatic civil service 外交文官

diplomatic corps (或 mission) 外交使团

diplomatic correspondence 外交文书

diplomatic courier 外交信使

diplomatic documents 外交文书(包括国书和领事证、条约、照会、备忘录外交函件等);外交证件

diplomatic envoy 外交使节

diplomatic evidence 文献上的证据

diplomatic immunity 外交豁免(权)

diplomatic institutions 外交机关(指国家对外进行外交交往的机关)

diplomatic intercourse 外交往来

diplomatic language 外交语言(指法、英、中、俄、西语为联合国法定的外交语言)

diplomatic list 外交官衔名录

diplomatic mail 外交邮件

diplomatic marriage 使馆婚姻(指驻外大使馆里举行婚姻仪式的婚姻)

diplomatic matter 外交事件

diplomatic means 外交手段

diplomatic negotiation 外交谈判

diplomatic organ 外交机构

diplomatic passport 外交护照

diplomatic personnel 外交人员

diplomatic practice 外交惯例

diplomatic privilege 外交特权,外交使节的治外法权

diplomatic privilege and immunity 外交特

权和外交豁免权
diplomatic protection 外交保护(权)
diplomatic protection of citizens abroad 对居住在外国的侨民的外交保护
diplomatic protocol 外交礼节
diplomatic reciprocity 外交互惠
diplomatic relations 外交关系
diplomatic representatives 外交代表;外交人员
diplomatic school 外交学派
diplomatic staff 外交人员
diplomatic visa 外交签证
diplomatist n. 外交官;外交家;有外交手腕的人
diplomatize (= diplomatise) v. 做外交工作,施展外交手腕,用外交手段处理
dipsomania n. 间发性酒狂[指有病理性心境恶劣(dysphoria)病人为摆脱负性情绪的困扰,"借酒消愁",呈发作性持续饮酒,称为间发性酒狂。见 dysphoria]
direct v./a. (法官)指示(陪审团);指导,导演;指挥;下令,对准(目标)/直接的;直系的;确实的;直率的
direct and verbal trial 直接言词
direct action 直接诉讼;直接行动
direct admission 直接承认;直接接纳
direct aggression 直接侵略行为
direct appeal 直接上诉
direct appeal for nullity 直接提起无效之诉
direct applicability (法律的)直接适用性(欧共体法中的一个概念)
direct arbitrage 直接套汇,两地套汇,两地套利
direct attack 直接攻击判决(指旨在以正当理由通过上诉或复审状等特有程序,为改变、撤销或推翻原有判决所提出的申请)
direct bill 直接汇票
direct bill of lading 直达提单
direct business 直接交易;直接买卖
direct causation 主要的因果关系,直接的因果关系
direct cause 直接原因
direct closing method 直接结算法

direct communication 直接表达
direct complicity 直接同谋(指跨国公司参与违反人权时为直接同谋受益)
direct confession 直接供认;直接坦白
direct consequence 直接后果
direct consumption tax 直接消费税
direct contempt of court 直接藐视法庭罪,直接侮辱法官罪
direct cost 直接成本,直接费用
direct county election 县级直接选举
direct damage 直接损失;直接损害
direct debt and overlapping debt 直接债务上的重叠债务
direct democracy 直接民主,直接民主政治
direct democratic system 直接民主制
direct draft 直接汇票
direct effect 直接适用(见 indirect effect),直接效果
direct election 直接选举
direct estoppel 再诉禁止,直接禁反言[指在英美法系国家,判决效力规则主要包括直接禁反言(也称诉因禁反言)(cause of action estoppel)和间接禁反言规则(collateral estoppel)。见 collateral estoppel]
direct evidence 直接证据
direct examination 直接诘问(指当事人或其诉讼代理人为了提供证词给法庭审理,向为其作证的证人进行的发问,使其就证据作出基本陈述。而对证人的诘问,即举证方的直接诘问应是第一顺序,另一方的反问则是第二顺序)(见 examination in chief)
direct exchange 直接汇兑
direct general election 普选
direct infringement 直接侵权
direct injury 直接伤害
direct intent 直接故意
direct invasion 直接入侵,直接侵犯
direct investment 直接投资
direct legacy 直接遗赠
direct legislation 直接立法
direct liability 直接责任;直接负债
direct line 直系
direct line of descent 直系亲属

direct loss　直接损失
direct national tax　直接国税
direct negotiation　直接协商,直接谈判
direct object　直接客体
direct placement　直接收养(见 private placement)
direct possession　直接占有
direct precautionary criteria　风险预防原则的直接标准
direct precursor　直接的先驱者
direct primaries　(美)直接预选
direct private rights of action　私人直接诉权(包括狭义的私人直接诉权与WTO协议直接适用方式)
direct proof　直接证明
direct repatriation　直接遣返
direct rule　直接规范
direct service　直接送达
direct subject　直接主体
direct subject of international law　国际法直接主体
direct subsidies　直接补贴
direct succession　直接继承
direct tax　(18世纪)直接税[指对财产所征收的税,直接税须由纳税人自己承担被确定的金额而不得转移(passed on)给他人。从价(ad valorem)税和财产税均为直接税,这区别于对权利或特权征税的间接税]
direct the jury　(法官)对陪审团作指示
direct trust　直接信托
direct universal suffrage　直接普选权(制)
direct universal suffrage over two ballots　直接的两轮投票制
direct verdict　(美)指示裁断,直接裁决(指负举证责任的当事人在举不出可供立案的证据时,法官指示陪审团按其指示作出有利于被告的裁决。从法律上讲,这种指示不容陪审团考虑,只能照做。在刑事案件中,此种裁决则由法官直接作出)
direct violence　直接暴力
direction n.　管理,监督,指挥,指导;指示;命令;方面,范围;倾向
direction of a verdict　给陪审团裁断的指示

direction to a jury　(法官)给予陪审团的指示
directive a./n.　指示的,管理的;起指导作用的/指令,命令,指示;(复)(欧共体的)指令
directive on taxation of interest　利息税指令
directive rules　规程
Directive to Approximate the Law of the Member State Relating to Trade Marks　《缩小成员国商标法差异的指令》[1988年欧共体理事会在总结和提炼《共同体商标条例(草案)》的基础上制定的]
directly applicable or application　直接适用性
Directoire n.　(法)(公元1795年至1799年期间5人的)执政内阁
director n.　董事;主任;理事;总裁,总监,处长,局长,署长,指导者,导演
director board　董事会
director of company　公司董事(长)
Director of Investigation and Research　(加)调查与研究总监
director of judicial services　司法事务署长
Directory of open access journals DOAJ　开放资源共享
director of public prosecutions　检察长;(英)检察官;(日)公诉官,公诉局长
director of the state bank　国家银行总裁
Director primacy　董事会决策优位[指趋同论者秉承古典经济学派的效率论和经济达尔文主义的教义,提炼并解释了美国公司法公司治理"股东利益导向"(shareholder-oriented model)与"董事会决策优先"两大主要特征]
director-general　董事长;理事长;总干事
Director-General of Fair Trading　(美)公平贸易总局长
Director-General of the WTO　世界贸易组织总干事
directorate n.　董事会,理事会,指导者(或处长,董事,导演等)的职位
directorial a.　指导的,指挥的,管理的;指挥者,管理者的
directory n./a.　姓名地址簿(录);工商行名

录,(美)董事会;(大写)(1795—1799年统治法国的)执政内阁/指导(性)的

directory provisions 指导性规定,指导性条款

directory service 名录服务(指因特网上根据用户的某些住处查找另一些住处的一种公共查询服务)

directory statute 指导性的制定法,指导性法规

directory trust 指导性信托

directress n. 女董事,女指导者,女导演,女指挥

diriment a. 使无效的,使作废的

diriment impediment of marriage 无效性的结婚障碍(尤指天主教使婚姻绝对无效的事实或状况)

dirty a. 脏的,污秽的;卑鄙的,淫猥的;凶狠的;下流的,黄色的,不洁的,污染的

dirty bill of lading 有债务提单

dirty industry (造成)污染的工业

dirty work 不法行为,欺诈行为

disabilities incident to coverture in general (英)一般已婚女子受丈夫监护的限制行为(能力)

disability n. 1.无行为能力,无资格 2.残疾,劳动能力丧失,无能

disability and infirmity allowance 伤残老弱津贴

disability certificate 残疾证明书

disability clause 丧失能力条款(亦称残疾附约,指人身保险中被保人残疾时可停止付保险费的规定)

disability compensation 残疾补偿(指不能工作的残疾人,应由公共基金或私人基金给予支付作为社会保障或工作的补偿福利。亦称为 disability benefits)

disability in line of duty 因公残疾

disability insurance 残疾保险

disability of mind 心神无能(又译"智力无能",精神病的一种)

disability pension 残疾金,残疾抚恤金

disable v. 使无行为能力,使(在法律上)无资格,致残,致失去战斗力

disabled a. 残疾的

disabled armyman 残疾军人

disabled military personnel of the revolution (中)革命残疾军人

disabled person 残疾人

disabled soldier 残疾军人;荣誉军人

disabled veterans 荣誉军人

disablement n. 残疾,无行为能力

disablement benefit (保险)伤残赔偿金;伤残救济金

disabling injury 致残伤害

disabling sentence (处以)剥夺资格的判决;剥夺资格的刑罚

disabling statute 剥夺资格法

disaccredit v. 撤销对……授权;撤销对……委任,对……不再信任

disadvantage n. 损失,损害(指名誉、信用等经济方面的);不利,不利条件

disadvantaged a. 被剥夺了基本权利的,生活条件差的;社会地位低下的

disaffection n. 挑唆背叛;叛离;不满,不忠;不友善,不满现政权

disaffirm v. 撤销以往的判决;否认,取消,反驳

disaffirmance n. 撤销原判;废除,否认,取消,反驳

disaffirmation n. 撤销原判;废除,否认,取消,反驳

disafforestation n. (英)不受森林法约束的普通地

disagree v. 抵触(尤指与法律相抵触);不同意;争执;不符合

disagreement n. 不一致;不同意;陪审团的意见不一致,异议

disagreement and mistrial 不一致和错误审判

disallow v. 拒绝接受,拒绝承认;不允许,否决

disallowance n. 不允许,否决

disallowance of appeal 不许上诉

disannul v. 废除,取消

disappear v. 失踪;消失;不在

disappearance n. 失踪;消失;不在

disappearance and declaration of death 失踪和宣告死亡

disappearance of insured person 承保人的失踪

disapprobative a. 不认可的,不赞成的,不满的
disapproval n. 不赞成,不认可;否决
disapprove v. 不赞成,不许可,非难,不同意
disarmament n. 裁军,解除军备
disaster n. 灾难;不幸;灾害;惨事
disaster area 灾区
disaster relief funds 救灾款
disaster relief provisions 救灾粮
disaster struck household 受灾户
disaster victims 灾民
disastrous in practice 实际上灾难性的,实际上会造成严重损失的
disavow v. 不承认,抵赖,拒绝对……承担责任;推翻(前言)
disavowal n. 拒绝承担责任;抵赖;否认
disband v. 解散;解除;遣散
disband martial law 解除军事管制(法)
disbar v. 取消(某人)律师资格,将某律师除名,(将某人)驱逐出律师界,取消(某人)的律师出庭资格
disbarment n. 取消律师(或出庭)资格,将(某)律师除名,驱逐出律师界
disbarring n. (英)取消律师资格
disbench v. (英)取消律师学院(原指英国14世纪的四大律师学院)主管人员的资格;使……丧失法学会会员资格
disburden v. 解除(责任,负担);摆脱;卸除(负担等)
disburse v. 支出,支付,分配
disbursement n. 付款;(复)船上开支,(船舶)费用
disbursement of payments 款项的支付
disbursements clause 船舶费用保险条款
disbursements insurance 船舶费用保险
discard v./n. 丢弃,抛弃,遗弃,解雇/丢弃,抛弃,垫牌
discern v. 目睹;认识;洞悉;识别;辨别;辨认出;分清
discern between right and wrong 分清是非
discern the false from the genuine 辨明真伪
discernment n. 认识;识别;洞察力

discharge n./v. 1.履行,清偿,完成任务;执行任务 2.撤销(法院命令)3.解除;释放;开除;解雇,解职,退役,免除;释放(或解职,退伍等)证明书 4. 卸货,卸载;发射/1.卸载〈discharge cargo from the ship〉(卸下船上的货物)2.射出,开炮等〈discharge a shot from a gun〉(用枪射击)3.排除(气体、液体等)4. 解雇,释放,离开〈be discharged from prison〉(从监狱离开)5.使免除,使卸脱〈discharge sb. from an obligation〉(特别指免除债务)6.履行,清偿〈discharge one's duty〉(清偿债务)7.(法律)撤销(法院的命令)
discharge a contract 履行合同(契约)
(to) discharge a defendant 释放被告;驳回对被告的指控,驳回对被告的诉讼
discharge afloat 船上卸货
discharge in insolvency 解除偿还责任裁定(指法庭对无力清偿债务者在交出其全部财产后解除其责任的裁定)
discharge of a jury 解除(某)陪审团职务
discharge of an attachment 解除对一项财产的扣押
discharge of contract 履行合同(契约)
discharge of debt 清偿债务
discharge of duty 履行职责
discharge of obligation 债的清偿,债的消灭
discharge of prisoners 释放囚犯
discharge of proceedings 履行诉讼手续
discharged a. 已解除的;已清偿的
discharged bankrupt 已解除债务的破产人
discharged by 由……执行,由……履行
discharged convicts 已被释放的罪犯
discharged obligation 已清偿的债务
discharged prisoners'aid societies (英)获释犯人援助社
discharged the jury 已解除的陪审团
discharger n. 履行者,卸货者,发射者,卸货工具,发射装置,排放装置
discharging expenses 卸货费用
discharging from floating 由驳船卸上码头
discharging port 卸货港口

disciple n. 门徒,信徒;追随者;耶稣十二门徒之一
disciplinable a. 应惩戒的,可训练的
disciplinarian n. 实施纪律者
disciplinary a. 纪律的,惩戒性的
disciplinary action 惩戒行为
disciplinary authority 惩戒权
disciplinary award 纪律处分
disciplinary barracks 军人惩戒所
disciplinary board 纪律(检查)委员会
disciplinary coercion 纪律强制
disciplinary control 纪律管制
disciplinary education 纪律教育
disciplinary examination committee 纪律检查委员会
disciplinary law 惩戒法
disciplinary law of seaman 海员惩戒法
disciplinary matter 惩戒性案件
disciplinary measures 纪律措施,惩戒措施
disciplinary offence 违反纪律罪
disciplinary power 纪律惩戒权
disciplinary procedure 纪律性程序,惩戒程序
disciplinary proceedings 职业惩戒程序,(指对某一行业或其他职业团体的成员因其不当的、不守职业道德的、非法的行为予以斥责,暂时其执业资格)
disciplinary proceeding 惩戒性诉讼
disciplinary punishment 纪律处分,纪律处罚
disciplinary rule (通常大写)惩戒性规则[指阐明职业行为的最低要求(minimum level)的强制性规定(mandatory regulation),一个专职人员(a professional)必须遵守,避免受到惩戒。对于律师来说,这个惩戒性规则主要可以在《示范职业责任法典》(Model Code of Professional Responsibility)中查到,缩略为 DR。见 ethical consideration]
disciplinary sanction 纪律制裁
disciplinary treatment 纪律处分
discipline n./v. 纪律;风纪;惩戒;惩罚;教规,戒律;训练/惩戒;惩罚;约束,控制;训育
discipline of labo(u)r 劳动纪律

discipline tribunal 纪律法庭
disciplined reason of the judges 法官惩戒的理由(或道理)
disciplined sense of justice 公平的惩戒意识,正义的惩戒意识
disclaim v. 放弃;否认;不索赔,不认领
disclaim liability 否认责任
disclaimer n. 放弃要求,不承认;放弃权利;放弃者,否认者
disclaimer by patentee 专利权人放弃专利权
disclaimer by trustee 受托人拒绝信托
disclaimer clause 弃权条款
disclaimer of onerous property 放弃负有法律义务的财产
disclaimer of peerage 放弃爵位
disclaimer of power 弃权
disclaimer of trustee 受托管理人的弃权书
disclamation n. 不承认,否认;放弃,不索赔,不认领
disclose v. 揭发,揭露;公开,透露;泄露(秘密)
disclose illegal activities 揭露非法活动
disclose or abstain rule 公开或戒绝交易规则,公开或禁止交易规则[亦译披露或弃绝交易规则,公布消息否则禁止买卖,戒绝交易否则公开规则等。该规则最早在内幕交易案件审理中应用,可见美国联邦最高法院 1909 年审理的斯壮诉锐派德案(Strong v. Repide),参见《美国联邦最高法院判例汇编》第 213 卷第 419 页(1909 年);凯蒂·罗伯特公司案(Cady & Robert Co.)后,该规则成为美国处理内幕交易案件的基本规则,要么公开该内幕信息,要么自我约束不得在信息公开前从事与该信息相关的证券交易。几乎每一个案件的审理都在讨论行为人是否违反该规则]
disclosed a. 揭发的,揭开的;透露的;公布的
disclosed agency 指名代理
disclosed agent 指名代理人
disclosed ballot 记名投票,无封投票,公开投票

disclosed contract 披露的合同
disclosed defect 发现的瑕疵
disclosure n. 揭发；披露，泄露；告知，通知；泄露之事
disclosure laws 披露法（规）
disclosure of information 泄露情报
disclosure regulation 公开规制，开示规制,强制披露制（指强制证券发行和交易中的特定当事人披露其相关信息,以供投资者进行判断的一种证券监管制度）
discommodity n. 无使用价值的东西；（古）不便
discommon v. （英）剥夺公地使用权；（将公地）占为私有
discontentment n. 不服；不安；不平；不满意
discontinuance n. 诉讼的撤销；诉讼程序的终止；中断；中止，停止，废止；放弃
discontinuance of action 终止诉讼，撤回诉讼
discontinuance of appeal 中止上诉，撤回上诉
discontinuance of counterclaim 撤销抗诉，撤回反要求（诉）
discontinuance of possession 占有中断，放弃占有
discontinue v. 撤销诉讼；中止，中断；废止，放弃
discontinuity n. 间断,不连续性,中断
discontinuous a. 中断的,不连续的,间断的
discontinuous easement 间断的役权
discount n./v. 折扣,贴现,打折扣；折息,扣息/折扣,折让；减价；贴现；（货物）没有销路,容易到手；不受欢迎
discount and allowance 折让
discount bank 贴现银行
discount bill 已贴现票据
discount broker 贴现经纪人,贴现掮客
discount house 贴现银行；贴现商店,廉价商店,折扣商店
discount interest 扣利
discount of bill 汇票贴现
discount of bills and notes 期票贴现
discount prices (act) 折扣减价(行为)

discount rate 贴现率
discount yield 折扣收益率,折价,以折扣方式销售的收益率,收益率
discountable a. 可贴现的,可打折扣的,不能全信的
discounter n. 折扣者；预扣利息的贷款人
discounting of book-credits 账面信用贴现
discourage v. 使失去信心,使泄气；劝阻
discouraging discovery abuse 防止披露程序滥用
discouraging discovery over-use 抑制披露程序滥用
discourse n. 论述,谈话；演说；讲道
discover v. 发现,暴露；显示,看出
discoverable and manageable standard 可发现的易操作的标准
discovered peril doctrine 见 last clean chance doctrine
discovering party 披露的一方
discovert n./a. 独身女子/无夫的；（女子）未婚的
discovery n. 证据披露,开示；(美)披露或调查取证程序[民事诉讼中的一种审前程序,一方当事人可以通过该程序从对方当事人处获得与案件有关的事实与信息,以有助于准备庭审。要求披露方式有：书面证词(deposition),书面询问(written interrogatories),请求承认(request for admissions),请求出示文件(request for admissions)。美国联邦法院民事诉讼流程之一,指代表民事案件当事人的律师,通过询问证人、调查物证以及构成对方案情的其他信息方法,尽力了解对方当事人事实的审理前程序]；(英)要求告知(指法院可以通知一方当事人,使他了解他方当事人或证人所知道的事实,以便准备受审的一种手续)；发现,发觉,被发现物；开示
discovery abuse 滥用开示,误用开示[指通过超出主要要求企图获取不必要的诉讼信息或超过允准披露的范畴,或为不适当目的去引导审前开示来妄用或滥用审前开示程序(Pretrial Procedure)。参见《联邦民事诉讼规则》,钥匙号1278]
discovery and inspection of documents （遗失）文据的发现和审查

discovery and occupation 先占发现和占有(领土)(指国家占有或获取领土的方法)
discovery device 披露手段;调查取证手段;披露程序方法,披露程序设置
discovery of documents 提供证件清单;(美)(民诉中)证据开示
discovery of law 法律开示(模式)[指把法律视为既存的,不容违背客观规则,解释者只能尽力去发现其真实(内)含义,并将之揭示出来以适用于具体个案]
discovery order (美)披露会议,调查取证会(民诉中的一项审前准备程序之一)
discovery plan 调查取证计划(指由案件当事人或他们的律师在调查会议前,应按《联邦民事诉讼规则》第26条第6款的要求,提交给法院的计划)
discovery process 披露程序,披露进程
discredit n./v. 不信任,丧失名誉,丧失信用,怀疑/诋毁;不相信,不信任,怀疑
discredited analysis 质疑的分析,不信任的分析
discrepancy n. 差异,不一致,不符,不一致之处
discrepancy in the documents 单据不符
discrete a. 分立的,无关联的,无联系的,不连续的,分离的,分裂的
discrete choice 离散选择
discrete probability distribution 离散概率分布
discrete set 离散集
Discretio est scire (or discernere) per legem quid sit justum. Discretion consists in knowing through the law what is just. 自由裁量权在于了解在法律上哪个是正当的
discretion n. 辨别,判断;自由酌情处理;自由裁量权,自由斟酌权,酌处权;任意决定权
discretion of costs 裁定讼费
discretion of punishment 量刑
discretion power of the judge 法官的自由裁量权
discretion statement 任意裁决陈述(指离婚请求人为了请求法庭运用任意判决,并批准其离婚而承认自己犯了通奸行为所作的陈述)
discretionary (=discretional) a. 有决定权的;自由决定的,任意的
discretionary act 任意决定的行为
discretionary allowance 特种补助金
discretionary authority 自由酌处权
discretionary costs 自由处置的费用
discretionary credit limit 自定信用限额
discretionary evaluation 自由心证
discretionary intervenor 自由行事的介入诉讼人
discretionary jurisdiction 酌情处理管辖权
discretionary licensing 酌情颁发证件权
discretionary matter 自由裁量性质事项(属自由裁量的事项)
discretionary portion 酌留份(指被继承人生前长期继续抚养的人,依其所受抚养之程度及其关系,由亲属会议商定的酌情所留给一定的遗产份额)
discretionary power 酌处权,自由裁量权
discretionary principle 擅断主义
discretionary reduction 酌减(尤指刑罚)
discretionary right (或 power) (法院的)自由裁量权,自由酌处权
discretionary trust 全权托管;任意决定处分的信托;自由裁量信托
discriminance n. 罪行辨别法,罪行判定法
discriminate v. 区别,辨别;有差别对待
discriminate against 歧视,对……歧视
discrimination n. 1.区别,辨别,识别 2.不平等待遇,差别待遇;歧视
discrimination in effect (美)效果歧视审查法(指法院用以审查州法是否构成地方保护主义立法的主要方法。如果一部法律的实施效果具有歧视性,则在隐性商业条款审查中,该法就可能被认定为歧视性法律。见 Dormant Commerce Clause)
discrimination treatment 差别待遇
discriminatory n. 区别对待
discriminatory law (为保护本国船只以对付外国船只的)有差别的法律;歧视性法律
discriminatory practices 歧视性(贸易)惯例
discriminatory tax 差别(对待的)税制,歧

视性税制
discriminatory terms 歧视性条款
discrown v. 废黜……的王位,使退位
disculpate v. 开脱……罪责;为……辩护
discursive practice 话语实践
discursive struggle 话语斗争(指"全球化"问题)并不是一个事实问题,而是一个话语问题,从法学目前的研究看,这个话语问题基本上被忽略,话语斗争介入全球化之中,实际也是"话语构建"问题。核心是话语争夺权的问题。)
discuss list (美)讨论(案件)目录;讨论(案件)清单(指联邦最高法院管理其承担案件的一种主要司法行政方法。这个目录也是许多小途径之一,通过它首席大法官可以掌握联邦最高法院的议事日程。由于"二战"后案件特多,大法官们便考虑如何选择其中一些重要案件来审理,采取由大法官的法律书记员尽力甄别筛选的一种机制,筛选只有少数被相信有价值的案件才被列入需经大法官周例会讨论的案件目录)
discussion n. 辩论,讨论,商议,论述,详述
discussion of judg(e)ments 裁判评议
disdemeanor fine 轻罪罚金
disease n. (身体或精神上的)疾病,伤害;(社会制度等)不健全状态,弊病
disease caused by public nuisance 公害病
disembededness n. 脱域[指英国 21 世纪著名社会学家吉登斯(Anthony Giddens)给"全球化"赋予经典定义:不能将全球化简单视为某种意识形态的推广,也不能将其看作经济或政治任何一种单项逻辑的扩张,而应从普遍相互联系的角度把握全球化的性质。吉登斯认为全球化是现代性的延伸,是"脱域"属性的深度扩展。"脱域"这一概念最早来自英国经济史学家波兰尼(Vrare Polanyi)。据考证,这一概念是最初是对矿物提炼的隐喻,指涉经济从社会中脱离而出,形成自主历史过程。吉登斯对此进行了创造性的发挥,主张"脱域"是社会关系从彼此互动的地域性关联中,从通过对不确定的时间的无限穿越而被重构的关联中脱离出来。"脱域"的内涵包括三个维度:首先,"脱域"意味着时间与空间的分离,即时间从过去时空一体化的状态中脱离出来,形成"虚化时间",使不同的功能系统形成彼此差异的时间感知,而不再与传统意义上的自然时间重合;其次,"脱域"意味着空间(space)与地点(place)的分离,即空间从它的物理地点的紧密结合中摆脱出来,形成"虚化空间",在"虚化空间"中,权力、符码与认同机制得以重组;最后,"脱域"意味着时间与空间的延伸,即分别"脱域"后的虚化时间和虚化空间在全球层面伸展,并以新的方式彼此结合,形成新的虚拟时空结构。要从这个意义上理解全球化]
disembowel v. 取出……内容;除去……内脏
disemployed a. 失业的
disencumber v. 解除负担,消除忧虑,排除障碍,使摆脱
disendow v. 剥夺(教会的)捐款(或基金);没收
disenfranchisement n. 褫夺公(民)权,剥夺选举权,剥夺特权
disengagement n. 解脱;解雇;解除;解除婚约
disentail v. 解除限定继承权,使(地产)免于限定继承
disentailing deed 解除限定继承权的契据
disentailment n. 限定继承权的解除
disentangle v. 解开,分清;解决(纠纷等)
disentitle v. 剥夺(尊号,头衔或权利等)
disentomb v. 挖墓,自墓中掘出
disestablish v. 使政教分离,解除(官职);废除……的既成状态
disestablishment n. 政教分离;解除官职,废除既成状态
disfavo(u)r v. 不赞成,不喜欢;轻视,蔑视
disfavored action (美)冷遇之诉(指普通法上欺诈是一种受冷遇之诉)
disfigure v. 损毁容颜,破相
disfigurement n. 损形,毁容,破相
disfranchise v. 褫夺公(民)权,剥夺选举权;终止特许权
disfranchisement n. 褫夺公民权,剥夺选举权;终止特许权

disgorgement measure 差价计算法（见 causation-in-fact approach 和 out-of-pocket-measure）
disgrace n. 不名誉,耻辱;罢黜,贬斥,失宠
disguise n. 假装,托辞,佯装;伪装(行为)
disguised cession 变相割让
disguised forms of corporal punishment 变相体罚
disguised gambling 变相赌博
disguiser n. 伪装者,假装者,假扮者
dishabilitate v. 取消(资格),使不合格
disherison n. 剥夺继承权
disheritor n. 剥夺继承权的人
dishonest a. 不忠实的,不诚实的,不正直的,欺诈的
dishonest behaviors 不法行为,恶意行为,欺诈行为
dishonest merchant 奸商
dishonest possession 不法占有,恶意占有
dishonest profits 不正当收益
dishonesty n. 不诚实;诈欺;不正直
dishono(u)r n./v. 1.拒绝承兑;拒付,退票,拒收 2.耻辱,不名誉 3.丢脸的人(或事)/1.无法偿付,拒绝承兑,拒付,退票,拒收 2.奸污;败坏(名誉)
dishono(u)r a woman 奸污(污辱)妇女
dishono(u)r of bill 拒绝承兑汇票
dishono(u)red a. 拒收的,拒付的,无法偿付的
dishono(u)red bill 拒绝承兑的汇票
dishono(u)red cheque 空头支票,拒付的支票
dishono(u)red note 拒付票据
disimprison v. 使自狱中释放
disincorporate v. 解散法人团体(或公司等)
disinfestation n. 防止骚乱,防止侵扰
disinflation n. 通货紧缩
disingenuously ad. 不真诚地,虚伪地,不坦率地,诡诈地
disinherit v. 剥夺继承权
disinheritance n. 剥夺继承权,废嫡
disinherited party 被剥夺继承权的人
disinterested a./n. 公正的,公平的;无偏见的;无私的,(美)漠不关心的,不感兴趣的/无利害关系的证人

disinterested assistance 无私援助
disinterested inquiry 无利害关系的调查,公正的调查
disinterested third party 无利害关系的第三人
disinterested witness 与案件无利害关系的证人
disjecta membra 不连贯的引文,片段
dislodge v. 把……赶出住处(有利地位,占有地方等);取出,移出;离开住处
disloyal elements (美)不忠诚分子
dismantle v. 摧毁,拆卸;脱下,分离;粉碎
dismembered body 碎尸
dismemberment n. 1.分解;肢解,死后分尸 2.(国际法)根据条约或领土合并致使一个国家被瓜分成为一个以上的多个国家;由于合并、割让或一部分分裂独立而造成一个国家领土的减少 3.(国际法)一个国家的消亡,从这个国家领土上产生出一个以上的新国家
dismemberment insurance 四肢残缺保险
dismemberment of nations 民族分裂,国家分裂
dismemberment of property 财产分割
dismemberment of ownership (罗马法)所有权的分解[指三个要素组成所有权的权利:使用权(usus)、孳息(用益权)(fructus)和处理(个人财产)权(abusus)。所有权的权利可以被分割开来,并以独立的物权形式转让,比如使用权、用益权以及财产担保权(right of security)。见 *usus; fructus; abusus*]
dismiss v. 1.让……离开,打发 2.解雇,开除,免职 3.驳回,对……不予受理 4.解散,遣散;消除,不考虑
dismiss a case 了结一个案件;驳回一个案子,不受理一个案子
dismiss a charge 不受理起诉,驳回控告
dismiss an accused 宣告一个被告无罪
dismiss an appeal 驳回上诉
dismissal n. 1.打发;罢免;免职;开除,解雇,解职 2.不予考虑 3.驳回,驳回诉讼(指原告如不在期限内递交索赔陈述,或不申请指示传票,或不披露文据,或不到庭受审,法庭有权驳回该诉讼);撤销诉讼

dismissal agreed 双方当事人无异议的撤销诉讼
dismissal for failure to prosecute 见 dismissal for want of prosecution
dismissal for lack of prosecution 见 dismissal for want of prosecution
dismissal for want of equity 公正的要求驳回起诉(因缺乏实体上的而非程序上的根据而驳回起诉。通常是因为发现原告陈述虚假或原告诉讼请求不充分)
dismissal for want of prosecution 驳回提起公诉要求(指因原告诉讼失败,案件趋于终止,故驳回起诉。缩略为 DWOP,亦称为 dismissal for failure to prosecute; dismissal for lack of prosecution)
dismissal from employment 解聘,解雇
dismissal from(或 of)**office** 撤职,开除公职,免职
dismissal from proceedings 免予起诉
dismissal in disgrace 撤职,革职
dismissal of action 驳回起诉
dismissal of appeal 驳回上诉
dismissal of law case 案件不受理,诉讼不受理
dismissal procedure 免职手续,解雇手续
dismissal statement 免职声明,解雇声明
dismissal with prejudice 有偏袒的驳回(诉讼)(亦称当事人受损害的驳回诉讼,一般指法庭作出带偏袒的裁决驳回诉讼后,排除在任何法庭以同一诉讼理由重新提起诉讼);不可再诉的驳回起诉
dismissal without prejudice 不带偏见的驳回起诉,无偏袒的驳回起诉(指原告有权重新提交起诉状,并使诉讼重新开始。如果被告未放弃送达,且原告在提交起诉状120天内未将起诉状送达被告,则由法院依职权或依申请驳回起诉。简言之,这种驳回诉讼准许以同一理由在再次起诉。见其反义词条 dismissal with prejudice)
dismissals of employees 职工解雇,职工下岗
dismissed for court martial 撤职查办
dismissible a. 可免职的,可解雇的;可不予考虑的
dismissing actions 终结诉讼,驳回诉讼

disobedience n. 不服从(命令);违抗(政令),反抗
disobedience to the award of a court 不服从法院裁定
disobedience to writ 不服从令状
disobedient child 见 incorrigible child
disobedient party 违令者
disorder in the court 法庭的无序,法庭的障碍,法庭的混乱,法庭的违规行为
disorder of intelligence 智力障碍,智力疾病
disorder of mind 心神错乱(精神病的一种)
disordered mind 神经错落的
disordered personality 人格失常
disorderliness in a public place 妨碍公共秩序,妨害社会治安
disorderly a. 妨害治安的,暴乱的,骚乱的;无法无天的,目无法纪的
disorderly conduct 扰乱社会治安行为;不规矩的行为,目无法纪行为
disorderly house 1.无序住房(指人们可在这类住房进行损害邻里的活动)2.妓院,赌场(人们在此进行犯罪和不道德的活动)。亦称(很少用)bowdy house; house of prostitution; house of ill fame; lewd house; assignation house; house of assignation
disorderly person 捣乱分子,危害治安分子
disown v. 声明(同子女)脱离关系,否认……是自己的(东西);否认……与自己有关系;否认……的正确性;否认……的权威性
disparage v. 轻视,贬低;诽谤;侮辱
disparagement n. 诽谤;贬抑;不相称
disparagement of goods 贬低物品质量
disparagement of property (以)诽谤(手段贬损他人)财产(的价值)
disparate impact discrimination 差别影响歧视(指就业歧视的一种,此为根据歧视结构分的)
disparate treatment discrimination 差别待遇歧视
disparate treatment 歧视待遇[美国联邦法律禁止基于种族、肤色、宗教信仰、性

别、国籍、年龄以及残疾等状况给予歧视待遇。但是,在特定情况下允许反向歧视对待,这些情况包括雇主根据有效的积极行为(affirmative action,即纠正以前存在的歧视惯例行为)、计划作出的或雇主能够证明基于宗教信仰、性别、国籍或年龄的区别对待是特殊商业或企业的正常运作所需要的、合理的职业资格的需要]

disparity n. 不同,不等,不一致,悬殊,差距,失调

disparity in age 年龄差别很大

disparity of sentence 判决的差别,量刑差异

dispassionately ad. 不带偏见地,冷静地

dispatch n./v. 1.调遣,派遣 2.就地正法,立即处死 3.迅速办理,迅速了结 4.速遣 5.发送 6.急报/调遣,派遣;杀死,迅速处决;迅速了结

dispatch days 速遣日

dispatch money 速遣费

dispatch money calculation sheet 速遣费计算单

dispatcher n. 发送者,调度员

dispensary system (美)专卖制度,中央配给制度

dispensation n. (教会法)赦免(权);特许权,豁免;执行,施行;处理,处置,统治;分配,分配物

dispense v. 执行,施行(法律等);(with)省却,免除,豁免;分配,给予

dispense with 省却,免除,准许废止;作罢,抛弃,不用

dispensing justice 执行法律,实施法律

dispensing with service 免除劳役;免于送达

disperse v. 退庭;解散(集会);传播;散布;消failure 散

displaced person 被迫流离失所者;难民

display v./n. 展示,表现,陈列,发扬/炫耀,显示,展览,陈列,表现

display of force 武力示威

disponer n. 分产人

disposable a. 可任意处理(或处置)的,可自由使用的;任意的

disposable capital 自由动用的资本

disposable income (或 **earnings**)(扣除所得税后)可自由支配的收入

disposable portion (遗产的)可处分部分

disposal n. 1.安排,布置 2.处理,处分(财产),自由处置权 3.出售,让与 4.财产处分方法(转让或出售)

disposal of criminal 对犯罪的处理

disposal of premises 房产处分权

disposal of stolen goods 销赃

disposal without trial 未经审讯即行终结案件

dispose v. 处理,处置,处分,支配;转让,卖掉,解决,办妥

dispose of a job 办妥一件事

disposing capacity 行为能力,处置能力

disposing capacity of juristic person 法人的行为能力

disposing capacity of the natural person 自然人的行为能力

disposing clause (美)处理条款[指美国联邦宪法(第4条)授予国会处理属于联邦政府财产权力的条款]

disposing judgement 妥当的判断,理性的判断

disposition n. 1.处置,支配,处分;处置权,处分权,支配(财产)权 2.安排,处理,让与;让与证书 3.(对少年的)判决 4.(诉讼)处分原则 5.科刑,宣判 6.庭外录音(调查证据所常用的方法,要求录取证言的律师向了解案件情况的当事人、证人或其他任何人发问,由提供证言者在宣誓后作答)

disposition contract 处分合同

disposition of goods 处理货物

disposition of land 土地处分

disposition of life-time 生前处分,使不再占有

disposition of property 财产权的处分,物权的处分;所有权的处分

disposition-contract n. 处分合同(契约)

dispositionsmaxim n. 处分权主义(大陆法系的一种诉讼理论,指举凡对在民事诉讼程序中有关起诉、诉讼终止、终结和诉讼标的等方面的决定,当事人拥有主动权的一种主义);职权探知主义

dispositive (dispository) a. 决定性的,结

论性的/不需改变的
dispositive facts 决定性事实(指引起法律关系变更或消灭的事实,即法律事实);决定性证据;处分性事实(指导致权利授予或丧失的事实)
dispositive issue (or fact) 决定性的问题(或事实)
dispositive law 任意法
dispositive matters (美)处置性事项(指诉讼中能够处置全部或部分案件的事件,诸如驳回案件或请求的动议。未经当事人双方同意,治安法官不得就处置事项作出最后决定,而必须向地区法官提出报告或建议。见 nondispositive matters)
dispositive power 处分权
dispossess v. 抢夺,霸占;剥夺;逐出
dispossess proceedings (美)腾让(房屋等)诉讼
dispossessed a. 无依无靠的;失去财产的;被逐出的
dispossession n. 剥夺;抢夺;强占;没收
dispossession of land 强占土地
dispossessor n. 夺取(他人财物,土地)者
disproof n. 反证,反证物;反驳,反驳证据
disproportionate control 不相称的控制
disproportionately ad. 不相称地,不均衡地,非比例地
disproval n. 反证,反驳
disprove v. 证明……不成立;反驳,驳斥;举反证
disputable a. 可争论的;可质疑的;可反驳的;不一定的
disputable presumption 可以反驳的推定,不确实的推定
disputant n. 争论者,辩论者,争执者
dispute n./v. 争端;争执;纠纷;争辩;争议;竞争/争执,争端;对……提出争辩(质疑),对……提出异议
dispute among the people 民间纠纷
dispute at law 法律争执,法律纠纷
dispute concerning private rights 民事权利的争议,私权争议
dispute concerning property 财产权的争议
dispute of competency 权限争执

dispute over obligation 债务纠纷
Dispute Resolution Board (DRB) 争议审查委员会,争议和解委员会
dispute resolution policy 争端解决政策
dispute settlement 和解协议;纠纷解决
dispute settlement mechanism (DSM) (WTO)争端解决机制
dispute the validity of a document 指出(对方提供的)文件有效性的争议
dispute to arbitration 提交仲裁,提交公断
disputed a. 有争执的
disputed debt 有争议的债权
disputed property 有争议的财产
disputes arising from discovery 因调查取证程序而产生的争议
disputes perse 自身的争议
disqualification n. 无资格,不合格;取消资格
disqualifications for voting 无投票资格
disqualified person 被取消资格者
disqualify v. 取消……资格,使不合格
disregard n. 不理,不顾,漠视,无视
disregard for 漠视,忽视
disregard of law 无视法律;置法律于不顾;违反法律
disregard the corporate entity (或 **personality**) 否认公司人格(英美国家称为 to pierce the corporate veil,指在具体法律关系中,基于特定事由否定法人的独立人格和股东的有限责任,对之重新配置义务或责任的法律制度,其适用的通常结果——使股东在某些情况下对法人债务人承担无限责任或撇开法人的存在重新确定股东应承担的法律义务)
disrepute n. 不名誉,声名狼藉,不受欢迎
disrupt v. 使崩溃,分张,互解,使混乱,破坏
disrupt the legal process 使法律程序混乱
disruption n. 破坏,分裂,瓦解
dissave v. 动用储蓄金
disseise (或 **disseize**) v. 强夺,强占(他人财产),霸占,侵占
disseisee n. 被强占地产者;被强夺者,被侵占者,被逐出者
disseisin (**disseizin**, 或 **dissasine**) n. 强占

地产;强夺,霸占;被强占状态
disseisor n. 强夺他人地产者;强占者,侵占者
dissemination n. 传播(思想,理论等);散布
dissension n. 异议;纷争,意见分歧;冲突
dissent n./v. (个别或少数法官对多数法官所持有的)异议(或不同意见);不尊奉国教/持异议,不同意;(英)不信国教
dissenter n. 持异议者(尤指不同政见的);反对者,老是唱反调者;(大写)(英)不尊奉国教者
dissentiente (个别或少数法官对多数法官所持有的)异议(或不同意见)
dissenting a. 不同意的,不赞成的
dissenting judg(e)ments 有分歧的判决
dissenting judges 不同意的法官
dissenting opinion 反对意见;(某法官的)异议
dissenting tradition 异端的传统
dissenting vote 反对票
dissertations n. 论述,(学位)论文;学术演讲
dissident n. 持不同政见者;唱反调者;背离国教者
dissident constitution groups 持不同政见的宪法团体
dissident element 持不同政见分子
dissociate v. (不赞成,不支持)分开,退伙,使分离
dissociation n. 解离(指一种症状,感觉某种东西在体内乱窜,伴有相应的负性情绪体验,更有重者会出现幻觉、妄想、思维紊乱、自言自语,行为失控或怪异精神状态。这种情况往往是练气功后的精神障碍。这种人不宜再练气功,具有限定刑事责任能力)
dissolution n. 1.解散(指议会,公司等);解散权 2.(合同,婚约等)解除 3.结束;取消,终止 4. 死亡;消亡;瓦解
dissolution of adoption 终止收养
dissolution of company 公司的解散
dissolution of contract 解除合同(契约)
dissolution of engagement 解除婚约
dissolution of injunction 取消禁(止)令
dissolution of juristic person 法人的解散
dissolution of marriage 婚姻的终止,解除婚姻关系(见 dissolving a marriage)
dissolution of parliament 解散议会
dissolution of partnership 终止合伙关系;拆伙,散伙
dissolution of responsibility 免除责任
dissolution of restitution 免除赔偿
dissolution of stock company 解散股份公司
dissolution of trade union 解散工会
dissolution of treaty 条约的终止,解除条约
dissolve v. 解散,解除,取消;废除;宣告无效
dissolved corporation 终止的公司
dissolving a marriage 解除婚姻关系,离婚(一般用 divorce,而不用 dissolution of marriage;但在美国,采用无过失或除"感情破裂而无法修复旧好"外的不列举具体离婚原因之"离婚",不称 divorce 而称 dissolution of marriage)
dissuade v. 劝阻,劝止
dissuading a witness 收买(贿赂)证人(为人作证)
distant a. 远的,远隔的;疏远的,冷淡的
distant bullet wound 远射枪弹创(伤)
distant defendants 远距离被告
distant fora 异地的法院,远距离的法院
distant relatives 远亲属
distant-water state 远海国(家)
distilled liquor 用蒸馏方法制成的烈性酒或含酒精之饮料
distilled spirits 见 distilled liquor
distinct a. 独特的,性质截然不同的;确定无误的,明显的
distinction n. 区分,区别,差别,特性,卓著,荣誉(称号),勋章
distinctions between the enemy and ourselves 分清敌我界限
distinctive a. 区别性的;鉴别性的,与众不同的,独特的,有特色的
distinctive circumstances 不同情节
distinctive innovations 区别性创新
distinctive nature of characteristics 不同

性质
distinctive quality （商标的）显著性
distinctiveness n. （商标的）显著性
distinguish v. 区别,辨别,识别;把……区别分类
distinguish among differing cases 区别不同情况(案件)
distinguishing n. （英美法）识别（指认定被作为先例的案件的事实问题与法律要点与正在审理案件有不同之处的一种处理技巧,也是新分析实证主义法学家拉兹改变现行英美法规则的三种办法之一。见 closure rule）;区别,辨别;区别分类
distinguishment of crime from noncrime 区别罪与非罪
distort v. 歪曲,曲解,篡改
distortion n. 畸变;歪曲,曲解
distortion of fact 歪曲事实
distortion of interest 利益的扭曲
distrain v. 扣押(动产);(为抵债而)扣押(财产)
distrainee n. 财产被扣押者
distrainer (= distrainor) n. 扣押他人财产者
distrainment n. 扣押财产
distraint n. 扣押财物,扣押;强制执行
distress v. 扣押(财产);使烦恼
distress （或 **distraint**）n. 扣押(通常指地主因租户欠租,将租户的东西扣押起来;有时指把侵害权利人的动产交给被侵害人来收管,使其得到被侵害权利的清偿);扣押物;痛苦,不幸;遇难
distress call 遇难呼救,求救呼号
distress (of) damage-feasant 牲畜损害赔偿的留置权(指对闯入他人土地造成损害的牲畜,土地占有人有权当场留置该牲畜,以便请求赔偿)
distress for rent 欠租扣押
distress sale 扣押物拍卖
distress signal 遇难信号;求救信号
distress warrant 财产扣押令
distributable pool account 可分配的共同基金账户
distribute v. 1.分配;分割 2.按类别排序;按序排列 3.交付 4.传播,散布

distribute the cargo 配载货物
distributee n. 被分配到财产的人
distribution n. （14世纪）1.遗产分配（指将私人财产分配给无遗嘱死亡者的继承人,特别是在实现动产支付抵偿其债务和其他人针对不动产提出权利主张之后分配财产的程序。见 descent 1）2.按比例分配或授予的行为或程序 3.(信托法)分配额,支付额(指向信托受益人支付或贷记款项) 4.(证券)发行,募集(指发行人自行或通过承销机构公开发行证券) 5.支付(指合伙以现金或财产方式向合伙人支付款项)
distribution cost （商品的）供销费用
distribution of assets 资产分配
distribution of judicial power to make rules of decision 制定判决依据的司法权的分配(或配置)
distribution of powers 权力的分配
distribution of profit and loss 损益分配
distribution of profits 利润分配
distribution of property 财产分配
distribution of surplus 剩余资产的分配
distribution of wealth and income 财富和收入的分配
distribution on the basis of labo(u)r 按劳分配
distribution system 分配制度,配给制度
distributional consequence 财产分配的后果
distributism n. 分产主义(主张把私人财产,特别是土地重新进行分配的一种主义)
distributist n. 分产主义者
distributive a. 分配的;分布的,分发的;普及的
distributive agreement 分配协定
distributive bargaining 分配性协商
distributive finding （美）寻找有利于每一方的陪审团
distributive function 分布函数
distributive justice 分配正义(指涉及团体对个人的义务,要求在个人间的权利与义务公平分配,根据个体的价值与行为与他人比较获得相当的权利与义务)

distributive trade 经销(行)业
distributor (=distributee) n. 经销商,分发者,分配者,货物配售人,商行;散布者;转播组织(见 originating organization)
district n. 地区;区域;地方,管区;(中)(直辖市和较大的市所辖的)区,县;(英)郡;(美)(各州的)众议员选区
district attorney (美)地方检察官(又译地区检察官)
district auditor 地方(区)审计官
district council 地方(区)议会
district court (美)(联邦系统的)地区法院,(州系统的)地方初审法院;地方法院,地区法庭(全国共94个)
district court-martial 地区军事法庭
district government 地区政府,地方政府
district judge (美)地区法官(指经参议院批准,由总统任命联邦地区的法官,亦称"第三条法官",因他们的审判权出自美国联邦宪法第3条)
district jurisdiction 地区管辖权,地方管辖范围
District of Columbia Code (美)《哥伦比亚特区法典》
District of Columbia 哥伦比亚特区(指美国首府华盛顿所在地的行政区)
district public prosecution's office 区检察院,(日)区检察厅
district registry 地方法院注册处,地区登记处
district tribunal 地区法庭,区法庭
distringas n. (英)强制到庭扣押令(指英国旧法庭所发出要求地方司法行政官扣押不到庭的被告人的财产,以便强制他到庭的一种命令)
distringas juratores (英)强制陪审员到庭扣押令
distrust n./v. 不信任,怀疑
disturb v. 滋扰,扰乱,妨碍,妨害
disturb(或 **break**)**the peace** 扰乱治安
disturbance n. 骚动,动乱;扰乱,(治安的)妨害,(权利的)侵犯
disturbance clause 内乱整治条款
disturbance of common 侵犯公有地,侵犯公有权

disturbance of coordination 干扰协作
disturbance of franchise 侵犯特许权;侵犯选举权;侵犯公民权;(美)侵犯(私人公司经营公共事业的)特许权
disturbance of public worship 妨害宗教信仰
disturbance of tenure 侵犯租借地
disturbance of the peace 妨害治安
disturbing the peace 扰乱邻居安宁,扰乱邻里生活秩序;妨害治安(罪)
disuse n./v. 不用;废弃/废弃,不用
disutility n. 负效用,反效用
divalgation n. 发表[指作者精神权利中的"发表权",在版权法中经常用 the Right of Divalgation (如西班牙1986年版权法)。它指作者对其作品是否公之于世的决定权,有的国家把发表权表达为"the right to make a work public"]
divan n. 1.烟馆,吸毒(品)馆 2.(土耳其等的)国务会议;法院
diverge v. 分歧,背驰,偏要(from),分义,分歧;离题,使发向
divergence n. 分歧,背驰,离题,异议
diverse citizenship to forum shop 不同籍公民选择法院,异籍当事人选择法院
diverse peoples 形形色色的不同民族
diversification n. 多样化,多种经营
diversified farm 多种经营的农场
diversify v. 使多样化,增加品种
diversion certificate 绕航证书
diversion clause 绕航条款
diversion law (美)转化法(指州的一种程序,即若毒品犯罪之初交付管教,如在管教期内,经教育、管教之影响而不再犯罪即可取消对罪犯之指控,并密封其罪行记录)
diversion model 转处模式(指刑事和解模式之一,即在罪犯被逮捕后起诉前,由和解中介机构进行和解。这种模式很大程度上依赖司法机关提供逮捕的和审判前的案件。见 community model)
diversion program 改邪归正(改弦易辙)计划
diversionary manoeuvres 转移目标的手法
diversion n. 转移,转向,绕航

diversity n. (刑事诉讼中,囚犯为阻止执行而提出的)其本人并非被所判该刑者的申诉;多样性;变更

diversity action 异籍诉讼

diversity action for personal injury 人身伤害的异籍诉讼

diversity case(s) (美)异籍案件(指涉及不同州公民的原告和被告的案件,或关系美国公民和外国人的案件)(见 diversity jurisdiction)

diversity jurisdiction (美)联邦法院异籍管辖权(指不同州的公民之间或州的公民与外侨之间所发生的诉讼管辖权,亦称 diversity of citizenship)

diversity of citizenship case (美)民事异籍案件(见 diversity case)

diversity of citizenship (美)异籍管辖权,联邦法院异籍管辖权

diversity of person (罪行判决者)囚犯因身份不同的答辩

diversity of status 身份(或地位)的变更

diversity litigation 异籍诉讼

diversity suits (美)异籍诉讼;(因囚犯关于自己并非受处刑判决的真正罪犯而)请求终止执行判决的申诉

diversity statute (美)异籍(管辖)制定法[指该制定法要求纠纷额超过75000美元,28USCA 1332 (a)]

diverso intuitu 以不同看法;以不同意图

divert v. 转移;转向;使转向;牵制

dives costs (英)较高的诉讼费用(这是衡平法庭的惯例,意思是应按通常公平原则负担诉讼费用。用以反对合格贫民起诉或上诉只用拿得出的钱来支付诉讼费用或免除费用)

divest v. 1.剥夺(他人地产或权益),抢夺,掠夺 2.放弃

divest (of) 剥夺某种权利

divestitive fact 剥夺权利性事实,消灭权利事实

divestiture n. (财产,权力等的)剥夺;放弃财产令(法院依照反托拉斯法向被告发出的一种令状,要求被告放弃自己的财产等以防贸易垄断);取消(称号、职位)

divestiture proceeding 放弃财产令状之诉(见 divestiture)

divide v. 分配(财产等),分担;分享;分歧(意见);分开,隔离

divide out the costs 补偿诉讼费用,分担诉讼费

divided a. 可分的,可离的,分裂的,意见分歧的

divided country 分裂的国家

divided court (美)(上诉法院中对特殊案件)法官意见不一致的法院,法官意见有分歧的法院;意见分歧的联邦法院大法官

divided custody (夫妇离婚后对子女的)分开监护制(在美国指离婚后子女的抚养监护由父母分开安排,其缺点是孩子来往于父母之间可能造成混乱和不安全;好处是子女都认父母。过去通常由母方监护或抚养,父方只有探视权利,而现在美国趋向于父母双方共同监护抚养,母方单方监护不再视为最好的方式)

divided government 分裂政府

divided panel of the Court of Appeals 上诉法院的不同意见陪审团名单

divided second circuit panel 有分歧的第二巡回上诉法庭合议庭

divided vote 分歧的表决,分歧的投票

divided world of state court personal and property jurisdiction 州法院对人和对物管辖的分裂状况

dividend n. 公债利息,股息;盈余;红利;破产债权人的偿金

dividend account 股息账户

dividend at a stated rate 按固定的股率

dividend cheque 股息支票,股息券

dividend coupon 股利券,股息票

dividend on preferred stock 优先股息

dividend payable 应付未付股息

dividend receivable 应收股利(息)

dividend reserve 股息准备金

dividend stock 股利(息)股份,股利(息)股票;红利股

dividend warrant 领取股息通知单,股息单

dividends on investments 投资股息

dividing strait 分水海峡

divine a./v. 神的;神圣的,敬神的;神学的;神授的;天才的/预言,批判
divine law 神圣法(指上帝制定的法律,不同于人制定的法律,有时也分自然法和神启法"revealed law"和实在法两类)
divine positive law 神的实在法(指圣经)
divine revelation 神圣的启示,神圣的新发现
divine right 王权神授
divine right of Kings 君权神授
divinely ordained state 神授法制国家
divining the correct limits of the stated test 推测(或预测)具体标准的正确界限
divinity n. 神性,神威,神德,上帝;(大写)神学,神学院;令人敬拜的人,令人崇拜之人
divisa n. (古英国法)1.裁决;判决 2.财产遗赠 3.(教区或农田的)界限
divisible a. 可分的,可分割的
divisible contract 可分合同(契约)(指一个合同为不同的履行规定了不同的对价者,称为可分合同)
divisible letter of credit 可分割信用证
divisible obligation 可分之债(指与indivisible obligation 相对而言)
divisible property 可分财产
divisible thing 可分物
division n. 遗产分割(配);意见分歧;区域,(英)选举区;专区,(法院)分庭;章节;部门,科室;(英)议会分组表决;(英)(对监狱犯人的待遇实行的)分别制;分部;部分
division of an ascendant's property 分割祖产
division of common property 分配共同财产
division of court 法院的分院(庭)
division of estates 遗产分割
division of functions and powers 职权的划分
division of labor 劳动分工,劳动部门,劳工分支机构
division of labo(u)r responsibility system 分工负责制
division of powers 权力分配;分权制

division of responsibility 责任分摊
divisional a. 分开的,分割的;分区的,分部的
divisional court 下属法院,分区法院;分庭
Divisional Court of the High Court (英)高等法院的法区分庭(指由高等法院各庭的 2 个或 3 个法官所组成的法庭)
divisional instruction 警察的分区训令
divisional system (英史)分级服刑制度
divisions of the high court (英)高等法院各庭(指英国 1925 年起高等法院组建的三个法庭:①衡平法庭;②后座庭;③遗嘱检验、离婚、海事庭)
divisions of the law 法的分类
division-separation of power 割裂式的权力分立
divisive issue 制造分裂问题,分裂问题
divisum imperium 分别的管辖权,可选择的管辖权
divorcé (法)离了婚的男子
divorce n. 离婚,分离,脱离
divorce a mensa et thoro (夫妻)分居(指保留夫妻关系,但不共寝食)
divorce a vinculo matrimonii (完全解除婚姻关系约束的)离婚
divorce by agreement 协议离婚
divorce by mutual consent 两愿离婚
divorce case 离婚案件
divorce certificate 离婚证书
divorce conciliation 离婚调解
divorce court 离婚法庭
divorce decree (美)离婚令[指离婚诉讼中的终局判决。离婚令终止婚姻关系,并通常解决所有涉及的财产问题和子女抚养教育问题。总之,如果在环境或情况方面有实质的改变,在离婚后诉讼(post-divorce action)中有关子女问题的规定还可修改]
divorce division 离婚法庭;(大写)(英)(高等法院的)遗嘱检验,离婚和海事法庭(即现在的家事法庭)
divorce from bed and board (夫妻)分居(见 divorce a mensa et thoro)
divorce from the bond of matrimony 解除婚姻关系的离婚(见 divorce a vinculo mat-

rimonii)
divorce mediation 离婚调解
divorce petition 离婚申请(书)
divorce proctor (美)离婚监护人,离婚代理人(指在离婚诉讼中被任命为代理人或监护人,目的在于保护州的利益和子女的利益,有时可简称为 proctor)
divorce proceedings 离婚诉讼
divorce racket 以敲诈勒索扶养费为目的的离婚案
divorce registry 离婚登记处
divorce requirement 离婚的要件
divorce shadowings 离婚纠缠
divorcée (法)离了婚的女子
divorcě(e) n. 离了婚的(人)
divorcer n. 提出离婚者
divortium 1.(罗马法)离婚(指已结合婚姻的分裂。古代传统法中对离婚并无什么条件要求。见 *repudium*)2.(教会法)允准夫妻离异的裁决令(decree)或宣告他们婚姻无效的判决(decree)
divortium a mensa et thoro (寺院法)分居
divortium a vinculo matrimonii (寺院法)离婚
divulge v. 泄露,公布,宣布
diyah (伊斯兰教法)人命赔偿(指杀人流血者按传统应支付的赔偿)
DLOP docket 同 DWOP docket, doowop docket
DNA identification (1987)脱氧核糖核酸鉴定,DNA 鉴定[指基于一个人的遗传基因结构进行科学鉴定的方法,特别是对一个人唯一的脱氧核糖核酸(Deoxyribonucleic acid,即 DNA)进行比较——验明遗传信息(genetic information)中的化学结构形式——即通过对生物标本(biological specimen)(如用血液,人体组织毛发等)的 DNA 进行鉴定确认该人是否是这个标本的来源。DNA 证据在刑事案件中常用来达到鉴定受害人的遗体(victim's remains)后再鉴别相关的犯罪嫌疑人,并且证明嫌疑犯无辜的目的。亦称为 DNA fingerprinting; genetic fingerprinting; DNA profiling; DNA typing。见 human-leukocyte antigen test]

DNA Deoxyribonucleic acid(脱氧核糖核酸)的缩写[核定或核元件(in cell nuclei)的双螺旋结构(double-helix structure)中带有绝大多数活着的人体组织(living organisms)的遗传信息]
do v. 做,干;作为,行动;尽(力),给予,照应
do away with(to) 去除,废除,去掉
do it all (美俚)服无期徒刑
do justice 公平对待
do justice to 公平对待,公平评判
do ut des 以物换物
do violence (to sb.) (对某人)施以暴力
do wrong 做坏事,作恶
do-it-yourself divorce (美)自助离婚(见 Do-It-Yourself Divorce Law)
Do-It-Yourself Divorce Law (= No-Hard-Feelings Divorce Law) (美)自助离婚法(指美国最先由加州 1978 年制定的作为家庭法中许多自由创新的一种法律。该法规定准允具有有限财产而结婚不满两年的无子女夫妻,只要交付 50 美元,就可以获准离婚,而无需请律师和法院解决)
dock n./v. 1.被告席;犯人栏 2.(美)码头,船坞;(英)站台/1.(惩罚性的)剥夺,扣去,减少(工资)2.停靠码头,拖入船坞
dock an entail 撤销限定继承权
dock brief (或 **dock defence**) (英)罪犯委托律师在法庭上辩护;律师在法庭上的辩护要点或答辩;(英)律师给无钱被告的免费辩护
dock receipt (海商法)码头单据,码头收货单[指由海运公司签发的一个临时单据证明货物已在码头,被指定人可凭此单据享有请求承运人向他签发提单、货运单和其他运输单据的权利。依据商业惯例,此单据亦被视为一种权利凭据(document of title)。亦称 dock warrant]
dock warrant 仓库凭单,码头单据(同 dock receipt)
dockage n. 1.码头捐,码头费;入坞费,船坞费 2.船坞设备 3.(薪给,供应,津贴,经费等的)削减,扣除
docket n./v. 1.摘要,概要 2.判决摘要书,备审案件目录表,议事日程 3.(英)法院积

案,诉讼摘录 4. 关税完纳证 5.货物上的签条/将……记入判决录;摘记;见证;附上签条

docket call (美)法院的会议,法庭的会议(指此种会议有律师和一些当事方出庭报告他们案情的情况。比如:他们可以宣布为审判已准备就绪或报告诉讼请求的安排,也常用简化语 to docket 来表示)

docket clerk 备审案件书记员

docket congestion 待审案件积压

docket fee 立案费,(美)律师费

docket judgment 记录判决

docket number 备审案件目录编号

dockmaster 船坞长;(英国法)指挥船舶停泊、开离以避免商务障碍的官员

doctor n. 博士;医生

Doctor of Juridical Science 法律科学博士,法学博士[指 J. D. 和 LL. M 之外的法学毕业生法律学位。缩写为 S. J. D.或 J. S. D.也可用术语: Doctor of Judicial Science; Doctor of the Science of Jurisprudence; Doctor of the Science of Law]

doctor of jurisprudence (或 laws) 法学博士

doctor of Muslim law 伊斯兰教法神学博士

Doctor's Commons 民法博士会(指 1511 年以来,在英国的大学里受过大陆法知识教育的法官和律师们形成的一个特殊的行会)

doctors of the civil law 罗马法学博士

Doctrina plecitandi (法)《判例评注》(1677 年出版)

doctrinairism n. 教条主义,空谈理论

doctrinal inquiry 理论咨询

doctrinal interpretation 学理解释

doctrinal shifts 理论的变迁

doctrinal writer 原理作者

doctrinal writing 原理的著述

doctrine n. (14 世纪)1.原则,原理,特别指法律原则或受到广泛支持的原理 2.(古)裁决、判决中获得的原理(见 holding ①)

doctrine of absolute equalization 绝对平均主义

doctrine of acceleration (较预期要)早获得的(财产权益)原则

doctrine of act of state 国家行为说(指否认地方司法部门可以合法审判外国国家行为和反对外事行为采用本国行政机构发表声明的一种理论)

doctrine of analogy 类推原则

doctrine of bilateral relation 双边关系说

doctrine of cannon range 大炮射程说(指主张领海宽度以大炮射程 3 海里为限)

doctrine of charitable immunity (美)慈善团体豁免权原则(指医院、学术机构及其他慈善团体对其成员所犯侵权行为不承担责任的旧原则。此原则来源于 Swift v. Tyson,现此判例已被联邦最高法院推翻)

doctrine of coercion 胁迫主义、威胁主义(指威胁要某人揭发某一秘密,以使某人受到憎恨、歧视或嘲弄或损害其良好信誉)

doctrine of common employment 共同雇员原则

doctrine of consideration (英美法)对价学说

doctrine of constitutional supremacy 宪法至上原则

doctrine of constitutive character of recognition (国家)承认构成说

doctrine of contiguity 毗连主义(指主张沿海国对其邻接领海之公海区内有行使必要的管制权的一种学说)

doctrine of *continental shelf* 大陆架原则

doctrine of continuous transportation 继续运输主义

doctrine of continuous voyage 继续航海主义(指主张第三国运输货物到中立港口再转运往敌方,视为单一航程或单一运输,以避免海上拦截的一种学说)

doctrine of *corpus delicti* 尸体证据原则

doctrine of equivalents (= equivalents doctrine) (专利法)等同论(指两项发明的功能相同,可以实质相同方式使用并产生实质相同结果);均等论

Doctrine of Erie Railroad Co. v. Tompkins (美)伊利铁路公司诉汤普金(见 Erie doctrine 及 Erie R Co. v. Tompkins)

doctrine of exhaustion 权利用尽原则

(the) doctrine of exhaustion of legal remedies 穷尽法律救济原则(亦称"穷尽原则",指将价值序列中更为重要的宪法救济,在时间序列中安置在相关救济被穷尽之后出场,换言之,即当事人通常须依循先法律救济后宪法救济的顺序救济)

doctrine of fellow-servant 同共雇员原则

doctrine of forum non-conveniens 不方便法院原则[亦称"非方便法院原则"或"不便管辖原则"]。学术界对此有不同主张。一种主张认为"不方便法院原则"是指在涉外民事诉讼中,当原告向某国法院对被告提起诉讼以后,有时被告认为他在该国应诉得不到公正对待。于是他以该国法院为不方便法院(forum non-convenience)为由要求终止诉讼。见 forum no competens]

doctrine of identification (诉讼)合一主义

doctrine of immunity from process 免于传票送达原则(指在美国,有身份和有地位的人如国会议员或立法机关的人可在民事上免于传票送达)

doctrine of incorporation 并入说(指 WTO 争端解决机制适用什么样的法律审理贸易争端,有两种学术观点:开放性法律体系的"并入说"与仅适用 WTO 涵盖协定的"自足说"理论)

doctrine of informed consent "告知后同意"法则(指医师有法律上的义务,用病人了解的语言主动告知其病情,可能治疗之方案、风险、后果,以利病人之选择,取得病人之告知后的同意后进行医疗之行为,医师应对此行为所产生后果承担责任)

doctrine of law 法律原理,法律学说

doctrine of liberal construction 从宽解释原则(说)

doctrine of limited government 政府权力有限说

doctrine of marshalling (处理破产、遗产时)按顺序分配原则

doctrine of materiality 重要性原则,重点原则

doctrine of mitigation 减轻损害原则,或者说是否允许被告提出"原告未减轻损害抗辩"(failure to mitigate defause)(所谓减轻损害原则是指原告受损害后,应采取合理努力,减轻被告违法行为给其造成的损害程度,否则扩大的损失部分不可获得赔偿)

doctrine of mutuality 相互性原理,相关性原则

doctrine of nationwide minimum contacts 国家范围最低联系原则

doctrine of natural rights 自然权利说

doctrine of necessity 必要原则

doctrine of non-equivalent 不均等论

doctrine of non-intervention 不干涉主义

doctrine of non-recognition (美)(国务卿史汀生于1932年所宣布的)不承认主义

doctrine of non-responsibility 无责任说,不负责任说

doctrine of *pari delicto* 同等过错原则(指法院不会帮助执行无效或非法合同的原则)

doctrine of part performance 部分履行原则

doctrine of perception 了解主义

doctrine of (judicial) precedent (司法)判例学说,(司法)先例原则

doctrine of primary jurisdiction 初审管辖权原则

doctrine of private rights 私权主义,私权原理

doctrine of privity 合同的相对性原则;合同的相互关系原理

doctrine of privity of contract 合同关系说(指合同上的损害赔偿,只能以合同关系为依据,例如消费者与制造商间无合同关系便不得提出损害赔偿之诉)

doctrine of reception 受信主义

doctrine of *res inter alios acta* 他人行为排斥主义

doctrine of *res ipsa loquitur* 事实推定原则;明显过失主义

doctrine of retroactivity (法律)溯及既往原则

doctrine of standing 正义(或正当)的原理

doctrine of *stare decisis* (英)遵循先例原则,判例约束说

doctrine of state immunity 国家豁免权学说(原则)
doctrine of strict construction 从严解释原则(说)
doctrine of subjective interpretation 主观解释原则
doctrine of supremacy of law 法律至上原则(说)
doctrine of the balance of power 均势主义
doctrine of the binding force of precedent (英)受先例效力约束原则
doctrine of the presumption of innocence 无罪推定原则
doctrine of the unity of the domicile of husband and wife 夫妻住所同一说
doctrine of ultra vires 能力外原则(指法人权利能力受目的事业范围的限制,在英美法被称为能力外原则。它是由Ashburg Railway Carriage & Iron Co. v. Riche 一案确立的,大陆法系各国多以法人目的事业范围制度严格规制法人的活动经营范围,法人的行为不得逾越目的事业范围)
doctrine of undisclosed principal 隐名代理原则
doctrine of unilateral relation 片面关系说
doctrine of uti possidetis 占有主义
doctrine of utterance 发言主义
document n./v. (15世纪) 1.文件,文书[指有文字记录和一些有含义的符号、标记的载体。参见《联邦民事诉讼规则》第34(a)条]/从传统来说,这个词(term)包含具有信息的一张纸,当今这个词也包含已被储存在电脑的信息
document a text 为正文提供文件(或旁证)
document against acceptance 承兑交单
document against payment 付款交单
document against payment after sight 远期付款交单
document against payment sight 即期付款交单
document collection 跟单托收
document draft 押汇汇票
document examination 文据审查
document for claim 索赔证件
document for service 送达文件
document issuing agency 发文机关
document of agreement 协议文据,协定文件
document of annuity 年金证书
document of control 统驭单(证)
document of international law 国际法文件
document of juristic act 法律行为文据
document of obligation 债权证书,债据
document of resolution 决议文件
document of search 搜查证
document of settlement 结算单据
document of the case 诉讼卷宗
document of title (英美法条的)提单(其法律性质可归结为有价证券,现代经济生活中是转让和流通);权利证据,权利凭证[指持有此凭证者(通常为受托人 bailee)有权接受、持有和处置该凭证中所列的货物,如提单、码头收据、码头提货单等。见 dock receipt]
document of title to goods 货物所有权凭证
document of value 价值证明书
document to land 土地权证,土地文据
document transaction 单据交付
documental a. 公文的,证书的,文件的,据的,证券的
documental credit 证券债权
documental obligation 证券债务
documentary a. 公文的,证书的,文件的,文据的;记录的,纪实的
documentary acceptance 跟单承兑
documentary bill 跟单票据,交换提单票据
documentary bill of exchange 跟单汇票
documentary collection 跟单托收
documentary collection through banks 银行跟单托收
documentary (letter of) credit 跟单信用证,押汇信用证(对比 clean credit)
documentary draft 跟单汇票
documentary evidence (18世纪)书证,书面证据,以书面文件为表现形式的证据在

被采信之前一般要经过认证(＝form of document)
documentary evidence of medicolegal expertise 法医鉴定(书)
documentary form 公文格式
documentary materials 档案材料
documentary negotiation 书面谈判
documentary promissory note 跟单期票
documentary proof 单据证明;文件证明
documentary sources of law 法的文件渊源,文件性法律渊源
documentation n. 证明文件(或文件证书等)的提供(或使用);备办文件(指代犯人填制的文件,如捺印指纹、照相、填写姓名、住址、登记罪行等项的文件)
documentation act 文据提供法
Dodd-Frank Act (美)《多德·弗兰克法》(指 2010 年联邦制定法,该法的旨意在于通过改善金融系统的责任性和透明度将促进美国金融的稳定性。此法规几乎影响到联邦的每一机构和覆盖金融或消费者保护的管辖区,甚至还影响到金融服务产业部门,亦称 Dodd-Frank Wall Street Reform & Consumer Protection Act)
Dodd-Frank Wall Street Reform & Consumer Protection Act 见 Dodd-Frank Act
dodge n. 推托、搪塞;躲闪,规避
dodger n. 推托者;规避者;用诡计蒙骗者;躲闪者
dodgery n. 推托;躲避;蒙骗;欺诈;施行诡计
dodgery John (英美法)诉讼中假设的当事人
doer n. 行为人,实行者;代理人,律师
doer of omission 不作为的人
dog-ear n./v. 书的折角/将书折角
dogma n. 信条,教条,教义;独断之见
dogmatic separation of powers 教条的分权,教条的权力分立
Doha Development Agenda 多哈发展议程
Doha Round Negotiation 多哈回合谈判[指 2001 年 11 月在卡塔尔首都多哈召开的世界贸易组织(WTO)第四次部长会议上,与会的 142 个成员方通过了《多哈部长宣言》,决定自 2002 年 1 月 31 日正式启动新一轮的多边贸易谈判,即多哈回合谈判]
doing a thing negligently 玩忽从事
doing business 经营事业,经营商业,做生意,经营
doing "businessnotion" of jurisdiction 管辖的"经营"概念
doing justice 匡扶正义
dole n. 失业救济;(苏格兰)犯意
dolesman n. 接受失业救济者
doli capax 应负责任的,应受惩罚的;有犯罪能力的,有犯意的
doli incapax 不应负责任的,不应受惩罚的;无犯罪能力的,无犯意的
dolo 欺诈,恶意,预谋
* ***Dolo malo pactumse non servaturum.*** An agreement induced by fraud is not valid. 靠欺诈达成的协议是无效的。
dolose(或 **dolous**)a. 欺诈的;有犯罪意图的
dolus (罗马法及大陆法)1.诈欺,欺骗;蓄意诈骗某人,恶意[诈骗包含有恶意(*dolus*),即使可能存有恶意而未诈骗]2.蓄意侵犯;有意或故意伤害,损害,特别是故意损害财产,亦称 dolus malus; fraus
dolus antecedens 事前犯意
dolus bonus 善意欺诈(罗马法)
* ***Dolus circuitu non purgatur.*** Fraud is not purged by circuity. 欺诈靠拐弯抹角的方法是洗刷不掉的。
dolus dans locum contractui 因诈欺或虚伪陈述产生的合同
dolus directus 直接欺诈行为
* ***Dolus et fraus nemini patrocinentur; patrocinari derent.*** Deceit and fraud shall excuse or benefit no man; they themselves need to be excused. 靠弄虚作假和欺诈是不会得到宽恕或有益于任何人的,倒是弄虚作假和欺诈本身需要获得人们的宽恕。
dolus eventualis 间接欺诈行为
dolus malus 恶意欺诈(罗马法)
dolus subsequens 事后犯意
dolus vel fraus 诈欺
Domain n. 1.可行使国家主权的领土 2.不动产,土地 3.完整的和绝对的土地所有权

4.范围,域名 5.国家对产业的支配权、征用权

domain name 域名[指已在互联网上被注册登记过的网站所有人设计的词和身份。所有的域名至少有两个等级。第一等级域名(first level domain name)认定注册人的类别,如商业网站(a commercial site)(.com)、政府机构(.gov)、教育机构(.edu)、非营利团体(.org)或协商团体(discussion group)(.net)。第二等级域名是特殊类别中用户的唯一识别人(unique identifier)(rhapsangel.com)(rhapsangel.org)。第二等级域名根据商标法受到保护,而第一级域名则无此等保护,在有些情况下,完整的域名可以有效被注册为商标,但商标权并非经登记或注册就自动创立而成]

domain name system 域名系统(简称 DNS)
domain of use 租地人的地上权
domain-state 领地国家
domaine prive 私产
domaine public 共产

Dombrowski doctrine 多姆布鲁斯基原则[指一条短暂的原则(short-lived rule),它可使一个人有权从联邦法院获得禁制令(injunction)以阻止州官员依据与美国联邦宪法第一修正案保证权利相抵触的州的笼统而又模糊的法规对原告提起诉讼。此原则来源于1965年美国联邦最高法院审理的多姆布鲁斯基诉菲斯特案(Dombrowski v. Pfister),参见《美国联邦最高法院判例汇编》第380卷第479页、第85卷第1116页(1965年)。此原则在6年之后已被宣布中止,联邦最高法院已规定,美国联邦宪法第一修正案"阻止权利效力"不得为联邦法院干预州的事务提供法律依据。见 Younger v. Harris 401 U.S. 37]

domestic a. (15世纪)1.涉及自己国家的,内政的(domestic affairs) 2.本地管辖范围的〈in Alaska, a domestic corporation is an Alaskan one〉(在阿拉斯加,本地管辖的公司是阿拉斯加人的一个公司) 3.家庭的;家事的;家务的〈domestic dispute〉(家庭纠纷)

domestic abuse 见 domestic violence
domestic accounting firms 境内会计师事务所
domestic affairs 内政,内部事务
domestic agreement 国内协定
domestic and foreign existing co. 国内和国外上市公司
domestic branch 国内分行
domestic calamity 内患
domestic corporation 本国公司;当地公司;(美)本州公司
domestic council 国内事务委员会
domestic courts 当事人居住地的管辖法院;当地法院
domestic disputes 内部争端,家庭纠纷
domestic driving permit 国内驾驶执照
domestic economy 国内经济
domestic exchange 国内汇兑
domestic fishing capacity 本国渔业能力
domestic government 国内统治
domestic industry 国内行业(指相同产品的国内各生产人全体或其集体产品数量构成该相同产品总量大部分者)
domestic institution 境内机构
Domestic International Sales Corporation (DISC) (从 GATT 对美国)国内的国际销售公司
domestic jurisdiction 国内管辖权
domestic law 国内法
domestic legal rules 国内法律规章
domestic legislative measure 国内立法措施
domestic loan 内债
domestic mandatory rules 国内强制性规范(见 International mandatory rules)
domestic policy 对内政策,国内政策
domestic premises 家庭房产
domestic price preference 国内价格优先
domestic proceedings 家事诉讼
domestic producers (产品的)国内生产者
domestic products 国产品,国货,土产品
domestic relation 亲属关系;家庭关系
domestic relations 家属关系法,家属法(亦称 domestic relation law;见 family law)
domestic relations cases 家庭关系案件
domestic relations court (或 family court)家庭关系法庭(指美国一些州中的一种法

庭。它对家庭事务具有有限的管辖权,包括对婚姻、扶养、抚养、赡养、离婚以及儿童教养等案件的审理)

Domestic Relations Law (美)《家庭关系法》(亦即《家庭法》)

domestic rent 住宅租金

domestic service 家庭服务

domestic subtenancy 住宅转租

domestic support 国内支持(国内支持作为一个固定的提法源于 WTO《农业协定》,但至今 WTO 规则体系对此未作明确定义。从《农业协定》及其附件相关内容看,"国内支持"可理解为一国政府在境内通过各种国内政策,以农业和农民为扶持资助对象所进行的各种直接、间接财政支持措施的总称)

domestic terrorism 国内恐怖主义[指①首先发生在美国领土区域管辖以内的恐怖主义。参见《美国注释法典》第 18 标题卷第 2331 节第(5)款。②对自己的政府和普通公民实行恐怖主义]

domestic system 家庭包工制(指曾盛行于 17 世纪西欧的一种生产制度)

domestic tenancy 住宅租赁

domestic tranquility 国内治安

domestic tribunal (英)自治法庭(指社团组织内建立的准司法机构)

domestic violence 1.家庭暴力[指家庭成员(通常为夫妻)之间的暴力,家庭的一个成员对另一成员所进行的侵害、伤害行为或暴力行为](见 battered child syndrome) 2.身体伤害的惩罚,或由其父母或孩子家庭的成员或以前的成员针对孩子或针对家庭的另一个成员创造一种适当的恐惧(reasonable fear)使其身体伤害或受到伤害之惩罚。亦称为 domestic abuse; family violence 3.(古代)暴动或非法武装在国内煽动暴乱行为

domesticate v. 使归化,使通俗化;采用(异族风俗等)

domesticator n. 使归化者

domicile n./v. (正式户口所在的)户籍;住所(指一个人永久居住或由法律推定永久居住的地方)/使定居,常住

Domicile and Matrimonial Proceedings Act (英)《住所与婚姻诉讼程序法》(1973 年)

domicile bill of exchange 注明汇款场所的汇票

domicile by operation of law 法定住所;合法户籍

domicile control 户口管制(理)

domicile law 住所法,户籍法

domicile of child 子女的住所

domicile of choice 选定住所,选择居住地

domicile of dependent persons 家属住所,家属所在地

domicile of origin 原籍(地),出生住所,原始住所,固有住所

domicile of the corporation 公司的住所地

domiciliary a. 适合定居的,与住所有关的;住所的;户籍的

domiciliary control system 户口管理制度

domiciliary register 户籍(簿)

domiciliary search 住宅搜查

domiciliary visit 住宅搜查;抄家

domicilium 住所

dominance n. 主控,统治,支配;控制

dominant a. 支配的,统治的;主要的;卓越的

dominant class 统治阶级,领导阶级

dominant company 主要公司

dominant motive 主要动机

dominant nation chauvinism 大民族主义,大国沙文主义

dominant owner 承役地所有人

dominant paradigm 主要范例

dominant party 执政党,主要政党

dominant powers 强权国家,列强

dominant strategy 上优战略;占优战略(博弈论中术语)

dominant tenement 承役地(指对毗邻土地享有地役权的一块土地),需役地

dominate n./v. (古罗马的)君主制时期/1.支配,统治,控制 2.处于支配地位,高耸

dominated strategy 劣战略,控制性战略

dominative a. 支配的,占优势的

dominator n. 支配者,统治者,占优势者

dominica potestas 家主权

Dominican divorce 多米尼加的离婚(见

Mexican divorce)

dominio (= *dominium*) （西班牙法）（财产）所有权

Dominion Law Report （起自1912）（加）自治领判例汇编（指唯一全国范围的连续性判例汇编。简称 DLR）

dominion n. 1.统治权,主权 2.统治,支配,管辖 3.领土,领地,领域 4.所有权,支配权 5.自治领;(大写)英国自治领

dominion register 所有权登记(注册)

dominium 所有权(罗马法中"所有权"称谓不一。早期称 *mancipium*；随后 *proprietas* 作为对物享有最高权利的技术性术语,主要相对于 *ususfrutus* 而使用；*Dominium* 则于罗马共和时代后期出现,主要指个人使用权形成过程中家父权或个人财产权的享有,因而 *dominium* 应为私人所有权的来源)；主人权

dominium directum （封建时代领主的或近代法上地主的）直接所有权;（大陆法）严格法上的所有权

dominium eminens 国家征用权

dominium ex jure quiritium （古罗马市民法上的）依法享有的所有权

dominium minus plenum 不完全所有权

dominium plenum 完全所有权

dominium utile 用益所有权;(罗马法)裁判官法所有权(凡要式移转物尚未按市民法规定方式买卖的,不生效力。该物所有权仍属出卖人,他可起诉追回。裁判官为维护公平正义,保护买受人之利益,特授予其以"物已出卖和交付之抗辩"驳回原告之诉,即裁判官法所有权)

domino theory 多米诺(骨牌)理论

dominus 封建领主

dominus legum 法学大师(指中世纪一种称号)

dominus litis 诉讼当事人(罗马法上指区别于诉讼代理人和法定代理人的案件当事人;英美法指能控制诉讼并按其意愿处分诉讼者)

domo reparanda （要求邻居）房屋修理令（以避免因房屋倒塌使自己受损害）

domus （英)房屋,住宅,住所

domus procerum （旧称)贵族院；上(议)院

* *Domus sua cuique est tutissimum refugium.* To every man his own house is his safest refuge. 对每个人来说,自己的家是最安全的藏身之处。

* *Dona clandestina sunt semper suspiciosa.* Clandestine gifts are always open to suspicion. 暗中送礼总是值得怀疑的。

donate v. 捐赠,赠送

donate blood 献血

donatio 赠与

donatio ante nuptias 婚前赠与

donatio divortii causa 离婚赠与

donatio inofficiosa 不履行道德义务的赠与(指一笔赠与因如此巨大以致可减少遗赠人财产的长子继承人的部分)

donatio inter virum et uxorem （罗马法）夫妻间的赠与[亦有极少例外情况（如周年纪念赠予）夫妻间赠予无效。但如果赠与人死亡而未撤销此赠予则仍被确认]

donatio inter vivos 生前赠与

donatio mortis causa 死因赠与(即临终前的赠与)

donatio propter nuptias 婚时赠与(指罗马法上结婚时丈夫决定给予妻子嫁资性质的赠与)

donatio testamento 遗赠

donation n. 捐赠,捐赠的东西,捐款;赠送;赠品

donation allowance 捐款

donation by will 遗嘱捐赠

donation *sub modo* 附条件捐赠

donative n./a. 赠品,赠送物/赠送的,捐赠的

* *Donator nunquam desinit possidere, antequam donatorius incipiat possidere.* A donor never ceases to possess, until the donee begins to possess. 在受赠人开始占有之前,(赠送物)终究还是归赠与人所有的。

donee n. 受赠人,受遗赠人;受役者(见 conservation easement)

donee beneficiary （第三当事人合同中的合同)受益人

donee of power 有权处理他人财产者,被指定授予权力者

donor n. 赠与人,捐赠人;遗赠人;授权

人;供役者(见 conservation easement)
donor of the power 权力授予人
doom n./v. 判决(尤指有罪的判决),定罪;毁灭;(历史上的)法律、法令;末日审判/判罪,判定有罪;注定失败(死亡等)
doombook 撒克逊法典[指由阿弗莱德(Alfred)主编的内容包括普通法准则,司法格式,以及刑法的一部法典。该法典一直使用到爱德华四世统治时为止]
doomsday n. 定罪日,审判日;世界末日
doomsmen n. (中世纪日耳曼民族当地自由人组成处理法律纠纷的)审判人
door-closing doctrine 补牢原则(指用制定法或法院判决弥补法律漏洞的原则)
door-to-door sale 上门销售
Door-to-Door Sales Act 《上门销售法》
doorkeeper (议会法)守门官员(指在审议会议期间,负责控制进入议会厅的守门官员。亦称护卫:guard)
doowop docket 见 DWOP docket
dope n./v. 黏稠物,胶状物;塑料;兴奋剂;毒品(如鸦片等);酒,软饮料;可靠的内部信息/服用麻醉剂或毒品,用黏稠物处理
dormant a. 休眠的,蛰伏的;暂停活动的;潜伏的,匿名的
dormant capital 未动用资本
Dormant Commerce Clause (美)休眠的"贸易条款",隐性商业条款(指美国法院对美国联邦宪法第一条第 8 项商业条款的反向解释。所谓"商业条款",是指美国联邦宪法第 1 条第 8 项关于国会有权"规定合众国与外国、各州间及印第安种族间之贸易"之规定,实质上是为专门解决美建国初期严重的地方保护主义而规定)
dormant fund 未动用基金;游资
dormant judg(e)ment 过期的判决,失效的判决
dormant law 不实施的法律,不执行的法律
dormant partner 隐名合伙人,隐名股东,外股
dos 嫁资
dos adventitia (罗马法)外来的嫁妆(指在新娘或其父之外的某人提供给新娘带给她丈夫的嫁妆)

dos profectitia (罗马法)嫁妆(指由新娘之父或新娘本人提供的嫁妆带给她的丈夫的嫁妆)
dos receptitia (罗马法)约还嫁资,约还嫁妆[指一种嫁资或嫁妆(无论是外来的嫁资或嫁妆)特别约定在结婚完成后归还给提供人或赠与人]
dosis n. 剂量
dosis lethal 致死量
dosis toxic 中毒量
dossier n. 有关文件;案卷
dot n. 妆奁,嫁资
dotage n. 老年昏聩;过度痴迷;痴情
dotal system 奁产制
dotalitium 嫁妆
doth (古)does 的古写
dotis dictio 寡妇地产口约
double a. 双重的;加倍的;两面派的
double actionability 双重可起诉性
double adultery 已婚男女间的通奸
double agent 双重间谍;双重代理人
double commission 双重佣金,双重酬金(指由买卖双方同时支付的佣金或酬金,或向不同身份的同一人支付的佣金或酬金)
double consciousness 双重意识
double contingency 双重偶然性
double criminality "双重犯罪"(原则)(指请求引渡的罪犯,其犯罪行为依请求国及被请求国双方法律均应处罚者,始得引渡)
double crossing 划双线支票
double damages 双重损害赔偿
(the) double derivative suit (美)二重代表诉讼[指在母子公司的架构中,当子公司的利益遭到损害,且母公司与子公司拒绝起诉追偿时,由母公司股东以自己名义代位子公司提起代表诉讼。当此种侵害发生在孙公司时,母公司股东代表孙公司提起诉讼时,该诉讼被称为"三重代表诉讼"(the triple derivative suit),依此类推,这些由母公司股东代表子公司、孙公司以及曾孙公司等而提起的诉讼,总称为"多重代表诉讼"(multiple derivative suit)]
double dividend 加倍红利
double entry 双重记录;复式记账法,复式

簿记

double entry bookkeeping 复式簿记

double federalism （美）双重联邦主义（该观点认为宪法是为主权州和主权州的人民为了给予新的全国政府一系列权力的有限目标而制定的契约。如果州不授予这些权力，它自己便享有作为一个有主权政治实体的各种权限，各州与全国政府是平等的，因为各州在自己的权力范围内——在他们所保留权力的行使方面——正如全国政府在其权力范围内一样，各州权力完全是至高无上的。在联邦成立时期和现在，许多人都认为美国联邦宪法第十修正案是这一观点的表述）

double financing 双重资金融通

double hearsay 两次传闻（指甲在法庭上证实听到乙说的某件事，而乙则说该件事是他听另一人说的）

double indemnity 双倍赔偿额（指根据人身保险合同条款在被保险人意外死亡时，可获得双倍保险金额的支付）

double insurance 复（式）保险，双重保险

double jeopardy （美）不得令其受两次生命或身体上的危险（见 Fifth Amendment）；同一罪名不受两次审理（指美法上禁止法院对同一罪行进行一次以上公诉的一个普通法和宪法原则。大陆法上称一事不再理原则）

double loop 双箕型线（纹），双箕

double nationality 双重国籍

double plea 两次答辩

double pleading 两次抗辩

double policy 双重性政策，双轨制政策

double possibility 双重可能性

double probate （对遗嘱的）两次认证（检验）

double reader （英国律师公会的）高级讲师

double rent 加倍租金

double rent and double value 双租双值

double social contract 双层社会契约

double talk 模棱两可的话，含糊其词

double tariff 双税则，双重税率制

double tax agreement 处理双重关税协定

double taxation （18世纪）重复征税，双重征税[指①在同一时间，因同一税收目的对同一财产或收益由同一税收机关进行两次征税，亦指同时征收附加法人税和个人所得税。②依据美国《国内税收法》规定可按合伙企业课税的公司（subchapter Co.）。税务机关按此规定对该公司收益两次征税。一次是对公司盈利收税，另一次是对股东分红的收益收税。③（国际法）两个或两个以上国家对同一纳税人，对相同标的（same subject matter）或相同物品课以两次相类似的税。亦称 duplicate taxation]

double unenforceability 双重不可执行性标准（英国法官区分两类公共政策：一是"基于普遍道德原则的"公共政策，二是"仅基于纯国内考虑的"公共政策。如果一个合同违反前一公共政策，英国法院将拒绝执行，而不考虑合同的准据法和履行地法规定；而当一个合同违背后一公共政策，只在合同既违反英国国内法的公共政策，又违反合同履行地的公共政策，它才会被英国法院拒绝执行。这即所谓双重不可执行性标准）

double value （英）加倍租值（指1730年的《业主租户法》规定的一种不执行规定的惩罚）

double veto 两次否决（又译双重否决）

double waste 双重毁损（指负有修好房屋义务的租借人，任凭房子毁坏而不去修理，后来又去砍伐树木来修理房屋，就叫双重毁损）

double whammy 双重打击

double will 相互遗嘱

double-crosser n. 骗子

double-deal v. 行骗，欺骗

double-dealing a. 狡猾的，欺诈的，伪善的；口是心非的，不诚实的，搞两面派的

doubly guilty 罪上加罪，双重罪

doubt n./v. 疑问；疑惑；疑惧，怀疑/怀疑，不相信

doubt a person's truth 怀疑某人的诚实

doubt the verity of sb. Statement 怀疑某人陈述的真实性

doubtful a. 怀疑的，有疑问的；不确定的，不可靠的；难以预测的；未定局的

doubtful case 疑案
doubtful jurisdiction 不可靠的管辖,有疑问的管辖
Doughnut Hole （美国阿拉斯加与俄罗斯堪察加半岛间的）"甜甜圈"水域
Dow Jones index （美）道琼斯股票指数（指表示美国证券市场一般涨跌情况的指数,由纽约 Dow Jones 公司所发布者,亦作 Dow Jones average）
dowager n. 受有亡夫遗产的寡妇,寡居贵妇人
dower n. 1.亡夫遗产（英国法上是指寡妇为维持生活和抚养子女应得她丈夫的遗产部分）2.嫁妆（罗马法指结婚时妻子给丈夫带来的财产）
dower by custom 寡妇依习惯法继承丈夫的遗产
down a. 向下的；现付的
down leg 发回信号（见 up leg）
down payment plan 押金制度
down time 窝工时间
down to the title of occupancy 单纯占有
down payment 定金[指用现金支付购买价格的一部分（或当销售协议执行时的等同价）。见 binder 2; earnest money]
down-payment n. 现付,已付定金；（分期付款的）首次付款
down-to-earth a. 切实的,实事求是的〈a down-to-earth style of work〉（实事求是的工作作风）,〈even to the down to earth scholar of stock corporation law〉（甚至股票公司法的实事求是的学者们）
Downing chair of law （英）（剑桥大学的）唐宁法学讲座职位
download 减轻负担,减低负荷
downright answer 坦率的答复,直爽的答复
downright evidence （罕用）占优势的证据（preponderance of evidence）
downright harmful 完全的伤害
downright lie 弥天大谎
(a) downright thief （一个）彻头彻尾的贼
downstate 州的最南部地区
Downstate Illinois Innocence Project （美）南伊利诺伊州无辜者行动,南伊利诺伊州无辜者专项立案（复审错案）
downtime n. 故障（发生到排除的）时间（计算机软件许可合同中有时要按软件运行时间收费,这种情况下,应排除故障时间；否则760许可人将不公平）；停工期
dowry n. 1.陪嫁物,嫁妆 2.（古）亡夫遗产,丈夫在婚前给予新娘的财礼
doyen n. 领袖；（外交使团）团长；首席
Doyen of Diplomatic Corps 外交使团团长
draconian a. （法律等）严厉的,残酷的
Draconian laws 德拉古法（指雅典立法者德拉古于公元前 621 年制定的一部载有罚则和程序规则的法典,以苛刑峻罚而闻名）
draft n./v. 1.汇票；本票,付款通知[指由出票人（drawer）签署的无条件书面付款通知（unconditional written order）,直接由受票人或付款人（drawee or payor）按要求或确定时间支付一定数额款项给予第三方（受款人 payee）或持票人（bearer）。支票（check）是最普通的本票例证。亦称 bill of exchange; letter of exchange。见 note 1] 2.征兵；强制征兵或服兵役〈his illness disqualified him from the draft〉（他的病使他失去服兵役资格）,亦称 conscription; military draft 3.草案,法案；草图（图样）〈the second draft of the contract〉（合同的第二草稿）/1.起草,组成,构成,排稿〈to draft a contract〉（起草一个合同） 2.征募,补充,选择〈to draft someone to run for political office〉（选某某人竞选政治职位）,〈to draft someone into the armed services〉（选择某人到部队服役）
draft amendment 修正草案
draft bill 法案草案,议案草案（亦可写为 draft of bills）
draft board （美）征兵局
draft card 征兵证
draft code 法典草案
Draft Code on Insider Trading （德）内幕交易守则草案
draft criminal code 刑法典草案
Draft Criminal Code for England and Wales 《英格兰和威尔士刑事法典草案》

draft decision 决议草案
draft declaration 宣言草案
draft dodger (美)逃避服兵役者
draft for collection 托收汇票
draft law 法律草案;(美)征兵法
draft of foreign currency 外币兑换券
draft on demand 即付汇票
draft regulation 法规草案
draft resister (美)抵制服兵役的人
draft resolution 决议草案
draft-age a. (美)应征年龄的
draftee n. (美)应征入伍者
drafting committee 起草委员会
draftsman n. 议(法)案起草人,起草人;制图员
drag out (on) 接近,使接近
drag out the proceedings for weeks or even years 使诉讼程序拖延数周甚至数年
dragnet n. 拖网,捕捞网;法网,天罗地网
dragnet arrest 大批逮捕(指可能关系到犯罪活动或民事干扰的情况下的大批逮捕犯罪嫌疑人。这种逮捕方式是非法的,因为它不是基于合理的根据,而只是建立在未经证实的怀疑或信条上。亦称 whole sale arrest, round-up arrest)
Drago doctrine 德拉戈主义(阿根廷外交部长德拉戈于1902年提出的主张,即国家负有不得对债务国使用强迫手段包括军事行动索债的义务)
dragon n. 凶恶的人;凶恶严厉的监护人(尤指老太婆)
dram-shop act 小酒店法令
dramatic arguments 戏剧性观点,鲜明观点,激动人心的观点,惹人注目的观点
dramatic effect 惹人注目的影响,显著的影响
drastic a. (法律等)极端的,严厉的
drastic measure 严厉措施
draw v. 草拟,制定;开立(票据等);支领,提取;获得;推论,引出;拉长,引长,拉紧;画线,制图;吸取(教训);吃水
draw on (upon) 利用或依靠(财力、智慧等);从中获得
draw out 1.拉长,拖长;掏出;引出 2.拟定(计划)等)3.(白昼)长起来

draw up a deed 草拟一份契据
draw up a writ 草拟令状
draw up an indictment 起草起诉书
draw upon you for assistance 依靠你的帮助
draw (of) votes 票数相等
draw-latches n. 盗贼
drawback n. 退款,退税;欠缺,弊端;障碍
drawback system 退税制度
drawee n. 付款人,受票人,汇票付款人
drawer n. 出票人,开票人,汇票发票人
drawer of bad cheek (或 cheque) 签发空头支票人,签发空头支票的客户
drawer of document 立证书人
drawing n. 提款;提存;抽签;草拟
drawing a cheek (或 cheque) without funds 签发空头支票
drawing and quartering (英史)四肢裂解(指对叛逆罪的一种刑罚)
drawing brief 草拟案情说明书
drawing of ballot 抽签,开票
drawing of bonds 提取债券
drawing of cheque 签发支票,以支票提款
drawing of profit 效益
drawing rights 提发权,提款权
drawn v. 办理支票汇款业务
dreit dreit 见 droit-droit
dress codes (美)衣着法规(指美国指定在公立中学校学生有关校服的规定)
drift n./v. 1.漂流,流速 2.漂流物〈drift harbour〉(港湾里漂浮的杂物)3.趋势,动向,倾向〈the general drift of affairs〉(事情的一般趋势,大势)4. 大意,要旨〈drift of argument〉(辩论的中心)5.坐观,放任自流〈a policy of drift〉(放任自流政策)6.(海、空)偏移;偏航(无)偏移,偏差(宇)(导弹的)航差 7.南非的浅滩/1.漂流,游荡;漂泊 2.放任自流〈don't let matters drift〉(不要听之任之)3.(价格等的)缓慢变动;渐渐趋向(toward)〈不知不觉地陷入〉〈(into) drift into collapse〉(渐趋崩溃),〈drift into a habit〉(逐渐陷入一种习惯);使漂流
drift-net n. 流刺网
drift-stuff 漂流木材(指在水上随意漂流的材料,而且无可发现之源。这种漂流木

材通常为湖水岸居民所有的财产)
driften n. 漂流物〈driften ice〉(漂冰)
drink n/v. 酒,喝酒,酗酒;饮料/饮;喝酒
drink from a spigot 喝(酒)过度
drink hard 大喝,痛饮
drink to excess 纵酒,狂饮
drinking frequency 饮用频率
drive v. 1.驱,赶,逐 2.驾驶,开(汽车等),开车 3.促进(交易),经营
drive a bargain 讲价,磋商交易
drive a hard bargain 讨价还价坚持成交条件
drive a roaring trade 生意兴隆
drive a wage-earning family to the impasse 将依赖工薪糊口的家庭逼至绝境
drive up price 抬高价格
drive-by download 路过式下载(又译"偷渡下载",是不希望用户知晓的下载行为,在用户不知道的情况下自动给用户电脑下载间谍软件、计算机病毒或者其他恶意软件。路过式下载可能发生在用户访问一个网站、阅读一封电子邮件或者点击一个欺骗性弹出式窗口的时候)
driver n. 驾驶员,司机,监工
driver-plaintiff 驾车人原告,司机原告
driving n. 开车;驾驶;力量,精力,能力
driving ability 驾驶能力
driving licence 驾驶执照
driving negligently 过失驾车(引起的交通事故)
driving permit 驾驶许可证
driving test order 驾驶考核令
driving to the public danger (驾驶汽车)违反交通法规
driving under the influence 有影响情况下驾车;有影响驾车[指在身体和精神上均受到伤害的情况下,尤其是在酗酒或吸毒之后驾驶机动车辆的犯罪行为或违法行为。总之,是比正酗酒驾车要轻些的罪行,但有极少数辖区将此二者(consuming alcohol or drugs 和 intoxicated)视为同义词,缩略为 DUI。亦称 driving while ability impaired (DWAT); driving under the influence of liquor (DUIL); driving while intoxicated (DWI); operating under the influence (OUI); operation while intoxicated (OWI); operating a motor vehicle while intoxicated (OMVI); operation a motor vehicle under the influence (OMVUI)。见 driving while intoxicated]
driving while intoxicated 1.酗酒开车[指在身体和精神上均已受到伤害的情况下,又在酗酒严重,血液中酒精含量超过法定限度(许多州为 0.8%)或在吸毒之后驾驶机动车辆的犯法或犯罪行为。处罚幅度很宽大,例如,在密苏里州和路易斯安那州最重处罚为 5000 美元罚金和 6 个月的监禁;而在纽约州,其罚金从 500 美元—5000 美元不等,监禁可高达 4 年 2.有影响下驾车(driving under the influence),缩略为 DWI,亦称 drunk driving。见 driving under the influence]
droit n. 1.法律上的权利,所有权 2.所有物,依法有权享受的东西 3.(复)税,关税 4. 法律;正义;衡平 5.(英)海军权(指国王授予海军的某些权力,包括战时在港口内捕获的船货,以及平时在管辖海域获得的弃船、货物、投海物等所得中的收入所有权)
droit absolut 绝对权
droit administralif 官法,行政法
droit commun (法)普通法(指地方或区域性习惯或特殊规定)
droit d'aubaine 外侨遗产没收权
droit de auteur 作者权
droit de chapelle (作为外交特权的)设礼拜堂礼拜权
droit de détraction 遗产出境税
droit de l'hotel (作为外交特权的)治外法权(指大使免受当地司法管辖和征税的豁免权)
droit de l'oeuvre 保护(作品)的完整性权
droit de poursuite 索取使用费权
droit de preseance 席次权,位次权
droit de quartier (作为外交特权的)警察管辖豁免权
droit de retraction 收回权(指作品发表后,因观点改变或其他原因而从传播领域中有收回作品的权利)
droit de seigneur (法)初夜权

droit de suite 债权人所设定物权的财产未被第三人占有时的追索权;(对不动产抵押物的)追及权;版税权;(版权法)(作品)追续权

droit international 国际法(又译国际公法,英文为 international law)

droit international privé 国际私法(英文为 private international law)

droit international public 国际公法(英文为 public international law)

droit maritime 海商法,海事法

droit moral (法)精神权利(主要指对作品的署名权及作品的不可侵犯权)

*** droit ne poet pas morier** right cannot die (法)权利不会死亡(注:这句法文的法律格言有两个字有误,一是 poet,应为 peut,原动词为 pouvoir,第三人称单数 il peut;另一为 morier,应为 mourir。这两个错字可能为"Black"之误,《元照英美法词典》亦按"Black"引用,未作改动,故应为 droit ne peut pas mourir)

droit of admiralty 海军(夺获敌国财产)权

droit relatit 相对权

droit-droit 双重权利(double right,双份权利,指所有权和财产权的统一,亦称 jus duplicatum; dreit dreit)

drop n./v. 滴剂;下降;落下;放下/(美)口服(麻醉品);扔(炸弹);遗漏;省略(美)开除;解雇;降低

drop shipper 直接发货批发商,承运批发商,出口中间商,向厂商直接进货的零售商

drop the reins of government 不再执政

drown v. 溺死,淹溺,淹杀

drown oneself 投水自尽

drowning n. 溺杀;淹死

drowning in unsorted information 埋头于未分类的信息之中,沉浸于杂乱的资料之中

drug n./v. 1.毒品;麻醉药(如鸦片、吗啡);药物,药材,药剂 2.(美)杂货店/使服麻醉药,使服毒品

drug abuse 毒品滥用

drug addict 吸毒者

drug addiction 吸毒癖;毒瘾

drug cartels 毒品卡特尔

drug control 毒品管制(又译麻醉品管制)

drug den 毒窟

drug driving 吸毒后驾车[指服食违禁物(例如大麻、迷幻药和可卡因)之后驾驶轿车、卡车或其他车辆的行为。这样的驾车者成为"drug driver"(吸毒后驾车者)。在英国,吸毒后驾车是一种犯罪行为。警察将使用类似于"breathalyser"(呼吸测试器)的设备"drugalyser"(毒品测定仪)对可疑驾车者的唾液进行检查。"drug driving"是基于20世纪60年代开始流行的词语"drink driving"(酒后驾车)创造的。在后一个词语中,"drink"是指含酒精饮品,例如"I really need a drink.""drink driving"是英国英语,美国英语是"drunk driving"]

drug enforcement 禁毒

Drug Enforcement Agency (DEA) 禁毒机构

drug habit (吸)毒(物)癖

drug laws 毒品法规

drug offences 贩卖毒品罪

drug on the market 滞销货

drug peddling 兜售毒品

Drug Price Competition and Patent Term Restorotion Act of 1984 见 Hatch Waxman Act

drug prohibition 毒品禁令

drug retailer 毒品零售商

drug smuggling 毒品走私

drug taking 吸毒

drug trafficker 私贩毒品者,毒品贩子

drug trafficking 毒品(非法)交易,贩毒

Drug Trafficking Offences Act, 1986 (美)(1986)《贩运麻醉品犯罪法令》

drug treatment center 毒品处理中心,戒毒中心

drug use 吸毒,毒品使用

drug users 吸毒者,毒品用户

drug-dependent n. 吸毒者,染有毒瘾者

drum up business 招徕生意

drumhead court-martial 战地临时军事法庭

drunk a./n. 醉酒的,兴奋的[指在酒类的

影响下使人的正常思维和行为达到损伤的程度。醉酒可分为四分之一醉酒(quarter drunk)、半醉酒(half drunk)和烂醉(dead drunk)三个阶段]/醉汉
drunk driving 醉酒驾车(见 driving while intoxicated)
drunk-driving arrests 醉酒驾驶被逮捕
drunken drive 酒醉开车者,酒醉驾驶者
drunkenness n. 酒醉,酩酊(大醉)
drunkometer 见 breathalyzer
dry a./n. 干的,枯竭的;不带偏见的;无预期结果的;禁酒的/禁酒主张者
dry check 见 bad check
dry goods container 干货集装箱
dry state (美)实施禁酒法的州
dry trust 消极信托
DSM-V (美国的)《精神障碍诊断与统计手册》(第五版)
du ut facias 以物换做,以物换劳,物劳互换
dual a. 双重的,二的,两体的
dual and unified system (政府会计的)双重(轨)制与单一(轨)制(做账方式)
dual chartering 双轨(重)执照
dual citizenship 1.双重国籍 2.(美)(同时为联邦和州)双重公民的资格
dual control 两国共管;双重管辖
dual distribution 双重销售,(美)双轨销售
dual effect of investment 投资的双重效应
Dual Federalism (美)(联邦和州分享主权的二元联邦制)
dual goal of doctrinal coherence and economy of judicial administration 原则的一致性和司法行政的经济性的双重目的
dual jurisdiction 双重管辖权
dual labor market theory 二元劳动市场理论
dual locking function 双锁功能(指把竞车锁在外面,而把投资锁在里面)
dual nationality 双重国籍
dual ownership 双重所有权
dual property rights 双重产权
dual purpose of the minimum contacts test 最低联系标准的双重目的
dual representation 双重代表权,双重

代理
dual system 双轨制,双重体制
dual system of court 法院的双轨制;双重的法院体制
dual system of enforcement of state-created right (美)州法权利实施的双重执行体制
dual taxation 双重课税,双重征税
dual-residential parent (美)双重(身份)的提供居住的父母[指与另一父母分担最先为孩子提供居住地的责任,而另一父或母提供实质最先的居所。在许多司法管辖区,双重提供居所涉及物质上共同监护(joint physical custody)。见 residential responsibility; custody ②; residential parent]
dualism n. 二元论,双重性,双轨制
dualist n. 二元论者
dualistic conception 二元论概念
dualistic doctrine 二元论
duality (或 **dualism**) **in the system of law** 法律制度上的双重性,法律制度双轨制
duality (或 **dualism**) **of court systems** 双重的法院体制;双规制的法院系统
duality (或 **dualism**) **of jurisdiction** 双重审判制,双轨的审判制度
duality of legal regimes (或 **systems**) 双重的法律体制,法律制度的双轨制
duality (或 **dualism**) **of modern law and traditional law** 现代法与传统法的双轨制(两重性)
duality (或 **dualism**) **of private law** 私法的双重性
duality (或 **dualism**) **of sources of the law** 两重性的法的渊源(又译:双重性的法律渊源);双轨制的法源
duality (或 **dualism**) **of status** 双重身份
dub v./n. 授予,授予……称号/(美俚)新手,笨蛋
dubious validity 未定效力,可疑的效力,含糊的效力,半信半疑的效力
dubitante 怀疑,可疑
duces tecum (随带证据)出庭受审令
duchy n. 公爵领地
ducking-stool n. 浸水刑凳(见 cucking stool)

due n./a. 应得权益,应得物;(复)应缴款,税款;税;(按期应缴的)费用/到期的,应付给的;适当的,正当的;预期的,应到的;充分的;约定的
due authority 适当的权限
due bill （美）(以服务抵偿债务的)借约;借据,到期票据
due care 适度谨慎（见 reasonable care）
due care and attention 应有的小心和注意
due care standard 应有小心的标准,适当注意的标准
due course 正当过程,正常过程
due course of law 正当法律手续;正当程序
due date (债务,税等)限定付款日期,应付款日期,支付日期
due deference 充分尊重
due diligence 应有(的)勤勉,适当(应有)努力,适当(应有)用功
due form 正当形式,正当格式合同;正当格式文件;正当(某种典型诉状,申请,法庭裁决或判决中陈述或请求的)格式
due notice （见 adequate notice）
due performance 适当履行,正当履行
due premium 到期保险费
due process (16 世纪)正当程序,正当法律程序（"due process of law"的缩略形式）[指为了保护和实施个人权利,包括对审通知和在有权判案的法庭前公平听审的权利,而确立规定(rules)和原则,依照这些规定和原则所进行的法律程序。亦称 due process of law; due course of law。见 fundamental fairness doctrine]
due process afforded 提供的正当程序
Due Process Clause (1890 年)正当法律程序条款[指宪法的条款,任何人无正当法律程序不得剥夺他人生命、自由或财产。美国联邦宪法中有两项"正当法律程序条款":一项为适用于联邦政府的第五修正案;另一项为适用于各州的第十四修正案,根据合并原则(incorporation doctrine),第五修正案的正当法律程序条款也适用于各州。见 Equal Protection Clause]
due process of law 见 due process
due process notice requirements 正当程序要求的通知,按正当程序的通知要求
due process requirements of notice and an opportunity to be hear 正当程序有关通知和听审机会的要求
due process right(s) （美）正当程序权利（指要求遵循公平与正义的正当程序标准）;正当程序条款权利
due process standard for jurisdiction 管辖的正当程序标准
due process standards 正当程序标准
due process test 正当程序检验标准
due proof 充分的证据,充分的证明[指足以恰当并有力支持某一结果或结论所提供的证据或证明,比如法定权利(entitlement)受到保险单支持的权益。此项证据不必是最佳可能的证明(best proof possible)]
due regard 应有注意,应有尊重;适当顾及
due share capital and dividends 到期股金和股息
due to changed conditions 因情势变迁
duel n. 决斗（指双方使用致命武器并按预定规则和事先安排,为解决纠纷或某种荣誉进行的格斗,作为诉诸司法外的另一种选择,最早形式为司法决斗）;(双方的)斗争
duel of wits 斗智
duel(l)ist n. 决斗者,斗争者
duello n. 决斗的全部规则
duke n. 公爵,(欧洲公国的)君主;(古罗马的)省督军
duke of Exeter's daughter "埃克塞特公爵之女"（指 15 世纪的一种类似拉肢刑架的拷问刑具）
dull brief 沉闷单调的诉讼要点
duly ad. 及时地,正式地,充分地,适当地
duly authorized 经正式授权的
dum 期间内;只要;规定为……
dum bene se gesserit 忠诚服务或品德良好期(间)（见 *durante bene placito*）
dum casta vixerit （英）贞居期（指分居协议中经常使用的一项条款,内容规定只有妻子过贞洁生活期间才付扶养费）
dum fuit non compos mentis 心神不健全期间

dum sola 独身期间
Duma n. 杜马(指俄罗斯经选举产生的立法机关)
dumb a. 哑的;沉默的;(车,船等)无动力的;缺乏某种特性的
dumb barter (若干未开化部落所进行的)物物交易制(指双方将交易货物置于指定地点,而不必做面对面的交付货物的交易)
dumb bid (拍卖时所有人所定而不做公开宣布的)拍卖底价,投标底数
dumb person 哑巴
dumb show 哑剧(与 pantominic work 含义相近,很多国家版权法明文规定哑剧享有版权保护)
dummy n./a. 哑人;经常沉默的人;名义代表;样本/假的,做幌子的;虚构的;傀儡的;不能独立行动的,没有发言权的,哑的
dummy company 秘密代营企业
dummy director 挂名董事,名义董事
dummy incorporators (美)名义公司创建人(指可依州法律创设公司,然后创建人再退出该公司)
dumping margin 倾销幅度
dungeon n. 土牢,地牢
dunnage n. 垫舱物料
* *Duo non possunt in solido unam rem possidere.* Two cannot possess one thing each in entirety. 两个人不能彼此排他地完全占有一个物品
duopoly n. 市场由两家卖主垄断的局面
duopsony n. 市场由两家买主垄断的局面
duoviri (= *duumviri*) 双司法行政官职制(指古罗马由两人担任一个司法行政官职务的制度)
dupable a. 易受骗的
duper n. 欺骗者,诈骗者
duplicate n. 复制品,副本;当票
duplicate (non-negotiable) bill of lading 副本提单
duplicate copy 副本
duplicate indorsement 复本背书
duplicate of services rendered 劳务账单副本
duplicate regulation 监管重叠

duplicate summary invoice 副本发货票
duplicate taxation 双重征税(见 double taxation)
duplicate will 遗嘱复本;遗嘱副本
duplication evidence 重复证据
duplicity n. 两重性;多重陈述或答辩(指诉状上包含一个以上的权利请求、指控或答辩);口是心非,言行不一;奸诈,欺诈
durante 期间
durante absentia 缺席期间,外出期间
durante bello 战争期间
durante bene placito 君主满意期间(与 *dum bene se gesserit* 相对而言)
durante lite 诉讼进行期间
durante viduitate 孀居期间(指把遗产给寡妇,一直到她再嫁为止的这段时间)
durante vita 毕生,一生中,活着的时候,在有生之年
duration n. 期间;持续时间
duration of contract 合同(契约)有效期
duration of detention 拘留期间
duration of employment 雇佣期,雇佣持续期间
duration of failure 故障持续期(与 downtime 意义相近)
duration of imprisonment 监禁期间
duration of insurance 保险期间
duration of licence 执照有效期
duration of residence 连续居住时间
duration of risk 危险期间
duration residency requirement 持续住所要求
durational residency requirement 持续住所要求
duress(e) n. 强迫,威胁;监禁,束缚;胁迫
duress(e) of imprisonment 以监禁相威胁
duressor n. 强迫者,威胁者,胁迫者
Durham rule (美)德拉姆规则(指被告因精神错乱或精神病情对其犯罪行为不负刑事责任的规则)
during good behavio(u)r 1.(法官等的保持)品德良好的任职期间 2.(美)(被告在其判决未决前)应规规矩矩(服从州的法律)期间
during legislature recess 立法机关休会期间

during marriage 婚姻关系存续期间
during the life of the cabinet 在内阁任期内
during the trial 审判期间(指自陪审团宣誓起至作出裁决时为止的审理期间或自大陪审团向法院提起公诉书时起至最后判决为止的审判期间)
(the) Dutch n/a. 荷兰人,荷兰语;(美)德国人;火气,怒气/荷兰的,德国(人)的
Dutch auction 荷兰式拍卖(指高标价拍卖而喊价逐步减价,直至有人愿买为止的一种拍卖)
Dutch courage 荷兰式的勇气[指为了实施犯罪,行为人借酒壮胆,被称为荷兰式的勇气。在此情况下,行为人实施了危害社会的行为却想按自愿醉态的基本原则,以便行为人有可能逃脱"特定故意犯罪"、甚至"一般故意犯罪"的刑事处罚。但英美刑法均确立了例外规则,认为这种自愿醉态不得作为辩护理由。此规则形成于"北爱尔兰总检察长诉加拉赫案"(A-G for Northern Ireland v. Gallagher)]
Dutch language 荷兰语[南非1909年法规定英语与荷兰语在南非联盟(Union of South-Arica)都是等同的]
Dutch judges 荷兰法官
Dutch law 荷兰法
dutiable a. (货物)应纳税的,应征税的
dutiable articles 应纳税物品
dutiable commodity 应纳税商品
dutiable goods (应)征税货物
dutiable price 完税价
duties created by private law 私法上义务
duties created by public law 公法上义务
duty n. 法律上的义务(指依照法律或约定应承担的责任,或自愿承担的责任,欠他人的应偿还的债务。享有相应的权利,如当事人有侵权行为违反注意义务,也会产生使其承担相应责任的法律关系,也可指官员和受托人的职责。在税收方面则指货物或交易应征收之税,尤其指关税)
duty allowance 职务津贴
duty bound to pay taxes 纳税的义务
duty drawback 关税退税,退税
duty free 免税
duty free goods 免税货物

duty in civil affairs 民事义务
duty of abstention 不作为的义务
duty of allegiance 效忠义务
duty of care 合理注意的义务
duty of care for safety (房产占有人)对住客安全应负的责任
duty of child to support parents 子女赡养父母的责任
duty of cohabitation (夫妻)同居义务
duty of contribution 出资义务,捐助义务
duty of disclosure 披露义务
duty of fulfillment 清偿的义务
duty of loyalty 忠实义务
duty of maintenance 扶养义务,赡养义务
duty of non-intervention 不干涉的义务
duty of performance 履行义务
duty of performing military service 服兵役的义务
duty of support 扶养义务,赡养义务,抚育义务
duty of vigilance 警戒责任
duty on value added 增值税
duty on wine 酒类税
duty set forth in the present section 本条所规定的义务
duty solicitor 责任律师
duty to mitigate (the) damage 减损义务,减轻损害的责任
duty to pay taxes 纳税的义务
duty to settle (保险)和解之义务,解决之义务(指承保人有义务协商、解决第三方对被保险人在诚信上的权利要求)
duty to support children 抚育子女的义务
duty to support parents 赡养父母的义务
duty-free a. (货物)免税的
duty-paid a. (货物)已纳税的
duumvirate n. 两人共同掌管,两头政治(统治);共同掌权的两人
Duumviri 双司法行政官制(古罗马人中对成双地选出去履行职责的司法行政官的普通称呼);(古罗马)两头政治中的一个统治者
Duumviri municipales (古罗马)在城镇、殖民地(具有司法审判权的)司法行政官
dwelling house (15世纪)1.住宅[指人们

生活居住的房屋或建筑物;居所或常住地(abode)]2.不动产(住宅以及所有附属于住宅的建筑物)3.(刑法)建筑物,部分建筑;帐篷,活动房;有意用来给人居住用的空地、庭园(enclosed space)[这个词原来涉及宅地、庭园(cartilage),但现在象征性地仅与建筑物相关,亦直接与住所或与围着的走廊相连,通常缩写为 dwelling,古代亦称 mansion house, 较广泛的称谓是 dwelling place]

dwelling place 见 dwelling house
dwindle v. 缩小,减少;衰落,退化
DWOP (dismissal for want of prosecution) 驳回提起公诉要求
DWOP docket 法院设置的案件目录[指法院设置可能驳回公诉要求的案件清单。亦称 doowop docket; DLOP docket。见 DWOP(dismissal for want of prosecution)]
dyarchy n. (罗马早期帝政时期的)两头政治(意指罗马统治由君主和元老院分享的)
Dyer Act (美)《戴尔法》[指 1919 年制定的联邦法,以下情况确定为非法行为:①在州际或国际贸易中运输(已知为盗窃的)盗窃机动车辆;②接收、隐藏或销售明知为盗窃的机动车车辆。参见《美国注释法典》第 18 标题卷第 2311—2313 节,亦称《全国机动车辆失窃法》(National Motor Vehicle Theft Act)]
dying a. 快要死的,垂死的,临终的
dying declaration 临终遗言,临终声明
dying evidence 临死证言
dying person 临终的人
dying testament 临终遗书(遗嘱)
dying without issue 一生无子女,死后无嗣
dynamic a./n. 动态的,原动力的,有火气的,有力的/动力,原动力,动态
dynamic relationship 有力的关系
dynamicism n. 实用主义;力本论主义,物力论主义
dynamics of pretrial negotiation 审前协商动机
dynamitard n. (为政治目的)使用炸药的人
dynast n. (世袭的)君主
dynastic(al) a. 皇(王)朝的,朝代的
dynasty n. 朝代,王朝
dysfunction n. 机能障碍,机能失调
dysfunctional a. 机能失调的
dysfunctional result 机能失调的结果
dysnomy n. 恶法;恶法的制定
dyspareunia n. 性交快感缺乏症,性交疼痛(尤指女性)
dysphoria n. 病理性心境恶劣[指癫痫性精神障碍类型中发作性精神障碍中的一种,另四种为精神性发作(psychic seizure),自动症(automatism),朦胧状态(twilight state),急性精神分裂症样发作(acute schizophrenia like episode)。病人意识清楚,无诱因地突发病,表现负性情绪:愤怒、恐惧、紧张、抑郁、苦闷等,有时无目的漫游。其在民事和刑事领域的法律关系均属癫痫性精神障碍对待]
dyvour (苏格兰法)债务缠身或破产者

E

E-borders 电子领土
e-business scofflaw 国际电子商务隐形违法人
e-check 电子支票[指由消费者提供给收款人(多为商人)的有价支票(paper check),他用此支票作为一项电子基金转账(An electronic funds transfer),同时以电子方式审视支票磁墨身份并识别编码(magnetic-ink character recognition coding),然后按银行常规(Bank-routing)、账户以编号(serial number),再进入支票账户。这通常是在销售点终端(a point of sale terminal)。此词亦称 electronic check;见 e-money]

E-Commerce Law 《电子商务法》
e-flight recorder n. 电子飞行记录仪,(俗)黑匣子[指飞机上的电子飞行记录仪。飞行数据记录仪(FDR)和舱声录音器(CVR)两个设备通常安装在飞机尾部,在那里当飞机失事时更易保存下来。FDR 记录飞机飞行速度、高度、垂直加速度和燃油流量等。黑匣子并非黑色而是深橘色,FDR 通常由钛和不锈钢包裹,能经受恶劣环境条件,包括记忆板的关键部分可承受带有钢铁的 227 公斤物体从 3 米高度砸到它的上面;在 1100 摄氏度高温下不被融毁;可以保存 25 小时的飞行数据。CVR 不仅记录机组人员之间的对话,还可以提供给调查人员关键线索的背景噪音,但只能保存两小时的驾驶舱声音记录]
E-Government 电子政府(中国官方文件多用"电子政务",国际社会大多用"电子政府",指目前特别是近几年多国推进电子政务进程,受互联网影响,对政府管理提出挑战,使其管理更先进快捷,服务周到、全面。目前对此还无确切定义,现各发达国家和发展中国家正在推进电子政府建议和电子政府立法)
E-Government Act 《电子政府法》
e-mail n./v. 电子邮件(指人们之间利用计算机进行交流的一种方式,通过本地区网络或互联网进行,亦可拼写成 email)/发出电子邮件,使用电子邮件,通过电子邮件(亦可写成 electronic mail)
e-mail listserves 电子邮件群,电子邮件讨论群(平台)[指电子邮件讨论群提供给其成员交流意见的一个平台(forum)]
e-marketplace n. 电子商贸交易平台
e-money 电子款项,电子现金(指货币或代games(money substitute)可被转换为信息,储存在电脑或电脑芯片(computer chip)上,因此它可以转入信息系统如互联网(internet)。见 e-check,亦称 digital cash; electronic cash; on-line scrip; internet scrip]
e-readiness 电子化准备度(2005 年经济学家智库运用的一种测试电子政府效率的排名办法)

E-signature 电子签名
* *Ea quae dari impossibilia sunt, vel quae in rerum natura non sunt, pro non adjectis habentur.* Those things which are impossible to be given, or which are not in the nature of things, are regarded as not added (as no part of an agreement). 凡不可能提供的或不属理所当然要提供的物可不视为附属物(即未包括在协议中之物)。
* *Ea quae raro accidunt non temere in agendis negotiis computantur.* Those things which rarely happen are not to be taken into account in the transaction of business without sufficient reason. 在处理事务时,对于那些罕有发生的事物如没有足够的根据就不应当去考虑。
each of the participants in barter 参加易货(贸易)的每一方
each session of parliament 每届议会
* *Eadem est ratio, eadem est lex.* The same reason, the same law. 同样理由,同样法律。
* *Eadem mens praesumitur regis quae est juris et quae esse debet, praesertim in dubiis.* The mind of the sovereign is presumed to be, coincident with that of the law and with that which it ought to be, especially in ambiguous matters. 统治者的意向得推定为与法律的意向相一致,而尤其对模棱两可的问题,就应当这样来推定。
eadem persona cum defuncto 如同被继承人
ealdorman n. (盎格鲁-撒克逊时代的)司法行政军事长官(亦为 ealderman)
ear-mark (=earmark) n. 特征;标记;(身份或所有权的)标记;可辨别的(财产);标注
ear-mark of a mortgage 抵押权标志
ear-witness n. 耳(传)闻证人(即以自己亲自听到的事作证的人)
eardom n. (英)伯爵的爵位或权限(现在仅留有爵位,而权限已被授予行政司法官 sheriff)
earl n. (英)伯爵,英国贵族等级的第三级,在公、侯爵之后
Earl Marshal 典礼官(指英国王室典礼官,

亦作 Earl Marshal of England)
earlier insurer 原保险人
earlier maturity rule 较早到期规则(指依此规则,当变卖担保的价款不足以清偿所有债务时,较早债务契约则享有优先权)
earliest possible convenience 最先的可能机会(指一种允诺支付期限,允诺人一旦有能力,即应给予支付)
early a. 早的;早熟的;及早的,早日的
early complaint 及早控诉(主要指被强奸的女人在罪行发生后,应及早向警方或其他人投诉。对此种投诉证词法院可作为不同意性行为的证据加以接受)
early history of divorce 离婚的最初经过
early marriage 早婚
early neutral evaluation (美)前期中立评估程序,早期中立评价[指 ADR 的一种。对争议的标的事项由有专门知识、经验丰富、公正的律师(中立者)向当事人双方提出无拘束力的案件评估,也可提供案件计划的指导与和解的帮助]
early postmortem phenomena 早期尸体现象
early retirement benefit 提前退休金
early termination 中止
earmark n./v. (亦可写作 ear-mark)特征,标记;(身份或所有权的)标记,可辨别的(财产)/标注;在耳朵上打戳记;指定(款项等)的用途;在……上做标记
earn v. 挣得,赚得,收入,博得,赢得
earn a reputation 赢得声誉
earned-income credit (1927年)劳务所得减免(指对于低工薪收入的职工且有子女负担的,则退还联邦税的减免部分。减免部分交还纳税人,即使超过应退税额)
earned income 劳动所得,工资收入
earned premium 已收保险费,实收保险费
earner n. 靠劳动收入者(指①靠个人的努力和资产的生产挣得收入的人;②靠资产或财产为自己产生的所得)
earnest money 定金[指预期的(特别是不动产的)购买者已经支付的款项,通常在信托账户(escrow)中,以表明诚信意图来完成这笔交易,而一般情况是买者违约(defaults)而丧失权利(forfeited)。尽管这一定金按传统方式曾是以很微小数目(比如5分镍币或美元)用作物品的买卖,可它不仅是不动产买卖中的象征,而且还相当于成千上万的美元。亦称 earnest;bargain money;caution money;hand money。见 binder 2;down payment]
earnest money 定金
earning assets 有收益资产
earning capacity 收入能力,挣钱能力[指一个人挣钱的能力和影响力,一个人的天赋、才能、技术、受训和经验。挣钱能力是在一个人伤害的诉讼中衡量恢复原状的损害赔偿中所要考虑的一个因素。在家庭法中,在判决子女的扶养和配偶的生活费(或扶养费)以及按离婚配偶之间财产分配时要考虑挣钱能力。亦称 earning power]
earning potential 收入的潜能(力)
earning power (公司或个人的)赚钱能力;(资本的)收益
earnings (复) n. 收入,所得;工资,薪水;报酬;利润,收益
earnings and profits tax 收入及利(润)所得税
earnout n. 挣利
earnout formula 挣利方式
earth-orbiting station 地球轨道站
earthly standpoint 世俗化的观点,现世的观点
ease of money 利率低;银根松
easement n. 地役权(指为图自己土地的利益而使用他人土地的权利);附属建筑物;舒适;安心
easement and profit 取益权(英美法上的地役权与大陆法系的似乎具有相同意义,而取益权则包括部分取得该土地以及产出物的权利,更类似于大陆法系的地上权)
easement by necessity 必要地役权(亦作 easement of necessity,指为合理使用需役地,而此又为必不可少的,故而成立地役权。如将地役权与道路相连所需的地役权)
easement of light 采光权(指光线不受邻居阻碍权)

Easex 东萨克森
easier cases 简易案件;简单案件
East African Community 东非共同体
East Anglia 东盎格利亚(即盎格鲁)
East Asian Common Laws 东亚普通法(指以古代中国法为基础、中日韩三国独特的交往为背景而形成的概念,它由法典化、儒教法文化、乡村村落法和法学四种要素组成,东亚普通法的发展有赖于东亚人的自觉与成熟)
East Greenwich (历史)(英)东格林维治[指英格兰肯特郡一个皇家领地(royal manor)的名称。历史上,这个领土(或采邑)在皇家特授权中作为自由免役土地保有(tenure of free socage)而备受关注]
Easter term (=Easter sittings) (英)(高等法院四个开庭期之一)复活节开庭期(见 four sittings)
Eastern Orthodox Church 东正教(会)
Eastphalian "伊斯特伐利亚"(此词是对"威斯特伐利亚"国际体系的揶揄;它的理念彰显亚洲国家已不再屈从于西方理念和利益,开始对国际事务拥有发言权)
easy position 头寸宽裕
easy-joinder n. 两审合并
easy-money a. 低息的,银根松的
easygoing attitude 轻松的态度,随和之态度;不严肃之态度
easygoing familiarity 松懈
eat inde sine die (被告)毋庸再到庭(意指诉讼已撤销)
eat no fish 不吃鱼[指原天主教规定教徒星期五只吃鱼。英伊丽莎白一世(Elizabeth I.1533–1603)统治时期,天主教与政府争权斗争,有些教徒为表示对政府忠诚,星期五不吃鱼,后即以"不吃鱼"泛指忠于政府]
eat one's terms (英)学法律,进修取得大律师资格的课程(指英国要取得大律师资格必须在律师学院每学期至少吃三次正餐)
eavesdrop n./v. 檐水权(一种地役权,亦作 stillicide)/窃听,偷听
eavesdroppers and the like 窃听者及其同类

eavesdropping n. 窃听罪;偷听
ebb(=ebba) n. (英)落潮,退潮;衰退,衰落
ebb and flow (12世纪前)潮涨潮落[指此术语早期用来指明海事管辖权的范围,潮水范围可以弃船(abandoned)。Genesee Chief v. Fitzhugh,参见《美国联邦最高法院判例汇编》(霍华德第12卷)第53卷第443页(1851年)]
ebb and flow of cases 案件的增减
ebook n. 电子书(亦可写 e-book)
EC Treaty 欧共体条约
eccentricity n. 怪僻,古怪
Eccles. Law 宗教法
ecclesia 寺院,教堂,牧师住所;(古希腊城邦的)公民大会;宗教集会
ecclesiastical commissioners (英)宗教管理委员会
ecclesiastical corporations (英)基督教会法人,宗教社团
ecclesiastical courts 宗教法庭,教会法院
ecclesiastical judge 宗教法官
ecclesiastical jurisdiction 宗教裁判权
ecclesiastical law 寺院法,教会法
ecclesiastical power 教权
ecclesiastical privilege 宗教特权
eclectic a. 折中(主义)的
eclectic approach 折中主义方法
eclectic penalty 折中刑
eclecticism n. (国际法上的)折中学派,折中主义(即格劳秀斯学派)
Ecloga n. 《利奥三世法律汇编》(指拜占庭皇帝利奥三世于公元740年发布的法律汇编)
Eclogue of Byzantine Emperor Leo Ⅲ and his son Constantin 拜占庭皇帝三世及其儿子康士坦丁对话录
ecocide n. 生态灭绝
ecologic(al) a. 生态的,生态学的
ecologic(al) balance 生态平衡
ecologic(al) disaster 生态灾祸
ecologic(al) disturbance 生态失调
ecologic(al) effect 生态效应
ecologic(al) system 生态系统
ecological rationality 进化理性主义

ecological forestry 生态林业
ecological zoning 生态城市规划(或称 eco-zoning)
ecology n. 生态学
ecology of crime 见 environmental criminology
ecology of law 法律生态学
ecology of public administration (美)行政生态学(指以生态学的方法来系统研究行政现象和事实的一门科学)
econometric n. 计量经济学
econometric technique 经济计量方法
economic a. 经济(上)的;经济学的;实用的;实际的;俭省的
economic accounting 经济核算
economic activity 经济活动
economic actors 经纪人;经济行为者
economic administration of justice 经济司法
economic affairs 经济事务
economic agent 经济代理
economic agreement 经济协定
Economic and Social Committee of European Communities 欧洲共同体经社委员会
Economic and Social Council (联合国)经济及社会理事会
economic arbitration 经济仲裁,经济公断
economic association 经济联合体
economic autonomy 经济上的自主权
economic behavio(u)r 经济行为
economic benefit 经济利益;经济补贴
economic blockade 经济封锁
economic boycott 经济上的联合抵制
economic cases 经济案件
economic chamber 经济法庭
economic code 经济法典
Economic Commission for Europe 欧洲经济委员会
economic compensation 经济赔偿;经济退赔;经济报酬
economic concession 经济特许协议;经济性之协议(指东道国政府与外国投资者根据东道国之国法签订的一种协议)
economic contract 经济合同(契约)
Economic Contract Law of the People's Republic of China 《中华人民共和国经济合同法》
economic control 经济统制,经济管理
economic council 经济委员会
economic court 经济法庭
economic crime 经济犯罪
economic data 经济数据
economic democracy 经济民主
economic determinism 经济决定论
economic discrimination 经济歧视
economic dynamics 动态经济学
economic effectiveness 经济效益
economic efficiency 经济效率(指经济学通常将"经济效率"界定为"消费者之间或生产者之间的均衡",而维持这种均衡一直是市场有效竞争的目标之一。分析互联网企业独家交易行为对经济效率之影响,成为判定该行为是否排除、限制竞争的重要环节。众所周知,资源利用率乃衡量经济效率的一个重要指标。因此,认定互联网企业独家交易行为对经济效率的影响,可将资源利用率作为考量标准。具体说,可从两个角度进行认定:一是考察互联网行业的资源配置效率;二是分析互联网企业内部资源配置效率。若互联网企业独家交易行为严重降低了资源配置效率,则会被认为损害了竞争机制,可能违反垄断法)
economic enterprise 经济企业
economic exploitation 经济剥削
economic forecasts 经济预测
economic formation 经济结构
economic function of goods 商品的经济功能
economic globalization 经济全球化
economic grounds 经济领域,经济基础
economic growth 经济增长
economic incentive 经济刺激(或鼓励),经济激励
economic independence 经济独立
economic indicator 经济指标
economic inducement 经济诱发,经济诱因
economic information 经济情报,经济信息
economic interest 经济利益
economic intervention 经济干预

economic interventionist 经济干预者
economic jurisdiction 经济审判权;经济管辖权;经济司法管辖区
economic jurisprudence 经济法学
economic jurist 经济法学家
economic law(s) 经济法,经济法则
economic legislation 经济立法
economic lever 经济杠杆,经济手段
economic liberties 经济自由
economic lifeline of the country 国家经济命脉
economic literatures on settlement 和解的经济学文献
economic litigation 经济诉讼
economic management system 经济管理体制
economic ministry 经济部
economic monopoly 经济垄断
economic order 经济秩序
Economic Partnership Agreement (EPA) 《经济合伙协定》
economic performance 经济成就,经济成效
economic persecution 经济迫害
economic plan 经济计划
economic planning act 经济计划法
economic planning agency 经济计划机构,(日)经济企划厅
economic planning board 经济规划委员会
economic plundering 经济掠夺
economic, political and legal integration 经济的、政治的和法律的融会
economic projection 经济预测
economic prosperity 经济繁荣
economic punishment 经济处罚
economic reform 经济改革
economic regulation 经济调整
economic relation 经济关系
economic responsibility system 经济责任制
economic right 经济权利(指在版权法中与作者精神权利相对的权利,有的国家称"物质权利"material right)
economic sanction 经济制裁,经济处分
economic sector 经济成分
Economic Stabilization Act 《经济稳定法》
economic status 经济地位
economic statute 经济法令;经济法规
economic strike 经济性罢工
economic structure 经济组织,经济结构
economic system 经济体系,经济体制
economic take-off 经济腾飞
economic theories of law 法律的经济学理论
economic theory of secession 脱离的经济理论
economic tort 经济上的侵权行为
economic transformation 经济的变换
economic treaty 经济条约
economic tribunal 经济裁判庭
economic trust 经济信托
economic U-turn 完全相反的经济政策
economic unit (国家征用)经济单位,经济统一性[指在部分土地征用(partial condemnation)的案件中,用来确定公平市场价格的部分土地是由国家征用权征用的部分。这块征用的土地是大或是小都是整个不动产的一部分。决定多少不动产在此经济单位之中,有三个因素可以衡量:①使用的共同性(unity of use);②所有人的统一性(unity of ownership);③毗连,其中最重要的是使用的共同性]
economic warfare 经济战
economical a. 经济上的,经济学的,节约的,节俭的
economics (复) n. 经济学;经济,经济情况
economics of crime 犯罪经济学
economics of legal procedure 法律诉讼的经济学
economics of scale 规模经济学
economics paradigm 经济学的范例
economism n. 经济主义
economist n. 经济学家;节俭的人
economy n. 1.经济,经济制度 2.节约,节约措施,经济实惠 3.系统,组织
economy game 经济博弈(指把经济看做一个"博弈",对于理解法律在经济学中的角色很有帮助,经济中每一市民都被认为博弈的参加者,他们可以采取一系列行为策略,经济中最终结果有赖于每一参加者对策略的选择,会导致每一个参加者的"收益",这种经济可被称为经济博弈)

Economy, Efficiency and Effectiveness 经济,效率和效益(亦称"三E",指工商管理理论的"管理主义"或"新公共管理",往往追求"三E")

ecoterrorism n. 生态恐怖主义、环境恐怖主义(指关系到环保和动物权利问题的恶劣状况,亦称 environmental terriorism, ecological crime, enviroterriorism, ecosabatage, ecovandalism)

ecosabatage 见 ecoterrorism

ecosystem(s) n. 生态系统〈climate charge is about ecosystems〉(气候变化关乎生态系统),〈climate change negotiations are about egosystems〉(气候变化谈判充斥的是利己主义氛围)

ecovandalism 见 ecoterrorism

EDI agreement (Electronic Data Interchange agreement) 电子数据交换协议[指规治数据交换或转让的一项协议,比如双方当事人之间利用电脑进行指令的买卖(purchase orders)。根据电子数据交换协议,被传送的电子数据(electronic data transmitted)通常按一个约定的标准(an agreed standard),如美国国家标准研究所(American National Standard Institute)X12标准或联合国 EDIFACT 标准,进行数据安排(formatted)]

edict n. (14世纪)正式的法令(decree) [指要求或由国家当局发行的公告(proclamation),在有些国家,法令(edict)具有和制定法同等的法律效力。关于罗马法的法令(edicts)。]见 *edictum*]

Edict Nautae, Caupones, Stabularii (罗马法)船主、旅店主、车行主的责任(指他们应对旅客带入船舱、旅店或马厩的财物安全负责原则)

Edict of Milan 《米兰敕令》(指罗马帝国313年宣布宽容基督教的公告)

Edict of Toleration 信仰自由令(指1781年神圣罗马帝国皇帝约瑟夫颁布的给予不信奉天主教的基督徒一定信仰自由的法令)

edicta 诏书,敕令,告示[指根据罗马帝国的权力等级体制,皇帝为最高行政司法长官,并享有所有行政司法长官所应享有的发布敕令的权力,其权力之广超越任何基层行政司法长官之权力,因此在罗马帝制背景下,皇帝所下达的诏书就是国家法律的主要渊源。皇帝下达的诏书涉及内容十分广泛,有一些不乏重要性;公元212年的安东尼法其实就是一则诏书。皇帝诏书具有永久效力,而不受其身后善恶之影响]

Edicta Justiniani 查士丁尼敕令

edictal a. (17世纪)法令的,正式发布公告的,一个或一个以上正式法令的(edictally ad.)

edicts of justinian (罗马法)查士丁尼敕令[指查士丁尼的十三部基本法律,以威尼斯式手稿附于《希腊新律汇编》(Greek Collection of Novels)之中;这种敕令被限定于罗马帝国各省的行政事务范畴]

edictum (罗马法)1.命令,敕令,法令[指在罗马帝国时期,一项敕令,一项训令;由皇帝宣布的命令或一项法规。一项敕令就是皇帝按照自己的意愿创制的重要或基本法律(constitution)。它不同于以回答方式而非退回的解释敕令(rescript),也区别于审判中并非被授予的裁决令(decree),也并非以请求(solicitation)为基础的,比如一项具有法律效力的皇帝宣告的基本法律]2.治安官的宣告[指涉及治安官的管辖权(jurisdiction)的宣告(declaration)或权限(competence)范围的宣告;特别是治安官对于他建议的公务行为的一些原则的宣告。复数为edicta。见 *edictum annuum; formula* 1]

edictum aedilicium (罗马法)罗马民政官员的告示(指一位显贵席位的罗马民政官对关于在公共市场销售或做买卖的敕令或告示,特别是对于次品、动物或奴隶的买卖给予补偿的告示。比如,一名民政官可以宣告销售人必须对货物内在的缺陷承担责任,并命令出卖的野生动物和狗应受到管制以保护公众。复数形式为 *edicta aedilicia*;亦可称为 *aedilitium edictum*)

edictum annuum 罗马的军事执政官在就职一年期开始发布的命令。复数为 edicta annua

edictum perpetuum (罗马法)永久性敕令

(指执政官和司法行政官颁布并在其任期内一直有效的敕令)
edictum praetoris (罗马法)裁判官告示(指罗马裁判官就职之初所颁布的宣言表明其在职之中所承诺遵守之规则或原则,以告示人民。亦称为 praetorian edict;见 *edictum annuum*)
edictum provinciale (罗马法)行政敕令,行政告示[指罗马帝国时期省的执政官 (provincial governors)按罗马裁判官告示的模式为司法审判(administration of justice)所颁布的告示或系统的规则。复数形式为 edicta provincialia]
edictum repentinum (罗马法)临时敕令(指颁布的补充敕令应对某种紧急情况。与 edictum perpetuum 相对)
Edictum Theodorici 迪奥多西法令集[指由奥斯特罗哥特(Ostrogoths)国王迪奥多西于公元 500 年在罗马颁布的法律汇集,共 154 条,适用于罗马和哥特。这可能是迪奥多西三世,维西哥特(Visigoths)在高卢(罗马帝国的一部分)的国王(公元 460 年)]
edictum tralaticium (罗马法)传袭性敕令(指能在下届执政官和司法行政官任期内继续有效的敕令)
editor n. 编者;主笔;编辑
Editor of Laws of the Department of State (美)国务院法律编辑局
editorial privilege 见 newsman's privilege 2
education n. 教育;教育程度;教育学;修养
education act 教育法
education allowance 教育津贴
education code 教育法典
education of legal system 法制教育
education policy 教育政策
Education, Science, Culture and Public Health Committee (中)教育科学文化卫生委员会(全国人民代表大会设立的专门委员会)
educational a. 教育的,有教育意义的
educational administration 教育行政
educational background 学历
educational legislation 教育立法

Educational Scientific and Cultural Organization (联合国)教育、科学及文化组织(简称"教科文组织")
educative reform 教育改革
effect n./v. 1.要旨,意义;作用,效能,效力,影响 2.结果;实施,实行,实现 3.(复)财产,动产/产生,招致,实现,实施,达到
effect arrest 执行逮捕
effect of appeal 上诉的效力
effect of bankruptcy 破产的效力
effect of criminal law 刑法的效力
effect of death 死亡的后果
effect of litigation costs on settlement terms 有关诉讼成本对和解条款的影响
effect of mortgage 抵押的效力
effect of obligation 债的效力
effect of rights over things 物权的效力
effect of sale 买卖效力
effect of the rigid concept of exclusive territorial sovereignty 排他领土主权的刚性概念的影响
effect of will 遗嘱的效力
effective a. 有效的,生效的;实在的,实际的,有力的
effective agency 有效机构;有效力量;有效作用
effective blockade 有效封锁
effective cause 直接原因
effective consensus obligation 实际一致的义务
effective control 有效统治,有效管制(理)
effective date 有效日期
effective government 有效率的政府
effective guarantee 有效担保
effective implementation 有效执行
effective instrument 有效文据
effective international control 有效的国际管制(监督)
effective judicial supervision 有效的司法监督
effective occupation (国际法)有效占领
effective operation of the litigation system 诉讼体系的有效运行
effective period of the contract 合同(契约)有效期

effective possession 有效占有
effective recourse 有效追索
effective relief 有效的(法律)救济
effective sovereignty 有效主权
Effective Trial Management Programme (英)有效审判管理机制
effectiveness n. 管辖效力
effects insured 保险财产
effects presuppose causes 有其果必有其因
effectuate v. 实现,实行,完成,使奏效
effete a. 枯竭的,虚弱的,无能的
effete communities 无力的社区
efficacy n. 功效,效能
efficacy of effort 努力的效果,努力的功效
efficiency n. 效力;效率;效能
efficiency considerations 效率对价
efficiency expert (研究如何取得人力、设备等最高效率的)效率专家
efficiency in governing 统治效率,治理效率
efficient a. (直接)生效的,效率高的,能胜任的,有能力的
efficient allocation 有效配置(指对资源配置中效率的分析,这是经济学理论的主要课题,亦是微观经济与理论的主要组成部分)
efficient breach 合理违反(指允许违约一方向对方支付损害赔偿,而不再履行该合同义务,这被称作"合理违反")
efficient capital market 有效资本市场
Efficient Capital Market Hypothesis (ECMH) 有效(率)资本市场假说(指现代金融市场理论中提供"欺诈市场理论"的一种系统理论基础)
efficient care 有效的小心
efficient care taking 有效的持有小心
efficient cause 有效起因,直接原因(与 immediate cause 意义相同)
efficient disposition 有效的处理
efficient equilibrium 有效均衡
efficient law 有效率的法律,有效法律
Efficient Market Hypothesis (EMH) 有效市场假说
efficient reliance 有效信赖
efficient remedy 有效救济方法
efficient working of free market 自由市场的有效运转
efflorescence n. (艺术事业)绝顶,开花
effluxion (=efflux) n. 1.满期;(时间的)消逝 2.(液体、空气等的)流出,散发;流出物
effluxion of time (许可证合同)正常履行完毕;一段时间;期限届满时,到期
effort n. 努力,艰难的尝试;成就;努力的成果
effractor n. 窃贼
effrontery n. 厚颜无耻(行为)
effusio sanguinis (古英国法)(国王准予领主进行强制的)放血惩罚;罚金
egalitarian analyze 主张平等主义的分析
egalitarianism n. 平等主义
egg donation (家庭法)卵子给予,卵子植入[指帮助再生产的一种治疗形式,可使一位妇女卵子移植到另一妇女的子宫(uterus)内。被移植的妇女接受卵子后可怀孕生子。在卵子植入期间,通常需试管内授精(fertilized in vitro)。见 in vitro fertilization]
eggshell plaintiff rule 蛋壳规则(源于一颅骨薄如蛋壳的原告在一事件中致颅骨破碎的案例,美国侵权法史上称之为蛋壳规则,又称 eggshell-skull rule。该原则规定,被告对原告的无法预见性以及对被告的过失或有意行为应该承担责任)
ego n. 自我,自己;自负;自私
ego-dystonic homosexuality 自压性同性恋(指一种精神疾病,患者不断抱怨异性对其缺乏吸引力,但对持续不断的同性需求却又产生罪恶感,日积月累成为内心无法承受之冲突的自然性同性恋精神疾病)
egosystem(s) n. 利己主义
egregious errors 极端的错误,惊人的错误
egregious situation 极端情况
Egyptian law 埃及法(指起源于公元前3100年米那王统一上下埃及时的法律,其形成发展一直延续到罗马人于公元前30年占领埃及为止)
ei et armis 使用暴力和武力
* *Ei incumbit probatio, qui dicit, non qui negat; cum per rerum naturam factum negantis probatio nulla sit.* The proof lies

upon him who affirms, not upon him who denies; since, by the nature of things, he who denies a fact can not produce any proof. 按事物的规律,否认事实的人是不可能提供任何证明的,因而证明的义务只能由确认事实的人,而不能由否认事实的人来负担。

eight-grade wage scale (中)八级工资标准

eight-grade wage system (中)八级工资制

Eight-Hour Law 《八小时工作法》

eight-hour work system 八小时工作制

Eighteenth Amendment 美国联邦宪法第十八修正案[这是唯一一个颁布之后被废止的宪法修正案。该修正案禁止"在合众国及其管辖下的一切领土内酿造、出售或运送作为饮料的酒类,禁止此类酒类输入或输出合众国及其管辖下的一切领土"。对酒类的禁令使联邦宪法第十八修正案成为全国性的禁酒令。该修正案于1917年12月在两院以两党中的大多数即超过2/3多数赞成而通过。到1919年1月16日,已有34个州批准了该修正案,并于1920年1月17日开始生效。经历了10年的争议后,以同样的一边倒的表决结果被1933年12月5日生效的联邦宪法第二十一修正案(Twenty-first Amendment)推翻。全国性的禁酒令是一个世纪里全国范围内的禁酒运动的产物。19世纪自愿戒酒运动极大降低了美国酒类的消费量。19世纪50年代12个州暂时通过了禁酒的法律,而从19世纪80年代到第一次世界大战,地方性法律以及州范围内的禁酒令开始扩展。在此胜利鼓舞下,宗教团体、女权组织、社会和政治改革者以及商界人们开始呼吁寻求一个整体的、永久性的全国性解决方案,即宪法禁令。参议员不愿投票通过禁酒的宪法修正案,但也不敢投票反对,所以提出了一个7年的批准期,希望以此计策阻止禁令批准的完成。然而在这以后的13个月就有44个州的立法机构批准了这一禁令。到1922年,除罗得岛外所有州都批准了该禁令,不过对全国禁酒的普遍抵制和有组织反对日益高涨,终于在1933年联邦宪法第二十一修正案废止了禁酒令。正如赫伯特·胡佛(Herbert Hoover)总统所说,禁酒令是"一个有着高尚目的的实验"]

Eighth Amendment 美国联邦宪法第八修正案[该修正案于1971年作为《权利法案》(Bill of Rights)的一部分被通过。它规定不得科处过多的保释金、过重的罚金和不得施加残酷而异常的刑罚(cruel and unusual punishment)。该规定为刑事判决的严厉性提供联邦宪法上的实体限制]

eigne 见 *aisne*

eindeutigkeitsregel 明白无误规则(指此规则要求解释遗嘱不得违反其明白无误的文义)

eirenicon n. 和解提议

* *Eisdem modis dissolvitur obligatio quae nascitur ex contractu, vel quasi, quibus contrahitur.* An obligation which arises from contract, or quasi contract, is dissolved in the same ways in which it is contracted. 由合同(契约)或准合同(契约)产生的债应以缔约时所采用的同样方式来解除。

eject v. 1.驱逐;排斥 2.(通过诉讼)排除(租户等的)占有权 3.免……的职

ejection of tenant 驱逐租户

ejectione firmae (普通法)逐出农庄诉讼;收回土地诉讼

ejectment n. 1.驱逐,赶走 2.收回不动产(土地或房屋)诉讼;收回地产占有权(或所有权)诉讼

ejectment of farm (= *ejctione firmae*)

ejector n. 驱逐者;收回不动产诉讼的原告;取消他人占有权者

ejuration n. (权利等的)放弃,(诉讼等的)撤回

* *Ejus est nolle, qui potest velle.* He who can will (exercise volition), has a right to refuse to will (to withhold consent). 谁可以表达意志(进行意思表示)也就有权拒绝表达意志(拒绝承诺)。

* *Ejus est non nolle qui potest velle.* He may consent tacitly who may consent expressly. 谁可以明示允诺也就可以默示允诺。

* *Ejus est periculum cujus est dominium aut*

commodum. He who has the dominion or advantage has the risk. 谁获得所有权或好处,谁就要承担风险。

* *Ejus nulla culpa est, cui parere necesse sit.* No guilt attaches to him who is compelled to obey. Obedience to existing laws is a sufficient extenuation of guilt before a civil tribunal. 任何罪行都不得加诸被迫服从的人。服从现行法规的行为足以在民事审判庭上减轻其罪责。

ejusdem generis 同一类别,同类性质的;同类解释规则(指一种解释规则,当用一系列含有特殊意义的词来解释一般意义的词汇时,该一般意义的词汇仅限于在与特殊意义的词语同种类的范畴理解,在一系列特定的人或物的如下单词或短语之后,总括性的单词和短句被解释为只包括列举的同类人或物。比如,短语中马、牛、猪、羊或农场的其他动物。其总括语言含义中不管"农场的其他动物"意义多广泛,但此时只能被解释为是四条腿的用蹄子走路的哺乳动物,而将鸡排除在外,亦称 Lord Tenderden's rule)

ejusdem generis rule 同类规则(即类似情况也适用的原则)

ejusdem negotii 同类交易的部分

elaborace 得到,获得;购得,通过劳动和勤奋赚得

elaborate v./a. 精心阐述;制作/详细说明的;制作的

elaboration n. 译述,尽力阐述,详尽阐述,精心制作

elaboratus 通过劳动获得的财产

elastic a. 1.有弹性的,可伸缩的 2.有活力的;灵活的;能适应的

elastic clause (法律等的)弹性条款(文)

elastic tariff 弹性关税

elasticity n. 1.弹性,伸缩性 2.活力;灵活性

elasticity of law 法律的灵活性

elasticity of ownership 所有权的伸缩性

Elden Brethern (英)领港协会会员[领港协会或航务管理所(Trinity House)会员的通称。经过选出的成员如主事(master)、代理主事,还有其他主事,其中包括荣誉主事等。该协会系1514年亨利八世统治时期

敕准设立的,承担许多海事任务,如码头与管理灯塔等。在海事诉讼中,1名法官和代理主事共同开庭,代理主事为法官提供海员和航海事项的咨询意见,还可作为陪审员在捕获法庭(prize courts)出庭]

elder a./n. 资格老的;地位最高的;年龄较大的;从前的/长者;(复)长者,前辈;长老;祖先,前人

elder law 年老法、老龄法(指处理年龄较长者范畴的法律,涉及遗产计划、退休福利、社会保障、年龄歧视以及健康关怀等问题)

elder statesman 政界元老(尤指已退休的)

elder time 昔日,往日

eldest judge 最年长的法官

elect v. 推选,选举;选择;决定;进行票选

elected n. 当选人,当选者,被选人

elected domicile 选定住所

elected government 当选的政府

elected local authorities 民选的地方权力机关

elected member (议会)当选议员,选举产生的议员

elected representative 当选代表

election n. (13世纪)1.选择;择取[特别是从好几个权利或救济中选择的行为,在某种程度上排斥其他权利或救济的适用〈the taxpayer's election to file jointly instead of separately〉纳税人选择联合申报来替代分别申报]。见 election of remedies]2.挑选,选定;愿意[指一项原则,据此某人按法律文件被强制接受一项福利或救助(benefit)或该人已具有资格保留某项财产权利,在两者之间挑选;具有债务的当事方在权利和权利主张之间挑选。如此,具有资格的当事方只能选择一项〈the prevailing plaintiff was put to an election between out-of-packet damages and lost profits〉(胜诉的原告被迫在赚钱赔偿损失和失去利益两者之间挑定一个),亦称 equitable election。见 right of election]3.选举[指选举某人担任某一职位(通常为公职)的过程,或选定会员或成员资格、奖金或其他头衔、地位等的程序〈the 2004 congressional eletion〉(2004年国会议员的选

举)。见 two-round voting]

election agent 选举代理人

election at large (美)大区选举[指选举政府官员(public official)的主要的或大的(全州或全市)选区,而非在大选举单位下的小区或分区的选举。亦称 at large election]

election auditor 选举费用审查官

election campaign 竞选运动

election commission 选举委员会

election commissioners 选举调查委员

election day 1.选举日 2.(大写)(美)总统及国会议员选举日(每隔四年或两年的11月第一个星期后的星期二)

election expenses 选举费用

election judge (英)审理选区选举案件的法官(被派往选区的高等法院法官,审理该区有关违法选举嫌疑的请愿书之类的案件)

election mechanism 选举机构

election meeting 选举会议

election mobilization 选举动员

election of remedies 1.救济的选择,补救的选定[指请求权人(claimant)在两个或两个以上共存但互不协调且基于简单系列事实的救济之间的选择行为] 2.积极辩护,阻止选择(指当另一救济已经被授予诉讼当事方且优于对方已造成损害时,则以积极辩护来阻止当事方寻求与另一已取得的救济不相一致的救济,这一准则已广泛地陷入不佳地,故当今已基本不再适用) 3.积极答辩,获得救济[指请求人不得同时重复获得两个不同的赔偿责任(liability)裁决的损害赔偿,如果两个权利请求均为同一损害,则创立双倍追索(double recovery)。见 alternative relief]

election of remedies doctrine 救济选择理论

election or appointment of liquidators 清算人的选任或指定

election petition (在选举时有贿赂双重投票情况所提的)选举请愿书

election petition court (英)选举请愿法庭

election precinct 选举区

election returns 选举报告

election system 选举制

election to an office 竞选官职

election tribunal 选举裁判庭

election year 选举年

electioneer v. 竞选,做竞选活动;拉选票

electioneering n. 竞选;助选

elections to parliament act 议会选举法

elective a. 选举的;由选举产生的,(职位等)选任的;有选举权的;可选择的

elective franchise 选举权

elective judge 选任法官

elective judiciary 选举法官制度

elective office 选任公职

elective share 选择的份额[指遗孀(或子女)可在接受其亡夫遗嘱中为其保留的遗产份额或其他保留财产份额进行选择。亦称 forced share; statutory share, statutory forced share 等]

Elector(s) n. 有选举权者,合格选举人,(神圣罗马帝国的)有权选举皇帝的诸侯;(美)选举团(electoral college)的成员[选举人(美国联邦宪法第2条规定:"各州应依照该州立法机关以规定的方式选派选举人若干名。其总数应与各该州有权派于国会的参议员与众议员的总数相等。但参议员、众议员、在合众国政府下受俸或任职人不得被派为选举人。")美国参众两院议员(100+435)共计535名,亦即国会议员数、选举人也是535名,由选举人选举总统和副总统]

electoral a. 选举的;选举人的;由选举人组成的

electoral act 选举法

electoral body 选举主体;选民

electoral boundary 选区范围

electoral circumscriptions 选举区

electoral college (美)(专门负责选举总统与副总统的)选举团(其代表由各州选举)

electoral council 选举委员会

electoral court 选举法院(庭)

electoral district 选举区,选区

electoral document 选举文件

electoral judge 选举法庭法官

electoral law 选举法

electoral lawsuit 选举案件;选举诉讼
electoral power 选举权,(大写)选举机构
electoral procedure 选举程序
electoral processes 选举程序
electoral program(me) 选举方案
electoral qualification 选举资格
electoral register 选民登记册
electoral roll 选举名册
electoral strength 选举力量
electoral system 选举制度
electoral tribunal 选举法庭
electorate n. 全体选民;选举团;选区;(神圣罗马帝国的)有权选举皇帝的诸侯的身份(或领地);(美国的总统)选举团(见 electoral college)
electorate perception 全国选民的概念
elector's certificate 选民证
electress n. 女选民;(神圣罗马帝国的)有权选举皇帝的诸侯的妻子
electric a. 电的,用电的
electric burn 电流烧伤
electric chair 电(刑)椅(指处决罪犯用的电椅)
electric failure 心衰竭
electric larceny 窃电(罪)
electrocute v. 施以电刑处死;触电致死
electrocution n. 施电刑
electronic a. 电子的
electronic agent 电子代理人(指由美国的 ATM 机和自动售货机在美国法律中被称为"电子代理人")
electronic authentication 电子印件
electronic bulletin board 电子公告牌
electronic cach 见 e-money
electronic chameleon 电子变色龙
electronic commerce 电子商务(简称 EC)(指通过电信网络进行的产品生产、广告营销、销售和流通的过程)
(The) Electronic Communication Private Act (ECPA) (美)《电子交易隐私法案》(见 reasonable expectation of privacy)
electronic correspondence 电子函件电子通信
Electronic Data Interchange (EDI) 电子数据交换(俗称无纸交易——paperless trading)
Electronic Data Interchange agreement 电子数据交换协议(见 EDI Agreement)
electronic data processing rights 数据的电子处理权[指属于新技术发展而产生的现代版权项目之一,即将文字或图(画、表)数据化后,储入计算机内的权利,以及借助计算机对原作复制、翻译或改编的权利]
electronic dissemination 电子传播
electronic eavesdropping equipment 电子窃听装置(=electronic eavesdropping)
electronic evidence 电子证据
electronic financial law 电子金融法
electronic fingerprinting method 电子仪器提取指纹法
Electronic Freedom of Information Act (EFOIA) (美)《电子情报自由法》(1996 年 9 月 17 日,美国众议院通过了关于修改 FOIA 的第 3802 号法案,第二天参议院也通过了这一法案,同年 10 月 2 日美国总统签署了这一法案,对"情报自由法"进行了历史上又一次重大修改,而成为《电子情报自由法》,主要是为解决随着政府记录电子化而来的电子情报公开问题及对公众关于情报公开申请答复迟缓的问题)
electronic funds transfer 电子基金转账[指由一个人或一个单位现金支付给另一个人,通过在计算机银行业务系统之间的一系列交易构成的支付程序。从最初的支付指令(payment order)开始到最后支付指令到达被受益人的银行(beneficiary's bank)接收为止。商业的或批发的基金转账均按照美国《统一商法典》(UCC)第 4 条 A 的准则操作。消费者基金转让(consumer funds transfers)则按联邦基金转让法(Federal Electronic Fund Transfer Act)进行管理。参见《美国注释法典》第 15 卷第 1693 节。同 funds transfer]
Electronic Fund Transfer Act of 1978 (美)《1978 年电子资金划拨法》
electronic information 电子信息
electronic mail 电脑通信;电子通信,电子邮件

electronic money 电子货币
electronic personalities 电子人格
electronic right 电子权
Electronic Signatures in Global and National Commerce Act (ESGNCA) 美国联邦政府通过《全球及国家商务电子签名法》（2000年6月）
electronic surveillance 电子监视
electronic trading facilities 电子交易设备
electronic warfare 电子战（一般指敌对双方争夺电磁频谱使用权和控制权的军事斗争,具体表现为敌对双方相互进行侦查、电子干扰、电子欺骗、电子隐身、电子摧毁等方面的斗争）
eleemosynary n./a. 受抚恤者,受人救济者/慈善（事业）的,施舍的,不收费的；受抚恤的,受救济的
eleemosynary corporation 慈善企业,慈善事业
elegit n. 扣押的执行令状（指授权原告占有被告的财产直至债务还清为止所发的执行令状）；土地扣押执行令状
elemency n. 赦免或减刑[特别是总统或州长有权赦免一个罪犯或减少刑事量刑（criminal sentence）,亦称 executive elemency。见 pardon; commutation 2]
element n. 因素；成分；分子；要素；（复）原理；基础
elemental a./n. 基本的,初步的；自然力的/1.（古希腊）四大要素（指土、木、气、水）2.（复）基本原理
elements deprived of political rights 被剥夺政治权利的分子
elements engaging beating, smashing and looting （中）打、砸、抢分子
elements of crime 犯罪要素；犯罪构成要件
elements released after serving a full term 刑满释放人员
elenctic a. 反驳论证的
elevated railroad 高架铁路
Eleventh Amendment 美国联邦宪法第十一修正案[该修正案于1794年3月4日由国会提出,于1798年1月8日批准生效。该修正案规定:"在普通法和衡平法上,凡另一州的公民或任何外国公民或属民控诉合众国任何一州的案件,不得由合众国法院受理。"这是一条限制联邦法院受理他州公民或外国属民起诉某一州权利的修正案。美国历史上仅有两个宪法修正案的通过明确是为了"撤销"美国联邦最高法院判决。其一为第十六修正案,另一为第十一修正案。它否决了1793年联邦最高法院对奇泽姆诉佐治亚州案（Chisholm v. Georgia）的判决。该案中,联邦最高法院认可了一州公民在联邦最高法院初审诉讼（origin action）中诉他州的权利。这一判决引起了共和主义者的愤怒和各州的强烈反对,认为破坏了各州的主权,在国会提出建议,国会接受建议于1793年4月提出第十一修正案,1795年2月7日该修正案获得3/4州立法机关的批准,直到1798年1月8日美国总统提出咨文后方被正式宣布成为宪法的组成部分。总体而言,联邦法院无权受理任何州（包括本州）公民、外国人、外国诉州的案件,但有权受理美国或代表本州利益的其他州起诉某一州的诉讼。对联邦法院审判权的限制可能威胁到那些重要的全民目标,美国联邦宪法第十一修正案以及州的主权豁免都属于那些重要的例外情况。国会可以在美国联邦宪法第十四修正案、第十五修正案的规定下,完全依据强制权理由提起对州的诉讼]
elicit v. 得出,引出（真理等）；诱出（回答）；使吐出（真情）
elicit the truth from a witness 使证人吐露真情
eliciting evidence 取证
elide v. 取消；不予考虑；削减,节删
eligibility n. 合格；合格性
eligible a. （15世纪）(for)合格的；符合被推选条件的,适宜的,法律上符合官员资格的
eligible for re-elected（或 **eligible for re-election**）得连选连任
eligible officer 合格官（职）员
eligible participants 符合资格条件的参加人
eliminate v. 消除,排除,消灭
elimination n. 排除,消除,消灭
elimination of counterrevolutionaries 肃清

反革命分子
elimination prints 排除嫌疑印纹
elisor n. (由法庭指派在某案件中)临时执行警长或验尸官职务者
élite status 优秀分子的身份(资格);优越的地位;高级地位
elitism n. 杰出人物统治论;(高人一等的)优越感
elliptical a. 椭圆的,省略的
eloin (=eloign) v. 移至远处,移走
elope v. 私奔;逃亡;弃职;私逃
elopement n. 私奔;逃亡;出走,卷逃;弃职
eloquence n. 善辩;口才;雄辩术
eloquent a. 有说服力的,雄辩的
eloqnent counsel 善辩的辩护人,雄辩的律师
eloquent proof 有力的证明
elucidation n. 阐明,解释
elucidation of facts 对事实的解释
elude v. 逃避,躲避(责任,危险等);难倒;使困惑(难以理解)
elude observation 掩人耳目
elusive a. 难以理解的,难以捉摸的,逃避的,易忘的
emanate v./n. 发源于(from),散发,发射/发出,发散
emanating from the sovereign 来源于主权
emanating power from 从……来源的权力
emancipate v. 使不受(政治社会、法律等)约束;使(孩子、妻子)摆脱亲权统治而获得自主的权利;释放;解放,自立
emancipated minor 自立的未成年人(指摆脱亲权而获得自主权利的未成年人)
emancipatio (罗马法)解放(又译:自立或摆脱管束。指家主可免除妻子、子女所受的管制);财产的转让
emancipation n. 自立;解放;释放;摆脱管束
emancipation acts 解放行为(见 married women's property acts)
Emancipation Manifesto (俄史)解放宣言(指俄皇亚历山大于1861年3月3日发布的附有解放农奴的17个法令的文件)
emancipation of children 子女自立
emancipation of woman 妇女解放

Emancipation Proclamation (美史)解放宣言(1863年林肯发布的解放奴隶的法令);解放黑奴宣言
emancipator n. 解放者
emancipatory a. 解放的
emancipist n. (澳)争取公民权者(指刑期已满的罪犯要求享有全部公民权者)
embalming n. 尸体防腐
embargo n./v. 禁运;禁止(通商);封港令,禁运令;扣船;禁止出(入)港/禁止(出)入港;禁止(通商);扣押(船舶、货物等)
embargo on ships 禁止船舶通行
embark v. 上船,上飞机;开始,从事(on, upon,in);搭载
embassy n. 1.大使的职务 2.大使的派遣 3.大使馆,特别使节团;大使住宅 4.大使馆全体人员 5.重任,差使
embed v. 埋置,嵌入,印入
embezzle v. 盗用(公款或公物);监守自盗;侵吞;盗用;贪污
embezzlement n. 贪污公款(罪);监守自盗(罪);侵吞,盗用
embezzlement of public funds 盗用公款(罪);侵吞公款(罪)
embezzlement of tax funds 侵吞税款(罪)
embezzler n. 贪污犯,盗用公款者;监守自盗者
embezzler of state funds 盗窃国库者
embezzling group 盗窃集团;贪污集团
emblem n. 标记;标志;纹章;徽章;象征
emblements (复) n. 收获庄稼权;耕作地的收获或孳息(见 away-going crop)
emblers de gentz 盗窃犯,窃贼(此词常见于古代英议会议事录中)
embodiment of property itself 财产本身的集体化
embody v. 体现,使具体化;包含,包括;合并,编入,收录
embolden sb. to do sth. 鼓励某人做某事
embrace v. 1.笼络,收买(陪审员等)2.拥抱;抓住;包围;着手;包括;领会;接受;信奉
embracer n. 笼络(或收买)陪审员(或法官)的人
embracer(or) n. 笼络(或收买)陪审员

(或法官)的人;犯有贿赂罪的人
embracery n. 笼络(贿赂)陪审员行为;贿赂陪审员罪
embryo n./a. 胎儿(尤指受孕后8周内的),胚胎;萌芽时期(状态)/初期的,未发达的;胚胎的
embryonic common law (英)萌芽时期的普通法
emendation n. 修改,校订,校改
emerge v. 冒出,出现,浮现,形成,(事实)暴露
emergence n. 浮现,出现
emergency n. 非常时刻,紧急情况,突然事件;遇险,紧急状态
emergency act 紧急法令
emergency action 紧急行动
emergency circumstances 非常情况,紧急情况
emergency closing of the border 紧急封锁边境
emergency conference (或 meeting) 紧急会议;非常会议
Emergency Court of Appeal (美国)紧急上诉法庭
Emergency Power Act 《紧急权力法》(英国议会1920年10月通过了世界上第一部《紧急权力法》。从此以后,"紧急状态"和"紧急权力"逐渐风靡全球,取代了传统的"戒严法"和"围困状态法"等称呼。1714年英国议会制定暴乱法是为了制止国内反对外来的汉诺威王室动乱活动。治安官可以国王名义宣告12人以上聚集暴动立即解散,否则可逮捕入狱,甚至可判重罪。法国1789年制定戒严法,即军法平抑暴动法。1791年法国又制定围困状态法,规定了紧急权力法律,以暴动法为原型的。近代紧急权力法的特征是:治理主体多为军事结构,治理对象基本限于战争与内乱,治理方式以强制为主。现代紧急法的特征是:治理主体以文官统领为主,辅以军队介入;治理对象扩展到经济、社会和自然环境各个领域;治理措施多种多样,出现各种社会保障措施)
emergency economic powers 非常时期的经济权;紧急(状况的)经济权
emergency engagement card 临时聘用证
emergency force 紧急部队
emergency legislation 紧急立法
emergency man (爱尔兰)诉讼代理人;递送通知的执达员
emergency measure 紧急措施
emergency penal ordinance 紧急治罪条例
emergency powers 非常时期的权力
Emergency Price Control Act (美)《物价紧急控制法》
emergency procedure 非常程序,紧急程序
emergency requisition 非常征用,紧急征用
Emergency Safeguard Measure (ESM) 紧急保障措施(指根据GATS第10条规定,成员应在非歧视原则基础上就ESM向问题进行多边谈判)
emergency session 紧急开庭;紧急会议
emergency unemployment compensation (美)紧急失业补偿金
emergent doctrine 非常理论(或原理)
emerging a. 出现的,发生的,形成的
emerging electronic trading systems 新兴的电子交易系统
emerging nation 新兴国家
emigrant n. 移民;侨民;移居国外者
emigrant ship 出境船只
emigrate v. 迁居,移居;移居国外
emigration n. 移民出境;移居国外,侨居;(总称)移民
emigration officers 移民局官员
emigration papers 出境证件
eminent domain 国家征用权;(国家对一切财产的)支配权;财产被收归公有;(美)征收权(指国家为了公共目的而占用私人财产的权力),征用权(指政府强迫不动产或私有财产的所有者将其财产或财产上的某些权利转移给政府。征用权都被认为是联邦和州政府也已将此权力扩展到了经营公用事业的私有公司,如铁路和公用事业的公司。英国在几个世纪里,国会已经在公共事业中实施了征用权)
eminent domain proceeding 国家征用土地之诉,国家征用土地诉讼
emit v. 发表(意见),发射;排出,排泄
emolument n. 薪金;津贴,酬金;利得,利润

emolled bill （美）国会通过的法案（指众参两院通过并经两院主持会议官员签署的法律）；待批法案（指经众参两院通过,送总统批签后,才正式成为法律）

emotional distress 精神折磨

emotional shock 精神骚扰

empanel (=impanel) v. （将陪审员姓名）登记入陪审员名册；从陪审员名册中挑选；召集（陪审员）

emparl (=imparl) v. 庭外调解；获准诉讼延期以便和解

emperor n. 皇帝

Emperor Justinian 帝国裁判官

emphatic a. 强调的,显著的,有力的,断然的

emphyteusis n. 永久租赁权；永久租耕权（指罗马法中地主长期或永久把土地给租户耕种,每年收租）；永佃权

emphyteuta n. 永久租赁人,永久佃户

emphyteuticary n. 永久佃户

empire n. 帝国；帝权；绝对统治；由一个集团（或个人）控制的地区（或企业）

empire-building discipline 皇家大厦戒律

empiric n. 经验主义者；江湖医生,庸医

empirical desert 经验性该当（指罚当其罪）

empirical investigation 以经验为根据的调查

empirical magnitudes 经验式的量

empiricism-pragmatism school 经验主义—实用主义学派（国际私法学派之一）

empiricist theories of justice 经验主义的正义论

employ v. 1.雇用,使用；聘请 2.使从事,使专心

employ one's substance 处分其财产,处理其财产

employed labo(u)r force 雇用劳动力

employed persons 在业人员

employed salesman 受雇的推销员；受雇店员

employee n. 受雇人,职员,雇员

employee authors 雇员作者,雇佣作者（亦称 employed authors 或 salaried authors,即"工资作者"）

employee benefit plan （1942 年）雇员福利计划 [指公司专为公司雇员、职员、顾问制定的书面福利计划,内容包括股票认购（stock purchase）、储蓄、期权（option）、红利、股票升值（stock appreciation）、利润分成、有利的职务（thrift）、奖励、养老金或类似计划。此术语还包含一个雇员幸福福利计划（employee-welfare benefit plan）、一个雇员养老金福利计划（employee-pension benefit plan）或此二者合二为一的计划。参见《美国注释法典》第 29 标题卷第 1002 节。但此术语排斥其他任何计划、基金或项目（而不是一项学徒或培训项目）,在此项目中,雇员是项目参与者。通常缩略为 Plan.]

employee stock 雇员股

employee's insurance fund self-donation 雇员自捐保险金

employee's welfare 劳工福利；员工福利

employer n. 雇主,雇用人；业主

employer-employee relationship 劳资关系

employer-identification number 雇主（纳税）认别号,缩略为 EIN。见 tax-identification number

employer's liability 雇主之法律责任

employers' association 雇主协会,业主协会

employers' liability insurance 职工伤害保险,雇主责任保险

employers' liability to an employee 雇主对雇员的责任

employment n. 1.使用,雇用 2.职业；就业；服务；工作 3.雇佣关系

employment agency 职业介绍所

employment agreement 就业协议；雇用协议

employment appeal tribunal （英）劳工上诉法庭,就业上诉法庭

employment case 雇佣劳工案件

employment contract 雇用合同（契约）

employment credential 录用证明

employment discrimination 雇用歧视,就业歧视 [指美国全国性的反就业歧视起始于 1964 年通过的一个内容广泛的《民权法》（Civil Rights Act of 1964）,该法案第 7 条规定禁止就业歧视。此前,对于工作场所中的种族、性别、歧视问题,几乎没有法律加以系统规范]

employment discrimination law 就业歧视法
employment discrimination suits 就业歧视诉讼
employment equity law 就业平等法
employment exchange (英)劳工介绍所
employment harassment 职业骚扰
employment injury insurance 工伤保险
employment law 雇佣法,就业法
employment permit 工作许可证,就业证
Employment Protection Act (英)《就业保护法》(1975年)
employment registration 就业登记
employment security 就业保险
employment service 就业介绍
employment structure 就业体制
employment system 雇用制度;(中)劳动就业制度
empoison v. 下毒,投毒
empower v. 授权,准许;转委
empowered person 全权代理人
emptio (罗马法)购买
emptio spei 机遇购买(指买方获得的只是取得货物的机会的一种买卖合同,例如购买彩票提供获得奖品的机会)
emption n. 购买
emptio-venditio (或 *emptio et venditio*) 买卖;(罗马法)买卖合同(契约)
emptor n. 购买人,买方
empty chair doctrine 见 adverse-interest rule
empty voter 空投票人
en autre droit 运用他人权利(指受托人对受托财产的掌管)
en banc 全体出庭法官听审(一件上诉案件)(在美国指巡回上诉法庭通常对一个重大案件的审理可扩大法庭审判官的人数,又称 sitting *en banc*),全院庭审;作为整体,全部
en banc proceedings 全院庭审程序
en bloc 全体,总
en bloc vote 全体票决
en ventre sa mère 腹中胎儿,待产胎儿
en vie 活着的
enable v. 使实现,使成为可能;授予……权力,使……有权
enabling act 权力(利)授权法(尤指行政机关实施各项被委任职能的国会立法);(英)(大写)《授权法》[指授权被限嗣继承的土地保有人(tenant in tail)等]
enabling power 见 power of appointment
enabling rules 赋予性规则
enabling statute 授权法[①见 statute。②(历史上)(大写)租赁法(Lense Act)(1540年),凭借此法,限嗣继承土地保有人,丈夫们依仗他们妻子的权利或其他人的权利被授权使租赁成为终身租赁或21年定期租赁。参见亨利八世第32个执政年通过的第28个法(St. 32 Hen. 8. Ch. 28)]
enact n./v. 1.法令;法规;条例 2.制定,规定;颁布/制定(法律);颁布(法律);通过(法案等);(法律所)规定
enactment n. (18世纪)1.制定法律的行为或程序〈enactment of a legislative bill〉(立法议案制定法律的程序)2.制定法〈a recent enactment〉(最新制定法)
enacted element 制定法律要素
enacted law 制定法
enacted rules 制定的规则,颁布的规定
enacting clause 说明(法案)制定经过的条文
enactive a. 法律制定的;有制定权的
enactment n. 1.制定,规定,颁布,通过 2.法令,条例;法规;法则
enactment of an oppressive statute 颁布一项苛刻的法规,颁布一项过分严格的制定法
enactment of law 制定法律,法的制定
encashment n. (英)兑现
enclave n. 飞地(指一国被包围在他国领土内的被包领土),在一国境内的外国领土
enclosed a. 围住的,圈起的
enclosed sea 内海
enclosure (=inclosure) n. 1.圈地(把公地圈为私有);围墙 2.(信函中的)附件
enclosure acts (英)圈地法令
encode n. 把(电文)译成电码(或密码);解密
encompass v. 包含;围绕,包围;包括;完成
encompassing interpretation 综合解释,包罗万象的解释

encourage v. 1.怂恿,煽动;助长,鼓动 2.援助;促进
encounter v./n. 遭遇,遭到;邂逅,意外,遇见/冲突,遭遇
encouragement n. 怂恿,煽动;助长,鼓励,帮助,支持
encouragement of competition 鼓励竞争
encroach v. 侵犯,侵入,侵占;侵略
encroachment n. 1.侵犯(权利),侵占(财产);侵入,侵略 2.侵占物,侵占地
encryption n. 加密技术(指一种可以防止非法翻录拷贝及黑客的加密技术)
encumber v. 1.使负(债) 2.妨碍,阻碍,阻塞(场所) 3.(财产)带有(抵押权)
encumbrance n. 累赘;(财产上设定的)负担(指抵押等);财产留置权(或抵押权);妨害,阻碍;障碍物
encyclic(al) n./a. (罗马教皇对教会的)通谕,通告/传阅的,广泛传送的
end n./v. 完结,结束;终止;限度,极顶;末端,尽头;目的,结局;死亡;废除/结束,终止,了结
end of each fiscal year 每届财政(会计)年度终了
end of the effective period of insurance 保险有效期终了
end of the law 法律目的
end of the punishment 刑罚的目的
end up 直立着,竖起,(俚)死;结束,告终
end-product n. 制成品
end-user n. 最终使用者(指产品设计的最终用户),目标用户
endamage v. 使损坏,使受损失;损害(=damage)
endanger v. 使危险,危及
endangered species 会造成危害的物件;濒临灭绝的物种
endangering the welfare of a child 见 child endangerment
endeavour n./v. 努力/尽力,力图,努力
endeavor to administer justice 努力行使审判职能,努力执法
endemic law on every hand 各方面的地方法律
endless opportunities for harassment 无休止的骚扰
endogamy n. 族内婚(姻),同族结婚
endorsable a. (票据)可背书的;可担保的;可承认的
endorse v. (或 **indorse**)批准,(票据)可背书;保证,担保;认可,赞同;签署(姓名);签注,批注
endorse over 背书……转让权利
endorse over a bill to another person 背书票据转让给别人
endorse writ 背书令状
endorsee n. 被背书人(指已背书票据的领受人);受让人
endorsement (=indorsement) n. 背书(尤指支票、票据背面的签字);批注;签名;认可;保证;(保险单上所加的)变更保险范围的条款
endorsement for collection 托收背书;委任取款背书
endorsement for credit 信托背书
endorsement for transfer 转让背书
endorsement in full 全名背书
endorsement in pledge 抵押背书
endorsement of claim 权利要求背书
endorsement of conviction 犯罪记录的批注
endorsement of patent 专利特许,专利背书
endorsement of service 送达背书(指将送达时间、地点、方法等批注在令状上)
endorsement on sea protest 海事报告附件
endorsement without recourse 无追索权的批注(背书)
endorser n. 背书人,转让人
endorser of a protested bill 拒兑汇票的背书人
endorsing the conclusion reached by Justice 赞同(或支持)大法官……得出(所作)的结论
endow v. 资助,捐赠遗产;分给寡妇一份遗产;授予,赋予(特权等)
endowment n. 捐款;捐赠;捐赠的基金;养老基金;才能,天资
endowment fund 捐赠的基金
endowment insurance 养老保险
endowment policy 养老保险(单)

Enduring Freedom （美）持久自由行动（指美国国防部把美反恐怖战争代号重新命名,原来命名为"无限正义行动"）
enduring value 持久的价值
enemy n. 1.敌人,仇人;敌军;敌国 2.有害物
enemy agent （=alien enemy） 敌国侨民,敌国人
enemy character 敌对身份
enemy currency 敌国货币
enemy goods, enemy ship（或 enemy ship, enemy goods） 敌船装敌货原则(指装载在敌船上的中立国货物,可当作敌货充公;同样,装载敌货的中立国船舶也可当作敌船充公。这个原则从 16 世纪争论到现在,在国际法上仍未被采纳）
enemy merchant ship 敌国商船
enemy national 敌国国民
enemy occupation zone 敌军占领区;敌占区
enemy property 敌产
enemy subjects 敌国国民
enemy territory 敌国领土
enemy's goods 敌国货物
enemy's ship 敌国船舶
energies of our courts 我们法院的精力
energize the administration 加强管理
energize v. 给予……力量,加强奋力而为
energy law 能源法
enfeeblings of punitive justice work 因果报应成果逐步减弱,惩罚性司法裁判工作的削弱
enfeoff v. 赐以封地;授予地产;让渡
enfeoffment n. 1.地产的授予;地产授予证书 2.封地,采邑
enfetter v. 给……上脚镣;束缚;使处于奴隶的地位
enforce v. 1.强制执行,实施;强制,强迫 2.强调,坚持主张,加强
enforce a blockade 实行封锁
enforce a law 实施法律
enforce discipline 执行纪律
enforce obedience to the law 强迫服从法律
enforce prostitution 强迫卖淫
enforce the law strictly 执法如山;严格执行法律
enforceability n. 强制性

enforceable contract 强制性合同(契约)
enforcement n. 实施,加强,厉行,执行,施行;强制执行
enforcement action 执行诉讼(指欧共体成员国的行为,包括欧共体成员国执行欧共体决定的行为和执行欧共体的法律措施的决定甚至是不作为。成员国的行为主要是履行欧共体义务的行为,包括作为和不作为。对之进行的审查,欧共体通常称为"执行诉讼"）
enforcement arrangement 强制措施
enforcement at law 用法律来强制执行
enforcement body 实施机构;执行机构
enforcement costs 使合同得以履行的费用（一般指一方违约时,另一方为使合同继续履行而付出的诉讼费)
enforcement formula （法院）强制执行判决令
enforcement machinery 执行机构
enforcement measures 强制执行措施
enforcement notice 实施通知书,强制执行通知书
enforcement of a new law 施行新法,新法律的实施
enforcement of an award 执行仲裁裁决
enforcement of claims established by judg(e)ment 行使已判决确定的权利
enforcement of guardian's liability 执行监护人责任
enforcement of judg(e)ment 执行判决
enforcement of maritime liens 行使海商法上的留置权
enforcement of right 行使权利
enforcement power 强制执行权
enforcement procedure 强制(执行判决的)程序
enforcement regulations 实施条例,实施细则,实施法规
enforcement staff 强制人员,执法人员
enforcer n. 实施者,强制者;(流氓集团内)为维护黑纪律设立的执法人
enforcing machinery 实施机制,执行机制
enfranchise v. 1.给予公民权(选举权或参政权);(英)给予自由土地保有权 2.释放(奴隶等)3.给(城、镇等)以政治权利(在

英国尤指选派议员权)
enfranchisement of African-Americans 给予非裔美国人选举权
engage v. 1.从事 2.保证,约束,束缚 3.雇用,聘请 4.预订(铺位等);允诺,约定;使订婚 5.使卷入其中,与……交战
engage in a lawsuit 进行诉讼;打官司
engage in conspiratorial activities 从事图谋不轨活动
engage in malpractices to selfish ends 进行营私舞弊
engage in speculation and profiteering 进行投机倒把
engaged a. 订婚的;约定的;预定的
engaged couples 已订婚的男女
engagement n. 1.约定;约束;雇用,雇用期;使用;预定 2.诺言,保证;订婚,婚约;义务 3.交战 4.(复)财务上的义务,财政承诺;债务
engagement clause 保证条款
engagement or employment 聘用或雇用
engagement to marry 婚约
engender v. 产生,造成,引起;形成
engineer n./v. 工程师,设计师/设计,管理,控制;策划;操纵
engineering interpretation 工程学解释
engineering type of mind 工程师式的心态(由"超人"重新安排社会的思维方式)
England n. 英格兰(英国的主要部分),(泛指)英国
England Courts Act 《英国法院法》(指1971年英国议会制定的改革司法机关的法律)
England Parliament Act 《英国议会法》(1911年)
English a. 英格兰的;英国的;英国人的;英语的
English barrister 英国(能出席高级法庭的)大律师
English bifurcated court 英国两分法审理法院,英国的分别审理法院
English bill 英语的起诉状(指衡平法庭的一般起诉状)
English civil war (英)(1642—1652)(议会党人与保皇党人的)内战

English common law 英国普通法,英国习惯法
English crown 英国王位,英国王权
English Evidence Act 《英国证据法》
English High Court 英国高等法院
English information 英格兰诉讼(指国王在王座法庭税务部提起衡平法诉讼程序,与 Latin informations 相对而言)
English Law 英格兰法(指在联合王国和不列颠岛组成之前的英格兰王国的部分,和威尔士一起发展起来并在那里适用的法律制度,但不包括苏格兰。由于相当早它就发展并适用整个英格兰的法律,英格兰法通常称作"普通法")
English Law Reports 《英国判例汇编》
English legal system 英国法律制度
English pale 英格兰特辖区
English Partnership Act 《英国合伙法》(1890年)
English solicitor 英国(办理案件事务,能在下级法院出庭的)撰状律师[又译:事务律师,这类律师可提供咨询、准备法律文件和承办每日法律事务,而不能出庭于高级法庭,如必须出庭于高级法庭时需要有大律师(barrister)代其出庭]
English style of parliament regime 英国议会政体的形式
English-styled court 英国式法院
Englishry n. (英史)英格兰人身份的抗辩,英格兰人身份的证明
engraft v. 灌输;附加;嫁接
engross v. 1.正式誊写,以大字体书写 2.囤积,垄断;占用
engrossing a. 1.誊清文件(指誊清契据或法律文据以备签名)的 2.囤积居奇的;垄断的;独占的 3.引人入胜的,非常令人注意的
engrossment n. 1.抄写文件;用大字写 2.垄断,独占,囤积居奇(罪);占用
engrossment clerk 书记员,抄写员
enhance v. 增进,增加,提高
enhance economic efficiency 增进经济效益
enhanced rights 增加的权利
enitia pars (英)长子继承份额(指共同继

承时属于长子继承的优先部分)
enjail v. 囚禁
enjoin n./v. 1.责成,命令,嘱咐 2.(英)衡平法院的强制令(指衡平法院发出的要求某人做某种行为或不做某种行为或停止某种行为的一种禁止令状),(美)禁止/禁止;命令,指示,责成
enjoinder n. 禁令,禁止令(见 enjoin)
enjoy v. 享受,享用,享有,获得某种利益
enjoy currency 到处流传(通)(指货币)
enjoy diplomatic immunities 享有外交豁免权
enjoyability n. 可享用性
enjoyment n. (权利的)享有和行使,享用(权);享受
enjoyment of land 土地享有权,土地使用权
enjoyment of personal property 个人财产享用(权)
enjoyment of public property 公共财产的享用(权)
enlarge v. 1.扩大;扩张;延期;增加 2.(美)释放
enlarged meeting 扩大会议
enlargement n. 扩展;扩张;延期;(英)权利扩展
enlightened terms of human existence 人类生存最有智慧的时期
enlightenment n. 启发,启蒙,the enlightenment(尤指 18 世纪欧洲的启蒙运动)
enlist v. 征募;征(兵);招(兵);应征;加入,赞助,支持;偏袒;利用;竞选
enlist in the army 从军
enlistment n. 征募,应征入伍;服(兵)役期;竞选
enlistment age 服役年龄
enormity n. 重罪,大罪,暴行,无法无天的行为,残暴
enormous caseloads 巨大的、沉重的案件负担
enounce v. 宣告,发表;清晰地读出
enquete par turbe (法)习惯法认可调查(指用以确认有争议或疑义的习惯的一种集团性调查的特别程序)
enquire (= inquire) v. 询问,调查;查究,质问
enquiring officer 调查官,调查员
enquiry n. 询问,查问;调查,查究
Enquiry Concerning the Principles of Morals 《道德原则的询问》[(David Hume)的名著,1751 年出版]
enregister v. 登记,记录
enriched person 受益人
enrichment n. 致富,丰富
enrol n. (英)英洛尔登记(指将文件记入或抄入官方档案)
enrol(1) v. 1.登记,编入,注册 2.入伍,服兵役,加入 3.最后澄清(议会通过的议案)
enrolled bill 见 emolled bill
enrollee n. 被征入伍者,入会者,入学者
enrollment n. 1.登记,注册 2.入伍,服兵役,参加;入会,入学 3.注册人数
enrollment of deed 契据登记
enrollment of vessels 船舶登记(海商法)(海事法)[指在沿海和内陆航行的商船登记和证明,以区别于涉外商业使用商船的登记。登记和商船注册(enrollment and registry)的使用旨在使两类允准的商船证书有明显区别。登记证明商船从事海岸贸易和国内交易的国有性质(national character);而注册是用来宣告从事对外贸易的商船的国籍。见 registry 3]
enrollment office (历史)登记处[衡平法院(或大法官法庭)的一个部门,负责保存已登记的契据(deeds)和判决书(judgments)。此单位已于 1879 年废除,其责任已移交中央办公室(Central Office)承担]
ens legis 法人(指法律的创造物,人为地与自然人相对。此词语描述一个实体,如一个公司,其存在完全来源于法律)
enslavement n. 奴役;征服;盲从;束缚
enslaver n. 奴役者,征服者
ensnare v. 诱捕,诱惑;使入圈套,陷害
ensue v. 接着发生,接着而来;追求;结果产生,结果是
ensure v. 保证,担保,保护,使安全;赋予
ensuring fairness for the accused 保证被告得到公正对待
entail n./v. 1.(地产等的)限定继承权;限定继承人的地产 2.预定继承人的顺序;世袭财产 3.负担,需要,惹起/限定继承(财

产);使负担;使需要;导致,惹起
entailed interest 限定继承的地产权益
entailer n. 限定继承的人
entailment n. 限定继承;世袭财产
ente di ragione (意)理性的实体[指意大利的二分理论。从犯罪是一种自在的危害,其存在与立法者的法律规定无关,即"理论的实体"这一前提出发,认为犯罪由两种本体性因素构成。这些因素被称为"力"(*forza*),包括犯罪的"物理力"(*forza visiza*)和"精神力"(*forza morale*)。这相当于现代刑法学中犯罪的"客观要件"和"主观要件"。"物理力"即主体的行为,"精神力"即指行为人的意志]
entente 友好;谅解(外交用语);协定,协约;有协定关系的各国(或各党派)
***entente* countries** (第一次世界大战时的)协约国,参加协约的国家
enter v. (13世纪)1.进入,加入,特别进入不动产[指通过进入租地权或收回租地权从而占有不动产。〈the landlord entered the defaulting tenant's premise〉(地主进入未得到土地保有人承诺的土地)] 2.正式提出,在法庭上正式提出〈the defendant entered a plea of no contest〉(被告提出无争辩的诉状或答辩状) 3.成为当事人(参加,加入)〈they entered into an agreement〉(他们加入了一项协议)(见 entry)
enter (an) appearance 出庭;投案
enter a complaint 提出控诉
enter a deficiency judgment for the difference 就其差额做出判决
enter a judg(e)ment 作出(成)判决
enter a motion (在议会、法庭等上)正式提出动议
enter a *nolle prosequi* 提出终止诉讼
enter a protest against 对……提出抗议
enter an action against 对……起诉
enter into 进入;参加;缔结,订立;受……约束;开始,从事,研究
enter into a bond (with) (与……)订立合同(契约);(与……)缔结条约;参加联盟(同盟)
enter into a contract 订立合同(契约)
enter into a treaty 缔结条约

enter into effect 生效
enter into obligations 签订合同,签订契约
enter into recognizances 具结(如向法院保证随传随到等)
enter into the rights of creditor 代替债权人的地位
enter the country 入境
enter up satisfaction 在法院备案表示债款已还
enter upon (或 on) 开始,着手;开始研讨;占有(土地,财产)
enter upon a property 占有财产
entering into marriage 结婚
entering judg(e)ment 正式登录诉讼判决入册
enterprise n. 企业,公司,事业[指①为商业目的的一个组织或风险经营单位,政府企业或国企业(government enterprise),由政府机关承办的一个企业,如创立的公共停车的停车部门(parks department),亦称 government enterprise。②根据联邦反诈骗法,虽然不是法律实体,但是一个独立个体、合伙、公司、协会、联盟或其他法人或事实上个体联合的团体。这个企业必须是正在发展中的而且必须作为一个实体存在,不得从事一些被认为的非法活动。参见《美国注释法典》第 18 标题卷第 1961 节。见 Racketeer Influenced and Corrupt Organization Act。③具有相关活动,联合经营或共同管理并有一个共同商业目的的个人、几个人或一个组织。根据《公平劳动基准法》(Fair Labor Standards Act),受该组织或公司雇用的雇员有权利或有资格获得最低工资和超时工作的福利(费),参见《美国注释法典》第 29 标题卷第 201 节以下]
enterprise budget allocation system 企业预算拨款制
Enterprise Entity Doctrine 企业整体说[(亦名同一体说 the identity doctrine)哥伦比亚大学伯乐(Berle)教授提出。该说认为股东如设立若干公司以经营同一事业或与公司之间存在着经营业务和利益一致性时,这些公司实质上为同一企业的不同部门。见 Agency Doctrine]

enterprise groups 企业集团
enterprise involved in labo(u)r reform (中)劳改企业
enterprise jointly managed by China and foreign countries 中外合资经营企业
enterprise law 企业法
enterprise liability 企业责任[指①对于生产的有害或有瑕疵的产品,产生的每一成员均应承担责任,因产业分配给每个生产商的市场份额(market's share)负有责任,亦称为 industry-wide liability。见 market share liability。②刑事责任,有关生意上的某种罪行,如公共福利罪(Public Welfare Offenses),对于此种罪行,立法机关专门特意施加刑事惩罚。参见《示范刑法典》第 2.07 节(Model Penal Code §2.07)]
enterprise management 企业管理
enterprise rights 企业权利
enterprise unionism (日)企业工会制(指一种企业范围的工会组织的制度)
enterprise units 企业单位
entertain v. 招待,款待;持有,怀着,抱着;容纳,接受,准备考虑
entertain a barrister 保证律师业务工作(的进行)
entertaining and informative account of the lawsuit itself 有趣的和内容广泛的诉讼本身
entertainment tax 娱乐税
enticed or induced 被诱(或被骗),诱使,怂恿
enticement n. 煽动;诱惑;引诱物
enticement of spouse 引诱他人的配偶
enticing a. 诱惑的,动人心神的
enticing the defendant 诱骗被告
entire a. 全部的,不可分割的,整体的;完整的
entire action 完整诉讼
entire agreement 合同完整性(指在许可证合同中经常是一个独立条款,不经一方同意,另一方不得修改),不可分合同,不可分协议
entire contract 不可分合同(契约)
entire controversy(doctrine) (美)全部争议原则[指一方当事人在诉讼第一阶段提出的争议必须是全部的,所以在第二次诉讼(后一阶段诉讼程序)中不得又提出]
entire courts 全体法官(大写时指联邦最高法院的大法官)
entire evidence 全部证据
entire liabilities 整体责任;全部债务
entire multi-modal journey 多种方式联运全程
entire obligation 全部债务
entire tenancy 整体租借(指单独占有的租借土地和房屋)
entirety n. (夫妻)共有制;整体,全部;共同占有
entitle v. 给……权利(资格),使有资格;称呼;给(书、文章等)题名
entitled party 有资格者;被授权的当事人;权利人,所有权人
entitlement n. (19世纪)法定权利,产权资格[指对某项利益(通常是金钱)的绝对权利(absolute right),比如社会保障或社会保险,一旦符合合法要件(legal requirement),即应立即授予。"rights"一词通常对应一种类型的权利,也即那些由所谓"财产规则"保护的权利,而"entitlement"(法定权利)是一种更宽泛的词语。在美国,法定权利有时被当作财产权(property),有时则被看作一种自由(liberty),但不管是哪种情况,美国联邦最高法院认为非经正当程序(due process)不得剥夺个人的这种法定权利]
entitlement with liability rules 责任法则的权利
entitlement with property rules 财产法则的权利
entity n. 实体;存在;统一体;本质;(工作)单位
entity law 实体法
entity of private law 私法人;私法上的实体
entity of public law 公法人;公法上的实体
entity ownership (美)(证券持有人对证券所代表的)资产的所有者(权益)
entrance n. 加入;进入;入场权;入港手续,入学,入会
entrance examination 入学考试,招生考试

entrance fee 入会费,入社费
entrance into office(或 **upon duties**) 就任,就职
entrance of citizens 公民入境
entrapment n. (1899年)1.设圈套诱人犯罪(指执行官员的或政府代理人的诱惑使人以诈骗或非法念头去实施犯罪,以达到以后对此人提出刑事指控之目的)2.已被如此受到诱骗的积极抗辩(affimative defense)[对于设立陷阱或圈套(在大多数州),刑事被告(他或她)必须表明既未实施犯罪,又未诈骗或提出非法主张(entrap v.)]
entrapment defense 诱陷抗辩[指过度的与非法的诱惑侦查可成立诱陷抗辩。刑事被告可凭借这种实体性抗辩获得无罪判决。而诱陷抗辩的成立条件即为诱惑侦查合法与否的边界。美国确立诱陷抗辩以来,从1932年美国联邦最高法院首例承认诱陷抗辩的索瑞斯诉美国案(Sorrells v. United States,参见《美国联邦最高法院判例汇编》第287卷第435页)至1992年的雅克布森诉美国案(参见《美国联邦最高法院判例汇编》第503卷第540页,1992年),主观标准始终是联邦法院系统以及多数州法院系统中的主流观点,诱陷抗辩所要回答的核心问题是,没有政府方的诱惑,受到指控的公民是否会实施被指挥的犯罪行为。以主观标准看,回答这一问题应求助被告方的而非执法机关的因素。具体而言,即在政府方使用诱惑之前,被引诱人是否有实施犯罪的意愿、打算或准备。这在美国被称为"犯罪倾向"。如果被引诱人本就有犯罪倾向或犯罪意图,那么,无论政府方的引诱多么过度,被引诱人自身对犯罪行为的实施都难辞其咎,其应当承担相应的刑事责任;诱陷抗辩不能成立。反之,如果能够证明若非政府方没有犯罪意图,就可以说明若非政府方的诱惑或鼓动,被引诱人根本不会实施被指控的犯罪,在此情况下,显然诱惑抗辩得以成立,从而免除被引诱人的刑事责任]
entrench v. 使处于牢固地位,巩固树立;侵占,侵犯(on/upon);深挖(壕沟)

entrenched clause (法律上的)刚性条款(文)
entrenched sections 特别维护条款
entreport n. 中转港,转运港
entrepôt 中转;转运口岸,保税仓库,仓库;货物集散地
entrepôt **trade** 转口贸易
entrepreneur n. 企业家;主办者;创业者;中间商;承包者
entrepreneurial lawyer 企业主的律师
entrust v. 委托,信任;托管
entrusted agent 委托代理人
entrusted organization 受委托的组织
entry n. (13世纪)1.权利,行为,进入不动产的优先权〈they were given entry into the stadium〉(他们被允许进入体育场)2.登记,记载,记下的(项目、账目等);批注,注释(notation)〈Forney made a false entry in the books on March 3〉(福尼3月3日在书中做了虚假批注)3.法庭上或档案上安排的一个位置或定位 4.(版权)所有权寄托[指将作品的所有权(title of work)寄托给美国版权注册官(Register of Copyrights)以保证版权得到保护] 5.(移民)进入(指任何侨民不管自愿或不自愿进入美国,均按移民法处理)6.(刑法)非法进入(指为进行犯罪活动而非法进入他人住宅或其他房屋)7.报送(指按海关法,将进口物品及其说明、发票等交海关税务官员侦查以便确定应交纳的关税)
entry certificate 入境证书
entry for consumption 进口货物报单
entry for free goods 免税货物报单
entry for search 入屋搜查
entry formalities 入境手续,进口手续
entry in log (look) 记入航海日志
entry into possession 强行占有;实施财产占有权
entry of appeal 提出上诉
entry of appearance 出庭,到案
entry of judg(e)ment 判决登记(指将判决记入法院文册,此为行政行为)
entry of motion 有利判决申请的登记
entry of satisfaction 偿清报单
entry of satisfaction of mortgage 抵押权的注销

entry passport 入境护照
entry permit 入境许可证
entry procedures 入境手续
entry visa 入境签证
entry word （章、节、项目中）开头的词
entry wound 射入创（伤），刺入创（伤）
entryman n. 进入公地并企图依法取得该公地的人
enumerate v. 逐条陈述，列举（事实），枚举；点，数
enumerated a. 明确提到的，明确列举的，明确指定的，详细说明的，（用在法律文件中）
enumeration n. 列举事实，逐条陈述
enunciate v. 确切说明，阐明（理论，原则等）；宣布；发表，公告
enure (＝inure) v. 有效力，生效，适用；有益
environist n. 研究环境污染问题专家；环境保护者
environment n. 环境，四周，外界；围绕，周围
environment (protection) law 环境保护法
environment court 环境法庭
environment degradation 环境退化
environment disruption 环境失调，环境破坏
environment hazards 环境危害
environment pollution 环境污染
Environment Program(me) （联合国）环境规划署
Environment Relief Fund 环境救济基金
environmental crime （美）环保罪行［指一项法定的有关危害环境的犯罪。诸如违反《1970年清洁空气法修订案》(Clean Air Act Amendment of 1970)中的刑事条例(crimninal provisions)，《1972年的联邦水污染防治法》(Federal Water Pollution Contract Act of 1972)（通常称作《净水法》(Clean Water Act)，《1973濒临灭绝的物种法》(the Endangered Species Act of 1973)。尽管最重要环保罪行法规是1970年代通过的，但实际从19世纪晚期就有了，比如《1896年的纯洁食品和毒品法》(Pure Food and Drug Act of 1896)和种法规最后都被统一整合为《1899年的江河、港口法》。亦称 crime against the environment］
environmental criminology 环保犯罪学（指对于犯罪在这些地区发生和为什么罪犯在这些地区如此活跃，进行学术上的研究，亦称 geography of crime, ecology of crime）
environmental economics 环境经济学
environmental externalities 环境外部效应
environmental finance 环境金融［指一种应对全球气候变化的新型金融模式，是一种金融创新。它是金融业和环境产业的桥梁，致力于通过分析金融业与环境产业的差异，寻求保护环境和生物多样性。对环境金融进行研究的美国学者索尼亚·拉巴特(Sonia Labatt)和罗德尼·R. 怀特(Rodney R. White)曾就环境金融的界定指出："环境金融是由金融机构主导的，将环境因素引入金融理论和实践之中，开发'为转移环境风险，以市场为基础的金融产品'；环境金融研究为提高所有环境质量、转移风险设计，以市场为基础的金融产品大致包括含绿色抵押在内的银行产品、天气衍生产品、社会责任投资中的绿色基金、可交易的减排信用、巨灾债券以及基于温室气体减排信用而创的金融产品。"］
environmental impact statement （美）环境影响报告书［指1971年环保法：①国家环保政策法(The National Environmental Policy Act)，《美国注释法典》第42卷第4332节第(2)(c)项要求联邦机构给市长的方案或立法的建议提供的一个文件，以便作出有关一项承诺的积极的或消极的环保效果的一些更为完美的决定；②在有些州，是指政府使用的一种官方文件，用以对于某一建议的方案的重要环保效果进行分析，鉴别，抉择，并公开可能的方法以减少或避免可能的环保损害。亦称 environmental impact report (EIR)］
environmental impairment liability insurance 环境损害责任保险（指美国环境责任保险额主要分为两类，除环境损害责任保险之外，还有：自有场地治理责任保险"own site clean-up insurance"）
Environmental Pollution Liability Insurance

环境污染责任保险
Environmental Protection Agency （美）环境保护署[指行政部门的一个独立的联邦机构,负责调整空气、水、固体废品、毒药、辐射、有毒物质等领域中的污染控制标准（pollution-control standard）强制执行已颁布的法律以保护环境,并与州和地方政府协调反污染成效。此项任务是根据1970年的第3号重组计划（Reorganization Plan No.3 of 1970）而确定的,简写 EPA]
environmental right 环境权[源于美国密歇根大学萨克斯（Joseph L. Sax）教授的公共信托理论（Public Trust Doctrine）]
environmental terrorism 环保恐怖状况,环保恐怖遭遇（见 ecoterrorism）
environmental-impact report （美）环保效力报告书（见 environmental impact statement）
envisage v. 面对,正视;设想,想象
envision n. 预期,预想;展望
envoy n. 使者,代表,使节;(全权)公使
envoy extraordinary 特派公使
envoy extraordinary and ambassador plenipotentiary 特命全权大使
envoy extraordinary and minister plenipotentiary 特命全权公使
envoy (minister) plenipotentiary 全权公使
ENVTL. L (Environmental Law) 环保法
eo instante (=*eo instanti*) At the very instant 立即,即刻
eo instanti 那时;立即
eo loci in that state; in that condition 在那种状态下,在那种情况下
eo nomine 以……名义
eo nomine By or in that name 以(或用)这个名字
Epanagoge 《法律入门》(指约公元879年在拜占庭皇帝巴西尔一世主持下编纂的一部法律典章)
ephemeral recording 短暂记录,短时录音(版权法)(指一个作品的短暂复制,作为广播员根据特许或法定豁免即无需获得版权所有人的允准的必要性来进行使用或制作。广播员必须仍然支付版税而且

在创制使用后法定规定的时间内必须毁掉该短暂记录)
ephor n. 执政官(指古代斯巴达最高级政务官)
epicontinental sea 大陆架上覆海
epicurism n. 享乐主义
epidemic victim 传染病人
epilepsia (=epilepsy) 癫痫
epilepsies n. 癫痫
epileptic dementia 癫痫性痴呆(指患者出现智能减退的概率远远低于癫痫性人格改变,以轻度智能减退多见。严重低下者少见。见 epileptic personality change)
epileptic personality change 癫痫性人格改变[指继发于慢性和严重的癫痫病人。就癫痫范围内,这一类型病人在司法精神医学鉴定中遇到很多。属于非发作性精神障碍的一种。另还有两种: epileptic dementia (癫痫性痴呆)和 chronic schizophrenia like psychosis (慢性精神分裂症样精神病)]
epinosic a. 不卫生的,有害健康的
Episcopal Charitable Society 主教派慈善会
episcopus 监督员;视察员;(中世纪基督教的)主教
episode n. 一段情节;插曲,(一系列事件中的)一个事件
episodic hearings 分割审理
episodic proceedings 分割断裂程序
epistatēs (古代希腊的)首席执法官
epistemic dynamics 认知动力学(见 belief revision theory)
epistemological a. 认识论的[epistemologically adv.; epistemology n.认识论(与本体论相对)]
epistulae (=*epistolae*) (罗马法上国王正式发送给总督、官员、地方议会或团体的)信函,谕书
epitome n. 梗概,节录,概括;缩影;集中体现
epitome of title (=abstract of title) 产权说明书;所有权证书摘要
epitomize v. 概括,集中体现,对……摘要
epoch-making (marking) a. 划时代的,开创新纪元的

epoch-making change 划时代的变化
equal a. 相等的,均等的;相同的;同等的;平等的;合适的;胜任的;平静的,平稳的
equal access to justice 司法平等
Equal Access to Justice Act (美)《司法平等法》(1980年通过,使涉及美国国家的诉讼中胜诉当事人获得诉讼和律师等费用的补偿,除非政府有正当理由)
equal and universal electoral system 平等普选制
equal authority 同等职权,同等权力机构
equal bargaining power 同等讨价还价(磋商)能力
Equal Credit Opportunity Act (美)平等信贷机会法[指禁止债权人以种族、肤色、宗教信仰、民族血统、年龄、性别或婚姻状况为基本条件歧视贷款申请人而不尊重各种信用交易(credit transaction)的联邦制定法规。缩略为 ECOA]
equal concern and respect 平等的关怀与尊重(指德沃金的主张——人最根本权利是获得平等的关怀与尊重)
equal conviction 同等信任,同等确信
equal effect (或 validity) 同等效力
Equal Employment Office (EEO) 平等就业单位
Equal Employment Officials (EEOs) (美)平等就业官员
Equal Employment Opportunity Commission (美)就业机会均等委员会
equal freedom 平等自由
* **equal in the eyes of law** 法律面前一律平等
Equal justice under law 法律面前人人平等(美国联邦最高法院大门口的庭训牌)
equal opportunities 机会均等,平等机会
Equal Opportunities Commission (英)机会均等委员会
equal opportunities in education and training 受教育和培训方面的机会均等
Equal Pay Act (英)《同工同酬法》(1970年)
Equal Pay Act of 1963 (美)《1963年同工同酬法》(主要条文规定,雇主对具有同等技能付出同等努力的雇员负同等责任,而在同一事业单位类似工作环境下从事大体相同工作的男性及女性受雇者,均应支付相同的报酬)
equal pay for equal work 同工同酬
equal per capital entitlement 人均平等排放权(见 contraction convergence)
equal protection (1866年)(美)平等保护[指美国联邦宪法第十四修正案保证政府对待个人或集体必然与对待另个人和另个集体在类似情况下完全相同。按照当今的合宪性法理(constitutional jurisprudence),平等保护意思是区别对待的立法必须有合理的基础(national basis)。如果该立法影响基本权利(fundamental right)如选举权和表决权等,或者涉及可疑分类(suspect classification)如种族等,除非它经受住严格审查(strict scrutiny),否则它是违宪性的。"平等保护不要求每个人或所有的人都受到同一的对待,但它要求提供与进行分类为目的相关联的特点。"亦称 equal protection of the laws; equal protection under the law。见 strict scrutiny]
Equal Protection Clause (美)平等保护条款(1868年采纳的美国联邦宪法第十四修正案明确表明在南北战争胜利之后,胜利的共和国部队承担的义务包括在宪法中的对新解放的奴隶平等权利的保护)
equal protection of the laws 法律(对公民)的平等保护
equal quantity exchange 等量交换
equal rates profit 同等利润率
equal representation 平等代表权
equal rights 平等权利
Equal Rights Amendment (美)平等权利修正案;男女平权修正案(指美国在1972年提出的一项修正案,主要规定:"合众国或任何州不得以性别为理由而剥夺或限制法律上的平等权利")
equal rights for both (the) sexes 男女平等权
equal share 同等份额;平均负担
equal status in the home 在家地位平等
equal suffrage 平等选举权
Equal Time Act (美)《同等时间法》(指该法规定有广播设备使用许可证的人允许一名法定合格候选人为公务使用该设

备进行广播的,那么也同样按联邦法必须提供一个平等机会给予所有其他为公务的候选人)
equal treatment 平等对待
equal treaty 平等条约
equal vote 平等表决权
equal-field system (中史)均田制
equal-management rule 平等管理规则[指夫或妻均可单独管理共同财产(community property)的原则,法律另有规定的除外]
equal-share clause (保险)同等份额条款,平均负担条款[指要求承保人支付权利主张损失(claimed loss)的相应份额或相应比例的规定条款]
equalitarianism n. 平均主义,平等主义
equality n. 同等;平等;相等;均等
equality and mutual benefit 平等互利
equality before the law 在法律面前(人人)平等
equality clause 平等条款
* **Equality is equity.** 平等即衡平法(衡平法原则之一)。
equality of (或 **between**) **the sexes** 两性平等,男女平等
equality of competitive opportunity 竞争机会平等
equality of men 人类平等,人人平等
equality of nationality 民族平等
equality of opportunity 机会均等
equality of persons 人人平等
equality of states (国际法)国家平等说(指根据国际法所有完全独立的国家都是平等的。当然这一原则并不意味着所有的国家在权力方面或影响方面都是平等的,但仅仅是作为国家,它们都具有相同的法律权利)
equalization n. 相等,均等;平等,平等化一律[指①评估价值的提高或降低以达到一致或合适;②税务:对一项评估的调整,或创立一个与另一项的统一税率。亦称为 equalization of taxes; fair and proper legal assessment]
equalization of landownership 平均地权
equalization of taxes 税务平等,税务平衡

(见 equalization)
equalization board (税收)平衡委员会(指美国地方政府的一个机构,负责调整不同地区的税率,以保证税务负担的平等分配。亦称 board of equalization)
equalize v. 使平等;使平均;使均等;补偿;补足;相等
equally authentic 同等效力的
equally between 彼此平等的(遗赠,赔偿中常用的词语)
equally binding 同等约束力
equally divided 平等分配[①指平等分配财产(按人数而不是按血缘关系)在遗嘱人死亡时,继承人之间的分配。法律明文规定遗嘱要求被分配的财产必须平均分配(share and share alike)才具有同样法律效力;②同等分配表决权:法庭上,立法机构或其他群体在系争点或争执的每一方均具有相同数目的表决权]
equally divided court 赞成票与反对票相等的法庭(指联邦最高法院法官对原判投赞成或投反对票的人数相等时,下级法院的判决应得到维持)
equate v. 使相同,使等同;同等对待
equation n. (对供应等的)平衡,均衡;平均,相等
equidistance line 等距线
equidistant collaterals of different levels 同辈分不同亲等旁系亲属
equidistant collaterals of the same level 同辈同亲等旁系亲属
equilibrium n. 平衡[在博弈论中,平衡常指"纳什平衡"(Nash equilibrium),通常用语中和在博弈论中使用一样均指一个稳定的结果(result),博弈中相似术语为(outcome)],均衡,平均,相称,均势;(判断上的)不偏不倚
equilibrium behavior 平衡行为
equilibrium of a game 对策(博弈)的均衡
equilibrium of supply and demand 供需平衡
equilibrium outcomes 均衡结果
equilibrium-selection norms 均衡的规范,选择均衡规范
equipment n. 装备,设备,器材,装置,配

备;(一企业除房地产以外的)固定资业
equitable a. 公平的,公正的;衡平法的;衡平法上有效的
equitable accommodations 公平调节
equitable action (英)(向衡平法院提起的)预防性诉讼(又译:衡平法上的诉讼。指以制止不法行为或伤害行为,以及防止违法行为为目的,依衡平法提起的诉讼,而根据普通法是得不到救济的)
equitable adoption 衡平法上的收养(见 adoption by estoppel)
equitable apportionment 衡平法上的分配
equitable assets (英)衡平法上的遗产(指死者所遗留下来的一种财产,如要求以此项财产偿债,只有依衡平法提起诉讼,而根据普通法是得不到救济的)
equitable assignment of debt (英)衡平法上债务的有效转让
equitable assignments by way of security 以担保方式作出衡平法上债务的有效转让
equitable charge 衡平法上的担保
equitable chattel mortgage (英)衡平法上的动产抵押权
equitable choses in action 衡平法诉讼上的财产权
equitable claimant 衡平法上的原告
equitable claims 衡平法上的请求权
equitable claims and defences (英)衡平法上的请求和辩护
equitable consideration 衡平法的对价原则
equitable counterclaim 衡平法上的反请求
equitable court 衡平法(上的)法院
equitable defence 衡平法上有效的辩护
equitable defenses 衡平法上的抗辩
equitable distribution 平等分配[指在离婚诉讼进程中,由法院依据法定准则(statutory guideline),即提供公平的但不必然平等的财产配置进行夫妻财产分配,而不管任何一方持有财产所有权。法庭在判决财产时考虑到许多因素,包括一方配偶对另一方的职业在金钱上的贡献,非金钱上的帮助,或在婚姻持续期间挣得的配偶双方潜能、成就以及婚姻期的延长。法院还考量夫妻双方的收入能力(earning capacity)和过失,平等分配在47个州适用(加州,新墨西哥和路易斯安那三个州除外)亦称 equitable division, assignment of property]
equitable distribution of landownership 平均地权
equitable division 见 equitable distribution
equitable doctrine of the marshalling of assets (破产中)债权清偿分配顺序原则
equitable duty 衡平法上的义务
equitable easement 衡平法上有效的地役权
equitable estates (and) interests 衡平法上的财产和权益
equitable estoppel 衡平法上的禁止翻供,衡平法上的不容否认,既有行为而不容否认[指①防衡性原则,即防止一方当事人采取不公正的有利条件通过假言假行对待他人。被禁止翻供者曾诱使他人进行一定程度的活动造成另一人在某种程度的伤害。这一原则是以欺诈原则(principles of fraud)为根据,不容否认型的五个要素是 A.对重大事实有虚假陈述或隐瞒; B.当事方所作的陈述为众所周知的虚假陈述,或当事方疏忽而不知其为虚假; C.相信该当事人所作陈述为真实的; D.为陈述的当事方意图其行为起到作用,或行为当事方欲证明其承诺的意图是正确的; E.主张不容翻供的当事方在某一点上进行陈述,除非不容否认的主张成功或继续否则会产生实质偏见。亦称 estoppel by conduct; estoppel in pais。②见 promissory estoppel]
equitable execution 公平执行,衡平法上的执行
equitable flaws 衡平法的瑕疵
equitable fraud 衡平法上的诈欺
equitable grounds 衡平法理由(或原因),衡平法上的根据
equitable interest 衡平法上的权益
equitable interest in real property 不动产(实产)上的衡平法权益
equitable jurisdiction 衡平法上的管辖权,衡平法上的裁判权
equitable jurist 衡平法学家
equitable liabilities 衡平法上的债务

equitable lien 衡平法上的留置权
equitable mortgage 衡平法上的抵押,衡平法上有效的抵押权
equitable owner 衡平法上的所有人
equitable ownership 衡平法上的所有权
equitable plea 衡平法上有效的抗辩
equitable presumption 衡平法上有效的推定
equitable principle(s) 衡平原则,衡平法原则
equitable procedure 衡平法上的诉讼程序
equitable relief 衡平法上的救济(或补助)(指签发禁制令或强制实际履行救济而非金钱赔偿。见 specific performance 和 legal relief)
equitable remedies 衡平法上的法律救济方法
equitable remedy 衡平法上救济[通常指非金钱的一种,诸如禁制令(injunction)或特定履行(specific performance),在适合于法律救济(legal remedies)时,通常于金钱赔偿时获得。而不适合于矫正侵害(injury),从历史上讲,衡平法上的救济只适于在衡平法庭解决。亦称 equitable relief]
equitable rights 衡平法上的权利
equitable seizin 依衡平法的占有
equitable sequestration 衡平法上的(争议)财产暂管
Equitable Society (英)(1762年设立于伦敦的)公平保险社
equitable solution 公平解决
equitable subordination 公平的从属求偿
equitable title 衡平法上的所有权
equitable tracing 追及效力的救济
equitable waste 衡平法上的毁损(指使用不当而发生的财产毁损)
equity n. 1.衡平法;衡平法上的权利 2.公道,公平;公平的事物 3.(美)财产超过其负债的所余价值;(押款金额之外的)财产价值 4.公司普通股所有人的利益 5.股份权益;(复)(英)(无固定利息的)股票,证券
﹡**Equity acts in** *personam.* 衡平法是依人行事的(衡平法原则之一)。
equity capital 1.自有资本 2.股东持有的证券或股票 3.投资于新企业的资本
equity cases 衡平法上的案件
equity clean-up "衡平法上的清白"原则
equity court 衡平法院
equity crowd funding 股权众筹[指以发行证券为融资手段的直接融资行为,与其他众筹类型不同,股权众筹中的筹资人(又称发行人,issuer)是以发行证券(securities)来募集资金的。而且,此种证券交易法律关系是在投融资双方之间直接产生的,金融媒介并不作为一方当事人参与其中]
﹡**Equity delegate equality.** 衡平法代表公平(衡平法原则之一)。
equity division 衡平(分)庭
﹡**Equity follows the law.** 衡平法依从法律(衡平法原则之一)。
equity holding 衡平法上的产权持有;衡平法上的裁决
equity if competitive opportunity 竞争机会平等
﹡**Equity imputes an intention to fulfil an obligation.** 衡平法将意图归诸履行义务。
equity investment 股票投资;公平投资
equity is equity 衡平法上的核心是平等
equity joinder procedures 衡平法合并程序
equity joint venture 股权式合资企业
Equity Joint-venture Law 有股权的合资经营法,中外合资企业经营法
equity jurisdiction 衡平法管辖权;衡平法上的审判权
equity jurisprudence 衡平法学
equity law jurisdiction 衡平法审理权;衡平法上的管辖
﹡**Equity looks on that as done which ought to be done.** 衡平法将要做的事看做应做的事(衡平法原则之一)。
﹡**Equity looks to the intent rather than to the form.** 衡平法注重含义不注重形式(衡平法原则之一)。
equity of a statute 制定法的公平(释义原则)
Equity of Arms 欧洲人权委员会最早提出

的"平等武装"

equity of redemption 衡平法上的赎回(担保物)权

equity of rights in litigation (中)诉讼权利平等原则

equity of subrogation 公平的代位行使,平等的代位权[指具有从属债务者(secondarily liable on a debt)以及偿清债务者的权利。个人坚持主张原债权人对债务人具有提起诉讼的权利,包括取消赎回债权人持有的任何相关担保物的权利,以及拥有债权人可能来自其他他从原债权人提供的偿债配额(contribution)的权利。亦称 right of subrogation;(苏格兰法)right of relief。见 subrogation]

equity ownership 业主产权,业主权利(益)

equity power 衡平权(力)

equity precedents 衡平法判例,衡平法先例

Equity Rules (美)《衡平法规则》(1912年通过并颁布,即衡平法诉讼程序规则"equity rules of practice")

equity securities 产权证券[指人们所说的公司股份(或股票),股票持有人被视为公司所有权人],股权证券,权益证券;认股证券(指类似证券权益的权证或证券)

equity share with loaded voting rights 有负担的投票权的股份

equity shares 股票(不论对红利或资产有无优先权的各种股票,均享有无限的红利权)

equity stock 普通奖金,普通股本,普通股

equity to a settlement (英)衡平法上的授予财产

＊**Equity will not suffer a wrong to be without a remedy.** 衡平法不容许对违法行为没有补救方法(衡平法原则之一)。

equity's interest 普通法上的利益

equivalence (= equivalency) n. 均等,相等;相当;等价,等值;同义;同类

equivalent caseload 同等案件负荷量

equivalent doctrine (专利法)等同论(指若两项发明的功能相同,即以实质相同方式使用并产生相同结果,即使在名称、形式和外形上有所差异,亦应认定该两项发明相同)

equivalent exchange 等价交换

equivalent treatment 同等待遇

equivocal a. 模棱两可的,含糊的;多义的;可疑的;未决的

equivocal behavio(u)r 可疑行为

equivocal reply 模棱两可的回答

equivocality n. (言语的)含糊,(语言的)多义性;(行为的)可疑性

equivocate v. 含糊其词,推诿,支吾,躲闪

99er n. 99 周失业者[指失业至少 99 周并且不再有资格领取失业保险金的美国公民。一般说来,美国失业保险金领取的期限最长为 26 周。如果仍然找不到工作,失业者还可领取最长 53 周的联邦政府资助紧急失业补偿金(Emergency Unemployment Compensation)。在一些高失业率的州,失业保险金可多领取 20 周。现行的 99 周失业保险金计划已经比 1974—1975 年经济衰退期间的最长失业保险期限延长了 34 周。失业 99 周仍未找到工作的人数大约 200 万至 400 万美国人已经超过了 99 周的失业保险金领取期限。2011 年 11 月又增加了 91000 人。面对这样的困境,失业者通过社交媒体自发地组织起来,成立了"美国 99 周失业者联盟"(American 99ers' Union),要求国会通过"美国人想工作法案"(Americans Want to Work Act)。该法案的意图是将现行的失业保险领取期限延长 20 周,即所谓的第五层(Tier V)失业保险。看来国会好像不愿意增加社会开支。一些观察家认为,国会延长现行失业保险计划的执行期限都可能遇到阻力]

eradicate v. 根除,消灭,歼灭

eradicate crime 根除犯罪现象

eradicate the old and foster the new 破旧立新

erase v. 擦掉,除去,删去

erect v. 设立,(法庭的)建立;树立;安装,装配

ergo 因此

ergo omnes 完全;全面

Erie doctrine (美)伊利(案)原则(指 Erie Railroad Co. v. Tompkins 即伊利铁路

公司诉汤普金斯案判决确定的原则:"凡在联邦法院进行的诉讼,除涉及美国宪法和美国国会法律所调整的事项外,任何事件所适用的法律都裁定为联邦法院所在地的州法")

Erie doctrine (美)伊利(案)原则[指伊利铁路公司诉汤普金斯案(Erie Railroad Co. v. Tompkins)判决确定的原则:"凡在联邦法院进行的诉讼,除涉及美国联邦宪法和美国国会法律所调整的事项外,任何事件所适用的法律都裁定为联邦法院所在地的州法。"]

Erie R. Co. v. Tompkins (美)伊利诉汤普金斯[指1938年美国联邦最高法院审理的一起具有里程碑意义的案件。该案件经联邦最高法院(由布兰代斯大法官代表联邦最高法院以8:0表决)裁定:凡在联邦法院所进行的诉讼,除涉及美国联邦宪法和美国法律所调整的事项外,任何案件所适用的法律都应是联邦法院所在地的州法。此案推翻了1842年斯威夫特诉泰森案(Swift v. Tyson)确立的在这类案件中应适用联邦普通法(Federal Common Law)的先例。后一案件造成近百年之错误,所以Erie案成为美国历史上唯一联邦最高法院承认自己犯有侵犯美国联邦宪法保留给州的权利的违宪案件]

Erie's constitutional grounds 伊利案的宪法依据

ermine n. 法官制服;法官职位
ermined a. 晋升法官的;被任命为法官的
erode v. 腐蚀,侵蚀,遭腐蚀,受侵蚀
erosion n. 侵害,侵蚀,腐蚀
erotic dancing 色情舞蹈,强烈性色情舞蹈
erotic insanity 色情精神病
erotic paranoia 色情妄想狂,情欲偏执狂
erotica (复)n. 色情书籍;色情画,淫画;淫书
err v. 弄错,犯错误;(不正确地)陈述;犯罪;作恶
err from the truth 违背真理
err on the side of mercy 失之宽大
errancy n. 错误;错误状态;违背常规的事
errata (复)n. 勘误表
erratic a. 疏忽不定的,不稳定的,无规律

的;古怪的,反复无常的
erring a. 做错事的;有罪过的;走入歧途的
erroneous a. 错误的,不正确的
erroneous application of the laws 错误适用法律
erroneous arrest 错捕
erroneous judgment 错判,误判[指由于适用法律不当造成错误判决,这种错判不可避免,但对案件和当事人具有完全充分管辖权(plenary jurisdiction)的审判法官可予以纠正。或直接上诉求得纠正。亦称judgment in error]
erroneous tendency 错误倾向
error n. 1.错误;罪过;违犯(行为);差错;谬误;错误思想 2.诉讼记录错误;诉讼手续不全 3.误审;违法;邪恶
error by good faith 善意的过失,善意(造成)的错误
error *coram vobis* ("*coram vobis*"意"在你们面前")在你们面前所犯的错误[指上诉法院发给案件原审法院的"纠错令状"(writ of error),因此 writ of error *coram vobis* 即"就是你们误审的令状"]
error *facti* 事实上的错误
* *Error fucatus nuda veritate in multis, est probabilior; et saepenumero rationibus vincit veritatem error.* Error artfully disguised (or colored) is in many instances, more probable than naked truth, and frequently error overwhelms truth by (its show of) reasons. 巧妙地伪装(或粉饰)起来的谬误在许多场合比明显的真理还要显得真实,而谬误常常用(它卖弄的)各种理由来压倒真理。
error in *corpore* 标的物的错误
error in *extremis* 紧急中的过失
error in law (= error of law) (法院审理案件时适用法律不当而构成的)适用法律上的错误
error in *negotia* 法律行为性质的错误
error in *persona* 主体错误
error in *substantia* 实质性的错误;重大错误
error in the face of the record 记录表面上错误

error of (或 in) fact　事实错误
error of judg(e)ment　判断错误
error of (或 in) object　标的物的错误,客体错误
error of omission　过失罪,不作为的过错
* *Error qui non resistitur approbatur.* An error which is not resisted or opposed is approved. 谬误若没有受到抵制和反对就意味着被认可。
error-free　随意的错误
erroris causes probatio　(罗马法)错误原因证明(见 *erroris probatio*)
erroris probatio　(罗马法)关于错误的证明[指罗马法制度中,身份问题具有十分重要的意义。当罗马市民在不知情的情况下娶了拉丁人(latini)或异邦人(peregrini)为妻,而误认为自己娶的是罗马市民,并且生下了儿子时,如果证明他自己犯了错误,就可使自己的妻子和儿子取得罗马市民籍]
errors and omissions excepted　错误或遗漏除外
errors excepted　错误不在此限
erudition n.　博学,学问
escalation n.　(军事或政治事件的)扩大,逐步升级;抬高;降低
escalation clause　调整条款,伸缩条款
escape n./v.　(14 世纪)逃脱罪[指①囚犯非法逃脱合法监禁其场所,但未使用暴力,亦称 actual escape(见 prison breach)。②为避免接受禁闭、限制或一项债务而逃脱的情况或行为。从技术意义上讲,escape 是未经允准而擅自离开合法监管;从宽松意义上讲,则用来指明既是非法逃离,亦是避免捕获。一般人使用均从广义。而法律上常常从狭义使用。③(普通法)由于治安官员(peace officer)的刑事犯罪行为而允准、放纵罪犯非法逃离法定监禁场所。亦称 voluntary escape]/(犯人)逃跑,逃脱,逃逸;流失;漏出
escape artist　屡次越狱的惯犯;善于越狱的囚犯;有脱身术的人
escape clause　(1945 年)(指 WTO 保障措施来源于美国贸易法中的)逃避条款;免责条款(亦译为例外条款,指合同、保险单或其他法律文件中载明在某种情况下当事人可不负责任的条款。见 excess clause; *pro rata* clause)
escape from prison　越狱
escape from the jurisdiction of the local state　规避当地国家的管辖
escape from the net　漏网
escape of dangerous things　危险物释放(指英格兰侵权行为法上的一项条款);危险物品失控
escape period　(劳动法)可退出期间(指根据签订的劳资合同"union contract",在合同规定的期将届满下一合同开始之前工人可以退出工会)
escape warrant　(对)逃犯通缉令
escape-valve　排泄阀说(指英美刑法学中刑罚报应论的一种变异流派,把复仇作为刑罚合理证明的主要理由,人们称之为刑罚复仇论,它分为三个不同学说:其一,排泄阀说,即认为法律制裁是攻击性或有序的排泄,要求以社会性的破坏方式得到满足,其二为享受主义说,其三浪漫说)
escaped a.　逃脱的;逃亡的;漏出的
escaped convict　越狱犯
escaped criminal　在逃犯
escaped prisoner　越狱逃犯
escapee n.　越狱犯人,逃犯;逃亡者;逃俘
escaping justice　逃避司法执行
escheat n./v.　(无继承人的土地、无主财产等的)收归国有,产业充公;(英史)土地归复(指佃户保有的土地因无人继承或被判重刑而归还领主)/归复土地(或其他财产);(无人继承的土地)转归国家(领主或国王)
escheat proceedings　土地征用的诉讼,土地复归诉讼
escheatable a.　收归国有的
escheated property　无人继承的财产
escheator n.　管理充公产业的官员
eschew v.　避免,避开(危害、恶事等)
escort n./v.　1.护送,押送 2.护卫;护航;陪同 3.护卫者,护送者,陪同者 4. 警卫队;护航舰(机)/1.护送,押送 2.护卫 3.陪同
escort under police　警察押送;警察护送
escrow n.　待条件完成的契据(指①法律文据、立约人交付的财产、金钱交给第三人

保管,确定相当的时间或在约定的条件实现时,才由第三者将法律文据和财产等交给受让人、受约人或债权人。②信托账户或担保账户。亦称 escrow account; impound account; reserve account)

escrow account 代管账户[指通常以储户(depositor)或代管人(escrow agent)之名义开立的银行账户,等待代管条件成熟或实现时交还给储户或第三方。亦称 escrow deposit。见 escrow]

escrow agreement 待条件完成后的转让协议
escrow bond 待条件完成后的转让债券
escrow fund 待条件完成后的转让资金
esoteric legal precedents 深奥的法律先例
especial a. 特别的,特殊的
espial n. 间谍,侦(探)察;窥探;监视;发现
espionage n. 谍报间谍活动;刺探;间谍,侦探
espionage activities 间谍活动
Espionage Acts (美)《间谍法》(指 1917 年国会首次通过的这一法律,是规定惩治间谍犯罪及处理有关国际战争事务的联邦法律。于 1940 年国会再次修订该法令,加大了触犯该法令的刑罚力度)
espionage agent 间谍
esplees (=explees) n. 土地上的生长物,土地收益
espousal n. 拥护,赞助;(复)订婚,订婚仪式;结婚,婚礼
espouse v. 1.娶,出嫁 2.袒护,拥护;赞助;信奉
essence n. 要素;本质,实质;本体,实体
essence of crime 犯罪构成要件,犯罪要素
essence of judicial duty 司法职责的要素
essence of law 法的本质(又译:法律的本质)
essence of offence 罪行要素
essence of the contract 合同(契约)的要件;合同(契约)成立要素
essence of the evidence 证据本质;证据的要素
essential a./n. 本质的,实质的;基本的;必要的,必不可少的/(复)本质,实质;要点,要素;必需品
essential condition 本质条件;主要条件;必备条件

essential facility doctrine 关键设施理论,核心设施理论[核心设施又称瓶颈设施"bottleneck facility",指反垄断法中历史悠久又富争议的理论。按欧共体的认定,核心设施可与消费终端直接连接,并可被竞争者视为对经营有价值的设施。在核心设施理论或原则中,当一个设施被认定为"核心"之后,设施的拥有者就在一定程度上承担以合理重要任务开放使用的义务,而不得拒绝交易。这在反垄断法理论上具有十分重要的意义。此理论或原则起源于 1912 年的 U. S. v. Terminal Railroad Association of St. Louis(即"终端铁路案"),但在此案 65 年后, essential facility doctrine 才再一次出现于美国法院的判决之中,在 1983 年的 Hech v. Profootball 案中联邦最高法院针对该原则提出了判断的四标准]
essential finding (军事法)(军事法庭对附带审前动议的)重要裁决
essential government duties (美)(美国联邦宪法规定的)联邦政府部门的主要职责
Essential Patent Pool 必要专利池[指专利联营组建常基于特定技术标准,如:欧盟 DVB 标准的必要专利池,3G 标准中的"必要专利平台"(Essential Patent Platform), MPEG-2 标准中的"必要专利组合"(Essential Patent Portfolio), DVD 标准的 3C 和 6C 专利联营]
essential point 要点;本质点
essential requirement 实质性要件;基本要件
essential stages in civil procedure 民事诉讼中的主要阶段
essential stages in criminal procedure 刑事诉讼中的主要阶段
essential term 主要条款,基本条款
essential to an effective defense 与被告防御(或辩护)有绝对关系
essentialia 要素(指法律行为要件)
essentialia feudi (苏格兰法)封建权利的重要条款(terms)
essentialia negotii 要件

essentiality n. 根本性,实质性;必要性;本质,实质,要素

essentially equitable 本质上属衡平法性质

essentials of marriage 婚姻的要件

essoin (=essoign) n./v. (古英国法)(在传票回执上提出这种不出庭的)宽恕请求/(没有服从传票的指定日期出庭而)请求宽恕

essoiner n. (英)代辩律师,请求宽恕人(出庭并为缺席一方作辩护。见 essoin)

*** Est autem vis legem simulans.** Violence may also put on the mask of law. 违法者也可能会戴着法律的假面具。

*** Est boni judicis ampliare jurisdictionem.** It is the role of a good judge to extend the jurisdiction. 掌握管辖权的实质范畴是一个好的法官,不拘泥于文字解释管辖权是一个称职法官。

*** Est ipsorum legislatorum tanquam viva vox.** The voice of the legislators themselves is like a living voice. That is, the provisions of a statute are to be understood and interpreted as practical rules for real circumstances. 立法者本身的声音就像一个活的声音(即成文法的规定条文需认真理解,根据实际情况解释为可行的实际规则)。

establish v. 1.建立,设立(公司等),创办 2.制定,规定 3.委任,安置,委派 4.确立,证实;认可 5.使开业,使营业 6.定为国教

establish an *alibi* 提供不在(犯罪)现场的证据

establish diplomatic relation 建立外交关系

establish (sb.'s) identity 1.证明(某人的)身份 2.验明正身,证实人的身份,认定同一

establish ownership in corporate shares 占有公司股份

established a. 建立的,设立的,制定的;确定的,既定的,确认的;固定的

established business 固定业务;固定的营业(如医生诊疗所,农产品农场等)

established case 案例,例案

Established Church 英国国教

established custom 确定的惯例,成规

established fact 既成事实

established practice 惯例,成规

established precedent 确定的先例,已成的先例

established principle 准则,既定原则

established principle of international law 公认的国际法准则

established religion (=established church) 国教

established right 既得权利;既得利益

established rule 成规

established rule of conduct 公认的行为规则

establishing identity (刑事技术鉴定的)同一认定

establishment n. 1.建立,设立;创办,开设 2.建立的机构;行政机关;军队;企业,公司 3.法规,法典 4.定员,编制 5.(大写)既定的权力机构(或体制);幕后统治集团

establishment circular 人事通告

establishment clause (美)正教分离条款(指美国联邦宪法第一修正案:国会不得制定关于确立某种宗教为国教或禁止自由信仰宗教的法律)

Establishment Department (英)编制部(指英国财政部内设立的一个专管除公务人员改选以外的其他一切有关人事行政事宜的部门)

establishment of a juristic act 法律行为的成立

establishment of basis fact 基本事实的确立,事实根据的成立

establishment of dower 寡妇财产转让书的制定

establishment of letter of credit 开信用证

establishment of paternity 父子关系的确认;父亲身份的确认

Establishment of Union 联盟(或联合)的建立

estate (15世纪)1.总额,等级,社会等级;性质,品质,特性[个人土地或其他财产权益的特性;特别是可能成为排他性所有的(possessory)不动产的权益(real-estate interest),所有权则按照存续时间来衡定。

见 periodic tenancy] 2.个人或部门的所有权,包括动产和不动产 3.遗产;死者清还债务的集中资产(collective assets)及义务
estate agent 地产经纪人;地产管理人
estate and interest 地产和收益;(总称)财产
estate at sufferance 经允许可继续占有的地产
estate at will 随意租借地产(见 tenancy at will)
estate bring(或 **brought**) **in** (夫妻)带来(家庭)的财产
estate by escheat 无人继承的遗产
estate by intestacy 依法继承的地产
estate by the curtesy 丈夫占有的亡妻地产
estate by the entirety 夫妻共有的财产
estate contract 地产合同(契约),不动产合同(契约)
estate duty(或 **tax**) 遗产税,继承税;地产税
estate executors 遗嘱遗产执行人
estate for life 终身占有的地产(权)
estate for years 有固定占有期限的地产,定期地产(权)(指非完全保有地产权的一种。权利人只能在双方约定的期限内占有土地和对土地享有权益的地产权。亦称 tenacy for a term; estate for a term)
estate free from encumbrance 无负担(指抵押等)的不动产
estate in a term of years absolute 按绝对规定年限承袭的地产(权)
estate in abeyance 所有人未定的不动产;无人继承的遗产
estate in common 共有不动产,共有地产
estate in coparcenary 数人共同继承的地产(权)
estate in dower 寡妇地产(权)
estate in expectancy 将来继承的遗产
estate in fee 世袭地产
estate in fee-simple 无限定继承权的地产(权)
estate in fee-tail 有限定继承权的地产(权)
estate in gage 已作抵押的地产(权)
estate in joint tenancy 共同租借的地产(权)
estate in land 地产(权)

estate in possession 占有上的财产权益;地产占有权
estate in remainder 余产;残余地产的收益(权)
estate in reversion 可望继承的地产(权)
estate in severalty 单独占有的地产(权)
estate in tail 限定继承的不动产(权)
estate income 遗产收益,产业收益
estate of deceased person 死者的遗产
estate of freehold 地产,不动产
estate of inheritance 被继承的遗产
estate of the realm 国有地产,国有不动产;(英)王国等级(指中世纪议会按地位划分的三种群体)
estate on condition (18世纪)附条件地产权[指地产权的设立、变更、终止取决于某个特定事件的发生或不发生。附期限地产权(an estate on limitation)不需通过让与人或让与人的继承人的任何诉讼,到约定期即应被归还。附条件地产权则要求在条件出现时,让与人和让与人的继承人为占有土地而进入诉讼(entry)终止该地产权。亦称 estate on conditional limitation; conditional estate。见 estate on limitation]
estate on conditional limitation 见 estate on condition
estate on limitation (18世纪)附期限地产权,到期归还的地产权[指根据规定条款,通常是有关经过的终止时期,该地产权自动归还让与人(grantor)。条款中的(during)"当……时",(while)"而当……时",及(as long as)"达……之久""长达……"为被指定用的词语。见 fee simple determinable; estate on condition]
estate owner 地产所有人;遗产所有人
estate planning 遗产计划[指①通过遗嘱的实现,考虑到信托、保险单以及其他安排,特别是减少遗产管理费用(administration cost)和遗产税责任(transfer-tax liability)。②有关对私人财产安排的相关法律部分(branch of law),考虑到遗嘱、税收、保险、财产和信托等法律法规]
estate pur autre vie 他人生存期的土地保有

estate tail 限定继承的不动产
estate tax (1728年)遗产税[指对因遗嘱或非遗嘱继承(intestate succession)而转移的财产所征收的税。亦称为 death tax; death duty。见 inheritance tax]
estate under a will 依遗嘱继承的遗产
estate upon condition 有条件继承的遗产
Estates-General n. (法史)三级会议(指法国大革命前君主制下教士、贵族、代表大多数人民的第三等级的三个等级的代议制会议)
estimate n./v. 估计;估价;估计数;预算;(承包人的)估价单;评价;判断;(大写)(复)(英)(财政大臣每年提交议会的)国家支出预算/估计;财政预算;评价;判断;估价
estimate tax (1926年)(美)估算税款,估缴税款[指不以预扣税款方式纳税的纳税人(如个体户"self-employed person")基于前一年的纳税金额(tax liability)或当年估计的纳税金额按季度缴纳的税款]
estimated a. 估计的,财政预算的,评价的,估价的,判断的
estimated assessment 预算税额
estimated cost 估计费用;估计成本
estimated expenditure 预算支出
estimated net profit 估计纯利
estimated revenue 预算收入
estimated surplus 估计盈余
estimated trial time 对庭审时间的估计(指美国民事诉讼审理前的程序之一,即当事人估计的庭审时间,包括陪审团遴选在内,需要3天的时间)
estimated value 估计价值
Estimates and Consolidated Fund Bills (英)预算和统一基金法案
Estimates Committee 预算委员会
estimative a. 作出判断的,被估计的,被判断的
estop v. 1.禁止,阻止,防止(from) 2.禁止翻供
estoppage n. 禁止翻供;阻止,堵塞
estoppel n. 不容反悔,不许否认,禁止改口,禁止翻供(即禁止翻供自己的供词和推翻过去所作的事实陈述),再诉禁止

estoppel by conduct 见 equitable estoppel
estoppel by deed (普通法上的)契据不容反悔
estoppel by election 因已选择不容否认(若某人有意识地在两个相互矛盾的选项中做出选择,将会阻止他从未选择的选项中获益)
estoppel by inaction 见 estoppel by silence
estoppel by judg(e)ment 既有判决不容推翻
estoppel by matter of record (estoppel by record) (普通法上的)记录在案的事实禁止翻供
estoppel by silence 因沉默而不容否认,因默认的事实而不容否认[指当事人在一定情况下有义务向他人明示陈述,但却未尽这项义务,从而致使他人向往某种事实的存在,并因此进行一定行为。此时,则禁止该当事人否认因其沉默导致他人相信该事实的存在。其实,这也是 estoppel in pais (不容推翻的事实/因既有行为而不容否认)的一种。亦称 estoppel by standing; estoppel by inaction]
estoppel by standing 见 estoppel by silence
estoppel by verdict 定案的判决不容推翻
estoppel equitable 衡平法上不容推翻的事实
estoppel in pais (衡平法上的)不容推翻的事实;因既有行为而不容否认(指当事人因其先前行为或不当沉默而自受制约,以后不得作自相矛盾的相反主张)
estoppel per rem judicatam 间接禁止翻供的事实,间接不容否认,间接再诉禁止,间接再诉否认[指①在一个诉讼中对于实际的争诉事实已经法院作了有约束力的判决和决定,当事人之间在以后涉及不同的权利主张的争论中,仍应以此原判决作为依据。而当事人不得以其他诉因为根据再次争讼。②该原则亦适用于刑事案件,亦称 issue preclusion; direct estoppel; estoppel by judgment; estoppel by record; estoppel by verdict; cause-of-action estoppel; technical estoppel; estoppel per rem judicatam。见 collateral estoppels]
estovers n. (法律上承认的)必需供给品

(如离婚时供给离婚妻子的扶养费等)

Estrada Doctrine 艾斯特拉达主义(指墨西哥外长艾斯特拉达于1930年所宣布的方针;墨西哥以后对外国新政府不作正式的承认表示,而只是决定彼此继续保持或不保持外交关系)

estray n. 无人认领的走失家畜,迷途家畜

estreat n./v. (关于罚款或保释金等的)裁判记录的副本或抄本;裁判记录、摘录或副本/摘录裁判记录以便执行;没收……以作罚金;抄录裁判记录

et al. 以及另一个人,以及其他人;……等人(et al 主要指人,而 etc 主要指物)

et alii (= et al) 以及其他人等,等人

et hoc genus omne and everything of the sort 诸如此类

et hoc paratus est verificare And this he is prepared to verify 并且他对证明此事的真实性有充分思想准备[这一术语传统上包括承认原告陈述之事,但又规避其法律效果的答辩(a plea in confession and avoidance)或是包含新的确认事项(affirmative matter)的任何答辩状。包括这一术语的答辩状从严格法律程序来讲,即以证明真实性推论(conclude with a verification),作为反对简单的否认(simple denial)]

et hoc petit quod inquiratur per patriam (古代)而且他请求国家(陪审团)调查此事[指原告申诉结束时的拉丁用语,请求:向国家(陪审团)提出争议的问题。见 conclusion to the country]

Eternal law 永恒法(根据阿奎那神学,宇宙间存在四种法律:①Eternal law,即永恒法;②Natural law,即自然法;③Divine law,即神授法;④Human law,即人类法。永恒法即上帝本身,自然法是上帝为自然立法,神授法即十诫,人类法即是我们今天的法律和社会体制)

ethereal realms 超凡王国

ethical a. 伦理的;伦理学的;道德的;合乎道德的

ethical blemishes 道德上的污点

ethical consideration (常大写)(英美法)道德对价[指律师界或法律界(legal profession)《模范职业责任法典》(Model Code of Professional Responsibility)中所提出的道德准则(ethical canon)的结构性部分,它包含意欲指导律师职业行为的道德准则或目的。道德对价通常被用来对《模范职业责任法典》进行解释或适用。缩略为 EC。见 disciplinary rule]

Ethical Culture 道德教育(运动)(指1876年出现的鼓吹社会力量促进社会福利观念的一种道德教育运动)

ethical ideas of good faith 诚信道德观念

ethical import 伦理上的意义

ethical jurisprudence 伦理法学

ethical laws 伦理的法则

ethics (复) n. 1.伦理学,道德学 2.伦理学论文(或书籍) 3.伦理观,道德观,道德标准

ethics opinion 道德的评价,合理决议(指具有执业纪律或惩戒的权威部门就有关律师执业责任的事宜所作的书面的合理决议),道德评价,道德评论,道德意见

ethics-based punishment 道德性惩罚

ethischer personalismus (康德创立的)"伦理人格主义"哲学

ethnarch n. (拜占庭帝国等的)总督

ethnic(al) a. 种族的;民族的;人种的;异教徒的

ethnic cleansing (1991年)种族净化,种族清洗[指官方采用暴力,系统地减少或消灭一个地区的少数民族,通常通过没收动产和不动产、命令(或安排)、不追究大规模屠杀和强奸以及驱逐存活者。理论上讲,种族清洗之目的就是一定要驱赶使受侵害之群体离开这一地区。实际上,种族清洗与种族灭绝(genocide)近乎同义词,如同大屠杀(mass murder)是这两者的特征。种族清洗还增加了包括培育的两条理由而大规模强奸(暴)(mass rapes):①受害者通常由其亲属处死或自杀;②所有出生的子女均被视为属于父亲的清洗群体(ethnic group),而不属于母亲的。这两者的行为(屠杀、强奸)意图减少或消灭使被侵害的少数民族(victimized minority)。见 genocide]

ethnic(al) national sovereignty 民族主权

ethnic(al) policy 民族政策

ethnic(al) prejudice 种族偏见
ethnic(al) rights 民族权利
ethnic discrimination 异教徒的歧视
ethnic group 民族团体,少数民族团(或群)体;种族集团
ethnic identities 种族身份
ethnic solidarity 种族集团,种族一致
etiquette n. 规则,成规;礼节,礼仪;典礼
etiquette of profession 职业道德
etiquette of service of process 诉讼书状送达的准则
eugenical community 优生社区
eugenical sterilization 优生的绝育
eunuch n. (中)宦官,太监;阉人
eupatrid n. (古雅典)元老(指古代雅典贵族成员,这一时期的公职可能由实际上的元老担任)
Euro Money 欧元
Euro-bond n. 欧洲债券(指美国公司在美国以外的地方尤指在欧洲地区,以美元买卖并计息的债券)
Euro-currency n. 欧洲货币
Euro-dollar n. 欧洲美元(美国在国外,尤指在欧洲使用的美元)
Euro-Market n. 欧洲市场
Euroclear 欧洲清算所(见 Depository Trust Company)
Europäischer Beschlu 欧洲决定
Europäisches Gesetz 欧洲法律
Europäisches Rahmengesetz 欧洲框架法律
European a. 欧洲的;欧洲人的
(The) European Agreement on the Transmission of Application for Legal Aid 在斯特拉斯堡通过的《关于转送诉讼救助申请的欧洲协定》(又称1977年《斯特拉斯堡协定》)
European Commission of Human Rights 欧洲人权委员会
European Common Market 欧洲共同市场
European Community 欧洲共同体
European Convention on Human 欧洲人权公约
European Convention on Human Rights 《欧洲人权公约》
European Court of Human Rights 欧洲人权法院
European Court of Justice 欧洲法院
European Defence Community 欧洲防卫共同体
European democratization 欧洲民主化
European Economic Community 欧洲经济共同体
European Extra-Judicial Network 欧洲司法外争议解决机制网(指目前欧盟非常重视运用的解决争议的机制)
European Free Trade Association 欧洲自由贸易联盟
European International Law 欧洲国际法
European Investment Bank 欧洲投资银行
European Jurisprudence of Interests 欧洲功利法学派
European Law 欧洲法
European Monetary Agreement 《欧洲货币协定》
European Monetary Institute 欧洲货币机构
European Parliament 欧洲议会
European Parliamentary Assembly 欧洲议会大会
European Patent Convention (EPC) 欧洲专利公约
European Political Co-operation (EPC) 欧洲政治合作(指在达成欧洲政治一体化中起作用的一种政策)
European System of Central Banks (ESCB) 欧洲中央银行体系
European Union (EU) 欧洲联盟(欧盟)
euthanasia n. 无痛苦的死亡;安乐死术(指为结束不治之症患者的痛苦而施行的无痛致死术)
Euthanasia Educational Fund (美)安乐死教育基金会
evade v. 逃避,躲避;回避,规避
evade acceptance 拒绝受领;拒绝承诺
evade doing a duty 逃避职责
evade foreign exchange 逃汇
evade tax 偷税,逃税
evading n. 规避,避免
evading justice 规避司法执行("司法执行"是要把犯罪者绳之以法,而规避司法

执行是一种"妨碍司法执行"的行为,意思是指帮助犯罪者,用以规避司法惩罚)
evaluate v. 评价,估价,定值
evaluating evidence 评价证据
evaluation n. 定值,估计;评价;评审
evaluation committee of academic degree 学位评审委员会
evaluation committee of academic ranks 学衔评审委员会
evaluation committee of professional titles 职称评审委员会
evaluation group 评审小组
evaluation of evidence 评价证据
evaluation of one's performance 考核(某人),对某人考核
evaluation of the consent theory of secession 渐进同意的脱离理论
Evarts Act (美)《埃瓦茨法》[指1891年的《巡回上诉法院法》(Circuit Court of Appeals Act),创设了联邦巡回上诉法院,从而改变了联邦法院系统的传统格局]
evasion n. 1.回避,规避;逃避;借口,遁词 2.(捐税等的)偷漏
evasion of foreign exchange 逃汇
evasion of labo(u)r reform (中)逃避劳动改造
evasion of law 法律规避,规避法律,法律规避行为[亦被称为"法律欺诈"(fraud à la loi; fraudulent evasion of law),是指涉外民事法律关系的当事人故意制造某种联结点,以避开原来的联结点所指引的准据法,从而得以适用新联结点所指引的准据法来实现对自己有利的结果。国际私法上不承认这种新联结点具有指引准据法的效力,而仍适用变更前的联结点所指引的法律,从而形成国际私法上的法律规避制度]
evasion of legal sanction 逃避法律制裁
evasion of liability by deception 通过欺骗而逃避债务或义务
evasion of registration 逃避登记
evasion of tax 逃税
evasor n. 逃税人,逃避者
evasive a. 逃避的,规避的;偷漏(捐税等)的;推托的;不可捉摸的

evasive answer 遁词;含糊其词的答辩
evenhanded a. 不偏不倚的,公正的
event n. 事件;事变;偶然时间;活动,经历;诉讼的(或判决的)结果,判决结果
event insured 被保险的事件
events at issue 诉讼系争点;诉讼争执点
eventual demise 最后的终止,终结
eventual intent 未必故意
eventual judgment 基于诉讼而遭受损失的判决
* *eventus varios res nova semper habet.* A novel matter always produces various results. 新事物(或新情况)往往产生不同的结果。
ever-living constitution 历史永存的宪法,永远的宪法
ever-present danger of inconsistent jury verdicts 各陪审团裁定不一致这一常见的危险
every jot of procedural advantage 每一诉讼的有利条件,每一诉讼好处,每一诉讼利益环节
evict v. (依法从土地上或建筑物中)逐出;驱逐(租户);没收;追回(财产);收回
evict property 收回财产,合法恢复财产所有
evictee n. 被驱逐者;被没收者
eviction n. 收回财产,收回租地;没收;逐出
eviction by title paramount 依绝对处分权的逐出(指在出租人无权出租的情况下所有人依绝对处分权逐出租户)
eviction principle 收回财产原则;恢复财产所有原则
evictor n. 驱逐者;没收者;收回者
evidence n./v. (14世纪)证据[指①一些事物,包括口供、文件以及实物都可以证明或反驳一件所主张的事实的存在〈the bloody glove is the key piece of evidence for the prosecution〉(血腥的手套正是检控方的一个关键性证据)。②见事实证据(fact in evidence)。③收集大量事物,特别是证言和出示的证物,在法庭上出现争议时出示〈the evidence will show that the defendant breached the contract〉(证据将表明被告违约)。④法律汇编(body of law)规

定,被提供证据(proof)进入法定诉讼程序中的可采性〈under the rules of evidence, the witness's statement is inadmissible hearsay that is not object to any exception〉(根据证据规则,证人陈述是不可采纳的,传闻亦不属于例外)。亦称 rules of evidence]/作证,证明,以证据支持
evidence act 证据法
evidence *aliunde* 旁证
evidence at assessment 课税根据
evidence both pro and con 正反两方面的证据
evidence by deposition 笔录供词
evidence *de bene esse* 由非审讯录取的证供
evidence documentary 书面证据
evidence for the defence 被告证人;答辩证据
evidence for the prosecution 原告证人;控告证据,检控证据
evidence in chief 主要证据
evidence in rebuttal (原告用以)反驳的证据
evidence in support of *alibi* 证明被告不在(犯罪)现场的证据
evidence in writing 文字证据,书面证据
evidence obtained by polygraph 由测谎器获取的证据
evidence of a crime 罪证
evidence of conformity 符合要求的证据
evidence of debt 借据;债务证据
evidence of fact 事实证据
evidence of guilt 有罪证据,罪证
evidence of identity 身份证据;鉴别(性)证据
evidence of innocence 无罪证据
evidence of negligence 过失证据
evidence of payment of duty 完税凭证
evidence of previous convictions 前科的证据
evidence of similar facts 相同事实的证据
evidence of subsequent repairs 事后修补的证据
evidence of title 所有权证据
evidence on a particular point 特定点上的证据
evidence on affidavit 宣誓证据
evidence on appeal 上诉证据
evidence on mitigation 减轻证据(指对损害赔偿金减轻的证据)
evidence on the AI model 关于攻击性(attack)和无罪性(innocence)模式的证据
Evidence Ordinance 《诉讼证据条例》
evidence outside the instrument 票据外的证据
evidence proving innocence 证明无罪的证据
evidence received by jury 为陪审团所接受的证据
evidence rules 证据规则
evidence to prove guilt 证明有罪的证据
evidence upon oath 宣誓证据
evidence-in-chief (18世纪)主要证据(指当事方在案件中采用的主要证据)
evidenciary fact (1855年)1.根本的事实(指关键的事实或必要的事实,亦称 predicate fact) 2.用以证明某些其他事实存在的事实证据(亦称 evidential fact)
evidencing feature 以证据支撑的特点,证明的特点[指一组情况在作为一个整体时就可形成一个综合特征(或特点),并能可靠地与单一客体相联系。此术语在刑事案件出现多于民事案件、刑事案件中,它常指一种可确定犯罪人身份(perpetrator's identity)的证据,在民事案件中它却常指一件发生或未发生的事件。此术语亦称 evidential mark; evidencing mark]
evidentia 证据
evidential (=evidentiary) a. 提供证据的;作证据用的;证据的;依证据的;证明的
evidential burden 举证责任
evidential effect 证据效力
evidentiary fact(s) 证据事实(指①确定案件主要事实所必需的事实;是以作为证据的事实;②亦指可证明其他事实存在的事实。亦称 evidential fact;predicate fact)
evidential function 证据作用
evidential item 证据物
evidentiary 见 evidential
evidentiary document 证明文件

evidentiary facts 证据事实
evidentiary formality 证据要式
evidentiary hearing 证据听证会
evidentiary material 证据材料
evidentiary privilege 证据上的特权
evidentiary requirement 证据性要求
evidentiary statement 口供证据
evil n./a. 1.邪恶,罪恶;恶行;弊病 2.不幸,灾难;祸害;痛苦 3.恶言,诽谤/邪恶的,罪恶的;有害的;中伤的
evil consequences 恶果
evil devices 奸计
evil intent 邪恶意图
evil man 坏人
evil practice (或 habit) 恶习
* **evil results of evil doing** 恶行恶果,恶有恶报
evil speaking 诽谤,中伤
evil thoughts 邪念
evil-doer n. 作恶的人,坏人
evitable a. 可以避免的
evocation n. (法)解体;提审;移送诉讼案件(指案件因上诉而由下级法院向上级法院移送),案卷移送
evocatory (=evocative) a. (上级法院)提审的;移送案件的
evoke v. (上级法院)提审;移送(案件至上级法院)
evolution n. 进展,发展,演变;展开;(气体等)放出;散出物;进化
evolution and creation science 进化论与创世论(此术语是用来描述地球及其物种长期渐进发展的理论)
evolution of law 法律的演进;法律的沿革
evolutionary social theory 社会演化论
evolutionary theories of law 进化论的法学,法的进化论
evolutive interpretation 演进解释[有学者认为演进解释与动态解释(dynamic interpretation)、累进解释(progressive interpretation)为同义语。有的国际公法学家以条约中"概念""术语""目的和宗旨""意图"等作为其主张演进解释的基础]
evolve the truth form a mass of confused evidence 从大量混杂的证据中推断出

事实
evolve v. 1.使发展,使进化,使渐进〈evolve a theory〉(发展一种理论)2.推论,引申出,推定(事实等)〈evolve the truth from a mass of confused evidence〉(从大量庞杂证据中推断出事实真相) 3.放出,发出 4.展开,演化,发达,发育,渐进
ex prep. 1.从,自;依据 2.在……交货 3.无,不;无权获得
ex abundanti cautela 由于过于谨慎
ex aequo et bono 公允和善良;出自公正善良;按良心和公平原则;按公平合理原则
ex animo 诚心诚意的(地)
ex ante 事前;根据经济上预期变化的
* ***Ex antecedentibus et consequentibus fit optima interpretatio.*** A passage will be best interpreted by reference to that which precedes and follows it./The best interpretation is made from the context./The context is to be considered in interpreting any phrase or clause, and not the mere isolated phrase./The best interpretation is made from what precedes and what follows. 解释法律的一段文字最好是通过参考其上下文来进行。
ex bond (纳税后)保税仓库(关栈)交货
ex buyer's godown 买方仓库交货价
ex cathedra 来自权威方面,权威方面宣称,命令式的,用职权的,用权威的
ex causa mendati (苏格兰法)由于命令;因为上级法院给下级法院的命令
ex causa potestatis because of his position of authority (罗马法)由于他的权位[某些人不得与受监护和监管的女人结婚,其理由据说是他们的权位]
ex consignment 由寄售货中拨销(交)
ex contractu 由合同(契约)引起的(诉讼);违反合同(契约)的(诉讼)
ex curia 法庭外的,双方一致的
ex debito justitiae 应得的补救权利(指法律上应得的权利,并非恩惠或任意决定)
ex delicto 由于违法、侵权、过失、犯罪或渎职所引起的(诉讼)
* ***Ex delicto non ex supplicio emergit infamia.*** Infamy arises from the crime, not from the punishment. 剥夺公权是由所犯罪行

引起的,并不是由刑罚引起的。
* ***Ex diuturnitate temporis, omnia praesumuntur solemniter esse acta.*** From length of time (after lapse of time) all things are presumed to have been done in due form. (经过拖延一段时间以后)只要在期限以内完成就应当认为是全部按规定完成。
ex dividend (英)无红利,无股息;红利未付;不包括下期红利
ex dock (或 **pier, quay, wharf**) 码头交货价格
* ***Ex dolo malo non oritur actio.*** Out of fraud no action arises. 不能出于欺诈的缘由来进行起诉。
ex facie (文件)从表面看,显然地
ex facie absolute disposition (苏格兰)形式上的绝对处分
ex facto 根据事实,事实上
ex factory 工厂交货价格
ex fictione juris 依法律的拟制
ex gratia 作为优惠的,通融的,出自恩惠的;宽018
ex gratia payment 宽限给付;没有法定对价的给付
ex hypothesi 就假定来说,根据假定
ex interest 无利息(不论到期与否)
ex leg 根据法律,法律上
ex lex (=outlaw) 法律之外的(指不受法律保护的)
* ***Ex maleficio non oritur contractus.*** A contract cannot arise out of an act radically vicious and illegal. 有效合同(契约)根本不能出自违法行为。
ex mero motu 出于自愿
ex mora (民法上) from or in consequence of delay 由于延误,由于迟延
ex more 根据风俗
ex new 无新股息
* ***Ex nudo pacto non oritur actio.*** Out of a nude or naked pact (that is, a bare parol agreement without consideration) no action arises. 无对价的口头合同(契约)不能诉请履行。
ex officio (=*ex-officio*) 依职权;当然(职务);前任(职务);依官职的;当然的

ex officio information 依职权提起的检控
ex officio justice 当然法官(即依职权取得的法官)
ex officio member 当然成员,当然议员,当然会员
ex officio oath 就职宣誓
ex officio principle (中)职权原则(刑事诉讼法原则之一)
ex officio reopening of decided cases 依职权重审定案
* ***Ex pacto illicito non oritur actio.*** From an illegal contract an action does not arise. 非法合同(契约)不能引起诉讼。
ex pacto nudo oritun actio et obligation "从简约中也可以产生诉权"
ex parte 单方诉讼,单方面的,片面的;偏袒的(拉丁文:"为了……利益")[该术语指不预先通知对方当事人或对方当事人不参加听审的诉讼。此术语用于一个案件标题时,如 ex parte young (1908)即"涉及杨的非诉案(1908)表明诉讼是为了标题所指认的利益而进行的"]
ex parte award 仅有一方当事人在场(时所作)的仲裁裁决
ex parte communication 单方面接触(指为了保证程序主持者和裁判者的独立性,当事人有权反对单方面的接触,即在复数以上当事人参与的程序中,程序主持者或裁判者在一方不在场的情况下与其他当事人的接触,即构成单方面接触)
ex parte injunction 单方面的强制令
ex parte inspection order 单方面检查令
ex parte proceedings 仅有一方当事人(参加)的诉讼;一造诉讼,单方程序
ex parte young (1908) 涉及杨的单方面诉讼案(1908)
ex post 事后;根据过去经济发展形势分析的
ex post facto 事后的,有溯及力的;追溯既往的
ex post facto clause 有追溯效力的条款
ex post facto laws 溯及既往的法律[指在某一事实发生或某一行为完成之后制定的并能适用于该事实或行为,且改变其法律后果和法律关系之法,亦如法律把一项

在行为时不宣布是犯罪的行为作为犯罪来惩罚。美国联邦宪法第1条第10款第1项禁止州通过任何溯及既往的法律;第1条第9款第3项同样禁止联邦政府通过这样的法律。联邦最高法院起先认定这些禁止性条款只适用刑法领域而不适用于民事领域。虽然如此,民事领域内溯及既往的法律在一定条件下也会违反契约条款或正当程序条款(contract or due process clause)。禁止溯及既往的法律禁令实际只是对立法权的限制。而不适用于法官对法律的改变。另外,溯及既往加重惩罚的法律也违反这样的条款。修改证据规则从而更易于判处被告有罪之法律也是宪法禁止的]

ex proprio motu 出自本意的,出于自愿的,出于自动的

ex rel 和……联系(见 *ex relatione*)

ex relatione 根据告发(用于检察官为了国家利益,以国家名义根据受害当事人的控告提起公诉)

ex rights 对新发行股票无购买特权

ex store (或 **warehouse**) 仓库交货

* *Ex turpi causa non oritur actio.* Out of a base (illegal, or immoral) consideration, an action does (can) not arise. 对非法或不道德的对价不能诉请履行。

ex work price 工厂交货价,即货物离开工厂时的价格(见 ex works)

ex works (EWX) 工厂交货[指以贸易术语表明买卖双方对于交货、支付、损失风险等的义务,当这些货物已备好在卖主选择的地点(location)而并未要求集装车辆运载交给买主时并交到买主指定的展览室,工厂或仓库,则卖主的交货任务已经完成(损失风险传给了买方)]

ex-convict n. 前科犯;出狱者;犯过罪的人

ex-judge n. 前任法官

ex-lord chancellor 前任大法官

ex-officio **magistrate** 兼任行政职务的司法官员

ex-parte application 单方面书面或口头申请(指要求法院制定特别规定或下达命令)

ex-parte contacts prohibited 禁止单方接触

ex-parte divorce proceeding 单方离婚程序

ex-parte hearing 单方听证

ex-parte investigation 单方调查

ex-parte prohibition 禁止偏向一方(即禁止单方接触之意)(见 *ex parte communication*)

ex-prisoner n. 前科犯;已出狱的囚犯

ex-soldier 退伍(复员)军人

ex-wife n. 前妻

exacerbate v. 使……恶化,使……加剧,使……更甚,使……加深

exact a./v. 确切的,正确的;精确无误的;严厉的;严格的/要求,强要;强迫;需要;急需

exact confession by torture 刑讯逼供

exact constitutional violation 确切违宪;确切地违反宪法

exact order 严厉的命令

exact satisfaction 强行履行义务

exaction n. 1.勒索,榨取,强取;勒索的物品(或金钱);无理要求 2.苛捐杂税,强征的税收;强索的费用

exactor n. 1.勒索者,榨取者 2.收税人

exaggerate v. 夸大,把……言过其实;使增大,使过大;夸张,言过其实

exaggerated abstract individualism 极端的抽象个人主义

exaggerated fact 夸大的事实

exalt v. 高举,升起;提升;提拔,晋升;赞扬,吹捧

exaltation of individual interests 个人利益的膨胀

examinable a. 在审查范围内的;可检查的

examinant n. 审查者;审查人;检查(察)官;审问人;主考人

examinate n. 受审者;受检查人

examination n. 1.检查;审查;审问,查问,讯问,询问(指在审判中采用双方当事人质问证人方式取得证供的程序) 2.考试

examination and approval 审批

examination candidate 应试生,考生

examination chamber (法院的)预审庭

examination in chief 主询问[亦称直接诘

问(询问)。见 direct examination]
examination of cargo 验关;货物检查
examination of conscience 反省
examination of document 检查证件,审查证件
examination of evidence 查证,复查证据
examination of invention 对发明的审查
examination of party (对方)当事人的查问
examination of the *voir dire* 对到庭的证人(或陪审员)预先所作的询问(见 *voir dire*)
examination of title 对所有权的审查;审查房地契
examination of witness 讯问证人,盘问证人
examination of witness on commission (法庭)委托他人录取证人供词
examine v. 1.审讯,审问;审查,查问 2.考试,考查;检查 3.验尸 4.研究,调查
examine and approve 核准
examine and distinguish evidence 审查和鉴别证据
examine the accused, collect and investigate evidence in court 对被告进行庭审调查
examine the charge 审查指控
examined copy 审定抄本,检定本
examinee n. 1.受审人,接受讯问者 2.接受考试者;考生
examiner n. 审查员,审问者;检察官;考试委员;验尸官;主考人
examiner of the court 法院讯问官,(英)法院预审官(指大法官委任的,并在法院以外录取证供的官员)
examiners of private bills (英)私法法案审查员
examining a. 1.审查的,审讯的 2.考试的
examining body 考试机构;审查机构
examining commission 调查委员会
examining court 预审法庭(院)
examining judge 检察官;预审法官
examining justice 预审法官;检察官
examining magistrate 地方预审法官,预审治安官
example n. 事例,范例,例证;样本,模范;儆戒

example in statutes 法规中(解释法律条文运用)的例证
example of case 案例
example of judg(e)ment 判例
example of legislation 立法范例
exarch n. (东罗马帝国的)总督;主教;主教特派使节
exasperate v./a. 激怒,触怒;使气恼;使(疾病、痛苦等)加剧;使恶化/恼怒的,被激怒的
exasperate sb. to do sth. 激怒某人去做某事
exaspirating obscurity 加剧了模糊性,更加扑朔迷离
excambium 交换
exceed v. 超过,胜过,越出
exceeding conventional rules 越出常规
exceeding one's authority (power) 越权
except prep. 除……以外,不计
except as the law otherwise provides 如法律未另行规定时除外
except for (sb.) 除了
except so far as the context otherwise requires... 除非上下文另有规定……
exceptant n. 抗告者,抗议者
excepted offense 不得缓刑的罪行
excepted risk (保险)除外风险
exceptio 除外,例外;(被告对原告陈述的)抗辩;抗议,异议
exceptio dilatoria (罗马法)以追诉为由的异议(指如根据一项在一定期限内不能起诉的协议,使提出的诉讼无效,从而使诉讼延期的答辩)
exceptio doli mali (罗马法)以欺诈为理由的异议(亦称 *exceptio doli*)
exceptio domili (罗马法)主张所有权的异议(指被告在诉讼中提出所有权的主张,要求恢复原告尚未占用的财产)
* *Exceptio ejus rei cujus petitur dissolutio nulla est.* A plea of that matter the dissolution of which is sought (by the action) is of no effect. 对已经(通过诉讼)得到解决的问题的抗辩是无效的。
* *Exceptio falsi omnium ultima.* A plea de-

nying a fact is the last of all. 拒绝承认事实的抗辩是无可奈何的最后一招而已。

* ***Exceptio firmat regulam in casibus non exceptis.*** An exception affirms the rule in cases not excepted. 在不属于例外案件中的一个例外可以证实规则(范)。

* ***Exceptio firmat regulam in contrarium.*** An exception proves an opposite rule. 一个例外可以证明一个相反的规则(范)。

exceptio in factum 基于事实的异议[指基于案件中特定的事实情况(circumstances)而提出的异议]

exceptio in personam 本人亲自提出的异议[指只能由法律允许的人才可提出的答辩(plea)]

exceptio in rem 不是必须本人提出的异议[指不具有个人性质而是与诉讼所基于的法律事实相关联,因此,任何利害关系人,如财产继承人、担保人和原始债务人(original debtor),均可提出异议]

exceptio iusti dominic 所有人的抗辩
exceptio juris jurandi 对事实已作过宣誓证明的抗辩,业经宣誓的异议
exceptio metus 以恐吓或胁迫为理由的异议或抗辩
exceptio non adimpleti contractus 以契约未履行为由提出异议,合同诉讼中涉及彼此义务或债务所提出的异议(指在涉及彼此义务或债务的合同诉讼中,被告以原告未履行合同义务而提出的异议。如果原告本身的义务未被履行,则原告无权提起诉讼)

* ***Exceptio nulla est versus actionem quae exceptionem perimit.*** There is no exception against an action that extinguishes the exception. 对不存在异议理由的诉讼提出的异议不成立

exceptio pacti 简约抗辩,例外异议
exceptio pacti conventi 以原告不同意起诉为理由的异议
exceptio plurium concubentium 除非与一人以上有奸情(在确定生父关系诉讼中的一种抗辩)

* ***Exceptio probat regulam de rebus non exceptis.*** An exception proves a rule concerning things not excepted. 例外证实不属于例外事件的规则;有关未被提出异议之事,异议证实规则。

exceptio quod metus causa 以被胁迫为理由的抗辩
exceptio quoque regulam declarat The exception also declares the rule 异议也表明了规则
exceptio rei judicatae 既判的抗辩
exception n. (14 世纪)1.(对法庭裁决或命令的)异议;反对[指当事人在诉讼中对法庭裁决(court's ruling)的正式反对,他意欲通过正式异议保留被推翻的反对意见或否决提出的诉〈the prosecutor stated her exception to the court's ruling disallowing the witness's testimony〉(公诉人陈述她正式反对法庭裁决拒绝证人的证明)];构成例外、除外或反对[有时律师说:"我例外"("I except")或"我反对"("I object")。严格地说,异议(exception)只关系到最初反对或提出保留上诉权利而被拒绝后形成的反对意见。大多数法庭现对于异议或例外不再被要求保留最先的异议或例外。实际上这种做法已基本被废除]2.除外的人(或物、事)[指人或某事物被排除在规则的执行之外〈employers with fewer than five employees are an exception to the rule〉(只有不到 5 名雇工的雇主对此规定实属例外)]3.保持既有的权利[指让与人或授予人将不动产让与他人时,保持既有的权利(existing right)或利益(权益)。见 reservation 1]
exception clause 免责条款;例(除)外条款
exception *d'illégalité* (法)除外异议权(指仅适用于申请人的对某项法律提出违法性异议的权利)
exception from liability 免责事项
exception law 例外法规
exception list 货物残损报告;批注清单
exception *quae firmat legem exponit legem* An exception that confirms the law expounds the law 确认法律的异议解释了法律
exception to bail 对保释的异(抗)议
exception to hearsay rule 传闻规则的例外
exceptional remedy 特殊补救办法,特殊

法律救济方法
exceptions to the principle of indemnity 损失填补原则之例外
exceptis *exceptio*之复数(见 *exceptio*)
exceptive a. 例外的,特殊的
excerpt n./v. 择录,选录,节录/摘,选,引用〈excerpt passages from a book (or an article)〉(从书中引用几段)
excess n. 1.超越,超过;过量,过剩;过度 2. (复)过度行为,暴行 3.超额,超过数 4. 免赔率,免赔额
excess clause 超额条款[指一项保险单的条款限制保险人的责任;对损失额超出其他保险范围的部分负赔偿责任(此条款特别要求其他承保人首先支付)。见 escape clause; *Pro rata* clause]
excess condemnation 过度征用[指按征用人(condemner)所规划的公共工程,过多地占用了相邻的土地]
excess fare 补票费
excess in luxuries 过度奢侈
excess luggage 超重的行李
excess of authority 逾越权限,越权
excess of export over import and import over export 出超和入超
excess of jurisdiction 超越管辖权;超越审判权(限);超越管辖范围
excess of liabilities over assets 资不抵债
excess of loss 超额赔款
excess of loss cover 超额赔款保障
excess of power 越权
excess profit 超额利润
excess-profits tax (1918年)(美)超额利润税[指征收超出商业正常利润的税款。这种类型的征税通常只是在国家处于紧急情况(如战争)下才征收,以达到劝阻商业暴利的目的]
excessive a. 过度的,过分的;额外的,超额的
excessive bail 额外保释金,过多保释金
excessive bank loans 额外银行贷款
excessive centralization 高度中央集权,高度集中制
excessive concern for the opportunity 对受听审机会的过分关注(或重视)
excessive cutting of trees 滥砍滥伐林木
excessive damages 超额损害赔偿(金)
excessive defence 防卫过当
excessive egotism 过分利己主义
excessive fine (美)(刑法)超额罚金(指与罪犯所犯罪行极不相称和不合理的过高罚金。美国联邦宪法第八修正案明文禁止超额罚金。如果罚金在规定限额之内,但明显超过被告人的支付能力,即使其付出一生之努力亦无法交清所定罚金,此金额亦为超额罚金)
Excessive Fines Clause 过多保释金条款
excessive imbalance between performance and counterperformance 给付与对待给付间显失公平
excessive interest 超额利息,过高利息
excessive leniency 宽大无边
excessive or inadequate 过当或不适当裁断
excessive power 过多权力
excetio est strictissimae interpretationis 例外规定,从严解释
exchange n. (14世纪)(商法)1.彼此权益之间的交易行为 2.作为支付提供的现金(货币)或票据;通货(见 medium of exchange) 3.通货交换或转换(conversion),(见 foreign exchange) 4.用汇票(bill of exchange)或信用证取款单(bill of credit)而不是现金支付债款 5.让证券、货物或类似商品的买卖商人集中的组织促使商人的惯例(customs and usages)统一,便于快速调解贸易争端,集中并传播有价值的商业和经济的信息,同时使该组织成员在他们合法追求的开展合作的权益得到安全保证(见 reciprocal exchange) 6.每个买卖营业日(business day),进行交易的成员们聚集的大厦或大厅,他们在那里如同经纪人一样,为了他们的顾客、为了现在和将来的交货进行贸易(见 security exchange)
1031 exchange 见 tax-free exchange
exchange action 外汇行动
exchange at (或 of) **equal value** 等价交换
exchange bank 汇兑银行
exchange broker 外汇经纪人
exchange clause 外汇条款

exchange commission 外汇兑换佣金
exchange contract 外汇兑换合同(契约), 外汇合同(契约)
exchange control 外汇管制,外汇管理
exchange control regulations 外汇管制条例(规定)
exchange fluctuations 外汇变动;汇价波动
exchange fund 外汇基金
exchange invoice 托运单
exchange loss 汇兑损失
exchange marriage 交换婚姻(指两个群体相互交换配偶的一种婚姻形式)
exchange memo (或 slip) (银行)外汇兑换水单
exchange of ambassadors 互换大使
exchange of goods between the city and the countryside 城乡物资交流
exchange of information 交换消息(或情报)
exchange of instruments of ratification (政府间、国家间就条约等)互换批准书
exchange of notes 交换照会,换文
exchange of pleading 交换起诉书或答辩书
exchange of POW 交换战俘
exchange of skills 技术交流
exchange of unequal values 不等价交换
exchange of views 交换意见
exchange parity 外汇平价
exchange price 行价,交易所价格
exchange proviso clause 外汇保留条款
exchange quotations 外汇行情
exchange rate 外汇率,汇兑率;汇价
exchange restriction 外汇限制
Exchange Stock (或 Stock Exchange) 证券交易所
exchange surrender certificate 外汇转移证
exchange tax 外汇税
exchangeable a. 可交换的;可兑换的
exchequer n. 国库;资财;资金;(大写)(英)理财法院(指英国高等法院的一个部门);(英)财政部(从前由税收部门和法院组成,现为管理政府税收部门);(英)政府债券
Exchequer and Audit Department (英)财政及审计署
exchequer bills 国库证券
exchequer bond (英)国库债券
Exchequer Division (英)理财法庭(指原高等法院一个分庭,1881 年并入王室法庭)
exchequer rolls 财政档案
excisable a. 应交纳货物税(或执照税)的
excise n./v. (15 世纪)(美)货物税、消费税;财产税;营业税[指对产品、买卖、货物收益(use of goods)等课的税,另还包括行业(occupation)或一些活动,如许可证税(license tax)或律师职业费。亦称 excise tax。见 income tax; property tax]/1.征收国产(货物)税;收税 2.索高价 3.割去;删除
excise law (英)酿(选)酒法
excise lieu property tax (美)保险许可证(或保险执业)税(指对于经批准经营业务的各类许可的保险公司所收到的保险费总额所征收的税)
excise tax (或 duty) (英)国产税;货物税;消费税;牌照税;烟酒税
exciseman n. (英)收税官
exclave n. 在外国境内的某一领土,飞地(指在他国境内的本国领土)
excludability n. 排他性
exclude v. 拒绝接纳(考虑),把……排除在外
excluded restriction 被排除的限制
excluded restrictions 排他性限制
excludendo fiscum et relictam To the exclusion of the rights of the Crown and of the widow 排除王室和遗孀的权利
excluding fault 排除在外的过错
exclusion n. 排斥;排除在外;拒绝;赶出;驱逐;负责条款,当事人不可为之事(指许可证合同中术语)
exclusion clause (保险合同中声明)不属保险事项的条款;除外条款
exclusion of penalty 不为罪
exclusion order (英)驱逐令(指依照1976 年《防止恐怖活动法》禁止具有恐怖嫌疑分子进入或滞留在英国)
exclusionary a. 排斥的
exclusionary practices 排斥性行为

exclusionary rule （美）证据排除（或例外）规则[指按此规则只要违反联邦宪法,非法搜查或扣押所取得的证据,庭审时均不得采纳。此规则1914年确立,1961年各州适用。1984年联邦最高法院在Leon v. United States, 468 U. S. 897(1984)案中创立了例外的规定,即增加了"最终和必然发现的例外"和"善意的例外"（good faith exception）。前者指非法取得的证据,只要能证明最终或必然会以合法手段取得即可采用。后者可参见 good faith exception]

Exclusionary Rule of illegally Obained Evidence （美）非法证据排除规则

exclusionary rules （美）排除规则,证据排除规则[指政府通过侵犯被告人的宪法权利而取得的证据不可用来对他提起控诉,被告可以通过在审判前提出"克服动议"（motion to suppress）请求法官作出此种证据不可使用于判决而达到阻止政府使用此种证据对其起诉的目的],非法证据排除规则

exclusive a. 1.专有的;独占的;唯一的;特有的;除外的;排他的;不公开的 2.(商品)高档的;第一等的 3.全部的

exclusive agency agreement(listing) 独家代理协议(指财产所有权人与代理人之间所订的协议,约定在特定时间内除财产所有权人之外,该代理是唯一有权销售该财产的人)

exclusive agency （1805年）独家代理[指具有被代理人的代理权,特别是在自由竞争的特定市场内享有独家销售被代理人产品的代理权,并可交付销售者的不动产代理人（agent）。严格地说,独家代理人只是排除所有其他经纪人（brokers）,但不包括销售的产品或财产的所有人。亦称 exclusive agency to sell; exclusive franchise; sole selling agency]

exclusive agency agreement 独家代理协议

exclusive agency to sell 独家专卖代理（见 exclusive agency）

exclusive agent 独家代理人

exclusive agreement 排他协定

exclusive authority 专有职权,专属权力

exclusive competency 专管;专属权限

exclusive dealing contract 排他性经营合同

exclusive dealing 独家经销

exclusive distribution 总经销

exclusive economic zone 单一经济区;（国际法）专属经济区

exclusive evidence （18世纪）排他性证据,独有证据[指仅有的事实或被法律所认可的事实在特定争议问题上具有完全的证据力（probative force）]

exclusive fishery zone 专属渔区

exclusive franchise 见 exclusive agency

exclusive holder of the executive power 独揽行政大权者

exclusive jurisdiction 专属管辖（权）;排他性的管辖（权）;专属审判权

exclusive licence（或 **license**） 专利许可证（旧译：专利执照）

exclusive licencing agreement 独占许可证协议;绝对许可证协议

exclusive license 专利执照,专利许可证;独占许可证(该证排斥包括权利人在内的任何人使用被许可人使用的权利。根据1990年我国著作权法规定,图书出版者与版权人签订的许可证合同,一般为10年独占许可合同,在此期间,版权人及其他出版者均无权出版同一部作品)

exclusive market 独有市场;专一市场

exclusive marketing rights 专有销售权

exclusive patent 独占专利权;绝对专利权

exclusive possession 独占（权）;专利品;排他性占有权

exclusive power 专有权力;特权

exclusive privilege 独占权;专有特权;专利权

exclusive reign 垄断地位

exclusive right 专有权;专利权

exclusive right to exploit the patented invention 利用专利发明的专有权

exclusive right to multiply publish 再版专有权

exclusive right to publish 出版专有权

exclusive right to use trademark 商标专用权

exclusive sales 包销;独家销售
exclusive sovereignty 排他主权
exclusive trader 独家营业;专利贸易商
exclusive use right 专用权
excogitation n. 设计,设法,想出;计划,计策,方案
excommunication n. 开除(党籍、会籍等);(教会法)绝罚(指禁止某人与信徒往来但不剥夺其成员身份)
excrescence of the common law 普通法之瘤(赘生物)
excruciation n. 1.酷刑;拷打 2.苦恼,磨难
exculpate v. 使无罪;申辩无罪,辩解,开脱
exculpation n. 免罪,赦罪;辩解,雪冤;开脱,申明无罪
exculpatory a. 开脱罪责的;申明无罪的;昭雪的;辩解的
exculpatory clauses 免责条款(指规定当事人对特定的不法行为免于承担责任的合同条款,其目的是使当事人免于因过错承担责任)
exculpatory evidence (18世纪)开脱罪责的证据,免责证据,昭雪证据[指倾向于确认刑事被告无罪的证据,参见《联邦刑事诉讼法规则》第16条。检控方在其拥有和控制的情况下,当该证据可能成为此案后果的关键时,有责任披露该免责证据。见 Brady material]
excusable a. 可辩解的;可原谅的;可免除的;言之成理的
excusable assault 可以原谅的殴打,可宽恕的殴打(尤指未遂的殴打)
excusable default 可原谅的违例,可原谅的失职
excusable homicide 可宽恕的杀人(指自卫杀人或疏忽杀人)
excusable neglect 可谅解的过失
excusable self-defense 可原谅的自卫
Excusat aut extenuat delictum in capitalibus quod non operatur idem in civilibus. That may excuse or palliate a wrongful act in capital cases which would not have the same effect in civil injuries. 在重大案件中能作为某一非法行为宽恕或减轻的借口,在民

事侵害案件中就有可能起不了同样的作用。
excuse n. 1.原谅,宽恕,赦免(指证明一个行为或作为是正当,或此理由可免除一个人的责任) 2.(刑法)辩护,答辩(由于被告已有的行为在某种程度上是犯罪,但并未受到责备而提起的辩护;以下的辩护或借口是传统的借口:强迫,胁迫;诱惑;未成年;精神错乱,非自愿,喝醉了酒等。亦称 legal excuse)
excuse and exemption for corrupt and illegal practice 对舞弊和不法行为的宽恕和赦免
excuse group (美)免除群体(指可请求免于从事陪审员工作,这里可能有医生、部长、企业主等)
excuse non-performance 作为不履行的借口
excused from a duty 免除义务
excuss v. 依法取得某物,依法扣押,依法扣留
excussio 依法追债(指向保证人要求履行保证义务前,应尽量设法向债务人讨债)
executable a. 可执行的,可实行的,可作成的
executant n. 执行者,实施者
execute v. 1.执行,履行,实施,实行;贯彻;完成 2.(经签名、盖章等手续)使(证书、契约等)生效,使合法 3.(英)(财产的)让渡 4.处决,处死
execute(或 **convict**)**summarily** 立即处死(决)
execute a deed 签名盖章使契据生效
Execute one man to warn a hundred. 杀一儆百。
executed a. 已生效的;已执行的;已完成的
executed agreement 已生效的协定
executed consideration (英美法)已履行的对价;已交付的补偿
executed contract 已履行的合同(契约)
executed covenant 已完全履行的合同条款
executed deed (完成签署手续而开始)生效的契据

executed estate 已确定的地产权;已让渡的财产权
executed remainder 已生效的继承权
executed treaty 已生效的条约
executed trust 已生效的信托
executed use 已生效的使用权
executed writ 已实施的令状
executing a sentence outside of jail 监外执行
executing agency 执行机构
executing agent 代理执行人
executing mortgages 经签署使抵押生效;抵押的生效条件
* *Executio est finis et fructus legis.* Execution is the end and fruit of the law. 实施乃是法律的目的和成果。
* *Executio juris non habet injuriam.* The execution of law does no injury./Execution of the law cannot work an injury. 执行法律不构成侵害。
execution n. 1.实行,实施,执行 2.处死刑 3.(经签名盖章等)法律文件的生效,合法;(授权将判决付诸实施的)执行令状
Execution Act (加)(安大略省的)《执行法令》
execution by shooting 枪决,枪毙
execution clerk 执行书记官
execution court 执行法院(庭)
execution creditor 债权执行人
execution debtor 债务执(履)行人
execution for the benefit of creditors (依追诉程序)为债权人请求的偿付
execution ground 刑场,法场
execution law 执行法规
execution of a criminal 处决罪犯
execution of an instrument of transfer 转让文件经签字生效;转让文件的生效条件
execution of arbitration decision 仲裁裁决的执行
execution of criminal judg(e)ment 刑事判决的执行
execution of decree 执行命令;执行判决
execution of deeds 契据生效条件(指契据经签署使生效)
execution of duty 履行职责
execution of judg(e)ment 执行判决
execution of obligation 债的履行
execution of power 行使权力
execution of punishment 刑罚的执行,执行刑罚
execution of testament 遗嘱的执行
execution of the death penalty 死刑的执行
execution of treaty 履行条约
execution of writ 令状的执行
execution procedure 执行程序
execution proceedings (强制)执行程序
execution sale 强制拍卖
execution stability 政府安定
executioner n. 死刑执行人,刽子手;行刑者
executive n./a. 行政机关;行政人员;执行者;高级官员;总经理;董事;社长;行政部门;(美)(大写)总统/执行的,实施的;行政上的
executive action 行政措施
executive administration 管理政府主要部门的高级国家公务官员,国家高级官员,高级行政官员,(英)行政机关;全体阁员
executive agencies (美)行政机构
executive agreement (美)行政协定(指政府与外国政府签订的,无须经国会批准的协定)
executive authority 行政权;执行权;行政当局
executive board (或 committee) 执行委员会,行政委员会
Executive Board (欧洲中央银行)执行理事会
executive body 执行机关
executive branch 行政部门
executive capacity 执行能力;执行人员的资格
executive certificate (国际法)行政机关证书
Executive Clemency (美)行政宽恕,行政宽大处理(这种宽大处理包括四种形式:pardon——特赦;commutation——减刑;reprieve——缓刑;remission of fine——免除罚金);(亦指行政首脑总统、州长有权

对已定罪者免除或减轻刑罚)
executive command 行政命令;行政管理
executive council 行政会议, 执行委员会
executive director 行政领导人,行政领导(指担任一个组织的行政和执行官员,并领导其部属的工作人员,亦为受薪的职员)
executive employment contracts 行政雇用合同
executive functions 行政职能;行政机关的职能
executive immunity 1.(美)行政官员豁免权,行政豁免[指美国总统或州长(state governor)在职权范围内的行为有绝对的豁免权(absolute immunity)。行政豁免通常要保护一位正当执行其已被确认的职责的官员,其职责是理性人所理解认可的]2.有资格从民事权利请求(civil claim)中得到豁免的较低级行政官员,如果他们的行为明显违反确立在宪法上和法律规定上的权利,则要承担责任。(见 executive privilege)
executive instrument 行政性文件
executive justice 行政裁决,执行正义(见 commutative justice; distributive justice; social justice)
executive measure 执行措施
executive meeting (中)(国务院)常务会议
executive office of the president 总统办公机构
executive officer 行政官;行政官员
Executive order (美)总统的行政命令;行政命令
Executive order No. 10988 (美)第10988号执行令(指美国约翰·肯尼迪总统1962年颁发的命令,该法令首次承认联邦雇员有与管理部门订立合同的权利)
Executive order No. 11490 (美)第11490号执行令(指1976年美国联邦法律授予总统在国家的紧急事件中有绝对的权力)
executive organ 执行机关
executive personnel 行政人员
executive plan 执行计划
executive power(s) 行政权,执行权,行政管理权;(大写)行政机关
executive privilege 1.行政特权[指美国法上的一个概念,行政特权既可作为判断国会法律是否侵犯行政权的标准,亦可作为抵制国会调查权的有力手段。虽然该权力很早被前几任总统华盛顿、杰斐逊行使,但并未形成一个确切概念,法院对此从未作过清晰界定。美国著名政治科学家罗奥尔·伯杰(Raoul Berger)在其著作《行政特权:一个宪法之谜》中指出:行政特权是"总统利用其宪法职权拒绝向国会提供情况的一种权利,是总统在履行义务时必不可少的法律手段"]2.执行优势[指基于美国宪法三权分立(separation of power)的原则,这种特权不受联邦政府行政部门的约束,当涉及国家安全或外交政策问题时,不得泄露任何秘密。见 executive immunity]
executive responsibility 行政责任
executive right (油气法)专有权,执行权利(指对规定土地或开矿权利的专有租借权。这种专有权是矿产利益的附带条件之一)
executive sale 行政出售,执行出售,强制出售[指由政府实施执行令(writ of execution)强行出售债务人的财产,亦称 forced sale; judgment sale; sheriff's sale。见 execution]
executive session (立法机构)内部会议,执行会议
executor n. 1.执行者,实施者 2.遗嘱执行人;遗嘱管理人(见 administrator)
executor dative (法院)指定的遗嘱执行人
executor de son tort (自封的)无权遗嘱执行人(指没有合法的授权,便自动来充当遗嘱的执行人,干预死者遗产处理的人)
executor fund 执行人基金[指为执行人支付继承遗产(estate)的最后一笔费用而设立的基金]
executor nominate (遗嘱中指定的)遗嘱执行人
executor testamentary 遗嘱执行人
executorial a. 执行命令的,实施法律的,执行法律程序的

executorship n. 遗嘱执行人身份
executory a. 有效的;实施中的;执行中的;行政上的;(将来)可生效(或实施)的
executory agreement 实施中的协定
executory consideration 应交付的补偿;(英美法)未完成的对价
executory contract 待履行的合同(契约),未经履行的合同(契约)
executory covenant 实施中的合同条款(指依然留有全部或部分未履行的合同条款)
executory devise 将来生效的财产遗赠
executory effect 执行效力
executory interest 未来有效的权益
executory limitation 限业(指普通法中在土地上创设将来利益的一种术语)
executory treaty 待履行的条约
executory trust 将来有效的信托
executory use 将来生效的使用权
executrix n. 女执行者;女遗嘱执行人
* ***Exempla illustrant, non restringunt, legem.*** Examples make the law clearer, and do not restrict it./Examples illustrate, not restrain, the law. 实例使法更为清楚,而非限制法律。实例乃法之例证,非法之限制。
exemplar n. 模范;典型;模型;样品;样本;范例;标本
exemplary a. 1.惩戒性的;超过实际损失的 2.示范的;典型的;模范的
exemplary case 专案
exemplary damages 惩戒性的损害赔偿(指判决的赔偿损失额超过实际所受的损害,亦作 punitive damages)
exempli causa 例如
exempli gratia 例如
exemplification n. 经盖公章核对的誊本;正式抄本;例证;范例;举例
exemplify v. 制作经公章证明的;例证;举例说明;作为例子
exempt n./v./a. 被免除义务者;免税者;特权者 / 免除;豁免(from);使……不受约束 / 被免除的,被豁免的
exempt boards of trade (美)豁免之交易所(指将期货交易市场分成指定的契约市场、衍生性交易执行机构、豁免之交易所等)
exempt commodity 豁免商品
exempt from... 豁免……
exempt from any fees or dues 免除一切税费
exempt from conscription 免役
exempt from penalty 免罚
exempt from tax 免税
exempt property (美)豁免的财产[指债务人的拥有物如股票、债券等以及依法所占用的财产,债权人不得扣押以清偿债务。而债权人竭力想合法取得的所有的财产均为不被豁免的财产(nonexempt property)。许多州明文规定家宅豁免,以此排除私人住宅和户主名下的各个项目。从大多数债权人的各种抵押物直至一定数额的款项均得豁免,不受债务影响。豁免之目的在于防止使债务人变为赤贫或无资力者]
exempt transaction 豁免交易[指销售已超出了某些法规规定的范围,正如《1933年的证券法》(the Securities Act of 1933)和《1934年证券交易法》(the Securities Exchange of 1934)]
exempt zone 豁免区
exemptible a. 可享受豁免权的
exemption (14世纪)1.免责,免除,豁免[指免除义务、免除责任或免除其他要求〈an exception〉(一项例外)。见 immunity; exception 2] 2.(法律允许的)财产豁免权(指法律允许判定债务人具有一种优惠或特权可被允准保留一定数量的财产,在执行、扣押、破产等程序中可免被扣押或变卖而不承担责任) 3.(税法)免税额[指从调整后的总收入中允准减免的总额,用以确定可征税收入或应纳税所得额(taxable income)。见 deduction 2]
exemption authority 豁免权
exemption clause 豁免条款;免责条款
exemption equivalent (美)最高免税转让财产额(指在承担联邦赠予税和财产税之前,可转让给他人的资产最高额)
exemption from customs duty 免征关税
exemption from execution 执行豁免;免予

执行
exemption from inspection 免验,免检
exemption from liability 免除责任
exemption from prosecution (刑事)免予起诉
exemption from punishment 免刑,免罚
exemption from the usual pollution standard 免除通常污染标准的检查
exemption law 免除法(指该法规定:债务人的财产在破产时不得被判决由债权人或受托管理人扣押以偿还债务)
exemption of aliens 外侨豁免权
exequatur n. 1.(驻在国发给的)领事(或商务官员)认可证书;领事证书 2.(法国惯例)(本国法院签署作出的关于)承认外国法院判决的裁定 3.仲裁裁决执行书
exercisable a. 可行使的,可实行的,可履行的,可运用的
exercise n./v. 行使,运用,实行,履行;训练;(复)仪式;传统做法;实施/行使,实施,履行;运用;施加;练习,训练
exercise a claim 行使债权,行使请求权
exercise discretion in light of the circumstances 酌情处理
exercise judicial power independently 独立行使审判权
exercise freely the will 自由地实现意志,自由地履行意愿
exercise of rights 权利的行使,行使权利
exercise taxes 营业税
exercise the faculties 行使权力
exercise the rights flowing from transactions 行使订立合同(契约)所生的权利
exercise yard 监狱中的囚犯操场
exercitor n. (船舶)所有人;船主;包租者
exert v. 行使(职权),尽(力),发挥(威力),施压,产生(影响等)
exertion n. 努力,尽力;行使;运用
exertion of power (或 authority) 权力的行使
exhaust v. 竭尽;耗尽;试尽;抽完,汲干;用完,花光
exhaustion n. 耗尽,用尽
exhaustion of administrative remedies 用尽行政救济方法

exhaustion of effect 有效期满
exhaustion of local remedies 用尽所有当地救济方法
exhaustion of remedies 救济穷竭[指美国的一项司法原则,即要求当事人在向联邦法院提起诉讼前先寻求别的救济方法。例如一个州的犯罪嫌疑人在未用尽州的所有救济方法之前通常不会获得联邦法院的人身保护状(habeas corpus)。如果原告还未用尽救济方法,联邦法院通常会拒绝给予司法救济]
exhaustion of right 专利穷竭(指专利权一次用尽,不能再行使之意。许多国家版权法对此均有规定)
exhaustion of state remedies 用尽所有政府救济方法(联邦法院只有政府的各种救济方法都业经使用无效后,才接受政治犯提出的人身保护令的申请)
Exhaustion theory (权利)耗尽论
exhaustive a. 彻底的,详尽无遗的,使耗尽的
exheredate v. 剥夺继承权
exhibit n./v. 物证,证物;证件;据据;展览;陈列品;显现;呈现/陈列,展出;正式提交(证据等);出示证据;表白,表示
exhibit presented at court as evidence 在法庭上出示的物证
exhibit register 物证登记册
exhibition n. 展览;出示证件(在苏格兰法律中有关出示契据来给人验阅的规定,而出示证件的诉讼则是请求强制对方把契据交出来接受验阅);提出,提示
exhibitionism n. 裸露癖,裸露的表现;露阴癖或露阴症(性心理障碍之一种,指反复在陌生异性面前暴露自己的生殖器,以满足引起性兴趣的强烈愿望,几乎仅见于男性。英国《1842年流浪罪法》第4条规定,"故意公开淫荡和猥亵地暴露他身体来意图侮辱女性的每个人,应被视为无赖或流氓"。《德国刑法典》对于露阴亦有规定(第183条),如"男子以暴露生殖器行为侵扰他人的处1年以下自由刑或罚金"。我国刑法对此无具体规定。见 sexual perversion)
exhibitionist n. 有露阴癖者;好出风头者;

风头主义者
exhibitor（或 **exhibiter**）n. 出示证物人；展览者；提供者
exhort v. 告诫,规劝,激励；提倡,主张
exhortation n. 激励,告诫,规劝；主张,提倡
exhorter n. 规劝者,告诫者；提倡者
exhumation n. 发掘；掘尸(罪)；掘尸检验
exigence（=exigency）n. 事变,紧急(状态),危急(关头)；(复)急事；苛求；迫切需要
exigent n./a. 催告书,勒令,限令/催促的；催告出庭的；紧急的,危急的；艰难的
exigenter n. 催告人,督促人；法院执达员(官)；刑事法庭中处理紧急事务的官员
exigi facias 催告令；督促；警告；勒令,限令
exigible a. 可催告的；可要求的
exile n. 流(放)刑；离乡背井；逃亡；流犯,逃亡者；充军者；离乡背井者
* *Exilium est patriae privatio, natalis soli mutatio, legum nativarum amissio.* Exile is a privation of country, a change of natal soil, a loss of native laws. 流放就是丧失国家,变更乡土,失去本国法律的保障。
existence n. 存在；存在状态；实体,存在物；生存；发生
existence of legal impediments to the marriage 法律上阻碍婚姻的原因
existence of the society 社会生活、社会存在
existimationis minutio (罗马法)令名减少(指普通名誉受限制)
existing a. 现行的,现存的,目前的,现在的
existing boundary line 现在的国境线
existing corporation 现存的公司,现有的法人(社团)
existing dispute 现有争议
existing evidence 目前的证据
existing goods 现货
existing law 现行法(律)
existing legislation 现行立法
existing practice 现行惯例
existing preferential duties 现行特惠关税

existing right 既存权利
existing text 现行条文
exit n./v. 出境；出口；退出；退出权；死亡/退出,离去
exit certificate 出境证书
exit formalities 出境手续
exit medical inspection certificate 出口检疫证书
exit permit 出境许可证
exit receipt 出境回执
exit the marriage 退出婚姻
exit visa 出境签证
exitus 子女；后嗣；租金；土地收益；诉讼结束
exitus acta probate 行为是否正当；应视其后果而定
exoculation n. 挖眼刑
exodus n. 退出；大批离去；成群外出
exodus of capital 资金外流
exogamy n. 异族结婚；族外婚
exogenous a. 外生的,外源的,外因的
exomeretur 免罪,免除(义务、责任)(指在法院已判决被告监禁之后法院命令免除保释义务的保释书通知)
Exon-Florio Provision (美)"艾克森—弗洛瑞奥条款"(指美国关于国家安全审查的规定)
exonerate v. 解罪,开释；免罪；免除(责任等)；证明无罪
exoneration n. 免罪；免除(责任)；解除；证明无罪
exoneration clause 免责条款
exonerative a. 免罪的；免责的；免除的
exorbitant jurisdiction（=excessive jurisdiction）过度管辖权
exorbition jurisdiction 过分管辖
expand v. 展开,扩充,扩大；推广,发展
expansion n. 1.伸展；辽阔 2.膨胀；(领土)扩充 3.扩充,发展 4.详细阐述
expansion of power 势力扩张
expansion of territory 领土扩张
expansionism n. 扩张主义
expansionist n. 扩张主义者
expansionist power 扩张主义政权
expansive a. 扩张的,广阔的,开阔的

expansive power　扩张力量,扩张权力
expansive construction（或 **interpretation**）扩大解释
exparte　单方面的(地);片面的(地);偏袒的(地)
exparte **lawsuit**　一方诉讼,一造诉讼
exparte **summon**　一方传票,一造传票
expatriate n./v.　脱离国籍者;移居国外者;被流放(国外)者/放弃原国籍;移居国外;流放,把……逐出国外
expatriate factor　脱离国籍因素
expatriation n.　移居国外;脱离国籍(指脱离原国籍而取得另一国籍),放弃国籍
expect v.　期待,期盼;预期;期望,要求,指望;(口)认为,想〈expect to pay〉(打算支付)(只是愿望、意愿,而不是承诺)
expectancy n.　期待,预期,期望,瞩望;期待的事物
expectancy of life　估计寿命
expectant n./a.　期待者;(有继承权而)期待占有者/(有继承权而)期待占有的;期待的,预期的;推定的
expectant estate　期待继承的财产
expectant heir　推定继承人;期待继承人(指他人死后,预期有获得继承权的人)
expectant interest　期待权益
expectant mother　待产妇,孕妇,待产母亲
expectant right　预期的权利;未来权
expectation n.　期待,预期,(复)前程(尤指晋升等希望);期待的事物;预期继承的遗产
expectation damages　预期赔偿金
expectation interest　预期利益(指因对合同履行获利的预期落空而产生的财产损失,即"使原告处于倘若被告履行了其允诺他所应处的处境。在这种场合下所保护的利益可称为期待利益")
expectation of life　(保险)平均寿命;预期寿命;生命预期收益
expectation of property　期待获得的财产
expected cost　预期成本;期望成本(指事故损失与发生事故可能性的乘积,事故可能性当然取决于参与人采取的特点战略组合)
expected judgment　预期裁决

expedient n.　紧急的手段(或办法),权宜之计
* *Expedit reipublicae ne sua re quis male utatur.* It is for the interest of the state that a man should not enjoy his own property improperly (to the injury of others).　任何人都不得不适当地(有损于他人)来享用其自己的财产,这是国家利益所要求的。
* *Expedit reipublicae ut sit finis litium.* It is for the advantage of the state that there be an end of suits. It is for the public good that actions be brought to a close. It is in the public interest that the decision of cases should be final.　为了有利于国家,为了公益和社会利益,就应当息事宁人,了结各种诉讼。
expedite v./a.　促进,迅速处理(事务);发出,派出／畅通的,迅速的,便利的
expedited procedure　紧急程序,加快程序
expel v.　驱逐,逐出;开除;打出,发射(子弹)
expellable a.　可驱逐的;应开除的;可击退的
expellee n.　被驱逐出境者;被开除者
expeller n.　驱逐者;开除者
expendable a.　可消费的;可消耗的,值得消耗的;可牺牲的
expenditure n.　支出额;支出,开支;经费,费用;使用
expenditure disbursements and non-expenditure disbursements　开支性支出与非开支性支出
expenditure for loan payments　借款支出
expenditure on national defence　国防开支
expenditure stream　支出线
expenditure vote　决定拨款的投票
expenditures for the benefit of another　为他人利益支付费用
expensae litis　讼费
expense n.　开支,支出;花费;经费,费用;损害;消耗
expense account　支出账;报销单
expense and receipts　收支
expense control　费用管制

expense in carrying on business 营业费用
expense incurred 所支的费用
expense of a lawsuit（或 of proceedings）诉讼费用
expense of administration 行政管理费用；遗产管理费用
expense of family 家庭费用(法定的家庭费用不仅指用于家庭的全部开支,而且包括夫妻一方所需用的医疗及丧葬费用)
expense of out-of-pocket 实际费用
expense of performance 清偿费用,履行(债务)费用
expense paid 费用已付,费用付讫
expensive a. 花费的；高价的,昂贵的；耗钱多的；奢华的
experience n./v. 经验,体验,阅历,经历/体现,遭受,经历
experience seriating 经验推敲,经验连续研究
experience table (根据人寿保险公司统计资料制成的)寿命估计表
experimental a. 实验(性)的,试验(性)的；经验上的
experimental evidence 实验证据
experimental law 实验法
experimental proof 实验证明
expert n./a. 专家,行家；有经验者；鉴定人/有经验的,熟练的,能干的；专家的,内行的,专门的；鉴定人的
expert advisor 专家顾问
expert conclusion 鉴定结论；鉴定意见
expert evidence 专家证据(指由具有资格证明的专家提供的有关科学的、技术的、专业或其他专门问题之证据,因专家对此项专业的通晓性,并在这个领域受过专门培训。如医生、精神病专家、药物专家、建筑师、指纹专家等。亦称 expert testimony)
expert legal advice 专家法律咨询
expert medical opinion 医疗鉴定意见
expert opinion 专家意见,鉴定意见
expert testimony 鉴定；司法鉴定；专家证词；鉴定证据
expert trial attorney 经验丰富的出庭律师,专家级的出庭律师
expert witness 专家证人；鉴定人

expert witness and lay witness 专家证人及普通证人
expert's disposition to prove sb.'s feeble-mindedness 专家决定证实对某人的低能(或弱智)
expert-reliance materials 专家证人信托的资料[指提供给一个专家证人(a expert witness)的数据和信息的事实、文件和其他资源(other sources)]
expertise n. 专门知识；专家鉴定；专家评价
expertise report 鉴定书
expertize (=expertise) v. 提出专门性意见(或鉴定),对……作(评价)鉴定
expiable a. 可抵偿的；可赎的
expiate v. 抵偿；补偿；赎；为(作恶,犯罪)而受罚；赎罪,抵罪
expiation n. 抵罪,赎罪
expiator n. 抵罪者,赎罪者
expilare (民法中的)抢夺；诈取；强占
expilatio (民法中的)抢夺；诈取；强占(为己有)(指非法分配继承中的财产的强占行为)
expiration n. (期间)终了,期满,届满,满期；出气；断气,死亡；完结(许可合同或合同履行完毕；在版权专利权等保护期方面则指保护期满)
expiration date of a time periods 期限届满的日期
expiration date of letter of credit 信用证有效期满
expiration of contract 合同(契约)期满
expiration of the agreed term 约定的期限届满
expiration of the concession 特许权有效期已届满
expiration of the imprisonment (徒)刑(期)满,监禁期满
expiration of the term of office 任期届满
expiration of the term of sentence 刑期届满
expire v. 终止,期满；开始无效
expired lease of premises 租赁期已满的租约
expiree n. 刑满出狱者,服满刑期者

expiring laws　失效法律
Expiring Laws Continuance Act　（英）《失效法律延续法》
expiry n.　期满,(期限届满而)终止;呼气;断气
expiry date　期满之日,失效之日
explain v.　1.解释,说明;阐明〈explain a difficult problem〉(阐明一个复杂的问题) 2.为……解释;说明……理由〈can you explain such conduct〉(你能对这种行为作出解释吗),〈that explains his hesitation〉(那解释了他的犹豫),〈explain away〉(把……解释过去)
explanation n.　解释,说明;辩解,辩明,讲明;为消除分歧(误会等的)交谈
explanation of policy　阐明政策;(中)交代政策
explanation of vote　对投票作解释性发言
explanatory a.　解释的,说明的;讲明的
explanatory evidence　例证
explanatory memorandum　说明书;解释性备忘录
explanatory reasons　说明性理由
Explanatory Report to the Arbitration Act　仲裁法的解释报告
explanatory rules　解说性规定
explanatory statement　解释性声明,解释性陈述;解说式报表
explanatory statement of financial condition　财务情况说明书
explees (=esplees)　土地收益
expletia (=expleta, explecia)　不动产的收益
expletive a.　填补的,补足的;附加的;多余的
explicable a.　可解释的,可辩明的,可说明的
explicate v.　详细解释,阐明;引申,发展（概念等）
explicatio　（大陆法系诉讼中的）第四次答辩(相当于普通法系诉讼中原告的第二次辩驳)
explicit a.　清楚的,明确的;详述的;不含糊的,显然可见的;(租金等)须直接付款的
explicit cost　直接以货币支付的成本
explicit directions　明确的指示

explicit language　明确表达,明确用语,明确措辞
explicit repudiation　明示拒绝履行(按英美判例法逐渐形成的理论:合同一方或双方若提出了与合同约定条件不一致的要求,要求本身不构成拒绝履行。但如正确理解,除非满足了超出合同约定的要求,提出要求的一方将不履行合同,则构成拒绝履行)
explicitly provided　明文规定的
explode v.　爆炸,爆发;破除(迷信等);戳穿,驳倒(论点等)
explode all fetishes and liberate the mind　破除迷信,解放思想
exploit v.　开拓,开发;剥夺
exploitation n.　剥削;开拓,开发,利用;宣传;广告
exploitation moratorium　暂缓开发,合法的延缓开发
exploitation of a work　对作品的使用(指版权领域中的复制、翻译等方式的使用)
exploitation of labo(u)r　劳工剥削
exploitation of man by man　人剥削人
exploitative relationship　剥削关系
exploited class　被剥削阶级
exploitee n.　被剥削者
exploiter n.　剥削者;开发者;(专利等)利用者
exploiting class　剥削阶级
exploiting entity　(专利等)实施单位
exploiting system　剥削制度
exploration n.　探索,考察,探究,钻研,勘查,测定,探险
explore v.　探索,探究;考察,探测
explosion accident　爆炸事故
explosive n./a.　炸药;爆炸物/爆炸(性)的;易爆炸的;爆发(性)的;易发脾气的;剧增的,急速扩张的
explosive substance　爆炸物
exponent n.　解释者,说明者,倡导者
export n./v./a.　出口,输出;输出品/输出,出口;运走/出口的,准备出口的;出口物的
Export Administration Act　出口管理法
export agent　出口代理商
export bill　出口汇票

export bill of entry 出口报单
export bill of exchange 出口押汇
export bounty 出口津贴;出口奖励金
export clause 出口条款
export commodity 出口商品
Export Control Act (英)《出口控制法》(2002年制定颁布)
export control rules 出口管理条例
export credit 出口信贷
export credit guarantee 出口信贷担保品
export credit insurance facilities 出口信贷保险业务
export declaration 出口报关
export document 出口单据
export duty 出口税,输出税
export label 出口标签
export letter of credit 出口信用证
export letter of guarantee 出口保证书
export licence 出口许可证
export listing 出口商品清单
export market 出口市场
export of capital 资本输出
export of complete industrial installation 成套工业设备的出口
export order 出口订单
export permit 出口许可(证),输出许可
export quarantine 出口检疫
export quota 出口限额[指出口到外国的产品的限制。在美国,出口限额由联邦政府根据不同目的包括国际价格支持(price support)以及经济稳定等来设定]
export regulations 出口条例
export surplus 出超;出口盈余
export tax 出口税(指对出口的商品和货物所征收的税)
export trade 出口贸易
Export Trading Company Act of 1982 (美)《1982年出口贸易公司法》(此法亦规定出口企业的限制竞争行为只要不严重损害美国境内的市场竞争就可以在反托拉斯法中得到豁免)
export value 外销价值
export-oriented interests 出口导向性利益
exportable a. 可输出的
exportation n. 输出;输出物资,输出品,出口物
exporter n. 出口商,输出者
exporting country 输出国
exports inspection law 出口商品检验法
exposé (事实的)陈述;引用;解释;暴露
expose v. 揭露,揭发;陈列;遗弃;暴露;使面临
exposing n. 陈列;遗弃(婴儿);露体(猥亵性暴露)
exposing child 遗弃婴儿
exposition n. 说明,解释,阐述;(对婴儿等的)遗弃;曝露;曝光;展览会;陈列
exposition de part 遗弃婴儿(法国法)(指将不能自理的婴儿遗弃在公共场所或非公共场所的行为)
exposition of idea 观念的阐明
expositor n. 说明者,讲解者,阐述者,评注者
expository statute 阐述性法规
expost instance of secession 事后的脱离
exposure n. 暴露;揭露,揭发;(对婴儿等的)遗弃
exposure of child 对婴儿的遗弃
exposure of person (在公共场合)裸露人体
expound v. 详述;陈述;解释,说明
expound the law 解释法律
express v./n./a. 表达,表示,表白;把……作快递邮件寄去/快信;快车;快运之物;(美)捷运公司/明示的,明白的;明确的,明显的;特殊的;快速的
express abrogation 明确废除;明文废除
express active trust 明示的积极信托
express actual knowledge 见 actual knowledge
express agency (18世纪)明示代理(指依据被代理人的口头或书面授权而成立的代理关系。见 implied agency)
express agreement 明示协定,明示协议;明文协议
express and implied consent 明示和暗示(默示)同意
express appointment 授权的代理
express arrangement 明示和解
express assignment (财产权利的)明示转让

express assumpsit （违约所造成损失的）明示赔偿诉讼
express authority 明示授权,明示权限;明示代理权
express bailment 明示保释
express condition 明示条件
express consent 明示同意
express consideration 明示对价
express contract 明示合同(契约)
express contractual consent 明示合同的同意,合同的明示同意
express covenant 明示的合同(契约)条款
express declaration 明确宣告,明示宣告;明文宣言
express delivery 明示交付
express derogation 明确减损
express extradition 明示引渡
express guaranteeship 明示担保
express malice 明显(犯罪)恶意
express notice 明示通知,实际通知
express objection 明示异议(或反对)
express offer and acceptance 明示的要约与承诺
express or implied 明示或默示
express partnership agreement 明示的合伙协议
express passing off 显形反向假冒(指美国的反向假冒与假冒一样,依据《兰哈姆法》第43条2款,反向假冒包括两种类型:①显形反向假冒,即行为人未经商标权人许可去掉其商标而以行为人自己的商标销售该商品的行为。②隐形反向假冒:即行为人未经商标人许可去掉其商标后没有使用任何商标而直接销售该商品的行为。美国许多法院认为隐形反向假冒不具有可诉性)
express power 明示权力
express proclamation 明示公告,明文公告
express promise 明示允诺
express provision 明文规定,明确规定
express recognition 明示承认,明确承认
express renunciation 明示(合同的)拒绝履行
express repeal 明显废止

express representation 明示代位继承;明示代理
express republication （对遗嘱的)明示重新公布
express request 明示请求
express reservation 明示权益保留
express reverse passing off 显形反向假冒（指甲购买乙的产品,然后贴上甲的商标出售。见 express passing off)
express rule 明示规定,明确规则
express terms 明示条件;明示条款
express trust 明示信托
express trustee 明示受托人
express waiver 明示放弃;明示弃权书
express warranty 明示担保;(苏格兰)明示保证
expressed intention 明示的意思表示
Expressio eorum quae tacite insunt nihil operatur. The expression of those things that one tacitly implied is of no consequence./The expressing of those things which are silently implied, has no effect. 将已经默示者予以明示则无济于事(指用来表达法律已经暗含之意的言语不过是多余的话)。
* *Expressio unius est exclusio alterius.* The expression of one thing is the exclusion of another. 明示其一即排斥其他。
* *Expressio unius personae est exclusio alterius.* The mention of one person is the exclusion of another. 提及一人即排斥其他人。
expression n. 表达,明确表示;措辞;表达方式
expression conduct 富于表情的行为,明示的行为
expression falsi 虚假陈述（这样的陈述可造成合同的撤销。见 allegation *falsi*)
expression of intention 意思表示
expression of regret 道歉
expressly prohibited by law 为法律所明文禁止者
* *Expressum facit cessare tacitum.* That which is expressed makes that which is implied to cease. 业已明示者则使默示者不复存在。

expromissio n. （债权人准许债务人）请人代为清偿债务

expromissor n. 替代债务人，代替他人还债者

expromittere （民法中）取而代之；代替他人承担责任

expropriate v. 征用；没收；剥夺……的所有权；把（他人财产）转移到自己名下，据为己有，侵占

expropriation n. 征用；没收财产；所有权的剥夺；让渡，转移（财产）；侵占，据为己有

expropriation of land 土地的征用

expropriation of property 财产的没收

expropriator n. 剥夺者，没收者，征用者

expulsion n. 驱逐出境，驱逐；开除

expulsion from academic status 开除学籍

expulsion from military service 开除军籍

expulsion from parliament 逐出议会

expulsion order 驱逐出境的命令

expulsive a. 逐出的；开除的

expunge v. 除去；删去；勾销；省略；消灭，歼灭；擦掉

expurgation n. 删改，订正

expurgator n. （书的）删改者，订正者

exputativa causa 误信原因

extant principle 现存的原则

extemporaneous a. 即席的，当场的；无准备的；临时的；权宜之计的

extemporaneous speech 即席演讲

extend v. 1.延长，延期，宽限；扩充，扩张 2.估价，评价；评价债务人的物业 3.没收（土地等）4.（将速记等）译出；详细写出 5.致以，给予，送达

extend a deed 草拟契据

extend a protest 送达抗议书

extend the right to counsel 扩充律师的权利

extended a. 展期的，延期的；延长的；扩大的；持久的，持续的

extended case method 扩展个案方法

extended credit 展期信用证

extended family 大家庭，家族（指①近亲属连同全部旁系亲属构成一个家族；氏族。②近亲属连同旁系亲属以及近亲属之朋友）

extended insurance 延期的保险

extended jurisdiction 广泛的管辖范围；广泛的管辖权；广泛的审判权

extended order "扩展秩序"（哈耶克认为，由经济学和生物学所揭示的惊人事实提出了我们的文明不管就其起源还是就其保持而论，无不依赖人际合作的扩展秩序……这种扩展了的秩序亦不源于人类的设想和意愿，而是自发地来到世间。它来自人们的对某些传统实践，尤其是道德实践的无意尊奉）

extended period 延长期

extended producer responsibility （EPR）生产者责任延伸[此概念是在1988年瑞典的环境经济学家 Thomas Lindhquist 给瑞典环境署提交的一份报告中提出的。他认为 EPR 是一种环境保护战略，旨在降低环境影响的目标。生产者延伸责任，亦有译为生产者责任延伸，延伸生产者责任，扩大生产者责任，延长生产者责任等，此概念提出已有20年左右，但其理论的界定仍未得到统一认识。1996年美国可持续发展总统委员会（The President's Council on Sustainable Development, PCSD）对"生产者延伸责任"修改为"产品延伸责任"提出在"延伸新产品责任"体系中制造商、供应商、使用者（公共和个人）以及产品处理者将共同承担产品及其废物对环境影响的责任。延伸产品责任的目标就是识别生产链条上那些最有能力改善产品环境影响的参与者。该责任主体视情况而定，或者是原料生产者抑或是最终用户或其他。欧盟的定义是：生产者责任延伸"主要指生产者必须负责产品使用完毕后回收、再生和处理，其策略是将产品废弃阶段的责任完全归于生产者"]

extended sentence 延长（刑期）的判决；加刑

extendible a. 可延长的；可扩张的

extending loan 延长贷款

extending of credit 信用证的展期

extending the incidence of tax 扩大征税范围

extension n. 1.延期；伸展；扩建 2.延期还

债认可书 3.(=denotation)外延
extension of a lease 延长租期,租约延期
extension of judg(e)ment 判决的延期
extension of note 期票延期,延期期票
extension of the term of the tenancy 延长租赁期
extension of time 延期
extension of time for payment 准许延期付款
extensive a. 扩充的,扩大的;广泛的;广阔的,广博的
extensive bodies of laws 广义的法律汇编
extensive democracy 广泛的民主
extensive interpretation 扩充解释,扩大解释
extensive order 大批订货
extensive practice 扩大的实务范畴
extensive report 详尽的报告
extent n. 1.范围,程度;广度,宽度;限度;长度 2.(古英国法中由理财法院直接给地方司法行政官发出的)收回债款执行令;收回债款扣押令(对收回私人债款有时用 writs of execution)3.(美)(债权人对债务人的财产可临时占有,直至债务人清偿债务为止的)临时所有权令 4.(英)(古时对土地等的)估价
extent for measurement of punishment 量刑幅度
extent in aid (古英国法)(为帮助或宽免债务人而发出的)宽待收回债款执行令
extent in chief (古英国法)(为皇室收回债款而发出的)首先执行的扣押令
extent of applicability 可适用的范围
extent of applications 适用范围;申请的范围
extent of authority 授权范围,代理权范围;权限
extent of compensation 赔偿范围
extent of competence 权限范围
extent of crime 犯罪程度
extent of damage 损害程度
extent of injury 伤害程度,损害程度
extent of judge's power 法官的权力范围
extent of jurisdiction 管辖范围
extent of liability (或 **responsibility**) 责任范围
extent of occupation 占有范围
extent of power 权力范围,权限
extent of repentance 悔改程度
extent of stipulated contribution 约定出资数额
extent of the agent's authority 代理人的授权范围
extent of the Gun Barrel Proof Acts (英)(1868年和1950年的)《枪支证明法》适用范围
extenuate v. (用偏袒的辩解或借口来)减轻(罪行);减弱;低估;藐视
extenuating a. 情有可原的;使(罪行)减轻的
extenuating circumstance 减轻情节(指在合同法中,因特殊情节阻却当事人在规定期限内履行义务。在刑事案件中指可以斟酌而处罚减轻的情节。见 mitigating circumstance)
extenuating circumstances 可(使罪行)减轻的情节
extenuation n. 减轻;偏袒的辩解
extenuation of a crime 减轻罪行
extenuatory a. 使减轻的;可原谅的
extenuatory defense 可使减罪的辩护
exterior inspection 外表观察,外观
exterminate v. 根除,消灭,灭绝,扑灭
external a. 外面的;外界的;外部的;外国的;对外的;外交上的;客观的;表面的
external affair 外交事务,(议会的)对外事务
external assets 在国外的投资,国外资产
external attribution of guilt 客观归罪
external borrowing 对外借款,外债
external cause 外因
external characteristic of a crime act 犯罪行为的外在特征
external debt 外债
external debt servicing 外债偿付
external evidence 外部证据
external intervention 外部干涉,外来干预
external law 外在法
external loans act 外债法
external objects 外部对象[指康德说的被意志支配的"外部对象"有三:外在于我的

有体物(A corporeal thing external to me);他人履行特定行为的自由意志(The free-will of another in the preformance of a particular act),他人在与我的关系中所处的状态(The state of another in relation to myself)。此三者的分类即相当于哲学上的本体(substance)、因果(causa-lity)、相互关系(reciprocity)]

external public law 国外公法[实在法学派学者佐恩(Zorn)认为,国际法是国内法的一个支系,单独构成为国外公法]
external representation 对外代表权
external self-determination 对外自决权
external solvency 对外偿付能力
external sovereignty 对外主权
external system of law 外部法律制度
external temptation 外界引诱
external trade 对外贸易
externalism n. 外在性,客观性;拘泥形式(或虚礼);(复)外部事务
externalities n. 外形,外表;外部事务;外在性,客观性
externalize the risk of hazardous activity 外化危险活动带来的风险
exterritorial(=extraterritorial) 治外法权的
exterritorial jurisdiction 治外法权,领事裁判权
exterritoriality (=extraterritoriality)
exterritoriality of diplomatic envoys 外交使节的治外法权
extinct a. 消灭了的;(希望、火等)熄灭了的;(法令等)过时的,无效的,废除了的;(贵族称号等)无合法继承人的;绝种的,灭绝的
extinct family 已绝嗣的家族(庭)
extinction n. 消灭;废除;灭绝;熄灭
extinction of claim 请求权的消灭
extinction of an action 诉讼时效的消灭(见 negative prescription)
extinction of crime 消灭犯罪,犯罪的消灭
extinction of mortgage 抵押权的消灭
extinction of obligation 债的消灭,废除债务
extinction of property rights 废除财产权,财产权的消灭
extinction of rights 权利的消灭
extinction of state 国家的消亡
extinction of terms 条件的消灭
extinctive prescription 消灭时效
* *Extincto subjecto tollitur adjunctum.* When the substance is extinguished, the incident ceases. 本质问题已解决,枝节问题也就不再存在了。
extinguish v. 1.消灭,熄灭,绝灭;压制,抑制 2.使无效;取消,废除 3.偿清(债务等)
extinguish a claim 使一项要求无效,取消请求权
extinguished by prescription 因时效而消灭
extinguishment n. 消失;(权利或义务的)撤销;无效;废除;偿清
extinguishment of common 共有权的丧失
extinguishment of copyhold (英)经官册(典籍)登记的土地保有权的撤销;依官册(典籍)享有土地保有权的撤销
extinguishment of debts 债务的偿清
extinguishment of obligation 债的消灭
extol v. 赞美;吹捧
extort v. 勒索,敲诈;逼供;强要
extort a confession by torture 刑讯逼供
extort under false pretences 讹诈
extorting confessions and believing such confessions easily (中)逼、供、信
extort money or other property from another 诈骗钱财
* *Extortio est crimen quando quis colore officii extorquet quod non est debitum, vel supra debitum, vel ante tempus quod est debitum.* Extortion is a crime when, by color of office, any person extorts that which is not due, or more than is due, or before the time when it is due. 任何人以执行公职为幌子向任何人勒索不应当要的,或超过了应当要的,或应当要而尚未到期的,都是一种犯罪。
extortion n. 1.勒索,敲诈,强取,恐吓索财罪(为普通法中的轻罪,指公务人员利用其职位,非法诈取财物或收受不应得的或逾额的酬金等)2.强取或勒索的财物
extortionate a. 勒索的,敲诈的;强夺的;过高的;太大的

extortionate and unconscionable term 苛刻而不公平的条件
extortionate transaction 勒索性交易
extortioner n. 勒索者,敲诈者,强夺者
extra a. 额外的,外加的;另外收费的;特别的
extra allowance 额外津贴
extra best quality 最优等品质
extra *commercia* 公用财产
extra dividend 附加股息,额外股息
extra duty 额外义务
extra judicial evidence 诉讼外证据,司法外证据[指不是在司法程序中所采用的而是私人为证明某项事实的证据。不属于司法认知(Judicial cognizance or judicial notice)的证据,但是却与司法证据和要求证明的事实之间构成中间联系。它包括法院通过司法证据所了解的全部事实。见 judicial notice; judicial evidence]
extra *judicium* 在法律范围外的;在法院外的;在司法程序范围外的
extra *legem* 法律之外的,法律保护之外的
extra statutory concessions 额外的法定特许(指严格法的放宽或对纳税者作有利的解释)
* *Extra territorium jus dicenti impune non paretur* The sentence of one adjudicating beyond his territory cannot be obeyed with impunity. One may safely disregard a judge administrating justice beyond his own country./One who gives a judgment outside his jurisdiction is disobeyed with impunity. 在管辖区域以外行使管辖权者不被服从而不受惩罚。
extra *vires* 越权,权力以外的
extra-budgetary a. 预算外的
extra-budgetary funds 预算外的资金(或基金)
extra-budgetary resources 预算外资金
extra-budgetary source 预算外来源
extra-contractual liability 合同(契约)外的责任
extra-contractual torts 合同(契约)外的侵权行为
extra-corriculum lectures 课外讲座
extra-costs n. 额外费用,附加费用
extra-economic factors 非经济因素
extra-judicial activities 审判外的活动
extra-judicial cases 非司法上的案件
extra-departmental organization 部外制的人事机构(指美国设立文官委员会和日本设立的人事院。它是一种独立于行政系统之外,管理一切人事行政事宜的机构。见 inter-departmental organization)
extra-legal 法律外,超法律
extract v./n. (用力)取出,拔出,抽出;提取;榨出;引出,推断出;吸取;摘录,选录;选取(精华)/摘要,选录,抽出物,精华,提取物〈extract a passage from a book〉(从书中摘出一段),〈extract a promise from sb.〉(迫使某人作出诺言)
extraction n. 摘录,摘要;血统,家世,出身,榨取
extraction of confession by torture 刑讯逼供
extractum 罚款裁判记录的副本(或抄本)
extracurial a. 法庭外安排(或和解)的
extraditable a. (逃犯、战俘等)可引渡的;可引渡逃犯的
extraditable crime 可引渡的罪名
extraditable criminal 可引渡的罪犯
extradite v. 引渡(逃犯),使(逃犯等)被引渡
extraditing state 引渡国
extradition n. 引渡(逃犯)
extradition crime 引渡罪
extradition *de facto* 事实上的引渡(遣返)(指将外籍不良分子,特别是出于政治原因而给予遣送或逐出)
extradition of aliens 引渡外侨
extradition proceedings 引渡诉讼
extradition treaty 引渡条约
extrahazardous a. 特别危险的,危险性特别大的
extrajudicial a. 法庭之外的,法院体系功能之外的(outside the functioning of the court system,亦称 out-of-court);在法庭审判程序之外,司法程序之外,非司法上的
extrajudicial admission 法庭外的承认;法庭外的供述和主张

extrajudicial assertion 审判外的主张
extrajudicial avoidance 由非诉讼方式宣告无效
extrajudicial confession 法院外的招供（指当事人在法庭外所作的有罪供述，或在司法调查或讯问程序以外对他人所作的有罪供述）
extrajudicial dispute 非司法上的纠纷
extrajudicial document 非正式文件，非法律文件
extrajudicial duties 司法外的任务
extrajudicial evidence 与诉讼无关的证据
extrajudicial function 司法外的职能
extrajudicial interpretation 非司法上的解释；司法外的注释
extrajudicial investigation 庭外调查；审判外的调查
extrajudicial oath 未按法律程序的宣誓
extraordinary remedy 特殊救济［指与通过诉讼而获得的普通救济相对而言的一种救济。其中主要的有如执行职务令状（writ of mandamus）或人身保护令状（writ of habeas corpus）——这种救济是一方当事人不可得到的，除非必须保持一种权利，而它又不能受到标准的法定和衡平救济的保护。因为没有特殊救济的合意清单（agreed list），作为特殊情况表述的某些标准救济则有预防性和永久性禁制令（preliminary and permanent injunctions）等，美国联邦最高法院和大多数州法院中多数此类令状已被废除］
extrajudicial statement 法院外的陈述
extrajurisdictional a. 管辖权以外的
extralegal a. 超出法律权限的；不受法律制裁的
extralegal detention 超越法律权限的拘留；违法拘留
extralegal imprisonment 违法监禁；私自监禁
extralegal punishment 私刑；违法的惩罚
extralegal search 超越法律权限的搜查，违法搜查
extramarital a. 私通的，通奸的

extramarital cohabitation 非婚同居
extramarital coitus 婚外性行为
extramarital relation 婚外性关系
extramural a. 市外的；城镇以外的；单位以外的
extranei heredes 外来继承人
extraneous a. 外部的；外来的；范围外的；无关系的；体外的
extraneous duty allowance 额外工作津贴
extraneous evidence 旁证，外部证据（见 extrinsic evidence）
extraneous offense （被告）审判之外的罪行
extraneous prejudicial information 无关联的偏见性信息
extraneous question （被）确定的论点之外的系争点
extraneous sources of law 法的外部(补充性)渊源（又译：外部的或补充性的法律渊源）
extraordinaria judicia 非常程序
extraordinary a. 特殊的，特别的，非常的；破例的；非凡的
extraordinary appeal 非常上诉，特别上诉
extraordinary average 特别海损，非常海损
extraordinary budget 非常预算
extraordinary case 特殊案件
extraordinary circumstances 特殊情况
extraordinary cost 特别费用
extraordinary court 特别法庭；非常法庭
extraordinary danger （职业上因为特殊环境而造成的）特殊危险
extraordinary election 特别选举；非常选举
extraordinary grand jury 特设大陪审团（指在宣告执行期内只限于进行调查的陪审团）
extraordinary meeting 特殊会议，非常会议
extraordinary remedies 特殊救济方法；特别补偿
extraordinary reopening of final judgment 特别重新终局(开庭)审理

extraordinary repair 特别修缮,特别维修
extraordinary resolution 非常决议案
extraordinary risk 特殊风险
extraordinary session 非常会议
extraordinary writs (= extraordinary remedies) 特别令状
extraterritorial (=exterritorial) a. 治外法权的
extraterritorial application 境外适用
extraterritorial asylum 域外庇护
extraterritorial criminal jurisdiction 域外刑事管辖权
extraterritorial effect 治外法权效力;域外的效力
extraterritorial effect of law 法律的域外效力
extraterritorial effect of the decree of nationalization 国有化法令的域外效力
extraterritorial jurisdiction 治外法权;领事裁判权;域外裁判权
extraterritorial service 境外送达,跨州送达,跨地区送达
extraterritoriality (=exterritoriality) n. 治外法权;领事裁判权;域外裁判权
extravagance v. 挥霍;浪费;过度,无节制
extravagance and waste 挥霍浪费,铺张浪费
extravagant interpretation 扩大(的)解释
extreme a./n. 极度的,极端的;严厉的,过分的;激烈的,激进的;末端的;最终的/极端,极度;激进行为,激烈手段,极端不同的性质(或事物)
extreme case 极端案件(指案件的事实或适用的法律或事实与适用的法律二者已达到可能性的极限)
extreme case only "只有极端情形"
extreme caution 严厉警告,最后警告
extreme commingling 过度混合
extreme cruelty (可以批准离婚的)极端虐待
extreme hazard 最大的危险;最大的公害
extreme measure 严厉措施
extreme offences to the marriage relationship 严重侵犯婚姻关系
extreme penalty 极刑,死刑
extreme theories of royal prerogative 王

室特权的终极理念(或极端理念)中最早的抵押(或质押)的一种形式(指通过拟制买卖或移诉而不移转占有权的一种抵押或质押)
extremity n. 极限;绝境,极危险的境地;极度;非常手段,激烈措施
extricate v. 解救,使解脱;(气体)放出
extricator n. 救出者,脱困者
extrinsic a. 外在的,非固有的,非本质的;外来的,外部的;附带的
extrinsic acceptance 票外承兑
extrinsic ambiguity 非(合同、协议之类本身)固有的意义不明确
extrinsic evidence (17世纪)外部证据,旁证[指①与契约有关但不是从契约中而是从其他来源所得的证据,如当事人的陈述、订约时的周围情况等。旁证通常不得采用反对或增加一个明确文件的条款。亦称 extraneous evidence; parol evidence; evidence aliunde。②旁证亦指未以合法方式在作裁决的审判庭上提出的证据。见 intrinsic evidence。③旁证还指故意质疑证人的可信性(credibility),并以对证人交叉询问之外的方法提出理由。这种手段可以包括在文件中的证据、记录以及其他的证人证言中。参见《联邦证据规则》第608(b)条和注释]
extrinsic fraud 外部性欺诈(见 intrinsic fraud)
Ey Strategic Growth Forum 安永战略性高增长论坛(指美国著名的企业家年会,有多名来自北美及全球各地的政商人士出席。论坛主办安永会计师事务所是全球领先的审计、税务、财务交易和咨询服务机构之一)
eye-witness n. 目击证人,见证人(指亲眼看见事情发生的证人)
eye-witness evidence 目击证人的证据
eye-witness identification 见证人的鉴定
eye-witnesser n. 目击者的报告
eyre (古法语 eire) "journey, march" (12世纪)(历史上)(英)巡回,巡回法庭[指经王室授权组派王家巡回法庭到各郡调查一些犯罪的指控(allegations of wrongdoing)并审理案件。同时征收罚金(levy of fine)为皇家提高财政收入的一种制度。

这种巡回制于 13 世纪被废止。见 articles of the eyre; justice in eyre。1176 年组成了 6 个巡回法庭(circuits)……这些法庭均有指派的法官,他们在 12 世纪 80 年代的数目达到 20 或 30 名,为当时众所周知的"巡回法官"(justiciae errantes),而后的巡回法官为 justiciarii in itinere, justice in eyre；法文"eyre","eire"变成了最久远形式的皇家法官(royal justice)。爱德华三世(Edward Ⅲ)最常用"总巡回法庭"或"大巡回审判"(general eyre)去巡访各个郡者,国王政府经常运用它,不仅是为了执行法律法庭的审判权,而且还对地方政府进行监督。该巡回法庭初创时每 5—7 年巡回审案一次,以后改为一年一次,现在由巡回审判法庭代替]

eyre(或 circuit) courts　(英)巡回法院(庭)

F

fabler n.　虚构情节者;编寓言者
fabricant n.　制造者,制作者
fabricate v.　制作,装配;创造;捏造;伪造
fabricated a.　制造的,装配的;捏造的;伪造的
fabricated evidence　捏造的证据
fabricated facts　捏造的事实
fabricated rumour　捏造的谣言
fabricating of evidence　捏造证据
fabricating of facts　捏造事实
fabrication n.　制造,装配;捏造,伪造;伪造物;谎言
fabrication of false evidence　制造伪证
fabricator n.　制造者,制造厂家;装配工;捏造者;伪造者
fabrics of law　法律的结构
face n.　面貌;票面;外表,表面;局面;额;面值
face amount　票面数额,面值;(保险)承保面额,保额
face of instrument　(票据的)票面
face off n.　敌对,对峙;面对面的会议
face recognition　面貌识别(警方用以抓捕罪犯的一种技术)
face up to the fact　承认事实
face value　票面价值;表面价值,面值(与 par value 同义)
face-to-face　面对面的;直接的
face-to-face meeting with witness　面对证人
face-to-face struggle against the enemy　面对面的对敌斗争
facet n.　(性格,思想,主题等)某一方面;方面
facilitate v.　使容易,使便利,推进,促进
facilitating agency　服务机构,提供便利的机构
facilitation n.　便利于他人犯罪的行为
facilitation of procedure　简化手续
＊Facility of pardon is an encouragement to crime.　轻易给以赦免就等于鼓励犯罪。
facio ut des　以做换物
facio ut facias　以做换做
facsimile n.　复制品,复本;传真
facsimile copy　(文件等的)传真本
facsimile of the entry in the register　登录登记处项目的副本
facsimile probate　(对遗嘱的)传真认证(书)
facsimile signature　传真签字(署)
fact n.　1.事实,实际;真情,真相 2.(犯罪)行为 3.论据
fact actually perceived with one's own senses　亲身见闻的事实
fact crammed　被塞进的事实
fact finding board　实情调查委员会
fact in contention　争议事实,争论中的事实
fact in evidence　(18 世纪)证据事实(指一个由法庭考虑得出的结论的事实,该事实已被采用在听审中作为证据。书面可写成 fact-in-evidence。亦称 evidentiary fact)
fact in issue　争执未决的事实;系争事实

fact judgment 事实判断[指只陈述大千世界客观存在的事实,即回答 what is(是什么)问题的逻辑思维。犯罪中的事实判断当然是指犯罪论评价体系中直接回答是否发生了法律规定的或已客观存在的犯罪事实,包括人、事、物及其过程等]
fact of legal case 案情
fact question 事实问题;事实审
fact relevant to penalty 与量刑有关的事实
fact situation 事实简况(指仅对案件的事实简要说明,并无任何评述或法律结论)
* *Facta sunt potentiora verbis.* Deeds (or Facts) are more powerful than words. 事实胜于雄辩。
fact-amount 事实与数额(指为消除可得利益损失不确定性的天然弊端,降低可得利益损失的证明难度,除引入"合理确定性"标准外,还须建立对可得利益损失的"事实与数额"加以区分的证明标准。见 reasonable certainty)
fact-finder (=finder of fact) 判定事实者,事实调查人(指政府、法庭或企业为了了解某一特定事件的情况或争议特指派调查、取证的人员或认定事实的人员。美国法院审案时通常由陪审团认定事实,民事审判和涉及轻罪的刑事审判由法官认定事实)
fact-finding a./n. 实情调查的/查明事实,事实认定(指法院通过审理证据推断和确认事实的过程);实情调查;调停
fact-finding agency (实情)调查机构
fact-finding meeting (实情)调查会
fact-oriented 导向性的事实,适应形势的事实
factio passiva 接受遗嘱权;受领遗嘱资格
factio testamenti 立遗嘱权;立遗嘱资格(亦称 *factio activa*)
faction n. 1.宗派,派别;小集团 2.派系斗争;内讧
factionalism n. 派别活动,派性
factionalist n. 搞派系斗争(活动)者
factionalist set-up 帮派体系
factious a. 宗派性的;好搞派系活动的;因搞宗派而产生的
facto 实际上,事实上

factor n. 1.因素,要素 2.代办人;代理商 3.(依法指定的)管理没收(或扣押)财产者 4.(苏格兰)地产管理人;管家
factorage n. 代理业;(代理商的)手续费(或佣金)
factoring n. 财务代理(指按合同方式将一家商行的应收账款售于财务代理商,以便在账款到期前取得现金)
Factors Acts, 1989 《1989年代销商法》(英、美两国规范代销业的立法)
Factors Lien Act (美)《代理商留置权法》
factory n. 1.制造厂,工厂 2.商行在国外的代理处
factory and commission (苏格兰)代理委托书
factory farm 工厂化农场
factory law 工厂法
factory legislation 工厂立法
factory manager 厂长
factual a. 事实的,与事实有关的;实际的,确实的,现实的;真实的
factual admission 据实招认
factual aspect 事实部分,事实方面
factual clusters 事实组群(指现代民事诉讼程序将各项请求归纳为法院便于处理各种事实组群)
factual evidence 事实证据
factual impossibility 事实上的不可能性(指某一非法行为在事实上不可能完成,如试图扒窃空的钱包。事实上的不可能性不能作为犯罪未遂的辩护理由。亦称 physical impossibility; impossibility of fact)
factual inference 事实的推断,事实推论
factual information 真实信息
factual materials 事实材料
factual mistake 事实错误
factual proof 事实证明;事实证据
factual works 事实作品
factualism n. 尊重事实;求实精神
factuality n. 真实性
factually incorrect or legal unjustifiable pleading 事实上有错误或法律上无理由的诉答文书
factum n. 事实,自己的行为;遗嘱的正式订立;事实的陈述书,呈文

factum 事实;自己的行为;契据;事实陈述书
factum juridicum 法律事实
factum probandum 待证事实
factum probantia 举证事实
facultative a. 授权的;任意的,可选择的;能力上的,才能上的
faculty n. 能力,才能;(授予的)权力;(大学)系;科;学院;(美)(任何学校的)全体人员;(从事某一专门职业的)全体人员;官能
faculty of advocates 律师联合会;(苏格兰)律师学院;状师公会
faculty of law 法学院,法律系
Faculty of Politics and Law (中)政法院系;政法学院
faggot vote (英)以变相合法手续取得(议会)的投票权(又译为"名义财产的议会投票权",指一个人因丧失财产而取消议会选举资格的时候,采取变相合法手段,如买入土地,又以原价抵押出去的办法以保持议会的选举资格)
Fagin 费金(英国小说家狄更斯的小说《雾都孤儿》中的人物,伦敦一贼窝中的头人,以教唆他人偷窃为生。后即以"费金"指小偷把头或教唆犯)
fagin n. 教唆犯(尤指教唆儿童犯罪者)
fail v. 1.失败;犯错误 2.缺少,不足(in) 3.未能,没能(to do) 4.使……失望 5.失去支付能力,破产
fail in a suit 败诉
fail in election 落选
fail in one's duty 失职
failed legacy 见 lapsed legacy
failing n. 失败;过失;缺点
failing to display an approved sign 未显示核准标记
failing to perform 不履行
failure n. 失败;不足;疏忽;不履行;破产,无力支付;衰竭;故障;衰退
failure of consideration 不加考虑;不予补偿,无报酬;(英美法)缺乏对价
failure of duty to educate and to supervise 对教育和监督权的失职
failure of evidence 证据不足,缺乏证据
failure of good behavio(u)r 行为不当,行为不端,错误行为
failure of issue 无子女,无后嗣
failure of justice 审判不公;审判失当,误判
failure of record 无法出示记录
failure of trust 信托过期(或失效)
failure to appear (当事人)未能出庭
failure to discharge debts as they become due 不能支付到期债务
failure to disclose 不通报;未能披露
failure to keep a promise 违约,未履行诺言
failure to make discovery 未能出示文据(或物证)
failure to plead 拒绝认罪辩护(指虽承认有罪事实,但又同时进行辩护或作无罪申辩)
faint a. 虚弱的,衰弱的;(行动等)软弱无力的;微弱的,不明显的,不清楚的
faint action (或 **feigned action**) 虚伪诉讼
faint pleader 欺诈答辩人,虚伪答辩人
fair a./n. 公平的,公正的;合理的;依法律可捕猎的;清楚的;无污点的;中等的;相当的;十足的,完全的;(财产等)丰富的;顺利的;美丽的/定期集市;商品交易会;(美)商品展览会;义卖市场
fair abridg(e)ment 合理节略
fair allocation of risk 风险的公平分担
fair and impartial jury 公正无私陪审团(指陪审团的每个陪审员必须是公正和无私的成员)
fair and impartial trial 公正而无偏袒的审判
fair average quality 平均中等品质
fair balance 公正的平衡
fair comment 正当批评,公正评论(指普通法赋予对官员、公务员行为的批评权利,只要评论公正善意,即使损坏别人名誉也不负构成名誉损坏责任)
fair compensation 合理补偿;公平补偿(原则)
fair consideration (英美法)合理对价,公平对价
fair construction (对合同的)合理解释
fair copy 誊正本,校正本,清样(稿)
Fair Credit Reporting Act (FCRA) (美)

《公正信贷报告法》(指联邦和州的法规,旨在管理消费者信贷信息组织机构);《公平合理信用报告法》(指1970年的联邦立法,要求各种信用报告应对消费者公正合理的方式进行,并应尊重其隐私权)

fair cross sections of community 公正社区

fair dealing 公平交易[指①经营或交易行为是完全透明的,通常由公司的高管和公司一道透露经营状况。②托收交易业务(fiduciary's transaction business)可以取得个人利益,只要所有利益关系人(all interested persons)完全知悉他们潜在的和所有的其他有关交易的实质性信息(见 self-dealing)。③(加拿大法)合理使用,正当使用(fair use)]

fair dismissal 合理驳回;正当解雇

fair employment statutes (美)公平就业法规

fair field and no favo(u)r 公正无私

fair forum 公正的审判地

fair forum for particular litigation 特定诉讼的公正审判地

fair hearing (美)公正听审(指根据司法的基本原则所进行的听审,旨在提供程序上的正当法律程序所进行的听审,使有权获得一个公正无私的判决,即有权出示证据并获得在出示的证据基础上所作出的判决)

fair inference 公平的推断

Fair Labor Standard Act 《美国公平劳动标准法》

Fair Labor Standard Act of 1938 (美)《1938年公平劳动基准法》[1974年虽加以修订,1979年后有关本法之执行由平等就业机会委员会(Equal Employment Opportunity Commission, EEOC)负责;该法规定国际贸易工厂最低工资标准,每周最长工时40小时,对少年工种也做了规定]

fair management of election 进行公正选举

fair market value 公平市场价格(指进行买卖交易双方都自愿接受的合理价格,而且是一种公平合理交易,符合供需双方利益。缩略为 FMV。亦称 actual value; actual cash value; actual market value; cash value; fair market price; fair value; full value; just value; market value; salable value; true value)

fair on its face 表面上合法

fair persuasion 以理服人,用道理说服

fair play 公平对待;条件均等,条件相同;公平竞争

fair play and substantive justice standard 公平对待和实体正义标准

fair practice 公平诉讼程序

fair preponderance of evidence 合理的证据优势(指负有举证责任的一方所提出的证据足以使审理事实的人们相信他所说的事实)

fair price 公平价格,合理价格

fair procedure 公平程序

fair quotation 合理引用(证)

fair rent 公平租金,合理租金

fair representation 公平代理

fair return 合理收益,合理利益,合理报酬

(the) fair (gentle; weaken) sex 女性

fair share of seats 一份公正席位

fair trade 公平贸易,公平交易

fair trade law 公平贸易法

fair trade practices 公平贸易惯例

fair trial 公正审判

fair use 合理使用,正当使用(指允许不经版权人许可或不给版权人费用而翻印,但上项使用必须合理且无损于版权人的权利,但什么是"合理"和"无损于",则不是信念所能判定的)

fair valuation 合理估价

fair value 公平市场价格,现时市场价,公平价值[美国民事法律中的重要概念和原则。美国建国之初,《独立宣言》中强调"人人生而平等"(All men are created equal),当时美国并非商业化国家,今日作为世界最发达国家,强调的不是"平等"而是"公平"(fair)。不管主体之间是否平等,但大雇主和小雇主之间所进行的交易应是公平的。如果有市场价,则公平价应以市场价为准;如果无法确定市场价,则应参考专家意见;如果估价对象是公司或企业,则应将公司或企业作为一个整体估其价值。"实际价值"(active value)、"市

fair wages clause (英)合理工资条款
fair warning 允许的警示,公正的警示
fair way (河流、海港)航道;(水上飞机升降用的)水面跑道
fair wear and tear (租借物等的)正常磨损
fair-minded a. 公正的,无偏见的
fair-trade v. 按公平贸易约定进行买卖
fair-trade agreement 公平贸易协议(指厂商规定代理商不得低于规定价格出售的约定)
fair-trade law 公平贸易法
fairground n. 集市(贸易)场所
fairness n. 公平性,合理性
fairness (或 **equal time**) **doctrine** (美)公正使用说(或等时使用说)(指对广播机构提供社会重大问题的影响范围所规定的责任,该范围应是广泛的且能反映不同观点,对于有关政治和社会争点问题的双方辩论人均应得到公正和等同的机会来广播他们的观点)
Fairness in Musical Licensing Act 1998 (美)《1998公平音乐许可法》
fairness to out-of-state defendants 对州外被告的公平
fait 契据;事实;行为
fait accompli 既成事实
fait juridique 法律事实
faith n. 信任;信仰;信念;保证,诺言;约定;忠于信仰;信条;守信;诚意
faithful a. 守信的;忠实的;忠诚的;可靠的,正确的;(诺言等)切实遵守的
faithless a. 背信弃义的;奸诈的;不忠实的,不可靠的
fake n./v. 伪装;伪造物;欺诈;赝品,假货;捏造的报道/假装;伪造,捏造
fake and shoddy commodities 伪劣商品
fake cash 假钞
faker n. 伪造者;捏造者;骗子;欺诈者
fakery n. 伪造,捏造;伪装;赝品,假货;欺诈
fakester n. 伪造者,冒名者,虚假制造者(指冒充名人等含有虚假或误导信息的社交网络账户,或谎称自己为某国某部长,甚至某国元首等。见 digital wildfire)
Falange n. (西班牙)长枪党
fall n./v. 落下,跌倒;垮台;失败/下落,跌落;崩溃,瓦解;垮台,坍倒;陷入,堕落;(事故)发生;出来;减退,减弱;变成,属于;适逢
fall a victim to 成为……受害者
fall back 退却,后退
fall back on (或 **upon**) 求……支持,求助于,转而依靠;退到;回过来再谈
fall due 到期
fall in 同意;(债务)到期;(租约等)期满,失效
fall into 1.落入 2.陷入,混乱,错误等,进入(某种状态) 3.(河流)注入〈the river of falls into the sea〉(河流注入海洋) 4.分成,(可)分成〈the story falls into three parts〉(这个故事可以分成三部分) 5.属于〈fall into the same category〉(属于同一范畴) 6.开始〈fall into conversation with sb.〉(与某人开始交流)
fall into (或 **in**) **abeyance** 被搁置,中止;暂缓实施,暂停生效
fall into error 陷入歧途
fall into temptation 受到诱惑
fall into the net of justice 落入法网;落网
fall of a government 政府的垮台
fall prices 价格下跌,跌价
fall to one's share 归某人负担;归某人的份额
fall under 属于,归类于,归入
fall vacant 缺位
fall within the general theft provision 属于一般盗窃(条文)规定
fall-out n. (原子弹爆炸后落向地面的)辐射性微尘;回降物,微粒回降
fallacy n. 欺诈;谬论;谬误
* *Falsa causa non nocet.* A false cause does not vitiate a document. 虚伪原因不影响文件效力。
falsa demonstratio (文据中对人或事的)虚伪描写(述)
* *Falsa demonstration non nocet.* A false description does not vitiate a document. 虚伪

描述不影响文件效力,错误表示不影响原则,错误不损真意。

* *Falsa orthographia non vitiat chartam, concessionem.* False spelling does not vitiate a deed. 拼写错误不影响契约效力。

false a. 假的,虚伪的;谬误的;欺诈的;伪造的;无信义的;违反意图的
false account 假账
false accounting 伪造账目,造假账
false accusation(或 **charge**) 诬告,诬陷
false action 虚伪的诉讼
false advertisement 欺骗性广告
false alarm 假警报
false answer 虚假答辩
false appearance 假象
false arrest 不法逮捕;非法拘留;假捕
false bill of lading 假提单
false character 假冒主人罪
false checks 使用支票骗取银行金钱罪
false claim 无根据的请求权,无理要求;虚假陈述请求;虚假的索赔
False Claim Act (美)《虚假陈述法》(指一项联邦法律,规定如故意向政府提供虚假陈述或申诉,或向政府少交应付金额,制造或使用虚假现象以减少对政府的义务的均应承担民事和刑事责任)
false coin 伪币,假币
false colour 假托,托辞
false confession 假坦白,骗人的供述
False conflict 虚拟冲突,假冲突
false debt 假债
false declaration 虚报;虚报税额
false declaration of domicile 假报户口
false demonstration 错误表达;虚伪表达
false documents 伪造(的)文书
false evidence 伪证,假证据
false fact 捏造的事实
false impersonation 假冒他人,冒充他人
false impression 虚假印象,假象
false imprisonment 私禁,非法拘禁;非法拘留,错误拘留;妨害他人行动自由罪(妨害自由罪),错误限制人身自由
false instrument 伪造(的)文书
false making 伪造
False Memory Syndrome Foundation(美)虚假记忆综合基金[指一个双亲组织,他们对于他们的成年子女(adult children)儿童时代受到性侵犯(childhood sexual abuse)的不公正的刑事指控而主张权利。这个组织形成的目的是帮助父母亲对于成年子女受到不公正的指控主张权利,如同恢复抑压记忆(repressed memories)的成果。缩略为 FMSF。见 Victims of Child Abuse Laws]
false money 伪钞,伪币
false negative 虚假否定的,假同意的
false news 谣言;假消息
false oath 伪誓,假誓
false papers (船只持有关于货物和目的港等的)假证件
false personation 假冒身份,冒名
false plea 伪辩;假答辩
false position 虚假立场,虚假主张;虚假态势,虚假职位
false positive 虚假确信,虚假自信
false pre-contractual negotiation 订约前谈判中弄虚作假
false pretense 欺诈
false report 假报告
false report of loss 虚报损失
false report to the police 向警察报假案
false representation 虚伪的事实陈述
false return (16世纪)虚假的回呈;错误的(所得税)申报表[指①传票送达人(process server)或其他司法官员对其执行令状的情况所记录的回呈与事实不符,或可给当事人或其他相关人造成损害,因而引起受害人提起损害赔偿之诉。②应纳所得税的纳税申报表上被错误填写申报或纳税额被错误计算。见 tax return]
false signals 假信号
false statement 虚假陈述
false step 错误;愚蠢的行为;不正当行为
false swearing 虚伪誓言;伪誓
false testimony 伪证,假证;伪供
false token 假文件(或假事实)
false trade description 虚假的商品说明书
false verdict 假裁决;不当裁决,不真实的裁决
false witness 伪证,作伪证人

false-coiner n. 制造伪币者
false-hearted a. 不忠实的;欺诈的
falsehood n. 虚伪陈述,谎言;谬误;不真实
falsely accused person 被诬告的人
falsereturna brevium (英格兰古法)虚假回呈之诉[指针对郡长(sheriff)制作回呈而签发的诉讼令状。若郡长制作虚假回呈,将面临公诉,同时因虚假回呈而遭受损害者可以索赔。见 false return]
falsi crimen 见 crimen falsi
falsification n. 弄虚作假;伪造,反证;篡改,曲解
falsification of account 伪造账目(罪),造假账
falsification of document 伪造文书(罪),作假文件
falsification of evidence 伪造证据
falsification of public seal 伪造公章(罪)
falsification of weights and measures 伪造度量衡(罪)
falsified sale 假卖
falsified scene of a crime 犯罪的假现场
falsifier n. 伪造者;伪证者;曲解者;弄虚作假者
falsify v. 1.窜改(文件),伪造,歪曲,捏造 2.证明……是假的,证明……是无根据的 3.误用,搞错;说谎
falsifying a record 窜改(法院)记录
falsifying a record judg(e)ment 撤销判决;窜改判决
falsity n. 虚假,不真实;欺诈,谎言;不正确
falsum n. (罗马法)1.虚假陈述(见 *crimen falsi*)2.伪造文书罪,篡改或弄虚作假罪[直至罗马帝国时代,此术语适用于"文件"和伪币(counterfeited coins)两者]
falsus 虚伪的;欺诈的,欺骗的;错误的
falter n./v. 犹豫,畏缩;支吾/摇摆;踌躇,犹豫,畏缩
* *Falsus in uno, falsus omnibus.* False in one thing, false in everything. 一事假,事事假。
famacide n. 诽谤;诽谤者,中伤者
familia (古英国法)家族;家长,户主;(罗马法)家族;家;家主权;(西班牙法)(包括奴仆在内的)家庭
familiae emptor (罗马法)(通过拟制买卖形式取得遗产的)遗嘱执行人
familial a. 家庭的,家族的;家庭(或家族)所特有的
familiar a. 熟悉的,通晓的;无拘无束的,放肆的;冒昧的;亲近的
familiarity n. 熟悉,通晓;亲近,顺便;放肆
families of laws 法系
familism n. 家庭主义(指强调家庭和家族感情的社会结构形式)
family n. 家庭;家属;亲属;氏族;家族;僚属;派别
family affairs determination law 家事裁判法
family allowance 家庭补助
Family and Medical Leave Act of 1993 (美)《1993年家庭及医疗休假法》[克林顿上任以来所正式签署的第一项重要的劳工法律。此法规定雇佣员工达50人以上之雇主应给予其雇佣期一年以上之正式受雇者(regular employees)为期12周的无薪特别假,以照顾新生儿、刚收养之孩童或罹患重病之近亲等。此法已于1994年2月正式生效]
family allowance tribunal 家庭扶养费裁判庭
family arbitrator 家事仲裁人
family arrangement 家产处分
family assets 家庭资产
family car(或 **automobile**)**doctrine** (美)家庭用车(替代责任)原则(见 family purpose doctrine)
family confidentiality (美)家庭秘密(指美国有少数州准许父母和子女对家庭关系中获得的情况在法庭上拒绝作证。但美国最高法院仍未承认这种新概念的合法性)
family corporation 家族公司(见 close corporation)
family council 亲属会议,家族会议
family court 家事法庭(院)(指不同类型的法院名称,这些法庭审理包括虐待儿童、过失、扶养、认定生父、离婚、分居等案件)

family dependents (=dependants) 家属, 眷属
family disintegration 家庭解体
family dispute 家庭纠纷
family dissension 家庭不和,家庭纠纷
family disturbance 妨害家庭(罪)(常用于表明家庭内部或有关对家庭的任何侵权、干扰或犯罪行为的一个术语)
family division (英)家事庭(指1971年设立的高等法院的一个分庭,管辖婚姻、子女、家庭财产案件与非讼的遗嘱检验工作,而将原属法庭的遗嘱检验诉讼移交给大法官法庭,将海事案件交给后座法庭的海事庭)
family dwellings 家庭住处,家庭寓所,家庭住宅
family expenses statutes 关于家庭费用的制定法
family group 家庭群体(指美国家庭用车的适用原则,包括车主和与其同住一处的人均有权用车)
family in distress 困难户
family income supplement 家庭收入补贴
family independence agency 见 Child Protective Services
family institution 家族制度
family law 家事法,亲属法
family law reform act 家庭法革新法例
family lawyer 家事律师,家庭律师
family maintenance 赡(扶)养家庭;家属赡(扶)养费
family maltreatment and desertion 家庭成员间的虐待和遗弃
family name 姓氏
family of a martyr 烈属
family of a soldier 军属
family of military personnel 军人家属
family of nations 国际社会
family of revolutionary martyrs (中)革命烈士家属
family of the suspect 嫌疑犯家属
family offense 家庭罪
family organization 家庭组织
family origin 家庭出身;祖籍
family planning 计划生育

family planning programs 计划生育方案
family policy 家庭保险单
family property 家产;家庭财产
family property law 家庭财产法
family provision 家庭供养(指法院有权从死者的遗产中拨出适当财产判给其困难的家属)
family purpose doctrine (美)家庭用车(替代责任)原则(指给家庭提供汽车使用并允许家庭任何成员驾驶的汽车持有人,对于任何成员经其允许开车而造成他人损害者,应负损害赔偿责任的原则)
family registration law 户籍(登记)法
family relation(s) 家庭关系,亲属关系
family reproductive behavio(u)r 家庭繁殖行为
family service rule 见 family car doctrine
family settlement 分授财产给家人的协议
family side occupations 家庭副业
family sidelines 家庭副业
family status 家庭地位;家属身份
family structure 家庭组织,家庭结构
family ties 家庭关系
family tree 家谱,家系图
family units 家庭(构成)单位
family voting 家庭投票;家庭选举制
family-oriented worker 家庭问题工作者
famosus 诽谤人格;诽谤名誉;造谣中伤的,诽谤性的
famosus libellus 损害名誉的诽谤;诽谤性文据
famous a. 著名的,出名的;非常令人满意的
famous trade-mark 名牌商标,驰名商标
famous trial 著名的审讯,有名的案件
fancy n./a./v. 想象力;设想;迷恋/根据想象的;(衣着、食品等)花式的;奇特的;品种珍贵的;供应高价品的,(美)最高档的;特级的/设想,想象;(无根据地)相信;认为
fancy fair (英)小商品商场
Fannie Mae 见 Federal National Mortgage Association
far-ranging a. 扩及远距离的,包罗万象的
far-reaching changes 深远影响的变化
far-reaching revolution 意义深远的革命
fare n. 车费;船费;乘客;伙食;精神食粮

fare dodger 不买票的乘客,混乘(车船)者

farm n./v. 农场,农庄;饲养场,畜牧场;(儿童等的)寄养场所;包出税款;包税区/1.耕种;出租,佃出 2.包出;(承包企业等的)收入 3.务农;经营农(牧)场

Farm Credit Administration (美)农场信贷管理局

farm for reform through labo(u)r (中)劳改农场

farm inheritance 农场财产继承

farm jail 农场监狱

farm labo(u)r[或 **labo(u)rer**] 雇农;农业工人,农场工人

farm property 农场财产

farm surplus 剩余农业品

farmer n. 农(牧)民;农(牧)场主;承包者;包税人

farmer's law 《农夫法》(指8世纪制定的规定有关农民及其所在村庄事项的一部拜占庭法典)

farming credit bank 农业信贷银行

farming lobbies 农业院外游说集团

farming-matter n. 农垦案件

Farmland Protection Policy Act (美)《农地保护政策法》(美国土地产权界定十分明确,或为联邦或州政府所有,或为私人所有。联邦一般不会干涉州或私人拥有的土地使用权,否则即可因构成"管制征收"而必须予以补偿。该法第658.3条明确规定,该法目的是尽量减少"联邦项目以没有必要和不同的挽回方式将农地转化为非农用途"并不授权联邦政府"以任何方式调控私人或非联邦土地的使用或以任何方式影响这些土地所有人的财产权")

farther on 认为,归……负责;更远些,在后面,在下面

farthing damages 象征性损害赔偿

fascism a. 法西斯主义

fascist dictatorship 法西斯专政

fascist legal thoughts 法西斯主义法律思想

fascist state 法西斯国家

fashion n./v. 样子,方式,流行式样;风气;风行一时的事物;红人;上流社会/形成;制作;改革,使适应,使适合

fashion a remedy for the breach 作出违约救济的判决

fast n. 禁食,斋戒;节食;禁食期

fast day 斋戒日

fast-tracking (1996年)1.司法速决处理(特别指法院采取措施让案件的争议迅速解决。比如法官可以命令所有的证据开示必须在90天内结束,而且审理推迟也许定为30日)2.(广泛)促进,促成(指迅速促进某事物发展,诸如议案或允诺成为专业人员)(fast track v.)

fat finger 乌龙指[也可写作 fat-finger 或 fatfinger,由 fat(肥胖)与 finger(手指)组合而成](是股票交易员、操盘手、股民等在交易的时候,不小心敲错了价格、数量、买卖方向的事件的统称。2004年9月,摩根士丹利公司的交易将一笔总额为数千万美元的股票买单错误输入为数十亿美元,结果罗素2000指数开盘就上涨2.8%,纳斯达克指数也随之上升)

fatal a. 致命的;毁灭性的;不幸的;重大的;决定命运的;宿命的

fatal accident 严重事故,死亡事故

fatal injury 致命伤

fatal wound 致命伤

fatalism n. 宿命论

fate n./v. 1.命运、天数〈decide/fix/seal sb.'s fate〉(决定某人的命运)2.毁灭、灾难、死亡〈go to one's fate〉(去死)3.结局 4.the fates(希腊神话中的命运三女神)/(常用被动语态)注定、命定

fateful decision 重大决议

fateful expansion 关键的阐述

father n. 父亲;父辈;父系,(复)祖先,前辈;创始人;创造者;源泉;长老;(议会)元老

father in law 岳父;继父

Father of Constitution (美)宪法创制人,宪法之父

father of the House 下议院元老

(the) father of the modern concept of human dignity 人的尊严的现代之父(指德国对法理学家康德的尊称。这来源于其

有关个人道德上的自治属性及价值尊重,特别是在法律上被作为目的而不能作为手段对待理论。人是目的是康德在《实践性批判》一书中被作为绝对命令而提出来的,所谓绝对命令是永恒的道德律令,其中核心含义是个人不能作为手段对待和使用。因这一命题蕴含个人的价值地位,故长期被作为尊严的法理基础)

father right 父权;父系继承权
father unknown 父亲不明
fatherless a. 没有父亲的,生父不明的
fatherly a. 父亲的;父亲般的;爱护的;慈祥的
fatherly duties 做父亲的职责
father's authority 父权
fault n./v. 过失;(民法)过错,缺点;错误的责任;毛病,误差,故障/挑剔,找……缺点;弄错,出毛病,有故障
fault liability 过失(赔偿)责任
fault-finder n. 挑剔者,找岔子的人
fault-finding n. 找岔子,吹毛求疵,挑剔
faultless a. 无错的,无可指责的,完美无缺的
faulty a. 过失的,有错误的,有缺点的,不完善的
faulty driving 过失开车
faulty goods 劣等货物
faulty merchandise 劣质商品
faulty packing 有缺陷的包装
faute de service 公务过失
Fauxsumerism 假消费主义[指随意浏览产品,关注并试图了解相关品牌,但不打算购买任何东西的做法。该词由 faux(假的、伪的)和 consumerism(消费主义)的后半部分组成。Fauxsumerist 为其形容词形式。Fauxsumer 可译为假消费者。美国商业调查和信息分析公司信息集团的报告最早使用这一表达方式。谈及虚假消费现象不断增多的原因,信息集团公司首席战略官杰米·古特弗罗因德说:"这并非表明前景黯淡,而是一种转变。经济衰退过后,这些消费者习惯于花钱时更加小心谨慎。"]
favo(u)r n./v. 偏祖;恩惠;庇护;赠与;赞同,喜爱;宠爱;礼物,纪念品;徽章;特别的权利/偏袒,偏爱;庇护;赠与;有利于;赞成
favo(u)rable a. 有利的,顺利的;优惠的;赞成的,称赞的;起促进作用的
favo(u)rable balance (surplus) 顺差;(贸易)出超
favo(u)rable condition 优惠条件;有利条件
favo(u)rable prognosis 预后良好
favo(u)rable tariff 优惠关税
favorable termination (刑诉)有利的结局(指在刑事指控上按法律规定,终审判决对被告有利。有利的结局是普通法蓄意侵权检控的要素)
favo(u)rable terms 优惠条件,有利条件
favo(u)rable treatment and pension 优待抚恤
favo(u)rable vote 多数(赞成)票
Favo(u)red area 最有利的区域(或范围),受优惠地区
favo(u)red beneficiary 优惠受益人
favo(u)red nation 受惠国
favo(u)rite n. 受宠爱的人,亲信,心腹;特别喜爱的人(或物)
favo(u)rite son 最宠爱的儿子;在故乡受称赞的人;(美)(党派代表大会上的)本州代表所拥护为总统候选人的人
favoritism (18世纪)1.偏祖,偏爱 2.任人唯亲(见 nepotism; patronage; cronyism; discrimination)
FDA Food Safety Modernization Act 2011年通过的美国《食品安全现代化法》[对《联邦食品、药品及化妆品法》(1938年)进行了大规模修订,授予美国食品和药品管理局以更大的监管权力和更高效的监管工具,旨在保证美国本土食品及进口食品的安全性。缩略为 FSMA]
fealty n. (英)宣誓效忠(指由封建土地保有人对其领主做出的尽忠誓言);孝顺
fear n./v. 害怕,恐惧,担心,敬畏
fearless reasoning 大胆的推理
feasance n. 作为;(责任、义务、条件等的)履行
feasibility study 可行性研究
feasible a. 可行的,可执行的;可完成的;

可用的;适宜的
feasible scheme 可行的计划
feasible set 可能解集合
feasible set of strategies 一套可行性策略
feasor n. 行为人,创造者;制定者
featherbed v. 担任闲职;要求(资方)雇用超过实际工作需要的人员;以政府补贴资助
featherbedding n. (工会迫使雇主超过工作实际需要,强迫雇用的)额外雇工
feature n./v. 1.特点,特色;特征 2.面貌,相貌 3.特写,特辑/1.以……为特色〈the U. S. Code in print features a number of research aides〉(美国法典印刷版以多种检索帮助为特色),〈round the clock service features the store〉(日夜服务是这家商店特色) 2.特写,特刊 3.起重要作用
federal a. 联邦的,联邦制的;联盟的;联合的;(大写)(美)联邦政府的;(美史)北部联盟的
Federal Administrative Procedure Act (美)《联邦行政程序法》(1846年)
federal agency (1859年)(美)联邦政府机关[指联邦政府行政部门中的一个单位或其他的一种媒介或"工具",包括政府公司(government corporation)和政府印刷所(Government Printing Office)。行政诉讼法(Administration Produce Act)界定"机关"(agency)这个词时否认是任何美国政府权力当局,其中也不包括国会、法院、哥伦比亚特区政府、任何领地或属地的政府(the government of any territory or possession)、军事法庭或军事权力当局,参见《美国注释法典》第5标题卷第551节。判例法上,这个词的意义上聚焦于权力当局(authority);总的说,实体(entity)是一个机构,如果它有权采取约束行为(binding action)。另外的一些联邦法规(statutes)界定机构(agency)包括任一行政部门、政府公司、政府已控制的公司和其他行政部门内或联邦管理委员会(federal regulatory board)内的机构]
federal aid (美)联邦帮助(指动用联邦基金帮助州的多种特殊困难)
Federal Aid in Wildlife Restoration Act of 1950 《1950年联邦帮助野生动植物恢复法》
federal assembly 联邦议会
Federal Bench 联邦法官,联邦法庭
Federal Bureau of Investigation (FBI) (美)联邦调查局[指美国司法部的一个部门,负责调查所有违反联邦法律、法规、条例的情况。特别指派给其他联邦政府机关的一些事项不在联邦调查局工作范围之内]
federal case 联邦案件
Federal Case News (美)《联邦判例消息》(指在各种联邦判例汇编先行本出现之前,作为每周先发行的单行本。由西方出版公司出版,概述重要的判决)
federal chancellor (德)联邦总理
Federal Charter 《联邦宪章》
Federal Circuit of Appeal (美)联邦巡回上诉法院
Federal Civil Justice Reform Law (美)《联邦民事司法改革法》(指1979年美国卡特总统为改善司法行政管理提出的一项对联邦司法重大改革的建议)
federal civil statute (美)联邦公民权利法规
federal common law 联邦普通法[指裁决联邦问题和其他联邦事项而产生的判例(决)依据法。见 general common law]
Federal Communication Law (美)《联邦通讯法》(1934年通过)
Federal Communications Commission (FCC) 美国联邦电信委员会(根据1934年联邦电信法设立)
Federal Congress (美)联邦国会
federal constitution 联邦宪法;(大写)(美)美国联邦宪法
Federal Constitutional Convention (美史)联邦立宪会议(1787年5月25日在费城举行)
Federal Constitutional Court (德)联邦宪法法庭
federal court (美国等的)联邦法院
federal court of appeal 联邦上诉法院
Federal Courts Study Committee (FCSC) (美)联邦法院研究委员会

federal courts system （美）联邦法院系统

federal crime 根据联邦法规的刑事犯罪［大部分这类刑事罪行均被编入《美国法典》第18标题卷(18 USC)之中］

Federal Declaratory Judgment Act of 1934 《1934年美国联邦宣告式判决法》《联邦确认判决法》(此法赋予被警告人一种主动的权利,即提起确认不侵权之诉,被控侵权人可以主动提起其行为不构成专利侵权的诉讼。确认不侵权之诉与大陆法上的确认之诉类似。此法颁布之前,专利权人可以滥用专利侵权诉讼,威胁竞争对手,从而使对方屈服于自己的利益。该法颁布后,竞争者不再坐以待毙,他可提起确认不侵权之诉,确认其行为是否构成侵权,从而排除这种不确定的法律风险)

Federal Digest （美）《联邦判决摘要汇编》(指联邦法院的一种单独判决摘要汇编。它包括的年代为1754—1939年)

federal discovery requests （在联邦法院提出披露要求的)联邦披露要求

federal district （美）联邦区

federal district attorney 联邦地区检察官

federal diversity court 不同(国)州籍当事人之间诉讼管辖权的联邦法院,异籍当事人诉讼管辖权联邦法院

federal doctrine 联邦的原理,联邦层面的原理

Federal Election Commission （美）联邦选举委员会［指10个成员组成的一个独立委员会,该委员会给予担保支付(certifies payments)以保证总统选举运动,起始和普选(general election)以及全国提名常规(national-nomination conventions)都符合质量,而且强化各种法规,要求总统大选的财务活动和各政党的财务活动必须公开透明。该委员会根据《1971年联邦选举运动法》(Federal Election Campaign Act of 1971)设立,参见《美国注释法典》第2标题卷第437c节。缩略为FEC］

federal employer's liability 联邦雇主责任

Federal Employer's Liability Act （美）《联邦雇主责任法》(FELA)

federal fiscal powers 联邦财政权

federal government 联邦政府

Federal Home Loan Bank Board （美）联邦内部贷款银行委员会(该委员会特许设立联邦储蓄和贷款协会并监督其遵守规定,同时控制联邦内部贷款银行系统)

Federal Home Loan Banks （美）联邦内部贷款银行(指根据1932年的联邦内部贷款银行法而创立的一些银行,目的在于保持长期为国内筹措资金,提供可得到的货币。这些银行均受联邦内部贷款银行委员会管制。储蓄和贷款、保险公司以及可进行长期抵押贷款的类似公司均可成为联邦内部贷款银行系统的成员,而且可以从全国12所地区银行中的任何一所借入款项)

Federal Home Loan Mortgage Corporation （美）联邦内部抵押贷款公司(指可从联邦储备系统和联邦内部信贷银行系统的成员单位购买第一批抵押品,包括常规承保和联邦范围内承保的一个联邦机构。通常称为"Freddie Mac")

Federal income tax 联邦所得税

Federal Indian Law （美）《联邦印第安法》

federal information processing standards （美）联邦信息处理标准

Federal Insurance Contribution Act 《联邦社会保险捐助法》

Federal Interpleader Act, 1936 （美）《1936年联邦确定竞合权利诉讼法》

federal judge （美国等国的)联邦法官

Federal Judicial Act （美）《联邦司法法》(1789年第一次制定)

Federal Judicial Center （美)联邦司法中心(系指隶属于联邦司法系统的研究和教育机构,1967年由国会根据美国司法联席会议的决定而建立,也是第三个全国性司法行政官僚机构,其主要任务是对联邦法官和联邦法院职员进行培训和连续教育以及为法院发展规划等,并促进对联邦司法程序、法院操作程序和历史方面的研究。该中心董事长由美国首席大法官担任)

Federal Judicial Circuits （美）联邦司法巡回法庭(按《美国法典》第28卷第41节的规定,有11个联邦司法巡回法庭区划。见本书附录)

Federal Judicial Code (美)《联邦司法典》[指包括有28项标题的美国法典。此法典涉及组织、管辖、诉因发生地和联邦法院系统的诉讼程序。司法部和法院的官职人员也包括在该法典所涉及的范围)

federal judicial supremacy 联邦司法至上

federal judiciary 联邦司法机关

federal jurisdiction (美)联邦管辖权,联邦管辖范围,联邦审判权

Federal Kidnapping Act 《联邦预防劫持法》[指一项联邦法规,惩罚那种使受害人被转移至州际或国际之间为求得赎金而劫持的行为,法律推定被害人在24小时内未被释放而被转移的,则为违法。《联邦预防劫持法》由于明示的条文(by express provision)不适用父母一方对未成年人(a minor)的劫持(the kidnapping),参见《美国注释法典》第18标题卷第1201节。亦称 Lindbergh Act。见 Parental Kidnapping Prevention Act]

Federal Land Bank (美)联邦土地银行(联邦农业银行,指由国会建立的专为农民提供抵押贷款的地区银行)

federal law 联邦法

federal lawyers (美)联邦律师(1978年约有20000名联邦雇用律师,国防部雇用律师5247名,而司法部雇用律师为3608名)

federal legacy tax 联邦遗产税

federal legislation 联邦立法

federal magistrate (美)联邦司法行政官(系委派的联邦官员,处理少量的联邦地区法院司法事务,是根据1968年联邦司法行政官条例所设立的)

Federal Maritime Commission (美)联邦海事委员会

Federal Mediation and Conciliation Service (美)联邦调解局

federal model 联邦制模式

Federal National Mortgage Association (美)联邦国民按揭协会(简称 Fannie Mae,是指美国20世纪二三十年代证券化时期出现的两家政府机构之一,当时就已买卖过按揭贷款,另一家政府机构为 Government National Mortgage Association)

Federal Obscenity Law (美)《联邦反淫秽法》

federal offense of criminal homicide (美)联邦杀人罪(指违反联邦法律的有关杀人犯罪行为)

federal organisation 联邦组织机构,联邦体制

Federal Parliament 联邦议会

federal popular jury (墨西哥)联邦陪审团

Federal Practice and Procedure by Wright and Miller (美)赖特和米勒的《联邦诉讼实务和程序》(一种多卷本专门领域的有深度的法学学术概论)

Federal Practice Digest Second (美)《联邦诉讼实务判决摘要汇编第二套丛书》(包括年代为1961—1975年)

Federal preemption (pre-emption) 联邦专有权(指美国联邦宪法和国会立法授权联邦政府在处理州际商务、骚乱等事务上有专有权,而排除州对这些事务的管辖权)

Federal Privacy Act (美)《联邦隐私法》

federal proceedings (美)联邦诉讼

federal question action (美)联邦问题诉讼(指涉及联邦宪法、法律和国际条约而引起的争议,此实质性争议可通过司法手段解决)

federal question actions take precedence over diversity cases (美)联邦问题诉讼应优先于异籍案件

federal question cases (美)联邦问题案件(指根据宪法、法律和合众国的条约所产生的案件)

federal question jurisdiction (美)联邦问题的初审权,联邦问题管辖权(指涉及美国联邦宪法、国会立法和条约及其解释的案件,通常称为联邦问题,由联邦法院管辖;案件涉及宪法和联邦法律及其条约适用时,联邦法院可依据联邦法律的授权审理该案件)

federal register 联邦日志,联邦公报[指每日出版包含有总统宣言(或宣告)和行政令的公报,内容还有行政机构普遍适用性和有效性的法规,建议的行政机构规则(proposed agency rules),而且这些文件要

求按照法律一样出版。《联邦公报》由国家档案和文献管理局 (the National Archives and Records Administration) 出版。缩略为 Fed. Reg]

Federal Register Act （美）《联邦日志法》（《联邦公示法》）[1935 年制定，它规定《联邦日志》为行政管理公告的每日公报。凡行政命令和行政法规如需具有法律效力者，都必须刊在该《联邦日志》上。1937 年经修订后成为《联邦法规汇典》(Code of Federal Regulations)]

Federal Regulatory Commissions （美）联邦管理委员会

federal removal statute （美）联邦移送管辖法

Federal Reporter （美）《联邦判例汇编》（又译：《联邦判决报告人汇编》，1880 年西方出版公司为出版地区法院和巡回法院的判决，创办了《联邦判例汇编》丛书，现在还包括美国临时紧急上诉法院的判决和许多专门联邦法院的判决。该汇编包括第一套和第二套丛书，并出版以下列出的联邦法院的案件判决理由：1880—1932 年巡回上诉法院，联邦地区法院，美国海关和专利权上诉法院；美国权利申诉法院，哥伦比亚特区上诉法院 1932 年至今；美国上诉法院，美国海关和专利权上诉法院 1942—1961 年，1972 年至今；美国紧急上诉法院，1960 年至今。见 Federal Supplement ）

Federal reserve system （美）联邦储备系统（根据 1913 年的《联邦储备法》建立，由该系统管理委员会、12 家联邦储备银行、联邦公开市场委员会、联邦顾问委员会所组成。1976 年还设有消费者咨询委员会，所有国民银行和州特批设立的银行均为该系统的委员银行，它在美国起中央银行的作用，并充当政府财政代理人而行使其职权，负责保管商业银行准备金，对商业银行发放贷款，并有权发行联邦储备券）

Federal Rule of Civil Procedure （美）《联邦民事诉讼规则》

Federal Rules （美）《联邦诉讼规程》（1938 年后，联邦地区法院统一实行最高法院制定的这一规程）

Federal Rules Decisions （美）《联邦诉讼规则判决汇编》（刊载有关法院程序规则的联邦法院判例汇编，该丛书由西方出版公司于 1940 年出版，也选择出版有限数目的较低一级联邦法院判决，这些判决在《联邦判例汇编》或《联邦补编》中均未刊载过）（属于美国全国判例汇编系统的一部分）

Federal Rules for the Trial of Minor Offenses before United States Magistrates 《美国司法行政官审理青少年犯罪的联邦规程》（指青少年违法或犯有轻罪，如果被同意不去地区法院而在司法行政官面前受审时所必须遵循的程序性的规则）

Federal Rules of Appellate Procedure （美）《联邦上诉规则》（向联邦法院上诉时必须遵循的诉讼程序规则。该规程于 1967 年经最高法院通过）

Federal Rules of Civil Procedure （美）《联邦民事诉讼规则》（联邦法院对处理民事案件的诉讼程序所制定的统一规则，该规程 1937 年经最高法院通过，次年生效）

Federal Rules of Criminal Procedure （美）《联邦刑事诉讼规则》（美国 1944 年由最高法院所通过的程序规则，对联邦法院在处理刑事案件、进行刑事诉讼过程中从调查、逮捕、提审直到最后审判，以及诸如有关保释和指定辩护人等的程序均做了详细规定）

Federal Rules of Evidence （美）《联邦证据法规》[联邦地区法院审案时，地区法院司法官（magistrates）面前可提出作为证据的事项。见 Civil Evidence Act]

Federal Securities Act （美）《联邦证券法》（1933 年）

Federal Securities Law Code （美）《联邦安全法典》

Federal Securities Trading Authority 联邦证券交易管理局

Federal Sentencing Guidelines （美）《联邦科刑指南》

federal service in force 联邦有效送达

federal state 联邦国家[指完整的国家主权复合国家（composite state），其内部分为中央政府或联邦政府和数个构成国家的地方政府。这种国家的联合,其对外关系的操控,所有的成员国家或子国家(member states)均服从于中央政府。所以唯有这个由联合而构成的国家才符合国际目的]

federal statute (美)联邦制定法,联邦法规

federal statutory forms 联邦法规形式

federal structure of government 联邦政府结构

Federal Supplement (美)《联邦补篇》(1932 年,随着联邦法院中的诉讼卷本日益增多,西方出版公司在《联邦判例汇编》基础上开始出版另一类名为《联邦补篇》的联邦判例汇编丛书,收集除联邦判例汇编之外的美国各巡回上诉法院——现称美国上诉法院的判例,还包括美国国际贸易法院以及根据地区铁路改组法和关于多地区诉讼的司法陪审团规定的特别法庭的判决。该补篇出版以下列出的联邦法院的案件判决理由:1932 年至今美国联邦地区法院;1932—1960 年美国权利申诉法院;1949 年至今美国海关法院,第 135 卷本。见 Federal Reporter)

federal supremacy 联邦至上

federal system 联邦制

federal system of prosecution (美)联邦检察系统(指包括司法部的刑事司和在联邦司法区代表联邦政府的美国检察官所构成的、承担对违反联邦法规的不法行为行使起诉职能的检察系统)

federal tax suits 联邦税务诉讼

federal territories 联邦地区

Federal Tort Claims Act (F. T. C. A.或 FTCA) (美)《联邦侵权赔偿法》[指限制联邦主权豁免并允准恢复在联邦诉讼中因联邦官员执行职务中的侵权行为造成的损害赔偿请求的制定法规。但仅限于州法规规定产生的侵害是占有职务的私人对此侵害承担责任。该法通过后,曾在 1966 年、1974 年和 1988 年等多次修改。《联邦侵权赔偿法》在很大程度上放弃了联邦政府承担侵权责任的豁免权,并规定因联邦官员执行职务中的过失、不法行为或不作为而产生损害的都应承担赔偿责任,而且赔偿额不受限制。不过该法仍有所保留,即规定美国对政府官员在执行职务范围内的故意侵权行为,对行政机关及公务员行使自由裁量权的行为等情形不负赔偿责任。该法汇编在《美国法典》第 28 标题卷第 2680 节。见 sovereign immunity; Bivens Actions]

Federal Trade Commission (美)联邦贸易委员会[指一个独立的 5 个成员组成的委员会,执行各种法规,预防商业垄断、贸易限制以及欺诈贸易交易(deceptive trade practices)。该委员会是根据《1914 年联邦贸易委员会法》(Federal Trade Commission Act of 1914)》建立的。参见《美国注释法典》第 15 标题卷第 41—58 节。该委员会的一些规定细节可以运用到很多按州法诉讼之中。因为许多被称为一些州的"小联邦贸易委员会"(Little FTC Acts)阐明 FTC 的解释应给州法院判决提供一个范例(model)。缩略为 FTC]

federal tribunal 联邦法庭

federal union 联邦

Federal-employer-identification number 联邦雇主(纳税)识别鉴定号,缩略为 FEIN(见 tax-identification number)

federalism n. (美)联邦主义(美国总统伍德罗·威尔逊在 1911 年写道,州和国家权力在美国联邦体制中的特有的平衡不是通过哪一代人的意见可以解决的。在社会和经济条件改变中,需要由政府提出全国选民概念的问题,同时在优越的政治价值观上要求处理好联邦和州的关系,如同一个"新问题"),联邦制

Federalist n. (美)联邦派[指 1787 年 5 月美国 13 个州的 39 名代表在费城开始进行制宪会议,9 月 17 日经他们签名通过宪法草案,交由各州批准,直到 1788 年 7 月 2 日联邦大会宣告美利坚合众国宪法正式生效。围绕宪法草案的批准,各州曾展开了激烈争辩,汉密尔顿、杰伊和麦迪逊三人以普布利乌斯为笔名在报刊上发表一系列文章,积极鼓吹这一草案,被称为"联邦派"(Federalist)]

Federalist Papers (美)《联邦主义论文集》[指由亚历山大·汉密尔顿、约翰·杰伊和詹姆斯·麦迪逊以共同的笔名普布

利乌斯写的85篇系列论文、评述并提倡采纳美国联邦宪法。大部分论文都是在1787—1788年出版。亦称 The Federalist]

federalist partisans 联邦制拥护党员
federalist president 联邦制的总统
federally created rights 联邦立法创设权利
federation n. 联邦,联盟;同盟,联邦政府;联合会
federation convention (德)联邦大会
Federation of Chinese Abroad (中)华侨联合会
federation of labo(u)r unions 工会联合会
federation of women 妇女联合会
federative a. 联邦的;联合的;(美)有关外交和国家安全的
federative republic 联邦共和国
fee n./v. 费(用);酬金;赏金,小费;税;会费;世袭土地,祖传土地;(英)可继承的土地;采邑,封地;聘金;权利权/付费
fee estate 可继承地产权
fee expectant 期待继承的地产
fee farm rent (英)保留的自由保有地的地租;非限定继承土地的永久地租
fee for acknowledgment of receipt 回执费
fee of permit 执照税,牌照税
fee shifting 费用改变
fee simple (英)非限定继承者身份的保有土地;无条件继承的不动产(权)
fee simple absolute 无条件继承的不动产;(英)非限定继承的保有土地;绝对所有权[美国财产法上最基本、最重要的问题是土地所有权。根据所有权人可获得土地的现实占有,土地所有权被分为现实所有权和将来所有权。现实所有权又依据是否有主体、时间、条件的限制而被分为绝对所有权(fee simple absolute)和附条件的完全所有权(defeasible fees)、终身所有权(life estate)、限定继承所有权(fee tail)及共有权(concurrent estate)]
fee simple absolute in possession (英)绝对占有权的不限制继承土地保有权;不限制继承的占有地产
fee simple conditional 附解除条件继承的地产权,(英)附条件继承的保有土地
fee simple determinable (18世纪)可终止的非限嗣继承地;(英)有期限的无条件继承的土地保有(权);(美)附停止条件的完全所有权(指土地所有权人将其土地所有权转让给受让人,并约定某特定事件发生时,受让人取得的所有权自行终止,土地所有权由转让人取回,受让人所受让的条件成熟时自行终止的土地权利为附停止条件的完全所有权。亦称 determinable fee; qualified fee; fee simple subject to common-law limitation; base fee estate on limitation)

fee simple subject to an executory interest (美)附转移条件的完全所有权(指转让人将其土地所有权转让受让人依契书约定,于某特定事件发生时,受让人所取得的所有权自行终止,但不回归转让人,而是自动转移给第三人。该完全土地所有权为附转移条件的完全所有权)

fee simple subject to condition subsequent and right of entry (美)附终止权的完全所有权(指受让人从转让人处所得的,于特定事件发生时经转让人行使终止权而终止的土地所有权)

fee tail (英)指定继承人继承的保有土地(权)(旧译:限嗣继承土地);(美)限定继承的完全所有权

fee-sharing 见 fee-splitting

fee-simple subject to common-law limitation 见 fee-simple determinable

fee-splitting 1.费用分开,分别费用,费用平分[指两个或两个以上的律师,尤其是办案律师与查询律师(the lawyer who handled a matter and the lawyer who referred a matter)之间代理人费用的部分。有些州认为这种分别费用的做法不道德]2.部分律师费用[指两个或两个以上律师(他们代表共同委托人,但不属同一律师事务所)之间的律师代理费。按多数州的道德准则(ethics rules),律师禁止与非律师职业者平分代理费用(splitting a fee)。亦称 fee-sharing]

feeble a. 虚弱的,无力的
feeble-minded a. 精神虚弱的;低能的;不果断的;意志薄弱的
feeble-minded persons 心神衰弱的人
feel aggrieved 感到不平,感到受委屈

feet of fines (英)土地产权诉讼协议存根(指一种形式上是自愿了结诉讼协议,实质上则是土地转让证书)

fehmgerichte (=hooded court) (中世纪在德意志和瑞士普遍存在的)戴面罩法官法院(亦称自由法庭)

feign v. 佯作,假装;虚构,捏造;伪造

feigned a. 伪造的;假装的;虚构的,想象的

feigned accomplice 假装从犯

feigned action 虚构诉讼

feigned case 假案

feigned diseases 假装的病

feigned matter 虚拟事项

feigned name 假名,化名

feigned recovery 见 common recovery

feint n. 伪装,佯装;假象;佯攻

Feist Case 菲斯特案(指美国联邦最高法院于1991年判决的一宗电话号码簿版权纠纷案。此判例中,法院认为受版权保护的作品应具有创造性——creativity)

Feist Publication, Inc. v. Rural Telephone Service Company, Inc. 费斯特出版公司诉乡村电话服务公司案[499 U.S. 340(1991)] [1991年1月9日辩论,1991年3月27日以9比0的表决结果作出判决。奥康纳代表美国联邦最高法院起草判决意见,布莱克表示赞同。乡村电话服务公司出版了地方性的白皮电话号码簿,费斯特出版公司则把乡村电话服务公司的电话号码清单编进了与乡村电话服务公司的服务区域相重叠的区域电话号码簿里。乡村电话服务公司主张版权(copyright)受到侵犯,美国联邦最高法院判决其版权无效。此举要性在于它重申了版权作为保护原作者的法律的历史性特征,并对后来另类版权主张予以拒绝,即版权不保护那些满头大汗(sweat-of-brow)或辛勤收集而完成的作品或其中一部。总之,版权只奖赏原创性而不是努力。美国联邦最高法院判决是根据宪法中版权条款作出的,该条款授权国会仅赋予创造性作品的"作者本人"以排他性权利,同时该判决也以美国联邦最高法院以前的判例为依据,包括哈珀与罗出版公司诉全国关系企业案(Harper & Rous v. Nation Enterprises)(1985)]

felicity n. 幸福,福气,幸运;(措辞等的)恰当,巧妙;恰当的语句

felificic calculus 幸福计算论

fellah n. (阿拉伯国家的)农民,农业劳动者

fellow n. 伙伴,同事,战友;(学术团体的)会员,(英)评议员(指某些大学管理委员会成员);(常用复数)同谋者,同伙

fellow Democrat (美)民主党同僚

fellow legal specialists 同伙法律专家

fellow partner 共同合伙人

fellow servant rule 承担雇员责任规则(指雇主不承担雇员为他人做事致伤的责任的规则)

fellow-heir n. 共同继承人

fellowship n. 伙伴关系,合伙关系;共同参与;团体,……会,联谊会

fellowship in crime 共同犯罪

fellowship in international law 国际法研究会

felo-de-se 自杀;自杀者

felon n. 重罪人,重罪犯

felonia 重罪

felonious a. 犯罪的,犯重罪的;罪恶的;凶恶的

felonious assault 严重暴力伤害人身罪

felonious entry (英)严重闯入(盗窃)罪[亦称现代法定闯入盗窃罪。普通法盗窃(burglary)罪的含义应是蓄意夜间破门而入他人住宅,而现代法定闯入盗窃罪则没有那样严格要求,只要蓄意闯入任何建筑,甚至进入汽车中进行盗窃即构成此罪]

felonious homicide 严重杀人罪,谋杀罪

felonious intent 犯重罪的意图

felonious larceny 重大盗窃罪

felonious murder 重大谋杀罪

felonious rioting 严重骚乱罪

felonious taking 具有重罪性质的窃取(用于抢劫罪和盗窃罪中的一个术语。意思是有蓄意盗窃目的,将财物取走)

felonry n. (总称)重罪犯;全体犯人

felony n. 重罪,重刑罪

Fem-crit 批判法学派(critical legal stud-

ies)的女权主义追随者
female a. 女性的,妇女的
female heir 女系继承人
female judge 女审判员,女法官(旧译:女推事)
female officer 女职员,女官员
female organization 妇女组织
female prisoner 女犯人,女囚犯
female suffrage 妇女参政权
female tail 限定女系继承的地产(权);(英)限定女性继承的土地保有(权)
feme n. 女子,妇人,妻子
feme covert 有夫之妇,已婚女子
feme plaintiff 女原告
feme sole (=*femme sole*) 独(单)身女子;未婚女子;已离婚的妇女;享有独立财产权的已婚女子
feme-sole trader (古英国法)可独立经营生意(不受丈夫限制)的已婚女子
femicide n. 杀害妇女;杀害妇女者
feminine persuasion 女性,母性
feminism n. 男女平等主义;争取女权运动
Feminist Approach to International Law 女权主义者的国际法方法
feminist legal scholars 提高女权论的法律学者
feminist plea 女权的辩解
femme 妻子;妇女
femme cevert 受丈夫保护的妇女(或已婚妇女)
fenagle (=finagle) v. 骗取,诈取,诱取;欺骗;使用欺骗手段
fence n./v. (14世纪)1.买卖赃物者(指接受盗窃来的物品,通常拿到合法市场销售的人)2.销赃地(见 receiving stolen goods)3.合法的栅栏(或篱笆等)4.(苏格兰法)以特定手势警示勿妨碍司法进程或立法程序(legislative proceeding) 5.(苏格兰法)根据法规或暂行规定进行没收的惩罚(penalty)6.(美)政治利益;政治地盘/1.销售赃物 2.(英格兰法)警示人们勿干扰立法部门或法院进行立法或开庭 3.(苏格兰法)以没收惩罚来震慑违法或违反契约承诺的行为
fence-month (或 fence season; fence time)

n. (古英国法)禁猎期,禁渔期
fencing n. 围栏;买卖赃物;辩论
fend v. 保护;挡开;供养;照料;努力,力争
fenus (罗马法)简单或单纯的利益(或权益)
fenus nauticum 见 *nauticum fenus*
feoff n. 采邑,封地
feoffee n. 不动产受让人;封地受领人;公共不动产管理人;(英)土地受益权的承受人
feoffee in trust 不动产受托人
feoffee to uses 享有使用权的不动产管理人;享有用益权的不动产的承受人
feoffment n. 赠与(或交付)不动产;不动产交付证书;封地授予;地产授予
feoffment with a covenant for reconveyance on payment 附一旦付款即可再让与条款的地产让与
feoffor (=feoffer) n. 不动产授予人;封地授予人,地产授予人
ferae bestiae 野兽
ferae naturae 不属于私产的;野生动物的
ferret n./v. 搜索者;侦查者/搜索;侦查;查获(秘密,罪犯等)
ferret out 查获
ferriage n. 摆渡;摆渡业;摆渡费
ferry n. 摆渡营业权;轮渡,渡口;飞机渡运
fertile a. 利于丰产的,丰富的,多产的
fertilizer n. 肥料;传播花粉之媒介
ferum (或 feudum, fief) n. 恩赐,采邑,封地
fesduca (古罗马人诉讼时手中握着的)木棍(象征所有权的标志)
festuca (古英格兰法)木棍,杖,棒,树枝 [指用交付树枝或棍、杖表示契约一方当事人的诚信担保完成了土地权利的转让。罗马法中,杖棒(fistuca=festuca)是所有权(ownership)的象征]
ferry franchise 摆渡特许权
fetation n. 怀孕,受胎
fetial n./a. (古罗马)监督外交谈判的祭司团成员/外交的,处理国家关系事务的
fetial law (古罗马)关于宣战和缔结和约的法律

feticide n. 杀死胎儿,非法堕胎
fetishism n. 拜物教,盲目崇拜
fetter n. 镣;脚镣;束缚
fetus n. 胎,胎儿
feud n. 1.争执;长期不和;世仇 2.采邑,封地
feudal a. 1.封建的,封建制度的;封地的,采邑的 2.世仇的,宿仇的,仇恨的
feudal court 封建法院;采邑法庭
feudal customs 封建习惯
feudal land tenure 封建土地占用制
feudal law 封建制法,封建主义法;(英)封建法(指中世纪在英格兰的财产法)
feudal patriarchism 封建宗法主义
feudal privileges 封建特权
feudal rules of succession 封建继承制;(英)采邑继承制
feudal separatism 封建割据
feudal system 封建制度
feudal tenure 封建的土地保有权
feudalism n. 封建主义;封建制
feudalist n. 封建论者;精通封建法的学者
feudality n. 封建性;封建政体;封地,采邑;封建诸侯或贵族(集体)
feudatory a. 臣属的;(国家)隶属于外国的
feudist n. 1.封建主义者;研究封建法的学者;封建法学家 2.结下世仇的人
feudum 可继承的土地;封地;世袭土地
feudum hauberticum 军役地产(权)[指在领主或国王发出出征召集令(arrière ban)后全副武装服军役而保有之地产]
feudum individuum 不可分割的地产(权)(只有长子方有权继承此地产)
few and far between 稀少,罕见
fiancé 未婚夫
fiancée 未婚妻
fiasco n. 大败,惨败,可耻下场
fiat (=*fiat*) n. 命令,法令;许可,批准;(英)指示(法官)完成令;(根据法规进行诉讼前的)检察总长的认可
fiat in bankruptcy (英)批准破产处理令(指由司法长官授权给破产行政官命令对经营商按破产程序处理,此令已由1949年的破产法所废弃。见 commissioners in bankruptcy)

fiat justitia (英)国王批准对错判案件的复审令(原意为公正审判,指国王在呈交的申诉书上批上此语,便授权议会作成复审令发出)
* *Fiat justitia, ruat coelum.* Let right be done, though the heavens should fall. 即使天塌下来,也要伸张正义。
fiat money (美)(不能兑换金银的)不兑换纸币;名义货币
fib n. 小谎
fibber n. 惯撒小谎的人
fictio n. (罗马法)法律上的拟制[法律上的假设或推定(legal fiction)(比如原告是公民)必须达到一定的法律效果而其他方法是不可能获得的。法律拟制允许罗马主管司法的裁判官(Roman magistrates "praetors")扩大市民法(jus civile)被严格允准法律范畴。在英国法中,这种实践(practice)也曾发生过,如阻止限嗣继承的拟制诉讼(action of common recovery),据此可允准土地拥有人(landowner)转让土地,但依照法律,这一土地不能转让,如限嗣继承保有的土地(fee tail),复数为fictiones]
fictio juris 法律上的拟制
* *Fictio legis neminem laedit.* A fiction of law injures no one. 法律上的拟制不会损害任何人。
fiction n. 虚构的事实;捏造;拟制,虚构,假设
fiction of implied consent 默示同意的虚拟
fiction of law 法律上的拟制(假设)
fiction theory (法人的)拟制说
fictional a. 拟制的,假装的,虚构的
fictional contract 拟制的合同(契约),假装的合同(契约)
fictional or nonfictional works 虚构或非虚构的作品
fictional parts of territory 拟制的领土(指西方有的国际法学家所主张的把一国在公海上及在他国领水内的军舰及其他公有船舶作该国领土的浮动部分,但这一主张并未为多数国际法学家所接受)
fictional presence for attachment 为扣押目的地拟制所在

fictional *"situs of the res"* **conception**　拟制的"物之所在地"概念
fictitious a.（习惯上的）假定的,假设的；虚构的；不真实的
fictitious action　假定的诉讼,虚拟诉讼
fictitious bill　假支票,假票据
fictitious blockade　虚拟封锁
fictitious capital　虚拟资本
fictitious declaration of intent　虚假的意思表示
fictitious defendant　假设的被告
fictitious ejectment　虚构的收回不动产诉讼
fictitious entry　虚拟进入
fictitious interest　拟制利息,虚利
fictitious name　假名,伪名
fictitious payee　虚拟付款人
fictitious plaintiff　假设的原告
fictitious price　虚价
fictitious relative　拟制血亲
fictitious return　（美）虚假报告（指一种犯罪行为,即美国政府官员或雇员对人口普查作虚假报告）
fictitious sale　拟制买卖
fictitious transactions　买空卖空
fictitious transfer　虚拟转让
fictitious value　虚构价值
fide iussio　同 *fide-jussio*
fide jubere v.（罗马法）（为他人债务）充任担保[此词由要式口头合同（*stipulatio*）的双方当事人的对话构成。此合同约束一方当事人成为另一方当事人的担保人,第一当事人问道："你愿为他人债务担保吗？"(Do you pledge yourself?)（"*fidejusbesne*?"）。第二当事人回答："我愿意为他人债务担保"（I do pledge myself）（"*fidejubeo*"）。见 *stipulatio*]
fide jussia　诚意负责保证,担保,保证
fide-jussio　（罗马法）诚意负责担保（见 *fidejussion*）
fide promissio　（罗马法）允诺担保
fide-jussor　（罗马法）（债务）担保人,保证人；担保,保证；保证金
fideicommissaria hereditas　遗产信托
fideicommissary n.（派生于拉丁语 *fideicommissarius* 一词）（经立遗嘱人指定的）受遗赠的非继承人
fideicommissor n.　指定受遗赠的非继承人的立遗嘱人（在遗嘱中指定继承人将财产的一部分赠与第三者的人）
fideicommissum　（罗马法和大陆法系）委托遗赠（指对继承人提出将财产的一部分赠与他人的要求）
fidejussion　（16世纪）（罗马法）诚意负责担保[指一个人为另一个人担保的行为,这一行为并不改变主债务人的责任（principal's liability）,但只添加了保证人的担保（surety's security）。*fidejussion* 是三种担保性质契约（*adpromission*）中的一种,而且是《查士丁尼法典》中唯一留下的形式,亦称 *fidejussio*；*fideiussio*。见 *adpromission*]
fidejussor　（16世纪）1.（罗马法）为另一人支付债务的担保人 2.（古）（海商法）在海事法院为被告充当保释人的人,亦可拼写为 *fideiussor*；*fidejussory* a.（见 *adpromissor*）
fidelity n.　忠诚,忠实；尽职；正确,精确
fidelity bond（=fidelity insurance）
fidelity insurance　忠实（尽职）保险（指对职工因不忠实或疏忽所致损失的保险）
fidelity to law　忠于法律
fides　诚实,信用,忠实
＊***Fides servanda est.***　Faith must be observed.　信用必须严格遵守。
fiducia　（罗马法中最早的）抵押（或质的）形式（指通过拟制买卖或拟诉而不移转占有权的一种抵押或质）
fiducia cum amico　（以管理财产为目的的）信托管理
fiducia cum creditore　（以担保债务履行为目的的）担保信托
fiducial a.　信托的,信用的；基于信仰的
fiduciant n.　受托人
fiduciary n./a.　1.忠于受托之事,信托事务 2.忠于信托职务的人；受信人（此词来自罗马法,原意是指一个具有信托应具备的信任和信用,以及信托所需要的谨慎诚实和公正的信托人的品格的人）/信用的；信托的,受信托的；受托人的
fiduciary bargain　（普通法）诚信责任,信

托责任
fiduciary bond 信用证券
fiduciary business 信托业务
fiduciary capacity 受托人资格(身份)
fiduciary certificate 信托证书
fiduciary contract 信托合同(契约)
fiduciary contribution 信用投资
fiduciary debt 信托贷款,信托放款,信用放款
fiduciary duty 受托责任;诚信义务;信托义务原则(指按普通法原则人和人之间应遵守信义,受托人应忠实应用其权利,为收益人谋求利益,衡平法则不准利用受托人身份谋求个人利益或使其义务与利益发生冲突,据此原则公司之董事、监事、经理和职员与公司之间为受托关系,在其与公司及股东发生关系时有受托义务)
fiduciary duty to share holder (对持股人的)信用责任(理论)(公司内部人和大股东有某种信用关系,此关系足以使他们了解公司内幕消息,当其购买本公司股票时,有向本公司或其他股东告知信息的义务)
fiduciary duty trump contract 信托义务胜于合同(指董事应将普通股利益优先于优先股合同规定特殊权利所产生的利益信义义务是英美判例法上的规则,即没有任何比立刻履行承诺者法律上或道义上的义务更为重要)
fiduciary guardian 受托监护人
fiduciary institution 信托机构
fiduciary money 信用货币,纸币
fiduciary obligation 信托义务
fiduciary position 受托人地位
fiduciary property 受托保管的财产
fiduciary relation 信托关系
fiduciary relationship 信任关系,信用关系,信义关系[指一种由受信(托)人对受益人承担的具有最大诚信、忠诚、信任和正直的义务]
fiduciary work 信用业务
fief n. (=feoff)
field n. 战地,战场;场地,实地;领域;原野
field army 野战军
Field Code (美)《菲尔德法典》[即最早

的纽约民事诉讼法典。指戴维·达德利·菲尔德(David Dudley Field)在18世纪60年代起草的《民法典》,曾于1878年经纽约州立法机关两院通过,但在律师坚持下为州长所否决。这部法典以后成为各州民事诉讼法规的模式]
Field Code of Civil Practice in New York 《菲尔德民事诉讼法典》(纽约州)(见 Field Code;New York's Field Code)
field general court-martial 战地军事法庭;军区军事法庭
field hand 田间农业劳动者;(美)干农活的黑奴
field investigation 实地调查
field marshal (英)陆军元帅,最高级的陆军将官
field offices (美)地区性机构(指美国平等就业委员会除在首都华盛顿特区设总部外,该委员会在美国各大地区及重要州内也分别设有50个各种地区性机构,以便与各州本身所设之州级公平平等就业机构共同合作,以消除各种不同类型的就业歧视)
field punishment 战地刑罚
field tax 场地税
fierce a. 猛烈的,残忍的,难受的
fieri facias 财物扣押令;扣押债务人动产令
fieri feci 执行报告(指执行扣押财物令的官员把执行后的情况向法院作的书面汇报)
Fifth Amendment (美)联邦宪法第五修正案(涉及人民不得为同一罪行而被两次置于危及生命或躯体之处境;不得强迫任何刑事案罪犯自证其罪,不得未经适当法律程序而被剥夺生命、自由或财产,以及人民私有产业如无公平赔偿不得被征用等规定)
Fifth Decennial (美)《第五个十年判决摘要汇编》(由西方出版公司出版的自1936年至1946年的判决摘要汇编)
fifth degree of kinship 五等亲属
fight violent crime campaign 扑灭暴力罪行运动
fighting n. 战斗,搏斗;打架(港译:打斗)
fighting position 拳斗姿势(指烧死尸体的

姿势）
fighting with weapons 械斗
fighting words 播弄是非的言辞；挑起争端的言词
figura humana 人的体态（指自然人的权利能力因出生而开始，但何种事实为出生，各国规定不同，因而产生"人的体态"一词，用于表示构成出生事实的一项条件。例如西班牙法律规定：胎儿必须具有"人的体态"，并与母胎分离后保持生命力24小时以上构成出生）
figure n./v. 外形，轮廓；图形，图案；人物，身份，地位；价格；（复）计算/描绘，想象，相信，估计，计算；表示
figure at crime scene （作案）现场图
figure out 1.合计（at）2.计算出，解决 3.领会到，断定
figure out a problem 解决了一个问题或算题
filacer n.（英史）令状归档官
file n./v. 文件夹；汇订的文件（或卡片）；档案，案卷，卷宗/1.归档 2.提出（申请等）；提起（诉讼）；呈请备案 3.（用电话，电报）发出稿子 4.排成纵队行进；（在预选中）备案作候选人
file a brief （律师向法院）提出辩护（或提交辩护状）
file a legal brief with the Court 向联邦最高法院呈交一份法律诉讼（要点）状
file a petition 呈交诉状；提出请愿
file a suit（或 **case**）**against sb.** 对某人提出控告
file a suit based on the same cause of action 以同一理由另行起诉
file an action 起诉
file an information 告发，诉讼
file clerk 档案管理员
file management 档案管理
file off（或 **away**） 排成纵队队外出发
file one's tax return 报送纳税申报表
file pleading （常用复数）呈递答辩状（起诉书）
file security 档案安全
file viruses 文件型病毒
file wrapper estoppel （＝prosecution history Estoppel）（美）专利申请记录不容反悔原则
filed case 被诉案件；起诉案件
filed date action 固定日期诉讼
filed law suits 归档的诉案
filed population （中）被诉案件总体
filiation n. 私生子生父的确定；父子关系的确定；收作养子；亲子关系；（社团等的）分支；起源
filiation order （美）私生子生父的鉴定（令）（指对私生子的父亲作法律上或其他官方的认定，在美国有些州可以此作为要求对私生子的抚养及其从生父那里继承遗产的条件）
filiation proceeding 私生子女的父亲认领诉讼程序，确认生父的诉讼程序
filibuster n. 海盗；掠夺兵；阻碍（议案）通过；阻挠议事的议员（指为阻挠议案通过而作冗长发言者）；擅自对外国进行战争者
filibustering n. 阻挠议事（指在议会中采取发表冗长演讲等拖延战术以阻挠立法活动的做法）
filicide n. 杀害子女罪；杀害子女犯；杀子（女）的行为
filing n. （18世纪）1.特定文件（如诉讼状 pleading）（指在法院书记员的文档或记录保管人处的诉讼文件，即诉讼状）〈the lawyer argued that the plaintiff's most recent filing was not germane to the issue before the court〉（在法庭上，律师辩护说原告最新的答辩状对系争点无关）2.文件归档，文件汇集
filing a court action 提起诉讼
filing a new action 提起一个新的诉讼
filing arrangement 档案分类排列
filing documents 注册申请文件
filing fee （1864年）申请费，登记费［指在诉讼程序开始之前，应支付给法院书记员的费用总额，亦称申请费；将诉状、文件等登记备案而由公职人员收取的费用或因申请宣告破产及申请破产案件中重组或债务人整顿计划（plan for-reha-bilitation）而向法院书记官交付的申请费用］
filing of suit 诉讼的提起

filing of unpaid 免费提起诉讼
filing requirement 注册申请要件
filing statement 归档文件陈述
filing system 归档制度
filing with court 向法院提交法律文件
filius families 家庭之子;(大陆法)尚未自立的儿子(指受他人的家父权支配的人)
filius nullius 非婚生子女;私生子女
filius populi 私生子
fill v. 充满;占满;填补;担任(职务);供应(订货);满足
fill an order 供应订货
fill in 填写;临时补缺,暂代
fill up 填补
fill up a vacancy 填补空白;补缺
filled with 备案
film censorship 电影审查
film n. 胶卷(指少数国家在版权法中电影仍用这个词)
film producer 电影制片人
film scripts 影片手稿,电影剧本手稿
filter n./v. 滤器,滤纸,过滤用多种物质(砂、碳、纸、布等)/1.过滤〈you can filter the results to view just the cases〉(你可以过滤这些成果以审视案件)2.透过,渗漏〈the news filtered through〉(消息走漏)
filth n. 污秽;污物;淫猥,猥亵语
filthy lucre 赃款,不义之财
finable a. 1.可罚款的;该罚款的 2.可提炼的,可精制的
finagler n. 骗子
final a. 确定的;最后的,最终的;决定性的
final accounts 决算
final accounts of all the income and expenditure of the state 国家的收支决算
final act (国际法)最后议定书,最后决议书(指为缔结一项公约而召开的国际会议的记录文件)
final address 结案陈词
final adjudication 终审判决
final administrative decision 行政终局决定(指 TRIPs 协定第 41 条第 42 款规定:"参与程序的当事人应当有机会对行政终局决定获得司法机关的审查,并在遵守一个成员关于案件重要的司法管辖权的法律规定的前提下,至少对案件是非的初步司法判决的法律内容进行审查。对有关知识产权的行政终局决定,应当提供司法机关进行司法审查的机会")
final agreement 最后协议,最后协定
final appeal 终审上诉,终审
final appeal in cassation 请求撤销判决的最终申请;请求再审的最终上诉
final approval 最后批准,最后通过
final argument 最后辩论(指审理中当事人双方均提供一份最后陈述给陪审团,各方表明其对事实和法律适用的看法)
final articles 最后条款
final authority 最终决定权
final award 最后裁决(断)
final ballot 决选投票
final clause 最终条款,最后条款
final composition 终局和解
final concord 书面和解协议(指当事方之间在诉讼进程中经法庭允准签订的协议,借以达成诉讼和解)
final costs 诉讼结束时的全部费用
final decision 终局判决,终局裁定(指案件事实审理清楚,涉及当事人的权利、责任赔偿等问题已经处理,争端已解决,无须作进一步审理判决;未对涉诉事实作出判断,终止案件或诉讼程序的裁定。与 final appealable judgment, final decree, definitive judgment, deterimininative judgment, final appealable order, final judgement 同)
final decree 最后判决令,离婚最后判决令
final disposition 最后供述
final dividend 末期红利
final election 终局选举,决选
final evidence 决定性证据,结论性证据
final hearing 终审,最后审讯
Final House(或 **Senate**) 参议院
final injunction 最后指令,最后禁令
final instance 终审
final judg(e)ment 最后判决,终审判决
final judgement 见 final decision
final jurisdiction 终审管辖(权);终审判权
final jurisprudence 目的法学
final order 诉讼终止时发出的命令,终局

命令,终局裁决
final passage (法令等的)最后通过
final pretrial conference (美)最终的审前会议(指一般由审理案件的法官根据《联邦民事诉讼规则》第 16 条第 4 款所召开的会议,旨在提高即将进行的审判的质量,并控制其进度和耗费。见 final pretrial order)
final pretrial order 审理前的最后命令(指通常由审理案件之法官根据《联邦民事诉讼规则》第 16 条第 4 款所召开的会议,旨在提高审判质量并控制其进度和耗费)
final process 最后诉讼阶段(指诉讼程序中最后执行的阶段)
final protocol 最后议定书
final provisions 最后条款
final reading 最后一读(指国会通过议案时的三读)
final recovery 诉讼的最终复决
final review (案件的)最后复审;终局复审
final ruling 终局裁决
final say 最终发言权
Final Selection Board (英)决选委员会(指英国文官委员会内所设的考选委员会和决选委员会的后一委员会,前者掌笔试,后者掌口试)
final sentence 终审判决
final settlement 最后的授予财产清算(指遗嘱认证诉讼中的一项直接宣告,即对遗产已被全部接管,遗产管理人已完全履行其受托责任,并按法律要求对接管的一切金钱开支作出说明的宣告)
final statement (法庭上的)最后陈述
final supervision 最后监督
final verdict 最后裁决;定论
final word 最后承认
finalis conordia (或 **fine**) 和解诉讼(英国中世纪通过当事人达成和解诉讼用作转让土地的一种手段)
finality n. 终结,定局;决定性;最后的言行(事物)
finality of verdict 已成定局的裁决
finance n./v. 财政,财务;金融;财政学;(复)财源,资金/供资金给;赊贷给;筹措资金;理财

finance bill 通融汇票;(英)财政法案
finance capital 金融资本
finance committee 财政委员会
finance company 信贷公司,金融公司(指向个人或企业提供贷款的非银行公司或向直接消费者给予小额贷款的金融机构,有时亦译财务公司)
finance court 财政法庭
finance theory's paradigm 金融理论范例
financial a. 财政的;金融的;财务的
financial account 财务账目
financial accountability system 经济核算制
Financial Accounting Standard Board 财务会计标准协会
financial administration 财务行政,财务管理
financial affairs 财政事务,财务
financial agent 财务代理人
financial aid 经济援助;财政资助
financial aid during unemployment 失业期间的财政救济
Financial and Economic Committee (中)财政经济委员会(全国人民代表大会设立的专门委员会)
financial and monetary crisis 金融货币危机
financial and mutual fund corporation 金融和互助基金组织
financial and trade system 财贸体制;财政贸易制度
financial arrangement 财产分配协议
financial asset 金融资产
Financial Asset Investment Trust (美)金融资产投资证券化信托(指用来证券化的一般债务,比如信用卡、应收账款、汽车贷款、住房贷款以及其他短期债务。见 Special Tax Entity)
financial autonomy 财政自主(权);财政独立
financial bond 金融债券
financial bonus 财政红利
financial burden 经济负担
financial business 财政事项
financial capital 金融资本
financial circular 财务通告
financial claim 债权
financial committee 财务委员会

financial community 金融界
financial condition 财政状况;财务状况
financial contribution 财政资助
financial control 财务管制;财务监督,财政管理
financial control system 财政管理体制,财务管理体制
financial deficit 财政赤字,预算赤字
financial delict 财政上的不法行为
financial derivatives contracts 衍生性金融商品契约
financial device 财政手段
financial discipline 财政纪律
financial disorder 金融混乱,财政混乱
financial estimate 财政预算
financial group 财团
financial guarantee 财政担保
financial indemnity 财务补偿
financial initiative 财政动议权
financial inspectorate 财政督察人员
financial institution 金融机关
financial instruments 金融工具
financial intermediarise 金融中介机构
financial law 财政法
financial laws and regulations 财政法规
financial legislation 财政立法
financial meltdown 金融危机
financial management 财务管理
financial motion 财政动议
Financial Ombudsman Service (FOS) 金融督察服务(公司);金融申诉专员(制度)[多元化纠纷解决机制(ADR)中的一种。ADR,即任择解决纠纷方法,可分为三种类型:①纯调解方式,即由第三方主持调解,其结果只有双方接受时才具有约束力;②第三方裁定方式,主要基于双方当事人自愿而采取的仲裁方式;③混合方式,既有调解又有裁定,在调解不成功的前提下由第三方权威机构作出裁定。申诉专员(Ombudsman)制度即属于第三种类型。其原是公共领域用于处理一般民众对政府部分申诉的制度,逐渐扩展到私法领域,在金融领域形成了一种重要的纠纷解决机制,即金融申诉专员制度。它结合了调解与裁决的优点]

financial panics 金融恐慌
financial penalty 罚款
financial perequation 财政调整制度
financial position 财务状况
financial power 财政权,财权
financial provision for injury or illness resulting from work 有关工伤和职业病的财政救济规定
financial provision for persons retired from employment 退休职工财政补助规定
financial reimbursement 经济赔偿
financial relief (离婚诉讼进行中的)财政救济
financial report 财政(年度)报告
financial responsibility 经济责任
financial revenue 财政收入
Financial Secretary (英)财务次官
financial security 经济担保;财政担保
financial standing 财务立场,财务状况,财务信誉
financial state 财政状况
financial statement 财政报告,财务报表;决算表,资产负债表,借贷对照表
financial strata 金融阶层,财政,或经济地位
financial stringency 银根紧
financial supervision 财政监督
financial taxonomy 金融分类
financial transactions 财务交易;财务事项
financial year 财政年度
financier n./v. 财政家,金融家;金融机构/(以欺诈等手段)从事金融活动,骗取,欺骗
financing n. 筹措资金,理财;筹集的资金
financing agency 融资机构[指银行、融资公司或其他正常商业经营业务中的实体。①以货物或权利凭证(documents of title)为据进行预付或贷款;②依据卖方或买方的协议参与支付或收取已到期或按销售合同所约定的货项,比如购买或支付卖方的汇票(seller's advances)或单纯为收款而取得汇票,而不顾汇票是否附有权利凭证。参见美国《统一商法典》第2-102节(a)(20)]
financing capital 筹措资金,提供资本

financing company 信贷公司
financing operation 筹措资金业务；资金供应业务
financing statement 筹资报表
find n./v. 拾得物，掘获物/1.查明，判定，认定 2.(法官)作出最后决定；裁决；判决 3.供给；支给；筹集(经费) 4.找到，发现
find a bill 控告，提起诉讼
find a true bill (陪审团)认为诉状应予以受理；提起公诉
find a verdict 作出裁判
find an indictment (宣告)起诉
find for the plaintiff 作出有利于原告的判决
find guilty 查明有罪，裁决有罪
find in damages 承认赔偿损失；(法官)判定赔偿损失
find innocent 查明无罪，裁决无罪
find out 找出，查明，发现；想出，认识到(that)；把(罪犯，坏人)揭发出来；使受应得惩罚
find sb. guilty 裁决某人有罪
finder n. 拾得人；无主物(一般指动产)的发现者
finder of goods 财物拾得人
finder of lost thing 遗失物拾得者
finder of treasure trove (由地下或他处掘出的)无主财富的发现者；无主埋藏物的发现者
finding n. 1.(复)调查结果；对事实的认定；判定(估计)的要素；验证；查明，察看 2.裁决，判决，决定(指审查事实所得的结果，例如陪审团的裁定) 3.拾得物；发现物
finding of a court 法院裁决
finding of a jury 陪审团的裁决
finding of fact 对事实的认定；对争论事实的认定
finding of law 适用法律的裁决
finding tools (美)查找工具(美国自有法律史以来，已发布无数判例和法规，且都按年代顺序出版。这里系指为大量法律资料提供便于进行查找的某些检索手段，包括检索工具书和计算机等)
fine n./v. (13世纪)1.协议诉讼[指(古英格兰法)友好最终协议或拟制或实际诉讼

和解(compromise of a fictitious or actual suit)以确定土地的真实的占有人。fine 以前常用来作为对非限定继承财产的转让形式，亦称 final concord；finalis concordia。见 foot of the fine] 2.土地转让费(fine for alienation) 3.在租佃降低租费开始时，承租人交纳给地主的费用 4.(历史上)来自承租人给其领主(lord)的支付款项 5.刑事罚款及民事罚款(civil penalty)，上交国库 6.结尾，终结/处……以罚金
Fine and Recovery Act 《废弃协议诉讼转让法》(指英国1833年颁布的制定法，该法废弃使用罚金协议诉讼作为转让土地所有权的手段)
fine arts 美术作品(见 artistic work)
fine at (或 left to) the discretion of the judge 法官酌处的罚金
fine for delaying payment 滞纳罚金
fine on admittance 承受金
finecomb (或 fine-tooth-comb) v. 仔细搜查
finesse n. 手段，手腕，策略，技巧
(the) finest (美俚)纽约的警察
finger n. 手指；指状物
finger language 手势语
finger man (美俚)(盗贼等的)眼线
finger prints 指纹，指印
finger ridge count 指纹嵴数
finger wear 指纹磨损
fingernail impression 指甲痕
fingernail injury 指甲伤，掐伤
fingerprint n./v. 指纹，指印/捺指(纹)印
fingerprint analysis 指纹分析[随着高科技的发展，指纹在法庭上不像过去那样起决定作用。20世纪90年代苏格兰法庭在对一名妇女被杀案的调查中发现被害人室内有警官拇指纹(随后认定为食指指纹)。这次失败表明，指纹鉴定中，有时会犯错误，如今指纹鉴定中，意大利要求16个相同特征，法国要求12个特征，而美国联邦调查局无此类标准，只要指纹鉴定人员认为两枚指纹相匹配则可以了，进一步解决此项问题正在研究之中]
fingerprint card 指纹卡片
fingerprint detective 指纹侦查
fingerprint evidence (查)指纹证据

fingerprint file 指纹档案
fingerprint identification 指纹鉴定
fingerprint pattern 指纹类型
fingerprint record 指纹记录;(复)指纹档案
fingertips n. 指尖
* *Finis rel attendendus est.* The end of a thing is to be attended to. 事情的结局(果)应当注意。
finish v. 结束,终结,完成;耗尽
finished a. 结束了的,完成了的;精致完美的
finished product 成品,产品成品(又译:产成品)
finite application 有限的适用
finite applications and limitations 有限的适用与限制
finium regundorum 境界线;边境所有权
finium regundorum actio (大陆法)土地边界的诉讼;调解土地边界纠纷
fink n. 内奸;告发者,告密者;工贼
Fiqh (伊斯兰教法)《教法学》(指伊斯兰教法学者对《古兰经》和《圣训》中的伊斯兰教法原理的解释和发展所通过的决议)
fire n. 火,火灾,失火;火刑;火刑拷问
fire alarm 火警;火警警报器,警钟
fire brigade 消防队
fire check 防火检查
Fire Chief 消防队长
fire company (英)火灾保险公司;(美)消防队
fire disaster 火灾
fire engine 救火车,消防车
fire fighter 消防人员
fire insurance 火灾保险;火险
fire lines 火灾现场的警戒线
fire loss adjustment 火灾损失评定
fire policy 火灾保险单
fire prevention regulation 防火规定
fire prevention safety inspection 防火安全检查
fire protection requirements 防火要求
fire risk 火险
fire sale (美)(火灾中损坏物品的)减价出售
fire station 消防站
fire wall 隔火墙(指国内外学者在研究金融业监督制度时常用的一个概念)

fire-bote n. 采伐权;燃料木
fire-brand n. 煽动叛乱者;挑起争执者
fire-bug n. 纵火者;放火狂
fire-raiser n. 纵火者,纵火犯
fire-raising n. (英)纵火罪
firearm fatality 枪杀死亡事故
firearm homicide 持枪杀人
firearm misuse 枪支滥用
firearm misusers 枪支滥用者
firearm n. 火器,枪炮;(尤指一人携带的)轻武器
firearm suicides 持枪自杀
firearms act 火器管理条例;枪支管理条例
firearms certificate 火器许可证,持枪许可证
firearms control 枪支管制
firearms deaths 枪杀死亡;死于枪杀
fireman n. 消防队员;司炉工
firing n. 点火;射击;司炉;燃料
firing area 射击区
firing squad (对军事法庭判处的犯人执行枪决的)行刑队,死刑执行部队;(军人葬礼时的)鸣枪队
firm n./v./a. 公司,商行/坚挺;变稳固,使牢固;确认(合同等)/稳固的,坚定的,确定的
firm brokerage 股票公司;经纪商行
firm in the undertone (行市)坚挺而稳定
firm name 行业名称;商店名称(旧译:商号)
firm offer 确定的要约(指要约人在要约确定的期限内不得撤回的要约),实盘
firm's emblem 行徽
firmware n. 固件(指固化软件的一种,亦称"半软体")
first a. 第一的;为首的;首要的;开始的;基本的
first aid 急救
First Amendment 美国联邦宪法第一修正案(即保证公民有言论、出版、集会、宗教、信仰的自由和请愿权的条款)
First Amendment Absolutism 美国联邦宪法第一修正案绝对论者(主要指首席大法官 Hugo Lafayette Black)
First Amendment freedoms 美国联邦宪法

第一修正案:自由(指第一修正案条款:"国会不得制定关于下列事项的法律:确定宗教或禁止信仰自由;剥夺人民言论或出版的自由;剥夺人民和平集会及向政府请愿的权利。")

first among equals (首相为内阁第一人)地位与其他阁员相当

first among unequals (首相为内阁第一人)地位高于其他阁员

first appeal 第二审;第一次上诉

first appointment 首任(职)

first appropriationist 先来先得[德国法学者 Grunebaum J. D. 将各家对财产权之论述分为三派:先占学派、追求人格圆满(natural perfection)之至善学派以及法政建制(the Conventionalist)之约定学派,同一学派之见解亦未必相同]

first approximation 初步近似值

first authentic copy (判决书,公证书的)第一副本

first ballot 第一轮(次)投票

first carrier 第一承运人

first cause 根源;主要原因

first chamber (荷兰议会的)一院

first charge 主要指控

first (second) class misdemeanant (英)一级(二级)轻刑犯[按英国监狱法,在郡、市、自治市监狱中判有轻罪而未判苦役的罪犯分为两个等级:即一级轻刑犯和二级轻刑犯,一级轻刑犯要受一级监禁(first division),二级轻刑犯受二级监禁]

first class paper 第一级文件;头等证券

first class wife 第一房妻子

First Commoner (英)下议院议长

First Continental Congress (美)第一次大陆会议(指1774年9月5日在费城召开的殖民地代表参加的第一次代表大会,除佐治亚州外,12个殖民地55名代表参加,通过"权利宣言"和一些抵制英货的议案)

first cost (利息等未计入的)原始成本

first Court of Appeal 二审上诉审法院

first cousin 第一代嫡堂(或表)兄弟姐妹

first crime 初犯

first day (一周的第一天)星期日

First Decennial (美)《第一个十年判决摘要汇编》(指西方出版公司出版的自1897年至1906年的判决摘要汇编)

first degree murder (美)一等(级)谋杀罪(指有谋杀故意,情节特别严重者。见 second degree murder)

first degree of imprisonment for a time 一等有期徒刑

first degree of relationship 一亲等

first devisee (按遗嘱)优先接受遗赠不动产者(见 next devisee)

first difficulties 首要的难题

first (second) division (英)一级(二级)监禁(指监狱中的监禁等级。见 first class misdemeanant)

first draft 初选

first election 初选

first federal judges 第一批联邦法官

first fruits (古)(封建法)1.直接分封保有土地的封臣去世后,其继承人必须向国王上缴一年的土地收益方可继承此地产。亦称 primer saizin 2.(英)(宗教法)神职人员[任职后第一年的全部圣俸(benefice)通过领圣俸者(incumbent)上交给教皇(Pope)。在与罗马破裂之后,则此圣俸献给国王。这项收入后来被"安妮女王基金会"(Queen Anne's Bounty)作为增加贫困神职人员圣俸的基金。此词有时可写成 firstfruit,亦称 primitae; primitive; annates; annats; Queen Anne's Bounty]

first hall 第一厅;第一室;(法院)第一庭

first hand knowledge 第一手的直接知识,第一手材料

first hearing 第一审

first heir 第一继承人

First House (美)众议院

first impression case 未有先例的诉讼事件

first instance 第一审,初审

First Instance (Court) 初审法院

first instance jurisdiction 一审管辖(权),初审管辖(权);一审审判(权)

First International 第一国际

first level of relationship 一亲等,亲等的第一顺序

first lien 优先留置权

first line of collaterals 一等旁系亲属

first listed plaintiff 第一被告
first marriage 初婚
First Monday in October 《十月的第一个星期一》(美国 Jerome Lawrence 和 Robert E. Lee 于 1978 年合写的剧本,它是按照美国最高法院每年首次开庭期的第一天这个日子命名的,内容是写一位被任命为高级法官的妇女)
first mortgage 优先抵押(权);首次抵押
first name 名字
first obligation 优先债务;首要责任
first offence 初犯;第一次犯罪
first offender 初犯者
first option 第一次选择权(指城市土地保有权人意欲出让时其亲属有首先收回的权利)
first papers (要求加入国籍的)初步申请书
First Peace Treaty 第一个和平条约[指 3000 年前,古埃及国王拉美西斯(Ramses)和赫梯族国王子哈吐西里斯(Hattusilis)之间订立的条约,表示决心建立"美好善意的和平和真挚的情谊"]
First President (法)首席院长(法国巴黎高等法院院长)
First Principles of Law 法学通论
first priority 绝对优先权
first publication 首次出版(指按许多国家版权法及两个版权国际公约获得"作品国籍"的前提);初版
first reading (通过议案时的)首读(又译:"一读",指法案印成后在议会第一次正式宣读)
first registration tax 首次登记税
First Report on Exemption Clauses in Contract (英)合同中免责条款的立法报告
first restatement 第一次重申
first restricted indorsee 第一限制背书人
First Sale Doctrine 首次销售说
first secretary of state 第一国务大臣
first selectman (美)某些地区的行政长官(如市长)
first solvent of individualism in our law 我们法律中个人主义的第一个助溶剂
first state arbiter 首席公断人

first ten amendments (美)前十个修正案(指美国联邦宪法前十个修正案,亦即 Bill of Rights "权利宣言",1798 年通过)
first termer 初次服刑者
first time selling 初次销售
first trial session 第一次审理开庭期
First World 第一世界
first-born n. 长子,长女
first-class paper 头等证券
first-degree a. 最低级的,最轻的;最高级的,一等的,最严重的
first-degree homicide 一等杀人罪,严重的杀人罪
first-in first-out 先进先出(法)
first-in-time priority 第一位的优先权
first-mentioned defendant 第一被告
first-past-the-post system 以简单多数获胜
first-person effect (媒体对)自己的影响
firsthand a. (来源,资料等的)第一手的,原始的,直接的
firsthand evidence 第一手证据
firsthand investigation 直接调查
firsthand investigation 直接调查,实地调查
firsthand material (或 data) 第一手材料,原始资料
fisc (= fisk) n. 国库,财库,金库;(古罗马)王室财库
fiscal n./a. 1.(苏格兰和某些欧洲国家的)地方检察官 2.印花税票 3.国库收入/国库的;国库岁入的;财政的
fiscal and monetary policy 财政与货币(金融)政策
fiscal and monetary powers 财政与货币权[指根据美国联邦宪法第 1 条第 8 款授权国会"规定并征服税金、捐税、关税和其他赋税,用以偿付国债并为合众国防御和全民福利提供经费",并按条款规定:不能对出口征收关税;依据各州人口分摊直接税;所有的关税,进口税以及消费税要全国统一。1985 年美国联邦最高法院认为按照《1894 年所得税法》(the Income Tax Act of 1894) 的规定没有分摊的直接税。因其来自不动产和个人财产收入征税,所

以国会有权无需分摊即可征收所得税。美国联邦宪法第十六修正案通过。联邦宪法第1条第8款授权国会借贷资金,制造钱币并调整其价值。同时国会还有权发放联邦国库券作为法定货币]

fiscal attorney (苏格兰)检察官
fiscal autonomy 财政自主权
fiscal court 财政法庭(院)
fiscal deficit 财政赤字
fiscal immunities 免除印花税
fiscal instruments 财政手段
fiscal levy 财政税收
fiscal officer (美)财务官员(指州或县的财务管理官员,负责征收和分配公共资金,这些官员包括财务主管,其职责为监管私法人或商业的财务)
fiscal or monetary action 财政或金融措施
fiscal period 纳税期;会计期
fiscal reserve 财政储备金
fiscal stamp (=revenue stamp) 印花税票
fiscal subsidies 财政补贴
fiscal year 财政年度,会计年度,营业年度
fiscus 国库
fisheries jurisdiction cases 渔业管辖权案
fisheries zone(或 waters) (国际法)渔区(或称专属渔区)
Fishermen's Protections Act of 1967 《渔民保护法》(1967)
fishery n. 捕鱼;捕鱼权;渔业,水产业;渔场
Fishery Affairs Chamber 渔业事务法庭
fishery law 捕鱼法
fishery licence 渔业许可证
fishing n. 钓鱼,捕鱼;渔业;捕鱼权
fishing entity 渔业实体
fishing expedition 1.审前盘问(或调查) 2.(为诬陷他人或搜集新闻材料而进行的)非法摸底调查;手段不当的调查
fishing port district 渔港区
Fishing Port Law 渔港法
fishing resources 渔业资源
fishing trip 超越诉讼范围的调查,非法手段的调查(见 fishing expedition)
fist n./v. 拳头;抓住;手迹,笔迹,手;(印刷品上)指标,见号/拳打;紧紧握住

fit v./n. (使)适合;(使)符合;(使)配合;(使)适应/适合,配合,适应(in with)
fitness n. 恰当,适当;合理;健康
fitness for a particular purpose (商品适用性的)默示担保
fitting description 相称的说明;适合的说明
Five Anti Campaign (中)五反运动
Five Interested Parties "五方利益集团"[指美国、欧共体、巴西和印度(代表 G-20)以及澳大利亚(代表凯恩斯集团)]
five principle of peaceful coexistence 和平共处五项原则(由中国政府最早于1954年1月8日在中印谈判中提出,经印度政府同意,同年6月29日周恩来总理访问缅甸又得到缅甸总理同意,而在中印、中缅的联合声明中确认下来的"互相尊重领土主权、互不侵犯、互不干涉内政、平等互惠、和平共处"五项原则。此原则已得到各国普遍确认。见"mutual respect for sovereignty and territorial integrity…"词条)
Five-power Constitution (中史)《五权宪法》(指孙中山先生倡导的立法、行政、司法、考试、监察五权分立原则)
five-year privilege 五年特权(指伯尔尼公约1971年文本术语,意指原公约成员国有权在5年之内不批准公约1971年文本的行政条款)
fix v. 1.安置;安装 2.决定(时,日;价格);固定 3.归罪,归咎,确定(责任) 4.惩罚,处罚 5.(美)贿赂,收买 6.选择 7.修理,修补
fix a jury 买通陪审团,贿赂陪审团
fix the venue 指定审判地点,决定审判地点
fixation n. 固定;(底片等的)定影,定相(见 fixed work)
fixed a. 固定的,确定的,不变的;固执的
fixed assets 固定资产
fixed bail 固定保释金
fixed bill 定期票据
fixed by law 法律规定
fixed capital 固定资本
fixed capital funds 固定资金
fixed charge 固定支出;固定负担(责任);固定担保
fixed condemnation 确定裁判;宣告有罪

fixed date 指定日期
fixed date of judg(e)ment 判决确定日
fixed deposit 定期存款
fixed duty 固定税
fixed fact 已确定的事实
fixed income 固定收入
fixed interest 固定利息
fixed investment trust 固定性投资信托
fixed labo(u)r norm 劳动定额
fixed law 定律
fixed liabilities 固定债务(额)
fixed loan secured 定期抵押贷款,固定抵押放款
fixed opinion 成见,定见(指陪审员对于罪行或责任的偏见)
fixed par of exchange 汇兑的法定平价,汇兑的法定牌价
fixed penalty 固定刑罚;定额罚款
fixed penalty scheme 定额罚款制度
fixed pitch licence 固定摊位执照
fixed price 固定价格,定价
fixed property 不动产,固定财产
fixed rate (of exchange) 固定汇率
Fixed Rules 固定法规,固定法则
fixed share capital 固定的股份资本
fixed tangible assets 固定有形资产
fixed term 固定期限,定期
fixed work 固定作品(指根据版权法,一部新的作品必须予以"固定"或"确立",然后进行保护,即使其具有稳定性和有形的形式,写在纸上或记录在胶卷上的也须加以固定)
fixed-interest securities 固定利息债券
fixed-term imprisonment 有期徒刑
fixed-term insurance 定期保险
fixed-term interest 定期利息
fixed-term sentence 有期徒刑判决
fixer n. 1.(美)向警察行贿或说情以求释放犯人者;向官方行贿(或疏通)者 2.(美)毒品贩 3.定影剂 4.修车工,保全工
fixture n. 1.(不动产的固定)附着物;固定物;附属装置 2.定期放款,定期存款
flag n. 旗帜;船籍
flag country 船旗国
flag desecration 亵渎国旗(在美国,公然侮辱国旗的行为如毁烧、玷污等,在宪法上受到言论自由的保护)
flag of truce 白旗,投降旗,休战旗
flagellate v. 鞭笞,鞭打
flagellation n. 鞭笞,鞭打
flagrancy n. 罪恶昭彰,明目张胆,臭名远扬
flagrant a. 公然的,罪恶昭彰的;现行的;臭名远扬的
flagrant and wanton 明目张胆,蛮横无理
flagrant crime 大罪;现行罪
flagrant delict 现行犯
flagrant offence 大罪,重罪;现行罪
flagrant violation 公然侵犯
flagrante delicto 犯罪当场;现行犯;正在犯罪
flam n. 诡计,欺骗,谎话,胡扯
flamen n. (古罗马)祭司
flash n. (总称)盗贼(的黑话)
(the) flash gentry 盗贼们,流氓们
flash-house n. 犯罪巢穴(盗贼、无赖及卖淫之巢穴)
flat n./a. (楼房的)一层;(英)(在同一层楼上的)一套房间;(复)公寓;断然的;一律的;(价格等)无涨落的;(市场)萧条的
flat commission 统一手续费
flat denial 完全否认
flat money 法定货币
flat rate 统一收费率;统售价格
flat tax (1952年)固定统一税,统一税率税[指不管计税依据(tax base)总额(amount),其税率保持固定的一项税种。绝大多数营业税均属固定统一税。亦称 proportional tax。见 progressive tax; regressive tax]
flaw n./v. 缺点,瑕疵;(使证件,程序等无效的)缺陷;裂缝/使破裂,使无效,使有瑕疵
fledg(e)ling n. 初出茅庐的人,尚缺乏经验者
fledgling central government 初出茅庐的(缺乏经验的)中央政府
fledgling law school 刚创立的法学院
flee v. 1.逃走(from),逃出(from) 2.损失,消散 3.抛弃;脱离
flee and hide 逃避,窜逃;消失,消散

flee from justice 逃出法网,畏罪潜逃,逃避审判
flee hither and thither 流窜
fleeceable a. 易受欺诈的
fleet n./v. 舰队(尤指有固定活动区的舰队);(汽)车队;河湾;(大写)佛里特监狱(指在英国伦敦的一个扣押欠债人的监狱,已于1842年关闭)/掠过,飞逝,腾飞
fleet policy 总括保险单
Fleet Street 舰队街(指英国伦敦的一条街,主要新闻报馆都坐落于这条街上,故又名新闻厅)
Fleet-Books n. 佛里特监狱书(指1686—1754年在伦敦佛里特监狱里秘密结婚的记录簿籍;亦称 Fleet-Registers)
Fleet-Registers n. 见 Fleet-Books
flemeswite 占有逃亡者的财物
Flemish n./a. 佛兰芒语;佛兰芒人/佛兰芒语的;佛兰芒人的
flesh wound 皮肉之伤,轻伤
flexibility of law 法律的灵活性
flexible a. 柔韧的,易弯曲的;可变通的,灵活的,有伸缩性的
flexible and dynamic medium 灵活有力的媒体
flexible approach 灵活方式
flexible constitution 弹性宪法;可修改的宪法
flexible measures 弹性措施;伸缩性措施
flexible rate (of exchange) 伸缩性汇率,可变动的汇率
flight n. 逃跑,溃退;(资金等的)外逃;抽逃;飞行
flight of thought 思维奔逸(指思维障碍的一种,思维障碍的种类甚多,大致可分为思维表达和思维内容障碍两大类。思维奔逸属于一种思维表达障碍。它表现思维的联想过快,思维量增加,思维内容丰富。患者表现话多,语速滔滔不绝,口若悬河,出口成章,句子之间常有音联、意联,话题易随环境改变而转移,即随境转移,让病患者沉默或充当听众均难办到。见 thought of insertion)
flightism n. 逃跑主义
flimflam n. 欺骗,诈骗;不正当行为;胡言乱语
flimsy a. 无价值的,不足信的;易损的,轻薄的
flimsy evidence 不可靠证据,无价值证据
flirt v. 玩弄,挑逗;不认真考虑
flirt with 调戏(妇女),调情,卖俏
float n. (计划的)付诸实行;(票据等的)流通;(谣言)传播;漂浮物
float capital 流动资本
floatage n. 漂浮物;漂浮物占有权;(吃水部分以上的)船身
floatation n. 漂浮,(船的)下水,(企业等)筹资开办,创立,(为创办企业)筹款
floater n. 1.(债券的)发行人;(公司的)发起人;流动证券;(有保险的)证券 2.漂浮物;浮尸 3.游民;流动工,临时工
floating a. 流动的;浮动的;不固定的;漂浮的
floating assets 流动资产
floating capital 流动资本;游资
floating charge 浮动抵押;浮动担保
floating currency 浮动货币
floating debt 短期债务;流动债务
floating island 浮动岛屿
floating lien 浮动留置权
floating loan 流动贷款
floating money 流动资金
floating policy 流动保险单;总保单
floating population 流动人口
floating prison 流动监狱
floating rate (of exchange) 浮动汇率
floating securities 流动证券
floating vote 流动票
floating voters 游离选民,流动投票人
floating wage 浮动工资
flogging n. 鞭打刑,笞刑
(the) floodgate argument 洪水之门理论(指英美法中商业机会利益法律保护的界限与内部损害商业机会的场合的基本依据——洪水之门理论。无论从单个侵权行为人的利益出发,还是为了自身生存的愿望,不确定的责任风险对注意范围的界定是正当的,侵权行为法都必须将那些过于"遥远"的利益损害从其体系中排除出去)

flooding n. 决水(罪)
floor (18世纪)1.(议会法)会议席[指大厅的部分审议机关的成员开会讨论问题并进行业务商谈,特别是在立法机关中心会议的地方,即立法成员的席位(sit)处理业务之处。此地不同于长廊(galleries)、走廊(corridor)或议会走廊(lobbies)⟨the senate floor⟩(参议员席),⟨nominations from the floor⟩(在议会席提名)。见 assignment of the floor; claim the floor; have the floor; obtain the floor; on the floor; privilege of the floor] 2.法庭上法官席与律师工作台之间的法庭部分 3.(股票)交易区,指股票和商品买卖交易地区⟨the broken placed his buy order with the trader on the floor of NYSE⟩(经纪人在纽约股票交易所的交易区将买单交给了交易人) 4.最低标准、底价、最低限价[指最低限制,如法律上允许的最低利率或根据合同的最少允许的支付(薪金)⟨the floor for that position is $25000 per year⟩(那个岗位的最低工薪为年金 25000 美元)]
floor amendment 见 amendment ③
floor approval in each House 获得两院的批准
floor broker (交易所内代客买卖的)场内经纪人;委任经纪人
floor leader (资产阶级议会中的)党派头目
floor of the court 法庭中的律师席;诉讼人席位
floor of the wound 创(伤)底,伤底
floor tax (美)最低标准税(指对储存于货栈的酒类饮料所课之税)
floppy disk 软盘
Florida Vacation Plan and Timesharing Act (美)佛罗里达州分时度假法
flotsam n. 漂流的船货(即失事船中漂出的货物或船只残骸)
flow n./v. 流动;流动物;流量;(资源等)丰富;(人车等)川流不息/流动;来自,是……结果;涌出
flow chart 流程图
flow from 来自,产生
flow of capital 资本的流动

fluctuating body 不稳定的主体
fluctuation n. 波动,涨落,起伏;动摇,不稳定
fluctuation of price 物价波动
fluid a. 流动的,流体的;不固定的;易变的
fluid capital 流动资金(本)
fluid population 流动人口
fluvial domain 领河
fly-by-night n. (美)夜逃的负债者;无信用的借债人;喜欢夜间外出的人
flying squad 机动警察(队),警察追捕队
FOB shipping point 起运点交货价
focal points 焦点
focus n./v. 焦点,注意中心;焦距/使聚焦,使注视;集中
focus on 关注,聚焦于
foedus (古罗马)盟约;(国际法)条约;合约,利息;有息贷款
foenus nauticum (大陆法)航海的或海上的权益(nautical or maritime interest)(指承担危险航行所收取的特高利益,亦称 usura maritima。见 nauticum fenus)
foeticide (=feticide) n. 堕胎(罪)
foetus n. 胎儿
fog n. 雾;大雾(二级能见度);迷惑,困惑
foist v. 骗售(假货,劣货);私自添加;把……强加于
folc-mote (=folk-mote, 或 folc-gemote) n. (英)平民大会(指盎格鲁-撒克逊时期,各州和各市处理司法和立法事务的人民集会)
folio n. 一定字数;单位字数;(法律文件的)一页
folk literature 民俗文学;民间文学
folk theorems 无名氏定理(指理解无限重复博弈的非常核心的定理)
folkland (=folc-land) n. (盎格鲁-撒克逊法的)依习惯法占有的土地,习惯土地所有制
folkways n. 社会习俗,传统习俗;民风
follo 终局判决(西班牙文)
follow v. 按照,遵奉;跟随,继续;贯彻;仿效,从事(职业等);做……后继人
follow from 是根据……得出来的;是从……得出来的

follow（或 practice）the law 当（做）律师；法律解决，诉讼
follow the robe 当（做）律师
follow the track 跟踪
follow the trust property 尾追信托财产（权）
follow up 追查，追向，追究
follow-up investment 后续资本
follower n. 追随者，拥护者，信徒，侍从；（契据的）附页
following assets （英）追索信托财产（衡平法的一项重要原则）
fondness n. 喜爱，嗜好
fons juris 见 source of law
Food and Agricultural Organization （联合国）粮农组织
food-poisoning n. 食物中毒
fool n. 愚人，傻子，白痴，莽汉；受愚弄的人
foolocracy n. 愚人统治；愚人统治集团
foot a bill 付账
foot of the fine （历史上）普通法上（协议诉讼）转让财产证书（fine of conveyance）的第 15 节是结尾部分（这部分包括整个事件的当事人姓名、诉讼时间、地点、见证人等，亦称 chirography。见 fine 1）
footprint n. 足印；脚印；鞋印
footprint identification 足印鉴定
for prep. 因为，为了，对于
for a time 一度，暂时
for all 尽管
for account of （1826 年）1.入……的账（指在票据或汇票背书时，用以指明收款人的程序用语）2.为……代销
for any sake 无论如何
for anything 无论如何
for cause 因可靠的法律上的理由
for coordinated or consolidated pretrial proceedings 以协调或统一审前程序
for future reference 备查
for sake of justice 为了公正的原因，为了公平之故
for hire 出租
for hire or reward 租用受酬，收取租金或酬劳（一般指收取旅客或货物承运人的费用）

for instance 例如
for life 终身
for one term 一届任期
for one thing 首先
for procedural reason 由于程序上的理由
for reference 备案
for the alienation of the other's affections （配偶一方）移情他人
for the Court （美）代表法庭，代表联邦最高法院（法庭和多数大法官）写裁决（意见）书
for the master 代船长
for the most part 就绝大部分而言；在极大程度上；多半
for the peace, order and good government 为了治安、秩序和有效治理
for the purpose of profit 以营利为目的
for the purpose of speculation 以投机买卖为目的；以承担风险为目的
for the record （登记）备案
for the satisfaction of one's doubts 为消除某人的怀疑
for value 具备合法代价，有偿的
for-profit organization 营利组织
fora n. (forum 的复数形式) 论坛，讨论；法庭
forbear v. 权利的暂不行使；克制，忍耐，宽容
forbearance n. 债务偿还期的延展；忍耐，宽容，克制
forbid v. 不许，禁止；阻止；妨碍
forbid bail 禁止保释
forbidden a. 被禁止的
forbidden degrees 禁止通婚的亲等
forbidden fruits 违禁收益
forbidden objects 违禁物品
forbidden under penalty of death 违者处以死刑
forbidding act 禁止行为
force n./v. 1.武力，暴力；效力；约束力 2.权力，强力，势力，压力；强制力 3.(总称)警察(the)；(复)军队；威胁；强迫，迫使；强加
force and arms 暴力
force auction 强行拍卖
force duty room 警员值班室

force entrance 闯入,闯进(民宅)
force establishment 警队编制
force from without 外界的强力
force harlotry 强迫卖淫
force into marriage 强迫成婚,逼婚
force *majeure* 不可抗力
force of bind 约束力
force of defense 防御实力
force of habit 习惯势力
force of law 法的效力(又译:法律效力)
force of public opinion 舆论压力
force of state 国家权力
force upon 强使接受,强加给
forced a. 强制的;法定的;强迫的,被迫的;用力的,竭力的;勉强的,牵强附会的
forced contract 强制性合同(契约),法定合同(契约)
forced heirs 特留份继承人;法定继承人
forced heirship 特留份继承权,法定继承权
forced insurance 强制保险
forced labo(u)r 强制(迫)劳动
forced labo(u)r farm 劳改农场
forced loans (英)强制借贷(指未经议会同意情况下筹款的方法)
forced marriage 强迫婚姻,包办婚姻
forced sale 强制出售,强行出售[指①见 executive sale;②因经济处于困境或债权人的起诉债务人急切出售(hurried sale)。见 voluntary sale]
forced share (继承的)强制份,特留份
forced widowhood 强迫守寡
forced withdrawal 强迫离职
forcible a. 强制的,强迫的;有势力的,用暴力的;有说服力的
forcible detainer 强行(继续)占有他人土地者;强行非法占有者
forcible entry 侵入家宅;非法侵入;强行进入他人住宅(罪)
forcible execution 强制执行
Forcible extraction of blood sample 强制抽血样
forcible felony 暴力性重罪
forcible invasion 武力侵犯
forcible rape 强奸(罪)

forcible repatriation 强制遣返
forcible resistance 强力抗拒
forcible speech 令人信服的讲话
forcing up price 哄抬物价
fore a. 先前的,预先的(常用做前缀)
fore-hand rent 预付租金
fore-mentioned a. 上述的,上面提到的
foreclose v. 取消回赎权(指取消抵押人抵押品的赎回权);排斥,排除,阻挡;预先了解,预先处理
foreclose the mortgage 了结抵押(指抵押权人依规定拍卖抵押标的物,以所得价金清偿债务)
foreclosed property (1984年4月12日)取消回赎权财产
foreclosure n. 取消(抵押)回赎权(手续)
foreclosure decree 取消抵押品赎回权令
foreclosure property 拍卖抵押物
foreclosure sale 抵押期满拍卖
foredated a. 倒填日期的
foredated cheque 倒填日期的支票(指支票上的出票日期早于实际出票日期)
foregift n. (英)租赁小费
forego (= forgo) vt. 走在……之前,发生……之前;摒弃;拒绝
foregoing counts 上述理由
foregone conclusion 未经讨论调查就作出的决定;预料中必然的结局
foreground n. 前景,突出地位
foreign a. 外国的;涉外的;在外国的;外国产的;外地的,外省的;(美)别州的;管辖外的;法律范围外的
foreign affairs 外交事务,外交,外事
Foreign Affairs Committee (中)外事委员会(指全国人民代表大会设立的专门委员会)
foreign agency 国外代理行
foreign agent 国外代理人
foreign aid agreement 外援协定
Foreign and Commonwealth Courts (或 Tribunals) (英)域外和英联邦法院(或裁判庭)(指按英国域外裁判法庭证据法的规定,可代外国法院或裁判庭录取证据的法院或裁判庭,以及依据录取证供的条例的规定,可代英联邦各法院或各裁判所

录取证供的法院或裁判庭)
Foreign and Commonwealth Office (英)外交和联邦事务部
foreign arbitral award 外国仲裁裁决书
foreign association 外国社团
foreign attachment (英)对诉讼外债务人财产的扣押(指英国许多城市沿用的一种诉讼程序。对于非参加诉讼的第三人欠判决被告债务人的债务,法院可应原告请求就此项债务对第三人的财物进行扣押,以偿还原告债权人)(港译:诉讼外债务人物业查封)
foreign bill (of exchange) 外埠汇票,外国汇票
foreign bills payable 应付外币汇票,应付外国汇票,应付外国票据
foreign borrowing 外债
foreign capital 外资,外国资本
foreign capital challenge 外资攻势
Foreign Capital Enterprises Law (中)外资企业法
foreign capital inducement law 外资引进法
foreign capital introduction 引进外资
foreign capital M&A 外资并购
foreign case 涉外案件
foreign company (或 **corporation**) 外国公司
foreign concession 租界
foreign consulate 外国领事馆
foreign corporation 外国公司,别(或他)州公司
foreign court 外国法院
foreign currency 外国货币;外国通货
foreign debt 外债
foreign deposit 国外存款
foreign domination 外国统治
Foreign Economic and Trade Arbitration Commission of the China Council for the Promotion of International Trade (中)中国国际贸易促进委员会对外经济贸易仲裁委员会
foreign element 涉外因素
foreign enlistment (英)应募当外国兵罪
foreign exchange (17 世纪)1.国际汇兑(指以国际货币转换程序特别转换成不同国家现钞)2.外汇[指以外国货币或票据如旅行支票(traveler's checks)用于国际结算的手段]3.外汇汇率(指两种货币的比价,即以一国货币表示另一国货币的价格)
foreign exchange arrangements 外汇安排
foreign exchange broker 外汇经纪人
foreign exchange control 外汇管制,外汇管理,外汇统制
foreign exchange firm 外汇商行
foreign exchange for incidental use 临时性外汇
foreign exchange instrument 外汇票证
foreign exchange market 外汇市场
foreign exchange receipt 外汇收入
foreign exchange regulations 外汇(管理)条例
foreign exchange reserve 外汇储备
foreign exchange restrictions 外汇限制
foreign exchange transaction 外汇业务,外汇交易
foreign exchange transfers 外汇的转移
foreign general agent 国外一般代理人
foreign general average 国外共同海损(险)
foreign goods 外国货
foreign guardians 外国人的监护人
foreign household 外侨户
foreign immigrant 外国侨民;外来移民
foreign immunity 外国人的豁免权
foreign intervention 外来干涉;外国干涉
foreign investment 外国投资;国外投资
Foreign Investment Commission (中)外国投资管理委员会
foreign joint venturer 外国合营者
foreign judg(e)ments 外国判决(指经过外国法院判决的案件)
foreign jurisdiction 外国裁判权,外国管辖权;涉外管辖权,涉外审判权
foreign juristic person 外国法人
foreign jury 外地人陪审团(指来自案件起诉地管辖以外地方组成的陪审团)
foreign law 外国法
foreign lawyer 外国律师;外国法学家(见 lawyer)

foreign loan 外债
foreign minister 外交部长
foreign mission 外国使团
foreign national exemption clause 外国人特权条款
foreign nationals 外国公民,外国人
foreign offender 外籍罪犯
Foreign Office (英)外交部
foreign office certificate 外交证明书
foreign passport 外国护照
foreign owned enterprises 外资企业
foreign pay-off law (美)防止外国公司贿赂(政府官员)法(指1977年国会通过的一部联邦法律)
foreign policy 对外政策,外交政策
foreign policy decision making 外交政策决策论
foreign policy school 对外政策学派
foreign principal 外国委托人(本人)
foreign private international law rule 外国国际私法规范(规则)
foreign process 外国诉讼(程序),管辖权以外的诉讼
foreign protection 外交保护
foreign public act 外国公证行为
foreign quarantine regulations 对外检疫规定
foreign registered judg(e)ment 外国登记在案的判决
foreign related enterprises 涉外企业
foreign relations 外交关系
Foreign Relations Committee (美)外交委员会
foreign resident 外来居民;外国居民
foreign revenue 海外收入;外国税收
Foreign Sale Corporations 外国销售公司
Foreign Secretary (英)外交大臣
foreign security 外国的基金证券
foreign service officer 外交官员,外交人员,外事人员
foreign settlement 外国人居留区
foreign settlers 外侨
foreign short-term claims 国外短期债权
foreign sovereigns 外国之首,外国君主,外国统治者

foreign spy 外国间谍
foreign state 外国国家
foreign tax credit (1928年)外国税收抵免[指纳税人在外国的劳务所得在外国按其所得已经纳税,则应将其在本国(美国)应纳税额中扣除]
foreign trade 国外贸易,对外贸易
foreign trade act 对外贸易法
foreign trade arbitration 外贸仲裁
foreign trade contract 外贸合同(契约)
foreign trade deficit 外贸逆差,入超
foreign trade mark 外国商标
foreign trade multiplier 对外贸易乘数(指凯恩斯的一部教科书中,哈罗德以最简化的形式介绍了人们所熟悉的与国际收支经常项目平衡相一致的国民收入流量决定的公式,即国民收入等于国家出口量与平均进口倾向倒数的乘积)
foreign trade policy 对外贸易政策
foreign trade power 外贸权
foreign tribunal 外国法庭,在外地的法庭,外省的法庭,(美)别州的法庭
foreign-funded enterprises 外商投资企业
foreign-owned enterprises 外资企业
foreign-related cases 涉外案件
foreigner n. 外国人;陌生人;进口货,外国货;外国船
foreigner's identity card 外国人身份证
forejudge (= forjudge) v. (15世纪)1.未审问而判决;未了解事实就断定 2.剥夺 3.(由法院判决)(驱)逐出(法庭)
forejudg(e)ment n. 驱逐出法庭的判决
forelady n. 女工头,女领班
foreman (= foreperson) n. 1.陪审团主席(又译陪审长,是陪审团的发言人) 2.领班,工头
foreman of the jury 陪审长,陪审团的主席
forenotice n. 预告,预先警告
forensic a. 法庭的;属于法庭的;适于法庭的;(法庭上)辩论的
forensic arena 法庭上,法庭辩论上
forensic argument 法庭辩论
forensic chemistry 司法化学,法医化学
Forensic Conditional Release Program 司法假释程序(指1985年美国联邦假释委员

会和州假释委员会经研究并经加利福尼亚州议会批准,启动了防止患者罪犯假释后再犯罪的司法假释程序。简称 CONREP)
forensic dentistry 司法牙科学,法医牙科学
forensic detachment 法院的独立性;法庭的超然性
forensic display 法庭辩论
forensic doctor 法医
forensic eloquence 辩护律师的口才;辩论的口才
forensic expert 法庭科学专家
forensic histology 法医组织学
forensic immunology 法医免疫学
forensic medical examination of living persons 法医学上的活体检验
forensic medical examination of material evidence 法医学上的物证检验
forensic medicine 法医学
forensic oratory 法庭演说
forensic pathology 法医病理学
forensic pharmacy 法医药学
forensic physician 法医(师)
forensic psychiatry 司法精神病学,法医心理分析学
forensic science 司法科学,法庭科学
forensic science examination 法庭科学检验,法科学检验
forensic serology 法医血清学
forensic speech 法庭演讲
forensic surgery 法医外科学
forensic thanatology 法医死因学
forensic toxicology 法医毒理学
foreperson (美)陪审团团长(指依据特定法院的惯例,由陪审员选举或由法官选任的主持陪审团评议的陪审员)(亦称 presiding juror; foreman; jury chancellor)
forerunner n. 先驱者
foreseeability n. 预见说(见 proximity)
foreseeability doctrine 可预见说(又称合理预见说,系英美法系重要的因果关系理论,以损害结果的可预先性为标准来确定因果关系的有无,进而确定有无赔偿责任)
foreseeability of breach 违约的可预测性
foreseeable a. 可预见的,可预料的
foreseeable consequence of unforeseeable **intervening cause** 不可预见的介入原因引发应当预见的损害结果
foreseeable damages 可料到的损失;可预见的损害
foreseeable intervening cause 应当预见的介入原因
foreseeable loss 可预见的损失
foreshore n. 涨滩,海滩
foresight n. 先见,预见;预见的能力,深谋远虑
forest n. 森林地带,森林;(英)王室狩猎的御林
forest act 森林法
forest carbon sink 林业碳汇(指利用森林的储碳功能,通过实施造林、再造林和加强森林管理,减少毁林、保护森林和恢复森林等活动,吸收和固定大气中的二氧化碳,并按照相关规则与碳汇交易相结合的过程、活动或机制。见 Carbon Sink)
forest court 森林法庭
forest fire 森林火灾
forest law 森林法
forest prohibiting on cutting and chopping timer 禁伐林
forest ranger 林警,森林保护员,(中)护林员
forest used for firewood and charcoal 薪炭林
forestall v. 先采取行动预防(或阻止);垄断,囤积
forestalling the market 垄断市场
forestry n. 林地;林学;林业
forestry act 森林法
forestry reserve 森林保护区
forethought n./a. 预谋,事先的考虑/预谋的,预先计划好的
forewoman n. 女陪审团主席(又译:女陪审长);女工头,女领班
foreword n. 前言,序,序言
forfeit n./v. (因犯罪、失职、违约等而)丧失(公民权利等);丧失的东西;没收物;罚金;惩罚/丧失,失去;没收;被没收,被罚
forfeit money 解约金
forfeit of civil right 公民权的被剥夺,丧失公民权

forfeitable a. 可没收的
forfeited recognizance 没收的(交法院的)保证金(或保释金,抵押金)
forfeited securities arising from loans 因债务而被没收的抵押品
forfeited stock 作废股
forfeiter n. 丧失者;受没收处分者
forfeiture n. 丧失,没收,没收物;罚金,罚款;权利的丧失;取消
forfeiture of an estate 丧失地产;没收地产
forfeiture of bail 保释权利的丧失
forfeiture of bond 不履行(保释)保证书的罚金
forfeiture of land 没收土地;丧失土地
forfeiture of marriage (被监护人)结婚(未征得监护人同意)的罚金
forfeiture of pay 停薪;罚薪
forfeiture of payment 取消付款;取消薪资
forfeiture of property 没收财产
forfeiture of shares 没收股份
forfeiture proceedings 没收程序,没收手续
forge v. 伪造;锻造;稳步前进;加速前进(ahead)
forge a signature 伪造签字
forged a. 伪造的
forged document 假造的文书;伪造的证件,伪造的单据
forged seal 伪造的印章
forged signature 假冒的签名,伪造的签名
forged stocks 伪造的股票
forger n. 伪造者;伪造犯
forgery n. 伪造;伪造罪;伪造品,赝品
forgery of document 伪造文件(罪)
forgery of household registry certificate 伪造户口证件(罪)
forgery of money note 伪造钞票(罪)
forgery of negotiable instruments 伪造票据(罪)
forgery of public document 伪造公文书(罪)
forgery of valuable securities 伪造有价证券(罪)
forgetfulness n. 疏忽,不注意;健忘
forgivable a. 可宽恕的
forgive v. 免除(债务);宽恕,原谅

forisfactura 应没收财产的罪行;罚金
forisfactus 重罪犯人;死刑犯
forisfamiliate v. 放弃对父母产业更多的继承;(使)脱离父母而独立;父母在世时使(儿女)继承产业
forisfamiliation n. 生前赠与的放弃(权);(子女)自立,解除亲权
forjudge v. 见 forejudge
Fork in the Road Provision 岔路口条款(指如果基础条约规定,当有多种争端解决途径可供选择时,外国投资者一旦选择了其中一种,就不能再选择另一种。如果条约中有"岔路口条款"规定,则外国投资者就不能援用最惠国待遇条款以第三方条约没有这样的限制为由,排除基础条约中"岔路口条款"的适用)
form n./v. 体制;形式;形状;形态;格式;方式;结构;类型;仪式;礼节/形成,产生,构成;(使)组成,建立;养成
form a conclusion (judgment) 作出结论(判断)
form a quorum 组成法定人数
form court's jurisdiction 审判地,法院辖区
form not forbidden by law 法律所不禁止的方式
form of a marriage concluded 缔结婚姻的形式,结婚形式
form of action 诉讼程序;诉讼形式(指美国民事诉讼中普通法诉辩下只有在同一令状或诉讼程式下提出的请求方可并入单一诉讼之中)
form of action system (英)诉讼格式制度(指令状制的又一称谓)
form of adoption 收养方式(形式)
form of contract 合同(契约)形式
form of conveyancing deed 财产转让契据的格式
form of delegated legislation 授权立法形式
form of detention 拘留方式
form of emancipation of a child 子女自立方式
form of execution 执行方式(形式);履行方式(形式)
form of extradition 引渡方式

form of government 政体
form of imprisonment 监禁方式
form of interpretative case-law 解释判例法形式,判例法释义方式
form of law 法律形式
form of legislation 立法形式
form of loan obligation 借贷债务的方式
form of marriage 婚姻形式;结婚方式
form of news reports 新闻报道的形式
form of obligation 债的形式
form of payment 支付方式
form of pleadings 诉状的格式
form of primitive law 原始形态法律
form of procedure 诉讼程序形式
form of proceeding 诉讼方式
form of prohibition 禁制方式;(上级法院对下级法院命令)诉讼中止程序
form of property 产权形式
form of proxy 委任书格式;委任方式
form of recommendation 建议的方式
form of state 国体,国家的形式
form of statute and regulation 制定法和行政规章的形式
form of talion 同态复仇惩罚的方式
form of treaty 条约的形式
form of trial 审判形式(方式)
form of will 立遗嘱的方式(形式)
form of wording 行文格式
form of writ 令状格式
form of written litigation 书面诉讼形式(方式)
forma pauperis 贫民诉讼(从前英国高等法院规程规定,以贫民身份诉讼者可免缴法院费用,并可得到免费状师为他出庭辩护)
formal a. 正式的,正规的;形式上的;合乎格式的;有效的
formal accusation of a crime 刑事控告书,刑事起诉书
formal act 正式行为;(复)正式法令
formal adjudication 正式裁决
formal admission 正式坦白,正式承认,正式供认
formal agreement 正式协议
formal announcement 正式公告;正式宣布

formal apology 正式道歉
formal capitalization of reserves 将准备金正式转为资本
formal charge 正式指控
formal civil law 形式民法
formal consent 正式同意
formal constraints 正式约束
formal contract 要式合同(契约)(指以当事人双方签名的书面文件为要件的合同)
formal criminal 形式犯
formal defect 形式上的瑕疵;手续上的漏洞
formal demand 正式要求
formal documents 正式文件
formal entry 正式进口
Formal Equal Opportunity (FEO) 形式上的机会平等
formal instrument 固定格式的文据
formal justice 形式上的公正,形式上的正义
formal law 形式法律
formal legal condition 正式法律状态
formal legitimacy 形式主义
formal litigation of a case 具体诉讼案件
formal mechanism 正式机制
formal meeting 正式会议
formal notice 正式通知书
formal official document 正式公文
formal organization 正规的组织
formal reciprocity 形式上的互惠
formal rationality 形式合法性,形式合理性
formal reentry 正式收回租地
formal relationship 正式关系
formal requirement 形式要件;正式要求
formal requirement for pleading 书写诉状的形式要件
formal rulemaking 正式规章的制定
formal sections 形式性条文;正式条文
formal separation 正式分居
formal source (法的)正式渊源;形式渊源;正式来源
formal source of law 法的正式渊源(又译为正式的法律渊源);法的形式渊源
formal summons 传唤通知,传票
formal validity of contract 合同(契约)的

形式效力
formal warning 正告,正式警告
formalism n. 形式主义,拘泥形式
formalism of real actions 不动产诉讼的形式主义
formalist jurisprudence 形式主义法学
formalistic a. 形式主义的
formalities in celebration 婚礼的规格;婚礼的仪式
formalities of customs 海关手续
formalities of incorporation 公司设立的手续
formalities of law 法律手续
formalities of legal transaction 法律行为的正式手续
formalities of marriage 结婚的正式手续
formalities required for the transfer of shares 股票转让的必要手续
formality (16世纪)1.礼仪,规格,格式(指虽然表面上看不重要,但实际上的小节必须认为达到法律上特定的后果)2.(古)(复)市政官员在庄严场合或时刻(solemn occasion)所穿的礼袍(Robes)3.(版权法)(常用复)法律手续,法律程序[指在获得美国版权保护之前的一种程序上的要求(procedural requirement)。法律程序(formalities)包括在作品上显示版权通告、实际出版(actual publication)、在版权局(Copyright Office)登记注册和将作品存放国会图书馆(Library of Congress)。20世纪这种方式已经不存在了(eroded),虽然当今在美国,著作登记注册仍然是侵权诉讼的先决条件(prerequisite)]
formality of consideration 约因的形式
formality of contract 合同(契约)格式
formalization of law 法律建设的正规化(形式化)
formant approach 形成方法
format n./v. 开本,版式;安排,形式/数据安排(形式)
formation n. 1.形成,组成,构成 2.形成物;构成物;结构
formation of a government 组建政府
formation of a union 合并;组成联盟
formation of contract 合同的形式

formation of federation 组成联邦
formation period of English law 英国法形成的时代
formative years 形成性格的时期
formbooks n. (美)格式文书(指可供律师咨询的法律文书和文据的样板形式,并在以后情况中用做准备类似文件的依据)
formed action 措辞方式固定的诉讼
formed design 预谋,故意
formedon n. (古英国法)追索限定继承的赠与土地权利(令)状
former a. 以前的,从前的;在前的
former adjudication 前判决,原判决,先前的裁决
former adjudication effect 先前裁判效力
former citizen 原公民,以前的公民
former convict 累犯;惯犯;前科犯
former conviction 前案判罪
former creditor 前债权人
former crime 原犯;原罪
former decision 原判
former jeopardy (=double jeopardy)
former marriage 前婚(初婚)
former office 前任职务
former owner 原所有权人
former ownership 原所有权
former proceedings 以前的诉讼,前诉
former proof 前证,以往的证明
former recovery 回复
former testimony 以前的证言
formerly known as 以前被认为是
formless a. 不定型的,无形状的,无定形的
formless contract 不定型合同(契约),非要式合同(契约)
forms and formulas of official documents 公文程式
forms of action 诉讼形式(指以前有关法庭的专门性、技术性的各种诉讼形式。若法律问题不适合这些条条框框,如不按照要求赔偿违约所造成的损失的诉讼、请求返还扣留物的诉讼、收回不动产的诉讼、追回原物之诉、侵害之诉、追索非法占用的诉讼等形式要求,则此法律问题不得提交法庭)
forms of evidence 证据的形式

forms of law 法的形式（常指法的渊源）。各个时期各种法的形式在不同的社会中的重要性各不相同。罗马法中法的形式有立法、法学家的咨询意见和论述。英美法系法的形式有立法、司法裁判、判例、协定、及权威著作等。大陆法系法的形式有立法、有权威的解释和法学著作,等等)

formula （17世纪）1.（罗马法）程式诉讼［指由裁判官（praetor）准备书面文件并交给审理事实的承审员（judex），该文件确认已被审理的系争点（issue）和由承审员所作的判决。这种程式诉讼是以裁判官在其法令（edict）中用公式表达的示范答辩申请（model plea）为基础的,并由裁判官或民事诉讼的其他地方司法官员（magistrates）改编（或改写）,让承审官员有些特权或优势（benefit）。承审员已经进行发布（issue）。这些示范答辩申请已经改写以适应案件的情节。程式诉讼通常包括：①请求的原因（*demonstratio*），其中原告提出权利主张的事实依据；②原告的请求（*intentio*），其中原告提出针对被告的诉讼救济要求；③判决要旨（*condemnatio*），其中主审司法官判决（通常支付原告一笔款项）或免除被告债务。（复数）*formulae*, 亦称 *verba concepta*］2. 普通法上的诉答程序,司法程序中通常使用的设定形式

formula instruction 程式化指示（指向陪审团作出的与案件有关的法律具体说明,指示陪审团在特定事实成立时应作出有利于原告或被告的裁断)（见 jury instructions)

formula of right 权利公式（萨维尼,历史法学派奠基人,把康德的权利公式变成一种法律)

formula rationality 形式理性,形式合理［指分析法学的传统观点,它从一个主权出发；这个主权以规则的形式发出命令,并且对不按"它的旨意"适用这些规则者施加制裁。韦伯把这称做西方法律的"形式合理"或"逻辑形式主义"（logical formalism)］

formulae n. 1.（法律文件、礼节、宗教等）惯用的语言程式；规程；准则；方案2.处方；配方；（罗马法）程式诉讼,诉讼中一种程式化语句

formulary resemblance 刻板的相似,极相似

formulary system （罗马法）语言程式（诉讼）制度

formulate v. 系统阐述；用公式表达；制定

formulate manner 公式化的态度,公式化的方式

formulating *legis actiones* 诉讼惯用的语言程式

formulation n. 制定,阐述,以公式表示

formulation of policy 政策的制定

formulism n. 公式主义

fornicate v. （一方未婚或双方均未婚者之间）私通

fornication n. （一方未婚或双方均未婚者之间的）私通

fornication laws （美）私通法规（它规定：如果私通的一方已婚,通常称已婚者犯通奸罪；而在有些州,只要女方已婚,则双方均犯有通奸罪)

fornication with an underage girl 奸淫幼女

fornicator n. 私通者,通奸者

fornix 妓院；私通（常指男女双方或一方未婚者而言）；宿娼；乱伦

forsake v. 遗弃,抛弃；摒弃

forswear v. 发誓抛弃；发誓否认；发伪誓；作伪证

forswear oneself 发伪誓,作伪证

forsworn a. 发了假誓的,作了伪证的

forthcoming a. 即将举行的,即将发生的

forthwith n. （美俚）必须立即执行的命令

forthwith paid 立即支付,立即付款

fortified port 军港

fortify v. 增强（体力,结构等）；设防于；使坚决

fortuitous a. 偶然的,偶然发生的；幸运的,意外的

fortuitous accident 意外事故

fortuitous causal relationship 偶然因果关系

fortuitous collision （船舶的）意外碰撞

fortuitous connection 偶然联系

fortuitous event 意外情况,意外事件

fortuna 命运；埋藏物

fortune n. 命运;好运;财产,大量财产
fortune-teller n. 用算命来欺诈的人(指用难以了解的技术、方法等进行欺骗的人);占卜者
forum n. 1.讨论会,专题讨论;公共论坛 2.法庭,诉讼地,管辖地 3.(古罗马)广场(或市场)
forum *actus* 行为发生地法院
forum *conscientiae* 良心法庭
forum *contentiosum* 一般法院
forum *contractus* 合同(契约)诉讼管辖地;立约地法院
forum *conveniens* 便于审理的法院;便于诉讼的司法区
forum court 诉讼法院
forum *domestium* 处理组织内部事务法庭
forum *domicilii* 住所地法院
forum *locus delicte* 不法行为所在地法院
forum no competens 无权法院原则[其为17世纪苏格兰法律中一项原则,不方便法院(forum non-convenience)的概念即由此而来,被称为无管辖权法院,其目的在于减少以扣押财产作为行使管辖权的依据引起的麻烦。20世纪初美国学者开始在理论上完整地进行总结和探讨,以后,英、加、澳等国法院也接受这一理论,并在司法实践中不同程度地采用这一原则处理相关案件]
forum non competence 非管辖法院(通常指在缺乏管辖权的情况下,承担"不方便法院"所移送的国际民事诉讼案件。见 forum non convenience)
forum of the harm 侵权地法院标准
forum non convenience **forum non** *conveniens* 不方便法院(指国际民事诉讼法中的"不方便法院"原则,即指一国法院根据其国内法或有关国际条约的规定,对国际民事案件有管辖权。但以当事人与诉因关系以及当事人、证人、律师或法院的便利或花费等角度来看,审理该案极不方便,而由外国法院审理更为适当。此原则最早出现在美国及苏格兰法院,亦称法院所在地不当)
forum *originis* 出生地法院
forum regis actum 行为地王室法院

forum *rei* 立案法庭;被告住所地法院(或诉争事物所在地)法院
forum *rei gestae* 行为所在地法院
forum *rei sitae* 诉争物所在地法院
forum shifting 场所转移
forum shopping 一方为自己利益挑选起诉法院,竞择法院,选择法院
forum state 诉讼地所在州,审判地所在州
forum state's interest in adjudicating the dispute 诉讼地州在审判这一纠纷中的利益
forum's long-arm statute 审判地州长臂法规
forum's laws 诉讼地法规
forward n./v./a. 期货/促进;发送(货物等);转递(信件等)/期货的;预约的;进步的,过激的;唐突的,动辄就……的;向前的;前部的;早熟的
forward (foreign) exchange 远期外汇
forward business 期货交易
forward buying 预购
forward contract 远期合同(契约),预约
forward dealing in securities 远期证券交易
forward delivery 远期交货,将来交货
forward policy 进步政策
forward price 期货价格,远期价
forwarded good 运送的货物
forwarder n. 交付人;运输代理人,转运商;报关行
forwarder MTO (multi-modal transport operator) 多式联运代理人
forwarder's receipt 运输商收据,转运商收据
forwarding a. 发送的,寄发的;运输的
forwarding agency 承揽运送,运输业
forwarding agent 货运承揽行,货运代理人,货物转运人[指①见 freight forwarder。②将小批量货物集中安排为整车货物装运,从运费率差价中获得利益的转运商]
forwarding agent's contract 承揽运送合同(契约),运输代理合同(契约)
forwarding agent's receipt 转运公司收据
forwarding contractor 承揽运送业;承揽运输人
forza fisica (意)物理力(见 *ente di ragione*)

forza morale (意)精神力(见 *ente di ragione*)
foster n./v. 养育,抚养/培育,培养,鼓励,扶养
foster care (1876年)1.领养,照管;照顾[指联邦为儿童福利规划提供基金,该规划对于通过法院裁决令(court decree)给予脱离其双亲或监护人关照的受虐待儿童以及由于家庭危机(family crisis)其父母安排由州临时照管自愿来的儿童实质性的照顾。参见《美国注释法典》第42标题卷第670—679a节)。州福利机关挑选、培训、监管并对这些作为领养父母(foster parents)的服务给予工资报酬]2.照顾区域(指有关适应参与这一类型福利规划的儿童需要的社会服务区域)
foster care drift 领养照管的放任自流[指在儿童被安排于领养照管的制度之中,处于法律的过渡(legal limbo)阶段,孩子们未与其父母在一起,或未被收养或未被安排在永久性的家中。许多年来他们在处于发育阶段的情况下所发生的这种放任自流现象。1997年通过的《收养和安全家庭法》帮助纠正了这个问题。见 Adoption and Safe Families Act]
foster child (12世纪)收养子女,收养的儿童[指照管和培育均委托给除孩子的生身父母或养父母以外的一个机构的成人来承担。收养的孩子可以接受由某人(通常为祖父母、其他的亲戚或邻居)给予非正式且自愿的照管。该人与孩子父母或父母代理人签订一项协议,作为对孩子的必要保护。更为正式的是:孩子即可成为联邦、州收养照管规划(federal-state foster-care program)的一部分。按该规划,对孩子进行识别、培养并支付对孩子提供家庭般关照的管理人的工薪。这些孩子有的无亲生父母,有的不能与其亲生父母在一起。亦称(古)fosterling。见 foster parent]
foster daughter 养女
foster daughter-in-law (中)童养媳
foster family 寄养家庭,收养的家庭
foster father 养父
foster home 照顾孤儿、不良儿童或精神病人的家庭(或场所)
foster home for delinquent children 违法儿童管教所
foster mother 养母
foster parent (17世纪)养父母,领养的父母[指对孤儿或受虐待的儿童、无人养育的孩子进行照管、培育的人,尽管他们之间无血缘或法律关系(blood ties or legal ties),通常是在一个机构的监督和指导下进行监督培育工作,以便获得补偿和福利。领养的父母有时是短期对孩子扶养、培育直到孩子被合法收养。见 foster care; foster child]
foster son 养子
foster-brother n. 奶兄弟,义兄弟
foster-children n. 养子女
foster-ling 养子(女)
foster-parent (foster parent) n. 寄父母
foster-parents n. 养父母
foster-sister n. 奶姐妹;义姐妹
fosterage n. 养育,寄养;养子(女)的身份(或地位);助长,鼓励
fosterer n. 养育者,教养人
fostering 见 foster child
fosterling 见 foster child
fostress n. 养母,保姆
foul a. 污秽的;邪恶的;险恶的;粗俗的
foul crime 邪恶之罪
foundation n. 1.基础,根据;基本原则 2.基金;基金会;(公司法)财团 3.创办,建立
foundation in fact 事实根据
foundation in law 法律根据
foundational a. 基础的,基本的
foundationer n. (英)领取基金会提供的薪金(或奖学金)的人
founder n. 创办人,创立者,缔造者;奠基者
founders' shares (公司法)发起人股,创办人股
founders' stock 公司创办人股
foundling n. 弃婴,弃儿
foundling hospital 弃婴堂,弃儿养育院
foundress n. 女创办人,女创立人,女奠基人
fountain of justice 公正的源泉;司法的源泉
four corners 十字路口;全部范围
Four Freedoms 四大自由(指1941年美国罗斯福总统提出的所谓言论自由、信仰自

由、免于匮乏、免于恐惧)

Four Fundamental Principles (中)四项基本原则[坚持社会主义道路,坚持中国共产党的领导,坚持无产阶级专政,坚持马列主义、毛泽东思想(adhere to the socialist road, adhere to the leadership of the Communist party, adhere to the dictatorship of the proletariat and adhere to Marxism Leninism and Mao Testung Thought)]

Four Horsemen 基督教《圣经》中的四骑士(战争、饥荒、时疫、死亡四大害)

four modernizations (中)四个现代化[农业、工业、国防和科学技术现代化(modernizations of agriculture, industry, national defence and science and technology)]

four seas (英)四海之内(指英联合王国境内)

four sittings (英)四次开庭期[指英国高等法院每年的四次开庭期:希拉里节(Hilary)开庭期,自1月11日起至复活节前一个星期三止;复活节(Easter)开庭期,自复活节后一周的星期二起至圣神降临节的星期天止(即复活节后第7个星期天止);"三位一体"日(Trinity)开庭期,自圣神降临节的星期天那周后的星期二起至7月31日止;米迦勒节(Michaelmas)开庭期,自枢密院命令中指定之日起至12月21日止。此四季开庭期在1875年已废,其中"Hilary"开庭期改定为每年1月11日起至1月31日止;"Easter"开庭期改为4月15日起至5月8日止(有时可延至5月13日);"Trinity"开庭期改为5月22日起至6月12日止。按1971年法院法四季开庭(期)法院全部被取消而由中央刑事法院系统"Crown Court System"所代替]

Fourteenth Amendment 美国联邦宪法第十四修正案[该修正案于1866年6月13日提出,经国会审议并于1866年7月28日批准生效,在各州颁布。第十四修正案表现出联邦共和国政府的决心,即南部各州如果不作出额外承诺,联邦和国会将不会重新接纳他们。第一款规定:"凡出生于合众国的人或入籍而受其管辖的人,均为合众国及其居住州的公民,各州不得制定或试行剥夺合众国公民的特权和豁免的法律,也不得未经正当法律程序,即行剥夺任何人的生命、自由和财产。并且在其辖境内,也不得否认任何人应享法律上的同等保护。"实质上,第十四修正案旨在把第十三修正案扩展为民权(civil rights)或权威(authority)的基础,目的还在于强调南方州遵从黑人新确立的政治权利。同时,禁止各州剥夺合众国公民特权(privileges)或豁免权(immunities)以及人们享有的正当法律程序(due process)的权利,更不能剥夺任何人应获得平等的法律保护。第十四修正案还规定国会中代表名额的分配,保护黑人的投票权。该法案现已成为美国民权(Bill of Rights)政策的奠基石和保障其一直扩展到各州的方式]

Fourth Amendment 美国联邦宪法第四修正案[该修正案是对政府的逮捕、搜查以及行政调查进行主要的法律限制,并通过(排除或例外)规则(exclusionary rule)来执行。排除规则禁止以违反第四修正案的要求所获得的文件或资料作为证据使用。第四修正案规定:"人民有保护其身体、住所、文件与财产的权利,不受无理搜查与扣押,此为不可侵犯之权利,除有可能的理由,以宣誓或郑重声明确保,并详载指定搜查地点、拘捕之人或押收之物外,不得颁发搜查证、拘捕证或扣押证。"在美国早期历史上,该修正案只适用于联邦政府,直到1868年第十四修正案通过(也通过其中的正当法律程序条款),第四修正案的适用范围才被扩大到州。联邦最高法院近来的判决放宽搜查的标准,削弱了第四修正案的执行力度,所以现在该修正案只能对个人自由与隐私提供很少的保护,并且联邦最高法院似乎并不会在不久的将来提交第四修正案的保障程度]

fourth branch of government 政府第四部门(即行政机关)

Fourth Decennial (美)《第四个十年判决摘要汇编》(指由西方出版公司出版的自1926年至1936年的判决摘要汇编)

fourth estate (英)第四等级(指新闻界在议会取得的边席)

fourth party 第四当事方,第四当事人

Fox Hunter's reason "猎人的根据"(边沁

的理论,即认为狐狸应有逃跑的机会,在狐狸没有跑到一定的距离之前,猎人不得开枪,否则就有失公平。但这种公平对于司法秩序是不适当的,因为司法程序中需要听取各方当事人的证词,以便判明事实真相)

Fox's Libel Act (1792)《福克斯文字诽谤法》或《福克斯书面诽谤法》(指英国18世纪时,对批评及政治讨论受到刑事诽谤法的限制,1731年后陪审团有权裁决是否构成诽谤,但曼斯菲尔德大法官坚持认为陪审团无权审判是否构成诽谤罪,这是应保留给法官的权利。1792年《福克斯法》终于授权陪审团就整个系争事项作出一般性的有罪或无罪判决)

fraction n. 小份额,百分数,小部分,零数

fraction of adjudicated cases 被判案件的比值

fraction of case tried 受审案件的比值

fractional a. 部分的,碎片的;分数的,小数的;零数的;(证券交易等)不足买卖单位的

fractional currency (总称)辅币

fractional stock warrant 零(星)股认股权证书

*** *Fractionem diei non recipit lex.*** The law does not regard the fraction of a day, when, therefore, a thing is to be done upon a particular day, all that day is allowed to do it in. 法律不承认一天的一部分(规定在某日作出的行为可在这一日的任何时间段完成)。

fragging n. (美)士兵杀伤军官的行为

Fragile Five 脆弱五国[指Brazil(巴西)、Indonesia(印度尼西亚)、India(印度)、Turkey(土耳其)和South Africa(南非)五国,根据其国名首字母缩写也可简称为BIITS]

fragment v./n. 分裂/断片,(作品)未完的部分,碎片

Fragment on government 《政府层论》(英国哲学家、法理学家边沁所作)

fragmental, no-system 零散的无系统

fragmentation n. 碎片化(指体系内部的各种要素之间缺乏有机联系和统一性。亦译"不成体系",将 fragmentation of international law 译成"国际法不成体系",直译则应译为"国际法碎片化")

fragmentation of international law 国际法碎片化,国际法不成体系问题(国际法碎片化是指近年来国际法学界讨论的热门话题之一。如在谷歌上检索中文的"国际法碎片化"可以搜索到约18000条相关信息。如在Westlaw International中检索"fragmentation of international law",可展示912篇相关文章。"碎片化"实际指国际法各领域日趋明显的专门化和板块化现象,即发展出越来越多分支或专门类别。这些类别、部门和板块无法用统一的上下级体系排列,加之各国法律关系主体不同领域交叉和变化涵盖国际法的诸多领域,法律原则适用等问题出现重叠、不协调和冲突)

frailty n. 虚弱;意志薄弱;因意志薄弱而犯的错误;弱点

frame v. 1.建造,塑造 2.设想,制订,拟出(计划) 3.诬害,陷害;捏造 4.讲出,发出

frame a case against sb. 捏造案情陷害某人

frame an accusation 诬告

frame-up n. 捏造;陷害,阴谋

framer n. (法律)制定者;创作者;构架设制者

Framers of the Constitution (美)宪法制定者

framework n. 结构;组织,机构;体制;框架

framework agreement 概要协定,框架协定

Framework of Standards to Secure and Facilitate Global Trade (美)《全球贸易安全与便利标准框架》(指9·11事件之后,作为回应,WTO开发出许多国际标准,其中就包括2005年6月通过的这一标准框架,并通过一种有力高效的能力建设项目来进一步支持成员海关当局贯彻实施。该标准框架不具强制执行力,对成员方没有约束力,但不能因此否认其作为国际法规范的性质。尽管它还未正式上升到国际法的硬法高度,但WTO大部分成员分别承诺对其若干或全部标准接受,实际上构成了一种国际法义务,从而带有国际法规范的性质)

framing document 草拟文件(书)
framing of issues 拟具要点；草拟诉讼纲要
framing pleading 拟具诉状
franchise n./v. 1.特权；特许；专营权；免税权 2.公民权(尤指选举权、参政权) 3.特许地，避难所 4.法人团体会员权 5.保险合同(契约)规定的免赔限度；免赔额/赋予选举权，赋予参政权；赋予特权
franchise clause 免费率(额)条款；(保险)免赔条款
franchise contracts 特许合同
franchise courts (英)特许法庭(指根据特许或国王的许可所设立的由私人掌管的法庭)
franchise tax 特许权税[指对商业(特别是公司)的一些经营项目的特许所课之税，通常根据经营收入计算]
franchising n. 特许，(包括商标权、版权、商誉等多种无形产权的转让，与一般许可不同)；特许专营权，出卖产销权
franco a. 免费的，邮资准免的，运费准免的
francophone citizen 法语公民
frank n./v. 免费邮寄权；免费/免费邮寄；准许免费通过；释放，豁免
frank-fee n. (英)自由保有的土地
frank-marriage (英)(因结婚而)给妇女的自由保有土地的赠与(或嫁资)
frank-tenant n. (英)自由保有土地权人
frank-tenement n. (英)自由保有的土地
Frankalmoin n. (英)教会土地保有
franking of letter 免费邮信权
frankpledge n. (英)十户联保制；十户联保制中的成员(指12岁以上的男子)；(实施十户联保制的)十户
frater consanguineus 同父异母兄弟
frater retraces 私生兄弟
frater uterinus 同母异父兄弟
frater uterinus 同母异父兄弟(见 *consanguineus frater*)
fraternal a. 兄弟的，兄弟般的；友好的；(美)互助会的，兄弟会的
fraternal benefit association (美)兄弟会，共济会[指为相互帮助、共同利益而自愿组成的非营利组织，其成员都具有共同的正义事业(common and worthy cause)、一致的目标和利益。这些组织通常具有分会系统、管理机关和一定的工作程序(rituals)以及会员福利制度。亦称 fraternal benefit society; fraternity; fraternal lodge; fraternal order。见 friendly society]
fraternal lodge 见 fraternal benefit association
fraternity n. 博爱，友爱，兄弟关系；(美)互助会，兄弟会；同一群职业的人，大学生联谊会
fratricidal a. 杀害兄弟姐妹的；杀害亲属(或同胞)的
fratricidal struggle (或 war) 内乱，内战，自相残杀的战争
fratricide n. 杀害兄弟(或姐妹)者；杀害兄弟(或姐妹)的行为
fraud n. 欺骗，欺骗行为；行骗的人，骗人之事，诡计，欺诈(罪)[指有意欺骗他人并给他人造成损害，可采取隐瞒事实真相、误导或不披露情况，原告必须证明被告有欺诈意图。与推断欺诈(constructive fraud)不同，只要有欺诈行为并给对方造成损失的，即构成欺诈行为，即使被告无欺诈意图]
fraud at common law 普通法上的欺诈行为
fraud in fact 事实上的欺诈
fraud in law (17世纪)法律上的欺诈(指根据情况所推定的欺诈，正如债务人转移财产而使债权人收不到应得的归还款项，由此而蒙受损失。亦称 constructive fraud)
fraud of representation 欺诈性不实表示
fraud on a power 使用权力的欺诈，仗势欺人
fraud relating to theft 与盗窃有关的欺诈行为
fraud squad 诈骗团伙
fraude à la douane 偷漏关税
fraude à la loi (法)规避法律
fraudulence n. 欺诈，欺骗性
fraudulent a. 欺诈的，欺骗的；骗取的；借以欺骗的
fraudulent abduction of heiress 欺骗诱拐嗣女(罪)
fraudulent act 诈骗行为

fraudulent agreement 恶意通谋
fraudulent alienation 欺诈让与
fraudulent alienee 欺诈让与的受让人
fraudulent appropriation（或 misappropriation） 欺诈性盗用（罪）；欺骗性的挪用（罪）
fraudulent assignment 欺诈性转让
fraudulent bankruptcy 欺诈性破产
fraudulent buying and selling 倒买倒卖，借以欺骗的买卖
fraudulent concealment of assets 欺诈性隐匿资产
fraudulent conduct 欺诈行为
fraudulent conversion 欺诈性侵占
fraudulent conveyance 欺诈性财产转让；欺诈性交付
fraudulent destruction 非法毁损（罪）
fraudulent intention 欺诈意图
fraudulent marking of merchandise 欺骗性的商品标记
fraudulent means 欺诈手段
fraudulent medicine 假药,骗人的药物
fraudulent mediums 欺诈手段,骗术
fraudulent misuse of funds 欺诈性挪用（侵占）款项罪
fraudulent person 骗子；欺诈分子
fraudulent preference 特惠欺诈（破产人在破产前3个月因要特别优待某一债主,而把欠款优先还清,或把财产优先让给他,使其他债主失去平均分配此项财产的机会,便是属于此类欺诈行为）
fraudulent proof 欺骗性证明
fraudulent representation 欺诈性陈述,诈称
fraudulent settlement 欺诈性家产授予
fraudulent statements in the sales of securities 证券销售中做出欺诈陈述
fraudulent stock deals 诈欺性的股票交易
fraudulent transfer 欺诈性转让
fraudulent use of the mails 对邮件的欺诈习惯
* *Fraus est celare fraudem.* It is a fraud to conceal a fraud. 隐瞒诈欺即是诈欺。
* *Fraus est odiosa et non praesumenda.* Fraud is odious, and not to be presumed.

诈欺可憎,但不得推断。
fraus omnia corrupt 欺诈完全无效
freak n. 1.任性的举动；怪诞的行动 2.(美俚)吸毒成瘾者
freak accident 特殊事件
Freddie Mac 见 Federal Home Mortgage Corporation
fredum 1.和解金（指罪犯支付一笔款项要求从检控中获得保释）2.罚款（指破坏治安求得宽恕而支付的罚款）3.献金（指为防止报复而付给治安官的钱）
free v./a. 释放；免除,解除,解脱/1.自由的,自主的；无拘束的 2.免税的；免费的 3.滥用浪费的；不检点的 4.丰富的,大量的；5.空闲的（指房屋等）
free a prisoner on probation 假释
free a prisoner under education with labo(u)r （中）解除劳役
free acknowledgment 自由认领（指由其生父自动对其非婚生子女的自由认领权）
free agent 自由行为人
free alongside ship 船边交货（价格）
free and clear 没有义务或牵连
free and easy 不拘仪式的,自由的；不拘仪式的集会
free and equal 自由与平等
Free and Hanseatic City of Hamburg 汉堡自由汉萨城（指国际海洋法制定的地址）
free bench （古英国法）寡妇的财产权,寡妇产
free business 自由营业,自由经营
free choice of occupation 自由选择职业
free choice of partners 自由选择配偶,婚姻自由,自由选择合伙（人）
free cohabitation 自由同居
free combination 自由组合,自由结合
free commodities 免税商品
free competition 自由竞争
free convertibility 自由兑换
free copies 样书（不是向行政机关交存的样书,而是指出版社免费赠送给作者的样书,也称 gift copies 或 presentation copies）
free course （船舶的）自由通行
free court 自由法庭（见 *fehmgerichte*）
free currency 自由货币

free deliveries 免费送货
Free Democratic Party （德）自由民主党
free education 免费教育
free egress and ingress 自由出入权
free election （美）自由选举［指由政治制度和程序保证的一种选举，即每个选举人或投票者均允许按自己的良心（conscience）投票］
free enterprise 自由企业，自由经营
free enterprise system 自由企业原则
free entry 免税报关单，免税品海关通知书；自由加入
free estate 动产
free evaluation of evidence 自由心证
free evaluation of evidence through inner conviction 大陆法系国家的内心确信证明标准（或证明要求）（指在1808年《法国刑事诉讼法典》第342条中第一次得到明确的规定，现行《法国刑事诉讼法典》第353条基本上沿袭了这一规定）
free exchange market 自由兑换市场
free exchange rate 自由汇价
free exercise clause 免除货物税务条款；（美）宗教活动自由条款（指遵照美国联邦宪法第一修正案规定）
free expression 自由表达，自由措辞
free fishery 自由捕鱼权
free flow of commerce 商业的自由流动
free from 不受什么影响
free from particular average 单独海损不赔；平安险
free goods 免税进口货物；中立货物（指国际法的一条原则，中立船的货物亦中立，不受交战国查获）
free hand 放手处理问题的权力，全权；无拘束
free institution 自由制度
free interpretation 自由解释
free judicial finding of law 无拘束适用法律进行司法裁决
free judicial methods of the classical jurists 古典法学家的自由司法方法
free law school 自由法学派
free legal aid 免费的司法救助
free list （美）免收进出口税的货单，商品免税单
free listing 免税商品表
free loan 无息贷款
free love 自由性爱（指无须结婚而发生性关系或同居）
free market 自由市场
free marriage 自由结婚
free medical care 公费医疗
free motion 自由申请，自由动议
free movement of goods 商品自由流动
Free movement of judg(e)ment 判决的自由流动原则（指欧盟有关冲突协调确定的一个总原则）
free movement of persons, services and capital 人员、劳务和资本的自由流动
free navigation 自由航行
free of capture and seizure 不负被拿捕和被劫责任（指海上保险的一种条款）
free of charge 免费的
free of duty 免税
free of ethical blemishes 无道德上的污点
free of general average 不赔偿的共同海损，不担保的共同海损
free of ground rent 免地租；免租
free of income tax 免付所得税
free of interest （或 bearing no interest）不计利息，无息，免息
free of marriage bonds 无婚姻约束
free on board 船上交货，离岸价格
free on rail （或 train）火车上交货（价格）
free pardon 赦免，特赦
free pass 免费通行（证）
free passage 自由通行权
free pay 免税数
free perimeter 免税地带，免税区
free port 自由港，无税港
free press 自由采访；不受政府检查（或控制）的出版，出版自由
free rein 自由控制，任意驾驭，随意统治
free rider "免费搭车"［指发达国家和发展中国家在MFN（最惠国待遇）原则上的不同主张和由此引发的争论，其根本原因在于发达国家认为适用无条件的MFN原则将产生"免费搭车"的问题］（见 incentive compatibility），无票乘车者

free rides 搭便车者
free riding 搭便车(指能获得另一个参与人所采取行动带来的收益的参与人,搭便车常常出现于存在公共物品的场合)
free school meals 免费供应校餐
free ship 中立国船只
free socage (英)封建时自由免役土地(保有)
free speech 言论自由
Free State 自由邦(如 Congo Free State 刚果自由邦)
free supply system (中史)供给制
free tenure 自由占有权;(英)完全(自由)土地保有制
free time 装卸时间(指货物运输合同当事人约定的装卸时间,而无须再支付费用);非工作时间
free to follow caprice 肆意妄为
free trade 自由贸易
free trade area 自由贸易区
free transit 自由过境
free use 无偿使用(各国认识不一,有的认为无偿使用可能合理,也可能不合理。有的认为该术语为"自由使用",即对已处于公有领域的作品的使用)
free voting 自由投票
free will 自由意志
(the) free will of another in the performance of a particular act 他人履行特定行为的自由意志(见 external objects)
free zone 免税区
free-surety 互保,连保,连环保
free-willing being 自由意志的人
freebench (英格兰法)寡妇对亡夫土地的保有权(指寡妇以守节为条件持有其亡夫的公簿地产)
freebooter n. 海盗,强盗
freeborn a. 生来是自由的
freedom n. 1.自由,自主;免除,解脱;放肆;2.自由权;特权(指城市、公司等的)
freedom from (civil) arrest (英)免受(民事)拘留的自由(指下议院特权之一)
freedom from being exploited 不受剥削的自由
freedom from discrimination 不受歧视的自由
freedom from fear 不受恐吓的自由,免于恐惧的自由
freedom from molestation (英)免于干扰的自由(指下议院特权之一)
freedom from subjection, serfdom or slavery 免受奴役、征服或苦役的自由
freedom from taxation 免税
freedom from want 免于匮乏的自由
freedom of access to courts 向法院申诉的自由
freedom of access to Her Majesty sovereign (英)晋见女王(君主)的自由(英国下院议员的特权之一)
freedom of action 诉讼自由;行动自由
freedom of assembly (and meeting) 集会(和开会)自由
freedom of association 结社自由
freedom of belief 信仰自由,信念自由
freedom of belief, worship and religious observances 信仰、崇拜和宗教仪式自由
freedom of business 营业自由
freedom of choice of residence 居住自由
freedom of commerce 贸易自由;商业自由
freedom of communication 通信自由,交往自由
freedom of competition 竞争自由
freedom of conscience 信仰自由
freedom of contract (美)合同自由,契约自由(freedom 是一种政治权利,即自身不受强制,依照自身意愿订立合同并确定合同条款内容的自由和权利,而且该合同以后之履行,除某先例和有限情况外,均由法院强制执行)
freedom of correspondence 通信自由
freedom of each House to conduct its proceedings 两院进行活动的自由
freedom of equal treatment by the law 受到法律同等对待的自由
freedom of establishment 设立机构自由
freedom of establishment and provision of services 确认(立)和服务提供自由
freedom of expatriation 出籍自由;放弃国籍自由
freedom of expression 言论自由
freedom of family rights 家庭权利自由

freedom of immigration 移民自由

freedom of information 新闻自由,情报自由,信息自由

Freedom of Information Act (FOIA) (美)《情报自由法》(指 1966 年国会通过,1967 年 7 月 4 日开始生效,其主要内容是规定民众在获得行政情报方面的权利与行政机关向民众公开行政情况方面的义务,该法律目的在于通过行政情报的公开,实现对人民"知情权"的保障。"知情权"是人民的重要权利之一)

freedom of marriage 婚姻自由

freedom of movement 迁徙自由,活动自由

freedom of movement with and from the state 在国内和出国迁徙自由

freedom of navigation 航行自由,航海自由

freedom of not believe in religion 不信仰宗教的自由

freedom of opinion 发表意见自由,言论自由

freedom of organizing 组织工会自由

freedom of parading and demonstration 游行示威自由

freedom of passage 通行自由

freedom of political conviction 政治信仰自由

freedom of property 财产自由

freedom of religion 宗教自由

freedom of religious belief 宗教信仰自由

freedom of sentiment 情感自由

freedom of speech (and express) 言论自由

freedom of speech, writing, the press and broadcasting 言论、著作、出版和广播自由

freedom of testamentary disposition (立)遗嘱处分(财产)的自由

freedom of the borough 自由市的自由

freedom of the city (英)城市自治;荣誉市民权

freedom of the person 人身自由

freedom of the press (美)(17 世纪)出版自由[指(宪法上)给予材料、资料的印制和出版的自由,政府不得加以干预,这是美国联邦宪法第一修正案赋予的权利。美国联邦宪法第一修正案规定:"国会不得指定关于下列事项的法律:确立宗教或禁止信仰自由,剥夺人民言论和出版的自由……"亦称 Liberty of the press]

freedom of the (open) seas (商船在)公海上的自由航行权(又译:海洋自由。指战时中立国船只要在公海上航行就不受交战国军舰干涉的自由航行权)

freedom of the will 意志自由

freedom of thought 思想自由

freedom of trade 贸易自由

freedom of transit 过境自由

freedom of worship 崇拜自由,做礼拜的自由

Freedom Party 自由党

freedom to bargain collectively (劳资)集体谈判自由

freedom to change one's residence 迁徙自由

freedom to co-operate, organize and combine in groups for manner of lawful purposes 合作、组织工会和一切旨在合法目的的结社自由

freedom to divorce 离婚自由

freedom to engage in import-export transaction 经营进出口交易的自由

freedom to engage in scientific research 科学研究自由

freedom to hold private property 拥有私有财产的自由

freedom to provide services 提供服务自由

freedom to strike 罢工自由

freedom to use one's own spoken and written languages 使用自己的语言文字的自由

freedom to use private radio broadcasting system 使用私人无线电广播系统的自由

freedom to vote 表决自由,投票自由

freedom to work 工作自由(指选择职业和专业的自由)

freedom under the law 法律下的自由[指英国丹宁勋爵(Alfred Thompson Danning)的一条哲学观点。即所谓自由是"每一个守法公民在合法的时候不受任何其他人干涉,想其所愿想、说其所愿说、去其所愿去的自由",也就是说个人自由必须受到法律的限制。这一直是西方政治和法律思想的一项重要原则,孟德斯鸠指出"自

由是做法律所许可的一切事情的权利,如果一个公民能做法律所禁止的事情,他就不再自由了……"]

freehold n. (英)自由(完全)保有土地权,终身(或世袭)保有土地权

freehold estate (英)自由(完全)保有土地权(指保全终身享有或可让与子嗣的地产权)

freehold interest 自由(完全)保有土地的权益

freehold of inheritance (英)继承的自由(完全)保有土地权

freehold of office 终身职务

freehold property (英)自由(完全)保有的财产(权)

freeholder n. (英)世袭土地保有人;自由(完全)土地保有权人

freeing administration 自由行政;任务执行

freeing child for adoption 让儿童能得到自由收养

freelance n. (美)自由职业者;个体企业家[指自由职业的升级版,就似一只八爪鱼,什么都要管,成本核算、行政管理、市场营销、客户服务等各项任务均需自己完成,几乎成了一个工作狂(workaholic)或工作极为努力的人。他拥有自由的"小小工作家庭办公室"(Small Office Home Office,缩略为SOHO)]

freeman n. (区别于奴隶或农奴的)自由民;公民,有公民权的人;荣誉市民

Freemason n. 共济会

freemen boroughs (英)自由民自治城市(指议会改革前在自由市所设立的选区)

freeze n. (工资、物价等的)冻结

freeze-out 排挤出去,排斥[通常为封闭性控股公司(closely held corporion)中的用语]

freezee n. 封闭性的控股公司或控股股东

freezing of property 冻结财产

freezing of rents on the housing 冻结房租

freight n. 运费;(运输中的)货物;货运,装货;负担

freight allowance 运输费用

freight and cartage 水陆运费

freight charge 运费(单)

freight forward 运费由提货人支付

freight forwarder 货运转运商;货物运输报关行(与forwarding agent同)

freight market 货运市场

freight paid 运费已付

freight policy 船货保险单

freight rate 运价,运费率

freight rebate 运费回扣

freight station 货运站,货运中转站

freight tariff 运费率表

freight to the destination 全程运费

freight transport contract 货运合同(契约)

freight-in (或 **inward**) n. 运入运费

freight-out (或 **outward**) n. 运出运费

freightage n. 运费;货物运输;运输的货物

freighter n. 货船;租船人;装货人;承运人;货主

Freirecht Movement 自由法学运动

French Community 法兰西共同体

French law 法国法

fresh a. 新的;新近的;新鲜的;重新的;年轻的;无经验的

fresh crime 新罪

fresh election 重新选举

fresh evidence 新证据

fresh fine (古英国法)已收缴上一年的罚金

fresh legislation 新近立法

fresh pursuit 1.(普通法上警官可越过管辖范围)立即追捕重罪犯权 2.立刻追寻(指对失物和走失鸟兽或对被盗的东西应立刻追寻)

fresh suit 1.立即追寻(= fresh pursuit) 2.(古英国法)立即追捕(指对正在逃跑的小偷须立即不停追捕)

friction n. 摩擦,冲突;不和

friend n. 朋友,友人;赞助者,支持者;同情者;助手;(用作称呼)老相识

friend and foe 敌与友

friend of the court 法庭之友(指与案件无关而被邀向法官提供意见的第三者。见 *amicus curiae*)

friendly a. 友好的,友谊的;赞助的,支持的

friendly amendment 友好的修订（指动议人的动议修订得到支持,对此并无其他议员反对）

friendly society （18世纪）在不列颠（in Britain）自愿组成的协会（指由赞助或捐献所支持的自愿组织的协会,其目的是对有病的成员以及一些濒临死亡的鳏夫和孩子进行救济。自愿组成的协会受制定法调整。见 benevolent association; fraternal benefit association）

friendly state 友好国家

friendly suit 友好诉讼（指双方同意的诉讼。目的是来到法庭通过诉讼而获得他们所要知道的法律要点的判定,以便妥当地进行他们的工作）

friendly treaty 友好条约
friendly troop 友军
friend's goods 友好国货物
friend's ship 友好国船舶
friendship n. 友谊,友好
fright n./v. 恐吓;恐怖/使恐惧
frigidity n. 缺乏性感,性冷淡（专指女性）
fringe benefits 小额补贴（指资本主义国家雇主给雇员的养老金及假日工资之类的小恩小惠）;附加福利
fringe firms 外围小企业
frisk n./v. 搜身;（俚）扒窃/1.遍身搜查,搜身 2.扒窃
frivolous a. 轻浮的,不重要的,无法律依据的,无法定基础的,没有合理意图的〈a frivolous claim〉（缺少法律依据的权利主张）
frivolous and vexatious proceedings 无意义和无根据的诉讼
frivolous behavio(u)r 轻浮的举动
frivolous case 轻浮案件
frivolous claims 轻浮的法律权利请求,缺少法律依据的权利主张
frivolous plea 敷衍推诿的抗辩
from and after sentence 前后（连续）判决,累积判决（见 consecutive sentence）
from ignorance 出于无知
from person 自（某人）身上
from spite 出自恶意,用心很毒
from the outset 从一开始,起始,最初

from the perspective of law 从法律的角度
from this date forward 从本日起
from time to time 有时,不时
front a. 前面的,前部的;正面的
front bench （英）下议院前座（有时称为下议院政府大臣席）
front bencher （英）（下议院的）前座议员
front man 公开的代表人;挂名负责人;出面人物
front office （机关等中的）全体决策人员
front page n./a./v. 1.标题页,书的封面页 2.（报纸）头版/头版的,轰动的,重要的/把……登在头条〈front-page an editorial〉（把一篇社论登在头条）
frontager n. 临街（河）土地所有人;临街的空地所有人
frontier n. 1.国境,边境,边界 2.新领域,尖端
frontier guards 边防部队;边防卫队
frontier inspection 边防检查
frontier pass 边防通行证
frontier science 尖端科学
frontier sentry 边防哨所
frontier society 边境社会,边区社会
frontier (inspection) station 边防（检查）站
frontier trade 边境贸易
frontier traffic 边境贸易
frottage n. 摩擦癖［与 frotteurism 同义,性心理障碍之一种。指男性患者在拥挤场合或乘对方不备之际,伺机以身体某一部分（常为阴茎）摩擦和触摸女性身体的某一部分以达到引起性兴奋之目的,其刑事责任能力可参照露阴癖。见 sexual perversion］
frozen a. 1.冰冻的;冻伤的 2.冻结的
frozen account 冻结账目
frozen assets 冻结资产
frozen capital 冻结资本
fructus （大陆法）收益,成果,产物,孳息
fructus civiles 法定孳息
fructus industriales 人工收获物;劳动成果
fructus legis 法律的效果（即执行）
fructus naturales 自然成果
* *Fructus pendentes pars fundi videntur.* Hanging fruits make part of the land. 未收

的产物构成土地的一部分。

* *Fructus perceptos villae non esse constat.* Gathered fruits do not make a part of the farm. 已收获的产物不能构成农牧场的一部分。

fructus rei alienae 他人财产的收益

fructuum perceptio 孳息的取得

fruit n. 水果;成果;产物;(复)孳息,收益;奏效;收获

fruit of crime 犯罪的后果

fruit of industry 勤劳的收获

fruit of the land 土地收益

fruit of the poisonous tree (美)毒树之果原则;"毒树之果"(指美国联邦最高法院通过的一种理论,将非法证据的排除扩展到从非法方式获得证据。按此理论,以违法方式收集到的证据为有毒之树,以这些证据为线索获得的其他证据为毒树的果子,毒树之果不可食,因而也应被排除)

fruitful a. 多产的;收效多的;富有成效的;富饶的;肥沃的

fruitful plan 富有成效的计划

fruitless a. 无效的,无益的,不结果实的

* *Frumenta quae sata sunt solo cedere intelliguntur.* Grain which is sown is understood to form a part of the soil. 业已播种的庄稼应构成耕地的一部分。

* *Frustra legis auxilium invocat (quaerit) qui in legem committit.* He vainly invokes the aid of the law who transgresses the law. 谁违反法律就休想得到法律的帮助。

frustrate v. 使无效,废除,废止;挫败,阻挠

frustrated contract 受挫失效的合同(契约)[又译:落空的合同(契约)、不能履行的合同(契约)。指因战争等不可抗力的意外事件而不能履行的合同(契约)]

frustration n. (合同或契约的)(指因不可抗力而使合同不可继续履行)受挫失效(又译:落空);无效,废除;挫折

frustration of purpose (doctrine) (合同)契约受挫原则(指因不可预见情况致使合同签订后不能得到履行,因而对承诺人给予宽恕的原则)

frustration of purposes (英)目的落空(指在英国法中,合同订立后如因法令的颁布或变更而导致合同履行违法,即构成"目的落空"。这足以解除合同,并可免除当事人不履行合同之责任。因此,嗣后违法是构成合同落空的免责事由之一)

fuel n./v. 燃料/供燃料,支持

fuer (古英国法)逃跑,不出庭

fuer in fait (或 *in facto*) 事实上的逃跑

fuer in ley (或 *in lege*) 法律上的逃跑(即不出庭)

fuero 1.(西班牙法)法律,法典;(西班牙)市镇特权(指中世纪由国王、贵族或主教授予市镇的地方性特权,包括征税、自治等);有法律强制力 2.特权和豁免的批准 3.对个人(或教堂、修道院)的赠与行为 4.地方司法行政官的一项有关税收、罚金等的宣告 5.法院的管辖

fugitive n./a. 逃亡者,亡命者/逃亡的;躲避的;流浪的;易消失的,短暂的

fugitive criminal 刑事逃犯

fugitive felon 逃亡的重罪犯(人)

fugitive from justice 逃犯

fugitive goods 窃贼所抛弃之赃物

fugitive landlord 逃亡地主

fugitive offender 逃犯

Fugitive Slave Acts (美)《逃奴法》(1793年和1850年的)

fugue n. 神游症(75%属癫痫症范畴,发作时有轻度意识障碍,反应较迟钝。见 automatism)

fulcrum n. 支撑点;支轴

fulfil(l) v. 1.履行(诺言、责任等)2.完成(计划、任务等)3.达到(目的),满足(愿望、要求等)4.执行(命令、法律),实施

fulfil(l) obligation 履行债务

fulfil(l)ment n. 履行;实现;完成;结束

fulfil(l)ment of treaty 条约的履行

full a. 1.完全的;正式的;详尽的,完备的 2.同父同母的 3.充满的;十足的

full access 全权使用

full adoption 正式收养,完全收养

full age 足龄,成年,达到法定年龄

full allocated cost 满打满算计入成本(指不仅包括固定和可变资本,还包括管理、销售等宏大的各种费用均摊入成本)

full answer 全面答辩

full appeal 完全上诉(指当事人就仲裁裁决的实体问题,不管是事实上的问题还是法律上的问题,向法院提起上诉,由法院进行全面审查,也就是二审,少数国家允许当事人提起此种完全上诉,但往往有严格限制)
full bench 合议庭
full blood 全血缘(亲),纯血统
full brother 同父母的兄弟,同胞兄弟
full capacity to act 完全行为能力
full chamber 综合法庭(指玻利维亚负责合宪性审查和其他案件的一种法庭)
full civil capacity 完全的民事行为能力
full compensation 全面赔偿
full container load (FCL) 整箱货(指集装箱)
full copy 完整文本
full council 全体会议
Full Court (澳大利亚)上诉法院
full court 全体法官(组成的)合议庭(指以全体出庭法官适当组织的法庭。它包括可允许补充的法官,以区别于法定的两人法庭。见 en banc)
full court at Westminster (英)威斯敏斯特合议庭
full court of divorce (英)离婚合议庭
full coverage 全保,总括保险
full defence 全面辩护;全面防卸
full dress (船舶等的)挂满旗;礼服;正式的
full dress talks (debates) 正式会议(辩论)
full employment 充分就业
full employment policy 充分就业政策
full endorsement 全记名背书
full faith and credit 充分诚信[指认可、接受并执行法规、法令和其他管辖的判决,特别是认可或承认一个州对另一个州的法律决议(legal decisions)]
Full Faith and Credit Act (美)《充分诚信和尊重法》[指一项联邦法规,它要求联邦法院给予州法院判决以相同的排他效力(preclusive effect),如同根据州法律应有的判决。参见《美国注释法典》第28标题卷第1738节, Migra v. Warrent City School Dist. Bd. of Educ 或《美国联邦最高法院判例汇编》第465卷第75、81页,第104卷第892、896页(1984年)]
Full Faith and Credit for Child-Support Orders Act (美)《对儿童扶养费命令法的充分诚信和尊重》[指1994年旨在便于州际儿童扶养费的收集而制定的联邦法规。根据该法,首先发布儿童扶养令的州需维持继续扶养,只要该儿童或一、两个诉讼当事人继续居住在这里,专属管辖就应明确该法令的含义,除非所有诉讼竞辩人以书面形式同意改变管辖。一个州的法令在另一个州执行可以登记注册。参见《美国注释法典》第28标题卷第1738B节]
full hearing 完全听证(会),充分听证
full in personam 完全的对人管辖权
full in personam jurisdiction 完全的对人管辖
full in personam liability 完全对人的责任
full indemnity 如数获得补偿
full insurance 足额保险
full jurisdiction 完整的管辖权
full jurisdictional power 最大的管辖权
full legal capacity 完全行为能力
full liability 完全责任
full line 全套货物,经销各种产品,货色齐全
full member 正式人员,正式成员
full modalities 细节方案;完整谈判模式
full name 全名
full of iniquities 恶贯满盈
full offense 已遂罪
full ownership 完全所有权
full pardon 完全赦免,彻底赦免
full (or general) partner 普通合伙人,无限责任合伙人;全体合伙人;合伙企业中负无限责任的合伙人
full partnership 无限公司,无限合伙
full person (罗马法)具有完全人格的人
full power 全权;(复)全权证书(指要求外交代表在进行有关国家间的条约谈判并签署条约时所应出示的证书);(复)全权书,全权代表书
full power to conclude a treaty 缔约全权证书

full prior knowledge 充分知情
full proof 充分的证明,全面证明
full recourse 完全追索权
full right of use 享有全部用益权
full satisfaction of the judgment 全部执行判决
full secured creditor 担保充分的债权人
full secured liabilities 担保充分的债
full session 全体法官会议
full sovereign state 完全主权国
full sovereignty 完整主权
full subject of international law 完全的国际法主体
full term 正式任期;完全任期
full text 全文
full title 全称;全权
full tort liability 完全侵权责任
full value 正式的价格(见 fair market value)
full-blown search 彻底全面搜查
full-budgeting approach 编制全面预算方法
full-funding basis 充分提供基金为基础
full-line forcing 全线需求
(a) full-scale trial 完整的审判
full-time judge 专职法官
full-time labo(u)r 全劳动力
full-time magistrate 专职治安官
full-time personnel 专职人员
full-time service 专任职务;(英)正规军的现役
full-time staff 专职人员
full-time working director 专职董事长
Fuller, Lon L. 朗·L.富勒(1902—1978)[美国合同法领域和纠纷解决替代领域的重要人物。在法哲学领域,他是美国现实主义早期有洞察力的批评者。他的程序自然法理论,以及他对法律实证主义的批评均有重大影响。富勒认为法律是人类的规划并隐含有道德目标——允许人们在社会中共存、合作。法律有自己的理想,不理解法律追求的道德理想就不可能真正理解法律。法律是"使人类行为服从规则治理的事业"。富勒的这一意味深长的名言和他对"法律的内在道德"的八个标准的严格检视,都暗示了他的关注点在

于立法。他认为"只有公民与官员相互合作、履行自己职能、法律才会起作用"。富勒提出了八个"合法性原则",作为检验一个政府的最低义务的标准,也作良好政府追求的目标。他的八个标准是:①法律应该具有普遍性;②法律应该广为人知;③溯及既往的立法或法律溯及既往的适用应尽量减少;④法律应易于被理解;⑤法律不能自相矛盾;⑥法律不能要求不可能做到的行为;⑦在时间流进中,法律应保持相对的稳定;⑧法律的规定和法律的实际适用应保持一致。富勒虽然对八个标准具有道德地位的论证不太清晰,但他还提出以下论证作为其著作的某些基础:①根据规则游戏或公正地游戏,其本身就是正义不可或缺的部分,即便不是全部(可以类推,许多人相信遵守诺言具有某些道德价值,即使承诺是坏事);②如果遵循了合适的程序,那么某些种类的邪恶就不大可能出现,比如:如果法官知道他们必须为他们的判决提供公开理由,那么法院更可作出公正判决(某些形式的腐败就难以合理化了);③富勒曾经写道,他不相信一个程序公正的法律体系会实质不公正。无论如何富勒对程序正义与实质正义的强强联系的信仰是他的理论的积极部分,但这也只是他的理论的边缘部分]
fully transaction information system 电子信息传递系统
fully-autonomous a. 完全自治的
fumage n. 烟囱税;肥料
function n./v. (16 世纪) 1.职能[指特定职务的适当行为或者一种专业的适当行为⟨court's function is to administer justice⟩(法院的职能就是执法、主持公道)] 2.职务、职责、职权(指一个职务的职权)⟨presidential function⟩(总统职权) 3. 履行职责;运行,起作用,工作,活动/履行职责,运行,起作用,工作,活动
function of administering justice 执法职能;执行司法任务
function of punishment 刑罚功能说(见 proximity)
functional a. 职能的,官能的;职务上的;

职责的
functional analyse 内涵分析；功能分析
functional classification 职能分类
functional concept 职能观念
functional department 职能部门
functional disease 官能病
functional equivalence 职责相当
functional equivalent approach "功能等同"模式(指美国《示范法》或《模范法》第7条中对书面签名和非书面签名的一视同仁,即功能等同模式。它基于对传统书面签名的目的和功能的分析,着眼于决定如何通过电子签名技术来满足其功能和目的)
functional illiteracy 半文盲
functional immunity (或 **immunity ratione materiae**) 属事理由豁免,职能豁免权,属事豁免
functional immunity of state 国家的职能豁免权
functional interpretation 功能解释;职能说明
functional jurisprudence 功用(能)法理学
functional kind 功能种类(指一种范畴的边界是由一个共享的功能决定的。许多法学理论家如迈克尔·摩尔(Michael Moore,1943—)主张最好的法律是为功能种类)
functional personality 功能性主体身份(指非政府组织积极广泛参与全球性事务,推进国际法律秩序的变革,在跨国区域中活跃是以一种功能性主体身份参与的)
functional regulation 功能监管
functional school of jurists 功用(能)法学派
functional tried 职能上的三分法
functional works 功能作品
functionalism n. 功能主义
functionalist style 功能主义模式(见 normalivist style)
functionalists n. 功能主义学派
functionary n. (机关等)工作人员,官员
functioning government (行使)职能的政府

functioning machinery 职能机构
functions and powers 职权
functions of the dictatorship 专政职能
functions of the state 国家职能
functus officio 职责已尽(指已完成任务,而其授权已终止的代理人,或者无权进一步行使职责,而其职权已终止的审判员或仲裁员)
fund n./v. (17 世纪)1.基金,一笔总额款项;(为特定目的)流动资产(liquid assets)⟨ a fund reserved for unanticipated expenses⟩(储备一笔款项以备未料之需)2.常用(复数)款项或其他资产比如股票、债券或流动资金(working capital), 适合支付债务、消费或类似的⟨ sue invested her funds in her sister's business⟩(在她姐妹的生意中对已投资的基金提出请求)3.为世袭土地共同拥有的投资联营(pool of investment)基金,共同基金(mutual fund)⟨ a diverse portfolio of funds⟩(各类基金的有价证券)/1.融资,(给个人)公司,合资企业,特别是专题项目提供资金,为……提供资金2.把短期借款转为固定利息的"长期借款"3.使用产生利息(或利益)的资源 4.(英)投资于公债
Fund Agreement 国际货币基金协定
Fund Claims Manual 国际油污索赔基金制定的《索赔手册》
fund deposition 存款
fund in court 法庭基金[指在法院储存的竞诉(或争诉、竞合权利诉讼)款项。见 interpleader]
fund-in-trust 信托基金
fundamental(s) a./n. 1.基础的,根本的,十分重要的 2.原始的,主要的/(常用复)基本原则(或原理);基本法则(或规律);纲要
fundamental change of circumstances 情势的根本变迁
fundamental division of the law 基本法律部门
fundamental duties of citizens 公民基本义务
fundamental fairness doctrine 基本公正原则(指将正当程序原则适用于司法程序的

一项法律原则,即保护受指控者合法权利的一种法律程序。美国联邦宪法第五和第十四修正案均包含否定联邦和州政府享有"未经正当法律程序剥夺个人生命、自由或财产"之权力的条款)

fundamental freedom 基本自由

fundamental human right 基本人权

Fundamental ILO Conventions 基本劳工公约

fundamental law (17世纪)根本大法,基本法,原则性法规[指一个民族或一个国家设定治理原则的建制法律或组织法(organic law)。特别是指宪法,亦称 Organic Law, Ground-law]

fundamental legal instrument 基本法律文件

fundamental norm 基本规范

fundamental object of the law 法律的基本目标

fundamental of our criminal law 我们刑法的基本原则

Fundamental Order of Connecticut (美)《康涅狄格根本法》(1639年)

fundamental principle 基本原则

fundamental proposition 基本主张,基本信条

fundamental provision (fundamental proviso) 基本条款

fundamental principle of governmental administration 国家行政管理的基本原则

fundamental provisions 基本条款

fundamental purpose 主要目的

fundamental right (17世纪)基本权利[指①来自自然或基本大法的权利。②宪法,自由的重要组成部分,侵犯权利则要受到法院的严格考查来确定政府所声称的合理性(soundness)是否正确。基本权利往往引起严格审查(strict scrutiny)来裁定该法律是否违反正当程序条款或美国联邦宪法第十四修正案的平等保护条款(Equal Protection Clause)。美国联邦最高法院确切公布的基本权利包括投票、表决、州际旅行等各种隐私(如婚姻和避孕权利),亦称 fundamental interest。见 strict scrutiny]

fundamental rights and duties of states 国家的基本权利和义务

fundamental source of law 基本法源

fundamental tenets (= primary source of law) 基本信条

fundatio founding or foundation 提供基金,基础,根本;设立,创立;(历史上)企业的基础,企业的创立(特别是慈善企业的设立)

fundatio incipiens 1.incipient foundation 原始基金 2.The incorporation or grant of corporate powers 法人权限的合并或转让

fundatio perficiens 1.perfecting foundation 完备的基金,法律上有效的基金 2.The endowment or gift of funds to a corporation 给企业或法人的捐赠或赠与的基金

funded a. 提供资金的;有固定利息的;长期借款的

funded debt 固定债务,长期借款

funded income 财产所得

funded indebtedness 担保负债

fundholder (英)公债持有人,证券持有人

funding n. (18世纪)提供基金,转成债务[指①通过发行长期债务(long term debt obligations)或通过将短期债务转成长期债务来筹措资金解决流动开支(current expenses)的程序,创立固定债务(funded debt)的程序。②旧债到期之前发行新债,亦称 refunding。③为了专用目的提供或配给款项,如养老金计划(pension plan)通过基金储备或投资来完成。④向一项专门活动或专项课题(如一研究项目)提供财源。⑤将财产转让到信托]

funding firewalls 融资防火墙(指限制集团内资本转移)

funeral expenses 丧葬费

fungible n./a. 可替代的物;(偿还债务用以)替代的财产;代替物;种类物/可替代的,可互换的

fungible things 可代替物;种类物

fungicide n. 杀真菌剂

funk money 为获取高利(或保障币值)而由一国转移到另一国的流动资金

furandi animus 盗窃意图

furca et fossa 绞死与溺死(指古代司法授

权证书常见的一个短语:"绞死男性重罪犯、溺死女性重罪犯")
furiosi 精神病人,疯子
furiosus 半痴
furious driving 超速驾驶
furnish v. 供应,提供;装备
furnish evidence 提供证据
furnished dwellings contract 带有家具的住宅租赁合同(契约)
furnished house 配备家具的出租房屋
furor n. 激励,狂怒;(宗教的)狂热
further a./v. 进一步的;深一层的;另外的,添加的/促进,推动
further appeal 申诉
further calls 未付金的催款缴付
further consideration 进一步审议,(法案的)再次审议
further direction (对陪审团的)进一步指示
further hearing 进一步审讯,进一步的审理
further instruction (=further direction)
further proof of 对……进一步证明
further provisions 添加的规定(条款)
further witness 其他证人
furtherance n. 促进,助长,推动
furtherance of offence 助长犯罪
furtive a. 鬼鬼祟祟的,偷偷摸摸的,狡猾的
furtive manner 鬼鬼祟祟的样子,狡猾的态度
furtum (罗马法)盗窃(罪);盗窃犯;盗窃物
furtum conceptum 赃物
furtum manifestum 现行盗窃犯;人赃并获的盗窃犯
furtum non manifestum 非现行盗窃犯;非即时人赃并获的盗窃犯
furtum oblatum 窝赃(港译:插赃)
furtum usus 物品使用盗窃
fustigation n. 笞刑,杖刑;猛烈抨击
FUTA tax (美)联邦失业保险税
futile trip 送出的货不被接受
futility n. 无益;无用
future n. 1.将来;未来;前途;远景 2.(复)期货;货交易
future acquired property 将来获得的财产(指构成目前拥有财产一部分的抵押品)
future advance 新债务;(复)未来金钱贷款(指以原先贷款的相同担保再借款项)
future advance mortgage 在抵押品上追加的新债务
future behavio(u)r 未来行为
future consideration 将来对价
future copyright 未来版权(指尚未开始或尚未完成创作的作品,将来可能享有版权。许多国家版权法规定:未来版权不可转让)
future delivery 未来之交割
future dispute 未来争议
future estate 将来的不动产物权;未来动产;未来地产权
future exchange contract 远期外汇买卖合同(契约)
future goods 期货
future husband 未婚夫
future interest 未来权益,远期权益
future interest in land 土地的未来权益
future interests in real property 不动产的远期利益
future lease 未来租地权
future property 未来财产
future wife 未婚妻
futures business 期货交易
futures contract 期货合同(契约)
futures exchange 外汇期货;期货交易所
futures quotation 期货报价单
futures trading 期货交易
futurology n. 未来学
fuzz n. (美)警官,刑警,警察,侦探
fuzzy a. 模糊的,失真的
fuzzy reasoning 模糊推理[指模糊理论的发展为司法证明提供的第三种推理方法。又称似真推理、推定推理或溯因(plausible reasoning/presumptive reasoning/abductive reasoning)。对于模糊推理,目前尚无统一定义;另两种为:演绎推理和归纳推理]
Fuzzy Sets 模糊系统[指美国加利福尼亚大学扎德(L. Zaden)教授1965年发表的一篇数学论文提出的模糊性。法理学家也借以提出法的模糊性进行探析]
fyrd n. (英史)民军

G

gabel 货物税,动产税,(法)盐务税(尤指1789年大革命前所课的盐务税)

gabelle n. 盐税(尤指法国1789年大革命前所课之盐税)

Gaceta Judicial de la Corte Suprema de Justicia 《最高法院司法公报》

GAFA 信息时代诞生的"帝国列强"(G—Google 谷歌,A—Amazon 亚马逊,F—FaceBook 脸书,A—Apple 苹果,这些超级企业组成的"帝国"。它们掌握了21世纪的最大资源,以及利用这些资源创造利润所需的技术。这种资源就是数据,GAFA 掌握无数用户的信息与用户沟通之渠道,又有强大技术优势)

gaff n. 欺骗,愚弄;滥用;(英俚)低级娱乐场所,杂耍场

gag n. 1.塞口物;对言论自由的压制 2.欺诈,哄骗 3.(口)闭会(指下议院闭会)

gag law (或 **gag rule**) 限制言论(出版)自由的法令;禁止发言规则(尤指限制议会继续辩论时间的规定);言论钳制令

gag order 司法限制言论令(指案件审理中的一种司法限制令,禁止律师、双方当事人、证人或陪审员在审判室外发表任何有关正式法庭活动的声明)

gag rule 见 gag law

gage n. 抵押品,担保物

gage of land (英)土地抵押(指为担保债务而转移土地占有)

gagee n. 受抵押人

gager n. 抵押人

gain n. 获取,挣得;赢利,所得,获利;增加,增添;(复)收益;利润;获得物

gain and loss 盈亏

gainer n. 获得者;得利者;得胜者

gainful a. 有利益的,有收益的;唯利是图的

gainful occupation 有报酬的职业

gainfully occupied population 有报酬职业人口

gainings (复) n. 收入;收益;赢得的东西

gainless a. 无利可图的;一无所获的;没有进展的

gains from corruption 贪污所得

gainsay v. (主要用于否定句或疑问句)否定,否认,反驳,反对

gale n. 定期交付的租金、年金、利益等

Gallagher Agreement (1977年)(美)加拉格尔协定[指给一个共同被告(codefendant)的一项对原告财产赔偿数额可调整的权利的协定。在审理时确定赔偿数额,并据此协定保证赔付调整后的数额而不管审判结果如何。据此,共同被告可减轻经济责任。在美国某些州,此类协定被认为违反公共政策而无效,但另一些州只要已向陪审团披露即被允准。该词条来源于图森城诉加拉格尔案(City of Tucson v. Gallagher),参见《太平洋区域判例汇编》第二套丛书第493卷1197页(493 P. 2d 1197)(亚利桑那州,1972年)。见 Mary Carter Agreement]

gallows n. 绞刑架,绞台;绞刑;该受绞刑的人

gallows bird 应受绞刑的人

gallows look 犯死罪的面相

gallows tree 绞刑架

gallows-ripe a. 应处绞刑的

Gallup Poll (美)盖洛普民意测验[指以美国统计学家盖洛普(George Horace Gallup 1901—1984)命名的一种民意测验方法,其特点是使用训练有素的调查访问员,深入民众进行调查征求对调查问题的意见,然后对收集数据进行统计及分析。盖洛普成功地预测了弗兰克林·罗斯福(1882—1945)将在总统选举中击败阿尔夫·兰登(Alf. Landon),一时名噪天下]

gamble n./v. 赌博,投机;冒险

gamble on the stock exchange 进行股票投机

gambler n. 赌徒;投机商人

gambling n. 赌博[指在意识到冒险和希望获得的情况下,以某些有价值的东西作为赌注所进行的竞赛,其结果全凭机会决定。英国法在赌博的这个一般范畴内,对于打赌(betting)、对赌(wagering)、游戏赌(gaming)和博彩(lottery)做了区分];投机,冒险
gambling case 赌博案
gambling device 赌具
gambling in group 聚赌
gambling-den n. 赌场,赌窟
game act 狩猎法(港译:狩猎法例)
game laws 狩猎规则
game of Prisoners' Dilemma 囚徒困境(或两难)博弈
game of secession 脱离博弈
game tenant 狩猎场(或渔场)的承租人
game theorists 博弈理论家
game theory 博弈论,对策论,策略理论,行业理论
game theory 策略理论
game-license(或 **game licence**) n. 狩猎许可(证);买卖野味许可(证)
gamekeeper n. 猎场看守人
gamester n. 猎棍;赌徒
gamete intrafallopian transfer (约1984年)卵子体内输卵管转移[指将成熟的卵子植入妇女体内的输卵管(fallopian tubes)并使之与精液结合而受精(fertilized),缩略为 GIFT,亦称 gamete-inytrafallopian-tube transfer。见 in vitro fertilization; insemination]
gaming 赌赛;(英)游戏赌(指以合约方式对游戏结果下赌注的一种赌博)
gaming act (英)赌博法(港译:赌博法例;旧译射幸法。见 wagering contract)
gaming and wagering (英)游戏赌和对赌
gaming contract 赌博合同(契约)(见 wagering contract)
gaming debt 赌债
gaming(或 **gambling**)**house** 赌场
gamut n. 全范围,全部⟨run the gamut of emotion⟩(百感交集),⟨run the gamut of a formal approval of a constitutional amendment⟩(成为宪法修正案的全面正式批准)

ganancial property (西班牙法)夫妻财产共有,夫妻共同财产(如果解除婚姻,则此财产可平均分割)
gang n./v. (犯罪)团伙,集团;帮(派);一伙囚犯/伙同行动;成群结队
gang employed 雇佣团伙
gang fighting 结伙斗殴
gang leader 帮会头目,帮派头目,团伙头目
gang of bandits 匪帮
gang of terrorist 恐怖分子集团
gang robbery 结伙抢劫
gang stealing 结伙盗窃
gang theft 集团盗窃
gang up with sb. 伙同某人;与某人联合行动
gang war (歹徒帮派之间的)打群架;聚众斗殴
gang-bang n. 流氓集团的集体淫乱行为
gangbuster n. 取缔流氓组织的执法人员
ganger n. 工长,领班,工作队长;工头,监工
gangland n. (有组织地进行罪恶活动的)黑社会,强盗世界
gangmaster n. 工头,把头
gangster n. (美)暴徒;恶棍,打手
gangster culture (美)黑板文化,恶棍文化(指20世纪50—70年代美国的有组织犯罪以及有关意大利裔美国人组成的黑手党组织这一具有浓厚种族色彩观念和意大利裔犯罪的刻板印象以及老套论调在发行量很大的报纸上试图为美国有组织犯罪寻求解释所表现出来的偏见和排外思想,并有专栏作家当时在174种报纸上每周刊载文章,读者多达1000万人)
gaol (= jail) n. 监牢,监狱;(英国文件中用"gaol",一般文字中与"jail"通用,美国则用"jail");拘留所;监禁
gaol bird 囚犯;惯犯;流氓
gaol break 越狱
gaol delivery (英)提审囚犯清理监狱;劫狱,越狱;强迫释放犯人
gaol sentences 徒刑
gaol session 监狱法庭
gaoler n. 监狱看守(员)
gaoleress n. 监狱女看守(员)
gap(s) n./v. 缺口,空白,缺漏,间隙/使豁开,使有间隙

gaplessness n. （法律体系的）没有漏洞性

garage n. 汽车修理商（厂）

garble v. 1.断章取义；窜改，歪曲 2.（非有意地）混淆

garden plots 菜园地，菜园基地

garner v. 警示；扣押；（garnishment 来源于 garner）

Garner doctrine（美）加纳原则[指公司代位诉讼中允许持股人原告披露在公司高级职员与公司律师间的特权私密通讯规则。此原则不适用于律师工作成果，而且请求人（或议者）必须表明有正当理由]

garnish n./v. 传讯；老囚犯向新囚犯勒索（金钱等）/1.（因甲、乙双方争讼）传讯（有关第三者）2.通知（受托人）扣押（债务人的财产）；（向第三债务人）下达扣押金；扣押债务人的财产，扣发债务人的工资3.（英史）入狱勒索金 4.警告（古法律用语）

garnishee n./v. 第三债务人（指代被告保管财产并接到法庭扣押令于诉讼未决期间不得处分所代保管财产者）；财产受人/通知（受托人）扣押债务人财产；向（第三债务人）下达扣押令；扣押（债务人的）财产，扣发（债务人的）工资

garnishee execution 案外债务人的财产扣押执行程序

garnishee order 扣押第三债务人保管的财产令

garnishee proceedings 扣押第三债务人保管财产的诉讼

garnisher n. 通知（第三债务人）扣押被告财产的人

garnishment n. 对案外债务人的扣押程序，传呼（第三债务人）出庭命令；发给（第三债务人的）财产扣押令；（对债务人）扣发部分工资的扣押令；（美国有的州称为）受托人程序（trustee process）

garnishment of wages （对债务人的）扣押工资令

garrison n. 卫戍部队；警备队；驻军；要塞

garrotte n./v. 1.（西班牙）绞刑；绞刑刑具 2.勒索抢劫；勒杀人用的绳索/1.（西班牙）处以绞刑 2.勒索并抢劫；用绳索勒杀

garrotter n. 进行勒杀和抢劫的匪徒

garrotting n. 绞杀；勒杀；（英）勒（杀）抢（劫）罪

gas and oil deposits 油料储存

gas chamber 毒气室（指美国一些州使用的一种死刑执行设施）

gather v. 聚集；收集；渐增；恢复；推断；概括；集中

gather a crowd 聚众

gathering n. 集会；捐款；聚集；收集

gauntlet n. 夹管刑（从前的一种刑罚，受罚者从两排人之间跑过而受夹道鞭笞）；执行夹管刑的两排人

gavel n. 1.（封建制的）贡奉，赋税或租金 2.议事槌；（法官、议长或拍卖人所用的）小木槌

gavelkind （14 世纪）（古代）（英格兰古法）1.农役土地保有[指一种农役土地保有引起的公平地遗传给死者的晚辈子孙的习惯。1066 年威廉征服以前，这种习惯已通行整个英格兰，一直到长子继承制（primogeniture）将其取代。但这种财产分配方法（Property-division technique）在肯特郡（Kent）受到很大限制。享有一些优先条件的持有土地所有人按普通法（common law）则不适用：土地可以根据遗嘱进行处分，但不得因犯有重罪而被没收，尽管在犯叛逆罪或无继承人（want of heirs）情况下将被没收，在继承人年满 15 岁时，可以转让该习惯保有之土地。这种农役土地保有的继承方式于 1925 年被废弃]2.封建时期的贡奉土地[指生产出产品多作贡奉服务（gavel service）的土地]

gay n./a. 同性恋者/淫荡的；同性恋者的

gay and lesbian issues 男女同性恋问题（见 homosexuality）

gay liberation movement 同性恋解放运动

gazanging n. 毁约[指英国房地产行业的一个新词，意指房屋卖家在与买家达成出售协议之后突然毁约之行为（其动词为 gazang），实际即价格议定后一种抬价的行为。Buyers may also get gazanged"买家也可能遭遇毁约"]

gazette n. 1.报纸；（大写）（用作报刊名称）……报 2.（英）政府公报（指政府出版的刊物，一般指伦敦的政府公报，登载法规、法案、公告、官员任命、政府命令等）

公报上登载过的文件,根据诉讼证据法,一般法院都可采纳,用作证据)
Gazette of the State Council (中)《国务院公报》
gazumping n. (卖主企图提高价格)撤回(其同意的)土地买卖的合同(契约)
gazundering n. 压价敲诈(指买家为压低房价威胁毁约的行为)
GDP per capita 人均国内生产总值
gefolgschaft (日耳曼部落的)军事随从制
gemot(e) n. 集会;(古英国的)立法(或司法)机构
gendarme (法)宪兵;(美俚)警察
Gendarmeria Pontifica 教廷警察
gendarmerie (= gendarmery) (法)宪兵队;(总称)宪兵警察
gender n. 性(中性,阳性)
gender budget (社会)性别预算[指从性别角度出发,对政府的财政收入和公共支出进行分析,看它对女性与男性有什么不同的影响。亦称社会性别敏感预算(gender-responsive budget)]
gender equality in employment 两性就业平等
gender neutrality 性的中立;中性
gender-based exclusion from jury service 性别为基础而排斥在陪审团工作
gender-responsive budget 社会性别敏感预算(见 gender budget)
gene n. 基因
genealogical a. 家系的,家谱的;系统的
genealogical tree 家系图
genealogy n. 家系,家谱;血统;家系图;系统图,家系学
gener n. (罗马法)女婿(A Son in Law)
general a. 一般的,普通的;全体的;综合的;全面的;总的;大众的;首席的;(用于职位)……长
general abandonment 一般遗弃(罪)
general acceptance 普通承兑;不带保留条件的承兑
general acceptance standard (科学证据的)公认标准
General Accounting Office (美)联邦政府审计局

General Action Program 一般行动方案[指现行欧共体环境领域的决策新增补的第1305(3)条,即欧共体为实现环保目标而计划采取的一系列行动的总方案,而不是实施具体环境指令的方案]
general act 一般法案
General Administration for Industry and Commerce (中)工商行政管理总局
General Administration of Aviation (中)民用航空总局
general advocate 总辩护人
general agency (18世纪)一般代理,总代理,全权代理(指一位代表主管的代理人,可代理主管人或委托人从事与委托相关的各项业务而不受限制,有权处理授权范围与特定业务相关的一切活动。亦称 universal agency)
general agent 总代理人;一般代理人
General Agreement on Tariff and Trade 《关税及贸易总协定》(为1947年签订的以统一税率、消除贸易阻碍和差别对待的限制政策的国际协定)
General Agreement on Trade in Services 《服务贸易总协定》(1986年由关贸总协定各缔约方在乌拉圭的埃斯特角城召开部长级会议,发表了乌拉圭回合部长宣言,发动了一轮空前规模的多边贸易谈判。经过7年谈判,发达国家和发展中国家找到了充分照顾双方利益的折中方案才达成了本协定)
general amnesty 大赦令
general appearance (美)一般应诉(与special appearance 相对);当事人到庭(表明接受法院管辖);一般性出庭(指同意法院管辖权,并声明不接受有权管辖以外的一切欠缺管辖的法院的管辖)
general applicability 普遍适用性
general application 普遍适应性
general armistices 全面休战
General Arrangement of Borrowing 借款总安排
General Assembly 总议院;(美)州议会;联合国会员大会;联合国大会;(苏格兰)长老会全会
General Assembly of the United Nations

联合国大会
general assets 资产总额
general assignment 共同分配(指债务人自动将其全部财产移交给一个受托人处理,以满足他的所有债权人的要求)
general assistance (或 **relief**) (美)普遍救助(指对穷人的地方福利帮助,通常为临时性的,并无联邦筹集资金)
general assumpsit 普通违约赔偿之诉(指根据允诺或合同在某些违约情况下造成损失而要求赔偿的诉讼)
general attorney 一般代理人;一般代理权
general average 共同海损
general average adjustment 共同海损理算
general average apportionment 共同海损分摊
general average deposit 共同海损保证金
general average loss 共同海损损失
general average statement 共同海损理算书
general bonded warehouse 保税仓库
general budget 总预算
general burden 一般举证责任
general calumny 一般诽谤罪
general cargo 杂货;普通货物
general character 共性;一般特征
general classification of offences 罪行的一般分类
general clauses 共同条款
general closing 普通决算;结账;总结算
general code 总法典
general committee 常务委员会;总务委员会
general common law (或 **federal common law, federal general common law**)(美)普遍适用的普通法(或联邦普通法,联邦遍适用的普通法)[指在 Erie R. C. (Railroad Co.) v. Tompkins 案(美国判例汇编第 304 卷第 64、78 页,1938 年)中,大法官布兰代斯(Brandeis)宣布:"没有联邦普遍适用的普通法。"(There is no longer a general federal common law.)除所谓普遍适用的普通法(general common law)外还有一个非常实际的关系到联邦利益的联邦普通法(federal common law),它是如此有力以致联邦法院可任意创制实质性的规定以保护那种利益。联邦普通法的适用范围包括联邦专利利益、海事及对外关系,在 Erie 案后,联邦法院受到制约必须适用其所在地的州法,即使有个别联邦普通法(federal common law),但不再有普遍联邦普通法(general federal common law)适用于联邦法院审理的所有争议]
General Conditions of Delivery (经互会的)《共同交货条件》
general conditions on the supply of goods 供货共同条件
general consent 一致认可
general consuming public 一般消费公众
general container 普通集装箱
general contract 普通合同(契约);总合同(契约)
general contractor 总承揽人;总承包人;建筑公司
general convention 公约
general cost of administration 一般管理费用
General Council 总理事会(指欧洲中央银行的总理事会)
General Council of the Bar (英)律师联合委员会
general court 1.一般申诉,陈述原告的权利主张而无任何不当特性 2.一般罪项
general court 常设法院;普通法院;(大写)(美国殖民地时代新英格兰具有立法与司法权的)地方议会;(美)马萨诸塞和新罕布什尔州的)州议会
general court-martial 普通军事法庭(指可审判任何违反军法案件的法庭,并有权处死刑或开除军籍)
general credit 一般信用,一般信誉(指对证人品性须具有一般人的道德信用要求,即具有规矩守法的公民的品格)
general creditor 普通债权人(指债权上无担保保证的债权人,与 particular creditor 相对而言)
general crime 普通犯罪
general crisis 总危机
general custom 一般习惯,通常惯例(指①在全国盛行的惯例或习惯,并构成本国的法律渊源;②商业经营认可并遵循的习惯或惯例。见 trade usage)

general damage (复)概括损失(指根据控诉的损害情节,由法庭采用法律推定的损失,这种损失原告无须在诉状里逐条说明。例如因疏忽行为而引起的损害,概括损失便包括身体所受痛苦、健康所受损伤、生活之不便等);一般损失;(复)概括损害赔偿金(指法律推定为侵害他人权利时所产生的损害赔偿金额);一般损害赔偿

general demand 概括请求,总需求

general demurrer 一般法律抗辩(指对一项起诉文书或答辩书的实体充足性提出异议称作一般法律抗辩),一般诉求不充分的抗辩

general denial 全部否认;概括否认

general deposit 普通存款;普通保证金

general deterrence 一般性抑制(指对侵权行为的一般性抑制,而非侵权责任的初始着眼点)

general devise 概括性财产转让

General Digest (美)《综合判决摘要汇编》(指西方出版公司将先行出版判决摘要汇编的梗概收集起来出版的累集卷本。见 American Digest System)

General Digest, Sixth Series (美)《综合判决摘要汇编,第六套汇编集成》(指由西方出版公司出版的自1981年至今的判决摘要汇编)

general direction (directive) 普通指令

General Directorate for Trade 贸易管理总署

general disarmament 普遍裁军

general education 普通教育

general elaboration 概述,阐明

general election (美)1.例行选举(指依照法律对应由选举产生的官员在规定的时间段进行选举。亦称 regular election)2.全部席位(seats)的选举(与议会的补充空缺席位选举相对应)

general endorsement 空白背书

general estimate 总概算

general exceptions 一般例外

general excise 普通消费税;普通货物税

general execution 一般执行令(指命令地方司法行政官或其他法院官员,将被告的个人财产用来偿清判决款项的法院执行令)

general executor 一般执行人

general export 总出口

general eyre (历史)一般巡回审判,总巡回法庭,大巡回法庭[指予予巡回法官以最广泛和重要的职权,享有巡回中各种案件的审判大权。巡回法庭任务有三项任务:刑事诉讼、陪审及咨审(assizes)诉讼和提审囚犯。巡回审判期间,所有地方法院全部停止审判活动,皇家民事法庭案件也要送交巡回法庭审理……随着议会兴起,大巡回法庭的审判权逐渐变得没有必要,这种总巡回审判权于14世纪初已不复存在。在13—14世纪,郡的管理中有巡回审判权,如郡长对百户治安区的治安巡视审判权(sheriff's tour)]

general fictions 普遍虚构

general final accounts 总决算

general finding (陪审团的)一般评议(或裁决)

general finding in favo(u)r of either party (陪审团作出的)当事人一方胜诉的概括裁决

general forum 普通法庭;一般管辖地

general free individual action 普遍的个人行为自由

general fund 常规基金[指①政府最初的运转基金:为支持政府并补助立法机构酌情配给而提供各种措施的国家资产。常规基金不同于特别性质的资产,如信托财产、担保账户(escrow)以及特定目的基金。②未指定用途的非营利部门的资产,具有特殊目的的资产]

general gaol delivery 监狱大出空;(英)提审全体囚犯出监

general good character 一般良好之品格

general grant 一般让与

general guaranty 一般保证;一般担保

general hearing list 普通听审目录(港译:普通聆讯录)

general heir 一般继承人

general imparlance 普通答辩的延期[指允准的时间为法院的下一个开庭期之前,任何被告不得例外;有关这种类型的答辩延期,请求的被告不得在以后对法院的管辖提出异议或以任何借口作妨诉答辩(plea in abatement）]

general income 总收入

general indorsement of claim 权利要求的一般背书

general information concerning patent 专利须知

general inspection of the administration 行政总监署

general inspector 总监；监察主任；监察长

general insurance 概括保险（指包括人身保险以外的一切险）

general intent 一般的故意

General Inter-American Convertion on Trademarks and Commercial Protection 商标和商务保护泛美公约（1929年2月）

general interest 大众利益，群众福祉

general international law 一般国际法（又译"普通国际法"，与区域国际法 regional international law 相对而言）

general interpretation 一般性解释

general issue 概括答辩（指被告没有说明理由的否认起诉或控告事实的一种答辩）

general jurisdiction （美）一般管辖（有两种含义：①法院有权审理其管辖地区内刑事、民事等广泛范围的案件；②法院有权在被告住所地或工作地审理针对被告的所有请求，而无须表明这些请求与审判地所在州之间的联系）

general jurisdiction 一般审判权；一般管辖权

general jurisprudence 普通法理学，法学通论

general jury 一般陪审团

general knowledge 普通知识，一般知识

general law （大陆法）普通法（又译"一般法"，指区别于特别法的法律，不是指英美法上的 common law）；总则（法）

general law on banks 银行总（则）法

general ledger 总账，总分类账

general legacy （18世纪）总资产遗赠［指①遗嘱人有意从总资产中提出一笔遗产作为个人财产的赠与，可以是支付的款项，或各不相同的赠与项目，如公开交易的股份。②（大陆法）遗嘱人的赠与部分，或在满足特定遗赠（particular legacy）以后所保留遗产按比例的部分。③（大陆法）遗嘱人的全部赠与（gift of all），按照制定法规说明的赠与部分的或按比例的某种类别财产的一种。参见《路易斯安那州民法典》第1586条。亦称 legacy under a general title。见 particular legacy; universal legacy］

general legal capacity 一般权利能力

general letter of hypothecation 一般质押书；押汇总质押书（港译：一般押汇负责书）

general liability insurance 一般责任保险

general lien 一般留置权（指被寄托人对寄托人的寄托物件有权扣留，直到寄托人所欠款项全部还清为止的一种留置权）

general manager 总经理

general mandate 全面委托；全面托管

general meeting 全体大会；股东大会；社员大会

general mobilization 总动员

general mortgage 一般抵押

general most-favo(u)red-nation clause 一般最惠国条款

general most-favo(u)red-nation treatment 一般最惠国待遇

general negligence 一般过失

general object 一般客体

general obligation 普遍性义务

general overall classification 总体分类

general pardon 大赦

general part 总则

general partner 普通合伙人（即无限责任的合伙人）

general partnership 普通合伙（即无限责任的合伙）

general patent 一般特许；普通专利

general plea 总括起诉

general police power 一般警方权力；一般警治权

general policy 总保险单

General Post Office （英）邮政总局

general power 总括的权限（指具有某种法律上的地位与职务的人才有的权力。见 general power of appointment）

general power of appointment （18世纪）一般指定权［指受赠人享有的指定权，即可以处理赠与人遗产的权力，选择或指定任

何人作为受益人,包括自己的或某人的财产或遗产。特别是一种授予可继承财产权(fee)给予受让人的权力。通常缩写为general power]

general power of attorney (18世纪)专项代理权,总代理权[指授予代理人(agent)为被代理人经营商业活动的代理权。见 special power of attorney]

General Powers 总揽大权者

general practice 通常惯例,一般诉讼程序

general preferential duties system 一般优惠关税制,普通优惠制

General Preferential System (GPS) 普惠制

general principles 总则,总纲

general principles governing jurisdiction over people and over property 适用对人和对物管辖的普通原则

General Principles of Civil Code (中)《民法通则》

general principles of justice 一般的公平原则

general principles of law 法律的一般原则,法的一般原则,法律的普通原则;法理

general profit rate 一般利润率

general program(me) 总纲

general property 普通财产;一般财产权

general protocol 总议定书

general provisions 总则,通则

general proxy 一般代理(权);一般代理人

general public 公众

general publication (美)公开发表和发行(指公开发表、发行的作品均取得制定法上的版权,受到法律保护)

general quarter sessions 四季开审的法庭;一般地方法庭

general receiver 破产财产总管理人

general recommendation 一般建议

general reference 一般提交审定[指法院将案件提交给审断人(通常要获得所有当事人各方的同意)来断决所有的争点系事实问题或法律问题。这个审断人的判决即意味着法庭的判决]

general register of sasines (苏格兰)土地象征转让总登记簿

general register office 登记总局,注册总局

general regulation 一般性规章,普通规章

general replication (原告对被告的)一般答辩

general reputation 一般信誉(见 general credit)

general reserve 普通储备金

general retainer 一般保留权;普通律师聘约

general revenue 总收入

general revenue balance 总收支余额

general revenue fund 总收入基金[指市政部门支付日常运转和偶发事件费用之外的基金。《法律百科全书》"市政企业"第1627节(C. J. S. Municipal Corporation § 1627)]

general rule 通则,一般规则,常规;(复)一般性的法规;一般性的法律规范

general sanction 全面制裁

general secretary of government 政府秘书长

general security 治安

General Services Administration (美)全国总务行政管理署(指管理政府财产、案卷记录的联邦机关,它也可对建筑物的建筑、施工、提供条件、通信系统等进行监督)

general session (英)一般法庭(指由两个或两个以上的治安官主持的记录法庭,1971年已废)

general ship 一般商船(指通常代客载物的商船,区别于合同租船包载货物的商船)

general special imparlance 全面的特别答辩延期(指保全所有对于令状、诉状、诉讼理由等的异议权的答辩延期的允准,因此被告以后不仅可以进行妨诉答辩,亦可对管辖权提出异议)

general staff 总参谋部(全体人员)

general standard for notice 一般通知标准

general state inspectorate 国家监察总署

general statute 普通成文法(规);一般性制定法(指普遍适用的制定法)

general statutory power of attorney 一般法定代理权

general strike 总罢工

general structure of state organs 国家机关的总体结构
general subject 一般主体
general superintendent of police 警察总监
general system of preferences （出口产品的）普惠制
general system theory 一般系统论
general tail 一般限定继承权（或地产）
general tariff 一般税率,普通税率
general tax （16世纪）（美）普通税收[指①国家征收的一税种,纳税人并不由此获得特殊利益回报,而政府的一些项目对全体人民有利;②财产税或从价税（ad valorem）除了提供国家财政收入,没有其他任何目的。见 special assessment]
general tenancy 普通租赁
general terms 通项,一般交易条款
general theory of law 法的一般原理
general tort 一般侵权行为
general trade warehouse 普通商业货栈（仓库）
general traverse 全盘推翻,全部否认;概括抗辩（指对所诉事实作一般性之概括抗辩,而不逐字加以反驳）
general treaty 公约（=convention）
general trustee 全面受托人
general verdict 一般裁决,总括裁断,概括裁定（从一般争点 general issue 导致一般裁决。美国的许多民事诉讼案件中,由陪审团作出的一种裁决,仅仅表明对案件的决定有利于何方当事人,如果有任何损害赔偿,则表明所判定的数额。见 special verdict。在刑事诉讼方面只裁定被告有罪或无罪,不同于 special verdict）
general warrant （英）一般扣押令（指以前出自国务大臣办公署的一种拘票,以逮捕淫秽的和妨害治安的书、画的作者和出版者）
general warranty 一般担保;一般保证
general warranty deed 一般担保契据（指一种土地转让的担保契据,包括正式的、书面的允诺保证买主免受他人对转让财产所有权的任何权利请求）
general welfare 公共福利;公益
General Welfare Clause （美）公共福利条款（指根据美国联邦宪法第1条第8款授予国会的权力"去偿付国债,并计划合众国的国防和公共福利"等）
general will 共同意志,公意,全意志
general words 例行文句
general, direct, free and secret election 普遍、直接、自由和无记名投票选举
general-liability policy 见 comprehensive general-liability policy
general-purpose a. 多种用途的
* *Generale dictum generaliter est interpretandum* A general dictum is to be understood or interpreted in a general sense. 一般性用语应作一般性解释
* *Generalia specialibus non derogant.* General things do not derogate from special things. 一般不得背离个别（指一般法不得损害特别法）。
* *Generalia verba sunt generaliter intelligenda.* General words are to be understood generally, or in a general sense. 通常用语只能在一般意义上来理解。
* *Generalibus specialia derogant.* Special things derogate from general things. 个别可以背离一般（指特别法可损害一般法）。
generalist n. 通晓多门知识者;多面手,有多方面才能的人
generality n. 一般（性）,一般原则;普遍性;概论;学说;通则;概括（性）,概念;主要部分,大多数
generalizability n. 可概括性
generalization n. 概括,普遍化,归纳,一般化,一体化;（贬）判断
generalize v. 概括出,归纳出,使一般化,形成概念
generalized formulas 一般性公式,概括的公式
generalized investigation 一般化侦查;一般性调研
Generalized System of Preference 普惠制[指1964年第一届联合国贸发会议期间,由77个发展中国家（即"77国集团"）发起,要求发达国家给予发展中国家的贸易在最惠国待遇基础上更加优惠的关税政策。后经多次协商,联合国贸发会议于

1968 年通过《对发展中国家出口至发达国家的制成品或半制成品给予优惠关税或免除关税的决议》,标志着"普惠制"原则正式确立]

generally accepted 公认的;普遍接受的

generalogical tree 系谱树形图

generate v. 生育,产生,导致,引起,形成

generation n. 生殖,生育,产生,发生;代,一代(30年),一代人,世代

generation-skipping tax (1977年)(美)隔代转让税(同 generation-skipping transfer tax; generation-skipping transfer; generation-skipping trust taxable distribution)

generation-skipping transfer tax 隔代转让税[指以隔代信托(generation-skipping trust)或隔代转让(generation-skipping transfer)方式征收赠与税或遗产税,参见美国《国内税收法》,《美国税收法典》第16卷第 2601 节。有时也可缩略为 generation-skipping tax; transfer tax]

generational right 代权(见 intergenerational equity)

generic a. 一般的,普通的;(商品名称)不注册的(如阿司匹林)

generic claim 见 patent claim

genetic child 见 natural child

generic term 通用名称(指商标法上的术语)

generlized amnesia 广泛性遗忘(指忘记了自己的全部过去,癔症性遗忘,非常见症状,主要见于大灾难性事件之后。见 hysteria)

genetic a. 创始的;发生的;遗传学的

genetic deficiency 基因缺损

genetic discrimination 基因歧视(见 genetic information)

genetic engineering 遗传工程

genetic fingerprinting 见 DNA identification

genetic information 遗传信息,基因信息,基因资讯[美国用来辨识哪些类型的人最容易遭到基因歧视(genetic discrimination),也是用基因检测办法,即用 DNA 检测出的一些信息,因而具有"基因素因"(genetic predisposition)。其副作用是会带来就业上的歧视]

genetic material 遗传物质

genetic predisposition 基因素因(见 genetic information)

genetic resources 遗传资源(指地球上各种各样的生物多样性与生物资源是人类赖以生存的基础。遗传资源是生物多样性的一个组成部分。随着遗传科学和生物技术的发展,遗传资源的经济价值越来越多地被世界各国所认识并进行大规模商业开发利用)

genetic variability of offender 罪犯遗传上的变异

genetic-marker test 遗传标记测试[指测试组织样本(tissue samples)用以在亲子鉴定(或父亲与非婚生子之间)时确定某人是否是孩子的生身父亲的一种医学方法。这种测试象征医学的进步,超过了血型检验(blood-grouping test),它分析 DNA 并可以在评估亲生父亲的可能性时更为确切认定。缩略为 GMT。见 paternity test; blood-grouping test; human-leukocyte antigen test]

Genetically Modified Organisms (GMO) 改变生物之特质(指为基因工程所创造出的产物,即基因物质被改变的生物体。包含 DNA 在未经基因改造之前无法自然存在)

Geneva Bar 日内瓦法庭

Geneva Convention 日内瓦公约(指《世界版权公约》,因在日内瓦缔结,故名)

Geneva Convention on the Protection of Civilian Person in Time of War 《关于战时保护平民的日内瓦公约》(第四公约,1949 年签订)

Geneva Convention on the Treatment of Prisoners of War 《关于战俘待遇的日内瓦公约》(第三公约,1949 年签订)

Geneva Law System 日内瓦公约体系

genital hallucination 性幻觉(指一些女病人会阴和阴道的黏膜会产生幻觉,在此基础上继而有被奸感,此种症状被称为性幻觉)

genius of constitution 宪法实质,宪法精神

genocide (约 1944 年)(国际法)种族灭绝

(罪),集团大屠杀(罪)[指一种国际罪行,以一种毁灭之意图,特别是完全造成全国的、全民族的或宗教群体的身心伤害。1948年广泛通过的《1948年防止种族绝灭罪行之约》(Genocide Convention of 1948)确定了此种罪行之含义。国际刑事法庭(International Criminal Court)有审判种族绝灭罪行之刑事被告的管辖权。许多国家也都有刑法法规规定对已定犯有绝灭种族罪的一些罪犯的惩罚。见 ethnic cleansing]

Genocide Convention 《惩治种族屠杀行为协定》

genotype (19世纪)基因型,遗传型;属模式种,属典型种;(专利)人体组织(living organism)的基因构成(genetic makeup) [关于现存事态(living matter)的专利必须公开其基因型(genotype),而不仅仅描述其有形的特征(physical characteristics)(表现型)(phenotype)或行为]

genro 元老(指古代雅典贵族成员,公元前594年以前,公职实际上都由他们担任,但公元前580年以后则实际上已无权力)

gens n. (古罗马或希腊的)氏族;氏族(尤指父系氏族)

genteel n. 上流社会的;绅士风度的;有教养的;时髦的

gentile 外邦人(犹太教名词,指非犹太人)

gentitial a. 国家的;民族的;部落的;家族的

gentium privatum 见 private international law

gentleman of long robe 律师

gentlemen's agreement (1886年)君子协定[指当双方达成的非成文协定,该协议或协定无强制执行的效力,其履行依赖于当事方的诚信和荣誉(honor)。如大写 Gentlement's Agreement]则指1907年美国与日本缔结的"美日移民协定"。日本停止向美国输出劳工,美国亦应停止歧视日侨。1924年美国国会禁止从日本移民,协定遂告终止]

gentrification n. (1973年)移民开发(指中产阶级或较富裕的人群向欠发达地区移民以促进或推动该地区经济发展,增加财富并常常提高较低收入的居民的生活。gentrify v.)

gentry n. 1.贵族们,绅士们(英)出身,地位低于贵族的中上阶层 2.(贬义)一类人,一批人

genuine a. (17世纪)1.(物品)可靠的,可信的,有根据的;真的,真正的[指该物品具有所提供物品意想达到的品质〈the plaintiff failed to question whether the exhibits were genuine〉(原告对物证并未提出是否真实的问题)] 2.(文件)真实的〈the bank teller could not determine whether the signature on the check was genuine〉(指假冒或伪造文件泛滥以致"银行出纳不可能确定支票上的签名是否是真实的")

genuine interpretation 忠实的注疏,实质性的解释

genuine issue of material fact 真正的重要事实问题

genuine suspicion 真正嫌疑

genuineness of documents 文件的真实性

geographic criterion 地点标准(指"作品国籍"标准,按两个版权国际公约,指作品的首次出版地)

geographical coverage 地域覆盖范围

geographical representation 地区代表制

geography of crime 同 ecology of crime

Gerichtsfreien Hoheitsakt 交权行为

german a. 同父母的;同祖父母的;同外祖父母的

German Institution of Arbitration 德国仲裁院

German law 德意志法,德国法

germane a. 有密切关系的;恰当的;切题的;合时宜的

Germanic doctrine 日耳曼法律学说

Germanic individualism 日耳曼个人主义

Germanic law 日耳曼法

Germanist movement 日耳曼语言运动

Germanization of the law of German empire 德意志帝国的法律日耳曼化

germanus 纯血亲;同一世系的,同一祖先的

gerontocracy n. 老人统治(指年长者进行统治的制度);长者支配(制);老人政府

Gerousia 长老会议(指古斯巴达克的元老院)

gerrymander v. (美)(为选举获胜而把某

地)不公正地划分选区;(捏造事实等以)谋取利益;弄虚作假

gersum(e) n. (英格兰古法)支付费用;(承租人给领主的)补偿;罚金;补贴(同 gersuma, grassum)

gesetzlicher vertreter 法定代理人

gesta per et aes libram 称铜式行为[早期罗马法的适法或法律行为(*negozio giuridico*)之一,表现为当事人一方用一定分量的铜块(作货币)向另一方换取相应的利益或偿还相应债务。由一名司称当着5名见证人的面对铜块过秤并将其交付另一方。根据不同目的,称铜式行为分为要式置卖、债务口约(*nexum*)和称铜式清偿(*solutio per aes et libram*)]

gestation n. 怀孕(期);酝酿

gestio 行为;管理,处理

get v. 1.获得,收获,得到;受到(处罚、打击等) 2.捕获;打击;击中;杀死;使受伤 3.(毒品等)使上瘾

get away with murder 谋杀(做坏事)而逍遥法外

get credit for goods 赊货

get one's fist on sth. (sb.) 抓住某事(某人)

get one's way 为所欲为,随心所欲

get out a vote 设法使有资格投票者都参加投票

get (a) patent for 获得……专利

get rid of 去掉,摆脱,除去

get rid of retributive theory 摆脱报应理论

get round 规避(法律等);说服,争取

get sb. to bail 取保

get-off n. (飞机的)起飞;获释;不受处罚

get-off (go) scot-free 安然逃脱,未受害;得无罪释放

get-out n. 逃脱,脱身

get-rich-quick a. 企图暴发致富的

get-up n. 格式,式样;装潢,装饰,包装;(书籍)版式

gett (或 **get**) (犹太教法)离婚书(尤指犹太教内的离婚文件)

ghetto n. 犹太人区;(城市中)少数民族聚居区

ghostwriter n. 代笔人(指由他人代笔创作的作品,由未动笔者署名,真正的作者为代笔。但如某人口述,他人记录整理,则不属代笔)

gibbet n./v. 绞刑台;断头台;绞刑;示众架/绞死,吊死;侮辱

gibbet law (英)私刑权(见 Halifax Law)

gift n. 赠与;赠品,捐赠,礼物;授予权;才能,天赋

gift by will 遗嘱赠与

gift copies 样书(见 free copies)

gift coupons (可换赠品的)赠券

gift in prospect of death 死因赠与

gift inter *vivos* 生前赠与(指生者之间的赠与)

gift *mortis causa* 死因赠与

gift on marriage 结婚赠与

gift over (英)可变的赠与(指某种特殊情况出现时,继承所确定给某人的赠与低于给另一人的赠与),(美)转赠(指赠与物由受赠人终身享有,受赠人死亡后,则转移给第三人)

gift subject to conditions 附条件赠与

gift tax (1925)赠与税[指在财产被自愿或无偿转让情况下的应征之税。根据联邦法,赠与税应强征赠与人(donor)的税,但有些州则征受赠人(donee)的税]

gift with obligation (或 **subject**) **to a charge** 附负担赠与

Gifts to Minors Act 见 Uniform Transfer to Minors Act

Gilbert Act (英)《吉尔伯特法》[指1782年,英国议会通过的规定贫民习艺所(Work House Act)不能收容体壮可就业的贫民,而只能收容那些贫困、年老、病弱者和孤儿以及随同离异、丧失母亲的儿童的《吉尔伯特法》]

gild 见 guild

gilt-edged a. (纸、书等)金边的;上等的

gilt-edged bonds 金边债券

gilt-edged securities 金边证券

gilt-edged shares 金边股票(尤指有政府担保的股票)

Ginnie Mae 见 Government National Mortgage Association

gist n. (诉讼的)依据;要旨,要点

gist of action 诉讼要点

gist of the offense 犯罪要点
give v. 1.给予,送给;授予;赐予;捐赠 2.付给,交付,出售;献出;交上,呈上(文件等) 3.作出;举出;表示出;提出(建议等) 4.对……施行(责罚等),惩罚;课以 5.产生,引起 6.发布,宣布,表明 7.让步,允许 8.举行,演出
give a fair trial 给予公正审判
give a ruling 作出裁决
give bail 交纳保释金
give credit 赊欠,赊账
give customs clearance 海关放行
give effect to 使生效
give evidence 证明,作证;提供证据
give false testimony 作假证,作伪证
give judg(e)ment 作出判决;定案
give notice 通知
give one the axe 给予斧子,发放斧子(指美洲印第安人习俗,如果谁违反了部落法规或作出有损部落的事情,部落酋长就会递给他一把斧子,命他拿过斧子去自寻出路。后即以"发放斧子"喻指解雇某人,与某人断绝往来;以"接到斧子"喻指被开除)
give one's pledge 作出保证
give oneself up 自首
give out 1.分发,发出(气味,热气) 2.发表,公布 3.用完,耗尽;精疲力竭
give over 1.停止,放弃 2.交,托(to) 3.give oneself over 或用被动语态,使沉溺于;使纵情于(to)〈give oneself/ be given over to drinking〉(纵酒)
give quarter 饶恕;饶命
give returning blows 还击,还手
give rise to 引起,导致
give sb. a demerit 给某人记过处分
give(或**get**)**sb. the benefit of the doubt** (在证据不足的情况下)假定某人无罪
give security 作保人;提供保证
give short shrift (to) 1.不理会,不予考虑 2.立即严厉处理;很快解决
give the reins to sb. 放纵某人
give time 给予(允诺)一个(延期履行债务的)期限
give (or pay) tit-for-tat 针锋相对
give up 放弃;停止;把……送交;使(自

己)投案;投降;泄露(秘密等)
give way 撤退;让路,让位;屈服;倒塌;(身体)垮掉;(股票)跌价
give witness on behalf of 为……作证
give-and-take n./a. 平等交换(的);互让(的);交换意见(的)
give-and-take policy 互惠政策
given deal 已准的商业(或交易)
given jurisdiction 特定的专辖区,特定的专门管辖区
given litigation 特定的诉讼,所受理的诉讼
given matters 特定事项
given monetary prices 特定价
given name(s) (美)1.(不包括姓的)名字 2.教名,受洗礼的名字
given proposition 给定的论点(主张或议题)
given that … 假定,设想
given under my hand this 10th day of May 2012 亲笔签名定于2012年5月10日
giver n. 赠与人,授予人
giving n. 给予物,礼物
gladiatorial a. 辩论的,论争的,格斗的
Glass Ceiling Act of 1991 (美)《1991年玻璃天花板法》[指1991年民权法的一部分,它特别规定应成立一"玻璃天花板委员会"(Glass Ceiling Commission),借以研究如何消除女性及少数族裔晋升至经理及决策阶层之人为障碍,并增进他们在这方面的机会及发展经验]
Glass-Steagall Act of 1933 (美)《1933年格拉斯-斯蒂格尔法》[指为保护存款人的权益,该法限制商业银行从事与证券有关的业务,并禁止其拥有经纪行或参与经纪业务。亦称《1933年银行法》(Banking Act of 1933)]
glebe n. (英)教会所属土地(教区牧师可享用的土地)
gli animali non sono cose 动物不是物
global a. 全球的,全世界的
global commons 全球公域
(the) Global Contract 全球契约
global disintermediation 全球的非中介化
global era 全球时代
(The) global intellectual property on ratch-

et （TRIPs 的最惠国待遇原则和双边自由贸易协议共同形成的）一种全球知识产权棘轮（效应）（推动国际知识产权保护水平不断提高）

Global Internet Jurisdiction 全球互联网管辖权

global mixed domain 全球混合场域

global positioning system 全球定位系统

Global Program of Action for the Protection of the Marine Environment from Land-based Activities 保护海洋环境免于陆源污染之全球行动纲领

(the) Global Reporting Initiative (GRI) 全球报告主动性

global society 国际社会

global village 环球村

Global Weirding 全球气候异变[不可数名词性词组,意指世界范围内极端或不可预测天气状况出现频率和严重程度的增加。这一表达方式最早出现于《纽约时报》2002年11月7日的刊文《大自然:后院的香蕉树》。2014年1月,40年一遇的超级暴风雪横扫美国22个州,部分地区遭遇创历史纪录的降雪和低温。人为致全球变暖论者(Warmist)认为,面对高昂的气候灾害,人类难辞其咎,人类自己沦为了气候难民(climate refugee)]

global world economy 全球经济化

Globalists 全球主义者(指相信经济的力量以及技术全球化,主张制定一项循序渐进的国际计划来解决恐怖主义根源问题。他们认识到对美国至高无上的权威侵蚀是不可避免的和不可容忍的。)

globalization of international laws 国际法的全球化

globalized localism 全球化地方主义

globalizes n. 全球主义学派

glom v. (俚)偷;抢;攫夺

Glorious Revolution (英)(1696年的)光荣革命

glory n. 光荣,荣誉;荣耀的事;壮丽,繁荣,昌盛;处于全盛时期

gloss n. 注解,注释,评注,集注;法律原本注释

glossator n. 注释法学家;(复)注释法学派,法律评论家

glove money 贿赂;手套里的钱财(指古代西方人行贿时把钱放在手套里;走的时候故意丢下手套。后即以"手套里的钱财"喻指贿赂物);(英)法院官员过去曾享受的特别津贴

Gmbhs 私营有限责任公司(德语的缩写)

GNI per capita 人均国民收入值

go v. 1.去,离去;走,驶;达到 2.归,属 3.诉诸,求助(于);查阅(to) 4.进行;行动;起作用;做 5.承距……责任 6.放弃,废弃 7.生产;出售;出价;花费

go around and make inquiries 查访

go (run, tread) away 出现差错;出现错误;失败

go back of (美)俚语(=go behind) 1.寻求 go behind sb.'s words 推敲某人话中含义 2.进一步斟酌,go behind a decision 对决定再斟酌一下,深入调查,探究

go back on 食(言),违(约)

go bail for sb. 为某人(保释)作保

go behind 深入调查,探究

go beyond one's authority 越权,超越权限(力)

go beyond one's commission 越权,超越(委任)授权

go beyond the law 违法,犯法

go by default 缺席裁判

(to) go counter 违反……规定,与……背道而驰

go for broke 全力以赴

go in for the law 进入法律界,投身法律界,从事法律工作

go into 调查;探讨;进入;考察,讨论;入

go into effect 付诸实施,施行;生效

go into liquidating (公司等)停业清理,破产

go on the scamp 趁火打劫,顺手牵羊

go over the wall 越狱

go over to the enemy 叛变投敌

go public 股票挂牌,股票上市

go round 四处走动;顺便去,非正式去;(消息)流传;足够分配,不够用

go scot-free 逍遥法外

go shares 分享,分担;合伙经营

go straight 改过自新
go through procedures 办理手续
go to 归于
go to court 1.起诉 2.朝见君主
go to law 诉诸法律
go to the bar 进入司法界;(英)走上法官席位(指任命为法官的人)
go to the chair (美俗)被处(上电椅的)死刑
go to the country 见 going to the country
go to the devil 堕落,毁灭,滚开,见鬼去
go to the polls 去投票处投票
go upon 以……为依据
go-between n. 中人,牵线人;媒人;掮客
go-slow n./a. 消极怠工/消极怠工的
goal n. 目标,目的,终点
God-given 神授
godown n. (亚洲某些地方的)货栈;仓库
godown charge 仓储费(又译栈租。港译:仓租)
godown warrant 仓单,栈单
God's truth 天经地义的事,千真万确的事
going n./a. 进行情况;工作条件;离去;(复)行为,行动/进行中的;营业中的;现行的,现存的;流行的
going and coming 没有出路,逃脱不了
going and coming rule (1927年)上下班途中规则,来去途中规则(指雇员在上下班途中所遭侵权的原则,即雇员在上下班途中受到伤害通常不得按劳工赔偿法获得补偿)
going armed 携带武器
going concern 兴旺企业,运营公司[指被证明为赢利的企业,其招牌、信誉等可获得一种无形价值,常与 value 联用,即 going concern value(运营公司价值),指公司整体价值,其前提是公司组织结构和财产不会发生变动,仍用来创造未来收入和现金收益。亦称 going business]
going concern value 持续经营价值[指商务企业价值或营业活跃企业本身的现有资产以及其未来赢利能力的价值,其对应词应是"企业或其资产的清算价值"。going concern value 包括如商誉(good-will)。亦称 going value]
going equipped for stealing 离家外出时备有偷窃工具
going price 时价(指普通市场上价格。见 fair market value)
Going private transaction 见 freeze-out
going project 进行中的项目
going rate 现行汇率
going through the bar (英)征询律师有无提出诉讼请求(指1873年以前普通法院的一种惯例)
going to the country (历史上)要求陪审团审理的行为[被告被告知:"请求陪审审理诉讼争议问题",用"根据诉答确定事实以备陪审团裁断"术语,而且"请求向国家(陪审团)提出争议的问题",亦称 go to the country。见 conclusion to the country]
going value 见 going concern value
going-over n. 核对;彻底审查;痛打;痛骂
goings-on (复) n. 1.行为,举止,品行 2.事件;发生之事
gold n./a. 金,黄金;金币;财宝,大宗款项/金的;金本位的,(货币等)可以兑换黄金的;用黄金作储备的;黄金般的
gold bloc 金本位国家集团(港译:金本价集团)
gold certificate 黄金证券
gold clause cases (1935) 黄金条款系列案件(1935年)[指美国"新政"(New Deal)时期三个相关案件的通用名称:Norman v. Baltimore & Ohio Railroad co.(294 U.S. 240), Nortz v. United States (294 U.S. 317), Perry v. United States (294 U.S. 330)。这三个案件均系1935年1月8日至11日辩论,18日判决。作为经济大危机复苏期间保存黄金储备的"新政"计划的一部分,1933年私人与公共合同中规定的以黄金支付的条款被废除。此三案中债权人对债务可以用贬值的货币进行支付的行为提出质疑,认为其构成对合同义务的违背,且未经正当程序,而剥夺了他们的财产权。虽然联邦最高法院事实上许可国会损害已存的合同,但是黄金条款案件重申了国会对金融系统的广泛权力。黄金条款(指在美国要求以黄金支付的条款,1933年已废除。此条款曾在合同、债

券和抵押契据中以黄金清偿债务适用过)]
gold coin 金币
gold coin clause (国际贸易)黄金硬通货条款
gold coin standard 金铸币本位制
gold cover 黄金准备金
gold draft 黄金支票
gold embargo 禁止黄金出口,黄金禁运
gold guarantee 黄金保证
gold holdings 黄金储备,金准备
gold price in U. S. dollars 黄金的美元价格
gold reserves 黄金储备
gold standard 金本位
gold standard system 金本位制
gold swap 黄金兑换
gold trafficker 买卖黄金者,黄金掮客
gold-exchange standard 金本位汇兑制(指本国货币兑换成在另一金本位国家提取的汇票的货币制度)
Golden Bull (英)金玺诏书(指皇帝钦用金玺颁布的法律或盖有金印或金玺的特许状总称)
golden calf 金钱;物质财富
golden key 贿赂(金)
golden rule 金科玉律,黄金规则(指制定法地位高于判例法,法官对法律的解释是对制定法的解释)
golden rule fallacy 谬误之推理
good n./a. 1.好,好事;利益,好处;(总称)好人 2.(复)有体动产;财产;私人财物(尤指动产);物品,商品,货物/有效的;良好的;有礼的;慈善的;风俗善良的;充分的;合适的;诚实的;有教养的;好的
good administration of justice 公正执法
good against general demurer 有效对抗一般法律抗辩
good and lawful 善良守法的
good and valid 充分并有效的
good approximation 极近似值
good as avail 良好效益
good behavio(u)r 规规矩矩;表现好,品行良好;(美国联邦宪法中司法官的)忠于职守;品行良好(有时用 during good behavior)

good buy 便宜货
good care 谨慎小心
good cause 正当理由,充足理由
good character 优良品德,优良的声誉
good conscience 问心无愧,公平(指与 unconscionable 相对而言,英国衡平法传统用语)
good consideration 与受益价值相符的酬报;(英美法)合适的对价,道德对价,感情对价(这种对价不可强制执行)
Good Earth Foundation (美)美好地球基金会(美国环保的民间组织)
good excuse 正当理由,合理原因
good fair 上等
good faith 善意,诚意,诚信[指一种思想意识的状态,包括:①忠诚于信任或目的;②忠实履行义务,承担责任;③在交易中严格遵守合理公平的商业标准;④不得欺诈或获取不当利益。美国《统一商法典》对商人的要求是,合同方在交易中以诚信为本,并遵守公平交易的准则。亦称 bona fides。见 bad faith]
good faith acquisition 善意取得
good faith exception 善意例外,诚信例外(指事实上进行侦查的人员有理由相信侦查程序是合法的,如侦查人员依照有签发权的官员签发的搜查证进行侦查,但最终却发现搜查证为无效)
good faith improver (美)善意不动产改进者[指在实际上和合理相信不动产确为其本人(他或他自己)所拥有时,为改进不动产的增值的善意改进者。见 improvement]
good faith purchaser 善意购买人
good faith residence 永久住所(见 bona fide residence)
* **good fenses make good neighbors** 好篱笆结交好邻居(西方谚语)
good government 良好治理;健全的政府机构
good jury (=special jury) 特别陪审团
good leasehold title 租借地保有权(登记)
good life (保险公司愿接受的)健康投保人
good location 优良场所

good lot 大量
good market 生意好,销路好
good money 高薪
good morals 良好的道德风尚;善良风俗
good neighborhood 睦邻友好
good office 斡旋
good order 良好秩序
good paper 可靠支票
good product 合格产品
good reputation 信誉
good result efficacy 好结果效应(指法律程序运作的结果符合和平、安全、正义等诸项实体价值标准,也即所谓的"程序的外在价值")
good round 巡回,巡逻;周期;巨额款项,一大笔钱,整笔巨款
good season 旺季
good sense 理性
good sense of court(s) 法院的理性,法官的高度判断力
good social customs 社会良好风尚
(a) good sport 堂堂正正的好汉
good title 完整的所有权,良好所有权,无瑕疵的所有权
good (ill) will 善(恶)意
good-neighbo(u)r policy 睦邻政策(又译:善邻政策)
good-neighbo(u)rship n. 睦邻关系;良好邻居关系
good-night n. (死刑罪犯临行刑前所作的)诀别词
good-will n. 善意、商誉(指公司基本净资产价值与另一家公司为了购置这些资产所支付价格之间的差额。商誉反映无形资产,如品牌的价值)(或写成 good will)
goods afloat 路货,在运途中的货物
goods and chattels 有体动产;杂物用品;私人财产;全部动产
goods attached 查封的货物
goods credit 货物抵押贷款
goods declaration 货物报关单
goods forbidden from import 禁止进口货物
goods forbidden to be exported 禁止出口货物
goods forming the subject matter in dispute 构成争议标的的货物
goods free from all rights and claims 不受他人一切权利和请求权限制的货物
goods imported and exported 进出口货物
goods in bond 保税货物
goods in stock 存货
goods in *transitu* 运送途中的货物
goods of first order 直接需要物品
goods of second order 间接需要物品
goods on consignment 受托寄售;受托寄售(货物)
goods out on consignment 寄售品(货物),委托寄售品(货物)
goods prohibited from mail 禁止邮寄的物品
goods received 收受的货物,已交付的货物
goods sold 出售的商品
goods sold on credit 赊销商品
goods with no known owner 所有人不明的货物
goods with no obvious owner 所有人不明确的货物
Goodwill n. 慈善组织
goof-off n. 屡犯错误的人,游手好闲者;失误
goon n. (受雇破坏罢工的)暴徒,打手,刺客
goose case 见 white horse case
(the) gospel of the futility of legislation 立法无效的真理
gossamer distinction 微妙区别
gouged wound 挖伤(眼睛),挖创(伤)
govern v. (先例所属的)支配,控制,治理,使成为准则[指控制争议点中的要点(control a point in issue)〈the Smith case will govern the outcome of the appeal〉(史密斯案成了上诉结果的准则或先例)]
governable a. 可统治的,可控制的
governance n. 治理,统治,管理,支配;统治方式,管理方法,治理结构
governance model 治理模式;统治模式
governing board 董事会,理事会
governing body (学校等的)理事会,董事会
governing by decree 命令统治

governing case 成为准则的判例,成为先例的判例〈under the doctrine of precedent, the holdings of governing case determine the resolution of issue in the subsequent controversies〉(根据先例原则,成为准则的判例的裁决决定后续具体争议中争论点的解决)
governing class 统治阶级
Governing Council (欧洲中央银行)首脑理事会
governing factor 支配因素
governing institutions 管理单位,管理机构
governing law 适用的法律,依据的法律
governing party 执政党
governing principle 指导原则
governing relationship 管理关系
government n. 1.政府,(英)内阁 2.统治;政体;政治;政治学 3.行政管理 4.统辖;政权,统治权 5.行政区
Government Accountability Office (美)政府审计署[指美国联邦政府立法机构内的一个部门,负责审计美国政府基金的收支情况和对国会及国会委员会的成员进行调查。由美国总审计长(Comptroller General)领导,它的前身为总审计署(General Accounting),是按照《1921年预算与审计法》(Budget and Accounting Act of 1921)创立的,重新命名于2004年。参见《美国注释法典》第31标题卷第702节,缩略为 GAO]
government agency 国家机关,机关
government agency defence (侵权)国家机关辩护(指一种积极性答辩,根据政府代理人或作为政府官员的行为的证明而免除承包人的责任,这种积极性答辩因为确立这种政府机关的关系有困难而受到很大的限制。)
government agent 政府代理人,政府代表
government appointment 政府任用,政府指派
government attorney 检察员,检察官;(美)政府律师(实指检察官)
government benefits 政府福利
government bond 公债
government budget deficit 政府预算赤字

government business 政府事务,政务
government by civilians 文治
government by law 法治
government by the people 民治
government chief whip (英)执政党首席组织秘书
government circular 政府通告(港译:政府报单)
government commissioner 政府专员,政府特派员
government copyright 政府版权(美国版权法中的术语。美政府文件虽不享有版权,但可经美国政府通过他人转让、赠与形式享有对非政府文件作品的版权,与英国版权法中的"皇家版权"相似)
government corporation 国营公司
government decree 政令
government departments 政府部门
government documents 政府公文
government employee 政府雇员
Government Employee Rights Act of 1991 (美)《1991年政府受雇者权利法》[本法为《1991年民权法》之一部分。它特别规定《1964年民权法》第七章禁止性别歧视之规定,应适用至参议院之雇者、总统任用人士(presidential appointees)以及过去未被适用之各州受雇者(previously exempt state employee),其特别保护对象更为完备]
government enterprise 国营企业
government finance 政府财政
government gazette 政府公报
government grants 政府拨款
government guarantee 政府保证
government impediments 政府干预
Government in Sunshine Law of 1977 (美)《1977年阳光普照法案》(指从媒体角度体现政府与公众的均衡利益,则可参照美国这一法案;亦可译为《阳光法中的政府》,《会议公开法中的政府》)
government in Sunshining Act 政府公开法
government instrumentality (或 immunity) doctrine 政府媒介(或豁免)说(指政府豁免税务负担的法律规则)
government interest analysis 政府利益分

析说(见 zero-sum games)
government land 政府土地;官地
government lawyer 政府律师
government litigation 政府的诉讼
government machinery 政府机构
government man 官员,公务员;支持政府者
government money 公款
Government National Mortgage Association (美)政府国民按揭协会(又简称 Ginnie Mae。见 Housing and Urban Development Act)
government notice 政府公告
government of laws 法治,法的统治
government of men 人治,人的统治
government office 政府机构,机关
government official 政府官员
government organization act 政府组织法
government owner 政府所有人,政府主管人
government papers 政府发行的有价证券
government party 执政党
government performance 政绩
government permission 政府批准
government policy 政府施政方针
government printer (英)政府印刷局(指皇家文书局及其他授权印刷法规和法令的印刷局)
government privilege 政府特权
government procurement 政府采购
Government Procurement Agreement (GPA) 《政府采购协定》(建立《世界贸易组织协定》的附件之一和世界贸易组织复边贸易协定之一,它是一个关于 GPA 成员对外开放政府采购市场,实现政府采购国际化和自由化的法律文件)
government promissory note 政府本票
government property 政府财产,公物
government regulation 政府调节,政府规定
government regulation of pornography 政府对色情文字等的规定
government representative 政府代表;官方代表;公方代表
government revenue collecting office 征收机关
government secret 见 executive privilege

government securities 政府发行的证券,公债券
government service 政府职能,行政职务,公职
government share (或 stock) 政府股份;公股
government subsidization (或 subsidies) 政府津贴,政府资助
government ticket 政府税单
government tort 政府侵权行为
government under law (=government of law) 法治政府
government's program(me) 政府施政纲领
government-in-exile n. 流亡政府
government-owned enterprise 国有企业
government-run factory 政府经办的工厂,国营工厂
governmental a. 政府的;统治的;政治上的
governmental accounting 政府会计
governmental arbitrator 国家公断人,国家仲裁人
governmental authority 政府权力
governmental budgets 政府预算
governmental functions 国家职能
Governmental Interests Analysis 政府利益分析说
governmental intervention 国家干预;(中国诉讼法上的)国家干预原则
governmental intrusion 政府的干扰(干预)(或侵犯)
governmental maternalism 政府中心主义
governmental organs 国家机构
governmental ownership 国家所有权
governmental power 政府权力
governmental property of all the people 全民的国有财产,全民财产
governmental responsibility 政府责任
governmental tool 政府工具
governmentalism n. 政府至上主义(指主张扩大政府职能、权限和作用的理论)
governor n. 统治者,管辖者;(美)州长,地方长官;(英)监狱长;(组织,机构的)主管人员;(英)(殖民地的)总督
governor of bank 银行行长,银行总裁
governor of the central bank 中央银行总裁

Governor's Council (美)州长政务会
governor-general (英)领地总督
gown n. (法官、律师、教士等所穿的)长外衣(礼服)
gowned war 法庭上的争辩
gownsman n. (职业上)穿长袍式外衣的人(尤指法官、律师)
grab n. 强夺;霸占;攫取;逮捕;掠夺
grabber n. 抢夺者;霸占者
grace n. 恩惠,赦免;宽恕,仁慈;(票据等的)宽限
grace period 宽限期,优惠期
grace theory 恩惠理论(指假释撤销的理论根据之一,其二为 contract theory 合同理论,其三为 continuing custody theory 继续监管理论)
graceless a. 堕落的,道德败坏的,邪恶的;不懂情理的,无礼貌的
gradation n. 分等,分级;(常用复)等级;阶段
gradation of crime 罪的等差,罪行的等级;犯罪的阶段
grade n./v. 等级,级别;阶段/给……分等级,给……分类;(美)给……评分;属于某等级
graded system 分级制,等级制
graduate diploma in law 法律研究生证书(见 Common Professional Examination)
graduated tax 累进税[指①利用附有较高边际税率(higher marginal rates)的税率表(rate schedule)对待较大的应纳税基线(taxable base)(收入、财产、转让财产等),实际即"税率随纳税人的收入提高而提高";②见 progressive tax]
graduated tax 累进税
graduated vote 递减投票法
graduation certificate 毕业证书
gradus 亲等
graffer n. 公证人;代书人
graffiti pollution 涂写污染(指在公共场所乱涂乱写的行为)
graft n. 渎职;贪污;诈取;贿赂;贪污获得物,不义之财
grafter n. (美)贪污分子;受贿者;骗子
grafter and thieves 贪污盗窃分子

Graham factors (1966年)(专利法)格雷厄姆要素[指按照《1952年专利法》第103节(§ 103 of the Patent Act of 1952),有三部分测试标准(three-part test)来决定显见性。这三部分是:先前技术(prior art)的内容和范畴、先前技术和专利权利请求之间的区别、相关技术中(pertinent art)中的普通技巧的水平。该词条来源于 Graham v. gohn Deere Co. of Kansas city,参见《美国联邦最高法院判例汇编》第383卷第1页和第86卷第684页(1966年)。见 non-obviousness]
grain n. 粮食;谷物
grain coupon (中)粮票
Grain Futures Act (美)《谷物期货法》(此法代替原先的期货交易法)
grain levies 征粮
grain supply certificate 粮食供应证
grain supply system 粮食供应制度
grain tax 粮食税
Gramm-Leach-Biley Act (Financial Modernization Act)(GLBA) (美)《金融服务现代法》
grammatical a. 语法上的,符合语法规则的
grammatical interpretation 字义解释
grammatical-logical interpretation 语法逻辑解释
grand a. 重大的;主要的;总的,全部的;伟大的,庄严的,最高级的;(亲属关系中的)(外)祖的,(外)孙的
grand and petty larceny 重大盗窃及轻微盗窃(罪)
grand assize (英史)大巡回法庭;大审(指亨利二世时所采用的一种陪审审判方式,1883年废除);(收回终身世袭领地等的)土地(占有的)裁判程序
grand bench of supreme court (日)最高法院大法庭
Grand Committee (英)常设委员会(指下议院审议法律和贸易法案的两个常设委员会之一)
grand conseil (法)大法院(指1497年建立的王室法庭,大革命时被废除)
grand corruption 大腐败
Grand Coutumier de France 《法国习惯法

大全》(又称《查理六世习惯法》,指约于1385年编撰的一部汇编,内容包括有关法令、法兰西地区采邑法、习惯规则、诉讼程序和形式)

Grand Customs of Normandie 诺曼底大习惯法

grand days (英)法律协会节

grand droits 广义权利,大权利[指一切音乐作品的表演权,与此相对应的为狭义表演权或小权利(*petits droits*)]

Grand Duchy 大公国

grand duke 大公,大公爵

grand inquest (总称)大陪审团

grand jours (法)临时大法庭(指由巴黎高等法院法官成立的临时审判机构)

grand judge 大法官

grand juror 大陪审团团员

grand jury 大陪审团(指由12—25名陪审员组成的陪审团)

grand justice 大法官

grand *kādi* (伊斯兰教法)大卡迪,首席卡迪(见 *Kādi*)

grand larceny 重大盗窃罪;大盗窃犯

Grand Panel (德)大陪审团

grand parents 祖父母

Grand Prosecutor (中)检察长

grand science approach 大科学观

grand sergeant 大警官

grand serjeanty (英)大服侍土地保有(又译大服役土地保有。指土地保有的一种形式,由于为君主做服侍的工作如随从君主执旗或剑等而获得土地保有者,而大小服侍本为土地保有的名誉上的附带条件)

grandchildren n. 孙辈,孙(子、女),外孙(子、女)

grandfather n. (外)祖父;祖先

grandfather-clause n. (新颁法律中的)不追溯条款;(美)老祖父条款(指美国1890年后南部某些州宪法中从财产和教育方面限制黑人选举权的一种条款。1915年已废除)

grandiose delusion 夸大妄想(思想内容障碍的一种:病人无中生有地夸大自己的出生、才能、社会地位、财富、知识和权力等。自己对其夸大的内容信以为真,他人和客观事实根本无法纠正其错误想法。这种病人爱夸大妄想驱使往往作案。见 delusion of reference;delusion)

grandiose temple 雄伟的圣殿

grandson n. (外)孙

grant n./v. 1.同意,准许 2.财产授予,转让;授予物,转让物;赠款,补助金;赠与 3.转让证书/同意,准许;许可;承认;授予,让与,租与

grant back clause 回授条款(在许可协议中,要求披露并分享被许可人对技术所进行的改良或改进的条款,称为"回授条款")

grant bail 准予保释

grant component 赠与组成部分

grant credit 给予赊欠,给予信贷

grant of letters of administration 遗产管理书的授予

grant of patent 专利权的授予

grant of personal property 个人财产的授予,动产的授予

grant of probate 遗嘱检验的认证

grant of probate wrongful obtained 不合法的遗嘱检验的认证

grant of representation 代表权的授予

grant reserving the reversion 保留归复权的转让

grant to the federal courts 批准联邦管辖

grant-aided a. 受补助的

grant-back 回授,回馈授权(简称回授,指被许可人同意知识产权许可人有权使用被许可人改进许可协议。回馈授权作为知识产权许可中的一种协议安排,要求许可方就其对许可技术的后续改进或通过使用标的技术所获得的新技术,应当向许可方报告或授权)

grant-in-aid n. 补助金;中央给予地方的拨款

grantable a. 可同意的;可授予的;可转让的

grantee n. 受让者,受助者;受役者(见 conservation easement)

grantee n. 受让人;受补助者

grantee of patent 被授予专利权者

granting of pardon 特赦

granting remedies 允准救济

grantor n. 让与人;授予者
graphic works 版刻作品
graphology n. 笔迹学(尤指以笔迹判断人的性格、才能等);图解法
grass-land law 草原法
grass-roots (复) n. 基层;基础;地面;(总称)农业区(指与城市工业区相对而言);基层群众
grass-roots court 基层法院
grass-roots organization 基层组织
grass-roots unit 基层单位
grass-widow n. 离婚(或分居)的女子;独守家中的女子;有私生子的女子;被遗弃的女子
grass-widowed a. 分居的
grass-widower n. 离婚(或分居)的男子;独守家中的男人
Gratian a. 格劳秀斯的
Gratian's Decretum 《格拉提安教令》(指大约于公元1140年涉及教会纪律和规则所有领域约3800篇文本的汇编)
gratification n. 满足,满意;可喜的事;奖金;报酬
gratis 无偿地(的),免费地(的)
gratis dictum 空言,仅仅是主张
gratitude n. 感激,感谢,感恩
gratuitous a. 无偿的,免费的;没有理由的
gratuitous act 无偿行为
gratuitous bailment 无报酬的委托;无偿委托
gratuitous contract 单方受益的合同(契约);无偿合同(契约)
gratuitous guest (美)宾客驾驶员(指不付费驾驶别人汽车的驾驶员,按照汽车法,即被车主当做客人看待驾驶车主汽车的驾驶员)
gratuitous legacy 慷慨遗赠;无偿遗赠
gratuitous loan 无偿借贷;使用借贷
gratuitous transaction 无偿法律行为
gratuitous trust 无偿信托
gratuity n. 退职金,退伍金;赏金,小费
gravamen n. 诉讼理由;控诉要点;冤情,委屈,不平,诉苦
gravamen of a charge 犯罪的事实;指控要点

grave a. 严重的;严肃的;重大的;沉重的
grave bodily injury 重伤
grave crime 重罪,严重罪行
grave error of judgement 严重判断错误
grave incident 严重事故,重大事故
grave negligence 严重过失,重大过失
grave procedural mistake 严重的程序上错误
Graviore culpa gravior poena 罪责越重,刑罚越重;罪越重,刑越重
gravity n. 严肃,认真;严重性;危险性;重要性
gravity of the circumstances 情节严重
gravity of the offence 罪行的严重性;严重罪行
gray market 半黑市(港译:灰市市场)
gray mule case 见 white horse case
grazier n. 放牧人;畜牧业者;牧场主
graziery n. 畜牧业
grazing n. 放牧;牧场;牧草
grazing land 森林草地
grease the hand of 买通……;向……行贿
great a./n. 大的;伟大的,重要的;重大的,主要的;长期的/全部,整体;(加 the)大人物;伟大的事物
Great Assembly (阿富汗)国民大会(见 *loia djerga*)
great bargain 廉价货物
great body of American Common laws 美国普通法的优大法律汇编体系
Great Britain 大不列颠(由英格兰及威尔士与苏格兰于1707年合并组成的政治实体,1801年又与爱尔兰合并成为联合王国)
great case-study reform 重大案件研究政策(指由哈佛法学院院长 Christophe Lengdell 所发起的一种政策)
great chamber (法史)大法庭(指高等法院向高级律师开放,受理上诉案的法庭)
Great Charter (=Magna Carta) (英)《大宪章》
Great Commandment 最重要的诫命(指《新约全书》规定,在教会所有的律法里,有两条最重要的诫命:"你要尽信、尽心、尽意受主宰你的神。这是诫命中的第一,

且是最大的。其次是相仿,就是要爱人如己。"这两条诫命是摩西律法和一切先知的道德总纲)

Great Contract (英史)大协约(指 1610 年提出的一项财政改革)

Great Council of the Realm 王国大会

Great Cultural Revolution (中)文化大革命

Great Depression (1929 年资本主义世界的)大萧条

great inquest 大审;陪审团;(大写)最后审判,(宗教上世界末日的)大审判

great inquest of the nation 国民大陪审团

great legal importance 重要的法律意义

Great London Council (英)大伦敦议会

great national assembly 大国民议会

great official 高级官员

Great People's *Khural* (蒙古)大人民呼拉尔(指最高权力机关和唯一的立法机关)

great personage 显贵人物

great seal 国玺,(国家)大印;(大写)(英)国玺大臣(加 the)

Great writ 大令状(指人身保护大令状。见 *habeas corpus*)

great-granddaughter n. 曾孙女、外曾孙女

great-power chauvinism 大国沙文主义

great-power politics 大国政治;大国外交

greater loss 较大损失

greater maximum penalty 最高刑(罚)

greater offender 重刑犯,重大案犯

greatest happying of the greatest number 最大幸福原理(指边沁把作为自己全部哲学基础的两大原理之一"最大幸福原理"直接运用到法学领域,他认为人类社会的一切活动都应以"最大幸福原理"为终极价值,即谋求最大多数人的最大幸福)

greediest of legal categories 法律范畴最急需的,法律范畴中最强烈渴望的

Greek law 希腊法

green a. 绿的;精力旺盛的;无经验的;未处理过的

green clause credit 绿条款信用证

green finance 绿色金融(即环境金融)(见 environmental finance)

Green Patent 绿色专利[绿色专利所保护的是绿色技术(Green Technology),也称为环境友好技术(Environmental Sound Technology),这是《联合国气候变化框架协议》(United Nations Framework Convention on Climate Change)除第 4、5 条外所规定的。由于与能源、气候变化紧密相关,"绿色技术"亦可称为"清洁技术"(clean technology)、环境技术(environmental technology)、气候相关技术(climate-related technology)以及减缓和适应技术(miligation and adaption technology)。1992 年《二十一世纪议程》将"绿色技术"定义为"保护环境的技术",与其所替代的技术相比,绿色技术污染更少,利用一切资源的方式更可持续能回收利用更多的废料和产品,处理剩余废料的方式更为合理。国际专利分类委员会(The International Patent Classification Committee)的国际专利绿色技术清单(IPC Green Inventory)将绿色技术分为"替代性能源生产技术、能源节约技术、核能发电技术、交通技术、废弃物处理技术、农林业技术以及管理、规制与设计方向的技术"七大类]

green power 绿色魔力,金钱力量

Green Haven 绿港监狱(美国纽约州的一个监狱)

Green shoe 绿鞋计划(证券监管合作的国际化经验)

green thumb(s) 园艺技能

greenback n. (美)美钞

Gregorian Code 《格列高里法典》(见 *Codex Gregorianus*)

Gretna-Green marriage (英)(违背父母意愿的)私奔结婚(从前英格兰结婚形式十分复杂,而苏格兰的婚姻法规定结婚手续很简单,故私奔的男女越境到苏格兰名叫 Gretna-Green 的小村庄举行结婚仪式,以取得合法婚姻手续)

Greyhound Corp. and its subsidiary Greyhound line (美)灰狗公司及其子公司;灰狗运输公司(主要经营地在亚利桑那,但在特拉华州成立,实际经营全国长途客运)

Greyhound line (美)灰狗运输公司(指全美的长途客、货运公司)

grievance n. 1.不满,不平;委屈 2.冤情,苦情
grievance arbitration process 冤情仲裁程序
grievance procedure 不满(或冤苦)诉讼程序
grievance procedures 诉怨程序(在美国绝大部分团体协约中,都有列入禁止因性别歧视或其他因素而加以歧视之条款,从而,如雇主有性别歧视之情形,则受害人得请求工会组织出面,根据协约中所规定之诉怨程序,加以处理,直至提交仲裁为止)
Grievance Resolution Committee (GRC) (美)诉怨解决委员会(纽约州)
grievous a. (罪恶)极大的;严重的;惨无人道的;痛苦的
grievous bodily harm 严重人体伤害,重伤
grievous crime 重罪,严重的罪行
grievous faulty 重大过失,严重过失
grievous injury 严重伤害,严重损害
grievous wounding 严重伤害,重伤
gross a. 1.严重的;显著的;粗野的 2.总的;毛重的;整个的,全部的 3.迟钝的;世俗的
gross adventure 冒风险的借贷(指以航行中的船只用作抵押的借贷)
gross amount 总额,总计
gross average (= general average) 共同海损
gross domestic product 国内生产总值
gross error 严重错误
gross estate 遗产的全部价值;全部地产
gross for net 以毛重作净重
gross income 总收入,毛收入
gross indecency 严重猥亵(罪)
gross injustice 沉冤;大冤案
gross liabilities 总负债额
gross loss 毛损
gross misbehavio(u)r 严重不法行为
gross misdemeanor (18世纪)严重的轻罪(虽非重罪,但严重程度高于一般轻罪。亦称 high misdemeanor)
gross mistake 重大错误
gross modo 大体上
gross national expenditure 国民总支出
gross national product 国民生产总值

gross neglect of duty 严重失职
gross negligence 严重过失,重大过失
gross overcharging 过重的指控
gross premium 毛保费,总保险费
gross professional negligence 重职业过失
gross profit 总收益;毛利润
gross receipts (美)(税法)总收入,毛收入[指在应纳税年度(taxable year)经营的纳税人因货物买卖或实行的服务在扣减(deduction)之前所获得的金额(total amount of money)或其他酬劳的总金额,参见美国《国内税收法》,《美国注释法典》第26标题卷第448节和《联邦法规汇编》第26卷第1.448-IT节]
gross sales 销货总额
gross value 总值
gross weight 毛重
gross-income tax (1916年)总收入税,总所得税(指一项全部收入的纳税,可能扣减销售货物成本费用之后而非净收益、不准抵扣或减除费用的所得税)
gross-receipts tax (美)总收入税(指对经营的总收入所课的税,而未减扣货物销售费用和允准的花费以及扣减金额,即不是对净收入征的税。见 gross receipts)
grotian 格劳秀斯的[英古典派杰出法学学者 Henry S. Nlaine (1822—1888) 曾说"格劳秀斯学派原理曾盛行一时"]
Grotius (Grotius, Hugo 1583—1645) 格劳秀斯(荷兰学者,法学家和政治家,为近代国际法莫基人)
ground n. 1.地,地面;场所 2.(问题涉及的)范围,领域;(研究的)课题 3.(常用复)根据,理由;论据,原因
ground of action 1.见 cause of action 1 2.见 cause of action 2
ground-law 基本法(见 fundamental law)
ground-rent n. 地租
groundage n. 进港费,停泊费,停泊权
groundless a. 无根据的,无理由的
grounds for divorce 离婚理由,离婚依据
grounds of action 诉讼原因,诉讼理由
grounds of appeal 上诉理由
grounds of claim 索赔理由,诉讼请求的理由;请求权的根据

grounds of decision 作出决定的理由；判决理由
grounds of defence 抗辩根据,抗辩理由
grounds of law 法律基础,法律依据
grounds to suspect （英）导致合理可疑的迹象(美国称为 reasonable suspicion,日本称为"合理判断后有相当理由足以怀疑"；德国法上称为"具体事实")
group n. 集团,团体,小组；群体；派
group gambling 聚赌
group home 教养院（一般指管教青少年违法者或有恶习过错的青少年的场所)
group in the community 社会团体
group insurance 团体保险
Group Legal Services （美）集团法律服务（指为一个组织的成员或公司的雇员进行法律帮助,但和健康保险一样须事先预付款项）
group life policy 集团人身（人寿）保险单
group marriage 群婚,集体结婚
group of claims 请求群,权力主张群,诉讼请求群
group of individuals 个人团体
group of persons 一群人,群体
group of persons or occupational class (美)多组人士或多组职业类别(指免于从事陪审团工作的人士之一)
group of religious systems 宗教法系
group order 分类订货；集体订货
group ownership 分时度假
group term life insurance 团体定期人身（人寿）保险
group therapy 集体治疗法（指现代美国的一种精神疗法）
group visa 团体签证
groups identity 集体同一性,集团特性
groups of accounts 账类
groups of enterprises 企业集团,联合企业
grow out of... 产生于……的
growth and use of Long-Arm Statute 长臂法的增加和运用（适用）
growth enterprise （风险企业通常被称为）成长企业(在风险投资中,它是投资的载体,是资金、管理、技术结合的产物)
growth of private right 私权的发生

gruel v. 使极度紧张；（用重罚或逼供等手段）使筋疲力尽
gruel(l)ing trial 疲劳审讯,车轮式的审问
Guangdong Province Committee for Administering the Special Economic Zones 广东省经济特区管理委员会
Guangdong Province Special Economic Zones Development Company 广东经济特区发展公司
guarantee n./v. 1.(统称)保证人(法律上用 guarantor) 2.接受保证人 3.保证；保证书；担保；保单；担保品；抵押物/保证,担保；抵押；作保证人
guarantee against double jeopardy (对刑事被告)一事不再理(原则)的保证
guarantee agreement 保证协议,担保协议
guarantee chain 担保系统
guarantee clause 担保条款,保证条款[指合同、契约、抵押等协议中的条款,约定保证人同意为债务人履行债务；(GC)指美国联邦宪法第4条第4款规定,联邦政府保证各州实行共和政体(Republican Form of Government),并保证在各州发生入侵和内乱时提供保护]
guarantee company 担保公司
guarantee deposit 押金；保证金
guarantee fund 担保基金；保证准备金
guarantee loan 抵押贷款
guarantee of consumer goods 消费品担保
guarantee of insurance 保险担保
guarantee of obligation 债的担保
guarantee of the debt 债务的担保
guarantee slip 保单
guarantee with one's property 以财产担保
guaranteed a. 被担保的,被保证的
guaranteed association 担保社团,担保协会
guaranteed bond 保证债券,担保债券
guaranteed loan 保证债款,担保债款
guaranteed minimum income 最低收入保证(指政府通过赋税制度所实施的维持收入的计划,按此计划来保障公民的最低标准的生活)
guaranteed note 担保票据,担保债券
guaranteed person 被担保人

guaranteed quality （物品）质量担保,保证品质

guaranteed stock 保证股,保息股

guaranteed suitable 保证适当,包用

guaranteed wage plan 保证工资计划（指雇主向被雇佣一定年限的工人保证每年最低雇佣时间或工资的制度）

guaranteeing litigants 有担保的当事人

guarantor n. 保证人,担保人

guarantor enterprise 担保企业

guarantor of treaty 条约担保人

guaranty n. 保证书；保证,担保；抵押物,担保品；担保人,保证人

guaranty fund 担保基金,保证基金[指私人的存储保险基金（deposit-insurance fund），最初由银行评估筹措,而且用于支付给相关银行的储户。保证基金先于1933年成立的联邦存款保险公司（FDIC）的存款保险,许多基金持续到20世纪80年代储蓄和贷款危机（savings and loan crisis）之前。马萨诸塞州有一种为未保险的存储（uninsured deposits）（存款100000美元以上）设立的保证基金,而此存储并不作为联邦存款保险（federal deposit insurance）]

guaranty money 保证金

guaranty of trust worthiness 可靠的担保,有信用的担保

guaranty period 保证期（间）,担保期（间）

guaranty trust company 担保信托公司

guard n./v. 守卫,警卫,保护；监狱看守,狱吏；监视,戒备；哨兵,卫兵 /1.警卫；防守；保护 2.看守,监视 3.谨慎使用（言辞等）

guard a prisoner 看守犯人

guard against deviation 防止偏差

guard personnel 警卫人员

guard room 禁闭室；哨所；卫兵室,警卫室

guarded a. 被保卫着的；被看守着的；被监视着的；谨慎的

guarded preference for constitutional government 对宪政的谨慎喜好

guarder n. 守卫的人（或物）,卫兵；看守人,监视人

guardhouse n. 警卫室

guardian n. （15世纪）监护人,监管人,守护人,保护人[指①对于幼年、无理解自控能力又不能处理自己事务或有残疾的人,有法定权利并有责任保护其人身、财产和其他正当权益的人。此监护人可以被指定为了全面各项目的监护,亦可指定于某项目的监护。缩略为 gdn.,亦可称 custodian。见 conservator; ward 1。②（历史上）封建领主为了各种实际目的有权处理幼年继承人（infant heir）的土地,当成领主自己的土地使用、收益。当该幼年继承人达到成年时,监护资格终止,但也不存在封建领主欠债问题]

guardian ad litem （18世纪）诉讼监护人（指通常由法院指定一名律师在诉讼期间代表无作证资格或未成年人的利益进行诉讼,缩写为 GAL,亦称 special advocate; special guardian; law guardian。见 next friend; attorney *ad litem*)

guardian allowance 监护津贴

guardian and ward 监护人与被监护人（之间的法律关系）

guardian by appointment of the court 法院指定的监护人

guardian by election 选择的监护人

guardian by estoppel 不容否认的监护人（指未经合法授权即履行监护人的职责。同 quasi guardian）

guardian by nature （历史上）自然监护人[指孩子在达到21岁之前,父母为其当然继承人的监护人。虽然普通法承认父亲为自然监护人,而母亲只有在父亲离世后才是自然监护人,但大多数州现已改变,即双亲有作为他们孩子监护人的同等权利。亦称 natural guardian]

guardian by nurture （历史上）养育监护人[指对孩子不是当然继承人的双亲监护人,其监护职责一直到孩子年满14岁,亦称 guardian for nurture。也有些自然监护人（guardian for nature）,当然是父亲或母亲,一直监护到孩子年满14岁。但由于父亲或母亲不在了,通常指定谨慎照顾孩子的个人财产,并负责提供孩子的养育、教育之费用,参见威廉·布莱克斯通：《英格兰法评述》第1卷449页（1765年）]

guardian by parental appointment 父母委

任的监护人
guardian by statute 法定监护人(见 statutory guardian)
guardian by testament 遗嘱指定的监护人
guardian de son tort 自任监护人,亦称准监护人(quasi guardian)(指未经授权而履行监护职责的监护人)
guardian for nurture 见 guardian by nurture
guardian in socage (纽约法)土地继承者的监管人(指因继承而获得土地的孩子的监管人。这个监管人通常由不能继承的亲属担任。这种类型的监管资格适用于对孩子的人身和财产两方面的监管。从历史上讲,只有孩子年满14岁方被允许选择监管人,而现今则要等到孩子18岁或到可摆脱亲人有自主权利时方可被允准选择监管人)
guardian of law 法律的捍卫者
guardian of mental patient 精神病患者的监护人
guardian of person 人身监护人
guardian of property (管理)财产监护人
guardian of the estate 财产监护人(指负责承担某人财产的监管人,该人因为未成年、无能力或残疾而不能管理自己的财产。亦称 guardian of property)
guardian of the peace 治安保卫人员
guardian of the person 人身监护人[指因为未成年、无能力或残疾而不能照管他(或她)自己本身,负责照管这样的人的监护人]
guardian's allowance 监护人津贴
guardian's authority 监护权
guardian's bonds 监护人的保证书
guardians by estoppel 无权推诿的监护人(指无权推卸,只能接受监护责任的监护人)
guardians in socage (英)租地权监护人
guardians of persons non compos mentis or spendthrifts 心神不健全者或浪费无度者的监护人
guardian's right to custody of ward 监护人对被监护人管领的权利
guardianship n. 监护,保护;监护人的职责(或身份);监护权

guardianship agency 监护机关
guardianship and curatorship agency 监护和保佐管理机关
guardianship as a trust 像信托一样监护
guardianship court 监护法院
guardianship judge 监护法官
guardianship proceedings 监护权诉讼,监护诉讼程序
guardianship right 监护权
gubernatorial a. 统治(或管辖)者的;地方长官的;州长的;总督的
gubernatorial election (美国、尼日利亚等国的)州长的选举
guerilla warfare 游击战
guest statute (美)宾客法规(指美国某些州法律规定搭车者因车主不慎而在交通事故中受到伤害,不得向车主要求赔偿;其目的主要是制止搭车者忘恩负义的行为以及防止车主和客人合谋制造事故,骗取保险索赔)
guidance n. 指导,指引,领导
Guide to the United States Treaties in Force 《美国有效条约指南》(提由 I. I. 卡瓦斯和 A. 斯普鲁兹编辑的商业性质出版的现行条约指南,第一部分1982年第一次出版,不同于有效条约,未将双边和多边条约分开,第二部分以多边条约为中心)
guideline n. 行动纲领,准则,指导方针;指导路线;指标
Guidelines for Sentencing (美)《量刑指南》
guiding cases 案例
guiding ideology 指导思想
guiding judicial decision 判例
guiding principle (指导)方针
guiding rule for behavio(u)r 行为指导规则
guiding standards 主导性标准
guild (或 gild) n. 协会;同业公会;中世纪的行会
guildhall n. 同业工会会所;(大写)(英)伦敦市政厅
guildhall sitting 伦敦市法院开庭期
guillotine n. 断头台,以斩首方式执行死刑的刑具[1789年法国吉洛蒂(Guillotione)

医生促进法国国民大会通过的法律,规定死刑由机器执行,断头台被广泛使用。1792年首次成为法国执行死刑的标准刑具];(英)审议截止程序

guilt n. 罪,犯罪,罪行,有罪;内疚

guilt by association 因(与犯罪者)有关联而被认为有罪

guilt of an office 犯罪

guilt of desertion 遗弃罪,遗弃配偶罪

guilt of contributory negligence 负有混合过失之(罪)责

guilt of instigation to crime 教唆罪;教唆犯罪之罪

guilt of supine negligence 犯有消极过失

guilt plea 认罪答辩[指刑事被告在法庭上正式承认已犯有所指控的罪行。在刑事被告被告知并了解其应享有的权利后,他必须是自愿地作出认罪答辩。这等同于法庭审理后的定罪,法律上的效力等同于有罪裁定。通常来说,认罪答辩是诉辩交易(plea bargain)的一部分]

guilt pleas 有罪答辩

guiltiness n. 有罪,罪恶;自觉有罪

guiltless a. 无辜的;无罪的;无知的

guilty a./n. 有罪的,犯罪的;自觉有罪的,内疚的/犯人

guilty act 犯罪行为

guilty belief 犯罪信念

guilty but insane (英)有罪但系精神病患者(精神病罪犯裁定方式)

guilty but mentally ill (GBMI) (美)"有罪但有精神病"[指美国密歇根州区分法律精神病(insanity)与医学精神病(mental illness)之间的区别。陪审团判"有罪但有精神病"必须依据三点:①被告人有触犯刑律行为;②被告人在行为当时正患精神病;③被告人患的是医学精神病,而不是法律精神病。1975年以来,密歇根州提出了"有罪但有精神病"的规则,这一规则的产生背景是:在该州被判有病无罪的人被安置在精神病院里,释放他们是根据普通民事委托的法律。该法规定,一旦病人不再有病和不再有危险性就得恢复自由。然而,病人的恢复是建立在继续服医生开的药的基础之上,如果他不坚持服药就会旧病复发,从而导致重新作案危及公共安全。而判"有罪但有精神病"就可将这部分犯人置于司法控制之下,又对他们有一个明显的约束,此为密歇根州主张"有罪但有精神病"规则的原因;(英)有罪但精神错乱指英国《1883年精神错乱者审判法》发生了变化,它规定应当裁决"被告被指控的作为或不作为有罪,但当时正处于精神错乱状态",这一裁决的更简单表述是"有罪但精神错乱"。这个改判是应维多利亚女王的要求而作出的,当时她对法院裁决刺杀她的凶手因精神障碍而无罪很不满意。另外,学者们认为"有罪但精神错乱"的裁决不符合逻辑。但直到20世纪60年代"因精神错乱而有罪"的裁决才在《1964年刑事诉讼(精神错乱法)》中得到重新认识]

guilty deed 犯罪行为

guilty intent 犯罪动机,犯罪意图

guilty intention 犯罪意图,犯意

guilty knowledge 犯罪意识;自知有罪

guilty looks 内疚的表情

guilty mind 犯罪心理,犯意

guilty of another impliedly charged 犯其他含有被指控的罪行

guilty of profane swearing 渎神宣誓罪者,亵渎宣誓罪者

guilty party 有罪一方当事人;有过错的一方当事人

guinea pig 供进行医学(或其他科学)试验的人

***(the) Guilty party files the suit.** 恶人先告状。

guilty place 犯罪地点

guilty spouse 有过错的配偶

guilty tools 犯罪工具

guilty verdict (由陪审团正式宣告被告有被指控罪行的)有罪裁决

guilty-conscious a. 内疚的;做贼心虚的

guinea n. 基尼(旧英币,现相当于1.05英镑,用于计算专业人员、律师、医生等收费)

guinea stamp of the state's authority 国家权力象征的基尼标记

gulf n. 海湾

gulf and bays 海湾

gulf state 海湾国家
gullible a. 易受骗的;轻信的
gultwit n. 侵入他人地产的赔偿(亦可写成 guiltwit),非法侵入他人土地或房产的赔偿
gum foot (美俚)(便衣)警察
gumption n. 通情达理;主动性;勇气;精明能干
gumshoe man (美俚)侦探,警察
gun n. 枪支;(美)手枪;带枪的暴徒;扒手
Gun Barred Proof Act (英)《枪支证明法》(1978年)
gun control 枪支控制
gun crime 持枪犯罪
gun killing 枪杀
gun robber 持枪抢劫犯
gun robbery 持枪抢劫(罪)
gun use and misuse 枪支使用和滥用
gun-control law (美)(1968年)《枪支控制法》[指对枪支的买卖、拥有和使用的管制条例或法规。《枪支控制法》在一些州均广泛存在,而且许多城市均制定有《枪支控制条例》。联邦法律也限制和管制枪支的非法买卖、拥有和使用,参见《美国注释法典》第18标题卷第921—930节。见 Brady Act]
gun-runner n. 军火走私贩
gun-running n. 私运军火,军火走私
gun-saturated US 枪支泛滥的美国
gunboat diplomacy 炮舰外交
gunman n. 1.持枪歹徒;持枪抢劫(或杀人)者 2.枪炮工人
guns and butter 大炮加黄油政策
gunsel n. (美俚)带枪的人,以杀人为业者;贼,罪犯,阴险狡猾的人
gunshot fracture 枪弹创骨折,枪伤骨折
gunshot trauma 枪弹创,枪弹伤
gunslinger n. 枪手;带枪的歹徒;被收买来行凶的人,杀手
gut n./v. 本质,内容主要部分,海峡,(复)效力,力量/毁坏,贪婪地吃,取出重要内容
gut question(或 **issues**) 关键,关键问题
gutter n. 贫民区,贫民窟;路旁沟渠
gutter-bird n. 声名狼藉的人
gutter-child (=gutter snipe) n. 街头流浪儿
gwalstow n. 刑场
gynecocracy n. 妇女执政;妇女具有法定最高统治权资格的国家
gyve n./v. 手铐,脚镣/使上手铐(或脚镣),钉镣

H

habeas corpora juratorum 强迫陪审员到庭令
habeas corpus 1.人身保护(令)状(= writ of *habeas corpus*)(指法院根据被军警机关非法拘留的人的申请,对军警机关发出应将该人即送法院处理的命令) 2.人身保护法 3.人身保护权
Habeas Corpus Act (英)《人身保护法》(1640年)
habeas corpus ad deliberandum et recipiendum (从一个监狱)解交被拘押者到另一监狱(另一郡)法院受审令
habeas corpus ad respondendum 1.移交民事被扣押人到另一法庭受审令 2.提押下级法院监禁的犯人到指定法庭受审令
habeas corpus ad subjiciendum 解交被拘押者并说明其拘押日期及原因令
habeas corpus ad testificandum 解交被扣押者到庭作证令
habeas corpus petition 人身保护令的申请,人身保护令之诉
habeas corpus writ 人身保护(令)状
habendum 契据的物权条款;物权合同(契约)中的转让条款(指契据中写明财产让与的权利有多少情况的条款)
habere facias (亦作 *hab. fa.*)为"habere facias possessionem"的略写
habere facias possessionem 收回土地占

有令
habere facias seisinam （英）恢复自由保有土地依法占有(令状)
habit n. 习惯,习性;特性;举止;毒瘾
habit and impulse control disorder 习惯与冲动控制障碍[又称意向冲动控制障碍,是指在过分强烈的欲望驱使下,采取某些不当行为的精神障碍,这些行为为社会规范所不容或给自己造成危害,其行为目的仅仅在于获得自我心理满足,不包括偏离正常的性行为。此类病患类型有:①pathological gambling 病理性赌博;②pathological fire-setting 病理性纵火（又称 pyromania 纵火癖）;③pathological stealing 病理性偷盗（又称 Kleptomania 偷盗癖）。以上三类均有完全或部分刑事责任能力]
habit and repute （英）公认的习俗婚姻(指苏格兰法承认的一种不依正规手续的结婚,只要男女有同居的事实,并被人们公认为夫妇,便成立婚姻关系)
habit evidence (1921年)习惯证据[指一个人对于重复特定的情况(repeated specific situation)的常规反映(regular response),参见《联邦证据规则》第406条(Fed. R. Evid. 406)]
habitability n. 可居住性,适宜居住(指经建筑卫生法规检测通过的居住房屋)
habitant n. 1.居住者 2.(法)祖籍法国的加拿大农民(亦可写作 habitan)
habitatio （罗马法）居住权(指免费居住他人住房的权利)
habitation n. 居住;住处;住宅;聚居地
habitual a. 习惯(性)的;习以为常的;惯常的,已成为规则的
habitual criminal 惯犯,累犯
habitual drunkard 酒徒,经常酗酒者;一贯酗酒,酒癖
habitual drunkard act 酒徒处置法
habitual intemperance 习惯性酗酒(指经常性过激饮酒,严重到足以影响家庭或职业,可作为离婚依据)
habitual loafer 游手好闲者,二流子;无业游民
habitual offence 惯犯
habitual residence 常居地,惯常居所
habitual robber 惯盗(犯),老抢劫犯
habitual thievery 惯窃
habitude n. 习俗,习惯;性情;气质
Habls （伊斯兰教法的)哈伯斯(见 *wakf*)
hack n./v./a. 1.(美)出租汽(马)车;出租汽车司机;(英)出租的马 2.(美俚)监狱看守;(美)唯命是从的政党工作人员 3.砍痕,伤痕 4.(对海军军官的)营房拘禁 5.苦役/l.出租(马等),驾驶出租汽(马)车 2.砍,劈;乱砍,乱劈/出租的,受雇的;陈腐的;平凡的
hacking the pie (年终股东)分红会议
Hadith （伊斯兰教法)《圣训》(指有关先知穆罕默德的传说或他的言语的记录,为伊斯兰教法及其道德规范的主要根据,其权威性仅次于《古兰经》,信徒必须遵守的和教法官据以断案的逊奈也由圣训产生)
haereditas 继承权;继承财产
haereditas ab intestato 无遗嘱继承权
haereditas jacens 无人继承的财产
* *Haereditas nunquan ascendit.* An inheritance never ascends. 继承权不向上溯。
haeres （罗马法）继承人,概括继承人
* *Haeres legitimus est quem nuptiae demonstrant.* He is a lawful heir whom marriage points out as such. 婚生子女才能作为法定继承人。
haeres natus 亲生的继承人(指当然之遗产继承人,与指定继承人有别)
haeres suus （罗马法）直系继承人,自家继承人;正统继承人
Haggadah n. 犹太教法典中的传说部分
haggle n. 争论不休,论价,讨价还价不休
hagiarchy n. 圣徒(或教徒)统治;圣徒等级组织
Hague Academy of International Law 海牙国际法学院(1923年成立)
Hague Conference on Private International Law 海牙国际私法会议
Hague Convention 《海牙公约》(指1899年和1907年两次海牙和平会议上通过限制作战手段和方法的重要条约)
Hague Convention for the Suppression of Unlawful Seizure of Aircraft 《关于制止非法劫持航空器的海牙公约》(1970年在

海牙签订)
Hague Convention on Law Applicable to Estate Succession 《关于不动产继承的法律适用海牙公约》(1988年)
Hague Convention on Service of Documents 《文件送达海牙公约》
Hague Convention on the Taking of Evidence Abroad 《关于海外取证的海牙公约》(1972年)
Hague law system 海牙公约体系
Hague Peace Conferences 海牙和平会议(指1899年和1907年在海牙举行的两次国际会议,目的在于解决国际争端)
Hague Regulations on Land Warfare 《海牙陆战规则》(1899年签订)
Hague Rules 《海牙规则》(指1923年布鲁塞尔会议通过并于1963年修订的有关海上货物运送的规则,全名为《统一提单若干法律规则的国际公约》)
Hague-Visby Rules 海牙-维斯比规则[实际指《修改统一提单的若干法律规则的国际公约的议定书》(Protocol to Amend the International Convention for the Unification of Certain Rules of Law Relation to Bills of Lading)的简称。由于讨论该议定书的会议期间,代表们曾对中世纪著名《维斯比海法》的发源地维斯比进行过访问,因此而得名]
hair trigger 一触即发的,即时的,一碰就坏的
haircut (证券)1.股票(折扣)差价[指美国全国证券交易商协会(National Association of Securities Dealers)要求的对股票价值(the value of stock)的折扣(discount),该折扣系经纪行业公司(brokerage firm)在呈交有关公司的净资产(值)状况(net capital condition)的月度报告时在其自身的折扣中所持有的].2.差价(指贷款额和附加以贷款担保的市场价值之间的差价)
haircut reorganization 剃头式债务重组,果断债务重组[指对于降低或减少欠债权人的债款的主要金额的重新调整。共同的习惯(common usage)多表示简单的折扣〈we took a haircut on that deal〉(在那笔交易中我们给予折扣)。见 reorganization 1]

Haitian divorce 海地的离婚(见 Mexican divorce)
hakim n. (伊斯兰教国家的)地方长官;法官;大学者;医生(亦作 hakeem)
hale v./a. 强拉,硬托/强壮的,有力的
half a. 一半的;不完全的,部分的
half blood 1.半血亲(同父异母或同母异父)亲,或同父异母(同母异父)兄弟,姐妹关系 2.混血儿
half brother and half sister 同父异母(同母异父)的兄弟姐妹
half seas-over (half-shot) a. (俚)半醉的
half sovereign state 半主权国
half-caste n. 半特权阶层
half-executed transaction 未履行交易
half-proof n. (大陆法)部分证据(指一方证人提供的证据或提供私人文书作证据)
half-quarter days (季节结账日之间的)中间日(指英格兰两个季度结账日之间的中间日期。全年有2月2日,5月9日,8月11日和11月11日)
half-sane (或 half-insane) **offender** 半疯癫罪犯
half-secret trust 半秘密信托
half-sister n. 同父异母(或同母异父)的姐妹
half-truth n. 只有部分真实的欺骗性陈述
half-way house (为长期住院的精神病患者或吸毒分子戒毒而设的)重返社会训练所(港译:过渡期宿舍)
Halifax Law (Halifax Gibbet Law)(英)《哈利法克斯缓刑法》(指英国古代的一种王室授权或领主在其领地上的一种私刑法律,即哈利法克斯自治市居民享有这种权利:在该市自治区内对被认定盗窃有超过13便士价值的财物者可处以绞刑,该法最后一次执行在1650年,此法为当时施行的《庄园内盗窃裁决法》)
hallmarking n. 金银纯度标志(指加在金银制品上表示其纯度的标志)
hallimote (或 **haligemot**) n. (撒克逊法)领主法庭
hallucination 幻觉(指虚幻的知觉体验,特点是没有相应的客观刺激存在,却出现了相关的知觉体验,属精神障碍词语),

幻象

Halsbury's Laws of England 《英国法大全》(亦称《霍尔兹伯里英国法大全》)

Halsbury's Statutes of England (英)《霍尔兹伯里英格兰法规汇编》(指巴特沃思公司出版的非官方版 1968—1975 年现行法判例的百科式法规汇编第 3 版,并附有司法判例注脚及索引。另有补编本《1952—1972 年,欧洲人的续编》,提供欧洲共同体条约和辅助立法)

halter n./v. 缰绳;绞刑;绞索/绞死;束缚,抑制

halfway house (1970 年)过渡住所,临时住所(或宿舍),过渡训练所(指旨在为刚离开监狱或医院者等返社会的人提供必要的适应性训练以便进入社会正常生活的一个机构,亦称 residential community treatment center)

Hamburg Rules 《汉堡规则》(为取代已过时的《海牙规则》,联合国于 1975 年 3 月在汉堡召开的有 70 多个国家参加的大会上通过的公约的简称,全名为《联合国海上货物运输公约》)

hamesecken n. (古英国法)破屋入室(罪),夜间侵入住宅盗窃(罪)

hamfare n. (撒克逊法)侵犯私宅安宁;住宅安全保卫权(见 hamsocne)

hammer v./n. 锤击;(英)交易所击锤宣布(某人)无力偿债;致力于,埋头于;重复论及;不断强调(会议主席或拍卖人等用的)小木锤;榔头;烙铁

Hammurabi Code 《汉谟拉比法典》(公元前 18 世纪古巴比伦国王颁布的世界上迄今完整保存下来的最早的法典)

hamper v./n. 妨碍;阻碍;牵制/阻碍物;平时不可少而在风险中成为累赘的船具

hamsocne n. (撒克逊法)(强行闯入私宅)侵犯私宅的安宁;住宅安全保护权(此词不同的拼写有:hamsoca, hamsocna, haimsucken, hamesaken, hamsocn)

Han chauvinism (中)大汉族主义

Hanābilah (伊斯兰教法)罕百里派(逊尼派的四种流派之一,为四大教派中最恪守原教义的派别,主张法学理论完全是真主的旨意,反对个人意见、类比和希腊化教义)

Hanāfiyah (伊斯兰教法)哈乃斐派(逊尼派的四种流派之一,此派承认《古兰经》和圣训是法律的基本依据,但又认为在无先例可援引下,可根据个人意见办案)

hanaper office (英)大篮子文件局(指一种与大法官法庭普通法管辖权相关联的办事机构)

hand n. 1.手;人手;字迹,手迹;(公文用语)签字;插手;经手 2.婚约;所有,支配;(罗马法)丈夫对妻子的控制权

hand down 宣布(判词);传递;传给(后代)

hand in 缴纳,上交

hand in glove 勾结着

hand in hand a. 1.手牵手的,亲密的 2.并进的

hand in one's business licence for cancellation 缴销营业执照

hand money 定金(亦作 earnest money)

hand(ing) over 交出,移交

hand-print n. 手印

hand-sale n. 握手买卖(指用握手表示成交);握手买卖合同(契约)

hand-vote n. 举手选举

handcuffs (复) n. 手铐

handexpert n. 笔迹鉴定人(专家)

handfasting n. 握手婚约(指英格兰和苏格兰边界地区的一种习俗,有时指虽服从教规约束但未受洗礼的结婚)

handgun (= handarm) n. 手枪

handicapped a. 有生理缺陷的,残废的

handicapped child 残疾儿童[指智力迟钝、耳聋或听力受到伤害、语音能力差、眼盲或视觉伤残、严重情感低沉、精神恍惚、形体伤害且由于专门学习无能而需特殊教育(special education)的儿童]

handicaps n. 障碍,不利条件

handle v. 处理,处置;管理;(美)经营,买卖;操纵,运用;对待(人)

handle a case 办案,理案

handle procedures 办理手续

handle wills 处理遗嘱,管理遗嘱

handling n. 处理(方法);管理;操纵;装卸,运用

handling cost 手续费,管理费,装卸费
handling of letters from the people (中)处理人民来信
handling of precedents 应用先例,先例的运用
handling operation 装卸作业
handling precedent 掌握先例
handling stolen goods 收受赃物(=receiving stolen goods)
handplay n. 互殴,殴打
hands clean 廉洁
hands off a./n. 不干涉的,不插手的/不干涉,不插手
hands-off policy 不干涉政策
handsel n. 1.定金;保证金 2.贺礼;新年赠品 3.试样;初次试用
handshow n. 举手投票(表决)
handwriting n. 手书;笔迹;手写稿
handwriting verification 笔迹鉴定
hang v. 1.使(陪审团)不能作出决定,搁置;悬而不决 2.附加;悬着,吊着 3.(被)绞死,(被)吊死
hang in doubt 悬而未决
hang oneself 自缢
hang the jury 使陪审团意见分歧而不能作出判定
hanged on the neck (宣判用语)处以绞刑
hanger n. 绞杀者,绞刑执行人
hanging n./a. 绞刑,绞死;悬而不决/应处绞刑的;意欲判绞刑的
hanging, drawing, and quartering (英)吊剖分尸刑(指古代对犯有叛国罪者所处的刑罚)
hanging cabinets (英)酌处(宽恕)绞刑的内阁会议(指19世纪在内阁会议上对死刑犯人是否宽恕作出决定,开始由国王独自作出,1837年移给内政大臣一人作出)
hanging case (或 matter) 以处以绞刑终结的案件;绞刑案件
hanging crime 应处绞刑的罪;死罪
hanging gale (英)欠交租金
hanging gear 绞刑具
hanging in chains (英史)吊尸示众(于1834年废除)
hanging jury 打算判(犯人)绞刑的陪审团
hanging offence 应处绞刑的罪行;死罪
hanging the process 搁置此项程序
hangman n. 执行绞刑者
hangwite (或 **hangwit**) n. 制裁(对非法绞死窃盗者或任其逃跑者所处的)罚金
hansard n. (英)议会辩论;(大写)《英国议会记事录》(指议会讨论事项的官方汇编)
hanse n. (14世纪)(中世纪北欧城市的)商人公会;(大写)汉萨同盟(指公元13—17世纪北欧城市结成的商业、政治同盟,以德意志北部诸城市为主)
Hanseatic Law of the Sea 《汉萨海商法》(1591年由汉萨同盟联系北欧各城而制定)
Hanseatic league 汉萨同盟(见 hanse)
hantelode (或 **hantetod**) n. (古欧洲法)逮捕,拘押
happen n. 投放要求立法机关讨论议案的箱子
happenchance n. 偶然事件
happy dispatch (hara-kiri) (日本式的)切腹自杀
harassment n. 折磨;骚扰,侵扰;烦恼;折磨人的东西
harassment of debtor 故意为难债务人
harassment of occupier 故意为难占有人(或房客)
harbo(u)r n./v. 隐匿,窝藏(罪犯等);港口;港湾;码头;避难所;碇泊税/包庇,庇护;隐匿,窝藏(罪犯);入港停泊
harbo(u)r a criminal 窝藏罪犯
harbo(u)r authority 港务局
harbo(u)r dues 入港税,港务费
harbo(u)r police 水上警察
harbo(u)rage n. 停泊处;躲藏处
harbo(u)ring n. 包庇,庇护;隐匿,窝藏(罪)
harbo(u)ring female 隐匿妇女
harbo(u)ring resentments and making false accusation 挟嫌诬告
Harbottle Principle 哈博特尔规则[指根据1843年福斯诉哈伯特案(Foss v. Harbottle)的主审法官威格拉姆(Wigram)爵

士对该案的判决理由所归纳出的哈博特尔规则,具体包括原告适格原则(principle of proper plaintiff)和司法不介入公司经营原则(principle of internal management of the company)]

hard a. 确定的,不容怀疑的;困难的,艰苦的;硬的;不友善的,含有敌意的;冷酷的;强烈的

hard and fast 严格的,不许变动的

hard and fast rules 固定和可靠的规则

hard bargain 极力讨价还价之交易,艰难的讨价还价

hard case 难处理的事情;(用于司法判决中的一个术语)棘手案件,疑难案件

* **Hard cases make bad law.** 难以处理的案件使法律徒具空名(或造成法律上的例外)。

hard cash 硬币,现金

hard cost 确实成本

hard currency 硬通货,硬币

hard drug 使人成瘾的毒品

hard evidence 铁证如山

hard labo(u)r (英)(囚犯的)强迫苦役;劳役;苦工

hard law 硬法(指一些经有关国家协商签订的国际性协约、公约和协定等,对有关国家具有较强的约束力,国际环境法学界称为"硬法")

hard loan 条件苛刻的贷款

hard look doctrine 不容置疑的原则(或原理),不容置疑

hard money (美)硬币;现金

hard paternalism 强式家长主义(指美国学者波普在德沃金的基础上进一步提出强式家长主义,即需四个构成要素:①干预者有意识地限制对方自由;②干预者主要是出于善意而限制对方自由;③干预者不考虑对方当下的偏向;④干预者或者不考虑对方是否愿意限制自己的行为,或者有意识地限制对方本来想实施的行为。见 paternalism)

hard swearing 假誓,伪誓;(委婉语)伪证

hard-and-fast a. 不可触犯的,非遵守不可的;严格的,不容变通的;(船)搁浅的

hard-core a. 长期失业需要救济的;坚定

的核心

hard-core restrictions 核心限制[指欧共体1996年发布的《技术转让协议集体适用欧共体条约》第81条规定和2004年第772号条例,将技术转让中的竞争限制分为两类:一为对竞争明显具有严重不利影响的核心限制;另一类为排他性限制(excluded restrictions)]

hard-line n. 强硬路线

hard-liner n. 持强硬路线者

hardened criminal 不知悔改的罪犯

harder cases 疑难案件

hardship n. 受苦,吃苦;苦难,困苦,困难

hardware n. 计算机硬件,计算机

harlot n. 妓女

harlotry n. 卖淫行为;娼妇(骂人语)

harm n./v. (12世纪之前)伤害;损失;损害,重大的或有形的损害(tangible detriment)/损害,伤害;危害〈harm set, harm get/harm watch, harm catch〉(损人反害己)

harm of a foreseeable kind 一种可预见的伤害

harm set, harm get (或 harm watch, harm catch) 害人反害己

harmed parties 命名当事人,名义当事人,形式当事人

harmful a. 有害的

harmful act 有害行为

harmful merchandise 有害商品

harmless a. 无害的;无恶意的;无损害的;无辜的

harmless error 无害的过错(指上诉法院认为下级法院在审判中所犯的错误对上诉人并无害处而无须判决)

harmonization or approximation legislation 法律的全面协调或趋同

harmonization of laws 法律上的一致(意译为法律协调,欧共体用语)

harmonization principle 协调原则(指电子商务立法既要与现行立法相互协调,又要与国际立法相互协调,同时还应协调好电子商务过程中出现的各种利益关系,如版权保护与合理使用、商标权与域名权之间的冲突等,尤其要协调好电子商家与消费者之间的利益平衡关系)

harms caused intentionally 故意所致的损害
harms caused negligently 过失所致的损害
harrier n. 抢劫者,蹂躏者
harsh a. 粗糙的;严厉的;苛刻的
harsh and brutal 残酷野蛮
harsh and uncompromising rules that governed actions 调整诉讼的严厉和难以通融的规则
harsh and unconscionable 苛刻的和违背良心的(此术语表示如果协议是苛刻且显失公平的,衡平法院可认定其有悖良心而不予强制执行)
harsh dissent 严厉的异议,深沉的异议
harsh forfeiture clause 苛刻罚金的条款
harsh rules 严格的规定
harsh terms 苛刻的条件
harshest punishment 最严厉的惩(刑)罚
harshest sanction 最严厉的制裁
Hart-Scott-Rodino Antitrust Improvement Act (HSR Act) (1976年)哈特-斯科特-罗迪诺反垄断改进法
Hatch Act 《哈奇法》[指1939年制定颁布的联邦法规,该法规限制联邦雇员参与政治竞选活动(political campaign activities),并且个人不得为政治竞选捐献(contribution),参见《美国注释法典》第5标题卷第1501—1508节)。参议员卡尔·哈奇(Carl Hatch)提倡的法规,连续披露工程兴办署(Works Progress Administration)的公务人员利用他们的职位为民主党(Democratic Party)参与竞选活动]
Harvard Ethical Society 哈佛道德协会
Hatch Waxman Act (美)《哈奇·韦克斯曼法》[指1984年普通名称的联邦法,该法规定激励发展普通药品(generic drugs)并允准这种药品专利拥有人(drug-patent owners)重新获得失去了的专利术语(patent's term)的时间,而等待食品药品行政管理署(Food and Drug Administration)对此药品的批准,亦称Drug Price Competition and Patent Term Restoration Act of 1984]
Harvard Law School (美)哈佛(大学)法学院(位于美马萨诸塞州剑桥城)

harvest yield 收获量
hashish(或 hasheesh) n. 麻醉品(用印度大麻制成的毒品)
hassle(或 hassel) n. 激战,激烈的争论;持久的辩论;混乱
hat-money n. 帽子钱(指船长酬金)
hatch v. 图谋,策划
hatch a sinister plot 图谋不轨
Hatch Act (美)《哈奇法》(指禁止联邦、州、和地方的雇员参与某种形式的政治活动的联邦法规)
hatch survey report 舱口检查报告
hatemonger n. 煽动仇恨者(尤指对少数民族)
hath (古)(等于)has
hatred n. 敌意;憎恨,憎恶,仇恨
haulage n. 拖运;搬运;拖运费
haulage contract 承包合同(契约);拖运合同(契约);搬运合同(契约)
haulage contractor 搬运承包人,搬运承包商
haulage equipment 搬运设备
haulier n. 运输工;拖曳者;(货物)承运人
haunt n. 1.常去的地方 2.(犯罪等的)巢穴
haunt of criminals 罪犯的巢穴
haunt of thieves 盗贼巢穴,贼窝
Haute mer 公海
have v. 有,包括有;持有;取得;经历;招致;进行,从事
have a case (=have an action)
have a deed witnessed 使字据得到证明
have(或 take) a fling at 试做(某事);嘲弄(某人)
have a spite against sb. 对某人怀恨在心
have a tussle 动武,开始打起来
have access to public service 参加公共服务
have all the say 有决定一切的权利
have an action (=have a case) 有起诉理由
have and hold (不动产的)占有和保有
have charge of 主管……
have (no) dealing with 和……有(没有)交往
have designs on(或 against) 对……抱不良企图;企图加害于(某人)

have good authority for starting that 有足够证据说……
have illicit relations with a foreign country 里通外国
have no precedent to go by 无先例可援
have no remedy at law 法律上无任何补救办法
have nothing on sb. (美)对某事不占有优势,不拥有表明某人确以有罪的证据
have one's licence endorsed (英)(驾驶员等)执照被注上违章记录
have one's own way 自主行事,为所欲为,随心所欲
have plenty of briefs (律师)生意兴隆
have precedence of (或 over) 优先于(或地位在……之上)
have relevance to 与……有关
have resource to law 诉诸法律
have sb. up 某人被起诉,使某人受到控告
have sex 性交
have the advantage of 胜过,占优势
have the best opinion 请教高明(律师、医师等)
have the corner on sth. 垄断某物
have the floor (1888年)(议会法)在被议长认可之后具有资格发言
have the last word 辩论中作最后辩驳;有决定权
have the law of sb. 控告某人,对人起诉
have the law on one's side 某一方为合法的
have the merits (在诉讼中)证明自己有理(或处于有利地位)
have the refusal of 对……有优先取舍权
have-not n. 无财产者;贫民;贫穷(或缺乏资源)的国家
having n. (常用复)财产;所有物
having a hand in sth. 插手某事
having tools for counterfeiting 持有伪造(票证等的)器具
havoc n. 大破坏,浩劫;大混乱,大杂乱
Hawala 哈瓦拉(指巴基斯坦古老的非正规银行网络,凭借一部电话、一台传真机即可调动数十亿的大量美元资金做进出交易业务,实质为一种非法金融机构)
hawk n. 鹰;鹰派成员,主战派成员;骗子

hawker n. 小贩,(英)执照商贩
hawker's licence 小贩执照
hazard n. 1.公害(指工业废气、废水等的危害);危险 2.机会;偶然的事
hazard beacon 警告灯标
hazardous substance 危险物品
hazardous substance reimbursement funds 危险物质补偿基金
hazardous substance superfund 危险物质超级基金
hazards to public (health) 公害
*He who comes into equity must come with clean hands. 到衡平法院来起诉者必须自己清白(衡平法原则之一)。
*He who seeks equity must do equity 寻求衡平法的人自己也应公平行事
head n. 1.首脑,头目;首长;主管;(中)县长,区长,乡长,镇长 2.头(部);生命 3.标题;项目 4.人;个人
head and front 主要部分;主要项目
head count 人口调查
head court 总法庭,主管法庭;(苏格兰)土地完全保有人法院
head downward 倒吊刑
head injury 头部伤害
Head Lama 大喇嘛
head lessee 主承租人,二房东
head of a family 家长,族长;一家之长
head of consular post 首席领事,领事长
head of government 政府元首,政府首脑
head of household 户主
head of proposal 提议要点;提案要点
head of the administrative area (行政区)区长
head of the armed forces 武装部队统帅,武装部队总司令
head of the state 国家元首
head off 阻挡,阻止,便于移动方向
head office 总行,总公司,总社;总部,总机构
head tax 1.见 poll tax 2.head money
head-money n. 人头税;为捕获俘虏(或犯人)所付的悬赏金;(移民的)入国(境)税
head-money cases 人头费系列案[美国国会试图在1882年《移民法》(Immigration

Act of 1882)中对移民实施更大控制。尽管各州在移民方面给予自由,但贫穷移民所带来的财政负担迅速使各大港口对船长征收人头费或保证金以便为贫困移民建立基金。此前的一系列案件,使联邦最高法院推翻这类法规,认为它们侵犯了联邦的商业权。国会为减轻各州财政负担,于1882年法案中规定了联邦人头费,每位移民50美分,将此费用用于各州资助贫困移民]

head-note n. 眉批;顶批;(判决书上面的)批注;判决提要(指由判例汇编人草拟的用以叙述案情的简明要点和理由来阐明法律要点的提要)

headborough n. (英史)十户长(指由采邑法庭选任的十人构成的十户连保首领,负本地治安责任)

heading n. 制定法、合同或其他书面文件的条款的标题;题目,题词

headman n. 1.酋长,头人 2.工头,监工 3.刽子手 4.村长

headquarters(复)n. 司令部,指挥部;(机构,企业等)总部,总店

heads of a charge 控诉要点,主要罪状

heads of a diplomatic mission 使馆馆长

headwords n. (书的章节前的)标题

headwork(s) n. 渠道(进水口)工程;脑力劳动,(复)准备工作

health administration 卫生管理

health and safety law 卫生与安全法

health and sanitary regulation 健康与卫生规定

health certificate 健康证明书

health code 卫生法典

health court 卫生法院

health hazard 损害健康的危险

health inspection 健康检查

health insurance 健康保险[指保险人负责赔偿由于疾病或意外伤害而带来的费用和损失。在此保险中,保险人同意在被保险人缴付保险费的基础上负责赔偿由于疾病或意外而带来的费用和损失,亦称意外及健康保险(accident and health insurance)或疾病和意外保险(sickness and accident insurance)]

health law 健康法,(复)卫生法规

health maintenance organization 保健组织

health measure 卫生处理,卫生措施

health quarantine regulations 卫生检疫条例

health station 保健站

health subsidies 保健费

health worker 保健人员

hear v. 审理,听审,受理;听,听取;同意,允准

hear a case 听审案件;审理案件

hear a case in private 禁止旁听的审案

hear a claim 受理申诉

hear a complaint 受理诉状

hear and decide a case 审理和判决案件,审判案件

hear both sides of the question 兼听双方意见(看法)

hear counsels on both side 听取双方当人的律师陈述

hear *de novo* 再审

hear evidence (议会或国会)听证

hear in private session 不公开审理

hear in the public 公审,公开审理

hear witnesses 听取证词

heard no testimony 未听证言

heares legitimus 合法继承人

hearing n. 审讯,审理,审问;听审,受理申诉(港译:聆讯);听力;(美)(政府组织的)意见听取会;(复)(美)听证资料;听证

hearing and final disposition of the case 听审和最后裁决案件

hearing examiners 听证官(指美国《联邦行政程序法》规定轮流审案的"听证官",他们不得履行与行政裁判不相干的职责,其独立性得到保障,不受长官直接控制)

hearing in presence (苏格兰)正式听审(指高等民事法院全体法官听审)

hearing of evidence by a judge alone 审判员单独听证(审案)

hearing of evidence by jury trial 陪审团听证

hearing of petitioners 听取请愿人申诉

hearing of the summon 听证传票

hearing officer (美)(组织意见听取会

的)政府特派调查员(见 administrative law judge)
hearing petition 受理请愿(书)
hearing record 审讯笔录;勘验记录
hearing room 审讯室;开调查庭用的房间
hearing time 审讯日期,开审日期
hearing trial 审理;听审
hearings on bill 议案听证
hearsay n. 传闻(证据),风闻,道听途说
hearsay evidence (或 **testimony**) 传闻证据(亦称传来证据、第三者证据。指证人听旁人传说所提供的证据,一般说这种证据不为法院所接受)
hearsay exception 传闻(证据)例外(规则)(指根据特别规定,即使一般被排除在外的传闻证据,如"临终声明"在审理中仍被作为可接受的证据)
*****Hearsay is no evidence.** 传闻不是证据。
hearsay statement 传闻陈述,传闻证据陈述
hearty puritanism 虔诚的清教主义
hearty Puritanism in view of humane nature (关于人性的)虔诚的清教主义思想
heat n. 热烈,激怒;性冲动;(美)(警察对罪犯的)穷追,大肆侦察;侦察活动的地区;(美俚)手枪;醉酒;强迫
heat of passion 激怒(指因暴躁和不可控制的情感状态所导致的愤怒,对过失杀人具有减轻罪行的法律含义)
Heart-Balm Acts (或 **Heart Balm Statute**) (美)哈特-巴姆法(指废弃或限制违反婚约诉讼的州法规)
heathen men's law 异教徒的法
*****Heaven's vengeance is slow but sure.** 天网恢恢,疏而不漏。
heavy a. 重的;重型的;繁重的;大量的;多的;较大的;严重的
heavy drinker 酗酒的人
heavy fine 巨额罚金
heavy forfeiture 巨额罚款;重大损失(指被没收)
heavy market 滞销市场,不活跃的市场;大量买卖的市场
heavy offense 重(刑)罪

heavy speculation 严重投机倒把(行为)
heavy taxation 课征重税
heavy use 重消费
heavy user 重消费者
heavy-headed Senate 严厉的参议院
Hebraic law 希伯来法
Hebrew Codes of the Bible 《圣经》中希伯来人的法典
Heddesorf Credit Union 赫德索夫信贷联会[指德国人弗里得里希·雷费森(Friedrich Raiffeisen)于1864组建的世界上第一个农村信用合作社。专门向农民提供信贷以便他们购置农具、种子、牲畜等]
hedge n./v. 1.保护或防御的方法(或工具);模棱两可的话2.套头交易(指为避免损失而买进现货、卖出期货或反之)/1.包围,限制,围困2.回避作正面答复3.隐藏,潜藏4.受到_____保护
hedge clause 免责条款;避险条款;套头交易条款;海琴条款
hedge funds 对冲基金,套头交易基金,有限合伙投机基金[指一个特殊的投资集团,通常由有限合伙或境外投资公司组成,通过风险买卖证券期权、进行套头交易获取权利。绝大多数对冲基金均未在证券交易委员会(SEC)登记注册,因此在市场上受到限制而不允许公开进行交易]
hedge sb. about (或 **round, in**) **with rules** 以清规戒律束缚某人手脚
hedge sb.'s path with difficulties 在某人道路上设置障碍
hedonist utilitarianism 享乐主义者的功利主义
Hegelian Philosophy of Law 《黑格尔法律哲学》
hegemonic(al) a. 霸权的;统治的
hegemonism n. 霸权主义
hegemonistic a. 霸权主义的
hegemony n. 霸权,盟主权
height n. (复)高地,高处;高度,顶点;海拔
heightened judicial scrutiny of genderbased classifications 增强对以性别为基础分类的司法调查

heinous a. 极可恨的;极凶残的
heinous crime 大罪,重罪;罪恶累累;十恶不赦的大罪;滔天罪行
heir n. 继承人;后嗣
heir apparency 成为有确定继承权者的条件,成为当然继承人的条件
heir apparent 当然继承人(指当然继承遗产的继承人,除非该继承人死于被继承者之先才被有效遗嘱排除。亦称 apparent heir)
heir at law 法定继承人
heir beneficiary 受益继承人
heir by adoption 收养继承人(指因曾被收养而成为死者的继承人。依据大多辖的制定法规,一个被收养的儿童对无遗嘱的遗产与死者亲生子女一样具有相同的继承权,除非死者有明确的相反意愿表示。一些管辖地区对于被收养儿童也可继承其亲父母或家庭遗产的规定不尽相同。绝大多数明确的观点是:依据收养,权利和义务完全分开,因此,被收养的孩子就失去继承其亲生父母遗产的权利)
heir by custom (古代)惯例继承人[指在英格兰,继承权依据特定的或当地惯例,如肯特斯土地保有习惯,即平均继承制的习惯(gavelkind)和英国的幼子优先继承地产(Borough English)。见 gavelkind; Borough English]
heir by devise 遗嘱赠与继承人
heir by institution 指定继承人
heir by proxy 代位继承人
heir collateral 旁系继承人
heir conventional (大陆法)惯例继承人,约定继承人[指依继承人被继承人之间的契约或财产授与契据(settlement)而继承遗产的人]
heir custom 习惯继承人
heir general 一般(法定)继承人
heir in tail 限嗣继承人;预定继承人
heir in the first order (rank) 第一顺序继承人
heir male (古)死者最近的男性血亲继承人
heir of divided share 份额继承人
heir of his body 直系继承人
heir of line 直系继承人

heir of one's body 直系继承人
heir of the blood (16世纪)纯血亲继承人[指与死者不是直系尊亲属(ascending)就是晚辈血亲(descending line)的亲属关系而继承遗产的继承人]
heir of the body (古代)直系血亲(系)继承人[生存的配偶、养子女和旁系亲属除外的直系血亲继承人。此技术性词条以前是用来创立一项限嗣继承权土地(fee tail)〈A conveys Blackacre to B and the heirs of his body〉(转让甲地给B和他的直系血亲继承人)。亦称 bodily heir]
heir of the second rank (order) 第二顺序继承人
heir of the whole 全部继承人
heir presumptive 假定继承人(指如果死者有更近的亲属诞生,他就不能作为继承人)
heir to property 遗产继承人
heirdom n. 继承权;继承人的地位;继承;世袭
heiress n. 女继承人;嗣女
heirless a. 无继承人的,无后嗣的
heirless estate 无人继承的遗产
heirloom n. 祖传动产;传家宝
heirs by operation of law 法定继承人
heirship n. 继承;继承权;继承资格,继承人的地位
heist n./v. (俚)持凶器抢劫,劫夺;偷窃/对……持凶器抢劫,劫夺;偷
held v. 已决定;已判决,裁定(见 hold)
Heliaea 赫利亚法院(指古雅典的一个司法组织)
heliborne a. 用直升机载运的
helicopter n. 直升机
heliport n. 直升机场
hell n. 1.地狱;困境;黑暗势力 2.地狱中的人
hell-or-high-water rule (1960年)1.克服困难规则[指一项原则,即除非承租人证明为不平等的交易范畴(unequal bargaining power)或违背良知性(unconscionablity),否则对于被承租的个人财产必须支付应付的全额租金,而不顾及任何对出租人的权利主张]2.(保险)一项原则(即指

被保险人的汽车政策包括使用属于他人所有的汽车的该被保险人,在其使用车辆时,某种程度上说必须在允准的范围)

Hellenistic law (古)希腊法

helmet n. 1.盔,钢盔 2.(美俗)警察

helot n. 农奴,奴隶;(大写)(古代斯巴达的)农奴

helotism n. 奴隶制,农奴制

helotry n. 奴隶阶级,农奴阶级;奴隶地位,农奴地位

help sb. out 帮助某人解决问题,帮助某人摆脱困境,帮助某人完成工作

helpmate (=helpmeet) n. 良伴,配偶

hem in 紧闭,受制约

henceforth adv. (14世纪)从现在起,从现在开始〈the newly enacted rule will apply henceforth〉(新颁布的法规从现在开始可以适用)

henfare (英格兰古法)对逃跑的杀人犯的刑事被告所科以的罚金

henchman n. 亲信,心腹;(政治上的)顺从者,仆从,狗腿子

henogamy n. 单一婚制(指家庭中只允许一个父系传宗的成员结婚的习俗,以维护家庭财产完整和限制继承人的需要)

Henry system 亨利分类法(指使用于英美法国家的一种指纹类型的分类方法)

Hepburn Act (美)《赫伯恩法》[指1906年联邦制定法规,它修订了《州际商业法》(Interstate Commerce Act),实现了以下目的:①扩大州际商业委员会(I. C. C.)的管辖权,并将管道纳入管辖范围。②除雇员外,禁止通行(prehibit free passes except-employees)。③禁止普通承运人运送除木材以外对其有利益的任何产品。④该法要求联合关税(joint tariffs)和统一会计系统]

heptarchy (英)1.七个统治者统治的政府,七头政治 2.七个政府统治的国家,七国之治[指在威廉征服英国(1066年Norman Conquest"诺尔曼征服")之前一个国家当时分割成七个政府统治,这七个是:肯特(Kent)的盎格鲁-撒克逊王国、苏塞克斯(Sussex)、埃塞克斯(Essex)、威塞克斯(Wessex)、东盎格里亚(East Anglia)、麦西亚(Mercia)以及诺森伯里亚(Northumbria)]

Her Majesty's Court of Common Pleas (英)女王陛下的民事法庭,皇家民事法庭

Her Majesty's dominions (英)(女王)陛下的自治领

Her Majesty's Forces (英)皇家三军

Her Majesty's Most Hono(u)rable Privy Council 英廷枢密院

Her Majesty's Overseas Judiciary 英属地的司法制度

Her Majesty's Privy Seal 英女王御玺

herald n. (13世纪)1.在英格兰和苏格兰分工负责登记保管宗谱名簿、校准纹章、盾微、管理皇室加冕、葬礼事宜的一些官员(纹章官员),在英格兰有6名,在苏格兰有3名 2.(古代)信使,使节(指宣布王室或国家的宣言、文告的信使以及在国王或国家之间送交外交信函,特别是宣战书、和平宣言或停战宣言等的使节)

Herald's College 纹章院[指1484年由查理三世创立,并由以厄尔·马歇尔(Earl Marshall)为首的3名纹章主管官、6名纹章官及4名纹章官助理治理该院。这是一座英国古老的皇家社团,负责颁授纹章,并记录扫描、保管记录宗谱,以及处理一些礼仪事宜(matters of precedence)。纹章院的家谱书籍都是以在全英国进行家族系谱调查为基础的,被认为是最确切的家谱(pedgrees)证据。该院的官员有权颁授纹章、更改姓名。亦称College of Arms]

herbage n. 放牧权

hereby ad. (用于公文等中)以此,特此,专此

heredes (市民法)继承人(为heres之复数形式)

hereditable a.(=heritable) 可遗传的,可世袭的;可继承的

hereditament n. 可继承的财产,世袭财产;继承的土地;继承

hereditary a. 世袭的,祖传的;遗传

hereditary diotinetion 世袭的荣誉,世袭的勋章

hereditary insanity 遗传性精神病

hereditary monarchy 世袭君主制

hereditary peerage 世袭贵族
hereditary property 世袭财产
hereditary revenues of the Crown 国王世袭俸禄
hereditary right 世袭权利,(王位的)世袭继承权
hereditary sheriff (苏格兰 1671 年前的)世袭司法行政官
hereditary succession 见 intestate succession
hereditas iacens (罗马法)尚未有继承人的财产
heredity n. 遗传;继承;遗传特征;传统
hereinafter ad. 在下文
hereinbefore ad. 在上文
heres 见 *heredes*
heresy n. (宗教上的)异端邪说;异端罪;异教;信奉(或主张)异教
hereto ad. 至此为止,至此
hereto annexed 在此附上,内附
hereunder ad. (书、文件等中)在下面
hereupon ad. (书、文件等中)于是,关于这个
heriot n. (英)(给领主的一种习惯上的)贡品;捐赠;佃户死时的贡献;(英)租借地继承税
heritable a. 可继承的,被继承的;可祖传的,被祖传的;可转让的;可遗传的
heritable bond (苏格兰)可继承的债券
heritable jurisdiction (英史)(封建领主的)世袭司法管辖权
heritable obligation 可继承债务;可转让债务
heritable property 可继承的遗产
heritable rights 可继承权利
heritable securities (苏格兰)可继承的担保物
heritage n. 遗产,继承财产;世袭财产;长子继承权
heritor n. 继承人;受让人
hermaphrodite n. 两性畸形人,阴阳人
hermaphroditism n. 两性畸形
hermeneutics n. 古文解释学;宗教经典解释学;解释学
Hermogenian Code 《海默根法典》(见

Codex Hermogenianus)
heroin n. 海洛因
hesitancy (=hesitance) n. 踌躇,犹豫
heterogeneity n. 异质性,不均匀性
heterogeneous communities 多元社区,情况复杂的社区
heterogeneous injurers 情况多异的加害人,不相同加害人
heterosexual a./n. 异性恋爱的;不同性别的/异性爱者
heterosexual sodomy 异性违反自然的性交行为
heterosexual twins 一男一女双胞胎
heterosexuality n. 异性恋爱,异性性欲
hiatus n. 空隙,脱字,漏句;中断,间歇
hidden counterrevolutionary 暗藏的反革命分子
hidden danger 隐患
hidden defect 隐藏着的缺陷,隐蔽瑕疵
hidden enemy agent 暗藏的敌特分子
hidden injury 内伤
hidden microphone 窃听器
hidden property 埋藏物
hidden tax (1935 年)隐蔽税,间接税[指一种由某人(如石油生产商等)以较高价格销售给消费者而获取暴利所要支付的税种,而不是正常被征税的个人或企业。对先前生产、分配阶段发生的最终销售收入所征的一种税]
hidden traitor 内奸
hide sb. from justice 隐(窝)藏某人使逃避审判
hide-away n. 隐藏处
hide-out n. 躲藏处(尤指盗匪的秘密藏身处)
hidegild n. (英格兰)(古)农奴或奴仆为了免受鞭刑而交付的赎金,亦可写成:hidegild;hydegeld;hudegeld
hiding n. 1.躲藏(指动作或情况);躲藏处 2.痛打,鞭打
hiding-place n. 躲藏处;储藏处
hierarch n. 1.大主教,司祭长 2.统治集团首领
hierarchic(al) a. 1.(等级森严的)僧侣统治(集团)的 2.统治集团的 3.等级(制

度)的
hierarchic(al) structure 等级制度结构
hierarchical court system 等级法院体制
hierarchy n. 等级;等级制度,等级体系;统治集团;僧侣统治;圣秩制度
hierarchy of norms 规范的等级体系,有阶层的规范
higgle v. 讨价还价;讲条件;争执
high a. 高的;高度的;强烈的;偏激的;高等的,高级的;严重的;重大的;主要的;价昂的
high bailiff 高级执达官(指送达传票和执行法院命令的人)
high bench 见 High Court
high boat 捕获鱼类、兽类最多的船
high command 统帅部,最高司令部;(机关中的)最高领导班子
high commission court (英)高等宗教事务法庭
high commissioner 高级专员;(英)自治领行政长官(指英联邦成员国间互派大使级代表的职衔)
high conservative 偏激的保守党人
high constables (英)村庄的警官(或治安官)
High council of judiciary 最高司法委员会,最高司法会议
High Court (high court) (在美国英语中High Court 或 High Bench 通常指)美国联邦最高法院,(英格兰和威尔士的)高等民事法院(通常缩写为 High Court),(苏格兰)高等刑事法院(可具有审理终局刑事上诉法庭的权力)
High Court in Chambers (英)高等法院内庭
High Court of Admiralty (英)高等海事法庭(1971年并入高等法院王座庭)
high court of appeal 高等上诉法院
High Court of Chancery (英)大法官法院
High Court of Chivalry 高等骑士法院
High Court of Delegates (英)高级特派专员法庭(指1833年前受理来自大主教法庭的及免受大主教监督的特殊管辖的上诉案件的法院)
high court of errors and appeals (美)高等上诉和复审法院;高等上诉法院
high court of impeachment 高等弹劾法院
High Court of Justice (英)高等法院
High Court of Justiciary 高等司法官法院(指苏格兰的高等刑事法院)
High Court of Parliament 英国议会;英国上议院(受理上诉的)法庭
High Court of Popular Justice (雅典)平民高等法院
high crime 重罪,大罪
high crimes and misdemeano(u)rs (美)重罪和轻罪(指按美国联邦宪法为检控基础的罪行,它可包括各种重刑罪,造成政治上有严重后果的反对美国罪,还可包括国会决定的一些罪行)
high degree of autonomy 高度的自治权
high degree of probability 高度盖然性,高度概率
high (或 great) diligence 高度勤勉;高度注意
high interest 高利息
high judicial office 大法官职;高级司法职务;司法要职;司法官员
high justice (具有)高级司法管辖权
high misdemeanor 1.(历史上)(英国法)严重罪行[指此类罪行等级仅低于重大叛逆罪(high treason)的严重性。在英格兰法(In English Law)上,这一术语与罪行(crime)是同义词。如称为 high misdemeanor 的范例是暴乱(riot)和共谋(conspiracy)。在早期的美国法中,这一术语已经具有与英格兰法相同的含义,而且还将此罪行界定为煽动暴乱罪(sedition)]2.见 gross misdemeanor 3.见 serious misdemeanor
high point 要点
high probability of guilt 有罪的高盖然率(指美国检察官在实务上决定起诉的证据标准一般要高于逮捕的证据标准,通常情况下,只有在可采的证据表明被告人有罪达到"高盖然率",即有充分证据相信能够获得有罪判决时,检察官才会提起公诉。见 probable cause)
high profile documents 高调的文档,高调的文件
high prosecution's office 高等检察院;

(日)高等检察厅
high purity drugs 纯度高的毒品
high purity gold 成色高的金子
high roller (美)挥金如土者,肆意挥霍者;狂赌者
high seas 公海,外海,外洋
high sheriff (英)高级执达官;高级司法行政官(指在英格兰和威尔士每年为各郡指定的司法行政官)
high stakes risks 高额赌注风险
high taxation on inheritances 高额遗产税
high treason 重大叛逆罪;叛国罪;杀君
high velocity shares 高速股
high-commission broker 高佣金经纪人
high-density urbanization 高密度人口城市化
high-handed 高压的,专横的
high-handed overriding of law 专横地凌驾于法律之上
high-living a. 生活豪华的,奢侈的
high-ranking officer 高级官员
high-risk individuals 高危人群
high-yield bonds 高收益证券
higher administrative office 上级行政机关;高级行政机关
higher authority 上级机关;较高权力
Higher Council (Committees) of Judiciary (法)最高司法委员会(会议)
Higher Council (Committees) of National Defence 最高国防委员会(会议)
higher court 上级法院;高级法院;高一级法院
higher court of justice 高等(司法)法院
higher executive 高级执行机关;高级行政机关;上级行政机关
higher law 高级法[在美国联邦最高法院的整个历史中,"高级法"被理解为一种限制政府或为(非书面形式的)制定法提供标准的法律。18世纪后期这种法律对美国人而言是既熟悉又复杂的思想。他们继承英国法律传统,产生理想的"古代宪法"或普通法律传统,对主权者的特权,对议会的立法权设定限制。多少年来有关"高级法"的种种争论在联邦最高法院的判决中保存下来,并一直存在争议,并继续影响联邦最高法院的判决]
higher leading organ 高级领导机关;上级领导机关
Higher People's Court (中)高级人民法院
highest administrative authority 最高行政当局(机关)
highest and best use 最好效果的使用,市郊的使用(指使土地获得更多收益的使用)
highest authority 最高权力机关;最高权威
highest bid 投标(出)最高价
highest comparable price 最高可比价格
highest court 最高级法院
highest decision-making organ 最高决策机关
highest degree of care 最高注意(指美国某些法域要求公共客运人须具有的一种注意标准;极度小心谨慎的人在相同情况下所采取的注意。)
highest federal tribunal (最高)联邦法院
highest judicial instance 最高审级
highest judicial organs 最高审判机关,最高司法机构
highest officer 最高级官员
highest order of counsel 最高级别的律师
highest organ of state administration 最高国家行政机关
highest organ of state authority power 最高国家权力机关
highest social import 最高社会意义
highest supervisory office 最高监督机关,最高监察机构
highest-bidder(或 **highest bidder**) n. 出价最高的投标人
highest-handed a. 高压的,专横的,目空一切的
highest-ranking judge 最高级的法官
highest-ranking public prosecutor 最高级的国家检察官
highlight v./n. 集中注意力于,着重,使显著,使突出/最重要的部分,精彩的场面
highly prudent person 见 reasonable person
highly publicized cases 过度曝光的案件
highly specialized society 高度专业化社会

highway n. 公路;大路;(英)公共通行权;(美)高速公路
highway code 公路法规
highway patrol 公路巡逻队
highway robbery 拦路抢劫
highway tax 公路税(指为修筑、修补公路筹集款项而征的税)
highwayman n. (拦路抢劫的)强盗
hijack v. 1.拦路抢劫(车、人等) 2.抢劫;绑架;劫持(指偷窃或武力劫持行驶中的交通工具,特别是劫持飞机的犯罪行为。见 skyjack)
hijackee n. 被绑架者,被劫持者;劫持事件的受害者
hijacker n. 劫持者;绑架者;抢劫者
hijacking n. 劫持;绑架
hijacking of aircraft 劫持飞机
hijacking of ship 劫持船只
Hilary Rules (英)希拉里规则(指法官根据1833年《民事诉讼法》制定的一套新的辩护规则,该规则于1834年在希拉里开庭期生效)
Hilary term (英)希拉里开庭期(指法庭的一个开庭期,每年开始于1月11日,结束于31日。1875年更名为Hilary sittings, 开始于1月11日,结束于复活节前的第一个星期三)

Himalayas Clause 喜马拉雅条款[指在单件货运合同的载货提单上有条款规定货主即使对运送人的受雇人、代理人或独立契约人(Independent Contractors)提出赔偿之诉——不论基于侵权之诉或违约之诉(Action in Tort or Action in Contract),他们亦主张该人依运送人依据契约上所主张的抗辩及责任限制的利益,但未提及仲裁合意。因此承租契约下所签发的载货提单能有效纳入喜马拉雅条款,对独立契约人等的索赔亦无法以此条款提出仲裁]
hinder v. 阻止;妨碍;阻碍
hinder and delay 阻止和拖延
hindrance n. 障碍,妨碍;妨碍的人(或物)
Hindu court of justice 印度法院
Hindu customary law 印度教习惯法
Hindu law 印度教法
Hindu law of marriage and divorce 印度教婚姻和离婚法
Hindu law of succession 印度教继承法
Hindu law system 印度法系
hinterland n. 内地;穷乡僻壤;物资供应地区(指从港口可供应到的内地贸易区)
hire n./v. 租用,雇用;租金,工钱/租用;雇用
hire charge 租费
hire charter 包租
hire of labo(u)r 雇工
hire of property 财产租赁
hire of service 雇用,服务
hire of work 承揽
hire purchase 分期付款租购[是一种赊购方式;指分期付款购买商品,但必须于最后一次付清款后,商品才归买主所有,在此之前,买主只有使用权,主要用于英国。应区别于instal(l)ments]
hire purchase agreement 分期付款租购协议
hire-purchase price 分期付款租购售价
hire-purchase system 分期付款租购制度
hiree n. 被雇者
hireling n./a. 佣工,单纯为金钱而听人使唤的人/被雇佣的,为了金钱而工作的
hirer n. 雇佣人,雇主;租借者
hiring n. 租用;雇用;(英)租赁合同(契约)
hiring hall (美)(航运业等工会举办的)职业介绍所
hiring of things 物件租赁
historic bay 历史性海湾[指由于海湾的外形(shape)(即海口宽度超过两岸领海宽度的海湾),因此除非该沿海岸国家在长期的历史中对这样的海湾坚持主张并连续行使主权,并具有传统的主权主张和实际保持控制,否则该海湾不被认为由该沿海岸国管辖]
Historic Bay: Memorandum 1957年联合国《历史性海湾备忘录》
historic bays (国际法)历史性海湾
historic preservation 历史(文物)的保护
historic right(s) (国际法)历史性权利(见historic title)
historic title 历史性所有权[与历史性权利(historic rights)含义无实质性区别,但目前尚无公认定义]

historic waters 历史性水域
historical a. 历史性的
historical anomalies 历史上的异常情况(或异常之事)
historical antecedent 历史先例
historical assessment 历史的评价
historical counterrevolutionary (中)历史反革命分子
historical cultural relics and remains 历史文化遗迹
historical document 历史文献
historical exposition 历史法学派阐释
historical interpretation 历史解释
historical jurisprudence 历史法(理)学
historical jurist 历史法(理)学家
historical legal scholarship 历史上的法律成就(或成果)
historical origin 历史渊源;历史根源
historical premises 历史的前提,历史的场所,历史基础
historical relics 历史文物
historical school of law 历史法(理)学派(19世纪初的一个学派,它代表封建统治者利益,支持旧的习惯法,反对新的、统一的法律,以后逐渐演变成为资产阶级的法学派别之一,其创始人为胡果及其学生萨维尼)
historical sources of law 法的历史渊源
Historically Underutilized Business Zone (HUB Zone) Program 历史原因欠发达商业地区计划(指美国《联邦采购规则》第19.13条规定这样地区通过优先提供联邦缔约机会给小企业,来刺激这些欠发达地区的城乡经济发展和增加就业机会)
historionic personality disorder 表演性(癔症性)人格障碍(人格障碍类型的一种,以女性较多,其特征是富于自我表演性、戏剧性、夸张地表达感情;自我为中心,自我放纵,不为他人着想;一味追求刺激,渴望受到赞赏,情感易受伤害;过分关心躯体性感,以满足自己需求。病人想人非非,常陷入"自欺欺人"迷茫之中。见 paranoid personality disorder)
History of Bills (美)议案历史
history of legal scholarship 法律学术史

hit n. 1.一击,击中;碰撞 2.讽刺 3.要求,达到
hit the bottle 酗酒
hit-and-run (=hit-run) a. (司机)肇事后即逃跑的;打了人后即逃跑的
hit-and-runner n. 肇事后逃跑的司机;打人后逃跑者
hit-run driver 逃逸的肇事司机
Hittite n./a. 赫梯人/赫梯人的
Hittite Law 赫梯法(指约公元前2000年中期小亚细亚中部或南部所建立的一个国家的法律)
Hlutdaw (缅甸)枢密院(指13—19世纪的大臣会议)
hoard n./v. 窖藏的钱财;秘藏的东西/贮藏,囤积;积聚
hoarder n. 贮藏者;囤积者
hoax n./v. 欺骗;骗局;戏弄/欺骗,戏弄
hoaxer n. 欺骗者
Hobbesians n. 霍布斯主义者
hock n./v. 典当,抵押;(美俚)监牢/当,抵押
hocker n. 典当者
hold n./v. 扣留,拘留,控制,掌握;擒拿法,监禁,监牢;货舱,底层舱;保留(或迟延)通知;预约/拿,抓住,握;支持;抑止,约束;认为,认定,持有(见解等),拥有,掌握;担任;举行;(美)扣留,扣押,拘留;裁定;用合同(契约)约束,依法占有;持续,保持;有效;适用,保留;开庭,开会;举行;包含有
hold a brief 当辩护律师
hold a court 开庭,开审
(to) hold a public office 担任公职
hold brief for sb. 为(代)某人承办案件
hold contract 抵押合同(契约)
hold court trial 审理;审案
hold down 压制,抑制;压低,缩减;牵制;保持住(职位等)
hold estate (依法)占有不动产
hold good for 对……适用(有效)
hold harmless 承担无辜(指同意支付可能控诉他人的索赔)
hold hearings 开庭审理
hold in custody 扣押

hold in fee (simple) 1.享有不限制继承者身份的人继承的土地,无限制条件继承的不动产(权)2.永远继承的土地
hold in one's own possession 个人持有
hold in pledge 抵押,持作抵押品
hold in suspicion 认为嫌疑;看做嫌疑
hold joint court trial 会审,合审
hold(keep, maintain, stand)one's ground 坚守阵地,坚持立场(或坚持论点,要求等)
hold one's judg(e)ment in suspense 迟迟不作判决(判断)
hold out v./n. 1.提出,提供〈hold out a promise〉(作出承诺),〈hold out unlimited prospects〉(有无限前途)2.伸出,端出 3.坚持,不退让〈hold out till victory〉(直到胜利绝不退让)4.支持,维持〈How long will the enemy's food supplies hold out〉(敌人的粮食供应可维持/1.(谈判等场合)不退让,坚持 2.坚持者,不让步的人(或物),坚持不合作者
hold over 1.逾期占有人 2.届满后留任的官员(同 holding over)
hold pleas 审理诉案
hold public sittings 公开审讯
hold sb. to bail 拘押某人直至交保释放
hold sb. to ransom 劫持某人勒索赎金,绑某人的票
hold to 坚持(说法,看法等),继续(想法,做法等),遵循
hold true 适用,有效
hold under duress 胁持,劫持
hold up 支撑,继续下去;(交通)阻塞;(美)拦路抢劫;提出;索高价;停止
hold water (论点等)站得住脚;说得通;有效的,真实的
holder n. 持票人,持证人;占有者;持有人;支持物
holder for value 有价证券(或契据)持有人
holder in bad faith 恶意占有人
holder in due course (正常)正当持票人(指已付对价的善意持有票据人有权实现其票据权利,而免于任何人对票据提出权利或抗辩);合法持有人
holder in good faith 善意占有人,善意占用人
holder of debt claims 债权人
holder of license 牌照持有人
holder of power 掌权者
holder of stolen goods 赃物窝藏人
holder of the thing 物的持有人
holder of value 等价物的持有人
holder on trust 受托人,保管人
holders of rights 权利主体;权利享有者,权利人
holding n. (15世纪)裁决[指①法庭就对其判决来说属于关键性的法律问题所作之裁决(见 *obiter dictum*)。②法官就庭审中提出的证据或其他问题所作之裁决。③(通常是复数)合法地拥有财产,特别是土地或证券。④从历史上讲,指的是封建法,保有封地(tenure)]
holding a discovery conference 召开披露会议
holding back 踌躇,阻止,隐瞒,抑制
holding charge (1949年)刑事指控[指尽管检察官正抓住时机确立较大案件和准备一些更为严重的指控罪行,可某些轻微罪行却被提起刑事指控并要求将刑事被告(accused)羁押]
holding company 控股公司(指以控制股权为目的的投资公司)
holding device 拥有的手段
holding of the court 法院裁定
holding office 任职
holding out 冒称,冒充(身份);谎报身份;自称;坚持
holding over 逾期占有[指①承租人在租期届满后仍继续占有土地的行为。逾期占有构成了容忍保有(a tenancy at sufferance)。见 tenancy at sufferance。②(议会法)留任,留用(指政府官员任期届满后,通常因为后继者还未被选出,无人承担其职之责,故他或她仍继续留任)]
holding period (1935年)(税法)资产有期,资产占有期(指在此期间纳税人持有的资本、资产在出售或交易中是盈是亏、时期是长是短,都属于持有期)
holding to jurisdictional matters 坚持管辖

问题

holding to situation such as… 坚持诸如……这样的情况

holding-company tax 控股公司税,(美)控股公司所得税(指在允许从个人控股公司的收入中扣除已支付的红利后,对于未分配的剩余所得征收的一种联邦税。亦称 personal-holding company tax)

holdout n. 勒索要挟;坚持不让步;坚持不合作者

hole n. 洞;缺陷,缺点,漏洞;牢房;躲藏处

holiday n. 假日;假期;(复)休假

holiday ownership 分时度假

holistic forestry 整体林业

Holland law 荷兰法

Holloway Prison (英)霍洛韦监狱[根据《后座监狱中止法》(1862年)第12条,在1870年怀特克罗斯大街监狱被取消后,作为债务人监狱。现已用于女子监狱]

Holmes, Oliver Wendell. Jr. 霍姆斯·小奥利弗·温德尔(1841—1935)[美国一位著名的大法官和法哲学家、不管在实践领域还是法哲学领域,他都是中心人物。霍姆斯的前半生是马萨诸塞州的最高法院法官和哈佛大学的法律学者。在当法官的任职期间,他以反对大多数其他法官支持保守解释宪法的方法而著称。他的异议特别有关表达自由和对经济的规制被后来的法院采纳并成为主流意见。许多人认为霍姆斯为美国历史上最伟大的法官。他的努力使得法律思维在很多普通法领域慢慢现代化,他的法学著作:《普通法》(1881年)、《法律的道路》(1897年,载《哈佛法律评论》),预示美国法律现实主义运动发生。在《法律的道路》一文中,霍姆斯写下了一句名言:"法律的生命始终不是逻辑而是经验。"他的实用主义,无论是革新的还是派生的,对美国的法律现实主义者均有相当重要的影响。最有影响的是他的主张:应当根据法律所服务的社会目的和社会利益看待法律,应当根据法律实现这一服务的功效进行判决。霍姆斯有关司法的作品和其他领域的作品反映出他倾向于一种外在的或"客观的"标准,如对合同的成立,他反对主观的"合意说"。这也说明他的两个观点:一是外在标准更适合社会目的(可使合同效力成为可以预测,可支持商业票据的流通性);另一较为抽象,法律针对的是人类的行为而不是人的内心]

holocaust archives 灭族大屠杀档案

holograph n. 亲笔文件;亲笔(书写签名的)遗嘱;亲笔(书写签名的)文据(或契据)

holographed testament 自书遗嘱

holographic will 亲笔遗嘱

holographo (西班牙法)亲笔自书(文件)(尤指遗嘱的亲笔自书,方为有效)

Holy Alliance 神圣同盟(指1815—1816年俄、普、奥三国君主所订的同盟)

Holy Office (罗马天主教的)宗教法庭

Holy See (罗马)教廷,教皇的地位(或权力)

Holy Week 复活节前周

Holyday 宗教祭日,法定假日(见 legal holiday)

homage n. (封臣对君主的)效忠;封建主与封臣的关系;尊敬,敬意

homage jury (英)(古)佃户陪审团[指贵族私人法院(Court Baron)中由佃户所组成的陪审团,以示对贵族或领主之敬意。见 Court Baron]

home n. 家;(美)住宅;本国;庇护所,收容所;产地;家乡

home (或 **construction**) **warranty** 见 home owner's warranty

home affair 民政;内务

home circuit (在伦敦附近各郡的)法官巡回问案;巡回问案,巡回审判

home civil service 国内文官

home confinement grant (英)家庭成员监禁补助金

home constituency 原选举单位,原选区

home country control 母国控制

home currency 本币,本国货币

home for discharged prisoners 出狱囚犯保护所

home government 本国政府

home law 国内法,本国法,住所法

home loss 家宅被征用而造成的损失

home market price 国内市场价
Home Minister （英）内务大臣
home mortgage lending 住宅抵押贷款
home office 总店,总公司;（大写）（英）内务部
home owner's insurance （美）户主的保险
home owner's policy （美）户主权益保单（指包括火、水、盗窃责任和其他损失的标准保险）
home owner's warranty （美）房主（建筑公司）担保（指根据国家建筑者协会所实行的担保或保险计划,或按国家法规对于新建几年的房屋缺陷,即新房提供保护）
home port 船舶注册港,船籍港
home rule 内部自治,地方自治
home state （美）（家庭法）本州［指在一项州际儿童监护争议问题在进入诉讼程序（proceeding）之前,立即由本州（即儿童与父母共同居住的州或代表父母的人至少连续6个月居住该州）按《统一儿童监护管辖与实施法》(the Uniform Child Custody Jurisdiction and Enforcement Act)来调整解决。见 home-state jurisdiction］
home trade 国内贸易
home trade ship （英）国内贸易船（指按1894年商船法,这类船只能在海峡岛屿、曼岛以及易北河和布雷斯特河之间的欧洲大陆航行）
home-produce firearms 自制枪支
home-state jurisdiction （美）（家庭法）本州管辖［指对于州际儿童监护争议问题,在进入诉讼之前,由该儿童连续居住6个月以上（含本数）的州迅速按《统一儿童监护管辖与实施法》来调整解决。见 home state］
homegrown a. 本国产的;土生土长的
homeless person 无家可归者
homeowner n. 房主,房屋所有人
* Homes of citizens are inviolable. 公民住宅不受侵犯。
homestead n. 宅基地;住宅;家园,田园;（美国或英国政府）给予移民开垦者的土地
homestead act （美）宅地法;家宅法;移居法

homestead exemption （美）家宅豁免（指有的州法规允许一家之长可保持家宅和某些不动产安全而不受一般债务的影响的法规规定）
homesteader n. 占有宅基地的人;承领（美国或英国政府给予）移民开垦公地的人
homicidal a. 杀人犯的;有杀人癖好的
homicidal act 杀人行为
homicidal arsonist 杀人放火犯
homicidal insanity 杀人狂
homicidal mania 杀人狂
homicidal poisoning 毒杀
homicidal strangulation 他人勒杀致死（指被人勒杀者）
homicidal wound 他杀伤（指被人杀伤者）
homicide n. 杀人（罪）;杀人者
homicide by misadventure 误杀;因突发事故而杀人
homicide by necessity 因不得已而杀人
homicide by omission 不作为杀人
homicide by poisoning 投毒杀人
homicide case 杀人案;人命案
homicide death 他杀（指被人杀死者）
homicide in self-defence 自卫杀人
homicide per infortunium 不幸事故致死（指非故意的行为不幸造成他人死亡）;横祸
homicide resulting from passion 情杀
homicide se defendendo 自卫杀人
homicide squad 凶杀案侦破队
homicide through negligence 过失杀人
homicide victim 被杀害者,被害人
homicidium 杀人（罪）;杀人者
homicidium ex casu 因事故杀人
homicidium ex justitia 执法杀人
* Hominum causa jus constitutum est. Law is established for the benefit of man. 法是为人的利益而立的。
homing pigeon 通讯鸽
hominess （历史上）封建的土地承租人,他们有资格从事他们的事业（cause）和其他工作（matters）,只有领主法院（Lord's court）方可就他们的这些事宜进行审理（见 homo）
homo 人类,人［在罗马法上,生物学意义

上的人称"homo",但它不一定是权利义务主体,权利义务主体被称为"caput";只有当"homo"具有"caput"(人格人)时,才是法律技术意义上的人(person)。这种人在法律上的地位称"personalita"。在罗马上法,人格只能为特定身份的人所享有。该词在历史上如下含义:①男人。②人类;人(不分性别)。③奴隶(罗马法上的奴隶不得为权利之主体,且为所有人之所有物)。④封臣;奴仆;封建时期的佃户。⑤保留者;依赖者;服役人(复) homines。见 homines]

homo alieni juris 他权人
homo economics 经济人;类似的经济学
homo politicus 政治人
* *Homo potest esse habilis et inhabilis diversis temporibus.* A man may be capable and incapable at different times. 一个人在某一个时间有行为能力,而在另一个时间也可能没有行为能力。
homo sui juris 自权人
homogeneity n. 同质性;同类
homogeneous a. 同种的;同质的;同性的;同源的;均匀的
homogenous community 相类似的居民区,相类似的社区
homogeneous function 齐次函数
homogenous individual interest 个人同类性利益(指一种个人利益的集合,和我们通常说的普通共同诉讼中个人享有的利益相似,集团成员因有相同的事实或法律争议而拥有相同或相似的诉因,在他们之间也仅仅存在相似的利益,为了简便才合并审理)
homogeneous population 同质化的人群
homogeneous society 同族社会
homologate v. 确认;同意;认可;批准;准执行
homologation n. 确认;同意;认可;批准;批准执行(判决)
homosexual a./n. 同性恋爱的;搞同性性关系的/搞同性关系的人
homosexual conduct 同性恋行为
homosexual relation 同性恋关系
homosexual sedomy 同性恋式的违反自然的性行为

homosexuality n. 同性恋爱,同性性关系,同性恋(指男性同性恋,女性为 lesbianism)
honest and conscientious 诚实和正当的,诚实和有道德的
honest and reasonable belief 诚实和合理的信念(指合法的自卫所需的诚实和合理的信念才能导致宣告无罪,诚实和合理的信念的条件需:①自卫者必须处于受到对方非法身体危害的紧急状态;②不使用强力不可避免这种危险)
honest possession 合法占有
honest wrong belief 诚实的错误信念
honeste vivere 以忠诚处世者
* *Honeste vivere, alterum non laedere, suum cuique tribuere.* To live hono(u)rably, to injure no man, to render to each his own. 体面生活,不伤害任何人,对每个人尽心尽力。
honestiores (罗马)高贵阶层
honestum non est semper quod licet. That is not always honorable which is lawful, or which the law allows. 法律允许的、合法的不一定总是体面的
Hong Kong Bill of Rights Ordinance 《香港人权法案条例》
Hong Kong Court of Final appeal Ordinance 《香港终审上诉法院条例》
hono(u)r n./v. 信用;功勋;荣誉;道义;名誉;尊敬(中世纪英格兰的)荣誉等级(大写)(对法官和某些高级官员的尊称)阁下/承兑;尊敬;给予荣誉;承认,实践,许诺
hono(u)r clause 不受法律约束的条款
honor est praemium vertutis Honor is the reward for virtue 荣誉是美德之报偿
honor matrimonii (罗马法)婚姻期待,婚姻期遇(指所有形式方法均以夫妻身份相待,以使配偶双方在社会上被看作夫妻。它使妇女获得丈夫的社会地位和妻子的身份,要从伦理上理解他们同居的体现,而不能单从物质意义上理解。)
hono(u)r one's liability 承担赔偿责任
hono(u)r system (监狱)无看守无监禁制;无监考考试制

hono(u)rable a. 荣誉的;正直的;体面的,高尚的;(大写)尊敬的(对英议员、法官、美国会议员及高级官员的尊称)
hono(u)rable duty 名誉职位
hono(u)rable peace 体面的和平
honoraria for experts 专家(证人)的酬金
honorarium (习惯上不应取报酬的或礼貌上未便定价钱的)酬金,谢礼,谢金
honorary a. 名誉的,荣誉的
honorary advisor 名誉顾问
honorary consul 名誉领事
honorary degrees 荣誉学位,名誉学位
honorary sheriff (苏格兰)荣誉司法行政官
honorary title 荣誉称号
honorary trust 名誉信托
honorary trustee 名誉受托人
honoris causa degree 荣誉学位
hood n. (美)流氓,地痞;贼
hoodlum n. (美)阿飞,无赖,恶棍,不良少年
hooligan n. 阿飞,(小)流氓,街头恶棍;不良少年
hooliganism n. 流氓行为
hoping extract a favorable settlement from a defendant 希望迫使被告作出有利的解决(方案)
horizon problem 前景问题,眼界问题
horizontal a. 水平的,横的;相类似产品(生产者、商人等)之间的
horizontal direct effect 水平直接效率,横向的直接效率
horizontal property 横向财产(关系)
horizontal trusts 行业组合,同业联合会
horizontal union 不同工业内同行业的职工工会(与 vertical union 相对而言)
horn n. 喇叭;警报器;角状物
Hornbook (16世纪)1.基础入门课本,解释本门科目的读物 2.基础法律教科书(指含有基本的法律领域中的原则的教材) 3.重要判例和法律观点综述
hornbook law 法律的(初级)基本知识;法学入门(书)
hors de la loi (法)法律上不受保护的,被宣布为非法的,法律上无效的,置于法律之外的
horsesense n. 起码,常识
hospice n. 收容贫病者的机构,济贫院;旅客招待所
hospital n. 医院;(钢笔等小东西的)修理商店,慈善院
hospital admission certificate 入院证书
hospital board 卫生局
hospital order (将罪犯扣留于特定医院的)入院令
Hospitia Cancellariae 衡平法学院
Hospitia Curiae (英)法律学院(见 Inns of Court)
hospiticide n. 杀害主人(或杀害客人)的人
host n. 主人;旅店老板;(广播、电视等)节目主持人
host country (state) 东道国;驻在国
hostage n. 人质,作抵押的人;抵押,抵押物
hostage murder 杀害人质
hostage trial 审讯人质
hostageship n. 充当人质;被抵押状态
hostes 敌人
hostes humani generis 人类之公敌
* *Hostes sunt qui nobis vel quibus nos belium decernimus*; *caeteri proditores vel praedones sunt.* Enemies are those with whom we declare war, or who declare it against us; all others are traitors or pirates. 敌人是指我们对之宣战的那些人,或那些对我们宣战的人;而所有其他的乃是叛徒或掠夺者。
hostile act 敌意行为,敌对行为
hostile attack 恶意攻击
hostile country 敌对国,敌国
hostile elements 敌对分子
hostile embargo 敌国船只的扣留
hostile international law 战时国际法
hostile nationality 敌国国籍
hostile policy 敌对政策,敌视政策
hostile possession 不动产的对抗占有
hostile propaganda 敌意宣传(指雇用或使用一个民族去操纵另一个民族的人民支持或反对他们的政府,亦称 ideological aggression。见 subversive propaganda)

hostile relations 敌对关系
hostile witness (对一方当事人怀有)敌意的证人,恶意证人
hostility n. 敌意;敌对行为;战争状态;抵抗
hot a. 1.热的;激动的;急躁的 2.紧迫的;极有利的 3.违禁的;非法的;被警察通缉的 4.(被窃物品)刚被盗窃的;淫秽的
hot bench (美)(受理上诉的法院的)"热庭"[指上诉法院在听审口头辩论之前,法官宣读法院诉讼记录和律师诉讼摘要这个阶段,对法庭的称谓。而在此之前,法官宣读由法庭书记官准备的案情概要这阶段,称为"温庭"(warm bench);法官在听审案件前既未宣读诉讼记录和摘要这阶段,称为"冷庭"(cold bench)]
hot bill 优良票据
hot cargo 1.争议的货物 2.偷来的货物
hot cargo clauses 热货条款
hot issue 热门股票,上市不久价格猛涨的股票
hot item 热门货
hot money 游资
hot money movement 游资移动
hot on the trail 紧跟踪迹追赶
hot pursuit 紧追不舍
hot seat (美俚)电椅
hot spot (美俚)1.麻烦地点;潜在危险的地区 2.电椅 3.低级下流的夜总会
hotchpotch (=hotchpot) n. 财产混同(指将各项遗产合并一起,以便在继承人中进行平均分配)
hotel's lien 旅馆留置权
hound n./v. 狗;猎狗;卑鄙的人/追逐;用猎狗追猎;追逼;追制
hound sb. to death 逼死某人
hounds of law 缉捕人员
hourly wages 计时工资
hours of labo(u)r 工时,工作时间
hours of work 工作时间,工时
house n. (12世纪)1.家;住宅;居所 2.立法机构或两院制的立法机构的下议院;这类部门的必到人数(a quorum of such branch) 3.(美)众议院 4.(议会的)众议院;下议院;代表会议(house of delegates)

house agent 房地产经纪人
House and Senate Journals (美)《参众两院公报》
house arrest 软禁
house chamber 众议院会议室,众议院审议室,众议院议事室
House Committee (美)议院委员会
House Committee on Un-American Activities (美)众议院非美活动调查委员会
house confinement 软禁
house counsel 专职法律顾问(指受雇于某公司,而非独自开业的律师)
house duty 房产税,房地产税
house expenses 家庭开支
house finding agency 房屋经纪业
house hunter 寻找出租房屋者
house manager 房屋管理人
house mortgage 房产抵押
house of assembly 立法议会;众议院
house of assignation 见 disorderly house
House of Burgesses 移民议会(指美国独立战争之前的弗吉尼亚或马里兰殖民地的代表会议)
House of Chiefs 酋长院(如博茨瓦纳,该院为议会的咨询机构)
House of Commons (英)下议院
House of Commons Papers (英)《下议院文件汇编》(指写有"下议院命令"印刷的、并按每届议会依次编号的文件汇编)
house of correction 感化院,反省院,矫正所[指①(美)少年感化院(reformatory)。②青少年罪犯的禁闭场所或犯有轻微罪行的青少年禁闭所。亦称 house of refuge]
House of Council(l)ors (日)参议院
house of delegates (18世纪)1.(通常大写 House of Delegates)代表会议[指许多博学的或专业的协会包括美国律师协会的代表的集会〈the ABA House of Delegates〉(美国律师协会代表会议),通常缩略为 House,也称为 house of representatives(大写 House of Representatives 众议院;下院)。见 convention 4] 2.(大写)马里兰州、弗吉尼亚州和西弗吉尼亚州的立法机构,也即下议院(lower-chamber)

house of detention 看守所,拘留所,收容所

House of Hanover (英史)汉诺威王朝(1714—1901年)

house of ill fame 1.妓院 2.赌场(disorderly house)

House of Keys (英国马恩岛的)下议院

House of Laity (英)世俗议会

House of Lords (英)(议会的)上议院;元老院,贵族院

House of Nation 国民议会

house of nobles 贵族院

House of Parliament (或 **Palace of Westminster**) (英)议会大厦(威斯敏斯特宫)

House of Peers 贵族院

House of Plantagenet (英史)金雀花王朝(1154—1399年)

house of prostitution 妓院(见 disorderly house 2)

house of refuge 见 house of correction

House of Representatives (美、日、澳、墨等国的)众议院

House of Saxe-Coburg (英史)萨克斯-柯柏克王朝(1901—1910年)

House of Stuart (英史)斯图亚特王朝(1603—1649年;1660—1714年)

House of the Nations 民族院

House of the People 人民院

House of Windsor (英史)温莎王朝(1910年至今)

house of worship 礼拜堂

house rental agreement 房屋租赁合约(协议)

house to let 房屋招租

house-agency n. 房地产经纪业

house-breaker n. 入屋行窃的人;(英)拆房子的人

house-breaking n. (为实施犯罪行为)侵入住宅(罪);入屋行窃;(英)拆房子

house-duty (历史上)(英国法)房产税[指1851年对于居住的房子(inhabited houses)第1次征收的税,见维多利亚第14、15个执政年通过的第36个法(1924年被废止)(14 & 15 Vict. ch 36.)(repealed 1924).此税种代替了窗户税(window tax),即有6个以上的窗户应交纳(5英镑/年)窗税。见 window tax]

house-owning company 房产拥有公司(指旨在拥有一幢多层大楼,以其中一半以上居住面积留做股票持有人居住所成立的公司)

house-renter n. 租屋者

house-to-house inspection 挨户检查

housebreaking 破门行窃[指破门进入住宅或其他安全大楼,并蓄意在房内实施犯(重)罪行为,侵入住宅罪(burglary)。"burglary"当今比 housebreaking 更为常用。在英国,虽然 housebreaking 这一术语仍在苏格兰法中使用,但 housebreaking 在1968年即被 statutory burglary 替代。在有些管辖地区,housebreaking 包括 breaking out of a house(闯出住宅),而不用 breaking(破门,破坏)。housebreaking(破门行窃)出自法律解释,即一个窃贼(burglar)采取威胁或诈骗手段进入宅门。亦称为 constructive breaking into a house。(英)拆房子]

houseburning (美)焚烧房屋(罪)[指普通法上的轻罪(misdemeanor),在城区范围内,有意烧毁任何个人的房屋或使十分邻近的其他房屋处于可能着火的危险境地(即使没有实际损害结果)。亦称为 combustio domorum。见 arson]

household n. 家庭;户;家属;家务

household goods 家庭全部动产,家庭财物

household head 户主

household management 家政,家务管理

household police (中)户籍警

household register 户口册,户口簿

household registration 户口登记

household registration book 户口本

household registration office 户口登记机关

household registry 户籍;户口登记

household registry certificate 户口证件

household registry jurisdictional area 户口管辖区

household troops 御林军

householder n. 户主,家长;住户;占有房产者

housework (= household work) n. 家务

劳动

housing n. （总称）房屋，住房；住房供给；住房建筑

housing allowance 住房津贴，房屋津贴

Housing and Urban Development Act （美）（指1968年国会通过的）《住宅及城市发展法》［该法授予政府国民按揭协会(The Government National Mortgage Association, 简称Ginnie Mae)有权购买以及处集按揭贷款，并有权出售由这些按揭贷款组合的股份给公众投资者］

housing association 房产建筑和管理协会

housing co-operative association 住宅建筑合作公司

housing corporation 房产公司

housing discrimination 住房歧视［在美国，住房歧视表现为适格公民由于其民族、性别、宗教、婚姻状况或残疾等原因在购房或租房时遭到拒绝。这是最严重且最难于处理的歧视问题。尽管联邦最高法院作了许多努力并与住房歧视持续斗争，但其努力多集中在歧视性意图以及歧视性行为上。同时美国联邦宪法第十四修正案禁止的歧视行为也适用于住房歧视案。尽管如此，仍然存在大量的种族歧视的现象］

housing dispute 房屋纠纷，住房纠纷

housing foreclosure 抵押房屋被收回

housing service 提供住房服务

housing subsidy 住房津贴

housing trust 房产信托

housing unit 住宅

hovering act 禁止船只在领海内逗留法；（规定3海里领海外的）外国船只应受检查法

hubus （伊斯兰教法）胡布斯（指北非国家对Wakf的称谓）

Hude Amendment 海德修正案［指一项联邦法规，该法规规定：除非必须保住母亲的生命，否则禁止使用医疗基金进行堕胎。同时，该法还禁止在全联邦范围建立基金的家庭计划项目（federally funded family-planning programs），不得提供堕胎咨询。此法条曾由伊利诺伊州众议院议员亨利·海德提倡］

Hudegeld 见hydegeld, hidegild

hue and cry 通缉文告；追捕犯人时的叫喊声；嘈杂声，（表示反对的）叫嚷

huggery n. （英）律师为抢生意而进行的活动

Huguenot descent 胡格诺派教徒（指16—17世纪法国加尔文派教徒的称呼）世系

hulk n. （英）囚船（指接纳流放囚犯置于停在美国沿海的旧战船上，1853年后不再使用）

hull insurance 船舶保险

human a./n. 人的；人类的；具有人文形体和属性的；有人情的；通人性的/人（等同human being）

human agency 人事代理

human being 自然人；人类

human bite 人咬伤

human development index (HDI) 人类发展指数［指以人均收入来衡量生活质量、学校教育、平均寿命以及其他指标等。2020年中国的人类发展指数为0.761，在全球189个国家和地区中位列第85位］

human development indicators 人文发展指标（其内容包括人口、教育、妇女就业比例、健康、信息利用、环境、经济等）

human dignity 人的尊严

human environment 人类环境

human institution 人类制度

human intellectual diversity 人类智慧的多样性

human law 人定法，人法

human machine 人性的机体

human magistrates 人类的法官，人类的司法官（或治安官）

human negligence 人的过失

human positive law 人的实在法，人定的实在法

human remains 人体残骸

Human Right Act 人权法

Human Right Commission 人权委员会

Human Right Day 人权日

human right to safe food（right to safe food） 食品安全权（或获取安全食品权）

human rights 人权

human rights legislation 人权立法

human settlements 人类居住区
human testimony and material evidence 人证物证
Human Tissue Act （英）《人体组织法》（指1961年颁布的对有关为治疗、教学及科研目的而使用死者身体器官所作的规定）
Human Use of Human Being 《人有人的用处》（罗伯特·维纳,1950年出版的《人有人的用处——控制论与社会》,不仅反复提到了自然界和人类的区别在于其是否具有"目的性",而且一针见血地指出法律控制的"道德性"）
human-leukocyte antigen test 人体白细胞抗原测试[指分析一个人的血液样本在父亲或（合法）婚生情况下对比子女血液的指数（indicators）来确定亲子关系的一种医学测试方法。缩略为 HLA test。见 blood-grouping test; genetic-marker test]
humane a. 人道的；仁慈的；高尚的
humane administration 人道主义行政
humane ingratitude 人性的忘恩负义
humane punishments 人道的惩处,人性化的惩处,人性化的处罚
humane studies 人文科学,人道研究
humane treatment 人道的处理,人道的待遇
humanism n. 人道主义；人文主义；人本主义；人性；古典学
humanist n. 人道主义者；人文主义者；人本主义者；人性学者；古典学者；（复）人文主义法学派（尤指1400—1600年间受古典文化复兴熏陶的法学家）
humanist movement 人文主义运动
humanistic a. 人道主义的，人文主义的；人本主义的；人情的；古典学的
humanitarian a. 人道主义者的；博爱家的
humanitarian activities 人道主义活动
humanitarian doctrine 见 last clean chance doctrine
humanitarian ideal 人道主义的理想
humanitarian law 人道主义法
Humanitarian Law of War 人道主义战争法
humanity n. 人类；人性；（复）人的属性（尤指美德）；博爱,仁慈,人道主义精神；（复）仁慈行为；（复）人文科学
humanity of socialist law 社会主义法的人道主义精神
humanizing globalization 全球化的人本化（迄今为止,对国际法的人本化尚未形成一致定义。根据有影响的西方国际法学者的观点,它主要指国际人道法和国际人权法的产生与发展给整个国际法发展带来的影响和变化）
humbug n. 欺骗；骗子；空话,骗人鬼话
humiliator n. 侮辱他人者,侮蔑他人者
hunch of judge 法官的预感
hundred （或 wapentake）n. （英）百户邑；（美）百家村
Hundred Courts （英）百户邑法庭（指古代较大型的采邑法庭"Court-baron",负责审理百户邑里的案件以代替一个领主的领主法庭）
hundred rolls （英）百户邑宗卷
hung jury （1854年）悬而未决的陪审团（或称意见分歧的陪审团）（指陪审员们在裁决书上不能取得意见一致的陪审团）
hunger-strike n. 绝食斗争,绝食示威
hunt v. 搜索,追寻；打猎
hunt down 追捕（犯人）；搜寻……直至发现
hunt down and seize 查获
hunting licence 狩猎特许；结婚特许（指由圣公会主教颁发的证书,准许一个由民庭解除婚约的人可在教堂内再行结婚）
hurdle n. （英）雪橇状囚笼（指1870年前用于将叛国罪犯押赴刑场的运送工具）
hurt n./v. 危害,损害；伤害；（精神、感情上的）创伤/危害,损害,伤害；使（感情）受到创伤
husband's authorization 夫权
husband's common law liability for wife's antenuptial debts 夫在普通法上关于妻婚前债务的责任
husband's liability for wife's funeral expenses 夫对妻的丧礼费用的责任
husband's marital authority 夫权
husband's right of unilateral repudiation of his wife 丈夫的单方休妻权
husband-wife immunity 夫妻豁免（指夫

妻因另一方的个人伤害的侵权行为而豁免。但到 1992 年,不管是依据司法判决理由或根据制定法,38 个州和哥伦比亚特区已废弃夫妻间侵权豁免。9 个州只是在特殊情况下,如有意侵权或车辆侵权中废弃这种规则。此词亦称 interspousal immunity;interspousal tort immunity;marital immunity。见 husband-wife tort actions)

husband-wife tort actions 夫妻间的侵权诉讼(指在美国,夫妻间的侵权诉讼是被禁止的。许多州的制定法均已采纳,但现行情况趋于废止此项夫妻间的豁免权,而允许因个人伤害夫妻间提起侵权诉讼。虽然如此,但不少州只是允许在汽车诉讼中取消这一规则。见 husband-wife immunity)

husbandage n. 船主付给船舶管理人的佣金
husbanding agent 委托代理人
husbandman n. 农民
husbandry n. 耕作;家政;节俭;家畜的科学管理
hush-hush n./a. 保密;极保密的事/秘密的,秘而不宣的
hush-hush policy 蒙蔽政策(指不公布战争损失等)
hush-money n. (封住他人嘴巴的)贿赂金,封口钱,遮羞钱
hustings (复) n. 1.选举程序 2.(英)议员竞选演说坛 3.地方法院
hustler n. 乱推乱挤的人(尤指与扒手同伙者);非法攒钱的人(尤指妓女等)
hybrid n. 混血儿;杂种;混合物
hybrid bill (英)(下议院的公私)混合法案
hybrid class action 混合的集团诉讼(见 true class action)
hybrid committee (英)(下议院)公私混合议案委员会
hybrid computer 混合计算机
hybrid product "混血"产品(指随着金融创新的不断推进,银行、证券和保险领域的产品及服务不再有截然的分野。兼具银行、证券、保险的金融"混血"产品不断问世)

hybrid system 混合法系(指苏格兰、以色列、路易斯安那、魁北克和南非的法律)
Hybrid trademark 见 composite trademark
hydegeld (英格兰)(古)1.免受鞭刑所交付的赎金(指对侵犯行为的雇工的殴打承担责任)2.hidegild,亦拼写为 hudegeld
hydrogen weapons 氢武器
hydrospace n. 海洋空间;海洋水域
hygeian a. 健康的,医药卫生的
hymen n. 处女膜
hymenal caruncles 处女膜痕
hymeneal a./n. 婚姻的/(复)婚姻;婚礼
hyperbole 夸张,夸张法
hyperlexis n. 极度法律热(指美国州和联邦制定了大量的法律)
hyperlink 超链接[指网址或电脑文件中的词语或图像,如果你点击它,它会提供你另一页或另一文件〈we should encourage hyperlinks to each other webpages〉(我们应该鼓励网页之间的超链接)〈A hyperlink from one work's subject heading can quickly retrieve a list of other items in the catalog with the same heading〉(点击一部著作的主题标题的超链接可以迅速检索获得包括相同标题的目录中的另一些项目),(亦可写作 haiperlink, hy-per-link)]
hypermarket n. (英)高级百货市场
hypermedia n. 超媒体(指超文本和多媒体在信息浏览下的结合,是超级媒体的简称)
hyperpower n. 超强国
hypertext 超文本
hypnotized person 进入催眠状态者
hypochondriacal delusion 疑病妄想(思想内容障碍的一种;指毫无根据地认为自己重病在身,四处求医,反复检查。如果他认为自己患病为某人使坏所致,则可能对某人进行攻击或报复。见 delusion)
hypodermic needle theory 皮下注射理论[指人们对大众传播信息的灌输是缺乏抗拒力的,媒介信息对于目标对象通常会产生皮下注射或子弹射击目标物一般的直接效果。这种为"皮下注射理论"或"输送带理论"(transmission belt theory)]
hypocrisy n. 伪善,虚伪

hypocrite n. 伪君子,虚伪的人
hypocritic(al) legal act 虚伪的法律行为
hypothec n. (罗马法)(不转移财产占有权的)抵押权,担保权;抵押物
hypotheca generalis 全部财产抵押权
hypotheca judicialis 审判上的抵押权
hypothecarius 抵押权人
hypothecary a. 抵押的,由抵押而获得的
hypothecary action 关于抵押财产索赔权的诉讼
hypothecary law 抵押法
hypothecate v. 担保,抵押(而不转移占有权)
hypothecated asset 质押资产
hypothecated loan 质押贷款
hypothecation n. 抵押;船舶或船货抵押;不交抵押品抵押(用财产来负担债款);对抵押财产的索赔权;(船舶或船货)货运抵押书;担保合同(契约)
hypothecation agreement 押汇担保书,押汇质权书,押汇负责书
hypotheque 抵押权,不动产抵押权
hypothesis n. 假设,假设(学)说,前提
hypothesize v. 假设,假定
hypothetic(al) 假设的,设想的;有前提的
hypothetical contractarianism 假象的契约论[罗尔斯力图把社会契约建立在道德契约论之上,意图以契约这个概念来导出道德或公正原则,表面上这是一种假象的社会契约论,根本不是一种社会契约论而是一种道德契约论(moral contractarianism)]
hypothetic(al) facts 假定的事实
hypothetic(al) law 假想的法律
hypothetic(al) question 假设的问题(指根据假设或已经证明的事实与环境相结合所作出有事实情况的说明,用以提出问题,征求专家意见)
hysteria n. 歇斯底里;癔病
hysteric n./a. 癔病患者;歇斯底里发作/癔病的,歇斯底里的
hysteric possession syndrome 癔症性附体综合征(指患者受刺激后急性发病,表现为由某个神、怪、精灵或死者亡魂附体,取代患者原来的人格或身份,以此身份讲话、行事。见 hysteria)
hysterical convulsion 癔症性抽搐发作(指病患具有戏剧性过程,无旁人不会发作,围观的人越多可能发作越厉害,发作时全身或局部肢体抖动,不像癫痫先有阵挛而后抽搐,有掀衣、抓头、翻滚和捶胸等动作,面色不改,意识清楚,持续时间长,无跌伤或大小便失禁现象)

I

ibidem (略作 *ib.* 或 *ibid.*) 出处同上,出自同一处
ICC's Commission on Banking Technique and Practice 国际商会银行技术与惯例委员会
icebox n. 1.冰箱 2.无名死尸安置处 3.(俚)单人牢房 4.无期徒刑 5.(美)保险箱
Icelandic law 冰岛法
Icelandic lawspeaker (中世纪的)冰岛法律代言人
ictus n. 猝发;发作;搏动
ictus epilepticus 癫痫发作
id est (i. e.) 即,就是
idea of decentralization 分权思想,地方分权说
idea of democracy 民主观念,民主思想
idea of law 法律的理想;法律概念;法律思想
idea of public service 公务观念
idea of relation and of legal consequence 关系及法律后果的观念(指贯穿英美法的每个方面的观念)
idea of the end of the legal order 法律秩序目的的观念
idea of the finality of the common law 普

通法的终极内容,普通法的终极概念
ideal a./n. 理想的,完美的,虚构的,不切实际的,唯心的/理想,观念,思想,完美的类型,规范
ideal element of law 法律的理想成分
ideal ought 理想应然(见 optimiza requirements)
idealistic interpretation 理想主义的解释
idealistic theory of state 观念(理想)主义的国家论
idem 同上,同前
idem genus 同类
idem sonans 同音姓名(指法庭不会因姓名的字母拼错而取消诉讼,即使因姓名读音相近而叫错了人,也如此)
identic(al) a. 相同的;(外交文件)同文的,(外交行动)方式相同的
identic(al) notes 同文照会,相同照会(指几个国家外交代表给驻在国政府对某事件发出相同的照会)
identic(al) trademark 相同的商标
identical treatment 同一待遇
identical with the law 与法律相同
identifiable a. 可证明为同一的,可以辨认的
identifiable fleet of vessels 可证明为统一的船队
identification n. 1.鉴定,识别;同一认定,确认,验明 2.证件,身份证明
identification by fingerprint 指纹鉴定
identification by hair 毛发鉴定
identification by palm print 掌纹鉴定
identification by photographs (以)相片认人(见 identification parade)
identification (或 identity) card 身份证
identification in disputed paternity 亲子鉴定,父权鉴定,亲权鉴定
identification of blood 血液鉴定
identification of bullet 弹头鉴定,枪弹鉴定
identification of (the) dead 尸体鉴定
identification of handwriting 笔迹鉴定
identification of immature fetus 未成熟儿鉴定
identification of law 法律的确认

identification of (the) living 活体鉴定
identification of poison 毒物鉴定
identification paper 身份证
identification parade 列队认人(指把嫌疑犯和其他的人混在一起,排列一行,让证人仔细辨认,认出了则可作证据)
identifier n. 鉴定人,检验人,认证人
identify v. 1.使等同于,认为……一致 2.认出,鉴定,鉴别;验明正身
identikit n. 拼图认人(指辨认人的面貌的一种方法,即把人的耳、口、鼻、目的图形逐件拼凑起来,成为一个完整面貌,给曾见过警方要寻找的人的人们来辨认,得出相仿的面貌后便印制成图,供追寻辨认)
identity n. 1.一致,同一(性);本人,本身;正身;本体 2.(表明姓名、职业等的)身份 3.个性,特征
identity certificate 身份证明书
identity document 身份证件
identity of an individual 对一个人的认定同一
identity of lost goods 失物(与失主所报的)相符
identity of organizational, budgetary, and accounting units 组织、预算、会计三位一体
identity of views 观点一致
identity test 鉴定试验
ideological a. 思想的,思想上的,意识形态的,观念形态的
ideological and political work 思想政治工作
ideological criminal 思想犯
ideological education 思想教育
ideological obstructions 思想障碍
ideological offence 思想罪
ideological remoulding (中)思想改造
ideological struggle 思想斗争
ideology n. 思想,思想意识,空论
idiocy n. 白痴,极端愚蠢;白痴行为
idiosyncratic a. 特殊的,习性的
idiosyncratic benefits 特殊利益,习性利益
idiosyncratic value 特殊价值
idiot n. 白痴(人),傻子
idiotic ordinances 愚蠢的条例

idiotism n. 白痴行为
idle a. 无用的,无效的,无根据的;懒散的,闲散的
idle and disorderly persons 游手好闲而爱闹事者,妨害治安者
idle exercise 无意义的行为
idle labo(u)r 闲散劳动力
idle rumo(u)r 毫无根据的谣言
idler n. 懒汉,游手好闲者
idoneis argumentis 适当的辩论,适当的论证
idoneitas 合适,(一个人的)能力,适应(性)(亦称 idoneity)
idoneity 同 idoneitas
Idoneous 见 *idoneus*
idoneum se facere; idoneare se. to make oneself sufficient; to clear oneself; to purge oneself; by oath; of a crime that one is accused of committing 以发誓洗涤自己被控的罪行
idoneus a. (罗马法)(人和事物)足够的,合适的;负责的,无疑的〈a responsible or solvent man was known as an *idoneus homo*〉(负责任的或有偿还能力的人是以他的负责任的人而出名),亦可称为 *idonea cautio*,英语拼写为 *idoneous*
(the) IEA Emergency Sharing System 国际能源机构"紧急分享机制"
If it comes to that... 假如事情真的到那种地步的话
ignis judicium (古代)蹈火判判法,火判法
ignominiosus (罗马法)不名誉[欺诈在罗马法上无疑为一种侵权,欺诈之诉(actio de dolo)是一种侵权之诉,受害人可以就其遭受的损害获得赔偿。欺诈人将会被处以"不名誉"之责,对其进行的谴责将会向市民公告]
ignominy n. 无耻行为,丑行;耻辱,不名誉
ignoramus 笨人,毫无知识的人;不予起诉(或译作不合起诉,指大陪审团查阅诉状后认为证据不足时,批用此语,以示反对控诉)
ignorance n. 无知,不知情;愚昧
* **Ignorance of the law is no excuse** 不知法律不是宽恕的理由

ignorant a. 无知的,愚昧的;不知情的;显示无知的;无知所造成的
ignorant error 出于无知(所造成)的错误
ignorant person 无知的人
ignorantia 不知情,特别不了解法律
* *Ignorantia eorum quae quis scire tenetur non excusat.* Ignorance of those things which one is bound to know excuses not. 凡人有义务应知道的事,就不能以不知道作为推卸责任的理由。
* *Ignorantia facti excusat.* Ignorance of fact excuses or is a ground of relief. 不知情可作为免责的理由。
* *ignorantia juris non* (或 *legis neminem*) *excusat.* Ignorance of law excuses not (or no one). (任何人)不得以不知法律为借口,不知法律不免责
* *Ignorantia juris sui non praejudicat juri.* Ignorance of one's right does not prejudice the right. 即使不知是某人的权利也不能损害该权利。
* **Ignorare legis** *est lala culpa.* To be ignorant of the law is gross neglect of it. 对法律的无知为重大过失。
* **Ignorance of law excuses no one.** 对法律无知不得作为抗辩理由,不得以不知法律为借口
ignoratio elenchi 用歪曲对方论点的手法驳斥对方
ignore v. 1.驳回 2.不顾,不理,忽视
ignore a complaint (法院)驳回无理起诉,拒绝无理起诉
ignore the bill (陪审团认为)诉状不予受理
ignore the facts 不顾事实,不承认事实
ignotum per ignotius 解释得比原来(需要解释的东西)更加难懂
ijmā (伊斯兰教法)公议(亦译《依默书说》,指穆斯林法学家们解释《古兰经》或《圣训》未规定的问题所确定的一致意见。为伊斯兰教法的主要渊源)
ill a. 1.有病的,不健康的 2.坏的,恶意的,邪恶的 3.拙劣的;不良的,不当的;难以处理的,麻烦的
ill-advised a. 鲁莽的,没头脑的

ill-disposed a. 存心不良的,坏心眼的;对……敌视的;不赞成的
ill-effect n. 恶果
ill-founded a. 无事实根据的,理由不充分的,无理由的
ill-gotten a. 非法获得的,来路不正的
ill-gotten gain(s) 非法所得,不当得利,不义之财
ill-judged a. 因判决不当所引起的,因判断错误所引起的
ill-timed a. 不适当的,不合时宜的
ill-treat v. 虐待,苛待,伤害
ill-use v. 虐待,滥用
ill-will n. 敌意,仇视;恶感
illegal a. 不合法的,非法的;违例的,违法的
illegal abortion 非法堕胎
illegal act 违法行为,不法行为
illegal action 不法诉讼,不法行为
illegal activity 不法活动
illegal arrest 非法逮捕
illegal association 非法结社
illegal condemnation 非法判罪
illegal confinement 非法监禁
illegal consideration (英美法)违法对价;非法报酬
illegal contract 非法合同(契约),违法合同(契约)
illegal decision 非法判决
illegal disposition 违法处分,非法处分
illegal electronic snooping 非法电子窃听(罪)
illegal encroachment 非法侵入,不法侵占
illegal exaction 非法勒索
illegal felling of trees 滥伐树木
illegal immigrant 非法入境者,非法移民
illegal imprisonment 非法监禁
illegal infiltration 非法闯入
illegal interest 不法收益,非法权益
illegal interrogation 非法讯问
illegal intervention 非法干涉
illegal knowingly 故意违法
illegal means 非法手段
illegal measures 不法措施
illegal migrant(s) 非法移民
illegal omission 非法遗漏;非法的不作为,非法不履行法律责任
illegal organization 非法组织
illegal payment 不当给付
illegal per se 当然违法,本身违法
illegal possession 不正当占用,非法占有
illegal practices 不法行为,非法行为
illegal procurement of foreign exchange 套汇
illegal profit 不当得利(指没有法律上或合同上的根据,或后来丧失了这种根据,使他人受到损害而获得的利益)
illegal punishment 非法惩罚
illegal racing 非法超速开车
illegal recruitment 非法征募
illegal regime 非法政权
illegal restraint 非法限制
illegal search and seizure 非法搜查与扣押
illegal transaction 非法买卖,非法交易
illegal transaction in foreign currencies 非法买卖外币(罪)
illegal trust 非法信托
illegal union (男女的)不合法的结合;非法联合
illegal vote 非法表决,非法投票
illegal weapon 非法武器
illegality n. 违法,不合法;非法;非法行为
illegalize v. 使成为非法,宣布为违法
illegally ad. 非法地,不合法地,违法地
illegally acquired money 赃款,非法所得款
illegally cross the national border 偷越国境
illegally obtained evidence 非法获得的证据
illegible a. 难以辨认的,字迹模糊的。
illegitimacy n. 非婚生,非嫡出;非法(性);不合理;不符惯例;违法(性)
illegitimacy of children (或 **illegitimate children**) 非婚生子女
illiberal decisions 持有偏见的判决,有偏袒的判决
illegitimate a./n./v. 非法的,违法的;非婚生的;不符惯例的/非婚生子女;没有合法身份的人(尤指私生子)/宣布为非法;宣布为非婚生子(女)
illegitimate child 非婚生子[指既非合法婚生子,亦非后来合法之子。按普通法,

这样的孩子被认为是私生子(nullius filias)(child of nobody),除非博得一个好名声,否则根本没有名字。由于非婚生子属无人的孩子,没有继承权,甚至不能从亲生母亲那里继承。但现在各州允准母系继承(maternal inheritance),诸如列维诉路易斯安那州案(Levy v. Louisiana),参见《美国联邦最高法院判例汇编》第391卷第68页,第88卷第1509页(1968年)和格洛那诉美国担保和责任保险公司案(Glona v. American Guar & Liab Ins Co.),参见《美国联邦最高法院判例汇编》第391卷第73页第88卷第1515页(1968年)。美国联邦最高法院坚持认为限制儿童从他(或她)母亲那里继承的权利是违宪的,因此,各州改变了它们的法律法规,允许有完全的母系继承。按照州的法律法规,如果孩子能证明父亲的渊源,则可允准父系的继承权(这种证明各州不一)。对于这种非婚生子唯一强求的举证是合宪的,此词亦可称为 bastard; child out of wedlock; nonmarital child(旧称) natural child

illegitimate filiation 非婚生子女的生父的确定

illegitimate income 非法收入

illegitimate warfare 非法战争,不符国际惯例的战争

illegitimation n. 宣告违法;宣布为非婚生子(女);不合法;不合理

illicit a. 违法的,违禁的,被禁止的;不正当的;私(卖、通、造等)的

illicit acts 违法行为

illicit and clandestine trafficking 非法和秘密贩运

illicit cohabitation 非法同居

illicit connection (或 **connexion**) 私通

illicit income 非法收入

illicit intercourse 私通,通奸

illicit market 黑市,非法市场

illicit money 赃款

illicit property 违法财产

illicit prostitution 秘密卖淫,暗娼

illicit sale 私卖

illicit sexual relations 不正当的关系

illicit trade 非法贸易

Illinois ex. rel. Mc Collum v. Board of Education. 333 U. S. 203 (1948) 麦克科勒姆引起的"伊利诺伊州诉教育理事会案" 333 U. S. 203 (1948) [此案是联邦最高法院有关联邦宪法第一修正案部分的早期判例之一,而该修正案禁止确立宗教(establishment of religion)。法院作出判决:公立学校不得允许传教士在校内提供宗教教导。多数意见及并存意见都属于严格的分离派,认为在国家与宗教活动之间应该存在一堵高墙]

illogical a. 不合逻辑的,无条理的,说不通的

illusage n. 虐待,苛待

illusion n. 错觉,幻觉(精神障碍的词语错觉是指歪曲的知觉体验,特点是首先有客观的刺激存在,但被完全错误地感知);假想,错误的观念

illusory a. 因错觉产生的,虚幻的,迷惑人的

illusory appointment 虚假处分[指依据处分权(power of appointment)对财产进行名义上的附加限制或有条件的财产转让]

illustrate v. 说明,阐明,举例

illustration n. 说明,图释,实例,插图,例证

illustrative case 解释性案件;用作说明的案例

(The) ILO Declaration on Fundamental Principles and Rights at Work 《国际劳工组织关于工作中的基本原则和权利宣言》

imaginative reconstruction 想象重构理论

imaginative reverence 想象的尊严,想象的威望

imbargo (古)(=embargo)

imbecile n. 禁治产者;低能者,心智能力极低者(近乎白痴)

imbezzle 见 embezzle

imbezzlement 见 embezzlement

imbibe v. 唱,饮;吸入(空气);吸收(思想,知识;光,热等)

imbue v. 使浸透,染;使充满,鼓舞(with)

imbue the courts with sense of power 以权力意识激励法院

imitation n. (商标)模仿,仿造,仿冒[指

对商标的仿冒,即与真正的商标非常相似,从而很可能使人信以为真(见similarity)。实际上,就是按照一物的形象制造另一物,如假币就是仿造真币而成的]
imitation brand goods 冒牌货
imitation firearms 假火器
immaterial a. 非物质的,无形的;非实质的;不重要的
immaterial averment 无意义的指证
immaterial capital 无形资本
immaterial injury 非物质性损害
immaterial issue 不重要的系争点(指诉讼辩论中,不能正确解决诉讼的一种非要点的争论点)
immaterial point 非要点
immaterial to the question 与此问题无关
immature a. 发育未全的,未成熟的;幼稚的;幼年的,未成年的;未完成的,不完全的
immature person 未成年人
immaturity n. 未成年,未成熟;未成熟行为;幼稚
immediacy n. 直接性,刻不容缓
immediate a. 直接的;即时的;最接近的
immediate antecedents to the law-and-economics 法经济学的前提,法经济学运动的直接前提[指英国经济学家科斯(Ronald Coase)执笔写的这场运动的奠基文章。这场法经济学运动是在一种经济学的传统中所发展而来的,它的意义在于为将来的法律和某种社会学特别是与经济学的结合开辟了途径]
immediate assets 流动资产
immediate breach 现时违约
immediate cash payment 立即付现,即时付现
immediate cause 直接原因,近因
immediate complaint 即时控告
immediate consequence 直接后果
immediate control (对机动车辆的)瞬时控制
immediate delivery 立即交付
immediate disciples 嫡系弟子
immediate evidence 直接证据
immediate execution 立即执行;立即处决

immediate family 近亲属[指①父母,配偶,子女,兄弟姐妹;②父母,配偶,子女,兄弟姐妹以及配偶的兄弟姐妹,继子女和收养的子女通常也属近亲属成员]
immediate gains 直接利益
immediate import of the decision 该判决的现实(直接)含义,判决的现实意义,判决的直接意义
immediate issue 子女,孩子
immediate object 直接客体
immediate possession 直接拥有权,直接所有权
immediate purpose 直接目的
immediate reply 即时答辩,立即回答
immediate sale 即时买卖,现货买卖
immediate shipment 立即装运,即期装运
immediate subject 直接主体
immediate will of the people 人民的迫切愿望,人民的急切要求
immediately pending motion 正在考虑中的悬而未决的动议;由议会主席最后阐明的未决的动议,接下来就将获得表决(见pending motion)
immemorial a. 无法追溯的;无法记忆的;太古老的
immemorial possession 自古占有
immemorial usage 古老的习惯,古老的惯例
immigrant n./a. (来自外国的)移民,外侨/(来自外国的)移民的,外侨的
immigrant visa 移民签证
immigration n. (来自外国的)移民;移居入境
Immigration and Naturalization Service (美)移民和归化局
immigration law 移民法
immigration office (或service) 移民局
immigration procedure 入境手续
immigration reform and control act 移民改革和控制法
imminence (或 **imminency**) n. 即将来临,逼近;紧迫的危险或灾祸;即将来临之事物
imminence of death 死亡的逼近,死亡的来临

imminent a. 急迫的,危急的;迫近的
imminent danger 迫在眉睫的危险
imminent death 濒临死亡
imminent infringement 即时侵权(指按某一活动发展必然构成侵权,但尚未构成侵权的情况)
imminently hazardous chemical substance 高度危险化学物质
* *Immobilia situm sequuntur.* Immovable things are governed by law of the place where they are fixed. 不动产受其坐落的所在地法管辖。
immobilis 不动产
immoral n. 不道德的,道德败坏的;邪恶的;猥亵的,淫荡的
immoral contract 不道德的合同(契约);有伤风化的合同(契约)
immoral nature 猥亵性质;不道德性质
immoral offence 有伤风化罪
immoral trade 不道德勾当,不道德交易
immoralist n. 不道德的人,鼓吹不道德行为者
immorality n. 不道德行为(尤指以不道德的性行为作内容的合同,这类合同是无效的);淫荡行为;不道德;伤风败俗的行为
immovable a./n. 不动的,固定的;无感情的;不可改变的;不屈不可移动的东西;(复)不动产
immovable by destination (法律上)预定的不动产
immovable goods (或 object) 不动产
immovable property 不动产
immovable property recording law 不动产登记法
immovable security 不动产担保
immovable thing in law 法律上的不动产
immune a. 免除的,被豁免的
immune from libel suit 免于诽谤性诉讼
immune from taxation 免税
immune to all pleas 不容申辩;对所有要求都置之不理
immunity n. 1.豁免;豁免权 2.免除;免疫 3.安全;安全性
immunity from arrest 不受逮捕
immunity from jurisdiction 司法裁判豁免权
immunity from litigation 免予起诉
immunity from prosecution 免予公诉
immunity from suit 免予起诉
immunity from suit of foreign states 外国国家司法豁免权
immunity from trial 不受审判
immunity of diplomatic envoys 外交代表豁免权
immunity of domicile 住所的豁免权
immunity of judge 法官豁免权
immunity of property of foreign state 外国国家财产的豁免权
immunity of state 国家豁免权
immunity of state-owned ship 国有船只的豁免权
immunity of the embassy from local jurisdiction and taxation (作为外交特权的)使馆人员的司法管辖豁免权和税收豁免权
immunity right 豁免权
immutability n. 永不改变,不变性,不易性
immutable forms 不可改变的形式
immunize v. 使免役;使免除(from)
impact n. 1.影响,效力;影响力 2.冲突,碰撞;撞击力
impact injury 碰撞伤
impacted area (美)(因人口激增导致公共设施不敷应用的)公共设施紧缺地区
impade v. 妨碍,阻止,阻碍
impair v. (17世纪)削弱,减少;降低,损害(指减少或降低财产或财产权的价值。这个词通常与损害合同义务的价值相关,损害达到合同变成无效的低点,或达到一方当事人损失合同中的利益。见 contract clause)
impairing the morals of minor (1931年)侵害未成年人的品德[指成年人与未成年人间的一种有关性行为,只是未发生性交的一种猥亵行为。这类行为例证就是抚弄、制作淫秽视频并展示这些色情资料。亦称 unlawful sexual conduct with minor; corrupting; corruption of a minor。见 contributing to the delinquency (of a minor)]
impairment n. 损坏;身体的损伤,伤害;损

失,削弱

impairment of a law 减低法律效力,削弱法律效力

impanel (=empanel) v. 把(某人)列入陪审员名单,编入陪审员名册;选任(陪审员等);召集陪审员

imparl (=emparl) v. 庭外调解;(获准)延期(诉讼,以便和解)

imparlance n. 1.答辩期的延长[指允准提出请求的当事人(通常为被告)对对方的最后诉状(特别是原告的提起诉讼令、诉状、控告理由)进行答辩的期间推延。这样,请求当事方则可有时间解决争端。英格兰于1853年废弃此项制度]2.答辩延期的申请3.同意答辩延期的允准4.庭外和解(指法庭允许双方当事人协商解决争端)

impartial a. 公正无私的,不偏袒的,公平的

impartial administration of justice 公正执法

impartial arbitrator 公正的仲裁人(或公断人)

impartial jury (17世纪)公正陪审团(指案件一开始,就不预先对其是非曲直作任何裁断,而只依据有法律效力的证据上所裁断的事实进行认定的陪审团。亦称为fair and impartial jury)

impartial third party 中立第三人,中立第三当事人

impartial trial 公正的审判

impartiality n. 公正无私,公平,公正

impartible a. (地产等)不可分割的,不可分的

impartible estate 不可分割的房地产

impartible feud 不可分割的封地(指此采单独的封地,不可分割。见 feudum individuum)

impasse n. 僵局,绝境,死路

impawn v. 典当,抵押;保证,立誓担保

impeach v. 1.控告,检举,弹劾 2.对……表示怀疑(特指怀疑证人的话),非难,责问;不信任

impeach sb. with (或 of) **a crime** 控告某人犯罪

impeach the testimony of a witness 对证人的可靠性提出异议

impeachable a. 可控告的,可弹劾的;可怀疑的

impeached for treason 被指控犯有叛国罪

impeaching witness credibility 弹劾主人可信性

impeachment n. 1.控告,检举 2.弹劾;弹劾权 3.责问,指责

impeachment case 弹劾案件,检举案件

impeachment evidence 质疑证据

impeachment of the verdict 对陪审团裁决的质疑

impeachment of waste 控告(某人)应负不动产的毁损责任;对毁坏租赁财产的责问

impeachment of witness 指责证人(指根据其他证人的证言所揭露的来指责某一证人所作证言不可信)

impeachment proceeding 弹劾程序

impeachment trials 弹劾审判

impediment n. 妨碍,障碍;法定婚姻障碍;身体缺陷;口吃

impediment to practice of law 实施法律的障碍

impedimento 禁止合同(契约)婚姻(指西班牙法中禁止某些人之间订立契约婚姻)

impediments to marriage 法定婚姻的障碍,婚姻障碍

impedimentum dirimens 无效性婚姻障碍
impedimentum impediens 禁止性婚姻障碍

impeding apprehension (英)(意图妨碍对应逮捕罪犯的)妨碍司法逮捕公务罪(亦包含妨碍起诉)

impel v. 推动,迫使

impending a. 就要来的,近在眼前的,紧急的,即将举行的

impending apprehension 听候拘押
impending danger 迫在眉睫的危险
impending invalidation 即将作废
impending judgment 即将举行的判决
impending prosecution (必须)立即进行的控诉

impenitent n. 顽固不化者,无悔改之意的人

imperative n./a. 命令,规则;必须履行的责任/强制的,命令的;必要的;紧急的

imperative character of enacted law 制定法的强制性
imperative element 强制性要素
imperative law 强行法
imperative necessity 紧迫的必要性
imperative theory of law 法律的命令说
imperfect a. 未完成的;不完美的;法律上不可实施的;未经批准的;不能履行的
imperfect competition 不完全竞争
imperfect gift 不完全赠与
imperfect independent state 不完全独立国
imperfect neutrality 不完全中立
imperfect obligation 道义上的义务,当然义务,不完全的义务(指不能用法律强迫履行,只具有道德上的义务,如做公益事等),不受法律约束的责任
imperfect ownership 不完全的所有权
imperfect procedural justice 不完全的程序正义
imperfect real right 不完全物权
imperfect right 非完整权利
imperfect self-defence 准正当防卫;正当防卫过当
imperfect self-defense doctrine 准正当防卫理论
imperfect trust 不完全的信托(指将来有效的信托)
imperfect usufruct 不完全用益权
imperfections n. 残次品
imperial a. 最高权力的;帝国的;皇家的,皇帝的;有属地的;威严的;(英)(度量衡的)法定标准的;特等的,特大的
Imperial Chamber (神圣罗马帝国的)最高司法法院
Imperial Chamber of Justice (德史)帝国司法法院
imperial chancellor 帝国首相
Imperial Court 皇家法院
imperial enactment 诏书
imperial envoy 钦差大臣
imperial household 皇室
Imperial Legislation 钦定立法
imperial ordinance 敕令
Imperial Parliament 英国议会
Imperial Privy Council (罗马)帝国枢密院
imperial standards (英)法定标准度量衡
Imperial Statute 英国制定法(指成文法)
imperialism n. 帝国主义
imperialist n. 帝国主义者;帝制拥护者
imperil v. 使处于危险,危害
* *Imperitia culpae annumeratur* Unskillfulness is reckoned as a fault (as a blameworthy conduct or neglect). 缺乏技能就是过失(亦称 imperitia enurneratur culpae)
imperium 主权;统治权;绝对统治权;司法行政管辖权;执法权;(古罗马)帝权
imperium limitatum 有限制的权威
imperscriptible a. 没有文件证明的;非官方的,非正式的
impersonal forces 非人力(指自然力等)
impersonality n. 与个人无关;客观,无人格,不具人格;非人格性的东西(指时空等);一般性
impersonate v. 体现;模仿;拟人,人格化
impersonation n. 模拟,扮演,假扮(角色);冒名顶替(计算机犯罪手段之一,指通过非法手段获取他人口令或许可证明之后,冒充合法使用者从事欺骗或其他犯罪活动)
impertinence n. 不切题,不相干(指陈述或答辩所提出的是与证据无关之事),不适合;无礼,失礼
implead v. 依法控诉,控告(尤指同案控告两个以上的),起诉
impleaded party 被引入诉讼的当事人
impleader n. 1.控告人,起诉人 2.要求诉讼第三当事人参加的诉讼
implement n./v. 1.履行,完全履行;执行,实施 2.家具,用具,工具,器具 /1.履行(合同,诺言等),贯彻;完成,实现,生效;实施,执行 2.供给器具
implement of gambling 赌具
implement of punishment 刑具
implement of robbery 打劫工具
implementation n. 执行,履行;实施,贯彻;生效;完成
implementation of law 法律的实施
implicate v. 使(某人)牵连(于罪行之

中);推断;涉及;暗示
implicated offender 牵连犯
implication n. 推断;含蓄之意;暗示,含义;牵连,牵涉
implication of law 法律上的默示;法律含义
implicative a. 言外之意的,暗示的;牵连的
implicit a. 暗示的,不言明的;绝对的,无疑的;无保留的
implicit assumption 暗含假定
implicit repudiation 默示拒绝履行(指在合同履行期届满前,当事人的某种行为造成合同不可能履行的结果,或在任何通情达理的第三方看来应是对合同义务的拒绝履行,即可构成默示拒绝履行)
implied a. 默示的,暗示的;不言而喻的
implied acceptance of risk 默示承担风险
implied actual authority 隐蔽的权力
implied actual knowledge 见 actual knowledge ②
implied agency (18世纪)默示代理[指依据当事人(principal)暗示创立一个代理关系而成立的实际代理(actual agency)]
implied agreement 默示协定,默示协议
implied answer 含蓄的答辩
implied assumpsit (可要求赔偿违约所造成的损失的)默示允诺
implied authority 默示授权;默示权限;默示代理权
implied condition (17世纪)默示条件(即没有明确表示的条件,但是由于交易的性质或当事双方的行为以及他们之间心照不宣的彼此了解正是协议的一部分,因而这构成法律归于它的责任。见 constructive condition, implied-in-fact condition)
implied consent 默许,默示准许,默示同意
implied consent theory 默示理论
implied contract 默示合同(契约)(或称准契约,指在合同关系中债务人所作的承诺,虽未明确表达,但依据他签订合同的行为或从法律上可予以确定的)
implied contract in fact 事实上的默示合同(契约)
implied contract in law 法律上的默示合同(契约)
implied covenant 默示合同(契约)条款

implied declaration 默示宣告;默示的意思表示
implied features 默示特征
implied intention 默示的意思表示
implied malice 隐含的恶意
implied objection 默示异议(或反对)
implied passing off 隐形假冒(指甲向买主出示乙的货样,但实际出售自己的产品)
implied power 默示权力
implied powers of Congress (美)国会的默示权力
implied promise 默示承诺,默示允诺
implied ratification 默示批准,默许
implied recognition 默示认可,默示承认
implied repeal 暗示废止
implied representation 默示代位继承;默示代理
implied reservation 默示权益保留
implied reverse passing off 隐形反向假冒(指甲购收乙的产品,然后在无任何标志的情况下出售。按美国学者看法,显形假冒应属商标侵权行为的一种,而隐形假冒、显形或隐形反向假冒行为均属不正当竞争,而非商品侵权)
implied term 默示条件(款)
implied trust 默示信托
implied waiver 默示放弃,暗示放弃
implied warrant 默示担保
implied warranty of quiet enjoyment 默示的享用担保
implied-in-fact condition 事实上的默示条件(指合同当事双方通过他们的行为和交易性质已默示同意的合同条件。见 constructive condition)
implied-in-law condition 见 constructive condition
imply v. 默示,暗示,暗指;含有……意思;推想;包含;必须具备
imply(implied) that... 意思是……
impolicy n. 失策;不明智
import n. 1.进口,输入;进口货,输入品 2.意义;重要性
Import and Export Commodity Inspection Bureau (中)进出口商品检验局
Import and Export Corporation (中)进

出口总公司
import and export declaration 进出口申报
import authorization 进口许可(证)
import cargoes 进口商品
import control 进口管制
import deposit 进口保证金,进口押金
import duty 进口税
import license 进口许可证
import permit 进口许可(证)
import procurement policy 输入品采购政策
import quantum 进口量
import quota 进口限额(指从国外进口某些产品的数量限制。在美国,总统可以设定有关项目的限额,此项目数额不得构成严重损害国内工业的威胁)
import quota system 进口配额制
import surcharge (或 surtax) 进口附加税
import surplus 入超
import tariff 进口税则
import trade bill 进口贸易票据
import-competing interests 进口竞争性利益
importance test 重要性标准
important a. 重要的,重大的;有权力的;有地位的;大量的
important case 重大案件
important conditions of appeal 上诉要件
important criminal 要犯
important event 重大事件
important figure 有地位的人,要人
important state interest 州的重大利益
importation n. 进口,输入;输入品,进口货
imported capital goods 进口生产资料
importee n. 从外国带进的工人
importer n. 进口商,输入者
importune v. 向……强求,纠缠;迫诱,(为不道德的目的而)强求,(妓女)拉客
impose v. 1.征(税)2.把……强加于;强制;加(负担,惩罚)于;设定,设置 3.利用 4.欺骗(on, upon)5.施加影响(on, upon)
impose liability in the absence of fault 承担无过错责任
impose sanctions against 处分,给……以处分
imposed a. 被强加的
imposed constitution 钦定宪法

imposed contract 标准合同
imposing judicial power 更庄严的司法权
imposing punishment 厉行惩罚;施以惩罚
imposition n. 1.课税,征税;惩罚,负担 2.强行进入 3.苛捐杂税 4.利用;欺骗
imposition of confiscatory 强行征服,强行没收
imposition of death penalty 死刑判决,判处死刑
imposition of penalty 判处刑罚
impossibilis condicio 不可能做到的条件,不能履行的条件
impossibilita fisica 物质不能(主要指标的的完全灭失)
impossibilita giuridica 法律不能(指标的不具有交易性)
impossibilitas facti 行为能力之不能(主要指人的能力不可能)
impossibilitas rei 事情本身之不能(指事情的本质上的不可能)
impossibility n. 不可能性;不可能的事
impossibility doctrine in contract law 合同法中的不可能学说
impossibility juridical 法律不能(指标的不具有交易性)
impossibility of fact 见 factual impossibility
impossibility of performance 无法履行,(合同等的)履行的不可能性
impossibility physical 物质不能(主要指标的的完全灭失)
impossibility without fault 无过失履行不能
* *Impossibilium nulla obligatio est.* There is no obligation to do impossible things. 对于做不到的事,就不承担义务。("以不能之给付为契约标的者,其誓约无效")——出自罗马法学家赛塞斯(Celsus)
impossible condition 不能做到的条件,不能履行的条件
impost n. 税,关税,进口税
imposter (= impostor) n. 冒名顶替者,骗子
impostor (同 imposter)(16世纪)冒名顶替者(指借他人之名欺骗另外的人,特别是接受流通票据的利益)

impost(h)ume n. 腐败,道德败坏
impotence (= impotency) n. 无力,虚弱;无能;阳痿,性交不能
impotentia n. 无能;阳痿,勃起不能
impotentia coeundi 男性交媾不能
impotentia erigendi 勃起不能
* *Impotentia excusat legem.* The impossibiity of doing what is required by the law excuses from the performance. 法律上规定必须做而不可能做到者,则免除履行责任。
impotentia generandi 生育不能
impound v. 充公,没收(物);扣押(人),保管
impound account 扣押财产,充公(资产)账户[指由贷方保管的累积基金账户,以便支付税收、保险或其定期的物权(不动产)债务。亦称 escrow account; reserve account]
impounding n. 充公,没收,扣押,保管
impounding fee 车辆扣留费
impounding of property seized 查封已抄没的财产
impoundment n. (总统对国会拨款的)扣押,保管
impoundment power 扣押权
impoverish v. 使陷入困境
impoverished a. 陷入困境的
impracticable a. 不能实行的,不切实际的;难以驾驭的;不适用的,行不通的
impregnate v. 使怀孕,受精
impregnation n. 受胎,怀孕
imprescriptibility n. 不受时效限制的
imprescriptible a. 不受法律约束的,不受惯例支配的;不可侵犯的,不可剥夺的;不因时效而消灭的
imprescriptible right 不受时效限制的权利,不因时效而丧失的权利
impress v. 强迫……服役;强征(费用、财产)等;(在辩论中)利用,引用
impress upon 牢记,铭刻
impression n. 印象;效果,影响;印痕,印记;盖印
impression of muzzle 枪口压印痕
impression of seal 印文

impressment n. (英)强制征用(指英王享有的为了保护王国利益,无需征得有关当事人的同意即可征得人员和财产的权利);强迫服役,强征入伍;强行征用
imprest n./a. 预付款,预付公款(指政府预付给某人执行公务的款项);垫款,备用金/预付的,借贷的
imprest fund 预付基金(指生意上作为小额常规费用使用的基金)
imprest holder 垫款受领人
imprest money 预付的公款,垫款
imprest warrant 垫款许可证
imprimatur (天主教对出版物的)出版许可;(官方审查后的)出版许可;批准,许可
imprimis 第一,首先
imprint n./v. 印,印记;痕迹;特征;版本说明/印,盖印,铭刻
imprison v. 关押,监禁;限制,束缚;入监,收押
imprisonable a. 应判处徒刑的,可监禁的
imprisonment n. 监禁,徒刑,拘禁,坐牢
imprisonment at forced labo(u)r 强迫劳役监禁
imprisonment for a definite 有期徒刑
imprisonment for a shorter term 短期徒刑(监禁)
imprisonment for debt 因负债而入狱(监禁)
imprisonment for life (或 **permanent imprisonment**) 无期徒刑,终身监禁
imprisonment in the first division (或 **ordinary imprisonment**) 警察局的拘禁
imprisonment in the second division (或 **rigorous imprisonment**) 轻罪拘禁
imprisonment with a suspension of sentence 缓刑
imprisonment with hard labo(u)r 苦役监禁(指监禁时服劳役)
imprisonment without forced labo(u)r 非强迫劳役监禁
imprisonment without the option of a fine 不能以罚款替代的徒刑
improbable a. 未必会有,不大可能发生的;未必确实的
improper a. 不适当的,不合适的,不正确的;不合理的;错误的;不道德的;下流的

improper act 不当行为
improper amendment 不正当的修改
improper arrest 不当逮捕,错捕(指把不应逮捕的人逮捕起来)
improper conduct 不良行为
improper feud(s) (英格兰古法)派生封地[指由服兵役而保有的封地(proper feud)派生而来的封地类型。即上级领主为了更好履行其军事方面的服役而分封出去一定土地作为代价使其在军中履行某种役务,此类土地可以转让,亦可继承。见 proper feud]
improper loan 非正规借贷(指非原本意义上的借贷,如消费借贷)
improper means of discovery (美)(商业秘密)不当的发现手段[指以一种错误的或非法的、不公正的方法断定竞争者的商业秘密。比如采取虚伪陈述(misrepresentation)、窃听(eavesdropping)或窃取(stealing)等手段]
improper motion 不合程序的动议
improper performance 不适当履行
improper person 名誉败坏的人
improper treatment of parents 不孝父母
improperly received profit 不正当所得的红利
impropriate v. 把(教会财产或收入)占为己有,把(教会财产)交给人保管
impropriety n. 不正当,不正确,不适当的举止,不正当的行为
improvement n. 改良,增进,改善,改进,改进措施,经营;(美)不动产的改进(指永久性或临时性的增加价值或效用,或改善其外观的措施)
improvement patent 改进工艺的专利
impuber 见 pubertas
impubes (未达青春发动期的)未成年人(大陆法用语,指男为14岁,女为12岁以下的未成年人)
impugn v. 驳斥,指责,非难;(对品质、道德等)表示怀疑
impugn a piece of evidence 对某一证据的怀疑
impugnable a. 可指责的,可非难的,易遭怀疑的,可驳斥的

impulse n. 冲力,推动,动力
impulsive insanity 冲动性精神病(指有富于暴力行为的倾向)
impulsive personality disorder 冲动性人格障碍(人格障碍类型的一种,又称攻击性人格障碍,其特点是以情感暴发,伴明显行为冲动,男性明显多于女性,容易产生人际关系紧张,导致情感危机;经常出现自杀、自伤行为。见 paranoid personality disorder)
impunity n. 不受刑罚;免罚;免罪;免责;不受损害
impure moralistic retributivism 不纯粹的道德报应主义
impure retributivism 不纯粹的报应主义
impure utilitarianism 不纯粹的功利主义
imputability n. 神志正常,能够负责,有归罪可能
imputable a. 可归罪于……的,可归因于……的(to)〈The oversight is not imputable to him〉(这个疏忽不能怪他)(imputability n.;imputably adv.)
imputation n. 归属;归罪,转嫁罪责;诋毁;非难;诬蔑
imputation of incompetence 诋毁(某人)无法定资格
imputation of payment (罗马法)债务人向债权人作出的直接偿还请求,特别是向两个以上的债权人的债务的偿付[可参见《路易斯安那州民法典》第 1864、1866 条(La. Civ. Code arts. 1984,1866)]
imputation of unchastity 诋毁(某人)不贞洁
imputazine oggetiva dell evant 结果的客观归罪(指根据刑法的需要来限制刑法中因果关系存在的范围,这种理论产生于刑法制度中尚未对因果关系作出一般规定的国家,如在德国)
impute v. 把……归因于,把……归咎于,归罪于,归责于;把……转嫁给(to)
imputed a. 被认为的,被归咎于关系方(人)的
imputed cost 估算成本,推算成本,应负成本,假设成本
imputed income 估算收入

imputed interest （按资本额）推（估）算的利息,应付利息
imputed knowledge 推测了解,推定认知,推定认识,推定了解
imputed malice 推定恶意
imputed negligence 关系人(方)受牵连的过失（又译:转嫁的过失责任,指可向与行为人有利害关系的人或有合同关系的另一方追究责任的过失。如雇员按雇主约定实施的行为的过失,可追究雇主的责任）
imputed notice 替代通知
imputed or implied consent 推论的或默示的同意
imputed rent 估算租金
imputive a. 归罪的,有归罪倾向的,归咎的,责难的,可归罪于……的(to)
in a dead hand 处于永远管业的情况下
in a given jurisdiction 特定管辖
in a manner 在一定意义上;在一定程度上
in a manner prescribed by law 依法定程序
in a nutshell 简括地说,一句话;简要,概括地说
in a public vote 采用公开投票方式
in a *quasi in rem* **proceeding** 准对物管辖程序
in a similar vein 依照类似思路,按相似脉络
in a（或 **one**）**way** 在某种程度上,在某一点上;稍微,有几分
in abatement 终止诉讼
in absentia 缺席
in accordance with practice 按照惯例;根据实践
in accordance with the law 依法
in accordance with the seriousness of the case 根据情节轻重
in action 在活动,在运转;在诉讼中
in addition to 除……之外
in advance of 在……前面;超过
in all likelihood 所有的可能,没有预料的;可能发生的

* *In ambigua voce legis ea potius accipienda est significatio quae vitio caret; praesertim cum etiam voluntas legis ex hoc colligi possit.* In an ambiguous expression of the law, the meaning will be preferred that is free of defect, especially when the intention of the law can be gathered from it./Where the words of a statute are capable of two interpretations, then it is better to adopt the interpretation which is unobjectionable, more especially if that interpretation is in accordance with the intention of the act. 法律表意不明或有歧义时,应采取符合公平正义之解释,立法原意如此时尤应如此。

in an interesting condition （英）怀孕
in any wise 无论如何
in arbitrim judicis **at the pleasure or descretion of the judge** 由法官自由裁量,由法庭自由裁决,由法庭裁决
in articulo 立即,即刻
in articulo mortis 临死时;濒死期,临终
in autre droit 凭他人权力;作为他人代表
in banc（或 **banco; on the bench**） 1.法庭全体法官出庭审理案件 2.法官席 3.(高级法院)在开庭中
in bankruptcy 在破产中,破产
in bar of 为禁止……
in behalf of 代表;为了……
in blank 有空白待填写的(适用于票据背后的用语)（见 endorsement）
in bond 1.保税(指进口货物尚未完税,而被放在保税仓库,以待完税)2.保税仓库交货(港译:关栈中交货)
in bond terms 保税仓库（或关栈）交货条件
in bonds 在拘留中,被奴役
in bonis habere 所有权
in business 营业;职责
in camera 1.秘密审议;非公开会议;不公开审讯 2.在法官工作室(指秘密审议的地方)
in camera declaration （美）"秘密陈述"(指在涉及国家安全的案件,法院通常采取秘密审查方式,必要时机关还可通过"秘密陈述"来解释不公开信息的原因。机关的"秘密陈述"只对法院作出,不向原告和外界公开)
in capita 按人头,每人

in capite　见 tenure in capite
in case　万一(见 in the event that)
in case of　(只跟名词)万一
in cassation　废除,取消
in chambers　在内庭,在法官个人办公室
in chancery　(英)与国王或政府有关的起诉案件
* In claris non est locus conjecturis.　In things obvious(or In obvious instance)there is no room for conjecture.　对显而易见之事,无猜测之必要
in close confinement　秘密地
in cold blood　蓄意地,残忍地
in collusion with　与……勾结,串骗
in Commendam　代为保管
in commission　1.现役的,服役中的 2.带有任务的,被委任的 3.委托代办的,代为保管的
in common　(两人以上的)共有,共同所有(或使用),共同的,共同地;共用
in common parlance　照一般的说法
in connection (或 connexion) with　1.与……有关;与……联运 2.关于
in conformity with (或 to)　依照,与……相一致
in conjunction with　和……在一起,与……协力,与……有关系
in consequence　结果是,因此
in consequence of　由于……缘故,基于
in consideration of　鉴于,考虑到
in consimili casu　在同类案件中
* In consimili casu, consimile debet esse remedium.　In a similar case the remedy should be similar.　类似案件应有类似救济。
in conspectu ejus　以他的观点,在他看来
in contemplation of death　死亡之际,在接近死亡的条件下
* In contractibus veniunt ea que sunt moris et consuetudinis in regione in qua contrahitur.　In contracts those things occur, which are of law and custom in the place in which the contract is made.　合同中出现的事情是属于法律和习俗在构成的合同中应有其地位。

in contradiction to　违反
in contrast with (或 to)　与……形成对比,与……形成对照
in contravention of　违反……
in contumaciam　藐视法庭
* In conventionibus contrahentium voluntas potius quam verba spectari placuit　In agreements, the intention of the contracting parties should be regarded more than their words.　协议的解释应追求双方当事人的真意,而非拘泥于文字
in corroboration of　为了证明……
in course of duty　因公
* In criminalibus pubationes debent esse luce clariores.　In criminal cases, the proofs ought to be clearer than light.　刑事案件中证据应是明确的
in criminalibus voluntas pro facto non reputabitur.　In criminal cases, the will will not be taken for the deed.　刑事案件中,意愿将不被当作行为
in critical condition　当在危急情况下
in curia　公开开庭;在公开审讯中
in custodia legis　依法保管(指文据或金钱处于法院或其他法定机关保管之下,表示业经官方查抄,可免第二次查封或扣押,在法律保管下,亦可称为 in legal custody)
in custody　被拘留,被监禁
in default of　因缺……,在缺少……时
in defense of　为……辩护,为保卫……
in deference to the books and proprieties　照本宣科,照章办事,服从教条
in deference to　遵从,服从
in defiance of　不顾,无视
in Dei nomine　(历史上)以上帝的名义[某种令状(writs)的开头语]
in delicto　有过失
in depth (in-depth)　深入地
in derogation of　背离……,无视
in doubt　怀疑,质疑,悬而未决,拿不准
in dubio　怀疑,有疑义的情况
* In dubio, pars mitior est sequenda.　In doubt, the milder course is to be followed.　遇有疑义时应遵循从宽方针。
in dubio, pro reo　遇有疑义时应有利于被

告原则(罗马法上的一个原则,即必须在有罪证明无疑义时才能处罚,否则将认为无罪。这就是现在"无罪推定"法律原则的渊源)

In dubio, sequendum quod tutius est. In doubt, the safer course is to be adopted. 在没把握时应采取比较稳妥的方针。

in due course 及时地,到(一定的)时候,在适当的时候

in due form 照例,正式地,按适当形式

in due time 在适当时间

in effect 有效;生效;实际上

in either case (在两种情况中)不论发生哪种情况

in equal proportions 按同等比例

In equali jure melior est conditio possidentis Where the right is equal, the condition of the party in actual possession shall prevail. Thus, also, when equities are equal, the laws shall prevail. 权利平等时实际占有当事人将取胜,同样衡平权益平等时,法律应占上风

in equality and good conscience 本着衡平和良知

in equity 公理上;依衡平法

in esse 实在地,确实存在

in essence 实质上

in evidence 明显的,显而易见的

in exchange for 交换

in excuse of 作为……辩解

in extenso 完全地;全文地;详尽地(指从头到尾没有遗漏的)

in extremis 临死时,濒死期;最后,临终

in fact the father 事实上的父亲

in facto et jure in fact and in law 在事实上和在法律上

In facto quod finitium et certum est, nullus est conjecture locus There is no room for conjecture where the fact is definite and ascertained. 只要事实确切清楚,则无需猜测(或质疑)

in fault 有责任,有过错

in favo(u)r of 1.赞同,支持 2.有利于,交付给

In favorem vitae, libertatis, et innocientiae omnia praesumuntur. Everything will be presumed in favor of life, liberty and innocence. All presumptions are in favor of life, liberty and innocence. 世界万物均有利于生命,有利于自由而天真无邪。

in fear of 唯恐

in fee simple 非限定继承的地产

in fieri 在履行(进行)的过程中

in fine 总而言之,总之

in flagrant delict 在作案(犯罪)现场,在作案时;现行(犯)

in force 1.(法律等)有效,生效 2.大批(地),大规模(地)

in force (或 **in-force**) **patent** 现行专利(指此专利并未过期,亦未被规定无效)

in forma pauperis (英)公民诉讼;贫民诉讼,以贫民的身份免付诉讼费(指法院准许对业经确认贫民身份的人进行诉讼,免去其诉讼费的负担)

in fraud of (或 **to the fraud of**) 为了欺骗,为了诈欺

in fraud of law 规避法律

in full 以全文,用完整的词;十足,充足;完全,全部;全船(运输合同用语)

in full accord 完全一致

in full agreement 完全同意

in full charge 负全部责任

in full freight 总括运费

in full operation 全面实施

in full settlement 全部偿还(债务)

in furtherance of 为促进……

in futuro 将来

in good faith 善意的,出于诚意的;诚实的

in good repair 修理完善(见 repair)

in gremio legis 在法律含义内,在法律保护范围内;延搁中

in (the) gross 1.大量的;总的来说 2.非附属于土地的权利

in haec foedera non venimus 我等并未订立此合同(契约)

In haeredes non solent transire actiones quae poenales ex maleficio sunt. Penal actions arising from anything of a criminal nature do not pass to heirs. 凡具有犯罪性质的行为引起的刑事诉讼不得转向(行为

人的)继承人提出。
in hand 处理中;受到控制
* ***In his quae de jure communi omnibus concedentur, consuetudo alicujus patriae vel loci non est allegenda.*** In those things which by common right are conceded to all, the custom of a particular district or place is not to be alleged. 凡按普通法上的权利已得到公认者,则任何特定地区或地方的惯例均不得用来作辩解。
in house counsel 内部顾问
in house funds 内部资金
in infinitum 无限制
in insuring risks 承保风险
in integrum 原有状态;以前的地位
in integrum restitutio (罗马法)恢复原状
in invitum 不管其意愿如何(此术语常用来反对对方当事人)
in issue 在争论中
in issue facts 争论中的事实
in its entirety 作为一个整体,全面,全盘
* ***In judiciis, minori aetati succurritur.*** In courts or judicial proceedings, infancy is aided or favored. 在法院或法律诉讼中,未成年人应该得到司法帮助或优待。
in judicio (apud judicem) (古罗马共和国政府时期民事诉讼的)诉讼第二阶段(即将案件提交法官审理阶段)
* ***In judicio non creditur nisi juratis.*** In a trial, credence is given only to those who are sworn. 在审判时,只能信任那些经过发誓的人。
in jure 在法律上,依照法律;(古罗马共和国政体时期民事诉讼的)诉讼第一阶段(即将案件提交民官的案件准备阶段)
in jure cessio 拟诉弃权(或称拟诉让让财产,指罗马法上假装当事人两方,一方为原告而起诉,他方为被告而应诉,并通过法院满足原告之请求的方式来求得抛弃其权利或转让财产的合法性)
* ***In jure, non remota causa sed proxima spectatur.*** In law, the proximate, and not the remote, cause is regarded. 法律只追究近因,不问远因。
in jus vocando (罗马法)传唤到庭

in justice to. . . 为了对……公正起见
in keeping with 与……一致,应遵照
in kind 以同类型的,同类型事物
in law 依法
lawyer parlance 按律师的说法
in legal custody 见 *custodia legis*
in legal parlance 按法律的用语,用法律上的话来说
in lieu of 代替,作为……的替代
in lieu of (或 **in addition to**) **a fine** 代替(或补充)罚金
in lieu tax 替代他人所课的税
in light of all existing fisheries knowledge 依据所有的渔业知识
in like manner 同样地
in like wise 同样地
in limine adv. (18世纪)开始,最初,初期(指在法官审理案件开始或之前,只提交给法官一项动议,以利于法官决定采纳某个证据)(a question to be decided in limine)(最初决定的问题)(见 motion *in limine*)
in line 一致,协调;成一直线;有秩序,受约束;与现行价格(或标准)一致
in line for (美)即将获得,可以得到
in litem 为了诉讼,对于诉讼
in loco 在适当地方,替代
in loco parentis 以替代父母的地位(指对未成年人负起同他父母一样的权利义务和责任);养父(母)地位
in lucro captando 努力获得优势,努力获得利益(见 *certans de captando*)
* ***In maleficiis voluntas spectatur, non exitus.*** In criminal acts, the intent is to be taken into consideration and not the result./In criminal offenses the intention is regarded, not the event. 在刑事犯罪中,需考虑其动机,而非其结果;在坏事中,要看其动机而非其结果。
* ***In maleficio ratihabitio mandato (equiparatur) courparatur.*** In offence against the law, a ratification is equal to command./In delict (or tort), ratification is equivalent to authorization. 在侵权案或渎职案中,批准相当于命令。

in matters of principle 在原则问题上
in loco tutoris 代替监护人的地位
In maxima potentia minima licentia. In the greatest power there is the least freedom. 权力越大者,越没有自由。
in medias res 在事物中心;在事件中
in my submission 根据我所持的(理论)论点;我认为
in naturalibus 暴露无遗
in nature 性质上;实际上;(在否定、疑问等句中)在任何地方,究竟
in no case 决不
in no way 决不,一点也不
in no wise 绝不,一点也不
in nomine 以……的名义
In novo casu, novum remedium apponendum est. A new remedy is to be applied to a new case./In a novel case a new legal remedy is to be applied. 新案件应适用新的救济方式。
in nullo est erratum 没有错误
in omnibus 在所有方面,在总的方面
In omnibus contractibus, sive nominatis sive innominatis, permutatio continetur. In all contracts, whether nominate or innominate, an exchange (of value, i.e., a consideration) is implied. 在所有合同中,不论是否有确定名称的合同,都暗含有某种(价值,即对价的)交换。
In omnibus fere minori etati succirritur. In nearly all respects a person under age is protected by the law. 未成年人几乎在各个方面均受法律保护。
In omnibus obligationibus in quibus dies non ponitur, praesenti die debetur. In all obligations in which a date is not put, the debt is due on the present day, the liability accrues immediately. 在所有未指明日期之债中,该债应按提出之日起算,偿债责任也随即自行增长(指利息)。
in open court 公开审讯,公开庭审
in operation 正在实施
in order to see how the offender confesses and behaves thereafter 以观后效
in order to warm against bad examples 以儆效尤
in overall charge 总负责,总管
in pais 无法律手续或文据(指未经过法律手续或订立文据的事实)
in pari causa 同一事由;同样事件,当事各方具有同等权利的案件
in pari delicto 同样过失,互有过失;同样有罪
In pari delicto potior est conditio possidentis (defendentis). In a case of equal or mutual fault (between two parties) the condition of the party in possession (or defending) is the better one. (当事人双方)互有过失时,则占有者(或被告)占优势。
in pari materia 在类似情况下,在类似事件中
in part 在某种程度上;部分地
in perpetuum 永久地,永久
in person 亲自
in personam 对人的;对人(请求)权;对人诉讼(见 action in *personam*)
in personam action 对人诉讼
in personam judgment 对人判决
in personam jurisdiction (或 **jurisdiction in personam**) 对人管辖权,对人诉讼管辖[指美国联邦最高法院根据美国联邦宪法第五以及第十四修正案的正当程序条款(due process clause)要求,必须对于被告人有管辖权,并且对于诉讼的标的物有管辖权.在早期"彭诺耶诉奈弗案"(Pennoyer v. Neff)中,斯蒂芬·菲尔德(Stephen.J. Field)坚持源自美国联邦宪法第十修正案的两条基本原则:"每个州对于其领域内的人和财都拥有专属管辖权和主权"及"任一州均不得对其领域外的人或财产行使直接管辖权与权力"。其中第一个原则确认了对于实际存在于一州领域内的人的所谓"标签服务",它已在"伯纳姆诉高级法院案"(Burnham v. Superior Court)(1990年)中得以全面重申]
in personam wing of jurisdiction 对人管辖的观点,对人管辖的派别
in perspective 1.显现脑海中的(地) 2.展望中的(地)3.观察正确的(地)(或以正确的观察方法观察事物)

in piecemeal fashion 一件件的方式,逐渐的方式
in place 在适当的位置,适当的,恰当的,相称的
in place of 代替
in pledge 在抵押中,在典当中
in pleno 完全
in point of law 依法律观点
in posse 可能的,可能存在
in possession 占有,持有
in practice 在实行中;在实施中;在执行中
in praesenti 出现,出面,现在
＊**In praesentia majoris potestatis, minor potestas cessat.** In the presence of the superior power, the inferior power ceases. 在上级权力当局出面时,下级权力当局就不再行使其权力。
＊**In pretio emptionis et venditionis, naturaliter licet contrahentibus se circumvenire.** In the price of buying and selling, it is naturally allowed to the contracting parties to overreach each other. 在买或卖的价款问题上,当然允许缔约双方讨价还价来相互压服对方。
in print 1.已出版的,在销售的(书籍等) 2.还能买到的(书等),书店有售的[与 out of print(已绝版的)]
in privity (=privty) 有利害关系,有相对关系的,有关系的
in propria persona 亲自(出庭)(指无律师帮助)
in public 公开地,当众
in pursuance of 执行,履行;根据,依照
in quasi in rem cases 在准对物的案件中
in question 正被谈论的;成问题的;被争论,被怀疑
in re 对于,关于(某事项);案由;对物(对事)诉讼,(拉丁语,就……而论),用于代表缺乏形式上的对方当事人的案件。它指的是作为诉讼主体的物(res)、不动产或实物
＊**In re dubia, magis inficiatio quam affirmatio intelligenda.** In a doubtful matter, the denial or negative is to be understood, rather than the affirmative. 对有疑问的事,加以拒绝或否定总要比加以肯定为好。
in re petagno 关于某一适当的案例
in real life 在现实生活中
in recognition of 为酬答
in record 记录在案
in red ink 以赤字表示
in (或 with) reference 关于,对于
in reference to 有关,指
in regard to 关于
in regular turn 依正常顺序
in relation to 关于,与……有关;相对于,和……成比例
in rem 对物权;对物诉讼
in rem judgment 对物判决
in rem jurisdiction (或 jurisdiction in rem) 对物(对事)诉讼管辖,对物(对事)管辖权[联邦和州法院所主张的三种管辖之一,其余两种为对人诉讼管辖(in personam)和准对物(对事)诉讼管辖。传统上将对物(对事)诉讼管辖理解为,管辖权是向位于法院管辖范围内的物(即实物与不动产)所作的延伸,而且这一概念在"彭诺耶诉奈弗案"(Pennoyer v. Neff)(1878 年)这一经典案例中得到解释。正如马萨诸塞州首席大法官奥利弗·温德尔·霍姆斯 Oliver Wendell Holms 所说:所有诉讼实际上都是针对人的。对物、对事诉讼管辖与准对物(对事)诉讼管辖的区别在于:对前者来说物本身被认为是诉讼标的;而对于后者物仅具有附属性,是为了满足涉及其他物之诉讼的可能判决而存在的。20世纪后随着无形财产,如信托以及财产流动性导致对物(对事)诉讼管辖和准对物(对事)诉讼管辖的主张变为复杂,美国联邦最高法院在(Shatter v. Heitner)(1977年)案中确定:关于对物(对事)诉讼管辖的主张必须与国际鞋业公司诉华盛顿案(International Shoe Co. v. Washington)(1945年)中有关对人诉讼管辖的主张一样,按正当程序要求,即被告必须与法院之管辖为最小联系]
in rem proceeding (= proceeding *in rem*; *in rem* action) 对物诉讼
**in rem proceedings for jurisdictional pur-

pose 对物管辖诉讼程序
in respect of 关于,就……而言
in response to 为响应;答复
in return 作为报答,作为回报
in right of 凭……权力
in session 在开庭,在开会
in setting the mutual accounts 作相互结算
in sharp contrast 成鲜明对比,鲜明对照,明显对比
in side tip 内部预测;内部秘密消息,内幕;内部行情
in situ 在原地;在原本情况下
in so far as 就……来说;在……范围内;到……的程度
in sober fact 完全就事实而言
in some sort 稍微,多少
in specie 1.特别的,专门的 2.同式样,同形式 3.按照说明
in statu quo 按原样,维持原状
in status pupillari 以受监护人的身份
in strict confidence 绝对机密,绝密
in subsidium 在……帮助下,通过帮助
in succession to 代替,继承
in system of equitable interests in land (英)衡平法上的土地权益制度
in tail 限定继承的产业
in terms of 1.用……话,以……措辞 2.按照,根据 3.在……方面,从……方面来说
in terrorem 威胁或警告性的,威胁或恐吓性的
in terrorem clause 警告条款(如遗嘱中有规定继承人应按遗嘱规定条件办事,否则即失去继承权的条款)
in testimony whereof 特引作证
in the absence of any other agreement 如无其他约定
in the absence of other provisions in the law or contract 法律或合同并无另外规定时
in the abstract 理论上;抽象地
in the act of preparing to commit a crime 正在准备作案
in the aggregate 合拼在一起
in the air 未定的
in the article of death 在临死时
in the capacity of 以……资格

in the case at trial 在受审案件中
in the case of 假使,如果发生
in the case of mutual objectivism (pessimism) 在双方持客(悲)观的案件中
in the dark 蒙在鼓里
in the dock 受审
in the event 结果,到头来
in the event of 如果……发生
in the event that... 万一……(引导的条件句通常指不太可能或不易发生的事。与 in case 同,但 in case 后不能跟 that)
in the eye of law 依法律观点
in the facts 当场
in the family way (英)怀孕(美作 in a family way)
in the first instance 起初,首先;在初审时
in the form required by law 用法定方式
in the guise of 在……幌子下,假借
in the hands of 掌管之中,支配之中;掌管支配
in the interests of 为……利益起见,为了
in the issue 结果,到头来
in the last 在最后;在终审时
in the light of 根据,按照
in the matter of 就……而论,在……方面
in the mean time 在此期间,同时
in the name of 假借……名义,以……的名义,代表……
in the opinion of 据……意见,据……的见解
in the order of 按……次序
in the outset 在开头时
in the person of 以……资格,代表……
in the presence of justifiable reasons 如有正当理由
in the process of committing a crime 正在作案,正在犯罪
in the public domain 不受版权限制,不受专利权限制
in the public eye 从公众的观点来看
in the shadow of 在……附近,与……接近
in the teeth 直接反对,当面,公然
in the teeth of 反对,抵挡的全部力量;对抗;面对;不顾
in the throes of sth./of doing sth. 处

于……痛苦之中
in the toils of the law 使人陷入法网
in the very teeth of legislative intent 与立法意图背道而驰;对抗立法意图,毫不顾及立法意图
in the vicinity of 在……附近
in the wake of 尾随(船),跟随,效仿
in the way 阻碍,妨碍人的
in the way of 以便,便于;关于,就,为……起见
in the wind 谣传
in this context 在此情况下;就这一点上
in toto 整个,全部,完全
in touch with 与……接触,与……相一致
in transit 在运送途中,在输送中
in transitu 在运送途中
in turn 依次,轮流
in utroque jure 在两法中(即民法和寺院法中)
in vain 徒然,无效
in ventre sa mere 在娘胎中,在怀孕中
in view of 鉴于
in vinculis 在强制下
in violation of criminal law 触犯刑律,违犯刑法
in viridi observantia (生动地)出现在人们脑海中,并充满了力量和能力
in virtue of 由于
in vitro fertilization 试管内授精(指妇女体外卵子授精的一个步骤,然后将授精卵放入妇女体内使其怀孕,缩略为 IVF。见 artificial insemination; Zygote Intrafallopian Transfer)
in vivo fertilization 体内授精(指在妇女体内放入精子的一个步骤。见 artificial insemination; Zygote Intrafallopian Transfer; gamete intrafallopian transfer)
in whole or in part (美)全部或部分地(指长臂法对合同之诉所规定的管辖范围如同侵权之诉,取决于立法所使用的特定语言和诉讼所在地州法院所作的解释)
in witness of 为……的证据
in witness where of 为……的证据,以资证明,特此作证明,兹为证明
in-group 内团体

in-house counsel 公司法律顾问(指一个公司雇佣的一个或多个法律顾问。亦称 home counsel。见 corporate counsel)
in-limine a. (1963年)偏见的[指一动议或申请、命令存在偏见,对一个证据的采纳存在争议,原因是提出申请者被认为有偏见〈*in-limine* motion〉(偏见的申请或动议)]
in-house counsels 法务人员
in-law n./v. (常用复)姻亲;外亲、外戚/将……置于法律的保护之下;恢复(犯人的)法律权益
in-state activities of defendant 被告在本州的活动
inability (或 **no-right**) n. 无能力(或无权利);不能
inability to pay 无力支付,无力清偿
inaccurate prophets 不准确的预言家
inaction n. 不作为,无行动
inadequacy n. 不充分,不足额;不适当;机能不全
inadequacy of consideration 不公平(或不适当)对价(指把衡平法明显不公平的对价往往视为诈欺或威胁的证据)
inadequate a. 不充分的;不适当的;机能不全的,反应迟钝的
inadequate capitalization 投资不足
inadequate damages 不足额损害赔偿费
inadequate judicial restraint 不够充分的司法制约
inadequate remedy 不足额补偿
inadequate sentence 过轻刑罚
inadmissibility n. 不能承认,不能允许,不能接受
inadmissible a. 不能承认的,不能接受的,不能允许的,不可作为证据采纳的
inadmissible evidence 不可接受的证据
inadvertence n. 粗心大意,漫不经心,疏忽;错误
inadvertent a. 非故意的,疏忽的,出于无心的,不经心的
inadvertent negligence 不注意的过失
inalienability n. 不可放弃性;不可让与性;不可分割性
inalienability of sovereignty 主权的不可

分割性
inalienability n. 1.不可让与性,不可分割性,不可放弃性 2.禁易规则(指卡-梅框架中的三项规则之一,是在明确法益归属的同时却"不许法益在即使自愿的买卖双方之间进行转让",也就是说,禁易规则承认一个私人主体拥有特定法益,但禁止或限制法益拥有者进行特定转让。实际上禁易规则可分两类:一是剥夺法益拥有者的转移自由,如禁止酒馆卖酒人卖酒给未成年人;二是剥夺法益相对人的转移自由,比如剥夺从事特定不法活动的人接受他人赠与的权利。究其实质,禁易规则旨在取缔特定市场,既涉及法益的客体标的,也涉及法益的主体资格。比如禁止人体器官私人买卖是关于法益客体的禁易规则,而禁止青少年或未成年人购买酒精饮料是关于交易主体的禁易规则)

inalienable natural rights 不能剥夺的自然权利,不能分割的自然权利
inalienable part 不可分割的部分
inalienable right 不可剥夺的权利;不可让与的权利;自然权利,天赋权利
inamorata 姘妇,情妇
inamorato 姘夫,情夫
inappealable a. 不能上诉的,不能申诉的
inappeasable a. 难以平息的;难以劝解的;难以满足的
inapplicable a. 不适用的,不适宜的
inappropriate a. 不适当的,不相宜的
inappropriate discrepancy 不适当的不一致之处,不适当的不一致
inaugurate v. 开始;为……举行开幕式
inauguration n. 就职;就职典礼;创始,开幕;开幕式
inauguration ceremony 就职典礼,开幕典礼,落成典礼
inauguration day 就职日;(美)总统就职日
inbound a. 归航的,开往本国的;入境的
incantations 咒语,咒符,妖术
incapability n. 无能力;无胜任;无资格
incapability of consent 无承诺能力
incapability of self-support 无力自养
incapability of work 无劳动能力
incapable a. 无能力的;无资格的;不能的

incapacitate v. 使无资格;使无能力;剥夺资格(权利)
incapacitated a. 丧失能力的
incapacitated shareholder 丧失能力的股东,无资格的股东
incapacitator n. 智能麻醉剂(指一种使人失去能力的化学剂或药物)
incapacity n. 无能力(包括无权利能力和无行为能力);无资格
incapacity based on physic-psychological condition 基于生理和心理状态的能力欠缺[通常能力欠缺依照两条基本思路构成其中之一,另一为出自组织地位或法律关系的能力欠缺(incapacity due to organizational status and legal relationship)]
incapacity of minors 未成年人的无资格(或无行为能力)
incarcerate v. 监禁,使下狱,禁闭
incarcerated individual 囚犯,被禁闭的人
incarceration n. 监禁,下狱,禁闭
incarnation n. 体现,化身,具体化
incendiarism n. 纵火,放火,煽动叛乱
incendiary n./a. 纵火者;放火者;煽动者,可引起燃烧的东西/纵火的,放火的,煽动的
incentive n./a. 激励,鼓励,刺激/鼓励的,激励的
incentive compatibility 刺激的协调性,奖励性协调(共存)
incentive stock option (ISO) 奖励性认股权(指公司给予公司雇员在特定时期的优惠价格购买公司股票特权);激励性股票期权
inception 开始,开端;(英)剑桥大学博士、硕士学位的取得
inception point 起点站
incertae personae 非特定人;未确定之人;未经指明的人
incest n. 乱伦(罪);血亲相奸
incestumiure civile 市民法上的乱伦(指与其女性直系尊亲或直系卑亲结婚的男人,构成万民法上的乱伦)
incestuous a. 乱伦的,犯乱伦罪的
incestuous adultery 乱伦通奸
inchoate a. 才开始的,初期的;不完全的;

未发展的
inchoate crime 犯罪未遂
inchoate instrument 空白单据；空白支票（汇票）
inchoate right 初期权利，期待权（指专利法中发明人申请待决时就其发明所享有的权利）
incidence n. 影响，影响范围，影响程度；发生率
incidence axiom 关联公理
incidence matrix 关联矩阵
incidence of crime 犯罪发生率
incidence of divorce 离婚的发生率，离婚的影响程度（或范围）
incidence of duty 关税的负担，关税负担转移
incidence of tax 税收负担转移
incident n./a. 事变；事件；附属于财产的权利或义务；附带条件，附属事物/附属的，附带的；有联系的
incident of tenure 土地保有附带条件，土地保有的附带权利义务
incidental n./a. 偶然事件，附带条件/附属的，附带的；非主要的；偶然碰到的；易发生的
incidental appeal 附带上诉
incidental causal relationship 偶然因果关系
incidental civil action 附带民事诉讼
incidental claim 附带请求权，附带诉讼请求
incidental crime 附带犯罪
incidental damages 附带损害赔偿
incidental effect 意外的后果（效力、作用、影响）
incidental judg(e)ment 附带判决
incidental losses 意外损失
incidental motion 临时动议，附议；临时申请
incidental revenue 附带收入
incidental to an appeal （上诉中的）附带诉讼
incidents of ownership 所有权的附属财产权利
incineration n. 焚化；火葬
incitation n. 煽动，煽惑，刺激
incite v. 鼓动，煽动

incite defection 策反
incite war 煽动战争
incitement n. 煽动（罪），刺激；怂恿犯罪，煽惑他人犯罪
incitement and attempt to commit conspiracy 煽动并企图谋反（罪）
incitement to disaffection 煽动（军人）背叛（罪）
incitement to disaffection act 煽动（军人）背叛法
incitement to incest 诱使乱伦（罪）
incitement to racial hatred 煽动种族仇恨（罪）
incitement to riot 煽动叛乱罪
inclination of human nature 人类本性倾向
incline v. 使倾向于；倾向于（to）；低头；赞同；喜爱
inclosure n. 见 enclosure
include v. 包括，包含
included offense 包含在内的罪行（见 lesser included offense）
* *Inclusio unius est exclusio alterius.* The inclusion of one is the exclusion of another. 包括其一，即排除其他。
inclusive growth 包容性增长（指亚洲开发银行首次提出这一概念，基本含义是公平合理地分享经济增长。参与、共享和亲贫乃包容性增长概念之要义。它不仅适用于宏观经济，也适用于国民经济细胞的企业）
incognito n./a. 隐匿姓名身份（者）/隐名的，隐匿姓名身份的，化名的
incola （罗马法）居民[指没有完全公民权的外国居民，外国殖民地的常住居民。此词尤指非罗马公民的外省居民或教省居民（provincial residents）。亦称 incolant。见 *peregrinus*]
income n. 收入，收益，所得，进款
income account （商业机构的）收支账；损益计算书，收益账
income average （或 **averaging**） 所得平均计算法；收入平均法
income beneficiary 遗产收益的受益人
income bond 收益债券

income from exploitation 剥削收入
income from royalties 版税收益
income refund notice 收入退还书
income statement 损益计算书;损益表,利润表
income stream 收入线,收入渠道
income tax 所得税
income tax bracket 所得税等级
income tax credit 所得税的抵免
income tax law 所得税法
Income Tax Law of the People's Republic of China Concerning Chinese-Foreign Joint Ventures 《中华人民共和国中外合资经营企业所得税法》
income tax return 所得税申报书(表)
income tax surcharge 所得附加税
income-and-expense declaration （美）（家庭法）收支公告,收支声明［指子女扶养（child support）诉讼中,有关其父母的收入、财产、消费以及应交税款等的信息文件］
income-bearing property 有孳息的财产
income-generating crime 因收入引发的犯罪
income-producing property 创收财产
income-tax deficiency 见 deficiency 2
income-tax return 所得税申报表,所得报税单(见 tax return)
incomer n. 侵入者;后继者;新任者;（英）移民
incoming 新来的,继任的
incomings and outgoings 收支
* *Incommodum non solvit argumentus.* An inconvenience does not destroy (or solve or demolish) an argument. 不便并不能解决争议(即不能因困难而认为已经解决争议)。
incommonsurability n. 不可用同一单位计算,无公度,不可相比性
incommunicable a. 不能表达的,不能传达的,不能以言语表达的;沉默的
incommunicado a. 被禁止与外界接触的;（犯人）被单独禁闭的
incompatible (with) 不相容,与……不一致
incompatibility n. 感情不和,不能和谐相处(尤指夫妇关系);矛盾
incompatibility of temper 性情不合
incompetence (= incompetency) n. 不胜任;不适合;无行为能力;法律上无资格
incompetence to stand trial 无诉讼能力者（主要指无受审能力者,这里指精神障碍的问题。法治国家将违法精神病分为四类,这属于第一类。另外三类是:not guilt by reason of insanity 无刑事责任者;mental disorder offender 精神障碍犯罪人;mental disorder sex offender 精神障碍性犯罪人)
incompetency from immature age or unsoundness of mind 幼年或精神不健全而没有资格(行为能力)
incompetent a./n. 法律上无行为能力的;法律上无资格的;没有法定资格的;法律上无效的;禁治产的/法律上无行为能力的人,禁治产者
incompetent evidence 不合法的证据(指不能接受的证据),不可采纳的证据,法律上无效的证据
incompetent judge 被回避的法官
incompetent person 无行为能力者
incompetent witness 无资格的证人
incomplete a. 不足的,不完全的;未完成的;不完善的
incomplete action 不完全行为;未完成行为
incomplete contract 不完全的合同
incomplete development of mind 智力发育不健全
incomplete information 不完全信息;不完整的资料
incomplete transfer （美）不完全转让［指死者生前的财产（inter vivos）转让,从联邦财产税的角度看这是不完全转让,因为死者对财产仍拥有控制和享用的权利。所以这种转让是不完全的,由此转让的全部或部分价值均包括在转让人的总财产（gross estate）之中。依照美国联邦死亡税（death tax）的规定,将按公平市场价值（fair market value）将其部分或全部财产计入转让人的总财产中作为税基来征收税款］
incompletion of extinctive prescription 消

灭时效未完成
inconclusive a. 非决定性的;不确定的;无结果的;无说服力的
inconclusive ballot 非决定性的投票(或选举)
inconclusive presumption 非决定性的法律推定
inconclusive vote 无结果的投票
inconsistency n. 前后矛盾(指自相矛盾的行为或言论);不一致(不一致的事物或行为)
inconsistent a. 矛盾的,不一致的,不协调的;多变的
inconsistent argument 前后矛盾的论据
inconsistent presumption 矛盾性推定
inconsistent statement 自相矛盾的陈述
incontestability clause (人寿或健康保险单上的)不容争议性条款(见 noncontestability clause)
incontestable a. 不可争辩的,无可否认的,不容置疑的
incontestable clause (=noncontestable clause)不可抗辩条款
incontestable evidence 铁证,不可否认的证据
***Incontinence** n. 不能控制,纵欲;放荡的人
incontractibus tacite insunt quae sunt moris et consuetudinis. Things which are warranted by manner and custom, may be tacitly imported into contracts./In contracts, matters of custom and usage are tacitly implied./A contract is understood to contain the customary clause, although they are not expressed.
一切契约毋庸明言,包括惯例与习俗在内。
incontrovertible a. 不可辩驳的,不容置疑的
inconvenience n. 不方便,麻烦,困扰之事;严重不公正
incorporales n. 无体财物
incorporate v. 编入;使组成法人(社团、公司等);合并(with),混合,结合,使具体化,体现
incorporated a. 组成法人(社团公司等)组织的,法人的,合并在一起的;一体化的

incorporated accountant 立案注册会计师
incorporated association 社团组织;组成法人的社团
incorporated company 法人公司;股份有限公司
Incorporated Council of Law Reporting 立案的判例汇编委员会
incorporated liability 合并责任;混合责任;附有的责任
incorporated mutual benefit association (具有公司组织性质的)互惠社
incorporated societies act 社团组织法
incorporated union 立案团体;立案工会;法人团体
incorporation n. 法人;社团;公司;结合,合并;(国际法)并入说;(美)并入理论
incorporation by reference 法律参并(指将原先法律中的章节或大部分采取参引方式并入未来的法律)
incorporation clause 并入条款
Incorporation Doctrine (美)并入原理[指联邦最高法院支持联邦《权利宣言》的大部分(并非全部),以保证通过第十修正案来限制州和地方政府以及联邦政府];(小写)设立说(按该学说公司成立地所在国家的法律是公司身份的准据法,这不仅意味着它具有这个国家的国籍,还意味着在公司内部组织关系上,也将适用该国的法律)
incorporation of law 法律的直接采纳(指国际商业贷款合同中,将合同签订之日或证券发行之日有关的现行法的具体规定,甚至整个民法典的规定写明在贷款合同或债券上,作为合同内容的一部分)
incorporator n. 合并者;公司创办人;社团成员
incorporeal a. 无形体的,非物质的,精神的,无形的
incorporeal capital 无形资本
incorporeal chattel 无形动产(指触摸不到的个人权利和利益,如个人年金、股份、版权等)
incorporeal hereditament 无形遗产
incorporeal heritable right 无形世袭权
incorporeal object 无形财产,无形客体,

无形物
incorporeal possession 无形占有(权)
incorporeal property 无形财产
incorporeal right 无形财产权,无形权利
incorporeality (=incorporeity) n. 无形体,无形性
incorrect a. 不正确的;错误的;不适当的
incorrect motion 错误动议
incorrect ruling 错误裁决
incorrect statement of law 法律陈述错误
incorrect transmission 误传
incorrigibility n. 严重持续的错误行为(指儿童或少年的一种严重并持续的错误行为,父母亦无法管教使其改正。见 juvenile delinquency),不能改正,不可救药
incorrigible n./a. 不改悔的人,不可救药者/难以纠正的,不可改造的,不可救药的,顽固的
incorrigible child 难以改悔的儿童,难以教育的儿童,不可救药的儿童(指拒绝听从父母或监护人的管教,亦称 disobedient child)
incorrigible rogue 惯犯;流氓成性者
incorrigible thief 惯盗
incoterm 标准海(或航)运术语[指由国际商会(International Chamber of Commerce)进行解释的标准海运术语,即在买方与卖方间按比例分配国际航运所承担的费用和责任。见 ex works; cost, insurance and freight; cost and freight; free alongside ship; free on board]
increase access to justice 增加取得公正的权利
increase of punishment (或 **penalty**) 刑的加重,加刑,加重刑罚
increased grand jury 增加人数的大陪审团
increment n. 增额,增值,增长
incremental a. 增加的,增收的;递增(工资)的;增值的
incremental credit 增加(的)信贷
incremental value 增加价值,增值
incriminate v. 1.控告;使负罪 2.连累(某人);牵连;归罪于
incriminate oneself 把自己牵连进刑事案件中
incriminating circumstance 证明犯罪事实的情节(指表明一个犯罪已经发生或某人已实施该犯罪行为的事实或情节)
incriminatory (或 **incriminating**) a. 归罪(于某人)的,牵连(某人)的;显示有罪的;归罪的,使负罪责的
inculpate v. 控告,连累(某人)受罪,归罪于
inculpation n. 控告,归罪,连累
inculpatory a. 可指控的,可归罪的,连累的
inculpatory evidence 定罪的证据
incumbency n. 职责,义务;在职;任期;职权
incumbent a. 成为责任的,要尽义务做的;在职的
incumbent president 在职总统
incumbrance n. 1.家累,拖累 2.(在不动产上设定的)债权,财产的留置权;财产的抵押权(见 encumbrance)
incumbrancer n. 对土地有他物权者
incur v. 招致,引起,惹气;遭受;负债;承担
incur a heavy loss 招致重大损失
incur a liability 应承担责任(指应支付给他人判决之款)
incur a reprimand 招致谴责
incur obligation 使负有义务
incurred obligation 承担债务,承付款项
incursion n. 侵犯,侵入,进入(into),对……侵入
* *Inde datae leges ne fortior omnia posset.*
　　Laws were made lest the stronger should have unlimited power. The laws are made lest the stronger should be altogether uncontrolled. 必须立法,以免强者为所欲为。
indebitatus assumpsit 被告承认负担债务之诉(普通法上一种要求赔偿违约损失的诉讼)
indebitatus counts 要求支付合同(契约)上的劳动报酬之诉
indebitum (大陆法)不应支付,未欠债
indebt v. 使负债
indebted a. 负债的,法律上有义务偿还的

indebtedness n. 处于负债中,所欠之款,(广义)所欠

indecency n. 粗野;粗鄙;猥亵,下流言行

indecent a. 粗野的;猥亵的,下流的,有伤风化的;不道德的

indecent assault 1.猥亵罪,猥亵侵犯他人身体(尤指按英国1936年性行为法规定,猥亵侵犯女人身体是有罪的) 2.强奸未遂罪

indecent assault on women 猥亵妇女,(企图)奸污妇女

indecent behavio(u)r 妨害风化,有伤风化

indecent books 黄色书刊,淫猥性书籍

indecent conduct 猥亵行为

indecent exhibition 淫秽展览品

indecent exposure 有伤风化罪,有伤风化的露体

indecent language 下流语言

indecent prints 有伤风化的印刷品,黄色印刷品;淫猥性印刷品

indecent publication 淫秽出版物

indecent publication act (取缔)淫秽出版物法

indecent publication court 淫秽出版物法庭(院)

indefeasibility n. 难以废止,不能废除,不能取消

indefeasible a. 难以废止的,不能废除的,不能取消的

indefensus n. (罗马法)诉讼中未经辩护或未进行答辩的被告

indefinite a. 不确定的,无限期的,模糊的

indefinite and definite permanent appropriation 不定额永久经费和定额永久经费

indefinite legacy 未确定数额的遗赠

indefinite limitation of time 不确定期限

indefinite payment 不指定(明)的还款 [指同一个债务人欠同一个债权人的多项不同债款,在还债款时并未说明还哪项欠款,此即称为不指定(明)的还款]

indefinite re-election 无限制的连选连任

indefinite shipment 不定期装运

indefinite tenancy 活租制,不定期租赁

indefinite term 不定期

indefinite thing 非特定物

indefinite third person 未确定的第三人

indemnification n. 赔偿,补偿;使免于受罚;保护;赔偿物,赔偿金

indemnification for loss 损失补偿,损失赔偿金

indemnify v. 补偿损失,赔偿;保障,保护;使免于受罚;偿付;使安全;使免受伤害损失;保险

indemnify sb. from (或 against) damage 保护某人不受损害

indemnifying measure 赔偿措施,赔偿办法;补偿措施,补偿办法

indemnitee n. 接受赔偿人,受补偿人

indemnitor n. 赔偿人,补偿人

indemnitory a. 补偿的,损害赔偿的

indemnity n. (15世纪)补偿,损害赔偿 [指①由他人引起的任何损失、损害、法律责任或赔偿责任的补偿义务;②受害当事方对于造成的损失、损害具有获赔偿责任的损害中有主张补偿的权利;③对于损失、损害或侵权责任的赔偿或补偿,特别是第二位有责任当事方有权利去弥补第一位有责任当事方因违反普通法义务(common law duty)而造成的伤害,支付给第三当事方(third party)赔偿费用。见 contribution; indemnitory]

indemnity act 赦免法(指特为免除因特定行为而招致刑事处罚的人的责任而通过的法律)

indemnity clause 赔偿条款

indemnity contract 赔偿合同(契约)

indemnity for defamation 名誉损失赔偿

indemnity of loss 损失赔偿

indemnity theory 赔偿请求原理

indent n./v. 合同(契约);(英)征用令,(英)国外订货单/用骑缝线(使证书等)一分为二(正副两份);(一式两份)承认证书;(英)(用双联单)订货;订合同(契约);正式申请

indented a. 订货的;订合同(契约)的;向国外订货的

indented deed 1.双联合同(契约) 2.订货合同(契约)

indentity of witness 证人的一致性(指当事人的陈述与证人的证言、证词或开示证

据的一致性),同一性

indenture n. 印据,凭单;双联合同(契约);定期服务合同(契约);(复)师徒合同(契约)

indenture of lease 租货合同(契约)

Independence n. (17世纪) 1.独立,自主[指独立的性质和状态,特别指一个国家自主(freedom)管理全部国家的内、外事务,而不受任何其他国家的控制影响] 2.足够维持闲居生活的收入(或资产)

independence constitution 独立宪法

independence lite 见 devo max

independence minus 见 devo max

independence of judicature (judiciary, court, judge) 司法(司法机关、法院、法官)独立

independence of protection 保护(著作权)独立(原则)(指伯尔尼公约三项重要原则之一)

independence of trial and decision 审判独立

independent a. (17世纪) 1.独立的,自治的,自主的[指不受其他人(或国家、部门、势力等)的控制或影响〈independent investigation〉(独立调查)] 2.自力更生的[指与其他(通常说较大的实体)无关联〈an independent subsidiary〉(独立的子公司)] 3.不依靠或不期待于某些条件的〈an independent person〉(一个独立自主的人)

independent accountability 独立核算

independent adjudication 独立审判

independent agencies 独立行政机关(构)

independent and adequate state grounds doctrine 独立与充分的州理由原则[指美国联邦最高法院根据两个案例宣布"独立与充分州理由原则,即在州法院的判决(已根据美国联邦法典第 28 章第 1257 节,现行版本《1789 年司法》》第 25 节,而被上诉到联邦最高法院)中,可适用两种法:一为联邦法,另一为非联邦法。如果非联邦法独立于联邦法,并有充分理由可支持该判决时,我们的管辖权无效"。这一原则理论基础十分清楚,但在适用上却很困难。假定现有一案件,根据 1257 节规定从州最高法院被上诉,其具有两种判决基础,一为联邦法律的解释,另一为州

法律的解释。如果联邦最高法院在联邦裁决中错误地否定了原则,则州法院对于发回的案件仍将基于州法律而重新肯定原有的判决。在此情况下,联邦最高法院的行为实际上只是一种咨询性质的意见。对此布朗代斯(Louis D. Brandeis)大法官在 Ashwander v. T. V. A(1936)(阿什旺德诉田纳西河流域管理局案)案中作出警告:对一个宪法性议题,规定了一个多余的规则,这将浪费两个法院的时间,并对州司法造成不必要的干扰。参阅 Mocrdock v. Memphis(1875)和 For Film corp. v. Muller(1935)两案]

Independent Commission Against Corruption Ordinance (香港)《廉政专员公署条例》

independent contractor 独立经营的承包商,独立经营的包工头;独立承揽人

independent country 独立国家

independent defence 自主辩护

independent democrat (中)无党派民主人士

independent evidence 独立证据

independent federal agency (美)独立联邦机构

independent figure (中)无党派人士

independent judg(e)ment 独立判决

independent legal norm 单行的法律规范

independent manager 独立经理

independent number 自变量,自变数

independent obligation 独立之债,主债

independent of... 独立于……的,不受……支配的

independent property 独立财产(权)

independent regulation agency 独立管制机构

independent regulatory commission 独立管制委员会

independent right 独立权利(又称主权利)

independent rule of letter of credit (美)信用证独立原则(信用证与可能作为其依据的销售合同或其他合同,是相互独立的交易;受益人在任何情况下,不得利用银行之间或申请人与开证行的契约关系)

independent sovereign state 独立的主权国家

independent state 独立国家
independent surveyor 独立验尸员,独立监督员,独立测量者
independent trade union 独立工会
independent trademark 自用商标
independent treasury system 独立公库制,独立金库制
independent witness 自愿证人
independent worker 独立劳动者
independently raise investment 自筹投资
indeterminate a. 不明确的;无定期的;不确定的;模糊的,含糊的;不会有结果的,未解决的,未决定的,无法预知的
indeterminate appropriation 不确定经费,特别经费(指各级政府为特殊目的而设置的特殊经费)
indeterminate guidance 不确定的指引
indeterminate sentence (服刑期)不特定刑判;不确定(刑期的)判决(指规定刑期限度的判决,即无确定的具体服刑期,但有最低和最高的服刑期,犯人服完最低期后,其余刑期则由执行机关根据法规规定和犯人表现而定)
index n. (14世纪)1.索引[指按字母顺序对于论题或其他项目包括单一的文件卷本或系列卷本的题目列表,通常在书卷的末了可以查到这样的索引〈index of authorities〉(判例汇编索引)]2.指数,指标,率[指一个数字,通常以百分比形式表示,以此指明或衡量一系列的观察资料,特别是关系到市场的经济方面〈cost-of-living index〉(生活消费指数),〈stock index〉(股票指数或证券指数)]
index crime 指数犯罪(指七种列入美国联邦调查局每年统一罪案报告书中的任何一种重大犯罪)
index number 指数
index of authorities (1881年)判例汇编索引[指一部按字母顺序编排的判例汇编列表,这些判例援引自著述或判例摘要(brief),通常还附有判例、制定法规、论文等细目,亦称 table of authorities; table of cases]
index of living 生活指数
index of prices 物价指数

Index to Foreign Legal Periodicals (美)《外国法律期刊索引》(1960年出版的季刊,由美国法律图书馆协会主办,在加州伯克利大学出版社出版的一种国际性法律期刊索引,它收集有约七十个国家和地区,近五百种重要法学期刊,编成主题、地区、书评、作者等综合性索引。1987年后中国有7种法学期刊索引编入该刊)
Index to Legal Periodicals (美)《法律期刊索引》(指始于1908年并自1926年起约有四百种法律期刊的索引)
Index to the Chemical Weapon Convention 《化学武器公约索引》
Index to the Statutes (英)《制定法索引》
Index to the United Nations Treaty Series (美)《联合国条约集索引》(此索引不限于有限条约,而且可以参考到已经修改或废弃的条约)
indexation 按指数增减(指在税收政策中从某一固定基期出发来衡量货币的"实际价值"以抵消通货膨胀或压缩对征税和支付救济金的影响)
indexed to securities market prices 证券市场价格指数论
indexer n. 索引员;索引工作者
Indian a./n. 1.印度的,印度人的;印度文化的 2.印第安人的,印第安文化的;西印度群岛的,西印度群岛文化的/印度人;印第安人;印第安语
Indian Claims Commission Act (美)印第安人权利请求审查委员会法,印第安求偿审查委员会法
Indian country 1.印第安人的家乡,印第安人的故土[指印第安人居留地(Indian reservations)边境之内土地范围。该地区由印第安社区所占有,而不管社区是否完全在被认可的居留地(recognized reservation),还包括由美国裁决成信托的土地,但可使印第安人或部落受益,亦为印第安人拥有。见 Indian Land]2.(历史上)印第安人地区(特别是在美国向西部移民时期很可能碰上的印第安人的地区)
Indian Land 印第安人的土地(指美国拥有的土地,但被裁定信托为美籍印第安人使用。亦称 Indian tribal property。见 tribal

land)
Indian law 印度法
Indian Law Legal Family 印度法系
Indian Treaties 印第安条约辑(指《法规大全》卷7,包括1778—1842年印第安条约的汇集)
Indian tribal property 见 Indian Land
Indian tribe 印第安部落[指一群、一帮、一个民族或其他有组织的土著美国人(indigenious American people),包括阿拉斯加土著村,由于印第安人的身份(Indian Status),他们是被承认有资格受到美国政府提供的特别规划(special programs)和服务。参见《美国注释法典》第42标题卷第9601(36)节。特别是这类群体已获联邦管理机构的承认,同时该机构正是实际上落实政府的义务并对这个地区具有管辖权。参见《美国注释法典》第42标题卷第300f(14)节,《联邦法规汇编》第40卷第146.3节。一个部落可以各种方式,特别是过去对待其他部落的方式来确认与联邦、州或地方政府的对待完全一致,或者以承认历史上的记载(historical records)办法来对待]
indicate v. 指明,暗示;表明,象征
indication n. 迹象,暗示,象征;指示,表示,明证
indication of origin 产地标记;原产地证明
indication systems 索引方式;索引系统
indicative a. 指示的;表示的;象征的
indicative character of the plan 计划的指导性
indicative evidence 象征性证据
indicative price 指导(性)价格
indicator n. (经济)标示,指标,指示数
indicia (复) n. 标记,记号;形迹,象征;(盖有代替邮票的邮戳的)签条;(表示作废的)戳记
indicia of personality 人格的象征
indicia of title 职衔标志
indict v. 控告;揭发;对……起诉
indict sb. for sabotage 控告某人的破坏行为
indictable a. 可被控告的(人或罪行),可提起公诉的

indictable criminal case 可提起公诉的刑事案件
indictable misdemeano(u)r 可予起诉的轻罪
indictable offence 公诉罪,可起诉的犯罪;适用陪审制的犯罪
indictable offender 可以起诉的罪犯,刑事犯
indicted person 被控告者(人)
indictee n. 被告,被起诉者(人)
indicter (=indictor) n. 原告,控告者(人),起诉者(人)
indiction n. 1.告发,控告 2.宣布,诏示 3.(罗马皇帝每隔15年规定财产价值宣布作为课税基础的)根据宣布征收的税
indictment n. 1.公诉书,刑事起诉书,(大陪审团对某人犯罪的)控告书 2.控告,告发,起诉,公诉,检控
indifference n. 中立,不偏袒;不重视,无足轻重;冷漠,不关心
indifferent a. 不关心的,冷淡的;不偏袒的,中立的
indifferent judge 铁面无私的法官
indigenous a. 本土的,土生土长的;生来的,固有的
indigenous customary law 本土习惯法
indigenous law 固有法
indigenous method 土方法,土法
indigenous people 本土人民,本土人;本土民族;本土百姓
indigent prisoners 贫困的犯人
indigents' claims 贫困人的权利主张
indignity n. 侮辱的言行,无礼,有伤尊严
indirect a. 间接的;曲折的;次要的;不诚实的;不坦率的
indirect agency 间接代理
indirect appeal 间接上诉
indirect compulsory guilt 间接(胁)从犯
indirect consequence 间接后果
indirect contempt 间接藐视(法庭或侮辱法官)罪
indirect cost 间接成本;固定负担(见 fixed charge)
indirect damage 间接损害
indirect democracy 间接民主政治
indirect duty (或 tax) 间接税

indirect effect 间接适用(指 WTO 协议在各成员方国内或域内的执行或适用由各成员方自主决定,如果将执行条的转化"transformation"和纳入"adoption"这两种方式应用于 WTO 协议的话,则将 WTO 协议的适用方式归纳为"间接适用",即"间接转化适用"与"直接适用"或"直接纳入适用")

indirect election 间接选举
indirect evidence 间接证据
indirect exchange 间接汇兑
indirect guilt 间接正犯
indirect infringement 间接侵权
indirect instigator 间接教唆者
indirect intent 间接故意
indirect invasion 间接侵犯,间接入侵
indirect legacy 间接遗赠
indirect legislation 间接立法
indirect losses 间接损失
indirect precautionary criteria 风险预防原则的间接标准
indirect possession 间接占有
indirect possessor 间接占有人
indirect pricing method 间接标价法
indirect private rights of action 私人间接诉权(包括传统的由国家或单独关税区代表私人行使外交保护与 WTO 转化或间接适用条件下国内行政程序性制度安排)
indirect protection 间接保护
indirect purchaser 间接购买者
indirect rate 间接汇兑率
indirect reply 间接答复,侧面答复
indirect route 非直达线
indirect subsidies 间接补贴
indirect tax (18 世纪)间接税[指课税的权力或特权(privilege),比如职业税(occupation tax)或特许经营权税(franchise tax)。总之,间接税通常是可以转移给其他人的税或那些由不负法定义务纳税的人所纳的税]
indirect vote 间接投票,间接选举
indiscretion n. 言行失检;轻率;不慎重,鲁莽
indiscriminate a. 不辨善恶的,不分青红皂白的;不加选择的

indiscriminate arrest 滥捕,乱捕
indispensable condition 必要条件
indispensable obligation 不可推卸的责任
indispensable parties 必不可少的当事人(美国民事诉讼中指拥有一种权益于终局判决中作出不能避免对该权益产生影响的,或使争议处于最终解决可能不符合衡平和良好的这一状况,这个主体才可被认为必不可少的。见 necessary party)
indisputable a. 不容争辩的,不容置疑的,确实的
indisputable fact 无可争辩的事实
individual n./a. 个人,个体,独立单位/个别的,单独的,个人的;特别的,有特性的
individual agreement 个人协议;单独协议
individual as adversaries 互为对手的个人之间
individual capacity 私人身份,私人资格
individual check 私人支票
individual citizen 个体公民
individual claim 个人请求权
individual communication procedure 个人申诉来文程序
individual contract of employment 个人雇用合同(契约)
individual data image 个人资料形象(指个人信息的收集与处理带来的结果被塑造成为"资料形象")
individual dispute 个人纠纷,个人的争议
individual dispute arising from employment contract 雇用合同(契约)所引起的个人争议
individual district judges 单个地区法官,个别地区法官
individual economy (中)个体经济
individual enactment 单行法规
individual enterprise 个体企业
individual entrepreneur 个体企业主
individual execution proceedings 单独执行程序(指抵押、质权和汇票等)
individual farmer (中)个体农户
individual handicraftsmen 个体手工业者
individual household (中)个体户
individual income tax 个人所得税
Individual Income Tax Law of the People's

Republic of China 《中华人民共和国个人所得税法》
individual initiative 个人的公民立法创议权;个人的主动性
individual inspection 单独检查
individual interest of personality 个人的人格利益
individual interrogation 个别讯问
individual justice 个案正义
individual justices 独任法官
individual labo(u)r 个体劳动
individual legal systems 单一的法律体系
individual license 个体营业执照
individual life policy 个人人身保险单,个人人寿保险单
individual litigant 单个诉讼人
individual members 个人成员,个体成员
individual naturalization 个别入籍
individual norm 个别规范;特别规范
individual notice 个人通知;单独通知
individual omnicompetence 个人的全权
individual operation 个体经营
individual ownership 个体所有制
individual privacy 个人隐私
individual private ownership 个体私有制
individual property 个人财产,固有财产
individual proprietorship (或 sole proprietorship) 独资
individual responsibility 个人责任
individual rights 个人权利
individual self-assertion 个人的自我主张,个人的自我断言,个人的自我权利主张
individual status 个人成分;个人身份
individual trademark 单独商标
individual type of contract 个人类型的承包合同
individual types of contracts 各种类型的合同(契约)
individual vote 个人投票
individual worker 个体劳动者
individual's guarantee 个人担保
individual's private rights 个人的私有权利
Individuals with Disabilities Education Act 《残疾人教育法》[指负责管理身心障碍(或残疾)儿童公共教育的联邦制定法,并

意图保证这些孩子都能受到他们唯一需求的免费公共教育。《全部残疾儿童教育法》(The Education of All Handicapped Children Act)(1953 年颁布),于 1990 年重新命名为《残疾人教育法》,又于 1997 年作了实质修订。美国所有州现今均适用该法。参见《美国注释法典》第 20 标题卷第 1400—1485 节,缩略 IDEA]
individualism n. 个人主义,利己主义;个性;个体;(在资本主义国家中政府对私营企业的)不干涉主义,自由放任主义
individualist crusade 个人主义运动
individualist idea of justice 个人主义的正义观
individualistic a. 个人主义(者)的
individualistic conception 个人主义概念
individualistic government 个人主义的政府,独裁政府
individualization in punitive justice 因果报应个性化
individualization of punishment 惩罚个性化
individualized application of law 法律分别情况的适用
individualizing comparison 个体化比较
individually defined thing 特定物
individually target 专门指向
indivisible a. 不能分的,不可分割的
indivisible obligation 不可分之债
indivisible thing 不可分物
indivisum 共有财产;共有
indoctrination n. 教育,教训,灌输
indoctrination centre 教养所
indoctrination through labo(u)r (中)劳动教养
indorser (=endorsee) n. 被背书人,背书票据受让人
indorsement (=endorsement) n. 背书(尤指票据持有人在转让票据时,在其票据背面批注和签章的行为);签名;认可;赞同
indorsement and delivery 背书与交付
indorsement before due or after maturity 到期前或到期后之背书
indorsement by mandate 委任背书
indorsement in blank 无记名背书(又译:

略式背书,空白背书)
indorsement in full 全衔背书,完全背书
indorsement of address 住址背书
indorsement of claim (英)权利请求背书(指英国最高法院的传令状需以原告提出权利请求性质的简短说明作为背书)
indorsement of pledge 质权背书
indorsement without recourse 免费背书;无追索权的背书
indorser (=indorsor, endorser) 背书人
indoxilyzer 见 breathalyzer
indoximeter 见 breathalyzer
indubitable 不容置疑的,明确的
indubitable proof 确证
induce v. 引诱,诱发;劝诱;招致
induced abortion 人工流产
induced offender 胁从犯
inducement n. 诱惑,引诱;诱因;主约诱因;(提出主张事项前的)陈述说明;(法律、条约等的)序言;犯罪动机;(诉状的)引言部分
inducement leading to confession 诱供,劝诱他人招供
inducement of breach of contract 引诱违约(英美法上的概念,即合同关系以外的第三人出于妨碍他人合同权利之目的,引诱债务人违反与债权人之间业已存在的合同,致债权人遭受损害的情形。大陆法也存在与引诱违约功能相似的设置——第三人侵害债权制度)
inducer n. 劝诱者,诱导者;诱导物;诱因
induction n. 1.就职;就职仪式;入会;入伍;入门 2.归纳(法);吸入;导致
induction of evidences 提供证据
induction of facts 列举事实
inductive a. 归纳的,归纳法的;引入的;诱使的;入门的
inductive inference 归纳推理
inductive questioning 诱导性发问
indulgence n. 宽容;纵容;赎罪券;付款延期;特惠
industria n. 工业化的行政形态(指从工业社会的经济背景、社会结构、意识形态、沟通系统、权力形式等因素来研究行政制度的组织及其行为方式)

industrial a./n. 工业的,实业的;产业工人的;劳资争议的;从事工业的;供工业用的;工业高度发达的/产业工人,工业(尤指制造业)的雇员;从事工业的公司;工业产品;(复)工业公司所发行的股票和债券
industrial accession 工业增益
industrial accident 工伤事故
industrial act 劳工法;劳资争议法
industrial actions 工业行动(指工会通过集体协商议定工资率和劳动条件,使用集体行动当做谈判武器,借以提高谈判力量和筹码,将劳动的买卖从市场中转移到谈判桌上来)
industrial and commercial administrative control bureau 工商行政管理局
industrial and commercial consolidated tax 工商统一税
industrial and commercial control regulations 工商管理规则(条例)
industrial and commercial tax 工商税
industrial and intellectual property 工业知识产权
industrial and provident societies (英)勤俭互助会
industrial arbitration 劳资(争议)仲裁,工业仲裁
industrial arbitration board 劳资争议仲裁委员会
industrial association 行业协会
industrial assurance (英)劳工人身保险
industrial award 劳资法庭判决
industrial bond 工业债券
industrial citizen 产业公民[美国劳资集体协商是工业治理的一种形态,工作场所中的统治权(sovereignty)是由资方和劳工代表来共同分享,它是建立产业民主的一种方式,劳工在产业中具有产业公民的身份]
industrial conciliation and arbitration act 劳资争议调解和仲裁法
industrial court 劳资争议法庭(又译:工业法庭,劳工法庭,劳资法庭)
industrial court act 劳资(争议)法庭法
industrial death benefits 工伤死亡抚恤金
Industrial Democracy 《产业民主》[指

1897 年英国韦伯夫妇(Webb S. and Webb B.)出版的一本书,其中界定了"集体协商"(collective bargain)一词,此词用来描述工会为了改善和维持劳动条件,争取经济和社会地位向上提升所采取的方法]
industrial design (and models) 工业品外观设计(指知识产权中一种较为特殊的智力成果,不仅涉及工商领域,也涉及文化艺术层面。法国对外观设计实行著作权和外观设计法的双重保护);工业品模型式样(和模型);工业品样式;工业设计
industrial design act 工业品外观设计法
industrial design register 工业品外观设计登记簿
industrial diseases benefits 职业病津贴
industrial dispute 劳资纠纷,劳资争议
industrial employment 劳工就业
industrial espionage 产业情报
industrial government 工业治理
industrial injuries benefits 工伤津贴
industrial injury 工伤
industrial insurance 产业工人人身(人寿)保险;简易人身(人寿)保险(即对被保险人免于体格检查以简易方法进行的一种人身保险)
industrial insurance company 产业工人人身(人寿)保险公司
industrial lien 工业留置权
industrial models 工业模型
industrial organizational theory 产业组织理论
industrial pollution 工业污染
industrial property (right) 工业产权(如专利权等)
industrial relation 劳资关系
industrial revolution (18 世纪 60 年代在英国开始的)产业革命,工业革命
industrial school (英)(管教违法青少年的)工艺劳作学校;(复)(英史)满席法官开庭(指古代普通法法院裁决法律问题的一种开庭形式,它不同于初审法庭、巡回法庭独任法官开庭形式)
industrial sector 工业部门
industrial tribunal 劳资争议裁判庭
industrial union 产业工会(指同一工业的跨行业的职工工会)
industrial worker 产业工人
industrial-enterprise law 工商企业法
industrial-revenue bond 工业收益债券(指目的在于提供工业设备出租,并按租项收益分期偿还及支付利息的一种债券)
industrialization n. 工业化
industriousness 辛德原则[在美国关于数据库是否享有著作权这一问题,1991 年前法院一般适用"辛德原则"和"前额出汗原则"(sweat of brow);1991 年联邦最高法院就该案作出判决后,法院对数据库的保护,一般均以"原创性"为标准]
industry n. 工业,产业;行业;勤劳,勤奋;有组织的劳动;(总称)工业(或产业)的资方人员
industry capital 产业资本
industry tax 产业税
industry wild liability 见 enterprise liability
indyref n. 苏格兰独立的全民公投
inebriate n. 酒徒,酒鬼,醉酒者
ineffective a. 失效的,无效的,效率低的;无能力的
ineffective contract 无效合同(契约)
ineffectual ways 无效的方法
inefficacy n. 无效果,无效力;不称职
inefficiency n. 低效率
inefficient a. 低效率的
inefficient gaming 低效博弈
inefficient management 低效管理,无效管理
inelastic demand 无弹性需求
inelastic supply 无弹性供给
ineligible n./a. 不合格的人;无资格者/无被选资格的,无资格的,不合格的;不可取的,不适当的
inept a. 不称职的,无能的;不符要求的;不适当的
ineptitude n. 不称职;无能;不适当,不适宜
inequality n. 不平等,不平衡;不平均,不相等
inequality of facilities 设施上不平等的
inequitable a. 不公正的,不公平的;偏私的;不一律的
inequitable exchange 不等价交换

inequity n. 不公正,不公平,偏私
inevitability n. 不能避免
inevitable a. 不可避免的,无法规避的;必然的
inevitable accident 不(可)能避免的意外,不可避免的事故
inevitable discovery exception 必然发现的例外[即一部分侦查人员虽偶尔进行违法侦查(即使不违法侦查),其他侦查人员通过合法侦查也必然会获得证据]
Inevitable Discovery Rule (美)必然发现规则,(刑事诉讼)不可避免的披露规则[此项规则实际是"毒树之果原则"(fruit of poisonous tree doctrine)的一个例外,即如果控方能够表明以非法手段获取的证据最终必然能以合法手段获得,则具有可采性。见 fruit of poisonous tree]
inevitable mistake 不能避免的错误
inexorable mechanical laws 不可改变的机械规律
inextricable a. (困难等)无法摆脱的;(问题等)无法解决的;(疙瘩、结)解不开的(inextricably ad.; inextricability n.)
infallible a. 无过失的,无错误的,确实可靠的;一贯正确的
infamia (罗马法)丧失名誉(或降低人格);破廉耻(指民会制定之法律以及大官法均规定令名减少之条规,凡有触犯条规而受令名减少者,谓之破廉耻)
infamia immediata 直接破廉耻
infamia mediata 间接破廉耻
infamous a. 罪大恶极的、声名狼藉的、不名誉的;犯有丧失廉耻的罪行的;(因犯重罪)被褫夺(部分)公权的;(普通法)被剥夺法律上作证权的
infamous conduct (美)行为不正(通常指医生因职业上的不诚实、不道德而被医药总会理事会判定的罪名);丑行
infamous crime 不名誉罪;丑恶无耻罪,丑行罪(指强奸、兽奸行为);重罪
infamy n. 1.(因犯重罪)丧失(部分)公权;(普通法上对证人能力的)剥夺 2.臭名昭著,声名狼藉,不名誉;出丑,丑事
infancy n. 未成年,幼年;幼稚期,婴儿期
* **Infancy is a shield, not a sword.** 未成年可作为抗辩之理由,但不作为防卫或攻击之剑
infangthef n. (早期中世纪法的)特定窃贼绞刑权(指可根据授予自己的管辖权,将在其土地上被当场抓获的窃贼吊死的权利)
infant n./a. 幼儿,婴儿;未成年人/未成年的,幼年的,婴儿的;初期的
infant heir 幼年继承人,未成年继承人
infant plaintiff 未成年的原告
infant son 幼子
infanticidal a. 杀婴的
infanticide n. 杀婴(罪),杀婴犯
infanticide act 杀婴处置法
infanticide by drowning 溺婴罪
infect v. 使受影响,感染;使(合同)无效
infect or pollute be unintentional 非故意的感染或污染
infected person 染疫人,受传染的人
infectious a. 有坏影响的;能使成为非法的;能导致充公的;传染的
infectious diseases 传染病
infer (that) v. 推论,推断;意味着,指明
inference n. 1.推论,推理,推断 2.推断的结果,结论
inference of law 法律(上的)推断;法律上的结论
inferential a. 推论的,推理的,推论上的,推理上的
inferential pleading 见 argumentative pleading
inferior a. 下级的;劣等的;初等的
inferior civil court 初等(级)民事法庭;下级民事法庭
inferior court (或 **lower court**) 初等(级)法院;下级法院
inferior court of record 初等(级)记录法庭(院)
inferior norm 下级规范,低级规范
inferior quality 品质低劣
infest v. 侵害,侵扰(with);寄生于
infestation n. 骚扰,扰害,横行;(盗贼、鼠、虫等的)成群出现
infeudation n. 分封土地
infirm a. 不牢靠的;不生效的(指证件

等);意志薄弱的;(身体)虚弱的
infirm person 心神耗弱者
infirmative a. 不可靠的
infirmative consideration (英美法)不可靠的对价,无效对价
infirmative fact 不可靠的事实
infirmity n. 1.(条例等的)无效;无力 2.残疾;虚弱,体弱 3.缺点
inflammable a. 易燃的;易激怒的;性情暴躁的
inflammable goods 易燃物品
inflammatory a. 使激怒的;煽动性的
inflammatory speech 煽动性言论
inflation n. 通货膨胀;信用膨胀;物价压力
inflation gap 通货膨胀缺口(这一术语来自凯恩斯在《如何筹措战费》中对通货膨胀的分析,如果在产品和劳务总需求水平与可得到的总供给量之间存在一个缺口,则会引起通货膨胀)
inflexible a. 坚定不移的,不屈的,不可动摇的
inflict v. 处(罚),加(刑);予以(打击);使遭受(损害)
inflict a punishment on a criminal 惩处罪犯
inflict punishment 处以刑罚
inflict the death 处以死刑
infliction n. 处罚,加刑,刑罚;伤害;打击;痛苦的经验
infliction of body 身体上的伤害
inflictor n. 科罚者;处罚者;加害者
influence n. 影响;势力;权势;感化
influence power 影响力
infocop n. (英)资深勇探(指依靠电脑、数据和人工智慧软件破案的警察)
inform v. 告发,告密;诉冤;告知,通知
inform probation system (美)观护制度
informal a. 缺乏法定形式的,非正式的
informal act 不要式行为
informal adjudication 非正式裁决
informal admission 非正式坦白
informal adoption 非正式收(领)养
informal agency action (1971年)行政机构的活动(指行政机构的活动而不是裁决或制定行政规则,诸如调查、宣传或监督。见 rule making)
informal composite negotiating text (ICNT) 非正式综合谈判条文
informal consultation 非正式磋商
informal contract 不要式合同(契约),非要式合同
informal constraints 非正式约束
Informal Draft Convention on the Law of the Sea 《非正式海洋法公约草案》
informal family 不要式(非正式)家庭(尤指美国目前很多的非婚同居的家庭)
informal hearing 非正式听证
informal justice 非正式正义
informal marriage 不要式的结婚
informal organization 非正式组织
informal rule (英)非正式规则[在英国,"非正式规则"名目繁多,有"操作手册"(a code of practice)、"指南"(guidance)、"指南要点"(guidance note)、"指南纲要"(Guidancelines)、"通告"(circular)、"白皮书"(white paper)、"纲要计划"(Outline Scheme)、"指导意见"(statement of advice)、"部门通告"(departmental circular)等等不一而足。有的是外在性的,直接规范相对人的活动,可以授予利益或课加义务或增进双方自愿合作。但有的只有内在性,仅规范行政机关的权力行使]
informal rulemaking 非正式规章的制定
informal single negotiating texts (ISNT) 非正式(资料)单一谈判条文
informal tribunal 非正式的法庭
informalization of law 法律建设的非正规化
informant n. 告发人;报告人;通知人;提供消息的人
informatics (复) n. 见 information science
information n. 1.(由检察官或普通合格的官员对一项刑事犯罪提出的)控告起诉书,公诉书 2.通知;报告;情报;资料;消息;信息;知识
information agency 新闻处,新闻发布室
information agreement 互相提供情报的协定
information and belief 根据信息和确信,善意的相信(标准法律用语,指事实主张

者并不基于第一手了解的材料而善意相信争辩的论点及其主张事实的真实性)
information asymmetry 信息不对称
information bureau 情报局
information channel 消息来源
information efficiency 信息效率(指金融学说中的有效市场学说,它认为市场价格能够完全反映可利用的信息,因而使获利的机会被充分利用,这就是所谓信息效率)
information fits 信息资料
information in chancery (英)与国王或政府有关的起诉案件
information interactivity 信息交往
information law 信息法
information location tools 信息定位服务提供者[指根据美国1998年《数字千年版权法》(DMCA)第512(c)条和512(d)条的规定,信息存储服务提供者(information residing)和信息定位服务提供者都不承担责任的主要条件是:①不实际知晓侵权内容的存在,无法从侵权想象中意识到侵权存在,在知晓或意识到之后立即移除相关内容;②在网络服务提供者有权利和能力控制侵权行为的情况下,未从侵权行为中直接获得利益;③在得到符合条件的侵权通知后,立即移除相应内容]
information media 新闻工具,新闻媒体
information on oath 起誓告发(指在裁判官面前经过发誓的告发)
information on paper 文件信息
information residing 信息存储服务提供者
information retrieval 情报(信息)检索
information science (复数形式为 informatics) 1.资料学(研究资料的收集、分类、储存等的学科) 2.信息学
information society 信息社会
Information Society Index 信息社会指数(指 IDC 公司所属的)
information storage 信息库
Information Super Highway 信息高速公路
information subject 信息权的权利主体
information warfare 信息战(指战争敌对双方之间为保持自身对信息的获取权、控制权以及使用权而对对方开展的一系列敌对活动,其内涵和外延要比网络战更广,可以包括网络战、情报战、电子战、心理战等)
information-only system 信息公开展示系统
informational advantage 提供信息的好处;信息优势
informational property right 信息权(此信息权既不是知识产权,又不是所有权,而是信息社会诞生的一种新类型的财产权。详言之,信息权是权利人直接支配特定的信息产品并排除他人干涉的权利。数字文化产品,又称信息产品,是信息权的客体。作为一项财产权,信息权的权利核心内容表现为支配与排他。指信息权人对自己的信息产品所享有的占有、使用、收益、处分的权利。见 digital cultural goods)
informational training 信息提供培训
informationalism n. 信息主义
informative a. 提供资料的,报告消息的,增加知识的
informative pleadings 提供资料(或信息)的答辩状(或诉答文书),实质性答辩状
informative treatments of substantive topics 扩增情况的实体课题的论述
informed a. 有知识的,见闻广的,掌握情况的,消息灵通的
informed consent 1.知情同意[指某人在充分了解某事一旦发生所涉及的风险和抉择情况下,同意做某事。在法律界,"知情同意"(informed consent)在《示范职业行为准则》(Model Rule of Professional Conduct)第1.D(e)条中已有界定] 2.病人知情选择[指在医生已作出医疗措施后,另一保健工作者(healthcare provider)不管透露什么信息,在医疗范畴(medical community)的理性谨慎提供人(a reasonable prudent provider)会将有关计划的医疗方案和医疗步骤所涉及的风险告知病人,病人在知情情况下作出选择。亦称 knowing consent]
informed mind 见闻广博者
informed player 拥有信息的参与人
informed settlement 了解情况的和解

informed sources 消息灵通人士
informer n. 控告人；通知者；告密者；报告者；检举人，揭发人
informer's case 告密者案件
infortunium 见 homicide *per infortunium*
infra 在下，以下
infra annos nubiles 未到结婚年龄
infra dignitatem curiae 法院不屑受理
infra dignitatum 有失身份，有失体面
infra metas 在范围内；在分界线内
infra quatuor maria 四海之内（指在势力范围之内）
infraction n. （法规等的）违犯，违反；违法
infraction of civil law 违反民法
infraction of law 违法
infraction of regulations 违犯规章，触犯规章
infrangible a. 不可破的；不可分离的；不可违背的；不可侵犯的
infrastructure n. 基础，（国家，社会等的）基础结构，基本设施
infrequent cases 非经常案件
infringe v. 破坏；侵犯，侵害；违背，违反
infringe a right 侵犯权利
infringe article 假冒商品
infringe personal or property rights 侵犯个人或财产权
infringe the copyright 侵犯版权
infringe the sovereignty 侵犯主权
infringe upon the prerogative of any political chauffeur 侵犯任何政客司机的特权
infringe upon the right of 侵犯……的权利
infringement n. 侵害；侵犯；触犯；违反；冒用商标；侵犯版权
infringement of copyright 侵犯版权，侵犯著作权
infringement of freedom 侵犯自由
infringement of patent（或 monopoly right）侵犯专利权
infringement of public order 侵害公共秩序
infringement of rights 侵犯权利
infringement of territorial sovereignty 侵犯领土主权
infringement of the law 违法，犯法

infringement of the same right by the same wrong 相同错误引起相同权利损害
infringement of title 侵犯所有权
infringement of trademarks 侵犯商标权
infringer n. 侵权人
infringing act 侵权行为
infringing copy 侵犯专利权的复印本
infringing label 假冒标签
infungible n./a. 不可替代的特定物/不可代替的，不可互换的
infuriosus 精神病人
infuse v. 向……注入，向……灌输；浸渍
infuse new life into the legal system 给这个法制注入生命力
infusion n. 注入，灌输；浸渍
infusion of ideas 思想的注入；观念的输入
infusion of morals into the law 道德注入法律
ingenious lawyers 机智的律师
ingenuus （古罗马的）自由人
ingestion n. 咽下，吞服
ingestion of dangerous drug 吞服毒品
ingrain n./v./a. 本质，固有品质/使根深蒂固；使遍体渗透/根深蒂固的，遍体渗透的，固有的，积习成性的
ingratitude n. 忘恩负义
ingredient n. 成分；因素；组成部分，配料
ingredients of crime （美国刑法中的可罚行为的基本要素被称为）犯罪要素（包括 *mens rea*）
ingress n. 进入（权），入境（权）；入口
ingress, egress and regress 出入自由（ingress 指入，egress 指出，regress 指回复，如租赁契约上载明出租人在租赁物上有进出回复之权）
ingross 见 engross
inhabitancy（=inhabitance）n. 居住；有人居住状态；住所；户籍
inhabitant n. 居民，常住居民；住户
inhabited house duty 住宅税
inhere in （生来即）存在于；（权利等）属于；固有
inherent a. 内在的，固有的；先天的，生来的
inherent cause 遗传因素；附带原因
inherent covenant 固有条款[指直接与土

地相关的条款,如安静享用条款(covenant of quiet enjoyment)。见 collateral covenant]

inherent danger 内在的危险,固有的危险

inherent defect 固有瑕疵,固有缺陷

inherent executive power 固有的行政权

inherent fallibility of human thought 人类思想的固有过错(或内在错)

inherent limitations 固有的局限性,内在的范畴

inherent power(s) 固有权力(首先,固有权力要区别于宪法或法律所明确规定的权力和另一种政府或政府官员基于主权或基于许可范围内通过宪法语言解释所实际拥有之权力。在美国宪法体系中,固有权力的存在一直是一个有争议的问题,固有权力实际上是源于主权而允许政府尤其是行政当局可在没有授权的情况下为国家利益和安全而进行活动的权力。由于该权力缺乏明示或默示的宪法根据,行使时的范围和程度难以确定);内在权利理论

inherent purposes of legal procedure 程序内在目标[指 1986 年美国法学家贝勒斯(Michael Bayles)提出"程序内在目标",此概念分析了程序中存在直接成本(DC),经济损害错误成本(EC),道德错误成本(MC)和程序利益(PB)]

inherent right 固有权利

inherent vice 固有瑕疵,内在缺陷,固有恶习

inherent vice of the goods 货物本身固有的瑕疵

inherently or through acquired distinctiveness "内在或者通过使用获得显著性"(2006 年美国联邦商标淡化修正案明确使用了这一"内在或通过使用获得显著性"表述。从逻辑上说,商标反淡化保护是商标的广告宣传功能。哪里发生了损害商标广告宣传功能的行为,哪里就应有商标反淡化保护,而不管商标"出身"如何)

inherit v. 继承;享有;接受遗产;成为继承人

inheritable a. 可继承的,有继承权的;可遗传的

inheritance n. 继承(财产);继承(权);遗产;遗赠;继承物;遗传

inheritance n. 继承(财产);继承(权);遗产(指按无遗嘱死亡法规定从先人得来的产业);遗赠(指遗赠得来的动产和不动产);继承物;遗传

inheritance act 继承法

inheritance agreement 继承合同(契约),继承协议

inheritance by operation of law 法定继承

inheritance law 继承法

inheritance of personal property 个人的财产继承(狭义又译:动产继承)

inheritance of property 财产继承

inheritance tax (18 世纪)继承税[指①对从另一个人身上继承到财产的人征收的税(类似于遗产税,是对死者财产所课的税),联邦没有继承税,但有些州有继承税(依据联邦遗产税规定,继承税是可减免或可扣除的),亦称 succession tax; death tax。②不严格地说,即遗产税(estate tax)]

inheritance under a will 遗嘱继承

inherited share 继承份额

inheritor n. 遗产继承人,继承人;后继者

inheritress (=inheritrix) n. 女继承人

inhibit v. 阻止,禁止,抑制,约束

inhibition n. 抑制;禁止,(英)制(禁)止令(指制止债务人订立有损于债权人的合同的禁令);中止诉讼令

inhibition of thought 思想迟缓(思维表达障碍的一种,即思想的联想受到抑制,想速度减慢,思维内容量减少,表现说话语速慢,语言表达困难,反应迟钝,语言低微,患者自感脑子生了锈似的转不动,思考问题吃力。此类患者缔约能力和受审能力均受影响。见 thought of insertion)

inhibitor n. 制止者,禁止者,抑制人

inhouse counsel 机构内部律师

inhuman a. 非人道的,不人道的;残忍的

inhuman act 非人道行为

inhuman treatment 非人道待遇

inhumanity n. 无人性,野蛮;残酷,残酷行为;非人道行为

inimical a. 敌意的,有害的,有碍的

iniquae leges 不平等之法律(如平民不能与贵族通婚等)

* *Iniquum est alios permittere, alios inhibere mercaturam.* It is inequitable to permit some to trade and to prohibit others. 只准许某些人经营而禁止另一些人经营,这是不公平的。

* *Iniquum est aliquem rei sui esse judicem.* It is wrong for a man to be a judge in his own cause. 在自己的案件中充当法官者是非法的(错误的)。

* *Iniquum est ingenuis hominibus non esse liberam rerum suarum, alienationem.* It is unjust that freemen should not have the free disposal of their own property. 自由民(或解除了法律约束的人)不能自由处分自己的财产,这是不公平的。

initial v./a. 标注;草签/创议的;最初的,开始的;词首的;首创的
initial a note 用缩写签署便条
initial appropriations 初步拨款
initial capital 创办资本
initial (budget) estimates 初步概算
initial jurisdiction 初审管辖权
initial maturity 原始期限
Initial Negotiating Right (INR) 最初谈判权
initial offers 初始出价
initial parties 最初的(或起始的)当事人
initial (或down) payment 首期付款;入门费加提成费(指签约后支付一笔入门费,以后按提成费计算)
initial pleading 起诉状
initial policy determination 最初政策裁定,最初政策判决
initial position of equality 原始的平等地位
initial public offering 最先公开发行[指一个公司的首次公开销售股票。发行人的产权证券(equity security)通过注册申请证券上市报告第一次公开发行,缩略为IPO]
initial public opening 见 initial public offering
initial screening survey 初步审查
initialed text 草签文本
initiate v. 创议;开始;创始;发动,发起;正式介绍;引进
initiate legal proceedings 提起诉讼
initiate proceedings against 对……提出控告
initiate the inquiry 提出质询,最初询问
initiation n. 创始;指引,传授;(会社等)加入
initiation of proceedings 提起诉讼
initiation of public prosecution 提起公诉
initiative n. 创制权;创始;主动,首创精神,积极性;动议权;优先权;公民立法创议权(与 referendum 不同)(指公民所享有的一种通常独立于立法机关的,在政治选举中提出法律议案和宪法修正案,并使这些议案修正案生效的权利,最早于 1898 年由南达科他州引进美国)
initiative in legislation 立法创制权
initiative of individual 个人的主创精神
initiative on the subject 创造性主题
initiative power 立法动议权
initiator n. 创议人;发起人,创始人;传授者,教导者
injudicial a. 不依照法律形式的;不符合法官身份的;判断不当的
injudicious a. 判决不当的
injunction n. 指令,命令;(由法院发出的带有强制性的从事或不得从事某种行为的)强制令;禁止令
injunction decree 禁制令判决
injunction hearing 停止听审,强制听审
injunctions and equitable remedies 禁令与衡平法上的救济(14世纪,英国有两套相互区别又有些竞争的法院系统:"普通法法院"和"衡平法法院"。前者特征是其在对普通法的发展、陪审团制度的运用,以及对普通法诉状与令状体系的依赖及解决法律纠纷之途径方面具有严格的形式要求。而后者则采取一种更加灵活的方式来审理案件,并提供多种救济方式。在普通法法院进行诉讼的当事人只能对人身伤害和财产损失要求金钱给付作为赔偿。与之相反,在衡平法法院的诉讼当事人则可在一系列强制救济措施中进行选择,包括要求或禁止某种行为的禁令,要求合同继续履行的强制令,或命令分割共有财产的禁令等。这些衡平法上的救济提供普通法法院所缺乏的灵活性。美

国的法院系统从英国传统中汲取了大量经验。立宪者的一项主要任务就是界定新的联邦法院的"司法权",他们写明:该权力"应及于普通法及衡平法上的所有案件",并授权联邦法院提供英国衡平法法院所形成的所有救济方式。美国所有州在殖民地时期都组建了衡平法法院,或独立存在或与普通法法院合并。在过去的一个世纪中,联邦法院积极运用衡平救济以强制适用联邦法律,而不是各州法律)

injunctive a. 禁令的,指令的,命令的
injunctive decree 强制性判决,强制性令
injunctive relief or damages 强制性的救济或赔偿;基金会性的救济或赔偿
injure v. 伤害,损害,毁坏,使受冤屈
injure the public interest to profit the private interest 损公肥私
injured a. 受害的,被害的
injured party 受害人,受害一方,受害者
injured person 受害人
injured state 受害国
injurer n. 加害者,伤害者,实害者,毁坏者,致害人
injuria 侵害;伤害;侵害权利(指可以控告的权利侵害。古罗马法上指以语言或文书毁损他人名誉,或殴打或以其他暴行加害于他人身体所犯的罪行)

*** Injuria non excusat injuriam.** One wrong does not justify another. 一事错不能证明另一事亦错(某一行为是侵权行为,并不证明另一行为亦是侵权行为)。

*** Injuria non praesumitur.** Injury is not presumed. 伤害不适用推定。(又译:Cruel, oppressive, or tortious conduct will not be presumed. 残暴行为、压制行为或侵权行为都不应当是推定的。)

*** Injuria proporia non cadet in beneficium facientis** No one shall profit by (or take advantage of) his own wrong./No benefit shall accrue to a person from his own wrong doing. 任何人不得从其侵害行为中获利

*** Injuria servi dominum pertingit.** The master is liable for injury done by his servant. 主人对其雇用的人所作的侵害行为负有责任。

injuria sine(或 **absque**)**domno** 没有造成损害的侵害(指没有造成损害、结果性伤害或损失的法定过错行为和违反职责行为)
injuries from high and low temperatures 高低温伤害
injuring party 加害人(方)
injuring person 加害人,伤害他人者
injurious a. 伤害的;有害的;不公平的;不法的;侮辱的;诽谤的
injurious act 侵害行为
injurious behavio(u)r 有害的举止行为
injurious experience 伤害经历
injurious reliance 有害的诈欺(指传播有害性的虚假陈述构成的行为,如商业诽谤)
injurious words 中伤的言论,侮辱的言辞
injury n. 侵害,伤害,损害;冤屈;受伤处
injury benefit (保险)伤害赔偿金;伤害救济金
injury by accident 意外伤害
injury from blunt utensil 钝器伤
injury from sharp utensil 锐器伤
injury in fact 实际上的损害
injury insurance 伤害保险
in jury margin 损害幅度(指确定反倾销税的一个条件,如果损害幅度低于倾销幅度,则按损害幅度而非倾销幅度确定反倾销税,如果高于倾销幅度,则按倾销幅度确定反倾销税。损害幅度是由世贸成员方决定,主管机关不仅定性分析倾销进口产品是否对国内产品造成损害,还定量分析倾销进口产品对国内产业所造成的损害程度,据此即可计算出损害幅度和倾销幅度,以后可将两者进行比较,确定征收反倾销税)
injury on job 工伤
injury through negligence 误伤,过失伤害
injury to credit 损害信用
injury to the right of spouses 损害配偶权利
injustice n. 不公正,不公平;侵害(他人)权利;不法行为;非正义(行为);不公正行为

*** Injustum est, nisi tota lege inspecta, de

una aliqua ejus particula proposita judicare vel respondere. It is unjust to decide or respond as to any particular part of a law without examining the whole of the law. 不考虑整个法律而只依据法律的某一特定部分规定或只对该特定部分的规定负责,都是不正确的。

inlagary(或 **inlagation**) n. 回复占有;恢复依法失去的权益;恢复法律的保护

inland n./a. 内地,国内,内陆/内地的,内陆的;国内的

inland bill (of exchange) 国内汇票

inland canal 内陆运河

inland contract of supply 国内的供应合同(契约)

inland departments 内地部门

inland duty 国内税

inland navigation 内河航行

inland revenue 国内收入

inland river 内河

inland sea 内海

inland trade 国内贸易

inland waters 内水,国内水域(见 national waters 和 internal waters)

inlawry n. 法律的保护,恢复(犯人的)法律权益

inmate n. 同屋居住者;同房病人;同狱犯人;居民;监犯

innate excellence of legal system 法律制度的天生优越性

inner a. 内部的;接近中心的(尤指权势);内在的;思想的;精神的;秘密的

inner barrister 内席律师(指英国准许在法庭上当辩护人的王室律师或大律师)

inner cabinet 核心内阁

inner circle 核心集团

inner continental shelf 内部大陆架

inner layers of the state 国家的内部机制

inner light 内在观念

inner morality (法律的)内在道德

Inner Temple (英)内殿律师学院(指英国最古老的四大律师学院之一。见 Inns of Court)

innocence(或 **not guilty**) n. 无罪;无罪的人,清白无辜者

Innocence Center (美)无辜者中心[指20世纪90年代中期美国很多州都接受了"无辜者中心",通过无辜者计划(innocence project)对可能错判的案件进行复查。这些中心是民间机构,复查案件的主要手段是 DNA 检验。]

innocence or guiltiness 无罪或有罪

Innocence Project (美)1.无辜者计划(指20世纪90年代以来美国兴起的民间冤案发现机构,最早由叶史瓦大学本杰明·卡多佐法学院于1992年创建,成立目的主要在于发现无辜者被判有罪的案件。无辜者计划是为那些自称的因犯提供法律代理服务或在案件调查方面提供帮助的非营利性组织。它通常为各大法学院内部设立的实践教学机构或附属法学院机构。其成员主要为法学院教授和其他人员。该组织依靠当地律师的推荐和在押犯人主动申请两种方式获得案例。这一组织还积极促进相关立法活动。2004—2010年就在全美范围推动制定或者完善了与无辜者有关的70项法案)2.洗冤联盟(指20世纪70年代成立的民权团体)

innocent n./a. 无罪者,无辜者/无罪的;清白;无知的;无害的

innocent agent 无辜的帮凶(指非出于故意而受他人的唆使或请求而犯了罪或做了非法的事的人)

innocent homicide 无辜杀人,非故意杀人

innocent infringer 无辜侵权人

innocent misrepresentation 善意的错误陈述

innocent omission 无意遗漏;非故意的不作为

innocent party 无辜方,受害一方

innocent passage 无害通过(见 right of innocent passage)

innocent purchase 善意购得(物)

innocent purchaser 善意买主(指许多国家芯片保护法中的术语;虽经营侵权产品,但进货时确实不知为侵权产品)

innocent spouse 无辜配偶

innocent-seeming provision 无误条款

innominate a. 无名的,匿名的

innominate contract (罗马法)无名契约[指不归属于任何有专门名称之契约之总

称,除当事人间的明示合意(express agreement)内容之外,法律对此不作任何补充。《民法典》(La Civil Code art.1914)第 1914 条,罗马法中无名契约分为:①给予与给予之交换 *do ut des*;②给予劳力之交换 *do ut des*;③劳力与给予之交换 *facia dut des*;④劳力与劳力之交换 *facia ut facias*。此四类为查士丁尼所认定。此词条亦可称为 innominate real contract]

innominate real contract 见 innominate contract

innovation n. 创新;改革;(技术)革新;新事物;新方案

innovation research 创新研究

innovative financial instruments 创新的金融手段

Inns of Court (英)(四大)律师学院(指英国 14 世纪时在伦敦组成的四大法律学院:林肯律师学院,格雷律师学院,内殿律师学院和中殿律师学院);四大律师协会(指英国伦敦有权授予律师资格的四大律师协会)

innuendo n. 文件中的附注句(尤指被称为诽谤性词句的注释);影射;暗指;讥讽;间接诽谤;(诉状中的)注释

inoffensive a. 无害的,不伤害人的;不触犯人的;不令人讨厌的

inoffensive navigation 无害航行

inoffensive passage 无害通行

inofficiosum 违背道义

inofficious a. 不尽道德义务的;无职务的;无效的;不近人情的

inofficious testament 不依道德义务的遗嘱(指立遗嘱时不顾妻儿亲属把遗产给外人,不给家儿,又未说明理由,依罗马法可将遗嘱取消)

inoperative a. 不起作用的;不能实行的;(法律、规章等)不生效的;不能使用的;无益的

inops consilii 缺少法律咨询(此术语指一个人在缺少法律咨询的情况下所为之行为,如立遗嘱人自己草拟遗嘱)

input n./v. 投入,投入资金/输入计算机

input-output analyse 投入量产出量的分析

inquest n. 验尸;勘查;审问;审讯(尤指陪审团参加的);审问后的判决;查询,(参加审讯的)陪审团;验尸团;调查;调查(判决)报告

inquest jury (1873 年)调查陪审团(指由行政司法官、验尸官或其他行政官员与从特别地区公民中招来的一些人组成陪审团出庭,一起共同调查与死亡相关的事实。亦称 jury of inquest。见 inquest)

inquire v. 询问;调查;查问;查究;审查

inquire into a matter 对某一事(或案件)进行调查

inquirer n. 调查人,询问者,审查人

inquiring limits 调查限制

inquiring party 调查的一方,询问的一方

inquiry n. 询问,打听;调查;探索;查究;审查

inquiry on the protection of secrets 保密审查

inquisition n. 1.勘验,讯问,审理 2.(宗教法庭)严厉刑罚 3.陪审团的判决 4.审讯,彻底调查 5.(大写)(罗马天主教的)宗教(异端)裁判所 6.调查报告,验尸结果报告,审讯结果记录

inquisition by torture 刑讯

inquisition per testes 证人询问

inquisitional a. 调查的,审问的,审理的;宗教(异端)裁判所的

inquisitional procedure 预审程序

inquisitoire n. 职权主义[来源于拉丁语形容词 inquisitorius,系动词 inquiere 的衍生词。19 世纪开始作为刑事诉讼的基本形态并与"accusatoire"(当事人主义)一起在不同时期学者的学术作品中出现。inquisitoire 最初含义系查清案件事实的方法,仅限于侦查阶段(包括预审),尚未对某种诉讼的整体描述;而"accusatoire"描述的则是法官受理案件的方式(当事人控告),也仅反映了某种程序特征。两个词汇在诉讼程序上并无对应关系。随着历史演进,界定"职权主义"应奉行三项准则:①准确性,准确反映当代职权主义国家的核心特质;②排他性,将"职权主义"与"当事人主义"清晰地区分开来;③契合性,和"职权主义"的称谓可高度融合。依此三项标准,"职权主义"的定义为:"诉讼以社会利

益优先为导向、国家权力为主导、实质真实为目标,审前程序凸显侦检机关的优势侦查权,审判程序凸显法官主导控制的正当程序模型。"]

inquisitor n. 审问官,调查官;(大写)宗教裁判官

inquisitorial a. 审问官(似)的,调查官(似)的;有关审问的,有关调查的,纠问式的

Inquisitorial System 纠问式审判制度[指大陆法国家所实行的审判制度,即由法官讯问,可依职权自己调查事实并直接提取证据,代表国家利益进行审判,区别于英美法系国家审判的对抗式审判制度(Adversary System)]

inquisitory procedure 纠问式诉讼程序

inreparable injury 无可挽回的伤害,无可弥补的伤害

inroad n. (突然)袭击;(突然)侵犯;(复)损害;侵蚀

inrollment (=enrollment) n. 登记;注册;入伍;入会

Inrollments of Acts of Parliament (英)《议会法规刊录》(指自1483年以来存放于档案馆的英格兰和不列颠制定法的原始材料,但1642—1660年不在此例)

ins and outs 详情细节,内情

insane a. 精神病患者的;疯子的,心神丧失的

insane asylum 收容所

insane at time of offence 犯罪时正患精神病的

insane person 精神病患者

insane wrongdoer 有精神病的违法者

insanity n. 1.精神错乱,精神病;疯狂;心神丧失 2.蠢行,蠢事

insanity defense 精神病不正常的辩护,精神错乱的辩护[指在评定刑事责任时的一个主要考虑精神失常状态的法律原则。这一辩护原则可回溯至基督之前的希腊,从中世纪的英国开始,英语系的国家就存在因"精神失常"而给予宽恕的案件书面记载。在美国精神错乱辩护一直被接受作为刑法原则的一部分。但这种辩护常存在争议,关键在于如何界定"精神错乱"。

美国联邦最高法院对这一领域一直行事谨慎。现代,它将"精神错乱"界定为一种智力损伤,妨碍了一个人理解他或他的行为之错误的能力("认知性"分支)或妨碍其控制行为的能力("意志性"分支)。联邦最高法院在 Leiand v. Oregon(1952)一案中指出:如一州选择了这种辩护,则联邦宪法并不要求运用比历史上麦克纳顿条例(或规则)(M'Naghten Rules)(由英国上议院于1843年所制定的检验标准,仅关注"认识性"损伤)更广泛的检验方式。至今,至少有五个州的法院用另外的规则取代了精神错乱辩护。这个替代规则是:只有在极少情况下,即被告故意犯罪的情况下,才考虑被告存在精神障碍的证据问题,甚至对那些精神疾病十分严重的人办是如此。见 M'Naghten Rules]

inscribed a. 记名的,登记的

inscribed debentures 记名债券

inscribed securities 记名证券

inscribed stock 记名股票

inscription n. 铭刻;标题;编入名单;注册;(复)记名证券

inscrutable a. 不可理解的,不可思议的,不可测知的

inscrutable fault 不明原因的过失

insecurity clause 不可靠条款,不安全条款(指如果有正当理由认为债务人将无力支付,则允许贷款债权人使其全部债务成为应得权益的条款)

insemination n. 人工授精;播种

insensibility and delirium "麻木和谵妄"(指对精神病人概括其病的术语,用此术语,不用解释大家即明白其内涵,也是判无罪的标准内涵)

inside directors 内部董事

inside job 内部人作的案,通过内应作的案

inside trading 内幕交易

inside-dealer market 内部(幕)交易人市场

insider n. 知情人;熟知(团体、组织等)内情的人;局中人;(德)(证券交易中的)内幕人[持有内幕信息的人均可被视为内幕人,包括:①公司董事会、监事会的成员、发行人、承销人;②能获得内幕信息的股东;③依雇佣关系、职业关系获得内幕信

息者)。美国法中的 insider 并非仅指公司内部人(corporation insider),有时也指证券市场内部人(market insider)]

insider dealing (trading) 内幕交易,秘密交易

insider trading prohibition 禁止内幕交易,禁止幕后交易

insight n. 洞察,见识,自知力(指患者对自己的精神疾病认识和判断的能力)

insignem (生殖器)不具者(此类人在罗马法中有完全行为能力,但无缔结婚姻契约之能力)

insignia 勋章,徽章;荣誉;光辉历程;商业印记

insignificant coefficienf 非重要的系数

insinuation n. 1.暗指,暗示;暗讽,间接讽刺 2.登记,备案;公证

insinuation of a will 遗嘱的公证

insist v. 坚决要求,定要(on,upon);坚持,坚决主张,坚决认为(on, upon)

insistence n. 坚决要求,坚持;坚决主张

insobriety n. 喝酒过度;无节制;头脑不清醒

insofar as the contract gives no indication 如合同(契约)上无约定时

insolence n. 无礼;蛮横;侮辱性言行

insolvency (bankruptcy) n. 破产;无力清偿债务,不足抵偿债务;濒临破产

Insolvency Act 1986 (英)《1986年无力偿债法》

insolvency assignee 破产清算人

insolvency guaranteed fund (美)破产担保基金(指联邦存款保险公司的担保)

Insolvency Law of 1811 (美)(纽约的)《1811年无力偿还债务法》

insolvency of debtor 债务人无偿付能力

insolvent n./a. 破产者,无力偿债者/破产的,无力还债的;破产者的,无力偿债者的

insolvent debtor 破产债务人,无偿债能力的债务人

insolvent estate 破产产业

insolvent law 破产法

insomnia 失眠症

inspect v. 检查;监察,视察,调查,审查

inspectio corporis 人身的检查(指实际为身体的检查,一般很少允许人身检查,除非极为特殊情况如隐瞒怀孕相关情况)

inspection n. 检查;监察;视察,调查;验尸

inspection bureau 检验局

inspection by judge 法官的审查

inspection certificate 检验证书

inspection of a will 查验遗嘱

inspection of books 查账

inspection of documents 对文据的审查,文据审查

inspection of material evidence 物证检验

inspection of property 查勘财产(指法官查勘所审理的案件中与争议有关的土地或建筑物,亦可授权给陪审团去查勘)

inspection office at the port 口岸检查机关

inspection on damaged cargo 货物残损检验

inspection report 检查报告,检验报告

inspection service 检查机关,监察机关

inspection station 检查站

inspector n. 检查员,检验员,观察员,监察员,稽查员,视察员;督察,巡官;督学

inspector general 总监察长,总监;监察主任;(军队)监察长

inspector general of administrative affairs 政务总监

inspector of administration 行政监察官

inspector of court 法院检验员(指法院中检验商品、食品、建筑物等质量的,并享有裁判权的官员)

inspector of ordnance 军械检验员

inspector of taxes 税务稽查员

inspector-general's department 监察处,监察署

inspectorate n. 检查员(监察员等)的职责(或身份);检查员(监察员等)的管辖区域;视(监)察团,监察署;视察人员;监察人员

inspectorate of administration affairs 行政事务监察署

inspectorship n. 检查员(或监察员等)的职位(或任期)

insta-cite (美)即刻援引(指利用计算机检索援引查对服务系统,即刻援引适用WESTLAW)

instability n. 不坚决,三心二意,不稳定性

installation n. 1.就任,就职 2.安装,安置; 设备,设施

installation ceremony 就职典礼;开幕典礼

installation fee 安装费

instal(l)ment n. 1.分期付款(指分期付款购买商品,在第二次付款后商品即归买主所有的一种赊购方式。见 hire purchase); 分期分批 2.就职 3.装设;安顿

instal(l)ment bond 分期偿还的债券

instal(l)ment contract 分期分批履行的合同(契约);分期付款合同(契约)

instal(l)ment contract act 分期付款合同(契约)法

instal(l)ment credit 分期付款信贷

instal(l)ment delivery 分期交货,分期分批给付

instal(l)ment mortgage 分期付还(贷款)的抵押

instal(l)ment payment 分期付款

instal(l)ment purchase and selling 分期付款买卖(指购买者购得货物,对支付出售者的全部或部分价金,在以后进行分段偿付的一种交易)

instance n./v. 1.例子,实例 2.要求,建议 3.诉讼程序(手续) 4.情况,场合;阶段,步骤;举……为例;用例子说明;获得例证;引证

instance of appeal 上诉程序,上诉审

instance(或 level) of court 法院审级

instance of judg(e)ment 判例

instance of legislation 立法例

instancy n. 紧急,紧迫;瞬间

instant a. 紧迫的,刻不容缓的;立即的,直接的;本月的(用于商业或公函中)

instant arbitration 即时仲裁

instant committal 立即关押

instant international custom 即时国际习惯(随着人类社会技术进步和国际法的发展,有的国际习惯形成甚至不需要长时期的国家实践,利益受到影响的国家只要不予以反对,一项原则被广泛接受,有可能形成"国际习惯"。苏联第一颗人造卫星绕地球轨道运转,各国对此并无异议,无人指责侵犯领土主权。因此,此事足以证明各国形成了外层空间不同于领空的法律确信)

instant international customary law 即时的国际习惯法

instantaneous death 瞬间死,猝死,即时死

instantaneous rigor 尸体痉挛

instanter ad. 立即,马上(指24小时内)

instate v. 授予(某人)职位(或资格);任命;安置

instigate v. 教唆,煽动,怂恿;鼓动

instigation n. 主使,教唆;煽动;怂恿

instigator n. 教唆犯,教唆者,煽动者

instinct n. 本能,天性

instinctive concern 本能的关心,内在的关注

institor 代理人;店员

Institut du Droit International 国际法学会

Institut International des Brevet 国际专利研究所

institute n./v. 1.法学著作;法学教科书;法学论文,评论,如 Coke's Institutes 柯克法学著作(卷本)全集(1628年出版) 2.(大写或复数)关于罗马法的四卷本的论文。这种论文是指《国法大全》或《民法大全》的4个部分,即《查士丁尼法典》或《法典》《法学阶梯》《学说汇纂》和《新律》之一,亦称 Institutes of Justinian, Justinian's Institutes 3.(大写或复数)罗马法学家盖尤斯(Gaius)所写的论文。公元2世纪所写的作为基础的论文集《查士丁尼法学阶梯》,亦可称 Institutes of *Gaius* 4.(大写或复数)由西奥菲勒斯(Theophilus)用希腊文写的《查士丁尼法学阶梯》的释义[他是君士坦丁堡(现今土耳其的伊士坦布尔市)的法学教授,帮助过《查士丁尼法学阶梯》的最初编写工作。此项著作是在6世纪准备完的,亦称 paraphrase of Theophilus; Institutes of Theophilus] 5.(大陆法)第一继承人[指按照遗嘱指定的继承人,但又依遗嘱指示(direction)将遗转让给特定的第三人(称为 substitute,代替人)。见 substitute 2] 6.法律研究组织(指致力于研究和改进法律的组织机构。见 American Law Institute; Institute)/(14世纪)开始,起始〈institute legal proceedings against the manufac-

turer〉[针对制造商提起(司法)诉讼]
institute an action 起诉
Institute for Court Management (美)法院管理学院
institute for sustainable development 可持续发展机构
institute(或 **take**) **legal proceedings against** … 对……提起诉讼
institute litigation 起诉,提起诉讼
Institutes of Chinese Law 《中国法通典》(指庞德对中国法律改革提出过编纂一套法学典籍的建议,其要旨是要把中国现代法作为一个有系统的整体呈现出来)
Institute of International Law 国际法学会(成立于1871年)
Institute of Justinian 《查士丁尼法学纲要》(亦译《法学阶梯》,是《国法大全》的构成部分,由东罗马皇帝查士丁尼颁布)
Institute of Mediation and Conflict Resolution (美)调停与冲突解决学院(或研究院)
institute of political science and law 政治法律学院;政法学院
institute penal proceedings 进行刑事诉讼
institute prosecution 提起公诉
instituted heir 见 testamentary heir
Institutes of Gaius 《盖尤斯法学阶梯》(见 institute)
institutio judicis (民选)法官的设定
institution (14世纪)1.(诉讼诸如民事,刑事等的)提起,开始 2.基本规则,原则;原理,实务(practice) 3.设立的机构,特别是具有公共性质的社会公共机构,如精神障碍者或心理障碍者治疗所(facility for mentally disabled person),亦称 public institution 4.(大陆法)遗嘱人(以遗嘱方式)指定继承人;第一继承人的指定(the designation of an institute)(见 institute 5) 5.(宗教法)授予牧师(cleric)圣职并享有圣俸(benefice),由此而成为教区宗教需要(spiritual needs)的负责成员(见 presentation 2; advowson)
institution functioning abroad 驻外机构
institution in dealing with offenders 管理犯人机关

institution of an action 诉讼的起始,诉讼的提出
institution of exemption from costs 诉讼费用豁免令
institution of marriage 婚姻制度
institution of proceedings 起诉
institution of regulations 制定条例
institution of republic 共和国建制
institutional a. 组织机构的;制度上的;公共机构的,社会事业的;惯例的
institutional accounting 公用事业会计
institutional affiliations 机构成员
institutional arbitration 由常设仲裁机构所作的仲裁
institutional arrangement 制度化安排
institutional books 制度性(或惯例性的)书籍
institutional changes 制度变迁
institutional competence 制度能力
institutional decision 机构的决议,机构的决定
institutional economics 制度经济学
institutional equilibrium 制度均衡
institutional fact 制度性事实[指1960—1980年英国法学家麦克密克(N. Mac Cormic)和奥地利法学家魏因贝格尔(Ota Weiberger)共同提出法律是一种"制度性事实"的观点,他们认为世界上的事实有两种;原始性事实(original fact)和制度性事实(institutional fact)。前者指与物质世界的有形存在有关的事实,后者则指以人类实践活动或其结果为条件的事实]
institutional framework 体制,组织机构
institutional interplay 制度互动(指一种制度的发展、运作和有效性,乃至更宽泛方面明显受到其他制度规则和程序的影响。国际法律制度互动是指一种国际法律制度与另一种或更多法律制度产生交互感应之关系。它既是对制度不可能彼此孤立存在的事实描述,也是对制度在功能和运作上彼此重叠或影响人的现象概括)
institutional investor (自然人投资者的)机构投资人
institutional jurisprudence 制度法理学

institutional law 组织法
institutional legislative positivism 制度法律实证主义
institutional regulation 机构监管
institutional setting 制度性调整
institutional theories of law 制度法学(指涉及将各种制度作为法律上人格化的一套社会关系的理论)
institutional unit 法人单位
institutionalism n. 制度主义,制度论
institutionalization n. 制度化
institutionalization of international community 国际社会的组织化
institutionalize v. 使制度化,使成惯常行为
institutionalized organization 常设的组织机构
institutiones (罗马法)法律的基础教科书,法律基础著作,如《盖尤斯法学阶梯》《查士丁尼法学阶梯》;总则性质的著作
institutions of government 政府机构
instruct v. 1.托办(指把事情告诉他人,委托他人办理。如托办人委托律师,律师委托状师去办理文据或诉讼辩护等)2.指导,指示;通知;命令;教育;训练
instruction n. 教育,训练,教导;(复)指令,命令;案情介绍,说明书,指示(指由法官就案件涉及的法律方面的问题给陪审团的说明或指示);(大陆法系诉讼程序中的)取证阶段(程序)
instructions on the reverse of form 表格背面的说明
instructive medical procedures 导入性医疗程序(指"事先知情同意"最初在医学中提出的"导入性医疗程序")
instructor n. 指导者,教员,(美)讲师
instrument n. 1.文据(指书面的正式法律文件,包括契据、遗嘱、合约、记录、汇票等);(正式)文件,证券 2.手段;工具
instrument *inter vivos* 生前(转让财产)所立的文件
instrument of agreement to sell 预卖书据
instrument of appeal 上诉文件,上诉书
instrument of commercial credit 商业信用证券
instrument of credit 信用证券,信贷工具(手段)
instrument of crime 犯罪工具
instrument of evidence 证据文件
instrument of government of the protectorate (英)摄政政府约法
instrument of justice 审判文件
instrument of law 法律文件
instrument of law to advance human potential 促进人类潜力的法律文件
instrument of payment 支付手段(工具)
instrument of ratification 批准书
instrument of succession 继承证书,遗嘱
instrument of torture 刑具
instrument of ratification (国际法)批准书(指对一个条约正式承认的签发国确认或同意的批准书,并由缔约方交换或交由指定国或国际组织保存。见 ratification 4)
instrument payable in foreign exchange 外国货币本位的付款证券
instrument to bearer (或 obligations to bearer; bearer paper) 无记名证券;凭票支付的票据
instrument to order 记名票据
instrument under hand 署名法律文件
instrumental case study 工具性个案研究
instrumental power 获得的权势[托马斯·霍布斯(Thomas Hobbes)将权势分为两类:自然权势与获得的权势,前者依靠身体与思想能力,后者则依靠财富、名誉或朋友等其他手段]
instrumentalism n. 工具主义
instrumentality n. 媒介;工具,手段
Instrumentality Doctrine 工具说[主要适用于美国公司法。即若一公司的组织、业务在很大程度上受另一公司控制而沦为后一公司之工具,前一公司则被视为后一公司之子公司,不具独立法人人格,而一公司对前一公司的债务承担责任。此工具说是由美国学者 Power 鲍威尔提出的,该说认为公司成为控股东的"工具"或者是"另一个自我(说) Alter Ego Doctrine"时,公司的面纱将要被揭开,由控股东对公司债务直接承担责任。见 Agency Doctrine]
instrumentary witness 公证书(文件等)的

见证人

instrumentum (历史上)文件,契约,文据;特别是指没有盖有印鉴的文件,如英庄园法庭的卷宗或租佃登记册(court roll)

insubordination (18世纪)1.有意忽视雇主的指示,特别是这种行为造成雇主有理由终止工人的雇用 2.不服其主管和领导的行为,特别是拒绝服从被授权的上级官员发布的命令

insubordination in the military 军中的反抗者,不顺从者

insufficiency n. 不足,不充分,缺乏

insufficiency of consideration (英美法)对价不充分

insufficiency of evidence 证据不足

insufficient a. 不足的,不充分的;不能胜任的;不适当的

insufficient evidence 不充分的证据

insufficient prestation 给付不足

insufficient quorum 不足法定人数

insular cases 海岛案件,岛民案件,海岛系列案件[指海岛系列案件是一组在1901到1904年间发生的涉及美国联邦宪法及《权利宣言》之海外领土适用的14个判例的总称,这些案件产生于美国结束西班牙——美国战争(1898年)之后,并依据战后条约获得领土之后。美国联邦最高法院为顺应民意,最终通过海岛系列案件把政治纠纷转变为联邦宪法上的条文]

insular courts (美)海岛法院(指国会设立对其岛属行使管辖权的联邦法院)

insulate v. 隔离,使孤立;绝缘

insult n./v. 侮辱;无礼,侮慢;凌辱;损害/侮辱;损害;冒犯;蔑视;攻击;刺激

insulting behavio(u)r 侮辱行为

insurability n. 可保险性;应当保险

insurable a. 可保险的,应保险的

insurable event 可保(险)事故

insurable interest 可保(险)利益,可保(险)权益,可保险的物,保险利益

insurable loss 可保险的损失

insurable person 可保险的人

insurable property 可保(险)财产(指可接受保险的财产)

insurable risk 可保危险

insurable value 可保(险)价值

insurance n. 保险,保险业;安全保障;保险(金)额;保险单(通常亦称做 policy);保险费(通常亦称作 premium);保证

insurance adjuster 保险调停人,保险理算人(指为保险公司决定和处理索赔的调解处理人)

insurance against all risks 保全险

insurance against death 死亡保险

insurance against litigation 诉讼保险

insurance agent 保险代理人,保险代理行

insurance amount 保险金额

insurance application 投保单;保险申请

insurance broker 保险经纪人,保险掮客

insurance business 保险业

insurance by way of indemnity 补偿保险

insurance certificate 保险凭证,保险证书;分保单

insurance claim 保险索赔,保险赔偿请求权

insurance company 保险公司

insurance contract 保险合同(契约)

insurance co-operative 保险合作社

insurance court 保险法庭(院)

insurance coverage 保险范围,保险项目

insurance in force 有效保险(单)

insurance indemnity 保险赔偿

insurance industry 保险行业

insurance industry antitrust exemption 保险业适用除外

insurance interest 保险利益

insurance law 保险法

insurance market 保险市场

insurance money 保险金

insurance obligation 保险义务

insurance of damage 损害保险

insurance of transport, by inland or by air 陆空运输保险

(The) Insurance Ombudsman Bureau 保险申诉(或调查巡视)专员署[指在英国,金融申诉专员(FOS)经历了一个由保险申诉专员署(IOB)到金融申诉专员服务公司(FOS)、由从业者自发组织设立到法律要求必须设立的变化过程。金融服务管理局(Financial Service Authority)任免

FOS 的董事会主席和董事会成员(任免董事会主席需经财政部同意),对 FOS 是否发挥法律上的申诉审查功能进行监督。见 Financial Ombudsman Service]
insurance on hull 船舶保险
insurance on life (=life insurance) 人寿保险,人身保险
insurance on the life of another 以他人生命投保的保险契约
insurance period 保险期
insurance policy (1869 年)1.保单,保险合同 2.评述此类合同的文件,常缩略为 policy(亦称 policy of insurance; contract of insurance)
insurance policy limits 对保险单(披露程序)的限制
insurance premium 保险费
insurance premium unexpired 未过期的保险费
insurance proceeds 保险收益,保险赔款
insurance receipt 保险收据,暂保单
insurance risk 可保风险,保险危险
insurance ship 保险单
insurance value 可保价值,保险价值
insurant n. 被保险人,要保人
insure v. 保险;保障,保证
(the) insured (=assured) n./a. 被保险人,要保人;投保人/保险的;保险范围以内的(the insured 或 assured 在美国不仅指以其存有保险利益的财产为保险标的的人,同时亦指提出投保申请的人及于危险的事故发生后享有保险金请求权的人)
insured amount 保险金额
insured exporter 被保险出口商
insured letter 保价信
insured liability 保险责任
insured object 保险对象,保险客体
insured person 被保险人
insured property 保险财产
insured sum 保险总额
insured unemployment rate 有保险的失业率
insured value 投保价值,保险价值
insurer n. 保险人,承保人;保险公司
insurgency (=insurgence) n. 暴动,起义;叛乱状态;造反(行动)
insurgent a. 叛乱的;起义的,反抗的
insurgent body 叛乱团体
insurgent clique 叛乱集团
insurrection n. 起义;叛乱,暴动,造反
insurrectionary a. 起义的;叛乱的;暴动的,造反的
insurrectionary officer 起义军官
insurrectionary personnel 起义人员
insurrectionist n. 起义者;叛乱者;暴动者,造反者;支持暴动者
intact a. 完整的,未受损的,未经触动的
intact family (父母与子女共同生活在一起的)完整的家庭
intake clerk 接待书记员
intangible a./n. 无形的,无实体的;不可捉摸的,难以确定的/无形物;不可捉摸的事物
intangible assets 无形资产
intangible damage 无形损害
intangible (personal) property 无形财产
intangible right 无形权利
intangible things 无形财产,无形物
intangible value 无形价值
integral a. 整体的,构成整体所必要的
integrate circuit (IC) 集成电路
integrated a. 成为整体的;综合的;全面的;统筹的
integrated agreement 整体协议,综合协议,全面协议
integrated bar 联合律师协会(指美国的一种律师体制,即在各地区法院的所有职业律师必须属于此组织,它受该地区的最高法院监督);统一律师协会(亦称 integration of the bar)
integrated contract 全面合同(契约)(指包括当事人全部协议范围的合同,由于当事人对合同作出他们协议的最后表述,不准许用口头证据加以辩论或修改)
integrated fund 综合基金
integrated (或 **integrative**) **jurisprudence** 整体法学,统一法理学
integrated product policy (IPP) 整合产品政策(指欧盟在 1992 年第五届欧洲环境行动方案中提出的一份"整合产品政策"绿

皮书,开始实施以产品为导向的环境对策——是一种着眼于持续改进产品生命周期全过程环境影响的政策)

integration n. (17世纪)1.整合,一体化,结合成为一个整体(指使组合成为一个整体的过程)2.(合同法)合同的完整性,合同的完整文本(指对当事方的协议的充分表述,故优先于当事方先前所有的合议,其法律效果在于任何一方当事人此后不得反对或增加此合同的条款。亦称 merger)3.(遗产和遗嘱)结合性的遗嘱[指一个以上的书面文稿结合在一个简单文件(simple document)中构成遗嘱的书面遗嘱或遗言(testament)。在执行遗嘱和了解遗嘱内所含意图时,其他相关多份文件必须出示。当关系到亲笔遗嘱时,不同时间可能有不止一份亲笔文件,因此结合性的遗嘱文件发表就更为复杂]4.企业一体化[指不同种族或民族结合在一起成立的现存的一个机构或一个企业。如公立学校(public school)的目的在于消除种族歧视。见 desegregation]5.(反垄断法)公司的履行职能[指一个公司可以在自由市场(open market)取得的履行职能。一个公司或企业通过公司本身进入市场,在次级市场(secondary market)获得一个公司或与一个次级市场经营的一个公司签订合同则可达到结合体。亦称 vertical integration。见 vertical merger]6.(证券)证券交易[指要求或规定所有的证券出售(security offerings),在指定时期均被视为单一出售(simple offerings),其目的在于免于注册登记(registration)。证券交易委员会(S.E.C)和法院应用五个准则或标准(criterion)来决定是否两个或更多交易标示证券的相同出售的一部分。这五个标准是:这些出售是否是单一财务计划的部分、这些出售是否与相同类别的证券的发行(issuance)有关、这些出售的组成是否在同一时间、相同型的对价(same type of consideration)是否可被接受、这些出售的组成是否为了一个相同的总目的(general purpose)]

integration grouping 一体化集团
integration of local government and commune management (中)政社合一(指农村经济体制改革前人民公社制度的一项组织原则,现政社已分开)
integration of manual and mental labo(u)r (中)体力劳动与脑力劳动相结合
integration theory (美)整体论,一体化理论(其目的是解决财产所有人住所地的州缴纳财产税的问题)
integration-requirements principle 一体化要求原则(指各项环保要求必须融入其他各项共同体政策的制定和实施之中)
integrity n. 1.完整(性),完善,无缺 2.正直,诚实⟨a man of moral integrity⟩(一个有道德的人)3.尊严;"原则一贯性[指不是在知识论和道德层面谈论融贯性,而是要去评估裁判理论中的具体含义,所以这个理论成为讨论核心。德沃金的"原则一贯性"主张具备双重前提:其一,相互支持的关系;其二,相互支持关系背后体现了特定道德原则。他将法律实践视为一种"诠释性实践"。诠释性实践有两个基本要素:第一,预设实践非但存在,而且必含有价值,亦即必适用于达成某种利益或目的或执行某项原则。简言之,必有某种本旨或要点(points)。第二,预设实践并不是一直以来被看成的那幅样子,反而敏感于本旨或要点,因此,该实践必须由那个要点或本旨来理解、适用、扩张、调整、修正或限制;也就是说人们必须赋予实践意义,然后再根据这个意义将实践重新构造出来。见(the) best justification]
(the) intellect and the conscience of free men 自由人的理性与良知
integrity of law 法律的完整性
integrity of the individual 个人的尊严
integrity right (版权)归属的完整权利(指作者和艺术工作者坚决主张他们的创作权利,未经他们授权不得改变。这种归属的权利在大陆法系国家包括欧洲大部地区是艺术工作者的一种道德权利。但美国大部分地区并不采用。见 moral rights)
intellectual n./a. 知识分子/智力,理智的,用脑筋的,需智力的
intellectual commitment 智力信奉,智力

投入
intellectual competitors 智力竞技者
intellectual education 智育
intellectual freedom 智力活动自由
intellectual leadership 智力领导
intellectual life 理性生活
intellectual property 知识产权,智力财产,版权
intellectual right 知识权利,知识产权
intellectual work 脑力劳动(工作);(复)智力作品
intelligence n. 情报,消息;智力,理解力;才智;情报人员;情报机构
intelligence agent 情报人员;谍报员
intelligence bureau 情报局,情报处
intelligencer n. 报道者;报信者;间谍,情报员
intelligible a. 可理解的,明白易懂的;仅用智力了解的,概念的
intemperance n. 饮酒过度,酗酒;无节制,放纵
intend v. 想要,打算;意指,意思是;打算使……成为
intendance n. 监督,管理;行政管理部门
intendant n. 监督人,管理人,经理人;(法、西、葡等国封建王朝时)总督,州长,地方行政官
intended a. 故意的,有意的;打算中的;预期的,未来的;未婚的
intended child 预期的孩子[指代孕生子合同(surrogacy contract)产生的孩子。见 surrogate mothers, intentional parent]
intended effect 预期效果
intended marriage 订婚
intended party 被状告的当事人
intended wife 未婚妻(见 betrothed)
intending spouses 未婚夫妻
intendment n. (法律文件上词句的)含义,意旨(指文件的真实意义及其目的)
intendment of law 法律含义,法律意图
intense pressure 强烈的压力
intensification n. 强化,增强
intensify v. 加剧,增强
intensive consultations "密集磋商"
intent n. 意图,故意;目的,计划,意义,

打算
intent and motive 目的和动机
intent before the fact 事前故意
intent theory 意向论
intent to kill 故意杀人
intentio n. 1.(罗马法)意图,目的;程式诉讼的部门(指原告在司法审理员前针对被告提出的权利主张在程式诉讼中陈述的部分。见 *formula* 1) 2.(古英国法)(物权诉讼中)原告对物权主张的诉讼声明[该词条是诉讼状(*narratio*)一词的早期名称。复数为 *intentiones*]
intention(或 **connotation**) n. 内涵,含蓄,含义,故意,蓄意;(文件等的)含义;意图,意向;目的;(复)结婚的意向(尤指婚娶背后隐藏的意图)
intention agreement 意向协定
intention of a clause 条款的意旨
intention of a document 文件的意旨
intention of company 公司意旨
intention of parliament statute 议院法规的意旨
intention of the legislator 立法者的立法要旨
intention to contract 缔约目的,意向书
intentional a. 故意的,有意(识)的
intentional act 故意行为
intentional concealment 故意隐瞒(事实真相)
intentional crime 蓄意犯罪,故意犯罪
intentional flooding 故意决水(罪)
intentional homicide 故意杀人
intentional infliction 有意伤害
intentional injury 故意伤害
intentional interference with property 故意损害财产
intentional interference with the person 故意侵害人身
intentional killing 故意杀人(罪)
intentional negligence 故意过失
intentional offence 故意犯罪
intentional offender 故意犯
intentional parent 预期(或蓄意)的父母(指有意拥有并抚养一个孩子,而与代孕母亲签订合同,代孕母亲接受法定母亲的丈夫的精子进行人工授精,怀孕生产,产

后将亲权转移给合法的、即预期的父母）（见 surrogate-parenting agreement）
intentional tort 故意的侵权行为
intentionality n. 目的性（见 creativity）
inter 中间
inter alia 除别的以外；在其他事物中；特别是；其中包括
* *Inter arma silent leges.* In time of war the laws are silent. 在战乱期间，法是无能为力的。
inter conjuges 夫妻间
inter nos 在我们之间；不得外传
* *Inter pares non est potestas.* Among equals, one has not authority over the other. 在（机会、责任等方面）同等地位者之间，谁亦无权支配另一方。
inter partes 在当事人之间
inter partes summons 对诉讼当事人双方的传票
inter se（或 **inter sese**） 在他们之间，在一组成员之间（以区别于在其他人之间）
inter virum et uxorem 夫妻之间
inter vivos 在世时；生者之间；生前（赠与）
Inter-American Court of Human Rights 美洲国家人权法院
Inter-American Juridical Committee 美洲国家司法委员会
Inter-American Multilateral Parts 美洲国家多边合约
Inter-American Treaties and Conventions (Organization of American States) 美洲国家之间的条约和协议（美洲国家组织）
inter-bank rate 银行间汇率，银行间利率
inter-departmental organization 部内制的人事机构（指欧洲大陆如法、德等国，在行政组织系统内各机关中设立人事机构组织的一种制度。它不同于美、日等国在行政机构之外，独立设立人事机构的制度）
inter-generational and intra-generational equity 世代衡平
inter-governmental a. 政府间的
inter-governmental cooperation 政府间的合作
Inter-Governmental Maritime Consultative Organization （联合国）政府间海事协商组织
inter-judge difference 法官之间的差别
interact v. 相互作用,相互影响
interaction n. 互相作用,相互影响
interactive multimedia works 互动多媒体著作（指具有数位化媒体时代的媒介特征，超出传统平面静态或动态的单一媒体形式，而成复数形式的互动多媒体著作，其著作权可归属于电脑程序著作、视听著作、语文著作、编辑著作等或创设新型类别著作如称"多位著作"）
interactive on-demand 互动索取式
interactivity of website 网络交换原则
interagenerational equity 代内公平（指代内的所有人，不论其国籍、种族、性别、经济发展水平和文化等方面差异，对于利用自然资源和享受清净好环境享有平等权利）
intercede v. 代为求情；从中调停,说情
intercept v. 窃听,侦听；截取
interception n. 窃听；侦听；截取；阻止
interceptor n. 窃听器；截取者；障碍物；阻止者；拦截人
intercession n. 仲裁；调解；说情；从中调停
intercessor n. 调解人；说情者,从中调停者
Interchange of Data Telecommunication 数据电传交换统一行为守则（1987年9月，国际商会执行理事会令第51届会议通过这一守则，旨在为EDI用户提供一套国际公认的行为准则）
interchangeability n. 可互换性,可交替性
interchangeably ad. 可交替地,可互换地
intercommoning n. 相互供用（指相连的两块领地,依习惯居民相互准许放牧者）；交际,来往,相互关系；交流
intercommunity n. 共用；共通性
interconversion n. 互相兑换,互相交换
intercourse （15世纪）1.交往,往来,联系（指生意、贸易间的往来,政府部门间的往来、联系以及类似情况）2.身体上的性接触,性交,特别是阴茎进入女子的阴道之中
interdependence school 相互依存学派
interdependent a. 相互依赖的,互相依存的
interdependent utility function 相依效用

函数
interdependent world　相互依存的世界
interdict n.　禁令;禁制,禁止;停止宗教教权的禁令
interdicted person　禁治产者
interdiction n.　禁止,制止;禁治产
interdiction of commercial intercourse　禁止商务交往
interdictor n.　受禁治产人
interdictory a.　禁止的,停止的,禁令的
interdictum n.　令状[指(罗马法中)长官在紧急情况下根据一方多数人的请求发布做或不做某事的命令,其目的在保护公共利益和公共秩序]
interdictum adipiscendae possessionis　占有权证明(令)状
interdictum exhibitoria　出示性令状(罗马法中的令状分为出示性、禁止性和恢复原状性;此出示性令状指为保卫某人的权利,要求另一人出示前者的子女或解放自由人)
interdictum guod vi aut clam　(罗马法)强制和秘密的禁令(指针对一个用暴力并秘密改变或占有权利要求请求人的财产所发布的禁令。该禁令要求被告将财产恢复到原先的状况。见 *actio vi bonorum raptorum*)
interdictum popularis　民众令状(罗马法中对于令状可分为保护私人利益的令状和保护公共利益的令状,后者人人均可申请,故称民众令状)
interdictum prohibitoria　(罗马法)禁止性的令状(指禁止人们做某种危害公共利益之事。见 *interdictum exhibitoria*)
interdictum recuperandae possessionis　恢复占有的令状
interdictum restitutoria　(罗马法)恢复原判性的令状(指命令已做危害公共利益事情的人恢复原状。见 *interdictum exhibitoria*)
interdictum retinendae possessionis　持续占有的令状
interdictum simplex　单独命令(指对当事者一方的命令)
interdisciplinary research　跨学科检索
＊*Interdum evenit ut exceptio quae prima fa-cie justa videtur tamen inique noceat.*　It sometimes happens that a plea which seems prima facie just, nevertheless is injurious and unequal. 表面上似乎公正的抗辩,常可能是有害而不公正的。
interesse　权益,利益,利息;收益
interesse termini　(普通法上)土地未来的租借权益
interessenjurisprudens(或 **jurisprudence of interests**)　利益法理学
interest n.　1.利息;利益;权益;股权;利害关系 2.重要性;影响 3.行业,势力 4.财产权益;所有权;附加物 5.关心,兴趣 6.(证据法)对(法庭可接受的)证据的死者声明
interest bill　附息汇票
interest clause　利息条款(指汇票上注明支付票款时须加付利息的字句)
interest coupon　债券,息券,息票
interest due　到期利息
interest free loan　无息贷款
interest group in court　法院中利益集团(指经常主动卷入诉讼中的利益集团,它们与法院有关系,能通过一定的途径影响法院判决)
interest in domestic relation　家庭关系利益
interest in expectancy　期待的权益,预期利息
interest in fee　祖传土地上的权益
interest in incorporeal property　无形财产上的权益
interest in land　土地上的权益
interest legitime　合法的利息
interest of substance　物质利益
interest on arrears　延期利息
interest on capital　资本利息
interest on condition　附有条件的权益
interest on deposit　存款利息
interest on public debt　公债利息
interest on rediscount　再贴现利息;转贴现息
interest on the loan　借款利息
interest or expectancy test　利益与期待标准(指认定公司机会是否存在的一个最早标准,该标准由阿拉斯加法院在1990年 Lagarde v. Anniston Lime & Stone Co.一案

中确立,其理论推导过程是:公司董事获取的财产具有推定信托之性质,公司机会也是一种具有信托性质的财产,如果公司在获取此种机会时对该种性质的机会享有有害或享有实体期待的话,则公司机会规则不应当被用来阻止公司董事购买任何可能对公司有用的财产,而仅用来阻止他们获得公司需要的或正努力取得的或者他负有为公司取得义务的财产。见 corporate opportunity rule)

interest per annum (周)年(利)息
interest policy 利息政策
interest rate 利率
interest rate swap 利率交换
interest rebate 利息回扣
interest representation model 利益代表模式
interest school of law 利益法学派
interest spread 利息差额
interest suit 决定遗产管理人的诉讼(指在遗产诉讼中为决定由谁管理死者的遗产而请求法院发给遗产管理证的诉讼)
interest surcharges 加收利息
interest tax 利息税
interest upon loans 放款利息
interest-bearing capital 借贷资本
interest-bearing debt certificate 计息负债证明书
interest-bearing loan certificate 计息贷款证明书
interest-bearing note 计息票据,附息票据
interest-free a. 无息的,免息的
interest-free loan 无息贷款
interest-group activity 利益集团活动
interested a. 有利害关系的;有股份的;偏私的,不公平的;关心的,感兴趣的
interested motive 不纯动机
interested party 利害关系人,有利害关系的当事人
interested person 利害关系人
interested witness 偏心的证人,与案件有利害关系的证人
interface 接口,接面(指一种计算机软件,但其版权保护仍有争议)
interface point (运送)交接点
interfere v. 干涉,干预;发生冲突;与……

抵触;妨害,妨碍;仲裁,调停;(美)对发明专利权提出争议
interfere with the course of justice 阻碍审判进程
interference n. 1.手段,干涉(指插手于他人的事务之间的行为)2.妨碍,阻碍,妨害 3.(专利)美国专利和商标局的行政诉讼在两个或两个以上申请人主张同一发明或者在一项申请涉及现行专利时以确定谁具有资格获得专利[具有以下情况,这种诉讼(proceeding)就会发生:在相同的发明声称①两个悬而未决的申请,或②一个未决的申请和另一发布在一年未决申请期内提出申请专利。亦称 priority contest]4.(商标)在美国专利和商标局的一件行政诉讼以确定一方当事人想注册的商标是否会造成在消费者之中与另一当事方的商标相混淆[可以举行行政听证(administrative hearing)以确定谁的商标战胜,但申请人往往撤销他们的申请并设计新的商标]
interference in election 妨碍选举(罪)
interference with airspace 侵犯领空
interference with contract right/relationship 妨害合同权利或关系
interference with family relations 妨碍家庭关系
interference with public function 妨碍公务
interference with right of privacy 妨害私人秘密,干涉个人隐私(罪)
interference with the exercise of public functions 妨害执行公务(罪)
interference with the liberty of another 干涉他人自由
interference with witness 干扰证人(尤指企图诱导证人改变证供或诱使证人提出某一证供或不出庭作证等)
interfund settlements 基金清账
interfund transfer 基金转账
intergenerational equity 代际公平[指美国著名国家法学家伊迪丝·布朗·韦斯(Edith Brown Weiss)教授于20世纪80年代提出的代际公平理论。1984年他在《生态法季刊》上发表了《行星托管:自然保护与代际公平》(The Planetary Trust: Conser-

vation and Intergenerational Equity) 一文,随后于 1989 年出版专著《公平对待未来人类:国际法、共同遗产与世代间衡平》,1990 年又在《美国国籍法杂志》上发表《为了环保,我国对未来各代的权利与义务》(Our Right and Obligation to Future Generations for the Environment),1997 年在《杜兰环境法杂志》上发表《对巴雷西(Barresi)的"对超越对未来的各代公平"的回答》(A Reply to Barresi's "Beyond Fairness to Future Generations"),全篇论述了代际公平理论,并回应有关学者的批评。其中,《公平对待未来人类:国际法、共同遗产与世代间衡平》一书是韦斯代际公平理论的集中体现。他借用全球性环境危机这一话语背景,在环境哲学、环境伦理学、环境政治学、环境法学等领域产生了全球性的深远影响。"代际公平"成为时髦学术用语,为众多学者接受,成为环保的正当理由,并加以使用。然而代际公平理论中的"后代人"是指"和现在的世代没有重叠的那些世代",即"那些将生活在未来,但是直到现在最后一个活着的人死亡以后还没有出生的未来世代"。实际上,有学者认为这种代际公平理论是建立在两个错误认识的基础上,即把集合概念的人类视为类概念的人类和把地球环境资源财产化]

intergovernmental conference 政府间内部会议

Intergovernmental Organization 政府间组织

interim a. 暂时的,临时的;间歇的;暂行的;期间的,期中的,过渡期间的

interim agreement 临时协定

interim attachment 临时扣押;暂行扣押

interim audit 期中审计

interim award 临时裁定

interim certificate 临时证书;临时股票证券

interim commission 临时委任

interim commissioner 临时专员,临时委员

interim custody 临时拘押,暂行拘押

interim damages payments order 中期支付损害赔偿令

interim dividends 期中股利,临时红利

interim injunction 中间禁止令,临时性强制令

interim interdict 临时禁令

interim interest 中间利息,中期利息

interim measures 临时措施

interim order 暂行法令;临时命令;(正式判决前的)临时裁决令

interim payment 中期付款

interim plan 过渡计划

interim president 临时总统,临时主席,临时议长;(银行)临时行长;临时院长或庭长,临时社长,临时校长,临时董事长,临时总经理

interim procedures 暂行办法

Interim Procedures for the Handling of Loans by the Bank of China to Chinese-Foreign Joint Ventures 《中国银行办理中外合资经营企业贷款暂行办法》

Interim Procedures of the State Import-Export Commission and the Ministry of Foreign Trade of the People's Republic of China Concerning the System of Export Licensing 《中华人民共和国国家进出口管理委员会、对外贸易部关于出口许可制度的暂行办法》

interim provisions 暂行规定

Interim Provisions of the State Council of the People's Republic of China for the Control of Resident Representative Offices of Foreign Enterprises 《中华人民共和国国务院关于管理外国企业常驻代表机构的暂行规定》

interim receiver 临时接收官;破产财产的临时管理人

interim regulations 暂行条例

Interim Regulations on Foreign Exchange Control of the People's Republic of China 《中华人民共和国外汇管理暂行条例》

Interim Rules on Transfer of Right to Use Land 1990 (中)《1990 年关于城市土地使用权转让的暂时规定》

Interim Rules to Prohibit Charging Enterprises with Duties of 28 April 1988 (Fq1177) 《1988 年 4 月 28 日禁止承担企业责任暂时法规》

interim statement 期中决算表
interim valuation 临时估价
interlineation n. 中间书写;写或印于行间的词句
interlocking director 兼任经理(又译:连锁董事),兼任主任
interlocking directorate (美)连锁董事会
interlocking transaction 连续交易,联销交易
interlocutory a. 1.对话的 2.临时的,非最后的,中间的 3.(法院在诉讼期间发出的)临时性命令的;中间裁决的(见 interlocutory decree)
interlocutory appeal 中间上诉
interlocutory application 诉讼中间(提交)的申请
interlocutory decree 中间裁决[指衡平法中的一种裁决,即在诉讼进行中并非对全案件作最终裁判,只是就某一方面的问题作出的一种裁决。对案件的全面问题所作的判决叫最终判决(final decree)]
interlocutory divorce decree 离婚中期(临时)裁决令
interlocutory injunction 中间(临时)禁令;中间(临时)强制令;临时性禁止令[在美国分为预备性禁止令(preliminary injunction)和临时性禁止令(temporary restraining orders)]
interlocutory judg(e)ment 见 interlocutory decree
interlocutory order 中间命令,中间裁决(指美国民事诉讼中法庭为给予临时救济而作出的命令,或依据当事人在诉讼中所提出的申请,根据是非曲直断案而作出的命令。见 appealable order)
interlocutory proceedings 中间程序
interlocutory writ 中间令状
interlope v. 1.侵占他人权益 2.无执照营业;妨碍他人事务
interloper n. 1.妨碍者;侵入者;(为营利目的)干涉他人事务者 2.无执照营业者
intermarriage n. 近亲结婚,族内通婚;近族间通婚
intermarry v. 近族通婚;不同种族、民族间由于通婚而结合

intermeddling n. 多管闲事;干涉他人(事务)
intermediary n./a. 中间人,调解人;媒人;媒介物;手段,工具/中间的,居间的;媒介的;中间人的,调解人的
intermediary-specialist 经纪人,专家
intermediate n./a. 居间人,调解人,中间物/中间的,居间的;中级的
intermediate appellate court 中级上诉院,(大写)(美)受理调解上诉法院
intermediate body 中间机构
intermediate court 中级法院
intermediate criminal court 中级刑事法院
intermediate law 过渡时期法律
intermediate people's court (中)中级人民法院
intermediate principles 中间原则(指约翰·菲尼斯在分析道德思想体系运用这条原则决定选择和协调基本善的可行方式——在一个较高层面上区分道德选择和不道德选择。见 basic goods)
intermediate scrutiny (美)中度审查标准(见 minimal scrutiny)
intermediate sentence 中间制裁;中间处罚
intermediate trial court (美)中间审理法院(指对初审及上诉案件均有一般管辖权)
intermediate witness 中间证人(指根据他人证词来作证的证人)
intermediated market transaction 市场间接型金融(金融是经济的血液,经济发展方式转变的首要核心在于金融发展方式,"第三金融"的市场间接金融市场是金融市场发展的一个趋势,是连接直接金融市场和间接金融市场的平台,是打通间接金融和直接金融的纽带)
intermediation n. 调解,调停;做中间人
intermediator n. 中间人,调解人,仲裁人
interministerial council 部际会议
intermittent dumping 间歇性倾销,短期的倾销
intermittent insanity 间歇性精神病
intermittent presidentialism (= alternating presidentialism) 交替式总统制
intermixture n. 混合物(指一种物品与另

一种物品的混合)
intermodal transportation 协调联运,联合运输
intern v. (尤指战时)禁闭;(在一定区域内的)拘留;扣留(交战国的人员、船只等)
internal a. 内部的;国内的,内政的;内在的;本质上的
internal affairs 内部事务
internal auditing system 内部(财务)牵制制度;内部审计制度
internal check system 内部(财务)牵制制度;内部(财务)复核制度
internal complaint procedure 内部申诉程序
internal connecting link 内在联系
internal contradiction 内部矛盾
internal control system 内部管制制度,内部监督制度
internal discipline 内部纪律
internal evidence 内证(指事物本身提供的证据)
internal injury 内伤
internal intervention 内部干预
internal labor force 内部劳动力
internal law 国内法,内部法
internal law of nations 内在的国际法(指主张国际法的性质及其约束力应以自然法为论据的一种学说,格劳秀斯学派称之为内在的国际法;有些学者则称之为自然国际法)
internal legislation 国内立法
internal loan 国内贷款
internal logic 内在联系,内在逻辑
internal point of view 内在观点(指持有此观点的人可接受一种法律规则,并以此指导人的行为。见 external point of law)
internal police (美)州的治安权(指各州具有有关维护公共安全、健康、道德等方面立法的权力)
internal postmortem examination 尸体内部检验
internal reactionary (中)国内反动派
internal relation 内部关系
internal revenue 国内税收
Internal Revenue Code (美)国内税收法,美国国内税务法则
Internal Revenue Service (IRS) (美)国内税务署[指美国财政部的一个部门,负责管理和实施国内税(务)收法规和其他税务法规(除涉及酒类、烟草、军火、爆炸物等之外)]
internal rules of labo(u)r 内部劳动规则
internal security 国内治安;内部安全
internal security force 国家保安部队
internal self-determination 对内自决权
internal trade 国内贸易
internal troubles 内讧
internal war 内战
internal waters 内水,国内水域(见 national waters)
international n./a. 取得一国国籍而长期侨居国外者;(大写)国际(国际社会主义者与国际共产主义者的国际性组织。例如:the First International 第一国际, the Second International 第二国际, the Third International 第三国际)/国际的,世界的
international accounting firms 国际会计师事务所
international act 国际行为
international adjudication 国际(法庭)裁判
international administration 国际行政
international administrative law 国际行政法
international affairs 国际事务
international agency 国际机构
international agreement 国际协定
international agreements of investment protection 投资保护的国际协定
international antitrust law 国际反托拉斯法
international arbitral award 国际仲裁裁决(书)
international arbitral tribunals 国际仲裁法庭
international arbitration 国际仲裁
international arena 国际活动场所
international aspect 国际层面
International Association for Penal Law 国际刑法学会(成立于1924年)

International Association for Philosophy of Law and Social Philosophy 国际法哲学和社会哲学协会(成立于 1909 年)

International Association of Comparative Law 国际比较法协会(成立于 1960 年)

International Association of Democratic Lawyers 国际民主法律工作者协会

International Association of Lawyers 国际法律工作者协会(成立于 1927 年)

International Association of Legal Science 国际法律科学协会(又译:国际法学会,成立于 1950 年)

International Association of Police Chiefs 国际警察局长协会

International Atomic Energy Agency (联合国)国际原子能机构(又译:国际原子能总署)

international authority 国际权威;国际机构

International Bank for Reconstruction and Development (联合国)国际复兴开发银行(亦称世界银行 World Bank)

International Bar Association (IBA) 国际律师协会(1947 年 1 月在纽约成立,非政府间国际组织,现设于伦敦)

international behavio(u)r 国际行为

International Bill of Human Rights (International Bill of Rights) 国际人权宪章(这只是一种提法,至今尚未形成任何法律文件,其中应包括哪些国际人权文书,各种提法不一)

International Bill of Rights 国际权利法案(指 1966 年的一项联合国协议)

international body 国际团体

international business transaction 国际商行为

International Bureau for the protection of Intellectual Property (版权)国际知识产权保护局[世界知识产权组织的前辈(predecessor),该局是将巴黎公约秘书处(Paris Convention's Secretariat),即巴黎公约国际局(the International Bureau for Paris Convention)与 1886 年《伯尔尼公约》合并而创立的,并受瑞士政府监督直至 1970 年该局已成为世界知识产权组织(WIPO)的一部分为止。该局亦称 Bureaux Internationaux Reunis pour la Protection de la Propriété Intellectuelle]

international canal 国际运河

international cargo transportation insurance 国际货物运输保险

international carriage 国际航运(或货运)

international case 国际案件

international case-law 国际判例法

International Chamber of Commerce (ICC) 国际商会

International Child Abduction Database (INCADAT) 国际儿童诱拐公约数据库

International Civil Aviation Organization 国际民用航空组织(为 1944 年《国际民用航空公约》的常设机构)

international civil jurisdiction 国际民事管辖权

international civil procedure 国际民事诉讼程序

international civil service 国际公务员制度,国际文官

international claims 国际求偿权

International Classification of Goods and Services for Registering Trademarks 《商品和劳务商标注册国际分类法》

international classification of patents 专利的国际分类

international clearing 国际清算;国际结算

international code 国际法,国际法典;国际电码

international code of conduct 国际行为准则

international comity 国际礼让

international comity theory 国际礼让说

international commercial arbitration 国际商业仲裁

international commercial contract 国际商事合同

international commercial law 国际商法

International Commission for Air Navigation 国际航空委员会(为《航空巴黎公约》的常设机构)

International Commission of Inquiry 国际调查委员会

International Commission of Jurists 国际

法学家委员会(成立于 1952 年)
international commitments 国际义务,国际承诺
International Committee of the Red Cross 国际红十字委员会
International Commodity Agreement 《国际商品协定》
international communist movement 国际共产主义运动
international community 国际社会
international competition 国际竞争
international conciliation 国际和解
international condominium 国际共管;国际共管区
international conduct 国际行为,国际行动
international conference 国际会议
international conflict 国际冲突
international congress 国会会议
International Constitutional Law 国际宪法
international context of this case 本案的国际背景,本案的国际来龙去脉
international contract 国际性合同(契约)
international control 国际管制,国际监督
international convention 国际公约
International Convention for the Unification of Certain Rules of Law Relating to Bills of Lading (1924) 1924 年《关于船舶载货提单法规的国际统一公约》[亦称《海牙规则》(1924 年)]
International Convention on Arrest of Ship (1999) 1999 年《国际扣船公约》(该公约于 1999 年 3 月 12 日在日内瓦定案,全文共 17 条。公约旨在规范有关船舶实施保全程序之各项问题)
International Convention on Civil Liability for Oil Pollution Damage 《国际油污民事责任公约》(1969 年在布鲁塞尔制定)
International Convention on Patents 《国际专利公约》
International Convention Relating to the Arrest of Seagoing Ships Brussels May 10, 1952 1952 年 5 月 10 日《(布鲁塞尔)扣押船公约》(《国际公约》,亦译《海船扣押国际公约》或《海船扣押公约》)

international cooperation 国际合作
international cooperation exploitation of natural resources 自然资源的国际合作开发
international copyright 国际版权
international copyright convention and agreement 国际版权公约和协定
International Copyright Treaties Implementing Rules (中)《实施国际著作权条约的规定》(指 1992 年 9 月 25 日国务院颁布的该项规定)
International Council for Commercial Arbitration 国际商业仲裁委员会
international court 国际法院(庭)
International Court of Justice (联合国)国际法院
international covenant 国际公约,国际专约,国际盟约
(the) International Covenant on Civil and Political Rights 《公民权利与政治权利国际公约》
international crime 国际罪行;违反国际法的罪行
international criminal clique 国际犯罪集团
International Criminal Code 《国际刑法典》
International Criminal Court 国际刑事法院
international criminal law 国际刑法
international criminal liability 国际刑事责任
International Criminal Police Organization 国际刑警组织(成立于 1923 年)
international custom(s) 国际习惯,国际惯例[《国际法院规约》第 38 条关于国际习惯(international custom)的表述为"作为通例之证明而经法律所接受的"。构成国际习惯需具备两个条件:一为通例(general practice),通常称为物质要素;二为法律确信(opionio juris),通常称为心理要素。这两者缺一不可。仅有物质要素存在,即使长期实行,也不能构成法律意义上的国际习惯,而会被视为国际礼让或国家实践。物质要素会随时间变化而变化,不存在法律约束力。心理要素的重要作用恰恰是使得所有存在着的国家实践改变原有的随意性成为必须遵守的法律义务。

因此,心理要素至关重要]
international delict 国际侵权行为
international delinquency 国际侵权行为,国际不法行为
International Development Association 国际开发协会(成立于1960年)
international development law 国际发展法(又译:国际开发法)
international direct investment 国际直接投资
international disarmament 国际裁军
international discovering procedure 国际调查取证程序,国际披露程序
international discovery 国际披露程序
international discovery procedure 国际调查取证程序,国际披露程序
international dispute 国际争端
international economic(al) law 国际经济法
international economic(al) order 国际经济秩序
international economic(al) organization law 国际经济组织法
international embargo 国际禁运
international environment law 国际环境法
international equilibrium 国际均势
international exchange crisis 国际外汇危机
International Express Carriage by Air 国际航空快递运输
International Federation for European Law 欧洲法国际联合会(成立于1961年)
International Federation of Accounts (IFA) 国际会计师联合会
International Finance Corporation 国际金融公司
international financial centre 国际金融中心
international financial institution 国际金融机构
International Food Safety Authorities Network (INFOSAN) 国际食品安全网络(2004年世界卫生组织为进一步开展与联合国粮农组织的合作而共同建立的)
international forum 国际讲坛
International Franchise Association 国际特许专营协会
international gendarme 国际宪兵

International Grotius Foundation for the Propagation of the Law of Nations 传播国际法格劳秀斯国际基金会(成立于1945年)
international guarantee 国际担保
international guardianship 国际监护(关系)
international humanitarian law 国际人道主义法
International Hydrographic Organization 国际海道测量组织
international indebtedness 国际负债
international insolvency 国际性的破产
International Institute for Unification of Private Law 国际统一私法学会
International Institute of Space Law 国际空间法学会(成立于1960年)
International Institute of the Unification of Private Law 国际统一私法研究所(成立于1926年)
international institution 国际机构
international instrument 国际文件,国际证书
international intervention 国际干预,国际干涉
international investment law 国际投资法
international investment trust 国际投资托拉斯
international issue of bonds 国际债券发行
international judicial review 国际司法复查
international judicial settlement 国际司法解决
International Juridical Institute 国际司法协会(成立于1918年)
international jurisdiction 国际管辖(权),国际裁判权;涉外管辖(权),涉外裁判权
International Labo(u)r Organization 国际劳工组织(1919年成立)
International Law 国际法(又称国际公法,古称万国法或万国公法。见 law of nations)
International Law Association 国际法律协会
International Law Association's Paris Mini-

mum Standard of Human's Rights Norms in a State of Emergency 《国际法协会紧急状态下人权准则巴黎最低标准》(1984年通过)
international Law Commission 国际法律委员会
international law doctrine of universal jurisdiction 国际法普遍管辖原理
international law in peace time 平时国际法
international law making 国际造法(指国家通过条约或习惯等方式,制定、承认、修改和废止国际法规范的活动;所谓国际法造法原则是指按国家在国际造法中所遵循的行为准则,它是国家据以进行国际造法的重要准绳,反映着国际造法的内在要求和精神品格)
international law of procedure 国际程序法
international law of transition 过渡国际法
international lawyer 国际法学者
international lease 国际租借
international legal assistance 国际司法协助
International Legal Centre 国际法律中心
international legal duty 国际法律义务
international legal order 国际法律秩序
international legal person 国际法人(又译:国际法律人格者,指国际法赋予法律上的人格并由此享受权利和承担义务的实体)
international legal personality 国际法人格
international legal process school 国际法律进程学派(主张探寻国际法作为一种法律在强制、判断和影响国际事务中的作用)
international legal relation 国际法律关系
international legal status 国际法律地位
international legal system 国际法律体系
international legislation 国际立法
international letting and hiring 国际租赁
international liability 国际责任
international licensing arrangements 国际发照办法
international liquidity 国际清偿能力;国际流通手段
international loan agreement 国际贷款协议
international mandate system 国际托管制度

international mandatory rules 国际强制性规范(指国际强制性规范要求不经冲突规范的指引或当事人的选择,无论涉外案件准据法为何都必须适用。而国内强制性规范服从于冲突规范的指引,作为准据法的组成部分得到适用)
International Maritime Bureau (IMB) 国际海事局
International Maritime Committee 国际海事委员会(成立于1897年)
international maritime law 国际海事法
International Maritime Organization (IMO) 国际海事组织
international market 国际市场
International Military Court (Tribunal) 国际军事法庭(院)
International Monetary Conference 国际金融会议,国际货币会议
International Monetary Fund 国际货币基金会,国际货币基金组织
international monetary law 国际货币法
international monetary system 国际货币制度
international money order 国际汇票,国际邮政汇票
international monitoring measures 国际监测措施
international morality 国际道德
international multilateral loans 国际多边贷款
international navigable waterway 国际可航水道
international obligation 国际债务;国际义务
International Opium Convention 《国际鸦片公约》
international order 国际秩序
international organization 国际组织
International Organization of Consumer Union (IOCU) 国际消费者组织联盟
International Patent Documentation Center 国际专利文献中心
International Patent Institute 国际专利学会
international payments 国际支付,国际

结算
international peace and security 国际和平与安全
International Pen 国际笔会(指国际间代表作者谈判集体许可证合同的组织之一,在不少国家设有分会)
international penal law 国际刑法
international personality 国际人格
international plant-engineering contract 国际工程承包合同(契约)
International Police 国际警察
International Post Union 万国邮政协会(又译:万国邮政联盟)
international practice 国际惯例,国际实践
international prestige 国际地位,国际声望
international private law (现多用 private international law) 国际私法
international prize court 国际捕获法庭(指决定战时在海上夺得船货等主权属何人的法庭)
international product liability law 国际产品责任法
international protection of copyright 版权的国际保护
international protection of human rights 人权的国际保护
international protection of intellectual property 知识产权的国际保护
international protection of patent 专利权的国际保护
international protection of trademark 商标权的国际保护
international public goods, service and policies 国际公共物品、服务和政策
international public law (现多用 public international law) 国际公法(通称国际法,称国际公法乃借以区别国际私法)
international public sector 国际公共部门
international reactionary 国际反动派
international recognition 国际承认
International Refugee Organization 国际难民组织
international regime 国际体制,国际制度
international regime theory 国际体制理论(指现代西方国际关系研究中涉及国际政治、经济、国际法、国际组织等诸多领域的较新课题)
International Regulations of Preventing Collisions at Sea 《国际海上避碰规则》(1960年)
international relation 国际关系
international remedies 国际补救方法
international remittance and exchange 国际汇兑
international restatement of general principles of contract law 合同法一般原则的国际重述
international right of correction 国际更正权
international rule of law 国际法治
International Rules for the Interpretation of Trade Terms (1990) 1990年《国际贸易术语解释通则》
international safeguard system 国际保障制度
international safety 国际安全
international sale of goods 国际货物销售合同(契约)(又译:国际货物买卖合同)
international sales transactions 国际间货物买卖
international sanctions 国际制裁
international sea areas 国际海域
International Sea-Bed Authority 国际海床管理局
International Sea-Bed Committee 国际海床委员会
international securities 国际证券
international service cooperation 国际劳务合作
international servitudes 国际地役权
international settlement 国际结算
international shipping legislation 国际航运立法
international shoe and its progeny 国际鞋业案以及其后遵循该案判决的判例
international shoe case 国际鞋业案(指美国 International Shoe Co. v. State of Washington 案,该案确立了一项规则,即若一外国公司被指定在某州诉讼,正当程序要求该外国公司在某州内的经营活动量必须

达到足以证明其在该州所在地最低限度联系的标准)
international shoe standard (美)国际鞋业案标准[指此标准应适用于所有形式的管辖(all forms of jurisdiction)]
international shoe test (美)国际鞋业判决中的标准(见 international shoe case)
international show down 国际性摊牌
international smuggling 国际走私(罪)
international sources of law 法的国际渊源
international specialization 国际专业化
international standard of justice 国际司法标准
international standard weights and measures 国际度量衡制
international standards 国际标准(规格),国际准则
international status 国际地位
international subcontraction 国际分包办法
international supervision 国际监察,国际监督
International Swaps and Derivatives Association (ISDA) 国际互换和衍生工具协会(1985年成立的国际互换和衍生工具协会是世界上最具权威性和代表性的场外衍生产品交易商协会,共吸收了来自58个国家的820多个会员机构。ISDA通过发布 ISDA 主协议、定义文件、交易确认书、信用担保文件等一系列场外交易文件群,制定了场外金融衍生产品交易规则。由于世界上绝大多数衍生产品的交易商均为其会员,其交易规则成为了实际上的全球交易规则)
international syndicated loans 国际银团贷款
international tax harmonization 国际税收协调[指一些国家或地区为了建立共同市场或经济集团,消除税收上对商品、资金、技术、劳力、人员流动的障碍,采取措施使集团内不同国家或地区的税收政策、税收制度(包括税种、税率)互助接近或统一,以减轻彼此之间的摩擦和冲突]
international telecommunication conflict 国际远程通讯(信)冲突
International Telecommunication Regulations (ITR) 国际电信规则
International Telecommunication Union 国际电信联盟
international terrorism 国际恐怖主义
international terrorist organization 国际恐怖组织
international tort 国际侵权行为(指包括违背国际义务的不正当行为或过错)
international trade charter 国际贸易宪章
international trade law 国际贸易法
international trade policy 国际贸易政策
international transaction 国际事务,国际交往
international transfer of payments 国际转账支付
international transfer of technology 国际技术转让
international transit 国际过境
international transportation fees 国际交通费
international treaty 国际条约
International Tribunal for the Law of the Sea 国际海洋法庭
International Tribunal of Arbitration 国际仲裁法庭
International Tribunals 国际法庭
international trusteeship system 国际托管制度
international unified regulation 国际统一规章
international uniform legal regime 国际统一法律体制
International Union of Credit and Investment Insurers (英、法、意、西的出口保险机构于1934年发起创建了)国际信用及投资保险协会(简称伯尼尔协会,目的在于增加国际合作,更好地对出口信用保险的承保、理赔及追偿技术进行信息交流)
international usage 国际习惯,国际惯例
international validity 国际效力
international visa 国际签证
International War Crimes Tribunal 国际战犯法庭
International War Crimes Tribunal for the

Far East 远东国际战犯法庭
international waters 国际海域,国际水域,公海
international waterways 国际水道,国际航道,国际水路
International Working Men's Association 国际劳工协会
international wrongful act 国际不当行为
International Year for Human Rights 国际人权年
internationalism n. 国际主义
internationalist n. 国际法学家;国际主义者;国际派
internationally wrongful act 国际非法行为
internecine a. 互相残杀的,两败俱伤的;杀人的
internee n. 拘留犯;(战争中被视为俘虏或敌侨而)被拘留者
Internet (或 internet work, interconnection network) n. (计算机)国际互联网络,互联网;因特网,国际信息(高速公路)网络,互联网络
internet banking 网络银行
Internet Corporation Assigned Names and Numbers (ICANN) (互联网)国际管理域名体系的机构[非政府的公益组织机构,在互联网范围内专门负责创造和分配域名设置规则的制定。控制互联网核心功能,包括 IP 地址和 DNS,其优势是居于互联网功能的中心,且能储存数据。目前,它负责对服务器的管理。全球互联网根服务器共 13 台,唯一的主根服务器在美国,其余 12 台辅根服务器中有 9 台也在美国。目前 ICANN 负责对根服务器的管理]
Internet governance 国际互联网治理
internet patent 互联网专利(指一种就一项发明被允准的实用性专利,此项专利将将商业方式与软件程序相结合以构成互联网的应用,亦称 cyberpatent)
internet payment 见 cyber payment
Internet Protocol 因特网协定(简称 IP)
internet search engines 互联网检索工具(指美国法律文献检索中电子检索的一种方式,可查找相关网站)
internet scrip 见 e-money
Internet service provider 网络服务提供者(见 DMCA)
internet user to control 控制因特网用户
internment n. 拘留;收容,禁闭;敌侨拘禁
internment camp (英)俘虏营;(拘留敌国人民的)拘留营
internship n. (美)(实习医生)见习期(或职务)
internuncio 教廷公使,使者;中间人
internuptial a. 同一人两次结婚之间发生的;近亲结婚的;异族通婚的
interoceanic canal 通洋运河
interpellate v. (议会中议员向政府官员的)质询
interpellatio 催告
interpellation n. 催告;质询,质问
interpellator n. 质问者,提出质询的议员
interpersonal a. 人与人之间(关系)的,需要与他人接触的
interplanetary law 星际法
interplead v. (提出债权等要求的)互相诉讼
interpleader n. 互相诉讼,互争权利的诉讼;互相诉讼者,确定竞合权利诉讼(指两个或两个以上主体对由第三人所有的财产提出同一权利主张时,确定该财产归属的诉讼)
interpleader issue 互争权利诉讼的系争点
interpleader summons 相互诉讼的传票
interpol (International Criminal Police) 国际刑警(组织)
interpolation n. 篡改(文件);添加,插入;添加物,添入的字句
interpolator n. 篡改(文件)者
interpose v. 干预,提出异议
interposition n. 提出(异议);干预,干涉,调停
interpret v. 解释,注释;说明;当译员,把……理解为;翻译,通译
interpretatio 解释
interpretatio critica 补正解释,更正解释
interpretatio extensiva 广义解释
* *Interpretatio fienda est ut res magis valeat quam pereat.* Such an interpretation is to

be adopted, that the thing may stand rather than fall./A document should be interpreted so that its intention is carried out and not defeated. 对文件之解释目的在使其实现而非被废弃。
interpretatio restrictiva 狭义的解释
interpretatio stricta 狭义解释
interpretation n. 1.解释,注释,阐明 2.解释条款,对法律的解释;法律上的解释 3.翻译,通译
Interpretation Act (英)《解释法》(该法律规定了成文法的一些解释原则,确定了大量成文法中常见的术语的含义)
interpretation clause (合同等的)释义条款
interpretation of constitution 宪法的解释
interpretation of contract 合同(契约)的解释
interpretation of law 法律阐释(模式)(指法律条文只提供一种供解释者在其中进行解释活动的结构,法律的含义最终取决于解释行动者与结构之间互动以及解释者之间的交流与共识)
interpretation of statute 法规的解释,(英)制定法的解释
interpretation of statutory language 法律文字(用语)的解释
interpretation of treaty 条约的解释
interpretation section (法律)条文解释,注释条款
interpretative decision 解释性裁决
interpretative quandary 解释上的困难
interpretative rules 解释性规则(指美国行政机构颁布的,用以解释、说服该机构实施的法律、法规)
interpreter n. 解释者;翻译者,译员;翻译器
interpretivism n. 解释主义
interpretivism and noninterpretivism (美)文本主义和非文本主义(文本主义和非文本主义的区别为当代关于宪法所规定的司法权之本质和范围的讨论核心。联邦最高法院必须受联邦宪法的条文及条文隐含之意图的约束呢还是超越文件的全面内容来确定其意义呢?这种讨论与宪法和法律解释中立法的原始意图的作用密切相关。文本主义与非文本主义不应和更传统的严格法律释义与自由的法律释义之间的区别相混淆。严格的自由法律释义为"文本解释"形式,其区别仅在于应如何解释联邦宪法是自由的,还是严格的。另外,非文本主义的观点即是否受其文本所约束内含及文本背后的隐含意思来解释宪法)
interpretivism n. 解释主义(所谓解释主义,意指法官在判决宪法案件时应当把他们自己限制于成文宪法所规定的或明确指示的效力规范之中;而非解释主义则与之相反,法院应当超越宪法文件,借助于文献资料,在宪法文本之外去发现所适用的规范);文本主义
interpretivist n. 解释主义者
interregnum n. 空缺位期(指两个国王统治期的间隔);(政府改组期间的)政权空白期间;中断,间歇
interrelationship n. 相互关系
interrogate v. 审问,审讯;质问,详问;提出一连串的问题
interrogate a witness 讯问证人
interrogation n. 讯问,审问,诘问;质问
interrogation of a criminal 讯问罪犯
interrogation of a defendant 讯问被告
interrogation of a indictor (或 **indicter**) 讯问原告
interrogation of a prisoner 讯问犯人
interrogation of a witness 讯问证人
interrogation record 讯问笔(记)录
interrogative a. 疑问的;质问的;讯问的
interrogator n. 讯问者;质问者;审问者
interrogatory (interrogatories) n./a. (美)质问书,询问书[美国民事诉讼审理前的程序之一,即调查取证的一种方法;由要求调查取证的当事人向另一方当事人提交书面问题,受询问的当事人应在宣誓后以书面回答];讯问,质问,疑问/讯问的,质问的,表示疑问的
interrupt v. 打断,中断;打扰,妨碍;使中断
interrupter n. 中断者,阻止者,妨碍者,障碍物

interruption n. 中断,阻碍;被中断的事物;中断期,休止期;时效中断
interruption of a right 权利的中断
interruption of prescription 时效中断
interruption of service 运行障碍
interruption of the extinctive prescription 消灭时效的中断
interspousal immunity 夫妻间豁免(见 husband-wife immunity)
interspousal tort immunity 见 husband-wife immunity
Intestate a./n. 1.死后未留有效遗嘱的〈having revoked her will without a new one, she was intestate when she died〉(没有新的,宣告她的遗嘱无效,她死时,未曾有遗嘱的)2.无遗嘱处分的(指关系到未留有效遗嘱的死者的财产)〈an intestate estate〉(一笔未留遗嘱的遗产)3.涉及未留遗嘱的死亡〈a spouse's instate share〉(夫妻一方的未留有效遗嘱的遗产分配)4.(古代)关系到没有有资格的人能证明〈the witness could not testify often being found intestate〉[证人在发现(死者)未留遗嘱之后无法也无资格证明(死者留有遗嘱)]
Interstate Agreement on Detainers Act (美)《有关扣押的州际协议法》[原为1956年颁布的法律,该法要求联邦政府、州以及哥伦比亚特区对临时羁押的犯罪分子进行审理,即使有的犯罪分子已在他地扣押。根据该法,如果罪犯分子书面申请要求在第二个法庭(second forum)处理其待审的被指控罪行,羁押该犯罪分子的政府(government)在其请求180日内必须对其罪行进行审判。参见《美国注释法典》第18标题卷附件第1—9条]
Interstate Commerce Commission (美)州际商业委员会[现已不存在的联邦行政机构,根据1887年的《州际商业法》设立的,目的在于通过监控质量和价格调节州际之间地面的运输以保证运输业和管道的畅通。1995年12月当国会废止此机构时,地面运输委员会(Surface Transportation Board),运输部(Department of Transportation)的三成员理事会的一个分部,承担此机构的大部分职责。见 Surface Transportation Board]
interstate commerce (美) 州际商业,州际贸易
Interstate Commerce Act (美)《州际商法》,《州际贸易法》(指调节各州之间陆上货运和客运的联邦法规)
Interstate Commerce Commission (美)州际商业委员会
Interstate Commerce Commission Regulation (美)《州际商业委员会条例》
interstate compacts (美)州际协定(指两个或两个以上的州之间的协议,这种协议属立法性质,其形式和效力如同条约,参加这些协定之前,该协定必须经国会同意)
interstate coordination and mutual assistance in judicial proceedings 国家间在司法程序上的协作与互助
interstate immorality (美)州际妨害风化(罪)
interstice of law 法律之不足,法律之漏洞或缺陷
intersystem n. 制度间,跨制度
intersystem problems of former adjudication 先例判决的制度间的问题
intertemporal BC (budget control) 各个时期的预算约束
intertemporal utility function 跨时期效用方式
intertwine v. (使)缠结;(使)缠绕在一起
interval n. (时间的)间隔,间歇,停止期间
intervene v. 干预,干涉;介入,插手,调停;(第三者为自己利益)参加诉讼
intervene in a dispute 调停争论
intervene in infringing proceedings (提起侵权之诉时)参与诉讼
intervener (= intervenor) n. 介入诉讼当事人;调停者;干涉者
intervenient (= intervening) a. 介入的;参加诉讼的,调停的
intervenient party 介入诉讼当事人;参加诉讼当事人
intervening n. 干预,干涉,介入;调停
intervening act 干预行为,介入行为

intervening cause 干预原因,妨碍诉因;介入原因;参加诉讼理由
intervening damages 延迟控诉引起的损害(赔偿)
intervening force 干预力(度)
intervening judg(e)ment 中间裁判
intervening party 介入诉讼当事人,参与诉讼当事人
intervention n. 介入诉讼(美国民事诉讼中一项准许不是诉讼当事人的某个人为保护其权益而加入诉讼之中的程序)
intervention as of right 作为权利的诉讼参加
intervention by right 依据权利的干涉,依权干预
intervention price 干预价格
interventionist n. 干涉内政者;武装干涉者;主张干涉的人
interweave v. 交织,使紧密结合
intestable a. 无资格立遗嘱的(如婴儿或精神病患者)
intestacy n. 未立遗嘱,无遗嘱的死亡(指死者没有留下遗嘱)
intestate n./a. 未留遗嘱的死亡者/未留遗嘱的;未按遗嘱处分的
intestate distribution law 无遗嘱析产法
intestate share 无遗嘱继承份额;法定继承份额
intestate succession (18世纪)1.无(有效)遗嘱继承(指无遗嘱死者拥有的财产分配的方法)2.依照普通法血统关系继承,法定继承(亦称 hereditary succession 或 descent and distribution)
intestates' estate 无遗嘱继承的遗产,法定继承的遗产
intestato (大陆法)未留遗嘱
intimacy n. (复)亲昵的行为(如吻或抚摸等);亲切,亲密;隐私,秘密;熟悉
intimate a. 亲密的;亲切的;私人的,个人的;内心的
intimate connection (或 **connexion**) 密切关系
intimate knowledge of the law 熟悉法律
intimate life 隐私,私生活
intimate social relations 隐私的社交关系

intimation n. 告知,通知;暗示,提示
intimidate v. 恐吓,威胁,使恐惧
intimidation n. 恐吓,威胁
intimidation and bribery 威胁利诱
intimidator n. 恐吓者,威胁者
intolerable acts (或 **coercive acts**) 不宽容的法令(或强制性法令,指美国历史上由美国议会颁布的针对当地人民反抗行为所采取的反击措施的统称)
intolerance n. 不容他说;偏执;不能容忍,不宽容
intoxicant n./a. 麻醉剂,毒药/麻醉的,使中毒的,使醉的
intoxicated a. 醉酒的,酗酒的
intoxicating dose 中毒量
intoxicating liquor 酒类
intoxication n. 醉酒,酒精中毒
intoxication of the tort-feasor 侵权行为人之醉酒
intra anni spatium 在一年的时间内
intra familiam 在家庭里(此术语表示在子女自立之前的情况)
intra fidem 在诚信的范围内;有公信力
intra fines commissi 在委托的范围内(此术语显示在代理关系范围内所做的一项代理行为)
intra luctus tempus 在哀悼的时间里,在悲痛的时间里
intra vires 在(法定)权限内(与 ultra vires 相对)
intra-company transaction 公司内部交易
intra-regional shipping 区域间航运
intrastate commerce (美)(一个)州内的商务
intrauterine death 子宫内死亡
intrench in constitutions 在宪法中扎根,在各宪法中得以确认
intrench (=entrench) v. 确立;确认;侵害(常与 on 和 upon 连用);(古)近乎,接近,在严格定义之内(与 on,upon 连用);用壕沟防御;牢固树立;使(自己)处于牢固地位;侵占,侵犯(on, upon)
intrenched oneself in a place 扎根于一个地方
intrenchment n. 堡垒;牢固树立;嵌入
intricacies n. 错综,复杂,缠结;(复)复杂

的事物
intricate a. 错综复杂的,纠缠不清的,头绪纷繁的;难懂的,难了解的
intricate case without a clue 无头公案
intrig(u)ant n. 阴谋者,私通者;奸夫
intrig(u)ante n. 女阴谋者;淫妇
intrigue n./v. 密谋,阴谋,诡计;私通/阴谋策划;用诡计取得;吸引,密谋;私通
intriguer n. 密谋者,阴谋者;私通者
intrinsic(al) a. 内在的;固有的,本质的
intrinsic case study 内在的个案研究
intrinsic(al) evidence 固有之证据,无需有其他的证据者;本身之证据(指书面证据而言)
intrinsic fraud 实质欺诈;内部性欺诈(美国学者和判例将欺诈分为外部性欺诈和内部性欺诈。内部性欺诈是指在案件审理过程中发生的欺诈;外部性欺诈是指妨碍或损害当事人诉讼权利而进行的欺诈,这种欺诈可以作为判决的依据)
intrinsic merit 内在的功过,内在的是非曲直,内在的实质
intrinsic value 内在价值(程序性权利的基础就是法律程序的内在价值),固有价值(指财产)
introduce v. 引进,输入;介绍,推荐;采用;提出(议案等)
introduce a question 开始讨论一个问题,提出问题
introduced evidence 采纳的证据(指当事人提出并由法庭采纳的证据)
introduction n. 介绍,推荐,引进,输入;传入;采用,使用;导言,导论;入门(书);说明书
introduction of bill 议案介绍
introduction of evidence 提交证据(指呈递证据以便在审理中可能接受)
introduction of foreign capital 引进外资
introduction to law 法学入门
introductive (= introductory) a. 介绍的,导引的;开端的,初步的
introductory law 施行法
introductory law to the civil code 民法典施行法
intromission n. 干预,插入,插手;准入

introspect v. 反省,进行思想反省,内省
introspection n. 反省,内省
intrude v. 侵入,闯入;侵扰;非法占领;强使他人采纳
intruder n. 闯入者,侵犯者;妨碍者
intrusion n. 侵扰,闯入,非法进入;干涉,妨碍,强使采纳
intrusive a. 闯入的,侵入的;干涉的,妨碍的
intrust v. 见 entrust
intuition n. 直觉,直观;直觉知识,直觉到的事物
intuitive appeal 直观上诉
inure (=enure) v. 1.生效,有效力,适用;有用 2.使坚强,使习惯于(不利条件)
inurement n. 生效,适用
invade v. 强入;侵犯,侵略,侵袭,侵害;干扰
invader n. 强入者,侵犯者,侵略者,干扰者
invalid a. (法律)无效的,无效力的,作废的;有病的,伤残的
invalid advice 过期无效通知
invalid ballot 无效选票
invalid charge 无效指控
invalid cheque (或 check) 无效支票
invalid contract 无效合同(契约)
invalidate v. 使无效,使无效力;使作废;使无价值
invalidating factor (合同的)无效原因
invalidation n. 无效,作废
invalidity n. 无效力;丧失工作能力(指病残);虚弱
invalidity benefit 病残津贴
invaluable a. 无法估计的,无价的;非常宝贵的〈invaluable service of sorting material by subject〉(按主题分类资料的宝贵服务/对于按主题分类资料进行十分有效的服务)
invariablely ad. 总是,不变,永恒,一律地
invasion n. 入侵,侵略;闯入,侵犯,侵害;干预
invasion of privacy 干预个人事务,干预他人私生活
invasion of sb.'s right 侵犯某人权利
inveigle v. 诱惑,诱骗,骗取

inveiglement n. 诱骗,骗取;笼络,勾引
inveigler n. 诱骗者,骗取者,勾引者
inventio (大陆法)发现(指一种用占有取得财产所有权的方式);(古英国法)发现物
invention n. 发明;创造;发明物;创作能力;虚构,捏造
invention bonus 发明奖
inventiveness n. 创造性(指专利的产品发明)
inventor n. 发明人,发明家,创造者
inventor's certificate system 发明人证书制度
inventory n. 详细目录,财产目录,存单,清单;盘存;存货
inventory certificate 存货证(书)
inventory of property 财产清单
inventory on seizure 查抄物品清单,没收清册
inventory searches 编目搜查(指警察扣押财物以后,可以基于保护财物所有人的权益、保护警察免受财物被偷盗或损坏的指责或控告、保护警察和公众免受危险和威胁三个理由,对扣押财物进行清理,列出清单。在美国称为编目搜查)
inventorying of property and auditing of capital (中)清产核资
inveracity n. 不诚实,谎言,虚伪
inverse comdemnation 1.回复控告,反征用诉讼(指诉因的一种,在政府实体涉嫌未进行任何正式的征用程序而直接占用财产时,财产所有者可提起这种诉讼。这是依据美国联邦宪法第五修正案的公平补偿条款;私人财产未经公平补偿不得征作公用)2.逆向征用(指国家征用土地而使邻近地块价值大减,该地块虽未被正式征用,但应推定为征用,其所有人可要求政府合理补偿。这是专门提供给财产所有人的救济手段)
inverse death knell doctrine 逆向丧钟原则或死亡钟声原则[美国民事诉讼中指拒绝作出一项集团诉讼认证的,被认为敲响诉讼的"死亡之钟"(death knell);反之,当集团诉讼获得认证后,其对方当事人借所谓"逆向死亡之钟"原则提出抗辩,要求对即将进行的上诉予以否决]

inverse/reverse passing off 反向假冒(指未经商标注册人同意,更换其注册商标并将更换商标的商品又投入市场的行为构成商标侵权,学理上称为反向假冒)(与 reverse palming off 同)
invert n./v. 同性恋者,颠倒了的事物/使颠倒,使倒转,使反向
inverted terms 同类术语
invest v. 授(权)给;投(资);花费,投入(时间,精力),(以正式仪式)使就职
invested capital 投资的资本
invested consensus 协商一致方式(或称为"倒协商一致")
invested money 股本
investigate v. 侦查,审查,调查;研究
investigate a crime 调查罪行,侦查犯罪
investigate and ascertain 查明,查清
investigate and prosecute 查办,查究
investigate and verify 查证
investigating n. 调查,调查研究;审查,侦查
investigating and prosecuting apparatus 侦查机关,检察机关
investigating committee 调查委员会
investigating judge 预审法官,调查法官
investigating magistrate (美)准司法官员(指负责审查并有时在案件开庭前,对刑事程序的某些方面作出调整。这种准司法官的制度是为了保持法律在执行上的尊严或完整性的一种手段。这种手段不是被指示用于避免执行中的不严格和放纵等弊病,而是相反地使其严格执行法律。)
investigating officer 侦查人员
investigation n. 调查,证据的调查;侦查;研究
investigation and verification 调查甄别
investigation at crime scenes 现场勘查
investigation grievances 审查冤情
investigation of cadres (中)(对)干部审查
investigation of evidence 调查证据
investigation of offences 侦查犯罪
investigation on crime scene 现场勘查
investigation report 调查报告书,侦查报告书

investigative (=investigatory) a. 调查的, 侦查的,审查的;受调查研究的
investigative fact 调查的事实
investigative power 调查权
investigative test 侦查实验
investigator n. 审查员,侦查员,调查研究员,预审员
investigatory apparatus 调查机关,侦查机关
investitive fact 授权性事实
investiture n. 授受;授职(旧译:叙任);授权;授权仪式,就职仪式,封地仪式
investment n. 投资,投入资本;正式授权,正式就职
investment association (英)投资协会
investment banker 投资银行家,投资银行业者
investment banking firm 投资银行
investment business 投资业
investment capital 投资资本
investment certificate 投资证书
investment climate 投资环境
investment company 投资公司
investment contract 投资合同(契约)
investment credit n. 投资信贷;投资信用
investment decision 投资决策
investment dispute 投资争议
investment enterprises 投资企业
investment firm 投资公司(欧盟与美国的 investment bank 和我国的 security company 相似,有证券包销内容)
investment funds 投资基金(组织),投资基金管理机构
investment in securities 证券投资
investment of capital goods and technology 生产资料和技术投资
investment or advertising function 投入或广告功能
investment performance 投资效果,投资效益
investment projects 投资项目,投资计划(方案)
investment providing revenue 提供收益的投资
Investment Related Trade Measures (IRTMS) 与投资有关的贸易关系(指投资与贸易具有密切关系。见 Trade-Related Investment Measures)
investment services directive (ISD) 投资服务指令
investment tax credit (1965年)投资税减免(或抵免)[此种税务减免目的在于激励以实物资产(capital goods)进行营业投资(business investment),允许将购买此实物资产价格按一定比例直接抵免纳税人的所得税款(as a credit against the taxpayer's income taxes)。《1986年的税改法》(The Tax Reform Act of 1986)自1986年1月1日起全面实施,有追溯效力地废止对于大多置于经营的资产的减免,缩略为 ITC]
investment trust 投资信托
investments in reputation for honesty 诚实信誉投资
investor n. 投资者,客商;授权者
investor beware 投资者(对证券市场)十分谨慎
inveterate a. 由来已久的,根深蒂固的,积重难返的,已成积习的
inveterate criminal 惯犯,屡教不改犯
invidious discrimination 嫉恨式歧视
inviolability n. 不可侵犯权,不可侵犯性;神圣不可侵犯
inviolability of consular premises 领事馆房产的不可侵犯权
inviolability of diplomatic envoys 外交使节的不可侵犯权
inviolability of domicile 住宅不可侵犯(权)
inviolability of frontiers 边界不可侵犯(权)
inviolability of personal freedom 人身自由不可侵犯
inviolability of property 财产(所有权)不可侵犯
inviolability of territory 领土不可侵犯
inviolability of the person 人身不可侵犯
inviolable a. 不可侵犯的;神圣的
inviolate a. 不可侵犯的,不可亵渎的,不被玷污的,无损的,纯洁的
inviolatity of treaties 条约神圣原则
invisible a. 隐蔽的,无形的;未列在账上的
invisible assets 账外资产
invisible balance 非贸易收支差额

invisible earnings 无形收益
invisible export 无形输出
invisible hand 看不见的手,无形的手,个人利益
Invisible Impire 无形帝国(指美国三K党活动初期的别称)
invisible import 无形输入
invisible loss 无形损失
invisible stock 无形股份
invisible trade 无形贸易(指国家之间无形项目的交换,有劳务的收支,海外投资收益的收支,以及由私人或政府从一国到另一国的货币转移等)
invisible waste 无形损耗
invitation n. 邀请,招待;请帖;吸引
invitation to offer 要约(的)引诱(亦称邀请要约)
invitation to submit an offer 要约邀请
invitation to tender 招标
invite oppression 施压,招致压力
invite subscription for a loan 申请批准贷款
invited error 招致错误(指诉讼中的一方当事人使用不可接受的证据时,另一方当事人也可使用类似证据反驳的规则)
invitee n. 被邀请人
inviter n. 邀请者
inviting a. 诱惑人的,动人的,吸引人的
inviting adultery and burglary 海淫海盗
inviting bids 招标
inviting country 邀请国
inviting suspicion 涉嫌
invito 不顾,未经同意;违反本意
* *Invito beneficium non datur.* A benefit is not conferred on one who is unwilling to receive it; that is to say, no one can be compelled to accept a benefit. 不得强迫接受恩惠。
invito debitore 违反债务人的意愿
invito domino 未经所有权人之同意
invocation n. 符咒,(法规中)援引;(法权中的)行使
invocation of constitution 宪法的援引
invoice n. 运单;销货发票;(货物托运的)收货清单

invoice discounting 发货单贴现
invoice of transfer 拨付凭单
invoice price 发票价格
invoice value 发票价值
invoke v. 援引;行使;实行;引起,产生;恳求
invoke a precedent 援例,援引先例
invoke economic sanctions 实行经济制裁
invoke the veto in the dispute 在辩论中行使否决权
involuntary a. 非故意的;偶然的;无意识的;非出于自愿的,非本意的
involuntary act 无意行为
involuntary bailment 非自愿保释
involuntary bankruptcy 非自愿的破产,强制破产
involuntary composition 强制性的和解协议
involuntary conduct 无意识行为
involuntary confession 违反本意的供述,非自愿招供
involuntary crime (= unintentional crime) 非自愿犯罪,过失犯罪
involuntary discontinuance 被迫中止;被迫中止诉讼
involuntary dismissal 强制(性)驳回诉讼
involuntary dissolution 强制解散
involuntary homicide 过失杀人
involuntary manslaughter 过失杀人罪,非故意(或蓄意)杀人(罪)
involuntary payment 被迫支付
involuntary servitude 强制劳役
involuntary transfer 非自愿转让
involuntary trust 非自愿信托
involve v. 包括;使卷入,使陷入;拖累,影响,牵连
involved testimony 复杂的证言(注意 testimony involved 则为有关的证言)
involvement n. 卷入,参与;牵连到的事物,复杂的情况;经济上的困窘
invulnerable a. 无懈可击的
Involution n. 卷入,纠缠;错综复杂;(功能的)衰退;复旧;"内卷化"理论[指一种社会或政治、经济、文化模式发展到某个阶段形成一定的形式后就停滞不前,只是在

内部变得越来越复杂而无法向新的、更高级的形式变迁的状态〈the involution of the subject matter of the litigation of theory〉(诉讼标的理论的"内卷化")]
inward a. 1.向内的,内部的 2.进口的;输入的 3.内陆的 4.秘密的
inward bill of lading 输入提单,进口提单
inward charges 入港费
inward documentary bill 进口押汇单
inward entry 输入申请书,输入记载
inward manifest 进口货物清单,进口仓单
inward remittance 汇入款;转入款
inword 口头上
iota 希腊的最小字母(第九个字母);小点儿,微小〈not change by one iota〉(丝毫也不变),〈have not an iota of〉(没有一点儿)
IOU (I owe you) (账单上签署的)我欠你(见 account stated)
IP protection 知识产权保护
ipissima verba 正如其言,确切的原文
ipse dixit 武断的话;亲口所述
ipso facto 根据事实本身,依事实
ipso facto ab initio by the deed itself, from (or at) the beginning 自始就根据事实本身
ipso facto et ipso jure by the deed (or the fact) itself and the law itself 根据事实本身和法律本身
ipso jure 根据法律,依法
ipso jure avoidance 依法宣布无效
ipsum matrimonium 婚姻本身
Iran-contra scandal (美)反伊朗丑闻(指里根解救人质事件)
ire ad largum 自由行动;逃脱;获得自由
iron n. 铁;铁制品;铁一般刚强;严厉;(复)镣铐
iron hand 铁腕(喻坚强严厉的手段)
iron house (美俚)铁窗,监狱
iron law 铁的法律,铁的规则;铁律
iron law of wages 工资铁律
iron rule 苛政;(美)(训练囚犯用的)严格处罚规则
ironclad a. 打不破的;装甲的,镶铁的
ironclad proof 铁证

irrational choice 非理性选择
irrational criminal 丧失理智的罪犯
irrationality n. 不合理,非理性
irrebuttable a. 不能反驳的(证据等);不容置疑的
irrebuttable(或 **conclusive**)**presumptions** 不容置疑的法律推定(又译不可反驳性推定,指不允许用任何证据反驳的一种推定,如8岁以下儿童推定为无犯罪能力,即限此类推定)
irreceivability n. 不可接受性
irreclaimable a. 难改造的(尤指坏得无法改造的人);不能恢复的;不能收回的;不能开垦的
irreconcilable difference 不能相容的歧见(又译难以和解的歧见,在不追究责任的离婚案中可作为离婚的根据)
irreconcilable disagreement (两者)不相容的分歧意见
irrecusable a. 不能拒绝的;排斥不了的;无法反对的
irredeemable a. 不能赎回的;不能偿还的;不可兑现的
irredentism n. 领土收复主义;民族统一主义
irrefragable a. 不能反驳的;不可争辩的;不能否认的
irrefutability n. 不能反驳
irrefutable a. 不可辩驳的;不可否认的
irregular a. 不规则的,无规律的;非正式的,非正规的;不合道德的,不合法的,不正当的;不正常的
irregular conduct 不正当行为
irregular consequences 非正常的后果
irregular death 非正常死亡
irregular endorsement 不当背书
irregular heir 非正式继承人(按美国路易斯安那州法律)[指在无遗嘱指定继承人或法定继承人的情况下,具有法定权利(statutory right)从可继承的地产(estate)中取得财产的个人或法人、实体(entity)]
irregular judg(e)ment 与(法院)惯例相反的判决
irregular marriage 非正式婚姻,非正式结婚;姘居

irregular succession 违规继承[指通过有利于某些人或国家而不利于按一般继承法的继承人(如按遗嘱指定的继承人)的特别法规的继承]
irregular summons 未依法传唤,非正式传唤
irregularity n. 不规则;无规律;形式上的瑕疵;违法;不正当行为;不符合司法程序(规则);违规行为
irregularity of judg(e)ment 判决不当
irrelevance (= irrelevancy) n. 无关联的事;离题;不相干,没关系
irrelevant a. 无关的,不相干的,离题的
irrelevant cost 非相关成本,无关成本
irrelevant evidence 无关证据(指在诉讼中既对证实无助,又不能有助于反证者)
irremediable a. 不可救药的;不可挽回的;医不好的;不可弥补的,不能改正的
irreparable a. 不可弥补的,不可挽回的;不能恢复的
irreparable injury 不能恢复之损害,不可弥补之损害;不能替代的侵害
irreplaceable a. 不能恢复原状的;不能替代的;无法弥补的
irrepleviable a. 不准保释的;不能领取被扣押物(或没收物)的
irresistible a. 不可抗拒的;不能压制的
irresistible cause 不可抗拒的原因
irresistible force 不可抗力
irresistable impulse 不可抗拒或不可控制的冲动条例(指 20 世纪 50 年代麦克·纳顿条例在美国受到来自精神病医生、法官、法学学者的严厉指责,他们批评该条例只注意认知功能而未考虑到意志力的受损。从 1986 年开始,美国一些州在麦克·纳顿条例中增加了新的内容,即不可抗拒的冲动条例。此条例适用于下述情况:"被告可能知道他的行为性质和他的行为是错误的,但他的行为是在来自精神疾病的强烈冲动的驱使下实施的,他不能抗拒这种冲动。"这是美国的第二个规则);不可抗拒或不可控制的冲动条例(指一类疾病成为一个人的真正行为动力,他不能抗拒或不能控制的一种行为冲动,则他不负刑事责任)[见 Thomas Denman (1779—1854)托马斯·登曼][美国颇有影响的三个团体 American Law Institute (ALI), American Bar Association(ABA), American Psychiatric Association(APA),即美国法律学会、美国律师协会、美国精神医学会,则建议废除这一规定]
irresolution n. 优柔寡断,摇摆不定,犹豫不决,不果断
irrespective a. 不考虑,不问的,不顾的
irrespective of percentage 无免赔率;单独海损全赔
irrespective of sex, age or education 不问性别、年龄或教育程度
irrespective of the consequences 不顾后果
irrespective of the values in question 不问争议价值多少
irrespective of underlying transaction 不顾优先交易
irresponsibility n. 不负责任,无责任,不承担责任
irresponsible n./a. 不负责任的人,不承担责任的人/不承担责任的,不需负责的,不负责任的
irretrievable a. 不能恢复的;无法挽救的;不能弥补的
irretrievable breakdown of marriage 不可挽回的婚姻破裂
irretrievable loss 不可弥补的损失
irrevocable a. 不可撤销的;最后的,不可废止的,不可改变的
irrevocable condition 不可取消的条件
irrevocable indictment 不可撤回的诉状
irrevocable judg(e)ment 不可撤销的判决
irrevocable offer 不可撤回的要约
irrevocable power of attorney (18 世纪)不可撤销代理人的权力(指被代理人不能撤销代理人的权力。亦称 power of attorney coupled with an interest)
irrevocable trust 不可撤销的信托
irrigation n. 灌溉;水利
irrigation dispute 水利纠纷
irritancy n. 无效;(合同)撤销;废弃;无效条款
irritant a. 刺激的;使无效的,使丧失效力的
irritate v. 激怒,使恼怒;使无效,使失效

irruption n. 侵入,闯进
Islamic and Near Eastern Law 伊斯兰教和近东法
Islamic extremism 伊斯兰极端主义
Islamic Law 伊斯兰教法
Islamic Law System(或 **Legal Family**) 伊斯兰教法法系
Islamic procedure 伊斯兰教法诉讼程序
Islāmic shari'a 伊斯兰沙里亚教法
Island of Palmas Arbitration 帕尔马斯岛仲裁案[1928年国际仲裁员胡伯(Max Huber)阐述了国际法上三个时间的原则:①法律事实产生时的法律;②该事实产生争议时的法律;③解决该争议时的法律]
isocracy n. 平等参政权;平等参政制度
isolate v. 隔离;孤立;脱离,分离
isolated case 与其他案件无关联的案件,孤立案件
isolation n. 隔离,孤立;脱离
isolation from the Court 从联邦最高法院中分离出来
isolation order 隔离令
Isonomia 伊索诺米(古希腊哲学家用来表达法治内涵的词汇,即"法律平等适用于各种人")
isonomy n. 政权平等
Israeli government 以色列政府
issuable a. 可争论的,可提出抗辩的,可进行辩护的;可能产生的;可发行的
issuable defence 尚有争议的辩护
issuable plea 尚有争议的答辩
issuance n. 发给,发行,颁布
issuance of writs of execution 发给执行令状
issue n./v. 1.(案件)系争点(旨在两个或两个以上的当事方之间存在的争点,有事实上的也有法律上的,或只有其中之一。既有具体法律问题又有事实分歧);争端;争议的问题(见 problem) 2.被扣押房地产收益(指对从前的土地房屋在被法庭强制扣押令执行后所得的收益) 3.出生;(合法)子女,后嗣,直系血亲,卑亲属 4.结果,结局 5.发行;发行物;流出 6.(法律、法令等)颁布,(票据、信用卡)签发/1.发表,发行;发布,发给 2.颁布(法律、法令) 3.收益,生成孳息⟨to accuse rents issuing from land⟩(从这块土地上获得)4.签发⟨without probable cause, the serch warrant will not issue⟩(无正当理由不得签发搜查令)5.送出,发行(issue process);送出传票;发行股票(issue stock)⟨at issue⟩(在争论中),⟨in the issue⟩(结果,到头来),⟨joint issue⟩共同提出争论点供裁决(双方提出或一方提出为另一方接受)
issue a policy 出立保单
issue a summon 发出传票
issue a warrant 发出逮捕证
issue a writ against sb. 传讯某人
issue an order 发布命令
issue at par 按票面发行
issue female 女性子孙
issue house 承销公司
issue in action 诉讼的系争点,诉讼争执点
issue in fact 事实上的争点
issue in (of) law 法律上的争点
issue male 男性子孙
issue of government bonds 发行公债
issue of share 发行股票
issue of share for less par 发行低于面值的股票
issue opinion 发表(尤指判决的)意见
issue pending decision 待决争点
issue preclusion 已判决的事项,既决案件;间接禁止翻供的事实;(既决)争点阻却(再诉)
issue price 发行价
issue roll 诉讼系争点(案)卷(登录册)
issue tax 发行税
issued a. 已发行的,已发出的
issued banknotes 已发行的钞票
issued(或 **shared**) **capital** 已发行的资(股)本
issued estoppel 已决问题的不得推翻
issued writ 发布的令状
issueless a. 徒劳的,无结果的;无争辩的;无子女的
issuer n. 发行人;发布人(机关)
issuer beware 股票发行人谨慎入市
issues and profits 孳息,不动产孳息(指地上及地下的孳息)

issuing(或 **opening**)**bank** 发行银行,(信用证)开证银行
issuing company 出保单公司
issuing date 开出日期
issuing long term debt obligations 发行长期债务
istisiāh (伊斯兰教法)公益(原则)(指对无法在《圣训》中找到答案的疑难问题作出判决所根据的一种原则)
it follows that ... 由此得出……,可见
It may be fairly asserted that ... 简直可以断定说……
It is agreed that 这成为共识……
It is not too much to say 毫不夸张地说
* *Ita utere tuo ut alienum non laedas.* Use your own property and your own rights in such a way that you will not hurt your neighbor, or prevent him from enjoying his. 使用你的财产和你的权利时,不应有害于你的邻居或妨害其享有他的财产和权利.
Italian law 意大利法
item n. 条,款;项,项目
item received in advance 预收项目
item vote 项目否决,分项否决
itemize v. 逐条记录,逐条列明
items(or **forms**)**of maritime lien** 船舶优先权的项目(这里应注意 items 和 forms 可译成类型或形式.对于英美法 lien 有种类或形式之分,但我国海商法并未以海事请求权的不同种类来划分船舶优先权的种类.因此海商法学界将产生船舶优先权的海事请求权称为船舶优先权的"项目",则混淆两种不同性质的权利,并模糊了它们之间原本清晰的界限,即海事请求权作为债权,系主权;船舶优先权,作为担保物权乃从权利)
iter 步行权(指罗马法上的地役权中的通行权),通行地役权(民法中归属于一个不动产上的一种权利,如行路权,骑马权);通过权;(古罗马法)巡回法官所作的巡回;(根据巡回法官个人的任务)审案;(海事法中的)海路,道路,航行方向
iterance(=**iterancy**)n. 重述,反复申说,重复
iterate v. 重述,反复申说

itinerant a./n. 巡回的/巡回工作者
itinerant judge 巡回法官
itinerant judge of the English royal court 英国皇家法院的巡回法官
itinerant justices (英史)巡游法官
itinerant royal judge (英史)皇家巡回法官
itinerate v. 巡回审判;巡回
itineration n. 巡回审判;巡回
iura novit curia 法官通晓法律(见 jura novit curia)
iure in personam 对人权
iure in rem 对物权
iudex 罗马审判官,亦作 *judex*(指一切享有审判权或行政权的官员)
Iudicium populi 人民审判(见 Lex Calpurnia de Precuniis Nepetundis)
iura in rebus alienis 他物权(指与所有权不同的抵押权、永佃权、地上权、地役权、用益权等)(同 *juna in rebus alienis*)
ius(=*jus*) 法律,权利
ius agris dandis adsignandis 土地分配权[指意大利法学研究人员玛塔·索蒂(Marta Sorti)推测的《韦斯巴芗谕令权法》铜表残片包含的规定有土地发展权、统帅设立与罢免权(*ius regibus creandis vel deponendis*)、设立殖民地、建立城市及毁灭城市权、台伯河河岸和河床定界权]
ius aliens rebus utendi salva rerum subslantia 使用和收益他人的物的同时不改变物的实质的权利(罗马法时代法学家保罗对用益权 *usus fructus* 下的定义)
ius civile 民法
Ius Commune 普通法,共同法
ius domini vel quasi 所有权和准所有权
ius in personam sire creditum 对人权或债权
ius praediorum 地役权
ius regibus creandis vel deponendis 统帅设立与罢免权(见 *ius agris dandis adsignandis*)
ius rtendi truendi 孳息的权利
iusta causa 合法原因
iusta causa traditionis 交付的正当原因
iustae nuptiae (罗马法)正当婚姻(*affectio*

martalis），婚意［指一个主观的和内在的要素，通过新郎、新娘自己的表白或其家人及友人的表白加以证明，当然最重要的是婚姻期遇（honor matriomonii）］

J

Jack Ketch （英）绞刑吏
jackal n. 帮凶；爪牙，走狗
jackals of the same lair 一丘之貉
jacketing n. 殴打，鞭打
jackpot n. （彩票等）头奖；（在冒险事业中获得的）最大成功
jackrolling n. （美）用酒灌醉后行窃
Jackson-denno hearing 杰克逊-丹诺听证（指法庭在外面有陪审团出席主持的程序，决定被告供认是否自愿或可采纳作为证据，亦称为 Jackson v. denno hearing）
jactitation n. 诈称；冒充
jactitation of marriage 冒充配偶罪诈婚（指诈称为某人的夫或妻者）；诈婚诉讼
jactitator n. 诈称者，冒充者
jactura （暴风雨中）投弃（货物）入海
jactura mercium 投弃货物入海
jail n. 监狱（见 gaol）
Jail delivery （= goal delivery） 1.监狱出空（即提审所有在押的未决犯出狱的程序）2.提审令状（给予法官提审在押未决犯的命令）3.提审法庭（指被委以一般刑事案件审判任务的法庭）
jail-bird n. （= gaolbird）
jail-break n. 越狱
jailbait n. （可构成法律上强奸对象的）未成年女子；（应负刑事责任的）诱奸；性ގ女子
jailer （= gaoler） n. 看守，狱卒，监狱管理员
jaileress （= gaoleress） n. 女看守，女狱卒，监狱女管理员
jailhouse n. 监狱
jailhouse lawyer （美）狱中法律行家（指有法律知识的罪犯）
Jainism n. 耆那教［这种教在印度有数百万人，渴望保护所有的生命。该教创始人为伐驮摩那（前599—前527），尊称

"大雄"］
James Hadfield 詹姆斯·哈德菲尔德［指1800年刺杀英皇乔治三世（George Ⅲ）的主犯。哈德菲尔德在参加法英战争中头部受伤，患有精神病后退役，伴有妄想精神症状。他病态地认为上帝要毁灭全球，只有自己以生命为代价才能拯救世界众生。但因坚持宗教信仰视自杀为道德上犯罪，而不得自杀。他认为向皇帝行刺肯定会被处以极刑，故找了个机会向皇帝身旁开枪（并不想真正打死皇帝）。英杰出律师托马斯·厄斯金（Thomas Erskin）抓住其妄想的证据，说服了英国陪审团将妄想作为一个精神病人无罪的评定标准，使詹姆斯被判无罪］
James Kent 詹姆斯·肯特［1763年—1847年，美国法学家，曾任法官和大法官25年。他的特点是能从判例的束缚中解放出来。其巨著《法律评论》（1826—1830）为美国普通法的经典著作］
Jamestown （美）詹姆斯城（指1606年英派出一支殖民军队在北美东海岸建立的第一个城市，以后发展为弗吉尼亚）
Jencks material （1961年）（刑诉）詹克斯证据资料［指检控方证人书面的或记录的审前陈述（pretrial statement），刑事被告根据证人已验证后提交的动议（filling a motion），有资格对证人准备进行交叉诘问。这种辩护可用作一种达到指责证言不可信的目的（for impeachment purpose）的一种陈述。见 Brady material］
Jane Doe （美）诉讼中隐匿真名的女方
Japanese law 日本法
Japanese Patent Office 日本专利局
javelin-men n. （英）法院（法官审案时的）警卫人员
jawbone n./v. （美俚）（财务上的）信用，赊

买,借贷,借到的款子/(美俚)赊卖给人,借贷给人;赊买,借到;利用职权企图使……就范,利用职权对……施加压力

jay-walker n. (不遵守交通规则)乱穿越马路者

jaywalking n. (不遵守交通规则)乱穿越马路

jealous of its rights 十分在意其权利

jealousy of the judge 对法官的戒备

jealousy n. 妒忌,忌妒;猜忌,谨慎戒备

Jeffersonian Republican 杰斐逊式共和党员

Jehovah's Witnesses 耶和华的目击者

jeofail (=*jeofaile*) n. 我失误(指诉状对答里有错漏而要求加以修改错漏的用语)

jeopardise (=jeopardize) v. 使受危害;使陷入危险,危及,危害

jeopardize the public order of resident country 危害驻在国的公共秩序

jeopardy n. 危险,危难;(刑事案件中被告的)危险处境;(对被告的)刑事追究

jeopardy assessment (美)预备征税,紧急征收[指一种国内税务署(IRS)无须经过通常审查程序的征税。应纳税人已经欠交纳税不足的欠额,由于拖延至将面临无法征收所欠税款的情况下,即采取此种紧急征收]

jeopardy clause 危险条款,危难条款

jeopardy of life or limb 受两次生命和身体上的危险

jerque v. 检查船上有无私货

jerque note 结关单,进口税检查证;海关检验单,输入检查证

jerquer (=jerguer) n. 缉私官员(英海关用语,指检查私匿物品、逃税等性质的海关官员)

jerry a. 草率的,偷工减料的,权宜之计的

jerry-builder n. 偷工减料的建筑师(或建筑商)

jerry-building n. 偷工减料的建筑(或工程)

Jesuit jurists 天主教耶稣会法学家

Jesuit jurists of counter-reformation 反对改革的耶稣会

jetsam n. (船舶遇险时)投弃的货物;沉入海底的(或冲到岸上的)投弃货物;被抛弃的东西

jettison n./v. (船或飞机遇险时)投弃货物(或行为);抛弃,放弃/抛弃,投弃(指投弃货物入海之行为,目的为减轻载重而避免沉没)

Jewish a. 犹太人似的,犹太人的

Jewish law 犹太人法,犹太教法

Jewry n. 犹太人;犹太民族;犹太人居住区

Jews n. 犹太人

jiggery-pokery n. (英)欺骗,诈骗

Jigsaw family 重组家庭,拼图家庭(又可写作 jigsaw puzzle family,指的是包括夫妻各自在前一段关系中生育的子女在内的再婚家庭。由已婚夫妇和自己平均生育的1.6个子女组成的传统家庭正被由夫妻二人以及各自在前一段关系中生育的子女所组成的家庭取代)

jihād n. 吉哈德(原意"奋斗",指穆罕默德与麦加多神教徒进行的战争,后指在伊斯兰旗帜下为宗教而进行的战争)穆斯林的护教战争,圣战;维护信仰的运动(for),讨伐(against)

Jim Crow (美俚)老乌鸦(指对黑人的污蔑称呼);(蔑称)黑人;对黑人的不平等待遇;种族歧视

Jim crow car 黑人专用列车

Jim Crow Law 歧视黑人的法律[指非法强制种族隔离的法律,此术语最早来源于19世纪名叫多玛斯·迪·瑞斯(Thomas D. Rice)的黑人话剧演员所唱"Jim Crow"的歌词]

Jim Crowism (美)种族歧视的做法(或政策),反黑人情绪;种族隔离,种族歧视

Jimmy Grant (美)对全部移民的(总)称呼

jingo n. 侵略主义者;沙文主义者,武力外交政策论者

jingoism n. 侵略主义,沙文主义

job n./v. 工作,包工,零活;职业,职位;职责,任务;(美俚)犯罪行为(尤指偷窃);(假公济私的)营利事业/批发;代客买卖;假公济私,营私;做零工,做包工

job action (对警察等的)抗议行动,临时性罢工示威;国家雇员或公职人员的罢工

job discipline 劳动纪律
job holder 有职业者;(美)公务员
job hunter (美)求职者,找工作的人
job lose from imports 进口导致职位丧失
job offer pendency 有条件给予工作
job lot 成批出售;分批出售
job responsibility system 岗位责任制
job restructing 职务再造
job security 就业保障
job splitting 一工分做制(指现代资本主义采取把全工日改为两半日工的做法)
job work 包工,散工
job-safety law 职业安全法
jobber n. 临时工人,做零活的人,散工;(英)股票证券经纪人,中间人;批发商;假公济私者
jobber's turn 中间人的赢利,赚头
jobbery n. 假公济私,营私舞弊,渎职行为
jockey v. 运用手段谋利益,比赛,驾驶;操作,欺骗
jockey club (英)(私营)赛马总会
jockeying among the judge and lawyers 法官与律师之间的技巧(或手段,谋略)
John Doe 原告(或被告)某甲(指诉讼程序中对不知道真实姓名的当事人的称呼)
John Marshall 约翰·马歇尔(1755—1835),生于美国弗吉尼亚曼敦(现在的米达兰),他的父母共有15个孩子,他为长子。边陲生活使马歇尔养成了平易近人而民主的品行。1801—1835年任首席大法官。约翰·马歇尔深受公众爱戴,他是解释美国联邦宪法的杰出代表,"伟大的首席大法官"。1901年奥利弗·温德尔·霍尔姆斯(Oliver Wendell Holmes)称:"他的伟大之处,部分在于他'存在'于联邦最高法院历史上的成型时期。马歇尔的保守的国家主义思想迎合了这个时期的要求。"他的个性和法学天赋使他超然胜任首席大法官的职责。约翰·亚当斯(John Adams)总统于1801年1月20日任命马歇尔为联邦最高法院首席大法官,以拯救宪法,使其免遭以杰斐逊为首的共和党人的破坏。战争年代铸就了马歇尔良好的职业观念。由于父亲的影响及个人在独立战争中的经历,他热爱联邦并将这种情感注入法学理念之中。1780年,他参加乔治·威思(George Wythe)(据说是美国第一个法学教授)的法学讲座之后开始了他的法学研究,继而又从事法律实务工作,作为法学巨匠所应具备的那些基本素质在他身上均有完美之结合。马歇尔自1801年3月5日担任联邦首席大法官后,即通过统一联邦最高法院而强化其地位。19—20世纪,他的判决意见经常被引用来说明联邦权力的正当性。他在联邦最高法院最有优势的时期是1801—1811年。1811—1823年是联邦最高法院最稳定和最有成效的时期。这一时期他与其他几位具有独立见解的同僚分享权力并在后10年进一步使自己的领导风格变得温和,以适应新时代。

John Wigmore 约翰·威格莫尔,美国证据法学家,他写的"A Treatise on the Anglo-American System of Evidence in Trials at Common Law"(《在普通法审判中的英美证据法学体系专论》)被认为是最经典的证据学专著

join v. 1.结合,参加;使缔交,使联姻 2.伴同,随同;毗连,接近
join force (with) (与)合作,联合行动
join issue 讨论;妥协;共同提出系争点供裁决;对一方或双方提出的系争点进行辩论;共同起诉
join(或 **take**)**issue with sb.** 与某人争论
join three (美)支持三位大法官签发调查令的投票[指在三位大法官同意对某一诉讼请求签发调令卷,而第四位大法官作出支持三位大法官签发调卷令的投票时则意味着可以签发,反之则视为拒绝签发。根据联邦最高法院的"四人规则"(rule of four),在四位大法官同意受理某上诉案时,法院可以行使管辖权。甚至在不足四位大法官投票受理这个案子时,也可能会签发调卷令。这种"支持三位大法官签发调卷令的投票"的确切起源无从知道,但这一惯例显然出现于"伯格法院"(即以Warren Earl Burger为首的大法官在任期间的法院)(1969年6月—1986年9月)]
joinder n. 1.联合,结合 2.共同诉讼,联合诉讼,合并诉讼;对他方提出的系争点的

接受(见 non-joinder)
joinder devices 合并方法,合并设计
joinder in demurrer 原告接受被告抗辩中所提出的法律上的系争点
joinder in issue 一方接受另一方提出的事实上的系争点
joinder in pleading 在答辩中接受对方的系争点
joinder of actions 联合诉讼,诉讼合并
joinder of causes of action 诉讼原因合并(指将几个诉因合在一起进行诉讼);同一诉讼有数项诉因
joinder of charges 合并检控
joinder of claims in the alternative 选择性请求合并
joinder of defendants 共同(刑事)被告
joinder of errors 1.对刑事复审令中所声称的错误所作的书面否认 2.对合并的系争事实所作的答复
joinder of indictments or informations 起诉书或控告状的合并
joinder of issues 双方系争事实的合并,相互坚持己见的系争点
joinder of offenders 共同(刑事)被告
joinder of offenses 数罪并合(指数种罪行合并在一起进行诉讼)
joinder of parties 多方当事人合并的诉讼,共同诉讼
joinder of persons needed for just adjudication 对公正审判所需的主体合并
joinder of proceedings 诉讼合并
joint n./a. 1.接合,连接(处)2.吸毒窝,下流场所/共同的,共有的;连带的;联合的;同时的,合办的
joint account 共同账户(指两人共有的银行账户),联合账户,合资账户
joint act (或 **conduct**)共同行为
joint action 联合行动;共同诉讼
joint action by the contracting parties 缔约国的联合行动
joint activity report 公共活动报告;联合活动报告
joint administration (破产财产)联合管理,共同管理(指破产法上,为了方便处理包括通知债权人在内的各项管理事务,以

便更有效地结案,通常将涉及多个债务人的两项或两项以上的破产财产置于一个案卷之中,进行并案处理。如果系属的两个或两个以上案件中涉及一对夫妻、合伙或至少一个合伙人、两个或两个以上商业合伙人或一个商业机构和一个附属机构,此时破产法院可以命令联合或共同管理破产财产。其目的在于提高办理两案之效率,债权人的实质权利并不受到影响。此术语亦作 procedural consolidation)
joint adventure 临时合伙,短期合伙,合资经营(企业)
joint agency 共同代理;联合经销处
joint and common (连带)共有的(财产)
joint and common property (夫妻)共同财产(制),(连带)共有财产
joint and mutual will 共同和相互遗嘱(指两人或两人以上为了对共同财产作遗赠处分而共同订立的遗嘱。joint will 是作出一个遗嘱文件共同在文件上签署,而 mutual will 则在各自作出的遗嘱上彼此加以规定)
joint and separate responsibility 共同连带责任
joint and several 共同的和个别的;连带的(见 jointly and severally)
joint and several contracts 连带合同(契约)
joint and several debtor 连带债务人
joint and several liability 连带责任,几个债务人的连带责任(见 jointly and severally)
joint and several obligation 连带之债
joint authors 合著者,共同作者,合作作者(指合作作者的所有作者,每位合作作者均有权按其意愿使用该作品,因此得到的收益应由合作作者按其在作品中所创作部分的比例分享)
joint cargo system 联合货运制度
joint cause of action 共同诉因
joint charges 联合(运输)费用
joint claim 共同权利,共同请求权,共同索赔
joint commission (或 **committee**) 议会(上下两院的)联合委员会;(几个组织

的)联合委员会
joint *communiqué* 联合公报
joint concealment of crime 共同隐瞒罪行
joint consignment 合伙寄销
joint conspiracy 同谋,共谋
joint consultation 共同磋商
joint contract 共同合同(契约)
joint covenant 盟约
joint credit 共同债权;共同信用
joint creditors 共同债权人
joint custody (美)共同监护(指父母双方同时获得对子女之监护权,但在法律和身体监护上加以分配)
joint debt 共同债务
joint debtors 共同债务人
joint declaration 联合声明
joint defence pact 共同防御公约
joint defendants 共同被告
joint determination 联合决定
joint doers 共同行为人
joint enterprise 合营企业
joint estate 共同财产;共有不动产物权
joint executors 遗嘱共同执行人;(两人或两人以上的)共同执行人
joint exploitation 联合开发;共同剥削
joint family (system) (几世同堂的)大家庭(制)
joint fiat 法官联合指令(指对两个或两个以上的贸易伙伴人发出的法官指令)
joint gains 共同利益
joint guarantee 共同担保,联保
joint habitation 同居,共同居住
joint hearing 会审
joint heir 共同继承人,合并继承人[指①共同继承人之一(coheir);②指该人是或将是指定的两人继承人之一并在该两人中的生存者死亡时才能发生继承]
joint illegal act 共同不法行为
joint indictment 联合诉状
joint industrial council 劳资联合委员会
joint inspection 双方会同检查
joint instigators 共同教唆犯
joint intervention 共同干预;共同调停
joint investigation 联合调查;共同侦查
joint investment company (venture) 合资公司
joint legal custody 法律上共同监护
joint lessees 共同承租人
joint liability 连带责任;共同责任
joint liability company 连带责任公司
joint lives 双方都活着的时候(使用)(指一项地产或权利授予两个或两个以上的人,在他们都活着这一持续期间使用,其中有一个人死亡,权益即告终止)
joint meeting 联席会议
joint mortgage 联合抵押
joint negligence 共同过失
joint nomination 联合提名
joint note 共同票据
joint obligation 共同之债
joint offence 共同犯罪
joint offenders 共犯,共谋者,同谋者
joint operating agreement 联合经营协议(指一种合资经营形式,具有共同投资、共同经营、共负盈亏的特点,但参加协议的各方并不共同组成一个独立的企业,在法律上仍保持各自的独立地位)
joint owners 共有人,共同所有人,有共同所有权的物主
joint ownership 共有,共有权
joint ownership of common space (建筑大楼的)公用楼层空间的共同所有权
joint participation (1971 年)(民权法)(Civil Rights Law)共同参与[指个人从事的职业与政府部门或国家公务人员相一致,这就导致个人履行公务(public functions)。因此,依照民权法,则应遵从权利请求(claims)。见 Symbiotic Relationship Test; nexus test]
joint parties 共同当事人
joint physical custody 物质上共同监护
joint plot 共谋,合谋,同谋
joint private enterprise 私人联合企业
joint property (夫妻的)共同财产(制)
joint purchase 共同购买(权)
joint resolution (17 世纪)(议会法)联合决议(指审议会或立法机构的一项正式的、主要的动议、意愿或一个法案,决议是主要动议的最高形式,通常含有一个序言和一个或一个以上的解决条款,其形式:

resoluted, that;它是参众两院通过的立法决议,具有法律效力,但须经总统批准方能成为法律)

joint return (1930年)夫妻所得税的共同申报,共同纳税申报[指夫妻一起共同呈递纳税申报单(return)。即使夫妻只有一方有收入,这种共同所得税纳税申报单仍然适用,但夫妻各方通常分别有责任纳税]

joint session (of both chambers) (议会上下两院的)联席会议

joint shareholders 共同股份持有人

joint signature 联合签字,联署

joint state-private enterprise (中)公私合营企业

joint statement 联合声明

joint stock 合股,合资

joint stock companies act 股份公司法

joint stock company 合股公司;合股殖民公司(指英国17世纪初以公司代替殖民者经营的主要殖民机构)

joint stock insurance company 合股保险公司

joint stock limited company 合股有限公司

joint stock limited partnership 合股有限合伙(公司)

joint sureties 连带保证人,共同担保人

joint suretyship 连带保证,共同担保

joint tax return (美)(夫妻)个人所得税合并申报表

joint tenancy 共同共有权[见 concurrent estate (财产)共有权];共同租借权;共同租赁;(英美)共同土地保有(权);(动产或不动产)共同占有(指由两人或两人以上共同占有的财产具有不可分割性,如一个共同占有人死亡时,则其份额直接归属于生存者占有。见 tenancy in common)

joint tenants 共同租借人;(英)共同土地保有人;(财产)合有人

joint terms for delivery of goods 交货共同条件

joint tort 共同侵权行为;共同过失行为

joint tort-feasors 共同侵权人,共同侵权行为人(指共同或分别单独侵害他人的人身或财产,而发生同一损害结果的人),共同过失责任人

joint trial 会审(指涉及两个或两个以上的当事方的审理,特别是两人或两人以上的同类或相似罪行的刑事审判)

joint trustees 共同受托(管理)人

joint venture 联合企业;(中)合营企业,合资经营企业;临时合伙

joint venture company 合资公司

joint venture with Chinese and foreign investment 中外合资经营企业

joint venturer (企业)合营者

joint verdict 共同裁决

joint will 共同遗嘱(见 joint and mutual will)

joint-welfare fund 共同福利基金[指经集体协议(collective bargaining)给工会雇员(union employees)提供健康福利而建立的基金。这项基金由劳资管理部门(labor and management representatives)共同管理,亦称 Taft-Hartley fund]

jointly acquired property 共同获得的财产(指夫妻在婚姻持续期间共同挣得的财产)

jointly and severally (或 joint and several) 连带责任(的)和各个负责(的);共同和个别(的)(指两人或两人以上的联合声明,表示他们共同和个别负责,即在不履行某契约或不偿还某笔欠款时,他们可由对方任意联合控诉或分开控诉。见 joint and several liability)

jointly and severally bound 连带责任,共同及个别负责

jointly and severally liable 负有连带责任的

jointly assess 评议商定

jointly cause an injury 共同导致(的)损害(或伤害)

jointly held 联合持有

jointrees n. 享有寡妇所得产(业)的女人

jointure n./v. 寡妇所得产(指丈夫生前拨给妻子的产业,通常指出租的房地产,作为丈夫死后妻子的扶养费)/指定死后由妻子继承财产

joker n. (美)(为意图歪曲本意使法案等

失效而在条文中埋下的)伏笔,曲笔;隐蔽的障碍

Jone(s) Act 琼斯法(美国 1920 年通过的联邦法;该法规定因船长、船主或其他海员过失使受雇佣海员在受雇佣期受到伤害的,受雇佣海员可索取赔偿金。现此法条可用于铁路员工)

Jone Doe 约翰·多伊;译"某甲"(可作虚拟的名义适用)

Joseph Story 约瑟夫·斯托里(1779—1845)美国法学家,曾任美国联邦最高法院大法官 30 多年,从 1832 年至 1845 年的 13 年中写过九本非凡的教科书,对美国法的形成有深远影响

jougs (joggs 或 juggs) n. 铁枷(指苏格兰、荷兰等地使用的惩罚器械)

journal n. (立法机关等的)议事录;日志;航海日记;杂志;日报;公报;日记账

journalism n. 报刊(总称);新闻业,新闻出版

journalist's privilege 新闻工作者的特权

Journals of Parliament 《国会议事录》

Journals of the Houses of Parliament (英)议会两院公报

journey n. 旅行,路程;历程

journey man 雇工,计日工;熟练工人

journey work 短工工作,雇用性的工作

joust(s) n. 比赛,斗争,参加比赛

joyrider n. 偷开车者

joyriding n. 疯狂驱车,偷开车

jubere (大陆法)命令,指挥;保证,承诺

Judaic law 犹太法(指尊重犹太人的宗教信仰、习惯和判例的犹太法典)

judex (= iudex) (大陆法)审判人员,法官;(古罗马)(保民官指定的)审判官;(古英国法)陪审员

judex a quo (大陆法)其判决被提出上诉的法官,原审法官,下级法官,与 *judex ad quem* 相对

judex ad quem (大陆法)受理上诉的法官,上级法官

Judex aequitatem semper spectare debet. A judge ought always to regard equity. 法官应当始终注意公平(衡平)

* *Judex bonus nihil ex arbitrio suo faciat, nec propositione domesticae voluntatis, sed juxta leges et jura pronunciet.* A good judge may do nothing from his own judgement, or from a dictate of private will; but he will pronounce according to law and justice. 称职的法官应依据法律和正义审理案件,而不受个人意愿好恶之影响。

* *Judex damnatur cum nocens absolvitur.* The judge is condemned when a guilty person escapes punishment. 有罪的人逍遥法外时,办案的法官应当受到谴责。

judex datus (罗马法)委任法官(指罗马的长官或省长委任审理案件的法官)

* *Judex debet judicare secundum allegata et probata.* The judge ought to decide according to the allegations and the proofs. 法官应当根据所提出的事实陈述和证据作出裁决。

judex delegatus (罗马法)特别法官,专门法官

* *Judex est lex loquens.* The judge is the speaking law. 法官是法律的代言人,法官是讲法律的。

judex fiscalis (罗马法)国库法官,财政法官(具有财产方面管辖权的法官)

* *Judex habere debet duos sales, salem sapientiae, ne sit insipidus, et salem conscientiae, ne sit diabolus.* A judge should have two salt: the salts of wisdom, lest he be foolish; and the salt of conscience, lest he be devilish. 法官应具有两种素质:一为智慧,使他不至受到愚弄;另一为良知,使他不至于邪恶。

* *Judex non potest esse testis in propria causa.* A judge cannot be a witness in his own cause. 法官不得在其受理的案件中当证人。

* *Judex non potest injuriam sibi datam punire.* A judge cannot punish a wrong done to himself. 法官不得对使自己蒙受损害的非法行为进行惩处。

* *judex non reddit plus quam quod petens ipse requirit.* The judge does not give more than the plaintiff himself demands. 法院之判决不得超出原告本身之请求的

范围。
judex ordinarius （大陆法）普通法官,常任法官
judex pedaneus （罗马法）助理法官（指①审理较小案件之法官；②下级法官,又称"judex specialis"）
judex selectux （大陆法）选定的法官（指刑事诉讼中被选定审理事实问题的法官）
Judex specialis （罗马法）（见 *judex pedaneus*）
judge n./v.　1.审判员,裁判员,法官,审判官（旧译：推事）2.鉴定人；审查官 3.裁判人,评判员；（大写）最高审判者（指上帝）/审判,裁判,审理,判决；裁定,判断,断定；鉴别,鉴定；作出裁判,作出判决；当法官
judge a case on its own merits　按事实真相（是非曲直）来审案
judge ad hoc　临时法官
judge advocate　军法官,军法检察官
judge advocate of the fleet　海军军法官,海军法律顾问
judge advocate-general　军法署署长,军法处长,高级军事法官；(苏格兰)代理检察长
judge advocate-general's department　军法署,军事司法部(门)
judge concurring in majority opinion　赞成大多数意见的法官
judge consul　领事裁判官,仲裁领事
judge de facto　事实上的法官
judge d'instruction　（法）预审法官,预审推事
judge in chambers　（英）内庭法官
judge in lunacy　（英）审理精神错乱案法官（系大法官分庭的法官,现称保护法官）
judge in reserve　（或 expectant judge）候补审判员,候补法官（旧译：候补推事）
judge in the first instance　一审法官,初审法官
judge interacts with jury　法官与陪审团互动
Judge Lynch　法官"私刑"（把私刑拟人化）
judge made law　见 judge-made law
judge of the trial bench　法庭审判员,承审法官,审判庭法官
judge ordinary　常任法官；（英）（高等法院的遗嘱检验、离婚、海事分庭的）庭长
judge pro tempore　临时法官（指常任法官缺席时,临时任命的法官履行整个开庭期和短时期内的法官职责）
* **Judge should be liable to no seducement.** 法官不应受诱惑。
judge with penal functions　刑事法官
judge writing dissent　书写反对意见的法官
judge writing majority opinion　书写大多数意见的法官
judge's chamber　（通常用复数）1.法官办公室或密室 2.在未举行开庭期时,法官处理公务之处（见 in camera）
judge's charge to the jury　法官对陪审团的指示（指法官听审完毕后,总结案中证据,向陪审员讲明他们有关判断该案件的责任,并指导他们如何作出裁定）
Judge's Code of Judicial Conduct　《法官司法行为准则》
judge's comment　法官的判断,法官的评价
judge's marshal　高等法院巡回法官的秘书
judge's mental impressions　法官心证
judge's note　法官笔录
judge's oath　法官的宣誓
judge's order　法官发布的命令
Judge's Rules　（英）《法官规程》（1712年高等院对法官制定的录取证供的一种规定,如违反规定,法庭可不接受证供）
judge's statement on decision　法官的判决陈述
judge's trials　法官的试办
judge-jury issue　（美）法官与陪审团争议[指伯德案（Byrd v. Blue Ridge Rural Electric Cooperative Inc.）中原告是否是法定的雇员,联邦最高法院裁定由联邦法院陪审团决定这一问题]
judge-made a.　由法官（或判决）制定的（指先例、判例等）
judge-made law（=judge made law）　判例法,法官（制定）法；法官造法（原则）
judge-made rules　判例法,法官造法

（原则）

judge-made standing rule （美）法官创制的诉讼资格规则（指可提交法院解决争议类型进行限制的一种控制机制）

judge-of-law n. 司法官

judges d'instance （法）初审法官

Judges Rule （英）法官规则（指指导警察询问犯罪嫌疑人或受刑事指控者的规则。现在这些规则已经被1984年的《警察和刑事证据法》和国务大臣的《程序法典》中相关的拘留、传唤、询问所代替）

judges sitting together 合议法官，合议庭审判员

Judges' Bill （美）法官法案

judges' private sitting 法官在判决前的评议，合议

judges' summons 法庭传票，法官传票

judgeship n. 法官（或审判员）的职权（任期或地位）

judging from the fact 根据事实判断

judging the law 评断法律

judg(e)ment n. 1.审判，裁判，裁决，判决（指刑事或民事诉讼的法庭的裁定、决定或判决）2.判断，鉴定，评价 3.意见，看法 4.批评，指责

judg(e)ment affirmed 维持原判

judgment against defendant 对被告不利的判决

judgment against the debtor 不利债务人（或被告）的判决

judg(e)ment against the plaintiff 原告败诉的判决

judgment as a matter of law 作为法律问题（或事项）的判决（指就特定请求没有提出足够可信的证据来让陪审团考虑而由法官作出的裁决。美国《联邦民事诉讼规则》第50条规定"在对方当事人的证据提供完毕之后，任何当事人均有权请求法院基于欠缺可靠证据的原因，作出不利于对方当事人的判决"）

judg(e)ment as prodigal 判为浪费者（浪子）

judg(e)ment book 判决记录簿

judg(e)ment by confession 根据（被告的）招供作出的判决

judg(e)ment by consent 合议判决；临时判决

judg(e)ment by default 缺席判决，缺席审判

judg(e)ment creditor 判定债权人，胜诉债权人

judg(e)ment debt 判决确定的债务，经法院裁定的债务

judg(e)ment debtor 判定债务人，败诉债务人

judgment docket （法院）判决登记簿（指法院书记官记录并保存的判决登记和记录的册子或一览表，提供有关各当事方所涉及的现行判决的相关事项的官方记载，供公众查阅。亦称为 judgment book；judgment file；judgment record；judgment roll）

judgment entered for the plaintiff 作出对原告有利的判决

judgment execution 判决执行（指命令执行官员没收判定债务人的财产来执行正式的或书面的偿还债务的判决）

judg(e)ment for the plaintiff 原告胜诉的判决

judg(e)ment in default 缺席判决

judgment in error 见 erroneous judgment

judg(e)ment in favo(u)r of the plaintiff 有利于原告的判决

judg(e)ment *in personam* 对人的判决

judg(e)ment *in rem* 对物的判决

judg(e)ment individual 经常犯罪者

judg(e)ment lien 法院判决的留置权，法院判决的财产扣押

judg(e)ment *non obstante veredicto* 不顾陪审团评断的裁决 [见 judg(e)ment not withstanding the verdict]，特别许可的裁决（见 direct verdict）

judgment of nonsuit 驳回诉讼的判决（见 nonsuit）

judg(e)ment not withstanding the verdict (JNOV) 无视裁决的判决，否定裁决的判决，与陪审团裁断相反的判决

judg(e)ment note （债务人未还债时，允许债权人不通知债务人）直接诉诸法院的条款

judg(e)ment of acquittal 判决无罪开释，

(宣告)无罪的判决
judg(e)ment of execution 执行判决;(刑事诉讼中)死刑判决
judg(e)ment of final instance 终审判决
judg(e)ment of first instance 初审判决
judg(e)ment of God 神意裁决
judg(e)ment of *non pros* 对不及时诉讼的判决(见 *non prosequitur*)
judg(e)ment of sentence 科刑判决
judg(e)ment on the merits 实质性问题的判决,根据案情和证据的判决(基于案情事实的)的最后判决
judg(e)ment on the pleadings 根据诉状作出判决
judg(e)ment payable 判定的应付款项
judg(e)ment proof (judgement proofness) 对于一切追索金钱的判决不生效者,无力履行判决者(亦称 execution-proof)
judg(e)ment record 判决记录
judgment roll 判决案卷[指美国一些州的书记官在登记判决时要作出案卷,内容有传票、判决、当事人自认书以及法庭命令等。在联邦多数州,判决分别记录在民事卷和刑事卷(civil docket and criminal docket)之中。在英国判决卷的全部诉讼程序的记录,均由法院存档]
judg(e)ment seat 审判员(法官)席;法院
judg(e)ment sum 判定数额
judg(e)ment summons 拘禁"判定债务人"传票
judg(e)ment thief 惯盗,惯偷
judgment without reasserting the jurisdiction point 没有管辖争议的判决,没有重新断定管辖权上的问题的判决
judg(e)ments extension acts (英)判决域外执行法(指 1868 年和 1682 年的一些法规)
judicable a. 可被审判的,应受审判的
* ***Judicandum est legibus, non exemplis.***
Judg(e)ment is to be given according to the laws, not according to examples or precedents. 判决应当根据法律而不应当按照案例或先例作出。
judicare (大陆法和古英国法)审判;判决;裁决

judicare model 司法保障模式(指加拿大称与专职律师相对的私人律师模式为 judicare model)
judicatio (大陆法)审判;(案件听审后)宣告判决
judicative a. 有审判权的;判决的;司法的;法庭的
judicator n. 审判官,裁判人
judicatory a./n. 审判的,裁判的;司法的/(总称)法院;司法行政;审判制度;裁判所
judicatum solvi 1.(罗马法)以判决方式来决定支付数额 2.(罗马法)为判决方式判定支付数额担保,在审理时当诉讼代理人以被告代理人身份出现时,可以适用
judicature n. 1.司法;司法权 2.(总称)审判员(法官);审判员(法官)的地位(职务、职权) 3.法庭 4.审判制度,司法行政 5.法官或法院的管辖权(或审判权)
Judicature Act (英)《司法组织法》;《司法制度(改革)法》[指在 1873—1875 年间对高等法院的组织和审判程序进行改革的法律。撤销了当时的最高司法组织,而组成了单一最高法院(Supreme Court)体系,下设高等法院(High Court of Justice)和上诉法院(Court of Appeal)。高等法院又再分为王座、民诉、财税、衡平以及遗嘱检验、离婚和海事 5 个分庭,从而奠定英国现代司法组织]
judicature fee stamp 裁判费印戳
Judicia Populi (罗马)平民法院
judiciability n. 可判决性;可裁决性
judicial a. 司法的;审判上的,法官的,法庭的,法院判决的;法官身份的;公正的;明断的;批评的
judicial abuse of sentencing power 司法(机关对)量刑权的滥用
judicial acquiescence 司法默认,司法默许,法院默认
judicial act 审判上的行为,司法行为(指司法官员执行司法职务的行为)
Judicial Act of 1925 (或 **Judges' Bill**)(美)《司法法》;《法官法》(指由于第一次世界大战后所激发的沉重案件负担而引起的《司法法》。该法的目的在于使备审案件数能适应联邦最高法院的判案能力)

judicial action 司法行为;(法院)审判行为;裁决行为(指法庭听审案件,确定当事人之间的权利与义务关系,并根据当事人的请求作出裁决)

judicial activism 司法激进主义(指美国一些主张法官超越他们特定的权力并致力于创造法律而不仅是解释法律的批评观点。与此相对的是司法保守主义观点,即主张法官应避免通过其判决和命令来影响公共政策。美国历史上很长一段时间都以保守的司法主义为特征,其表现就是联邦最高法院不允许各州或国会制定调整社会或经济事务的立法);司法能动主义(主要指鼓励法官摆脱遵照先例的束缚,允许法官在作出判决时考虑其个人对于公共政策的观点以及其他因素。另外还适用司法经济原则来解决WTO法的内部冲突)

judicial administration 司法管理(主要涉及两个领域——法院组织、人事的管理以及诉讼的运行管理)

judicial administration of justice 公正司法审判;主管司法审判

judicial administration of punitive justice 惩罚性的公正司法审判

judicial administrative authority 司法行政权;司法行政当局(机关)

judicial administrative organs 司法行政机关

judicial administrators 司法行政长官

judicial and juristic experience of the rules and principles 规则和原则的司法和法理的经验

judicial apparatus 审判机关,司法机关

Judicial Appointed Committee (英)司法任命委员会(此机构为布莱尔在政组内阁时期三年内新设立的机构,包括Supreme Court, Department of Constitutional Affairs & Judicial Appointed Committee。见Department of Constitutional Affairs)

judicial appointment 司法职务,司法任用

judicial approval 司法认可,司法允许

judicial arbitration 司法仲裁,法院仲裁

Judicial Arbitration & Mediation Service Inc. (JAMS) (美)(设立在洛杉矶南部的)司法仲裁和调解服务有限公司(由退休法官沃伦奈特在1977年建立,依靠200名退休法官进行调解、仲裁或案件鉴定工作)

judicial area 司法管辖范围;司法管区

judicial arrogance 司法傲慢

judicial assembly 审判大会

judicial assertion 司法主张

judicial assessor 司法陪审员;司法顾问

judicial assistance 司法援助

judicial attachment 法院扣押

judicial authority 司法权威

judicial authority of the federal government 联邦政府的司法权限(权力)

judicial auxiliaries 司法辅助人员;司法机关的附属机关

judicial avoidance 经司法机关(法院)宣布的无效

judicial banishment 司法放逐

judicial behavior 司法行为

judicial bench (总称)法官

judicial biography 司法发展史

judicial body 司法机关

judicial branch 司法部门

judicial business 司法业务

judicial cadre (中)司法干部

judicial canton 司法片区

judicial capacity 司法职能,司法权力

judicial chamber 司法庭

judicial chauvinism 司法沙文主义

judicial circles 司法界

judicial circuits 巡回审判

judicial clerkship 法院书记员职位

judicial clout 司法影响,司法势力

Judicial Code (美)《司法法典》(见Federal Judicial Code)

judicial cognizance 司法知识,审判知识(见judicial notice)

judicial combat 司法决斗

judicial comity 司法礼让(指法院之间的相互尊重)

judicial committee(或 **commission**) 审判委员会,司法委员会

Judicial Committee of the Privy Council (英)枢密院司法委员会

Judicial Committee of the Supreme People's Court (中)最高人民法院审判委员会
judicial competence 司法权限
judicial composition 司法和解(指具备破产原因的债务人为避免破产清算,而与债权人团体达成让步方法了结债务的协议,但须经法院认可后方能生效的一项法律程序)
judicial concentration 司法审讯;司法检查;司法研究
judicial conference 司法会议(指法官检讨诉讼程序等有关法院问题的会议)
Judicial conference of senior circuit judges 司法高级巡回法官大会
Judicial Conference of the United States 美国司法大会[指1922年设立的高级巡回法官大会(Judicial Conference of Senior Circuit Judges),由首席大法官任主席,每一巡回法庭首席大法官、国际贸易法庭首席法官以及每一巡回区的地区法院的一名法官组成]
judicial confession (被告在法庭上的)自供,坦白,当庭供认
judicial control 司法监督,司法管制
judicial cooperation agreement 司法合作协定
judicial council 司法委员会,司法会议
judicial counsel(l)or 法律顾问
judicial court 法院,法庭,司法法院
judicial decision 司法裁决
judicial decision-making 司法裁决
judicial declaration (原告的)司法申诉;(苏格兰)法庭上的承认(等同于英国的judicial admission)
judicial declaration of nationality 国籍的司法宣告
judicial declaration of right 司法上的权利宣告
judicial defender 司法辩护人
judicial deference 司法遵从,司法确认
judicial deliverance 司法判决,司法法官判决意见
judicial democracy 司法民主
judicial department 司法部门
judicial dicta judicial dictum 的复数

judicial dictum 法院(或法官)对判决的意见,法官审判时表示的意见
judicial discoverable and manageable standards 司法上可发现的和管理的标准
judicial discretion 司法酌处权,法官的自由裁量权;(英)司法自由裁量权(指法官对当事人是否给予衡平法上的救济,有自由决定权)
judicial dissent 司法分歧
judicial district (巡回法院的)审判区域,司法辖区
judicial divorce 法院判定的离婚
judicial doctrine 司法原理
judicial document 司法文件
judicial duty 司法职责;司法义务
judicial economy 司法节制,司法经济性
judicial empirism 司法经验
judicial entity 法律实体;法人,法人单位
judicial errors 司法错误,审判错误
judicial establishment 司法机构
judicial estoppel 司法上的宣誓陈述不容推翻原则,司法上的陈述不容否认(指防止一方当事人否认在同一或以前的司法程序中所作宣誓的陈述。因为如果以后立场观点改变会不利地影响诉讼程序并在法庭上构成欺骗,所以禁止其以后涉及同一争点和相同当事人之诉讼进程中予以否认或推翻。亦称 doctrine of preclusion of inconsistent positions; doctrine of the conclusiveness of the judgment)
judicial ethics (美)司法职业道德准则,司法伦理准则[该准则关系到司法行为的三个方面:①法官作为法官应有的行为;②什么情况下法官应当避免参与审理案件,即应回避(recusal)问题;③法官的非司法活动的恰当范围。这些控制着司法职业道德的规则和原则来源于习惯或传统以及正当程序的宪法保证(见 due process, procedural)、国会通过的各种制定法以及司法系统采用的各种自律规则。联邦最高法院的大法官也受那些控制低级联邦法院和州法院法官的司法伦理原则的约束。这些基本原则规定在法官行为法典之中。该法典由美国律师协会起

草,并在 1972 年公布。尽管法官行为法典不能控制联邦最高法院的法官,然而其规定反映了习惯法和普通法的内容,并且在实际上也适用于联邦最高法院的大法官们]

judicial evidence 司法证据(指法院出示认定的证据或被法庭采信的证据);诉讼证据

judicial examination 司法审讯

judicial experience 司法经验

judicial experiment 司法实验

judicial experimentation and experience 司法实践和司法经验

judicial expertise 司法鉴定

judicial finding of law 适用法律的司法裁决

judicial function 司法职能,审判权能;法院职能

judicial functionary 法院工作人员,司法工作人员

judicial game 司法竞技;司法博弈

judicial guarantee 司法担保;法律保证

judicial guardianship 司法监护权

judicial guideline 司法指导

judicial head 司法官员,法官

judicial hearing 司法听证

judicial hierarchy (法院)审级制度,法院的等级制度;司法系统

judicial highlights 司法上的重要部分,司法上的要点

judicial history 司法历史,司法史

judicial homologation 司法部门的同意;司法部门的认可

judicial hypothec 司法上的不转移财产占有权的担保;法院判定的不转移财产占有权的担保

judicial ideas 司法意见;司法观念

judicial immunity (美)司法豁免(指法官对其履行司法职能的行为免于承担民事责任。见 judicial immunity from civil damages)

judicial immunity from civil damages (美)民事损害赔偿的司法豁免[指法官对因其公务行为造成的民事损害赔偿享有豁免权。这起源于 16 世纪早期,并在普通法和美国判例中得以确立。美国联邦最高法院在兰德尔诉布里汉姆(Randell v. Brigham)(1869 年)案中判决"个人不能因法官的司法行为而对其提起诉讼,哪怕这些行为是有害的或应受谴责的"。三年后,在布拉德利诉费希尔(Bradley v. Fisher)(1872 年)一案中,联邦最高法院宣布"豁免是一个'最重要'的'原则'"。然而,在"普利亚姆诉艾廉"(Pulliam v. Alien)(1984 年)一案中,联邦最高法院判决"司法豁免既不适用于司法官员在法定权限内的行为违反以后颁布的禁令而应给予的赔偿,也不适用于依据民事权利律师费偿还法所应赔偿的律师费"]

judicial impression 司法效果

Judicial Improvement and Access to Judicial Act (美)1988 年通过的《司法改进和获得司法行为权》[此立法实际旨在消除所有法院无自由裁量权的管理上诉管辖,使联邦最高法院只需审理强制性上诉案,以减轻联邦最高法院沉重的案件负担]

judicial independence 司法独立

judicial indication 司法信号,司法标志

judicial indulgence 司法宽容

judicial inquiry 司法调查(指调查过去和现在发生的事实,据此依据法律宣布某人应承担的责任)

judicial instance 审级

judicial interdiction 司法上的禁治产

judicial interpretation 司法(上的)解释

judicial intervention 司法干预

judicial inventiveness 司法创造性

judicial investigation 法院调查;司法调查

judicial judgment 司法判断

judicial justice 司法公正

judicial knowledge 审判(上的)知识(见 judicial notice)

judicial latitude 司法范畴,司法幅度,司法自由

judicial law 审判法

judicial law finding 审判法裁判

Judicial Law for Laymen 《俗人判例法》[指东欧各国采用最早的(10 世纪)《查士丁尼法典选编》中的不同于斯拉夫文的一种译本,内容主要涉及刑法]

judicial law-making 司法立法,审判立法,司法法官制定法,法院创立法

judicial legislation 司法立法;(英)有关法院的立法(常用来表示根据"遵循先例"原则作出的实际上是重申或修改众所周知的法律原则的判决)

judicial lien 法律上的留置权,法院判定的留置权(见 status lien)

judicial limitation of time for argument 辩论的司法时效(对辩论的司法有效期限)

judicial limits 司法管辖范围

judicial liquidation 司法清算,经由法院的清算,法定清算

judicial machinery 司法机构

judicial magistracy 司法行政官,司法行政官法庭

judicial magistrate 司法行政官,地方司法官

judicial making 司法发展,司法形成

judicial management device 司法管理措施

judicial matter 诉讼案件

judicial member 司法人员

judicial member of House of Lord (英)上议院法官议员

judicial methods 司法方法说(美国现代冲突法学者桑德勒将自己的学说称为"司法方法说");审判方法,司法方法

Judicial Mind 《司法心态》(常指美国法学家舒伯特所著的《司法心态》)

judicial minimalists (美)司法极简主义[指从个人身份来讲,法官慎言义务基于法官职业角色的特殊性,他几乎没有行为动作上的职责,只有判断言论的职责,所以人们关注法官言论表达不亚于对法官行为的注意。法官对自己言论的约束比对自己行为的约束更难。法官地位尊贵无比,受到人们"神"性般的尊敬。他是法律的嘴巴,法官是说话的法律。一个公正的法官是一个冷冷的中立者。英美的法官通常是"金口难开",法庭上尽量少发表自己的观点,因此易于困,有的被误认为是睡觉的法官(Sleeping Judge)。当然,法官的沉默不等于没有判断力,法官在法庭上只要带耳朵和大脑就可以了。西方司法界所谓"司法沉默",美国采取的就是"司法极简主义"的司法态度和司法哲学,正是司法消极性态度]

judicial mortgage 法院判定的抵押

judicial murder 合法但不公正的死刑判决,法律上的杀人(指错判死刑)

judicial notice 司法认知,审判(上的)认知(亦称司法上的知识,指法庭审判时运用审判上的知识,对若干事情无须证明,如习惯法上车辆靠右行驶等)

judicial oath 司法上的宣誓(指在司法程序中,在公开法庭上于法官面前所作的宣誓,区别于法庭外在其他官员面前所作的非司法上的宣誓 non-judicial oath)

judicial office 司法机关;司法职务

judicial officer (或 **official**) 审判(官)员,司法人员;司法官员

judicial opinion 司法见解;法官意见,(美)司法判决理由

judicial order 裁决令;司法体制

judicial organ 司法机关,司法机构

judicial organization (或 **organisation**) 司法组织

judicial panel (美)合议庭(指上诉法院经选定的3名法官组成的合议庭)

judicial panel on multidistrict litigation 多地区诉讼合议庭,多地区诉讼司法小组

judicial passivism 司法消极主义

judicial person 法人;(复)司法人员

judicial personnel 司法人员

judicial philosophy 司法哲学

judicial plain 司法阵地

judicial police 法警,司法警察

judicial power 司法权(①指法院和法官被授予的审理和判决案件的权力和对案件作出有拘束力判决的权力。美国联邦宪法第3条授予联邦法院"合众国的司法权",这使得联邦法院和法官依法享有审理、裁判案件并作出有约束力的判决的权力。宪法还确定了联邦法官行使权力的限制,联邦法院不能代替州法院的作用。司法权由美国联邦最高法院和国会设立的下级法院行使,政府的另外两个大的权力为立法权和行政权。②指政府官员在涉及影响人身和财产权益的案件中,可在裁决权利问题上行使判断和自由裁量权。

在此意义上讲,此术语与行使的行政权力形成对比)
judicial practice 司法惯例;判例;司法程序;司法实践
judicial pragmaticism 实用主义法学
judicial precedent 司法先例,司法判例,判(决)例
judicial preference 司法偏见,司法偏好
judicial principle 司法原则
judicial procedure 司法程序
judicial proceeding(s) 司法程序,司法进程,法庭程序
judicial process 法院传票,司法程序,审判程序
judicial protection 司法保护;司法监护
judicial question 司法问题
judicial reasoning 司法理性,司法推理
judicial records 法院记录,诉讼记录(或摘录),审判记录
judicial redress 司法矫正;司法修正
judicial reference bureaus 司法协议仲裁署(或局)
judicial remedy 司法救济方法,司法补偿
judicial reports (美)司法判例汇编
judicial responsibility 司法任务,司法责任
judicial review (美)司法审查(指法院审查法律是否合乎宪法及政府官员的行为是否违宪);司法检查
judicial review of administration action (英)行政行为的司法审查(指高等法院审查行使行政权的人和机关的行为,以及决议的合法性和有效性)
judicial right 司法权,审判权
judicial robes 法官服
judicial role 司法作用,司法任务,司法角色
judicial rules 司法裁决;司法准则
judicial sale (经法院判决的)强制出售,法院授权的拍卖
judicial security 法院(判决)指定的担保
judicial seizure 法院查封;司法扣押;司法没收
judicial self-restraint (美)司法的自我制约(根据三权分立的原则及其共和党政府的原则,联邦最高法院限制司法审查的使用权);法官自我制约(指法官在审理案件时应自觉避免与判例和制定法不符的观点)
judicial separation 法院判决的(夫妇)分居
judicial sequestration 司法上的扣押或保存(指在诉讼过程中对有争执的财产由法院命令保管)
judicial service 司法机关,司法事务署;司法人员
judicial settlement 司法解决
Judicial Settlement of International Dispute 国际争端的司法调解(或调停)
judicial slot machine 司法自动机
judicial solution of a dispute 通过司法途径解决纠纷
judicial statistics 司法统计学
judicial structure 法院的组织结构;司法体制
judicial style 司法方式;司法文本
judicial supervision 司法监督
judicial supremacy 司法主权,司法最高权力
judicial system 司法制度,审判制度;法院系统,司法系统
judicial system of decision making 司法决策体制
judicial temperament 法官心态,法官气质
judicial title 司法头衔,司法职务
judicial transformation 司法变革,司法改造
judicial tribunal 裁判庭,法庭,审判庭
judicial trustee (英)(依司法受托人法委任的)司法受托人
judicial tyranny 司法专横,司法擅断
judicial valor 司法价值;司法勇气
judicial world 司法界
judicial writ 法院(所发的)令状,司法令状(指由起始令状"original writ"之后法院发出之令状,目的在于处理已开始之诉讼中的一些相关事务)
judicial-type a. 审判式的
judicial-type investigation 审判式的调查
judicialization n. 法院化
judicially created federal law 联邦法院创

立的联邦法(相当于 judicial lawmaking)
judicially developed doctrines　审判实践中发展起来的原理
judicially developed standard　审判过程中发展起来的标准
judiciary a./n.　审判员的,法官的;法院的,司法的/(大写)司法部;(总称)法官,审判人员;法院系统;司法机关;司法制度
judiciary act　法官法,司法法;(复)(美)司法制度法(案)
Judiciary Act of 1789　(美)《1789 年司法法》[此法为美国国会制定的最重要的法律之一。它创立了一个创造性的法院系统,设立了除联邦最高法院以外的下级联邦法院,使宪法规定得以实现,这样就形成了一个三层等级制度的法院系统结构。该结构底部为地方法院,每一法院有一名独任的地方法官,除马萨诸塞州和弗吉尼亚州之外,每个州都有一个这样的地方法院;结构的顶端为联邦最高法院;结构的中层则为三个巡回法院:南部巡回法院(当时由南卡罗来纳州和佐治亚州组成,北卡罗来纳州于 1790 年参加联盟后划入这一区域)、东部巡回法院(包括纽约州、康涅狄克州、马萨诸塞州、新罕布什尔州、罗得岛州和佛蒙特州在它们参加联盟后分别于 1790 年和 1791 年划入这一地区)以及中部巡回法院(包括弗吉尼亚州、马里兰州、宾夕法尼亚州、特拉华州和新泽西州)]
Judiciary Acts of 1801 and 1802　(美) 1801 年和 1802 年《司法法》[指 1799 年联邦主义者开始努力扩大《1789 年司法法》创制的全国法院的组织系统及其管辖权。他们主导的国会通过了《1801 年司法法》,它废除了现存的巡回法院并免除联邦最高法院法官们担任巡回法院法官的职责(见 circuit riding)。它将联邦最高法院的人数从 6 人减少至 5 人,并创制了 6 个新的巡回法院,并授予即将离职的亚当斯政府权力任命 16 名巡回法官,即所谓午夜法官(见 Midnight Judge)。另外联邦管辖权也急剧地扩大了。1801 年的立法给予巡回法院在 1789 年中曾被取消的联邦问题管辖权(federal question jurisdiction)。它拓宽了州际管辖权,并扩大了转移管辖权。尽管国会通过《1802 年司法法》废除了《1801 年司法法》,但联邦司法系统并未发生根本性的改变。不过宪法授予的对联邦问题案件的充分管辖权直到 1875 年才得以实现。联邦最高法院认为 1802 年的废除法是合宪的,关于司法审查制合法性的讨论一直持续到现代]
judiciary committee　(国会)司法委员会
judiciary organization law　法院组织法
judiciary proceedings　审判程序
judiciously ad.　明智地,有见识地,审慎地
* ***Judicis est jus dicere, non dare.***　It is the province of a judge to declare the law, not to give it.　法官的职责在于阐明法律,而不是立法。
judicium　(= *iudicium*)　(罗马法)诉讼第二阶段;司法权,管辖权;法院,法庭;判决,裁决;审讯
judicium capitale　判处死刑(亦作 *judicium vitae amissionis*)
juggle v.　欺骗,诈欺;歪曲;篡改;耍花招
juggle black and white　混淆黑白
juggle with the law　玩弄法律,歪曲法律
jugglery n.　欺骗,诈欺
jugulate v.　扼杀,勒死,割喉致死
jumble n./v.　(英)旧杂货义卖;(总称)旧杂货义卖品,杂乱,混乱/搞乱,混乱
jumble sale　(英)旧杂货拍卖(尤指义卖)
jumble shop　(英)(廉价)杂货店
jump v.　1.跳越 2.非法侵占(采矿权等) 3.(因欠债等)逃离 4.匆匆作出(结论) 5.欣然接受 6.(价格)暴涨,猛增
jump a claim　(美)强占已为他人所取得的土地(或矿场等)
jump bail　弃保潜逃(指在保释中逃跑)
jump to a conclusion　(未经调查或未得证据而)轻易断定,妄自断定,过早下结论
Jumpstart Our Business Startups Act　(美) (2012 年签署生效的)《初创期企业推动法案》(JOBS)(该法案第三节规定,众筹只有满足项目发起人发行总额限制、单个投资者投资额限制、交易方式限制以及发行人的行为要求等几个要件方可豁免。《1933 年证券法》第 5 条项下的注册

要求。互联网融资适用这些规定,对于借款金额或集资人数超过限额的互联网融资行为,因其潜在危险大,不应给予全面豁免,而需纳入监管体系之中)

jungle justice 私刑

jungle law 无法无天;弱肉强食法则

junior n./a. 未成年人;年少者;晚辈;职位低者;资历浅者/年少的;等级较低的;资历较浅的;由青少年组成的

junior barrister 1.(英)资浅高级律师(又译初级出庭律师,指王室律师King's counsel以外的高级律师)2.(英)后参加的高级律师(指在同一诉方的两个律师中后参加的一个)

junior counsel 初级律师

junior execution (根据不同判决给同一被告的)后一执行令状

junior magistrate 资浅司法行政官,低级地方法官

junior minister 资浅部长(大臣)

junior mortgage 次级抵押(权)

junior partner 新合伙人

junior party 劣势一方(指诉讼中不利的一方,与senior party对立)

junior prosecution counsel 低级公诉人

junior rank 资历浅者身份

junior writ 后发令状,后签令状(指针对同一被告,该令状签发迟于另一方发出的或依不同请求而发出的类似令状)

juniority n. 年幼;幼子继承权;(资历或等级上)辈分在后

junk n./v. 旧货,破烂物;冒充物,假货,废话,哄骗;毒品,麻醉品/把(废物)……丢弃

Junktimklausel 唇齿条款[指法律规范就某一事项予以规定时,必须同时就与该事项相关联的其他事项进行规定。就财产权规范而言,意味着征收规范和补偿规范相互联结、相互依存,规定征收的法律必须同时规定补偿。最早使用这一术语为德国学者益普生(Ipsen)]

junk man 废旧品商人

junk value 残值;成本以下的价值

junker n. (美)吸毒者;废弃可丢之汽车

junta n. 1.政务会(尤指西班牙、意大利、拉丁美洲等国的立法、行政机构,或夺取政权后的政权机关)2.(=junto)

junto n. 秘密政治集团,小集团;派系

jura (=*iura*) *jus*的复数(见*jus*)

jura in re aliena 对他人财产上的权利

jura in re propria 对自有财产上的权利

* *Jura naturae sunt immutabilia.* The laws of nature are unchangeable. 自然法(规则)是不可以改变的。

* *Jura novit curia.* The court knows the laws. 法院是通晓法律的;法官知法。

jura personarum 人权,人身权利

jura quaestia 法律上的既得权利

jura regalia 王权(指君主的权力,特别指刑事、民事的审判权);王权标记

jural a. 法律上的;关于权利义务的

jural act 法律行为;权利义务行为

jural materials 法律资料

jural order of nature 自然的法律秩序

jural postulate 权利与义务的原理,法律上的原理;法律假设(指罗斯科·庞德在其法学原理中提出的一个法律秩序所必需的一系列基本假设)

jural relation 权利义务关系;(复)法律上的一般关系(指用一般方法观察法律人格者之间的法律关系的术语)

jural revolution 法律变革

juramentum (=*iuramentun*) (大陆法)(法庭)宣誓,誓词

* *Juramentum est indivisibile, et non est admittendum in parte verum et in parte falsum.* An oath is indivisible; it is not to be held partly true and partly false. 誓词是不可分割的,对它不能认为部分真诚,部分不真诚。

jurant n./a. 宣誓人/宣誓的

jurat (*jurare*) n. 1.(英)(Chinque Ports的)市政官;(英)(海峡群岛终身职务的)治安司法官2.宣誓书末尾的记载(包括宣誓场所、地点、日期及监视人姓名等的记载)

juration n. 宣誓;监督

* *Juratores sunt judices facti.* Juries are the judges of fact. 陪审员是事实的裁判者。

juratory a. 宣誓的,以誓言表达的

juratory caution 宣誓保证(或宣誓的警告)1.(海商法)免费承诺[指法院承诺因贫困可免交登记费(filing fees)和诉讼费(court costs)。根据宣誓警告或宣誓保证的诉讼是相当于贫民诉讼(forma pauperis),这一权利是第一次在美国海事法庭(admiralty court)的布拉德福德诉布拉德福德案(Bradford v. Bradford)中首次被承认。参见《联邦案件集》(1789—1880年)第3卷第1129页(1878年)。见 in *forma pauperis*]2.(苏格兰法)宣誓担保(指对到期债务用宣誓进行担保)

jure civili 按照民法
jure divino 按照神律,按照天律
jure emphyteutico (罗马法)根据永佃权;根据永佃权法
jure gentium 按照国际法;(罗马法)按照万民法

* *Jure naturae aequum est neminem cum alterius detrimento et injuria fieri locupletiorem.* By the law of nature it is not just that any one should be enriched by the detriment or injury of another. 依照自然法,任何人都不得以损害他人来达到致富的目的。

jure officii 依法律职权(能)
jure representationis 根据代表的权利,根据他人的权利
jure sanguinis (= *jus sanguinis*) 血统主义,血统原则;父母国籍国法(见 *jus soli*)
jure uxoris 根据妻子的权利

juridic(al) a. 司法上的,审判上的,法律上的,法学上的
juridic(al) act 法律行为,审判行为
juridic(al) action 审判行为,法律行为
juridic(al) aggravation 裁判上的加重(罪责)
juridic(al) association 社团法人
juridic(al) business 司法事务,审判业务
juridic(al) day 法院开庭日
juridic(al) divorce (或 **divorce by judicial decree**) 判决离婚
juridic(al) entity 法人,法人单位,法律实体
juridic(al) expense 审判费用,诉讼费用
juridic(al) extenuation 裁判上减轻(罪责)
juridic(al) fact 法律事实
juridic(al) organization 司法组织
juridic(al) person 法人
juridic(al) personality 法律人格
juridic(al) practice 司法惯例,司法实践,审判实践
juridic(al) status 法律地位
Juridical idealism 司法上的唯心主义,法律上的理念;司法上的理念;合法的理念;司法理想主义;司法观念论
juridicus (= *iuridicus*) 有关法院的,执法上的,司法的,合法的/最高裁判官(指罗马法上具有执政官身份的司法人员);法院,执法
juries act 陪审团法
jurimetrics n. (1949年)法律统计学[指运用科学和经验的方法,包括衡量来研究,分析一些法律问题(legal matters)。jurimetrician, jurimetricist n.]
juris (= *iuris*) 权力的,法律的

* *Juris affectus in executione consistit.* The effect of the law consists in the execution. 法律的效力在于执行。

Juris Doctor (或 **Doctor of Jurisprudence**) 法学博士[在美国指最基本的法律学位,从20世纪60年代起代替法学学士(Bachelor of law),在其他国家一般指比硕士高一级的学位]
juris divini (罗马法)神权,遵守神圣法(divine law),依据神权。此术语与教会、宗教相关
juris et de jure 合理合法(而不得反驳的)(又译:于法于权)
juris possessio 权利占有
juris possessor 权利占有人

* *Juris praecepta sunt haec: honeste vivere; alterum non laedere; suum cuique tribuere.* These are the precepts of the law: to live honorably; to hurt nobody; to render to every one his due. 法律的格言是:让人们体面地生活;不伤害任何人;使每个人都做自己应当做的事。

juris privatum 私权的;私有财产的主体
juris prudentia 法律知识;法(理)学

juris publici 共同权利的;共同使用的(如高速公路)
juris scientia 法律科学
juris tantum 法律上的推定,可举证予以反驳
Juris Utriusque Doctor 民法及教会法博士
juris vinculum 法律上的连锁关系(又译:法锁)
jurisconsult n. 法学学者(尤指国际法、公法学者)
jurisconsultus (罗马法)法律学家;法律顾问
jurisdictio contentiosa (罗马法)争议事项的管辖权[指与自愿管辖(voluntary jurisdiction)相对立引起争议事项的管辖权]
* *Jurisdictio est potestas de publico introducta, cum necessitate juris dicendi.* Jurisdiction is a power introduced for the public good, on account of the necessity of dispensing justice. 司法审判权是为了公共利益而考虑到执法需要所产生的一种权力。
jurisdiction n. (14世纪)1.权力,职权,管辖权[指政府在其本国领土上对所有人或行使的权力或职权,尤其指一个州创造权益的权利(power to create interests),根据普通法原则(common law principles)在其他州应得到有效的承认〈New Jersey's jurisdiction〉(新泽西州的创益权)]2.法院对案件的判决权或发布判决令(decree)的权力〈constitutional grant of federal question jurisdiction〉(宪法授予的联邦问题管辖权)3.行使权力的地区[指可行使政治权和司法权的地区范畴〈the accused fled to another jurisdiction〉(这个刑事被告人逃到另一个管辖区)]4.政治的、司法的分区范畴的小区范围内(管辖权)〈other jurisdictions have decided the issue differently〉(其他管辖已经对此争点作出了不同的判决或决定)(jurisdictional a.)(见 venue)
jurisdiction n. 1.司法(权),裁判权,审判权 2.管辖(权);管辖区,管辖范围 3.权限,控制
jurisdiction allegation 管辖权主张
jurisdiction(al) amount 司法管辖的请求金额(指案件中构成诉讼请求的金额,有些法庭规定只受理一定金额请求范围的案件),管辖金额
jurisdiction at first instance 一审管辖权
jurisdiction disputes 管辖争议(指工会之间就其代表的工人和各自工人有权从事的特定工作所生争议)
jurisdiction facts 确定管辖权的事实;可使(法院)取得管辖权的事实
jurisdiction fictions 管辖拟制
jurisdiction in cyberspace 电脑空间的管辖
jurisdiction in error 纠正错案管辖权
jurisdiction *in personam* (= personal jurisdiction) 对人管辖权
jurisdiction in prize 捕获管辖权
jurisdiction *in rem* 对物管辖权
jurisdiction of civil cases involving foreign element 涉外民事案件管辖权
jurisdiction of state over air space 国家的制空权
jurisdiction of the court 法院管辖(权),法院管辖范围(或区域);法院审判权,法院权限
jurisdiction of the court of crown cases (英)刑事案件的法院管辖权
jurisdiction of the subject matter (=subjective matter jurisdiction) 事物管辖权,诉讼标的管辖权
jurisdiction on appeal 上诉审管辖权
jurisdiction over a nondomiciliary in the forum 对在诉讼所在地州无住所地者行使管辖
jurisdiction over an absent domiciliary 对主人不在住所地行使管辖
jurisdiction over constitutional questions 宪法(争议)问题的管辖权
jurisdiction over contractual claims 对合同诉讼请求行使管辖,对合同纠纷的管辖
jurisdiction over customary affair 习惯事务的审判权,习惯事务的管辖权
jurisdiction over people and over property 对人和对物管辖权
jurisdiction over property 对财产的管辖权

jurisdiction over things 对物的管辖权
jurisdiction overlap 管辖权的重叠
jurisdiction *quasi in rem* （或 **quasi-jurisdiction** *in rem*）（对）准物权的管辖权,（对）准物权的审判权
jurisdiction *ratione loci* 属地管辖权
jurisdiction to control inferior courts 对下级法院的监督管辖权
jurisdiction to handle all steps in the processing of civil case 对民事案件处理过程中的所有阶段之事项有（处理）管辖权
jurisdiction *voluntaire* 自愿管辖权
jurisdiction within territorial space 领空管辖权
jurisdiction within territorial waters 领海管辖权
jurisdiction within territory 领土管辖权
jurisdictional a. 司法权的,裁判权的;审判权的;管辖的;管辖范围的;管辖的,权力的,权限的
jurisdictional agency 司法代理;管辖机构
jurisdictional amount requirement 管辖金额标准,管辖金额要求
jurisdictional area 管辖区域
jurisdictional defect 管辖的瑕疵
jurisdictional dilemmas 司法（管辖）困460
jurisdictional dispute 管辖（上的）争执
jurisdictional error 管辖权错误
jurisdictional fact(s) 管辖权事实,管辖范围的事实（指法院在受理案件之前必须知道的一些事情,或指提交法院可使其取得该特定案件管辖权所存在的那些案件事实,如被告是否已收到专门送达的法院公报或文件等）
jurisdictional fetter （英）司法管辖权的脚镣[1278年法案规定,侵害诉讼必须先诉至郡法庭,除非当事人发誓标的额超过40先令或请求权利属实,否则他不能获得侵害令状(trespass writ),这一限制似乎成为束缚王室法庭司法管辖权的脚镣]
jurisdictional immunity 管辖豁免（权）
jurisdictional immunity of foreign heads of states（或 **diplomatic representatives**） 外国国家元首（或外交代表）的司法管辖豁免

jurisdictional immunity of foreign state vessels 外国国家船舶的司法管辖豁免
jurisdictional immunity of foreign states 外国国家的司法管辖豁免
jurisdictional law 管辖权法律
jurisdictional limits 管辖限度,管辖范围
jurisdictional objection 管辖的异议
jurisdictional plea 管辖权答辩（指法院对被告人或诉讼标的是否有管辖权的问题所作的答辩）,管辖抗辩
jurisdictional principle 管辖权准则,司法权准则,司法原则
jurisdictional privilege 管辖（上的）特权
jurisdictional property 管辖区的财产,管辖区所属的财产
jurisdictional provision 管辖权规定
jurisdictional *quid pro quo* 法院间的互让互惠
jurisdictional reach 管辖权范围所及
jurisdictional requirements 管辖权的要求
jurisdictional ruling 管辖权上的决定,管辖（权上的）裁定,管辖（权上的）细则
jurisdictional sleight-of-hand 管辖把戏,管辖花招,管辖骗术
jurisdictional sweep of modern long-arm statute （美）现代长臂法的管辖飚风（指其目的在于确保本州居民在因非本州居民的活动而产生的诉因能在当地进行诉讼）
jurisdictional system 管辖制度;管辖系统
jurisdictional vehicle 管辖通道,管辖媒介,管辖机制
jurisdictional water 管辖水域
jurisdictional wrangling 司法争论
jurisperitus （罗马）精通法律的
jurisprudence n. 1.法学,法理学,法哲学,法律学（指研究法律原理和现象的科学）2.法学的一个部门（如民法、刑法、诉讼法等）;一种法律制度 3.法律的一个分支 4.(法院的)审判规程;判决录;判例法 5.法院的裁定（尤指复审裁定）
jurisprudence of concepts 概念法学（派）
jurisprudence of interests 利益法学
jurisprudence of labels 标志法学,标示法学

jurisprudence of legal realism 法律现实主义的法理学
jurisprudence society 法学会
jurisprudent a./n. 精通法学的,精通法律的,专攻法学的/法学家,法理学家
jurisprudentes n. (罗马)法学家,法理学家
jurisprudentia (= *iurisprudentia*) (罗马法)法理学,法学
　＊*Jurisprudentia est divinarum atque humanarum rerum notita, justi atque injusti scientia.* Jurisprudence is the knowledge of things divine and human, the science of what is right and what is wrong. 法学是有关神道和人类事物的知识,是研究什么是正当和什么是不正当的科学。
jurisprudential a. 法学上的,法理学上的
jurisprudential circle 法学界
jurisprudential doctrine 法理
jurisprudential scholar 法学家
jurisprudential study 法学研究
jurist n. 法(理)学家;(中)法家;律师;法官;法律学者,法律工作者
jurist-theologians of the preceding century 世纪前的法神学家
jurist-theologians 法神学家
juristic(al) a. 法律的,法学的,法科的,法学家的;合法的,法律上所承认的;法理学的,法理学家的,法家的
juristic(al) act 法律行为(见 act in the law)
juristic(al) act of real right 物权行为
juristic(al) act subject to conditions 附条件的法律行为
juristic(al) act subject to stipulation of time limit 限定期限的法律行为
juristic(al) action 法律诉讼,法律行为
juristic edifice 司法大厦
juristic(al) fact 法律事实
juristic(al) hypothesis 法学上的假设
juristic literature 法学文献
juristic(al) method 司法方法(指建立和利用使一切法律工作人员和机制出色地进行工作的技能)
juristic movement 法理学的运动
juristic(al) person 法人
juristic(al) personality 法人人格,法人资格
juristic pessimism 法律的悲观主义
juristic philosophical method 司法哲学方法,法哲学方法
Juristic Philosophy of Roscoe Pound 《论庞德的法律哲学》[指美国法学家罗斯科・庞德(Roscoe Pound)于 1924 年发表在《伊利诺法律评论》上的一篇论文。该论文受到了高度评价,认为庞德的社会利益理论意义重大,"重点以法律条文本身为中心,转移到社会对条文生效的要求"]
juristic reasoning 法律上的推理
juristic science 法科学、法理学
juristic superfluity 司法越权
juristic(al) theory 法学理论
juristic theory of natural rights 自然权利的法学理论
juristic thought 法学思想,法理学思想,法律思想
juristic tradition 法学家的传统,法学的传统
juristic(al) work 法律著作,法学著作
juristic(al) writing 法律文献
jurists' law 法官(创造的)法
juror n. 陪审员,陪审官;宣誓者;审查员,评判员
juror on trial 出庭(审案的)陪审员
juror qualification questionnaire 陪审员资格调查问卷
juror testimony 陪审员证言
juror's book (美)陪审员名册(指每年每个州将有资格担任陪审员的人员编成名册,法院需要时可按名册召集)
juror's oath 陪审员的宣誓
juror's seat 陪审员席
jury n. 1.陪审团(指依法选出一定数目的男女陪审员组成的各种陪审团,其职能是经过宣誓,调查案件的事实;根据证据,宣布事实的真实性。陪审团有:大陪审团"grand jury"、小陪审团"petty jury"、普通陪审团"common jury"、专门陪审团"special jury"、司法行政官的陪审团"sheriff's jury"、验尸官的陪审团"coroner's jury"等)2.(行政上的)评判委员会
jury array 陪审团成员名册

jury as impartial finder of fact 作为公正事实认定人的陪审团
jury as witness-adjudicator 作为证人——裁判者的陪审团
jury box 陪审团席(指法庭上陪审员的座位)
jury case 陪审团参加的案件
jury challenge 陪审团陷入僵局,申请陪审团回避
jury chancellor 陪审团长(见 foreperson)
jury charge 法官对陪审团的指令
jury commissioner 陪审团审选官,陪审团推选官(员)
jury court 陪审法庭
jury deliberation (美)陪审团审议
jury demand 陪审团要求,陪审团审理请求书
jury de medietate linguae (古代英格兰)双语陪审团(jury of halfness of language)[指当当事方中之一人为外侨时,允许陪审团半数人用母语(英语),半数人用那个当事人国籍的语言]
jury duty (1829年)1.在陪审团的服务义务 2.陪审团的实际服务(actual service)。亦称 jury service
jury fixer 收买(或胁迫)陪审团的人
jury impartiality 陪审团公正无私性
jury instructions 对陪审团的指示(指法官就案件的有关法律问题向陪审团作出的指示)
jury list (具备)陪审员(资格的人员)名单
jury matters 陪审团事项(指美国民事诉讼审理前的程序之一,即应指示律师于审判前5天,向法院递交其所请求的陪审团指示及请求法院预先核陪审团的问题)
jury nullification 陪审团的拒绝(指陪审团在拟就某一超出本案的社会问题传送信息,或者按法律意志的结果有违陪审团的正义感、道德感和公正感时,故意拒绝证据或拒绝适用法律)
jury of indictment 见 grand jury
jury of inquest 验尸陪审团;专门事实调查陪审团(见 inquest jury)
jury of matrons 妇女陪审团(亦称受胎讯陪审团,指负责确定判处死刑的女犯是否有孕的陪审团)
jury of peers 贵族或与被告同等地位的陪审团(指由与被告同等地位组成的陪审团。在普通法上,对被指控犯有罪行的贵族被告人则要由与其同等身份或地位的人,即贵族组成的陪审团进行审判)
jury of vicinage 1.在普通法上,来自犯罪实施地区的公民中遴选的陪审团 2.从法院判决地的公民中选出的陪审团(见 vicinage)
jury packing (1887年)策划好的陪审团[指一种事先安排好(在这方或另一方)的一些人员组成陪审团的策划行为。亦称 packing a jury。见 embracery;jury-fixing]
jury panel 预期陪审团名单(指一组预期陪审员将按规定日期出面,以便从中选择大陪审团或陪审团)
jury pardon (1974年)陪审团赦免(指在有足够证据对两个刑事被告之一定罪的情况下,允准陪审团裁定一个被指控犯有较轻罪行的刑事被告的规则)
jury process (18世纪)1.陪审团召集令,陪审员召集令(指由法院发出给陪审员召唤他们出庭的程序)2.给预备陪审员要求其出庭的通讯或告知令
jury question (18世纪)1.陪审团裁决的问题[指由陪审团裁决的事实上的争点(issue of fact)。见 question of fact]2.法庭要求陪审团特别裁断的特别问题(见 special interrogatories)
jury room 陪审团休息室(指陪审员在此讨论决定审判事项的房间)
jury secrecy 陪审团保密(能力),陪审团的秘密
jury sequestration 看管隔离陪审团(见 sequestration ⑧)
jury service 见 jury duty
jury system 陪审制
jury trial (陪审团审理、参加的)陪审
jury wheel 陪审团旋转装置(指为了储存和任意选择预备陪审员的鉴定号码和姓名而使用的一种物理装置或电子系统)
jury's domain 陪审团工作范围
jury-awarded damages in a diversity action 陪审团在异籍诉讼裁决的损害赔偿

jury-fixing (1887年)非法手段操纵陪审团,笼络陪审团(指某个人或数个陪审员合作进行非法行为在实际上达到影响审判的后果。见 embracery;jury packing;jury fixer)

jury-packing n. (律师)非法影响陪审团的做法

juryman n. 陪审员

jurywoman n. 女陪审员

jus (=*ius*) 1.法;法律;权力;权利 2.法庭,(罗马的)裁判法庭;诉讼程序 3.法律和道德的责任 4.法律原则;法律所保证的权利

jus abstinendi (罗马法)抛弃权利(如抛弃遗产的权利)

jus abutendi 滥用权,随意处分财产权

jus accrescendi (在共有财产中生存者对死者共有权的)取得权利,增添权

jus ad bellum 诉诸战争权

* ***Jus ad praeteritum trahi nequit.*** The law prefers to let off for one's past wrongdoings. 法律不溯及既往。

jus ad rem (大陆法)物权(指根据契约或债务可取得的对物权)

jus aequum 公正法,衡平法;特赦权,依个别案件的案情来适用法律(古罗马使用的术语,指依个别案情来适用法律,与 *jus strictum* 相对而言)

jus albinatus (古代法国法)没收外侨遗产权

jus altius non tollendi 禁止建筑物加高的地役权

jus angariae 非常征用权,战时船舶征用权(见 angary),(国际法)中立国财产征用权

jus aquaeductus (大陆法)引水权;(在他人土地上的)饮畜权

jus avocandi 召还权(指召还侨居在他国的本国人民),引渡权

jus banci (古英国法)审判权

jus belli 战争法

jus belli et pacis (罗马时代的)战争与和平论;国际法

jus bellum dicendi 宣战权

jus canonicum 寺院法,宗教法规

jus civile (罗马法)市民法,民法

* ***Jus civile est quod sibi populus constituit.*** The civil law is what a people establishes for itself. 民法是一国人民为自己制定的法律。

jus civitatus 公民权

jus cloacae mittendae 排水的地役权

jus cogens 强行法(指具有强制性的法规);绝对法(指在国际法之外存有一项不容违反的"最高规范")

jus collectandi 审慎考虑的权利(民法中的术语,指继承人的继承是否拒绝或接受的深思熟虑)

jus commune 共有权;(大陆法)普通法(规)(指与 *jus singulare* 相对而言)

jus connubu (或 *connbi*) 通婚权

jus contrahendi 缔约权

jus criminale 刑法

jus curialitatis (古英国法)亡妻财产收益享有权(见 curtesy of England)

jus dare 制定法律;立法部门的职能与特权

jus de non appellando 拒绝上诉的权利,不上告的权利

* ***Jus dicere, et non jus dare.*** To declare the law, not to make it. 宣布法律者并不制定法律。

jus disponendi 处置权,处分权

jus dispositivum 容许法(指法律上有某要件存在时,许可为某一行为的法律规范)

jus distrahendi (在不支付情况下)享有抵押物品拍卖权

jus domicilic the law of the domicile 居住法,住所法

jus duplicatum 双重权利(指连同财产权一起的占有权,亦称 droit-droit)

jus edicendi (罗马法上的)告示权

* ***Jus est ars boni et aequi.*** Law is the science of what is good and just. 法乃善良公平之道。

* ***Jus est norma recti; et quicquid est contra normam recti est injuria.*** The law is the rule of right; and what ever is contrary to the rule of right is an injury. 法律是公正的规则,与公正相违反的则是侵害。

* ***Jus et fraus nunquam cohabitant.*** Right

and fraud never dwell together. 权利和欺诈绝不(能)共处。
* **Jus ex injuria non oritur.** A right does (or can) not rise out of a wrong. 不法行为是不(或不会)产生权利的。
jus fluminum 江河的使用权
jus fruendi aut fructus 收益权
jus futurum 未来权利
jus gentilicium 氏族法律
jus gentium (=law of nations) 万民法(国际法的最早名称,原属罗马法的一部分,系市民法的对称)
jus habendi 财产保有权,财产实际占有权
jus haereditatis 继承权
jus honorarium (罗马法)大法官法(又译:司法行政官法)
jus honorum (罗马法)任职权
jus immunitatis (大陆法)豁免权
jus in personam (大陆法)对人权,债权
jus in re (或 **rem**) (大陆法)对物权,物权
jus in re aliena 他物权
jus in re propria 自物权
jus inter gentes 国际法
jus legitimum 合法权利
jus mariti 夫权(尤指男子由于结婚而取得他的妻子的准动产所有权)
jus mercetorium 商人法
jus naturae 见 *jus naturale*
jus naturale (或 *naturae*) 自然法
* **Jus naturale est quod apud homines eandem habet potentiam.** Natural right is that which has the same force among all mankind. 自然权利在全人类中间具有同等的力量。
jus navigandi 航行权,航运权
jus necis (罗马法)处死权,死权(指古时父亲对孩子享有的处死权)
* **Jus non habenti tute non paretur.** One who has no right can not be safely obeyed. 无权的人不会安稳地受到人们遵从。
* **Jus non patitur ut idem bis solvatur.** Law does not suffer that the same thing be twice paid. 法律不能容忍同一事物作两次支付。
jus non scriptum 不成文法,约定俗成的法律

jus novum 新教会法(指1075—1122年间所谓格列高利改革与授权之争达到顶点而导致了一个西方近代法律体系,即罗马天主教的"新教会法"的形成)
jus offerendi (罗马法)代位权,代位求偿权
jus oneris ferendi (罗马法)建房的靠壁权(一种城市役权)
jus pascendi (在草地上的)放牧权
jus perpetuum 永佃权
jus personarum 人身权(指大陆法中诸如父母与子女间、主人与仆人之间、与人身有关的不同性质与关系的权利)
jus portus (海事法)港口权,停泊权
jus possessionis 所有权,占有权
jus postliminii (罗马法)(俘房回国后的公民资格)恢复权,(国际法)(战犯财产或公民资格的)恢复权
jus praetorium (大陆法)裁判官自由裁量权;裁判官法
jus primae noctis 初夜权
jus privatum 私法
jus projiciendi 突出栏杆及其他物件于邻地的权利
jus proprietatis 财产权
jus publicum 公法(指涉及宪法、政府职能以及其官员和刑事执法的法律)
* **Jus publicum privatorum pactis mutari non potest.** A public law or right cannot be altered by the agreements of private persons. 公法或公权不得通过私人协议而加以变更。
jus quaesitum tertio 为第三者的权利
jus recuperandi 恢复(土地)权
jus relictae (苏格兰)遗孀继承权
jus relicti (苏格兰)鳏夫继承权
jus representationis 代表权
jus representationis omnimodae 全权代表权
jus rerum 物权;物权法(指调整人对于物的权力和权利的关系,即调整物权关系。例如,如何取得财产、享用财产和转让财产。见 law of things)
* **Jus respicit aequitatem.** Law regards eq-

uity./The law pays regard to equity./Law bears equity in mind. 法律尊重公平。

jus respondendi （罗马法）解答法律权[指当传出法律意见书(Legal Opinion)时,某些法学家得到授权进行解答。现代研究古罗马法律者不同意此词条的确切含义]

jus sanguinis 血统主义(指以父或母的国籍为子女的国籍的原则)

jus scriptum （英）成文法,制定法

jus singulare （大陆法）特别法(规)[区别于普通法(规) *jus commune*]

jus soli 出生地主义(指以出生地的国籍为出生婴儿的国籍的原则)

jus stillicidii vel fluminis recipiendi （罗马法）在邻人土地上方砌接屋檐或开通房屋排水沟的权利(一种城市役权)

jus strictum 严格法（或称绝对法,指不能作任何修改解释或极其严酷的法律）

jus suffragii （罗马法）选举权,投票权

jus tertii 第三者权利,第三当事人的请求权

jus tigni immittendi （在邻人墙上）架屋梁权(一种城市役权)

jus transitus innoxii 无害通行权

jus utendi 财产使用权

jus venandi et piscandi 狩猎权和捕鱼权

jus voluntarium 意志法

Jusis ignorantia nocet （古罗马）不知法为有害

jusiurandum (= *iusiurandum*) （罗马法）诉讼宣誓

just *a.* 正义的,公正的,正直的,公平的;合法的,有充分根据的;正当的;确当的,精确的;应当的;应得的;有正当理由的

just and amicable settlement 公平友好地解决

just and equitable 公正和衡平的

just and equitable winding-up 公正合理清盘令[现代公司法起源地英国,保护小股东合法权益长期以来便是英国公司法关注的焦点之一。1948年英国公司法(Companies Act 1948)第210条规定,如果公司中存在"压迫"(oppression)小股东的情况,小股东可请求法院解散公司。如法院认为解散公司是正当公平的,即可颁发公正合理清盘令,这作为对小股东权益保护和救济的一种手段,而被保留下来并继续有效]

just and true account 真实账目(指准确真实的账目)

just authority 合法权力,合法授权

just cause 合理诉因;正当理由;合法理由

just compensation （16世纪）公平补偿,合理补偿,合理赔偿[指美国政府运用征用权征用财产时,必须支付该财产所有人一定数目的金钱,此项支付即为"公平补偿"。美国联邦宪法第五修正案的占有条款(taking clause)限制了征用权的行使,其中的重要之处即"公平补偿",支付给被征用财产的人。美国大多数州的宪法均使用类似语言。见 taking clause]

just debts 合法或正当债务(指在遗嘱和制定法中,那些合法有效、并无可争议的债务,但不包括因诉讼时效原因受阻的债务或由于当事人选择可撤销之债务)

just decision 公正决定,公正的裁定

just final disposition of the litigation 诉讼的最终公正解决,公正地最终解决诉讼

just indignation 义愤

just justices 公正的审判

just man 公正的人

just opinion 合理意见

just powers 正当权力

just punishment 应得的惩罚

just social order 正义的社会秩序(当法律旨在创设一种正义的社会秩序时,它才是良法)

just solutions 公正解决

just suspicion 有充分理由的怀疑

just title （依时效取得的）合法所有权,合法权利

just war 正义战争

justa causa 正当原因,合法理由;合理诉因

justae nuptiae （或 ***justum matrimonium***）正当结合,正式婚姻,合法婚姻

justice *n.* 1.正义,公正,公正原则,公平;公道,公理 2.(英)高等法院法官,(美)最高法院法官 3.司法审判,法律制裁 4.法官,治安官 5.正当理由;合法;正确,确实 6.公平处理,公平待遇;应得的奖赏（或惩罚） 7.司法,审判

justice as fairness 作为公正的正义
Justice before Truth 正义先于事实
justice court 审判法院(美国法院制度)
justice from above 自上而下的正义
justice from below 自下而上的正义
* **Justice has long arms.** 天网恢恢(疏而不漏)。
justice in eyre (历史)巡审法官(指中世纪巡回审问法官,负责调查被指控的违法行为、审理案件、征收罚金,亦称 *justicia errante*; *justiciar in itinere*。见 eyre)
justice *itinerantes* (古英国法)巡回法院(区别于在威斯敏斯特的住地法院 *justicii residentes*)
justice manager 公正管理人
justice model 司法模式(指刑事和解模式之一,它重视被害人的利益,把刑事和解作为提高犯罪人责任的一种手段,使向被害人的赔偿公正合理。见 community model)
Justice must not only be done, but must be seen to be done. 正义不但要伸张,而且必须眼见其被伸张(英国一句古老法律格言)。
justice of appeal 上诉法院法官
justice of assize (英)巡回审判法官(旧称)
justice of jail delivery 负责提审全体在押犯人的法官
justice of (the) peace (英)治安官(又译治安法官,指兼理一般司法事务的地方官员。有的是无薪给的);(美)(州初级法院处理非重大案件的)治安官(负责 justice's court)
justice of peace court 治安官法院
justice of the high court 高等法院法官
justice's court (美)下级法院,审理法院,治安官主持法院(该类法院无记录,仅有有限管辖权,民事、刑事案件均可审理,由治安官主持,现已有趋向废止此类法庭,将其权力和职能转移给其他法院,如城市或地区法院)
justice's judg(e)ment 治安官的裁判
justice's justice 执法不当的裁判(讽刺治安官裁判不当)

justicer n. (古语)法官
justices council 法官委员会,审判委员会
justiciability n. (美)联邦司法权的范围(指按美国联邦宪法第3条界定的根据案件和争议确定联邦司法管辖权的范围);可辩解性,正当,有理,可辨明(性)
Justices of the Peace Act 《治安官法》
justiceship n. 法官的任期(职位或职能)
justiciable a. 应受法院审判的,应受法院管辖的
justiciable case 应受法院管辖的案件
justiciable controversy 可受法院裁判的争执,可由法院管辖的纠纷(指真正的而非假定的法院可以处理的争执)
justiciable criminal 应受法院审判的罪犯
justiciable dispute 可(由法院)审判的争议(纠纷)
Justicia(r) n. 1.中世纪(12世纪)英格兰皇家司法官员,高级法院的司法法官 2.见 Justiciary 2,亦可拼写为 justicier
justicia errante 见 justice in eyre
justiciar in itinere 见 justice in eyre
justiciary n. 1.法官,审判官 2.(历史上)政府与司法两方的行政司法长官(Chief Administration of Both Government and Justice)[1066年起直到亨利三世统治时期(1216—1272),法官(judiciary)主持王座法庭和财务法庭(King's court and in the exchequer),监督所有政府部门,同时在国王离开时充任摄政官(regent)。后来在几类官员,如御前大臣(Lord Chancellor)(亦译大法官)、首席大法官(Chief Justice)和首席财务大臣(Lord High Treasurer)之间分担摄政官的这些职能。亦称 justiciar; chief justiciar; capitalis justiciarius] 3.(苏格兰法)司法审判(Administration of Justice),特别是刑事法律方面(criminal law)的审判
justiciary court (苏格兰)刑事法院
justicii residentes 固定地点的法院,住地法院(见 justice *itinerantes*)
justifiability n. 有理,正当;可辩解性,可辨明(性)
justifiable a. 正当的,不可非议的;可辨明的;有理由的

justifiable abortion　合法堕胎，正当堕胎（指怀孕将危及母体健康而进行的堕胎）
justifiable defense　正当防卫
justifiable homicide　正当杀人（指执行任务或防止残杀时因自卫所导致的杀人，一般不负刑事责任）
justifiable reliance　合理信赖
Justification n.　1.正当理由，充分理由，合法理由[指一个人的行为或不作为的合法理由或充分理由；可以防止错误或不法(wrongful)行为的任一事实]2.辨明在法庭上充分理由的陈述，为何对被告行为提出指控要求被告应承担的责任[根据《示范刑法典》，刑事被告必须相信为了避免伤害或灾难(harm or evil)，该行为是必要的(necessary)，还应相信这种被避免的伤害大于已犯罪造成结果的伤害。亦称 justification defense; necessary defense。见 lesser-evils defense]3.担保的证明[指具有足够的金钱或信贷(money and credit)，可提供当事人所要求的担保(security)。justify v.; justificary a.]
justification defense　正当理由辩护（或防卫）(指在刑法和侵权法上，被告证明其受到控告是正当的并有合法理由的)
justification for the Erie decision　对伊利案判决的正当性（合理性）
justification of arrest　正当逮捕，合法逮捕
justification of civil society　市民社会的正义
justification of detention　正当拘留，合法拘留
justification of judg(e)ment　正当判决，合法判决
justification of punishment　刑罚的合理证明，刑罚的正当理由
justification of war　战争的正当理由，正义战争
justification selecting　管辖选择
justificator n.　宣誓证明他人无辜（或无罪）者
justificatory (=justificative) a.　认为正当的；辨明的，辩护的
justificatory material　申辩材料
justifier n.　辨明者，证明者，提出充分法律依据者；释罪者
justify v.　1.证明……是正当的（或有理由的）行为；证明合法 2.为……辩护 3.证明确有其事 4.认为无罪 5.为……提供法律根据
justifying bail　合法保释（指具有足够保释资格与财产担保能力的保释）；宣誓证明（自己）有财力作保
justifying reasons　正当化理由
Justinian Code（或 **Coder Justinian**）《查士丁尼法典》[指指查士丁尼任命的一个百人委员会(commission)起草的皇家法典(imperial constitution)，于公元 529 年正式公布、出版。以特里波尼安(Triborian)为首的 10 名法学家于公元 528 年 2 月开始实施这个项目，于 529 年 4 月完工，它代替了以前所有的皇家法律，在公元 534 年之前有效，其后则修订的《新查士丁尼法典》所替代，但第一部的准确内容无人知晓，第二部（修订法典）包括 12 卷本，其中有格里高列(Gregorian)皇家法典、海默真尼安(Hermogenian)法典和西奥多西安(Theodosianus)法典，这三部法典集中一起，经过修订协调一致而成为一个完整的法律体系。它论及宗教、寺院法、刑法、行政法和私法。在这些示范的著作(modern writings)中，公元 534 年的释义(Version)就是根据查士丁尼法典工作的成果。亦称 Justinanean Code; Code of Justinian; Code Vetus (Old Code); Codex Iustinianus Repetitae Praelectionis]
Justinian Roman texts　查士丁尼罗马法文本
Justinian's codification　《查士丁尼法典》
Justinian's Digest　《查士丁尼学说汇纂》
Justinianean Code　见 Justinian Code
justitia　公平，正义；管辖权；法官职位
* *Justitia non est neganda, non differenda.*
　Justice is neither to be denied nor delayed./Justice is not to be denied or delayed.
　公正既不应拒绝给予，又不应拖延给予。
justitia（= *iustitia*）　公正；法规，法律；条例；管辖权；法官职位
* *Justitia non novit patrem nec matrem; solam*

veritatem spectat justitia. Justice knows not father nor mother; justice looks at truth alone. 审判的公平是不认父母而只看真理的。
justitium (= *iustitium*) （罗马法）暂时中止行使审判权
justum matrimonoum 合法婚姻
juvenile n./a. 少年，未成年人/少年的，未成年的
juvenile adult 青少年
juvenile case 少年违法犯罪案件
Juvenile Court （1903年）少年法庭［指①具有涉及通常在18岁以下少年的案件的管辖权。伊利诺伊州于1899年第一次颁布全州范围(statewide)的《少年法庭法》(Juvenile Courts Act)。现今每个州都有专门的少年和家庭法院，并具有特别原有的少年犯罪、违法的管辖权。此词亦可称为children court。②具有对孤儿少年、不能独立的个人、无人管养的儿童等特有的管辖权。这种类型的少年法庭是根据制定法和关系到虐待、收养、身份犯罪(status offenses)以及少年犯罪等案情的由原有管辖法规的专门措辞授予权力而创设的。总之，少年法庭是父系性质的对孩子关怀、监护、管理（如制定法所界定的定义）等的管辖权。少年法庭的管辖权是在孩子所在州(state for the child)和孩子的父母之间行使，并不涉及监护的争议，也不影响孩子的道德、健康和幸福。少年法庭不是刑事法院，它首先关怀的是孩子的实际幸福。见 Uniform Juvenile Court Act］
Juvenile Courts Act 《少年法庭法》
juvenile crime 少年犯罪
juvenile criminality 少年犯罪（问题）
juvenile delinquency 未成年人违法行为（指未成年人的反社会行为，特别是，如果行为人是成年人，这种行为是要受刑事惩罚的，但对未成年人则通常适用于未成年人的特别法规来替代这种惩罚。见 incorrigibility）
Juvenile Delinquency Prevention Act 《少年违法行为预防法》［指一项联邦制定法，其目的包括帮助州和当地乡镇为处于违法危险境地的少年提供一些预防措施(prevention services)；帮助个人就业培训、

准备就预防措施方面的工作就业；在预防违法领域提供技术性帮助。参见《美国注释法典》第42标题卷第3801节及以下］
juvenile delinquent （1816年）少年犯（指有犯罪行为的少年，通常要受不同于成人的专门法律惩处，有时缩略为 delinquent。亦称 juvenile offender；youthful offender；delinquent minor。见 offender；delinquent child）
juvenile dependency 少年保护
juvenile justice （美）未成年审判，少年审判（自19世纪末在芝加哥建立了分开的少年法庭起才有此概念，运用具有监护人资格的家长权利的普通法原理来授权立法机关保护儿童和他们的父母。刑事被告的罪行和记录犯罪的污点均当以"挽救儿童"的法官以必要的轻罪和过失犯罪的判决来替代保护措施）
Juvenile Justice and Delinquency Prevention Act 《少年司法和预防违法行为法》［指一项联邦制定法。它提供资金、帮助、培训以及支持各州运作少年司法计划、创议和法院体系。参见《美国注释法典》第42标题卷第5601—5785节］
juvenile law 少年法
juvenile-justice system 少年司法系统，少年司法体制［指对于青少年罪犯的各种指控均得以处分或进行量刑的一些公共机构。这个体制包括少年法庭（法官和律师）、执法（警察）、惩治教养（缓刑监督官、社会工作者）］
juvenile offender 少年犯
juvenile offender correctional institution （中）少年犯管教所
juvenile under age 幼年人
juvenility n. 年少，年轻；幼稚；（复）幼稚的行为，（总称）少年人
juvenocracy n. 由年轻人管理的国家
juxta 靠近，跟随；根据
juxta conventionem 根据公约，按照协议，按照惯例
juxta formam statuti 根据法律形式，根据制定法形式
juxta ratam 在该比率或在该比率之后，在该等级或在该等级之后

juxta tenorem sequentem 按要旨办,遵循要旨,按其大意
juxtapose v. 使连接;毗连;并列
juxtaposition n. (17世纪)1.并列;(事物、土地的)毗连(见 juxtapose) 2.(专利)见 aggregation
juzgado 1.法院,特别指由1名法官主审的法院 2.法院,法院大厦

K

Kādi (=*Qādi*) (伊斯兰教法)卡迪(亦译做教法官,指根据伊斯兰教法断案的教法官。理论上讲,卡迪可审理民事和刑事案件,但实际上仅审理财产、继承、宗教捐赠、结婚、离婚之类的案件)
Kādi court (伊斯兰教法)卡迪法庭(亦译做教法官法院,指由卡迪主持的一种穆斯林法院)
kādi's courts act 卡迪法院法
kaiage (或 *kaigium*) 船舶之停泊费,入港税
kangaroo closure (英)限制议事法(亦称跳议法或抽议法,指议会中结束辩论的一种方法,议长就修正案中选出若干付诸讨论,以此删去其余的修正案)
kangaroo court 袋鼠法庭(指采取完全漠视犯人的权利,并因法庭偏见预先作出结论,而不按司法程序进行审判的法庭);私设法庭(如囚犯在监狱中私设的模拟法庭)
Kantian Philosophy of Law 康德法哲学
kanun 法规(指奥斯曼帝国补充伊斯兰教法的行政规定)
kapo n. (集中营或劳动营中)管理其他犯人的犯人,犯人头目
Kappler, Indian Affairs, Laws and Treaties 卡普勒的《印第安事务、法律和条约》(指印第安条约及其有关法规的最好的一套汇编)
kashrut 饮食教规(指犹太教关于饮食的规定)
keelage n. 入港税;停泊税
keelhaul v./n. 把(某人)用绳子缚在船底拖(作为一种刑罚)/船拖刑(指英国海军曾用过的一种刑罚)
keep n./v. 守护,看守,管理;保持;保有生活费,生计/1.保持;保有;保留 2.履行,遵守;保守(秘密) 3.看守;拘留 4.赡养,扶养 5.经销;管理,经营 6.防止,预防(from)
keep a close watch over 监视
keep afloat 免于破产
keep back 留在后面;阻止;隐瞒;留下
keep down 镇压;压服;控制;缩减;卧下,蹲下;保留(食物等)
keep from 阻止,抑制;隐瞒
keep in custody 管押;拘押
keep intact the scene of a crime (或 accident)保护犯罪(或事故)现场
keep (或 **hold**) **one's peace** 闭口不说
keep one's promise inviolate 坚守诺言
keep one's words 遵守诺言
keep shady 隐匿,躲藏
keep (或 **hold**) **sth. in check** (prevent sth. from advancing or increasing, control sth.) 抑制,约束,制止
keep strict watch 严密监视
keep the law 遵守法律,守法
keep the left 靠左行驶
keep the peace 维持治安
keep to the record 不谈与本案无关的事;依记录
keep under detention 看押
keep under strict supervision 严格监督
keep under surveillance 看管
keep up 继续,支持,保存;忍受,忍耐
keep up appearance 虚饰外表
keep up with 追上,跟上;赶得上
Keep up with the Joneses "赶上琼斯家"(指1913年至1940年《纽约世界》等报刊连载的漫画主人公,麦查尼斯一家为挤进上流社会而拼命仿效富有的邻居琼斯家,

后来这就成了一个习语,指的是想方设法要像周围人一样有钱或成功。琼斯这个姓也就用来指代喜欢炫富的邻居,时髦的圈里人)

keep (或 remain) within the four corners of the law 在法律范围内

keeper n. 保管人;看守人;管理人;开设人,经营人;监护人

keeper of prison 监狱长,(美)监狱看守人员

Keeper of the Great Seal (英)国玺掌玺大臣(1563年以后英王国玺由大法官保管)

Keeper of the King's Conscience (英)国王良心的维护者(指大法官行使早先属于英王而未作解释的正当或合法的剩余权力。历史上的大法官具有衡平法上向英王申诉的王权,这种权力产生于衡平法制度。也就是说,具有国王良心的维护者的特性,大法官在行使早先属于英王而未作解释的剩余权力被认为是正当的或有法律依据的);(英)负责(代表)国王听审的大法官;国王良心的守护者;早先属于国王剩余权力的行使者

keeper of the peace 治安维持(员),治安官

keeper of the Privy Seal (或 Lord Privy seal)(英)玉玺保管官 (又译石玺掌玺大臣,指敕书、敕令等在加玉玺之前,均由玉玺掌玺大臣保管并由他办理,1884年被撤销,但仍保留此职位,现此职由内阁大臣担任)

keeper of the wardrobe (英)王室保管库总管(指13世纪英格兰王室主要事务官)

keeping n. 保管,保护,管理;保存,维持;开设,经营;协议,一致

keeping false account books 伪造账目

keeping house 匿居避债(系一种破产行为)

keeping terms (英国四大律师学院学员的)按期修业

keeping the peace 维持治安

keepwell n. 必要条款

Kennedy Round 肯尼迪回合[指关贸总协定(GATT)范围内于1964—1967年在日内瓦举行的第六次多边贸易谈判,因由美国肯尼迪总统发起而得名]

Keogh Plan (美)基奥计划(指个体经营纳税人的退休计划,即每年所得税费扣减到一定数额,即 HR 10 计划)

kermess (=*kermis*) n. (荷兰等国的)定期露天集市;(美)义卖集市

kern(e) n. 流浪汉,无业游民,盲流;(爱尔兰、苏格兰的古时)轻步兵

ketubba (犹太教法)婚书(婚前订立,用以保证新娘一部分未来权利)

key n./a. 1.钥匙 2.(解决问题的)线索 3.秘诀;关键,要害 4.答案/主要的,关键的,基本的;额外的

key contract 关键合同(契约)

key criminal case 刑事要案,重大刑事案件

key enterprises 骨干企业

key instruction (计算机)引导指令

key issue 关键问题;重要争点

Key man (或 person) insurance 关键人员保险

key man system "要人"制度(指陪审团专员从社区候选人中挑选陪审员的一种制度)

key money 额外租金(指为了取得租赁权而暗中送的钱);预付房租(主要用于欧洲);押租,(房地产经纪人索取的)额外小费

key number digest system (美)钥匙号判决摘要汇编系统(指西方出版公司编制的一种用钥匙号分类系统检索全部判决摘要汇编的方法)

key number system (美)钥匙号系统[指美国西方出版公司编制的一整套检索判例和判决摘要的手段。该系统有四百多判决摘要汇编的标题(Topics),均按字母顺序编排。每一标题在判决摘要汇编中都作为一章,一般概括本章内可找到的一些法律争点。这一标题又进一步分成几个副标题(Subtopics),每一副标题又冠上含义较广泛的标题名称和指定其特别子目的钥匙号]

key numbers (美)钥匙号(指通过专门标题和副标题进行分类,并带有钥匙号的法学主题参考系统,用钥匙号均可检索到每一标题,从而可以查到在美国判决摘要汇

编系统和全国判例汇编系统中按主题分编的判例)

key person 重要官员或职员,成功商业的首要负责人

key players 最具实力的比赛对手

key point 要点

key research projects (或 **items**) 重点攻关项目,重点科研项目

key witness 主要证人;关键证人

keycite n. 关键援引,钥匙援引(指美国的一种计算机检索法律文献或判例、制定法等方法)

keying ads 链接式广告

keyword 关键词[指美国法律文献检索的一种方法,通过它可检索到数据库(datebase)中成千上万的判例或文件]

Khairi (伊斯兰教法)哈里(指卧各夫的一种形式,以慈善目的设立的卧各夫)

Khural 呼拉尔(指蒙古的代表会议)

kibbutz n. (以色列的)集体农庄(或聚居区)

kick n./v. 踢;(意外的)反抗(或抗议);抱怨;解雇,撤职/踢开,(用强硬手段)赶出,驱逐(out);使汽车加速

kick the wind (或 **clouds**) 被绞死

kickback n. 1.(美)退赔的赃款 2.佣金(酬金);回扣

kicker n. 顽固者;叛党者;好踢人之马;老是唱反调的人

kickout clause 合同解除条款,合同变更条款(指在特定事件发生时允许一方当事人解除或变更合同条款,根据这种合同解除条款,如果新的公司总部不能完成其财产所得,则公司可拒绝出售土地)

Kid Credentialing 为子女升学攒资历(指让子女参加各种活动和比赛、考取证书、积累经历,以此为今后申请大学做准备的现象。哈佛大学肯尼迪政治学院马尔科姆·维纳社会政策研究中心成员希拉里·利维·弗里德曼 2013 年 11 月为美国《大西洋月刊》网站撰文时首次用到该词)

kiddie tax (18 世纪)(俚语)(美)儿童非劳动所得税,儿童份外所得税(指对儿童的分外所得课以联邦税。如果孩子在 18 岁以下,父母的税率较高,则按父母税率

纳税。亦称 child's income tax)

kidnap v. 拐带,诱拐(儿童);绑架;勒赎,绑票

kidnap and sell people 拐卖人口

kidnap(p)er n. 诱拐者,拐骗犯,绑架者

kidna(p)ping 绑架罪(早期普通法中的一种罪行,指违反他人意志将其劫持或偷运至他地或他国秘密隐藏的犯罪行为。在普通法上属轻罪)

kidnap(p)ing by terrorists 恐怖分子的绑架

kill n./v. 杀,杀伤;猎获物/1.杀死,扼杀 2.阻拦,否决议案等 3.取消,删去 4.压制,制服 5.中和,抵消

kill a bill 使议案搁置,使议案通不过

kill a petition 断然拒绝请求

kill for money 谋财害命

kill in revenge 仇杀

kill oneself 自杀

kill ratio 杀伤率

killer n. 杀人凶手,杀人者

killing n. 杀死,屠杀

Killing by accident 意外杀人

killing by misadventure 意外杀人

killing by somebody 他杀

kin n. 家族;门第;家属;亲戚;亲戚关系

kind n. 种,类属;性质,本质;实物

kindly tenancy (苏格兰)优惠土地保有

kindred n. 血缘关系,亲属关系;家属,亲属;相似;血亲;宗族

kindred offence 同类罪行,同类犯罪

kindred science 相关科学

kinds of punishment (或 **penalty**) 刑罚的种类

kinfolk (= kinsfolk) n. 家属,亲属,亲戚;血缘

King n. 君王,君主;国王;最高者

King at (或 **of**) **Arms** 纹章主管长官,(英)纹章长官,纹章院长

* **(the) King can do no wrong.** (英)国王无错事(原则)

king (或 **prince**) **consort** 女王的丈夫

King de facto (= de facto king) 事实上的国王

King de jure 合法英(国)王,王位的合法继承

King of Kings 1.万王之王(指耶稣基督) 2.(古代东方国家的)皇帝

King of Terrors 死神

King's advocate (英)(在大陆法或教会法占优势的法院中次于检察长地位的)王室律师(或检察官)

King's Bench (或 **Queen's Bench**) (英)(高等法院的)王座(后座)法庭(=Banc le roy)

King's Bench Division (英)王座法庭

King's briefs (或 **letters**) (英)国王特许状

king's chamber (英)国王议事厅

King's conscience 行使早先属于英王而未作解释的剩余权力(见 Keeper of the King's conscience)

king's council 王室会议,御前会议;(英史)国王法律顾问团(指1250年前的咨询性质的议会,为现代枢密院或上议院的前身)

King's counsel (或 **King's sergeant, Queen's counsel**) 王室法律顾问,王室律师(指专门研究法律并被任命为皇家律师者。其实,这是一种荣誉称号,并不对王室履行具体的法律职责。一般资深的出庭律师经本人申请、大法官推荐和经英王批准,方可被授予这一称号。获此称号之律师出庭可身穿丝袍坐在审判席上,故亦称"丝袍")

king's custom 国王的习惯[指 Constitution of Clarendon(《克拉伦敦宪法》)所宣布认可的国王的习惯。"对祖先享有的习惯、自由以及尊严的认可和记录。"]

King's enemy (英)敌国;敌国人;公敌

King's evidence (英)求英王宽恕的证据(指刑事案件中,同案犯为求得宽赦而供出的对共犯不利的证据)

king's justice (英)刑事法官

King's omnibus (英)警察局用的囚车

King's peace (英)国家治安,社会秩序,公共治安

King's printer (英)国王特许印刷者(所)(指经君主授予特许状而拥有印刷制定法的独占权者)

King's proctor (英)(家事法庭中代表国家的)公诉人(或律师)

king's procurator 皇家检察官

king's serjeant 国王的高级律师

King's Silver (英)(古)国王的罚款(指意图以协议诉讼方式转让土地者在获法庭批准后应向国王交纳的费用)

king's solicitor (英)国家检察官

King's widow (英)国王土地保有人的遗孀(指国土第一级土地保有人的遗孀)

kingdom n. 王国;领域;(大写)英国;神政

kingless a. 无国王的,无君主的;无政府的

kinglet n. 小国的王;小王

kingly a. 国王的;君主地位的;适合君主身份的;国王似的;君主政体的;适于君王的

kingly form of government 君主政体(的统治)

kingmaker n. (有足够的权威或影响力而能)选择国王者(或选择其他公职人员者)

kingship n. 王权;帝王统治;君王的身份

kinless a. 无家属(或亲属)的,无亲戚的

kinship n. 亲属关系,家属关系,类似家属(或亲属)的亲密关系

kinship family 大家庭(指由直系亲属的小家庭共同组成的家庭)

kinship inheritance 亲属继承

kinship relations 亲属关系

kinsman n. 男性亲属

kinsmen of the fourth (或 **sixth**) **degree** 四亲(或六亲)等的男性亲属

kinswoman n. 女性亲属

Kippers 啃老族["花父母的钱、逐渐消耗其退休储蓄金的子女"的简称(kids in parents' pockets eroding retirement savings),指的是仍与父母住在一起的成年子女,尤指30岁或30岁以上的人群,单指一个人时则用 Kipper]

Kirby's Reports 《克尔比判例汇编》(最早的一部美国判例汇编。美国判例汇编早期发展依照英国模式,冠以姓名的判例汇编在英国还很普遍时,第一部美国判例汇编就冠以报道、纪录法院判决的个人名义出版,即1789年康涅狄格州的《克尔比判例汇编》)

kissing the book (英史)吻(圣经)宣誓

(指英格兰法院曾采用过的一种诉讼特别程序)

kitchen cabinet 食厨,碗橱;政府首脑的顾问团(在美国指非官方的、非正式的、非内阁的顾问团体,通常他们比真正的内阁具有更多行政影响力。这个词最初用来对待美国第7任总统安德鲁·杰克逊的顾问团中的某个成员,由于他的声誉和粗鲁态度而受到嘲弄,但顾问团在白宫正规会议室开会时并不给予足够重视)

kite n. 1.骗子;流氓 2.空头支票;抵用票据

kiteflying n. 胡乱发布政治新闻(事后又否认);开空头支票

kitemark n. 标准印记(指在英国工业标准协会注册证明的商标)

kith n. 邻居,(熟悉的)朋友;亲属

kiting n. 用空头支票骗钱,开空头支票,移挪补空

kiting cheque 空头支票

kittum u mêarum 法律(指古代西亚地区,楔形文字中"法律",实为阿卡德语,相当于"真理和权利"之意)

kitty n. 共同的资金(如储金);全部赌注;(从赌注中抽出的)头钱

kiyas 吉雅论(指穆斯林法官在司法实践中通过类推而得到的司法结论,为伊斯兰教法的一个渊源)

Klaxon principle (美)克拉克森原则(一种冲突法原理,即要求联邦地区法院行使跨州管辖权时适用法院所在地的原则来确定准据法)

kleptomania n. 盗窃癖,盗窃狂

kleptomaniac n. 有盗窃癖的人;见东西就偷的精神病患者

knack n. 诀窍,窍门;技巧;需要熟练技巧的工作

knave n. 流氓,无赖,恶棍

knavery n. 流氓行为,无赖行为;欺诈,欺诈行为

kneel-in n. 祈祷示威(指美国黑人抗议种族歧视,进入白人教堂做礼拜进行示威)

knife money (中)(古时的)刀币(硬币)

knife robber 持刀抢劫犯

knight n. 骑士

knight marshall (英)(管辖并审理王室或管辖区内犯罪案件和签订契约的)审理警务官;皇宫警官

knight of community 州选议员

knight of the collar 应处以绞刑的犯人

knight of the parliament 州选议员

knight of the post 被缚于柱上处以笞刑的囚犯;以受贿作假证的人;以作假为职业的人

knight-service n. (英史)服役土地保有(指封建采邑制中的一种主要土地保有形式,1600年废除后,转为农役土地保有形式)

knighthood 骑士身份

knights of the shire (古英格兰)(不列颠议会中的)郡选议员

knobstick n. (英)罢工时上工的工人,工贼

knock down (或 **knock off**) 敲槌(指拍卖拍板成交);迫使降价

knock for knock agreement 汽车互撞免赔协议

knock-on knells n./v. 钟声、丧钟,(喻)死亡、灭亡/敲丧钟;发出悲哀之声

knock-out n./a. 垄断拍卖,勾结拍卖(指公开拍卖时,预先串谋,以便得以低价成交,此种行为合视为非法行为);致命打击/勾结拍卖的;使昏迷的

knock-out agreement 相互勾结(低价买进拍卖品并加以瓜分)的秘密协议

knock-out drops (投入酒中的)昏迷药,蒙汗药

knot n. 难题;结合(指婚姻);涅

know all men by these presents 见礼知人

know as 所知,已知

know one's way around 熟悉业务知识

know-how n. (专利上的)技术秘密(又译:技术诀窍);专门知识;技能;技艺;秘诀;方法

know-how license contract 技术诀窍许可合同(契约)

knowing a./n. 故意的,知道的,世故的,有知识的,机灵的/知道,认识

knowing consent 明知同意(见 informed consent)

knowingly ad. 心照不宣地;故意地;有意地

knowingly and wilfully 明知而故意地
knowledge n. 性交(carnal knowledge); 明知, 知道(指对事实和情况的认识, 反义词为 ignorance); 知道[包括实际知道(actual knowledge)和推定知道(constructive knowledge), 与故意 intent 不同的是, knowledge 基于认识, 而 intent 则基于目的]; 信息, 了解
knowledge economy (know what, why, how, who) 知识经济(知识经济是建立在以知识和信息生产、分配和使用之上的经济)
knowledge-based economy 知识经济
known danger 已知危险
known heir 已知的继承人[指在无近亲属(closer relative)情况下, 主张继承的继承人]
known heirs 已知的继承人(出售无人继承之遗产的用语, 必须指明确实无已知继承人时方能进行此种出售)
known loss 已知损失

known market 技术知识(技术)市场
known party 已知的当事人
known practice and expedient 已知的惯例和手段
Koran n. 《古兰经》(也可译做《可兰经》, 伊斯兰经典, 是穆罕默德在传教中作为安拉之神对诸穆斯林信徒发布经文的启示集, 为伊斯兰教法最重要的渊源)
Koranic a. 《古兰经》的
koshuba (犹太)结婚契约, 结婚时分授财产给妻子的文件
Koranic law 古兰经法
Koranic precept 古兰经教义
Koranic rules 古兰经教规
kotwal (亦做 cotwal) (英、印度城市的)警察局长
kotwalee (亦做 kotwali) (英、印度的)警察局
Kreis (神圣罗马帝国的)行政区
Ku Klux Kian n. (美)三 K 党(指用私刑迫害黑人和进步组织人士的美国恐怖组织)

L

L'état, c'est moi 朕即国家
la commune intention des parties contractantes 合同当事人共同的意思
* *La conscience est lá plus changeante des règles.* Conscience is the most changeable of rules. 良心是行为规范中最容易变化的。
* *La ley favour l'enheritance d'un home.* The Law favors the inheritance of a man. 法律顾及个人继承。
* *La ley favour la vie d'un home.* The Law favors the life of a man. 法律爱护人命。
La vente en droit belge (1960) 《比利时销售法》(1960 年)
label n./v. (文件等的)签条, 标签; 标记, 标志, 符号; 称号, 绰号; (古)附在文件上带有封印的丝带; (苏格兰)标签证据(指刑事诉讼中对实物证据如武器上系有一个标签的称谓)/贴标签于……; 指名; 给……戴上帽子; 称……为; 把……列为
labeling acceptance of a directorship as consent 接受董事同意的标签
Labeling Theory (美)标签理论[指美国的 4D 政策和标理论。该理论始于 20 世纪 70 年代的美国少年司法改革, 并逐渐影响了多数法治国家的少年司法改革。"4D"是指"due process"(正当程序)、"division"(分流)、"decriminalization"(非犯罪化)和"deinstitutionalization"(非机构化), 标签理论颠覆了传统犯罪理论, 旨在研究控制犯罪的机制, 在促成犯罪中起的作用。标签理论的代表人物克拉伦斯·施拉格(Clarence Schrag)、埃德温·M. 莱蒙特(Edwin M. Lement)、弗兰克·汤南鲍姆(Frank Tannenbaum)等研究认为, 刑事

司法活动将犯罪人贴上社会遗弃者和坏人的标签,犯罪人会逐渐形成心理暗示而按标签模式去行为,由此提出分流、补偿、非机构化和非犯罪化等政策建议]

label(l)ing regulations 标签条例

labes realis (苏格兰)真实瑕疵(指影响财产所有权的内在瑕疵,如被窃物)

labo(u)r n./v. 1.劳动;工作;(总称)工人;劳动力;劳方 2.(大写)(英)工党 3.分娩,阵痛/1.劳动,劳作 2.分娩,阵痛 3.过于详细地分析(解释)

labo(u)r a jury 对陪审团施加影响(指以不正当手段去左右陪审的裁决)

labo(u)r affair 劳工事务

labo(u)r agitator 为劳工谋利益鼓吹者(指正当地为增进劳工福利而言)

labo(u)r and capital 劳资(关系)

labo(u)r camp (犯人)劳动营;劳改场所;流动工人的营地

labo(u)r capacity 劳动能力

labo(u)r chamber (法院的)劳工庭

labo(u)r charter 劳动宪章

labo(u)r code 劳工法典;劳动法典

labo(u)r contract 劳动合同(契约);劳工合同(契约)

labo(u)r cost 人工成本;劳工成本

labo(u)r court 劳资争议法庭(又译:劳工法庭)

Labo(u)r Day (五一国际)劳动节;(美)劳工节(9月的第一个星期一)

labo(u)r discipline 劳动纪律

labo(u)r disputes (between employers and employees) (雇主和雇员间的)劳资纠纷,劳资争议

labo(u)r education and rehabilitation school (中)劳动教养所

labo(u)r employment 劳动就业

labo(u)r evaluating committee 劳动鉴定委员会

labo(u)r exchange (大写)职业介绍所;(英)(劳工部门的)劳工介绍所;产品交换

labo(u)r force 劳动力

Labo(u)r Government (英)工党政府

labo(u)r hero 劳动英雄

labo(u)r injunction 劳动禁令

labo(u)r insurance 劳动保险,劳保

labo(u)r insurance regulations 劳保条例

labo(u)r intensity 劳动强度

labo(u)r judge 劳工法官

labo(u)r law (中)劳动法,劳工法

labo(u)r legislation 劳动立法,劳动法规

labo(u)r management (department) 劳动管理(部门)

labo(u)r management co-decision act 劳资共议法

Labo(u)r Management Reporting and Disclosure Act (美)《劳资关系报告和揭发法》

labo(u)r market 劳动力市场,劳工市场

labo(u)r norms 劳动定额

labo(u)r organization 劳工组织

labo(u)r pact 劳动公约

Labo(u)r Party (英)工党(1900年成立,初称"劳工代表委员会")

labor pension n. 劳工退休金

labo(u)r problem 劳工问题

labo(u)r productivity 劳动生产率

labo(u)r protection 劳动保护

labo(u)r reform (中)劳动改造(指对违法犯罪者通过实施教育和强制劳动,使改造成为新人)

labo(u)r reform committee (中)劳改委员会

labo(u)r reform regulations (中)劳动改造条例

labo(u)r reform site (中)劳改场所

labo(u)r reform team (中)劳改队

labo(u)r reform under surveillance (中)监督劳动改造

labo(u)r relation 劳资关系

labo(u)r relations adjustment law 劳资关系调整法

labo(u)r safety 劳动安全

labo(u)r service charge 劳动服务费

labo(u)r service company (中)劳动服务公司

labo(u)r service contract 劳务合同(契约)

labo(u)r standards law 劳动基准法

labo(u)r tribunal 劳资争议裁判庭(又

译:劳工裁判庭)
labo(u)r trouble 劳资纠纷
labor troubleshooter 劳务调解人
labo(u)r union 工会
labo(u)r union organization 工会组织
Labo(u)r vote 支持工党的选票
labo(u)r wages 劳动工资
labo(u)r's right to participate in management decisions 劳工参加(企业)经营决策权
labor-management relations 劳动管理关系
Labor-Management Reporting and Disclosure Act (美)《劳资关系报告暨公开法》(1959年)
labo(u)r-saving a. 节省劳力的,减轻劳动的
labo(u)rage n. 工资,工钱
labo(u)rer n. 劳动者,工人
labo(u)ring a. 劳动的,劳工的,劳资(争议)的
labo(u)ring clause 劳工条款,劳资争议条款
labo(u)ring people 劳动人民
laboring population 劳动人口
Labo(u)rism n. 工党政策,工党原则;(集合名词)工党;(大写)工党党员
labo(u)rite n. 工党支持者,工党追随者;劳工派成员;(大写)(英)工党党员
lace v./n. 用带子束紧,鞭打,加少量,使有活力/系带,鞋带,精细织品
lacerated wound 破裂伤;碎裂伤(指软组织受到伤害)
laceration n. 脑裂伤(指脑组织、软脑膜和脑血管破裂,组织失去连续性,出血严重,伴有脑组织坏死和严重脑水肿者称脑裂伤。脑挫伤可单独出现,而脑裂伤常合称脑挫伤)
laches n. (对行使权利的)疏忽,懈怠;迟延,迟误
lachrymator n. 催泪性毒气;催泪物
lack n./v. 缺乏,不足;缺少的东西;需要的东西/缺少,没有;需要
lack a *quorum* 不足法定人数
lack of competence 无权;缺乏管辖权
lack of consideration 缺乏对价
lack of evidence 缺乏证据,证据不足

lack of maturity 未成年
lack of title 欠缺权利根据
lacking of redeeming virtue 欠缺补偿价值
lacta (古英国法)重量不足(指钱币分量不足)
lacuna (复数 *lacunae*, *lacunas*) n. 空白;缺陷;空隙;脱漏;疏漏
lacunae in the legislative structure 立法结构上的空白
lading n. 装载(之货);船货,客货
lady day (英)春季结账日(新历3月25日)
laenland 租赁土地所有制
laesio enormis 最低标准(说)
laesione fidel 不守信用,违约
lag n./v. (俚)因犯,犯人;旧犯;徒刑期限,苦役期限;滞后,迟延/把(犯人)押往监狱,送去做苦役;(英)逮捕
lagan (或 **lagend**, **ligan**) n. (船只遇险时)系有浮标的投海货物
lagged in the forum state 被锁定在判决地州,被锁定在本州
lagger n. (俚)囚犯,旧犯
lagniappe n. 免费赠品,商人给顾客的小赠品
laicism n. 政权归还俗人主义
laid out (美)喝醉了的
laird n. (苏格兰)地主
lairdship n. 地主身份,领地
laissez-aller 放任,自由
laissez-faire (或 *laisser-faire*) 放任;自由竞争;自由放任主义,不干涉主义,政府对工商业的自由放任(政策)
laissez-faire **capitalism** 自由资本主义
laissez-faire **constitutionalism** 放任自由的立宪主义(指的是一种思想态度,它表现了从美国内战到新政期间联邦最高法院的一些法官的思想特征,这种思想反映了古典经济学的特点,即赞成由市场来控制经济,主张企业自由,反对政府管制经济;在社会生活中提倡达尔文主义;在经济领域采取适者生存原则,以形式主义的方法来审视法院的判决;喜欢抽象概念和形式逻辑、传统的美国价值观、个人主义和机会均等;反对限制竞争;对于由移民、工业化以及有组织的劳工斗争所引发的社会

不稳定感到恐惧)
laissez-faire era 自由放任时期(主要是19世纪和20世纪初期,国家职能有限,政府不干预经济和商务时期,奉行政府不干预理论)
laissez-faire et laisser-passer 任其所作为(的自由放任主义思想)(是民事诉讼的辩证主义思想的根源所在)
laissez-faire theory of government 放任主义的政府论
laissez-passer (联合国职员出外所持的)通行证,护照
laity n. (集合名词)世俗人(用以区别于僧侣或教士);外行
lam v. 打,鞭打(越(狱),逃跑
lama n. 喇嘛(藏、蒙等佛教的僧侣)
lame a. 跛的,残废的;有缺陷的;站不住脚的
lame duck (俚)1.(美)(任期快满但未重新选上的)落选官员(或议员)2.(交易所投机失败后)无力偿债的人 3.残疾人,无能的人,引起周转不灵而经济困难者
lament over 悔改;痛惜,悲伤
Lammas n. (英)秋季结账日(新历8月1日);收获节
lammas lands 收获季节的开放地
lamster (=lamister) n. 逃亡者(尤指逃避法律制裁者);(美)逃犯
land n./v. (12世纪前)1.(作为一个法律概念是指不可破坏的三面立体的面积,包括地表、地表之上和地下的整个空间以及永远附着于其中的或生长的任何事物)土地 2.陆地;国土,国家;地带,境界 3.(复)地产,田产,所有不动产中的权益/使上岸,使登陆,使(飞机)等降落;使到达;把……送到;使陷入,使处于;(罪犯等)落网;登陆,上岸,降落,(终于)到达,(船舶等)靠岸,歇脚
land administration 土地管理
land agency 地产经纪
land agent 地产商,地产买卖经纪人;公有土地管理官员,(英)田产管理人
land allotment 土地核配
land and thing so attached thereto 土地及其附着物

land bank (经营土地抵押业务的)土地银行
land board 土地局
land carriage 陆上运输,陆运
land certificate 土地证,地契
land charge (英)土地负担;土地抵押
land concession 土地特许权
land condemnation 土地征收
land condemnation cases 在土地征用案件(中)
land court 土地法院(庭)
land disputes 土地纠纷
land domain (或 territory) 领陆,领土
land fall (因近亲突然死亡而发生的)土地所有权的获得;初见陆地;地崩
land free of any effective occupation 完全未经有效占有的荒地
land grants (美)土地授予[指历届政府都取得了对土地的所有权并将大部土地分配给私人以作定居与生存发展之用。在早期案例中,联邦最高法院承认,作为美国政治、经济制度组成部分的土地是受宪法保护的私人财产(权)。美国联邦宪法的财产条款授权国会可以将联邦所有的土地进行"分配"。依此法律条款,国会可将大部分联邦土地出售给或授予各州、公司和个人。其中许多授予都是为了支付教育事业、铁路运输以及其他公益事业。分配公共土地的权力属于国会而非各个法院]
land holder 土地所有人;土地租用人
land in abeyance 所有权未定的土地
land increment value duty 土地增值税
land jobber 土地投机商,地皮经纪人
land lady 女房东;女业主;(旅馆的)女店主
land law 土地法
land lease 土地租赁;土地租赁合同(契约)
land legislation 土地立法
land let to lease 仅供租借的土地
land levelling project 土地平整工程
land lot 地段
land mark 地界,界标;(历史的)里程碑
land occupied under customary tenure 传统的占有土地

land of uncertain ownership 所有权不明的土地
land office 土地局,地政局
land patent 公共土地转让特许证
land pollution 土地污染
land power 陆军强国;陆军力量;地面力量
land price 地价
land proprietor 地产所有人;地主
land reform (law) 土地改革(法)
land register 土地登记簿
land registration 土地登记
land registry 土地登记处
land rent 地租
land requisition 土地征用
land right 土地权,地产权,地亩权
land sale 土地买卖,土地出售
land surveyor 土地测定(量)员
land tax 见 property tax
land tenant 土地实际占有人;(英)土地保有人
land tenure 土地占有制;(英)土地保有制
land the troops at the beachhead 把部队送上滩头阵地
land title 土地所有权
land transaction 土地交易
land transfer 土地转让
land transfer act 土地转让法
land transfer system 土地转让制度
land transit insurance 陆上运输保险
land transport 陆上运输(送)
land trust 土地信托
land under the sea (陆地领土在海底的)自然延伸原则
land use certificate 土地使用证(书)
land use planning (美)土地使用计划(指可表示城市区划法规、不动产开发、环保影响研究的州和地方主事官计划等的一般用法)
Land Use Planning & Zoning Law (美)《土地使用计划与分区规划法》(美国的土地使用受到三种限制,即直接的政府法规、私人土地使用协议或者说地役权以及普通法上的私人妨害原则。其中,直接的政府法规主要表现为土地使用计划与分区规划法)

land valuation court 土地估价法院
land value 地价
land values duties 地价税
land warfare 陆战
land warrant 土地转让证(书)
land-grabber n. 霸占土地者,侵占土地者
land-grant n. 政府赠与地
land-locked lake 内陆湖泊,陆锁湖泊
land-locked seas (国际法)陆锁海,内陆海
land-locked state 内陆国
land-ownership n. 土地所有制;土地所有权
Land-ownership Law 《土地所有权法》
land-poor a. 因持有大量无利可图的土地而周转不灵的(或经济困难的)
land-to-the-tiller 耕者有其田(指孙中山学说民生主义中的一个重要原则)
land-waiter n. (英)海关税务检查人员
landed a. 不动产的;拥有土地的;地皮的;由土地构成的
landed class 地主阶级
landed estate court 地产法院
landed men (苏格兰)土地拥有者
landed price 卸岸价格
landed property 地产;不动产
landed servitude 土地的地役权
landed terms 目的港岸上交货价格
landing n. 着陆,登陆;码头上装卸货处
landing account 起货单
landing book 起货细单
landing certificate 卸货证书
landing charge 卸货费
landing force 登陆部队
landing pass 登陆证
landless a. 无地的
landlord n. 地主;地主分子;业主,房东,(旅馆的)店主
landlord and tenant 地主和佃户(土地租借人)
landlord class 地主阶级
landlord of writ 法庭审定的地主,法庭审定的业主
landlord-comprador class (中)地主买办阶级
landlordism n. 地主所有制

landmark n. 界标;里程碑;陆上的标志
landmark case 标志性判例
landmark decision 标志性的判决
landmark opinion 标志性的判决意见
Landmark Preservation Law (美)(1968年纽约市的)《界标保护法》
landowner n. 土地所有人;地主
landowner and despotic gentry 地主豪绅
landrecht 邦区法(指中世纪某一个邦国或地区的普通法或立法)
Landrum-Griffin Act (美)《兰德勒姆-格里芬法》[1959年通过的联邦法规,给予个体联合会会员一些新的权利,如要求联合会应有公正的章程,该法也在某些方面修改了《塔夫特-哈特利法》(Taft-Hartley Act)]
lands tribunal (英)土地裁判庭(指英国按1949年土地裁判庭法规定所组成的法庭)
landslide n. 压倒的优势(尤指竞选中选票的一边倒);山崩;塌方
landsman n. 本国人,同胞;未出过海的人,不懂航海的人
language n. 语言,语文;使用语言能力
Lanham Act 《兰哈姆法》[指美国联邦商标成文法规,1946年制定颁布。该法规为全国商标注册体制和保护联邦注册的商标的所有人并预防类似商标混用,如果任何(商标)滥用产生,或有实力的商标的力量冲击,则立即禁止。《兰哈姆法》是独立的,而且与州普通法一样为现行法。参见《美国注释法典》第15标题卷第1051节及以下。亦称 Federal Trademark Act; Trademart Act of 1946]
language of the court (或 **legal language**) 法庭用语(法律用语)
Lanham Act of 1946 《1946年兰汉姆法》(指《1946年商标法》)
lapse n./v. 1.(未履行义务所引起的)权利终止,权利失效 2.失效(一般指在立遗嘱人未死亡之前而受遗赠人先死亡时遗赠的失效) 3.失误;失检,小错/背离,陷入;因失效而转归;权利终止,消失
lapse of a stated period 过了规定期限,过了上述期限

lapse of attention 一时疏忽
lapse of legacy (遗产承受人比遗嘱人先死时的)遗产承受权的终止(或失效)
lapse of memory 记忆错误
lapse of patent 专利权的终止
lapse of the pen 笔误
lapse of time 时效终止
lapsed a. 失效的,过期的
lapsed cheque (或 **check**) 过期支票
lapsed devise 失效的不动产遗赠(亦称 failed devise, failed gift)
lapsed gift 因失效而转归(他人)的赠与
lapse statute 见 antilapse statute
lapsed legacy 失效的遗产承受人[指遗赠承受人(legatee)或死于遗赠人(testator)之前或死于遗赠付予之前。除非该管辖地区具有反失效成文制定法规(antilapse statute),否则对于剩余遗赠也会失效。亦称 failed legacy; failed gift。见 antilapse statute]
lapsed policy (1873年)1.失效保单[指保险支付费用(premium payments)已经失效的保单]2.保险政策(保险人以保险费为对价)因制定法上的规定在未履行交付保险费情况下而仍继续有效 3.制定法对未支付保险费之后补交通常提供30或31天的宽限期(grace period)
lapsed writ 过期令状
lapsus 错误,失误,差错
lapsus calami 笔误
lapsus linguae 失言,口误
lapsus memoriae 记忆上的错误
larcener n. 盗窃犯,窃贼
larcenist n. 盗窃犯,窃贼
larcenous a. 构成盗窃罪的;犯盗窃罪的;偷窃的
larcenous intent 盗窃意图
larceny n. 盗窃罪;非法侵占(他人)财产
Larceny Act (英)《盗偷法》
larceny by trick 玩弄诡计而非法侵占(他人)财产
larceny from the person 从(被盗)人身上窃取财产(见 compound larceny)
larceny of public property 盗窃公共财产罪
larceny suspect 非法侵占他人财产嫌疑犯

larceny theft 非法侵占他人财产的盗贼
large amounts 大量的
large degree of autonomy 高度自治
large exposures 大额风险
large industrial 大型工业
large stakes （案件中的）重要问题，重要的利益攸关问题
large-scale pelagic drift-net 大型流刺网
large-scale systemic responses 大规模的系统回应体系
larger estate 大宗房地产；大宗产业；大宗遗产
larger stakes cases 风险大的案件
largess(e) n. 慷慨，大度；慷慨的赠与，慷慨的赐予；赏赐物
laron （古）小偷
larrikin n. 地痞，街头恶棍，无赖；二流子
Las partidas 《阿方索条例》[又称《七章法典》，指西班牙的一部有七个部分的法典，于1250年依罗马法、习惯法和教会法合编，1384年被正式公布。该法典部分内容在美国佛罗里达、路易斯安那和得克萨斯等州具有法律效力]
lascivious a. 淫荡的，好色的
lascivious cohabitation 非法同居
laser n. 激光（又译：莱塞）；激光器
laser weapons 激光武器
lash n. 鞭笞刑；鞭打，抽打
last a. 最后的，最终的；临终的；结论性的；权威性的；极端的；最新式的
last argument 最后的论据
last clean chance doctrine （侵权）最后明显机会原则[该原则规定损害虽由本身具有过失的原告造成，但他仍可从被告那里获得赔偿，如果被告已有最后机会阻止伤害或损害发生，但却未这样做而让其发生。换句话说：即被告的疏忽过失迟于原告，仍应负赔偿之责任。这一原则允准原告反驳自身存在过失(contributory negligence)，几乎没有哪个管辖区的被告会全力阻止对自身存在过失的赔偿。亦称 discovered peril doctrine; humanitarian doctrine; last opportunity doctrine; sulsequent negligence doctrine; supervening-negligence doctrine]

last clear chance doctrine 最后明显机会原则(指交通法中损害虽由于原告过失造成，但被告驾驶员见到原告处于危险境地，有最后防止损害的明显机会，而让其发生，仍应负赔偿责任的原则)
last court （英）权威法庭(指建立在英格兰东南海岸五港同盟地区的一个行政机构)
last day for the deposit of the petition and bill 提交申请和法案的截止日期
last event 最后事件地
last heir 最后继承人
last illness 致命疾病
last instance 终审
last judg(e)ment 终审判决；（大写）上帝的最后审判日（亦称 last day）
last mile （被判死刑者赴刑场的）最后路程
last opportunity （原告获得赔偿的）最后机会
last opportunity doctrine 见 last clean chance doctrine
last residence 经常居住地
last resort 最后手段；终审，终审判决
last will 临终遗嘱
last will and testament （处理身后财产的）临终遗嘱
last word 最后一句话；最后决定权；决定性的说明；定论
lasting significance 持久的定义
lata culpa 重大过失
* *Lata culpa dolo aequiparatur.* Gross negligence is equivalent to fraud. 重大过失等于诈骗。（英格兰法称此格言并不适用：无论过失多少，并不能构成诈骗）
late a. 晚的；新近的；已故的；前任的
late childbirth 晚育
late fee （英）过时补加费(指在邮局规定的时间之后投递邮件时所付的费)
late marriage 晚婚
late *postmortem phenomena* 晚期尸体现象
latency n. 潜伏，潜在；潜伏物；潜伏因素
latency period 潜伏期
latent a. 潜在的，潜伏的；隐而不见的
latent ambiguity 隐晦不明处(指法律文件

的文句隐晦不明、暧昧不清)
latent capital 潜在资本
latent criminal 潜在罪犯,潜伏的罪犯
latent deed 秘密保存(达二十年以上)的契据
latent defect 隐蔽的瑕疵,隐蔽的缺陷
latent evidence 无色(隐)印痕证据
latent fingerprints 无色指印(纹);潜指纹
later intervention 介入因素(指因果关系理论中限制的具体理由,哈特、奥若尔认为责任限制有5个因素,即necessity 必要性、later intervention 介入因素;probability 可能性、the scope of the rule of law in question 规范范围和equity 衡平。前两个属于正常意识上的因果关系,后三者属于非因果关系类型。另有学者将限制因素归纳为行政管理因素 administrative factor、价值阶层因素 the superior value factor、环境因素 environmental factor 和责任保险因素 liability insurance factor)
later will 后立的遗嘱
lateral a. 侧面的,旁边的;横向的;系统外的;从侧面的,从旁边的,从系统外的;次要的;副的
lateral entry 系统外选拔制(指美国的现行人事制度,即各种人员不管有无学历均可参加公务人员选拔考试而为政府机关所任用);公开选任制
lateral judge 副法官,副审判员
lateral support (土地所有者的土地有)受相邻土地自然支撑的权利
latifundium n. 大地产,大庄园,大领地
latifundus n. 拥有大量地产者,大地产商
Latin information (英)拉丁诉讼(指用于侵权或动产债务纠纷,或者损害赔偿的诉讼。见 English information)
Latin side of chancery (英)大法官法院拉丁语分庭(指旧大法官法庭的一个分庭)
latini colonarii (罗马法)殖民地拉丁人(指罗马殖民地之居民)
latini juniani (罗马法上的)布衣阶层
latini veteres (罗马法)古拉丁人(指组成拉丁同盟之市的人民)
latitat 共同管辖程序(指英15世纪王座法院创立的一项程序使其具有与高等民事法院共同的管辖权)
latitude n. (言论、行动等)自由;范围;幅度;纬度
lato sensu in a wide sense, in a broad sense 广义上讲,从广泛的意义来说
launch v. 发射;开办;使投掷;使下水;发动,开展;提出;开始,着手;发起,发出(命令)
launching aggressive war 发动侵略战争
laughing heir (1943年)(俚语)可笑的继承人[指一位毫不悲伤的远房继承人。当亲属死亡并留下一笔遗产,通常被视为意外之财或横财(windfall),得此遗产者为很远很远的远房继承人]
law n./v. 1.法;法律,法令 2.法学;法律知识 3.司法界,法律行业 4.诉讼;法律解决 5.法则,定律,规律 6.(英)成文法和习惯法 7.(复)法规;法治/诉,控告;对……起诉
law abiding 遵守法律的
law against unfair competition 反不正当竞争法
law agents (苏格兰)法律代理人(现称为撰状律师);律师
law and decree 法令,法律和政令
law and discipline 法纪,法律和纪律
law and economy 法与经济(又译:法律与经济)
law and equity (英美法)普通法和衡平法
law and morals 法与道德(又译:法律与道德)
law and order 治安;法律和秩序
law and regulation 法规,法律和规章
law and the surrounding social science 法律及其相关的社会科学
law applicable in the state 国内现行法律;(美)州内适用的法律
law as generic 一般的法律
law as integrity 整合法学
law as it is 法的实然领域,实然法,实际上是这样的法
Law as it ought to be 法的应然领域,应然法,应当是这样的法
law as it stands 现行的法律
law at the owner's domicile 所有人的住所

地法
Law Blogs （美）（有时称为 Blawgs）法律书面重大信息[指广泛范畴的论题的书面信息,有时则成为最新信息的主要资源,比如 SCOTUSblog（www.scotusblog.com）通常具有联邦最高法院特大新闻的第一报道]
law book　法律学书籍,法学课本
law by analogy　法律类推
law career　律师业,律师生涯,律师工作
law case　法律案件,诉讼案
law centre　法律中心
law chosen by the parties　双方当事人选定的法律
law circle　法律界
law clerk（美）律师助手;大法官的书记员（指被指派到联邦最高法院大法官办公室协助大法官处理司法业务的书记员）;法律书记员（指在美国,在法官指导下对具体案件涉及的法律问题进行研究并起草有关法律文件者,这些人不能转为法官）
Law Commission　（英）法律委员会（指英国司法改革的专门组织）
Law Committee　（中）法律委员会（指全国人民代表大会设立的专门委员会）
law concerning bankruptcy　破产法
law concerning employer-employee relationships　劳资关系法
law concerning international carriage of goods by sea　国际海上货物运输法
Law Concerning the Prohibition of Private Monopoly and the Maintenance of Fair Trade　（日）《关于禁止私人垄断及确保公平交易法》（1947 年）
law correspondence course　函授法律课程
law court　法庭,（大陆法）司法法院（指与习惯法法院相对而言）;（英美法）普通法法院（指与衡平法法院相对而言）;（英）（伦敦）皇家司法法院
law court for public trial　公开审判法庭
law court of appeals　上诉法院
law day（或 date）　（美）法律日,法庭处置日（指法律规定每年 5 月 1 日为法律日,亦指支付债款之日,此日之后,则对不动产的抵押不再清偿债款,也不再可能获得

土地抵押的赎回权）
law department　（大学的）法律系;法律部门
law division　（英美法）普通法（分）庭
(The) law does not allow a captions and strained intendment, for such nice pretence of certainty confounds true and legal certainty.　法律中不允许过度矫情,这种做作的稳定性会扰乱真正的法律稳定性;法律中不允许含义含糊,这样伪装的确定性会干扰真正的法律确定性。
＊Law does not reach such case.　法律不适用于这种案件。
law draftsman　法律撰拟人,法案起草人
law enforcement　法的实施（又译:法律的实施）,法（律）的执行
law enforcement agency　执法机关
law enforcement apparatus　执法机构,执法部门
law enforcement office　治安机关,执法机关
law enforcement officers（或 official）　治安人（官）员,执法人（官）员
law enforcement resources　执法资源,执法财力物力
law evasion costs　逃避法律诉讼费
law factory　（美）法律工厂（此词在美国是用来称呼大型的律师事务机构的,1963 年美国只有 10 家这样的机构,各雇有一百多个律师,现在约有六十家,其中 11 家各雇有二百多个律师）
law fallen into desuetude　已废除的法律
law firms　法律事务所,律师事务所
law for the preservation of antiques　文物保护法
Law French　法律法语（指几个世纪以来在英格兰法律中使用的诺尔曼法语,很多词语现在仍然常用）
law governing application　实施法
law governing the foreigner's personal relation　管辖外国人身份关系法
law guardian　见 guardian ad litem
law improperly so-called　不正确称呼的法律
law in action　行动中的法（指法律现实主义从庞德的社会学理念出发,强调完全认识"书本上的法"与"行动中的法"之间的

差距,主要通过司法实践认识法与社会及公共政策之间的关系)
law in book　书本上的法律
law in force　现行法(指正在实施中的法律)
law in operation　现行法,正在实施中的法律
law in(或 of) the member states　会员国之法律
law in the slavery society　奴隶制法
law information network　法律信息网络
* **Law is subordinate to the state.**　法从属于国家。
law is the law　法律毕竟是法律
Law is wholly a conscious product of human will.　法律完全是人们意志的有意识产品。
Law Latin　法律拉丁语(指在英国法庭中拉丁语演变的形式,许多词语现在仍然适用)
law latin tag　法律拉丁语的附加语,法律拉丁语的标签
law library　法律丛书;法律图书馆
law list　(英)《法律指南》(指英国半官方性质的法律出版物),(出版物中编辑的)开业律师人名录
Law Lord　(英)上诉法院常任高级法官(正式职称为 Lord of Appeal in Ordinary);(英)(指执掌最高司法职务的议员)上议院高级法官
law merchant　商业习惯(指中世纪有关商人、商业事务方面的习惯、规章和原则的总称);商人法
law monger　讼棍
Lawmaker　制法人,造法者[指选出的公务人员(或公职担当人,official)负责制定法律,与 legislator(立法者)同意]
Lawmaking　造法,立法[指行使该项职能的政府部门按照正式程序和成文形式制定实在法(positive law),亦指立法程序或立法活动]
law of act　行为法
law of actions　(罗马法)诉讼法
law of admiralty　海事法
law of adoption of and wills　收养与遗嘱法

law of advocate　律师法
law of aliens　外国人法,外侨法
law of *Amalfi*　《阿玛斐法》
law of application　适用法,施行法
law of armed conflict　武装冲突法
law of arms control　武器管制法
law of arrest　逮捕法,拘捕法
law of association　联合法(亦译:结社法)
law of aviation　航空法
law of bankruptcy　破产法
law of bills　票据法
law of carriage (of goods)　(货物)运输法
law of causality(或 causation)　因果关系法则,因果律
law of citations　引证法
law of civil administration　民政法,内政法
law of civil procedure　民事诉讼法
law of civil responsibility　民事责任法
law of co-existence　共处法[指国际法被界定为"共处法",有时被描绘成"合作法"(law of co-operation),有被认定为"共进法"(law of co-progressivence)的趋势]
law of co-operation　合作法(见 law of co-existence)
law of co-progressivence　共进法(见 law of co-existence)
law of commercial transaction　商业交易法
law of compensation for wrong detention and conviction　冤狱(错捕错判)赔偿法
law of competing principles　冲突法则
law of conscription　兵役法
law of consideration　对价法则
Law of Consolato　《康苏拉底法》[指《海事习惯法汇编》,首次在巴塞罗那(Barcelona)洽塔兰(Chatalan)出版,亦称 Code of Barcelona 或 Book of Jurisdiction of the Sea]
law of contract　合同法(又译:契约法)
law of corporation　公司法
law of creator　造物的法则
law of criminal procedure　刑事诉讼法
law of cultural relics　文物法
law of damages　损害赔偿法
law of diminishing returns　报酬递减律(资产阶级经济学的一种理论),(土地)

收益递减律
law of distress　财产扣押法
law of domestic relation　亲属法,亲属关系法
law of donations　赠与法
law of each party's antenuptial domicile　各当事人的婚前住所地法
law of economic contract　经济合同法(又译:经济契约法)
law of economic planning　经济计划法
law of education　教育法
law of England　英国法
law of enterprises　企业法
law of environmental protection　环境保护法,环保法
law of equity　衡平法
law of evidence　证据法
law of family　家庭法;家事法
law of family planning　计划生育法
law of Finland　芬兰法
law of forestry　森林法
law of God　上帝法
law of guarantee　担保法
law of health　健康法,卫生法
law of infancy　未成年人法
law of inheritance　继承法(旧译:嗣继法)
law of insurance　保险法
law of insurance contracts　保险合同法(又译:保险契约法)
law of international bills　国际票据法
law of international civil procedure　国际民事诉讼法
law of international patent　国际专利法
law of international trade　国际贸易法
law of international transfer of technology　国际技术转让法
law of intestate distribution　遗产处分法
law of investment securities　投资担保法
law of invoices　发票法
law of (the) jungle　弱肉强食法则
law of labo(u)r　劳工法,(中)劳动法
law of land　土地法
law of liability for accidents　事故责任法
Law of Libel (Libel Law)　诽谤罪法
law of (ancient) lights　(老窗户)采光权法

Law of Majestas　(罗马)大法,王法,国法
law of mariners　海员法
law of maritime (commerce)　海事法,海商法
law of maritime prize　海上捕获法
law of market control　市场管理法
law of marque　(英)捕拿抵偿法(又译:报复法,该法规定受害人在侵害人所在的境内无法得到公平的审判时,可夺取侵害人船只或货物来抵偿。已废)
law of marriage　婚姻法
law of mass media　新闻工具法
law of material management and supply　物资供应管理法
law of merchant　商法,商人法
law of morality　道德法,道德准则
law of morals　道德法则
law of mortgages　抵押法
law of Moses　(基督教《圣经旧约全书》前五章中的)摩西律法(亦称 The Mosaic law)
law of national land　国土法
law of nationality　国籍法
law of nations　万国公法[为国际法(international law)的旧称]
law of nature　自然法,自然法则
law of nature school　自然法学派
law of navigation　航海法;航运法
Law of Navigational Channel　《航道法》
law of neutrality　中立法
law of nuisance　防止危害(公众利益)法,公害法
law of obligation　债法,义务法
law of ocean-going trade　海上贸易法
law of outer space　外层空间法;太空法
law of ownership　所有权法
law of persons　(罗马法)人法
law of place of the court　法院地法
law of population registration　户籍法,人口登记法
law of ports and harbo(u)rs　港口法
law of post　邮政法
law of press　新闻出版法
law of procedure　诉讼法,诉讼程序法
law of property　(英)财产法;(大陆法)所有权法

Law of Property Act 1925 (英)《1925年财产法》(以后于1926、1929、1932、1964和1969年均有修改,主要统一并修订了英国土地法律,简化了土地转让手续)
law of property in a strict sense 严格意义上的财产法
law of public economy 公共经济法
law of publication 出版法
law of quasi-contract 准合同法(又译:准契约法)
law of railway transportation 铁路运输法
Law of Regional National Autonomy (中)《民族区域自治法》
law of remedies 法律救济法(指权利受到侵犯时寻求法律救济的办法)
law of restitution 赔偿法
law of retaliation (古代法)同态复仇法
Law of Return 《归回法》[以色列法规定,允许每个犹太人有权回到以色列,并作为一名犹太人的移民(Oleh),每个犹太人的移民只要一进入以色列国,根据以色列国籍法,即自动获得以色列国籍]
law of road 公路法
law of Scandinavian countries 斯堪的那维亚国家的法律
law of sea treaty 海洋条约法
law of securities 担保法
Law of Ships 《船舶法》
law of social relief 社会救济法
law of succession 继承法
law of supply and demand 供求法则,供需规律
law of surety (law of suretyship) 担保同法,担保法,保证法
law of tax 税法
law of testamentary succession 遗嘱继承法
law of the burden of proof 证明责任法,举证责任法
law of the case 判例的法则(指由以前审理的或上诉法院所作的有关案件的任何判决或法则,在以后案件的相类似的人和相类似案情中得到适用)
law of the cases 案例法
law of the flag 船籍国法(律)
law of the forum 审判地法
law of the intended matrimonial home 意想中的婚姻住所地法
law of the land 国法;当地法律,国内(的)法(律)
law of the Middle Ages 中世纪法
Law of the People's Republic of China on Chinese-Foreign Joint Ventures 《中华人民共和国中外合资经营企业法》
law of the place of contracting 缔结地法
law of the place of dispatch 起运地法
law of the place of domicile 住所地法
law of the place of performance of contract 合同(契约)的履行地法
law of the place of tort 侵权行为地法
law of the place where ceremony take place 婚姻仪式举行地法
law of the place where the corporation is registered 法人注册地法;法人登记地法
law of the planned economy 计划经济法
law of the realm 国法,王法
law of the Saxons 撒克逊法
law of the sea 海洋法
law of the stronger 强权法则
law of things (罗马法)物权法,财产法
law of tort and quasi-delict responsibility 侵权和准侵权责任法
law of torts 侵权行为法,民事侵权法
law of town planning 城市规划法
law of trade 贸易法
law of transportation 交通运输法
law of treaties 条约法
Law of Twelve Tables 十二铜表法(指罗马在纪元前5世纪公布的成文法。见 Lex Duodecim Tabularum)
law of value 价值规律
law of vendor and purchaser (英)卖主和买主法(指土地买卖法的传统称呼)
law of war 战争法
law of waters 水法,水流法
Law of Wisby(i) 威斯比法
law of wrong 过错行为法[西方法学家布莱克斯东(W. T. Blackstone)将17世纪的权利观引入普通法的一个显著成就是过错行为法,即规定国家可对私人做什么的规则]

law offender 罪犯;犯法分子
law office （美）律师事务所;法律顾问处
law officers 司法人(官)员,法律官员
law officers of the Crown （英）政府法律官员(指英国法务总长和法务次长)
law on accidents at work 工伤事故法
law on bails for bad cheques 空头支票法
law on compulsory social security 强制社会保障法
law on court organization 法院组织法
Law on Environmental Protection of the People's Republic of China 《中华人民共和国环境保护法》
law on judicial organization 法院组织法,司法组织法
law on land reform 土地改革法
law on paternal authority 亲权法
law on public administration 公共行政法,行政管理法
law on public prosecutors 检察长法,检察官法
law on separate property in the space in building 大楼内楼层面积分别产权法
law on the organization and jurisdiction of courts 法院组织和管辖权法
law on the sale and mortgage of a business 企业出让和抵押法
law practice 法律实务,律师事务（实习）所
law practitioner 开业律师(= legal practitioner)
Law Practitioners Act 《开业律师法》
law presumption 法律推定
law properly so-called 正确称呼之法律
law reform 法律改革
law relating to rights over things 物权法
law reporters 判例汇编;(美)判决发布人汇编(指对法院的判决发布人发布的判决所编纂成的汇编)
law reports 法律判例汇编(指由法院判决的案例汇编出版的丛书);(英)《法律判例汇编》(指由英格兰和威尔士法律判例汇编联合委员会出版,包括1865年至今来自上院和枢密院司法委员会的上诉判例、高等法院的法庭分庭、大法官法庭和家事法庭1972年以前称为遗嘱检验、离婚和海事法庭的判例的汇编)
law review 法律评论
law revision committee 法律修订委员会
Law Revision Council of The House of Representatives （美）众议院法律修订委员会
law school 法学院,法律学校;法律学派
Law School Aptitude （或 Admissions） Test （美)法学院入学考试
law school curricula 法学院课程
law should be king 法律应当为王,法律高于一切
law society 律师协会;法律学会;(英)律师公会(指按议会法或法院命令来管理司法教育和律师考试、编制律师名册、签发律师执照、管理律师等项业务的组织)
law student 法律学校学生
law term 1.法律用语 2.(法庭）开庭期
law theory 法律理论,法学理论
Law Week （美）《法律周报》(亦称《美国法律周报》,它是一种服务资料,提供来自最高法院、其他法院和某些立法机关的"辛辣、轰动"的新闻)
law's constitutionality 法律的合宪性
Law's Empire 《法律帝国》[1986年罗纳德·德沃金(Ronald Dworkin)著]
law-abiding a. 守法的,安分守己的,守秩序的
law-adviser n. 法律顾问
law-agent n. 诉讼代理人
law-and-economics from the perspective of laws 从法观点看法经济学
law-and-economics in action 变化中的法经济学
law-and-order a. 严肃法纪的;宣扬法治的
law-as-action n. 作为行动的法律;行为法
law-breaker n. 违法者
law-breaking a. 违法的
law-breaking capitalist 违法资本家
law-costs （复）n. 诉讼费用
law-court n. 见 law court
law-creating agency 造法机构
law-creating body 创制法律的机构(见 law-finding body)

law-declaring agency 法律宣布机构
law-enforcing power 执法权
law-executor n. 执法者
law-finding n. 法律裁决
law-finding body （中世纪晚期，英国议会都一直被视为一个）发现法律的机构[而非创制法律的机构(law-creating body)]
law-giver n. 立法者，制定法律者，制定法典者
law-giving a. 制定法律的
law-giving body 制定法律的部门(单位)，制定法律的机构
law-governing n. 法治
law-hand n. （英旧时）（法律文书的）书写法
law-jobs n. 法律工作(指美国法学家卢埃林的法律功能论，认为法律是一种制度，而制度是围绕一项工作或一连串工作的有组织的活动，因此法律功能就是法律工作)
law-maker n. 立法者
law-making body 立法机关，立法机构
law-making convention 造法公约
law-making organ 立法机关
law-making power 立法权
law-making process 立法程序
law-making stipulation 立法条款；立法规定
law-making treaties 造法条约[又译：立法式条约或称多方（边）条约（multilateral treaties）]
law-man n. 执法者，(美)执法吏；(复)"法律通"，司法人员
law-of-war tribunal 战争法法庭
law-related issue 有关法律的争议(或系争点)
law-writer n. 法学家；法院的复本制作者
lawburrows （苏格兰）保护救济，法律预防
lawful a. 合理合法的，法定的；守法的；法律许可的；依法的(lawful 意为"合乎或不违反国家的法律、教会的戒律或道德的标准"，与 legal, legitimate 有一定差别)
lawful action 合法行为
lawful adoption 合法收养关系，合法领养

lawful age 法定年龄
lawful arrest 合法拘捕，依法拘捕
lawful authority 合法权限，合法权力；合法当局（政府），合法政权
lawful bearer (holder) 合法持证人，合法持票人
lawful cause （大陆法）合法诉因，合法理由
lawful condition 法定条件
lawful damages 法定的损害赔偿额
lawful day 有效日期，法定日期；（审理）开庭日期
lawful discharge 合法免除（债务）；合法释放
lawful document 合法证件，合法文书
lawful duties 法定职责；法定义务；法定的税
lawful entry (17世纪)1.合法进入[指一个人尚未占有的不动产(real property)的进入，是根据其权利主张或表面权利(color of right)而非以暴力或欺诈方式进入不动产] 2.根据免搜查证(search warrant)进入他人房屋(premises)（见 search warrant)
lawful goods （战时)中立国船只上的货物
lawful heir 合法继承人
lawful homicide 依法杀人(尤指依法执行死刑判决的杀人)
lawful issue 合法子女，合法继承人
lawful man 有宣誓资格者；自由人
lawful means 合法手段
lawful money 法定货币(旧译：法币)
lawful occupier 合法占有者；合法居住者
lawful operations 合法经营
lawful order 合法命令
lawful party 合法政党
lawful possession 合法占有（权）
lawful principal wife （法律上的）正妻(旧译：原配)
lawful prize 合法捕获物
lawful property 合法财产
lawful relict 合法遗孀
lawful revenge 合法复仇
lawful rights and interests 合法权益
lawful savings 合法储蓄

lawful seat 合法席位
lawful self-defence 合法自卫
lawful sovereign 合法主权
lawful spouse 合法配偶
lawful wedlock 合法婚姻
lawful woman 有宣誓资格的妇女
lawfully earned income 合法收入
lawfully wedded 合法结婚的
lawless a. 无法律的,失去法律控制的;法律无法实行的;目无法纪的,违法的,不法的,非法的
lawless landlord 不法地主
lawless person 不法之徒
lawless practices 违法行为,不法行为
lawlessness n. 不法,非法,无法无天
lawlike a. 似法律的
lawmakers on the international level 国际一级的立法者
lawmaking n./a. 立法,造法,制定法律/立法的,造法的,制定法律的
lawnmower parent 割草机父母[该词由 lawnmower(割草机)与 parent(父母)两词组合而成,是指试图为子女解决所有问题,帮助他们扫清人生道路上一切障碍的父母]
laws and customs of war 战争规则和惯例
Laws about Rented Oxen 《租牛法典》[指苏美尔法律教本的一部分,其大量内容涉及对租借耕牛的伤害和损失的法律规定。该泥板每一法律条文均采用苏美尔人习惯"倘若"(tukum-bi)体例,列举了租借耕牛的契约在履行中可能遇到的种种情形,规定了租牛者应当承担的相应民事赔偿责任]
laws and regulations of economic development 经济建设法规;经济开发法规
Laws for Civil Societies 《市民社会法》(指社会团体的立法,对其权利、义务和行为进行法律规范,有的国家称其为非政府组织法,或营利组织法)
Laws for Non-governmental Organizations 《非政府组织法》(见 Laws for Civil Societies)
Laws for Non-Profit Organizations 《非营利组织法》(见 Laws for Civil Societies)
laws obtaining in natural liberty 获得自然自由的法规
Laws of Indies 《西印度群岛法》(指 16—18 世纪西班牙王国为治理欧洲以外的地区,主要是美洲殖民地而颁布的法律);《西印度群岛法律汇编》
Law of Lawyering 《律师业法》[指美国杰弗·C. 哈泽 Jr.(Geoffrey C. Hazard, Jr.)和 W. 威廉姆·霍迪斯(W. William Hodes)合著,于 2000 年出版(第三版)的两卷本图书。主要为律师工作怎样应对紧急情况,实务中遭遇两难境地该如何解决的实务工作专著或工作手册]
laws of legal and social evolution 法律和社会之进化法则
Laws of Oleron, Rules of Oleron, *Rôles ou judgements d'Oléron* (1100-1200 A.D.) 《奥勒伦海法》[指被欧洲各国作为本国海商法依据并予以接受的一部海商法法典。因该法典于 12 世纪在英国西海岸奥列隆(亦称奥勒伦)岛颁布,故名《奥列隆法典》]
laws of the *Visigoths* (或 **Roman Law of the *Visigoths***) 西哥特法(西哥特罗马法)(最古老的一种原始蛮族法,约在公元 5 世纪至 6 世纪间)
laws of things (罗马法)物权法(指从属于物之法律。由物之性质改变而被决定的法律。亦众所周知的"*jus rerum*")
Laws of Visby 维斯比法[指一部海事习惯判例法。15 世纪以波罗的海地区哥德兰岛(Gothland)的维斯比为主要港口命名的海事法集。此法在奥列隆法(Laws of Olecon)之后,影响了整个北欧。维斯比协议书(Visby Protocol)经修订后成为在维斯比签订的海牙规则(Hague Rules),该规则一直治理着世界航运贸易]
laws *pari materia* 相同(主题的)法规,相关法规
lawsuit n./v. 诉讼(见 suit)(衡平法上的民事诉讼通常用 suit, action 则为普通法的民事诉讼,现 action 已替代了 suit)诉讼案件;(俚)官司/提起诉讼,(俚)打官司
lawsuit sounding in tort 侵权诉讼
lawyer n. 律师,辩护律师;法学家;(英)

法律工作者
lawyer of the corporation　法人(聘请)的律师,公司(雇佣)的律师
lawyer's association　律师协会
Lawyer's Code of Professional Responsibility　律师行(职)业责任准则
lawyer's discipline　律师纪律
Lawyer's Edition　律师版(是《美国联邦最高法院判例汇编律师版》的通称。它是由律师合作出版公司出版的联邦最高法院判例的一个非官方系列。1882年开始首次发行,重印了之前联邦最高法院所有的判例,包括许多官方从未报道过的判例,如《美国判例汇编》第131卷和第154卷附录中的判例。其后发行的卷本也保留了一些以前没有公开报道的判例)
Lawyer's Edition Supreme Court Reports (L. Ed. 2d)　(美)(律师合作出版公司出版的)《最高法院判例汇编》第二套丛书
lawyer's fee　律师费
lawyer's jargon　律师的行话(术语)
lawyer's law　"律师的法律"(在美国一般指各州保留其传统上所掌握的大量律师法,即私法、商法、刑法和诉讼法)
lawyer's lien　律师留置权
lawyer-client　律师与委托人
lawyer-client privilege　同 attorney-client privilege
lawyer-client relationship　律师与委托人的关系
lawyeress n.　女律师;女法学家
lawyering n.　律师业
lawyerlike (或 **lawyerly**) a.　似律师的,适于律师的
lawyerly a.　法学工作者的,律师的
lax a.　松弛的;不严格的;马虎的;不严肃的,放纵的;不明确的
lax judg(e)ment　轻(宽)判;马虎的判决;不明确的判决
lay n./v./a.　1.位置,地形 2.行业,职业 3.行动计划,着手 4.(销售)条件;价格 5.打赌,赌注 6.抽税;加罚/1.放,置,使处于某种状态 2.拟定;策划;提出(要求,主张等) 3.消除(疑虑等) 4.归罪于……,把……归于 5.课(税);加(罚)/外行的;非专业的;世俗的;平民的
lay a fine on sb.　处某人以罚金
lay a heavy tax on land　对土地课以重税
lay a question before a committee　把问题提交委员会
lay a scheme　起草方案(计划等)
lay a trap　设圈套(或陷阱)
lay advocate　助理律师,尚未通晓法律业务的见习律师
lay an information against a person　控告某人,对某人起诉
lay assessors　兼职法官,非专业法官,非专业技术顾问
lay (fast) by the heels　逮捕(住),监禁
lay corporation　世俗法人(非宗教法人的总称)
lay day　港口耽搁日,(租船合同所允许的)装卸货物日期中的第一日
lay down　1.规定,制定,立法 2.放下,交出,献出 3.主张,断言 4.计划,设计
lay down the law　制定法律,立法
lay intermediary　置身于律师与当事人之间的中间人
lay judge　(未经过专门法律训练的)非专业法官;陪审员(官),世俗法官
lay jury　非专业的陪审团(指未经专业培训的陪审团)
lay magistrate　非专业治安官(指英美没有薪俸,不一定受过法律教育的治安官)
lay notion　外行想法(或见解)
lay observers　非专职观察员
lay on the table　搁置(议案等)
lay open　揭发;伤及
lay opiniontestimony　非专业人员的意见证据(指不具专家资格的证人提供的证据,但他可对意见或推断作出证明。联邦法院将这种证据的可采性限定为作为证人认知的理性基础的意见和推断,这些有助于对证人证据的了解和对有争议事实的确定)
lay out　布置,设计,安排;投资;展示
lay participation　普通民众参与司法审判
lay people　陪审员
lay tenure　(英)世俗土地保有制
lay the venue　指定审判地点

lay violent hands on a person　用暴力对待某人；猛击某人，强迫某人

lay witness　外行证人（亦译做普通证人，与 expert witness 相对而言,指缺乏有关专门知识的证人）

lay-off(s) n.　暂时裁员,解雇,临时解雇,失业期间

lay-off agreement　解雇协议

lay-out n.　布局；陈设；安排,设计

laye　法律（古法语）

layer n.　层次,阶层

layering n.　离析（指洗钱一般所经过的第二阶段,即通过复杂的金融操作,如以假名或受托人名义开立银行账户,虚拟贸易收支、买卖无记名证券等,掩盖犯罪资金的来龙去脉和真实所有权关系,模糊其非法特征。见 placement）

laying court　世俗法院（指相对宗教法院而言）

laying foundation　（美）设置（指根据证据法,在提出或引入证据的实践和要求中确立一些必要的初步证据为以后作证,同时也确立更重要的和可接受的证据）

layman n.　外行人,门外汉

lazaretto　检疫船,检疫所

le contrat fait la loi　契约（合同）构成法律

le mort saisir le vif　The dead seizes the living　死亡将权利赋于生者（原则）（指占有人死亡之时,其法定权利即归属于死者继承人。此项原则并不排除占有人死亡时不在场的继承人和未知的继承人）

le principe du non-cumul　（法国法上基于契约责任与侵权责任的）不竞合原则；（诉讼上的）非并合原则

le Reine le veult　（英）女王愿意（指对公共和地方性法案的御准用语）；女王同意接受（法案）

le Reine s'avisera　（英）女王拟考虑（拒绝御准的用语,指英女王拒绝批准国会法案）

le roi le veut　The king wills it.　国王的意愿,国王愿意如此。[指国王（或女王）批准议会通过的公法案（public bill）所使用的格式化语言]

* **Le Roy remercie ses bons sujets, accepte leur benevolence, et ainsi le veut.**　The king thanks his loyal subjects, accepts their bonevolence, and therefore will it to be so.　国王感谢其臣民接受他们的捐献,并愿其如此。[此为对以拨款预算为公共目的法案的御准（royal assent）的格式用语]

* **Le salut du peuple est la supreme loi.**　The safety of the people is the highest law.　人民安全就是最高的法律。

lead n./v.　领导；带头；领先,领先的程度（或距离）；首位；提示,暗示/领导,指挥；用诱导法询问（证人等）；导致（to）,致使；（尤指在选举时）压倒（对手）

lead a witness　（向证人提出有倾向性问题）诱导证人回答

lead counsel　首席律师

lead evidence　诱导（某人）拿出证据

lead plaintiff　首席原告

lead solicitor　首席律师

lead time　从产品设计至实际投产间的时间；从订货至交货的时间

lead underwriter　牵头承保人

leader n.　1.领袖；首领,领导者 2.带头人 3.首席状师,（一个案件中的）主要法律顾问,主要辩护人

leader of the House　议院议长

leader of the largest（或 **majority**）**party**　多数党领袖

leader of the (main) opposition party　（主要）反对党的领袖

leadership n.　领导；（总称）领导人员；领导能力

leadership abilities　领导才干

leading n./a.　引导,指导；诱导/第一位的,最主要的；指导的,领导的

leading bodies　领导机关

leading cadre　（中）领导干部

leading case　首要判例；指导性判例；成为判例的案件；有判例效力的案件

leading counsel　主管律师,主要法律顾问

leading firm　主要厂商

leading force　领导力量

leading judge　首席法官（旧译：首席推事）,审判长

leading market　主要市场

leading motive 主要动机
leading object rule (=main propose doctrine) （美）主要目的的规则(指如果一个人对他人债务负责的允诺是为要约人自己的利益,这类允诺可不按欺诈法要求,无必要写成书面文件。这一规则有时被称为主要目的学说或理论)
leading plaintiff 主要原告
leading proponent 主要辩护者,主要支持者
leading prophet 首创者
leading question 暗示性讯问,诱导证人回答的讯问,诱导性问题(指律师在对证人提问时,通过他们的措辞,暗示证人如何作答,在交叉询问中允许提出这类问题,但直接询问则不允许)
leading to summary judgment for the opposing party 导致НА判决判决对方胜诉
leaf readers 见 tea readers
league n. 同盟,联盟;盟约,联合会;种类;范畴
League of Arab States 阿拉伯国家联盟（1945年建立）
league of armed neutrality 武装中立同盟
League of Nations 国际联盟(简称"国联",1920—1946年)
League of Nations Treaty Series 《国际联盟条约丛书》(此书现已停止出版,已由《联合国条约集》接替。见 United Nations Treaty Series)
leakage n. 漏损;（商业上许可的）漏损率;漏出量
leakage clause 漏损条款
lealte 合法性;法人的条件;有宣誓资格的条件
leapfrog procedure （民事诉讼中的）越级程序
learned doctors of law 法学博士
Learned Hand Rule 伦德·汉德规则[指在比较潜在过失和可能期望利益的基础上,指出过失的一种方法。这种方法是根据20世纪美国知名法官伦德·汉德的名字命名的,他在1974年的卡罗尔拖船公司案(Carrel Towing Case)中提出这一标准]
learned profession 须有学识的职业(指律师、医师、会计师等职业)
learned supreme court 博学的高等法庭
learning n. 知识,学问
learning effect 学习效应(指当一个系统被使用的越来越频繁时,在使用过程中操作者相应地积累起越来越多经验,而这种经验也会形成一种自下而上的反馈,使系统本身变得更有效率,其有效性与其他替代机制相比也会不断增加)
learned a. 1.博学的,有学问的;精通法律的(well-versed in law and its history, the judge be learned in the law)2.同 erudite[一个律师在对抗制中可能遇上"learned colleague"(博学的同行,法律同行)或"learned opponent"(博学对手,善辩的对手)]
leasable a. 可出租的;可租借的
lease n./v. 租,租约;租借期限;租借权,租地权;租借物/出租(土地等),租借
lease agreement 租约
lease and release （英）租借和放弃（指以前采用的先借出租后放弃回复权,用以让与自由土地保有权的一种方法）
lease by estoppel 不得废止的租借,无可反悔的租借
lease contract 租赁合同(契约),租契
lease for lives （英）终身租赁
lease in perpetuity 永租权,永佃权
lease of agricultural land 农用土地租赁
lease of commercial premises 商业性房屋的租赁
lease of property 财产租借
lease on premises to professional men 出租给职业人员的房屋租赁
lease on shop premises 商店用房租赁
lease purchase 租用购买,租购
lease term 租期;（复）租借条件
lease timeshare interest 租赁型的分时度假拥有权
lease with option to purchase （承租人）有权购买（所借租财产）的租赁
lease-back n. 回租(指产权人先将产权产业出售,然后再同时长期租用该产业)
leased enterprises 租赁企业
leased house law 房屋租赁法
leased land law 租地法

leased reprint rights 租版重印权(指出版社"版式权"项下的一项版权,亦即出版社出租纸型或其他印刷版面材料给别的出版社出书的权利,但在行使此项权利时不得损害作者的权利)
leased territories 租借地
leasee n. 承租人,租借人
leasehold a./n. 租借的;租赁的/租赁权;租借的土地(或建筑物);租借期;(复)(英)租借土地保有权
leasehold interests 租赁权益
leasehold ownership 租借地所有权
leasehold property 租赁财产
leasehold relation 租赁关系
leaseholder n. 租借人,承租人,租地人
leaseholding nation 承租国
leases of live quarters 住房租赁
leasor n. 出租人,租让人
least advantaged country 处于困境的国家
least dangerous branch 危险最小的部门 [指美国的律师和政治家亚历山大·汉密尔顿(Alexander Hamilton)(1757—1804)在他著名的《联邦党人文集》(Federalist Papers)的第78篇中预言:司法部门应当总是联邦政府中"危险性最小的部门",因为司法部门"对军队和财政都没有影响力",而且"既无力量又无意志,仅仅只有裁判"];最不危险的部门(指司法部门为最不危险的部门,因为司法权是消极性权力,权力启动程序由利益相关人自治,且司法权运作程序最为公正公开)
least developed among the developing countries 发展中国家中最不发达国家
least favo(u)red area 最不利的区域(或范围)
least restrictive alternative 最小限制性替代措施
least restrictive means test (美)最低限制手段标准[美国联邦宪法第一修正案所规定的对自由进行限制绝不能超过对州的特定利益进行保护所必需的限制,所以这一规则要求任一法律和政府规章应尽可能以保护公民个人自由(individual civil liberties)的方式精心制定。只有为合法政府的目的所必需时才可对公民自由加以

限制。联邦最高法院认为,只要存在可选择的方法,政府就必须选择那些禁止言论时危害最小的方法]
least-cost accident avoider 最低成本意外事故逃避人
least-cost avoider 最低成本逃避者
least-fault divorce 判断基本正确的离婚,失误最少的离婚
leave n./v. 许可,同意;准假;休假;假期;离去,告别/留置,遗忘;听任;离开;(死后)遗留,遗赠,传下;托付,委托;剩余;遗弃;放弃;停止;经过
leave and licence 允许和许可(指在诉讼中提出非法侵犯行为为原告所允许的辩护)
leave of absence 假释,暂时离狱;请准休假
leave of court 法院的准许,经法院许可
leave the country 出境
leave the matter open 把事情搁起来暂不解决
leave to defend 准许辩护
leave with pay 工资照付的假期,有薪假期
leave without pay 留职停薪;无薪假期
leaving certificate 毕业证书;修业证书
Lebach Case 刑满出狱报道案(指德国联邦宪法第一法庭1973年6月5日的判决,联邦宪法法院判例集第35目第202页及以下)
lecher n. 好色之徒,色情狂者
lecherous a. 好色的,淫荡的
lechery n. 淫荡,淫荡行为
lecture method 讲演式教学法
lecturer n. 讲演人,讲课人;讲师
ledger n. 总分类账
ledger account 总分类账,总账(簿)
ledger credit 赊账
ledo n. 海上升起的水位,海水的增长
lee n. 庇护,保护;庇护所;避风处
leet n. 1.(英)领地刑事法庭;刑事法庭管辖区(见 court leet),1997年在英格兰废除 2.(苏格兰)修候选人名单
leeway n. 可允许的误差,余地,灵活性
left n. 临终遗留,传下;遗赠;(坐在议长左侧的)左派议员(们)
left-handed marriage 见 morganatic mar-

riage
left-leaning standard 左倾标准
lefty n. 左派的人,左倾的人;用左手的人
leg n. 腿;(桌子的)支撑物;(任务的)部分完成;一段航程(行程,旅程……);一局,一盘
leg bail 逃狱;逃亡
leg of a straddle position 跨期买卖的一个过程,跨期买卖的状况
leg-iron n. 脚镣
legabilis a. 根据遗嘱赠与的财产或物品,作为与"bequeathable"一词(可被遗赠的"财产"同义)
legable a. 可被遗赠的(财产)
legacy n. 遗产;遗赠产(一般指动产);祖先传下来的东西
legacy tax 遗产税,继承税[指根据遗赠财产所课之税,通常按规定,受赠人的关系要是与遗赠人(testator)太远,税率则要增加。英国法中这个税则被认为是动产遗产税(legacy duty),1949年已经废弃。见 collateral-inheritance tax]
legacy hunter 为图遗赠而向人谄媚者
legacy under a general title 见 general legacy
legacy under a particular title 见 particular legacy
legacy under a universal title (美国路易斯安那州法)全部不动产或动产的遗嘱处分(testamentary disposition);全部不动产或动产按固定比例的遗嘱处分[参见《路易斯安那州民法典》第1612条(La. Civ. Code art. 1612.)。见 general legacy; particular legacy; universal legacy]
legacy with obligation 有负担的遗赠
legacy with terms 有期限的遗赠
legal a./n. 依法的;法定的,法律承认的;合法的;律师的;正当的;法律(上)的(legal 意为"合乎国家正式颁布的法律的,或经法律许可的",可参看 lawful 与 legitimate)/法定权利;法定声明(指必须依法登报的声明);(复)(储蓄公司或信托公司等)依法可以用来投资的证券
legal abode 合法住所
legal abortion 合法堕胎
legal abuses 法律弊端

legal accountability 法律责任(或经营、经济责任)
legal act 法律行为
legal action 合法行为;诉讼,争讼,法律诉讼
legal actor 法律促进者
legal address 法定地址
legal administrator 合法管财人,法定财产管理人
legal advantage 合法利益
legal advice 法律咨询;法律劝告
legal adviser 法律顾问(律师)
legal advisory office 法律顾问处
legal affairs 法律事务,司法事务
legal age 法定年龄
legal agency 法律机构;法定代理
legal agent 法定代理人
legal aid 法律援助
legal aid certificate 法律援助证书
legal aid society 法律援助协会;诉讼救助协会
legal aid system 法律救助制度
legal aider 律师助理(手)
legal aliment 法定扶养费
legal and disciplinary education 法纪教育
legal and judicial information 法律情报,法学信息
legal annotation 法律注释
legal anthropology 法人类学
legal appointment (财产受让人等的)合法指定
legal approach 法律方法,法律入门,法律研究
legal approbation 依法认可
legal arbitration 法律仲裁
legal arena 法律界,法学活动场所
legal argument 法律辩护,法律论据,法律论点
legal arm 法权
legal assessor 法定评税人;法定估价人
legal assets 法定(偿债)资产(指遗产执行人或管理人掌握的死者资财,此资财依法应偿还债权人者)
legal assignee (财产)合法受让人
legal assignment 合法让与

legal assistance 辩护律师的帮助；司法协助
legal assistant 律师的专职法律助手（见 paralegal）
legal attachment 依法拘捕，依法扣押
legal authority 法律许可，法律授权
legal autonomy 法律上的自治权，依法自治
legal axiology 法律目的论
legal, absolute, and unitary condition 法律的，绝对的和一体的状态
legal bargaining 合法议价，法定议价
legal basis 法律根据
legal benefit 见 benefit 2
legal bibliography 法律文献目录，法律文献学
legal blizzard 法律暴风雪（见 hyperlexis）
legal blood 准血亲，准血族
legal body 法人
legal bound 法律范畴，合法的范围
legal brief 诉讼案情摘要
legal burden of proof 法定举证责任（= persuasive burden of proof）
legal burdens 法律上担负的义务；法定责任
legal bureaucrats 司法官僚
legal business 法律事务，司法业务
legal business status 合法经营资格
legal cap （一种长的）法律业务专用信纸（左页边空白宽而右页边空白窄）
legal capacity 权利能力，行为能力；法定身份（或资格）
legal capacity of juristic person 法人的权利能力，法人的行为能力
legal capacity of psychopaths 精神病人的权利能力和行为能力
legal capacity to commit crimes 刑事犯罪能力
legal capacity to make contracts 缔（立）约的权利能力，缔（立）约的行为能力
legal capacity to sue 诉权，（向法院）起诉的权利（或资格）
legal career 律师职业
legal case 法律案件
legal cause 法定原因；近因；法律原因，（大陆法）法定诉因
legal centralism 法律中央集权制，法律中央集权主义
legal certainty 法律的确定性，法律上的确定性
legal chain 法系
legal character 法律性质
legal charge 法定土地负担（契据）
legal chattels 法律上的无体动产（如金钱，债权等）
legal check 法律检查，法律控制
legal chemistry 法律化学（指用来解决法律问题的应用化学）
legal chooses in action （英美法）普通法诉讼上的财产权，制定法诉讼上的财产权
legal chose 普通法上的无体动产（如金钱，债权，票据等）
legal claim 合法的诉讼请求，法定请求权
legal clinical course 法律实务课
legal clinics 法律事务所，律师实习事务所；法律诊所
legal code 法典
legal community 法律界，法学界
legal compensation 合法赔偿，法定补偿
legal competence 法律权限，法律权利
legal competition 合法竞争
legal computer technology 法学计算机技术（指现代的电子数据程序处理设备在法学上的应用，如诉讼文件准备、报表、法学的调研、情报等）
legal concept 法律概念
legal consciousness 法的意识（又译：法律意识）
legal consequence 法律后果
legal consideration 法律上的有效对价（与 illegal 或 immoral consideration 相对）
legal constraint 合法扣押，合法拘押（指按合法程序对人身进行拘押或对财产进行扣押）
legal construction 法律解释，法律释义
legal contentions 法律争点
legal context 法定场合；法律上的上下文
legal continuity 法的连续性（又译：法律的连续性）
legal control 法律控制
legal costs 诉讼费用；法定费用
legal counsel 法律辩护人，律师；法律顾问

[attorney 一词广泛应用于美国,指授权为当事人代理案件的律师或代表或协助客户处理法律事务。而在英格兰,此词则指威斯敏斯特地区普通高等法院(庭)的公职人员。counsel 指接受指派专门为个人、公司和政府公务部门提供法律服务的人,称为法律顾问或律师]

legal criticism 法律评论
legal culture 法文化
legal currency 法定货币
legal curriculum 法律课程
legal custody 法律监督,合法拘禁,合法监护
legal custody of child 对未成年人的合法监护
legal custody of property of a debtor 依法扣留债务人财产
legal damages 1.法定损害赔偿(指法律承认的损害赔偿,即不法行为所造成的损害中为法律允许给予赔偿者)2.法律损害赔偿(指一种由于违反国际法义务而产生的损害。中美洲人权法院曾经裁决受害者的孩子、父母以及其兄弟姐妹同样享有精神损害赔偿金)
legal data 法学资料
legal death 宣告死亡(指法律上的死亡,区别于自然死亡)
legal death of missing person 失踪人的(法定)宣告死亡
legal debate in court 法庭辩论
legal debt margin 法定债务限额,合法债务差额
legal debts (能收回的)合法债务
legal decision 法律决议
legal deed 法定契据
legal defect 法定瑕疵,法律的欠缺
legal defect of the petition 诉状有法定瑕疵
legal defence 合法辩护
Legal Defense and Education Fund. Inc. (美)法律辩护和教育基金公司[由美国有色人种促进委员会(NAACP)于 1909 年成立,是为了改善美国黑人地位而致力于院外游说、政治教育以及法律诉讼的组织,其目的在于疏通议员和官员,通过政治教育和法律行为改变非美国籍人的政治地位,并招募新成员,出版公报和一份杂志,依靠志愿律师为有色人种提起诉讼]
legal definition n. 法律定义,法律说明,法律上的含义
legal demand 合法要求
legal demarcation of state action 国家作为的合法界限
legal deprivation of civil rights 依法褫夺公权
legal description 土地的正式说明,土地的法定说明(指包括对土地中没有地役权或作为保留部分所作的说明,以此足以说明某一特定土地所在的位置。此说明可参考政府土地勘测、地界,亦称 land description)
legal detention 合法扣留
legal detriment 见 detriment 2
legal dictionary 法律词典
legal dilemma 法律疑难
legal disability 无行为能力,无法定能力,法律上无资格
legal discipline 法纪,(古)法律学科
legal discretion 见 judicial discretion
legal dispute 法律纠纷;(国际)法律争端
legal doctrine 法律学说,法律原则(理)
legal doctrine and public values at stake 法律原理和(危险中)公众价值
legal document 法律文件;合法文书
legal dogmatics 法律教条论
legal domicile 法定住所
legal draftsman 法案撰拟人,法规拟人
legal dress 法衣(指法官和律师在法庭上穿的专用服装)
legal duty 法定职责,法律上的义务,法定义务
legal duty to take care 法定的注意义务
legal easement 法定地役权
legal education 法制教育,法律教育
legal effect 法的效力(又译:法律效力)
legal effectiveness 法律效用
legal empowerment 法律激发权能,法律赋能[根据贫穷人口法律赋能委员会和联合国开发计划署的定义,是指使穷人受到

保护并运用法律来推动其在国家和市场中的权利和权益的过程。亦即利用法律服务及相关活动增进弱势人群掌控自己生活的能力的超越传统法治(rule of law orthodoxy)的另一种形式]

legal encyclop(a)edias 法律百科全书

legal enforcement of Confucian dominant morals 儒教支配道德之法律强制执行

legal enforcement of morality 道德的法律强制(指特定种类的道德义务强制,无人真正主张法律应该永远不支持道德规范所禁止的行为,大多数刑法、侵权法、合同法和财产法等都涉及道德准则的法典化。这一术语通常指不以任何明显方式影响公共秩序和商业活动的正常运行的法律规制)

legal entitlement 法益(指比"权益"较窄而介于"权利"和"利益"之间的一个概念。"权利"当然意味着法律保护,而"利益"则并非一定能够获得法律保护。介于两者之间的"法益"指的是所有受法律保护的权利和利益,既包括私有权利,也包含公有权利;既包括财产权利,也包含人格权利;既包括受到绝对权利保护的"权利化"的利益,也包含有待法院在具体情形加以确定的绝对权利保护之外的"纯经济利益"。同时,"法益"并不限于物质利益,精神利益亦同样受到法律保护)

legal entity 法律实体,法人

legal estate 合法不动产;法定财产(权);(英美法)普通法上的财产(权)(指与衡平法上的财产 equitable estate 相对而言)

legal ethics 律师的职业道德[指律师职业行为应符合最低限度可接受的标准。英格兰律师总会(General Association of the Bar)和美国律师协会(American Bar Association)都有自己的行业行为道德规范,起着十分重要的作用]

legal etiquette 法律礼仪(指法律职业界的荣誉和习惯行为规则的准则)

legal evidence 合法证据,法定证据

legal excuse 合法理由,合法借口

legal executive (英)初级撰状律师(指雇用的撰状律师助手),事务律师助理

legal existence 合法存在;法律生活

legal expenses insurance 法律费用保险[指投保人通过购买确定的险种(法律费用险或诉讼险),在自己与他人发生民事诉讼时,由保险公司通过理赔方式向投保人支付诉讼费用的保险制度]

legal expert 法律专家,法学家

legal explanation 法律解释,法律释义

legal expression 法律上的表达,法律措辞

legal facility 法律上的便利

legal fact 法律事实

legal fee 司法费用,法定费用

Legal Fee Arbitration Board (美)司法费用仲裁委员会(1974年最早建立于马萨诸塞州,以后各地效法建立,由律师仲裁解决诉讼委托人和他们的辩护人之间诉讼费纠纷的机构)

legal fiction 法律拟制,法律上的假定或推定

legal fiction of "presence" as the test for asserting jurisdiction 作为主张管辖标准的"在场"法律拟制

legal force 法的效力,法律拘束力,法的力量

legal form 法定方式,法定形式

legal formalities 法律手续,法律程序

legal formant 法律的部分

legal formulas (罗马法)法定的程式诉讼[由裁判官 Praector 指定审理事实的承审员(judex),并告知其审理案件的有关程式,包括:①请求的原因 *demonstralio*;原告说出要求事实及依据;②原告请求(*intentio*);③分析裁判(*adjudicatio*);④判决要旨(*condemnatio*)]

legal framework 法律体制(又译:法律结构)

legal fraternity 法律界,律师界

legal fruit 法定孳息

legal glossators 注释法学派

legal government 合法政府

legal ground 法律上的依据,合法理由

legal(或 statutory)guardian 法定监护人

legal guilt 合法认定的有罪(指建立在事实基础上的认定被告人犯有被指控的罪行)

legal hegemony 法律优势

legal heir 法定继承人
legal heir of the first rank 第一顺序法定继承人
legal hermeneutics 法律解释学(指对法律文件、法规和学说的解释和注释的艺术)
legal history (18世纪)1.法制史(指在一个法律体制之内记录和解说所发生的事件的知识部分或是在此法律体制内文化发展进程中所发生的事件)2.法律大事件(指一些大事涉及法律事实部分的主要大事件问题)3.法律史(指系统地表述所发生的历史事件,通常以哲学观点解说事件的专著)
legal holiday 法定假日(指由法律设定的假日,法庭不开庭、不发送传票等,州与州之间关于法定假日的实际不尽相同,有时缩短这种假期,亦称 nonjudicial day)
legal humanism 人文主义法学派
legal hypothec 法定不转移财产占有权的担保
legal identity 合法身份
legal impediment 法律上的障碍(见 impediment)
legal imprisonment 合法监禁
legal incapacity 无权利能力,无行为能力;无法定身份(或资格)
legal incapacity to marriage 无结婚行为能力
legal income 合法收入
legal informatics 法律信息,法学信息(学)
legal information 法律信息,法学信息(学)
legal infrastructure 法制的基础结构
legal injury (18世纪)法律上的侵害(指违反合法的权利)
legal insanity 法律精神病[与医学精神病(mental illness)相对而言。见 guilty but mentally ill"有罪但有精神病"规则]
legal institutions 法律制度;法律机构
legal instrument 法律文件,法律文据,(常用复)法律文书
legal intercourse 法律上的往来
legal interdiction 法律上的禁治产
legal interest 法定利息;法定利益,合法权益
legal interpretation 法律上的解释
legal interpretation developed by the panel 专家组展开的法律解释
legal investigation 法律调查,合法侦查
legal investment 合法投资(目录)(有时亦称 legal lists)
legal issue 法律问题;法律争点
legal jargon(或 **lingo**) 法律专用术语(或行话)
legal jointure (丈夫生前指定的)妻子的合法遗产,寡妇合法所得产
legal jurisdiction 法定管辖(权),合法审判权;(英美法)普通法上的管辖权[指与衡平法上的管辖权(equitable jurisdiction)相对而言]
legal justice 法的公正原则
legal justification 法律上的正当理由,法定的不罚行为
legal keeping 合法持有
legal language 法律用语,法律语言
legal legacy 合法遗赠(物)
legal level 法律层次
legal liability 法律责任
legal liberalism 法律的自由主义
legal lien 法定留置权
legal limbo 法律的中间过渡状态
legal limit (车辆等行驶的)法定速度
legal limitation 法定限制,法律上的限制;法律的局限性;法定时效
legal liquidation 合法清算,法定清算
legal list (国家批准的银行等的)合法投资目录(见 legal investment)
legal literature 法律著述,法律文献;法文化
legal logic 法律推理;法律逻辑
legal loophole 法律漏洞
legal loose leafs in print (美)已出版的法律活页资料
legal maintenance 法定扶养(责任);法定赡养费
legal malice 法律上的预谋,故意
legal malpractice (法律上的)渎职罪
legal marriage 合法婚姻
legal materials 法律事务
legal maternalism 法律上的母系家族,法

律上的母系权威,法律如母式的管教
legal mathematics 法律数学
legal matter 法律事件,法律问题,司法案件,司法问题
legal maxims 法律格言,法律谚语;法律准则
legal maximum 法定最高限额
legal meaning 法律意义
legal means 法律手段
legal measure 法律措施
legal mechanism 法律机制,法律手段
legal medical expert 法医
legal medicine 法医学
legal memorandum 法律备忘录
legal memory 法律上的记忆;法律上的追溯期限;(英)法定追溯日
legal merits 法律上的依据,法律上的是非曲直
legal methodology 法律方法学,法律方法论
legal mode 法律模式
legal monks 法律僧侣
legal mortgage 合法抵押,法定抵押,(英)普通法上的抵押
legal mother 合法母亲(旧译:嫡母)
legal muck-raker 专门暴露丑闻的法律记者
legal myth 法律神话
legal name 合法名称(指依法登记的公司或社团法人名称;依法登记的个人姓名)
legal nature 法律性质
legal negligence 法律上的过失,法定过失
legal nexus 法律关系
legal nihilism 法律虚无主义
legal norm 法律规范
legal notice 法律通告,法律通知,法律告示
legal objection 合法的反对(意见)
legal obligation 法定义务
Legal Office (美)法律事务所(指联邦最高法院1937年设立,由首席大法官任命两名辩护律师负责,至少工作四年,主要为联邦最高法院咨询各类法律事务问题的机构)
legal officer 法律上的官员[指拥有职位、法定职衔标志(legal indicia of title)的个人];(美)军事司法官,军事顾问,军法助理

Legal Officers Ordinance (中)(香港特别行政区)《律政官员条例》
legal official 司法行政官员
legal ontology 法律的本体论
legal operation 法律实施,法律操作
legal opinion 法律意见书(指司法官员或律师就其对适用于特定事实的法律的理解所发表的书面意见,它能否为依此意见行事者提供保护,则取决于该意见书的性质和调整该意见书的相关法律规定)
legal or judicial security 法定的或法院判决的担保
legal order 法律秩序,法令
legal ordering 法律排序
legal ordering of society 社会法律秩序
legal organization 法律组织
legal orthodoxy 法律正统观念,法律的正统做法
legal owner 合法所有人,法定所有权人
legal ownership 合法所有权,法定所有权
legal parental authority (美)法律上的亲权(指对于子女长期利益、教育、医疗照顾、宗教教育或对于子女生活有重大影响的事件有决定权)
legal paternalism 法律上的家长,法律上的父系家族,法律如父式的管教
legal person 法人
legal person of private law 私法人
legal person of public law 公法人
legal personality 法人资格;法律上的人格,权利能力(亦译:权利主体的资格)
legal personalty 合法动产,合法的个人财产
legal pettifogger 爱打官司者;非正式的律师;卑劣的律师(旧译:讼棍)
legal phenomenon 法律现象
legal philosophy(或 **philosophy of law**)法理学,法哲学
legal phraseology 法律术语
legal pigeon hole 法律上的条条框框
legal pluralism 法律的多元主义(指在一定的情况下,在一个国家里不同的法律体制共同存在,并且每一种都适宜不同群体中的个体)
legal polity 法律的政治团体(亦即宪政

团体)

legal position 法律地位

legal positivism 法律的实证主义[在说英语的国度里,法律实证主义指18世纪末19世纪初由吉瑞米·边沁(Jeremy Bentham)及约翰·奥斯汀(John Austin)所提出的对法律本质的两种见解:所有国内法都是假定的,即由人类精心创造出来的,人们把它称为"精心创造理论";人们通过经验的调查可以发现任何事物的规律,但这种规律并不能满足任何实质性的道德检验,那么法律就可能会常常偏离法律的本质,这就是"分离理论"]

legal possession 合法占有(权),法定占有(权)

legal power 法定权力

legal practise 见 practice of law

legal practitioner 开业律师(= law practitioner)

legal precedent 判例,先例

legal precept 法律格言;法律规则;法律令状;法律箴言

legal prerequisites and consequences of matrimony 婚姻的法定条件和后果

legal prescription 法律时效;法律手段;法律规定,法律指令,法律处方

legal presumption 法律推定

legal price 法定价格

legal principle 法律准则;法律原则;法理

legal problem 法律问题

legal procedure 法定程序,(英美法)普通法程序

legal proceedings 法定程序,诉讼程序;诉讼,(英美法)普通法诉讼

legal process 诉讼方法;诉讼程序;法律手段;法律过程

legal profession 律师界;法律界;法律专业

legal professional 法律专业人士,法律专业者

legal professional privilege 合法的职业权利

legal professionals 法律工作者;律师职业;律师界(美国的法律职业由律师、法官、检察官和法律教师组成,这几种人均可称为 lawyer)

legal profit 合法赢利,合法利润

legal property 合法财产,法定财产(权)

legal protection 法律保护

legal protest 法律上的拒绝证书

legal provision 法律条文,法律规定

legal provision to the contrasting 相反的法律规定

legal pseudo-science 传统法律的伪科学

legal psychiatry 司法精神病学

legal punishment 合法处罚,法律处罚;依法惩处

legal pursuits 法律上的追求

legal qualification 法定资格

legal question(或 **law question**) 见 question of law

legal rate of interest 法定利率

legal realism 法律现实主义[通常指美国现实主义思潮。其代表人物为美国联邦最高法院大法官霍尔姆斯(Oliver Wendell Holmes)和哈佛大学教授 J. C. 格雷、卢埃林与弗兰克。它是以实证主义、实证主义哲学作为理论基础,受到心理学、弗洛伊德的精神分析学、统计社会学等思想的影响,反对美国传统的法学概念论。强调从人的行为特别是司法官员的行为中探求现实的法律规则]

legal realism intellectual mood 法律现实主义知识思潮

legal reason 法律理由

legal reasoning 法律推理[广义来说法律推理涵盖了在法律过程中把法律适用到事实上的人(法官以及由此派生的想对司法判决产生影响的辩护人、评价司法判决的法律学者)所运用的各种形式的分析。从狭义来说,仅指从法律原材料中引导法律后果。例如法官能够或应参考法律外的规范,那么这些学者就会把"法律是什么""法律要求的是什么"与"法官应该/将要怎样作出判决"区分开来]

legal recognition 法律上承认

legal red tape 法律文书(指司法公文之类)

legal redress 法律(上的)补救,法律(上的)赔偿

legal reference 法律证明,法律咨询

legal reform 法律变革;法律改革

legal regime 司法体制,法律体制;合法体制
legal regime of Jim Crow 歧视黑人的法律制度
legal regulation 法律规定;法律条例;法律调整
legal relation 法律关系
legal relief(或 **liability rule**) 法定救济;责任规定(指法院对违约方判处一笔补偿金以赔偿受害方履行合同的损失)
legal remedy 法律救济,法定救济[指从历史上讲,适合于普通法庭上申诉获得的救济,以区别于仅在衡平法上的救济,但在普通法与衡平法合并以后,在相关的某些方面保留了这种区别,比如决定陪审团审理的权利和选择性的救济(alternate remedies)之间的选定]
legal representative 法定代理人,合法代理人;法定代表,合法代表
legal requirement 法律要件;法律要求
legal research (18世纪)1.法律文献检索[指查找或检索和收集有关某一法律的法律根据(authorities);亦指对某一法律问题的法律根据进行有效的整理编排并进行研究以利于检索]2.法律研究(指对法律问题及其相关问题进行系统研究和考察。法学院校和专门法学研究机构将其研究成果提供给司法部门,供改革参考)3.(美国)法学院校的一门基础课程之一
legal reserve(requirement) 法定储备金(要件)
legal reserve fund 法定基(公积)金,法定储备金
legal residence 法定住所;依法登记的住所
legal responsibility 法律责任
legal restraint 法律(的)约束,法律(上的)限制
legal reversion 合法继承权,合法未来所有权,合法的归属(权利)
legal rhetoric 法律雄辩术
legal right 法定权利,合法权利;(英美法)普通法上的权利;(苏格兰)法定遗产请求权;(复)权利能力
legal right doctrine 法律上的权利原则
legal right for natural objects 自然的法律权利
legal rule 法律规范,法律规定,(复)法律规则
legal rulings 法律裁决
legal safeguard 法律保障措施
legal sanction 法律制裁;法律认可
legal sanctity 法律尊严
legal scholar 法律家;法学学者
legal scholarship 法律学术
legal science (18世纪)法律科学,法学(同 science of law)[指作为社会科学的一个研究领域,讨论研究特定社会已经发展的制度和原理:①界定人们在各种不同情况下对于他人的权利主张和承担的责任;②在符合公平与正义(fair and right)可接受的原则下于特定时间和特定社区内和平地解决争端和纠纷。法律科学从广义上讲,亦可称为法哲学(jurisprudence)。从哲学、历史、比较研究、分析、评论等诸多角度对广义的法律及其演变、转型、形成、阐释、应用等方面系统化、体系化的知识。法律有理论法学和应用法学,前者为法学家所从事的研究工作,后者则属于立法者、法官、律师等实际法律工作者的工作范畴]
legal secretary (英)(以前殖民地的)司法官
legal sense 法律意义,法律意识,法制观念
legal sentence 法定刑期;合法判决
legal separation 合法分居,依法分居(指法院判决的夫妻分居)
Legal Services Corporation (美)法律服务公司(指提出基金为展开联邦法律援助项目的联邦政府机构)
legal servitude 法定地役(权)
legal sinking(或 **reserved**)**fund** 法定公积金
legal situation 法律处境;法律条件
legal situs 法律处所,法律位置,合法地点,合法的所在地
legal sociology 法(律)社会学
legal sovereignty 法律上的主权,合法主权;合法统治者
legal speed limit 法定时速
legal staff 司法人员
legal standard 法律标准,合法标准

legal standard of care 法律上的注意(小心)标准(指人们通常运用两种方法引来潜在的伤害者采取对社会的注意,一则是注意减少受害者受到伤害的可能性,另一则是减少受害者受到伤害的程度,或两者兼顾。法律标准则是指人们可引导一位伤害者采取使社会满意的注意措施,其方法是通过建立他的行为标准并使他明白如有违反就要承担责任)
legal state 法治国家
legal station 法律地位
legal status 合法地位;法律地位,合法身份
legal status of a person 个人的法律地位;自然人的法律地位
legal status of earth-orbiting station 地球轨道站的法律地位
legal status of the Antarctica 南极洲的法律地位
legal status of women 妇女的法律地位
legal structure 法律结构
legal subject 法律主体
legal substitute 法定候补人,法定代理人
legal succession 合法继承,法定继承(指按照法律,通常按最有利于死者的最亲的亲属法律确定的继承)
legal superstructure 法律的上层建筑
legal supervision 法律监督,司法监督
legal supplement 法律补遗;法律附则
legal system 法律制度;法的体系(又译:法律体系)
legal talent 法律才能,法律才干
legal taxation system 法定税收制度
legal technicalities (of the case) (案件的)法律细节
legal techniques 法律技巧
legal tender (paper money) 法定货币(指在境内具有强制流通的效力)
legal tender act (美)法定货币法
Legal tender cases (美)法定货币系列案[是19世纪70年代三个案例的总称。三个案例分别是赫伯恩诉格里斯沃尔德案(Hepburn v.Griswold,75 U. S. 603,1870)、克劳斯诉李案(Knox v. Lee)以及帕克诉戴维斯案(Parker v. Davis,79 U. S. 457,1871)。法定货币系列案代表了一种主张,即认为合众国可以强制债权人收受纸币以作为对债务的偿付]
legal term 法定期限;法定支付期;法律术语,法律名词
legal terminology 法律术语
legal theorists 法学家,法理学家
legal theory 法律理论;法理
legal theory of parliamentary sovereignty 法律的国会主权说
legal thought 法律思想
legal thought of ancient Greeks 古希腊的法律思想
legal thoughts in Chinese history 中国法律思想史
legal time 法定时间,法定日期
legal time limit 法定期限
Legal Times of Washington (美)《华盛顿法治时代报》(1978年于首都华盛顿创刊的全国性周报)
legal title 法定所有权,合法所有权;名义所有权
legal toxicology 法医毒理学,司法毒理学
legal tradition 法律传统
legal training 法律培训
legal transaction 法律事务处理;法律上的交易;法律行为
legal transaction of processing a public calling 以公众需要的法律交易
legal transplant(s) 法律移植
legal treatises and textbooks 法律专著和教科书
legal treatment 合法对待;法定处理
legal uncertainty 法律的不确定性
legal utilitarianism 法律功利主义(指法哲学的一种流派)
legal validity 法律效力,合法性
legal value 见 benefit 2
legal value of computer records 计算机记录的法律价值(指 1985 年联合国国际贸易委员会发表的一份"计算机记录的法律价值"。该报告建议各国政府采取措施承认计算机记录作为诉讼中的证据)
legal warranty 合法担保
legal word 法律用语
legal work 法律工作

legal worker 法律工作者
legal writ 法律令状
legal writing 法律文书写作
legal wrong 违法行为(以区别于 moral wrong 不道德行为),法律上的过错(行为),法定过错(行为),法定侵权行为
legal year 法定年度
legal-unity doctrine (历史)法定统一性原则(指普通法上规定妻子不得离开其丈夫单独生活。亦称 doctrine of legal unities; unities doctrine of marriage。见 married women's property acts; spousal-unity doctrine)
legalese n. 深奥的法律用语,法律涩语,高深难懂的法律用语
legalglobalization 法律全球化
legalis homo (=lawful man) 有宣誓资格的人;自由人;奉公守法的人
legalism n. 条文主义,文牍主义,墨守法律条文;合法主义;法律术语(尤指空洞无内容者);(中)法家学说
legalist n. (1829年)法律学家,法学家[指从法律和法律方式的立场(或观点)(standpoint)观察事物的人,特别是法学人相信严格的法律字面含意甚于其背后内含]
legalist school (中)法家
legalistic a. 墨守成规的
legalistic approach 遵法派(见 rule-oriented approach)
legalistic retributionism 法律报应主义
legality (15世纪)1.合法性,合法的性质(指法律所允准的质量、状况、和条件) 2.严格守法(指严格忠于法律,忠于法规,忠于原则)3.根据以前尚未出版的刑事制定法:一个人不得被提起公诉的原则(亦称 principle of legality)
legality of administrative decision 行政决定的合法性
legality of search 合法搜查
legalization n. 合法化;合法;法律认可;公证
legalization of documents (合同等)法律文书的公证手续
legalize v. 使合法化,法律上认可;使符合法律,使成为法定

legally ad. 法律上,合法地,法定地
legally admissible in evidence 法律上可取证的
legally binding instrument 具有法律约束力的文件
legally competent to contract 有法定缔(立)约资格
legally constituted authority 法统
legally impossible 法律上不可能的(如四岁签订合同)
legally named contract 具名合同(契约)
legally performed 合法处理的
legally registered enterprise 依法登记的企业
legally sovereign 法律上的主权,合法主权
legally trained persons 受过法律专业训练的人员
legally valid record 有法律效力的记录
legatary a. 遗产的,遗赠的
legate v./n. 作为遗产让与,遗赠/使者,使节(尤指教廷使节)
legatee n. 遗产承受人,遗产继承人,受遗赠人
legation n. 1.使节的派遣;使节负有的使命;使节的职权 2.公使馆;公使馆全体人员
legation abroad 驻外公使馆
legator n. 遗赠人;立遗嘱人
* *Legatos violare contra jus gentium est.* It is contrary to the law of nations to injure ambassadors. 伤害使节是违反国际法的。
legatum (大陆法)遗赠,遗产
legatum liberationis 债务免除的遗赠
legatum nominis 债权遗赠
legatum optionis (罗马法)选择遗赠
legatum per damnationem 间接遗赠
legatum per praeceptionem 先取遗赠(指罗马法上共同继承人中的一个人,在继承财产前,以受遗赠人资格,于应继份外领取的遗赠物)
legatum per vindicationem 直接遗赠
legatum poenae nomine 有条件的遗赠,限制性遗赠
leges (罗马法)法令(指由主持议会的司法行政官建议并为平民大会通过的法

令);法律,法规
Leges Angliae 英格兰法(区别于大陆法和其他外国法)
Leges Barbarorum 蛮族法;蛮族法典;中古式的欧洲人法典
***Leges Barbarorum* of the Continent** 欧洲大陆的蛮族法典(受罗马法之影响,全是用拉丁文写成的)
* ***Leges figendi et refigendi consuetudo est periculosissima.*** The practice of fixing and refixing (making and remaking) the laws is the most dangerous one. 惯于制定和修改法规是最有害的做法。
Leges Henrici Primi (英)《亨利一世法令》[约1118年汇编的英国法原则综述,内有盎格鲁-撒克逊时期(449—1066年)的一些法令、习惯、法规、法律等]
Leges Marchiarum (英)边境领地法,边界地区法(一部古代法典,记述苏格兰和英格兰接壤地区的法律、习惯,以及诉讼的判决)
* ***Leges non verbis, sed rebus, sunt impositae.*** Laws are imposed, not on words, but things. 法不是由文字决定的,而是由事物决定的。
* ***Leges posteriores priores contrarias abrogant.*** Later laws abrogate prior laws that contrary to them. 后法废止与之相抵触的前法(又译:后法优先适用于前法)。
Leges Romanae Barbarorum 蛮族罗马法
* ***Leges vigilantibus, non dormientibus, subveniunt.*** The laws aid the vigilant, not the negligent. 法帮助的是兢兢业业的人,而不是粗心大意的人。
Legibus solutus 受法律约束
Legion of Merit (美)军团荣誉(指美国军团 American Legion,美退伍军人组织);全国退伍军人协会荣誉
legis 立法,法规
legis actio (罗马法)口头诉讼制度(指两种由司法行政官使用的第一诉讼程序制度中的较古老的一种)
legis action (罗马法)法定的或合法的诉讼[指一种法律上要求使用固定的格式语言(fixed form of words)的诉讼]

* ***Legis interpretatio legis vim obtinet.*** The interpretation of law obtains the force of law. 法律的解释可获得法律效力。
* ***Legis minister non tenetur in executione officii sui, fugere aut retrocedere.*** The minister of the law is bound, in the execution of his office, not to fly nor to retreat. 司法部长(大臣)在执行自己的公务时负有不得逃避或放弃公务之责。
legislate v. 制定法律,通过法律,立法
legislation n. 立法;制定法,法规,法制;立法机关审议事项
legislation act 法律的制定;立法机关制定的法律
legislation committee 立法委员会
legislation districts 立法地区,法定的议员选区
legislation futility 立法无效,立法无用
legislation interfering with an individual's liberty 干涉个人自由的立法
legislation law 立法法
legislation motion 立法动议
legislation on economic matters 经济立法
legislation on labo(u)r protection 劳动保护法规
legislation on wages 工资法规
legislation to levy money 征税立法
legislative n./a. 立法机关;立法权;立法/立法的;有立法权的;立法机关的;由立法机关成员组成的;根据法规执行的,起立法作用的;立法机关创立的
legislative action 立法行为
legislative acts 立法性法规
legislative apportionment 立法分配权(亦译做议员名额分配权,指代议机关选举时在选区内分配代表权的程序)
legislative assembly 1.(一院制的)立法院 2.(两院制议会的)下院 3.(美)(州或领地的)两院制议会 4.(加拿大等国的)立法议会
legislative authority 立法权;立法机关的权力;法律依据;立法当局(机关)
legislative bill 法律草案,法案
legislative body 立法机关
legislative branch 立法部门

Legislative Calendar of the Senate Foreign Relations Committee （美）参院外交委员会的立法日程表
Legislative Calendars （美）立法议事日程表（指众参两院和大多数委员会均出版有悬而未决事项日程表,为其成员使用）
legislative chamber 立法议院(会)
legislative commission 立法委员会
legislative competence 立法权限
legislative control on administration 立法对行政的控制
legislative council 1.立法委员会 2.(英)议会上院 3.一院制议会;立法议会 4.(美)州议会常设委员会
legislative council resolution 立法委员会决议案
Legislative Courts （美）由立法机构按议会立法设立的法院(不同于按宪法设立的法院)
legislative debates 立法辩论
legislative districting （美）(为分配议员席位的)立法机构的选区划分(美国联邦宪法要求议会代表按照人口数选举产生,但州的立法机构可不受宪法模式约束,不仅按人口,而且按地域大小、特殊利益和区县等行政区域等因素划分选区,由各区选出代表各该区的立法机构成员)
legislative drafting 立法起草
legislative economics 立法经济学
legislative effect 立法效力
legislative enactment 立法性法规
legislative encroachments 合法的占用
legislative explanation 立法说明;立法机关的解释
legislative facts 立法的事实(指有助于行政机构决定法律和政策的一般问题,并可制定法规的事实。见 adjudicative facts)
legislative filibustering 立法的阻挠,阻碍议会通过法案
legislative function 立法功能,立法机构的职能[指①确定立法政策的职责;②制定和决定未来权利和职能。见 legislative power]
legislative futility 立法无用论
legislative hearing 立法听证

legislative history 立法史
legislative immunity （美）国会议员之豁免权
legislative initiative 立法创制权
legislative instrument 立法文件
legislative intent (rule) 立法意图(原则)(指法院应决定立法者的意图,或表明何时通过该项法律记入立法史册,这只是解释法规的几种可能方式之一)
legislative intervention 立法干预
legislative investigative power 立法机关的调查权
legislative justice 议会审判
legislative law making 制定立法法
legislative law-making 立法机关的立法,立法机关产生的立法
legislative mandate 立法委任权
legislative meets 立法会议
legislative officer 立法官员,立法机关成员
legislative organ 立法机关
legislative power (17 世纪)(宪法法)立法权[大写为立法机关(或议会)权][指制定、修改或废除法律专有的权力,根据联邦法(federal law),这个权力被授予给由参议院和众议院组成的国会(congress)。立法机关可以将部分制定法律的权力授予行政部门内的代理机构以便制定法规和章程,但立法机关不得授权给司法部门,而且司法部门不得侵犯立法机关的职权(legislative duties)]
legislative privilege （美）法定特惠,立法机关的特权(指此种特权目的在于保护:①任何由立法机关的某一成员在立法机关内所做的陈述;②立法机关的业务上所出版的任何文件。亦称 parliamentary privilege)
legislative procedure 立法程序
legislative process 立法手续;立法程序
legislative progression 立法进程
legislative purpose rule 立法目的原则(指法院应该在现法律通过之前关注立此法律的目的是什么,并据此判断该法律试图修改些什么)
legislative reciprocity 立法上的互惠
Legislative Reporting Service （美）《立法

报告汇编服务》(指由美国商业情报交换印刷所提供的包括国会的和州的立法服务)
legislative review conference 立法审议会议
legislative rule (美)立法性法规(指行政机关行使授予的准立法权限而制定的法规,目的在于补充制定法。这些规则具有法律效力,对法院具有约束力)
legislative series 法规汇编(丛书)
legislative session (美)立法会议
legislative source 立法渊源
legislative spirit 立法精神
legislative stalemate 立法的僵持(僵局)
legislative standing 立法者诉权(立法者诉权是诉讼原则下的概念,指的是国会议员向法院起诉行政官员和行政机构的能力)
legislative steps 立法步骤
legislative subjects 立法事项
legislative supremacy of parliament 议会的最高立法权
legislative thinking 立法观点,立法思想
legislative trends 立法趋势
legislative veto (美)立法否决[指1932年国会和总统赫伯特·胡佛(Herbert Hoover)的行政机构同意在起草立法进程中可有一个较大范围新的越轨诉讼行为。总统或行政机构根据授权所制定的法规或采取的行动必须得到国会同意方可生效。从半个世纪看来,国会在二百多部法规上均寄希望于立法否决权的规定]
legislative vote 按法规执行的选票
legislative-executive agreement 立法—行政协定(指如今的条约已被立法—行政协定所取代,而在过去条约曾是国际承诺的主要工具。条约需要2/3的绝大多数参议员同意,但协定只需众议院和参议院多数通过即可。立法—行政协定始于18世纪90年代,那时协定只用来获取国外贷款偿还债务、建立国际邮政协议。最近美国联邦最高法院始终支持协定的合宪性,至于是否反对协定而追求条约,这一选择法院认为应留给总统和国会去斟酌)
legislative steam-roller 立法的高压手段;专制立法

legislator n. 立法者,立法机关成员;立法委员;议员
legislatorial a. 立法者的,立法委员的
legislatorship n. (立法委员或议员)的身份(地位或资格)
Legislature (17世纪)立法机构,立法机关(指负责制定成文法规的政府部门。联邦政府和大部分州都有两院制的立法机构,通常是众议院和参议院。亦称 Legislative Assembly。见 executive;judiciary)
legislature-made law 议会的立法
legist n. 法律学者,法(律)学家(尤指精通罗马法或民法者);(大写)(中)法家
Legistimate privacy interests do not exist in public place. 公共场所不存在合法的隐私利益(是20世纪60年代以前美国权威的法律信条,但随着时间推移,事态的发展对此信条提出严峻挑战。偷拍、跟踪事件以及秘密侦查手段的广泛使用使越来越多的人相信在私人空间之外的公共场所也存在合法的隐私利益)
legitim (苏格兰)特留份,遗留份(与 bairn's part of gear, bairn's part 或 legitime part of gear 同)
legitima portio (苏格兰)特留份,遗留份
legitimacy n. 婚生;合法性(指实践、制度或整个体系的道德价值。主要在讨论政治行为人的行为和制度时使用此词。但有时此词的使用更为宽泛,适用所有或大多数的受规则管理的实践。一些理论研究者在"合理性"与"合法性"之间作出区分。前者指对实践做的道德评价,而后者则适用于一个行为是否与被实践接收的规则相一致)
legitimacy declaration (英)婚生宣告(旧译:嫡出声明,指法院宣布申请人为合法婚姻出生者,其父母、祖父母、本人的婚姻均为有效;或宣布其出生以来即为英王臣民)
legitimacy of children 婚生子女,嫡生子女
legitimacy of government 统治的正当性(或合法性)
legitimacy status of children 子女的合法地位
legitimacy-democracy deficit problem 合

法性与民主性赤字问题(指完全由主权国家作为传统国际法主体与单独关税区作为现代有限国际法主体主导的多边贸易条约的谈判与执行给成员方域内及域外的贸易商,特别是跨国公司对此条约的缔结与执行机制会造成"合法性与民主性赤字问题")

legitimate v./a. 使合法;宣布……为合法;给……合法地位;为合法婚姻所生,立为嫡嗣;证明……有理/合法的;正统的;婚生的;合理的,正当的(legitimate 指根据法律、公认权威与准则为正当的。见 lawful; legal)
legitimate authority 合法职权
legitimate birth rate 合理的出生率
legitimate business 正当业务,合法营业
legitimate children 婚生子女
legitimate claim 合法的请求(权)
legitimate defence 合法防卫,正当防卫
legitimate democratic rule 民主规则的合法性
legitimate descent 合法世系,正统的世系
legitimate expectation 合法可得权益,合法期望权益(指依法可以期望得到的利益,如继承等);合理期待(指从国内行政法中借用的术语,不少国内法要求政府机构在对私人及公司行使行政力时尊重其"合理期待")
legitimate father 合法父亲
legitimate filiation 合法的父子关系
legitimate freedom 合法的自由;正当自由
legitimate government 正统政府,合法政府
legitimate guideline 法定准则
legitimate hegemony in legislation and politics 立法与政治中的合法权威
legitimate hegemony 合法的霸权,合法的权威;合法的统治
legitimate heir 合法继承人
legitimate income 合法收入,正当收入
legitimate interests 正当利益,合法权益
legitimate mode of acquisition 合法的取得方式
legitimate objects of regulation 合法的异议,否决权
legitimate portion 合法的遗赠;合法的嫁妆;合法的配额;法定应继份,特留份
legitimate private property 合法私有财产
legitimate reasons 合法理由
legitimate religious activities 合法的宗教活动
legitimate right 合法权利
legitimate self-defence 正当自卫,合法自卫
legitimate son 婚生子,嫡子
legitimate sovereign 合法主权
legitimate status 合法地位,合法身份
legitimate trade interest 合法的贸易利益
legitimate warfare 合法战争
legitimating function (国家行为的)正当化(指美国联邦宪法判断的重要功能是实现对国家公权力行为的正当化,而非颠覆性的国家行为。另外对美国联邦最高法院宪法判断的一个重要功能是对执政者的某些基本政策进行正当化。法学家罗伯特·达尔认为:这种正当化不仅为占据统治地位的联盟具体政策提供正当性,从长远来看,也为民主制度所必需的基本行为方式提供正当性)

legitimatio (罗马法)认领[指使不正当子归于家父权下之方法。按罗马法规定,凡妾所生之子为不正当子(*liberi non justi*),与其父无法律关系。其父对不正当子亦不能发生家父权。如欲对于妾出子行使家父权,则必须采取"认领"之方法。此法可独用于妾出子。有三种"认领"方法:①因日后结婚之认领(*legitimatio per subsequens matrimorium*),妾出子之父若日后娶其妾为正妻,则虽婚前所生之子取得嫡子身份,其父对于此子亦取得家父权。②因皇帝敕令之认领(*legitimatio per principis*)"父无嫡子而仅有妾出子者及妾死亡或失踪或无结婚之价值时,实际上不能适用第一认领方法。于是优帝复以新敕令七十四号规定:凡父对于妾出之子,得向皇帝请愿给予认领之许可。纵令父未请愿而死亡,若其遗嘱书中载明认领之意旨,则其子得以遗嘱书而代替请之。但父有嫡子存在或未经其子承诺者,不在此限"。③因充地方官之认领(*legitimatio per oblationem curiae*)。此认领方法与前二者不同,前二者以更正其子身份,此则因充地

方官而后认领,但当时地方官纯属义务,还需代以金上税和充实地方国库。故罗马人视为畏途,而不乐意为此名誉,而无权利。若一旦就职,终身不能辞退,子孙复世袭之,故各府地方官无正妻,无嫡子,而蓄妾生子,断绝父子之法律关系比比皆是。戴奥多帝(Theodosius)为矫斯弊,于公元443年下敕令曰:"凡妾出子充当地方官以嫡子论。"此认领方法需三个条件:父无嫡子、给予一定土地以及经其子承诺是也。至于妾出女儿,则仅与地方官结婚足矣]

legitimation n. 1.使合法,合法化;正统化 2.婚生,嫡出 3.认领为婚生子女;立为嫡嗣

legitimation by father (非婚生子女)经父亲认领为婚生子女

legitimation by subsequent marriage (或 le-gitimation *per subsequens matrimonium*) (非婚生子女因父母)事后结婚的认领(为婚生子女)(指允许非婚生子女在他们父母以后结婚时取得合法身份)

legitimation of a natural child 私生子的认领

legitimation of illegitimate child 对非婚生子女认领为婚生子女

legitime (大陆法)(父母的遗产无法定原因不得剥夺的)子女的应继份

* *Legitime imperanti parere necesse est.* One lawfully commanding must be obeyed. 凡依法发布命令或进行指挥的人,都应予以服从。

legitimi 婚生子女

legitimi haeredes (罗马法)合法继承人

legitimism n. 正统主义(尤指封建王位的继承)

legitimize v. 使合法化;给予法律保障;认领为婚生子女,立为嫡嗣;给以合法地位;证明……合法

legitimum imprimum 合法的权利

legistimo modo (苏格兰法)以合法形式

legistimo modo acquietatus 依法宣判无罪

legitimum tempus restitutionis 归还原状的法定时间,归还原物的法定时间;要求恢复原状的诉讼之法定时间

lego (罗马法)余以遗嘱赠与(遗嘱中用语)

Legum Doctor 法学博士
Legum Magister 法学硕士
leipa n. (古英国法)逃犯
leisure a. 空闲的,有闲的
leisure activities 业余活动
leisure time 业余时间
lemon law (美)次品汽车买主保护法,产品质量法(旨在保护购有低于汽车标准的消费者的制定法规)
Lemon Test 莱蒙案标准[美国联邦最高法院在 Lemon v. Kurtzman 一案中,由伯格(Burger)大法官代表多数提出的判决意见,确立了莱蒙标准。根据莱蒙标准,如果一部法律不侵犯禁止确立宗教条款的规定,必须满足以下三个条件:①必须出于非宗教的世俗目的;②其主要原则和主要作用既不能促进也不能限制宗教的发展;③它未鼓励对宗教的过度参与。虽然多年来经历了不少来自各方的反对意见,但莱蒙案标准仍旧是"禁止确立宗教"条款的核心]
lemons market 次品市场
lemons type market failure "柠檬"类型市场缺陷(指难以区分高质量可信之信息与低质量的信息)
lend v. 借出,提供,贷(款);出租;贷给
lend-lease n./a./v. 租借(指美国在第二次世界大战时期向盟国提供战争物资的一种方式)/依租借法批准的,租借法批准借给的/根据租借法借给
Lend-Lease Act (1941年3月11日美国制定的)《租借法》
lend-lease administration 租借管理
lend-lease agreement 租借协定
lendable a. 可供借贷的
lender n. 贷与人,贷方,出借人
lender of last resort arrangement 最后求助贷款人安排
lending n. 出借,出租;借出物,租借物
lending a chattel 出租动产
lending money to customers 向客户发放贷款
lending upon consideration 有偿借贷
length n. 长,长度,(时间的)长短;期间

length of protection 保护期限
length of residence 居住期限
length of sentence (服)刑期,徒刑期
length of the limitation period 时效期限
lengthy residence 长期居住
leniency n. 宽大;宽恕,仁慈
leniency policy(或 **program**) 宽恕政策
(是英美法中"从宽处理制"的一种表述,亦译为"量刑折扣制度""减免制度"或"从宽处理政策")
 * Leniency toward those who acknowledge their crimes but severe punishment of those who stubbornly refuse to do so. (中)坦白从宽,抗拒从严(系刑事政策中的量刑原则)。
lenient a. 宽大的;仁慈的
lenient disposal of a criminal 对罪犯的从宽处理
lenient sentence 宽大的判决,宽大的定刑
lenient treatment 宽大处理
lenity n. 宽大,宽大的行为
lenocinium (苏格兰)纵容(指丈夫纵容其妻子通奸或参与她卖淫获利的行为)
leonine a. 1.狮子似的 2.一方独占最大部分 3.对某一方片面有利的
leonine convention 对某一方片面有利的合约
leonine partnership 狮子合伙(指合伙人中某一个人赚钱分利,赔本不认账的一种合伙)
 * *Les animaux ne sont pas des choses.* 动物不是物。
les eaux intérieures 内水
 * *Les lois ne se chargent de punir que les actions extérieures.* Laws charge themselves with punishing overt acts only./Laws undertake to punish only outward actions. 法律只惩罚明显的外在行为。
lesbian n. 女同性恋者
lesbianism n. (女性)同性恋
lese majesty n. (对君主、元首的)不敬罪,叛逆罪
lèse-majesté 见 lese majesty
lesion n. 损伤,损害(程度);侵权(行为)
less material elements in affairs 事态中的次要因素
less recognizable 不怎么被承认,较少被承认
less restrictive alternative 较少限制选择
less than a container load (LCL) 拼箱货,拼箱装载
less-developed contracting party 欠发达的缔约方
less-formal a. 非正式的
less-formal agreement 非正式协定
less-than-carload a. (铁路运输中的)零担的
less-than-truckload a. (卡车运输中的)零担的
lessee n. 承租人,租用人,租户;租地人
lessen v. 减少,减轻;变小
lesser duty 次要义务,次要责任;轻税
lesser evils defense 见 defense 1
lesser included offense (1908年)被包括的较轻罪行[指这一罪行是对较重罪行构成要素(但不是所有要素)中的某一较轻罪行,而且这一罪行是实施较重罪行所必需的条件〈battery is lesser included offense of murder〉(殴打罪是被包括在凶杀罪的较轻罪行)。被包括的较轻罪行与较重罪行被视为同一罪行,按一事不再理的原则(double-jeoparady)处理,所以不得一个审判无罪释放,另一个判为有罪,而是不得重复审判。亦称 included offense; necessarily included offense; predicate offense; predicate act。见 cognate offense]
lesser standard 次要标准
lesser-contaminated properties 微污染的土地,极少污染的不动产
lesser-evils defense 见 defense 1
letter of attorney 委托书,授权书,委托状(见 power of attorney)
letter of the law 法律的字面含义
letter ruling n. (1950年)(税法)答复函[指由美国国内税务署(IRS)对咨询的纳税人作出的书面陈述,解释特定交易的税收内含,亦称 private letter ruling]
lesson by negative example 反面教材
lessor n. 出租人
let v. 1.出租,租给;交付(承包等) 2.允许,(表示建议、请求、命令等)让……3.解散,

开释 4.认为,假设
let alone 不干涉,不管束;更不用说,不碰
let go on bail 交保
let off 免除,免罚;放掉,对……从轻处理
* Let right be done, though the heavens fall. 秉公理办事,何惧天塌下来。
* Let the purchaser beware. 购买者注意! 购买者留意!
lethal a. 致命的,致死的;毁灭性的
lethal chamber 毒气行刑室
lethal firearms 致命火器
lethal injection 致命性药物注射(美国死刑执行方法之一)
lethal weapon 致命凶器
lethality n. 致死性,毁灭性
lethe n. 健忘,记忆丧失
letter n. 1.证书;许可证;书信;通知书;字母;字面意义 2.(英)出租人
letter ad clligenda bona 收集遗产状
letter bomb 书信炸弹;邮件爆炸物
letter close (英)密令(指国王向臣属个人发出的非正式指令)
letter credential (= letter of credence) 国书
letter missive 传达上级命令,任命,许可,(英)公文函件(指大法官给诉案中贵族被告发出的要求他出庭的信函)
letter of accusation 检举信,控告信
letter of administration 遗产管理委任书
letter of administration de bonis non (遗产管理人死后)新遗产管理人委任书
letter of advice (汇票、发货等)通知书(单)
letter of allotment (股票红利等)分配通知书
letter of apology 悔过书
letter of appointment 委任书;委任状
letter of assignment 转让书,过户书;分派书
letter of attorney 委托书;委任状;授权书
letter of authorization 授权书;委托书
letter of cancellation 解约书
letter of commendation 奖状
letter of commitment 公证委托书,承担义务书

letter of confession 自首书,悔过书
letter of confirmation 确认书,证实书
letter of countermarque (或 countermarque) 报复追偿海事损失的行动指令
letter of credence 国书;信任状
letter of credit 信用证,信用状
letter of credit with red clause 红线条款信用证
letter of delegation 代理收款委托书;委托书
letter of denization 外侨入籍证书
letter of guarantee (海运)保证函,信用保证书
letter of guarantee for production of bill of lading 提货担保书,出示提单保证书
letter of hypothecation 抵押权证书;质押书,(货主将载货)质押(给银行的)证书
letter of identification (信用证的)签字式样证明书;证明信
letter of indemnity (海运)赔偿保证书
letter of indication 印鉴证明书;(一国银行委托外国银行)承兑(其)本票的信函
letter of instruction 指示书,采购委托书,购买汇票指示书
letter of intent (合同的)草约,意向书
letter of introduction 介绍信
letter of licence 延期索偿同意书
letter of lien (财产)留置权书
letter of marque and reprisal 向敌方追偿海事损失命令书;捕拿(敌船或货物)特许证,报复许可证(指战时国家授权人民及武装船只,为采取报复行动而俘虏对方人员或抢夺其财产的特许证,亦做 letter of marque 或 letter of reprisal)
letter of notice 通知书
letter of patent 专利证书;(英)(国王颁发的)特许状
letter of procuration 委任状
letter of ratification 批准书
letter of recall 召回(大使等)国书;解任状
letter of recommendation 推荐书,介绍书
letter of subrogation 权益转让书,债权代位证书,保险代位证书
letter of transfer (权利)转让证书
letter of trust 信托书

letter of undertaking 担保书,承诺书,承诺保证函

letter overt 特许证

letter requisitorial (一国法院)委托(他国法院对于诉讼案件就地)调查证据的公函;(一法院给另一法院对某一诉讼案件)请求(就地)调查的公函

letter rogatory 1.调查委托书(指一个法院寄给另一独立管辖的法院要求按附去的问题向一证人调查的委托书);盘问证人委托书;代讯证人委托书 2.(一国法院委托他国法院)协助调查证据的委托书

letter ruling (美)函件规则(指美国税务署给纳税人关于税务法规适用特定的原则事项的函复)

letter testamentary (法院或官员颁发的)遗嘱执行授权书(状)

letter transfer 信汇

letterhead n. 信纸的上端所印的文字(包括姓名、商号、地址、电话等)

letters of business (英王)提议书

letters of safe conduct (英)通行许可证(指授权敌国侨民在公海航行、进入国境或运送货物不被没收的证书)

letters of the law 法律的字面意义

letters patent 专利权书,专利特权许可证

letting n. (英)租金;出租

lettre d'avis 发货通知单

lettre de credit 信用证

lettre de provision (法)领事委任书

lettres de cachet (或 **lettres du petit signet**, 或 **lettres du roi**) (法史)国王签署的监禁令;拘票

lettres de creance (法)国书

lettres de provision 委任状(指任命领事、总领事之本国政府委任状)

lettres de rappel (或 **recreance**) 召回国书,辞任国书

levant v. (英)躲债(尤指逃避赌债);躲避

levanter n. (英)躲债者

levari facias 拍卖(判定的债务人的)财产抵偿债务的执行令

levee n. (中)(帝王的)早朝;(英)王宫接见会(在午后举行);(美)总统(或高级官员)招待会

level n./v. 1.级别;地位 2.标准;水平(线);高度/把……对准,瞄准;击倒

level a charge against sb. 控告某人(的罪责)

level change value 位级切换值

level of adaptation 适应能力

leveleaged buyout (LBO) 杠杆作用买下全部产权

leveling and rating 评定和调整

leveling factor 评定因素

leveling of income 收益平衡

leveller n. 平等主义者;(喻)伟大的(美国用 leveler, death, the great leveler)

levels of relationship 亲等等级

leviable a. 可课税的,可课的(税)

leviathan n. 有财有势的人,(大写)极权主义国家

levier n. 强征人(尤指征税人)

levirate marriage 转房婚(指死者的兄弟优先成为其遗孀配偶的古希伯来习俗或法律)

levissima culpa (亦做 **levis culpa**)轻微过失

levitical degrees (英)利未亲等(指《利未纪》第18章列出的英格兰和苏格兰立法中有关禁止结婚的亲等,但现已放宽限制)

leviticus 《利未记》(指《圣经旧约》第三卷,该卷基本上是法律汇编,但也包括几段叙事)

levy n./v. 1.扣押;扣押财产 2.征集;征(集)的兵额 3.征收,征税;征收额/1.扣押(财产);征收 2.征税,抽税;强索;征集(兵员) 3.发动(战争)

levy blackmail upon 恐吓取财,敲诈,讹诈

levy en masse 国家战时总动员,民兵征集

levy execution (=levy of execution) 扣押;扣押拍卖得到的金钱;执行判决扣押财产

levy on 扣押

levy taxes on 对……抽税,征税

lewd a. 淫荡的,猥亵的

lewd and lascivious cohabitation 姘居

lewd house 见 disorderly house 2

lewdness n. 淫乱;公开姘居

lex 法,法律;法律实体

Lex Angliae 英格兰法;普通法

Lex Aquilia 阿奎利亚法[指自罗马建城时起,根据当时有名的护民官嘉路斯·阿魁琉斯(C. Aquilius Gallus)的建议所通过的著名的法律,该法代替了早先的十二铜表法的一部分]

Lex Atilia 阿提利亚法[指罗马在公元前2世纪中叶制定的法律,实际是由古罗马保民官阿提利乌斯(L. Atilius Regulus)提出后通过的法律,该法授予执法官(magistrate)以指定监护人的权利。此法仅适用于罗马城]

Lex Atinia de Rebus Subreptis 《关于盗窃物的阿提尼亚法》(公元前150年)(该法规定对盗窃赃物不能因时效取得权利)

Lex Barbara 《巴比伦法》

lex causae 诉因地法

Lex Calpurnia de Precuniis Nepetundis (罗马法)《关于搜刮钱财罪的卡尔布尔尼亚法》[指公元前149年颁布,该法设立了审理搜刮钱财罪的常设刑事法庭(Gqaestio perpetuae),取代过去的人民审判(Iudicium populi)刑事诉讼程序]

Lex Comelia 《考麦利亚法案》(指公元前81年罗马制定的成文法律,规定订立遗嘱能力的丧失,不影响在有能力时订立的遗嘱,同时规定了侵害之诉)

lex commercii 商法,商事法

lex commissoria (罗马法上的合同)解除条款

Lex Consolato 《康索拉度海法》(是10世纪海商习惯法发展的海事惯例集之一。还有 Lex Oleron, Laws of Visby 等)

Lex Danorum 见 Dane-Law

*** Lex de futuro, judex de praeterito.** The law provides for the future, the judge for the past. 法是为未来而制定的,而法官则是为过去而设置的。

Lex de Imperio Vespasiani 《韦斯巴芎谕令权法》[指爱好收藏古董的公证人科拉·李恩佐(Cola di Rienzo,1313—1354年)于1347年在罗马的圣乔万尼拉特兰诺大教堂的一个祭坛上发现被嵌在墙上的刻有《韦斯巴芎谕令权法》的铜表,其长为164厘米,厚4.5厘米,宽113厘米。同年5月,李恩佐发起了一场革命,短暂地建立了罗马共和国,他自任保民官,力图恢复古罗马共和国的辉煌并统一当时破碎的意大利。李恩佐以铜表唤起民众对光荣过去的骄傲。他领导的罗马共和国于1350年终结,其本人于1354年被罗马暴民杀害,但他留下了宝贵遗产《韦斯巴芎谕令权法》。1576年,根据教皇格里高利十三世的谕令,该铜表被移至卡皮托尔山展出,如今它被保存在卡皮托尔山博物馆的 Fauno 厅]

Lex delationes semper exborret. The law always abhors delays. 法律永远憎恨推延。

Lex delicti commisi 犯罪地法

Lex domicilii 住所地法

Lex Duodecim Tabularum 《十二铜表法》(Tabula 1. De in jus vocando 第一表:提传;Tabula 2. De judiciis 第二表:审问;Tabula 3. De aere confesso rebusque judicatis 第三表:偿债;Tabula 4. De jure patrio 第四表:家长权;Tabula 5. De heareditatibus et tuelise 第五表:财产继承及监护;Tabula 6. De dominio et possessione 第六表:所有权及占有;Tabula 7. De jure aedium et agrorum 第七表:家属及土地;Tabula 8. De delicto 第八表:私犯法;Tabula 9. De jure publico 第九表:公法;Tabula 10. De jure sacro 第十表:宗教法;Tabula 11. supplementum 5 priorarum tabularum 第十一表:前五表的补遗;Tabula 12. supplementum 5 posteriorarum tabularum 第十二表:后五表的补遗)

*** Lex est norma recti.** Law is a rule of right. 法是权利的规范,法是正义的准则。

*** Lex est sanctio sancta, jubens honesta, et prohibens contraria.** Law is a sacred sanction, commanding what is right and prohibiting the contrary. 法律是神圣的约束力,是命令要求做正当的事,禁止做不正当的事。

*** Lex est summa ratio.** Law is the highest reason. 法是最高的理性。

*** Lex est tutissima cassis; sub clypeo legis nemo decipitur.** Law is the safest helmet; under the shield of the law no one is deceived. 法律是最安全的钢盔,在此法律的庇护下,无人会被欺骗。

Lex Falcidia 发尔企第阿法案(公元前40年罗马颁布此法,规定继承人的特留份为全部遗产的1/4,这样遗嘱人所为的遗嘱,其总数不得超过全部遗产的3/4等)

* **Lex facit regem.** Law makes the king (i. e., makes the monarch king). 法律造成君主统治。

* **Lex favet doti.** The law favors dower. 法律保护寡妇从亡夫那里获得的财产。

lex ferenda 拟议法,应有法

lex fori 审判地法,法院(庭)地法

lex generalis non derogat legi speciali 特别法优于一般法(或通用法)

* **Lex injusta non est lex.** Any interpretation of the law which makes the law work injustice is bad law. 法之解释构成法律工作不公正者实为坏法。

* **Lex intendit vicinum vicini facta scire.** The law presumes that one neighbor knows the actions of another. 法律推定邻人了解其邻人的行为。

Lex Iulia Iudiciorum Publicorum 《关于公共审判的优利亚法》(是罗马法中的一种法,于公元前17年制定,规定一个人除非自己是受害人,不得同时提出两个控告,主要是为了减少职业控告人的机会)

* **Lex judicat de rebus necessario faciendis quasi de re ipsa factis.** The law judges of things that must necessarily be done as if actually done. 法律判断之事项,一定是必需作为之事项,如同其已经作为。

lex Iulia de bonis cedendis (罗马法)《关于财产让与的优流斯法》[指允许债务人自愿将其全部财产让与债权人,从而避免任何人身性措施(如强制执行)并避免破廉耻,拍卖财产制是导致债务人破廉耻的。该法还允许破产债务人在能够证明自己遭受不可抗力事件而导致财产毁损时,减少其财产让与的额度]

lex lata 现行法

Lex Licinia Sextia 李锡尼亚(乌斯)—赛克斯提亚(乌斯)法案(公元367年罗马制定的民事成文法律,内容为取消平民不能与贵族通婚的限制)

lex loci 属地法,本地(适用的)法(律)

lex loci actus 行为地法

lex loci celebrationis 婚礼举行地法

lex loci contractus 缔约地法

lex loci delicti commissi 侵权行为发生地法

lex loci delictus 罪行发生地法

lex loci domicilii 居住地法

lex loci executionis 合同(契约)履行地法

lex loci rei sitae 物所在地法

lex loci solutionis 合同(契约)履行地法,支付地法

lex mercatoria 商法;商事法,(欧洲中古通行的)商习惯法

* **lex merciorum** 见 Mercen-Lage

lex nationalis 本国法,所属民族的本国法

lex naturale 自然法

* **Lex necessitatis est lex temporis, i. e., instantis.** The law of necessity is the law of time, i. e., time present. 必要的法律即适时的法律。

* **Lex neminem cogit ad vana seu inutilia peragenda.** The law forces no one to do vain or useless things. 法律不强迫任何人做徒劳或无益之事。

* **Lex neminem cogit ostendere quod nescire praesumitur.** The law forces no one to make known what he is presumed not to know. 法律不强迫任何人说出他被推定不了解的情况。

* **Lex nemini facit injuriam.** The law does injury to no one. 法本身并不伤害任何人。

* **Lex nemini operatur iniquum.** The law works injustice to no one. 法的实施不会对任何人不公平。

* **Lex nil facit frustra, nil jubet frustra.** The law does nothing in vain and commands nothing in vain. 法律不为徒劳之事,也不命令人做徒劳之事。

* **Lex non a rege est violanda.** The law is not violated by the king. 国王不可违反法律;法律不可被国王违反。

* **Lex non cogit ad impossibilia; Lex neminem cogit ad impossibilia.** The law does not compel the impossible. 法律不强人所难。

Lex non curat de minimis　法律不计较琐事
* *Lex non debet deficere conguerentibus in justia exhibenda.*　The law aught not to fail in dispensing justice to those with grievance.　法律不应对有冤情的人失去公正。
* *Lex non deficit in justitia exhibenda.*　The law does not fail in showing justice.　法律不容丧失公正面貌。
* *Lex non exacte define, sed anbitrio foni viri permitet.*　The law does not define exactly, but trust in the judgment of a good man.　法律并不作详尽规定，而委诸优秀之人进行裁判；法律规定并不精细入微，它信任公正之人的判断。
* *Lex non favet delicatorum votis.*　The law does not favor the wishes of the fastidious.　法律不能满足挑剔者的愿望。
* *Lex non intendit aliquid impossible.*　The law does not intend anything impossibile.　法律不强求任何不可能之事。
* *Lex non novit patrem, nec matrem; solam varitatem.*　The law knows neither father nor mother, only the truth.　法律知道既非父亦非母而只是真理。
* *Lex non patitur fractiones et divisiones statuum.*　The law does not tolerate fractions and divisions of estates.　法律不容忍肢解财产；法律不允许肢解财。
* *Lex non requirit verificari quod apparet curiae.*　The law does not require that to be verified (or proved) which is apparent to the court.　法对于法庭认为明显的事，并不要求加以证明或证实。
lex non scripta　不成文法，习惯法，普通法
lex onginis　本地法
lex patriae　本国法，国内法
lex personalis　属人法
* *Lex plus laudatur quando ratione probatur.*　The law is more praised when it is consonant with reason.　法律愈加理性愈受到赞扬。
Lex poetetia de nexis　波提利阿法案（指公元 326 年罗马制定的民事成文法律，内容为废除债务奴役制）

* *Lex posterior derogat priori.*　A later statute takes away the effect of a prior one.　后法废除前法。（又译:后法优于前法。）
* *Lex posterior generalis non derogat legis priori speciali.*　后制定的普通法不废除原有的特别法（大陆法原则，这里普通法亦可译做一般法或普遍适用的法，指与特别法相对而言）。
lex praetoria　裁判官法
* *Lex prospicit, non respicit.*　The law looks forward, not backward.　法是向前看的，而不是向后看的（即法不溯及既往）。
* *Lex punit mendacium.*　The law punishes falsehood.　法惩罚虚假和不诚实。
lex regia　王权法（根据此法罗马人民授予皇帝最高权力）
lex rei sitae　物所在地法
* *Lex rejicit superflua, pugnantia, incongrua.*　The law rejects superfluous, contradictory, and incongruous things.　法律拒绝多余的、互相矛盾的和不一致的事物。
* *Lex reprobat moram.*　The law disapproves of delay.　法律不允许迟延。
* *Lex respicit aequitatem.*　The law regards equity.　法律尊重公平。
Lex Rhodia　《罗得海法》（最早的海上习惯法）
lex Rhodia de jactu　罗得弃货损失分担规则（指源自《罗得海法》中的一项规则，是现代共同海损分担请求权的基础。见 Sea-Law of Rhodes）
Lex Ripuaria　《利浦安法》[现残存的古老的日耳曼法典，约在公元 600 年编纂，亦译:墨普利安法典（Les Ripuaria）]
lex salica　《萨利克法》（现残存的最古老的日耳曼法典）（约在公元 500 年）
lex saxonum　（古代的）撒克逊法（为古代撒克逊法律汇编，于公元 800 年前后编成。共 20 章，内容包括刑罚问题）
lex scripta　成文法，制定法
* *Lex semper dabit remedium.*　The law always gives a remedy.　（普通法上的箴言）法律总是给予救济；法律在于救济。
Lex semper intendit quod convenit rationi.　The law always intends what is agreeable to

reason. 法律总是指望合理之事。
lex situs (= *lex rei sitae*) 物所在地法
lex situs to **immovables** 不动产依物之所在地法
lex solutionis （合同）履行地法
lex specialis 特殊法
* *Lex specialis derogat generali.* 特别法优于普通法（大陆法原则）。
* *Lex spectat naturae ordinem.* The law regards the order of nature. 法律尊重自然秩序。
* *Lex succurrit ignoranti.* The law aids the ignorant. 法帮助不知情者。
* *Lex succurrit minoribus.* The law aids minors. 法帮助未成年者。
lex talons (talionis) 同态复仇法[即以眼还眼、以牙还牙的治罪方法，最早存在于"旧约"(Old Testment)问世时代]
lex terrae 国内法（相当于 law of the land）
Lex Theodosii 《狄奥多西法典》
* *Lex uno ore omnes alloquitur.* The law addresses all with one (the same) mouth or voice. 法对一切（人）都是用同一个声音讲话的（意思是指法律面前人人平等）。
* *Lex vigilantibus, non dormientibus, subvenit.* Law aids the watchful, not the sleeping. 法律帮助有警觉者，而非昏沉者。
lex voluntatis 当事人自己选择的法律；当事人选择适用的法律
Lex, Rex 法即王[中世纪欧洲提出的法律至上(the supremacy of law)和法即王的观念，其权威甚至高于国王]
lexer n. （美）法科大学生
lexicon n. 字典（尤指拉丁、希伯来、希腊语等）
Lexis （美）莱克西斯计算机系统[指 1923 年起即由 Mead Data 中心公司在全国范围销售的计算机检索服务系统。这些服务包括 1970 年直至最近的所有联邦最高法院的判决和裁定，它是以最快速度提供联邦最高法院的判决（判例）的检索通道]
Lexis Nexis （美）Lexis Nexis 数据库[指米德数据中心（Mead Data Central）公司于 1973 年创建的数据库，是面向全国的法律文献检索服务系统。它包括联邦最高法院自 1970 年至今的所有判决的全文。联邦最高法院的判决在宣判以后均以电子传输方式立即送到该检索系统，所以，通过 Lexis Nexis 数据库可以检索到联邦最高法院当天的判决。这些判决也可通过 Lexis Nexis 数据库的综合联邦图书馆（GENFED）在一个名叫"USLED"的文档下进行查询。用户还可通过因特网进入 Lexis Nexis 数据库。通过布兰(Boolean)连接，以关键词、短语和单词组合等方式搜索、查询判决引文或全文并可打印下载。Lexis Nexis 是美国两大商业数据库系统之一，另一为 Westlaw，它们都被法学院和法律实务部门作为综合检索工具广泛地应用]
lewd house 见 disorderly house 2
ley 法律；宣誓
ley de nature 自然法
ley escripte 成文法
ley gager 宣誓断讼法；法律担保
leze majesty 叛逆罪；叛乱罪
liability n. 责任；义务；负担；不利、缺点；(复)债务；负债；资产负债表上的债务；赔偿责任；不利条件
liability accident 责任事故
liability and asset 负债与资产
liability clause 责任条款；债务条款
liability company 责任公司
liability for acceptance 承兑责任
liability for auxiliaries 辅助人责任（指《欧洲侵权法原则》中第六章"替代责任"中规定的"辅助人责任"）
liability for breach of non-contractual duties 违反非合同义务的责任
liability for damage by animals 因动物所造成损害的责任
liability for damage caused by means of transport 由运输工具所造成损害的责任
liability for defective equipment 提供有缺陷设备的责任
liability for defective premises （租让）有缺陷房产的责任
liability for delay 迟延责任，延误责任

liability for endorsement 背书责任
liability for failure to act 不作为的刑事责任
liability for fault 过失责任
liability for injuries caused by an agent 代理人造成的损害责任
liability for loss 对损失所负责任
liability for reduced chance 减少有机会的责任
liability for satisfaction 清偿责任
liability for the risk of loss 损失险责任
liability for tort 侵权责任
liability for unavoidable accident 对不可避免事故的责任
liability for wrong 不法行为责任,侵权责任
liability insurance 责任保险(指预防投保人可能产生损失和损害的保险)
liability insurance factor 责任保险因素(见 later intervention)
liability insurance premium 责任保险费
liability insurer 责任保险承保人
liability limits 责任范围,责任限度;债务限额
liability of drunken person for crimes 酗酒者对犯罪行为的责任
liability of drunken person for torts 酗酒者的侵权行为责任
liability of guardian 监护人的责任
liability of handling vehicles to other road-uses 驾驶车辆对其他公路使用人的责任
liability of infants for torts 未成年人对侵权行为的责任
liability of insane persons for torts 精神病患者对侵权行为的责任
liability of motor-vehicle operator 机动车辆司机的责任
liability of occupiers of land to visitors 土地占有者对观光客的责任
liability of suppliers to consumers 供应者对消费者的责任
liability rule 责任规则[指卡—梅框架的三项规则之一,另两项规则为财产规则和禁易规则。卡—梅框架的所谓责任规则是指只要愿意支付一个客观确定的价值,就可消灭一个初始法益。也就是说,法益的转移不再仅仅取决于当事人之间的自愿定价,而是由法律设定"买断"或"卖断"价格。这时,法益实际上被划分为两半,一半是法益拥有者的求偿权,即法定情形发生时,可以从法益剥夺者那里获得赔偿的权利;另一半是法益相对人的征用权,即法定情形发生时,可以通过支付法定价格,从法益拥有者那里合法取得法益的权利。法益拥有者的求偿权和法益相对人的征用权往往规定在同一条文或判例规则之中,但常各自表述,彼此独立。法律上规定的法定情形,不仅包括意外事故或紧急情况,也包括公共利益需要格外保护的常规情况。这里的"法定价格"在法律上常为如下类型:损害赔偿金、无因管理合理赔偿、不当得利之返还、征用的合理赔偿,等等。既然责任规则剥夺了法益拥有者的自愿定价权利,就只能由其他机构(常常是法院)进行强制定价。对于法益的"法定价格"(客观价格)如何评估,责任规则通常由法院在具体案件的审理中适用,但有时政府的特定部门,乃至个人自己,都可能被法律赋予评估"客观价格"的职责或权力。法律上适用责任规则的典型例子甚多,如不当得利、无因管理、过失侵权、征用和征收、添附、紧急避险、法定许可、强制缔约,等等。从权利的剥夺和补偿的相互顺序来看,不当得利、无因管理、过失侵权、添附和紧急避险,适用的都是先剥夺后补偿型的责任规则,而征用、征收、法定许可、强制缔约,则是先补偿后剥夺型的责任规则。与财产规则不同的是,责任规则之下,一个私人主体拥有的不再是一项完整的无限权利,而是一个在法定情形下可以被他人以法定赔偿强行剥夺的有限权利]
liability to give evidence 提供证据的责任
liability to national taxation 国税的纳税义务
liability to pay compensation 赔偿责任
liability to punishment 受惩罚的责任,刑事责任
liability to rates (地方税的)纳税义务
liability without fault 无过失责任(见

strict liability)
liable a. 1.有(法律)责任的;(财产等)可受(法律)处理的 2.应受罚的;应付税的(to);有义务的 3.可能遭受的 4.易于……的;有倾向的(to)
liable jointly and severally 负共同连带责任
liable on bill of exchange 承担汇票上的义务
liable on conviction upon（或 **on**）**indictment** 被检控罪名成立
liable to（**a fine** 或 **a term of imprisonment**） 应科(罚金或徒刑)
libel n./v. 1.诽谤,诽谤罪;文字诽谤,书面诽谤 2.(海事法)原告的诉状 3.侮辱,对人不公/1.诽谤;用文字诽谤 2.(向海事法庭或宗教裁判所)起诉
libel action 诽谤诉讼,诽谤行为
libel cases 诽谤的案件
libel suits 诽谤的诉讼
libel with big character posters (中)用大字报诽谤
libel(l)ant n. 1.诽谤者 2.(向海事法庭或宗教裁判所提出控诉的)控告人(原告)
libel(l)ee n. 1.被诽谤者 2.(在海事法庭或宗教裁判所)被控告者(被告)
libel(l)er n. 诽谤者
libel(l)ist n. 诽谤者
libellus famosus 文字诽谤;毁损名誉之印刷品
Libellus inscriptionis (检举人)制作起诉书
libellus repudii 离婚证书
libel(l)ous a. 诽谤的,诽谤性的,中伤的;受诽谤的
liber 簿册,契据登记册
Liber Assisarum 《判例大全》(见 Book of Assizes)
Liber Judiciorum 《民法大全》(指西哥德人的法典,由雷塞斯温国王于 654 年颁布,后成为中世纪西班牙法的基础)
libera 自由,免税,豁免
libera batella 自由捕鱼权
liberal a. 自由主义的;宽大的;慷慨的;充分的;不严格的,不受拘束的,无拘束的;不拘泥字句的;(大写)自由党员
liberal activist 自由的激进者

liberal approach 宽松处理方法,自由方式,轻松方法
liberal construction（或 **interpretation**） 任意解释,扩大解释,广义解释
Liberal Democrats 自由民主党人[在美国,民主党(Democrats)人中,有的敢于称自己为自由民主党人。但第一大中间偏左政党的成员也被称为自由民主党人(Liberal Democrats)。然而这两个组织的准确称呼应分别为: Democratic Party 和 Liberal Democrat Party]
liberal end of the Court 联邦最高法院的自由主义残余
liberal exemption 自由豁免
liberal intellectual system 自由智力体制,开放的理性制度
liberal justice 自由主义的大法官
liberal legalism 自由主义的法条观(指美国学者杜鲁贝克和加兰特对其理论预设进行的概括:①社会由个人组成,国家基于个人的同意而存在,并以实现个人的福祉为最高目的;②国家基于法律而控制个人行为,国家本身也受法律控制;③法律旨在实现目标,平等保护全体成员的核心利益,所有人都有权参与法律制定过程;④在法律适用上,人人平等;⑤立法机构负责立法,行政机构负责执法,法院负责司法,法院是法律秩序的中心;⑥社会成员应普遍遵守法律,官方行为尤其应符合法律规定。他们称这些理论预设为"自由主义的法条观")
liberal licensing 自由许可制
liberal notice pleading rules 自由告知诉辩规则
Liberal Party (英)自由党(其前身为当年的辉格党)
liberal state 自由国家,自由主义国家
liberal voting 自由表决记录
liberal-democratic a. 自由民主的
liberal-democratic government 自由民主政府
Liberal-Democratic Party (日)自由民主党
liberalism n. 自由主义[在政治理论和法律对策的讨论中,该词具有广泛的意义,即指那种强调个人权利的政府理论和社

会政策。与之相反的为保守主义(conservatism)理论,它强调的是传统、习惯和权威的重要性。另外,从狭隘上理解,"自由主义"也指一种特殊的左派观点和激进的政治观点(通常它支持平等主义,认为政府有责任赞助贫困人群,支持收入的再分配以及类似的政策)]

liberalist n. 自由主义者
liberalistic a. (倾向于)自由主义的
liberalization n. 自由化,放宽范围
liberalization of exchange 外汇自由化
liberalization of interest rates 放宽利率
liberalization of trade 贸易自由化
liberalize v. 1.使自由主义化,使自由化 2.放宽……范围(或限制);解除(官方对)……控制
liberalize the conditions of loans 放宽贷款条件

* *Libertas est potestas faciendi id quod jure licet.* Liberty is the power of doing that which the law permits. 自由是法律允准范围行为的权力。

* *Libertas est res inestimabilis.* Liberty is an inestimable thing. 自由为无价之宝;自由无价。

Liberate (英)利勃雷特令状
liberate rolls (英)令状档案(指国家档案局保存的1201—1436年的大法官发出的令状档案)
liberation n. 1.解放;取消合同(契约);免除责任 2.支付
liberation front 解放阵线
liberation on parole 宣誓释放
liberationism n. 政教分离主义
liberationist n. 政教分离主义者
liberi 1.(撒克逊法)自由民;自由土地保有人 2.(大陆法)子(包括女、孙子、孙女)
liberi justi 婚生子
liberi non justi 非婚生子
libertarian n. 自由意志论者,鼓吹思想和行动自由的人
liberte' d' opinion 意见自由(相当于 freedom of expression)
liberticide n. 扼杀自由;扼杀自由者
liberties of the subject (联合王国的)臣民的自由权利

liberty n. 自由,自由权,特许权;自由区域,特许区域(尤指英国一些城市中享有某种司法、行政特权的区域);(复)特权,特典;特惠;(对规章等的)违反行为
liberty in perpetuity 终身特许权;(英)永久性的特许辖区
liberty man 获准上岸的海员
liberty of assembly 集会自由
liberty of association 结社自由
liberty of commerce 商业自由
liberty of conscience 宗教信仰自由
liberty of prisoners (囚犯的)狱外居住地
liberty of speech 言论自由
liberty of the press 出版自由
liberty to apply 自由实施令
liberty to marry 婚姻自由
liberty to move within the country 国内迁徙自由
liberty under the law 法律下的自由
liberty within the family 家族成员自由
liberum maritagium 见 frank-marriage
liberum tenementum (普通法程序中的)自由保有土地权的请求
liberum veto 自由否决权
library lending right 出借图书作者受偿权
libration n. 天平动(空间法)
licencable (=licensable) a. 可获准许可的,可被认可的;放纵的;准许的
licence (=license) n./v. 许可,特许,认可;许可证,特许证;执照;牌照;特许权;放纵,准许/准许,批准;发给许可证
licence by estoppel (一经颁发就)不得退回的特许证
license cases 许可(证)系列案[是"瑟诺诉马萨诸塞州案""弗莱彻诉罗得岛州案"和"皮尔斯诉新罕布什尔州案"的合称。许可系列案涉及马萨诸塞州、罗得岛州和新罕布什尔州有关对进入该州的酒精饮料征税或进行管制的法律的合法性问题。这些法律对当地的零售商予以照顾。该案的问题是,这些法律侵犯了联邦对州际商业活动的控制,还是其治安权的正当行使。联邦最高法院一致同意维护各州的权力。许可系列案件形成了托尼时代联

邦最高法院被称为"选择性排斥"(selective exclusiveness)原则的妥协政策的构架,直到"新政"(New Deal)时期联邦权力取代州权力为止,这一原则都影响着商业权力(commerce power)的运用]

licence contract (或 **agreement**) 许可合同(契约)(或特许权协议)(指具有专有权的无形财产转让的主要形式)
licence duplicate 执照副本
licence duty 牌照税,执照税
licence fee 执照费,牌照费
licence for the export of commodities 出口货物许可证
licence for use 使用牌照
licence of export 出口许可证
licence of import 进口许可证
licence plate (或 **tag**) (汽车)牌照
licence system 许可证制度
licence to conduct trade and industry 经营工商业的执照
licence to engage in trade 营业许可证
licence to exploit the patented invention 利用专利发明许可证
licence to practice 开业执照
licence to sell excisable liquids 应纳执照税的酒类的销售许可证
licence to use land (英)土地使用许可状
licenced (= licensed) a. 领有执照的;特许的
licenced broker 特许经纪人
licenced dealer 持证交易人,特许交易人
licenced gambling 公共赌博业
licensed jurisconsult 特许的法律学者,特别授权的法学家
licenced practical nurse 持照护士,持牌护士
licenced premises (英)特许的卖烟酒处
licenced prostitution 公娼(制度)
licenced technology 许可转让的技术
licenced warehouse 持有执照的货栈(或仓库)
licencee (=licensee) n. 许可证接受人,被许可人;领有执照者
licencee estoppel 许可证接受人不得推翻原议;权利人无提出异议之权
licences to use patented processes 使用专

利工序的许可证
licencing agreement 许可证协议
licencing jurisdiction 特许裁判权;特许管辖权
licencing operation 颁发许可证业务
licencing system for MTO 发给联运人执照的制度
license tax 特许征税
license to use software 软件使用许可证
licensing (15 世纪)1.许可证交易[指许可证销售授权他人使用(如同计算机软件),该许可是知识产权(版权、专利或商标权)的保护]2.颁发许可证执照(指由政府部门颁发执照的程序,亦称为 licensure)
licensing scheme 颁发许可证计划
licensor (=licenser) n. 许可者;颁发许可证(或执照)者,有权批准执照的人
licensure n. 发给执照(尤指开业执照)(见 licensing 2)
licentiate n. (专门职业)有开业资格者;领有开业执照者
licentious a. 放纵的,无法无天的;不守法的
licentiousness n. 无法无天,放任不拘;放荡淫秽
licit a. 合法的,正当的
licit traffic 合法买卖
lictor n. (古罗马)侍从官(按现代方式持束棒和斧子为长官清道,并协助处罚罪犯的小吏。斧子象征执法官拥有对民众生杀和肉体惩罚大权。见 *imperium*)
Lidford (或 **Lydford**) **justice** 私刑(指英国旧时有 Lidford law, Jedwood justice, Jedburgh justice 和 Jeddart justice 者,与美国的 Lynch law 相似。见 lynch law)
lie v. 1.展现,伸展 2.处于某种状态;存在,所在,位于 3.(船)停泊 4.成立;给予;(案件)可受理 5.说谎,欺骗,作假
lie at sb.'s door (过失,罪责)归于某人
lie detection technique (或 **brain fingerprinting**) 测谎技术
lie detector 测谎器
lie in franchise 专项特许处理(指不用法院帮助,即可将遗弃赃物、迷途牲畜等没收)

lie in grant 依授予文据转移处理(无体遗产)
lie in livery 按让渡处理(有体遗产)
lie in one's teeth 撒大谎
liege a. (封建制度)君主的,有权受臣服的;有臣服义务的;忠诚的
liege lord 君主,王侯
liege man 臣子;忠诚的追随者
liege subjects 臣下
lien n. 留置权,质权,抵押权;优先权(指债权人在债务人的特定财产上设置的一种权益担保,到债务清偿时止,如债务人逾期清偿,则债权人可通过变卖留置物等按法定程序优先得到清偿。见 pledge)
lien creditor 有抵押(财产)权的债权人
lienholder n. 留置权人,留置权的持有人,留置权的所有人
lien of covenant 合同(契约)留置权
lien on cargo 对船货的留置权
lienor n. 有留置权者,有抵押权者
lieu n. 场所;(一般用于 in lieu of)替代
lieu and substitution 替代和更换(指文件内容之更换,如遗嘱条文的更替)
lieutenant governor (省或地区的)代理总督(亦译省督或副总督);(美)副州长
life n. 生命,性命;一生;生存;生计,生活;寿命;人生;无期(徒刑)
life annuity 终身年金(生存时每年可得的养老金)
life appointment 终身任职
life assets 终身资产
life assurance (英)人寿保险
Life Assurance Act 《人身保险法》(指英国国会1774年制定的人身保险法)
life cycle assessment 生命周期评价
life cycle hypothesis 生命周期假说
life estate 终身地产;终身财产(指限于本人生存时管理产业,而不允许继承者)
life expectancy 平均寿命
life history 生活史,生活经历
life imprisonment 终身监禁,无期徒刑
life in being (1836年)生存期(与perpetuities相对)[(在普通法和制定法中)按禁止永久权的规则,某人生存期对未来的权益是成立的,不管该人的利益是否存在于不动产之中。在契约或遗嘱生效时期,某人生命存续期间即为生存期。见 measuring life]
life insurance 人寿(身)保险
life insurance in the event of death 人寿(身)保险中的死亡保险
life interest 终身权益;非世袭终身财产拥有者的财产权
(the) life of a free-willing being 一个自由意志人的生命,一个自由意志人的生活
life of a person 人的生命
life of agreement 合同期
life of an execution (令状)执行期
life of assets 资产寿命
life of franchise (美)特许期限
life of loan 借款期限
life of parliament 议会任期
life of the community 社会生活
life of writ 令状有效期
life office 人寿(身)保险公司,人寿(身)保险办事处
life peerage 终身贵族的爵位,非世袭贵族
life policy 人寿(身)保险单
life senator 终身参议员
life sentence 无期徒刑(判决)
life sentence with parole 有假释的终身刑
life sentence without parole 没有假释的终身刑
life tenancy 终身租赁
life tenant 终身租借人,土地终身占有人
life tenure 终身租用;终身职,终身任期;终身占有
life termer 无期徒刑犯
life-force n. 生命力
life-qualified jury (刑法)生命合格陪审团[指在死刑案件中,如果刑事被告被判决有罪,法官在陪审团名册(venire)中已经剔除任一不可能或不愿意考虑替代死刑的终身监禁的人而挑选组成的陪审团。见 death-qualified jury]
life-saving n. 救生,救生用品
life-support machine 生命维护器官,生命支持器官
life-sustaining procedure 生命维持程序

（指运用医疗或人工方法维持、恢复生命活力，主要在于延缓死期）

lifer n. 无期徒刑犯；无期徒刑；职业军人

lifelong capacity 毕生的行为能力，终身的行为能力

lifestyle (=life-style) n. 生活方式

lift v. 1.提高，使升góng 2.(美)赎(典当物)；清偿，偿付 3.扒窃；剽窃 4.解除(禁令)，撤销 5.运送，空运 6.耸立

lift a curfew 撤销宵禁

lift up one's voice 叫嚷，抗议

lifter n. 小偷；起重机

ligan 见 lagan

ligature strangulation 勒死，绞死

light n./a. 1.光，光线，日光 2.采光权(又译光线不受阻碍权，指他人不得用建筑物等遮蔽权利享有人的窗户光线) 3.白天，白昼 4.明白，见解 5.名家，权威，著名的人 6.信号灯，灯塔/轻的；轻微的；容易担负的；少量的；不重要的

light house due 灯塔税

light industry enterprise 轻工企业

light offense 轻罪

light punishment 轻刑，轻刑罚，轻的惩处

light sentence 轻判

lighter n. 驳船；点火的人（或物）

lighterage n. 驳运费；驳船装卸；驳运

ligula 法庭案卷或文件副本或复印件

like a./prep./n. 相似的，相同的，同类的/(好像)就要，可能；像，如同样的人或事物

like cases treated alike 同案同判[指"同案同判"原本就是"同等情况同样对待(like treated a like)"在司法领域的具体化。理论家也会以同样的方式来辩护自己的主张。见 integrity(原则一贯性)]

like product 同类产品[GATT/WTO 的长期司法实践中对同类产品的判定逐渐形成了一些特定标准：在既定市场上的产品最终用途；消费者的品位、喜好、习惯，对产品的认知及行为反应等；产品的物理特性、性质和质量等；产品分类的关税分类表。这些因素可用以确定产品的同类性，亦可称为确定产品同类性的传统标准(traditional criteria)]

like service providers 同类服务提供者(指 GATT 第 17 条第 1 款规定的"同类服务提供者"。根据该款规定，中国需要对同类服务的外国服务和服务提供者给予与本国服务及服务提供者相同的待遇)

like situation 相似情形

like-kind exchange (1963年)同类的贸易交易，同类的商业交易；同类的投资财产交易；一种不征税的交易[指贸易、商业或投资财产的交易(盘存存货或证券除外)，以便于同类、同级别、同性质的财产交易，除非收到现金或其他财产，否则此类交易不应征税]

like-kind property 同类的财产[(税务)与其他财产相比属于相似类别、等级或性质的财产，从此类财产交易中获得的利益不征收美国联邦所得税。见 like-kind exchange]

likelihood n. 可能性，可能

likelihood of confusion (商品)混淆的可能性

likelihood-of-confusion test (商标)商标混淆可能性测试[指基于一种可能性，即实质性的数码对于一般谨慎的买者来说存在被误导或被混淆的可能性，而产生的对商标侵权(trademark infringement)进行测试]

likelihood-of-confusion test (商标)混淆的可能性标准(是判定冒用商标侵权的标准。即当某商标侵犯了较早产品的商标权时，是否有相当多的正常谨慎的消费者有可能在产品来源等方面被误导或产生困惑)

likelihood-of-success-on-the-merits test (民诉)案件是非曲直的成功可能性测试，案件的实质依据成功可能性检验[指在上诉时，寻求预防禁制令(preliminary injunction)或寻求阻碍有效判决的诉讼当事方的一项法规(rule)，它必须表明在诉讼或上诉过程中成功的合理可能性]

Likonomics 李克强经济学[当今时代，经济状况决定着一国的发展水平，而领导人所推行的经济政策则往往对国家的经济走向产生重大影响。由此，一些以领导人名字命名的词应运而生，前有"Reaganomics"(里根经济学)和"Abenomics"(安倍经济学),如今有"Likonomics"(李克强经济学),是由英国巴克莱资本公司在其发表的一份报告中创造的新词,表示李克强总理为中国制定的经济增长计划。该词条代表着用短痛换取长期的益处,它有三个重要支柱:"no stimulus"(不出台刺激措施)、"deleveraging"(去杠杆化)以及"structural reform"(结构性改革)。前两大支柱可能正在造成痛苦,但它们对于为中国的结构性改革铺平道路却有重要作用]

limb n. 四肢;顽童;身体
limb of the law 执法人员(指警察、律师或法官)
limbo n. 1.监狱,拘禁 2.忘却,遗弃 3.中间过渡状态
limine out 不采纳,排斥[指法院一开始允准动议,即不采纳证据。如审理法官不采纳大多数原告的医疗记录(The trial judge limined out most of the plaintiff's medical records)]
limine 见 in limine
limit n./v. 界限,界线,限定,限制;范围,限度,极限/限定,限制;确定,确切指派
limit an estate over to sb. 将一份产业明确判给某人
limit down (价位)跌幅
limit for the use 使用范围
limit of authority 权限
limit of competency 权限
limit of debate 辩论范围
limit of financial capacity 财力负担限度
limit of liability 责任限额(指限定负担责任的最高限额)
limit of one's functions and powers 职权范围
limit of stay 逗留期限
limit on detention 羁押范围
limit on state power 州权的范围
limit price 限定价格
limit up (价位)涨幅
limitable a. 可限制的
limitary a. 有限的,有界限的;限制的;界限的
limitation n. 1.(法定的)提起诉讼的限期;诉讼时效;时效,(法律规定的)有效期 2.限度;限制,局限;限制因素
Limitation Act 《时效法》
limitation clause 责任限制条款,责任范围条款
limitation fund 处理船主责任范围以外的索赔基金
limitation in law 法律时效
limitation limit 责任的最高限度
limitation of action 诉讼时效
limitation of births 生育限制
limitation of claims 诉权时效,请求权的时效
limitation of copyright 版权限制(指法定许可、强制许可、合理使用的版权限制,与restriction of copyright同义,在《伯尔尼公约》中指一国对另一保护水平低的国家或非公约成员国版权保护上的保留)
limitation of debate 辩论范围
limitation of estate 财产限制
limitation of liability 责任限度,责任范围
limitation of prosecution 追诉时效
limitation of sanction 制裁时效,处分时效
limitation of time 时效
limitation on all authority 对所有权利的限制(或制约)
limitation on government 有限政府
limitation on sovereignty 主权限制
limitation on strategic nuclear weapons 限制战略核武器
limitation period 时效期限
limitative a. 限制(性)的
limited a. 有限制的,有限度的;有限责任的;特别的
limited administration 有限制的遗产管理
limited agency 有限代理
limited appearance 部分时间出庭,有限的出庭
limited but unambiguous right of transit 有限但明确之过境权利
limited capacity to act 限制行为能力
limited circumstance in 特定情况下,有限情况下
limited commitment 有限的使命
limited community of property 有限的

夫妻共同财产制
limited company 有限公司
limited court (由法律规定的)专门法院(庭)
limited divorce (判决不规定扶养费的)限制性解除婚姻关系;(无权重婚的)有限制(夫妻)分居
limited executor 有限制的遗嘱执行人(指被限制在某种范围或时间内来执行死者遗嘱的人)
limited fee 限制继承的地产
limited government (美)立宪政治,立宪政体,有限(权力)政府(指该政府仅仅拥有并行使那些为宪法所明和规定的权力,而这些权力均为美国人民所赋予的)
limited immunity 限制(性)豁免
limited in private rights 民事权利的限制,私权的限制
limited interest 有限权益
limited judicial review 有限的司法审查
limited (或 special) jurisdiction (由法律规定的)特定(或专门)管辖权,特定(或专门)裁判权
limited legacy 有限制的遗赠
limited legal capacity 有限制的权利能力;有限制的行为能力
limited legal personality 有限制的法律人格
limited liability 有限责任
limited liability company (law) 有限责任公司(简称有限公司)(法)
Limited Liability Company (美)有限责任公司(指一种起源于美国的依据有限责任公司法设立的新型企业组织形式,是迄今为止将传统公司的有限责任屏障和合伙的税收待遇结合起来的最完美形式。作为一种制度,有限责任公司可视为数种传统公司的杂交产品,除具有有限责任公司的基本特征,如投资者的责任有限以外,其在税法上的重要特点是不需要双重纳税,即有限责任公司本身不是一个纳税主体,其税负仅从所有人的个人报税单上体现出来;另一个特点是公司内部管理机构设置比较灵活,公司内部的权利、义务主要基于公司章程的规定。缩略为LLC)
limited means 有限方法,有限经费(资金);特定手段
limited monarchy 有限君主制,君主立宪政体
limited or qualified utilitarianism 有限的或限制的功利主义
limited owner (英)有限制的所有人(指终身土地保有人享有限定继承权;或者丈夫对亡妻的收益权;或者不拥有可绝对处分的有条件继承的财产权)
limited ownership 有限制的所有权
limited participation 有限参与
limited partner 有限责任合伙人,有限责任股东
limited partnership 有限合伙,两合公司;(英)《有限合伙法》(1907年);隐名合伙
limited partnership certificate 两合公司证书,有限合伙证书
limited partnership on (或 with) **shares** 股份有限合伙,股份两合公司
limited payment 有限支付
limited period of imprisonment 有期徒刑
limited personal easement 有限人役权
limited policy 有限赔偿保险单(指载明某项损失不予赔偿的保险单)
limited political power 有限政治权力
limited power of appointment (1830年)限定委托权,限定指定权(指要么不允许转让全部资产,要么限制转让资产给某人的指定权或委托权。该权力的行使只能由被指定授予权力者指定给有利于创设该权利的文件中所指定的人员,而不能指定某人或某人的资产。该词亦可缩略为 limited power,亦称 special power of appointment)
limited probate 有限制的遗嘱检验
limited prohibition 有限制的禁令
limited property right (大陆法)有限物权
limited recognition 有限制的承认
limited recourse 有限追索权
limited responsibility 有限责任
limited sovereignty 有限主权
limited state 受限制的国家
limited succession 限定继承
limited suffrage 有限制的选举权
limited territorial sovereignty 有限领土主权

limited tort liability 有限侵权责任
limited war 有限战争
limiting retributivism 限制性报应主义[刑罚的一种理论,正义之该当(just desert)对于刑罚常具有基础性的作用,不论是决定性的还是限制性的,抑或仅仅是限制性的,正义之该当至少是限制性的原则,正如美国法律协会对《示范刑法典》进行修正所确立的"限制性报应主义"的刑罚分配原则一样,对于其他功利性目的的考虑不能超过正义之该当。刑罚不能重于必要性之要求]
limitless a. 无限制的,无限的
limitrophe a. 位于边界上的;有相邻边界的
limitrophe countries 相邻国
limits of the constitution 宪法所允许的范围
limping family law relationship 跛脚家庭法律关系[指由于各国法律关于当事人婚姻家庭权的内容和实现程度之规定各异,必然会导致所谓"跛脚家庭法律关系",为了避免由此导致对当事人不利影响,《欧洲人权公约》第8条采取"尊重私人和家庭生活的权利"(right to respect for private and family life)]
limping marriage 不稳定婚姻(指需经乙国法院承认甲国法院所作认婚姻效力的判决的婚姻,否则婚姻可能在甲国有效,而在乙国无效)
linchpin of the constitution (美)《宪法的关键》
Lincoln's Inn (英)林肯律师学院
Lindbergh Act 见 Federal Kidnapping Act
line n. 线,界线(土地)边界;路线;界线,方式;运输路线;(固定路线的)运输公司;血统,家系,亲系;行业;皮肤上的条纹,皱纹;掌纹;设计草图(复)外形,轮廓;(复)运气,命运;(复)结婚证书
line haul (由启运地至目的地的)陆地运输(包括公路和铁路)
line of actual control on the border 边界实际控制线
line of business 商业范围,营业范围
line of business test 经营范围标准(1939年,该标准在 Guth v. Loft Inc.一案获得说明,接着又在一组相关案件中得到适用。之后又由《哈佛法学评论》作了论述,从而使该标准扩大影响,成为检验某种机会是否为公司机会的最重要标准。美国特拉华州法院认为:"公司从事某种行业,如果面临这样的机会,即公司对于从事此项活动拥有基本的知识、实际经验和能力,或就其财务状况而言,理所当然地适宜从事此项业务,并且该机会符合公司的实际需要和扩展业务的愿望,那么该机会就可以恰当地视为该公司的经营范围")
line of credit 信用透支额,通融额度,信用额度
line of duty 值勤;公务
line of least resistance 最简便的方法
line-item veto 逐项否决(又称:部分否决)
linea 血统,家系,亲系;继承血亲(见 descent)
linea ascendantiun 祖辈血亲,祖先系,尊血亲;直系尊亲属,直系长辈
linea descendantium 卑血亲,卑族系;直系卑亲属,直系晚辈
linea descent 直系,直系血亲,直系继承
linea obliqua 旁系,旁系血亲
linea recta 直系,直系血亲
linea superior 尊血亲,祖先系,祖辈血亲
linea transversalis 旁系,旁系血亲
lineage n. 血统,世系
lineal a. 直系的;世袭的;继承的;属同一世系的
lineal ascendants 直系尊亲属
lineal consanguinity 直系亲属
lineal descendent 直系卑亲属;直系后裔
lineal descent 直系后裔;直系血统
lineal heir 直系继承人(指既是直系亲属,又是死者后裔如父母或子女。见 collateral heir)
lineal kin 直系亲属
lineal relation by blood (up to the third degree relationship) 三代以内旁系血亲,直系血亲
lineal relative 直系亲属
lineal warranty 直系亲属担保;被继承人的担保书
linear (lineal) descendants 直系卑亲属,

直系晚辈
Liner Conference 班轮工会(指两个或两个以上的航运公司为在特定地理范围内同一或数条航线上提供货物运输的国际班轮服务,通过任何协议或安排,按统一的运费及任何其他有关提供班轮服务的协议条件经营业务而组成的国际海运垄断组织)
linger v. 逗留,徘徊;拖延;苟延;把……推延
linkage n. 联系,联销,联动;联动装置
linked transaction 连环交易,连锁贸易
L'institut de Droit International 国际法学会
lion's share 最大的份额
lip print 口唇纹,口唇印痕
liquid a. (1879年)1.流动的(资产),可以变换成现金 2.(人或单位)拥有的资产可以变换成现金
liquid assets 流动资产
liquid capital 流动资本,活动资本
liquid fund 流动资金
liquid reserve 流动储备金
liquid securities 流动证券
liquidate v. 消灭,清除;清偿;取消;了结(债务);清算,(破产企业等的)清理;将资产变换现金
liquidated a. (18世纪)1.已清偿的,已结清的(指按合同清偿的债务或一笔款项) 2.可变换成现金的一项资产或一笔财富
liquidated account 清偿的账户(指账户的财产通过协议或法律已被清楚地查清确认)
liquidated damages 已判定的损害赔偿金,约(协)定的损害赔偿金
liquidated damages provision (合同的)预定损害赔偿条款
liquidated demand 清偿债务的要求
liquidated obligation 已清偿的债权
liquidated sum 实得还款数,已清偿金额
liquidating partner (合伙企业的)清理合伙人
liquidation n. 清理,(公司)清算;清偿,了结;(资产的)变现;消灭
liquidation holdings 清理人所掌握的债券(或股票)

liquidation of a judicial person 法人的(财产)清算
liquidation of debt 偿还债务
liquidation of partnership business 合伙经营的清算
liquidation of property 变卖财产换为现金
liquidation reserve 清偿准备金
liquidation sale (停业)清理大拍卖
liquidation value 清算价值
liquidationism n. 取消主义
liquidator n. 财产清算人;破产管理人;清算人,(公司的)账目清算人
liquidity n. 清偿能力;流动性
liquidity risk 流动性风险
liquor n. 酒,酒类;汤药
liquor head 醉汉
liquor laws 酒精法;酒类法律
liquor licence 卖酒执照
lis 诉讼案件;争执;诉讼行为,起诉
lis alibi pendens 诉讼在另案进行(抗辩用语)
lis mota 诉讼进行中;争执已开始
lis pendens (或 lite pendente) 悬案,未决诉讼;有待法律解决
lis seriatim 分诉诉讼
lis sub judice 争议的案件;有争议之物
list n./v. 1.(13世纪) 表,清单;目录;名单;表册 2.备审案件目录,议事日(同docket) 3.(税)上市证券表/(12世纪之前) 1.将(人、事信息等)汇编成表 2.把……编入目录 3.将(房地产……)登记入册(并进行许可交易) 4.根据与不动产代理人或经纪人的协议列出销售财产(清单)
list of balances 余额表,差额表
list of candidates 候选人名单
list of casualty 伤亡名单
List of Chemicals with Quantities for Application of Public Liability Insurance Act (1992年3月24日印度环境部公布的)《适用公共责任保险法的化学物质名录和数量限值》
list of digest topics (美)判决摘要汇编标题目录
list of document 文据清单,文件登记表
list of exchange rate quotations 外汇牌价表

list of members 成员花名册
list of signatories and parties 签署国和缔约国名单
list price 厂价,批发价;目录价格
list procedure 名册程序(指选定仲裁员的方法。根据荷兰仲裁规则,以名册程序选择仲裁员。仲裁协会具有一份对外保密的,拥有 500 多名不同专业仲裁员名单,如果是独任仲裁员,协会将提供 3 名仲裁员进行选择,如果指定 3 名仲裁员,则应至少抽 9 名仲裁员供当事人选择)
list system 按名单选举制(指在选票所列候选人名单上画记号选定若干名候选人的选举法,候选人通常是同属一政党的成员)
listed a. 挂牌的;已列表的
listed bonds 挂牌债券
listed buildings 登录入册的名胜古迹建筑物
listed companies 上市公司,登记合格公司,注册公司
listed firms 挂牌公司
listed securities 上市证券,挂牌证券
listen v. 听,留神听;倾听,听信,听从
listen in 1.收听,监听 2.偷听,窃听
＊**Listen to both sides and you will be enlightened, heed only one side and you will be benighted.** 兼听则明,偏信则暗。
lister n. 制表人,编目者
listing n. 上市,上市股票登记;(证券交易所)挂牌;列出计划;制表;(不动产代理人)出租或出售土地的权利(指依据不动产的所有权人与不动产的代理人之间的一项协议,代理人担保买主或承租人按规定的条款给予佣金或一定费用作为报酬)
listing agreement 上市合同(契约);上市(债券或股票)同意书
lit de justice (法史)国王立法仪式(指国王作为最高首席法官御临法院以敕令制定法律的一种仪式)
litany n. 祈祷,祈祷词
lite pendente 见 *lis pendens*
litem suam facere 自诉
litera excambii 汇票(即 bill of exchange)
litera legis 法规的文字
literae recognitionis 提单,提货单(即 bill of lading)
literal a. 文字上的;字面的,逐字的;刻板的
literal application 按照字面含义的适用
literal construction(或 **interpretation**) 字面释义;文字释义;书面解释
literal contract (罗马法)成文合同(契约);书面合同(契约)
literal infringement 字面侵害
literal method (法律文件的)字面解释方法
literal proof 书面证据
literal rule 字义规则(见 golden rule)
literalism n. 拘泥于字面意义的倾向;忠实于字面意义
literalist n. 拘泥于字面解释的人
literalize(或 **literalise**) v. 照字面解释;对……作字面直译
literarum obligatio(或 *expensilatio*) (罗马法)书面(形式)之债;文书合同(契约)
literary a. 文学的,从事文学的;从事写作的;文人的,书本的
literary and artistic property right 文学艺术产权
literary executor 遗稿保管人
literary property 版权;著作权
literary sources of law 法的文学渊源(又译:法律的文学渊源)
literary works 文学作品,文字作品
literatim 逐字地,照原文
literator n. 作家,文人
literature n. 文学;文献;作品
literature of legal information 法律信息文献
litigable a. 可诉讼的
litigant n./a. 诉讼当事人,诉讼参与人/诉讼的;有关诉讼的;诉讼中的;好争讼的
＊**Litigant loves lawyers who locate loopholes.** 诉讼当事人喜欢会钻法律条文空子的律师。
litigant participant 诉讼参与人
litigant parties 诉讼双方当事人(又译:诉讼两造)
litigant right 诉讼的权利
litigant's statement 诉讼当事人的陈述
litigate v. 诉诸法律;(俚)打官司;诉讼,

争讼
litigating party 诉讼当事人
litigation n. (民事)诉讼,起诉,(俚)打官司,争讼(有时可作 law suit 的同义语)
Litigation Autonomy 当事人诉讼自治(指保证当事人对自己的诉讼权利的掌控和控制)
litigation bar 民事诉讼律师
litigation cost 诉讼费用
litigation for the sake of litigation 为诉讼而诉讼
litigation lawyer 见 trial attorney
litigation procedure 诉讼程序
litigation process 诉讼进程
litigation-ending penalty 结束诉讼的惩罚,终止诉讼惩罚
litigator (16 世纪)1. 诉讼代理人(trial lawyer)(指专门出庭办理诉讼的律师) 2. 庭审律师(指为庭审准备案件,如进行证据开示、审前动议、审理案件和处理上诉等。律师代理诉讼当事人进行诉讼,不管是在法庭或其他与诉讼相关地点) 3. (古代)诉讼当事人(同 litigant)
litigious a. 关于诉讼的,可引起诉讼的;好诉讼的,(俚)好打官司的
litigious matter 可引起诉讼的案件
litigious right 诉讼权利
litis aestimatio 损害赔偿的幅度,损害赔偿金的估计(评定)
litis contestatio (或 contestatio litis) 1.(罗马法)诉讼,争议程序[指诉讼双方当事人就诉讼的最后合意(final agreement)以程序诉讼由裁判官(praetor)发给审判官(judex)。在古罗马请求权体制下,当事人关于诉讼的"合意"制,即所谓"认诉"制,"认诉"是诉讼成立基础。如果一个案件再度诉讼就违反了当事方间的"诉讼合意"] 2. 诉讼中的争点(contested point);诉讼当事方交替表述展示的诉讼系争点(litigable issue) 3. 诉讼的争辩
litis contestation n. (罗马法)辩护陈述阶段
litis denunciatio 告知参加,告知第三人(参加诉讼)(指当事人于诉讼中因自己将败诉而告知在法律上有利害关系之第三

人来参加诉讼)
litispendence n. 诉讼期间
litterbug n. (在公共场所)乱丢废物者,破坏清洁者
littering n. 乱丢废物,乱扔废杂物的行为
Little Collection of Six Codes (日)《袖珍六法全书》(有斐阁出版)
little content 未予关注,不满意,未达到满意程度
little(或 **nothing**) **short of** 简直不比……差,简直可以说
littoral a. 沿岸的,沿海岸的
littoral rights 海滨产权(指有关海洋、海、湖的财产权,此词常涉及海岸的享用权)
littoral state 沿岸国,沿海国
live entertainment 实况播送表演,有活力的(表演)文娱活动
live issue 尚在争论中的问题
live on capital 靠吃资本,资本消耗,靠资本过活
live separate 分居
live up to 履行;达到预期目标
live-in circuit judge (美)旅居巡回法官(根据现行规定,要求巡回法官住在巡回地区,其推事室设在哪里即应住在哪里,但可将推事室设于他们所希望的地方)
livelihood n. 生活,生计
Liverpool Court of Passage (英)利物浦航行法院(指 17 世纪经特许建立的法院,具有一般管辖权和海事管辖权。1971 年已取消)
livery n. 财产所有权的让渡(批准书);交付;(英)同业公会;公会的特权;(总称)同业公会会员
livery of seisin (普通法上的)移转土地占有权的适当方式,转让法定占有的财产;(英)让渡自由保有土地
liveryman n. (英)同业公会会员
livestock n. 牲畜,家畜
livestock insurance 牲畜保险
livestock trading tax 牲畜交易税
living a. 现行的,现存的;起作用的;使用着的;生活的,维持生活的;适于居住的
living allowance 生活津贴
living apart (夫妻)分居

living condition 生活状况;居住环境
living constitution 现行(的)宪法
living force 现实力量,真实的权力
living index 生活指数
living law 活法(指埃利希的"活法"论,认为"活法"的知识来源于二:一为现代法律性文件;二为直接的具体事物)
living on earning of prostitution 以卖淫为生
living organism 活的机体,生命的机体
living organs 现存的机构;有生气的机体
living person 有生命的人
living pledge 活质(权),活抵押(权),(以土地收益偿债的)典质权(见 vivum vadium)
living space 居住面积
living trust 有效信托,现行信托
living wage 最低生活工资,糊口工资
living will 活遗嘱,安乐死志愿书(该词出现于20世纪70年代早期。实际为误称,因其与遗嘱无关。它是由某人给某亲属、医生或律师和牧师的一份声明书,表示如果本人将来患不治之症而康复无望时,不要采用延长生命之手段,而让其在较短时间内死亡,这与遗嘱是不同的)
living witness 人证
living-together agreement 见 cohabitation agreement
livor mortis 尸斑
Llewllyn Karl N. 卢埃林·卡尔·N.(1893—1962)[最为杰出的、最为雄辩的美国法律现实主义者,同时他也是最具有实践影响力的法学家。他参与起草了《统一商法典》(UCC)的第2篇。这部法典几经修改,至今仍然规制着美国社会中的货物买卖。他在起草此法典过程中,把很多法律现实主义者的思想都变成了现实,特别是法官应关注法律之下的公民的感受和需求,以及少一些对法概念的形式主义理解和机械的适用。在《普通法传统》一书中,卢埃林建议法官在判决案件时运用其"情形感"(situation sense),即除考虑法律的推理因素之外,同时考虑政治和经济因素,追求一种"宏大的判决风格"(grand style),发展法律以适应变化的环境]

Lloyd's (英)劳埃德保险社(旧译劳合社,指设在伦敦的保险商和保险经纪人的公会,是按1871年劳埃德法组成的法人社团);劳埃德债券(指公司用作担保付款的债务)
Lloyd's class 劳氏船级
Lloyd's form "Average Bond" 劳氏海损合同(契约)格式
Lloyd's Standard Form of Salvage Agreement 劳氏标准海难救助合约,劳氏海难救助合约标准格式
Lloyd's Standard Salvage and Agreement Clause (简称 LSSA Clause) 劳氏标准海难救助及仲裁条款
Lloyd's underwriters 劳氏承保人
load n. 担子,重担,重任;装载量;工作量;自重,负荷
load line 吃水线
loaded a. 有负载的,装着货的,加重的
loading n. 装载;(车船)装载的货
loading charges 装船费,装货费
loading manifest 装货清单,装车清单
loafer n. 无业游民;不务正业者,二流子
loan n./v. 借,借入,借出;贷款,贷金;公债;借出的东西;借贷/(美)借出
loan account 贷款账户
loan agreement 借贷合同(契约),借款合约
loan and saving company 借贷储蓄公司
loan bears interest 有利息的借贷
loan bill 借款票证
loan capital 借贷资金,放息资金,借贷资本
loan chattel 以动产为担保的借贷
loan contract 借贷合同(契约)
loan creditor 贷款债权人
loan for consumption 消费借贷
loan for consumption with consideration 有偿消费借贷
loan for the settlement of accounts 结算贷款
loan for use 使用借贷
loan interest 贷款利息
loan money 借贷款项
loan notice 贷款通知(书)
loan of fungibles 可替代物的借贷,种类物

借贷,消费借贷
loan of infungibles 不可替代物的借贷,特定物借贷
loan office (向私人放贷的)贷款处;当铺;公债经募处
loan on actual estate 不动产抵押放款
loan on security 担保借款
loan relations 借贷关系
loan repayment 归还贷款
loan secured by credit 以信用担保的贷款
loan secured by mortgage (on landed property) 抵押(地产)贷款
loan secured by thing 以物品担保的贷款
loan services 放款业务
loan shark 高利贷者(指以超过法定利率的高利借款给借贷者并使用恐吓诈骗以取得偿还)
loan society 信用合作社;互助储金会
loan tied to an index 按指数偿付的贷款
loan without security 无担保的贷款
loan worthy 有偿付能力
loan-sharking n. 放高利贷
loanee n. 借入者;债务人
loaner n. 借出者;债权人
loanholder n. 公债持有人,债券持有人;押款受押人
loansin default 拖欠的贷款,违约的贷款
lobby n./v. 休息室;(英)下议院民众接待室;(美)院外活动集团(亦称"第三院",指美国垄断组织为收买或胁迫议员使立法为其服务所派的专人和所设的专门机构,因活动在走廊、休息室而得名)/对议员进行疏通活动,游说,疏通
lobby correspondent 驻议会记者
lobby-fodder n. 走廊食客(指在议会外进行游说等方式影响议员投票者)
lobbying n. 游说拉票,院外活动
lobbyism n. (美)院外活动
lobbyist n. 院外活动集团成员
local a./n. 地方的,当地的;本地的;局部的,一部分的/当地居民,当地律师(或医生,教士);本地新闻;(美)地方分会(尤指工会)
local acceptance 本地承兑
local accounting firm 地方(性)会计事务所
local act 地方性法规,(英)地方法令(指适用于某地区的法令)
local actions 属地诉讼,当地诉讼(指只能在与案件直接有关的特定地方才能提起的诉讼,如涉及不动产纠纷案件应在不动产所在地进行的诉讼)
local administration 地方行政管理;地方政府
local administration unit 地方政府单位,地方行政单位
local affairs 地方事务
local agent (美)当地代理,地区代理人
local agreement 地方协定,局部协定
local allegiance (英)当地效忠,居留地的效忠
local and special legislation (美)地方立法,特别立法[指适用于特别地区或特别个人的立法。如果这种立法在相同属性(The Same Class)人之间,根据专断的和不公平的划分,则属于违宪,亦称为 class legislation]
local Assembly 地方议会
local assessment 地方征税金(为地方公益之用)
local authorities 地方政权,(英)地方当局(指被授权在特定地区执行特定的制定法职能的人员或机关);地方政权机关
local authority by-laws 地方权力机关章程
local autonomous government 地方自治政府
local autonomy (law) 地方自治(法)
local body of administration 地方行政机关
local body of state power 地方国家权力机关
local collection authority-in-charge 当地征收机关
local community 地方社区,市镇
local competence 地方权限
local constable (英)地方警察
local constituency 地方选区
local courts 地方法庭;初级法庭;地区法院(指只对某一地区有审判权的法院,如州法院、治安官法院等);本地法院
Local Criminal Justice Board (英)地方

刑事司法委员会
local custom 地方习惯,当地惯例
local customary measures 地方性习惯计量标准
local customs 地方习惯法,当地惯例
local debt 地方债务
local deeds registry 地方契据登记处
local despot (中)恶霸
local economic construction 地方经济建设
local executive 地方行政机关
local government (美)地方政府(指比州小的等级的市、县或其他政府管理机构。地方政府对不动产、城市规划和其他当地事务有最大的控制权)
Local Government Antitrust Act (美)《地方政府反垄断法》(1984年通过)
local government area 地方行政区
Local Government Board (英)地方管理委员会
local income tax 地方所得税
local inferior courts for petty causes 处理小型案件的地方初级法院
local inquiry 地方调查
local judge 地方法官;本地法官
local jurisdiction (美)地方管辖权(指对联邦管辖权而言)
local law 本地法,当地的法律
local law theory 地域法学说
local laws and ordinances (美)地方法规和法令(指属授权立法的法规和法令。此立法权由州立法机构授予地方政府某些制定法律的部门)
local legislation 地方立法
local legislature 地方立法机关
local nationalism 地方民族主义
local negotiation 局部谈判
local option (美)地方(人民)抉择权(例如关于禁酒问题,亦做 local veto)
local ordinances 地方法令,当地法令
local organ 地方机关
local organ of state power 地方权力机关
local peace magistrate 地方治安法官;地方基层司法官员
local people's congresses at different levels (中)地方各级人民代表大会
local people's courts at different levels (中)地方各级人民法院
local people's governments at different levels (中)地方各级人民政府
local people's procuratorates at different levels (中)地方各级人民检察院
local police station 当地警察派出所
local prejudice 地方偏见
local prosecuting attorney (美)地方检察官
local prosecutor (美)地方检察官
local public prosecution's office 地方检察院,(日)地方检察厅
local public prosecutor 地方检察长,地方检察官
local public security force (中)地方公安部队
local rate 地方税
local regulations 地方规章,当地规章
local remedy 当地补救方法,本地救济方法
local revenue officer 当地税务官员
local rights 本地利益,地方权利
local rules of court 法院的地方规则
local self-administered organ 地方自治机关
local self-government 地方自治
local statute 地方法规
local tax 地方税
local time 地方时间
local treaty 地方性条约
local tyrants and evil gentry (中)土豪劣绅
local unit 地方单位
local usage 地方性惯例
local venue 限定的审判地(与 transitory venue 转换审判地相对)(指案件诉因只能在一县或一郡内发生,从而此案只能在一县或一郡审判地审理)
local veto 见 local option
local war 局部战争
local-nationality chauvinism 地方民族主义
locale n. (事情发生的)场所,地点
localism n. 地方主义,地方观念;地方风俗;思想闭塞

locality n. 位置,场所,地区,所在地;方向
locality of a crime 犯罪地点,犯罪场所
localization n. 地方化
localization of law 法律本地化,法律地方化
localization policy 地方分权政策
localization rate 国产化率
localized globalism 地方化全球主义
locally elected officials(或 **prosecutor**) 地方选举官员(或地方选举检察官)
locate v. 确定……的地点(或范围);设置;居住;找出,探出;(美)设计,计划;追查
locate loopholes 找到(法规等)漏洞所在
locatio 租赁;借出
locatio conductio (罗马法)租赁行为(指租赁物品或劳务雇佣)
locatio custodiae (罗马法)保管物的租赁
locatio operarum (罗马法)劳务借出,劳工雇用
locatio operis 佣工合同(契约);劳务合同(契约),因劳务的借出
locatio operis faciendi (罗马法)因物的维修或与维修有关的借出,提供劳务合同(契约)
locatio operis mercium vehendarum (罗马法)因完成货物运输工作的借出
locatio rei 物的租赁
location n. (16世纪)1.位置、地点(指一个人或事物的特定位置或地点)2.定位、安置;定位的行为;寻找、查明、勘定 3.对于不动产中特定分界线的勘定 4.(采矿法)适当的采矿区的勘定行为;地上显著位置设的告示,标明勘界人的姓名,勘定的事实及矿地范围 5.(大陆法)临时的租赁合同或协议或临时雇佣合同
location of a crime 犯罪地点
locative calls 地界(位置)标记(指地契或其他文件中使用界标或有形客体对土地的描述)
loci celebrationis 缔约地(国)
lock n. 拘留所;阻塞;(格斗时的)揪扭
lock hospital (英)性病医院,花柳病医院(亦称 lock venereal hospital)
lock stepper 囚犯

lock-in-clause n. 锁住条款
lock-in-effect 锁入效应(见 Network Effect)
lock-out n. 停工,停业,闭厂(指劳资纠纷中雇主拒绝工人,把雇工关在厂外的一种策略)
lock-step pricing 定价一致行动,紧跟定价
lock-step procedure 因循守旧过程,陈旧古板做法
lock-step system 因循守旧制
lock-up n. 拘留所,(资金)搁死
lock-up for prisoners awaiting trial 待决犯的看守所
lockage n. 船闸通行税,通过船闸;船闸系统
loco 卖方当地交货价格;交货地点
loco citato 在上述引文中
loco parentis 代替父母(见 in loco parentis),代替双亲
loco **terms** 当地交货条件,现场交货条件
locum tenens 代理人,代替人,代表,助理人
locus 地点,所在地,场所
locus contractus 缔(立)约地,合同(契约)地
locus criminis 犯罪地点,罪行发生地
locus delicti 侵犯行为地;犯罪地点
locus in quo 现场;事情发生地
locus poenitentiae 1.悔改地;改变主意的机会 2.反悔可能性 3.(市场交易中)推翻前言
locus publicus 公共场所
locus regit actum (国际私法)行为依行为地法;"场所支配行为"(原则),行为地法
locus regit formam actum (国际私法)行为形式依行为地法
locus sigilli 盖印处
locus standi 出庭,出庭资格;发言权;陈述权;立足点
locus-off-the-tort-ambiguities n. 侵权含混的所在,侵权所在地的含混侵权行为地(规定中的含混)
lodemanage(或 **loadmanage**) n. 领港员
lodge n./v. 门房,传达室;出租房屋;(秘密社团或联谊会的)分会/寄宿,租房给某人

住,存放;提呈,提起(诉讼);监禁;授(权)予某人

lodge a complaint 投诉,控告
lodge a proof 出示证据,举证
lodge a protest against court judg(e)ments 抗诉
lodge an appeal 提出上诉
lodge an objection 反对,抗议;反抗
lodge sb. in goal 监禁某人于监狱
lodge the subject matter 标的物提存
lodger n. 寄宿人
lodging n. 提起(诉讼),申(诉);住所;存放处
lodging contract 租房合同(契约)
lodging house 住宅,宅第
lodgment n. 告发,控告;交付,存放;住所;住宿
lodgment in court 向法院起诉
log v. 1.记录,记入 2.飞行;航行;以……的速度航行
log-book n. 航海日志;飞行日志
logging in 记入日志(指被带入警察局的人的姓名等的最早记录,可与 booking 综合一起。见 booking)
logic (logical) bomb 逻辑炸弹(指破坏计算机程序的一种形式,与病毒的区别是逻辑炸弹没有传染性,不自我复制)
logic equation 逻辑方程
logic in legal contexts 法律中的逻辑
logical a. 逻辑的,符合逻辑的
logical formalism 逻辑形式主义(与"形式合理"同义。见 formula rationality)
logical inference 逻辑推理,逻辑推断
logical interconnection 逻辑关联
logical interpretation 逻辑解释
logical positivism (neo-positivism) 逻辑实证主义(新实证主义)
logical reasoning 逻辑推理
logically impossible 逻辑上的不可能(例如,60 美元一顶帽子的售价,买主却给 90 美元)
lognitio extra ordinem 非常诉讼程序
logroll v. 互投赞成票(促使)议案通过;互相捧场
loi d'application imméeiate 直接适用的法

(指法国法院在实践中,法院地国的一些法律由于其实体内容在冲突规范的双边体系中获得特殊地位,可排除一般冲突规范的指引而得到直接适用,弗朗西斯卡基斯在 1958 年发现此种情况,故将此类规范定义为 loi d'application immédiate,并将此情况写于其所著的《反致理论与国际私法制度》中)

loi fondamentale 根本法
loia djerga (阿富汗)大支尔格会议(亦称大国民议会,由议会议员和省议会议长组成)
lois de police 警察法
Loislaw (美)罗易斯网(指法律文献检索中的一个检索网址,适用于法律大学生免费检索,全称为 www.loislaw.com)
loiterer n. 游手好闲者,不务正业者
loitering n. 游荡
lok sabha 人民院(指印度两院制议会的下院)
lombard n/a. (英)放款人;银行家/放债人的
Lombard Street (英)伦巴第街;英国金融界;英国金融中心
Lombrosian a. 龙勃罗梭犯罪论的(Lombroso Cesare 为意大利精神病犯罪学家)
Lome Agreement 洛美协定
London Process 伦敦进程[指随着互联网的迅猛发展和网络攻击、网络犯罪等问题的凸显,网络安全在各国安全战略中的地位不断上升,并逐渐成为晚近国际关系中一个重要议题。在此背景下,各国不仅纷纷加强网络安全领域的国内法律和政策制定,还越来越多地谋求通过各种国际组织和国际会议来协调相关政策。发起于 2011 年的"伦敦进程"就是围绕网络安全相关问题的一个颇为独特和重要的国际磋商和对话进程。2011 年 11 月 1—2 日,由英国外交和联邦事务部主办的网络空间会议在伦敦举行。这是国际上第一次以网络安全和网络治理为主题的大规模会议,共有来自 60 多个国家的 700 余名代表与会。此会的重要特点是与会代表除各国政府官员和国际组织代表之外,互联网企业如谷歌、脸书、华为等非政府组织、各国智库以及学界人士也占有相当比例,

体现了网络空间治理中的"公私伙伴关系"(public-private partnership)(PPP)。为期两天的会议中,与会代表主要围绕"经济增长与发展""社会福利""网络犯罪""安全可靠网络接入"以及"国际安全"这五大议题展开治理和规则制定的辩论,这标志着"伦敦进程"的起点]

lone star state (美)孤星州(得克萨斯州)

long a. 长的;长久;长期的;多头的;看涨的;众多的;高的;变更大的

long arm jurisdiction (**long-arm jurisdictions**) (美)长臂管辖权[指对不需要其同意接受,也不居住在那里的人和公司行使管辖权,也就是对原来没有管辖权的人(包括法人)行使管辖权][亦指当非法院地区居民与法院地区间存在某种限度的联系,同时原告提起的诉讼又产生于这一联系时,法院对被告所主张的网络(Internet)案件的管辖权。在实践中美国法院提出很多是依据长臂管辖权理论对网络案件行使管辖权;如被告在他州内有侵权行为,则该州法院可对其行使管辖]

long arm of the law 法律远及之力量
long bill 长期汇票,长期票证
long credit 长期信用
long exchange 长期汇兑
long handnote 普通笔录
long lease 长期租赁;永佃权
long parliament (英史)长期国会(1640—1660年)
long position 多头;超买;多头寸,长盘(指银行资金头寸用语)
long price 高价,昂价
long robe 律师业;书记(记录)业;律师长袍
Long Shore and Harbo(u)r Workers' Compensation Act (美)《码头和港口工人补偿法》
long term of years 长期租借(权)
long term sustainability 长期持续可产量
long term tenancy 长期租约
long title (法令的正式)详细标题
long vacation (英)休庭期(指每年8月至9月这段时间法院不正常开庭);大学暑假
long-arm statute (美)长臂法规(指允许

本州法院要求涉及其他州的人或财产的管辖权的州法规)

long-continued possession 长期继续占有
long-continued questioning 长时间继续审问
long-dated a. 远期的
long-dated bill 远期票据
long-distance road transport 长途公路运输
long-run dumping 长期的倾销
long-standing (美)长期诉讼资格;长期存在
long-standing case 旧案(又译:陈案)
long-standing custom of judge 长期存在的审判惯例
long-standing dispute 长期存在的争端
long-term a. 长期的
long-term (或 **range**) **agreement** 长期合同(契约),长期协定
long-term bonds 长期债券
long-term capital gain 长期资本收益[指持有资产长于规定时期(通常为一年)内出售或交易所获取的收益或利润]
long-term co-existence and mutual supervision (中)长期共存,互相监督(指共产党和民主党派合作共事的准则)
long-term credit 长期贷款,长期信贷
long-term creditor 长期债权人
long-term debt 长期债务,长期债款(指通常超过一年,不得要求在第二年内偿还)
long-term imprisonment 长期徒刑
long-term interest-free loan 长期无息贷款
long-term loan 长期贷款,长期放款
long-term plan 长期计划
long-term planning 长期规划
long-term prospect 远景规划,长期规划
long-tested a. 久经考验的
long-term foster care 长期领养照管[指安排儿童在较长的时间里得到照顾关照,甚至可能包括儿童的整个少年时期(entire minority),以替代家庭的重聚、终止、收养或监护。尽管大多法院一般不作出让孩子处于最佳利益的安排裁决,但有时只是唯一的可能性,即在孩子因年龄或无行为能力,被领养亦不可靠,或父母与孩子不可能长期在一起的情况下,只得从孩子的最佳受益考虑与其父母订立专门合同

(limited contract)。根据《收养和安全家庭法》(Adoption and Safe Families Act)最终安排长期领养照管]
long-timer (美)长期徒刑犯
*** Longa possessio jus parit.** Longpossession begets right. 长期占有会导致产生权利。
longer-term forward contract 远期合同(契约)
longevity n. 长寿;长期供职,资历
longi temporis praescriptio 土地取得时效
longshore a. 海岸边的,在海岸工作的
longshoremen n. 码头装卸工人
longstanding business relationship 长期存在的商务关系
look v. 1.看,注意,留神 2.显得,好像 3.朝向,倾向 4.寻找,搜查
look forward to 期待,盼望
look into 调查
look up 涨价,繁荣,查阅,探访;锁定[指公司兼并中的手段。"王冠宝珠"(crown jewel)指目标公司的最好资产或子公司。目标公司可以将其卖给第三方。敌意收购中待敌意收购者收购目标公司一定比例的股份后,允许第三方购买"王冠宝珠",此作法亦称"锁定选择"(look up option)。此外,向友好的第三方出售目标公司的股票或股票的购股权,成为股票锁定(stock look up)]
looker n. 观众;(英)检查员
looking for 1.寻找〈looking for clue to interpret specific language in a code section〉(查找关键来翻译法典条款中的专用词语),〈look first for an explanation and ananysis of governing legal doctrine〉(首先查找支配法律原理解说与分析) 2.期待〈looking for sb.'s arrival〉(期待某人的到来)
looking through approach 透视法(指防范滥用税收协定的措施之一)
lookout n. 看守;看望;留心观察,警戒,监视;守望者,放风者
loom v./n. 隐隐出现;逼近;隐隐呈现的形象
loop n. 箕型线,蹄型纹
loophole n. (法规等的)漏洞(空子)
loops and whorls on a finger 指纹

loose a. 松散的,宽大的;散漫的;放荡的,荒淫的;无拘束的,自由的;释放的
loose construction 扩大解释
loose money 头寸松
loose woman 放荡的女人;淫荡的女人
Loose-leaf Services (美)活页服务资料(在美国有两种以活页形式出版的非官方商业性出版物,在最高法院判决宣布之日后即行出版,即国家事务出版局出版的《美国法律周刊》和商业情报交换所出版的《最高法院公报》,这两个出版单位也出版有其他法学课题的活页服务资料)
loosen up price 放开物价
looseness of thought 思维散漫(思维表达障碍的一种。此种思维指其思维的指向性、连贯性和逻辑性障碍。说话缺乏中心,东拉西扯,不着边际,答非所问。显然,这类患者缔约能力、刑事责任能力、作证能力和受审能力均丧失。见 thought of insertion)
loot n./v. (俗称)赃物;掠夺物;非法收入;战利品/强夺,掠夺,抢劫;洗劫
looter n. 掠夺者,抢劫者
looting of assets 资产的掠夺
Lord n. 贵族;勋爵;君主;领主;地主;阁下(对贵族、议长、高等法院法官等的尊称);(一行业的)巨头
Lord Advocate (苏格兰 15—17 世纪)法院院长,大法官;检察总长;(苏格兰 1746—1885 年)国务大臣;(苏格兰,当代)政府法律总顾问,总检察长
Lord (High) Chancellor (英)兼任上议院议长的大法官(集集立法、司法、行政大权于一身的首脑人物)
Lord (High) Constable (英)高级警官
Lord Chamberlain (英史)宫廷大臣
Lord Chancellor's Office (英)大法官事务部
Lord Chief Baron (英)理财法院首席法官(称谓)
Lord Chief Justice of England (英)高等法院院长[指高等法院后座法庭的首席法官(chief judge)。这个勋爵首席大法官(Lord Chief Justice)也是上诉法院任职的首席大法官,其地位仅次于英国司法等级

制度(English Judicial Hierarchy)中的大法官、上议院议长(chancellor)。以前此词亦称 Chief Justice of England。见 Chief Justice of Common Pleas]
Lord Chief Justice of the Common Pleas (英)高等民事法院首席法官(1881年前称谓)
Lord Chief Justice of the Queen's Bench (英)后座法庭首席法官(1881年前称谓)
Lord Clerk Register (苏格兰)档案主事官
Lord Great Chamberlain (英)掌礼大臣
Lord High Admiral (英)海军大臣
Lord High Steward (英)上议院特别刑事审判长(指对贵族的叛国等罪行进行审判的主持人)
Lord Justice Clerk (苏格兰)法院的陪审法官、助理法官(或副院长)
Lord Justice General (苏格兰)法院院长、巡回法庭庭长、最高刑事法官
Lord Justice in Chancery (英)大法官、大法官法庭法官
Lord Justices of Appeal (英)上诉法院常任法官
Lord Lieutenant (英)郡最高军事长官
Lord Lyon King of Arms (苏格兰)纹章院长
Lord Mansfield's rule 曼斯菲尔德规则[指不管夫妻任何一方都不能证明丈夫是否在妻子怀孕时曾有过性行为,所提供证言均不具可采性的原则。实际上,这项规则已被许多州摈弃,而且它也不可能判定婚姻期间出生的孩子为非婚生子。]
Lord mayor (英)伦敦市长、大市长[指①伦敦组合城市的重要官员、大市长,之所以这样称呼,是因为爱德华三世的第四个特许授权(the fourth charter of Edward Ⅲ)授予拥有手持权杖的荣誉的官员。②这个城市的主要司法官员的头衔,其职位已被授予专利特许证(letters patent)]
Lord Mayor's Court in London (英)伦敦市长法院
Lord of Admiralty (英)海事法庭最高官员
Lord of Appeal (英)上议院议员,上诉审判官[指上议院议员,听审和判决上诉案件时至少有三位议员出庭:包括上议院议长(chancellor)、常任高级法官(Lords of Appeal in ordinary)和具有高级司法职位的贵族上议院议员,诸如前任议长、大不列颠和爱尔兰高级法院的法官]
Lord of Appeal in Ordinary (英)上诉法院常任高级法官[指受任命并有薪水负责帮助上议院(House of Lords)听审上诉案件的人。这些贵族作为终身有爵位者在上议院占议席、有投票表决权(sit and vote),甚至退休后亦是如此]
Lord of Misrule (英史)宫廷庆典总管
Lord of the Great Seal 国玺掌玺大臣
Lord of the Manor 采邑领主
Lord Ordinary (苏格兰)最高民事法院独任法官
Lord President of the Court of Session (苏格兰)最高民事法院院长
Lord President of the Privy Council (英)枢密院长,枢密大臣
Lord Privy Seal (英)(御玺)掌玺大臣
Lord Provost (苏格兰大城市的)市长
Lord Steward (英)王室事务长
Lord Steward of the Queen's Household (英)王室总管
Lord Tenderden's rule 见 *ejusdem generis*
Lord (High) Treasurer (英)财政大臣
Lord's Chancellor's Department (英)大法官办公厅(指大法官下设的大法官办公厅,属文官机构,办公厅内设常任秘书 Permanent Secretary,或皇家书记官 Clerk to the Crown,还有两名副手,分掌立法和司法大权)
Lords Commissioners of Justiciary (苏格兰)高等司法法院常任法官
Lords Commissioners of the Great Seal (英)国玺专员
Lords Justices 高等法官
Lords Marchers 边境领主
Lords of Council and Session (苏格兰)最高民事法院法官
Lords Spiritual (英)上议院圣职议员
Lords Spiritual and Temporal (英)上议院神职议员和世俗议员

Lords Temporal （英）世俗贵族（亦称不居僧职的上议员，或上议院世俗议员，指除宗教贵族以外一般在上议院有席位的贵族）

Lordship 1.领地,贵族领地,领主权 2.公爵(duke)以外的贵族常用的一种荣誉称号 3.对法官或其他官员的习俗头衔

lose v. 遗失,丧失；失败；浪费,损失；迷失,错过；赔钱；输掉

lose an action （或 lose the case, lose in lawsuit） 败诉

loser n. 失败者；失物人；遗失者；（美）刑事犯；损失者；损失物

Loser's Justice 失败者的正义（指美国著名法学家弗里德曼在《选择的共和国》一书中以此词条来表述"通过国家的介入为弱者提供相对完善的制度保护，以使他们可借以重新获得发展之可能"这一含义。实际上，"失败者正义"原则是在"选择的多样性"和"失败的可能性"前提下为弱者提供一种重新出发的"第二次机会"，使其能恢复到社会上正常人的能力与地位的法律制度安排。"选择的多样性"用弗里德曼的话说："在人们能够或人们确实可以控制的情况下，法律应当允许、提供和授予一个广泛的选择空间，只有这样，人们才能以适合他们自己的方式生活得充实而自由；只有这样，他们才能富有成效地发展他们自己的人格和个性。""失败的可能性"按弗里德曼的理论："在生活和法律中——每一项诉讼，每一个主张，每一次选择——都必然有成功者和失败者。"可以说生活中没有任何人敢断言自己每一次决策都是正确的，也不存在一生都不会犯错的永恒胜利者。正因如此，在生活、工作中招致失败的概率也就更大，其主要原因按弗里德曼所述，是因为科学革命所带来的人类社会的不可预知。选择是多样性的，失败是可能的，那么，应如何应对？弗里德曼认为在法律上为了减少错误选择的风险，就必须允许给予失败者"第二次机会"，弗里德曼以破产法为例对此问题进行说明："在破产法领域……如果无破产制度或其他类似制度安排，那么一个经营失败者或因其他原因而债台高筑的企业家，也就无可避免地完全被毁了。破产制度是一种复杂安排，但其目标之一是确保无论破产之后还留下多少财产，都要在债权人之间公平分配，但同时也让破产者有一个干净、全新的开始。这对于作为弱者的失败者来说，是获取第二次机会，不啻是解救其脱离困厄境地的唯一路径。"）

loser of a lawsuit 败诉人

losing a. 失败的；输的；折亏的，招致损失的

losing a suit 败诉

losing defendant 败诉的被告

losing effect 失效

losing party 败诉当事人

losing self-control 失去自控能力

loss n. 灭（损）失,遗失,丧失；灭（损）失物,丧失物；亏损；伤亡；损毁；浪费

loss of possession 占有权的丧失

loss and damage through negligence 因过失所致的灭失和损害

loss apportionment 损失分摊

loss assessment 损失额评定

loss assessor 损失评定人

loss in weight 损耗,缺量

loss leader(s) 为吸引顾客亏本卖出的东西

loss limitation act 损失限定法

loss list 伤亡名单,死伤名册

loss of body temperature 体温下降；尸冷

loss of civil right 褫夺公权

loss of consortium 配偶权利的丧失

loss of expectation of life 生命期望的丧失

loss of faculty 官能的丧失

loss of future expenses 预期费用损失

loss of future income 预期收益损失

loss of liberty 丧失自由,剥夺自由

loss of nationality 国籍的丧失

loss of ownership 所有权的丧失,所有权的消灭

loss of parental authority 亲权的丧失

loss of privilege 特权的丧失

loss of profit 利润损失

loss of profits insurance 利润损失保险

loss of property 丧失财产,剥夺财产

loss of realization 变产损失

loss of self-control 失去自我控制
loss of service 丧失劳务,丧失服务
loss of the case 败诉
loss of the document 证件的遗失
loss of the private right 私权的消灭
loss of exchange 汇兑损失
loss or gain on exchange 外汇损益
loss order 损失赔偿支付令
loss paid 已付赔款
loss ratio 损失比率(亦称赔付率,指保险公司在一定期间赔偿保险损失额与所收保险费的比率)
loss shifting 损害移转
loss spreading 损害分散
loss-making n. 造成损失
lost a. 1.失去的(失去的财产已不在自己的掌握之中,努力搜寻无法找到)〈lost at sea〉(海上丢失的),〈lost papers〉(丢失的文件)2.(人的)丢失,丢失的(人),失踪,下落不明(missing)〈lost child〉(丢失的儿童/失踪的儿童)3.(议会法)动议的拒绝,被拒绝的,不采纳的〈the motion is lost〉(动议是不采纳的)
lost and found 失物招领
lost and lost (海上运输保险单上的用语)已灭失
lost at the polls 落选
lost check 遗失支票
lost document 原件已丢失
lost earnings 失去收入[指如果他或她未失去职业或工作岗位,即可以挣得工资、薪金或其他收入;如果致残受伤或死去则失去此种收入。失去收入在人身伤害和非法终止就业(wrongful termination)案件中象征性地被判损害赔偿。此词意指可能过去失去收入和将来失去收入]
lost gain 失去的赢利,失去的利润
lost grant 转让证书已丢失
lost judge 失踪的法官(指纽约最高法院某法官饭后失踪,成为传闻)
lost policy holder 失踪的保险单持有人
lost profits 失去的收益
lost property (或 goods) 拾得物,遗失物
lost property office 失物招领处
lost things 遗失物

lost will 遗失的遗嘱
lot n. 1.签,抽签;命运;运气 2.份额,份;地段 3.(商品、拍卖品或人的)一批,一摊;某一类的人
lot money 拍卖(佣)金
lot number 地段号码
lot production 成批生产
lot quality protection 分批质量保护
loth=loath a. 不愿意的,厌恶的
lottery n. 奖券(或彩票)的发行;偶然之事;博彩(指以抽签给奖方式进行的一种赌博)
lottery bond 中奖券;中签债券
lottery drawing 奖券抽签;彩票抽签
lottery ticket 彩票,奖券
love day (英古法)爱心日(这一天邻里间相互无偿帮助,有纠纷平心静气和平解决)
love matches 恋爱婚姻(指出自真正爱情的婚姻),爱情的结合(美国佐治亚州1859年通过一条法规禁止"恋爱婚姻",坚信"恋爱婚姻"只存在于小说家的幻想之中。凡各种违反此条法规行为均由主持法官的判决予以惩处)
low a. 低的;浅的;少的;低下的
low diligence 不勤勉;不留意
low firearm prevalence 低枪支普及率
low interest rate 低利率
low justice (具有)低级司法管辖权
low politics 低级政治
low quality (货物)品质低劣
low velocity shares 低速股
low-cost arbitrage 低成本套利
low-down n. 内幕,真相
low-income housing 低租住房
low-interest loan 低息贷款
low-level uniform liability 低标准统一赔偿责任(制度)
low-speed or high-speed 低速或高速的
low-volume shipper 小批量托运人
low-water line(或 mark) 低潮线(标)
lower a./v. 较低的;较低级的/放下;减低;减弱;贬低
Lower Chambers (或 House) (英)下议院,(美)众议院

lower classes（或 orders） 下层社会
lower competitive price 较低竞争价格
lower court 下级法院,低级法院,初等（级）法院
lower court appealed 被上诉的下级法院
lower federal courts 低级别联邦法院[美国联邦法院体系依照《1789年司法法》(the Judiciary Act of 1789)确立。一系列的初审法院(一审)形成金字塔式基础,上面是中间的上诉法院(Courts of Appeal),顶端为联邦最高法院。联邦系统的初审法院是联邦地区法院,有权审理所有宪法允许联邦法院解决的案件。每个州的管辖区域内至少有1个联邦地区法院,其地区管辖范围都不超出一个州的区域。除怀俄明州的联邦地区法院管辖区包括爱达荷州和蒙大拿州在黄石公园的地区外,还有50个州和哥伦比亚特区的90个地区法院。此外,国会还为美国的准州地区(territories)如关岛、波多黎各、北马里亚纳群岛、维尔京群岛设立了4个地区法院。纽约州、得克萨斯州和加利福尼亚3个州各有4个地区法院,另有9个州各有3个地区法院。有些较大的州有不止一个地区法院,分别以北、南、东、西和中心或中间来描述。联邦地区法院约有600名法官,由总统经参议院同意后任命。地方治安法官负责协助联邦法官,负责审前程序以及审理轻罪,担任破产案件的鉴定人。联邦地区法院法官每8年任命一次地方治安法官。地区法院只有1名法官审理案件,以前国会曾要求由三名法官(1个来自地区法院,另2个来自上诉法院)组成的法庭审理,20世纪70年代中期几乎主张民事权利受侵犯案件均从3人法庭存审理了。到1990年,这种方式几乎不复存在了。美各州及其尚未成为州的地区共有11个上诉巡回法院,另还有哥伦比亚特区上诉法院。国会在这些上诉巡回法院设有150个法官席位。任一法院至少有6名法官,多的则有26名法官。此外,还有大量的专门上诉法院;海关专利上诉法院、1982年改名为联邦巡回区的上诉法院(即以前的海关法院)以及军事上诉法院。所以美国的司法体系概括了全国的管辖区]
lower limit 下限
lower officeholder 低级公职人员
lower people's court （中）下级人民法院
lower price 低价
lower the boom (on) （俚）惩罚,采取严厉措施;禁止
lower the price 减低价格
lower-middle peasant （中）下中农
lowest a. 最低的;基层的
lowest bidder 出价最低的投标人
lowest court 最低一级法院,基层法院
lowest level of the local people's congress （中）基层人民代表大会
lowest level of the local people's court （中）基层人民法院
lowest level of the local people's procuratorate （中）基层人民检察院
lowest perigee 最低点(指太空距地球的最低点)
loyalism n. 忠诚,效忠
loyalty n. 忠诚,忠心
loyalty agreement 忠诚信约
loyalty duty 忠实义务
loyalty examination 忠诚审查
loyalty oath 忠诚宣誓,效忠宣誓
loyalty system 忠诚信约制度
loyalty to the people 忠于人民
* *Lubricum linguae non facile trahendum est in poenam.* A slip of the tongue ought not lightly be subjected to punishment. 口误不受罚,不因失言而受罚。
lucid a. 清醒的;易懂的;神志清醒的,头脑清楚的
lucid interval （精神病的）神志不乱的间隙;神志短暂清醒期
lucrative a. 有利可图的,生利的,赚钱的;可获利的
lucrative business 赚钱的买卖
lucrative title 有利资格(指接受赠礼或遗赠财产的接受权)
lucre n. （贬义词）金钱上的收益,钱财
lucreative succession （苏格兰法）见 *praeceptio haeredictatis*
lucri causa 1.以获利为目的的 2.（美国刑

法)从前这是盗窃的主要要件,即盗窃财产主要意图。但是现今只有剥夺了物主所有权方能构成盗窃罪(见 larceny)
lucri grati 以获利为目的(同 lucri causa)
lucro captando 1. 见 certans de captando 2. 见 in lucro captando
lucrum cessans 持续性利润的损失(见 damnum emergens)
luetic n. 梅毒患者
luggage n. (总称)行李;(美)(店家出售的)皮箱;皮包
lumen n. 采光权(地役权的一种)
lump-sum n./a. 总额,总数;总结算;整批/总额的,总数的;(金额)一次总付的;整批的
lump-sum alimony 一次总付的离婚生活费
lump-sum award (损害赔偿的)总裁定额
lump-sum basis 一次兑付的方法
lump-sum contract 总清算合同(契约);一次性付款的合同(契约)
lump-sum payment n. (金额)一次总付时的/总价,运费总额,一次支付(清算);总额支付(清算)
lump-sum tax 一次总付的人头税
lumpen-proletarian n./a. 游民无产者,流氓无产者(的)
lumper n. 装卸工,码头工人;(英)小包工头,小承包商
lumpy a. 凹凸不平的,笨拙的,波浪起伏的
lunacy n. 精神错乱;疯狂行为
Lunacy Act (英)《精神病人法》(1890年)
lunatic n./a. 精神丧失者,精神病患者;疯子;狂人,怪人/心神丧失的,精神错乱的;精神病的
lunatic asylum 精神病院
lunatic criminal 精神病罪犯
lunatic fringe 极端分子,极端主义
lunatic so found by inquisition 经讯问才发现的精神病患者
lure v./n. 引诱,诱惑/魅力,诱惑物
lurker n. 潜伏者,间谍;小偷
Lusaka Declaration 《卢萨卡宣言》(1970年)
lustmurder n. 杀人淫虐狂
luxembourg compromise 卢森堡妥协方案(1960年通过)
Luxembourg Law 《卢森堡法》
luxury tax 奢侈品税
lying in franchise 专项特许处理(见 lie in franchise)
lying in grant 依授予文据转移处理(无体遗产)
lying in livery 按让渡处理(有体遗产)
lying in wait 埋伏,伏击,诡计
lynch n./v. 私刑,私罚;处私刑/以私刑处死,处以私刑,私刑拷打
lynch law(或 **Lynch's Law**) (美)私刑(1686年美弗吉尼亚州的当地人选出的保安官查尔斯·林奇,他主张对敢于触犯奴隶制的黑人及其他犯法分子均施酷刑直至处死)
lynch law court 私刑法庭
lyncher n. 施用私刑者
lynching n. 私刑(指群众暴力的一种形式,暴民以执行法律为名,不经审判就把他们认为是罪犯的人处死,往往还采用拷打和肢解等残酷手段)
Lyons Law (= Residency Law) (美)《居住地法》

M

M'Naghten Rules (英)麦克纳顿条例(1843年制定,专门解决精神障碍者刑事责任能力问题的法律规定。它对英美法系和大陆法系国家的相关立法都产生了巨大深远的影响。在英国,该条例自1843年确立后,一直单独适用至20世纪60年代。该条例的内容是:"应该假设每一个被告人是心神正常的,并且有足够理由认定

他应对犯罪负有责任,除非证明了是相反的情况。如果被告以精神错乱为理由进行辩护时,那么必须清楚地证明他在进行危害行为的当时,由于精神疾病而处于精神错乱状态,例如他不了解自己行为的性质,或者他虽了解但却不知自己行为是错误的或违法的")

M'Naghten Daniel　(英)麦克纳顿·丹尼尔[指1843年1月20日在伦敦,麦克纳顿的偏执型精神(病)分裂症患者将保守党领袖兼首相罗伯特·皮尔(Robert Pear)的秘书爱德华·德拉蒙德(Edward Drumond)当作皮尔杀害]

Maastricht Treaty　《马斯特里赫特条约》(指关于欧洲联盟条约)

Mace n.　权杖

machination n.　诡计,奸计;阴谋,图谋不轨

machine　对……起诉;对……发出传票;处理;办理加工⟨to process data⟩(处理数据),⟨to process polluted water⟩(处理污水),⟨to process a loan⟩(办理贷款手续)

machine franked　机器盖印的

machine language　机器(计算机)语言

machine voting　机器投票

machinery n.　机制(与 mechanism 同义)

machinery for consultation　咨询机构

machinery insurance　机械保险

macro virus　宏病毒(指电脑病毒)

macrocontract n.　总合同(契约)

macroeconomic direction　宏观经济指导

macroeconomics (复) n.　宏观经济学

mactator (古欧洲法)谋杀犯,凶手

mad a.　发疯的,疯狂的

made a.　人工制造的;虚构的;捏造的;拼成的;成功的

made over the common law　改造了普通法

made-to-order product　按订货生产的产品

made-up a.　虚构的,捏造的;编制的;决定的

made-up story　捏造的情节

madman n.　疯子,狂人

Madrid Arrangement (1891)　1891年《马德里协定》,有关商标方面的协定

Maf(f)ia n.　1.黑手党(指20世纪初一些在美国的意大利人的秘密犯罪组织)2.政治恐怖分子的秘密团体3.(全球性从事贩毒等非法活动的)秘密犯罪组织

mafioso n.　黑手党成员;秘密犯罪集团成员;秘密恐怖集团成员

Mafiya　黑手党(区别于意大利西西里黑手党 maffia 名称)

magazine n.　杂志,期刊;星期刊(报);仓库;弹药库;库存弹药

magdalen(e) n.　从良妓女;妓女收容所

Magill Case　马吉尔案(指20世纪90年代欧洲法院审理的一起最有名的电视节目时间表的版权纠纷案)

* *Magis de bono quam de malo lex intendit.*
The law favors a good rather than a bad construction. (Where the words used in an agreement are susceptible of two meanings, the one in accordance with law, and the other not so, the former should be adopted.)　法律倾向于善意而非恶意解释(合同用语可有两种解释时,其一为合法,另一为不合法,法律则采用前者)。

magister *cancellariae*　(英古法)衡平法官助理(之所以如此称呼,因为这种法官助理均为教士 priest)

magister *libellorum*　(罗马法)书面请求的助理法官(指帝国的主要存卷主事官负责将书面请求或控诉状呈交皇帝)

magister *litis*　承办案件的官员(即司法官,检察官)

magister *navis*　(罗马法)船长;商船船长;[亦指船长的贸易债务,包括船只的维修保养费用,以及涉及对船主或包船者提起的诉讼(an action exercitoria)]

magister *palatii*　(大陆法系)皇宫的主管[类似于英国的宫廷大臣(Lord chamberlain),其主要职责是参加王室的加冕典礼,威斯敏斯特宫廷保管和议会大厦房屋管理装修,以及出席贵族和主教册封、宣誓效忠仪式等]

magister *populi*　最高权力(独裁的意见)

magisterial a.　长官的;司法行政官的;有权威的;专横的;执法者的;硕士的

magisterial discretion 司法行政官的酌处权或自由裁量权
magisterial ineptitude 判处失当
magistracy n. 裁判司(署);地方法庭;司法行政官法庭;(英)治安官法庭;司法行政官(总称);司法行政官辖区(职权或任期)
magistrate n. 最高统治者,首席官员,司法行政官,司法官员(美国许多州的司法系统中均有此类基层司法官员,常冠以"magistrate""justice of peace""police justice"等称呼);(英)治安官;地方法官(港译:裁判官);高级市政官;(苏格兰)自治市市长;地方法院
magistrate grade I 一级司法行政官(亦译做一级地方法官)
magistrate judge(s) (美)治安法官(指通常由各地区法院的法官委任,协助地区法官进行工作的司法官员,他们协助地区法院法官做开庭前的案件准备工作和和解工作)
magistrate on the commission 在职(任)治安官(或司法行政官)
Magistrates Courts Act 1980 (英)《1980年治安法院法》
magistrate's clerk n. 治安官的书记官
magistrate's court (英)治安法官法庭(刑事审判系统的最低审级),司法行政官法庭;(美)(州的)地方法院(具有对成年人的刑事初审管辖权,类似市法院或治安官法院)
magistrature n. (=magistracy)
magistratus (大陆法)司法行政官,(有权听审和决定案件的)司法官员
Magna Carta (1215年)(英)《大宪章》(见 Great Charter)
magna cum laude 优异学业成绩
magna negligentia 重大过失
* *Magna negligentia culpa est*; *magna culpa dolus est*. Gross negligence is fault; gross fault is fraud. 重大过失(疏忽)就是失误,重大失误就是欺诈。
magnanimous a. 气量大的,宽大的;高尚的
magnate n. 大官,权贵;大资本家,巨头
magnifico n. 高官,权贵,贵人;(古威尼斯)贵族

magnitude n. 重大,重要性,数量
magnitude of error 错误量
magnitude of the operation 业务工作量
magnitude of traffic flow 交通流量
magnitude of transaction costs 交易成本量,交易费用量
magnitude of value 价值量
Magnum Concilium (英史)大议事团
Magnuson Fishery Conservation and Management Act (美)《马格纳森渔业保护(区)和管理法》(1976年)
Magnuson-Moss Act (美)《马格纳森—莫斯法》(指为消费者产品担保而订立质量标准的联邦法规)
maiden n. 1.少女,未婚青年女子,处女 2.(苏格兰16世纪使用过的)断头机
maiden assize (英)形式上的开庭(即无效果的开庭,开始指没有人被判处死刑的巡回法庭,后来指无犯人受审的刑事法庭开庭,亦做 maiden circuit, maiden sessions)
maihem n. (强暴)致人残废;残害
mail n. 1.邮件;(美)邮递;邮递员;邮递工具;邮政制度(英国一般用 post) 2.(古苏格兰法)租金
mail confirmation 邮寄电报证实书,邮寄证实书
mail credit 邮寄融资
mail day 邮件截止日
mail fraud 利用邮件的欺诈活动;邮件欺诈案
mail order 函购,邮购
mail order divorce (1922年)邮函离婚[指配图获准离婚的夫妻双方未亲身出庭,亦无隶属的居住管辖,而却欲获得在管辖内批准离婚。这样的离婚在美国不被承认,因为缺少通常管辖需要的根据(usual base for jurisdiction)。见 Mexican divorce]
mail transfer 信汇
mail-bomb n. 邮寄炸弹
mail-order business 邮购业
mail-order divorce 邮件离婚(指由一个既无人居住又无人旅游的国家来允准的离婚,在美国无法律效力)
mail-order firm 邮购公司

mail-order house （以函购为经营方式的）邮购商行
mailbox deposit 通讯存款，邮政存款
mailbox rule 邮箱规则（指通过信件对要约作承诺，从投入邮箱寄出时有效合同即告成立，此为司法实践的合理原则）
maim v. 残害，使人残废，使负重伤
maimer n. 残害他人者，给人重创者
maiming n. 伤害他人身体；伤害物体
main a. 主要的；最重要的；总的；全力的
main body of assets 主体财产，主体资产
main channel 主航道
main clause 主要条款
main contract 主合同（契约）
main culprit 主犯，首犯
main evidence 主要证据
main fact in issue 争执中的主要事实
main interests center 主要利益中心[在跨国破产案件管辖权最近的发展中，以《欧盟破产程序条例》(Council Regulation on Insolvency Proceedings)和1997年《国际破产合作示范法》(Model International Insolvency Cooperation Act)为代表，进一步发展的管辖权标准——主要利益中心]
main issue of the suit 诉讼的实质系争点
main judg(e)ment 判决主文
main motion 主要动议，主要请求
main office 总行，总办事处
main residence 主要居所
main stem （铁路的）干线；（河流的）主航道；（美俚）大街
main suit 主诉，主案
main things 主物
main types of contract 合同（契约）的主要类型
main war criminal 主要战犯
mainframe computer 计算机主机
mainland n. 大陆
mainline v./n. （美）把毒品直接注入静脉／主血管；对主血管的海洛因注射
mainovre（或 **mainoevre**）直接侵权，直接犯罪
mainour（或 **manour, meinour**）n. （在盗窃犯身上找到的）被窃物品，赃物
mainpernor n. （英）（保证被保释人随传随到的）具保人；（复）保释
mainprise (=mainprize) n. （英）（保证被保释人随传随到的）保释；具保罪犯释放令
mainspring n. 主要动机；主要原因；主要动力
mainstream economics 主流经济学
mainstream of the original action 原诉的主流问题
mainswear v. （英）立伪誓，立假誓言；发假誓，作假证
mainsworn n. 发假誓；作假证；发假誓者，作假证者
maintain v. 1.供养，扶养 2.维护（纪律等），维持（秩序等），主张；强调；坚持 3.资助诉讼
maintain discipline 维护纪律，严肃纪律
maintain strict neutrality 严守中立
maintain the law 执法，维护法律
maintain the people's right 维护人民的权利
maintain vigilance 保持警惕
maintainable a. 可维持的，可保持的；可修的，可供养的；可坚持的；可主张的
maintainor n. 非法帮助诉讼的人，插手资助与本人无关的未决案件者
maintenance n. 1.扶养费，赡养费，生活费；扶养；抚养 2.维修，保养，维持 3.唆讼行为，非法帮助诉讼，包揽诉讼；助讼罪 4.依法应负的扶养义务
maintenance agreement （丈夫付给妻子的）扶养费协议
maintenance and cure （在船上供职期间受伤或有病船员应获得的）供养和医疗（权）
maintenance and education clauses 抚养和教育条款
maintenance cost 维修费
maintenance of actions 包揽诉讼；对诉讼的非法资助
maintenance of children 子女抚养费；对子女应负的抚养义务
maintenance of deserted wives and children 被遗弃的妻子儿女的扶养费
maintenance of justice 维护正义，维持

公道
maintenance of law and order 维持法律和秩序
maintenance of membership (美)(劳资合同或契约中)工会会员资格保留条款
maintenance of peace 维持治安
maintenance of possession 继续占有
maintenance of premises and equipment 房屋和设备维修
maintenance of public order 维护公共秩序
maintenance of social order 维持社会秩序
maintenance of social stability 维持社会安定
Maintenance Order 赡养令
Majalla 《马亚拉法典》(指奥托曼帝国时期的一部民法典,以《沙里亚法典》为基础,但受欧洲法典影响,若干年后奠定了奥托曼帝国及其后继国的民法基础)
majestas (罗马法)最高权力,君权
majesty n. 1.君权,最高权力 2.(大写)陛下 3.尊严,(帝王的)威仪 4.庄严,崇高
major n./a. 成年人,长者;陆军少校/重要的;主要的;较大的;较多的;成年的;较年长的;较大范围的
major accident 重大事故
major act of smuggling 重大走私行为
major case prints 主要印痕(包括手掌纹印、手掌尺骨一侧印痕、完整的滚压手指印痕,以及中间的、贴近指骨纹线部位和从手指中心到指甲和从指甲一侧到另一侧的滚压指尖印痕)
major casualty 主要灾害,严重伤亡事故
major civil liberties (美)重大公民自由权(指大法官布莱克对商业言论、外侨权利以及堕胎等权利方面维护的贡献)
major construct in Pound's thinking 庞德思想中的主要构想
major counter-revolutionary case 重大反革命案件
major crimes 恶性犯罪,重罪
major criminal 重大刑事犯,重刑犯
major criminal case 重大刑事案件
major critical component 主要关键部件
major department of government 政府的主要部门
major engineering 大型工程

major executives 高级职员,高级主管人员,上层管理人员
major freight station 主要货运站
* *Major haereditas venit unicuique nostrum a jure et legibus quam a parentibus.* A greater inheritance comes to every one of us from right and the laws than from parents. 对于我们每一个人来说,从权利和法(律)中获得的比从父母那里继承的要多得多。
major issue 主要系争点;主要事件
major legal families 主要法系
major offence 主要罪行,重罪
major offender 主犯
major party (有竞选力量的)主要政党
Major Peace Treaties of Modern History 《现代史上的重要和平条约》(由弗雷德·L.依斯雷尔编辑的一部5卷本的1648—1979年和平条约汇编)
major punishment 重罚,主刑
major smuggler 大走私犯
major suspect 重大嫌疑犯
major thief 巨盗,大盗贼
major war criminal 主要战犯
majores (英)(古代)伟人,富有财产者;(罗马法)六代以上的男系(祖先)尊亲属
majori inest minus (=majori summae minor inest) The less is contained in the greater/ The lesser is included in the greater sum 大额包含小额;更大包括更小(亦等于 *majus continet minus* = the greater contains the less)
majoritarian democracy 多数主义的民主,多数说了算的民主
majoritarianism n. 多数主义派
majority n. 1.多数,大多数,半数以上 2.得票多的党(集团);(选举中)多得的票数;多数党 3.成年,法定年龄
majority ballot 多数票
majority consensus 多数一致意见
majority control 多数控制(指经营者拥有公司过半数的股权,并据此控制公司。见 Control through almost complete ownership)
majority decision 多数议决
majority holding 多数股权
majority in parliament 议会中的多数派

majority interest 多数股权,控制股权
majority joint-venture 多股合资
majority judg(e)ment 多数判决(定案)制
majority leader 多数党领袖
majority opinion 多数意见(指受理上诉法院参加成员的大多数人意见或在案件中半数以上的多数法官同意判决结果及判决理由)
majority party 多数党
majority party or coalition in the legislature 议会中占多数席位的政党和政党联合
majority representation 多数代表制,多数表决制
majority rule 多数裁定原则,多数通过制(原则)
majority shareholder 多数股东(指控制公司50%以上股份的股东,类似中国说的"大股东""多数股东",它不同于"控股股东"。如果公司在外发行的股票分散在多人手中,则控股公司远不需要掌握50%的股份。在封闭公司中,控股股东对少数股东负有特殊责任,相当于合伙人之间相互所负的责任)
majority verdict 多数裁决
majority vote 多数票决(制)
majority voting over two ballots 两轮多数票(当选)制
* *Majus dignum trahit ad se minus dignum.* The more worthy draws to itself the less worthy. 重要的吸收次要的(如企业兼并)。
* *Majus est delictum seipsum occidere quam alium.* It is a greater crime to kill one's self than (to kill) another. 自杀比杀害他人罪行更重。
majus jus (英)较多权利(指旧时对物诉讼中的一种抗辩)
make v. 1.作出,制定,订立 2.构成,组成,造成;变成,成为 3.认为;抱有 4.进行,实行 5.产生;制造 6.获得,净得;立下(合同、遗嘱等)7.引起,产生;迫使 8.总计;等于
make a clean breast of 坦白供认,完全承认(秘密等)
make a complaint against… 控告……,控诉……

make a corner in (sth.) 垄断;囤积(某物)
make a difference between 区别对待
make a false countercharge 进行诬告,倒打一耙
make a getaway (美)逃跑,逃掉
make a killing 赚大钱
make a law 制定法律
make a loss 亏损
make a noise at night 夜间发出高声(指夜间发出大噪声,干扰他人安宁,也是一种犯罪行为)
make a play for 想取得,挖空心思,想尽办法
make a point 立论;证明论点
make a point of 强调,认为重要
make a power point 演示实力,显示实力
make (或 give) a present to sb. 送礼给某人
make a pretense of ignorance 假装不知道;假装无知
make a protest against 提出抗议
make a raise 筹款,凑钱
make a remittance 汇款
make a reparation for an injury 赔偿损失
make a ring 联合操纵市场
make a ruling 裁决
make a ruling by summary 简易作出裁决,即决裁定
make a scrutiny into sth. 对某事进行详尽研究
make a settlement on sb. 给予某人财产
make a stand against 反对,反抗
make a virtue of necessity 把非做不可的事装成出于好心而做的
make a will 立遗嘱
make advances to sb. 为交友或求爱而接近某人
make allowance 留余地
make allowance for 体谅,顾及
make amends for one's crimes by good deeds 将功赎罪
make an advance to sb. 贷款给某人
make an affidavit (或 swear) 作宣誓供状
make an offer 提供出售;要价
make away with 杀掉;摧毁;用完;卖出;

偷走
make away with oneself 自杀
make believe 假装;佯为借口,托词
make both ends meet 量入为出;收支相抵
make cargo 接货
make certain 弄清楚,弄确实
make default 缺席;不履行法律义务
make for a loss 弥补损失
make for certainty 毋庸置疑
make good 兑现,补偿
make head 向前进(尤指迎着阻力);武装起来反抗
make his law 自律(指当某人履行约束他的法律义务时称为自律)
make inroads into a country 侵袭某一个国家
make interest with… 施加影响于……
make little difference 无关紧要;没大区别
make little of 不重视,轻视
make money 赚钱
make much of 认为极重要;重视
make no bones about 不加挑剔,毫无顾忌
make no exceptions 不容许有例外,无例外,照办
make of 了解;明白;用……制造;对待,处理;批准,解释
make off with 偷出;拿走,拐走
make offer and counter offer 出价和杀价
make one's case 证明自己有理
make one's market 出售(存货)
make one's option 进行选举
make one's own bargain 对自己同意成交的交易负责
make one's testament 立遗嘱
make out 1.书写,填写〈make out a chaque〉(开支票),〈make out a document in duplicate〉(将文件缮写一式两份),并列;2.(企图)证明,说明;把……说成〈I don't see what you are trying to make out〉(我不明白你试图要说明什么),〈this is not such a wasteland as some people make out〉(这块地方绝不是像有些人所说的那样的荒地),3.拼凑,完成〈make out a sum to settle the account〉(拼凑一笔款了结账目)4.理解,了解〈I can't make out the meaning of this passage〉(我不理解这段文章的含义)5.辨认出〈I can't make out his handwriting〉(我不能辨认出他的笔迹)6.详细勾画出 7.设法应付(美)进展,过活〈he made out with a defective tool and still got the job done〉(他使用一件不完善的工具,但仍然完成任务)
make over 转让(财产),让与;移交;修改,更改
make overall arrangement 统筹兼顾
make painstaking investigation 做艰苦的调查
make (a) profit (＝make interest) 获利
make promise 作出承诺
make provision for 为……采取措施
make real 兑现
make replacement and technical innovations 更新改造
make reprisal 进行报复
make sense 有意义
make shift 设法,想尽办法
make such order as it is just 依公平原则下达指令
make sure of fact 确查事实,弄清事实
make the bull's eye 取得成功;打中靶心的一击
make the plaintiff whole again 使原告恢复如初
make unwarranted arrest 擅自逮捕
make whole 补发工资令
make up 1.弥补,补偿,补足;补考〈we must make it up to him somehow〉(我们得想个办法赔偿他);修改;修订(议案,法规等)2.拼凑成;配制;包装〈make up books into bundles〉(把书包成几包)3.编排(版面等);编制 4.虚构;捏造(谎言,故事等)5.缝制(衣服等)6.组成〈a mobile medical team make up of ten doctors〉(由10名医生组成的流动医疗队)7.调停(纠纷等),和解〈make it up with sb.〉(和某人讲和),〈shake hands and make up〉(握手言和)8.结算;标高(商品)价目;整理,准备 9.化妆(演员化妆),打扮 10.缔结(协定等),安排(婚姻等)11.加燃料使(炉火)不熄 12.洗牌

make up to 1.接近(a fishing boat make up to us)(一艘渔船驶近我们)2.巴结,奉承;向(女子)求爱
make…of… 用……做;使……成为
maker n. 立借据人;出票人;制造者(商)
maker of bill 出票人
maker's certificate 制造商证书
maker-of promissory note 期票出票人
makeshift a./n. 权宜的,临时凑合的/权宜之计;临时凑合的代用品
makeshift arrangement 临时安排
makeshift policy 权宜政策
makeup n./v. (1916年)1.提示物品销售价格(指对一个项目所增加的价值且以决定其出售价)(见 profit margin)2.国会委员会的会议中修改立法议案,使其在呈交适当议院之前已成最后的形式/(1865年)1.增价(增加货物的价格)2.修订(指修订立法的议案、规定等)3.置于安排(指将一个案件置于审理日历或安排一个案子于某个日期审理)
making law 造法,制定法律
making of article to order 物品定做
making of law(或 **decree**) 制定法律(或法令)
making of peace 媾和,调停
making off without payment 赖账逃跑
making public 发表(可采取口头方式,而出版则必须以物质固定形式,并达到一定数量,在国际公约中出版为关键行为,发表则不是)
Mala fede supenveniens non nocet. 后来失信不影响占有效力(罗马法格言)[只要求占有人在取得占有时具有初始诚信(*bona fides*),在占有取得后出现的失信则一般不予考虑]
mala fides 恶意(指与 *bona fides* 相对而言)
* *Mala grammatica non vitiat chartam.* Bad grammar does not vitiate a deed. 语法不通不影响契据效力。
mala in se 自然犯,自然罪行;本质不合法
mala per se 本质罪恶
mala praxis 医疗失误,医疗不当(受损伤病人有权要求赔偿)

mala prohibita 法律所禁止的行为(指不法行为或犯罪行为)
maladministration n. 管理不善,弊政
malapportioned a. 分配不均的,代表性不够理想的
malapportioned governmental bodies 代表性不理想的政府机关,分配不均的政府机关
malappropriate v. 侵占,非法据为己有;误用,乱用
malappropriation n. 侵占,非法占为己有;误用,乱用
malconduct in office 见 official misconduct
malcontent a./n. 不满的,对政治现状不满的,反叛的/不满者,反叛者
male n. 男性;公,雄;男人,男孩
male ascendant 男性尊亲属
male chauvinism 大男子主义
male chauvinist 大男子主义者
male heir 男性继承人
male issue 男性子嗣
male officer 男职员
male supremacist 大男子主义者
male tail 限于男性为继承人的遗产继承,限定男嗣继承(权)
malefaction n. 犯罪,犯罪行为;罪行;罪恶
malefactor n. 罪犯,作恶者
malefactress n. 女罪犯,作恶妇女
maleficence n. 坏事,罪行,恶行,邪恶性
* *Maleficia non debent remanere impunita; et impunitas continuum affectum tribuit delinquenti.* Evil deeds ought not to remain unpunished, and impunity affords continual incitement to the delinquent. 罪恶的行为不应当不受惩罚,而不受惩罚就会继续唆使发生违法犯罪的行为。
* *Maleficia propositis distinguuntur.* Evil deeds are distinguished from evil purposes, or by their purposes. 罪恶行为是从罪恶的目的或依其目的来识别的。
malevolence n. 恶意,恶毒;敌意;用心狠毒的行为
malfeasance n. 渎职(罪);滥用职权;违法乱纪,胡作非为;恶行
malfeasant n./a. 渎职者,违法乱纪者,犯罪

者/渎职的,违法乱纪的,犯罪的
malfeasant administrative act 违法的行政行为;行政渎职行为
malfunction n./v. 失灵,故障/失灵,发生故障,运转不正常
malice a. 预谋;蓄意(犯罪或害人);恶意,恶毒
malice action 恶意行为
malice aforethought 预谋的恶意;预谋不轨;预谋罪
malice in fact 事实上的恶意(指明示的或实际的预谋非法行为)
malice in law 法律上的恶意(亦称隐蔽的恶意,指依法推定的预谋非法行为,以区别于事实上的恶意。见 malice in fact)
malice intention 恶意
malice prepense (= malice aforethought) 预谋的恶意
malicious a. 预谋的,蓄意的;恶意的,有敌意的;心毒的;任意的
malicious abandonment 非法遗弃
malicious abuse of civil proceedings 恶意滥用民事诉讼
malicious abuse of process 蓄意滥用诉讼程序
malicious accusation 恶意控告,诬告
malicious act 恶意行为,任意伤害他人的行为
malicious arrest (不合乎法律手续的)非法拘捕,任意逮捕;(民事)非法扣押
malicious damage 蓄意损害
malicious damage to property 恶意毁损财物罪
malicious destruction of property 恶意破坏(他人)财产(物)罪
malicious falsehood 恶意诽谤(指故意诽谤他人的权利、物品或对财产作不真实的陈述使造成或正在造成损害者)
malicious imprisonment 非法监禁
malicious injury 蓄意伤害(罪)
malicious intent 恶意,犯罪意图
malicious mischief 蓄意毁损(财产)罪
malicious motive 恶意动机
malicious nonperformance 蓄意不履行
malicious omission 蓄意懈怠,蓄意遗漏,蓄意不作为
malicious prosecution and defamation 诬告和诽谤
malicious trespass 蓄(恶)意损害(他人财产或公共财物的)行为;蓄意非法侵害
malicious waste 蓄意毁损
malicious wounding 蓄意伤害(他人身体)
maliciously false accuser 诬告人,诬告分子
maliciousness n. 恶意
malign v./a. 中伤,诽谤,污蔑/恶意的,邪恶的,有害的,恶性的;致命的
malignancy (= malignance) n. 恶意,恶毒,恶意行为;邪恶;恶性;恶性肿瘤
malignant a. 恶意的,恶毒的,有害的,邪恶的;恶性的
malignant inflation 恶性通货膨胀
maligner n. 诽谤者,中伤者
malignity n. 极端憎恨,极大的恶意,恶言恶行
maliki school 马立克派(见 *Malikiyah*)
Malikiyah(伊斯兰教法)马立克派(指逊尼派的四种流派之一,强调麦地那地方教团的传统习惯,断案时根据传统意见和类比推理,而不依据圣训)
malingerer n. 装病者,诈病不出勤者,装病以获取救济物者
malingering a. 诈病的,装病的
militia supplet aetatem 构成蓄意(行为要求)的最低年龄(指达到刑事责任能力的最低年龄)
malo animo 恶念,蓄意,恶意
malpractice n. 1.不当行为,渎职,营私舞弊,玩忽职守 2.治疗错误,治疗失当 3.业务技术事故(此词常用于医生、律师、会计师在业务上的不端行为)
malpractice insurance 医疗事故保险(现此词亦用作律师、会计师等业务上的事故保险)
maltreat v. 粗暴对待,虐待;乱用,滥用(机器等)
maltreatment n. 虐待,粗暴对待(多指外科医生对待病员)
maltreatment and desertion 虐待和遗弃
maltreatment of animals 虐待牲畜

maltreatment of family members 虐待家庭成员

maltreatment of prisoners 虐待囚犯

maltreatment of the aged（或 **old people**）虐待老人

maltreatment of women 虐待妇女

malum in se 不法,不法行为

＊**Malum non habet efficientem, sed deficientem, causam.** Evil has not an efficient, but a deficient, cause. 罪恶除了某种软弱无力的理由外,不会有什么充分有力的理由。

malum non praesumitur Evil is not to be presumed. 恶意不得推定

malum prohibitum 法律所禁止的不法行为

malus fide 恶意,恶信（与 *bona fide* 相对）

＊**Malus in uno malus in omnibus** bad in one respect, bad in all 恶习渗入一方面,即会渗入全部

＊**Malus usus abolendus est.** A bad or invalid custom is (ought) to be abolished. 坏的或无效的惯例应予废止。

malversation n. 贪污;受贿;营私舞弊;渎职;(公职人员的)不法行为;腐败的行政

mammonism n. 拜金主义

mammonist n. 拜金主义者

Mammoth n./a. 庞然大物,巨物/庞大的,巨大的、盛大的〈mammoth enactments〉(大量的法规条例)

Mamn Act (美)《曼恩法》(为了提高美国的道德水平,1910 年通过此法,它也被称为"禁止贩卖白人奴隶法"。根据《曼恩法》,"为了卖淫及淫逸或其他不道德之目的,或旨在引诱、教唆或强迫妇女"从事不道德的活动而跨州或在对外贸易中运输或帮助运输妇女的行为应定为重罪)

man n. 1.人,个人;成年男子 2.(史)封臣;佃户;侍从;男仆 3.(复)雇工;雇员;士兵;水手

man and wife 丈夫和妻子,夫妻

man at the wheel 舵手,驾驶员;负责人

man higher up (美)政界巨头

man of action 活动家,实行家

man of blood 杀人成性的人

man of business (商业或法律上的)代理人

man of law 法律界人士(指法官、律师等)

man of means 有门路的人,有办法的人

man of property 物主

man of resources 足智多谋的人

man of sin 罪人,堕落的人

man of straw 稻草人(指已无实际财产可供执行,因而对其没有起诉价值的人)

man on the Clapham omnibus "克拉彭公共汽车上的人"(用以喻作"有理智的人")

man with plain clothes 便衣警察

manacle n. 束缚,约束;(复)手铐

manadate n./v. 命令,训令;(上级法院给下级法院的)命令(训令);(英国法)财产委托;(罗马法)委任合同(契约)(指委任受托人无偿代理的合同);(美)(刑诉中由一个法院或一个司法官要求某一适当官员执行一项裁决或法令的)指令,执行令;委托办理;(国联的)委任制度;委托统治权;选民对议员或公职人员的要求(或授权);(大陆法)授权书/托管,将(某地区)置于委任制度之下,授权;命令

manage v. 管理;处理;经营;安排;运用;操纵,驾驭;控制

manageable a. 易管理的,易操作的,易驾驭的

management n. 管理,经营;安排,支配,处理;资方;经理,管理人员;经营才能;(工商企业的)管理部门

management agreement 管理合约,管理协定

management committee 管理委员会

management consultant (企业)管理顾问

management control 经营者控制,经营控制权(指经营者所拥有的股权微不足道,原本无法控制公司经营,但因公司股权极为分散,没有任何人或任何集团持有足够股份可控制公司,或给予经营者以有力威胁,经营者从而可获得公司的控制。见 Control through almost complete ownership)

management in enterprises 企业管理

management levels 管理层次

management of affairs of state 总理国务,掌管国家事务

management of the economy 经济管理

management personnel 管理人员
management processes 管理过程
management system 管理制度,管理体制
manager n. 经理;干事;业务管理人;(英)(高等法院指定的)财务管理人;经纪人;(英)(议会中)处理两院共同事务的议员
manager of the deceased property 遗产管理人
managerial a. 经理的;管理人的;管理上的;经营上的
managerial contract system 经理承包制
managerial control 管理监督,经营监督
managerial decision-making 经营决策
managerial direction (form) 管理指挥(美国著名法理学家富勒将哈特等人的法律实证主义和他本人的学说归结为两种不同"社会指导形式",哈特等人代表的是"管理指挥"形式,而富勒本人代表的则是"法律"形式)
managerial personnel 管理人员
managerial prerogatives 经营管理权
managerial skill 经理人技术
managing a. 管理的;主管的;善于经营的;节俭的
managing adjudication 管理裁判方面
managing agent 代管人
managing clerk (英)(初级律师办公室的)常务书记官(员)(工作十年后可成为初级律师)
managing director 总经理;常务董事
managing for results 目标管理,目标经营法
managing partner 有全权处理合伙事务的合伙人
managing underwriter 代理认购人,代理承包人;代理承诺支付者;代理保险商
manbote n. 杀人赔偿金(指因杀人支付的赔偿金,特别是指向被杀死的农奴的领主所支付的赔偿金)
mancipatio (或 **mancupatio**, **onis**, **mancipatus**) 拟制买卖(指罗马法上一种重要的交易形式,后来常用以使遗嘱通过这种形式转让他的全部财产)
mandamus n./v. 1.(给下级法院的)命令书;命令状 2.(上级法院要求下级法院或官员执行某一特殊行为的)指令(或执行令)/(上级法院对下级法院或官吏)发出(履行责任或执行令的)命令(或执行令)
mandata 皇帝训令(敕示);司法训令(命令)
mandatary n. 受托人;委托统治国;受命者;受托国
mandate n. 1.命令,训令;(上级法院给下级法院的)命令(训令) 2.(英国法)财产委托;(罗马法)委任合同(契约)(指委任受托人无偿代理的合同) 3.(美)(刑诉中由一个法院或一个司法官要求某一适当官员执行一项裁决或命令的)指令,执行令 4.委托办理;(国联的)委任制度;委托统治权 5.选民对议员或公职人员的要求(或授权)
mandate of presidency 总统任期
mandate system 委托统治制度;委任制
mandated area 委托统治地
mandated care 法定的谨慎,法定的小心
mandated state 受委托统治国,受托国
mandated territory 委托统治下的领土,委托统治地
mandator n. 委托者,委任者,命令者
mandatory n./a. 受托人,受命者;受托国(=mandatary)/强制的;命令的;训令的;委任的;受委托统治的;无选择自由的
mandatory administration 委托管理
mandatory application 强制适用
mandatory arbitration 强制仲裁,强制公断
mandatory authority 强制权力,有约束力的权力;委托授权
mandatory cumulative voting 强制性累积投票
mandatory disclosure system (美)信息披露义务制度;强制性出示制度
mandatory franchise 强制性特许权
mandatory injunction (法院)指令性强制令
mandatory instruction (1895年)(对陪审团)命令性的指示[指法官要求陪审团必须裁断当事人何方胜诉,何方败诉的指示,如果依据证据优势(preponderance of the evidence)为基础裁断一系列事实的存在,则可对上述要求作出裁断。亦称 bind-

ing instruction]
mandatory insurance　强制保险
mandatory insurance on accidental injury to railroad passengers　铁路旅客意外伤害强制保险
mandatory judg(e)ment　委托裁(判)决
mandatory law　强制法
mandatory marine insurance　船舶强制保险
mandatory marriage statutes　婚姻强制施行法
mandatory mediation　强制性调解
mandatory order　委托令
mandatory plan　指定性计划
mandatory presumption　强制性推定(与conclusive presumption 同),不容辩驳的推定,结论性推定,决定性推定
mandatory provisions　强制性规定,约束性条款
mandatory quotas　指令性指标
mandatory review　强制性审查
mandatory right　委托统治权
mandatory right of appeal　受托上诉权
mandatory rules　强制性规则
mandatory rules of law　强制性法规,强制性法律规范
mandatory rules of national statutes　国内法上的强制性规范
mandatory sanction　强制(性)制裁
mandatory sentence　强制判决,确定刑事判决
mandatory sentencing guidelines　(美)委托科刑指南(见 United States sentencing commission)
mandatory take-over bid　强制性收购要约(见 take over)
mandatory term　强行条款,强制性条款
mandatum　委任,托管,(大陆法)委任合同(契约);(英)财产委托
mandle child　(历史上)出生为非婚生子,以后父母结婚为婚生子女。传统地说,这个身份是以父母正式婚姻仪式为依据的
manerium　(古英国法)采邑,领地,庄园
manhood n.　(男)成年身份(或资格);成年;成年期男子(的总称)

manhood suffrage　男公民选举权
manhunt n.　(美)搜索逃犯
manhunter n.　搜索逃犯者
manic-depressive n.　躁狂抑郁症患者
manifest destiny　昭昭天命(这是美国的历史名词,广义指美国人是上帝派去建立模范社会的选民;狭义指 19 世纪美国扩张主义者把疆土从大西洋扩张到太平洋的意图)
manifest injustice　明显不公正(指在初审法院发生的直接明显错误,如被告作出的有罪答辩是出于非自愿的等),重大不公
manifest n.　1.声明,宣言;表明;证明;出现,显露 2.(飞机、船上的)货物清单,(陆上的)运货单 3.快运货车
manifest of cargo　运货清单
manifest phenomenon　明显的现象
manifest tenor of the constitution　宣告宪法的旨意
* *Manifesta probatione non indigent.* Things manifest do not require proof.　明显的事情无须找证据。
manifesto n.　(英)宣言,声明(指主权国家或其政府发布的正式文件)
manifestation n.　表明;显示;(政府或政党的)公开声明;示威运动,表现形式,现象
manifestation of dishonesty　虚假现象
manifestation of right　权利声明(见 *monstrans de droit*)
manifestly unsuitable　明显不合理
manifesto n.　宣言,声明
manipulation n.　篡改(账目);操纵,使用;应付,处理
manipulator n.　篡改者;操纵者
mankiller n.　杀人者
mankilling a.　可置人于死地的,可杀死人的;令人精疲力竭的
Mann Act　(美)《曼法》(指反对为不道德目的,通常为娼妓目的运送女人穿越州界的联邦法规)
manner n.　方式,方法,样式;举止,态度;习惯,风俗
manner assuring the safety of goods　确保货物安全的方法
manner of execution　执行方法(式)

manner of negotiation 协商方式,谈判方式
manner of payment 付款方法
manner of proof 证明的方法
manner of reaching agreement 达成协议方式,订立协定的方式
(the) manner of service in federal court action 在联邦法院诉讼的送达方式
manners and customs 风俗习惯
mannopus（=*mainour*）（古英国法）赃物
manor n. （英）（封建贵族的）采邑,庄园；（美）领地
manor law 采邑法,（美）领地法
manorial court （英）（封建时代的）领主法院,领地法庭；采邑法庭
manpower n. 人力
Manpower Services Commission （英）人力服务委员会（1973年设立）
manpower utilization survey 人力利用调查
manrent n. 役租
Mansfield Rule 曼斯菲尔德规则（指18世纪英国曼斯菲尔德制定出具有历史意义的规则,规定关于陪审团裁决并不因其个别陪审员的不当行为而受到质疑）
manslaughter n. 过失杀人(罪)，误杀(罪)
manslaughter in self-defense 自卫杀人
manslayer（或 **man-slayer**）n. 杀人凶手,杀人者,杀人犯
mantrap n. 罪恶场所（如赌场）；危险场所；捕人陷阱（指用以捕捉侵入私宅者）
manual a. 手的,用手（操作）的；实际占有的；体力的
Manual for Complex Litigation 《复杂诉讼手册》（美国民事诉讼中可供法官有效管理集团诉讼的众多程序参考）
manual industrial property 手工工业产权
manual instruction 指导手册
Manual of Discipline 《会规手册》（指犹太教艾赛尼派教团的重要文件）
Manual of Patent Examining Proceeding 《专利审查作业手册》
manual strangulation 扼颈,扼死
manual worker 体力劳动者
manufacture n./v. （16世纪）制造；制造业；制造品,产品（专利法）[指由人工或机器制造的物品,区别于自然产生的物品。产品可被授予专利的发明为法定类别之一。产品的范例是座椅和梳妆台,参见《美国注释法典》第35标题卷第101节。亦称 article of manufacture。见 machine；process 3]/制造,加工；粗制滥造（文艺作品等）；捏造,虚构（证据,借口等）
manufactured goods 制成品；工艺制成品
manufacturer n. （17世纪）制造商,制造[指从事制造或生产产品或组装新产品的制造商或生产组装部门。联邦法已扩大了这一界定含义,包括由个人或部门控制新产品的分配,以及控制新产品进口销售的进口商,均可称为制造商。参见《美国注释法典》第42标题卷第4902(6)节]
manufacturer's certificate 厂商证明书
manufacturer's liability 制造商的责任
Manufacturers Aircraft Association (MAA) （美国组建的）飞机制造商协会（见 Mega Pool）
manufacturing activity 加工生产
manufacturing process 生产过程,制造过程
manumissio censu （古罗马）（用）注册（方式）解放（奴隶）
manumissio in ecclesia （罗马法的）寺院解放
manumissio testamento （古罗马）（用）遗嘱（方式）解放（奴隶）
manumissio vindicta （古罗马）（用）执棒仪式解放（奴隶）
manumission n. （罗马法）"我释手"（I send out of hand）,即（奴隶）解放[指允准奴隶获得自由。在共和和早期帝国时期有3种常用方法可使奴隶得到自由而成为公民（citizen）,这些方法是：①*manumission vindicta*（by the rod）执棒解放,即利用拟诉（fictitious lawsuit）弃权（in jure cessio）。涉及自由的奴隶持棒在裁判官（praetor）前并声称他自由了。②*manumission censu* 注册解放,即将奴隶姓名注入户口册中,即可取得自由之身份。古罗马时期每三年调查一次户口。此时,主人将其奴隶之姓名注入户口册,这些奴隶即可获自由,为自由身份。③*manumission testamento*（by will）遗嘱解放,根据《查士丁尼法典》,任何形式的遗嘱（债权人的欺诈除外）均可使奴隶解

放,使其获取自由人或公民身份。亦称 manumission。遗嘱解放有两种:直接遗嘱与间接遗嘱,前者即主人以遗嘱允准其奴隶自由之谓,该遗嘱有解放之效力;后者为主人委托自己的继承人解放奴隶之谓,故又谓信托解放(*manumission fideicommissoria*),与直接解放不同]

manumission censu (罗马法)(奴隶)注册解放(指奴隶经过在户口册注册登记,即可获得自由人之身份。见 *manumission*)

manumission sacrorum causa (通过)主人庄严宣告解放奴隶[当奴隶持着木棒,并且承诺如果成为自由人后脱离家庭仪礼常规,将支付一笔款项,主人庄严宣布该奴隶已获自由。然后,主人绕了一圈,并释放奴隶,使其获得自由,但仍受一定约束去履行家庭的礼仪常规(family rite)。亦称 *manumissio sacrorum causa*]

manumission testamento (罗马法)(奴隶)遗嘱解放(by will)(指奴隶通主人之遗嘱允准其奴隶获得解放或自由而成为自由人。见 *manumission*)

manumission vindicta (罗马法)(奴隶)执棒解放[指一种有仪式的奴隶解放。仪式上,第三当事方在审判官或裁判官(praetor)面前将木棒(a rod, vindicta)执于奴隶的上方同时宣称该奴隶已是自由了,此后均承认奴隶的自由,裁判官宣布奴隶获得自由。这种仪式实际上是法律上的虚拟诉讼(fictitious action at law)。见 manumission]

manumit v. to free (a slave)使(或给)奴隶自由

manumitter n. 给予奴隶自由者

manung (古)官方的(或正式的)管辖地区(或管辖权地区;官方的审判权地区,正式的司法管辖地区。亦可拼写为 monung)

manus n. (罗马法)1.手;权力,夫权(指家长对家庭的所有成员和奴隶行使的权力。特别是丈夫对妻子行使或享有的权利,即夫权。这是早期罗马时代大多数婚姻期的状态)2.(历史上)宣誓助诉人(compurgator)或宣誓人(该宣誓惯例起源于宣誓人在宣誓进程中一只手放在《圣经》上)

(见 compurgator)

manus capere 争取;一手交钱一手交货

manus iniectio 拘押[指在债务口约订立过程中,当事人要说这样的套语:"若某某债务人到期不将某款项归还,应将他收为奴隶,使役之、出卖之、杀戮之"。此等套语中规定的"三之"违约后果为拘押,其内容体现在《十二铜表法》第三表的规定之中。根据规定,拘押的第一步为催告还债,30 天的恩惠期过后债权人可将债务人带到长官前,此时后者有机会提出推迟应诉保证人(*vindex*)。如不能提出此等保证人,债权人可监禁债务人 60 天。其间,让他戴上枷锁强制劳动,此即为"使役之",此时的债务人成为 *addictus*(债奴)。60 天的监禁期过后,债权人有杀死或出卖债务人两个选择,此为"出卖之、杀戮之"。如此,债务人以他的人身作为债的担保,尽管十分残酷,但相较于《汉穆拉比法典》第 117 条的规定,《十二铜表法》尚未把债务人家属的人身作为债的担保,属于"残酷中的人道"]

manuscript n. 原稿,手稿,底稿

Manu-smrti《摩奴法典》(指传统上被认为最具有权威性的印度教法典)

man-year n. (按每周一般工作日标准的)一人一年的工作量

many-sided a. 多方面的

map out 规划,策划

maraud v. 抢劫,掳掠,攫夺

marauder n. 抢劫者,掳掠者

Marbury v. Madison, 5 U. S. (Cranch) 137 (1803) 马伯里诉麦迪逊,卷 5《美国判例汇编》(克兰奇 1 卷)第 137 页(1803 年)[指确定司法审查(Judicial Review)、国会法案的合宪性的一个重大判例。联邦最高法院不仅有权确立审查州政府和其他部门的行为是否符合美国联邦宪法,而且还有权审查其是否符合美国联邦宪法第 3 条第 2 款所规定的其他联邦法律和条约的判例原则,还包括审查州刑事法庭诉讼程序是否与美国联邦宪法相一致的权力以及美国联邦法院确认立法和行政行为违宪而宣告其无效的权力]

march-in rights (专利)政府对融资发明

的权力[指如果联邦融资发明的拥有人（或拥有人的许可证接受人）在合理的时间内没有充分地发展或应用此项发明,则政府有干预或授予新人的许可或撤销现有许可证的权力。参见《美国注释法典》第 35 标题卷第 203 节（35 USCA § 203）]

Marches n. (英)边境地区(指英格兰和威尔士、英格兰和苏格兰之界地区)

marchet (或 **merchet**) n. (佃户对其女儿出嫁给主人的)婚嫁纳金

marchioness n. 女侯爵,侯爵夫人(女性的丈夫为侯爵;或对她的尊严,高贵而称谓)

mare 海

mare clausum 领海,闭海,公海封锁

mare liberum 海洋自由；(大写或斜体字)《海洋自由论》[指格劳秀斯(Grotius)于 1609 年发表的论著]

Margagao 画押

margin n. 1.(纸)页边的空白；边缘；界限 2.(成本与销售的)差额；盈余；利润 3.幅度 4.保证金

margin money 保证金

margin(s) of dumping 倾销差额

margin of judicial action 司法行为之范围

marginal a. 记在页边的,由旁注的；边缘的,边际的；界限的,边境的；介乎两者之间的

marginal ability 勉强合格的能力

marginal accident reductions 边防意外事故减少

marginal belt 边缘带

marginal benefit 边际收益

marginal capital costs savings 边际资金成本节约

marginal clause 边列条款(保险),边际条款；保险单主文外的特别条款,栏外条款

marginal compliance cost 边际补偿成本

marginal constituency 边际选民

marginal cost 边际成本

marginal credit 边际信用,信用限度

marginal deposit 开发信用证的保证金,保证金

marginal deterence 边际阻遏(效果)[美国芝加哥大学法经济学家波斯纳(Richard A. Posner)在用经济学观点来分析刑法时,提出了"边际阻遏"的效果,他认为刑事责任也仅仅是价格行为的一种方法。刑法若能对非法行为有一种合理的代价表(schedule of price),那么当一个罪犯不是被判监禁,而是被课以相同价值的法外处罚时,其他人为何在意该罪犯会不会有进一步犯罪行为？从本质而言,低成本有拘束力之交易的普通法罪行该强调的应是预防]

marginal disclosure costs 边际披露成本

marginal effect 边际效力

marginal gains 边际收益

marginal notes (英)旁注(指写在议会法案正式条款前空白处,与法案主题无直接关系的不视为法案内容的文字说明,在法庭上也不得援用)；附注

marginal product 边际产品

marginal profits 边际利润,界限利润

marginal rate (of tax) 边际税率,限界税率

marginal revenue 边际收入

marginal sea 边缘海,陆缘海,领海

marginal seat (竞选中双方票数接近)可能为任何方争得的席位

marginal tax rate (1939 年)边际税率(指在税率表中,适用于纳税人所得的最高金额的税率。这一概念在计收受增加所得税或主张增加、扣减中是有实际用处的。见 tax bracket)

marginal waters 沿海

margrave n. (神圣罗马帝国的)侯爵；(德国边境各省的)总督

marijuana n. 大麻(＝marihuana),大麻中的毒质；粉兰烟草

marijuana cigarette 大麻香烟

marijuana consumption 大麻消耗

marine n./a. (总称)(一个国家的)船舶；海运业；(大写)(法国等国的)海军部/海上的；海事的；海船的；航海的；海运的；海产的

marine adventure 海上冒险业

marine agency 船舶代理,海运代理

marine cargo insurance 海运货物保险

marine court 海事法庭

marine environment 海洋环境
Marine Environment Chamber 海洋环境法庭
marine hull insurance 船舶保险
marine insurance 海上保险(旧译:水险)
marine insurance action 海上保险诉讼
marine law 海事法(又译:海商法)
marine life 海洋生物
marine magistrate 海事裁判官
marine police 水上警察,海上警察
marine product liability 海运产品责任
marine resources 海洋资源
marine risk 水险
marine salvage 海上救助(亦译:海难救助)
Maris et faeminae conjunctio est de jure naturae. The union of male and female is founded on the law of nature. 雄性与雌性结合就奠定了自然法则基础;雄性与雌性结合构成自然法则
maritagium 嫁资,妆奁;对未成年人的婚姻监护权
marital a. 婚姻的;(古)丈夫的
marital abode 婚姻的常住地,婚姻住所
marital agreement (1866年)夫妻(财产)协议[指结婚后配偶之间根据婚姻期间或因死亡、离婚、婚姻终止后涉及夫妻财产的所有权和分割所达成的任何协议,尤指婚前合同(premarital contract)或分居协议(separation agreement)。因其主要涉及离婚时如何分割夫妻财产的问题,亦称marriage settlement; property settlement。见 prenuptial agreement; postnuptial agreement]
marital autonomy 婚姻自主(权)
marital communications privilege (美)婚姻上通讯(交谈)特权(指夫妇双方在某些事情上有彼此保密的权利,同时彼此在刑事审判中亦不能用作证据来反对方)
marital crime 婚姻上的犯罪
marital deduction (夫或妻的)遗产减税
marital dispute 婚姻纠纷
marital exchange 姻亲换婚制(指必须从指定的某些家庭、家族、部落或部落的分支择偶的制度)

marital feelings 婚姻感情
marital fertility rate 婚生率
marital immunity 夫妻豁免(见 husband-wife immunity)
marital obligation 婚姻上的义务,丈夫的责任
marital offences 婚姻上的罪行(过错、违法等)
marital partnership assets 婚姻共同财产
marital privacy 婚姻隐私权
marital privilege 丈夫特权
marital property 夫妻财产,婚姻财产[指婚姻期间所获得的财产,在婚姻终止时方可进行分配或分割,一般来说,多指结婚日期以后和配偶一方提出分居或离婚以前所取得的财产。此术语"夫妻财产"用于平等分配(equitable distribution)的一些州,也就大体等于夫妻共同财产,即community property,亦称 marital estate]
marital rape 婚内强奸
marital relations 婚姻关系
marital rights 婚姻权(即同居权);夫权
marital status 婚姻状况
marital status classification 婚姻状况分类
marital testimonial privilege 婚姻证言特权(亦称不利婚姻事实之特权,指在刑事诉讼中证人有权拒绝作不利于其配偶的证言,以及刑事被告人有权阻止其配偶提供不利于自己的证言)
marital violator 破坏、妨碍他人婚姻者
maritime a. 近海的;海上的;海生的;航海的;船用的;海事的;海运的;海员的;海军陆战队的
Maritime Administration 海事管理局[美国运输部的一个部门,负责资助在美国国旗下一些运营船只的费用;为美国政府组织,监督商业型船只;运作战争风险保险规划(War Risk Insurance Program);管理培养商船高级职员的商船学院(Merchant Marine Academy)。缩略为 MARAD]
maritime arbitration 海事仲裁,海事公断
Maritime Arbitration Commission 海事仲裁委员会;海事公断委员会
Maritime Arbitration Commission of the China Council for the Promotion of Inter-

national Trade 中国国际贸易促进委员会海事仲裁委员会
maritime belt 领海带
maritime casualty 海上事故
maritime cause 海事讼案
maritime claim 海商法上的请求权,海商法上的债权
Maritime Code 《海商法》
maritime commerce 海上贸易
maritime contract 海事合同(契约)
maritime convention 海洋公约
maritime court 海事法院
maritime custom 海关
maritime dispute 海事争议,海事纠纷
maritime domain 领海权
maritime flag (每个国家的)海上公用的国旗;航海旗帜;海商旗
maritime insurance 海事保险,海上保险
maritime international law 国际海事法,国际海洋法
maritime jurisdiction 海事管辖(权)
maritime law 海商法,海事法
maritime lien 海上留置权,海事留置权,海上优先权,海事优先权,船舶优先权(英美法上的 lien 是指物上的负担,其内涵相当于我国法上的担保物权加上诉讼保全等强制措施。该词条是 lien 在海上的特殊表现形式,即设定在海上财产的法定非移转占有型担保。但应注意在相关国际公约中该条的法文相对应概念应是 privilege maritime,可译船舶优先权,海事优先权)
maritime matter 海事案件
maritime negligence 海上过失
maritime partnership 海上合伙
maritime peril 海上遇险,海难
maritime power (或 state) 海洋国家,海上强国
maritime sovereignty 海洋主权
maritime supremacy 海上霸权
maritime tort 海上侵权行为
maritime trade 海上贸易
maritime transaction 海事行为;海上贸易
maritime transport service 海运服务
maritime transportation insurance 海上运输保险
maritime warfare 海战
maritime mortgages 海事抵押,海事抵押权
mark v. 1.留痕迹;作记号;表明;明显表示 2.记下,记录;标志,表示……特征;在……上贴价目(或尺寸等)的标签 3.注意,留心
mark down 减价;标低(商品)价目
Mark System (澳)记分制(指一种鼓励已决犯的制度)
mark up v./n. (1865年)1.加价,标高(商品)价目(指对一件物品或项目增加价目以决定其出售价)2.赊欠(账项);弥补,补偿;虚构,捏造(谎言、故事等)3.调停(纠纷等)4.结算(账目等)5.缔结(协定等)6.修改或修订立法议案,法规等;将案件列入审理日程/1.(1916年)加价,标高的价目(见 profit margin)2.法案的审议过程(指国会委员会会议期间对议案进行修订并在其最后形成之前报送至对其审查的一院)
marked a. 有标记的;显著的;被监视的;受人注意的
marked improvement patent 显著的改良专利
marked man 可疑的人;被监视的人;受敌视的人
market n./v. 市场;市场设置权;行情;推销,销路;行业/销售,(市场上)买卖,赶集
market access 市场准入
market administration 市场管理
market angel 天使融资市场
market-augumenting government 强化市场型政府(是美国经济学家奥尔森提出的在民主体制下的政府,即强化市场型政府,它有足够权力去创造和保护私有产权,并可强制执行合约,与此同时,它还受到约束,不可剥夺或侵犯个人权利)
market authority 市场设置权
market condition 行情;市场状况
market control commission 市场管理委员会
market day 赶集日,定期集市日
market discipline 市场的纪律,管理规定
market discount rate 市场贴现率

market displacement 市场取代
market economy 市场经济
market emergency 市场紧急状态
market factor 市场因素;市场代理人
market failure 市场失灵,市场失效
market garden 以供应市场为目的的菜园
market house 市场管理所
market instinct 市场本能
market integrity theory 市场完整性理论
market leading business 市场导向业务,主要市场经营
market letter (股票等)市场消息(指证券行等所印发的有关市场的行情、展望、消息的印刷品)
market maker 市场撮合者
market mechanism 市场机制,市场功能,市场结构
market overt 公开市场;(英格兰)公开市场原则
market period 营销期
market place 市场,集市;商业界;商业中心
market power 市场力量;市场支配力
market price 市价,市场价格,出售价格
market price for entrepreneurial skill 企业家技术的市场价格
market price for managerial skill 经理人技术的市场价格
market quotation 市场报价,时价(指证券和商品交易的最近报价)
market rate 市场利率,市场汇率
market research 市场调查
market research study 市场调研
market share liability (1980年)各个成员自负其责[指基于每个生产商的市场份额或置于市场的各产品百分比,产生的每个成员通常各自所应承担的责任。这种责任理论(theory of liability)通常只适用于当有些产品含有代替物质时,原告无法探索特定产品的伤害问题(harmful exposure)的情况,比如原告通过显示石棉使其受到伤害而应提出权利主张。见enterprise liability]
market share threshold (market share ceiling) 市场份额阈值
market stand-off agreement (证券)市场锁定协议[指在股份认购合同(stock purchase contract)中有一项规定,其中股份持有人承诺在公司进行公债发行(public stock offering)之后的限定时期内不出售证券也不转移证券]
market structure 市场结构[指美国哈佛大学经济学家贝恩(J. S. Bain)、谢勒(F. M. Scheren)等为代表的哈佛马派倡导旧产业组织理论作为结构主义的立法基础];亦指广义上的市场组织结构特点;销售的密集性、产品的差异性和市场进入壁垒等
market town 集镇
market trading 集市贸易
market value 市场价值,市面价值
market volume 1.市场交易量,股票交易总额(指证券交易所一天内股票交易的总额)2.一天内交易股票份额的总数,亦称market activity
market-making n. 做市
market-oriented industry 市场定位产业
market-oriented model law 市场导向模式的法律
market-oriented mode 市场导向型(见global era)
market-preserving federalism 市场保护型联邦主义
marketable a. 可销售的,适合市场销售的,有销路的;市场买卖的
marketable grain 商品粮
marketable securities 流通证券,挂牌证券;上市证券
marketable share 上市股票,上市股份公司股东的股份,上市股份公司资本的份额
marketable share company 上市股份公司(又译:上市股票公司)
marketable share company act 上市股份公司法(又译:上市股票公司法)
marketable title to land 具有土地销售资格;具有对土地出售的所有权
marketable value 市场价值
marketeer n. 市场上的卖主,市场商人;(英)(20世纪60年代)主张加入欧洲共同市场的人
marketer n. 市场上的买卖人

marketing n. （在市场上）销售,经营,推销;市场学,营销学
marketing arrangement 市场经营（或销售）安排
marketing contract 供销合同（契约）
marketing of product 产品销售
marketing price 销售价
marketing research 销售调查
marketman n. 在市场销货（或购货）的人
markets and fairs 市场与集市;行情,市价
marking board （股票市场上的）揭示牌
marking exhibit 编号证件
marking up （美）法案审议程序[指①国会的法制委员会(legislative committee)逐条逐条地审议法律议案(a bill),并审视修改其语言文本,同时根据要求对内容也进行修改;②案件列入审议日程的程序]
marking up loans 提高贷款利息,标高贷款利息
marks of origin 原产国（地）标记
Marks rule 马尔克斯规则[指美国联邦最高法院的多数法官的判决意见(plurality opinion),但少数法官对此判决有不同的保留理由——并存——狭义的依据。多数判决意见即为法院同意的法定标准(legal standard),也是法院所持的原则]
marksman n. 按手印者;不能用笔署名者
Markush claim 见 patent claim
Markush doctrine （专利法）马尔库什原则[指对于专利申请不得使用选择性语言的一项例外。据此,在某些专利申请书中（特别是涉及化学合成物的发明）,申请人在没有找到通常适用的商标上的专用表达或系属性的表达方式(generic expression)时,则可使用选择性和亚属性(subgeneric)的词语。通过词语陈述出特性,比如"从组成的小组(group)中挑选",这个专利授权请求包括实体小组(a group of substances),小组中的任一成员在进程中均提供同一功能。术语"马尔库什"来源于博士尤·A. 马尔库什(Dr. Eugene A. Markush),他于1923年被授予染料制剂专利(dye preparation patent)。见 Markush group]
Markush group （专利法）马尔库什组[一种限定形式的系属性专利授权申请书,陈述一个要件(element)。说明此要件是这个组的一个成员,同时也举出这个组另一些要件的名字,其中任何一个要件均可能替代第一个陈述的文件。所有马尔库什组的成员至少必须具有共同的财产,主要负责在被专利授权请求关系中承担它们的功能。虽然在小组中,每一材料均有区别,但每一材料必须能够提供同一功能。见 Markush doctrine]
marleet share liability （1980年）各个成员自负其责[指基于每个生产商的市场份额或置于生产商的各自产品百分比,产业的每个成员通常各自所应承担的责任。这种责任理论(theory of liability)通常只适用于当有些产品含有代替物质时,原告无法探索特定产品的伤害问题(harmful exposure)的情况,比如,原告通过显示石棉使其受伤害而应提出权利主张。见 enterprise liability]
marque n. 1.商品的型号（或样式）（尤指汽车等的）2.报复性的捕拿（见 letter of marque and reprisal）
marque and reprisal 报复特许（指一个国家统治者提出要求扣押另一国家的公民或货物。见 letter of marque and reprisal）
marquess （或 **marquis**）n. 侯爵
marriage n. （13世纪）婚姻[指男女成为夫妻的法定结合。有效婚姻的要件是:①双方具有法定能力的订约结婚;②双方同意或赞成;③根据法律规定实际订约(actual contracting)的形式要件。婚姻在法律的许多方面都会产生重要的,诸如侵权,刑法,证据,债权人—债务人关系,财产和合同等问题。亦称 matrimony; conjugal union]
marriage act 婚姻法;（大写）（英）《婚礼法》(1753年)
marriage after divorce 再婚
marriage agency 婚姻介绍所
marriage and divorce records 结婚和离婚登记
marriage and family relation 婚姻和家族关系
marriage application 结婚申请（书）

marriage articles 结婚合同(契约)条款(如婚前对于财产权的协议等)
marriage as a consideration (英美法)以婚姻为(合同的)对价
marriage bed 新婚床;夫妇关系;夫妻床第之事
marriage between cousins (中)中表婚
marriage between families 亲属通婚
marriage between minors 未成年人结成的婚姻
marriage bonds 夫妻关系
marriage brokage 职业的婚姻介绍
marriage brokage contracts 婚姻介绍合同(契约)
marriage broker 婚姻介绍人,媒人
marriage broking 婚姻介绍活动
marriage by capture 抢婚;掠夺婚姻
marriage by certificate 结婚证明书,有证明的婚姻
marriage by purchase 买卖婚姻
marriage ceremony 结婚仪式,正式婚礼
marriage certificate 结婚证书
marriage consideration (构成)婚姻(的)对价(指结婚聘礼)
marriage contract (婚前确定财产权、继承权的)婚姻合同(契约)
marriage counselling (第三人对不和谐的夫妇提出的)婚姻忠告
marriage custom 结婚习俗,婚姻上的习惯
marriage dispute 婚姻纠纷
marriage failure 婚姻破裂
marriage *in articulo mortis* 临终时的结婚
marriage law 婚姻法
Marriage Law of the People's Republic of China 《中华人民共和国婚姻法》
marriage licence 结婚登记证,结婚许可证
marriage lines (英)结婚证书
marriage notice book 婚姻申报册,婚姻登记册
marriage of convenience 基于利害关系的结婚(亦称政略结婚、权宜结婚,指封建社会和资本主义社会中为追求社会地位或政治、经济利益的结婚)
marriage of property 基于财产的婚姻,"门当户对"的婚姻
marriage pacts 婚姻合约(指男女双方在婚前订立婚后处置财产问题的合同)
marriage *per verba de praesenti* (苏格兰法)自双方同意之时间起即可结婚的非正式婚姻(原先的中世纪宗教法,这种形式的婚姻在苏格兰一直到1940年都是被承认的。见 Scotch marriage)
marriage portion 嫁妆,妆奁
marriage promise 婚约
marriage property 婚姻财产
marriage registration 结婚登记
marriage registration office 婚姻登记处
marriage regulations 婚姻条例
marriage service (教会的)婚礼
marriage settlement 见 premarital agreement; prenuptial agreement
marriage system 婚姻制度
marriage termination rule (美)结婚终止规则(指残疾人领取社会保险补助的结婚终止规则)
marriage ties 婚姻关系
marriage upon arbitrary decision (by a third party) (中)包办婚姻
married a. 结了婚的(指未丧偶或离过婚的);有配偶的;夫妇的,婚姻的
married couple domicile 已婚夫妇的住所
married life 婚后生活
married man 已婚男子,有妇之夫
married state 结婚,婚姻生活(状态)
married woman 已婚妇人
married women's property acts 已婚妇女财产法(有时开头字大写)[该制定法正式规定,摒弃已婚妇女无行为能力的问题,特别是去除普通法上禁止已婚妇女签订契约、应诉、应诉以及获取、保有、转让等属于自己权利的财产,不应受到丈夫的限制。例如这些行为摒弃了配偶共同性原则(spousal-unity doctrine)的当今惯例。这个词(act)总是用复数形式(acts),而不用单数(act),除非涉及特殊的法律规定。亦称为 married women's acts; married women's acts; married women's property acts; emancipation acts; married women's e-mancipation acts。见 legal-unity doctrine]
married women's settled property (英)已

婚妇女的限定授予财产

marrier n. 结婚(的)人;为他人举行结婚仪式的牧师(或官员)

marriage de convenance 基于利害关系的结婚,权宜婚姻(见 marriage of convenience)

marry v. 结婚,嫁,娶;结合

marry *per verba de futuro* (寺院法)根据许诺的婚姻(其效力相当于订约或婚约)

marry *per verba de prassenti* (寺院法)根据现诺的婚姻(其效力相当于结婚合约)

marry the partner of one's choice 婚姻自主,自由结婚

marshal n./v. (13 世纪)1.与行政法官(sheriff)相类似的职责的执法官员 2.司法官员(为法院提供安全、实施诉讼进程、必须履行其基本任务)(marshalship n.) 3.(美)联邦法院的执行官;市警察局长;消防队长 4.(英国中世纪)宫内司法官;典礼官 5.元帅;最高级指挥官 6.法警/(15 世纪)安排,排列〈the brief effectively marshaled the appellant's argument〉(诉讼要点有效地被安排为上诉人的辩护);整理,调度;(整理破产或决定遗产分配等的)次序;集合

marshal facts 整理事实

marshal of court 法院执行官;法警

Marshal of Queen's Bench (历史上)1.后座法院监狱典狱长。此职位根据《1842年后座监狱法》(the Queen's Prison Act of 1842)已被废弃。维多利亚第 5 个和第 6 个执政年通过的第 22 个法(St. 586 Vict. ch 22)

Marshals of the Court 联邦最高法院执法官[美国的执法官制始于《1789 年司法法》,乔治·华盛顿(George Washington)总统依据该任命首批 13 名执法官 。他们在联邦法院审判中保护法官和其他参与人员,并送交令状、实施逮捕,以及执行法院判决和联邦法律。联邦最高法院援引美国联邦宪法第 2 条第 3 款的规定:总统享有广泛的权力,以"保证法律被忠实地执行"。总统经参院批准后任命联邦最高法院执法官,任期四年。司法部长对其进行监督。今天美国 94 个司法管辖区各自均有 1 名执法官,并且总共约有 2100 名

职业助理执法官(career deputies)]

Marshal of the King's Household (古英国法)王室司法官(区别于纹章院长的一个古老官职)

Marshal of the Queen's Bench 后座法院执行官

marshal the assets 排列债权人顺序;按顺序分配资产

marshal(l)ing n. (对遗产或破产财产的)分配(或分摊)

marshal(l)ing area (集装箱运输)整理场区

marshaling doctrine 确定债务人财产分配次序原则[指其原则是当优势的债权人(senior creditor)要求就其债务的两笔或两笔以上的财产(funds)进行清偿,而劣势的债权人(junior creditor)要求仅就其债务的一笔财产进行清偿时,优势债权人则必须就劣势债权人所不能求偿的那笔债务人财产得以清偿,而不是取走劣势债权人唯一能求偿的那笔财产,从而避免劣势债权人的债权落空。见 rule of marshaling assets]

marshal(l)ing of assets 资产的分配(或分摊)

marshaling the evidence (1892年)1.安排证据,确定证据(指安排当事方的全部证据,以便庭审时举证)2.法官对陪审团指示(jury charge)的格式程序的实践。因此,安排证据要对特别解释提供更好的可信度

Marshalsea n. (历史上)1.安排皇家诸官职的席位或法官(court)2.在皇室内务法庭(Court of Marshalsea)管辖下关押债务人的监狱(在伦敦)(见 Court of Marshalsea)

Marsilius of Padua (in middle Ages) 帕多亚的马西里乌斯(1270—1342)[意大利学者,与简顿的约翰(Jone of Jandun)合著《和平保卫者》,竭力主张人民自己选择对人民负责的政府首脑,反对不应有的宗教管辖]

martial a. 军事的;战争的;军人的;尚武的
martial appeal court 军事上诉法院
martial court 军事法院,军事法庭

martial judge 军法官,军事审判员
martial justice 军事审判;军事司法
martial law 戒严法,戒严令;军法,军事管制法
Martindale-Hubbell Law Directory (美)《马丁代尔法律指南》(在律师指南中较全面的一种律师指南,它提供美国各州、许多城市、镇以及外国律师名册,并对提供的律师及律师事务所作全面介绍)
Martindale-Hubble (美)《马丁代尔—哈布尔手册》(一套列有许多律师姓名以及其工作地点和业务类型的丛书,其中还有一卷提供各州主要地区法律概况简述)
martinet n. 厉行严格纪律的人,严厉的军纪官
marvel v./n. 对……感到惊异,惊奇(at)/奇异的例子,惊异,惊奇
Marxism n. 马克思主义
Marxism Leninism n. 马克思列宁主义
Marxism Leninism Mao Tse-tung Thought 马列主义毛泽东思想
Marxist (或 **Marxian**) a./n. 马克思的;马克思主义的/马克思主义者
Marxist jurisprudence 马克思主义法学
Marxist jurist 马克思主义法学家
Marxist views 马克思主义观点
Mary Carter Agreement (1972年)《玛丽·卡特协定》[指适用于原告和部分共同被告(不是全部被告)之间达成的共同协议,若此协议可减轻达成协议的共同被告的经济负担。其减轻的部分往往比原告从未达成协议的共同被告处所获得的赔偿额成反比。此种协定在美国有些州认为违反公共政策而无效,但另一些州只向陪审团披露则被允准。此协定来源于1967年的玻斯诉玛丽·卡特油漆公司案(Booth v. Mary Garter Paint Co.)(202 So. 2d 8 Fla. Dist, ct. app. 1967)(《南方区判例汇编》第二套丛书第202卷第8页,佛罗里达地区上诉法院1967年)(见 Gallagher Agreement)]
Mashall Court (美)以马歇尔为首席大法官的联邦最高法院
mask work (版权法)掩膜作品[指金属设置或半导体材料的三维模型(three-dimen-sional patten)存在或可移动于计算机芯片层(layers of computer chip)。依照《1984年半导体芯片保护法》(the Semiconductor Chip Protection Act of 1984),掩膜作品应受到保护,参见《美国注释法典》第17标题卷第902节及以下]
masochism n. 色情受虐狂(一种以受性虐待为快的病态色情狂);性受虐狂(与 sadism 性虐待狂相对应。见 sadism 和 sexual perversion)
mass a. 大批的,大量的;大规模的;群众的,民众的;群众性的;总的
mass armed uprising 聚众持械叛乱
mass communication 有广泛影响的宣传工具(指报纸、广播、电视等)
mass control 群众管制
mass crime 大量犯罪(案件)
mass democracy 大民主
mass destruction 大规模杀伤;大破坏
mass line 群众路线
mass media 大众传播媒介,大众媒体,舆论工具
mass meeting 群众集会,群众大会
mass movement 群众运动
mass observation (英)民意调查
mass organization 群众组织,群众团体
mass produced product 工业化生产的产品,大批量生产的产品,大规模生产的产品
mass security defense organization (中)群众性治安保卫组织
mass transit 公共交通
mass-based a. 有广大群众基础的
mass-produced a. 成批生产的
mass-run enterprises 民办企业
massacre n. 大屠杀,残杀
Massive Open Online Course 大型互联网公开课(指在互联网上向所有人免费提供的受众极多的课程。该词于2008年首次出现,据说是加拿大爱德华王子岛大学网络革新专家戴夫·克米尔谈及该国两位教授开设的课程时创造的。缩写是MOOC,为可数名词)
massive program 大量方案计划
massive repudiation 大量拒绝履行合同;(宗教方面的)不断拒绝接薪俸

master n. 主人;雇主;户主;(大写)硕士;(学院的)院长;(法院的)书记官;助理法官;(最高法院的)司法主事官;船长;师傅
master and servant 雇主和雇员
master BL 主提单
master contract 主合同(契约)
master copy 标准本,原本
master file 主文件,主资料;主外存储器
master in chancery 衡平法院的助理法官(或主事官)
master in lunacy (大法官委派的)调查(声称曾是)精神病患者的司法官员;精神病患者的主事官
master lease 主租约
master letter of credit 主信用证
master list 总清单
master mariner 商船船长,(经验丰富、有资格做商船船长的)老海员
master of a ship 船长(指商船的船长,持有运输部长的证明书,一般称为 captain)
master of ceremony 司仪
master of chamber 法院(或司法机关)议事室的书记官
master of facts 掌握事实
master of the bench (英)律师学院主事官,律师主事官
master of the court 法院主事官
master of the court of common law (英)普通法法院主事官(从前普通法法院都设有五名主事官负责记录诉讼程序,监督发出命令,收取法院费用等事宜)
Master of the Court of Protection 保护法庭主事官
Master of the Court of Wards and Liveries (古英国法)王权实施法院主事官
Master of the Crown Office 王座法庭公诉人
master of the high court (英)高等法院主事官
Master of the Household (英)王室主管
master of the litigation 诉讼当事人
Master of the Revels (英史)宫廷游艺总管(亦译:节庆典礼官)
Master of the Rolls (英)案卷保管主事官(指高等法院各分院中主管文牍等事务的

官员,如保管案卷的法官);卷录主任,录事主任
Master of the Supreme Court (英)高等法院的高级司法官(指原大法官法庭司法官)
master policy 总保险单
master printing 原版
master wheel 候选名册(指用作未来陪审员来源的某一地区经注册的选民名单。有的地区还补充其他来源。书记员处向候选名册上的每一未来陪审员发一份问卷。这是美国民诉审理前的程序之一)
master-key n. 万能钥匙
master-servant rule 见 respondeat superior
master-slave computer 主从计算机
masterman n. (英)家长;丈夫
mastermind n. 具有极大才智的人;出谋划策的人
masterpiece n. 杰作,名作;杰出的事(与 master work 同)
Masters Extraordinary (或 Masters Extraordinary in Chancery) (古英国大法官法庭的)特命宣誓主事官
Masters of Requests 权利请求法院法官
mastery n. 统治权,控制权;征服;精通;知识;优势
mastery of the air (或 sea) 制空权(或制海权)
Matecalfe's Law 梅特卡夫法则[指网络价值的用户数量的平方速度增长,网络价值等于网络节点数的平方,即 v=n 的平方(v 表示网络的总价值,n 表示用户数),网络外部性是梅特卡夫法则的本质]
matching basis 以较量为基础,以竞赛为基础
mate n. 配偶(夫或妻);伙伴,同事;一对中的一个;大副
material a./n. 决定性的,(对案件有)决定性影响的;实质性的;重要的,重大的;物质的;有形的;实体的/材料,原料,资料,事实
material allegation 实质性主张;重要事实陈述
material alteration 实质性变更;重大修改
material award 物质奖励

material basis 物质基础
material breach 重大违反;实质性违反
material circumstances of a crime 犯罪具体情节
material contract 重要合同(契约)
material damage 严重损害;物质损失
material date (罪行的)确定日期;实施日期;罪行的日期(用于刑法上,表达那个罪行的发生或形成的那一天,类似的还有 material period 罪行确定的时期)
material difference 本质上的区别;实质性的分歧
material element (或 substantial factor) rule 重要因素法则
material elements 具体要件;具体因素;物质要件
material elements in the establishment of a concrete crime 构成具体犯罪的具体要件
material evidence 实质性证据;物证,对审理的事实有影响的证据
material fact 重要事实,决定性事实;(合同中规定的)对等给付物,(合同中的)实质性约因
material fact in pleading 诉状(或答辩状)中的重要事实
material fact of the case 要件事实
material incentive 物质刺激
material injury 实质伤害,实质损害;重大损伤(指倾销时对国内相同产品行业造成的重大损害),物质性损害
material interpretation 实质性解释
material issue 实质性的系争点
material law 实体法
material matter 重要事项
material misrepresentation 实质性的虚伪陈述
material misrepresentation and omission 重大不实陈述和失职行为
material omission 重要遗漏;重大懈怠
material particulars 重要事项;重要细节
material piece of evidence 实质性的证据
material point 要点
material property 有形财产
material reciprocity 实质性互惠;物质上

的互惠
material remains of a crime 犯罪遗留物
material representation 重要事实的陈述,实质性陈述
material requisites 物质要件
material sphere of validity 属事效力范围,实质的效力范围
material term 实质性条款
material time 关键时间;重要时间
material witness 重要证人
materiality n. 实质性;重要性原则;重点;重要性;重大;具体性;物质性;实体性
materiality of facts 事实的重要性
materialization n. (形式理性法律的)实质化
materialman n. 材料供应人(指为建筑和修缮而供应建筑材料者)
materials processing 材料加工
maternal a. 母系的;母亲的;母性的;从母方继承的
maternal and child hygiene 妇幼保健
maternal grandchildren 外孙子女
maternal grandparents 外祖父母
maternal line 母系
maternal property 母系遗产(或财产)
maternity n./a. (17世纪)1.母亲的身份,母性(见 filiation)2.妇产科医院;医院妇产科 3.归属权[指版权法中的归属权(attribution right)]/产妇的,怀孕的,即将成为母亲的,产后的(特别是生理上的)〈maternity nurse〉(产科护士)
maternity allowance 产妇津贴;孕妇津贴
maternity benefit 产妇分娩津贴
maternity grant 产妇补助金;孕妇补助金
maternity leave 产假
maternity pay 产假工资
mate's receipt (商船)大副收据
mathematical a. 精确的;毋庸置疑的;可能性极小的;数学的
mathematical chance 极小的可能;很少的机会
mathematical evidence (或 proof) 毋庸置疑的证据
mathematical mechanical law 精确的机械规律

mathematical property 数学特征
matriarchy n. 母权制;母系氏族制
matricidal a. 犯杀母罪的;杀母的
matricide n. 杀母罪;杀母者
matrilineal a. 母系的
matrilineal family 母系家族
matrilineal society 母系社会
* *Matrimonia debent esse libera.* Marriages ought to be free. 婚姻应该是自由的(大陆法原则)。
matrimonial a. 婚姻的;婚礼的
matrimonial action 离婚诉讼
matrimonial age 结婚年龄
matrimonial case 婚姻案件
matrimonial cause act 婚姻诉讼法
matrimonial causes 婚姻诉讼(案)
matrimonial cohabitation 夫妇同居(权)
matrimonial domicile(或 home) 婚姻住所(指夫妻共同居住的地方,被遗弃的妻子在衡平法上有权留在婚姻住所居住)
matrimonial guardian 婚姻监护人
matrimonial guilt 破坏婚姻罪
matrimonial home 婚姻住所
matrimonial offence 有关婚姻的罪行
matrimonial order 夫妻分居令
matrimonial proceedings 婚姻诉讼程序
matrimonial proceedings act 婚姻诉讼法
matrimonial property 婚姻(所得)财产(又译:夫妻财产)
matrimonial regime 婚姻财产制(又译:夫妻财产制);婚姻制度
matrimonial remedies 婚姻救济方法
matrimonial res 婚姻状况
matrimonial rites 婚礼
matrimonial suit 婚姻诉讼
matrimonial tort 婚姻上的侵权行为,婚姻过失罪
matrimonial vows 婚姻的誓约,婚约
matrimonium (罗马法)合法婚姻
matrimonium cum manu 有夫权的婚姻
matrimonium per usum (罗马法)时效婚(姻)
matrimonium sine connubio 非正式婚姻
matrimonium sine manum 无夫权的婚姻
matrimony n. 婚姻(生活);结婚;婚礼;婚姻关系

matrix n. (大陆法)(须从一切复本取得的)法律文件草约(或初稿);渊源资料(判刑表,判刑目录);发源地,策源地;母体组织,子宫;模型
matron n. 主妇,已婚妇女;(监狱等)女看守;(学校等的)女舍监;护士长
matronymic n. 取自母(或女祖先)名的名字
matter n. 1.事实,事件,案件 2.问题,事态;情况 3.事项(除一般用法外,在诉讼中可分:matter in deed 有文据事项,可用契据证明其事实; matter in *pais* 无文据事项,需要证人证明其事实; matter of record 有记录事项,可用记录证明其事项) 4.实质,实体 5.资料,材料 6.理由,根据
matter for petty criminal affair 轻微的刑事案件
matter in deed 有文据事项,文据上的事实(见 matter)
matter in dispute 诉讼事件;纠纷案;争议事项
matter in issue 争执不决的事件,有争议的案件;争执点
* *Matter in ley ne serra mise in bautche del jurors.* Matter of law should not be put into the mouth of jurors. 法律问题不应由陪审团决定。
matter in *pais* 无文据事项(见 matter)
matter of aggravation 增加损失事项,严重事件
matter of concern 有关事项
matter of course 理所当然的事
matter of customary law 习惯法案件
matter of defence 答辩事项,抗辩事项
matter of domestic jurisdiction 国内管辖事项(或案件)
matter of fact 事实(上的)问题
matter of federal law 联邦法律问题
matter of good faith 诚信的标的物,诚信的对象,诚信的客观物
(a) matter of great import 重大事情
matter of inducement 诉状引言,案由
matter of law 法律(上的)问题
matter of modern law 现代法案件(与 matter of customary law 相对而言)

matter of opinion 看法有分歧的事项;有争论余地的问题
matter of personal status 个人身份案件
matter of procedure 有关诉讼程序的事项
matter of public knowledge 家喻户晓的事件
matter of record 备案事项,有案可查的事项,有记录的事项(见 matter)
matter of substance 实质性事项
matter on the merits 根据案件事实的是非曲直
matter pertinent to 有关……事项
matter under final appeal 终审上诉案,终审案件
matter within the domestic jurisdiction 国内管辖范围内的案件
matters in hand 手头的案件
matters of general knowledge 一般知识的事实,一般知识的一些问题
mature v. (商业上的票据等)到期;使成熟;慎重地完成
matured note 到期票据
maturing liability 将到期的债务
maturity n. 成熟;满期,到期;完成;偿还期
maturity date 到期之日,期满日
maturity of bill 票据到期
maturity of law 法律的成熟
maturity of notice 通知到期
maturity of obligation 债务到期之日
maxim n. (法律)格言;准则;原则;谚语
maxim of equity 衡平法准则
* *Maxima illecebra est peccandi impunitatis spes.* The greatest incitement to wrongdoing is the hope of impunity. 期待不受处罚是实施犯罪的最大动因。
maundering 胡言乱语、呓语
maximal a. 最大的;最高的;最全的;最总括性的
maximalist n. 最高纲领派
maxims and usages 准则和惯例:原则和习俗
maximum n./a. 最高限度,最高额/最大的,最多的,最高的,顶点的
maximum amount 最高额
maximum and minimum tariffs 最高和最低税率(表)
maximum legal rate on interest 最高法定利率
maximum liability 最大限度的责任
maximum limit 最高限额
maximum of individual self-assertion 最大限度个人的自我权利主张
maximum possible loss 可能的最大损失额
maximum royalties 最高使用费,最高版税(指版权合同中规定:某作品成书后无论销量多少,向作者支付的版税额将不超过某数额。此数额即为"最高版税",与此相对的为 minimum royalties "最低版税")
maximum sentence 最高刑期(判决)
maximum working hours 最长工作时间
mayhem n. 暴力伤害罪,致人残废罪;(英)重伤害罪(普通法指伤害他人的手足齿目等致残);故意伤害罪
mayor n. 市长
mayoralty n. 市长职位;市长任期
mayoress n. 女市长;市长夫人
Mayor's Court (of London) (英)(伦敦市)市长法庭(英国有些大城市也有这种法庭)
Mc Carthyism n. (美)麦卡锡主义(指采用法西斯手段迫害民主和进步力量的反动主张)
McNaghten Rules 麦克·纳顿规则(刑法)[该规则指一旦认定一个人在精神上有智力障碍或精神病,就不应承担其行为的刑事责任。亦即"如果行为人在实施行为时由于精神之疾病导致缺乏理智而不知其行为性质,或不知其行为是正确与否,则不负刑事责任"。美国联邦法院和大多数州均以某种形式采用此项准则。见 McNaghten's case & Eng Rep. 718 (H. L1843 例)即 McNaghten Rules,亦称 right-and-wrong test, right-wrong test]
McCarran Act 《麦卡伦法》(指 1950 年《国内安全法》。该法旨在控制共产党在美国国内活动,要求受共产党控制的组织向司法部长登记备案,并公布其官员和成员姓名、收入来源及开支情况,还禁止与共产党关系密切的外国移民进入美国。

该法还有有关紧急拘留的规定,设有"拘留中心",于1971年被废除)

McCarron-Ferguson Act (美)《麦卡兰—费古森法》(授权州政府对保险业进行规制的法律,自1945年通过之后,美国保险业基本不受联邦反托拉斯法的规制)

McCarthy Era (美)麦卡锡时代

McDonnell Douglas test (美)麦克唐纳·道格拉斯准则(就业法)[是适用于就业歧视案件的举证责任原则。该原则要求原告(雇员)证明雇佣歧视行为的存在,还要求被告(雇主)用证据表明涉诉的雇佣行为是基于非歧视理由。具体而言,该测试要求:①原告(雇员)必须足以使歧视案件成立;②被告(雇主)必须为其行为出示合法的、非歧视的证据,如果证据成立,那么对歧视的假定被推翻;③原告(雇员)必须提供事实表明歧视确实存在。见 burden-shifting analysis]

McNabb-Mallory rule 麦克纳布—马洛里规则(美)(刑事诉讼)[此规则指如果犯罪嫌疑人在被逮捕后至预审前超过了合理的羁押时间,在此时间内获取的犯罪嫌疑人的有罪供述不可采信。其根据是米兰达规则(Miranda rule)提供的广泛的保护。这一刑事诉讼规则来自麦克纳布诉美国(McNabb v. United States)(美国《联邦最高法院判例汇编》第318卷第332页,和《最高法院判例汇编》第63卷第608页)(1943年)和马洛里诉美国(Mallory v. United States)(美国《联邦最高法院判例汇编》第354卷第449页,《最高法院判例汇编》第77卷,第1356页)(1957年)两个判例。简称 Mallory rule]

me judice 依我的意见

mea culpa (是)本人过失

mean v. 表达……的意思,作……的解释;意指,意谓;意味着,意欲,打算

meaning n. 意思;意义;含义,词义;目的,意图

meaning and nature of administration efficiency 行政效率的意义和性质

meaning in extension 外延

meaning in intension 内涵

means (复) n. 方法;手段;工具;财产;资力;收入

means of adjudicating the controversy 判决纠纷的方式(方法,手段)

means of bribery 贿赂手段

means of communication 通信方法;通信工具;运输工具

means of conveyance (财产)转让方式

means of creating manus 作为创设对他人的权利(如夫权)的手段

means of defence 辩护方式;防御手段

means of discipline 惩戒手段

means of payment 支付手段(或工具)

means of production 生产资料

means of proof 证明方法;举证方法

means of relief 救助方法;救济方法

means of subject access 主题检索手段,用主题检索的方法

means of subsistence (或 livelihood) 生活资料;谋生手段

means of transport 运输工具

means of warfare 战争手段(指用以作战的武器、工具和方法)

means test (英)(在发放救济金前对申请人的)家庭经济状况调查

means to punishment 惩罚手段

means to reformation (对罪犯的)改造手段

measure n./v. 1.措施,办法 2.(英)长老会法案,议案 3.量度;标准;计量制度,度量法 4.程度;范围,限度;分寸;估计/1.测量;估量;衡量;计量 2.酌量,权衡;调节 3.配给,分派

measure of attachment on property in litigation 诉中财产保全

measure of damages 损害赔偿估算量,损害赔偿额

measure of discrimination 歧视性措施

measure of economic coordination 经济调节工具

measure of sentence 量刑幅度

measure of value 价值尺度

measure punishment 量刑

measure to obtain revenue 取得税收的措施

measure to protect the right 保障权利的办法

measurement n. 度量衡;测量,衡量;度量制

measurement of cargo 货物体积
measurement of penalty 量刑
measures for investigation 侦查措施
measures of stake asymmetry 预期不对称量度指标
measuring life （1922年）衡量赋予权利［根据禁止永久权规则(rule against perpetuities)，最后受益人死于留有遗嘱人之后，通常并持有先有利益(preceding interest)。衡量赋予权利(measuring life)常用来按禁止永久权规则决定是否赋予权利。见 rule against perpetuities; life in being］
measuring rod 测量的尺标
measuring the costs 成本的计算
mechanic's lien 建筑物上优先权，技工留置权［指法律上的一种对建筑物的建设、维修、改造提供劳工、服务和材料优先权的规定(见 lien)］
mechanical apparatus 机械
mechanical asphyxia 机械性窒息
mechanical injuries 机械性损伤
mechanical jurisprudence 机械法理学
mechanical mode of trial 机械的审判模式
mechanical reproduction (right) 录音重制(权)
mechanical rights 录制权
mechanical sociologist 机械社会学派
mechanical solidarity 机械的连带关系
mechanics n./a. 结构，技巧/机械似的，机构式的
mechanics of fingerprints 指纹技术
mechanics of law-making 立法技巧
mechanism n. 机制，方式，机构，手法
mechanism for retaining power 维持权力机制
Med-Arb 先调解后仲裁（即双方先进行调解程序，如果调解不成，再进行仲裁程序；如调解成功，可通过仲裁程序裁决）
medal n. 奖章，勋章，纪念章
medal of honor 荣誉勋章
meddle v. 干预，干涉，插手；乱弄
meddler n. 干预者
médecin des morts 法医
media (=medium 的复数) n. 新闻(或传播)工具(或手段)；媒介；传导体；环境，自然条件；调解人，中间人；巫师
media of communication 交通工具；交流工具，交流媒介
media credibility 媒体可信度
media neutrality 媒介中立原则，媒介中性原则［指法律对无论是采用纸质媒介还是采用电子媒介（或其他媒介）的交易都应一视同仁，不因采用不同媒介而区别对待或赋予不同的法律效力］
media of information 新闻工具，信息传递工具
mediacy n. 中间状态，媒介；调解
mediaeval law 中世纪法
median rule 调解规则；中间规则，斡旋规则
mediate a./v. 间接的；居间的，介乎中间的；中间人的/处于中间位置；调停，调解
mediate evidence 第二手证据，间接证据
mediate facts 中间事实
mediate possession 委托占有
mediate testimony 间接证据
mediated cases 调解的案件
mediation n. 仲裁；调停，居中调停；调解
mediation and conciliation （国际法）调停和调解（前者指第三国直接参与当事国间的谈判；后者指当事国将争端提交调解委员会以求得公正的解决）
Mediation Committee 调停委员会
mediation committee of neighborhood (中)居民调解委员会
mediation of disputes 调解纠纷
mediation out of court 院外调解，庭外调解
mediation personnel 调解人员
Mediation-Arbitration 调解—仲裁（指美国解决争议非诉讼方式之一，即 ADR 之一，此方法为政府和劳资部门所采纳，在劳资双方发生纠纷时先行调解，不成时则申请仲裁）
mediator n. 仲裁者；调解者，调停人；调停国
mediatory a. 调解的，调停的；斡旋的；调解人的
medicaid n. 公费医疗补助制；(政府开办的)医疗保健业；(美)医疗补助方案(或

项目)
medical a. 医学的;医药的;医疗的;内科的(与 surgical 相对)
medical accident 医疗事故
medical and hospital care 医疗和住院补助
medical assistance 医疗救助
medical benefit 医疗福利
medical care 医疗上的照顾
medical certificate 健康证明书;诊断书;医疗证
medical committee 医务委员会
medical diagnosis on death 死亡诊断
medical doctor's certification 医生证明
medical ethics 医疗道德
medical evidence 医疗证据(尤指医生提供的证据)
medical examination 体格检查;验尸
medical examination at the port 口岸药检,港口药检
medical examiner 1.验尸官;法医;体检人员 2.(保险公司、工厂等的特约)医师
medical examiner's death certificate 法医死亡证明书
medical expert 法医;法医鉴定人
medical fee 医疗费
medical jurisprudence 法医学
medical law 医疗法
medical malpractice 医疗失当,医疗错误,医疗过失
medical negligence 医疗事故(一般指医务人员因业务上过失引起的病人死亡事故)
medical parole 保外就医
medical practitioner 开业医生
medical report 医生检查报告书
medical witness 医学证人
medicare n. (美、加)公办的医疗保险制
medicinalis toxicosis 药物中毒
medicine n. 药;医学;医术;内科;医生(行业)
medicolegal (= medico-legal) a. 法医学的,法医的
medicolegal autopsy 法医学尸体解剖
medicolegal examination 法医学检验
medicolegal expert 法医鉴定人
medicolegal expertise 法医鉴定

medicolegal investigation 法医学检验
medicolegal pathology 法医病理学
medidas provisories 临时措施
medieval common law system 中世纪普通法体系
medieval law and institution 中世纪法和机构
medium n./a. 媒介物;中间人,调解人;手段,工具/中等的,中间的
medium of exchange 货币;支票
medium of legislation 立法手段,法律手段
medium term loan 中期贷款,中期信贷
medium term plan 中期计划
medius 中间的
meet n./v. (美)会,集合;集会者;集会地/1.会见,会谈,应付;如期偿付,付(债务、账单等)2.集会,开会;遇到,迎接 3.满足,适合;同意 4.互撞,与……对抗
meet (with) one's death 死去
meet a bill 准备支付到期的票据
meet halfway 折中;让步
meet one's engagements 履行合约;偿还债务
meet with an accident 遇到事故
meeting n. 会议,会谈;集会,聚合,会见;汇合点
meeting of minds 意见一致
meeting of representative of the employees 职代会
Mega Pool (巨型)专利联营(指飞机、汽车等行业出现的巨型专利联营)
megacorporation n. 特大企业
megalomania n. 妄自尊大狂(指精神病患者妄想权势、财富、尊贵等)
megalopolitan a. 特大城市的
Megan's Law (美)《梅甘法》(指 1995 年新泽西州立法机关通过的,说明累犯对社会安全的危害,并要求有关当局在有前科的性罪犯返回社会时,应告知其邻里居民注意安全的一项法律。这是由于 1994 年 6 月有一名 7 岁女孩被奸污后勒死,而在公众要求下才制定此法律,因该女孩名叫 Megan 而命名)
Meiji-period Japan 明治维新时代的日本
melancholia n. (精神病)忧郁症

melancholiac n. 忧郁症患者
melancholic a. 患忧郁症的；令人忧伤的
* *Melior est conditio possidentis, ubi neuter jus habet.* Where neither has a right, the condition of the possessor is the better. 各方均无权时，占有地位更为有利。
* *Melior est justitia vere praeveniens quam severe puniens.* That justice which absolutely prevents (a crime) is better than that which severely punishes it. 从根本上防止犯罪的司法审判总要比严厉惩办犯罪的好。
* *Melius est in tempore occurrere, quam post causam vulneratum remedium quaerere.* It is better to meet a thing in time than after an injury inflicted to seek a remedy. 及时处理总要比造成损害后寻求补救办法好。
* *Melius est jus deficiens quam jus incertum.* Law that is deficient is better than law that is uncertain. 有缺点的法总要比含糊不清的法好。
* *Melius est omnia mala pati quam malo consentire.* It is better to suffer every ill than to consent to ill. 宁受多种恶行而不同意恶行为。
melon n. （美俚）额外红利，横财，赃物
member n. （团体、组织等的）成员，会员，社员；（联合国的）会员国；（安理会的）理事国；（大写）议员；（国际法委员会等）委员；组成人员
member above the gangway （英）观点与所属政党政策较密切的下议员
member below the gangway （英）观点与所属政党政策不密切的下议员
member government 会员国政府
Member of Congress （美）国会众议院议员
member of family 家属；家庭成员
Member of Parliament （英）下议院议员
member of partnership 合伙人
member of religious orders 宗教界人士
member of state administration 国家行政管理工作人员
member of the armed forces 武装人员
member of the Bar 律师公会会员；司法界成员
member of the court-martial 军法官
member of the government 政府成员
member of the police forces 警察部队成员，警务人员
member of the United Nation 联合国的会员国
member organization 成员组织
member-driven organization 成员驱动型组织（指 WTO 是一个成员驱动型国际组织。它没有要求各成员方加入并享有权利、承担义务，而是各成员方自愿要求加入该国际组织的）
member-state n. 成员国；（联邦制国家中的）成员州
member-states judiciary 州司法机关
members as of right 当然成员，当然委员
members of the judiciary 司法人员
membership n. 会员资格，成员资格；会籍；全体会员，会员人数
membership by accession 加入国
membership card 会员证
membership committee 会员资格审查委员会
membership corporation 会员公司（指为社会的、慈善的或政治等目的而创立的非营利、非股票的公司）
membership of parliament 议会议员职务（位）
mémoire （外交上的）备忘录；摘要，节略
Memoranda of Understanding 双边谅解备忘
memorandum n. 备忘录；摘要；节略，便函，非正式记录；买卖合同（契约）书
memorandum clause （海上保险中）减免责任条款，备忘（录）条款
memorandum decision 节略判决书，未说明判决理由的判决书
memorandum in error （附有宣誓的）指出事实错误的备案书
memorandum in writing 合同书；证书；书面契据
memorandum of agreement 协定备忘录，协议备忘录

memorandum of appeal 上诉摘要;上诉备忘录
memorandum of appearance 出庭通知
memorandum of association (公司)组织简章,社团简章
memorandum of complaint 民事起诉书;抗告状;控诉书
memorandum of payment 缴款通知
memorandum of satisfaction 清偿债务备忘录
Memorandum of Understanding 谅解备忘录
memorandum of writings 文据摘要
memorandum opinion 一致的节略意见(指判决上法官判决意见)
memorandum record 备忘记录
memorial n. 纪念物(品);纪念日,纪念仪式;(国际法院的)诉状;(向政府或当权者请求执行某事的)请愿书,抗议书,(英)契据摘要,(文件)提要;(复)(外交上的)备忘录;纪要(书),节录
memorial of re-entry (英)回复土地所有权契据摘要
memory n. 记忆;记忆力;回忆;记忆期间,追忆得起的年限
men's natural right 天赋人权(说)
menace n./v. 胁迫,威胁,恐吓;威胁者;危险物
menacing a. 威胁的,恐吓的;险恶的;胁迫的
mend v. 修补;改良;改正错误,纠正
mend one's ways 悔改
mendacious a. 不诚实的,好说谎的;虚假的,捏造的
mendacity(或**mandaciousness**) n. 谎言;说谎癖;虚伪
mender n. 改良者,改善者,修理者
menial n. 住家佣工,仆人;下贱的人
menopause n. 更年期,绝经(期)
mens rea 犯意,犯罪意图(构成刑事犯罪的要件之一)
mensa et thoro 见 *a mensa et thoro*
mental a. 精神的;智力的;精神病的
mental aberration 心理失常
mental activities 智力活动

mental age 智力年龄
mental association 精神上的联系(指美国联邦最高法院认为"联系"的一种可能解释是:它使相关公众以为在后使用人与驰名商标所有人之间存在"精神上的联系")
mental capacities of parties (当事人)双方的意识能力
mental capacity 1.意识能力 2.智力,能力
mental competence 精神上的行为能力;智力资格
mental creation 智力创作
mental cruelty 精神虐待
mental defective 心智不健全(美模范刑法典"MPC rule"将其界定为"有精神疾患而不能辨认自己行为的性质")
mental deficiency 智力(或心理)缺陷,精神不健全
Mental Deficiency Act (英)《智力不健全法》(1913年)
mental derangement 精神错乱
mental disability 精神上的缺陷,精神上的无能力
mental disease 精神(疾)病
mental disorder 精神错乱;精神失常
mental disorders after cranic cerebral trauma 颅脑创伤后精神障碍(指遭受各种颅脑创伤后发生的精神障碍。颅脑损伤所致精神障碍的病人的刑事责任能力评定要根据情况处理)
mental examination 心理检查
mental faculties 智力,智能
Mental Health Act (英)《精神保健法》(1959年)
mental health review tribunal 智力健康复查法庭
mental hospital(或 **home, asylum**) 精神病院,疯人院
mental illness 心神错乱;精神病
mental illness of an intermittent nature 间歇性精神病
mental immaturity 智力不成熟
mental injury 精神损伤(指遭受物理、生理和心理等损伤后直接或间接引起的精神障碍。它涵盖功能性和器质性的精神障碍,而精神伤残仅指器质性的精神障

碍,即指脑器质性损伤所致的精神障碍。)
mental laborer 脑力劳动者
mental makeup 精神特质
mental patient 精神病人
mental power 精神力量,智力
mental processes of the jurors 陪审员的智力过程
mental reservation 心理保留,(对某项声明的)未明言的保留
mental responsibility 主观责任
mental restriction 意中保留(指说话人在思想上保留的意思和嘴里说出来的不同)
mental retardation (MR) 精神发育迟滞(又称为精神发育不全、弱智、智力残疾等。指生长发育阶段的儿童由遗传基因、环境因素或社会心理因素等原因引起的上述情况,以智能发育不全或受阻为特征)
mental scales 心如天平(公正之意)
mental shock 精神损害,精神上的打击,精神震惊,精神的强烈刺激,大悲大伤
mental skill required 用脑程度
mental specialist 精神病专家
mental suffering 精神痛苦,精神折磨
Mental Treatment Act (英)《精神病治疗法》(1930年)
mental type 心理型
mental worker 脑力劳动者
mentality n. 精神,思想;智力
mentally ad. 精神上,智力上
mentally competent 智力上健全的
mentally defective person 智力上有缺陷的人
mentally disordered offender 精神障碍犯罪人(1930年起,美国不少州就已将"性犯罪者"视为精神异常者并规定了长期治疗的处分。但现在这种看法和做法已有改变,美国不再将大多数性犯罪者当作精神障碍者对待,而是作为具有反社会性质的犯罪者,收容在普通监狱,在获得假释时才获得附加治疗的命令)
Mentally Disordered Offender Law (美)《精神障碍犯罪者法》(指1985年美加利福尼亚州制定的法)
mentally disordered person 精神失常者
mentally incompetent 智力不健全者

mentally retarded person 智力迟钝者
mente captur 惯发性精神失常者;精神全部失常的人
mention v. 提到,说起,提及
mention sb. in a will 在遗嘱里提及某人
mentioned above 如上所述
mentition n. 撒谎行为;欺诈
menu n. 菜单(指计算机领域的选择单)
mercantile a. 商业的;贸易的;商人的;重商主义的
mercantile agency 商业代理机构
mercantile agent 代理商,代办商
mercantile contract 商业合同,贸易合同
mercantile credit agency 商业资信咨询机构
mercantile law 商法,商事法
mercantile marine (总称)(一个国家的)商船;商船队
mercantile paper 商业票据,商业流通证券
mercantile partnership 贸易伙伴
mercantile thing 商业事务;商事
mercantile transaction 商行为,商业交易
mercantile usages 商业惯例,商业习惯
mercantilism n. 重商主义;商业活动,商业理论;商界习俗;商用术语
mercantilist n. 重商主义者
Mercen-Lage 麦西亚法[指在11世纪盛行于英格兰中部地区三大法系之一,中部地区的郡及其邻近以及威尔士边区均适用此法。这是麦西亚人的法(Law of Merciens),亦可拼写成 Merchenlage,亦称为 Lex merciorum。这个法据说是不同习惯法的混合体]
mercenary a. 为钱的,唯利是图的,贪财的;雇佣的
mercenary marriage 着眼实利的婚姻,买卖婚姻
mercenary system 募兵制,雇佣兵役制
mercenary troops 雇佣军
merchandise n. (总称)商品,存货
merchandise marks 商品标识
merchandising right 商品化权利(主要指真实的或虚构的人物或动物形象,在贸易活动中产生的一种"类版权"或"准版权",有的版权中将此权利称为形象公开权 right of publicity)

merchant n./a. 商人;零售商;店主/商人的;商业的
Merchant Adventurers （英国中世纪的）商业冒险者协会
merchant bill 商业汇票
merchant contract 商业合同(契约)
merchant guild 商业公会(指欧洲中世纪从事国际贸易的商人组成的协会)
merchant marine （一个国家的)商船;商船队;商船船员
Merchant Marine Act 《商船法》(美 1936)[见 Jones Act 琼斯法(1920年通过)]
merchant prince 富商,豪商
merchant rate 商业汇率
merchant ship 商船
merchant shipping 商船运输
Merchant Shipping Act （英)《商船海运法》(1894年);(美)《商务海运法》(1915年)
merchant shipping code 商船运输法典
merchant status 商人地位
merchant's good faith 商人的善意(指在经营中遵奉公平交易、诚实信用的商业准则)
merchant-usurer n. 商业高利贷
merchantable a. 适于销售的,可卖的,有销路的
merchantable quality 适合销售的质量
mercheta mulierum （苏格兰)女性失贞罚款;初夜权赎金
Mercians 莫西亚法(见 Danes 丹麦法)
mercy n. (法院的)权宜处置权,决定权;宽恕,仁慈,恩惠
mercy killing 1.安乐死(指促使患剧痛的绝症病人死亡,须由司法部门会同医师进行,否则应负法律责任,与 euthanasia 同) 2.(使受刑者)减少痛苦的处决
mercy stroke 致命的一击(=*coup de grâce*)
mere a. 只不过的,仅仅的;纯粹的
mere declaration of unconstitutionality 单纯违宪判决
mere right 纯权利(指只有财产的权利,而没有财产的占有)
mere right of property 纯财产权
mere shipment rule 单纯交货规则

mere-color rule 纯色原则(指美国联邦最高法院确立单纯由颜色组成的商标能获得注册之前,美国法对颜色商标的注册采纯色原则,此原则亦称颜色本身原则 the color *per se* rule)
merged a. 合并的,被合并的;(美)结了婚的
merged company 合并公司
merger (18世纪)1.联合或统一行为,联合或统一请求(instance) 2.(契约或合同)合并,合二为一,指高一级的格式合同代替低一级的格式合同,如同用书面合同替代所有口头协议和先前协定(prior understanding)一样(见 integration 2) 3.(契约、合同)替代约定义务(contractual duty)或替代以相同当事人之间的新义务去补偿的义务,基于不同的有效事实(operative facts) 4.(财产)吸收合并、兼并、吸收兼并较少的地产(estate)并入更多的地产,最终两者都成为同一个人的财产(见 surrender 3) 5.(刑法)重罪吸收轻罪[指在一个人犯有两种或更多罪行时,重罪吸收轻罪,只能就重罪追诉。所以,一个人不得受到双重追诉(double jeopardy)。例如:一个被告不得被判未遂罪（或怂恿罪）(attempt or solicitation)和已遂犯罪(completed crime)两种罪行,即使数罪合并(merger)也不能适用共谋罪和已遂罪行,此术语亦称 merger of offenses] 6.(民事诉讼)因判决导致诉讼请求的消失[指对原告的有效判决使其诉讼请求融合(absorb)于判决之中。所以在执行判决中,原告的权利是受到限制的。见 bar 6] 7.普通法与衡平法程序方面的结合（或合并）8.兼并[尤指一个公司组织被兼并到另一个公司之中而成为一个公司,被兼并的公司不存在了,而另一个公司(兼并者)保留下来,并具有自己的名称、法律人格,而且获得前者的资产、权利和义务。公司兼并必须履行法定程序,通常需经未清股份(或已发行的股份)(outstanding share)的多数的批准或同意。此术语亦称 corporate merger。见 consolidation 4; Buyout] 9.权利和责任(或义务)的融合、合并,引起债务的废除,特别是债权人与债务人权利的融合

(blending)导致债权人收集欠债权利的消失[在罗马法原先发展时,债务人与债权人可以婚姻结合的融合或债务人成为债权人的继承人。此词条亦称为 confusion; confusion of debts; confusion of rights。见 confusion of titles]10. 合同融入法院令,因此当事双方协议(常指夫妻财产协议),附有离婚,分居财产问题解决,该协议就失去独立性特征(separate identity),因该合同并入法院令时即成为强制可执行的合同。
merger doctrine of husband and wife (见 married women's property acts)
merger clause 合并条款,混同条款(合同用语,常指以完整的协议制成书面合同来结束以前的口头协议)
merger of offenses 数罪并合,重罪吸收轻罪
merger of states 国家的合并
merger transaction 合并交易
merging of the rights of creditor and debtor 债权人和债务人的权利混同
merit n./v. 价值;功绩;(复)(惩、奖的)事实真相,事件实质;(案件的)是非曲直;功过;法律依据,法律意义/值得,应受赏(或罚)
merit of the decision 判决的法律依据
merit rating 人事考核,职工考绩
merit system (美)文官的考绩制度,量才录用制
Merits System Protection Board (美)择优录用制保护委员会,功绩制度保护局,功绩制度保护委员会[指独立的联邦机构,它负责监督联邦政府全体职员的实务(personal practices),并对针对联邦雇员提起人事诉讼的申诉进行听证、裁决。该机构拥有 5 个区域性办公处(regional offices)和 5 个专业办公室(field offices)。它的功能是根据1978年重组计划2号(Reorganization Plan No. 2 of 1978)前文官委员会(former Civil Service Commission)转让过来的。缩略为 MSPB。见 Civil Service Commission]
meritorious a. 有功的;值得称赞的;善意的;有法律价值的;有权利的
meritorious case 有法律权利的案件
meritorious cause of action (大陆法)有价值的诉因;(英美法)权利性诉因
meritorious consideration (英美法)有价值的对价
meritorious defence 击中要害的答辩
merits n. 功过是非,(案件的)是非曲直;当事人的法定权利;(诉讼或答辩的)实质依据
Merits don't matter 价值无关
merits of case 案件的实质问题;(诉讼中的)实体权利(指诉讼当事人拥有的法律权利,以区别于法院可以自由裁量的问题和程序问题)
merits of the plaintiff's claim 原告诉讼请求的法律依据
mesalliance 不相称的婚姻,门户不当的婚姻,与社会地位低下的人结婚
mesne 中间的
mesne assignment 中间转让
mesne landlord 二房东;二地主;中间业主
mesne lord 封建领主
mesne notice 中间通知
mesne process 中间诉讼阶段(亦译做中间程序,指诉讼程序中开始诉讼阶段和最后诉讼阶段之间的这一阶段。见 original process 和 final process);中间传票;中间令状(见 writ of *mesne*)
mesne profits 中间收益(指土地非法占有期间所获得的利益)
message n. 文电;通讯;祝词;差使;电报;(美)咨文;消息
messenger n. 信使;通信员
messenger-at-arms n. (苏格兰)高等法院执法官
messuage n. 住宅及其宅基
meta-legal doctrine 基本法律原理
meta-national level 越国,跨国
meta-strategy n. 总战略
metagame theory 连续博弈论,在后的博弈论
metage n. 计量检查(权);容量的官方检定;(容量检定的)检定费
metagovernance 元治理[指在杰索普(Bob Jessop, "国家理论"state theory 的作者)看来,一个多元权威并存的治理体系

确实正在形成。但国家与其他治理主体的作用是不相同的,国家首要要承担元治理的角色,即国家既是社会中的一个组成部分,也是保证该社会的机构制度完整和社会凝聚力的责任承担者,它必须平衡地方、国家、地区、全球多层次的治理,并相互协调它们的行动]
metal detectors 金属探测器
metalaw n. 星际法
metaphor n. 隐喻、比喻的说法
metaphorically ad. 含有隐喻地
Metaphysical Elements of Justice 《法的形而上学原理》,《正义的形而上学要素》(康德的法哲学著作)
metaphysical jurisprudence 形而上学法理学
metaphysical laws 形而上学的法则
metaphysical meaning 虚拟的含义,抽象微妙的含义
metaphysical principle of individual liberty 个人自由的形而上学原则
metaphysical school 形而上学学派
metaphysical world of electron 抽象的电子世界,超自然的电子世界
metaphysics n. 形而上学,空理论
Metaphysics of Morals (1797) 《道德形而上学》(1797年出版)[康德(1724—1804)的著作。在此书中,他主张违反刑法的人应根据其罪行本身的应受惩罚性给予惩罚。这与功利主义相对立,后者主张将威慑和改造作为刑罚性的正当理由]
metatag n. 网站元标签
metayage 折半佃法(指供给耕地、农具的地主与佃农均分收获的制度)
metayer 折半佃法的佃农
mete n./v. 边界;分界;边界标志,界石/给予,派给;加以(惩罚,奖励等)
mete out rewards 给予报酬
mete out severe punishment to sb. 给予某人严惩
meteorology n. 气象学
meter maid 处理违章停车的女警察
meter mail 收费邮件
metes and bounds 区划,边界;分界;(土)地(分)界(线)(土地转让中的用语,=butts and bounds)
method n. 方法,办法;做事的条理、秩序、计划
method *ad valorem* 从价法,按值计算法
method of deduction 演绎方法,推导方法
method of delivery 交付方法
method of disposition 处理办法
method of execution of judg(e)ment 执行判决的方法
method of figuring interest 计息方法
method of infliction the death penalty 死刑的执行方式
method of interrogation 审讯方法
method of proof 举证方法
method of redress 补救方法
method of sampling 抽样方法
method of service 送达方式
method of voting 投票方法,选举方法
methodology n. 方法论,方法学;课程
methods of economic intervention 经济干预方法
metric a. 公制的,米制的
metric system 公制,米制
metric system of weights and measures 公制计量标准,公制度量衡标准
metrological law 计量法
metropolis n. 1.大城市,主要都市 2.大都会(常指首都、首府或经济文化等中心城市) 3.(殖民地的)宗主国 4.大主教教区
metropolitan n./a. 1.大城市人 2.大主教/1.大城市的,主要都市的;大都会的 2.宗主(国)的;大主教教区的
Metropolitan County (英)都市郡(指一些人口集中的城市地区)
metropolitan government (大)城市政府;大都会政府
metropolitan homeland 宗主国本土
metropolitan police 都市警察
metropolitan state (或 country) 宗主国
metropolitan stipendiary magistrates 都市领薪专职治安官
metropolitan territory 本土
mettrèa large 释放,使自由
metus 恐惧,忧虑,担心,胁迫
metus vis impusive metus 精神胁迫

metus vis physica 身体胁迫

meum 我的(指财产所有权而言)

Mexican divorce 墨西哥式离婚[指通过邮寄方式或从未在墨西哥有过住所的夫妻一方出庭在墨西哥获准离婚。不管以上两种方式中任何一种离婚在美国均不被承认。亦称 Dominican divorce(如果在多米尼加共和国被允许);Haition divorce(如果在海地被允许)]

MIC(Microwave Communications Inc) (案)微波通讯有限公司[即 MCI Communications v. AT&T Co. 708F. 2d 1081(1983)案。此案与关键设施(essential facilities)理论的发展有关。此案中,法院提出四个标准:第一,MCI 案标准(法院提出四个要件认定网络构成核心设施:①设施为垄断者控制;②竞争对手无法合理复制这一设施;③竞争对手使用设施被拒绝;④提供设施是可能的)。第二,竞争者标准。第三,公共利益标准。第四,消费者偏好标准]

Michaelmas sittings (英格兰)米迦勒节开庭期(term),从 11 月 2 日至 11 月 25 日[1875 年之前,它也叫"Michaelmas term"。(英格兰古法)四个开庭期之一,即英国法院自 13 世纪以来沿用四个开庭期:春季开庭期(Hilary)、复活节开庭期(Easter)、三一节开庭期(Trinity)和米迦勒节开庭期。根据《1873 年司法法》(Judicature Act of 1873)或《司法组织法》(已被废止),亦称 Michaelmas term。见 Easter term; Hilary term; Trinity sittings]

Michaelmas term (=Michaelmas sittings) (英)(高等法院的四个开庭期之一)米加勒节开庭期(即最末一个开庭期,按照枢密院命令的开庭日起至 12 月 31 日止)

miche (mich) v. (英格兰古法)小偷,小摸,以隐藏方式实施犯罪。亦称 mich

(the) micro-nationalism and localism 微型国家主义与地方主义

micro-organisms n. 微生物

microbiological organism 微生物有机体

microbiological process 微生物学进程

microcode n. 微码(指固化在硬件上的计算机程序,是否应列入版权保护客体,尚有争议)

microcomputer n. 微型(电子)计算机

microdata n. 微观数据

microeconomic implications of sexual harassment 性骚扰的微观经济含义

microfaction n. 小宗派,小集团

microfiche n. 缩微平片

microfilm n. 微缩胶卷,缩微胶片

microform n. 缩微制品,缩微资料(过程)

microprint n. 缩微复印品

microprocessor n. 微信息处理机

microstate n. 微型国家

mid a. 中部的,中间的,居中的,当中的

mid channel 中(间)航道

mid election 中期选举

mid point rate 平均价格,平均汇率

mid review 中期复查

mid-range theory 中间理论(指美国犯罪学者 Paul McCold 提出的中间理论,以否定泛化理论为前提,对纯化理论的发展做出自己的贡献,其基本内容为:①适用领域;②理论框架)

mid-term n. 中期

Midcal test (反垄断法)密得卡尔准则[指私方当事人(private party)的反竞争行为的准则将被认为是州的行为(state acts)。而且根据反垄断法,如果这些行为是在"清晰的与州所表述的政策密切,确切相关的范围"之内,同时这种行为还受到州的实际监督。借此,这种私方当事人反竞争行为可受到保护而不承担责任。见(the) state action doctrine; active supervision]

middle a. 中部的,中间的;中等的,中级的

middle class 中产阶级

middle of the proceedings 诉讼过程中,诉讼过程中,诉讼中期

middle peasant (中)中农

middle rate 平均价,中间价

Middle Temple (英)中殿律师学院(古时英国的四大律师学院之一。见 Inns of Court)

middle tier (法院系统的)中间审级(法院)

middle way 中间路线

middle-term plan 中期计划

middleman (17 世纪)居间人;中间代理人;转卖人[指双方当事人之间,特别是经

销人(如批发商);他从生产商那里买来,然后又卖给零售商或消费商]

Middlesex Registry （英）米度息斯登记局（英国以前办理土地契据和遗嘱登记的地方,现已迁至伦敦）

Midnight Judge （美）午夜法官(指杰弗逊共和党人执政前,随着 1800 年大选胜利联邦党国会通过了 1801 年的《司法法》。该法废除了现行巡回法院,因而解脱了联邦最高法院大法官作为巡回法官的职责;将大法官从 6 名减为 5 名,而创立了 6 个新的巡回审判区。这样使得亚当斯能够任命 16 名巡回法官,就是所谓"午夜法官")

Midnight Judges Acts of 1801 （美）《1801 年午夜法官法》(指联邦党控制的国会颁行的午夜法官法,该法授予联邦法院以联邦问题管辖权,但经审后即被废除)

midpoint of settlement range 和解范围的中点

midway house 感化院

midwife n. 助产士;接生婆

mifepristone n. 堕胎药(1980 年法国教授埃米尔·波列尤等人研制开发成功,Ru-486 和 misoprostol 两种药共同服用,成功率大于 95%)

might n. 强权;权力;势力;能力

migrancy n. 居无定所

migrant n. 移居者

migrant labor （美）农业季节工人的劳动

migrant labor system 流动劳工制

migrant worker 流动工人,移民工人

migrate v. 迁移,移居;使移居,使迁移

migration n. 迁居;移居国外;移民群

migration date 移居日期

Migratory Bird Hunting Stamp（Duck Stamp）**Act of 1934** （美）《1934 年候鸟追猎标记(鸭子标记)法》

migratory divorce （1911 年）迁移离婚(指夫妻一方为达到离婚目的的迁居到另一个州或到另一个国家以求获得其结婚居所以外的管辖获准离婚)

mild sentence 轻判

milder form of realism （美）现实主义中的温和派（即社会法学派 so-called sociological jurisprudence）

mileage n. 里程;英里数;按英里计算的旅费;(为法官等支付的)旅费

Miliangos （外币债务判决中的）密利安戈斯规则[由 1975 年英国上议院的密利安戈斯诉乔治·弗兰克(纺织品)有限公司案确立。此后一系列相关案件形成判决密利安戈斯规则,即法院可用外国货币作出判决或按实际支付国的汇率,折算成本国货币判决。根据英美法系传统规则,法院必须以本国货币判决,所有涉及外国货币的判决都必须依照原债务到期日（即违约日）的汇率折算成本国货币作出。密利安戈斯案改变了这种状况,它允许法院可直接用外国货币判决。密利安戈斯规则首先在英国确立,随后影响到美国、加拿大、澳大利亚、新西兰等众多英美法系国家,及法国等大陆法系国家]

militarism n. 军国主义;尚武精神,好战精神

militaristic a. 军国主义的,穷兵黩武的

military a. 军事的,军用的;军人的;战争的

military action 军事行动

military adventure 军事冒险

military age 兵役年龄

military aggression 军事侵略

military agreement 军事协定

military air-traffic control 军事航空管制

military alliance 军事同盟

Military Appeal 军事上诉法院

military *attaché* （大使馆）武官

military base 军事基地

military bloc 军事集团

military blockade 军事封锁

military cause 军事案件

military charge 军事费用,军事负担

military code of criminal procedure 军事刑诉法典

military commission 特别军事法庭(指特别审理违反军法或戒严法的公民的法庭)

military committee 军事委员会

military control 军管,军事管制

military *coup d'état* 军事政变

military court 军事法庭

military crime 军人违反职责罪

military delegate 军事代表

military dependents 军人家属
military deserter 逃兵
military dictatorship 军事独裁
military discipline 军纪,军事纪律
military district 军区;军事地区
military draft law 征兵法
military duty 军人职责,军事义务
military emergency regime 军事非常时期体制
military flag 军旗
military government (国际法)(对军事占领区的)军事管制政府,军人政府
military governor (行政区政府的)军事长官
military guard 军警,警卫
military indemnity 军事赔款
military intelligence 军事情报
military judge 军法官
military jurisdiction 军事裁判权,军事管辖权,军事审判(管辖)范围
Military Justice Reporter 军事审判判例汇编
military law 军法;陆军法
military legal officer 军法官(员)
military legislation 军事立法
military levy 征兵
military might 军事实力
military necessity 军用必需品,军需品
military objective 军事目标
military occupation 军事占领
military offence 触犯军法的行为,军事罪行
military order 军令
military organization 军事组织
military penal code 军法典
military personnel 军人;军事人员
military personnel on active service 现役军人
military police 军事警察;宪兵
military posts 军职人员
military power 军权,兵力
military power of the executive 行政首长的军事权
military preparation 备战,战备
military prison 陆军监狱

military procurator 军事检察官
military procuratorate 军事检察院
military prosecutor 军事公诉人
military provocation 军事挑衅
military public prosecutor's office 军事检察院
military register 军人登记册
military regulation 军规,军事条例
military requisition 军事征用
military salvage 对交战者财产的救护
military sanction 军事制裁
military secret 军事机密
military service 军籍;兵役,军役
military service law 兵役法
military severance pay 转业费
Military Staff Committee (联合国)军事参谋团
military sub-district 军分区
military target 军事目标
military tenures (英)兵役土地保有权
military testament 军人(口头)遗嘱;服兵役时所立遗嘱
military threat 军事威胁,军事恫吓
military title 军衔
military treaty 军事条约
military trial and martial law (美)军事审判与军事法(军事审判通常被称为军法审判,是在军事机构而非普通机构控制下进行的司法程序。在美国法律史上,军事法庭是最古老的联邦法庭,其运行规则由大陆会议1775年制定,也就是在《独立宣言》发表的前一年和联邦宪法颁布的前12年。联邦最高法院一直拒绝受理军事审判的上诉案件,并认为美国联邦宪法第1条规定已明确授权国会制定规则和法规以管理武装力量,包括军事审判);军事法,或称军事管制法(指战争时期从必要的军事安全、国家安全考虑军队替代国内权力机构治理国家的法律);戒严令(指军队保证控制局面旨在使国家权力机构能够恢复正常)
military tribunal 军事裁判庭
military will 军人(口头)遗嘱
military writ 军令状
militia n. 民兵组织;(总称)民兵;(美)

(18—45 岁未入伍的)全体青壮年;民团;全体国民警卫队,国民自卫队
milk v. 挤;榨取,压;套出(消息等);窃取(电话、电报线上的)消息
milk the market (美)操纵市场,从中牟利
Miller Act (美)《米勒法》[指一项联邦制定法(40 USCA 270a.-270f.),该法要求履行过账和支付一定数额债券为公共建筑物的建设、改修或修缮之用]
millionaire n. 百万富翁,巨富
millionairess n. 百万富婆
minacious a. 威胁的,恐吓的
minacity n. 威胁(性),威吓(性)

* *Minatur innocentibus qui parcit nocentibus.* He threatens the innocent who spares the guilty. The learning of law-breakers unpunished is a menace to a law-abiding persons. 放纵违者等于惩罚守法者;放纵坏人就是惩罚好人。

mind n. 心意;智力;思想;记忆
mind and memory 心意与记忆
mindful a. 留心的,注意的,不忘的(of)
mindful one's duty 认真对待自己的责任
mine n. 矿藏、矿山;宝库;源泉
mine register 矿藏登记册(簿)
mineral n./a. 矿物/矿物的
mineral concession 采矿特许权
mineral right 采矿权
mineral wealth 矿藏
minhag n. (犹太教法)成俗(指具有与哈卡拉同等法律效力的宗教习惯,哈卡拉本身以习惯为依据,因此成俗如与过去法律抵触,也可执行)
Mini-trial n. 小型审判(此方法由争议当事人各自选派的有授权的高级职员充当公断人,与当事人各自委托的律师一起研究如何解决争议)
minifundium n. 小庄园,小领地,小地产
minimal diversity 最低程度的异籍
minimal principle 最低程度原则(指电子商务立法仅是为电子商务扫除现有的障碍,并非全面建立一个有关电子商务的新的系统性的法律,而是在最低程度上对电子商务订立新的法律,尽可能将已存在的法律适用到电子商务中)

minimal scrutiny (美)最小审查标准[指美国联邦最高法院行使司法审查过程中并非对所有宪法问题适用统一的审查标准,而是逐渐发展形成三重审查标准。这三重审查标准并不存在于宪法文本之中,而是联邦最高法院创造性的解释宪法的结果。这三重审查标准分别是:①最小审查标准,又称为合宪性审查,此时联邦最高法院对政府的立法分支和行政分支表现出极大的服从性,并秉持司法克制的宪政理念。最小审查标准正是司法克制在司法审查标准中的具体体现。但随着人权保护的呼声及民权运动的日益强烈,联邦最高法院意识到最小审查标准并不适合于所有的司法审查对象。②联邦最高法院因此发展出了严格审查标准(strict scrutiny),它适用于宪法明确表达或隐含的基本权利、可疑分类等。与最小审查标准正好相反,它不是假设政府的调控为合宪,而是它假定它违宪。③伯格法院发展出了司法审查标准的第三种标准,即中度审查标准(intermediate scrutiny),此时联邦最高法院的立场是中立的,既不支持政府一方,也不支持挑战者一方。如果政府行为与一个重要的政府利益实质相关,联邦最高法院就会支持它。反之,则会推翻它]
minimalist n. 最低纲领派
minimalist approach 最低限制模式(指采取"最低限制模式"以基本的安全性给予所有电子签名以法律认可,这是联合国国际贸易法委员会制定第 7 条时的唯一选择)
minimax regret rule 最小最大后悔法则
minimum n./a. 最低额,最小量,最低限度/最少的,最小的,最低限度的,最低(额)的
minimum age 最低年龄
minimum age for marriage 结婚的最低年龄
minimum authorized capital 法定的最低资本额
minimum bill of lading charge 最低提单费,起码提单费
minimum contact requirement 最低联系

minimum contact with the state 与该州最低程度的联系
minimum contacts （美）最低限制联系（指美国联邦最高法院在 International Shoe Co. v. State of Washington 一案中已确立关于非本州民事被告行使对人管辖权的最低法律要求原则,既然被告与诉讼地州有足够的或实质性联系,从而对该案审理不违反传统公平和实质公正原理,则州法院对不在该州居住的民事被告有对人管辖权)
minimum contacts analysis 最低联系分析
minimum contacts standard 最低限度联系标准(见 minimum contacts)
minimum contacts test （standard）（1983 suits） （美）最低联系标准（1983 诉讼）[指依据民权法（1871 年）（Civil Right Act）第 1983 条规定提起诉讼,该条规定任何人对以任何州和地区的法律为借口剥夺其宪法权利或法定权利的行为均可提起诉讼。见 minimum contacts]
minimum contacts threshold （美）最低联系标准,最低联系的门槛(指管辖的要求,即被告必须与诉讼所在地的州在某种经营或其他方面有最低程度的实体性的联系,该州法院方对其有管辖权)
minimum content of natural law 自然法的最低限度的内容
minimum fine 最低罚款额
minimum harmonization 低标准协调,最低限度的协调
minimum permissible amount of capital stock 核定的最低资本额
minimum prescribed penalty 法定最低刑
minimum prices 最低价格
minimum punishment 最低刑(罚)
minimum safety standards for products 产品的最低安全标准
minimum sentence 最短刑期(判决)
Minimum Statutory Grievance Procedure （英）法定最低申诉程序[是 2002 年雇佣法案（Employment Act 2002）引入的程序。申诉是指雇员针对雇主已经采取或将要采取的行动而要求双方协商解决分歧的救济方式]
minimum tax 见 alternative minimum tax
minimum wage 最低工资
minimum wage payable 最低工资限额
minimum-maximum employment conditions 最高最低的雇佣条件
mining n. 采矿;矿业
mining bank 矿业银行
mining code 采矿法典,矿业法典
mining concession 采矿特许权
mining court 矿务法院
mining permit 开矿执照,采矿许可证
mining right 采矿权
mining superintendent 矿务督察员
mining-matter n. 矿务案件
Minister of Gospel 福音牧师
minion of the law 警察;监狱看守
minister n. 部长,大臣;公使;外交使节;教长;执行者;执法者;代理者
minister of agriculture 农业部长
minister of civil administration 民政部长
minister of economic 经济部长
minister of economic affairs 经济事务部长(大臣)
minister of foreign affairs 外交部长,外交大臣
minister of international trade and industry （日）通产大臣
minister of justice 司法部长
minister of justice's authority 司法大臣
minister of legal affair （日）法务大臣
minister of police 治安部长,治安大臣
Minister of Public Security （中）公安部长
Minister of State （英）国务大臣；(复)内务部长
Minister of the Crown （英）王室大臣
minister of the interior 内政部长,内务大臣
minister plenipotentiary 全权公使
minister resident 驻办公使
minister without portfolio 不管部部长;(英)不管大臣(指不兼部长职务的阁员),无任所大臣;政务委员
ministére public （法）检察院;检察机关
ministerial a. 部长的;部的;公使的;行政

上的;(大写)内阁的
ministerial benches 部长席;(英)(下院的)执政党席位
ministerial colleagues 部长的同僚们
Ministerial crisis 内阁危机
ministerial decree 部长命令
ministerial duties 政府成员的职责
ministerial function 行政职能
ministerial level 部长级
ministerial portfolio 部长职务
ministerial procedure 行政性程序,执行性程序
ministerial responsibility 部长负责制;部长责任制
ministerialist n. 内阁的支持者
ministry n. 部;(大写)内阁;全体部长;部长职务;公使的任期;部的办公楼
ministry for industry and trade 工商业部
ministry for overseas (英)海外领地部
Ministry for the Government of the People (中)民政部
ministry of civil administration 民政部,内政部
ministry of communications 交通部
Ministry of Consumer and Corporate Affairs (加)消费者与公司事务部
Ministry of Defence (英)国防部
ministry of finance 财政部
ministry of foreign affairs 外交部
ministry of foreign economics and trade 对外经济贸易部
ministry of foreign trade 对外贸易部,外贸部
ministry of international trade and industry (日)通产省
ministry of justice 司法部
ministry of national security 国家安全部
ministry of public security (中)公安部
minitreaty regime 小型条约体系(又称 Reciprocating States Regime)
mino author 第二作者(指国际上多年版权实践,第二作者虽与主要作者一道署名,但版权仅属主要作者)
mino translator 第二译者,次要译者
minor n./a. 1.未达到法定年龄的人,未成年人,未成年;儿童或未成年者,亦称 infant(见 adult)2.(罗马法)过了青春期(16岁以上)但尚不到25岁的人。亦称 minor guam 25 annis

* *Minor ante tempus agere non potest in oasu proprietatis, nec etiam convenire.* A minor before majority cannot act in a case of property, not even to agree. 未成年人无处理财产之行为能力,甚至无权表示同意。

minor case (或 **matter**) 较轻微的案件
minor children 未成年子女
minor confinement 轻刑监禁
minor criminal case 轻微刑事案件
minor defects 枝节性瑕疵
minor defence 轻微犯罪
minor details of performance 履行细节
minor fine 轻微罚金
minor in need of supervision 见 child in need of supervision,缩略为 MINS
minor injury 轻伤(害)
minor issue 枝节问题
minor judge 初级法官,低级法官
minor jurare non potest A minor cannot take an oath 未成年人不得举行宣誓

* *Minor non tenatur respondere durante minori aetati, nisi in causa dotis, propter favorem.* A minor is not bound to answer during his minority, except as a matter of favor in a cause of dower. 未成年人在未成年期无答辩之义务,但对其有利的寡母财产的继承问题除外。

minor offence 轻罪,小罪
minor offender 轻刑犯;未成年罪犯
minor orphan 未成年孤儿
minor penalty 轻微的刑罚
minor psychoses 轻微变态心理

* *Minor qui infra aetatem 12 annorum fuerit uteagari non potest, nec extra legem poni, quia ante talem aetatem, non est sub lege aliqua, nec in decenna.* A minor who is under 12 years of age cannot be outlawed nor placed beyond the law, because before that age he is not under any law nor in a decennary. 12岁以下的未成年人不能被剥夺法律的保护,也不能置于法律之外(或

也要受到法律约束)。因为这样年龄的未成年人既无任何专门法律保护,亦不处于10岁以下的保护期。

* *Minor septemdecim annis non admittitur fore executorem.* A person under 17 years of age is not admitted to be an executor. 17岁以下未成年人不被允许承担执行人。

minores 适婚的未成年人
minority n. 少数;少数票;少数民族;少数党(派);未成年;不到法定年龄的状态
minority areas 少数民族地区
minority control 少数控制(即个人或少数人集团持有充分的股票权益,通过自身的股票权益控制公司。见 Control through almost complete ownership)
minority holding 少数股权
minority in parliament 议会的少数派
minority language 少数民族语言
minority leader 少数党领袖
minority opinion 少数意见(指用书面写出的不同意多数法官的判决意见的异议。见 dissenting opinion)
minority party 少数党
minority position 少数人的见解,少数人的主张
minority problem 少数民族问题
minority representation 少数代表制
minority shareholder 少数股东(指"多数股东"相对而言,即我们所说的"小户""散户"或"公众股东",其所持股票占公司发行在外的股票总数中所占比例极小,不足以控制公司的管理或选举自己的董事。亦可称为"minority stockholder")
mint v./n. 铸造(钱币);制造;伪造;创造/造币厂;制造所;伪造物;巨额;富源
MINT 薄荷四国[指2001年末,时任高盛公司首席经济学家的吉姆·奥尼尔首次在报告中使用了"金砖四国"(BRIC)这一缩略词,引发了人们对正在崛起的巴西、俄罗斯、印度、中国以及南非的巨大关注。这些国家以高速经济增长、丰富的原材料资源和人口红利著称,吸引着投资者的目光。但近年来,金砖国家的经济增长由于不同原因而明显减速。此外还有如下事实:一旦达到某种水平,就不再那么容易实现两位数的经济增长。因此,很多投资者已经在四处寻找其他新兴市场,比金砖国家小因此具备更大增长潜力的国家。吉姆·奥尼尔介绍了自己的最新研究对象:薄荷四国(MINT)、即墨西哥(M)、印度尼西亚(I)、尼日利亚(N)和土耳其(T),这些国家值得受到同金砖国家一样的重视。他指出,这些国家在未来20年有着非常不错的人口前景,经济前景也很具有吸引力。彭博社的另一名专栏作家指出,信诚投资公司早在2011年就已使用过"薄荷四国"的表述]

mint of money 巨款
mint of rumo(u)rs 谣言制造所
mint par 法定价格,官价
mint par of exchange 汇兑平价,汇兑的铸币平价
mintage n. 铸币(权);造币(权);造币费
minute n. (时间)分;瞬间;备忘录;(复)会议记录;审判记录
minute book 备忘簿,记事簿(指一些法院的书记员列出所有以案号表示的每一案件的全部指令概要的记录本)
minutes of judg(e)ment 判决记录
minutes of proceedings 议事记录
minutes of trial 审判记录
Miranda rule (美)米兰达规则(指警察在对拘押嫌疑人讯问前应告知其可享受权利的规定,这些权利为:1.他具有保持沉默权利 2.他所作的任何陈述均可用来作为反对他本人的证据 3.他有权见到律师 4.如果他不能提供律师,在对他讯问之前,如果他有此要求,可为他指定一名律师)
Miranda Warning (美)米兰达忠告(或警告)(见 Miranda rule)
mirror image "镜像"标准(对信用证进行审单的代表性学说,曾经是英美法院所援用的主要审单标准之一)
mirror image reciprocity 镜像互惠(指要求第三国对欧共体信用机构给予的待遇须与欧共体对该第三国银行所给予的待遇完全相同)
Mirror of Justice (英格兰古法)正义宝鉴(一部英国法律著作,爱德华二世1307—

1327 年期间写成,亦有 1285—1290 年期间写成之说,又译《司法之镜》)

mirror rule 镜像原则(指英美法采用的一种订立合同的原则,即承诺如同照镜子一般应照出要约的内容,承诺必须与要约内容一致,合同才能成立)

misadministration n. 管理不善,管理失当

misadventure n. 意外事故,不幸遭遇,灾难

misallege v. 虚伪陈述,错误举证

misalliance n. 不适当的结婚(例如年龄相差悬殊)

misallocation n. 不当分配

misallocative costs 不当分配成本

misapplication n. 误用;滥用;错用;挪用罪

misapplication of law 法律的误用

misapprehension n. 误会,误解

misappropriate v. 侵占;私吞;盗用;挪用,挪作他用;滥用

misappropriation n. 侵占;私吞;贪污;挪用;滥用

Misappropriation Doctrine 非法盗用学说(指知识产权领域的法官造法在很多国家都不同程度和不同形式地存在,如美国法院可能依据普通法判例中确定的"非法盗用学说",对联邦立法保护范围之外的一些知识产权主体提供保护,如时事新闻、名人形象、未出版的作品等)

misappropriation of public funds 挪用公款

misappropriation theory 盗用理论(指即使信息获取者与上市公司或其他股东无任何信用关系,基于合同或其他关系获得信息者,若利用工作职务之便,盗用他人信息或资料,对他人也有法律责任。见 temporary insider theory)

misbegotten (=misbegot) a. 非法产生的,不正当手段取得的;私生的;可鄙的

misbehaved a. 行为不正当的,不规矩的

misbehavio(u)r n. 行为不端,品行不良,不正当的举止,举止失检

misbehavior in office 见 official misconduct

misbelieve v. 误信;信异教

misbirth n. 堕胎,流产

miscarriage n. 1.失败 2.错报;误送 3.小产,流产,堕胎 4.审判错误 5.(英)不按合同(契约)规定运送货物

miscarriage of goods 货物未曾送过

miscarriage of justice 审判不公,错判,误判(指在司法程序中极不公的后果,在缺乏重要犯罪证据的情况下,毫不顾及犯罪要件的证据而作出刑事被告有罪的不公正的判决)

miscegenation n. 异族通婚(尤指美国黑人与白人通婚);种族混淆;混血,(异种)杂婚

miscellaneous a. 各种的,不同性质的

miscellaneous cases 杂项案件

miscellaneous charge order 杂费支付通知

miscellaneous disputes 各种不同性质的争议

miscellaneous docket (美)其他案件,杂项案件[通常与"appellate docket"上诉案件、"original docket"一审案件等术语并列出现。杂项案件的材料都用红色文件夹存档,其他交付了相关费用的而被列入上诉案件表的案件材料则通常用蓝色文件夹存档。可参阅 28 U.S.C 1915(a)]

miscellaneous forms of conversion 各种方式的侵占行为

miscellanous itemized deduction (1955 年)各种名目分项扣减额[指一般来说,对批发(job)或投资支出(investment expenses)的分项扣减;美国《国内税收法》所指定的那些可作为计算调整后总收入(adjusted gross income)之外的扣除(或扣减),参见《美国注释法典》第 26 标题卷第 67 节以及个人的减免税额。这种扣减的形式只是分项纳税人(itemizing taxpayer)在其调整后的总收入总的逐项扣减超过了法定的百分比时方可允许]

miscellaneous tort 各种侵权行为

mischance n. 不幸,横祸,灾难

mischarge (1939 年)错误指示(指法官对陪审团作出错误的指示,可作为撤销陪审团裁决的依据。亦称 misdirection)

mischief n. 1.损害,伤害,危害,毒害;造成损害的行为(或人);祸根 2.恶作剧 3.不明的文字(指在制定法中的含糊不清的文字,要靠法官来推定或解释)4.不和,争执

mischief of statute 条文晦涩(指法规中的不明确处)

mischief rule 不确切文字解释规则(指法院在解释其成文法条文时,应先了解此条文制定之前的有关法律概况及其弊端,从而明白其针对何弊端而设,为解决何种问题而订,以便于更有针对性地解释,指在解释制定法中,对于制定法中不明确之处,应从有利于实现制定法的目的出发进行解释,以弥补制定法的不足);消除混乱规则

mischievous effects 危害后果
mischief rule 不确切文字释义规则
miscolor v. 作歪曲陈述,颠倒黑白
misconceive n. 误解,对……有错误看法
misconduct n. 处理不当;渎职;行为不端;通奸
misconduct in office 渎职,玩忽职守(见 official misconduct)
misconduct offence 渎职罪
misconstruction n. 曲解,误解;结构不对;错误句法
misconstrue v. 曲解,误解,误会
miscreancy n. 不道德,卑鄙
misdeed n. 不端行为;犯罪;恶行
misdemeanant n. 轻罪犯(人);行为不端者
misdemeano(u)r (16世纪)1.(美)不轨行为,轻罪[指联邦或州法将重罪以外的罪行均归入轻罪,且通常受到罚款,惩罚,没收处分或禁闭(短暂期间)。亦称为 minor crime; summary offense。见 felony] 2.(古代)任何罪行,包括重罪(felony)
misdemeanor in office 见 official misconduct
misderive v. 作错误的推论(或溯源)
misdescription n. 错误描述
misdirect v. 对……作错误指示,瞎指挥
misdirect a jury (法官)给陪审团下达错误指令
misdirection n. (法官对陪审团的)错误指示;错误指导,瞎指挥
misdoing n. (常用复)坏事,恶行,罪行;犯罪
mise n. 1.(英)(普通法上土地权利令状中的)系争点 2.协定,协约 3.(英)税(指从前威尔士地方的税);费用(指诉讼费用的开

支) 4.赌金
* *Misera est servitus ubi jus est vagum aut incognitum* (or *incertum*). Obedience to the law is hardship, where the law is vague or unknown (or uncertain)./It is miserable slavery where the law is vague or uncertain. 法律不确定或不清楚时,如令遵守,实属苛求。
misfeasance n. 错误行为;不法行为;滥用职权(尤指以不法手段做合法的事);不正当的行为,违法;过失;犯罪
misfeasance and nonfeasance 违法与渎职
misfeasor n. 行为不法者,违法者;滥用职权者
misfile v. 把(文件等)归错档案
misfortune n. 不幸事故;不幸,灾祸
misgotten a. 用不正当手段取得的
misgotten treasure 不义之财
misinformation n. 错误的消息,误传
misinformer n. 提供不正确消息者;误报者,误传者
misjoinder n. 错误的共同合并,错误的共同诉讼,不同诉因的错误合并;错误参与诉讼,诉讼主体错误,错误联合诉讼人(指错误参加联合诉讼的原告或被告,但诉讼不得因此无效。不过法院有权命令其停止参加诉讼)
misjoinder of causes 不同讼案的错误合并
misjoinder of parties 诉讼当事人的不当联合
misjudge v. 判断错误,判断失当;错误地判决,误判
misjudged a. 判决失当的,错判的
misjudged case 错判案,冤案
misjudg(e)ment n. 审判错误;判断错误
misjudg(e)ment failure 从属故障(指因判断错误而出现的故障)
mislabelling n. 错误标示,错误标志
mislaid property 错置财产
misleading a. 误写姓名的;误称的;(易)令人误解的,导致错误的
misleading actions 错误诱导性作为(欧共体条约指令第 6 条规定错误诱导行为"misleading practice"包括两种:①错误诱导性作为;和②错误诱导性遗漏"mislead-

ing omission")
misleading advertisement (advertising) 误导性广告(指使消费者产生误解的广告)
misleading conduct 令人误解的行为
misleading omission 错误诱导遗漏(见 misleading actions 和 misleading practice)
misleading practice 错误诱导性行为(指如果商业行为含有不真实或夸大陈述的虚假信息,错误诱导或可能诱导"一般消费者",这种行为被认定为"错误诱导行为";或者即使信息正确,但其所涉及的一些因素会导致或可能导致消费者作出在其他情况下不会作出的交易决定,这种行为也将被认定为错误诱导行为。见 misleading action)
misleading question 错误诱导询问(指询问证人时,用暗示方法使证人发生错觉而作出和记忆相悖的供述)
misleading trade description 令人误解的商品说明(书)
mismarriage n. 不相配的婚姻,不美满的婚姻
mismatch v. (婚姻方面的)错配,(尤指不适当婚姻)配合不当
misnomer n./v. (文件中)指定人名的错误、地名的错误;名词或名字的误用/叫错姓名(指诉状、诉词里把人名叫错了);用词不当,使用不当名称(名词)
misperception n. 错误的感知
misplead v. 不正确地辩护
mispleading n. 诉词中的错误;不当申述;不当辩护
misprision n. 1.渎职,玩忽职守 2.知情不报,包庇,隐匿(罪) 3.轻视,蔑视 4.(反对政府和法院的)煽动行为 5.误会,错误
misprision of felony 藏匿重罪犯的罪行
misprision of treason 隐匿叛国犯的罪行,隐匿叛逆犯的罪行
misprize v. 轻视,蔑视
misread v. 看错,误读
misrecital n. 错误陈述事实
misreport n. 谎报,误报,报道不实
misrepresentation n. 讹传,谎言;虚伪的陈述;与事实不符的陈述、谎传、误述、歪曲、不正当的代表;不称职的代表;不诚实表示

Misrepresentation Act 1967 (英)《1967年误述法》;《1967年不实陈述法》
misrepresentation and omission 虚假陈述和失职行为
misrepresentation of age 虚报年龄
misrepresentation of health 误述健康状况
misrepresentation of identity 诈称身份
misrepresentation of law 曲解法律
missi (法)皇家巡回法官
missi dominici (法)(查理曼大帝时代的)钦差
missile n. 投射物,发射器;火箭;飞弹
missing a. 行踪不明的;失踪的;遗失的;不在的;缺少的
missing person 失踪人
missing spouse 缺席配偶,失踪的配偶
missioin bona (罗马法)财产占有(指通过执行使债权人占有债务人的财产。实际上,即裁判官授权原告对逃跑未履行债务的被告的全部财产的占有,以督促被告参加诉讼程序,使之继续。因原告并无出售财产权利,因为占有制就是给占有的原告这个权利)
missio in possessionem (罗马法)财产的占有(指裁判官允准债权人取得对债务人财产的占有。此等占有的安宁受裁判官令状的保护,如同执行判决一样)
mission n. 使命,任务;使节团;负有特殊任务的团体
mission allowance 出差补贴,出差津贴
missionary n./a. 传教士/传教的,教会的,传教士的
missive n. 公文,公函
misspend 滥用,浪费,虚度
misstate or omit certain information 虚假陈述或遗漏特定信息
misstatement n. 虚报;错报;错误表述,伪述
misstep n. 失足;过失;失策;(少女的)失身
mistake n./v. 错误;过失;失策;误解/搞错;误解
mistake as the parties 作为当事人的错误
mistake as to the nature of obligation 作为债务性质的错误

mistake declaration of intent 错误的意思表示
mistake in communication 传达错误
mistake in judg(e)ment 判决错误
mistake of competency 管辖错误
mistake of fact 事实(上的)错误
mistake of kill 误杀
mistake of law 法律(上的)错误
mistaken a. 错的,弄错的;判断错误的;犯错误的,意见错误的
mistaken accusation 误告
mistaken identity 判断错了的(人的)身份
mistreat v. 虐待,苛待
Mistress of the Robes (英)女王的女侍长
mistrial n. (因违反诉讼程序的)无效审判;误判;审判失误;(因陪审团意见不一致的)未决审判;(美)无效审判(指在法官确信不可能作出一个公平的裁决而终止诉讼程序之时,若陪审团不能就裁决达成共识,而法官认为即便他们再作评议,也不存在达成一致的合理意见可能性,法官则宣布此乃无效审判,此后,此案可能另定日期,由另一陪审团审理)
mistrust v. 不信任,怀疑
misunderstanding n. 误解,误会;不和,争执
misusage n. (文字等)误用;滥用;苛待,虐待
misuse n./v. 误用,滥用;苛待,虐待;[①产品责任诉讼中的控辩理由,是指非以生产者之意图或合理预见的方式使用产品;②专利方面:专利使用不正当的侵权扩大到垄断的非专利产品或违反反垄断法之产品]/滥用、误用,虐待
misuse of authority 滥用职权
misuse of drugs 滥用药物
misuse of legal procedure 滥用诉讼(程序)
misuse of legal process 滥用法律程序(手续)
misuse of powers 权力滥用标准(是由美国教授谢弗提出的,其内涵是:当董事获得某种机会或其他商业优势,无论这个机会或优势是否可由公司获得,如果董事在事实上通过滥用其权力而获得了这种商业或其他商业优势,即可推定董事滥用公司赋予其权力这一事实存在。公司董事除非能证明其所取得的这种商业机会或其他商业优势不是通过其受信人的权力的运用,否则他就应对此承担法律责任。见 Corporate opportunity rule)
misuser n. 权利滥用;滥用权利者(指政府公职人员滥用职权、企业滥用特许权,均足以引起权利的丧失。见 user)
mitigate v. 缓和;减轻;安慰
mitigated injury 轻度伤害
mitigated penalty 减轻刑罚
mitigated responsibility 减轻责任
mitigating circumstance (17世纪)减刑情节[指①不能证明合法或不能宽恕不法行为或罪行,但具有可减轻应受惩罚程度的一些情节或事实,而且这样可在民事案件中减轻损害赔偿,在刑事案件中减轻惩罚。②对于不承担被告罪责的问题之事实和情节,法院在给予惩罚时考虑到这种情节,特别在减轻严惩上(severity of sentence)予以考量。法院或陪审团考虑减轻情节的权力是不受制定法限制的,见洛克特诉俄亥俄州案(Lockett v. Ohio),《美国联邦最高法院判例汇编》第438卷第586页。对于因罪杀人案件(a capital-murder case)减刑情节的目录,可参见《示范刑法典》第210.6(4)节。③(合同法)一个意外的,不可预测的,如工人罢工而阻合同的履行,亦可称为 extenuating circumstance (见 aggravating circumstance)。④(刑事)比如一个人被合法地激怒,一时气愤杀人,可作为减轻情节,将杀人罪(homicide)降为非预谋杀人罪(manslaughter)]
mitigating contaminated soil for urban gardens 减轻城区菜园污染的土壤
mitigation n. (刑)减轻,缓和;安慰;(英)减轻其他证据效力的论据;减轻责任的辩护
mitigation of damages 损害赔偿的减轻,减轻损害赔偿金
mitigation of penalty 减轻惩罚
mitigation of punishment (18世纪)(刑法)减刑[指由于降低刑罚应受惩的程度(criminal's level of culpability),如无前科定罪(no prior conviction)等减轻情节(mitigating circumstance)而减刑。见 miti-

gating circumstance]
mitigation of sentence 缩减刑期(判决)
* *Mitius imperanti melius paretur.* He is better obeyed who commands leniently./The more mildly one commands, the better is he obeyed. 以仁施政,其令易行。
mittimus n. 1.徒刑执行令;(法院)移送案卷令;收监令 2.解雇通知,免职,解聘;(英)地方行政官
mitzvah (犹太教法)戒条(广义指《托拉》所载一切犹太教徒必须遵守的全部戒条、律例、律法和典章)
mitzwot ma'asiyyot (犹太教正统派的)成俗(指必须遵守的行动成规。见 *minhag*)
mixed a. 混合的,混杂的
mixed accomplices 复杂共犯
mixed action 混合之诉(见 *actio mixta*)
mixed arbitral tribunal 混合仲裁法庭
mixed-motive discrimination 混合动机歧视(见 theory of social discrimination)
mixed arbitration 混合仲裁
mixed chamber 混合法庭
mixed claim 混合索赔,混合请求权
mixed claims commission 混合索赔委员会;混合诉讼委员会
mixed code 混合法典
mixed commission (法)(议会的)混合委员会
mixed committee (某些国家议会参、众两院由同等数额议员组成的)混合委员会
mixed court 会审庭,会审公堂
mixed duties 混合税
mixed economy company 混合经济公司
mixed fact-law questions 混杂的事实与法律问题
mixed fund 混合资金(包含动产和不动产的资金)
mixed government 混合政体,混合政府
mixed holding company 混合控股公司
mixed insurance 混合保险
mixed jury 混合陪审团
mixed larceny 混合盗窃罪(见 compound larceny)
mixed law and fact 法律和事实的混合
mixed marriage 混合婚姻,杂婚,异族通婚
mixed personality 混合动产
mixed policy 混合保险单
mixed possession 混合占有
mixed presumption 合并推定(指法律与事实兼顾的推断)
mixed private/state company 公私合营公司
mixed process 混合程序
mixed property 混合财产(权)(指不动产附带有一些动产的财产权利)
mixed punishment (多种刑罚的)合并处罚,合并论罪
mixed questions 混合问题(指涉及事实和法律两方面的法律问题或涉及本国法律和外国法律两方面的问题)
mixed questions of fact and law (涉及)事实与法律的混合问题
mixed stock company 股份混合公司
mixed stock company organized without participation of foreign capital 无外国资本的股份混合公司
mixed subjects of property 动产和不动产的混合
mixed ticket 混合选票
mixed tribunal 混合裁判庭
mixture n. 混合,混合物;混合状态
ML clause 超过与不足条款
mob n./v. 民众;一群流氓;暴民,暴徒;一群罪犯/聚众闹事;成群结伙搞袭击(骚扰);结伙惹事
mob law 私刑;暴民法
mob violence 暴动
mob-rule n. 暴民统治制
mobbing and rioting 暴乱
mobbish a. 无纪律的;如暴徒般的
mobbist n. 暴徒
mobile a./n. 活动的,运动的,流动的/(美)汽车
mobile patrol 流动巡逻队
mobile phone 移动电话
mobile pollution source 流动污染源
mobile shop license 流动商店执照
* *Mobilia sequuntur personam.* Movables follow the (law of the) person. 动产随人(动产遵循所有人住所地法)。

mobility n. 1.运动性;流动性;变动性;灵活性 2.民众
mobilization n. 动员;流通
mobilization order 动员令
mobilize v. 动员;使(不动产)变为动产;使流通
mobocracy n. 暴民政治,暴徒统治;(总称)取得统治地位的暴民阶级
mobsman n. (英)打扮时髦的扒手;暴民,暴徒
mobster n. (美)暴徒,盗匪
mock a. 假的;模拟的
mock auction 假拍卖
mock court 假设法庭;模拟法庭
mock marriage 假婚
mock trial 模拟审判,假审判
modal a. 规定执行(或应用)方式的;形式的,形态的;典型的,一般的
modal legacy 有条件的遗赠
mode n. 方式,方法;样式;模式;时式,风尚
mode of acquisition 取得的方式
mode of commission 授权方式,委托方式,任命方式
mode of execution 执行方式
mode of imprisonment 监禁形式
mode of living 生活方式
mode of normal navigation 正常航行模式
mode of payment 付款方式
mode of proof 证明方式;证据形式
mode of punishment 惩罚方法
mode of rule 规则模式
mode of settlement 结算方式;(英)财产授予方式;和解方式
mode of subsistence 生存模式(指孟德斯鸠界定特定法律的决定因素)
mode of thought 思维模式
mode of trial 审讯形式,审讯方式
mode of voting 投票方式
model n./v. 实用新型,式样,模型;模范,典型;时装模特儿;示范,模式/模仿,使模仿(on, upon after),做……的模型
Model Act (美)示范法[指由美国统一州法委员会起草的法规,并建议作为各州立法准则(guideline legislation),便于借用或采纳以适合它们各自的需要。比如示范法规,包括《模范雇用终止法》(Mode Employment Termination Act)和《示范(州)惩罚性损害赔偿法》(Model Punitive Damages Act)。见 Uniform Law; Uniform Act]
model acts (美)示范法[亦译做建议的法规,指向立法机构建议采纳的法规,如《示范遗嘱检验法》(Model Probate Code)即由全国统一州法规委员会大会建议的]
Model BIT (美)1982年制定的"双边投资条约的范本"
model building 建筑模型,建造模型
Model Business Corporation Act (美)《示范公司法》[亦译为《标准公司法》《典范商业公司法》,它是由美国律师协会(ABA)1950年起草,总结美国各州的公司法,代表公司法发展趋势,虽不是立法机构制定,但颇有权威性,美国绝大多数州公司法在很大程度上采用此法作为蓝本]
model case(**model action**) 示范性诉讼(案件)
model clauses 示范条款
Model Code of Evidence (美)《示范证据法典》
Model Code of Professional Responsibility (美)《示范职业责任法规》[指以准则、惩戒性规定、道德方面对价(ethical considerations)的形式构成的律师的一系列道德行动纲领(ethical guideline)。此法规于1969年由美国律师协会正式公布,但它在许多州中已为《律师职业行为示范法规》(Model Rules of Professional Conduct)所替代]
model contract 模式合同(契约);标准合同(契约);合同(契约)范本;(大写)(美)示范合同(契约)
model convention 示范公约,公约范本
Model Law on Electronic Commerce 《电子商务示范法》
Model Marriage and Divorce Act 见 Uniform Marriage and Divorce Act
model of a poster 招贴样本
model of dialectical reasoning 辩证推理模式
model of government 规范的政府

model of law 规范的法律
Model Penal Code (美)《示范刑法典》
Model Penal Code rule (MPC rule) (美)《示范刑法典规则》[又称实际能力规则(substantial capacity rule)。它是由美国法律学会(ALI)于1962年在《示范刑法典》中制定的一个规则,是美国有关精神病方面的第4个规则。主要内容是:①因精神疾病或有缺陷,被告人在实施犯罪行为时缺乏识别其行为的犯罪性(非法性)或缺乏使其行为符合法律要求的实际能力时,被告人对该行为不负责任;②这里所使用的"精神疾病或缺陷"不包括仅由反复实施犯罪行为或其他反社会行为所表明的变态人格;③1984年前,除一个联邦上诉法院外,其他联邦上诉法院和半数以上州法院均采用这一规则,该规则否定了纯医学的德赫姆规则,整合了麦克·纳顿条例和不可控制的冲动条例;④有里但有精神病(Guilty but mentally ill GBMI)的规则(见 Durham rule;guilty but mentally ill 英、美两个词条)]
Model Probate Code (美)《示范遗嘱检验法》
Model Public Defender Act (美)《示范公设律师法》
Model Putative Fathers Act 见 Uniform Putative and Unknown Fathers Act
Model Rules of Professional Conduct (美)《律师职责行为示范法规》,《模范律师职业行为法规》[指由52条规定对律师构成的一系列道德准则(ethical guideline),有的是强制性的(mandatory),有的是酌处自由决定的(discretionary),全部都有解释性评注。此行为法规于1983年由美国律师协会正式颁布出版。这些行为法规代替了《示范职业责任法规》(Model Code of Professional Responsibility),而且已为许多州作为法律采用。缩略为 MRPC]
Model State Punitive Damages Act (美)《(示范州)惩罚性损害赔偿法》
model statute 示范法规,制定法范本
model treaty 示范性条约
model worker (中)劳动模范;模范工作者

(the) Model Written Obligation Act (美)宾夕法尼亚州《标准书面债务法》[该法前身是统一州法全国委员会制定的1925年的《统一书面债务法》(Uniform Written Obligation Act),目前只有宾州无条件采用,其他州均有条件采用]
modeling n. 模拟,模型建立
modeling behavior 模拟行为
modeling method 标准方法
modeling process 模仿建立的过程,模仿进程
models of two sided asymmetric information 以全面不对称信息为内容的模型
moderamen inculpatae tutelae 正当防卫(指罗马法规定为防卫自己的身体或财产安全,对侵犯者之暴力可使用防卫,于必要时可置侵犯者于死地)
moderate a./n./v. 花费不多的,公道的,中等的,适度的,有节制的/温和主义者,稳健派/使温和,使减轻,节制;主持(会议等),变温和
moderate price 适度价格
moderate sin taxes 中等罪税
moderate wage 低工资
moderatism n. (政治宗教方面的)温和主义,中庸主义,稳健主义
moderatist n. 温和派,稳健的人,中庸主义者
moderator n. 1.仲裁人,调解人 2.(辩论会)主席;议长 3.监考员,主考员
moderatorship n. 仲裁人的职权;(辩论会等)主席的职权
modern code 现代法典
Modern Commerce Power Tests (美)现代商务权力检验标准
modern constitution 现代政府体制
modern court 现代法院
modern delegation of power doctrine 现代授权法则
modern democratize states 现代民主国家
modern equal protection jurisprudence (美)现代平等保护法理学
Modern Federal Practice Digest (美)《现代联邦实践判决摘要汇编》(指为增补《联邦判决摘要汇编》的连续汇集的一种,包

括年代为 1939—1961 年)
modern law 近代法,现代法
Modern Law Report 《现代法律判例汇编》
modern legal armory 现代法律武器库
modern limitation on warfare 关于现代战争的限制
modern long-arm statute (美)现代长臂法
modern pleading 现代诉辩
modern regulation 现代规则
modern system of courts 现代法院体制
modern western legal thoughts 现代西方法律思想
modernitas 当代时期(见 modernity)
modernity n. 现代性(来源于 11 世纪的拉丁词汇"*modernitas*")
modernization n. 现代化;维新;现代化之事物
modernization of law 法律现代化,法的现代化
modernization of traditional administrative law theory 传统行政法理论的现代化
modernize v. 使现代化,使适应现代化需要
modes of payment of wages 支付工资方式
modification n. (17 世纪)变更,改变;更改,修改;缓和,减轻;意义的限制[指①对某些事物的改变,变更,更正〈a contract modification〉(合同契约的变更);②某种事物合格性或限制〈a modification of drinking habits〉(对饮酒习惯的限制);③(议会法)动议的变更或更改(指通常在议长开始介绍动议之前,动议人提出并认可动议的变更),动议人控制动议只能在议长陈述此问题之前,在陈述动议之后,则它属于议会(assembly),如不经议会同意或允准,动议人是不能更改的。见 request for permission to modify a motion]
modification of motion 修改动议
modification of the data contained in the original declaration 原申请书记载事项的变更
modify v. 变更,修改;限制(意义);明确(意义)
modify one's registration 变更登记

modify the terms of contract 修改合同(契约)条款
modo 方法上
modo et forma 方法上和形式上(的抗辩)(指采取方式和形式上否定对方答辩中事实的一种古老诉讼形式)
modus 负担;手段,方法,方式;习惯
modus acquirendi 所有权的取得方式
Modus et conventio vincunt legem. Custom and agreement overrule law. 惯例和协议(在一定限度内)优于法。
modus habilis 有效方式
modus operandi 惯技;作案手法;办事方法,做法
modus vivendi 临时解决办法,过渡办法;临时协定,权宜之计
moerda 谋杀,秘密杀害
Mohammedan (Mohan) a./n. (伊斯兰教创立人)穆罕默德的,伊斯兰教的/伊斯兰教徒,穆斯林
Mohammedan court 伊斯兰教法法院(亦译作穆罕默德法院)
Mohammedan law 穆罕默德法(即伊斯兰教法)
Mohammedan marriage, divorce and succession act 伊斯兰婚姻、离婚和继承法
moiety n. (财产等)的一半;二分之一;部分,约一半
mold(=**mould**) v./n. 对……产生影响,形成;用模子做;浇铸/模子,模型;铸型;类型
molecular biology 分子生物学(指从分子水平上研究生命现象物质基础的学科。除此之外,尚有 genetics"遗传学"、environmental biology"环境生物学", physical authropology"人体人类学"、evolutionary biology"进化生物学"、population genetics"群体遗传学"和 statistics"统计学"等领域)
molest v. 调戏,作弄;恶意干涉,妨害;骚扰
molest a female 调戏女性
molestation n. (15 世纪)骚扰,伤害,残害[指①对某人的骚扰或残害〈molestation of a witness〉(在对证人的骚扰残害);②特别是为了性满足而进行的对某人的非自愿的求爱的接近行为〈sexual molestation〉

（性骚扰）。molest v.; molester n.]
molliter manus imposuit （警官在制止妨害治安案件中所提出的）手掌轻按抗辩（意指未施暴力）
momentary a. 顷刻的,瞬息的,短暂的;时时刻刻的
momentum n. 势头,力量,动力,要素,契机（复）momenta
mommy track （美）母亲轨道（指女性受雇者在管理和决策阶层代表性偏低的情形迟迟难以改善,有部分人力资源专家将此现象归责于所谓"母亲轨道"理论,即认为女性受雇者通常同时都必须负担母职,而影响其晋升机会）
monandry n. （婚姻上的）一夫制
monarch n. 君主,最高统治者
monarch's region 君主的统治
monarchal a. 君主的,君主政治的,君主政体的
monarchism n. 君主制,君主主义,君主政治
monarchy n. 君主政体;君主国;君主制
monetarism n. 货币主义（指货币数量对经济活动和价格水平有重要影响,货币政策的目标可以通过控制货币供给增长率指标而得以很好实现）
monetary a. 货币的;币制的;金钱的;金融的,财政的
monetary authorities 财政当局（机关）
monetary circulation 货币流通
monetary equivalent 折算金额
monetary law 货币法
monetary liabilities 货币债务
monetary limits of the insurance policy 保单的金额限制
monetary loss 金钱损失
monetary obligation 金钱债务
monetary penalty 罚款（处罚）
monetary reform 货币改革
monetary relationship 金钱关系
monetary reserves 货币储存,货币储备
monetary settlement 金钱和解
monetary standard 货币本位
monetary system 货币制度,币制
monetary unit 货币单位

money n. 货币;款项;金钱;金额;财富;金融界
money bill 财政法案,拨款法案
money broker 代办短期借款的经纪人;兑换商;放款收息的人
money changer 货币兑换商;货币兑换机
money claim 金钱索赔,金钱债务诉讼;金钱请求权,金钱债权
money counts （普通法上的）金钱之诉
money damages 金钱赔偿
money down 现金支付
money had and received （原告针对诸如代理人等所提出的）收受金钱的诉由
money income 金钱收入
Money Laundering Control Act of 1986 （美）《1986年控制洗钱法》
money laundries（或 **laundering**） 洗钱（指为了掩盖收入的存在、非法来源或非法使用,而将这些收入设置假象使其具有表面合法性的过程）
money lender 放债者,放款人
Money Lenders Act （英）《金钱借贷者法》(1900—1927年)
money loan 金钱借贷,货币借贷
money market 货币市场;金融市场
money matter 金钱问题,财政问题;财政案件
money obligation 金钱债务
money of account 记账货币,结算通货;虚位通货（如英国的 guinea）
money order 汇款单,汇票;邮政汇票
money payments 金钱给付
money penalties 金钱处罚
money supply 货币供应量
money verdict 金钱裁断（决）（见 quotient verdict）
money's worth 合算的买卖
money-exchanging n. 外汇兑换,货币兑换
money-maker n. 会赚钱的人;赚钱的东西（或计划）
money-man n. 投资者;金融家;财政家
money-market n. 金融市场
money-monger n. 放债的人,放利者
money-purchase plan 退休金计划（指雇员每年交出定额款项的一种退休金计划,

根据投入的情况,享受不同的福利)
moneyed a. 金钱上的;有钱的,富有的
moneyed classes 有产阶级
moneylending n. 金钱借贷
Monisim n. (国际法)一元论,一元
monist n. 一元论者
Monistic Doctrine 一元论
monition n. 通告,告诫,警告;(法院的)传票,传唤
monitor n./v. (美)国会监察员;监听器;告诫者/监听,监视,监控
monitoring n. 监测
monitoring cost 控制成本
monitoring of rivers 河流监测
Monitoring the Digital Divide 监测数字鸿沟(属 Orbicom 公司的)
monitoring urban soil quality 检测城区土壤质量
monocracy n. 独裁政治
monocrat n. 独裁者;君主制度主义者
monoculture n. (农业的)单一经营
monogamous a. 一夫一妻制的,主张一夫一妻制的,实行一夫一妻制的;一生一婚制的
monogamous marriage 一夫一妻制婚姻
monogamy n. 一夫一妻制,一生一婚制
monogram n. 交织文字,花押字,字母图案
monographs n. 专题著作,专题文章,专著
monogynous a. 一妻制的
monogyny n. 一妻制
monomania n. 偏僻,偏执狂
monomark n. (英)注册代号,注册标记(由字面或数字组成代表商号或商品名称)
monometallic a. 单本位制的,单一金属本位币制的;使用一金属的
monometallic country 单本位制的国家
monometallic currency 单本位币制度
* *Monopolia dicitur, cum unus solus aliquod genus mercaturae universum emit, pretium ad suum libitum statuens.* It is said to be monopoly when one person alone buys up the whole of one kind of commodity, fixing a price at his own pleasure. 当某人买下全部某种商品,并且自己任意决定

价格,这就叫垄断。
Monopolies and Mergers Commission (英)垄断企业和合并企业委员会
monopolies and restrictive trade practices 垄断和限制性贸易惯例活动(措施)
monopolism n. 垄断主义,垄断制度
monopolist n. 垄断者,独占者;专利者;垄断论者
monopolistic concession 垄断特许权
monopolistic license 垄断许可证
monopolize v. 垄断,独占,专利,专营
monopolizing the market 垄断市场
monopoly n. 垄断,独占,专利;垄断商品;专利事业;垄断权,独占权,专卖权,专权;享有专卖权的公司
monopoly agreement 垄断协议;专利协议
monopoly capital 垄断资本,独占资本
monopoly capitalist class 垄断资产阶级
monopoly commodities 专卖商品
monopoly company 专卖公司;垄断公司
monopoly enterprise 专卖企业;垄断企业
monopoly in foreign trade 外贸垄断
monopoly of bringing prosecution 提起公诉的专属权
monopoly of exploitation 利用垄断权;利用专利权;专用权
monopoly over smuggling 专营走私,包揽走私
monopoly power 垄断力
monopoly price 垄断价格
monopoly right 垄断权;专利权;专用权
monopoly trademark 专用商标;垄断商标
monopsony n. 买主独家垄断(指市场情况)
Monroe Doctrine 门罗主义(美国总统门罗于1823年致美国国会咨文中,声明美国政府不干涉欧洲事务,也绝不容许欧洲国家干涉南美新兴共和国的独立)
monster n. 怪物;怪胎(按英国法无权继承);恶人,残忍的人
monstrans de droit (普通法)权利声明(指从王室不动产或私人财产中取得所有权或恢复原状的一种方法)
monstrous a. 巨大的;异形的,畸形的;荒诞的
monstrous crime 恐怖的罪行,暴行

monstrous fetus 怪胎(见 monster)
monstrum 怪胎
montes pietatis (=*mont-de-piété*) （发放小额动产抵押贷款的）公共典当机构
Montevideo Convention on Rights and Duties of States （1933年）《蒙得维的亚国家权利与义务公约》
Montevideo Declaration on the Law of the Sea 《海洋法蒙得维的亚宣言》(1970年阿根廷等九个拉丁美洲国家在蒙得维的亚签订)
monthly a. 每月的,每月一次的,按月计算的
monthly and probate court 每月开庭的遗嘱检验法庭
monthly instal(l)ment 按月摊付;按月付款
monthly tenant 按月租赁的租户
Montreal Convention for the Suppression of Unlawful Acts against the Safety of Civil Aviation 《关于制止危害民用航空安全的非法行为蒙特利尔公约》(1971年在蒙特利尔签订,简称《蒙特利尔公约》)
Montreal Protocol on Substances that Deplete the Ozone Layer, 1987 1987年《关于消耗臭氧层物质的蒙特利尔议定书》
monument n. 纪念碑;不朽的著作;标石,界石
moocher n. 招摇撞骗者;小偷;流浪人
mood disorders 心境障碍[又称感情性障碍(affective disorders),国际上均采用心境障碍的称谓,指以显著而持久的情感和心境改变为主要特征的一组疾病。司法医学评定根据其行为对社会危害程度可评定为无刑事责任能力和具有部分刑事责任能力]
moor v. 使(船)停泊,下锚;使固定
moorage n. 停泊;停泊处;停泊费
moored in safety 海上保险(水险),安全停泊[指为了在码头上装卸货物,通常停泊在一定位置的船只的海上保险,免除用任何紧急投保险抵付(imminent peril insured against)]
mooring n. 船舶停泊(海商法名词)
moot n./a./v. （司法判决）未(解)决事项;(法学院学生实习采用的)模拟审判,练习辩论;(古英格兰)国民咨议会/有讨论余地的;未决定的;怀疑的,假设的/(在模拟法庭上)进行辩论,提出讨论,辩论
moot a case 提出一个案件供辩论
moot case 未决案;模拟审判案件;提出讨论案件
moot court （法律系学生实习采用的）模拟法庭(又译:假设法庭或实习法庭)
moot men 模拟法庭辩论者
moot point （假设案件讨论会上）讨论要点,未决要点
moot question 假设的问题,纯理论问题(指无现实存在的事实依据或权利、争议而引起的问题)
mootness n. 未决性,争论未决性,可讨论性,不切实际性,无实际价值(指无实际价值就由美国联邦宪法第3条限制联邦宪法管辖"案件"和"争议"而引起的几个问题之一。本应诉讼解决但已通过某种方式处理,因而原告处于无现实依据请求状态,即所谓无实际价值问题)
mop-up n. 排除
mopery n. （美）轻微的违法行为;莫须有的罪名
mora 迟延;非法延误;疏忽,过失
mora creditoris 债权人的迟延
mora debitoris 债务人的迟延
* ***Mora debitoris non debet esse creditori damnosa.*** The delay of the debtor should not go to damage of the creditor. 债务人的推延不得损害债权人;承担义务的一方的迟延不得损害另一方。
mora reprobatur in lege Delay is disapproved of in law 法律不允许推延
mora solvendi 履行迟延;给付迟延
moral n./a. 教训,寓意;(复)品行,风化;道德;(复)伦理学,道德学/品行端正的;公正的;道德上的,精神上的,心理上的,道义上的
moral action 道德诉讼;心理活动
moral blackmail 精神威胁
moral capacity 道德能力
moral character 品德
moral claim 道义要求(指根据道义而提出的请求)
moral clarity 道德上的透明

moral code 道德准则

moral coercion 道德胁迫,道德威胁[指一种非正当影响(undue influence),即不正当使用经济权力去威胁或强制他人屈服于控制经济权力者的愿望。见 undue influence,亦称 economic coercion]

moral consideration (英美法)道德上的对价;无物质价值之报偿;无合同(契约)约束力的对价(与 legal consideration 及 valuable consideration 相对)

moral culture 德育

moral damages 精神上的损害赔偿

moral degeneration 道德败坏

moral delinquent "道德犯"

moral duty 道德义务

moral education 道德教育,德育

moral fraud 心理欺诈;有意欺诈

moral hazard 道德危险(指因保险而引起的幸灾乐祸的心理,即受有保险契约上利益者或被保险者在内心深处所潜伏期望危险发生或损失之扩大的私愿);道德风险(最早它是保险学中的一个概念,指投保人投保后,对其保险标的的注意程度会降低,从而增大了保险标的风险程度。见 asymmetry of information)

moral judg(e)ment 道德判断

moral justification 公正的正当理由

moral law 道德法律

moral legislation (有关)道德立法

moral liberty 道德自由

moral makeup 道德风貌

moral norm 道德规范

moral obligation(s) 道德责任;道德义务,道德义务说

moral order 道德秩序

moral personality 道德个性

moral philosophy 伦理学;道德哲学

moral responsibility 道德责任

moral responsibility of corporation 企业道德责任

moral right to reference 注明权

moral rights 精神权利[指《伯尔尼公约》及多数承认作者精神权利国家的用语,亦称为著作人身权。1990 年我国著作权法中使用的是"人身权"(personal rights)];道义上的权利

moral science 伦理学

moral statute (有关)道德(的)法规

moral *suasion* 道德上的劝告,道德说服

moral terminology 道德字眼

moral theory of secession 脱离的道德论

moral thesis (分析实证主义法学的)道德论

moral turpitude 反公德行为(指和公认的权利义务原则不相容的行为)

moral value 道德价值

moral wrong 道德上的过错

moralism n. 伦理主义,道德主义;(道德方面的)格言,箴言;道德教育;说教

moralistic retributivism 道义报应主义

morality n. 道德,道义

morality and practices 道德风尚

morality of aspiration 愿望的道德(见 morality of duty)

morality of duty 义务的道德(指美国著名法学家朗·富勒在论证法律与道德不可分时所提出的两种道德概念:愿望的道德和义务的道德)

morality of law 法律的道德

morally better 道德上更要好

morally fitting 道德上适合于

morals court 道德法庭,道德判决

moratorial a. 延期偿付的

moratorium n. 1.(依法给债务人的)延期偿付(权);(法律义务上的)延缓履行(权);延期偿还期;合法迟延 2.(使用或制造)禁止(或暂停);(某种行为的)暂停 3.停止兑现 4.延期偿债协议,延期付款命令

moratory a. 延期偿付的;(规定可以)延期履行义务的

moratory law 延期偿付的法规

more and more 越来越多〈More and more questions lead to statutory research.〉(越来越多的问题关系到制定法的检索)

more conduct-specific long-arm statutes (美)长臂法中具体的规定,特定行为长臂法

more likely than not 可能大于非可能性(的证明标准)

more or less 左右(指用以表示合同或转让证书的说明或上下文间有轻微不精确性)
mores 习俗,惯例;道德态度
Morgan presumption 摩根推定(指1933年埃德蒙得·摩根提出的推定,即转移证明的推定。见 Thayer presumption)
morganatic a. 上层社会男子与下层社会女子结婚的
morganatic marriage (历史上)门第悬殊的婚姻,贵贱婚(指高地位的男方与低贱地位的女方之间的婚姻,并订有契约规定妻子及其子女不得享有其丈夫的地位或拥有财产。广而言之,此后这个术语也运用到高地位的女方与低贱位的男方之间的婚姻。此概念现在只限于皇室婚姻。亦称 left handed marriage; marriage of the left hand; salic marriage)
morgue (待人认领尸体的)陈尸所;(报社等的)资料室;(资料室)收藏的参考资料
Mormon 1.摩门教信徒(1830年创立于美国的一个教派,初期实行一夫多妻制)2.一夫多妻主义者
morphine n. 吗啡毒品
morphinism n. 慢性吗啡中毒,吗啡瘾
mors omnia solvit Death dissolves all things. 一死百了(适用于诉讼一方当事人死亡)
mort civil 被褫夺公权的人
mort civile 法律死亡(在法国法中,指被判犯有重罪者在法律上即视为死亡。在普通法上指丧失权利,诸如选举权、表决权、订立合同权、继承权、起诉权,即一个被剥夺公民权者或被判定有严重罪行者或被认为即将去世者。见 civil death)
mortal a. 1.致命的 2.临死的,终有一死的 3.不共戴天的,你死我活的 4.世间的,人类的
mortal(或 **fatal**)**wound** 致命伤
mortal disease 致命疾病
mortal injury 致命伤害
mortal sin 不可宽恕的大罪
mortality n. 致命性,必死性;死亡数;死亡率;人类
mortality insurance 死亡保险
mortality rate 死亡率

mortgage n./v. (15世纪)1.抵押,抵押权;抵押品[指作为担保支付债款的财产所有权的转让,如果未按约定清偿条款应予支付,或履行义务则抵押失效。亦称(古) dead pledge(死质)] 2.质,质权,留置权[指财产的质权,它允准担保一项债务(如一笔欠款),根据约定条款进行支付或履行则欠债消除] 3.抵押契据,文据(如字据,合同),详细说明交易条文的契据 4.非严格含义,抵押贷款,贷款就是基于这类交易 5.抵押权(指受抵押人就是通过这类交易,即抵押财产而被授予的抵押权) 6.物权担保,宽松地说任何不动产(物权)担保交易(real-property security transaction),均包括信托契据(deed of trust)。缩略 M./抵押;把……作抵押;使有义务,把……许给
mortgage action 抵押诉讼
mortgage agreement 抵押协议
mortgage assets 抵押资产
mortgage bank 抵押银行
mortgage bond 抵押债券(据)
mortgage by deposit of title deeds 以房地契作抵押品的抵押
mortgage certificate 抵押证书
mortgage clause 抵押条款
mortgage condition 抵押条件
mortgage contract 抵押合同(契约);质权合同(契约)
mortgage credit 抵押信贷
mortgage debenture 抵押债券,有抵押品的公司债券
mortgage debt 抵押债务
mortgage deed 抵押契据;质权契据
mortgage document 抵押文据
mortgage for record 制作抵押记录
mortgage holder 抵押权人
mortgage in the stage of processing 加工中货物的质权
mortgage instrument 质权证书,抵押证书
mortgage insurance 抵押保险
mortgage liability 抵押债务
mortgage loan 有抵押的贷款;抵押借贷
mortgage money 抵押款项
mortgage of(或 **on**) **land** 土地抵押
mortgage of a business 企业抵押

mortgage of chattels 动产抵押
mortgage of chose in action 可依法占有（而未实际占有）的动产质权
mortgage of goods in flow 流通中的货物抵押权，流通中的货物质权
mortgage of property 财产抵押，财产质权
mortgage of share 股份抵押
mortgage operation 抵押业务
mortgage registers 抵押登记处
mortgage relief 抵押救济
mortgage term 抵押期
mortgage things 抵押品
mortgage undertaking 抵押事项
mortgage warrant 抵押契据
mortgaged a. 抵押的，作抵押的
mortgaged land 已抵押的土地
mortgaged property 已抵押的财产
mortgagee n. 受抵押人，抵押权人；质权人
mortgagee following next 次位抵押权人，次位质权人
mortgagee of shares 股票抵押权人，股票质权人
mortgagee's rights 受抵押人的权利，受质人的权利
mortgages-backed securities（**MBS**） 按揭证券；不动产抵押债权证券；（美）住房抵押债券
mortgagor n. 抵押人，出质人
mortgagor's rights 抵押人的权利；出质人的权利
mortis causa 死因；临终时所作的
mortmain （原意"死手"）(15世纪)永久管业权,不可转让的法人财产[指由宗教或其他法人团体持有的土地或房地产状况是永久性的。转让的土地处于"死手"之中则不能转让，而且它将永不归入产业充公(escheat)或由继承接受。这样就没有继承税的支付,因为法人团体没有死。见 amortize 3; dead hand control]
mortmain act 见 mortmain statute
mortmain statute (1839年)永久管业制定法[指限制对土地的赠与或安排给予法人(特别是慈善机构或部门)的制定法规,同时该法规还禁止法人特别是慈善机构永久管控土地。在英格兰,一些法规诸如威斯敏斯特条文(Provisions of Westminster)和大宪章(Magna Carta)主要要求皇家授权将土地赐予慈善机构,其主要目的是防止土地被教会永远占有。虽然,一般来说这种限制方式在美国并非普通法的一部分,但它影响了某些州制定颁布的法规限制了法人或团体为宗教和慈善目的而持有的财产数额。亦称 mortmain act; statute of mortmain]
mortuary n. 停尸所,太平间；殡仪馆；验尸所
mortuum vadium 死典（权）（指在债不履行的情况下,债权人把担保的抵押物没收的一种抵押。它是典质的一个起始概念）；死抵押（权）
mortuus civiliter 法律上的死亡,法律规定的死亡（指不受法律保护的人）；民事死亡
mos 习俗（罗马法中与神法 fas 相对,是调整家庭内部关系的）
Mos Gallicus 高卢法律研究风格（指16世纪人文主义法学家研究罗马法的一种比意大利法律老式更新颖的风格）
Mos Italicus 意大利法律研究风格（指意大利法律学派探讨罗马法所采用的一种风格）
Mosaic Code 《摩西法典》(常指最早的新英格兰法规汇编的名称)
Mosaic Commandments 摩西十戒
Mosaic Law 摩西律（摩西制定的古代犹太人的法律）
Moses 摩西（《圣经》人物,希伯来的领袖,率领希伯来人走出埃及,又在西奈山上接受上帝的律法戒命,遂以"摩西"喻指领袖、立法者）
mosques n. 清真寺
most a. 最多的,最高程度的,大部分的
most cost efficient forms 最有效的成本形式
most favored-nation clause 最惠国条款（①两国间条约中的一项条款,规定任何一方将给予第三方的优惠或利益给予对方；②扩大意义为在合同中的这类条款,特别是石油和天然气合同亦按①处理。可缩写为 favored-nation clause）
most significant relationship 最重要联系说（指美国现代冲突法学说有影响的学者里斯的一种学说）

most significant theory 最密切联系说(指国际私法上的一种新的法律选择,效力以及履行等问题,法庭应适用与争议问题最密切的法律)
most suitable forum 最适当审理地
most-favo(u)red-nation n./a. 最惠国/最惠国的
most-favo(u)red-nation clause 最惠国条款
most-favo(u)red-nation rates 最惠国税率
most-favo(u)red-nation-treatment (clause) 最惠国待遇(条款)
mother n./a. 1.母亲;母爱 2.根本;泉源/1.母亲的 2.本国的 3.根源的
Mother Godess 母亲神(埃及人认为她是掌管生育和繁殖的女神伊希斯)
mother land 祖国
mother right 母权
mother tongue 本国语言,本民族语言
mother's relatives 表亲
mother-in-law n. 岳母,婆母
motif n. 主旨;主题;动机
motion n. 申请,请求;动议(指法庭或法官提出的对申请人有利的裁决命令或指示的行动。有些动议只能在一定的时限内提出,有些则可在诉讼的任何阶段提出。亦指议会中由议院提出简易或解决方法以及议会考虑及采取措施所用的一种方式)
motion day 动议听审日(指美国民事诉讼审理前的程序之一,即法官确定的就动议予以听审和辩论的日期)
motion firm 录像证据(见 movies)
motion for a bill of particulars 申请详情诉状(与 motion for more definite statement 同义)
motion for a direct verdict 直接裁决的申请(书)
motion for a more definite statement (美)详情说明的申请
motion for a new trial 再审申请,提出重新审理的申请
motion for debate 请求辩论的申请(动议)
motion for decree 申请作出判决
motion for dismissal 撤销案件的申请
motion for judg(e)ment 请求作出于己有利的判决的申请
motion for severance 分别审判的申请(指在有许多被告的情况下,为了分别进行审判而提出的申请)
motion in arrest of judg(e)ment (美)停止裁决的申请(指在裁决后可以提出申请,以指出刑事案件中起诉或告发的证据不足)
motion in error 请求改判(或复审)的申请
motion in limine 防止偏见动议[指一项审前要求,即在庭审时不要提交或提出某种不可采纳的证据。当事方认为在审理时提及的证据可能具有高度偏见,且法庭上的引导对消除偏见无任何帮助,因此提出这种申请。如果这种申请得以批准以后,对方当事人提及或企图在陪审前提供证据,那无效审判(mistrial)则会发生]
motion of strike (美)要求删节的申请(指原告的诉状如果含有不相关的、存有偏见的和其他不适当的事实,可要求法庭命令删去这些事实)
motion of urgent necessity (议会)紧急动议,紧急申请
motion on appeal 上诉申请
motion picture 电影作品(见 cinematographic work),录影
motion to compel 强制动议
motion to dismiss (美)异议,抗议,抗诉,抗辩(美国许多法院以此术语代替 demurrer 一词);驳回的请求,驳回(诉讼)的请求
motion to quash 请求驳回(或宣告无效)的申请
motion to quash service of summons (美)宣告所发传票无效的申请(此项申请为被告呈递答辩状的一个内容,它涉及已送交被告的传票存在不符合法律规定的一些问题而要求取消传票)
motion to remand 发(或返)回(民事诉讼中转移诉讼的)动议(或申请)
motion to remind 驳回(民事诉讼中转移诉讼的)动议(或申请)
motion to revive the lapsed time period 回复期间的申请
motion to set aside the judgment 撤销判决的动议,请求撤销判决的申请

motion to vacate sentence （囚犯申请）要求撤销判刑的动议
motion-paper n. 动议书,申请书
motions on discovery 调查程序中的动议[美国民事诉讼审理前的程序之一,与调查程序各个阶段有关的动议(包括但不限于强调调查的动议或请求保护令的动议)应不迟于该阶段截止期而提出]
motivate v./a. 作为…动机,促进,激发/有动机的,动机的
motivating reasons 动机性理由
motivation n. 动机说明,引起动机,动机的形成
motivational psychology 动机心理学
motivational structure 动力结构
motive n. 动机;主旨,目的;动因,行为理由
motive of a crime 犯罪动机
motive of lucre 贪财动机
motor bandit 驱车行窃的盗匪
Motor Carrier Act 《汽车运输业法》
motor guarantee fund 机动车辆担保基金(会)
Motor Insurers' Bureau （英）车辆保险局
motor vehicle product liability 机动车产品责任
motor vehicle repair establishment 机动车辆的修理厂
motor vehicle theft 摩托(机动)车盗窃
motoring offense 违章驾驶汽车
motto n. 箴言,格言,座右铭;疑词;警句
motu proprio （罗马教廷）教皇自动诏书;教皇（某类）诏书的开头语
moulage n. （刑事侦查用以复制实物作为证据的）印模,印痕;印模术
mould v./n. 浇铸,形成,对……产生影响/模子,模型,类型,形状,气质
mount the scaffold 上断头台,被处绞刑
mountebank n. 江湖医生(指走江湖卖假药的人);江湖骗子
mouthpiece n. （俗语）律师,刑事辩护人
mouthpiece for the popular will 公众意志的代言人
movable (= moveable) a./n. 可移动的,活动的,不定的;动产的(与 immovable 相对)/(可移动的)家具;(复)动产

movable and immovable property 动产与不动产
movable goods (或 object) 动产
movable property 动产
movable security 动产担保
movable type printing 活字印刷
movables by anticipation 预期可得收益的动产
movant n. 作出动议的人,提出请求的人
move v./n. (15世纪)1.申请[指向法院申请作出裁决、命令或某司法措施〈The appellant moved the court for a new trial.〉（上诉人向法院申请要求重新审判。）] 2.提出动议〈The senator moved to that a vote be taken.〉（参议员提出采取表决的动议。）3.转移,让渡[指将合同的对价(consideration)从一方当事人转移到另一方] 4.移动,搬迁,改变位置 5.开动,运行;使运行 6.感动,激起/1.搬家,移动;步跋 2.(走棋)一着〈one careless move loses the whole game〉（一着不慎,满盘皆输）,〈a clever move〉(妙着)(喻)机智的一着;活动〈free move〉(关节)自由活动
movement n. 运动;活动;动向,倾向;（价格）变动,迁移,迁居;（军队、舰队等）调动;输送
movement for shield laws 庇护法运动(见 shield law)
movement of goods 货物流动
movement of goods document 运货单据
movement of personnel 自然人流动（服务贸易的基本概念之一,指允许外国单位的个人入境来本国提供服务。如外国教授、高级工程师、医生来中国从事个体服务）
mover n. 1.(俚语)不稳定价的股票(指感受到一种特别市场波动的股票)2.提动议者,作出动议的人(movant)
movies (motion film) 录像证据(英美证据法中叫 motion film"电影"。其可采性需要满足相关性、真实性和证明性三个要件)
moving party 提出申请的当事人
moving pictures 影视作品(指著作权的客体,录像制品则为邻接权的客体,这是大陆法系国家如德、意等采用的两分法,对

于体育活动、自然活动、军事活动的拍摄、谈话节目、戏剧或歌剧等的拍摄等不能构成影视作品,只能属于"活动影像"。与此相反,英美法系国家未对照片、录像采取"两分法",而从实用主义哲学出发,未经许可使用的照片尽可能进行版权保护。英美法系的版权法理论认为,很小程度的个性就足以符合独创性的要求)

MPEG LA (MEPG Licensing Administration) 专利联营的专门管理机构(该机构汇集了美国加州大学、飞利浦、东芝、索尼、法国电信公司、富士通、佳能等在内的多家高校及企业的技术)

MPEG-2 (专利联营特定技术的一种基础)标准(以实施该技术标准为目标的专利联营)

muckrake v. 揭发贪污腐化

muckraker n. 揭发贪污腐化者(尤指记者)

mudor šsuan 成家礼(指沃尔加克人宣布成家的典礼)

mufti n. 伊斯兰教法典解说者;伊斯兰教法学家(或法律顾问)

mug (=mugg) n./v. (俚)罪犯;暴徒;(警察局档案中的)嫌疑犯照片/抢劫;(为罪犯)拍照存档

mugger n. 行凶抢劫者,谋财害命的盗匪

mugshot n. 面部照片;(警察局档案中的)嫌疑犯(或通缉犯)照片

mugwump n. (政党中的)独立分子,政治上的超然派,骑墙派;大人物,头子

mulct n./v. 罚款;罚金,惩罚/诈取;抢夺;处以罚款

* **Mulcta damnum famae non irrogat.** A fine does not involve loss of character. 罚款并不牵连到个人身份上的损失。

mulier 1. (罗马法)女子(指未出嫁之成年女子),(旧英国法)妇人;妻子 2. (旧英国法)婚生子女,嫡生子女

mulier puisné 第一个婚生子女(指其父母在婚前已有一个非婚生子女,实际上是第二个孩子)

mulierty n. (旧英国法)婚生

Mullum crimin sine jure. 不违背正义要求不为罪。

Mullum crimin sine poena. There should be no crime without punishment. 无惩罚者不为罪。

* **Multa fidem promissa levant.** Many promises lessen confidence. 许诺多了会降低(人们的)信任。

* **Multa in jure communi contra rationem disputandi, pro communi utilitate, introducta sunt.** Many things contrary to the rule of argument (i. e. inconsistent which sound reason able) are introduced into the Common Law for common utility./Many things have been introduced into the common law, with a view to the public good, that are contrary to logical reasoning. 为了公共福利,许多不合事理之事项引入了普通法。

* **Multa non vetat lex, quae tamen tacite damnavit.** The law forbids not many things, which yet it has silently condemned. 许多事虽不受法律的禁止,但却受其无声谴责。

* **Multi multa, nemo omnia novit.** Many men know many things; no one knows everything. 多人知多事,但无一人可知所有的事。

multi ownership 分时度假

multi-diplomacy n. 多部门,多学科

multi-disciplinary accounting firms 多部门会计事务所

multi-faceted discussion 多元讨论,多方面讨论

multi-industry n. (工业的)多种经营

multi-judge appellate court 多位法官(开庭)制的上诉法院

multi-national river 多国河流

multi-partism n. 多党制(政体)

multidistrict consolidation (美)多区合作(诉讼)

multidistrict litigation (美)(MDL)(民事诉讼)跨区诉讼,多地区诉讼(指涉及1个或多个共同事实问题的民事案件同时在几个不同联邦地区法院诉讼,则可将这些案件移送至其中一个地区法院以便统一审理。该多地区诉讼由多地区诉讼的合

议庭审理。合议庭是由联邦最高法院首席大法官任命的 7 名巡回和地区法院法官组成。见 28 USLA §1407 即《美国注释法典》第 28 标题卷第 1407 节）
multifarious pronouncement 多种公告
multifariousness n. 不适当的合并控诉(指衡平法诉讼中,把应分开的诉因不适当地在一张诉状中提出控诉)
multifariousness of claims 不适当的合并控诉的请求
multilateral a. 多国的,多边的,多国参加的,涉及多方的
multilateral agreement 多边协定
multiple case study or collective case study 多个案研究
Multilateral Agreement on Investment (MAI) 多边投资计划,多边投资协议
multilateral barter transaction 多边易货贸易
multilateral clearing 多边清算
multilateral contract 多边合同(契约)
multilateral convention 多边协约,多边协议
multilateral international agreement 多边国际协定
Multilateral Investment Agreement (MIA) 多边投资协议
multilateral mechanism 多种机制
multilateral political treaty 多边政治条约
multilateral talks 多边会谈
multilateral tax treaty 多边税务条约
multilateral transaction execution facility 多边交易执行机构
Multilateral Treaties Deposited with the Secretary-General 联合国秘书长受委托主持的多边条约(指限于联合国秘书长作为受委托人在联合国主持下订立的约约)
multilateral treaty 多边条约
multilateralism n. 多边性;多边贸易
multilation n. 删改,修改 (此词多在消极意义上使用,而 modification 则多在积极意义上使用)
multilevel distribution 多层次销售
multilevel distributor ship 见 pyramid Sales Scheme

multilevel system theory 多级系统理论,多层次系统理论
multimedia n. 多媒体
multimedia work 多媒体作品
multimember district system 多数选区制
multimillionaire n. （拥有数百万的）大富豪
multimodal transport 多种方式联运
multimodal transport user 联运使用人
multimodal transportation system 多种模式运输系统
multinational n./a. 多国公司,跨国公司/多民族的,多国家的
multinational area 民族杂居地区
multinational corporation 多国公司
multinational state（或 country） 多民族国家
multipartite a. 多方的,多方参加的;分成多份的
multipartite action 多方参与的诉讼
multipartite contract 多方参与的合同(契约)
multipartite convention 多边协约
multipartite national entities 国际法团
multipartite treaty 多边条约
multiparty action 多方当事人的诉讼
multiparty litigation 多方当事人参加的诉讼
multiparty system 多党制
multiparty-multiclaim actions 多当事人—多请求诉讼
multiperson accident 多人事故
multiple a. 复合的,多重的,多样的;并联的
multiple admissibility （证据）多重可接受性
multiple agreement 复合协议
multiple cause （事实上的)复合原因
multiple claims system 多项请求制
multiple derivative suit 多重代表诉讼(见 double derivative suit)
multiple entry-exit visa 多次往返有效的出入境签证
multiple litigation 多个诉讼;重复诉讼
Multiple Nash Equilibrium 多重纳什均衡
multiple party obligation 多方当事人之债

multiple personality 多重人格(指一种罕见的精神障碍)
multiple poinding (苏格兰)多重(财产)扣押诉讼
multiple rates 多种汇率,复汇率
multiple relationship 多重亲属关系
multiple shop(或 store)(英)联号商店
multiple succession rights 多重继承权
multiple texts 复合的法律文本
multiple tort-feasors 多重侵权行为的人
multiple voting 重复投票
multiple-claim context 多诉讼请求案件
multiple-claimant phenomenon 多数请求现象
multiple-party system 多党制
multiple-use-forestry 多效益林业

Multiplicita transgressione crescat poenae inflictio. As transgression is multiplied, the infliction of punishment should increase. 由于犯罪成倍增加,处刑也因此予以加重。

multiplicity n. 重复,复合;多重性;繁多
multiplicity of actions (同一案件的)重复诉讼(指不适当地以同一案件多次重复提起诉讼);缠讼
multiplicity of fora (fora 为 forum 的复数) 法庭的多重性
multiplicity of legal proceedings 繁多的法律程序
multiplicity of suits 重复诉讼
multiplaintiff n. 多方原告
multishift working 多班工作制
multispecies(或 multiproduct)**resources** 多物种(或多产品)资源
Multistate Bar Exam (美)多州律师资格考试
(a) **multitude of statutory offences** 大量法定罪行
multitudinem decem faciunt Ten make a crowd 十人为众

Multitudo errantium non parit errori patrocinium. The multitude of those who err gives no excuse for the error./The multitude of those who err does not produce indulgence for error. 众人所犯之错误仍是错误,众人所犯的错误仍不容宽恕。

multiunit residential properties 多单元住宅产业;多单元住宅所有权
multum in parvo 大寓于小,小中见大,小而containing
mumbo-jumbo 深奥的法律用语和(专业)行话
mundane a. 1.世俗的,庸俗的 2.宇宙的 3.世事(mundane affairs)(mundanely ad.; mundaneness n.; mundanenessly ad.)
mundbryce n. (盎格鲁-撒克逊法上的)滋扰(治安)赔偿
mundium (法律拉丁语)教会或修道院所进的贡品[法国古法,是教会或修道院交给其所承领地的辩护官(*avoues*)或主教代理官(*vidames*)的物品,作为保护他们的代价]
Munich Agreement 《慕尼黑协定》(指 1938 年 9 月英、法、德、意四国在慕尼黑签订的出卖捷克民族利益的协定)
Munich Code 《慕尼黑守则》(指德国慕尼黑马普协会的学者们拟定的一个"国际竞争法"草案,通称为"慕尼黑守则")
municipal a. 市的,都市的;市政的;内政的
municipal administration 市政管理
municipal assembly 市政会议;审议会
municipal auditoriums 城市剧场,城市音乐厅听众席;(美)城市礼堂
municipal bankruptcies 地方的破产程序,属于市(或当地)的破产
municipal bond 市政债券
municipal charters 市政规章
municipal corporation 市政法人(指美国通常以特许状的形式,将某一地区居民联合起来,建立具有一定公权力的法律实体,以便于地方政府的管理;而在英国则指由国王颁发特许状将英格兰或威尔士自治市的居民联合起来构成法人团体,由市长、市高级官员和市民组成);市属社团;自治团体
municipal council 市议会,市政委员会
municipal council(l)or 市议会议员;市议员
municipal court 市镇法院(在美国只有某些州有这类法院,相当于治安官法院,是一种管辖权很小的低级法院);自治市法

院;国内法院
municipal district （中）市辖区
municipal government 市政府
municipal immunity 市政豁免原则
municipal law 国内法(与国际法相对);市政法
municipal law of the ships registry 船旗国法律
municipal ordinance 市政法令
municipal people's congress （中）市人民代表大会
municipal people's court （中）市人民法院
municipal people's government （中）市人民政府
municipal people's procuratorate （中）市人民检察院
municipal prosecutor （美）市检察官(按美国检察系统,州和市检察官均属地方检察官)
municipal prosecutorial system （美）市检察系统(该系统包括城镇一级的公诉人)
municipal public security bureau （中）市公安局
municipal resources 市政资源
municipal rule 国内法规范
municipal sources of law 法的国内渊源（又译法律的国内渊源）
municipality n. 市;自治市;自治地区;市政当局(机关),市政府
municipality directly controlled by a provincial government （中）省辖市
municipality directly controlled by an autonomous region （中）自治区辖市
municipality directly under the central government （中）中央直辖市
municipalize v. 把……归市有,把……归市管
municipium （罗马法）地方自治市镇
muniment n. 保护;保护的手段;(复)档案;不动产权利证书;契据;(复)(证明权利或特权)证书;单据
muniments of title 产权证书
muniments room 档案室,契据保存室
munition n. (常用复)军火;军需品
munus （古罗马公民对国家的）义务;职

守,本分
murder n./v. 谋杀(罪);谋杀案;凶杀(罪);凶杀案;(战争中的)屠杀/屠杀,犯谋杀罪;凶杀;扼杀(真理等)
murder case 谋杀案
murder of the first degree 一等谋杀(大多数国家将谋杀分为一、二等两个类别。凡采用蓄谋、预谋、毒杀等手段在犯有或企图进行纵火、强奸、抢劫、盗窃等罪行中杀人者,均属于一等谋杀,其余为二等谋杀)
murder of the second degree 二等谋杀（见 murder of the first degree 和 second degree murder）
murder suspect 谋杀嫌疑,凶杀嫌疑犯
Murder will out. 杀了人终究要暴露。
murderee n. 被谋杀者
murderer n. 谋杀犯,凶手
murderess n. 女谋杀犯,女凶手
murderous a. 谋杀的,杀人的;残酷的,凶狠的
murderous villain 杀人恶棍
murderous weapon 杀人凶器
murdrum n. （旧英国法）秘密杀害
murrain n. 兽疫;农作物病害
muscle n./v. （美）大力士,打手;实力,势力/使具有力量,强推
museum piece 博物馆珍品;老古董
music compulsory license 音乐强制授权
music work 音乐著作
Muslim court 穆斯林法院
Muslim law 伊斯兰教法（亦译:穆斯林法）
Muslim teaching 伊斯兰教义
muster n./v. 聚集;样品,拆验;人员清单/召集,聚集;收集,搜集,征召;合计,组成
muster-roll n. 船员名册;(海商法)花名册或账目(指某一船舶公司的名册或账目)
mutatis mutandis 细节上作必要的修改
mute n./a. 故意拒绝答辩者;哑巴/故意不答辩的,沉默的,哑的
mute and deaf 聋哑人
mute appeal 无言的控诉
mute by visitation of god 先天性的哑巴
mute of malice 故意缄默者
mute testimony 无言证据

mutilate v. 1.使断肢,使残废,使四肢不全 2.使残缺不全 3.删改
mutilating punishment 断肢刑
mutilation n. 1.使他人肢体残缺的行为;肢体残缺 2.使文件残缺不全(用于书面文据、文件,如遗嘱、法庭记录等由于缩减重要部分或被删节、撕毁、焚烧或抹去等原因而造成文件残缺不全)
mutineer n. 反叛者,叛变者
mutiny n. 叛乱,兵变
mutism n. 缄默症(医学检查不能找到器质性病变依据,与失音症 aphonia 类似)
mutual a. 彼此的,相互的;共同的,共有的
mutual agreement 共同协议
mutual aid 互助
mutual and equitable benefit 平等互利
mutual assent (17 世纪)合意[指双方当事人表示一致的意思,特别是在合同法上,通常要约和认可(offer and aceptance)格式被视为合同成立的标志,是使合同具有拘束力的基本要求,不过在英美法上则还要附加对价要素。见 consideration; meeting of minds]
mutual assistance 互助,互相援助
mutual benefit 互利
mutual check 相互制约
mutual club 互保协会
mutual coercion 相互强制
mutual company 合股公司
mutual concealment 互相包庇,互相隐瞒
mutual concession 互相让步;双方认可
mutual confrontation 互相对质,互相对证
mutual consent 协议;双方同意
mutual conspiracy 共谋,同谋
mutual contracts 双务合同(契约)
mutual contradiction 相互抵触
mutual corroboration 相互印证(确证)
mutual covenants 互相赔偿损失的协约
mutual credit 相互债权(对相互之债务而言)
mutual credit facility 互惠信贷
mutual debt 相互债务(对相互之债权而言)
mutual defence 联防,共同防御
mutual defence treaty 共同防御条约

mutual election 互选
mutual encroachment 相互占用
mutual exemption of visa 互免签证
mutual fund 共同基金,单位信托公司,股份不定公司,股票投资(公司)
mutual gable 共同山墙
mutual indemnification 相互补偿
mutual insurance company 互保公司
mutual insurance society 互助保险社
mutual intent 共同故意
mutual investment company 合股投资公司,发行后随时可换成现款的股票投资公司
Mutual Legal Assistance Treaties (MLATS) 司法互助协定
mutual limitation of cause and effect 因果制约性
mutual mistake (或 error) 相互过错
mutual most-favo(u)red-nation clause 双边的最惠国条款
mutual non-aggression (pact) 互不侵犯(条约)
mutual noninterference 互不干涉
mutual obligation 共同义务
mutual office 相互保险社
mutual preferential duties 互惠关税
mutual promises 相互允诺
mutual recognition 相互承认
mutual relation of children and parents 父母子女间的关系
mutual requirement (夫妻双方的)共同要件(指与 unilateral requirement 相对而言)
mutual respect for sovereignty and territorial integrity, mutual non-aggression, non-interference in each other's internal affairs, equality and mutual benefit and peaceful coexistence 互相尊重主权和领土完整,互不侵犯,互不干涉内政,平等互利,和平共处(见 five principles of peaceful coexistence)
mutual restraint 互相牵制
Mutual Security Act (美)《共同安全保障法》
mutual settlement 相互财产授予

mutual succour　相互救助
mutual supervision　互相监督
mutual transaction　互相交易,互易
mutual transfer　互相转让
mutual understanding　相互谅解
mutual will(或 testament)　相互遗嘱(见 joint and mutual will)
mutual-aid and cooperative treaty　互助合作条约
mutual-aid committee　互助委员会
mutual-aid society　互助会
mutual-aid team　(中)互助组
mutual-benefit society for housing credits　住房建筑信贷互助社
mutual-benefit society for saving　互助储蓄会
mutualism n.　互助制度;互惠共生
mutuality n.　相互性,相互关系;相关;相互依存;相își义务;感情的共鸣;亲密
mutuality of advantage　互利性质,相互有利
mutuality of assent　双方同意
mutuality of contract　合同(契约)上的相互关系
mutuality of obligation　债之相互关系
mutually beneficial agreement　互惠协议
mutually responsible　连环保

mutuum　(罗马法和苏格兰法)种类物借贷合同(契约);消费借贷;借贷;无偿消费借贷
my learned friend(或 brother)　我精通法律的同行(英国法院律师间的称呼)
My Lord　尊敬的阁下,老爷(对高等法院法官的尊称)
my uncle's　(俚)当铺
myopia (myopy) n.　近视;缺乏远见
myopic consumption　无辨别能力的消耗
myriad n./a.　无数,极大数量;千变万化(myriad of change)/无数的,含有无数因素,极有才能的(myriad minded)
Myrmindon of law　法律的密尔弥冬(希腊神话中的蚁民。埃癸那岛瘟疫后,人口大减,主神宙斯把蚂蚁变成人。这些蚁民后来迁至忒萨利国,跟随大英雄阿基里斯,唯命是从。后遂用 Myrmindon 喻指坚定不移地严格执行一切命令的部属,以 Myrmindon of law 喻指"警察、警官和执法官")
mystic faith　神秘的信仰,不可思议的忠实信仰
mystic testament　密封遗嘱
myth system　理想主义体系(指属于巴丹斯基所说的国际环境法行为被视作习惯国际法的一部分)

N

N. D. Cent. code　《北达科他世纪法典》(全称为 North Dakota Century Code)
naam(或 nam, namium)　1.(撒克逊时代的)扣押(指用合法扣押或其他方法取得他人的动产)2. 动产扣押
nab v.　(俚)逮捕,捉住(尤指对现行犯等);猛然抓住;攫夺(东西)
nabbing n.　逮住,抓住
Naiba court　(伊斯兰教法)乃巴法院(指一种初级穆斯林法院)
nail n./v.　指甲;趾甲;钉/钉住;抓住,捉住;捕获,(美俚)逮捕

nail down　束缚(to);确定(合同等);使成定案
naive expectation　简单预期
naive rationalism　天真的理性主义
naked a.　1.裸体的;无保护的 2.直率的,坦白的 3.无证据的;无保证的;未经证实的;无对价的
naked authority　无偿委任
naked confession　未经证实的供词
naked contract　无保证的合同(契约);无偿合同(契约)
naked debenture　(英)无担保的债券

naked facts 赤裸裸的事实
naked law 无保护（或无保证）的法律(law without enforcement in naked law)
naked possession 无保证的占有
naked power (18世纪)单纯代理权,即仅有代理权限者[指对某些事项具有行使的权力(如委托),而在此事项上却无相应利益。见 power coupled with an interest]
naked promise 无效诺言;(英美法)无对价的允诺;未经证实的字据
naked short sale 裸卖空(指证券的无交收保障的卖空)。见 covered short sale)
naked trust 无担保信托;单纯信托,不处理事务之信托(亦称 dry trust 或 passive trust,指受托人除交还受托之财物外不须处理信托上之事务)
naked truth 真相
Nam qui haeret in litera, haeret in cortice.
　　He who considers merely the letter of an instrument, goes but skin-deep into its meaning. 拘泥于文字的人做的是表面文章。
name n./v./a. 名字,姓,姓名;名称;名义;名声,名誉;族姓/命名;提名,任命;指控,指责;指定,说出;(英)(下议院议长因议员不服从裁决等的)点名警告/姓名的;(作品的)取某人名字的,据以取名的;有声誉的
name and address 姓名和地址
name and arms clause (英)(在财产转让和遗嘱中时有出现的)姓名与纹章条款(常用于遗嘱和授产书内,遗产和财产之接受人必须承袭遗嘱人或财产所有人的姓氏纹章,否则丧失此种权利)
name brand 名牌
Name Law (美)《姓名法》(指1972年教育修正法案第四部分)
name of counsel 辩护人的姓名
name of origin (商品)原产地名称
name of the punishment 刑名
name-sake n. 同姓名的人,同名者
named a. 记名的;提名的;指定的;著名的
named bill of lading 记名提单
named consignee 指定收货人
named insured 记名被保险人
named partner 具名合伙人

named party 被指明的当事人
named peril 指定(保)险
named person 被指定的人,被提名的人
named plaintiff (defendant) 记名原告(或被告)已知原告人;任命的原告,名义上代表人,名义上的原告
nameless a. 1.无名声的;不知名字的;没有名字的;故意不提名的 2.(罪恶等)坏得说不出口的 3.无合法名义的;非法的;私生的
nameless child 非婚生子(女),私生子(女)
nameless dead 无名死者
nameless death 死刑
naming a member (经下议院议长指责的)指责议员(又译点名警告议员,指议长对拒绝收回其冒犯性言论的议员可令其退出会场的一种程序)
nap v. 打盹;(乘人不备)抓住其疏忽之处;攫取;偷窃
Napoleonic Codes 《拿破仑法典》
Napoleonic system 拿破仑制度(指以《拿破仑法典》为基础的法律制度)
narc (=narco) n. (专门取缔吸毒的)便衣警察
narcotic n./a. 麻醉剂;吸毒者/麻醉(性)的,麻醉剂的;精神上有麻醉作用的;吸毒成瘾者的
narcotic addict 吸毒成瘾者
narcotic bureau 毒品调查局
narcotic control 麻醉品管制
narcotic drug 麻醉品
nark n. (英俚)(警察机关雇用的)密探;告密者
narratio n. (历史上)原告的申诉,原告陈述事实或上诉[指原告陈述案件的事实或原告对事实作出口头陈述,并基于权利主张提出法律论据(legal argument),此词亦被称为"Conte"或"tale"。缩略为 narr.]
narrative n. (苏格兰法)事实性陈述条款(指合同或誓约中的一项条款)
narrative jurisprudence 叙述法学
narrator (=narrater) n. (出庭)辩护人;陈述者;辩述者
narrow a./v. 窄的;有限范围的;勉强的;褊狭的;精密的;仔细的/弄窄,缩小……两者

之间的差距
narrow definition 狭义解释
narrow scrutiny 细审,详审
narrow seas (复)英吉利海峡和爱尔兰海
narrow versions of no fault liability (美)无过错责任的有限版本(即为分娩过程中遭受神经系统损害的婴儿提供无过错赔偿,而无须考虑医疗机构或医务人员是否存在过失)
narrower view 少数人的观点,少数派观点
nascent company 新筹办的公司
nasciturus 胎儿(区别于 *natus*,已出生婴儿)
Nasciturus pro iam nato habetur, quamdiu agitur de eius commodo. one about to be born is held as already born as long as the issue is to his benefit; a child conceived is treated as born to the extent that it is to his or her benefit. 只要对胎儿有利,就应将胎儿视为已出生。
Nash Equilibrium 纳什均衡
natality n. 出生率;出生
nation n. 民族;国家;(总称)国民
nation-state n. 单一民族国家,民族国家
national n./a. 国民/民族的;国家的;国有的;国立的;国民的;全国性的;国家主义的;爱国的;各党联合的
National Academy of Science (美)国家科学研究院
National Academy of Sciences' Panel on Common Property (National Research Council 1986) (美)共同财产全国科学小组
national affairs 国家事务
national anthem 国歌
national assembly 国民大会,国会,(大写)(法史)国民会议
national assets 国家资产
national assimilation 民族同化
National Assistance 国家救助,国家补助[英国1948年国家补助法 National Assistance Act, 1951, 1959 National Assistance (Amendment)Acts; 1966 the Ministry of Social Security Act; 1975 the Social Security Act]
National Association for the Advancement of Colored People 全国有色人种协进会[缩写 NAACP,这是美国最大的民权组织,成立于1909年,随后20年间参与了大量扩大非洲裔美国人权利、由联邦最高法院审理的案件。在 Guinn v.United States (1915)一案中提出法庭之友陈述(*amicus brief*)推翻了祖父条款(Grandfather Clause)剥夺黑人选举权的做法。在 Buchanan v. Warley(1917)一案中成功挑战居住隔离法令。另,在 Moore v.Dempsey(1923)案中,联邦最高法院认可了该协进会可以介入保护在暴民控制的州接受审判的被告诉讼权利的主张。1934年该组织任命霍华德法学院院长 Charles Hamilton Houston 作为第一位专职律师,以统一方法解决歧视、种族隔离和种族暴力等问题。1939年该协进会法律辩护基金 Legal Defense Fund (LDF)的成立进一步增强了该组织按宪法诉讼的策略能力]
National Association of Bar Executives (美)全国律师常务协会
National Association of Legal Secretaries (英)(殖民时期)全国司法官协会
National Association of Securities Dealers (NASD) 美国全国证券交易商协会
National Association of Securities Dealers Automated Quotations (NASDAQ) 全美证券交易商协会自动报价系统(纳斯达克)(前身为美国 OTC 市场,隶属于美国全国证券交易商协会,于1971年2月8日开始交易)
National Association of Working Women (9 to 5) (美)朝九晚五全国职业妇女协会
national autonomous area 民族自治地方(区)
national autonomous region (中)民族自治区
national autonomy 民族自治;民族自治权;民族自治区
national bank 国家银行
National Bankruptcy Act (美)《全国破产法》
National Bar Association 国家律师协会

(美国包括大部分黑人法官和律师的组织)
National Biological Diversity Conservation and Environmental Research Act (美)《国家生物多样化保护区和环境研究法》
National Board of Trial Advocacy (美)全国审判辩护委员会(私人集团)
national boundary 国界,国境
national bourgeoisie 民族资产阶级
National Bureau of Criminal Identification (美)国家刑事鉴定局
National Bureau of Economic Research (美)国家经济调查局
National Center for State Courts (美)国家州法院中心
(The) National Childhood Vaccine Injury Compensation Act 《国家儿童疫苗伤害法》[美国1986年11月14日国会通过的此法,该法确立了对疫苗受害者的无过错补偿制度。依据该法,疫苗受害者无须证明任何人对于疫苗伤害存在过错,就能顺利获得一笔数目可观的国家赔偿款。为此,国家还建立了疫苗伤害补偿信托基金(the Vaccine Injury Compesation Trust Fund),补偿费统一由该基金负担]
national code 全国性的法典
National Committee on Governmental Accounting (美)全国政府会计委员会
national company 国营公司
National Computerized Legal Information Retrieval System (CLIRS) (澳)全国计算机法学信息检索系统(1984年建立此系统)
National Conference of Black Lawyers (美)全国黑人律师会议(指成立于1969年的非洲美籍律师的一个组织,特别在民权方面,非常活跃)
National Conference of Commissioners on Uniform State Laws (美)统一州法律委员全国会议,统一州法委员会[指目的在于促进各州之间各类项目法律统一的组织,它起草并建议各种法律供各州采纳。该组织建立于1892年,由来自五十个州的代表组成。该会议起草了200个以上的统一法规法律,其中包括《统一商法典》(Uniform Commercial Code)。缩略为NC-CUSL,亦称 Uniform law, Commissioners。见 Uniform Act; Uniform Law; Model Act]
National Congress 全国代表大会;国民代表大会;国会,国民议会
National Conservation Commission (美)国家资源调查委员会
National Constitution 国家宪法;国宪
national constitutional conference 国家制宪会议
National Consumers' League (美)国家消费者联合会;全国消费者联合会
National Convention (法史)国民公会,(美)全国修宪大会
national council 全国议会,全国委员会
National Council on Land Reform 全国土地改革委员会
national court 民族法院
National Crime Information Center (美)全国犯罪情报中心
National Criminal Justice Board (英)全国刑事司法委员会
national currency 国家货币
national customs 民族习惯
national customs territory 国家海关辖区
National Day 国庆日
national debt 国债
National Debt Commissioners (英)国家债务委员会
national defense 国防
National Democratic Party (德)国家民主党
national determinism 民族决定主义
national diplomacy 国民外交
national discord 民族纠纷
national domain 国家领土;国有土地
national domicile 国内住所;国籍
national economic plan 国民经济计划
national economic system of socialism 社会主义国民经济体系
national economy 国民经济,民族经济
national emblem 国徽
national emergency 全国处于紧急状态
national enterprise 国营企业
National Environmental Policy Act (美)《国家环保政策法》(1969年通过)
national equality 民族平等

national expenditure　国家开支
national flag　国旗
national forests　国有森林
national front　民族阵线
national government　国民政府,国家政府
National Guard (N. G.)　(美)国民警卫队
national health insurance　(英)国民健康保险(指英国 1912 年实施的国民健康保险)
National Health Service　(美)国民保健署
national heritage　国家(民族)遗产
national holiday　国定假日
National Homestead Act　(美)《一般家园法》
national honor　民族尊严
national ID cards　国民身份证
national identity　民族主体(国际法用语)
national income　国民收入
national income accounting　国民收入核算
national independence　国家独立
National Industrial Relation Act, Wagner Act　(美)《国家劳资关系法》(又称《瓦格纳法》,此法确立了雇员保护制度,规定雇员不因参加合法组织或从事产业行为而被解雇,1935 年美国会通过并颁布此法)
National Industrial Relations Court　(美)全国劳资关系仲裁法院
national industries　民族工业
National Information Infrastructure (NII)　(美)全国信息基础结构(框架)
National Information Infrastructure　(美)国家信息基础设施计划(指美国政府 1993 年上半年提出的建设一个能给用户提供大量信息,由计算机通信网、数据库以及各种日用电子设备组成的完备网络,这一巨大网络即信息高速公路)
national insignia　国徽
National Institute for Dispute Resolution (NIDR)　(美)争端解决全国协会(设立于首都华盛顿特区)
National Institute of Corrections　(美)国家矫治局,国家矫治研究所[指一个联邦组织(属监狱局),其主要责任是帮助联邦、州和地方当局改进矫治规划(program),进行矫治问题的研究如预防犯罪,和办各种法律执行人员、社会工作者、法官以及其他正在处理和正将释放的罪犯(rehabilitating of offenders)的培训班(workshops)。参见《美国注释法典》第 18 标题卷第 4351—4353 节(18 USCA §§ 4351—4353)。见 Bureau of Prisons]
national institute of industrial property　国家工业产权局
National Institute of Justica　(美)司法部国家研究院
national insurance　(英)国民保险(指 1948 年实行的对国民实行健康保险、失业保险等强制保险的总称,1973 年为社会保障津贴所取代)
national insurance contributions　国家保险捐款
national insurance surcharge　国家保险附加税
national judges　(国际法院的)本国法官
national judicial conference　全国司法会议
national juristic person　本国法人
National Labor Relation Act　(美)国家劳资关系法(指瓦格纳、塔夫特和兰德勒姆三法的混合法规)
National Labor Relation Board (NLRB)　(美)国家劳工关系委员会
National Land Reform Service　全国土地改革署
national law　国内法,本国法,国家法
National Lawyers Guild　(美)全国律师公会(于 1937 年组成,主要对付美国律师协会的保守势力)
national legal order　国内法律秩序
national legal system　全国法律体系,全国法律系统
national legislation　国内立法,国内法规
national legislative assembly　全国立法会议
national legislature　国民议会,全国议会
National Liberation Front　民族解放阵线
national maternity leave system　全国职业妇女产假制
national monument　国家保护区

national mythologies 国家神话
National Nuclear Security Agency (NNSA) (美)国家核安全局
national ocean space 国家海洋空间
national open port 国家对外开放口岸
national optimal tariff 国家理想关税税则
National Organization for Victims Assistance (美)全国受害人救助组织
national origin 特定地国;民族血统
national ownership 国家所有制;国民所有制;全民所有制
National Panchayat (尼泊尔)全国评议会
National People's Congress (中)全国人民代表大会
National People's Party (德)国家人民党
national personality 国家人格,国格
national personnel authority 国家人事机关;(大写)(日)人事院
National Pollution Control Foundation (美)全国污染控制基金会
National Program for the Development of Agriculture (中)《全国农业发展纲要》
National Public Radio (NPR) (美)国家公共广播电视台
national purse 国库,国富
National Quotation Bureau (美)全国行情局
National Reemployment Service (美)全国再就业事务局
national regional autonomy 民族区域自治
national registration 国家登记
National Registry of Exonerations 全美无罪开释案件统计处
National Reporter Blue Book (美)《全国判例汇编蓝皮书》(指一种已知官方援引,而旨在查找非官方援引的工具书,西方出版公司为此目的每年出版此书)
National Reporter System (美)全国判例(发布人)汇编系统(该系统将全美国划分7个区域;大西洋区、东北区、西北区、太平洋区、东南区、南方区和西南区。这些区域中每个区域的州受理上诉法院的判决,均被汇集出版成为一整套卷本丛书。该系统还包括《最高法院判例汇编》、《联邦判例汇编》、《联邦补篇》、《联邦法规判决》、《西方破产判例汇编》、《纽约补篇》、《西方加利福尼亚州判例汇编》、《西方伊利诺伊州判决》,以及《西方军事司法判例汇编》)
national revenue 国民收入
national rivers 国有河流,国内河流,内河
national sanction 国家制裁
national sanctity 民族尊严;国家的尊严,国家的神圣不可侵犯性
national savings certificate 国家储蓄证书
national scum 民族败类
national secessionism 民族分裂主义
national security 国家安全
National Security Act (美)(1947年通过的)《国家安全法》
national security agency 国家安全局
national security clause 国家安全条款
National Security Council (美)国家安全委员会
National Security Exchange 国民证券交易所,(美)国家证券交易所,全国证券交易所
national self-determination 民族自决
national self-preservation 民族自我维护,国家自我维护
National Shipping Line 国家航运公司(指主营业所和有效控制机构位于该国境内并经主管机关认可的合资航运公司)
National Society for Clean Air (英)全国空气净化学会
national solidarity 民族团结
national sources of law 法的国内渊源(又译:法律的国内渊源)
national sovereignty 国家主权
national strength 国力
national tariff 国家税率;自主税率;自主关税
national tax tribunal 国家税务法庭
national treasury 国库
national treatment 国民待遇(原则)
national trust 国家信托(指依国家的信托法律规定组成的国家信托机构)
national union of workers 全国工人联合会
national united front 民族统一阵线

national unity 国家统一
national utility 国家公用事业
National Visa Center 美国国家签证中心
National Water Council (英)全国水质委员会
national waters 国内水(或称内水、内地水、内陆水,包括国家的湖、内海、河流,连同其河口、港口、运河以及海湾和海峡内的水域)
national well-being 全民福利
National Women's Law Center (美)全国妇女法律中心
National Work Rules for Workers 《全国职工守则》
nationalism n. 民族主义,国家主义;民族特征;工业国有化主义;爱国心
nationalism sentiments 民族感情
nationalist a./n. 民族主义的,国家主义的;(大写)民族主义(国家主义)政党的/民族主义者,国家主义者;(大写)民族主义(国家主义)政党成员
nationalities affairs 民族事务
Nationalities Committee (中)民族委员会(指全国人民代表大会设立的一个专门委员会)
nationality n. 国家;民族;国民;国籍;船籍;国情;民族性;国民身份;独立国地位
nationality act 国籍法
Nationality Affairs Commission (中)民族事务委员会
nationality areas 民族聚居地区
nationality autonomous region 民族自治地区
nationality by birth 依出生地取得的国籍
nationality by domicile 依居住地取得的国籍
nationality by parenthood 依父母国籍而取得的国籍
nationality *de facto* 事实上的国籍
nationality *de jure* 法律上的国籍
nationality effective 实际国籍
nationality law 国籍法
Nationality Law of the People's Republic of China 《中华人民共和国国籍法》
nationality of origin 原国籍,原始国籍

nationality of registry of a ship 船舶所属国;船舶登记国籍
nationality papers of ship 船舶国籍证书
nationality township (中)民族乡
nationalization n. 国有化,收归国有;民族化;具有某国国籍
nationalization acts (或 law) 国有化法(令)
nationalization of American economy 美国经济一体化
nationalization of enterprise 企业国有化
nationalization of land 土地国有化
nationalize v. 归化,使具有某国国籍;使国有化,把……收归国有;使组成国家;使民族化
nationalized a. 收回国有的,国有化的
nationalized land 国有土地
nationalized railway 国有化铁路
nationally unifying force 全国性一体强力措施;国家性统一化的强力措施
nationhood n. 成为国家的地位(事实或状态)
nationwide a. 全国的,全国范围的
nationwide census 全国人口普查
nationwide proclamation of martial law 全国宣布戒严法(令)
nationwide serve 全国范围送达
native n./a. 本国人;本地人;土人,土著/出生地的;出生的;本国的,本土的;土著的;天生的,天然的;朴素的
native ability 天赋才能
native Americans 土著美国人
Native American Law 《土著美国人法》[指调整或处理美国印第安(人)部落(tribes)以及他们与联邦和州政府之间,与公民之间和他们彼此之间关系的全部法律。亦称 American Indian Law; Indian Law]
native and tribal affairs court 土著和部落事务法院
native appellate court 土著上诉法院
native court 土著法院
native court of appeal 土著上诉法院
native goods 国货;土产
native law 本地法;土著法
native place 原籍;本地

native ruler 当地统治者;土著首领
native witness 本地证人
native-born a. 本国生的,本地生的;土著的
nativism n. 排外主义;地方主义
* *Natura appetit perfectum, ita et lex.* Nature desires perfection, so does the law. 自然追求完美,法律也一样。
* *Natura non facit saltum, ita nec lex.* Nature takes no leap, so neither does the law. 自然不能跳跃发展,法律亦然。
natura rerum 事物的本质(或本性、事理)
nativist n. 排外主义者;地方主义者
natural a. 1.自然的,自然界的;天生的,野生的 2.惯常的;正常的 3.生来的;私生的;不合法出生的;(父母)生身的,有血统关系的
natural accretion(或 accession) 自然添附
natural affection 自然感情(在合同中常出现的术语,表示赠送财产、报酬等是出于亲属关系的自然感情)
natural allegiance 与生俱来的忠诚(指本国出生的国民应对其君主的永久忠诚);对祖国的忠诚
natural and man-made disasters 天灾人祸
natural and probable consequences 自然并可能的结果(指以一个谨慎之人的预见力所能预见的、实施某一行为后可能造成之结果。因该行为往往导致该结果,从而以此经验可对此结果作出预测。这是"proximate cause"近因的测试标准。)
natural body 自然人
natural boundary 自然疆界,天然国境
natural calamity 自然灾害,天灾
natural capacity 本能
natural child 私生子[①区别于收养的孩子,亦称为 biological child; genetic child;②从遗传学上讲,此子女与父母相关而不同于人工授精或卵子移植;③私生子女按旧的说法,要父亲确认;④按旧时说法为非婚生子女]
natural capacity of persons to contract 签约人的本能
natural children 私生子女,非婚生子女
natural condition 自然条件

natural consequences 自然的后果(即当事人所约定并希望发生的后果,如要求履行,因为这种问题本属合同的实质问题,故应适用合同缔结地法)
natural consequences of acts 行为的自然结果(指一个人的行为应负其所产生的自然结果的法律责任)
natural corollary 必然结果,必然推断;自然定理
natural counterparts 惯常的相应部分
natural day 白天(指日出到日落的全天)
natural death 自然死亡;正常死亡
natural descent 私生子女;私生的世系
natural destruction 自然毁损
natural duties 自然义务
natural entity 自然实体(与 legal entity 相对而言)
natural environment 自然环境
natural equity 自然衡平(通常与自然正义同义)
natural evidence 自然证据
natural father 生父
natural fixture 自然的定着物
natural fool 天生的白痴
natural force 自然力
natural freedom 天生的自由(指人性中固有的自由,包括理性思考、综合说话能力等。这是人类特有的,称为天生的自由)
natural fruits 天生孳息
natural goods 天然物(品)
natural growing or common nucleus of operative facts 产生法律效果的事实的自然群体或共同内核
natural guardian 自然监护人,法定监护人[指①(历史)长子的父亲为长子的监护人直至长子年满 21 岁。②在无制定法的情况下,婚子女的父亲为监护人直到孩子年满 21 岁。非婚生子女的父亲在其身后可被指定为他们的监护人。③最普遍地或按照法规或是未成年人的父亲,抑或母亲作为监护人,同时每人都有资格承担监护人。如果双亲中一位去世,另一位为当然的或法定的监护人。见 guardian by nature]
natural harbor 天然码头;天然港

natural heir 自然继承人(指因血缘关系而存在的继承人,区别于收养继承人或如配偶等法定继承人)

natural incapacities 自然能力丧失,自然的无行为能力,自然的行为能力丧失

natural infancy 自然幼年期,幼年

natural justice 自然公平,(古罗马时的)自然正义,自然公正(指西方社会的一条最基本的法则。法律上它适合于一切案件的审理,包括法官在审案时不得偏袒任何一方,必须给予被告以充分的辩护和申诉的权利等),自然裁断(指负责裁判的官员要公正行事)

natural law 自然法[自然法学是一种哲学学说,认为自然界存在一种特定的秩序,规定了人类行为的规范。自然法是人法的标准,非正义的法原则上没有约束力。早期的政治哲学家托马斯·霍布斯(Thomas Hobbes)和约翰·洛克(John Locke)认为,自然法的根源不是一系列人类福利和满足的自然安排,而是自我保护的内在需要,因而在此基础上创立了新的"自然权利"学说。自我保护需要订立社会契约,建立市民社会。根据洛克的《政府论》(Two Treatises of Government)(1690年)(或译《关于文官政府的两篇论文》),政治主要义务是保护生命权、自由权和财产权。现代自然权利理论对美国政府建立者颇有影响,"独立宣言"的原则已有体现。通过普通法(common law)的不同概念和"城市共和国"的传统教义,古老自然法教义的某些方面仍嵌在美国法律和政治思想之中。19世纪中期到20世纪初期自然法理论和社会契约理论遭到拒斥、诘难而处于低潮,法律实证主义、功利主义等法学理论取代了其地位。"二战"后出于对法西斯罪恶的批判、反省,自然法理论得以复兴,而对"恶法亦法"的法律实证主义进行批判,以美国的朗·富勒(Lon Fuller)为突出代表的学者指出,法律的道德基础为非神学的自然法思想确立了理论基础。古典自然法思想及近代自然法理论,对近现代以来的政治、国家理论等造成深刻影响。其推演出的天赋人权、有限政府论,以及追求平等、自由、财产与幸福的权利,为民众提供了斗争利器和有力依据。这些对法国大革命、美国宪法的制定以及国际法的制定都有很大影响]

natural law device 自然法方法

natural law jurisprudence 自然法学

natural law method 自然法方法(按照自然法学者菲尼斯的学说,自然法不仅指有关人类幸福的基本形式的实践原则,而且还指实践理智性的基本要求,对这些幸福的承诺、方案和行动进行选择的方法便称为自然法方法)

natural law of nations 自然国际法(见 internal law of nations)

natural law school 自然法学派

natural liberty 天赋自由权,自然的自由(西方法理学家麦考密克将自由分为公民自由与自然自由两种,后者即在自然状态下实行的自由,而这种人类状态是哲学家们假设在人类没有制度化的法律和政府时的状态。见 civil liberties)

natural life 寿命;自然生命

natural loss 自然损耗

natural mother 生母

natural object 自然目标(客体)(指如果没有遗嘱,具有继承权的人将是遗嘱法中一个人遗赠的自然目标)

natural obligations 自然债,自然义务

natural parents 生身父母

natural paternity 私生子的父亲身份

natural perfection first appropriationist 人格圆满(见 first appropriationist)

natural person 自然人

natural person physically present 自然人客观出现,客观出现的自然人

natural physiologic(al) behavior 自然生理行为

natural possession 自然占有

natural power resources 自然动力资源

natural price 自然价格

natural proclivity of judges 法官的天生癖性,法官的自然倾向

natural reason 天赋理性

natural representative 当然代表

natural reserves 自然保护区,天然景物保

护区
natural resources 自然资源
natural rights 自然权利,与生俱来的权利;(大写)天赋人权
natural rights of abstract individual man 抽象个人的自然权利
natural servitude 自然地役(权)
natural succession 当然继承,法定继承
natural transition 自然变迁
natural use (或 **user**) 自然使用
natural wrong 自然错误(指根据道德标准被认为不正当或应受谴责的)
natural-born a. 生来的,生来就有……权利的;本国生的,本地生的
natural-born citizen 本国出生的公民(区别于改变了国籍的公民)
natural-born subject (英)生来籍民(又译生来臣民,指一生下就取得英国国籍的人,即凡在英联合王国及其殖民地、保护地出生的人以及在任何地方出生的君主和大使的子女均为生来的英籍人)
naturales liberi 非婚生子女
naturalia 常素(指法律行为的通常要件)
naturalia negotii 通常条件
naturalis obligatio 自然债
naturalis possessio 自然占有
naturalist(s) n. 自然法学家(派)
naturalization (=naturalisation) n. 入籍;归化;采纳
naturalization paper (或 **certificate**) 入籍证书
naturalization procedure 入籍手续,入籍程序
naturalization proceedings 入籍程序,入籍手续
naturalization right 入籍权,归化权
naturalize (=naturalise) v. 授予……国籍,使入籍;归化;采纳;使摆脱习俗
naturalized (=naturalised) a. 入籍的;归化的;采纳的
naturalized alien 归化的外国人,入籍的外侨
naturalized citizen 已归化公民,入籍公民
naturalized person 归化人,入籍者
naturalized subjects (英)已归化臣民

naturally accrues (自然添附)孳息
nature (14世纪)1.(事物的)本性,本质 2.自然状态,未接触到文明的原野状态 3.人格,品格;性质 4.纯洁,真实(区别于人工的,或设计制造的事物)5.本能,本性 6.万物,自然界(如山,树林,卫星,星球等)
nature catastrophes 自然灾难(害)
Nature Conservancy (英)自然保护协会(1949年成立)
nature increase (人口)自然增长
nature justice 自然正义(与美国的正当程序概念相似,英国则称"自然主义")
nature of a thing 事物的本性
nature of an abstract isolated individual 单个的抽象的个人品性
nature of agreement 协议的性质
nature of an incident 事故的性质
nature of contradiction 矛盾的性质
nature of crime 犯罪(的)性质;犯罪本性
nature of law 法的性质(又译:法律的性质)
nature of libel 文字诽谤的性质
nature of man 人(类)的本性
nature of mistake 错误的性质
nature of the case 案件的性质
nature of the evidence 证据的性质
nature of the lawsuit 诉讼的性质
nature of the offence 犯罪性质
nature of tort 侵权行为的性质
nature power 自然权势(见 instrumental power)
nature presumption 自然推定[是英美证据法学中的一对推定的范畴之一,另一为人造推定(artificial presumption)。自然推定是指按照事物的自然规律所作出的推定。这里"自然"的含义是事物自身的固有特性或依其自然,而非自然界或自然科学]
nature reserve 自然保护区
nature rights 自然权利(观)
natus 已出生婴儿(见 *nasciturus*)
nauta (罗马法)船的雇主
nautical a. 航海的,海上的;船舶的;海员的
nautical assessor 海事案件技术顾问
nautical miles 海里(1海里=1.852公里)
nauticum fenus (*foenus*) (希腊文 nautikon

+拉丁文 fenus,即 nautical 海上的+interest 利益)(罗马法暨大陆法)海上权益[指为海运物资提供资金的贷款;特别是与船运货物的运输当事方订立押船贷款合同(bottomry)所贷之款。这笔贷款属高利贷(extremely high rate of interest),因为要是航船未到达目的地,则这笔贷款不需偿还。这个术语既是"贷款"(loan),又是"海上保险"(marine insurance)。这个利率最开始是不受限制的,因为海上航行风险最终才能确定为12%。所以,被贷之款为"向海外转运费款"(precunia trajectitia)(money conveyed overseas)。亦称 fenus nauticum; nautica-pecunia; fonus nauticum]

naval a.　海军的;军舰的;船的;海上的
naval blockade　海上封锁
naval court　(英)海军海事法庭(指在国外停泊的英国皇家军舰舰长或领事官员所召集组成的法庭)
naval court-martial　(英)海军军事法庭
naval criminal law　海军刑法
Naval Discipline Act　(英)《海军军纪法》
naval law　海军法
naval prison　海军监狱
naval prize　海上捕获
naval station　军港
naval supremacy　海上霸权
naval warfare(或 war)　海战
navicert n.　航海证明书(战时由交战国在中立国的外交官发给该国商船的证明书,证明该船系友好或中立国的船只,并未载运违禁品)
navigable a.　可航行的,可通航的,具备航行条件的
navigable ship　适航船舶,具有航行条件的船舶
navigable water　可航行的水域
navigable waterway　可航水道,通航水道
navigation n.　航行;航海;航空;导航;航行术;海上交通
Navigation Acts　《航海条例》(17世纪中叶英国颁布的一条例,旨在禁止欧洲殖民军队来北美进行航运和贸易)
navigation area(或 region)　航(行)区(域)

navigation law　航海法
navigation mark　航(行)标(志)
navigation right　航海权,航运权
navigation risk　航行过失,航行风险
navigation rules　航行规则
navigation safety　航行安全
navigation satellite　导航卫星
navigation warning　航行通告,航行警告
navigational a.　航行的;航海的;航空的;航行用的
navigational accidents(或 casualty)　航行事故
navigational aids　助航设施
navigational buoy　航行浮标
navigational hazard　航海威胁,航行危险
navigational route　航行通道
navigational signals　航行信号
navigator n.　领航员;驾驶员;航海者;导航仪;海洋探险家
navy bill　(英)海军部出的票据;海军军票
Navy Intelligence Agency　(美)海军情报局
naysay n.　否定,否认;拒绝;投反对票
naysayer n.　否定者,投反对票者
nazir n.　(印度)法院本籍官员;(伊斯兰教国家的)官员,公务员
ne baila pas　尚未支付[指在请求返还非法扣留物之诉(in action for *detinue*)中,被告提出否认争议物已将会的辩词(他或她尚未交付)]
ne bis in idem(=*res judicata*) a thing adjudicated; an issue that has been definitively settled by judicial decision　既决案件,一事不再理
ne exeat　扣留令,禁止离境令(指为禁止某人离开国境或法院管辖区域所发的令状)
ne exeat regno　(英)禁止出国令(指为禁止一个人离开英国国境所发的令状)
ne limit order　无限制令(指对价格无规定的证券买卖令)
Neagle, Ie re, 135 U. S. 1(1890)　尼格尔对物(对事)诉讼案
near a.　近的;近似的;近期的;接近的,关系接近的;亲密的
near delivery　近期交货,近期交割

near kin 近亲
near-bank n. 准银行
near-money n. 准货币,近似货币
nearest relative 最近亲(属)
nec vi, nec clam, nec precario （罗马法）非暴力、非隐秘和非许可(或非欺瞒和非勉强)(指对某物的占有必须依据非暴力、非隐秘和非许可的方式才能取得)
nec manifestum 并非声明、并非明证;(罗马法)(此术语常指在行窃中未被抓到的窃贼)已遂盗、暗盗
necessarii heredes 当然继承人
necessarily included offense 见 lesser included offense
Mecessarium est quod non potest aliter se habere. That which is necessary cannot be otherwise. 别无选择即为必要;必要者即不可能有其他选择。
necessary a./n. 强制的、被迫的;必需的、必要的/(常用复)必需品,生活必需品
Necessary and Proper Clause 必要和适当条款(指美国联邦宪法第1条第8款第18项授权国会制定法律、行使宪法授予国会的各项权力,联邦最高法院已经广泛解释此项条款,暗许国会具有此项默示权力可制定任何法律,以明确刑事宪法权力。亦可称之为 Basket Clause、Coefficient Clause、Elastic Clause 或 Sweeping Clause)
necessary consent 必需的同意
necessary damages 必要的损害赔偿
necessary defense 见 justification 2
necessary formality 必要程式;必要手续
necessary heir 特留份继承人,当然继承
necessary if feasible 在可行情况下应当是必要的
necessary law 必然法则;强制法
necessary law of nations (国家间的)必要法,国际强制法
necessary party 必要的当事人(指对争议具有利害关系,而应成为诉讼当事人,以便法院可依照这样的规则行事:要求法院进行裁决并最终解决整个争议,以此调整所涉的所有权利来实现完全主义)
necessary repair 必要补偿
Necessitas est lex temporis et loci. Necessity is the law of time and of place. 必须就是法律,但应依时间和地点而定。
Necessitas non habet legem. Necessity has no law. 必须的情况下考虑不到法律。
Necessitas quod cogit, defendit. Necessity defends or justifies what it compels. 必须可以用来为做事不择手段辩护或证明它是正当的(此谚语适用于中下层行政、司法官员执行公务的行为)。
necessitate v. 使必须,迫切要求,迫使
necessity n. (美)紧急避险[①(刑法)指一个人在紧急情况下的正当防卫(justification defense)行为,这种紧急情况并非由他(或她)自身引起,但他(或她)也造成了损害,这种损害比以前曾发生过的要轻。只是对人诉讼(person's action)而已。比如,一名登山者在暴风雪中迷失,因而在附近小屋中窃取食品和毛毯,为了他的生命和健康,他可主张紧急避难进行抗辩。这个词亦称 choice of evils; duresse of circumstance(见 lesser-evils defense)。②(侵权)如果一个人没有任何选择、为了保护自己的生命和健康而去损害他人的财产,此时他具有免除其侵犯他人土地或侵犯他人财产的侵权责任的特权]
necessity for life 生活必需品
necessity in defence 必要自卫,正当防卫
necessity of confidentiality 必要信任
necessity of self-protection 必要自卫,正当自卫
neck tie party (美俚)绞死(尤指私刑)
necrology n. 死亡者名单,死亡人姓名录;死亡通知,讣告
necrophilia n. 恋尸癖(属性心理障碍的一种,多见于男性,以迷恋尸体或奸尸为特征。其实女性偶尔也可遇见。此类患者均具有完全刑事责任能力。见 sexual perversion)
necropsy (或 **necroscopy**) n. 验尸,尸体剖验
n'ee (=nee) (法)娘家姓……的(放在已婚女子姓后,表示婚前的娘家姓)
need n. 1.需要,必要;(复)必需品;需求 2.困窘;危急
needle time 唱针时间(指被许可人可录制有关作品的全部时间。许可合同中常见

的术语)
needs allowance 生活必需津贴
needs test 经济情况调查(指对申请救济者)
needy a. 贫困的,贫穷的
needy parents 贫困的双亲
negate v. 使无效;使无价值;废弃
* *Negatio duplex est affirmatio.* A double negative is an affirmative. 两个否定就是一个肯定(否定的否定,就是肯定)。
negative n./a./v. 1.(摄)底片〈Not only the pictures, but also the negatives, were required to be neatened.〉(不仅需要消除图片,还需要消除底片。)2.否决权〈two negatives make an affirmative/one positive〉(负负得正)/1.拒绝的(指与坏事物的属性相关联的),否定的〈no and not are negative〉(no 和 not 都是否定的),〈a negative answer〉(否定的回复)2.负面的,消极的(与 positive 相对)〈a negative attitude〉(消极态度)3.反面的〈negative evidence〉(反证)/1.否决,拒绝(指否决或拒绝的一个词语);驳斥、否认 2.使无价值、使无效〈the jury negatived fraud〉(陪审团使诈骗败诉)
negative (state) servitude 消极(国家)地役权
negative act 不作为;不行为;消极行为
negative agency 消极代理
negative averment 否定指证,反证供,反面证明,(诉状中)否定性的事实主张
negative capital 消极资本,负资本(借款、存款等)
negative clearance 豁免结关(或出港)证明
negative condition (规定某一状况或行为不得发生的)消极条件
negative consensus 否定式共识,以共识作出否定表示
negative crime 不作为犯罪
negative covenant 禁止协议,禁止合同(指要求当事方不得从事某些行为的协议或合同,尤其在不动产的筹资交易中,借方向贷方允诺,在贷方未还清之前,不得对不动产设置负债或进行交易。见 affirmative covenant)

negative doctrine of equivalents 消极均等论
negative duty 消极义务;不作为义务
negative evidence 消极证据;反证
negative externalities 负面外部效应
negative factor 消极因素;负因素
negative guarantee 消极保证,消极担保
negative income tax 负所得税
negative indirect history 消极间接史
negative infinity 负无穷
negative instrument 消极工具(指传统模式把行政法视作控制政府权力的一种消极工具)
negative interest 逆利率,倒利息
negative investment 负投资,减少投资
negative liberty 消极自由
negative list 不准进口商品单,限制进口商品表,负面清单(指列举法律、法规禁止的事项,对法律没有明确禁止的事项,都属于法律之许之事项。负面清单作为一种国际通行的外商投资管理办法,其特征在于以否定性列表的形式标明外资禁入的领域)
negative means 消极方法,消极手段
negative misprision 消极隐瞒罪行(指犯罪行为的包庇隐匿)
negative plea 否认原告指控的抗辩
negative pregnant(s) 隐含确认的否认,含蓄否定(指从字面上否认所受指控,但不谈其实质内容或本身包含对部分内容的默认的一种答辩),蕴涵肯定的否认
negative prescription 消极时效,消灭时效
negative proof 反面证据,反证
negative punishment 消极惩罚
negative reaction 消极反应
negative rights 消极的权利(如个人居住、迁徙、言论、出版、信仰、通信、集会、结社等权利)
negative savings 减少储蓄
negative sovereignty 消极主权
negative statute 反面法规;消极法规
negative testimony 反面证据,反证供
negative vote 反对票
negative wage tax (美)负工资税(美国对于工资低于某一水平者的补贴)
negativing *mens rea* 否认有犯意

negativism n. 怀疑主义,否定态度
neglect n./v. 疏忽,玩忽,忽略,忽视/忽略,疏忽;忽视,玩忽;弃置不顾
neglect business 旷工
neglect of duty 失职,过失责任;玩忽职守
neglect of one's official duties 玩忽职守
neglected a. 未被好好照管的;被忽视的
neglected child (17世纪)受虐待的孩子(指①孩子的父母或法定监护人没有适当照管,反而十分残忍、不道德而无资格地虐待孩子;②孩子父母或其法定监护人没有提供应有的、必需的关照,没有提供孩子必需的医疗服务。见 deprived child)
neglected children 无人照管的儿童
neglected discount 放弃的折扣
negligence n. 过失;疏忽,玩忽;怠慢
negligence clause 提单上免除船舶公司责任的条款;(保险业上的)疏忽条款,免责条款
negligence defence 过失辩护
negligence formula of judge Learned Hand 伦德·汉德法官的过失公式
negligence general average clause 共同海损疏忽条款
negligence of duty 失职
negligence per se 自身的过失
negligent a. 玩忽的,疏忽的,粗心大意的;因疏忽造成损害的;依民法应负赔偿责任的;过失的
negligent act 过失行为
negligent bankruptcy 过失破产
negligent crime 过失罪
negligent damage 过失毁损,过失损害
negligent debtor 有过失的债务人
negligent driving 疏忽驾驶
negligent escape 乘隙逃脱罪,由于疏忽成(罪犯乘隙)逃脱[指由于治安人员(peace officer)的刑事犯罪行为玩忽地放纵罪犯逃离法定监禁场所(legal custody)。"逃脱"(escape)既有放纵(voluntary),亦有玩忽或疏忽(negligent)。"放纵"正是看守人的明示同意(express consent),在这之后,看守人不可能再重新捕获(retake)该囚犯(即使原告可于任何时间重新抓到他),但行政司法官(sheriff)必

须对"债务"承担责任(answer for the debt)。因疏忽造成(囚犯)逃脱(negligent escapes),即囚犯是在看守人不知情或未同意的情况下逃脱,然后急追可能重新捕获,在控告该司法行政官造成逃脱的玩忽行为之前,则该司法行政官受到宽恕]
negligent harm 过失伤害
negligent homicide 过失杀人
negligent injury 过失伤害
negligent interference (依法应负赔偿责任的)消极妨害行为
negligent misrepresentation 过失误述
negligent misstatement 因疏忽而引起的错误陈述
negligentia 过失
∗ *Negligentia semper habet infortuniam comitem.* Negligence always has misfortune for a companion. 过失(或懈怠)常与不幸为伴。
negligible quantity 无足轻重的人;可忽略的因素
negotia inter vivos 生前行为,生时行为
negotia mortis causa 临死行为,死因行为
negotiability n. 可转让性;可流通性;可谈判;可协商
negotiable a. 可转让的;可流通的;可谈判的,可协商的
negotiable amount 可议付的金额
negotiable bill 流通汇票
negotiable bill of lading 可转让提单
negotiable CD 可转让的定期存单
negotiable credit 可流通的信用证,可转让的信用证
negotiable document 流通契据,可转让的契据
negotiable instrument 流通票据,可转让票据
negotiable instruments law (流通)票据法
negotiable order of withdrawal account 可转让提款单(或称指令账户,指能开出可转让支付的活期存款账户)
negotiable paper 流通证券,可转让票据
negotiable promissory note 可转让期票;流通借据;可转让的本票
negotiable securities 流通的有价证券

negotiant (=negotiator) n. 交涉者,磋商者;交易人

negotiate v. 议定;谈判,协商;出售,转让;兑现;处置,解决

negotiate purchase 议价购买

negotiated a. 可谈判的,可协商的;可转让的,可流通的

negotiated amount 议付金额

Negotiated Rulemaking Act (美)《法规制定协商法》

negotiated settlement 协商解决,协议解决

negotiating bank 议付银行,让购汇票银行

negotiating date 汇票让购期限

negotiation n. 让与,转付;流通;交涉;谈判;商议

negotiation against guarantee 凭保证议付

negotiation credit 议付信用证,让购信用证书

negotiation for settling a dispute 解决争议的协商;协商解决争议

negotiation of a bill 转付票据

negotiation of contract terms 磋商合约条款

negotiorum gestio (罗马法)无因管理;未经授权的代理(指未获授权在他人不在时,基于友好善意而代为干预某项事务)

negotium (19世纪法律体系中最为重要的)义契约(庞德的译著中译为"法律交易""法律事务")

negozio giuridico 适法行为(罗马法上的契约概念,指法律允许当事人在规定的条件和限度内按个人意愿确定其后果的行为)

negro suffrage 黑人选举权

negrophobe n. 强烈厌恶黑人的人;畏惧黑人的人

neighbo(u)rhood n. 四邻,邻居;邻近的地区;街坊,街道;邻居关系

neighborhood committee (中)居民委员会

neighborhood court (或 **Neighborhood Justice Center**) (美)邻里(调解)法庭(或称邻里司法调解点,指非正式的、非官方的调解邻居中父母与子女、同房间的住客、夫妻、朋友以及房主与租户等之间的民事纠纷的机构,于1978年创立)

neighborhood law centre 居民法律咨询处

neighborhood mediation committee (中)居民调解委员会

neighborhood planning 住宅区规划

neighbo(u)ring a. 邻近的;附近的;接壤的

neighboring country 邻国,邻邦

neighboring relations (中)相邻关系

neighboring right 类似权利

neighbo(u)rship n. 四邻关系

nemesis n. 给以报应者,复仇者;难以对付的敌手;公正的惩罚;报应;(大写)复仇女神,报应女神

nemine contradicente 一致同意,无人异议(常用于法庭、立法机构对于一项判决、决议、表决或动议所表示的一致意见)

nemine dissentiente 无异议地,全体一致地

* **Neminem oportet esse sapientiorem legibus.** No man, out of his private reason ought to be wiser than the laws. No one ought to be wiser than the laws. 任何人无须贤明过法律。

nemo 无人,没有一个人

* **Nemo agit in seipsum.** A man cannot be a judge and a party in his own cause. 在自己的诉案中不能既充任法官又作当事人。

* **Nemo alieno nomme lege agere potest.** No one can sue at law in the name of another. 任何人不得以他人名义起诉。

* **Nemo allegans suam tunpitudinem audiendus est.** No one who alleges his own guilt ought to be heard. No one testifying to his own wrong is to be heard as a witness. 任何声称自己为不法者(或卑鄙者)不得作为证人。(这非证据规则,但适用于当事人请求强制执行基于非法之上的权利时)

* **Nemo bis punitur pro eodem delicto.** No one can be punished twice for the same offense. 同一罪行不受两次刑罚。

* **Nemo damnum facit nisi qui id fecit quod facere jus non habet.** No one is a wrongdoer, but he who does what the law does not allow. 任何人只要不做法律不准做的事即不会成为违法者。

* **Nemo dat qui non habet.** He who hath (i.e.has) not cannot give. 不能给付自己没

有的东西。
* *Nemo debet aliena jactura locupletari.* No one ought to gain by another's loss. 任何人不得损人利己。

nemo debet bis vector 任何人不应受两次磨难

* *Nemo debet bis vexari pro eadem causa.* No one should be twice harassed for the same cause. 同一案件不受两次处理（一事不再理）。

* *Nemo debet esse judex in propria causa.* No man ought to be a judge in his own cause. 无人能为自己案件充当审判官。

* *Nemo debet ex aliena jactura lucrari (nemo debet ex alieno damno lucrari).* No person ought to gain by another person's loss. 任何人不得因他人受损而得益。

* *Nemo est haeres viventis.* No one is the heir of a living person. 任何人不能充当活着的人的继承人。

* *Nemo est supra leges.* No one is above the law. 任何人不得凌驾于法律之上。

* *Nemo ex dolo suo proprio releveur, aut auxilium capiat.* Let no one be relieved or gain an advantage by his own fraud. 任何人不得因自己之欺诈而免除义务或获取利益。

* *Nemo ex suo delicto meliorem suam conditionem facere potest.* No one can improve his condition by his own misdeed. 任何人不得靠自己的不端行为来改善自己的状况。

* *Nemo in propria causa testis esse debet.* No one ought to be a witness in his own cause. 任何人不得在自己的案件中充当证人。

* *Nemo judex in causa sua.* Nobody can be a judge in his own case. 任何人不得成为自己案件的法官。

* *Nemo judex in re sua.* 当事人不得审判自己的案件。

* *Nemo jus sibi dicere potest.* No one can declare the law for himself. No one is entitled to take the law into his own hands. 任何人无权为自己的利益而确定法律（任何

人无权操纵法律）。

* *Nemo moriturus praesumitur mentire.* No one about to die is presumed to die. 任何人不得将即将死亡者推定为死亡。

* *Nemo plus juris ad alium transferre potest quam ipse habet.* No one can transfer more right to another than he has himself. 任何人不得转让超出自己原有的权利。

* *Nemo potest esse simul actor et judex.* No one can be at once suitor and judge. 任何人不得同时作原告和法官。

* *Nemo potest facere per alium, quod per se non potest.* No one can do through another what he can not do through himself. 任何人不得通过他人为自己不得为之事。

* *Nemo praesumitur malus.* No one is presumed to be bad. 任何人不得被推定为恶人。

* *Nemo prohibetur pluribus defensionibus uti.* No one is prohibited from making use of several defenses. 不能禁止任何人使用各自不同的辩护。

* *Nemo sibi esse judex vel suis jus dicere debet.* No man ought to be his own judge, or administer justice in cases where his relations are concerned. 任何人不得在自己或与自己有利害关系的案件中自行审判或执法。

* *Nemo tenetur accusare ipsum* （或 *Nemo tenetur seipsum accusare*）. No one is bound to accuse himself. 任何人无义务控告自己。

* *Nemo tenetur ad impossibile.* No one is bound to an impossibility. 任何人都不受做不可能做的事的约束。

* *Nemo tenetur divinare.* No one is bound to foretell. 任何人无预测之责（指任何人对意外事件无预测、预告之责任）。

* *Nemo tenetur edere intrumenta contra se.* No man is bound to produce writings against himself. 任何人均无义务出示文据来反对自己。

* *Nemo tenetur informare qui nescit sed quisquis scire quod informat.* No one who is ignorant of a thing is bound to give information of it but everyone is bound to

know what he gives information of. 自己不知之事无义务提供情况给任何人,但一旦提供情况必须为自己所熟悉之事。

Nemo tenetur prodere seipsum. No one is bound to betray himself. No one can be compelled to criminate himself. 任何人无坦白自己有罪之义务。

nemo tenetur respondere 无须应诉(指被告在未见到王室令状时无需出席在封建法庭开始的针对他的自由保有地的诉讼,即需王室令状才能开始的诉讼。见 praecipe 和 writ of right)

Nemo tenetur seipsum accusare. No one is bound to incriminate himself. 任何人无起诉自己的义务(任何人不得受拘束控告自己)。

Nemo videtur fraudare eos qui sciunt, et consentiunt. No one seems (is supposed) to defraud those who know and assent (to his act). 任何知情且已同意者不为被诈欺。

neo-colony n. 新殖民地

neo-functionalists n. 新功能主义学派

Neo-Hegelian Philosophy of Law 新黑格尔法(律)哲学

neo-Hegelian school of law 新黑格尔主义法学派

Neo-Hegelian theories of justice 新黑格尔正义论

Neo-Kantian Philosophy of Law 新康德法(律)哲学

neo-Kantian school of law 新康德主义法学派

neo-Natural school of law 新自然法学派

neo-Thomist school of law 新托马斯主义法学派

neoclassicism n. 新古典主义

neocolonialism n. 新殖民主义

neodoxy n. 新学说,新观点

neofascism n. 新法西斯主义

neofascist n. 新法西斯主义者

neoimperialism n. 新帝国主义

neoimperialist n. 新帝国主义者

neologism 语词新作(思维表达障碍的一种,指概念的融合、浓缩以及无关概念的拼凑。患者自创一些新的符号、图形、文字或语言并赋予其特殊概念。本症状引起作案的概率极低,主要是帮助鉴定人诊断和鉴别诊断。发现这一症状依靠的是病人的书面语言,所以警方需注意收集被鉴定人平日亲自写的书面材料。见 thought of insertion)

Neomercantilism n. 新重商主义

neoscholastic theories of law 新经院法学

nepotism (17世纪)裙带关系,任人唯亲(nepotistic a.)(见 cronyism)

neritic province 浅海区,近岸区

nervous lesion 神经损害

nervous shock 神经震颤(现如同人身伤害一样可作为侵权行为的一项诉理由)

net a./n./v. 净的;净的;最后的/净利;净值;实价;净数;净重;要点,要旨/1.净得;净赚;得到 2.用网捕,张网

net amount 实数,净额

net assets 资产净额

net available assets 可利用的资产净额

net balance 净差额

net book agreement 净账面协议

net capacity 净载货量

net chargeable income 应纳税的纯小息;诉讼进行中的入息额

net cost 净价

net deficiency 净亏损

net earnings 净收益,实得报酬

net effect of prohibition 禁令的净效应

net estate 纯地产,纯不动产,纯资产

net income 纯收入,净所得,纯收益

net interest 纯利,净利

net investment 净投资,投资净额

net liquid assets 流动资产净额

net loss 纯损,净损

net national product 国民生产净值

net of tax 纳税后净额,纳税后净入额(指许可合同中常作为支付使用费的底数)

net output 净产值;净产出(量)

net premium 净贴水,净保(险)费

net price 实价,净价

net proceeds 净收益;实得额

net profit 净利,净利润,纯利润

net registered tonnage 净注册吨

net result 最后结果

net sales 产品销售净额,销售净额
net selling price 净销售费
net single premium 一次性交足保险费[指保单持有人必须一次性将保险费缴足,以保证有足够金额支付给签订保险的赔偿金(claims)。这个金额保证利息增长达到预期比率(expected rate),而且是建立在某种赔偿金的可能性预测基础之上]
net tare 净皮重
net value added to taxable product 应税产品的净增加值
net weight 净重
net worth 净值
Netherlands Arbitration Act 1986 《1986年荷兰仲裁法》
Netherlands law 荷兰法
nettoyage de la situation verbale 语词情境之清洗(指对语言的精心关注,对语言会成为迷惑之源的意识,是边沁思想特征之一)
network n. 网状物;网状系统;网络;广播网,电视网;广播网(电视网)联播网
network commerce 网络交易,网络贸易
Network Effect 网络效应[指在经济学中一项技术的用户增加时,其价值也就随之增加,最典型的例子是电话的效用会随着电话网络接入范围的扩大与电话用户的增加而提升。在公司治理的领域,该理论也可适用。东亚(除朝鲜)的主要经济体都引入大量盎格鲁-美国式的治理规则。如日本,韩国分别在1998年和1999年引入独立董事制。2003年日本经治理改革后选择适用盎格鲁-美国式的以董事会为中心的单层公司治理模式,或选择适用日本传统的包含监事会的双层公司治理模式。我国台湾地区2003年修订的"公司法"中引入了英美法中董事受信义务;我国香港特区作为英美法系的一个地区,同样保持着大量英美公司法系的传统]
network firewall 网络防火墙(指能阻挡99%的黑客恶意刺探的网络预防技术,但并非绝对安全,黑客还可通过目标公司与合伙人、供货商以及客户之间不设防的因特网连接渗入公司的网络)
network radio 无线电通讯网

Networked Readiness Index 网络准备度指数(属世界论坛的)
Neumeier n. (美)勒迈耶规则(指1972年 Neumeier v. Kuehner 案中,针对侵权案件中"宾客法规"的适用,纽约州上诉法院提出了三个具体化的现代冲突规则,通称为 Neumeier 规则)
neuropathic a. 患神经病的,神经病的
neuropathy n. 神经(系)病
neuropoison n. 神经毒药
neutral n./a. 中立国;中立国国民;中立者;非彩色(尤指灰色)/中立的;中立国的;非彩色的
neutral alien 中立国侨民
neutral asylum 中立国庇护
neutral concern 中立的动机;立场中立
neutral debtor 中性债务人
neutral forum 中立论坛;中立国法庭
neutral goods 中立国货物
neutral inhabitants 中立国居民
neutral port [或 harbo(u)r] 中立港
neutral ship 中立国船只
neutral ships acting in an unneutral manner 非以中立方式行事的中立国船舶
neutral state 中立国
neutral subjects (或 national) 中立国国民
neutral waters 中立国领海;中立国水域
neutral zone 中立区,中立地带
neutralism n. 中立主义,中立政策,中立
neutralist n. 中立主义者,采取中立主义的政府
neutrality n. 中立,中立地位
neutrality law 中立法
neutrality pact 中立公约
neutrality proclamation 中立宣告,宣告中立
neutrality regulations 中立规则,中立条例
neutralization n. 中立化;变为无效;抵消
neutralize v. 使中立化;使成为无效,抵消
neutralized states 永久中立国
never ad. 永不,绝不;从来没有;不,没有
never dying 连续不断
never indebted 无依据的债务
never seek hegemony 永不称霸
never sober 从未清醒过;常常醉酒
never-never system (英俚)分期付款制

new a. 新发现的;新的;重新开始的;新生的;新就任的;新开发的(土地);不熟悉的
new analytical jurisprudence 新分析法学
new analytical school of law 新分析法学派
new analytical-positivist jurisprudence 新分析实证主义法学
new assets 新资产
new assignment (普通法上辩论中的)新的陈述;新的转让
new auction 新拍卖
new cause of action 新的诉因,以前未提及的诉因
new commerce clause 新商业条款[指在新政(New Deal)复苏过程中的商业条款,联邦最高法院认定国会可以对州际经济活动和州际商业产生"实质影响"的州内活动进行管制。同时国会对于这些事务拥有自实际上的自由处置权。不过,考虑到新联邦主义实际上以牺牲联邦权力为代价而强化州权力,所以国会必须小心翼翼,并时刻留意尊重州的主权]
New Commercial Policy Instrument (NCPI) 新商业政策工具(1984年欧共体理事会颁布的对抗美国1974年贸易法310条款的第2681/84号条例,又称新商业政策工具)
new consideration (英美法)新对价
New Deal (美)新政(指罗斯福总统于1933—1939年间所实施的对美国经济与社会进行改革的内政纲领,目的在于加强政府对经济的控制)
New Deal Recovery Plan 新政恢复(经济)计划
New Dealer (美)主张实行新政者
new departure 新政策,新方针
new duties incident to increased tasks 随着新增加的任务而来的新的职责
new economic policy 新经济政策
new enough 新颖性,进步性
new evidence 新发现的证据,新证据
new evidence scholarship 新证据学
new fact 新事实
New Federal Sentencing Guideline (美)《新联邦科刑准则指南》
new federalism 新联邦主义

new for old 新换旧,以旧换新
new forestry 新林业
New Freedom (美)新自由政纲(指美国第28任总统伍德罗·威尔逊竞选时的政纲,主张解散大垄断企业,以利于小企业发展)
new generations of lawyers 新一代的律师,新一代的法律人
new humanism 新人道主义
New Inn (英史)纽律师学院
New Institutional Economics (NIE) 新制度经济学
New International Economic Order (NIEO) 国际经济新秩序
new issue 新发行(证券、纸币等)
new issue of shares in the company 新发行的公司股票
new ius commune 新欧洲普通法
new judg(e)ment 重新审判;重新判决
new legal orthodoxy 新的法律正统性,新的法律正统观念
new legal pluralism 新法律多元主义(见 classic legal pluralism)
new matter 新的事件;新的案件
new mortgage 新的抵押
new mortgage 新质权人
New Natura Brevium (英)《新令状选编及其评注》(1794年再版本)
new online investor 在线投资新手
new online trader 在线交易新手
new order of ideas 新秩序化的理念[伊曼纽尔·康德(1724—1804)挖掘17、18世纪法哲学的基础,并代之以一种新秩序化的理念,在使众多法律现象秩序化的过程中,以把握普遍性中的特殊性的认识能力为基础的观点]
new orthodoxies 新的正统性,新的正统观
New Pragmatism 新实用主义
new problem of extradition 引渡新问题
new property (美)新财产(美国学者弗里德曼认为本世纪已经出现了"新财产"的概念,应将就业机会、养老金、政府特许作为新财产对待)(耶鲁大学Charles Reich教授分别于1964年和1965年发表了两篇论文,呼吁法院承认并保障个人通过政府

福利而获得的利益,即新财产权)
new public management 新公共管理(英国知名公共行政学者克里斯多夫·胡德 Christopher Hood 认为新公共管理强调竞争性、使用者的选择、透明以及诱因结构,其原因不同于传统的官僚性概念。也是以目标导向代替过去的规则导向)
new rates of the annual taxes (英)年度内各税的新税率
new realism 新现实主义
new rich 暴发户
new share 新股
new states 见 territories and new states
new stories 新闻报道
New Style (英)新历(即现在通用的阳历)
New Testament 《新约全书》(《圣经》两大部分中成书较晚而内容较少的一部分)
new trade agenda 新的贸易议事日程
new trial 再审;重新审判(指由于判决不当、不公平或有错误,向上级法院上诉,经裁定撤销原判决,而引起的重新审判)
new visitor counting 再次造访次数记录软件
New World 新世界;新大陆(指美北美洲);西半球,美洲(见 Old World)
New York City Charter And Administrative Code (美)《纽约市规章和行政汇典》
New York Clearing House Association (美)纽约票据交换所(美国最大的票据交换所)
New York Convention for Recognition and Enforcement of Foreign Arbitrational Awards 《承认和执行外国仲裁裁决的纽约公约》
New York Court of Appeals (美)纽约上诉法院
New York remains in the cross-hairs 纽约仍是袭击目标
New York Stock Exchange (NYSE) 纽约股票交易
New York Supplement (美)《纽约补篇》[指美国"全国判例汇编系统"中的一部分。《纽约补编》(1888 年至今)内容:①康斯托克(Comstock);②受理上诉法

庭;③各种不同的案件和许多其他现在中断的下一级法院判例汇编。该补篇的特点:①每一判例的司法判决意见书(judicial opinion)均有眉批(headnote)和钥匙号;②西方版钥匙号系统(West Key Number System)指引查找法律并帮助找到相关判例;③概要概括了程序和最重要的司法判决意见的裁决;④编辑好的眉批诠释了司法判决意见的每一要点,纳入关键事实和推理;⑤西方版的法典或法规注释(codenote)指明一项特有制定法或联邦法规违宪或无效的意见]
New York's Field Code 《纽约州菲尔德法典》(见 Field Code)(该法典旨在简化民事诉讼程序)
New Zealand law 新西兰法
New-Kantian theory of justice 新康德主义正义论
Newgate n. (英)新门监狱(伦敦一监狱的名称)
newly-discovered facts 发现新事实
newly-discovered evidence 新发现的证据
news (复) n. 新闻,消息,新闻报道
news conference 记者招待会,新闻发布会
newsgathering n. 新闻采集,新闻收集
newsletter n. (定期出版的)时事通讯;时事信札;(公司印发的)业务通讯
newsman's privilege (美)新闻工作者的特权,新闻记者的特权(指①根据宪法和制定法对新闻工作者的保护规定避免强制透露其新闻的秘密来源,与 journalist's privilege, reporter's privilege 意思相同;②在国家公务人员处理公务时,出版物作出公正评论时要保护出版商以避免诽谤性诉讼,同样含义的词条有 editorial privilege、common interest privilege、common-interest exception 等]
newspaper right 报刊使用权(指将某部作品在报刊上转载或摘登的权利。与 shot periodical rights, single issue rights 同)
Nexi (罗马法)受到(法律上)约束的人(用于表示债务人对债权人的债务关系);合同(契约)的双方当事人
next a. 最近的;紧接的;其次的
next budgetary year 下一个预算年度

next devisee 剩余遗产受赠人(见 first devisee)
next friend 次代理人(指虽非正式监护人而充当未成年人或其他无行为能力者的诉讼代理人、监护人或保护人的人,一般都是近亲属)
next host thing 欠佳之事
next of kin 最近亲;最近的血亲(常见于死后无遗嘱,而遗产由其最近的血亲继承时所使用的用语)
next settlement period 下一个结算期
next succeeding term 继续连任期
next-of-kin card 家属证
Nexue Approach (美)"联结"方式(基于最近实证社会科学证明男女同性恋者均能真正教育出心理健康之子女,且强调法院在证明同性恋父母是否适任时无须适用特殊假设,亦无须专家评估)
nexum (罗马法)尼克萨姆借贷合同(契约)(指早期罗马法上一种贷款的要式合同,需有一位负责金钱度量的人和五位证人以及相对方在场,合同才能成立。其条件十分苛刻,债务如未能偿还,可使债务人完全处于债权人支配之下),债务口约(一种古老契约形式,类似要式买卖)
nexus n. 关系,联系;结合
nexus of contracts 契约链(指英美公司法对公司本质理解的一种理论,即从契约责任来"肢解"设立中公司的责任)
nexus test (1975年)联结准则[指个人行为的准则(standard)被认为是国家行为(state action),而且这一准则可能会引起违反某人的(someone's)宪法权利的责任承担,即如果该行为与政府的行为(governments conduct)如此紧密或纠缠一起以致进行选择它可能造成是国家行为的。尽管相似于共生关系准则(symbiotic relationship test),但联结准则却聚焦于特定行为(particular act)只委屈地聚焦到代替的全部当事方的关系(overall relationship of parties)上。有的法院使用一些术语(terms)并作互换(使用)地分析。亦称 close-nexus test。见 Symbiotic Relationship Test; joint participation; state-compulsion test]

Niagara of words 尼亚加拉大瀑布式的词条
niche fame 特殊市场驰名(指1996年美国《联邦商标反淡化法》明确规定只有驰名商标才受该法的反淡化保护。法院适用此条时创造了"特殊市场驰名"标准,该标准认为尽管对一般公众来说商标并不驰名,但只要原告和被告在同样的或相关联的市场经营运作,而原告商标在特殊市场已有很高知名度,则该商标有权获得反淡化保护。但2006年的商标淡化修正法案否定了"特殊市场驰名"标准,规定了商标淡化中驰名商标的定义,当商标作为商标所有人的商品或服务来源标识而为美国一般公众广泛认可时,商标为驰名)
niche market 有利可图的市场
nickname n. 别号,外号,绰号,诨号
nient (法)无,没有
nient comprise (法)无所依据;未列入
nient culpable (法)无罪(侵权行为的一般争议或刑事诉讼中的用语)
nient dedire (法国古法)无答辩(的判决)(指因未加否认或未提出答辩致受到不利于自己的判决)
nient le fait (法国古法)否认(是他的契据)的答辩
nigger n. 被歧视者;有黑人血统者
night n. 夜,黑夜;黑暗;罪恶
night court (大城市中办理即决刑事案件的)夜间法庭
night man 更夫;清扫厕所的工人
night shift 夜班;(总称)夜班工人
night stick (美)警棍
night walker 夜间扰乱治安者;晚上行窃者;妓女
night watch (man) 守夜(人),值夜(者)
night-watchman state 守夜人似的国家
nightrider n. (美)(南部)夜间骑马为非作歹的人
nihil 无,无物(此术语单独用时,为司法行政官回复令状的用语,意思是"无物"执行);无价值的东西,无关紧要之物
nihil ad rem 不相干的,牛头不对马嘴的,不切合的
nihil capiat per billam 驳回诉状的一种判

决格式(见 *nihil capiat per breve*)
nihil capiat per breve 不满足诉状请求的一种判决格式(拉丁文原意为:根据他提出的诉状什么都得不到,即不管是诉讼或中止诉讼,对原告都是败诉的一种判决格式)
nihil dicit (= *nil dicit*) 无答辩(见 *nient dedire*)
nihil est 无法送达(拉丁文意思是那里什么都没有。这是司法行政官在无法送达令状作回复手续时的用语)
* **Nihil est tam populare quam bonitas.** Nothing is so popular as goodness is. 没有什么比美更受欢迎。
* **Nihil facit error nominis cum de corpore constat(e).** An error as to or in a name is nothing when there is a certainty as to the person. 只要能确定何人,姓名无关紧要。
nihil habet 无法通知(拉丁文意思是他什么也没有。这是司法行政官在送达预告令状或其他令状找寻被告无着作回复手续时的用语)
* **Nihil habet forum ex scena.** The court has nothing to do with what is not before it. 法院不过问未诉诸法庭之事项;不告不理。
* **Nihil in lege intolerabilius est (quam) eandem rem diverso jure censeri.** Nothing is more intolerable in law than that the same matter, thing, or case should be subject to different views of law. 法绝不容许用不同的法律观点来处理同一问题、同一事情或同一案件(此谚语适用于不同法院在处理特定案件时持有不同的法律观点)。
* **Nihil majis justum est quam quod necessarium est.** Nothing is more just than what is necessary. 没有比必要更为正当了。
* **Nihil perfectum est dum aliquid restat agendum.** Nothing is perfect while anything remains to be done. 任何事在未完成时都是不完美的。
* **Nihil possumus contra veritatem.** We have no power against the truth. We are not able to stand against the truth. 我们无力对抗真理。

* **Nihil quod est contra rationem est licitum.** Nothing is permitted which is contrary to reason./Nothing that is against reason is lawful. 不合理即不合法。
* **Nihil simul inventum est et perfectum.** Nothing is invented and perfected at the same moment. 任何创造出的新事物不可能同时是完美的,新生事物不可能同时完美。
* **Nihil tam munitum quod non expugnari pecunia possit.** No fortification is such that it cannot be vanquished by money. 再坚强的堡垒也敌不过金钱之侵蚀。
* **Nihil tam proprium imperio quam legebus vivre.** Nothing is so becoming to authority as to live according to the law. 没有什么比依法生活更为高尚的了。
* **Nihil tam proprium est imperio quam legebus vivere. / Nihil tam proprium imperio quam legibus virere.** Nothing is so much the property of sovereignty as to live according to the laws./Nothing is so characteristic of the royal power as the fact that it is exercised in accordance with the laws./Nothing is so becoming to authority as to live according to law. 依法而治乃政府最重要之举。
nihilism n. 虚无主义;恐怖手段;(大写)(19世纪后期俄国的)民粹主义
nil n. 无,零,(什么都)没有
nil admirari 没有什么东西能使之惊奇的,漠然的
* **Nil (或 Nihil) consensui tam contrarium est quam vis atque metus.** There is nothing so opposed to consent as force and fear (coercion and threat)./Nothing is so opposite to consent as force and fear. 决不能以胁迫和威逼使人同意。
nil debet 否认债务的抗辩
nill v. 不愿意,拒绝
* **Nimia subtilitas in jure reprobatur, et talis certitudo certitudinem confundit.** Too great subtlety is disapproved of in law, and such confounds certainty. 法律不宜过于细微,否则会使确定的事产生混淆。
Nimia certitudo certitudinem ipsam destru-

it. Too great certainty destroys certainty itself. 过分确定反有损其确定性;极度确定反有损其确定性。
Nine Old Men 《九个老头》[指由于联邦最高法院反对用"新政"(New Deal)应对大萧条时期经济危机,许多人批评大法官以偏见代替说理。罗斯福(Franklin D. Roosevelt)总统支持这一看法并对联邦最高法院年迈大法官提出"重组计划"(Court-Packing Plan)。由记者皮尔逊(Drew Pearson)和艾伦(Robert Allen)所著的《九个老头》,即为一本批评性著作]
nine-squares system (中史)井田制度
Nineteenth Amendment 美国联邦宪法第十九修正案(该修正案于1919年6月4日由国会提出,1920年8月26日批准公布,生效。1878年后赋予妇女选举权的支持者,涉及给予妇女的选举权,即合众国公民的选举权不得因性别缘故被合众国或任何一州加以否认或剥夺。该修正案是为争取妇女选举权而长期努力的产物。直至1838年,美国尚无一个州在任一选举中允许妇女有选举权。但在同年,肯特基州允许妇女在学校选举中享有选举权)
Ninth Amendment 美国联邦宪法第九修正案(指宪法中列举的某些权利不得被解释为否认或轻视人民拥有的其他权利。这一规定也意味着一种权利,即使未在联邦宪法中列明,也应受到司法保护)
Ninth Decennial Part I (美)《第九个十年判决摘要汇编》(第1部分)(指由西方出版公司出版的自1976年至1981年的判决摘要汇编,第1部分)
NIPLECC (美)"全国知识产权协调委员会"(指1999年国会通过立法,宣布成立。作为贸易代表办公室、司法部、海关、商务部、专利商标局等部门之协调机构。根据2000年《财政及政府总拨款法》成立该委员会,其职责是在联邦和驻外机构之间协调国内国际知识产权执法,并就各部门协调情况向总统及参众两院的拨款和司法委员会提交年度报告)
nisi (=unless) 除非;不然则,为最后的,非绝对的(见 decree *nisi*)
nisi prius 初审,事实审

nisi prius court 初审法庭(指区别于上诉审、由陪审员和一位法官所组成进行事实审的法庭)
nisi prius trial 初审法庭的审判,事实审的审判
nitty-gritty n. 事实的真相,本质
nix n. 无,无物;无法投递的邮件
no accusation, no trial 不告不理(见 no trial without complaint)
no aggregation 不累计规则(美国集团诉讼中有要求达到诉讼标的额,是否可累计到多种纠纷的诉讼标的额,由联邦最高法院判定,对每一集团成员必须拥有能满足纠纷标的额的请求,而不累计规则对标的额一定抑制作用)
no arrival, no sale 无(货物)抵达即无买卖(指买卖合同中的条款)
no bill 无依据(或证据不足)的诉状
no case 不构成案件
no case to answer 无须答辩
no comment letter 无异议函
no confidence vote 不信任(投)票
no consequence 无足轻重
no consideration 无偿;(英美法)无对价
no contest 见 *nolo contendere*
no cure, no pay 无效果,无报酬
no defence 不能用的辩护
* **No deputy to the National People's congress may be arrested or placed on criminal trial without the consent of the Presidium of the current session of the National People's Congress or, when the National People's Congress is not in session, without the consent of its Standing Committee.** (中)全国人民代表大会代表非经全国人民代表大会会议主席团许可,在全国人民代表大会闭会期间非经全国人民代表大会常务委员会许可,不受逮捕或者刑事审判。
no double taxation 税不重征,免征双重税
no effects 无存款;无财产;无效
no entry 不准入内,不准驶入
no generalization or law remains final 概念和法律都不是永恒的
no go 不行,失败

no jail time sentence 不监禁的判决
* **No law or administrative or local rules and regulations shall contravene the Constitution.** （中）一切法律、行政法规和地方性法规都不得同宪法相抵触。
no lawyer（或 **poor lawyer**） 不懂法律的人,法盲
no legislative basis 无法律根据
no less favorable than 不低于……的待遇
no margin allowed 金额需全数收取
* **No one should be judged without a hearing.** （当事人有陈述和被倾听的权利）任何人未经听证不得受到判决
* **No organization or individual may enjoy the privilege of being above the constitution and the law.** （中）任何组织或者个人都不得有超越宪法和法律的特权。
no par share 无面值股票
* **No person and no act is beyond law.** 任何人和任何行为不得超过法律
no person shall 一个人不得,没有人应,任何人不得
* **No person should be twice vexed by the same claim.** 同一请求不得两次无根据缠诉。
no record 无案可查
* **No rights pass without physical delivery.** 无实物交付便无权利转移（原则）。
no taxation without representation 无代表则无税（以经典性表述揭示税收法定主义的基本含义）
no thoroughfare 不准通行
no trial without complaint 1.不告不理（原则）2.告诉乃论,亲告罪
no waiting 不准停车等候
no-action letters （美）(1959年)不起诉意见书[指政府机构工作人员所提交的函件,说明如果当事人为了请求该机构就某事项作出的裁决而提供的事实与实际情况相符,该工作人员建议政府机构不对当事人提起诉讼。传统地说,这个不起诉函意见书是来自证券交易委员会(SEC)就一些事项进行诸如持股人申请、建议、股票再售出以及市场销售技巧的这类有关问题,提起的请求］

no-claim n. 无请求权
no-donor-controlled foundations 非捐赠者控制基金会
no-evidence n. 无证据
no-fault n. （美）不追究责任的事(1.汽车保险术语,指肇事事故中的受伤者由他的保险公司负责赔偿损失及费用,不管此意外是否系他的过失 2.一种离婚法则,指男女双方皆不需负婚姻破裂的责任)
no-fault divorce 无过错离婚[指对于这种离婚,当事双方除表明不可挽回的婚姻破裂和不可调和的裂痕之外无须证明任何一方有无过错或理由。在20世纪的美国,这种离婚风行全境。1974年,有45个州采纳了无过错离婚,1985除纽约州采用某种方式的离婚,即离婚错误理由的最后堡垒就是在一年法定分居(legal separation)或法定分居协议(legal separation agreement)之后,进行有条件的离婚(conversion divorce)外,每州均采纳无过错离婚]
no-fault insurance 不追究责任的保险（见 no-fault）
no-fault liability 无过失责任
no-fault medical liability 无过错医疗责任
no-fault system of motor vehicle insurance 不追究责任的机动车辆责任保险
no-go a. 1.不宜开展的;不宜通过的 2.(英)治外法权的;只准特许人士进入的
no-go area 禁区
no-good a. 无价值的,无用的,无希望的
No-Hard-Feelings Divorce Law （见 Do-It-Yourself Divorce Law）
no-harm rule "禁止损害"规则(指跨国损害方面,最为核心的习惯国际法规则莫过于"禁止损害"规则,即一国境内或一国管辖、控制下的活动不得对他国造成损害）
no-industrial building 非工业用建筑物
no-justice, non system 不公正,而无系统（指有些美国学者批评美国的刑事司法系统用语）
no-knock n./a. 破门而入的强行搜捕/(搜查,逮捕等)强行闯入进行的
no-knock search 强行搜查(指警察进家前不经敲门并宣告他们的到来和到来目的——搜查财产。强行搜查证只能根据

有限的情况签发,比如事先宣告会导致要搜查的标的物的灭失,或者警察和他人的安全会因此陷入危险处境)

no-lockout clause 不关闭工厂条款

*** Nolumus leges Angliae mutari.** We decline to have the laws of English changed. 没有人能改变英国的法律。(指普通法被嵌入了其自身的技术、实践和制度,并已创制了自己的框架,产生了一种技术性很强、具有相当复杂性和精确性的术语,能持续许多世纪从而构成对罗马法影响的一道屏障,足以满足当时社会需求。见 statute of Merton)

no-man's-land n. 无主土地;所有权争议未决的土地;荒地

no-par a. 无票面价值的

no-par stock 无票面价值的股份

no-right n. 无权利

no-show n. 1.订了飞机(或火车,轮船)票不来取票的人 2.不到场的人;未露面者

no-value stock 无票面价值的股份

No. 1 Veto man 头号反对派,专投反对票的人

Noahide Laws 《诺亚律法》(指犹太教法典中七条出自《圣经》的法律)

nobble v. 1.(英)捉住;逮住(罪犯) 2.偷;诈骗

nobility n. 贵族(阶层);高位;高贵

noble n./a. 贵族;(美俚)雇来破坏罢工的工贼头子/高尚的,崇高的

nobody n. 无身份;小人物,无足轻重的人;没有人

nocent a. 有害的;(古)有罪的

noise n. 声音;高声;噪音

noise abatement 噪声消除

noise pollution 噪声污染

nol pros 见 *nolle prosequi*

nolens volens 不论是否同意;不论愿意与否

noli me tangere 禁止接触(或干涉)的警告

nolle prosequi 撤回诉讼;不予起诉(尤指检察机关所作的决定,常用于民事中的原告,特别是刑事中的检察官在诉状中正式记载:不予起诉,简写为"nol pros",以示撤回诉讼的一种形式)

nolo contendere 被告不抗辩之声明,被告不申辩(指刑事被告对诉讼书,可作不争执之声明,但不承认有罪,法官据此作判决,但须注意变相之认罪,其效力仅限于公诉之范围)

nol-pros v. (美)(原告)撤回起诉;(原告同意)中止诉讼(见 *nolle prosequi*)

nom de plume 笔名

nomad group 游牧部落

nomadism n. 游动生活(指不总是在同一地区生活而是周期性定期迁移的生活方式)

*** Nome punitun pro alino delicto.** 任何人不因他人不法行为而受处罚。

nomen juris 法律名称,法定名称

*** Nomen non sufficit si res non sit de jure aut de facto.** The name is not sufficient if the thing be not by law or by fact./A name does not suffice if the thing does not exist by law or by fact. 如果一个事物在法律上和事实上都不存在,那么仅有名称是不够的。

nomen transcripticium 债权誊账

nomenclature n. 名称,术语

nominal a. 名义上的,挂名的;有名无实的;票面的;名称上的;记名的;按计划进行的

nominal account 名义账目;虚账

nominal amount 面额

nominal and virtual 名义与实际(名义意味着没有把通货膨胀考虑在内进行调整;实际意味着通货膨胀被考虑在内。经济学家在描述国内生产总值时往往使用后者)

nominal capital 名义资本

nominal damages (法院或陪审团指明被告过失而给予原告)名义上的损害赔偿,象征性的损害赔偿

nominal defence 指名的抗辩

nominal defendant 名义上的被告

nominal defendant procedure 名义被告程序(某些机动车辆保险制度规定,遇到肇事司机逃跑或未保险车辆时,受害人可采取这一程序请求从储备基金中取得赔偿)

nominal director 挂名董事,挂名主任

nominal expulsion 名义上的开除

nominal fine 轻微的罚金
nominal list of the personnel 人员名单
nominal par 名义票面价格
nominal partner 名义合伙人,挂名合伙人
nominal party 名义上的当事人(指根据辩护的专门规定,需要在记录中作为当事人或被告出庭的人)
nominal plaintiff 名义上的原告
nominal price 名义价格,虚价
nominal profit 薄利
nominal punishment 象征性处罚
nominal quotation 名义牌价;虚牌价(港译:名义挂牌)
nominal rate 名义汇价,名义汇率
nominal share capital 额定股份资本,名义股份资本
nominal shipper 名义托运人
nominal sovereignty 有名无实的主权
nominal sum 微小数额
nominal total value of the company 公司的名义财产总值
nominal value (股票等的)票面价值
nominal wage 名义工资,货币工资
nominate v./a. 提名……为候选人;指定;推荐;任命;命名/有名的;命名的;具名的;名义上的;微不足道的(数额);按计划进行的
nominate obligation 具名的义务,有名之债
nominate right 有名的权利,具名的权利
nominate theory of contract 指名合同(契约)说
nominated contract 指名合同(契约),具名合同(契约)(或译:有名合同)
nominated member 被提名者;被任命的人员;(议会)指定议员
nominating ballot 提名投票
Nominating Committee 提名委员会
nomination n. 提名(为候选人);任命;提名权;任命权;指定;推荐
nomination procedures 任命程序;提名程序
nominative certificate 记名证券
nominative member 任命的成员;任命的议员
nominative reporters 命名的判例(发布人)汇编

Nominative Reports (美)冠有名字的判例汇编(即将法院的判例汇编冠以记录整理者或编辑者的姓名。英国最早有名的判例汇编者可能是詹姆斯·戴尔。他整理的判例汇编大约在1550年出版,包括直到1537年的判例)
nominator n. 提名者;任命者
nominee n. 被提名的候选人;被任命者
nominee buyer 指定买主
nominis delatio 正式检举(罗马法中,非经这一程序,长官不得依职权启动审判,也不得置任何人于被告之地位)
nomocracy n. 根据法律成立的政府
nomography n. 法律制定论
nomological a. 法律学的
nomology n. 法律学
nomos (古希腊哲学中的)惯例(在法国指经人们一致同意而形成的)
nomothetic(al) a. 立法的;法律的;根据法律的
* *Non alio modo puniatur aliquis quam secundum quod se habet condemnatio.* A person may not be punished differently than according to what the sentence enjoins. 任何人除根据判决所施加的惩罚外不应再受其他的惩罚
non assumpsit 提出未承诺或否认有合同(契约)上的义务的答辩
* *Non bis in idem.* Not twice for the same. 同一罪行不受两次审判(一事不二罚;禁止双重处罚原则;一事不再理)。
* *Non capitur qui jus publicum sequitur.* To insist upon a rule of a public law is not to overreach. 坚持公法规则并非超越。
non cepit 无扣留动产答辩(指收回非法扣留诉讼中被告人作没有扣留如原告人所说的东西的答辩)
non commodity-based form 非产品形式
non compos mentis 精神不健全,精神失常
non consentit qui errat 陷于错误者,不为同意(指因对合同标的有误解而订立合同的当事人不能被视为已同意订立合同)
non constat 不显明,非顺理成章,不够明白,欠明确,尚不明确,难以断言
* *Non culpa nisi men sit rea.* There is no

guilt unless there be a guilty intention. 除非有犯罪意图否则无罪。

non culpabilis 无罪

* ***Non debet actori licere quod reo non permittitur.*** A plaintiff ought not to be allowed what is not permitted to a defendant. 不允许被告者也不得允许原告(民法的一项原则)。

* ***Non decipitur qui scit se decipi.*** He is not deceived who knows himself to be deceived. 明知受骗者不属受骗。

non detinet 未拘留,未扣留

non est factum 否认订立合同(契约)的答辩

non est inventus (被告)所在不明,未查获(司法行政官在辖区内未查获被告时用此术语回复)

* ***Non est regula quin fallet.*** There is no rule but what may fail. 任何规则不可能没有不足之处。

non facere 不作为之债

* ***Non facias malum ut inde veniat bonum.*** You are not to do evil (so) that good may come from it. 做恶事不要期望有好结果,或不应为追求好的结果而做恶事。

non faciendo 不作为

non hearsay 非传闻

non jure factum not made by law 非法律所为

non juridicus 不合法,不依法律的

non jurisdiction 非管辖权,非司法管辖权

non lapse statute 见 antilapse statute

non licet 不准许的;不合法的

non liquet 责任不明确;案情不清(指在罗马法院中,任何一个法官经过审理裁决时,认为案情不清可用此术语表示自己的意见进行裁决)

non litigation 非诉讼

non obstante 否定裁决;不赞成;不核准;虽然;纵使(有法律之规定)(＝notwithstanding)

non obstante veredicto 但是裁决,否定裁决,相反的裁决

Non omne quod licet honestum est. Not everything which the law allows is honorable./Not everything that is allowable is morally right. 合法的并非都是体面的,合法的并不一定是符合道德的权利。

non performing loan 不良贷款

* ***Non pertinet ad judicem secularem cognoscere de iis quae sunt mere spiritualia annexa.*** It belongs not to the secular judge to take cognizance of things which are merely spiritual. 纯粹宗教上的事情不由世俗法院法官管辖。

non placet 不批准,否决票,不赞成票(见 placet)

* ***Non possessori incumbit necessitas probandi possessiones ad se pertinere.*** A person in possession is not bound to prove that the possessions belong to him. 占有者无须证明自己为物主。

non possumus 1. 我们不能 2. 我们无权(指对某事不能考虑或不能采取行动的一种表示)

non prosequitur (或 **non pros**) 不(及时继续)追诉(指原告未能按法定程序及时采取适当行动,参加诉讼,此时被告可要求法院作出不追诉判决,撤销诉讼)

* ***Non quod dictum, sed quod factum est***, (in jure) inspicitur. Not what has been said but what has been done is regarded./Not what is said but what is done is regarded in law. 在法律应考虑所做的而不是所说的,也即在法律上应观其行而非闻其言。

non random sample of filed cases 被审案件的非随机抽样

* ***Non refert quid notum sit judici, si notum non sit in forma judici.*** It matters not what is known to the judge, if it is not known in judicial form, i. e. if he has not judicial cognizance of it. 如果法官不是在司法上知道某事,那么他知道什么也无关紧要。

non securities markets 非证券市场

non sequitur 不根据前提的推理,不合理的推论(指结论不合逻辑)

Non sibi , sed toti 不是为己而是为公(not for himself, but for the whole community)

* ***Non solent quae abundant vitiare scripturas.***

Superfluities do not vitiate a written instrument. 冗词赘语不会影响书面文本的效力。
non sui juris 无法律行为能力
* *Non temere credere est nervus sapientiae.*
Not to believe rashly is the nerve of wisdom. 不轻信为智慧之枢。
non valentia agere 无诉讼能力
* *Non verbis sed ipsis rebus, leges imponimus.* 不是针对言词而是针对事实本身实施法律。
* *Non videntur qui errant consentire.*
Those who are mistaken are not deemed to consent. 错误同意者不应视作同意。
non vult contendere 被告不抗辩(刑法用语)
non-abuse of right 权利不得滥用
non-acceptance n. 不接受(履行);拒绝承兑
non-access n. 无接触(指丈夫与妻子于某一段特定时间内不可能发生性关系情况);合法同居的不可能性;(夫妇)不能性交
non-active partner 不参加业务经营的合伙人
non-admission n. 不接纳,不准加入
non-age (或 **nonage**) n. 未到法定年龄;未成年,青春期,未成熟
non-aggression n. 不侵犯,不侵略
non-aggression treaty 互不侵犯条约
non-agricultural individual laborers 非农业个体劳动者
non-agricultural population 非农业人口
non-aligned countries (或 **nations**) 不结盟国家
non-alignment n. 不结盟
non-alignment policy 不结盟政策
non-antagonistic a. 非对抗性的
non-antagonistic contradictions 非对抗性矛盾
non-apparently infirm person 不明显的心神丧失者
non-arrestable offence 不受逮捕的犯罪;不构成逮捕的罪行
non-assignable a. 不可转让的,不可让与的,不可移转的

non-assignable duty 不可转让的义务
non-attendance n. 缺席,不到场(庭)
non-attesting witnesses 非见证人
non-autocrative government 非专制政府,非独裁政体
non-bailable a. 不得被保释的
non-belligerent a./n. 非交战的/非交战国;非交战状态
non-binding arbitration 无拘束力仲裁(此方法由仲裁员作出决定,是否执行仲裁员的决定,则依靠当事人的信用,且该决定不能向法院申请强制执行。见 ADR)
non-business day 非营业日
non-business expenditure 营业外支出
non-capital murder (加拿大)不判死刑(只判无期徒刑)的谋杀罪
non-carrier MTO 非承运人的联运人
non-claim (在规定期间内)未提出要求
non-cohabitation order (夫妇)不同居令
non-combatant (或 **noncombatant**) n.
1.非战斗人员(如军医);(战争期间的)平民 2.非交战方
non-commercial activity 非经营性活动,非商业活动
non-commercial agreement 非商业协定,非商业性协议
non-commercial enterprise 非商业性企业
non-commercial group 非商业团体
non-commissioned a. 无委任状的,未受任命的;未委托的;未授军官衔的
non-committal a. 不置可否的,不明确表示意见的,含糊的;不承担义务的
non-complying judge 不遵照办理的法官
non-compulsory heir 非强制性继承人,非特留份继承人
non-concession alien 无特许权的外国人
non-conclusory factual allegations 非推断性的事实主张
non-confidence motion 不信任案,不信任动议
non-confidence voting 不信任投票
non-conformity n. 和规则等不适合,不一致(with, to);非国教徒
non-consensual a. 非经双方同意的
non-consenting nonresident 不同意的非本

州居民
non-consenting nonresident defendant 非同意非居民被告,不同意非居民被告,不被同意为非本州居民被告(实际是非本州居民被告不同意)
non-consumer sale 非(向)消费者(的)销售
non-content (或 **noncontent**) n. (英)(在上议院)投反对票者
non-contentious a. 非讼的;非争论性的
non-contentious business 无争执之事件;非讼事(案)件
non-contentious jurisdiction act 非讼事(案)件管辖法
non-contentious law 非讼事(案)件法
non-contentious matter 非讼事(案)件
non-contentious probate business 非讼的遗嘱认证事务
non-contentious proceedings 非讼(事件)程序
non-contraband n. 非违禁品
non-contraband goods 非禁制品货物,非违禁货物,非禁运货物
non-contractual a. 非合同(契约)的
non-contractual claims 非合同(契约)的索赔,非合同(契约)的请求权
non-contractual liability 非合同(契约)性责任
non-contractual obligation 非合同(契约)上的责任(或义务),非合同(契约)之债
non-convertible currency 不可兑换的货币
non-cooperative game theory 非合作博弈论
non-criminal charge 非刑事指控
non-criminalizing n. 非犯罪化(指将曾经作为犯罪认定的行为不再作为犯罪对待)
non-cumulative preferred stock 非累积优先股
non-current assets 非流动资产
non-custodial measures 非监禁措施(见 non-custodial penalty)
non-custodial parent 非抚养父亲(或母亲)(指在离婚诉讼中不承担抚养未成年子女的一方)
non-custodial penalty 非监禁刑
non-custodial sanction 非监禁制裁
non-delivery (或 **nondelivery**) n. 未交付;无法投递;不引渡;未送达
non-departmental function 非部门性的职能
non-deterrence function 无威慑力量功能
non-direction n. 未指导(尤指法官对陪审团作指示时遗漏了对陪审团作必要的法律要点的指导)
non-dischargeable debt 不可撤销的债务,必须履行清偿之债,不可免除的债务(指不可通过破产程序免除的债务。这种债务包括纳税之债,以欺诈方式取得财产而生之债,因故意伤害而生的侵权之债,因赡养、扶养而生之债等)
non-discrimination (或 **nondiscrimination**) n. 不歧视
non-discrimination treatment 不歧视待遇,无差别的待遇
non-discriminatory a. 无差别待遇的,无不公平待遇的,不歧视的
non-discriminatory administration of quantitative restrictions 非歧视地实施数量限制
non-dumped import price method 非倾销进口价格法(指非损害价格根据国内产品的价格计算。此方法通常在非倾销进口产品占据市场重大份额以致对市场价格具有重大影响时采用。在此情况下,通过对倾销进口产品征收反倾销税,使之达到非倾销进口产品的价格,非倾销进口产品将与倾销进口产品竞争,倾销进口产品的损害性影响将消失。)
non-employed persons 无业人员
non-employment n. 非就业性;无职业;未雇用
non-entitled party 非所有权人,非权利人
non-essential a. 不需要的;非本质的;不重要的
non-essential stipulation 非主要条款,非主要规定
non-essential term 非主要条款,非基本条款
non-examination system 不实行审查的制度
non-exclusive jurisdiction 非专属管辖权
non-execution n. 不执行
non-executive directors 非执行董事,非常务董事

non-exempt property （破产时的）非除外财产
non-exercise of entitlements 不行使应享权利
non-existent marriage 不存在的婚姻
non-fatal firearm injuries 非致命枪伤
non-fatal robberies 无致命抢劫（案）
non-fault condition 无过失情形
Non-Ferrous Metals Corporation 有色金属公司
non-financial commodity 非金融商品
non-financial matter 非财政性事项
non-flagrant delict 非现行犯罪
non-flagrant delictor 非现行犯
non-forcible felony 非暴力重罪（见 forcible felony）
non-free tenure （英）不完全自由的土地保有制
non-fulfillment n. 不履行,不执行
non-full sovereign state 非完全主权国
non-fundamental breach 非重大违约
non-fungible thing 不可代替物
non-government agency 非政府机构
non-gratuitous act 有偿行为
non-gratuitous transaction 非无偿法律行为,有偿法律行为
non-holographic wills 非自书的遗嘱（指不是亲笔书写的遗嘱）
non-hostile relation 非敌对关系
non-indictable a. 不起诉的
non-indictable offenses 不予起诉的轻罪
non-individual interest 非个人利益
non-institutional treatment 非机构性处理（见 non-custodial penalty）
non-intercourse n. 不通商（指国际间停止贸易往来,相当于 embargo）;夫妻间断绝性行为
non-interest bearing note 无息票据
non-interference n. 不干预;不干涉
non-interference in each other's internal affairs 互不干涉内政
non-intervention n. （国际间的）不干涉（内政）;不干预
non-intervention will 不干预（的）遗嘱（有时应用于遗嘱的一个术语,意思是授权给遗嘱执行人处理和分配不动产,不要法庭干预）
non-issuable a. 非辩护的;非争议的
non-issuable plea 无须置答的抗辩,无系争点的答辩
non-judicial day 非开庭日
non-judicial discretion 非司法化的自由裁量权
non-judicial divorce 非司法性离婚
non-judicial matters 非司法性案件
non-judicial oath 非司法上的宣誓（见 judicial oath）
non-judicial punishment （军事法）非法性惩处,非司法性惩处[指由指挥官对于必须统一遵循《统一军法典》(Uniform Code of Military Justice)的轻刑犯 (minor offender) 实施惩罚的一项程序。在海军和海岸警卫队中,非司法性惩处 (nonjudicial punishment) 亦称 captain's mast;在海事部队或海事团体 (marine corps) 内,它被称为 office hours;在陆军和空军中,它则涉及第 15 条,即非司法性惩罚不在法庭（court martial）处理]
non-jurisdictional fact 非管辖权事实
non-juror （=nonjuror）n. （英）不宣誓者,拒绝宣誓者
non-jury a. 不要陪审团的
non-jury cases 无陪审团审理的案件
non-justiciable （= nonjusticiable）a. 不可裁判的（尤指国际争端）
non-justiciable dispute 不应由法院裁决的争端（纠纷）
non-justiciability n. 不可裁判性
non-legal a. 与法律无关的
non-legal duty 非法律上的义务;非法定义务,非法定职责
non-lethal weapons 非致命武器（包含反人员武器和反装备武器两种）
non-lieu （根据不足或无根据而）不予诉;无足够理由起诉
non-literal infringement 非字面侵害
non-litigated case 非讼事（案）件
non-litigation service 非诉讼服务
non-litigious procedure 非诉讼程序
non-market dichotomies 非市场二分法学
non-market economy country 非市场经济

国家
non-Marxists n. 非马克思主义者
non-material term 非实质性条款
non-member state 非成员国
non-military a. 非军事的
non-military objective 非军事目标
non-military personnel 文职人员,非军事人员
non-molestation clause (分居期间)互不妨害条款
non-monopoly n./a. 非垄断(的),非独占(的)
non-moving party 非提出申请的当事人
non-national crime 非国事犯
non-native species legislation 外来物种立法,非本土物种立法
non-navigable river 不可通航的河流
non-negotiable a. 不可磋商的,不可谈判的,无商量余地的;不可转让的,不可流通的
non-negotiable bill 不可转让的票据,非流通票据
non-negotiable bill of lading 不可转让的提单,非流通提单
non-negotiable claim 不可转让的请求权
non-negotiable property 不融通物
non-negotiable receipt 不可流通的收据,不可转让的收据
non-notoriously insane person 非众所周知的精神病患者
non-nuclear n. 非核国家(指只拥有常规武器的国家)
non-objection procedure 无异议程序
non-obligatory act 非债权行为;非责任行为
non-obliviousness n. 非显而易知性
non-observance n. 不遵守,违反
non-operating company 非自营公司
non-owning possessor 无权占有人
non-participating a. 无分红权的;不参加的
non-participating preference share 非参加分红的优先股
non-participation n. 无分红权;不参加
non-participation stock 无分红权股份
non-party intervention 非当事国形式的参加(或干预)(见 party intervention)

non-party state 非缔约国,非当事国
non-patrial n. 无居住权的人(见 pa-trial);移居受到限制的人
non-payment n. 不支付,拒绝支付,无力支付
non-pecuniary loss 非金钱损失
non-pensionable supplements 不计抚恤金的补助(金)
non-performance (或 **nonperformance**) n. 不履行,不践约,不清偿,不给付,不完成;违约行为
non-performance of duty 不履行义务(责任)
non-performance of obligation 债的不履行,不履行义务
non-performing loans 无赢利效力贷款
non-physical a. 非实体的,无形的
non-physical assets 非实物资产
non-physical loss 无形损失
non-political condition of mankind 非政治化的人类状态
non-political treaty 非政治性条约
non-possessor n. 非占有人,非所有者
non-possessory security interest 非占有的担保权益
non-prescritive nature 无时效性质
non-production n. 未出示(证据等)
non-productive a. 非生产的,与生产无直接关系的
non-productive personnel 非生产人员
non-professional a. 非专业性的,与专门工作无关系的;无职业的
nonprofit a. 非营利的;无利可图的
non-profit corporation 非营利公司
non-profit-making organization 非营利性组织(或 non-profit organization, non-profit association, non-profit corporation)
non-profit enterprise 非营利性企业
non-profit-making organization 非营利组织
non-proliferation n. 不扩散,防(止)扩散(尤指防止核扩散)
Non-Proliferation of Nuclear Weapons 《核武器不扩散条约》(1968年)
non-prosecution (或 **nonprosecution**) n. 不予起诉(指检察机关或检察官员对于没有犯罪或依法不予追究刑事责任的人所

作出的决定)
non-prosecution order 不予提起公诉的决(裁)定
non-protestable bill 无追索权的汇票
non-qualified stock option 不合格的股票期权,无附加条件股票期权;非法定股票期权(见 stock option 和 incentive stock option)
non-random sample 非随机抽样
non-realized assets 未变卖资产
non-reciprocal agreements 非互惠协议
non-reciprocal reinsurance 单方面无互惠业务分保
non-recognition n. 不承认;否认
non-recorded vote 无记录表决
non-recurrent cost 临时费用
non-recurring gain 偶生盈利
non-recurring gain and loss 临时损益,非经常损益
non-renewable resources 不可再生资源
non-renewal n. 不更换
non-resident n. 非本地居民,非本地居住的人
non-resident alien 过境侨民(外国人)
non-resource-dependent development 非依赖天然资源选择(开发)
non-responding party 不应答的当事人
non-restricted preference 无限制优惠
non-retroactivity ratione personae 对人不溯及既往
non-retrospection n. 不溯及既往
non-retrospective a. 不追溯的,不溯及既往的
non-reviewable discretion 不受审查的自由裁量权
non-sane memory 不健全的记忆力
non-screem time 无屏幕时间
non-self-executing treaties 非自动执行条约(指除非美国国会对其制定了转化实施的立法,否则在美国法院中不得被直接援引的条约。见 self-executing treaty)
non-self-governing territories 非自治领
non-sequitur n. 不根据前提的推理
non-service invention and creation 非职务发明创造

non-sovereign act 非主权行为
non-standard condition 非标准条件
non-state entity 非国家实体
non-statutory law 非制定法,不成文法
non-statutory legal materials 不成文法律,非成文的法律资料
non-stop a. 直达的
non-storability n. 不可存储性
non-sub transactions 非买卖的交易
non-sudden accidental occurrence 非突发事故性事件(如渗漏和地下水的渐进性污染)
non-support n. 不按规定负担抚养费,不(认真)履行抚养义务,不尽赡养义务
non-suspendable innocent passage 不得停止无害通过
non-tariff barrier 非关税壁垒
non-tenure n. 否认占有(指被告提出并未占有原告声称的全部或部分土地的答辩)
non-term n. (法院)不开庭(假)期
non-testifying experts 不出庭作证的专家
non-testimonial evidence 证言以外的证据
non-time-critical 非时间紧迫性
non-trader n. 非商人
non-transferable a. 不可转让的
non-trivial question 重要的问题
non-union employee 非工会会员的员工(劳工)
non-vanishing party 非消失性当事方
non-verifiable information 不可核实的信息
non-violation complaint 不以违法为诉由,非违法之诉
non-visible property 无形财产
non-voting a. 不投票的;无投票权的,无表决权的;弃权的
non-voting equity share 无投票权股份
non-war armed conflict 非(战争)武装冲突
nonadverse party 非对方当事人
nonappealable a. 不能上诉的
nonappealable judg(e)ment 终审判决(又译:不能上诉的判决)
nonappearance (或 **non-appearance**) n. 不出庭;不出席
nonappearance certificate 不出庭证书
nonassessable a. (股份的)(除投资额外)

nonbinding clause 非约束性条款
noncapital felonies 不判死刑的重刑罪
noncausal juristic act 不要因的法律行为
noncausal relationship 无因果关系;非因果关系
Noncode state (1926年)(历史上)普通法州(指在一定的时间段,这个州未曾在程序上将普通法与衡平法合并。所以,衡平法仍以单独的体制实施。这个词早在20世纪中期就已流行。亦称 common-law state。见 code state)
noncoercive form of administrative action 非强制性行政行为
noncommunity property 非夫妻双方共同财产,(夫妻一方的)个人财产(见 community property)
noncompletion n. 不履行(合同等)
noncompliance n. 不承诺,不顺从,不让步
nonconfinement n. 不关押
nonconforming a. 不符合的,不遵从的,不适合的
nonconforming goods 不符合合同(契约)规格要求的货物
nonconforming lot (美)不适合的小块土地(指城市区划法所不允许的大小、形状和位置的小块土地)
nonconforming use 违反规范的使用(指根据规划法规在此地区不允许使用这种类型土地,但因在规划法规制定之前或因情况变化而允准的这类土地的使用)
nonconformity 不墨守成规的行为,非墨守成规的行为
noncontestability clause (= incontestability clause) 不容争议性条款(指人寿保险单规定,保险单经过一段时间,一般为二至五年的实施之后,承保人不得再对申请中所作的陈述提出异议的条款)
noncontestable clause 无争议条款;不可抗辩条款(= incontestable clause)
noncorporal punishment 非体罚
noncrime n. 非罪
noncriminal a. 非(犯)罪的
nondeadly force 非致命暴力,非致命力量
nondestructive a. 无破坏性的;无害的

nondisclosure (= non-disclosure) n. 不披露;单纯沉默;不泄露;不揭发;不告知
nondiscretionary a. 无酌处权的,无裁量权的
nondiscretionary appellate jurisdiction 无酌处权的受审上诉管辖
nondispositive matters (美)非处置性事项(指诉讼中不起全部或部分决定作用的事件。见 dispositive matters)
nondistribution constraint 非分配约束
nondiverse party 州籍相同当事人;非异籍当事人
nondollar a. 非美元的;非美元地区的(指不以美元为兑换基础者)
nondomiciliary a. 无住所地的
noneffective a. 无效力的,不起作用的;无战斗力的
nonetheless 仍然
nonextradition n. 不引渡
nonextradition of own nationals 本国国民不引渡
nonextradition of political criminal 政治犯不引渡
nonfeasance n. 失职,未履行,未履行责任[指一个人不论是否出于故意、无知、疏忽或其他主观原因,无正当理由根本不履行法律规定的职责或合同要求的义务。常指政府官员、代理人、雇员怠于或疏于履行职责或义务。注意"未履行"不同于失职行为或不当行为(misfeasance)和不法行为、违法行为(malfeasance),前者是指以不适当的方式履行职责或义务;后者则指一个人做出根本不应做的行为]
nonfeasant a. 失职的,未履行的
nonfeasor a. 未履行的人,失职者
nonhabitual offender 偶犯,非惯犯
nonimmigrant n. 非移民入境的外国人;出境后又回来的外国侨民
nonimportation n. 不进口,禁止进口
noninstal(l)ment a. 一次付清的,非分期付款的
noninterpretivism n. 非解释主义(见 interpretivism)
noninvolvement n. 不介入,拒绝介入
nonjoinder (或 **non-joinder**) n. 非共同诉

讼;(应参加而)未参加共同诉讼;应参加诉讼的当事人的不参与(指被告应有两人,而只对一人起诉)
nonjoinder of necessary and indispensable parties 未合并的必需和必不可少的当事人
nonlawyer n. 非律师职业者
nonmarital cohabitation 非(未)婚同居
nonmoral a. 与道德无关的
nonmovant n. 非申请人,非请求人,非请求裁决的人
nonmarital child 见 illegitimate child
nonobviousness (专利法)非显而易见性[专利(权)(patent-ability)的三要素之一。①指一项发明的质量不足以区别于发明构成当时的先前技术或现有技术(prior art),对于在相关发明的技术中拥有普通技能(ordinary skill)的人来说,这种发明的质量仍不具有显见性。②一项发明的质量必须经过证实显示其达到可以取得专利权的要求。这种非显而易见性可以用相关的现有技术证据证明,或以其他的客观证据(objective evidence)诸如商业上的成功或专业批准来证明。非显而易见性的测试或检验标准关系到检查现有技术的范围和内容,和现有技术和专利立法之间的区别,以及在技术中普通技能(ordinary skill)的水平。参见《美国注释法典》第 35 标题卷第 103 节。见 Graham factor; novelty; obviousness]
nonofficeholding a. 不任(官)职的;在野的,下台的
nonoriginalism 非原旨主义(见 originalism)
nonowner n. 非所有人
nonpartisan election 无党派选举
nonparty (nonparties) n. 非当事人;非当事人一方
nonpenetration n. 未(能)奸入(强奸罪中的术语)
nonperson n. 被认为不在的人,被认为失踪的人;(因政策等原因而)被排除在考虑之外的人
nonprincipled a. 非原则的;非道德的;与原则无关的

Nonproliferation Bureau 见 Bureau of Nonproliferation
nonpros v. 不及时继续诉追;对(原告)作缺席判决
nonpublic information 非公众信息
nonrecourse loan (美)无追索权贷款(指放款人不得收取超过担保金额以清偿贷款)
nonrefund annuity 不再归还的年金(指在年金享有权人还活着时享有被保证的支付年金,该享有人去世,此年金则不再归还给任何人。亦称 straight life annuity; pure annuity)
nonregistered foreign equities 非注册的外国股票
nonrepudiating party 非拒绝履行当事方
nonresident corporation 非居民公司
nonresident defendants 非本州居民被告
nonresident individual 非本州居民个人
nonresident nature person 非本州居住的自然人
nonresident person 非本州居民
nonresident plaintiff 非本州居民原告
nonresidential land parcels 非宅基地块
nonresident n./a. 暂居的人,不住各种地点的人/不寄宿的
nonresistance n. 不抵抗(主义)
nonrestrictive a. 非限制性的
nonsegregation n. 非种族隔离
nonskip person (1988 年)(美)(税法)非隔代人[对于隔代转让税(generation-skipping transfer tax)来说,该人不是隔代人(skip person)。见 skip person]
nonsense a. 荒谬的
nonspecialist n. 非专家,不属于专家
nonstaple article 非常用物品(指除实施某种专利方法之外无其他实质性商业性用途的"非常用物品")
nonstriker n. 不参加罢工的人
nonsuit (non-suit) 终结诉讼,驳回诉讼[①指由于程序上的无效(procedural infirmity)或缺少证据且达不到是非曲直的判决,也提不出合法的诉讼理由的情况下法官宣布诉讼终止。②原告自愿撤诉,在美国民事诉讼程序中,该词与 dismissal 同

义。驳回诉讼的判决(judgment of nonsuit)分为原告自愿的(voluntary)和原告非自愿的(involuntary)两种,前者指原告自行撤诉并同意法院作出对其不利的判决,并负担诉讼费用;后者表示由于原告经传唤不出庭或怠于诉讼程序,无充分诉讼理由或举不出证据让陪审团作出裁断等原因而由法官主动或应被告请求驳回其诉讼,终止诉讼]

nontrespassory nuisance 非侵入式滋扰
nonunanimous majority 非一致同意的多数
nonunion a. 不属于工会的,未加入工会的;反对工会的
nonuse n. 不使用;未形成习惯
nonuse of force 不使用武力
nonuser (或 **non-user**) n. 弃权;不行使权利;权利消失
nonverbal testimony 非口头证据(指照片、图画、图样、素描、地图、海图、航图或其他可帮助证人证明的描绘、描述。证人无须制造图画等,而这些必须准确被提供给证人看。见 demonstrative evidence)
nonviolence n. 不诉诸武力的主张(或政策);非暴力主义
nonviolent offender 非暴力罪犯
nonvoter n. 不投票者,弃权者;无投票权者
nonwork-caused disability 非因公致残
noodle n. 傻子,笨蛋
noose n./v. 绞索;束缚;圈套/把……处绞刑;使落入圈套
Nordic Consumer Ombudsmen (北欧)消费者监察委员
Nordic Council 北欧理事会(1952年成立)
Nordic country 北欧国家
norm n. 标准,规范;典型;限额,定额;模范
norm of court unanimity 法院全体一致的标准
norm of international law 国际法规范
norm of law 法律规范
norm of lending 贷款标准
norm of morality 道德规范
norm of the civil law 民法规范,民事法律规范
normal a. 正常的,标准的,正规的
normal civil obligation 公民正常义务
normal court 正规法院
normal distribution 正常分布
normal existence 正常生存
normal form game 标准形式博弈(亦称:战争形式博弈)
normal inter-state relations 国家间正常关系
normal law 正常人法(现代法理学上的术语,指对正常人有效的法律)
normal legal safeguards 正常法律保障
normal legislative process 正规的立法程序
normal loss 自然损耗,正常损耗
normal persons 正常人(指身心健康,有行为能力的人)
normal price 正常价格
normal residence 永久住所
normal rivalry 正常竞争
normal value 正常价值
normal working hours 正规工作时间
normative body 规范体系
normalivist style 规范主义模式(指欧美行政法学术传统的两个主要源头之一,另一为功能主义模式)
normalization n. 规范性,规范化,标准化
normalization of law 法律的规范性
Norman Law 有关正常人的法律,正常人法
normative a. 标准的,规范的,合乎规范的
normative statements 规范性陈述
normative connection 规范关系
normative criteria 准则
normative decrees 规范性法令
Normative Economics 规范经济学
normative functions (法律的)规范作用
normative jurisprudence 规范法学
normative predisposition 规范的预先安排
normative reasons 规范性理由 rule of law 之下
normative reference group 规范参照群体
normative rule of law 规范性法律规则
normative theory 规范理论
normative treaties 规范性条约
(the) Normativist style 规范主义模式(指欧美行政法学术传统的两个主要源头之一,即以 A. V. Dicey 为代表的规范主义模式,另一为以 Leon Dugout 为代表的功能主义模式)

norme fondamentale　基本规范
norme supérieure　最高规范
norms for decision　裁决规范
norms of non-law　非法律规范
Norris-La Guardian Act　（美）《诺里斯-拉·瓜迪亚法》(1932 年制定的联邦法,旨在禁止许多类型的强制令,反对罢工和禁止以受雇人不加入工会为条件的雇佣契约)
North American Free Trade Agreement　《北美自由贸易协定》(1992 年)
North Atlantic Treaty　《北大西洋公约》(1949 年 4 月 4 日签订)
North Atlantic Treaty Organization　北大西洋公约组织(也称"北大西洋联盟"或"北大西洋集团",为履行《北大西洋公约》而建立的一个组织,西欧国家主要集体防卫协议机构)
North Eastern Reporter　（美）《东北区判例汇编》(东北区包括纽约州、伊利诺伊州、印第安纳州、俄亥俄州和马萨诸塞州)
North Sea Continental Shelf Cases　北海大陆架案件
North Western Reporter　（美）《西北区判例汇编》(西北区包括北达科他州、南达科他州、内布拉斯加州、明尼苏达州、艾奥瓦州、威斯康星州和密歇根州)
Northern League　北部同盟(意大利的一个政党)
Northwest Atlantic Fishes Organization (NAFO)　西北大西洋渔业组织
Northwest Ordinance　（美）《西北法令》(由联邦大会于 1787 年 7 月 13 日颁布,该法令确立了美国领土体系的基本框架)
Norwegian law　挪威法
noscitur a sociis　文理解释(指字义应根据前后文连贯起来解释),依相关文字解释
nostrum n.　秘方;江湖医生所卖的药;(解决社会、政治等问题的)得意方案(又译：灵丹妙药,指反对者常用的一种反语);有专利权的药品
not a *scintilla* of truth　一点真实性也没有
not for sale　非卖品
not forbidden by law　法律所不禁止的
not found　见 *non est inventus*
not guilty　（自认）无罪(指被告对起诉书中全部事实的否认,并声明自己无罪的惯用语)
Not Guilty by Reason of Insanity (NGRI)　因精神障碍而无罪(指英国《1800 年精神错乱者刑事法》规定陪审团应宣布被告因精神失常不构成犯罪的内容);无刑事责任能力者(见 incompetence to stand trial)
not guilty of the crime charged　未犯有刑事指控的罪(行)
not guilty of theft but guilty of receiving　未犯有盗窃罪但犯有窝赃罪
not guilty plea　无罪答辩
not in session　休会期间
not involved with　没有致力于,与……无关
not less favorable to trade　不次(低)于受惠贸易
not misdemeano(u)r　（非轻罪的）违法行为(指具有犯罪性质的行为,但可处以罚金等)
not negotiable　不可转让的,不流通的
not negotiable cheque（或 check）　非流通支票,不可转让支票
not nominated contract　未命名合同(契约),不具名的合同(契约)(或译:无名合同)
not proven　（苏格兰）证据不足
not risk after landing　船到港后解除责任
not risk after shipment　起运后解除责任
not satisfied　未清偿的;不令人满意的
not self-induced　非自陷性的(醉酒者),非自愿的(醉酒者)
not subject to cassation appeal　不得上诉
not to be called to legal account　不受法律追究
not to be taken as an evidence　不足为证
not to constitute a crime　未构成犯罪
not to go into past misdeeds　不咎既往
not to injure another　不损害他人
not to the public　（法院）不公开审理
not tolerated by law　为法律所不容
* Not what is said, but what is done, is to be regarded.　重在行为而不在言词
not without reason　不无理由
not worth the candle　得不偿失
not worth litigating　不值得诉讼;无诉讼

价值
nota bene 注意,留心
notable a. 1.值得注意的,显著的;重要的 2.可觉察的;有相当分量的
notandum 备忘录,(拟)记录事项
notarial a. 公证的;由公证人经办的
notarial act 公证行为
notarial attestation 公证人的证词
notarial certificate 公证(证)书
notarial certification 公证证明
notarial deed 公证书
notarial document 公证文件,公证证书
notarial form 公证形式,公证手续
notarial instrument 公证文据
notarial office 公证处,公证办公室
notarial practice 公证业务
notarial procedure 公证程序
notarial procedure on inheritance 继承的公证程序
notarial supervision 公证监督
notarial verification 公证鉴证,公证认证
notarially ad. 经公证;由公证人证明
notarially certified 经公证证明的
notarially certified transaction 由公证人证明的法律行为;由公证人证明的交易
notarization n. 公证人的证实;(附在文件上的)公证书
notarize v. 公证,以公证人资格证实
notarized a. 由公证人证实的
notarized contract 经公证的合同(契约)
notarized document 经公证的文件
notary n. 公证人;公证员;公证
notary organs 公证机关
notary public (=notary) 公证人
notary public office 公证处
notary system 公证制度
notary testament 公证遗嘱
note n./v. (17世纪)1.本票[指当事一方,即本票签发人(maker)承诺支付款项给另一当事方,即提款人(payee)或持票人(bearer)的书面承诺票据。本票是双名流通票据(two-party negotiable instrument),不同于汇票(draft),它是三名流通票据(three-party negotiable instrument)。亦称 promissory note。见 draft 1]2.法律文章[指学术上短于正式论文(article)的法律文章(essay)。该文章被限制在一定的范围,说明或批评分析特定的一系列案件或法律的一般领域,而且通常是由法律专业的大学生所写,并在《法律评论》上公开出版。亦称 comment; lawnote。见 annotation]3.备忘录,会议或审判记录(目的便于以后参考),非正式记录,备忘摘要(见 memorandum)/(13世纪)1.细致观察或带有详细说明〈the defendant noted that the plaintiff seemed nervous〉(被告注意到或表明原告似乎神经质或胆怯不安)2.书面记下〈the court reporter noted the objection in the record〉(法院的判例汇编员记下对诉状中的异议)3.(古)打了个烙印,铭记〈as punishment, the criminal was no-ted〉(作为惩罚,该罪犯已被打了个烙印)
note a bill (公证人)记录拒兑汇票
note broker (股票等)有价证券经纪人
note circulation 钞票流通
note for 以……著称
note for a term 期票
note holder 持票人
note of a fine (历史上)(英国法)协议诉讼节录(指转让土地的司法程序的一个步骤,在转让文据正式誊写之前,还包括有亲笔书写的程序摘要。亦称 abstract of a fine。见 fine 1)
note of acceptance 承诺书;承兑书
note of allowance (英国法)批准通知[指诉讼当事任何一方均可向主事官(master)提交一份案件在程序和法庭记录方面存在错误的备忘录(memorandum),主事官则据此开出一份收据,它被称为批准通知,诉讼当事一方可将备忘录和批准通知一并同达给对方当事人,以此作为取得纠错令(writ of error)的依据,允准根除错误的依据]
note of approval 同意的照会
note of convocation 召开会议的函件(或通知书)
note of decisions (美)判例注释,判例说明(指注释法规卷本中刊出的讨论法规的案例参考)
note of dishono(u)r 退票通知(书)

note(s) of hand 本票,期票,手头票据(见 promissory note)
note of protest 海事报告;(公证人对汇票等的)拒付(证明)通知;(国际法)抗议照会
note on demand 即付票据
note on discounted 贴现票据,票据贴现
note payable 应付票据
note receivable 应收票据;给债权人的期票
note renewals 转期票据
note to bearer 不记名票据
note to order 记名支票
note verbale 照会(指用第三人称而未签名的外交文书,介于 note 和 aide-mémoire 之间)
notes in question 有争议的注释,对这些注释有异议(表示质疑)
noteworthy a. 值得注意的,显著的
nothing on this agreement shall be construed 本协议不得解释为
notice n. 1.声明;通知,通告(通知书);短评 2.布告,告示 3.标记,招牌;预告 4.警示;注意 5.开审通知书
notice and takedown regime (美)通知移除制度[指对于通知移除制度的法律性质,美国《数字千年版权法》中认为在互联网之前,依据美国传统理论,版权侵权分为直接侵权责任(direct liability)和第三人侵权责任(third part liability),即只要存在侵权事实,无论侵权人的主观意图如何,都需对此承担侵权责任。第三人侵权责任包括促成责任(contributory liability)和替代责任(vicarious liability),其认定要件依据相应的构成要件进行。互联网产生后,法院选择依据直接侵权的严格责任原则来认定网络服务提供者的侵权责任,其典型判例是 1993 年的弗雷那(Frena)案,即被告 BBS 网站的经营者弗雷那,其网站用户未经原告授权擅自上传了原告出版物上的图片,并将图片上配文字材料删去,代之以被告的文字、广告及地址。尽管被告辩称并未上传侵权内容,法院仍判决被告侵权,并认为:"认定构成版权侵权无需侵权之意图,主观上的故意或实际知晓并非构成侵权的一个要件,即使是无由

之错的侵权人也应对其行为承担法律责任,有无过错只是影响法院判决的法定赔偿金数额。"]
notice board 布告栏
notice day 通知日
notice in lieu of *distringas* 代替财产冻结的通知(指下达给银行或公司停止股票交换或停付股息的通知)
notice in writing 书面通知
notice of a call 催款通知
notice of abandonment 放弃(权利等)通知(书);(保险上的)委付通知(书)
notice of acceptance 承兑通知(书)
notice of action 诉讼通知(书)
notice of appeal 上诉通知(书)
notice of appearance 出庭通知(书)
notice of arrival 到货通知(书)
notice of avoidance 撤销(法律行为的)通知
notice of cancellation 撤销通知
notice of compliance with the award 愿执行仲裁裁决的通知
notice of criticism (中)通报批评
notice of defence 申辩通知(书)
notice of discontinuance 中止诉讼通知(书)
notice of dishono(u)r 拒付通知(书);拒绝承兑通知(书);退票通知(书)
notice of disposition 处理通知(书),处分通知(书)
notice of expiry 期满通知(书)
notice of hearing 听审通知(书),开审通知(书)
notice of institution of the action 起诉通知
notice of intended prosecution 预期起诉通知(书)
notice of intent 意思公告
notice of judg(e)ment 判决通知书;判决通告
notice of lawsuit 诉讼通知书
notice of loss 损失通知(书)
notice of motion 提出动议通知(书)
notice of opposition (专利的)异议申请书
notice of pendency (或 **notice of lis penders**) 案件待决通知(指向公众公告正在

审理的案件所涉及财产的产权有瑕疵的通知,通知上应由当事人或其诉讼代理人签字)

notice of proceedings 诉讼通知

notice of question 质询通知(书),提出问题的通知

notice of refusal to pay 拒付通知(书)

notice of rescission 解约通知(书)

notice of resignation 辞职通知(书)

notice of sanction 处分通知(书);制裁通告

notice of settlement 和解通知,协议通知(书)

notice of the commencement of the action 诉讼开始的通知书

notice of the conversion 对转化的通知,转化告知

Notice of the General Administration for Industry and Commerce of the People's Republic of China Concerning the Handling of Registration Matters by Resident Representative Offices of Foreign Enterprises 《中华人民共和国工商行政管理总局关于外国企业常驻代表机构办理登记事项的通告》

notice of the institution of proceedings 诉讼程序开始的通知

notice of title 产权通知

notice of transfer 过户启事,过户通知

notice of trial 开庭通知(书),开审通知(书)

notice of violation 违法通知,犯规通知

Notice Paper of Public Business (英)议会公法事务议程通知

notice period 通知期限

notice to admit 确认通知书(指要求对方承认文据或事实的通函)

notice to appear 要求被告出庭(并说明理由)的(简便)通知(或传票)

notice to plead 要求被告(在规定期限内)答辩的通知

notice to produce 要求出示文据(或提供证据)的通知

notice to produce for inspection 要求出示文据以便审查的通知

notice to quit (领主给佃户的或佃户给领主)退佃通知

notice to treat 强制征用(收回)土地的通知(书)

Notice-and-comment period (1974年)通知和评论的时期(指行政法上的用语,当制定法规计划时期行政机构出版建议的制定法规,并接受公众对这些法规的评述,这个法规一直到此时期过后仍未生效。通常缩略为 comment period)

Notice-and-Demand (美)通知与请求(程序)[指控方就是否在审判中将实验检验报告作为证据使用事先通知被告,在给予被告合理的考虑期后,被告可以请求传唤实验室专家出庭。如果专家不出庭,则被告可以提出证据排出动议。参见《佐治亚州注释法典》第35节3.154(Ga. Code Ann.§35-3-154)]

notifiable a. 应具报的

notification n. 公告,通报,告示;通知书(单)

notified party 被通知人

notifier n. 通知人,通告人

notify v. 1.宣布,宣告 2.通知

noting n. 拒付记录

noting a bill 记录(拒兑)汇票;在票据上加附注

noting and protest (公证人作成汇票)拒绝承兑(或拒付的)证书

noting for protest 通知拒付

notion n. 概念;观念;看法;意见;信仰;见解;意图

notion of foreseeability 有预见性的概念

notion of justice 司法概念

notion of risk 风险概念

notional amount 名目金额

notions of fair play 公平竞争的观念

notions of fairness 公正概念

notions of fairness require that 出于公平考虑……

notions of federalism (= federalism notions) 联邦制观念

Notitia Dignitatum (古罗马)《百官志》(指罗马帝国4世纪末至5世纪初的文武百官职名录)

notorious a. 自明的;公然的;臭名昭著的,声名狼藉的,众所周知的

notorious bankrupt 众所周知的破产者

notorious insolvency 众所周知的无力清偿
notorious murder trial 众所周知的谋杀案审判
notorious possession 公然占有
notorious scoundrel 劣迹昭彰的人
notoriously insane person 众所周知的精神病患者
notwithstanding the verdict (= *non obstante verdicto*) 否定裁决
nova n. 新事物;政治变革;进化,革命,改革
nova causa interveniens 新的妨碍诉因
* *Nova constitutio futuris formam imponere debet, non praeteritis.* A new state of the law ought to affect the future, not the past. 一项法律的新规定只适用于未来,不溯及过去(法律不溯及既往原则)。
nova statuta 新法规
novatio 更改;债的变更
novation n. 债的变更,(债务、义务等的)更新;新债替代旧债,新合同(契约)代旧合同(契约)
novation of contract 合同(契约)的更新
novation of loan 贷款变更
novel n./a. (常用复)(罗马法)新律(见 *novellae*);附律的;新奇的,新颖的
novel assignment 新的转让
novel case 无先例可循的案件
novel constitutional claims 新的宪法权利
novel design 新设计
novel disseisin (对他人土地)新近强夺(或侵占)诉讼(见 assize of novel disseisin)
novellae (罗马法)新律(指查士丁尼及其继承者所颁布的新律的总称,后并入《民法大全》)。见 *Corpus Juris Civilis*
novelty (14世纪)(商业秘密)新颖性[指 ①商业秘密:通常未使用过或不知道的一种新性质的信息,而且它还在商业领域给其拥有人以竞争优势(competitive advantage)。在商业秘密的法律方面,新颖性并不要求独立(independent)的概念,甚至独创性(originality)。一项具有市场畅销实用性的重新发现的技术可以证明其新颖性,而且作为商业秘密受到保护。②(专利法)一项发明在形式上、功能或实践上

(in function or performance)的新性质(newness);严格的法律要求是:这种独创性(originality)在一项发明可取得专利权之前必须经过证明(demonstrated)。证实新颖性是严格和昂贵的检查程序的目的。如果这项发明以前已获得专利,对它的描述业已公布,他人已经知道并且使用或被销售,就不存在新颖了。参见《美国注释法典》第35标题卷第102节(35 USCA §102)。见 nonobviousness]
novigild (益格鲁-撒克逊)九倍赔偿金(指一个人必须支付给另一人财产的损害赔偿金,此数额相当于九倍的财产损害的买价)
* *Novo damos.* We grant anew. 我们同意重新审议;我们允准延续(延续特许状)(指特许状中的条款,延续允准某些权利更新)
novodamus (苏格兰法)我们同意延续,[是特许状(charter)中的条款:渐进允准某些权利的延续]
novoting a. 不投票的;无投票权的,无表决权的;弃权的
novus actus interveniens 新的干预行为,新行为的介入,新的妨害行为,新的妨碍诉讼的行为
now comes the plaintiff 兹有原告
nowhere ad. 任何地方都不
* *Noxa caput sequitur.* (= noxa sequitur caput) The injury follows the principal or the head person. 由奴隶或动物造成之损害,由其主人负责赔偿(或承担赔偿之责)。
noxal action (对奴隶主因其奴隶致人伤害所提出的)伤害诉讼(见 noxal liability)
noxal liability 伤害责任(指罗马法上主人对奴隶伤害他人的责任)
noxious a. 有害的;有毒的;不健全的;不卫生的;有罪的;使道德败坏的
noxious substance 有害物
noyade 溺水刑,溺死刑(尤指1794年在法国把大批人溺死的处决)
nub n. (故事)要点
nubility n. 女子的适婚性(指在年龄或身体发育条件方面)
nuclear n./a. 1.核武器(尤指装有原子弹头

的导弹)2.核国家(指拥有制造核武器工厂的国家)/核子的;基本的;原子能的;原子弹的;核动力的
nuclear blackmail 核讹诈
nuclear deterrent 核威慑力量
nuclear energy 核能
nuclear family 基本家庭,核心家庭(指已婚夫妻俩及其社会承认的子女所组成的家庭)
nuclear monopoly 核垄断
nuclear power 核国家
nuclear regulatory commission 核管理委员会,核管制委员会
nuclear superpowers 超级核大国
nuclear test cases 核试爆案
nuclear tests 核试验
nuclear umbrella 核保护伞
nuclear warfare 核战争
Nuclear Weapon Test Ban Treaty 《禁止试验核武器条约》
nuclei n. 核子(nucleus 的复数)
nuclear-free zone 无核区
* *Nuda pactio obligationem non parit.* A naked promise does not create a binding obligation. 无对价的允诺并不产生有约束力的债务(义务)。
nuda possessio 虚有占有权
nuda proprietas 虚有财产权
* *Nuda ratio et nuda pactio non ligant aliquem debitorem.* Naked intention and naked promise do not bind any debtor. 无保证的意思表示和无对价的允诺,都不约束任何债务人。
nuda traditio 虚有转让(交付)(指罗马法上不能转让的所有权的转让)
nude a./n. 裸体的,光秃的;无效的;(合同等)无偿的;无证据的(这个词常用于各种不同问题的"隐喻",表明它们缺乏某些法律要件)/裸体者
nude cargo 裸装货
nude contract (英美法)无对价合同(契约),无偿合同(契约),无报酬合同(契约)
nude matter 无证据事项,无证据案件
nude pact 无对价的合约
nudie n. (美俚)廉价的黄色电影

nudism n. 裸体主义
nudity n. 裸体;裸体画
nudo consensu 单纯的合意
nudum jus 虚名权
nudum pactum (罗马法)无诉权的特殊协议,无约因合同(契约),无偿合同(契约)
* *Nudum pactum ex quo non oritur actio.*
   Nudum pactum is that upon which no action arises. 无偿合同(契约)不产生追诉权。
nugatory a. 不起作用的,无效的;无价值的;琐碎的;无力的,无益的
nuisance n. 妨害、公害、损害,滋扰罪,妨害行为[此词具有广泛含意,其含义不十分确切,但主要指一种条件、一个行为或一种环境(如噪音或污秽气味)妨害资源、财产的使用和享用,特别是不可选择的情况或持续的行为既损害毗邻土地的客观条件,又损地役权的享用或妨害某些公共交通的使用。亦称 annoyance]
nuisance at law 法律上的妨害(指与 nuisance *per se* 含义相同,即法律上本身构成的妨害行为)
nuisance case 滋扰案件
nuisance in fact 事实上的妨害(指由于使用的环境,或位置而产生妨害,而非不动产使用本身构成妨害)
nuisance or public nuisance 公共滋扰罪,公害(罪)
nuisance order 清除障碍令,清除公害令
Nuisance per se 本身(或自动)妨害(指建筑物、设施或某一行为本身构成的妨害,与使用的环境或位置无关,如核废气贮藏设施泄露。亦称 nuisance at law 或 absolute nuisance)
nuisance raid 滋扰性袭击
nuisance suits 公共滋扰罪诉讼
nuisance tax (美)(直接对消费者征收的)小额消费品税(亦称烦扰性捐税,指征收方法使人感觉头痛)
* *Nul ne doit s'enrichir aux depens des autres.* No one ought to enrich himself at the expense of others. 任何人不得以损害他人而自己得益。
* *Nul prendra advantage de son tort de-*

mesne. No one shall take advantage of his own wrong. 任何人不得从其不法行为中获益。

* *Nul sans damage avera error ou attaint.* No one shall have error or attain unless there has been damage. 未遭受损害者不得申请复审令(writ of error)或撤销陪审团裁决的令状(writ of attain)(或只有遭受损害者方可申请复审令状或撤销陪审团裁决令状)。

nul waste 无毁损

null v./a. 使无效/无效的,无价值的;无意义的,无拘束力的

null and void 无效,失效(指法律文件而言)

null and void vote 废票,无效票分

nulla bona 无财物(供执行)(执达官回复执行令状的用语,意思是找不到被告任何财物可供执行)

* *Nulla intelligitur mora ibi fieri ubi nulla pititis est.* No delay of payment is meant to have been made when there has been no demand. 没有强求就没有退付。

* *Nulla poena sine lege.* No penalty without law making it so. 法无明文者不罚(罪刑法定主义原则)。

nulla poena sine lege parlamentaria 没有来自议会的法律(侵权)就不受惩罚

* *Nulli enim res sua servit jure servitutis.* No one can have a servitude over his own property. 任何人除对其自己的财产外,都不能享有役权。

nullification (= impairment) n. 抵消或损伤;无效,废除,废弃;(美)州对国会法令的拒绝执行,州废除联邦法令的行为(亦称否认原则)

nullification process 无效程序

nullifier n. 取消者,废弃者;使成为无效者

nullify v. 使无效,使无拘束力;废弃,作废,取消,注销

nullify one's registration 注销登记

nullity n. (尤указ法律上的)无效,作废;无效行为;无效东西(尤指无效的法案、文件等);无;不存在;不足道的人(或物)

nullity of contract 无效合同(契约)

nullity of judg(e)ment 无效判决
nullity of juristic act 无效法律行为
nullity of marriage 无效婚姻
nullity plea 无效申诉
nullity proceeding 要求宣告无效的诉讼
nullity suit (英)要求宣判结婚无效的诉讼;请求合同(契约)无效的诉讼
nullius filius 私生子
nullius juris 无法律拘束力的

* *Nullum crimen majus est inobedientia.* No crime is greater than disobedience. 没有任何犯罪比不服从更严重。

* *Nullum crimen sine lege.* No crime without law making it so. 法无明文者不为罪。

* *Nullum crimen sine lege, nulla poena sine lege.* 没有法律就没有犯罪,没有法律就没有刑罚。

* *Nullum crimen sine poena.* 没有刑罚,就没有犯罪。

* *Nullum iniquum est praesumendum in jure.* No inequity is presumed in the law./ Nothing injust is to be presumed in law. 法律上不得推定不公正之事。

* *Nullum simile est idem.* A thing which is similar to another thing is not the same as that other thing. 类似者未必即为相同者。

* *Nullum tempus occurrit regi.* Time never runs against the Crown. 对国王无时效。

* *Nullus commodum capere potest de injuria sua propria.* No one can take advantage of or profit by his own wrong. 任何人不得从自己的非法行为中得益。

* *Nullus dicitur accessorius post feloniam, sed ille qui novit principalem feloniam fecisse, et illum receptavit et comfortavit.* No one is called an accessory after the fact but he who knew the principal to have committed a felony, and received and comforted him. 在犯罪事实之后,只有知道主犯已犯有重罪,而仍接纳并安顿他者才能称该人为从犯。

* *Nullus jus alienum forisfacere potest.* No man can forfeit the right of another. 任何人都不得剥夺他人的权利。

number address 数码地址(即真正的网址)

number of headnote 眉标号,眉批号
number of justice 法官人数[美国联邦宪法没有具体规定联邦最高法院的人数规模。《1789年司法法》(Judiciary Act of 1789)将联邦最高法院与对低级联邦法院(lower federal courts)的控制联系起来。它创设了3个巡回法院(circuit courts),由两名联邦法院法官和地方法官掌管。那时6人的联邦最高法院成为必然。自1793年起,巡回法院改为1名单独法官,联邦最高法院仍为6人。1801年,国会使法官们不再到巡回法院任职,此时联邦最高法院的法官削减为5名。杰斐逊主义者对《1801年司法法》不满,于1802年将之废除,并恢复了6人的联邦最高法院规模。随着国会意识到国家向西部扩张的需求及法院案件量大增,在建立额外的巡回法院的同时又于1807年将联邦最高法院法官增至7人;1837年增为8人和9人,1863年曾增为10人。国会在《1869年司法法》中确定法官人数为9名。尽管富兰克林·D.罗斯福总统的联邦最高法院扩充计划中提到扩充法官数目,但联邦最高法院法官人数仍保持在9人]
numbers game 数字彩票赌博
numerical ceiling 最高限额
numerous family 子女众多的家庭
nunc pro tunc 追溯既往;现在代替过去;事后补正;追补过去
nunciature n. (罗马教皇的)教廷公使职位(或任期);(罗马教皇的)教廷使团
nuncio n. (罗马教皇的)教廷公使,使节
nuncupate v. 口头宣布,口述(证词、遗嘱等)
nuncupation n. 口述(证词、遗嘱等)
nuncupative(或 **nuncupatory**) a. 口头的,口述的
nuncupative will 口述遗嘱
nune pro tune amendment 追溯既往效力的修正[通常出于法院令(court order)]
* *Nunquam crescit ex post facto praeteriti delicti aestimatio.* The estimation of past offense is never increased by an after fact. A later fact will not be allowed to extend or amplify a past offense./The valuation for a past offense is never increased by what happens subsequently. 犯罪之轻重程度不能因后来发生之事件而加重。
* *Nunquam nimis dicitur quod nunquam satis dictur.* What is never sufficiently said is never said too much. 从未充分说明的,绝非过多说明的。
nuptial a. 婚姻的,婚礼的
nuptial day 结婚之日
nuptialis tabulae 结婚证书
nuptials(复) n. 婚礼
* *Nuptias non concubitus sed consensus facit.* Not cohabitation but consent makes the marriage. 婚姻的构成不是由于同居,而是由于双方同意。
Nuremberg laws 纽伦堡法(指德国纳粹政府1933年制定的迫害犹太人的法律)
Nuremberg Trials 纽伦堡审判(指1945年11月20日至1946年10月1日纽伦堡国际军事法庭对第二次世界大战纳粹战犯的审讯)
Nuremberg War Crimes Tribunal 纽伦堡战犯审判法庭(第二次世界大战胜利后设立审判纳粹战犯的法庭)
nurse n./v. 1.奶妈;护士 2.保护人;养育人 3.保育;养育/1.喂奶 2.守护;看护;照料;培育 3.小心操纵 4.怀有(希望、仇恨)
nurse a constituency 对选区的选民进行笼络
nurse hatred against sb. 怀恨某人
nursing women 哺乳妇女
nurture n. 营养物;食物;教育;教养
nympholepsy n. 妄想狂
nymphomania n. (女子的)色情狂
N. Y. Correction Law (美)《纽约州教养法》(1975年8月9日州议会通过的州法)

O

oath n. 誓言,誓约;宣誓
Oath Act 《宣誓条例》
oath against bribery 立誓不受贿;(英)(在选举中)不进行贿赂活动的宣誓
oath capacity 宣誓资格
oath ex officio (古英国法)无罪宣誓
oath of administration 遗产管理委任宣誓
oath of allegiance 忠诚宣誓(亦称效忠宣誓,指政府官员或获得归化的人对国家或君主表示忠诚的宣誓)
oath of fidelity 宣誓诚实(尤指对君主忠诚的宣誓)
oath of indigency 贫穷的誓言,贫穷的宣誓
oath of office 就职宣誓,宣誓就职
oath of secrecy 保密宣誓
oath of verity 真实宣誓
oath supremacy (英)承认(英王具有政治、宗教)最高权威的宣誓
oath-helpers n. (英)(宣誓断案中的)宣誓帮助人
oath-rite n. 宣誓仪式
obdurate a. 执迷不悟的,毫不悔改的;无情的,固执的
obedience n. 服从;顺从,遵从
obedient a. 服从的,顺从的,恭顺的
* *Obedientia est legis essentia.* Obedience is the essence of the law. 服从是法的要义。
obey v. 服从,顺从,遵奉;执行;按照……行动
obey the law 遵从法律
obit n. 死亡;葬礼仪式,葬礼;周年忌辰(指某人死亡的周年纪念日),周(年)祭(奠)
obit sine prole 死后无子女
obiter 顺便,附带
obiter dictum 附带意见,(something said in passing)(18世纪)判决附言[指法官在作出判决过程中就某一案件所作的评论,并不必然与该案判决相关,因此不具有先前判例的约束性,纵然它可被视为有说服力(persuasive)的。通常缩略为 dictum。复数为 *obiter dicla*]
object n./v. 物体,客体(物质的客体为物,知识产权的客体为智力成果,版权的客体为作品),标的物;对象;目的,目标;客观/提出……作为反对理由(根据);反对,抗议,拒绝
* **Object cannot be analogized.** 客体不能适用类推。
object code 目的码
object excluded from trade 不得买卖的物品
object given as a pledge 抵押物
object in contention 系争物
object of a legal claim 合法请求权的标的;法定请求权客体
object of a legal right 法定权利客体;合法权利的标的
object of a power 指名权受益人(指行使指名权时接受财产并受益的人)
object of a sale contract 买卖合同(契约)的标的
object of action 诉讼标的
object of adjudication 审判对象
object of civil legal relationship 民事法律关系的客体
object of connection (国际私法)联结对象
object of crime 犯罪客体
object of equivalent value 等价物
object of general concern 大众所关注的事物
object of gift 赠与物
object of insurance 保险标的
object of international law 国际法客体
object of legal relationship 法律关系的客体
object of litigation 诉讼标的
object of obligation 债的标的
object of pledge 抵押物,质权标的物

object of private right 私权客体,民事权利的客体
object of procedure 诉讼标的
object of proof 证明对象(指在诉讼中需要运用证据予以证明的事实情况)
object of property 财产权的客体,所有权客体
object of right 权利客体
object of the legal relations of ownership 所有权法律关系的客体
object of the right of ownership 所有权客体
object of the trust 信托的客体,信托的标的
object pledged in security 担保客体,担保中作为抵押之物
object sold 买卖标的物,出售的商品
object to this proposal 反对这个决议,反对这一提议
objecting on the other grounds 以其他理由提出异议
objecting party 提出异议的一方
objection n. (1837年)1.异议,反对[指对已经发生的某种事情表示反对的正式陈述,或是在法庭上当法官即将对某种观点进行裁决时的正式异议。表示异议的当事方通常必须陈述反对的根据以便维护对不利裁决(adverse ruling)的上诉权利] 2.(议会法)抑制动议[指一项抑制主要动议(main motion)的动议,特别是一项可加剧争议的动议,可能会立即停止或取消辩论。由于安排了主要动议,这样的抑制动议通常要求绝对多数通过方能有效。亦称 question of consideration; objection to consideration of a question]3.(议会法)反对票[指一张反对票或否决票(a negative vote),特别是一张可击败普遍认可要求(requst for general consent)的反对票] 4.(专利)鉴别行为,识别行为,审定程序[指审查人员鉴别专利申请格式(form)中瑕疵的行为或程序(action),通常体现在绘图或技术参数说明书中。这种识别异议并不会引起权利主张的实质问题,审查员可以反对并对不完美的誓约(defective oath)或对商标绘图上显示的商标表示异议。见 rejection]
objection stands 持续反对,继续持反对意见
objection sustained (法官宣告)异议(或抗议)成立
objection to consideration of a question 见 objection 2
objections to payment 拒付抗辩,对支付有异议
objective a./n. 客观的,真实的;目标的;如实的;无偏见的/目标,目的
objective actuality 客观实际
objective aspects 客观方面
objective aspects of crime 犯罪的客观方面
objective cause 客观原因
objective circumstance 客观环境
objective commercial act 客观的商行为
objective condition 客观情况,客观条件
objective connection 客观联系
objective contradiction 客观矛盾
objective correspondence 同客观相符合,名副其实
objective criteria 客观标准
objective criterion(或 **standard**) 客观标准
objective elements of crime 犯罪客观方面的要件
objective existence 客观存在
objective factor 客观因素
objective facts 客观事实
objective impossibility 客观上的不可能
objective increase 客观的加重
objective incrimination 客观归罪
objective law 客观法(则)
objective motive 客观动机
objective probability 客观概率
objective reality 客观真实
objective requisites of crime 犯罪的客观要件
objective standard of reasonableness 客观理性标准
objective tax 客体税,对物税
objective territorial principle 客体领土原则
objective truth 客观真实
objectivism n. 客观主义
objectivity n. 客观性,客观现实
objector n. 反对者,表示异议者

objects clause 标的物条款
obligate v. 负有责任,负有……义务;(道义上或法律上)强制……做某事
obligatio n. (罗马法)债,合同范畴,注销(legal bond);债权,债务[有时指法律关系。债则为"当事人之一方依法得请求他方为一定给付之法律关系"。有时则指注销(legal bond)。《查士丁尼法典》将"债"的定义为:"债者,依国法而应履行义务之法锁也"。后来人们也用它表示债务人的义务和债权人(或权利人)享有的权利]
obligatio alternativa 选择之债
obligatio certa 特定之债(指以特定物作为标的之债)
obligatio civilis 法定债务,民法上之债
obligatio dividua 可分之债
obligatio ex contractu 合同(契约)之债,由合同(契约)所生之债
obligatio ex delicto 侵权行为所发生的债
obligatio generis 种类之债(指以种类物为标的之债)
obligatio individua 不可分之债
Obligatio mandati consensce contrahentium consisti. The authority of an agent to contract for his principal rests on the consent of his principal. 为代理其委托人签约之权仍需其委托人之同意。
obligatio mora debitoris perpetuatur 债务不因迟延而消灭
obligatio naturalis 自然之债(指非靠诉讼强制执行之债,如依万民法设定而未被市民法所承认之债等)
obligatio quasi ex contractu 准合同(契约)之债,由准合同(契约)所生之债
obligatio quasi ex delicto 准侵权行为所发生之债
obligation n. 1.义务,职责,责任 2.债,债务;债权关系 3.合同(契约)证券 4.(法令、承诺、义务等的)束缚 5.偿付债务的款项 6.恩惠
obligation arising from a judg(e)ment of a court 因法院判决所产生之债
obligation arising from contract 合同(契约)所生之债
obligation arising from delict 不法行为所生之债
obligation arising from injury caused to another 因损害他人所生之债
obligation arising from the provisions of a statute 因法律规定所生之债
obligation arising from the relationship of trust 因信托关系所生之债
obligation arising from tort (tortious conduct) 侵权行为所生之债
obligation arising from unjust enrichment 因不当得利所生之债
obligation arising out of the instrument 票据法上的义务,由票据所生之债
obligation assumed 负担的义务
obligation barred by prescription 时效已过之债,消灭时效已完成的债
obligation created by administrative orders (中)行政命令所发生的债
obligation establishing joint and several 连带责任的债务,连带之债
obligation in general 一般之债
obligation in general average 共同海损之债
obligation in the absence of a contract 非合同(契约)之债
obligation of a party 当事方之债(义务),当事人的责任;当事人的债权债务关系
obligation of compensation for losses 赔偿损失的义务,损失赔偿之债
obligation of contract 合同(契约)义务,合同(契约)之债
obligation of giving claim notice 通知索赔义务,请求权通知义务
obligation of guarantee 保证责任,担保之债
obligation of restitution 返还原物之债,恢复原状之债
obligation relating to civil law 民事责任,民事义务;民法上之债
obligation relation 债的关系
obligation to bearer 无记名证券
obligation to disclose 说明义务,告知义务
obligation to educate children 教育子女的责任
obligation to pay salvage 支付海上救助费

用之债
obligation to pay tax 纳税义务
obligation under bond 担保责任,担保之债
obligation under condition precedent 根据事先条件所生之债
obligation under condition subsequent 根据事后条件所生之债
obligation under resolutive condition 附解除条件之债
obligation under suspensive condition 附停止条件之债
obligation with several creditors (或debtors) 多数债权人(或债务人)之债
obligation-oriented 义务本位
obligationes verbis (罗马法)口头形式之债
obligations *erga omnes* 普遍义务(又译"对一切"义务,是指一国对所有国家、整个国际社会的义务,对一切的义务。该概念首次出现于20世纪70年代,它不同于一国对某个特定国家或对象承担的义务,普遍义务所对应的权利主体是所有国家、全人类和整个国际社会),对一切的义务(指一国因违反有关国际法义务而承担的责任不因他国违反相应的义务而免除。这是现代化国际法上出现的"对一切的义务")
obligations-contract n. 债务合同(契约)
obligatory a. (法律上或道义上)必须履行的,强制性的;有约束力的;应尽的
obligatory annual contribution 每年度必须交纳的会费
obligatory arbitration 强制性仲裁,强制性公断
obligatory contract 债权合同(契约)
obligatory judicial settlement 强制司法解决
obligatory jurisdiction 强制性管辖(权)
obligatory military service 义务兵役(制)
obligatory notification 有约束力的公告
obligatory provision 强制性条款
obligatory reinsurance 固定分保
obligatory right 债权
obligatory rules 强制性法律规范;强制性

法规
obligatory term 义务年限,义务期限
obligatory voting (＝compulsory voting) 义务投票(强迫投票)
oblige v. 迫使;责成;施恩于;使满足,答应……的请求;以誓言(或合同等)约束(某人)
obliged to 必须;有义务……;责成,迫使
obligee n. 1.债权人,权利人;债主(与obligor相对)2.受惠人(与obliger相对)
obligee in the maintenance 享有抚育(扶养或赡养)权利的人
obliger n. 施惠于人者,施惠人
obligor n. 义务人,债务人,欠债者;有责任者
obligue reference 偏差
obliterate v. 灭迹,消灭;涂抹,擦去;去掉痕迹;使消灭;除去,删去;使被忘却
obliterate traces of murder 杀人灭迹
obliteration n. 灭迹;涂抹;消灭;删除
obliteration of accounts 涂改账目
obliteration of name 涂改姓名
oblivion n. 1.忘却,被忘却的事(或状态)2.大赦,赦免
oblivious a. 忘却的;健忘的;不在意的
obnoxious a. 令人非常不快的,引起反感的;应负责任的;应受谴责的
obnoxious matter 应受处罚的事(案)件
obrogation n. (通过另一项法律来)废除一项法律(的全部或部分)
obscene a. 猥亵的,诲淫的;污秽的;令人厌恶的
obscene articles 淫秽作品;淫猥物品
obscene language 污言秽语
obscene libels 淫秽诽谤罪;(英)(普通法)出版淫秽作品罪
obscene literature 诲淫文学,败坏风化的文学作品
obscene picture 淫画,春宫图
Obscene Publication Act (英)《诲淫刊物处理法》
obscene, lewd or lascivious publication 淫秽、下流色情出版物
obscenity n. 淫秽,猥亵,下流(猥亵)的言语(或行动)

obscenity in theatre 演出(或指挥演出)淫秽剧目(罪)
obscure rule of law 含糊不清的法律规范
obscurity n. 暗淡;模糊,含糊不清;不引人注目;偏僻;隐匿;无名(的人);微贱(的人)
observable a. 应遵守的,可遵守的;可庆祝的;值得注意的;看得见的
observance n. 1.(法律、习俗、规章的)遵守,奉行 2.惯例,习惯;仪式 3.注意,观察 4.纪念,庆祝
observant a. 注意的,留心的;严格遵守的
observant party 守约一方
observation n. 注意,观察;观察资料,观察报告;评论
observe v. 奉行,遵守(法律、命令等);观察,监视;陈述(意见);评述;庆祝,纪念
observer n. 观察者,观察员;监场员,监视人;见证人,目击者
observer-representative n. 列席代表
observing that… 注意到……
obsession n. 着迷,缠住,摆不脱的思想感情
obsession-compulsive syndrome 心神困扰强制综合征
obsolescent a. 逐渐被废弃的,处于逐渐过时中的
obsolete a. 1.(法律等)过时的;已废弃的;陈旧的 2.发育不健全的
obsolete decisions 陈旧的判例
obsolete legal science 陈旧的(老套的)法律知识
obstacle preemption (美)优先的障碍(指可以替代或优先于州地方法规的联邦或州法律的原则,这意味着一种障碍阻止至上的联邦法律或州法律的全面计划或目标的完成。同 conflict preemption)
obstinate conflict 公然的冲突,难分难解的冲突
obstinate desertion 公然遗弃(指这种遗弃是配偶一方长期拒绝回到婚姻居所,因此另一方配偶有理由离婚,在不追究责任的离婚到来之前。这一术语通常在离婚的成文法中使用。亦有较长的术语是:willful, continued and obstinate desertion)

obstruct v. 阻碍,妨碍,阻挠;设置障碍(尤指在议会中)
obstruct wilfully 故意阻挠
obstructed channel 渠道堵塞
obstructing n. 阻碍,妨碍,阻止,阻挠;设置障碍
obstructing (public) justice 妨碍司法公正;妨碍司法执行(罪)
obstructing mail (美)妨害邮政罪
obstructing proceedings of legislature 妨碍立法机关活动(罪)
obstructing process 妨碍诉讼程序(罪),阻止发出(或执行)传票(或命令)(罪)
obstruction n. 1.妨碍;阻碍,阻塞,障碍 2.(对会议议事所采取的)妨害(或拖延手段) 3.阻塞道路交通(罪)(按英国习惯法是一种公共妨扰罪行,违反公路或效能法规的一项罪行) 4.(对警官执行任务的)妨害罪
obstruction of police 妨害警察执行任务(罪)
obstructionist n. 妨碍会议议事者
obstructor n. 阻碍者,妨害者;阻碍物
obtain v. 获得,买到,得到;达到(目的);应用;流行;得到公认
obtain an order for enforcement 得到法院执行判决的命令
obtain money or goods by false pretence 诈取财物(罪)
obtain or strengthen dominant status 取得或加强主导地位(见 detriment to competition)
obtain satisfaction of a claim 索赔获得圆满解决,胜诉
obtain the floor (1820年)(议会法)接受议长认可被认为有资格发言
obtainable a. 可获得的;可取得的;可买到的
obtained a judgment 胜诉,赢得诉讼
obtained mean 实得平均数
obtaining n. 获得,得到,买得
obtaining a guarantor and pending trial 取保候审
obtaining by deception (英)诈取财物(罪)(按1968年盗窃法,凡用诈欺方法取

得他人财物并意图长期据为己有,即属此罪
obtaining by false pretences 伪装骗取
obtaining credit by deception (或 fraud)骗取信用
obtaining evidence to determine guilt 取证定罪
obtaining pecuniary advantage by deception (英)诈骗金钱利益(罪)(按1968年盗窃法,凡用欺骗方法为自己或为他人取得金钱上利益,即犯此罪)
obtaining testimony by deception 骗供
obtaining the floor 获得发言权
* *Obtemperandum est consuetudini rationabili tanquam legi.* A reasonable custom is to be obeyed as a law. 一项公道的习惯(惯例)应视为法律来服从。
obtest v. 恳求;传唤作证,请求作证;抗议
obtestation n. 请求作证;抗议;恳求,恳请
obtruder n. 闯入者;莽撞者;强加者
obtrusion n. 闯入;强行提出;强迫接受,莽撞
obviate v. 排除,消除(危险、困难等)
obvious a. 显而易见(现已成为专利法的用语);明显的,显著的
obvious inappropriateness of the specific administration act 具体行政行为明显不当
obviousness n. (专利法)显而易见性[指对于一个在特定技巧(given art)中掌握普通技能(ordinary skill)的人来说,这种质量和状况都是显而易见的,由于考虑到在先技术(prior art)的范围和内容,所以该人会有理由相信,这个被设计的发明是可以期待的/虽然显而易见性(obviousness)要求是在事实问题上十分流行(rife),但很明显的决定一项发明并不能获得专利,最终的决定还是法律问题,参见《美国注释法典》第35标题卷第103节。见 nonobviousness; obvious]
occasion n./v. 1.时机,场合,机会 2.近因,偶因,原因,诱因 3.特殊事件/引起,惹起
occasion of trouble 纠纷的起因
occasional a. 偶然的;特殊场合的;非经常的
occasional cause 偶因,诱因

occasional dealer's licence 临时商贩执照
occasional offender 偶犯
occupancy n. 1.占据,据有;占用;占有;占有期间;居住期间 2.先占(指把从前没有物主的东西占为己有)
occupancy agreement 占用性协议
occupancy expense 占用费
occupancy of resort 胜地的入住率
occupancy permit 占用许可证
occupancy right 占用权,租佃权;先占权
occupant n. 占有人,占据者;占领者;居住者;因占有而取得所有权者,实际占有人
occupantis fiunt derelicta Things abandoned become the property of the (first) occupant. 遗弃归先占有人所有
occupatio 先占(指因占有而取得所有者),占领,征服
occupatio bellica 军事占领
occupatio pacifica 和平占领
occupation n. 占据,占领;享用,占用,占有;占有权;占有时间;居住时间;占领状态;占领军(当局);职业;工作;消遣
occupation franchise (英)租地人投票权
occupation in war 战时占领
occupation of enemy territory 占领敌国领土
occupation statute 占领法规
occupation tax 职业税
occupation troop 占领军
occupational a. 职业的;职业引起的;军事占领的
occupational disease 职业病
occupational hazard 职业性危害(指由业引起的危害,如事故、疾病等)
occupational licenses 职业许可
occupational negligence 职业性过失
Occupational Safety and Health Act (美)《职业安全和保健法》
occupational safety/health 职业安全/健康
occupational tax 开业税,开业许可税
occupationist n. 军事占领者
occupied territory 被占领土
occupier n. 占用者;居住者;军事占领者
occupier's liability 住户的责任
occupier's tax 农民所得税
occupy v. 占领,占据;占有,占用;充任;住

(房子等);处于(某种地位);使从事
occupy by force 武力占领,强行占据
occupying power 占领国
occupying tenant 占用租户
occurrence n. 出现,发生;事件;突然发生的事件,意外事件(保险法上指导致人身伤害或财产损失,这既非投保人有意行为亦非其预期的)
occurrence of crime 罪行的发生
occurrence rule (民事诉讼法)时效开始的有效规则(指当违法行为或不作为发生时,时效规则即开始有效,而非原告发现伤害之时。此规则适用于如大多数违背契约的权利主张。见 statute of limitation)
occurrence-based liability insurance 基于保险责任的事故(见 insurance)
occurrent a. 目前正在发生的;偶然发生的
ocean n. 海洋,海
ocean carriage 海运
ocean freight 海运费用(旧译:海运水脚)
ocean insurance 海上保险
ocean liner 远洋(客)班轮,定期远洋船
ocean route 远洋航线
ocean shipping agents 海运代理商
ocean space 海域,海洋区域
ocean thermal energy conversion 海洋热转换能源
ocean trade 远洋贸易
ocean transport 远洋运输
ocean transportation insurance 海洋运输保险
ocean way-bill 海运提单
oceangoing commerce 海外贸易
oceangoing transportation 远洋运输
oceanic and coastal system 海洋和海岸系统
oceanic coastal state 沿海国
ochlocracy n. 暴民政治,暴民统治
OCP bill of lading 水陆联运提单
octavus subscriptor 署名证人
octroi (法)货物入市税,入市税征收所(处);入市税征收人员
odd jobs 零活
odd lot sale 散股交易
odds (复) n. (形势)敌我力量对比的差距;不平等

odium n. 憎恨,愤怒
of age 成年的
of counsel (美)1.助理律师 2.特邀律师(①指案件中当事人雇用的律师,虽非记录在卷之主要律师,但他是受雇准备或掌控案件或进行上诉陈词的律师;②指附属于一个律师事务所的律师,但非该所的成员,亦非合伙人或助理律师)
of course 当然,事实上,实际上(指在诉讼中一个人可以既不需要请示法官允准也无须通过请求得到批准而采取的行为)
of good repute 信誉良好的
of grace 宽限的;赦免的;(法院)允许的
of no fixed abode 无固定住所的,居无定所的
of one's own accord 自愿的,自动的,心甘情愿的
of one's word 守信的
of purpose 故意的,有意的,蓄意的
of record 记录在案的
off v. 无限地推迟,无限地延期;宣布中止(谈判,合同等);取消与……约定;(美俚)杀掉;走开,离开
off balance-skeet 资产负债表外的
off balance-skeet financing 不根据资产负债表的筹资
off issue 枝节问题
off job 离职,失业
off the book payment 不登账的支付
off the docket 不在受理中;不予受理;审理完毕
off the equilibrium path 不在均衡途径
off the peg 现成的,非定做的(一般指服装)
off the track 误入歧途
off year (美)非大选年
(an) off year election 中期选举
off-balance transaction 资产负债表外的交易(在美国,公司从事资产负债表以外的某些交易是完全合法的,如从银行开信用证,或利率套购。现在此种交易的会计规则是处于大众监管之下)
off-budget n. 预算外
off-budget year 非编制预算年度
off-described as the Courts "liberal" 难以

描述成联邦最高法院的"自由派"
off-duty n. 下班,休假
off-exchange futures trading 地下期货交易
off-limits a. (美)禁止进入的
off-line 离线
Off-shore Group of Banking Supervisisors 离岸银行业监管集团
off-shore market 离岸金融市场,又称境外市场(相对在岸金融市场而言,系指经营可自由兑换货币,交易在货币发行国境内或境外,在非居民之间进行,基本不受市场所在国法制和税制限制,同时享受一定优惠待遇的独立自由交易市)
off-the-books deal 黑市交易
off-the-books quotation 秘密交易价格,账外交易价格
off-the-court activities 法庭外活动
off-the-record a. 秘密的,不公开的;非正式的;不许发表的,不许引用的
offence (= offense) n. 1.犯法(行为);罪过;过错;罪行(英国法中这个词一般指公共错误行为,不仅指刑事罪行或可检控的罪行,还包括那些用简易程序审判的罪行)2.攻击,冒犯;侮辱
offence against an individual 危害个人罪
offence against constitution 违宪罪
offence against dead bodies 残害尸体罪
offence against election 妨碍选举罪
offence against marriage and the family 破坏婚姻家庭罪
offence against morality 有伤风化罪
offence against neutrality 妨害国家中立罪
offence against person 侵犯人身罪
offence against public order 危害公共秩序罪
offence against social order 危害社会秩序罪
offence against the bankruptcy law 妨害破产法罪
offence against the law 违法行为
offence against the socialist economic order (中)破坏社会主义经济秩序罪
offence of abandonment 遗弃罪
offence of absorbing property 侵吞财产罪
offence of arson 纵火罪
offence of betraying state secretes 泄露国家机密罪
offence of bigamy 重婚罪
offence of bribery 行贿受贿罪,贿赂罪
offence of conspiring to overthrow the government 阴谋推翻政府罪
offence of conviction 判定有罪的罪行,判决的罪行
offence of corruption 贪污罪
offence of counterfeiting bank notes 伪造钞票罪
offence of counterfeiting valuable securities 伪造有价证券罪
offence of counterrevolution 反革命罪
offence of covering up the criminals 包庇(罪犯)罪
offence of defacing public property 毁坏公共财物罪
offence of dereliction of duty 渎职罪
offence of detrimental to public moral 危害公共道德罪
offence of disclosing military secrets 泄露军事机密罪
offence of disrupting the money and banking 扰乱货币金融罪
offence of disturbance of public order 扰乱公共秩序罪
offence of extorting confessions by torture 刑讯逼供罪
offence of fleeing 脱逃罪
offence of forging national currency 伪造国家货币罪
offence of graft and embezzlement 贪污盗窃罪
offence of handling stolen goods 销赃罪
offence of harboring criminals 窝藏罪犯罪
offence of harboring the stolen goods and contrabands 窝赃罪
offence of homicide by conspiracy 同谋杀人罪
offence of illegal infringement of citizens 非法侵犯公民权利罪
offence of indecent activities 流氓(活动)罪

offence of intentional killing 故意杀人罪
offence of interference with the freedom of marriage 干涉婚姻自由罪
offence of libel 诽谤罪
offence of misconduct in office 失职罪
offence of murder 谋杀罪
offence of plotting an armed rebellion 阴谋武装叛乱罪
offence of poisoning 投毒罪
offence of prosecuting false charges 诬告陷害罪
offence of rape 强奸罪
offence of robbery 抢劫罪
offence of smuggling 走私罪
offence of splitting the state 分裂国家罪
offence to the public 公开性的犯罪
offence triable summarily 可简易审判的犯罪
offence-reporter n. 检举人
offences against property and possession 对财产所有权和占有权的犯罪
offences against public safety and order 妨害社会安全和公共秩序罪
offences against the safety of the state 危害国家安全罪
offend v. 犯法, 犯罪; 触犯; 伤害, 开罪, 忤逆; 冒犯
offender n. (15世纪) 1.成年后犯有罪行的人 2.犯有罪行的青少年犯 3.犯有罪行的未成年犯, 作为成年犯而不是未成年犯审理的违法者[此词尤指初犯(first offender)、逃犯(fugitive offender)和少年犯(juvenile offender)等]
offender in corruption 贪污犯
offender released from labor camp 劳改释放犯
offender resisting arrest 拒捕犯
offender subject to arrest 人犯
offender under labor reform (中)劳改犯
offender with old records 累犯, 积犯
offending against 触犯(法律等)
offending articles 违法条文
offending mark 假冒商标
offending party 攻击当事方
offending ship 对标的船舶之扣押

offendress n. 女罪犯, 女犯人
offense (=offence)
offense in question 有争议的犯罪, 争议中的罪行
offenseful a. 有罪的; 冒犯的
offensive a. 攻击的, 进攻的; 冒犯的, 侮辱的
offensive and defensive league (国际法)攻守联盟
offensive cargo 违禁货物
offensive enforcement 攻击性执行(德国《反限制竞争法》规定, 私人当事人执行竞争法有三种方式: 一是提起损害赔偿诉讼; 二是提出禁令诉讼; 三是提出反竞争协议无效诉讼。其中前两种执行方式被称为"攻击性执行", 最后一种被称为defensive enforcement"防御性执行")
offensive in nature 进攻性
offensive language 污言秽语, 令人讨厌的语言
offensive matter 令人讨厌的东西, 激怒人的物质
offensive missile system 进攻性导弹系统
offensive odo(u)rs 臭味
offensive trade (英)厌恶性的营业(英国法把制革、溶脂等营业列为厌恶性的营业)
offensive war 进攻性战争; 侵略性战争
offensive weapon 进攻性武器(指目的用来伤害他人或使人体无能力防卫的任何武器)
offer n./v. 要约(指提出缔结合同之要求); 报价; 发价; 出盘, 提供, 贡献, 给予; 提议; 求婚; 意图/出价; 提供; 提议; 提出; 试图; 呈现; 奉献; (公司)招(股)
offer (或 **make**) **a proposal** 提出建议; 求婚
offer a reward 悬赏
offer an apology 赔礼道歉
offer (或 **produce**) **an exhibit** 出示证件(证物)
offer attractive condition 提供优惠条件
offer by description 附说明书的要约, 附说明书的发盘
offer faked evidence 提供伪证

offer for sale 开价销售
offer letter (document) 报价书;建议书
offer of proof (主动)提供证据
offer of settlement rules 和解(要约)的规则
offer on sale or return 准许退货报价,准许退货的发盘
offer quoted price 报价
offer shares to the public (公司的)公开招股
offer without engagement 虚盘,不受约束的要约
offer-to-sell n. 贩卖要约
offeree n. 受要约人;被发价人;受盘人
offering n. 提供,提出;礼物;捐献物;出售物;祭品;发行证券
offering bribe 行贿
offering for sale 推销
offering memorandum 发行备忘录[指涉及公司发行证券的一种备忘录。公司首次发行证券(initial public offering)通常须有股票招股说明书,但有些公司或企业发行股票或其他证券时并不面向整个市场,更不在股票交易所交易。这类企业发行证券时并无招股说明书,只需发行备忘录(initial public of offering memorandum)]
offering of bonds 出售债券
offering price 发行价格(指股票新股发行或二级发行时每股的价格,提供的价格,要价)
offering to sell 许诺销售
offeror (=offerer) n. 要约人;发价人;发盘人
offhand ad./a 立即,当下;事先无准备地;临时的,简慢的
office n. 1.办公室,办事处,事务所,营业处 2.处,局,社,行,公司 3.(大写)政府机关(旧译:官署);(英)部;(美)司,局 4.公职,职位;职责,任务;礼仪,祭礼 5.(复)照料,帮助
office accommodations 办公用具
office action 审定通知程序(指专利审查后,以书面通知申请人的程序);审定通知行为
office copy 正式文本;誊本;公文

office employees 职员
Office for Harmonization of Internal Market (OHIM) (欧盟)内部市场协调局
office hours (军事法)办公时间,营业时间(见 non-judicial punishment)
office hunter (或 office seeker) (美)谋求官职者,希望就任官职者
office in charge of the commercial register 主管商业登记机关
office lawyer 顾问律师
office management 机关事务管理
Office of Management and Budget (美)管理和预算办公室[指美国总统办公室内的一个管理预算的办公室,负责帮助总统准备年度预算并监督其执行。原来是按1939年第1号重组计划设立,作为"预标局"(Bureau of Budget)。缩写为 OMB]
office of associations 社团局
Office of Drug Abuse Policy (美)毒品滥用政策管理局
office of examining and documentation control 审查与文件管制处
office of execution 执行办公室
Office of Federal Contract Compliance Programs (OFCCP) (美)联邦契约(合同)遵循署
Office of General Counsel (美)法律总顾问室
office of honor 荣誉职位
office of legal advisers 法律顾问处
office of legal affairs 法律事务所
Office of Legal Counsel (美)(联邦最高法院)法律顾问处(创建于1972年的联邦最高法院行政结构中的一个非法定单位。该顾问处有两名律师,履行的职责繁多,有研究、分析以及为非普通令状和请求原审管辖权的申请提出建议。它也是最高法院的总顾问处,它将应首席大法官之要求而承办一些特殊事项,也可协助法官完成他们的巡回审判工作)
Office of Management and Budget (美)管理和预算局
office of president 总统职位(务)
Office of Science and Technology Policy (美)科学和技术政策局

office of speaker （议会的）议长职位(务)

office of the charge d'affaires （外交）代办处

Office of the Chief Justice （美）首席大法官的职务（或职位）[《1789年司法法》创设了首席大法官职位,但其职务的本质、功能和权限仍未得到界定。首席大法官是"平等者之间的第一人"（first among equals）。与其他大法官的形式差别包括薪水和人事上的不同,1995年以后还有制服上的差异。首席大法官履行传统的司法功能:主持法院公开性和封闭性的程式,偶尔也主持总统弹劾案的审理。依据惯例,首席大法官最显著的义务是主持联邦最高法院的审判。早期,首席大法官还要在被分配到的巡审中担任巡回法官。另外,在联邦最高法院审判闭庭后,就案件的选择和有争议的问题召开会议。尽管其投票权只占1/9,但其名义上的职位为其领导地位提供了机会。首席大法官在完全复审的案件中主持审查的,对法院日程安排起关键的作用。根据其是否认为案件有发调卷令的价值,决定列入"讨论清单"或列入"死名单"。首席大法官还承担法院的各项管理义务]

office of the clerk （美）书记官办公室(负责美国联邦最高法院的行政事务。依据1790年2月最高法院首次正式的规则而建立。至今仅有19位书记官服务于联邦最高法院)

office of the curator 美国联邦最高法院文史室(指1973年由首席大法官建立的文史室,以记录和保存最高法院的历史和重要纪事。其职员对范围极广的主题以及与联邦最高法院有关的各种档案文献一直进行着研究,并对来源于社会公众、学术团体和法官的大量信息需要作出回应)

Office of the Marshall of the Court （美）联邦最高法院首席大法官马歇尔办公室

office of the master in lunacy 精神病主事官办事处

office of the military procurator 军事检察院

Office of the President 总统府

office of the prime minister 总理府,首相府

office of the procurator-general 最高检察院,检察总署

office of the public prosecutor 检察院,检察机关

office on a non-political basis 无党派人士（担任的）职务

office practice （美）法律实务(指法庭外首先应处理的一些事务,比如协商、起草合同、准备遗嘱以及信托;清理私法人和合伙人债务或有关税务、就业问题的咨询;贸易上的法律实务等)

office practitioner （美）顾问律师,办公律师(指不做诉讼的律师,该律师首要任务是坐办公室完成工作,而不出庭。亦称 office lawyer、transactional lawyer)

office premises 公用建筑物

Official Residence System 官邸制[据维基百科网站解释,official residence(官邸)通常指的是国家元首、政府首脑、地方长官或其他重要人物的居所。比较有代表性的包括美国总统的White House(白宫)和度假胜地Camp David(戴维营)、法国总统的Elysee Palace(爱丽舍宫)、韩国总统的 Cheong Wa Dae(青瓦台)、英国首相的No. 10 Downing Street(唐宁街10号)以及俄罗斯总统的Kremlin(克里姆林宫)等。简而言之,该词条就是国家为一定级别官员在任期内提供住房的制度,已在国外实行多年。各国官邸制的范围、对象和标准不尽相同。例如,加拿大政府除为总理、国家机构负责人等准备官邸外,还为各个区域的长官、外国驻加拿大大使及来访的国外政要提供官邸。而德国主要为在职的高级公务人员设立了官邸。但这些制度也有共同点,即官员对官邸只有居住权(right of habitation),没有产权(property right);官员任期期间入住,卸任后搬出;官邸基本归国家所有或由国家租用,按照规定配置内部设施,费用由国家承担。许多国家还规定官员的住房、薪酬等待遇必须公开透明]

office romance 办公室恋情

office-bearer n. 在职人员;公务员;职员,官员

office-block ballot 顺序选票(指将候选人

名字按 A、B、C 顺序写在拟竞选的职务下的一种选票）

office-clerk n. 职员,办事员

office-copy n. （经官方认证的）文书;复本;公文

office-holder n. 公务员,官吏

officer n. (14 世纪) 1.官员,办事员 高级职员,司令官,军官(持有一个授权、命令或委任的职务。在公共事务或国家事务中,这一术语特涉及某人持有公务人员职位,是国家、州或地方政府的官员以及政府授权行使特别职能。在公司法中 该术语特别指由董事会选出或任命的管理公司日常业务的高级职员。如 CEA、首席执行官、主席、秘书长或财务主管) 2.(军法)军官,司令官(支持有军队的职务或高一级军官职位。亦称 military officer)

officer of criminal prosecution 刑事检察官

officer of justice 政府司法官员;法院的司法人员

officer of law 执法官员,执法人员

officer of the court 法庭官员(指法官、书记官、见习行政官、法警、法院执达员、治安官以及其他法院雇员;律师也属法庭官员,但必须遵守法庭规定,忠实于法庭而且根据法律需要进行广泛性服务)

officer of the guard 警卫军官

officer on agreement 签约聘任的职员

officer on probation 试用职员

officer on the active list 现役军官

officer on trial 试任职员

officer-in-charge n. 主管官员

officers of the state 政府各部部长

official a./n. 官方的,法定的;正式的,公家的;职务上的/1.行政人员,公务员,官吏;高级职员 2.(复)(政府)任职人员 3.(宗教法院)推事

official act 正式行为,官方行为

official assignee 法定受托人;指定受让人

official assigneeship 法定受托人的身份,指定受让人的身份

official authority 法定效力,官方权威,法律效力

official bank 国家银行,官方银行

official banned books 禁书

official bond 任职保证书[指 1.由公职官员授予的保证书要求踏实履行职责,由保证人对其失职行为承担赔偿责任 2.由一名遗嘱执行人、监护人或受托人(trustee)或其他受信托人(fiduciary)提交的保证书]

official bulletin 正式公报,官方公报

official capacity 公职权力,官方权力;法定资格

official certificate 正式证书

official character 公务性质

official charges payable upon exportation and importation of the goods 货物进出口应交纳的官费

official circles 政界

official citation 官方援引,正式援引

official collection 官方汇编;正式汇编

official comment 官方评论

official commission 正式委托

official communication 正式照会;官方公文

official confirmation 正式确认

official confiscation 官方没收;充公

official copy 正式文本

official correspondence 公函

official court 正式法院,依法设立的法院

official custody 正式拘押

official declaration 正式公告,官方公告

official deed 正式契据

official devaluation 法定贬值

official document 公文(即公文书),政府文件

(The) Official Documents System 正式文件数据库(指收集联合国 1993 年以来发行的文件及 1946 年以来大会、安理会、经社理事会和托管会的决议全文,2004 年起可提供汉语查询)

official emoluments 职位薪酬

official exchange 法定汇率

official family (前加 the President's) （总统的）内阁

official files 官方档案

official fixed price 公价,官价

official form 正式格式

Official Gazette (或 Journal) 《政府公

报》(又译:《官方公报》)
official holidays 例假,法定假期
official idealogy 官方意识形态,法定的意识形态
official information 官方消息
official inheritance certificate 正式继承证书
official instruction 正式指令
official language 法定语言;正式语言,官方语言
official law 正式法律,政府颁布的法律
official lawyer 正式律师,官方律师
official letter 公函,公文
official liability 官员承担责任[指一名官员或涉诉财产管理人(receiver)在其任职期内因违反合同或犯有侵权问题而承担的责任,但不涉及任何个人责任(personal liability)]
official liquidation 官方清理(算),法定清理(算)
official liquidator 清理官(指贸易委员会委任的官员,或由破产事务官担任来办理公司结束事务的官员),法定财产清算人
official managers (英)管理公司解散事务官(指从前指定在大法官法院控制下主管无偿还债务能力的公司解散事务的官员)
official map 官方地图,分区划的地图
official minimum rate 法定最低利率
official misconduct (1830年)渎职,公务不当行为[指公务人员因其恶行(malfeasance)、滥用职权(misfeasance)或失职(nonfeasance)而腐败,违反了委任的职责,亦称 misconduct in office; misbehavior in office; malconduct in office; misdemeanor in office; corruption in office; official corruption; political corruption 等]
official name 官方名称,正式名称
official notice 官方知识(与Judicial notice 相类似,但不是对法官的要求,而是对行政机构的要求)
official oath (官吏)就职宣誓
official of local authority 地方政府官员
official par of exchange 法定汇兑平价
official petitioner 正式(破产)申请人
Official Principal (英)(宗教法)教务总长[指由一名大主教、主教或副主教(arch-

deacon)任命的教务总长行使管辖和主持一所宗教法庭]
official privilege (美)公务特权,公务特惠,官员特惠,职务上的特惠[指免除一个州的官员对另一州的官员在执行职务过程中所作的陈述有关诽谤诉讼的特权,亦可称为诽谤豁免权(privilege in defamation)]
official procurator 官方代诉人,公诉人
official quality standards 法定质量标准
official rank 官衔
official rate of exchange 法定汇率,官方汇率
official receipt 正式收据
official receiver 正式涉讼财产管理人;清算管理(财产的)官员
official recognition 正式承认;官方认可
official record 正式记录,官方记录
official referee (高等法院的)咨询官
official religion 国教
official report (美)官方的判例汇编(指由官方出版的判例汇编)
official responsibility 公务上的责任
official sanction 正式认可,正式批准
official seal 封印,公印
official secrecy (或 **secrets**) 国家机密,官方机密,工作机密
(The) Official Secrets Act (OSA) (英)《公务机密法》
official signature 正式签署;官方签署
official solicitor 最高法院律师;(英)(最高法院指定的为无行为能力者的)代诉人(或临时监护人)
official stamp 官方印记,官方印章
official standing 法定地位,正式地位,官方地位
official statement 正式声明
official strike (受工会支持的)正式罢工
official system 职权主义(指当今世界上存在两种主要的民事诉讼模式:职权主义与当事人主义或对抗制)
official text 正本,正式文本
official trustee 官方受托人,正式受托人
official trustees of charitable funds 慈善基金官方受托人
official trustee of charity lands 慈善用土

地官方受托人
official use 正式使用权
official version of Supreme Court decisions and opinions （美）联邦最高法院的判决和判决意见的正式（官方）文本
official visa 公务签证
officialdom n. 官场,公务员界；（总称）官吏；公务员；官僚作风
officialese n. 官话；公文用语,公文体
officialis n. （罗马教区婚姻法庭的）首席法官
officialism n. 死板的机关作风,文牍主义；官僚作风；官员；官场
officialize v. 使成为正式的；使经过例行手续；置……于官方控制下
officials' rule （政府）官员统治
officiate v. 行使职务,执行公务
officina justitiae 法庭,衡平法院的法庭，（英）大法官法庭
officious a. 非官方的,非正式的
officious statement 非（官方）正式声明
officious will 非正式遗嘱
officius 义务
off-line a. 脱（离主）机（单独工作）的；不在铁路沿线的
offset n. 1.后裔；分支 2.抵消,补偿
offset credit 抵消信贷
offset guilty by merit 立功赎罪
offset to the loss 对损失的补偿
offsetting change 补偿变更；抵消变更
offshoot n. 分支,支流,支族,旁系
offshore area 近海地区
offshore berth 离岸泊位
offshore loan 海外贷款
offspring n. 后辈,子孙,后裔,后嗣；结果,产物
offspring or product of mental disease 精神病的产物或结果
offspring outside a marital union 非婚姻结合的后嗣
oil and gas law 油气法
oil embargo 石油禁运
oil pollution damage 油污损害
(The) Oil Weapon 石油武器
old age pension 养老金

Old Age Pensions Act （英）《养老金法》（1971年）
old age welfare scheme 老人福利规划
Old Bailey （英）老贝利（伦敦中央刑事法院的俗称）
old common-law pleadings （英）旧普通法上的书面申述程序（如声明、被告答辩状、原告对被告答辩的驳复、被告对原告的第二次答辩状、原告的二次驳复、被告的第三次答辩、原告的第三次辩驳状等,都是如此刚性,以致一个技术上的错误就可能导致诉讼的全部后果）
old lag 老犯；惯犯；累犯
old liner 守旧者,政治上保守的人；（大写）（英）保守党党员
old natural law 古代自然法 [指 Gratian 格拉提安（宗教主义之父）将古代自然法与神法（Law of God）统一起来中,认为自然法是神法的一部分,永恒不变,超越习惯法和实在法]
old（或 repeated）offender 累犯,老犯
old rules 陈旧的规则,老的规则；传统的规则
Old Testament 《旧约全书》（基督教和犹太教的正典经书）
old timer n. 老资格的人,老前辈；守旧的人；上了年纪的人；老式东西
Old World 旧大陆 [指与美洲新大陆（New World）相对而言的东半球旧大陆,尤指欧洲],旧世界（指欧、亚、非洲）
old-line a. 老资格的,老牌的
old-line counter-revolutionary 历史反革命分子
old-line imperialists 老牌帝国主义
old-money a. 继承祖先遗产的
older generation of lawyers and judges 老一辈的律师和法官
oligarchy n. 寡头政治（制）；寡头政治集团；寡头政体,实行寡头独裁的政府（国家）；少数人垄断的组织
oligopolists n. 对市场进行控制的少量制造商
oligopoly n. 寡头垄断（指在大量买主情况下仅有少数卖主为特征的市场状况）；少数制造商对市场的控制

oligopsony n. （在有大量卖主的情况下）少数买主对市场的控制

olograph (= holograph)

ombudsman n. 欧洲监督专员；调查专员（指专门调查官员舞弊情况的政府官员，或指机关组织内专门负责听取批评、搜集意见的人）；监察专员（指民众可以向其反映冤情的官方或半官方的人员）；（斯堪的纳维亚国家的）巡视官；调查专员制度

ombudsman for justice 司法官员

ombudsmanship n. 调查（或监察）专员的职权（或身份）

ombudsperson n. （美）监察使（指联邦契约遵循署内设置的若干监察使，负责调查承包商是否有违反总统行政命令之行为。见 Office of Federal Contract Compliance Programs)

ombudswoman n. 女性调查专员，女性监察专员

omissible a. 可以删掉的，可以省去的

* *Omissio eorum quae tacite insunt nihil operatur.* The omission of those things which are tacitly implied is of no consequence. 对那些默示的（心照不宣的）事采取不作为态度是无足轻重的。

omission n. 懈怠；不履行法律责任，不作为；遗漏，省略；删除

omission of date 漏写日期

omissive a. 遗漏的；删节的，省略的；失职的；疏忽的

omit v. 遗漏，省略，删去；忽略，忘记；失职；疏忽

omit to do any act 忽略去做某事；不注意去做某事

omittance n. 债务清偿期的延迟；遗漏；不作为

* **Omittance is no quittance.** 债务清偿期的延迟不等于免除债务（遗漏不等于注销）。

omitted population 遗漏的人口

* *Omne actum ab intentione agentis est judicandum.* Every act is to be judged by the intention of the doer. 每个行为应按行为人的意图来作出判断。

* *Omne jus aut consensus fecit, aut necessitas constituit aut firmavit consuetudo.* Every right is either made by consent, or is constituted by necessity, or is established by custom. 每项权利都或是经同意取得，或是由于必需或依惯例而产生的。

* *Omne majus dignum continet in se minus dignum.* The more worthy contains in itself the less worthy. 较有价值的东西本身就包含着较无价值的东西（好中有坏）。

* *Omne principale trahit ad se accessorium.* Every principal thing draws to itself the accessory. 任一主物本身都带有从物（有主就有从）。

* *Omne quod solo inaedificatur solo cedit.* Everything which is built upon the soil belongs to the soil. 建立在土地之上的一切都属于该土地。

* *Omne testamentum morte consummatum est.* Every will is completed by death. 任一遗嘱都因（立遗嘱人）死亡才告成立。

* *Omnes actiones in mundo infra certa tempora habent limitationem.* All actions in the world are limited within certain periods. 世界上一切诉讼都要受一定的时间限制。

* *Omnes homines aut liberi sunt aut servi.* All men are freemen or slaves. 所有的人不是自由人，就是奴隶。

* *Omnes licentiam habere his quae pro se indulta sunt, renunclare.* All persons shall have liberty to renounce those privileges which have been conferred for their benefit. 凡属授予其利益的特权，均可自由抛弃（古代法的规则）。

* *Omnes licentiam habere his, quae pro se introducta (or indulta) sunt renunciare.* Every man may renounce a benefit which the law has conferred upon him. All have liberty to renounce these things that have been granted in their favor. 任何人均享有抛弃法律赋予其有益之物的自由。

* *Omnia delicta in aperto leviora sunt.* All crimes that are committed openly are lighter. 一切公开犯下的罪行都（要比秘密犯下的）较为轻。

* *Omnia praesumuntur contra spoliatorem.* All things are presumed against a despoiler or wrongdoer. 一切事情都应推定是打击不法行为者的。

* *Omnia praesumuntur legitime facta donec probetur in contrarium.* All things are presumed to be lawfully done, until proof be made to the contrary. 一切事情在未证明不合法前均应推定为合法。

* *Omnia praesumuntur rite et solemniter esse acta donec probetur in contrarium.* All things are presumed to have been rightly and duly performed until the contrary is proved. 若无反证,一切行为均作为正常、合法并以正当之方式完成来推定。

* *Omnia praesumuntur solemniter esse acta.* All things are presumed to have been done rightly. 凡事均应推定其已经过正当处理。

omnibus clause (1880年)1.总括条款(指汽车保险单的一项条款,规定其保险不仅包括驾驶被保险的汽车驾驶人员,还包括对该汽车负法律责任的拥有人)2.(遗嘱中)剩余财产处理条款(residuary clause)

omnibus bill 混合法案(即包含多项条款的法案)

omnibus clause 总括(保险)条款

omnibus credit 总括放款(指多种不同性质的贷款)

omnibus hearing 混合听审(指同时受理与案件无关的其他许多事项)

Omnibus Trade and Competition Act 1988 (美)《1988年综合贸易竞争法》[美国是最早实施知识产权边境保护的国家,(美)《1930年关税法》第337节对"进口贸易中的不公平做法"予以规范,成为知识产权边保的雏形。国家实施知识产权边境保护的执法主体主要是美国海关与边境保护局(CBP)和美国国际贸易委员会(ITC)。美国海关与边境保护局于2003年3月1日成立,隶属于国土安全部,统管边境执法,包括对知识产权实施边境保护。美国国际贸易委员会则是在国会领导下的准司法机构,负责对违反"337条款"的案件作出终局判决,并采取相应的救济措施。"337条款"是指1994年修订的《1988年综合贸易竞争法》的第1342条,即《美国法典》第19标题卷第1337条。"337条款"是美国贸易法中的一条特殊条款,针对不公平的贸易行为采取一种行政救济措施。"337条款"中规定的非法行为包括:①所有人、进口商、承销人(及其代理商)将货物(非下属②③④所指货物)进口美国或销售中存在不公平竞争方法和不公平做法,其效果破坏或实质损害美国产业,阻止美国产业建立和限制垄断美国贸易和商业;②所有人、进口商、承销人(及其代理商)对下属物品向美国进口,为进口而销售,或进口后在美销售侵犯有效可执行的美国专利或有效可执行的美国版权的物品或利用有效的可执行的美国专利请求权包括的方法制造、生产、加工或开采的物品;③物品所有人、进口商、承销人(及其代理商)以侵犯有效可执行的美国注册商标的物品向美国的进口,为进口而销售或进口后在美销售;④有半导体芯片产品所有人、进口商、承销人(及其代理商)以侵犯按照《美国法典》第17标题卷第9章注册的掩膜作品(mask work)的方式,向美国进口、为进口而销售或进口后在美销售]

omnicompetence n. 有全部权力
omnicompetent a. 有全权的;全能的
omniparity n. 一切平等
omnipotence n. 无限权力;无限威力;万能
omnipotence of law 法律万能

* *Omnis exceptio est ipsa quoque regula.* Every exception is itself also a rule. 每一项例外,其自身也是一条规则。

* *Omnis interpretatio si fieri potest ita fienda est in instrumentis, ut omnes contrarietates amoveantur.* All the interpretations of instruments, as far as possible, are to be such that every inconsistency is removed. Every interpretation of instruments is to be made, as it is can be, so that all contradictions may be removed. 所有的解释,如果可能,必是通过文本中消除矛盾而实现。

* *Omnis regula suas patitur exceptiones.* Every rule is liable to its own exceptions.

一切规则皆有其例外。
omnishambles 一塌糊涂[流行于英国本土,形容词为 omnishambolic。该词首次出现在英国广播公司 2009 年热播的讲述英国政府内部运作的电视连续剧"幕后危机"(The Tick of It)中。剧中虚构人物马尔科姆·塔克对虚构议员尼古拉·默里大发雷霆,说他是"an omnishambles"。工党领袖埃德·米利班德在议会辩论中抨击保守党政府的预算建议,对政府准备征收"馅饼税"不满,说这样会将预算提高到"omnishambles status"。该词很快成为英国社会中的一个热词,广泛用于英国的政治评论中,描述被视为混乱、无效的政府活动]
omnium n. 担保证券的总额;全部,总额
on a charge of 以……罪名
on a preponderance of probability 概然性居上或占优势,概然率居上
on a roll 归入卷宗,归入案卷
on account 赊账;部分偿还账款;分期付款
on account of 因为,由于,为了某物
on agreement 按合约,按协议,根据协定
on all fours (=of a law case) (法律案件或诉讼案件的)完全一致[指在事实上和法律上两方面同先例完全一致,几乎在所有重要范畴完全相同〈our client's case is on all fours with Supreme Court's most recent opinion〉(我们的委托人的案情与联邦最高法院的最近判决意见完全一致)。见 white horse case]
on and off (或 off and on) 断断续续的,(船)时而靠岸时而离岸
on appointment 任职期间
on bail bond 具保在外候审
on balance 总的来说
on behalf of 代表……;为(某人的)利益
on call 即期支付的;已经准备妥当的;待通知的;待召回的
on carrier 陆地承运人,(集装箱运输)陆地承运人
on commission (受)委托
on credit 赊账
on deck risks 舱面险,甲板装货险
on default 如有过失;如未出庭;有疏忽

遗漏;未履行责任
on demand 根据要求(立即支付);见票即付(亦称 demand notes)
on (no) evidence 有(无)证据
on file 存档,归档
on going case 正在进行的案件
on good authority 有确实可靠的根据
on hand 现有的;现存的
on its own initiative 依职权,按职权
on lease 租用
on line transaction 网络贸易,联机交易
on (its) merits 按其是非曲直,按实情
on oath 发誓
on one's own account 自负其责;后果自负
on one's own terms 根据自己的主张,根据自己的条件
on or about 大约,大概,约
on/upon/under pain of (death) 违者处(死)
on parole 假释,在假释中(时)
on point 直接适用(指一项法规或先例如果直接适用于当前案例事实,则可称为 a law on point;a case on point)
on purpose 故意地
on record 在案
on relief (根据法律的)救济方法
on remand pending 押候审判
on sale or return (对供试用的商品)买下或退货
on second thoughts 经仔细考虑之后
on shares 分摊盈亏,分摊
on sufferance 出于容忍,出于宽容
on suspicion 因受怀疑
on the alert 戒备,留意
on the bench 任法官,在法院
on the books 载入名册;有记载;有案可查
on the complaint of 根据……的控诉
on the contrary 正相反,相反的
on the courthouse steps 在法庭的阶梯上
on the defendant's behalf 被告之代理
on the docket 在审理中;在审查中;在执行中;在考虑中
on the face of 就表面看
on the face of it 从表面判断,乍看起来
on the floor (议会法)待决动议(根据考

虑此动议待决)(见 pending 2)〈The motion ison the floor〉(此动议处于待决之中)
on the ground 当场
on the ground of 以……为理由;以……为借口
on the happening of an insurable event 发生保险事故时
on the horizon 已露端倪,临近的,即将发生的
on the information of 根据……的告发
on the merits 依据是非曲直,依据法律(指依据法律实质性问题提出的抗辩),实体审判,基于案情实质,基于法定权利
on the motion of sb. 经某人的动(提)议
on the national level 在国家一级
on the part of 就……而言
on the point 在那个问题上
on the quiet 秘密地,私下地
on the record 有记录的
on the regional level 在地区一级
on the run 在逃
on the scene 当场,在出事地点,在现场
on the spot 当场,立即;在危险中(尤指被暗杀的危险);处于负责地位;处于必须行动的地位
on the stand 在法院的证人席
on the subject of 关于……问题
on the table 摆在桌面上;在考虑中;被搁置
on the track of 追踪
on time 1.准时,按时 2.按时付款,分期付款
on trial 受审
on-dit (法)据说,传闻,道听途说,谣传,流言
on-licence n. 不许外卖(只许堂饮)酒类的执照
on-line n. 联机
on-line scrip 见 e-money
on-line service provider 网络传输中服务供应商,联网中服务供应商
onomastic a. 签字款式与原文件笔迹不同的
on-site examination 现场检查
on-the-job professional training 在职专业人员培训
on-the-spot a. 现场的,当场的
on-the-spot investigation 现场调查,现场勘验
on-the-spot mediation 就地调解
on-the-spot meeting 现场会议
on-the-spot trial 就地审判
once a mortgage 一次抵押
＊Once a mortgage, always a mortgage. 一次抵押总归是抵押。
once for all 一劳永逸地,彻底地
one among the equals 平等者中平等的一员
one clean-cut rule (美)同一明确规则
one contracting party 合同(契约)当事人的一方
one day of 7 hours 一天之内的 7 个小时
one dimensional man 单向度的人(指在高度发达的工业文明中,人从生产到物质生活和精神生活的自由度被社会强制剥夺,人的精神家园已完全丧失。生活在这种环境的人丧失了个人的独立性,是一种被社会机械整合的——西方马克思主义学派代表人物美国哲学家郝伯特·马尔库塞称之为——"单向度的人")
one man company 一人公司(指只有股东一人的公司)
one man grand jury 一人大陪审团(指对美国一些州将类似于大陪审团的调查权授予一名司法官或其他代理人的称呼)
one nation (或 country), two systems (中)一国两制(即一个国家两种制度)
one of the parties 当事人的一方
one party 一方当事人
one person acts for another person or group 一个人替他人或团体而作出各种行为的(一种制度)(指代议制)
one person, one vote 一人(只投)一票
one shot litigants 一次性诉讼当事人
one size fits all 一个尺寸所有人穿[指工业化国家强迫后进国家接受与其经济条件不合的保护(如知识产权等)标准]
one time special price 一次性处理价格
one vote majority 一票领先

one way intervention 一条道的诉讼参与(1966年美国《联邦民事诉讼规则》第23条修订后和州集团诉讼条款比较被解释为允许一道的诉讼参与,即允许缺席集团成员直到有利判决后才参加进来)
one way or two way 单向或双向
one whose acts related to a crime 牵连犯
one word will suffice 一句话就够了
one year's notice 一年的通知
one-claim, one-enforcement method 一请求权一执行方法(指德国民事强制执行方法的原则之一)
ONE-HALF "温哈夫"计算机病毒
one-level system of reconsideration 一级复议制
one-party principle 一党制原则
one-party state 一党制政府
one-party states 一党制国家
one-shot 一次性成功的,一次性使用的,一次性通过
one-shot game 一次有效的对策,一次完成的博弈
one-shot litigants 一次性成功的诉讼当事人
one-shot payment 一次支付
one-side offer of settlement rule 单边和解要约规则
one-sided most-favo(u)red-nation clause 单边(片面的)最惠国条款
one-step investigation 一步式侦查(指整个侦查过程没有明确的阶段划分和相应的职责分工,一个犯罪案件的侦查工作由一个部门的侦查人员从头至尾负责,又称为一贯式侦查)
one-time a./ad. 一度的/从前
one-time deals 一次性交易
one-trial assessor system 一审陪审制
one-way ratchet theory 见 ratchet theory
onerari non debet 否认原告所提债款的存在
onerous a. 负有义务的;艰巨的,繁重的
onerous act 苛例
onerous contract 有偿合同(契约)
onerous gift 负有义务的遗赠
onerous property 负有义务的财产(权)
onerous test of admissibility (负有义务的)可接受性的繁重试验
onerous title 负有义务的所有权
oneself action 自诉
ongoing claims 现行的权利要求
ongoing consulting 日常咨询
ongoing enterprise 现有企业
ongoing project 施行方案
online dispute resolution 线解决纠纷机制,在线争端解决(指利用电子邮件、电子布告栏、电子聊天室、语言设备、视频设备、网站系统软件等网络信息技术进行资讯交流,实现当事人在电脑屏幕前完成纠纷解决的协商、调解、仲裁等程序。实现在线争端解决裁决书的最佳方式当然是当事人自愿履行,但如果当事人不自愿履行在线争端解决裁决书,该裁决书的强制执行则成为在线争端解决实务中面临的两大难题之一,有的学者甚至认为这是最大的难题。因此,完善的裁决书执行机制乃是在线争端解决能否发展壮大的关键)
online sale 在线销售(指交易双方通过互联网进行的以提供某种数据化产品或服务为标的的交易活动,亦称直接电子商务,是电子商务的一个专用术语)
only as a matter of form 形式了事
only too 非常
ontological element 本体论要素(自然法包括的两要素之一,另一为认识论要素 gnoseological element)
ontology n. 本体论
onus 1.责任,义务,负担,举证责任 2.过失,耻辱
onus of maintaining an illegitimate child 非婚生子女的抚养义务
onus of proof 举证责任
onus probandi 举证责任,证明责任
open v./a. 开始;揭开;开放,开办,开设,开张,展现/1.空旷的;敞开的 2.开始工作的,在营业的;活动着的 3.开放的;不受禁止的;无法律限制的 4.公开的;坦率的 5.悬而未决的,未决定的 6.无冰冻的;温和的
open a case 开始审理案件
open a court 开庭
open a debate 开始辩论
open a judg(e)ment 保持有效的判决(指

在法庭进行复查之前保持判决一直生效)
open access 开放存取(指国际社会的一些团体或个人采取"亚政治"运动,其中最有代表性的即为"开放存取与知识共享",前身是国际学术界、出版界、图书情报界为了推动科学成果利用互联网自由传播而采取的运动。按照2011年"布达佩斯开放存取协议"的说法,"对某文献的'开放存取',即意味着肩负在互联网公共领域里可免费获取,并允许任何用户阅读、下载、复制、传递、打字、搜索超链该文献,也允许用户将其通览并建立索引用作下载软件载入数据或其他任何合法用途")
open access initiatives (OAI) 开放获取计划
open account 来往账目;记账交易,赊账
open an account 开户
open an embassy 开设大使馆
open and notorious adultery 公然通奸罪
open and peaceful possession 公开与和平的占有(或占领)
open and tangible 公开而且确实
open and undefended city 不设防城市
open ballot 公开的无记名投票
open bid 公开投标
open career system 公开考选制,(美)开放职业制(指美国政府的机关人员补充,不受教育程度、年龄、社会阶层的限制,均可凭其知识、能力,经考试合格进入政府)
open cemetery 公共坟场
open check (或 **cheque**) 普通支票(即非线支票)
open contract 不订明条件的合同(契约),简略合同(契约)
open corporation (面向公众的)开放股份公司
open court 公开法庭(指准许群众参加旁听的法庭)
open cover 预约保险单,承保单
open credit 无担保信贷
open crossed check 无记名画线支票
open debt 未清欠账
open diplomacy 公开外交
open door doctrine 门户开放主义
open door policy 门户开放政策

open election 公开的选举
open entry (18世纪)公开进入,公开占有不动产(指明目张胆进入并占有不动产;这种进入既非秘密,亦非诡计或施展计谋实施,而是在两个证人在场情况下公开进入)
open fiduciary loan 信用借款
open general license 公开一般许可,无限制一般许可
open housing 自由售租的房屋
open judgment 将判决公开
open letter of credit 公开信用证
open license 公开营业执照
open (或 **general**) **listing** 对不动产经纪人的开放性登记;一个以上代理的销售权
open market 公开市场,自由市场
open market operations 公开市场业务
Open Method of Coordination 开放协商机制(指构成软法结构的核心,因此民主协商性在软法的制定与实施过程中能够得到更为充分的体现,简称OMC)
open mortgage 开放抵押,可以清偿的抵押,未足额的抵押
open of position 空缺
open policy 1.不定值保险合同(契约);开口保险单,未确定保单 2.开放政策
open port 通商口岸,对外开放口岸,开放港;不冻港
open possession 公开占有
open pricing 公开定价
open principle 开放原则[亦称开放、兼容原则,指电子商务立法对所涉及的诸如电子商务、签名(字)、认证、原件、书面形式、数据电文、信息系统等有关范畴应保持开放、中立态度以适应电子商务不断发展的客观需要,而不能将其局限于某一特定的形态]
open prison 不设防监狱
open question 待决的问题,容许争议的问题
Open Range (美史)自由放牧区
open record 未建的诉讼记录卷
open registry 开放登记(国际海事上用语)
open sea 公海
open season (渔猎等)开放期
open secret 公开的秘密

open session 公开会议
open ship 敞舱船
open shop (美)自由雇佣(制)企业(指不论是否属工会会员均可招雇的企业)
open skies 开放领空(指裁军时双方允许对方从空中侦察军事设施的一种做法)
Open Source Software 开源软件[开源软件是开源代码软件的简称,一般认为开源软件是指遵循某种开源许可证协议,其源代码在不同程度上向公众公开,并允许用户在许可证协议约定的许可"条件"内自由地使用、修改和分发的计算机软件。开源软件最主要特征在于软件开发者通过通用许可协议(GPL)的方式规定使用者免费使用软件的前提条件和所承担的义务]
open tender 公开招标
open texture 开放结构(指语言边界上的不确定性,在此边界上会产生争议,这与司法证明语言上的模糊性有关。见 fuzzy reasoning);空缺结构(指大量的法律漏洞和在一定程度上可有效弥补的种种规范缺失的判例制度,即哈特所言的空缺结构)
open the pleadings 在抗辩前作简单陈述
open to judicial exploration 让司法考察公开
open town 不禁赌、不禁酒等的城市(镇)
open trade 未完结交易
open treaty 开放条约
open trial 公开审讯;审判公开(原则)
open union 可自由加入的工会
open university 开放性大学
open up 吐露真情,揭露;展现,开始;开放,取消对……限制
open verdict 1.存疑裁决(指陪审团仅确定有罪而不能确定何人犯罪所作的裁决) 2.死因未详的裁决(指验尸陪审团所作的一种裁决)
open vote 记名投票
open voting 公开投票
open wound 有裂口的伤
open-account terms 按记账方式交易
open-end a. 开放的,无限制的,可广泛解释的,不固定的
open-end contract 开口合同(契约)(指在一定期间内不改变价格和条件,买受人可随时购买的合同)
open-end investment company 发行可随时换成现款的股票的投资公司
open-end mortgage 无限制的抵押(亦译做开放抵押,指允许抵押人在同一抵押财产上可以追加抵押借款数额的一种抵押,比较 closed-end mortgage)
open-ended anti-trust law 无限制的反托拉斯法
open-ended claim 开放式请求
open-fields doctrine (刑事诉讼)敞(开)地(方)搜查原则[该原则允准警方在个人拥有的财产,如住宅外面露天空地,进行无证搜查。这一原则必须排除住宅和住宅相邻近的土地,如庭院。这些都是圈围地或受治安(public scrutiny)保护的,除非警方具有一些其他法律依据,否则不得进行无证搜查。亦称 open-field doctrine 或 open-field rule。见 plain view doctrine]
open-mindedness 开放的心胸
opener n. (信用证)开证人
opening n. 1.开始,初步 2.空缺的职位;机会;空地(场) 3.(提出证据前辩护人的)开始陈述 4.开幕
opening bank (信用证)开证银行
opening (of) credit 无担保贷款;开立信用账户
opening price 开盘价,开价
opening rate 开盘价,开盘汇率
opening section 开头条文;首条
opening statement 开场陈述(指在美国民诉案件中,提出证据之前审理时,律师向陪审团就案件性质和预计提供的证据作简要的陈述。目的在于使陪审团对案件事实及所涉及争议有一个概括了解,便于其理解随后提出的证据)
opening statement of counsel (审讯开始时)辩护人(对陪审员提前举证并就案件性质等)所作的概述
opening stock 初期库存
opening the case 开始陈述案情
opening the pleadings (英)开庭陈述(指庭审开始,原告律师向陪审团简要介绍诉状实质内容);(律师的)开始陈述

opening transaction 开始交易
openness n. 空缺性
openness of the data of declaration 申报资料的公开
operae servorum et animalis 奴隶及家畜的劳役使用权
operate v. 操作;工作;施行手术;作战;从事投机(指证券、商品等);经营;管理;完成;运行;营运;引起
operating a. 营业上的;操作的;工作的;(权力)实施的
operating activities 经营活动
operating capital 流动资本,营业资本
operating cost 营业成本,营运成本
operating expenses 营业支出,业务开支,营业费用
operating holding company 经营性控股公司(欧洲国家和地区很普遍)
operating income 见 ordinary income
operating profit 营业利润
operating rules 操作规程
operating table 手术台
operation n. 运用;作用;实施;生效;经营,管理;交易,买卖
operation agreement 经营协议
operation of foreign investment 外资运营阶段
operation of law 法律的实施,法律的运用
operation of legal system 法制的运作
operation of payment 支付业务
operation of the civil registry 办理民事登记业务
operational a. 操作上的;业务上的;可起作用的,可使用的;作战上的,现役的
operational command 实施令
operational expenditure 业务费用
operational period 缓刑期内;现役期内
operational staff 执行人员
operations manager 操作管理员
operations research 运筹学(通常被称为 OR,亦称为 operational research)
operative a./n. 有效的,生效的,实施的;起作用的;工作的,生产的/技工,工人,操作人员;特务;侦察人员;地下工作人员;私人侦探

operative clause 生效条款
operative fact(s) 产生法律效果的事实,有效事实;发生效力的事实
operative mistake 执行中的错误
operative norm 行动准则,行为规范,执行标准
operative part 正文;有关部分;主要部分;(条约、议定、合同等)执行部分
operative part of a deed 契据的履行部分
operative words (契据等中的)有法律效力的词,重要的词
operator n. 1.经营者;厂主;经纪人;投机商 2.执行人 3.司机,操作人员 4.善于以巧妙手段达到目的的人(如善于钻法律空子的人)
opiate n./a./v. 鸦片剂,麻醉剂/含鸦片的,安眠的,麻醉的,安神的/使安神,使麻醉
opiniojuris 法律确信
opinio juris ef recessitatis 法律和必要的确信
*Opinio quae favet testamento est tenenda. The opinion which favors a will is to be followed. 有利于遗嘱的意见应该遵从。
opinion (14 世纪)1.法院(或法官)判决意见书[指法院的书面陈述表明在特定案件中其判决结果,通常包括案件事实、本案适用的法律观点、判决的法理以及附带意见(dicta)等,缩略为 op.;亦称 judicial opinion。见 decision; judgment 1; ruling 1]2.正式判决的表达(指根据专家的特别知识或专有知识,又应委托人的要求,通常是准备的一份文件对判决的正式表述或告知内容,包括律师对特定案件适用法律的理解。亦称 opinion letter)3.个人的理想,信念,推断,尤其是在争议中对有关事实证人的观点,以区别于事实本身的一些专业知识(在意义 3 上),亦称 conclusion(见 opinion evidence)
opinion evidence (1995 年)意见证据[指证人的思想、信念和推断或有关事实或一些事实的结论,参见《联邦证据规则》第 701—705 条。见 opinion 3; opinion rule]
opinion letter 见 opinion 2
opinion of the court 1.(仲裁过程中的)法庭判定(裁定)2.法庭意见(指导致法庭判

决的绝大多数法官的意见)
opinion poll 民意测验
opinion rule (1896年)(证据)意见规则[指证人对一些事实的证明的原则,而不是判决意见,而且非专家证人的意见通常被排除在证据之外。传统地说,这一原则在证据法中被认为是重要排除规则之一,它是基于这样的观念:即已观察到的理论数据(data)的证人应提供更可能的事实证据,而弃掉陪审团根据证据草拟的推断或结论,根据这一体制,证人的意见(opinion)就没有必要。当今,如果理论性基于证人的观念并有助于事实调查人(factfinder),则这些意见都是可以采纳的]
opinion testimony 意见证言(指就争议的问题陈述个人的观点、看法而区别于就自己了解案件事实而作的客观陈述。意见证言不管出自非专家证人或一个专家证人,仅在一定条件下方可被允准作为证据)
opium n. 鸦片
opium addict 吸食鸦片者
opium offender 鸦片犯,毒品犯
opium smuggling 鸦片走私,私运鸦片(罪)
opium trade 贩毒,贩卖鸦片
opium trafficker 私贩鸦片商
opium trafficking 私贩鸦片(罪)
* *Oportet quod certae personae, terrae, et certi status comprehendantur in declaratione usuum.* It is necessary that given persons, lands, and estates should be comprehended in a declaration of uses. 有必要在受益权声明中将特定的人、土地、产权等都包括在内。
Oppeuiheim (Oppenheim, Lassa Francis Lawrence) 奥本海(1858—1919)[德国国际法学家,先后在德国的弗赖堡大学和巴塞尔大学讲授法学,后又在英国研究和讲授国际法。主要著作有《国际法》(1905年)和两卷本的《国际法的前途》(1911年)。其中,《国际法》已数次修订再版,迄今为止仍是一本权威性很高的著作。奥本海为实证主义者,他主张国际法的渊源是习惯、国际判例以及准立法文件。他是国际联盟的强烈拥护者]
oppidan n. 城市居民

oppignerare (大陆法)保证,担保;抵押
opponency n. 反对的行为;敌对状态
opponent n. (诉讼)对方当事人;反对者;抗辩人;对手,敌手
opponent's pleading by new matter 对方带有新事实的答辩
opponents to a bill 方(议)案的反对者
opponent's witness and evidence 对方的证人和证据
opportunism n. 机会主义
opportunistic post-contractual manipulation 机会主义的后合同操纵
opportunity cost 机会成本(或备择成本)(表达稀缺与选择二者之间的基本关系,特指拒绝备择品或机会的最高价值的估价)
opportunity cost of capital 资本的机会成本
opportunity on the law 《法律中的机会主义》[指1916—1939年美国大法官布朗代斯(Brandeis)在哈佛道德学会演讲稿名称]
opportunity to defend 答辩的机会
opposable a. 可反对的,可对抗的;可提出的
oppose v. 反对,反抗;阻挠
oppose an action 抗诉
opposed a. 反对的,敌对的,对抗的,对立的,相对的,相反的
opposer n. 反对者;反对注册某一商标者
opposing case 相反的判例
opposing claim 对方请求,反对方的请求
opposing counsel 抗辩者,对方律师
opposing position 对方立场
opposing traffic 对向交通;双向通行
opposing vote 反对票
opposite a. 反对的;对立的,相反的;相对的
opposite faction 反对派
opposite (或 **opposing**) **party** 对方当事人
opposition n. 1.对抗;反对 2.反抗;对立 2.相反 3.抗诉 4.(大写)反对党
Opposition benches (议会中的)反对党席位
Opposition chief whip (英)反对党首席组织秘书
Opposition Party 反对党
opposition to payment 拒付
Opposition whip 在野党议员首领

oppression n. （非法）抑压;压制;压迫;高压手段;（刑法）滥用职权（公职人员出于不正当目的滥用职权造成他人伤害之行为）;（合同法）强迫签订非法合同

oppression leading to confession 逼供

oppression of majority by minority 少数股东对多数股东的压迫

oppressive a. 压迫的,压制的;沉重的

oppressive contracts 胁迫性契约

oppressor n. 压迫者,压制者,强迫者

opprobrium n. 1.轻蔑,责骂 2.不名誉,耻辱,羞耻 3.非难,诽谤 4.不名誉的事（或人）

oppugn v. 反驳;质问;攻击

oppugner n. 反驳者;质问者;抗击者

opt v. 抉择,选择

opt in （1966年）选择加入（某事）〈when the choose of setting or not setting came, the Joneses opted in, hoping to avoid a length trial〉（在安排选择或没有安排选择到来时,琼斯选择加入,希望避免漫长的审理）

opt out 宣布放弃选择（权）;退出;选择退出（指消费者使用的"选择退出"权利,明确通知信用报告机构将自己从此类促销名单中删除）

opt out of action 退出诉讼,放弃诉讼选择权

opt-in election 选入式

opt-out election 选出式

opt-out class 退出选择的群体,放弃选择的群体[指《联邦民事诉讼规则》规定的原告群体。据此书面证明,该群体成员只要不想受到案件判决或调解所及范畴的束缚,即可选择将他们自己排除在外。该规则第23(c)条允准法庭不考虑要求排除在外的群体成员。该群体成员在选择退出之前可以等待调解安排的条款（settlement's terms）宣布]

opt-out clause 选出的条款（指公司明确其股东之间就拟让股权的事先同意权和优先购买权）

opt-out provisions 宣布放弃选择的条款,放弃选择性条款

optant n. 抉择者,选择者

∗ *Optima est legis interpres consuetudo.* Custom is the best interpreter of the laws. 习惯是对法律的最好解释。

∗ *Optima est lex quae minimum relinquit arbitrio judicis; optimus judex qui minimum sibi.* That law is the best which leaves least to the discretion of the judge; that judge is the best who leaves least to his own. 留给法官以最小的自由裁量权的法律是最好的法律;留给自己以最小的自由裁量权的法官是最好的法官。

∗ *Optima legum interpres consuetudo.* Custom is the best interpreter of the laws. 习惯（惯例）是法律的最好解释者。

optimal capital structure 最佳资本结构

optimal care 最令人满意的谨慎

optimal firearm regulatory regime 最佳枪支管理制度

optimal royalty rate 最佳版税率

optimal size of a governmental unit 政府单元的最优模式

Optimates （古罗马）贵族党

optimistic(al) criminal 存有侥幸心理的罪犯

optimiza requirements 极佳化诫命[指原则上给予法律和事实的可能性要求尽最大可能实现其内容的规范,为此,德国法理论者阿列克西把此原则定义为"极佳化诫命"和"理想应然"（ideal ought）];最佳化诫命（基于既有法律与事实现状的需求尽可能实现某一目标的规范）

optimum n. （生长繁殖的）最适宜条件,最适度

optimum exploitation 最适当之开发

optimum sustainability 最适当持续能力

optimum yield 最适度产量,最适宜条件的收益

option n. 1.选择权,自由选择;选择的事物 2.期权,买卖的特权（指在合同或契约期内按规定价格买卖指定的股票、货物等的权利）3.（在规定时间内要求履行合同的）优先权,特权 4.（被保险人对赔款方式的）选择

option agreement 选择权协议

option of domicile 居住选择权

option of nationality 国籍的选择（权）

option of profession 职业选择权

option of removal （美）移送选择权

optional a. 可选择的;非强制的,任意的
optional clause 任择条款,任意条款;选择权条款(一般出版合同中常见的术语,希望作者如果以后出书,应先选择原出版社为合作谈判人)
optional compulsory jurisdiction 可选择的强制裁判权,任选强制管辖(权)
optional nature 选择性,非强制性,任意性
optional obligation 任意之债,选择之债
optional port 选择港
optional stipulation 可选择的合同(契约)条款
optional writ 诉讼开始令(指旧英国惯例中的一种原始令状,亦称 *praecipe*,即命令被告必须做某事或陈述不做此事之理由的令状)
optionee n. 取得优先买卖权的人;有选择权的人
oracle n. 神谕,预言者,大智者
oral a. 口头的,口述的
oral accusation 口头控诉
oral agreement 口头协议
oral argument 口头辩论
oral character of proceeding 带有口头方式进行的诉讼
oral communication 口头表达
oral complaint 口头起诉
oral confession 口供
oral contract 口头合同(契约)
oral declaration (合同的)口头宣告,口头声明;口头申报;口头供述,口头陈述
oral (或 parole) evidence 口头证据
oral examination 口头审问;口试
oral form 口头方式
oral instruction 口头指示,口头说明
oral judg(e)ment 口头判决
oral pleading 口头答辩
oral procedure 口头式诉讼程序
oral question (议会上的)口头质询(程序)
oral sex (美)(嗜性交)口交
oral statement 口头声明,口头陈述
oral summons 口头传唤
oral testament 口授遗嘱
oral testimony 口头证词,证言
oral trust 口头信托

oral will 口述遗嘱
oral work 口头作品
orality n. 口头陈述
Orange Book (美)(专利)橙色书本名册[指有关药材或药材产品的专利名册,其中普通药品申请(generic-drug applications)部分申请应属美国食品药品管理署(Food and Drug Administration,缩略为 FDA)。专利的保护有效期均被列出,申请人于任何时候均可将普通药品申请呈上,但申请人必须或是接受 FDA 在专利保护期届满前延期批准,或是接受对专利有效性(validity)的争议。这个橙色书本名册的正式名称为《已核定具有等同价值疗效的药材产品》(Approved Drug, Products With Therapeutic Equivalence Evaluation)]
oration n. 演说,演讲
orator n. 请愿人;原告;雄辩者,演说家
oratress n. 女演说家,女雄辩家
oratrix n. orator 的女性
ordain v. 1.任命,委任;颁布命令 2.(法律等)制定,规定;注定
ordeal n. 1.神(明)裁判法(指古时的一种判罪法,使抱灼烧之物或服毒等以视其结果,而认为这是神之裁判)2.严酷的考验,痛苦的经验
ordeal by battle 决斗神判法
ordeal by fire 探火神判法
ordeal by water 探(沸)水神判法
ordeffe (或 ordelfe) n. (自己土地下的)矿藏特许使用权
order n./v. 1.顺序,次序;条理,整齐 2.制度;(议事)规程,(程序)规则;秩序;治安 3.命令;法院的决议,法院指令 4.(转让产业的)许可证,授权证明书 5.订货单;定购;汇票,汇单 6.等级;种类 7.阶层,界,团体/命令,指令;定购,订货;安排,整理
order bill of lading 指示提单,指定人提单
order blank 订货单
order book 动议(或议事)登记簿,订货簿
order check (或 cheque) 指定人支票,抬头支票,记名支票
order confirmation 订货确认书;(印好的)订货单

order entry 委托进入
order flaw and trade interaction 委托和相互交易
order for account （法院发出的）调查双方资金账目的命令
order for arrest 通缉令
order for attachment 逮捕令,拘捕令
order for delivery up of infringing articles 上缴侵权商品令
order for deprivation of political rights 剥夺政治权利令
order for discharge 释放令(又译:开释令)
order for ejectment 驱逐令
order for enforcement 强制执行判决的(法院)命令
order for eviction 搬迁令
order for foreclosure absolute 绝对判决的取消赎回权令
order for foreclosure nisi 非绝对判决的取消赎回权令
order for maintenance 支付赡养费令
order for payment 支付命令
order for seizure of property 查抄财产令
order for the administration of trust 财产管理委托令
order form 订货单
Order in Council （英）枢密院(在院)令(亦称女王在枢密院命令,指英女王依据枢密院的建议,运用特权或制定法授权,会同枢密院颁发的命令。见 Order of Council)
order nisi 限期内无人提出反对则法庭判决生效令
order nunc pro tunc 追补令
order of acquittal 释放令,清还令,解除令
order of adducing 引证程序,援引程序
order of business 议程,议事程(次)序
order of calling witnesses 挑选、召集证人令
order of certiorari （调取案件）复审令(见 writ of certiorari)
order of commendation 嘉奖令
order of committal 收监令,拘押令
Order of Council （英）枢密院(不在院)命令(这种命令和女王在枢密院命令 Order in Council 大致相同,不同的只是枢密院运用女王权力,在她外出或有病时颁发的而无须女王同意的命令)
order of course （英史）当然令状(指申请人以自己的申请并自己承担风险依适当形式取得法院发给的令状)
order of detention 拘留令
order of discharge 解除破产命令(破产被告人经过公开审讯之后,如果获得免除其债务的决定,则破产被告人可向法院申请颁发这种命令)
order of disposition 处分令
order of expulsion 驱逐令
order of filiation 私生子女的父亲确认令
order of general amnesty 大赦令
order of goods 商品等级
order of mandamus 履行责任令(见 mandamus)
order of martial law 戒严令
order of nature 自然规律
order of payment 付款凭单,付款委托
order of preference 优先程序
order of presentation 陈述顺序
order of priority 优先顺序
order of procedure 进行程序;程序顺(次)序
order of prohibition 禁止令
order of question （议会的）质询程序
order of reference of accounts 审查账目令
order of reference to arbitration 提交仲裁令,提交公断令
order of release 释放(犯人)出狱令
order of removal 案件移送令(指由一个法院发出指示将案件转移到另一个法院的命令)
order of restitution 发还令,回复原状令
order of revivor 重新审理讼案令,(英)恢复诉讼令(指要求恢复因一方死亡而中断的诉讼的命令)
order of serjeants 高级律师界
order of severity 严重程度
order of specific performance （英）具体执行令
order of succession 继承顺序
order of suppression 中止令,抑制令
order of the coif 白帽阶层(指英格兰律师

界的高级律师阶层)
order of the day 议事日程
order of the line of appeal 上诉的程序
order of transfer 移送案件令
order on a bank 银行汇票,银行汇票单
order on reconsideration 复审决定
order paper 订货证券;订货票证(字据)(又译指示票据,指一个票据文件中有付款给持票人"Pay to bearer"或"To the order of"字样者)
order placing meeting 订货会议
order public (大陆法)公共秩序
order refusing to proceed in the case for want of jurisdiction 因管辖错误而拒绝进行诉讼(程序)的裁定
order sb. arrested (美)下令逮捕某人
order sheet 订货单
order the arrest of a criminal at large 通缉逃犯
order to cease-fire 停战令
order to pay 指示付款票证
order to release 释放令
order to show cause 陈述理由令
order to suspend production or business operation 责令停产停业
ordered a. 有安排的,安排好的
ordered liberty 命令享有自由
ordering conference 订货会议
ordering discovery 命令性披露程序
ordering entry of judgment 命令作出判决登记
ordering of provisional measure (法院)下令采取临时措施
orderly litigation 有序诉讼
orders of heirs 继承人的顺序
ordinance n. 1.命令;法令,法规;布告 2.(英)条例(指从前的制定法的一种,因为它未经过上议院、下议院、君主的三重通过或赞许,而只经过一重或二重通过,所以不叫法,只叫条例)3.传统的风俗习惯
Ordinances of the Holy Apostles Through Clement 《克莱蒙神圣使徒法令》(或称《使徒法令》。见 Apostolic Constitutions)
ordinance power of executive 行政首长的命令权

ordinarily prudent person 见 reasonable person
ordinary n./a. 1.审判员(旧译:推事) 2.(美)(审理遗嘱检验或监护案件的)法官 3.(罗马法)常任法官(指无须指派可依自己职权进行案件审理的法官)4.(英)罪犯的忏悔牧师;(普通法上的)具有推事管辖权的宗教推事(指担任教区主教职务,并具有教会审判权的人)/普通的,一般的;平常的;常任的;编制内的;有直接管辖权的;直隶(属)的
ordinary accident 一般事故
ordinary agent 普通代理人
ordinary annuity 常规年金(指每次支付期末给予支付的年金。见 annuity due)
ordinary appeal 普通上诉
ordinary assembly (议会法)一般审议会 [指立法机构之外的审议机关(deliberative assembly)]
ordinary care 见 reasonable care
ordinary cause of trade 正常贸易情况
ordinary check 普通支票
ordinary civil disputes 一般民事纠纷
ordinary co-litigation 普通共同诉讼
ordinary conviction 一般性定罪
ordinary court 普通法院,普通法庭(与特别法庭或专门法庭相对而言)
ordinary criminal case 普通(一般)刑事案件
ordinary criminal offender 普通(一般)刑事犯
ordinary criminal offenses 普通(一般)刑事犯罪
ordinary deputy 普通代表(即下院议员),(国民议会的)下院议员
ordinary destruction 一般毁损
ordinary diligence 通常的勤勉
ordinary election 通常选举
ordinary hazard principle 通常危险原则
ordinary homicide 一般杀人(罪)
ordinary gain (1945年)正常收益,正常获利(指非资产的出售或交易所获取的收益。见 capital gain)
ordinary income 1.经营收入(在缴纳商业税方面,在商业经营的正常活动中所得的

收入,亦称"operating income")2.一般收入,在个人所得税方面[指来自工资、佣金、利息等收入(与资本利益所得相对而言)]
ordinary judge 常任法官,普通法官
ordinary judg(e)ments proceedings 普通判决诉讼(程序)(即书面判决程序)
ordinary jurisdiction 普通审判权,普通管辖权
ordinary jury 普通陪审团
ordinary language 普通语言
ordinary language analysis 日常语言分析派
ordinary larceny 普通(一般)盗窃
ordinary law 一般法;(大陆法)普通法(与特别法相对而言,非指英美法上的普通法"Common Law")
ordinary lawsuit 普通诉讼案件
ordinary legal action 普通诉讼
ordinary life assurance 普通人身(寿)保险
ordinary Lord (苏格兰)最高民事法院法官
ordinary meeting 常会,例会
ordinary(或 general)negligence 普通(一般)过失
ordinary of assize and sessions (由主教任命的)巡回法庭和法庭的(行刑前的)罪犯忏悔牧师
ordinary out of court casual remark 一般性庭外偶然议论
ordinary partnership 普通合伙
ordinary proceedings in first instance 第一审的普通程序
ordinary prudent man 通常谨慎的人
ordinary removing (苏格兰)普通驱逐租户之诉
ordinary residence 通常居所,通常住所
ordinary revenue 经常收入
ordinary senator 常任参议员,普通参议员
ordinary session 例会
ordinary share(或 **stock**) 普通股
ordinary shareholder 普通股持有者,普通股股东
ordinary skill 普通技能(①见 skill;②见 ordinary skill in the art)
ordinary skill in the art (专利法)普通技能水平(指有代表性的工程师、科学家、设计师等在有关一项发明的技术中所拥有的技术知识、经验和专门技术的水平)
ordinary trustee 普通(一般)受托人
ordinary visa 普通(一般)签证
ordinary written law 一般(普通)成文法
ordination n. 分类,排成等级;委任,受委任;颁布法令;圣职授任
ordine delle istanze successive 顺序审理原则
ordinis beneficium (大陆法)保证人的先诉抗辩权(指债权人须先向债务人追偿,到追偿不足或追偿无着时,方可向保证人要求代偿)
Ordo Judiciarius 《司法程序》(指12世纪早期德国的一本关于罗马寺院法程序的教科书)
ordo judiciorum (寺院法)判决程序
ordo judiciorum privatorum 私诉程序
ordonnance (法)命令,法令,条例
ordonnance n. 命令,法令;安排,配置
ordre publique 公共秩序
ore resources law 矿产资源法
ore tanus 口头送达
organ n. 机关,机构;器官;喉舌;报刊
organ of authority 权力机构
organ of conciliation 调解机关
organ of judicial control 司法监督机关
organ of legal supervision 法律监督机关
organ of local self-government 地方自治机关
organ of military justice 军法机关
organ of non-contentious jurisdiction 非讼事件裁判机关
organ of public opinion 舆论的喉舌
organ of self-government 自治机关
organ of self-government of national autonomous area (中)民族自治地方的自治机关
organ of state 国家机关,国家机构
organ of state power 国家权力机关
organ of supreme power 最高权力机关
organ of the corporate body(或 **the legal entity**) 法人机关
organ of the executive 行政机关
organ of the prosecution 检控机关;检察机关

organ of the state administration 国家行政管理机关
organ of the United Nation 联合国机构
organ of violence 暴力机关
organ transplant 器官移植
organic a. 器官的;组织的,构成的;建制的;有组织的
Organic Act (美)构成法,组织法,组织条例
organic constitutional law 基本宪法,建制的宪法
organic law 基本法;建制法,组织法
Organic Law of the Local People's Congresses (中)《地方人民代表大会组织法》
Organic Law of the Local People's Governments (中)《地方人民政府组织法》
Organic Law of the People's Courts (中)《人民法院组织法》
Organic Law of the People's Procuratorates (中)《人民检察院组织法》
organic law on customs and excise 关税与国产税基本法,关税与货物税基本法
organic life forms 器官生命结构,器官生命体制
organic rules 组织条例,组织细则
organic solidarity 有机的连带关系
organicism n. 生物主义
(The) Organisation of African Unity 非洲统一组织
organism n. 生物体,有机体,社会组织,机关
organization n. 体制,编制;组织,团体,机构;设置,设立
organization control 机关管制
Organization for Economic Co-operation and Development (DECD) 经济合作与发展组织(1960年成立)
Organization for European Economic Co-operation 欧洲经济合作组织(1948年成立)
Organization of African Unity 非洲统一组织(1963年建立)
Organization of American States 美洲国家组织

Organization of American States Treaty Series (美)《美洲国家组织条约丛书》[即从前的《泛美联盟条约丛书》(Pan American Union Treaty Series),系该组织的某些个别国家和一些地区组织出版的它们自己的条约丛书,包括美国加入的多边条约的全文]
Organization of Central American States 中美国家组织
organization of courts 法院组织
organization of labo(u)r 劳动组织,劳工组织
organization of stock company 股份公司的设立
organization of the socialized sector 社会化部门
organization theory (法人的)有机体说
organizational a. 组织的,编制的,机构的
organizational law 组织法
organizational principle 组织原则
organizations for international marketing 国际市场经营组织
organized crime 有组织的犯罪,集团犯罪
organized crimecontinuum 有组织犯罪统一体(美国学术界提出了"有组织犯罪统一体"这一全新概念。在此概念之下,有组织犯罪作为一个统一的犯罪形态被细分为三个不同层次:第一层次,成熟的有组织犯罪,如黑手党型犯罪集团的犯罪;第二层次,欠缺某些典型特征的半成熟有组织犯罪;第三层次,即街头团伙和其他处于较低发展阶段的有组织犯罪。这种将有组织犯罪分为成熟的高级形态、半成熟的中级形态以及尚未成熟的低级形态,既揭示了有组织犯罪由低级形态不断向高级形态发展的趋势,也体现了美国对有组织犯罪的认识彻底摆脱预设模式而趋于理性和务实)
organizer of uncertainties 不确定因素的组织者[指美国学者曼恩(Manne)的理论。他对企业家的概念进行了一番甄别,认为企业家具有对生产的诸因素进行新的组合的功能,因而企业家是不确定因素的组织者]
oriental justice 导向性司法体制

origin n. 缘由,起因;起源;血统;出身;(出口商品时向进口国提供的)商品原产地(证明书)
origin and limit of risk 危险的生成与界限
origin function 来源功能
origin of a dispute 争议的起因
origin of law 法的起源(又译:法律的起源)
origin of product 产品的原产地
origin of state 国家的起源
original n./a. 原物;原作品;原文;来源,起因/最初的,最早的,原先的;原始的;独创的;未来的;原有的
original acquisition (所有权的)原始取得
original agreement 原始协议,原有协定
original and derivative estate 原始取得和继受的地产
original assigner 原有让与人;原有委托人
original bill 原法案,法案正本;汇票正本
original bills of lading 提单正本
original certificate 原始证书;原始凭证;原始单据
original civil jurisdiction 初审民事管辖权
original claim 主请求,原始请求
original conveyance 首次转让
original copy of the deed 正契;原始文件
original court 原判法庭
original criminal jurisdiction 初审刑事管辖权
original document 原本,正本,原始文件
original document rule 见 best evidence rule
original domicile 本籍,原籍,原始住所
original draft 原始汇票,汇票正本
original estate 原始地产(与 derivative estate 相对而言)
original evidence 1.原始证据[指证人他(或她)凭自己五官之一的感受或领悟在争点中的陈述,或证人是处于特有身心健康状态(particular physical and mental state)。亦称 direct evidence] 2.见 best evidence
original fact 原始性事实(见 institutional fact)
original game 原博弈

original insurance(或 **direct insurance**) 原保险(相对再保险而言,若无再保险也就无所谓原保险)
original insurer 原保险人
original intent 立法者本意,立法本意(对宪法解释和法律解释的一种方法,力图辨明文句的立法者本意,按照立法者在创设宪法和法律的相关规定时的意图进行解释。美国传统上的立法本意常指"法律制定者的意图""原来意思"或"本来的理解"。立法者本意作为审判的指导原则,法官解释法律时要受到立法本意的约束)
original inventor 最早的发明者
original invoice 正本发货票
original issue 原始发行
original judg(e)ment 原(审)判(决)
original jurisdiction 原始管辖,初审管辖权,联邦最高法院的初审管辖权[指最先听审诉讼的法院所行使的司法管辖权,作为一审法庭,法庭必须进行审判,确定争论的事实,对认定的事实适用法律,从而断结该案。美国国会创设了联邦地区法院并将其作为联邦司法的初审法院。美国联邦宪法第3条授予联邦最高法院对涉及大使、公使、领事等外国使节的案件或州为当事人的案件以初审管辖权。这种授权并不排除国会对其他法院给予同样的授权]
original lease 原始租赁,原租约
original leasee 原始承租人,原承租人
original leasor 原始出租人,原出租人
original main motion 原主(议)案,原来的主要动议
original manuscript 原稿
original member-state 创始会员国
original mortgage 原抵押
original nationality 原有国籍
original of the treaty 条约正本,条约原文
original offer 原要约,原提议;原发价
original owner 原业主,原始所有人
Original Package Act (美)《原包装法》(见 license case)
original package doctrine (美)"原始包装"原则,原装原则[是在布朗诉马里兰案(Brown v. Maryland, 12 wheat, 25 U. S.

419, 1827)中确立的原则。在本案中,马尔兰州的法律要求所有销售外国进口商品者均需购买特许证,外国货物进口商认为该项州法律违反宪法第1条第10款禁止征收进口税的规定,同时也干预了联邦在州际和对外贸易方面的权力。联邦最高法院首席大法官约翰·马歇尔(John Marshall)支持这两点主张,并系统阐明了"原始包装"原则:州的税收权不得扩大到海外进口领域,只要进口货物保持了原始包装;只有当这些货物在州内与一般财产相融混之后,州才能将其按当地货物一样对待并销售。联邦最高法院支持"原始包装"原则不适用州际贸易中流通的货物]

original payee 原提款人,原受款人
original plaintiff 原诉原告,原先原告
original position 原有地位
original possession 原始占有
original proceeding 初审程序
original process 开始诉讼阶段(指诉讼程序中从诉讼提起到强制被告出庭的这一阶段)
original proposal 原提案,最初提案
original proprietor 原业主,原物主;原财产所有人
original publication 初版
original record 原始记录
original rent 原定租金
original responsibility 原始责任
original scene 原始现场
original sentence 原判,原科刑
original sin 原罪(指旧约记载,人类始祖亚当及妻子夏娃违上帝禁令,偷吃禁果,被逐出伊甸园,罚亚当终生劳作,夏娃遭受分娩之苦。此后亚当之罪父传子,子传孙,所有的人都天生有罪,遂以"原罪"喻指罪恶之源头,最初之犯罪)
original source of law 法的最初渊源(又译:法律的原始渊源)
original sources 原始资料(见 primary sources)
original state 创始国
original suit 原诉(案)
original tenancy 原定租约
original text 原始文本,正本

original title 原本房(地)契;原来的名称;原始权利
original trademark 正商标
original work 原著,创作作品;(文学作品)手稿
original work and authorship 原创著作,原创著作品
original writ (英)起始令状[指普通法制度的王室令状分为两大类:起始令状和司法令状(judicial writ)。而起始令状又分为三大类:①*praecipe* 指令令状(其标准的范例是针对土地权利的令状(writ of right),也是被认为最早出现的起始令状)。②trespass writs 侵害令状(指并非单独诉讼格式,而是以令状为前提的一群令状,命令被告依法为某一行为或为自己辩解;该令状传唤被告出庭并解释其为何为侵害行为。见 jurisdictional fetter)。③trespass on the case 特殊侵害令状(指1285年《威斯敏斯特法Ⅱ》认可了的令状格式,同年法案最终承认了著名的类案诉讼。但文秘署的官员至少花了50年才认清自己的权力:即根据既存的令状类推可创制新的令状。这一情况通常针对的是非暴力侵害的案件);(英)原始令状,起始令状(将被直接分配权利义务的"命令书"演变成启动诉讼的司法文书,即为起始令状)](又译诉讼开始令,亦称初审令,指从前按普通法提起民事诉讼的传讯令)
original writing rule 见 best evidence rule
originalia rolls (英)原始案卷(指1236—1837年间大法官法院编撰的案卷)
originalism 原旨主义(指在宪法裁判中给予宪法文本或制宪者意图以具有约束力的权威。nonoriginalism 为非原旨主义,则指在宪法裁判中,虽假设宪法文本和原初历史具有重要性,但并不认为它们具有权威性和约束力)
originality n. 原创性;创举;独创性;创见;新颖;初创性
originate v. 引起,发源,发生,发起
originality (18世纪)(版权法)独创性[指①独立创作(independent creation)产品的状态或质量,并具有最低程度的创造性(creativity)。独创性是版权保护的要

件,但这是次要标准(lesser standard)而非专利法中新颖性(novelty)的标准,作为一项作品的独创性(original)不一定必然要具有新的(novel)或独一无二的(unique)的要求(见 novelty)。②一个主张版权的产品的独创性的程度就是作者独立创作完成的结果(见 creativity)]

originating motion 原动议

originating notice (加)(适用于司法审查的)传唤通知

originating organization 来源组织(指版权领域的卫星公约中播出有关节目的广播组织,以示区别 distributor"转播组织")

originating summons (由高等法院的一名法官在议事室进行调解的)传唤令(依法必须送还议事室)

originator n. 创始人,发明人;起源,来源,起因

*** *Origo rei inspici debet.*** The origin of a thing ought to be regarded. 事情的起因应予重视。

ornamental a. 装饰的

ornamental fixtures 装饰附着物

orphan n. 孤儿

orphan asylum 孤儿院

orphan's court 孤儿法庭

orphanage n. 孤儿身份;孤儿(集合称);孤儿院

orphanagehood n. 孤儿状态,孤儿身份

orthodox practice 传统惯例,固有方法

orthodox view 传统观点

orthodoxy n. 1.正统性;正统观念;正统做法 2.(宗)正教

Osaka Shosen Kaisha (日)大阪商船会社

ossify v. 使硬化,使僵化

ostensible a. 可公开的;显然的;外表的;名义上的

ostensible agency 表见代理(见 apparent agency)

ostensible agent 名义代理人

ostensible authority 名义代理权,名义上的授权

ostensible partner 名义合伙人,挂名合伙人

ostracism n. 1.流放,放逐;排斥 2.(古代雅典的)贝壳流放(指对威胁城邦安宁的公民由公众在会议上采用贝壳投票的方式来确定是否流放的制度,即将被流放的人名写在贝壳上,如够规定数目,应于十日内离开雅典流放十年)

other a. 另外的,其他的

other contracting party 缔约的另一方当事人

other person related by blood 其他亲属,其他血亲

other income (美)其他收入(指非来自主要经营实体的或商业的收入。而是比如股息或红利等收入)

other side 对方(另一方)当事人

other than offending ship 对标的船舶以外之船舶之扣押(见 offending ship)

Ottoman Constitution 《奥斯曼宪法》(又译:《奥托曼宪法》,指中东的第一部宪法)

Ottoman Empire 奥托曼帝国

ought to behave in a certain way 应当如何行为(表现)

oust v. 驱逐;剥夺;取代;免职,罢黜(港译:横夺)

oust courts of jurisdictions 取代辖区法院

oust the jurisdiction 恶意主张管辖,取代管辖

ouster n. 1.驱逐,撵走 2.(非法)剥夺;免职,罢黜

ouster of franchise 剥夺选举权,剥夺参政权

ouster of jurisdiction 剥夺裁判权

out of 在……外,离开;出于,由于;缺乏;没有,丧失,放弃;越出……外;来自;用……制成

out of any contract made this state or to be performed in this state 来自在本州签订或在本州履行的合同

out of bounds 范围外;禁区

out of control 不受控制

out of court 1.(英)没有诉讼支持(口语,指诉讼当事人一方在诉讼上的失败,即他的主要证人所提供的证词已被对方驳倒) 2.在法庭外面;私了,不经审判

out of court agreement 不受法庭干预的协议;法庭外(和解达成的)协议

out of court confession 法庭外的自认,

坦白
out of court settlement 法庭外和解
out of court statement 法庭外的(声明)陈述
out of danger notice 出险通知
out of date check 过期支票
out of habit 出于习惯
out of hand 无法约束,失去控制;立即,无准备
out of line 越轨,不合规定
out of one's sense 精神失常
out of order 不适合;出毛病;违反……规程;乱套;损坏,失修
out of packet 现金支付,实体
out of place 不在适当位置,不适当的,不合适的
out of pocket a. 赔钱,无钱的,无产业的;现款支付的
out of pocket rule 买卖差价的损失赔偿规则[此原则是指受欺诈的买方可以买价和市价间的差(价)额要求赔偿]
out of pocket rule 受损金额规则
out of print 绝版(不再发行的书刊)
out of proportion 不相称;不成比例
out of repairs 失修
out of stock 脱销,无现货
out of term (在法院)开庭期以外的
out of the question 不可能
out of the way 把……移开,把……除掉
out of work 失业
out-clearing n. (英)票据交换额
out-group 外团体
out-of-packet expenses 零星杂项费
out-of-pocket-measure 现金支付方法(又称实物价值计算法,指内幕交易造成损失赔偿之计算方法)
out-of-state tuition program for African-American 州外非裔美国人的讲授规划
outbreak n. 暴发;暴动;反抗
outbreak of fire 发生火警
outbreak of hostilities 敌对行动的爆发
outbreak of war 战争爆发,战争开始
outcast a./n. 被遗弃的;被放逐的;无家可归的/被遗弃者;被放逐者;流浪者
outcaste n. (印度)被剥夺了种姓者,无种

姓者;贱民
outcome (=outlet) n. 结果,后果,成果
outcome test (美)诉讼结果标准[在美国,民事诉讼程序中有一条重要原则,即所谓的伊利原则(Erie doctrine)。根据该原则,一个享有多样管辖权(diversity jurisdiction)的联邦法院在不涉及联邦事务的问题上,必须适用法庭所在地州的实体法。该测试将同一问题分别适用联邦法与州法,检验结果是否存在差别,是否会违反伊利规则]
outcome-determinative test 见 outcome test
outcome-impact test "影响结果"标准[是美国各法院判断是否为"无害"之标准。有两种不同类型:显著权利标准(substantial right test)和"影响结果"标准]
outcome-oriented a. 结果导向的
outcomer n. 外来人;外国人;陌生人
outcry n. 1.喊叫;叫卖;拍卖 2.强烈抗议(against);强烈要求(for)
outcry market 喊价市场
outdate v. 使过时
outdo v. 超过,胜过,战胜,制服
outer a. 外部的,外面的;远离中心的
outer bar 见 utter bar
outer barrister 见 utter barrister
outer boundaries of jurisdiction 管辖的(外部)边界,管辖的外缘
outer continental shelf 大陆架外缘
Outer Continental Shelf Land Act (美)《大陆架以外土地法》
outer harbo(u)r 外港
outer man (人的)外貌,外表
outer space 太空,星际空间,外层空间
Outer Space Treaty 《太空(外层空间)条约》(1967年)
outer-space law 外层空间法(又译:太空法)
outfangthief n. (英)(封建领主)对(英采邑内的任何居民在英封地以外任何地方犯有重罪的)领地外犯罪人的审判特权,对领地外盗窃的绞刑权
outflow of foreign exchange 外汇外流
outgiving n. 公开声明,公开发言
outgo n. 外出,出发;出口;支出;消耗

outgoing a. 即将外出的,出发的;即将离职的,开朗的;对人友好的
outgroup n. 外集团,非自己人集团(见 in-group)
outlaw n./v. 歹徒;逃犯;亡命之徒;被剥夺公民权者;被放逐者/1.剥夺(某人的)公民权;将某人放逐;取缔 2.使失去法律上的效力;宣告……为不合法
outlaw strike (美俚)未经工会批准同意的罢工
outlawed debt 已失时效的债务
outlawry n. (英)公民权的剥夺,剥夺权益;已失时效;宣布为非法;逍遥法外;不受法律保障,驱逐令
outlawry of war 宣布战争为非法
outlay n. 支出,费用
outlet n. 出口,出路;销路;市场;出售某种产品的商店
outlet for export produce 出口商品的口岸
outlets of states on the sea 国家通海之路
outline v./n. 概括,提示,略述,提出的纲要/外廓,大纲;概要;草案;(复)主要原则
outline of video program 录像内容概要
outlive v. 在(某人)死时尚未死;度过(风暴、危机等)而健在,(比喻某物)经久
outlook n. 眺望处;(政治、经济的)前景;眼光;展望;看法,观点;景色,风光
outlying territory 海外领地
outmoded a. 过时的
outpensioner n. (救济院,慈善机构等的)院外领受年金(或津贴的)人
outperform v. 超额完成,超额执行
outpoll v. 得到的选票超过(某人)
outport n. 输出港,外港(指位于大港口附近而在行政上独立的小港)
outpost n. (警戒部队)前哨,前哨基地
output n. 1.生产额,产量,输出量 2.发挥,发出;用电脑求出的解答
output capacity 生产率,产生率
output coefficient 产量系数
output contract 产量合同(契约)(指生产厂家同意将所有商品卖给买方,买方也同意购买的一种协议,即使数量没有限定,但这是有效合同)
output cost 产品生产成本
output decision 生产决定,生产产量决定
output digit 输出数字
output norm 产量定额
output quota 产量定额
outrage n./v. 暴行,蛮横逞凶;伤害,蹂躏;严重违法行为(道德败坏等)/对……施暴行;伤害;凌辱;强奸;公开违犯(法律等)
outrageous behavio(u)r 强暴行为
outrank v. 在级别(或身份、地位)方面比……高
outré (法)越出常规的,失当的;激怒,愤慨
outreach v. 越出……的范围;胜过;伸出去;走得太远
outrelief n. (英)对不住在贫民院的贫民施舍
outright gift 完全赠与;全部赠与
outrospection 外省[律师助手阿比盖尔·达尼莱科和从商的丈夫从加拿大多伦多搬到美国路易斯安那州的杜拉克,创办了一家慈善组织。据美联社报道:"他们的非营利组织名为'犹太人免费回收组织'。不过它不是用来传播宗教信息,而是向有需要的人提供帮助,鼓励人们进行外省(outrospection)。" outrospection 为 introspection(内省,自我反省)的反义词,意指以思考的方式关注自身以外事物的做法,尤其是通过观察或审视他人的思想和情感来完成的行为。美联社 2014 年 6 月 23 日报道称,达尼莱科夫妇采取对物品升级改造、回收利用和转送礼品等方式帮助别人。阿比盖尔说:"如果我们忙于把注意力集中到自己身上,就会忘记我们可以向整个世界学习。走出我们的舒适区(comfort zone),向他人表示'我们想向你学习'——这是该非营利组织的关注重点。"]
outsell v. (比别的货)更畅销,更能推销
outset n. 开端(见 from the outset)
outset of the action 诉讼开始,诉讼起始
outside a. 外部的;外国的;外界的;超出……的;最高的;最大的
outside casual labo(u)r 临时工人
outside child (美)私生子

outside contracting approach 采用外界承包的方法
outside director 公司外董事,外聘董事[指公司董事会成员,但不担任任何职务,也不是公司的控股股东,他可以是律师、投资银行家或其他对现行管理提供建议和服务者,抑或是虚设的闲职人。亦称独立董事(independent director)或加盟董事(affiliated director)]
outside evidence 外部证据
outside parties 案外当事人
outside port 因码头设备缺乏不得不用驳船上下货的港区(或海港);(某公司的)船只不去的海港
outside the law 超出法律范围的
outside the protection of law 在法律保护范围外的
outside the purview of 在……范围之外
outside wedlock 婚外
outsider n. 外人,局外人;非会员;外行,门外汉;案外人
outspeak v. 公开宣布;在讲话方面胜过
outspoken a. 直言的;坦率的;毫无保留的
outspoken editor 直言的编者,坦率的编者
outstanding a. 1.著名的,显著的,突出的 2.未付的;未决的;未完成的
(a great of work) outstanding 许多尚未完成的工作
outstanding account 未清账目,未清账款
outstanding achievement award 杰出成果奖
outstanding balance 待结款项,未清余额
outstanding capital 未偿本金
outstanding capital stock 见 outstanding stock
outstanding check (或 cheque) 未兑现支票
outstanding claims 未决索赔(案),待理请求权
outstanding credit 未偿付的信贷
outstanding debt 未偿债务
outstanding drawing 未偿还的提存
outstanding expense 未付费用
outstanding issue 悬而未决的问题(争点)
outstanding loan 未偿贷款
outstanding obligations 未了债务
outstanding question 未决问题

outstanding share/stock 投资者持有且未经发行公司回购的股票;在外股票,流通股票(亦称 outstanding capital stock, shares outstanding)
outstanding sum 未付款额
outtrade v. 买卖中占(某人的)上风;占(某人的)便宜
outvalue v. 价值大于;比……更可贵
outward a. 外面的,外表的;向外的,外部的;肉体的
outward documentary bill 出口押汇
outward form 外部形式
outward processing 外(运)加工
outward reinsurance 分出再保险
outward remittance 汇出汇款
outweigh v. 在价值上超过,在重量上超过
outworker n. 室外工作者;在所属机关外工作的人员(港译:外工)
over prep. 1.横过,越过 2.超出,高于;关于,由于
over age 超龄
over insurance 超额保险(指超过保险价值的保险)
over interest 过期利息
over protest 虽有异议,但……(比较 under protest)
over the counter contraceptive 自买避孕剂
over the property of another 他物权
over-assessment n. 估价太高
over-individualization 高度个人主义化
over-investment n. 过度投资(如果一项有风险的投资不能对应于预期的回报,在金融行业中称"过度投资")
over-the-counter a. 场外交易(指证券买卖经过经纪人而不在交易所的买卖)的;买卖双方直接交易的;非挂牌证券的;场外的
over-the-counter (not prescribed) drug 自买药物,非处方药物,非医生处方的药物
over-the-counter market 场外交易市场(亦称交易所外市场或未挂牌市场,指不在交易所内进行的证券交易)
over-the-counter trading 场外交易,现货交易

over-wide scope for discretion 自由的广泛空间,广泛的司法自由裁量权,过于广泛的司法自由裁量权

overall a. 包括一切的;全面的;综合的;所有的

overall adjustment of the economy 经济的重大调整

overall balance 综合平衡

overall control 全面管制,全面监督

overall efficiency 总效率,综合效率

overall employment policy 全面就业政策

overall financial plan 综合财务计划

overall supervision 全面监督

overall synthesis 全面综合

overbearing a. 自大的;专制的;压倒的;极重要的

overbearing conduct 压迫行为;傲慢行为

overbearing the will of the defendant 压服被告人意志

overboard ad. 向船外,从船上落入(或抛入)水中

overbreadth (doctrine) n. (美)超范围说(亦译做超宽度说,指企图惩治或禁止由宪法保护的行为或语言的部分法规)

overburdened judicial system 负荷过重的司法制度

overcharge v. 过高索价,要价过高,索费太多;装载过多;过多要价(指超过法律规定的要价)

overcome v. 1.克服;战胜;压倒 2.(通过反证)推翻;(用来推定的事实或结果的)推定证据

overcoming of the will 违背意志

overcompensation n. 过分补偿

overconfident a. 过于自信的,过于自恃的

overconfident negligence 疏虞过失(指因过于自信而造成的过失)

overcrowding n. 过分拥挤

overdeterrence n. 过度防止,过度威慑;过度制止

overdraft n. 透支;透支额

overdraw (=over-drawn) v. 超支,透支;夸大

overdue a. 过期的,延误的;过期未付的;过大的,过量的

overdue bill (或 **note**) 过期(未付)票据

overdue tax payment 积欠税款,滞纳税款

overexpenditure n. 超支

overhaul v./n. 彻底检修(检查);追上,赶上;解松(船的缆绳)/详细检查,大检修

overhauling n. 彻底检查

overhead n. (税、租金、保险费、电费等)经常开支;(企业)管理费用;间接费用;行政费用

overhours n. 加班工作时间;空余的时间

overing commission 包销佣金,转分保手续费

overinsurance n. 超额保险

overissue n. (钞票,债券等)过度发行;滥发

overland freight 陆路运输(费)

overlap v. 交错;重叠;与……部分相一致

overlapping consensus 重叠共识[美国哲学家约翰·罗尔斯(John Rawls)在20世纪80年代末提出的"重叠共识"观念,这个概念在其1971年出版的《正义论》中就出现了,其共识的逻辑含义即"不同之前提有可能导致同一个结论"]

overlapping insurance 重复保险

overlapping interests 重叠权益

overlapping protection 重叠保护

overload n./v. 超载,过载;超负荷/使负载过重,使超载

overlook v. 放任,宽容,忽略,监督,俯视,检查

overlord n. 霸权;霸主地位;封建君主;大地主;最高统治者

overlying right (土地所有人)使用(其土地的)地下水权利

overman n. 监工,工头,头头;仲裁者;裁判者

overpayment n. 多付,超付;逾额付款

overpowering drug 迷药

overrate v. 对……估计(或估价)过高

overreaching n. 欺诈得利(指通过欺诈或基于不道德行为获取不正当的商业利益);(英)权益不随产转移(一项衡平法原则)

overreaching in the market-place 市场上的诈骗

overrent v. 以过高租金出租(土地、房屋等)
override n./v. 代理佣金/制服,压倒使无效
overriding a veto 使否决无效
overriding force 包销力量
overriding interest 压倒一切的权益,优先的权益;(复)(英)不可废弃的权益
overriding public interests 优先的公共权益
overriding reason 压倒一切的理由
overridingstatute 优先条款
overring factor 决定性因素,压倒一切的因素
overrule v./n. (上级权力机构的)否决,驳回(指在审判过程中,法官驳回律师提出的反对意见);批驳;推翻;变更;宣布……无效;统治;制服;对……施加影响/驳回
overrule a decision 驳回判决,推翻判决
overrule sb.'s claim 对某人的诉讼要求不予受理,驳回某人的请求
overruling n. (英)推翻(原判)(由于下级法院的判决所引用的判例或以前的判决出现了对法律的错误说明而应予变更);推翻(新分析实证主义法学家拉兹改变现行英美法规则的三种办法之一。见 closure rule)
overruling precedent 推翻先例,否定先例
overrun commitment 超支承诺
oversea(s) a. 海外的,外国的;与外国有关的;向海外的;在海外的
overseas accounting firms 境外会计师事务所
overseas Chinese (中)华侨
Overseas Chinese Association (中)华侨联合会
Overseas Chinese Committee (中)华侨委员会(指全国人民代表大会设立的一个专门委员会)
Overseas Chinese Investment Corporation (中)华侨投资公司
overseas Chinese ventures 侨资企业
overseas company 海外公司
overseas contract 海外合同(契约)
overseas investment 海外投资
overseas investment guaranty program 海外投资保证制度(方案)
overseas obligation (或 debt) 外债
overseas principal 海外委托人
overseas remittance 侨汇
oversee v. 监察,监视;俯瞰
overseer n. 监察人,监视人,监工
overseer of the poor (英)济贫监督官
oversight n. 失察;忽略,疏忽出错,监督,看管
oversman n. (苏格兰)最后裁决者
overstep v. 违犯,逾越
overstep one's authority 越权,逾越授权(范围)
overt act (刑)外在行为;明显的行为;公开的行为(指由此行为可以推出一个人的意图)
overt behavio(u)r 外表行为
overt discrimination 公然歧视
overt hostility 公开的敌意
overt provocation 公开挑衅
overt word 明白的话,不会被误解的话
overtaking and passing 追赶与超车
overtaking cause 超越因果关系(指侵害人的行为导致损害的发生,受害人因此受有损害,然而即使无此侵害行为,同样的损害也会因其他独立于该侵害行为的事由发生)
overtax v. 超额征税;使负担过度;对……要求过高
overtime n. 额外时间,加班;超时薪金,加班费
overtime allowance 加班津贴
overtime cost 加班费用
overtime service 超期服役
overtime wages 加班工资
overture n. 提议,提案;主动的表示;开端
overturn v. 推翻,颠覆(政权)
overturning of vehicle (机动车辆,尤指汽车)翻车
overview n. 总的看法,一般观察

overvote 多选(指选民在选票上选定的人数超过了规定的人数。该词条通常只发生在人工统计或机器扫描的纸质选票上。选民通常在无意之中或因为没弄清规则而在选票上选定了超出规定人数的候选人,结果造成选票无效。电子计票系统通常可防止这种情况的发生。2000年11月大选中,美国佛罗里达州曾因这种情况发生过争议,乔治·布什当时以微弱多数票战胜民主党候选人阿尔·戈尔,有人认为选民在选票上选定的人数超过了规定的人数影响了选举结果。该词条既可以作为动词也可作为可数名词,主要在美国英语中使用)

overwhelm v. 1.打翻,倾覆;覆盖 2.制服,压倒;使不知所措

overwhelming evidence 压倒性证据

overwhelming majority 压倒的多数,绝大多数

owe v. 欠债,负债;负有义务;应把……归功于

owing a. 未付的,欠着的,应给予的

owl n. 走私

owler n. (尤指夜间的)走私者,走私船

owling n. 违禁品的走私

own v. 占有,拥有;承认,自认

own as you earn scheme (公司)雇员分股计划

own immediate advantage 自己的切身利益

own risk 自负责任

Own site clean-up insurance (美)自有场地治理责任保险(见 environmental impairment liability insurance)

own up to a crime 坦白承认罪行

owner n. 所有权人,物主

owner of a corpse 尸主

owner of copyright 版权所有人

owner of dominant land 地役权人

owner of goods 货主

owner of lost property (财产的)失主

owner of property 物主,财产所有人

owner of the surface 地表所有者

owner of title 产权所有人,所有权人

owner-farmer n. 自耕农

owner-state 自产国家

ownerless a. 无主的

ownerless animal 无主动物,无主畜

ownerless articles 无主物

ownerless immovables 无主不动产

ownerless land 无主土地

ownerless movables 无主动产

owners of collective property 集体财产所有人

owners' capital 业主资本

owners-in-common n. 共同所有人

ownership n. 所有权;所有制;物主身份;所有权人身份

ownership by the individual labo(u)rer (中)个体劳动者所有权

ownership by the whole people 全民所有制

ownership in a mark 商标所有权

ownership in horizontal divisions of a building 大楼分层建筑物所有权

ownership of flats in a building 建筑大楼分楼层所有权

ownership of interest in land 土地收益所有权

ownership of land 土地所有制;土地所有权

ownership of land by state 土地国有制

ownership of mines 矿山所有权

ownership of mountains 山林所有权

ownership of personal property by citizen 公民个人财产所有权

ownership of property 物权,财产所有权

ownership of rivers 河流所有权

ownership of territorial sea 领海所有权

ownership of trademark 商标所有权

ownership relation 所有制关系,所有权关系

ownership system of land 土地所有制

ownership timeshare interest 拥有型的分时度假权益

ownership without usufruct 虚有权

ownership-in-common n. 共同所有权,共有权;共有制

oxymoron n. 矛盾修饰法,矛盾用语

oyer n. 1.(刑事案件的)审理,听审 2.=oyer and terminer

oyer and terminer 1.(英)就地听审裁判

委任令(指示巡回法庭法官开庭审判刑事案件的一种命令)2.(英)听审裁判庭(指英国审理刑事案件的一种巡回法庭)3.(美)(某些州的)高等刑事裁判庭

oyes (=oyez) n. (法庭用语)肃静;听,静听(指法庭作出宣告时由传呼员大声连呼三次,以引起大家注意,一般呼做"O oyes")

P

P-phonogram n. 录音制品邻接权保留标记
pacemaker n. 起搏器;标兵,定步速者
pacific a. 和平的;平时的;爱好和平的;(大写)太平洋的
pacific blockade 平时封锁
Pacific Reporter (美)《太平洋区判例汇编》(太平洋区包括华盛顿州、俄勒冈州、内华达州、加利福尼亚州、蒙大拿州、爱达荷州、犹他州、亚利桑那州、怀俄明州、科罗拉多州、新墨西哥州、堪萨斯州、俄克拉何马州和阿拉斯加州、夏威夷州)
pacific settlement of international disputes 和平解决国际争端
pacification n. 绥靖;媾和;和约
pacificator n. 调解人;平定者;使和解的人
pacifism n. 和平主义;非战主义;不抵抗主义
pacifist n. 和平主义者;非战主义者;不抵抗主义者
pack n./v. 包装;包装材料;容器;包装货物的标准重量(或数量)单位;包裹,包,捆;一大堆/收买,笼络(陪审员等)
pack a jury 挑选(纠集)偏袒某一方的陪审团;收买陪审团
package n. 包裹;一揽子交易;合同上的利益(如福利条件、养老金等)
package deal 一揽子交易
package transfer 成套转让,一揽子转让
package veto (美)全案否决〔总统仅能将法案整体当成一个包裹,一起退回国会,国会复议时可推翻总统的否决(即再否决);但"再否决"需要参众两院各 2/3 以上的多数票〕
packaging n. 包装
packet part (美)袋装部分(指一些法律丛书在封三处设有一小纸袋,可将最新补充材料装入以备参考研究)
packet-veto (美)口袋否决(亦称搁置否决议案,指总统对国会通过的议案拥有暂时搁置的否决权。即国会通过的议案送交总统签署时如被总统搁置至国会休会后十日不予签字,则该议案即被否决而不能成为法律。此否决权只有经过国会三分之二的多数票才能予以推翻)
packing n. 包装,打包;(美)操纵选区技术(指主要政治团体或种族团体通过在极少地区通过尽可能地集中少数票的方法使之减少到最少的代表)
packing charges 包装费,装箱费
packing credit 打包放款
packing list 装箱单
packing mark 包装标志
pact n. 合约,公约;盟约;合同,契约
Pact Banning Chemical and Bacteriological Weapons 《禁止化学和细菌武器的公约》
Pact for Protection of Accidents 《防止事故公约》
Pact of Locarno 《洛迦诺公约》(1925年10月5日至16日,英、德、法、意、比、捷、波七国代表在瑞士洛迦诺举行的会议上签订,是第一次世界大战后西方国家扶植德国军国主义复活的国际公约)
pacta 无形约束,公约,合约,协议
pacta adiecta 附加简约
*Pacta dant legem contractui. The stipulations of parties constitute the law of the contract. 当事人协议构成具有法律效力的合同。
pacta legitima 合法简约
pacta praetoria 裁判官简约
*Pacta quae turpem causam continent non

sunt observanda. Agreements founded upon an immoral consideration are not to be observed. 不应遵守依据不道德的约因签立协议。

* **Pacta sunt servanda.** Agreements (and stipulations) of the parties (to a contract) must be observed. 当事人的合约必须守信执行。公约必须信守。有约必守。条约(协议)必须遵守。

* **Pacta tertiis nec nocent nec prosunt.** Contracts do not impose any burden nor confer any benefit upon a third party. 条约不损害第三国利益(原则);合同(契约)不损害第三者利益(原则)。

pacta vestita 穿衣简约
pacte d' association 合伙,(契)协约
pactio (罗马法)一般协议(不同于 pactum)
paction n. 合同,契约;合约,公约,盟约,短période的国际协定
pactional damages 约定违约金(=liquidate damages)
pactum n. (罗马法,大陆法)协议,协定(通常指简短契约、合同、协定、简约,亦称 *pactum conventum*,复数为 *pacta*)
pactum de constitio 履行债务协议[指一项非正式协议,即在确定的时间支付或偿还某人或另一人欠的现有债款。此协议是由执政官(praetor)强制执行的。查士丁尼扩限任何债务的履行债务协议。该协议亦可用来担保,主要不具备合法形式中区别于诚意允诺保证(*fidejussion*)。亦称为 *pactum constitutae pecuniae*。见 *constitutum*; *fidejussion*]
pactum de contrahendo 缔约承诺
(a) *pactum de negotiando* 预约谈判原则 (指在国家间协调中可以发挥作用的原则,即对于有关事项的处理,"当事方有义务以达成一项协议为目的进行谈判,而不是仅仅为了完成一个正式的谈判程序……它们负有义务有所作为,使谈判具有意义,而不会沦为各方固执己见、不愿考虑对方立场以作任何调整的情形"。依该原则,还要在合作中善意做出有法律意义的努力,争取达成产生国际法规范的相互协议)
pactum de non petendo 不受债权人请求权约束的协议;不起诉的协议
pactum de retrovendendo 回购协议
pactum illicitum 非法协定,非法协约
pactum legis commissoriae 逾期无效条款
pactum reservati dominii 保留所有权的合约
pactum subiectionis 替代协议
pactus (日耳曼法)君民协定
pad n. 1.(俚)警察接受的赃款;为免祸而付给讹诈犯的钱 2.(美俚)汽车硬牌照
paddy n. 警察
paddy wag(g)on 囚车;警车
pad(i)shah n. 君主,国王;(大写)伊朗国王;(从前欧洲称的)土耳其苏丹;(从前印度称的)英国国王
paederactia n. 鸡奸(尤指成年男子对男性青少年的反常行为)
paediaphilia n. 恋童癖[指心理障碍的一种。患者喜欢的性对象是儿童,对成年异性反而没兴趣,所恋的儿童一般为异性,有的为同性,也有的两性都喜欢。要注意,精神发育迟滞或老年人(尤其痴呆症患者)与女性儿童发生性关系或猥亵行为,不属恋童癖。我国刑法规定对儿童实施性行为的要加重处罚。见 sexual perversion]
page image 页面图像,全文图像
page(s) v./n. 标出……页码;给……标页码/1.页(缩略为 P) 2.(常用复)记录 3.(值得记载的)事件,插曲 4.(报刊的)专页、专栏〈editorial page〉(社论栏),〈sports page〉(体育专栏) 5.版面〈fat page〉(空白多的页面),〈full page〉(全满的页面)
page-image 页面图像,全文图像
pagination n. 标记页码,页码,页数
paid a. 支薪金的,受雇的;已付清的,已兑现的
paid advisor 支薪顾问
paid and satisfied 实际支付(见 satisfaction of judgment)
paid case 付费案件
paid check 已兑现的支票
paid debt 已还清的债款

paid docket (美)付费的待决案件[指联邦最高法院每年都要受理4000件以上的上诉申请,这些申请都是由希望联邦最高法院对案件进行复审的当事人提出的,这些上诉申请被分成"贫民诉讼"(*in forma pauperis*)和"付费案件"]

paid maternity leave 照付工资的产假

paid off 付清,付讫

paid on the time 按时计酬

paid-in a. (由物主)已供应的,已供给的,已缴纳会费的

paid-in capital 已缴资本

paid-in fund 已提供的基金,已储备的基金[指由互保公司(mutual insurance company)所设立已储备的一笔现金基金用来支付不可预见的损失。这笔基金是代替股本账户(capital stock account)]

paid-in surplus 股票溢价,非利润盈余,缴入盈余

paid-up 已付清的,已付足的

paid-up capital 已缴资本

paid-up loan 还清的贷款

paid-up policy 已付足款的保险单

paid-up share 已缴足款的股份

pain n. 痛苦;惩罚;努力;苦心

pain and suffering (肉体上的)痛苦与(精神上的)创伤

pains and penalties 刑罚

pair n. 1.一对(已婚)夫妇,成对,配偶 2.(会议中)相互约好放弃投票权的两个对立派会员

pais (=*pays*)国家陪审团,陪审团候选人;(从被告邻人中选出的)陪审团;邻居;国家

palace n. 王宫;宫;宫殿;豪华的公共娱乐场所,宏伟建筑物

Palace Court (英)宫廷法院[指白厅(White Hall)12英里之内发生的所有对人诉讼的案件具有管辖权的宫廷法院。此法院是詹姆斯一世(James Ⅰ)颁发特许建立,以对诉讼人对于宫廷侍臣法院(Court of the Marshalsea)不便之回应。此法院之管辖权与宫廷侍臣法院相似,但该院一直保留在白厅地区(White Hall)。1849年此法院与宫廷侍臣法院一起被废弃。以后此词被称为 curia palatii。见 Court of the Marshalsea]

Palace of Westminster 威斯敏斯特宫(指英国伦敦的议会大厦)

palam (罗马法)公开,不隐匿

palatine a. 宫廷官吏的;有王室特权的

palatine court 宫廷法院,特权法院

pale n. 1.界限,范围 2.(英)栅栏区

pale of law 法律范围;法律界限

palimony n. (未结婚而有同居关系者之间的)赡养费,(=alimony)生活费

palliate v. 掩饰;减轻,缓和;辩解;减罪

palliate a crime 减罪

palliation n. 辩解;掩饰的言辞;缓和,减轻

palliator n. 掩饰罪过者,辩解者

palm off 骗售;卖假货(指以欺诈手法,达到伪货混售目的)

palm tree justice 棕榈树审判(指在棕榈树下开庭审判解决民事纠纷的一种古老的审判形式)

palming off 哄骗,欺诈(与 passing off 之意近似)

palmprint(或 **palm print**) n. 掌纹,掌印

palpable a. 明显的,显而易见的(常用于形容错误、滥用权力或其他一些错行为等)

palpable mistake 明显错误

paltry inducements 轻微诱因

paltry sum 微不足道的款项

pamphlet laws 法规小册子

Pan American Union Treaty Series 《泛美联盟条约丛书》(见 Organization of American States Treaty Series)

Pan-Africanist n. 泛非主义者

Pan-American a. 泛美的;全美洲的

Pan-American Convention (版权)泛美公约[《伯尔尼公约》之后西半球国家之间举行了一系列协商仿造的条约,第一个协约是在1902年,最后一次是在1946年,规模最大的一次是在布宜诺斯艾利斯协商制定的1910年泛美公约]

Pan-American Union 泛美联盟(指21个美洲国家所组成的联盟)

Pan-Americanism n. 泛美主义

Pan-German a. 泛德意志的,泛德意志主

义的
panacea n. 治百病的灵药
Panama Canal Treaty (1977) 巴拿马运河条约(1977年)
panchayat n. (印度)乡村行政委员会(由5人左右组成),乡村自治委员会;评议会
panchayat system 评议会制度(指尼泊尔的保证公民参与国家管理的一种形式,有四级评议会,即村、县、地区和全国评议会)
Pandeatae 《学说汇编》(《学说汇纂》的别称)
pandect (罗马法上的)《学说汇纂》(指6世纪查士丁尼一世所命令编纂的《民法大全》的一个组成部分,共50卷。见 *Corpus Juris Civilis*);(复)法令大全,法典
Pandect-science 潘德克特法学[指对罗马法经过净化而成为高度概念化的一种法律数学(legal mathematics)]
Pandectists n. 学说汇纂派;潘德克特派学者
pander n. 淫乱之事的勾引者,拉皮条者;为妓女拉客者;怂恿人做坏事者
Pandora's box 潘多拉盒子[(希腊神话)喻指:①带来不幸的礼物;②灾难的渊薮]
Panduit test (专利)"潘迪义"标准[指由于专利的侵权,有4个要素可测利益损失。专利权人必须证实:对此产品有需求、专利权人具有制造和销售该产品的能力以适应需求、不接受市场上非侵权的替代品(non infringing alternatives)和收益上有多少损失]
panel n. (14世纪)1.候选陪审员名单;(选定的)陪审团;全体陪审团;全体陪审员 2.(美)合议庭(英)国民健康保险名单,愿意提供法律援助的职业律师名单 3.组成少年法庭法官名单 4.(苏格兰)受审被告人(刑事被告)(该意义上亦称 pannel)
panel discussion 讨论会,座谈会
panel doctor 医治投过保险的病人的医生
panel for criminal matter 刑事案件的合议庭
panel of jury 陪审团名单
panel of three judges 三名法官组成的合议庭

panel on complaints 诉讼专家组
panel on takeover and mergers (德)公司收购与兼并委员会
panelist n. 专门小组成员,陪审团成员
panic n. 恐慌,经济上的恐慌
panic attack 惊恐发作[一种精神疾病,出现短期或阵发性的控制障碍,典型的即惊恐发作和焦虑症。惊恐发作常见于患有恐惧症(phobia)的病人,亦称恐怖性神经症,是一种以过分和不合理地恐惧外界某种客观事物或情境为主要表现的神经症,惊恐发作很少涉及刑事责任能力,但有时会造成民事赔偿]
panic-monger n. 制造恐慌的人
panicky a. 恐慌的,由恐慌引起的
pannage n. (英)林中放猪权;为取得林中放猪权所交纳的费用
panopticon n. 圆形监狱(指监狱设计成将犯人关在一个圆形建筑中,使永远处于矗立在圆形建筑中心的一个警戒塔监视下)
Pantomimic Work 哑剧作品
Papacy n. 1.罗马教皇的职位(或权力、任期)2.教皇的继承、教皇世系 3.(大写)罗马天主教教会制度,教皇统治
papal a. 罗马教皇的;罗马教皇职位的(或权力、任期的);罗马天主教教会的
papal arbitration 教皇仲裁(指国际仲裁的一种)
papal brief 教皇敕令
papal documents 教皇文件
papal encyclic(al) 教皇通谕
paparazzi n. 追踪摄影队(此名词出现于1958年,指专事偷拍的追踪摄影队)
paper(s) n. 票据;证券;纸币;(复)文件;身份证;(有时作)正式公诉状;论文;文章
paper blockade 纸上封锁,封锁宣告(指在实行封锁前之封锁宣告)
paper book 讼案、证据、答辩、物证、令状等的汇编本
(a) paper copy of the summons and complaint 纸面传票和诉状
paper credit 信用证;信用债权
paper currency 纸通货;不兑换的纸币
paper gold "纸黄金"(即国际货币基金的特别提款权)

paper hanger (美)开空头支票者,用假钞票的人

paper hanging (美)伪造支票(罪)

paper mill (英)档案保存所(指1578年设立保存朝廷档案的地方;现又指王座法院保存档案的地方)

paper money 纸币,钞票;票据;支票

paper office 记录保存处;档案保存所(见 paper mill)

paper patent 从未实际利用的专利权

paper profits 账面利润(指实际尚未到手的利润)

paper rule 纸面规则[指美国现实主义法学家卢埃林和弗兰克进一步发挥其先驱格雷和霍姆斯的"行为中的法律"的观点,提出了彻底的规则怀疑论和事实怀疑论。卢埃林将规则分为纸面规则(paper rule)和实在规则(real rule),认为后者才是具体案件起决定作用的"真正规则"。纸面规则仅意味着有适用的可能性,这种可能性是重要的,被视为决定裁判的众多法律渊源之一,但是作用有限,有决定意义的是实际适用]

paper standard 纸币本位

paper title 纸面资格;纸面权利(指有资格或有权利的文件,它可能有效,也可能无效)

paper to bearer 不记名票据

paperless trading 无纸贸易(见 Electronic Data Interchange)

papers and documents 文件

papinian 帕比尼安(见 papinianistae)

papinianistae 帕皮尼安门徒(是查士丁尼时期对进入第三学年的法律学士的称呼,因在此学年要学习帕比尼安的著作而得名)

par a./n. 与票面价值相等的,平均的/同等地位;定额;(公债、票据、股票等的)票面价值

par delictum 同等罪行

par excellence 典型的,卓越的

par example 例如

* *Par in parem imperium non habet.* An equal has no dominion over an equal. 平等者之间无统治权(指国际法的一个原则,基于国家平等原则,应相互豁免管辖权)。

par of exchange 汇兑平准率,汇兑平价

par value 票面价值,面值[指在股票、债券的票面上载明的价额,这与实际价值(actual value)有较大差异。票面金额适用于优先股和公司债券,优先股和债券的股息均按票面价(金额)计算,缩略语常用"to par"。亦称 face value; nominal value; stated value]

par value stock 面值股份,票面金额股份

paraclete n. 辩护者,调解人,安慰者

Paradigm n. 范例,示范,范式(范式概念是美国科学哲学家托马斯·康恩最早提出的,是康恩历史主义科学哲学的核心。他认为科学界是由一个流行的范式所控制的,那个范式代表科学界的世界观,它是指导和决定问题、数据和理论的选择,一直到另一个范式将其取代)

paradigm of mechanistic rules of law 机械主义的法律规则的模式

paradigm shift 典范转移[指美国法哲学家孔恩(Kuhn)近半世纪前提出的概念,指人们习以为常的思维模式或背景假设:科学的发展是一系列思维旧有模式被新的思维模式所取代,往往是旧的典范无法应对现实发展而崩溃后新的典范才有生机取而代之]

paradigmatic procedures 标准诉讼程序,示范诉讼程序

paradise of (the) philistines 市侩的天堂

paradox n. 自相矛盾现象;似是而非的论点;谬论,怪事

parage n. 条件相等;同等地位;同等血亲

paragium n. 平等之血亲(或地位)(= parage,亦指继承人之间财产之均等分配)

paragraph n. (法律条文和制定法、诉讼文件条文中的)项;段落;节

paral evidence rule 非正式证据法则

paralegal n. 律师的专职助手

paralegal workers 律师辅助人员

paralled citation 平行援引(指同一判例分别记载于两份或两份以上不同的判例汇编之中)

paralled procedural directives 平行程序指令

paralled proceeding 平行诉讼

parallel a./n./v. 平行的,并行的;相同的,类似的/类似的事(或物、人、情况等)比较;纬线/比较(with);与……平行;配得上
parallel action 并行诉讼,平行诉讼,同时进行的诉讼
parallel citation 并列援引(指一个判例或其他法律文件不止刊载在一处的援引)
parallel import 平行进口(指与"权利穷竭"原则相联系的术语,承认该原则只具有地域性的国家认为平行进口属于侵权行为)
parallel proceedings 平行诉讼(亦称平等诉讼,指在国际民事诉讼活动中常常会出现相同当事人就他们之间的相同争议分别在两个国家的法院提起诉讼,而且这两个国家的法院都有适当的管辖权,并据此受理案件,这就构成国际民事诉讼中的诉讼竞合,有些国家称为平行诉讼)
paralogism n. 不合逻辑的推论;谬误推理
paralogism thinking 逻辑倒错性思维(思维表达障碍之一,指思维推理缺乏逻辑性,或推理离奇荒唐,或无前因后果或因果倒置。只要逻辑倒错性思维的病理推理中不含恶意成分,便应考虑辨认能力丧失,评定无责任能力丧失。见 thought of insertion)
paralogize v. 做谬误推理,做不合逻辑的推理
paralysis n. 无能为力,无能
paralyzation n. 无能为力;瘫痪
paralyzation of the force of law and order 治安机关的无能为力
parameters n. 参项,参数
paramount a./n. 最高的,至上的;首要的,卓越的/最高掌权者,元首
paramount chiefs' court 最高酋长法院
paramount clause 首要条款
paramount equity 衡平法上的优先权
paramount jurisdiction 最高管辖权
paramount lien 优先留置权
paramount ownership 最高所有权
paramount right 首要权利
paramount title 最高所有权,最有优先权(指被盗财产,其真正所有人应具有最高所有权;在不动产法规中"paramount title"

原意为原先所有权,但现已具有较好或优等所有权之含义)
paramountcy n. 至上,首要;最高,优越
paramour n. 奸夫;奸妇;情夫;情妇
paranoia n. 患狂想症的人,妄想狂,偏执狂
paranoid disorder 偏执性精神障碍(指一组以系统妄想为主要症状而病因未明的精神障碍。偏执性精神障碍的患者认知能力比偏执型分裂症患者好得多,除诉讼能力外,其他民事行为能力很少受到本病影响)
paranoid personality disorder 偏执性人格障碍[对于人格障碍的分类各家看法不一,美国的《精神障碍诊断与统计手册》(DSM-Ⅳ-TR)列出 10 种人格障碍的分类类型。涉及法律问题较多的有:①偏执性人格障碍(指以猜疑和偏执为特点,始于成年早期,男性多于女性);② schizotypal personality disorder 分裂性人格障碍;③ antisocial personality disorder 反社会性人格障碍;④ impulsive personality disorder 冲动性人格障碍;⑤ histrionic personality disorder 表演性(癔症性)人格障碍;⑥ borderline personality disorder 边缘性人格障碍]
paraph n. (用以防止签名伪造的)签名后的画押;花押
paraphasia n. 语言错乱症
parapherna (罗马法)随嫁物品(指婚姻中妻方除妆奁以外的随嫁动产,其所有权属于女方本人,可由妻遗赠与人)
paraphernal property 已婚妇女可自由处理的动产
paraphernalia n. 已婚妇女可自由处理的动产(主要指衣服、首饰);私人财产,妻子所有物
paraphilia n. 性欲倒错
paraphrase n./v. 释意,意译/释意,意译;将……译意为……将……意译为(paraphrastic a.)
paraphrasis 释义
parapraxis (复数-xes, -xia) n. (心理学上的)动作倒错,错误行动
paraprofessional n. 辅助专职人员的人(如 paralegal 等)
parasexuality n. 性欲倒错

parasitic stage (美)"寄生阶段"[指美国学者卢萨(Lupsha)1996年提出的有组织犯罪可能对国家影响的三个阶段之一。见 predatory stage]

parastatal n. 半国营

paravail 下等,从属(指旧时对低等租户之称)

parcel n. 一小片(土地);一宗(货物);包裹

parcel post (总)邮包,包裹邮件;邮政包裹业务

parcel post insurance 邮包保险

parcenary n. 共同继承

parcener (或 **coparcener**) n. 共同继承人

parchment 羊皮纸文稿

pardon n./v. 宽恕,赦免;免罪;赦免特许(特赦)状/原谅;宽恕;赦免

pardon attorney (美)负责审议和实施特赦的司法官员

pardon power 赦免权(指美国联邦宪法第2条第2款对总统的授权,赦免权扩展适用于"对合众国的犯罪,但弹劾案件除外"。即有权宽恕罪犯的罪责,免除其全部刑罚,恢复其因犯罪被剥夺的权利和特权。在英国,英王发布特赦令。在美国,如触犯非联邦法律的罪犯,则州长有权决定特赦)

pardonable a. 可赦免的;可宽恕的

pardoned criminal 被赦免罪犯

pardoner n. 赦罪者;宽恕者

parens patriae 1.(parent of his or her country)"一国之父" 2.政府监护(指政府对没有行为能力而需要保护的人所进行的监护);国家监护人权

parens patriae suit (美)"国父诉讼"(指一个州代表全体州的公民向联邦法院提起的诉讼)

parent n. 父亲,母亲;根源;根本;(复)双亲;祖先

parent and child 父母与子女(的法律关系)

parent and subsidiary corporations 母子公司

parent body 上级机构

parent by adoption (或 **adoptive parent**) 收养人,养父母

parent company (或 **corporation**) 母公司,总公司(见 holding company)

parent government 母国政府

parent patrial (英王的)国家监护权(依文字为"parent of the country",即国家父母,是英王的一种固有权利,为确保其封建统治稳定,对其统领下的未成年人、精神和心神弱者及无行为能力贵族有照顾之义务)

parent subsidiary relationship 母子公司关系

parent's duty to educate children 父母教育子女的责任

parent's duty to protect children 父母保护子女的责任

parent's duty to support children 父母抚养子女的责任

parent's liability for child's torts 父母对于子女侵权行为的责任

parent's responsibility for child's crime 父母对于子女的犯罪行为的责任

parent's right to child's services and earnings 父母获得子女的服务及工资的权利

parent's right to punish child 父母惩罚子女的权利

parent-in-law n. 配偶的父母(如岳父或岳母)

parentage n. 来历,出身,家系;父母身份

parental a. 父母的;父的;母的;双亲的;似父母的;为父母的

parental appointment 父母委任

parental authority (或 **power**) 亲权

parental control 父母(对子女)的照管权

parental home (有问题的儿童)教养院

Parental Kidnapping Prevention Act 《防止父母劫持法》[指 1980 年制定颁布的一项联邦法。该法规定对于无法定监护权的父母将子女"劫持"给予惩罚,并要求各州均承认并执行他州法院所作的符合该规定的关于子女监护令的判决。参见《美国注释法典》第 28 标题卷第 1738A 节、第 42 标题卷第 654、655、653 节。缩略为 PKPA。见 Uniform Child Custody Jurisdiction Act; Federal Kidnapping Act]

parental patriae 家长式统治权(指对各类人具有一种家族式的监护统治权,包括实行无能力人,如未成年人、精神病者,他们需要保护)

parental priority doctrine (美)父母优先原则(指父母往往被推定为最佳利益之监护人)

parental relation 亲子关系

parental right 亲权

parental rights and duties 父母的权利与义务

parentela n. (复)(15 世纪)出自同一祖先的人们

parentelic group 亲等群

parentelic system 亲系(指将特定人的继承人都包括在各种亲等内构成的群体系谱)

parenthood n. 父母的身份

parenticide n. 杀亲罪;杀害父、母罪;杀亲犯;杀害父、母犯

parentless a. 无父母的

parentless child 孤儿

parents and relations 直系和旁系亲属

* *Parentum est liberos alere etiam nothos.* It is the duty of parents to support their children even when illegitimate. 父母有抚养子女之义务,对非婚生子女亦然。

pares n. (英)地位平等者(指按《大宪章》规定,只有与被告同等地位的人所作出的判决,才能给被告定罪)

Pareto, Vilfredo 帕累托·维尔费里多(1848—1923)(经济学家)

Pareto efficiency 帕累托效率(指经济学中"效率"一词概念应用最为广泛,主要指不浪费,尽可能好地应用可用资源)

Pareto Improvement 帕累托改良(理论)

Pareto Optimality 帕累托最优

Pareto-optionality Criterion 帕累托最优原则

pari 等同,相同

pari causa 同等权利,同等地位

pari delicto 相同过错,同类罪行,相似罪行

pari materia 性质相同的,同类事件的,彼此依赖的,相关的

pari passu 公平地;按比例地;不分先后;没有选择地

pari ratione 基于同样的理由

pari-mutuel 派利分成法(指一种赛马彩票的赌博方法)

* *Paria copulantur paribus.* Like things unite with the like./Birds of a feather flock together./Similar things unite with similar. 物以类聚。

Paris Commune 巴黎公社(指 1871 年 3 月 18 日,法国巴黎的无产阶级和革命群众建立的历史上第一个无产阶级政权)

Paris Convention (Stockholm Revision as of 1967) 《巴黎公约》(1967 年斯德哥尔摩文本)

Paris Convention for the Protection of Industrial Property (1883) 《保护工业产权巴黎公约》(1883 年)

(The) Paris Peace Conference of 1919 (1919 年召开的)巴黎和会

parish n. 救贫区;教区

parish council (英)农村教区行政团体

parish court (美)(路易斯安那州行政)牧区法院

Parish Poor Rate (英)《教区救济贫民税法》

parish register 教区记事录(指记录教区居民的洗礼、命名、婚丧等事的册子)

parity n. 同等,均势;价值对等,平价;平价制度(指美国政府通常采用价格补贴和限额生产以调节农产品价格的一种制度)

parity clause 平价条款

parity commission for wages and prices 工资和物价协调委员会

parity of treatment 同等待遇

park n. (英国王特许的)猎园;(汽车等的)停车场;园林

parenting function 父母似的关照职责[指对孩子的或孩子家的每日需求或直接需求进行服务的任务。父母似的关照职能包括为了孩子的幸福提供必要的事项或金钱(necessaries)并维持孩子的家庭住所。见 caretaking function]

parking (1983 年)1.证券销售,证券买卖[指出售人在晚些时候可以同样价格买回

证券的协议(agreement)。销售证券。如果有阻止证券交易规定或税法执行力,则证券销售为非法(Parking is illegal)。这通常是规避(evading)美国证券业协会(National Association of Securities Dealers,缩略为 NASD)的净资本规定(net-capital requirement),该规定要求当经纪业公司(brokerage firm)呈递其关于净资本状况月报告时降低其账户上持有的任何股份价(value of stock)。为了与美国证券业协会的净资本规定协调一致(compliance),经纪业公司从自己的账户上以市场价"销售"(sells)股份给客户,借以避免为报告目的而(证券)折价发行(discount)。因为已经呈递公司报告,公司可以卖出给客户的相同价从客户手中将股份"买回"(buy back)。在此意义上亦可称 stock-parking] 2.考虑其他投资机会短期投资时资产的安全安置

parking lot 露天停车场
parking meter (计算汽车停放时间的)停车计时器
parking ticker (警察给)违反停车规则(者的)传票
parking-lot rule 劳工赔偿保险原则[劳工赔偿保险(Workers'compensation insurance)原则包括雇员在雇主的建筑物及其相连的基地来工作或刚离工作时所受到的侵害。亦称 premises rule]
parlance n. 用语,说法;(尤指正式辩论或谈判中的)发言,讲话
parlement (法史)(旧)大理院;立法机关的议会,最高法院的权力范围,最高法院的会议期;(大写)国会,议会
parlementaire 最高法院的,议会的;(法)军事谈判代表
parley n. 会谈,谈判;商议;辩论
parliament n. 议会,国会;议院;(法国革命前的)高等法院,立法机构;(大写)(英)议会
Parliament Act (英)1911 年《议会法》,Act of Parliament;(英)议会立法,(亦称议会制定法,指 1949 年《议会法》对 1911 年的议会法"Parliament Act"修订后的规定。该规定主要对财政法案和非财政法案等进行了修改)
Parliament House (英)议会大厦
parliament journal 议会公报
parliament rolls 议会档案,(英)议会案卷(指从14世纪早期开始的议会会议记录)
parliamentarian n. 议会法规专家;国会议员;议会中的雄辩家
parliamentarianism n. 代议制政体,议会制政府
parliamentarism n. 议会政治;议会制度
parliamentary a. 国会的,议会的;根据议会法的;国会或议会制定的;国会或议会特有的;议员的
parliamentary agent 设法使议会通过有关局部权益的法案的律师;受托在议会中为某党派效力的议员
parliamentary authority 议会的权威[指某一部门已经采用议会的手册(parliamentary manual)以便对其审议,该权威的手册条文在各种情况下只要与法律相符,与组织部门治理文件相一致,均可适用于治理这个部门。见 parliamentary manual]
parliamentary bar 议会律师业
parliamentary borough (英)议会议员选举区
parliamentary commissioner for administration (英)议会行政专员
parliamentary committee 议院委员会
parliamentary congress 议会(两院)联席会议
parliamentary constituency 议会选举区
parliamentary control 议会(对政府的)控制
parliamentary counsel 议院律师
Parliamentary Counsel to the Treasury (英)议会财政顾问
parliamentary decision 议会决议
parliamentary democracy 议会民主制度
parliamentary draftsman 议会起草人
parliamentary election 国会选举,议会选举
parliamentary franchise 议会(国会)议员选举权;议会(国会)给予(个人、公司、社团)的特许权
parliamentary government 议会政体;议会政治;代议政府

parliamentary immunity 议员豁免权,议会豁免权
parliamentary language 议会特有的措辞,慎重有礼的言辞
parliamentary law 议会法(总称)
parliamentary legislation 议会立法
parliamentary manual 议会手册[通常指商业性出版的法律或咨询手册,其中包括议会规则(parliamentary rules)和提供的一些规则作为议会的权威为一些组织采用。该指导性的议会手册(美国印制的)均为《罗伯特指令规则》(Robert Rules of Order),为非立法部门(nonlegislative bodies)新修订的版本,以及为州的立法部门提供的《麦逊的立法程序手册》(Mason's Manuel of Legislative Procedure)。见 parliamentary authority]
parliamentary ombudsman 议会监察专员;议会调查专员
parliamentary papers 议院公文,国会文件
parliamentary private secretary (英)议会私人秘书
parliamentary privilege 立法机关特权,议会特权[(美)见 legislative privilege。(英)为从法律方面保障议会及议员履行其职能而赋予议会和议员以不受国王、法院、议会以外的其他机构及公众的干涉的特权,包括:①免受民事拘禁权;②言论自由及集体觐见君主权;③内部程序性权利,如决定议事程序等;④对侵犯或蔑视议会特权者的惩治权]
parliamentary procedure 议会(国会)程序(指遵照议会法的程序);议院法程序
parliamentary questioning 议会质询
parliamentary secretary (英)政务次官(指位于大臣和国务大臣之下作为大臣助理的初级大臣,由首相任命)
parliamentary sovereignty 议会主权
parliamentary statute 议会法规
parliamentary system 议会制;议会政体
parliamentary system of government 议会制政体
parliamentary under-secretary (英)政务次官
parliamentary vacation 议会休假期

parliamentialism n. 内阁制
parochial school 教区的学校
parol n. 口头答辩书
parol agreement 口头协定,口头合约
parol arrest 凭口头命令逮捕;口头逮捕令(指犯了妨害治安罪的人,由保安官发出口头命令,将其逮捕)
parol contract 口头合同(契约)
parol/parole evidence 口头证据(见 extrinsic evidence)
parol(或 parole)evidence rule 口头证据规则(指在人们进行书面协议时,除非正准备的书面合同中有错误或欺诈,否则其含义不能因以前口头协议而产生矛盾)
parol lease 口头租借
parol promise 口头允诺
parole n. (美)假释,有条件的释放;准许在狱中有条件的自由;诺言,宣誓(尤指战俘所作誓言);特用暗号(或口令)
parole v. 假释;使(俘虏)宣誓后释放
Parole Board (英)假释委员会
parole of honor 誓言
parole officer 假(保)释官
parolee n. (美)获假释者,假释犯
parquet (法)检察机关,检察院;(古法院)法官或律师席
parricidal a. 杀父母的;犯杀亲罪的;杀尊长的,犯杀尊长罪的
parricide n. 1.杀父母,杀父母罪;杀亲罪 2.叛逆罪;杀尊长罪 3.杀父母者;杀尊长者
parson n. 教区牧师
part a./n. 部分的,局部的/1.(法律条文中的)一部分,项,篇 2.(契约交易等)一方(辩论中的)一面 3.本分,职责 4.区域,地方
part and parcel 重要(组成)部分
part owners 共有人
part payment 部分支付,部分付款
part performance 局部履行,部分履行
part sovereign state 部分主权国
part-time adjudicator 兼职仲裁人;兼职公断人
part-time duty personnel 兼职人员
part-time judge 兼职法官,(英皇家刑事法院)兼职法官(指由国王根据大法官的

提议,从具有 10 年以上工作实践的律师中任命的,有任期,不执行法官职务时,仍可操律师业务)
part-time staff 非全日制工作人员,兼职人员
parti pris 先入之见,偏见
partial a. 不完全的,部分的,局部的;偏向一方的,偏袒的,不公平的
partial acceptance 部分承兑;部分承诺
partial alteration 局部变更,部分变更
partial armistice(s) 局部休战
partial award 部分仲裁裁决
partial collective ownership 部分集体所有制
partial condemnation 部分征用(指征用一块完整土地的一部分)
partial defense 局部答辩;非全面辩护
partial delay 局部延误
partial delivery 部分交付,部分交货
partial delusion 部分错觉
partial disarmament 局部裁军
partial enjoyment 部分享有(权)
partial evidence 部分证据(材料)
partial guarantee 局部担保,部分担保
partial guardian 部分监护人(指监护人的权利、义务和权力都受到法院命令中对其特别规定的严格限制)
partial incapacity 局部丧失能力
partial intestacy 局部未立遗嘱
partial invalidity 部分无效
partial loss 部分损失(指海上保险所保的物体,一部分遭受损失)
partial mobilization 部分总动员,局部动员
partial neutrality 局部中立,不完全中立
partial no-fault liability 部分的无过错责任
partial occupation 部分占有;局部占领
partial opinion 偏见,不公正的意见
partial payment 部分支付
partial performance 部分履行
partial remission of debt 部分免除债务
partial retort 部分的反驳,部分的反对
partial revisions 部分修订
partial societies 部分性社会(见 spontaneous suborders)
partial succession 部分的继承(指国际法上国家一部分脱离母国或自行独立或与他国合并,通称部分的继承)
partial transfer 部分转让,部分转移
partial verdict 部分裁决
partial veto 部分否决
partiality n. 偏袒,偏见;不公平
partially secured creditor 部分担保的债权人
partially secured liability 部分担保的债务
partibility n. 可分性;(财产)分割
partible inheritance 可分的遗产
particeps criminis 共犯;伙同犯(指共谋或参加罪行行为的人)
participant n. 参加者,参与者,共享者
participant in a crime 共犯
participant state 参加国,参与国
participants in criminal proceeding 刑事诉讼参与人
participating preference share 参加优先股
participating a. 由多人(或多方)发起的,由多人或多方一起参加的;(股票等)使持有人有权参与分享的
participating bonds 分担债券
participating countries 参加国
participating loan 共同放款
participating preferred stock 参加优先股权
participating sponsorship 多人(或多方)参加的集体发起
participation n. 参加,参与;分享,共享
participation agreement 参与协定
participation certificate 参股证券
participation company 参股公司
participation in business activities 参与商业活动
participation in homicide 参与杀人
participation of workers in business like management 职工参加企业管理
participator n. 分享者;参与者,参加者
participatory democracy 分享民主制
participatory governance 参与性统治[指将直接言词(direct and verbal trial)纳入民诉程序基本原则系列。不仅在程序意义上促进了两造到庭、现实参与,而且将当事人的庭审陈述落到实处,使庭审更具有实质参与感和参与性。另外,直接言词可以在对方视角意义上形成参与满足感,实

现当事人到庭的参与性统治的程序正义]
participatory merchant court 分享的商业法庭,观众可参加的商业法庭
particular n./a. 分列细节的原告起诉书(或被告答辩书),单独事项;个别部分;详细说明;(复)细目,要点/单独的,个别的;特殊的;特别的,特定的;各个的;特指的;特有的;分项的;详细的
particular average (=petty average) 单独海损
particular average loss 单独海损损失
particular case 特殊案件,特定案件;个案
particular cause of action at issue 有争议的特定诉因
particular charge 单项费用,特别费用
particular commodity rate 特定货物运费率
particular crime 特定罪行
particular custom(s) 特定习惯(指贸易惯例或行业惯例),特殊习惯
particular degree of relatedness required by the minimum contacts doctrine 最低联系理论所要求的某种程度的联系
particular estate 特定地产(权)
particular evidence 特定证据
particular facts of the case 案件的特定事实
particular forms of evidence 证据的特定形式
particular international law 特定国际法
particular issue of fact 某一事实争点,特定事实争点
particular jurisprudence 特别法学,专门法学(指民法、刑法、宪法、国际法之类)特殊法理学
particular jury 特别陪审团
particular kind of cases (美)特定(种)类型案件(指涉及外交人员的案件以及涉及海事、海商事务的案件和破产案件等)
particular legacy (大陆法)特定遗赠[指一项遗嘱赠与,并未明示何一部分或按何比例,而是不低于全部遗产(estate);任何遗嘱赠与(testamentary gift)均不适用一般遗赠(general legacy)或全部遗产遗赠(universal legacy)的定义或概念(definition)。参见《路易斯安那州民法典》第1587、3506条。亦称 legacy under a particular title。见 general legacy; universal legacy]
particular (special) lien 特别留置权(与概括留置权相对,指特定物留置权)
particular of amendment 单独修改事项
particular of appliant 申请人详细说明
particular offense 特别罪行
particular opinion 特别判决意见书,特别律师意见书;特别意见
particular period 特定阶段
particular point 特点,特别争论点,特定观点,特殊论点
particular presumptions 具体的推定[指澳大利亚证据法学家威特和威廉姆斯主要根据澳大利亚法院判例分析推定原理和运用而讨论出的具体的推定。在其司法实践中运用比较广泛的推定包括:①婚姻子女合法性推定(the presumption of legitimacy);②婚姻合法性推定(the presumption of the validity of marriages);③生存推定(the presumption of life or continuance);④死亡推定(the presumption of death);⑤存活推定(the presumption of survivorship);⑥合法性和常规性推定(the presumption of regularity);⑦科学仪器准确性推定(the presumption of accuracy of scientific instruments)]
particular remedies 特殊救济方法
particular rules 特殊裁决,特别规定
particular successor 特定继承人
particular tenant 特定租借人,特定地产占有人
particular texts 单行的法律文本
particular thing(s) 特定物
particular writ 特殊令状
particularim n. 排他主义;自觉主义;各邦自主独立主义
particularism-nationalism school 特殊主义—国家主义学派(又称个别主义学派,指19世纪末代替普遍主义—国家主义学派兴起的国际私法学派)
particularity n. (诉讼文书中的)详情叙述,细节说明;精确;特性,个性
particulars of charges 控告要点;主要罪状
particulars of offence 罪行细节

particulars of sale 买卖摘要(指概述等待出卖的货物的要点和交易条件等);招标细则;拍卖物品说明书
partie civile 民事诉讼当事人
parties in action 诉讼当事人
parties of contract 合同(契约)当事人
parties to a contract 合同当事人
parties to civil suits 民事诉讼案件当事人
parties to dipute 争论的各方,争论的各当事方
parties to litigation 诉讼当事人
parties to offences 和罪行有牵连的人,和罪行有关的当事人
parties to treaties 缔约国
parties' actual course of dealing 当事人的实际交易过程(见 two-step "minimum contact" analysis)
parties' prior negotiation 当事人以前的协商(见 two-step "minimum contact" analysis)
partisan n. 有偏颇(袒)之人;帮伙,同党
partisan advocacy 偏袒性辩护
partisan troop 游击队
partition n./v. 分配;分割;瓜分;区分;区分物/分配;分割;瓜分;区分
Partition Act 分割法(通常指财产的分割规定)
partition deed 分割契约
partition of chattels 动产分割
partition of inheritance 分配遗产
partly-autonomous a. 半自治的,部分自治的
partner n. 1.分享者,分担者;合伙人,股东,伙伴,合作者 2.配偶,夫或妻
partner by estoppel 不得否认为合伙人
partner for life 终身伴侣,配偶
partner's interest in partnership 合伙企业中的财产份额
partnership n. 1.合伙,合股;合伙企业 2.伙伴关系,合伙关系,合股关系
Partnership Act (1890) (英)《统一普通合伙法》(1890年)
partnership affair 合伙事务
partnership agreement 合伙协约
partnership assets 合伙资产
partnership at will 不定期的合伙关系,随意合伙
partnership bankruptcy 合伙企业破产
partnership by shares 股份公司
partnership capital 合伙资本
partnership contract 合伙合同(契约)
partnership contribution 合伙出资
partnership debt 合伙的债务
partnership instrument 合伙文据
partnership of marriage 婚姻的结合,婚配
partnership property 合伙财产
partnership with limited liability 有限责任公司
partnerships in crime 共犯
patrician (罗马早期的)贵族
parts of a set 复本(见 bill in a set)
party n. 1.诉讼当事人;关系人;参与者 2.团体,政党 3.会,(社交、游戏等的)集会,宴会
party appointment 各方指定仲裁员
(the) party at fault 有错误的一方当事人,负责任的一方当事人
party autonomy 当事人(意思)自治原则(其内涵是:除强制性法律规范外,其余条款均可由当事人自行协商制定。见 functional equivalence)
party caucus in congress (美)国会预选会,国会党派秘密会议
party causing the injury 加害方
party concerned 有关当事人
party constitution 党章
party government 政党政治
party in a lawsuit 诉讼当事人(旧译:事主)
party in bankruptcy 破产当事人
party in breach (=party in default) 违约的合同当事人
party in delay 迟延方
party (parties) in interest 利害关系人,(亦称)利益当事人(real party in interest)
party in office 执政党
party in opposition 反对党
party in power 执政党
party initiating a private prosecution 自诉人
party injured 受损害的一方

party injuring　损害他人的一方
party institution　党的机构
party insuring (=policy holder)　要保人
party intervention　当事国形式的参加(指1922年《常设国际法院规则》中的用词)
party joinder　当事人合并
party line　政党的路线
party losing the lawsuit　败诉方
party man　政党的忠实支持者,政党党员
party of the first part　赘词(指用来替代重复在文件上的当事人姓名的多余词语)
party of the working class　工人阶级政党
party or coalition having a majority in the legislature　议会中占多数席位的政党或政党联盟
party out of office　在野党
party platform　政纲
party politics　政党政治
party privilege　政党特权
party system　政党制度
party to a case　诉讼当事人
party to a contract　合同当事人,立约当事人
party to a dispute　争议当事人
party to a lawsuit　诉讼当事人
party to a treaty　缔约当事国
party to the court proceedings　诉讼参与人
party vote　(美)根据政党政策所投的票
party-wall (或 party wall) n.　界墙,共有墙(指两个不同的所有人的建筑物或房屋连在一起的墙)
* *Parum proficit scire quid fieri debet, si non cognoscas quomodo sit facturum.*　It avails little to know what ought to be done, if you do not know how it is done.　仅知道应做什么,而不知如何去做,则毫无用处。
parvenu　暴发户
pas n.　先行权;优先权;上席
pascua publica　公共使用的牧场
pasha n.　巴夏(指伊斯兰国家高级官员的称谓)
pass n./v.　护照;执照;通行证;经过;及格证书;招待券/(14 世纪)1.宣布,宣判;判决,作出判决;裁决,裁定;规定〈the court refused to pass on the constitutional issue, deciding the case instead on procedural grounds〉(法院拒绝裁决宪法上的争议 却基于程序上的理由对案件作出判决)2.(财产)转让或被转让〈the woman's will passes title to the house to her nephew, much to her husband's surprise〉(这位妇女的遗嘱转让该房屋所有权给其侄女,使其丈夫十分惊讶)3.裁定,颁布(法律,法案或决议);采纳〈Congress has debated whether to pass a balanced-budget amendment to the constitution〉(国会经过辩论是否采纳符合宪法的平衡计划修订)4.批准或证实(某些事)以适应特定要求〈the mechanic informed her that the car had passed inspection〉(机修工告知她小车已被证实通过审查)5.出版,发行;转移,转让;或流通,流动(一个事物,通常为赝品)〈he was found guilt of passing counterfeit bills〉(他被判发行伪造单据罪)6.生 在……之前,走在……之前;或进行,超出范围的进行,放弃〈the case was passed on the court's trial docket because the judge was presiding over a criminal trial〉(此案已在法院备审案件表上放弃了,因为法官要主审一件刑事案)7.放弃;弃权;戒除;避免(见 abstain 1)
pass a law　通过法律
pass a sentence　宣判
pass book　(银行)存折;(顾客)赊购(货物)的折子;(前南非白人政府发给有色人种的)身份证
pass book custodian certificate　存折保管证
pass down　传下来
pass judg(e)ment on　对……作判决
pass key　万能钥匙
pass law　(前南非白人政府为推行种族隔离而制定的)通行证法
pass off　1.(感觉)终止,停止〈has the pain passed off〉(疼痛已经终止)2.(事件)发生进行到最后〈the transaction passed off with out a hitch〉(此笔生意顺利做成) 3.故意忽略 4.(专利)出卖假货,假冒
pass off the patent　假冒(他人)专利
pass on　给,给予,转交,转递〈property or death benefits pass on the death of one survived by the other〉[财产和人身保险金给予相对于另个人后死亡者(或幸存者)]

pass (a sentence) on (somebody) 对(某人)作出(某种刑罚的刑事判决)
pass upon a case 宣判案件
pass-through n. [美国住房抵押贷款证券(MBS)中最基本的抵押权]转手债券
pass-through of the character of income 所得性质的上传[指合伙企业的税收问题,其与所得和亏损的分派(allocation of income and loss)这两组问题的解决是确立合理的对企业及外商合伙人所得税制的前提]
pass-through securities 转手型证券
pass-through taxation (1998年)转手债券税[指一个企业所得的纳税不是由企业本身而是由企业的所有人进行纳税。合伙企业和S公司都是按同一方式纳税。因此,除非有限责任公司(limited liability companies)和有限责任合伙企业(limited liability partnership)就有关它们的所得税申报单选定成被以法人(corporation)通过"核查票箱"(checking the box)身份纳税,那它们则属于按转手债券税方式。这种选择是依8832形式(实体类别选择)(Form 8832)(Entity Classification Election)制定的。参见"财政法规"第301.7701节。亦称conduit taxation]
passage n. 1.航行权(指河流、水道的自由航行的权利);自由通过权 2.(议案,法案的)通过 3.(海上,空中的)航行 4.经过,变迁
passage at arms 比武,交战;互殴,吵架
passage broker 旅运经纪,航行经纪
passage in transit 途中通过
passage ticket 通行证
passenger n. 乘客,旅客,过路人
passenger liability insurance 旅客责任保险
passenger-plaintiff n. 乘客原告
passim 各处;遍及
passing of title 所有权转移
passing off 冒充,蒙混;假冒(指普通法的专用语,专指假冒他人商品,但并非假冒他人商标),卖假货,骗卖
passing over 不注意,忽略,省略
passing-on-defense 转嫁抗辩
passive a. 消极的;被动的;无利息的;不抵抗的
passive bond 无息债券
passive breach of contract (大陆法)消极违约[指未履行合同上承诺之要求。根据直到1984年的路易斯安那州法律,消极违约与积极违约成为鲜明对比。它在履行合约义务过程中疏于履行(negligence in performance),而积极违约则会引起合同的或因侵权的请求权,消极违约通常不会引起因侵权的请求权。见active breach of contract]
passive citizens 消极公民
passive concealment 消极隐匿,被动隐瞒
passive contact 被动联系
passive crime 被动犯罪,被动性罪行
passive debt 无息债款
passive depositary 消极受寄人
passive income 消极所得,非劳动所得(与工资、薪水、贸易或经营的收入相对而言的一种非劳动收入,如来自有限合伙股权的收入、租金收入等。积极收入为"active income")
passive (permissive) investment income 消极投资收入,被动投资收入(美国《国内税收法》中的名词,指不涉及或不需要积极行为而获取的投资所得,特别指从版税、某些租金、股息权益、年金以及出售或成交换股票或证券所得的毛收入)
passive investor 消极投资人(指通过购买证券等方式进行投资者)
passive loss(es) (美)消极损失(指纳税人实际未参与活动的损失、来自租贷活动的损失以及来自避税活动的损失,这三种情况均为消极损失。这种损失通常为部分损失)
passive negligence 可谅解的疏忽(或缺陷);房产上存在的隐患;应完成的事而未完成
passive operation (银行的)无息业务
passive right 消极权利
passive shareholder 消极股东
passive support 被动支持;消极支持
passive title 消极所有权
passive trust 无利息信托;被动信托;消极信托

passive trustee 消极受托人
passive use 消极使用权
passive waste 非人为毁损;消极毁损
passive website 被动网址(在美国,涉及互联网纠纷管辖权的原则在不同州、不同的发展阶段均有所不同。互联网发展初期,有些公司在某一州拥有被动网址而被该州法院行使管辖权。随着互联网的发展,这种确定管辖权原则被新的管辖权原则所代替)
passive work slowdown 消极怠工
passivism n. 消极主义;被动行为(或态度等)
passport n. 通行证;护照
past a. 过去的,以往的;前任的
past consideration 既往对价
past due note 过期票据
past (或 beyond) redress 无法补救的,无法挽回的
pasthumous publication 去世后版权(指作者死亡后出版的作品)
pasties and G-string (为应付禁止裸体暴露的法律规定而穿的,贴乳房较紧或遮乳中和下身的)遮羞布
pasture n. 牧场
patchwork of provisions (英)多种救济混合制
patent a./n. 1.专利的,专利权的,专卖的 2.公开的,开放的 3.显著的,明显的/(美)根据联邦宪法第1条第8款授予发明者和作者"特定期间的排他权"以促进科学和艺术的进步之规定,国会规定"发明或发现任何新的有用的程序、机械、制造或物质组合的任何人"都能获得专利;(政府给予的)公有地让渡证书;专利,专利权;专卖权;专利发明物;特许状
patent v. 取得专利;特许专卖;给予专利
patent act 专利法
patent agent 专利代理人
patent ambiguity (法律文字上的)明显暧昧不清的语言或文句;显著不明处
Patent and Trademark Office (美)专利商标局
Patent and Trade Mark Law Amendment Act 见 Bayh-Dole Act

patent application 专利申请(书)
patent claim 专利的权利申请,专利的权利主张[指描述一项发明的新颖性(novel)和界定该专利的保护范畴的正式陈述〈Claim #3 of the patent describes an eletrical means for diving a metal pin〉(3 号的专利权利请求描述一项电动方法来驱动金属探头)。见 specification 3]
Patent Cliff 专利悬崖[最近,制药业专利保护到期的话题引起媒体和业内人士的极大关注。未来几年被人们戏称为"专利悬崖"(Patent Cliff)时期,即一旦迈出悬崖(药品失去专利保护),大型制药企业的销售额和利润就会一落千丈,而这些企业将无一幸免。Wordspy 网站对"Patent cliff"的解释是企业的收入在一项利润丰厚的专利失效后大幅度下降]
Patent Corporation Treaty (PCT) (1990)《专利权合作条约》
patent defect 显著的瑕疵(指一望而知的瑕疵)
patent eligibility 专利适格性,可专利主题范围(指判断一项研究工具是否可以授予专利的形式要件。美国《专利法》第 101 条将专利主题范围界定为"任何新颖且有用的方法、机器、产品或组合以及任何新颖且有用的改良物"。美国联邦最高法院也曾将该法条宽泛地解释为"阳光下的任何人造之物")
patent fee 专利费
patent holder 专利持有者,专利权人
patent infringerment 侵害专利权
patent interference 专利权的争议
patent law 专利法
Patent Law of the People's Republic of China 《中华人民共和国专利法》
patent legislation 专利权立法
patent license 专利许可证,专卖执照
patent medicine 专利药品
patent methods 专利方法
patent misuse 专利滥用(指专利设置原本是期望通过对专利权人的激励来促进技术创新和应用,但一些专利权人却凭借专利的垄断来牟取暴利,限制市场竞争,既妨碍技术的应用,又损害消费者的

利益)
Patent Misuse Reform Act (美)《专利权滥用改革法》[指1988年美国国会通过的一项法律,对专利滥用进行了更进一步的限制,补充了两项不构成专利权滥用的行为,即(4)(5)两项:(4)拒绝许可或使用专利权;(5)在对专利权许可或专利产品销售中附加条件,要求获得另一项专利授权或购买一件单独的商品,除非专利权人在附加条件给予许可或销售该专利产品的相关领域拥有市场权力]
patent of invention 发明专利(权)
patent of precedence 先卖权;专利权授予证书;(英史)位次特许状
patent office 专利局
patent office journal 专利局公报
(The) Patent Office of the People's Republic of China 中国专利局
patent owner 专利(权)所有人
patent pool 专利联营,专利权共享互用的一组企业
patent pooling 专利联营制,专利共同使用制度
patent register 专利登记簿
patent right 专利权
Patent Rolls (英)特许状案卷(指从1202年迄今的大法官法庭案卷);(小写)(美)专利登记册;(英)专卖特许登记簿
patent royalty 专利权使用费
patent search 专利调查
patent ticket 专利入场券(指只有获得专利权人的一个授权,才能"买"到生产这个产品的入场券,只有这样才能合法生产)
Patent Troll (美)"专利流氓"(指源于美国巨额专利侵权赔偿制度中的一种现象。"专利流氓"本身并不制造专利产品或提供专利服务,它们通常从公司、科研院所或个人发明者那里购买专利,然后凭专利诉讼赚取巨额利润,它们将大量专利打包组合起来,往往就能形成十倍、百倍于原先专利的威力,产生所谓"专利恐怖主义",给市场竞争秩序和后续带来巨大威胁)
patent writ 空白令状(指未盖章或未予密封之令状)

patentability n. 专利性,能否授予专利
patentability conditions 授予专利(权)的条件[指授予专利的实质性条件:新颖性(novelty)、实用性(utility)和非显而易见性(nonobviousness);在美国还需发明或创造人的身份(inventorship)或其合法代表]
patentable a. 可给予专利权的,可以取得专利的
patentable device 可授予专利的发明,可授予专利的设计
patentable novelty 可授予专利的新产品
patentable process 可授予专利的新方法(见 process patent)
patented a. 有专利权的
patented goods 专利产品
patented invention 专利发明
patentee n. 专利权人,专利取得者,专利权所有人,专利权获得者
patently ad. 显然地,一清二楚地
patentor n. 授予专利的人或机关
patents appeal tribunal 专利上诉法庭
patents court 专利法庭
patents pool 专利联盟
patents registration 专利登记
pater n. 父亲(大陆法上有时包括祖父)
Pater est quem nuptiae demonstrant. The father is he whom the marriage indicates. 婚后所生子女当以婚夫为父。
paterfamilia 一家之父;户主
paterfamilias (罗马法)家长(男性)
paterfamilias's agnatic family (罗马法)男性家长的父系家庭,男性家长的同族家庭
paternal a. 1.父系的;父亲的,像父亲的 2.传自父亲的
paternal acres 自父系继承的土地
paternal authority 亲权;父权
paternal family 父系家族,父系家庭
paternal line 父系
paternal power 父权,(对子女的)家长权(可包括母权)
paternal property 父系遗产
paternal society 父系社会
paternalism n. 家长统治,家长作风,父爱主义,家长主义(家长主义研究的代表人

物为美国学者吉诺德·德沃金,他在其著作《剑桥哲学辞典》中的"家长主义"词条中提出 p 对 q 的行为构成家长主义的三个条件:① p 的行为是出于为 q 避免某种危害或维护某种利益的意图;② p 的行为与 q 当时的偏好、意愿或价值观相反或无关;③ p 的行为是对 q 的自由或自主的限制。见 hard paternalism)
paternalist n. 搞家长式统治的人
paternalistic a. 家长式的,家长作风的,家长式统治的
paternalistic government 家长统治式的政府
paternalistic position 家长式的统治地位
paternity （15世纪）1.父亲的身份;父权;父性(见 filiation)2.归属权(版权)(attribution right)3.来源,根源
paternity exclusion 父权否定
paternity of an illegitimate child 非婚生子(女)的生父身份
paternity right 确认身份权;指明出处权(指精神权利的一种)
paternity suit 确认生父的诉讼(指确认非婚生子女父亲的诉讼)
paternity test （1926年）亲子鉴定[指通常运用 DNA 鉴定(DNA identification)或组织分型(tissue-typing)的测试来确定某人是某子女的亲生父亲(biological father)。见 DNA identification; human-leukocyte antigen test; blood-grouping test]
path dependence "路径依赖"[指诺贝尔奖得主诺斯(D. North)教授提出的著名理论;强调初始的条件或选择对一国经济发展的特殊影响]
path-dependence theory 路径依赖理论[指通过"积极的反馈"与"累进增长的回报"把某一系统的发展"锁定"在一种特定模式中,并不断"自我强化"的现象。按罗伊(Roe)理论,公司治理语境中路径依赖可分为两种:一为结构驱动的路径依赖(structure driven path-dependence);另一为法律规则驱动的路径依赖(rule-driven path-dependence)。见 convergence of corporate governance]
pathological category 病理类

pathological feeling 病理性情绪(在犯罪心理结构中,无意识因素占重要位置。它以不为犯罪人觉察到的方式影响着其犯罪心理和行为。病理性情绪实质含有一种"无意识",即主体对客观的一种不知不觉的认识功能,不是对客观对象根本没有一点认识反映,而是一种不自觉的模糊不清的反映,是未被意识到的认识,无意识不等于无认识。有病理性情绪患者易产生消极心情,挫折情绪和激情状态,这些均可导致无意识的体验,从事违法、甚至犯罪活动。)
pathological fire-setting 病理性纵火(又称 pyromania 纵火狂,指病人有纵火烧物的强烈欲望和浓厚兴趣,并有行动前的紧张感和行动后的轻松感,经常思考纵火行为及其周围场景,纵火并非为了政治目的、报复或经济利益。见 habit and impulse control disorder)
pathological gambling 病理性赌博(属习惯与冲动控制障碍的一种)
pathology n. 病理学;病理;病状
patria (从被告邻人中选出的)陪审团;邻人,近邻,邻居
patria potestas (罗马法上的)父权,家长权(与 paternal power 同)
patrial n. （英）（根据1971年的《移民法》)有居住权的人
patriarch n. 家长,族长;创始人;元老
patriarchal a. 家(族)长的,家长制的;主教的
patriarchal society 宗法社会
patriarchal style of work 家长作风
patriarchal system 宗法制度
patriarchalism n. 宗法制社会或国家
patriarchism n. 家长主义;族长政治
patriarchy n. 家长制;父权制;父系社会
patrician n. 贵族
patricidal a. 弑父罪的;弑父者的
patricide n. 弑父罪;弑父者
Patrick Henry's Stamp Act （美）《帕特里克·亨利印花法》(S. A.)
patrilareral a. 父系亲属的
patrilineage n. 父系
patrilineal society 父系社会

patrimoine （法）广义财产（指民事主体拥有的财产和债务的总和）；祖产，遗产，家财，家业；宝贵遗产；全部财产（包括权利与义务）
patrimonial a. 祖传的,世袭的,世袭财产的
patrimonial law 承袭法（继承法）
patrimonial rights 世袭权（指与人身权不同的从属于世袭财产或继承财产的权利）
patrimonial sea 承袭海
patrimony n. 祖传财产（亦称世袭财产；继承财产,家庭世代相传下来的财产；又指宗教会所基金）
Patriot Act 见 USA Patriot Act
patrioteer n. 打着爱国旗号牟私利者
patriotic a. 爱国的,有爱国心的
patriotic democratic personages （中）爱国民主人士
patriotic oversea Chinese （中）爱国华侨
patriotism n. 爱国主义,爱国心,爱国精神
patrocinium （罗马帝国晚期的）庇护地产制
patrol n. 巡逻（队）；巡查；巡逻兵
patrol boat 巡逻船,哨艇
patrol dog 警犬
patrol wagon 警车；囚车
patrolman n. 巡逻人；（美）巡逻警察
patron n. 保护人,庇护人；赞助人,资助人；有圣职授予权者或圣职推荐权人
patronage n. 1.保护,庇护 2.赞助,资助 3.授予官职或特权的权力
patronage practice 保护的惯例,保护的家族
patroness n. 女保护人,女庇护人
patronize v. 庇护,保护,赞助,资助；光顾,惠顾；对……恩人自居,对……提出屈尊俯就之志
patronymic n. 源于父名；姓
Pattern n. 模式:指一种行为(behavior)方式(mode)或一系列动作(或作为)都是公认或终如一的〈A pattern of racial discrimination〉(种族歧视的模式/种族歧视的始终如一)
pattern of estate in land 地产权的形式
pattern of shipments 出货方式
paucital rights 对人的少项权利（指与 multital right 相对而言）
paucity n. 少量,少许；缺乏,贫乏
pauper n. （可免除诉讼费用的）贫民；穷人
paupers' cost 贫民(起诉)支付的诉讼费用
paupries （罗马法）由于家畜所造成损害赔偿之诉
pawn n./v. 抵押品；典当的状态；人质/典当；抵押；以……保证
pawn receipt 抵押凭据；抵押收据；当票
pawn ticket 当票；抵押凭据
pawnage n. 典当；典当物
pawnbroker n. 当铺老板,经营当铺者；留置动产典押并收取法定利息的贷款业者
pawnbroking n./a. 典当业/经营典当业的
pawned property 典当财产
pawnee n. 承典人,收当人；质权人,接受抵押品的人
pawner (pawnor) n. 交当人,抵押人,出典人,典当人
pawning n. 典当,抵押
pawnshop n. 当铺
pawnshop dispute 典当纠纷
pay n./v. 1.支付；工资(旧译:薪俸)；报酬；报偿；偿还 2.有支付能力者,按期付款者/支付；付款；缴付；付清偿还,补偿；抵偿
pay as you earn (PAYE) 按收益征收的税项；(英)付工资时扣缴所得税制度
pay as you go 1.账单到期即付 2.领到薪金即付所得税 3.量入为出
pay back 偿还(借款等),偿付
pay code 付款账号
pay demand note 收费单
pay dispute 工资纠纷
pay down 用现金支付
pay in advance in quarterly instalments 分季预缴
pay in cash 现金支付,付现款
pay in cheque 以支票付款
pay in kind 以实物支付
pay instalment 分期付款
Pay Master-General (Paymaster-General) (英)主计大臣(指由陆军军需部长和海军司库两个职位于 1835 年合并而成的官职,现为一个政治性官职,只有很少的财

政职能,即具有对永久编制人员掌握的公款的支付职能。另外,该职位还具有特殊的和非部门性的职权。通常这种职位由内阁大臣担任,有时初级大臣亦可担任)
pay money down 现款支付
pay off 1.付清,偿清 2.给薪解雇 3.贿赂 4.进行报复
pay on a consolidated basis 汇总缴纳
pay on term 定期付款
pay on the line 立即付款
pay one's way 支付自己应承担的费用,支付生活费;勉强维持,不负责
pay order 支付凭证
pay pause (英)工资冻结
pay regard to 注意到
pay scale 工资标准
pay scot and lot 纳税人应纳的税;分担财政负担
pay supplement 工资补贴
pay tax 纳税
pay warrant 支付命令,付款委托书
pay-day (payday) n. 发薪日;交割日;结账过户日
pay-master-General (英)主计大臣
pay-through securities 受偿型证券
pay-up n. 现金损失;付高价;全部按时付清
payable a. 可支付的;应付的;到期的;可获利的
payable agent 付款代理人
payable at maturity 到期付款
payable at sight 见票即付
payable at usance 远期付款
payable on demand 见票即付
payable to bearer 见票即付持票人
payable to order of 凭指定付款;付款给指定人……
paycheque n. (付)薪金(用的)支票
payee n. 受款人;提款人,收款人;收票人
payer n. 付款人,交付人,支付人
payer for honour 参加付款人
paying bank 付款银行
paying certificate 付款凭单
paying enterprise 有效的企业
paying public domain 为进入公有领域作品付费

paying system 传唤系统(指利用声和光来传唤要找的人,通常由电话总机的电话员兼管此事,在美国机关、单位内常使用此种设备)
payload n. (企业的)工资负担;最大负荷量
paymaster n. (发放工资的)出纳员;军需官
paymaster general 军需部长;(英)财政部的主计长;(美)海军主计总监
payment n. (14世纪)1.支付,偿还(指用交付现金或某些可接受的贵重物品部分或全部还清债或债款) 2.现金支付[或可使满意地偿还"债"(obligation)的贵重物品] 3.合同债务或其他义务的履行
payment against document(s) 凭单付款
payment against presentation of shipping document 凭运单付款
payment agreement 支付协议,支付协定
payment by intervention 第三人参加付款
payment by mistake of fact 误付
payment by post 邮寄支付
payment by remittance 汇拨支付
payment card 交纳证,缴款
payment credit 付款信用证
payment forward 预付货款
payment imbalance 收支不平衡
payment in advance 预付,预付货款
payment in arrears 拖欠款项
payment in due course (票据)按期支付
payment in full 全部付款,全部照付
payment in international trade 国际贸易支付
payment in lieu 以付款代替
payment instrument 支付凭证
payment insufficient 付款不足
payment into court (被告)向法院交存的保证金
payment notice 缴款通知
payment of compensation 支付赔偿金;特别赔款,抚恤赔款
payment of damages 支付损害赔偿金
payment of deposit 支付押金;支付定金
payment of inherited and testamentary obligations 继承上的债务和遗嘱上指明的债务的清偿
payment of interest 利息支付
payment of money into court 向法院付款

(指在索取赔偿或债务的诉讼中被告人把应付还款项交给法院或银行作为清偿用,以减少继续进行诉讼的费用)
payment of rent 支付租金
payment of royalty 版权费,专利权税
payment of the price 支付价款
payment on a fixed day after sight 见票后定期付款
payment on deferred terms 分期付款,分期支付
payment order 付款通知书,付款委托书,支付命令
payment out of court 从法院提取的款项
payment procedure 支付手续
payment remuneration 支付酬金
payment respite 延期付款
payment stopped 止付,停止付款
payment undertaker 支付担当者,付款承担人
payment voucher 付款凭单
payoff n./a. 支付;发工资;分配盈利;分赃;营利;报酬;报应;(事件的)高潮;决定因素;过分/得出结果的,决定的
payoff function 支付函数
payoff matrix 支付矩阵,赔付矩阵
payoff table 成果表,结算表,偿付表
payola n. (美俚)暗中行贿;私下给予的贿赂
payout n. 花费,支出
payroll n. 工资名单,饷金名单
payroll tax 工资税
payroller n. (美)领薪者;受津贴者(尤指政府雇员)
pays 见 pais
Pays du Droit Coutumier 习惯法区域(或国家)
Pays du Droit Ecrit 成文法区域(或国家)
peace n. 和平;治安,社会秩序;安宁;(大写)和约
peace and order 公共秩序;治安
peace and security 和平与安全;治安
peace bond 治安保证书;安宁保证书(指在一定时期内保证良好的行为的保证书)
peace conference 和会
peace court 治安法庭

peace envoy 和平使者
peace fraud 和平骗局
Peace Keeping Force (PKF) 维和部队
peace negotiations 和平谈判,和谈
peace of God 上帝和平令(指中世纪天主教制止私斗和暴力行为的一种措施)
peace of the state 国家安全;国内和平
peace offensive 和平攻势
peace offering 和平建议;和平仪式;和解礼物;谢罪之礼物;(古犹太人的)谢恩祭
peace officer 治安官员
peace rally 和平集会,反战集会
peace settlement 和平解决
peace talks 和平谈判
peace treaty 和平条约,和约
peace zone 和平区
peace-breaker n. 扰乱治安者;肇事者;破坏和平者
peace-breaking n. 扰乱治安;破坏和平
peace-making n. 调解;调停争端
peaceable and quiet possession 继续和平地占有(取得土地所有权)
peaceable conduct 温和行为;规矩行为;缓和行为
peaceful a. 和平的;爱好和平的;和平时期的;平时的;安静的
peaceful co-existence 和平共处
peaceful evolution 和平演变
peaceful production 民用生产
peaceful settlement reached in court 诉讼上的和解,法院内和解
peaceful solution of international discords 和平解决国际争端
peaceful transition of political power 政权和平过渡
peaceful unification 和平统一
peacekeeping a. 维护和平的,执行停火协定的
peacekeeping forces 维持和平部队(指联合国为行使其维护世界和平的权限所建立的部队)
peacemaker n. 解调人;调停人;和事佬
peacenik n. (美)反战运动分子
peach v. 告发;出卖;告密
peasant association (中)农会

peasant movement 农民运动
peasant proprietor 自耕农,占有土地的农民
peasant uprising 农民起义
peasantry n. (总称)农民;农民的地位;小农阶级;自耕农阶层
peccable a. 易犯罪的;易有过失的
peccable human nature 容易犯罪的人性
peccadillo 轻罪,小过失
peccancy n. 有罪,犯罪;罪行,罪过;违章
peccant a. 有罪的;犯罪的;违章的;有过错的
peccatophobia n. (精神病学上的)犯罪恐惧
peccatum 罪行;恶行;错误行为
peccavi 认罪,认错
peculate v. 挪用;盗用;侵吞
peculation n. 挪用(公款),盗用(公款、公物),侵吞(公款、公物)
peculator n. 挪用公款者;盗用公款者
peculiar n./a. 专有的特权或私产;(不受当地司法机关管辖的)特殊教会(或教区)/个人的,私人的;特有的,特殊的,特别的
peculiar jurisdiction 特殊管辖(权),特殊审判权,特殊管辖范围
peculiar(或 **separate**)**property** 特有财产
peculium (罗马法)特有产(指准许妻儿拥有的或主人准许奴仆拥有的私产);私产
peculium adventitium (罗马法)家子自家父以外的人取得的特有产
peculium castrense (罗马法)军功特有产,参军所取得的特有财产
peculium profectium (罗马法)家子自家父取得的特有产
peculium quasi-castrense (罗马法)(为国家服役的收益取得的)准军功特有产
pecunia n. (英)有体动产
pecuniary a. 金钱的;应罚款的
pecuniary aid 资助
pecuniary benefits 有金钱价值之利益
pecuniary claim 索赔案件;索债案件
pecuniary compensation 金钱补偿
pecuniary damages 用金钱支付的损害赔偿
pecuniary damages in compensation 损害赔偿金
pecuniary donation 金钱捐赠,捐款
pecuniary embarrassment 财政困难
pecuniary fine 罚金
pecuniary interests 罚金的利益
pecuniary legacy 金钱遗赠
pecuniary loss 金钱损失,经济损失
pecuniary obligation 金钱债务
pecuniary offence 应罚款的违法行为;应科罚金的罪
pecuniary penalty 罚款
pecuniary promise 金钱上的允诺
pecuniary punishment 科以罚款的处分
pecunia trajectitia (罗马法)(向)海外转运货款(money conveyed overseas)[指所贷款项与货物由与船运相连的,贷方承担损失风险。见 nauticum fenus]
pecuniary sentence (处以)罚金的判决,罚金刑罚
pecuniary value 金钱价值
pecuniary unit 货币单位
pedage (古)通行费(指支付一笔钱为了通行他人土地的通行费)
pederast n. 鸡奸者
pederasty n. 鸡奸
pedigree n. 1.家系;出身;血统 2.(美俚)(警察局留存的)犯人身份调查书 3.前科
pedigreeman n. (美俚)有案可查的惯犯,有前科的罪犯
pedlar hawker's licence 流动小贩执照
pedophilia (1906 年)1.性流氓[指性乱(sexual disorder)的成年人,为了满足性欲而伤害孩子,甚至刚发育的少年] 2.伤害儿童的成人恶劣行为。这个词可以但不一定必须与性交相关联
peeler n. (爱尔兰)警察,(美俚)警察
peep culture 窥探文化[peep 的意思是"窥视""偷看",该词条指的是许多人乐此不疲地展示自己日常生活的点点滴滴,另一些人则津津有味地阅读或观看。不用说,这当然以博客、微博以及 YouTube 等视频网站为典型表现形式,此外还有 QQ 签名、人人网状态栏、网上论坛的发帖等。该词条是借鉴 pop culture(流行文化)一词产生的,最早见于 2007 年 9 月 3 日的美国《出

版者周刊》。报道称,多伦多作家兼社会评论家哈尔·涅季维茨基写了一本书,题目叫《窥探文化:"流行"变"窥探",我们学会了以窥视邻居为乐》(这本书在 2009 年正式出版时定名为《窥探日记:我们学会以观察自己和邻居为乐》)。窥探文化中涉及两类人,一类人热衷于通过各种渠道传播自己的想法,另一类人喜欢在各种渠道上发现别人的信息,他们分别在"被窥探"和"窥探"之中。然而,数字时代"有话就说,有图就秀"的窥探文化造成的不良社会影响也是显而易见的,比如削弱了对隐私的保护。"过度分享",也就是泄漏过多个人信息的行为,还会招致不必要的风险]

peeper Peeping Tom 的同义词

Peeping Tom (18 世纪)窥视者汤姆,窥视的汤姆[指通过窗户偷看他人以获得性快感的人(*voyeur*),亦称 peeper。实际为英国传说中的人物,因偷看戈黛娃夫人(Lady Codiva)裸背骑马过市,被打瞎双眼。现通常以此指那些追求性满足而爬窗偷看他人裸体或性行为的行为,侵犯他人隐私权的人]

peer n. 同等的人,同等地位者(见 pares);(英)(可成为上议院议员)贵族

peer review 共行评估

peerage n. (总称)贵族;贵族爵位,贵族名册

peers n. (英)贵族;贵族院议员;上议院议员;同等的人;同等地位者

peine forte et dure (古英国法对重罪犯的)严刑逼供,酷刑审讯

pejorative a. 轻蔑的,贬低的,恶化的

pelf (pelfe, pelfre) n. 不义之财,劫掠物,阿堵物(对金钱的轻蔑语)

pen v. 监禁,关闭

penal a. 刑事的,刑法的;受刑罚的,应受处罚的;用作处罚的;用作罚金的

penal act 应受处罚的行为,违法行为

penal action 刑事的民事诉讼(以罚款来惩罚的罪行,控告人可领得罚款的诉讼)

penal bond 罚金保证金(指允诺未办成一件事则愿付规定数额罚金的保证)

penal case 刑事案件

penal chamber (法院的)刑庭
penal clause 罚则;刑事条款;刑法条例
penal code 刑法典
penal colony (海外)流放地,充军地
penal consideration 刑罚上的考虑
penal damages 惩罚性的损害赔偿(相当于 punitive damages)
penal deduction 罚款扣除额
penal detention 刑事拘留
penal farm 劳改农场,劳役农场
penal institution 刑罚机构
penal jurisdiction 刑事管辖权
penal jurisprudence 刑法学
penal jurist 刑法学家
penal law 刑法
(a) **penal limbo** 刑罚拘禁(所),服刑监狱
penal matter 刑事案件
penal offence 刑事(犯)罪
penal practice 刑事程序
penal procedure 刑事诉讼程序
penal prosecution 刑事检控;公诉
penal provision 刑罚条款,刑法(条文)规定
penal sanction 刑事制裁
penal section 刑罚条文部分
penal sentence 徒刑;刑事判决
penal servitude (英)监禁和劳役合并的一种惩罚;劳役刑
penal servitude for a fixed-term (或 **definite period**) 有期徒刑
penal servitude for life (**imprisonment**) 无期徒刑
penal statute 刑事法规;刑法的制定法
penal sum 罚金,罚金总额
penal theory 刑罚理论;刑罚学说
penal treatment 刑罚,刑事处分
penalizable a. 可处罚的;应受处罚的
penalization n. 处罚,惩罚
penalize v. 处罚;对……处以刑事惩罚;使处于不利地位
penalize unlicensed driver 惩罚无照驾车者
penalized litigants 受惩罚的诉讼当事人
penalty n. 惩罚,处罚;刑罚(特别指罚款)
penalty clause (美)私人冒用者必罚(印在政府免费邮件上的字样)

penalty default 受惩罚的不应诉行为,惩罚性缺席行为
penalty for a fixed time 定期徒刑,有期徒刑
penalty for a short time 短期徒刑
penalty of perjury 对伪证罪的处罚
penalty provision (合同)违约罚金条款
Penant n. 《佩南氏汇编》(指一种收集大量非洲法律文献资料的非洲国家法律杂志的名称,创刊于1891年)
pendency n. 悬而未决,未定;悬挂,吊垂
pendency of action 未决诉讼
pendens 未决的,待决的
pendens lis(或 *lis pendens*) 未决诉讼案
pendent a. 悬而未决的;即将发生的,即将来临的
pendent jurisdiction (doctrine) (美)待决管辖权原则(指对于非联邦争点诉讼请求的联邦法院判决权,如如果此项权利请求取决于一些相类似于联邦争点的事实,则管辖权属联邦地区法院的原则)
pendent party jurisdiction 未决当事人管辖
pendente lite 在诉讼中(亦称待决诉讼期间,指民事诉讼在开始之后至判决之前这一期间);待决案件
pendentia litis 权利拘束
pending a./perp. (17世纪)1.悬而未决的,等待判决的,如等待判决的案子(a pending case)2.(议会法)(有关一项动议"motion")正在考虑中的;由1名议员作出动议并由任议会主席或议会主持人(chair)阐释而作为一个问题提交会议考虑(见consideration),即松散的、有价约因(valuable consideration)、对价,这适合支持交易双方已达成的允诺交换磋商〈his agreement to pay the offering price was good consideration for sale)(他们支付发行价格的协议正是销售的道德冲价);最低价(on the floor)。这个动议可能是正在等待决定的,意即它正被考虑之中,由于是议会主持人最后陈述的一项动议,下一步即将获得表决;或者可能是等待服从于另一些比它具有优先性的较高类别的动议(见immediately pending motion;pending motion)/在……以前

pending action 未决诉讼
pending case 待决案件,未决案件,悬案
pending cause 待决诉讼
pending claimant 候人认领
pending decision issue 未决争点,待决的争点
pending matter 待决事项,待决案件
pending motion 未决的动议(指即使其他较高类别的未决动议可能已具有优势,而这一动议也正在考虑之中。见 immediately pending motion)
pending proceeding 未决诉讼
pending question 未决问题
pending suit 待决诉讼案件
pending the negotiation 在谈判期间
pending trial 待审,候审
penetration n. 侵入,渗透;奸入(刑事强奸案中的一个术语,与 non-penetration 相对)
penetrator n. 侵入者;渗透者;识破者
penitence n. 悔罪;悔过;忏悔
penitential a. 悔罪的;悔过的
penitentiary n./a. 1.(罪犯)教养所;(美)妓女收容所 2.(美)州(或联邦)监狱 3.(天主教)宗教裁判所;宗教裁判员;罪犯忏悔所(古英格兰和现代美国对监狱的称呼)/教养的;监禁的;应予惩罚的;悔罪的
penitentiary misdemeanor 见 serious misdemeanor
Pennoyer Rule 彭诺耶规则(指对被告无对人管辖权的法院不得对其作出对人的判决)
Pennoyer rule of presence (美)彭诺耶的在场规则[按该规则,被告本人只要在诉讼地即成为法院对其行使对人管辖权的充分基础,亦即人身在场规则(rule of physical presence)或彭诺耶规则(Pennoyer rule)]
Pennsylvania system 宾夕法尼亚制度(指以单独监禁可以鼓励忏悔、促使悔改的一种行刑方法)
penological a. 刑罚学的;监狱学的;监狱管理学的;典狱学的
penologist n. 刑罚学家;监狱学家
penology n. 刑罚学;监狱学;监狱管理学;典狱学

pension(s) n. 抚恤金;年金;养老金,退休金;津贴
pension appeal tribunal 退休金(养老金)上诉法庭
pension commissions 养老金的委托,抚恤金代办权
pension(s) for the disabled and for survivors 抚恤金
pension fund 抚恤基金;养老基金;互助福利金
pension trusts 退休信托
pensionable a. 有资格领退休(或养老)金的;有资格领抚恤金的
pensionable age 领退休(或养老)金年龄
pensionary n. 为金钱所收买的人;傀儡;受年金者;领取退休(或养老)金者
pensioner n. 领取退休(或养老)金者;领取抚恤金者
Pentagon n. 五角大楼(指美国防部的办公大楼)
Pentagon Force Protection Agency (美)五角大楼武力保护局[指美国国防部的一个部门,负责管理(operating)五角大楼的警察部队并为基本法律强制执行作准备,同时保证五角大楼和首都华盛顿地区的军事设施的安全。此机构为五角大楼在2001年9·11事件后成立的,缩略为PFPA]
pentarchy n. 五国联盟;五头(国)政治
Pentateuch 《摩西五经》(指《旧约全书》的首五卷)
penumbral situation 弱化的周围环境,弱化的边缘环境
penury n. 赤贫;缺乏
peon n. 被强制执行劳役以抵偿罚金的人;(印度的)警察;仆从
peonage n. 劳役偿债(制);雇用日工;做日工
people n. 1.人民;平民;公民;居民 2.民族;国民;人类 3.家族,家人;随员
people's assembly 人民代表大会,人民议会
people's assessor (中)人民陪审员
(The) People's Charter (英)人民宪章
people's committee 人民委员会
people's congress (system) (中)人民代表大会(制)
people's council 人民委员会
people's court (中)人民法院
people's democracy 人民民主(制度)
people's democratic dictatorship 人民民主专政
people's democratic self-government 人民民主自治
people's democratic system 人民民主制度
people's democratic united front (中)人民民主统一战线
people's government 人民政府
people's law 一个民族的法律
People's Law School (美)大众法律学校(指加州免费提供为人们法律教育的私人团体)
people's judge (中)人民审判员
people's mediation commission (中)人民调解委员会
people's organization 人民团体
people's (christian) party 人民(基督教)党
people's police (中)人民警察
people's power 人民政权
people's procuratorate (中)人民检察院
people's property 全民财产,人民的财产
people's public security (forces) (中)人民公安(部队)
people's representative (中)人民代表
people's right to know 人民的知情权
people-to-people a. 人民之间的
pepoudrous n. 集市法院[指商人法(Lex Mercatoria)时代的集市法院,其审判应在商人脚上尘土未掉之前完结,故又称"泥足"法院(pie-poulder court)]
peppercorn rent (以胡椒子交付房屋出租人的)象征性租金,名义租金
per 每,按,依,通过,由,因
per annum 按年度,每年
per autre vie 在他人生存期间(享有不动产物权)
per capita (per caput) 按人数,按人口平均计算,每人
per capita income 按人口平均计算的收入
per capita tax 见 poll tax
per cent 百分率

per centum 每百
per contra 对比;反之,相反
per curiam (Lat, by the court) 依法院,按法院,由整个法院或法院多数法官所作的判决意见而不是由个别的法官所作的;(美)依法院,有时已成为多数判决意见的媒介
per curiam (或 ***per cure***) 依法院,由法院所定;引用法官判词
per curiam decision 依法院所作的判决
per curiam opinion 法庭(无异议的)意见,一致的意见
per decree dum 绝对命令
per diem 按天,每日
per epistelam (罗马法)以证书(代之)(指奴隶主以解放状给予其奴隶,作为解放之证据)
per incuriam 疏忽所致,因失误所致
per infortunium 失误,过失;意外之事故
per legem terrae 按国家法律,经适当法律程序
per mensem 按月,每月
per mill (或 ***mille***, ***mil***) 每千
per my et per tout 按部分和全部
per pais (或 ***pays***) 由陪审团审理
per pro (***per*** procuration) 代理,委任代理,授权为代理人
per pro indorsement (P. P. indorsement) 代理背书
Per Procurationem (P. P. 或 ***Per Pro***) 由(某某)代表(指用来表示签名的人,是优惠他人的,如在汇票上代表他人的签署)
per quod 由于,因此;归咎于
per quod consortium amisit 因他人(伤害等)的原因,使其失去(妻子或丈夫作为)伴侣
per quod servitium amisit 因他人(过失)的原因,使其失去(仆从的)服侍
per rescriptum principis (罗马法)按帝王的敕令;根据皇帝对请求的书面答复
per saltum 以跳跃方式,迅速地,快速
per se a./ad. (16世纪)1.本身的,自身的;本质上的;固有地,单独地;孤立地(见 actionable ***per se***) 2.由于法律的原因(as a matter of law)

***per se* offense** 自身犯罪
***per se* rule** (反托拉斯法)本身违反谢尔曼法规则,单独确认规则[指只要贸易实务是受到限制,无须考虑它实际上是否给他人造成伤害,即可认定这违反谢尔曼法(Sherman Act)]
***per se* violations** (反托拉斯法)自身违法,实务本身违法[指贸易实务(如固定价格)被认定为其本身反竞争并有损公众利益,而无需举证其实务是否伤害市场竞争]
per stirpes 按家系(指按继承人的家系来分配无遗嘱的遗产)
per subsequens matrimonium 后来结婚(使非婚生子女合法化的一种方式)
per totam curiam 由整个法庭(常用来指由整个法庭一致作出的决断)
per verba de futuro 根据对将来的诺言(婚约中应用的术语)
per verba de praesenti 根据诺言,根据现在诺言(婚约中应用的术语)
perambulation n. 步533地界
perceive v. 1.察觉,发觉,看见;看⟨perceive the danger⟩(察觉危险) 2.理解,领会,领悟
percentage n. 百分率;(以百分比率计算的)利息,佣金,折扣,罚款;部分
percentage defendant victories 被告胜诉率
percentage lease 分成租借
percentage of voter turnout 投票率
perception n. (地租的)征收;(农作物的)收获;感知,观念,概念,感受
Perching 蹲守停车位(指驾驶员在拥挤的停车场里坐在车中等待另一位司机驾车离开,从而为自己空出一个停车位的过程。等候某人腾出车位的表达方式是 perching on someone)
perduellio (罗马法)叛国罪[指对祖国有敌意之罪行,叛逆行为如投敌、放弃阵地,与英语中的重大叛国罪(high treason)同意。在罗马共和国中,有些行为可构成叛国罪,如篡夺王权(assuming regal power)、试图颠覆(try to subvert)、暴动(violence)组成国内叛逆政府,与境外敌人相勾结。这些都是更广泛地反对国家的犯罪类型,(the) crimen laesae majestatis,亦称为perduellion。见 crimen majestatis]

peregrinus （罗马法）非罗马公民的自由人，自由外国人，异乡人，外国侨民
peremption n.　诉讼驳回
peremptory a./n.　绝对的，最后决定的；断然的，紧急的；强制的/断然，绝对，最后决定
peremptory call　（对债务人的）正式催告
peremptory challenge　无因回避，强制回避（指律师从陪审员名单中剔除的某一准陪审员而不说明任何理由。在任何案件中，律师都有权提出一定次数的强制回避。提出强制回避可能有包括预感在内等的几种原因，但不能基于种族、性别。见 challenge for cause）
peremptory charge　终局控（告）诉
peremptory challenge　无因异议，无因回避（美国民事诉讼或刑事诉讼中的当事人可以不说明理由而拒绝某人担任本案陪审员。法院即应更换。民事诉讼中无因回避权有数额限制，在英国刑事诉讼中当事人或其辩护律师均有权提出无因回避，英国1988年的《刑事司法法》最终废除了这一制度）
peremptory day　绝对（不能延期的）审判日
peremptory exception　完全否认诉讼原因的辩护
peremptory instruction　（陪审团）必须执行的指令
peremptory judgment　终审判决，不能上诉的判决
peremptory *mandamus*　强制履行令；强制执行命令书
peremptory norm　强制规范
peremptory plea　断然的抗辩[与延讼的抗辩(dilatory plea)相对而言,指被告驳斥原告无权提起诉讼所作的答辩,亦称 plea in bar]
peremptory provision　强制性规定
peremptory rule　不可更改的原则（指审判的法官或听审的司法行政官"当场"所作的规定）
peremptory writ　（在原告向司法行政官作出保证后司法行政官发出的）强制被告出庭令
perfect a.　1.完美的，无瑕的；完全的，完备

的 2.绝对的，不容置疑的 3.熟练的，正确的 4.法律上有效的
perfect and imperfect right　有效的与无效的权利
perfect case　无懈可击的证据和争辩
perfect copy　精确文本
perfect court　完全的法院，可强制执行的法院
perfect game-theoretic models　完善的博弈理论模式
perfect information　完美信息
perfect instrument　有效证件
perfect mobility　完全的流动性
perfect neutrality　完全中立
perfect obligation　合法的债务，具有完备手续的债务
perfect procedural justice　完善的程序正义
perfect right　完整权利
perfect self-defense　合法的正当防卫（指要求具有诚实和合理的信念，才算合法有效的正当防卫，才能导致宣告无罪）
perfect sovereignty　完全主权
perfect subject of international law　完全的国际法主体
perfect title　有效所有权；完全所有权
perfect trust　法律上有效的信托
perfect usufruct　完善的用益权
perfecting bail　手续完备的保释（令）
perfection n.　圆满，十全十美；无缺；完成；（复）美德
perfidy n.　叛变，出卖；背信弃义，不忠，不诚实
perforating wound　穿扎伤，刺穿伤
perform v.　履行，执行；完成；进行
perform duties　履行职责；负担义务
perform in person all acts of agency　亲自处理委任事务
perform meritorious service to atone for one's crimes（或 **misdeed**）　立功赎罪
perform shoddily　劣质履行
performance n.　1.履行，执行；完成；清偿 2.行为，行动；表现；表演
performance bond (margins)　履约保证（金）
performance budgeting　绩效预算（指西方发达国家在新的公共管理理念和财政民

主化背景下追求政府资金效率的一种预算管理方式,即通过设定有意义的绩效目标,衡量进度情况,为决策者在配置有限资源和审议优先次序时提供信息,从而在公共服务中创造价值)

performance criteria 实施标准,绩效标准(指解决根源性国际收支失衡问题是绩效标准的核心内容)

performance guarantee 履行保证(书),履行担保;履行合同保证人

performance in part (或 **on installment**) 部分履行

performance of a contract 合同(契约)的履行

performance of a definite act 特定行为的履行

performance of budget 预算的执行

performance of debt 债务清偿

performance of duty 执行任务,履行职责

performance of obligation 债的履行,履行债务

performance requirements 履行要求

performance right (电影,戏剧等)上演权

performer n. 表演者

performing arts 表演艺术,演奏艺术

performing badly 不适当履行

performing late 迟延履行

performing party 应为给付方当事人,应履约方

performing right 上演权

performing right tribunal (英)上演权裁判庭

performs substantially the same function 实质上同一结果

peril n. 危险

peril clause 海难条款;危险条款

peril insured 所投保的危险

perils of the sea 海上危险(指海上保险中包括一切海上的危险。亦称 perils on the sea);海难

perils of the sea exception 海难例外条款

period n. 期间;时期;期限

period bill 定期汇票

period for bring an action 起诉期

period for presenting claim 提出请求的期限

period for redemption of the mortgage 抵押的回赎期

period normally necessary to receive an answer 得到承诺的正常必要的时间

period of adjournment 休会期;休庭期

period of "articles" (律师)见习期(因律师见习生除称"apprendice"之外,习惯称"article")

period of delay 延迟期

period of employment 雇佣期间

period of existence 存续期间

period of gestation 妊娠期,怀孕期间

period of grace (票据等到期后的)宽限期

period of limitation (或 **prescription**) 时效期限

period of notice 预告期间

period of stay 居留期间

period of the creditor's delay 债权人受领迟延期间

period of the Empire (古罗马)帝国时期

period of the monarchy (古罗马)君主时期

period of the Republic (古罗马)共和时期

period of time 期间

period of transition 过渡时期

period of validity 有效期

period spent in detention 羁押时间,已监禁的时间

period stipulated for delivery 约定交货期

period under review 审核期

periodic a. 定期的;某一时期的;周期的;不时发生的

periodic audit 定期审计

periodic insanity 间歇性精神病

periodic payment 定期付款

periodic pension 周期性养老金

periodic performances 定期给付;定期履行

periodic prestation 定期给付

periodic report 定期报告

periodic tenancy 定期租借(权)

peripheral definition 界定主义

perjure v. 作伪证;发假誓

perjured a. 作了伪证的;发了假誓的;犯了伪证罪的

perjured witness 作了伪证的证人；作伪证者，伪证证人；伪证
perjurer n. 犯伪证罪者；发假誓者；作伪证者
perjurious a. 伪证的，假证的；伪证罪的
perjury n. 伪证；伪誓；伪证罪
perlustrate v. 仔细巡视；彻底调查
permanence n. 永久性，持久性
permanency n. 长久不变的人、物或地位
permanent a. 永远的，长期的；不变的；常设的
permanent abode 永久住址，常住地址
permanent agreement 长期协定，永久性协定
permanent alimony 终身扶养费，终身供养费
permanent alliance 永久性同盟
permanent ambassador 常驻大使
permanent appointment 长期任用
permanent assets 固定资产
permanent commission 常设委员会
permanent committee 常务委员会，常设委员会
Permanent Court of Arbitration (Hague) （海牙）常设国际仲裁法庭（1900年根据1899年《海牙公约》设立的）
Permanent Court of International Arbitration 常设国际仲裁法院（国际上第一个常设仲裁法院于1900年成立）
Permanent Court of International Justice （国联）常设国际法庭（1922年成立，1946年宣告解散）
permanent delegate 常驻代表
permanent deprivation of political rights 剥夺政治权利终身
permanent diplomatic mission 常驻外交使团
permanent disability 终身残疾
permanent embassies 常驻使节
permanent envoy 常驻使节
permanent financing documents 长久性财务文件；常用财务文件
permanent injunction 长期禁制令
permanent legal advisor 常年法律顾问
permanent magistrate 终身任职的司法行政官
Permanent Mandates Commission 常设委任统治地委员会
permanent military tribunal 常设军事裁判庭
permanent neutrality 永久中立
permanent nuisance 长期妨扰，长期干扰
permanent population 常住人口
permanent property 固定财产
permanent public service 常任公务员
permanent repairs 大修理，大修
permanent representative 常驻代表
permanent requirement 固定要求（与 fixing requirement 相近，但较此严格）
permanent residency 永久居住权
permanent sovereignty over natural resources 对自然资源的永久主权
permanent staff 在编人员
permanent transfer 长期转让
permanent treaty 永久性条约
permanent (institution) tribunal of arbitration 常设仲裁机构，常设仲裁法庭
Permanent United Nations Force (PUNF) 联合国永久部队
permanent, court-ordered alimony 法庭判决的永久性赡养给付
permanently acting body 常设机构
permanently depriving 永久剥夺，终身剥夺
permanently neutralized states 永久中立国
permanently resident outside China 常驻中国以外
permissible a. 可允许的，许可的，准许的
permissible decision 允许的决议，允许的决定
permissible level of human exposure 人体允许裸露的程度
permissible sanction 允许的制裁
permission n. 允许，许可；批准；同意
permissive a. 表示许可的；随意的；纵容的
permissive counter claim 任意性反请求，任意性反诉
permissive cumulative voting 许可(性)累积投票
permissive intervention 任意性诉讼参加
permissive intervention provisions 现代介

入诉讼规则,当代介入诉讼规则(规定)
permissive joinder 许可性(当事人)合并;允许合并(《美国联邦民事诉讼规则》第20条)
permissive jurisdiction (一个国家行使)许可管辖权
permissive legislation 非强制性法规;(授权地方当局可自行斟酌执行的)任意法规
permissive party joinder 许可性当事人合并
permissive provision (下级机关可随意实施的)任意条款,灵活规定
permissive statute 任意法规
permissive use 获准使用权
permissive waste 通常损耗;(英)消极毁损(指侵权法上的放任建筑物自行破损达到不能修缮的地步。见 waste)
permit n./v. 执照,许可证/允许,许可
permit of residence 居留证
permitted only in cases especially provided by law 仅以法律上有特别规定的情形为限
permitted rent 核准的租金
permittee n. 持证人,持照人
permitting person 承诺人
permutatio 交换,互易
permutation n. 变更;(与他人)交换;(动产)互易;取代
pernicious a. 有害的(指倾销是有害的),有毒的,致命的
pernor of profits (土地等的)受益人
perpetrate v. 犯(罪);作(恶);行(诈);为(非)
perpetrate a crime 犯罪
perpetration n. 行凶;作恶;犯罪
perpetrator n. 作恶者;行凶者;犯罪者
perpetual a. 永久的,永远的;终身的;永续的;不断的;长期的
perpetual debate 长期辩论
perpetual debenture 永久债券
perpetual guardianship 终身监护制
perpetual injunction 永久禁制令;最后(决定性)禁令;长久性禁令,持续性假处分
perpetual interdict 永久性禁令

perpetual lease 永久租借;永租权
perpetual provision 永久性条款;永久性的规定
perpetual statute 永久性法规,长期有效的法规
perpetual succession 连续存在,继续存在(指一个公司即使其所有人或董事更换,但公司仍继续存在)
perpetual tutelage of women 妇女终身监护
perpetuating evidence 永久保存的证据(指可保证此证据在以后审理中适用)
perpetuating testimony 永久保存的证据(亦称永久保存的证言,指衡平法诉讼程序中,准许将证言录取下来,以供将来审判需要时用作证据,以防止在审判前有失去的危险)
perpetuation of evidence (或 **testimony**)证据保全,证据保存(备案)
perpetuity n. 永远不得转让性;永远不得转让的产业;永久持有权(指限嗣继承土地的赠与)
perplex v. 困惑,使复杂化;使纠缠不清
perplexed question 纠缠不清的问题,错综复杂的问题
perplexing issue (最)令人困惑的问题
perquisite n. 1.额外补贴,津贴 2.奖金;赏钱,小费;因(为身份、地位等)特权而享有的东西 3.额外收入;自得物(与世袭物相对而言)
perquisition n. 彻底搜查;详细询问
persecute v. 1.迫害;虐待 2.烦扰;为难
persecutee n. 受迫害者(尤指受迫害的难民)
persecutio (罗马法)根据非常诉讼程序(*cognitio extraordinaria*)所进行的诉讼或民事请求(civil claim)
persecution n. 迫害;虐待;困扰
persecution mania 被迫害妄想症(指一种精神病)
persecutor n. 迫害者;虐待者
persepective of law 从法律角度
persequi (罗马法)通过司法程序提出权利主张
persistence n. 持久性,持久
persistent a. 坚持的;固执的;持续的,持久

的,不断的
persistent cruelty 经常性虐待
persistent offender （英）惯常犯（指曾因犯检控罪而被判刑三次以上的超过 21 岁的人,如现在所犯的罪,又可判处 2 年以上监禁者,则允许法庭权宜处理,延长监禁时间。如应判 5 年的可加判 10 年监禁;5 年以下的,可判到 5 年）
person （13 世纪）1.人（亦称 nature person）,自然人,普通人 2.普通人的生活主体（living body of human being）〈contraband found on the smuggler's person〉（走私者的同伙被认定贩卖走私烟行为属犯联邦罪）3.法人[按法律组成的主体（entity）（如一个公司）,它具有大多普通人的权利与义务。就这个意义上讲,该词包括合伙企业和其他协会,不管是合并组成或非法人组成的均在其内]
person accused of having committed crime 受刑事犯罪指控的人
person acquiring possession 取得占有的人
person acquiring the property 财产受让人
person admitted to practice of law 准许执行律师事务的人
person arrested 被逮捕的人
person assuming the debt 债务承担人
person born outside wedlock 婚外所生的子女,私生子女,非婚生子（女）
person bound to furnish support (obliger in the maintenance) 负扶（扶、赡）养义务人
person capable of disposing 有行为能力人
person causing the injury 加害人
person charged 被指控的人,被告人
person civilly dead 民法上死亡的人
person concerned 关系人
person conveying 财产转让人
person dealing with the firm 与商行有业务关系的人
person declared dead 被宣告死亡的人
person delivered 被释放的人
person detaining another 拘禁他人者
person directly responsible 直接责任人（员）
person duly authorized to practice physic and surgery 有执照的医师和外科医师
person enjoying a given right 享受特定权利者
person entirely incapable of legal transaction 完全丧失行为能力人
person entitled to possession 有权占有的人
person giving the child adoption 送养人
person having actual possession 实际占有人
person having legal authority 具有合法授权的人
person having property inexpectancy 享有期待财产权的人
Person holding an Office of Trust or Profit under the United States 合众国政府下受俸或任职人或官员
person in active military service 现役军人
person in authority 当权人士,权威人士
person in charge 主管人;代表
person in custody awaiting trial 关押候审的人
person in *loco parentis* （未经正式收养而被认为）有父母身份和义务的人
person in need of supervision 见 child in need of supervision,缩略为 PINS
person in the know 知情人
person incapable of disposing 无行为能力人
person indispensable 必不可少的人
person injured 受害人
person intending to develop land 意图开发土地的人
person involved 有关人员,关系人
person involved in lawsuit 涉讼人
person legitimated *per subsequens matrimonium* 依后来结婚认领为婚生子女的人
person limited in disposing capacity 限制行为能力人
person mentally deranged 精神病人
person *non compotes mentis* 心神不健全者
person of full age 成年人
person of mental infirmity 心神耗弱人
person of standing 有地位的人士
person of suitable age and discretion 适龄和适智者
person of uncertain nationality 国籍不明

的人
person of unsound mind 精神不健全者
person on trial 受审人
person outside the jurisdiction of that court 该法院管辖权(范围)以外的人
person passing off the patent of another person 假冒他人专利的人
person proposed in the motion 动议的提议人
person qualified to dispose 有权处分的人
person represented 被代理人
person responsible 责任人,(复)责任人员
person retired from employment 退休职工,退休雇员
person sanctioned 受制裁者,受处分者
person seised 土地占有人
person serving such sentence 服刑的人
person serving the decision 裁决书的送达人
person summoned 受传唤者,接受传票被传唤的人
person suspected of having committed the crime 有犯罪嫌疑的人
person transferring possession 移转占有的人
person uncommitted to another marriage 未同他人缔结婚姻关系的人
person under a legal disability 法律上无行为能力的人
person under age 未成年人
person under curatorship 被保佐人
person under disability 无行为能力人
person under guardianship 被监护人
person under public surveillance (中)被管制分子
person undergoing sentence 服刑者
person without title 无权利的人;无头衔的人
persona 人,人格,(人的)身份
persona designata 指定人
persona grata 受欢迎的人;可接受的人
persona nongrata 不受欢迎的人;不能接受的人
persona standi in judicio 人的法律地位;诉讼资格

persona standi in judicio of enemy alien 敌侨的法律地位
personal a. 个人的,私人的;本人的,亲自的;人身的;有关个人的;攻击人的;属于个人的;可动的/(美)报纸上有关个人的简讯
personal abuse 人身攻击
personal accident insurance 人身意外伤害保险,人身事故保险
personal act (英)个人法令(指只涉及特定人的地位、权利、财产等的议会法令,如判决离婚法令)
personal action 对人诉讼(见 action in personam)
Personal Acts of Parliament (英)国会关于(限制)个人的法(指国会对特定人员的一些限制性法规,如授权给人更改姓名等)
personal administration 人事行政,人事管理
personal allowance 个人免税额;个人津贴
personal assessment 个人总入息估税
personal assets 私人资产
personal association for profit 营利性的私人社团
personal autonomy (私有财产制社会中体现的)个人自治
personal characteristics 个人特征
personal claim(s) 个人的诉讼请求,个人的权利主张
personal column (报上登载的)寻人、离婚等通告的专栏
personal conduct 私人行为,个人行为
personal credit 个人信用;私人信贷
personal data 个人数据(指有关个人身份、财产、身体健康状况等数据)
personal dignity 人格尊严
personal document 个人文件
personal donation 个人捐助
personal effects 私人财产,个人财产(指非商品)
personal equation 人差;个人观察上的误差
personal estate 动产
personal evidence 人证
personal exemption (1920年)个人的减

税额(指从单个的纳税人在调整后的总收入中允准减免的总额)
personal freedom 人身自由
personal hereditament 私人家产
personal income 个人所得,个人收入
personal income tax 个人所得税
personal injury 人身损害;人身伤害
personal injury-Med malpractice 人身伤害—医疗事故
personal injury-product liability 人身伤害—产品责任
personal insult 人身侮辱
personal insurance 人身保险
personal insurance contract 人身保险合同(契约)
personal integrity 个人的尊严
personal inviolability 人身的不可侵犯性
personal judgment 对人判决(指判令被告个人负责,以其个人财产交付的判决,而不等同于从某项基金或财产支付的判决,亦指法院对当事人有管辖权)
personal jurisdiction (=jurisdiction in personal) 对人管辖
personal jurisdiction dispute 对人管辖争议
personal jurisdiction over a corporation 及于公司的对人管辖,对一个公司的对人管辖
personal knowledge 直接所知(指非因传闻而知),亲身所知
personal law 属人法
personal legel relationship 人身法律关系
personal liability 个人责任
personal liberty 人身自由(权)
personal liberty law (美史)人身自由法
personal loan 个人借款
personal matter 人事问题;人身案件
personal nonproperty relations 人身非财产关系
personal ownership 个人所有制
personal performance 个人表现
personal probability (=subjective probability) 个人概率
personal profile 个人简介
personal property (有时用于包括动产和住宅的)个人财产,动产

personal property in mortgage 抵押动产
personal property right 动产权;个人财产权
personal property tax (1863年)(美)动产税(指州或地方政府征收个人财产诸如首饰、家具等的税)
personal relations between spouses 配偶间的人身关系(又译:夫妻间的人身关系)
personal representative 私人代表;遗产代表人;遗产执行人;遗产管理人;死者(遗产的)代理人
personal reputation 个人名誉
personal right 人身权;人格权(包括名誉权,姓名权,人身自由权)
personal rights 人的权利(又译:人权。指个人的安全权利,即生命、四肢、健康、名誉、自由等安全和保障的权利);公民权利
personal security 人身安全
personal service (=actual service) 个别送达,个人劳务;个人送达;直接送达;个人专属服务
personal service on the defendant 对被告的个人送达
personal service of the writ 令状直接送达当事人
personal servitude 人身地役权
personal sphere of validity 属人效力范围
personal stake 私人(个人)赌注
personal status (=statut personnel) 个人地位,个人身份
personal strain of litigating 为孩子抚养的个人
personal suretyship 个人担保
personal taxation 个人所得税
personal testimony 人证(一般指由证人提供的有关案件事实的证据)
personal tort 个人侵权行为
personal union 君合国(亦称人合国,身合国;通常指两个国家由一个君主统治而形成的联合,如1714—1837年英国和汉诺威的联合)
personal violence 个人暴行
personal warranty 个人担保
personal wealth 人身财富(指才能、精力等)
personal wrong 个人不法行为
personal-holding company tax 见 holding-

company tax
personalism n. 个人人格至上(或不可侵犯)论,人格主义(一种哲学派别)
personalismo 个人统治(指拉丁美洲抬高领袖人物使政党、意识形态和宪政利益都受其控制的做法)
personality n. 人格;品格;个性;(常用复数)人身攻击,诽谤;人法(指与人的身份、人身相关的法律)
personality cult 个人迷信(指对个人偶像式的崇拜)
personality disorders 人格异常;人格障碍
personality of judge 法官的个性
personality of women 妇女人格
personality principle 人格原则
personalty n. 动产(与 realty 相对);个人财产(主要指动产,有时也包括个人住房等不动产)
* **Personalty has no locality.** 动产无场所(指动产没有场所,按准据法应依所有权人的所在地而定)。
personalty in possession 所占有的动产
personam jurisdiction 对人管辖权
personate v. 假扮,假装;冒充
personation n. 假冒;假冒人名罪;冒名,化身
personation of a policeman 冒充警察
personation of a voter 冒充选民
personator n. 假冒者,冒充者,冒名者
personification n. 人格化
personnel n. 全体人员
personnel administration 人事行政,人事管理
personnel agency 职业介绍所
personnel department 人事部
personnel engineering 人事工程(指以科学的知识、技术与方法谋求对工作人员的体力、心力、智力作最适当的利用与最大的发挥的学科)
personnel file 个人档案
personnel retirement papers 退休人员证明书
persons hold office 担任公职的人
persons retired 退休人员
persons to be joined 被合并之人
persons under legal custody or control of a party 法定监护之下或当事人控制下的人员

perspective n./a. 1.透视,透视图 2.正确观察事物相互关系的能力;眼力〈lack perspective〉(缺乏眼力) 3.远景,前景;展望,前途;景象 4.观点,看法 5.事物相互关系的外观;整体各个部分的比例(或关系)〈look at things in their right(or wrong)perspective〉[正确(或不正确)地观察事物]/透视的,透视图的
persuade v. 唆使,说服,劝诱;使相信
persuade to murder 唆使(他人)谋杀
persuader n. 1.说服者,劝诱者;说客 2.用以胁迫人服从的东西;手枪
persuasion n. 说服,劝说;说服力;劝说的论点;主张,见解,信念;教派;性别
persuasion and education 说服与教育
persuasive authority 有说服力的法律根据,令人信服的权威(典籍);永久的权威,有说服力的权威(指法官为确立对一个案件的思考可使用的全部法律渊源资料,比如法律百科全书或其他州的有关判例。一个判例如果出自一位知名法官和权威甚至更高的法庭就可能更有说服力。与"有约束力的法律依据"相对)
persuasive burden 担负的说服责任
persuasive burden of proof 有说服力证据的,承担有说服(责任)的举证责任
persuasive decision 有说服力的裁决
persuasive effect 说服性的效力
persuasive precedents 有说服力的判例,说服性先例
pertain v. 1.属于,从属,附属 2.关于,有关 3.合宜,适于
pertinency of question 与问题相关
pertinent a. 恰当的;有关的
pertinent art 1.见 analogous art 2.见 relevant art
pertinent certificate 有关证件
pertinent provision 恰当的条文规定,相应的条文规定
pertinent questions 相关问题,有关问题
peruse v. 1.细阅,细读〈peruse news paper〉(细读报纸)2.仔细察看(perusal n.)
pervade v. 遍及,弥漫,渗透
pervasive a. 充满的;普及的

pervasive feature of a legal system 充满特色(特点)的法制
pervasiveness of private power 私人权利的普及
perverse a. 1.邪恶的,罪恶的,堕落的 2.(判决等)不合法的;不正当的;固执的
perverse behavior 反常行为
perverse verdict 反常的裁定(亦称不合法的裁定,指陪审团不遵守法官的法律要点指示,而按自己的意志所作出的裁定)
perversion n. 1.曲解,歪曲;误用,滥用 2.反常,变态;性反常行为;颠倒,倒置
perversion of aristocracy 贵族制的非正常形式
perversion of truth 歪曲真相
pervert n./v. 堕落的人;性变态者/1.诱惑,引入邪路,使堕落 2.歪曲,曲解;误用,滥用于 3.使反常
perverting the course of justice 使审判不能正常进行,破坏审判
pest n. 1.令人讨厌的人或物 2.疫病
pest of society 害群之马;社会败类
pesticide n. 杀虫剂,农药;毒药,毒物
pesticide control law 农药管理法
pestilence n. 传染病,流行病,瘟疫,鼠疫
pestilent a. (对社会、道德等)有危害性的,致命的;讨厌的;有传染性的
petit 小的,轻的
petit assize 见 petite assize
petit average 小海损(指船长支出的拖拉、装卸等费用)
petit cape (在旧时的诉讼中司法行政官)收回租地的令状(指用于佃户被传到案后不再参加后来诉讼的令状)
petit juror 小陪审团的陪审员(区别于大陪审团中的成员)
petit jury 小陪审团(通常由12人组成,但有时可少至6人,在许多案件审理中,他们只决定事实问题,亦称 trial jury, petty jury)
petit larceny (英)轻盗窃罪(指从前偷盗12便士价值以下的东西的罪行,现已废)
petit treason (英)小叛逆罪(指杀夫或弑主罪,亦作 petty treason)
petite assize 小巡回法庭;小陪审团(指只

裁决占有问题的陪审团,以区别于裁决财产权问题的大陪审团——grande assize)
petitio 1.(英)申请,请求 2.(大陆法)(对物诉讼中原告的)诉因陈述
petition n./v. 1.请愿,请求,申请;祈求 2.诉状;上诉状;请愿书;申请书/请愿,申请,请求,呈请
petition against final decision 对终审判决(提出)的申诉
petition copy 诉状副本
petition creditor 出具请求书的债权人(指向法院要求宣告债务人破产而提出请求书的债权人);破产申请债权人
petition for appeal 上诉状,起诉状
petition for certiorari (上级法院向下级法院)调取案卷复审令申请书
petition for divorce 申请离婚
petition for naturalization 入籍申请书
petition for probate 遗嘱检认申请书
petition for rehearing 复审请求书
petition for sequestration 请求查封状,申请扣押状
petition for winding up 停止营业申请书
petition in bankruptcy 破产申请书
petition of revision 请求复审状;申诉状
Petition of Rights (英)权利请愿书,民权宣言(指英国1628年由社会向查尔斯一世提出并得其承认关于人民权利的国会宣言);权利申请书(指向政府请求归还或赔偿违约损害的文书,通过此权利请求书,法院将给予公正处理,由于1947年颁布了人民可对政府起诉的法律而废止)
petition on unconstitutionality 违宪性申诉
petitionary a. 请愿的,请求的
petitioner n. 诉愿人;上诉人;请愿人;请求人
Petitioning Immunity (美)请愿行为适用除外(指企业或企业联合组织要求联邦政府或州政府采取措施,限制贸易等游说行为,豁免请愿行为的反托拉斯法责任的主要依据是 Noerr-Pennington doctrine,亦称 Noerr doctrine)
petitory a. 提出所有权要求的
petitory action 确认物的所有权的诉讼,确认权利的诉讼

petits droits 狭义(表演)权利,小权利(除去"音乐—戏剧"作品中的音乐之外的音乐作品表演权)
Petri Exceptiones Legum Romanorum 《罗马法摘编》(指12世纪法国南部地方法官编纂的法律手册)
petroleur (法)用石油放火者
pettifog v. 1.以诡诈手段从事法律事务,作讼棍;从事琐碎的法律事务 2.对枝节问题进行诡辩;吹毛求疵
pettifogger n. 讼棍;卑劣的律师;非正式律师;小题大做的人;诡辩者
pettifoggery n. 讼棍伎俩;奸诈手段;欺瞒;诡计
pettifogging a. 讼棍般的;诡计多端的
petty a. 小的;次要的;低下的,下级的;卑贱的
petty assize (assise) 小巡回审判
petty average (= particular average) 单独海损
Petty Bag Office (英)小袋子文件局(指过去大法官法院普通法机构系统中的主要办公机构)
petty bench of supreme court (日)最高法院小法庭
petty bourgeosie 小资产阶级
petty cash 小额现金收入;零用钱
petty civil court 简易民事法院;小额民事纠纷法院
petty constable 小巡警
petty crime 轻微罪行
petty criminal offence 轻微的刑事犯罪
petty criminality 轻罪;微罪
petty current deposit 小额活期存款
petty forms of criminality 小型犯罪(指扒窃之类),轻罪
petty juror 小陪审团成员
petty jury 小陪审团(由6人或12人组成,判决审理、评定事实)
petty larceny 轻盗窃罪
petty loan 小额贷款
petty loss 轻度损失
petty misdemeanor 轻罪;过失
petty offence 过失;轻罪
petty patent 见 utility model
petty private owner 小私有者
petty proprietor 小业主
petty seasonal court (或 division) 简易季审法庭,即决法院分庭,即决审判分庭(= petty sessions)
petty sergeant 小服侍(土地保有人对领主的私人服役)
petty serjeanty (英)小服役土地保有,小劳务土地保有
petty sessions (英)小治安裁判法庭(指由保安官、受薪裁判官或伦敦市长、市议长主持审判刑事案件的简易法庭);即决法庭
petty theft 小偷
petty treason (= *petit* treason) 小叛逆罪,轻叛逆罪
petty trial courts (美)小审判庭(指州的基层法院)
phantom ship "鬼船"[指那些具有"影子"身份的船舶,它似"幽灵"(phantom)一样出没无常,虽然它始终以合格船舶身份出现,但无固定船名,身份令人难以摸清,这些注册登记资料多为假的,包括船名、吨位、体积和船东的身份]
pharaoh n. (古埃及君王的尊称)法老;暴君
pharmaceutical a. 药物的,药用的,药剂师的
pharmacist n. 药剂师
pharmacy and poisons board 药剂和毒品管理局
phase n./v. 状态;方面,侧面阶段,时期/使分阶段进行,使按协议计划进行
phenomenological jurisprudence 现象法理学
Philadelphia Code of Ordinances (美)《费城法令汇典》
Philadelphia Convention (美)费城会议(指1786年由大陆会议召集的会议,旨在修订《联邦条款》来巩固联邦政府。1787年5月至1787年9月在费城召开,各州均有首脑参加,普遍要求加强中央政府,要求立法、司法、行政三方面平衡的政府,在联邦政府与州政府的权力、大小州的权力划分上均有争议,最后通过宪法草案,经各州会议批准于1789年生效。见 First

Continental Congress)
Philadelphia lawyer （美）费城律师（1735年纽约市一名德国移民——约翰・彼得・曾格在自己创办的报上抨击英国皇家总督威廉・科斯比横征暴敛。科斯比因此逮捕了曾格,指控他犯有诽谤罪。纽约的律师慑于总督淫威,不敢为曾格辩护,但当时已80岁的费城高级律师安德鲁・汉密尔顿却挺身而出,以无可辩驳的证据为曾格辩护,终使曾格被判无罪。后即以"费城律师"寓意有正义感的律师、能力杰出精明善辩的律师、能坚持正义为民请命的人)
philander v. 追求女性；调戏妇女；玩弄(with)
philanderer n. 淫棍,追求女性者
philanthropic a. 博爱的,仁慈的；慈善事业的
philanthropism n. 仁爱,慈善,博爱主义
philanthropist n. 慈善家,博爱主义者
philosopher n. 哲学家,哲学研究者
philosophical jurisprudence 法哲学,法理学
philosophical jurists 哲理法学家,法哲学家
philosophy of distributive justice 分配正义思想(哲学)
philosophy of language 语言的哲学(指主要从哲学视角看语言中的一些基本组成部分；其中包括语言的研究意义、语言的基本特征、语言的逻辑性以及言语的行为等方面。正因如此,语言哲学又称为语言分析哲学。语言分析哲学创始人是德国著名哲学家弗雷格,其后的罗素、胡塞尔、摩尔、维特根斯坦也作出巨大贡献,并将语言分析哲学从本体论的角度转向了日常语言的分析,使语言分析哲学重新回到鲜活的现实生活中来)
philosophy of law （狭义的)法哲学(法理学的同义词)
phone tapping 窃听电话
phonomania n. 杀害狂,嗜杀狂
phony n. 骗子,假冒者,假货
phony stuff 虚假材料,伪造的材料
photocopy n. 影印,影印件
photography on crime 刑事照相
photoreconnaissance n. 空中照相侦察
phraseology n. 措辞,用语,术语

phraseoplerosis 诉诸补缺
phyle n. （古希腊）政治划分单位,部落,宗族
phylogenetic 种族发生的；系统发育的
physical a. 肉体的,身体的；有形的；物质的；自然的
physical and mental examinations 身体及精神检查
physical and mental health 身心健康
physical assault 身体伤害；行凶
physical assets 实物资产,有形资产
physical capital 实物资本,有形资本
physical check up 健康检查,体格检查
physical child endangerment 儿童身体上处于危险境地(指由于不小心的行为,给儿童造成或可能造成其身体上的严重伤害。有时可缩写为 physical endangerment)
physical control over the defendant 对被告的人身控制
physical custody 身心监护,实物保管
physical damage to the goods 货物遭受的物质损失
physical delivery 实际交货,实物付给
physical disability 生理(上的)缺陷
physical distribution system 物质分配制度
physical effort 体力
physical endangerment 见 physical child endangerment
physical environment 自然环境
physical evidence 物证,确凿证据
physical evidence at the scene 现场物证
physical evidence technology 物证技术学
physical examination 体格检查
physical examination of judicature 司法物理检验
physical exhibit 物品展示(指证据形式中的实物证据,它包括实在证据和示意证据)
physical fact 客观事实,外界存在的客观事实；科学的事实；不可争辩的自然法则；可以见到的、听到的或通过感官可以"理解"的一些事物
physical force 体力；暴力；强制
physical goods 实物
physical harm 人身伤害

physical impossibility 事实上的不可能性（见 factual impossibility）
physical impossible 身体上的不可能,实际上的不可能(指如果实际上不可能,如一个人同时在两个地方,则合同没有约束力并不能执行)
physical injury 肉体伤害,人身伤害
physical market 现货市场
physical nature 物质的性质
physical object 物
physical parental authority （美）身体上的亲权(指享有监护权的一方父母对影响子女日常生活的活动,如夜宿朋友家、参加舞会、使用父母汽车等日常生活的细节有决定权)
physical parents 生身父母
physical person 自然人
physical planning legislation 自然环境规划立法
physical possession 物质占有;实质占有
physical power 实际权力
physical power over defendant 对被告的实际权力
physical presence 人身在场,亲自到场,人身到场,有形存在
physical presence alone 人身在场,客观出现
physical presence in court 亲自出庭
physical presence of the defendant in the forum 被告在当地的人身在场(客观出现)
physical protection 人身保护
physical punishment 体罚,肉刑
physical relations 物质关系
physical seizure of the written instrument 对书面文契的实际扣消
physical setting of a crime 犯罪环境
physical surrounding of court 法院的自然环境
physical traces of a crime 犯罪痕迹
physical tradition 实际交付,实物交付
physical unit of goods 货物有形计算单位
physical volume of foreign trade 对外贸易量
physically and mentally handicapped 生理上和精神上有缺陷的
physiocracy n. 重农主义

physiologic(al) a. 生理的,生理学的
physiologic(al) sterility 生理性不孕
pia causa 财团
piacle（或 piaculum）n. 恶性罪行,恶性犯罪,重大罪行
pianola n. 自动钢琴
picaro n. 1.坏蛋,亡命之徒 2.流浪汉
picaroon n. 海盗;海盗船
pick v. 1.选择,挑选 2.撬开,撬;扒窃;窃取 3.找,寻求 4.挖;凿;采
pick a lock 撬锁
pick a pocket 扒窃,摸包
pick (seek) a quarrel 寻衅,挑衅
pick and steal 扒窃,小偷小摸
pick on 挑剔;作弄人;选读
pick up （偶然地）获得（收益,生计等）；中途搭客（或带货）；拾起；逮住（盗贼或犯）；提审（罪犯）
picked ports (P. P.) 被选择的港口
picker n. 扒手
pickers and stealers 扒手和窃贼
picket n./v. 警戒哨,哨兵,步哨;执行警戒的飞机或船只;在建筑物示威的群众;站桩刑(指古代刑法,使犯人以一只脚站在桩上)/护围,用警戒哨保卫;担任纠察
picket line 警戒线
picketer n. 纠察员,警戒哨
picketing n. 警戒,监视;执行纠察任务
picking n. 1.选择;掘 2.扒窃;（复）赃物,扒窃物
picklock n. 撬锁工具;撬锁人;撬锁贼
pickpocket n. 扒手
pickpurse n. 扒手(指偷皮夹者)
pickup tax （美）（俚语或行话）（州的）遗产税(指所课税数额相当于联邦遗产税信贷金额的州的遗产税。亦可称为 sponge tax; slack tax)
picquet（=pickct）n. 哨兵,步哨
picture patent 图像专利
picture quality 影质
picture transmitter 传真电报发送
pie wag(g)on 押送囚犯的警车
pie-poulder court 泥足法院(见 pepoudrous)
piece rate wage 计件工资
piecemeal appeals 零碎上诉

piecemeal fashion 一件件的方式,逐渐的方式

piecework n. 计件工作(按工作量付报酬的工作)

piecework remuneration 计件给酬制

piecework wage system 计件工资制

pier dues 码头费

piercing the corporate veil 揭开公司面纱,刺穿法人的面纱[指在某些(如欺诈)案件中,法庭不赞同公司结构中固有的有限责任原则,而是要强使它的股东、官员和经理承担个人责任。见 disregard the corporate entity]

pigeonhole n./v. 文件架,文件柜的分类架;条条框框,取信处;把文件分类储存,把文件归档;搁置

pignorate v. 抵押,典当

pignorative contract 典押合同(契约),抵押(或不动产抵押)合同(契约)

pignus 质押

pignus in causa judicatio praetorium 裁判官判定的扣押质权

pignus legale 法定的出质契约,合法的质押(由法律运用引起的留置权,如土地出租人对承租人财产的留置权)

pignus praetorium (罗马法)裁判官法上的质权(指在进入让与财产程序的债权人取得裁判官法上的质权。此等权利保障他们优先于一切后来的债权人得到满足,如果由于自己的过失而丧失了对财产的占有,则可以依据此等裁判官法上的质权得到占有之回复)

Pigou Arthur Cecil 庇古·阿瑟·塞西尔(1877—1959年,英国著名经济学家)

pike n. 收税栅;收税门;通行税(费);收税路;关卡

pikeman n. 收税(费)栅看守人

pilfer v. 小偷小摸,偷窃

pilferage n. 轻微偷窃,小偷行为;失窃物

pilferer n. 小偷,扒手;窃贼

pilfering n. 偷窃行为

pillage n./v. 掠夺,抢劫;掠夺物/抢劫,抢夺

pillager n. 掠夺者;抢劫者

pilliwinks n. (古代)钳夹拇指的刑具

pillory n./v. (颈、手)枷(古时的一种刑

具);示众受辱/上颈手枷;处以枷刑;使示众受辱

pilot n./a. 1.领港员,领航员;引水员;向导 2.机师;飞行员;驾驶船者/1.实验性的,示范的,用于实验的 2.引导的,领航的 3.总的

pilot census 试验性人口调查

pilot house (船上)驾驶室

pilot lamp (light) 指示灯,信号灯;领航灯

pilotage n. 1.领港(权),领航(权);引水(权) 2.领港费,领航费

pilotage dues 领港费,领航费

pilotage inwards 入港领港费

pilotage water 引水区

pilotless aircraft 无人驾驶飞机

pin sb. down 使某人具体或确切说明意图,明确说明或确定某事物

pin-money n. (丈夫给妻子或父亲给子女的)零用钱

pinch v. 紧急,紧急关头;挟,挤;(俚)偷;(俚)逮捕

pinfold n. 1.收留迷路家畜以待认领的畜栏 2.监禁地;关闭或约束的地方

pink slip (俚)解雇通知书

Pinkerton n. (美)平克顿私家侦探公司;平克顿私家侦探公司的侦探;便衣侦探

Pinkie n. 平克顿私家侦探公司的侦探;便衣侦探

pioneer patent 首创性专利

pioneering international conference 首创性的国际会议

pioneering law 首创的法律

pinpoint n./v./a. 1.针尖,极尖的顶端 2.琐事、微物、一点⟨pinpoint of light⟩(一点灯光),⟨a pinpoint of difference⟩(微小差别)/1.指出,确认为;为……准确定位 2.突出,强调 3.精确地从空中拍摄/针尖的;极小的;细致的;详尽的

pinpointing contamination sources 微弱的传染源

pipe rolls (或 **great rolls of Exchequer**)卷筒宗卷(指英国财政部大档)

piracy n. 1.海盗行为,海上掠夺;海盗罪 2.侵犯版权,非法翻印;侵犯专利权

* ***Pirata est hostis humani generis.*** A pi-

rate is an enemy of the human race. 海盗是人类的敌人。
pirata non mutat dominium 海盗行为不变更所有权
pirate n./v. 1.海盗,掠夺者;海盗船 2.侵犯版权者,非法翻印者;非法广播者/掠夺;从事海盗活动;非法翻印
pirate jure gentium 国际法上的海盗
pirate radio station "海盗"电台
piratic(或 **piratical**)a. 海盗的,海盗行为的;剽窃的,侵害著作权的
piratical vessel 海盗船
pis aller 最后的手段;应急措施;权宜之计
piscary n. 共渔权(=common of piscary,指在他人水域内捕鱼的权利);捕鱼权;捕鱼场
pistol n. 手枪,信号手枪
pistol wound (手)枪弹创(伤)
pit and gallows (授予封建领主设立)地牢和绞架的授权条款
pitch n. 1.投掷;投掷物 2.商贩摆摊处 3.推销商品的广告或宣传
pitch card 小贩摊位卡
pitching stalls 摆摊售货
pivotal a. 关键性的,决定性的
pivotal legislative actors 决定性的立法者(行为人)
Pivy Signet (英)御玺(由英王幕府掌管)
pixilated a. 精神有些失常的;有点怪僻的
place v./n. 1.放置,安置 2.寄托(希望等);给予(信任等) 3.安抚;任命;完全认定 4.投(资);存(款);发出(订单等)/1.场所,地方,地点;位置 2.住所,寓所 3.地位,处境 4.职责,职权
place bills (英)席位条款(指用以排除王室官员在下议院席位的法案)
place for holding offenders 羁押犯人的场所
place for performance 履行地点
place for punishment 惩罚场所
place of abode 住所
place of acceptance 受领地;承诺地
place of commission 犯罪地点
place of contract (合同的)缔约地
place of crime 犯罪地点,犯罪场所

place of custody 羁押场所
place of delivery 财物交付处;投递处;发货地点
place of detention 拘留所
place of establishment (公司等的)设立地,创办地
place of execution 刑场;执行(死刑)地
place of payment 付款地点,支付地点
place of performance 清偿地点,履行地
place of the act 行为地
place of the birth 出生地
place of the court session 审判地点,开庭地点
place of the offence 犯罪地方
place of tort 侵权行为发生地
place of wrong doing 不法行为发生地
place on record 记录在案,公开宣布
place reliance in(或 **on**) 信任……;依靠……
placement n. 处置(指"洗钱"即对洗钱款进行初步处理,与其他合法款项混同或转做金融机构存款);(美)职业介绍;配置;部署
placet 赞成(票)(与 non placet 相对);许可;认为
placid career 平静的职业生涯
placing n. (未经申请等手续将公司全部或部分)出售(出盘),私自直接发行(证券)
placit 命令,决定
placita communia 民事诉讼
placita coronae 刑事诉讼
placitum nominatum 指定罪犯出庭辩护的日期
plagiarism n./v. (17世纪)抄袭;剽窃;剽窃作品,剽窃物[指有意明知呈现他人的原作品的思想或创作的表达(original ideas or creative expression)作为自己的作品。一般说,抄袭是不道德的,但不违法。如果表达的创作者对其表达的使用给予无限制的允准(unrestricted permission),使用者索取的如同原始的表达,使用进行了抄袭,但不违反版权法规(copyright laws)。如果原始表达(original expression)未经允准而被拷贝,则该剽窃者违反版权法规,即使荣誉(credit)归属创作人。如果这种

剽窃导致重大盈利则会被视为售假活动（passing-off activity）且违反《兰哈姆法》（Lamham Act）。见 infringement。plagiarize v.; plagiarist n.]
plagiarist n. 剽窃者,抄袭者
plagiarize v. 抄袭,剽窃(著作等)
plagiarizer n. 剽窃者
plagiary n. 抄袭者,剽窃者;抄袭,剽窃;剽窃物
plague v./n. 使染瘟疫;使得灾祸,折磨,烦扰/瘟疫,鼠疫,黑死病,天灾,灾害
plain a. 1.平的;简单的 2.清楚的,明白的;坦白的,直率的 3.(指纹的)弧形的,平弧形的
plain arch 弧形纹
plain bond 无担保债券
plain error 明显错误
plain error rule (美)显然错误规则(指在审理时,纵使一方当事人未提出存在一种错误,而这种错误如果是明显、有偏见又影响实质性权利并涉及审理的根本公正问题,如果不予纠正,将会有辱法院的整体和名誉,在此情况下,受理上诉法院可以推翻这一判决)
plain meaning 本义(文本)(指要求解释者或法官按照同一语言共同体中普遍成员所理解的法律条文的意思去解释法律,追求的是一种共识意义上的形式正当性)
plain meaning of legislation 立法的明确含义
plain meaning rule 显明含义规则(指解释法规的几种可能方法之一,即:如果一项法规似乎很清楚,那么,词语的最简单含义不需深入阅读即可领会)
plain statement 简单陈述;使人容易明白的陈述
plain view doctrine 显明观点说(指警察执行任务时,偶然遇到与犯罪有关的东西,他无须授权即有权没收该项物品并在刑事审判中作为证据提供)
plain whorl (指纹)斗,螺形斗,普通斗形线;平斗
plain-clothes n. 便衣(常用于警探);便服
plain-clothes investigation 便衣稽查
plain-clothes man 便衣警察

plaint n. 控告,起诉,告状;起诉状
plaintiff n. 原告,检举人
plaintiff corporation 原告公司
plaintiff favoring rule 有利于原告规则说(韦乔伯的一种学说)
plaintiff in error 提请复审的当事人,取得复审令状的当事人
plaintiff lawyer 原告的辩护律师
plaintiff sues in person 原告自诉
plaintiff win rate 原告胜诉率
plaintiff winner and losers 胜利原告和失败原告
plaintiff's interest in obtaining convenient and effective relief 原告获得方便有效救济
plaintiff's overall cost of going to trial 原告的整个诉讼成本
plaintiff's restate and reallege 原告重申并再次主张
plan n. 计划;策略;方法;设计图;方案
plan concerning manpower and pay scales 劳动工资计划
planless a. 无计划的,未计划的
planned a. 有计划的,计划的;有秩序的;安排的
planned annual profits 年度计划利润额
planned contract 计划合同(契约)
planned deliveries 计划供应
planned economy 计划经济
planned parenthood 计划生育
planned products 计划产品
planned spacing of birth 计划生育间隔
planning n. 计划的制订;规划;设计
planning and management of the national economy 国民经济的计划和管理
planning authority 规划机关,规划当局
planning board 计划委员会
planning estimate 计划概算
planning law 计划法,规划法
planning permission 规划许可证
planning personnel 规划人员
planning policies 计划化政策
planning-programing budgeting system 设计计划预算制度
plans of project and products 设计和产品

图纸
plant breeder's rights　植物培育者的权利
plant patent act　植物专利法
plant quarantine (law)　植物检疫(法)
plant variety rights tribunal　植物品种权利裁判庭
plantation forestry　人工林林业
plastic works　塑造的艺术品
plat (=plot) n./v.　小块土地;地图/密谋,策划
platform n.　1.站台;月台;讲台 2.(政党的)政纲,党纲
platform committee　政纲草拟委员会
platform container　平台集装箱,平板集装箱
plausibility n.　花言巧语;似乎有理
plausible a.　花言巧语的;似乎有理的
play v.　假装;嘲弄;赌博;玩弄;利用;摆布
play a trick on a person　诈骗某人,开某人玩笑
play around　对配偶不忠,乱搞两性关系
play booty　(赌场中)做诱子通同作弊;勾结,朋比为奸
play fair and squarely　表现正大光明
play hard　不择手段;行为卑鄙
play (make 或 raise) havoc with　大肆破坏,对……造成严重破坏;使陷入大混乱
play on the human reaction of jury　利用陪审团的人性反应
play politics　玩弄权术,搞阴谋诡计
play the market　投机倒把
playing field　活动领域,活动空间
playing for hire　见 playing (或 standing) for hire
playright n.　表演权
plea n.　(13 世纪)1.辩诉,抗辩[指刑事被告对其刑事犯罪(criminal charge)的有罪、认罪(guilty)、无罪、不认罪(not guilty)或无争议、不服争辩(no contest)的正式回答。亦称为 criminal plea,刑事被告答辩状。在英国 pleas 已由 statement of defence 代替]2.答辩书(普通法)民事诉讼中被告的答辩书
plea agreement　见 plea bargaining
plea and direction hearings　(英)答辩和

指示听证程序
plea bargaining (=cop a plea)　诉辩交易,诉辩磋商(经法庭批准被告为了避免受到较重的处罚与控诉人达成的认罪认情协议),控辩交易(指一套独特的程序,借以来确定刑事诉讼被告有罪或无罪,并适用对犯罪者适用的刑罚)
plea for aid　请求援助
plea for mercy　恳(要)求宽恕
plea in abatement　妨诉答辩;起诉不当答辩(指一种提出对于维护原告权利主张的地点、时间和方法的诉辩或异议,但不涉及原告的诉求。原告可以在另一地点、时间提起诉讼。起诉不当答辩仅仅是推迟或拖延诉讼进程,或成功地主张妨诉答辩的被告在出现有瑕疵情况下,让原告请求继续在新近的诉讼中公开透明或在以后的诉讼中再次提出权利主张。亦称为 abater)
plea in bar　诉讼进行中(对原告的诉讼所作的)抗辩,法庭上的答辩(见 peremptory plea);原告无权之抗辩
plea in bar of a prosecution　中止公诉的答辩(抗辩)
plea in bar of trial　中止审判请求
plea in confession and avoidance　承认但无效答辩(见 confession and avoidance)
plea in discharge　表明诉讼原因已排除的答辩
plea in law　法律提述(指原告据此作为提起诉讼之依据);法律上的抗辩
plea in mitigation of damages　请求减轻损害赔偿(责任)
plea in reconvention　(罗马法)反请求诉讼[指被告在答辩中提出新的事实,这不是作为抗辩,而只是作为反请求(cross-complaint)、抵销(setoff)或反诉(counter in claim)的依据]
plea in suspension　请求暂时中止诉讼
plea of "act of state"　"国家行为"的抗辩
plea of *autrefois acquit*　前经宣告无罪不应再受审判的抗辩
plea of confession and avoidance　见 confession and avoidance
plea of duresse　以被胁迫为由,请求宣告

行为无效
plea of general issue 全部否定原告申述之抗辩
plea of guilty 表示认罪
plea of guilty by post (不出庭而)通过邮寄方式认罪
plea of military necessity 出于军事上需要的答辩
plea of *non set factum* 非其所为的抗辩
plea of not guilty 不认罪
plea of nullity 请求(宣告判决)无效的抗辩
plea of pardom 免罪辩护(指前经开释或前经定罪等辩护)
plea of pregnancy 以怀孕为理由的抗辩
plea of privilege 特许抗辩;特权抗辩(指抗辩人或被告寻求在其住所地进行诉讼而指出的抗辩,除非法院另有规定,对被告提出的特许抗辩不得驳回)
plea of self-defence 出于自卫的抗辩
plea of superior order 职务行为的抗辩(指自己的行为是为了执行上级命令的抗辩)
plea of tender 提存抗辩
plea side (英)民诉部(前王座法院的一个部门,专门审理普通民事案件)
plea to indictment 对起诉书的答辩
plea to jurisdiction 认为法院无权审判的抗辩
plead v. 辩护,抗辩,答辩;请求;以……为借口
plead against sb. 反驳某人
plead as a defence 以……作为辩解
plead before the court 在法庭上辩护
plead for mercy 恳求宽恕
plead for the accused 为被告辩护
plead guilty (刑事被告)表示服罪,服罪
plead ignorance 借口不知情;以不知情为理由
plead not guilty (刑事被告)表示不服罪
plead over 未注意到对方当事人诉答中有缺陷之陈述;被告人提出追诉答辩被法庭驳回后的
pleadable a. 可抗辩的,可辩护的,可作为辩护理由的

pleader n. 抗辩人,答辩人;辩护律师;代为求情者
pleading n. (16世纪)1.诉讼文件,诉状[指诉讼程序(legal proceeding)(特别是民事诉讼)中当事人一方呈交给法院的正式法律文件或者是针对宣称的某事权利主张、驳回或辩护(allegation; claims; denials or defense)的答辩状。在联邦民事诉讼流程中,主要的诉讼文件(main pleadings)是原告的起诉状(plaintiff's complaint)和被告的答辩(defendant's answer)] 2.诉答,诉答程序[指在民事诉讼中,确定和缩小诉讼争点(issues)范围的制度。当事人在此阶段呈交正式书状(documents)阐明各自的主张] 3.诉答规则[指规范调整原告权利主张的起诉和被告答辩的法律规则〈today, pleading is a much simple subject than it was in former years〉(今天,比起前些年,诉状中的主题更为简单)。旧时普通法诉讼中:①原告的起诉状中叫"declaration",被告的答辩状中叫"plea";②原告的次答辩状叫"replication",被告的次答辩状叫"rejoinder";③原告次轮答辩状叫"surrejoinder";④原告三轮答辩状叫"surrebutter",被告三轮答辩状叫"rebutter"。衡平法诉讼中的诉状:原告的起诉状为"bill of complaint";被告的答辩状为"demurrer, plea; answer or disclaimer"或其混合形式。原告的答辩状为"replication"等。目前在英国高等法院诉讼程序中,起诉状、被告答辩状以及原告答辩状分别为: statement of claim, statement of defense 和 reply。其后的诉状仍用普通法诉讼中的名称。在美国,这种诉状体系已大大简化,其作用也有所降低。对事实和争议点的限定通过披露程序(discovery)和审前会议(pretrial conference)来完成。根据《联邦民事诉讼程序规则》,诉状包括起诉状(complaint)、答辩状(answer)、交叉诉讼答辩状(reply to a counterclaim)、交叉诉讼答辩状(answer to a cross-claim)、第三方起诉状(third party complaint)以及第三方答辩状(third party answer)。在诉讼进程中提交或使用的申请书(motions)、律师辩论意见书(briefs)、宣誓书(affidavits)等均属广义上的法庭文

件(court papers),而不属于诉状]
pleading failing health 以健康不佳为由
pleading of evidentiary facts 证据事实的诉辩
pleading of the accused 被告申辩
pleading the baby act 为未成年(的法律)行为的抗辩(见 baby act)
pleadings n. 正式书面的答辩状;正式书面的申述、反诉;反请求;被告的反诉状
pleadings by written notes 用书面记录进行的诉讼程序
pleas by confession and avoidance 采取自认但又主张无效的抗辩
pleas by way of traverse 采取反驳方式的抗辩
pleas in abatement 妨碍抗辩
pleas of guilty 有罪答辩;认罪
pleas of the Crown 1.(英)刑事诉讼及程序;公诉,刑事诉讼 2.(苏格兰)抢劫、强奸、凶杀及纵火等的刑事诉讼
pleas rolls (英)诉讼案卷(中世纪法院的诉讼记录)
pleasure appointment 随意指派,随意任命(指任某人就业或就职,任何时间,不需任何理由,不需公告或听证。亦称 at pleasure appointment)
plebeian n. 平民,庶民;(复)(罗马时代的)平民团
plebiscitary a. 公民投票的;(古罗马法上)平民表决的
plebiscite n. 公民投票;(古罗马法上)平民表决,公民表决
plebiscitum (罗马法上的)平民制定的法律;公民投票
plebs (罗马法上的)平民,公民
pledge n./v. 1.抵押;抵押权,质权;抵押品;典当物 2.保人,保证人 3.誓言,誓约;保证;保证物/质物,抵押,典当;发誓,保证;以……作担保
pledge assets 出质资产,抵押资产
pledge certificate 质押凭证
pledge holder 受质人
pledge of movables 动产质押权
pledge of obligation 债权质押,债权质
pledge of secrecy 保密宣誓
pledge on immovables 不动产质权
pledgee n. 接受抵押人,抵押权人,受质人,质权人
pledgery n. 担保,保证;发誓
pledging n. 抵押物(品),典当物
pledgor (pledger) n. 出质人,抵押人,典当者,设定抵押权人
pleine jurisdiction (法国行政法院的)完全管辖权
plena adoptio 完全收养
plena aetas 足龄,成年
plena probatio 充分证据;补充宣誓
plenary a. 1.完全的,充分的;绝对的;全权的 2.全体出席的;无限制的
plenary action 完整诉讼(指按全部合法诉讼程序进行审理的诉讼,与简易诉讼相对。见 summary proceeding)
plenary causes 完整诉案(指按全部合法的诉讼程序进行审理的诉案)
plenary competence that states prima facie possess 国家所假定享有的完整权力
plenary confession 全部供认,彻底坦白
plenary decision 法官全体会议的判决
plenary docket 完整的备审案件目录
plenary jurisdiction 完全审判权;全部管辖权
plenary meeting 全体会议
plenary powers 全权
plenary session (最高法院全体法官组成的)全体会议
plene administravit 遗产全部处理(已无资还债的)答辩(指遗产管理人代表死者被人控告负债所作的答辩)
plenipotentiary n./a. 全权大使/有全权的;完全的,绝对的
plenipotentiary credentials 全权证书
plenipotentiary delegate 全权代表
pleno jure 有充分(完全)的权利
plenum n. 全体会议;充实,充满
plenum dominium 绝对所有权,完全的所有权
plenum of the supreme court 最高法院全体会议
plethora n. 过量,过剩,过多
plethora of asset backed instruments 资产

支撑工具层出不穷
plethora of money 货币过剩
plevin 担保,保证;令状;证书
pliable a. 能适用的,柔顺的
pliable framework of Merchant Law 商法的灵活框架,商法可适用的结构
plight n./v. 1.困境,境况 2.誓约,婚约 3.保证/发誓,立誓
plight one's faith 宣誓
plight one's truth 矢其忠诚
plight one's words 担保
plight oneself to sb. 和某人订婚
plot n./v. 1.小块土地;地区 2.秘密计划,阴谋/密谋,策划
plot in (或 **of**) **secret** 暗算,暗中策划
plot of land for personal needs (中)自留地
plot sabotage 阴谋破坏
plot treason 谋反,谋叛
plotter n. 搞阴谋者,策划人,密谋者
plough back profit 把利润再投资
plough land 耕地
Plowden's Reports (英)《普洛登的判例汇编》(于 1571 年首次出版,被认为是最好、最确切的一种汇编)
plumber n. (美国调查政府人员泄密情形的)堵漏防漏人员
plunder n./v. 抢劫,掠夺;掠夺物,赃物;战利品/掠夺,抢劫
plunder bund (美)掠夺者的组织或集团(尤指侵占或盗用公款的)
plunderage n. 抢劫,掠夺,盗用船货;掠夺品,盗用的船货;赃物
plunderer n. 掠夺者,抢劫者,盗贼
plunge v./n. 使投入,使遭受,使陷入,下降,陷入/投入,陷入
plunge sb. into debt 使某人负债
plunger n. 1.跳入者,潜入者 2.冒险的投机家;滥赌的赌徒
plural a. 复数的
plural laws 多重法则
plural marriage 一夫多妻或一妻多夫
plural nationality 多重国籍
plural offices 兼职,兼任
plural society (由多人种组成的)多人种社会,多人种社交组织(单位);多元社会

plural vote 一人多选区投票(权);一人多选票制
plural wife 一夫多妻制下的任何一妻,属于同一丈夫的妻妾
pluralism n. 复数,多种;兼职;多元论
pluralist n. 多元论者;兼职的人
pluralist doctrine 多元论
plurality n. 复数,多种;兼职;多元化,多元
plurality elections 相对多数决定的选举
plurality of creditors 复数债权人,多数债权人
plurality of debtors 复数债务人,多数债务人
plurality opinion (1908 年)相对多数判决意见,多数判决意见[指没有足够法官表决构成的多数,但是接受了比任何其他判决意见更多的表决意见。多数法官同意判决的结果,但不附有理由的书面法律文件,亦译为多元意见(指宣布联邦最高法院判决,但并未保证参与大法官大多数同意的判决意见。20 世纪 70 年代以后,随着联邦最高法院在原则理解上走向分裂,多元意见也越来越多)]
plurality system 得票最多者当选制;相对多数当选制
plurality votes 相对多数票;较多票数
plures rei 多为被告(连带债务)
pluri-national river 多国河流
pluries fi. fa. 第三次财产扣押令(见 *pluries writ*)
pluries summons (在第一、第二次传票未曾送达时所发出的)第三次传票
pluries writ (法院在第二次令状未产生效果时发出的)第三次执行令
plurilateral trade agreement 多边贸易协定,复合贸易协定
plurilateral treaty 多边条约
plus and minus factors 有利和不利因素
* *Plus exempla quam peccata nocent.* Examples hurt more than crimes. 老是警戒比犯罪还要伤害更多的人。
plus or minus clause 增减条款
* *Plus peccat author quam actor.* The originator or instigator of a crime is a worse

offender than the actual perpetrator of it. 策谋犯或教唆犯比实行犯罪恶更大。
plus side 贷方
* *Plus valet unus oculatus testis quam auriti decem.* One eye-witness is of more weight than ten ear-witnesses (or those who speak from hearsay). 一个目击证据比十个耳闻证据要有分量。一个目击证人比十个道听途说的证人更强。
* *Plus vident oculi quam oculus.* Seceral eyes see more than one. 众人所见要比一人所见更加明了。
plus-petere（或 **plus-petitie**） （罗马法）分外的诉讼请求
plutocracy n. 财阀统治
plying（或 **standing**）**for hire** （汽车行驶着或停着的）招租(指任何车辆,在任何道路上行驶着或停着,显出标记或信号表示可以出租)
pnigma n. 绞死, 勒死
poach v. 1.偷猎; 偷渔 2.侵犯他人权利
poacher n. 1.非法偷猎者,非法偷渔者 2.侵犯他人产业者;抢夺他人顾客的商人
poaching n. 偷猎(指侵入他人地区,非法打猎)
pocket n. 1.钱袋; 衣袋 2.袋
pocket borough （英）（议会改革前由个人或一个家族、集团）操纵的选区或政治团体
pocket defendant 与原告相串通（勾结）的辩护人
pocket part （美）袋装部分［指美国的法规汇典和法律百科全书以及一些法规判例汇编的书背面(封三)设有一个小袋,以便装置一些补充资料页］
pocket sheriff （由王室指定的）司法执行官
pocket veto 袋中否决或口袋否决（见package veto）
pocket-picking n. 扒窃
pocket-veto v. 用搁置手段否决议案
podesta （中世纪意大利的）主要行政官,法官,市长
poena 惩罚,处罚,刑罚,罚金
* *Poena ad paucos, metus ad omnes perveniat.* If punishment be inflicted on a few, a dread comes to all. 惩一儆百。
poena arbitraria 擅自判刑,任意定刑
poena capitalis 死刑
poena conventa 违约惩罚
poena corporalis 体刑,身体刑罚,身体刑,肉刑
* *Poena ex delicto defuncti haeres teneri non debet.* The hair ought not to be bound by a penalty arising out of the wrongful act of the deceased. 继承人不应负因被继承人的错误行为所该受惩罚的责任。
poena legitima 正刑
* *Poena non potest, culpa perennis erit.* Punishment can not be, crime will be, perpetual. 惩罚不能是永久的,但罪行将是终身的。
poena pecunialia 金钱刑,罚金
poena sanguinis 死刑
* *Poena suos tenere debet actores et non alios.* Punishment ought to bind the guilty, and not others. 惩罚应限制罪行,而不限制其他。
* *Poena tolli potest, culpa perennis erit.* The Punishment can be removed, but the crime remains. 惩罚可以变更,但罪行仍然存在。
poenae exasperatio（或 **aggrevatio**） 刑的加重
poenae moderatio 刑的减轻
poenae ordinaria 正常刑,常刑
poenae pilloralis （古英国法）一种颈手枷刑罚,枷刑示众
* *Poenae potius molliendae quam exasparandae sunt.* Punishments should rather be softened than aggravated. 惩罚宁轻勿重。
* *Poenae sint restringendae.* Punishments should be restrained. 惩罚应受限制。
poenae stipulatio 违约罚金(指契约规定的违约罚金)
* *Poenae suos tenere debet actores et non alios.* Punishment ought to be inflicted upon the guilty, and not upon others. 处刑应根据罪行而不应根据其他。
poenitentia （大陆法）悔改,悔悟,反思,重新考虑

pogroist n. 组织或参加大屠杀者
pogrom n./v. 有组织的屠杀;集体屠杀;对少数民族的迫害/集体迫害;大屠杀,杀戮
poind n./v. 扣押;/收押;(苏格兰)没收并拍卖(债务人的财产)
poinding 财产扣押(指苏格兰法律上扣押财产之形式)
poinding of the ground 财产扣押令;地上财产扣押之诉
point n./v. 1.要害;要点;论点;细目 2.地点,方位,场所 3.警察固定岗位 4.特点,特质 5.意义,目的;一项单独的法律建议;(诉讼中引起的)论点;百分点/指向,面向,表明(to, at);暗示(to, at, towards)
point at issue (诉讼)系争要点
point constable (英)交通警察
point expectation (相应变量的)主观点预期(指消费选择理论中的消费计划基础)
point in dispute 争执点
point of contact 联结点(指国内法与外国法相冲突情况下,对涉外民事关系指出一个适用的法律,而此适用法律的指定,在规范形态上一般是通过一个标志来表现的,国际私法术语中将此标志称为"联结点")
point of contract 合同(契约)要点
point of defence 辩护要点
point of disagreement 不同意见,异议
point of entry 入境地点
point of fact 事实观点,事实证明(指在案件中对于争论点的事实的具体意见)
point of law 法律观点,法律主张(指在案件中对争论点的具体法律上的主张)
point of liberation 天平动点(宇航法中的术语,指宇宙空间中,两个或两个以上天体,在零点速度时,它们之间的吸引力得到平衡而等于零,被发射到那里的太空装置可以长久停留)
point of order 关于议事程序问题
point of plea 抗辩要点,答辩要点
point of pleadings 诉抗要点,答辩要点
point of rejoinder 再答辩要点,第二次答辩论点
point of view 论点,见解,立场
point to point 定向之

point-duty n. (英)(交通警的)站岗,值勤
pointer(s) n. 1.指示物,指示者 2.指针 3.暗示,线索;点子,主意〈give us some pointers on how to do the job〉(给我们出点主意如何做好这项工作)
pointless a. 无意义的,不得要领的,空洞乏味的,未得分的
points and authorities 关键与权威(指在诉讼中为采取支持的法律立场而准备的文件名称,如支持或反对一项动议)
points not challenged 未提出质疑的论点;未提出质疑的问题
points of claim 要求要点,求偿要点;(商业案件中的)诉讼请求(要点)
points of law 法律条文或条款,法律要点
pointsman n. (有固定岗位的)交通警察
poison n./v. 1.毒;毒药;毒物 2.败坏道德的事/1.投毒,下毒;毒害,毒杀,使中毒 2.摧毁;败坏
poison-pen a. 匿名而有恶意的,匿名而有恶意的信的,诽谤作品的
poison-pen letter 匿名信
poisoned food 有毒食品
poisoner n. 投毒者,毒害者
poisoning n. 中毒;毒害
poisonous a. 1.有毒的;有害的 2.有恶意的;败坏道德的
poisonous materials 剧毒物品
poisonous substance 有毒物
polarization n. 极化;两极分化
polaroid photo 偏振片相片(指拍照后可立即冲洗出来的相片)
police n./v. 警察;警察当局;警察组织;警务人员;公安,治安/1.维持治安;整顿;警备 2.设置警察,实施警察制度 3.管理,管治
Police Academy 警官学院
Police Act 《警察法》
police action 警察行动(指霸权主义国家镇压殖民地国家的民族解放和革命的行动)
police advisory board 警察咨询委员会
police agency 警察机构
police agent (法国的)警察;警员
police apparatus 警察机构
police arrest power 警察逮捕权

police authority 警察权;警察当局
police bail 警察保释(在英国刑事诉讼程序中,执法官员,如警察等,有权允许被检控人自己用金钱担保,或准许他人用金钱或提供担保而给以保释)
police blotter (=blotter) 警察逮捕人员记录簿
police box 警察岗亭
police bureau 警察局
police cadet 实习警员
Police Cadet School (英)青少年警察训练学校
police car 警察巡逻车
police cell 警察局拘留室
police constable (英)普通警察,警员
police court 违警罪法庭,治安法庭
police custody 警察拘留
police doctor 警医
police dog 警犬
police force 警察(总称),警察部队
police force ordinance 警察部队条例
police inspector 巡警官
police investigation 警方调查
police investigative power 警察调查权
police judge (或 justice) (= police magistrate) 违警罪法庭法官
police jury (美)(路易斯安那州县属教区的)管理机构或警察组合
police lock-up 警察局拘留所
police magistrate 违警罪法庭法官或裁判官,警务司法官
police matter 违警事件;违警案件
police offence 违警罪
police offences act 违警法
police office 警察局
police officer 警察,警官;内务军官
police patrol 警察巡逻
police post 派出所,警察分所
police power(s) 警权,治安权,警力机关,警力范围[指①一个主权国家享有内在的充分权力维护公共安全、公共秩序、公共道德和公共卫生以及维护司法而制定各项必需的适当的法律。这是十分重要的属于政府的基本权力,不可能为立法机构将此权力放弃或从政府中将此权力转移。

②根据美国联邦宪法第十修正案授予州的权力,州有权制定并实施保护公共卫生、公共安全和社会福利的法律,或将此权力委托给地方政府,但行使此权力应受正当程序和其他规定的限制。③泛指政府有权干预私有财产的使用,比如将该财产予以征用(eminent domain)]
police precinct 警察管区
police record 违警记录
police regulation 警察条例
police reporter 采访警方消息的记者
police science 警察科学(指寻求着手实施法律作为职业的人们所追求的研究领域)
police security team 警备队
police sergeant 警长,警佐
police stand 警察岗
police state 极权国家,警察国家(指该国公民的政治的、经济的和社会的生活均受到极权政府控制和统治集团的专权虐待,该极权政府运用警察工具控制整个极权国家)
police station 警察分局,派出所
police sub-station 派出所
police superintendent 治安官,警官
police the street 维持街上秩序
police training school 警察训练学校
police wagon 警车
police witness 警方证人
policeman n. 警察
policeman in disguise 便衣警察
policewoman n. 女警察
Policies Complaints Board (英)控警委员会
policy n. 1.政策,方针;权谋 2.保险单 3.法律的总目的
policy decision 政策决定
policy declaration 政策宣告
policy holder 保单持有人;投保人;保险客户
policy in force 有效保险单
policy limitation 政策界限
policy loan 保险单贷款
policy of assurance 保险单
policy of atomic blackmail 原子讹诈政策
policy of benevolence 仁政

policy of conciliation 和解政策
policy of containment 遏制政策
policy of controlled procurement and distribution （中）统购统销政策
policy of decolonization 非殖民化政策
policy of educating and redeeming the juvenile delinquents 教育和挽救少年罪犯的政策
policy of expansion 扩张政策
policy of grab 掠夺政策
policy of insurance 保险单
policy of lenient treatment 宽大政策
policy of life insurance 人寿保险单，人身保险单
policy of maritime insurance 海上保险单
policy of neutrality 中立政策
policy of nonentanglement 不介入政策
policy of nonresistance 不抵抗政策
policy of opening to the outside world 对外开放政策
policy of redemption 赎买政策
policy of reforming the criminals （中）改造罪犯的政策
policy of terrorism 恐怖政策
policy of the big revolver 用报复关税威胁他国的政策
policy of totally barring in-person solicitation of clients 完全禁止（律师）亲身招徕客户政策
policy oriented 定向政策（美国现代冲突法学主张以政策定向为主轴灵活地解决法律冲突）
policy premium payments 保单保险费
policy proof of interest 保险单证明可获利益；凭保险单证明的保险利益
policy rescission 政策目的消除；保单撤销
policy science 政策科学
policy surveillance 政策监督
policy year 保险单年度
policy-oriented approach 政策法学派
policy-science of law 政策法学（法国的维莱和美国拉斯韦尔等为该法学学派创始人，在西方法学中该法学被认为属于价值论法学，以某种价值观而轻视民主社会共有的价值，同时，以人的尊严作为民主的

最高价值）；政策法学派
policy-selecting rule 政策选择规则说
policymaker n. 政策制定者，决策人
policymaking n. 制定政策，决策
policymaking body 决策机构
poligraph n. 测谎器
polis 城邦制
politburo n. （共产党的）政治局；（资本主义国家类似政治局的）决策控制机构
politic arithmetic 政治算术［由威廉·佩蒂爵士（Sir William Petty）创造的"政治算术"一词比政治经济学出现得早。它指的是"一种根据与政府事务诸如国家收入、人口数量、土地规模和价值、税收贸易等有关数据资料论证的技艺"］
political a. 政治的，政治上的；党派政治的
political accountability 政府负责
political advantage 政治利益
political aim 政治目的
political animal 政治动物
political appearance 政治面目，政治表现
political assassination 政治性暗杀
political asylum（或 refuge） 政治避难，政治庇护
political authorities 政府部门
political belief 政治信仰，政治信念
political body 政治机关，国家机关，政府机构
political bureau（=politburo） 政治局
political centralization 政治上的集中制
political code 政治守则，政治准则
political conceptions 政治概念，政治观念
political constitution 政治宪法
political corruption 见 official misconduct
political economy 政治经济学［指研究处理（或应对）政府的经济问题和政治政策与经济过程之间的关系的社会科学］
political crime 政治罪
political criminal 政治犯
political crisis 政治危机
political demonstration 政治示威（或游行）
political discourse 政治论述，政治演说
political dispute （国际）政治争端
political ends 政治目的；政治结局
political entities 政治实体

political envoys 政治使节
political establishment 政治(体制)建制
political evolution 政治演进
political executive 政治行政部门
political foes 政敌,政治反对者
political force 政治力量
political freedom 政治自由
political fund 政治基金
political genocide 政治性大规模屠杀
political in governing 统治效率,政治上的治理
political independence 政治独立
political intrigue 政治阴谋
political jurisdiction 政治管辖;政治管辖权
political jurisprudence (美)政治法学(指基于法律现实主义和社会学的法的概念化,以法律和法律学说为根据的一个学科)
political jurist 政治法学家
political law (通常用 science)政府组织和管理学,政治学
political liberties 政治自由
political life 政治生活
political morality and fidelity 政治道德与忠诚
political offence 政治罪,政治罪行(指与政治叛乱有关的罪行,英国 1870 年的引渡罪人法例规定不得引渡犯有政治罪行的逃亡者)
political offender 政治犯
political opponent 政敌
political order 政治秩序
political organization 政治组织
political party 政党
political party life 政党活动
political persecution 政治迫害
political philosophy 政治哲学
political power 政治权力,政权
political prerogative 政治特权
political programme 政纲
political protection 政治保护
political question 政治问题[指法院不能决定的问题,因为它涉及只能由执行机关(executive branch)专门作出决议的问题]
political refugee 政治流亡者,政治避难者

political remedies 政治性救济方法
political responsibility 政治责任
political revolution 政治革命
political rhetoric of social compact 社会契约的政治辩术
political right 政治权利,参政权
political sanction 政治制裁
political self-determination 政治自决
political settlement 政治解决
political situation 政局,政治局势
political society 政治社会
political solution 政治解决
political sovereignty 政治上的主权
political state of nature 政治自然状态
political status 政治地位
political structure of state 国家政体
political suspect 政治嫌疑犯
political system 政治体系;政治制度
political testament 政治的信仰声明
political text 政治文件
political thought 政治思想
political treaty 政治性条约
political trial 政治性审判
political view 政见,政治观点
political whipsaw 政治锯子
political-legal a. 政治法律的,政法的
political-legal cadre school (中)政法干部学校
political-legal circle (中)政法界
political-legal departments (中)政法部门
political-legal functionaries (中)政法干部,政法人员
political-legal organs (中)政法机关
Political-Military Affairs Bureau 见 Bureau of Political-Military Affairs
politically organized society 政治组织社会
politician n. 政客;政治家
politicize v. 搞政治,谈论政治;使具有政治性
politicking n. 政治活动(尤指竞选等活动)
politics n. 政治;政治学;政纲,政见;政治活动;政治生活
(The) Politics and Law Association of China 中国政法学会(1983 年正式改为中国法学会)

politics of neutral concern 中立政治
polity n. 政府;政治制度;政治形态,政体;国家组织
poll n./v. 1.选举投票;投票结果;投票记录 2.投票人的名册;民意测验 3.(复)(美)投票及点票处/1.投票,查票,收受及登记选票;得到……选票 2.对……进行民意测验
poll a jury 逐一询问陪审员,逐一征求每个陪审员对裁决的意见
poll results 投票结果;民意测验结果
poll tax (17世纪)人头税(指在收税管辖权内对每个人头所课的固定税收。美国联邦宪法第二十四修正案禁止联邦或州政府以未交人头税为名剥夺选举权、投票权。亦可称为 *per capita* tax; capitation tax; capitation; head tax)
poll-clerk n. 选举投票工作人员;计票人
pollbook n. 选举人名册
pollcard n. 选举卡;登记卡
polldeed (或 **deed poll**) n. 单边契据,单方面的契据
pollicitation n. 要约;(罗马法上)(为感谢政府给予荣誉时所作的)致谢许诺
polling a. 投票的,选举的
polling agent 投票代理人
polling booth 选举场所,投票站
polling day 选举日
polling station 投票所,投票站,投票点
polling the jury 征求陪审团的意见;要求陪审团员表明自己的判断(即分别询问每一个陪审员是否曾经并且仍然同意陪审团作出的判决书);陪审员裁决投票(指分别询问每一个陪审员并要求表明自己的判断的方式)
polltaker (或 **pollster**) n. 民意测验者,民意调查人
polltax n. 人头税
pollutant n. 污染物(质)
pollute v. 污染;玷污;败坏(道德等)
polluter-pays-principle n. 污染者补偿原则
pollution n. 污染;亵渎;败坏
pollution of a river 污染河流
pollution of air 空气污染
pollution of atmosphere 大气层污染
pollution of water 水污染

pollution right 污染权(指环保法必须明确界定的一项重要权利,指权利人在符合法律规定的条件下向环境排放污染物的权利)
pollwatcher n. (投票所的)监票人,监察人(指监督是否有违法竞选的人)
polyandrous a. 一妻多夫的
polyandry n. 一妻多夫制,一妻多夫
polygamist n. 多配偶的人;多配偶论者;主张或实行一夫多妻或一妻多夫的人
polygamy 一夫多妻制,一妻多夫制,多配偶
polygraph n. 多产作家;复写器;测谎器;谎言侦查员,伪探子
polygynous a. 一夫多妻的
polygyny n. 一夫多妻制
polymetallic nodules 多金属结核(指海床下之矿物资源之一)
pontage n. (英)养护桥梁税;过桥费
pontifex n. (古罗马)大祭司团成员,大祭司,主教
pontifical a./n. 教皇的;大祭司的;主教的;(古罗马)(pontifical college)最高祭司团/1.主教法衣与标志 2.主教仪典书
Pooh-Bah n. 显要人物,大官,居高位的人;公私兼职很多的人
pool n./v. 1.垄断性联营;合伙经营;联营;运价协定联营 2.集团分保 3.共同使用的物或金钱/合伙经营,联营;共同组织基金;共享,分享
pool of available assets 可用的资产总量
pooling equilibrium 混用均衡(指博弈的一种解,其中不同类型的参与人选取相同的战略,从而防止不拥有信息的参与人能从拥有信息参与人的行动中得出关于他们类型的任何推论)
pooling of conscience 共同经营,联合经营
pooling of land 土地入股
poop sheet 官方的书面声明(或材料汇编等);书面的详细指示
poor a. 贫民的,贫穷的,需要救济的
poor house 贫民院,教养院
poor law (英)(简称)济贫法,贫民救济法(指1601年在英国女王伊丽莎白一世的授权下,英国政府制定并颁布《伊丽莎

白 43 号法案》)
Poor Law Act of 1601 (英)《1601 年济贫法》
Poor Law Amendment Act (英)《济贫法修正案》(英国保障法史上的重要的《新济贫法》)
poor peasant (中)贫农
poor performance 软弱的履行,执行不力
Poor Prisoner's Defence Act (英)《保护穷苦贫民犯人法》(1908 年)
poor quality 质量差
poor quality product 质量差的产品
poor rate 济贫税,贫民救济税
Poor Relief Act (英)《贫民救济法》(1601 年)
poorer class 穷苦阶层
pop-up menu 弹出的菜单
popery n. 教皇制度
popular a. 人民的,大众的;普及的,流行的;大众化的;受欢迎的
popular action (英)请求判处罚金的诉讼(指一般人或第三人对一定的刑事案件可以民事诉讼方式,请求判处被告罚金,胜诉后罚金的部分可给予原告,此种方式已于 1951 年被废除)
popular chamber (英)下院,众议院
popular conscience 大众的良知
popular council 人民委员会
popular election (或 suffrage) 普选
popular feelings 民心
popular front 人民阵线
popular government 民众的政府
popular group 群众团体
popular jury (墨西哥)群众陪审团
Popular Name Table (美)《普通名称目录》[指以谢泼德(Shepard)命名出版的案件名称检索工具书,此目录也以法规的名称列出许多法规以便参考]
popular opinion 民意
popular opinion poll 民意测验
popular organization 群众组织
popular participation in 人民参政;人民参与国事
popular referendum 全民公决,公民投票
popular sense 普遍的意义,普遍的含义;常识

popular song 流行歌曲
popular sovereignty 人民主权;人民主权论(指美国南北战争前的一种政治见解,主张各州人民有权处理其内政)
popular verdict 公众的意见
popular vote 民众选举;普选
populares n. (古罗马)平民党
population n. 人口;全体居民;殖民
population census 人口普查
population control 人口控制
population density 人口密度
population fluctuation 户口波动,人口波动
population pressure 人口压力
population pyramid 表示人口分布的统计图表;人口金字塔
population statistics 人口统计
population surplus 人口过剩
populism n. (美)(19 世纪末)人民党的主义
Populist Democrat (美)人民党的民主党党员
(the) Populist Movement (19 世纪末美国的)人民党运动
populus n./a. (罗马法)民众,人民,罗马公民的全体或整体总称,包括贵州与平民(patricians and plebeians)
Populus Romanus 罗马民众
porne (希文)色情
pornographic a. 色情画的;色情文字的
pornography n. 色情画;色情文学;黄色读物
porrect v. (宗教法律中用语)提出(公文);出示
port n. 港口;港市;口岸
port activities 港口作业
port authority 港务局
port charges 港口费,港务费;港税,入口税
port clearance 港口结关
port dues (=harbor dues) 港口税,港口费
port efficiency (=port speed) 港口装卸效率
port investment 港口投资
port of arrival 到达港
port of call 停泊港,停靠港
port of delivery 交货港
port of departure 始发港,起运港

port of destination 目的港
port of discharge 卸货港
port of dispatch 发货港
port of distress 避难港
port of embarkation (或 embarcation) 装载港,起运港
port of entry 进口港,输入港;报关港口
port of registry 登记港口,船籍港
port of transshipment 船运中转港,转运港
port tax 港口税
port-to-port contract 港至港合同(契约)
portability estimates of a given benefit 一个给定利益的概审估计
portage n. 1.水陆联运;(两水陆间的)陆上货物运送 2.运输,搬运;运费,搬运费
Porte n. (帝制时代)土耳其政府
porterage n. 搬运业;搬运行李;运费
portfolio n. 1.公文包,文件夹 2.阁员(或大臣)职务,部长职务 3.未满期责任4.有价证券;(保险上的)业务责任
portfolio approach 投资组合法(指使用现代投资组织理论来评价投资组合价值的波动性。见 building block approach)
portfolio effect 整宗投资效果,风险的均衡效应
portfolio foreign investment 国外证券投资
portfolio investment 有价证券投资;证券投资,间接投资
portfolio management 有价证券管理
portfolio theory 投资搭配理论
portio hereditaria 继承份
portio legitima 法定特留份
portio statutaria 寡妇的特留份
portio virilis 平均继承份
portion n. 嫁妆;分与遗赠财产(指父母婚姻赠与财产所得的部分或全部,留给子女的财产);一部分,一份;(单)命运
portion of the estate (遗产)应继分
portioner n. 获得遗产、嫁妆的人;分得财产的人
portionist n. 获得一份遗产(或嫁妆)者
portionless a. 没有遗产份的,无承继份的
portray v. 描写;扮演
portreeve n. 城市中区的治安法官,执达官;(英)副市长

Portuguese law 葡萄牙法
* *Portus est locus in quo exportantur et importantur merces.* A port is a place where goods are exported or imported. 港口是货物进出口的地方。
pose a grave danger to other 对他人构成威胁
posit v. 安置,安排;论断;假设,假定
position n. 位置,方位;地位,身份;职位,职务;形势,状况;姿态;见解,立场;阵地
(a) position paper 表明立场的文件
positive a. 实证的,确实的;肯定的;明确的;积极的;正面的;绝对的
positive act 积极行为
positive causal relationship 必然因果关系
positive coexistence 积极共处
positive condition 肯定条件,积极条件
positive conditions of an action 积极诉讼条件
positive connection 必然联系
positive consensus 肯定式共识,以共识做出肯定表示
positive contract 已证实的合同(契约),已确认的合同(契约)
positive denial 明确否认
positive development 正面发展
positive duty (或 obligation) 积极义务
positive economics 实证经济学
positive evidence 直接证据,确证
positive factor 正面因素,积极因素
positive general prevention 积极的一般预防(指通过刑罚适用实现对刑法的忠诚;消极的一般预防指在刑罚的威吓下又分两种形态:肉体威吓和以心理威吓为特征的一般预防)
positive guarantee 积极的保证,积极的担保
positive harmonization 积极协调
positive implication 实证含义,实证的言外之意
positive international law 实在国际法(又译:实证国际法)
positive jurisprudence 实在法学(又译:实证法学)
positive law 实在法(又译:实证法);制定法;成文法;现行法

positive liberty 积极自由(权)
positive misprision 侵占(挪用)公款;贪污渎职
positive misrepresentation 正面的虚伪陈述
positive morality 实证道德
positive political theory 实证政治理论(P. P. T.)
positive prescription 确定时效,积极时效
positive probability 正概率,实证概率
positive proof 直接证据;肯定(的)证据(与 negative proof 相对)
positive redes 明确的计划;明确的劝告(建议)
positive resale royalty rate 积极的转销版税率
positive rights 积极的权利(指个人要求国家采取积极行为的权利:如各种社会福利、工作权、受教育权、社会救济权、保证权、休假权等,对于这些权利,国家不得消极地不作为)
positive servitude(s) 积极地役(指一国准许他国或其人民对其领土的一部分进行有限控制)
positive settlement 肯定和解
positive sovereignty 积极主权
positive theory of litigation and settlement 和解和诉讼的确定理论
positive waste 积极损耗,积极损毁
positive wrong 蓄意的不法行为
positivism n. 实在法主义(又译法律实在主义、法律实定主义、实证法学说);实证主义
positivist n. 实在法学派(又译实证法学派,这一派认为国际法的基础,几乎完全建筑在惯例和条约之上);实证主义者,实证论者
positivist jurisprudence 实在主义法学(又译:实证主义法学)
positivist philosophy of law 实证主义法哲学
* *Posito uno oppositorum, negatur alterum.* One of two opposite positions being affirmed, the other is denied. 两个相反的主张其一被肯定时,则另一应该加以否定。
posse 可能性
posse comitatus (州长或郡的司法行政官可随时召集用来维持治安或帮助强制执法的)武装力量;地方武装团队(又译:民团。指古代英国郡内公民组成的维持地方秩序的一个机构)
possess v. 1.持有,占有,具有 2.支配,控制;保持 3.使获得(财产)
possess landed property 拥有地产
possessed things 占有物
possessing arms 持有凶器
possessio 占有,拟据为己有的占有
possessio bonorum (=*bonorum possessio*)资产占有
possessio civilis (罗马法)合法占有,善意占有
possession n. 1.有,持有,占有 2.所有权,所有物 3.(常用复数)财产;领地,属地,殖民地
possession by entireties (二人共同的)全部占有(所有权),不可分割的所有权;共同占有
* **Possession is nine points of law.** (=Possession is nine-tenths of law.) 占有者在诉讼中总占上风。现实占有,败一胜九。
possession money 保管费(指执达官完成执行令后暂时代为保管财产的费用)
possession of drug (私)藏有毒品,私藏毒品
possession of housebreaking implements 持有入屋行窃的工具
possession of right 对权利的占有
possession of thing 对物的占有
possession of unexplained property (英)持有无法解释的产业(按防止贿赂条例,指公务员拥有财产与其现在和过去职位、薪酬不相称的,除非他能够向法院作出圆满的解释,否则是犯罪的)
possession of unlawful objects 持有非法物品
possession theory 占有理论(指占有内幕消息者有向交易对方公开信息的义务,而且信息未公开前不得买卖公司股票,也不得以牟利为目的散布虚假信息。见 temporary insider theory)
* ***Possession vaut titre.*** Possession is deemed to be ownership. (动产的)占有视为所有

(原则)。
possessive a. 占有的,所有的,占有欲的
possessor n. 拥有者,所有者,持有人,占有人
possessor *bona fide* 善意占有人
possessor *mala fide* 恶意占有人
possessor of a double nationality 具有双重国籍者
possessory a. 所有的,占有的;所有者的;由占有而产生的
possessory action 确定占有权的诉讼;(土地等所有制的)占有诉讼
possessory assize(或 **assise**) 占有(权)性诉讼审理
possessory interest (无所有权的)单纯占有权
possessory judgement (对某人)继续占有土地的判决
possessory lien 占有留置权
possessory remedies 占有权上的法律救济
possessory right 占有权
possessory right by finding 因发现所取得的占有权
possessory things 所有制,占有物
possessory title 占有取得的土地产权
possessory title to land 土地占有权
possibility of credit 偿债能力的可能性;信贷可能性
possible father (私生子的)可能的父亲
possible object 疑似物体,怀疑的可能物体
post n./v./ad. 1.邮件;邮政;邮寄 2.职位;职守 3.哨兵;岗位;哨站 4.(交易所)交易台 5.(会计)过账/1.贴(布告等),公布,提示 2.使列入公布名单内 3.公告不得侵入/在后
post a reward 公告悬赏
post acceptance 事后承兑
Post CLS (美)后批判法学
post date 迟签日期
post diem 日后
post factum 事后,事后行为
post hoc 此后,因此
post hoc, ergo propter hoc 倒果为因,把发生在后的事实或现象作为发生在前的事实或现象的原因
post import financing 进口后资金融汇

post judgment 判决后
post liberalism 后自由主义
post litem motam 诉讼开始后,起诉后
post mark 邮戳
post no bill 不准张贴
post obit bond 以第三者死亡为清偿期的债券
post office 邮局
post responsibility system (中)岗位责任制
post voting 通讯投票
post-act n. 事后行为
post-audit n. 事后审计
Post-Brexit 脱欧后的英国〈it's the firmst sign yet of the seeming in exorability of Brexit...〉(在看似不可阻挡的英国脱欧进程中,这是迄今为止最明确的迹象说明……)
post-conviction remedies (PCR) 判罪后的补救(指对于判罪表示异议的程序)
post-date v. 1.把日期填迟;预填(支票等)日期 2.时间上后于……
post-date bill of exchange 迟填日期的汇票
post-dated instrument 在文据上填迟日期(指按汇票法例规定,汇票和支票等均可填迟日期)
post-establishment n. 投资设业后[《多边投资协议》(MAI)草案将国民待遇原则扩大到投资设业前(pre-establishment)的阶段,而不仅限于"投资设业后"阶段]
post-free a. 免付邮资的;邮费付讫的
post-modern approach to international law 后现代国际法研究方法
post-modernism n. 后现代主义(指20世纪60年代产生于西方发达国家的一种法文化思潮,它涉及人文社会科学诸多领域。后现代法学是指后现代主义立场和方法渗透到法学领域后形成的诸多新说新论)
post-obit n./a. (他人)死后(高利)偿还的借据(指某人以其将来所应得的遗产或期待获得的财产作为抵押而签订的高利借据)/死后生效的
post-obit bond 死亡偿还借据(指以某人

或某一指定人死亡后应得遗产作抵押的借据);(他人)死后清偿的协约(又译:太子账协约,指向人借款签立借据,说明等到其被继承人死后才能按高于法定利率并多还的契约)
post-office inspectors 邮政视察官(员)
post-paid a. 邮资付讫的
post-sale confusion of non-customers 售后非买卖人的混淆
post-trial motion for judgment 审(判)后作出判决的动议
postage n. 邮资,邮费
postage-due stamp 欠资邮票
postal a. 邮寄的;邮政的,邮局的
postal address 通信地址
postal ballot 邮寄选票
postal forbidden articles 邮政禁寄品
postal insurance 邮件保险
postal item 邮件
postal law 邮政法
postal (money) order 邮政汇票
postal remittance 邮政汇款
postal savings certificate 邮政储蓄凭证
postal service agreement 邮政协定
Postal Union 万国邮政协会
postea (初审的)诉讼笔录;(初审的)正式陈述
posteriores 后裔
posterity n. 子孙,后代;后裔
postglossators (或 **commentators**)(复)n. 后注释法学派(指12世纪罗马法复兴后以罗马法为研究对象,继注释法学派第二批法学家)
postgraduate professional education (美)研究生一级的(律师)专业教育(指美国大学法学院招收考生以已在其他院系获得学士学位为限,故称 postgraduate education,其培养专业目标为律师,亦称 professional education)
posthouse n. (旧时)驿站,驿栈;(古)邮局
posthumous a. 1.死后的,身后的;父死后出生的,遗腹的 2.死后(作品)出版的
posthumous adoption 遗腹子出生后的领养
posthumous birth 遗腹出生(子女)
posthumous child 遗腹子女(指父或母死

后出生之子女。通常此词多指父亲死后出生的孩子,但至少有一种情形:合法的要死的怀孕妇女必然保持其生命维护器官直至孩子安全出生,这样才有可能成为母亲的遗腹子。见 after born child)
posthumous works 遗著
postiche n./a. 代替物;伪装物;仿制品;伪装/伪造的,假冒的,假的,人工的;补加的,不适当的
posting n. (会计)过账;登入(总账)
posting audit 过账审计
postliminium n. (罗马法)(罗马人进入不友好的其他国被剥夺权利后,如又返回罗马时的)权利恢复;(罗马法)复境权(指恢复公民的权利或身份时,视为未陷于奴隶,而取消其自为奴隶所生之一切后果之含义);(国际法)战后(敌人侵占的)财产恢复权,战后恢复公民权
postliminy n. 战后财产恢复权;(俘虏等回国后)战后公民资格恢复权
postman n. 1.邮递员 2.(英)理财法庭的初级律师
postmodern n. 后现代
postmortem n./a. 1.验尸;尸体解剖 2.事后评价或检讨/死的;验尸的;事后的
postmortem cooling 尸冷(死后体温下降)
postmortem delivery 死后分娩,棺内分娩
postmortem dismemberment 死后分尸,死后碎尸
postmortem examination 尸体检验
postmortem fingerprinting 尸体指纹捺印,死后指纹捺印
postmortem injury 死后伤
postmortem inspection 验尸
postmortem interval 死后经过时间,死后间隔时间
postmortem lividity 尸斑
postmortem phenomena 尸体现象
postmortem putrefaction 死后腐败,尸体腐败
postmortem rigidity 尸僵
postnuptial a. (结)婚后的
postnuptial agreement (1834年)婚后协议(指结婚期间所达成的当事双方协议,确定在离婚,分居或死亡时夫妻一方对他

方财产所享有的权利。更常称为 a property settlement or marital agreement。常缩略为 postnup., 亦称 postnuptial settlement。见 prenuptial agreement）
postnuptial settlement 见 postnuptial agreement
postpone v. 延搁,延期;迟误
postpone a sentence of punishment 缓刑
postpone without day 无限延期
postponement n. 延期;延迟
postponement of execution 延期执行
postponement of trial 延期审讯
postponement subordination of a lien, mortgage 抵押权的延期（指具有一般的优先权）
postremogeniture n. （英）（遗产的）幼子（女）继承权制（1925 年已废，= borough-English）
postscript (P. S.) n. （信件中的）附笔；（书中的）附加资料
posttraumatic a. 创伤后的,继发创伤的
posttraumatic neurosis 创伤后神经官能症
postulate n./v. 假定,假设/要求,假象,以……为出发点
potent a. 有力的,强有力的,（药方）有效力的,（男性）有性交能力的
potentate n. 当权者;统治者;君主;有权势的人
potentia 1.可能性 2.权力
* *Potentia dedet sequi justitiam, non antecedere.* Power ought to follow justice, not go before it. 权力应依正义行使,而不得超越正义。
* *Potentia non est nisi ad bonum.* Power is not confered but for the public good. 权力只为公益而授予。
potentia propinqua 有希望的可能性;按常理可能实现者
potentia remota 可能性太小,渺茫的可能性
potential n./a. 潜势,潜能,潜力;隐痕迹,无色印痕;潜在性,可能性/潜在的,有可能性的,隐存的
potential criminal 可能犯罪者;潜在的罪犯
potential damage 潜在损害,潜在损失
potential danger 潜在危险

potential evidence 可能的证据
potential intervener 潜在的介入诉讼,潜在的介入诉讼人［指①必须拥有与作为诉讼标的产权或交易相关的一项权益；②当没有介入诉讼人时对诉讼处理可能会损害介入诉讼人保护该权益的能力；③必须证明现有的诉讼当事人并未充分代表介入诉讼人的权益］,潜在的参加诉讼人
potential investor 有意投资者,潜在的投资者
potential jurors 可能性的陪审员,预备陪审员
potential lawsuit 潜在的诉讼,可能的诉讼
potential multiple liability 可能的多重责任,潜在的多重责任
potential utility 潜在效用
potential witness 潜在的证人,可能的证人
potentiality for international navigation 国际航行可能性
potestas 权力,权限;统治权;支配,统治
* *Potior est conditio defendentis.* The condition of a defendant is the better. 被告处于较有利地位。
* *Potior est conditio possidentis.* The condition of a possessor is the better. 占有者处于较有利地位。
Potomac n. （美）波托马克河（位于美国首府华盛顿）
Potsdam Proclamation 《波茨坦公告》（又称《波茨坦宣言》,全称为《中美英三国促令日本投降之波茨坦公告》,于 1945 年 7 月 26 日发表,苏联后来也加入）
potwalloper n. （英）成家后才有选举权的人,为获得选举权而成家的人（亦作 potwaller）
pound n. 1.（收留迷失牲畜的）兽栏 2.监牢;拘留所 3.（扣留财产的）待领所,待赎所 4.磅
pound of flesh 一磅肉（原出自莎士比亚《威尼斯商人》）（合法但极不合理的要求）,全部数额
poundage n. 1.磅税 2.（走失家畜的）待领场;家畜赎领费 3.监禁
poundbreach n. 破门而入从没收财物存放所盗走没收的货物（罪）;破门而入从收

留迷失牲畜圈栏盗走待领的牲畜(罪)
pour-over trust 遗嘱信托(指遗嘱中的一项条款指明将不动产中之剩余财产予以信托)
pour-over will 信托遗嘱(见 pour-over trust)
pourparler 预备性谈判,谈判前磋商
pourvoi en cassation 向最高法院上诉
poverty n. 贫困,贫穷;缺乏
poverty affidavit 贫穷起诉人的宣誓书(同 IFP affidavit)
poverty law (美)贫困法,济贫法
poverty of thought 思维贫乏(思维表达障碍的一种,即思维内容空洞,抽象思维能力几乎丧失殆尽,表现概念与词语贫乏,说及简单和具体事物语速正常,但只要一问到与抽象思维有关的内容便回答不出来,与这样的患者交流十分困难。与思维迟缓的病人有相似之处,但思想贫乏病人对自己状况浑然不觉,表现也麻木与冷漠。见 thought of insertion)
power n. 1.权力;政权;势力;权限,权力范围;能力;(复)职权 2.强国,大国 3.有权力的人;有影响的机构 4.授权证书
power broker 政治掮客,权力掮客
power coupled with interest 附有利益的权力
power coupled with an interest (18世纪)兼有产权的代理权[指被授权人具有一定行为的代理权,而且是被授予标的本身的某项权益或产权的权力。这种兼有产权的代理权并不为了被代理人的权益而持有权益,而且如果因争议财产(subject property)中代理人利益(agent's interest)原因,这种代理权会被终止。因此,有些权威人士认为这不是"真正的代理权"(true agency power)。此术语亦称 power given as security; proprietary power。见 irrevocable power of attorney; naked power]
power elite 权力精英,权力上层人物
power given as security 见 power coupled with an interest
power in deciding 裁决权
power of absolution 赦免权
power of acceptance 承诺权
power of administering law 执法权
power of administration 行政管理权
power of advancement (受托人)预付(部分)托管财产(给受益人之)权
power of agency 代理权
power of alienation (财产)转让权
power of appointment (决定财产归属的)指名权,任命权,委任权[指一个人被授予并保留拥有财产分配的权利(power),他有权将财产给指定受让人或使受赠人享有将得到的份额,特别是有权通过遗嘱授予受赠人(donee)或通过根据选择或决定一个或一个以上的受领人获得赠与人(donor)的房地产(或遗产)或收入。如果这个权力行使于受赠人死亡前,则此权力行使完全有利于受赠人。如果这个权力采用遗嘱赠与,则这种行为是完全支持受赠人的遗产赠与。亦称 enabling power;常缩写成 power]
power of appointment and removal 任免权
power of appointment as to remainder in the trust 指定分配此信托中剩余财产的权力
power of arrest 拘捕权
power of attorney (美)委托书,授权(书),(民法意义上的)委托,权利转移证书[指①保证某人为授予人作为代理人或事实上的受托人(attorney in fact)的授权书或委托书。这个一般的委托书是根据委托人的死亡后无行为能力(incapacity)的情况可以撤销,作废或自动终止。亦可称为 letter of attorney。②授权,在契约或协议说明中阐明如此授权,其法定能力可在通过授权的行为改变法律关系,即授权可限定在一定范围,也可是一般的和全权代表]
power of attorney coupled with an interest 见 irrevocable power of attorney
power of attorney endorsement 委任背书
power of attorney to manage property 管理财产的委任书
power of attorney to perform operation 办理业务的委任书
power of commercial agent 商务代办权

power of compulsory purchase of land　强制购买土地权;土地征购权
power of conciliation　调解权
power of contracting a treaty　缔约权
power of delaying bills for a short period of time　短期延迟法案通过权
power of demand and supply　供需能力
power of detention　拘留权;扣押权
power of disallowance　驳回权;驳复权
power of disciplinary control　纪律监督权
power of disposition　处分权
power of government　统治权
power of interpretation　解释权
power of law-making　立法权
power of leadership　领导权
power of legislature to validate marriage　立法机关(议会)宣告婚姻有效的权力
power of life and death　生死予夺之权
power of police order　警察命令权
power of preventive arrest　防范性拘捕权
power of procuration　委任权
power of pit and gallows　(苏格兰)(贵族)淹死或绞杀(罪犯)的权力
power of punishment　惩罚权
power of random search　任意搜查权
power of recognition　承认权
power of redemption　赎回权
power of representation　代表权,代理权
power of reservation　保留权
power of revision　修改权
power of revocation (=power to revoke)　(行为的)撤销权
power of sale　买卖授权书;销售权
power of self-government　自治权
power of self-management　自行管理权,自主权
power of signature　签署权
power of termination　终止权
power of the American Supreme Court to declare a law unconstitutional　美国最高法院宣布某项法律违宪的权力
power of the head of the house　家长权
power of the keys　教皇享有的最高权力;(基督教)司钥权;钥匙使用权(指妻子在家事方面有代表其丈夫的权力)
power of the purse　(美)(国会具有的)财政大权(指government行政部分不得开征任何捐税和增加税源,未经国会表决不得开支任何费用)
power of the sword of justice　司法权,裁判权
power of validation　确认权
power of veto　否决权
power oriented　权力型,导向权力
power politics　强权政治
power right　权力,权
power structure　(社会、组织等)权力结构
power struggle　权力斗争
power to adjudicate　审判权
power to adjudication　审判权
power to arrest without a warrant　无逮捕证的有权逮捕;无证逮捕权
power to charge tolls　掌管通行税的权力
power to execute instruments　签署书证的权力
power to forbid　阻止性权力
power to interpret the constitution　解释宪法权,宪法解释权
power to interrupt the legislative progression　中断立法程序权
power to intervene　干预权
power to make by(e)-laws　制定实施细则的权力
power to make claims at international level　国际索偿权
power to make treaties　缔约权
power to proclaim war　宣战权
power to promulgate law　颁布法律权
power to prosecute　追诉权
power to reduce a charge　降格起诉的权力(指检察官有权对被告人提起一项比证据所能证明的罪行要轻一些的指控)
power to replace　撤换权
power to sign　(代表)签字权
power to supervise through auditing　审计监督权
power-holder n.　实权派;掌权者
power-monger n.　角逐权力者,争权者
powerful a.　强有力的,有权威的,有影响力,有实效的

powerful counter 强有力的回击
powerful drip on political realities 强有力的控制政治现实
powerful interests 可观的利益
pracdatio 掠夺,缴获
practicable a. 可通行的,可实际使用的,可适合的
practical a. 事实上的,实际上的;接近……的;实用的;实践(上)的
practical case 具体案件;特定案件
practical effect 实际效力,实际使用效力
practical limitation 惯例上的限制
practical owner 事实上的所有人,事实上的物主
practical politics 可实施的政治;实用政治
practical reasonableness 实践理智性(自然法学者菲尼斯认为,人类基本幸福或基本价值有七种形式;生命、知识、游戏、美感、社交、宗教及实践理智性)
practical sovereignty 事实上的主权
Practical Training Institute 实习训练学院(指澳大利亚绝大多数州规定法学学士获得者在正式执业前必须在实习训练学院学习一定时间或在执业律师事务所担任一定时间的培训律师或助理律师)
practical unanimity (意见的)几乎一致
practical wisdom 实践智慧(指既体现于了解何者对自我及一般意义上的人有益,又涉及"合乎逻辑的、真实的能力形态",并以此"为人的利益而行动"。与利益相并,意味着实践智慧以价值的关切为题中意义。亚里士多德又指出:"实践智慧指向'一种好生活',并关乎人'总体上的有益生活'合乎逻辑体现理性的品格";为人的利益而行动"则是与价值追求相联系的实践活动。实践智慧所内含唯一目的,内在地规定了实践和行动的方向,从心物关系看,目的关乎内在理想、意向与外在的存在法则)
practice (美亦作 practise) n./v. 1.实际;实行;惯例;实践 2.(律师、医生等)开业手续;诉讼手续,诉讼程序;常规;律师业务/实行,实践;开业;办理手续;习惯于
practice and public companies 上市公司和非上市公司,公营公司和私营公司

practice court 诉讼程序法庭(亦称保释法庭,指从前英国王座法院附设的法庭,专办保释事务及决定特殊诉状和诉讼程序)
practice direction (法院的)程序指示、指导;诉讼程序指南
practice law 执行律师职务,做开业律师
practice master 诉讼程序主事官(指英国王座法院轮流一人出庭回答有关诉讼程序疑难问题的主事官)
practice of advocacy 律师业务
practice of law (17世纪)1.律师执业,执行律师业务[指包括广泛范围的服务,诸如在法庭上处理案件(conducting cases)、准备必需的文件以便各种交易防止土地有效合并、以不同的法律观点准备法律意见书(legal opinion)、起草遗嘱和其他不动产计划文件以及对于客户的有关法律问题的咨询等。这个术语也包括一些很少律师从事但要求法律专家知识的法律实务(legal expertise),比如起草立法或法庭规则,亦称 legal practice。practise v.]
practice of the court (法院的)诉讼程序
practice orders 诉讼程序的次序
practician n. (医生、律师等)开业者;熟练者
Practicing Law Institute (美)实践法律学会(指一个非营利性组织,它出版书籍并办学习班培训律师);执业律师学会(英)(1933年成立,主办过许多法律刊物)
practicing lawyer 开业律师,执业律师
practise at the bar 挂牌做律师,开业做律师
practise bribery at election 贿选
practise fraud 行骗
practise intimidation and bribery 威迫利诱
practise law (=practise the law) 开业做律师,(律师)开业
practise usury 放高利贷
practising accountant 执业会计师
practising certificate (律师、医生)开业证书;执照
practising legal profession 开业的律师界
practising solicitor 开业撰状律师
practitioner n. 开业者(尤指律师、医生等);从业者

practization of theory　理论的实践
praeceptio haeredictatis　(苏格兰法)无偿取得的继承(指一种消极的权利,如果继承人愿义务承担偿付被继承人的全部债务,则该继承人有资格无偿接收死者遗产,即使份额很少)
praecipe(=precipe) n.　1.原令状,诉讼开始令(指法院要求被告做某事或不做某事所发出的命令)2.(英)申请便笺(指法院的便条,诉讼当事人可在条上书写他需要法院代他办理或发出文件的请求)
praecipe quod reddat　(令被告)归还占有土地原令状
Praector n.　古罗马选出的执政官,掌握军权的执行官
praedatoria navis　掠夺船;缉私船
praedial a.　土地的,不动产的;农业的;应提供地役的
praedial servitude　地役权
praedium　土地,不动产
praedium dominans　需役地,应提供地役的土地
praedium serviens　承役地
praefectus urbi　(古罗马)城市行政长官
praemium　报酬,补偿
praemunire(或 **premunire**) n.　(英国法律)王权侵害罪(亦称主张教皇为最高权力罪,指不服从国王而服从教皇,认为教皇的权力比英王权力更大的罪名)
praenomen　(除姓以外的)名
praepositura　(通过合同)使丈夫负责(承担维持家庭生活的财产义务)
praepositus　(英)掌权者
praescriptio　时效;取得时效,(由于长期占用等而)获得权利
praescriptio acquisitiva　取得时效
praescriptio dormiens　时效停止
praescriptio extinctiva　消灭时效
praestare　给付
* *Praestat cautela quam medela.*　Prevention is better than cure.　预防胜于治疗,防止胜于纠正。
praesumptio　推定,推断
* *Praesumptio, ex eo quod plerunque fit.* Presumptions arise from what generally happens.　推定应从普遍发生的情况中产生。
praesumptio hominis vel facti　事实的推定
praesumptio juris　法律上的推定
praesumptio juris et de jure　法律和权利上的推定,不容反证的法律推定
praesumptio juris tantum　可用反证否定的法律推定
praeter legem　(古罗马)(超越)法律以外
* *Praetextu liciti non debet admitti illicitum.*　Under pretext of legality, what is illegal ought not to be admitted.　借口合法并不能认定他人为非法。
praetor(或 **pretor**) n.　(古罗马每年选出的)军事执政官;主管司法的保民官;裁判官
praetor peregrinus　(罗马法上的)外事法官,外事裁判官
praetor tutelari　(古罗马)监护执行官
praetor urbanus　(罗马法上的)内事法官,内事裁判官
pragmatic a.　1.独断的,固执己见的 2.实用主义的,实用的 3.好事的
pragmatic approach　务实取向;务实的方法,务实的态度
pragmatic consideration　务实的考虑,注意实效的考察
pragmatic jurisprudence　实用主义法学
pragmatic sanction　国事诏书(指罗马帝国后期调整国家重要事务的法律文件)
pragmatica n.　(西班牙殖民地法)国王敕令
pragmatically expedient　务实上的权宜之计,务实便利
pragmaticism n.　实用主义
pragmatism n.　实用主义;干涉主义;独断;自负
pratique n.　(船只检疫后发给船长的)检疫通行证
praxeology n.　人类行为学
praxis　使用;惯例
* *Praxis judicum est interpres legum.*　The practice of the judges is the interpreter of laws.　法官的审判实践就是在解释法律。
prayer n.　祈求,恳求(常指原告希望法院准予求助等请求的表示);诉讼请求

prayer for relief 救济请求
pre-action protocols （英）（民事诉讼中实施的）诉前议定书（制度）[指当事人在提起诉讼之前，首要要按照诉前议定书的要求进行一系列活动。到目前为止，英国已制定10个诉前议定书，分别是：人身伤害诉前议定书（1999年4月26日起实施）、医疗过失诉前议定书（1999年4月26日起实施）、建筑和工程诉前议定书（2000年10月2日起实施）、诽谤诉前议定书（2000年3月4日起实施）、专家责任诉前议定书（2001年7月16日起实施）、司法审查诉前议定书（2002年3月4日起实施）、疾病纠纷诉前议定书（2003年12月8日起实施）、房屋破损诉前议定书（2003年12月8日起实施）、基于购置自住房欠款的占有权请求诉前议定书（2008年11月19日起实施）、基于抵押欠款的占有权请求诉前议定书（2008年11月19日起实施）。诉前议定书制度总的目的在于鼓励当事人尽量在起诉前通过替代诉讼的纠纷解决机制解决纠纷，将诉讼作为最后的救济手段。如果不能避免的话，促进对案件有效管理，这一目的主要通过当事人交换争议的有关信息和考虑适用ADR（Alternative Dispute Resolution）来实现]
pre-action seizure 诉前扣押
pre-answer motion 答辩状之前的申请
pre-charge case screening （美）提起指控前的案件过滤[指当警察将犯罪嫌疑人被捕的刑事案件移送至检察官办公室后，案件就进入过滤阶段。美国各版本的《国家公诉标准》中均专章规定如何在此阶段进行案件过滤。其一，检察官可以在正式审查时"拒绝"（reject）受理案件。通常而言，那些被拒绝之案件"不会再有任何针对犯罪嫌疑人的后续追诉行为"。其二，检察官还会对符合特定条件的案件采取转处程序（diversion）。转处程序通常与延缓起诉结合使用，从而使被告人免受起诉之耻辱，并积极回归社会。见case screening]
pre-contractual negotiation 订约前的谈判
pre-empting state 优先购买国
pre-establishment n. 投资设业前（见post-establishment）
pre-existing work 已有作品，原作（一般指"演绎作品"）
pre-indictment case screening （美）正式起诉前的案件过滤[指美国联邦宪法规定，在嫌疑人被捕后，必须"无必要延迟地"接受首次聆讯。在绝大多数司法管辖区中，检察官若决定对案件提出指控，便会尽快将其移送法院接受聆讯。首次聆讯通常在限制管辖权的初级法院进行。审理者可以是法官，也可以是治安官或司法官。此时，司法官对于"合理根据"（probable cause）的单方面审查是对于被告人是否在"事实上有罪"的第一道司法过滤（judicial screening）。如果法官（治安官或司法官）认为证据不足以支持指控的话，则会驳回对嫌疑人的指控。当然，由于该环节的审查是行政性的（ministerial），而非对抗性的。因此，初级法院法官或治安官几乎不会（seldom）履行对案件的过滤职能。另外，针对警察以重罪名义移送之案件，检察官并不会不加区别地提起重罪指控。有些案件则以轻罪加以指控。见case screening]
pre-investment project 投资前项目
pre-judgment seizure 判前扣押，审判前进行扣押
pre-modern states 发达前国家
pre-packed articles 预先包装条款
pre-performance n. 履行前
pre-performance bargaining advantage 履行前协商的优势
pre-printed standard form contract 制式合约
pre-trial reviews 审理前审查
preach v. 布道，宣讲，劝诫；鼓吹，宣扬
preach down 贬损，（用说教或讲话）当众折服
preamble n. （法规、条约等的）序言，导言，序文，绪言
preappointed evidence 预先指定证据（指法律所要求的特定举证）
preaudience n. （英）（法庭上一方辩护律师的）优先发言权
precarious a. 不稳定的；不安全的；前提有

问题的;不确定的;根据不足的
precarious right 不确定的财产权;不确定的权利
precarium 无偿占有;随时可被收回的假占有
Precation 任前带薪假期[为可数名词,亦可写作 pre-cation,意指新员工在开始工作前获得的带薪假期。该词由前缀 pre-(先于,在……前)和 vacation(休假,假期)的后半部分组成。产品设计师阿尔·阿布特2013年4月14日在为艺术工作者和设计师提供作品在线服务的 Dribbble 网站上首先使用这一表达方式。身为多家初创公司创始人的弗里德曼一直专注工作,无暇休假。基于自己的经历和感受,他推出了一项政策:"在42Floors公司,我们强烈建议所有新员工休假两周,从此他们第一天入职开始……任前带薪假期无法解决一切问题,但它至少是一种以良好方式开始新工作的方法。"]
precatory (=precative) a. 恳求的,请求的
precatory trust (遗嘱的)恳求的信托
precatory words (遗嘱中)请求的话,拜托的话
precaution n. 预防;预防措施;警惕
precautionary measures 预防措施
precautionary patent 预告专利,预防性专利
precautionary principle 预防原则
precede v. 先于,位于……之前,(地位等)高于
precedence (=precedency) n. 领先;在前(的状态,行为);优先权
precedent n./a. 先例;判例,惯例;/在前的,在先的;优先的
precedent case 先例案件
precedent condition (=condition precedent) 先决条件
precedent in point 与先例切合的
precedent not in point 与先例不切合的
precedent on all fours 与先例完全一致的
precedented a. 有先例的,有先例可援引的
precedential support 判例支持
preceding a. 在前的,在先的,前面的
preceding article 前条
preceding cases 前面的判决,先前判例

preceding clause 前项,前款
preceding mortgagee 前抵押权人
preceding paragraph 前段,前节,前款,前项,前目
preceding president 前任总统(或主席)
preceding years 以前的年份
precensor v. (新闻、书刊、影片等)预先审查
precinct n. 区域(在美国指地理上的一个单元,如"选区""警区""司法管辖区"等等。在英国则指皇宫、法院、教堂等紧邻周围的土地)
precinct n. (美)管辖区;(美)选区;分界,分区;范围内
precipitate v. 促使,加速;使突然发生,猛损
precipitate recognition 过急的承认
precise a. 精确的,准确的;恰好的;拘泥的
precise mathematical equality 准确的数学均等
preclude v. 预防;排除,消除;阻止;杜绝
precludi non debet 不排除[指针对被告提出的终结诉讼答辩(plea in bar)原告所进行的驳辩或答辩状(reply)的起始语,对于答辩状中所提的各种理由均不能排除原告对被告的诉讼。有时该术语缩略为 pre-cludi non]
preclusion n. 预防,排除;阻止,妨碍
preclusion order 排除令(指在诉讼中禁止一方以未发生的事实为基础构成论据的法官令)
preclusive effect 排除效力
precognition n. 预见,预知;(苏格兰)预审时提出的证据
precognition of witnesses (苏格兰)预审证人;预审时提出的证据
precommitment n. 预先羁押
preconceived ideas 先入之见,成见;预想
preconception n. 先入之见,成见,偏见
precondemn v. (不调查或审讯地)预先确定有罪
precondition n. 前提,先决条件
precontract n. 前约(指一合同签订之前,已签订的另一相同性质的合同);(尤指婚约方面的)预约;婚约
precursors n. 先驱者,先锋;前辈,前任

predate v. (在日期上)先于,把……日期填早
predatory a. 掠夺性的;掠夺成性的,以掠夺为生的
predatory price discrimination 掠夺性价格歧视
predatory pricing 用低价销售撵走竞争者以支配市场的行为;低价以求垄断行为,掠夺性定价
predatory stage (美)掠夺阶段[指美国学者卢萨(Lupsha)1996年提出关于有组织犯罪可能对国家的影响三个阶段的理论模式。第一个阶段是"掠夺阶段"(predatory stage),犯罪组织以特定的地区为根据地并试图保持在该地区非法使用强力的垄断地位。第二个阶段是所谓的"寄生阶段"(parasitic stage),在此阶段,有组织犯罪通过腐败与权力的经纪人建立联系,这个阶段常依赖于某种"机会之窗"(Windows of opportunity),如美国历史上的禁酒时期(prohibition era)以及哥伦比亚普遍存在的贩毒时期,此时腐败成为有组织犯罪与权力经纪人建立联系的黏合剂(Glue),有组织犯罪通过腐败的手段向经济、政治领域渗透。第三阶段为"共生阶段"(symbiotic stage),在这个阶段,有组织犯罪与政治体制之间形成相互融为一体的紧密关系,卢萨举了卡利贩毒集团(Gali drug cartel)对哥伦比亚立法和司法体制的影响以及意大利黑手党与基督教民主党40年勾结关系的例子,卢萨指出:"到了共生阶段,国家传统的执法工具不再起作用,因为有组织犯罪已是国家的一个组成部分,成为了国家中的国家。"]
predatory war 掠夺性的战争
predecease v./n. 死在(某事件)之前,比(别人)先死/早死,先死
predeceased parent 已故父母
predeceased spouse 已故配偶
predecessor n. 1.前辈,祖先;被继承人 2.前任者 3.原主;(被取代的)原有事物
predecessor in title 原始财产所有权人
predeprivation hearing 执行剥夺前的听证(会)
predetermined amount 预定全额

predial(或 **praedial**) a. 土地的,不动产的;与土地有关的,附属在土地上的
predial servitude 土地劳役
predial tithes (征收田产的)什一税
predicate v./n. 断言,论断……;使基于,使依据;意味着,具有……的含义/本质,属性,宣布,声明
predicate act (1977年)1.见 predicate offense 2.见 lesser included offense 3.依据 RICO,两个或两个以上相关勒索行为(racketering)中之一种行为,必须是合谋的这一行为 4.附属性的行为[指在法律后果(legal consequences)之前一项必须完成的行为可能附属于法律后果的,或附属于另一行为或在未来发生行为之前]
predicate offense 见 lesser included offense
predictability of law 法律的可预测性
prediction n. 预测,预言
prediction studies 预测研究
predictions for the trial rate 预测案件受审率
predictive theory of law 法律的预测说
predidential commission 总统授权,总统委任
prediscovery meeting 调查前会议(指美国民事诉讼审理前的程序之一,即根据《联邦民事诉讼规则》第26条第6款要求所召开的会议。双方当事人或其律师可在会上讨论各自的请求和抗辩,以探求和解的可能性,并按上述第26条第1款之规定进行证据披露。当事人在会议过程中将制定并提交发现计划给法院)
predisposition n. 事先安排(处理);犯罪倾向(指被告人实施受指控罪行的准备犯罪的心理倾向)
predominant a. 占优势的;支配其他的(over);主要的;突出的;流行的
predominant factor test 决定性因素测试
preduction of witness (英)证人举证
preelect v. 预选;预先选举
preelection n. 预选;预定
preeminent guardian 杰出的监护人(保护人)
preempt v. 先取,先占;以先占(土地)而取得先买权

preemption n. 优先购买权[指①抢先占用取得的公共土地的优先购买权(preemption right);②根据这一权利优先购买的物品;③(国际法)早先扣留或占用的物品;④占有公共土地以确立优先占有权(preemption title);⑤(宪法)美国至上条款原则:即联邦法律可高于或取代与美国宪法相抵触的州法或法规,即联邦专有权(federal preemption)。见 complete-preemption doctrine]

Preemption Act of 1830 (美)《1830年预先占有法》(见 Preemption Laws)

preemption claimant 优先购买土地权的请求人(指已先占有优先购买的条件的土地目的在于善意采用满足合乎法律规定的条件来取得该土地的所有权)

Preemption Laws (美)《先占先买权法》(指《1830年预先占有法》以来颁布一系列有关土地的出售、分配的联邦法律)

preemption right (美)土地先购权(指持有者或政府给予土地的移居或开垦者的特权,即有权以规定价优先购买这块土地。见 preemption)

preemptive a. 有优先购买权的;优先购买的;先发制人的

preemptive action 先发制人的行动

preemptive rights 优先权,优先购买权[指每次发行新股时,现有股东有权按其持股比例在其他人之前优先购买新股。优先之目的是防止因公司发行新股导致现有股东所持股票的淡化(dilution)而影响其对公司的控制]

preengagement n. 预约;订婚约束;先得,先占

preestablish v. 预先设立,预先制订

preexisting claim in the property 财产上原有权益的诉讼请求

prefect n. 1.(古罗马的)长官;高级文武官员;地方行政长官;司令官 2.(法国的)县长;(巴黎的)警察局局长 3.(某些国家的)省长;(专区)专员

prefect of police (法)警务总监

prefecture n. (法)县长的职权(或职位、官邸);(古罗马)地方长官的职权(或职位、官邸);大行政区;府;县;专区;地区

prefecture de police (法)行省警察部队;(巴黎)警察局

prefer v. 1.宁愿,宁可;更喜欢〈the heroine preferred death to surrender〉[女英雄宁死不降(屈)],〈I should prefer you not to stay there too long〉(我宁愿你在那不要待太久) 2.提出(声明,请求,控诉)〈prefer a charge against sb.〉(对某人提出控告),〈the defendant claimed he was innocent of the charges preferred against him〉(被告对于对他提起指控,而他主张自己是无辜的) 3.(古)提升,提拔(to),推荐,介绍 4.优先偿付,给予优先权〈the statute prefers creditors who are first to file their claims〉(制定法给予债权人以优先权,他们可以最先提出权利请求) 5.(美)"preferred stock"优先股(指持有者可优先提取股息,并有权在公司清理时优先取回股金)

prefer a boll of indictment 提出起诉书
prefer a charge against some one 告发某人,对某人提出控告
prefer a complaint(或 charge) 控告,起诉;提出控告
prefer public charges 提起公诉
preference n. 1.优先得到偿还的权利 2.优先;优先权;(关税等的)特惠 3.选择机会;选择权;偏爱
preference bond 优先公债券
preference changing norms 改变偏好的规范
preference clause 优惠条款,特惠条款
preference dividend 优先股息,优先股利
preference function 优先函数
preference shareholder 优先股股东,优先股持有者
preference shares 有优先权的股份,优先股
preference stock 有优先权的股票,优先股(票)
preference system 特惠制
preferences in force 现行优惠
preferential n./a. 优先权;特惠/优先的;特惠的;先取的
preferential assignment 特惠转让;优先转让
preferential ballot 选择投票法的选票
preferential clause 特惠条款
preferential creditor 优先债权人

preferential debt 优先债务
preferential debtor 优先债务人
preferential duty 特惠税
preferential interest rate 优惠利率
preferential measure 优惠办法
preferential order of voting 选择次序的投票(指可在选票上指明对几个候选人的优先选择次序的投票)
preferential payments 优先付(款)给(指在宣布破产、公司结束、遗产管理的案件中,获得优先支付的债款)
preferential rates 优惠税率
preferential right 优惠权;优先权
preferential right to renew the contract 更新合同(契约)的优先权
preferential shop 优惠商店(指工会会员可享受先租用的商店)
preferential surcharge 优惠的附加税(费)
preferential system 择优(投票)制;选择投票制
preferential tariff(或 agreement) 优惠关税(协定),特惠关税(协定)
preferential tariff cut 优惠减税额;特惠减税
preferential tariff system 特惠关税制
Preferential Trade Agreements (PTAs)《优惠贸易协定》
preferential trading agreement 特惠贸易协定
preferential transfer 优先转让;优惠转让
preferential treatment 优惠待遇,优待
preferential voting 选择投票法(指利用投票结果来表示选举人对候选人支持程度的一种选举方法)
preferment n. 1.(购置财产等的)优先权 2.(控告等的)提出 3.晋升,升级;有利可图的职位
preferment of claims (根据优先权)提出索赔;提出请求
preferred a. 优先的;选择的
preferred creditor 优先债权人
preferred income 优先收入
preferred liability 优先债务
preferred share/stock (without voting rights) (无表决权的)优先股,(美)优先股(持有者优先享受股息,并在公司清理时有权优先取回股金)

pregnancy n. 怀孕;孕期;充满,富有意义
Pregnancy Discrimination Act of 1978 (美)《1978年禁止怀孕歧视法》(指禁止雇主因女性受雇者怀孕、分娩或其他相关之医疗情况而给予任何歧视待遇的法规。目前该法已被并入1964年《民权法》第7章)
pregnancy outcome 丰富成果
pregnant a. 怀孕的;含蓄的;有意义的
pregnant negative (= negative pregnant) 暧昧的否认;含蓄的否定
pregnant woman 孕妇
prehistory n. 史前史;史前考古学;史前背景
prejudge v. 预决,预先判断;未获充分证据而作判断,未经详究而判断
prejudgment n. 未经审讯的判决;预断;臆断
prejudgment attachment 未决之前的扣押,预先判断的扣押(指在案件判决前的一项扣押令。见 provisional attachment)
prejudication n. 预先判决;预先判断;判例
prejudice n./v. 偏见,成见;损害;侵害;不利/使受损害,侵害;不利
prejudice of judge 法官(对两造中一方)的偏见
prejudicial a. 有损害的;不利的;有偏见的
prejudicial act 侵(损)害行为
prejudicial error 可以更改的错误(指上诉法院可以推翻的原有的错误裁决, = visible error)
prejudicial to security 妨害安全
prelaw a. (学制上)法律预科的
prelaw student 法律预科生
preliberation n. 解放前的
preliminarily approve 初步审定;初步核准
preliminary a. 预备的;初步的;开端的
preliminary act 预备诉讼行为(指因船舶相撞索取赔偿的诉状在未交法院前,应先将船舶相撞的情形用文件密封送交法院)
preliminary action 预备诉讼
preliminary advice 初步建议
preliminary agreement 预约
preliminary arrest 预先逮捕

preliminary complaint （1833年）起初控告书,初步控告书[指为获得犯罪嫌疑人(criminal suspect)的管辖权而由法院签发的犯罪控告书,并据此听审有关合理根据(probable cause)或是应对嫌疑人羁押交付审判]
preliminary contract 预备性合同(契约)
preliminary criminal procedure 刑事预审程序(指庭审前的所有程序)
preliminary detention 候审羁押
preliminary enquiry 预审调查
preliminary examination 预审;预考
preliminary expenses （公司成立的）创设费
preliminary hearing 调查庭;预审（刑事诉讼法中同 preliminary examination）
preliminary hearing binding over 预审(听证)具结(指主持预审听证的法官要求被告具结保证出庭受审或不再犯罪的一种司法行为)
preliminary hearing court 预审庭;预审法院
preliminary injunction(s) 预防性禁制令,临时禁制令(起诉后判决前法院发出的禁制令,禁止被告实施或继续某项行为)
preliminary inquiry （英）预先审查(指将被指控罪犯带到治安官法庭预先审查,以决定是否将其交付审判);初步调查
preliminary investigation 预先调查,初步调查;(检察员的)侦查,临时调查
preliminary investigator 侦查员
preliminary (examining) judge 预审审判员,预审法官(旧译:预审推事)
preliminary matters （美国民事诉讼中）预备性事项(指在最终的审理前会议上未能得到解决的法律或实际问题,要求在审判之初引起注意)
preliminary motion before trial 审前预备性申请,审前前期申请
preliminary objection （国际法院的）初步反对意见
preliminary preparation of the case 案件的准备程序
preliminary procedure of conciliation 审判前的调解程序
preliminary proof 初步证据

preliminary question （国际私法）先决问题
preliminary ruling(s) （欧洲法院对欧共体和有关条约的解释等所作的）先决裁定,先行裁决
Preliminary Screening Board (PSB) （美）预审委员会
preliminary trial 初审,预审
premarital agreement 婚前协议,婚前协定,亦称 premarital contract（见 prenuptial agreemen）
premarital contract 见 premarital agreement; prenuptial agreement
premature n./a. 早产婴儿/过早的,不成熟的,提前的
premature action 过早诉讼,提前诉讼
premature birth 提前出生(指未足月出生的孩子)
premature delivery 提前交货
premature tax write-off 过早的税收冲销
premeditate v. 预先计划;预谋;预先考虑
premeditated a. 经预先计划的;预谋的
premeditated design （杀人案的）预谋
premeditated homicide 谋杀
premeditated intent 预谋;故意;蓄意
premeditated murder 谋杀,故意杀人
premeditation n. 预谋;预先计划;预谋犯罪
premier n. 首相;总理
premier fine （古）（英格兰）令状获得的基本费用[指在向法院申请开始转让财产(to begin a conveyance)的原始令状而向国王交纳的基本费用]
Premier of the State Council （中）国务院总理
premiership n. 总理职位(或职权);首相职位(或职权)
premise n./v. （14世纪）前提[指从中推断出结论的先前陈述或争议。英国英语(in BrE)亦拼写为 premiss]/提出,前提
premises （15世纪）1.上述各点,前述各点[指同一文书或文件中的前面部分通常提到的各个事实或观点〈wherefore, premises considered, the plaintiff prays for the following relief〉(因此,考虑到上述各点,原告祈求获得下救助)]2.(土地转让契据的)部分(指陈述土地转让契据中的部分,以及说

明交易当事人,确认相关事实和解说交易原因等)3.房屋,建筑和房屋连地基〈smoking is not allowed on these premises〉(在一带房屋连基地之处禁止吸烟)
premises open to general use 公共场所
premises rule 见 parking-lot rule
premises to let 出租房屋
premium n. 贴水,升水;利息,红利;报酬,佣金,酬金;奖品,奖赏,奖金;额外补贴;额外费用;补付地价;保险费;期权费[指为购买证券期权(option)而支付的费用,又叫 option premium];溢价
premium bonds (英)政府的有奖债券
premium due 到期保险费
premium loan (人身保险公司借给投保人付)保险金的贷款
premium pay 加班工资;假日工资;奖金,额外酬劳
premium quality 一流质量,优质
premium rates 保险费率;(外汇)升水率
premium returns 额外收益,额外利润
premium system 奖金制度
premium tax (美)保险税(指保险人就其对受保人缴纳保险总收入交纳的保险税)
premunire n. 见 praemunire
prenatal a. 出生前的,胎中的
prender be baron (英)获得丈夫,已婚
prenotice seizure 通知前扣押
prenup. n. 见 prenuptial agreement
prenuptial a. 结婚前的,结婚前订立的,婚前产生的,亦称 antenuptial(见 postnuptial)
prenuptial agreement (1882 年)(美)预备婚姻协议,预备结婚协定,婚前协议[指男女双方在结婚前订立的协议,通常是为了解决因离婚或配偶一方死亡而终止婚姻所引起的扶养和财产分配(property division)问题。亦称 antenuptial agreement; antenuptial contract; premarital agreement; premarital contract; marriage settlement,有时亦缩略为 prenup。见 postnuptial agreement; cohabitation agreement]
prenuptial gift (1921 年)婚前赠与[指前将财产从一方转移到另一方。在共同财产状况(community-property states)下,婚前赠与通常使其保持为"单独财产"

(separate property)的类别。亦称 antenuptial gift]
preoccupancy n. 1.先占,先取;先占权 2.全神贯注
preoccupation n. 1.先占,先取 2.偏见,成见,先入之见 3.急务
preparation n. 准备,筹备
preparation of the budget 编制预算
preparatory a. 预备性的;准备的;筹备的;初步的
preparatory committee 筹备委员会
preparatory crime 预备犯罪;预谋犯罪
preparatory hearings (英)准备性听证程序
preparatory judge 预审法官
prepayment n. 预付费用
prepense a. 故意的;预谋的;蓄意的
prepense malice 犯意
prepetition a. (1938 年)预先申请[指在呈递申请(特别是破产申请)前即已存在。"预先申请追偿债务之诉"(prepetition debts)]
prepetition agent 见 custodian ②
preplan v. 预先计划(规划)
prepolitical society 前政治的社会
preponderance n. (17 世纪)分量上的优势,重要性的优势,影响上的优势(preponderate v.; preponderant a.)
preponderance of the evidence (18 世纪)占有证据的优势,证据优势[证据的较重大分量并不必然取决于证人的多寡来试图证明事实,而是由最有说服力(convincing force)的证据;优势的证据分量虽不能足以解脱心中全部的合理怀疑(all reasonable doubt),但它仍足以让你心中倾向于公平、公正的一边,而不是另一边。这是大多数民事案件审判中的举证责任(burden of proof),审判中陪审团受指示裁定具有强有力证据的当事方胜诉,而另一则可能为败诉了。亦称 preponderance of proof; balance of probability。见 reasonable doubt; clear and convincing evidence]
preponderance of probability 盖然性占优势
prerequisite n. 先决条件;必要条件;前提
prerogative n./a. 特权;天赋特权;(英)君

权,帝王的特权/有特权的;有优先投票权的
prerogative court (英)特权法院(指保留给国王行使自由裁量权、优惠特权和法定豁免权的法院);(审查遗嘱等的)大主教法庭;(美)(英殖民地统治时期的)总督委任组织的法庭
prerogative law 特权法
prerogative legislation (英)(皇家的)特权立法
prerogative of mercy 特赦权,赦免权
prerogative of the Crown (英)王室特权
prerogative order 命令书;禁令;令状
prerogative writ 紧急令;(英)(君主)特权令(指英高等法院限制下级法院超越权限的法令)
presbyter (大陆法和宗教法上的)长者;祭司;长老;牧师
preschool education 学龄前教育
prescient opinion 有预见的意见;判决意见中所预见的
prescribe v. 1.命令,指示;规定 2.(通过长期占有等而)要求(权利等)(to, for) 3.使(过期限而)失效(或不合法) 4.(因时效而)消灭(或失效)
prescribed a. 法定的;规定的
prescribed examination 法定检验;法定审查
prescribed limit 规定范围
prescribed penalty 法定刑罚;规定的罚款
prescribed period for litigation 诉讼时效
prescribed procedure 法定程序,法定手续
prescribed supervision 法定监督
prescribed time 规定期间,法定期间
prescript a./n. 命令的;指示的;规定的/命令;训令;法令;指示;规则
prescription n. 1.时效;因时效而取得的利益 2.命令;指示;规定;法规 3.惯例;传统 4.处方,药方
prescription act 诉讼时效法
prescription for execution (刑罚)执行的时效
prescription in criminal law 刑法上的时效
prescription of action 诉讼时效
prescription term 规定的时限
prescription with the right to take polls and dues 享有通行税和收取费用权而取得长期占有
prescriptive a. 1.规定的;指示的;命令的 2.因时效而取得的;长期使用而获得的 3.惯例的;约定俗成的
prescriptive period 时效期
prescriptive right 因时效而取得的权利
prescriptive right to property 因长期使用而获得的财产权
presence n. 在场(指行为或事件发生在所处的地点或在听、视所及范围之内)
presence of an officier 警察面前
presence of court 法庭上,到庭,当庭
presence of defendant 被告到场
presence of the court (在)法庭面前(藐视法庭罪用语)
presence of the defendant's property within the forum 被告财产在审判地(州)的存在
presence of the testator 遗嘱人面前
present n./v./a. 现在,目前;(复)本证书,本文件,本契据(用作表示证书、文件、契据的本身);赠礼,礼品/1.介绍;引见;出席;出庭 2.控告,告发 3.出示,提出 4.赠送/目前的;现在的;在场的,出席的
present a plea 提起诉讼
present ability 现场行为能力(常用来说明侵犯人身罪构成要素的术语,用以表示被告造成伤害的行为能力)
present authorities 当局,现政当局
present capital value 资本现值
present enjoyment 现时的占有和享用
present estate 现时占有的地产,现有地产
present interest 现时占有的财产收益
present law 本法
present oneself 出席,到场
present promisee 当下受约人
present promisor 当下(本契据)立约人
present recollection recorded 暂时回忆的文件(指可帮助证人恢复或唤起对过去事件的记忆,此文件证据为证人之证据)
present recollection revived 暂时回忆的恢复
present regime 现行体制
present section 本条,本节,本条文
present sense impression 当场印象

present sitting 现在审理,现在开庭期
present statutory authority 现行的法规性权威
present term 现开庭期,现期限,现任期
present the court with … 向法院提出……
present use 即时使用(权)
present value 现值
present value index 现值指数
present value of income from investment 投资收入现值
presentation (15世纪)1.(根据信用证)提起诉讼[指根据信用证,将文件交付给签发人(issuer)或指定的人以达到提起诉讼之目的;正式提交票据必须承兑或付款(acceptance or payments)。见 presentment 3]2.(宗教法)圣职推荐[指有圣职推荐权人或圣职授予权人(patron)向主教推荐圣职候选人以充职空缺。如果主教拒绝被提名人(appointee),有圣职授予权人可依据妨碍圣职推荐令或妨碍圣职推荐之诉(quare inpedic)在普通民事诉讼法庭(Common the Court of Plea)强制执行此项充职空缺的权利]
presentation copies 见 free copies
presentation of credentials 递交国书
presentation of evidence 出示证据
presentation of the case 案件的陈述
presentation of the cheque 支票的提示(付款)
presentee n. 受赠者;被推荐者
presentence a. 判决以前的
presentence hearing 判决前审理(指法官在正式判决前审阅案卷的全部有关材料的程序)
presentence investigation (PSI) 判决前调查(指法院对已判定有罪的罪犯进行有关其背景的调查,作为量刑的依据)
presenter n. 告发者;提出者;推荐者;任命者;赠送者
presenting public prosecution 提起公诉
presentment n. 陪审员的直接控告书(报告书)(指大陪审团在没有接到控诉状的情况下,根据他们自己的了解或观察认为已有犯罪事实而向法院提出的说明书或报告);公诉;大陪审团提出的公诉,控诉状;陈述,表示;(依规定时间、地点)提出票据提示(指收据、汇票以及要求付款)
presentment for acceptance 承兑提示
presentment of a bill for acceptance 出示票据要求承兑
presentment of a bill of exchange 汇票提示
presentment of a case 对一案件的陈述
(by these) presents 根据本文件(或本契据)
preservation n. 保管,保存,保护;维持;维护
preservation of environment 环境保护
preservation of peace 维护和平
preservation of physical evidence 保存物证
preservation of the public domain 公共领域保留(指将知识产权限制在一定期间和范围之内,公共领域是典型的"知识共有物",即知识产品的非专有领域,根据规定专利权和著作权的保护期限届满后,原受保护的知识产权即进入公共领域。后来美国联邦宪法在著名的知识产权三项政策中专门规定"公共领域保留")
preservation of public peace 维持治安
preservation of rights clauses 权利保留条款
preservation order 保存令,维持令[指给予财产拥有人的一项命令,要求维护历史建筑,或保留自然的产地(habitat)]
preservative measures of property 财产保全
preserve v. 保护,维护,维持;保存,保藏;使流传;禁猎
preserver n. 保存者,保管人;保护人,维护者
preshipment inspection 装船前检验
preside (at, over) v. 主持;负责;指挥;管理
preside at lawsuit 听讼,主持诉讼
presidency n. 1.(美)总统直辖的政府机构(包括决策机构等)2.总理的职位(或职权、任期)(中)(国家)主席的职位(或职权、任期)3.院长、庭长、董事长、总经理、社长、会长或大学校长的职位(或职权、任期)4.管辖区 5.主宰,支配
president n. 1.(美国等)总统;总裁;大臣,议长;会长;(中)(国家)主席;(联合国大会)主席 2.院长;庭长 3.(银行等)行长(总裁);社长,大学校长;董事长;总经理
(the) president elect (尚未就职的)当选

总统;当选的下届议长、会长
president judge 主持法官
president of law court 法庭庭长;法院院长
President of Supreme People's Court (中)最高人民法院院长
president of the council of ministers 部长会议主席
president of the Family Division (英)(高等法院的)家事法庭庭长
president of the government 政府总理,政府主席
president of the national assembly 国民议会议长
President of the People's Republic of China (中)中华人民共和国主席
president of the Republic 共和国总统;(中)国家主席;(美)共和党主席
president pro tempore 临时议长[指在美国参议院议长(副总统为参议院的当然议长)缺席时,主持参议院的参议员]
President's Assistant for National Security (美)总统国家安全事务特别助理
president's cabinet (美)总统的内阁[指此内阁只对总统负责,而不对国会负责。总统内阁是习惯和传统的创举,起始于乔治·华盛顿时期。美国联邦宪法提到一组总统顾问(presidential advisers),"总统可令各行政部门主管长官,以书面发表关于其职务任何事项的意见"(第2条第2款)]
President's Council on Competitiveness 总统竞争力评议会
(the) President's official family 政府内阁
president's running mate 总统的选择伙伴(指与总统一起竞选的副总统的人)
presidential a. 1.总统的;议长的;(中)主席的;院(庭)长的;总经理的;董事长的;社长的;会长的;大学校长的 2.统辖的;主宰的;支配的
Presidential Assassination Statute (美)《(防止)行刺总统法》
presidential bid (美)总统投标;总统竞选
presidential campaign 总统选举运动
presidential candidate 总统候选人;(独立机构)主席候选人
presidential democracy 总统制的民主政体
presidential documents (美)总统文件
presidential election 总统选举
presidential election campaign fund 总统竞选基金
presidential electoral college (美)总统选举团(见 presidential electors)
presidential electors (美)总统的选举人(美国总统选举又名选举人制度,是间接选举,即首先由州的选民投票选出本州的总统选举人,然后由各州的总统选举人投票选举总统、副总统);(美国各州选出的)总统和副总统选举团
presidential government 总统制政体
presidential immunity (美)总统免责权
presidential inauguration 总统就职典礼
presidential mandate 替任总统,代总统
presidential meeting 总统会议
presidential message (美)总统向国会提出的国情咨文
presidential nominating conventions 总统提名会议
presidential primary (美国大选的)预备选举
presidential primary candidates 总统选拔候选人,总统首要候选人
presidential proclamations 总统公告
presidential regime 总统制
presidential system of government 总统制政体
presidential term 总统任期
presidential type 总统制
presidential veto message (美)总统否决说明
presidential year (美)总统选举年
presidentialism n. 总统制
presider n. (会议的)主席,主持者
presiding a. 主持的,执行的
presiding arbitrator 仲裁庭长
presiding chairman 执行主席
presiding judge 审判长;主持法官(亦为某些州一审法院的院长,亦称 chief judge 或 chief justice);法庭庭长;审判长;首席法官(旧译:首席推事)
presidium n. 主席团;常务委员会

presidium of the federal assembly 联邦议会主席团
presitious legal practice 有声望的法律实务,有威信的律师开业所
press n./v. 出版;新闻;印刷;新闻界;出版界;通讯/贯彻,迫使接受(on, upon);复印
press and printing 出版印刷
press censor 新闻检查官(员)
press communique 新闻公报
press conference 记者招待会
press law 出版法;新闻法
press release 新闻发表
press room (政府机关中的)记者室
pressing to death 酷刑致死
pressure n. 1.压力;强制 2.紧迫,紧急,艰难;困苦 3.电压
pressure group 压力集团(指用游说、宣传等手段对议员们施加压力,以便左右立法或政策来维持自身利益的集团)
prestable a. (苏格兰)可履行性的
prestation n. (古英国法)给付;履行;付款
pretended intoxication 佯装醉酒(与actual intoxication 相对)
prestige n. 威信,威望
presuit(或 **prelitigation**)**discovery** 诉前披露程序
presuit examination 诉前检查
presumable a. 可假定的,可推测的,可推定的;可能的
presume v. 推定,假定,假设;擅自,敢于;滥用,利用;意味着
presume on one's position 滥用职权
presume someone innocent 推定某人无辜
presumed agency 推定代理
presumed consent 推定同意
presumer n. 1.推定者,假定者 2.冒昧的人,放肆的人
presumption n. 1.假定,推测,设想,推定;推断 2.作出推论的根据(或理由、证据);事实的推定
presumption as to the place of endorsement 背书地点的推定
presumption favoring pretrial release 有利审前释放推定
presumption from habit 根据习惯推断

presumption of accuracy 准确性的推定
presumption of death 死亡推定(尤指无确实证据说明某人失踪的原因而达到一定时间者,法律上可推定其已死亡)
presumption of fact 事实推定
presumption of good faith 善意推定
presumption of guilt 有罪推定
presumption of innocence 无罪推定
presumption of law 法律上的推定(指根据法律的规定,法院和法官应从一项特殊的事实或证据中引申出一项特殊的推断)
presumption of legitimacy (婚生子女的)合法性的推定
presumption of liability 推定责任
presumption of life 生存推定
presumption of marriage 婚姻的推定
presumption of negligence 过失推定
presumption of proof 推定证据
presumption of survivorship(或 **life**)(在共有财产中)生存者(对死者权利的取得权的)的推定,生存推定
presumptive a. 可推定的,假定的,由推定得到的
presumptive death 推定死亡
presumptive disappearance 推定失踪
presumptive disappearance and death act 推定失踪和死亡法
presumptive evidence 推定证据(指不是由实际上争论的事实来推出结论,而是凭一般道理来推出证据,和情况证据相同)
presumptive exist 推定存在
presumptive heir 假定继承人(在继承人出生时即失去继承权的人)
presumptive privilege 推定的特权
presumptive title 推定产权
presupposition n. 预想(的事);预先假定(的事);先决条件
pretax income 税前所得
pretax profits 税前利润
pretence n. 假装;借口,托词;(无事实根据的)要求;虚假
pretence of ignorance 假装无知
pretend v. 借口,托词;假装,装作;妄求;自称
pretended legal transaction 虚假的法律行

为,假装的法律行为
pretended right 伪称的权利,虚假的权利
pretender n. 佯装者,冒充者,妄求者
pretension n. 要求,主张;意图,借口
preterition n. 遗漏,忽略;遗嘱内遗漏合法继承人
preterlegal a. 无法律根据的;超过法律范围的
pretermission n. 忽略,遗漏;置之不问;省略;怠忽
pretermission of duty 玩忽职守
pretermit v. 忽略,遗漏(常指遗嘱中未提及的子女)
pretermitted heir 被遗漏的继承人(指遗嘱人因无意中的遗漏在其遗嘱里未被提及的配偶或子女或遗嘱后才出生的子女)
pretext n. 借口,托词
pretium 价金,价格,销售价
pretrial n./a. 预审;(美)审前预备会议/审判前的
pretrial conference (美)审前会议
pretrial discovery 审前披露程序
pretrial discovery procedure 审前披露程序(指普通法系国家民事诉讼中的证据由当事人及其律师自行收集,并在庭审时全部出示给法官和陪审团,不允许为补充新的证据而终止审理。为此,必须有适当手段和途径帮助当事人和律师在审理之前获得所需证据,这一手段和途径即"审前披露程序")
pretrial hearing (英美法)预先(审判前)的听证
pretrial meeting 审前会议[原本指在美国法庭审理之前,法官传唤双方当事人(实际为双方当事人的律师)为了顺利进行法庭审理而整理争点的会议。早在《联邦民事诉讼规则》规定审前会议之前,1926年密歇根州地方法院就已开始适用这一程序,即在诉答程序(pleading)结束后,法院传唤当事人试行和解。后来联邦民事诉讼规则咨询委员会将这种做法规定在《联邦民事诉讼规则》第16条之中]
pretrial motion(s) 审前动议,审前请求
pretrial order (美)审前决议(指民诉中包括审前会议各方同意的条款和项目,审

前决议引导审判的进行,双方当事人必须遵守)
pretrial probation 审前考察监督制(指美国20世纪50年代引入的一种对犯罪行为的审前考察制度,即经过一定考察如果认为犯罪行为人表现良好,可不予起诉)
pretrial procedure 审判前的程序
pretrial proceedings 审理前的程序
pretrial purposes 审前事项
prevail v. 胜,优胜;胜诉;流行,普遍;劝服(on,upon)
prevailing a. 占优势的;盛行的,通行的;有力的;主要的;当前的
prevailing costs 现行成本
prevailing economic ideology 现行经济意识形态,主流经济意识形态
prevailing opinion 占优势的意见,最普遍的意见
prevailing party 胜诉的一方
prevailing price 现行价格,时价
prevailing U. S. rule of conflict laws 美国现行的冲突法规
prevailing wage 现行工资
prevalent a. 盛行的,流行的,普遍的
prevarication n. 推诿,支吾其词,搪塞
prevaricator n. 推诿者,撒谎人
prevent v. 预防,阻止(from),制止,妨碍(from);预先应付(问题等),预先迎合(愿望)
prevent the new legislation from taking 1976 election 阻止新立法使不致采取1976年的选举办法
preventing justice 歪曲司法执行(指妨碍司法执行的一种罪行)
preventing wrongful imprisonment 防止非法监禁
prevention n. 预防,防止;阻止,妨碍;预防法
prevention costs 预防费用
prevention of accidents 防止事故发生,预防事故
(the) Prevention of Bribery Ordinance (英)《防止贿赂条例》
prevention of burglary 防盗
prevention of corruption 防止贪污
prevention of crime(s) 预防犯罪,防止犯罪

prevention of cruelty 防止虐待
prevention of disease 疾病防治
prevention of enemy agent 防特,预防特务(破坏)
prevention of epidemics 防疫,预防瘟疫
prevention of estoppel 防止翻供
prevention of fire 防火
prevention of fraud 防止欺诈
prevention of thievery 防盗
prevention principle 防止原则
preventive a. 预防的,防止的,妨碍的
preventive action 预防性行动
preventive attachment 假扣押,预防性扣押
Preventive Coastguard Service (英)海关缉私署
preventive composition 预防性和解
preventive detention 防护关押;预防性的监禁(尤指按英国1967年刑事审判法例,授权法院,可将惯常犯的服刑期延长,以防他继续犯罪)
preventive detention person without trail 未经审判对人进行预防性拘押
preventive detention warrant 防护关押令
preventive diplomacy 预防外交
preventive injunction 防范性禁令
preventive justice 预防犯罪的司法,(采用)预防措施的司法
preventive law 预防法(指专门对一些回避法律问题的人在法律问题发生之前给予法律帮助和法律信息的规定)
preventive measures 预防措施
previous a. 以前的;生前的;前述的,上面提及的
previous case 以前发生的案件
previous conviction 以前判的罪;有前科的人
previous crime 以前犯的罪,前科罪
previous election 上届选举
previous judg(e)ment 以前的判决,前判(决)
previous owner 原物主,以前的所有人
previous question (议会中的)先决问题(指对正在讨论的某议案应否立即投票表决的动议)
previously convicted 前科犯

prevot (法国革命前的一种低级)王室法官
price n. 价值;价格;代价;(对杀死或捉拿某人的)赏金;(贿赂的)金额
price agreed upon 约定的价金
price commission 物价委员会
price control 价格控制,物价控制,物价管理
price difference 差价
price discrimination 差价销售(即在两个市场上同一货物以两种不同价格出售)
price duty paid 完税货价
price elasticity 价格弹性
price exposure 价格披露
price fixing 限价,价格确定,定价
price fluctuations 价格波动
price for the goods 货物的价格
price index 物价指数
price law 价格法
price level 物价水平
price line 价格相同的一批货物
price list 价目表
price loco 当地价格
price maintenance agreement 维持物价协定(制造商和零售商之间订立的一种协议,该协议约定零售商保证不得以低于协议所规定的价格出售商品)
price markdown 减价
price markup 加价
price most advantageous 最有利的价格
price negotiated 议价
price of commodity 物价,商品价格
price of money 贷款利率
price of the shares not already paid 未缴股款
price packing (故意提高开价,以便削价出售,而仍大赚其钱的)噱头
price range 价格变动幅度
price stability 稳定物价
price standard 价格标准
price supports (美)(联邦政府用补贴或收购手段)保持价格的措施
price tag 价格(目)标签
price tribunal 价格裁判庭
price war 价格战(指采用一再削价的商业竞争)
pricing n. 定价,估价

pricing of capital asset 固定资产的估计（估价）
pricing policy 价格政策
priest-rule n. 僧侣统治
Priestly Code 《祭司法典》（指古希伯来法律汇编）
prima facie 初步的,表面的,表面看来
prima facie case 有表面(或初步)证据的案件,有希望立案的案件
prima facie case of damage 初步推定的损害案
prima facie evidence 表面证据(一般指对举证人有利的表面证据,除了将来再有证据把表面证据推翻之外,法庭可接受作为事实的证明)
prima facie presumption 初步推定,有表面语气的推定
prima facie void 初步无效,表面无效
prima（或 primae）impressionis （英美法）初见案件(指无确切权威典据可依,因而需按情理裁决的案件,亦即无先例可援的案件)
primacy n. 第一位,首任；大主教的职责；教皇的最高权力
primacy of right theory 权利优先论
primage n. 小额酬金；运费补贴；运费外的小费；船长酬金(指货主或收货人送给船长的小额酬金)
primarily ad. （美）1.首先,原先；起初；原来 2.主要地,根本上
primary n./a. 1.（美）（政党的）预选,初选；初选制；候选人选拔会 2.最主要者；居首地位/1.主要的,首要的；基本的 2.初步的；原来的,初级的
primary allegation （宗教法庭上）（诉讼中）一开始的答辩,首次答辩(亦称 primary plea)
primary argument in favor of a different standard 倾向于不同标准的主要论据,赞同不同标准的主要依据
primary assembly 公民大会；预选会
primary authority 首要权威(指①具有约束力的机构；②法规、法庭判决、规定和其他类似的法律渊源资料,而不是百科全书、论文等)

primary boycott 第一次联合抵制；直接抵制；初期抵制,第一次杯葛(指通过联合抵制试图劝说人民不使用、购买或运输雇主的货物)
primary caretaker 主要照护人,主要照顾人
primary cause 主因,根本原因
primary claim 支配基础权；主要权利主张,基本权利请求
primary court 初级法院,初审法院,基层法院
primary culprit 主犯,首犯
primary data 原始资料,原始数据
primary debtor 主要债务人
primary dependent 主要受扶(抚)养人
primary deposit 现金存款
primary election 预选,初选
primary evidence 原始证据；基本证据(亦叫最佳证据,指文件本身或文件原本的副本)
primary exporting country 初级产品出口国
primary fact 主要事实,基本事实
primary functions 第一位的作用(法律的直接作用可分为第一位作用和第二位作用)
primary industry 第一产业(包括农、林、渔、采矿、采石业等)
primary language analysis 日常语言分析派
primary legal norm 基本法律规范
primary liability (on bill of exchange) （汇票的）第一位责任
primary market 初级市场
primary material 原始资料,主要资料
primary of international law 国际法的首要地位
primary of national law 国内法的首要地位
primary parentelic group 第一亲等群
primary party 首位当事人
primary plea 首次答辩（见 primary allegation）
primary pollution source 主要污染源
primary powers （委托人授予代理人的）基本代理权,主要代理权
primary product 初级产品
primary purpose test 主要目的检测规则
primary right 优先权；主权利,原始权利；

原有权
primary right to exercise jurisdiction 实施管辖优先权,优先管辖权
primary rule(s) 初级规则,原始法则,原始规则,主要规则
primary scene 第一现场
primary source of law 基本法源
primary sources (美)原始资料(指可界定为将由国家强制执行而被记载下来的有关人们行为规范的规则。它们包括立法机构通过的成文法、法院的判决、颁布的法令和执行令以及行政机构的条例和规定)
primary sources of law 主要法的渊源(又译:主要法律渊源);主要法源
primary virtue 主要优势,主要优点,主要美德
primate n. 首席主教,大主教
prime v./a. 1.事先给……以指导;事先为……提供消息 2.装火药/首要的;最初的;原始的;基本的;头等的
prime a witness 开导证人(使他来作证)
prime cost 1.原始成本;主要成本 2.(善意购买货物所付的)原价
prime culprit 首犯,罪魁,正犯
prime maker (协议、文据的)签署人
prime minister 总理;首相;内阁总理;内阁大臣
prime minister's office 首相府;总理府
prime mover 1.首要煽动者 2.发起人
prime rate 最优惠利率;(银行贷款给信用极好的大公司所定的)最低利率
prime seisin (或 **seizin**)(=primer seisin) 初继承;(英)(土地保有人死亡时国王收取的)土地初继承捐赋;最先的土地占有
prime serjeant (英国法上国王的)高级御用状师
primer n./v. 1.入门书;入门;初级读本 2.第一 3.雷管,引火药/超载,胜过,优先于……占先,领先,居首位;奖偿,给以奖金
primer election 首选,首先进行选择(特别指:"共同继承人中,年老者有权挑选应得的一份土地遗产。")
primer statutory provision 以前的法律条文,旧法律条文
primi n. primus 的复数形式
primitiae (=primitae)(古)(英格兰)最先果实收获(见 first fruits 2)
primitive (=primitae) 见 first fruits
primitive accumulation 原始积累
primitive communes (或 **society**) 原始公社(或原始社会)
primitive economic systems 原始经济制度(指原始社会的经济制度)
primitive law 原始法
primitive state 原始国家(指文化人类学理论上的人类社会组织类型)
primo fronte at first sight 乍一看(之下),乍看起来
primo loco 第一位的
primo venienti 给先来者(指以前的遗嘱遗产执行人对债务清偿请求时,只要一经提出,即予偿付,而不管遗产是否足够清偿所有债务)
primogenitary a. 长子继承的
primogenitary succession 长子优先继承
primogenitor n. 始祖;祖先
primogeniture n. 长子身份,长子继承制[①长子身份(指兄弟姐妹之间最先出生的身份);②长子继承制(指长子继承先辈的土地和不动产的权利,并排除较幼的兄弟姐妹)。亦称 primogenitureship。见 borough-English]
primogeniture ship 长子继承制性质(见 primogeniture ②)
primum decetum (教会法)初步判决[指①作出原告胜诉的判决,即使原告未出庭应诉;②(海事法)临时判决]
primus n./a. 苏格兰监督教派之监督长/首位的,第一的;最年长的(常常与姓氏连用)〈Jone primus〉(最年长的约翰)
primus inter pares 贵族中的第一位;同辈中的带头人
prince n. 亲王;王子
princeps (罗马法)领导人,皇帝,元老
princeps senatus 首席元老(又称做"坐象牙圈椅的"元老)
princess regent 女摄政王;摄政王夫人
Princess Royal 大公主

principal n./a. 首长,长官,主管人;本人;当事人;委托人;主犯,正犯,(共犯的)首犯;第一被告;被保应付款的本人,主债务人;本金,母金,资金;祖传动产(指家族相传的物件)/主要的,重要的;为首的,第一位的
principal act 主行为;主犯行为
principal action 主诉
principal advisor 主要顾问
principal agent 委托代理人,主要代理人
principal and accessory 主犯和从犯,首犯和胁从犯
principal and agent 本人(指委托人)和代理人;雇主和代理人(指职工)
principal and interest 本和利,本息
principal and surety 主债务人和保证人
principal attorney 主要辩护人;第一代理人
principal cause of crime 犯罪主因
principal (general) challenge 主要(总的)回避(指因安排陪审团名单的司法行政官与一方有利害等理由所提出的要求回避);一个陪审员或全部陪审员的回避
principal channel 主航道
principal clause 主要条款
principal conspirator 主谋者
principal contract 主合同(契约)
principal debt 主债务
principal debtee 主债权人
principal debtor 主债务人
principal fact related to the crime 主要犯罪事实
principal goods 主物
principal governor 首席行政长官,行政首脑
principal in the first degree 第一主犯,首犯,一级主犯
principal in the second degree 第二主犯,主犯,二级主犯
principal legal adviser to the government 政府的首席法律顾问
principal legal system 主要法律体系,主要法律制度
principal murderer 主凶,谋杀主犯
principal obligation 主债务;主要义务
principal offender 主犯,正犯

principal office 总部,总店,总社
principal officials 主要官员
principal party 主要当事人;主要部分
principal penalty 主刑
principal plotter 主谋者,首谋
principal punishment 主刑
principal real right 主物权
principal right 主权利
principal sentence 判决主文
principal source of international law 国际法的主要渊源
principal sum secured by a mortgage 抵押所担保主债的金额
Principal Supplying Interest 主要供应利益
principal tax 正税
principal thing 主物
principal town 首府
principal trial 主审,主判
principal wife 正妻
principal's representative 委任人的代表人,委任代理人
principal's successor in interest 委托人的权益承受人
principal-to-principal transaction 买卖双方直接交易
principalis 1.本人,当事人 2.主债务人 3.主犯
principality n. 1.公国;侯国;封邑 2.公国君主的权力(或职位、领地)3.首长(或校长的职位或权力)
principate n. 最高权力;公国;封地;首领;王侯;(复)(古罗马保留主某些共和体制的)早期帝政;(罗马帝国)执政者的权力(或任期)
* *Principiorum non est ratio.* No argument is required to prove fundamental rules. 基本原则无须论证。
* *Principium est potissima pars cujusque rei.* The principle of anything is its most powerful part. 任何事物的原则是最有权力的部分。
principle n. 原理;原则;方针;政策,要素;主义,委托人[指股东与管理人之间构成了委托人(principle)与代理人(agent)的关系]

principle law office of crown （英）国王的主要法条官员
principle of a prescribed punishment for a specified crime 罪刑法定主义,罪刑法定原则
principle of advancing socialist culture and ideology （中）有利于社会主义精神文明建设原则
principle of assumed jurisdiction 裁量管辖原则(指在特定情况下,即使被告不在管辖国内,管辖国仍得依裁判权对其行使裁判管辖)
principle of centralization 中央集权原则
principle of checks and balances （权利的）制约和平衡原则
principle of collective leadership 集体领导原则
principle of comity 礼让原则
principle of concentration of preliminary hearing 预审集中原则
principle of *contemporaneas exposito* 以文件拟就时的意义为解释的原则
principle of correct application of the law 正确适用法律原则
principle of cross examination （诉讼中间向对方询人）诘问原则
principle of democratic centralism 民主集中制原则
principle of direct trial 直接审理原则
principle of dispatch （诉讼法）迅速（结案）原则
(the) principle of "double criminality" "双重归罪"原则
principle of effective nationality 有效国籍原则
principle of equal value exchange 等价交换原则
principle of equality 平等原则
principle of equality and mutual benefit 平等和互利原则
principle of equidistance 等距原则
principle of equitable burden sharing 公平分担原则
(the) Principle of Evolving Standards of Decency 发展中适宜标准原则(指这一原则属美国联邦宪法解释的重要原则,是为第八修正案注入时代活力的一项重要原则,核心是强调根据当代价值观念解读宪法。联邦最高法院在对第五、六、十四等修正案的适用中均采用过本原则进行解释)
principle of fairness 公正原则
principle of free intention 自由心证原则
principle of freedom 自由原则
principle of good faith 诚信原则,善意原则
principle of humanitarianism 人道主义原则
principle of immediacy （诉讼法）直接（审理）原则
principle of individual liberty 个人自由原则
principle of international law 国际法原则
principle of legality 法制主义,法定原则（见 legality 3）
principle of Islamic jurisprudence 伊斯兰教法学原则
principle of judical investigation 司法调查原则
principle of just law 法律的公正原则
principle of laches （权利人）及时主张权利的原则
principle of laissez-faire 放任主义原则;（政府）不干涉原则
principle of law 法理;法律原则
principle of legality 法制原则;法定主义
principle of legitimacy 正统原则
principle of market economy 市场经济原则
principle of marshalling （美）分配原则（美国破产法中的一种原则）
principle of monetary nominalism 唯货币名称论原则
principle of mutual loyalty between the contracting parties 合同当事人相互忠诚约原则
principle of mutual respect for sovereignty and territorial integrity 相互尊重主权和领土完整原则
principle of national self-determination 民族自决原则
principle of new interfering act 新介入行

为原则(见 ordinary hazard principle)
principle of non-discrimination 无差异原则[指对于存储在计算机中由计算机生成的数据信息,只要能保证首次是以最终"可视"或"可读"的完整形式表现出来的,就可将这种数据信息视同"原件"而将其采纳为证据,亦称功能等同法(function equivalence)]
principle of non-extradition 不引渡原则
principle of non-intervention 不干涉原则(不干涉别国主权范围内的事项,是现代国际法上一个公认的基本原则)
principle of non-reciprocity 非互惠原则
principle of occupier's liability 占有人责任原则
principle of operational independence of the enterprise 企业独立经营原则
principle of oral and written argument (诉讼法)口头辩论和书面辩论原则
principle of orality (诉讼法)言词审理原则,口头审理原则
principle of parliamentary immunity 议员豁免权原则
principle of party autonomy 当事人意志自由原则
principle of party control over allegation and proof 当事人掌握陈述和证明原则
principle of party initiative 当事人起诉原则
principle of perpetual allegiance 永远尽忠原则(指国际法中有些国家采取的国籍原则)
principle of personal jurisdiction 属人管辖原则
principle of presumption of innocence 无罪推定原则
principle of proletarian internationalism 无产阶级国际主义原则
(the) principle of proportionality 比例原则[指美国联邦宪法第八修正案禁止"残酷而异常的处罚"的规定本身就包括比例原则的要求。在立法原意上"残酷而异常的处罚"(cruel and unusual punishment)包含三层含义:未经授权的处罚、有失比例的处罚及折磨或野蛮的处罚。1976 年的

格雷格(Gregg)案中,联邦最高法院明确第八修正案应包含两层意思:一是刑罚不涉及不必要的或随意施加的痛苦;二是防止刑罚与犯罪的严重程度显失比例。前者涉及人性尊严原则,后者则属于比例原则的范围]
principle of public administration 行政原则
principle of public hearing 公开听审原则
principle of public opening 公开审判原则
principle of punishing the few and reforming the many (中)惩办少数,改造多数的原则
principle of reliance 信赖原则
principle of remoteness of damage 损失间接性原则
principle of remoteness of injury 伤害间接性原则
principle of representation 代位继承原则
principle of restitution 赔偿原则;恢复原状原则
principle of retroactivity 追溯效力原则,溯及既往原则
principle of securing the individual against harm 保障个人不使遭受损害的原则
principle of selecting the best qualified 择优原则
principle of separating investigation and judg(e)ment 侦查与审判分开原则
principle of separation of function, coordination and mutual check of judicial organs (中)(审判机关的)分工负责,互相配合,相互制约原则(刑事诉讼上的一项职权原则)
principle of specification 根据指定原则
principle of surrogation (保险过程中)承保人的代位原则(指保人付出赔偿给被保险人之后,继承受保险人的权利)
principle of taking facts as the basis and the law as criterion (中)(诉讼法)以事实为根据,以法律为准绳(原则)
principle of territoriality of criminal law 刑法的属地原则
principle of territory 属地原则,属地主义
principle of the autonomy of will 意志自由原则

principle of the decision 判决的原则
principle of the personality of the law 法律的属人原则
principle of the relativity of rights 权利相对论原则
principle of the separation of powers 分权原则
principle of the territoriality of law 法律的属地原则
principle of the utmost good faith and disclose honestly all facts relevant to the risk （保险法上保险人必须遵守的）最高诚信和真实披露一切有关危险的原则
principle of two instance 两审制原则
principle of uninterrupted trial （法庭）审理不间断原则
principle of universality 普遍性原则,世界性原则
principle of using native language （中）使用民族语言原则
principle of value 价值原则
principle of voluntariness in the conclusion of contracts 订合同（契约）的自愿原则
principle pacta sunt servanda 合约守信原则
principle-agent impediments to settlement 本人代理人和解不能
principled a. 原则（性）的,有原则的
principled argument 原则性的争论
principled process of enunciating 宣布有原则的程序,阐明有原则的程序
principles and maxims 原则与准则
principles of corporate finance 公司财务理论（原理）
Principles of International Commercial Contracts 《国际商事合同通则》（指国际私法协会制定的《国际商事合同通则》）
principles of judicial proof 司法证明机理（指美国证据学家约翰·威格莫尔在他1913年出版的《司法证明机理》一书中提出的"证明机理"概念。书中系统地提出了"司法证明机理"思想,并主张把这一思想视为与证据可采性规则并列的知识领域。甚至认为:"所有人为设定的可采性规则都可能被废除,但只要审判依然是为

解决法律纠纷而寻求真相的理性活动,证明机理便会永远存在。"亦可译为"司法证明原则"）
principles of public law 公法原则
print n. 1.纹印;痕迹 2.印刷（品）;相片;图片
printed document 印刷品
printed form 印制格式,印制形式
printer n. 1.打印机;印刷机;印相机 2.印刷者;排版者;排版工人
printer form 印成格式
printout n. 印出,用打印机印出;打印输出;以打印方式表示的计算机的处理结果
prior a. 在先的;在前的;优先的;更重要的
prior agreement 事前合意
prior art （专利法）先前技术,在先技术,现有技术,现在技术[指众人皆知的,为他人使用的技术知识（knowledge）,或是一个在技巧中掌握普遍技能的人在发明之时丹所包含的来自技术知识中的明显技术。在先技术包括以下要素:对以前取得专利的发明的应用信息（information in application）、专利应用已被提出申请之前一年以上或对其正式公布的信息、专利应用被提出申请之前一年以上。其他专利应用和发明人的合格证明文件已呈上的信息。美国专利和商标局和法院在对可比的（或相似的）发明（comparable invention）是否授予专利（patentability）判决之前要对在先技术进行分析。参见《美国注释法典》第35标题卷第102节]
prior authorization 事先核准
prior claim 优先受偿请求权;优先请求权
prior condition 先决条件
prior conviction 前科,前科的定罪
prior criminal record 前科
prior decision 事先裁决
prior endorser 前手背书人
prior hearing （美）先前听审（指对人伤害提起诉讼之前,在有些情况下,必须由行政机关对伤害人进行的听审）
prior heir 优先继承人
prior inconsistent statement 与先前不一致的陈述
prior investigation 初步调查;初步侦查;

预审
prior measures of attachment on property 诉前财产保全
prior probability approach 优先可能性方式
prior restraint （美）优先制约,在先制约,预先制约(指制止事先制约有关言论和出版,此为美国联邦宪法第一修正案的核心)
prior restraint law 预先制约法规
prior sale 先前售价(专利)(指一项专利被应用之前,其发明的售出报价或售价。如果出现的售价大于一年前应用申请时价格,此专利申请则按法规终止)
prior right 优先权;优先继承权
* *Prior tempore potior jure.* He who is first in time is preferred in right. 谁首先按时谁就会被认为站在正确的一边(捷足先登者有优先权)。
prior to the date due 到期前
prior to the expiration of the term 在期限届满前
prior warning （解雇,辞职等的)预先警告通知
priori a./ad./n. 一开始,刚接触时,先天的,先验的/先验地,先天地/先天论者,先验论者
priority contest 优势竞争(见 interference 3)
priority date of claims 请求专利的优先日
priority in the purchase 优先购置权
priority of adoption （商标)采纳优先权[指设计或创新商标中的优先权。如果有他人在商务中首先使用它,采纳优先权本身并不授予商标专用权(right to exclusive use of a mark)。见 priority of use]
priority of debts 优先偿付的债务
priority of exercise 行使管辖的优先权[指数个法院享有并存管辖权(concurrent jurisdiction)的情况下,首先取得行使管辖权的法院可继续审理案件独占管辖权]
priority of liens 留置权的优先权,留置权的顺序(指留置权顺序按其设定的排列顺序,先设定的留置权具有优先权)
priority of repayment 优先受偿
the priority of right over good 正当优先于善(指罗尔斯在涉及自由主义的一个论点)
priority of use （商标)优先使用权(指实际商务中商标使用的优先权,此权决定谁具有保护的权利。见 priority of adoption)
priority share 优先股
priory n. 小修道院,小女修道院
prison n. 监狱,牢狱;看守所,拘留所;监禁(见 gaol; jail; penitentiary)
prison act 监狱法
prison bird 囚犯
prison breach (17世纪)越狱罪,打破监狱罪[指囚犯运用暴力冲破并离开合法监禁他的地方。这是逃脱监狱或看守所的罪行。越狱罪与逃脱罪(escape)的区别传统上看法在于是否运用暴力,但现在一些司法管辖区已抛弃这一观点。亦称 prison breaching; breach of prison。见 escape]
prison breaker 越狱犯
prison breaking 越狱
prison camp 囚犯集中营;战俘集中营
prison cell 监房,囚室
prison doctor 监狱医生
prison escapee 越狱逃跑犯
prison factory 犯人劳动场所,监狱工厂,囚犯工厂
prison for women 女监
prison *forte et dure* （古英国法对重罪犯)残酷监禁
prison garb 囚衣,犯人衣服
prison guard 监狱看守,狱卒
prison house 牢房,监狱
prison labour （狱中)劳役
prison law 监狱法
Prison Litigation Reform Act （美)《监狱诉讼改革法》[指为了减少囚犯上诉,1995年美国出台此法,该法规定囚犯提出诉讼之前必须耗尽行政救济手段,要求法官甄别所有囚犯上诉案件并采取直接驳回轻率诉讼等措施(有效)减缓了案件增长度,大幅降低其审判率]
prison of convicts 已决罪犯的监禁
prison official 监狱官,狱政官员,(监狱)管教人员
prison raid 劫狱
prison ration 囚粮

prison reform 监狱改革
prison regime 监狱制度
prison regulation 监狱规则
prison sentence 徒刑判决,监狱刑罚(见 non-custodial penalty)
prison staff 监狱工作人员
prison van 囚车
prison violence 监狱暴乱
prison visitors 探监者;探视囚犯的人
prisoner n. 犯人,囚犯;羁押犯;罪犯;俘虏;刑事被告
prisoner at the bar 刑事罪犯;刑事被告
prisoner awaiting trial 候审犯,未决犯
prisoner granted parole 获得假释的犯人
prisoner of conscience 政治犯
prisoner of war 战俘
prisoner of state 政治犯,国事犯
prisoner of war 战俘
prisoner on remand 在押犯;未决囚犯
prisoner pending sentence 待判犯
prisoner pending trial 候审犯
prisoner petitions 刑事被告申诉,囚犯申请
prisoner under public surveillance (中)被管制犯(人)
prisoner under sentence of death 死刑犯
prisoner's box 被告席
prisoner's statement 罪犯的供词
prisoner's dilemma 囚犯两难,囚犯困境(指对策论进入成熟阶段的主要成就表现;策略对策均衡问题、重复对策问题、随机和动态对策、囚犯两难问题、讨价还价问题、对策解的值、公理体系的形成等七个方面)
privacy n. 1.(个人)秘密;隐私 2.隐退;隐居
Privacy Act of 1974 (美)《1974年隐私权法》[指政府创立的规定,即收集、利用和传播有关个人信息以及其他人事信息均作出明确规定,参见《美国注释法典》第18标题卷第5522页]
Privacy Law (1936年)1.《隐私权法》[指联邦或州的制定法规,旨在保护个人和生活权利(person's right to be left alone)或限制公众取得个人信息诸如纳税人申报单(tax return)和医疗档案等。亦称 Privacy Act] 2.保护隐私权(指法律研究在处理或对待个人和生活权利的领域受到法律限制,同时亦限制公众获取诸如个人信息、纳税申报表以及医疗档案等个人信息)
privacy of correspondence 通信秘密
privacy of individual 个人的私生活;个人隐私
private a. 私人的,个人的;私有的;私营的;私设的;秘密的;平民的
private accident insurance 私人意外事故保险
private act (英)私法法令(指议会关于个人利益和特定地方利益方面的法令)
private action 私诉
private acts of parliament 议会私法法例(指议会中涉及地方或私人权益性质的法例,如离婚法例、归化法例等)
private adoption (未经法院批准的)私自收养
private agent 私人代理人
private and public companies 私营公司和公营公司;非上市公司和(股份)上市公司;私人公司和公众公司
private annuity 私人(或私方)年金[指来源于私人(或私方)的年金,而非来源于公方或人寿保险公司的年金]
private arbitration 私方仲裁,不公开仲裁
private arbitrator 私人仲裁员
private association 民间团体
private attorney 私人律师;私人代理人
private attorney general (美)私人出庭检察官(指可出庭为每个公民实施公共权利的个人检察官)
private bail bondsmen 私人保释,(保证书)提供人,私人保释保证人,(美)私方保释保证金提供人
private bank 私营银行
private benefits of control 控制权的私利(指控股股东在与其他股东分享公司共有收益的同时,其自身对企业的控制权往往使得控制权的私利变得可能。也就是说,控股股东可以排他性获得其他中小股东所无法分享的利益)
private bill office (英国议会的)私法法案处
private bills 私法法案(议会中涉及私人、民营公司的私利所提出的法案)

private business 私营企业
private businessman 私人经营者
private capitalist sector 私人资本主义成分
private carrier 私人运输业;私人运输行
private citizen 平民
private code 私用密码;私人密码
private commercial law 私商法
private company 私营公司;股份不公开发行的公司
private compromise (或 agreement) 私下和解;私了协议
private contract 私人合同
private corporation 私法人
private custody 秘密拘禁;私设的拘禁
private debtor 私人债务人
private defence 自卫,个人防卫
private defense lawyers 私人辩护律师
private detective 私家侦探;秘密侦探
private direct investment 私人直接投资
private distribution 私人分配
private document 私文书
private economy 私有经济,私人经济
private enemy property 敌国私有财产
private enterprise 私营企业
private entities 私人实体
private foundation 私人基金会
private freedom 个人自由
private gaol 私设的监狱
private goods 私人产品
private hatred 私仇
private income tax 个人所得税
private individual 私人
private industry and commerce 个体工商业
private information 非公开信息,私方信息,私人信息
private international law 国际冲突法,国际私法[法学学者通常对"国际冲突法"这个名称感到悲哀,因为它误导地推断法律体系(a body of law)在某种程度上与国际公法或国际法(public international law)是并行或类似的,而事实上,它仅仅是每一法制的私法的一部分。国际私法实际上是解决两个或两个以上国家有关交易诉讼或一些事件方面冲突性法律间的适用的冲突法。亦可称作 international private law; jus geutium privatum; intermunicipal law; comity; extraterritorial recognition of rights。见 conflicts of laws 2]
private investor 私人投资者
private labourer 个体劳动者
private land 私人土地,私有土地
private law 私法
private law arbitration 私法仲裁
private lawyer 私法律人(指律师的规制方面以西方式的"职业自治"为实质理想,以行业自律为发展目标,进行管理体制改革,这就是英美所称"私法律人")
private legal entity 私法人
private legal scholar 民间研究法律的学者
Private Letter ruling (美)个别回复(指纳税人在特定交易中所涉及的税法解释和具体适用问题,国内税务署应该对纳税人的请求给予的适当答复。亦称 Letter ruling)
private libel 秘密文字诽谤(罪)
private litigants 私诉当事人
private maritime law 海事私法
private means of investigation 秘密的调查手段,私下的调查方法
private member's bill (英)议员个人议案
private municipal law 国内私法
private nuisance 私人妨扰;妨害私人利益的行为;妨害个人的事物
private officer 私职(指遗产管理人与遗嘱执行人之类只有有限的职权范围的职务,与 public officer 相对而言)
private ownership 私人所有(权);个体所有制
private ownership of the means of production 生产资料私有制
private ownership system 私有制
private parties 私人当事人,个别当事人,私诉当事人
private person 1.普通人(指未担任公务,亦未在军中服役者)2.(大陆法)私法主体(指由私法进行规范的公司或合伙企业)
private placement 私下交易;私人收养[指不通过收养机构而直接由养父母由律师或医生中介收养,亦称直接收养(direct placement);(证券)私募(指不公开发行,不公开发售,发行的股票或债券直接向部

分人群或投资机构发售而非公开发售,亦称 private offering)]
private placement of convertible debentures 转换债券私下交易
private plot (中)自留地
private power 私人权力,个人权力
private practice 民间惯例
private practitioner 个体开业者(尤指律师、医生等)
private professional activity 私人职业性活动
private property 私有财产
private prosecution 自诉
private prosecutor 自诉人
private Roman law 罗马私法
private seal 私章
Private Securities Litigation Reform Act of 1995 《1995年私人有价证券诉讼改革法》
private self-employed economy 私营个体经济
private settlement (不经过法院的)私下解决
private settlement behavior 私下和解行为,私了行为
private statute (英)私人性制定法
private trust 私人信托
private use 私人使用[有些国家将个人使用(individual use)与私人使用认为是一回事,但多数国家将其分开,私人使用只在专门限定范围内才属于合理使用]
private watchman 私人警卫,保镖
private way 私人通行权
private wrong 个人错误行为;侵犯个人权利的不法行为,私人的犯罪;侵权行为(侵犯公共利益和私人利益时,应承担民事责任)
privateer n. 私掠船;私掠船长(或船员)(用于战时当局准许私船武装起来,缉捕敌船)
privateering n. 私掠制
privatisation n. 私有化
* ***Privatum commodum publico cedit.*** Private good yields to public. 个人利益服从公共利益。
* ***Privatum incommodum publico bono pensatur.*** Private loss is compensated by public good. Private inconvenience is made up for by public benefit. 个人损失受到公共利益补偿。个人的困难靠公共利益来弥补。
privigna 前夫或前妻的女儿
privignus 前夫或前妻的儿子
privilege n./v. 特权;特惠;特殊利益;免责特权/授予特权;特许;(美)秘密特权
privilege against compulsory self-incrimination 反对强迫自我归罪的特权
privilege against self-incrimination (被告享有)不受强迫自证其罪的特权
privilege and obligation 权利与义务
privilege from arrest 不受拘捕的特权
(the) privilege of clergy 神职人员的特权(前教士犯罪时,不受普通法院的审判)
privilege of order (保证人的)后诉的权利(见 *beneficium ordinis*)
privilege of self-defence 自卫权
privilege of silence 沉默权
privilege of termination 终止权
privilege of the floor (1854年)(议会法)入席权,入场权利,会议期间入席
privilege of witness 作证权
privilege tax (美)特许权税(指对经营一项事业或专业而要求的特权或许可证而征收的税)
privileged a. 特许的;有特权的,受特权保护的
privileged and immunities (美)优惠和豁免(特权与特免)(指美国联邦宪法第4条第2款要求任何州不得以不公正态度处理来自另一州的人)
privileged audience 特许立法质询,特许听政,特许陈述意见
privileged class 特权阶级
privileged communication 特许不泄露的信息(指证人在法庭作证时,不得强令其揭露因夫妻关系、律师与当事人关系、医生与病人关系、牧师与忏悔者关系而获知的内情与信息);特许保密通讯(指在法律上特许若干负有特定忠诚和保密义务的人彼此进行保密通讯)(见 confidentiality);法律上特许可能泄露的内情;有特权的通信;免责通信

privileged creditor 享有优先权的债权人
privileged debt 应优先偿还的债务(指遗产管理人所支付的医疗费、丧葬费等)
privileged deed 特许契据
privileged estate 保留财产
privileged matter(s) 特权事项,特惠事项,特许事项
privileged motion 先决的动议案
privileged places 庇护场所
privileged relationship 受特权保护的关系(指某些特定主体之间建立信任基础之上的关系,受法律的特别保护。见 privileged communication)
privileged statement (不受一般法规制约的)特许声明
privileged ville(i)nage (英)特权的农役土地保有权;(英中世纪的)特权农奴身份
privileged will (现役军人和海员所立的)特别遗嘱
privileges and immunities (美)优惠和豁免(指宪法要求任何州不得以不公正态度处理来自另一州的人)
Privileges and Immunities Clause of the U. S. Constitution 美国联邦宪法的特权和豁免条款
privilegiarius 特权占有者
privilegium (罗马法上的)特别宪法;特别权利;特权
privilegium clericale 神职人员(不受普通法院审判)的特权
* *Privilegium est beneficium personale, et extinguitur cum persona.* A privilege is personal benefit, and dies with the person. 特权是某一个人的利益,并随该人的死亡而消失。
* *Privilegium est quasi privata lex.* Privilege is, as it were, a private law. 特权就其本身来说不过是私法的权利。
privity n. 1.共同与闻的秘密;暗中参与;秘密,私事 2.默契;私人知悉 3.(由法律或契约规定的对同一权利的)有关当事人的相互关系(也称"合同连接关系",即传统上就任何合同起诉的前提是原告与被告就相关事宜必须有连接关系。现在美国《统一商法典》有关于担保的法律,按其

"严格责任",在涉及合同和侵权的诉讼中,原告与被告之间没有连接关系则不能成为抗辩理由)
privity in deed 合同(契约)上的债务(关系)
privity in law 法定债务的相互关系;法律上的相互关系
privity in representation 代理关系
privity of blood 血缘关系;血亲关系
privity of contract 合同(契约)有关当事人的相互关系;(与合同当事人一方有关系而产生的)非合同当事人的权益
privity of estate 地产保有相互关系(指两宗地产来自同一保有人和同一时间,在法律上,它们被当做一宗地产看待。因此这两宗地产保有人就有着保有的相互关系);(不动产)出租人与承租人的互助关系
privity of tenure 租地的相互关系;租地保有相互关系(指地主和他的直接租户之间的相互关系)
privy n./a. 当事人,利害关系人/1.秘密的,机密的;暗中参与的 2.私有的;君主私有的;君主私用的
privy council 1.(英)(大写)枢密院 2.智囊团;顾问团
privy councillor (或 counselor) (英)枢密院官员或顾问;(大写)伦敦枢密院的审讯法官
privy seal (英)御玺(仅用于一般政府公文)
privy verdict 秘密裁决
prize n./v. 战时捕获;俘虏;俘获品,战利品;奖(品)/1.捕获 2.估价;认为有大的价值
prize action 捕获诉讼
prize case 捕获案
prize court (处理战时在海上捕获敌方船舶、货物等的)捕获法庭(或称捕获物法庭、战利品法庭)
prize crew 押解船员(指执行押解捕获船命令的船员)
prize law 捕获法(处理海上捕获物的专门法规)
prize master 捕获船只的押送官员

prize money 捕获物奖金

prize of war 战利品(指战时海上捕获的敌船及敌产)

pro 为了,按照;代表;为……利益;由于,因为

pro(s) and con(s) 赞成与反对;正反论据

pro bono 为了(某人的)利益;慈善的(指免费提供帮助等)

pro bono legal assistance (美)慈善性法律帮助(指法律界一些成员为公众服务不收费用的行为)

pro bono publico 为了公共利益,为了全体的利益

Pro bonos lawyer 提供社会公益性法律服务的律师,免费提供服务的律师

pro confesso (罗马法)如同承认(指由于被告已承认或承担责任,故要求其出庭而未出庭。对未回答衡平法提交诉状的被告,通常按如同承认诉状属实对待)

pro consilio impendendo 为了给予劝告(for counsel to be given)[这一术语说明以承诺付款(commitment)形式作为对价(consideration)提供法律咨询以换取年金(annuity)]

pro consilio impoens 为了提供建议,为了劝告

pro convicto 如同已判定罪的,如同已被判刑的

pro corpore regni 代表整个国家;为整个国家利益

pro derelicto 作为遗弃物或无主物,按大陆法,这可适用时效而取得财产(见 *usucapio*)

pro dignitate regali 考虑到王室的尊严

pro et contra (赞成)拥护和反对

pro forma 作为惯例,形式上(的);估计(通常指对上诉的裁判并非一定正确无误,而只便于对案件作进一步审理);数据代码

pro forma invoice 形式发票

pro forma vote 形式上的表决

pro hac vice 只此一回,仅限于这一特殊场合

pro indiviso 共有的,共用的;不可分开的(常用于共有租借或合有租借的土地文据里)

pro interesse suo 为本身利益

pro legato 作为遗赠,视如遗赠

pro memoria 备忘录

pro rata 按比例计,成比例地

pro rata average clause 按比例分摊海损条款

pro rata clause 按比例条款(指一项保险单的条款,被保险人重复保险时,承保人的赔偿责任是按照其保险金额与保险金额总和的比例来确定,或承保人的赔偿责任只限于相对于全部保险的保单面值的损失部分。亦称 *pro rata* distribution clause。见 excess clause)

pro rata distribution clause 按比例分配条款(同 pro rata clause)

pro rata liability 按比例计算的责任

pro rata tax system 比例税制

pro re nata 临时的(地);须即时处理的事

pro se 亲自,自行;代表自己,为自己

pro se representation 自己代理(指在法庭上自己处理自己案情而不需要律师)

pro solido 整个,整体,全部

pro tanto 至此,到这个程度,以此为限;力所能

pro tempore 暂时,临时

pro tutors 代理保佐人

pro-active investigations 主动型侦查

pro-choice n. (美)自由选择派(指在主张生育问题上,妇女理应享有选择的自由权利。只有她们才能决定是继续妊娠,还是终止妊娠,对此任何政府不仅无权干涉,而且有义务提供必要的服务和保障。见 Roe v. Wade 和 pro-life)

pro-emptive bids 优先投标

pro-life n. (美)生命权利派(该派认为:怀在母体内的胎儿是生命的体现,不管妊娠是如何开始的,生命本身必须受到保护。堕胎等同于谋杀,等同于剥夺天赋的权利,堕胎也是对妇女的一种侵害。因此,政府必须对堕胎实施严厉管制。见 Roe v. Wade 和 pro-choice)

Pro-Northern justice (美)拥护北方的司法审判

probabilistic 概率的,不确定性的,随机性的

probability n. 可能性,或然性;机会;概然率,概率
probability estimates of a given benefit 一个给定利益的概率估计
probability function 概率函数
probability of plaintiff victory (success) 原告胜诉的概率
probability of ruin 破产的可能性
probable a. 大概的,很可能的;似乎确有的,或有的
probable candidate 大有希望(当选)的候选人
probable cause 合理的理由[指美国检察官提起公诉所适用的标准与合法逮捕的证据标准一样,即只要求有合理的根据(probable cause)];相当理由(指对于运用卧底警探之证明标准,德国法上是"充分的事实根据",美国判例法的标准是"相当理由"。"充分的事实根据"相对于"相当理由"而言证明度较高,不但要求卧底侦查的事实有证据证明,而且要求证据证明力能充分证明犯罪事实存在的高度可能性);可能的原因;(相信被告有罪的)合理根据
probable evidence 可能成立的证据(亦称推定的证据 presumptive evidence)
probable reasoning 似乎可信的推理
probate n./v. 遗嘱的检验;经过检验的遗嘱;遗嘱认证/检验遗嘱;处(犯人)以缓刑
probate, divorce and admiralty division 遗嘱检验、离婚和海事法庭(指高等法院中的一个分庭)
probate action 遗嘱检验诉讼
probate business 遗嘱检验事务
probate code 遗嘱检验法规
probate copy 遗嘱检验文本
probate court (=the court of special probate jurisdiction) 遗嘱检验法庭(指有权认证遗嘱与管理死者遗产的特种法庭)
probate division 遗嘱检验(分)庭
probate duty 立遗嘱人死后的动产税;遗嘱检验税
probate judge 遗嘱检验法官
probate judge (18世纪)遗嘱检验法官,遗产继承,监护资格,以及类似的情况的

检验法官(亦称 judge of probate; surrogate; register; registry)
probate jurisdiction 遗嘱检验裁判权
probate of codicil 遗嘱附录检验(书)
probate of will 遗嘱检验,遗嘱认证
probate of will in common form 用通常方式检验遗嘱
probate of will in solemn form 用庄严方式检验遗嘱
probate proceeding 遗嘱检验程序
probate registry 遗嘱检验登记处
probatio minus plena 不完全(或不充分的)证据
probatio mortua 物证;证件;字据
probatio per documenta (或 *instrumenta*) 书面证据
probatio plena 充足证据;由两个证人提供的证据;由政府文件提供的证据
probatio probatissima et plenissima 直接和充足的证据
probatio viva 人证
probation n. 1.检验,验证;鉴定 2.见习,试用;见习期;试用期 3.察看(以观后效);感化犯人 4.缓刑考验(指对判处轻刑的犯人根据犯罪情节,认为适用缓刑可保不再危害社会的,可以宣告缓刑,用缓刑考验来代替原刑),缓刑监督
probation agency (美)青少年教养所
probation home 缓刑犯的教养所
probation hostel 缓刑犯收容所
Probation of First Offenders Act 《初犯缓刑条例》(指英国1887年在监狱改革家霍华德的努力下参照美国马萨诸塞州缓刑立法而指定的明确的缓刑法律)
probation of offenders (一种对罪犯实行缓刑考验以观后效的)判决缓刑,缓刑判决
Probation of Offenders Act (英)《犯罪人保护观察法》(1907年)
probation of will 遗嘱检验,遗嘱认证
probation officer 试用官;(美)监护官,监视缓刑犯的官员
probation system 1.试用制度 2.缓刑制度(指英美法对判处轻刑的犯人,尤其是少年犯,常暂缓执行其刑,将其交给负责监

护的官吏监护以观后效的一种制度)
probational a. 缓刑中的
probational criminal 缓刑犯人
probationary a. 1.试用的,见习的 2.缓刑的
probationary appointment 试用
probationary employee 试用人员
probationary lawyer 见习律师
probationary period 试用期间;缓刑期间;考验(缓刑犯)期间;试养期(现代国际社会的收养法一般规定为6个月到1年)
probationary sentence 缓刑判决
probationer n. 1.试用人员,见习人员 2.缓刑犯,感化犯
probative (=probatory) 提供证据或证明的;证明的;检验的,鉴定的
probative effect 证明效力
probative evidence 提供证明的证据
probative fact 提供证据的事实
probative force 证明力
probative similarity 见 substantial similarity
probative term 鉴定期,检验期
probative value 证据力;证明价值
probativeness n. 证明性;鉴定性
probatory term 立证期限
probe v. 调查;查究;探索;彻底调查
probe a matter to the bottom 对案件进行彻底调查
problem n. 问题,难题[与英语中的"issue""question"同意,但三者有区别:issue是法律用语,常指事实问题和法律问题,这是律师的口头禅,常译"争点""系争点"。而 problem 则指需要解决的难题,"question"是指提问的问题,也可指需要讨论的事项(matter),也可指需要解决的问题(problem)]
problem child (尤指性格古怪难以处置的)成问题的儿童;难管教的儿童
problem of classification (国际私法)识别问题
problematic(al) a. 成问题的,难题的,有疑问的;未定的
probondence of probability 盖然居上或占优势,概率居上
procedendo 1.强制判决令(用作高级法院命令下级法院将延搁的案件进行判决的催办令状) 2.(民事诉讼中上级法院将案件)发还(给下级法院)再审令
procedendo ad judicium 强制进行判决令(见 *procedendo*)
procedural a. 诉讼程序的,诉讼程序上的;有关诉讼程序的,程序性的
procedural capacity (to action) 诉讼能力
procedural constitutionalism "程序宪政"(有两方面基本内容:以正当程序为规范原则的宪政构建和以宪政原理为构成内容的程序法治)
procedural cost 诉讼程序成本
procedural devices 程序方法
procedural document 诉讼文书
procedural due process (美)程序上的正当法律程序(指依据美国联邦宪法第5条、第十四修正案关于正当程序条款的规定,保证程序上的公正),程序性的正当程序,程序上的正当手续,程序上的正当过程
procedural fairness 程序的公平性
procedural justice 程序公正;程序正义
procedural law 程序法,诉讼法
procedural legislation 程序立法
procedural matter(s) 程序事项
procedural nature law 程序的自然法(美国法学家富勒将法律的内在道德称为程序的自然法,外在道德称为实体的自然法)
procedural posture 程序态势(指听诉的性质和状态)
procedural presumption 程序性推定(可反驳的推定)
procedural problem 程序问题
procedural protection 诉讼程序上的保护
Procedural Republic 程序共和制
procedural right 程序性权利(源于法律程序和行政性程序),诉讼上的权利
procedural rights theory 程序权利理论
procedural rule of the forum 审判地的诉讼原则
procedural safeguards 程序保障
procedural step 诉讼步骤
procedural value 程序价值(指法律程序是为保证一些独立于判决结果的程序

价值)
procedure n. (16 世纪) 1.诉讼程序(指一项诉讼进程或特定的方法) 2.有关民事诉讼或刑事检控实施的司法规或方法(matters), 亦称 rule of procedure (见 criminal procedure)
procedure alteration 诉讼程序的改变
procedure equity 程序平等原则
procedure *extra ordinem* 特别诉讼程序
procedure for appeal 上诉程序
procedure for concluding a contract 签订合同的程序, 签约程序
procedure for default 缺席判决程序
procedure for establishing proof 确立证据程序
procedure for granting, revoking, or restoring citizenship 授予、取消或恢复公民身份(国籍)程序
procedure for labo(u)r disputes 劳工争议程序, 劳资争议程序
procedure for levying execution (扣押)财产执行程序
procedure for obtaining enforcement 申请执行判决的程序
procedure for obtaining judg(e)ment 判决程序
procedure for review of death sentence (中)死刑复核程序
procedure for sequestration 财产扣押程序
procedure for small bankruptcy 小额破产程序
procedure for supervision upon adjudication 审判监督程序
procedure for the acquisition and loss of citizenship 公民身份的取得和丧失程序
procedure governing adjudication 影响裁决的程序
procedure in administrative tribunals 行政法庭的诉讼程序
procedure in civil litigation 民事诉讼的程序
procedure in equity (英美法)衡平法诉讼程序
procedure in law (英美法)普通法诉讼程序
procedure of a criminal case 刑事案件的诉讼程序
procedure of attachment 拘留程序
procedure of bankruptcy 破产程序
procedure of conclusion of treaties 条约的缔结程序
procedure of first instance 第一审程序
procedure of investigation 侦查程序
procedure of judg(e)ment by default 缺席审判程序
procedure of mediation 调解程序
procedure of putting a case on file 立案程序
procedure of second instance 第二审程序
procedure of sentence 宣判程序, 判决程序
procedure of the House 议院议事程序
procedure of trial 审判程序
procedure of verification 鉴证程序
procedure of wager of battle 决斗断讼程序
procedure process innovation 程序创新
procedure rules 诉讼规程
Procedures of the People's Republic of China for the Registration and Administration of Chinese-Foreign Joint Ventures 《中华人民共和国中外合资经营企业登记管理办法》
proceed n./v. 所得;(复)收入;收益;变卖所得的钱/进行;继续进行;发生;起诉;进行诉讼程序
proceed against (sb. for sth.) (为某事对某人)提起诉讼
proceed from interests of the people 从人民的利益出发
proceed in a case 开始进行诉讼程序
proceed in taking a deposition 开始录取证言
proceed of a pawn 抵押品变卖所得
proceeding n. 行动, 经过; 处置; (诉讼)程序; (复)诉讼; 纪录; 会议录; 事项
proceeding for nuisance 排除妨害的诉讼
proceeding for trespass 排除侵犯行为的诉讼
proceeding in admiralty 海事程序
proceeding in error 复审程序, 依纠错令将案件移送上级法院进行复审的程序
proceeding *in personam* (= in personam ac-

tion) 对人诉讼
proceeding(s) *in rem* 对物诉讼
proceeding of relative formality 相对正规程序
proceeding related to action pending 对有关未决诉讼提出的诉讼
proceedings (16世纪)1.程序,诉讼程序(指完整正规的诉讼程序,包括从诉讼开始到作出判决,其间所进行的全部行为和步骤)2.寻求救济(指向法庭或其他官方机构求得救济的任何程序和手段)3.较大诉讼过程中的一个程序和步骤 4.听证,听审(指法庭或其他官方机构所处理的事务)5.(破产法)诉讼进行期间未决案件中所引起的特定争议或问题,正好与整体案件本身相反
proceedings at first instance 第一审程序
proceedings for declaration of legitimacy 婚生宣告程序
proceedings for revision 复核程序
proceedings in contentious-administrative appeal 行政性争议的申诉程序
proceedings in error 复审程序;复审诉讼
proceedings *in personam* 对人诉讼
proceedings of granting of probate 遗嘱检验程序
proceedings of non-contentious jurisdiction 非讼裁判程序
proceedings pending 未决程序
proceedings prior to trial 庭审前的程序;审前准备程序
proceeds of policy 保险收益,保险所得
Proces Verbaux 逐字记录,会议记录
proces-verbal (法)事实陈述会议记录(见 protocol)(经过情况的)官方纪录;(案件的)笔录;(控告时)提出的书面说明
process n./v. (14世纪)1.诉讼程序,诉讼进程(指任何诉讼或检控的进程或程序)〈due process of law〉(正当法律诉讼程序)2.传票,令状(指法院的传票或令状命令被告到庭受审)〈service of process〉(诉讼书证送达)"传票送达"。亦称 judicial process;legal process 3.(专利)方法,工艺,手段(指为达到某种新的有用的目的

或结果,而改变必要材料的化学或物理性质,采用一系列工艺或手段)进程(process)是可以取得专利发明的一种法律范畴(见 manufacture;machine)/1.处理,办理;加工〈to process data〉(整理数据),〈to process polluted water〉(处理污水),〈to process a loan〉(办理贷款手续)2.对……起诉;对……发出传票
process a loan 办理贷款手续
process against a defendant 传唤被告
process against third parties 传唤第三人
process attorney 诉讼代理人
process before right 程序先于权利
process benefit (value) 程序价值(指通过法律程序本身体现出来的独立于裁判结果的价值如尊严、公平、参与等。见 procedural justice)
process costs 分步成本
process costs accounting 分步成本会计
process costs system 分步成本制度
process *in rem* 对物诉讼程序
process of criminal proceedings 刑事诉讼程序
process of impeachment 弹劾程序
process of import (export) 进口(出口)手续
process of interpretation 解释程序
process of law 法律程序
process of payment 付款手续
process of sequestration 财产扣押程序
process patent 制造方法专利权
process registering land 土地登记手续
process roll 传票登记册;诉讼登记册
process server 传票送达员(即递送传票的司法人员)
process serving 传票送达
process value 程序价值[指萨莫斯(Robort S.Summers)用以判断法律程序本身是否为善的价值标准称为程序价值。见 inherent purposes of legal procedure 和 good result efficacy]
process value efficacy 程序价值效应
processing industry contract 加工订货合同(契约)
processing on order 来料加工

processing tax （农产品的）加工税
processor n. （情报数据等的）分理者；加工者；处理人，信息处理化
processus causarum minutarum 小案的诉讼程序
processus verbalis 口头诉讼
prochain ami 次代理人（见 next friend）
prochronism n. 早记日期的错误（指将事实等误记在实际发生日期之前）
procidential history 神意历史（西方宗教的一种信仰）
proclaim v. 1.宣布,宣告,公布 2.以法律制止、宣布、禁止；对……以法律管制 3.表明,显示
proclamation n. 1.宣告,宣布,布告,公告 2.宣言书,声明书
proclamation of emancipation 解放宣言
proclamation of neutrality 宣告中立
proclamation of peace 恢复和平公告
proclamation of the accession of a new sovereign （新君即位的）登基公告
proclamation of war 宣战公告,宣战
proclamator n. （英）高等民事法庭的（司法）官员
proconsul n. （罗马法）1.留任执政官［指前执政官在其离职后,其执政权由元老院（senate）给予近期或由罗马皇帝赐予延期］2.元老院某个行省的总督（governor）
procrastination n. 拖延,耽搁；因循
procreation n. 生育,生殖；产生
proctor n. （美）1.代理人,被指定管理他人事务的人 2.诉讼律师（指在宗教学院的诉讼代理人,即 procurator）3.离婚代理人 4.海事诉讼律师［指在地区法院代表海事当事方的律师（advocate）］
procul dubis （=without doubt） 无疑
proculians (school) 普罗库卢斯派（古罗马帝国时期多数法学家追随的两派之一）
procuracy n. （授权）检察官的授权书；代诉人授权书；代理；代理人的职务
procuration n. 1.代理（权）；委任状赋予权力；（对代诉人等的）委任 2.介绍费,佣金 3.淫媒业；淫媒
procuration of signature 代理签名（字）
procuration of women 介绍妇女卖淫

procurator n. 1.（罗马法）诉讼代理人（指在司法程序中被任命的代理人。见 *cognitor*）2.（罗马法）代理人［指一种政府官员,通常是代理行政府总督的助理官员；罗马帝国的一个官员受托管理行省财务,并通常在行省中具有行政权来作为皇帝的代理人（agents）］3.（历史）（英国法）代理人（agent）,诉讼代理人（attorney），或雇员 4.（教会法）宗教机构（religious house）诉讼代理人或律师（代表牧师的或教会社在法律方面的事务。亦称 proctor）5.代理人或事实代理人（attorney-in-fact）6.（苏格兰法）事务律师在低级法院代理诉讼委托人（client）；正式的,作为法律代理人或律师（law agent）
procurator fiscal （= procurator of the fisk）（苏格兰）财务检察官；地方检察官；公诉人；律师
procurator general （法）检察总长
procurator general's office （或 **chamber**）检察总署；最高检察院
procurator in reserve 候补检察官
procurator *litis* 受任代诉人,代理人诉讼
procurator *negotiorum* 受委托的代理人（指在法庭外者）
procurator of parliameat 下议院院长
procurator of republic （法）国家检察官
procurator of St. Mark 威尼斯共和国部长
procurator's office 检察部门,检察官职务
procuratorate n. 代理人（或代理人、检察员、检察官）的职业；检察机关,（中）检察院
procuratorate general 总检察长、首席检察官；（中）（最高人民检察院）检察长
procuratorial a. 代诉人的；代理人的；检察的
procuratorial action 代理人诉讼
procuratorial authority 检察权；检察机关；检察当局
procuratorial committee 检察委员会
Procuratorial Committee of the Supreme People's Procuratorate （中）最高人民检察院检察委员会
procuratorial function 检察职能
procuratorial investigation 检察侦查
procuratorial personnel 检察人员

procuratorial powers 检察权
procuratorial protest 代理人的抗诉
procuratorial responsibility system 检察长负责制
procuratorial supervision 检察监督
procuratorship n. 代理人（或代诉人、检察官等的）职位（=procuratorate）；检察官的职位；代理人
procuratory n. （对代理人的）委任
procure v. 1.(努力)取得，获得 2.实现，达成；完成 3.促成，诱使；引诱妇女卖淫 4.(设法)提起诉讼
procure a quorum 达到法定人数
procurement n. 取得，获得；达成；促成
procurement of credit 取得信贷
procurement price 收购价格
procurer （女性用 procuress）1.取得者，获得者 2.引诱妇女卖淫者
procureur （法）代理人，律师；检察官
procureur general （法）检察总长
procuring (causing or encouraging) prostitution 引诱(唆使或怂恿)妇女卖淫
prodding 刺激，激励，促进，推动
prodigal n. 浪子，浪费人(指大陆法系上的一种人，由于他挥霍、浪费及恶劣行为，因而其一切事务均由监护人管理。在罗马法上，这种浪人或浪费人的父系家属将使该浪人不得从事合法的交易，他的财产必须由监护人监管)
prodigus （罗马法）浪费人，浪费者（受监护的精神病者、纵欲者、嗜酒者、挥霍者等。见 prodigal)
produce v./n. 提出(理由)；展现；出示(证据)；引起；生产，出产，制造／农产品(总称)产品，结果，成果
produce evidence 提出证据
produce evidence at trial 在庭审中举证
produce marketing corporation 生产销售公司
produce one's papers 出示证件
produce proof to the contrary 提供(出)相反证据
produce reason 提出理由
producent n. （英）(旧宗教法庭制度中的)呼唤证人出庭的一方(当事人)

producer of motion picture 电影制片人(许多国家为行使版权方便依法将电影版权的大部分授予制片人)
producer price 出价，生产者价格
producers of phonograms 录音制品制作者
product (1825 年)1.产品，制成品 2.智力成果 作品，创作 3.产物，结果 4.劳动成果 5.产量(见 manufacture; product liability)
product costing 产品成本计算
product disparagement 产品诽谤,产品毁誉
product liability 产品责任
product liability law 产品责任法
product malfunction 有毛病的产品，有问题的产品，次级产品
product mix 产品搭配，产品组合
Product Process Methods (PPM) 产品加工标准(指除了要求产品本身符合环境保护标准外，还进一步要求其整个生产过程使用的技术和方法也必须符合环保标准，以确保产品生产过程中污染物排放的浓度与数量不危害人体健康和自然生态环境)
product quality law 产品质量法
product reliability 产品可靠性
product substitution 商品替换
product-driven regulatory structure 产品驱动管理结构
production n. 1.生产，制作；工作；著作 2.提出；提供 3.生产物,制品；著作，作品
production accident 生产事故
production cooperative（或 society） 生产合作社
production cost 生产成本，生产费用
production function 生产函数，生产职能
production fund 生产基金
production materials 生产材料
production of document 出示文件,出示证件
production of evidence 提供证据,出示证据
production of suit 提起诉讼；起诉
production permit 生产许可,生产许可证
production team (中)生产队
productive a. 生产的，多产的；有生产价值的；生产性的；丰产的
productive capital 生产资本
productive judge 多结案的法官

productivity n. 生产率,生产能力;富饶,多产
productivity of judicial system 司法系统的效率
productivity of superior beings (人口)优质生产率
produralist n. 程序主义者
profane swearing 渎神宣誓,渎神宣言
profanity n. 渎神;(复)亵渎语言
profer =proffer;profert
profess v. 1.表示,声称;承认 2.自称;冒充,假装 3.公开声明,公开说明
professio juris (当事人的)自认权利(合同法和法律冲突用语,指在文件中规定调整整个合同所适用的法规方式来确认合同当事人的权利)
professing a public calling 所谓公共行业;所谓公共行业名称
profession n. 1.职业,专门职业;专业 2.宣言;自白,表白;自称,自认
professional a./n. 职业上的;专业上的;从事专门职业的/行家里手,专业人员
professional accountant 专职会计师
professional activity 业务活动,专业活动
professional advisor 专业顾问
professional affiliation 专业认定,专业确认
professional aid 职业援助,专业援助
professional association 行业协会(旧称:行业公会),专业协会
professional autonomy 职业自治(见professional projects)
professional card 职业证
professional category (联合国秘书处)专门人员职责
professional chamber 同业公会
professional company 专业公司
professional consul 职业领事
professional corporation 职业性公司
professional criminal 职业犯
professional ethics 职业道德
professional group 专业团体
professional judge 专职法官
professional judiciary 专门司法系统
professional knowledge (skill) 专业知识(或技术)
professional lawyer 专业律师;法律专业工作者;职业律师
(a) Professional Legal Secretary (PLS) (已通过全国司法官协会考试的)专业司法官
professional liability insurance 职业责任保险
professional licence 职业证明书
professional man (person) 专业人员(尤指医生、律师等)
professional misconduct 渎职,失职,失职行为
professional morality 职业道德
professional negligence 业务过失
professional obligation 行业义务;职业义务
professional personnel 专职人员;专业人员
professional plaintiff 职业性原告
professional privateers 职业私掠者(指以勒索多数股东为业者)
professional privilege 职业上的特权
professional projects 职业蓝图[西方各国法律界普遍认可的概念。主要指法律人共同体以实现"职业自治"(professional autonomy)为前提,试图以"自我规制"(self-regulation)的方式来有效控制职业准入(对法学教育和法律职业资格的有效规制)、有效监督其成员行为(与大众道德不同,有效的职业伦理规范)、保护法律服务的市场垄断地位(法律服务的独占性)以及共同体享有较高社会地位(法律作为一个整体在社会中享有较高声誉和政治地位)的一种职业理想]
professional register 职业登记簿
professional representative function (全国性)职业代表的职务
professional responsibility 职业责任
professional witness 专业证人,懂得(某一)专门知识的证人
professionalism n. 职业特性,职业作风;职业化
professionalize v. 职业化,专业化
professor n. 教授;(美)教师(泛指)
professors' law 教授(创造)法
proffer n./v. (正式)提供,提出;贡献/提出,提供

proficua 收益;地产收益
profile n./v. (1989年)1.(刑法)形迹可疑(指个人的一连串特点引起警察注意而实施目标侦察程序,比如一个中止旅行者的行为或其他品质特性使产生刑事嫌疑) 2.外形,轮廓,外观,形象,侧面 3.传略,简介/1.显出(描绘出……)轮廓;给……画侧面图 2.写某人传略
profit n./v. 益处,收益;受益权;盈余;利润;红利;利润率/得益,得到;有益,有益于,有利
profit and loss account 损益账
profit and loss statement 损益表,损益计算书
profit from retention system 利润留成制
profit in common 共同采取权
profit margin (1868年)利润率,销售利润率[指①销售价与成本价之间的差别;②表明差价百分比的比率,比如零售商花了10美元买的小工具,而销售15美元获利率比33%(即以5的差数除以15)]
profit maximization 利润极大化,最大利润点
profit motive 利润动机
profit rate 利润率
profit sharing 利润分成(制)
profit taking (靠买空卖空)获得利润
profit target 利润指标
profit tax 利得税
profit-and-loss responsibility 自负盈亏
profit-making enterprise 营利事业,营利企业
profit-making year 获利年度
profit-maximizing strategy 理论利润最大化策略
profit-seeking corporation 营利法人
profit-sharing agreement 分红协议(指资本家与雇员订立的分享企业利润的协议)
profit-sharing system 利润分成,利润提成,利润留成;分红制
profitability n. 获利能力,有利,有用
profitable a. 有益的,有用的,有利的;有利可图的
profitable business 赚钱生意
profitable insurance 营利保险

profiteer n. 奸商(尤指发国难财者),投机商人,牟取暴利者
profiteering n. 暴利行为;不当得利行为;牟取暴利
profiting from one's wrong 从自己的错误中得利
profitless a. 无利可图的;无益的;无用的
profits à prendre (土地)收益权(指从他人的土地役地上获取产物的权利)(亦称 right of common)
profound impact 深远影响
progenitor n. 原本,正本;先驱,前辈,祖先
progeny n. 子孙,后裔;后继者;(喻)结果,成果
prognosis n. 预后;预测;预告
program(me) n. 课程(表);程序(表);计划;节目;节目单
program appropriation 计划拨款
program budgeting 按计划编制预算
program data 程序数据
program outline 计划纲要
program-carrying-signal 载节目信号
programmed cost 计划成本
programmed guidance system 程序指导系统
programmed market economy 计划市场经济
programming manager 程序管理员
progressist n. 革新主义者;提倡进步者;进步分子;进步党派成员;改良主义者
progressive a./n. 累进的;渐进的;进步的;先进的;(美)(P)进步党的/进步党党员
Progressive Era (美)进步党时代
progressive liberalization 逐步自由化
progressive stage system 渐进阶段制(指一种给予囚犯以希望的鼓励,即只要表现良好和勤奋,可获得早日释放的监狱的管理制度)
progressive tax (1886年)累进税[指这种税型的税率随着纳税人的收入增加其所应纳所得税亦按百分比增加。绝大多数的所得税均属累进的,所以收入越高应纳税率也越高。税收可以是累进的,然而不得使用(超级)累进率(graduated rate)。亦可称为 graduated tax,与 regressive tax 相对。见 graduated tax]
progressive total 累计额,累计总额

Progressivism n. （美）进步党的主义；政党人士的意见；进步党人的主张
prohibit v. 取缔；禁止；阻止，妨碍
prohibited a. 被禁止的,违禁的
prohibited area 禁区
prohibited articles 违禁品
prohibited bargaining 禁止协商
prohibited bargaining subjects 禁止协商议题
prohibited degrees of marriage（或 relationship） 禁止结婚的血亲等级
prohibited immigrant 禁止入境的移民
prohibited military zone 军事禁区
prohibited publication 被禁止的出版物
prohibited weapon 被禁用的武器
prohibition n. 禁止；禁令，禁律；禁制（令），抑制令（上级法院禁止下级法院对无权审理的案件的）诉讼中止令；禁酒；禁酒时期
prohibition against self-incrimination （美）禁止自我归罪原则
prohibition era 禁酒时期
prohibition law （美）禁酒法
prohibition of books 禁书
prohibition of gambling 禁赌
prohibition of illegal use of force 禁止非法使用武力
prohibition of opium 禁止鸦片；禁毒
prohibition of physical punishment 禁止体罚,禁止肉刑
prohibition of private rights 私权禁令
prohibition of slave trade 禁止奴隶贩卖
prohibition of the imprisonment of children 禁止监禁儿童
prohibition of use 禁止使用
prohibition on drug-traffic 麻醉品贩运禁令
prohibition order 禁制令
prohibition-induced crime 禁令降低犯罪
prohibitions del *roy* （英）对国王禁令案（指1607年宣布国王不得亲自审理任何案件）
prohibitions of ex parte communications 禁止单方接触
prohibitive (= prohibitory) a. 禁止性的；限制性的；抑制的

prohibitive duty（或 **tariff**） 禁止性关税
prohibitive impediment of marriage 限制性婚姻障碍（指虽不道德,并不合法但仍可使婚姻有效）
prohibitive right 禁止权
prohibitory order 禁制(处分)令
project n. 方案；计划；规划；工程；(工程、科研等)项目
project budget 项目预算,工程预算
project implementation 项目的执行
project of the state plan 国家计划方案
project programming 制订项目计划
projection n. 投影；反映；预测；估计
projet （条约等的）草案；设计,计划
proletarian a. 无产阶级的
proletarian democracy 无产阶级民主
proletarian dictatorship 无产阶级专政
proletarian jurist 无产阶级法学家
proletarian party 无产阶级政党
proletariat(e) n. 无产阶级
proletay n. （古罗马）最下层阶级的公民
prolicidal a. 杀婴的；堕胎的
prolicide n. （产前、产后）杀害自己的婴儿,堕胎罪；杀婴罪
proliferation n. 扩散,激增
Proliferation Bureau 见 Bureau of Nonproliferation
prolixity n. 冗长失当(指冗长无礼的诉讼对答,法院可对行为者处以罚款)；冗长的答辩,冗长的陈述；冗长,累赘
prolocutor n. 代言人,发言人；教士会议议长,会议主席
prolong v. 延期；延长；拖延
prolong a bill 推迟票据付款期
prolongation n. 延期；延长
prolongation of a bill 汇票延期
prolonged interrogation 延长的审讯
prominence n. 显著,凸出,声望
prominent examples 突出的例证
promise n./v. 1.许诺,诺言；约定；允诺；字据；允诺的东西2.(有)希望,(有)指望；预示/订约,立约；约定；许诺,允诺,作出保证；有希望
promise enforceable at law 可由法律强制执行的允诺

promise to make a gift 赠与的允诺
promised insurance benefit 承诺的保险利益
promised performance 约定之履行,约定之给付
promisee n. 受约人;承诺人
promiser (= promisor) n. 约束者;订约者,立约人;要约人
promisor's promise 允诺人的允诺
promissio insurata 禁言
promissory a. 表示允诺的;约定的,订约的
promissory estoppel 允诺后不得否认的原则
promissory estoppels 允诺禁反言原则,允诺不容否定,允诺后不容否定的原则(指允诺人相信被允诺人由于信赖其允诺而做出某项实质性的作为或不作为,被允诺人确实因此作出某项作为或不作为,且作出后的允诺不得取消或否定,以免给对方造成损害。见 equitable estoppel)
promissory note (18世纪)本票,期票[指一纸无条件的书面承诺票据,由出票人签名,不管发生任何事情,见票绝对支付给持票人或指定的人(designated person)一定数额款项。亦称 note of hand]
promissory warranty (保险法上的)按约定承担(保险责任)
promote v. 促进;发扬;引起;提升;发起,创立;推销(商品);设法通过(法律、议案等);(用不正当手段)获得
promoter n. 1.(企业)发起人,创办人;推销商 2.(恶意的)煽动者;带头者(人) 3.(古代政府告发罪犯的)公众告发人 4.(宗教裁判的)起诉人;揭发人
promoter of disorder (或 treason, crime) 带头作乱(叛国、犯罪)者
promoter's share 发起人股份
promotion n. 促进,增进;提升,晋升;(商品的)推销;(企业的)发起;创设
promotion according to seniority 年资晋升制,以服务满规定年限为标准的晋升制度
promotion by merit 功绩晋升制;以功绩为标准的晋升;量才晋升制
promotion money 开办费,创办费
promotion through examination 考试晋升制(指以考试成绩为公务人员晋升的依据

的一种人事制度)
promotional activities 促销活动,业务推广活动
promotional allowance 推销津贴
prompt a./v. 立即行动的;迅速的;干脆的;果断的;当场交付的/激励,鼓励
prompt cash 立即付现
prompt goods 现货,当场交付的商品
prompt punishment 即时惩罚,就地惩罚
prompt shipment 即期装运
promulgate v. 颁布,公布(法律、法令);散播;传播(信仰,知识等)
promulgate a decree 颁布法令
promulgation n. 颁布,公布;散播;传播
promulgator n. 颁布者,公布者
prong n./v. 尖치,叉子,尖齿/刺,戳,耙开(泥土)
pronoia **system** (拜占庭的)赐地制(一种封建制度)
pronotary n. (美国宾夕法尼亚州某些法院)首席书记官的尊称;首席公证人(见 prothonotary)
pronounce v. 宣布,宣判;宣称,宣告;表示;作出判断
pronounced a. 显著的;明显的,明确的;决然的
pronounced opinion 明确的意见
pronounced sentence 已宣判的判决
pronouncement n. 宣判;宣布;宣告;声明,文告,公告
pronouncement of judgment 宣告判决,宣判
pronouncing a judgement 宣判;宣告;宣称;断言
pronunciamento n. 宣言;檄文;公告;声明
proof n. 1.证据,物证;(口头或书面)言词,证明 2.(苏格兰)法官单独审理证据(以便与陪审团的相对比)3.校稿,校样
proof beyond (a) reasonable doubt 可靠证据,证实无可置疑,无可置疑的程度(证据)
proof by documentary evidence 以书证举证
proof by facts 事实证明
proof of a crime 罪证
proof of a crime beyond a shadow of doubt 罪证确凿

proof of abduction （美）（冤案中的实践证明过程）设证或证明［指相对归纳（induction）与演绎（deduction）证明而言，亦被译为猜想性"推断"，是指裁判者将两种以上的先验性假定视为相互竞争关系，如果有罪假定能令人信服地解释法庭中的已有证据，则作出有罪判决，反之则宣告被告人无罪。定罪证明的过程亦是"设证式证明"的过程，裁判者有"逆向推理"的过程］
proof of age 年龄证明
proof of conviction 判罪的确证
proof of damage 证明损害的证据
proof of death 死亡验证，死亡证明
proof of evidence （英）证据证明
proof of handwriting 笔迹证明
proof of highlypreponderance （美）高度盖然性证明（指在司法实践中法官或陪审团作为定罪的根据；能否排除合理怀疑的证明度未必高于"高度盖然性证明"。依据排除合理怀疑或根据高度盖然性证明标准而定罪，其结果大同小异无本质区别）
proof of innocence 证明无罪
proof of loss 损失证明（指投保人向保险公司提出损失赔偿的书面要求）
proof of marriage 婚姻证明
proof of obligation 债的证明（据）
proof of ownership 所有权的证据
proof of will 遗嘱证明，遗嘱认证
proof on a balance of probabilities "盖然性与优势的证明"要求，盖然性与优势（指被告人负担证明责任时，其证明需达到盖然性占优势的程度），或然性权衡证明
proof of service 送达证明（同 certificate of service）
proof to the contrary 反面证据，反证
proofless a. 无证据的，缺乏证据的，未予证明的，无法证明的
propagandasheet n. 传单
propensity n. （性格上的）倾向，嗜好，癖好
proper a. 适合的，适当的，恰当的，正当的
proper authority 合法委任；有关当局
proper balance between public and private interest 公共利益和个人利益之间的恰当平衡

proper care 见 reasonable care
proper consumer protection measure 消费者正当保护措施
proper defendant 适格被告
proper evidence 适当的证据，正当证据
proper evidence and testimony 正当证据和证言
proper faculties 职能，权力
proper feud 真正的封地或领地［指通过服兵役（on military service）而保有的封地。见 improper feud］
proper jurisdiction 真正管辖权，适当管辖权
proper law （国际私法）准据法（指根据冲突法的原则治理交易的实体法）
proper law of the contract 合同（契约）准据法
proper legal basis 适当的法律依据，正当法律依据
proper loan 正规借贷（指原来意义上的借贷，即使用借贷）
proper means 正当手段
proper name 专有名称
proper party 适当当事人［指与诉讼标的物有利害关系的人，区别于必需当事人（necessary party）］
proper plaintiff 适格原告
proper procedure 正当手续
proper punishment 主刑；适当处罚
proper return port 返航港
property rule 财产规则［指卡—梅框架的三个规则之一，另外两个为责任规则和禁易规则。财产规则意味着国家允许和保护法益的自愿交易："要想从拥有者那里得到法益（legal entitlement），必须通过自愿交易，也就是从拥有者那里以卖方同意的法益的价格加以购买"。就是说："一旦法益归属得到了初始决定，国家不再试图决定其价值……财产规则涉及的是一个有关初始法益归属而非法益价值的公共决定。"至于法益的交易价格则由私人决定："让每一方当事人自己决定这一法益对他价值几何，并且在买方出价不足时给予卖方否决权"。简言之，财产规则赋予法益拥有者的权利，实际上是法益的定价权，

法益拥有者有自愿决定法益交易价格的充分而完整的权利。见 legal entitlement; C & M Framework]
proper third-party claim 适当的第三人请求
proper trial 正当审理
propertied a. 有财产的,有产的(尤指证券等方面的);使用道具的
properties community 有产的社区
properties of nature 自然的特性
property n. 物(权);财产权;所有权;财产(指一切合法的动产和不动产)
property acquired during marriage 婚姻存续期间取得的财产
property adjustment order (离婚或分居后的)财产处分命令
property claim 产权要求
property collectively owned 集体财产
property constable 保管财产的警察
property conveyed 转让的财产
property (in) dispute 系争财产,财产纠纷
property division deed 分产契据(又译:析产契据)
property entrusted 受委托的财产
property in a chattel 动产
property in action 无体物权(与实际占有的物权相对言,指现在不能享用和占有的,如存款、债券、股票、版权等。这类物权如果对方拒绝交出,所有人只有用诉讼方式才可取回)
property in common 共有物;共有财产
property in copyright 版权所有权
property in *custodia legis* 在法院管理下之财产
property in expectancy 期待财产权;预期所有权
property in goods 财产所有权
property in land 土地财产权,土地所有权
property in mortmain 永久营业的财产;不可能转让的产业
property in reversion 归复(财产)权
property inherited 继承财产
property insurance 财产保险
property insured 被保险的财产
property law (英美法系)财产法;(大陆法系)物权法

property liability 财产责任
property loss 财产损失
property market 财产市场
property of all the people 全民财产
property of cooperative 合作社财产
property of dissolved company 已解散公司的财产
property of legacy 遗产
property of military value 具有军事价值的财产
property of ownerless 无主财产
property of social organization 社会组织财产
property of succession 应继承遗产
property owner 财产所有人
property ownership 财产所有制;财产所有权
property pawned 典当财产
property protection 财产权的保护,所有权的保护
property register 财产登记员;财产登记册
property relationship 财产关系
property right 物权,财产权,产权
property right of husband (或 **wife**) 丈夫(或妻子)财产权
property rule 财产规则(见 specific performance)
property settlement 财产协议(书)(指夫妻离婚的产权协议,这种协议包含夫妻婚姻期间所拥有财产的公平分配)
property status 财产状况
property stolen and recovered 被盗已追回的财物
property suit 财产诉讼
property tax (1808年)(美)财产税[指对于私人拥有的财产(特别是不动产),通常基于其财产价值征收的一个税种。地方政府通常对学区(school districts)、市政工程(municipal project)以及类似项目征收财产税。亦称 land tax。见 income tax; excise]
property title 财产契据
property torts 财产毁坏,财产损坏;侵犯财产
property transfer deed 授产契据,过户契据

property unfit for use 已不适用的财产,无用财产
property-owning test for voting 投票的财产资格审查
prophet n. 预言家,先知者[the Prophet(伊斯兰教创立人)穆罕默德;the Prophets(基督教《圣经》中的)各种预言书]
propinquity n. 1.(时间、地点上的)接近;邻近 2.(血统上的)近亲关系 3.(性质、观念上的)类似,近似
proponent n. 提议者;辩护者;支持者;提出认证遗嘱者
proportion n. 1.比;比例;比率 2.均衡;相称;调和 3.部分
proportional a. 按比例的;相当的;相称的
proportional representation 1.比例代表;比例代表制(法)2.人口比例主义
proportional representation in various forms 各种形式的比例代表制
proportional sampling 比例抽样
proportional tax 同 flat tax
proportionality principle in self-defense doctrine 正当防卫说中的相称原则[指理性的信念与理性的行为应该相匀称,相一致,使正当防卫中的理性信念(reasonable beliefs)与理性行为(reasonable acts)得到统一]
proportionality *stritu sensu* 严格意义的相称性
proportionate a./v. 成比例的,均衡的,相称的/使成比例的,使均衡
proposal n. 1.申请;方案;动议,建议,提议 2.求婚 3.(英)投标
proposal form 投保单
proposal of insurance 要保书
propose v. 1.申请,提议;提出 2.提名,推荐 3.求婚 4.计划;打算
proposed contract 草约
Proposed Final Draft of Complex Litigation Project (美)《复合诉讼规程最佳建议草案》(简称《规程草案》)(指关于美国联邦法院系统内部、州法院系统与联邦法院系统之间以及州法院系统内部复合诉讼的移送及相关的诉讼合并的一套标准)
proposed law 审议中的法律,法案

proposed legislation 立法提议
proposed piece of legislation 立法建议
proposed regulation 试行办法,试行规则,试行条例
proposer n. 要保人;提议人;提名人
proposer and seconder 建议人和附议人
proposition n. 建议,提议;计划;陈述;主张
proposition of law 法律命题,法律建(提)议,法律主张
propositus 1.祖先 2.被推荐的人,被提名的人
propound v. 1.提出建议;提出(问题、计划等)供考虑 2.(为求确定合法性而向有关方面)提出(遗嘱等)
propounder n. 提出遗嘱者;提议人,建议人
propria persona (= *in propris persona*)亲自
proprietarianism n. 独占主义
proprietary n./a. 所有权;(指个人或总称)所有人,业主;(美国独立前,英王特许占某一殖民地的)领主;专卖药品/所有人的;有财产的;专有的,独占的
proprietary article 专利品,专卖品
proprietary company 控股公司,持股公司;(英)土地兴业公司;(英)独立公司
proprietary limited 有限所有权
proprietary medicine 专卖药品
proprietary power 见 power coupled with an interest
proprietary right 所有权,所有权权利(指依靠所有物而取得的权利)
proprietary technology 专有技术
proprietary water 专有水域
proprietas nuda (或 *proprietas deducto usufructu*) 虚有权,没有收益的所有权
proprietate probanda (下达给地方行政司法官要执)查清扣押财物的物主的令状
proprietor n. 所有主;业主;专利权人;所有人
proprietorship n. 所有权
proprietory interests 所有人的权益
proprietress n. 女所有主;女业主;女专利权人;女所有人
propriety n. 适当,妥当,正当,得体;礼貌;

(复)礼仪,礼节
propriety of defendant 对被告行使管辖正当性
prorate v. 按比例分配;摊派
proration n. 按比例分配
prorogated jurisdiction (授予法院的)扩大管辖权
prorogatio de loco in locum prorogation (esp. of jurisdiction) from one place to another. (古)处处服从管辖
prorogatio de tempore in tempus proogation (esp. of jurisdiction) from one time to another. 时时服从管辖
prorogation n. 议会等的休会,闭会(尤指英国君主行使特权使议会闭会);(苏格兰)法院扩大管辖权;服从管辖(指当事人同意接受法院管辖);(美)合同中的约定管辖(指合同双方约定一个制定解决有关合同的有争议的州或县法院);诉讼延期
prorogation of parliament 议会休会
prorogue v. 使(议会)休会,使(立法会议)闭会(见 prorogation)
prosaic non-doctrinal form 如实的非教条形式
proscribe v. 1.(古罗马)公布(死囚)的姓名;剥夺……的公权 2.摒弃于法律的保护之外;禁止 3.放逐;充军
proscription n. 剥夺,剥夺公权;禁止;放逐;排斥;(古罗马)判刑公告(公布杀死或放逐某人)
proscriptive a. 1.剥夺公权的 2.禁止的;排斥的
prosecutable a. 可提起公诉的
prosecute v. 1.告发,检举,对……提起公诉 2.实行,进行,执行,彻底执行 3.做检察官
prosecute an action 起诉,提起诉讼
prosecuting a. 告发的,检控的;控方的
prosecuting a claim 提出诉讼请求
prosecuting attorney (美)(州或地方的)检察官(又称 state's attorney 或 district attorney)
prosecuting counsel 控方律师
prosecuting of offenders 检控罪犯
prosecuting officer 公诉人

prosecuting witness 控方证人
prosecution n. (多指刑事诉讼)起诉,检举;告发;被告发;(总称)原告及其律师;检察当局;(偶用于民事)提起诉讼;进行,实施;从事,经营
prosecution case 控方的证据和争论(与 defence case 相对而言)
prosecution counsel 原告律师;公诉律师
prosecution fee 控诉费
prosecution of offences 罪行检控
Prosecution of Offense Acts, 1985 (英)《1985 年罪行公诉法》;《罪行起诉法》
prosecution of writers accused of literary offence 指控用文字进行违法犯罪的作者;文字狱
prosecution order 提起公诉的裁定
prosecutor n. 原告,起诉人;检举人;(通常指)检察官(员)(见 public prosecutor)
prosecutor general 总检察长
prosecutor of the pleas (美)(新泽西州的)区(或县)检察官(与其他州的"district attorney"或"county attorney"相一致)
prosecutor's detectives 检察官侦探队
prosecutor's office 检察院
prosecutorial discretion 检察官的酌处权(指检察官决定是否对某人提起公诉、对新闻界发表有多大的影响、给予何等惩罚、什么类型的抗辩方可接受等的酌处权)
prosecutorial quirks 检察权的争论,检察管辖的争执;检察管辖的借口
prosecutrix n. 女起诉人;女原告;女检察官
prospect v./n. 勘探;勘察;找矿/展望,期望;(美)可能成为主顾的人;有希望的候选人;(复)前景;前程
prospecting permit 探矿许可证
prospective a. 未来的;预料中的,预期的
prospective borrower 贷款的对象
prospective damages 可预见的损害赔偿
prospective heir 预期继承人[指可以排除其他人继承财产的当然继承人,或为当然继承人(heir apparent)或为推定法定继承人(heir presumptive)。见 expectant heir]
prospective juror(s) 准陪审员,预期担任的陪审员

prospective law (statute) 适用于将来的法律(法规),将会生效的法律(法规)
prospective pilots 预备飞行员
prospective purchaser 未来的买主
prospective value 预期价值
prospective yield 预期收益
prospectus n. 1.招股章程;(募债)说明书(指公司撰写股份或募债的说明书)2.意见书;计划书;发起书
prosperity in common 共同富裕
prostitute n./v. 1.妓女,娼妓 2.出卖灵魂者;贪墨者(尤指为了图利而粗制滥造的文人)/1.使沦为妓女;卖淫 2.滥用(才能等);出卖(名誉)
prostitution n. 1.操淫业;卖淫 2.滥用
protagonist n. 提倡者,拥护者
protanto (pro tan to) 就那么多,尽可能多,力所能及
protean topics 多种多样的课题;变幻莫测的课题
protect v. 1.庇护,保护;警戒;防护 2.备款(以应期票的)支付
protect...from 保护……不受;使免于
protected a. 受保护的,被保护的
protected building 受保护的建筑(物)
protected child 受保护的儿童
protected goods 受保护的财物
protected internee 受保护的被拘留者;受保护的被扣留物(如船只等)
protected offendress 受保护的女罪犯
protected person 1.被任命的监护人(conservator)或制定的其他保护令进行保护的人 2.(国际法)按国际法受到保护的人,特别是在冲突中落入占领军之手的人,有资格受到保护的人受到标准对待的,按照《关于战时保护平民的日内瓦公约》(1949年)(包括禁止暴力威胁和肉体惩罚) 3.(英国法)英联合王国(United Kingdom)的保护国(protectorate)的居民[虽然他们不是不列颠的臣民,但他们受到王国政府(Crown)的外交保护]
protected prisoner of war 受保护的战俘
protected state 受保护国,被保护国
protected tenancy 受保护的租借权
protected tenant 受保护的租户

protected territory 保护地
protected trade 受保护的贸易
protecting state (或 power) 保护国
* *Protectio trahit subjectionem, et subjectio protectionem.* Protection draws with it subjection, and subjection protection. 保护导致服从,服从导致保护。
protection n. 1.保护,庇护;保护者,保护物;通行证;护照 2.保护贸易制度 3.(美)(罪犯通过贿赂而取得的)免予起诉
protection and indemnity clause 保赔保险条款;保护及赔偿条款
protection and indemnity club 保赔协会
protection and indemnity insurance 保赔保险
protection and indemnity liability insurer 保赔责任承保人
protection of infant industry 幼稚产业保护,新兴产业的保护
protection of one's personality 人格保护
protection of the environment 环境保护
protection of the interests of minor 保护未成年人的利益
protection of trustee (法院)对受托人的保护
protection of women and children 保护妇女与儿童
protectionism n. (贸易)保护主义;贸易保护制
protectionist a. 保护(贸易)制的
protectionist policy 保护贸易的政策
protective a. 保护的;保护贸易的
protective custody (1929年)保护性监管[指①因为一个人的安全和健康处于危险境地诸如证人或无行为能力人可能会伤害自己或伤害他人,所以政府将这类人实施保护性的监管、控制或将他们隔离开来;②(家庭法)将孩子从家中或从以前负责监护的人的手中转移之后,为了保护孩子免受虐待、遗弃或危险处境的一种安排,将孩子安置在环境安全收养家庭(foster family)之中;③因为一个人受到会伤害他的刑事威胁,而由执法机关安排他在某地(而不是他家)并进行安全保护]
protective device 保安装置

protective export (或 import) duty 保护出(进)口税
protective legislation 保护贸易立法
protective measure 保护措施,安全措施,保安措施
protective order 保护令(指法院为保护某一个人不受干扰的命令);告知出庭的令状
protective provisional measures 临时措施,临时办法
protective provisions 保护性法律条款,保护性法律规定
protective rule 保护性规范
protective settlement 保护性的财产授予
protective tariff 保护性税则,保护性关税
protective trade 保护性贸易
protective trust 1.受保护信托 2.保护信托(终生或比终生短一点的信托)
protector n. 1.保护人 2.保护装置;保护物 3.(英)摄政
protector of the settlement (英)地产保护人
protectorate n. 1.保护国;保护权;保护制度;保护关系 2.摄政职位;摄政时期;摄政政治
protégé 被保护人;门徒,女性被保护人,女门徒
protest n./v. 1.明言,主张 2.抗议;异议;反对;抗议书 3.船长海事报告书;船长证明书(通常指证明船的损坏是由灾难造成的证明书);货船损失证书(指因货物或船舶受损失而由船长写的证明,备以后赔偿纠纷使用) 4.(对票据等的)拒付证书;(缴付人对苛捐等的)抗议书/明言,断言,主张;抗诉,抗议;不服,反对;拒付(票据等)
protest a decision 反对一项决定,对裁决提出异议
protest expenses 拒兑费用
protest for non-acceptance 拒绝承兑证书
protest for non-payment 拒绝付款证书
protest of negotiable instrument 流通票据的拒付
(a) protest strike 表示抗议的罢工
protestant n. 1.抗议人;抗诉人;异议人 2.基督教徒;新教徒
protestation n. 抗议,异议,反对;声明,断言

protested bill 拒绝承兑的票据,拒兑汇票
protester (=protestor) n. (期票等的)拒付者;抗议者;提出异议者;反对者
prothonotary n. 1.=pronotary 2.(英)(从前的民事诉讼和王座高等法院的)首席书记官;(美)(某些法院的)首席书记官
protocol n./v. 议定书;条约草案;草约;外交礼节;会议记录,备忘录;外交文书的首尾程式;礼仪,外交礼节/拟定草案(议定书),拟定条约草案
protocol of arbitration 仲裁议定书
protocol of authentication 认证备忘录
protocol of statelessness relating to a certain case (1930年的)关于某种无国籍情况认定书
Protocol thereto on Matters Specific to Aircraft Equipment 《与航空器设备有关的议定书》(该协定书与《移动设备国际利益公约》均为国际统一私法协会和国际民航组织密切合作的产物)
prototype n. 样品,样本,原型;典型;范例
protract v. 延迟,拖延,延长
protract a debate 延长辩论
protracted cases 拖延的案件,长时间的案件
protutor 代理监护人
provable a. 可证明的,可证实的
provable debt in bankruptcy 可证实的破产债务;宣告破产时确认的债务
prove v. 1.证明,证实 2.检验;试验;考验;认证(遗嘱等)
prove a will 认证遗嘱(有效)
prove an *alibi* 提出不在犯罪现场的证据
prove sb.'s honesty 考验某人是否诚实
proved damage 已证实的损害
prover n. 证明者,证实者;证明物;招供(同案犯)人
provide v. 提供;抚养(for);赡养(for);提供生计(for);备装;供给;预防(against);做准备(for);规定,订立;提供(with)
provide for 提供生计
provided conj. (that)以……为条件,假如,只要,但
provided by law 按法律(或法规)所规定
provided (that) circumstances permit 假

如情况允许
provided that 只要,但
provider n. 供应者,供养者;准备者
province n. 1.省;地方;(学术的)领域;部门;活动范围 2.职权;(法官、法院、陪审团的)司法管辖(或职权)范围
province of government 政府的职权
provincial a. 1.省的,外省的;地方(性)的 2.粗野的
provincial administration 省级行政机关
provincial assembly 省议会
provincial board 省委员会
provincial council 省议会,省委员会
provincial courts 省法院;(英)大主教辖区法院
provincial estates (法史)外省三级会议(指14世纪出现的省的代表制议会制度)
provincial government 省政府
provincial governor 省长
provincialis 在省里(或当地)有住所的人
proving a will 认证遗嘱(有效)
provision(s) n. 1.条文,条款,规定 2.供应,给养;粮食;供应品 3.预备;防备;措施;准备
provision of law 法律条文(旧译:法条),法律规定
Provision of Oxford 《牛津条例》(指从贵族议会中推选24人的委员会于1258年制定的法律,旨在限制亨利三世的权力)
provision of the treaty 条约的条文规定
provisional a. 暂时的,暂时性的,暂行的
provisional agenda 临时议程
provisional agreement 临时协议,临时协定
provisional apprehension 拘留;暂时拘捕
provisional assessment 临时估值;临时估税额
provisional assignee 临时受让人
provisional attachment (案件)判决前的扣押(prejudgment attachment) [指在未判决前扣押中债务人的财产已被扣押,所以债权人具有优势,通过变卖已扣押之财产,债权人将获得保证在判决时重新取得补偿。一般来说,听审必须在扣押之前进行,而大多数法庭要求债权人交纳保证金(to post a bond)以备由财产扣押所扣

任何损害赔偿(damages)。特别是如果最终债权人败诉。见 prejudgment attachment]
provisional certificate 临时证书;临时执照
provisional charter 临时执照;临时包租(机、船)
provisional committee 临时委员会
provisional constitution 临时宪法,临时约法
provisional court 临时法庭
provisional domicile 临时住所
provisional government 临时政府
provisional injunction 临时禁令;临时指令
provisional institution (或 tribunal) of arbitration 临时仲裁机构
provisional measure 临时措施
provisional notice 临时通告
provisional order 临时(性)命令;(法院)临时裁定;临时(性)程序
provisional regulation 暂行条例
Provisional Regulations on the Governance of Populations (中)《城市户口管理暂行条例》
provisional remedy 1.立即补偿;临时补偿 2.特别紧急补救办法(指民事诉讼中一个适用于原告的临时手续,在诉案悬而未决时,可用来保证他不致受到不可弥补的损害和财产的耗费)
provisional seizure (美)临时(财产)扣押(指路易斯安那州法律的一项补偿,实际上与其他州的一般性财产查封具有相同的性质)
provisional sovereignty 临时主权
provisional specification 临时说明书
provisional statutory effect 临时的法定效力
provisional treaty 临时条约,暂行条约
provisions in contracts for choice of law 合同(契约)中的法律选择条款
Provisions of Rule 144A 144A号法令条款(指"合格机构购买者"条款,它允许足够数量的非注册证券持有者在二级流通市场进行交易)
Provisions of the Peoples Republic of China for Labour Management in Chinese Foreign Joint Ventures 《中华人民共和国中外合资经营企业劳动管理规定》

proviso n. （合同等的）附件；（法律的）但书，条件
proviso clause 保留条款（亦称限制性条款，指法规或合同上限制若干权限或行为的保留条款）
* *Proviso est providere praesentia et futura, non praeterita.* A proviso is to provide for the present or future, not the past. 但书不是为了过去而是为了现在或将来规定的。
provisory a. 有附文的,附带条件的；一时的,临时的,暂定的
provisory clause 除外条款；限制性条款
provocable (=provokable) a. 易受刺激（煽动、挑拨）的
provocateur n. 挑衅者；挑拨者；煽动者
provocateur agent 煽动分子
provocation n. 挑衅,刺激,激愤,激怒（指①刺激他人做些事情,特别是进行犯罪行为；②由于某种言语或某种行为致使他人丧失理智,以致失去自我控制,甚至造成该人冲动犯罪）
provocation of disorder 煽动骚乱
provocative act 挑衅行为
provoke v. 刺激；煽动；激怒；惹气；引起
provoke dissension 挑拨离间
provost n. 监督者；负责官员；监狱看守；宪兵司令；院长；（苏格兰）市长
provost court （在敌国占领区设立的审理非重大案件的）宪兵法庭
provost guard 宪兵纠察队
provost marshal 宪兵主任；宪兵司令；军法官
provost sergeant 宪兵中士
prowl n. 徘徊（潜行（想偷窃等）
prowl car （警察用的）巡逻车
prowler n. 小偷；徘徊者；暗巡者
proximate a. （场所、时间、次序等）最接近的；贴近的；近似的；前后紧接的
proximate cause 近因,最近原因（指时间和空间上与损害结果最接近的原因）
proximate damages 最接近的损害赔偿
proximate estimate 概算
proximity n. 近因（英美刑法理论中的法定原因）；近似,最近
proximo 下月的（商业或公函用语）；最近

proxy n. 1.代理；代理（权）,代表（权）2.代理人,代表人 3.（对代理人的）委托书；委托代表 4.代理投票
proxy contract 代理合同,委托合同
proxy executor 代理执行人
proxy marriage 代理举办婚礼,代理婚姻,代办婚姻[指婚姻当事人一方或当事双方通过代理人缔结婚姻并举办婚姻仪式。婚姻是一种按法律规定的实际缔结婚姻的形式(in form),在法律的许多方面来说婚姻具有十分重要的后果,涉及比如侵权、刑法、证据、债务人-债权人关系、财产、契约等]
proxy signature 被授权人签字,代表签字
proxy statement 委托说明书,授权委托说明书[指伴随委托书要求(proxy solicitation)的一个信息文件,该文件说明由公司建议的行为,比如合并等,或根据证券交易委员会之要求上市公司在为股东大会征集委托书时,按规定应向股东披露股东大会所表决事项等]
proxy voting 代理投票
prude n. 过分拘谨的人,装作正经的人（尤指女人）
prudent person 见 reasonable person
prudent person rule 智虑者规则（指受托人可以进行传统安全性投资、信托投资,但亦冒风险承担损失责任）
prudent trustee 谨慎的受托人
* *Prudenter agit qui praecepto legis obtemperat.* He acts prudently who obeys the command of the law. 谁依法行事,谁就精明、谨慎。
prurient a. 1.好色的,荒淫的,淫欲的,色情的 2.渴望的
psephologist n. 选举学家
psephology n. 选举学（对选举结果等的评估等）
pseudograph n. 伪书,伪作；冒名作品
pseudohermaphroditism n. 假两性体
pseudology n. 谎话
pseudonym n. 笔名,假名
pseudonymous work 假名作品（不少国家版权法把假名作品与匿名作品归为一类,与笔名作品分开,假名作者往往难以找

到,而笔名作者则比较明确)
psychiatric(al) a. 精神病学的;医治精神病的
psychiatric a. 精神病学的,医疗精神病的(指涉及或关系到对精神上、感情上或行为上的错乱,经过在精神病学领域培养有素的医生对此进行研究、处理)
psychiatric evidence 精神病学上的证据
psychiatric expert certification 司法精神病鉴定
psychiatry n. 精神病学
psychological a. 心理上的;心理学的
psychological block 精神障碍,心理障碍
psychological depression 精神衰弱
psychological function 心理效能
psychological parent 心理上父母
psychological test 心理测验
psychological theory of law 心理(学)法学
psychological treatment of prisoners 囚犯的心理治疗
psychologist n. 心理学家
psychoneurosis n. 精神(性)神经病
psychopath n. 精神病人;精神变态者;心理病者
psychopathic a. 心理变态的,精神变态的
psychopathic disorder 精神错乱,心理混乱
psychopathology n. 精神病理学,心理病理学
psychopathy n. 精神变态
psychotherapy n. 心理疗法,精神疗法
psychotic n. 精神病患者
ptomain(e) n. 尸毒碱
ptomaine poisoning 尸碱中毒;食物中毒
ptomatopsia n. 尸体剖检
ptomatopsy n. 尸体剖检
Pub. L. (Public Law) 公法
pubertas (罗马法)适婚期(指人的生理成熟适宜生育,已具备足够智育、发育阶段,则被认为取得民事行为能力并可缔结婚姻关系。查士丁尼法将适婚年龄定为男14岁,女12岁。见 puberty)
puberty n. 青春期(英国1926年法律规定自16岁两性儿童进入青春期;美国和大多数国家规定为男孩14岁、女孩12岁)
public n./a. 群众,大众,民众;公众(the public)/1.公共的,公众的,公有的,公用的 2.政府的,公家的,公立的 3.公共事务的;为公的 4.知名的,突出的
public accommodation 公众优惠的地方,公众方便之处
public accountant 公共会计师
public accounts 公共账目
public act 公众行为;(英)公法法令(指处理有关事务以及关于公共利益和一般利益方面的法令,与私法法令相对而言)
public action 公诉
public adjuster (或 appraiser) 保险公证人(指向保险人收取费用,为其办理保险标的查勘、鉴定和估价以及赔偿的理算、洽商并给以证明的人)
public administration 公共行政;行政管理;行政
public administrator 公定遗产管理人
public advantages 公共利益
public affairs 公共事务;国家事务
public announcement 公告
public appointment 公职的任命
public arbitrator 公设仲裁人
public assent 公众意见,公众赞许
public attitude 公众态度,公众看法
public attorney (英)检察总长,公诉律师
public auction 公开拍卖
public audit 公开稽核;公开审计
public authority 公共机构;政府机构
public benefit 公益
public benefiting foundation 公益基金会;公益财团
public bidding 公开投标,公开招标
public bill (国会提出的)有关公开利益的法案;公法案(指英国提交议会的有关国家政策事务的法案)
public body 公共团体;民意机关
public bond 公债券,公债
public building 公共建筑物;国家建筑物
public calling 公共名称;公共行业
public cemetery 公墓,公共坟场
public character 知名人物
public charge 受政府救济者(指靠政府救济以维持生活的穷人);受公众监管者
public choice theory 公共选择理论
public civil officer 政府文职官员,政府官员

public coercion 公开胁迫;公开压制
public comments 公共评论
public company 公营公司;(美、英、法等国)公益公司(指基于公益的、由政府投资并控制的公司)
public contract 公共契约;公约;公用事业集资合同(契约)
public control (中)管制(指对罪犯不予关押只限制其行动自由的一种刑罚)
public corporation 公法人;公共事务行政机构;公众公司(指相对"封闭公司"而言,其股票由公众持有并可进行交易)
public credit 政府贷款,政府信用
public danger 国难
public debate 公开辩论
public debt 公债,国家债务
public decency 公共礼仪;社会风化
public deed 公文据
public defamation 公开毁坏他人名誉(罪)
public defender 公设律师;(美刑事案件中的)公设辩护人
public document 公文,国家文件
public domain 公有产业;(美)国有土地;不属专利范围;不受版权保护的财产
public domain citation system 公共所有(版权)援引系统(指一种援引检索体系)
public domain works 公共所有著作(指大众均可任意使用的属公共所有的著作,除须注意著作人格权保护外,不存在着作权的授权问题)
public duty 公共职责;公务;公共责任
public economy of socialism 社会主义公有经济
public election 公开选举
public employee 公职人员
public enemy 公敌
public enemy number one 头号公敌;第一号罪犯
public enforcement of law 公开执法
public enterprise 公营企业
public examination 公开审讯;公开审查;公开检查;公开考试
public expenditure 政府开支
public facilities 公共设施

public finance (国家或地方的)公共财政,财政
public franchising 公共经营特许权;公共特许
public functionary 公务人员,公职人员,国家职员
public fund 公共基金[指①政府部门的收入或款项(常用复数),这个词条不仅包含硬币、纸币还包含银行存款,和代替公款(public money)投资的文据(instruments)。②州或国民政府发行的证券]
public gallery (法庭上的)公众旁听席
public gathering 公共集会
Public General Acts and Measures (英)《公共普通法和措施》(指由皇家文书局1831年起出版的一种按年代顺序编排的单行法汇编)
public general bills (美)公共普通议案
public good 公益;社会利益;社会风尚
public good or common good 公共的善,公益
public goods 公共产品,公共物品
public harm (或hazard) 公害
public health 1.公共健康;公众的健康及卫生状况 2.很多城市设有公共卫生,或公共健康部门[负责维护公共健康,联邦法规对于健康的行政管理规定由健康与人类服务部(Department Of Health and Human Services)管理]
public health services 公共卫生事业
Public Health Service (美)公共卫生部(或局)(原为美国卫生部与人类局的一个机构,负责提高美国公民体力智力的健康水平)
public hearing 公开听审
public hearings (美国国会的)公众听证
public held corporation 大型公开公司
public holiday 公休假日
public house 酒馆;旅店,客栈
Public Housing Administration (美)公众房产管理局
public indecency 公共猥亵(罪);公然猥亵(罪);公开的粗野言行
public indictment 公诉书
Public Information Officer (美)公共信息

官(指联邦最高法院于1935年增加的一名公众信息官,主要目的在于提高法院的判决工作透明度,但不得解释判决意见)
public institution 公共机构
public interest 公共利益,公众利益[指①授权公认和保护的公共利益;②符合政府规定的与公众利益相关的事物。法学界认为:国家利益、社会利益,以社会公众为利益主体的利益,不包括国家利益;③不仅包括国家利益、社会利益,还包括其他不特定法人和自然人的利益]
public interest action 公益诉讼[指美国公益诉讼最早就是通过法律授权的形式产生的。1890年美国国会通过了反垄断的《谢尔曼反托拉斯法》(the Sherman Anti-Trust Act of 1890)。该法规定,针对违法的垄断公司,司法部门、联邦政府、团体乃至个人均可提起诉讼。这项法案的出台标志着民事公益诉讼制度在美国诞生]
public interest lawyer 公共利益律师
public interest organization 公益组织
public international law 国际公法,国际法
Public International Union 国际公会
public intervention (中)社会干预原则(诉讼法上的一项原则)
public investment 公共投资
public issure of shares 公开发行的股票
public jail 监狱
public job 公职
public juristic person 公法人
public land 公有地,公地
public law 公法
public lawyers 公法律人,公设律师(指法官、检察官所在的司法机关,英美称为公法律人。见 private lawyer)
public legal entity 公法人
public legal notice 法定的公告
public legislation 公共立法
public libel 公开文字诽谤(罪)
public liquidator 公共清算人
public maritime law 海事公法;公海法
public market 公共市场
public meeting 公众集会
public mischief 公众妨害(指故意干扰司法实施、干扰警察执行任务,如虚报被窃使警察白费调查时间等)
public money 公款
public morality 公共道德;社会风纪
public morals 公共道德
public mortgage society 公共抵押协会
public notary 公证人
public notice 公告
public nuisance 公害;(法律上禁止的)妨害公共利益的行为;妨害大众的事物;妨害公益罪
public offense 公罪(指侵犯公共利益的犯罪);违法行为;轻罪行为;法律禁止并予以处罚的行为或不作为
public offering 公开上市的
public office 公职;公务机关;国家机构
public officer (或 **officials**) 公职人员,公务员;国家官员
public officials act 公职人员法,公务员法
public offense 公罪(指侵犯公共利益的犯罪);违法行为;轻罪行为;犯罪行为;法律禁止并予以处罚的行为或不作为
public opinion 舆论,民意;公众意见
public opinion poll 民意测验,民意调查
public order 公共秩序
public order theory of law 法律的公共秩序论
public organization 公共组织,社会团体
public ownership 公有制;公有权
public ownership of the means of production 生产资料公有制
public ownership system of socialism 社会主义公有制
Public Papers of the Presidents (美)《总统公文》(指1958年由联邦注册部出版的一个官方成套卷本总统文件的汇集,对于D.罗斯福总统和胡佛总统以后的历届总统,均按年代顺序编排)
public parking 公共停车场地
public pawnshop 公共典当
public peace 治安,公安
public performance 公开演出
public place 公共场所
public policy 公共政策
public policy exception 公共政策例外(指英美法系国家对外法域法律适用的限制,

即对国际私法上的公共政策机制的称谓。大陆法系国家则称为 reservation of public order)
public policy underpinnings 公共政策基础
public power 公共权力
public press 公共印刷所
public pressure 公众压力
public proclamation 公告,公开宣告;公开宣言
public procurator 公诉人;检察官
public procurator-general (=public procurator- in-chief) 首席检察官,总检察长(又译:检察总长)
public proceedings 公开的程序
public property 公有财产,公产
public prosecuting authority 公诉机关,检察机关
public prosecution 公诉;公诉机关
public prosecutor 检察官,公诉人
public protector 公共保护人
public readiness 公众准备就绪
public reason 公共理性[指美国著名法哲学家罗尔斯(John Rawls)(1921—2002),在其后期关于"政治自由主义"的论说中基于现代社会的"合理多元论事实"(the fact of reasonable pluralism)所构建的"最低纲领的自由主义",为深入认识现代法律秩序的形成机制提供理论参照。其中,他关于"公共理性"(public reason)的论说更是这种"最低纲领的自由主义"的核心理论构件。从法哲学视角探究公共理性的启示与限度,对于深入认识"现代法律秩序"的形成机理具有重要意义。"公共理性"具有丰富内涵,主要有三个方面:第一,现代社会的"合理多元论事实"构建的一个政治自由理念;第二,其对立面不是"私人理性"或康德—哈贝马斯意义上的"理性的私人运用",而是非公共理性;第三,公共理性所适用的主题具有公共性,即只适用于与所有公民都息息相关的"宪法实质"和"基本正义"问题]
public record 政府机构(依法保存备查的可作证据用的)备案材料
public record office 国家档案局,政府档案局

public register 公设登记簿
public registry of commerce 国家商业登记局,国家商业注册处
public relation 公共关系
public relief 社会救济
public revenue 国库收入,财政收入
public right 公权;(英)公共权利(普通法和制定法上的一项权利,它属于公众全体,任何成员均可行使,在此项权利被侵犯后,由受害人本人或其家属提起诉讼,请求检察官颁发禁止令)
public right of passage (或 way) 公共通行权;公共道路通行权
public right to know 公共知情权
public river 有共同航运权的河流
public safety 公共安全(指国家可行使警察权力制定法规予以保护的公众安全)
public sale 公开买卖;公开出售;拍卖
public seal 公章
public security 公安;治安
public security assistant (中)公安助理员
public security authority 公安当局,公安机关
Public Security Bureau 公安局
public security commissioner (中)治(安)保(卫)委员
public security detainee (因)违反治安规定而受拘留者
public security harbor precinct station 水上公安派出所
public security household registry section 公安户籍段
public security inspectorate 公安侦查机关
Public Security Ministry 公安部
public security officer 公安人员,公安机关官员
public security organ 公安机关
public security railroad precinct station 铁路公安派出所
public security school 公安学校
public security sector 公安部门
public security subbureau (中)公安分局
public servant 公务员,公职人员;公仆;官员;(英)公用事业的职员
public service 公共事业,公用事业;(大

写)公共(用)事业单位(或其职员)
Public Service(或 **Utilities**)**Commission** 公用事业委员会(指管理具有公益事务章程的私有商业之间的公用事业委员会,它履行公共职能并对于政府部门有帮助)
Public Service Commission Ordinance 《公务员叙用委员会条例》
public session 公开开庭期
public sexual activity 公开的性行为
public ships 国有船舶,公有船舶
public statute (英)公法性制定法
public subscription 公开认购;公开捐助
public surveillance (中)群众管制,群众监督
public surveyor 公共验证人,公共鉴定人
public tender 公开投标
public things 公有物
public trial 公开审理;公判;公审
public trial meeting 公审大会
public trust 公众信托,公开信托;团体信托(见 trust corporation)
public trustee 公共受托人
public undertaking 公营企业,国营企业
public use 公共使用,公用[指美国联邦宪法第五修正案规定:非经正当补偿,私有财产不得征收充作公用(…nor shall private property be taken for public use, without just compensation)。据此可知,美国联邦宪法不是用"公共利益"而是用"公用"(public use)的概念来表述征用的目的。按字面含义,"公用"应当是公众可以直接使用被征收的土地,但在美国的司法实践中,"公用"的含义被扩展为包括"公共利益"或"公共目的"(public purpose)的概念。即使公众不能直接使用被征收的土地,如果公众能够从被征收土地的使用中获益,征收土地就是正当的]
public utility 公用事业;(复)公共设施
public utility facilities 市政公共设施
public value 社会价值
public verdict 公开裁决
public virtue 公德
public waters 公海
public waterway 公共水道
public weal 公共福利

public welfare fund 公益金;公共福利基金
public welfare legal entity 公益法人
public welfare undertaking 公益事业
public will 公证遗嘱
public work contract 公共工程合同(契约);市政工程合同(契约)
public works 公共工程,市政工程
Public Works Administration (美)公共工程署
public wrong 侵犯公众利益的不法行为(指侵犯国家和社会的罪行,并非所有侵犯公众利益均为犯罪,例如因违反与政府签订的合同而犯有违法行为,侵犯公众利益,这种违法行为属于民事,而非刑事)
public-law controversy 公法上的争议
public-private joint operation (中)公私合营
public-private partnerships 公私合伙人资格
public-welfare offense 见 offence 1
publican n. (古罗马)承办人(指承包公共事务,如兴建或维修公共建筑供应海外军队征收什一税和关税工作的人);(税务、贡物的)征收员(英)酒店(或客栈)老板
publication n. 1.出版物,发行物;出版,发行;发表,公布 2.散布(指有损他人名誉之类的"小广播")
publication contract 出版合同(契约)
publication of a will 遗嘱正式宣告
publici juris 公共权利的
publicist n. 国际法学家,公法学家;政治家;时事评论家
publicity n. 宣传;广告
publicity campaign 宣传运动
publicity requirements 公示要件
publicly ad. 1.当众地,公开地 2.由公众、由政府(出资或持有等)
publicly certified acknowledgment 公认证书
publicly elected body 民选机构
publicly owned merchant ship 国有商船
publicly owned property 公有财产
publicly traded securities 公开交易证券
publicness n. 公开性(用于审理、辩论等)
publish v. 出版,发行;发表,公开
publish (to ask, put up) the banns (英)结婚预告,结婚周知(=call the banns)

published edition of works 已出版的作品版式(这种客体享有版权或邻接权。我国1991年著作权法实施条例中规定它享有邻接权)
publisher n. 1.发行人;出版者;报刊发行者 2.发表者,公布者
publishers act 出版法
publishing right 出版权
Publius n. 普布利乌斯(美)[亚历山大·汉密尔顿(Alexander Hamilton)和约翰·杰伊(John Jay)共同使用的笔名,创作《联邦党人文集》,为议会制政府的经典著作]
Puerto Rico (美)波多黎各[指位于北大西洋和加勒比海(Caribbean Sea)之间,大安的列斯岛的东端,按1952年美国国会立法成为美国的一个自由联邦],波多黎各人,波多黎各的
puff n./v. (对作品、商品等的)言过其实的(地)吹嘘;夸张;(作)广告
puffer n. 吹捧者;(拍卖场中人)抬价人;加价人
puffery n. 吹捧;鼓吹;吹捧的广告
puffing n. (对作品、商品等的)言过其实的吹嘘
puis darrein continuance (普通法)自延后期追加辩诉理由(指自上次讯问后,持有新事由,须追加辩诉理由);追加辩诉意旨书
puisne n./a. 助理法官(旧译:陪席推事,= puisne judge)/后辈的;年轻的;资历浅的;职位较低的
puisne judge 年轻资浅的法官;合议庭审判长以下的法官;高等法院之陪席法官
puisne justices 高等法院的普通法官
puisne mortgage (英)普通抵押(指没有交出地产文件为抵押品的抵押)
puissance publique 公共权力
pull down 1.拉倒,推翻,摧毁 2.使降低,下跌 3.使体质减弱,使精神不振 4.领取(工资等)
Pullman Strike of 1894 1894年普尔门式火车罢工
pulsator n. 原告;行为者
pump v. 1.用抽水机打水 2.盘问,探问,审问;以追问(或奥妙方式)探出(秘密)
pump a prisoner 审问罪犯

punch v. 1.用拳猛击,拳打;用力击,用力按 2.(用棒)戳,刺
pundbrech 1.(古英国法律上)越监;越监犯 2.非法从牲畜栏内取走牲畜
punish v. 1.罚;惩罚;处罚 2.痛击;折磨;损害
punish by law 依法惩处,法办
punish capitally 处以死刑
punish not in keeping with the crime 罚不当罪
punishable a. 该罚的,可受惩处的
punishable offence 应受惩处的罪行
punisher n. 处罚者,惩罚者
punishment n. 罚,处罚;刑罚;痛击;折磨;损害
punishment by exile 流放刑;处以流放
punishment by labor service 处以劳役,罚役
punishment conditions 处罚条件
* **Punishment does not fit the crime.** 罚不当罪。
punishment exceeding the crime 罚不当罪
* **Punishment fits the crime.** 罪有应得(又译:罪刑相当)。
punishment of control 管制处罚,管制处分
punishment of deprivation of liberty 剥夺自由的刑罚
punishment of detention 拘役处罚;拘留处分
punishment of imprisonment 监禁处罚
punishment of war criminals 对战争罪犯的惩罚
punishment with a warning 警告处分
punitism n. 惩办主义
punitive a. 刑罚的;惩戒性的;给予惩处的
punitive damages 惩罚性的损害赔偿费(见 exemplary damages)
punitive damages update 惩罚性损害赔偿新资料
punitive expedition (为)惩罚叛乱者的征伐,讨伐
punitive intervention 惩罚性干预
punitive justice 因果报应
punitive law 刑罚法,刑法
punitive measure 惩罚措施

punitive power 惩罚权
punitive sanction 惩罚性的制裁
punitory a. =punitive
pupil n. （有监护人的）未成年人；被监护人；（中、小学）学生；学徒
pupilage [=pupil(l)age, pupil(l)arity] n. 未成年期（指自出生至青春期以前的时期）；学徒身份；（中、小学）学生身份
pupilius 男（性）被监护人
pupilla 女（性）被监护人
pupillary a. （受监护的）未成年人的；（中、小学）学生的
puppet n. 1.木偶 2.傀儡；受他人操纵的人
puppet government 傀儡政府
puppet regime 傀儡政权
pur autre vie 为他人的终身利益
pural postulates of life 生命的权利义务原则；生命的权利义务基本原理
purchase n./v. （15世纪）1.购置行为或购买程序 2.通过意愿、转让、抵押或赠与等而获得一个人拥有的而非从另一个人世传或继承方式所获得的不动产（见 descent）3.奖偿，奖金；战利品 4.土地的年租，年收益/1.购买，取得，通过（非继承方式）获得，占有 2.使用起重装置，举起
purchase accounting 进货会计
purchase an anchor 起锚
purchase and sale 买卖
purchase and sale at fixed date 定期买卖
purchase and sale by installments 分期付款买卖
purchase and sale by sample 货样买卖，样本买卖
purchase and sale by will 任意买卖
purchase and sale contract 购销合同（契约）
purchase compensation 购买赔偿，购置赔偿
purchase discounts and allowances 进货折让
purchase money 买价；购买费用
purchase money commission 代购佣金
purchase money mortgage 购买财产抵押，置产抵押
purchase money obligation 购买财产债务，置产债务
purchase note（或 confirmation） 购货确认书

purchase on credit（或 account） 赊购，赊买
purchase order 订单，订购单，订货单
purchase price 买价，价金
purchase rebates and allowances 购货回扣或折让
purchase returns 进货退出
purchase tax （英）消费品零售税
purchase voucher 购货证，购买证
purchase-money n. 价金
purchaser n. 买主，购得人
purchaser for value 等价物的购买人
purchaser for value without notice 善意第三人，不知情购买者
purchaser in good faith 诚信买主，善意买主（见 innocent purchaser）
purchaser's lien 买方留置权
purchases basis and consumption basis 采购基础与耗用基础
purchasing（或 purchase）power 购买力
pure a. 纯粹的，单纯的，纯洁的；无瑕的，无错的；完全的，纯理论的
pure accident 纯粹事故（指事故是由某种不可预见和不可避免的原因造成的，任何一方都无法控制的）
pure annuity 纯粹的养老金，纯净的年金（见 nonrefund annuity）
pure best procedural justice 完善的程序正义
pure commercial act 纯粹商业行为
pure economic loss （英）纯粹经济损失，（美国称为）金钱上的损失（pecuniary loss），德国法称其为"纯粹财产上的损失"（reines vermögensschäden）（指受害人直接遭受经济上的不利或金钱上的损失，而该不利与损失并非由受害人的人身或有形财产遭受损害而引起的）
pure holding company 纯粹控股公司
pure moralistic retributivism 纯粹的道德报应主义
pure obligation 纯债务
pure personalty 纯动产，与土地无关联的动产
pure power theory 纯粹权力说
pure private goods 纯私人产品
pure procedural justice 纯粹的程序公正

（正义）
pure public goods 纯公共产品
pure question of fact 纯粹的事实问题
pure question of law 纯粹的法律问题
pure reason 纯理论缘由；纯理论理由
pure theory of law 纯粹法学（派）
pure ville(i)nage （英）纯粹的农役土地保有权
purely judicial power 纯司法权（指与quasi-judicial power 相对而言）
purely political offences 纯粹的政治犯罪
purgation n. 1.洗净，清洗 2.洗罪；以自行发誓等证明无罪；洗冤
purge v. 1.使净化，清洗，清除 2.证明无罪，洗罪；辩白 3.服满刑期；以认错（或承担责任）作为……的补偿
purge an offence 以认错（承担罪责）作为补偿
purge company 净化公司
purge one's contempt 在藐视法官或法庭后认错
purge oneself of a charge 为自己辩解，证明自己无罪
purging a tort 以认错来纠正侵权行为
purification n. 1.洗净；净化；提纯 2.宗教上的斋戒；洗罪
puritan ancestry 清教世系
purlieu n. 1.(归原主所有的）森林边缘的空地 2.(复）界限 3.常到的地方 4.范围；环境
purloin v. 偷窃
purloiner n. 小偷，盗窃者
purple heart （美）紫心勋章（授予战争中受过伤的战士）
purport n./v. （文件等）意义，含义，主旨，主旨目的，企图/意味着，大意是；号称，声称；意图，意欲
purported a. 声称为，声称是
purpose n. 目的；意向；决心；宗旨
purpose of the Charter （联合国的）宪章宗旨
purpose of the crime 犯罪目的
purpose theory （法人的）目的说
purposeful a. 有意图的，有目的的，故意的
purposeful affiliation 有目的的关联，有目

的的确认
purposeful conduct 有目的的行为
purposeful direct contact with the forum state 与诉讼地所在州有目的的直接联系
purposive a. 1.有意图的，有目的的；为一定目的服务的 2.果断的；有决心的
purposive entities 有目的的实体
purposive sampling 立意抽样，有目的的抽样
purpresture n. 侵占公产（如阻塞公路或航道等）；被非法侵占或圈用的公地
pursuance n. 1.追求；追赶；追踪 2.进行；实行；从事；继续进行
pursuant a. 1.追赶的；追求的 2.依据的，按照的(to)
pursuant to an act of Congress 依照国会法令
pursuant to law 依法，按照法律
pursue v. 1.控诉，起诉(for) 2.追赶；追踪；追捕；追击；追缴 3.追求，寻求 4.进行，从事，实行，继续
pursuer n. 原告，起诉人；进行者，从事者；追捕者
pursuer's pleading （苏格兰）原告的诉状
pursuit n. 追捕；追求
pursuit of profits 利润追求
purveyance n. （英史）王室用品征购权
purview n. 1.权限；职权范围；范围，领域 2.(某一法律）条款部分；法规（例）的前言；法规本文
push for 奋力争取，力图取得
Push Technology 见 Agent Technology
push-button warfare 按钮战争，现代化战争
put v./n. 1.放；摆；装；使处于（某种状态） 2.使从事；把……用于；使受到（to）3.驱使，追使，促使/股票/股票出售期权，卖出期权，看跌期权[指允准股票持有人在规定期限内即使在市场下降情况下仍以固定价格出售规定数量的股票或商品的期权。此权利需向同意购买股票或商品者支付一笔费用方可买得（买入期权则为call）。卖出期权的购买者则期望股票或商品价下跌以便交割后可以盈利，如价格上升则无需履行卖出期权。此词亦称"择期或约期

出售选择权"]
put a matter in the hands of a lawyer 委托律师办理
put a tap on sb.'s telephone at sb.'s home (office) 窃听电话;搭线窃听某人电话;话侦
put a veto upon 否决,禁止
put a wrong interpretation on 对……作错误解释
put across 使被理解;作成,搞成(尤指不正当手段),欺骗
put and call options 特权交易,期货抛出和买进选择权
put away 1.把……收起来,放好;储存……备用 2.处理掉;放弃(想法等),抛弃 3.吃掉,喝掉 4.(口)把……送进监狱,或将……送进疯人院 5.(俚)把……处死,杀掉 6.离掉,丢掉
put down 1.放下,拒绝 2.平定,镇压,取缔(put down, rebellion) 3.制止,使安定下来〈put down the gossip〉(制止流言蜚语)4.记下〈to put down in writing〉(写下来),〈the court reporter noted the objection to the record〉(法院的判例汇编员记下对诉状中的异议),〈put the purchase down to sb.'s account〉(把买的货物记在某人的账下)5.贬低、轻蔑、羞辱、使降职 6.削减(开支等)7.贮藏(食物等) 8.估计(as, at),认为(as, for) 9.把……归因于(to)〈put the dispute down to some misunderstanding〉(把争议归因于误解)
put forth 1.放出、长出(树叶、嫩芽)2.发表、颁布 3.提出(理由意见等)4.使用,用出
put forward 放出,提出(理论,意见等)
put in force 施行
put in issue 提出问题,提出异议
put/ lay (sth.) in pledge 以(某物)作抵押
put in (into) practice 实行
put in suit 就……提起诉讼
put (carry) into execution 实行,实施,执行
put into operation 实施
put into words 以语言文字表示
put (或 lay) it on the line (美)付款;坦率地说;提供证据
put off 1.拖延,推迟,延期;阻止,劝阻

2.用欺骗手段卖掉 3.混用(伪币)
put on record/file 备案,立案;提出意见
put on the black cap (法官)戴上黑色法帽(指准备宣判死刑)
put on trial 交由法院审判;将案件移交法院审理
put (sb.) out of court 使(某人)失去诉讼权利
put the claw on sb. (美俚)逮捕某人;向某人借钱
put to a right 拥有一项权利
put to death 处死
put to execution 处以死刑,执行枪决
put to the proof 作为证据,举证
put to vote 付诸表决
put together 把……放在一起,组合
put under arrest 拘禁
put up for auction 交付拍卖
put up with 不计算;容忍
put upon 欺骗,使成为牺牲品;占便宜;利用(多用于被动)
put-call parity 卖出买入期的平价
put-pay-contract n. 照供不议合同(指项目公司为了减少原材料供应数量和价格变化的风险,可以与供应商签订照供不议合同。可得到供应商以固定价格、质量品质为建设项目提供长期稳定的建设用品)
putative a. 被公认的;推定的,假定的
putative father 推定的父亲,公认的父亲(指被认证私生子女的父亲的人)
putative marriage 受到公认的婚姻(指善意缔结的,但一方或双方未意识到因存在婚姻障碍而成为非法的婚姻)
putative proper law 推定的准据法,被公认的准据法
putting in prison 投入监狱,入狱
putting into effect of statute 实施法律
puture (或 **pulture**) n. (英史)实物征收权(习惯法上的一种权利)
puzzle n./v. 谜,难题;困惑/使为难,使迷惑
puzzling behavior 费解行为,令人困惑的行为
PV ratio 利润对销售额比率
pyramid n./v. 金字塔现象/用累进式方法扩大交易

(a) pyramid of credit 信贷的层层加大
pyramid sales scheme （美）多层次销售方法
pyramid selling 金字塔式销售法，多层次传销
pyromania n. 放火狂，纵火癖

Q

Qādi n. 穆斯林法官；卡迪（见 *kādi*）
qua 以……的资格，视为，作为
quack n./a./v. 庸医，江湖医生；骗子；冒充内行的人/庸医的；骗人的；假的；冒充内行的；作伪骗人的/用骗术行医；胡吹；做夸大宣传
quack doctor 庸医，江湖医生
quack medicine 假药
quackery n. 庸医医术；欺骗行为；骗术
quacksalver n. 庸医；骗子（＝quack）
Quadragesms （英）爱德华三世年鉴的第三部分（从1366年起始）
quadriennium n. （法科学生的）四年级必修课（指按罗马法，法科学生须修满四年课程方可修读法典）
quadriennium utile 四年有效期（指苏格兰法律规定，在四年期限内，未成年人成年后可对其在未成年时所订的与其不利的契约的效力提出异议）
Quadripartite Agreement （英、美、法、苏于1971年9月3日签订的）《四方协议》
Quadripartitus 《四章法》，四论说[指英国王座法庭一名受雇文牍员温切斯特（Wenchester）1111—1118年间编的小型文集，有四个部分，现仅存拉丁文译的"盎格鲁-撒克逊"法律部分和作者所处时代的重要文件两部分，另两部分——法律程序与盗窃——已遗失]；四部分组成的，四方参加的

∗ *Quae ab hostibus capiuntur, statim capientium fiunt.* Things which are taken from enemies immediately become the property of the captors. 自敌手处取得之物，即属夺得者财产。

∗ *Quae ab initio inutilis fuit institutio, ex post facto convalescere non potest.* An institution void in the beginning can not acquire validity by a subsequent act./That which was a useless institution at the commencement cannot grow strong by an after fact. 自始无效者，不得因其后之行为而有效。

∗ *Quae accessionum locum obtinent, extinguuntur cum principales res peremptae fuerint.* Things which hold the place of accessories are extinguished when the principal things are destroyed. 当主物已被消灭，从物也就被消灭。

∗ *Quae communi legi derogant stricte interpretantur.* Things which derogate from common law are to be strictly interpreted. 对限制普通法之成文法，须从严解释。

∗ *Quae contra rationem juris introducta sunt, non debent trahi in consequentiam.* Things introduced contrary to the reason of law ought not to be drawn into a precedent. 违反法之原理所提出者，不应列为先例。

∗ *Quae dubitationis causa contractibus inseruntur, jus commune non laedunt.* Clauses inserted in contracts to take away all ground for doubt, hurt not the common law. 为消除疑点而插入合约者，不违反普通法。

∗ *Quae dubitationis causa tollendae inseruntur communemlegem non laudunt.* Things which are inserted for the purpose of removing doubt, hurt not the common law. 为消除疑点而插入者，并不违反普通法。

∗ *Quae in testamento ita sunt scripta ut intelligi non possint, perinde sunt ac si scripta non essent.* What has been so written in a will as to be unintelligible is to be regarded as though it had not been written. Things that are so written in a will that they can not be understood are as if they had not been written. 遗嘱所写之事物,如不可能理解时,视为自始未写。

Quae mala sunt inchoata in principio vix bono peraguntur exitu. Things bad in principle at the commencement seldom achieve a good end. 坏的开始,鲜有好的结局。

Quaecunque intra rationem legis inveniuntur intra legem ipsam esse judicantur. What things so ever appear within the reason of law are to be considered within the law itself. 凡符合法之原理者,应被视为存在于法律之中。

quae est eadum 与前相同,与前述者同

Quaelibet jurisdictio cancellos suos habet. Every jurisdiction has its own bounds. 每一种司法裁判权都有自己的管辖范围。

Quaelibet poena corporalis, quamvis minima, major est qualibet poena pecuniaria. Every corporal punishment, although the very least, is greater than any pecuniary punishment. 每一种肉刑,即使是最轻的,也比罚金的刑罚为重。

Quaeras de dubiis legem bene discere si vis. Inquire into doubtful points if you wish to understand the law well. 如果你想深刻理解法律,你就得对疑点进行一番调查研究。

quaere 有疑义,有问题(案例常用语,指"有疑义""待考"诸如此类);问题,质问,疑问

quaerens 原告

Quaerere dat sapere quae sunt legitima vere. To inquire into them, is the way to know what things are truly lawful. 要想了解事情是否真正合法,其方法就是去调查一下事情真相。

quaestio (罗马)审判处;(中世纪法律)问题;询问;严刑拷问;由一委员会询问刑事问题

quaestio de adulterilis (罗马)通奸审判处

quaestio facti 事实问题
quaestio juris 法律问题
quaestio perpetuae 常设刑事法庭(见 *Lex Calpurnia de Precuniis Nepetundis*)
quaestio vexata 争执的问题;难解决的问题
quaestiones 1.(早期罗马法)刑事审判庭 2.法律问答(指罗马法或寺院法学者采用问答式辩论形式来探讨法律问题的一种写作方法)
quaestiones perpetuae (古罗马)刑事审判庭
Quaestor (罗马)司法行政长官(具有集中财政收入的职责)
Quaestores Parricidii (questores parricidii) (罗马)弑亲和谋杀案审判官
Quai d'Orsey (法)法国外交部;法国司法警察总署
quaker meeting 贵族会的教友聚会
qualification (或 **characterization**) n. (国际私法)识别(又译定性,指法院决定涉外民事案件所涉及的民事关系的性质,以确定所适用的准据法);资格;合格性;合格证明;限制条件;限定;赋予资格
qualification for election 当选资格
qualification of a martyr 烈士资格
qualification test 合格测试,合格检查
qualifications for voting 有投票资格
qualifications statutes 限制法
qualified a. 有资格的;能胜任的;合格的;有限制的;合适的;可采用的
qualified acceptance 附条件承兑,有限制承兑
qualified accounts 保留账目
qualified covenant 限制性的合同(契约)条款
qualified delegation 合格的代表团
qualified elector 合格选举人
qualified endorsement (或 **indorsement**) 附条件背书,有条件背书,无担保背书,限制性背书
qualified estate 有限制的不动产(权)
qualified expert 合格的鉴定人,合格的专家
qualified fee 有条件的世袭地产(见 base fee)
qualified foreign institutional investors (简称 QFII)合格境外投资者

qualified good-faith immunity 有限的诚信豁免权
qualified institution 主管机构,主管机关
qualified institutional buyer 合格机构买家
qualified job-seeker 有资格就业者
qualified majority 特定多数,合格多数
qualified majority vote 有效多数表决制
qualified neutrality 有条件中立
qualified notary 合格公证人
qualified opinion 有保留的意见书(指对财务报表审计持保留意见)
qualified pardon 有限制赦免
qualified person 合格人(指在版权领域有资格受版权法保护的人)
qualified privilege 特有权
qualified property 有限制的物权,有限制的财产权
qualified purchaser 合格购买人
qualified right 相对权利(见 common right);附条件的权利
qualified stock option 合格的股票期权,附加条件股票期权
qualified title 有限制的所有权,有限制的产权(如有年限规定之产权),受限制的土地产权
qualified to inherit 有资格继承
qualified ultimatum 附条件的最后通牒
qualified veto 有限制的否决权
qualified voter 合格投票人
qualified voting 合格投票,有条件的表决
qualified wheel 合格名册(指未从陪审员的候选名册中免除或豁免的一组准陪审员,他们由此被认为有资格充任陪审员。该名册上的任何人都可以基于实际困难而请求免当陪审员)
qualify v. 1.(使)合格,(使)具有资格 2.证明……合格;授权予,准予 3.限制,限定
qualify a jury 授权于陪审团
qualify a statement 限制声明的范围
qualify as a witness 有资格作证人,具有证人资格
qualify for the bar 取得律师资格
qualify for the vote (依法)取得选举权
qualifying clause 限制条款
quality n. 1.质,质量;优质;品质 2.性质;种类
quality as per buyer's (seller's) sample 凭买(卖)方样品交货
quality control 质量检查制;品质管制
quality license 质的许可;质量许可证
quality of estate 地产的特质(指某一地产的性质、如何开始和享有利益等);地产权的限定范围
quality of the crime 犯罪性质
quality or guarantee function 品质或保证功能
quality requirement 质量要求,品质条件
quality standard 质量标准
qualm n. 疑虑;不安;内疚
quamdiu 迟至,……期间,达……之久;只要
quamdiu se bene gesserit 品行端正期间(指具有一种特权职位的人,在任职期间只要行为良好,就不会被免职,直至他自愿辞职或死亡为止)
quamdiu tenure 终身任期;终身任职
quando 当……时,任何时候;因为
* **Quando abest provisio partis, adest provisio legis.** When the provision of the party is wanting, the provision of the law is at hand. 无契约之规定则依法律条文规定.
quando acciderint 将来发生的时候(法院的一种判词,如死者的遗产管理人向法院提出死者的遗产经过全部处理已无剩余来还清死者的债务,等候死者再有财产的时候,由代理人来清还)
* **Quando aliquid prohibitur, prohibitur et omne per quod devenitur ad illud.** When anything is prohibited, everything which tends towards it is also prohibited. 禁止某一行为时,亦禁止与之同一归属之行为.
* **Quando aliquid prohibetur fieri, prohibetur ex directo et per obliquum.** When the doing of anything is forbidden, then the doing of it either directly or indirectly is forbidden. 凡法所禁止做的事,不论直接或间接均在禁止之列.
* **Quando les aliquid alicui conceddit, concedere vedetur et id sine quo res ipsa esse non potest.** When the law gives a man any-

thing, it gives him that without which it cannot exist. 法律向某人让与某物时,与该物之存在不可分离者亦被视为让与。
* *Quando lex est specialis, ratio sutem generalis, generaliter lex est intelligenda.* Where a law is special, but its reason general, the law is to be understood generally. 一个专门的法律,只要其根据或理由具有普遍性,就应当理解为普遍性法律。
Quangos n. 昆格斯(准自治国家政府组织)
quantitative a. 量的,数量的;定量的
quantitative change 量变
qualitative difference 质的差异,质的区别
qualitative economics 定性经济学
quality n. 质,质量;优质;品质;性质;种类;使……有资格;限制,约束
quality of the trial process 审判程序质量
quantifiable benefits 能计量的利益
quantifiable data 可量化数据
quantifiable function 可量化函数
quantity n. 量,分量;数量;(复)大量,大宗
quantity license 量的许可
quantity of an estate 地产权的持续期
quantity of contribution 分担额
quantity of employment 就业人数
quantity theory of money 物价随货币流通量的多寡而升降的理论
quantum n. 量,定量,分量;总量
quantum damnificatus 损害估计额,损害额
quantum leap 量的跳跃
quantum lucratus (不当得利诉讼法中作为恢复原状标准的)应按得益额返还
quantum mechanics 量子力学
quantum meruit 按照服务计酬;相当的付给;(无合同规定时)按合理价格支付
quantum meruit **claim** 按照服务计酬请求权;相当给付请求权
quantum **of damages** 相当损害赔偿额
quantum **of international trade** 国际贸易量
quantum valebat 按值付价
quarantine (或 **quarentaine**, **quarentine**) v./n. 检疫;封锁;隔离;使孤立/1.(在港口对船舶等的)检疫;检疫所;检疫期 2.(因传染病、流行病对人等的)隔离;隔离区 3.

(在政治、商业上的)隔绝 4.(英)寡妇居留期(以前在丈夫死后,寡妇可留住亡夫的住宅直至获得亡夫产业的分配期止)
quarantine agency 检疫机关
quarantine buoy 检疫地浮标(黄色)
quarantine certificate 检疫证明书
quarantine conditions 检疫条件
quarantine declaration (船舶)检疫申报(单)
quarantine doctor 检疫医生
quarantine flag 检疫旗(表示船上未发生疾病的黄旗,作为请求入港许可的信号)
quarantine law 检疫法
quarantine notice 检疫通告单
quarantine of animals and plants 动植物检疫
quarantine of sea port 海港检疫
quarantine of the exporting country 输出国检疫
quarantine period 检疫期间
quarantine port 检疫港
quarantine range 检疫范围
quarantine signal 检疫信号
quarantine station 检疫所
quare 所以,因此;因……理由;为何原因,理由(常用于拉丁文式普通法令状)
quare **actions** (中世纪的)诉讼理由令状
quare clausum fregit 侵入私地,为什么进入原告围场(这个词组用于非法侵入他人土地的诉讼中,具有一切不正当进入他人土地的含义)
quare ejecit infra terminum 在租期内逐出租户的理由(令状)
quare impedit (英)妨碍圣职推荐令(指一种属不动产占有之诉性质的诉讼及其令状。在圣职推荐权发生纠纷时,一方起诉所用的令状,由此开始诉讼,源于令状中要求被告说明他为何妨碍原告推荐圣职的语句),妨碍圣职推荐之诉(指强制执行圣职推荐人的权利的令状或诉讼,即圣职推荐权人有权推荐一个人去填补空缺的圣职。亦称 writ of *quare impedit*。见 *de clerico admittendo*)
quarrel n./v. 争吵,争论,口角;争吵的原因;怨言;责备,挑剔;不和/争吵,吵架;

与……不和
quarry n./v. 石场,石矿;采石矿;泉源;追求物(或目标)/发掘,搜索(资料、证据等),探索
quarta antonina (quarta divi pii, quarta D. pii.) (罗马法)继承遗产 1/4(曾为遗嘱人收养过的孩子,后因解除收养关系或被不公平的剥夺继承,依法律规定可继承 1/4 的遗产)
quarter n. 1.四分之一,四等份;季度,付款的季度 2.区域;方位 3.(复)住处 4.(受刑者被肢解后的)四分之一尸体
quarter session courts (美)四季法庭(指以前有些州建立的法庭,每年开庭 4 次,对较轻刑事案件具有管辖权,有时亦审理行政案件诸如公路、桥梁之类毁损);(英)季审法庭(指英国一年开 4 次的地方法庭,现已废除。根据 1971 年的法院法已与巡回法院合并改组为刑事法院)
quarterage n. 1.每季付款;每季收入;季度税;季度津贴 2.兵营
quartering of troops 供部队住宿
quartering punishment 四肢裂解刑
quartermaster n. 军需官,后勤官,军需主任
quartet n. 4 人一组,4 人一套,四重唱、四重奏
quarto die post 4 日后(指按英国旧制,被告于收到送达传票后 4 日须到案)
quash v. 撤销(一项传唤或控告状);废止;宣布(判决等)无效
quash an indictment 撤销起诉
(to) quash the array 废止陪审团名单;抗议陪审团名单(指对陪审团名单表示异议)
quasi a. 准;类似;半
quasi ex contractu 准合同(契约)
quasi ex delicto 准私犯
quasi guardian 准监护人(指没有有效权限即承担起监护人的职责。此人可以被考虑作为监护人。亦可称为 guardian by estoppel; guardiann de son tort)
quasi in rem action 准对物诉讼
quasi in rem concept 准对物管辖观念
quasi in rem judgment 准对物管辖,准对物法规,准对物判决
quasi in rem jurisdiction 准对物管辖(权)
quasi in rem jurisdiction over specific property 对特定财产上的准对物管辖
quasi in rem proceedings(＝quasi in rem action) 准对物诉讼
quasi judicial act 准司法行为(指非法官之司法行为)
quasi judicial proceedings 准司法程序
quasi mutuality treatment 准相互性对待
quasi-adult n. 准成年
quasi-arbitrator n. 准仲裁人;准公断人
quasi-automatic adoption 准自动通过,准自动通过程序
quasi-burglar n. 准盗窃犯
quasi-composite state 准复合国
quasi-contract n. 准合同,准契约
quasi-contract 准合同[英美法系又称不当得利,指在创意情况下,当创意当事人与创意接受人之间不存在合同和保密关系时,法院有权基于公平正义目的,要求使用了创意的被告(创意接受人)向原告(创意人)支付一定报酬。此含意与大陆法系国家的不当得利含意基本一致。见 confidence relationship]
quasi-contractual obligation 准合同(契约)义务
quasi-copyright n. 准版权(指依传统版权理论因不具有独创性而不能受保护,但却有投入,应予一定保护的"作品",如编排上不具有独创性的某些汇编作品)
quasi-corporation n. 准法人,准公司
quasi-crime n. 准犯罪(指行为虽具有犯罪性质,但并未经法律规定需处以刑罚者,包括所有非犯罪、轻罪劣行,多以没收或罚款论处)
quasi-delict n. 准侵权行为
quasi-delictum 准私犯
quasi-diplomatic relation 准外交关系
quasi-dwelling-house 准住宅,准居所;(历史上)外屋(指诸如谷仓之类的任一外屋,近似用来住人的建筑物。见 burglary 1)
quasi-full employment 接近充分就业
quasi-general average 准共同海损
quasi-government nature 半政府性质

quasi-guardian n. 准监护人
quasi-incompetency n. 准法律上资格
quasi-interdicted person 准无行为能力人(旧译:准禁治产人)
quasi-international agreement 准国际协议
quasi-judicial a.准司法的,具有某些司法权的(可处理版权侵权纠纷、合同纠纷的行政管理机关以及仲裁管理机关之类均属于准司法机关),行政裁决
quasi-judicial decision 准司法裁决
quasi judicial function 准司法职能(指类似于法官的职能、职权)
quasi-judicial government commission (英)准司法性的政府委员会
quasi-judicial jurisdiction "准司法"裁判权(指审理和裁决有关行政诉讼的国家权力,又叫行政裁判权)
quasi-judicial personnel 准司法人员
quasi-lawabiding a. 半守法的
quasi-lawbreaking a. 半违法的
quasi-legislative a. 准立法的
quasi-legislative action 准立法行为
quasi-legislative discretion 准立法性的自由裁量权
quasi-legislative powers 准立法权
quasi-liquidation n. 准清算
quasi-neutrality n. 准中立
quasi-paternal jurisdiction 准家长权
quasi-penal n. 准刑罚性
quasi-personalty n. 准动产
quasi-piracy n. 准海盗行为
quasi-possession n. 准占有
quasi-possessor n. 准占有人
quasi-posthumous child (大陆法系)准遗腹子(指由于孩子的父亲已经去世,该孩子即成为其祖父的直接继承人或其他男性尊亲属的直接继承人)
quasi-presidentialism n. 准总统制
quasi-private international law 准国际私法,区际私法
quasi-proprietary right 准所有权
quasi-public a. 私有但属公共性质的;(公司、企业等)私营公用事业的
quasi-public international contract 准公共(或准公法上)的国际合同(契约)(指国家和外国公司所订的合同)
quasi-real right 准物权
quasi-realty n. 准不动产
quasi-rent stream 准纯利;准租金
quasi-rents n. 准租金,近似租金(或纯利)
quasi-son-in-law n. (男方为女方家庭成员的)女婿(旧译:赘婿)
quasi-sovereign a. 半独立的;半主权的
quasi-sovereignty n. 准主权关系
quasi-sovereignty of the state 各州的准主权关系
quasi-state n. 半独立国;半主权国;准国家
quasi-tort n. 准侵权行为
quasi-traditio 准占有人(大陆法用语,指在所有人知情况下的占用他人财产者)
quasi-trustee n. 准信托人(指未受委托而行使受托人职务者)
quasi-ususfructus 准用益权
quay n. 码头(指与岸平行的码头)
queen n. (与 king 相对应)1.(英国)女王;王后(国王的配偶);王太后(指已故国王的遗孀);(大写)英国政府 2.搞同性恋的男子
Queen Anne's Bounty 见 first fruits
queen consort 王后
queen dowager 王太后(已故君主的遗孀)
queen in Council (英)枢密院会议
Queen Mary's cushion 假妊娠
queen mother 王太后(在位君主之母)
queen regent 摄政女王,女王;女皇
Queen's advocate 女王法律顾问
Queen's ancient serjeant (英)女王的元老高级律师
Queen's (或 King's) Bench (英国高等法院三个法庭之一的)王(后)座法庭;(英国旧译的)王(后)座法院(亦译:女王座法院或女王法院)
Queen's (或 King's) Bench Division (英)高等法院王(后)座法庭所属分庭
Queen's Case 英国判例
Queen's consent (英)女王同意(与 Royal assent 不同,女王同意必须有枢密顾问签名,通常要经三读程序)
Queen's coroner and attorney (英)政府

验尸官
Queen's (或 King's) Counsel　(英)皇家律师,王室法律顾问
Queen's enemies　(英)国王的敌人(租船运货合同的传统用语,意指国家的敌人)
Queen's (或 King's) evidence　政府的证人(英政府准许犯人为政府作证,证明和他一同犯罪的人的罪行,如果所举供证未能使政府满意,就有可能判他已承认的罪行)
Queen's key　(苏格兰)准许侵(进)入债务者住宅的令状
Queen's peace　(英)国家治安
Queen's premier serjeant　(英)女王的首席高级律师
Queen's printer　(英)国王特许印刷者
Queen's prison　(英)国家监狱
Queen's (或 King's) proctor　政府代表官(亦称政府律师,代表政府检验遗嘱、婚约和海事组工作)
Queen's recommendation　(英)女王建议(指因君主享有行政权,并对所有岁人与支出负责,如无女王建议不得提出财政性议案)
Queen's Regulations　(英)《皇家军事条例》
Queen's remembrancer　(英)政府债务征收官;高等法院的官员
Queen's serjeant　(英)国王高级律师
Queen's shilling　(英)军饷
Queen's ship　(英)女王的舰艇
Queen's Speech　(英国议会期间开始时)女王(宣读的)内政外交说明(或致词,施政演说)
quell v.　镇压,平息;消除,减轻
querela　向任何法庭提起诉讼;原告的控告书或声明
querela inofficiosi testamenti　遗嘱违背道义之诉(指对非法剥夺未成年人继承遗产的一种诉讼)
querens　原告,告发人,检举人
querist n.　询问者,质问者,讯问者
query n.　质问,讯问,疑问
quest n.　1.寻求,追求,探索 2.验尸陪审团;验尸调查

question n./v.　1.发问,询问;问题议题;疑问 2.(法庭上的)争端;争论点 3.(对问题的)投票表决;(待表决的)提案,提议/询问;讯问,审问,审查;争论;提出异议
question at issue　争论中的问题
question for decision　有待裁决的问题
question in dispute　争执的问题
question in parliament　议会中的质询
question of consideration　见 objection 2
question of dispute　争议问题
question of fact　事实问题[指①法律上未事先确认或作权威性回答的争点,比如特定的刑事被告(particular criminal defendant)是否有罪,或承包商是否无理推迟大厦的建筑;②不涉及法律所提出观点的争点;③应由陪审团审判时解决的争议问题或由无陪审团参加的法官审判(bench trial)时解决的争议问题;④只有通过开示证据的方法可回答的一个问题,与无法证实的判定的问题(question of unverifiable opinion)相对]
question of guilt　是否有罪的问题
question of law　法律问题[指①涉及法律解释或适用法律的,并由法官决定的争点问题,陪审团不能决定法律问题;②法律本身具有权威性回答的问题,所以法院可以自由酌处问题(matter of discretion)不予回答(一项仲裁条款"an arbitration clause"的强制性法律问题);③关于法律是特别争论点的问题,在此法律问题上双方当事人进行辩论,法院必须作出决定,法律的公正规则(true rule of law)是什么,是双方当事人共同诉诸的法律问题(both parties appealed on the question of law);④虽然这一问题可能转为事实上的争论点(factual point),但此问题仍由法院保留并拒绝陪审团参与;这是一个在法官特有的职权范围内的问题,而非陪审团的职能范畴(不管存在合同的含糊不清如何都是法律问题)。亦称 legal question, law question]
question of procedure　程序问题
question of punishment in consultation　量刑问题
(a) question of the first importance　首要问题

(a) question of the last importance 极其重要的问题
question requiring written answers 需书面答复的质询,(议会的)需要答复的书面质询
question time 议会的质询时间
question to Ministers （议会)向内阁(提出)质问
questionable a. 可疑的;有问题的;不可靠的
questionable person 可疑的人
questioner n. 质问者;询问者
questiones perpetuae （罗马法上的)常设刑事法庭
questioning n. 审问,讯问,质问
questioning of suspects 讯问嫌疑犯
questionnaire 调查表,征询书
questman (或 questmonger) n. 诉讼发起人;咨询量刑者;教会执事
* *Qui accusat integrae famae sit, et non criminosus.* Let him who accuse be of clear fame and not criminal. Let the one who accuses be of honest reputation and not implicated in a crime. 具有诚实名声的控告人不会被卷入罪行之中;控告人应具诚实之名声,而不应为罪犯。
* *Qui aliquid statuerit parte inaudita altera, aequum licet dexerit, haud aequum facerit.* He who decides anything, one party being unheard, though he should decide right, does wrong./ One who has decided anything without hearing the other party, even though he has said what is right, has done wrong. 未听取另一方当事人意见而作出裁决者,尽管可以作出正确裁决,但其做法不正当。
* *Qui approbat non reprobat.* He who approbates does not reprobate. 既接受就不得回绝。
* *Qui facit per alium facit per se.* He who acts through another is deemed to act in person. 通过他人去做的行为视同自己亲自做的一样。
* *Qui facit per allu, facit (or est prinde ac si faciat) per se.* He who acts through another (is in the same position as if he) acts through himself. 通过他人做事的人,是在为自己做事(这是一条代理关系的基本格言。在讨论雇主对雇员行为所负责任时也常适用)。
* *Qui jure suo utitur, neminent loedit (or nemini facit injuriam).* He who exercises his right does an injustice to nobody. He who exercise his right injures no one. 行使自己的权利不会侵害任何人。
* *Qui jure suo utitur, nemini facit injuriam.* He who uses his legal rights harms no one. 行使自己的合法权利不得损害别人。
* *Qui molitur insidias in patriam id facit quod insanus nauta perforans navem in qua vehitur.* He who betrays his country is like the insane sailor who bores a hole in the ship which carries him. 背叛祖国的人就像把自己所乘的船挖个洞的发了疯的水手。
qui ne dit mot consent 沉默即为同意
qui nimium probat mihil probat 证明过多等于没有证明
* *Qui non improbat, approbat.* He who does not blame (or disapprove), approves. 不责备,即赞成。
* *Qui non negat fatetur.* He who does not deny, admits. 不否认等于承认。
* *Qui parcit noncentibus innocentes punit.* He who spares the guilty punishes the innocent. 不处罚罪犯等于惩罚无辜者。
* *Qui sentit commodum sentire debet et onus.* He who receives the advantage ought also to suffer the burden. 得到好处就应承担责任。
* *Qui per fraudem agit, frustra agit.* What a man does fraudently, he does in vain. A person who acts fraudulently acts in vain. 诈骗行为无效。
* *Qui prior est tempore, potior est jure.* He who is first in point of time is more powerful in law. He who is prior in time is stronger in right. 时间在先者其权利在法律上优先。

* *Qui sentit commodum sentire debet et onus; ete contra.* A person who enjoys the benefit ought also to bear the burden. He who receives the advantage ought to suffer the burden,and on the contrary. 获利者,亦应承受负担,反之亦然。

* *Qui tacet, consentire videtur.* He who is silent is supposed to consent. 沉默即可视为同意。

qui tam action(s) 公私共分罚款之诉(指私人和政府根据制定法规定,用共分罚款的办法提起诉讼)

Quia Emptores (英)土地完全保有法[指爱德华一世第18个执政年在威斯敏斯特议会通过的一项法规,亦称威斯敏斯特法规Ⅲ(或第三威斯敏斯特法规, Statute of Westminster Ⅲ)]

quia sunt duae animae in carne una 夫妻在法律上视为一人

quia timet 由于畏惧或疑虑(亦译:预防,指因畏惧而请求法院帮助、保护,以防他人滥用权力而损害疑虑者的权益)

quibble n./v. 诡辩,遁词;吹毛求疵;双关语/诡辩;使用遁词;用双关语说出,模棱两可地说

quibbler n. 诡辩者,狡辩者

quibbling n. 诡辩,吹毛求疵

quick a. 迅速的;流动的,敏捷的;性急的

quick assets 现钱;即可兑换成货币的资产;流动资产

quick condemnation 快速征用,立即征用[指立即取得私人拥有的财产归公使用。因此,评估的补偿费存储于法院或补偿实际数额一经确定即支付给被征用者(condemner)。亦称 quick-take。见 eminent domain]

Quick Index (美)《快速索引》(指将判决摘要汇编的引词和事实上的词语引词合并成为一种按字母顺序的有效检索方法。现有,它是整个美国法律判例汇编系统中关于注释的标准检索方法)

quick liabilities 短期债务

(The) Quick Text (美)快速文本(指美国许多法规在颁布或颁布后不久即行生效,而不管是否有效,即尽快出版这类新法规文本)

quick-take 见 quick condemnation

quickie divorce n. (俚语)快速离婚(指允准的最少文书手续的离婚。亦称 quick divorce)

* *Quicquid est contra normam recti est injuria.* Whatever is against the rule of right is a wrong. 违反正当规则之行为为不法行为。

* *Quicquid in excessu actum est, lege prohibetur.* Whatever is done in excess is prohibited by law. 过分行为,为法律所禁止之行为。

* *Quicquid plantatur solo, solo cedit.* Whatever is affixed to the soil belongs to the soil. 凡土地上的定着物,归属于土地。

quid pro quo 一物对一物,一事对一事;(用于合同中指)对价

quid pro quo What for What 相等的补偿或报酬;交换条件;对价

quid pro quo sexual harassment 回报式性骚扰

quiet n./a. 平静;(社会政治状况的)安定/安静的;静止的,温和的,平静的

quiet beneath the surface in judicial decision 略损司法判决之尊严

quiet enjoyment 安静享受,安静享用[指具有不受任何上位产权(superior title)干扰的土地;房屋租赁合同的一项条款,指保证承租人安静使用租赁的房屋,不受任何人的干扰]

quiet possession 平静占有权

quiet title (法院)判决产权属谁

quiet title action 确定产权诉讼(指一种确认不动产的产权诉讼)

quietus 1.(债务的)偿清;(义务等的)解除,清除 2.收据 3.死 4.平息;制止

* *Quilibet potest renunciare juri pro se introducto.* Every one may renounce or relinquish a right introduced for his own benefit. 人人可放弃有利于己的权利。

quint-exact (= *quinto exactus*) (英)第5次催告出庭(指如再不出庭,即置于法律保护之外)

quinto exactus (英)第5次传唤(指5个

郡的法院公告或传唤被告仍不到庭时,郡验尸官据此可宣告其不再受法律保护)
quirky a. 诡诈的;颇为曲折的
quirky lawyer 狡诈的律师
quisle v. 卖国,做卖国贼;当傀儡政府的头子
quisling n. 卖国贼,内奸,通敌分子,傀儡政府的头子
quit v. 1.离开,放弃(思想、行动、职业等) 2.解除,免除;偿清(债务等) 3.(美)停止 4.离开,选出
quit claim 放弃权利
quit rent 免役地租;免役税(封建时代不动产所有者为代替劳役而向其封建主交纳的代偿金)
quitclaim n./v. 放弃要求,放弃权利;(产权或其他权利的)转让合同(契约)/放弃或转让(对……的合法权利),放弃(对权利或财产的)要求
quitclaim deed 产权转让契据;放弃权利证书
quittance n. (债或义务的)免除;赦免;免除债务的证书;收据;赔偿;酬报;偿还
quiz n./v. 测试;戏弄;小型考试/挖苦,盘问;嘲弄
quiz answer key 测试答案
quo animo 动机何在,意欲何为
quo jure (英)依何权限(用于法院要求被告人拿出依据来说明在原告的土地上有共同放牧权的一种传讯令)
* *Quo ligatur, eo dissolvitur.* By the same mode by which a thing is bound, by that is it released.如何系之,则如何解之。
quo minus (英)(中世纪发给理财法院的)一般管辖权令
quo minus sufficiens existit by which he was less able to pay the king his debt or rent (英)提起不能支付王室现有债务理由之诉(指向理财法院提出的声称原告为王室债务人,以能从被告方获得偿还借款或损害赔偿金为理由,以致不能完全偿付王室债务的诉讼)
quo non est in actis 不告不理
quo warranto (美)公职质疑令状(拉丁语"以得到保障的")(起源于中世纪的特殊令状,经过长期发展,已形成一种质疑一方当事人的职业或其行政职权或特权的民事或刑事的程序。其目的在于阻止连续地不法地使用权力。由州或联邦政府针对任何"没有合法地履行公职和权力"的人提起);1.(旧时英国法庭所发的)责问某人根据什么行使职权(或享受特权)的令状 2.(旧时)收回被占的职位(或特权)的诉讼 3.为收回被僭占的职位(或特权)而提起的公诉;疑权诉讼(指对其法人人格提出质疑)
quoad hoc 到此程度(或范围);在这一点上,就此而论,关于这件事
quod n./v. (英俚)监狱,牢狱/关押,监禁
quod 关于;因为
* *Quod alias non fuit licitum necessitas licitum facit.* Necessity makes lawful what otherwise was unlawful. 原来不合法的,必要时亦合法。
* *Quod approbo non reprobo.* I cannot approve and reject at the same time. 我不能同时又接受又回绝。
quot articuli tot libelli As many points of dispute as libels 正如诽谤(或诉状)一样有许多争点
quod erat demonstrandum 这就是所要证明的
quod erat faciendum 这就是所要做的
* *Quod est necessarium est licitum.* What is necessary is lawful. 需要即合法。
* *Quod fieri non debet (or debuit) factum valet.* What ought not to be done, when done, is valid. What should not be done, yet being done, shall be valid. 本不应为之事,于其完成后或可有效。
* *Quod necessitas cogit, defendit.* What necessity compels, it justifies. 必要性是被迫所为者的辩护。
* *Quod non apparet non est.* That which does not appear does not exist.That is to say, the court knows nothing except what is proved in the case. 未出现者,不存在(法院只认定在案件中已证实的事实)。
* *Quod non est in actis, non est in mundo.* 未转化为书面形式之物不存于世。
* *Quod per me non possum, nec per alium.*

What I cannot do by myself, I cannot do by another. 凡我不能做的行为,也不能通过他人去做。

Quod principi placuit, legis habet vigorem; utpote cum lege regia, quae de imperio ejus lata est, populus ei et in eum omne suum imperium et potestatem conferat. A decision of the emperor has the force of law; for, by the royal law that has been made concerning his authority, the people have conferred on him all their sovereignty and power. 君主决定之事具有法律效力,而君主得作出这样的决定只因人民依法的授权或君主旨具有法律效力,因为民众已依法授予其主权和一切权力。

Quod pro minore licitum est et pro majore licitum est. what is lawful in the lesser is also lawful in the greater. 在小合法的,在大也合法。

Quod vanum et inutile est, lex non requirit. The law requires not what is vain and useless. The law does not require what is vain and useless. 法不要求空洞无用之事。

quod vide (q. v.) 见该项;见该条
quorum 1.法定人数 2.(英)(总称)治安法官 3.治安法官法定人数(指英国法庭开庭时必须达到的治安法官人数)
quota n. 1.定额,配额,限额,规定的数额(指按比例份额给一个人或一个团体);分配,配额〈the university's admission standards included a quota for in state residents〉(大学入学允准的标准包括有州的居民的配额)2.规定的数量,限定的数量(指最大或最小数量)〈Faldo met his sales quota for the month〉(法多满足了他这个月的销售额)
quota allocation 配额分配
quota limit 限额范围
quota tax 定额税
quota system 定额分配制;(进口)限额制
quotation n. 1.引号;引证 2.牌价,行市,行情,报价单;估价;价位
quote v./n. 引用,引证,引述;复述;把……放在引号内;报……价/引文,引语
quoted company 上市公司(股票或证券),报价公司
quoted expressions 引用短语
quoted material 引用的材料
quoted price 报价,牌价
quoted securities 挂牌证券
quotient verdict (陪审团)以金额平均数作裁决(指每一陪审员提出他自己认为应满足原告请求的数目,然后加起来,并以陪审员人数除之所得的平均数,作为裁决的数额);平均数裁决

Quoties in verbis nulla est ambiguitas ibi nulla exposito contra verba expressa fienda est. Wherever there is no ambiguity in the words, then no exposition contrary to the words is to be made. If there is no ambiguity in the words,then no exposition contrary to the expressed words is to be made. 如词句中无模棱两可之意,则不能作出与词意相悖之解释。

quousque 多久;多远;直至
quovis modo 以任何旋转,无论何种方式
quovis tempore 任何时候

R

rabbi (=rabbin) n. 犹太教的法学博士;老师;犹太教教士
rabbinic(al) a. 犹太法学博士的,犹太法学博士的教义(或著作)的
Rabbinic(al) Court 犹太教法庭
rabbinical divorce 拉比式离婚[指按犹太教法学博士(rabbi)的权威(authority)允准的离婚。这种方式的离婚按犹太教的宗旨是影响当事双方的关系,它特别影响犹太妇女符合犹太法(Judaic Law)的再婚

能力。在美国,这种离婚在民事法庭上一般是得不到认可的]
rabbinic(al) scholar 犹太法学博士;犹太教教士;(犹太人的尊称)先生
rabbinism n. 犹太法系博士的教义(或风格)
rabbit n. 野兔(指破坏计算机程序的一种形式,即通过无限制地复制自身来耗尽系统资源,它与病毒的区别是它不感染其他程序)
rabble n. 暴民,乌合之众;(蔑)下层民众
race n. 人种,种族;民族;家族;血统,家系,门第
race bill 为兑款而签发的支票
race conscious gerry-mandering (美)种族有意识地不正当地划分选区,种族有意识地不公正划分选区
race for president 总统竞选
race hostility 种族敌意
race of murder victims 种族(歧视)谋杀受害者
race prejudices 种族偏见
race recording statute (美)优先登记法规(指一项州法规,规定登记土地转让文据的当事人具有优先请求权,可以置以前未登记的文据于不顾)
race relations 种族关系
Race Relations Board (英)种族关系委员会(现已为社会关系委员会取代)
race statute 优先通知登记法规
race to judg(e)ment 竞相获得判决
race to bottom 竞争到底部(指跨国公司已经将其生产环节转移到许多不发达国家以降低成本或增加利润,这种对更便宜的劳动力和原材料的转移追逐通常被称为 race to bottom)
race to the bottom 追底竞赛(全球化时代,某些国家以剥夺本国劳动阶层的各种劳动保障、人为压低他们的工资、放任自然环境的损坏为代价,从而赢得竞争中的价格优势)
race-riot n. 种族暴乱(指不同种族间因种族偏见引起的暴力敌对行为)
racial a. 人种的,种族的,种族间的
racial abhorrence 种族憎恶(指不同种族间的相互憎恶)
racial balance 种族的平衡
racial boundaries 种族界限
racial differentiation 种族差别
racial discrimination 种族歧视
racial disfranchisement 种族的剥夺选举权
racial empowerment 种族授权(指给予受歧视的种族更多的权利,从而使他们摆脱受歧视的地位)
racial equality 种族平等
racial exclusion 种族排斥
racial groups 种族团体
racial law 种族法
racial mixing 种族混合
racial moderate 种族间的稳健派,温和主义者
racial persecution 种族迫害
racial prejudice 种族偏见
racial quotas 种族的限额,种族的超额
racial segregation 种族隔离
racial strife 种族冲突,种族竞争,种族斗争
racial supremacy 种族至上
racial unrest 种族动乱不安;种族动荡不安
racial unsound 种族的不健全
racial war 种族战争
racially restrictive covenant 种族限制条款(指在不动产契据中规定不得将其财产出售或转让给属于某一种族或某种宗教信仰的人,使其占有契约中指定的不动产)
radical element 激进分子;根本要素
racism (或 **racialism**) n. 种族主义;种族歧视(或偏见、隔离等)的主张
racist (= racialist) a. 种族主义的,种族歧视(或隔离、迫害等)的
racist regime 种族主义政权,种族主义制度
rack n./v. 1.拷问(指笞打使被告招认有罪);拷问逼供 2.拉肢刑具(指拷问犯人时拉其四肢使关节脱开的一种刑具) 3.折磨;记号,痕迹;毁灭/拷问(指笞打使被告招认有罪);使遭受极大痛苦
rack jobber 高级经纪人,送货促售商;供应超级市场的批发商
rack-rent (或 **rack rent**) n. 高额租金;极高的地租;全额地租(指与地产年产值相

等或相接近的地租)
rack-renter n. 勒索高额租金的人;索取高地租者;受高地租剥削者
racket n./v. 放荡生活;(以勒索、欺诈等手段进行的)有组织的非法活动/过放荡生活;忙于社交
racketeer n./v. 诈骗者;敲诈勒索者,以威胁手段诈财者/诈骗;敲诈,以威胁手段勒索
Racketeer Influenced and Corrupt Organization Act (美)《反勒索及受贿组织法》[指旨在打击有组织犯罪的法规并通过调查、控制以及对一些图谋参与勒索的一帮人提起控告以保持市场的整体性或尊严。该法于 1970 年正式制定颁布,联邦的《反勒索及受贿组织法》只适用于州际或对外商业的活动。参见《美国注释法典》第 18 标题卷第 1961—1968 节。此后,许多州基于联邦法规采纳此法,有时称为"小反勒索及受贿法"(little RICO acts)。联邦的和大多数州的《反勒索及受贿组织法》为了强制执行还规定不仅可进行刑事起诉,还可采取民事诉讼,甚至原告可提起三倍损害赔偿的诉讼,缩略为 RICO]
rada (伊斯兰教法)共奶血亲(指其同受一个妇女哺育的子女之间的法律关系,有此种关系的人禁止通婚);(大写)(乌克兰共和国的)议会
radia 反箕形纹
radiation damage 辐射损伤
radiative forcing (大气中)辐射强迫[用于衡量某个因子改变地球大气系统中入射和逸出能量平衡程度的一种度量,它同时也是一种指数,反映了该因子在潜在气候变化中的重要性。正强迫使地球表面增温,负强迫则使其降温。IPCC 报告中的辐射强迫值是指相对于 1750 年工业化之前各种条件之变化,用瓦特/每平方米(w/m2)表示]
radical a. 1.基本的,根本的;彻底的 2.激进的,激进派的
radical innovation 根本性创新
radical loop 桡骨箕,甲种蹄状纹,反箕
radical principle 基本原则
radical property-right-in-gross 激进的完整的财产权
radical right 基本权利
radicalism n. 激进主义
Radio Act 无线电法
radio-play n. 广播剧
radioactive pollution (contamination) 放射性污染
radiodetector n. 无线电探测器,雷达
radiologic(al) safety protection 辐射安全保护
radiophone work 广播作品(仅指广播作品而不包括电视作品)
raffle n. (常为义卖等实行的)抽彩售货(方法)
rag-picker n. 拾破烂的人
rags of despotism 专制体制残余
raid n./v. 1.(警察的)突然搜查;搜捕;袭击;侵入 2.(对公款等的)非法盗用;抢劫公款 3.故意造成股票猛跌的行为/袭击;侵入;搜查;搜捕;抢劫;压低股票价格
raid the market (制造恐慌气氛)扰乱市场,冲击市场
raid the sinking 挪用偿债基金
raider n. 袭击者;侵入者;劫掠商船的武装快船
rail v. 埋怨,谴责
rail transportation of goods and persons 铁路货物和旅客运输
railroad register 铁路登记册(簿)
railroad traffic regulations 列车运行规章
railroad-rate 铁路系统运价
Railway and Canal Commission (美)铁路运河委员会
Railway Labor Act 《铁路劳动法》
railway statute 铁路运输条例
railway-transport court 铁路运输法院(或法庭)
Rainbow Ceiling 彩虹天花板[指美国公司首席执行官蒂姆·库克近日首次公开承认自己是同性恋者(same-sex person)。一年前,他曾呼吁美国国会支持并通过《就业非歧视法案》,保护员工免受因性倾向和性别认同而产生的歧视。他认为美国职场没有给予同性恋者公平待遇。其实,许多国家的职场都存在着彩虹天花

板。彩虹旗被视为 LGBT(lesbian, gay, bisexual and transgender)(女同性恋者、男同性恋者、双性恋者和跨性恋者)的标志,多种颜色代表了该社群的多元性。该词条指的是为同性恋雇员的个人晋升设置非官方的隐形障碍的商业行为和歧视做法。Pink Ceiling(粉色天花板)与其含有相同的意思。《澳大利亚人报》2002年10月3日刊登的文章《研究发现为同性恋、双性恋和跨性别员工设置的职业"粉色天花板"》最早使用了 Rainbow Ceiling 这一表达方式。文章称,澳大利亚对上述人群展开调查发现,900名受访者中有超过52%的人因自己的性取向而在工作中受到过骚扰或歧视。倡导同性婚姻权利的Workers Out 组织副会长马克·多拉亨蒂说:"对女性而言存在着 glass ceiling(玻璃天花板),我想我们这里还有粉色天花板或彩虹天花板。"记者约翰·卢奇尤2013年8月11日为美国《哈里斯堡爱国新闻》撰文时也提到了"彩虹天花板"的问题。他写道,婚姻不是同性恋者、双性恋者和跨性别者唯一担心的问题,他们在职场中更为脆弱,能否找到工作、赚到钱和拥有保险,这些都是面临风险的问题]

rain and freshwater damage 雨淋淡水损失
rain water damage 雨淋损失
raise v. 提出;举起;引起;增加,提高;筹措,产生;惹起;使出现;涂改支票;结束;解除;养育,培育
raise a claim 提出(索赔等的)要求
raise a disturbance 引起骚乱
raise a loan 借款
raise a plea 提出抗辩
raise a plea of lack of jurisdiction 提出关于无管辖权的抗辩
raise a presumption 提出假定,提出抗辩
raise a protest 提出抗议
raise an action 提起诉讼
random acts of violence 随意的暴行
raise an embargo on 对……解禁
raise an issue 提出争论点
raise funds 筹措资金
raise money 筹款
raised to the bench (英)升任法官的职位

raison d'être 存在的理由
raj n. (英、印)统治;支配;主权
rake n. 浪子,放荡的人;流氓
rake-off n. 佣金,回扣(尤指交易中非法所得)
rally n./v. 召集,重振旗鼓,集合,大会,振作/集合,团结,振作,恢复
ram an argument home 反复说明论点使充分了解
ramp n. (对租金等)勒索高价;敲诈;诈骗
rampancy n. (指言行的)过激;猖獗;猖狂;不法
rampant litigation 过量的诉讼
ran with the land (土地上的利益和负担)随土地转移;(给购买人或其他受让人的)约定
random a. 随意的,无目的的,胡乱的
random action 轻率行为
random assignment of cases to judges 对法官随机分配案件
random audit (定期的)任意(账目)审查(指美国不宣布地检查一个律师的财政收入,以确定雇主的钱是否稳妥地分别立账保存)
random event (计算机)随机事件
random sampling 随意抽样
random selection 随机选择程序(指书记员处使用计算机编制程序,以确保通过随机的程序将案件安排给地区法官和治安法官)
range n./v. 限度,范围,程度,幅度;距离,射程;(动植物)分布区,生态区/使并列;使系统化,沿(海岸)巡航;解开;探寻;涉及;测距
rank n./v. 1.秩序;社会阶层 2.身份;地位;等级/1.把……分等,分类,列于 2.对破产者的财产有要求权
rank and file 1.武装部队应征的士兵,区别于军官 2.一般协会或工会、公会(union)的会员
rank and file employees 普通雇员
rank and file officer 一般官员
ranking n./a. 等级,顺序;高级官员,地位高的,第一流的,首位;资历仅次于会长(议长等)〈ranking minority members of Committee

equally divided and controlled.〉(在委员会中的少数派成员排名均等并且受到控制)
ranking member of the embassy　大使馆的高级官员
ranking of creditors　排列债权人的顺序；依次偿还债权人的债款
ranking of the justice　(美)大法官的排名[指半个世纪以来,许多独立学者、学术专家对坐在全国司法宝座上担任联邦最高法院大法官者所取得的司法成就作出的评价。尽管缺少特定的或可接受的标准,但以堪称"伟大"大法官来评估。1938 年著名哈佛法学教授罗斯科·庞德(Roscoe Pound)提出了他个人所列的美国司法历史上排名一流的4位法官名单(涵盖联邦和州法官):约翰·马歇尔(John Marshall)、约瑟夫·斯托里(Joseph Story)、奥利弗·温德尔·霍姆斯(Olive Wendell Holmes)、本杰明·内森·卡多佐(Benjamin Nathan Cardozo)。20 年后,任威斯康星州最高法院首席大法官的乔治·R. 柯里(George R. Currie)以"空前的、全明星的美国联邦最高法院"为标题进行筛选。同庞德相比,他在 1964 年删除了卡多佐,同庞德保留马歇尔、斯托里和霍尔姆斯,另加上6名法官名字:威廉·约翰逊(William Johnson)、罗杰·B. 托尼(Roger Brooke Taney)、塞缪尔·F. 米勒(Samual F. Miller)、詹姆斯·布拉德利·塞耶(James Bradley Thayer)、路易斯·D. 布兰代斯(Louise D. Brandeis)和查尔斯·埃文斯·休斯(Charles Evans Hughes)。1972 年罗伊·默斯基(Roy Mersdy)列出了新名单,即在庞德所列4位法官之后,加了8位法官名字:雨果·拉斐特·布莱克(Hugo Lafayette Black)、布兰代斯(Brandeis)、费利克斯·法兰克福(Felix Frankfurter)、约翰·哈伦Ⅰ(John Harlan Ⅰ)、休斯(Hughes)、哈伦·菲斯科·斯通(Harlan F. Stone)、托尼(Taney)和厄尔·沃伦(Earl Warren)。1983 年汉布勒顿(Jim Hambleton)作了概括,只选了9名法官,删除了法兰克福特、哈伦和斯托里]
ransack v.　洗劫,抢劫,掠夺；彻底搜查
ransom n./v.　1.赎金；赎身；赎；(宗教的)赎罪法；赎出；赎回 2.敲诈,勒索/绑票,勒赎；赎回；赎救；取赎金后释放
ransom bill　(国际法)赎偿契约；赎偿证书(尤指海上被俘捕的船舶于赎偿之后所获的证书,亦作 ransom bond)
ransom money　赎款,赎金
ransom note　勒索信；勒索赎金信
rap n./v.　敲击,责备；(美俚)判刑；刑事责任；罪名；罪犯身份的验明/敲击；责备；(美俚)逮捕；处以……刑罚；判决；判刑
rape in marriage　婚内强奸(英国著名法学家 Mathew Hale 认为妇女在婚礼上的誓言已表明她自动承诺在婚姻期间将无条件接受来自丈夫的性交要求。根据这一论点,丈夫不能被指控犯有强奸罪,因为夫妻之间的"婚内强奸"不构成强奸罪)
rap sheet　(美)逮捕(名单)活页(指列有被捕人员和判罪记录名单的警察部门文件)
rapacity n.　1.强取,掠夺,掠夺性 2.贪婪,贪欲,贪得性
rape n./v.　(15 世纪)1.普通法上的强奸罪[指男子强行与一个不是他妻子的女子,并违背她的意愿发生性行为的犯罪。普通法上这一强奸罪的构成要求阴茎至少按入阴道(vagina),而且普通法上明确规定丈夫不能被指控成为强奸其妻子的犯罪主体。正式称为 rapture; ravishment] 2.非法的性行为[特别是以暴力威胁,违背妇女意愿实施性交(intercourse)的犯罪。大多州的现代制定法对该犯罪构成的含义已予扩展,强奸包括在实施犯罪者(perpetrator)通过在受害者不知情和未同意的情况下,使其吸(毒)或饮ь醉酒类以达到预防反抗目的,实质上已使其受到伤害之后违背意愿地进行非法性交。它还包括与一个无意识到的人发生非法性交关系。现在婚姻身份和受害人性别已与该罪的犯罪构成无关。亦称(有些制定法)unlawful sexual intercourse; sexual assault; sexual battery; sexual abuse; cimen raptus。见 sexual assault] 3.劫掠,强夺 4.蹂躏,破坏
rape-murder n.　强奸杀人
rape under age　见 statutory rape
raper n.　强奸犯

rapid charge processing system (美)加速处理控诉事件制度
rapid transit 城市高速铁路;高速交通
rapina 抢劫,掠夺;(罗马,大陆法)强劫他人动产为自己所用[rapina 是以暴力手段掠夺财产(thing),它引起向裁判官(praetorian)提起返还被抢劫财产之诉]
rapine n. 1.抢劫,掠夺他人财产 2.(古)强奸
rapine and red ruin 劫掠和纵火焚烧
rapist n. 强奸犯
rapparee n. 土匪,强盗;(17世纪爱尔兰的)海盗;无业游民
rapper n. 1.敲门人 2.(美俚)控告人,检举人;证人
rapporteur (法史)汇报法官(指给法院其他法官就当前案件提供书面报告的法官);告发人;负责整理编辑报告者;(国际会议商谈条约时的)主要起草人
rapture (古代)1.强夺,强行扣押;劫持他人(尤其妇女);诱拐 2.强奸(见 rape 1)
rapuit (历史)被强奸的[以前此词用于大陪审团的公诉书(indictment)中的强奸。见 ravishment]
rascal n. 流氓,无赖;恶棍
rascaldom n. (总称)流氓,无赖,恶棍;恶性
rascality n. 流氓行为,卑鄙行为;恶事,坏事
rash n./a. 大量出现的事物,大量/急躁的,急性的,鲁莽的
rash of disputes 大量的争论,大量的争端
rasure (=erasure) n. 1.消灭,消除 2.抹去,涂改(指在契约或其他文件字据的涂改、删节的痕迹)
ratable (=rateable) a. 可估价的,可评价的;按比例的;应课税的
ratable property (英)(应负担地方税的)应课税的财产
ratable value 估定价格;征税估价
ratal n. 纳税额,征税价(格)
ratchet theory (1977年)(宪法)棘齿轮理论,拉奇特理论[指国会根据美国联邦宪法第十四修正案行使其执行的权力能够增加而不致冲淡或减少由联邦最高法院原先所确定的保证第十四修正案的权力范围。强调这一术语的思想是使得这

个条款有权只按一个指示方向工作,如同棘齿轮一样。这一理论已由大法官布伦南(Brennan)在卡岑巴赫诉摩根案中阐明(Katzenbach v. Morgan),参见《美国联邦最高法院判例汇编》第 384 卷第 641 页、第 86 卷第 1717 页(1966年),布伦南认为:"国会制定法律只需具备合理理由即可……"亦称 one-way ratchet theory]
rate n./v. 1.比率,利率;价格;等级 2.(复)(英)地方税,捐税/1.对……估价,评价;认为 2.征地方税;定税率 3.定(船或海员的)等级 4.申斥,斥责
rate charged by state banks 国家银行收息的利率
rate of assessment 分摊比率
rate of conversion 兑换率
rate of depreciation 折旧率;贬价率
rate of duty 关税税率
rate of exchange 汇率,汇兑率;货币兑换率;比价
rate of gross profit 毛利率
rate of inflation 通货膨胀率
rate of interest 利率
rate of margin 毛利率
rate of occurrence of criminal cases 刑事案件发案率
rate of payment 付款率
rate-payer n. (英)纳(地方)税人
rateability n. 纳税义务,可纳税性(=rata-bility)
rateable a. =ratable
rater n. 估价人;定等级人
rates of guilty findings at trial 判定有罪率
ratification n. (15世纪)1.认可或通过[特别是指一个法在经过一系列程序中的最后一个步骤或同意认可(consent)时〈the ratification of the conventions of nine states, shall be sufficient for the Establishment of this Constitution between the States so ratifying the same〉(九个州对修宪协议的认可足以确立州之间的宪法成立,类似的州必以同样方式认可或批准)(注:这句话是美国联邦宪法的最后一条,即第 7 条。1789 年 9 月 17 日该宪法草案由 39

名代表签名通过,并交由各州批准。特拉华州于该年12月7日最先批准。1788年6月21日新罕布什尔州作为第九个州批准这一条。但由于当时最大的弗吉尼亚州和纽约州尚未批准,所以直到1789年3月4日这一条才宣告正式生效),就此意义上讲,此项认可成为宪法修正案的全面正式批准,相当于工会就管理问题的集体谈判协议(collective bargaining agreement)的一般批准(rank and file approval)] 2.确认,接受,同意。对以前的法规"act"的确认,使其从正式有效时日起有效〈the board of director's ratification of the president's resolution〉(董事委员会确认主席的决议)。就此意义包括立法机构所采取的作为使得经协商的条约在执行具有约束力 3.(合同)个人对一个行为的约束承诺(binding adoption)已经完成,但在某种程度上说原有所引起的法律义务(legal obligation)还未履行,抑或第三当事方此时还无权限充当个人的代理人〈an adult's ratification of a contract signed during childhood is necessary to make the contract enforceable〉(幼年签署的合同需要成年人的承诺方可使合同有效执行) 4.(国际法)批准[指缔约方同意接受条约的约束而对此最后的确认。通常包括批准文件的交换与保存〈the ratification of the nuclear-weapons treaty〉(核武器条约的批准)(见 instrument of ratification; confirmation)]

ratification of contract 合同(契约)的追认
ratification of judicial act (国际私法)司法行为的批准(或认可)
ratification of treaties 条约的批准
ratifier n. 批准者;认可者
ratify v. 批准;承认,认可;追认
ratify a motion 批准动议,批准请求
ratify a treaty 批准条约
ratihabitio (大陆法)(对合同目的)确认,同意或批准,尤指委托人对代理人执行事务的认可(复数为 ratihabitiones)
rating n. 1.评价;估价 2.定额;等级 3.申斥,责骂
rating and valuation (英)征税和估产
rating and valuation act 定额和估价法例

rating and valuation of land 土地的定级与估价
rating area 征收区
rating authority 地方税收机关
ratio 比,比率;比例
ratio decidendi (rationes decidendi) 判决理由(指法官判决一个案件所根据的理由),法律原则(含义是"判决的理由"或"本案的法则",它对今后案件具有约束力。)
* **Ratio est formalis causa consuetudinis.** Reason is the formal cause of custom. 理由是习惯或惯例的有效的起因。
* **Ratio est legis anima; mutata legis ratione mutatur et lex.** Reason is the soul of law; the reason of law being changed the law is also changed. 理由是法律的灵魂,法的存在理由变了,法律也就变了。
* **Ratio et auctoritas, duo clarissima mundi lumina.** Reason and authority, the two brightest lights of the world. 理由和权威,是世界上两个最明亮的灯塔。
ratio essenti (自由诚然是道德法则的)存在理由, **ratio cogroscendi** (道德法则确实自由的)认识理由[康德的这一表达在今天可以被诠释为:法是自由的认识根据,自由是法的存在根据]
ratio legis 立法的理由
* **Ratio legis est anima legis.** The reason of law is the soul of law. 立法的理由是法律的灵魂。
ratio of space allotted to buildings 分配给建筑物的空间比例
ration n. (食物等的)定量,配给量;(复)粮食,口粮,食物
ration allowance 粮食补贴,粮贴
rationabile estoverium (离婚后或诉讼期间一方给另一方的)合理扶养费(相当于 alimony)
rational a. 合理的;理性的;推理的
rational act 合理的行为
rational actor 理性行为人
rational basis (或 **purpose**) **test** 合理基础(或目的)说(指如果法律或行政判决具有某种合理基础,则法院不应猜测立法机关

或行政机构的法学理论)
(The) Rational Basis of Trademark Protection 《商标保护的理性基础》(1927年美国学者弗兰克·施凯特 Franc Schechter 在《哈佛评论》上发表的文章)
rational bubbles 理性泡沫
rational calculators 理性的计算者
rational criterion 理性标准
rational doubt 合理的怀疑
Rational Expectation (RE) 理性预期
rational individual 理性个人
rational intuitions 理性的直觉
rational justice 理性司法
rational maximizer 理性最大化者
rational relationship 理性关系
rationale n. 基本原因;基本原理,理论基础,全部理由,原理阐述;理论说明;阐释
(the) *rationale* of the decision in the case 此案判决的理由说明
rationales of a more interventionist state 国家干预主义(见 regulatory era)
rationalism n. 理性主义,唯理论
rationalism constructivism 理性建构主义
rationality-limiting norms 限制理性的规范
rationalization n. 合理化
rationalization proposal 合理化建议
rationalize v. 使合理,使合理化;使理性化
rationalizing legal philosophy of Grotius 格劳秀斯合理化法哲学
ratione loci 属地理由
ratione materiae 属物理由
ratione personnae 属人理由
ratione pro et contra 基于正反两方面的理由
ratione soli 仅有的理由
ratione temperis 属时理由
ratione tenurae 租期理由
rationes decidendi 判决依据(见 *ratio decidendi*)
rationing n. 定量配给
rationing system 定量配给制
rattening n. (英)(工人)扰乱(指部分罢工工人夺取或破坏机器等使工厂主或不参加工会的工人同意工会要求的行为,这在英国是一种犯罪行为)
rave n. 胡言乱语,狂骂;叫嚣,怒吼

raving n./a. 胡言乱语,疯话/语无伦次的;胡言乱语的;疯狂的
raving lunatic 狂躁性的精神病患者
ravish v. 强夺,抢去;强奸;将(妇女)掳走
ravisher n. 强夺者;强奸者
ravishment n. 强奸;强夺,掠夺
raw equity 原始衡平法
raw land 未开垦过的土地,素地
re 关于……;就……而论;在……案件中(意指 in the matter of,常用于只有一方当事人的诉讼程序);理由
re immobiles 有关不动产
re, verbis, liteus, consensus (罗马法)通过履行[即处理(handing over)、语言(words)、书面文件(writing)和合意或允许(consent)。这一术语显现出相关的四个层次的罗马契约(four class of Roman contract)]
re-affirmation of the standard 标准的重申,标准的重新确认,标准的再次证实
re-examination clause (美)重新审查条款(指美国联邦宪法第七修正案内容)
re-registration n. 重新登记,重新注册
reach n./v. 能及的范围,抵达;伸出,到达;区域;(上、中、下)游;海峡;横风行驶/抵(到)达,伸出,影响,与……取得联系;深入,竭力想得到
reach of judicial discretion 法官自由裁量权的范围
reaching agreement 达成协议
reacquisition of citizenship 重新取得公民身份
reacquired stock 见 treasury stock
react (to) v. 起反应,有影响,履行
reaction n. 反应;反作用;反动
reaction of animals 动物的反应
reaction of human body 人体的反应
reaction of the offender to the training given him in prison 罪犯在监狱中的改造表现
reactionary n./a. 反动派;反动分子/反动的;复古的;保守的
reactionary class 反动阶级
reactionary clique (或 circle) 反动集团
reactionary element 反动分子

reactionary force 反动势力
reactionary organization 反动组织
reactionary parties and groups 反动党团
reactionary regime 反动政权
reactionary slogan 反动标语
read v. 读,阅读;攻读,学习;解释;宣读;规定;书写
read out 宣告开除;宣读;读出(指把计算机存储器中的资料取出等)
readily available 易于得到
readiness n. 警觉;准备就绪;愿意;迅速,敏捷
readiness is all 有备无患
reading n. (议会的)读议案,(议案的)宣读;解释;校阅
reading of bill 宣读法案
reading report 书面报告
reading stage (议会中)宣读(议案)阶段
readings stages of Bill 法案宣读程序
readjust v. 再整理,再调整
readjustment n. 再调整
ready frame of mind 警觉的思想状态
ready identification (=unique identification) 独特性的确认[指在物证的鉴真问题上,美国证据法确立了两种方法:一是"独特性的确认",二是"保管链条的证明"(chain of custody)。第一种主要适用于对特定物质的鉴真,也即某一物证具有独一无二的特征或具有某些特殊的造型或标记,并说明法庭上该项物证具有相似之处。由此,证人通过当庭提供证言对该物证与原来看到的物证的同一性作出确定的证明。另一种鉴真方法是"保管链条的证明",主要适用于物证为种类物的情形,即某一物证并不具有任何明显特征,即便组织证人当庭辨认,也无法说清楚它具有的特殊造型、标记或其他特征。在此情况下,"独特性的确认"就无法适用了。而取代之的鉴真方法就只能是对该物证从提取到当庭出示的完整过程的展示。所谓"保管链条的证明",其实是指从该物证被提取之后直到法庭出示它的整个期间,所有持有、接触、处置、保管该项物证的人都要就其真实性和同一性提供令人信服的证言,以便证明该项证据在此期间得到妥善保管,其真实性不容置疑]
ready money (或 **cash**) 现金
ready up 用现金支付,即付
ready wit 机智
reaffirmation n. 再断定,再肯定,再证实;重申
Reagan Administration (美)里根政府
real n./a. 实在的东西;(the~)现实/不动产的;真正的;现实的;实际的
real action 物权诉讼[指为返还或被别人占有但属于自己的土地的诉讼,特别是对自由保有地产权在不动产的占有或占用中收回的诉讼。这是对物权的诉讼,大陆法中这区别于对人相关权利的诉讼。(美)路易斯安那州法指为保护占有人、所有人和其他不动产物权而提起的诉讼。亦称 action *in rem*]
real and demonstrative evidence 物证与确证
real bargain 合算交易,真便宜
real basis of jurisdiction 管辖权的真正基础
real capital 有形资本;实际资本
real chattels 不动产;物的准动产
real connection with a contract 与合同真正的联系
real contract 物权合同(契约),要物合同(源于罗马法,指债的成立不仅需要当事人的合意,还需有物的交付,如消费借贷、使用借贷、典质、寄托等)
real cost 实际成本
real credit 实际信用
real defences (被告)基于物权的抗辩
real domicile 实际住所
real earning 实际收入,实际收益
real economy 现实经济
real estate 不动产;房地产
real estate agency 地产公司
real estate agent 不动产代理人;地产经纪人
real estate binder 买卖不动产定金收据
real estate bond 不动产债券(据)
real estate broker 地产经纪人
real estate investment trust 不动产投资信托
Real Estate Investment Trust Act (REITA) (美)《不动产投资信托法》(1960年国会制定,用于证券化不动产投资)

real estate limited partnership （美）不动产合伙
real estate mortgage 不动产抵押
Real Estate Mortgage Investment Conduits (REMIC) （美）不动产按揭投资管理（指用于证券化不动产投资。见 Special Tax Entity）
real estate purchase price 地产征购价格
Real Estate Settlement Procedures Act 《不动产清理程序法》
real estate tax 不动产税,房地产税
real estate title deeds 房地契
real estate transaction 不动产交易
real evidence （17世纪）物证,实物证据,实证[指①实物证据(如衣服、刀伤),其本身在有争议的事件中充当直接证据部分,亦可称 physical evidence。②见 demonstrative evidence]
real exchange 商业汇兑价
real extra 上等产品
real GDP 实际国内生产总值
real hereditament 不动产遗产,可继承的不动产
real income 实际收入
real injury 实际伤害;非法行为所引起的伤害[有别于口头的语言伤害(verbal injury)]
real international public policy 真正的国际公共政策[指引申自那些必须强制(执行)实施的国际性原则,是对"国际礼让"(international comity)的某种新表述]
real law 不动产法;(大陆法上的)特种财产法
real life a. 真实的,非想象的
real life test 真实的试验,非想象的试验
real likelihood of bias 真正可能的偏见
real money 资金;硬通货;硬币[有别于纸币(paper currency),支票(check)和汇票(drafts)]
real party 真正当事人,实际当事人
real party in interest 具有利益关系的真实当事人(根据实体法有权提起诉讼的人,对诉讼标的具有实际和实质性利益的当事人,但不一定是最终获得利益的人。亦称 party in interest。见 nominal party)
real person 现实人（指非假设的经济人economic person）
real points of controversy 争议的真实要点
real price 实际价格
real property 不动产(指土地房屋可继承的财产)
real physical matter 实质物体
real physical matter of which a person or thing consists 组成个人或事物之实质物体
real representative 不动产的代表人(又称不动产代理人,指死者的不动产的代管人,也就是指他的继承人或土地受遗赠人)
real right 物权
real right for a definite period of time 有期限物权
real right for an indefinite period of time 无期限物权
real right for security 担保物权
real rule 实在规则,真正规则(见 paper rule)
real security 物保;物的担保,不动产担保(指抵押担保或债权人在债务人的特定财产之上设置的一种权益担保,抑或附加于土地上的负担担保。见 collateral 2)
real securities 作保不动产(用于以地产或租金作保证物的抵押)
real servitude 对物地役权,不动产地役权
real tare 实际皮重
real thing 真品,上等货;(复)不动产,房地产(=things real)
real union 政合国(指两个或两个以上的国家联合于一个君主之下,内政各自独立,外交关系则合为一体,以共同统治者之名义进行,这种联合形成一个新的国际法主体)
real voice of law 真正的法律之声
real wages 实际工资(指不以钱之多寡而以购买力为准的工资)
real-dollar value 不变美元价值
real-property easements appurtenant 从属于不动产的地役权
real-property security 不动产担保
realign v. 给……重新定位,使重新组合,重新列名

realignment n. 重新组合,改组
realignment of legislative district 重新组合法定的议员选区
realism n. 现实主义
realism jurisprudence 现实主义法学
realist n. 现实主义者;现实主义作家;实在论者;采取现实态度的人
realist intellectual mood 现实主义思潮
(the) realist movement 现实主义法学运动(指在美国,与利益法学和自由法学相对应的法学派,是现实主义法学运动和庞德的社会学法理学)
realist school of law 现实主义法学派
realist theory （法人的)实在说
realistic jurisprudence 现实主义法学
realistic prospect of convictions 现实的定罪预期(指英国《1994年检察官守则》明确规定提起公诉的证据标准,同时要求检察官必须确信对每一个被告人提出的每项指控有足够的证据提供"现实定罪预期"。这是一个客观标准)
realities of the day 当前的现实
reality n. 现实;实在存在的事物;实在性;实体,实物
reality of laws 法律的实在性
reality, the novelty or the merit of the invention 发明的实用性、新颖性或优越性
realizable a. 可实现的,可实行的;可变卖的;可变为现钱的
realization n. 1.实现;现实化;实在化;成就 2.变卖;把钱变成不动产;把(证券、产业等)变卖(为现钱)
realization and liquidation 变产清算
realization of an insolvent estate 变卖破产产业
realization of assets 变卖资产
realization of property 变卖财产
realize v. 1.认识到,了解 2.实现;(把证券、产业等)变卖为现金;(因出售、投资等而)获得(利润等)
realized assets 变卖的财产(指变卖资产所得的现金)
realized profit 到手的现金;库存现金[与账面利润(paper profit)相对而言]
realm n. 王国;国土;领土;地区;领域;范围
realm of jurisprudence 法学领域
realpolitik 现实政治(指国际关系上各国旨在谋求扩张权力并在这过程中依靠武力胁迫和经济压迫)
realtor n. (美)房地产经纪人(尤指全国房地产同业公会成员)
realty n. (与 personalty 相对。见 personalty)不动产,房地产
realty tax 不动产税,房地产税
reapply v. 再申请;再运用
reappoint v. 重新任命;重新委任;重新约定;重新指定;复职
reapportion v. 重新分配
reapportionment n. 重新分配;立法机构中代表之重新分配(指由于人口变化众议院或州立法机关的选区应定期重新划定以符合宪法规定的选举权的平等原则);反映人口变化的立法地区边界的改变
reapportionment revolution (美)议席重新分配革命(指美参议员名额分配。见 reapportionment)
reappraisal n. 重新估价,重新评价;重新鉴定
reappraisal of property 重估财产
rear v. 抚养;培养;树立,建立
rearrest n./v. 再拘捕,再拘留(或扣留)/再拘捕(指依法拘捕后脱逃,再拘捕时就无须拘捕状);拘留(或扣留)
reason n./v. 理由,原因;道理;理性;情理;理智;明智;前提/推理,推想;思考;辩论,讨论
reason and conscience 理性和良心;理性和良知
reason and reason 以种种理由
reason(s) for appeal 上诉理由
reason for dismissal 解雇理由
reason(s) for findings 裁决理由
reason(s) for rejection 不接受的理由
reason for the decision 判决理由
reason man 有理性的人(指法律所拟定具有正常精神状态、普通知识和经验及处事能力的人,是一项抽象的客观标准)
reason of state (或 raison d'état) 国家利益说

reasonable a. 合理的,公道的;正当的,适当的,理智的
reasonable act 合理行为,正当行为
reasonable act requirement 理性行为要求,理智行为要件
reasonable allowance 合理之分配额,合理减免额;合理生活费
reasonable amount of force 合理的力度,合理的强力范围
reasonable and probable cause 合理及可能的理由(指原告深信被告有犯罪可能的事实,即使任何明智者处于原告的地位,审核当时的情况,加以理性判断亦会得出合理及可能的理由);相当的原因(常用来进行非法拘留或恶意控告的诉讼的辩解,就是说被告那样做是有相当原因的)
reasonable balance 合理的平衡
reasonable basis 合理的根据
reasonable being 理性的人
reasonable beliefs 理性信任(见 probable cause)
reasonable care (17世纪)适度谨慎,适当注意,合理注意[指对过失责任的一种测试(test),即在相同或相类似的情况下,从事相同专业的具有行为能力,慎重而理智的人所持有小心或注意程度。亦称 due care; ordinary care; adequate care; proper care。见 reasonable person]
reasonable cause 合理原因(见 reasonable and probable cause)
reasonable certainty (美)合理的确定性(指违约可得利益损失本身就是假设的,具有天然的不确定性,即使让原告倾其所能提供相关所有证据也不一定能够证明可得利益损失的完全确定性。因此,严格要求确定性标准会严重损害非违约方的利益。因此,美国法院后来对确定性标准进行了改进,降低了非违约方的证明标准,提出了合理的确定性这一颇具灵活性的标准。现已成为美国法院判断违约可得利益损失的实践原则)
reasonable consideration 合理考虑;合理约因
reasonable creature in being 活着的人(指要构成谋杀罪必须证明所谋杀的人为活着的人,如初生婴儿要脱了娘胎独立地活着,才能算活着的人)
reasonable deviation 合理的绕航
reasonable diligence 合理的勤勉
reasonable dismissal 正当驳回;合理解雇
reasonable dispatch clause 合理运送条款
reasonable distribution of national income 国民收入的合理分配
reasonable doubt (18世纪)合理怀疑[指对被告是否有罪产生合理的怀疑,或相信被告无罪亦有真实的可能性。"无可置疑的原则",或排除合理怀疑或超出合理怀疑之外(beyond a reasonable doubt)是一项标准,依此由陪审团来审定刑事被告是否有罪。参见《示范刑法典》第1.12节(Model Penal Code §1.12)。在决定刑事被告是否有罪时如已经得到无可置疑或排除合理怀疑的证明,则陪审团必须推定该被告为无辜的。亦称 rational doubt。见 burden of persuasion; preponderance of the evidence]
reasonable equipment 合理配置,配置(船舶)之相当设备
reasonable excuse 合理解释(用于因含义不清所引起的辩论)
reasonable expectation of privacy 合理隐私期待[指美国司法部颁布的《刑事侦查中搜查、扣押计算机获得电子证据》(Searching and Seizing Computers and Obtaining Electronic Evidence in Criminal Investigation)中认为,用户对不同系统计算机"合理隐私期待"是不同的,放在用户家里没有联网的计算机,相当于用户自身的私有财产,用户对其有最大的隐私期待,因而在一般情况下,只有取得搜查证才能对其进行侦查。与此相反,放在开放系统(因特网)内的计算机数据,其合理隐私期待相对要小,因而只要法庭给网络服务运营商签发一张传票或特别法庭令即可,并不需搜查证。在美国,此两者有严格区别:用户家中计算机拥有的权利是美国联邦宪法第四修正案《电子窃听法案》保护的专利;而因特网上的信息拥有的权利不是宪法权利,其拥有的权利是有限的,通过《电子交易隐私法案》(The Electronic

Communication Private Act,简称 ECPA)来保护,一般情况下,无须搜查证]
reasonable expectation of privacy 对隐私的合理期待
reasonable expense 合理开支
reasonable fact finder 理性的事实认定者
reasonable force 正当的武力(指为保护自己或一个人的财产而使用的适当的力量)
reasonable foresight principle 合理预见原则(见 ordinary hazard principle)
reasonable grounds 合理的原因,正当的理由(见 reasonable cause);合理依据
reasonable grounds to suspect 怀疑的合理根据
reasonable judg(e)ment 公正的判决
reasonable legislation 合理的立法,合理的法规
reasonable man 正常人,理性人(现已改用 reasonable person,以免有歧视女性之嫌。见 bon pere de famille)
reasonable man doctrine or standard 有理性的人的原则或标准(见 reason man)
reasonable mind 有正常理性的人,正常理性(者)
reasonable nexus 合理的关联
reasonable norm 合理定额
reasonable notice of abandonment 适当的委付通知(保险)
reasonable parts (英)(遗产的)合理份额
reasonable period of time 合理的期间,相当期限
reasonable person 理性人;有理智的人[指用法律标准(legal standard)所拟制的人,特别是判定某人是否有过失行为;其规格是:具有谨慎办事能力、有知识、有智力、有判断能力,符合社会对其成员的要求能保护他们自己的和他人的权益。理性人明白事理地做事,不推迟做事,适当地小心,但不过度。参见《侵权法重述》(第二次)第 283(B)节。亦称 reasonable man; prudent person; ordinarily prudent person; reasonably prudent person; highly prudent person。见 reasonable care; bon pere de famille]
reasonable person standard 理智者标准,理性人标准
reasonable punishment 合理处罚
reasonable regard test 合理考量原则
reasonable rent 合理租金
reasonable suspicion (美)合理怀疑(见 grounds to suspect)
reasonable suspicious of bias 合理怀疑的偏见
reasonable time (提示票据的)合理的时间
reasonableness n. 相当,正当;合理;合理性,合情合理
reasonableness of provision for wife 对于妻子的合理的供养
reasonably prudent person 见 reasonable person
reasoned decision 合理裁决
reasoning n. 推理,推论;论证,论据
reasoning from analogy 类推
reasoning in laws 法律中的推理
reasoning that 理由是……;根据是……
reasonless a. 不合情理的,没有道理的,不讲道理的,无理性的
reasonless arguments 强辩,毫不讲理的争辩
reassemble v. 再开庭;再召集会;重新聚集;重新装配
reassert v. 再断言;再宣称;再坚持
reassessment n. 再估价;再确定;再征收(税款等)
reassignment n. 再分配;再委派,再指定
reassure v. 重新保证;再保险;使清除疑虑
reattachment n. 重新逮捕(或重新拘留、扣押、查封)
reave v. 劫掠,抢走;剥夺;偷窃
rebate n. 回扣;折扣;(付款总额的)减少;部分款项的退还;部分减免的款项
rebate of income tax 所得税退还部分
rebate on interest rate 利率上的回扣
rebeldom n. 全体造反者;叛徒;造反者控制的地区
rebellion n. 造反;反叛,叛乱,反抗,对抗
rebellious a. 造反的;反抗的,反叛的;叛乱的
rebuild v. 重启创制,重新建立
rebuke n. 指责,非难,责难
rebus sic stantibus 情势变迁原则(指在国

际法中缔约后发生未及预料之环境之重大变迁);在此情况下
rebut v. 辩驳,反驳,驳回;揭露,戳穿;举出反证
rebutment n. 反证,反驳;驳回
rebuttable a. 可反驳的,可辩驳的,可驳回的;举出反证的
rebuttable presumption 可予反驳的推定;推翻的推定
rebuttable presumption of law 可予驳回的法律推定
rebuttal n. 辩驳,反驳,驳回;反证,驳回的证据
rebuttal evidence 反驳证据
rebutter n. 辩驳(或揭露)的人;(被告的)第三次答辩状;反驳的论点
rebutting evidence 反驳证据(指用于反驳法律或事实的推定而使推定不能发生效力所举的证据)
recalcitrant n./a. 顽抗者,拒绝者;不服从的人,倔强的人/顽抗的,不服从的;难对付的,难管束的
recalcitrant witnesses 难以对付的证人,顽抗的证人
recall n./v. 1.(尤指由公民投票对官员的)罢免,罢免权 2.召回,撤回 3.撤销,取消 4.回收(指制造商对于有缺点的商品自动要求回收) 5.回想,回忆/1.召回;取消,撤销 2.召回,叫回 3.回忆起;恢复记忆 4.罢免
recall a decision 取消决定,撤销裁定
recall a judgment 撤销判决
recall an ambassador from his post 召回大使
recall an order 撤销订货单
recall by popular vote 投票罢免
recall of judicial decisions 撤销判决
recall of products 回收产品
recall of witness 撤销证人资格;再召回证人
recall to life 使苏醒
recallable a. 可撤销的;可召回的;可回忆的
recant v. 宣布放弃(信仰、主张等);宣布撤回;撤回声明;公开认错
recanter n. 抵赖者;变节者
recapitalization n. (企业的)调整资本,资本结构重组,资本结构调整(指通过母公司或子公司的合并或公司条款的修订以及改变公司的股票、债券或其他有价证券的比例,以调整资本结构。)
recapitulation n. 扼要的重述
recapitulation of salient points 复述要点
reception n. 取回;复取行为;再扣押,再扣押令;自行夺回
recapture n. 1.夺回;收复;收复物(指收复被掠劫的船只、财物),再获得之物 2.政府的征收(指超过定额的部分收益) 3.重新占领;再获得 4.合法收回(从前的领土、财产等)
recast v. 重新铸造,再铸造;彻底改动,重做;重算,重计
recast the notion 重新改变,改变观念
* *Receditur a placitis juris , potius quam injuriae et delicta maneant impunita.* We surrender the forms of law rather than allow injuries to remain unpunished. 即使实体法律规则弃之不用,也不能使罪过逃避制裁。
receipt n./v. 1.收到;收条,收据 2.(复)收到的物(或款项);收入 3.(古)税务局(= recipe) /开……的收据,在……上注明收讫(或付清)
receipt a bill 在账上签字或盖章
receipt and expenditure 收入和支出
receipt book 收据簿
receipt for cargo 货运收据
receipt of goods 对货物出具的收据
receipt of payments 钱款的受领
receipt of policy premium payments 支付保单保险费收据
receipt of stolen goods 收藏盗窃货物,窝赃
receipt rolls (英史)收入(钱款的)账目(后为收入和支出账簿取代)
receiptor n. 收受人
receivable n./a. 应收票据;应收款项;可收到的账目或账单;(复)可领取的账目或账单/可收到的,可接受的;应收的
receivable bill 应收票据;收款票
receivable discounted bill 贴现应收票据
receivable negotiated bill 转让应收票据
receivable testimony 可接受的证据

receive v. 1.接到,收到(与 accept 一般同义,但在欺诈法中 receive 为占有,而 accept 则为"推定占有"的含义);接受,承认 2.接见;受理;听取
receive a petition 受理请愿书(或诉状)
received a. 被普遍接受的,标准的,公认的
received corpus juris 公权的法令大全
received law 继受法
receiver n. 1.接受人;收款人;接待人;收货人 2.接受赃物者;赃物商 3.接管官(指法院委派来接收财产然后向法庭报告的人)4.破产事务官(亦称破产管理人,指破产诉讼中临时接收破产人的财产的法院官员)5.收管人(指按精神卫生法由法官任命的保护精神错乱者的人)
receiver and manager 继承财产管理人
receiver in bankruptcy 破产程序中的财产管理人
receiver of bribes 受贿者
receiver of the metropolitan police 城市治安财产监管人
receiver of wrecks (沉船后的)漂流物的看管人;遇难船舶管理人
receiver pendente lite 指定的诉讼中财产管理人
receiver system 破产管理办法
receivership n. 破产案产业管理人的职务(或职位)
receiving account 收入账户
receiving areas (土地)受让区
receiving order 法院宣告破产并指定破产财产管理人的命令;接管令
receiving quotation 接受报价;接受行市
receiving state 接受国
receiving stolen goods (或 **property**) 收受明知为盗窃的物品,窝藏赃物或财产(的罪行)(见 handling stolen goods);窝赃(罪)
recension n. 修订;修订本;修订版
recent and sudden enough 时间上的最近、突然(指上诉机构之所以提出"最近、突然"这两个标准,主要出于两个方面考虑:一是对《保障措施协定》和 GATT1994 的具体条文考量的结果;二是从保障措施的性质和基本原则中推断出来。)

* **Recent law prevails over prior law.** 新法优于旧法。
reception n. 接待,接见;接收,接纳;招待会;(对罗马法等的)继受(一般指西欧日耳曼各国法律体系对罗马法及对教会法和封建法的摄取,尤指在1400—1700年间的这一过程)
reception department (中)信访部门
reception of Roman law 罗马法的继受
reception office for letters and visits from people (中)人民来信来访接待处
reception order (对精神错乱者的)接受监护令
reception procedure 接受程序;继受程序(指欧洲共同体法须经各会员国内部之接受程序始能成为会员国法律秩序之一部分,而产生法律上之约束力)
receptiveness n. 感受性,接受性
receptum indebiti 不当得利(指无法律上的依据而受利益,致他人蒙受损害)
recess n. 休息;休会(有时立法会议持续休会许多周);休庭(通常 1—2 小时)
recess appointment 休会期间的任命(指当参议院不在会议期间总统所作的任命,包括司法官员任命,均需报参议院以后追认或批准)
recession n. 退回;撤回;(领土的)归还;交还原主;经济衰退现象
recessional a. 撤回的;后退的;(英)议会休会期的
rechanneling n. 再引导
recharge n./v. 再袭击;再控告
recharter v. 再次特许
rechte an rechten 权利上的权利
Rechtsstaatsprinzip 法治原则;依法治国原则
recidivism n. 累犯;再犯(行为或倾向)
recidivist n./a. 累犯者;惯犯;常习犯者/惯犯的,再犯的
recipient n. 受领人,接受人;受援者;受援国
recipient country 受援国
recipient of the earnest 收受定金的人
recipient of the mail correspondence 邮寄物的受领人
reciprocal a. 1.相互的,互惠的,交往的;对等的 2.相应的;相互补充的

reciprocal admission (美)相互认可(指订有协议的州与州之间的相互认可,对通过律师考试,获准在一个州开业的律师,通常过几年以后,又可根据其申请,认可到另一个州开业)
reciprocal agreement 互惠协定
reciprocal authorization 相互批准书
reciprocal benefit 互惠利益
reciprocal blockage 互相封锁
reciprocal causation 互为因果
reciprocal contract 互惠合同(契约)
reciprocal credit 对开信用,互惠信用
reciprocal enforcement of maintenance orders 赡养令的相互执行
reciprocal exemption statutes 互免(税)法规
reciprocal exchange 相互保险协会(指一个交换合同的会员组织,他们为了自身保险和相互保险目的,通过代理人并支付佣金达到此目的。相互交易包含个人、合伙、受托人或公司,但交易本身是非法人的。亦称 interinsurance exchange;reciprocal insurance exchange;reciprocal interinsurance exchange。同 reciprocal insurance association)
reciprocal insurance exchange 见 reciprocal exchange
reciprocal interinsurance exchange 见 reciprocal exchange
reciprocal laws (美)互惠法规(指一个州同意以同样的优惠和权利对待他州的公民,则两州之间可达成的互惠法规)
reciprocal letter of credit 对开信用证,互惠信用证
reciprocal rights and duties 相互的权利和义务,相应的权利义务
reciprocal tariff 互惠关税
reciprocal tax 互惠捐税
reciprocal tax immunities (美)互惠税收豁免
reciprocal trade 互惠贸易
reciprocal trade agreement 互惠贸易协定,最惠国通商协定
reciprocal treatment 互惠待遇,对等待遇
reciprocal treaty 互惠条约
reciprocal will 两人相互订立的遗嘱,互惠遗嘱
reciprocity n. 1.相互关系,交互作用;交换,交流 2.互惠;相互的权利与义务
reciprocity clause 互惠条款[互惠条款的内容主要为互惠国民待遇(reciprocity treatment),即授予国给予外国人国民待遇要以该国人所属国也给予该国的国民以国民待遇为条件,也就是两国约定互相把给予本国人的民商事权利也同样给予对方国家的人。最惠国条款内容主要为最惠国待遇,即授予国给予某外国的待遇,不低于或不少于授予国已给予或将给予任何第三国的待遇]
reciprocity in trade 商业上的互惠,贸易上的互惠
recision =rescission
recital n. 1.叙述,评述;列举 2.(契约等中)陈述(或证明)事实的部分;(证书的)说明部分;引述语
recitation n. 叙述,评述;书面陈述;援引
recitation right 朗诵权(有些国家的版权法中列为一项单独权利;有的国家将其编入表演权中。我国著作权法实施条例即将其归入表演权中)
recite v. 1.书面陈述(事实) 2.叙述,列举 3.援引,引证,引用
reckless a. 不注意的,粗心大意的(指有意识地无视重大、不顾风险、不顾后果的,严重有悖常人做事的标准和遵纪守法者的行为);鲁莽的
reckless conduct 疏忽大意行为
reckless cycling 鲁莽骑车
reckless driving 鲁莽驾驶,乱开车
reckless homicide 恣意杀人罪(按英美刑法,行为人没有和一般具有理性的人的谨慎,对自己行为或不作为的必然结果不加注意,非法致人死亡,应令负恣意杀人罪责);有意的过失(或任意)杀人(罪)(见 vehicular homicide)
reckless litigation 轻率的诉讼
reckless negligence 重大过失
recklessly caused loss 出于轻率造成的损失
recklessness n. 鲁莽,粗心大意
reckon v. 计算;估计;推断;把……看做;断定

reckon with 和……算账(向……算账);认真对付,将……加以考虑
reckoning n. 清算,结算,计算;估计;结账
reclaim v. 1.开拓;开垦 2.改造,纠正;使悔改,感化(指对犯错误或犯罪者而言) 3.对……提出要求;要求将……归还
reclaim of juvenile delinquents 少年犯罪的感化
reclaim sb. from vice 改邪归正
reclaimable a. 可改造的,可悔改的,可感化的
reclaimed animal 驯养的动物(可作为一项合法财产)
reclaiming (苏格兰)(最高民事法院的)再诉(指从外庭上诉到内庭)
reclaiming motion (苏格兰)再诉动议书
reclamation n. 1.要求归还,收复;再生;回收 2.改造,感化;开拓
reclusion n. (大陆法)单独监禁;幽禁
recognition n. 1.认出;识别;认识 2.承认,认可;公认
recognition and enforcement of foreign arbitral award 外国仲裁裁决的承认与执行
recognition and enforcement of foreign judg(e)ment 外国(法院)判决的承认与执行
recognition by the family 家庭承认
recognition *de facto* 事实上的承认
recognition *de jure* 法律上的承认
recognition in international law 国际法上的承认
recognition of a new government 承认新政府
recognition of a new state 承认新国家
recognition of belligerency 对交战团体的承认
recognition of insurgence 对叛乱团体的承认
Recognition of Trust Bill 信托承认法案
recognitor n. 1.被认可的(列入巡回法庭陪审团名单的)陪审员 2.具保人(=recognizor)
recognizable a. 可被认出的;可辨认的;可被承认的

recognizance n. 1.保证(书);保释;具结 2.(交付法院的)保证金,保释金;抵押金
recognize v. 具结;备案;认识;承认;自认;公认;认可;准许
recognize a claim 承认(对方的)债权
recognized document 认可的文据
recognized gain (1951年)已确认的收益[指属于所得税的部分收益,参见美国《国内税收法》及《美国注释法典》第26标题卷第1001节。见 boot 1]
recognized principle 公认的原则
recognized right 公认的权利
recognized state 被承认国
recognizee n. 被具保人,受具结保证的人
recognizor n. 具保人;取保候审的人
recollection n. 回忆,追忆,记忆;(复)记忆起的事物
recommend v. 介绍,推荐;劝告,建议;托付
recommendation n. 建议;推荐,保举,介绍
recommendation to mercy (苏格兰)(陪审团提出的)赦免建议,宽恕建议
recommit v. 再委托;重提(议案等);再犯,重犯;再入狱
recommit a criminal to prison 将犯人再关入监狱
recommitment (=recommittal) n. 再委托;(议案的)重提再犯(罪);再入狱
recompense n./v. 1.报酬;偿还补偿;赔偿 2.(赔、补)偿金/给以补酬;偿还;给以补偿;赔偿
reconcilable a. 可调解的,可和解的,可调停的
reconcile v. 1.使调解,使和解 2.调解,和解
reconciliation n. 媾和;和解;调停,调解
reconciliation agreement 调解(和解)书;调解(和解)协议
recondition v. 使恢复良好状态;修复;改革,纠正
reconfirm v. 重新证实;重新批准;重新确认
reconfirmation n. 重新确认;重新证实
reconnaissance n. 侦察;搜索,勘察,勘查
reconnaissance in force 实(武)力侦察,强行侦察
reconsider v. 重新考虑,复议,重新讨论

（决议案）
reconsideration n. （行政）复议，（议会）重新审议，重新考虑
reconsideration decision （中）复议案件
reconsideration office （中）（行政）复议机构
reconsignment n. 再委托；再托卖；改变原提货单（的交货地点、运输线路、收货人等）
reconstitute v. 重新构成；重新组成；重新设立；使还原
Reconstruction n. （美）(1865—1877年)原退出联邦的南方各州改组并重新加入联邦；(南北战争后原退出联邦的南方各州的)重组与重建或重制（加入联邦，建立宪法关系，恢复在国会的代表权，并在政府内部进行必要变动的过程）
reconstruction of company 公司的重建
reconstructions n. （美国南北战争后）重建运动；犹太教复兴运动
reconvention n. （大陆法）反诉；交叉起诉，交叉诉讼
reconversion n. 再转变；恢复；恢复原状；再次信仰；再改政党
reconveyance n. 1.归还；取回 2.再让与（亦称复让与，指财产抵押欠款还清之后，受押人把财产用再让与契据归还抵押人）
reconviction n. 再次定罪，再次判罪
record n. 1.记录，记载；登记；诉讼记录（指保存在法院里书面的真正的证供和文件）2.履历，经历；报告 3.案卷，档案；诉状；公判录 4.录了音的磁带；（美）犯罪记录，前科记录
Record Commission （英）法律文献委员会（指1800年根据下议院特别委员会建议成立的一个机构）
record date 记录日期
record disposition 档案处理
record of births 出生登记
record of conviction 犯罪前科
record of deaths 死亡登记
record of investigation （或 examination）勘查笔录，调查记录
record of penalty charges 罚款记录
record of previous crime 旧罪记录，前科记录
record of proceedings 诉讼程序记录
record of trial 审讯笔录，审讯记录
record of words 笔录
(The) Record Office （英）伦敦档案局（又译：伦敦档案署）
recorded instance 记载的实例，记录的判例
recorder 1.书记；记录员；掌卷官。（英）1个城市或自治市的首席司法官；2.记录器，录音器；3.(某些英国市、自治市具有刑事管辖的)司法官员；(具有刑事司法官员管辖的)市法官或(具有有限民事管辖的)违警罪法庭法官(police judge)，(四季法院或自治市法院的)法官，(美)地方司法官(类似 police justice 治安法官)；4.保管政府机构的档案材料(public records)如契据，留置权、判决等的市或县的官员
recorder of deeds 契（文）据登记保管的官员
(the) Recorder of London （英）伦敦市首席法官；伦敦市中央刑事法院法官（根据1971年法院法）
recordership n. 记录员或法官(推事)的职位(或任期)
recording n. 记录；录音
recording acts 案卷法；（美）记录法规（指不动产中相同利益的权利请求人之间建立优先原则的国家法规）
recording at election 选举记录
recording of ballots （唱票的候选人）得票记录
recording of changes of name 变更姓名的登记
recording officer 见 secretary ③
recording secretary 见 secretary ③
recording secretary （会议、档案的）记录秘书
records disposition 档案处理
records management 档案管理
records of testimony 口供笔录，口供记录
recoup v. 扣除；赔偿；补偿；偿还；补偿损失；扣留（应给付的一部分款项）
recoupment n. 扣除；补偿；付还；付还之款；补偿物；求偿权；补偿损失
recourse n. 追索权(亦译：求偿权，其含义

与 droit de suite 同),求偿权;偿还请求
recourse action 追索诉讼
recourse to courts 诉诸法院
recourse to force 诉诸武力
recover v./n. 1.重新获得;重新找到;收回 2.恢复 3.(根据法律程序)取得;获得补偿,胜诉;追缴/收回债权
recover booty 追赃
recover damage 补偿损失,取得补偿损失
recoverable damage 恢复原状的损害赔偿
recoveree n. 被追索财产者
recoverer n. 追索财产者;财产收回取得者
recovery n. 恢复;追索;财产收回(指用诉讼收回被非法占据或扣留的土地或财产);取得某权益
recovery action 追索(财产)诉讼
recovery in kind 复还原物
recovery of defaulted student loans 收回违约学生贷款
recovery of nationality 国籍的恢复
recovery of one's reputation 恢复某人名誉
recovery of overpayment of veteran's benefits 收回多支付的退伍费
recovery of payment made by mistake 追还错付款项
recovery of possession 恢复占有
recovery of premises 收回房产
recovery of right 恢复权利,回复权利
recovery of the original 恢复原状
recriminate v. 反控;反诉;反责
recrimination n. 反诉(罪行);反控(告);反责;相互控告
recross-examination n. (对证人)反复盘问;(对证人)再复诘问(指对方当事人或律师在己方当事人或律师对证人再直接询问后的诘问)
recrudescence (病)复发;(内乱等)再发作
recrudescence of executive justice 执行正义的复兴
recruiting system 征兵制
recruitment n. 招募(新兵等);补充,充实;恢复(健康)
recruitment examination 征聘考试
recta ratio 直接理由,(日)常理
rectification n. 纠正,矫正;调整;校正,改正
rectification convention 修正案,修正协议
rectification of boundaries 调整边界,修正边界;修正地界
rectification of instrument 校正文据
rectify v. 纠正,改正,调整
rectitude n. 公正,正直;严正;判断正确
rectitudo 权利;公正;法定费用;纳金或付款
recto de dote 寡妇向亡夫的继承人请求归还部分应得的房地产的权利状
recto de dote unde nihil habet 寡妇向亡夫的继承人请求全部应得 1/3 的房地产的权利状
rectum 权利;公道要求的义务;公正,审判,指控
rectus 权利
rectus in curia 恢复权利;恢复法律权利(指被剥夺法律权利的人,在恢复法律权利后才能得到法律的保障)
* *Recuperatio est alicujus rei in causam, alterius adductae per judicem acquisitio.* Recovery is the acquisition by sentence of a judge of anything brought into the cause of another. 恢复原状(复得)是由法官就他人案件所涉及的任何事物作出判决而取得的。
recuperatores (罗马法)合议法官(指诉讼第二阶段代替独任法官的审判人员)
* *Recurrendum est ad extraordinarium quando non valet ordinarium.* We must have recourse to what is extraordinary, when what is ordinary fails. 当通常的办法行不通时,必须求助于非常的办法。
recurrent account 经常性开支账目
recurrent reference 经常性参考;经常性关联;经常职权范围;经常查询,新近审断
recusant n/a. 不信奉国教者/不服从权威的
recusatio 回避,拒绝;抗辩
recusatio judicis (大陆法系)法官的回避
recuse v. 回避,拒绝,不服
recuse v. 回避,法官的回避[此词来源于拉丁文 recusare(拒绝)](指在对案件进行审理或判决时,因为对相关事项的利益或偏见的原因法官可能回避,如首席大法

官马歇尔在马丁诉亨特租户案中因早期曾担任过该案法律顾问,因而回避),拒绝,不服
red n./a. 赤字,亏空,负债/红色的
Red Army 红军
Red Books (美)红皮书
Red Cross 红十字会
red herring 要求计划书的样本;借口;证券说明书;证券销售书
red herring issue 非正式上市的股票
red light 红灯理论(美国印第安纳大学 Alfred C. Aman 教授认为行政法发展有三个阶段,这是第一阶段的主要理论,其功能被界定为以司法审查为中心对行政权力的控制,旨在最大限度地保护公民个人权利免受权力侵蚀。见 *laissez-faire era*)
red light abatement laws 红灯区废除法规(指一项条例或一项制定法规旨在取缔或禁止性导向买卖)
red tape 官样文章;繁杂;拖拉公文程序
red tapery (=red-tapism) 官僚主义的行政制度;文牍主义
red-cow case 见 white horse case
red-handed a. 1.沾满鲜血的手的;正在犯罪的现行犯的 2.当场的;流血的;暴动的
red-letter day 纪念日
red-light district 红灯区(指包括很多妓院等的一些淫秽地区)
reddendo (苏格兰)租金条款;贡赋条款
reddendo singula singulis 各对各;各从其文字的本义
reddendo singular singulis 同 *referendo singula singulis*
reddendum (写明租赁金额及付款期限的)租约条款;应付租金
redditus 收入,利润(尤指租金)
redeem v. 1.买回;赎回;偿还,偿清;履行(诺言)2.补偿;弥补(过失);补救 3.恢复(权利,地位)4.挽回荣誉
redeem a mortgage (或 pledge) 赎回抵押品
redeem one's obligation 履行义务
redeemable (=redemptive) a. 可赎回的;(证券等)可换成现金的;能改过自新的;可补救的;可拯救的

redeemable preference shares 可赎回的优先股
redeemable right 赎回(土地)权
redeemer n. 赎买者;(诺言等的)履行者;偿还者;回赎者;补救者;拯救者
redemise n. 交还,归还(指土地、财产)
redemption n. 1.买回;赎回;回赎权 2.偿还,还清 3.补偿;(诺言等的)履行;(证券)变卖成现金 4.改善;修复
redemption action 清偿债务诉讼;赎回抵押物诉讼
redemption annuity 补偿年金
redemption date 偿还期;偿还日
redemption fund 偿还公债基金会;偿债基金
redemption of a promise 诺言的履行
redemption of capital contribution 赎回出资额
redemption period 回赎期[指定法规定的一个期间,在此期间内未履约之抵押人通过支付尚欠债务重新获得其被抵押或税产拍卖(tax sale)之财产]
redemption rate 兑换率
redemption system 回赎制度
redemptiones (古英国法上)重的罚金(有别于 *misericordia*)
redemptive a. 赎回的;赎买的;(宗教上)赎罪的
redhibition n. (由于发现货物有瑕疵以致不能使用而)取消购货合同(契约)
redhibitory action 因货物有瑕疵要求取消合同的诉讼
redimere (罗马法)买回
redintegration n. 恢复完整,使再完善
redirect v./a. 1.更改(信件等上的)姓名、地址 2.(对证人)再直接询问(指己方当事人或律师对己方证人受对方反诘问的再询问)/对方对己方证人查问后之查问的
redirect and subsequent examination (对证人)再直接及连续询问
redirect examination (对证人)再次主询问,再次直接询问(指由对证人实施过直接询问的律师对该证人再次作出的询问。再次提出询问紧接在交叉询问之后提出,并集中在交叉询问中首次提出的问题上)

(英国人常用 reexamination)
redirection n. (己方当事人或律师在对方向己方证人诘问后的)再询问
rediscount n. 1.再折扣;再贴现 2.再贴现票据
rediscount operation 再减价交易
rediscount rate 再贴现率
redistribute v. 重新分配
redistribution of land 土地重划;重新分配土地
redistrict v. 把……重新划区(尤指重划选取)
redistricting cases (美)重新划区的案件
reditus albi 用现金付租(亦称白租,指用白银付租)
reditus nigri 用谷物付租;用劳役付租(亦称黑租 black rent,以区别于用现金付租)
redivide v. 重新划分;再分配,再划分
redline v. 确定(飞机)安全速度;画红线以注销;使飞机停飞
redlining n. (美)红线禁飞,画红线地区拒贷(用红线在地图上划出一个经济不景气的地区范围,在此范围内的金融机构可拒绝抵押贷款,通常认为这是一种经济歧视,是非法行为);画红线注销(将某些顾客划出贷款范围)
redo v. 重做(作);修补;改进;组织
redound v. 有助于;增加;提高;有损于;归之于
redraft n. 重新起草,再次起草,重开票
redress n./v. 改正,矫正,纠正,补偿;调整;平反/补救;矫正;纠正,改正;平反;处理,再整理
redress abuses 矫正流弊
redress damages 赔偿损失
redress of a grievance 纠正冤情,平反冤案
redress of wrongs 损失赔偿,补偿损失
redress the scales 作公平的调整
reduce v. 1.减少,减轻;降低 2.使变为(to);改变(状况等)3.使沦为;使降级;降职
reduce a penalty 减刑
reduce a rule to practice 使规定付诸实现
reduce the amount of the contribution 减少出资数额

reduce the cost 降低成本
reduce the duty 降低税收,降税
reduce them to discipline 迫使他们服从纪律
reduce to writing 草拟;写入;书面委托
reductio ad absurdum 反论证法(亦称归谬法,指借说明某一命题的反面为不可能或荒谬,以证明该命题为正确;或借说明某一命题的逻辑上的结论为荒谬或不可能,以证明该命题为错误的方法)
reduced the punishment to censure 降低惩罚为谴责
reduced to material form 以物质形式体现
reduced to writing 以书面形式体现
reduction n. 1.减少;(刑罚等的)减轻 2.折扣 3.还原,回复
reduction at judicial discretion 酌情减刑
reduction in force 大量减员,大规模解雇
reduction in prices 减价
reduction into possession 复归所有
reduction of armament 裁军
reduction of capital 减少资本
reduction of punishment 减轻刑罚
reduction of the purchase price 降低售价
reduction to absurdity (= *reductio ad absurdum*) 归谬法,反证论法
reduction to practice 付诸实施
redundancy n. 多余事项(指诉讼答辩中与诉讼无关的事项);冗长,累赘,多余的东西
redundancy fund (英)多余雇员解雇基金
redundancy payments (英)多余雇员解雇金
redundant population 过剩的人口
Redwood Library (美)雷德伍德图书馆[指殖民地时代北美大陆的慈善事业很发达,从剑桥的哈佛学院(Harvard College)到纽堡特(Newport)的雷德伍德图书馆等都是私人捐赠建立起的慈善机构]
recriminative (= recriminatory) a. 反控的,反诉的,反责的;互控的,互诉的
reeducation n. 再教育,重新教育
reeducation through labour (中)劳动教养,劳教
reelection n. 再选,重选;再次当选;改选
reeligible a. 有资格再度竞选的;再度获得

资格的;再度合格的
reemploy v. 再度雇用
reenact v. 重新制定;再用法律规定;使(法律、措施等)再度生效
reenforce (= reinforce) v. 增强,加强;再执行;使再生效
reengagement card 续聘卡
reengagement order 重新雇用令
reenter v. (出租地产者)重新占有(出租的地产);再进入;再登记
reentry n. 1.再进入;重新登记 2.收回租借物(指收回被承租人所租借的房屋、土地);回复土地所有权;再获所有权
reentry permit 批准(或准允)外籍侨民重新迁入(本国);国境证;回乡证
reestablishment n. 1.使复位;使复职;恢复 2.再建,重建
reestablishment of marital relationship 恢复夫妻关系
reeve n. 1.(执行某种规章的)地方执行官 2.(英)(市镇的)地方治安法官 3.(加拿大)(乡会的)议长;(英)(从前代表皇家的)高级官员
reexamination n. 再审问;再调查;再检查;再审查,重审
reexchange n. 1.退汇费(指汇票在遭到拒绝承兑时,发票人应负担的费用) 2.再交换;再交易 3.回汇;回兑
reexchange bill 退回的汇票
refashion v. 再作;重制;改变
refer v. 1.把……归诸于;认为……起源于⟨the invention of the compass is referred to China⟩(指南针的发明应当归诸于中国) 2.把……归类于,把……归属于⟨refer this flower to the rose family⟩(将此花归入蔷薇科) 3.把……提交;把……委托⟨refer a question to a committee⟩(把问题提交委员会) 4.指点,请求助于;使向……请教 5.提到,涉及,谈到;有关
refer a matter to a tribunal 把某事提交法院审理(解决)
refer to drawer 请给出票人
referee n. (受法庭委托的)鉴定人;仲裁人,公断人;裁判官(指在法院负责审理证人作证和当事人提交的报告,向法院报告

结果。裁判官是法院为特殊目的而指定的准司法人员,可行使某些司法权)
referee for inquiry 调查事实的鉴定人
referee in bankruptcy (破产债权团的)法定代表;破产审定人
referee in case of need 需要时的受托人;(票据)预备支付人(指在汇票上加上名字,作该汇票的预备支付人)
reference n./v. 1.参考(指以信息、服务思考提供人考虑)⟨this is for your reference only⟩(仅供你参考),⟨reference material⟩(参考资料) 2.出处、参考目录、参照⟨the author does not give references⟩(作者未注明所引用资料的出处),⟨the list of reference⟩(参考书目) 3.参考符号(reference mark) 4.提及,涉及⟨make references to the decision of the case⟩(涉及该案的判决) 5.关系、关联⟨the parts of the Digest all have reference to each other⟩(《判例摘要汇编》的各个部分都是互相关联的) 6.提交、委托⟨the reference of a bill to a committee⟩(向委员会提交议案) 7.(品行、能力等的)证明,证明书;介绍,介绍书,证明,证明人和介绍人⟨referencs from sb.'s colleagues⟩(某人同事给予的证明) 8.(关于品行、能力等间)查询、了解⟨make a reference to sb.'s friend⟩(查询某人朋友的情况) 9.职权范围⟨keep to the terms of reference⟩[不超越职权(或调查、审查)范围] 10.(专利)信息,比如:这一刊载出版物上的信息包括另外的专利或另外专利的申请。专利审查员认为这是先期在先技术(anticipatory prior art)或是在技术中不可预测性的证据,它将形成一个或一个以上的权利申请被驳回的根据(见 citation 4) / 给……加上参考图书目录;without reference to 不论,与……无关;with reference to 关于
reference clause 仲裁条款
reference group 参照群体
reference in case of need 需要时的保证人
reference on consent 同意审断
reference price mechanism 参考价格制度
reference source 参考资料
reference statute 参考性法规,参引性制定法

reference to European Court 诉诸欧洲法院
reference to the law 适用法律
reference to the record 案卷编号(指诉讼开始时案卷按年份、原告姓氏的第一个字母、地区用数码编入记录簿,以后有关此案均用此编号)
reference-over n. (国际私法)转致
referenda n. (见 referendum)
referenda on judicial decision 司法判例的复决权
referendarius (罗马法)向皇帝陈述接受请求(或诉状 petitions)的官员(该官员对请求者已给予回复);宫廷官员
referendary n. 1.(英)(中世纪宫廷、教廷的)大臣(具有顾问、调查、发布外交文件的职能)2.＝referee
referendo singular singulis 不同的词指不同的事物(这是一种词句结构规则,目的是对当事人起草的文件的意图产生效力。同 *reddendo singular singulis*)
referendum (复 referenda, referendums) n. 公民投票;公民投票权;复决(权);国民复决;(外交官对本国政府的)请示书
referendum and dissolution powers 公民复决及解散国会权
referendum on sovereignty 公民就主权投票
referent n. (神圣罗马帝国高级法院的)法庭顾问(其职责为分析案件证据,提出问题和处理意见)
referential a. 参考的,参照的;指示的;供参考用的
referral, reference n. 分派事项[指美国司法部长可要求分派给独立检察官的调查事项,提交问题(给董事会);被分派职务者//两词的含义均为"提交的行为"(act of referring);reference 意思更为广泛。"referral"早在20世纪初,开始如同美国用词或美国词意,但现在一般属于英国英语的使用。其含义特别指〈the referring to a third party of personal information concerning another.〉(提交给第三当事方有关另一个人的信息);〈the referenring of a person to an expert or specialist for advice〉(委托某人向专家或专业者咨询)]
referral fee 律师介绍费(指律师介绍顾客给另一律师时所收的手续费)
referral order (美)委任令(指民事案件中委任给治安法官处理审前事项并确保当事人严格遵守案件准备日程的命令)
referral sales plan 连环式销售计划
referred to 提交
refinancing n. 发行新债券取代旧债券;资本的再筹划
refinancing credit 再筹资金信贷
refinancing of debt service payments 为偿付债务开支再筹划资金
refine upon (或 on) **the wording** 字斟句酌
refinement n. 精心安排;精炼,精制;细微改进;详尽的阐述
reflation n. 通货再膨胀
reflect v. 归咎于;损害(名誉)(与 on 连用)
reflective equilibrium 反思平衡(指用于道德、伦理和正义理论的一个术语,表示一种道德推理的研究进路,道德直觉和道德理论通过它而相互检验)
reflexive modernization 自反性现代化[指所谓的"向风险社会转型的过程",首先是一种"自反性现代化"来消解工业社会,而且另一种现代化(即风险社会)也正在形成之中]
reform n. 改革,革新,改良;改造;使改过自新;感化
reform and opening up 改革开放
Reform Bill (英国1832年制定的)《改革法案》(其主要内容为扩大公民选举权、改革议会代表制)
(to) reform criminals 改造罪犯
reform law 改革法
reform of the constitution 修改宪法
reform prison 改良监狱
reform school (＝reformatory school,英国为 approved school)少年管教所;感化院
reform through labor (中)劳动改造
reformable a. 可改造的,可改过自新的;可革除的;可改革的
reformation n. 1.改革,改善,改良;修订(指法官修改或重写一个书面协议以吻合双方交谈人的意愿)2.重新组成,重新形成 3.改过自新
reformation of criminals 改造罪犯

reformatory n./a. 感化院;(美)少年感化院;(中)少年管教所(见 reform school)/意在改变的,意在感化的
reformatory education 感化教育;教育改造
reformatory school 教养院;工读学校
Reformatory Schools Act (英)《感化院法》(1854年)
reformer n. 1.改良者,改革者,革新者 2.改过自新者
reforming legislation 改革性立法
reformism n. 改良主义
reformist statute 改良主义的制定法
reformulated theory 重新系统阐述的理论
refractory a. 难驾驭的,顽强的,固执的;难治疗的
refractory prisoner 屡教不改犯;顽固犯
refrain v. 抑制,制止(from);忍;戒;禁止
refrain from crime 抑制犯罪
refrain from prosecution 抑制控告
refresh v. 1.使恢复精力,恢复记忆;补充,补足 2.提神,恢复精神
refresh sb.'s memory 使某人重新想起,使某人恢复记忆
refresher n. 使人恢复记忆的事物;(诉讼进行中付给律师的)额外费用
refresher fee (律师收取的)额外诉讼费用
refreshing the memory (使证人查阅文件、书籍等以)恢复记忆
refreshment of recollection 记(回)忆的恢复
refuge n. 安全,保护;避难处,避难所;慰藉物
refugee n. 避难者,流亡者;难民;逃亡者
refugee camp 难民收容所,难民营
refugee government 流亡政府
refund v. 归还,偿还;(用销售债券收入)偿还债务;发新债券取代旧债券;退款
refund annuity 偿还年金(指按照合同,如果年金受益人在领取分期支付年金前死亡,则该年金的金额应归入其遗产,或给予其指定的受益人)
refund of duty(或 tax) 退税
refunding n. 发行新债券取代旧债券;偿还(债务)
refunding of bond 公债偿还

refundment n. 资金偿还
refundment bond(或 guarantee) 偿还保证书
refunds and rebates 退款和回扣
refusal n. 1.拒绝,谢绝 2.取舍权;先买权
refusal of enforcement 拒绝执行
refusal of justice 拒绝审判
refusal of recognition 拒绝承认(外国判决等);否认
refusal of registration 拒绝登记
refusal of the Royal assent 拒绝御准
refusal of visa 拒发签证
refusal to accept 拒绝承兑(汇票)
refusal to accept office 拒任公职(罪)
refusal to follow the precedent 拒绝遵循先例
refusal to pay 拒付
refusal to release 拒绝释放
refuse v. 拒绝;拒受;拒给;不愿
refuse bail 不准保释;拒绝保释
refuse to pay tax 抗税
refusing inspection of books 拒绝查账;拒绝验证
refusing to perform 拒绝履行
refutable a. 可驳斥的,可驳倒的
refutation n. 反驳,辩驳
refute v. 反驳,驳斥
refute the testimony 反驳(驳斥)证据
regain v. 收回,重新获得;恢复(原职,健康,智力等)
regain consciousness 恢复知觉;苏醒
regain possession of 重新获得……所有权,恢复……占有
regal a. 国王的,王室的
regal office 王位
regal title 国王的称号
regalia n. 1.王权;王室的特权;王权的标记(如王冠等) 2.(等级、社团等的)标记,(社团)徽
regalia majora (英)主要王权(指不能移交给臣民的各种君王特权)
regalia minora (英)次要王权(指可通过明示授权移交给臣民的)
regalism n. 王权至上(尤指国王有控制教会的论说);帝王教权论

regalist n. 君主主义者
regality n. 王位,王权;君主国,王国;王土;国王特权;(国王赐予的)地方管辖权,管辖区
regard n./v. 1.(英)(对升任高级律师者奉送的)礼金;护林官 2.注意,注重;尊重,尊敬;敬意 3.关系/看待,对待;注视;与……有关;把……认为
regency n. 摄政;摄政权;统治;摄政时期
regent n. 摄政;摄政(统治)者;董事(如大学董事会成员)
regicide n. (英)弑君;弑君者;参与宣判查理一世死刑者;(法)判处法王路易十六死刑者
regie n. (法)政府对烟酒等的专卖;专卖的烟草及其产品;政府对公用事业的直接管理;专卖局;税吏;税务局
regime n. 政体;政权;统治;制度
regime matrimonial 婚姻财产制
regime of centralism 集权制度
regime of innocent passage 无害通过制度
regime of justice 司法制度
regime of law 法律制度;法制
regime of liability 赔偿责任制度
regime of movables and immovables 动产和不动产制度
regime of non-suspendable innocent 不得停止之无害通过制
regime of the international seabed 国际海底制度
regimen n. (古)政权;政体;统治(方式);社会制度
regimentation n. 组成,编组;编制
regina (=Regina) n. (英)女王,(用作英国女王当政时的公告签署或王室对某一讼案的)女王称号
Regina(略作 Reg.; R.) **Versus**(略作 v.) **sb.** 女王诉某人案(见 *Rex*)
region n. 1.地区,地带 2.范围,领域 3.层;行政区
region of war 战区
regional n./a. (美)地区交易所(指分布全国各地的小型证券交易所)/地区的,局部的;区域性的
regional agencies 区域机构

regional agreements 区域协定
regional alliance defence treaty 区域性同盟防御条约
regional autonomy 地区自治;(中)区域自治
regional autonomy of minority nationalities (中)少数民族区域自治
regional circuit courts (美)区域性巡回法院(全美国共有 12 个)
regional commissioner 专区专员,地区专员
regional cooperation tax system 区域合作税收制度
regional development programme 地区开发规划
Regional Economic Integration Organization (REIO) 区域经济一体化组织
regional fisheries organizations 区域渔业组织
regional international law 区域国际法(见 general international law)
regional international organization 区域国际组织
regional national autonomy 民族区域自治
regional oceanography 区域海洋学
regional organization 区域性(国际)组织
regional preferential duties 地区特惠税
regional security 区域安全
regional system of law 区域性法律体系
regional understanding 区域性谅解,区域性协议(国际法用语)
regionalization n. 地区化
regionalization of the law of sea 海洋法的区域化
regionalize v. 把……分成地区,使区域化;把……按地区安排;使地区化
register n./v. (16 世纪)1.担任正式记录的政府官员〈each county employs a register of deeds and wills〉(每个县都雇用契据和遗嘱的注册记录员)(见 registrar)2.遗嘱检验法官(probate judge)3.诉讼登记册[指所有各种案件备审目录均在此册内,亦称(意思 3)register of actions] 4.(教会法)记事册(指在教区内发生的重大事件如结婚、出生、洗礼和洗礼命名以及葬礼等均记载该于该记事册。此记事册对英格兰十分需要,其起始年约为 1530 年。缩略

为 Reg.)/(14 世纪) 1. 走进公共注册处〈public registry〉登记〈register a new car〉(在公共注册处登记一部新车) 2.(正式地)登记为选址〈five voter registered yesterday〉(五个选民昨天正式登记) 3.作记录〈counsel registered yesterday three objections〉(律师对于三个异议的依据作了记录) 4.(律师 当事人或证人)在诉讼开始之前向法院书记官登记〈please register at the clerk's office before entering the courtroom〉(在进入法庭之前,请先在书记官办公室登记) 5.申请发行新证券〈a new security issue〉(指向证券交易委员会或类似国家机关申请发行新证券),〈the company hopes to register its securities before the end of the year〉(该公司希望在本年前申请发行本公司的证券)

Register General (Establishment) Ordinance 《注册总署署长(人事编制)条例》
register in bankruptcy 破产事项登记册
Register of Copyrights (美)版权注册(或登记)官 [指联邦官员,负责美国版权局(U. S. Copyright Office)的工作。该局发布版权申请注册、登记的规定和法定程序。亦称(不正确的) Registrar of Copyriths]
register of debates (1824—1837 年)《国会讲演录》(指 1824—1837 年在美国国会发言的非官方记录)
register of births, deaths and marriages 出生、死亡和结婚登记簿
register of copyrights 版权登记(册)
register of deeds 契据登记(册)
register of judg(e)ments 判决登记(册)
register of marriages 结婚登记(册)
register of M. P. s' interests (英)议员(对议案有关的)利害关系登记制(有关下议院议员的一项古老规则,指与问题有直接金钱关系的议员不可就该议题参加投票。M. P. 指 Member Pecuniary)
register of patents 专利登记(册)
register of pending actions 未决诉讼登记(册)
register of stock transfer 股票过户登记(册)

register of trademark 商标注册簿
register of trust companies 信托公司登记册
register of wills 遗嘱登记(册)
register of writs 法院令状登记(册)
register office 登记处,注册处
register the changes (in one's registration) 变更登记
register with the police 在警察局登记
registered a. 已注册的;已登记的;挂号(邮寄)的
registered association 已登记的社团;注册社团
registered ballot 记名投票;登记票
registered bond 登记债券;注册公债券
registered capital 注册资本
registered certificate of shares 注册股票;记名股票证书
registered company 注册公司
registered contractor 注册承包商
registered designs 注册的外观设计
registered juristic person 注册法人
registered land 已登记的土地
registered luggage 托运的行李
registered mail insurance 挂号邮件保险
registered marriage 已登记的婚姻,正式婚姻
registered matter 已备案事件
registered partner 注册合伙营业股东
registered proprietor (房地产、专利等的)注册所有人
registered share 记名股票
registered trader 场内交易商,证券交易所注册的直接经营人
registered trademark 注册商标
registered voter 已登记的投票人
registering court 登记法庭
registry of commerce 商业登记;(大写)商业登记局(处)
registrable a. 可注册的,可登记的;可挂号(邮寄)的
registrant n. 负责(管)注册的人;被登记者;登记人;注册人;被注册者
registrar n. 注册主任;登记官员;负责登记股票转让的信托公司(或银行)的人;注

册官
registrar of copyrights 见 register of copyrights
registrar police 户籍警
registrar's office 登记处
registrar-general n. 总注册官;注册总局局长
registrar-general of births, deaths and marriages （英）生、死、婚姻注册总局局长(指在英国,生、死、婚姻的办事处叫注册总局,现隶属财政部)
registration n. 登记;注册;登记证
registration certificate 登记证明书;注册证书
registration fee 登记费,注册费
registration for execution （苏格兰）(相当于具有法院判决效力的)执行登记
registration for preservation （苏格兰）登记保存
registration for publication （土地契据的)公开登记
registration law of industrial and commercial enterprises 工商企业登记法
registration numbers 登记编号,注册号码
registration of an award 仲裁裁决登记
registration of birth 出生登记
Registration of Business Names Act 商号名称注册法
registration of charges on land 土地负担登记
registration of commons 公地登记
registration of crimes 刑事资讯
registration of death 死亡登记
registration of juristic persons 法人登记
registration of land transfers 土地转让登记
registration of marriage 婚姻登记;结婚登记
registration of patents 专利登记
Registration of Patents Ordinance 专利注册条例
registration of residence 居住登记
registration of title 产权登记
registration of trade marks 商标登记,商标注册
registration of treaties 条约登记
registration of voters 选民登记;投票人登记
registration of writs 令状登记
registration on the electoral lists 在选民册上登记
registration paper 登记证件
registration statement （美）注册报告书(指公司对公众发布的大多数证券交易商所要求的财政和所有权方面的报告书),注册说明书;有价证券申请上市登记表
registration system 登记制度
registration tax 注册税
registry n. 1.见 probate judge 2.见 register 2 3.(海商法）商船国籍的登记,或列表遵照该特定国家的海事规定行事。根据商船悬挂的旗帜国籍被列入名录（见 certificate of registry; registry of ships; enrollment of vessels)
registry anew 重新登记
registry of ships 船舶登记
registry office 1.(英）保存公共记录的户籍以及监管非教堂结婚的机关;出生、死亡、结婚登记处;用工介绍所 2.法院的诉讼档案(保管)室
regius chairs of law （英）钦定法律讲座(指由国王在几所古老的不列颠大学所设立的教授职位)
regius professor 钦定教授(指牛津、剑桥大学的神学、希腊文、希伯来文、法学、医学五种中由国王指定所设讲座的教授或讲师的教席)
regnal year(s) （英国法）国王即(在)位纪元;帝王就(在)位之年;国王执政年
regnant a. 统治的;占优势(地位)的;流行的
regnum 统治
regrant v. 复准;回让财产给原主
regrating n. （收购粮食)以便再出售获利;零售,转售;囤积居奇
regrator n. 囤积居奇者
regress n./v. 复归权;回归,退回/退回;倒退
regressive a. 税率递减的
regressive rate 累退(减)率
regressive tax （1893 年）递减税[随着纳税基数的增加,指有效税率降低的一个税种。此类型之税是随着纳税人收入的增

加,而纳税的百分比减少。固定统一税(flat tax),如典型的营业税(sales tax),通常被认为是递减的而不顾其固定率(constant rate)。因为比起高收入的纳税人,低收入的纳税人更难于负担,随着不断地增加免税(exemption),即发生递减税务效果。见 progressive tax; flat tax]
regressive tax rate 累退(减)税率
regressive taxation 累退(减)课税
regret n./v. 懊悔;悔恨;表示遗憾;(复)歉意/懊悔;悔恨;抱歉
regrets only (如不能出席)谨请告知(用于国际礼仪中宴会请帖)
* *Regula est, juris quidem ignorantiam cuique nocere, facti vero ignorantiam non nocere.* It is a rule, that every one is prejudiced by his ignorance of law, but not by his ignorance of fact. 不论谁,其所以受害并不是由于对事实无知,而是由于对法律无知,这算作一条规则。
* *Regula ex jure, non jus ex regula, sumitur.* The practice is taken from the law, and not the law from the practice 实务来自法律,而非法律来自实务
regulae generales 一般规程(指各个法院随时宣布的诉讼程序和司法手续;亦指高等法院规程)
regular a./n. 通常的,正常的;依法的;遵循的;有秩序的;正式的,正规的;习惯性的;常备的;有规则的;(美)忠于政党领导的,政党领导选定的/常客,(美)忠于领导的某一党派成员
regular account 正规账户
regular army 正规军,常备军
regular budget 正常预算
regular course of business 正常业务,一般业务(指公司或企业的一般出售,相对"大宗出售"而言。"大宗出售"则指公司、企业出售其拥有的大宗物资或产品。美国《统一商法典》对大宗出售有专门规定,以保护债权人的权益)
regular court 普通法院
regular diplomatic relations 正常外交关系
regular donation 定期(给付的)赠与
regular election 见 general election

regular indorsement 正常背书
regular insurance 定期保险
regular judge 正规(式)法官;合格法官
regular law 常规法(指具有统一化和专业化的特点的英格兰普通法)
regular long form bill of lading 正常样式提单
regular magistrate 正规(式)司法行政官;合格的司法行政官
regular marriage 正规婚姻(尤指合乎宗教仪式的)
regular meeting 常会,例会
regular merchant 正规商人
regular military 正规军,常规军
regular party nominee 正规的党派被提名候选人
regular payment 定期付款
regular practitioner 挂牌律师
regular procedure 例行手续,正规手续
regular proceedings 正常程序
regular receipt 正式收据
regular session 例会
regular tax and additional tax 正常税和附加税
regularity n. 规律性,规则性;正规,定期,经常;一致性
regularity of a referendum 公民投票是否符合规定
regularity of electoral proceedings 选举手续是否合乎选举程序
regularize v. 使有规律,使规则化;使合法化,使正确;使系统化;调整
regularize one's position 使某人的地位合法化
regulate v. 管理;管制,控制;调整;使遵守规章;调节;整顿;规定
regulated contract 调整合同(契约)(与planned contract 相对)
regulated markets 管制性的市场
regulating output 控制产量;调节产量
regulation n. (17世纪)1.管理,管制,控制,调整,规制(指通过规则或限制控制或规制某些事项)2.规章;管理规定;规则;条例。规章如同众所周知的规则(rule)一样,在美国行政法中这两个术语可以互换

使用〈the federal regulation of airline industry〉(联邦对航班人员的规定),内部章程〈the CEO referred to the corporate regulation〉(首席执行官提交公司规章) 3.官方的规则,命令,[指通常由一个行政机构发布的有法律效力的正式规则,命令〈treasury regulations explain and interpret the Internal Revenue Code〉(财务规则表明并解释国内税收法)。缩略(特别)大写 REG。亦称(第3个意思上)〈agency regulation〉(行政机构规定),〈subordinate legislation〉(辅助法规);〈delegated legislation〉(授权立法,授权法规)]4.(欧洲法)一项常规的立法(指直接适用于欧盟成员国的一项常规立法,而无需单独的成员国去实施或执行法规) (regulatory a.; regulable a.)
regulation in force 现行规则
regulation light 规定号灯(指根据国际海上避碰规则设置的号灯)
regulation of conduct 行为规范
regulation of monopoly 垄断的规定,垄断的控制
regulation of registration 登记(注册)规则
regulation of stock 股票价格规定;股票管理
regulation of traffic 交通管制
Regulation on Computer Software Protection 计算机软件保护条例
Regulation on the Trade Mark (1993年12月欧共体委员会正式通过的)《共同体商标条例》
regulation size 法定尺寸,法定规格
Regulation S-K S-K 规则[指美国1934年《证券交易法》第402节S-K规则,以表格方式列举了要求公司披露的特定信息范围:一个表格"薪酬总表"(Summary Compensation Table),内容包括一年度内公司的薪酬总额诸如薪酬和红利,长期薪酬诸如有限股票奖励和长期激励计划;另一表格要求公司提供有关股票期权授予的信息、长期激励薪酬信息以及养老金收益信息]
regulation Z (美)Z 条规定(指联邦储备委员会一条规定,即实施贷款条件表示法的规定)
regulation-making power 制定规章权
regulations concerning civil appointment 文官任用条例
Regulations for Preventing Collisions at Sea (国际)《海上避碰规则》(1662年)
regulations for the carriage of goods by sea 海运规章
regulations governing the organization 组织条例
Regulations of Navigation 航行规章
regulations on academic degrees 学位条例
regulations on maintenance of social order 社会治安条例
regulations on the exercise of autonomy 自治条例
regulative a. 管理的,调整的,调节的
regulative agency 管理机构
regulator n. 管理者;调整者,校准者
regulatory a. 规范的;章程的;制定规章的
regulatory acts 行政规章性法规(令)
regulatory agencies (或 bodies) 行政管理机构,管理机构(指根据立法法令设立的独立的政府委员会);(美)准司法性的政府委员会
regulatory arbitrage 规章制度性的套利
regulatory barriers to communication 通讯的常规障碍
regulatory compliance defense (=defense of regulatory compliance) 合理抗辩(进行辩护)
regulatory capture 规定夺得
regulatory capture theory 管制俘获论(与公共利益相反,该理论认为"俘获"政府管制即促使政府管制的利益方,是财力雄厚或有助于政治选票的利益集团;政府管制与其说是为了公益目的,毋宁说是特殊利益集团"寻租"结果。因此,管制无助于解决市场问题,还导致社会财富浪费,对社会有害无益)
regulatory commissions 规章制定委员会;管理委员会
regulatory data bases 规范性数据库
regulatory era 管制时期
regulatory framework 规章制度
regulatory gap 监管真空
regulatory interest 规制的利益

Regulatory Negotiation (简称 Reg-Neg)(美)行政立法协商(程序)
regulatory offense (美)规章性犯罪[指①违反规章、条例所规定的轻罪罪行,及普通法上规定的犯罪。②见 public offenses]
regulatory oversight 规范性监督,看管
regulatory power 制定规章的权力;管理权;行政管理权
regulatory reform 规章制度的改革
regulatory regime 管理制度
regulatory rules 规范性的规则
regulatory taking (美)管制征收,管制性占用[指虽然所有者的权利未受侵害,但当土地使用限制实质上妨碍了所有人享有受益时,管制性占有就产生了。根据联邦宪法第五修正案的占有条款(taking clause)应给予公平补偿的财产占有]
regulatory takings (美)管制性征收(指管制行为对土地使用的限制,即使达不到完全排除其经济效益的程度,仍然可能构成征收)
regulatory theory 管制理论
rehabilitate v. 1.恢复(原有职位;地位;权利;名誉等)2.使恢复心理健康 3.修复
rehabilitate a witness 恢复证人名誉
rehabilitation n. 1.恢复;修复 2.复权;复职;复位;恢复名誉 3.身心康复
Rehabilitation Act of 1973 (美)《1973年(残疾人)康复法》,《1973年(残疾人)正常活动法》(指禁止联邦雇主对残障者加以歧视的法规,同时规定承包联邦政府契约者及接受联邦政府财政补助者,都有义务对残障者提供就业机会)
rehabilitation n. 恢复,修复;复职,复位;恢复名誉;(犯罪的)再教育,改造;(证据法中对证人信誉提出异议后的)证人名誉恢复;(破产法)恢复权利;(伤残和吸毒成瘾者戒毒后独立生活)恢复健康
rehabilitation home 教养院
rehabilitation of offenders (或 **criminals**)前科消失(指罪犯释放后,经几年前科消失期未再犯任何严重罪行,就应像未判过刑的人同样看待)
rehabilitation of the bankrupt 破产人的

恢复权利
rehabilitation period (已释放犯人)名誉(或社会活动等的)恢复期,前科消失期
rehabilitative a. 改过自新的,重新做人的;恢复正常生活的;恢复名誉的;复职的;复权的
rehabilitative principles 恢复正常生活的原则,复权(或复职)的原则;重新做人的原则,改过自新的原则
rehear v. 复审,再审问
rehearing n. 复审;再审;重新审理
rehearsal n. 详述;列举事实;复述
rehire n. 再雇用
rehumanize v. 使再有教养;再教化;再赋予人性
rei interoventus (苏格兰)不得变更的行为
* *Rei turpis nullum mandatum est.* The mandate of an immoral thing is void. 对不道德的事所作的委托无效。A contract of mandate requiring an illegal or immoral act to be done has no legal obligation. 要人履行非法行为或不道德行为的委托契约不产生法律效力。
rei vindicatio 所有权收回之诉;请求返还物的诉讼;(罗马法)主张物权之诉
rei vindicatio utilis 所有物返还扩用之诉
Reichskammergericht (神圣罗马帝国的)枢密法院(1495年设立)
Reichstag n. (神圣罗马帝国的)国会(起源于中世纪),德意志帝国国会
reign n./v. 王权,君权;君主统治,统治;统治时期/为王,为君;统治;盛行,占优势
reimbursable a. 可收回的;可补偿的
reimbursable expenditure 可收回支出;可报销的开支
reimburse v. 偿还,赔偿
reimbursement n. 补偿,赔偿;偿还;偿还款项
reimbursement account 补偿账户,补偿理由(或根据)
reimbursement credit 偿付信用证
reimbursement of capital 资本的退还;退还资本
reimbursing bank 偿付银行
reimpose v. 重新开始征收(曾停收的税

等);再强加(负担,义务和统治等)
reimprison v. 使重新入狱,再囚禁
rein(s) n. 驾驭;统治;控制;权势
reincarnate v. 使新生,改造好,(赋予)新生
reindict v. 对……再提起诉讼
reinforce v. 增援;加强;加固
reins of government 统治权,政权
reins of office 职权
reinscribe v. 再登记;再印,再刻写;铭记
reinstate v. 恢复原状;恢复原职;恢复原位
reinstate a case 恢复审理案件(指对驳回案件的恢复审理)
reinstated of reopened cases 被恢复的或重开举证的案件
reinstatement n. 恢复权利;复原;复职;复位
reinsurance n. 再保险;转保险;分保;再保险金额
reinsurance agreement (保险)分保合约
reinsurance company 再保险公司
reinsure v. 再保险
reinsurer n. 再保险人
reinsuring for common account 共同利益再保险
reintegration n. 重新统一,重新结合
reintegrative justice 融合性司法
reinterrogate v. 重新审问,再审问
reinvest v. 再投资;重新投资;再授权;再赋予(与 with 连用)
reinvest profits 再投资利润
reinvested earning 再投资的收益
reinvestigate v. 再调查,重新调查
reinvestigation n. 重新调查
reinvestment n. 再投资
reissue n. 重新发行;再版
reiterate v. 1.重述,重申 2.反复地做;反复
reiterate one's view 重申己见,反复说明自己的观点
reject v. 抵制,拒绝;驳回,否决;驱出;丢弃
reject a complaint 不受理申诉
reject a proof 驳回证据
reject an appeal 驳回上诉
rejectamenta 漂浮物
rejected check 拒付支票

rejecting cabinet's proposals 否决内阁决议(常导致内阁垮台)
rejection n. (16世纪)1.拒绝接受合约要约 2.拒绝接受提供的货物作为合同之履行。根据美国《统一商法典》,买方对不规范的货物(nonconforming goods)的拒绝接受必须在交付后合理时间内做出,并且还必须将拒绝接受的通知送达给卖方(见 repudiation 2; rescission; revocation 1) 3.(议会法)未采纳,未批准(见 lost 3) 4.(专利法)专利审查后在审定通知程序(office action)中的裁定,其权利主张的申请是不可取得专利的(见 objection 4; restriction 4)(reject v.)
rejection of offer 要约之拒绝
rejection of payment 拒绝付款
rejection slip (出版社附在退稿上的)不采用通知,退稿通知
rejector (或 **rejecter**) n. 否决者,拒绝者,抛弃者
rejoin v. 1.再参加,再加入;再结合 2.(被告对原告作)第二次答辩,再答辩
rejoinder n. 答辩;反驳;(被告对原告的)第二次答辩,被告次轮答辩状
rejoinder to the defence (原告)对被告抗辩的答辩
rejuvenescence n. 返老还童,活力的恢复,重获新生,复活
relapse n. 复发;故态复萌;旧病复发,恶化;再犯罪
relapse into crime 重犯,重新犯罪
relapse of the stock (或 **share**) **market** 股票(市场)行情(回升后)再下跌
relate v. 讲,叙述;使联系,显示出;涉及(to),与……有关(to)
relate back to 溯及
related case(s) 相关案件
related patent 相关专利
related right 相关权利
relating to civil law 与民法有关的;民法上的
relation n. 1.关系;家属;亲属;亲属关系 2.(复)(特殊的)关系;性行为 3.叙述;(英)(向检察长告发而使其起诉的)告发 4.追溯效力
relation arising from the employment of la-

bor 因雇佣劳动所生的关系
relation back 追溯效力(指法律的一种原则,认为后一行为可有追溯前一行为的效力)
relation back principle 溯及力原则
relation by blood 血亲(关系)
relation by marriage 姻亲(关系)
relation in public law 公法关系
relation of private right 私权关系
relational investing 关系投资
relations between parents and children 父母子女关系
relations of production 生产关系
relationship n. 亲属关系;关系
relationship by (或 of) affinity 姻亲关系
relationship by consanguinity 血亲关系
relationship in law 姻亲关系
relationship of agnation 男系血亲
relationship of the blood 血统关系,血亲关系
relationship of the half-blood 半血亲关系
relationship of the wholeblood 纯血亲关系
relationships through marriage 姻亲关系
relatival a. 亲戚的,亲属的
relative n./a. 亲属,亲戚/有关系的;相对的;比较的;相应的;有关的
relative advantage 相对利益
relative availability 相对有效性,相对有用,相对适用性
relative by blood 血亲亲属
relative by marriage 姻亲
relative claim 相对请求权
relative comfortable life 小康
relative conditions of an action 相对诉讼条件
relative contraband 相对禁制品
relative cost 相对成本
relative cost control 相对成本控制
relative deprivation 相对剥夺;相对短绌
relative exclusion of issues of process 相关独有的程序问题
relative fact(s) 有关事实,次要事实;客观环境
relative impediment (禁止亲属结婚的)相对障碍
relative in the direct line 直系亲属
relative in the direct line of descent 直系

尊卑亲属
relative legal incapacity 相对无行为能力;相对无权利能力
relative majority 相对多数
relative nullity 相对无效
relative nullity of marriage 相对无效的婚姻
relative of the same rank 同辈亲
relative of the wife 妻亲
relative political offences 相对的政治犯罪
relative price 比价,相对价格
relative reduction 相对的减轻
relative rights 相对权利
relative to 关于……
relative total loss 相对全损
relatively incapacitated person 相对丧失能力的人;相对无行为能力的人
relatively inexperienced lawyer 缺少经验的律师
relatives up to the sixth degree 六亲等内的亲属
relativism n. 相对主义
relativist n. 相对主义者,相对论者
relativist jurisprudence 相对主义法学
relator n. 1.叙述者,陈述者 2.原告,告发人
relator action (英)相关人诉讼(指当某公共机关的行为违法并妨害公众利益,却又没有给任何人造成特别损失时,国王的代表——总检察长可根据相关人的"告发"或"检举",授权或许可该人以自己的名义提起诉讼,这即为"相关人诉讼")
relatrix n. 女告发人,女原告
relax v. 1.放松;放宽;缓和 2.减轻(处罚,课税等);解除疑虑
relaxation n. 放松;放宽;减轻(处罚,课税等)
release n./v. 1.释放;免除 2.解除(合同);弃权;让渡 3.发表,发行/1.解放,开释 2.解除,免除 3.准予发表 4.让与(财产等);放弃(权利等)
release a prisoner 释放囚犯
release after the sentence expires 延期释放
release an article for publication 准许一篇文章发表
release before the sentence expires 提前释放
release certificate 让渡证书;释放证书

release fee 遣散费
release from confinement 释放
release from guilt 免罪,赦罪
release from liability to penalty 免除刑事责任
release from the contract 免除合同(契约)义务
release of bank accounts 银行存款解冻
release of debt 免除债务
release of distress 解除扣押;发还扣押物
release on bail 保释
release on own recognizance (ROR) 具结后释放,被告提供保证之后释放
release on parole 假释
release on probation 缓刑释放
release procedure 释放程序(手续)
released bill of lading 放行提单
released by court 被当庭释放
released on bail for medical treatment 保外就医
released time (美)宗教教导时间[指允许公立学校的学生在校期间接受宗教教育的一种实践。在左拉奇诉克卢森(Zorach v. Clauson)(1952年)一案中,联邦最高法院同意纽约州的做法,让学生到宗教中心去接受他们所选的宗教课程教育。不参加宗教课程的学生会被通报,但未真正受到惩罚,仍留在学校。此案开创了政府援助宗教教育机构的活动得到宪法许可的可能性]
releasee n. 被免除债务人;(权利、财产等的)受让人
releasor n. 放弃权利的人;(权利、财产等的)让渡人
release on licence 释放许可证
relegate v. 1.流放;判流放刑;驱逐,放逐;贬谪 2.使……降级(降位);把……归于 3.把……委托(移交)给(to);使归于(某类……)
relegate a question to a committee 把问题委托给一委员会研究
relegation n. 放逐;贬谪
relevance of specific evidence 具体证据的关联性
relevancy (=relevance) n. 关联性;中肯,

恰当
relevancy and admissibility of evidence 证据的关联性和可采性
relevancy of evidence 证据的关联性
relevant a. 有关的,相关的
relevant action 有关诉讼;相关诉讼
relevant art (专利法)相关技术[指人们可以合理期待指望问题解决方案的一项技术,而这一方案正是有专利权的设施试图去解决的。这个术语包含不仅有关特殊产业中一些问题的知识,而且还包含科学领域中已累积的知识,其技术已普遍得到使用并解决问题。亦称 pertinent art]
relevant competent authority 主管机关
relevant counterpart 相关的对应物
relevant date 有关日期
relevant document 证明字据;有关字据,有关证件
relevant evidence (与案情)相关的证据
relevant facts 有关事实
relevant market 相关市场(指美国反垄断法上的市场,即相关市场为三维市场,包括产品市场、地理市场和时间市场三个向度。反垄断法市场的界定就是以一定的方法揭示涉案企业所处市场的三个向度)
relevant testimony 有关证据
relevant court 有关法院,适格法院
reliability n. 可靠性
reliable a. 可靠的,可信赖的;确实的
reliable account 可靠账户
reliable applicability 可靠的应用性
reliable document 可靠证件
reliable guaranty 可靠担保,可靠保证
reliable witness 可靠证人
reliance n. 信任,信赖,信心;依赖的人(或物);可靠的人
reliance interest 信赖利益
reliance interest (1936年)信赖利益[指在违约时要求损害赔偿之专用语。无过错的一方基于对双方履行合同的信赖而支付的资金费用和消耗或转移的财产。某些事物中合法部分;对于财产权的权利主张的部分或全部。信赖利益是指因实施行为而导致的财产损失以及因信托合同而发生的损失。基于对被告之允诺的

信赖,原告改变了其处境,用富勒(Fuller)的话说,"可以判给原告损害赔偿以消除他因信赖被告之允诺而遭受的损害。"其目的在于使恢复到与允诺前一样的处境,在这种情况受保护的利益才叫信赖利益]
reliance on(或 in)**his promise** 信赖他的诺言
relict n. 1.寡妇 2.生存者;残存者;残余物
relicta verificatione 诉讼之认诺(指被告在诉讼中承认原告所诉之事实,因而接受败诉之判决)
reliction n. 遗物,纪念物;遗风,遗俗;遗迹,废墟;(复)遗体,尸体
relief n. 减轻;免除;免责;救济;(损害赔偿上的)法律补救方法(指英美法上的原告在损害赔偿诉讼里,请求衡平法庭给予救助补救);土地继承的缴纳(指继承土地时缴给领主的财物);换班,接替
relief against forfeiture 免予没收;免除罚金
relief for work-caused injuries 因工负伤救济
relief from action 免予起诉
relief from income tax 减免所得税
relief from taxation 免税;减税
relief fund 抚恤金;救济金
relief in the form of money 金钱赔(补)偿[普通法的两种救济方法之一;另一为返还财产(restoration of property)]
relief laws 救济法规,补救法规
relief of the poor 救济贫民
relief payment 救济金
relief sought 救济要求
reliefer n. 接受公共救济者;暂时接替他人者
relieve v. 免除;减轻;救济;使免除,使解除
relieve from obligation 免除义务
relieve sb. of liability 免除某人责任,使某人免责
religion n. 宗教;宗教信仰;信仰
religion-based punishment 宗教性惩罚
religious a. 宗教的;宗教上的;宗教信仰的
religious belief 宗教信仰
religious bigotry 宗教的偏执
religious conviction 宗教信仰
religious court 宗教法庭
religious customs 宗教习惯
religious dissenters (英)不信奉国教者
religious faith 宗教信仰
religious foundation 宗教基金(会)
Religious Freedom Restoration Act (RFRA) (美)(1993年国会通过的)宗教自由恢复法
religious group 宗教团体
religious law 宗教法
religious liberties 宗教自由
religious marriage 宗教婚姻
religious rite 宗教仪式
religious teaching 宗教教义
relinquish v. 1.让与(权利、财产等);把……交给 2.放弃;撤回;停止;弃权
relinquishment n. 放弃;放弃权利(财产);放弃继承(财产)权;撤回
relocate off-shore 离岸设立
relocatio 续租(民法用语。指租约展期,经明示或暗示同意依原有租约续展)
relocation n. 1.更换(新)租约 2.重新安置;迁移
reluctance (= reluctancy) n. 不愿,勉强;因勉强而行动迟缓
reluctant a. 不愿的,勉强的;难以处理的;难驾驭的;顽抗的
reluctant communities 反对派;对立团体
reluctant follower 胁从分子
rely (on) v. 依赖,依靠,仗着
rem jurisdiction 对物管辖权
remain v. 1.停留,居住 2.继续,依然 3.剩下,留下
remain in suspense 悬而未决,停而未决
remain neutral in a war 战争中保持中立
remain with 属于,归于
remain within the four corners of the law 在法律范围内
remainder n. 剩余物;余产;剩余遗产;剩下的人;其余的人;地产的指定继承权,继承替代;存货
remainder of opinion 其余的判决意见者
remainder of the life time 未来余生
remainderman n. 剩余遗产继承人;最终受益人(见 ultimate beneficiary)
remainderman in trail (英)限定继承的

剩余财产继承人
remaindership n. 继承权;残留权
remains n. 1.遗体,尸体,遗骸;残存者 2.剩下的东西,剩余,余数 3.废墟,遗迹;遗稿,尚存之著作
remand n./v. 1.送回,还押,送回一案件重审(指送回某一事物如一案件、一个请求或一个人重新审理的行为) 2.发回一个案件,一项诉求或一个人下至下级法院重审
remand centres 未成年犯羁押候审中心
remand for retrial 发回重审
remand home (英)(8—16岁的)少年拘留所
remanded from Appellate Court 从上诉法院移送(或发回案件)
remanent a./n. (苏格兰)附加的,添加的;残留的,残余的/1.残存;残留 2.延期审理的诉讼案件 3.(英)留待下届议会讨论的议案
remanent pro defectu emporium 1.Remains unsold for want of buyer 未售出之剩余物品为买主之需;2.在司法行政官未能售出被没收的财产时,这种语言常用于执行令"a writ of execution"的回执中。
remark n./v. 1.注意,觉察,看⟨a report worthy of special remark⟩(值得特别注意的一篇报告) 2.评论,议论,谈论,陈述,话⟨pass remark about (or at) sb.⟩(议论某人),⟨make no remark⟩(不加评论),⟨make a few remarks⟩(说几句)(同 remarrque)/1.注意,觉察,看见⟨he remarked the changes of his hometown⟩(他已觉察到他的家乡的变化) 2.评论,谈论,议论⟨i would like to remark that...⟩(我认为……)
remark n./v. 注意,觉察/注意,谈论,评论,议论
remark right 重编权(指以同一方式重新改编原作的权利)
remarkable consequence 显著后果
remarriage n. 再婚,再娶;再嫁,改嫁
remarry v. 再婚,再娶;再嫁,改嫁
remedial a. 补救的;补偿的;矫正的
remedial action 补偿性诉讼,补救性诉讼[①(环保法)旨在使环境质量得到长期恢复而意欲提起的诉讼,尤其是根据 CERCLA 即 Comprehensive Environmental Response, Compensation, and Liability Act of 1980.,《1980 年环境综合性反应、赔偿和责任法案》的规定,在危险物质已经释放并可能污染环境时采取的一种目的在于永久减少污染的治理,或使危险物质达到最低程度的排放。因而不致影响公众健康,并使危害减少到最低限度。②旨在恢复或收回债款、个人财产或损害赔偿等任何诉因而提起的诉讼,亦称补偿性诉讼 remedial action。其实,即以补偿受害人为目的而由受害人提起的民事诉讼]
remedial acts 补救性法令
remedial measure(s) 补救措施,补救方法
remedial right(s) 法律救济性权利,补救性权利,纠正性权利
remedial statute 补救性法规
remediate v. 去掉错误(改正文本);补救;修订,校订;纠正,整顿;矫正,消除;修复,更新;改善,超过;调节,校正;改革,赔偿,补偿,使纠正错误;重启,重铸;治愈
remediation (环保法)补救性、补救解决(指让被污染的土地、水或空气恢复以前的状态,或几乎可以适用的状态)
remedy n./v. 1.法律补救方法;补救;补偿 2.司法救济(《伯尔尼公约》中与 redress 含义相同) 3.纠正;改善;去除弊病/补救;纠正;抵消;消灭
remedy a mistake 纠正一个错误
remedy an abuse 矫正弊端
remedy an evil 根绝罪恶
remedy claimable as of right 依法当然可予救济的补偿
remedy for breach of contract 因违反合同而要求补偿
remedies praetoriis 裁判官的救济
remedium extraordinarium 特殊救济(见 extraordinary remedy)
remember v. 记得,想起;送礼给……;遗赠给
remembrancer n. 1.记忆唤起者;提醒者 2.(大写)(英)王室征收债款的官员;(英)高等法院的法官
reminder n. 提醒者;助人记忆的事物
remise v. 放弃;让与;让渡(权利,财产

等);立契出让
remissible a. 可宽恕的,可赦免的
remissio 免除,延期支付
remissio injuriae (古苏格兰)通奸宽恕
remissio pignoris 放弃质押(导致质押关系解除的事实之一)
remission n. 1.宽恕;赦免;免罪 2.(债务、捐税等的)免除;豁免;减轻 3.发还下级法院 4.(国际私法中的)反致
remission of crime 免罪,赦罪
remission of debt 免除债务
remission of fine 免除罚金
remission of one-third of prison sentence 减三分之一刑期
remission of punishment 免除刑罚,免刑;减刑
remission pardon 赦减刑罚
* *Remissius imperanti melius paretur.* A man commanding not too strictly is better obeyed. 谁在指挥时不过于严格,谁就会更加得到人们的服从。
remissive a. 赦免的;豁免的;减免的
remissness n. 粗心大意;疏忽,懈怠
remit n./v. 案件的移交(尤指高级法院将案件送回原审法院);呈交当局解决的事项/1.宽恕,赦免;豁免;(债务、捐税等的)免除 2.免予(处罚);减轻;缓和;减退 3.提交,移交(问题等) 4.汇款;汇拨 5.(将案件)发回下级法院重审;还押;将……呈送某人请求裁决
remitment n. 还押;撤销,废止
remittance n. 汇款;汇款额
remittance man (侨居外国的)依靠国内汇款生活的人
remittance operation 汇兑业务
remittance slip 汇款通知单
remittee n. (汇票的)收款人
remitter (或 **remittor**) n. 1.汇款人 2.将案件移送下级法院审理 3.以某人的两份所有权证中更有效的一份代替另一份;恢复权利 4.赦免者,宽恕者
remitting agency 承办汇款机构,承办汇款单位
remitting bank 汇款银行
remittitur n. 案件发回原审法院重审;减

轻,减免赔偿额(指审理的法官有减少由陪审团判给原告金额的权利,或如果原告同意拿出低于审理提出的一定金额,则上诉法院有拒绝重新审理被告的权力)
remittitur damna (= *remittit damna, remittitur damnum*) 减免损害赔偿
remittitur of record 案件复位发回(指将上诉的案件返回到原审法院来执行上一级法院的判决)
remnant n. 残余,剩余,残迹,痕迹
remonetize v. 把(某种金属)重新用作货币
remonstrance n. 抗议;抗辩;规劝,告诫,忠告
remonstrate v. 抗议;抗辩;规劝,告诫,忠告(与 with 连用)
remorse n. 悔恨,自责,懊悔;同情心
remortgaging of property 财产的转质
remote a. (15世纪) 1.(在时间,空间和关系上的)远离的,远的 2.轻微的 3.(财产法)迟于死后21年,遗产必须转让处理(vest)(见 rule against perpetuities)
remote cause 远因;间接原因
remote damage 间接损害
remote kinsman 男性远亲
remote possibility 两面可能性;极小的可能性
remote online sale 远程在线销售[通常指位于不同地域(国家)的交易当事人之间进行的在线销售活动,有时亦称"跨国在线销售活动"。见 online sale]
remoteness n. 遥远;间接(原因、影响等);疏远
remoteness of cause 远因
remoteness of damage 间接损失;间接损害
remoteness of evidence 间接证据
remoteness of foreseeability 极少预见性
remoter degree 较远亲等
removable a. 可免职的,可去除的,可移动的
removal n. (16世纪) 1.解除;撤换;免职;转移(人或物)(指将人或物、事从一处转移至另一处,或居所转移至另一处) 2.(美)转移案件[指允许被告将州法院的案件转移至联邦法院。在转移案件至联邦法院时,诉讼当事人必须及时呈交转移的文件(removal papers),还必须出示或表明转移至联邦法院的有效根据(valid ba-

sis)。参见《美国注释法典》第 28 标题卷第 1441 节。见 remand 1]
Removal Act of 1875 (美)《1875 年管辖转移法》[由于 1875 年管辖转移法的重要性,有时被称为《1875 年司法法》(the Judicial Act of 1875)。它第一次授予联邦法院原审和转移管辖权。这两种管辖权与宪法授予联邦法院对联邦问题(federal questions)的管辖权相并存。美国联邦宪法第 3 条(Article Ⅲ)授予司法权的管辖范围包括宪法、合众国法律和合众国已订的、将订的条约之下发生的一切涉及普通法和衡平法的案件]
removal of cases 案件的转移(美国联邦主义的特色正是双重的司法体制并存。每个州都有自己的法院体制,包括初审法院、中级的上诉法院以及最高法院。联邦体制有着类似结构的司法体制。一般情况,由原告决定在州法院或联邦法院提起诉讼,只要被选择的法院对该案件有管辖权,原告的决定不受妨碍。案件转移则是一般规则的例外,允许被告将案件从州法院转移到未决案件所在地区的联邦法院。因此,案件转移使被告得以变更原告对州法院的选择。一个案件被转移之后,州法院则失去对该案之管辖权,而联邦法院则获得决定这一案件的所有方面的权力。根据现行制定法,只有当案件属于联邦法院的司法管辖范围,并且经由原告诉诸法院时,案件的转移才被允许)
removal certificate 迁移证
removal expense 搬运费
removal from office 解除职务,撤职
removal jurisdiction 案件移送管辖;移送管辖
remake rights 重播权,复制权。(版权)(指制造一部或更多部电影片或剧本的权利,这些电影或剧本实际上与原先的都是相同故事情节,而且已被授予复制权的)
removal of action 诉讼案件转移,诉讼转移(指诉讼案件在法院间的转送)
removal of articles from places open to the public 从对公众开放的地方取走(陈列)物品
removal of causes (把一法院的)诉讼案件转移(到另一法院)审理
removal of judge 审判员的回避
removal of matrimonial bond 解除婚姻关系
removal of wrecks 清除航道
removal order 案件移送令
removal power 免职权
remove v. 1.移动,搬开,消除,去掉 2.免职,撤去 3.(美)移送(指允许被告将州法院的案件移送至联邦法院的程序,如果案件提起时存在联邦问题或异籍问题管辖权,大多案件适用此种程序,《美国法典》第 28 标题卷本第 1441 条确立了联邦移送的规定,允许被告将案件移送至联邦法院);移交(案件)4.杀掉,暗杀
remove an arbitrator 更换仲裁人
remove case for trial 提审
removed a. 1.(亲族关系)相隔一等(代)或多等(代)的 2.无关的;远的,远离的
removing (苏格兰)驱逐租户之诉
REMT 物权抵押信托(全称为 real-estate mortgage trust)
remuneration n. 报酬,酬金;补偿,赔偿
remuneration for personal services 劳务报酬,报酬,酬金;补偿,赔偿;稿酬
remuneration for work 工作报酬,劳动报酬
remuneration of labor 劳动报酬
remunerative price 报酬性价格
(the) Renaissance n./a. (欧洲 14—16 世纪的)文艺复兴,文艺复兴时期;文艺复兴的
render v. 1.作出(判决、裁决);判处 2.表示;汇报;开出(账单等);提供,提出(理由);呈递 3.执行;实行,实施 4.放弃,让与;给予,给付,纳贡
(to) render a decision 作出判决,作出决定
render a verdict 交付宣判(指一种正式程序,将已同意的裁决交宣判法官在公开开庭时宣判)
render an account of 答辩;报告
render an account of one's action 说明某人的行为
render joint liable 使有连带关系,使有连带责任

render judgement 宣判,宣布判决;作出判决
render justice 进行审判
render useless 致使无用
rendering services 提供劳务
rendezvous n. 公共场所;聚会的地方(尤指军队聚集的、舰队集中的或船舶会聚的指定地点);约会
rendition n. 1.施行 2.给予,让与;放弃;引渡 3.译述,翻译
rendition of a fugitive 逃犯的引渡,让渡
rendition of judg(e)ment 判决,宣判[区别于 entry of judg(e)ment——将判决记录在案。rendition of judgment 是宣判行为,而 entry of judg(e)ment 是上诉前的司法行政行为]
renegade n./a. 叛徒,变节者,逃兵/背叛的,变节的,叛教的
renege(或 **renegue**)v. 食言,背信,违约;否认;放弃;拒绝
renegotiation n. 重新谈判,重新协商(尤指为了超额利润)
renew v. 更新;重新开始;焕发;准予(合同)展期
renew a contract 使合同(契约)展期
renewable a. 可更新的;可继续的,(合同等)可展期的
renewable clause 可更新的条款
renewable nature resources 再生自然资源
renewal n. 1.重订,续订(合同等的)展期,更换 2.恢复,复原;更新;重新开始 3.补充,加强,修补,重申;重新确定
renewal of insurance 续保
renewal of negotiation 恢复谈判
renewal of registration (商标)续展注册
renewal of the obligation 债的更新
renewal of treaties 条约的展期
renewal of writs 传讯令更新(指法院传讯令有效期为 12 个月,到期可更换新的,更新的最多只有 6 个月有效期,但可继续更新下去)
renewal plan 重新计划,更新计划
renewed deliberation 复议
renominate v. 重新提名;提名连任
renounce v. (14 世纪)1.正式放弃(权利或利益),否认,不认领⟨renounce an inheritance⟩(放弃继承)2.拒绝[指拒绝遵守或拒绝承认⟨renounce one's allegiance⟩(拒绝一个人的忠诚义务)]
renounce an action 放弃诉讼
renounce right 抛弃权利
renouncement of a succession 放弃(遗产等)继承权
renouncer n. 放弃人,放弃继承权的人;拒绝承认人
renouncing probate 放弃遗嘱检认(认证)
renovate v. 整修;革新;恢复,刷新,净化
renown n. 名望,声誉
rent n./v. 租金(指为使用土地、劳动、设备、思想甚至货币等资源所作的支付。一般来说,劳动的租金称作"工资";对土地和设备的支付称作"租金";对使用一种思想而支付的称作"专利使用费";对使用货币的支付称作"利息"。经济理论中如果一种可供使用的资源量长久地不受使用这种资源所作的支付额多少的影响,这种支付称作"经济租",如果可供的资源量只是暂时不受支付额多少的影响,这种支付称作"准租金");1.租,租费,房租,地租 2.(任何生产事业的)纯利 3.租入,租用/出租,租用
rent act 租赁法(例)
Rent Assessment Committee (英)租金评定委员会
rent charge 租费;(依遗嘱或合同)土地所有权的继承人应向第三人缴纳的定期给付
rent control (政府对)租金控制
rent dissipation 租金耗散(指任何寻租过程都必然伴随"租金耗散",即只要存在对租金的竞争,就会引起租值的减少,就是租金耗散)
rent in kind 实物地租;实物租金
rent insurance 房租保险
Rent Judge 租借法官,借用法官(指争议当事人在法院办理登记手续后,借用已退休的法官主持审理程序,该法官与普通法院法官的决定具有相同的效力,败诉方不服决定的可向当地法院上诉)
rent lease and ejectment 租赁和驱逐

rent of assize　法定地租；法定租金
rent of dwelling-house　住房租金
rent recovery index　租金追偿指数
rent restriction act　租额限制法（例）
rent roll （收入）租金登记册；租金账册
rent service （英）（代替租金的）劳役
rent strike （美）抗租行动（指房客抗议房租增加和服务太差而拒付房租的行动）
rent tribunals（或 **rents tribunal**） 租金裁判庭（指1968年英国租金法案设立的裁判庭），租金法庭
Rent-a-judge (= private judge, temporary judge)　私人裁决（在这种裁决中，法定程序和规则得以遵守，但裁判者非正式法官，而是熟悉法律程序和规则的人，多数是律师、退休法官等）
rent-a-robber n.　雇（佣）请的强盗；抢手
rent-day n.　租金付款日
rent-free a.　不收租金的
rent-party n.　（房客为自己）筹措租金（而举办）的集会（舞会等）
rent-roll n.　房（地产）租账；租折
rent-seck n.　（从前通行的佃户虽未能缴纳田租，也不能强取佃户的财物作为补偿田租的）租约
rent-seeking n.　租金谋取，寻租［指以一种激励方法进行超额的商品生产意图获得比生产成本（cost of production）大得多的回报。这样一种动机的经济行为，按Bouvier Law Dictionary（P.942），此术语通常用于法律和经济领域。"寻租"是指通过市场拓展（market exploitation）寻利。"'寻租'是经济学中的一个术语，用来表示追求纯利（pursuit of rent）（一般意义上：利润和收入而不是对租赁的支付）"，通过市场拓展而不是通过商品生产和服务，或通过贸易来寻求利益，比如通常讨论寻租（rent seeking）的例子都是拓展垄断（exploitation of monopolies），免费搭车机会（free-rider opportunity），以及优惠规则与纳税（preferential regulation and taxation）。该词条亦可描述负面外部效应（negative externalition）蓄意产生（deliberate generation）。寻租亦指1974年由安·奥·克鲁格提出的概念和1976年由戈登·塔洛克对相关理论作的阐述］

rentable a.　可租的；可收租金的
rental n.　出租，出租业；租费，租金（额），租金收入；租金登记期；租册；出租的财产
rental agreement　租赁协议，租赁合同（契约）
rental allowance　房租津贴
rental and maintenance　租金和维修费
rental charges　租赁费
rental expenses　租金费用
rental for housing　承租住宅的租金，房租
rental for living quarters　房租
rental income　租金收益
rental management agreement　租赁管理协议
rente （法）定期利息；定期租金；定期收益；岁入，年金；（复）统一公债券；统一公债券的利息
rented property　租赁财产
renter n.　租赁人，租户
rentier n.　领年金的人；有固定的地租、利息收入的人；靠租、息收入生活的人
renunciation n.　（14世纪）1.放弃（权利）（指明示或默示将权利放弃而不将它转让给他人）2.（遗嘱和遗产）放弃继承［指依据遗嘱放弃继承权利的行为。以前，一个人曾宣布放弃根据无遗嘱继承而未处分的财产或根据遗嘱而放弃赠与。今天，这两种情况，这种放弃是普遍或正常的。根据2的意思亦称disclaimer。见right of election；disclaimer］3.（刑法）犯罪中止［指完全、自愿放弃刑事犯罪目的，有时在进行犯罪之前即使中止或未遂。该词条可以是对犯罪未遂（to attempt）、同谋或共谋（conspiracy）以及类似的一个肯定性答辩（affirmative defense）。参见《示范刑法典》第5.01（4）节。亦称 Withdrawal；abandonment 4。见 anticipatory repudiation。renuncidive a.；renunciatory a.］
renunciation of children　与子女脱离关系
renunciation of right　放弃权利
renunciation of succession　放弃继承权
renunciative (renunciatory)　1.放弃的，抛弃的 2.拒绝承认的，拒绝的 3.克制自己的
renvoi 1.驱逐外国人（尤指外交官员）出境 2.（国际私法中的）反致

renvoi au permier degré (国际私法中的)一级反致
renvoi au second degré (国际私法中的)二级反致,转致
reoccupy v. 再占领;收回;再用
reopen v. 重开;重新进行;再开始;继续
reopen a discussion 重(新进)行讨论
reopen closed case 重审审理已结案件
reopen the door to foreign countries 重新对外开放
reopener clause (英)(工会与公司所订合同中规定在合同期满前任何一方得要求)重开谈判的条款
reopening clause 重新谈判条款
reopening nomination 再行提名
reopening of a case 再审某案
reopening of the trial 再继续审讯
reorder v./n. 再订购(货品);再命令;再整理/(同一订购者对同一货品的)再订购(单)
reorganization n. 1.(破产法)改组,重组。公司的经济结构的调整(restructing of a corporation)或重组(见 chapter Ⅱ) 2.(税法)税收调整[指根据美国《国内税收法》,因企业结构调整,合并,资本结构重组,为达到改善其税收待遇而进行税收调整。该法将各种类型的调整,重组以不同字母(different letters)分类。参见美国《国内税收法》,《美国注释法典》第 26 标题卷第 368 节。见 recapitalization]
reorganization of the court 法院改组
reorganization plan(s) (美)改组计划(指总统改组部级以下执行机构的建议。按授权法规,该建议应提交国会,如国会未否决此项计划,则此项计划在通常立法程序变更过程中自动成为法律,并在《国会记录》上刊出)
reorganize v. 改组,改编;改革;整顿
repair n./v. 1.修理;补救;恢复;(复)修理工作 2.补偿;补救;赔偿 3.修理完善(从法律方面讲与 in good repair, sufficient repair 无大差别)/赔偿(损失等);补救;纠正;修理;修补;使恢复
repair a wrong 补偿自己对别人的过错
repair of article 物品修理
repair order 修理通知单

repair the injury 赔偿损害
repairing charges 修缮费
reparable a. 可修补的;可补救的;可纠正的;可补偿的;可赔偿的;可治愈的
reparable injury 可补偿的伤害(指可用金钱补偿的错误)
reparable loss 可补偿的损失
reparation n. 补偿;(常用复)赔款,赔偿;弥补,补救
reparation by equivalent 相应赔偿
reparation of injury 损害赔偿
reparations in kind 实物赔偿,物质赔偿
repartition n. 划分,分配;(国家等的)瓜分;重新分配
repass v. 重新通过(法案等);再经过;折回
repatriate n./v. 被遣返国者/遣送;遣返(回国);调回;调入
repatriation n. 恢复国籍(指恢复失去的国籍);(把外国人)遣送回国,遣返
repatriation of prisoners of war 战俘遣返
repay v. 偿还,付还;补偿;报复
repayment n. 偿还;赔偿;报答;报复;偿付的款项(或物)
repayment guarantee 偿还款项担保,偿还保证金
repayment of debt 清偿债务
repeal n./v. (法律、法令、判决等的)废除,撤销,撤回/撤销,取消,废止[有收回或作废的意思。指一制定法全部或一部被另一制定法废掉。一般来说废除(rescind)是用在废除合同方面,撤销(revoke)是用在撤销契据方面,取消(cancel)是用在把文件某一部分画线注销方面,取代(replace)是用在以甲文件取代乙文件方面]
Repeal Amendment 废止修正案(指美国联邦宪法第二十一修正案。因该修正案废除第十八修正案,故名)
repeal by implication 默示作废,默认作废
repealed ordinance 已废除的条例
repealer n. 1.废止者;撤回者;撤销者 2.(美)废止某一条早期法律的议案
repealing provision 废除旧法的条文
repeat n./v. 重复/重做

repeat appearances 重复出现
repeat litigation 重复诉讼
repeated a. 反复的,再三的,屡次的,重复的
repeated game 重复博弈(指一个单独博弈依次重复多次形成的博弈,它是没有终点的重复博弈,一个具有不确定终点的博弈可以模型化为一个无限重复博弈)
repeated offender 累犯
repeated prisoner's dilemma game 重复囚徒困境博弈
repeater n. 惯犯;常坐牢的人
repent v. 悔悟,懊悔,悔改;后悔
repentance n. 悔改,悔悟;后悔,忏悔
* **Repentance is good, but innocence is better.** 悔罪虽好,无罪更佳;与其悔过,不如无过。
repentance right 收回权(= droit de retractation)
repetition n. 1.重复;重做 2.副本,复制品 3.要求归还不当给付的金钱财物的诉讼
repetitious lawsuits 重复性诉讼
replace v. 撤换;替换,取代
replaceable a. 可归原处的;可替换的;可撤换的
replaceable thing 可替代物
replacement n. 取代,替换,重置
replacement cost 重置成本[从厂房或建筑物角度来讲,则指其再生产成本;购置一项具有相同收益或服务功能的资产的公平市价。指相当于一项拥有的流动资产的替代资产(substitute asset)的成本,这种新的资产具有相同收益,而并非由一个相同产业可替代]
replacement insurance 重置保险
replacer n. 代替者;复原者;代用品
replead v. 重新申诉;进行第二次申诉;进行第二次答辩
repleader n. 第二次申诉(答辩);第二次申诉(答辩)权;法院要求诉讼双方再次申诉令
repledge v. 转质,转押
repledging n. (古代法)(要求把罪犯转交另一法庭管辖的)转押权
replegiare facias 恢复占有的诉讼
replete a. 充实的,充分供应的,饱满的,充满的《laws revised are usually replete with footnotes citing to primary source》(修订法律因有援引原始资源注释而通常很充实)
replevin n. 1.(英)追回原物的诉讼(指要求返还被非法取走的动产及要求赔偿由此造成的损害,是一种古老的诉讼形式) 2.(被扣押等的)财产的发送;要求发还被扣押财产的诉讼;发还被扣押财产的通知书
replevin bond (追回原物之诉中)执行扣押令时所提供的保证金
replevisable a. 可具结取回的;可发还的
replevish n. (古英国法)保释
replevisor n. 要求发还扣押财产诉讼的原告
replevy n./v. (= replevin) /1.以诉讼收回(被押物);凭令状取回(被押物) 2.保释,准许保释
replicatio (大陆法或古老的英国诉讼中)原告对被告抗辩的回复(回答);原告的答辩
replication n. 1.原告的答辩状;原告对被告抗辩的回复 2.复制品;回答,答复
reply n./v. (原告对被告答辩的)回答,(原告对被告抗辩的)答辩;答复;应诉/1.回答,答复 2.(原告对被告)答辩
reply brief 答辩书
repo 1."买回协议"(指交易人同意在规定时间和规定价格买回证券) 2.恢复占有
répondez s'il vous plaît (= please reply) 请答复(用于国际礼仪中宴会请帖,询问能否出席,常简写为 RSVP)
repone v. 代替;恢复;更换
repone in an office 恢复职务
report n./v. 1.报告,汇报,记录;判例汇编 2.告发,揭发,控告 3.写报道;报到/1.报告,汇报,记录;判例汇编 2.告发,揭发,告 3.写报道;报道
report and recommendations 报告和建议(指由指派而未经当事人同意而听审的治安法官向地区法官提出的一系列有关事实认定的建议和案件处理意见)
report form balance sheet 报告式资产负债表
report form profit and loss statement 报

告式损益表
report of parties' planning meeting 当事人计划会议报告(指美国民事案件审理前的程序)
report on sentences 判刑报告
report on the closed accounts 决算报告书
report out (立法机关的专门委员会)将法案提交大会并附审查报告
report stage (英)议会在议案三读前对议案的讨论与处理阶段
report to the court 请求法院裁(决)定
reported cases 1.被告发的案件(指刑事上的报警案件)2.收入判例汇编的案件
reported decision 判例,汇编过的判决
reporter n. 法院判决记录发布人;整理和编辑法庭各个判案记录人;法院判决汇编;新闻记者,作者,编者,调查人员;判例汇编;法律专题活页汇编
(the) reporter's privilege 记者的特权,记者拒证权(指美国记者在司法活动中,有一项法律权利,即拒绝作证提供消息来源的权利)
reporter's seat (法庭)新闻记者席
reporting contract 申报式保险合同(契约)
reporting judge 记录法官
reporting obligations 报告义务
reporting pay 付与报到上班而无工作可做的人的报酬
reporting properties by public office personnel 公职人员财产申报
reporting rate 告发率
reports n. (美)法庭判决意见汇编卷本,判决(例)汇编;行政判决意见汇编卷本
reports of case-law 判例法汇编
reports of judgments 判例汇编
reporting of opinions 判决意见的报道,判决意见的汇编[美国的司法判决早先极少被系统出版,伊夫雷姆·柯比(Ephraim Kirby)出版了第一卷州判例汇编。不久后,亚历山大·达拉斯(Alexander Dallas)出版了宾夕法尼亚最高法院的判例汇编。1970年该判例汇编第一卷名为《达拉斯 I 》,是美国判例汇编(United States Reports)系列的第1卷。而达拉斯则继续出版了宾夕法尼亚的判例其他系列。以与第一卷相同的标准开始了标有美国联邦最高法院的《达拉斯 II 》的出版工作。到1874年,他的继任者威廉·克兰奇(William Cranch)、亨利·惠顿(Henry Wheaton)、本杰明·霍华德(Benjamin Howard)、杰里迈亚·布莱克(Jeremiah Black)、理查德·彼得斯(Richard Peters)、约翰·华莱士(John Wallace)同样具名地编辑了联邦最高法院判例汇编。1816年,国会正式创造判例汇编机构。次年为此职位建立1000美元的年金。1817年2月,首席大法官约翰·马歇尔提出所有联邦最高法院大法官都认为准确、迅速地对判例进行汇编"对于在美国所有法院中判决的正确性与统一性是必要的"。继亨利·惠顿之后,从1816年到1827年汇编人首次开始注释联邦最高法院判决,其出版亦很及时。当彼得斯出版了更为便宜的判例汇编而削弱惠顿的出版市场时,惠顿便控告他的继任者理查德·彼得斯侵犯了他的权利。1834年法院在Weaton v. Peters一案中判决认为判例汇编不享有权。这样,就允许联邦最高法院的判例汇编存在着相互竞争的版本。1874年司法拨款25000美元用于官方的判例汇编,开始了91卷不再注明汇编人姓名的《美国判例汇编》工作。到1921年政府才授权私人出版者出版判例汇编。1883年,西方出版公司开始了《美国联邦最高法院判例汇编》系列的出版工作。它收录了始于1882年度10月所判决的案件。它所出版的判例汇编一直持续到今天。律师联合出版公司于1901年开始《美国联邦最高法院判例汇编》律师版(Lawyers' Edition)的编辑工作。第一系列100卷本,包括从联邦最高法院第一次开庭期至1955年10月的判决。第二系列开始于1955年10月,此项工作仍在继续。国家事务委员会1931年起已经出版了《美国法律周刊》(United States Law Week),每期刊载联邦最高法院的大部分近期判决全文。同样,联邦最高法院的判决也出现在West Law和Lexis等在线网络服务上。1991年10月,判决的电子版开始出现在联邦最高法院的网络站上(http://www.supremecourtus.

gov)]

Reports of the U. S. Supreme Court 美国最高法院判例汇编[美国最高法院判例汇编始于1790年的亚历山大·J.达拉斯的判例汇编(1790—1800),经过克兰奇(1801—1805)、惠顿(1816—1827)、彼德(1828—1842)、霍华德(1843—1860)布莱克(1861—1862)以及最后的华莱士(1863—1874)等人的冠以姓名的判例汇编,共90卷本,在此(1874年)以后,判例援引一般只按《美国判例汇编》(U. S. Reports)的卷号]

repository n. 1.贮藏所,仓库,贮物容器(箱,柜等)⟨this book is a repository of useful information⟩(这本书内有许多有用的知识),⟨he is a repository of curious information.⟩(他知道许多稀奇古怪的事情) 2.博物馆,陈列室;店铺 3.资源丰富地区 4.墓地 5.亲信,知己

repossess v. 重新占有;重新获得;使重新占有;收回

repossessed goods 收回货物

repossession n. 重新占有,收回;恢复占有

reprehensible a. 应受严责的,应受谴责的;应受申斥的

represent v. 表示,象征;代表,描述,陈述(事实),主张,声称;充任(他人律师)

representamen (要素的)符形[指符号的三个要素构成的一个要素,另两个为object referent"要素的对象"和interpretant"要素的符释"。这是美国著名实用主义哲学家皮尔士(1839—1914)最早系统阐释符号现象的基础思维。与索绪尔的"能指""所指"等均有心理效应和符号的适当效果]

representation n. 1.陈述,事实上的陈述[指以语言或行为所表达的事实陈述,以便他人与之订立合同或实施其他行为。将这种意向,即包括精神状态(state of mind)的事实传给对方⟨the buyer relied on the seller's representation that the roof did not leak⟩(购买者依赖销售者的不使房顶渗漏,意无懈击或十分真实的陈述)。见 misrepresentation];担保的陈述[在美国法的合同中,陈述与担保(representation and warranty)是不可缺少的内容,合同方就事实部分作出陈述与担保,担保陈述内容的真实性。这里的担保实际是一种承诺,如果陈述的内容与事实不符,承诺方将赔偿损失。在普通法上,如果某项陈述并未在事后订入合同,则陈述不实(有欺诈等情况除外),不产生实质性法律后果;但如果该陈述被订入合同并成为合同的条件(condition),则受损一方可撤销合同,如果陈述只构成附属性允诺(即合同的warranty),则当事方可据此提出损害赔偿之诉,但不能撤销合同。如果一项陈述与实际情况略有差别,则根据买主自慎原则(caveat emptor,亦货物出门概不退货,买主小心),买受人不能据此而请求撤销合同或提出损害赔偿之诉] 2.替代行为,替代陈述[指替代行为或替代陈述要求替代他人诉讼,特别是通过律师来替代客户提起诉讼⟨Clarence Darrow's representation of John Scopes⟩(克拉伦斯·达罗为约翰·斯科普斯作为代理人替代诉讼)] 3.诉讼中的密切利益组合[指诉讼当事人与另一在诉讼中正要出庭的人具有密切利益组合的事实⟨the named plaintiff provided adequate representation for the absent class members⟩(被指定的原告为了缺席的集体成员的利益以诉讼中的密切利益组合为先决条件)] 4.推定的继承权[指由继承人对其先辈具有的继承权⟨each child takes a share by representation⟩(每个孩子根据推定继承权均取得应继承的一份遗嘱)。见 **per stirpes**] 5.(国际法)外交声明[指友好的但又是坚定的对一项误解(perceived wrong)的声明。这是一个国家对另一国家不满(complaint)的最温和的形式]

representation of interests 利益代表制
representation of parties in court 诉讼代理
representation of reality 真实描述的代表
representation of the people 人民代表制
Representation of the People Act (1918) (英)1918年《民选代表制度法例》
representational a. 代表性的
representative n./a. 代表;(代位)继承人;诉讼代理人;(大写)(美)众议院议员;立法机构成员/1.表现的,表示的 2.代表的;

代理的;代议制的;代表性的;典型的
representative abroad 驻国外代表
representative action 代表人诉讼,代理诉讼;代表诉讼
representative assemblies 代表大会;议会
representative body(或 **organ**) 代表机关;代理机构;代议制机构
representative(s) by special invitation 特邀代表
representative capacity 代理人资格;代表资格
representative democracy 间接民主政治;代议民主政治;代议民主制
representative democracy system 代议制民主制;间接民主制
representative deputy ministers 代副部长
representative cost plus profit method 代表性成本加利润法(指非损害价格根据国内产品的具有代表性的每单位生产成本、利润所构成的价格计算。这种方法适用于倾销产品之影响,国内同类产品的价格降低了,或本应提高而未提高。由于此种方法存在滥用之可能性,故应对决定国内同类产品的代表性利润、生产成本的方法进行严格规制)
representative government 代议政府
representative heir 代位继承人
representative(或 **key**) **industries** (= window industries) "窗口行业"
representative institution 代议制机构
representative legislature 代议制立法机关
representative of the people 人民代表
representative office 代表处
representative organ of the people (中)人民代表机关
representative parties 当事人代表
representative peers (英)贵族代表
representative suit 见 derivative suit
representative system 代议制
representative theory 代表说[法国人简称代表式的委托说,此学说发源于16世纪中叶的英国,以杨(Sir Yonge)、布莱克斯通(Sir W. Blankstone)、柏克(Edmund Burke)为代表;此学说由19世纪英国代议制理论家 J. S. 密尔确立。见 delegated

theory]
representee n. 陈述的相对人
representor n. 表意人
repress v. 镇压;压服;阻止;抑制,约束(行为)
repressive government 专制政府,极权政府
repressive measures 镇压措施,镇压手段
reprieval n. 缓刑
reprieve n./v. 暂缓,暂止;缓刑/缓刑,暂缓行刑(指中止执行刑事判决的刑罚。见 reprieval)
reprimand n. 惩戒;申斥;谴责(指伊斯兰刑法中的一种惩罚)
reprisal n. 1.复仇,报复(被侵害的国家对侵害国家的报复);(除战争外所施行的)报复性暴力行为 2.(复)赔偿;报复行为
reprise n. 1.(英)(复)(从地产中支付的)年金;租金 2.(古语)夺回;赔偿
repristinate v. 使恢复原状
reprobate n./v. 恶棍;堕落者;放荡者/1.谴责,斥责,指责 2.拒绝;摈弃
reprobation n. 谴责,指责;拒绝;摈弃
reproduction n. 再生产;复制
reputation capital theory 声誉资本理论
Reproductive Health Service (美)生殖健康服务部
reproductive investment 再生产投资
reproductive materials 生殖性细胞
reproductive technology 再生殖技术学
reproof (=reproval) n. 谴责,申斥,责备
reprove v. 责骂;谴责;指责,非难
republic n. 共和国;共和政体;(其成员享有平等权利的)社团;(职业)界
republican a./n. 共和国的;共和政体的;共和政体论(者)的,共和主义者的;(大写)(美国的)共和党的/拥护共和政体者,共和主义者;(大写)(美国的)共和党员;拥护共和党的人
Republican National Convention (美)共和党人全国大会
republican form 共和政体
republican form of the state 共和政体的形式
Republican Party (美)共和党
republicanism n. 1.共和政体;共和国政

府;共和主义;共和论 2.(大写)(美)共和党纲领;共和党;共和党人(总称)
republication n. 1.恢复撤销遗嘱;重新执行已撤销的遗嘱 2.再版;重新公布;再版本
republish v. 1.再版;再印刷;再发行;重新发表(公布);再颁布(法令等)2.重(恢复)订立遗嘱
repudiate v. 1.与(妻)离婚;遗弃(妻子);抛弃(孩子);断绝(与某人的)关系 2.拒绝接受;否认……权威(或效力);否定 3.撤销(合同,协议等)
repudiation n. (16 世纪)1.(宗教法)拒绝接受圣俸 2.拒绝履行合同[指立约方的语言或行为表明在未来不履行合同的意图;预示违约(threatened breach of contrast)的风险。见 rejection 1、2;rescission;revocation 1]3.遗弃(订婚女子或妻子)
repudiation of estate 放弃遗产;放弃财产
repudiator n. 1.休妻者;离婚者 2.拒付(债务)者;拒绝承担(义务等)者 3.赖债者,国债废弃者
repudium (罗马法)取消婚约[指男方或女方废弃婚约。在奥古斯都时期之后,则必须有一封解除婚约函给对方(男方或女方)以终止婚姻。见 *divortium*]
repugnance (=repugnancy) n. 1.不一致,矛盾;不一致之处,矛盾之处(指同一法律文书中条款之间的相互矛盾和不一致或事实陈述中的矛盾和不一致) 2.嫌恶,厌弃;深恶痛绝
repugnance of statement 说法不一致
repugnant a. 1.不一致的;不相当的;矛盾的 2.令人反感的;敌对的;相斥的
repurchasable (或 **repurchase**) **agreements** 回购协议
repurchase n. 再购买,再买;购回
repurchase agreement 回收(货物)契约,购回契约;买回协议(见 *repo*)
reputable a. 声誉好的,可尊敬的
reputable citizen 好公民,有声誉的公民
reputation n. 名声;名誉;(英)公认证据(指英国证据法准许的在涉及公共利害的案件中采用旧文件或提起诉讼时已死人物的陈述作为证据)

reputed a. 1.好名誉的;驰名的;号称的;挂名的 2.一般公认的;一般认为的,公众舆论承认的
reputed father 公众推测的(私生子的)父亲
reputed marriage 公认婚姻[按婚姻应经法定程序,未具备者为非法婚姻,但亦有欠缺一定仪式的或善意的因未明应具备之手续而以正式夫妻相处,为众所周知的婚姻,即所谓公认婚姻,也称为普通法上的婚姻(common law marriage)或事实上婚姻(*de facto* marriage)]
reputed owner 大家可以推测的所有者,人所共知的所有者
reputed ownership 推定的所有权
reputed thief 共知的盗贼,大家可以推测的盗贼(指根据其行为、举止、生活方式、交往人物可以推测为干盗窃这一行的人)
request n./v. 要求,请求;请求书;请求得到的需求/请求得到;要求
request defective (美)申请瑕疵(指向机关提交的申请本身和提交申请方式存在缺陷。如申请书不合要求,申请过于广泛,没交纳申请费)
request for admissions 要求自认(指美国民事诉讼审理前的程序之一,即调查取证的一种方法。依此,一方当事人要求另一方当事人提供就事实的真实性和文件的正确性作出承认或否认),自认要求书,请求承认书
request for permission 请求批准
request for permission to modify a motion 请求允准更改动议[指在议会主席阐述动议之后,该动议的提议人(mover)要求更改他(或她)提的动议。提动议人只能在议会主席阐述动议之前控制动议,在主席阐述之后,该动议属于议会,如未经议会允准,动议人是不能更改动议的。见 friendly amendment]
request for production of documents 要求提出文件(指美国民事诉讼审理前的程序之一,即调查取证的一种方法。按此方法,一方当事人要求另一方当事人提供一定的文件和其他实物,以便检查和复制)
request for proposals 请求建议;为提案而

请求
request for waiver of service of summons 放弃传票送达请求书
request permission to 请求,恳请(允准)
requested in complaint 起诉中的要求
requests for admission(s) 请求承认,要求认可;(美)自白要求
requests for production 请求出示文件;出示证物的请求
requests for production of documents and other things (美)要求提出文书及其他证据
require v. 需要;要求;命令
required course 必修课
required majority 法定多数
required procedure 法定程序
requirement n. 1.需要;要求 2.命令;规定 3.需要的事物;要求的事物;要件
requirement for division 见 restriction 4
requirement for restriction 见 restriction 4
requirement of exchange 交换的要求
requirement of form 形式要件
requirement of formalities (含同等的)形式要件
requirements contract 需要物件合同;按需供货合同(指合同中对供货量并无确切规定,但在合同有效期内买主所需要的只要真实、合理即应供给)
requirements of law 法律的规定,法律的要求
requisite a./n. 需要的,必要的,必不可少的/必需品;要件
requisite document 必备文件
requisites of a crime 犯罪的必要条件,犯罪要件
requisites to constitute a crime 构成犯罪的要件
requisition n./v. 1.需要;征用;请购单;调拨单 2.正式请求,正式申请,书面请求;申请单 3.引渡犯人的要求 4.必备条件/要求;征用
requisition by purchase 征购
requisition for payment 请求付款书
requisition form 请购单
requisition in kind 实物征用

requisition of land 征用土地
requisition order 征用令
requisitions on title 请求消除产权瑕疵
requital n. 1.报答,回报;报复 2.清偿;报答之物(事) 3.报仇,报复,处罚
res 物;事件;财产;标的;有体物;无体物;权利的客体
res accessoria 从物
* *Res accessoria sequitur rem principalem.* The accessory follows the principal. 从物随(从)主物。
res adjudicata 经判决的事件;(最高法院)已作最后判决的案件(见 *res judicata*)
res alienae 属于他人的财产,他主物
res allodialis 自由让与的财产
res anticipitis uses 战时及平时两用的物品
res caduca 转归的财产;无继承人的土地
res capitalis 主物
res certae 特定物
res communes 共用物(共同使用物);共有物(空气,光线等)
res communis 公共财产,公有物
res consumptionis 消费物
res controversa 争议物;争议事项
res corporales 有体物
* *Res denominatur a principaliori parte.* The thing is named from its principal part. 事物是以其主要部分来命名的。
res derelicta 抛弃了的财物
res divisibiles 可分物
* *Res est misera, ubi jus est vagum et incertum.* It is a miserable state of things where the law is vague and uncertain 法律不安定,不确定时,事态就不幸。(法律谚语)
res extra commercium 不可流转物;非交易物
res extra nostrum patrimonium 不可占有物
res facti 事实
res fungibiles 可代替物
res furtivae 赃物,盗窃物
res gestae 1.成就之事,真实事(指案件的确切事实,与传闻的事实相对);有关物 2.犯罪构成要件
res habiles 因时效而取得的物
res immobiles 不动产
res in commercio 可流转物

res in nostro patrimonio 可占有物
res in transitu 运输途中之物
res incertae 不特定物,非特定物
res inconsumtibiles 不可消费物
res incorporales 无体物
res indivisibiles 不可分物
res integra 未决定的要点(指无法律根据亦无先例可援,只有用法理来解决的新事项);完整无瑕的物品
* *Res inter alios acta alteri nocere non debet.* Things done between strangers ought not to injure who are not parties to them. 他人之间的行为不应损害无关的第三者。
res inter alios actas 他人之间的行为;与本案无关的第三者的行为
res inter alios acta 他人之间的行为,与本案无关的第三者的行为[①合同上指普通法原则坚持合同不得不利于与合同无关的第三方;②证据上此原则禁止采纳间接事实(collateral facts)作为证据]
* *Res ipsa loquitur.* The thing speaks for itself. 事情本身说明,事情不言自明。(一般用于因疏忽而引起损害的诉讼中,指事件发生的本身已足以证明疏忽的行为)
res judicata a thing adjdicated (既判案件)1.已由司法判决明确地解决了的争议 2.一事不再理[指一案件经合法司法作出终局判决后,则原当事方不得就同一请求、同一事项、同一诉讼标的或另外一系相同于第一次诉讼的事项再次提起诉讼。三个基本要件是:对于案件的系争点(issue)较早已有判决、依据法律作了终局判决(final judgment on the merits)、涉及相同当事方或涉及与原来当事方相关的共同关系当事方(parties in privity)。参见《第二次判决重述》第 17、24 节(1982 年)。亦称 res adjudicate;claim preclusion;doctrine of res judicata。见 collateral estoppel;double jeopardy]
res judicata effect 既判事项效力,既判效力
* *Res judicata pro veritate accipitur* A matter adjudged is taken for truth 既判事项视为真实,立案即视为事实;A matter adjudged is taken for correct 既判事项视为

正确
res judiciaria 司法行政,司法部门
res litigiosa 争议物,诉讼争议物
res mancipi 要式移转物
res merae facultatis (苏格兰)绝对权利(指不因长期不行使而丧失的权利)
res mobiles 动产
res naturales 自然物
res nec mancipi 非要式移转物(略式移转物)
res non fungibiles 不可代替物
res nova 新事;新案;待决的问题;未决定的事
res nullius 无主物,无主财产
* *Res nullius naturaliter fit primi occupantis.* A thing which has no owner naturally belongs to the first finder. 无主物归先占者所有。
res patrinonio 可有物
res perit domino 损失归所有人(指损失应由所有人承担)
res principales 主物
res privatae 私有产,个人私有之财产
res publicae 公有物,公共财产
res publici juris 公法物
res quotidianae 日常事务;熟悉问题
* *Res sacra non recipit aestimationem.* A sacred thing does not admit of valuation. 神圣的东西是不承认人们的评价的。
res sic stantibus 保持原状(指签订和约或合同各方同意保持现状作为基础而不作变更)
res singolorum 私有物,个人所有物
* *Res transit cum suo onere.* The thing passes with its burden. 物的负担随物而转移。
res turtivae 被偷窃之物
res universitatis (大陆法)社会所有物;社会、团体共有物
res vindicatio 所有物之返还请求权
resale n. 再卖;转卖;出售旧物
resale price maintenance 维持再销售价格
resale price maintenance contract 维持转售(卖)价格合同
resale prices act 转卖价格法;(大写)(英)《再销售价格法》(1964 年)
resale royalty law 再销售征税法

resale royalty right 追续权,重售版税权(与 *droit de suite* 含义相同)
resale service (国际电信)转台服务
resaonable doubt (18世纪)合理怀疑[指排除人们坚决认为被告人有罪的怀疑,相信被告无罪的真实可能性(real possibility);根据案件审理中提出的证据,虽不足够,但使正常谨慎的人们对被告是否有罪产生合情合理的怀疑。排除合理怀疑(beyond reasonable doubt)是刑事诉讼中陪审团认定刑事被告有罪时适用的标准,参见《示范刑法典》第1.12节(Modle Penal Code §1.12)。只有在控方提出的证据对刑事被告的有罪事实的证明足以达到可排除合理怀疑的程度,陪审团方可裁定被告有罪,但陪审团在适用此标准之初必须首先推定该被告人无罪。亦称 rational doubt。见 burden of persuation; preponderance of the evidence]
resceit of homage (英古)接受效忠宣誓(指承租人对其领主进行效忠宣誓,佃户与领主之间的租赁契约因而得以确认)
rescheduling debt 重定还债期
rescheduling of payment 重定付款期
rescind v. 废除,取消,撤回,撤销;解除;宣告无效(见 repeal)
rescind a judg(e)ment 取消判决
rescind a law 废除法律
rescind an agreement 取消合同
rescind the contract 撤销合同
rescind the unreasonable rules 废除不合理的规定
rescinded action 已撤销的诉讼
rescinding a judg(e)ment 撤销判决
rescinding the contract 解除合同(契约)
rescinding the unreasonable rules 废除不合理的规章
rescissible a. 可废止的;可取消的
rescission n. 1.废除,取消,撤回,撤销 2. 解除;解约
rescission of a contract 合同(契约)的废止
rescission of a permit (或 license) 吊销许可证(或执照)
rescission of contract 终止合同
rescissory a. 撤销的,废除的,解除的

rescissory damages 解除(或撤销)合同的损害赔偿,恢复性损害赔偿[指一种损害赔偿的方式,让受害方恢复到交易前的状态,可采用返还原物方式,如不可能返还原先的财产,则可以等价金额(如股票价值)进行赔偿]
rescous 劫夺犯人;夺回扣押物(见 rescue)
rescript n. 1.(罗马皇帝或教皇的)(解答)敕令,诏书 2.命令,法令,政令;处理案件的法庭命令 3.(法律文件的)副本
rescripta 皇帝解答(敕令);诏书
rescue n./v. 1.救济;援救 2.(对被拘留的人或物的)暴力夺回;(对被围困的)武力解围(见 *rescous*)/1. 援救,营救 2. 暴力夺回(被拘留的人或物);(对被围地)以武力解围 3. (国际法)暴力夺回(敌人的掠夺物)
rescuee n. 被施救者
rescuer n. 1.营救者;援救者 2.劫夺犯人者;非法释放犯人者;非法劫夺扣押物者
rescussor n. 劫夺犯人者(指犯了劫夺犯人的罪行的人)
rescyt 窝藏重罪犯人
resealing n. (英)遗嘱检验的重新论证
research n. 调查,研究;研究工作
research attorney 法官助理(见 briefing attorney ②)
Research Committee on Sociology of Law of the International Sociological Association 国际社会学协会法社会学研究委员会
residential community treatment center 见 halfway house
research grants 研究补助金
research steps 研究步骤,检索步骤
reseize v. 夺回,取出;使恢复;使再具有
reseizure n. 再捕获;再占有;夺回,复位
resell n. 再卖;转卖(商品)
reselling goods at cut prices 削价(廉价地)转售货物
resent v./n. 对……有怨恨,对……不满/怨恨,不满
resent sb.'s action 对……人行为不满
reservation n. 1.(让与或租赁财产时的)权益保留;(高级圣职人员)敕罪权保留

2.(美)居留地;专用地;保留地;禁猎地
3.保留;预订 4.限制条件;保留条款
reservation clause (国际私法)保留条款
reservation of intention 真意保留(指做意思表示的人故意隐匿其心中的真实意志,而做与其真实意思不相符合的表示,亦称心里保留,或称单独的虚伪表示)
reservation of power 权力保留
reservation of power to amend and repeal 修改和废止权力保留
reservation of public order 公共秩序保留(见 public policy exception)
reservation of right 权利保留
reservation value 保留价值
reserve n./v. 1.储备(物),保存(物)2.(复)后备军,预备役 3.保留;专用地 4.未透露的消息;秘密 5.储备金;公积金;保留;限度/1.储备,保存 2.推迟,延迟 3.保留,留给
reserve a decision (法官)推迟判决
reserve account 见 impound account
reserve bank 储(准)备银行
reserve capital 储备资本
reserve currency 储备货币
reserve for accidents 意外损伤储备金
reserve for bond redemption 偿债储备
reserve for taxes 纳税储备
reserve fund 储备基金,准备金
reserve price 内定最低价;最低拍卖价格
reserve the user of 保留受益权,保留使用权
reserved a. 用作储备的;保留的;预定的
reserved clause 保留条款
reserved estate 保留财产;保留的遗产
reserved fund 公积金
reserved heir 享有特留份的继承人
reserved judgement 有保留的判决
reserved point 保留要点
reserved portion(s) 应得分
reserved powers (= residuary power)(美)(非宪法赋予的,但为国家或人民)保留的权力
reserved rights 保留权利理论(指政府的征收权存在的两种理论)
reserving points of law 保留法律要点(指过去普通法上一种常见做法)
reserving state 保留国(指对条约提出保留条款的国家)
reset n./v. (苏格兰)接受(赃物)/(苏格兰)接受(赃物);窝藏(赃物)
resettlement n. 重新定居;重予安置
resgestae 成就;一切有关情况;附随状况
reship v. (将货物)改装其他船只
reshuffle n. 撤换(官员等);改组
(a) **reshuffle of cabinet** 内阁的改组
resiance 居住,逗留
reside v. 居住
residence n. 1.住宅,居所(一般指一个人继续居住下去的地方)2.居住;居留;居住期间,居留期
residence abroad 居住海外
residence certificate 居留证件
residence of obligee 债权人所在地
residence permit 居住证;居留证
residency n. 1.住处 2.(驻扎在保护国的)管辖区
resident n./a. 居民,居住者;驻外(国的低于大使级的)政治代表/居住的,居留的,常驻的;定居的
resident aliens 外籍居民,外侨
resident certificate 居民证
resident commissionor (美)(派驻众议院的)属地代表(可发言但无投票权);驻节专员
resident country 驻在国
resident magistrate (爱尔兰)受薪治安官(常缩写为 R. M.)
resident minister 驻外公使,常驻公使
resident office 常驻办事机构
resident population 常住人口
resident representative (office) 常驻代表(机构)
resident representative office registration certificate 常驻代表机构登记证
resident requirements 居住要件
residenter n. 居民
residential a. 有关居住的;房产的;居所的;适于居住的
residential lease 住宅租赁
residential mortgage 住宅抵押债款
residential occupier 房产占有人;居住者
residential parent (美)提供居住的父母

［指他们对孩子具有最先提供居住责任,但他们并非双重提供居住的父母(dual residential parent)。见 residential responsibility; dual-residential parent］
residential quarters 居民区
residential qualification 居留资格,居住资格
residential responsibility 整夜守护孩子的责任［见 custody; dual-residential parent; residential parent. (primary residential responsibility predominant overright responsibility for a child)］
residents' committee (中)居民委员会
resider n. 见 resident
residual n./a. 1.剩余物,残留物 2.重演版权费(电视、广告等,每次重演给作者或演员的报酬)/剩余的,残留的
residual assets 剩余资产
residual clause of territorial competence 地域管辖剩余权限条款
residual income recipients 剩余收入接受人
residual inheritance claim (国家的)剩余遗产的继承权
residual jurisdiction 剩余管辖权
residual legislative function 剩余的立法职能
residual legislative powers 剩余立法权
residual property 剩余财产,余产
residual right 剩余权利
residual rights doctrine 剩余权原理(指美国随着劳资集体协商政策及工会力量的增强,雇主对工会的要求加以善意回应并让步。因而丧失部分原来资方所固有的权利。资方所剩的权利即所谓的剩余权利)
residual sovereignty 剩余主权
residuary a. 1.剩余的,残留的 2.接受剩余财产的,剩余财产的
residuary account 剩余财产账,余产账目
residuary bequest 剩余动产的遗赠,余产遗赠
residuary clause (遗嘱和遗产)剩余财产处理条款(指遗嘱中的一项条款,按该条款所满足的所有其他赠与之后的剩余财产的分配处理)
residuary competence 剩余权限

residuary devisee (legatee) 剩余遗产承受人,余产承受人(遗嘱中指明在不动产的特别遗赠分完之后,可以领得剩余的不动产的人)
residuary power of the *parens patriae to do justice* 国家作为监护人拥有实施正义的剩余权力
residue claimant 最后索取人(指股东表决权应当配置给公司剩余财产的最后索取人)
residuary estate 剩余遗产(指扣除债务、赠与、遗赠之外的财产)
residuary legacy 剩余财产的遗赠
residuary legatee (= residuary devisee residue) 残余,剩余;残留物;(偿债;纳税;遗赠等后的)剩余财产;遗产剩余(指除还清欠债和特别遗赠之外剩余的动产);剩余动产受遗赠人
residue of property 剩余财产
residuum 剩余;剩余;剩余财产
resign v. 1.放弃,辞去;把……交托给 2.辞职;屈从(于);听任(于)3.再誊;再签字
resignation n. 放弃,辞职,辞职书;辞呈
resignation from office 辞职
resignation of the government 政府辞呈
resignation on bloc 全体辞职
resigned partner 退伙人
resipiscence n. 悔改,认错;悔过自新
resist v. 抵抗,抗拒,反抗,对抗
resist a temptation 抗拒诱惑
resist arrest 拒捕
resist the authority of the court 抗拒司法当局
resist the evidence 不接受证据,拒绝接受证据
resistance n. 抵抗;反抗;抵制;反对;(大写)(被占领国家的)地下反抗组织
resistance movement (反侵略的)抵抗运动
resistance to search 抗拒搜查
resisting n. 抗拒
resisting arrest 拒绝逮捕(指抑制或反对警官正在执行逮捕任务的罪行,亦可称为 resisting lawful arrest)
resisting lawful arrest 拒绝合法逮捕［指反抗警官执行合法逮捕任务,多数管辖已

接受现代刑法典(Model Penal)的观点,在被拘捕人知道警官在执行拘捕任务时,禁止使用暴力抑制一种合法的拘捕,但有些管辖允许被拘捕人使用非致命性暴力(nondeadly force)阻止逮捕,参见《现代刑法典》第3节]

resmancipi 要式物,要式移转物(罗马法上指非经要式买卖不得转让的物,如土地、房屋、奴隶、牲畜等)

resolution n. (17世纪)(议会法)1.决议[指正式表示一个主要动议、一个意愿或者是审议会(delibrative assembly)的一个法案(action),决议是一个非常正式的主要动议,通常包括序言和一个或一个以上解决问题的条款(resolving clause)];决定,法院之判决,裁决;议案 2.正式或合法作为(指由公司董事会或其他部门授予一项特别法令、一笔交易或一项任命) 3.文件,文书,公文(指含有陈述、表达、或授权的文件) 4.法院正式的判决或裁决 5.(民法)(合同的废除)决定

Resolution Concerning Conflict of Laws in the Law of the Air 《关于航空法中法律冲突的决议》(国际法学会于1963年在布鲁塞尔年会上通过)

resolve v. (14世纪) 1.解决(指认定一项可接受的或满意地处理一个问题或难题的方式)〈they resolved their conflicting claims〉(他解决了他们的矛盾权利主张) 2.分解;解析(指通过智力分析使其服从一些原理或关系)〈he resolved the geometry problem〉(他分解了几何难题) 3.使明白,使了解清楚(指使易于了解,明白,以:"0"的困惑方式表明)〈the hieroglyphics were finally resolved by a clever puzzle expert〉(这个难解的符号终于被聪明者解谜/这个难解的符号终于被专家弄明白了) 4.决心,决意(指明确决定做或不做什么事情)〈he resolved never marry again〉(他决意永不再结婚) 5.做出正式决议,如通过举手表决、投票表决〈the board members resolved to accept their colleague's resignation〉(委员会成员作出正式决定接受同事的辞呈) 6.决意、决定、坚决目的(指在目的上使更为坚定以便判决或决定)〈the defeat re-solved him to try even harder〉(胜诉更坚决地使失败者尝试更为艰难的处境) 7.归结为,归结为改(resolve into)[指组织形式上的变更,特别在审议会(delibrative assembly)可能以另一种程序(灵活之会议)去代替一种程序方式.〈the standing committee resolved itself into a style committee of the wholes〉(常务委员会决定改组其本身的整体委员会模式)] 8.解析,分解[指分解一个事物的构成部分,细分后进行分析〈the DNA sample were obtained and then resolved DNA〉(样本已经获取,接着就是进行分析了)] 9.(大陆法)成为无效,权利失效〈the gift resolved by ademption〉(此赠与已被撤销遗赠而失效) 10.(古代)咨询、请教〈she resolved with her lawyer about the problem〉(有关这个问题,她请教了她的律师)

respective obligations were legally implied 彼此负有法律上所暗示之义务

Resolution Concerning the Legal Regime of Outer Space 《关于外层空间的法律制度的决议》(国际法学会1963在布鲁塞尔年会上通过)

resolution expressing lack of confidence in the government 对政府不信任的决议案

resolution of doubt 疑团的消除;消除怀疑

resolution of majority 多数决议案

resolution passed 已通过的决议案

Resolution Trust Corporation (美)清算信托公司

resolutioner n. 附议人;支持决议案的人(亦做 resolutionist)

resolutions committee 决议案草拟委员会

resolutive a. 解除的

resolutive clause 解除条款

resolutive condition 解除条件

∗ ***Resoluto jure concedentis resolvitur jus concessum.*** The right of the grantor being extinguished, the right granted is extinguished. 授权者自身的权利被取消时,其所授予的权利也就被取消。

resolvability n. 可表决性,可议决性,可决定;可改变

resolvable a. 可表决的,可议决的,可决定

的;可改变的
resolve n./v. 决心;决定;决意;坚决,刚毅/ 1.解决,解答;消除 2.决心;决定;决议
resolve into 改组
resort n./v. 1.凭借的方法,手段 2.常去的地方,聚集地/求助,凭借;诉诸;采取(某种手段等)
resort of thieves 贼窝
resort to 诉诸,借助
resort to force 诉诸武力
resort to proceedings 向法庭起诉,诉诸法律
resort to sophistry 狡辩
resort to war 诉诸战争
resource n. 办法,对策;智谋,机智;(复)资源,物力,财力;资金
Resource Conservation and Recovery Act (美)《资源保护与再生产法》,或译为《资源养护与权利恢复法》
resource gap 资金差额
resource(s) preservation 资源复原;资源保育(指对稀有的动植物和濒临灭绝的动植物种的保护、保存与合理地经济利用,以保护环境,形成"多种利用机制")
resource(s) restoration 资源增长
resource units 资源单位
resourceful a. 足智多谋的,机智的,智慧的
resources survey 资源勘察
respect n./v. 尊重;考虑;重视;关心;遵守;方面/尊重;考虑;重视,关心;遵守
respect for treaties 遵守条约
respect the law 尊重法律
respite n./v. 1.暂缓,延期;中止 2.(死刑等的)缓期执行/(死刑等)暂缓执行;延缓(处分等)
respite of appeal 中止上诉
respite of sentence 缓刑
respond v. 回答;答复;承担责任;反应
respond in damages 承担赔偿费用;对损失负责
respond the judg(e)ment 履行判决
respond to action 应诉
respondeat ouster 准再答辩(指从前法官准犯人或被告再行答辩,然后判决)
respondeat superior 1.准委托人答辩(指由于雇佣关系,雇主应对雇员服务时所犯错

误行为负责。因此对雇员的诉讼,雇主有答辩的必要,此时雇主以委托人身份出现,亦称 master-servant rule) 2.长官负责制(指长官应对下属职务范围之内的行为负责)3.优势责任(指英美国家使用的概念,包括被强加的过失责任,其意义都是一样的。即行为人不是就自己的侵权行为引起的损害对他人承担的个人责任,而是就第三人实施的侵权行为对他人承担的侵权责任)
respondent n. 1.回答者,响应者;(学位论文的)答辩人 2.答辩人(指对请求书、传票、上诉书,应作出答复的人);被告(尤指上诉及离婚案件的被告)
respondentia n. 冒险借款;货船抵押贷款
respondentia bond 货船抵押债券
respondere 答复,回答(指古罗马法学家对法律问题之答复,当时法学家职责有四:答复、编撰、办案和著述)
responsa prudentium 法学家之解答(在罗马法中,十二铜表法后之惯用语,指法学家之意见与判断形成民法的一部分)
responding party 应答当事人
response n. 回复,回答;反应,反响
response costs 答辩成本
responsibility n. 责任;责任感;负担;职责;任务;能力;可靠性
responsibility contracts (中)责任承包(合同)
responsibility for a crime 犯罪责任
responsibility of infants for crime 未成年人的刑事责任
responsibility of insane person for crime 精神病患者的刑事责任
responsibility system 责任制
responsibility without of fault 无过失责任
responsible a. 应负责任的;有责任的;能履行责任的;可靠的
responsible *accessoire* 附属的责任,次要的责任承担者
responsible cause 责任原因
responsible cabinet 责任内阁
responsible government 责任政府;责任政府制
responsible only to law 只服从法律,只向

法律负责
responsible organ 主管机构;主管机关
responsible person 负责人
responsible political minister 负责政务之大臣,政务部长
responsible protectorate 责任制保护国(地)
responsible stakeholder 负责任的利害关系人(原意为赌局里代管赌金的人,在管理学上成了关照面较广的"利害关系人",在政治上可解释为负责任处理"国际事务大局"的利害关系人)
responsabilité accessoire 附属的责任,次要的责任
responsabilité directe 直接责任
responsabilité du fait d' autrui 因他人的行为承担的侵权责任(指行为人应当就其控制的第三人实施的侵权行为对受害人承担侵权责任)
responsabilité indirecte 间接责任(指行为人就别人实施的侵权行为对受害人承担的侵权责任。见 *respondeat superior*)
responsive a. 回答的;答应的;敏感的
responsive brief 应答理由书;应答判词摘要;应答词书
responsive investigations 回应型侦查
responsive pleading 答辩书(指直接回答由另方辩护书提出的一些要点的法庭文件);(美)应答答辩(指对对方当事人的前次答辩的回应)
responsiveness n. 响应能力
rest n./v. 1.休息;安静;停止;住宿处;休息处 2.剩余部分;盈余;盘存结算 3.(复)结算期(指账目结算期间,例如半年结算一次等)/1.休息;安心;停止 2.依据;信赖 3.自动停止向法庭提出证据 4.静候处理(英美诉讼中的惯用语,一方当事人提出他的全部证据以后,常说 rest,或 rest my case,意思是静候处理我的案件)
rest day 休息日
rest on 依赖,取决于,建立在
rest on the self-reliance 依靠自力更生
rest the case 1.停止对该案提出证据 2.静候处理此案(件)
rest upon 以……为基础(依据)
rest upon considerations of right and justice 权利和公正为补偿作为基础
restart v. 重新开始
restate v. 重新陈述;再声明;重申
restatement n. 重述;再声明、(对前次的话以新方式)再作重述 [(美)《重述》即《法律重述》(Restatement of the Law),是美国法学会(American Law Institute)一项努力的结果。其目的是将已存的大量判例法进行系统化、条理化、简单化,重新整编、重述。第一次重述(1923—1944)内容包括代理法、州际冲突法、合同法、判决法、财产法、担保法、侵权法等;第二次重述于 1952 年出版,内容包括代理法、合同法、州际冲突法、对外关系法,判决法、土地租佃法、财产法、信托法、侵权法等。1986 年第三次重述,即《美国对外关系法重述》(Foreign Relation Law)。1988 年为新的法律领域重述,亦即出版律师法与不公平竞争法的重述。这些重述使用一种黑体字规则(black-letter rules)的独特版式、官方评述、实例以及判例汇编的注释。虽然《重述》在判例和评述中经常被援引,但除非它们已被相应管辖区的最高法院适用的法律所采纳,重述的条文在法庭上不具有约束力]
Restatement (second), Foreign Relations Law of the United States 《美国涉外关系法重述》
Restatement in the Courts (美)《法庭重述》(指为法院判例提供注释的丛书,由西方出版公司出版)
restatement of agency 代理的重新陈述
Restatement of Agency 《代理法案重述》[美国法学会(ALI American Law Institute)编纂的。2006 年 4 月公布第三版《代理法案重述》,其中涉及表见代理定义,判断和效果的成文规定就达到 15 条之多,规定十分详尽。表见代理制度适用范围广泛,似乎又脱离了禁止反言原则而自成体系。有学者将表见代理称为一项普通法重要原则,在构成要件上美国法也采用与大陆法系相近的标准,即采用外观(appearance)、合理依赖(justifiable reliance)和可归责性(responsible for the appearance they create)要件。在每项要件背后,均有

许多案例积累已形成了相当成熟的判断规则]
Restatement of (the Law of) Contracts (美)《合同法重述》
Restatement of Law (美)《法律重述》(指由美国法学会著并由西方出版公司出版的系列多卷本丛书,包括10个专题范围:代理权、法律的冲突、契约、对外关系法、审判、财产、偿还、保证、侵权行为、委托。学者、研究人员和司法人员可以从该丛书中得到关于美国法律的一些最重要的评述)
Restaterments of Law 3d. Restitution and Unjust Enrichment (美)《不当得利法重述》(第三版)[指2011年美国法律协会《第三次返还不当得利法重述》。美国、英国和欧洲三四年间先后公布了不当得利示范法。2009年《欧洲私法的原则、定义和示范规则,共同参照框架草案》(Principles, definitions and Model rules of European Private law; Draft Common Frame of Reference);第七编"不当得利" "Book VII Unjust enrichment",简称"欧洲不当得利法草案";2012年牛津大学安德鲁·伯罗斯(Andrew Burrows)教授个人著有《英国不当得利重述》(A Restatement of English law of Unjust Enrichment)。这三部示范法几乎集中了全世界私法学智慧,很大程度代表了不当得利的最高研究水平。见restatement]
Restatement of Torts (美)《侵权法重述》
Restatement Second of Conflicts of Laws 《第二次冲突法重述》
Restatement Second of Judgments 《第二次判决重述》
Restatement standard 重述标准
restater n. 《重述》的作者或判例汇编者
resting time 休息时间
restitute v. 恢复;复原;偿还,归还;赔偿
restitutio in integrum 回复原状;恢复原状
restitutio in integrum 回复原状;恢复原状(罗马法中由罗马执政官根据受害方之申请,按公平原则批准撤销依法有效之合同或交易,或者批准恢复当事人原有之地位或法律关系。另外,也指接受败诉方之申请,将案件恢复原状,以便重审)
restitution n. 1.归还(指将非法取得他人的东西归还所有人。在习惯上常表示将非法占据的房屋、土地归还给所有人)2.恢复原状;追复原物 3.要求恢复原状的诉讼;赔偿
restitution in kind 实物复原
restitution law 归还法(指将非法所得归还给被占有者)
restitution of civil rights 恢复公民权利
restitution of conjugal rights (英)要求恢复夫妇同居权的诉讼;恢复夫妇同居权
restitution of personal freedom 恢复人身自由
restitution of property 财产的归还
restitution order (英)归还(赃物)令
restitution rationale 补偿论
restitutionary relief 恢复原状的救济
restitutionary remedy 恢复原状的补救方法
restoration n. 复原;恢复;返还;复位;复职;复辟
restoration of a marriage 复婚
restoration of civil rights 恢复公民权利
restoration of diplomatic relations 外交关系的恢复
restoration of goods taken in distraint 归还被扣押的货物
restoration to the original state 恢复原状
restoration to the roll 恢复登记
restorative justice 恢复司法,恢复正义,修复正义;修复性司法[指20世纪70年代以来世界范围内的刑事司法的最新发展,是积极性刑事司法的三个支柱之一(另两个主社区警治和社区矫治),这些支柱被认为代表了21世纪的刑事司法的发展方向]
restorative justice program 恢复性司法(指运用恢复性司法过程或目的实现恢复性结果的任何方案)
restore v. 返还,归还,把……交还;(使)恢复;(使)回复;(使)复辟;修复
restore order 恢复秩序
restoring and maintaining environmental quality 恢复和保持环境质量
restrain v. 1.抑制,遏制;制止 2.管束;监禁

（疯人、犯人等）；限制；约束
restrained from anticipation　预支限制的财产（指英国已婚妇女自己执管的，不得处分，也不得预支财产收益的一种财产）
restraining order(s)　（法院的）禁止令；（英）抑制令（指英高等法院对苏格兰银行或其他公共公司发出的禁止买卖抑制令中所指定的股票的命令）；管制命令（指美国在事实婚姻中的同居双方如果发生家庭暴力，受害方可以请求法院制定管制命令，包括占有双方住所的命令）
restraining order on goods　限制处理货物令
restraining power　禁止权
restraining statute　禁止法令
restraint n.　限制，遏制；监禁，羁押；约束力；管束
restraint of alienation of an absolute interest in possession　对绝对占有权益转让的限制
restraint of alienation of lesser interests　对次要权益转让的限制
restraint of labour　劳工管制
restraint of liberty　限制自由
restraint of marriage　限制结婚（指用订立合同或让与财产为手段，以此来限制某人终身不能结婚或和某人结婚无效）
restraint of trade　限制贸易；贸易管制
restraint of trade doctrine　贸易限制原则
restraint on alienation　（财产）让渡限制；转让限制（指对人的财产转让权利的限制）
restraint upon anticipation　预支限制
restraints of princes　出入港禁止（常见于提单、海上保险单及类似契据上的用语）；封港；限制航行
restrict v.　限制，约束
restrict a road　限制（车辆）在公路上的速度
restricted a.　1.受限制的；受约束的 2.仅限于某一团体或人群的 3.（美政府、军队）（最低的）密级［其他为机密（confidential），极机密（secret），绝密（top secret）］
restricted ballot　限制投票
restricted loyalty oaths　受制约的忠实宣誓（或誓言）
restricted message　密电
restricted most favoured nation clause　附条件的最惠国条款
restriction　（15世纪）1.限制或限制条件，资格，合格证明；带有限制性的条件和规则 2.限制条件［指特别是在契据(deed)中着重在财产的使用和享有上。见 restrictive covenants］3.（军法）剥夺道德上或法律上的自由，而不是对人身体上的拘禁或约束、限制［这种强制实施的军事限制或惩罚是作为军事指挥官的非司法惩罚（nonjudicial punishment）或由普通军事法庭进行简易程序的审理（summary）；限制是一种较轻的约束（restrain），因为它允许受约束者可以尽力履行其职责］4.（专利）限制条件［指专利审查员的规定：即专利申请应包含两个或者两个以上可取得专利权的明显的或独立的发明（inventions）；这项要求是要申请人根据原有的或最先的申请通过放弃某些原有的权利要求而继续提出选定的一个发明。申请人可以通过全面研究这一要求，辩证保护权利主张，而放弃任何非选择的发明（nonelected invention）或根据单独的部分申请（separate divisional application）继续提起任一非选择发明。亦称 requirement for restriction；requirement for division；restriction requirement；division。见 objection 2；rejection 4］
restriction of birth　节制生育
restriction of copyright　版权限制（见 limitation of copyright）
restriction of import　输入限制，进口限制
restriction of personal freedom　限制人身自由
restriction of right　权利限制
restrictionism n.　（对贸易、移民等的）限制主义；商业（尤指银行）限制政策
restrictions on marriage　结婚之限制（指亲属间结婚之限制，英美法对亲属之限制亦有限制，男女双方受限制之亲属如下：对男方之限制为 daughter, wife's daughter, son's wife, son's daughter, daughter's daughter, son's son's wife, daughter's son's wife, wife's mother, wife's father's mother, wife's mother's mother, wife's son's daughter, wife's

daughter's daughter, brother's daughter, mother, mother's mother, mother's father's mother, mother's sister, father's sister, father's wife, father's father's wife, and father's mother; 对女方之限制为 son, son's son, daughter's husband, brother, brother's son, sister's son, husband's son, husband's father's father, husband's mother's father, husband's son's son, husband's father, mother's brother, mother's mother's husband, mother's husband, mother's father, father, father's father, father's brother, father's mother's husband, daughter's son, daughter's husband, and daughter's daughter's husband)
restrictive a. 带有限制性的,约束性的
restrictive business clauses 限制商业条款
restrictive business practice 限制性商业措施
restrictive condition 限制条件
restrictive covenants (美)某一地区业主间相约不得随意使用产业的公约(主要用于种族或宗教歧视上);不作为条款;限制性证据(指英国于19世纪出现的一种新的地役权形式,即所谓限制性证据,是根据土地买卖合同而产生的,经登记而对任何取得供役地的人生效,供役地所有人有不违反城乡规划,不实施有损环境行为的不作为义务,地役权人有权请求强制执行)
restrictive endorsement 限制性背书
restrictive immunity 有限制的豁免权
restrictive injunction 禁制令
restrictive interpretation 限制解释;缩小解释
restrictive policy of a discriminatire nature 歧视性的限制政策
restrictive practice 限制性商业惯例
restrictive practices court (英)限制贸易实施法庭(指按1956年限制贸易实施法规定建立的法庭),限制商业惯例法院
restrictive provisions 限制性条款
restrictive regulation 限制性的规章,限制性的规范
restrictive trade practices 限制贸易的实施

Restrictive Trade Practices Act (1968) (英)《限制贸易实施法》(1968年)
restrictive trading agreement 限制贸易协议
restructuring n. 改订;重新组织
restructuring the economy 经济改革
result n./v. 结果,效果;(美)(议院等的)决议;决定/发生,产生(from);结果,终归,导致(in)
result from 由于;由……引起
result in 产生;导致
result in the court's entry of a default judgment 导致法院作出不应诉的判决
result selection 结果选择(美国现代冲突法理论学者卡弗斯的学说)
resultant uncertainty 综合的不定性,作为结果而产生的不定性
resulting of trust 归复信托(指因信托物失去价值而复归财产所有人)
resulting trust 推定信托,自益信托
resume v. 恢复;重новый占用;重新开始
résumé 梗概;摘要;简历
resume the exercise of sovereignty 恢复行使主权
resummon v./n. 再传唤,再传讯;重新召集/(复)再传唤;重新发出的传票
resumption n. 1.复活;恢复;修复 2.重新收回土地 3.重新开始;再继续;再取回;重新占用
resumption of marital relation 恢复夫妻关系,恢复婚姻关系
resumption of nationality 恢复国籍
resumption of one's duties 重新履行职责
resumption of residence 重返原来住地居住
resurrectionary a. 复活的;盗尸的
resurrectionist n. 掘尸的人,盗尸贼;(秘密的)暴露者
resurrectionman n. 盗尸者
retail n./a. 零售/零售的,零售商品的
retail clients 散户
retail dealer 零售商
retail price 零售价格
retail sales tax 零售税(见 sales tax)
retail trade 零售交易,零售买卖
retailer n. 1.零售商 2.(流言等的)传播人
retain v. 1.留存,保留 2.聘雇(律师等) 3.留

住;不忘;记忆
retain a counsel 聘请撰状律师
retained earnings 保留收益
retainer n. 1.保留者;保留职务 2.(律师等的预聘)辩护费;律师聘请费 3.(遗产)保留权(指遗嘱执行人或遗产管理人有权保留死者财产来还清死者债务);保留物 4.聘请状师或(大)律师
retaining fee 预约聘请(律师等的)辩护费
retaining possession 保留的占有权
retaliate v. 1.报复;反击 2.征收报复性关税
retaliation n. 报仇;报复;回敬
retaliation claim 报复性诉讼请求
retaliative a. 报复性的;回报的
retaliatory a. 见 retaliative
retaliatory eviction (美)报复性地逐出租户(指房东因房客未经协议参加房客联合会或类似活动而对房客提出收回房产的诉讼,在某些州是禁止的)
retaliatory tariff 报复性关税
retallia n. (英国古法用语)零售
retard n./v. 阻碍,延缓/使停滞;阻止,妨碍
retardate n. 智力迟钝者
retarded a. 智力迟钝的,身体或(尤指)精神发育迟钝的
retention n. 1.保留,保持 2.扣押,拘留 3.留置;(保险)保有额;自由额 4.记忆;记忆力
retention money 保留款项;扣付金额
retention money bond 扣付金额担保;保留金保证
retention of dower right 寡妇(对亡夫遗产的)保留权
reticent a. 言不尽意的;沉默寡言的;有保留的
retinue n. (总称)(高级官兵的)随员;随从
retire n./v. 1.收回(指将到期股票、汇票、证券等清付收回) 2.退休;退职;退役 3.撤退;辞退/1.隐居,隐退 2.退休;退席 3.收回(票据等);撤销
retire a bill 见票即付;赎票
retire from office 退职
retired a. 退休的,已退休的;隐蔽的
retired judge 退休法官
retired partner 告退股东,退出的合伙人

retired pay 退休金;退役金;退职金
retired persons 退休人员
retired stock 见 treasury stock
retiree n. 退休者;退职者
retirement n. 1.退休金;退股,退隐之所 2.赎回;收回(股票、债券等) 3.退职
retirement allowance 退职补助金;退职补助费
retirement annuity 退休养老金,退休年金享受权(指年金享受权人只有在退休之后才能开始获得年金的支付,如果年金享受权人在退休前即已离世,已批准的数额通常要归还到年金享受者的财库中)
retirement benefit 退休金
retirement from the court (或 bench) 退庭
retirement insurance 退休保险
retirement of a partner 退伙
retirement of jury 撤退陪审团
retirement pay 退休费
retirement pension 退休年金
retires to deliberate 退庭详议,退庭细审
retiring age 退休年龄,退职年龄
retiring benefit 退休福利
retiring pension 退休金,养老金
retorno habendo 返还(扣押财物的)令状(指法院根据要求发还扣押财物之诉,令实施侵权行为人将非法扣押的财物归还给请求人所作出的令状)
retorsion (=retortion) n. 1.返回,折回 2.报复;(国际法)报复行为
retort n. 反击;反驳;回报
retour n. 回报书(指古苏格兰程序法规定要求其他法院向大法官法院提交陪审团调查事件情况的报告书)
retract v. 撤回,收回,取消(声明,诺言,意见等)
retract a confession 翻供
retractation n. 收回;撤销;(约束、意见、陈述等的)取消
retractile a. 取消的,收回的
retraction n. 1.(放弃遗嘱检证的)撤回(指收回拒绝接受做遗嘱执行人的决定) 2.收回,撤销;撤回否认声明;撤回解约声明
retraining program 再培训计划

retrait féodal (英)(城市保有土地的)业主收回
retrait lignager (英)(城市保有土地的)亲属收回
retreat n./v. 撤退,退却;避难所;(酗酒者和疯子的)收容所;退避,逃避/退却,放弃
retreat from a controversy 退出论战
retrial n./v. 复审;再审/再审;复审
retrial on appeal 上诉审
retribution n. 1.惩罚 2.报应;报答;报酬
retribution theory of punishment 报应刑论,绝对理论,正义理论(指一种绝对主义为基础的刑法理论)
retributive punishment 报应性惩罚
retributive theory 惩罚报应论
retributivist a. 惩罚主义的
retributory civil action 惩罚性民事诉讼
retrieval n. 1.收回;恢复;补偿;挽回 2.恢复或挽回的可能性
retrieval system 检索(数据库)系统
retrieve v. 1.重新获得,收回,恢复〈he retrieves his spirits〉(他恢复了精神) 2.挽回,补救;补偿 3.纠正〈retrieve an error〉(纠正一个错误),〈retrieve one's honour〉(挽回某个人的荣誉) 4.追溯,回忆〈beyond/ past retrieval〉(不可挽回、不可恢复) (retrieval n.)
retroact v. 1.追溯既往;有追溯效力 2.反动
retroaction n. 1.追溯效力;追溯既往 2.反作用;反动;反应
retroactive a. 1.追溯的,追溯既往的,有追溯效力的 2.可补发增加工资的
retroactive amnesia 逆行性健忘症
retroactive effect 追溯效力
retroactive inference 追溯的推论,追溯的推断
retroactive law 溯及既往的法律,追溯法
retroactive policy 有追溯效力的保险单
retroactivity n. 溯及既往,追溯效力
retroactivity of payments 补付款项的追领;补发工资
retroactivity of recognition 承认的追溯力
retrocede v. 交还;归还;恢复(领土、司法权等);退回
retrocession n. 交还;归还;收复(领土、司法权等);再保险;转分保
retrocession treaty 转分保合同;再保险合同
retrospect n. 回顾,回想;追溯;追溯力
retrospectant evidence 事后证据
retrospective a. 溯及既往的,有追溯效力的;追溯的
retrospective effect 追溯效力
retrospective index 追溯索引
retrospective law 有追溯效力的法律,追溯法
retrospective legislation 有追溯效力的立法
retrospective research 追溯检索
retry v. 再审;再试;重新审讯,重新审理
return n./v. (向法院)送还(传票等);归还;报答;(复)收入,退货,利润,成果;补偿,红利;(复)报告书;统计表;(选举)结果报告;选出;申报所得/归还;回答,反驳;报告,汇报;宣告,正式宣布;(选区)选举,选出;(令状等)回呈
return a deposit 退押金
return a prisoner guilty 宣告被告有罪
return a verdict of guilt (陪审团)宣告有罪裁决
return and refund 退货及还款
return cargo 回运货物;回程货;回头货
return commission 回佣,回扣(佣金)
return day (或 **date**) 公布选举日;传票送还日;被告呈交抗辩书日(指被告接到要求出庭传票后必须呈交抗辩书的日子)
return of capital 资本收益
return of service (传票)送达回证
return of stolen goods 退赃
return of writs 令状的退还
return offer 回复要约
return performance 补偿(或报酬等)给付
return (of) premium 退回保险费
return promise 回复允诺
return sb. to parliament 选举某人为国会议员
return to power 重新执政
return visit (中)(诉讼法)回访制度
returna brevium (历史上)对于令状(writ)的回复,这是由司法执行官在令状上签署或由其他与令状执行相关官员签署的回执

returnable a. 1.可以退还的;应报告的(指定时间、地点)2.依法必须送还的;依法必须答辩的
returned a. 已回来的,已归还的
returned convict 释放的流刑犯(苦役犯,徒刑犯)
returned guilty 被宣告有罪
returned overseas Chinese (中)归侨
returned unexecuted 送达未完成,返回
returnee n. 1.(流放、服刑等后)释放回来的人 2.从国外回来者;海外服役回来的军人
returning board (美)(某些州里的)选举监察所;选举监察委员
returning note 复照
returning of stolen goods 退赃
returning officer (英)选举监察官员;选举管理官(指负责管理选举事务的官员);选举主任
returns to scale 与生产规模成比例的收益;规模报酬
re-up v. 1.重新入伍〈the soldier re-upped the day after being discharged〉(该士兵在执行任务完成之后这天又重新入伍)2.签署延期合同,特别是一项就业协议〈the star athlete re-upped in a three year deal worth $ 12 million〉(星级运动员已再行服役但在三年期内索高价达1200万美元)
reus 1.(大陆法、宗教法中的)诉讼中的报告;被控犯罪的人 2.诉讼当事人;原告或被告 3.合同(契约)当事人
reus promittendi (罗马法)(订立契约时的)承诺一方当事人,承诺人[指从罗马法要式口头契约(stipulation)中的回答者,亦称为 promissor。见 stipulation 3]
reus stipulandi (罗马法)订立契约时的要约,一方当事人,要约人[指罗马法要式口头契约(stipulation)中的提问人(questioner),亦称 stipulator。见 stipulation 3]
revalorization n. 货币价值的恢复
revaluation n. 重新估(评)价,再估价;币值的重新调整(贬值或升值)
revanche n. 复仇
revanchism n. 复仇主义
reveal v. 揭示,露出,呈现,披露

revel n. 狂欢;纵酒;闹饮
revelation n. 新发现;启示
revendication n. 1.要求收复;正式要求;收复 2.(外交上)收回失地的正式要求;(经要求后)收复失地
revenge n./v. 报仇心,复仇心;报复,报仇/报仇,替……报仇
revenge murder 报复杀人
revenger n. 报仇者,报复者
revengism n. 报复主义
revenue n. 1.(国家的)岁入;税收;收入;收益 2.(复)总收入;收入项 3.税务署(或局)
revenue above reprises 净收入;(从地产收入中)支付租金之外的收入
Revenue Act of 1971 (美)《1971年税收法》,(亦为)《岁入法令》[指美国国会依据联邦宪法第1条第8款授权征收直接税(taxes)、间接税(exercises)而制定之法律]
revenue agent 税务员
revenue and expenditure (国家的)岁入和岁出;收支
revenue bond 收益债券(指政府或公用事业机构授权建设、收购或改善一项公用事业所发行的债券)
revenue charge 营业支出;收益支出
revenue collection agency 税收机构
revenue cutter 缉私船,海关缉私船
revenue from loans 放款收入
revenue from tax 税收
revenue law 税收法,赋税法
revenue officer 税务官员,缉私官员
revenue paper 税单
revenue receipt 税收
revenue side (英)财政岁入诉讼部(指理财法院一个专门审理财政岁入案件的部门)
revenue stamp 印花税票
revenue tariff 财政关税,收入关税
revenuer n. 1.(美)财政部缉私酒的官员;税务官员 2.(海关)缉私船
reversal (15世纪)1.推翻,撤销(指受理上诉法院推翻或撤销下级法院的判决,或宣布其无效)2.(证券)逆行(指证券交易市场或期货市场行情变动方向的术语)

如道琼斯工业平均指数持续由 1100 上升到 1200 之后又跌回至 1100)
reversal of a miscarriage of justice 撤销错案;平反冤狱
reversal of court decision 撤销法庭判决
reversal of decision 撤销裁决,撤销决定
reversal of judgment 撤销判决,废弃判决
reversal of procedure 诉讼程序的撤销
reverse n./v. 1.颠倒,反转 2.不幸,逆运 3.背面,反面;反向/1.逆行,反转,颠倒 2.取消,废弃;翻过来,颠倒过来;否定
reverse a judgment 撤销原判
reverse compensatory adjustment 反向补偿
reverse consensus (知识产权)反向一致原则[指根据"与贸易相关知识产权"(Trips),在争端解决的程序中,不应将争端当事双方的协议呈交世贸组织合议庭(World Trade Organization Panel)来审判裁决。在 Trips 之前,任一当事方可推选 WTO 合议庭的组成或采用其报告(report)而拒绝合意(consensus)。根据 Trips,除非所有当事方均不同意,否则该报告则自动通过]
reverse conviction 取消定罪
reverse discrimination (1964 年)反向歧视原则(指一般通过确定性的行为项目对于少数群体给予优惠待遇,从而使多数群体的成员的利益受到消极影响。见 affirmative action)
reverse doctrine of equivalents (或 **inverse doctrine of equivalents**) 逆均等论
reverse engineering 反向工程(指美国等许多国家把在研究某产品构造后,返回其设计构想的活动视为"合理使用"。在芯片保护法中即是)
reverse/inverse passing off 反向假冒(与 reverse palming off 同。见 reverse/inverse passing off)
reverse the decision of a lower court 否定下级法院的判决
reverse the procedure 取消诉讼事程序
reverse the verdict 翻案;撤销裁决
reverse-confusion doctrine (知识产权)反向混淆原则,反向混合原则[指不正当竞争的规则。如果被告使用的专利名称(ti-tle)与原告所使用的具有混同性的类似,因而这导致公众相信原告的产品与被告的是相同的,或它是出自被告或在某种样式上与被告相关联。根据传统的不正当竞争的假冒伪劣形式,专利名称的相似点(similarity of title)导致公众相信被告的产品相同于原告的产品(work),或者其样式方面来源于原告,但是因混淆而产生的不公平竞争创设了在反向混淆中有关原告的产品的原产地(origin)]
reversed a. 被撤销的,被推翻的
reversed and remanded 撤销原判并发回重审(指上诉审法院撤销初审法院所作的判决,并将此案发回初审法院重审)
reversement (= reversal) n. 撤销原判,变更
reversibility n. 可逆(性);可撤销(性);(命令等)撤销可能
reversible a. (判决等)可撤销的,可废弃的
reversible error (= prejudicial error) 可更改的(裁决)错误(指上诉法院有理由可以推翻原有裁决,改正错误),可撤销判决的错误
reversing n. 撤销判决(指上级法院撤销下级法院的判决)
reversion n. 1.(地产等的)归还,归属;继承权 2.隔代遗传;未来所有权 3.租权恢复
reversion ad dominum 返还所有主(指被盗物或强占物重新回到所有主控制下,此种情况发生使占有状态消除,从而使物品不再构成时效取得的对象)
reversion of copyright 自然返还版权
reversion to justice 恢复正义,恢复公正
reversional a. (=reversionary)
reversionary a. 复归(原主或其继承人)的;应继承的;将可继承的;将来享有(占有)的;隔代遗传的
reversionary interest 期待权,可回复的权利(指不动产或动产的租权回复或残留权的权利);将来应享有的权益
reversionary interest in chattels 动产的期待权
reversionary interest in land 不动产的期待权

reversionary right 归复(原主)权;期待权;应继承权
reversioner n. 将来享有继承权者;具有未来所有权者
revert v./n. 1.恢复原状,回复 2.(财产等的)归还;归属(to);继承/归属;继承;反回者
revertible a. 可恢复原状的;可复归的;可归属的
revest v. 1.使恢复原状(原位);再赋予(某人)所有权(职权等) 2.重新投资
revesting n. 物归原主
review n./v. 1.回顾,检讨;检查,检阅 2.评论;(高等法院等的)复查(案件)/1.复阅,回顾;细察,观察 2.复查(案件),复审 3.评论,批评
review a case 复审案件
review and appraisal 审查和评定
review by the legislature 立法机关的审议
review of constitutionality 合(违)宪审查制度
review of decision 复查判决
review of final decision 终局判决的复审(查),终局裁定的复审
review of legal question 法律争议的复审
review of not final decision 非终审判决的复审(查)
review of taxation 复评讼费(指法院命令法官对不满讼费的人的讼费再行评定)
review of the merits 审查案件的实体方面,查清是非曲直
review on appeal 上诉复审
reviewability n. 可复审性
reviewal n. 再调查;评论;批评;校阅
revisable a. 可修改的;可订正的
revisal n. 修订;修正
revise v. 修订;修正;校订;修改
revised reports 判例汇编修订;(大写)(英)《判例汇编》修订本(指 1785—1865 年英格兰普通法法院和衡平法法院判例汇编的再版本)
revised statute 经修订的成文法
revised text 修订文本
revised version 修订本
revising assessor (英)(每年校勘选区议员选举人名单的)校勘陪审员,校勘律师
revising barrister (英)(每年修订各区议员选举人名册的)校勘律师
revision n. 修订;修正;校订;修改
revision of bylaws 修改章程
revision of judg(e)ment 更改判决
revision of treaties 修改条约
revisionism n. 修正主义
revisionist n. (对法院判决的)修正论者;修正主义者
revisionist views 修正主义观点
reviso in jure 法律审
revitalize v. 使新生,使恢复元气
revival n. 重振,恢复,复苏;回复;复兴;苏醒,复活,再生;(契约的)再生效
revival of barred claim 恢复已失时效的债权
revival of contract 合同(契约)的重新生效
revival of wills 遗嘱的重新生效
revive v. 1.苏醒;复活;复兴 2.使(法律、契约等)再生效;再提出;恢复
revive an old charge 再提起控告
revivor n. 诉讼程序中止后的再恢复;(英)复诉(指要求恢复一方死亡而中断的诉讼)
revocability n. 可撤销性
revocable a. 可撤回的,可废除的,可取消的
revocable adoption 可撤销的收养
revocable letter of credit 可撤销的信用证
revocable transfer 可撤销财产转移
revocable trust 可撤销的信托
revocable trusts to the settlor 对财产授予者的可撤销信托
revocable undertaking 可撤回的义务承担
revocation n. 1.撤回;废除;撤销;失效 2.取消或撤销(要约等)
revocation of a law 废止法律
revocation of a testament 遗嘱的撤销
revocation of a will 废除遗嘱(如一个人另立遗嘱则废除原有遗嘱)
revocation of an offer 要约的撤回
revocation of order 撤销命令
revocation of patent 撤销专利权
revocation of probate 撤销遗嘱检认
revocation of treaty 废除条约

revocation of will 撤销遗嘱
revocatory a. 撤销的,废止的,解除的
revocatory action 合同(契约)解除诉讼
revoke v. 收回,撤回;撤销;废除;废止,取消(法律、允诺等),宣告……无效(见 repeal)
revoke a decision 取消决定
revoke commission 撤销委托
revoke verbal evidence 翻供
revoked licence 已吊销的执照
revoking party 撤销方当事人
revolt n. 谋反,叛变,造反,反抗,背叛
revolter n. 谋反者,叛变者;造反者;背叛者
revolution n. 1.革命;剧烈变革;彻底改变 2.循环,循环一周
revolutionary a. 革命的
revolutionary command council 革命指挥委员会
revolutionary committee (或 council) 革命委员会
revolutionary humanitatianism 革命人道主义
revolutionary military personnel (中)革命军人
revolutionary tribunal 革命裁判庭,革命法庭
revolving charge 周转费用,周转支付(指通常由信用卡或百货公司提供的一种信贷,借此可以分期付款购买,新的购买也可在同一时期内分期支付)
revolving charge account 循环收费账;限额赊销账户;循环赊账户
revolving credit 循环信用;周转信用
revolving funds 周转基金[指其款项用于继续消费,以后又再消费,如小额现款基金(petty-cash fund)]
reward n. 报酬;报答;酬谢;奖金,奖赏;赏金
reward and punishment 奖惩;赏罚
reward payment 奖金
rewards and costs of litigation 诉讼收入和成本
rewrite v. 书面答复;改写
rewriting contract 修改合同

Rex (R.) 国王(指作为刑事案件中进行诉讼的一方当事人)
* Rex datur propter regnum, non regnum propter regnem. A king is given to serve the kingdom, not the kingdom to serve the king. 国王应为王国服务,而非王国为国王服务。
* Rex non potest peccare. The king cannot do wrong. 国王无过错(指英国封建时代的一条法律原则,一直应用到 1947 年的政府诉讼程序法颁布为止)。
rhadamanthine a. 像阴间判官似的;严峻的;公正的
rhadamanthus (=rhadamanthys) n. 严峻的法官,公正的法官,铁面无私的法官
rhetoric n. 修辞学,运用语言技术,辩术
rhetorical question 措辞上的问题
rhetorical reasons 措辞上的原因
Rhodian Law (300-400 B.C.) 古代罗得法,罗得海法(指最早的海事法法典或汇编)或罗地斯法(该法就"船体之航行能力""船舶之运行能力""船舶之载货能力"虽无具体规定,但已有船舶适航能力之担保义务的概念)
Rhodian Sea Law 《罗得海法》(1909)
ribaldry n. 下流;猥亵;猥亵语
Richard Roe (Jane Doe) 被告某乙[诉讼程序中对不知真实姓名的当事人(尤指第二当事人)的称呼。见 John Doe];某甲(指诉讼中或公文和合同中用以代表不知姓名的当事人的用语。见 John Doe)
rid v. 免除;清除;摆脱;去掉
rid oneself of debt 结清债务,清偿债务
ridden a. 折磨的;受虐待的;受支配的
ridden per prejudice 受偏见支配
ride v. 1.骑;乘(车、船、飞机等);控制,驾驭 2.绑架谋杀,诈骗 3.欺压,压制
ride backwards up to Holborn Hill 倒坐马车上霍尔鲍山(英国旧时常在泰伯恩刑场处决犯人,押犯人赴刑场时途中需翻越霍尔鲍山。山路陡峭,罪犯通常背朝马匹,坐或站马拉的囚车上。后随以"倒坐马车上霍尔鲍山"喻指赴刑场或上绞刑架)
ride circuit 在审判区管辖范围内作巡回

审判
ride herd (on) 监督;监视;管教
rider n. 1.骑马者,骑车者,乘车者 2.附加条款;(文件上的)附加补充(或修正),附文,附件;(陪审团对其裁定的)附加意见
rider to a bill 议案上的附加条款(指在立法程序中的新附件且常与该议案无关)
ridicule n. 耻笑,嘲笑,讥笑
riding n. (英)(约克郡的、英国本部及其自治领的)行政区;选区
rien culp 无罪
riens en arriere (或 in arrear) 任何过期未付款不得拖欠
riens per descent 无继承资产
riffraff n. 暴徒,流氓
rifle n./v. 来复枪,步枪/抢劫;搜劫;偷去;掠夺
rifle the tomb 挖墓;挖坟
rig n./v. 1.(英)骗局;欺诈;恶作剧 2.荡妇,娼妓/(用欺骗手段)操纵,控制;匆促凑成
rig an election 控制选举
rig the market 操纵市场
right n./v. 1.公正;正当;正义,公理 2.权利;权;认股权,购买新股特权 3.(复)实况,实情,真相 4.右方,右翼/纠正,补偿;为……申冤;公正对待
right a. 正确的,对的;合法;正义的;正当的;合适的,正常的
right a wrong 矫枉;雪冤
right against double jeopardy 同一罪行不受两次审判的权利
right against self-incrimination 不得自证其罪的权利;(美)拒绝自证其罪行权
right against spouse and children 对配偶和子女的权利
right against the world at large 对世权
right against trespass to the land 禁止侵入土地权
right akin to land 类似土地的权利
right an error 纠正错误
right and duty 权利与义务
right and might 公理和强权
right and remedies 权利和法律救济方法
right and (或 from) wrong test 辨别是非说[指陪审团审判时推定被告在实施犯罪

时心神正常,具有犯罪能力的一种原则。如被告以犯罪时心神丧失为理由作为推卸责任的抗辩,必须提出具体证据。见 M'Naghten Rules]
right at work 工作中的权利
right based theory 权利基础说
right heir 法定继承人[指①将限定继承某项财产的指定继承人与一般法定继承人相区别,这是在土地限定继承权(estate tail)取消之前;②只是在优先继承(preferred heir)及其血系无效的情况下,才具有一般法定继承人(general heir)进行土地限定继承权]
right holder 权利持有人
Right Hono(u)rable (英)对高级官员(或有爵位者)的尊称
right in action 诉讼财产权;可依法赢得但尚未实际占有的动产
right in civil affairs 民事权利
right in court 法庭上的权利(指运用法律为自己辩护的权利)
right in dispute 争执中的权利
right in foreign territory 在外国领土上的权利
right in immovable property 不动产上(设定)的权利
right in land 土地上的权利
right in personam 对人权
right in property 财产权,物权
right in rem 对物权
right inherent in an individual 人固有的权利
right intervention 权利性介入诉讼
(the) right legal order 正当法律秩序(指罗尔斯的观点:国家及其立法应遵循"中立性"原则,应致力于正当法律秩序的构建,而不能偏袒任何一方宗派性的善观念。见 public reason)
right of abandonment 委付权;受领被弃财物权
right of abode 居住权,住所权
right of access 出入权;使用(人、地或物)权
right of action 1.起诉权,诉讼的权利[指向法院提起特定案件(special case)的权

利]2.通过诉讼可得到强制执行的权利;诉讼中的财产(chose in action)(见 cause of action)
right of amendment (法案等)修正权
right of ancient light 采光权,(英)老采光权(按1959年采光权法例,窗户光线不受阻碍经过27年后才有老采光权,开始获得法律保护)
right of appeal 上诉权
right of approach (国际法)靠近权,临检权(检查权)(指战船在公海上靠近另一船只以确定该船舶的国籍)
right of archipelagos seaplanes passage 群岛水域通行权
right of arraignment 提审权
right of arrest 逮捕权
right of assembly 集会权
right of asylum (国家的)庇护权;(个人的)要求避难权
right of attendance 出席权
rights of attribution 见 attribution right
right of audience 发言权,发表意见的权利;出庭申述权
right of author 著作权
right of authorship 著作权(世界各国保护因著作或作品的创作和传播而产生的立法。由于强调的保护重点不同,因而有不同的称谓,英美法系国家强调保护权,故称 copyright,大陆法系国家强调保护它的人身权,故将其称为"著作权"),作品创作人的署名权
right of autonomy (中)(民族自治地方的)自治权利
right of autonomy for enterprises 企业自主权
right of cancellation 注销权,撤销权
right of capture (海上)捕获权
right of choice 选择权
right of citizen 公民权利
right of claim 请求权;求偿权;索赔权
right of collective self-defence 集体正当防卫权,集体自卫权
right of commercial property 商业产权
right of common 共有权,公用权
right of communication to the public 传输权,公开传播之权利,向公众传播的权利[指1996年12月20日为解决国际互联网环境下应用数字技术而产生的保护问题,由 WIPO 主持120多个国家代表参加缔结了《WIPO 版权条约》与《WIPO 表演与唱片条约》。在前一条约中明确发行权为一项独立的权利(第6条),增加了网络时代产生问题的传输权(第8条)、技术保护权(第11条)和权利标示权(第12条)]
right of complaint 控告权
right of compulsory process 强制取证权
right of confrontation 对质权(指英美宪法通常规定刑事被告有与检方证人对质的宪法权利)
right of consortium 配偶的权利
right of contribution 分摊权,分配权(见 contribution 1)
right of creating port and harbo(u)r 开设港口和码头权
right of creditor 债权;债权人的权利
right of curtesy 鳏夫产取得权
right of denunciation 宣告条约无效权
right of detention 拘留权,扣押权
right of diplomatic protection 外交保护权
right of discovery 发现权
right of disposition 处分权利
right of election 选择权;选举权
right of entry 收回租地权;进入租地权(指以和平方式进入土地,来恢复占有的权利)
right of equality 平等权
right of establishment 设立权(指欧共体一项规定,某一成员国的法人或非法人都有权在另一成员国设立工商企业、代理机构或分支机构的权利);创业权
right of existence 生存权
right of exoneration 免除权
right of fishery 捕鱼权
right of habitation 居住权
right of heirs 继承人的权利
right of hereditary lease (英)世袭土地租赁权(亦译做永佃权,此种权利有严格的人身限制,并不得转让)
right of holding and acquiring territory 拥有和取得领土权

right of homestead 宅地权,地基权
right of hot pursuit 紧追权(指警察为追捕重罪犯人有权跨越管辖界线,警察或官员为此可追入他国,=fresh pursuit);当即追回(财物)权;(国际法)紧追权(指一船或船上的人在一国领海内违反该国法律,该国船只有权对该船紧追,直至公海捕获为止)
right of immunity 豁免权
right of independence and self-determination 独立自主权
right of independent trial 独立审判权
right of individual 个人权利
right of individual self-defense 个人自卫的权利
right of industrial property 工业产权
right of initial examination 初审权
right of initiative 创制权
right of inland navigation 内河航行权
right of innocent passage 无害通过权(他国船舶均享有无害通过沿海国领海权利,是国际法的一项习惯规则)
right of integrity (保护)作品的完整性权
right of intercourse inter se (国家间)彼此交往权
right of interpellation 质问权
right of intervention 干预权
right of invention 发明权
right of invention and discovery 发明与发现权
right of judicial review 司法复查(审)权(见 judicial review)
right of jurisdiction 司法管辖权
right of know 知情权
right of labo(u)r 劳动权
right of legation 使节派遣权
right of lien 留置权
right of light 采光权(见 right of ancient light)
right of litigation 诉讼的权利
right of maritime capture (战时)海上捕获权
right of mining 采矿权,开采权
right of monopoly 专有权;专卖权
right of national autonomy 民族自治权

right of national self-determination 民族自决权
right of nationality 国籍权
right of navigation 航行权,航运权
right of obligation 债权
right of option (民法上的)选择权
right of ownership 所有权
right of ownership in a thing 物的所有权
right of ownership in immovables 不动产所有权
right of ownership in movables 动产所有权
right of passage 通行权,通过权
right of passive resistance (国际法上的)消极抵抗权
right of people to self-determination 民族自决权
right of personal freedom (或 liberty)人身自由权
right of personal security 人身安全权
right of personality (=rights to personal existence and freedom) 人格权(亦称著作人身权,指作者对其作品享有一系列权利,包括发表、署名、修改、保护作品完整等权利)
right of petition 请愿权,申诉的权利[指美国联邦宪法第一修正案,保障"向政府申诉以获赔偿"的权利。该权利源于英国宪法。1688年光荣革命之后,议会制定了《1689年民权宣言》(Declaration of Right of 1689),同年即被批准为《权利法案》,力图赋予公民请愿权。即作为一项宪法性权利,公民有机会请求政府纠正冤案或批准一项请求。这也是美国《1776年独立宣言》和《1791年权利法案》的奠基石。其中很自然地包括请愿权。同时美国绝大多数州的宪法也规定有类似的保护条款]
right of pledge 抵押权,质权
right of possession 占有权
right of pre-emption 优先购买权
right of primogeniture 长子继承权
right of priority 优先权
right of privacy 私生活秘密权;私人秘密权,隐私权
right of property 财产权

right of prosecution　检控权,起诉权,公诉权
right of prospect　眺望权
right of prospecting　探矿权,地质勘探权
right of public meeting　公共集会权
right of publication　出版权
right of publicity　形象公开权(准版权的一种。见 merchandising right)
right of pursuit　追捕权
right of recall　罢免权
right of reciprocity　互惠权
right of recourse　追索权,请求返还权,求偿权
right of recovery　追索权,请求归还权
right of redemption　回赎权,买回权,赎回权
right of reduction　回复权(指未成年人在未成年期所行使的法律行为,此后有撤销其原有行为之权)
right of reentry　(美)重占土地的所有权,或终止权(这是转让人的将来权利);重新占有权
right of relief　(苏格兰法)见 equity of subrogation
right of reply　答辩权
right of representation　代理权
right of reprieve　暂缓行刑权
right of repudiation　休妻的权利
right of resale　转卖权
right of rescission　撤销权
right of retainer　(遗嘱执行人或遗产管理人的)财产保留权
right of retention　拘留权,保留权,留置权
right of reverter　土地归复权,土地归属权
right of sanctuary　庇护权,居留权
right of search　见 right of visit and search
right of security　财产担保权(亦称 security on property,也称物保 real security。财产担保或物保则是在特定财产或权利上设定的担保,以补偿债务人履行债务之允诺,并在债务人未履行债务时可以优先于其他债权人实现其债权)
right of seeing the witness face to face　目睹证人的权利(指被告于审判时有在场目睹证人之权利,美国通称"面对面权利")

right of self-defence　自卫权
right of self-help　自助权
right of self-preservation　自保权,自卫权
right of servitude　地役权
right of set-off　抵消权
right of silence　沉默权
right of states　公共权利
right of stopping the goods in transit　运送途中商品的停止发送权
right of subrogation　1.见 subrogation 2.见 equity of subrogation
right of succession　继承权
right of succession by the child *en ventre sa mere*　胎儿继承权
right of succession on intestacy　无遗嘱继承的继承权
right of supervision　监视权;监督权;管理权
right of support　抚养权;赡养权;土地支撑权
right of survivorship　生存者取得权(见 survivorship)
right of taxation　征税权
right of territorial sea　领海权
right of the accused　被告(人)的权利
right of the obligatory claim　债权请求权
right of the real claim　物上请求权
right of things　物权
right of transit　过境权
right of transit passage　过境通过权
right of unborn children　未出生子女的权利
right of use and habitation　使用和居住权
right of user　连续使用权
right of using public property　公共财产使用权
right of using water in the current area　水流地用水权
right of usufruct on the community's goods　村社财物的用益权利
right of veto　否决权
right of vindication　维护(自己财产权的)权利;辩护权
right of visit　见 right of visit and search
right of visit and search　(交战国在公海上对中立国船舶的)搜查权,搜索权,临检

及搜索权
right of visitation （国际法）(对商船的）检查权
right of war 战争权
right of water 土地水利权
right of watercourse 水流权
right of way 通行地役；(道路)通行权；（某些车辆或船只依法的）先行权
right of withdrawal 撤销权
right of withdrawal from a partnership 退伙权利
right of work 工作权
right over another's property 对他人财产的权利
right over body 人身权
right over immovables 不动产权
right over movables 动产权
right over one's own property 对自有财产的权利
right over things 物权
right quality 适当的品质,适当的质量
right reason 正当理由
right related to work 工作有关的权利
right relating to civil law 民事权利
right system 权利体系
right to a fair trial （当事人依法获取的）公正审判的权利（指排除制度适用可能构成了对公民宪法性权利侵犯,当事人因此可以提起宪法诉讼）
right to a living wage 享有取得维持最低生活的工资权利
right to a pension 领取养老金权
right to abstention from injury 免受伤害的权利
right to abuse 滥用权利
right to access to work 获得工作机会的权利
right to acquire and alienate property 受让及让与财产的权利
right to address questions 质询权,质问权
right to alienate 转让权
right to an impartial tribunal 受公正法院管辖之权
right to appeal 申诉权（指当事人对于已作出的决定应有提出申诉的权利,此权利表达了一个关于程序公正的基本思想）
right to appoint and dismiss 任免权
right to art proceeds 艺术收入权
right to bail 保释权
right to bar trespasser 阻止侵犯者的权利
right to be elected 被选举权
right to be eligible for public office 担任公职的权利
right to be informed 被告知的权利[指当事人的实体权利在可能受到政府权力的不利影响时,他(她)有被告知的权利]
right to bear and keep arms 携带和保存武器权
right to bear arms 武器持有权（指美国联邦宪法赋予人们拥有武器的权利。美国联邦宪法第二修正案规定：“管理良好的民兵是保障自由州的安全之所必需,因此人民持有和携带武器的权利不得侵犯。”）
right to begin 首先在法庭陈述权（指诉讼中带头辩论的权利,一般属于负有举证责任的一方,在刑诉方面则是指控方先陈述）
right to bequeath 遗赠权
right to bring an action 起诉权
right to claim damages 要求损害赔偿的权利
right to compulsory execution 强制执行权
right to confer 授予权
right to confrontation 对质诘问的权利
right to consume 消费权
right to convey 财产转让权
right to convoy 护航权
right to counsel 聘请律师之权利；辩护权
right to demand a block vote （英)要求冻结投票权
right to determine family domicile 决定家庭住所权
right to dissolve the parliament 解散议会权
right to due process of law 要求按法定程序审判的权利
right to education 教育权
right to elect 选举权
right to equal and fair treatment 享受平等和公正待遇的权利
right to equal concern and respect 受到同

等关心和尊重的权利
right to equal pay for equal work 同工同酬的权利
right to equal treatment 平等对待权(指行政机关对相同情况应作出相同处理,实质是对行政自由裁量权的一种限制,也是对权力行使理性化所表现的一致化)
right to equitable and satisfactory working conditions 享受公正和合适工作条件的权利
right to establishment 开业权
right to exact payment 求偿权
right to exact toll 强制征收通行费权
right to exclude all others 排除他人的权利
right to exclusive use 专用权
right to exist 生存权
right to expel a member 罢免议员权
right to exploit the work 利用作品的权利
right to fair trial 要求公正审判的权利
Right to Financial Privacy Act of 1978 (美)《1978年对金融秘密的权利法案》
right to financial support 经济补偿的权利,经济抚养、资助、抚养或赡养的权利
right to fly a flag (船舶的)悬挂国旗权
right to free choice of employment 自由选择职业的权利
right to free medial treatment 享受免费医疗权
right to freedom in buying and selling 买卖自由权
right to fructus 收益权
right to get payment for labour 获得劳动报酬的权利
right to get work 获得工作的权利
right to gift 赠与权
right to grant as security 设定担保权
right to habeas corpus 人身保护权
right to harvest 收获庄稼的权利
right to health 享受卫生保健的权利
right to hold public office 担任公职的权利
right to hono(u)r and reputation 荣誉权和名誉权
right to hono(u)rs, dignities and official position 享受礼遇、尊严和官职的权利

right to impeach 检举权,弹劾权
right to information 取得情报的权利,了解情况权
right to inheritance 继承权
right to initiate legislation 立法创制权
right to insurance 领取保险金权
right to interpret 解释权
right to introduce legislation 立法创议权
right to join a family 参与家庭的权利,共同在家庭生活的权利
right to jury trial 受陪审员审判的权利;(要求)陪审团陪审的权利;享受由陪审团审理的权利
right to just and favourable remuneration 获得公平优厚报酬的权利
right to know 知情权
right to labor 劳动的权利
right to lease published works 出租出版作品权
right to lend 出借权
right to let on hire 出租权
right to make a will 立遗嘱的权利
right to make peace 宣布和平权
right to make treaties 签订条约权
right to make war 宣布战争权
right to marriage and choice of spouse 婚姻和选择配偶的权利
right to matrimonial fidelity 忠诚婚姻的权利
right to move about freely 自由迁徙的权利
right to performance of a contract 履行契约的权利
right to petition (英)(向国会或国王的官员或法院的)请愿权,请求权,申请权
right to possess 请求占有权;占有权
right to present petition 呈递请愿书的权利
right to priority in fixing the agenda 决定议程的优先权
right to privacy 隐私权
right to product distribution 产品分配权
right to protection of laws 受法律保护的权利
right to protest 抗议权
right to publish the work (著作人)发表作品的权利

right to reason-giving （要求决定者为决定）说明理由的权利(指当事人要求裁判者对其所作出的决定给出理由的权利,乃是基于权利必须理性地行使这一基本法律精神延伸而来的)
right to recover 追索权
right to recover goods in transit 追回在运途中的货物的权利
right to redeem 赎回不动产的权利
right to redemption 赎买权,回赎权
right to relaxation 休息权
right to rely on lack of conformity 因货物不符合同而主张的权利
right to remain silent 沉默权
right to repurchase 买回权
right to request compensation 请求赔偿权
right to rescind the contract 解除合同(契约)的权利
right to resell 转卖权
right to rest and leisure 享受休息和休假的权利
right to sell 出卖权,销售权
right to silence 沉默权
right to social security 社会保障权
right to speak out 发表言论权
right to stand for election 被选举权
right to strike 罢工权
right to sue 起诉权
right to support of buildings 建筑支撑权（一种城市地役权)
right to take hostages 扣押人质权
right to take residence 居住权利
right to the benefit 收益权
right to the use of a site 场地使用权
right to unemployment benefit 领取失业救济金权
right to use 使用权
right to use up 用尽权
right to usufruct 收益权,使用权
right to vote 选举权;表决权;投票权[美国联邦宪法并未对选举权作出明确宣示,最初将选举权的规定留给各州。但在美国,选举权是由立法机关规定调整且不能为美国和州宪法明示或条款所禁止的权利。实质上它是与民事权利、财产权或人

身权(right of person)相区别的一项政治权利或特权,指赋予某一组织、国家或团体成员投票支持某一议案或候选人的权利;从广义上说,是投票支持或赞同某一有争议的问题或任命的权利。1870年美国联邦宪法第十五修正案禁止各州基于"种族、肤色以及先前的奴役状态"而否认其投票权。1913年美国联邦宪法第十七修正案规定对合众国的参议员实行普选。1920年美国联邦宪法第十九修正案给予妇女投票权(为妇女规定了最基本的公民权——选举权)。1964年美国联邦宪法第二十四修正案禁止征收人头税(poll taxes)。1971年美国联邦宪法第二十六修正案指示各州给予18岁以上的公民以投票权后,1868年美国联邦宪法第十四修正案中的平等保护条款(equal protection)和正当程序条款(due process)被解读为禁止州制定与公平、民主和自治原则相冲突的选举法。联邦最高法院在1964年的Reynolds v. Sims一案中裁决联邦选举中的投票权存在于美国联邦宪法的第1条第2款有关众议院的代表"由各州人民选举"的规定中,而涉及参议员的选举规则规定在联邦宪法第十七修正案中。1965年《投票权法》(the Voting Rights Act)对非裔美国人的投票权产生很大影响并于1970年、1975年和1982年分别进行修订。该法第四节宣布文化考试等做法不合法,第二节则禁止州依据种族来进行投票稀释,该法的其他部分规定一些新的法律救济方式以及联邦政府为了保护非裔美国人在州的投票权而具有干预的权利]
right to wage 获得劳动报酬的权利
right to watercourses 水道通行权
right to work 工作权利
right-and-wrong test 对与错准则（见 M'Naghten Rules; McNaghten Rules）（同 right-wrong test)
right-of-way 1.通行地役权(指通行他人拥有的土地的权利);通行权[可以根据合同、惯例、或政府企业(如高速公路)可以通行] 2.建筑权和营运一条铁路线权(或)在他人土地上的或已使用土地上的高速公路 3.交通的优先权 4.(无权占有人的一条

土地)通行权
right-oriented 权利本位,权利导向
rights-management information 权利管理信息(知识产权)[指有关知识产权信息,当此信息传递到公众时,附加在主题上的,特别以电子形式(electronic form),可鉴别出产权的拥有人。使用的条款(terms of use)、索引号或编码以及其他识别信息,此信息便于与产权拥有人签约。在数字技术中,作为一种知识产权的保护形式,各种法规均可禁止对知识产权管理信息进行修改或取消]
right-to-know act (美)知情权法[指联邦或州制定法要求生产危险物品(hazardous substances)的企业(如化工厂等)在生产或储存它们的社区和处理它们的雇员中公开这些危险物品的信息;亦称为 right-to-know statute]
Right-to-Know Act(s) (美)《知情权法》(指法律要求化学品制造商等工商企业向该企业工人及公众公开危险物质的有关信息,使其了解对生活危险度)
right-to-work a. (法律等)禁止强行要求(企业雇用的)工人加入工会的
right-to-work law (美)工作权利法(指一项州法,它禁止各种工会保障措施,特别禁止那些要求所有工人都必须在受雇后一定期间内参加工会的企业或禁止劳资合同和类似条款要求工会成员优先雇用的法规)
right-winger n. 右翼分子
righteous a. 正直的;正当的;正义的;公正的
righteous defence 正当防卫
rightful a. 正当的;合法的;依法有要求权的;公正的
rightful exercise of legislative authority 立法权的正当行使
rightful heir 合法继承人
rightful notice 正式通知
rightful owner 有合法(财产)所有权者
rightful position 合法地位
rightism n. (常大写)右派纲领,右派言论(观点);赞同右派观点
rightist n. 保守分子,右派分子,右倾分子

rightness of the party's case 当事人的证据的正确性
rights and duties of relatives 亲属间的权利义务
rights and obligations in civil actions 民事诉讼中的权利与义务
rights arising out of the bill 票据上的权利
rights assignments 转让权;陈述权;指派权
rights at law 按法律授予的权利
rights candidate 候选人(或候补人)的权利
Rights Consciousness in Contemporary Society (美)当代社会的权利意识(1955—1990)
rights in civil affairs 民事权利
rights in rem 物权
rights in security 担保权
rights of a tenant 租赁权
rights of accused 刑事被告人权利(指为保障刑事被告人获得公正审判所赋予的各种权利和特权)
rights of credit 荣誉权
rights of guardians 监护人的权利
rights of husband 夫的权利
rights of mankind (或 man) 人权,人的权利
rights of minorities 少数民族的权利
rights of nonparties 非诉讼当事人的主体权益
rights of redress 补偿性权利
rights of the collectives 集体权利
rights of the individual 个人权利
rights of wife 妻的权利
(the) rights thesis 权利论(指当代美国法理学家罗纳德·德沃金的学说核心)
rights to and upon instrument 根据票据主张的权利
rights to succeed 继承权利
rigid a. 刚硬的,坚硬的,刚性的;僵硬的,严峻的,刻板的
rigid and absolute enforcement 强制施行
rigid constitution 刚性宪法(指非经一定程序不得加以修改的),硬性宪法
rigid doctrine of absolute right 绝对权利的刚性原则
rigid economy 严格节约

rigid limitations 刚性限制;刚性时效;僵硬的限制
rigid planning 刚性计划,硬性计划
rigidifying process 固定化过程
rigidity n. 刚硬,刚性;不变;僵化,刻板,严峻
rigidity of assets 资产刚性
rigidity of law 法律的硬性(或刚性),法律的严格性
rigjacker n. 海上油钻劫持者
rigjacking n. 海上油钻劫持
rigo(u)r n. 严峻;严格;严密;严厉
rigor juris 法律的严谨性(有别于 gratia curioe)
rigor mortis 尸僵;死后僵直
ring n. 1.交易场;垄断集团;圆形竞技场 2.恶党;一群坏人,犯罪集团 3.竞争
ring-lock n. 环形锁,暗码锁
ringleader n. 头目;魁首;叛国头子;叛党首领;元凶;首要分子
riot n. 放肆;暴动;骚乱;扰乱治安罪;暴动引起的危险
Riot Act 《取缔暴动法》(指 1715 年英国通过的一项法令,规定 12 人以上不法集会扰乱治安,经过宣读此项法令后,应行解散,否则科以重刑)
riot control weapon 防暴武器
riot police 防暴警察
riot squad 镇压暴乱队
rioter n. 暴徒;骚乱者;暴动者
riotous assembly 暴乱性非法集会
rip v. (美俚)偷;抢掠;诈取
rip off 抢劫;盗窃;诈骗(财物)
riparian n./a. 河岸居住者;河岸权/河岸的,沿岸的
riparian nation(或 **state**) 沿(河)岸国家(指用河岸作为边境的国家)
riparian proprietor 河岸土地所有人
riparian right 河岸权
ripe a./v. 成熟的,年长的;足够的,十分的/(英)搜查;调查
ripeness and immediacy 案件的成熟性和紧迫性,案件的成熟性和直接性
rise v./n. 反抗,叛乱;休会,闭会;增加,提高,增长;晋升;起始,开始;发生/升起,上涨,升高,兴起,出现,起源

rise clause 上涨条款(指运保费上涨归买方负责的条款)
rise to (a point of) order 议员起立质询有关违背议事规则的事
rising n. 上升;叛乱,暴动;起义;休会,散会
rising market price 行情上涨
rising of court 开庭或休庭(指任何法院活动的起始和终了)
risk n./v. 1.危险;冒险 2.(保险业中的)……险;危险率;保险金(额);保险对象(人或物) 3.风险;(复)险类;冒……之险;使冒险;作赌注
risk assessment 风险评价,风险评估
risk averse 风险不愿承担
risk capital 作冒险投资的资本,风险资本
risk control 危险控制
risk factors 风险因素
risk in transit 运输途中的风险
risk liability 风险责任
risk neutral 风险中性
risk note 暂保单,保险凭条
risk of accidental loss 意外损失险
risk of breakage 破碎险,破损险
risk of carriage 运输的风险
risk of collision 碰撞危险
risk of confusion (商品)混淆的风险
risk of contamination 致污险
risk of dissension 异议风险
risk of fresh water damage 淡水险
risk of hook damage 钩损险
risk of jury doubt 陪审团怀疑风险(见 burden of persuasion)
risk of leakage 渗漏险
risk of mischance 意外风险,灾难风险
risk of mould 发霉险
risk of non-delivery 提货不着险
risk of non-persuasion 不能说服的风险
risk of oil damage 油渍险
risk of rust 锈损险
risk of shortage 货差险
risk of shortage in weight 短重险
risk of sling damage 吊索损险
risk of sweat damage 潮腐险

risk of theft and (or) pilferage 盗窃险
risk of warehouse to warehouse 仓库至仓库险
risk preference 风险偏好
risk premium 风险补贴,风险溢价(指对于从事超出正常危险程度工作的职工的额外补贴或工薪;对高风险贷款的债权人支付的额外利息);风险溢价(指美国财政部发行的联邦债券的利息为基准。如该利息为6%,而债券的利息为10%,则该公司证券的风险溢价为4%)
risk return analysis 风险收益分析
risk sharing 风险分担
risk surcharge 风险超载
risk-bearing entity 保险实体,保险单位
Risk-Management Agency (RMA) (美)风险管理局[指美国农业部的一个机构,负责管理联邦农作物保险公司(the Federal Crop Insurance Corporation)的各种项目以及监督有关农作物或农产品的其他项目的风险管理]
risk-shifting activity 风险转移业务,风险性转移活动
risqué 淫秽的,败坏风俗的,猥亵的
risky a. 冒险的,投机的;危险的;淫秽的,有伤风化的
ritual n./a. 仪式,典礼;宗教仪式或程序/典礼的,仪式的
rite n. 仪式,典礼;习俗,惯例;宗教礼拜式
ritual mutilation 残毁礼俗(指以切除、劈裂或其他方式损毁人体一部分使社会承认其社会地位或身份有所改变,多行于婚礼、成年或葬礼)
rival firms 竞争公司
rival gangs 竞争者伙
rival models 竞争者模式
rival system of law 竞争的法律体系
rival tradition 竞争的传统
river n. 河流,江河,内河
river bill of lading 内河提单
river freight 内河水运运费(即货物交内河承运人运输的费用)
river police force 水上警察队
river pollution 河流污染
river *prima facie* 河流表面

river transport 内河运输,水上运输
rivers in international law 国际法上的河流
rivers in municipal law 国内法上的河流
Rivers Pollution Prevention Act (英)《河流防污法》
RMB banknote custodian certificate (中)人民币现钞保管证
RMB foreign exchange instrument (中)人民币外汇票证
Ro-Ro vessel 驶进驶出船
road n. 公路;道路;行车道;途径
road accident 交通事故
road agent (美)沿大道抢劫的强盗;拦路抢劫犯
road capacity 道路通车量;道路运输能力
road carrier 陆运承运人
road closed to passage 禁行路
road death 因交通事故而造成的死亡
road safety act 公路安全法
road show 路演制度(指证券监管合作的国际化经验)
road traffic 道路交通
road traffic offences 破坏交通罪
Road Traffic Reports 《公路交通判例汇编》
roadway n. 道路,路面;快车道;车行道;路线
rob v. 抢劫;盗取;偷取;剥夺
robber n. 强盗,劫匪
robberbaron n. (英)抢劫路过其土地的旅客的贵族;(美)19世纪后期不择手段致富的资本家
robbering ring 抢劫集团
robbery n. 1.强盗(罪)2.抢劫,劫掠;抢劫案
robbery suspect 抢劫嫌疑犯
robbery under arms 武装抢劫
robbery with violence 暴力抢劫
robe n. 1.法衣 2.(the robe)律师业
Robert n. (英俗)警察
Robert's Rule 罗伯特规则 1.议会指南,标题为:《罗伯特指令规则》(Robert's Rules of Order)[最先由亨利·M.罗伯特(Henry M. Robert)(1837—1923)于1875—1876年写的。按原先的名称该手册发行过三版(开始于1915年),三版后则按《罗伯特指令规则》(新修订版)出版,自1970

年起,已是新修订版的名称,甚为畅销,且在美国普遍采用议会手册(parliamentary manual)]2.任一议会手册均包括着"罗伯特规则"这一篇名。先前几版的版权已经到期,许多伪造者采用各种不同程度的背叛原作的版本 3.(单数)见 rule 3;parliamentary manual

robing room 律师(或法官)更衣室

Robinson Patman Act of 1936 (美)《1936 罗宾逊—帕特曼法》[指 1936 年通过的一项联邦法律,旨在禁止阻碍竞争或形成垄断价格行为,实际是对克莱顿法(Clayton Act)的修改]

robot n. 机器人;自动机

robotry n. 机器人的状态;机器人(总称)

rodenticide n. 杀鼠剂

Roe v. Wade (美)罗诉韦德案[1973 年 1 月 23 日作出该案的著名判决,从那时起每年这一天都会成为支持堕胎的人和反对堕胎的人激烈交锋的日子。美国对堕胎的看法分为"自由选择派"(pro-choice)和"生命权利派"(prolife)。罗(Jane Roe),是白人女性诺尔马·麦科维(Norma Mccorvey)的化名,年仅 21 岁的她已经三次怀孕,希望堕胎,在律师帮助下向美国最高法院起诉。9 名大法官以 7 比 2 作出里程碑式判决,裁定禁止妇女堕胎违反美国宪法。这引起全美轩然大波]

ROG dating 货到日起算

rogatio testium (罗马法中的)证人(证据)(指要作口头遗嘱的人要求一个人对此遗嘱作证)

rogation n. (罗马法)法案的提出;提出的法案

rogatory letter (一法官请求另一法官询问证人的)调查委托书

rogo (罗马法)请求,我请求(指常用于遗嘱中的具有恳求的表示)

rogue n. 流氓,无赖;歹徒,恶棍;欺诈者;骗子

rogue trader 恶棍交易员[指专业交易中未经雇主同意进行未经批准的金融交易。"恶棍交易"的著名典型案例就是尼克·里森(Nick Leeson)进行未经授权的股指期货和债券期货投资,最终导致巴林银行破产]

roguery n. 奸诈,诈骗;流氓行为;歹徒团伙

rogues and vagabonds 流氓团伙;盗窃集团

rogues' gallery 罪犯照片陈列室

roguish a. 不诚实的;流氓的;恶作剧的

roket-docket (1987 年)1.争议速决程序 2.闻名的司法管辖区(指其闻名缘由是速决处理案件)3.(相似的)行政程序(在此程序中有特定的时间"60 天内"争议必须得到解决。见 fast-tracking)

role of fault 错误的关键

role of judge 法官的作用

role of suspects 嫌疑人所起的作用

roll n./v. 1.名册;目录;公文;案卷;档案 2.(货物的计算单位)卷 3.(复)记录卷(指古代用羊皮纸书写的记录,然后缝合,不用时可卷起来的)/l.滚转;摇摆 2.发展,进展 3.行驶;用车运载;(俚)盗窃(睡着、喝醉的人等)

roll book 出席登记簿;出勤簿

roll call 点名;点名时间

roll in 纷至沓来,蜂拥而至

roll of attorneys for the district 该地区的律师名册

(to) roll over a debt 再筹划资金清偿债务

roll-back v. (政府)把(价格)压低到原来(或标准)水平;击退,使退却

rolling over (短期贷款的)时间变更

rolling stock (铁路或汽车公司的)全部车辆;(运输业者所有的)车辆

rolling stone 无固定职业者

rolling strike 持续的罢工

rollover paper 可更换时间支付的短期贷款票据

rolls court (英)案卷法庭

rolls of court 法院案卷,法院记录卷

rolls of parliament (英)议会的(会议)记录卷

rolls office of the chancery (英)衡平法法院档案室

Rolls Series (英)《卷丛》(指从 1858 年开始汇编的系列卷宗,包括大不列颠和爱尔兰中世纪编年史中一切有重大意义的著作,为研究中世纪英国不可缺少的资料)

roly-poly CD 转期存单
Roman n./a. 古罗马人,罗马人;罗马天古教徒(蔑);(复)古罗马基督教徒;罗马字;罗马人讲的意大利语;/古罗马的;古罗马人的;罗马天主教的,罗马教徒的
Roman catholic 罗马天主教徒,罗马天主教(亦称罗马公教。1054年基督教分裂为东西两派,东派以君士坦丁堡为中心,称为东正教;西派以罗马为中心即天主教)
Roman Curia 罗马教廷
(the) Roman Empire 罗马帝国
Roman jurisprudence 罗马法学
Roman jurist 罗马法学家
Roman law 罗马法
Roman law 罗马法[指古代罗马人的法律体制,形成了现代大陆法系(民法系)的基础。罗马法是一系列的法规体系。在最早的史前时代到公元1453年之间的一些时间,它调整欧洲、亚洲和非洲等许多民族、人民的社会关系,甚至到现今对整个美国普通法也影响很深。广义的罗马法指罗马人中普遍适用的所有法律,包括优士丁尼大全(Collection of Justinian)。狭义的罗马法,在德国仅指优士丁尼的法律。在英、美习惯使用"罗马法"一词以区别"大陆法"(civil law),以表示包括优士丁尼大全在内的罗马法体系。美国法发展既不同于其他普通法(common law)系国家,亦不同于民法(civil law)法系国家。它深受罗马法的影响,如在佛罗里达州和得克萨斯州,在一段时间内罗马法的确发挥了主导作用。但从总体上来看,罗马法要取代普通法是不可能的]
Roman legal procedure 罗马法诉讼程序
Roman legal school 罗马法学派
Roman materials 罗马法资料(如博茨瓦纳继受下来的那一部分好望角殖民地的法律)
Roman polity 罗马行政制度
Roman texts 罗马文本
Roman-canon system 罗马寺院法律制度
Roman-Dutch law (Roman Dutch law) 罗马—荷兰法(指融合了中世纪荷兰法而形成的一个法律体系,主要来源于日耳曼部落习惯和罗马法运动中所接受的查士丁尼罗马法。17、18世纪传入南非)
Romance language 罗马语言
Romanesque legal system 罗马法系
Romanism n. 古罗马体制;古罗马精神
Romanist n. 研究古罗马法律(或文化,语言)的人
Romanistic a. 罗马法的;罗马文化的
Romanized Law of Germany 德国罗马化法律
Romano-Germanic family 罗马—日耳曼法系,大陆法系(亦称民法法系)
Rome Act (版权法)《罗马法规》《罗马规约》[指《伯尔尼公约》1928年修订增加了对于保护最低标准的道德权利的归属性与完整性,参与签署国必须承认,并创设强制许可(compulsory license),记录履行情况公开播放,并详细说明对于合作作品(joint works)的保护条款必须以最后合作存活者(surviving coauthor)到死亡来衡量考虑。亦称Rome Act of 1928; 1928 Rome Act]
rook n./v. (以赌博营生的)赌棍,骗子/以赌博骗取;敲诈
Rooker-Feldman doctrine 罗克尔-菲尔德曼原则[指联邦法院不考虑实际上已由州法院判决的权利请求的规则,或者对于与一项早先州法院的判决纠缠在一起而不可能解决的权利申请不予考虑的原则。此原则排除了州法院的败诉方实质上去寻求因州法院判决本身违反了败诉者的联邦权利(loser's federal rights)而要求上诉复审(appellate review)的可能性]
room trader 交易所自行投机的掮客
roomer n. 房客,寄宿者
roorback (或 roorbach) n. (美)(中伤候选人等的)诽谤性谣言
root n. 根,地下茎;根源,来源;祖先
roots of crime 罪源,犯罪根源
root of title 契据的存根(指已登记注册的土地交易,通常至少是40年了,才开契据检索。见 chain of title; title search)
Root-Takahira Agreement 鲁特-高平协定[20世纪初期日本和美国政府订立,由日本自行阻止日本移民去美国,而美国方面则不直接禁止日本移民。此协定又称"君子协

定"(the Unwritten Gentleman's Agreement)]
rope n. 1.粗绳;绞人用的绳索;吊死 2.(the ropes)内情;门道;秘诀
rope's end 一种笞打罪犯的刑具
Rose's Note on the United States Reports 《罗斯的美国判例汇编诠释》[《罗斯美国判例汇编诠释》(1899—1901),共 13 卷,从最初出版到 20 世纪 30 年代中期一直是一套颇受欢迎的注释援引汇编。沃尔特·马林斯·罗斯(Water Malins Rose)(1872—1908),一位年轻的加州律师,以编年体系整理存在于美国联邦最高法院从两个达拉斯系列到 172 卷美国判例汇编中判决的法律原则,并对其所引用的每一案例均增添了引证。罗斯的注释援引汇编提供了在谢泼德(Shepard)的援引汇编中简单的援引目录所缺少的讨论分析。查尔斯·L.汤普森(Charles L. Thompson)的修订版(1917—1920 年)将该诠释扩大到 20 卷和两个增订版(1925 和 1932 年),同时将援引案例延伸至 283 卷美国判例汇编]
roster n. 名册,花名册;逐项登记表;履行某种职责的人员名单
roster of candidates 候选人名单
rostrum n. (复)演讲台,讲坛〈Tian An Men Restrum〉(天安门城楼)
rota n. 1.(英)花名册;值勤人员名单;轮值表 2.(大写)天主教的最高法庭,教廷法院
rota court (古老的)宗教法庭
Rotating savings and credit associations (Roscas) 滚动储蓄信贷协会
rotten borough (英)1.某些只有少数投票人但仍在议会有代表的市镇 2.居民减少而仍保持选举议员权利的市镇
rough and ready (方法)粗糙但尚能顶用的;(估计)大致差不多的
(old) Rough and Ready 美国第十二任总统扎卡里·泰洛(Zachary Taylor)(1849—1850)的绰号
rough and ready community 简单而完备的社区
rough n./a. 无赖;莽汉/粗糙的;初步的;大致的;粗陋的;笨重的;艰难的;未加工的

rough copy 草稿
rough justice 简易判决,简易裁决
rough numbers 概数
rough-house n./v. 室内殴斗与喧闹行为,大吵,大打出手/用暴力对待,用暴力对付;粗鲁地逗弄;参与打闹
roughly proportional 大致相当
round(s) n. 回合(指关税减让的谈判)
round of multilateral trade negotiations 多边贸易谈判回合
round out 圆满完成,完成
round table conference 圆桌会议(指双方代表人数相等的会议)
round-up arrest 见 dragnet arrest
roundsman n. 巡官;看夜人;(英)商业推销员(旧译:跑街)
roup n. (苏格兰)拍卖
rout n. 聚众骚扰(罪);骚动(罪);(意区)聚众闹事;非法集会
route n. 路,道路;(城镇间客货运输的)路线;航线
routine n. 例行公事;惯例,常规
routine cases 惯例案件,惯常案件,日常案件
routine contracts 日常合同
routine order 例行通令
routine procedure 例行手续,例行程序
routine remedy 常规的救济
routine searches 例行搜查(指不需事实理由或合理怀疑,就可进行无证搜查,如在边境上或与边境功能类似地点即可进行例行搜查)
routine traffic stop 例行路检
routing n. 行程的安排;货物路线的安排;依排定次序交货
routinism n. 遵循惯例常规
routinize v. 使惯例化
rover n. 流浪者;海盗;海盗船
roving ambassador 巡回大使,无任所大使
roving commission (英)(海军部给予舰长的)自由航行权,(给调查员的)自由航行权
royal a. 1.王的,王室的 2.(大写)英国的,英国皇家的
Royal Advisory Council 皇家(王室)咨询委员会

Royal arms 皇家纹章(指专用于君主的纹章标志)
Royal Assent (英)御准(指君主对议会两院所通过的法案,加以赞同批准。法案获得御准之后,即成法例)
royal authorities 皇室当局,皇家授权
Royal authorization (英)皇室授权
Royal Charter (英)皇家特许状
Royal Command 皇家敕令
Royal Commission (英)皇家委员会
royal court of justice 皇室法院
Royal declaration (英)王室宣言
royal decree 敕令
Royal demesne (英)王室私有产业
royal edict 敕令,圣旨
royal family 皇族,王室
Royal fish (英)王室的鱼(指英格兰法律上规定鲸和鲟搁浅或被捕均归王国所有,也可通过惯例转让他人)
Royal forces (英)皇家武装力量
Royal grant (英)王室特许权
Royal household (英)王室诸官职
royal instruction 谕旨,圣旨
Royal Law(s) (英)王室法(律)(指公元5世纪由各日耳曼封建王国的王室所颁布,在王国境内普遍适用的世俗法,为大陆法系的第四种法律渊源)
royal letters patent 皇家特许证(状)
Royal Mercantile Law Commission (英)皇家商业法律委员会
royal power 王权
royal prerogative 王权;君主特权;王室特权
royal proclamation 王室公告
Royal Society (英)皇家学会
Royal Style and Titles 英王的称号和头衔
Royal veto (英)君主否决权(现已不再使用)
royal warrant (英)英廷委任状
royalism n. 保皇主义,君主主义;忠君,保皇
royalist n. 保皇主义者,保皇党人;(美)保守的实业界巨头
royalty n. 1.使用税;特许税;租金;版税;专利权税;上演税;专利权使用费;特许权使用费;提成费 2.王位,王权 3.(常用复数)王的特权 4.(常授予私人或公司的采矿等)特许权
royalty as to know-how 技术知识使用费,技术秘密使用费
royalty clearance (美)特许批准;版税特许
royalty of patent right 专利特许使用费
royalty payment 权利金,特许使用金
rozzer n. (英俚)警察
rubber stamping 橡皮图章
rubbish n. 垃圾,废物(指体积较小,破碎的已经无用的垃圾)
rubout n. (美俚)谋杀
rubric n. 红标题;(法律、法令或法典某一部分的)标题;成规
rudiment n. (复)基础,基本原理;初步,入门。(复)雏形;萌芽;培育未全的器官
rudimentary doctrinal apparatus 起码的教条组织;基本教条模式
rudiments of legal education 法律教育的基本原理,法律教育的基本理论
ruffian n. 流氓;暴徒;恶棍,无赖
ruffianism n. 流氓习气;暴徒行为
rule n./v. (13世纪)1.规则,准则,细则[总的说,已制定权威的标准或原则(standard or principle);一般指导行为为准则,或典型环境中的行为准则]2.规定[指治理法院或行政机关(agency)内部程序的规定]3.(议会法)程序的规则(procedural rule)(见意思 1)[可使在审议会(deliberative assembly)中有序地进行实务(business),亦称 rule of order(常用复数)]/(13世纪)1.命令;要求;统治,治理〈The dictator ruled the country.〉(专政者统治了这个国家。)2.(法官)裁决,判决一个法律要点〈The court ruled on the issue of admissibility.〉(法院裁决有关证据可采性的争点。)
rule absolute 确定性命令,(终止否定裁决的)确定性裁决(与 rule nisi 相对);绝对规则,绝对规范
rule against accumulations 限制积累规则[指只有在财产永久持有权期限内(perpetuity period)其收益才合法有效,否则无效。此规则即是有关从财产所得收益的范围即对于一些受益人的所分配获得的收入只能是在规定的期限内才有效,超出

期限收益则无效。见 rule against perpetuities]
rule against bias 防止偏见的原则
(the) rule against hearsay 传闻规则(指英美法系国家相当重要的证据规则,美国著名证据法学家威格莫尔曾说:"它是英美证据法上最具特色的制度,其受重视程度仅次于陪审制,是杰出的司法体制对人类诉讼程序一大贡献。"它的主要含义是如果提交法庭的证据是传闻证据,除法定例外情况外,在审判中不具有可采性)
rule against perpetuities (有时大写 Rule Against Perpetuities)(18世纪)(财产法)禁止永久权规则[指普通法上的一项规则;禁止允准财产转让,除非其权益必须转让或赋予(vest),如果是全部权益,则不得迟于立遗嘱人死后21年(另加上怀孕期间,涵盖死腹子)包括死者存活时所创设的权益必须转让。此规则之目的是限制财产所有权(title to property)终止商业活动的时间(suspended out of commerce),因为没有此财产之所有权人,谁可以销售它或谁可行使其他方面的所有权。如果合同或赠与中的期限(terms)超过了该规则的时间限制,则此赠与或交易无效。见 measuring life; accumulation; rule against accumulations]
rule against splitting causes of action 防止诉讼原因分割规则
rule applicable 可适用的原则,可适用的规范
rule by generals 军人统治
rule by law 法治
rule by special privilege 特权统治
rule by trade-union bosses 工会领袖统治
rule concerning risk 有关风险的规则
rule conferring power 授予权力的规则
rule conferring right 赋予权利的规则
rule day 被告出庭日[要求说明理由(rule to show cause)的回呈日]
rule for testing quality 质量检验(查)制度
rule imposing duty (或 **obligation**) 设定义务的规则
rule in one's favor (最高法院)对他(或某人)庇护

Rule in Shelley's Case 谢利案中的规则(指一项适用于契约和遗嘱的古老的英格兰原则,该原则已于1926年被废除。"如果在同一份文据中保有地产给予该人有限定授予某人,并将遗留地产给予该人的继承人或给予保有人自己的继承人,则该遗留地产以非限定的继承地产赋予文据上记名的被继承人,或在后一情况下,赋予其以限定继承的地产。")
rule interpleader 确定竞合权利诉讼,规则上的确定竞合权利诉讼
rule making n. (1926年)行政规则制定程序(指行政机关制定、修订或废止一项规则或规章所运用的程序。亦称为 administrative rulemaking。见 administrative adjudication; informal agency action; rulemaking)
rule making power (美)规则制定权(指国会授予联邦最高法院制定基层法院和上诉法院审理案件应当遵循的程序规则的权力)
rule nisi (或 **rule to show cause**) 1.(法院)否定(付给赔偿金的)裁决(指美国法院根据当事人说明理由的动议而作的裁决)2.提审裁决(指英国凡被不法拘禁的本人或其亲友可向高等法院法官请发"提审裁决",将被拘禁的人移送到该法院);非确定性命令,非确定性裁决;非绝对规则
rule of adjudication 审判规则
rule of cabinet solidarity 内阁一致原则
rule of civil law 民法规范
rule of conduct 行为规则
rule of constitution 宪则
rule of court 1.法庭规则(常用复数,指有法庭资格管辖权的法院所作出有关判例、程序或某项特定问题的规定)2.法院案例;法院的判决;支配法院活动的规则
rule of criminal law 刑法规范
rule of debate 辩论规则
rule of decision 判决依据(指法律规则,制定法,法律汇编,先前判决等均为裁决案件的根据)
rule of double criminality 见 double criminality

rule of doubt 质疑原则[①(版权)存放在美国版权局(US Copyright Office)的难于辨认或难于全面鉴别的资料根据版权法不受保护,因为不易于鉴别其是否合格。此原则亦常适用于计算机目的码(computer object code)②(专利)放弃司法原则,认为一个创新是否可取得专利受到质疑时,该专利应成为争点,故发明者可在法庭上进行争辩测试以证明其合法性]

rule of elders 长老统治

rule of equity 衡平法规则

rule of evidence 证据法规则(见 evidence ④)

rule of exclusion (证据法)除外规则(指将传闻证据等排除在外的规则)

rule of execution 执行规则

rule of four 四个原则(指美国联邦最高法院在1990年代为减少沉重案件负担的一种方法,即经联邦最高法院审理的四个案件中都有普遍性重要法律问题方可复审,其中请求上诉的将予以复审。另外,在每周秘密会议讨论备审案件目录的案件时,至少有4名大法官必须一致同意某个案件值得听审,并经全体大法官充分考虑方可听审)

rule of four A (美)四A法规(指如果有四个美国最高法院审理发现案件引起普遍性的重要法律问题,则此案值得复审)

rule of international law 国际法规则

rule of jurisdiction 管辖权规则

rule of justice 正义原则

rule of law 法律原则;法律规则;法治

rule of life 生活规律,生活规则

rule of literal interpretation 字面解释原则

rule of *locus regit actum* 法律行为符合行为地法律所要求的形式原则

rule of law (18世纪)1.实质性法律原则⟨Under the rule of law known as respondent superior, the employer is answerable for all wrongs committed by an employee in the course of the employment.⟩(按照被认为是长官负责制而闻名的实质性法律原则,雇主对于1名雇员在执行任务中所犯下的全部错误应承担全部责任。)2.法治[指相对于专权的正规至上权力(supremacy)⟨Citizens must respect the rule of law.⟩(公民必须遵守法治。)]3.正常法律原理[指在管辖范围内,人人需遵守常规法律(ordinary law)的原理⟨All persons within the United States are within the American rule of law.⟩(在美国内所有的人都在美国的法律管理之中。)]4.宪法的原则[指普遍的宪法原则是司法判决的结果决定在法庭中的个人权利⟨Under the rule of law, Supreme Court case law makes up the bulk of what we call "constitutional law".⟩(在实质性法律治理下,联邦最高法院判例法构成了大量我们所称的"宪法法"。)]5.法律裁决[指宽松地解释一项法律裁决,按法律的某一观点裁定⟨The ratio decidenti of a case is any rule of law reached by judge as a necessary step in the decision.⟩(一个案件的判决依据或判决理由是法官达到任何法律裁决在判决中的必要步骤。)]

rule of market overt 公开市场原则

rule of marshaling assets 债权清偿顺序规则[指一项衡平原则,要求享有优先偿权的债权人(senior creditor)有两项或者两项以上的资金(funds)来满足其债务清偿。首先应以后顺位债权人(junior creditor)无权受偿的那项获得清偿。该原则旨在防止享有优先偿权的债权人选择以后顺位债权人以唯一可受偿的资金来获取清偿,从而造成后顺位债权人得不到任何清偿的不公平后果。亦称 marshaling doctrine; rule of marshaling securities; rule of marshaling remedies]

rule of marshaling remedies 见 rule of marshaling assets

rule of marshaling securities 见 rule of marshaling assets

rule of mortmain 永久管业原则

rule of non-discrimination 非歧视原则

rule of obligation 债务规则

rule of origin 原产地规则

rule of pleading 辩护规则

rule of practice 诉讼程序规则

rule of preference for males over females 男性优于女性原则

rule of primogeniture 长子继承制原则

rule of procedure 议事规则
rule of reason (美)合理规则,理性规则合理原(准)则(指通过衡量案情的各方面要素,如限制的历史、存在的弊端、采取特殊补救的理由以及要达到的目的等,来确定有关贸易限制的合法性的反托拉斯原则)
rule of reasonableness 合乎常理的准则
rule of recognition 承认规则
rule of remoteness (英)远因规则(指法院判决损害赔偿时对造成损害的行为与结果关系距离太远者,则不予考虑)
rule of speaking 发言规则
rule of standing to sue 起诉资格规则
rule of statutory interpretation 法规解释规则
rule of technique for security 安全技术规程
rule of the relative effect of contracts 合同(契约)相对效力规则
rule of the road 公路法规
rule of thumb 单凭经验来做的方法,比较粗糙的方法;约略的衡量或估计
rule of transitory presence "暂时停留"规则,"短暂在场"规则
rule of universal inheritance 见 universal inheritance rule
rule oriented 规则型,导向规则
rule out 划去,排除,取消,拒绝考虑
rule outside state law 国家法律以外的准则
rule paterna paternis, materna maternis 从父方得来的财产由父方的人继承,从母方得来的财产由母方的人继承原则
rule relating to debates 辩论规则
rule relating to internal discipline 内部纪律规程
rule skeptics 规则怀疑论
rule to show cause 见 rule nisi
rule-bound 规则束缚的,遵守规则的
rule-following models 循规模型
rule-governed system 依法而治的制度
rule-making power (美)法规制定权(指联邦政府颁布法规与规章的权力。大部分美国法律以行政法规的形式出现);规则制定权(指国会授予联邦最高法院制定基层法院和上诉法院审理案件应当遵循的程序规则的权力)
rule-oriented approach 赞成派,规则导向派(或 legalistic approach 遵法派)(指 WTO 专家出于对争端解决机制下私人利益诉求的关注,对能否赋予私人直接向争端解决机制提起诉讼的权利形成了对立的两派意见:一派为赞成派或规则导向派或遵法派;另一派为反对派即外交导向派"diplomacy-oriented approach"或实用派"pragmatic approach")
ruleless a. 无约束的,无法无天的,无规则的
rulemaking n. 规章制度,规章制定
rulemaking power (美)规程制定权(指某些受理上诉法院的权力,通常是最高受理上诉法院具有此种规定权力,可以制定应由其下级法院执行的程序规程)
ruler n. 统治者;管理者
rulers of England 历代英王(指以盎格鲁-撒克逊王朝起直至伊丽莎白二世)
rulership n. 统治权;统治地位及职权
rules against double portions 一人不能受两份遗产的原则
rules and doctrines of common law 普通法的规范和原理
rules and regulations 规章制度
rules as to the authority of precedents 先例权威原则
Rules Enabling Act of 1934 (美)《1934年规则制定授权法》(该法授予联邦最高法院广泛诉讼规则制定权的一项联邦法律)
rules for implementation 施行细则;实施细则
rules of absolute exclusion 绝对排除规则
rules of adjudication 审判规则[指哈特的法律理论,他认为法律制度存在两个标准:一是大众遵守法律;二是这个法律体系中的官员们实际上接受这个体系作为共同的公共准则,即承认规则(the rules of recognition)、改变规则(the rules of change)和审判规则(the rules of adjudication)。哈特认为接受一条法律规则高于对规则的外在服务,但低于这样的信念——认为规则创设了有约束力的道德义务]
rules of adjective law 程序法规则

rules of choice of law 法律选择的规则
rules of claim preclusion 请求权排除规则
rules of conditional exclusion 附条件排除规则
rules of conduct 礼仪,礼节
rules of conflicts 冲突法(即国际私法)
rules of construction 解释法律的规则
rules of court 见 court rules
Rules of Decision Act (美)《裁判规则法》或《裁判依据法》[(指《司法法》第 34 条规定)可见 rule of decision(即在审理州际间公民纠纷案件时,除美国宪法、条约和制定法外,一些州的法制应被视为判决依据)]
rules of etiquette 礼法;仪礼规定
rules of evidence 举证程序法规
rules of expedited arbitration 快速仲裁规则
rules of forum 审判地法
rules of good seamanship 良好海员规则(指根据海员在驾驶船舶过程中的习惯和经验来衡量其行为习惯上的规则)
rules of interpretation 解释(法律、合同等的)规则
rules of jus common 普通法规则
rules of labor health 劳动卫生规程
rules of law 法律规范,法律规则;法治
rules of navigation 海上避碰规则;(公海航行时避免船只碰撞的)航行规则
rules of order 程序规则;会议规则
rules of organization 组织规程
rules of origin 原产地规则
rules of practice 业务规则,实务规则
rules of prison 监狱规则
rules of private international law 国际私法规则[指冲突规范(conflicts rules)]
rules of procedure 诉讼程序规则(程),程序规则
rules of procedure of arbitration 仲裁程序规则(程)
rules of recognition 确认性规则
rules of standing to sue (美)起诉涉及管辖的规则(见 standing to sue)
rules of substantive law 实体法规范,实体法规则
Rules of the Court 美国联邦最高法院规则(指联邦最高法院用规则规范自己的行为。这种规范行为规则最早产生于1790年。此规范行为规则进行了多次修订。最近一次修订于 1990 年元旦生效。联邦最高法院确立这些规则的权力规定在《美国法典》第 28 标题卷第 2071 节。改变这些规则可由律师提出要求,或由联邦最高法院专为此目的而设的委员会提出,也可由一名或一名以上大法官提出。传统上由全体大法官一致同意而非绝对多数同意获得通过。现在共有 48 条规则规范联邦最高法院的活动。第 1 条到第 9 条规定法院官员,第 10 条到第 20 条规定法院管辖权,第 20 条至 40 条规定出庭律师应遵循的形式和程序,第 41 条到 46 条规定案件作出判决后法院和当事人可能采取的行动)
rules of the law of merchant 商法通例
rules of the road at sea 海上避撞规程(亦译做海道规则,指一种国际协议的海上交通规则。最近一次修订是在 1965 年)
Rules of the Supreme Court (英)《最高法院规程》
rules of war 战争法规;战略;策略
Rules on Administrative Reconsideration 行政重组规则;行政重建规则
rules on air warfare 空战法规
rules on (或 of) procedure 程序规则(程);程序性法规;程序性规范
Rules Publication Act (美)《行政法规公布法》
rules to plead 答辩通则
ruling n./a. 1.裁决,裁定;规定 2.统治;支配;管理/管理的;支配的;统治的;主要的;流行的
ruling against a motion 否决动议
ruling case law 《重要判例法》
ruling cases 首要案例(又译指导性案例,指其原则对后来的案件具有约束力)
ruling class 统治阶级;控制阶层
ruling elite 统治集团,统治领导层
ruling of final instance 终审裁决
ruling of first instance 初审裁决
ruling on evidence 证据之裁定
ruling on the burden of proof 举证责任的

裁决
ruling party 执政党
ruling passion （支配行为的）主导情绪
ruling price 市价,时价
rulings of acquittal 释放裁定书
rum n./a. 酒;甜酒;/(英)可笑的,奇异的;难对付的
rummage n. 翻动;搜查;(海关)检查
rummager n. 搜查者,(海关)检查者
rumo(u)r n. 谣言;谣传;传说,流言
rumo(u)r mongering 造谣,散布谣言
rumo(u)r-monger n. 传布谣言者;造谣者
run v. 1.逃;跑;进行;(机器等)运转;追溯;追赶;追捕(查)2.延伸;延续;成为,变为;散布 3.(美)竞选;提名;经营;举办4.通用;有效;一再出现;连续重现 5.偷运,走私;运送 6.赊欠
(to) run a candidate in the presidential election 提出竞选总统的候选人
run a rumour 追查谣言
run a rumor back to its source 追查谣言的来源
run a taxi 驾驶出租汽车
run (up) a score 赊账;欠债
run aboard a ship 船相撞
run (fall) afoul of 与……纠缠;与……发生冲突;(船只)与……相撞;
run after shadow 捕风捉影
run amuck（或 **amok**） 乱砍乱杀;胡作非为,横行霸道
run away 潜逃,私奔,失去控制
run away demand 迅速增加的需求
run away with 1.偷;携带……潜逃;同……私奔 2.匆忙接受 3.失去控制
run back over 回顾
run（或 **go, act**）**counter to** 违反,与……背道而驰
run down 1.停止 2.诽谤;搜捕 3.撞倒;毁坏 4.找寻后发现
run for mayor 竞选市长
run for office 竞选(职位)
run foul (afoul) of the law 触犯法律
run off 1.逃跑,逃脱 2.出版,印出 3.决定;获胜
run off election 见 election 3

run out 背弃;遗弃;逃避
run out to sea 出海
run over 过去;溢出,超出限度;扼要复述;匆匆读过;(车辆)辗过
run riot 肆无忌惮,无法无天
run sb. into difficulties 使人陷入困境
run scared （因恐落选而）尽力拉票
run the risk of 冒……的风险
run with land 随地而动,随地而动原则 [指地役权是"以他人土地供自己土地的方便和利用的权利"。从立法技术构造来看,地役权这种用益物权的独特之处在于其从属性与不可分性之特性,大陆法上称主体属物,英美法上则称随地而动(run with land)。这样的制度安排使得大量役权在经济上会有正外部性,不但对需役地、供役地所有权人有效果,而且对其利益在协议中未得到代表的第三方也有效果。随地而动原则在美国经历了一个从难到易的过程,主要原因在于其所依据的合同自由原则]
run-off primary （美国南部诸州在政党预选会中举行的）第二次预选(就第一次投票中得票最多的两人中选定一名)
run-up n. 涨价
runaway n./a. 逃亡,逃跑;私奔;逃亡者,逃跑者;私奔者;亡命之徒;脱离控制/1.逃亡的,私奔的,逃的 2.由私逃者做的 3.迅速增加的
"runaway" grand jury （美）"私访的"大陪审团(指大陪审团脱离检察官自己进行调查);自行查访的大陪审团
runaway inflation 急速增加的通货膨胀
runaway marriage 私奔结婚
runaway prisoner 逃犯
runner n. 1.走私者;走私船;偷越封锁线者 2.推销员 3.信差
runner-up n. （在竞选等中）得票名列第二位的候选人;亚军
running a. 持续的;流动的;跟随的
running account 流水账
running cost 日常费用,经营费用;运行成本,运转费;操作费用
running days 连续工作日(包括假日和星期日)

running down cases 1.撞车事件损害赔偿的诉案 2.诽谤引起的诉案
running with the land (土地买主的)义务;跟随土地转让
running with the reversion 一切随地产的归宿而定
running-down clause 船舶碰撞条款
ruptio 伤害
rupture n. 破裂;决裂;敌对;断绝(关系)
rupture of diplomatic relations 断(绝)交,断绝外交关系
rural a. 农村的,乡村的;有关农业的
rural code 农业法,(大写)《农业法典》
rural collective 农村集体
rural community 农村社区,农村公社,乡镇
rural constable 乡警
rural expansion zone 农业开发区
rural households 农村家庭,农户
rural leases 农业租赁
rural policy 农村政策
rural political power organization 农村政权组织
rural population 农村人口
rural responsibility contracts (中)农村责任承包(制)
rural sector 农业部门
rural servitude 乡村地役权
rural sociology 农村社会学
rural-urban migration 农村向城市移民,农村人口流入城市
Rurales n. (墨西哥)乡警
ruran a. 住在从事农业的居住区的,住在郊外(但不在农场)的
ruse n. 诡计,计策
rush v./n. 急进;猛攻;向……索高价/突进;匆忙;抢购
rush hour 交通拥挤时间
rush order 紧急订货;加急订单
Russian Revolution 俄国革命(指1917年11月7日推翻沙皇政府,建立苏维埃政权的革命,又称十月革命)
rust bowl 生锈地区(指美国东北部和中西部日益衰落的工业区)
rusticate v. 下乡,到农村去;住在农村
rusticum judicium (海事法上的)(两船相碰撞引起损害赔偿的)简易裁决
rustium n. 耕作地
rustler n. 偷盗牲畜犯
rustling n. 偷盗牲畜罪;偷牛
ruta 地下挖出的财产
ruthless a. 无情的;残忍的
ruttish a. 淫乱的,好色的
ryot n. (印度)农民

S

S corporation (1961年)(美)S公司[指该公司的所得非通过公司本身而是由其股东个人纳税。美国《国内税收法》第S分章(subchapter S)规定:只有公司的股东符合限定的人数方可被选定享有S公司税收身份(S corporation tax status)。亦称 Subchapter S corporation; tax-option corporation。见 C corporation]
sabinians (school) n. 萨宾派(指古罗马帝国时期多数法学家追逐的两学派之一)
sabotage n./v. 破坏行动(指工人在劳资纠纷中所从事的毁坏机器、浪费材料及怠工活动,也指被占领国人民对占领军的破坏活动)/进行破坏,从事破坏活动;怠工,怠业
saboteur n. 破坏者,破坏分子;怠工者
sac n. (古代英国法中的领主法庭的)审判权
sacaburth (sacabere, sakabere) n. (古英国法中)被抢劫或被偷盗钱财的人;被抢劫者,被偷盗者
sack v. 1.劫掠,掠夺 2.解雇
sacker n. 抢劫者,掠夺者
sacramentum (最古老的罗马法上誓金诉

讼中的)誓金
sacred a. 神圣的,不可侵犯的;郑重的
sacred promise 郑重的诺言
sacred territory 神圣不可侵犯的领土
sacred texts 经典
sacrifice n. 牺牲(品);损失;亏本出售的商品
sacrifice of property 牺牲财产
sacrifice sale 亏本出售,认赔抛售
sacrilege n. 撬门入教堂行窃(指撬门进入教堂在做礼拜的地方行窃。在英国,从前构成盗窃罪,现已废止);窃取圣物
sacrilegious children 渎圣所生的子女
sacrilegious person 盗窃圣物的人;撬门入教堂行窃者
sacrilegium 盗窃圣物(罪)
sacrilegus 犯撬门入教堂行窃罪者
sad sack (美)不中用的人,无能者
sadism n. 性虐待狂,性施虐症(与masochism相对应,性受虐症是,以向性爱对象施加虐待或接受对方虐待作为性兴奋的主要手段。这种手段有捆绑、引起疼痛和侮辱等,甚至可造成伤残或死亡。而以接受虐待行为来达到性兴奋者为性受虐症。它们均属自诉类刑事案件。需注意区分虐待罪。施虐者有完全的刑事责任能力。见 sexual perversion)
sadist n. 性虐待狂者,虐待狂者
sadistic surgeon (患)虐待狂的外科医生
sado-fascist a. 法西斯虐待狂的
sado-sexuality n. 性虐待狂
safe n./a. 保险箱;冷藏柜/1.安全的,没有危险的2.确实的,可靠的;可信赖的
safe cracker 撬开保险箱的盗贼
safe custody 保管
safe harbor 安全港口,安全港湾(指符合法规且经批准的港口)
safe harbor provision 安全港规定
safe harbor rules 避风港规则
safe load 安全载重
safe operation 安全操作
safe place to work (雇主必须为雇员提供的)安全工作场所
safe pledgs 可靠的抵押保证(或担保)
safe retreat 收容所,救济所;庇护所
safe stopping distance 安全停车距离

safe-conduct n. 安全通行证(指交战国发给敌对国国民或其他人的安全通行证明,允许其进入或离开一个管辖范围,否则他会遭受逮捕、拘留或被夺其他权利,对于船舶和货物也可颁发此类通行证,但必须由交战国之间安排颁发),通行许可证,护照;护送持有安全通行证者的卫兵
safe-cracker n. 同 safe cracker
safe-cracking n. 打开保险箱抢劫
safe-deposit n./a. 保险仓库;安全仓库;信托仓库,贵重物品保管处/安全保管的
safe-deposit box (银行的)保管箱,保险箱
safe-deposit company (出租保管箱、保险箱的)保管公司
safeblower n. 以炸药炸开保险箱抢劫者
safeblowing n. 以炸药炸开保险箱抢劫
safebreaker n. 打开保险箱进行抢劫者
safeguard n./v. 1.保护措施,保证条款2.安全装置,防护设施 3.(= safe-conduct)(尤指战时的)安全通行证,护照 4.保护者,护送者,警卫员/保护,维护,捍卫
safeguard clause 保障条款;保护条款;保证条款
safeguard mechanism 保障办法
safeguard practice 保护性措施
safeguarding duties (对进口货征收的)保护关税
safekeeping n. 妥善保护,妥善保管
safety n. 1.安全,平安;确实,稳妥 2.安全设备,保险装置
safety belt 救生带,(高空作业或飞机乘客用的)安全带
safety check 安全检查
safety code 安全条例
safety devices 安全设施,安全装置
safety factor (或 coeffcient) 安全系数
safety in production 安全生产
safety insurance 安全险
safety island (或 zone) (交通)安全岛;(公共汽车上下车的)站台
safety lock 保险锁;(武器的)保险机
safety measures 安全措施
safety of civil aviation 民航安全
safety of goods 物品安全
safety of life or property 生命财产安全

safety of person 人身安全
safety operating rules 安全操作规程
safety pact 安全公约
safety principle 安全原则(指电子商务必须以安全为其前提,它不仅需要技术上的安全措施,同时也离不开法律上的安全规范。安全性原则要求与电子商务有关的交易信息在传输、存储、交换等整个过程不被丢失、泄漏、窃听、拦截、改变等,要求网络和信息应保持可靠性、可用性、保密性、完整性、可控性和不可抵赖性)
safety regulations 安全条例,安全规章
safety responsibility system 安全责任制
safety rules 安全规则,安全规程,安全条例
said a. 上述的;该(人或事物等)
(the) said contract 上述合同,上述誓约
said circumstances 上述情形
said party 上述当事人
"said to be" clause "据称"条款
said to weight 申请重量,据称重量
(the) said witness 该证人,上述证人
sail n./v. 航行,航海;驶行,驾驶/航行,航海;起航,驾驶
sail near (或 close) to the wind 几乎违法
sailing cards 起航通知单
sailling day 开航日,(客轮的)起航日
sailor n. 水手,船员,海员
sailor's shore pass 船员登陆证
Saint Hilary sittings (英)最高法院开庭期(1月1日至3月23日),希拉里开庭期(根据1873年的《司法法》第26条,此开庭期已被废止),春季开庭期(见 Hilary Rule)
saisie-arret 扣押第三人占有的债务人财产
salable a. 可销售的,易卖的
salable price 易卖的价格
salable value 可出售的价格(见 fair market value)
salacious a. 淫秽的,黄色的;淫荡的,好色的
salacity n. 黄色,淫荡
salariat n. 工薪阶层
salary n./v. 工资,薪酬,薪金,薪水/给……工资,发薪金给……
salary savings insurance (雇主从雇员薪金中扣除保险费直接付给保险公司的)人身(寿)保险制

salaried lawyer 领薪律师(英国常用此称谓)
salaries of the justices 联邦最高法院大法官的薪金[指为确保司法独立,联邦宪法规定禁止削减法官报酬。《1789年司法法》(Judiciary Act of 1789)确定首席大法官薪金为4000美元,大法官的薪金为3500美元,二者之间有500美元差距,这差距一直持续到1969年。到2005年,这个差距已增至8900美元。这反映了首席大法官在行政管理方面承担了不同的责任(见 Office of the Chief Justice)]
sale n./a. 买卖;出售;拍卖;销售(常指零售)/大量制售的
sale afloat 运输途中销售
sale against the box 见 short sale against the box
sale agreement 销售合同
sale allowances 销货折让(扣)
sale and leaseback 出卖产业并租回该产业
sale as per origin 凭产地买卖
sale as per specifications 规格买卖
sale at an exchange 在交易所出售
sale breaks lease (罗马法)出售中断租赁(原则)
sale by auction 拍卖
sale by authority of law 根据法院命令出售,根据合法当局的命令出售
sale by sample 照样品销售,凭样出售
sale by standard or type 凭标准销售
sale by trade mark or brand 凭商标、牌记买卖
sale by way of execution 强制执行判决中的售卖
sale confirmation 售货确认书
sale contract 销售合同(契约)
sale discounts and allowances 销货折让(扣)
sale for cash 现金交易
sale for the account (或 the settlememt) 赊销
sale in (on) execution 强制执行判决中的售卖
sale in market-overt 在公共市场售卖

sale of a business　企业出让
sale of an expectancy　期待(事物的)买卖
sale of chattel　动产买卖
sale of chose in action　无形财产买卖,权利上的财产买卖
sale of commodities　商品买卖
sale of drugs　毒品买卖
sale of goods　货物销售,货物买卖
Sale of Goods Act (SGA)　(英)货物买卖法
sale of immovable　不动产买卖
sale of land　土地买卖
sale of securities　出售担保品;出售证券
sale of trade name　商号的出让(又译:商业名称的出让)
sale on (open) account　赊销,赊卖
sale on approval　试销
sale on availability　现销
sale on clearance (或 clearance sale)　减价买卖,清仓出卖
sale on commission　寄售,委托销售,代售
sale on condition　附条件的买卖,附条件的销售
sale on consignment　委托销售
sale on credit　赊销,信用买卖
sale on documents　凭(按)证买卖
sale on stock exchanges　证券交易所买卖
sale on time　定(按)时销售(实际指分期付款销售)
sale or return　可退货经售(指转手买卖无法销售时,可以退货的一种销售方式)
sale premium (act)　有奖销售(法)
sale price　廉价
sale promotion　推销
sale ring　拍卖人周围的顾客
sale short　见 short sale
sale tools　大量制售的工具
sale upon inspection　通过检验的买卖
sale upon judicial order　根据法院裁定的出售
sale with all faults　残缺商品出售(声明售出商品有各种缺陷的一种销售方式)
sale with obligation to forward the thing　期货买卖
sale with ownership reserved　保留所有权的买卖
sale with right of redemption　附有买回权之销售(指卖人保留原出售物以原价购回之权)
Salem witch trials (1692)　塞勒姆巫婆审判案(1692)
saleman n.　(德国法)财产转让官(据认为是受托人概念的起源)
sales a.　售货的,有关售货的
sales agency　经销处
sales agreement　售货合同
sales and purchase commissions　买卖经纪
sales department　门市部
sales duplicate　销售(发票)副本(指为订立商业买卖合同所开具的发票副本)
sales law　买卖法
sales people　推销人员
sales returns　售货退回
sales slip　发货账单
sales tax　(1921年)营业税,销售税(指根据货物销售及其服务所课之税,通常以其价格的百分比来衡定。亦称为 retail sales tax。见 flat tax)
sales transaction　销售(事务),交易
sales voucher　售货凭证
salesman n.　推销员,售货员,兜售员,店员
Salic (或 Salique) Law　萨利克族法律(又译:舍利法典,萨利克法。指古代法国的基本法规,不准子女继承遗产和王位)
salic marriage　(古)(法国法规不准子女继承遗产和王位)萨利克婚姻(见 morganatic marriage)
salus　健康;安全;兴旺
* Salus publica supremea lex esto.　Let the safety of the people be the supreme law.　公益优于私益;人民之安全高于法律。
* Salus populi suprema lex.　The welfare of the people is the supreme law.　人民的福利是最高的法律。公众利益高于法律,人民之安宁高于法律。
salutary effect　有益健康的效果,有益的效力
salva rerum sustantia　不毁坏物的实体
salvage n./v.　1.海上救助,海上打捞,救难;救助费 2.被救财物,被救船舶或船员 3.救助,救济 4.财产的抢救/救难,救助;营救;打捞

salvage act 海难救助法
salvage agreement 海难救助合约
salvage charges (SC) 救助费用,海难救助费用,海上打捞费,施救费用
salvage clause 救助条款
salvage company 海难救助公司,沉船打捞公司
salvage corps (保险公司的)救火队,消防队
salvage gear 救助船具
salvage loss (扣除援救费外水险商必须承担的)海难损失,救助打捞损失
salvage money 救难偿金,营救费,救助费用(=salvage charges)
salvage prize 海上捕获偿金
salvage service 救助机构
salved value 被救价值(指海上被救出船舶及货物的价值)
salvo n. 1.保留条款;但书;托辞 2.不使(合法权利等)受损害,(名誉等的)保全手段
salvo jure 不影响,不妨害;对法定利益或要求无影响,无损害
salvor (=salver) n. 救助人员;打捞船;救难船
Samaritan(s) (复)撒玛利亚会(慈善组织);慈善的人;愿做好事的人
same a. 同一的,相同的;上述的(与 this, that, these, those 等连用)
same blood 同血缘,同族
same poll 同一次投票
same "quantum" of contacts 相同"量"的联系
same term in office 相同的任期
same-sex family 同性家庭
same-sex marriage 同性恋婚姻
same-sex sexual harassment 同性间性骚扰
same-transaction test 同一交易检测标准
sample n. 货样,样品;实例,标本
sample contract 样品合同(契约)
sample drawn by owner 货主自抽货样
sample order 照样品订货
sample survey 抽样调查,样品检验
sampled offer 附样品的要约,附样品发盘
sampling n. 取样,抽样;提取或试验样品的程序
sampling investigation 抽样调查
San Domingo Declaration 《圣多明哥宣言》(指 1972 年 10 个加勒比海国家于 6月 9 日之圣多明哥宣言,界定领海外线为 12 海里)
san-ad n. (英国和印度)许可,认可;让渡证书
sanae mentis (古英国法上)神志正常的,心智健全
Sanctio pragmatica "国事诏书"(优士丁尼皇帝通过此"诏书"使其法典适用于意大利,因而《国法大全》中所记录的帝国晚期的非常诉讼程序成为意大利法定诉讼程序)
sanction n. (15 世纪)1.正式批准或授权〈the committee gave sanction to the proposal〉(该委员会已对此方案已正式批准),〈the court will sanction the trust disposition if it is not against public policy〉(如果与公共政策无抵触,法院则批准信托处分)(见 ratification 1) 2.刑罚惩戒或其后果造成与法律、法规或命令不一致的强制措施[即使法律、法规命令得到遵守的附加条件(如偿、罚等)〈the court sanctioned the attorney for violating the gag order〉(因违反司法禁言令,法院判决惩处该律师),〈a sanction for discovery abuse〉(因滥用开示程序而受到的惩处)(见 discipline 惩戒)。《联邦民事诉讼程序规则》(the Federal Rule of Civil Procedure)第 37 条规定,没有正式批准或授权,开示程序总是无效的]
sanction of a law 法律的制裁,法律的认可
sanction of custom 按惯例的制裁
sanction of expulsion 开除处分
sanction of marriage 批准结婚
sanction of suspension from office 暂行停职的处分
sanctionative a. 制裁的,认可的;约束的
sanctioned by usage 约定俗成,习惯(使用上)认可
sanctiones pragmaticae (罗马皇帝的)国事诏书
sanctioning authority 处分权
sanctioning right 制裁性权利
sanctionist n. (对违反国际法的国家实行制裁的)制裁国
sanctity n. 1.神圣不可侵犯性 2.(复)神圣

的义务(或权利)
sanctity of treaties 条约神圣原则
sanctuary n. 1.庇护所,避难所 2.教堂,寺院
sane a. 健全的;神志正常的;明智的;合情合理的;稳健的
sane memory 健全的记忆
sane person 神志清楚的人
sane policy 稳健的政策
sane proposal 合理的建议
sanguinary a. 血淋淋的;残忍的;动辄处以死刑的;残虐的;死伤甚多的
sanguinary conflict 流血冲突
sanguinary rule 血腥统治
sanguis 1.血;血亲 2.领主对流血案件的审判权
sanitary a. 卫生的,关于环境卫生的;清洁的
sanitary and fire-protection regulation 卫生及消防规章
sanitary code 卫生法规
sanitation n. 环境卫生,公共卫生;公共卫生设施;卫生科学的实施
sanity n. 精神健全,头脑清醒;公正
sanity hearing 对精神状态问题的预审
sanity trial 对精神状态问题的隔离审讯
sans 没有,无
sans frais 免费
sans nombre 没有限制(数)
sans phrase 直率之言,直截了当
sans recours 无追索权
＊*Sapiens omnia agit cum concilio.* A wise man does everything advisedly. 智者每做一事均慎重考虑而为之;智者做事,慎veatherbr 为之。
＊*Sapienta legis nummario pretio non est aestimanda.* The wistom of the law cannot be measured by money. 法律名言不能用金钱衡量。
＊*Sapienta supplet aetatem.* Wisdom supplies the want of age. 老年需要智慧。
sapphism n. 女子同性恋爱
Sarbane-Oxley Act (美国2002年制定的)《沙氏法》(该法关于公司治理制度之强化,采取改善措施,以及对董事独立性

与审计委员会之制度加以规范均有论述)
satellite n. 1.卫星 2.附庸国;附属品;随从人员
Satellite Convention 《卫星公约》(在版权领域指"关于播送人造卫星传播载有节目的信号公约")
satellite Litigation (美民事诉讼中的)管辖的属地原则诉讼(亦译卫星诉讼)
satellite reconnaissance 卫星侦察
satellite rules 推论的规则,附属的规则
satellite state 卫星国
satellite surveillance 卫星监视
satisdare (大陆法)对委任人的债的担保
satisdatio (由一方对诉讼作出的)担保
satisfaction n. 1.赔偿,偿还;履行义务;补偿,赔偿物 2.满足,满意;清偿(指可用其他东西来代替约定的东西以清偿欠债) 3.报复;决斗
satisfaction of judgment 执行判决书;(指1.根据判决完全清偿了债务;2.存档或归入记录的文件指明判决已被执行支付)
satisfaction on the roll 按记录账目清偿
satisfaction piece 债已做清偿的清单;履行义务证明书
satisfactory a. 令人满意的;(合同)令当事人满意的;(证据)充分的
satisfactory evidence 充分证据
satisfactory remedies 充分的救济,满意的救济
satisfied term (18世纪)偿还期,履行期;土地年限(指土地年限,即在此限期届满之前使其创设目的得以实现或履行)
satisfy v. 1.偿还,补偿,赔偿 2.履行;满足,解决 3.确信
satisfy the liabilities 清偿债务
satisfy the prescriptive period 完成时效期
＊*Satius est petere fontes quam sectari rivulos.* It is better to seek the source than to follow the streamlets. 寻找源头胜于沿着小溪走穷途末路(办案要看主流不要看支流。应追根求源,而不应舍本逐末)。
satrap n. 1.(古波斯帝国的)行省总督 2.(属地的)统治者,殖民总督 3.暴吏,爪牙
saturnine a. 铅的

saturnine poisoning 铅中毒
saturnism n. 铅中毒
satute of mortmain 永久营业法
Satyr 萨蒂尔(指希腊神话中的森林之神,酒神的侍从,总是吃喝玩乐,生活淫荡,和神女们一起鬼混。后遂以萨蒂尔喻指性欲无度的男人、色情狂)
satyriasis n. 男性色情狂
saucerman n. 星球人,外太空人
sauvegarde de justice 司法保护(法国1968年1月的法律对成年人免受无行为能力而引起的伤害的保护方式做了改革。以前主要通过司法程序取消成年人的缔约能力,这一策略已被新的保护方式所代替)
save v. 1.救,挽救,搭救 2.储存,储蓄;节省 3.保全,保留;不失……时机
save harmless 免受无辜(=hold harmless。见 save harmless clause)
save harmless clause 免受无辜条款(指一方当事人同意对方关于可对他主张的权利请求或诉讼同意补偿并免受无辜的文据条款)
save(或 surrender to) one's bail 保释后如期出庭
(to) save one's face 保全面子
save one's neck 免受绞刑
saving a./n. 保留的,除外的;救助,补偿的;节约的,储蓄的/1.搭救,挽救 2.节约,节俭 3.(复)储蓄,存款
saving account trust 储蓄账户信托(指以一个名义开立而以另一人为信托受益人的储蓄账户。见 totten trust)
saving bargain 保本交易
saving clause 但书;(美)保留条款[指在保持某些权利、救济和(特权)优惠的法规中的一种限制,法规中条文规定如果部分法规被宣布违宪,其余法规如果可以自立并不违宪仍属有效。见 separability clause]
savings account book 银行存折
savings and loan association 信用合作社,储蓄放款协会(指一种储蓄和住宅贷款机构),(美)储蓄贷款协会
savings bank 储蓄银行
savings deposit 储蓄存款
savings of society 团体储蓄
savings stamp 储蓄印花(存款单)
savour v. 具有……的特点,与……相近
saw n. 格言,名言,谚语
Saxon-lage n. 西撒克逊人法律(=West Saxon-lage)
say n. 意见,发言机会,发言权(常用 the say);决定权
say about 估计;大约;未定的数
say that 据说……
say-so n. 无证据的断言,并无证据的个人声明,最后决定权,权威,权威性判断,随口一说的话
sb.'s goods and chattels 某人的全部财产
scab n. 不加入工会的工人,不参加工会或罢工而接替罢工工人工作的工人
scaffold n. 断头台,绞刑架
scald n./v. 烫伤/烫,烫伤
scale n./v. 1.标准刻度,标度;等级 2.比例;比率;规模 3.(复)天平/1.调节,衡量 2.过磅,用秤称
scale down (按比例)缩减,降低
scale economic 按比例的经济
scale free 任意尺度的,无标尺的
scale merit 规模适当所产生的利益
scale of assessment 评定,估价比例
scale of penalty 刑罚等级,刑罚标准
scale variable 按比例变量
scallywag (=scalawag) n. 恶棍,流氓,无赖
scalper n. 投机倒把者(指倒卖门票的人)
scamp n. 流氓,坏蛋,无赖;拦路强盗
scan v. 细察,审视,浏览;(用电子装置)核验;扫描
scandal n. 1.丑事,丑闻;干丑事的人 2.流言蜚语;恶意诽谤
scandal sheet 揭人隐私的报纸或杂志;黄色报刊
scandal-monger n. 恶意中伤者,传播丑闻者
scandalous a. 恶意中伤的,诽谤的,丢人现眼的;令人反感至极的
scandalous matter 诽谤性事件
scandalous statement 诽谤性陈述,诽谤他人名誉的声明
scandalum magnatum 诋毁权贵
Scandinavian jurisprudence 斯堪的纳维

亚法学
Scandinavian law 斯堪的纳维亚法(中世纪日耳曼法的一部分,最初创于挪威、瑞典和丹麦,并由此扩展到冰岛、格陵兰岛、法罗群岛、芬兰、大不列颠和爱尔兰部分地区以及诺曼底)
Scandinavian legal realism 斯堪的纳维亚现实主义法学(简称斯堪的纳维亚法学,创始人是瑞典乌普萨拉大学教授海耶斯特勒姆)
Scandinavian school of law 斯堪的纳维亚法学派
scanty knowledge of the law 对法律一知半解,法律知识贫乏
scapegoat n. 替罪羊,代人受过
scapegoatism n. 抛出替罪羊,透过,卸罪
scapegrace n. 恶棍,无赖,流氓
scar n./v. 伤疤,伤痕;(精神上的)创伤/结疤,愈合;使留有伤疤
scar-face n. 脸上有刀伤的人,脸上有伤疤的人
scarcity value 缺货价格
scare n./v. 惊恐,恐慌/恐吓,受惊
scare a confession 吓得招供
scare buying 恐怕物资缺乏而大量购买;抢购
scare-monger n. 散布骇人谣言的人
scarcely adv. 仅仅,刚刚;几乎不,简直不,几乎没有;绝不,不很,大概不
scarlet-letter 红A字(美国在殖民地时期用此标志通奸罪,常将此符号戴在有此罪的妇女身上)
scarlet-letter punishment 见 shame sanction
scarlet-letter sentence 见 shame sanction
scathing a. 严厉的,尖刻的
scathing liability with a defense of contributory negligence 保护受伤者疏忽的严格责任
scatology n. 淫秽的作品;淫书的研究
scavenging n. 废品利用(计算机犯罪手段之一,指有目的、有选择地利用在废弃的资料、磁带、磁盘中搜寻具有潜在价值的数据、信息和密码等来达到犯罪目的)
scenario n. 剧情说明,方案;电影剧本
scene n. 出事地点,(犯罪)现场;情景,实况

scène à faire (法)戏剧的精彩部分(按法国著作权法,这部分并无特殊的著作权保护,因为它是剧作中的一部分的自然表现)
scene of a traffic accident 交通事故现场,交通事故发生地点
scene of crime 犯罪现场,作案现场
scene of death 死亡现场,尸体现场
scenic sites 名胜风景点
sceptre n. 君主的节杖(权位的象征);君权;统治权
schedule n./v. 1.一览表,目录;明细表;程序表,议事日程 2.附表(指附在法例和法律文件里的表格、清单等);/列表;列入计划表(或程序表、时间表);(美)安排,排定
schedule of cases 诉讼案件(开)庭(日)期表
schedule of charges 官方税率
schedule of concessions 关税减让表
schedule of terms and conditions 税率表;收费率表
scheduled period (民事时效的)预定时间(亦称除斥时间,指法律对某种权利所规定的存续期间)
scheduled prices 按预定价格
scheduled rotation system 按期轮换制
scheduled time 指定时间
schedules of concessions 减让表
scheduling order 发布日程安排命令,日程安排令(指美国民事诉讼审理前的程序之一,案件中各项设定时限的命令。按《联邦民事诉讼规则》第16条要求法院就地方规则予以免除外,所有案件均应发出日程安排令)
scheme n. 1.计划,方案;系统体制;配合,组合;摘要,图解 2.诡计,阴谋
scheme for collective settlement 清偿债务的共同方案
scheme for power 阴谋夺权
scheme of arrangement 债务协议(指债权人和债务人商量清偿债务的协议,以避免债务人宣告破产);(公司法)债务和解方案
scheme of composition 偿还部分欠款而了结债务的协议

scheme of compromise or arrangement 和解或偿债安排协议
scheme of liquidation and reconstruction 清算与重建协议
schemer n. 1.阴谋家 2.计划人,设计人
scheming a. 1.诡计多的,诡诈的 2.计划的,设计的
schism n. (组织)分裂(为几个小派系);分裂宗教(或教会)罪,宗派
schizophrenia n. 精神分裂症(该症是以基本个性改变、思维、情感及行为的分裂、精神活动与环境的不协调为主要特征的一类常见精神病,对于这类病人刑事责任能力的评定,国内外司法精神医学鉴定实践评定为有完全刑事责任能力)
schizophrenosis n. 精神分裂症,早发痴呆症
schizotypal personality disorder 分裂样人格障碍(指人格障碍类型中的一种,它是以观念、行为和外貌装饰的奇特、情感冷漠及人际关系明显缺陷为特点。男性多于女性。见 paranoid personality disorder)
scholar n. 学者
scholarship n. 学术成就
scholastic theories of law 经院法学
scholastical school 宗教哲学派
scholasticism n. 宗教哲学(派)
school n. 学派;流派;理论;学院;书院;经院;(复)学术界
school desegregation 学校取消种族隔离
school district (美)学区[指由立法机构创设的一个州的政治分区,并授予地方自治权(local power of self-government),在这个地域范围,可以建设、维修、提供资金来支持公立学校,并在其他方面资助州尽其管理教育的职责]
school of commentator 评论法学派(见 school of post-glossators)
school of comparative jurisprudence 比较法学派
school of experimentation 实证学派
school of judicial realism 实在主义法学派
school of law 法学院
school of natural law 自然法学派
(the) school of post-glossators 后期注释法学派(亦称评论法学派),评论法学派(指ección大利14—15世纪的一个法学学派)
school of social utilitarianism 社会功利派
school segregation 学校种族隔离
school-age child 学龄儿童
schools of jurisprudence 法理学的学派
science n. 1.科学,学科;科学研究;自然科学 2.专门技术;技术,知识,学(问)
science of civil law 民法学
science of civil liberty 公民自由科学
science of criminal investigation 刑事侦查学
science of criminal law 刑法学
science of human nature 人性科学(指早期苏格兰的法学中不少法学者研究人性世俗化和试验化)
science of international economic law 国际经济法学
science of international organizations 国际组织学
science of law 法学,法律科学
science of positive law 实证法学,实在法学
science of public administration 行政学
science of training police dogs 警犬学,训练警犬学
scienter n. 明知,知情;故意(指在若干民事或刑事诉讼中,原告必须证明被告的行为或罪行是出于故意,才能构成违法或犯罪);诈欺的故意
scientia fraudis 欺诈知情(指提起撤销转让行为之诉的基本条件之一)
scientia rei alienae 明知物为他人的
* *Scientia sciolorum est mixta ignorantia.* The knowledge of smatterers is diluted ignorance. 一知半解的人的知识只不过是被冲淡了的无知。(处理法律问题)一知半解等于无知。
scientific a. 科学的,学术的;精通学理的;有系统的
scientific association 科学协会
scientific body 科学团体
scientific community 科学团体;科学界
scientific method of hypothesis 科学的假设方法
scientific verification 科学鉴定

scientism n. 科学态度,科学方法,唯科学主义
scilicet 就是说,即
scintilla 火花;一点点;极少;痕迹;微粒
scintilla juris 法定占有的可能性;法律拟制的微薄占有权益
scintilla of evidence (一点点)微弱的证据,无力的证据
scintilla of evidence rule (美)微弱证据规则(指普通法上的一项规则,案件中只要有任何证据,即使微弱,也可产生一定的法律后果。各法庭对于什么样证据为微弱证据主张不一,目前美国已摒弃这一原则)
scintilla test (美)微弱证据测评(见 *scintilla of evidence rule*。亦称 *scintilla rule*)
sciolist n. 一知半解的人,冒充博学者
scion n. 子孙,后裔
scire facias 告知令状(指法院指示司法行政官告知曾在法院记录在案取得裁决或特许证的人为何原因得不到裁决或特许的利益以及使之无效的原因的令状)
scission system 分割制
scofflaw n. 藐视(或违犯)法律(法令)者[尤指一些违反法律者在车上携带人体模特儿,旨在以合伙用车(carpool)驱车于背道上];故意违犯禁酒法者
scold n./v. 干扰邻里的妇女,好骂街的泼妇/骂詈,叱责
scope n. 界限;范围;视野;机会
scope of application 适用范围
scope of authority 委托权限;授权范围
scope of cover 责任范围
scope of delegated authority 代理权限
scope of employment 就业机会,就业范围
scope of judicial latitude 司法自由的范畴
scope of law 法律界限
scope of official duty 职责范围
scope of validity 效力范围
scopolagnia n. 窥阴症,窥阴癖(见 *voyeurism*;*sexual perversion*)
score n. 1.刻痕;伤疤 2.账record;(复)大量,许多 3.理由,根据
scot n. 税款;分配的负担(额),负担;应分担的给付

scot and lot 普通税;分担财政负担,按能力支付教区税
scot-and-lot borough (英)按能力纳税的自治市
Scot's Charitable Society 苏格兰慈善会
scotch n./v. 刻痕;砍痕;划伤/弄伤;镇压;制止
Scotch n. 苏格兰人
Scotch cousin 远亲
Scotch law 苏格兰法律
Scotch marriage (苏格兰法)苏格兰式结婚,苏格兰式婚姻[指经过双方同意的(订约或)诺成合同(consensual contract)而无必要的正式仪式的婚姻。直到1940年,苏格兰法保留了中世纪宗教法的婚姻体制(forms of marriage),即自双方同意之时立即成为夫妻的婚姻(marriage *per verba de presenti*)和婚约后肉体接触构成的婚姻(marriage *per verba futuro subsequente copula*)。这些允诺构成非正规但有效的婚姻。苏格兰法现仍保留通过习惯式同居并为公众承认的(cohabitation with habit and repute)同居而构成的非正规婚姻。没有仪式需要证明的这种婚姻,但夫妻一方去世后,存活的一方或其任一子女均可获得法院对婚姻存在的确认(confirmation),这完全基于邻居、朋友以及家庭的普遍信任或相信]
Scotch verdict 1.苏格兰式判决(虽无证据,但不判"无罪",而暂判"未证实")2.非最终的决定;未最后定局的事
scot-free a. 1.免于受罚的;未受损害的;免税的 2.逍遥法外(和 *go* 或 *get off* 连用)
Scots law 苏格兰法
Scottish Enlightenment 苏格兰启蒙运动(指18世纪初期,苏格兰的法学文化繁荣情况)
scoundrel n./a. 恶棍,流氓/卑鄙的,恶棍般的
scoundrelism n. 恶棍性格,恶棍行为,无赖
scour v. 搜索;追寻;擦洗;惩罚
scour after sb. 追寻其人
scour the city for the thief 全城搜索盗贼
scour the country 四处搜索;八方寻找
scource of obligation 债的发生根据

scourge n./v. 鞭,笞;刑具;惩罚;灾难根源/鞭打;严斥;惩罚
scout n./v. 侦察,侦察兵/侦察;寻找,蔑视地拒绝(提议、意见等)
scout-car n. 警察巡逻车
scrag v. 掐住……脖子;(俚)勒死,绞死
scramble v. 争夺,抢夺(for);改变频率使(电话)不被窃听
scrambler n. 扰频器,保密器
scrap n./v. 1.(俚)吵嘴,打架,斗殴 2.少许,点滴/1.打架,斗殴,吵嘴 2.拆毁,废弃
scrap certificate 拆毁许可证
scrap value 残值
scrape v. 1.刮,擦;擦伤 2.积蓄,凑集 3.擦过,勉强通过
scratch v. 1.搔伤,抓伤,擦伤 2.勾销,画线涂掉 3.(美)支持本党大部分候选人,但将若干票投给党外人士;在(政党候选人)名单上勾去一些名字以示反对
scratch one's head 搔头皮;(对某事)迷惑不解(over)
screed n. 1.(古法律中的)事故陈述书;呈文;冗长文章 2.要求收回(物等)的清单
screen v. 筛,筛分;甄别,审查;包庇,掩护
screen credit 因发行电影拷贝而支付的版税
screen offender 包庇罪犯
screen visa applications 审查护照签证申请书
screening n. 甄别,审查;调查
screening committee 甄别委员会
screw n. (英)(监狱)看守员,拇指夹(旧时刑具);吝啬鬼,守财奴,心狠手辣的卖(或买)主;(英俚)薪水
scriba 书记官,秘书,大臣
scriba regis 国务大臣,大法官
scribe n./v. (古时)犹太法学家;文牍,书记;作家,新闻记者/书写,铭刻;刻以标记
* *Scribere est agere.* To write is to act. Treasonable words set down in writing amount to overt acts of treason. 写下文字即行为。/写下叛逆文字即构成叛逆行为。
scrip (=scrip certificate) n. 1.临时收据,凭证,股单 2.字条(指收条、表格等) 3.临时通货(证券)

scrip dividend 以后兑现的股票红利证书
scrip-holder n. 凭证持有人
script n. 1.手迹;笔迹;手稿 2.原件;正本
scripture n. 权威性著作,手稿,文件;经文,经典,(大写)圣经
scrivener n. 代笔人;代书人;公证人
scroll n. 名册;(在签名后的)画押
scruple n./v. 迟疑不安,踌躇/有顾虑,感到迟疑不安
scrupulous a. 严格认真的,审慎的,拘泥细节的,多顾虑的
scrutator n. (古英国法上的)(护卫皇室利益的)水上监督员;观察者,调查者,检查者
scrutineer n. (英)选票检查人,监票人;检查人
scrutinize v. 细看,细阅;仔细检查
scrutiny n. 细阅;详尽研究;监视;对选票的复查,调查投票(是否正当合法),仔细检查
scrutiny of character 品德审查
scrutiny of state regulations 对州法规的监察
scum of a nation 民族败类
scurrility n. 粗鲁的语言,庸俗下流,漫骂
scurrilous a. 语言粗鄙的,庸俗的
scurry off 窜逃,匆忙逃开
scutage (或 **escuage**) n. (中世纪采邑法)免兵役税
scuttle v. 1.(船底钻孔)使船沉没,凿沉;全部毁坏;全部放弃 2.急促奔跑(away,off)
scuttling n. 故意弃船
scyra (英旧时的)郡;郡民,郡的居民
se defendendo 防御,自卫
sea n. 海,海洋
sea bed 海床
sea board 海岸线;沿海地区
sea captain (商船)船长
sea carriage 海洋运输
sea damage 海损
sea farer 海员,水手
sea going vessel 远洋船舱
Sea-Law of Rhodes 《罗得海法》(指公元600—800年间在罗得编撰的法典,其中包括《罗得弃货法》。根据此法,如果船舶遇

难,需保船舶安全及必要物资,因而将部分货物投弃。这样,所有船主及货主则应分担损失。此为共同海损之渊源)
sea laws 海洋法
sea lawyer 好争辩的水手;懂法律的水手
sea letter 海上通行证;中立国船舶证明书
sea line 海岸线;海平线
sea marks 航海标记(指灯塔、浮标、指向标等)
sea mile 海里
sea port 海港,港市
sea power 海军强国;制海权;海上力量,海权
sea protest 海事报告书
sea ridge 海脊
sea rights 领海权
sea robber 海盗,海贼
sea rover 海盗;海盗船
sea warfare 海战
Sea-Bed Disputes Chamber 海底争端法庭
sea-carrier n. 从事海运者
sea-dog n. 有经验的海员(或水手);海豹
sea-fishing n. 海洋捕鱼
sea-going a. 海上的,航海的,从事航海事业的
sea-going ship (vessel) 远洋轮
sea-jet-one n. 海空联运
sea-launched ballistic missile 海上发射的弹道导弹
sea-launched cruise missile 海上发射的巡航导弹
sea-lift(或 **sealift**)(=seahaul) n. 海上运输
sea-pass(=sea letter) n. 海上通行证
sea-risk n. 海险(海上保险)
Seabed Committee of United Nations 联合国海底委员会
seaborne a. 海运的
seaborne trade 海运贸易,海运
seafarer n. 海员,水手;海上旅行者
seafaring a. 海上旅行的,航海的
seafaring class 海员级别
seafaring man 海员
seal n./v. 盖印;印章;火漆;封条,封铅;密封;保证/1.盖印;密封 2.确证,保证;批准
seal a bargain 成交

seal envelop trick 密封的信封圈套(指海事贸易利用单据的欺诈行为之一)
seal of the state 国玺
seal of the court 法庭印鉴
sealed a. 盖印的;经盖章批准或证实的;密封的
sealed commission 经盖章批准的授权
sealed contract 正式合同(契约),有法律效力的合同(契约);有签署(或盖章)的合同(契约)
sealed instrument 有签名盖章的文据
sealed orders 密封命令
sealed promises 正式承诺
sealed verdict 密封裁决,经签字盖章的裁决
sealer n. 盖章人;检查度量衡的官吏
sealing n. 盖章,盖印
sealing of contracts 合同(契约)的签署盖印
sealing of records (罪犯)案卷的密封(未经法庭同意不得启封)
sealing oneself 闭关锁国;自我封闭
sealing up, distraint, or freezing of property 对财产的查封、扣押或冻结
sealless a. 未盖印的(文件等)
seaman n. 海员,水手,精通海事者
seaman's papers 海员证书
seaman's status 海员的身份,海员资格
seamanship n. 航海技术,良好船员之能力
Seanad Eireann (爱尔兰共和国的)参议院
search n./v. 搜寻,搜查;探求;调查,研究;检查/搜寻;搜查;探查;调查,研究
search a house 搜查住宅
search and seizure 搜查与扣押
search book 检索书
search for smuggler 缉私;搜索走私犯
search for violations of ban 查禁
search in workplace (美)工作场所的搜查(指雇主对雇员的办公室、写字台、柜子、邮件以及人身侵入和检查的一种行为。在美国曾经出现过许多因雇主搜查而产生的侵权案件)
search incident to arrest 逮捕时的附带搜查(指警官只要有权逮捕某个人,不管有无搜查证,为了搜查凶器都可对该人人身

及在实施逮捕的附近地区进行搜查)
search into a matter 调查事件
search upon arrest 搜捕
search warrant 搜查令(状);(住宅等的)搜查证
search warrant rules, exceptions to 搜查令规则的例外(指美国联邦宪法第四修正案保护民众不受不合理的搜查,而且联邦最高法院已作出结论:无搜查令的搜查,即使有相当理由,也是"本身不合理"的。不过也有例外情况,如无法取得搜查令或明示、暗示不同意搜查。同样,如果事实和情况排除了任何合理的侵犯隐私的预期,那么无须搜查令。搜查令规则的例外包括但不仅限于以下情况:合法逮捕所附带的搜查或者为确保安全所必须的搜查,诸如"令停与搜身"程序;海关、边境和机构官员的检查;经嫌犯同意进行的检查;依照政府的合法行为所进行的检查;一眼就能看出的证物的检查;对学生所带物的检查。这一标准同样适用所有的搜查令或无搜查令的搜查)
search without warrant 无证搜查
searcher n. 搜查者,检查者;搜寻者
searches n. 调查地产负担(指通常购买地产的人向地产登记处去打听该地有无负担,如抵押等)
searches incident to lawful arrests 附带搜查
searching enquiry 深入调查
searching examination 彻底考察,彻底审查
searching question 追究,追查到底
seashore n. 海岸,海边地带
seasonable a. 合理时间范围的,及时的,适合时机的
seasonable business 季节性营业
seat n./v. 位置,所在地;席位;合法资格;住宅/就职,登记,入座
seat(ed) belt (系于飞机座位上的)安全带,汽车座位上的安全带
seat doctrine 住所说[亦称本座说,该学说其实有很多变种,例如总部所在地标准、实际管理地标准等。与设立说(incorporation doctrine)相反,该学说不考虑公司在哪个国家设立,而只看公司总部或实际管理机构所在地,然后以此地国家的法律作为公司的身份法]
seat in parliament 议会里占有议席
seat of business 营业所
seat of government 政府所在地
seat of justice (古英国法中)(御猎林场)法庭
seated magistracy 坐着的治安官(指法庭上坐着听审的法官)
seating capacity 载客人数(定员)
seaward boundary 向海界(限)
seaworthiness n. (船只的)适航性,适航能力,适航状态,适航,适航安全能力
seaworthy a. 适于航海的(船)(指按照商船法,船舶的构造、设备、海员均符合该法的要求标准)
secede (from) v. (从宗教、政治等组织中)退出;脱离
seceding unit 脱离单位
secession n. 分裂(指国际法上国家的一部分脱离母国而独立)
secession convention 脱离协定,脱离会议
seclusion of chambers 隔开法官室
seclusionist n. 闭关自守者
seck a. 不生产的;无利益的;无结果的
second a. 第二的,次要的,次等的
Second Amendment 美国联邦宪法第二修正案[该修正案作为《权利法案》(Bill of Rights)的一部分获得批准。该修正案规定:"管理良好的民兵,是保障自由各州的安全所必需的,因此人民持有和携带武器的权利不得侵犯。"这一规定引起对枪支管理的广泛争议,主张严格管理枪支者认为该修正案本意是保护各州维持军事系统的集体权利,而反对者则认为该修正案旨在保护个人权利。但联邦最高法院对该修正案的解析中却对此项权利进行了严格地限制,旨在使美国国会享有对枪支的占有和买卖进行限制的自由。该修正案仅适用于联邦政府,并不可阻止州制定符合其意愿的任何枪支控制的立法。有关武器控制的争论已经成为并将在未来很长一段时间里成为美国政治生活的一部分。一方面拥有武器的人增多,另一方面要求更为严格地管控枪支,这就使得美国联邦宪法第二修正案的争论继续下去,

也是联邦最高法院必须面对的问题]
second appeal 再上诉
second arrest 第二次拘捕(指拘捕释放后,不得就同一罪名来另请发拘捕状而做第二次拘捕)
second auction 再拍卖
second ballot 第二轮(次)投票(指投票人在获票最多的两名预选候选人之间进行一次选择,以避免候选人以少数票当选)
Second Banking Coordination Directive (SBCD 1989) 第二银行协作指令
second benefiary(或 beneciary) 第二受益人
second brief 第二次(律师的)辩护状
second chamber (荷兰议会的)二院;(大写)(荷兰)众议院
second chief judge 次首席法官
second class wife 第二房妻子
second cousin 从兄弟姐妹;从表兄弟姐妹;远房堂表兄弟姐妹
Second Decennial (美)《第二个十年判决摘要汇编》(系指由西方出版公司出版的自1907年至1916年的判决摘要汇编)
second degree 二亲等
second degree burglary 二等夜盗(指在白天带着犯罪意图,打开并进入无人或当时有人居住的住宅的行为)
second degree crime (美)二级犯罪[指根据罪行严重程度和相应的量刑,将犯罪分成的等级。二级犯罪指轻于一级犯罪(first degree crime)的犯罪情节。许多州将犯罪分为一、二、三三个等级,并有相应的量刑]
second degree murder (美)二级谋杀罪(指无谋杀故意、情节不及一等谋杀罪严重者。见 murder of the first degree)
second dimensions in the argument 第二层次的理论,论点上的第二层次
second deliverance 发还扣押财物的再次通知书
Second Development Decade (联合国)第二个发展十年
second distress 第二次扣押;从属扣押物
second division (英)监狱中的中等待遇(指监狱中对犯人的分级待遇)

Second Employers' Liability Cases 第二雇主责任案件(见 223U. S. 1, 169, 56, L, Ed. 327,1912)
second estate (英)上议院全体贵族议员;(欧洲封建时代的)二等贵族
Second Financial Markets Promotion Act (德)《第二金融市场促进法案》
second hall 第二厅,第二室,(法院)第二庭
second house (戏剧)第二场
second instance 二审
Second Institute(Coke's) 柯克的第二本《法理概要》(主要对大宪章和其他中世纪成文法及一些后期成文法的评论)
(the) Second International 第二国际(1839年成立于巴黎的国际共产主义组织)
second level dilemma 第二层次两难的选择
second lien 留置权
second marriage 再婚
second mortgage 第二次抵押
second of exchanges (一式三份中的)第二张汇票
second offence 再犯,第二次犯罪;重犯
second option 第二选择权(指业主收回城市土地保有人出让其土地保有权时的权利)
second party 第二方,乙方
second petition 再次诉请
second reading (议会提案的)二读
(the) (first) second secretary of embassy 大使馆(一)二等秘书
second stor(e)y (或 floor 或 second-storey man) 夜盗,窃贼(尤指从楼上窗口进入行窃的)
second stor(e)y man 窃贼(尤指从楼上窗户进入的小偷)
second thought(s) 重新考虑(而得出的意见)
(the) Second World 第二世界
second-guess(ing) v. (在劝告或批评人或解决过去问题时)用事后聪明;放马后炮;预言,猜测
second-hand a./n. 1.用过的,旧的;经营旧货的 2.中间的,媒介的,间接的;第二手的/ 1.媒介人,中间人 2.旧货
second-hand evidence 第二手证据,间接

得来的证据,传闻证据
second-hand market 旧货市场
second-hand witness （陈述听来的事实的）间接证人,陈述从他人听到的证言的证人,根据他人证言作证的证人
second-home tourism 别居旅游
second-rate justice 次等正义
second-tier patent 见 utility model
second-timer n. 第二次犯罪的人
secondary n./a. 副手,次要人物；代理人；（英王座法庭与高等民事法庭的）副书记官/次要的；从属的,附属的；非原始的,间接的
secondary abuse 见 abuse
secondary abuse 间接虐待[指因虐待受到痛苦的儿童,虽然他们的身体未受到虐待,但他们证明在他们的家庭内有家庭暴力(domestic violence)]
secondary authority 次级权威,附属权威（指既是能说服的权威又是对法律的详述的一种注释）
secondary benefits 次位补助金
secondary boycott 间接的联合抵制,第二次联合抵制,第二次杯葛（指涉及经营的公司及人工会的雇员的联合抵制。见 primary boycott）
secondary cause 次要原因
secondary caution 第二次警示
secondary credit（或 **secondary L/C**）从属信用证
secondary embargo 二类禁运
secondary evidence 辅助证据；间接证据；次要证据（指主要证据外的证据,如果可得到主要证据时,它即可被摒弃）
secondary financing 间接融资,次要贷款,间接筹措资金
secondary functions 第二位作用（见 primary functions）
secondary heir 次等继承人
secondary income 次要收益,非营业收入,非营业收益
secondary industry 第二产业（又称制造业）
secondary infringement 二次侵权
secondary legislation 辅助立法；第二次立法
secondary liability 从属债务,第二位责任
secondary market 次级市场
secondary materials 二次文献
secondary meaning of words 法律词句的引申义；(商标法中保护业主使用某一商标名的)引申义说
Secondary Mortgage Market Enhancement Act (美)1984年制定的《二级按揭市场加强法》
secondary motion 先入为主的动议；再次（向法院提出诉讼的）申请
secondary party （流通票据的）出票人（或背书人）,次位当事人
secondary performance 从属给付
secondary products 次级产品,副产品
secondary register 登记簿副本
secondary right 次位权利；从权利
secondary rule 次要规则,次级规则
secondary scene 第二现场
secondary sheriff （英）（伦敦城的）副司法行政官
secondary signature 副署
secondary source of law 从属法源,派生法源；法的次要渊源（又译：次要法律渊源）；次要法源；二次法律文献
secondary sources （美）二次文献（二次文献资料是法律文献目录中的一个重要部分,其中包括教科书、论文、律师业务手册、评论、重述以及为开业律师、学者和学生解释或评述法律的期刊等）
secondary use 第二用益权,次位用益权
secondary wife 妾,偏房
seconded officer 调用人员,调派官员
seconder n. 附议人,赞成（某项议案的）人,赞助人
seconding of a motion 附和动议
secondment n. （英）暂调,调用（指由一个机构调另一机构,资历不受影响）
secrecy n. 秘密；秘密状态；保密；保密习惯,保密能力；守秘密,不坦白
secret a./n. 秘密的,机密的；隐蔽的,暗藏的；暗中进行的/秘密,机密；隐藏[指①保持不让他人知晓的某些事或只让相关的人知道（见 state secret; trade secret）；②不得

违背信托义务(breach of trust)去泄露信息,特别是律师与当事人之间的关系所获得的信息,并且当事人曾经要求保守秘密(keep private)或律师认为如果信息披露会给当事人带来麻烦,或可能带来损失。根据美国律师协会的《职业责任法规》,律师不得泄露当事人的秘密,除非充分披露得到当事人的同意,参见《惩戒性规则》第4-101条(DR. 4-101)。见 confidence 3]

secret agent 特工人员,特务,间谍
secret alliance 秘密同盟
secret arrest 秘密逮捕
secret ballot 无记名投票,秘密投票
secret clause 秘密条款
secret code 密(电)码,暗号
secret company 不公开公司
secret diplomacy 秘密外交
secret document 机密文件
secret election 秘密选举
secret errand 密使
secret inquiry 秘密调查
secret investigation 秘密调查,秘密侦查
secret judg(e)ment 秘密宣判
secret language 密语
secret law 秘密法
secret lien (出卖人已将出卖物交付给买受人后为了保证获得价款,并不让任何第三人知情而设置的)秘密留置权
secret matters 秘密事件
secret police 秘密警察
secret poll 秘密投票
secret process 秘密制造方法(指一种虽非专利但受法律保护的产品的制作方法)
secret prostitution 暗娼,私娼
secret protocol 秘密议定书
Secret Service United States Secret Service 的缩略,见该词条
secret service fund 政府的机密费
secret society 秘密会社,帮会
secret testament 密封遗嘱
secret treaty 秘密条约
secret trust 秘密信托(立遗嘱人要把产业遗赠给一个人,要他为另一人的利益作信托保管,被信托人要表示他愿接受这一任务,并表明交给他的产业是信托的)

secret voting 秘密投票
secretarial staff 秘书人员
(the) Secretariat n. (联合国)秘书处
secretary n. 秘书,书记,大臣,部长,干事,文书[指①行政助手;②负责公司往来公函、董事会议记录,以及股票拥有和转让的记载档案的公司高级职员,亦称为 clerk of the corporation;③议会法(parliamentary law)负责审议会审议事项记录(deliberative assembly's proceedings)的官员。亦称 clerk; recorder; recording secretary; recording officer; scribe]
Secretary for Foreign Affairs (英)外交大臣
Secretary General (联合国)秘书长
Secretary of Agriculture (美)农业部长(指美国总统的内阁成员,领导美国农业部工作)
Secretary of Commerce (美)商业部长(指美国总统的内阁成员,负责领导美国商业部工作)
Secretary of Defense (War) (美)国防部长
Secretary of Department of State (美)国务卿
secretary of embassy 外交官员[指任命为秘书或助理的外交官员,通常是为大使或全权公使(minister plenipotentiary)担任秘书或助理]
Secretary of Health and Human Services (美)卫生与公共服务部长
Secretary of Interior (美)内政部长
Secretary of Justice (英)司法大臣
Secretary of Party Committee (中)党委书记
Secretary of State (英)国务大臣;(美)国务卿;州的高级行政长官
Secretary of State for Employment (英)就业大臣
Secretary of (或 for) State for Foreign (Home) Affairs (英)外交(内政)大臣
Secretary of State for War (英)国防大臣
Secretary of Treasury (美)财政部长
Secretary of Veterans Affairs (美)退伍军人事务部长

secrete v. 窝藏;隐匿;私行侵吞
secretion n. 隐匿,隐藏
secta 随同原告作证者(指随同原告一起到法庭为他作证的人或随他一起出庭的人);(英)(古代法律中)审理中的案件;诉讼,到庭
section n. 1.(条文中的)条(指制定法中经常分章、条、款、段、项等的条)2.地区,地段;切开;断面
section eight 1.(美俚)(由于身心不适服役的)退役(也指由此而退役的军人)2.精神不正常者
sector n. 扇形,扇形面;部分,成分;部门
sector of the economy 经济成分
sector principle 扇形原则(指有些国家依据扇形原则,对其靠近南北极的一块扇形陆地或冰冻的海洋主张主权要求)
sector search 地段搜查(见 zone search)
secular a. 现世的,世俗的,非宗教的
secular and social state 政教分离的国家
secular court 非宗教法庭,世俗法庭
secular law 世俗法(律)
secular power 非宗教权力,世俗的权力
secularization of the civil law 民法世俗化
secundum 根据,依照,按照;由
secundum bonos mores 依历来惯例,照例
secundum formam doni 按照赠与或财产赠与的方式
secundum forman statuli 照法令,依法规
secundum juris 根据法律
secundum legem 根据法规
secundum legem communem 依普通法
secundum legem domicilli, vel loci contractus 依照住所法或缔约地法(见 *lex loci contractus*)
secundum naturam 依照自然,顺其自然
secundum norman legis 依照法规
secundum ordinem 依次,按次序
secundum probata 依照证据(指按照审理时提出之证据)
secundum quid 只在某一方面
secundum rationem legis 类推解释
secundum regulam 按照规定
secundum subjectam materiam 根据主旨(重要事实),按照标的物

secundum usum 根据惯例
secundum usum mercatorum 依照商务习惯
secundum vires hereditatis 根据遗产的临时所有权令
secure v./a. 获得;使安全,保卫掩护;保证;为(借款等)作保;向(债权人)提供保证找到/有保证的,有担保的;保险的,安全的
secure a declaratory judgment 获得确权判决
secure an obligation 保证债权
secure claims 保证债权
secured and recognized boundaries 安全和得到承认的边界
secured claim 有担保的债权
secured credit 担保信贷,抵押信贷
secured creditor 有保证的债权人(指具有债权担保品的债权人,如握有抵押品或留置权者)
secured debts 有担保的债务
secured liability (有)担保的债务
secured loan (有)担保的贷款
secured transactions 担保交易,可靠交易
securing of the profit 取得利润
(the) Securities Act (或 law) 《证券法》
Securities and Exchange Commission (美)证券交易委员会
securities and exchange law 有价证券和交易所法
securities borrowing 证券借用(人)
securities exchange 证券交易所
Securities Exchange Act (美)《证券交易法》(1934)
securities in the trust fund 信托基金证券
securities issued 已发证券
securities issued by affiliated companies 联合公司发行的证券
securities regulatory regimes 证券管理体制
securities trading 证券交易
securities without certificates 无单证券
securitization n. 安全性,可靠性
securitization by substitution 替代证券化(即债务证券化)
securitization of cash flows 现金流量的证券化

security n. （15世纪）1.抵押,担保[指用抵押作为担保,以满足债务。特别是对于债权人采取的附加利息偿还或扩大给债务人的信贷(credit)来担保(assurance)] 2.担保人[指受到某种类型担保的约束者,担保人(surety),保证人]3.担保的性质、状态,情况(特别是遇到风险或冲击时)4.文据,产权证明[指持有人在公司(股票)的所有权身份的证明,持有人的债权人(证券)与公司或政府(债券)关系或与持有人的其他权利(买卖的特权或选择权)的关系证明] 5.证券[指美国法语境下,证券的种类繁多,在美国《1933年证券法》(Security Act of 1933)中对证券作了相当宽泛的规定,包括任何票据、股票、库存股票、债券、公司信用债券、债务凭证、盈利分享协议下的权益证书、以证据作抵押的信用证书、组建前证书、可转让股票、投资合同、股权信托证、证券存款单、石油煤气或其他矿产小额矿产利益滚存权,或被普遍认为是"证券"的任何权益和票据或上述任一种证券的权益或参与证书、暂时或临时证书、收据、担保证书或认股证书或订购权、购买权。参见《1933年证券法》第77b节。这个词条表明基于在普通公司或企业的一项投资利益,而不是参与企业。根据一个重要的法定定义(statutory definition),证券是任一项利益或一个与金融相关的文据,包括票据(note)、股票、国库券(treasury stock)、债券(bond)、无抵押债券或关税凭券(debenture)、负债凭证(evidence of indebtedness)、利息凭单(certificate of interest)或参与分红的协议(profit-sharing agreement)的证明、附属担保信托(collateral trust)的证明、预先组织或预约资金(preorganization certificate or subscription)、可转让的股票或股份(share)、投资合同、表决信托(voting trust)证明、为担保的保证金(deposit)证明等等在油、气、采矿权中部分不可分割的权益的证明或是对于以上的这些事项中任何一项的参与权益的证明或临时的参与证明以及收受、担保、保证取得押金或购买的证明文件等。证券(security)还包括:从事兑、采购、买卖(option)证券或授予任一证券,押金证书,证券系列或特权,或对任何可进入与外国通货相关的国家证券交易所(nation security exchange)设置(device)授予特权。参见《美国注释法典》第15标题卷第77 b(1)节。亦称为(在意义4上) evidence of indebtedness; evidence of debt。见 share 2;stock 1]

security administration 治安管理
Security Administration Punishment Act (中)《治安管理处罚条例》
security agreement 担保合同(契约)
security and protection systems 安全保卫制度
security arrangement 保安措施
security body 保卫部门,保卫机关
security cadre (中)治保干部
security classification 保密级
security clearance 忠贞调查(指选派某人或机构参与国家机密前,调查其是否忠贞可靠)
security company 证券公司
Security Council of the United Nations 联合国安全理事会
security defence 治安保卫
security deposit 身份保证金,不动产租赁押金
security detention 治安拘留
security exceptions 安全例外
security (securities) exchange （1909年）证券交易所[指①有组织的证券特别是股票买卖市场(marketplace)或交易便利之处(facility);②一个有组织的群体或集团创立的交易市场(见 exchange);③此术语通常缩写为 exchange,有时用 stock exchange]
security for costs 讼费保证(指被告可向法庭申请要求原告具备讼费保证。一般理由是原告居住地不在审判管辖范围内,地址不确,而且只是为他人利益提起诉讼等。保证金多少,则由法官判定)
security for debt 债务担保
security for default 不履行义务的担保
security for good behavio(u)r 良好品行保证
security for keeping the peace 保证安分

守己
security for the costs of litigation 诉讼费保证金
security for the performance of an obligation 履行债务的担保
security forces 保安部队
security guards 安全防卫,安全警卫
security in litigation 诉讼担保
security information 机密资料
security instruction 安全指令
security interest(s) (in real property) 物权担保;担保利益(国际贷款担保可分人的担保和物的担保。大陆法系多称物的担保,英美法系则称担保利益),(不动产的)担保物权
security market 证券市场
security measures 保安措施
security mediation committee (中)治安调解委员会
security mom 安全妈妈[系指2004年美国总统选举中的特殊选民群体,她们都是已经结婚的白人母亲,自从9·11恐怖袭击之后,她们就对恐怖威胁、安全问题和伊拉克战争问题格外关注。这一词条构成政治分析家自20世纪60年代以来一直称为"swing group"(关键群体)的成员,这部分选民能使选举结果朝某个特定方向发展。"安全妈妈"即总统竞选中发现的一系列"swing group"中的一个。"安全妈妈"一词来自1996年大选期间出现的词语"soccer mom"(足球妈妈),指的是居住在郊区的有小孩的白人女性,她们经常观摩自己孩子参加的足球比赛。1998年的中期选举中出现了"waitress mom"(服务员妈妈),指的是依靠低收入来养活一家人的妇女,她们大多数都从事服务生工作。在2000年的总统大选中,WMWM(White Married Working Mom)(白人已婚工作妈妈)成为人们关注的焦点。然而,9·11事件之后,WMWM很快变成对恐怖威胁极度关注的群体,这些人后来被称为"security mom"]
security of obligation 债的担保
security of society 社会治安
security of tenure 1.(土地)保有权的保障,租用权担保 2.任期保障
security of tenure employment 雇佣期保障
security of transactions 交易安全
security organ 治安机关
security package "担保篮"(指为了弱化项目风险,贷款人一般要求项目发起人与政府、原材料供应方、承包商、经营者、产品购买者等当事方签订一系列协议、合同,组成"担保篮"将风险划分给有关当事方,以有效权利、义务约束机制划定风险界限)
security pact 安全条约
security personel 治安保卫人员(总称)
security police 治安警察,秘密警察
security price 证券价格
security regulations 治安条例;保密条例,安全条例
security rights 担保权
security risk 可能危及国家安全的人物
security section (中)保卫科,保卫组
security system 国家安全制度,国际安全制度
security transaction 担保交易
security-graded a. 机密的
secus 另外,否则;相反;与相反
sed vide (=But see) 但见[此标号意即后面跟有援引,指导读者注意到一个权威法律根据(authority)或是与给定的原则与陈述相冲突、相矛盾]
sed quaere 深入调查(指进一步审查事实上或法律上的系争点)
sedente curia 开庭期
seditio 暴动
sedition n. 煽动;煽动叛逆罪;暴动;动乱教唆罪
Sedition Act of 1798 (美)《1798年煽动罪法》或《惩治叛乱法》[指1798年7月14日通过的《1798年煽动罪法》。因当年发生"x. y. z"事件。该法为约翰·亚当斯(John Adans)政府企图平息颠覆政府的暴乱和反抗而采取的措施。该法规定对那些阴谋反对和妨碍联邦政府举措的人(多为英格兰、爱尔兰和法国移民)施以严惩,对那些书面反对的人也要进行严惩](x. y. z事件,是指1798年美国亚当斯总

统接到新派往法国特使发来急电,揭露以"x. y. z."为代号的法国特务人员向美国外交使节勒索贿赂,否则法外交部长塔利兰德拒不接见。亚当斯一怒之下,原拟对法宣战,后经克制,打消战意,将该密电秘而不宣,只要求国会对华盛顿的中立政策稍加改动,以后将"x. y. z."事公之于众,引起全国群情激愤)

seditionary n./a. 煽动分子,煽动叛乱者/煽动暴乱的;骚动的

seditious a. 妨害治安罪的;煽动性的;危及治安的

seditious libel (美)煽动性诽谤[煽动性诽谤最早形成于17世纪的英格兰,任何削弱政府、法律或公共官员的威望及险恶的政治批评均列入此项罪行。该法产生于星室法院(Star-Chamber)而改进于普通法法院(common law courts)。它授权法院对批评是否具有诽谤性作出裁决,并不允许被告作任何辩护。依传统观念:"越是真实,越是诽谤。"北美殖民地时期,煽动性诽谤罪曾引发争议和异议,并通过1732年对约翰·彼得曾格的控诉而对上述传统观念提出了挑战。18世纪中期,自由主义者认为应由陪审团(而非法官)对表达的诽谤性作出裁决,并允许被告以事实真相进行辩护。直到1791年,美国联邦宪法第一修正案对言论自由和出版自由的保障才得以通过并上升为法律。1919年之后联邦最高法院开始审理有关煽动罪方面的上诉案件,包括对政治言论的控诉。大法官奥利弗·温德尔·霍姆斯在艾布拉姆斯诉合众国(Abrams v. United States)(1919)案中提出著名的异议:美国联邦宪法第一修正案已摒除煽动性诽谤普通法,指出政府只能根据他所提出的明显、现实危险标准(clear and present danger test)对政治言论提起公诉。有影响的法学研究学者则坚持煽动性诽谤罪不符合言论自由的基本解释。"诸多的言论都已被排除在煽动性诽谤罪之外,那么还剩下何种言论可定为煽动性诽谤罪呢?"从一些案件及1969年的"布兰登堡诉俄亥俄州案"(Brandenburg v. Ohio)中推翻一项犯罪集团法(criminal syndicalist law)。其理论根据为:即使是偏激的政治言论,其本身也不能受到惩罚——联邦最高法院最终似乎已铲除对涉及政府及其法律的一般性批评提起煽动性诽谤公诉的理论和宪法依据]

seditious meetings act 危及治安集会处置法

seditious propaganda 煽动性宣传

seditious publication 煽动性出版物

seditious speech 煽动(用暴力推翻政府的)言论

seditious writings 煽动性作品

seduce v. 勾引,诱惑;诱奸;诱使……堕落(犯罪)

seducement n. 勾引,引诱,诱惑;笼络手段;诡计

seducer n. 勾引者,诱奸者

seducible a. 可诱惑的;易被勾引的

seduction n. 1.诱奸;勾引;引诱 2.诱拐妇女;诱奸 3.诱惑军人(指恶意引诱军人离开工作,属于煽动背叛的罪行)

seductress n. 具有勾引力的女人;勾引男性的女人

see n./v. 主教教座(或教区),主教的地位(权威或管辖权)/察看,看见,遇见,会见,参看;领会,参观,得悉,看中,同意,经历;目睹;设想;任凭;照料,注意,考虑;(美俚)收买,贿赂

seed law 种子法

seek v. 1.寻找;探索;追求〈seek truth from facts〉(实事求是)2.在……中探索;搜查遍(through) 3.试图,企图(后接不定式)〈seek to kill sb.〉(试图谋害某人),〈be much to seek〉(还未找到);seek after/for 寻找,追求,探索;seek out 寻找出;挑起;竭力找(某人)做伴

seek a quarrel 寻衅

seek damages caused by non performance 请求因不履行所致的损害赔偿

seek employment 找职业

seek enforcement of the judgement 请求执行判决

seek recognition (或 enforcement) of an award 请求承认(或执行)仲裁裁决

seek redrese 要求赔偿

seek sb.'s life 谋害某人
seek the opinion of the masses 征求群众意见
seek truth from facts 实事求是
seeker n. 搜索人,搜查人
seeking asylum 请求庇护
seeking truth from facts 实事求是
seemingly a. 表面的,似乎真实的
Sega Case 塞加判例(指1992年美国的"威兰"判例,被否决版权的判例;也指1994年美国联邦法院判决网络经营人对侵犯版权要负"无过错责任"的又一起著名判例)
segment n./v. 部分,段,节/分裂,裂开
segmented labor market theory 分割劳动市场理论
segregated state (美)实行种族隔离的州
segregation n. 分离,被隔离部分;种族隔离
segregation of assets 资产分隔(指经验明并将一人之财产从共同资产中分开)
segregation of fixed items principle 固定项目分开原则
Segregation of Negroes form white people (美)黑人同白人隔离
seignior n. 庄园主,封建领主;贵族;显贵;绅士
seigniorage n. 1.对铸造银币或金币所用的银块或金块所课的税;硬币面值与相当金属块的价值加上铸造费后的差额 2.君主特权,统治权
seigniorial (=seignorial) a. 庄园的;庄园主的,封建领主的
seignory n. 君权,领主权;领地
seisable a. 可依法占有的;可没收的;可占领的;可扣押的
seise v. 占有(尤指终身或世袭领地);扣押;强夺
seised a. 有所有权的
seisin n. (=seizin)
seisine n. 法定占有权者
seizable offence 可被拘捕的罪行
seize v. 捉住;逮捕;俘获;占有,夺取;抓住(时机),掌握;依法没收,查封,扣押
seizer n. 捕获者;夺取者;查封者;没收者
seized upon (on) 占有,利用;抓住(机会)

seizin n. 土地的占有;占有土地;占有物;依法占有的财产
seizin in deed (英)(保有土地的)实际占有
seizin in fact (英)(保有土地的)事实上的占有
seizin in law (英)(保有土地的)法律上的占有
seizor n. 占有人,扣押者,查封人,没收人
seizure n. 1.依法占有;充公;没收(物) 2.占领,夺取;捉住,捕获
seizure for unlawful use 为非法使用而占有,非法扣押(使用)
seizure goods 没收货物
seizure of contraband 没收违禁品
seizure of property 扣押财产
seizure of public land 强占公有土地
seizure or some equivalent act 扣押或某些强制行为(或措施)
seizure quousque (英)暂时没收土地
seizure under legal process 依法律手续扣押
seldom a./ad. 仅有的,难得的/很少的;很少,难得
Seldon Society (英)塞尔登协会(指1886年梅特兰和其他同仁创办的目的在促进英国法律史研究的一个协会。它出版过一系列有价值的著作,其中主要有三套:①法律史有重要意义的旧法律文本再编;②章程文件选和年鉴;③法院裁判汇编)
select n. 1.选择,挑选 2.被挑选者
select committee (英)(立法机关为某一案件或问题所组成的)特别委员会;调查委员会(亦作 special committee)
Select Committee on Public Expenditure (英)特别经费开支(调查)委员会
select for employment on the basis of one's qualifications 择优录用
Select Pleas in Manorial Court (英)《采邑法院的专门诉讼》
Select Vestries Bill (英)选择议事案(指每届上议院就女王讲演致答词进行辩论前第一次所宣读的议案)
selected forum 合同(协议)指定的法院
selecti judices (罗马法)选任法官
selection n. 选择,挑选,选拔;挑选物

selection board 遴选委员会

selection of justices 大法官的遴选[美国联邦最高法院的大法官的遴选极为重要。美国联邦宪法第2条规定:"总统应提出人选,并在咨询参议院和取得其同意后任命……最高法院法官……"联邦最高法院作为一个相对不受约束的机构,法官遴选是一个政治程序。由总统提名经参议院批准后再由总统任命。甚至没有规定被提名者必须是律师,当然总统不会提名,参议院也不会批准未经过法律培训的人担任法官。总统是唯一由宪法授权任命法官的个人。他当然要广泛征求意见,与低级别联邦法院提名相比,联邦最高法院的提名候选人很可能为总统个人很熟悉,并由总统本人作出的选择]

selective a. 选择的,挑选的;有选择性的,淘汰性的

selective buying 拒买(旧译:杯葛。见 Boycott)

selective domicile 选择住所

selective employment tax (英)选择就业税(1966年开征,后为增值税所取代)

selective justice 有选择的正义

selective preparation 选择性准备(指从心理学含义上说注意的本质是选择性的准备)

selective service system 义务兵役制,遴选兵役制

selectman n. (美)(某些地区市政行政管理委员会的)成员,行政委员

self accusation 自责,自首

self preservation n. 自卫,自保;自卫本能

self rule 自治,国家自治权;独立,解放

self standing legal claims 独立的普通法请求,独立的合法诉讼请求,独立的合法权利主张

self-abandoned a. 自暴自弃;放肆的;为所欲为的

self-abuse n. 自暴自弃;手淫

self-accusation n. 自责,自首

self-accusing guilt 亏心事

self-administered a. 自治的,自己管理的

self-appointed a. 自封的;自己任命的

self-assertion n. 一意孤行;坚持自己的权利(或要求);自我权利主张

self-assumed a. 僭越的,专断的;自负的;自封的

self-authentication n. 自我认证[指一种证明的行为,即某些事物,通常指文件是真实的,确切的,而无需使用外部证据(extrinsic evidence),比如经认证过的文件和经证实的政府机构备案(public record)的复制品,这些通常均被视为自我认证]

self-betrayal n. 自我暴露

self-burning n. 自焚

self-centred (= self-centered) a. 自私自利的;自给自足的

self-command (= self-control) n. 自我控制,自制,克己

self-confessed a. 自首的,自我坦白的,自供的;公开承认的

self-confession n. 自供,自供状

self-confrontation 自我对抗,反身性现代化,自反性现代化(指德国社会学家提出的风险社会理论中的用语,就是"现代化利用自主的现代化的力量挖现代化的墙角",所以译成"自反性现代化"或"反身性现代化"更为准确。简言之,贝克所说的反思性现代化是与第一次现代化不断深入,科学将宗教解为神秘化人类了解征服自然,第一次现代化的预设客体逐渐消失。它所创造的一些不可控的毁灭性的全球风险却正在撼动和消解第一次现代化的基础)

self-contained a. 1.有自制力的,能克制自己言行的 2.自足的,独立的

self-contained regime doctrine 自足说(指WTO争端解决机制只适用WTO涵盖协定解决实体争议。见doctrine of incorporation"并入说")

self-contained regimes 自含机制(指国际监督机制通常由多边条约建立起来,并以常设机构或例会形式开展的机构性和连续性活动,这种机制通常称为条约的"自含机制")

self-contradictory a. 自相矛盾的

self-control n. 自我控制;自制(力),自我克制

self-convicted a. 自判有罪的,自遭的

self-correcting processes 自我纠正程序,自我更改进程
self-criticism n. 自我批评
self-dealing n. 自私对待(指应考虑别人利益时却只想到自己,负有依托责任或依托关系者将他人财产作为己用,如受托管理人为自己利己做交易而牺牲托管人的利益或公司因公务之便,以牺牲公司利益为代价,牟取私利。见 fair dealing ①、②)
self-deception n. 自欺,自欺欺人的行为
self-defense n. 自卫,正当防卫
self-denial n. 自我牺牲;无私;克己
self-dependence n. 自力更生,依靠自己
self-destruction n. 自毁;自杀
self-determination n. 自决;民族自决
self-discipline n. 自律;自我约束;自我修养
self-education n. 自我教育;自修
self-employed a. 自雇的(如作家等不受雇于别人的)
self-employed persons tax 自营职业者税
self-employed persons 自雇人员
self-employment n. 个体经营
self-employment tax 自营人员税;(美)个体经营税(指个体经营所得的社会保险税)
self-enforcing a. 自我实施
self-enforcing market 自我实施型市场(指没有社会制度安排,但只要交易收益相当显著,只要不愿从事互惠行为的危险并可通过种种非官方方式而消除此种危险,一般情况下均可形成交易市场)
self-entering right 介入权
self-esteem n. 自尊
self-evident a. 不证自明的,不言而喻的
self-executing a. 不需补充立法即可生效的,直接生效的(指无须立法手续即能实施的)
self-executing agreement 自执行协定(= executing agreement)
self-executing judgement 自动执行的判决(指无须法院采取措施或发布执行令即可实现的判决)
self-executing provision of treaty law 直接生效的条约法条款
self-executing provisions 自行生效的条文;直接生效的法律规定
self-executing treaty (不需要通过立法手续)即刻生效的条约;自动执行条约(指无需美国国会的转化实施立法,即可在美国法院中被个人援引的条约)
self-explanatory a. 不言而喻的,不言自明的
self-financing a. 自筹资金的
self-fulfilling prophecy 自圆其说的定理
self-governed common-pool resources 共有资源自治
self-governing a. 自治的;自制的
self-governing state 自治州
self-governing dominion 自治领
self-government n. 自治;自治制;自制;克己
self-government ordinance 自治条例
self-help n. 自助,自立;以自己的正当行为维护自己权利
self-help eviction 主动收回房产(指房主将房客财产从公寓房搬出,并将门锁上不让房客进屋,有些情况为合法,有的情况则为非法)
self-help group 自助组(见 self-help)
self-help remedy 自助救济 同 extrajudicial remedy
self-imposed limitation 自律约束
self-incrimination n. 自证其罪(美国联邦宪法第五修正案规定任何人"不得在任何刑事案件中被迫自证其罪"。该权利不仅适用于调查程序、审前证据开示程序以及审判程序本身,而且也适用于民事、行政和立法诉讼中的证人证言。自证其罪规则的保护是以普通法的沉默权为基础而构建的,必须坚决予以实现);自认犯罪;自我牵连(于刑事案件中);自咎;自我归罪
self-indulgence n. 自我放纵
self-inflicted a. 自使蒙受的;自己造成的
self-inflicted injury 自伤
self-injury n. 自害,自伤
self-insurance n. 自家保险
self-interest n. 自身利益,自私自利
self-interested utility maximizers 最大功利追求者
self-judgment n. 自己审判;对自己的判断
self-jurisdiction n. 内部管辖权

self-justifying a. 自己辩白的
self-limiting rules 自我限制规范
self-liquidating a. 能把货物迅速变成现款的;自身能生利还本的
self-liquidating loan 自动清偿贷款(指能将货物迅速变为现金的贷款,或自身能生利还本的贷款)
self-liquidating trust fund 自行生息偿还的信托基金,自偿信托基金
self-management n. 自治,自我管理
self-murder n. 自杀(罪)
self-mutilation n. 自残,自伤,自毁
self-neutralization n. 自行中立化
self-opinioned a. 固执的,执迷不悟的;顽固的,固执己见的
self-organization n. 组织工会,加入工会
self-policing function 自我管辖职能
self-preservation n. 自我维护
self-protection n. 自卫
self-questioning n. 反省
self-redress n. 自救
self-regulating control 自动调节装置
self-regulation of the bar 律师的自动调节;自动遵守规章
self-regulatory organization (SRO) (美)自我规制组织[指美国的一个非政府组织,依法被授权通过采用或执行行为规范(rules of conduct),特别是以公正的、道德的以及有效实务的这些管理做法来调整规制其成员]
self-reinforcing a. 自我巩固,自我施行
self-reliance n. 自力更生(港译:自靠)
self-reliant man 自立人
self-remo(u)lding n. 自我改造
self-reported drug use 自我报告的毒品使用
self-respect n. 自尊
self-restraint n. 自我克制,自我约束
self-righteous a. 伪善的,自以为公正善良的
self-rule n. 自治
self-sacrificing n. 自我牺牲的,不自私的,献身的
self-seclusion n. 闭关自守
self-seeking n. 追求私利
self-service n. 自助,顾客自理,无人售货
self-serving a. 求私利的,自私的;无人售货的
self-serving declaration 私下陈述的声明(指诉讼当事人在法庭外所作的用以证明其案件要素的陈述)
self-slaughter n. 自杀
self-slayer n. 自杀者
self-stultification 自我宣告智力不健全而无行为能力(指一种证明有关自己不健全的行为或请求。见 stultify)
self-sufficiency n. 自给自足
self-supporting a. 自立的
self-torture n. 自我折磨
self-validating a. 可自己(我)确认的(不需外来的证实或批准)
self-wounding n. 自伤(身体)
selfie 自拍照[为可数名词,也可拼写成 selfy,是指用智能手机或其他手持设备为自己拍摄的照片,通常包括人物的头和肩膀等部位。不同于普通证件照,拍摄对象会摆出某种造型或选取别出心裁的拍摄角度令自拍照看起来与众不同。该词最早作为 self-portrait(自画像)的网络缩写出现在 2004 年,起初被用作照片分享网站的标签]
selfless a. 无私的,忘我的
selfless labo(u)r 忘我劳动
sell v. 1.卖,销售,经售,出卖 2.背叛,(俚)欺骗(常用被动态)
sell at a sacrifice 亏本出售
sell by auction 拍卖
sell on credit 赊卖,赊销
sell one up 变卖(债务人的)财产偿还(债权人)
sell out 1.卖出,出售货物;卖完;产品脱销 2.(俚)出卖,背叛;受贿 3.为清偿债务出卖(债务人)的货物;(出卖商品,股票等)抵偿欠债
sell short 卖空;低估
sell sth at a profit 出售某物而获利
sell-off n. 证券跌价,打折扣销售,廉价出货;售出
seller n. 出卖人,卖方,销售者;出售物
seller in good faith 善意出卖人
seller's failure to perform 卖方不履行合同(契约)

seller's price 卖价;售价
sellers' market （对）卖方（有利的）市场
selling a. 卖的,出售的;可出售的
selling broker 推销经纪人
selling operation 销售业务
selling point （推销商品时）被大肆宣传的特色
selling price 卖价,售价
selling rate 卖出价;卖出汇率
selling short （=short sale）
selling the same property twice 同一财产两次出售
semantic theories（或 thesis） 语义理论（指法律实证主义的一种主张）
semantics n. 语义学
semble（=it seems）v. 似乎是（那样）（表示对法律上的一种怀疑）
* Semel major semper major. 曾为成年人者,恒为成年人。（德国民法施行法第 7 条第 2 款采取此原则,承认可依本国法来确定行为能力）
semen analysis 精液分析
semi-autonomous entity 半自治实体,半自治单位
semi-autonomous public institution 半自主的公共机构
semi-bankruptcy n. 半破产
semi-closed sea 半闭海
semi-colony n. 半殖民地
semi-commercial a. 半商业性的,试销的
semi-container n. 半集装箱
semi-finished product 半成品
semi-free class 半自由阶层
semi-independent state 半独立国家
semi-inflation 半通货膨胀
semi-invalid n. 半病残人
semi-judicial character 半司法性质
semi-legislative body 半立法机构,准立法机构
semi-legislative power 半立法权,准立法权
semi-literate a. 半文盲的（指能读而不能写的）
semi-matrimonium 不完备之婚姻,准婚姻（罗马法名词,有纳妾之意）
semi-official a. 半官方的

semi-official organization 半官方组织
semi-plena probation （拉）不完全证据（见 half proof）
semi-plena propatio （大陆法）属推定的证明,补充证据,部分证据
semi-presidentialism n. 半总统制;准总统制
semi-privilege n. 半特权
semi-proletariat n. 半无产阶级
semi-state banking institution 公私合营的银行机构
semi-subsistence n. 半自治
semi-tenant peasant 半自耕农
seminal power 生殖力;创新能力
seminar(s) n. 研究班,大学研究班讨论会,（美）专家讨论会,讨论会
seminary of vice and crime 罪恶的渊薮
* Semper in dubiis benigniora praeferenda sunt. In doubtful cases the more favorable constructions are always to be preferred. 有疑义时常作有利解释。
semper paratus （永远）随时准备（指防卫者的一个口号,向来犯者宣布"随时准备迎击";也指美海岸警备队的口号）
* Semper praesumitur pro matrimonio. The presumption is always in favor of the validity of a marriage. 法律推定总是支持婚姻有效的。
senat conservateur 护法元老院
senate n. 1.（美、法等）参议院;上议院;立法机构;（古罗马的）元老院 2.立法机构的全体成员 3.立法程序 4.大学评议会
senate campaign 参议院竞选活动
Senate Committee on Finance （美）参议院财政委员会
Senate Executive Documents （美）《参议院行政文件》[现已改为"条约文件"（Treaty Documents）]
Senate Executive Reports （美）《参议院行政报告》（指包括参议院外交委员会有关条约的报告）
Senate Judiciary Committee （美）参议院司法委员会（或 Senate Committee on Judiciary 可提出联邦最高法院大法官候选人的名单）
senate version of bill 参议院对议案的意见

senator n. 参议员,上议员
senator of the college of justice （苏格兰）法官
senatorial a. 上议院的;参议院的;参议员的
senatorial courtesy 对参议员的优待(礼貌)
senatorial district 参议员选区
senatus （古罗马的）元老院
senatus decreta （古罗马）元老院的(民事)判决
senatus consultum （罗马法）元老院决议[指元老院在公共事务方面之决议,虽然通常遵循,但无法律约束力(force of law)。在公元1世纪,这些决议代替了古罗马的民众大会(comitia)的立法,但到了2世纪末期,这些决议只是元老院(senate)对罗马帝国意愿(imperial will)的正式明确表示。元老院通常采用罗马皇帝的讲话原文(text of a speech "oratio")。此词有时可写成 senatus consultum,亦可称为 senatus consulta(复)]
Senatus placuit 元老院决定
senatus-consulto (=senatus-consultum)（古罗马）元老院的决议(或法令)
send v. 派遣;打发;呈递;施与;赐给
send into exile 放逐
send off 发出,派遣;解雇
send out of the country under escort 递解出境
send to the gallows 处以绞刑
sending areas （土地）转让区
sending country 派遣国
sending state （外交人员等的）派出国
senile dementia 老年痴呆
senile person 精神衰弱者(从法律上讲,与正常人相反,无能力签约或设立遗嘱)
senility n. （因年迈而）精神衰弱或精神损伤
senior (counsel) n. 高级律师,（英）高级法律顾问(指区别于初级法律顾问或出庭律师的王室法律顾问)
senior citizen （美）（65岁以上已退休或依靠退休金生活的）高龄公民
senior interest 优先的利益,优先的权益(指优于他人而获得或取得的有效权利与利益)
senior judge 资深法官,高级法官
senior magistrate 高级司法行政官（又译：高级地方法官）
senior officer 高级职员,高级军官
senior partner 大股东,主要合伙人
senior party 优势一方(指诉讼中占优势的一方,与 junior party 相对立。见 junior party)
senior procurator 资深检察官
senior prosecution counsel 高级公诉人
senior securities 优先证券,有优先分红权利的证券
senior shares 优先股
senior state attorney 高级地方检察官
seniority n. 年长,资历深,职位高,年资
seniority rule （美）资历规则(指国会中由多数党资历深的议员任委员会主席的规定)
sensational cases 轰动性案件
sensationalize v. 使引起轰动;耸人听闻的报道
sensationalized crime report 耸人听闻的犯罪报道
sense n. 感官;感觉;辨别力;观念,意识
sense of discipline 纪律性,纪律观念
sense of justice 正义感
sense of legal 法制观念
sense of security 安全感
sense stricto 狭义上的
sensitive a. 敏感,灵敏的;感光的
sensitivity n. 敏感,感受性
sensory inspection 感官检查
sensu lato 广义上的
sensu politico 政治意义上的
sensus n. 意义,意思
* **Sensus verborum est anima legis.** The meaning of words is the spirit of the law. 语词之含义乃法律之精神
sentence n./v. 宣判,科刑,刑罚,判决(专指刑事判决,教会案件亦同)/宣判,判决;科刑,定刑
sentence discretion 量刑
sentence in absence 缺席判决
sentence in stocks 脚枷刑罚

sentence of bankruptcy 判决破产
sentence of death by hanging 绞刑
sentence of imprisonment 判处徒刑,判处监禁
sentence of life imprisonment 判处无期徒刑
* Sentence the accuser to the punishment facing the person he falsely accused. 诬告反坐。
sentenced offender 已决犯
sentenced person 已判过刑的人
* *Sentencia interlocutoria revocari potest, definitiva non potest.* Any interlocutory judgment may be revoked, but not a final one. 任何中间判决均可被撤销,但终局判决则不可被撤销。
* *Sentencia non fertur de rebus non liquidis.* Judgment is not given on matters that are not clear. 对于不清楚的事项不作判决。
sentencing n. 判决,宣判;判刑,科刑
sentencing disparities 科刑差异,判决(科刑)不一致
sentencing concessions 量刑折扣;科刑特许,量刑让步
(the) sentencing judge 宣判的法官,主判法官
sentencing policy 判决政策
(the) Sentencing Reform Act of 1984 (SRA) (美)《1984年科刑判决改革法》(1984年10月12日由里根签署批准)
sententia n. 意义,含义;(法庭或法官的)判决
* *Sententia a non judice lata nemini debet nocere.* A judgment pronounced by one who is not a judge should harm no one. 不是法官宣布之判决应不伤害任何人。
* *Sententia contra matrimonium nunquam transit in rem judicatam.* A sentence against marriage never becomes a final judgment(i.e. *res judicata*). 反对婚姻之判决绝不会成为终局判决(即已判决案件)。
* *Sententia facit jus, et res judicata pro veritate accipitur.* The judgment creates right, and what is adjudicated is taken for truth. 判决创造权利,因被判的事项被视为真实。
sententia legis 法规的意义
sentiment n. 感情,情绪;意见,观点
separability clause 可分性条款(指合同中一项或一项以上条款被宣布无效时,其余部分条款仍保持有效,也就是说无效条款是可分的条款。见 saving clause)
separable a. 可分离的,可分隔的,可分开的,可区分的
separable controversy (美)可分性争议(见 separate and independent cause of action);关于讼案是否可分开审理的争论;(美国)关于讼案移送联邦法院审理与否的争论
separable obligation 可分的债务
separate a. 单独的,个别的;分开的,分离的
separate account 专账
separate action (共同原告中各个原告对同一被告的)单独诉讼(与 joint action 相对),独立诉讼
separate acts (或 statutes) 单行法规
separate and apart 别居,分居(离婚的依据)
separate and independent (美)可分且独立(指民事诉讼中有关移送诉讼请求问题的一项要求。见 separable controversy; separate and independent cause of action)
separate and independent cause of action (美)可分和独立诉因(指可单独将其从州法院移送给联邦法院的独立诉讼请求或诉因被合并于一个诉讼中,按《美国法典》规定,一案存有可分性争议,即可全案移送法院审理,不可移送事项可发回原法院裁决)
Separate and Unequal (美)隔离且不平等原则
separate application 分别申请,单独申请
separate but equal (美)隔离但平等原则(指美国最高法院在"Brown v. Board of Education"一案判决前均依赖自1896年Plessy案所揭示的"隔离但平等"的原则,将南部各州的种族隔离政策加以合法化。但1954年,在Brown一案中,美国联邦最

高法院却用联邦宪法第十四修正案来推翻"隔离但平等"的原则,宣告亚拉巴马州的教育隔离政策违宪,因而促进黑白种族融合)

separate charter 单独的特许状
separate code 特别法典,单独法典
separate compensation 特别报酬
separate confinement 分别禁监,隔离监禁
separate count 单独罪行,独立罪状(指在一件刑事起诉书中两项或两项以上的刑事指控之一项罪状。每项指控均构成单独的刑事起诉书,据此,刑事被告均应受到审理)
separate customs territory 独立关税地区
separate debate 分别辩论
separate edition 单行本,单行版本
separate electoral roll 单一的候选人名单
separate entity 单独实体,独立单位;分离实体论
separate estate 独有财产(指属于妻子独立支配而不属于丈夫的财产)
separate examination (目的在于了解妻方承认契据或文据是否出于自愿或出自其丈夫迫使而对妻方的)个别讯问;(对证人的)单独询问
separate existence system 夫妻分居制
separate instrumental and organic elements of his thought 分离他思想中的工具性的和结构性的因素
separate interest in space in a building 大楼楼层面积的分别权益(制)
separate jurisdiction 分别管辖权
separate legal regime 个别法律制度
separate maintenance 分居的扶养费(指1.尚未离婚而实行分居的夫妻一方所给予另一方及其子女的生活费 2.丈夫给妻子作为分居的条件的扶养费)
separate maintenance by decree without divorce 未离婚时夫妇分居的扶养费判决
separate opinion 单独意见,个别意见[指美国在由多数法官组成的法庭中,某一法官赞成或反对多数意见(majority opinion);但在英国则指上诉审法院的某一法官同意多数法官对上诉处理结果但持有不同理由的意见]

separate or individual verdict 个别或单独裁决
separate ownership of each portion (建筑大楼的)每一楼层单独所有权
separate ownership of things on the land 单独地上权;分别地上权
separate panel 单独的合议庭,单独的审判组,单独的专门小组
separate payment 单独支付
separate property (18世纪)单独财产[指①夫妻双方婚前共有的财产,或婚姻存续期间由遗产所得或由第三方之赠与所得之财产。在美国有些州,指婚续期期间所得之财产,即使夫妻双方已签订分居协议(Separation Agreement)或已开始分居,或夫妻一方已开始进行离婚诉讼时的共同财产。亦称 individual property。见 community property; marital property。②在有些共同财产状况(community-property states)下,以配偶一方的名义的财产或婚姻存续期间配偶一方单独获得的财产。③婚姻续期间所获得的财产,进行交换的单独财产]
separate regulation 单行规则,单行条例
separate return (1913年)夫妻分别报税单,夫妻所得税的分别申报单[指夫妻各方分别呈交纳税申报单,表明其收入和义务。与共同纳税申报(joint return)不同,夫妻各方以分别报税单方式承担应纳税之责任]
(a) separate sentencing trial 独立量刑审判程序
separate statement 独立的陈述
separate system (监狱的)隔离监禁制
separate transactions 独立事项,独立的处理办法
separate trial 1.(刑事诉讼)分别审理,单独审讯[指被指控共同犯有同一罪刑的数名被告中的任何一人进行审理。(联邦刑事诉讼规则第14条"Fded. R. Crim. p 14")]2.(民事诉讼)单个诉讼(single action),分别审理[通常为了节约资源或避免偏见,由审理的法官命令,指对分别的权利主张或争点进行单独审理,或对一个群体的权利主张或争点进行单独审理美

国联邦民事诉讼规则第42条(b)"Fed. R. Civ. P. 42(b)"]
separate votes 单独表决,分别表决
separate-property regime (婚姻)分别财产制
separated examination 分别讯问
separated joint owner 被分出的共有人
separated-institution competing for shared powers 不同的权力部分竞逐共有权力
separating equilibrium 分离均衡(指博弈的一种解,其中不同类型的参与人选取不同战略,从而使得不拥有信息的参与人能从拥有信息参与人的行为中推论出其类型)
separating securities 分离证券业
separation n. (夫妇)别居,分居;脱离;分开,分离期间
separation a *mensa et thoro* 单方解除婚姻关系(指法院判决的夫妇分居)
separation agreement 分居协议(书)
separation allowance 军属津贴(指对军人的妻子的津贴)
separation clause 隔离条款
separation deed (夫妻)分居协议
separation from service 离职
(the) separation of corporate ownership and management 公司所有与公司经营分离原则(指股份公司的股东虽然是公司资本的所有者,但对公司经营权无法介入,公司经营权完全掌握于董事会——美国学者Berle与Means于1932年分析公众公司中存在的共存所有与公司经营相分离的现象)
separation of power 1.分权原则,指将政府分为立法、司法、行政,即三权,每一支均为按宪法规定的职责范围,不得相互侵犯。2.分权与制衡原则(checks and balances) [分权的同时必须划分责任,但一个部门的所有权力不应由另一部门的所有权力的同一双手所掌握。大法官路易斯·D.布兰代斯(Louis D. Brandies)认为,"分权原则之所以被1787年的制宪会议采纳,不是为了提高政府效率而是防止独断专行,其目的不是避免矛盾而是通过分配政府三部门的权力的方法来保证人民免受暴政和独

裁专政之苦"]
separation of property regime 分别(开)财产制(见 separate property)
separation of territory 领土分割
separation of witness 证人退庭令(指除原告和被告外,所有证人留在法庭外待分别召唤出庭作证)
separation order (夫妇)分居判决令
separation pay 见 severance pay
separation payment 离职(偿)金,遣散费
separatism n. 分裂主义;分离,脱离,隔离,分裂
separatist movement 分裂主义运动
seppuku n. (日)切腹自杀
sepulchral customs 丧葬习俗
sequence of discovery 披露的顺序;出示的顺序
sequentia 以下
sequential definition 相继的意义,相继的释(定)义
sequential equilibrium 序贯均衡
sequential shifts in legal arrangement 法律安排中的相继转变,法律调节中的序贯手段
sequester v. 1.扣押(债务人的地产等);查封;没收 2.把系争物交第三人保管
(to) sequester property 扣押(或查封)财产(指在诉讼期间将有关财产搁置一边由指定人管理)
sequestrable a. 可查封的,可没收的,可扣押的
sequestrate v. 1.扣押(债务人地产等);没收 2.把系争物交第三者保管
sequestratio n. (罗马法)寄托,寄存[指与持有人(也是扣押人,不管是自愿的或是按法庭命令的)有争执的一件东西的寄托或寄存。复数为 sequestrationes]
sequestration n. 争执物的移走或保管[指①在双方或多方对一项财产争执的结果之前,已将此财产从其拥有人手中移走的进程。见 attachment 1; garnishment。②当无人自愿充当遗产的执行代理人(personal representative)时,则可将个人财产拨留(setting apart)。③诉讼过程十分希望他(或她)已知有关放弃的事情;遵照

公司法安排放弃利益和按遗嘱人之意愿进行分配。④命令司法行政官(sheriff)或其他官员扣押令状中指明的人的财物的一项司法令状(Judicial Writ),这种令状有时是针对不出庭或藐视法庭的民事被告的。⑤为了债权人的利益,法院命令扣押破产的产业(estate)。⑥(国际法)交战国(belligerent power)对于敌对国资产的合法占有,参见《法律判例汇编大全》(C. J. S.)"战争与国防"(War and National Defense)第 8、13、16-22、84-85 节。⑦政府机构基金的冻结。⑧隔离看管小陪审团(trial jury)以防止干扰或暴露公开化,或看管隔离证人以预防他们听到其他人的证言,亦称为 jury sequestration。参见《法律百科全书》或《法律判例汇编大全》《刑法》(Criminal Law)第 1195 节、第 1163 节,审判(trial)第 774 节]

sequestration of jury 隔绝陪审团

sequestration of witness 证人隔离(指在证人作证之前,法院将他们排除在法庭之外,以免其证词受到前一位证人所作证言之影响。如律师有此要求,此一做法通常可采纳)

sequestrator n. 系争财产保管者,查封财产者;扣押令执行者,假扣押财产保管人

sequestro habendo (历史)(宗教法)国王(sovereign)给主教的令状(writ),命令清偿对于圣职收益(benefice's profits)的没收

*** Sequi debet potentia justitiam non praecedere.** Power should follow justice, not precede it. 权力应当遵从公道与正义,而不应当高于公道与正义。

serf n. 农奴;受压迫者,做苦工的人

serfdom n. 1.农奴制 2.农奴地位 3. 奴役

serfhood n. 1.(总称)农奴 2. 农奴地位

sergeant n. (= serjeant)

sergeant-at-arm n. (=serjeant-at-arms)

sergeant-at-law n. (=serjeant-at-law)

seriatim ad. 逐条地,依次地,逐一地

seriatim opinion 分述判决意见[依照英国在美国独立时的法律传统,上诉法院以每位参审法官各自的判决意见的形式宣布案件审理结果。直至今日这一惯例在英国仍然普遍。美国联邦最高法院秉承其法律渊源,初期亦采纳分述判决作为宣布判决的一种方式。首席大法官约翰·马歇尔终止了这一做法。1801 年马歇尔主持联邦最高法院之时,司法系统在政府三大机构中最为薄弱。他致力于将联邦最高法院建设成与行政、立法平等之机构。他认为终止分述判决的做法是达到此目标之第一步。为了提高联邦最高法院的威望,他认为必须用一个声言说话,因而采纳一个判决意见宣告联邦最高法院判决的做法。但这一改革遭到托马斯·杰斐逊(Thomas Jefferson)的强烈反对。20 世纪 40 年代中期以来,并存意见和不同意见呈激剧上升之势。如在纽约时报公司诉合众国案(New York times co. v. United States)(1971)、五角大楼文件案和弗曼诉佐治亚州(Furman v. Georgia)(1972)案的死刑案件中 9 位大法官均发表了各自的意见]

series n. 系列,连续;丛书,辑

serious a. 严重的,危急的;真诚的,彻底的,重要的

serious accident 严重事故,重大事故

serious case 重大案件

serious crime 严重罪行

serious defect 严重瑕疵,严重缺陷

serious illness (人寿保险用语)重病

serious injuries resulting in death 重伤致亡

serious irregularity 重大不法行为

serious loss 重大损失

serious misdemeanor (1893 年)严重的轻罪,严重的不当行为[指轻罪中的一个等级,比起其他的轻罪具有更为严厉的惩罚。构成达到严重轻罪等级的行为在有些管辖区被指控既是重罪也是轻罪(be charged as either a felony or a misdeanor),亦称为 high misdemeanor; indictable misdemeanor; penitentiary misdemeanor; aggravated misdemeanor]

serious offense 严重违法犯罪

serious warning 严重警告

serjeant (=sergeant) n. 警官,宪兵队长;(从前在英国皇家法庭具有特权的)律师

serjeant-at-arms n. (议会、法院等的)卫士;法警;警官

serjeant-at-law n. 1.民法博士 2.高级(撰状)律师;(英)御用状师
Serjeants Inn 律师法学院
* *Sermo est index animi.* Speech is the index of the mind. 语言为智力之标准。
* *Sermones semper accipiendi sunt secundum subjectam materiam, et conditionem personarum.* Language is always to be understood according to its subject-matter, and the condition of the persons. 人们对语言总是根据其所反映的论题和人们所处的条件来理解。
* *Servanda est consuetudo loci ubi causa agitur.* The custom of the place where the action is brought is to be observed. 诉讼地的惯例应该得到遵守。
servant n. 受雇人;服务者;公务员
servant's security agreement 雇员保安合约
servato juris ordine 遵从法庭命令
serve v. 1.服务;服役;为……服务,为……效劳 2.送达(传票等);向……送交(令状等);3.可作……用(for, as)
serve a judgement 正式通知一项判决
serve a process on 对……发出传票
serve a sentence 服徒刑
serve a sentence on bail 保外执行判决
serve a subpoena on 将传票送达
serve a summon on sb.(或 **serve sb. with a summon**) 向某人送传票
serve a time 服刑
serve a writ on sb. 将令状送达某人
serve as a guardian for sb. 为某人作监护人
serve as a witness at court 出庭作证
serve on the jury 属陪审团的(成员)
serve sb.'s purpose 符合某人的目的
serve to 足矣,足够
served with process 被送达传票
server(=servant) n. 服务员;传票送达员;送达者
server-side geolication 服务器端定位(见 client-side geolocation)
service n. 1.服侍(指从前土地租借人对领主应尽的义务,雇员对雇主应尽的义务);效劳;雇佣;公职;服务(业) 2.(传票等的)送达 3.帮助;贡献
service abroad of documents 文书的域外送达(指将司法文件或司法以外文件送达域外的本国人或外国人)
service by publication 公告送达,公示送达,公示催告
service by substitution 代理送达
service charge 服务费(用)
service contract 劳务合同(契约)
service fee 手续费
service industries 服务行业,服务产业
service industry 服务行业
service intermediaries 服务中介人
service invention-creation 职务发明创造
service judgment 传达判决
service life 使用期限,服务期限
service mark 使用标记,服务标记(指在广告和销售中的一种标记或标号,通常是以设计、名称、性质等来区别于另一个生产公司)
service of charges 控告的罪状
service of defence 防卫服务,服兵役
service of documents 文书送达
service of legal process 送达法律令状
service of notice 送达通知书
service of order 送达命令
service of paper 传票送达,送达传票
service of process (美)诉讼开始文书的送达;传票送达手续(指将法院传票的内容告有关人员知晓的手续,通过递送传票或起诉的通知,使司法程序引起受其影响的人的关注)[在美国,指将令状、传票、诉状等送达当事人的行为。送达的主要方式有:①直接送达(personal service),即直接将诉状或副本传票交受送达人,或送到其住所或经常居住地的负有责任人(responsible person),或送交受送达人所指定的人;②推定送达(constructive service)或替代送达(substitute service),指直接送达方式以外的任何送达方式,有邮寄送达(service by mail)和报纸上公告送达(service by publication)。在英国有:①直接送达(direct service);对传唤令(writ of summons)及某些文件要求直接送达,送达对象为人时则

称对人的送达(personal service),送达对象为物时则称对物送达(real service);②还有一种叫接受送达(accepting service),即由受送达人的律师在令状上注明,代表被告接受令状的送达]

service of process statute 诉讼事状送达法规,诉讼书状送达立法

service of summons 送达传票(在美国民事案件一般由原告或原告律师负责送达传票)

service of summons and complaint 送达传票和诉状

service of writ 令状送达

service on the in-state official 对本州官员的送达

service out of the jurisdiction 管辖区外的送达

service performed 劳务

service policy 劳务保险单

service regulations 服役条例

service rendered 劳务账单

service unit for foreigners 外事服务单位

service worker 服务行业人员

service works 雇佣作品

services in aid of crime 为帮助犯罪效劳

servient a. 从属的

servient tenement 供役地(指为接邻土地的地役权服务的土地)

servilis cognatio (罗马法)奴隶的血亲关系

serving n. 服务,服役,服(刑);送达;招待,上菜;一份食物(或饮料)

serving a sentence 服刑

serving of process 传审,传讯;发出传票等;(美)诉讼开始文书的送达

serving officer 现任职员

serving person outside the state 外州送达人

serving prime minister 在职总理

serving sentence outside the prison under surveillance 监外执行(刑罚),监外服刑,监外监督执行

servitude n. 1.苦役,劳役 2.奴役,奴隶状态 3.地役(权) 4.徒刑

servitutes 役权[古罗马法上,役权可分为地役权(servitute rerum)(亦称物役权),与人役权(servitude personarum)。地役权的

意思是为他人的利益或便利在某一财产上设立的负担;人役权是指为特定人的利益所设立的役权,甚至在特定人死亡时终止的役权:用役权(usufruct)、使用权(use)、居住权(habitation)]

servitutes dividinon possund 地役权不可分割

servitutes juris gentium naturals 国际法上的自然地役

servitutes juris gentium voluntariae 国际法上的自愿地役

servitutes personarum 人役权

servitutes praediorum 地役权

servitutes praediorum urbanorum 市府地役

servus 奴隶

servus terrae 土地奴隶;土著农民

sess (英)税,税率

session n. 1.开会,开庭;开会期,开庭期(指法官们受委任,开庭审判诉讼的日期) 2.治安推事定期会议 3.(复)英法官开庭(审理小案件等),法庭 4.一场(盘)交易

session cases 开庭期审理的案件

Session Law Services (美)《会期法汇编服务》(指美国有些州为了使其法规及时跟上形势,而采取对法规及时补充的方式,在立法机构会议期间还提供汇编服务的先行本)

Session Laws (session laws) (美)(一年或两年的)定期汇编的法规(有别于 compiled laws 或 revised laws),《会期法》(美国法规出版的另一种形式,系指按年代顺序编排的法规集成,在每年或在立法会议期间分别出版单独卷本。在每卷本内,法规依照通过的日期顺序编排,末尾附有索引,各州出版有自己的《会期法》,而名称各州不一)

session of parliament 议会会期

session of the peace 治安法官开庭

sessional a. 法庭的,开庭的;会议的

sessional programme 会议议程

sessions court (英)法官开庭的法院(亦译:属审法院)

set v./n. 放,安置;签(字);盖(章);写;记录;定(日期,限度,价格等);制定(规则等);颁布;估计;评价;分配;提出;调整/套,批,部,副

set（或 **crest**）**a precedent for** 为……创先例

set a price on one's head 悬赏通缉某人

* **Set a thief to catch a thief.** 以贼捉贼，让坏人惩治坏人。

set about 着手，开始

set apart (for…) 留出，拨出

set apart a sum for damages 留出一笔款作损害赔偿

set aside v./n. （18世纪）1.（法院的）撤销，驳回，宣布（判决、命令等）无效〈the judge refused to set aside the default judgment〉（法官拒绝宣布缺席判决无效），〈set aside a claim〉（驳回一项权利请求）2.留出，拨出〈set aside ample reserve grain〉（留出充足的储备粮）3.不顾，把……放在一边，略去〈set aside all objections〉（不顾一切反对）/留出一笔款子

set aside of the arbitral award 撤销仲裁裁决

set aside proceeding 搁置诉讼程序

set at defiance 蔑视，反对

set at large 放宽，释放，释放囚犯

set at the law naught 蔑视法律

set at variance 不同意，使不一致；使不协调

set by 留作将来之用，把……搁开

set by for further consideration 留待进一步审议

set down 1.放下，卸下 2.写下，填入（表中）3.视为，归之于 4.制定，规定 5.（飞机）降落

set fire 纵火

set forth 陈述，阐明；宣布；提出

set free 释放，使获自由

set of (parts) 一套，一批，一副，一部

set of parameters 参数组合

set of provisions 成套规章，成套规定

set off v./n. 1.出发，动身 2.使爆炸，爆发；使（某人）开始（做某事）3.衬托，使更明显，点缀 4.抵销 5.分开，划分 6.（未干油墨）粘脏（另一印张）/1.装饰品，陪衬物 2.（债务的抵销）；用以抵销债务的权利 3.粘脏 4.墙壁突出部分

set off a barred claim in defence to an action 以债权的时效期满作为（对原告诉权的）辩护

set off receipts against expenditures 以收入抵作支出

set one's hand to a document 在文件上签字

set one's seal 盖章

set oneself against 坚决反对，坚决与……对立

set out 发表；宣布；打算，计划；出发；解释；描述；整理，开始，着手（to）

set price 固定价格，确定价格

set right 恢复正常，使……纠正错误

set the record straight 澄清是非

set up 1.设立，创立，建立；开始 2.提出，提议；供应 3.宣称；假装 4.计划，装置，方案，机构，安装，建立，装配

set up（或 **enter, raise**）**a protest against** 对……提出抗议

set up an action 起诉，进行诉讼

set up an *alibi* 提出不在犯罪现场的辩护

set up for 兹认为，自称为

set-off n. 抵销，债务抵销；相抵（指在反索偿的诉讼里，如被告有反索偿时，可先承认原告索偿，然后要求法庭把自己的反索偿和原告的索偿的两笔账相抵，法院则须考虑情况一并审讯）

set-off a claim 抵销债权

set-off in equity 衡平抵销［指同一交易内或相关联交易的抵销。从发展历史看，法律较早就承认并保护衡平抵销。在英国，成文法未规定法定抵销（set-off by statute）时，大法官法院（court of chancery）便承认衡平抵销。此类抵销在英国法上又被称为减抵（abatement），在美国法上称为抵扣（recoupment），在法国和德国法上称为具有"关联关系"的抵销。当然，在同一双务合同中，互为对价的义务是不能"抵销"的（如买卖合同中，买方不得以其价款义务抵销其对卖方的货物交付请求权），因其与当事人缔约之本意不符（当事人当然可以约定的形式摆脱合同的拘束，但那已构成合同解除而不再是抵销）。见 transaction set-off］

setback n. （美）缩进地段（指街边的一段空地，也叫建筑线或财产线，即在此限之内城市规划或法规均禁止有任何建筑物）

setdown n. 申诉,辱骂
setentia legis 法规的意义
setting n. 安装,调整;环境,背景;定位
setting aside the case 要求驳回诉讼
setting off explosive 进行爆破
setting the mutter privately 私下和解,私下了结
settle v. 1.指定(财产的处理、分配等);授予 2.决定;解决;安排,定居;安置 3.调整;和解;了结 4.偿付,清算,清理
settle a document 处理文件
settle a lawsuit 断案;结案
settle area (殖民地的)定居区
settle by compromise 以和解了事
settle claims 理赔
settle claims and debts 清理债权债务
settle once a month 每月结算一次
settle one's score 清账,结账
settle out of court 在法庭外和解
settle the claim 解决争端
settle up 清偿,结清,了结,付清
settle with creditors 偿还债权人
settled a. 1.已结算的,已付清的;已解决的 2.一定的,固定的
settled account 已结清的账目(款)
settled between the parties 双方已和解
settled conviction 已判定的罪行,已确定之罪行
settled country(或 **state**) 定居国,拓殖国家
settled intention 预谋;已确定的意图
settled land 1.租出或租入的土地 2.限制授予土地(指受继承限制的土地,如限定由几个人来继承的土地,使取享有土地利益的人不能剥夺他人未来享有该土地的权益)
Settled Land Act, 1925(英)《限制授予土地法》(1925 年)
settled population 定居人口
settled principle 固定原则
settled property 被限制授予财产(土地)
settled social standard of justice 固定的社会正义标准
settled tendency 大趋势,稳定趋势
settlement n. 1.解决,和解;决定,了结 2.(通过法律手续的)财产授予;依法设定的财产 3.整理,安排;安置;定居 4.清理;清偿,清算
settlement agreements 清偿协议,和解协议
settlement allowance 安置费
settlement behavior 和解行为
settlement by amicable arrangement 以友好和解解决争端
settlement by conciliation 以和解方式解决
settlement by force 以武力解决
settlement conference 和解会议
settlement cost 和解成本
settlement fee (德)和解费(见 Cost Amendment)
settlement for minor (英)对未成年人的财产授予
settlement *inter vivos* 生前的财产处分,(英)生前的财产授予
settlement netting 结算轧差(指双方当事人互负相同之义务。该义务同时到期,此时双方只需结算两项业务的净差额即可。例如:在外汇交易中,一方应向另一方支付 100 美元,另一方需向该方支付 101 美元,则双方的净差额将变为 1 美元。而无需按原先各自的债权额履行,以减少各自面临的破产风险)
settlement of action 诉讼了结;诉讼和解
settlement of claim 理赔
settlement of exchange 结汇
settlement of international disputes by mediation 通过调停解决国际争端
settlement of international investment disputes 国际投资争议的处理
settlement of litigation 诉讼和解
settlement of loss 赔付损失,损失处理
settlement on account 记账结算
settlement process 和解进程
settlement relation 结算关系
settlement to minimize tax (英)使税额减至最低额的财产授予
settlement warrant 财产授予令
settlements based on antenuptial agreements 婚前合议的财产授予协约
settler n. 1.居留者,定居者 2.赠与者;调停者 3.移民;殖民者;开拓者
settler regime 移民政权

settling n. 1.固定,移住,殖民;居留 2.决定,解决;和解;了结
settling accounts 结算
settling agents 理赔代理人(保险标的物受损失时,被保险人应通知保险人或其指定的海损查勘员或理赔代理人进行检验,有检验报告方能索赔)
settling day 清算日,结账日
settling dispute 解决争议
settling fee 理赔费
settling up 结算,了结,清理
settlor n. 信托创立人,赠与产业者;财产授予人,财产让与人
setto n. 争论,争斗
Seven Hills (City) 罗马城的别称
Seventeenth Amendment 美国联邦宪法第十七修正案[指美国联邦宪法第 1 条第 3 款规定参议员由各州立法机构选出,这显然希望参议院所代表的选民不同于众议院。但到 1900 年,随着民主观念的不断发展,这一体制越来越不合时宜,有些州要求立法机构提名以前由公众投票同意的候选人担任参议员从而规避该项条款。这给国会造成了很大压力,(包括要召开一次制宪会议)以修正条款。国会针对这一情况拟议了一个修正案,各州于 1913 年批准,国会于 1912 年 5 月 12 日提出该修正案,于 1913 年 5 月 31 日批准生效。该修正案第 1 款规定:"合众国参议院由各州人民选举的参议员二人组成,参议员任期六年,参议员各有一票表决权,各州选举人应具有各州立法机关中人数最多一院的选举人所需具的资格。"该修正案逐渐削弱了政党的权力,因为它绕过了行使该权力的政治机制]
Seventh Amendment 美国联邦宪法第七修正案(该修正案规定"在普通法上的诉讼,关于价额超过 20 元的案件,有受陪审团陪审的权利。凡经陪审审理的事实,非依普通法的规定,不得在合众国任何法院中再加审理",故涉及在习惯法的诉讼中其争执所涉及者有权要求陪审团审判)
Seventh Decennial (美)《第七个十年判决摘要汇编》(系指由西方出版公司出版的自 1956 年至 1966 年的判决摘要汇编)

sever v. 分割(产业);区别;使分离;中断,断绝
(to) sever a trial 分别审理,隔离审理[指对同一案件的参与人逐个分别审理,亦称分离(审)]
sever diplomatic relation with 与……断绝外交关系
sever hand 断指(刑)
severability of contract 合同的可分性(指当一部分合同条款无效时,不影响其他条款的继续有效)
severable a. 可分离处理的,可断绝的,可分开的;独立部分中易受影响部分的法规的可分割部分的,可分部分的
severable contract(s) 可分开执行的合同,可分的合同
severable statute 可分的法规(指一项法规即使它的部分已被废除,法院认为无效,但其他部分不受影响仍为有效法规)
several a. 1.数个的;个别的,各自的;专有的,独占的 2.有连带责任的
several contract 可分合同
several estate 各自的财产
several guarantee 按份保证
several inheritance (两人以上的)各自的继承产
several issues 几个争执点
several judg(e)ment 分别判决
several liability 多数的债;分别债务,分担的债
several offences 数罪
several property 个人独占财产,各自的财产
several tenancy 单独管理之产业(指对共有产业而言),独占的租地
severally ad. 分别地,个别地,有连带责任地
severally liable 分别的责任,单独的责任
severalty n. 各自,各个,单独制,(土地的)单独所有,单独租用
severalty ownership 仅为个人所有,个人所有权
severance n. 1.切断行为,割断;断绝 2.(民事诉讼)诉讼分离[指通过法院,对多个当事方的权利请求分离,允准根据各个请求分别诉讼或者允准一定的中间裁决(cer-

tain interlocutory order)而成为终局裁决，亦称 severance of actions; severance of claims。见 bifurcated trial; consolidation 3] 3.共同共有权(joint tenancy)的终止，通常通过占有它而成为共有租赁或按份共有(权)(tenancy in common) 4.任何事物的转移[指附属于不动产的，比如农作物或矿物的转移，成为动产而不属于土地的部分。采矿权通常从地上权(surface rights)被分离开，而分离后的财产可能含有油、气或其矿物质]

severance allowance 补贴,经济补贴,离职补贴[国际劳工组织的公约称为离职补贴,我国台湾地区称为"资遣费",英国称为"遣散费"(redundancy pay)]

severance damages 可分的损害赔偿(指对土地拥有人因降低其应予征用或没收的剩余遗产价值而作的补偿裁决)

severance of action 诉讼划分,诉的分离(指民事诉讼中可根据诉因或审理中争议事项进行划分)

severance of diplomatic relation 外交关系断绝

severance pay 退职金;解雇金;离职金,解职金(指雇主支付给被解职雇员的所欠工资和薪金。这种支付可构成雇员对雇主的权利主张放弃。有时可缩略为 severance，亦称 separation pay; dismissal compensation)

severance tax 采矿税;森林物产税;自然资源税

severe a. 严厉的,苛刻的;严重的,酷烈的

severe injury accident 重伤事故

severe judg(e)ment 重判,严判

severe penalty 严惩;严刑;重罚

severe reprimand 严重警告

severe subnormality 严重失常(精神病的一种)

severity and extensivity of punishment 惩处的宽严轻重

severity of the sentence 判刑的轻重

sewage n. 污水,污水

sewage disposal 污水处理

sewage farm 污水处理场

sewage system 污水系统

sewer service 使送达通畅(指当法庭得知法庭公报未能送达时派专人送达)

sex n. 性,性别;性欲,性行为;性交

sex change 见 sex reassignment

sex discrimination 性别歧视(指在提供服务、就业、报酬、教育和设施方面所普遍存在的一种性别和另一种性别的歧视,通常为对妇女的歧视)

Sex Discrimination Act (英)《性别歧视法》(1975年)

sex discrimination in employment 就业上的性别歧视

sex obsessed 性纠缠

sex of murder victims 性谋杀受害者

sex offenders 性犯罪者,性罪犯

sex outside marriage 婚外性行为

sex pervert 性反常;同性恋

sex reassignment 性别的再确定(指目的在改变性别的医疗措施、手术和事先计划好的选择人的性别的荷尔蒙处理。亦称 sex change)

Sex-offender registry (美)性犯罪者注册登记簿[指记录从监狱释放的性犯罪人的姓名和地址,并可公开查阅的登记簿。此登记册起始于一个州的公众熟知的"梅甘法"(Megan's Law)。这些名册清单经常在互联网上公布,而且有些州还要求在当地报纸刊登罪犯的姓名,照片和住址。见 Megan's Law]

sexage specific death rate 分性别、年龄的死亡率

sexist perception 性主义者感知

sexting 性短信(指用手机发送与性有关的信息或图片)

sexual a. 性的,性欲的

sexual abuse 性侵犯(尤指成年人对未成年人的非法行为);强奸

sexual access 性交能力

sexual assault (美)性侵犯[指①未经对方同意的性交行为,有些州的制定法废弃了强奸罪(crime of rape)而以性侵犯代替。②强奸以外的无礼、侮辱性性行为。《示范刑法典》列出了8种情况属于性接触(sexual contact)而引起的侵犯:如在罪犯明知受害人缺乏意识能力来判断接触

的性质或者由于受害人智力障碍或精神病,或由于罪犯使受害人服用麻醉药而失去抵抗力。③根据《示范刑法典》第213—214节,亦称 indecent assault; indecent assault by contact; sexual assault by contact。见 rape]
sexual capacity 性交能力
sexual commerce 性交(=sexual intercourse)
sexual crimes against the person 侵犯人身罪
sexual equality 男女平等,不分性别
sexual favoritism 性徇私
sexual gratification 性满足
sexual harassment 性骚扰(指利用权势、地位对个人的职业、工资等施加影响以获得性的允诺或对拒绝允诺者给以惩罚)
sexual harassment in the workplace 工作场所性骚扰
sexual intercourse 性交
sexual molestation 性骚扰,性摧残
sexual offense 性犯罪[指有关非法的性行为,如卖淫,有伤风化罪(indecent exposure)鸡奸和兽奸等]
sexual orientation 性导向
sexual perversion 性心理障碍(又称性变态,传统精神医学对性变态最早定义与分类指是:患者满足性欲的对象不正常,如同性恋、恋童色情、恋兽癖等;其满足性行为的方式不正常,如露阴癖、目淫癖、恋物癖等;患者性别认同倒错并违背自然,如易性癖。此类障碍有:①transsexualism 易性癖;②fetishism 恋物癖;③transvestism 异装癖;④exhibitionism 露阴癖;⑤voyeurism, scopalagnia 窥阴癖;⑥frottage, frotteurism 摩擦癖;⑦sadism and masochism 性施虐症与性受虐症;⑧paediaphilia 恋童癖;⑨necrophilia 恋尸癖;⑩homosexuality 同性恋]
sexual psychopathy 性心理变态
sexual revolution 性革命(见 Roe v. Wade)
sexual stereotype 性模式,性旧陈规
sexuality n. 性欲,性过ность行为;性别,性的特征;性欲发展
sexuality transmitted diseases (STD) 性传播疾病,传播性疾病(罪)
sexually importence man 无性交能力的男人
Sexually Violent Predator Act (美)(堪萨斯州制定的)《性暴力侵犯者法》(1994年)
shackles n. 镣铐,手铐;脚铐;羁绊物
shadkhan n. (犹太教法)媒人
shadow n./v. 影子;黑暗;庇护;忧郁/秘密尾随,盯梢
shadow banking system 影子银行体系[指此概念由太平洋管理公司董事保罗·麦考利(Paul McCulley)提出,意指游离于金融监管体系之外,从事类似于传统银行业务的非银行机构。2008年美联储和国际货币基金组织(IMF)相继提出了与影子银行类似的平行银行系统(paralled banking system)和准银行(near-bank)概念]
shadow cabinet 影子内阁(指在野政党计划的预备内阁);总统或首相的智囊团
shadow price 影子价格(推算价格),核算价格
shadow zones 盲区(指收不到节目信号或收到信号不清晰的高山、高层建筑等影响的地区)
shady a. 成问题的,令人怀疑的
shady business 非正当买卖
shady looking customer 形迹可疑的人
shady transaction 不正当交易
Shafi'iyah (伊斯兰教法)沙斐仪派(逊尼派四种流派之一,主要探讨伊斯兰教法的来源及其如何运用这种原始资料解决当代法律问题)
Shafit rite (伊斯兰教法)沙斐仪教派的惯例
shake n./v. 解雇,撵走;(美俚)敲诈,勒索;贿â赂;动摇,握手/摇动,挥动,使震动,(俚)抛弃,摆脱,握手
shake down 1.(美俚)敲诈,勒索 2.(美俚)搜查,搜身
shake one's fist 挥拳威胁
shake person 令人怀疑的人
shake-up n. 把……打散后,重新组合,大改组;权宜之计的办法;震动,激励
shackles n. 镣铐,手铐;脚铐;羁绊物;束缚,枷锁;羁绊
shall v. 应(此字常用于法令或契约中)
sham n./a./v. 赝品,假物;骗子,假冒者/假

的;虚假的;仿制的,假装的/假装,佯作
sham company 假公司,伪公司
sham defense 假辩护,虚伪的答辩
sham marriage 假结婚
sham officer 冒充官员,假官员
sham plea 虚伪的答辩(指明显不忠实和不合理的答辩,这种答辩法官可命令把它删去或修改)
shaman n. 巫师
shame n. 羞耻,羞辱;可耻之事,羞辱心
shame sanction (1991年)羞辱惩罚[指旨在对已判罪的罪犯打上羞辱烙印的一种刑事惩罚,并通常就罪犯的罪行以警示公众。羞辱惩罚通常公开化的,并与他(或她)所犯罪行相关联。比如在某个天井贴上一个标牌,上面写上:"已判罪少年 Molester 居住于此。"亦称 shame sentence; shaming sanction; shaming sentence; scarlet-letter punishment; scarlet-letter sentence]
Shaming sentence 见 shame sanction
shammer n. 说谎者,骗子,冒充者
shape v./n. 形成,体现;计划,策划,想出;使具体化;使适合(to)/形状,外形,字形;具体化;未来的情况;模型
shape an answer 作出回答
shape one's plan to this condition 使某人计划符合某种情况
shape public opinion 影响(左右)舆论
shape the common law 塑造普通法,使普通法具体化
shaping of law 对法律的影响(或形成、决定)
share n./v. 1.一份,份额 2.股份,股票 3.贡献,参与/分享,分担;分配,共有
share and share alike 平均分配
share balance 股票结存
share broker 股票经纪人
share capital 股本,股份资本
share certificate 股票;股票证券
share charged hand 股票撸手,股票监督人
share company 股份公司
share contract note 订购股份单
share cropping contracts 分成制合同
share draft account (SDA) 股金提款账户
share in company 公司股票
share in profits 分享利润,分红
share list (英)股票行情表
share loan (信用合作社等的)存款抵押贷款
share losses expenses 分担损失费用
share of foreign exchange 外汇分成,外汇留成
share of investment 股份投资
share of stock 股份,股票
share of the market 市场份额
share of trade 货载承运份额
share options 优先股票权,股票选择买卖
share orders 分配订货单
share (或 stock) premium 股票发行溢价
share pusher 硬推销不值钱股票的掮客,股票贩子
share register 股票登记过户
share remittance system 提成制度
share repurchase 股票回购
share rights 股权
share sb.'s view 与某人看法相同
share transfer 股票过户,股票转让,转股
share warrant 股票证书,股份保证书
share-issuing company group 股份制公司集团
share-issuing enterprises 股份制企业
shared principles 共同原则
shared value 共同价值观
shareholder n. 股东,股票持有人
shareholder derivative suit(s) 股东代位诉讼;股东派生诉讼[美国民事诉讼中指当通常负责维护公司权利职责的人(一般是公司经理)拒绝履行该职责的,股东为维护公司利益提起的诉讼](见 derivative action)
shareholder equity 股东产权,股东权益,股东拥有的资产净值,股东自有资本
shareholder general meeting 股东大会
shareholders' meeting 股东大会
shareholders' voting rights 股东表决权
shareholder-oriented model 股东利益导向(见 Director primacy)
shareholding commercial enterprises (或 contribution) 商业企业股份制
shareholding (或 stock) system 股份制度

sharer in an estate 可分得遗产的人
shares offered 已开盘的股票
shares outstanding 见 outstanding share/stock
shares system 股份制度
Sharia **chief court** 沙里亚酋长法院
Sharia **Court** (伊斯兰教法)沙里亚法院(亦译作伊斯兰教法法院。指一种处理穆斯林继承中的有关身份、家庭法院)
Sharia **Court of appeal** 沙里亚上诉法院(见 *Sharia* Court)
Shariah 沙里亚(指伊斯兰教法的基本概念)
sharing of information 信息分享
sharing profits and losses 共负盈亏
sharing system 分成制度
shark n./v. 1.骗子 2.(俚)专家;杰出者/诈骗,敲诈,骗取
sharp a./n. 1.线条分明的,明显的 2.锐利的;机警的;精明的 3.狡猾的,不择手段的/骗子;(美俚)专家,内行
sharp clause 严厉条款(指在抵押或其他担保字据中订明在债务人迟延给付时,债权人可立即采取法律行动)
sharp contrast 鲜明对比
sharp instrument injury 锐器伤
sharp split of authority 对依据的严重分歧,对依据的尖锐分歧
sharper n. 欺骗者;欺诈犯
sharper practice 不正当的行为;不择手段的行为;欺骗
sharpie(或 **sharpy**) n. (美俚)骗子,狡猾的人
shear v. 修剪;切断;剥夺(of)
shear[**sheared**,(古) **shore**, **shorn**] v. 修剪,切断,剥夺;收割
shed v. 流出,流下,散发,放射,溢出,摆脱,放弃
shed light on 使某(物)事情明白显示出来
shedding risk 摆脱风险
sheer determination 彻底的决心,完全的决心,果断的决议
sheet n./v. 1.纸张,页;表格 2.被单 3.(美俚)罪犯档案,(俗)酒醉;/用裹尸布包;覆盖

sheet anchor 1.紧急时使用的大锚 2.紧急时可依恃的人或物;最后的依恃
Shelley's case 谢利判例,谢利案件(见 Rule in Shelley's case)
shelter n./v. 1.掩护,庇护,保护 2.隐匿 3.供住宿/1.庇护 2.庇护所;避难所;庇护物
shelter belt 防护林带
sheltered trades (英)不受外国竞争影响的行业(指建筑、国内运输等行业)
shelve v. 搁置(建议),暂缓考虑;将(某人)解雇,让(军人)退役
Shepard's Citators (美)《谢泼德援引集》[此援引集是美国最为完整的判例援引系统。通过该援引可列出官方或非官方判例汇编中出版的每一判例,根据该援引还可列出每个已援引了有争议判例的判例。此援引集可用于每个州、哥伦比亚和波多黎各地区、全国判例汇编系统(U. S. National Reporter System)的每一地区、低一级联邦法院、联邦最高法院以及一些行政机构的判例汇编。该集使用有助于律师达到以下目的:①对判例提供相同援引,查出官方或非官方判例汇编中每一判例的司法历史;②鉴定每一判例现状,明确此判例现在是否有效,抑或已被推翻,或宣告无效;③查出已援引的主要凑合的后来的一些判例,并对期刊文章、检察长意见以及判例注释提供线索]
Shepard's Northeastern Reporter Citations (美)《谢泼德的东北区判例汇编援引》
Shepard's Restatement of the Law Citations (美)《谢泼德的法律重述援引》
Shepard's State Citations (美)《谢泼德的州援引》(指一种查对官方援引和非官方援引的对照资料,如《谢泼德俄亥俄州援引》等)
Shepard's United States Citations—Statutes Edition (美)《谢泼德美国援引——法规版》(指一种援引集,仅限于原联邦法院的判决,但除了那些实际上是解释条约的判决外,还包括所有提及的条约判例)
shepardize v. 1.(通常大写)以谢泼德援引法核查(判例)[指通过出版的或电脑处理过的谢泼德援引汇集(Shepardize's cita-

tors)来决定(判例)的后续历史]2.(不严格的)通过如与含义1相同的方法核查一个判例的先例价值(Shepardization, Shepardizing)

shereef (=sherif) n. (阿拉伯国家的)王子,酋长,首领;麦加的行政长官

sheriff n. (英)(州、郡)司法行政官,郡长,执行吏;(美)县司法行政官,警官

sheriff principal 首席司法行政官

sheriff substitute (苏格兰)行政司法官助理

sheriff's court 州法院;郡法院

sheriff's jury (=sheriff's panel) (美)司法行政官的陪审团(司法行政官的陪审团名单)(指1684年建立于纽约的富翁私人俱乐部,其成员随时碰头审议有关资格的事情,但他们没有正式陪审员的责任)

sheriff's sale 1.见 execution sale 2.见 judicial sale

sheriff's tourn 郡长治安巡回法庭 郡长裁判庭(指1887年已被撤销的由郡长主持的郡内百户区巡回法庭,每年开庭两次)

sheriff-officer n. 执达官(员)

sheriff-principal n. (英)郡督

sheriffdom (或 **sheriffalty, sheriffship**) n. 司法行政官的管辖区或职务

sheriffwick n. (州、市、县)司法官员的管辖区或职务

sheristadar n. 档案或记录保管员

sherlock n. 私家侦探

Sherman Act (美)《谢尔曼法》[指联邦政府通过的第一个反托拉斯或反垄断法,1890年通过,后经克莱顿法修正,旨在摧毁"贸易限制联合"(combination in restraint of trade)]

Sherman Anti-trust Act (美)(1890年的)《谢尔曼反托拉斯法》(遏制和削弱卡特尔)

shew cause (或 **show cause**) 说出理由,表明理由(常用于法院依据申请作出命令或宣判时,保留让另一方向法庭表明反对的理由,而后才根据表明理由作出最后判决)

Shi'ah (伊斯兰教法)什叶派(亦称异端派,与逊尼派对立而居于少数的一种学派;两派分歧在于对伊马目的作用和《古兰经》经文的理解上)

shibboleth n. 1.(《圣经》中)考验的词,任何考验的词;口号,口令 2.(党派、行业、集团等的)行话,术语,口头禅,习俗,习惯 3.陈词滥调,过时的信仰(或教义)

shield n./v. 盾;保护者;庇护者;(美)警察徽章/庇护,掩盖,避开(off),保护

Shield Law 《庇护(新闻秘密)法》(指美国一半以上的州通过的一种立法,该法保护新闻记者和其他新闻工具的报道人员,倘若不能透露新闻来源时,不被监禁、不被罚款、不被控告,使他们分享律师、医生和牧师的豁免权利)

shift v./n. 1.变更,移动,转移 2.推托;欺骗;策划;图谋/1.变更,移动,转移 2.推托,欺骗;设法应付 3.手段,权宜之计;瞒骗,图谋;变换,更易 4.工作班,轮班

shift for oneself 摆脱困境

shift the burden of proof 逃避举证责任,转移举证责任

shift the responsibility upon 把责任推卸给(别人),转嫁责任

shifting n. 狡赖,通词诈术(的使用);移动

shifting clause (财产授予中的)转换条款

shifting facts 政变的事实

shifting of a delinquent 罪犯的抵赖

shifting population 流动人口

shifting tax consequence 转嫁税收后果

shifting use 转移用益权

shiftless a. 无能的,无力谋生的

shifty a. 善于应变的,多策略的;诡诈的;不正直的

shifty behaviour 可疑的行为;诡诈行为

Shinto n. 神道教(指纯粹的日本宗教,该教崇拜"Kami"——代表一种"神灵"和"概念")

ship n. 船舶,船只

ship abandoned 弃船

ship chartering 租船

ship inspection 船舶检查

ship license 船舶牌照

ship master 船长

ship money (英)造船税费(指英格兰中世纪末经议会通过的一种税收)

ship mortgage　船舶抵押权
Ship Mortgage Act　(美)《船舶抵押法》[指规定有关已登记船舶(如美国船舶)抵押的联邦法规,1920年国会通过]
Ship Owners Mutual Protection and Indemnity (P & I)　船主互保与赔偿
ship ownership　船舶所有权
ship registration　船舶登记
Ship Safety Convention　《船舶安全公约》
ship's articles　雇用船员条例
ship's company　一船之全体水手、船员(不包括官员)
ship's creditor　船舶债权人
ship's husband　船舶管理人,船舶代理人;随船押货人,船舶所有人的代理人
ship's manifest　轮船载货清单
ship's papers　船舶文件(指用来证明船舶的性质和所载的货物的文件,包括有注册证明书、提货单、卫生报告书、租约、航行日记等等);船证,船照
ship's passport　船舶执照,船照
ship's protest　船长海事声明(报告)
ship's warrant　船舶保证书
ship-owner n.　船主,船东
shipbroker n.　海运经纪人;船舶经纪人
shipbuilder n.　船舶制造商;造船工人
shipbuilding corporation　造船公司
shipload n.　船货,船舶运载量,(喻)大量
shiploads of merchandise　整船商品,大量商品
shipmaster n.　船长
shipment n.　装货,装船,装运;装载货物(量)
shipment inward　承销,承销品
shipment request　装运申请书
shipowner n.　船舶所有人
shipowner's lien　船舶所有人的留置权,船东留置权(指为了获得海事债务清偿、运费和滞期费,船东享有的留置权)
shippable a.　可装运的
shipper n.　托运人,发货人
shippers' contract　托运合同(指托运人与承运人之间的合同或契约)
shippers' order　托运人的指定人
shipping n.　1.船运;航运;运输 2.船舶的总称(=ships) 3.船舶的总吨数 4.某一国家、城市、企业界等船舶的集合称;运送,海运,装运
Shipping Act of 1984　(美)《1984年海运法》
shipping agent　船公司代理人,海运代理人,水陆运输业者
shipping articles　船员雇用合同(契约)
shipping bill(s)　海运单据;装货通知
shipping business　船运业
shipping by rail, water, and air　铁路、水上及空中的运输
shipping casualty　海难
shipping charges　装运费
shipping clause　装运条款
shipping country　海运国,装货国
shipping document　装运单据,货运单据
shipping exchange　海运交易所
shipping frustration　航程中止
(the) shipping industry　航运业
shipping inquiry　航运调查(指对航运事故的调查)
shipping law　海运法
shipping line　航线
shipping note　装船通知单,装货通知,装运通知单
shipping of freight　货载的发运
shipping office　货运业事务所,海运监事务所
shipping ring　海运同盟
shipping weight　装船重量,(船)离岸重量
shipwreck n.　船舶失事
shipwreck affidavits　轮船失事记录
shire n.　(英史)郡(指英格兰非常古老的行政区划);郡府所在地;县(行政区)
shire court　(英)郡法院
shire town　(英)郡府所在地(或县政府);高一级法院所在地
shirk v.　规避,逃避(义务,责任等);躲避
shirk one's duty toward　逃避……的责任
shock n./v.　震动,地震;震惊;撞击;休克,中风;精神损害/使震动,使休克
shock interrogation　突击审讯
shock probation　休克缓刑(美国运用非常广泛的一种缓刑类型,又称"休克假释"和

shock

"间歇性刑罚",它是指将犯罪人监禁一定时间后释放,并重新宣判缓刑和执行缓刑的刑罚措施。)

shock the conscience of the court 震惊了法庭的良知

shocking evidence 令人震惊的证据,可怕的证据

shoddy n. 粗制滥造,虚饰外观的劣等货

Shoe Standard of Fairness 国际鞋业案判决中的公正的标准[指 International Shoe Company v. State of Washington 案的判决,即使用最低联系分析法以评估行使对人管辖权的正当性与保留拟制的"物之所在地"(*situs* of the *res*)概念以决定准对物管辖的有效性之间存在不当的矛盾]

shoes n. (喻)地位,境遇;轮胎,外胎

shoot v. 1.发射,射出;抛出 2.开枪,射击,射中 3.拍摄 4.使爆炸

shoot off one's own (或 face) 轻率地说出(秘密等)

shoot on the spot 就地枪决

shooting n. 射击,射杀;持枪杀人;(英)射猎权,猎场

shooting iron (美)火器;(尤指)手枪

shop n./v. 商店,店铺;工厂,修理厂;职业;业务/逮捕,拘捕,告发(同犯)使入狱;选购

shop assistant 店员,售货员

shop book rule (美)(1998年)(证据法)账簿规则(指一种传闻规则的例外,如果账簿的记载是通常商业活动中作出的,且由保管账簿者证明,那么则允许原始账簿记录可被采纳作为证据)

shop books 账簿,账册(指商人用以记录业务活动的簿记,亦称 books of account; account books)

shop card (工会发给按劳资协议经营的商店)营业证,营业卡;车间工作卡

shop commitee (资本主义国家)厂矿中代表劳方与资方谈判的委员会

shop hours 营业时间

shop right (专利法)雇员发明实施权(指雇主可在其业务中免费使用雇员的发明权利),不排他使用权

shop rush 抢购

shop steward (美)(一个企业部门中选出的代表雇员的)工会官员;工人谈判代表

shop-lifter (或 **shoplifteer**) n. 冒充顾客进商店行窃者

shopkeeper n. 店主,掌柜

shoplifting n. (17世纪)入店行窃[指从商店窃取出售之商品,特别是蓄意从仓库或商店或商业机构盗窃或非法占有那里的商品,并隐藏起来变换交给其他人使用而不付款项。入店行窃是盗窃罪(larceny)的一种形式,但不是一个独立罪名。事实上根据盗窃罪法规,很难证明这种非法窃取与犯罪意图要件来定罪。所以在英国一般对入店行窃均多采用简易程序,适用监禁刑]

shopper n. 商店顾客,购物者;(商店雇用的)打听行情的人,代客选购的人;(美)当地商店的广告传单

shopping list 购货单

shopping mall (车辆不得入内,只限行人活动的)商业区

shore n. 滨,岸;涨潮线与低潮线之间的地带

shore lands 岸滨地;沿岸地带;可通航线与高水位线之间的地带;涨潮线与低潮线之间地带

shore line 滨海线

shore rights 停泊权

shore-side superintendent 岸上管理员

short a. 1.短期的;短的;简略的 2.卖空的,无存货的 3.不足的,缺少的

short ballot 短票选举(指限于对少数主要官员或议员等的选举)

short bill 短期汇票

short bonds 短期债券

short cause (或 **calendar**) 简易案件(指简单无难处的诉讼,一般审讯在两小时左右的案件);(无陪审团参与,只要一名法官审理的)简易诉讼

short cause list 简易案件表

short contract 卖空合同(契约)

short date (**bill**) 短期的(票据)

short exchange 短期汇票

short form 简易格式

short lease 短期租借

short list 压缩的最后候选人(或谋职者)名单

short run 短期的,小生产量

short run consumption function 短期消费函数

short sale (证券)卖空(指卖方并不拥有自己的股票来销售也未签合同约定出售时间。卖方必须借入股票进行交付。这样的卖空通常是在卖方期望股价下降时进行,如股价降了,卖方则以低价股票还给借方而从差价中获利,亦称 sale short)

short sale against the box (证券)以保险柜抵卖空[指一种证券卖空交易。即卖方拥有足够证券可供交易,但由于出售人想保持自己拥有证券的秘密,或者因为自己拥有的股票难以从信托机构取到,所以无论如何必须借入股票提供交易(这种信托保管在华尔街俚语中被称为"以保险柜为抵")。供交割的股票可用自己拥有的,亦可用借入的股票。因此,这种交易较之一般形式卖空而言风险较小。亦可缩写为 sale against the box]

short saller 卖空者

short salling 卖空行为

short sea trade 海上短程运输

short shipment 短货,装载不足

short shrift 1.临终忏悔 2.将死(或处死刑)的短暂时间

short summons (美)速达传票(指对潜逃、诈骗或无定居的债务人所发出的传票,要求比一般传票早几天得到回复)

short supply 供应不足

short time horizons 目光短浅

short title 简略标题(指法律的条、项等的简略标题,便于人们引用);简称

short-cause trial 简易案件审理(指要求抓很短时间审理的案件,通常用半天或更少些时间,亦称 short cause)

short-form merger 简易式兼并[指当母公司拥有子公司绝对多数股权时(如90%至95%),母公司强制收购子公司少数股东股权,并把少数股东排挤出去的兼并(Parent-Subsidiary)]

short-handed a. 人手不足的

short-list n. 精选的名单

short-run production 小批生产

short-shipped a. 退关的;(货物)已报关但未装船(或重新起岸)的

short-shipped goods 短装货

short-term assets 短期资产

short-term bonds 短期公债

short-term credit 短期信用

short-term capital gain 短期资本收益[指持有资产短于规定时期(specified period)内出售或交易所获取的收益。依据最近联邦税法,这是作为正常收益(ordinary gain)来对待]

short-term imprisonment 短期徒刑

short-term loan 短期借贷,短期借款

short-term orders 短期指令

short-term plan 短期计划

short-term prisoner 短刑期罪犯,短刑犯

short-timer (或 short-termer) 服短期徒刑的犯人

shortage of qualified judge 不够合格的法官

shortcut n. 近路,捷径

shortest route algorithm 最近路程算法,最短路程算法

shortfall n. 缺少,亏损

shortfall freight 亏舱运费

shorthand n. 速记法,速记;记录文字

shorthand writer's notes 庭讯速记记录,案件速记记录

shot n. 1.弹丸;炮弹;发射,射击;一发 2.射手;炮手 3.试图,试为 4.应付之款 5.照相,摄影

shot periodical rights 报刊使用权(见 newspaper right)

shot-proof a. 防弹的

shotgun n. 滑膛枪,(美俚)机关枪

shotgun agreement (用武力)强迫达成的协议(或缔结的协定)

shotgun marriage (或 wedding) 1.由于怀孕而被迫结婚,勉强的结合或同意 2.为需要而作妥协

show v./n. 1.显示,表现 2.解释,说明;告知 3.证明,表明 4.指示,引导;陈述,辩护/1.显示;展览,表示 2.迹象,痕迹,象征 3.借口

show bill 广告,招贴

show cause 说出理由,表明理由(见 shew

cause); 陈述案情, 为一案件作辩护
show of hands 举手表示(赞成, 反对或志愿等), 举手表决
show one's right 显示某人的权利; 表明某人的权利
show-up n. (=show up line)(被警察)排起来供检查和辨认的一队人; 揭露
showing n. 陈述, 显示, 展开
shrew n. 悍妇, 泼妇
shrewed lawyers 厉害的律师, 善辩的律师
shrievalty n. (英)(州、郡)司法行政官, 执行吏或郡长的职务(任期或职权); (美)县行政司法官的职务(任期或职权)
shrift n. 1.忏悔; 赦免; 临终忏悔 2.承认, 招认
shrink-wrap contract 拆封授权合同(指软件厂商在销售其产品时, 在软件产品的外包装上印明, 如购买者打开包装, 须受在该包装上面或里面的协议约束的合同, 此拆封授权合同源于美国)
shrink-wrap license 启封许可证 (见 box top license)
shuffle n./v. 支吾; 暧昧; 闪烁其词; 模棱两可; 可疑, 诡计/支吾; 弄乱; 乱堆
shuffle off 推卸(责任等); 除去
shuffle off responsibilities 把(自己的)责任推卸到别人身上
shuffling a. 支吾的, 含混的; 可疑的, 躲躲闪闪的; 规避的
shuggism n. 暗杀, 杀人, 暴行, 凶暴
shun v. 避开, 回避, 推延, 搁置(计划等), 把某人撇在一边, 来回运行, 往返
shut v. 关闭; 拒绝; 排出
shut a criminal into a prison 将一罪犯关入监狱
shut down (工厂、车间等)停工; 关闭, 停业
shut down cost 停工成本, 停产成本
shut down inspection 停工检查
shylock n. 狠毒无情的; 放高利贷者; 勒索者; 冷酷无情的(商)人
shyster n. 奸诈的律师; 讼棍; 不择手段的人(尤指政客等); 奸诈的人
* *Si duo in testamento pugnantia reperientur, ultimum est ratum.* If two conflicting provisions are found in a will, the last is observed. 如果在一个遗嘱中发现两个相互冲突的意思表示时, 后一个应该得到遵守。
* *Si quis praegnantem uxorem reliquit, non videtur sine liberis decessisse.* If a man dies, leaving his wife pregnant, he shall not be considered to have died without children. 一个男子死亡时, 如果留下的妻子已经怀孕, 则不应当看作无子女死亡。
* *Si vis pacem, para bellum.* If you wish for peace, be prepared for war. 如果你要和平, 就必须做好战争的准备。
siamese twins 连体婴儿, 连体胎
sib n. 氏族, 血亲亲属(尤指同胞兄弟姐妹); (总称)亲属
sibling n. (常用复)兄弟, 姐妹; 同胞; (同父异父同母或异母同父的)兄弟姐妹
sic 原文如此
sic in originali 原文如此
sic ut alias 第二次传票, 再次传票
* *Sic utere tuo ut ulienum non laedas.* Use your property so as not to damage another's, so use your own as not injure another's property. 使用自己的财产应不损及他人财产。("禁止损害"规则 no-harm rule 与此罗马法格言一脉相承, 是国家主权原则在国际关系中的具体体现)
sic volo sic jubeo 我的原意如此, 我的命令如此
sicker road 安全的道路
sickness n. 疾病
sickness allowance 医疗津贴
sickness and ill-health 疾病和健康状况不良
sickness benefit 疾病救济金, 疾病津贴
sickness insurance 疾病保险
* *Sicut nature nil facit per saltum, ita nec lex.* Just as nature, does nothing with a leap, so neither does the law. 如同自然, 法律也不能一蹴而就。
side n./a. 1.边, 侧; 河岸 2.集团, 政党, 派系; 方面, (当事人一方的)方 3.血统, 家系, 世系/侧的, 旁的, 不重要的; 枝节的
side arms 随身武器
side effect 副作用, 负面影响

side issue 次要问题,次要争点
side judge 陪审法官,陪审员
side light 偶然启示,间接说明
side line 副职,副业;兼职;支线
side note 旁注,附注
side product 副业产品
side reports 非官方报告(与 official reports 相对而言)
side witness 旁证
side-bar n./a. (英)法庭旁厅,陪席律师/兼职的,次要的
side-bar conference 单方法庭会议(指法官要求律师走近法官席,并与其直接交谈而不让陪审团听到的会议。它常常涉及复杂的争论和重要证据的争议)
side-bar lawyer 兼职律师
side(s)-man n. 教区副执事,(英)辅助教会委员
side-step v. 闪开,规避
side-step a responsibility 逃(规)避责任
sieve of cases 筛选案件,案件的筛选
sift v. 筛;细审;详查;盘问
sight n. 1.视力,眼界;瞥见 2.情景;意见;即场
sight bill 即期票据,见票即付汇票
sight credit 即期信用证
sight draft 即期汇票,见票即付
sight letter of credit 即期信用证
sight unseen (美)(购物时)事先未看现货,未经查看,未经查验,不看现货
sigil (古英国法)封铅,火漆,封蜡,封印;图章,玺,印章;用作图章的缩略签署
sign v./n. 签名,署名,签字/符号,记号;迹象,足迹
sign a statement of repentance 具结悔过书
sign away 签字让渡,签字让与财产
sign bill 签署法案
sign field 商标标识域
sign manual 亲笔签名;君主亲笔签名;文件上君主或行政长官的签字
sign on (或 up) 签字于雇佣合同(契约);签字于……
sign out 用签名(或考勤卡打卡)方式记录离去时间
sign over 签字移交(财产等)

sign up 1.签约参加工作(或组织);报名从军;〈sign up for〉(签约承担义务)2.签约雇佣(工人等);使签约者承担义务
sign value 标记价值
signal n./v. 信号/v.暗号/用信号通知,标志,向……发出信号
signal code 通信密码
signal flag 信号旗
signal of distress (或 distress signal) (船只等的)遇难信号
signaling mechanism 信号机制
signalment n. 1.有关通缉犯特征的描述 2.特殊记号
signatories n. 签署国
signatory n./a. (协议、条约等的)签署者;签署国;签署人/签署的,签约的
signatory of a bill of exchange 汇票上签署的人
signatory representative 签约代表
signatory state 签字国,签署国
signature n. 签名,签署,署名
signature ad referendum 暂签(指对条约正本的认证,如果条约正本未经其他方式认证的话,对条约正本的一种临时签字或听候政府指示期中的一种临时签字)
signature bond (美)签署保释保证证书(指一种保释办法的证明,可以邮寄不要求交付现金,但被告如未按法庭要求出庭,则必须支付证书上的金额的现金),签署承诺保证金
signature by facsimile 穿空签字,传真签字
signature by symbols 符号签字
signature loan 无担保贷款,不需抵押品的贷款
signature of witness 证人签署
signature specimen 签署式样
signature subject to 待核准的签署,附条件签署
signature-less a. 未经签字的
signboard n. 招牌,广告牌
signed check 记名支票
signed receipt 签收
signed return receipt 签名的回执,签名的收到凭据
signer n. 签字人

signet n. 小图章;御玺(指女王的印章)
significance n. 重要,重大;意义,意味
significance of law 法律含义
significative a. 1.有意义的;表示的 2.为……提供推定证据的
signified 所指(见 signifier "能指"条)
signifier 能指[指商标三元结构及其符号学分析中的一个术语,瑞士语言学家索绪尔(1857—1913)提出了被后世奉为圭臬的符号学思想:可以设想建立一门研究社会中各种符号生命的科学,这将成为社会心理学的一部分,我把它称为符号学。符号学是研究符号构成及其规律。"能指"与"所指"是符号组成的二元实体,指可以被感知的形式,如单词读音,可代表特定心理构成]
signify v. 表示,表明,意味;要紧,有重要性
signing n. 签署,签名
signing authority 签字权,签署权
signing by command 奉命签署
signing judg(e)ment (英)判决签字(指获得判决的当事人准备两份判决书交法院主管官员签字)
signing-bonus n. 签约酬金
signoria eminente sullacosa 对物显要的主宰
signpost n. (十字路口的)路标
* *Siguid universitati debertur singuli nin debetur, nec quod debet universitas singuli debent.* If anything be owing to an entire body (or to a corporation), it is not owing to the individual members, nor do the individuals owe that which is owing by the entire body. 团体债务与其成员债务各不相干。
silence n. 缄默,沉默,静默,无声;无音信,无联系;沉默权
Silence gives consent. 沉默即表示同意。
silent a. 沉默的;不作声的;未说出的;未作记述的
silent complicity 沉默的共谋(见 corporate complicity)
* *Silent leges inter arma.* The power of law is suspended during war. 战争时期法律不彰(战时法律失去效力)。
silent partner 隐名合伙人,无经营权(或发言权)的合伙人

silent system (美)沉默制度,(禁止犯人相互交谈的)监禁制度,禁言制(又称 Ausburn 制,指监狱的一项管理制度,起源于波士顿,即犯人在劳动中禁止交谈,后为许多州监狱所采纳)
silent trade (古代一种将交换物置于一定地点彼此不见面而各取所需物品的)物物交换,无声交易
silent vote 不记名投票;(有资格投票而)不投票者的票数;(对候选人、政见等事先)不表示意见者所投的票
silicon valley (美)硅谷(指尖端技术生产中心)
silent witness 静默证人(指关于美国对于录像带在何种情况下具有可信性基础的两种不同理论之一,另一种为图像证词"pictorial testimony"。它的观点是:录像本身就相当于一个"哑巴证人",放映录像与听取证人评议两者获得的证词没有任何区别,而且在某些情况下,录像带甚至优于证人证言。因此,"静默证人"理论认为,即使没有目击证人,只要录像带操作正常,中途无人移动,录像带仍然具有独立的证据作用)
Silk n. (英)王室律师,王室法律顾问
silk gown 王室律师(见 Silk)
silver n./a. 银;银币/银的;银质的;银制的
Silver Platter Doctrine 银盘原则(指美国各州的警察治安人员,对被控犯州法律的人,非法搜查其住宅或人身而取得的联邦证据,得于联邦法院加以应用,但需以联邦治安人员未参与该非法搜查为限)
silver standard 银本位
silviculture n. 造林,林垦;造林学
similar n/a. 类似物,类似者/相似的,类似的
similar accidents 类似的意外事件
similar case 类似案件,类似情况
similar case should be treated similarly. "同案同判"(指德国法理学家考夫曼曾经说过的"同案同判"的哲理—正义的核心是平等。法律被认为是不分轩轾地援用到一切情况,一切任务,不论贫富,无分贵贱。法律能这样毫无差别地适用才可称得上是"正义的实践")
similar facts 同类事实

similar legislation 类似立法,类似的法规
similar sales （美）类似销售（国家征用）[指在依法征用引起的诉讼（condemnation action）中,对于特定财产在市场价格上存在争议情况下,则可依据类似财产在相同地区和时间范围（time frame）内销售状况作为依据来确定价格]
similar situation 类似情形
similarity n. （知识产权）类似性,相似性[指一个商标或版权所有的作品（copyrighted work）与另一件相似（resemblance）。一个商标与另一个很可能极为相似等同于侵权（infringement）,这取决于产品的性质（nature of product）,而且买主要更加小心期待在特定的市场上作出选择,这是一个全面的印象问题（question of overall impression）而不是两个商标（marks）的一个要素和一个要素的比较问题。亦称 imitation; colorable imitation。见 substantial similarity]
similiter 依然,同样（方式）（普通法抗辩用语）
similitudinary bigamy 类似重婚罪
simon-pure a. 真正的,货真价实的;不受贿的,清白的;伪装纯正的
simoniac n. 买卖圣职的人
simony n. 买卖圣职;买卖圣职罪;卖圣物牟利
simple a. 普通的,简单的,简易的,单纯的,单一的,完全的
simple adoption 单纯收养
simple agreement 简单的意思表示一致
simple assault 单纯强暴罪（指行为人企图以暴力施加有形的伤害于他人的一种罪行）
simple average (=particular average) 单独海损
simple bastard 单纯的私生子;普通私生子
simple contingency 单纯偶然性
simple contract 1.口头契约（合同）;无签名的合同（契约）2.简单合同（契约）（指按口头诺言订立的但无完备形式、未加盖印记的非正式合同）,简式合同
simple contract creditor 普通债权人（指无担保债权人）

simple contract debts 简式合同（契约）债务,简式合同（契约）之债
simple formalistic framework 简单的形式主义框架
simple guarantee 单独保证
simple insurance 单保险
simple interest 单利（息）
simple larceny 单纯的盗窃罪（指不带有任何威胁的盗窃,古英国法中分单纯盗窃罪为大、小两种;盗窃12便士以上的为大的单纯盗窃罪,10便士以下的为小的单纯盗窃罪。见 compound larceny）
simple legacy 单纯遗赠
simple legal charge 单纯法律负担
simple licensing agreement 普通许可证协议（指被许可方和许可方及经同意后的第三方都可在一定地区内享有专利、商标使用权的协议）
simple majority vote(s) 简单多数票
simple negligence 简单过失
simple obligation 单纯债务;无条件的义务
simple organ 单一机关
simple partnership 单纯合伙,普通合伙
simple resolution （18世纪）单一决议（指国会参众两院中只有一个院通过,它表明通过的议院的意见,并影响其内部事务,但该决议没有法律效力）
simple（或 unitary）states 单一国（具有代表国家意志及权力的唯一最高当局称单一国,或一个统一的主权国家）
simple trust 单一信托
simple warrandice （苏格兰）单独保证
simplification of procedure 简化诉讼程序（手续）
simplified pleading 简式诉状
simplified procedure 简易普通程序
simplify v. 精简,简化,使单纯,使易懂
simplify the administrative structure 精简行政机构
simplistic a. 过于简单的
simplistic explanation 过于简单的解释
Simply Acta 《每日纪闻》（见 Acta Diurna）
simply ad. 坦率地,单纯地,简单地,直率地;只是,仅仅,只不过
simply tribunal 单一的裁判庭

simulate a./v. 伪装的,模拟的/假装,伪装,冒充;模仿,模拟
simulate bomb 假炸弹
simulated contract (大陆法)虚假合同 [指经过相互意愿一致订立的合同,但并未表示当事双方的真实意图(true intent),参见《路易斯安那州民法典》第2025条(La. Civ. Code art. 2025)。在双方当事人意图该合同不强加任何义务时,该虚假合同是绝对的;根据此种合同,双方没有任何义务需要履行。如果当事双方意图该合同强加的义务不同于合同中陈述的义务时,则虚假合同是相对性的(relative);如果所有相关条件得以满足,那么意图的义务可强制执行。虚假合同影响第三当事方的权利。亦称 simulation。见 action en declaration de simulaed]
simulated death 装死
simulated fact 伪造的事实
simulated scene 伪造的现场
simulated training 模拟训练
simulated trials 模拟的法庭
simulation n. (通谋)虚伪表示;模拟,假装
simulation (或 false) declaration intention 虚伪表示,假装的表示(为故意的不一致的一种。表意人为欺骗第三人而与相对人通谋,故意作非真意的表示,因此又称通谋虚伪表示 false declaration of intention known to other party conspiracy)
simulation of disease 诈病
simulation of injury 伪伤
simultaneous a. 同时发生的,同时的
simultaneous death 同时发生的死亡
simultaneous distribution 联合分布
simultaneous equation 联立方程式
simultaneous interpretation 同声传译,同声口译,同声翻译
simultaneous publication 同时出版(指按"两约"规定,30天内先后在两个或两个以上国家出版某作品,应视为同时出版。我国亦有同样规定)
simultaneous verification 同时论证
sin n./v. 罪,罪恶,罪行;犯罪,犯法;不该做的事/犯罪;犯法;违背,违犯
sin money 赎罪金

(a) **sin unpunishable by law** 法律不能处罚的罪
sinallagma 双务契约(来源于希腊语,包括两个双向给付义务的协议),相互给付之债
sine 无
sine anno 日期不详,无注明年代
sine causa 无原因的
sine die 无限期,不定期
sine legitima prole 无法定子女,无嫡出后代
sine mascula prole 无男性后代
sine mora sine mora 立即,不迟延
sine prole 无子女
sine prole superstite 无后代,无子孙
sine qua non 绝对必需(的条件或资格),必要条件;必要事物;不可缺,必要者
sinecure n. 挂名职务;闲职;只领工资不干活
sinere 容许
sinful a. 有罪的,罪孽深重的;罪重的,不道德的
sinful thoughts 充满罪恶的思想
sing out (美俚)(向法院或警方)自供,告密
Sing Sing 新新监狱(美国纽约州的一所大监狱)
singe n./v. 损伤,损害;烧焦,烤焦
single a. 单一的,单独的,个别的;独身的,未婚的
single account 个人账户
single action 单个诉讼
single adultery 一方未婚的通奸(或和好)(指未婚者与有配偶者之间的通奸)
single agency 单独代理
single agreement 简单协议,单一协议
single analytical framework 单一分析框架
single Assembly 一院制的国民会议
single ballot 一次投票
Single Banking License 单一银行许可(指欧共体银行法的一项独有原则。据此原则,凡在欧共体一成员国内取得许可证的信用机构,有权在其他成员国内自由设立分行并提供经许可的服务,而无须经东道国的另行许可或授权)

single body of law 单一的法的体系；单一法体
single chamber （议会的）一院制
single combat 一人对一人的斗殴；两人之间的战斗
single contract 统一合同
single convention 单一公约
single currency peg 单一货币挂钩
single defendant 单一被告
single dimension 一维方式
single election 一次选举，直接选举
single entity 单一的实体
single entry 单式记账
single escheat 单独没收；(英）个别没收（指因某人被宣布为叛乱者而将其所有动产没收归国王）
Single European Passport 单一欧洲护照（指欧共体运用相互承认的法律技术要求各东道成员国承认银行母国的现行银行许可制度的效力，借以使其母国颁发的银行护照在整个欧共体有效，由此创立这一通行于整个欧共体的单一欧洲护照）
single finger dactylography 单指指纹法，单指指纹分析
single folio book 单页对开本
single form of civil action 单一的民事诉讼形式
single government fee 一次缴纳的费用
single heir 单一继承人
single insurance 单独保险，个别保险
single issue rights 报刊使用权（见 newspaper right）
single（或 sole）judge 独任法官
single juror charge 单一陪审员反对指示（指法官向陪审团说明，如果有任一陪审员不能根据证据合理确信原告应该胜诉时，则陪审团不能作出原告胜诉的裁断的指示）
single law 单一法
single legal entity 单一法律实体
single letter 一页纸的信
single license principle 单一执照原则
single legal system 单一的法律制度，单一的法的体系
single life 独自生活

single list of candidates 单一的候选人名单
single loan 单一借款(债款)
single majority 简单的多数
single man 独身男子
single market 统一市场
single member company 一人公司
single memorial 唯一记载
single national constituency 单一的全国选区
single nationality 单一国籍
single negotiating text 单一协商文本
single offender 偶(然)犯
single one 单一的个人(无政府主义从"单一的个人"，即具体的自我出发的个人主义，它否认任何国家和法律)
single or multifactor variants of the capital assets pricing model 资本资产定价模式的单一或多因素变量
single original 单一的原始文件
single party government 一党政府
single payment 整笔(款)支付
single plaintiff 单一原告
single practitioners 单独开业者(或律师)
single proprietor 独资(企业)
single（或 sole）proprietorship 一个人所拥有的商业，个人所有权
single res 同一标的物，单一标的物
single right 单项权利，单一的权利
single shipowner 唯一所有人；只有一条船的船舶所有人
single standard 1.统一标准；单本位制 2.全体适用的道德标准
single state 单一的国家
single system of government 单一的政府体制
single tax 统一税，单一税
single transferable vote 一次性转移性投票(指选举人所选的候选人未能取得绝对多数当选时，将他的一票转给另一候选人的一种投票方式)
single uniform body of law 单一的统一的法的体系
single vote 单一投票表决
single woman 独(单)身女人
single-act statute （美)单一行为法规，单

一行为制定法(该法规将州法院对人的管辖权扩大到"正当程序条款所允许的程度")

single-aspect methods 单点要素方法(英美法系国家的传统理论和实践是通过所谓"单点要素"方法让法官对案件的性质进行识别,然后根据一审的"连结点"把该案件同连结点所指向的法域连接起来以适用该地法律,达到判决趋于一致的目的)

single-candidate system 单一候选人制

single-chamber a. 仅有一院的(国会);一院制的

single-chamber legislature 一院制立法机构

single-child policy 独子女政策(中)(一对夫妇只生)一个孩子的政策

(the) single-eye to the subsidiary's interest test 关注子公司利益标准

single-handed a. 独立的,无助的,单枪匹马

single-head system 首长制,一长制

single-member company 一人公司

single-member district plan 单数选举区制

single-member constituency 单个议员选区(指一个选区选出一名议员)

single-name paper 只有开票人背书的期票

single-party system 一党制

singlehood n. 独身,未婚状态

singrafe 约据

singular a. 单一的,独特的,奇特的;非凡的,卓越的

singular sample 独一无二的样本

singular successor 单项继承的继承人,特定继承人

sinister a. 凶兆的;阴险的,凶恶的,邪恶的,不幸的,不吉利的

sinister design 阴谋

sink v./n. 1.沉没,堕落;降低(名誉、地位等)2.偿还(债务)3.隐匿(证据等),掩饰 4.忽视,把……放在一边;弃置不用;投资失败,投资受损/阴沟;藏污纳垢的地方

sink evidence 掩饰证据,隐匿证据

sinking n. 偿还债务,投资

sinking damages 偿还损害赔偿

sinking funds 偿债基金,减债基金(指以常规存款并累积利润而构成的基金用来支付长期法人或公债或国债,简称 SF.)

sinking-fund debenture (1893年)偿债基金担保债券[指担保设立的退休长期债务(retire long-term debt)的基金做担保,定期偿债的债券或凭证]

sinking spell 跌价期间(指股票等)

sinless a. 无罪的,无辜的,清白的

sinner n. (宗教和道德上的)罪人;无赖

Sino-British Joint Declaration on the Question of Hong Kong, 1984 1984年《中英关于香港问题的联合声明》

Sino-British Joint Liaison Group 中英联合联络小组(指依中华人民共和国政府和大不列颠及北爱尔兰联合王国政府关于香港问题的联合声明成立的小组)

Sino-foreign cooperative accounting firms 中外合作会计师事务所

Sino-US Joint Economic Committee 中美联合经济委员会(1975)

Sino-US Trade Agreement 《中美贸易关系协定》(1980)

sint-in demonstrations 静坐抗议示威

siphon v. 吮吸(民脂民膏)(off)

sirdar n. (印度等国的)酋长,贵族;工头;佃农

sist n. (苏格兰)中止案件(指诉讼程序中中止案件审理一段时间,也指使某人成为案件一方当事人)

sister n. 姐妹,姐,妹;同父异母(同母异父的)姐妹;姑子,姨子,嫂子,弟媳;修女,女教士;尼;女会员;女社友;(英)护士长,护士

sister nations 姐妹国家

sister ships 姐妹(船)舰,同类(船)舰

sister-in-law n. 1.夫或妻的姐妹 2.兄或弟的妻.姻兄、姻弟的妻

sister-state conflict of laws (美)州际冲突法,州际抵触法

sit v. (14世纪)1.就位,就法官之位〈Judge Wilson sit on the trial court for the Easten District of Arkansas.〉(威尔逊法官担任阿肯色州东区审理法院法官职位。)2.主持(法官主持)(指主持开庭或履行职务的功能)〈Is the judge sitting this week?〉(法官

本周开庭吗?)3.(法庭或立法部门)开庭,开会〈The Supreme Court sits from October to June.〉(最高法院从六月到十月开庭。)

sit at session 听审;开审

sit in cases of summary procedure 紧急(或即决)裁定

sit in judg(e)ment 审判;判断;(自告奋勇)评判他人(行为)

sit in panel 组成合议庭开庭(美国、加拿大将 panel 作合议庭解,指挑选出一组法官来裁决某案件,尤指上诉法院开庭的由3名法官组成的合议庭)

sit on/upon 1.(为陪审团、委员会等的)成员;调查,询问 2.开会讨论〈the jury sat on the case〉(陪审团开会讨论案件)3.扣押(新闻,提案等)4.责备,压制〈He wants sitting on〉(得好好责备他一顿才行)

sit on a fence 持观望态度,采取骑墙态度,保持中立不偏

sit on the case 开会讨论案件,调查案件

sit on (upon) the jury 参加陪审团,作为陪审团成员

sit on thorns 如坐针毡,局促不安

sit-down n. (美)静坐罢工;座位

sit-down strike 静坐罢工,在工厂罢工

sit-in n. 静坐示威(指一种工人非暴力的反抗或斗争的方式)

sit-in demonstration 静坐示威[20世纪60年代静坐示威席卷美国南部,其目的在于铲除公共膳宿场所的种族歧视。国会依据美国联邦宪法第十三和第十四修正案的权限行事,在《1875年民权法》中已禁止了这方面的歧视。但该法在民权系列案(Civil Rights Cases)(1883年)中被联邦最高法院推翻。联邦最高法院裁定联邦宪法第十三修正案的禁止奴隶制度或强迫性奴役的禁止性规定并不适用于公共膳宿场所的歧视;同时也裁定第十四修正案并未授权国会直接禁止私人歧视行为,而仅仅是禁止歧视性的"国家行为"。这一判决和 Plessy v. Ferguson (1896年)一案的判决将"隔离但公平原则"(separate but equal)合法化,作为平等保护条款(the Equal Protection Clause)的合法注释。依此两个判决,南部诸州重新制定了它们各自的宪法,要求隔离公共设施和膳宿场所。这样,"平等性"内涵几乎被完全忽略了。"二战"之后,反对公共膳宿方面的种族歧视运动高涨。1947年哈瑞·S·杜鲁门总统领导的民权委员会建议"由各州的法律规定保障所有人平等进入公共膳宿场所的权利,不论种族、肤色、宗教信仰和国家来源如何"。直至1962年,已有28个州制定了这样的法律,但南部无一州制定此法。北部也依然存在种族歧视,而南部诸州要求隔离公共设施。1960年2月1日格林斯博罗(北卡罗来纳)市4名黑人大学生为抗议一校园快餐馆拒绝为他们提供服务而"静坐示威"数日,以后引起不断有学生参加,静坐示威席卷全国,约有7000黑人大学生和白人大学生(多来自北方)投入运动,约3600人被捕,并以破坏和平、非法侵入、拉皮条、流氓等各种罪名被定罪,并对其家人施加暴力和经济制裁。联邦最高法院很快受理了静坐示威的上诉案件。这些案件的最基本争议是:是否存在完全的"国家行为",从而可推翻认定为私人歧视的裁决,转而认定为州支持种族歧视的行为。前一行为并未违反宪法而后一行为则是第十四修正案所禁止的。联邦法院推翻了这些定罪,裁定市镇官员言论属州行为,等于一项政令。联邦最高法院裁定以侵入罪(对 Bell v. Maryland)(1964)案完全"中立"的逮捕示威者是推翻所定罪名的充分依据。大多数大法官不愿让第十四修正案演变为公共膳宿场所法。《1964年民权法》(Civil Rights Act of 1964)第二编在 Heart of Atlanta Model v.United States (1964)一案中被联邦最高法院裁定有效。该法禁止公开膳宿场所的种族歧视。国会已经承认静坐示威的权利主张和此政策的合法性]

sit-in strike 静坐罢工

site n. 地点,场所,工地;位置;遗址

site-audit n. 就地审计

sitting after term 开庭期(限)后开庭

sitting duck 易于欺骗的对象(目标),易于射中的目标

sitting en banc 全体法规审理

sitting in banc (或 banco) 全体法官出庭

（见 en banc）
sitting in camera　秘密开庭,非公开审讯（亦译:内庭聆讯）
sitting in chamber　庭内审理
sitting in diversity　审理异籍案件
sitting in term　开庭期(限)内开庭
sitting judge　现任法官
sitting magistrate　审判官
sittings　法院开庭期[指法院一年中处理司法事务和开庭审理案件的期限。英国以前不管普通法或衡平法均用"terms"表示开庭期,并区分开庭期内的开庭期和开庭期后的开庭期。1873—1875年《司法组织法》或《司法法》(Judicature Act)废除了开庭期(terms),而代之以开庭期(sittings)。最高法院每年有四个开庭期。见four sittings]
sittings of magistrate's court　治安法庭开庭期
situated　a.　坐落……的,位于……的,处于某种境地的
situation　n.　形势,政局;位置,地位,处境,境遇
situation ethics　应变道德观(指道德标准须依情况而定),实用主义的道德观
situation of alien　外国人的地位
situation of danger　危险处境(见 last clear chance doctrine)
situation of legal entity　法人的地位
situation offences（或 situational offences）　状态犯;状态犯罪(见 state of affairs offences)
situational approach　情境研究方法
situational thinking　情境思维
situs　地点;部位,位置
situs conception　所在地的概念(指以此概念作为管辖根据)
situs of account payable　付款场所,应付款项场所
situs of corporate securities　公司债券的处所
situs of crime　犯罪地点
situs of stock　股票的所在,股票的所处
situs of the agreement　协议(或合同)的地点

situs of the res　物之所在地,物之地点,诉讼标的物的(财产)所在地
situs rules　按财产所在地征税的规定
situs test　所在地标准
Six Acts　(英)《关于保卫英国治安的六个法令》(1819年)
six and eight (pence)　(英)六先令八便士(指以前付给律师的一般费用)
six codes　六法全书(国民党政府的主要法规汇编。亦指法国在颁布《民法典》《商法典》《民事诉讼法典》《刑事诉讼法典》《刑法典》后又颁布《宪法》,日本将其译为日文,称为公法,在日本广为流传)
Six Libres de la republique　《论共和国》[或译《国家六论》,法国的博丹(Jeon Bodin 1530—1590)首次将主权一词引入政治学,并创主权学说,他的名著《国家六论》中首次提出主权,并对主权进行系统阐述]
six-day licence　(英)六日许可证(指允许星期日全日关闭的场所的许可证,是按1964年许可证法例所规定的附带条件发给的)
Sixteenth Amendment　美国联邦宪法第十六修正案[该修正案于1909年7月12日由国会提出,1913年2月25日批准生效。"国会有课征所得税之权,不必问其所得之来源,不必分配于各州,也不必根据户口调查或统计,以定其税额。"该修正案是对联邦最高法院对"波洛克诉农场主贷款与信托公司案"(Pollock v. Farmer's Loan & Trust Co.)(1895)的判决回应。该案中联邦最高法院认为这种税属直接税(direct tax),只能按人口调查或统计比例分摊于各州而征收,故宣布1894年联邦税法违宪。这一判决迅速引发了推翻它的努力,随着联邦政府规模不断扩大,传统税源收入匮乏,另一方面公众对因工业化而使贫富悬殊日益不满,最终导致第十六修正案产生。这一逐步形成的所得税很快成为联邦政府的主要财政税源,并一直持续至今]
Sixth Amendment　美国联邦宪法第六修正案[该修正案赋予刑事被告数项重要权利,在刑事案件中,被告人有权要求罪案

发生地之州或区的公正的陪审团迅速公开审判,要求获悉被控罪名和理由,要求与原告的证人对质,要求以强制手段促使对被告有利的证人出庭作证以及要求律师协助辩护。该修正案不仅适用于联邦政府,也适用于各州。同时,该修正案已合理地融入联邦宪法第十四修正案的正当法律程序条款(Due Process Clause of The Fourteenth Amendment)之中]

Sixth Amendment phrase 美国联邦宪法第六修正案的内容宣告

Sixth Decennial (美)《第六个十年判决摘要汇编》(系指由西方出版公司出版的自1946年至1956年的判决摘要汇编)

sizable a. 大的,相当大的

sizable antitrust judg(e)ment 相当严重(大)的反托拉斯判决

size n. 规模,尺寸,大小,身价,声望,才干,真相,实佳,巨大

skeleton n./a. 骷髅;骨骼;(建筑物的)残骸;骨瘦如柴之人(或动物);(文学作品等的)梗概;骨干/骨骼的,概略的;基干的

skeptical a. 怀疑的,不信的;怀疑论者的,多疑的

skeptical of arguments 证据的质疑

skepticism (=scepticism) n. 怀疑主义,怀疑论

sketch n./v. 草图,概略/描述,草拟

skill grades 技术等级

skill standard 技术标准

skilled a. 有经验的;有训练的;熟练的;有技术的

skilled (unskilled) labour (worker) 熟练(不熟练)工人,技术工

skilled witness 技能证人(指法院聘请有专门知识的人运用他的专门知识对案件的专门性问题进行鉴别和判断来认定事实)

skilled workers' school 技工学校

skimming n. 赌场(少报收入)瞒税

skin n. 皮,皮肤;(美俚)骗子

skin flick 裸体黄色影片

skin game 骗局

skin magazine 裸体杂志,色情刊物

skinner n. 皮革商;剥皮者;(俚)骗子

skip v. 1.跳过,略过;悄悄离开(某地);匆匆离开 2.漏过,遗漏

skip bail (或 **jump bail**) 保释中逃跑

skip person (1988年)(美)(税法)隔代人[指示转让人(transferor)更多隔一代的受益人及其在隔代转让税中资产已被转让,参见美国《国内税收法》,《美国注释法典》第26标题卷第2613节。见 generation-skipping transfer tax]

Skull & Bones (美)骷髅会(指1833年在耶鲁大学校内秘密成立的团体,许多耶鲁出身的政商界名流均为其成员)

skul(1) duggery n. 诡计;(美俚)欺骗,诈骗

skunk n. 1.卑鄙的人;下流 2.赖账,欺骗

sky n. 天,天空;(复)气候,天气

sky jacker 空中劫机的人

sky jacking 空中劫持飞机

sky man 飞机驾驶员;(美俚)伞兵

sky marshal 空中警官

sky master 巨型客机

sky pilot 飞机驾驶员

sky truck (大型)运输机

skyjack n./v. 劫机事件/劫机

skyjacker n. (空中)劫机者

skyway n. 航路;高架公路

slack tax 见 pickup tax

slacking at work 怠工

slacktivism n. 懒人行动主义

slammer n. 监狱

slander n. 诽谤,言词诽谤,诽谤罪;中伤;谩骂行为;造谣

slander and libel 口头和书面的诽谤罪

slander of business 商业诽谤

slander of goods 商品诽谤(诉讼)

slander of property 财产诽谤(诉讼)

slander of title 权利诽谤;诋毁(他人的财产)所有权(指一种恶意诽谤他人的物业或权利,使其蒙受损失,例如,说人家住宅闹鬼,以致租不出去)

slanderer (=slander-monger) n. 诽谤者,造谣中伤者

slanderous a. 诽谤的,造谣中伤的,诋毁的

slanderous *per se* 本质性侮辱(指语言本质属于侮辱,无须证明)

slang n. 1.俗话;(盗贼等的)行道话;隐语 2.(美俚)欺骗,诈骗
slang for fingerprint 潜指纹
slap additional taxes 任意加税
slap on the wrist 略予申斥
slash v. 乱砍,猛劈,鞭打;挥(剑,鞭等);(大幅度)削减;减低(工资),减少(犯罪)等
slate n./v. (美)候选人(提名)名单,内定用人名单;(操行等)记录/(美)提名……为候选人,内定……任某职
slate club (英)(成员每周缴少量钱的)互助会
slaughter n. 屠杀,杀戮;屠宰
slaughter man 刽子手,杀人者
slaughter of the innocents (英)(议会中乘会期快满而作出的)撤销某些议案的决定
slaughterer n. 屠夫;屠杀者,刽子手
slave n. 奴隶;苦役
slave labour 奴役性劳动,强迫劳动
slave trade (或 **traffic**) 奴隶贩卖,贩卖奴隶(罪)
slaver n. 奴隶贩子;诱骗女子为娼者(= white slave)
slavery n. 奴隶制度;奴役;苦役;束缚
slavish a. 奴隶的,奴隶性的;缺乏独创性的;盲从的
slavish thinking 奴才思想
slavocracy n. (美)(南北战争前南方的)维护奴隶制的统治集团
slay n. 1.砍死,斩死,杀死;杀害 2.克服,压倒
slayer n. 杀人者,凶手
sleep around 随便发生性行为,乱搞男女关系
sleeper n. 睡眠者;懒人;死人;长期潜伏的特务
sleeping draught 安眠药
Sleeping Judge (英)睡觉的法官[指17世纪英国一位名叫多德里奇(Mr. Judge Doderidge)的法官常常在法官席上闭上眼睛以免被周围事物打扰,这样来聚精会神地听取辩论,被民众误认为"睡觉的法官"]
sleeping partner (dormant, silent, partnership) 隐名合伙人;隐名股东(指不参与实际业务的股东)
sleeping partnership 隐名合伙(指合伙的一种特殊形式,当事人双方约定一方对他方出资,不参加执行业务但可分享收益,并仅以其出资额为限承担责任的合伙。其中负责合伙事务执行的一方为出名营业人,只出资而不执行业务的一方为隐名合伙人)
sleeping pill 安眠药丸
sleeping rent 固定的租金
sleight-of-hand n. 戏法,花招,魔术
sleuth n. 一种嗅觉敏锐的警犬,(美俚)侦探
slicker n. (美俗)骗子,油腔滑调的人
slickster n. 骗子
slide v. 滑动;潜行,溜进;使滑动
sliding scale approach 滑动标尺法(指根据被告通过网络所从事的行为与法院地的密切程度来决定法院是否有管辖权的方法,也是美国长臂管辖应用到涉及互联网的国际民事案件中确定管辖权的方法)
sliding scale of probable cause 滑动的相当理由(指美国对卧底警探之证明标准。"相当理由"可以根据罪行的轻重程度在一定范围内浮动,并无统一标准)
sliding scale price 滑动价格,浮动价格
sliding scale tariff 滑动关税,浮动关税
sliding scales (按市场等情况调整工资、价格、税收等的)滑动计算法,浮动比例
sliding-scale approach 可调整范畴的方法,浮动制的办法
slight a./v. 轻微的;不稳固的,脆弱的/轻视,蔑视,怠慢
slight fault 轻微错误
slight negligence 轻微过失
slight presumption 弱力推定(见 strong presumption)
slip n./v. 1.接枝,(喻)后裔 2.纸条,片条 3.滑,滑跌 4.错误,失误/1.失足,滑倒;滑脱,溜走;失误,犯错误 2.无意中说出,脱口而出
slip a cog 犯错误,做错事
slip bill 单行本议案
slip copy versions of law 法律的单行(译)文

slip decision (或 sheet, opinion) （美）判决原文单行本(系指非官方的活页服务资料出现几个星期后,官方的最高法院判决原文由法院自己出版单行本,这是第一个官方的权威性的判决原文)

slip law (1922年)单行法;议案单行法[指国会通过后并经总统签署的议案法单行本(活页小册子),是美国法规三种出版形式之一。以前,单行小册子还包括有如:《定期法律汇编》(session laws)或美国《制定法大全》(U. S. Statutes at large)。亦称 slip-law print]

slip of the pen 笔误

slip of the tongue 口误,舌音的误会

slip out of one's memory 被遗忘

slip rule 错漏规程(指法院的判决或命令如果有文字上的错误或遗漏,在接到询问或申请时,可随时更正)

slip treaty publication （美）条约单行本出版物

slip up 犯错误,失误,疏忽

slip-and-fall case (1952年)1.失足造成损伤案件(指因失足造成伤害而提起诉讼,通常针对被告的财产)2.广泛地说,轻微的侵权案

slip-law print 带注释的单行法(指国会制定的每部公法或私法经总统签署后即出版发行并附有注释。见 slip law; session laws)

slippage n. （美）降等(指在美国司法统计中被称为"降等"的,即在未被过滤案件首次传讯后在两周至一月内进行预审,或由大陪审团审查。其间,检察官还会撤销部分已经提出的指控。类似于我国刑事诉讼中将刑事案件改立为治安案件)

slippery a. 1.狡猾的;不可靠的 2.不安定的;不稳固的 3.含糊其词的,难以解释的

slot machine 投币式自动赌博机(俗称"吃角子"老虎)

slot-machine theory 投币机理论(一种讽刺性的术语以比喻将现存、已确定的法律原则直接运用到一系列新事实上去的做法)

Slow Journalism 慢新闻(为了获得点击率、阅读率和收视率,不少新闻媒体只顾发快讯、抢头条,报道重时效轻深度。该词条意指有意回避即刻写成的文章和肤浅的观点,倾向于采取用时较长的报道方式,并重点关注深度调查、深入分析的新闻报道。英国《先驱报》2004年7月10日发表《为堕落的媒体浇一桶冷水》一文时最早使用这一表达方式。文章写道:"这篇写得极好的短文相当于发出了对'慢新闻'的号召。"普利策新闻奖得主、美国记者保罗·萨洛佩克是一位典型的从事慢节奏新闻报道的记者。萨洛克计划从2013年至2020年完成名为"走出伊甸园"的报道。他从埃塞俄比亚的东非大裂谷徒步出发,沿7万年前离开非洲的古人足迹,渡过红海进入中东地区;穿越中国和西伯利亚,再从白令海峡进入美国阿拉斯加,随后沿着北美洲西海岸一路南下,直至南美洲智利,全程3万多公里,预计至少需迈出3000万步。旅行途中,他定期为美国《国家地理杂志》撰写文章,并在互联网通过文字和音视频记录自己的见闻)

slow-down n. 减退,减速;怠工

sludge n. 污物,污垢;(美俚)卑鄙,下流,废话,黄色东西;废弃物

slum(s) n. 贫民窟,贫民区;赤贫

slum clearance 拆迁,贫民区拆迁(指将贫民区危旧房拆除而建新房给予贫困居民或低收入者居住)

slump n. 物价等暴跌;下降;(市场等)不景气,萧条,衰退

slur v. 忽略;含糊地发(音),模糊不清地写(字);诽谤,玷污;掩盖(罪行等)

sly a. 狡诈的,躲躲闪闪的,偷偷摸摸的

sly answer 闪烁其词的答辩

sly question 狡黠的问题

small a. 小的,小型的;琐细的,微不足道的

small arms (便于随身携带的)轻武器(如手枪、步枪等)

small business 小生意(指管理机构根据雇工人数、销售量以及股东和售货员等情况来确定是否属于"小"生意的范畴)

Small Business Act （美）《小企业法》

Small Business Administration (SBA) （美）小企业管理署(指通过提供咨询、贷款并协助获得签订政府购买和服务合同

等方式帮助小企业的联邦机构)
Small Business Job Protection Act （1996年美国国会制定的)《中小企业保护法》
small but significant non-transitory increase in price 小幅度但很重要且非临时性涨价
small claims 小权利请求索赔(美国的"小额"一般指 500 美元以下的索赔,而英国则指不超过 100 英镑的索赔),小额诉讼请求程序
small claim(s) court 小额索赔法院,小额权利主张法院[指在美国的许多较大的市镇均设有这种小额索赔法院解决房租纠纷、经营与消费间的商品服务纠纷,实质上它是一个程序上非正规,但是依法高效裁决损害赔偿和小额权利主张(总额低于500 美元)的法庭。亦称 small debts court; conciliation court; people's court]
small debt 小额债务
small debts court 小额债务法庭
small denomination bonds 小额债券
small holding （英)出卖(或出租)50 英亩以下的小农田
small invention 见 utility model
small land holder 小量土地持有者,小农
small land lessor 小土地出租者
small loans 小额贷款
small packet 小包邮件
small peasant economy 小农经济
small pecuniary claim 小额金钱请求索赔,小额金钱诉讼
small private economy 小私有经济
small proprietor 小业主
small trader 小商
small-scale a./n. 小规模的/小规模,小批量
small-scale decentralized socialism 小型分散化的社会主义
small-scale production sector 小生产成分
smart-money n. 1.罚款;赔偿金 2.(英)伤兵抚恤金
smash v./n. 捣碎,使破碎;击败,使瓦解/粉碎;碰撞;破产;灾难;假硬币;硬币
smash-and-grab a. （英)打破窗子将屋中陈列的贵重品偷走的
smash-and-grab raid 打破(商店等)橱窗的抢劫
smash-and-grabber n. （英)打破窗子盗窃屋中陈列的贵重品的人
smashed a. 酒醉的
smasher n. 使用假钞票者;收买赃物者
smear v./n. 涂抹;弄脏;诽谤;贿赂;打垮;杀死/污点,污迹,污蔑,诽谤
smear word 污蔑性字眼
Smith Act 《史密斯法》[指由弗吉尼亚州的众议员霍华德·W. 史密斯(Howard W. Smith)提出的,由国会于 1939 年通过的数个反颠覆阴谋的议案之一,于 1940 年 6 月修改后由两院通过,作为外国人登记法的第一章。该法实质是政府反对国内共产主义分子的斗争中最重要的武器。另外,该法第 1 条规定:对于削弱武装部队士气者可处 1 万美元罚金以及 10 年监禁;第 2—3 条规定:任何人如有下列行为,如"鼓动、唆使、建议或教导"暴力推翻政府、出版或散发印刷品鼓动暴力颠覆政府、基于该目的组织任何社团、故意参加此类社团或企图从事上述任何一项,则处以与第 1 条相同的惩罚]
smoking gun （美)烟枪,有力证据[指可毫无疑问地指挥对方当事人有关诉讼结果的问题(an outcome-determinative issue)或毁掉对方当事人的可信性的一件物证或一纸书面证据]
Smoot-Hawley Tariff Act 《斯穆特—霍利税务法》[指 1930 年的一项保护贸易的制定法规(protectionist statute),该法规对于进口到美国的绝大多数商品提高关税税率(tariff rates)而导致美国贸易合伙人制定类似的关税增长。这个法通常作为一个要素被援引进入突然陷入扩展成1929 年资本主义世界的大萧条。该法的命名是因有几位议员或立法者为该法发起人,他们是:犹他州参议院议员里德·斯穆特(Reed Smoot)和俄勒冈州的众议院议员威利斯·C.霍利(Willis C. Hawley)。有时该法被称为格伦迪关税(Grundy Tariff),因约瑟夫·格伦迪(Joseph Grundy)是宾夕法尼亚州制造业协会(Pennsylvania Manufactures Association)的主席,而且院外活动集团的主要成员

(Lobbyist)都支持这个法。此法亦称 Tariff Act of 1930]
smooth v. 使光滑,使弄平;消除;掩饰
smooth a./ad. (=smoothly)平坦的(地),平稳的(地),平静的(地),平和的(地),顺利的(地)
smooth things over 把事情掩饰过去
smooth transfer of government 政权的顺利交接
smother n./v. 1.抑制;遏制,掩盖;掩饰2.窒息,使窒息之物/闷死,使窒息;被窒息;把……掩盖起来
smother up a scandal 掩盖一件丑闻
smotherer n. 1.尘、烟,雾气等2.使人窒息的事物3.窒息;混乱
smuggle v. 偷运;私运;走私
smuggle out (或 **away**) 掩盖,回避;逃避税
smuggle tax 偷税
smuggled a. 走私的
smuggled goods 走私物品
smuggler n. 走私者;偷运者;走私船
smuggling n. (17世纪)走私(指进出口非法商品的罪行,或未交纳应缴的海关税款)
smuggling case 走私案件
smuggling of drug 毒品走私
smuggling ring 走私集团
smurf n. (俚语,行话)洗钱人,洗钱贩子[指①参与洗钱经营(money-laundering operation),在每一银行至少进行10000美元交易。这个名称来源于1980年代的卡通漫画人物。②见 currency-transaction report]
smut n./v. 1.污物,污处,污点2.猥亵之词,淫词/弄脏,污染
smut shops 妓院,淫秽场所
smutiness n. 猥亵
smutty a. 污染的;猥亵的
snatch v. 攫取;(俚)绑架
snatcher n. 抢夺者,绑架者
sneak n. 1.行为鬼祟2.鬼鬼祟祟的人,偷偷摸摸的行为,小偷
sneak v./a. 偷偷摸摸地行动;潜行;鬼鬼祟祟地干/偷偷的,鬼鬼祟祟;暗中进行的;突如其来的
sneak attack 突然的袭击

sneak in 潜行进入
sneak landing 偷渡登陆
sneak out of 偷偷地逃避(责任,工作等)
sneak-thief n. 小偷
sneaking a. 隐秘的;鬼祟的;卑怯的
snide n. 假珠宝,伪钱币
snidesman n. 使假钱币流通的人
snitch n. 告发者,告密者
snob n. 势利的人,诸上欺下的人;假内行
snuff v. 1.嗅、闻;吹熄 2.动怒;镇压 3.(俚)死;杀死
so as 只要
so as to 为的是,以便,使得;结果是,以致
so...as to 如此…以致
so ordered 特此命令
so to speak/say 可以这么说,打个比喻说(拟人语)
so-called a. 所谓的,据称的
so-called dead-man statute 所谓对于死亡人的制定法(证据法),所谓死亡者生前口头承诺法(见 dead man's statute)
so-called ex-officio oath 所谓职权上当然宣誓
so-called John Doe proceedings 所谓某甲(不动产回复)诉讼程序
sober a. (14世纪)1.未喝醉的;清醒的 2.严肃庄重的;审慎的;有节制的 3.冷静的;有理智的;合理的
sober facts 毫不夸张的事实
sober judg(e)ment 冷静的判断
sober truth 无偏见的事实真相;事实真相
soc (或 *sok*, *soka*) 司法管辖权,司法特权(指执行法律和审判案件的特权)(撒克逊法用语)
socage n. (英)停役租地(指佃户所不服兵役的一种封建土地制)
socage tenant (英)免(停)役土地保有人(亦称农役佃户)
social a. 社会的,有关社会的;社会性的,社交的
social action litigation 社会性民事诉讼
social action programme (欧共体)社会行动纲领
social and moral order 社会和道德秩序
social and welfare services 社会福利事业

social aspects of old age 老年人的社会问题
social assistance 社会救济
Social Bankruptcy 社会破产[指因使用社交媒体而感到应接不暇,不知所措,以致唯一的解决办法就是关闭自己所有社交媒体账户的情况。为小企业提供咨询和服务的 IttyBiz 网站创始人娜奥米·邓福德 2011 年 10 月 19 日向上述商务人士提供建议时最早提及这一概念:"至于你实际上做些什么才能实现社交破产,你有两种选择:当机立断关闭账户或不露声色慢慢淡出社交网站。"拥有大量追随者的美国励志演说家、企业家史蒂夫·帕夫林纳曾有过类似经历。他认为社交关系就像是礼物一样。数量不多时,它们显得很珍贵,令人心生感激,但数量过多就会带来麻烦。2012 年 1 月 26 日,他在个人网站撰文宣称:"接受这个需要花些时间,但最终我意识到,自己不得不宣告社交破产。"]
social bond 社会结合,社会联系
social business 社会型企业[孟加拉国经济学家、诺贝尔和平奖得主穆罕默德·尤努斯是社会型企业的主要倡导者。他在《创建一个没有贫困的世界——社会型企业和资本主义的未来》(Creating a World without Poverty—Social Business and the Future of Capitalism) 一书中提出,社会型企业需要有积极的社会目标,例如帮助解决保健、教育、贫困、环境或气候等问题。维基百科给出的进一步解释是:在一个社会型企业,投资者和企业主可逐渐收回投入的资金,但是除此之外不能获取红利。企业必须支付所有成本并获得收益,同时实现社会目标。尤努斯在孟加拉国创立的格莱珉银行(Grameen Bank)是全球最著名的社会型企业。它开创和发展了"小额贷款"(microfinance)服务,专门提供给因贫穷而无法获得传统银行贷款的创业者,帮助穷人摆脱贫困。据美通社报道,尤努斯参与创建的格莱珉基金会最近与我国一家社会型企业建立合作关系,为我国的贫困人口提供小额贷款]
social category 社会阶层
social chamber 社会裁判庭
social climber 向上爬的人(尤指企图与权贵、富人交往的人)
social closure 社会屏障(指二元户籍制度导致农民工待遇不平等,实质是一种社会屏障,将农民工屏蔽在城市社会资源之外)
social compact 社会契约(合同)
social consensus 社会合意
social context 社会的来龙去脉;社会背景
social contract (或 compact) 社会契约
social contract theory 社会契约论,民约论
social contradiction 社会矛盾
social control 社会控制
social controlling force 社会强制力
social cost(s) 社会费用,社会代价,社会成本
social court 社会法院,社会法庭
social credit 社会债权说(指工业利润应归于整个社会的一种学说)
social Darwinist legal system 社会达尔文法系
social defence 社会防卫(原则)
Social Democratic Party 社会民主党
social disadvantaged group 社会弱势群体
social disharmony 社会失调
social disorganization 社会解体,社会秩序崩溃,社会失控
social division of labor 社会分工
social duty 社会义务
social ecology 社会生态学
social economic order 社会经济秩序
social effects of pollution 公害
social engagement 社交约定
social engineering 社会工程
social entitlements 社会受益权(指以社会保障权为核心的权利为社会受益权)
social environment 社会环境
social ethics 社会主义道德观;社会公德;社会伦理学
(the) social evil 社会邪恶,对社会有害的事情(指贩毒,盗窃活动等);卖淫
social facts 社会事实
social function of property 财产的社会功能
social functions (法律的)社会作用,社会功能
social group 社会团体,(复)社会群体

social harm 社会危害
social idealism 社会理想主义
social identity theory 社会认同理论
social ills 社会弊病
social imperialism 社会帝国主义
social import 社会的含义,社会的重要性
social instinct 社会本能
social institution(s) 社会习俗,社会机构,社会制度
social insurance (agency) 社会保险(机关)
social insurance institute 社会保险局
social integration 社会一体化
social intelligence test 社会智力测验
social interest 社会利益
social jurisprudence 社会法学
social justice 社会正义
social law 社会法
social legislation 社会立法
social life 社会生活
social liquidation 社会清算(指使私有财产成为社会的公有财产)
social logical science of law 社会法哲学
social matter 社会事件
social morality 社会道德
social morals 社会公德
social norm 社会规范
Social Networking Fatigue 社交网络疲劳(亦可写作 social network fatigue)[指因创建和维护使用过多的社交网站账户而产生的脑力透支和精神压力。路透社记者亚当·帕斯克 2004 年首次指出这一问题:"每周都有新的社交网站推出,一些用户的收件箱中塞满了这些网站发出的大量邀请信,他们已深受"社交网络疲劳之害。"从 Chinaren 校友录到开心网,从博客到微博,一些社交网站在 10 多年里经历了大起大落。正如普林斯顿大学的坎纳雷拉和斯佩克勒所言,使用社交网站像是一种传染病,波及范围达到顶峰后就会经历消退。中国互联网信息中心曾报告称,45.8% 的用户认为,社交网络"浪费时间";40.4% 的人对社交网络"失去兴趣";39.9% 的人觉得社交网络用处不大。"好友"和"关注"对象发布的海量信息容易令人产生信息疲劳综合征(information fa-

tigue syndrome)。上班时间为"摸鱼"登陆社交网站而自我干扰(self-interrupt)无疑得不偿失。晒出过多个人行踪的过度分享信息者(diarrheaist)有可能面临安全风险。无论原因如何,社交网络用户流失问题在许多国家都已不容小觑]
social optimum 社会的最适度
social order 社会秩序
social organization 社会组织
social origin of crime 犯罪的社会根源
social phenomenon 社会现象
social philosophical school of law 社会哲理法学派
social policy 社会政策
social position 社会地位
social practice 社会实践
social problem 社会问题
social protection 社会保护
social relations 社会关系
social research 社会调查(研究)
social revolution 社会革命
social righteousness 社会公正,社会正义
social rights 社会权利
social risks 社会风险
social sanction 社会制裁
social science (人文科学之外的)社会科学
social security 社会保障,社会保险
social security act (或 code) 社会保障法(或法典)
Social Security Act (美)《社会保障法》,《社会老年保险法》[指 1935 制定颁布的一项联邦法律,以回应大萧条(great depression)而创设一个福利制度,包括老年人和幸存者(survivors)的福利,并设立社会保障署(Social Security Administration),参见《美国注释法典》第 42 标题卷第 401—433 节]
Social Security Administration (美)社会保障署[缩写为 SSA,指美国行政部门中的联邦机构,其职责是执行国家的退休计划(retirement program)及退休人员和残疾人的保险计划。此机构是依据 1935 年《社会保障法》(Social Security Act)设立的,并于 1995 年成为独立机构(判例:Social Security

and Public Welfare 钥匙号5)]
social security benefits 社会保险补助金
social security institute 社会保障局
Social Security Number (美)社会安全号 (指每一美国公民不管怎样迁移流动,必须始终带着一个终身无法伪造的社会安全号,有了这个卡即可易于办理各种信用证和驾驶执照等)
social security tribunal (英)社会保障裁判庭
social service (agency) 社会服务机构(尤指慈善事业),社会工作,社会服务
social setting 社会环境
social solidarism jurisprudence 社会连带主义法学
social solidarist school of law 社会连带主义法学派
social solidarity 社会连带关系
social stability 社会稳定
social standard of justice 社会的正义标准
Social Statics 《社会静力学》[赫伯特·斯宾塞(Herbert Spensen)的作品,美国法庭深受其影响]
social strata 社会阶层
social structure 社会结构
social survey 社会调查
social system 社会制度,社会体系
social theories of law 社会法学理论,法社会学理论
social thesis (分析主义法学的)社会论
social transformation of law 法律的社会转型(指现代法治从形式法治转向实质法治的标志。韦伯将这种转型称为近代法的"反形式倾向";哈贝马斯则将其名为"法律的社会转型",并进一步将其概况推定为从"自由主义范式"向"福利国家范式"的转型)
social unrest 社会动荡,社会动乱局面
social usage 社会习俗
social utilitarian jurisprudence 社会功利主义法学
social utility 社会功利
social vulnerable group 社会的弱势群体
social welfare (court) 社会福利(法院);社会福利救济

social welfare function 社会福利函数
social work 社会工作,社会救济工作
social-minded a. 热心于社会福利事业的,关心社会的
social-philosophical jurists 社会哲理法学家
social-utilitarian criterion 社会功利主义标准
socialism with Chinese characteristics 中国特色的社会主义
socialist a./n. 社会主义的/社会党人
socialist accumulation 社会主义积累
socialist civil law 社会主义民法
socialist collective ownership 社会主义集体所有制
socialist collectivization 社会主义集体化
socialist constitution 社会主义宪法
socialist construction 社会主义建设
socialist criminal law 社会主义刑法
socialist culture and ideology 社会主义精神文明
socialist democracy 社会主义民主
socialist discipline of labor 社会主义劳动纪律
socialist economic (system) 社会主义经济(制度)
socialist enterprise 社会主义企业
socialist jurisprudence 社会主义法学
socialist jurist 社会主义法学家
socialist labor emulation 社会主义劳动竞赛
socialist law 社会主义法律
socialist law systems (或family) 社会主义法系,社会主义法律体制
socialist legal order 社会主义法律秩序
socialist legality 社会主义法制
socialist market economy 社会主义市场经济
socialist marriage and family system 社会主义的婚姻和家庭制度
socialist material civilization 社会主义物质文明
socialist mode of production 社会主义生产方式
socialist morals or customs 社会主义道德风尚
socialist nationalization 社会主义国有化

socialist ownership by the entire people 社会主义全民所有制
socialist ownership by the state 社会主义国家所有制
socialist party 社会主义政党,(大写)社会党
socialist political power 社会主义政权
socialist public economy 社会主义公有制经济
socialist public ownership 社会主义公有制
socialist public property 社会主义公有财产,社会主义的公共财产
*Socialist public property is sacred and inviolable. (中)社会主义的公共财产神圣不可侵犯(宪法原则之一)。
socialist relations of equality 社会主义平等关系
socialist revolution 社会主义革命
socialist road 社会主义道路
socialist sector of economy 社会主义经济成分
socialist society 社会主义社会
socialist spiritual civilization 社会主义精神文明
socialist state 社会主义国家
socialist state ownership 社会主义国家所有权
socialist superiority 社会主义优越性
socialist system 社会主义制度
socialist transformation 社会主义改造
socialist unity front 社会主义团结阵线
socialization of law 法律的社会化
socialized court 社会化的法院
socialized medicine 社会化医疗制度,公费医疗
socially contrived market 社会规划型市场(指通过政府和社会制度安排的市场。它通过法律体系和社会秩序提供一系列关于生产和交易的制度安排,使个人拥有产权和生产贸易及创新的自由,得到公正的法庭服务,从而保障社会能获得市场的全部好处)
socially dangerous homicide 有社会危险性的杀人

socially organized sanction 社会有组织的制裁
socially regularized 社会规制的
socida 寄存合同,委托合同[指一项寄存或委托合同,据此被委托人(bailee)保证不得有损失风险,如委托人将一些动物卖给另外的人,如果动物死亡,被委托人将承担损失责任]
societas 合伙
societas civilis 民间合伙
societas delinquere non potest 法人不能违反可罚行为
societas leonina 狮式合伙(指合伙人中之一人仅分担损失而无权分享红利,如被狮子吞食一样)
societas publicanorum 租税征收合伙
societas totorum bonorum 并产合伙
societas unius alicujus negotii 特业合伙,特定事业的合伙
société anonyme (法)股份有限公司
société de capital(或 *capitaux*) (法)资合公司,合伙公司(指出资人负无限责任)
société de personnes (法)人合公司
société en commandite (法)两合公司
société en commandite par actions (法)股份两合公司
société en commandite simple 有限合伙,(法)普通两合公司
société en nom collectif (法)普通合伙
société par actions (法)股份公司
société par interets (法)合伙公司
society n. 1.社会,团体;社团;会,社 2.交际界,社交界
society at large 社会整体
society decline 衰落社会
society of friends 教友会(指贵族会的教友会)
society of nations 国际社会(指国际法产生的社会基础)
sociological jurisprudence 社会学法学,社会法学[在美国,社会法学的拓荒者包括霍姆斯(O. W. Holms)大法官、卡多佐、庞德等人,庞德认为社会法学应着重研究以下内容:法律制度、规则及理论的社会功效;立法准备;什么途径使法律规则在实

践中的产生功效;司法途径;法律社会史;正义的实施如何实现法律秩序更为有效。他们将重点放在了对个人利益、社会利益和公共利益的保护上。社会法学的一个分支是现实主义法学,代表人物主要为美国的格雷(Gray)、霍姆斯·弗兰克(Frank)和卢埃林(Llewellyn)等,他们主要将法律视作是法庭或实际上在特定案件中的所作所为。社会法学与法社会学不同,后者为一门实践性科学,研究法律在特殊背景下的运作。庞德呼吁用他所命名的"社会学法学"取代形式主义。这将承认法律并不是相互独立、自我指认的当然组合。相反,法官从法律之外的原则(包括政治学和社会学)获得启迪,将会更敏锐地把握法律原则的实际影响,他们会力争在具体案件中公平适用法律以达到公正结果]

Society of Maritime Arbitration (SMA) 海事仲裁员协会
socio-cultural a. 社会文化的
socio-economic a. 社会经济的
socio-economic composition 社会经济构成
socio-economic system 社会经济制度
sociological a. 社会学的;针对社会问题的
sociological jurisprudence 社会法学
sociological jurist 社会法学者;社会法学家
sociological legal history 社会学法制史
sociological positivism 社会实证主义
sociological school 社会学派
sociological school in jurisprudence 法理社会学派
sociological school of law 社会法学派
sociological science of law 法社会学
sociologist n. 社会学家
sociology n. 社会学
sociology jurisprudence 社会法理学
sociology of law 法律社会学
socius 同伙,同事,会员
socius criminis 共犯
Socratic method 苏格拉底式(或问答式)教学法
sodomite n. 鸡奸者;兽奸者
sodomy n. 1.鸡奸(又译:男奸。一般指男人间的性行为)2.兽奸(指违反自然的性交行为)3.猥亵行为(罪)
soft budget constraint (SBC) 软预算约束
soft currency 软货币(亦称软通货,指准备金不足的货币,或与其他货币兑换时须打折扣的货币)
soft law 软法(起源于西方国际法学。学术著述中软法有多种表述形式,如"自我规制""志愿规制""合作规制"和"准规制"等。作为现象的软法在国内公法中早已存在,对软法的界定,引用法国学者Francis Snyder 于 1994 年对软法概念,即"软法是原则上没有法律约束力但有实际效力的行为规则")
soft law communication conclusion action program act (欧共体中的)软法[其形式多样,既有欧共体条约第249(189)条所列举的意见和建议,也有通报(communication)、结论(conclusion)、宣言(declaration)、行动计划(action programme)等。见 act]
soft loan 软贷款(指可用软货币偿还的优惠贷款或利息低而偿还期长的优惠贷款),用本国币偿还外汇贷款
soft market 疲软市场
soft money 纸币
soft regime 软性制度
soft-liner n. 实行(或主张)温和路线者;支持温和路线者
softening process 软化处理
softest possible terms 最优厚的条件
software n. (计算机)软件,程序设计
software legal protection 软件法律保护
Software Patent Institute (美)软件专利协会[指基于堪萨斯的非营利协会,收集并组织非专利的现有技术(prior act)软件参考进入为研究人员使用的数据库中]
(a) software-cryptography system 软件密码体系
soil n. 土壤,土地,地面;国土,国家;务农
soil conservation 土壤保持
Soil Conservation and Domestic Allotment Act (美)(1936年)《水土保持和国内生产配给法》
soil contamination 土壤污染,土壤玷污

sojourn v./n. 逗留;寄居
sojourner n. 逗留者;寄居者
soke n. (英史)地方司法权;法院的管辖区;裁判权
sola bill of exchange 单份汇票,一纸汇票(指汇票通常作成二纸,一纸为第一汇票 first bill of exchange,另纸为第二汇票 second bill of exchange)
solarium 租金
solatium n. (苏格兰)慰藉金(指给予受害者一定金额作为对其感情所受伤的一种抚慰);赔偿费;慰问金;赔偿
soldier n. 战士,士兵,军人
soldier in active service 现役军人
sole a. 1.(常指女子)独身的,未婚的 2.单独的,唯一的;专用的
sole agency 独家代理;独家代理机构
sole agent 全权代表;独家代理人(商)
sole cause 唯一的原因
sole consensus 简单的意思表示一致,单一承诺
sole corporation 单独法人
sole custody (美)单独监护(指由父母其中一方单独行使的监护权,即父母之一方同时获得子女法律上和身体上的监护权,而另一方则完全无监护权,充其量仅有与子女会面交往的探视权)
sole discretion 全权处理;单独
sole draft 单张汇票
sole entrepreneur (法)独资企业
sole heir 唯一的继承人
sole justice of the peace 独任治安官
sole legatee 概括遗赠财产承受人
sole legitimate government 唯一合法政府
sole license 排他许可证(指在一定地区和时间内,被许可方享有专利商标等使用权,任何第三方不得享有,但许可方仍可保留使用权的许可证)
sole licensing agreement 排他许可证协议(见上条);专用许可证协议
sole power 全权
sole proprietorship 独资经营,独资企业
sole proprietorship with limited liability 有限责任的独资企业
sole responsibility for one's own profits and losses 自负盈亏
sole right of use 专用权
sole selling agency 独家专卖代理(见 exclusive agency)
sole solicitor (诉讼中的)唯一律师
sole trader 个体营业者
sole-practitioners n. 个体开业者
solemn a. 1.正式的;庄严的,郑重的,严肃的,神圣的 2.(格式、仪式等)合格的,法律上正确的
solemn decision 神圣判例
solemn form 严格格式检证证明书(指遗嘱检证的一种,这种证书的发给,是经过法庭公开传讯那些与遗嘱检证有利害关系的人,然后作出宣判,一般情况是不可取消的,与可取消的普通格式证明书有别)
solemn oath 正式誓言,庄严的誓言
solemn statement 庄严的声明,郑重(的)声明
solemn war 经过公开宣告的战争
solemn warning 严重警告
Solemnes legum formulae 法定程式,合法程式(罗马法名词,即 Solemn forms of laws)
* *Solemnitates juris sunt observandae.* The solemnities of law are to be observed. 法律的严肃性应当得到重视。
solemnity n. 1.要式;(复)庄严的仪式,严肃(性) 2.(使文件、合同等生效的)必要的手续
solemnization n. 仪式,举行(宗教)仪式;庄严化;监督
solemnization of marriage 结婚仪式的举行
solicit v. 1.谋求;恳求;要求;恳求给予〈solicit sb. for help〉(恳求某人给予帮助),〈The situation solicits the closet attention.〉(这种情况需密切予以关注。) 2.征求〈solicit opinion from sb. or mass〉(从某人或群众中征求意见) 3.诱惑,勾引……做坏事 4.引发,诱发
solicit for immoral purpose (勾)引人干不道德的事
solicitation n. 1.诱人犯罪,教唆(罪);(妓

女)拉客 2.恳求,请求 3.律师招徕生意
solicitation of business 商业招揽
solicitation of clients (律师)招揽生意
solicitation to bribery 诱使他人行贿或受贿
solicitation to larceny 诱使他人为盗
soliciting passers 招揽顾客(指停留在街上的人向过路人兜生意或为妓女"拉客")
solicitor n. 1.(英)(初级)律师(指为当事人所聘请的一般辩护律师,承办案件起诉和辩护等事务性工作,地位低于有资格出席高等法院法庭辩护的 barrister),诉状律师 2.(美)法务官(指在政府部门或一城市中负责法律事务的官员)
Solicitor General (英)副检察长;(美)副司法部长(由总统经参议院建议并同意后任命);(美国若干无检察长的州的)首席检察官,大律师
solicitor general (of all the nation's officials) (美)首席检察官(指导国家全部官员的首席检察官)。1870年创立此职位和检察机构。负责甄别来自联邦政府各个部门所有方面的上诉或请求案件,并决定什么上诉或请求由联邦最高法院审理。他是唯一制定法所要求的"精通法律者",又是法庭上行政部门的大律师,并在司法部任职的副部长,但他在联邦最高法院也有接待室,事实上他在每个机构中任职,并强调其特殊作用。他的非正式头衔"第十大法官");(大写)(英)副检察长;(美)副总检察长,副司法部长(由总统经参议院提议并同意后任命);(美国若干无检察长的州的)首席检察官;大律师
solicitor's act 律师法例
Solicitor's Disciplinary Tribunal (英)(诉状)律师纪律法庭
solicitor's lien 律师留置权
solicitor-trustee n. 律师信托人
solicitress n. 女初级律师,女诉状律师;女法务官
solid a. 稳固的;有根据的,可靠的,确实的;资金雄厚的
solid arguments 有根据的论点
solid business firm 殷实商号
solid consideration 全面的考虑,有根据的考虑

solid defence 有效的辩护(答辩);有效的防卫
solid evidence 实证,实据
solid majority 有效的多数
solid man 有钱人
solid vote 全体一致的投票
solidarity n. 团结一致;共同责任;休戚相关
solidarity by similitude 共同连带关系
solidarity through division of labour 分工连带关系
solidum 合力负担(指一个人和他人一起或分开共同负担一整笔债款,而并不是按人数的比例负担份额);连带责任
solipsism n. 唯我论,唯我论者
solitariness n. (=solitary confinement)
solitary a./n. 独居的,无伴的;单独的,唯一的/隐居者;单独监禁;被遗弃的人
solitary confinement (监狱的)单独监禁(制),单独拘禁
solitary custody 单独羁押
solitary example 独一无二的例子
solitary life 独居生活,孤独生活
solitary obligation 单独责任,单独债务
solo-practitioners n. 个体开业者
solon n. 贤明的立法者;(美)议员
solopreneur 个体企业家[为可数名词,由 solo(单独)和 entrepreneur(企业家)合成,意指独自经营生意的企业所有者。他们可能会在某些情况下把一些工作外包出去,但要对自己的企业全权负责。该词最早出现在2010年。为个体企业家提供资讯服务的"个体企业家生活"网站负责人拉里·凯尔托认为,向往独立、自由和充满弹性的工作环境是人们选择自立门户的主要原因。互联网的飞速发展对此大有神益。任何人只需用一台计算机连接上互联网就能建立起自己的"办公室"]
solum 1.土地,地 2.单独,仅
solutio 清偿债务,清偿
solutio indebiti 错债清偿,错债给付
solutio per aes et libram ("称铜式"的)要式行为(见 gesta per et aes libram),要式清偿
solutio sine causa (因错误而)偿还不存在

之债
solution n. 1.解决，了结 2.解答，解释 3.偿付,清偿 4.溶液
solution concepts 解概念(指求解博弈的工具。解概念是关于理性的当事人在给定目标后将可能选取战术以及关于当事人可能选取战术特性的一般性要求)
solution to game 博弈解
solve v. 解释,解决;付给,偿付;博弈求解
solve a case 破案
solvency n. 有清偿能力,偿付能力,支付能力;溶解力
solvency of the debtor 债务人的支付能力
solvendi causa 清偿原因
solvent (solvency) a. 有偿付能力的;有溶解力的
solvit ad diem 被告宣称可随时偿还债务（以此作为辩护的手段),可按期给付
* *solvitur adhuc societas etiam morte socii.* A partnership is also dissolved by the death of a partner. 合伙关系也会因一方合伙人去世而终止。
solvit ante diem 被告宣称可在指定之日前偿还债务(以此作为辩护的手段)
solvitur in modum solventis 依付款者的意思,指定给付之标的(指付款人有数项债务)
some genuine interest of public 重大公共利益
some kind of hearing 某种形式的听证
somewhat different proposition 不同陈述,不同主张,不同意见
somnambulism n. 梦游症(此症患者一般均有癫痫病史,指患者在夜间熟睡后突然起来活动,在屋内或室外无目的地行走或移动物品,呼之不应。对外界事物与人物不能正确辨认,持续数分钟后又回到床上继续睡眠。醒后对这段经历不能回忆。见 automatism)
somnambulist n. 患梦游症者
son n. 儿子,女婿,养子;(复)后裔,子孙
son by another venter 异母子
son of Bacchus 酒鬼
Son of Liberty "自由之子社"(指美国在北美殖民地时人民成立的群众性的反对英国殖民统治的革命团体)
son of no-body 没有身份的儿子,私生子
son-in-law n. 女婿
sonless a. 无后嗣的
sooner n. 抢先而获得不正当利益的人；(美)(政府开放西部地区前)抢先占有土地者
sophisticated a. 1.尖端的,高级的 2.非常有经验的;老练的 3.精致的
sophisticated and experienced businessman 老练和经验丰富的商人
sophisticated criminals 老练的罪犯,"高级"罪犯
sophisticated market participates 精明的市场参与者
sophisticated professional criminals 老练的职业罪犯
sophisticated technique 尖端技术
sophisticated weapon 尖端武器;现代化武器
sophistry n. 诡辩,辩术,诡辩法
sorcerer n. 男巫师;魔法师
sorcery n. 巫术
soroptimist n. 职业妇女会会员
soroptimist club 职业妇女会
sororal a. 姐妹的,姐妹关系的
sororate n. 填房婚(指男人与他妻子的姊或妹的婚姻)
sororicidal a. 杀害亲姐妹的
sororicide n. 杀害亲姐妹罪;杀害亲姐妹者
sort v./n. 1.把……分类,整理,拣选〈sort letter〉(将信件分类),〈sort out enemies from friends〉(分清敌友);2.交往(with) 3.一致,协调(with)/1.类similar,种类 2.样子,举止 3.品质,性质 4.(复)一套
sorts of crimes 犯罪种类
sostituzione processuale 替代诉讼(指原告以自己的名义为实现他人的权利起诉,诉讼后而由被替代人承担的诉讼)
sot n./v. 酒鬼,酒糊涂;嗜酒;滥喝酒/嗜酒,喝酒浪费
sottish a. 饮酒过多而糊涂的,滥喝酒的,酒徒的
sound a. 有效的;健康的;合理的,正确的;明智的,稳妥的

sound advice 忠告
sound alarm 有效警告
sound argument 理由充足的论据
sound discretion 合理裁量(指依据美国《联邦民事诉讼规则》第 60 条第 B 款规定,当事人以意思表示不真实为由向法院申请取消该行为判决,必须服从法院的合理裁量)
sound in body and mind 身心健康
sound lawyer 可靠的律师
sound marks 声标,声音标志
sound mind 健康的,成熟的
sound policy 明智稳妥的政策
sound reasoning 正确的推理
sound recording 录音
sound recording intended for electronic distribution 为电子分销而制作的录音制品[美国认为,所有录音制品,不论进口或国产均应属 GATT 第 3 条第 4 款意义上的同类产品。特别是其内容同类(音乐或其他录音)、吸引同类型的听众,甚至为产品目标市场也相同,均适合于通过电子网络渠道进行产品分销]
sound recording works 录音著作
sound thinking 合理的思想,正确的理念
sound title 合法有效的产权
sound title to land 土地合法的所有权
sound view 正确的观点
sounding in damages 要求损害赔偿的(常用于索赔诉讼,指要法庭来确定实质上的损害赔偿,目的只是为了请求获得因合同和侵权等而产生的损害赔偿,而不是为要求收回土地、货物等)
sounding promise 夸口的允诺
soundness n. 健康,健全;可靠性,正确性,合理性
soundtracks n. 胶带声片(指电影两边的声槽。许多国家版权法专门规定:将作品录在声带中,不能列入录制品"如唱片等"中)
soup n. 1.(美俚)浓雾;显影剂;炸药 2.(英俚)委托资历较浅的律师承办的刑事起诉案件
source n. 来源,渊源,出处,根源
source n. 1.来源,渊源;出处,根源〈The side business was the source of income.〉[旁边的(附带的)商业是收入的来源。]2.提供信息者(informed sources),消息灵通人士〈She was the source of the information.〉(她是此信息的提供人。)3.原始资料〈legislative historical sources〉(立法史史料来源,或立法史原始资料)4.source(s) language 被译语言;source(s) book 原始资料(集)
source and object code 数据来源与结果代码
source book (有关历史等)原始资料集
source credibility 信(息)源的可信度
source code 原始码,源码(指计算机术语)
source distinctiveness 来源显著性(指商标有两个显著性:来源显著性,差异显著性 differential distinctiveness)
source du droit derivé 派生法源
source material 原始资源
source of capital 资本来源
source of decision making 作出裁决的依据
source of finance 经济来源
source of income 收入来源
source(s) of law (1892 年)法律渊源[指有些东西(诸如宪法、条约、制定法或习俗惯例)提供的立法,司法判例的法律根据(authority);还对法律或法律分析提供最早的法律要点。亦称 fons juris (source of law)。"法律渊源"这一术语通常更多地用于狭义。在法理学文献中"渊源"的问题是指:法官判案是根据什么规定? 从这一意义上讲,法律渊源中有成文法规、先例、习俗惯例、专家意见、道义(morality)以及衡平法(equity)。在通常讨论中,这些不同的法律渊源是要受到分析,而且有的是意图阐述一些情况,根据这些情况,各个渊源在法律争辩的判决之中可能被适当地吸收进来。罕见的是,立法机构制定颁布法律时,不必谈论它来源于判决中的"渊源",就是将来的法律。虽然,分析这些术语中可以获得多于法官履行有限职能的启示。至于比通常法理学渊源更为广泛的"渊源"(sources)含义更受关注,与我们利害相关的不是法律汇典或法典的渊源(source of laws)而是法律的渊源

(source of law)。从何处何因法律不仅引出它的具体内容,而且它的权威还在一直存在人们的生命之中。根据法律文献检索(legal research),"法律渊源"(source of law)这个术语是指 3 个不同的概念:法律渊源可指法律概念和法律思想(legal concept and ideas)的起源、法律渊源可指构成一些法律规则(legal rules)的政府的法律原则(institutions)、法律渊源可指正式出版的法律公告或法律声明(manifestations of law)。图书、电脑数据库(computer databases)、缩微资料(microforms)、光盘(optical disks)以及其他媒体(出版物)其中所包含的法律资料(legal information)都是法律渊源]

source of obligation 债的发生根据
source of order in international trade 国际贸易中的订货源
source of potential energy 潜在的能源
source of war 战争的根源
source version 原本
Sourcebook of Criminal Justice Statistics, 1994 (美)《刑事司法统计原始资料集》(1994 年)
sourcehood n. 来源性(见 creativity)
sources of Anglo-American Law 英美法法源
sources of international law 国际法的渊源
sources of private international law 国际私法的渊源
sources of written law 成文法渊源
sources thesis 渊源论(指实证主义法学的社会论,也可称为"以渊源为基础的法律概念",简称渊源论)
South 美国南部,(美史)南部联邦
South Coordination Commission 南方协调委员会(指由南方首脑会议主席、不结盟运动主席、东南亚国家联盟主席、阿拉伯联盟主席、加勒比海共同体主席、非洲统一组织等南方国家各大区域性组织的主要领导人共同组成的机构,成为一个比较稳定的核心领导机构,统一协调和组织实施《哈瓦那行动纲领》和有关南南合作的各项决定)
South Eastern Reporter (美)《东南区判例汇编》(东南区包括西弗吉尼亚州、弗吉尼亚州、北卡罗来纳州、南卡罗来纳州和佐治亚州)
South Western Reporter (美)《西南区判例汇编》(西南区包括密苏里州、阿肯色州、肯塔基州、田纳西州和得克萨斯州)
South-South Cooperation 南南合作
southern particularism (美)南部的特殊主义
Southern Reporter (美)《南方区判例汇编》(南方区包括路易斯安那州、密西西比州、阿拉巴马和佛弗里达州。第一套丛书包括 1887—1941 年的判例,第二套丛书为最近一套)
sovereign n./a. 1.君主,国王,统治者 2.独立国 3.主权 4.金镑(英国的金币)/拥有最高权力的;主权的;君主的;独立的
sovereign act 主权行为
sovereign council (法史)最高评议会(指具有最高法院类似职能机构)
sovereign court 最高法庭
sovereign equality 主权平等
sovereign government 主权政府
sovereign immunity 主权豁免,国家主权豁免;政府豁免权,政府机关豁免,国家管辖豁免(此项主权豁免原则,最早起源于英国的普通法,即国王不受其臣民的诉讼。其原则的理论依据为:既然法律源自主权,那么国王不能被自己所创设的法院裁定而对自己行为负责。在美国,主权豁免原则在 19 世纪时用于限制个人对州和联邦政府提起诉讼,美国联邦宪法第十一修正案于 1795 年批准禁止联邦法院受理对任何州的诉讼,各州最高法院也都承认该原则。今天,主权豁免这一观念已经得不到支持。许多州的制定法及司法判例均限制豁免。主权豁免原则已在逐渐衰落,即使在禁止起诉政府的情况下,受害当事人仍可从对该决定负有个人责任的官员处获得损害赔偿)
sovereign nations (或 state) 主权国家
sovereign people 统治者,主权主宰者,统治集团;臣民,拥有最高权力的人民
sovereign political power 主权;国家政权(指在其所及的范围内具有绝对性和不受控制的权力)

sovereign right over territory 领土主权
sovereign society 主权社会
sovereign statehood 主权国家属性
sovereign status 主权地位,主权状态
sovereignty n. 主权,主权国家,统治权;君权;独立国
sovereignty association 主权联盟
sovereignty discourse 主权学说,主权论
sovereignty of parliament 国会主权
sovereignty of the right of ownership 所有权至高无上(原则)
sovereignty over air space 领空主权
sovereignty right 主权上权利
sovereignty-of-the-air theory (国家)空中主权原则(国家对其领土上空,即全部空气空间拥有完全的主权)
space n. 1.空间 2.(常指空气空间以外的)外层空间,太空,星际空间 3.时间,一段时间 4.间隔,距离
space aeronautics 宇宙航空学
space charge 空间费;占地费,占用场地费
space charter 舱位租价
space jurisdiction 空间管辖(权)
space law 空间法(亦称外层空间法,太空法,星际空间法)
space man 太空人,宇宙航行员
space object 空间飞行器
space power 航天国家
space rocket 宇宙火箭;太空船
space ship 太空船,航天飞船
space vehicle 航天器
space war 外层空间战争
space writer 以稿件所占篇幅计酬的作家(尤指新闻记者)
spacial (=spatial) a. 空间的,存在于空间的;占有空间的
spacial extent 空间范围
spacial scale 空间范围
spado 无生育能力的人,无性能力的人;阉者
Spanish law 西班牙法
spank buttocks 打屁股(刑)
spare v. 赦免(刑罚);免除;节省;匀出
sparseness of substantive general law 实质性的一般法的稀少
spawn v. 酿成,引起

speak v./n. 说话;表示意思;请求,要求;代表;表明/(美俚)贩卖私酒的酒店,秘密酒店(=speak-easy)
speak evil of sb. 诽谤某人
speak for 代表……谈话,充当……代言人;为……辩护,要求得到
speak for oneself 为自己辩护
speak of (常用于否定句)(不)值得一提的
speak one's mind 直言不讳
speak out 大胆地说,清楚和响亮地说
speak volumes for sb./sth. 足以证明某人某事
speaker n. 1.发言人,演讲者 2.主席,(大写)议长(指英国下议院议长或美国众议院议长) 3.扩音机,扬声器
Speakers of the Houses of Parliament 国(议)会两院议长
speakership n. 议长的职务,议长的任期
speaking a. 1.发言的,交谈的 2.雄辩的,能说明问题的 3.逼真的
speaking demurrer(s) 提出新事实的诉求不充分的抗辩,叙事性异议(指一种特殊抗辩,与针对起诉状中的主张而指出其不足的抗辩不同,它是提出了原告诉讼中所未有的新事实,并以此反驳原告的请求权)
speaking for the court 为法庭辩护说,代表法庭辩护说
speaking witness 有力的证明
special n./a. 1.特殊的人;特派员,特使;特别护士 2.特别考试 3.专车 4.新闻;号外 5.特制品/1.特别的,特殊的;专门的,专用的 2.临时的,特设的
special acceptance 有条件承兑
special account 特别账户
special act(s) 特别法(令)
special ad hoc agreement 特别临时协定
special administration 特别遗产管理[与一般遗产管理(general administration)相对,指对死者某一部分财产而非全部遗产进行管理或在某一期间进行遗产管理]
Special Administrative Region (中)特别行政区
special administrative tribunal 特别行政裁判庭
special advocate 见 guardian ad litem

special agreement 特别协定,特别协议
special agent 1.特别代理人;特定代理人 2.特务分子
special agency (1808年)特别代理,特定代理[指此项代理人只是被授权进行单一交易或一系列交易,而不涉及持续性的服务或活动(service)]
special allowance 特别津贴,专项津贴
special ambassador 特使
special appearance 特别诉讼,(仅为有限或专门目的,如对法院管辖权提出异议的应诉),特别出庭,临时出庭(与 general appearance 相对)
special appropriation 专用拨款
Special Arbitration Tribunal 特别仲裁法庭
special area (英)长期不景气的工业地区;特别地区
special assessment 特种课税(评估)(指选定一些土地所有人交纳不动产税以改善人行道等设施,这至少在理论上有利于这些公益事业,但不是普遍有利于纳税人);特别受益费,捐税,特别捐税,特别摊派
special assumpsit 根据明示契约或明示允诺而要求违约所造成损失的赔偿之诉;由于不履行契约而请求赔偿损害的诉讼
special bastard 特别非婚生子女(指父母未婚时所生而结婚后成为合法的子女)
special bequest 特定遗赠
special bill 特别法案;特别诉状
special branch of the law of procedure 程序法的特别分歧(指证据法)
special budget 特别预算
special burden 特殊举证责任
special case 诉讼事实陈述(指诉讼双方或多方协议,把事实写成事实陈述书呈交法庭,请求依据所述事实作出法律上的裁决;亦指公证人或仲裁人依据他们裁定案件的事实写成陈述书请高等法院作出法律上的裁决,有时也可作判案要点解。见 case stated)
special chamber (法院)特别法庭
special charge 1.(法官对陪审团就法律方面的)特别指示 2.特别费用
special city 特别市
special civil court 特别民事法院,民事专门法院
special commercial court 特别商事法院,商事专门法院
special commercial privilege 商业特权
special commissioners 特别专员署
special committee 专门委员会,(国会)特别委员会(见 select committee)
special conditions of an action 特别诉讼条件
special constable (特殊场合的)临时警察;纠察
special constabulary 特别警察队,特警队
special constitutional guarantee 特别的宪法保证
special contract 专约;特约(指当事人间对于契约中某种事项的权利或义务另外作出的免除或限制的特别规定);特别履行的契约(合同)
special councillor 特别顾问,特别咨议
special counsel (美)特别律师(指州或一定程度上享有地方政府权力的选区雇用的专门办理与公共利益相关案件的律师)
special court 专门法院,专门法庭,特别法院(庭)
special criminal case 特种刑事案件
special criminal court 特别刑事法院,刑事专门法院
special custom 特别惯例
special customs privileges facilities 关税特惠设施
special damage 专项损失(指原告需在诉状中逐条说明如医药费、工资损失等,并加以证明,否则得不到赔偿,如交通事故、工伤、口头诽谤等所受的损失均属此类损失)
special damages 特别损失赔偿(指被害人所受金钱上的损害的赔偿)
special data dissemination standard (SDDS) 数据公布特殊标准
special decision 特别决定,特别决议,专门决定
special defence (苏格兰)特别辩护理由(包括不在现场、无罪、自卫和犯罪时精神错乱等辩护理由)
special delivery (美)快递邮件
special demurrer 特别抗诉(指以特别理

由来抗辩对方的控诉),特别异议
special derivative action prerequisites 特殊派生诉讼条件
special devise 特别不动产遗赠,专项不动产遗赠
special disability 特别无行为能力,特别无能
special disposing capacity 特殊行为能力
special divident 额外红利,特别股息
special division (法院的)特别庭
special drawing rights (SDR) 特别提款权〔指国际货币基金组织(IMF)创设的一种储备资产和记账单位。它是 IMF 分配给会员国的一种使用资金的权力。会员国发生国际收支逆差时,可用它向 IMF 指定的其他会员国换取外汇,以偿付国际收支逆差或偿还 IMF 贷款,还可与黄金、自由兑换货币一样充作国际储备。但由于其只是一种记账单位,不是真正货币,使用时必须先换成其他货币,不能直接用于贸易或非贸易的支付。特别提款权定值和"一篮子"货币挂钩,市值不是固定的〕
Special Economic Zone (中)经济特区
special election 特别选举
special embassy 特别使团;特使
special enactment 单行法规
special endorsement 记名式背书,特别背书,后注
special envoy 特使
special error (对误判的)专案复审
special expertise 特殊专长
special fund 特种基金
special grand jury 高级专案陪审团(指审理特种案件或专门处理某一类犯罪案件的高级陪审团)
special guarantee contract 特别保证契约
special guaranty 特别保证,特别担保
special guardian (17 世纪)特定监护人〔指①对被监护人人身(ward's person)或财产具有特别的或有限的权力的监护人。比如一些监护人,仅对财产具有监护但对人身没有监护职责,有些只对人身而非对财产具有监护职责。亦可称(在大陆法中)curator ad hoc。②见 guardian ad litem〕
special heir 特别继承人

special imparlance 特别答辩延期(指仅保全被告人对于令状、诉状、诉讼理由等的异议权的答辩延期,但不得对法院的管辖权有异议)
special income tax 特别所得税
special indorsement (英)特殊背书(写在传唤令状背面,写明原告的诉讼请求是一项债务或已清偿的请求权的背书)
special industrial copyright 特别工业版权(指一些国家中的外观设计、半导体布图设计、计算机软件等的专有权)
special injunction 特别禁制令
special instance 特别实例;专门请求;特定审级;特殊情况
special interest (=special interest group) (借口与公共利益攸关而要求立法机关给予特权的)特殊工商企业集团
special interrogatories 专门诉案质询书(指提交给陪审团的一个或数个系争事实的书面问题答复书,此答复书对于作出裁决是必需的)
special investigators 特别侦察员,专门调查人员
special investment 特种投资,特定投资
special judge 特别法官,任命法官(指在特定案件中被任命或被选出去开庭的法官,或常任法官不合格或缺席的情况下被任命的法官,或按制定法规定指定合格法官)
special jurisdiction 特定管辖(权),特定审判(权)(见 Court of Limited Jurisdiction)
special jury (17 世纪)(美)特别陪审团〔指①专为此案件特制的候选陪审员名单(panel)中遴选的陪审团。这类陪审团通常是在一个非常重要或很复杂的案件应一方当事人的要求从候选陪审员名单选出而组成的陪审团,亦称 struck jury(见 striking a jury)。②在普通法上,陪审团是由一般自由地产保有人(freeholder)以上阶层的人员组成,被召唤出庭审判较为重要的问题而不是一般陪审团所听审的一些问题,亦称为 good jury〕
special kind of criminal offender 特种刑事犯

special kinds of purchase and sale 特种买卖
special law 特别法
special leave 特许
special legacy 特别遗赠(见 specific legacy)
special legal status 特殊法律地位
special licence 1.特别许可证 2.特许结婚(指可免除公告的结婚)
special lien 特别留置权
special majorities 特定的多数
special master 特别主事
special mission 专门使团,特派使团;特殊使命
special mortgage 特别抵押
special most favoured nation clause 特定的最惠国条款
special object 特殊客体
special orders (英)上议院特别命令(指生效前须得两院赞成决议的立法文件)
special ordinance 单行条例,特别法令
special pardon 特赦
special part 分则
special (或 limited) partner 特别合伙人,有限合伙人(指对公司债权责任仅以投资额为限的股东)
special partnership 特别合伙
special performance (衡平法院强迫一个违反合同者的)特定履行令或强制履行令;实际履行令
special permission 特许(证)
special personal jurisdiction 特定对人管辖权
(a) special plea 特殊抗辩(指被告接受原告的指控,但提出特殊的或新的情况使诉讼不能成立)
special pleader 诉状草拟人(指代人们起草诉状和答辩的人),专为人撰状之律师
special pleading 自圆其说的议论;诉状拟学(指中世纪有过的研究诉状写作的一种学术);间接答辩法(不直接答复对方,而提出新事实以抵消对方论点效果);诡辩法
special policy 单独保险单,特殊保险单
special post allowance 特别职位津贴
special power 特别权力
special power of appointment 特别委托权,特别指定权(见 limited power of appointment)
special power of attorney (18世纪)特别代理权(指只授予代理的指定的事项具有代理的权限。见 general power of attorney)
special presumption 特别推定
special prevention 特殊预防
special privilege 特权,特殊权益
special procedure 特别诉讼程序
special procedure orders (英)特别程序令(指大臣对某些事项发布的命令)
special proceedings 特别诉讼(程序)
special property 特有物权(指具有指定或限定的物权,如租用房屋作营业用途,则对该房屋具有供营业用的特有物权)
special proviso 特别但书
special proxy 特别代理(权)
special purchase offer 特价购买要约
special purpose check 专用支票
special purpose entity (SPE) 特殊目的工具(指2006年十国集团国家开始实施的《资本计量和资本标准的国际协议:修订框架》第516条规定,对传统型证券化提出的6项操作性要求之一:承接被转让资产的应当是特殊目的工具)
special purpose trust (SPT) 特定目的信托
special purpose vehicle (SPV) 特殊目的公司(指美、日等发达国家中购买抵押贷款债权的机构)
special referee 特别仲裁人,特别公断人
special reference 特殊提交审定[指法院将案件提交给审断人(referee),由其就特别事实问题作出决定。特别审断员可以对这些事实问题做出认定或报告,并呈交给审理法官。法官则将这些认定和报告仅作为参考咨询,而不作为有约束性的裁决]
special replication 原告对被告在答辩中提出的新事实所作的答辩
2008 Special 301 Report (美)《2008年度特别301报告》(指涉及网络服务者在收到权利人通知后应履行及时移除义务以及移除制度如何适用网络用户利用网络服务提供者等的免责问题的一些规定)

special reserve fund 特别准备基金
special resolution 特别决议(案)
special responsibilities of a prosecutor (美)检察官的特定责任[《美国律师协会职业操守规范规则》第3.8条专门注明了"检察官的特定责任"。指出检察官如果违反其特定责任应当按照律师惩戒的标准进行处罚。具体包括吊销律师资格、暂停执业、谴责、不公开谴责以及留用察看等类型。联邦最高法院也曾建议,对检察官的不轨行为最适宜由州律师协会给予纪律处分。但目前由州律师协会对检察官做出纪律惩处的案例实际上凤毛麟角。为此,美国司法系统正在积极制定规则和法案拟对检察官的不轨行为实施提出指控或特别审查等更为严厉的惩戒措施]
special retainer 特殊律师聘约
special revenue funds 特别收入基金
special rules 特别规范,特别规定;特殊规则
special sentence 特别刑罚;特别判决
special service vessel 专用船
special session 1.(美)(国会)特别会议:(立法机关召开的)特别会议 2.(英)特别法庭(亦称临时法庭,指在四季法庭开庭时之外,由两个或两个以上司法治安官主持的开庭,审理一些小的案件或批准执照等)
special sphere of responsibility 特殊的责任范围
special statute 特别法规
special subject 特殊主体
special subject of a crime 犯罪的特殊主体
Special Subject(或 **Topical**)**Reporters** (美)《特别主题(或标题)判例汇编》(指一种非官方出版的法院判例汇编的重要形式,它将全部判例纳入一个特定主题范围,如《美国海事判例》《公用事业注释判例汇编》和《美国专利季刊》等)
Special Supplementary Agreement 《专门补充协定》(指自《联合国海洋法公约》签署以来,国际社会已就该公约中的某些缺陷制定了此《专门补充协定》以弥补该公约的不足。例如:《联合国海洋法公约》第11部分,"区域"中的开发制度是海洋法的新问题,广大发展中国家和发达国家对此有重大的立场和利益分歧。因此1994年7月美、英、法、德等发达国家共同参与,联合国大会制定并通过了《关于执行1982年12月10日〈联合国海洋法公约〉第11部分的协定》,对《海洋法公约》第11部分作了根本性修改)

special survey 特别检验
special tariff concession 特别关税减让,特种关税减让
Special Tax Entity 特种税务实体[指美国联邦税法通过创设的特别税务实体,对所有的证券化交易施以非常深刻的影响。目前,这类特别税务实体主要有:不动产按揭投资管理(REMIC);不动产投资信托(REITS);金融资产投资证券化信托(FASIT)];特种工具[美国证券法中的一个概念,指一个仅为从事发展、拥有以及运作某一个大型复杂之项目而设立的商业实体]
special traverse 深入抗辩,特别抗辩(指对对方所提出之事由给予详尽解答或反驳)
special treatment 额外待遇;特别待遇
special treaty 特别条约,专门条约
special trial court 特别审判庭,专门审判庭(旧译:特种刑事法庭,简称特刑庭)
special tribunal 特别法庭,专门法庭
special trust 特别信托;自动信托
special use permit 特别使用允准(指在符合城市规划情况下经政府允准使用财产)
special verdict 特别裁断,特别裁决(在比较复杂的民事审判中,法院可以指示陪审团作出的一种裁决,包括对案中的争议事实的书面认定)
special warranty deed 特别担保(产权转让)契据
special witness 特别证人
special-facts rule (公司)特别事实原则,特殊情况规则(指公司董事或高级管理职员在特殊情况下进行股票交易时具有一种信托义务,即对股东披露内部真实信息。这种特殊情况包括:股东缺乏商业敏锐或技能;股份为少数人拥有而不能确定其市场价值;或者董事或高级职员唆使进行股票交易等。亦称 special-circumstances

rule)

special-needs child 特别需求的孩子[指①具有医疗上的问题,或具有情感上或身体上的不利因素(emotional or physical handicap);②由于医疗问题或身体上、情感上的不利因素或者是由于年龄或种族背景,而似乎成为不可收养的孩子。见 Adoption Assistance and Child Welfare Act]

special-purpose entity 特种实体(见 special purpose vehicle)

special-purpose vehicle(SPV) 特种工具[指美国证券化中对特种机构的一个重要概念。特种机构在美国有不同称呼,大多数称其为 SPV,也有人称 SPE(special-purpose entity),即特种实体。不管称呼如何,其表达核心内容均一致,指仅为一个从事发展、拥有以及运作某一大型复杂之项目而设立的商业实体。其主要原因是限制对该项目具有求偿权的债权人的人数,亦指美、日等发达国家购买抵押贷款债权的机构,也称特殊目的公司。见 special purpose vehicle]

specialised agencies of the United Nations 联合国专门机构(指根据协定与联合国建立关系的或根据联合国决定而成立的对某一特定业务范围负有国际责任的政府间的专门性国际组织)

specialised chamber 专门法庭;特别法庭

specialised commissions (或 committees) 特别委员会,专门委员会

specialised court 专门化法院;专门法院

specialised law 专门法

specialist n. 专业律师;专业证券商

speciality 1.特性;特质;专门研究,特长;专业 2.盖印合同(契约)或契据 3.(复)细节,特点

speciality contract 书面要式合同(契约),盖印合同(契约)

speciality debt 书面要式合同(契约)之债

speciality of criminality 特定罪行(原则)(指请求国不得以犯被请求引渡的罪名以外之罪来处罚该犯)

specialization n. 专门化,专业化;局限化

specialization of police service 警务专业化

specialize v. 特加说明;限制在……范围内,把……用于专门目的;专门研究

specialize one's studies 使研究专门化

specialized a. 专门的,特别的

specialized agency 专门机构

specialized berth 专用泊位,专业泊位

specialized body 特别团体,专门机构

specialized company 专业公司

specialized corporation 专业公司

specialized court 专门法院

specialized federal tribunals (美)联邦特种法院

specialized form of jurisdiction 特定形式的管辖权

specialized investigation 专门化侦查

specialized police forces 特种警察部队

specializer n. 专家,专业者

specially elected member 特别选举产生的议员

specially endorsed writ 特别背书令状

specie n. 钱币,硬币

specie par 铸币平价,法定平价

specie payment 硬币支付,铸币支付

specie reserve 硬币储备,铸币准备

species n. 式样,形式,种类

speciesism n. 物种歧视(见 animal right,即"动物权力论")

specific n./a. 1.特性;细节 2.(复)(计划、建议等)详细说明书 3.特定用途的东西;特效药/1.特有的,特定的 2.具体的,明确的

specific administrative act 具体的行政行为,特定的行政行为

specific bequest 特定的动产遗赠

specific charge 特别费用

specific commitment 具体承诺

specific contract (与约定书合成完整合约的)特定合约

specific devise 特定土地的遗赠

specific duty 从量税

specific evidence 特定证据

specific goods 特定货物;特种货物

specific implement 特别履行

specific insurance 特定保险

specific intent 特定故意

specific jurisdiction 特殊管辖(在美国当被告与当地只有零星联系,但诉讼起源于

这种联系,则适用特殊管辖)
specific legacy 指定遗赠,特定遗赠(指特定物或投资等馈赠)
specific negligence 特定过失
* **Specific norms prevail overmore general ones.** 特别法规范优于普通法规范。
specific object 特殊客体
specific order 正式命令;特别订货
specific performance (衡平法院强迫违反合同者的)特定履行令或强制履行令;实际履行(英美法系对违约履行合同者的两种判决救济方法之一,即命令违约方履行合同义务。见 legal relief)
specific performance of contract 强制照约履行
specific policy 1.特定保险(契约);(水险中填入承运船名的)船名确定保单 2.特殊政策
specific provisions (of criminal law) (刑法)分则
specific quotation in question 有争议的特别引文
specific regulation 特别规章,专门规章
specific relief 特殊的法律救济
specific sample survey 典型抽样调查
specific statute 特别法规
specific unit taxation 从量计税
specific wording 专门措辞,专有用语
specific wording of the statute 法规的专门措辞,制定法的特别用语
specificatio 加工
specification n. 1.详述;(性能、使用等)说明书,发明说明书(指详细描述新发明物品的性质,向政府请求专利的说明书) 2.范围,规格;明细表 3.对来料加工成新产品所取得的所有权 4.技术条件
specification cost 规定成本
specification error 规定误差,规格误差
specification limit 规定极限
specification of quality 质量要求;质量规格
specification of quality 质量要求;质量规格
specified a. 限定的,规定的
specified over-all limit 规定的总限额
specified period 规定的时期
specified time for suit 起诉的规定时间

specify v. 指定,详细说明,列入说明书
specimen n. 1.样本,样品,标本 2.实例,例子 3.(贬义)怪人,怪事
specimen computation 抽样计算
specimen of draft 汇票样本
specimen signature (= facsimile signature) 印鉴样本
spectators n. 听众,观众
spectra n. (spectrum 的复数)系列,范围;光谱
spectrum n. 频谱系列;系列,范围;光谱
speculate v. 投机;推测
speculate in stocks (或 shares) 做股票投机生意
speculation n. 投机买卖,投机交易,投机事业,推测,推断
speculation on stock market 股票投机
speculative a. 投机的,投机买卖的,投机交易的
speculative activities 投机倒把活动
speculative efficiency hypothesis (SEH) 投资效率假说
speculative damages 推测性损害赔偿(指一种可能未来成为的伤害请求,这里指一种不确定性的,亦无合理证明的损害赔偿,一般法院不能予以裁决);相当于 punitive damages
speculative enterprises 投机事业
speculative lawyer 推断法学家
speculative profiteer 投机倒把获暴利者,暴发户
speculative sale 投机买卖
speculative trade 投机买卖
speculative trader 投机商
speculator n. 投机者,投机商 (= speculative trader)
speech n. 言论,说话;语言,方言;讲话,演说
speech and print 言论与出版
speech and the press 言论与出版(美国联邦宪法第一修正案宣布:"国会不得制定法律……剥夺言论自由或出版自由。"联邦宪法的言论和出版条款还包括了政府官员不得禁止公开讨论公共事务之含义。言论自由已经成为合众国制定政策程序

的基础。亦称 speech clause)
speech clause 言论条款(同 speech and the press)
speech from the throne (英)议会开幕时国王所作(或委托宣读)的国情与施政演说
speech reading n. 视话法(聋哑人观察对方嘴的动作而了解所表达意思的一种方法)
speech related conduct 与行为相关的言论
speechless a. 哑的;说不出话的;无言的,非言语所能表达的
speechmaker n. 演讲人,发言人,致辞者
speechway n. 某民族(或地区,集团)特有的言语方式
speed n. 速度,快速
speed cop (美俚)监督汽车速度的警察
speed limit 速度极限,受限制的最高速度
speed trap 汽车超速监视区(如在该区中超速将受严厉处罚)
speed way 高速车道,高速公路
speeding n. 超速行驶
speedster n. 超速驾驶者;高速双人座汽车
speedup n. 加速,增加速度;(雇主对雇员提出)增加产量而不增加工资的要求
speedy a. 快的,迅速的,敏捷的
speedy trial (美)迅速审判,快速审判(指在遵守法定规则和法定程序,同时又在法定期限或无不合理拖延情况下进行审判。联邦宪法第六修正案规定:"在一切刑事诉讼中,被告享有下列权利:由犯罪行为发生地的州和地区的公正陪审团予以迅速和公开的审判……"此修正案迅速审理的保障规定曾多次在联邦最高法院审理案件中被提到,且在 Klopfer v. North Carolina(1967)案中将它与第十四修正案中有关正当程序的条款联结在一起,以得到法律保护)
Speenhamland system (英史)斯宾汉姆兰德制度(英格兰大部分地区曾实施过的贫民救济办法)
spell v. 认真研究,琢磨,招致,带来,意味
spell out 理解,讲清楚,清楚说明
spell over 考虑,思考
spend v. 花费,消费,消耗,耗费,用尽

spendable earnings (=spendable income)(工资扣除所得税及保险费之后的)净收入
spender n. 挥金如土者,挥霍钱财者
spending n. 经费,开销,消费
spending boom 消费高涨
spending money (美)零用钱
spending public money in campaign 公费选举
spendthrift n. 消费无度者,挥金如土的人
spendthrift trust 浪费信托,消费信托,禁止挥霍信托
spent a. 用尽的;失去效能的;精疲力竭的
spent bullet 乏弹(指冲力已尽的子弹),死弹(指超射程、无杀伤力的子弹)
spent conviction 失效的判决
spes successionis 继承的期望,有希望继承
sphere n. 1.范围,领域 2.地位,身份 3.圆体,球体
sphere of activity 活动范围
sphere of application 适用范围
sphere of influence 势力范围;影响范围
sphere of jurisdiction 管辖范围
sphere of legal validity 法律效力范围
spill over 溢出;溢出量,因某种商品供应不足而引起的其他有关商品的需求
spin-off 股份转移(指母公司用子公司的股份向股东换回母公司的股份),分营
spinning one's wheels 无功而劳(美国习用语,意为一个人采取多种行为而毫无后果)
spinstor (=spinster) n. 未婚女子;老处女;纺织女
spiral of silence 沉默的盘旋(指借鉴西方媒介成ква,持不同观点的人们不愿发表与媒介所提供的舆论相悖的看法)
spirit n./v. 1.精神,真意,要旨 2.(复)酒,酒精;/1.使精神振作;鼓舞,鼓励 2.拐走,偷走
spirit of law 法的精神,法律真意,法意
spirit of legality 法制精神
Spirit of the Common Law 《普通法的精神》(美国法学家罗斯科·庞德,1921年著,现已有中文译本)
spiritism n. 招魂术,招魂论
spiritual a. 精神的;神的;宗教的;崇高的

spiritual court 宗教法庭
spiritual encouragement 精神奖励
spiritual incest 同受洗礼者间的逼奸行为
spiritual law 宗教法规
spiritual temporalities 教权
spiritual tenure (英)宗教土地保有制
spite n./v. 恶意,怨恨;(from/out of...)出于恶意/恶意对待,刁难;使烦恼
spite homination 恶意任命
spiteful tongue 恶毒的舌头,说话尖酸刻薄
split n./v. 1.(英)告密;告密者;便衣警察 2.分裂,分离,分摊 3.派别,派系/1.分离,破裂;断绝关系 2.均分,分割 3.告密
split action 分别诉讼(只能恢复单一的权利请求的诉讼,一般来说,其余部分在以后诉讼中也不能进行权利请求)
split check 部分兑现支票
split custody (美)分割监护(父母双方各自对不同之子女取得单独的监护权)
split of total freight 运费分摊
split on an accomplice 告发同案犯
split personality 精神分裂;双重人格,有双重人格的人
split sale 分割销售
split sentence 复合刑罚(该制度1883年起源于比利时,1927年引入美国司法体系)
split share 分散股
split tax 股本分散转移税
split the difference 妥协,折中;相互让步
split ticket 分裂票(指投给不同党派的候选人的选票);包括非党员在内的政党提名的候选人名单
split votes 分开选举制(指各政党分别选举的制度)
split-up n. 1.(股本的)分散转移;(母公司向子公司)转移全部股本 2.(美俚)吵架;离婚
splitrate n. 股本分散率
splitting 股本分散转移
splitting appeal 反复上诉
splitting cause of action 分割诉讼标的,分割诉因(指将单个诉因分割成若干部分,并提起单个诉讼)

splitting commission 分制委托
splitting of the Soviet Union 苏联解体
spoil n./v. 1.掠夺物;抢劫物;赃物;战利品 2.废品;次品 3.(美)(常用复)获胜政党分到的官职/1.损坏;糟蹋;伤害 2.抢劫;掠夺
spoil an orphan of his inheritance 掠夺孤儿的遗产
spoils of war 战利品
spoilt vote 废票
spokesman n. 发言人,代言人
spokeswoman n. 女发言人,女代言人
spoliate n./v. 1.抢劫,掠夺 2.因损坏而受到的损失;损耗率,损坏率;抢劫
spoliation n. 1.抢劫,掠夺 2.(战时交战国)抢劫中立国船舶;(使人不能用作证据为目的的)毁灭文件,篡改文件
spoliator n. 1.抢劫者,掠夺者 2.毁灭文件(证据)者,篡改文件(证据)者
spoliatory a. 1.掠夺的,抢劫的 2.毁损文件的,篡改文件的
spondeo 承担;着手做,从事
sponge v./n. 乞讨;骗取;过寄生生活/海绵;过寄生生活者;大酒量的人
sponge tax 见 pickup tax
sponging-house (英)债务人拘留所(将债务人拘留于此24小时后,如不还债,即送入狱)
sponsa 婚约女方
sponsalia (或 *stipulatio sponsalitia*) (大陆法)婚约
sponsalia per verba de futuro 口头同意将来结婚的婚约
sponsalia per verba de praesenti 口头同意即时结婚的婚约
sponsalia publica 正式婚约
sponsio (罗马法上最古老的)要式口头合同(契约)(其订约方式为口头提问和回答,即一方说:"订约吗?",另一方回答:"订约",合同即告成立);(罗马法)保证
sponsio ludicra (苏格兰)随意性的赌博协议
sponsion n. 1.(为他人)作保,私人担保,保证 2.越权或无权协定(指代表未经授权所作的约定或行为)
sponsor n./v. 发起者,倡办者;资助者;保

证人,负责人/主办,提倡,发起;提出
sponsoring a. 发起人的,倡办的
sponsoring power 发起国
sponsus 婚约男方
spontaneous declaration 本能的陈述,出于自然的陈述(指个人在突然事件发生当时或受该事件制约的状态下,大脑尚未及考虑而出于本能地反映当时情况的陈述,这种陈述是传闻证据的一个例外,可作证据采纳)
spontaneous exclamation 本能的叫喊(见 spontaneous declaration)
spontaneous statement rule 自发(或自动)陈述规则(指作出关于一个事件或可接受作为证据情况的大多陈述的规则,必须该陈述在事件或情况发生后不久即已作出)
spontaneous suborders 次级秩序[指英国社科哲学和历史学家哈耶克强调大社会中存在重合的若干"部分性社会"(partial societies)个人除了作为大社会的成员,还可能是众多自生自发的次级秩序(spontaneous suborders)的成员]
spontaneous utterances 本能的表达,出于自然的陈述(见 spontaneous declaration)
spoof n. 开玩笑,骗局
spoorer n. 跟踪者
sporadic dumping 偶见的倾销
sporadic or casual activities 零星或偶然性的活动
sporting a. 光明正大的,公平的;有体育道德的,体育运动的
sporting house (美)妓院;赌场
sporting theory of justice 光明正大的司法理论,公正的司法理论;司法竞技理论[指美国法学家罗斯科·庞德(Roscoe Pound)轻蔑地称对抗诉讼为"司法竞技理论",认为法官为理所当然的裁判员,而当事人在他们的比赛项目中以其自由的方式搏击,法官不予干预,他提出法官应有独立寻求客观真实和正义的义务。可当时庞德的这一观点被视为谬论时,他坚持普通法诉讼程序是"设计最精巧、凝聚着人类智慧的科学态度"]
sports antitrust exemption (美)体育运动

的适用除外(主要指棒球)
spot n./v. 1.(交易所)现货;当场交货价 2.认出(犯人)3.污点,瑕疵 4.夜总会,酒吧间;(美俚)小面额钞票 5.(美俚)(常在数词后构成复合词,指短期徒刑,如 a one-spot 一年徒刑)/1.玷污,把……弄脏,变污 2.记认(惯犯,嫌疑犯)
spot assets 现金存款
spot audit 见 random audit
spot cash (或 **payment**) 即付,即期现款,(当场交付的)现金
spot contract 现货合约
spot delivery 当场交付,当场交货
spot exchange 即期外汇
spot price 现货价格
spot test 当场抽样,当场试验
spot transaction 现货交易
spot zoning 临时(或短期)城市区划(指不顾地区城市规划而改变一块土地的城市规划)
spotter n. 私家侦探;(对银行公司职员的)秘密监视人
spousal(s) (古英国法)结婚,婚礼(指双方允诺的结婚)
spousal disqualification 配偶丧失资格规则(指在诉讼中配偶无权给对方作证,因此最初并不存在配偶有权拒绝作证的问题)
spousal support law 配偶扶养法
spousal-unity doctrine (历史)夫妻一体主义,夫妻统一体原则[指①(家庭法)普通法上的规定:丈夫与妻子是法律上的统一体。根据夫妻统一体原则,丈夫具有拥有、管理、控制和转让财产的所有权利,而妻子对财产毫无权益。亦称 doctrine of spousal-unity。见 legal-unity doctrine; married women's property acts。②(税法)规定,个人及其配偶(或丈夫)被视为一个整体对待。此规定已被废除,亦称 spousal-unity rule]
Spousal-unity rule 见 spousal-unity doctrine ②
spouse n. 配偶(指夫或妻)
spouse's benefit (或 **allowance**) 配偶津贴
spouse's inheritance 配偶继承
spouse's objects 配偶的反对

spouse's share 配偶的应继份额
spread v. 延伸,开展,扩大,传播
spreadeagle 见 straddle
spree n./v. 狂欢;狂饮;无节制的狂热行为/狂欢,狂饮
spring(s) n. 根源,原动力,动机
spring up 产生,实现,建立
Springboard n. 1.跳板 2.出发点(for, to) 〈It lacks editorial summaries such as introductory synopsis or headnotes to provide research springboards to other cases.〉(它缺少编者的概要诸如梗概或眉批以便提供判例检索的起点。)
springes n/v. 圈套,陷阱;/设圈套,设陷阱;用圈套抓住
springing use 有条件的使用权或收益权;未来使用权
Springing power of attorney 见 power of attorney
springs of conduct 行为的动机
sprited controversy 鼓励争议
spuilzie n. (苏格兰)非法骗取财产,掠夺财物
spur v. 推动,激励,刺激
spurii 私生子,非婚生子(罗马法名词)
spurious a. 1.假的;伪造者;欺骗性的;(证据等的)不合逻辑;谬误的 2.私生的;庶出的
spurious accusation letter 诬告信
spurious bank-bill 伪造的纸币;伪钞
spurious bicameral system 虚设的两院制
spurious certificate 假证书
spurious class action 虚假的集团诉讼(见 true class action)
spurious coin 伪币
spurious document 伪证件,假文件
spurious drug 假药
spurious interpretations 《虚拟的解释》(指1907年罗斯科·庞德 Roscoe pound 在《哥伦比亚法律评论》上发表的第二篇论文。它揭示庞德的法律分析思想,探究人类的道德性)
spurious marriage 伪装婚姻
spurius 私生子
spurt n. 物价的暂时上涨;(商业的)突然兴隆
spurt in prices 价格暴涨
spy n./v. 侦探,侦察者;密探,间谍,特务/暗中监视,侦察;做间谍
spy aeroplane 间谍飞机
spy out 秘密监视;秘密侦察而发现
spy satellite 间谍卫星
spying n. 间谍活动,侦探
spy-in-the-sky n. 侦察卫星
spy-master n. 间谍首脑,特务头子
squabble n./v. 争吵,口角/争吵,口角,(with sb.) 与某人争吵;(about or over sth.)为某事争吵
squad n. 班,小队,小组
squad-car n. 警察巡逻车
squander n. 浪费,挥霍;滥用;漂尽
squanderer n. 挥霍浪费者
square a. 1.公正的;适合的;断然的 2.收支相抵的;清算的
square deal (俗)公平交易,公平待人
square John (美俚)守法良民
square refusal 断然的拒绝
square shooter 公正诚实的人
squarely ad. 对准地,正方地,面对面地;成直角地
squat v. 蹲;擅自占地,非法占空屋,依法在政府公地上定居(以图取得该地所有权)
squatter n. 擅自占地(或空屋)者;公地擅占人,无权而定居公地者;合法居住政府公地而图获得该地所有权者
squatter(或popular)sovereignty (美史)人民主权论(南北战争前主张各州人民都有处理其内政权,并决定是否容许奴隶制的一种政治论点)
squatter's rights 擅自占地有权
squatter's title (英)占据土地人的所有权(指非法长期占据他人土地,不交地租而取得的所有权,承认他人有优越的所有权,但经过相当时间占有而获得的不可废除的土地所有权)
squeal n. 1.尖而长的叫声 2.大声诉苦 3.告密
squealer n. 发出尖叫声者;告密人;大声诉苦人

squeeze v. 榨取,压榨;勒索;逼迫
squeeze money out of sb. 向某人榨取钱财
squeeze the shorts 轧空头(指迫使卖空者用高价补进)
squeeze-out 排斥[指在公司中采取一种企图排除或降低小股东的利益(minority interest)。见 freeze-out]
squeezer n. 敲诈者;压榨者;勒夺者
squelch n. 镇压,压服,压制
squire n. 1.(英)大地主,乡绅;地主 2.(美)治安官;律师;法官 3.护卫,妇女的护卫
squirearchy n. (英)地主势力,地主政治,地主阶级
stall peddler 摊贩
stab n. 刺伤的伤口;刺,伤心,剧痛
stability n. 稳定(性),稳固,永恒性,耐久性
stability of law 法律的稳定性
stabilize v. 稳定,安定
stabilize a security (通过大量买进)维持一种证券的最低价格
stabilize the market 稳定市场
* *Stabit praesumptio donec probetur in contrarium.* A presumption will stand until proof given to the contrary. 在提供反证之前,推定仍然成立(有些推定是不可反驳的)。
stabit presumption proveritate 推定表明了事实真相
stable government 稳定政府
stabutarii (罗马法)车行主
staff n./v. 全体人员,职员,参谋/为……配置工作人员
staff allowance 工作人员津贴
staff and worker 职工
staff attorney 1.法院律师、法官助理,工薪律师[指为法院工作,通常为长期岗位,涉及的事项诸如复审法庭或法官提出的动议(motions),审查备审案件目录的陈述,准备好发布日程安排等以及审查人身保护令案件的申请书。工薪律师并不掌管有关动议或判决案件,但是他们复审和研究事实上和法律上的论点,并对法官提出建设性的裁决意见以及起草一些执行裁决的命令。一个组织,特别是非营利性组织,有时是企业的律师]

内部律师或法律顾问。见 in-house counsel;briefing attorney ②]
staff counsellor (公司)顾问
staff in post 在职工作人员
staff lawyer 专职律师(加拿大常用此称谓)
staff members' regulations 职工守则,工作人员条例
staff on official business 公务出差人员
staff shares 职工股
staffer n. 职员;报刊的编辑;采访人员
stag n. 股票投机商,非正规证券商;新股套利者,非会员股票经纪人
stage n. 1.时期,阶段 2.舞台
stage of equity or natural law 衡平或自然法阶段(指欧洲大陆一般的法律基础是由古罗马法学家著作的摘要编辑而成的《查士丁尼学术汇纂》,它代表了法律发展的这一阶段,称为衡平或自然法阶段)
stage of the strict law (美)严格法阶段(指19世纪美国法官们制定的控制美国人生活的法律,以日耳曼法作为根基。不仅有学术意义,还意味着是美国法律依据的素材)
stage of trial 审讯阶段
stage organs 国家机关
stage performance contract 舞台演出合同(契约)
stage right 上演权
stages of commission of a crime 犯罪阶段
stagflation n. 停滞性通货膨胀
stagger n. 1.犹豫的人,摇摆不定的人 2.难题,难事
staggered term 间隔式任期
stagnation n. 停滞
stagnation of 19 century law 19世纪法律停滞不前
stagnation of law 法律的停滞不前
stain n. 1.污染;玷污 2.污点,瑕疵,耻辱;污辱,受辱
stake n./v. (公元前12世纪)1.争议财物[指由双方或双方以上的当事方保管的财物(如财产)与第三方争议需解决时,则成了相互起诉(interpleader)的标的(subject matter)]2.商业风险(business venture)中的利益和股份 3.以金钱为赌注,打赌,竞

争 4.土地测量的标桩/打赌,保留,要求(土地,利息,功劳……)
stake out 1.(警察)盯梢(嫌疑犯)2.派警察监视(看管)嫌疑犯或某一地方
stake out a claim 立界标标明(土地等的)所有权;坚持要求(获得某物)
stake-out n. (因预知有罪犯或通缉犯出现)警察埋伏或监视某一地方;监视
stakeholder n. 赌款保存人,赌金保管人,赌注保管人;保存保证金的人(指保存签订合同购买物业的保证金的人,但不是卖者的代理人);争议财产保管人
stale a. 1.精力丧失的 2.(权利等因多年未行使而)失时效的;过期的
stale bill of lading 过期提单
stale check 过期支票[指超过支付日期一段时间(通常为6个月)的支票,并非无效支票。开出支票者重新填写一个日期或者开出一张新支票后即可向银行兑换]
stale claim unrelated 无关的失时效权利主张或请求
stale debt 失时效的债务
stall n./v. 1.厩,分隔栏;汽车停车处 2.牧师座位,牧师职位;教堂内的长排座椅 3.(复)前排座位(复)前排观众;(空)失速/l.(将动物等)置入厩中 2.使停车〈stalled traffic〉(阻塞了交通)堵车;阻塞,使停止 3.〈Even if a bill appears to be stalled in committee, news stories and press releases can provide leads to what is happening behind the scenes.〉[即使一项议案出现了在委员会被搁置的情况,新闻报道和媒体传播也会提供新闻提要(leads)告知你幕后发生了什么。]
stall licence 货摊执照
stall-holder (= stall-keeper) (英)摊贩;(商场中)摊位所有人或出租者
stallage n. 摊贩,摆摊权;摊位费
stamp n./v. 印花;邮票;标记;图章/盖章于,贴邮票(于);打上(标记等);标出,表示
Stamp Act 《印花税法例》(英 1765年通过的法案,规定美洲殖民地于公私文件上必须贴印花,后遭反对,于 1765 年废止);《印花税法》

stamp duty (或 **tax**) 印花税(指各种文件利用贴印花来交应缴纳的税,如租约、收据等的印花税)
stamp office n. 印花税务局
stamp out 扑灭,毁掉,拒绝
"stamped" money "盖印戳的"货币
stamped shares (或 **stock**) 加盖戳记的股票
stamped signature 签字盖章
stampede v. 1.逃窜 2.使(大群人)冲动行事 3.使(投票人、代表等)一下倒向某候选人
stamper n. 盖印者,打印人,邮票盖销员
stance n. 姿态,态度,(苏格兰)位置
stand n./v. 1.(美)法院的证人席 (=witness stand) 2.站立位置,立场 3.台,架 4.(苏格兰)(衣服等的)一套;(英)(一个士兵的)全套武装 1.站,立;位于;停住不动 2.坚持,主张,站稳立场 3.维持原状,继续有效
stand above all other laws 高于其他法律
stand alone in… 在……方面独一无二
stand and deliver (古)(拦路强盗用语)留下买路钱!
stand and neuronal distribution 标准正态分布
stand as 意味着,主张,做(候选人)竞选
stand aside (候选人)自行退出竞选,让开,避开
stand between 阻挠,阻碍
stand by 旁观,遵守;保持;准备行动
stand by letter of credit 备用信用证
stand by one's promise 遵守诺言
stand convicted of 被认定有……罪;被确证有……罪
stand down 1.离开证人席 2.退休,撤退,退出竞争
stand for 1.代替,代表 2.拥护;赞成;为……候选人 3.容忍,允许
stand for election 参加选举
stand for Parliament 竞选议员
stand in 杰出,替代
stand(s)in the shoe of sb. 取代某人之位置;处于某人的境遇
stand mute (对控告)不作答辩[①被告对

于刑事指控(criminal charge)拒不答辩,
以沉默对待作为无罪(no guilty)的答辩。
②任何当事人提出无异议(no objections)]

stand mute of malice 故意不作答辩
(a) stand of arms 全副武装
stand off 1.避开,不接近 2.(英)临时解雇
stand one's ground 坚持立场
stand order 长期订单
stand out 突出,坚持,杰出,替代
stand over 1.延缓,展期;悬而未决 2.密切注意,严格监督
stand surety for sb. 为某人做保证人
stand to 遵守,守约;坚持,固守;坚决主张;坚持原则
stand to one's assertion 坚持自己的主张
stand to one's post 坚守岗位
stand to one's word 遵守诺言
stand trial 接受审判
stand up for 坚持,维护,护
stand up-speak up-shut up 直立——直说——勿乱说(法庭用语,三个词连在一起,用来指导那些在证人席上的人应怎样向法庭供证,即要站好,不要左顾右盼,照事实直说)
stand with 支持
(a) stand-alone legal research component 独特的美国法律文献检索构成部分
stand-by arrangements 备用安排
standard n. 1.标准,准则 2.本位,官本位 3.模范,范本 4.(复)道德(伦理、习惯等的)标准
standard agreement 标准协议,标准合同
standard annual rate 标准年利率
standard arbitration clause 标准仲裁条款
standard blanket policy (保险的)标准统保单
standard C & P form 标准型租船契约格式
standard charter 示范章程
standard charter party 标准租船合同
standard coin 本位货币
standard condition 标准条件
standard contract 标准合同(契约)
standard contract provisions 标准合同(契约)条款

standard cost of entry 标准的进入成本
standard court reporters (美)标准的法院判例汇编
standard deduction 标准扣除额(此词组现已由"零级额"zero bracket amount 所代替)
standard economics 标准经济学
standard economics theory 标准经济学理论
standard efficiency criteria 普通效率标准
standard equilibrium theory 标准均衡理论
standard error 0 标准误差为0
standard evidence rule 实质证据规则[指按美、日法律规定,其享有准司法权的反垄断执法机关在行政裁决中认定的事实,有此实质证据证明时,对法院具有约束力,即该执法机关享有专属事实认定权,法院应尊重执法机关的事实认定。这是其外在效力的表现。美国《联邦贸易委员会法》第5(c)条规定,在联邦上诉法院审查时,委员会发现的事实经证据证实的,即是确定的,美国称为实质的证据法则]
standard for asserting jurisdiction 行使管辖的标准
standard form contract 固定格式合同(契约);标准合同
standard gold 标金
standard judicial behavior 司法行为的标准
Standard Juvenile Court Act 《标准少年法庭法》(美国一些州所颁布的法律,根据此项法律设立的少年法庭对16岁以下少年犯有绝对管辖权,对16岁到18岁的青少年犯除所犯的是重罪外,亦有管辖权)
standard microeconomic model 标准微观经济模式
standard of care 注意的标准(指侵权法上的标准:1.在有关过失的法律中,相同或类似情况下,一个理性和谨慎的人应达到的注意程度。如果行为人的注意低于这一注意程度的标准,则有可能对其行为造成的损失或伤害承担责任 2.在涉及专家诸如医师、律师等责任案件中,运用这一标准衡量专业能力)

standard of care in negligence cases 过失案件中的注意标准（指一个理智者在相同情况下会持有的小心程度），（法律对应负注意义务的人要求所应达到的）注意标准
standard of conduct 行为准则，行为标准
standard of international law 国际法准则
standard of living 生活水准（水平）
standard of proof 提供证据的准则
standard of weight 衡量标准
standard policy conditions 标准保单条件
standard set by ministry 部定标准
standard set forth in international shoe and its progeny 国际鞋业案及受其影响的判例所确立的标准
standard set of representation 代表定的标准
standard trade terms 标准贸易条件（贸易术语）
standard-bearer 掌旗者，旗手；杰出的领导者（倡导者）
standardization law 标准化法
standardization measures 标准化措施
standardize v. 标准化，使与标准一致
standardized contract 标准化合同
standardized products 标准化产品
Standards for Owner and Operators of Hazardous Waste Treatment, storage and disposal facilities 危险废物处理、贮存和处置设施的所有者和经营者的标准
standards of fairness and justice 公平和公正的标准
standards of normal output 工作定额
standards of proof 提供证据的准则
standby n. 备用品，备用设备；可依靠的人（物）；一级战斗准备；准备（收）报
standby agreement 备用协定，支持协定
standby credit 备用信贷，支持信用；担保信用证
standby guardian 可依靠的监护人［指如果孩子的父母成为无能力照管孩子，则父母可指定监护人，让其承担在未来监护孩子的职责，但不能剥夺父母对孩子的监护权（custodial rights）。有几个州已经制定了法规规定在孩子父母处于晚年病状时应提供可靠监护人，该监护人在孩子父母无行为能力或死亡时期承担监护孩子的职责］
stander-by (=bystander) n. 旁观者
standing n./a. 司法审判；持续；地位，身份，申诉人身份，名望，诉讼资格，诉权；资质/已为法律（或习惯）所确定的；固定的，经常的；常备的；常务的；常设的
standing alone 孤立地讲
Standing and Procedural Committees （联合国）常设和程序委员会
standing army 常备军
standing aside juror （英）排除陪审员（过去英国的一种判例，在刑事审判中，检察官可以把1名以至全体陪审员排除出陪审团而无须说明理由）
standing body 常设机构
standing circular 例行通告
standing civilian court （英）常设文职人员法庭
standing committee 常务委员会，常设委员会
Standing Committee of the National People's Congress （中）全国人民代表大会常务委员会
standing institution 常设机构
standing doctrine 诉权原则（指美国联邦宪法第三条之受案范围原则，旨在确立合理的司法决策必要的功能。其中最重要的原则即诉权原则。它要求只有自身受到属于法院审判权范围内损害的人才可提起诉讼。诉权原则要求具体的诉讼参与人把以对抗的方式提出问题作为启发法院决策的手段）
standing magistracy 站着的治安官（指法庭上站着
standing mute 保持沉默（指刑事被告人拒绝在刑事指控中的答辩，在此情况下应被视作无罪答辩）
standing of inanimate objects 无生命的诉讼资格
standing operating procedure （美）标准操作规定；标准做法
standing or plying for hire （汽车）非法招揽顾主（指违反交通法规的车辆在马路上边行驶边招揽顾主的出租行为）
standing order committee 议事规则委员会
standing orders 现行通令；议事规则（英

国上、下议院议事程序的规章);现行规定(指美国的一些特别法庭为指导诉讼程序所采取的一些现行规定);确定的要约,长期有效的要约
standing point 立场
standing resolution 现行决议(案)
standing to protect their own interests 保护它们自己利益的诉讼资格
standing to sue 起诉权,起诉资格,原告资格,司法救济请求权[指一方当事人因与某项纠纷有密切的利害关系,从而具有可向法院寻求司法解决的权利或资格,若要取得这个资格,美国联邦最高法院要求:当事人所反对的行为已给自己造成实际损害;当事人寻求保护的权利属于宪法或制定法所保护的范围。起诉权是确定案件可诉性(justiciability)的原则之一。这个原则衍生于美国联邦宪法第三修正案。对"案件与争议"(cases and controversies)的要求,简言之,起诉权确定谁可以就某些违反了宪法的政府行为提起诉讼。到20世纪60年代,诉权原则几乎没有对原告进行限制。Flast v. Cohen(1968)和Association of Data Processing Services v. Camp(1970)两个案例可证明这个原则]
standing vote 起立表决
standing water 死水
standout n. 杰出的人(或物),坚持己见者
standpatter n. 固执的保守分子(尤指政治上的),顽固地反对变革的人
standstill n. 停止,停顿;停滞不前
standstill agreement 暂停偿债协议
standstill cease-fire 就地停火
stangulation n. 扼杀,勒死
stante matrionomio 保持未取消的婚姻
staple n. 大宗出产,主要产品(商品);原材料;原材料来源(地);主要成分;(古)贸易中心城镇
staple article 常用物品(见 nonstaple article)
staple courts 商事法庭
staple legal analogy 主要的法律推理
staple of litigation before the Supreme Court 联邦最高法院的诉讼主题,联邦最高法院的最多诉讼(或主要诉讼)

staple remedy 主要救济
stapler n. 主要商品批发商,羊毛商
* *Star decisis et non quieta movere.* Literally to stand by previous decisions and not to disturb settled matters; To adhere to precedents, and not to depart from established principles. 按字义,遵循先例而勿改变已确立之原则。
star paging (美)星记标号页码(系指非官方出版的最高法院判决版本所采用的一种援引官方文本的方法,运用边注参考,在非官方出版的判例汇编文本上附加官方出版的这个文本页码)
star witness 主要证人
Star-Chamber(或 **camera stellate**) n./a. (英)星室法院(1487年根据亨利七世制定的法规组织起来的法院,以擅断、酷刑著称,1640年废止)/进行星室法院秘密审讯的
stare decisis 服从前例(原则),遵照先例(指法院对某一类事实确定一项原则,在以后的案件中可适用于同一类的事实);根据判例
* *stare decisis et non quieta movere.*
1.Literally, to stand by previous decisions and to disturb settled matters. 照词句原义,遵照先例原则,不得扰乱已确立之事项。2.To adhere precedents, and not to depart from established principles. 坚守先例,不得违反已确立的原则。
stare in judicio (原告或被告)出庭
stark a. 僵硬的,严格的;彻底的,完全的;赤裸裸的,贫瘠的
stark exposure 彻底揭露
stark fact 极其明显的事实
stark poor 赤贫
stark reality of Jim Crow 种族歧视的真实性
stars and stripes 美国的星条旗
start up cost 创办成本
start-up 起步阶段(指风险企业的起步阶段,风险资本往往是其唯一的资金来源,而这一阶段正是一个烧钱的过程,大量资金投入后,结果可能是完全失败)
start-up cost (高科技产品的研制或)创办费用

starting point 起点

starting point for theoretical analysis of litigation 诉讼的理论分析出发点

starting-point of the limitation 时效期的起算点（日）

startup(s) n. 新企业（尤指互联网公司）

starvation n. 饿死, 饥饿

starvation wages 不足温饱的工资

* *Stat pro ratione voluntas.* The will stands in place of a reason. 意志代表法理。

* *Stat pro ratione voluntas populin.* The will of the people stands in place of reason. 人民的意志就是根据, 人民的意志就是法理。

STAT-USA 美国商业部的一个单位[指属经济情况和统计情况行政管理部的一个部门（An Agency Within the Department of Economics and Statistics Administration）, 负责传播经济情况（economics）和贸易信息。这些均由其他联邦机构编辑并通过订购发行给商业部门、个人以及联邦指定的出借政府出版物图书馆]

state n. （16 世纪）1.国家[指经过政治组织的人民主体（body）的政治制度；通过多种法规制度对于人民的主体行使管辖和权力（authority）〈separation of church and state〉（宗教与国家的分离）。亦称 political society。见 nation。"国家是人们在其领土的范围内生活的共同体（community），这个永久的组织, 目的在于保障法律自律的正义优势（prevalence of justice）, 国家与其他国家保持关系的运作是通过国家机构（organ of state），这就是政府。"] 2.内部具有相当大政治实体的一个自治机构（An Institution of Self-government），特别是具有构成国家部分 50 个州的联邦政府] 3.（常大写）公众, 民众[国家的人民, 集体被认为作为被犯罪行为受害当事方代表国家的人民提起公诉〈The State rests its cases.〉（国家的人民停止对其案件的举证。）]

state a claim for relief 提出需要救济的诉讼请求

state action （1893 年）（美）州行为；国家行为[指任何由政府实施的行为；特别是在宪法法中, 一种干扰个人权利特别是民权的行为不管是由政府部门所为或由私人需求所为, 都只能由政府来强制执行（比如种族限制条款则要求司法强制执行）解决。美国联邦宪法第十四和第十五修正案主要在于保护解放了的奴隶, 确保法律的正当程序、法律的平等保护以及否决国家侵权的投票权。在民权系列案（1883）中, 联邦最高法院认为第十四修正案只适用于由国家法律直接授权或批准的行为, 对于国家行为要件的狭义解释是除了任何私人的源于联邦权限之外非政府组织的种族歧视行为。至于州行为则指直接由州实施的或与州有密切关系的而被认为是州实施的行为, 如果该州行为侵犯了美国联邦宪法第十四修正案所保障的正当程序和平等保护的权利, 则将受到司法审查。公民对其不当侵犯的政府行为可根据正当程序和《民权法》请求损害赔偿。另外, 州以法规或国家监管的垄断行为来排除竞争, 此种行为则不导致承担反托拉斯责任]

(the) state action doctrine （美）州行为学说[指依该学说那些可归之于州本身的行为（state itself），可获得反托拉斯豁免]; 国家行为学说[美国联邦最高法院在 1943 年"帕克诉布朗案"（Parker v. Brown）中提出的这一学说。即国家主权行为可以得到反垄断法的豁免。亦称 Parker doctrine]

state action immunity （美）州行为适用除外

state adjudicatory 国家审判机关

state administration 国家行政管理, 国家行政机关

state administrative agencies 国家行政机关, 国家管理机关

state affairs 国家事务, 国务

state agency 国家机关

state aid （美）州政府用于地方公共事业的补助费；国家（补）帮助

State Anti-Monopoly Committee 国家反垄断委员会

state approval 国家批准

state arbiter 公断人

state arbitration 国家仲裁机关；公断机关,（国家）公断（局）

state arbitration tribunal 国家公断庭
state attorney 国家检察官
state attorney general （美）州总检察长，州检察长
state attorney office 检察院
state auditor （美）州审计长
state authority 国家权力机关，国家当局
state bank 国家银行，国营银行；（美）州立银行
state bar association （美）州律师协会[指允准在某一州执业的律师全体的团体或协会。该协会组织是州一级范畴。州律师协会通常依据制定法建立。会员资格通常为强制性的。在该州执业的均为会员。与自愿性的促进行业发展的律师协会如美国律师协会（ABA）不同，州律师协会通常有权管理本州律师行业，如给予律师惩戒，对参与未经授权的律师执业活动提起诉讼等]
state based (statebased) 国家为基础的
state budget and the final state accounts 国家预算和决算
*State can do no wrong. 国家不会做错事。
state capitalism 国家资本主义
state capitalist sector 国家资本主义成分
state claim 已丧失时效的请求权
state code procedure （美）州法典程序
State Commission of Correction (SCC) （美）州教养委员会
state compulsion test (=state-compulsion test) （1978年）（民权法）国家强制行为准则[指国家对于歧视行为或区别对待(discrimination)负有责任的规则；当餐厅老板按国家法律(state law)的要求而拒绝为少数民族服务时，该个人当事方的作为是根据国家法律要求之作为。"阿迪克斯诉克雷斯公司案"(Adickes v. S. H. Kress & Co.)，参见《美国联邦最高法院判例汇编》第398卷第144页、第90卷第1598页（1970年）。见 Symbiotic Relationship Test; nexus test]
state conflicts doctrine （美）州的冲突法理
state conflicts principle （美）州的冲突法原则
state constables （美）州警

state constitution （美国等联邦国家的）州宪法；国家宪法
state contract 国家契约
state control 国家监督，(大写)国家监督机构
state control board 国家监督署(局)
state controlled trade country 国家控制贸易的国家，非市场经济的国家
State Council （美）州议会；(中)国务院
state councillor (中)国务委员
state counsel's chamber 检察署
state court decision(s) （美）州法院判例，州法院判决
state court system （美）州法院体制
state courts （美）州法院[美国的州法院系统，可见本词典附录Ⅱ。各州法院系统是独立的，在设置和名称上也极不一致。多数州实行三级制，少数州实行二级制，也有的州设有不列入审级的小型法院。州的案件可从各州的最高上诉法院进入联邦最高法院审理，联邦最高法院依据它享有的受理的自由裁量权以及维护它自己的诉权规则，受理的案件不超过所有各州上诉案件的10%。州的案件也可以因为低级别联邦法院对来源于州法院的案件作出了裁决而进入联邦最高法院审理。这种情况包括从州法院转移到联邦法院的争议、联邦法院中止州法院审理程序的禁令以及联邦法院对那些声称被侵犯了联邦权利的各州犯罪嫌疑人签发的人身保护状(habeas corpus)]
state courts to "step into the breach" （美）州法院"担当责任"，州法院"承担责任"
state crime （美）触犯州法罪
state criminal 政治犯，国事犯
state decisional law （美）州判例法
state defendant （美）州被告人
state demesne 国有土地
(the) State Department (=Department of State) （美）国务院
state despotism 国家专制主义
state direction of trade 国家对贸易的管理
state discipline 国家纪律
state district attorney （美）州检察官

state door-closing statutes （美）州的补牢制定法，州的弥补法律漏洞的法规（见 door-closing doctrine）
state economic organization 国家经济组织
state enterprise 国营企业
state farm law 国营农场法
state functionaries 国家工作人员
state gazette 国家公报，政府公报
State General （荷兰）总议会（又译三级议会，指荷兰共和国 1579 年至 1795 年各省代表组成的机构；现为荷兰国会名称）；（法）总国会（大革命前由国王召集，由贵族、僧侣、平民三个等级代表组成，以处理批准诸如征税等重要问题，产生于 14 世纪）
State General Administration of Exchange Control （中）国家外汇管理总局
state government （美）州政府
state guarantee 国家保证
State House （美）州议会
State Immunity Act （英）《国家豁免法》
State Import-export Commission （中）国家进出口管理委员会
state in breach 违约国
State Indemnity Law （中国 1994 年制定的）《国家赔偿法》
state institution(s) 国家制度，国家体制
state insurance system 国家保险制度
state interests 国家利益
state intervening in running of the economy 国家干预经济管理（问题）
state intervention in trade 国家对贸易的干预
state investment 国家投资
state judicial organs 国家司法机关
state jurisdiction 国家管辖权
state land 公地，国有土地
state law 国内法，（美）州法（美国各州或州政府制定的法律，有别于联邦法律，联邦法律为最高法律，但联邦法律未规定的事项，亦参照州法实行）；国家法
state law on the topic （美）州法上的有关细目，州法的有关纲要，州法的有关标题；可适用的州法
state legal service 国家司法机构，国家法律机构
state legislative district （美）州的法定议员选区
state legislator （美）州立法者
state legislature （美）州立法机构
state liability 国家责任
state machinery 国家机器
state medicine （国家的）公费医疗
state monopoly 国家垄断，国家专营
state name 国名，（美）州名
state notarial organ 国家公证机关
state of affairs 事态，形势，事实状态
state of affairs offences 状态犯（英美刑法中的一种罪行，亦称 situation offences 或 situational offences）
state of anarchy 无政府状态
(the) state of another in relation to myself 他人与我关系中所处的状态（见 external objects"外部对象"）
state of bankruptcy 破产状态
state of belligerency 交战状态
state of case 诉讼中的情形，案情陈述
state of emergency 紧急状态
state of intoxication 醉酒状态
state of landing 着陆国
state of mind 精神状态
state of nature 自然状态
state of origin 产地国
state of peace 和平状态
state of perfect freedom 安全自由的状态
state of permanent neutrality 永久中立国
state of registry 登记国
state of siege 戒严状态
state of source of copyright royalty 版税来源国
state of the forum 审判地（所在）国
state of the union message （美总统每年 1 月向国会提出的）国情咨文
state of unconsciousness 心神丧失状态
state of war 战争状态
State Office for Administration of Industry and Trade （中）国家工商行政管理局
state organ 国家机关
state organs of legal supervision 国家监察机关，国家法定监督机关

state ownership 国家所有制,公有制
state paper(s) 国家文件,官方文书(如白皮书、蓝皮书类),政府公文
state parties reporting procedure 缔约国报告程序
state party 缔约当事国
state plan 国家计划
state planning commission 国家计划委员会
state police (美)州警察
state policy 国策
state political power 国家政权
state power in areas not expressly delegated to the federal government (美)未明确授权联邦和政府权力的领域的州权
state power organ 国家权力机关
state practice (美)州的诉讼程序
state president 国家总统;(中)国家主席
state price 规定价格
state prison (=state's prison) (美)州监狱
state prisoner 政治犯(人),重罪犯(人)
State Privacy Act (美)《州隐私法》
state property (right) 国家财产,国家(财产)所有权
state prosecutor 国家公诉人
state prosecutorial apparatus 国家检察机关
(the) state prosecutorial system (美)州检察系统
state prosecutors (美)州检察官(见 municipal prosecutor)
state reapportionment (美)州重新分配(指州议会中议员名额的重新分配)
state relations 国家关系
state relief laws (美)州的救济法规
state replevying procedure (美)州追还原物之诉的程序,州追回原物之诉程序
State Reports (美)州判例汇编(美国的州判例汇编以两种形式出版:官方的判例汇编和非官方的判例汇编,前者由法院自己出版,作为其判决的权威文本。有两个全面的非官方判例汇编系统——西方出版公司的综合全国判例汇编系统和律师合作出版公司选编的《美国法律判例汇编》系统。至于联邦的判例汇编,也有许多其他专门的更多受到专题范围限制的判例汇编,其中包括州法院的判决,以及两个计算机法律文献检索服务系统——LEXIS 和 WESTLAW,这两者均提供范围广泛的州的判决)
state requesting extradition 请求引渡国
state responsibility 国家责任
state right (=state's right) (美)(宪法赋予)州的权利
State(s') Rights (美)州权
state rights of action 国家诉权
state rivers 国有河流
state rule of in-hand delivery (美)州的亲手送达规则,州法亲手送达
state secret 国家秘密,国家机密(指如果泄露这一秘密,则可能对美国国际和外交利益受到威胁。政府、军事或外交部门所掌握的信息,如被泄露,亦会损害公众利益。国家机密通过证人在正常的司法程序上是有不受泄露的特权。亦称为 governmental secret;government secret。见 executive privilege)
state secretary 国务秘书
state sector 国营部门
state security (court) 国家治安,国家安全(法院)
state security-for-expenses statutes (美)州的诉讼费用担保法(要求在允许诉讼继续进行之前提供保证金,被告败诉时由担保公司承担其诉讼费用)
state sequestration statute (美)州的扣押法规,州的扣押制定法
state servitude 国际地役(或称国家地役)(指为了他国的利益,根据条约,对一国领土所加的特殊限制)
state socialism 国家社会主义
state sovereignty 国家主权(或外部主权 external sovereignty)
state statute (美)州法规
state statute of limitations (美)州的时效法
state statutory law (美)州立法
state structure 国家结构(指国家整体与组成部分之间的关系)
state succession 国家继承
state superintendent of banks (美)州银监会
State Supreme Court (美)州最高法院
state system 国家制度,国体

state tax commissioner （美）州税务专员，州税务专员署
state territory 国家领土
state the case 陈述情况和理由
state the facts of a case 阐明案情真相
state tobacco monopoly 国家烟草专卖公司
state tortuous liability 国家民事侵权责任
state trading enterprise 国营贸易企业
State Transfer of Development Right Act （美）（新泽西州颁布）《土地发展权移转法》
state treasury 国库
state('s) trial 国家审判（由国家起诉的案件，尤指政治案件的审理）
state under protectorate 被保护国
state visit 国事访问
state's attorney 公诉人；（美）州检察官
state's evidence 知情人的证据（刑事案件中的罪犯对同案犯自动揭发的证词，以证实其他犯人有罪而减轻自己的罪证）
state-centric views 国家中心观
state-chartered bank 国家特许银行
state-contingent contract 国家或有合同
state-contingent contracting 国家（不确定的）签订
state-created rights （美）州法制定的权利，州法规定的权利
state-mandated a. （美）州（委托）法定的
state-owned enterprises (SOEs) 国营企业
state-run industrial enterprise 国营工业企业
state-to-state enforcement 国家对国家执行（指根据传统国际法原理，国际条约的执行主要由主权国家来完成，这种执行机制被称为国家对国家执行或公力执行 public enforcement）
state-treason n. 叛国罪，国事罪
stated a. 规定的；固定的；定期的；被宣称的
stated capital 设定资本
stated case 判决要点陈述（见 case stated）
stated day 规定日期
stated period 规定的期限
stated value 设定价值，面价（与 par value 同）
statehood n. 国家属性，国家的地位；（美）州一级；州的地位

statehouse n. （美）州的首府；州议会大厦
stateless a. 无国籍的；无国家地位的
stateless persons 无国籍人
stateless refugee 无国籍的难民
stateless world 大同世界
statelessness n. 无国籍；无国家主权
stateman n. 政治家；国务活动家
statement n. 1.陈述，声明；声明书 2.（法庭的）供述；（商业上的）计算书，报告书，报表
statement anteo mortem 遗言
statement in answer to the charge （英）答辩控罪陈述书（亦称控罪答辩书，指犯人在警察通知他被控的罪行后，并经过警官按规定对其进行指导和警告的手续后，该犯人对所控罪发表的意见，经记录，并由警方人员和犯人签名，有法律效力）
statement obscure the proceedings 故意蒙混的陈述
statement of account 结账单，对账单；计算书；收支报告书
statement of accused 刑事被告（人）的陈述
Statement of Administration Action (SAA) 《政府行政声明》
statement of affairs 1.债务清册（清单）（指破产债务人列出的债权人、债务人名单和财产的清单），资产负债结算表 2.事务报告，业务报表
Statement of American Administration （美）《行政行动声明》（指 1999 年欧盟诉美国"301 条款"案中专家组认定该条款违反 WTO 协议的相关规定而迫使美国联邦政府通过"行政行动声明"来确保国际法的适用性）
statement of assets and liabilities 资产负债表
statement of being guilty 作有罪陈述
statement of being not guilty 作无罪陈述
statement of case 案情陈述，案情报告
statement of charges 起诉书
statement of claim 索赔清单；起诉书；索偿陈述书（指原告向法院申诉请求他应得补偿及其理由的陈述书）；诉讼的陈述；原告的诉讼标的
statement of confession 坦白书，认罪书，

自供状
statement of defence 被告的抗辩声明;答辩陈述(指答复原告索偿陈述的陈述书)
statement of expenses 费用清单
statement of fact 事实陈述
statement of final accounts 会计决算报表
statement of general average 共同海损理算书
statement of grounds 申诉
statement of income and expenditure 收支报告书
statement of insufficient fund (银行)存款不足声明书
statement of law 法律(上的)陈述,法律(上的)申明
statement of non-law 非法律陈述
statement of offence 罪行摘要
statement of particulars 情节详细的诉状
statement of physical symptoms 身体症状的陈述,体征陈述
statement of profit and loss 损益计算书
statement of reasons for court's decision 法庭判决理由的陈述
statement of reasons for judicial decision 司法裁决理由的陈述
statement of receipts and payments 收支报告书
statement of repentance 悔过书
statement of resources 资产来源表
statement of service 履历表
statement of service fee 送达费陈述(指包括差旅费、送达费总数)
statement of the accused 被告陈述
statement of the case 案情记录;案情陈述
statement unconformable to previous accounts 与以前说明不符的供述
＊States are judicially equal. 各国法律上一律平等。
States Generals (1789年法国的)议会;(15、16世纪时荷兰的)国会
States' Right Republicans (美)州权共和党人,州权维护的共和党人
States' Rights (美)州权(指有利于维护州权不受联邦政府侵犯的一种政治权利)
states' rights sentiment (美)州的权威性

statesmanlike a. 政治家的,有政治家才能(或风度)的
statesmanship n. 治国之才,政治家的才能(或风度)
statewide a. 全国范围的
static a./n. 静态的,固定的,变化小的/静电
static approach 静态方式
static meaning 静态含义,静态意义
static model 静态模型
static rule 静态规则
static system of norm 静态规范体系
stating time 规定时间
station n. 1.车站,所,局;岗位,位置 2.地位,身份
station agent (美)火车站管理人员,(铁路)站长
station house 火车站;警察所;消防站
station in life 身份
station-master 火车站站长
stationery n. (总称)文具
Stationery Office (英)文书局(英国印刷出版和发行政府文件、法例、书籍的机构)
statism n. 国家主义
statist n. 国家主义者,中央集权下经济统治的主张者;统计学家,统计员
statistic law 统计法
statistical a. 统计的,统计学的
statistical compilation 统计汇编
statistical data 统计资料
statistical inference 统计推断
statistical model of plaintiff win rates 原告胜诉率的统计模型
statistical sampling 统计抽样
statistics n. 统计学;统计表;统计数字
statistics of population 人口统计
statistics of prices 物价统计
statolatry n. 中央集权论
statue n. 塑像,雕像
statue of liberty (美)(纽约)自由女神铜像
statuer à titre préjudiciel (法)先行裁决权
stature n. 身材,高度;(精神,道德)发展成长状况
stature of named parties 名义上的当事人的道德水平
status n. 1.地位,身份 2.状况,情形 3.法律

地位

status and capacity of persons 人的法律地位和权利能力

status civitatis (罗马法上的)市民权

status crime 身份罪(指基于被告人的特定情况或状态,如流浪罪等)

status crime or offense 基于身份的犯罪(指受控人并非由于他的作为或不作为,而是基于他拥有某种身份状况或特定人格的犯罪)

status familiae (罗马法上的)家族权

status in quo (= *status quo*) 现状

status libertatis (罗马法上的)自由权

status lien 身份留置权[指《美国商法典》第9条规定中的担保权益(其中包括法典制定前为人们熟悉的担保方式,诸如质权、抵押权、附条件的买卖以及信托收据等)属于自愿留置权范畴。非自愿留置权主要有两类:一为身份留置权(status lien)(为保护建筑工程商、物料供应商以及诸如此类的当事人的利益而产生);另一类为法定留置权(judicial lien)]

status maximizers 最大利益追求者

status of a natural-born citizen 公民生来的身份

status of alien 外籍人的地位,外侨身份

status of illegitimate children 非婚生子女的地位

status of the judge 法官的地位

status of women 妇女的地位

status offense or crime (少年法院管辖的)身份罪错;基于身份的犯罪(指①受控人并非由于他的作为或不作为而是他拥有某种身份和状况或特定人格的犯罪。比如身份犯罪是流浪罪,无所事事。②指未成年人做了某事而违反未成年人法,如系成年人所做时并不被认为非法,但这事ь说明未成年人已超越父母之管教,比如从家中逃跑,恶性不改等。见 juvenile delinquency)

status penalty 身份制裁

status quo 现状

status quo ante 原状,以前的状态,旧状

status quo ante bellum 战前状态

status quo on the border 边界现状

status quo post bellum 战后状态

status table 议案情况纪要目录[指为探究和追踪国会议案和它们的立法史的重要查找工具,它以不同方式出版,该目录是待决议案和决议的记录,并附有采纳相关法案(action)说明和对该法案反应的文件参考。此目录按议会案号排序,通常还会有对议案的简明摘要]

status-offense jurisdiction 身份罪错管辖权(指法院听审有关青少年的非犯罪行为事项的权利。参加 status-offense)

statuta odiosa 令人厌恶的法则

statuta personalia 人法

* *Statuta pro publico commodo late interpretantur.* Statutes made for the public advantage ought to be broadly construed. 为公众福祉所制定的法规应作广泛解释。

statuta realia 物的法则,物法

* *Statuta suo clauduntur territorio, nec ultra territorium disponunt.* Statutes are confined to their own territory and have no extraterritorial effect. 法律限于主权范围内有效;主权范围外则无效。

statutable a. 符合法律的,依法的;法定的

statute n. (14世纪)制定法[指立法机构通过的法律,特别是由造法单位(lawmaking body),包括立法机关、行政署以及地方法院所制定颁布的立法。术语 act 与 statute 可以互换使用,亦可谓同义词。缩略 S; Stat.]

Statute at Large 《法规大全》,《制定法大全》[指美国国会定期法规汇编的名称或称《会期法》。按年、月顺序汇集编纂。大量的《法规大全》形成以后按50个标题分类汇编的《美国法典》(U. S. C.),州的《会期法》样本是《纽约法规》(Laws of New York)和《马萨诸塞州的法令和决议》(Acts and Resolves of Massachusetts),所有的州出版有自己的《会期法》,而其各州不一。个别州还有商业版的]

statute barred coupon 有法定时间限制的息票

statute book 法典;法令全书

statute journal 法规公报

statute labo(u)r (英)法定劳务(指法律

规定教区居民在由该教区负责的公共事务方面所应完成定额的无偿劳动)
(the) statute law 成文法,制定法
Statute Law Commissions (英)制定法委员会
Statute Law Committee (英)制定法汇编委员会
statute law repeals act 修正制定法性法令,废除制定法性法令
Statute Law Revision (英)《制定法修订汇编》,(小写)制定法修订程序
Statute of Anne 《安娜法》[英国第一部版权法(1790年)]
Statute of Citation (英)(1531年)《传讯法》(亦译《传唤条例》)
(the) Statute of Charitable Uses 《慈善使用法》(1601年英国议会制定的,该法亦被称作"现代慈善法的开端"。至今仍是英美法中界定慈善的基础之一)
statute of descent and distribution 见 statute of distribution
statute of distribution (18世纪)遗产分配法规[指州的制定法规,规定无遗嘱继承遗产在继承人和亲属之间的分配。从历史上看,分配一项无遗嘱继承的不动产和动产的方式按阐明的法规是分开的且常常不同的。一般来说,土地传给继承人,动产则给最近的血亲继承。亦称 statute of descent and distribution]
Statute of Fraud 1.(历史)《防止欺诈法》[1677年美国制定法宣称某些合同在司法上并非强制执行的,但并非无效,如果这些合同没有由承担责任的当事方书面签署。该制定法原名为《Act for the Prevention of Fruads and Perjuries》(29 Can, 2ed 3),亦称"Statute of Fraud and Perjuries"。该法规的制定是在证据法不发达的年代,所以为了减少欺诈在当事人无法提供合格证人的情况下涉及地产权益转让、不动产遗嘱、信托证明等制定了防止欺诈法规或转让某些特定类的合同签订时,必须采用书面合同。但是此法一出,就遭到广泛批评,并有大量的判例对其进行辩称。美国继受了《防止欺诈法》而制定了自己的法律。同时各个州均采纳这部法规]

2.(1828年)《防止欺诈法》[要求书面合同 并由承担履行职责的当事方签署。凡涉及以下问题必须采用书面合同:①土地权益销售或转让之类;②一年内合同无法履行的;③销售货物价格超过500美元或多于此数额的;④执行或管理补偿死者债务的合同;⑤担保债务或其他义务;⑥婚姻的对价。参见美国《统一商法典》第2.201节(UCC§2.201)。缩略为S/F;SOF]
statute of general application in force 普遍适用的现行法规
statute of limitation 诉讼时效法规,追诉权时效法,时效法
statute of merchant (英)商业约定(指根据1285年《商业法》规定在城镇首席治安官前认可的约定)
Statute of Merton (英)《默顿法》(一般被认为是最早的英国制定法,是在萨里的默顿小隐修院通过的,故而得名。该法允许庄园主圈占公地,并宣布婚前所生子女为私生子女。主教们希望修改该法而与寺院法相一致,但贵族们一致反对。因而该法直至1926年才被修订)
statute of monopolies 专卖权法
statute of mortmain 见 mortmain statute
statute of presumption 时效推定
statute of Quia Emptores (英)《土地完全保有法》(爱德华一世时所实施的法律,亦称《封地买卖法》,是1290年通过的英格兰古法)
statute of repose (= repose statutes) 时效休眠,时效法,除斥期间法(其目的在于除斥当事人对失效请求权提出主张)
Statute of the International Court of Justice 《国际法院规约》(指关于机构设置及其权限范围的国际性文件)
Statute of the Staple (英)(1353年)《贸易中心城镇法》;贸易中心城镇的法定记录
Statute of Uses 《用益权法》或《受益权法》[指1535年英格兰的法律,由受益人(cestui que use:beneficiary)持有衡平法上的所有权(equitable title)转移给法律上的所有权人(legal owner)。目的是使受益人有责任缴纳税款,来达到法定所有人

(feofee to uses:受益的让与人)之所有功能。该法规定:"信托就是让渡财产,即受益人实际上是完全合法的所有人,而不仅仅是受益权人。"该法既无废除所有的受益权之意图,也没有适用于所有的受益权。它使土地所有人负有法律上所有权的义务,并剥夺土地所有人以遗嘱让与其土地的权力,尽管这种状况已由 1540 年《遗嘱法》得到恢复,但大法官法院的辩护律师通过信托制来阻止适用该法,该法是由监护人设想的一系列法规来阻止在土地上创设用益权的实践,这就剥夺了封建地主对封建土地保有所产生的有价值的附属财产权利。见 cestui que use]

Statute of Westminster 《威斯敏斯特条例》(英国制定的关于加拿大、澳大利亚、新西兰、南非、爱尔兰自由邦和纽芬兰等英属自治领实现完全立法独立的法律)

Statute of Westminster Adopted Act 《威斯敏斯特条例适用法》

statute of wills 遗嘱法

statute on adoption 收养法

statute on collection proceedings 托收程序法

statute on commercial registration 商业登记章程

statute on condominium 公寓成套房间个人所有权法

statute on declaration of death 宣告死亡法

Statute on Farm Inheritance (奥地利)《农场财产继承法》

Statute on Freedom of Transit 《自由运输规约》(1921 年国联主持下的巴塞罗那运输会议制定的两项法规之一,另一法规为《国际可航水道规约》)

statute on government liability 政府责任法

statute on inland water transport 国内水运章程

statute on instal(1)ment sales 分期付款销售法

statute on landlord and tenant 土地租佃关系法,地主和佃户法

statute on limitation of action 诉讼时效法

Statute on Navigable Waterways of International Concern 《国际可航水道规约》(见 Statute on Freedom of Transit)

statute on non-contentious proceedings 非讼事件程序法

statute on regulation of markets 市场管理法

statute on stock company 股份公司章程

statute on the expropriation for purposes of railway construction 铁路建设征用土地法

statute on the press 出版法

statute on trade marks 商标法

statute on unfair competition 反不正当竞争法

statute on usury (取缔)高利贷法

Statute Roll (美)《制定法档案》(指保存在政府档案局的,包括从 1278—1431 年和 1445—1468 年美国国会的各种制定法及许多文件卷宗,1466 年后为《国会法令刊录》取代)

statute-barred a. 因时效而被废除的(债务等),已逾时效规定的

statute-barred debt 已逾时效期而免除的债务

statute-like norm (准)类法律标准,(准)类法律规范

Statutes 制定法〈Statutes revised〉(修订的制定法),〈U. S. Statutes at large (Official)〉[《美国法规大全》(官方版),《美国制定法大全》]

Statutes at Large (美)《制定法大全》,《法规大全》(美国法规出版的第三种形式,系指美国国会定期法规汇编的名称);(英)《制定法大全》(为私人汇编,有几种版本,最早的为克里斯托弗·帕克出版的 1215—1587 年的英格兰制定法汇编)

Statutes in Force: Official Revised Edition (英)《现行制定法》,《现行法规:官方修订版》(指由皇家文书局出版的 1972 年至今的官方汇编,取代《修订法规》第三版,可与《美国法典》或《哈尔斯伯里法规》相比)

Statutes of Kingdom (*Ordenagoes do Reino*) (1603 年的)《王国法规》(指葡萄牙国王菲利浦二世即"西班牙菲利浦二世"通过的强调中世纪精神的旧《王国法规》)

statutes of reposes 见 statute of limitations

statutes revised 修订的,制定法

Statutes Revised (英)《制定法修订汇编》(初版于 1870—1878 年出版;第二版于 1888—1901 年出版;第三版于 1950 年出版,1972 年为《现行制定法》所取代)
statutes theories 见 *Bartolus de Saxoferrato*
statuto Albertino (意史)《阿尔贝特宪法》(指 1848 年皮埃蒙特-撒丁国王阿尔贝特颁布的宪法)
statutory a. 1.法令的,法规的;法律的 2.法定的,依照法令的;合乎法令的 3.依法应惩处的
statutory abolition of action 依法取消的诉讼
statutory acknowledgement 法定认领
statutory action 制定法诉讼
statutory advisory body 法定顾问机构
statutory age 适龄,法定年龄
statutory agent 法定代理人
statutory allowance 法定津贴,法定补助费
statutory arbitration 法定仲裁
statutory assaults (英)法定法所规定的殴打(又译:制定法上的殴打,指制定法所规定的侵犯行为,和习惯法的侵犯行为不同)
statutory assignee n. 法定受让人
statutory (或 **legal**) **auction** 法定拍卖
statutory authority 法定权限,制定法授权
statutory authorization 法律授权,法定的诉讼委托,立法授权
statutory basis 法定基础,法定准则
statutory beneficiary 法定继承人;法定继承的受益人
statutory burglary 见 burglary 2
statutory cause of action 制定法上的诉因,法定诉因
statutory claims 公法诉求(或公法争议)
statutory classes 法定分类
statutory code 法规汇典
statutory company 合法公司(即依法登记成立的公司)
statutory compilations 法规汇编
statutory construction 法律解释
statutory copyright 法定版权
statutory corporation 法定法人
statutory crime (或 **offense**) 依成文法规可惩罚的罪行
statutory damages 法定损害赔偿
statutory debt 法定债务
statutory defense 法定抗辩
statutory declaration 宣誓声明;书面声明,证明书;制定誓证(指按英国 1835 年誓证法例规定,将一种事实写成书面供述,誓证人只需在监督委员或政府委员的官员面前签名并庄重声明所供述事实是真实的,再经监督人签名后,即成法定文件)
statutory domicile 法定住所
statutory duty 法定责任
statutory duty of maintenance 法定赡养义务,法定扶养义务
statutory ejectment suit 法定收回不动产诉讼
statutory employee 法定的雇员,合法的雇员,制定法上雇员的身份(或地位)
statutory enactment 法规之颁布,法的制定
statutory exception 法定例外
statutory executor 法定遗嘱执行人
statutory exemption 法定豁免
statutory extinctive prescription 法定消灭时效
statutory failure 制定法上的异议
statutory force 法定效力
statutory foreclosure 法定取消(抵押人)的抵押品赎回权
statutory form 法规形式
statutory functions 法定职能
statutory general meeting 法定股东大会
statutory guarantee 法定担保
statutory guardian 法定监护人(指具有专有法定管辖权的法院所指定的监护人或监管人。亦称 guardian by statute)
statutory heir 法定继承人
statutory immunity from prosecution 制定法上追诉的免除
statutory instruments 法定文件,(英)制定法文件(指次级立法这一类的法律文件,其法定含义含糊不清),(大写)(英)《制定法文件》(指每年根据制定法委员会授权汇编成卷的汇编本)

Statutory Instruments Act (1946) (英)《法定规范法》[替代 1893 年由议会制定的《行政法规公布法》(Rule Publication Act)]

Statutory Instruments Revised (英)《经修订的制定法文件》(一套多卷本的法律文献汇编)

statutory interpleader 制定法上的确定竞合权利

statutory interpretation 法定的解释

statutory jurisdiction 法定管辖权

statutory (statute) law 成文法,制定法

statutory legacy 法定遗赠

statutory legatee 法定遗产受赠人

statutory license 法定许可(对版权限制的一种制度)

statutory limitation 法定时效

statutory majority 法定多数

statutory mandate of Congress (美)国会的法定授权,(美)国会的法定命令

statutory matrimonial property regime 法定婚姻(夫妻)财产制

statutory maximum (minimum) 法定最大(最小)限度

statutory notice by publication 法定的公告通知

statutory oath 法定宣誓

statutory obligation 法定债务,法定义务

statutory offense 法定罪行

statutory order 制定法上的法令,法令

Statutory Orders (Special Procedure) Acts (英)《法定命令(特别程序)法》

statutory ordinance 法定条例

statutory owner 法定所有人

statutory penalty 法定处罚,法定罚金

statutory period 法定期间

statutory power 法定权限(力)

statutory presence of stock 法定的股份所在地

statutory proclamation 法定公告

statutory prohibition 法律上的禁止

statutory protection 依法保护,法定的保护

statutory provisions 法律规定;法定条文

statutory punishment 法定处罚,法定刑罚

statutory qualification 法定资格

statutory rape (1873)制定法上规定的强奸罪[指与不满合法年龄(under the age of consent)的少女进行非法的性交行为,(正如法规所明确的定义)而不顾该少女是否愿意。总的来说,只要是一个成年人就可被判强奸罪,亦可称为 rape under age。见 age of consent]

statutory release 法定转让,依法释放

statutory rent 法定租金

statutory representative 法定代理人,法定代表

statutory requirement 法定条件,法规要求

statutory reserve (继承)特留份

statutory retirement of partner 法定退伙

statutory right 法定权利

statutory right of succession 法定继承权

statutory rule (英)制定法上的规章

Statutory Rules and Order (英)《制定法文件和命令》(1948 年改名为《制定法文件》。见 statutory instruments)

statutory salary increase 法定加薪

statutory scheme 法定方案,立法方案

statutory seat 法定所在地(2002 年 12 月 12 日欧盟理事会和欧洲会议通过的《布鲁塞尔条例》第 60 条规定,确定法人住所有三条可供选择的标准:法定所在地;管理中心地;主要营业地)

statutory share 同 statutory forced share (见 elective share)

statutory share of estate 遗产的法定应继份

statutory standard for judicial review of jury-awarded damages in diversity action 对陪审团在异籍诉讼中仲裁损害赔偿的司法审查的法定标准

statutory subject matter 法定的诉讼标的,法定的权利主张

statutory successor 法定继承人

statutory system of marital property 法定婚姻财产制(又译法定夫妻财产制)

statutory tariff 法定税则

statutory tenant 法定租户(指按照租金限制法例的权限,在租约期满后,有权占用受管制房屋的租户)

statutory text 法定文本

statutory time bar 法定时效已过
statutory time limit 法定期限
statutory tribunal 制定法上的裁判庭,法定裁判庭
statutory trustee 法定受托人
statutory trusts 制定法上的信托(指英国依据1925年遗产管理法例规定的信托)
statutory undertaker （英）执办人(指经法律授权创办水、电、气等公益事业的人)
* *Statutum affirmativum non derogat communi legi.* An affirmative statute does not take away from the common law. 确定之制定法不得违背普通法。
staunch defender 忠诚的捍卫者
staunch opponent 坚定的对手
stave off 避开,延缓,避免
stay n./v. 1.停留;阻止;延缓;延期执行 2.中止诉讼程序 3.妨碍,抑制 4.耐久力,持久力/1.停留,停止,逗留,耽搁 2.阻止,制止,抑制 3.延缓,延期
stay enforcement 停止执行(判决或仲裁裁决)
stay in (strike) （英）静坐（罢工）
stay (of) judg(e)ment 延缓审判,延期审判
stay of action 诉讼中止
stay of appeal 中止上诉
stay of collection 延期收款,延期征收
stay of execution 延期执行,停止执行(判决或命令),暂停执行(指判决不强制执行的时间阶段)
stay of trial 延期审判
stay of winding up 暂缓停业,暂缓解散
stay on 继续停留
stay (of) proceedings 停止进行诉讼(程序)
stay-down strike （矿工）留在井下罢工;静坐罢工
steading n. 小农场,(苏格兰)农庄
steadying factors 稳定因素
steal v./n. 偷,窃取;潜行/窃,窃得物;不正当的政治交易;以极其低廉价格买得的东西
steal into a house 潜入房屋
stealage n. 偷窃;失物;偷窃的损失
stealer n. 小偷
stealing n./a. 窃取,偷窃行为;（复）赃物/

有偷窃行为的,偷窃的
stealing children 诱拐儿童(罪),有偷窃行为的儿童
stealing ring 盗窃集团
stealth n. 秘密行动,鬼祟
stealth juror 隐秘的(或暗中的)陪审团员(指为了成为陪审团成员而隐藏潜在取消资格的偏见或利益冲突的陪审员;亦指企图影响审理结果或计划在陪审团审议中获得经济上的好处的隐秘陪审员)
stealthy a. 隐秘的,暗中的
stealthy murder 暗中谋害,阴谋杀害
steaming goods 转口货物,过境货物
steamline v. 1.把……设计成流线型 2.把……集为一个整体 3.使现代化,使合理化;精简……使效率提高
steams of payment 一连串的支出
steel n. 钢,钢铁,坚硬;炼钢工业;（复）钢铁公司股票(或债券)
steering committee 指导委员会,程序委员会
steersman n. 司机,轮机手;操纵转向机的人
stellionate n. 诈欺(指将同一物卖给数人的行为);欺骗性销售;欺骗行为
stem v./n. 堵塞,顶住,挡住,止住/堵塞物,坝
stem cells 干细胞
stem from 由……引起(产生)
stem from Article Ⅲ of the Constitution 源于《宪法》第3条
stench n./v. 恶臭/使发臭
step n./v. 1.脚步;步调;脚印,足迹 2.步骤,手段,措施/步行,跨入,踏进;介入
step in 走进,插手,干涉;作短时间的正式访问
step in the shoes of sb. 取代某人位置;步某人之后尘
stepbrother n. 继父与其前妻(或继母与其前夫)所生的儿子;继兄弟
stepchild n. 妻与前夫(或夫与前妻)所生的孩子;继子女
stepdaughter n. 妻与前夫(或夫与前妻)所生的女儿;继女
stepfather n. 继父
stepmother n. 继母
stepparent n. 继父(或继母)

steps in the social scale 社会等级
stepsister n. 继父与其前妻(或继母与其前夫)所生的女儿,继姊妹
stepson n. 妻与前夫(或夫与前妻)所生的儿子,继子
stereotype n. 1.陈规,老套;旧框框 2.铅版
stereotyped a. 已成陈规的,老一套的;用铅版的
stereotypes n. 刻板印象(指一个国家国民对于其他国家的国民大都持有一种固定看法,一个地区的人对其他地区的人,普通群体也会形成一种固定看法,这些看法被称之刻板印象)
stereotyping of the law 法律的陈规,法律的老一套,法律的千篇一律
sterile a. 不生育的
sterile negotiations 无结果的谈判
sterile woman 不生育的妇女
sterility n. 不孕不育症;不孕状态
sterilization n. 使不孕,绝育;消毒,灭菌
sterling a./n. 英币的,用英币支付(或计算)的,纯银制的;(金银)标准成分的/英国货币,标准纯银
sterling area 英镑区
sterling bill 英币汇票
sterling price 以英镑计算的价格
stern a. 严厉的,严格的,苛刻的;坚定的
stern rebuke 严厉的谴责
stern resolve 坚强的决心
stet 无需删改,仍用原文(指原稿或校样上删改后,再欲保留原文的注释)
stet processus 同意停止诉讼(指诉讼双方同意停止诉讼,也和判决一样,要记录在案卷里)
stevedorage n. 码头工人搬运费
stevedore n./v. 码头装卸工人/装货卸货(船),从(船)上卸货;装卸货物
steward n./v. 乘务员,服务员;(学校、旅馆、医院等的)伙食管理员;(美)车间(或部门)工会代表/当乘务员(或服务员等)
stewardship n. 乘务员(或服务员)的职位
stick-up n. 抢劫,拦路抢劫
stiff penalty 重罚,重刑
stiff sentence 严厉的有罪判决

stiffening process 呆板的程序,强硬的程序,变得僵硬的程序;硬性过程
stifle v. 扑灭,遏制,使窒息
stifle a rebellion 镇压叛乱
stifling a prosecution 免诉协议(对于重罪案件这种协议是无效的)
stigma of divorce 离婚的污名(或耻辱)
stigmatize v. (古)给……打上烙印;污辱,诬蔑
still n./a. 非法酿酒场所;蒸馏室,蒸馏器/寂静的,静止的,不动的,平静的
still alarm (以电话等非一般性报警系统所作的)火警警报
still-birth n. 死产;死于胎中的婴儿,死胎
still-born a. 死产的,流产的
still-born child 死婴
still-born scheme 流产计划
still-existing duty 还在的义务,仍存在的现行义务
stimulate v. 刺激,激发,促进;起刺激作用
stimulating action 推动工作
stint n. 吝惜,限制;定额工作,定量,停止
stipend n. 定期生活津贴;薪俸,薪给
stipendiary judge 支薪法官
stipendiary magistrate 受薪裁判官(指任的和有薪的具有七年状师资历且比一般裁判官的权力大的司法官员)
stipulate v./n. (法规、条约或合同)规定;约定;订定;保证;坚持以……作为协议的条件(for)/协定(就未真正形成的纠纷分歧点达成的有拘束力的协议,达成协定的事项需视为业经证明任何一方当事人均不再被要求对它们提供证据)
stipulated a. 合同规定的,约定的
stipulated damages (= liquidated damages)了结的损害赔偿(金);清偿了的损害赔偿(金)
stipulated form 约定方式
stipulated jointure 预先定下的亡夫遗产
stipulated price 约定的价金
stipulated quality 约定的品质
stipulatio (罗马法)要式口约,要式口头契约(合同)(指要求经过正式问答的口头契约。该契约约束回答者履行被询问的承诺。最关键的是双方当事人的直接问答。

其回答必须符合发问之内容,且回答目的在于由此承担合同义务,而不要求任何对价。复数为 *stipulationes*。见 action ex stipulatu)

stipulatio alteri 为他人的要式口约

stipulatio juris 口头契约,口头要约,承诺,要约(常指当事人先约定法律争议及其适用的协议)

stipulatio juris civilis 市民法的要式口约

stipulatio poenae 罚金合同(契约)

stipulation n. (18世纪)1.约定合同中的实质条款[指协议中关键的或实质性条款,或重要要求,特别是事实上的表述(factual representation)并入契约(合同)之中的术语(term)〈breach of the stipulation regarding payment of taxes〉(违背有关纳税之重要条款)。这类合同或约定术语(contractual term)通常出现在契约条款当中,被称为"事实陈述与担保"(Representations and Warranties)]2.自愿协议[指双方当事人就争点的某个争点的自愿协议(voluntary agreement),特别是由代理对方当事人的律师制订的诉讼程序的协议〈the plaintiff and defendant entered into a stipulation on the issue of liability〉(原告与被告就承担责任的争点订立协议)。由诉讼当事人或当事方代理人制订的关系到待决司法程序的协议中的实质性条款,具有约束力而无需对价(consideration)] 3.(罗马法) 要式口头契约[指由允诺人(promisor)(而且只有允诺人)通过口头问答而订立具有约束力的契约。公元3世纪,这种要式口头契约通常以书面文件证明](stipulate v.; stipulative a.)(见 reus promittendi; reus stipulandi)

stipulator n. 约定者,规定者,订定者

stipulatory a. 合同的,契约的,规定的,条款的

stir v. 动,摇动,激起,挑起,鼓动,煽动,轰动;传布,流通,流行

stir up strife 挑起争端

stirp(s) (或 **stirpes**) n. 族,祖先,家系,世系,血统,家族;种

stirp in blood 血亲

stock n./a. 1.证券,股本,股票(股份)总额

2.库存品,存货,贮存 3.储蓄,积蓄 4.足枷,手枷(旧时的刑具);估计;放任/(美)股票的,证券的,库存的,管理存货的,现有的,常备的;饲养牲畜用的;普通的,平凡的

stock account (英)股份账;存货账

stock arbitrage 股票套利

stock argument of strict law 严格法的根本论据

stock association 股份公司(见 joint stock company)

stock book 存货簿

stock boy 理货勤杂工

stock broker 股票经纪人,证券经纪人

stock certificate 股票

stock clearing corporation 股份清算公司,股票清算公司,股票成交公司

stock company 股份公司

stock divident(s) 股份分红,股票的股息

stock draft 股票汇票

stock exchange (broker) 证券交易所(经纪人)

stock holds activism 股东积极主义

stock issue cost 股票发行费用

stock ledger 股东名册;存货簿

stock market 股票市场,证券市场,证券交易所,证券行情;证券交易

stock of a company 公司股票

stock of capital (SC) 股本,资本储存,资本存量

stock of real capital 全部实际资本

stock of money 现金储备

stock of wealth 财富股

stock option 股票特权(指发行公司给本公司职工优先购买其股票的特权,又称"股票期权"或"认股期权")

stock owner 股权所有人

stock ownership 股权,股权所有制

stock ownership register of the corporation 公司股票所有人登记簿

stock power 股票转让授权书

stock preferred as to dividents 优先分配股息的优先股

stock price (index) 股票价格(指数)

stock redemption fund 收回股份基金

stock register 股份登记册

stock retirement plan 赎股计划
stock room (旅店中供旅销推销员用的)商品展览陈列室;贮藏室
stock split 股票分股
stock split-up 股份分割,析产分股,析股
stock swap 证券交易,股票交易,股票交换
stock to bearer 无记名股票
stock watering 过多发股;掺水股
stock-broker n. 证券(股票)经纪人
stock-brokerage n. 证券交易,证券经纪人的业务
stock-broking n. 证券交易
stock-generating resources units 待开发的资源单位
stock-in-trade n. 存货;生财(指企业的全部营业用具);惯用手段
stock-jobbing n. 证券交易,股票买卖
stockbreeder n. 牲畜饲养员
stockbreeding n. 畜牧业,牲畜饲养
stockholder n. 股东,股票持有者,股票所有人
stockholder's derivative suit 公司股东以公司名义提起的公司权利的诉讼
stockist n. (英)现货出售商(指备有存货准备出售的商人)
stockjobber (stock-jobber) n. 盘存,清查存货;证券经纪人,证券交易者;投机者;(美)证券经纪人;(英)(以证券经纪人为买卖对象的)证券批发商;场内股票经纪人
stockman n. 牧场主;饲养员;仓库管理员
stockpile v. 储存,堆集
stockpile nuclear weapon 储存核武器
stockpiling agreement 存货协定
Stoic philosophy 斯多葛哲学(指公元4世纪创立于雅典的哲学派别)
stolen a. 被盗的,失盗的;窃取的
stolen goods 赃物
stonewall v. (英)(用辩论等拖延手段)阻挠议事
stonewaller n. (英)阻挠议事者
stonewalling n. (英)阻挠议事
stony-arm a. 强迫的;暴烈的;用体力的
stooge n. 助手,傀儡,走狗;暗探,奸细
stool of repentance (宗教)悔罪席

stool-pigeon 1.(用来诱引他鸽入罗网的)媒鸽;用以引诱他人入圈套的人(或手段) 2.密探,探警
stop n./v. 1.阻塞,塞住 2.中止,停止,停下/中止,停止;阻塞,障碍
stop a case 中止诉讼
stop a cheque (或 stop payment on a cheque) (通知开户银行)止付支票
"stop and frisk" law "不准动并接受搜身检查"规则(指对怀疑有犯罪意图似乎带有武器的人,警察有权实施临时搜身检查的规则)
stop clause (规定在某种情况下允许提前)终止合同的条款
stop list (英)(贸易协会保存的)被禁止交易者名单
stop loss (订单上的)免损限度(又译:限损)
stop loss cover treaty 超额赔款分保合同(契约)
stop order 停止交易令;限损订单;依限买卖指令(指投资人对证券经纪人发出当股票涨跌至某一限度时,即应售出或买进股票的指示)
stop payment 止付,停付
stop-and-search campaign 搜查(战役)运动
stop-notice statute 停止支付通知法规[指对建筑物上的优先权或留置权(mechanic's lien)的一种选择的法律,即允准承包商、材料供应商、劳动者就未支付的建筑贷款对建筑物的出租人或所有人提出强制请求。见 mechanic's lien]
stop-payment notice (或 order) 止付通知书
stopgap n./a. 权宜之计;补缺者,临时代替的人(或物)/补缺的,暂时的
stopgap loan 过渡性贷款
stopgap measure 权宜措施,临时措施
stopgap tax 临时替代税,替代税[指在预算期间对于未预料到的赤字(deficit)所征收的临时税种]
stoping the company's operation 停止公司营业
stoppage n. 停止,中止;停付;扣留;停工,罢工
stoppage in transit (卖方)中途停运权

（指卖方享有的一项权利）
stoppage of all further payments　停止一切继续支付
stoppage of interest　停止利息
storage n.　保管；仓储；栈租；存仓费
storage charge(s)　栈租
storage life　保存期限，储存寿命
store n.　1.商店，仓库 2.储藏，(复)储存品 3.备用品；必需品
store warrants　仓储提单
Story school　斯托里学派（一种国际私法学派,亦即英美的属地主义学派）
stowage n.　1.储藏处；储藏费 2.装载；装载物；装载费
stowaway n.　偷渡者,揩油乘客；隐藏的地方
straddle n./v.　跨期买卖[指在证券与货物交易中,投资者持有买卖相同的证券与货物的合同,从而保证其中的一种合同不受损失。这种战略目的在于推缓收益并利用亏损以抵销另一应税所得(taxable income)，此词条亦可称为 spread eagle；combination]/跨期买卖；对敲；套购
straddle year　跨税率变化的财政年度（指一部分处于税率变化前而另一部分处于税率变化后的企业或公司财政年度）
straddling option　套购选择权
straight a.　直的；直接的,连续的；有条理的；正直的,正确的；彻底支持的；单价固定的
straight annuity　直接的年金,纯粹的年金（指固定数额,定期的间隔时间给予支付的年金或养老金。见 variable annuity）
straight ballot　彻底支持某政党所有候选人的投票
straight baseline system　（测定领海）直线基线法（制度）
straight bill of lading　记名提单,不得转让的提单
straight letter of credit　一次使用信用证
straight life annuity　终身支付的年金享受权（见 nonrefund annuity）
straight life insurance　投保人终生支付保险费的人寿保险
straight loan　无担保贷款
straight paper　由个人签发（或背书）的流通票据
straight ticket　(美)只选某一政党所有候选人的选票
straight trespass action　直接侵害诉讼（见 trespass on the case）
straight waist coat　(囚犯用的)紧身衣
straight-out n.　（对某一政党或政策）支持到底的人
straightforward a.　1.直接的,一直向前的 2.正直的；老实的；坦率的〈a straightforword reply〉(坦率的回复) 3.易做的,易懂的,简单的〈a straightforward problem in law〉(一个简单的法律问题) 4.明确的,肯定的〈your responsibility is straightforward〉(你的责任是明确的)(staightforwordly ad. 坦率地,直截了当地, straightforwordness n.)
strain v.　歪曲,曲解；牵强附会；滥用
strain one's authority　滥用权力,滥用职权
strain the law　歪曲法律
strained a.　牵强附会的；勉强的,紧张的；不自然的
strained interpretation　牵强附会的解释
strained relations　（两国或两团体间的）紧张关系
strait(s) n./a.　海峡/（受）束缚的,限制的；窘迫的；严密的
strait jacket（或 **waistcoat**）　（束缚疯子或囚犯用的）紧身衣
stranding n.　搁浅
stranger n.　外国人,陌生人；第三者,局外人；非合同当事人（指不参与合同交易的人,对债务不承担责任,合同内容对其无法律约束力）；自愿付款人（亦指自愿替他人债务的付款人,即使该付款人并无承担债务的法律责任,而且他的财产亦不受债权人权利之影响）（另代位"subrogation"并不适用非合同当事人,如债务人不同意或不指派代位权利）
stranger in blood　非血亲（指无血统关系的人）
stranger to the action　案外人；与诉讼无关者
strangle v.　勒死,扼死,绞死
strappado n.　吊坠刑（亦称"老鹰飞"刑,指旧时将犯人用绳缚住后将其吊起,并坠下的一种刑罚）；吊坠刑的刑具

strata n. (复)(社会的)阶层;层;地层
strategic (或 **strategical**) a. 战略的
Strategic Arms Limitation Treaty 《战略武器限制条约》
strategic behaviour (或 **behaviors**) 策略行为;对策行为
strategic blockade 战略封锁
strategic build-up 战略集结
strategic material 战略物资
strategic nuclear force 战略核力量
strategic trusteeship 战略托管
Strategy Environmental Impact Assessment (SEIA) 战略环境影响评价制度[(或战略环境评价制度) Strategy Environmental Assessment (SEA)(环境与发展综合决策的一项重要制度)]
strategy space 战略空间
stratified sampling 分层抽样
stratify v. 使成层,使分层
stratocracy n. 军人专政
stratum n. 地层;阶层
straw a. 无意义的,无价值的;假的,假想的
straw bail 空头保释(指无恒产而又假装有财产的人所提供的保释)
straw fiduciary 虚假的财产信托人
straw man 稻草人;替别人作伪证者;不重要的事实;易驳倒的相反论点;(非法交易中)被用作挡箭牌的人
straw polls 稻草选举[源自美国第一次民意测验。1824年,宾夕法尼亚州的一家报纸决定举办一次民意测验,特派记者到威尔明顿和特拉华两市向选民调查,预测四位总统候选人中哪一位最有可能获选。选举结果印证了调查结果:安德鲁·杰克逊(Andrew Jackson, 1767—1845 年) 当选美国第七届总统。人们认为这种民意测验就像举起一根稻草来测风向一样,因而称为"稻草选举"。后用以喻指民意测验,非正式投票]
straw vote (美)测验民意的假投票
straw-splitter n. 讲歪理者;诡辩者;爱钻空子的人
stray n./v. 1.流浪者;迷路人 2.因无人继承而归公的财产/迷路,走失,走入歧途/流浪
strayed children 迷失的儿童

strayer n. 迷失者
stream of commerce 商业的洪流
streamline n./v. 流线,流线型/使合理状,使现代化,精简,使效率更提高
streamlined rules 合理化的规则
street n. 街道;马路
(the) Street (指市内)从事某行业(尤指金融界)的地区;(美)纽约的华尔街(Wall Street);(英)伦巴第大街(Lombard Street);(英)伦敦金融中心,伦敦的舰队街(新闻业集中的地区 Fleet Street)
street betting (或 **gambling**) 街头聚赌
street clash 街头冲突
street crime 街头犯罪
street criminal at bay 穷途末路的街头罪犯
street name 经纪人名下,经纪人名义[证券业的行话,是指由他人注册登记在经纪人名义之下拥有证券,而非顾客名下,证券上只有经纪人和银行之名义(按顾客要求)。此类证券是"不记名背书"(black endorsement),即在转换票据背书时不记受让人的名称。这是因为此类证券是以保证金购买的,或是顾客希望此类证券由经纪人持有,从而可以通过由经纪人加具空白背书后仅凭交付而自由转让,这可掩盖真正拥有人的身份。该词条中的"street"与"Wall Street"有关联]
street offences 街道上罪行(指根据英国1839年首都警察法例和1847年城市警察条款法例所指定的各种在街上实施的罪行,共有47种,如狂暴地骑马、驾车、妓女游荡、勾引人宿娼等)
street office (中)街道办事处
street price (交易所)场外行情
street ruffians 流氓
street value 成交价格
street walker 娼妓
street walking 卖淫
street worker n. (美、加)街道工作者(指亲近并设法帮助一个街区中有问题的或曾犯罪的青年人的社会工作者)
streetcar franchise 电车专营税,电车专营
strength n. 力,力量,实力;人数,兵力;(美)股票市场价格上升(或稳定)的趋势
strepitus judicialis 在法庭上实施的骚扰行为

stress v./n. 着重,强调;使受压力/压力,紧迫;紧张,重压;重点,强调
* Stress must be on the weight of evidence and confessions should not be taken on trust. (中)重证据而不轻信口供。
* Stress should be laid on evidence, investigation and study and one should not be too ready to believe confessions. (中)重证据,重调查研究,而不轻信口供。

stress-related disorder 应激相关障碍[亦称反应性精神障碍。指一组主要由心理、社会环境因素引起的异常心理反应导致的精神障碍。以青壮年居多,性别差异不明显,主要有三种精神症状:①意识障碍;②情绪障碍(抑郁,焦虑);③妄想,幻觉。这类障碍在民事索赔案件中经常遇到,多为抚慰性的精神赔偿]

stretch n./v. 1.伸展,展开 2.夸张;滥用;曲解 3.(俚)刑期;徒刑/1.伸张,展开中 2.曲解;滥用 4.(俚)绞死,吊死;被绞死

stretch of authority 超越权限
stretch the fact 夸大事实
stretch the law 滥用法律
stretch-out n. (美)增加劳动强度的工业管理制度(指不增或略增加工资,使工人劳动强度增加的制度)

strict a. 严格的;精确的;绝对的;完全的
strict application of territorial power 领土主权的严格适用,严格的属地管辖权适用
strict construction 严格解释,狭义解释
strict discipline 严格的纪律
strict guaranty 严格保证;绝对保证
strict inquiry 详尽调查
strict law 严格的法律(严格法,严正法)
strict liability 后果责任(指制造特别是销售有缺陷的危险品使消费者人身安全受到侵害时应负的责任);严格赔偿责任;严格责任(制)[指刑法中即使没有犯罪意图仍然有罪,必须承担犯罪的责任和专门法规规定的罪责,如污染环境,制造污染等。与"无过错责任"(liability without fault)同义]
strict liability with a defence of contributory negligence 受害人有过失时的严格责任
strict neutrality 严守中立

strict rule interpretation 严格的规范解释
strict scrutiny (美)严格审查标准(见 minimal scrutiny)
strict secrecy 绝密
strict settlement (英)严格的土地授予(旨在将地产保留在男系血统之内的一种土地授予)
strict settlement and resettlement of land 严格的地产授予和再授予
strict settlement of settled land 严格限制授予土地的财产处分
strict surveillance 严格监视
stricti juris 依照严格法律;严格意义;严格地说
strictly document 严格占优(博弈论术语)
strictly obligatory 严格强制性的
strictus sensu 严格地说,严格地感受
strike n./v. 1.打击,攻击 2.罢工,罢市,罢课 3.意外成功/1.罢工;打击;殴打 2.缔结;拍板(定约等),成交 3.清算,结算 4.结束
strike (= settle) **a bargain** 成交;达成协议;订立合同,谈妥交易
strike a blance 结账,结算余额
strike a docket 结束案件的审理
strike a jury 挑选陪审团成员
strike an agreement 缔结合同(契约)
strike an appropriation from the budget 从预算中取消一项拨款
strike clause 罢工条款
strike down 击倒,杀死;去除,消除,废除
strike fund 罢工基金(指当工会会员在罢工时,提供给会员福利的工会基金,特别是当他们未领到工资而为生计罢工所需时)
strike home 击中要害,取得意想的结果
strike leader 罢工领导人
strike off 1.勾销,取消,抹去 2.斩下(人头) 3.轻易地做或生产 4.(拍卖时)卖(给出价最高者) 5.(法院因无权审理,指示将某一个案件从备审案件目录表中)取消(或勾销)
strike off the roll 从名册上除名(指英国高等法院出于律师的自愿或由于其行为不端而将其除名)
strike one's name off 除名
strike out 1.打击 2.搞出,设计出 3.勾销,

划掉

strike out pleadings 除去诉状(指法院或法官在诉讼进程的任何阶段,如发现有中伤他人的诉状,或不依从法官命令披露文据给对方检验等,可命令剔除诉状或修改诉状,作为惩罚)

strike pay (工会在)罢工(期间发给工人的)津贴

strike pleading 排除诉状,剔除诉状,修改诉状

strike, riot and civil commotion risks 罢工、暴动、民变险

strike suits (美)(公司法)恶意股东诉讼(指由不具善意请求的人提起的诉讼,其原理是通过负担沉重的审前程序来困扰公司以谋求有利可图的庭外和解)

strike-breaker (或 **strikebreaker**) n. 罢工破坏者,工贼

strikebound a. 因罢工而停顿的

strikebreaking n. 破坏罢工

striking a. 1.罢工的,罢市的,罢课的 2.打击的,攻击的 3.显著的,引人注目的,惊人的

striking a docket 结束案件的审理

striking a jury 挑选陪审团成员(见 struck jury)

striking distance 射击距离;有效距离

striking of local discovery rule 从地方披露程序规则的出庭陪审员名单中将他们划出

striking proof 明显的证明,明显的证据

string citation (美)一系列援引(指在法律结论之后所刊出的一系列判例名称或援引)

stringency n. 1.严格,严厉 2.紧迫;手头很紧 3.说服力

stringent a. 严格的,严厉的;(银根)紧的,(货币与信贷数量)缺少的;有说服力的

stringent laws 严苛的法律

stringent rules 严格的规定

strip v./n. 1.剥去,剥夺;夺去,掠夺 2.拆卸,拆去 3.抢劫/1.条纹,条子 2.(复)犯人穿的横条服,囚衣 3.鞭痕;(一记)鞭打;(一记)抽打

strip search 赤膊搜查(指脱去一个人的衣服以后进行搜查,目的通常是发现该人有无藏匿违禁物品)

strive v. 努力,奋斗;斗争,反抗

strong a. 牢固的,坚决的;强烈的;强大的

(the) strong arms of the law 法律的威力

strong box 保险柜

strong claim 强烈请求权

strong evaluation 强调评价

strong evidence 强有力证据;真凭实据

strong man 有实力者,实权派;铁腕人物;大力士,有才干的人

strong measures 强硬措施

strong partisan discipline 强有力的政党准则(纪律)

strong presumption 强力推定(指英美法系国家学者描述不同推定在效力上的差异的一种说法。slight presumption 弱力推定也是同类的一种说法)

strong protest 强烈抗议

strong room (保藏贵重物品的)保险室,保险库

strong-arm v./a. 强制,威胁;迫使/强制的,迫使的,威胁的

strong-arm methods 强迫的方法(手段)

strong-arm provision (美)强制规定(联邦破产法的一部分,规定最有权的、有担保的债权人的全部债权给予破产受托人,因此使受托人能集中全部破产的财产)

stronger sex 男性(同 tougher sex)

strongly worded statement 措辞强烈的声明

struck a. 因罢工而关闭的,受罢工影响的

struck down this provision 去除这个规定

struck jury (18世纪)1.用排除法选定陪审团[指从名单中允准当事双方选出一些人,然后又将其不乐意的人排除而组成的陪审团。陪审团人数达到适当数(通常为12人)为止。见 striking a jury] 2.见 special jury ①

structural estimates 结构推断

structural functionalism (功能)结构主义

structural realism 结构现实主义

structuralism n. 结构主义

structure n./v. 体制;结构;建筑;建筑物/构造,组织,建造

structure of criminal procedure 刑事诉讼程序的结构
structure of government 政府组织结构, 政府体制
structure of incentives 诱因结构
structure of party control 政党控制机制
structure of society 社会结构
structure of the law 法律结构
structure of the state 国家机构
structured finance 结构性金融
structuring sentencing discretion 构成科刑的酌处权, 构成科刑宣判的酌处权
structuring the public interest debate 构成公共利益论坛
struggle v./n. 斗争, 奋斗, 努力
struggle for national independence 为民族独立而斗争
struggle for supremacy 争夺霸权, 争霸
struggler n. 斗争者, 奋斗者, 挣扎着的人
stub n. (票据、支票等)票根; 存根
stubborn fact 难于对付的事实, 棘手的事实
stubborn problem 棘手问题
stubborn theory 顽固不化的理论, 顽强的理论
stubs of a checkbook 支票存根
studbook n. 优良畜种登记簿
student aid 学生补助金, 助学金
students' regulations 学生守则
study n./v. 学习, 研究; 研究的项目, 研究的对象; 学科, 论文/学习, 研究; 考虑; 细察; 细想
Study Group on International Payments (联合国法律委员会)国际支付研究小组
study market needs 调查市场需要
study of criminology 对犯罪学的研究
stuff gown (英)1.(旧时)资历较浅的律师穿的绒质礼服 2.资历较浅的律师, 普通律师
stuff gownsman 年轻的律师, 资历浅的律师
stultification n. 愚弄, 被愚弄
stultifier n. 声明精神错乱者
stultify v. 1.宣告某人精神错乱不负法律责任, 或宣告某事荒谬无效 2.声明自己智力不健全而无行为能力 3.否定自己, 自行提起要求撤销其所有契约或其他合同之诉, 并提出无行为能力履行他人提起强制履行合同之诉的请求
stultify oneself 自己声明精神错乱
stumbling block 障碍物, 绊脚石
stumer n. 1.假钞票; 假支票 2.错误, 大错
stun v. 使不省人事的行为, 使吃惊的行为; 昏晕, 目瞪口呆
stunner n. 假支票; 惊人的事
stupefy v. 使昏迷; 使失去知觉; 使呆若木鸡
stupor n. 恍惚; 昏迷, 不省人事
stuprum 同居关系
stuti 上帝的明示(指印度教徒信仰和尊敬的教义)
style n. 1.方式; 风格; 作风 2.式样, 款式 3.时式, 时尚
style book 样本
style of cause 案件的名称
style of "government commerce" "官商"作风
style of law 法律的样式, 法律的型式, 法律风格
style of living 生活方式
style of offence 犯罪方式
sua sponte 出于本人自愿, 自愿地; 法官个人的动议(并非来自哪一方的请求); 主动的
suability n. 可起诉, 可控告
suable a. 可起诉的, 可控告的
suasion n. 劝告, 劝说
sub n./v. 1.代替者, 代替物 2.代替, 代理/ 1.做替补 2.向……借支 3.审阅(稿件)
sub 在……之下, 靠近; 在……内, 内
sub colore juris 在合法外衣下
sub curia 依法, 依照法律
sub finem 见本章末
sub judice 在法庭中, 在审判中; 尚未决定
sub modo 附有条件, 在条件限制下
sub nomine (或 **sub nom**) 在……名义下
sub pede sigilli 在密封下, 在盖印下
sub poena 违犯者处以刑罚
sub potestate 在他人权力的支配下
sub rosa 秘密地, 机密地; 不公开地

sub sigillo 极端秘密
sub silentio 在沉默中,沉默,私下地
sub spe rati 尚待批准
sub spe reconciliationis 尚待调解
sub specie 假装
sub suo periculo 自我承担危险
sub voce(或 *sub verbo*) (词典的参看用语)在……词下;见……条
sub-agent 副代理人,分经销处,分代理人
sub-clause 副条款
sub-constitutional a. 亚宪法性的,仅次于宪法的
sub-contract n. 转包合同,分包合同
sub-contractual selling 分销
sub-court n. 法院分院,附属法庭
sub-delegated legislation 次级授权立法
sub-delegating legislative powers 次级授权立法权
sub-department n. 分处,分部
sub-district n. 分区
sub-division(或 subdivision) n. 分区;再分成的部分;再分,供出卖再分成的小块土地;(复)下属地区
sub-divisional court 分区法院
sub-function n. 次功能
sub-game perfect Nash equilibrium 子博弈精炼纳什均衡
sub-game perfection 子博弈精炼
sub-glacial water 冰下水
sub-heading n. (报纸、文章上的)副标题
sub-inspector n. 副检查员
sub-lease v./n. 转租,分租(土地或房屋)/转租
sub-lessee n. 转租租户,承受转租者
sub-lessor n. 转租人,分租人
sub-license agreement 可转让的许可证协议
sub-manager n. 副经理
sub-minister n. 助理部长
sub-paragraph(或 subparagraph) n. (法律条文等的)段,项,款,目
sub-partners(或 subpartners) n. 附股合伙人
sub-prefect n. 县长,(法)区长
sub-prefecture n. 县
sub-province n. 分省,专区

sub-purchaser n. 转购人
sub-regional fishery organizations 分区域渔业组织
sub-routines n. 次常规
sub-section n. 款,项
sub-transferee n. 再转让人
subadult a. 接近成年的
subagency(或 sub-agency) n. 分经销处,分代理人
subaltern cosmopolitanism 次级世界主义
subarea n. 分区
subcabinet n. (美)(总统私人选用的)非正式顾问团
subchapted S-corporation 见 S corporation
Subchapter n. (美)按合伙企业课税的公司地位(指某些少数所有权人的公司选定的法律地位,按关税法规定可按合伙企业对其课税,免交公司所得税)
Subchapter Corporations (美)美国《国内税收法》规定可按合伙企业课税的公司
Subchapter-C Corporation 见 C corporation
subcharter n. 转租租船合同(契约)
subcoalition n. 子联盟,附属的联盟
subcommission n. (委员会所属的)分会(或小组)
subcommissioner n. (委员会下的)分会(或小组)委员;副专员,副地方长官
subcommittee n. (委员会下的)分会,委员会的小组,小组委员会
subcon offer 附条件要约
subcovering license 综合分批输入许可证,分批输入许可证
subdelegation n. 特权,权力委任,授权[见 delegation of power(或 authority)]
subdivide v. 再分,细分(尤指分割土地)
subduct v. 1.撤回(指遗嘱检证程序中表示把申请检证撤回)2.抽去,减去
subdued a. 被征服的,屈从的,被抑制的
subgame n. 子博弈(扩展式博弈的一个子博弈,使博弈中满足三个条件的部分:①从一个单结信息集的决策结开始;②它包括博弈中该决策结之后的所有决策结和终点结而不包括其他结点;③没有结点属于一个不是该子博弈起始决策结的后

续结点的信息集)
subgroups n. 次群体
subinfeudation n. 分封采邑制
subjacent support 受其土地支撑的土地权利(不同于 side support or lateral support)
subjacent waters 下层水域
subject n./a./v. 1.国民,(君主国)臣民;主体 2.题目,主题,问题;学科,科目 3.理由,原由/受制于……的,服从的,从属的,易受的;依照……的,听候……的,争议中的/依照,使从属;使服从;使受到;使遭遇;使隶属;使遭受;提出,呈交
subject and object 主体与客体
subject classification 主题分类
subject country 属国
subject for registation 登记事项
subject matter 标的物;主题;主旨;主体;争诉事项,权利主张
subject matter competence (of a court) 按标的物确定的管辖权
subject matter insured 保险标的
subject matter jurisdiction 对事的管辖权;诉讼标的管辖权
subject matter of an action 诉讼标的物;诉讼的争诉事项
subject matter of contract 合同(契约)标的物
subject matter of the litigation 诉讼主题(要点),诉讼标的
subject matter of the proceeding 诉讼标的
subject of a duty 义务主体
subject of civil legal relationship 民事法律关系主体
subject of crime 犯罪主体
subject of dispute 争执事由
subject of international law 国际法主体
subject of law in the contract responsibility system 承包制法律主体
subject of obligation 债的主体
subject of punishment 刑罚主体
subject of the action 诉讼主体
subject of the right 权利主体
subject property 争议的财产
subject to approval (SA) 以批准为条件
subject to contract 以签订合同(契约)为条件
subject to cross-examination 受讯问,受诘问
subject to damage 易受损伤
subject to discipline 受纪律约束
subject to entry in the land register 载入土地登记簿的事项
subject to financing clause 融资条件条款
subject to the law 依照法律,受法律管辖,服从法律
subject-matter jurisdiction (或 **competenses**) 诉讼标的事物管辖权,事物管辖权,诉讼权的管辖权的管辖权
subject-matter of the suit 诉讼标的
subject-object dichotomy 主客二分法
subjection n. 隶属;服从;屈从;征服,镇压
subjective a. 主观的
subjective aspects of crime 犯罪的主观方面
subjective contradictions 主观矛盾
subjective elements of crime 犯罪主观方面的要件
subjective fact 主观事实(指法官、陪审官所发现的事实,并不是在初审以前在特定时间、地点的实际的"客观事实")
subjective factor 主观因素
subjective impossibility 主观上不可能
subjective individualization 主观个性化
subjective initiative 主观能动性
subjective law 实体法
subjective probability 主观概率
subjective requisites of crime 犯罪的主观要件
subjective right 主观权利
subjective standard (或 **criterion**) 主观标准
subjective standard of reasonableness 主观理性标准
subjective theory of contract 主观的契约理论
subjectivism n. 主观主义
subjects of law 法律主体
subjects reserved to legislative competence 属于立法机关所保留的立法权限项目
subjoin v. 附加;增补,添
subjoin an example in a statement 在陈述中附加一个例子

subjugation n. 征服,镇压,克制
sublet (sub-let) v./n. 转租,分租;分包(工程、任务等);把工作转包出去/转租(或分租)的房屋;转包,分包
sublicensing n. 转授使用许可,分让专利权
Submerged Land Act (1953) (美)《浸没土地法》,《水淹地法》(系联邦制定法,规范州境内可航行水域水流下的土地以及大陆架土地上的权利等)
submerged lands 淹没的土地
submission n. 1.递呈,提交,提出;提交公断;提交仲裁 2.建议,看法,意见;向法官及陪审员提出的意见 3.屈从,降服,服从 4.辩护词,论点
submission of a law to a referendum 将一项法律提交公民投票
submission of credentials 呈递国书
submission of tenders 投标
submission to arbitration 提交公断,提交仲裁;仲裁协议书(指争议发生前或发生后由双方当事人表示同意将争议交付仲裁的一种协议)
submissiveness n. 顺从,服从,柔顺,谦恭
submit v. 1.使屈从,使受到(to) 2.呈交,提交;提出 3.认为,主张,建议 4.服从,屈从,顺从,忍受(to)
submit a case to court 向法院起诉
submit a question to 将问题提交给……
submit for approval 呈核;呈请批准
submit to trial 交付审判
submittal n. 建议,条呈
submitting court 移送案件的法院
submortgage (或 **sub-mortgage**) n./v. 转抵押;副抵押权/转(抵)押
subnormal a. 低于正常的,智力低于正常的
subnormality n. 智力低于常人者
suboffice n. 分办事处,分理处;分局,支局
subordinate n./a./v. 部属;部下;下级服从者/从属的,下级的;次要的/使……服从
subordinate body 下级机构
subordinate court 下级法院
subordinate debenture (1929年)次级债券,附属债券[指这种债券属于一般债券(ordinary debenture)和其他处于负债中的

优先支付(prior payment)债券]
subordinate government 下属政府机关
subordinate legislation 次位立法,辅助性(附属)法规,辅助(从属性)立法
subordinate legislature 辅助性(附属性)立法机构
subordinate magistrate 助理裁判官,助理治安官
subordinate officer 下属官员
subordinate political corporations (英)附属政治法人(指英殖民主义时期一些法学家把殖民地看成是一种附属政治法人,因而英国会和王室对它们行使最高统治权)
subordinate relationship 从属关系
subordinate unit 下属单位,下级单位
subordinated debt(s) 附属债务
subordination n. 放在次级,使从属;次级,次等;服从,附属;附属关系
subordination agreement 降位协议(指根据合同自由、意思自治原则,如当事方同意,完全可以变更权利顺位,对于当事方自愿协商达成的这种协议,法律予以承认并加以保护。当事方之间订立的这种合同在法律上称降位协议)
suborn v. 1.以贿赂或其他非法手段取得;贿买 2.使作伪证,使发假誓 3.唆使(他人)犯法
subornation n. 使人作伪证,贿赂他人作伪证;贿赂人犯罪,教唆犯罪
subornation of perjury 唆使发假誓,唆使(他人)作伪证罪
subornative a. 发伪誓的,作假证的;教唆的,唆使的
suborner n. 唆使者,唆使发假誓者
subpart n. 较小的问题,较小的部分
subpoena n./v. 传票(指要求某人出庭审理、听审或者作为证人录取证言的法庭命令;传票分两种:出庭作证传票和提交书面文件传票),衡平法上的传票[每一起诉由命令被告出庭的传唤令(writ of supoena)开始,如今则由"writ of summons"开始]/传审,以传票传唤
subpoena a witness (用传票)传唤证人;传唤证人出庭

subpoena ad testificandum 出庭作证的传票
subpoena docus tecum 携带书证出庭传票（指命令证人不仅到庭，而且应携带相关文件的传票。这也是美国民事诉讼审判前的程序之一）；提交书面文件的传票
subpoena for documents 提交书面文件传票
subprime mortgage crisis 次贷危机，次级抵押贷款危机
subrent n. 转租人所付的租金
subreption n. 1.隐瞒事实真相，虚报事实 2.由隐匿或虚报事实而非法获利
subreptitious a. 隐瞒事实的；隐瞒事实而骗得的
subrogate v. 代替；取代（别人）；代位取得（指担保人代偿债务后取代债权人获得对债务人的债权的地位）
subrogate country 替代国
subrogation n. 1.代位行使，代替，代位权（指当事人一方代理，替代债务方清偿债务，同时亦指有资格替代原债权人享有的一切权利），如保证人代债务人清偿债务（通过代位权）使其有资格对债权人所持有的债务和对债权人对债务人赢得判决的利益作任何担保，另外还可（如债权人一样）对债务人提起诉讼 2.衡平法上的救济，通过这种救济，这种代位行使则会产生(take place) 3.保险上的原则[指根据一次保单已经支付损失费的承保人(insurer)有资格处理属于投保人(the insurer)针对涉及保单覆盖的任何损失，包括第三方的所有权利和救济]（见 equity of subrogation；anti-subrogation rule）
subrogation form 权利转让书
subrogation of compensation 代位赔偿
subrogation to right under a contract 代位取得合同（契约）上的权利
subrogation-exception n. 接替性例外情况，代位性例外
subrogee n. 被取代者
subrogé-tuteur 代位监护人（指为未成年人指定的第二监护人；当未成年人与第一监护人发生利益冲突时，则第二监护人可行使监护权）
subscribe v. 1.签署（文件）；签名 2.捐助，捐款 3.订购（阅），认购 4.同意，赞成
subscribe to share 认股
subscribed capital 已认股本，认购资本
subscriber n. 认股人，（公司债）应募人，（公债）认购人；捐助人；签名者；订户
subscriber information 用户信息
subscribing state 签署国
subscribing witness 文据上的证人（亦称证明的证人，指在文据上签名，证明该文据签订的证人）
subscription n. 1.签署，同意，赞助；亲笔签名 2.预订，预订费；认购；预约金 3.捐助（金），捐款；会费
subscription agreement 认购协议
subscription datebase 认购数据库，预订数据库（指一种援引检索的数据库）
subscription of shares 认购股份
subscription period 认股期限，认购期限
subscription promise 认购（或认股，认捐）允诺
subscription quota 认购份额，认缴份额
subscription record 认股记录
subscription register 认股登记（簿）
subsection n. （法律条文的）款
subsequence n. 后来，随后；随后发生之事
subsequent a. 后起的，后继的，后来的
subsequent acceptance 附条件承兑
subsequent act 后来发生的行为，后继行为
subsequent changes of beneficiary 后来代替的受益人
subsequent condition 解除条件
subsequent conduct 后续行为
subsequent courts （美）后继法院（指下级法院或同级的以后处理同类纷争问题的法院）
subsequent decision 随后的判决
subsequent endorser 后手背书人
subsequent estate 后继财（地）产权益
subsequent insurer 后续保险人
subsequent investigation 事后调查
subsequent marriage 后续婚姻
subsequent mortgage 后续抵押，次抵押
subsequent mortgagee 次质权人
subsequent order 后补令
subsequent ratification 事后追认

subsequente capula 随后的性交,随后的肉体交合
subset of alternatives 抉择的子集
subset of firearms 枪支的部分集中
subsidia 辅助,次要;附属
subsidiary n./a. 子公司,附属物/补足的,辅助的;附属的
subsidiary body 附属机构;辅助机构
subsidiary civil action 附带民事诉讼
subsidiary coin 硬辅币
subsidiary company 从属公司,子公司
subsidiary conditions 附加条件,附属条件,辅助条件
subsidiary credit 从属信用证
subsidiary ledger 明细分类账,辅助账
subsidiary legislation 辅助立法,附属立法
subsidiary money 辅币
subsidiary of the borrower 借款人的分支机构
subsidiary production 副业生产,辅助生产
subsidiary remedy 补充性法律救济
subsidiary source of law 法的补充渊源(又译:法律补充渊源)
subsidiary statute 辅助性法规,补充性法规,从属性法规
subsidies in general 一般补贴
subsidize exports 出口补贴,出口津贴
subsidized v. 以金钱辅助,资助,津贴;收买
subsidized credit 信贷津贴
subsidized housing 住房补贴
subsidized legal aid 法律援助补贴
subsidized price 补助价格
subsidy n. 补助金,津贴;奖金,援助
Subsidy Code (英)《政府辅助规例》
subsidy for leave of absence from work 离职补助费
subsidy *pro rats* 按比例补助
subsidy program 补贴计划
subsigilo 极机密也
subsistence n. 生存;生计;生活
subsistence allowance 生活津贴,生活补助;工作津贴
subsistence cost 生活费
subsistence wages 维持最低生活的工资
subsisting a. 维持生活的;存在的,继续存在的;有效的
subsisting contract 现存合同(契约),有效合同(契约)
subsoil n. 底土,下层土
substance n. 1.实质,实体;物(质);本质,本体 2.主旨,要义 3.资产,财产,资金,财物 4.内容
substance of common law 普通法要旨
substance of dispute 争执的实质性问题
substance of legal act 法律行为的实体内容
substandard a. 低于法定标准的,低于标准规格的
substandard life 低于标准寿命(尤指健康较差使保险公司人寿保险承担风险较大者)
substandard products 等外品,次品
substandard risk 低于标准的险(指保险公司认为风险可能大于同类保险的对象)
substantial a./n. 真实的,实际的,实体的,物质的,实质的;有重大价值的,内容充实的;巨大的,大量的/重要部分,要领;实质性的东西,实际存在物;有实际价值的东西
substantial agency findings & reasons for agency action 对行政行为的实质性行政机构裁决及理由
substantial and continuous relationship (美)实质性和持续的联系关系(见 minimum contacts 和 two-step "minimum contact" analysis)
substantial argument 重要的论证
substantial body of research 实质性的研究机构
substantial connection 实体联系,实质联系
substantial convergence 实际的聚焦
substantial damages 实质的损害赔偿(指由陪审团裁定损失的数额和项目,它和纯粹名义上的损害赔偿相反)
substantial defence 实体法上的抗辩
substantial economic effect 实质经济效应
substantial equality among districts 地区间的实质性均等
substantial evidence 主证据,实质性证据(指为某一争议事实提供证据,使得凡理性者均能相信它足以支持某一结论,高于

微弱证据 scintilla 并排除其他含糊不清的不相关成分);定案证据
substantial evidence test (美)实质证据测评(见 substantial evidence)
substantial financial burden 重大经济负担
substantial injustice 实质性的不公正或不公平
substantial interest 实质利益
substantial justice 实体正义,实质正义(与程序正义对,依照实体法规则所确立的正义,而不考虑程序上的问题)
substantial justification 实质性正当理由
substantial law 实体法,本体法,主法
substantial likelihood 实质可能性
substantial measure 实际范围,实际措施
substantial measure of sanctuary 实际庇护措施
substantial nexus 实质性联系
substantial performance 实质给付(指可以满足债权人的愿望所为的一种给付),实际履行
substantial performance of the contract 合同的实质性履行
substantial portion of the trust 信托中大部分(财产)
substantial prejudice 实质性的偏见
substantial similarity (版权)实质上的相似性[指在一个版权所有的作品与一个被指称的侵权(作品)之间极为相似(strong resemblance),由此而推定其为未经授权的拷贝(unauthorized copying)。对于实质上相似性的标准,是一般人(ordinary person)均可判断出这个被指称的侵权(作品)是否已经侵占了版权所有作品(copyrighted work)所表达的重要价值或成果(nontrivial amounts)。亦称 probative similarity。见 derivative work]
substantial things 实际存在的东西
substantiality n. 实质性的部分,实际有价值的东西;重要部分;要领
substantiality doctrine (美)实质性原则
substantially connected 实体上联系
substantially the same result 实质上同一结果
substantially the same way 实质上同一方式

substantially unrelated 实质(体)上无关
substantiate v. 1.证实,证明,(控诉、陈述、主张等)有根据 2.使具体化,使实体化
substantiate a charge 提供指控事实
substantiate a claim 确立一项请求的依据
substantiator n. 证人,立证据者;证明人,证实者
substanting taking 实质性照搬,(版权领域的)抄袭
substantive a. 1.独立存在的,真正的;实际的;实质的,本质的 2.规定权利与义务的 3.大量的,巨额的
substantive body of law 实体法
substantive claim 实体法上的请求权
Substantive Common Law 实体性的普通法
substantive court 事实审法院
substantive crime 实质性犯罪;实体罪
substantive defence 实质性辩护,可确定的实质性问题的辩护
substantive degree 实质性程度
substantive due process 实质性正当过程,实体正当程序[指不仅包括在美国联邦宪法中的理念,还包含有对隐私的保护以及个人民权(civil right)的基本理念,即包括第十四修正案中的规定,以保护任何人享有法律上的平等。见 due process]
substantive evidence 实质证据[美国学者对于录像带在何种情况下具有可信性基础,有两种不同理论:①图像证词(pictorial testimony 理论),在此理论下,录像证据为示意性证据(demonstrative evidence);②在静默证人(silent witness)理论之下,图像证据为实质性证据。见 silent witness],主证据,可确定系争实质性问题的证据
substantive failure 实质上的未能,实质上的失职,实质上的失效,实质性失败
substantive felony 独立重罪(指不依赖于另一人的另一罪行而独立的重大罪行)
substantive hearing 实体审理
substantive issue 实质性问题
substantive justice 实体正义
substantive law 实体法(又称主法、主体法系,程序法的对称,指规定主体间或人们在政治、经济、文化和家庭婚姻等事关系的权利、义务和责任的法律)

substantive legislation 实体立法
substantive matter 实质问题
substantive motion 实质性动议
substantive natural law 实体自然法
substantive obligation 实体债,主债
substantive offense 实体罪,主罪行
substantive policies 实体规定,实体政策
substantive provision(s) 实质性规定
substantive punishment 主刑,实体刑
substantive requirements of form (法律行为的)形式要求
substantive resolution 正式决定(议)
substantive right 实体权利,实质性权利
substantive right even in equity 甚至在衡平法上的实质权利
substantive rights even in equity matters 甚至包括衡平法事项在内的实体权利
substantive rules 实体法性质的法规(规则)
substantive rules for federal courts 联邦法院的实体规则,联邦法院的实质性规则
substantive rules of common law 普通法的实体规则
substantive source 实质渊源
substantive validity 实质性效力;实体法上的效力
substate entity 次国家实体
substituent n. 取代者,替代者
substitut (或 ***substitut général***) (法)代理(总)检察官(长)
substitutability n. 可置换性,替代性
substitutability of input 投入的替代可能性
substitute n./v. 1.代替者,代理人[指代替他人位置的人〈a substitute for a party〉(当事方的代理人)](见 subrogation] 2.(大陆法)第一继承人[指遗嘱中指定的继承人继承遗产(estate),但该遗产已被决定并转移至特定的人(称为 institute)。见 institute 5]3.(议会法)修订动议或修订申请的一种形式[指以另一些文字替代原有的词语提出修订申请(motion to amend)。见 amendment ③] 4.(苏格兰法)代表,代理人/代理(某人),代替(某人或某物)
substitute *ad interim* 临时代理;代理
substitute arbitrator 替代仲裁人(员),替

代公断人
substitute deputy 候补代表,候补(下院)议员
substitute father 代父(指与孩子的母亲未结婚而同居者)
substitute for personal service 替代性直接送达
substitute for sb. 代替某人
substitute resolution 替代决议
substitute security 替代担保
substitute service by publication 替代性公告送达
substituted a. 代替的,代理的
substituted complaint 见 amended complaint
substituted contract 替代合同(指代替旧合同的新合同)
substituted executor 代位执行人
substituted service 代替送达(指在无法把传讯、传票、诉讼通告等文件交给受件人本人时,即用代替的办法,把文件交给一个可能通知受件人的人,如受件人的妻子、代理人或采用邮寄、刊登广告等办法通知受件人。见 service of process)
substituted service of process 传票的替代送达
substituted service of writ 代理送达令状
substitutio 设定补充继承人
substitutio pupillaris 未成年人的补充继承人
substitutio vulgaris 通常补充继承
substitution n. 代,代替,替换;继承的代理
substitution of debt 债务的更新
substitutional a. 替代的,替换的
substitutionary a. (=substitutional)
substitutionary evidence 替代的证据
substitutionary gift 取代他人接受的赠与
substitutive a. 可以替代的,代用的;取代的
substratum n. 根据,基层;基础;下层
substratum of the law 法律之根基
subsystem n. 子系统,分系统,分支系统;(社会制度的)子制度
subtenancy n. 转租,转借,转佃
subtenant n. 转租人,次承租人
subterfuge n. 遁词,托词,借口,狡猾手段,诡计
subtitle n. 副标题,小标题

subtle a. 微妙的,精微的;狡猾的,诡谲的;聪明的
subtle scheme to get money 骗钱诡计
subtopia n. 城乡一体化的趋势;(由于都市化)丧失自然风景的乡村(或市郊)地区
subtract v. 减少,扣除;缺少
subtraction n. 减去,扣除;不履行义务(指疏忽或拒绝履行义务)
subtraction of conjugal right 放弃配偶权利(指夫妻无合法理由而分居的行为)
subtransferor n. 再转让人,再转移人
subtreasury n. 国库(或金库等)的分库
suburb n. 郊区,郊外;近郊;(复)边缘
suburbani (古英国法上的)农民,庄稼汉
suburbanite n. 郊区居民
suburbanize v. 使市郊化
suburbia n. (总称)都市的郊区,郊区居民,郊区居民特有的风俗习惯
subvention n. 补助金,津贴
subversion n. 颠覆,灭亡,败坏;促使灭亡
subversion of the government 颠覆政府(罪)
subversive n./a. 颠覆分子,搞颠覆阴谋的人/颠覆性的,促使灭亡的
subversive activities 颠覆活动
subversive propaganda 颠覆性宣传(指蓄意图谋挑起内战或革命,而煽动者往往是另一个民族。亦称 hostile propaganda 或 ideological aggression)
subvert v. 颠覆,推翻;灭亡
subverter n. 颠覆者,破坏者
succeed v. 1.继……后,接替,继承;继续,继任 2.成功
succeed oneself (美)重新当选,连任,留任
succeed to a fortune 继承大笔遗产
succeed to the Crown (或throne) 继承王位
succeeder n. 继承人;嗣子
succeeding in the vice 不当接替
success n. 成功,成就,胜利
successful a. 成功的;结果良好的,有成就的
successful at the polls 当选
successful bidder 得标的投标人
successful party 胜诉当事人
successful plaintiff 胜诉原告
successful tenderer 得标人

successio 继承
successio ab intestato 无遗嘱的继承,法定继承
successio moris causa (罗马法)死因继承[指在被继承人(*de cuius*)死亡的情况下,其遗产向继承人(*heres*)的转移,从广义上说,死因继承的形式还可表现为遗赠(*legatum*)和遗产依托(*fidei commissum heredictatips*)]
successio per universitatem 概括继承
successio tra vivi (罗马法)生者间继承[这与死因继承(*successio moris causa*)不同,此种继承发生在活着的当事人之间,这一般表现为某一主体取得对另一主体的支配权(见 *potestas*)从而接替后者享受和承担一切原有的权利和义务。较典型的例子是自权人收养(*adrogatio*)和作为自权人(*sui iuis*)的妇女归顺夫权]
succession n. 1.继承;继承权;继位;继权;连续 2.一系列继承人;继承顺序
succession *ab intestato* 无遗嘱的继承,法定继承
succession by subrogation 代袭继承,代位继承
succession by testament 遗嘱继承
succession by the eldest son 长子继承
succession during life time 生前继承
succession duty (英)遗产税;继承税(美国称为 inheritance tax)
succession *ex testamento* 遗命继承,遗嘱继承
succession *morits causa* 遗产继承原因
succession of governmental forms 政府体制的继续
succession of state in respect of treaties 关于条约的国家继承
succession on intestacy 无遗嘱的继承
succession relations 继承关系
succession tax 见 inheritance tax
succession to property 财产继承
succession to status within the family 家庭地位的继承
succession to the Crown 王位继承
succession to the family headship 户主继承,家督继承(日本的一种继承制度,家督即户主)

succession upon death 死后继承
successional a. 继续的,连续的,继承的
successional portion 应继份
successive a. 继续的,连续的
successive action 连续诉讼
successive carrier 连续承运人
successive election 连续选举
successive estate 连续的财(地)产权益(指将财产权益或地产权分为两个或两个以上,其中的第一、第二的权益所使用的术语)
successive government 历届政府
successive injury 连续伤害
successive interest 连续性权益;可继承权益
successor n. 继承人;继任者;后继者;接班人
successor guardian 继任监护人(指父母的遗嘱中指名的继任或候补的监护人,以应对第一个指定的监护人未能履行其职责)
successor in interest of the commission agent 经纪人的权利承受人
successor in title 权利继承人
successor in total 完全的继承人
successor regime 接着上台的政权,政权更迭后的继任统治集团
successor state 继受国
succinct a. 简易的,简洁的;贴身的,紧身的
succinct statement of the case 案情的简洁阐述
succo(u)r n./v. 救济,援助;救急的东西,救助者/帮助,救助
succumb v. 屈服,屈从(to),死于(to)
succumbed to temptation 受诱惑
* *Succurritur minori; facilis est lapsus juventutis.* A minor is (to be) aided; a mistake of youth is easy. 要帮助未成年人,因为他们是容易犯错误的。
such being the case 事实既然如此
suck in (俚)欺骗,失望,失败
sucking barrister 初出茅庐的律师;年轻的状师;无生意的律师
sudden a. 突然的,忽然的
sudden accidental occurrence 突发事故性事件,突发性事件
sudden death 猝死,急死

sudden emergency 紧迫事件
sudden heat of passion 突然的感情冲动
sudden huge probits 暴利
sue v. 起诉,控告;提起诉讼;提出请求;上诉(用于民事诉讼)
sue and be sued in court 在法院起诉和应诉
sue and labour charges 施救费用,损害防止费用
sue and labour clause (保险)施救条款,防止损害条款;事故防止条款(海上保险)
sue at (the) law 提起诉讼,起诉
sue for a divorce 要求离婚之诉
sue for a writ of recovery 请求法官宣告恢复权利的令状(或裁定)
sue for damages 起诉要求赔偿损失
sue for one's livery (向法院)请求将某人财产交监护人
sue in a civil action 进行民事诉讼
sue out 经向法院请求而得到(赦免,赔偿等)
sue out a pardon 求得宽赦
sue sb. for civil injury 控诉某人要求民事上的损害赔偿
suffer v. 1.蒙受;遭受;忍受 2.受苦;惩罚;被处死刑 3.受损失,受损害(from) 4.患病
suffer a loss 遭受损失
suffer for 因……而受到惩罚,因……而遭受
suffer from 患……病;苦于;因……损害;因……受困扰
suffer from floods 遭受水灾
sufferance n. 容许,容忍
sufferance wharf 许可码头(指关税和消费税委员所指定的应纳税的装卸码头)
sufferer n. 受害者,受难者
suffice v. 满足……需要,满足,足够,有能力
suffice it to say that 只要说……就够了
sufficiency n. 充分性,足量性,(财产、收入、能力等)充足
sufficiency of the security 充分的担保,足够的担保
sufficiency of the service of process 诉讼书状送达的充分性(指该送达符合法定要

求,正确及时送达到被告手中)
sufficient a. 充分的,足够的
sufficient acceptance 充分承诺
sufficient condition 充分条件
sufficient consideration 充分对价(又称 due consideration;legally sufficient consideration)
sufficient evidence 充分证据;证据充足
sufficient madness (英)"足够的疯狂"(指野兽条例的标准)(见 wild beast test)
sufficient notice of the pending action 未决诉讼的充分通知
sufficient publicity 布告周知
sufficient reason 充足的理由
sufficient repair 修理完善(见 repair)
sufficient writing 充分的书面
suffocate v. 窒息;闷死
suffocation n. 窒息
suffragatte n. 鼓吹妇女参政的妇女
suffrage n. 1.选举权,投票权,参政权 2.投票,所投的赞成票;同意
suffragist n. 扩大参政的主张者(尤指妇女参政的)
suffragium 选举权
suffragium et honores 选举权和名誉权
sufism n. (伊斯兰教)泛神论,神秘主义
suggest v. 1.建议;提出,提议 2.暗示,间接表明
suggestio falsi 假声明(指不忠实的话或暗示),虚伪的提示或暗示
suggestion n. 建议,意见
suggestion for rationalization 合理化建议
suggestive a. 1.建议性的;启发性的 2.暗示的;示意的 3.猥亵的
suggestive interrogation 诱导性的讯问
suggestive mark 暗示性商标(指给予购买者一些有关商标所表述商品或服务暗示的商标。如"微软"等需要想象、思考和理解才能得出的该商品性质的结论)
suggestive matters 提示性的事实(指民事违法行为或犯罪行为之前或之后的相关有争议的事实)
sui causa 由于自己的原因
sui et necessarii heredes (正统)必然继承人
sui generis (of its own kind) (18世纪)自成一类的(of or class),特殊的、独特的(unique or peculiar)[这个词条常用于知识产权法,说明旨在保护权利的体制,如对于权利不符合传统专利、商标版权以及商业秘密等原则进行保护。比如:数据库如其内容不是原始的则不受版权法的保护,但可受到旨在保护这类权利的独特法规(*sui generis* statute)的保护]
Sui Generis **Law** 特别法,专门法(指不属于版权法又不归入版权法的有关法律。独立于版权法之外的计算机软件保护法均为"特别法")
sui generis **rights** 特别权,专门权(指不属于版权,又与版权有密切关系的一些专有权,如芯片法中的集成电路布图设计专有权等)
sui haeredes 第一顺序继承适当继承人
sui juris (iuris) 主权人[指有法律能力,可以和他人签订合同、买卖物业、提起诉讼或被诉讼的人;自主(权);具有完全行为能力的人;(罗马法)自权人(指称家父)]
suicidal a. 自杀的
suicidal behavior 自杀行为
suicidal death 自杀死
suicidal hanging 自缢
suicidal policy 自杀政策
suicidal strangulation 自勒
suicidal wound 自杀伤
suicide n./v. 1.自杀,自杀罪(从前在英国,规定自杀为犯罪,1961年自杀法例施行后,废止自杀罪,但有共谋"自杀"罪名,如帮助、教唆、诱导他人自杀,都是有罪的)2.自杀事件,自杀者/自杀
suicide act (英)自杀法例(见 suicide)
suicide bomber 自杀性爆炸
suicide clause 自杀条款(指人寿保险合同中声明,如投保人在保险期内自杀,则保险公司偿付保险金等于他所交保险费的总额)
suicide note 绝命书
suicide oneself to escape punishment 畏罪自杀
suicide pact 自杀协议
Suicide Pacts and Internet 自杀协议与互联网

suing and being sued 起诉和应诉
suit n./v. 诉讼;起诉;控告;讼案;请求;恳求;求婚(现一般 action 已代替 suit, suit 指衡平法上的诉讼, action 指普通法的诉讼)/使适应,配合
suit against state 通过向国家诉讼而求得法律救济的案件
suit at law 诉讼,诉讼案件,民事诉讼[指根据普通法或衡平法进行的诉讼,区别于按法定条文(regulatory provision)进行之诉讼。按联邦和大多数州法院新近的诉讼程序规则(rules of practice),"民事诉讼"(civil action)这个术语包括普通法上和衡平法上的两类诉讼。参见《联邦民事诉讼规则》第 2 页(Fed. R. Civ. P. 2.)。见 action at law]
suit between corporations 公司之间的诉讼
suit for contract 关于合同(契约)的诉讼
suit for contribution 平均分摊债务之诉(指一项债务本应数人共同平均负担,但因法律或某种关系,一个人先代表这几个人把债务还清,然后可根据衡平法来提起诉讼向其他人追还他们名下应分摊之款)
suit for damages 损害赔偿之诉
suit for the collection of money 请求给付金钱的诉讼
suit in equity 衡平法上的诉讼(指起因于衡平法上的请求权并寻求专项特有的衡平法上的救济,亦称 action in equity)
suit in *forma pauperis* 以贫苦人身份参加诉讼免付诉讼费的案件
suit in marriage 婚姻诉讼
suit money 1.(离婚案件中)诉讼期间(丈夫给妻子)负担的费用 2.法院判当事人支付的律师费用
suit of civil nature 民事诉讼
suit on clouds on title 可疑权利之诉
suit pending 案件正在审理中
suit to remove a cloud 澄清产权之诉
suitability n. 适当性,适宜性,适合性
suitability texts 适宜性测试(见 appropriateness texts)
suitable a. 合适的,适宜的,适当的,相对的(to, for)
suitable age and discretion 适当年龄和可酌处事务,适当年龄和负责任年纪适当能够负责(在美国只能由送达官员决定谁是年龄适当并能够负责的人)
suitable alternative accommodation 合适的选择供应
suitable marriage 合适的婚姻,很相配的婚姻
suite n. (一批)随从人员;套,组,(一套)房间(家具)
suited to 适于
suitor n. 起诉人,原告;求婚者,请求人
suitor's fee fund (英)衡平法院的起诉费基金(指起诉人向法院缴付的费用,用于支付法院各种官员的薪金)
suitress n. 女起诉人,女原告
suits against parents for the maintenance and support of children 要求父母抚养子女的案件
Sultan n. 苏丹(苏丹国国王的称谓,某些伊斯兰国家最高统治者的称号)
sultanate n. 1.苏丹国 2. 苏丹的职位(权力或统治)
sul-sequent-negligence doctrine 见 last clean chance doctrine
sum n./v. 金额,款项;总数,全部/总结,概括
sum insured 保险金额
sum of claim 索赔额
sum of indemnity 补偿金
sum of insurance 保险金额
sum up (诉讼中法官对证据辩论等)的总结,概述
sum up the evidence 概述证据
sum up the main points (在陪审团退席商讨裁决前向陪审团陈述证据的)概述要点,总结要点
Sumerian Laws Exercise Tablet 《苏美尔法律研习本》[指一位名为贝尔舒努(Belshunu)的中级学生学习、临摹的教本,也可能是别人口述由他写下的泥板残片。该泥板共有文字 5 行,仅存其中最后两行的法律内容。该"研习本"又释为《苏美尔亲属法》,是拉尔沙王国的另一部残片,是阿卡佐译文的苏美尔原文,也是"智慧之家"(也译为"法律家")所用的苏美

尔教本。该泥板教本包含了苏美尔、阿卡佐双体文字典、文法、法律格式以及法律内容各种样式的原文,反映了拉尔沙王国的法律实践]

* *Summa caritas est facere justitiam singulis , et omni tempore quando neccesse fuerit.* The greatest charity is to do justice to every one, and at any time whenever it may be necessary. 最大的慈善是对每个人都公正,这在任何时候都是需要的。

summa cum laude 以最优异的学习成绩
summa divisio rerum 对物的基本划分
summarize v. 概括,概述,总结
summarizing judge 简易法庭法官
summary n./a. 摘要,概要,概略,一览/概括的,扼要的,简易的;即时的,速决的,即决的
summary action 简易诉讼
summary arrest 当场逮捕;即时逮捕
summary bail 简易保释
Summary Compensation Table (美)(一年度内公司的)薪酬总表(见 Regulation S-K)
summary conviction 即决裁定,简易判罪(指不经过陪审团的判罪)
summary court 简易法院,即决法院
summary court-martial (美军)(只以一名法官组成的)审理轻罪的军事法庭
summary dismissal 即决驳回;即决撤职
summary hearing 简易程序的听审
summary judg(e)ment 即决审判(指未经陪审团听审而作的判决,如债权人提出足够证据即可据此判决),简易判决
summary judg(e)ment motion 即决(简易)判决动议
summary jurisdiction 简易审判权(指有权立刻判决或作出决定或命令的法院的审判权,特别是指刑事案件,裁判官有权直接判案,不必将案件送高等法院)
Summary Jurisdiction Act (英)《即决裁判法》(1879年)
summary jury trial (美)简易陪审团审判(适用于将面临长时间陪审团审判的案件的审判前程序后期,它要求短暂的审理,由律师以简易方式向陪审团提交证据,没有证人出庭,而由陪审团作出无拘束力的参考性判决作为以后和解的基础)
summary justice 即决裁判;简易程序裁判
Summary of Case Law 《判例法摘要》(巴西联邦最高法院的一种具有告诫性的判例摘要)
summary of leading cases and decisions 主导判例和判决汇集;简要判例汇编
summary offences (或 **offenses**) 即决犯罪(英国对刑事犯罪概括分为即决犯罪和可起诉犯罪,前者由一个或一个以上地方法官审理,后者由巡回刑事法庭的一个法官和陪审团审理);可迅速判决的犯罪(行为),可以简易程序审判的罪行
summary procedure 即决裁判程序,简易程序
summary procedure chamber 简易程序法庭
summary proceeding (或 **procedure**) 简易诉讼(即不经辩论只根据法律条文所作的审判);简易程序(与 ordinary proceeding 相对)
summary process 简易听审程序(法庭听审的简易形式,适用于因不付房租而收回财产之类的简单案件)
summary punishment 惩戒性惩罚;纪律处分
summary record 摘要记录
summary recovery 简易收回(指通过诉讼收回被侵占的权利或财产)
summary removing (苏格兰)简易驱逐租户之诉
summary statement 简要供述,简要声明
summary trial 即决审讯,简易审判
summation (=summing up) n. 证据总结,判决前法庭辩论的总结
summer time act 夏令时间法
summing up 证据总结(见 summation)
summing up evidence 证据结论(指法官把经过辩论的证据作出一个结论,也指当事人的辩护律师将所提出的证据作出总结)
summing-up n. 1.证据概述(指法官综述证据提请陪审员注意)2.总结,结论
summit a./n. 政府首脑的,最高级的/顶点,极点;最高官阶(尤指外交上所称的政府首脑),最高级会议

summit meetings（或 conference） （政府首脑就国际重大问题进行外交活动的）最高级会议,首脑会议
summon v. 召唤,传唤,传讯,传证人（出庭）作证
summon exhortation 催告（出庭等）
summon the defendant 传唤被告出庭
summon to appear in court 传唤出庭
summon to proceed 传唤继续诉讼
summoned in person 受送达人
summoned party 被传当事人
summoner n. 传唤者,送法院传票的人
summoning of creditors （破产）召集债权人
summoning of parliament 召开国会
summons n. 传唤,传票
summons ex-parte 一方当事人传票,给一方当事人传票
summum bonum 至善
summum jus 极权,峻法,苛法
* *Summum jus, summa injuria; summa lex, summa crux.* Extreme law (rigor of law) is the greatest injury; strict law is great punishment. 法越严对无辜者伤害也就越大。（通常指普通法过严,约束一人也就有害于他人,如无衡平法来调节,则不公道）
sumptuary a. 规定个人费用的；禁止奢侈浪费的,限制费用的
sumptuary laws 节约条例,禁止奢侈的法令
sunday closing laws （亦称 blue laws,指在若干管辖范围内）禁止星期天营业的法规
sunday legislation 星期日立法（指禁止在星期日从事各种工作、娱乐或其他活动的立法）
Sunday Morning Conference （英）星期日上午会议（指 1612 年 11 月 10 日星期日上午。应坎特伯雷大主教的奏请,詹姆士一世国王会见英格兰的法官们,会议主题为针对在司法上强调至上原则情况下,有人建国王按自己意愿收回案件审判权以征求法官意见。实质为王权与司法权较量与辩论的会议）
sundays and holidays excepted 星期日和假日除外
sundays and holidays included 星期日和

假日包括在内
sundry a. 杂的,各式各样的
sundry expenses 种种费用；杂费
sundry revenue 杂项税收
sunk commitment 滞留承诺,旁置承诺
sunk costs 沉没成本（指来自经济学的概念,即那些已经付出或已经投入但却无法收回的费用。在特定情况中,成本已经"沉没"的事实会明显影响各方做出的选择,以及他们所选择使用的策略）,滞留成本,旁置成本,已垫支成本
sunk fund 沉没资金
sunna（或 sunnah） 《圣训》（亦译《逊奈》,或《圣行》,指穆罕默德的言行传诉作为穆斯林社会的行为典范,也是伊斯兰教法的重要渊源）
sunni （伊斯兰教法）逊尼派（正统派）
sunset clause 落日条款［指限制"事故基础制"下的期后索赔,按"落日条款",如果环境侵权行为发生在保险期间,但由此引起责任索赔在期后的,保险人只对期后一定期间（如 30 年）内的索赔承担保险责任。］
Sunset Law （美）《夕阳法》（科罗拉多州的规定,除非有法律明文要求重新成立,否则所有新的政府机构均应关闭）
Sunshine Act Meetings （美）公开法案会议
Sunshine Law （美）《公开法》（指要求政府机关和部门召开众人参加会议的法律）
super dispatch 特别迅速处理；特急急件；特别发送
super majority 超额多数,特别多数
super microcomputer 超微型计算机
super *visum corporis* 尸体观察（指法庭的陪审团为对死因进行研究,观察被研究死因的尸体）
super-national 超国家的
super-strong state 超强国家
superable a. 可超越的,可胜过的
superannuate v. 因年老体弱使之退职,给养老金而辞退的官吏；退休
superanuation n. 年老（或体弱）退休,退职,退休金；淘汰,废弃
superanuation benefit 退休金
superbusiness n. 超级公司

supercargo(es) n. 押货人,(复)商船上货物管理人;经管船运货物的外国代理商;监运员

supercriminal n. (美)罪魁

supererogatory a. 职务以外的;分外的;多余的

supereragatory act 职务以外的行为

superette n. 小规模的超级市场,小型自选商店

superficial a. 表面的,表面性的;肤浅的,浅薄的;平方的

superficial aspect 表面现象

superficiary n./a. 有地上权的人,租地造屋者/1.表面的 2.有地上权的

superficies n. 1.表面外观,外貌 2.地上权,地上建筑物

superficies solo cedit 附着于土地者为土地的一部分

superfluity n. 多余物,过剩品;奢侈;多余,过剩

Superfund n. (美)超级基金,舒泊尔基金[①指为治理并清除危险废弃的处置场所而提供或设置的信托资金(由石油、化工以及某些公司的税款作为筹措的资金),创立此基金是支付由承担责任的当事方归还的治理清污费用;②这一名称源自1980年《综合环境治理、赔偿与责任法》(the Comprehensive Environmental Response, Compensation and Liability Act of 1980) (CERCLA)所创设的一个基金项目]

Superfund Law (美)《超级基金法》,《舒泊尔基金法》[指1980年国会通过的《综合环境治理、赔偿与责任法》(the Comprehensive Environmental Response, Compensation and Liability Act of 1980) (CERCLA),通常称为《超级基金法》。其目的是解决环境中的"化学毒物"问题,主要手段是运用超级基金治理全国范围内闲置不用或废弃物处理场所,并对危险物质泄漏做出紧急反应。美国国会之所以在1976年通过《资源保护与回收法》(the Resource Conservation and Recovery Act) (RCRA)之后又制定《超级基金法》,是因为《资源保护与回收法》中有关危险废弃物产生与处理的规定并未解决在其之前排放或处置的危险废弃物的责任问题,而这些闲置的危险废弃物处理场所被视为威胁公众健康的重大隐患]

supergovernment n. 国际政治;超政府政治(指政府外之组织控制政权的政治)

superhuman dogmas 超人的信条

superimposed tax 特别附加税

superimposition n. 附加物,加上,添附

superinduce v. 另加,外加;另娶(以取代原配偶);另立……为继承人

superintendence n. 监督;管理,指挥

superintendency n. 主管人(监督者或指挥者)的职位(管区等)

superintendency of banks 银行监理

superintendency of companies 公司监理

superintendent n./a. 监督者,指挥者;管理者;警(察)长;/监督的,管理的

superintendent of customs 海关监督人

superintendent of documents 档案室主任

superintendent of state police 州警察总监

superintendent registrar 注册监督(官员)

superior n./a. 长者,上级,长官/优越者/超越的,优质的;较高的;上司的,上级的,长官的

superior council of institutions 高级机构委员会

superior council of the public service 公务员高级协议委员会(指法国1945年10月设立的,解决有关公务员的待遇及工作条件等纠纷的仲裁机构)

superior court(s) 上级法院;(美国一些州内有概括管辖权的)高级法院

superior force 不可抗力量,不可抗力

superior instance 高一级审判(级)

superior officer 上司,上级官员

superior order(s) 上级命令

superior people's court (中)高级人民法院

superior people's procuratorates (中)高级人民检察院

superior title 更高的权利根据,更高的头衔

superiority n. 优越性;优势,卓越;优良

superliberalism n. 超自由主义

supermarket n. 超级市场,自选市场

supernational corporation 超国家的公司

supernational government 超国家的政府
supernational law 超国家的法律
supernumerary a. 额外的,多余的;候补的
supernumerary judge 候补法官
supernumerary magistrate 候补司法行政官
superpower n. 超级大国
superprofit n. 超额利润
superscription n. 1.信封上的姓名、地址 2.铭文;题字
supersecret a. 绝密的
supersede v. 1.替代,替换;充任,接替,取而代之 2.优先次序于……,比……优先
supersede an official 解除一官员职务
supersedeas （在提起上诉时暂不执行裁决的）中止执行令;中止诉讼令状
supersedeas **bond** 暂停执行保证书,判决中止执行保证书(指上诉人要求目的在于中止初审判决时应提供的保证书,可以由正在对判决提起上诉的被告人提供)
superseding cause 替代原因
supersession n. 代替,取代;废弃;废撤;罢黜
superstate n. 超级大国,超国家
superstition n. 迷信;迷信行为
superstitious a. 迷信的,由迷信引起的
superstitious objects 迷信品
superstitious uses and trusts 迷信的受益和信托(指用法律所不允许的宗教仪式来交接动产或不动产是无效的)
superstructure n. 上层建筑
supertax n. 附加税;附加所得税
supertoxic agent 剧毒剂
supervene v. 1.附带发生,并发,附加 2.起于……之后;续……之后
supervening cause 后发原因（见 intervening cause）
supervening impossibility of performance 嗣后的履行不(可)能性
supervening negligence 后发介入的过失（见 last clear chance doctrine）
supervening-negligence doctrine 后发过失原则（见 last clean chance doctrine）
supervise v. 监督,管理,指导
supervised access 受监督情况下接触（数据）
superviser (=supervisor) n. 监督者;管理者;监察人
superviser of guardianship 监护监督人
supervision n. 监督,监察;管理
supervision of election 选举监督(人)
supervision of judicial service 对司法机关的监督
supervision of prison 对监狱的监督
supervision of residence 监视住所（一种刑事强制措施）
supervision of the estimate 监督（财政）预算
supervision order （英）监督令（指受缓刑监视官监督的令状）
supervision over juristic person 对法人的监督
supervision over the exact legality of the acts of application of law 对适用法律的合法性进行监督
supervision prescribed by law 法定监督
supervision system 监察制度
supervisory a. 监督的,管理的
supervisory authority 监督权,监察权;监督当局,监察当局
supervisory board 监事会
supervisory body 监督机构
supervisory council (或 **committee**) 监察委员会;(公司的)监事会
supervisory jurisdiction 司法监督权
supervisory organ 监察机关
supervisory personnel 监督人员,监察人员
supine a. 消极的,懒的
supplant v. 替代,取代,把……排挤掉
supplement n./v. 增补物,补遗;补编;附件/增补,补充
supplement reserve facility 补充储备贷款
supplement to the votes (英)(议会)表决意见补充
supplemental (=supplementary) a. 补充的,增补的,追加的
supplemental agreement 补充协议
supplemental answer 补充答辩
supplemental bill 补充诉状(指以前衡平法的诉状有不足之处,用补充诉状补充前诉状之不足)
supplemental calls 追加股款;追加保费

supplemental claim 附加要求
supplemental complaint （美）补充起诉状[根据《联邦民事诉讼规则》第15(d)条,指原告并非修改原起诉状中的错误,亦非增加一些事实,而是在诉讼后发生的就可能其权利主张的一些事项提请法院和对方当事人注意的诉状。一般来说,这必须经法院允准后原告可提出申请此种诉状。见 amended complaint]
supplemental deed 补充契据
supplemental jurisdiction （美）补充管辖
supplemental jurisdiction statute （美国1990年颁布的）补充管辖权法规(28 USCA 1367)
supplemental personal jurisdiction 补充的对人管辖
supplemental pleading （1841年）补充答辩[指既是改正以前答辩状的缺点又是纠正以前提出诉状中产生的事实。不同于修改过的诉状（ amended pleading）,补充答辩是补充说明初次诉讼提交后才发生对诉讼争点的新的事项而提出的诉答。而修订的事项只是在寻求修订提交诉状时曾经单纯答辩过的事项。但在诉状中存在被忽略的错误或疏漏以及虚假陈述之处,这两者是不同的。见 amended pleading]
supplemental provision 附则
supplemental subject-matter jurisdiction （美）补充事物管辖权（这一概念扩展至包括《民事诉讼规则》第14条项下的大多数请求）
supplemental wage 辅助工资,附加工资
supplementary n./a. 附则;补充物/补充的;附属的;追加的
supplementary appropriation 追加拨款
supplementary benefits （英）（发给16岁或16岁以上有收入的人的）追加补贴
supplementary civil action in criminal proceedings 刑事诉讼附带民事诉讼
supplementary civil compensation 附带民事赔偿
supplementary contract 补充合同（契约）
supplementary election 补选
supplementary estimates 追加概算
supplementary income tax 追加所得税
supplementary item 补充项目
supplementary judg(e)ment 补充判决
supplementary ordinances 补充法令
supplementary proceedings 补充程序、辅助程序（指①未决诉讼可以独立审理的程序,据此终局裁决可立即上诉;②涉及制定法规定的民事上的救济或规则而非依据一般程序规则可获得的救济或规则。实质是制定法和诉讼规则中规定的一种判决后的救济措施。通过它可了解债务人的财产所在地及相关情况,以便将这些财产可用于清偿判决所确定的债务。因此,它是一种协助执行判决之程序。判决令签发后,债权人可借此程序来实现债权)
supplementary provisions 补充规定,附则
supplementary punishment 附加刑
supplementary question （议会中的）补充质询
supplementary registration 补充登记
supplementary regulations 补充规章,补充规定,补充条例,补充办法
supplementary rules 补充性规则
supplementary source of law 法的补充（辅助）渊源（亦译作补充的法律渊源）
supplementary statement 补充陈述
supplementary tax 附加税
supplementary terms 补充条款,补充条件
supplementary verification 补充鉴定
supplicant n. 恳求者,哀求者
supplicate v. 恳求,哀求,祈求
supplicate the judge to spare 恳（请）求法官赦免
supplicatio 1. 要求撤销判决的申请;赦免初犯的申请 2. (= duplicatio)（大陆法上的）被告对原告的第二次答辩
supplication n. 恳求,祈求;祈祷
supplicavit n. （英）法院通知令（指法院通知治安法官,要求取得某人不再扰乱治安的保证）
supplier n. 供应方,供应者,补充者
supplier's export credit 卖方出口信贷
supplimentary budget 追加预算
supply v./n. 供给,供应,提供;代理,暂代;弥补,补充/1. 供给（量）,供应（量）,补给

2.(复)存货,供应品,生活用品,(储备)物资,生活费用,议会对政府的拨款
supply and credit 供应方和信贷方
supply and demand 供需
supply and valuation contract 供应与估价合同(契约)(即寄售合同)
supply demand functions 供需函数
supply of product 产品供应
supply services or things (美)提供服务或货物(指长臂法所规定的对合同之诉所管辖范畴取决于立法的特定语言和法院解释。见 in whole or in part)
support n./v. 1.抚养;扶养;赡养;支持;援助;扶助;资助 2.抚(扶)养者;援助者 3.证明,实证;证实/1.供养,抚养,扶养,赡养,赡(抚)养费 2.支持;援助;扶助,资助 3.为……提供证据,证实 4.经受,忍受
support a charge 支持(一项)控告
support a conviction 承认刑罚,承受罪罚
support claim 抚养请求权
support money 补助金
support obligation 抚养义务
support of children 抚养子女
support of official safety net 官方安全网支持
support of parents 赡养父母
support payments 赡养费,抚育费
supporter n. 支持者;资助者;赡养者,抚养者
supporting document 证件,单据
supporting material 支持材料(指计算机软件领域中程序之外的如文档、说明书等辅助材料)
supporting right (美)支撑权(美国法上有较为完善的不动产支撑权制度。支撑权是指相邻所有人维护其土地自然状态的一种权利,是指获得侧面支撑或地下土壤对土地提供支撑的权利)
supporting witness 支持证人
supposed a. 推测的,想象的,被信以为真的,误传误信的,被期望的
supposed mechanical laws 想象的机械法则
supposed to 被期望,应该,(口)获准
supposition n. 假定;推定,推测;臆测
supposititious (或 suppositious) a. 1.伪的,伪造的;冒充的,顶替的 2.想象的,推定的

supposititious child (非法充作财产继承人的)抱来的孩子,顶替的孩子
supposititious name 假名字;冒充的名字
supposititious will 冒充的遗嘱
suppress v. 1.镇压,平定 2.禁止出版,扣留 3.隐瞒,隐匿 4.禁止,以命令废止
suppress (the) evidence 隐匿证据
suppress smuggling 缉私,通缉走私
suppress the news 扣发消息
suppress the rebellion 镇压叛乱
suppress the truth 隐瞒真相
suppressio veri 隐瞒真相,隐瞒事实
* *Suppressio veri, expressio falsi.* Suppression of the truth is the expression of what is false. 隐瞒真相就是虚伪的表示。
suppression n. 隐瞒,隐匿;镇压,压制;禁止,制止
suppression hearing 查禁审;(美)排除证据的诉审(刑事诉讼中的一种审前程序,被告人于此阶段可以请求对其认为是以非法手段取得的证据禁止在以后庭审中提出,法庭就此作出裁决在以后庭审中有效)
suppression of document 毁改文件[一种欺诈(deception)罪行,包括将有价值的文件和契约、遗嘱等进行销毁、涂改、隐匿等]
suppression of evidence 隐匿证据
suppression of free expression 禁止自由意思表达
suppression of intermediate bodies 取缔中间组织
suppression of violence 残酷镇压
suppressor (=suppresser) n. 镇压者;扣留者;隐瞒者;禁止者
supra 在上,在前,上述
supra compensary 超过补偿的
supra protest 参与承兑(指付款人拒绝付款后第三者为维护发票人的信誉而代为承兑)
supra-class a. 超阶级的
supra-national agreement 跨国协议
supra-national authority 超国家的权力,(复)超国家的权力机关
supra-national institution 超国家机构

supra-national law 超国家法
supra-national legislation 跨国立法
supra-national organization 超国家组织
supra-national supranational a. 超国家的;跨国的
supraeconomic administrative measures 超经济的行政手段
supraexploit v. 超剥削,极度剥削
supranational judiciary 超国家司法机关(如欧盟法院等)
supranational law 超国家法
suprem court of appeal 最高上诉法院
* *Suprema potestas seipsam dissolvere potest.* Supreme power can dissolve itself. 最高权力机关可以自行解散。
supremacist n. 至上主义者
supremacy n. 1.至高权力;无上权力;霸权 2.至高,无上
supremacy clause 至高权力条款(美国联邦宪法规定,美国联邦宪法、法规、条约优于与之发生抵触的州宪法、法规)
Supremacy Clause of the Federal Constitution, Article VI 美国联邦宪法的至上条款,第6条
Supremacy of (the) Law 法律至高无上,法律的至高权威(指一个政府的最高权威是法律,而不是人);最高法律
Supremacy of Parliament 国会至上
supreme a. 最高的,最重要的
supreme administrative court 最高行政法院
supreme authority 最高权力,(复)最高权力机关
supreme clause (美)最高法条款(指美国联邦宪法前言中关于美国宪法是国家最高法的规定)
supreme command 最高指令
supreme commander of the armed forces 武装部队最高统帅
Supreme Constitutional Court 最高宪法法院
supreme council 最高委员会
Supreme Court (美国联邦、州)最高法院,最高法院
Supreme Court bar (美)最高法院法庭
supreme court costs rules 最高法院诉讼费规则

Supreme Court (of) Judicature (英)最高法院(又译最高司法法院,由衡平法法院、王座法院、民事诉讼高等法院、财务大臣上诉法院等合并而成)
supreme court justices (美)最高法院大法官
supreme court of appeal 最高上诉法院
supreme court of errors (美)(康涅狄格州以前的)终审法院(现名 supreme court)
(the) Supreme Court of Judicature Act 《最高法院制度法案》(指1873年和1875年英议会通过的法案及修正案原提案名称)
Supreme Court of Justice (英)最高司法法院,最高法院
Supreme Court of Law and Equity 普通法和衡平法最高法院(事实上在英美并不存在这样一个法院)
Supreme Court of the United States 美国最高法院
Supreme Court on Appeal (美)最高法院上诉庭
Supreme Court Reporter 《最高法院判例汇编》[美国两大非官方出版的判例汇编之一。以《美国判例汇编》的106卷为开始,并归入西方出版公司的钥匙号判决摘要汇编系统(Key Number Digest System),该系统用广泛的法律标题和详细的副标题的独特分类表作出索引,其统一援引缩写为 U. S.,即 United States Supreme Court Reports]
supreme court rules 最高法院规程
supreme executive power 最高行政权
supreme executive organ 最高行政机关
Supreme Federal Court of Justice (美)联邦最高法院
supreme judicial court (美国缅因州和马萨诸塞州)最高上诉法院
supreme law 最高法律
supreme law of the land (美)国家最高法(指美国联邦宪法)
supreme legal authority 最高法律权威
supreme legislation 最高立法(与 delegated legislation 相对而言)
supreme legislative power 最高立法权

supreme organ of state power 最高国家权力机关
(the) Supreme People's Court （中）最高人民法院
(the) Supreme People's Procuratorate （中）最高人民检察院
supreme political authority 最高政治机构,最高政治当局
supreme power of state 国家最高权力
Supreme Public Prosecutor's Office 最高检察院,(日)最高检察厅
Supreme Soviet 最高苏维埃(苏联的最高立法机构)
supreme state conference 最高国务会议
supreme supervisory power 最高监督权
sur (=on the basis of) prep. 根据
sur disclaimer 对否认承租的佃户要求收回土地的(权利)令状
sur disseisin 根据强占(土地)(见 writ of entry)
surcharge n./v. 1.超载 2.附加费;附加税;索高价;附加罚款 3.附加责任(指核算师对于政府官员动用公款用于非法定用途时,有权要求动用款项的官员,由个人承担归还用于非法定用途的款项的责任)/1.使超载,使负担过重;处以罚款,额外索款 2.表示账目漏记,指出(对方在账上)漏记贷方款项
surcharge and falsify the accounting party 提供对方当事人的不精确的结账单的证据
surcharge for overdue tax payment 滞纳金
sure a. 确信的,有把握的;可靠的,确实的;稳固的;必定的;(美)一定成功的
sure evidence 确凿证据
surete generale （法国的）秘密警察
surety n. 1.保证人;担保人 2.保证;担保 3.可靠性,确实性
surety company 担保公司
surety-bond n. 保证金;担保,担保保证金;保证债券;担保书
suretyship n. 1.保证,担保合同(契约) 2.保证人的地位或责任
suretyship contract 保证合同(契约)
suretyship obligation 保证债务

surface n./a./v. 表面,外观/表面的,外观的/呈现,出现,使出现,进行表面处理
surface movement 水陆运输
surface right 地上权
Surface Traffic Law 《陆上交通法》
surface transport 地表运输,水陆运输
Surface Transportation Board （美）地面运输理事会[指美国运输部(Department of Transportation)下属的一个单位,负责州际地面运输,主要是铁路系统运输的经济调整。它管辖范畴包括铁路系统运价、服务争端、铁路系统的公司合并以及相关劳务纠纷。某些货车和海洋运输的运价;某些城市间巴士公司体制以及由联邦能源管理委员会(Federal Energy Regulatory Commission)来规制的某些管道事宜]
surface water 地表水;地面水,淤水
surge of withdrawals 提款浪潮,提款风潮
surmise v. 臆想,猜度,推测,揣度
surname n. 姓,别名,别号
surplus n./a. 盈余,过剩;盈余额/过剩的,剩余的,多余的
surplus account 盈余账户
surplus allowable catch 剩余可捕量
surplus at liquidation 清算盈余
surplus capacity 过剩生产力
surplus from consolidation 企业合并盈益
surplus labo(u)r 剩余劳动力
surplus of assets 剩余财产
surplus personnel 编余人员
surplus product 过剩产品,长线产品
surplus receipts 剩余收入
surplus value 剩余价值
surplusage n. 1.过剩;盈余;多余 2.(法律文件如诉状等)多说出的事情;(辩护时所作的)多余的辩解
surprise n./v. 惊骇,惊奇;意外事件/使惊愕,使感到意外,突然袭击,突然发作;出其不意地使某人做某事
surprise a witness into telling the truth 使证人于不知不觉中说出实话
surprise witness 突如其来的证人(指美国民事、刑事案件审判辩论中,原告提出反驳证据时,用原来没有提供出的证据,包括新的证人,对被告证人进行反驳,这个

新的证人即所谓突如其来的证人)
surrealism n. 超现实主义
surrebut v. (原告)对被告的第三次答辩作辩驳
surrebuter n. (旧普通法上的)原告的第三次辩驳
surrebuttal n. 原告第三次辩驳中的举证
surrebutter n. (原告)对被告的第三次答辩作辩驳
surrejoin n. 原告的第二次辩驳
surrejoinder n. 原告的第二次辩驳
surrender n. (15世纪)1.让与,交出(指让与或交出给另一个的权力或控制的行为2.放弃权利或权利请求(claim)(见release 1)3.返还,归复[指将地产返还给具有归复土地权(reversion)或剩余地产权(remainder)的人。见merger 4]
surrender at discretion 无条件投降
surrender by bail 保释人将罪犯交回
surrender clause 投降条款,放弃条款
surrender of fugitive 引渡逃犯
surrender of leases 放弃租赁
surrender of mortgage 放弃抵押
surrender of one's claims 放弃自己的权利要求
surrender of the thing 返还原物
surrender one's insurance policy (取得保险金后)将保险单退回(保险公司),交回保险单给保险公司
surrender one's privileges 放弃特权
surrender oneself to justice 投案,向司法机关自首
surrender to custody (犯人)自动归押
surrender to one's bail (犯人)交保期满后自动出庭,保释后如期出庭
surrender to the police 向警察局自首
surrender value (被保险人中途解约而以回)剩余保险费额,退保金额
surrenderee n. 受让人,受让者
surrenderor n. 让与人;投降者;自首者
surreptitious a. 鬼鬼祟祟的,秘密的,欺骗的;偷偷的
surrogacy n. 代位(指①履行代位功能的行为;②给别人代领孩子的过程),监护代理

surrogacy contract 见 surrogate-parenting agreement
surrogate n./v. 1.代理者(尤指主教的代理者)2.(美国某些州的认证遗嘱及管理遗产等事的)地方法官(或司法官员)/代替;代位;使继任;使代理
surrogate court (或 orphans' court)(美)(宾夕法尼亚州)遗嘱检验法院(或叫孤儿法院);(纽约主管检验等事的)地方法官(推事)法院
surrogate guardian 监督监护人
surrogate mother 代母(代指不育女子生育的女子),代孕母亲(该妇女接受另一妇女丈夫的精子进行人工授精、怀孕、生产,并在产后将亲权移转给该孩子的父亲及其妻子)
surrogate-parenting agreement 代孕生子合同(指一位妇女和典型不生育夫妇之间的合同,按该合同,该妇女接受对方丈夫的精子进行人工授孕并在生产后将其亲权转移给孩子的生父及其妻子。合同目的是使孩子与其生母永远分离,而由孩子生父及其妻子成为孩子永远的父母。见surrogacy contract; surrogate mother; intended child)
surround v./n. 围绕,包围/围绕物;地毯
surrounding facts 周围事实,关联事实
surtax n. (1881年)附件税[指在基本税收(primary tax)本身的基础上再按一定的税率附加征收的税]
surveillance n. 1.监视,看守 2.监督,管理
surveillant n. 监督者,监视者,看管人,密探
survey v./n. 1.考察;视察;调查 2.通盘考虑;逐点说明/1.概观,概括研究,通论,调查 2.测量,查勘 3.(复)测量记录,测量图,被测量的地区
survey data 调查资料
survey evidence 调查证据
survey land 测量土地
survey marker 测量标志(物);测量标志者
survey of personal income (SPI) (英)个人收入调查
surveyor n. 1.土地测量员;海关检货员;鉴定人 2.公证行;总监,主管
surveyor general (某部门、某地区或某项

任务的)总检查员,总监;(美)某地区公地的测量主任
surveyor of highway 公路总监
surveyor of the port 港口验关员
surveyor's certificate 公证人证明书
surveyor's report 鉴定书;检验报告(书)
surveyorship n. 测量员或检验员的职位
surviable a. 可生存的,可免死亡的
surviable accident 免于一死的意外事件
survival n. 1.幸存,残存,遗留;生存 2.幸存者;残存物;遗留物
survival of action 诉讼中的幸存者(另一方为死亡者)
survival statute (=survival cause of action) (美)幸存者法规(指允许受害的死者亲属提起诉讼的国家法规),遗存诉因法(指原告或被告死亡后仍存在的诉因)
survive v. 比……活得长,幸免于,从……中逃生,活下来,幸存
surviving a. 继续存在的,未死的;依然健在的
surviving parent 健在的父母,未亡父母,幸存父母
surviving partner 幸存合伙人
surviving spouse 未亡配偶,幸存配偶,健在配偶
surviving widow 遗孀
survivor n. 生还者,生存者,幸存者;残存物
survivorship n. 1.生存者取得(权)(指在共有财产中生存者对死者名下享有权利的取得权)(见 joint tenancy);(美)共有财产的享有权[简称"享有权",此权并非来自死者,而是来自产生共同共有权(joint tenancy) 的转让行为。见 concurrent estate]2.生还,生存,幸存
survivorship annuity 生存者的年金享受权[指提供给生存者的专门持续支付的生活费用,如原年金享受权人(的妻子或丈夫)已经去世,(妻或夫)仍可享有。亦称 continuing annuity]
susceptible a. 1.易感的,易受影响的 2.能容许……的,可受……影响的(of)
(be) susceptible of proof 能证明的
suspect n./v. 1.嫌疑,怀疑,猜疑 2.(泛指和某些罪行有关的)嫌疑犯,嫌疑分子,被怀疑的人/嫌疑,怀疑,猜疑

suspect a. 令人怀疑的,不可信的
suspect a person of a crime 猜疑某人犯罪,认为某人有犯罪嫌疑
suspectable a. 可疑的
suspected a. 嫌疑的,涉嫌的
suspected criminal 嫌疑犯
suspected grafter 贪污嫌疑犯
suspected murder 杀人嫌疑犯
suspected of being guilty 有犯罪嫌疑,涉嫌有罪
suspected offence 可疑罪行
suspected offender 嫌疑犯
suspected person 可疑人物(指某些法律所规定的"形迹可疑"人物)
suspected smuggling 走私嫌疑
suspected thief 盗窃嫌疑犯
suspend v. 中止,推迟;悬而不决;暂时停办;无力支付,宣布破产
suspend a motor licence 吊销汽车执照
suspend an action 中止诉讼
suspend diplomatic relations 中止外交关系
suspend judg(e)ment (sentence) 缓期宣判(处刑)
suspend payment 宣告无力偿还欠债;破产
suspend proceedings 暂停起诉;中止诉讼
suspend production 停产
suspend talks 中止谈判,中止会谈
suspendatur per collum (S. P. C.) 绞首,缢首(即绞杀,从前法官在判处死刑的囚犯姓名后面写上这个词,作为给执行官行刑的命令),处以绞刑
suspended a. 缓期的
suspended animation 人事不省;假死
suspended sentence 缓刑(判决),缓期处刑
suspending power (英史)中止法规(效力)权(一项王室的权力)
suspense n. 1.中止,停止 2.悬而不决;未决,不定 3.权利中止,权利停止
suspense account 暂记账目,中止(的)账目
suspensible a. 可中止的;可缓期的,可延缓的
suspension n. 中止宣判,中止处刑;无力偿债;停止支付
suspension for the completed prescription

时效完成的中止
suspension from duty 停止任用,停职
suspension in the action （法庭的）中止诉讼权
suspension of a treaty 中止条约
suspension of arms 停战
suspension of business 停止营业
suspension of civil right 停止（享受）公民权利
suspension of detention 中止羁押
suspension of execution 停止执行
suspension of licence 吊销执照(亦译:停牌)
suspension of litigation 诉讼的中止
suspension of payment 停止支付
suspension of proceedings 诉讼程序的中止
suspension of sentence 中止处刑
suspension of the constitution 停止行宪
suspension of the extinctive prescription 消灭时效的中止
suspension of the prescriptive period 时效期中断
suspension of treaty 中止条约
suspensive a. 未决定的,未确定的;停止的;悬搁的
suspensive condition 停止条件(亦称先决条件)
suspensive veto 致使停顿的否决
suspensory a. 中止的;悬搁的
suspicion n. 怀疑;疑心;嫌疑
suspicion case 疑案
(on) suspicion of theft （因）偷窃嫌疑
suspicious a. 怀疑的,令人怀疑的;可疑的
suspicious action(s) 可疑的行为
suspicious character 可疑的人物
suspicious movement 可疑的行迹
sustain v./n. 支撑,支援,承受住;供养,赡养;维持,继续;证明,证实;认可,准许,准于支持;蒙受损失,遭受/维持,统一,准许(指法官作出律师异议有效的裁决,而且该裁决受异议证词的影响);供养,赡养
sustain a family 扶养家属
sustain a great loss 蒙受重大损失
sustain an injury 遭受伤害,负伤
sustain an objection 支持异议
sustainable development 可持续发展,永续发展（当前世界环境保护原则的一个理念）
sustainable forestry 持续林业
sustainable resource development 永续资源的发展
sustainer n. 证实者;认可者;扶养者
sustenance n. 1.营养物 2.维持,支持;生计,食物
suttee n. （印度）寡妇在亡夫火葬堆上自焚,殉夫自焚的寡妇(旧时习俗)
Suum cuique tribuere. To render to everyone his own. 各人应得的归于各人。物归原主。
suus judex 合格的法官
suzerain state 宗主国
suzerainty n. 1.宗主权,宗主地位 2.保护（权）
Svengali-like 斯文加利式(指 Svengali 是英国小说中的人物,善于运用催眠术,使人唯命是从。后来人们用斯文加利式的人物来形容某些心怀叵测,用操纵他人的方式达到自己欲望和目的者)
swag n./v. 赃物,珍贵物,钱财,大量/交换;交流;用……做交易
swamp v./n. 击溃,淹没,沉陷;压倒,清除/沼泽,沼泽地
swap agreement 互换协议,交换契约
swap arrangement 互惠信贷协议
swap credits 互惠信贷
swap market 互换市场
swap meet 旧货物物交换会,交流会
swap transaction 互惠信贷交易
swapper n. 1.互换者;交易者 2.谎言
sway n. 支配,统治,势力,权势,影响,摇动
swear n./v. 誓言,诅咒/宣誓,立誓,发誓
swear a crime against sb. 发誓控诉某人犯罪
swear a person to secrecy 使某人誓守秘密
swear a witness 使证人宣誓
swear an oath 立誓,宣誓
swear for 担保,保证
swear in 使宣誓就职
swear off 立誓弃绝
swear out 由宣誓而得到;通过宣誓控告使法院发出（对被告人的拘捕证）

swear the jury 使陪审团宣誓就职
swearer n. 发誓者,宣誓者;证实者
swearing n. 发誓,宣誓(自己不说假话)
sweat-of-the brow doctrine （版权法)前额出汗原则[指现已抛弃的(now discarded)版权可以保护对于作品付出的辛劳和费用(labor and expense)的原则,而非独创性(originality)。美国联邦最高法院在拳头酒吧公司诉乡村电话服务公司案(Feist Pubs. Inc. v. Rural Tel. Servs. Co.)中否决了"前额出汗原则"。参见《美国联邦最高法院判例汇编》第 499 卷第 340 页。见 sweatwork]
sweat-shop （俚语)血汗工厂(指雇工工作时间长、工资低、工作条件极差的工厂或营业部门。用律师的话来说,一个要求联合的律师事务所,即使这个所作为回报可以支付较高工薪,工作如此辛苦以致无法养活家庭或参与社会交际)
sweatwork （俚语)汇编[指可检索的计算机数据库(database),但它不能为美国版权保护提供合格理由,这本事实是不可享受版权保护的,而且汇编也不是一项重要安排(nontrivial arrangement)。知识产权法规的新形式目的在于保护"前额出汗"(sweat of the brow)投资进入编排数据库。见 sweat-of-the brow doctrine]
sweep v. 扫除,打扫,扫荡,消灭,环视,猛力移动
sweeping a. 范围大的,连续的,彻底的,总括的
sweeping generalizations 总的归纳
sweeping operation 彻底全面的运作,彻底的办法
sweeping overhaul 彻底清查
sweeping powers 范围扩大的权利,大权
sweeping reform 彻底的改革
sweeping statement 彻底的陈述,彻底的声明,全面宣称
sweetheart deal 甜心交易;私下签订的交易(例如:雇主与工会代表私下达成协议,允许雇主支付较低工资,而工会代表因此获得额外的酬劳)
swell n. 1.增大,增加的部分 2.名人,名流
swell mob （俚)衣着时髦的扒手,骗子

swelldom n. 上流社会;一群时髦人物
swift a. 快的,迅速的,反应快的;突然发生的
Swift doctrine （美)斯威夫特原则(指 Swift v. Tyson 一案的判决结果,即限于州宪法、州制定法和法院对宪法和立法的解释被视为《司法法》第 34 条所规定可以用作联邦法院判决依据的法律)
swift punitive justice 立即进行惩罚性司法制裁
swift witness 偏心于召请自己一方的证人,回答问题时有偏袒的证人
swindle n./v. 行骗,诈骗,欺骗,欺诈;骗术/骗子,诈骗者
swindling n. 欺骗,诈骗
swing v./n. 摆动,摇摆;动摇,改变态度,获取,完成,处理;吊,挂;经营,操纵/经济趋势,行情涨落;(竞选等的)巡回旅行
swing credits 摆动信贷,互许贸易差额;额度高低变化的贷款
swing district （美)摇摆选区
swing of the pendulum 政党间执政的交替,盛衰,消长
swing round the circle 1.论及一个问题的不同方面 2.(候选人)巡回选区 3.连续地抱不同看法和态度 4.(美)政治性的旅行
swing the lead （英俚)以欺骗或伴称病而逃避责任
swing vote 操纵选票表决
swinger n. 乱搞男女关系的人,时髦人物;惊人的事物
switch v. 鞭打;转变;转换
switch operation 转手交易
swiz(z) n. （英)欺骗,诈取
sworn a. 宣过誓的;宣誓证明的;绝不改变的
sworn brothers （或 **friends**） 结义弟兄,盟兄弟
sworn enemies 不共戴天的仇人
sworn evidence 宣誓之证言(指相当于具结后之证言,但如发现有虚伪的陈述,则构成伪证罪)
sworn inquest （英)宣誓调查制度[指陪审团的起源有两种说法:①陪审团起源于盎格鲁-撒克逊社会。认为是亨利二世

1166年《克拉伦敦法》所确立的控诉陪审团的起源,但997年到1166年间无连续使用该制度的相关证据,因而人们产生最大质疑。②认为陪审团起源于加洛林王朝的宣誓调查制度(sworn inquest),这一说法的主要代表为海因里希·布伦纳(Heinrich Brunner)和 C. H. 哈斯金斯(C. H. Haskings)。布伦纳将陪审制的起源追溯到了加洛林王朝,而哈斯金斯的考证则在加洛林和后来的英格兰之间建立了联系,使陪审制起源于欧洲大陆的说法在证据上得以连贯。梅特兰接受了该理论,它逐渐成为陪审制起源的正统理论。陪审制经历了宣誓调查(sworn inquest)再到咨审(assize)(现称大陪审团、咨审团、巡回裁断等)再到陪审(jury)三个阶段]

sworn jury 宣誓陪审团
sworn witness 宣誓证人
SWOT analysis 优点、弱点、机会、威胁分析
syb and som (撒克逊人的祝贺语)和平和安宁
sycophant n./a. 谄媚者,拍马者;追随者/谄媚的,拍马的
syllabus n. 摘要,提纲;(判决书的)判决理由概述
syllabus by the court 法院判决理由的概要
Symbiotic Relationship Test (1973年)共生关系准则[指当政府与个人之间的行为关系如此紧密以致可公平地说是行为纠缠在一起(acting jointly)而构成一种标准(standard),个人按此标准则被认为是国家行为者(state actor)。这可能承担违反某人的宪法权的责任。个人进行的个人行为通常并不构成违反某人宪法权利(constitution rights)的责任,但若从事国家行为时,如果个人违法某人的宪法权利,那么个人和政府可能承担责任。国家行为已由个人行为和国家具有一种相依共生(symbiotic)关系得以表示。比如在公共停车库的一个餐厅采取拒绝服务于非籍美国人来坚持从事区别对待的国家行为(discriminatory state action)。伯顿诉威尔明顿停车管理局案(Burton v. Wilmington Parking Authority),参见《美国最高法院判例汇编》第365卷第715页、第81卷第

856页(1961年);《牛津美国联邦最高法院指南》(The Oxford Companion to the Supreme Court of the United States,北京大学出版社2009年版)第116页。在那里美国联邦最高法院判决共生关系(symbiotic relationship),因为该餐厅依赖于此车库而得以存在,并对市政泊车管理局能保持车库做了贡献,但这个共生关系准则(Symbiotic Relationship Test)的解释十分严格。比如:一个单位接受来自政府的经济支持的事实或受到政府严格规制的事实可能不足以表明一种共生关系。这样,虽然国家已经授予(granted)公用事业部分专卖权,但美国联邦最高法院则拒绝判决它们之间的共生关系。杰克逊诉都会爱迪生公司案(Jackson v. Metropolitan Edison Co.),参见《美国联邦最高法院判例汇编》第419卷第345页、第98卷第449页(1974年)。见 joint participation; state compulsion test; nexus test]

symboleography n. 法律文件起草法;合同(契约)书写法
symbolic a. 用作象征的,用作符号的;象征的
symbolic(al) annexation 象征性的兼并
symbolic delivery 象征的交付(指移交小的东西来象征移交让与物的仪式)
symbolic mark 象征性标章
symbolic speech 象征性的说话,象征性的语言
symbolic thinking 象征性思维(思维表达障碍的一种。此种属于概念转换,以无关的具体概念代替某一抽象概念,不经患者解释,他人无法理解,如某患者常反穿衣服,以表示自己"表里合一,心地坦诚",见于精神分裂症。见 thought of insertion)
symbolic(al) tradition 象征性交付
symbolum animae 停尸房,太平间,验尸所,殡仪馆
symmetries stakes 对称预期
symmetry n. 对称(性),匀称,对称美
Symond's Inn (英)古时大律师法官学位之一;衡平法学会;西蒙学会
sympathetic a. 有同情心的,和谐的,合意的,赞同的

symposium n. 座谈会,专题会,(正式宴会后的)酒会;专题论文集
symposium on court management 法庭管理(治理)专题讨论会
symptom n. 症候,症状
synagogue n. 犹太教会堂(源于希腊语 Synagein,意为"集合或聚集",后来从动词转化为名词。指犹太教徒聚集在一起,为自己和被迫害者祈祷,他们聚集之地即犹太教会堂之前身)
synallagmatic n. 双务性(指双方当事人都承担义务和责任)
synallagmatic contract 双务合同(契约)
synchronization right 同步录音权
synchronous or asynchronous 同步的或不同步的
syndic n. 1.经理人;理事;董事 2.政府官吏;地方行政长官
syndicalism n. 工团主义,工联主义
syndicate n. 1.辛迪加联合企业,企业组合;银行团 2.理事会,董事会 3.(美俚)罪魁集团
syndicate state 工团国家
syndicated loan 银团贷款,联合贷款,辛迪加贷款(人们习惯将银团贷款称为辛迪加贷款)
syndrome n. 综合征;同时存在的事物;症候群
synergism n. (专利)结合体,联合体;协作体[指①已知的一些零件和功能的结合体,它创造出比单独一些零件或单独的功能总和更大的效果。"结合体"(synergism)的存在表明有时虽不明显但却是实用的、有益的。美国联邦最高法院在审理大西洋和太平洋茶叶公司诉超级自动销售设备公司案(Great Alt. & Pac. Tea. Co v. Supermarket Equip. Corp.),参见《美国联邦最高法院判例汇编》第 340 卷、第 147 页(1950 年)中认为:"结合体"是结合体专利(combination patent)的需求。但是这种裁定(holding)被 1952 年的专利法(Patent Act of 1952)推翻,参见《美国注释法典》第 35 标题卷第 103 节(25 USCA §103)。②提出一项新的或不一样的功能或一种很不寻常、成果惊人、可授予专利的发明。亦可称为 synergy; synergistic result]
synergistic a. (专利)结合体的,联合体的(见 synergism)
synopsis n. 提要,概要,梗概
synergy n. 协同作用
synopsize v. 作……的提要,作……摘要
syntagma canonum Antiochenum 《安提阿寺院法汇编》(包括 341 年到 800 年间的寺院法规)
syntagma canonum et legum 《寺院教规和法律大全》(指 1335 年罗马帝国的一部汇编)
synthesis n. 综合,综合物、综合性(复数为 syntheses)
synthesist t n. 综合者;(化)合成法使用者
synthesized a. 被综合而成的
synthetic securities 合成证券
syphilitic n./a. 梅毒患者/患梅毒的
Syro-Roman Law Book 《叙利亚-罗马法律全书》
system n. 1.制度;体系,体制;系统 2.方式;方法 3.人格 4.社会结构;按规律结合为一体
system approach 系统方法,系统思路,系统研究法,制度化
system engineer 系统工程师
system engineering 系统工程,系统工程学
system of a fixed distribution of business among the judges 法官的固定分工制
system of administration 管理制度;行政制度
system of advocacy 辩护制度
system of appeal 上诉制度
system of boot sector virus 引导型病毒
system of budget and financial statement 预算决算制度
system of burghs 自治市制度
system of capitalist ownership 资本主义所有制
system of centralization (中央)集权制
system of civil justice 民事审判体制
system of civil law 大陆法系
system of cluster virus 链式病毒
system of collective security 集体安全体系

system of common law 普通法系(即英美法系)
system of compensatory financing 补偿贷款制度
system of competition by merit 择优录用制
system of compulsory arbitration of labor disputes 劳工争议的强制仲裁制度
system of contracts 合同制,契约制度
system of courts 法院制度
system of credit insurance for exports 出口信贷保险制度
system of criminal justice 刑事审判体制
system of cumulative voting 累积投票制
system of decentralization 分权制
system of democratic centralism 民主集中制
system of deposit (样品)存贮(档)制度
system of direct election 直接选举制
system of economic management 经济管理体制
system of economic regulation 经济规范体系
(the) system of estimating increases and decreases 实额增减法
system of exploitation 剥削制度
system of exploitation of man by man 人剥削人的制度
system of export licensing 出口许可制度
system of fixed output to households (中)包产到户制
system of forced reform through labour (中)强迫劳动改造制度
system of formalized dispute resolution 正式纠纷解决体系
system of government 政体,政制
system of government by decrees 依政令的统治制度
system of hands off 不干涉体系
system of inquisitions 纠问制度(见 Inquisitorial System)
system of international civil jurisdiction 国际民事管辖权制度
system of international law 国际法体系
system of judicial oversight 司法监督体制
system of jurisprudence 法学体系
system of justiciars 法官制度

system of labo(u)r protection for the worker under age 未成年工人劳动保护制度
system of labor protection for woman workers 女工劳动保护制度
system of law 法律体系,法律制度
system of legal evidence 法定证据制度
system of legal rules 法律规则体系
system of licensing 许可证制度
system of majority representation 多数代表制
system of matrimonial property law 婚姻(夫妻)财产法律制
system of mediation 调解制度
system of multi-member (single-member) constituencies 多个(单个)代表(议员)选区制
system of national insurance 国家保险制度
system of ownership by individual workers 个体劳动者所有制
system of ownership of the means of production 生产资料所有制
system of people's assessors 人民陪审员制度
system of people's congress 人民代表大会制
system of people's juror 人民陪审员制度
system of personal responsibility for profit and loss 自负盈亏制度
system of primogeniture (英)长子继承制
system of prior censorship of press 出版事先检查制度
system of prior examination 事先审查制度
system of prize 奖励制度
system of probationary suspension 缓刑制度
system of proportional representation (众议院)议席比例制
system of public bidding 招标承包制
system of public procuration (或 public prosecution system) 检察制度
system of public service 公务员制度,国家公务员制度
system of publicity for immovables 不动产公示(告)制度
system of publicity for movables 动产公示(告)制度
system of recourse 求偿制度
system of registration of deeds 契据登记

制度
system of registration of title 土地产权登记制度
system of responsibility in production（或 **system of production responsibility**） 生产责任制
system of rewards and penalties 奖惩制度
system of separation of three power 三权分立制度
system of share coorporation 股份合作制
system of sheriffs （英）郡长制度
system of social security 社会保障制度
system of special resposibility for each person 个人专责制
system of state ownership 国家所有制
system of tax division（或 **allocation**） 分税制
system of the court of first instance being the court of last instance 一审终审制
system of the court of second instance being the court of last instance 两审终审制
system of titles and ranks （军人和外交人员等的）衔级制度
system of tribal courts 部落法院制度
system of universal election 普遍选举制
system of vocational and technical training 职业培训制度
system of weights and measures 度量衡制
system on the nation's economy 有关民族经济的体系
system program 系统程序,控制程序（见 control program）
system programmer 系统程序员
system risk 系统风险（指除无法预见的科技水平发展责任风险外,还有一些已知却无法以现有技术克服的缺陷）
systematic a./n. 1.系统的,有系统的 2.分类的;有规则的,成体系的 3.有计划的;故意的/1.分类学;分类法;组织学;组织法 2.结构;体制
systematic account 体系化（系统化）的思考
systematic deviation 系统偏差
systematic interpretation 系统解释
systematic management 制度管理
Systematically Important Financial Institutions (SIFIs) 系统重要性金融机构[指全球金融危机的产生的新概念,业务规模大,业务复杂程度高,一旦发生风险事件除给地区或全球金融体系带来冲击性的"太大而不能倒"的金融机构。SIFIs 监管制度的核心是如何平衡所涉及各主体之间的利益冲突,它的监管涉及各方面的利益冲突与平衡：①SIFIs 与非 SIFIs 之间的利益平衡；②SIFIs 与金融消费者之间的利益平衡；③SIFIs 管理层与 SIFIs 之间的利益平衡；④SIFIs 股东及债权人与 SIFIs 之间的利益平衡；⑤SIFIs 母国与东道国之间的利益平衡。实现平衡的法律路径是重新调整监管所涉利益主体的权利与义务,以及实现金融安全、金融效率与金融公平之间的法价值平衡]
systematist n. 维护制度者,订立制度者,照章办事者；分类学者
systematize v. 使系统化,使成体系,使有秩序,使组织化,把……分类
systemic a. 影响全身的,全身的,内在的
systemic perspective 全面观点

T

T square T 字尺
tab n. 票据；开票；账单
tabernacle n./v. （临时）住所；教会,神灵/使居住于临时住处
table n./v. 1.表,项目表；一览表；账单；目录；文献 2.工作台 3.会议；同席人员；（复）刻于石上的法律条文（与 the 连用）,（大写,加 the）十二铜表法（= the Twelve Tables）/（美）1.搁置（动议或议案）2.提出；（英）把……列入议事日程

table a motion （美）搁置动议；（英）提出动议,将动议列入议程

table for annuity 年金计算表

table of authorities 见 index of authorities

table of cases （18世纪）1.判例目录,判例表,案例一览表（指将法律书籍,判例汇编,论文摘要等中所援引的判例按字母顺序排列在书前或书后,并分别注明所在的章节,页号段落）2.见 index of authorities

table of precedence 品位次序表（指英国王公贵族的地位高低的顺序）

table time 时间表

tabloid n./a. 小报；文摘；药片/摘要的,节略的；轰动性的

taboo n. 禁止,禁忌,忌讳；戒律

Tabula Amalphitana (1300-1400 A.D.)《阿玛尔非海法》[一部海事法汇编,由阿玛尔非人11世纪编纂完毕,在地中海沿岸国家实行至16世纪末,为古代海法的权威,亦名 Amalphita Code (Table)]

Tabula in naufragio 失事船上的木板（指船只出事时,人们会争夺船上木板作为求生的工具,喻指第三抵押权人未通知第二抵押权人而直接抢占抵押物,并于第二抵押权人之前出售抵押物以满足其抵押权）

tacit a. 1.缄默的,默想的；默示的（法律认可的一种表示方法）2.心照不宣的,不言而喻的 3.由于法律的执行而产生的

tacit acceptance 默示的承诺

tacit accomplice 默认同谋

tacit admission 默认,默让

tacit agreement 默契,默示协议

tacit approval 默认,默准

tacit consent 默许,默示同意

tacit declaration 默示宣告

tacit knowing 默会知识；隐性（同 tacit knowledge）知识

tacit law 习惯法

tacit mortgage （美）路易斯安那州法定抵押（=legal mortgage）

tacit promise 默示允诺

tacit recognition 默认,默示承认

tacit relocation （苏格兰）默示延期租约,租约默示展期（展期期限和前租约租期相同）

tacit understanding 默契

taciturnity n. （英）缄默（在可提出诉讼请求的情况下,如保持长期缄默,得推定其已放弃索赔）

Tacitus (c.56-120) 罗马历史学家,全名是帕伯里乌斯或盖依乌斯·柯赖利乌斯·塔西乌斯（Publics/Gaius Cornelius Tacitus）。他的《编年史》（囊括14—68）和《历史》（囊括69—96）是罗马帝国时期的主要历史著作。罗马帝国的元老院议员、雄辩家、高级官员、历史学家。用拉丁文写作的最伟大的历史学家和散文作家,公元77年与阿格里科拉的女儿结婚,次年任执政官,后出任不列颠总督。97年任罗马帝国执政官司。《历史》是他的巨著。从公元69年加尔巴当政开始写起到公元96年图密善进世为止。全书12—14卷,和《编年史》共30卷。

tack n. 1.行动步骤；政策 2.（苏格兰）借贷合同（契约）；租借合同（契约）；租借的牧地合同 3.（英议院用语）附带条款（尤指为保证某提案通过,将该提案作为财政提案的附加条款,因上议院无权修正财政提案,这样即可使上项提案能与财政提案一起顺利通过）

tacking n. 抵押优先清偿（指不根据抵押品的先后来确定清偿顺序,而用加添抵押品或抵押款的方法取得的优先清偿）；附加,添加

tacking mortgage 优先清偿的抵押（见 tacking）

tackle n./v. 1.用具,装备 2.卸货索具,吊钩/1.处理,应付,解决 2.捕捉,格斗,抓住

tackle adifficult problem 对付难题

tackle a task 着手进行一项任务

tackle the thing before you 处理眼前的事

tactic a./n. 顺序的,排列的,有规则结构的/（一个）战术,（一个）策略

Taft-Hartly Act （美）《塔夫特—哈特莱劳资关系法》（1947年通过的联邦法,是对《瓦格纳法》"Wagner Act"的修正,主要是对有组织的劳工施加限制,并企图平衡劳资双方的谈判权利）

tags n. 简单引语,附加语

tahsildar n. （印度的）税务员,税收人员

Taiho Code (日史)《大宝律令》(指奈良初期所制定的行政和刑事法典)
tail n./a./v. 1.财产继承的限制;限定继承权;限定继承的产业;限定所有权(见 fee tail) 2.侍从人员/继承有特定限制的,限制继承的/跟踪,尾随
tail female 限定女嗣继承(的产业)
tail general 一般限定继承权,一般限定继承(的产业)
tail male 限定男嗣继承(的产业)
taille n. (英法等国封建时代君主及领主征收的)租税
tailler n. 限嗣继承地(见 fee tail)
tailless a. 无财产继承之限制的;无尾随的;无跟踪的
tailling n. 尾随,跟踪
tailor-made to the case at hand 个案裁量
tailzie n. (苏格兰)遗嘱继承的顺序
taint v./v. 1.污点,腐败;病毒 2.犯重罪;重罪犯人/使感染;使腐败;污染
taints consent 有瑕疵的同意
tainted a. 有污点的,污染的
tainted heredity 有污点的继承权,被诽谤的继承
tainted with fraud 受欺诈影响,受欺诈损害
Taiwan Relation Act (美)《(与)台湾关系法》(1979 年制定,实质为侵犯我国主权行为之法)
take v. 1.拿,取;享有,享受 2.攻取,占领;占用;偷取;逮捕;羁押 3.接受;采取,采纳;获得 4.奏效,有效 5.记录;履行
take a bath 投资失败
take a brief 接手承办案件
take a decision ultra petition 超过(当事人的)申请范围作出判决(或裁决)
take (或 make) a vow 立誓
take advantage of 利用,运用
take advantage of sb. 欺骗(捉弄)某人
take advantage of sth. 乘机利用某事(或某物)
take after 1.像,相似 2.追赶,跟随
take an affidavit 录取宣誓供状
take an instrument for value 以合法代价取得票据
take an oath 发誓,宣誓
take away 剥夺
take back 1.撤销,撤回 2.重新获得,取回 3.退回调换 4.准许回来;接受 5.证券收回
take blame for others 代人受过
take by stealth 偷窃,盗窃
take care of 抚养,赡养,扶养,照料;处理;应付
take charge of... 1.负起管理之责 2.负责
take (或 have) cognizance of 认识到,注意到;承担对……审理权
take count of votes 计算票数
(to) take decision 作出决定
take delivery 收货
take down 1.记录 2.拆毁 3.病熄
take drastic measures 采取严厉措施
take effect 生效,实施
take exception to (against) 对……表示反对(或抗议),异议
take for 当作,误认为
take for granted 认为当然,认为理所当然,不成问题
take from the table (美)(将搁置的议案)重新(提出)讨论
take home 实得工资(指扣除捐税外)
take home pay 实得工资
take in 1.收容;了解;接受 2.欺骗;笼络;干预 3.包括;注意 4.轻信 5.拘捕
take in charge 逮捕(罪犯)
take into account 考虑
take into camp 骗过,瞒过
take into custody 逮捕;羁押,拘留;拘禁,实行保管,实行监护;进行拘留
take (或 come) into effect 开始生效
take issue 采取反对立场,持反对意见,不同意
take law as the criterion (或 yardstick) 以法律为准绳
take legal action 起诉
take legal proceedings against sb. 对某人起诉
take no notice of sb.'s comments 不理会他人的议论
take notice 注意,理会
take off 1.脱去,离开 2.复制 3.杀死,致死
take office 就职

take on 呈现,具有,增加,承担;对付
take on extra work 雇用临时工
take on refusal 坚持
take or pay contract 提取或支付合同;照付不议合同
take out 取出;发出;领得;申请取得(许可证、专卖权等)
take out a summons against sb. 派人传唤某人
take out of pledge 赎回抵押品,赎回押品
take over (或 **takeover**) 接管,接收;让受,收购;兼并;公司收购(指通过公开收购要约取得对一家公司的控制权的行为)
take over bid (英)公开收购要约(美国叫 tender off。见 take over);收购竞争,合并出价,兼并要约
take over for use 征用
take over target 收购目标,合并目标
take part in 参加
take part in the conduct of public affairs 参加公共事务
take place 出现,发生
take possession 取得所有权;住进
take prisoner 俘虏,使……成俘虏
take proceedings 提起诉讼,起诉
take sb. at advantage 乘某人不备
take sb. into 把……当作(taking coworker into confidence)(把同事当成知己)
take sb. up 提携某人,扶持某人
take sb.'s advantage 对某人有利
take sb.'s notice 得到他人的通知
take side with 偏袒
take silk (英)被任命为王室律师,王室律顾问
take step 设法处置,办手续;采取步骤
take sth. out of pledge 赎回某物
take sth. up 拿起,举起,提起
take stock of 估量,观察(take stock of the public opinion/the situation)[估量公共(众)舆论/观察形势]
take the chair 担任会议主席
take the consequence 承担后果
take the evidence 保全证据
take the floor 发言(尤指辩论中发言)
take the law into one's hands 不顾法律,肆意妄为;违法处罚;私自处罚;畏罪自杀;自惩
take (have) the law of sb. 控告某人
take the place of 代替
take the rap (for) 承担刑事责任,(常指为别人)受责备
take the stand 站在证人席上作证
take the witness stand 站在证人席上作证
take (或 **call**) **to task** 找麻烦,责备;指责
take (a woman) to wife 娶(某女)为妻
take turns to rape a woman 轮奸妇女
take up 逮捕;阻止,抓住;偿清;承兑(汇票);认购(公债等),接受(抵押品);继续(占用);拿,举起,提起,提出
take up a case 受理案件
take up challenge 接受挑战
take up with 忍受;接受;采用;与……同居;与(人)相交;赞成,同意
take vengeance on (或 **upon**) 向……报仇(或报复)
take-care cabinet 看守内阁
take-home pay 实得工资(指扣除税金、保险费等后所实得的)
take-it-or-leave-it "要么接受,要么放弃"
taken as a whole 作为一个整体来看
taken into consideration 在考虑之中
taken together 加在一起,一并考虑
taker n. 接受者,(车票等)收票人,接受打赌的人;捕获者
taking n. 1.(刑事及侵权)占有,夺取(指夺取商品之行为,不管将物品运走与否都毫无疑问是动产占有的转移或控制) 2.(宪法)没收;征用(指政府可采取没收,摧毁或削弱私人财产的效益达到事实上或实效的对私人财产的占有。当政府的行为直接干预或实质上扰乱财产拥有人对财产的享用或使用时为政府征用之意。亦称 constitutional taking。见 condemnation 2; eminent domain)
taking and carrying away 窃取行为
taking clause (1955年)(美)征用条款,公共占用条款,宪法占用条款[指征用权条款(Eminent Domain Clause),它是美国联邦宪法第五修正案的组成部分,该修正案规定禁止政府征用私人土地公用而不

给予土地所有人公平补偿。实际上占用条款是关注司法问题的,《权利法案》(Bill of Rights)不可分割的一部分,当政府实质上强迫所有者向政府转移所有权时,财产即被占用。宪法并没有明确授予征用权,这被认为是政府的固有权力。占用条款只是对这一权力的行使作出限制。即出于"公共使用"目的方可征用财产,并规定对所有者应给予公平补偿。占用条款的目的在于保证政府执行公共政策的财政负担能被全体公众分担,而不致不公正地施加于个体财产所有人。这一占用条款不仅适用于联邦政府,也适用于州政府。亦称 just compensation clause。见 eminent domain]

taking conveyance without authority 未获准许而私用运输工具(按英国 1968 年盗窃法规定,如未获物主或其他合法权力机构的同意,任何人私取运输工具为自己或他人使用,或明知他人此运输工具为非法仍然驾驶,便构成犯罪,但自行车例外)
taking effect (=put into effect) 生效
taking notice 提起注意
taking of evidence 记录证据
taking of hostage 扣留人质
taking of oaths 进行宣誓
taking possession 占有
Taking Rights Seriously 《认真地看待权利》(美著名法学家德沃金的一本著作)
taking the oath 手抚(圣经)宣誓
taking without due process 未经正当法律程序的夺权
Takings Clause 公共占用条款,征用条款
takkana (犹太教法)拉比法令(指为增进公益事业或提高教民宗教修养而颁布的教法法令)
tale n. 虚语,荒语,谣言
tale quale 按现状,现有条件
talebearer n. 搬弄是非的人
talented a. 天资高的,有才能的
tales n. (复)应召补足陪审员缺额的人;(用作单数)召集补足缺额陪审令
tales de circumstantibus 补缺陪审员召集令
talesman n. 补缺陪审员
taleteller n. 告密者;逸言者;说谎行骗者

taletelling a. 告密的;逸言的
talio 以牙还牙式处罚
talion n. 应得的处罚;以牙还牙的报复
talk n./v. 1.(常用复)谈话;会谈,会议 2.讲话,演讲,报告;空谈,谣言,小道消息;话题/谈话;讨论;表示;劝使
talk against time 在规定时间内尽快讲完;(为阻挠议案通过)用讨论消磨时间
talk of 谈到,说到,说及
(the) talk of the town 街谈巷议
talk out 通过商谈消除分歧;(英)把讨论拖到议会休会以便搁置议案
talk over 以口才使改变立场;商量,讨论
talk round 兜圈子谈(问题),说服……同意自己,说服
talk sense 讲有道理的话
talk tall 吹牛,说大话,自吹自擂
talk to death 以长篇演说扼杀(议案)
talk with 与……交谈,与……讨论,试图说服
talkathon n. (美)冗长的讨论,(为拖延讨论时间而作的)冗长演说;候选人长时间广播回答选民的一种竞选方式
talkfest n. 漫谈会,(非正式的)讨论会,冗长的讨论(辩)
talking n. 讲话,讨论
talking point 论据
tallage n. (封建领主向佃户所收的)地租;(封建时代英皇向皇室领地强征的)税
tally n. 1.账;记账;记录;计算 2.结果 3.符合,符合物 4.复制品,副本 5.古时记载欠账或付款数目的木块(上划刻痕)
tally card 记数卡
tally plan (英)分期付款
tally shop (英)以分期付款方式售货的商店
tally system 分期付款的赊卖制度
tally trade 分期付款的赊卖
tally-clerk n. 1.理货员(指清点货物的人) 2.计票员(指计算选票的人)
tally-sheet n. 1.投票数记录纸 2.计数单;理货单
tallying document 点数单据,理货单据
tallyman (=tally-master) n. 1.(英)经营赊销商品的商人;带样品销售的售货员;以

分期付款方式销售商品的商人 2.记账员,理货员;记数员

talmud n. 犹太教的法典(指收录犹太人的民法和教会法的法律书籍总体,包括本文与注释。有时仅指注释部分)

talmudist n. 犹太教法典编撰者,遵守犹太教法典的人,犹太教法典研究者

tamper v. 1.(用不正当手段)影响,干涉,干预 2.伪造;篡改;削弱;损害 3.贿赂

tamper with (a witness) 向(证人)行贿
tamper with a document 窜改文件
tamper with a lock 撬锁
tamper with other's business 干预别人的事
tamper with voters 收买投票人,以不正当手段影响投票人

tamperer n. 阴谋家,伪造者,假冒者;收买证人的人,诱骗者

tampering n. 贿赂,收买
tampering with jury 贿赂陪审团(行为)
tampering with witness 收买证人
tanadar n. (印度)警察所长,哨所所长
tangible a. 1.有形的,实体的,实质的 2.确实的,真实的,实在的
tangible assets(或 **property**) 有形资产,有形财产
tangible cultural goods 实物文化商品(指储存介质和介质附着的载体作为一个整体而存在的文化商品,如纸质和美术作品。这种和载体结合为一个整体的数字文化商品在交易时被当作有体物对待,由物权法调整,而受知识产权法的权利穷竭原则限制)
tangible evidence 实物证据
tangible goods 有形货物,有形财产
tangible ground of complaint 确实的申诉,有根据的申诉
tangible injury 有形伤害
tangible medium of expression 具体的表达媒介
tangible personal property 有形动产,实体动产;有形个人财产(除动产外包括住房等一些不动产)
tangible personality 有形动产
tangible proofs 确凿的证(明)据
tangible results 确实成效,实效

tangible things 有形财产
tangibles n. (复)有形资产,有形财产
tangled a. 复杂的,缠结的,繁乱的
tangled case 复杂的案件
tangled traffic 繁乱的交通
tanistry(或 **tanistria**)n. 选长男制(爱尔兰一种古代所有权的法制。欧洲野蛮时代选家庭中最年长的男性成员来继承财产,于詹姆斯一世执政时已废)
tantamount a. 相等于……的;相当于……的(to),相等的,同等的
tantamount to a refusal 相当于拒绝
＊*Tantum bona valent, quantum vendi possunt.* Things are worth what they as much as can be sold for. 货真价实。
Taoism n. 道教
tap v./n. 1.(在电话线上搭线)窃听 2.任命,指定 3.轻敲,轻扣/线带,狭带;卷尺;磁带,录音带;纸带,胶布
tap a telegraph wire to intercept the message 私接电报线截取消息
tap bond (美)(为吸收游资而发行的国库)债券
tap phones 窃听电话
tap stock (英)政府(通过银行直接发行的)债券
tape recording (美)磁带录音[指联邦最高法院公开开庭时进行磁带录音。在法官和每位律师面前放有麦克风,庭审情况均被记录在开盘式录音系统之中。自1955年10月开始50多年未作大的变动。开庭结束后,录音带即被放入国家档案馆。根据联邦最高法院与档案馆之协议,这些录音带不供公众使用。2000年以后随着时代的发展,录音档案可由联邦最高法院将口头辩论的文字记录传到网上。网址为 www.supremecourtus.gov.,还可通过西方出版公司(Westlaw)查询1990年以来的文字记录。也可通过 Lexis 检索1979年以来的文字记录。联邦最高法院图书馆保存了1968年以来录音的文字记录,最早的文字记录可追溯到1935年。未经编辑的录音包括判决意见可从 www.oyez.org 网站上的 OYEZ 栏目上获得]
tape-record v. 用磁带录音机录音

taped interview 用磁带录音机录音的会晤谈话
taper v. 逐渐减少
taper off 逐渐衰亡,逐渐消失,逐渐减少
tapering n. 窃听(电话或电报)
tapering device 窃听器
tapering system (税收等的)递减制度
tare n. 皮重(指货物包装、物品容器、货车车身等重量)的扣除;扣除的皮重
tare and tret 皮重和添头
tare weight 皮重
target n./v. 目标,目的;标的/把……作为目标,定指标,订定
target consumers 目标消费者
target corporation (或 **company**) 目标公司
target date 预定开始或完成的日期
target of dictatorship 专政对象
target of no military importance 非重要的军事对象
target offense (在共谋罪中的)阴谋罪
target witness (调查团主要寻找的能在大陪审团调查的案件中提供需要的证言的)目标证人
targeting approach 目标指向方法(指如果被告通过互联网所从事的行为是明确指向法院地,且该行为对法院地造成了可遇见的后果,则法院有管辖权)
targeting of the forum 目标法院地原则
tariff n. 1.税,关税;税则,关税率;关税表 2.价目表;运费表;价格
Tariff Act of 1930 (美)《1930年税务法》(见 Smoot-Hawley Tariff Act)
tariff agreement 关税协定
tariff autonomy 关税自主
tariff barrier 关税壁垒
tariff ceiling 关税最高限额
Tariff Commission (美)关税委员会,海关税则委员会
tariff de favour 特惠运费率
tariffless a. 无关税的
tariff negotiations 关税谈判
tariff nomenclature 税则分类表,税则目录
tariff policy 关税政策
tariff preference 关税特惠
tariff quota 关税限额,关税配额
tariff range 关税幅度
tariff reform 关税改革(美国历史上指要求削减关税率,摆脱保护主义;英国历史上指反对"自由贸易",要求征收进口税)
tariff regulations 税则
tariff schedule 税率表,税则
tariff union 关税同盟
tariff wall (或 **barrier**) 关税壁垒,海关税卡,关税障碍
tariff-free zone 自由关税区,免税区
tariff-rate quota 关税率限额,关税率配额
tariff-state 关税国家
tariff-walled a. 关税壁垒的
tarnish v. 污损(名誉),玷污,使失去光泽
tarnishment n. 丑化(指商标淡化的两种形式之一);污染;败坏名誉(见 blurring),玷污,污点;污损
tart n. 妓女,举止轻浮的女子
task n. 任务;职务;工作
task force (美)特遣部队,(非军事性质的)特别工作组
task of day-to-day administration 日常的行政管理工作
task-master n. 工头,监工;派遣他人做繁重的工作者
task-work n. 派定的工作;包工(即以件计酬的工作)
taskmistress n. 女工头,女监工
tautology n. 同义语的重复;无谓的重复
tax n./v. 税,租税;重负;税收,税款(公社、团体等的)会费/评定(诉讼费等);征税;斥责;(俗)指控
tax abatement 减税
tax accounting 税务会计(指常用于确定纳税人应纳税额的会计规则和方法)
tax *ad valorem* 从价税,按值征税
tax advantage 税收优惠
tax assessment ledger 税收查证底册
tax assessment rolls 税额评定表
tax assessor 税收评定人,估税员
tax audit 税收查账,税收审计
tax (或 **taxation, taxing**) **authority** 税务机关
tax avoidance (1927年)逃税,规避纳税(指利用一切合法手段及逃税机会尽量减

少个人的纳税额而得到好处的行为,该词条与 tax evasion 不同,后者是不采取非法手段的逃税。见 tax evasion)

tax base 税基,纳税依据,课税基准[指特定税务管辖范围内属于应课税的全部财产、收入、钱财。财产的累计(或总)价值以特定税种(particular tax)纳税。见 basis]

tax basis (美)税基,基准数[指税法中的术语,即以纳税人的财产投资(investment in property)指明的价值(assigned value)和从财产转让(transfer of property)中计算的盈亏作为基数]

tax bearer 纳税人

tax bracket (1923年)(美)税率等级[指按照联邦和州法规(28%税率等级),属于专项税率(particular tax rate)收入的分类等级]

tax bureau 税务局

tax certificate 欠税不动产拍卖成交证书,税产拍卖成交证书(指颁发给欠税不动产拍卖的买主的文件,证明成交买卖及买主有产权资格以抵税收契据,并在回赎期届满期内拥有财产权。如果财产被赎回,则此税产拍卖成交证书失效。见 redemption period; tax sale; tax deed)

tax code (英)免税代码(指雇员收入免税部分的代码)(大写)《税收法典》

tax collector 收税官,税务员

tax concession 税收减让

tax court (1841年)税务法院(指①美国税务法庭;②在有些州,听审非联邦税收上诉案件的法庭,该法庭可更改或变更估价、评估类别、税额或作上诉后的终局裁决)

Tax Court Act 《税务法院法》

Tax Court U. S. (=United States Tax Court) 美国税务法院[指联邦法院,听审由纳税人对国内税务署(IRS)就税款差额(tax deficiencies)作出的决定提起的上诉案件。该法院于1942年创立,代替原来的税务上诉委员会(Board of Tax Appeals),缩略为 T. C.]

tax credit (1946年)税额减免(或抵免)[指从一个人总的应纳税额(total tax liability)中直接扣除额]

tax deduction 免税额

tax deed (为偿付欠税而由公家主持的私有房地产拍卖中发给买主的)税务当局永久契据

tax deficiency (deficiencies) (美)税值评估差价[指缴纳税款的不足,即应纳税财产总额超出了纳税人在其申报表(return)中所示出的总额。亦可称为 deficiency in tax; income-tax deficiency]

tax delinquent 拖欠税款者,税收滞纳人

tax denier (=tax protester) 见 tax protester

tax dodger 偷税人,逃税人

tax equity 课税公平

tax equity and fiscal responsibility act 产权和财政责任课税法

tax evader 偷税人,逃税人

tax evasion (1922年)逃税,偷税漏税(指有意不交或想方设法绕开税法以非法减少一个人的纳税义务。逃税要受到民事和刑事两方面的惩罚)

tax evasion and refusal to pay taxes 逃税抗税

tax exemption 免税,(一部分或全部)缴税义务的免除

tax exemption card 免税证

tax exemption regulation 免税条例

tax farmer 包税人(商),租税包税人,税收包办人

tax feret 搜查逃税财产者(指搜查应纳税而未纳税人的人)

tax form 纳税申请书

tax fraud (=tax evasion) 逃税,偷税

tax free a. 免税的,不征税的,已付税

tax gatherer 收税官,税务员

tax haven (18世纪)(美)避税区,避税天堂,避税港(指对其管辖范围的交易盈利只课以极少的税或不征税的国家或地区)

tax holiday(s) 免税期

tax home (18世纪)(美)纳税地(指纳税人的主要营业地点、场所、贸易站。只要纳税人离开其纳税地,其旅行费用纳税可以扣除)

tax immunities (美)税收免除,税收豁免(指为了保持联邦体系的活力,各州政府之间相互豁免税收的原则。虽然在20世纪30年代要求税收豁免观念日益高涨,

但联邦最高法院的判决限制这一原则的适用范围。20世纪30年代到40年代,大多数对第三方的税收免除被推翻。此后,随着联邦及州收入增加,政府间税收免除原则已经变化了）

tax in kind 实物税,以实物缴纳的税

tax incentive （18世纪）（美）税收激励[指政府通过税收利益(tax benefit)去激励一种特殊活动,如捐助或奉献金钱或财产给予有资质的慈善事业]

tax injunction act （美）税务禁止介入法,税务禁止干预法[指一项联邦法规,对于各州的州税务评估或征收过程中产生的纠纷,如果该州可以提供正常、快速、有效的救济,则联邦法院不得干预或介入。参见《美国注释法典》第28标题卷第1341节]

tax item 税目

tax jurisdiction 税务管辖权

tax law （美）(18世纪）税法,税务法[指①国内税务法,国内税务法则;②法定的、规范的、合宪的、普通法的规章、条例构成适用于税务的法规;③法学涉及税务的一个研究领域]

tax levy 纳税付款通知书,完税总额核定（书）;征税所依据的法案、法律

tax liability （1932年）纳税义务,纳税责任[指纳税人(taxpayer)根据适用税法之规定在计算收入总额、应纳税款以及抵免之后的应缴纳税款之总额]

tax lien （美）（州或地方政府）对不动产征税的留置权[指①由联邦政府具有对未缴纳联邦税款的财产留置或全部财产留置的权力;②如果不动产所有人未依法纳税则州或政府税务机构具有将其不动产留置的权力,同时通过法院判决还可出售该不动产而取消对留置财产的回赎权;③绝大多数州已采用《统一联邦税务留置注册法》(The Uniform Federal Tax Lien Registration Act)]

tax list 应纳税财产清单[指在税务管辖范围内的纳税项目清单,应纳税的人和财产的官方(或正式)的造册或清单]

tax on animal husbandry 牧业税

tax on commerce 商业税

tax on luxuries 奢侈品税

tax on price of land 地价税,地值税

tax on profits 利得税

tax on property 财产税

tax on remission 减免税

tax on rents 租金税

tax on sales 产品销售税金,销售税

tax payable 应纳税额,应付税款

tax payer n. 纳税人

tax payment 税款

tax payment receipt 纳税凭证

tax planning 逃税伎俩,税务计划

tax policy 税收政策

tax protest （美）税务抗议书,纳税异议申明[指纳税人在其（他或她）未得到法定的应纳税的基数(basis)或义务纳税款数通知的情况下通常提出的正式书面申明。其目的是:清楚表明任何纳税支付均在"抗议之中"(under protests),如果以后这项税款无效则有权收回已支付之税额]

tax protester 税收异议者,税收反抗者[指①提交税收抗议书的人;②反对纳税法规并寻求或使用各种不法手段逃避法律执行的人,特别是那种以政府无职权课税为理由而拒缴税款的人,亦可称为tax denier]

tax rate 税率(指税额和应税收益或应税财产之间的比率)

tax rebate 见tax refund

tax receipt 税票,税单

tax reduction 减税

tax reference price 税收参考价格

(the) Tax Reform Act of 1986 1986年美国会制定的《税收改革法》

tax refund 退税,退税款(指纳税人超额所支付之税款,由税务机构向纳税人退还之款项)

tax registration 税务登记

tax regulations 税务条例

tax reimbursement 退税

tax report 纳税报告书

tax reserve certificate 储税券

tax return （美）(1870年)所得税申报表,报税单[指一项所得税的格式文件(income-tax form),一个个人或实体在其上

填写收入、减免额以及免除税款(exemption)等内容,并计算出应纳税额。通常缩略为"return",亦可写为"income-tax return"]
tax roll 税册
tax sale (美)(为偿付欠税而由公家主持的私有房地产拍卖的)税产拍卖
tax saving 节税
tax shelter 逃税,避税(指在合法范围内以合法手段逃避可交纳之税,属合法)
tax shield 避税,逃税(见 shelter)
tax situs 课税地,纳税地(指与应纳税资产具有实质联系的州或其他税务管辖区)
tax stamp 纳印花税
tax surcharge 附加税
tax system 税制,税收制度
tax table 税率表(见 tax-rate schedule)
tax title (购买因欠税而由公家拍卖的不动产)税产买主所有权
tax verification 税务稽核
tax warrant 追缴欠税令状(根据此令状可扣押和拍卖财产)
tax year 纳税年度,完税年度,征税年度
tax-anticipation bill (美)抵税国库券[指由美国国库(U. S. Treasury)发行的短期债券(short-term obligation)以适应政府的现金流通之需求。一些公司按照国库券面值支付其构成的 1/4 税收来偿还(tender)这些国债券。该词条缩略为 TAB]
tax-apportionment clause (美)税务分担条款(指一项遗嘱条款之指明继承和遗产税应如何交付)
tax-benefit doctrine 见 tax-benefit rule
tax-benefit rule (1942 年)(美)税收利益规则[指按此规则:在上一纳税年度内,作为费用开支(expense)或损失,纳税人应获得损害赔偿(recover),这种赔偿应计入在本纳税年度已扣减上年损失的总收入所得之中。亦称 tax-benefit doctrine]
tax-deductible a. 在计算所得税时可以扣减的
tax-deferred a. (1948 年)纳税延期的[指到将来的日期或判决结果(event)之前可不纳税]
tax-exempt a. (1923 年)免税的[指①根据法律不需交税⟨a tax-exempt charity⟩(免税的慈善机构)。②收益免税的,指免收所得税的收益⟨tax-exempt municipal bonds⟩(免税的地方政府公债收益),亦称 tax-free]
tax-exempt import 免税进口,免税输入,免税进口货物
tax-exempt security 免税证券
tax-free a. 免税的,已付税的
tax-free allowance 免税津贴,免税宽减额
tax-free exchange (1927 年)免税财产转让,免税交易[指经税法特别规定推迟(defer)或可能免交所课税而进行的财产转让,比如依据美国《国内税收法》,参见《美国注释法典》第 26 标题卷第 1031 节,亦可称为 1031 exchange。见 1031 exchange]
tax-free profit 免税利润
tax-gatherer n. 收税官,税务员
tax-identification number (美)税务鉴定号,税收认定号[指由美国国内税务署制定的 9 位跟踪数码作为经营商户的税收依据,同时这个数字也给予需要提交经营纳税申报(business tax returns)的个人和实体。此术语缩略为 TIN,但常缩写为 tax i.d.。亦称 employer-identification number (EIN);federal-employer-identification number(FEIN)]
tax-increment financing (美)税收增值信贷[指政府提供资金或信贷激励商业发展的一种方式,通常是由政府采取放行公债向土地开发或其他较高费用(up-front costs)的产业提供资金,然后以这些新的开发产业增加的财产税来偿还债务(to service the debt)。缩略为 TIF]
tax-option corporation 见 S corporation
tax-preference items (美)(1971 年)纳税优惠项目[指在计算纳税人的最低替代税(alternative minimum tax)时所必须考虑的一些特定项目,在为规范税收目的而进行常规计算税收时这些项目应合法地予以扣除]
tax-rate schedule (1951 年)税率表[指通常用来决定有关特定的应税收益水平的税收,而且以纳税人的法律身份(status)为基

础,比如结婚者要提供双方收入所得纳税申报表。亦可称为"tax table"]

tax-state 税收国家

tax-straddle rule 双重期权税收原则[指防止非正当延期所得税缴纳的一项原则,或改变正常所得,或因不愿接受买卖损失提前扣减而将短期资本收益改变为长期资本收益,或放弃其中一项而保留另一项以补偿一部分,比如在跨期买卖的情况下允诺销售可通过允诺买进(a promise to buy)来补偿,又比如期货合同(futures contract),由于货物交易上的盈亏要求必须基于年终对于它们的价值评估作出报告,参见美国《国内税务法》,《美国注释法典》第 26 标题卷第 165 节]

taxability n. 应纳税,可纳税性

taxable a. (16 世纪)应纳税的,有税的,应课税的[指①属于税收(核查账户所挣得的收益为应税所得);②属于法律上的费用、规费(legal costs & fees),可以纳税,专家证人的费用不属于可纳税的法庭费用(taxable count costs)]

taxable distribution (1927 年)(美)可征税的信托分配额[指对给信托受益人,即隔代人(skip person),的信托分配额缴纳隔代转让税(a generation-skipping transfer),这种税既不是直接避开(direct skip),也非可纳税终止(taxable termination)。见 generation-skipping transfer tax;skip person]

taxable gift (1922 年)应税税赠与[指在调整年度之外的和申请扣除的之后,该项赠与应遵照联邦统一转让税缴纳,参见美国《国内税收法》,《美国注释法典》第 26 标题卷第 2503 节]

taxable income (1856 年)应税所得,应税收益[指税益总额减去允准的扣除额之后的余额。应税所得是由可适用税率(applicable tax rate)成倍增加来计算一个人的纳税义务(tax liability)的]

taxable product 应纳税产品

taxable termination (1988 年)(美)可征税收终止[指在以下情况下,即发生可征税事件(taxable event):①隔代转让信托财产(generation-skipping trust property)中

的利益终止,如拥有利益的隔代人(skip person)的父母死亡;②被非隔代人(non-skip person)所持有的信托中没有利益(interest);③可对隔代人制定信托分配额(distribution)。于 1976 年创立可征税收终止之前,纳税人可创立一项给予孩子终生收入(income to a child for life)的信托,以后让孩子的孩子都终生享有,而且在每代受益人死亡时不会招致遗产税或赠与纳税之义务。见 generation-skipping transfer tax]

taxable transaction 应税交易,纳税的交易行为

taxable transfer 应缴纳赠与税的财产转让(见 taxable gift)

taxable year 课税年度

taxation n. 1.税,征税,纳税,课税;租税;估价征税,税制 2.清算诉讼费用

taxation administration 税务管理

taxation bureau (或 office) 税务局(署)

taxation of added value 增值税

taxation of costs 评(核)定诉讼费

taxation of profit 利润税

taxation of turnover 营业税

taxation on inheritance 继承税,遗产税

taxation power 税权

taxation proceeding 税务诉讼

taxation standard 计税标准

taxation system 税收制度

taxed bill of costs (由法官)核定过诉讼费用的诉状

taxed costs 可征收的诉讼费用(指依据法官或书记员的命令,败诉当事人被要求补偿胜诉方的诉讼费用)

taxer n. 缴税人,纳税人

taximeter n. (出租汽车等上的)车费计算表

taxing a. 征税的;评定(诉讼费等)的负担颇重的

taxing costs 按法定要求一方支付给另一方的诉讼费用

taxing district 征税区域[指居民应当交纳或按比例交纳特定税收(particular tax)的区域,这个区域可以是整个国家、一个县、一个市或其他更大的区(unit)]

taxing master (英)法院(诉讼费)审计官,讼费评定官;最高法院评定官
taxing officer 税务官员,讼费评定官
taxing officer's certificate 税务官员执照
taxing power (18世纪)课税权,征税权,稽税权[指授予政府部分课税的权力,特别是国会课税和征税的权力,美国联邦宪法第十六修正案规定:"……国会有课征所得税之权,不必问其所得税的来源,其收入不必分配给各州,也不必根据户口调查或统计以定其税额……"见 Sixteenth Amendment]
taxing power of congress 国会征税权
taxing the cash surrender value of the policy 退保所得的现金征税
taxless n. 无税,免税
taxonomy n. 分类;分类学
taxpaid a. 已纳税的;用税款支付的,用税款付薪的
taxpayer n. 纳税人,纳税义务人(在美国常作为"公民"的同义词)
taxpayer personally filing returns 自行申报纳税人
taxpayer suit 纳税人的诉讼(指个人因对为特定目的花费公款不满而提起的诉讼)
taxpayers' bill of rights (美)(1988年)纳税人的权利法案[指一项联邦法规允准纳税人在面对国内税务署时具有的一些特别权利,比如申诉(representation)权利和在征收税款强制执行30天前获得书面通知的权利]
taxpayers' lists (美)纳税人的申报表[在某些税务区要求纳税人提供的书面申报单据(written exhibits),列出他们所拥有的应税财产,实际上也是应纳税的人和财产的清单,以此作为征税评估的依据]
taxpayer-standing doctrine (1977年)(宪法法)纳税人长期有效原则,纳税人常设原则[指纳税人除能证实有个人争议财物(personal stake)并表明某种直接伤害(direct injury)外,没有资格起诉并指控政府滥用公共税款(public's tax money)]
taxpaying obligations 纳税义务
tea bagger n. 茶包[在美国指参加茶会的人(贬义)]

Tea Party 茶会;波士顿倾茶事件;暴力反抗[①指美国1773年通过茶叶条例(Tea Act)给予英东印度公司以茶叶专卖权,引起美国人民愤怒而不允许该公司茶叶在美港口卸货,从而在纽约、波士顿等地开始反殖民主义的斗争,将该公司运来港口茶叶全部倒入海中。②指美国反税、反政府或反奥巴马的抗议者参加的有组织的聚会]
tea readers 茶占卜读者,茶占卜释者[指源于西方17世纪的茶占卜爱好者(tea readers)。当时欧洲人流行喝完茶后利用杯中茶叶来预测前程,亦称 leaf readers]
teach v. (专利)指导[指①对于专利的性能、使用,指导某人如何制造和使用发明的技术方面的普通技能(ordinary skill)。②(与现有技术或先前技术相关)预先否认(刚经过检验的发明)。通过讨论、描述或分析该发明的主要因素或技术来预先否认刚检查过的发明。就此意义上讲,先前技术(prior art)劝阻发明者去追求发明,指其远离发明。这种指导对于一项发明的专利性(patentability)展示出一种法定障碍]
teaching(s) n./a. 教导,学说,主义;教义/教导的,教学的
team n. 小队,组,(中)生产队
team design 成套设计
team management 协作管理
team production 协作生产
team work 协作,配合,工作小组
teamster n. 卡车驾驶员;运输工会会员;驾驭一队牲畜者
teamwork n. 联合工作;联合行动;协调工作
tear down 扯下,拆毁;逐条驳斥(论点等);诋毁,毁坏(名誉等)
tear open license 启封许可证(见 box top license)
tearaway n./a. 暴徒,流氓/行动莽撞的
tech-life balance 技术与生活平衡[指技术的使用不会降低生活质量或影响人与人之间的关系。过去,普通百姓的所有时间都用于解决温饱,自由时间无从谈起。到了20世纪,随着社会的进步,人们有了一定的闲暇时间,随之出现的问题是工作与

生活的平衡(work-life balance)]

technical a. 1.技术的,工艺的,技巧的,专门性的 2.严格依法律意义的,根据法律的 3.市场内部因素(如投机,操纵等)引起的 4.用工业方式生产的(指化工产品)

Technical and Miscellaneous Revenue Act of 1988 1988年美国会制定的《技术与多种收入法》

technical assault 法律上认为的攻击
technical assistance 技术援助
technical body 技术团体
technical defect 诉讼程序上的不足;技术上的缺点
technical difficulty 诉讼程序问题;技术性的困难
technical documentation 技术资料
technical error (审判上的)技术性错误(亦称诉讼程序性的错误,指审判过程中所犯无损于当事人的利益因而不能作为撤销裁定的根据的错误)
technical examination of crime 刑事技术检验
technical expertise 技术鉴定
technical innovation 技术改造
technical irregularity in the trial 审判技术上不符合司法程序规则
technical know-how (专利用语)专门技能,技术秘诀
technical legal meaning 专门的法律含义
technical loss 推定损失,估计损失
technical meaning 专门意义
technical rule of law 技术的法律规则
technical service 技术服务
technical terms 专门名词或术语
technical total loss 推定全损
technical visa 技术签证
technicality n. 1.专门的事项;细节;用语,术语;表现 2.专门性;技术性 3.(诉讼)程序或形式上的问题
technique element of law 法律的技术成分
technique of law 法律技术
technocracy n. 专家政治,技术统治
technocrat n. 专家治国论者,专家政治论者
technological supervision 技术监理,技术监督

technological transformation 技术改造
technology neutrality 技术中立原则,技术中性原则(指法律对电子商务的技术手段一视同仁,不限定使用或不禁止使用何种技术,也不对特种技术在法律效力上进行区别对待)
technology transfer 技术转让
technology-intensive investment 技术密集的投资
technostructure n. 技术专家体制
tectonic legal thought 条款法律知识,构成的法律思想
teenagers n. (13～19岁的)青少年,十几岁的年轻人
Tehren Conference 德黑兰会议(指苏、美、英三国于1943年11月28日到12月1日在德黑兰举行的首脑会议,讨论了加速击溃德国法西斯和战后有关问题,发表了德黑兰宣言)
teind court (英)什一税法庭(1925年以后,此法庭职权大减,现其大部分事务均属非诉讼性的)
teinds n. (苏格兰)什一税
tel quel 按现状
tele-politic n. 电视政治(尤指竞选运动中候选人利用电视进行活动)
Telecommunication Competition and Deregulation Act of 1996 (美)《1996年电讯竞争和不规则法》
Telecommunication Law (Act) 电信法
telecommunication lines 电信线路
telecommunication mugging 电信走私
telecommuting n. 通讯,电讯,电讯联络
telecon n. 电话会议,(用电传打字机的)电报会议
teledesic n. 全球卫星通信
telegraph n. 电报;电信;电报机,讯号机
telegraphic a. 电报的,电送的
telegraphic authority 电信代理,电信当局
telegraphic code 电码
telegraphic transfer (美)电汇
telephone n. 电话,电话机
telephone box 电话亭
telephone directory 电话(用户号码)簿
telephone tapping 电话窃听

Telephone-directory Yellow Pages （美）《黄页电话指南》(指美国的一种黄皮页的电话簿,其中多为公用电话)
television n. 电视;电视接收机;电视广播事业,电视业,电视广告事业;电视机,电视学
television ads. 电视广告
television broadcasters 电视广播机构
television transmission 电视播放
televising trials 电视直播审判
tell v. 1.讲述,告诉 2.吩咐,命令 3.分辨,辨别 4.泄露(机密),吐露 5.告发(on) 6.产生效果,发生影响 7.作证,表明,说明
tell on sb. 告发某人;说某人坏话
tell one's own tale 不言自喻
tell tales 泄露秘密;讲他人坏话;告密
teller n. 1.讲述者 2.(议会等的)点票员 3.出纳员,收款官员
tellers in parliament （英）议会点票人(指议会中选出的清点分组表决票数的议员)
telnet n. 远程登录(指因特网的远程登录服务,它允许一个用户登录到一个远程计算机系统)
temper n./v. 1.气质,性情,心情;特征 2.趋向,倾向,趋势/调剂,缓和,调和
temper justice with mercy 恩威并施,宽严并举
temperament n. 气质,性格
templar n. （英）（伦敦的）法学家,律师;（大写）圣殿骑士(团)
temples n. （英）（四大法学院中的）内殿（寺）和中殿（寺）法律学院（见 Inns of Court）
temporal a. 暂时的;时间的;世俗的,现世的,世间事物的
temporal affair 俗事,俗务
temporal and spiritual jurisdiction （世俗）普通司法管辖和宗教司法管辖
temporal or spiritual injury, **damage**, **harm** 物质上或精神上的妨害,损害,伤害
temporal sphere of validity 时间的效力范围
temporalis 临时的,有期限的,时间的
temporality (=temporalty) n. 1.临时性;一时的事物 2.(常用复)物质方面的权利与财产

temporary a./n. 临时的,暂时的/临时工
temporary absentee 临时缺席者;临时不出庭者
temporary administration （法院指定的）临时管理遗产(者)
temporary alimony （或 support） 临时扶养费(指离婚诉讼悬而未决时给配偶方临时的扶养费)
temporary association 暂时合伙
temporary budget 假预算
temporary cessation of business 暂停营业
temporary committee 临时委员会
temporary control 临时管制
temporary detention 临时拘留
temporary disability 暂时丧失工作能力
temporary disposal of question 问题的暂时处置
temporary domicile 假住所,临时住所
Temporary Emergency Court of Appeals （美）临时紧急上诉法院
temporary employment 临时雇用;临时性职业
temporary imprisonment（或 **punishment**） 有期徒刑,有期刑
temporary injunction 临时禁止处分命令
temporary insanity 暂时性精神错乱
temporary insider 临时内部人员(指除公司内部人员外,与公司人员有特殊关系且对获取证券信息有一定优势的人员)
temporary insider theory 临时内部人理论(指相关"外部人"因特殊原因而知悉公司情况,若从事内幕交易就应承担责任)
temporary interest 临时性权益
temporary investment 短期投资,临时投资
temporary judge 临时接任的法官,临时法官(指通常在常任法官不在的情况下由一个行政区域特定法庭临时开庭的主审法官任命或指定的法官。履行常任法官职责以区别于特别法官,亦称 judge pro tempore)
temporary laws 临时性法规
temporary letter of credence 临时国书,临时信托状
temporary licence 临时执照
temporary loan 暂时借款,短期借款

temporary neutrality 临时中立
temporary officer 临时官员
temporary orders 临时限制令(指法院庭审前为保护原告权利,避免在诉讼进行中不可挽回的伤害而发出的命令)
temporary policy 暂保单
temporary prohibition 临时禁制令
temporary punishment 有期徒刑
temporary receipt 临时收据
temporary receivers 临时财产管理人
temporary respite 暂缓执行
temporary restraining order(s) (法院)临时制止令,(英)临时抑制令,临时禁止令
temporary restraint 临时约束(限止)
temporary settlement 临时协议
temporary sheriff 临时司法行政官
temporary treaty 临时性条约(指条约非属永久性质,如赔款条约等)
temporary tribunal 临时法庭
temporis exceptio 时效抗辩;法定时效届满的抗辩
temporization n. 顺应时势,拖延应付,见风使舵
temporizer n. 顺应时势的人,见风使舵的人
temptation n. 诱惑;诱惑物
tempter (temptress) n. 诱惑者,引诱者(指诱人作恶的女人,迷惑人的妇女)
tempus 期间,限期
tempus continuum 持续期间
tempus fatale 不变期间(指法律所规定的时间,如上诉期间)
tempus semestre (古英国法)半年期间(合182天)
tempus utile 盈利期间;使用期间,有用期间(指休假日不计算在内)
Ten Commandments 十诫(指《圣经》上的十诫)
Ten Principle of Banclung Conference 万隆会议十项原则(和平共处五项原则的引申和发展)
ten-year regime 十年保留制(指《伯尔尼公约》允许成员国只给外国作品的翻译权以10年的保护期)
tenacity n. 坚毅,顽强,固执

tenancy n. 1.租用,租赁,租借;租赁期限;占有 2.任职,任职期间
tenancy agreement 租借合约,租赁合约
tenancy at will (17世纪)任意租赁[指经土地所有人的同意,承租人对保有不动产可保持占有,但无确定期限。关于存续期或租金(as for duration or rent)不管是地产转让人还是受让人要是想终止地产租赁而且不再有存续期,须经各方同意后任何一方通告即可终止。亦称 at-will tenancy; estate at-will]
tenancy at sufferance (18世纪)逾期租赁,容忍保有[指某人曾经合法占有财产(不动产),但其地产权益(interest)已经届满后仍作为逾期占有者(holdover)继续保有而引起的逾期保有。亦称为 holdover tenancy; estate at sufferance。见 holding over]
tenancy attendant on the inheritance 继承上的伴有保有地产权(指为了继承财产所有人的利益,授予受托人的保有地产权的期限。这个地产保有权是指私人财产交付受托人的一种形式,亦称 tenancy attendant on an inheritance; term attendant on the inheritance)
tenancy by entireties (entirety) (英)土地整体保有(权),不可分的租赁(权),共同租赁(权),(夫妻之间的)整体租赁(如夫妻一方死亡,则生存的另一方可取得该项全部的租赁权),(美)夫妻共同保有财产权,夫妻一体所有,夫妻共同所有,夫妻财产共有权(指配偶双方的任何一方不分份额地对全部财产享有的所有权),夫妻一体保有财产
tenancy card 租用证
tenancy for a fixed period 定期租用
tenancy for a term 定期保有地产,定期租赁地产(指从地产产生效益开始,其期限是众所周知的按年、月、周计。)
tenancy for life 终身租赁(权);(英)终身土地保有(权)
tenancy for years 定期租赁(权);(英)定期土地保有(权)
tenancy from month to month 逐月租借(赁),按月租借(赁)

tenancy from year to year 逐年连续的租借(赁),按年租借(赁)
tenancy in common (美)共有租借;按份共有权(指两个以上共有人对不可分割的同一土地有份额地共同享有的所有权。见concurrent estate),普遍共有,混合共有
tenancy in gross (1860年)独立的地产保有,独立的不动产保有[指地产保有期限是独立的(in gross, outstanding),也就是说它与遗赠或继承遗产无关]
tenancy in partnership 合伙租赁
tenancy in perpetuity 永佃权
tenancy system 租佃制度
tenant n./v. 承租人;房客;佃户,租户/租赁;居住;持有
tenant at sufferance 宽容土地租借人(指租借土地已期满或合法占有权已终止,但出于业主的宽容仍继续占有租借土地的人)
tenant by copy of court roll (英)(在领地)法庭案卷中有副本可查的土地保有人(见 copyholder)
tenant by curtesy (或 courtesy) 继承亡妻遗产的男人
tenant by socage (英)根据停役租地法租借土地的人
tenant farming 租佃制(亦称谷物分成制)
tenant for life (英)终身租户,终身土地租借人(指地产租期的长短以租借人生命的长短来计算的租借人)
tenant for years (英)以若干年为期的土地租借人
tenant from year to year 按年计期的土地租借人(指租借期限按年计算,习惯上租出、租入两方都需要提前半年预先通知,然后才能把一年的租借权终止,而耕地则需提前一年预先通知)
tenant in chief (英)第一土地保有人(指由国王直接分封土地的人)
tenant in capite (英)英王直辖的承租人,从王室那里直接保有土地的领主
tenant in fee simple (或 tenant in fee) 单纯继承土地保有人
tenant in possession 占有人,持有人;正式任职者
tenant in tail 限嗣继承地保有人
tenant of the demesne 中间地主的承租户
tenant pur autre vie 终身租户
tenant right (土地房屋)租借人的权利(指房屋或土地租借人在租借权终止时,有权要求他对房屋或土地一些改进的补偿,但这必须是在他离去时,这些改进仍然留着且并未用尽的部分)
tenant's repairs 租借人的修理(见 tenantable repair)
tenant-builder n. 建筑权人
tenant-farmer n. 佃户,佃农,租地自行经营的农民
tenant-peasant n. 佃农
tenantable a. 可租赁的;可居住的
tenantable repair 维持可租住的修理(指租借人应把所租的房屋加以修理,使具有适合人们居住的良好状态)
tenantry n. (总称)承租人;出租的财产,租赁;占有
tenants by entireties 共同财产占有人;共同不动产租赁人
tenants in common 保有人,不动产共同租赁人,共同土地占有人;共同财产的共有人,共同财产的;(财产)共有人,混合共有;混合共有人;普通共有人;混合共同承租人
tenants in coparcenary 共同继承财产的承租人
tenants in dower 继承亡夫遗产的女人
tend v. 1.走向,走向,有助于(to/towards)〈tend to the same conclusion〉(趋于相同的结论)2.服务,做贡献(to),出一份力;导致 3.倾向
tendency n. 趋势,倾向
tender n./v. 1.提供,提出,提供物 2.投标;招标 3.偿还,偿付债务的手段 4.货币/提供;提出;偿还;投标
tender a bail 提出保释
tender a plea (或 a plea of tender) 提出准备偿还的答辩(指被告人诉说他随时准备有足够款项,来清偿对原告的欠款,并把款项带到法庭)
tender an oath 尊重誓言;效忠誓言
tender bidding 投标买卖

tender bond 投标担保
tender evidence 提出证据,出示证据
tender for 对……投标
tender guarantee 投标担保;提供担保,投标保证书
tender money 偿还(或提供)款项
tender of amends 金钱赔偿
tender of issue 提出争论点
tender offer (美)公开收购要约(见take over;take over bid),招标,提出要约;收购股权
tender(of) performance 准备履行(合同),提供给付(指一方当事人用来约束不履行合同的对方当事人使负违约责任所采用的一种手段)
tender price 投标价格
tender procedures 投标手续
tender year doctrine 襁褓原则
tendered ballot paper 已投选票
tenderer n. 投标人;偿还人;提供者
tendering party 投标人
tenement n. 1.住宅;一房客所租的一部分房屋;分租房屋 2.共同住宅;多家合住的房屋 3.地产;保有物,享有物(指由他人授予并在一定期间或终身享有的房地产、特权等)
tenement-house n. 共同住宅;多家合住的房屋;分租房屋
tenemental a. 地产的;住房的;出租的;分租的
tenementary a. 地产的;住房的;供出租的;供分租的
tenendum (英)土地保有方式条款(土地转让中的一项条款);不动产契据上有关租期的条款
tenet n. 信条,宗旨,原则
tenno n. (日)天皇
tenor n. 1.(文件)要旨,大意 2.一般趋势,进程 3.抄本,誊本 4.(支票的)期限
tenor of a deed 契据要旨
tense a. 紧张的
tense situation 紧张局势
tension n. 紧张,紧张状态
tension in foreign relations 外交上的紧张状态

tentative n./a. 1.试验性提案;推测;试验 2.未遂罪/假定的,推测的,试验的
tentative plan 暂时(试验性)的计划
tentative rules 试行规定,暂行规定
Tenth Amendment 美国联邦宪法第十修正案[美国联邦宪法第十修正案于1971年批准成为《权利法案》的一部分,被称为"被保留权力的修正案"(reserved powers Amendment):"举凡宪法未授予合众国政府行使,而又不禁止各州行使的各种权力,均保留给各州政府或人民行使之。"增加此条主要为了减去人们对联邦政府侵蚀州权力的担心,但并未解决联邦与州权力的划分]
tenth justice (美)第十大法官(指首席律师,首席检察官总检察长,副司法部长。见 Solicitor General)
Tenther n. 美国联邦宪法第十修正案论者(指认为联邦政府基本上可以说是违法的人,因为它篡夺了属于各州的权利,违反了美国联邦宪法第十修正案)
tenure n. 1.任期;保有期间 2.保有地,租借地;保有权 3.保有的条件 4.永久保有
tenure ad vitam aut culpam 终身职(只要不犯错误的)
tenure by divine service 敬神土地保有权(教会所有权之一)
tenure for life 1.土地终身保有权 2.终身任期
tenure in aumone 施舍的土地(指施舍给教堂的土地)
tenure in capite 直接分封保有,第一土地保有(指封臣从国王那里直接领受土地的保有方式)
tenure in free socage (英)自由(完全)免役土地保有(指自由人享有的自由土地保有);土地自由保有制
tenure in serjeanty (英)服役土地保有,劳务土地保有
tenure in (common) socage (英)免役土地(共同)保有(指通常由佃户向领主土地提供劳务或缴纳地租的土地保有)
tenure in villeinage (英)佃农土地保有
tenure of office 在职;任期
tenurial a. 依赖于保有权的;土地保有的

terce n. （苏格兰）夫产三分权（指以前寡妇可享有其已故丈夫可继承的遗产的1/3,现已废除）
tergiversation n. 变节,背叛;完全改变意见;（言语）自相矛盾,支吾
term n./v. (14世纪) 1.术语,专门用语(指某一领域具有的固定含义)〈term of art〉（艺术术语) 2.(合同)条款,约定〈The delivery term provided for shipment within 30 days.〉(提供装船交货约定在30日之内。)（见condition 3) 3.(复) terms [法院开庭期;界定协定范畴的规定,条款;条件〈terms of sale〉(销售的条件)] 4.确定的时期;特别授予财产的期限〈term of years〉(几年的期限/年限) 5.时期或开庭期[指法院处理司法事务(judicial business)〈the most recent term was busy indeed〉(最近大部分开庭期确实很忙)。在5的含义上亦可称 term of court]/把……称为
term annuity 期限年金（见 annuity certain）
term day 1.付款日期,(租金)支付日 2.(苏格兰)法定季度结账日 3.开庭日
term for appeal 上诉期限
term for deliberating (1843年) 斟酌或考虑的时间[指给予受益人(beneficiary)决定是否接受或拒绝一笔遗产或其他继承(财产)的慎重考虑时间]
term implied by law 法律默示的条款
term in gross (1852年) 独立的地产或继承遗产的保有年限(见 tenancy in gross)
term insurance 定期保险
term life insurance 定期人寿保险
term loan 定期贷款
term mortgage 定期抵押
term of active service 现役期限
term of commitment 禁闭期;监禁期;债务期
term of contract 合同(契约)条款
term of detention 拘留期限
term of disappearance 失踪期间
term of employment 就业条件
term of imprisonment 监禁期;刑期
term of lease 租赁期限
term of loan 放款期限
term of office 任期,任职期间
term of payment 清偿期,付款期
term of penalty 刑期
term of public summons 公告期间
term of redemption 偿还期限,回赎期
term of residence 居住期限,驻在期限
term of service 任期;服役期
term of tenancy 租赁期
term (或 limitation) of time 期限
term of validity 有效期间
term of years 1.年限(指确切年数的固定时).亦称 tenancy for a term 2.(英国法)不少于1年的固定期或特定的年数及几个月。根据现代英国《1925年财产法》适用上述含义 3.定期地产权(指在一定期限内将土地租给他人保有、使用)
term of years absolute 绝对年限
term of years in land (英)有期保有土地权益
term policy 定期保险单
term-time n. （苏格兰)(利息或租金的)法定支付期;学期
termagant n. 泼妇,嘴碎的妇女
termbill n. 期票,定期汇票
termer n. 刑期中的囚犯,服刑者
terminable a. 可终止的;可撤销的;有期限的
terminable annuity 有年限的年金,有期限的养老金
terminable contract 有期限的合同(契约)
terminable legacy 有期限的遗赠
terminable property 有限期的财产权
terminal n./a. 末端,终点/终止的,最末的;按期的,定期的;致命的,致死的
terminal engineer 终端工程师
terminal expenses 起点、终点费用
terminal market (农产品)集散的中心市场
terminal operating system 终端操作系统
terminal port 起讫港
terminate v. 1.限定;终止 2.完成;满期;结束,了结
terminate contract before the date of expiration 提前终止合同
terminate the action 终止诉讼

terminate the pleadings 辩论终结
terminating the contract 终止合同(契约);解除合同(契约)
termination n. 1.终止,终点,结束;结局,终局 2.末端
termination forthwith clause 立即终止生效条款,立即终止马上执行的条款
termination of a treaty 解除条约;条约的终止
termination of business 停业
termination of employment 解雇
termination of guardianship 监护关系的终止
termination of hostilities 停止敌对行动
termination of labor contract 劳动合同终止
termination of litigation 诉讼终结;诉讼终止
termination of risk 保险责任终止
termination of tenancy 租赁期满
termination of the lease 租赁终了
termination of the marriage 婚姻关系终止
termination of the partnership 合伙解散
termination of the power of attorney 撤销委任书
terminative a. 终止的,结束的,限定的
terminer n. 决定;判定
terminology n. 专门术语
terminus n. 1.界标,界牌,界石 2.目的地;终点 3.(铁路线或公路汽车线的)一端(起点或终点)
terminus *a quo* 开始,出发点,起点
terminus *ad quem* 目标,到达目的地;终点;结论
termless a. 无限期的;无限的;永不终止的;无条件的
termor n. 在某一时期内或终身占有财产者;定期租户;终身租户
termor's interest 有期限(土地)占有人的权益;定期租产的权益
terms and conditions 限制性规定
terms and conditions for optional secession 最优化脱离的条件和限期
terms and conditions of employment 其他劳动条件
terms cash 须用现金支付

terms of a written permit 书面允许条款(或条件)
terms of an agreement 协定条款,协议条款
terms of contact 合同(契约)条款(见 two-step "minimum contact" analysis)
terms of credit 信用证条件
terms of employment 雇用条件;待遇
terms of peace 媾和条件
terms of reference 1.委托的规定说明 2.(委员会等的)受权调查范围(或事项);职权范围;工作范围
terms of reference of UNCITRAL 联合国国际贸易法委员会的审查事项说明
terms (condition) of sale 买卖条件
terms of settlement 解决办法;和解办法,和解的条款
terms of shipment 装运条件
terms of the law 法律条款,约定
terms of the opinion 观点性术语
terms of the statement 陈述性术语
terms of trade 贸易条件(即交换比价);进出口交换比率
termtime 法庭这年中的开庭期的时间
termtnum 给予被告的一天时间
terpan n. 诱惑者,诱惑物;计谋、圈套,陷阱
terra 地;土;地球
terra incognita 未知领域,未知的土地
* *Terra manens vacua occupanti conceditur.* Land lying unoccupied is given to the first occupant. 未被占有的土地应属于第一个占有者。
terra nullius 不属于任何人的土地,无主地
terra putura 森林地
terra salica 屋地
terra transit cum onere 土地与其负担一起转移
terra wainabilis 可耕地
terra-tenant n. 土地的实际占有人
terrae dominicales regis 历代皇室占用的土地
* *Terrae dominium finitur, ubi finitur armoram vis.* The dominium of the land ends where the power of arms ends. (根据大炮射程规则)陆上国家的权力以其武器所及范围为限。

terrier n. 地籍册

terris catallistentis ultradeditum leva-turn a judicial writ for the restoring of lands or goods to a debtor who is distrained above the amount of the debt 归还超过债款所扣押的债务人土地或财产的令状

territorial a. 土地的,领地的;区域性的,地方性的;(大写)美国领土的;(英)保卫本土的,为本土防卫而组织的

territorial acquisition 领土取得

territorial administrative unit 区域性的行政单位,地方行政单位

territorial air (space) 领空

territorial assembly 领地议会

territorial asylum 领土庇护,域内庇护

territorial authority 地方政府机关

territorial boundaries 边缘,边界

territorial claim 领土要求

territorial commission theory 犯罪地主义,犯罪地说

territorial court (美)属地法院

territorial department (美)海外领土部(负责组织与协调海外领土范围内的军事行动)

territorial division 行政区划

territorial entity 地方实体

territorial governor (美)地方行政长官

territorial gulf and hay 领湾

territorial integrity 领土的完整

territorial inviolability 领土的不可侵犯性

territorial jurisdiction 属地管辖权,区域管辖

territorial jurisdiction premised on physical presence 以人身在场为基础的属地管辖

territorial law 属地法;领地的法律

territorial legal unit 法域

territorial maritime belt 领海带

territorial power 领土主权

territorial property 地产,(美)州属财产

territorial sea 领海

territorial security 领土安全

territorial sky 领空

territorial sovereignty 领土主权

territorial sovereignty by adjudication 依裁决而取得的领土主权

territorial sovereignty by prescription 依时效而取得的领土主权

territorial space 领空

territorial *status quo* 领土现状

territorial strait 领峡

territorial subsoil 地下领土

territorial supremacy 属地优越权,属地最高权

territorial system (=territorialism)

territorial title 全民所有权,领土所有权

territorial under the trusteeship system 托管制度下的土地

territorial unit 地区单位

territorial water(s) 领水(包括领海和一国的内水域、内海)

territorial waters (或 **maritime**) 领水、领水带(海岸线以外及特定距离以内,通常指从落潮点算起的一定距离加 3 英里海面而言)

Territorial Waters Jurisdiction Act (英)《领海管辖权法》(1878 年)

territorialism n. 地主阶级统治权;地方政府权力高于教会的制度;(大写)鼓吹建立犹太自治区的主义(或运动)

territoriality n. 领土权,领土性质或状态

territoriality of criminal law 刑法属地性(原则)

territoriality of laws 法律属地原则(与 **personality of laws** 相对而言)

(the) territoriality principle 地域性原则

territorialization n. 扩张领土;区域化,地区化

territorialize (=territorialise) v. (通过扩张)使成为领地(或领土);按区域分配,按区域组织

territories and new states 美国准州和新州[指美国联邦宪法第 4 条第 3 款授权国会为联邦准州制定专门条例和规章,并规定新州"可经国会准许而加入联邦"。后一条款的许可性质曾引起大的争议。尽管《西北法令》(the Northwest Ordinance)(1787)规定,国会显然无任何宪法义务去设立新州。准州权的拥护者抵制这一意旨,强调国会只是作为将来新的各州的受托人管理准州。19 世纪,准州内居民拥有

全面的宪法保障,因此可有效地限制国会的"主权"。同时,国会放松了对准州的政治管制,扩大了自治范围。《威斯康星州组织法》(1836)取代了《西北法令》,成为国会法律规则的基本模式。联邦权力增长使准州权力的认可及国会权力的限制成为可能]

territories of co-ordination 领土协调说(该学说试图摆脱传统理论的束缚,用一种新的观念阐释国际法与国内法的关系,其代表人物为著名英国国际法学家、前国际法院法官 G. Fitzmaurice)

territories of U. S. 美国的准州(指尚未正式成立为州,但有本地立法机构的地区)

territorium 领土,区域,领域

territory n. 领土;领域;地方;区域

territory of a judge 法官管辖区域

territory under the jurisdiction 管辖区域

terror n. 1.恐怖,令人恐怖的人或事物 2.恐怖分子集团或其政策 3.(大写)恐怖时代

terrorism n. 胁迫;暴政,恐怖政治;恐怖主义

terrorist n. 恐怖分子,恐怖主义者

terroristic a. 恐怖行为的;恐怖主义的

terroristic act 恐怖行为

terroristic means 恐怖手段

terroristic organization 恐怖组织

terrorization n. 胁迫,威吓,恐怖统治

tertiary industry 第三产业(又称服务行业),三次产业

tertium quid 第三者,中间物,第二物

tertius 第三的

tertius gaudens 渔翁得利者

tertius interreniens 中间介入的第三人;涉讼第三方

test n./v. 试验,考验,测验;化验,化验剂;试验石;检验标准,考察/试验

Test Act 《宣誓条例》(英国规定出任官吏、议员必须信奉国教的法律,1828 年废除)

test action 选定作为判案标准的诉讼

test ban 禁止核试验协定;对核子武器试爆之禁止

test case 试验案件(指一个组织以一个可能发生纠纷的事件作为案件向法院起诉,以便试验法庭做如何处理,将来实际发生纠纷时即可按此为例作出处理);选定作为判案标准的案件

test oaths 测试宣誓[指带有强迫意味的排他测试宣誓,通常要求宣誓告别过去的组织、行为或信仰,但对将来的行为的强制性承诺也被认为是非正式测试宣誓的基础。美国联邦宪法制定者对宣誓表示怀疑,因此禁止在就职时进行宗教性测试宣誓。但为求团结,特别规定总统就职宣誓(第2条第1款),并要求所有联邦及州政府官员宣誓拥护宪法(第6条)。1832年至 1833 年在有关否认原则(nullification)争议中,南卡罗来纳州要求其官员首先对州而不是对国家宣誓效忠。1865 年将宣誓效忠扩大到联邦法院的律师、立约者和欲取得养老金者。经过林肯总统和国会同意将这一宣誓适用到南部地区拟任官员和特许执业的专业人员身上,并从整体上重新确认公务人员的一项政策]

test of personnel qualification 个人品格测验

test-tube baby 试管婴儿

testable a. 1.可试验的 2.有资格做证人的;有资格立遗嘱的;可依据遗嘱处理的

testacy n. 留有遗嘱

testament n. 遗言,遗嘱;确实的证明;实证;信仰声明

testament mystique 密封遗嘱

* ***Testamenta latissimam interpretationem habere debent.*** Wills ought to have the broadest interpretation. 对遗嘱应作广义解释。

testamental a. 遗嘱中写明的,遗嘱的

testamentarius 遗嘱执行人

testamentary a. 遗嘱的;由遗嘱给予或指定的;按遗嘱作的;包含于遗嘱中的

testamentary action 遗嘱诉讼

testamentary bequest 按遗嘱的遗赠

testamentary capacity 遗嘱能力;立遗嘱的法定资格

testamentary class (1865 年)遗(嘱)赠受益人群体[指一群数目未定的受益人,他们究竟有多少,将来方可以定。即他们每

个人都可获得等额的或其他比例不等的遗赠份额]
testamentary disposition 遗嘱处分
testamentary document 遗嘱证书
testamentary freedom 立遗嘱处分财产的自由
testamentary gift 遗赠
testamentary guardian 遗嘱上指定的监护人[指父母遗嘱上指定的监护人,对于其子女的人身和财产进行监护直至其子女达到成熟年龄(18岁)]
testamentary heir 遗嘱指定的继承人(大陆法)(指死者遗嘱中指定的继承人,亦称 instituted heir)
testamentary intention 立遗嘱的意图
testamentary obligation 遗嘱上指明的债务
testamentary paper 遗嘱书
testamentary power 立遗嘱的权力
testamentary property transaction 遗嘱财产转让
testamentary script 遗嘱原本,遗嘱正本
testamentary succession 依遗嘱继承
testamentary trust 遗嘱委托财产
testamentary trustee 遗嘱指定的受托管理人
testamentary will 遗嘱
testamenti factio (罗马法)遗嘱能力(指按市民法规定有为遗嘱或有为遗嘱证人或依遗嘱而继承财产之权利)
testamentum 遗嘱,遗言
testamentum allographum 他笔遗嘱
Testamentum Domini 《我主遗言》(指早期基督教会教规著作之一)
testamentum holographa 自书遗嘱,亲笔遗嘱
testamentum in procincto will made before the army a will made by a soldier before fellow soldiers while preparing for battle 军人的遗嘱,(罗马法)一个士兵准备参加战役在战士们前的遗嘱
testamentum inofficiosum (=inoffcious testament) 违反义务的遗嘱,无理剥夺继承人继承权的遗嘱
testamentum numcupativum 口头遗嘱
* *Testamentum omne morte consummatur.*
Every will is perfected by death. 任何遗嘱只有在立遗嘱人死亡后才能成立。
testamentum tripertitum 书面遗嘱
testamur n. (英国大学的)考试及格证
testate n./a. 留有遗嘱而死者,遗嘱人/留有遗嘱的
testate disposition 遗嘱处分
testate succession 遗嘱继承
testatio mentis an expression of a testator's mind; a testament 遗嘱人理智的表示;遗嘱
testation n. 证人;证据
testator n. 遗嘱人,留有遗嘱者
testatrix n. 女遗嘱人,立遗嘱的人
testatum 1.(法院)向另一郡(或县)的司法行政官发的令状(指一个郡、县法院在其所在地找不到被告,而向其他郡、县的司法行政官所发的令状总称)2.契据开头部分(指让与契据中,用"立约为证"字样作为开头的契据部分)
testatum capias ad satisfaciendum (英)向另一郡、县司法行政官发的拘捕债务人的令状(见 *testatum*)
testatus 遗嘱人,已立下遗嘱者
teste n. (英)(法院令状的)终结部分(指令状的日期、发出地点部分)
testee n. 测验对象,接受测验者,被试验者
tester n. 执行测验者;试验者;检验器,测定器
testes n. 证人,证据
* *Testes pondearantur, non numerantur.*
Witnesses are weighed, not numbered. 证据在于分量,而不在于数量。
testfy v. 1.证明,表明 2.作证,证实;提供证据 3.确言,宣称
testifiable a. 可作证的,可证明的,可表明的
testificandum 立证
testification n. 证据,证言;立证,作证,证明
testifier n. 证人,作证者,证明者
testify v. 证明,证实,作(见)证
testify a fact 证实一个事实
testify against (on behalf of) a person 作不利(有利)于某人的证明

testify at trial 出庭作证
testify to sb.'s innocence 证明某人无罪
testify under oath 宣誓作证
* *Testimonia ponderanda sunt, non enumeranda.* Evidence is to be weighed, not enumerated. No particular number of witnesses should be required for the proof of any fact. 证据贵在其证明力的大小,而非其数量之多寡。
testimonial n./a. 1.(品格、资格、行为等的)证明书;推荐书,介绍信;鉴定书 2.奖品,奖状;纪念品/有关证明(或鉴定书等)的,表扬的,纪念的
testimonial evidence 证人证言(区别于书证、物证),证据
testimonial letter 证明书
testimonial limits 证人证词的限制
testimonial privilege 证据的特惠,证据的特免权
testimonial proof 口供证据,证人证据
testimonium 签名前条款(指在契据或遗嘱末尾引出签名的一句话)
testimonium clause 合同(契约)的末了条款(或条文)(指契约或文件的部分包括签署人和签署时间、地点)
testimony n. 1.证据(指证人以誓言口头提供证明);口供,证明;证言 2.(基督教刻在两块石板上的)摩西十诫
testimony of a witness 人证
testimony of accomplice 同案犯证言
testimony of the accused 被告供述,被告口供
testimony of witness with knowledge 知情证人的证言
testing and licensing of person to drive vehicles of different classes 对驾驶不同种类车辆的人进行考核和颁发驾驶执照
testing certificate 检验证(明)书
testing clause 验证条款(苏格兰法中在正式生效的契据结尾处的一项条款)
testis 证人,见证人,作证人
* *Testis de visu praeponderate aliis.* An eyewitness is preferred to others. 见证人优于其他证人。
* *Testis nemo in sua causa esse potest.* No one can be a witness in his own cause. 任何人都不得在自己的诉讼案件中充当证人。
* *Testis oculatus unus plus valet quam auriti decem.* One eye-witness is worth more than ten ear-witnesses. 一个见证人胜过十个道听途说者。
* *Testis unus, testis nullus.* 一个证人等于没有证人。
testmamenti factio activa (罗马法上的)立遗嘱的能力
testmamenti factio passiva (罗马法上的)依遗嘱受领物件的能力
testmamenti factio relativa (罗马法上的)做遗嘱证人的能力
* *Testmoignes ne poent testifier le negative, mes l'affirmative.* Witnesses cannot testify to a negative, they must testify to an affirmative. 证据不证明否定的东西,而必须证明肯定的东西。
tests for efficiency and convenience developed by the chancellors 衡平法院法官所创制的效率和方便的标准
tête à tête (两人在一起)私下地,秘密地
Teu Codes 《条顿法典》
text n. 主文,正文,本文;原文;题目;主题;课文,课本,教科书
text actually in force 现行法律文本
text of court's decision 法院判决主文
text of the judgment 判决主文,判决正文
text of treaty 约文,约本
textbook law 教科书法
textbound n. 文本合订本
textual a. 原文的,本文的,文字上的
textual error 原文错误
textual interpretation 文本解释
textualism n. 文本主义
thalassocracy n. 制海权
thalassocrat n. 拥有制海权者
thalweg n. 航道分界线(指两国国界之河流航道的中线)
thanatology n. 死亡学,死因学
thanatopsy n. 尸体剖检
that (it) depends n. 要看情况而定
Thayer presumption 塞耶推定(指 1898

年詹姆斯·塞耶提出的推定,即只转移先行举证责任但不转移证明责任的推定。见 Morgan presumption)
The Federalist 见 Federalist Papers
the said board 本(或联系上下文时的前述)(州)政府部门
The said witness 该证人,上述证人
the state rests its cases 国家的人民停止对其案件的举证;国家(代表人民)停止对案件的举证(见 state;rest)
the sterner (stronger, rough) sex 男性
thearchy n.神权统治
theatre of war 战场,战地,战区
theatrical performance 剧场上演,舞台演出
theft n. 1.盗窃行为,偷窃 2.失窃,被窃
theft by false pretex 诈称取财
theft from the person 盗窃他人身上财物
theft insurance 偷窃保险
theft of consigned goods 偷窃托运货物
theft of data 盗窃数据
theft of state economic information 盗窃国家经济情报
theft of state property 盗窃国家资财
theft of state secrets 窃取国家机密
theft of wild creatures 偷猎野生动物
theft or larceny 窃盗罪
theftbote n. 私了窃案(指被盗窃人收回失物或得到赔偿,私下谈妥了结案子,不进行告发)
theism n. 有神论
thematic dialogue 主题对话
theme n. 主题,题目
Themis n. 忒弥斯(希腊神话中的一位神明,此神为主管法律和正义的女神)
theocracy n. 1.神权政治,僧侣政治 2.神权政治国家,掌握政治的僧侣集团
Theodosiantheft Code 《狄奥多西法典》(见 Codex Theodosianus)
Theodosiantheft Law of Citation 《狄奥多西引证法》(指公元 426 年狄奥多西二世所颁布的规定引证罗马法学家的许多著作时确定其权威性效力的法律)
theological 神学的
theoretical remedies 理论救济
theoretical sampling 理论抽样
theology n. 神学
theorem n. 定理;原理,原则
theoretical disagreement "理论性"争论(指法律依据的理论性争论)
theoreticaltheft disagreement 理论上的争议
theorizing n. 推理
theory n. 理论,学说;原理;意见;推测
theory and practice 理论与实践
theory of adequate relationship 恰当关系说
theory of adjudication 司法判决理论,裁判理论(指致力于描述、解释或规定法官如何判案的一个特定法律体系,试图放之四海而皆准的理论)
theory of balance 平衡论[指英国丹宁勋爵关于自由的定义没有超出前人孟德斯鸠的《论法的精神》中自由的思想和界定。但他不断强调"个人的自由必须用个人的责任予以平衡",并提出一个重要概念,即"平衡论"。1953 年丹宁在他的《变化中的法律》一书中指出:英国的宪法的特征在于"自由和责任是平衡的,权利和义务是平衡的,既不能滥用权利(力)和自由,也不能不承担义务和责任"。他认为法官的责任在于使自由和责任之间的天平平衡,使权利(力)和义务之间的天平平衡。见 freedom under the law]
theory of case 当事人对案件的主张(指诉讼当事人在起诉和答辩时应说明其对案件的主张,还要有事实予以支持。此为必要之内容)
theory of chaos 混沌理论
theory of corporate presence 公司在场的理论(见 corporate consent theory)
theory of criminal law 刑法理论
theory of elimination of the right of action 诉权消灭主义[指德国萨维尼(Savigny)首倡,他认为诉讼时效完成后当事人的实体权利本身仍然存在,仅诉权归于消灭,因而不能请求法院为强制执行,即成为自然债,这也是罗马法时效的本旨]
theory of excess demand of inflation 需求过多引起通货膨胀的理论
theory of expiation 赎罪说(一种刑罚

学说)
theory of fiction juristic person 法人拟制说
theory of formal act 要式行为说
theory of governmental interests 政府利益说
theory of human capital 人力资本理论
theory of inflation induced by monopoly 垄断引起通货膨胀的理论
theory of interests 社会利益说
theory of inherent moral qualities of persons 人们固有的道德品性理论
theory of joint act 共同行为说
theory of jurisdiction 管辖说,管辖理论
theory of justice 正义论
theory of law 法律原理,法律理论
theory of law as social engineering 法律社会工程论
theory of limited sovereignty 有限主权说
theory of localization of contracts 合同场所化理论
theory of most real connection 最实际关联说
theory of negating juristic person 法人否认说
theory of personal rights 人身权理论
theory of pleading doctrine （美）辩护理论原则(普通法原则,即诉讼人必须切证明所提起诉讼的案情,如果常以不同的辩词证明,即使事实方面可以获胜,但也构成败诉。大多数法庭认为,此种理论不再有效,因为辩护可以常常修改以适应举证);"以诉辩意义为准"的原则
theory of practization 实践之理论
theory of profit maximization 最大利润理论
theory of rational decision 理性决定论
theory of real juristic person 法人实在说
theory of responsibility without fault 无过失责任理论
theory of retribution 报复说(一种刑罚学说)
theory of seat of legal relation 法律关系本座说
theory of separate powers 分权学说
theory of social contract 社会契约论(又译民约论)
theory of social discrimination 社会歧视理论(由于就业歧视产生原因多种多样,不同领域的学者从不同角度提出许多理论,主要有社会风俗及管理理论,亦称社会歧视理论)
theory of space 外层空间学说
theory of state self-limitation 国家自限说
theory of statistical discrimination 统计歧视理论
theory of statutes 法则区别说(一种为国际私法发展奠定基础的学说)
theory of secession 脱离理论
theory of state organ 国家机关说(此学说认为选民团体与代表机关都是国家的一种机关,各有其责,各行其职。前者的职责为选举;后者的职责为协助议会作出各种决定。两者不存在法律上的委托关系或代表关系。它们的职权来自宪法。见 delegated theory)
theory of taste for discrimination 偏好歧视理论
theory of the act by agent 代理人行为说
theory of the act by principal 本人行为说
theory of the contractual meeting 合同(契约)洽谈说
theory of the divine right 神权说
theory of the enterprise entity （法人的）企业实体说
theory of the fiction of legal personality 法人拟制说(该学说以"权利义务为主体,应以自然人为限"为其独立论的基础,认为除自然人之外无权利义务主体。法人取得的法律人格不过是法律将国家主权特许的团体拟制为自然人而已。此学说为极端个人主义思想在法理上的反映)
theory of the place of the first effect 最先作用地说
theory of the presumption of innocence 无罪推定论
theory of the reality of legal personality 法人实在说(该学说认为法人并非法律上虚幻的拟制,而是具有独立的存在和独立的意思能力,有独立的意思机关和独立的人格,完全区别于公民个人独立存在的社

会有机体。与此相对应的为法人拟制说)
theory of ultimate popular sovereignty 人民主权论
theory of ultraimperialism 超帝国主义论
theory of vital change of circumstances 情势变迁说
theory theoretical principle 理论原则
therapy n. 疗法,治疗;治疗性
there are indications that ... 有迹象表明……
there-in-after ad. 在下文,在下(一部分)文中
there-in-before ad. 在上文,在上(前)(一部分)文中
there-under ad. 遵照,在其下
* **There is a right, there is a remedy.** 有权利就有补救方法;有补救方法就有权利,有诉求才有救济。
thereabout(s) ad. 在那附近;(表示数目、数量、时间、程度等)大约,左右、上下
thereby ad. 借此
thereof ad. 1.由是;由此 2.属于它的,关于它的
Theresiana (或 *Constitutio Criminalis Theresiana*) 《特莱西亚刑法典》(1769年制定的一部奥地利刑法典)
thereupon ad. 1.于是,因此 2.随即,立即 3.在其上
thesaurus n. 词库
thesaurus absconditus (英)埋藏物;隐藏物
thesaurus inventus (英)埋藏物;发现物
thesaurus thesauri (复)(或 *thesauruses*) 埋藏物,宝库;词典;汇编;百科全书
these rules flow from principles 这些规则产生这些规则,这些规则来自这些原则
thesmothete 立法者
thickening jurisdiction 强化管辖权
thief n. 窃贼;小偷
thieve v. 偷,窃
thievery n. 偷窃行为;被窃之物;偷窃事件
thieves latin 窃贼的隐语,黑话,切口
thievish a. 1.盗窃的;有盗窃习惯的;像贼的,有贼性的 2.偷偷摸摸的,隐秘的
thievish living 盗窃的生涯
thievish look (一副)贼样子

thievishness n. 盗窃成性;鬼鬼祟祟
thimblerigger n. 骗子
thin-spuelled rule 见 eggshell plaintiff rule
thing n. 1.物;事物;东西 2.事,行为 3.(复)所有物,衣服;用品;情况,事情 4.工作;目标,目的;细节
thing in action 诉讼上的物,诉讼上的财产,无形准动产(英美法系财产法中往往指包括版权在内的无形产权)
thing incapable of physical transfer 不可实际转移的物
thing owned 所有物
thing pawned 典当物(品)
thing pledged 质押物(品),担保物
thing possessed 占有物
things n. (英美法上的)物(法定权利的客体,指可以保存的东西或物业,通常分为:1.不动产或不能移动的物件,如房、地产等 2.动产或可移动的物件,如货物 3.混合物件,如契据、若干年的租赁权等)
things concealed 隐蔽物
things confiscated 没收物品
things corporeal 有体物,有形物
things immovable 不动物
things in action 无体所有权(指那些不能实际享用和占有的财产权利,如果对方不把权益归还,只能用诉讼来实现,如债券、银行存款、股票等)
things incorporeal 无体物,无形体之物
things mixed 混合物
things mortgaged 抵押品
things movable 动物
things personal 动产,个人财物
things real 不动产
things with defects 有瑕疵物
things with no defects 无瑕疵物
things without owner 无主物
think better of 改变……的念头
thinkable a. 想象中可能的,能加以思考的
thinker of the judicial organization 调整司法组织
thinking n. 思想,思考;想法,见解
third n./a. 1.第三;三分之一;(月份的)第三日;第三人 2.(复)(英)归寡妇所得的亡夫遗产的三分之一/第三的;三分之一的

Third Amendment 美国联邦宪法第三修正案[指《权利法案》之一，它规定除在战时作为军事必须外，禁止和平时期士兵未经房主同意，强制驻扎民房（quartering of soldiers）。该修正案原文："未经户主许可，平时不得驻扎军队于民房。除依法律所规定的手续外，战时也不得在民房驻扎军队。"该修正案反映了公民的住宅不受侵犯的极端重要性。与第四修正案相关联，它们共同确立对个人隐私权的基本保护，这对于现代宪法来说具有重大意义]

third arbitrator 第三仲裁员

third ballot 第三轮（次）投票

third conviction 第三次定罪（指对重罪犯人而言）

third country price 第三国出口价

third debtor 第三债务人

Third Decennial （美）《第三个十年判决摘要汇编》（由西方出版公司出版的自1916年至1926年的判决摘要汇编）

third degree （美）拷问，刑讯逼供，疲劳讯问（指对嫌疑人延长审讯以获得案情的手段）；第三亲等

third degree criminal sexual conduct （美）第三等级刑事性行为（见 criminal sexual conduct in the third degree）

third degree of relation 第三亲等

third ear （俚）告密者

third estate 平民阶级（亦译作第三等级，区别于贵族、僧侣而言）

third flag carrier 第三国承运人

third holder 第三占有人

Third House （美国会的）第三院，院外活动集团；对立法机关施加压力的集团；游说团

(the) Third International 第三国际（即共产国际）

third party （或 person） 1.第三人，第三当事人 2.（英、美）第三党

third party acting in good faith 善意第三人

third party admitted to join in the case 准许参加诉讼的第三人

third party beneficiary 受益第三人

third party claim 第三人诉讼请求

third party claim proceeding 决定债权人对判给原告的产权中有无权益的诉讼

third party clause 第三者条款（指信用证上规定，可由信用证受益人以外的第三人出面，作为装货人的条款）

third party complaint （美）被告向当时不是诉讼当事人的第三方所提出损害赔偿的请求书；对第三人的起诉（指被告对本案当事人以外第三人的起诉）

third party defendant 第三人诉讼中的被告（见 third party plaintiff）

third party having a limited title 拥有有限产权的第三人

third party in litigation 诉讼中的第三当事人

third party motor insurance 汽车（致使）第三者（损害的）责任保险（见 third party risk insurance）

third party plaintiff 第三人诉讼中的原告（指本诉中的被告向应对自己承担责任的第三人提起诉讼，从而取得原告地位）

third party practice 第三人引入诉讼（指美国民事诉讼中当被告试图向未被原告起诉的第三人转移责任时，让第三人参与到诉讼中来的程序）

third party risk insurance 第三者保险（根据交通法例规定要求使用汽车的人向保险公司投保，当第三者受到该汽车伤害时，可得到保险公司的赔偿）

third party state 第三国

third party summons in a civil action 民事诉讼中第三当事人的传票

third reading （议案）第三读（通常为表决前最后一读）

Third Reich 第三帝国（指1933—1945年纳粹统治的德国）

Third Republic 法兰西第三共和国（1870—1940年）

third sector 第三部门（指当政府失灵时，由其来弥补）

third sex 同性恋者

(the) Third World 第三世界（主要指亚洲、非洲和拉丁美洲的发展中国家和地区）

(the) Third World Network 第三世界网

third world views 第三世界观点

third-class a. 三等的;低劣的;平庸的(相当于 third-rate)

third-party attachments 债权人扣押(欠债务人债务的)第三人的财产

third-party claim 第三方请求,索赔涉及第三方的诉讼

third-party claimant 涉讼第三方(见 third party claim proceeding; third party complaint)

third-party complaint 第三当事人的起诉(指被告对本案当事人以外的第三人的起诉,即本案原告向其主张的损害赔偿将可能由第三人承担全部或部分,因而起诉)

third-party verification system 第三方认证系统(电子商务中通过数字签名进行网络交易的一种安全技术)

third-person effect (媒体对)第三人的影响

third-person perception 第三人效果认知(指一种衡量媒体对他人和自己影响的区别)

third-rater n. 劣等的物(成人)

Thirteenth Amendment 美国联邦宪法第十三修正案[该修正案于 1865 年由国会提出,于 1865 年 12 月 18 日批准生效。共两款:"第 1 款 合众国境内或受合众国管辖的任何地区内,不准有奴隶或强迫劳役(involuntary servitude)存在,惟用以惩罚业经定罪的罪犯者,不在此限。第 2 款 国会有权为实施本条而制定适当的法律。"美国联邦宪法第十三修正案实质是废除美国的奴隶制和强迫劳役制。各种力量的结合促使这一修正案得以通过。它具有自行的强制力,是唯一一条可直接作用于人民和各州的修正案。它规定除处罚犯罪外,禁止使用苦役,也禁止允许和实施奴役的法律。该修正案授予国会执行这些规定的权力]

this day six months (将议案推迟)6 个月后的今日(指议会推迟某议案的二读辩论日期,实际上不再进行辩论而否决该议案)

this matter 本事,本案,本项

Thomas Denman (1779—1854)托马斯·登曼[英国著名法官。1840 年发生了 18 岁的侍者奥克斯福德(Oxford)刺杀维多利亚女皇和凯塞堤王子的案件。奥克斯福德因精神错乱而被宣告无罪。法官登曼向陪审团指出:如果有一类疾病是一个人行为的真正动力,他不能抗拒,那他则不负刑事责任。登曼肯定了不可抗拒的冲动的存在及意义。登曼主张被称作"登曼裁决"(Lord Denmans Ruling of 1840),是不可抗拒冲动规则(irresistable impulse rule)]

thorny problems 棘手问题,难题

thorough grounding in the law 十分扎实的法律基础

thorough scoundrel 大流氓,彻头彻尾的坏蛋

(a) thoroughgoing conviction 确信,深信,十足的信念,彻底信服;坚定的信念

thought of insertion 思维插入(思想表达障碍之一,指病人感到有某种思想不属于自己,不受他的意志所支配,是别人强行插入其脑中。思维障碍大致可分两类,即思维表达与思维内容障碍。思维表达障碍共有 9 种:①flight of thought 思维奔逸;②inhibition of thought 思维迟缓;③poverty of thought 思维贫乏;④looseness of thought 思维散漫;⑤splitting of thought 思维破裂;⑥symbolic thinking 象征性思维;⑦neologism 词语新作;⑧paralogism thinging 逻辑倒错性思维;⑨thought insertion 思维插入。至于思维内容障碍,可见 delusion of persecution 被害妄想等)

thoughtlessness n. 疏忽,不注意

thral(l)dom n. 奴隶身份或地位;奴役

thrall n. 奴隶,奴仆,农奴;奴隶状态,奴役;束缚

threat n./v. 胁迫,恐吓;威吓;凶兆/威胁,恐吓,可能发生

threat of force 武力威胁,以武力相威胁

threaten v.威胁,恐吓;预示……的恶兆,使有受……之虑

threaten proceedings 以起诉恐吓(威胁)

threaten sb. with lawsuit 以诉讼威胁某人

threatener n. 威胁者,恐吓者,恫吓者

threatening a. 威胁的,恐吓的;危险的,险恶的

threating language 威胁语言,恫吓
threating letter 威胁信,恐吓信
threats to murder 以凶杀相威胁
three degree (美)三等审问(一种强迫他人认罪的非法审问方法)
(the) three important principles of the Berne Convention 《伯尔尼公约》的三项重要原则
three point arbitrage 三角套汇,三地套汇
three R's 三个"R"运动[指 Maitland 所称的三"R"运动,即文艺复兴、基督教改革、对罗马法的继受(Renaissance, Reformation, and Reception of Roman Law)(见 reception of Roman Law)]
three readings (议案的)三读制;三读会
(the) Three Services 海陆空三军
Three Strike You're Out (美)三振出局[指美国20世纪60年代盛行对犯罪人的挽救与矫正,但效果不佳;80年代中期被放弃并回归报应主义(罪刑该当);90年代中期,以加利福尼亚州的"三振出局"法案为标志,刑事司法实践中的刑罚政策开始转向剥夺犯罪能力和较低层次的威慑(deterrence)。到了1997年,24个州和联邦法律均制定出台了"三振出局"法案,各州的惯犯法也不同程度地加强对惯犯的惩罚力度。这一刑罚思想和刑事政策在美国一直维持至今。见 Three Strikes Law; Three Strikes and You're Out Law]
Three Strikes and You're Out Law "三振出局法""三击出局法"(指美国1984年对累犯加重判刑的制定法,特别对于累犯的三级重罪定罪犯,多判终身监禁。半数以上的州均制定有类似法律。亦称 Three Strikes Law)
Three Strikes Law "三击出局法""三振出局法"(见 Three Strikes and You're Out Law)
three-card trick 用三张纸牌的猜牌赌博
three-court hierarchy 三审级制
three-dimensional trademark 三度空间的商标(立体商标)
three-fifths compromise (制宪会议中)五分之三妥协案
three-in-one n. 三结合,三位一体

three-judge court (美)合议三法官法庭[指特设的一种由三名法官组成的法庭,其中至少有一名巡回法官。该法庭代替习惯的一个法官的地区法庭,以防止一名法官擅断,根据1903年《从快法》(Expediting Act)规定,它可以审理一些应属最高法院上诉的案件。亦指根据联邦法规有限的一些类型案件而专设的联邦地区法庭,或称三法官联邦地区法庭(three-judge federal district court)]
three-judge district court (美)三法官地区法庭(见 three-judge court)
three-judge section 三位法官组成的合议庭
three-mile limit 三海里的领海界限
three-miles strip 三英里地带(指美国独立时13个殖民地州获三英里地带所有权)
three-part test 三步法(见 three-step test)
three-party argument 三段博弈分析模型(指芝加哥学派提出的不带任何倾向性的经济分析文件,通过对独家交易双方和潜在竞争者的三方博弈分析来认定独家交易行为的经济效益)
three-step test (美)三步法(指法院用来决定行使特定对人管辖是否合宪的方法。第一步,被告是否有目的地使自己从诉讼所在州获益;第二步,诉因是否产生于被告与最低联系州的联系;最后一步,行使管辖是否合理。亦称 three-part test)
three-tiered system 三(级)审(判)(体)制
threshold n. 起点,门槛,入门,开端
threshold character 起码特征,开端特征
threshold defense 起始答辩,开始辩护
threshold of patent protection 专利保护的界限,专利保护的起始
threshold question 基本的问题,起码的问题
threshold returns 起码利润
thrift payment 储蓄报酬(指雇主根据雇员的储蓄计划而对其支付的报酬)
thriftessness n. 挥霍,不节俭;无价值,无用
thrifty shop (美)旧货店(指专为慈善事业而收购旧货出售的店铺)

throne n. 宝座,御座;王(帝)位,王(君)权;皇上
throng n. 群,人群;群集;事务紧迫;众多
through a. 直达的,过境的;可通行的,对穿的
through bill of lading 联运提单,全程提单
through carriage 全程运输
through document 全程单据,直达单据
through multimodal transport 全程多种方式联运
through rate 联运运费率,全程运费率
through the agency of a broker 由经纪人介绍,由经纪人经手
through transport 联运
through water pollution 水源污染
throughout the European Union 全欧盟,整个欧盟
throw v. 投掷;推倒;使陷入
throw down one's brief (律师)拒绝接受案件
throw good money after bad 为了小钱丢大钱
throw into 投入
throw light on sth. 把光芒放在某物上;(喻)有利于帮助理解某物
throw off 扔掉;摆脱掉;推翻;发出,放出,使犯错误;使产生偏差;开始(讲话);
throw one's weight around (或 about) 仗势凌人;过分夸耀自己的地位;专权,弄权
throw out 否决(议案等);发表;拒绝,摈斥;提出讨论;说出,提出;抛出;解雇,不予考虑;显示,展示;发出;建造;打乱,打扰
throw out a bill 否决一项议案
throw out a suggestion 提出建议
throw over 放弃,遗弃;拒绝,拒绝接受
throw the blame on sb. 将责任和错误推给他人
throw the book at 1.把罪名尽量加在……身上 2.给予严厉的惩处
throwster n. 赌徒;掷骰子者
thrug n. 凶手,刺客,暴徒,恶棍,(从前印度的)暗杀团员
thrust n./v. 口头攻击,讽刺;激烈辩论;攻击,戳,刺/插入;刺,猛推,冲,力推
thrust a dagger 用匕首刺入

thrusting n. 用力推,强拉,猛拉
thuggee n. (从前印度暗杀团员的)暗杀抢掠行为
thuggish a. 暗杀的,杀人的,暴行的,凶暴的
thugs n. 恶棍,凶手,暴徒
thumb impression 拇指印
thumb in, fingers out (拇指从内向外,四指从外向内;擦印的口诀)拇指内,四指外
thumb print n. 拇指纹;拇指印
thus far 至今,迄今
thus worded 如此措辞,这样措辞
thwaite n. 开垦地,(英)新开地
thwart v. 挫败,使失败
tibetan monastic education (中)西藏寺院教育
tick n. (俗)账目
ticket n. 票,车票;(美)某一政党在一次选举中所提出的候选人名单;(俗)(因违反交通规则而收到的)通知(书)单;高级船员和飞机驾驶人员执照;(银行的)临时登记账
ticket agency (车、船、飞机和戏院等的)售票代理处
ticket agent (车、船、飞机和戏院等的)售票代理人
ticket day (英)(交易所的)发票日,决算日
ticket of leave (英)假释许可证(指根据1967年的刑事审判法例,把终身监禁的囚犯附有条件地予以释放的证书)
ticket office 票房,售票处
ticket-of-leave man 假释犯(见 ticket of leave)
tidbits (=titbits) n. (新闻界)珍品
tide-waiter n. 1.旧时海关负责上船监视卸货的人员,海关检查员 2.骑墙主义者
tide-water(s) n. 水位受潮汐影响的低洼地区,受涨潮影响的地区
tie v. 1.结,捆,绑 2.约束,限制 3.(俗)结婚 4.联结 5.冻结(遗产,资本)
tie a person's tongue 使某人闭口不言
tie down 限制,约束
tie one on 喝得大醉
tie sb. down to a contract 使某人受合同约束

tie the knot (俗)结婚
tie up (美)罢工;停滞
tied aid 限制性援助
tied house (英)酒厂自营或与酒厂有合同的酒店,专售该厂出品者;雇主租给雇用人员的房屋(亦作 tied cottage)
tied loan 有条件贷款
tied selling 联号经销
tied-insale clause 搭买条款
tierce opposition 第三人抗辩制度
tiere sind keine sachen 动物不是物
tiers etat 第三身份
tiff n. 小争吵,小争执;小口角
tight a. 紧的,紧密;紧张的;困难的;处于困境的
(a) tight corner (或 place) 困难或危险的处境
tight market 供不应求的市场
tight money 银根紧
tight money policies 高利率政策,银根紧缩政策,信用紧缩政策
tight position 头寸短缺
tight rope dancing 在绳索上跳舞(喻在危险形势中艰难地应付)
tigni immittendi (大陆法)架屋梁权(一种城市地役权)
tillable a. 可耕种的
tillage n. 耕种,耕地,耕地上的作物
Tim Rice of Action Aid (英国)行动援助组织
timber n. 木料,木材;森林
timber resource 森林资源
timber right 伐木权
time n. 时间,时期,时刻,时代;时机;次数
time after sight 见票后若干日
time and half provision (美)超过原工资标准半倍加班工资
time bargain 定期交易(买卖)
time barred 丧失时效
time bill 期票;(英)(火车等的)时刻表
time bomb 定时炸弹
time book 工作时间记录
time certificate 定期存款单
time charter 定期租船契约(合同)
time deposit 定期存款

time determined by law or contract 法律或合同规定的期限
time discount 贴现
time draft 定期汇票,远期汇票
time endowment 时间资源
time factor 时间因素
time for adjudication 宣判日期
time for performance 履行时间
time for protest 作出拒绝承兑(或拒绝付款)证书的期限
time for usucaption 取得时效的期限
time horizon 时间基准,时间范围
time hull insurance 船舶定期保险,定期船身保险;定期船体保险
time immemorial 1.不能记忆的时期 2.(英)法律不能追溯的年代(指英国1276年颁布的法律规定,法律可追溯的年代只能到英王理查德一世开始执政之年,即1189年为止,超过这个年代即不能追溯)
time insurance 定期保险
* Time is of the essence. 时间是关键,时间是实质(指合同中如有此用语时,表示对合同指定的时间有特别要求,必须按时履行,若未做到则属违约)。
* Time is the essence of the contract. 时间是合同的要件(主要指合同必须按时履行)。
time lag 时滞
time limit 限期,期限
time limit expires 满期,到期
time limit for acceptance 承诺期限
time limit of contract 合同的期限
time limit required for an answer 承诺的期限
time loan (或 money) 定期贷款
time of crime 犯罪时间
time of delivery 交货期,交付期限
time of duration 持续期间
time of effect 有效期间
time of entering employment 就业期间
time of legal memory (英)法定追溯期(指理查德开始执政的时间,因为1275年威斯敏斯特第一条例将该日作为某些对物诉讼的时效时间)
time of life 年龄

time of memory 1.能追忆到的时期 2.(英)法律可追溯的年代(见 time immemorial)
time of payment 付款期
time of performance 履行期限
time of prescription 时效期间,时效期限
time of the act 行为时间
time of the court session 审判时间
time out of memory 追忆不出的时期
time pay 被分成若干次的支付
time periods 期限,时间间隔,时期
time periods governing the procedure 诉讼期间
time policy 定期保险单;期间保险单(指水险中订明保险有效期的保险单)
time purchase 分期付款的购买
time shipment 定期装运,限期装运
time sight bill 见票后定期付款票据(或汇票)
time spirit 时代精神
time unity 见 unity of time
time wage 计时工资
time-consuming a. 耗时的
time-critical 时间紧迫性
time-work n. 计时(或计日)的工作
timeless a. 无时间限制的,无日期的,长期有效的,永恒的
timeshare n./v. 分时段享用权[指共同所有财产的一种,如数人(或更多的人)合资购买度假村一幢房屋,按出资多少规定每人每年居住时间,即分时段享用此房之权利]/按时间段享用
timeshare estate 分时度假房地产权
timeshare interest 分时度假权益(指不动产分时度假权益)
timeshare license 分时度假许可
timeshare n. 分时度假
timeshare right 分时度假权益
timeshare use 分时度假有期物权
timetable n. 时间表
(a) timely manner 只争朝夕的态度
timing n. 时间的选择,计时,定时
timocracy n. (柏拉图的)以荣誉至上为原则的政体;(亚里士多德的)根据财产分配权力的政体

tip n. 1.小费;赏钱 2.(关于赛马,证券交易的)秘密消息;暗示;劝告 3.尖端
tippee n. 受密者,消息领受人[①指信息泄露理论(Tippen-Tippee Theory)是"私取(亦称不当取胜,misappropriate)理论"的另一面,该理论及其信息的领受人可作案件裁判之依据。②(证券法)不适当地获取内幕消息的人(指获取非公开信息的人,其信息来自与公司相关的悉知内幕信息的受托人)]
tipper-tippee n. 信息泄露理论(指内幕人若基于私利不适当地向外界泄露信息,并从事交易,则应负法律责任;即使泄露者不从事交易,但使他人从事交易,二者均应承担连带法律责任。见 temporary insider theory)
tippling house 酗酒店,饮用烈酒的地方
tipstaff n. 1.法庭警官(指负责在法庭上扣押被判监禁的犯人的法庭官吏);法院的执达员 2.(旧时法警所执的)金属包顶的手杖(亦指执此手杖的官吏)
tipster n. (在赛马等投机事业中的)通报秘密消息者,泄露内情者
TIR Carnet 国际公路运输证,国际路运放行证,免检通关卡
tire mark 车轮压痕
TIRM Trade Policy Review Mechanism (WTO的)"贸易政策评审机制"
tiro (tyro) n. 没有经验的人;新手
tirocinium n. 学徒期限,学徒身份,技艺入门
tissue-typing 组织分型(见 paternity test)
tit-for-tat n. 针锋相对
Titan n. 泰坦(传说中统治过世界的巨人族一员,巨人、巨物、大力神式导弹)
titans of the law 法律的巨人
tithe n. 1.什一税 2.任何小额的赋税 3.十分之一
Tithe Commutation Act (英)《什一税税折现法》
tither n. 付什一税者;收什一税者;提倡什一税者
tithing n. 征什一税;付什一税;什一税;(英)旧时英国民政管辖的单位,十户区(百户邑的下属单位)

tithing-man 旧时英国村镇官吏(类似现在的警察)

title n. 1.权利,资格,权利的根据 2.称号;头衔(官衔,学衔) 3.题目,书名,篇 4.契据;产权书;房地契;所有权

Title Ⅶ 《第七权利条款》(指 Civil Legislative History of Title Ⅶ, Rights Act of 1964。禁止基于种族、性别、宗教、民族血统进行就职歧视和侵扰,并禁止对雇员歧视、非法骚扰或在工作地点进行报复)

title and escrow arrangement 产权和第三者保存契据(指由第三者保存,待所定条件具备后再交付受让人的契据或证书等)

title and rank 职衔,职位级别
title by descent 因继承而获得的所有权
title by limitation(或 **prescription**) 因时效而取得的所有权
title by occupancy 因占有而取得的所有权,占有权
title clear of defects and encumbrance 产权无瑕疵和无负担
title division (古代法)产权分割,产权分配(指有关婚姻时所取得的财产及根据解除婚约财产分配的普通法体系,这种分配是基于谁持有合法的财产权利。根据财产分配,当离婚即婚姻终止时,在结婚时所购买的财产判决给具有财产所有权的一方。见 community property; equitable distribution)
title document 所有权证书,所有权文件
title in personal property 动产所有权
title insurance 产权保险(不动产买卖时的产权保险)
title insurers 产权保险人
title of a cause 案件名称
title of a patent 专利名称(指说明发明标的物的简短名称)
title of an act 法律的名称
title of entry 进入土地权
title of honour 荣誉称号
title of nobility 崇高的头衔,高贵的称号
title of ownership 所有权凭证,所有权状
title of penalty 刑名
title of position 职位
title of record to land 经过备案的土地产权书(契据)
title of state 国家称号
title of the absolute owner 绝对所有权人的地产
title of the subsidy program 补贴计划名称
title search 注册证件、契据的检索(用以了解契据登记证件是否良好或有瑕疵)
title theory jurisdiction 契据理论上的管辖
title to debt 债权证书
title to individual floors in a multi-story-building 多层建筑大楼各楼层所有权
title to land 土地所有权
title to property 财产所有权
title to real estate 不动产所有权
title to the goods 货物所有权
title to the provision (法)优先受偿权
title-deed n. 土地证,地契,房契;所有权契据;产权契约
title-deed for house 房契,房户权证
titled a. 有官衔的,有爵位的
titled to high praise 值得高度赞扬
titular n./a. 有爵位或称号的人/1.名义上的,有名无实的 2.有正当权利的,享有所有权的,持有所有权的 3.有爵位的
titular judge 有头衔的法官,(英)有爵位的法官
titular possessions 有权持有的财产
titular property 合法占有的财产
titulus 名义
Titus Flavius Vespasianus 韦斯巴芗[为了理解《韦斯巴芗谕令权法》的规定,必须了解韦斯巴芗的人生简历。韦斯巴芗公元9年生于罗马的小城列提(Rieti,古名 Reate)。他未出生在罗马,构成他皇帝路的第一障碍,第二障碍是他属于骑士阶级而不是高级贵族。成年后,他加入军队,36年他在色雷斯担任军团司令官,后来又在昔兰尼加和克里特行省担任财务官员。38年当上了营造官,在卡里古拉帝制时期当过裁判官,43年在不列颠战役中立有战功。51年担任备位执政官,63年任阿非利加省总督,67年被尼禄启用镇压犹太起义,68年率军攻陷耶路撒冷。同年,尼禄暴政引发民变,是年6月9日,尼

禄自杀,恺撒开创的优流斯—克劳狄王朝覆灭,出现了一年的混乱局面。69年,维特流斯被元老院确认为唯一的皇帝,但他治国无能,又出现群雄逐鹿,其中就有韦斯巴芗及其党人。当时的叙利亚总督穆恰努斯(Gaius Licinus Mucianus)和埃及总督亚历山大(Tiberius Iulius Alexandrus)和韦斯巴芗三人于69年6月底在贝鲁特商定,穆恰努斯率兵前往意大利夺取政权,韦斯巴芗前往埃及待机而动。韦斯巴芗于69年7月1日被埃及的罗马军队拥立为皇帝,12月穆恰努斯进入罗马。《韦斯巴芗谕令权法》是在韦斯巴芗不在罗马的情况下由其盟友穆恰努斯等筹划制定的。70年11月,韦斯巴芗从埃及回到罗马才真正统治其国家。他不在期间,均由穆恰努斯代理他当皇帝]

to aid and abet 教唆
to all appearance 显然
to all intents and proposes (法律文件上的常见用语)事实上,实际上,无论如何
to arrive price 在途货物报价
to be at one's wit's end(s) 穷于应付,不知所措
to be in abeyance 暂停,未定;缓办
to be on trial 在审判(理)中
to be open to conviction 服理
to be proof against bullets 不为子弹所穿入
to begin with 首先
to boot 除此之外,再者
to brief counsel 向律师(作提供案情的)指示
to call out the militia 征召民兵
to credit...to... 说明……把……归于……
to deal with a case 与案件有关
to do justice 公平对待,公平审判,公正司法
to end up in police court 在治安法庭(直立着)受审
to execute an obligation 应履行一项义务[指契约(合同)设立的义务应该履行,亦可简称execution]
to execute the laws 实施法律,执行法律
to geno in(on) 集中力量于,聚焦于,集中注意于……〈Limiting a search to headings are often a productive way to geno in (on) the most relevant material.〉(将搜索限制在标题经常是聚焦于最相关材料的有效方式。)
to give a false colo(u)r to... 曲解,曲解原意
to give to each his own 每个人各得其所
to give to everyone his due 待人公平
to have and to hold 具有并持有(在作土地转让要求时,许多契据中仍最常发现这种无必要的词语)
to have eye to 着眼于
to induce foreign investment 引进外资
to let 招租
to live by one's end(s) 靠小聪明混日子
to live honorably 为人诚实
to my mind 在我看来
to plead ignorance 以不知为托词,以不知情为借口
to present (汇票等的)提示
to remedy an abuse 革除弊端
to remind (请帖中)请(届时参加)勿忘(用于国际礼仪中)
to secure the payment of money (英)担保付款(债券)
to see eye to eye 完全同意
to share chambers 合用办公室(习惯上称律师或法官办公室为chamber,而不称office)
to stand in a white sheet 忏悔,悔改
to sue for the wrong done 不正当行为之诉
to suffer justice 遭受审判,承受司法审判
to the best of my knowledge and belief 据我所知和所信的(制定誓证或宣誓声明的开头语)
to the best of one's memory 就记忆所及
to the detriment of... 有损于……;对……不利
to the effect that 大意是……
to the order of 支付给执票人
to the same effect 相同意义
to toll a statute of limitations 使法规时效延期
to vindicate justice 明辩审判,维权审判;

求得公平处理
to vote the budget　通过预算，投票表决预算
to wield influence (control)　施加影响（控制）
to wit　即，就是(不必要的词语，用冒号可以替代)
to zero in (on)　聚焦于，集中力量于，集中注意于〈Limiting a search to headings is often a productive way to zero in on the most relevant material.〉(限定检索主题通常是有效的方法去集中关注大多相关资料。)
tobacco tax　烟草税
tobar Doctrine　托巴主义(厄瓜多尔外长托巴在1907年发表的主张，认为凡用宪法外的手段掌握政权的政府不应该被承认)
tocher n.　(苏格兰)嫁妆
toe print　趾印
toft n.　(英)屋基；宅地；小丘
together to comprise the court　组成合议法庭(美国的各州地区法院根据工作量可设有1—27名联邦地区法官，通常要求其中1名听审，判决案件，有时复杂案件则要3名法官组成合议法庭审理)
toil n.　劳苦；辛苦工作
toiler n.　劳动人民，劳动者
toils of law　法网
token n.　1.象征；记号 2.纪念品，货币；(英)民铸货币，指明权利的金属牌，有票面价值的东西(如纸币)
token money (=coin)　代用货币
token payment　象征性的偿付(指还给所欠的小部分，作为承认该债务的象征)
token vote　(英)议会对于支出预算草案的决议
Tokyo Convention on Offences and Certain Other Acts Committed on Board Aircraft　《东京公约》(全称为《关于在航空器内的犯罪和其他某些行为的公约》，是国际民航组织于1963年9月在日本东京召开的国际航空会议上签订的，到1980年已有一百多个国家参加这个公约)
tolerance n.　1.宽容；容忍的精神 2.(货币重量和机械上允许的)公差；合理的偏差额
tolerate v.　容忍，宽恕，默认
toleration n.　1.容忍；容许；忍受；宽恕；默认 2.信仰自由
toll n./v. 1.通过税，通行税(指通过公路、桥梁、渡船等应缴纳的税)，过境税；通行费 2.代价；(事故等)伤亡数目，损失；征收捐税；夺去；使遭受伤亡
toll bar (或 **toll gate**)　(征收公路、桥梁等通行税或通行费)征收关卡
toll booth　(苏格兰)监狱
toll bridge　缴纳通行税后才能通过的桥
toll charge　通行税，通行费
toll collector　收费人，收费机
toll gate　通行税的征收关卡
toll gatherer　收费人；收通行税人
toll house　收费处，征通行税所
toll in gate　入城税
toll of road　公路税
toll on transit　通行税
toll road (=**toll way**)　缴纳通行税后才能通行的道路
toll television　收费电视
toll thorough　(英)道路或桥梁的通行税
toll traverse　(英)私有地通行税(或通行费，指通过私人土地应缴纳的税或费)
toll turn　(英)牲畜市场税
tollage n.　税；通行税；征税，纳税
toller n.　收费人，征税官
tollkeeper n.　收通行税人
tombstone ad (或 **advertisement**) n.　股票(或证券)或土地销售通知；基石，墓碑；(美)报纸上的证券发行广告(指宣布安排一笔信贷或债券发行广告，因此种广告带框以黑色而得名)
tommy n.　抵工资的面包(或食物)；实物工资制
tommy shop　面包店；厂内商店，实物工资制商店(指供雇员凭雇主所发代价券购物的商店)
tonnage n.　(航船的)吨税，吨位
tonnage dues　吨税
tonnage hatchway　量吨舱口
tonnage tax　吨税
tonnage-rent　矿产采掘税

tontine n. 联合养老保险法（又译:唐提式保险法）;联合养老保险

tontine mortgage 联合养老保险的抵押

* **Too great subtlety is disapproved of in law, and such certainty confounds certainty.** 过分的细微在法律上是不允准的,因为这种不确定性混淆其稳定性。

took and carried away 盗取并拿走,窃得

tool for criminal purpose 作案工具,犯罪器械

tool mark 工具痕迹

tooth n. 1.起损害（或折磨、毁坏）作用2.强迫（或惩罪等）的有效手段

toothless a. "无牙"

top bond （英、美）国库债券

top drawer 最高权威阶层,社会最上层

top secret 绝密

top-drawer a. 最高级别的,社会最上层的,头等重要的

top-drawer socialites 交际界知名人士

top-level a. 最高级的

top-level conference 最高级会议

top-secret document 绝密文件

toper n. 醉汉,酒徒

topic n. 论题,话题,题目;格言,通则

topical access 标题查找,标题检索（指美国法律文献检索的一种方式）

topical approach 标题查找,标题检索

torah(tora) （犹太教）教训,神论,法律;（大写）摩西正经;全部宗教文献（包括Scripture Talmud）

torment n. 折磨;曲解,歪曲;痛苦,烦恼;（古）刑具,拷打

torpidity n. 麻木不仁,迟钝

Torrens system of land tenure 托伦斯土地保有制（见 Torrens title system）

Torrens system of registration of land titles 托伦斯土地所有权登记制（见 Torrens title system）

Torrens title system 托伦斯（土地）所有权制度（托伦斯于1857年任南澳大利亚总理,为南澳土地改革者）（美）托伦斯土地权利制（一种土地所有权注册制度,有些州已经使用此种制度）

torrential sea straits 领海峡

Torrins Act 《托伦斯法》（见 Torrens title system）

tort n. 侵权行为,轻罪,过失罪,违法（侵权行为指侵犯法律规定而非合同约定的权利而导致诉讼产生的不法行为或损害行为。故侵权行为与违约行为及犯罪行为有所区别;违约是基于当事人之间的协议而产生的;犯罪行为是侵犯国家主权所追求的公共利益;而侵权行为所侵害的是被侵害人所追求的个人利益。torts 复数形式指侵权法和侵权行为法。即 law of torts 或 tort law）

tort action 侵权诉讼

tort action of deceit 欺诈性侵权行为

tort affecting economic right 与经济权利有关的侵权行为

tort affecting property 与财产有关的侵权行为

tort affecting reputation 与名誉有关的侵权行为

tort affecting the family 与家庭有关的侵权行为

tort affecting the person 与人身有关的侵权行为

tort(s) against married women 对已婚妇女的侵权行为

tort(s) between husband and wife 夫妻间的侵权行为

tort(s) between parent and child 父母子女间的侵权行为

Tort(s) Claims Act 《侵权求偿法》

tort containing foreign elements 涉外侵权

tort involving intention 故意的侵权行为

tort involving negligence 过失的侵权行为

tort liability of insane person 精神错乱者的侵权责任

tort litigation 侵权诉讼

tort of conspiracy 共谋侵权

tort of negligence 过失的侵权行为

tort-feasor n. 侵权行为人,不法行为人

tortious a. 不法占有的;民事上侵害的;侵犯行为的

tortious act 侵权行为,不法行为

tortious action 加害行为,侵权行为

tortious liability（或 **responsibility**） 侵权

行为的责任
torts to land 土地侵权
tortuous a. 欺骗的,不正当的,曲折的,居心叵测的
tortuous act (conduct) outside the forum 诉讼所在地外的侵权行为,本州外的侵权行为
* *Tortura legum pessima.* The torture or wresting of laws is the worst. 对法律的歪曲是极端恶劣的(侵权和不法行为)
torture n./v. 拷问,拷打;刑讯;(复)(身体上或精神上的)痛苦或苦恼;歪曲/拷打,拷问,折磨,使扭曲,曲解,歪曲
torture chamber 刑讯室,拷问室,用刑室
torture memo (美)酷刑备忘录(指布什政府秘密准许对恐怖主义嫌犯实施酷刑的文件)
torture of animals 虐待动物(罪)
torture of children 虐待儿童(罪)
torture of disables 虐待残疾人(罪)
torturer n. 拷问者,虐待者;酷吏
tortus 侵权行为
Tory n. 1.英国昔日的保守党员 2.(美独立战争时)倾向英国的美国人 3.很保守的人
Tory Maps (Tory Mps) 英国下议院中的保守党员(Tory member of Parliament)
tota curia (古代审判记录中的用语)全法院,合议庭
total a. 完全的;全部的;总的
total abolition 全部废除
total discontinuance of an action 诉讼完全撤销
total eviction (在所有人完全丧失房产权时的)全部逐出(俗称扫地出门)
total fulfilment (或 performance) 全部清偿
total incapacity 完全无行为能力
total insurance 全部保险,全保
total loss 全损,完全损失(指被保险的船舶或货物全部受到损失,承保人对物主应负全责)
total loss control 全损控制
total loss of part 部分全损
total loss only 全损担保
total offense level 全部罪行程度,全部罪

行等级,总的罪行程度,犯罪总水平
total payment for honor 全部参加付款
total production 总生产量
total (或 universal) succession 全面继承,全部的继承(国际法上整个国家为他国或一联合国家所合并,称为全部的继承)
total sum 总额
total war 总体战争,全面战争
total waste (对财产的)全部毁损
total will 总意志
total wreck (保险)船舶全部沉没(毁损)险
totalitarian government 极权主义政府
totalitarian state 极权主义国家
totalitarian technological society 极权技术性社会
totalitarianism n. 极权主义
totality n. 总数,总额,事物的全部
totalizator n. 总额计算器;(英)赛马赌金计算机
totidem verbis 明确的,直截了当的;原文照抄,正是如此
totis quoties 经常发生,每次,每回
totis viribus 竭尽全力,尽全力
toto caelo 正相反,差距极大的
totten trust 临时信托(指某人为他人而用本人名义作为受托人在银行存款上所设立的信托)
touch and go 触礁之势;不确定的或危急的情况
touch-and-go a. 急速的,危急的,草率的;一触即发的,危险的
touchstone n. 试金石,标准;准则,措施
touchstone of jurisdiction 管辖的试金石
tough minded courts 强硬的法院,讲究实际的法院,现实的法院
tough-policy 强硬政策
toughen v. (使)变坚硬,(使)变强硬,(使)变强;变困难
toughie (=toughy) n. 1.(美俚)土匪,恶棍 2.难题;劲敌
tour n. 旅游;参观;巡视;巡回
tour of duty 值班,出差,值勤期间
tour of service 任职期间,服务期间
tourist n. 旅游者,观光者

tourist agent 旅游代理商,旅行社(常用 tourist agency)
tourist attraction 旅游胜地
tourist card (有期限的)旅游护照
tourist hotel 旅游宾馆
tourist party 观光团
tous les biens 所有财产
tout n./v. 1.招徕顾客;拉生意;争取选票等 2.侦探,侦探者;(英)侦探赛马的情报(者)/招徕顾客,拉生意;拉选票等;侦查,暗查;(英)探听有关消息;暗通(探)赛马情报
tout à fait 完全,全然
tout de suite 立即
tout for votes 拉选票
tout le monde 全世界;每个人
tout temps prist 早已准备,随时准备(以对偿债答辩词的术语,即被告声称他早已准备偿付债务,故无起诉必要)
tow n. 被拖船舶
tow-truck operator 拖曳车辆驾驶员
towage n. 1.拖船,拖带 2.拖船费,拖船费
towage contract 拖船契约(合同)
towage dues 拖带费用
towards brinkmanship 破裂边缘
town n. 城镇;城市,闹市;镇;市民
town and country planning 城乡规划
town clerk 镇执事,镇书记官(指掌管一镇的案卷的官员并作镇民代表会的法律咨询)
town collector 城镇收税员
town council 城镇参议会,镇民代表会
town father 城镇官员;城镇士绅
town girl (或 woman) 妓女,都市女郎
town hall 镇公所,市政厅
town house (主要住所在乡间的)市内住所
town planning 城市规划
town police 城镇警察
town (或 **township**) **prosecutor** (美)城镇检察官
town toll (旧时的)入市税
town-councilor n. 镇民代表,镇参议会议员
township n. 1.(美及加拿大的)镇区(county 以下的行政区划,享有若干行政权)2.(中)乡
township government (中)乡政府
townsman n. 镇民,市民,城里人,同乡,同镇人
toxic a. 有毒的,毒性的;中毒的
toxic effect 毒效
toxic ground 有毒性的土地
toxic pollutants 有毒污染物
toxic substance 有毒物
Toxic Substances Control Act 《有毒物品控制法》
toxic symptoms 中毒征候
toxic tort case 毒品侵权案
toxic waste (美)有毒废物
toxicant n.毒药,有毒物;麻醉剂,酒
toxicity n. 毒性
toxicity criterion 毒性标准
toxicity determination 毒性测定
toxicologist n. 毒理学者,毒物学者
toxicology n. 毒理学,毒物学
Toxics Release Inventory 有毒物质排放清单(即美国的 TRI 制度,通过环保团体和大众传媒介入,TRI 公开的信息流动到希望了解风险信息的主体,通过专业知识和公众常识双向交流,相互补充,风险交流强调交涉性,协商性,而非单纯信息传递,最终达到民主的技术控制)
toxin n. 毒素,毒质
trace n./v. 痕迹,足迹;遗迹/追踪;跟踪;追溯,探索
trace a rumour to its source 追查谣言来源
trace back 追溯〈Many judicial doctrine can be traced back even farther.〉(许多司法原则甚至可以追溯到更为遥远。)
trace back to 追溯,回溯到
trace the thief 追踪盗窃犯
traceable a. 可追踪的;可追溯的;可归因于……的,由于……的(与 to 连用);可查出的
traceless a. 无踪迹的,无痕迹的
traceless crime 不留痕迹的犯罪
tracer n. 追踪者;失物追查者;失物追查单
traces of a crime 犯罪痕迹
tracing n. 追踪,追查,探索;描绘;(衡平

法上的)信托追溯(指在受托人错误交付信托财产的情况下,受益人可追回财产的原则)

tracing the consideration 追溯约因,追溯对价

track n./v. 1.足迹,痕迹 2.行为的方式;路;途径,轨道,线路;进程 3.一连串的事或观念;形成痕迹的事物(如车轮等)/追踪;曳(船);循足迹而行

track down 追踪至捕获;探索至发现;追查到底

track down a criminal 追获罪犯

track out (根据遗迹等)探索出

trackage n. 铁路使用权;轨道使用所交的费

tracker n. 追踪人,探索者,追踪空中移动物体的仪器(如雷达)

tracker dog 追踪逃犯用犬

tracking n. 跟踪

trackless a. 无足迹的,不留踪迹的;无路的,无轨道的

tract n. (土地、森林等的)一片,地带,(时间的)一段,系统/(宗教和政治宣传的)小册子,传单

tradable good 可贸易的好处,可贸易的利益

trade n./v. (14世纪)1.买卖交易,销售商品或互易商品,营业服务;商业 2.商品交易或互惠交易 3.工商业;税;同行业/贸易,交易,经商,经营

trade acceptance 商业承兑(汇票)

trade act 交易行为,贸易行为;商业行为;(大写)《贸易法》

trade agreement (国际)贸易协定,劳资双方(有关工资、工作时间等)的协定

Trade Agreement Act of 1979 《美)《1979年贸易协定法》

trade and commerce 商贸,商业贸易,(亦指)商贸营业活动

trade and payments agreement 贸易支付协定

Trade and Tariff Act of 1984 (美)《1984年贸易及关税法》

trade association 同业公会

trade association labels 贸易协会标签

trade barrier 贸易壁垒;(关税、禁运等)国际贸易的障碍

Trade Barrier Regulation (TBR) 欧盟1994年第3286/94号《反贸易壁垒条例》

trade bill 商业汇票

trade bloc 贸易集团

Trade Board (英)劳资协商会(1945年为工资委员会取代)

trade by agreement 协定贸易

trade cartel 贸易卡特尔

trade circular 回单,营业传单,商务布告书

trade combinations 贸易联合

trade creation 贸易创造

trade creation effect 增加贸易的作用

trade credit 贸易(商业)信贷,同行信贷

trade custom 贸易惯例;商业惯例

trade cycle (英)商业盛衰的周期

trade data bank 贸易数据库

trade defence instruments 贸易防御措施

trade deficit 贸易逆差

Trade Description Act (英)《商品说明法》(1968年)

Trade Description Ordinance 《商品说明条例》

trade descriptions 商品说明

trade discount 同业间的折扣,批发折扣

trade discrimination 贸易歧视

trade disease 职业病

trade dispute 劳资纠纷;商业争执

Trade Disputes Act (英)《劳资争议法》(1906年)

trade down 以高价物品交换廉价物品

trade dress 产品包装,装潢[普通法和兰汉姆法(即1946年的商标法)所保护的如未注册的商标,最早保护的包装,容器以及标签等]

trade effluent 工商业污水排除(指由工商业房屋排出之污水、污物流入河流要受防止污染等法例所管制)

trade embargo 贸易禁运

Trade Expansion Act (美)《贸易扩展法》;《扩大贸易法》

trade fair 交易会(指为发展贸易而组织的临时性市场)

Trade Fair Act (美)《联邦商品交易会

法》(1959年通过之联邦法律)(指美国举行的商品交易会可获得优惠,参与展览商品国家可免关税和国内税)
trade fixtures 工商业设备
trade flows 贸易流向
trade guild 同业公会;(中世纪的)行会
trade in 1.(以旧换)折价换取(同类新物) 2.经营,做买卖
trade in credit 商业信贷,商业信用
trade in deal 旧换新
trade in value 旧换新折价
trade law 贸易法
trade licence(或 **trade plate**) 试车牌照
trade loan 商业贷款
trade mark court 商标法庭
Trade Mark Law(或 **Trademark Act**)《商标法》
trade mark privileges 商标权
trade mark registration fee 商标注册费
trade ministry 贸易部
trade name 商店、商业或商品的名称,商号
trade off 权衡,折中方案;利益或让步的交换;交替换位,交替使用,条件交换;卖掉
trade on commission 委托贸易
trade organization 同业公会
trade pact 贸易协定
trade paper 商业票据;短期商业票据
trade pledge 商业质押
Trade Policy Committee (美)贸易政策委员会
trade practice (tribunal) 商业惯例,贸易惯例(法庭)
trade Practice Act Review Committee 贸易惯例法审查委员会
trade Practices Tribunal (澳大利亚)商业法院
trade preference 贸易优惠
trade price 同行价,批发价
trade promotion centre 贸易促进中心
trade protocol 贸易议定书
trade reference 查询资料处(个人或公司)
trade regulations 贸易条例,通商章程
trade relation 贸易关系

Trade Remedy Assistance Office (美)贸易救济服务台
trade route 商业航线,贸易航线,商人路线
trade sale 同行买卖,合伙竞买
trade secret (1862年)(美)1.商业秘密,贸易秘密[指经营方案、进程,设置以及其他保持机密的经营信息,这些都是战胜竞争者的商业秘密,包括营业方案(formula)、合伙、汇编资料、规划、设置、方法、技术以及进程。这些秘密:①可衍生单独的经济价值,或明或暗地一般都不为他人所知晓或为他人易于察觉,如让他人获得该秘密并加以利用,亦可获得经济价值。②根据情况,保持其机密状态,可以是理性奋斗的目标。这表明大多数观点的定义在《统一商业秘密法》(Uniform Trade Secrets Act)中可以见到]2.信息[①并非普遍可以知道或可以查到的。②可提供竞争的优势。③在原告的费用上(at the plaintiff's expense)上可被发展并继续使用由原告来经营。④原告保持特定机密的意图及目的。这种少数观点的界定可在美国的《侵权法重述》(Restatement of Torts)第757节评论b.(cmt. b.)(1939年)中见到。亦称 undisclosed information]
Trade Secrets Act (美)《商业保密法》(1994年制定1996年修订)
trade surplus 贸易顺差
trade terms 交易条件,商业术语
trade union(或 **trades union**) 工会,职工会
Trade Union Congress (TUC) (英)工会大会,英国职工大会
trade union federation 工会联合会
trade union law 工会法
trade unionism 工会主义,工会制度
trade unionist 工会会员,工会主义者
trade up 1.以廉价物交换高价货物 2.经营高档商品以求得高利润
trade usage (1864年)贸易惯例,行业惯例,商业惯例[指在一个地区、在行业上具有一种常规的惯例作为交易的方法和惯常做法。在现行的交易中,这个惯例得到遵守,以致使人相信这个交易是合法的和

可以期待的。这一系列习惯或惯例都与特定的商业和贸易相关且为人们所熟悉。比如在抵押贷款交易(in mortgage loan transaction)中,习惯于先评估抵押的财产来支付给贷款人。履行的过程或贸易的过程可由当事双方的证言(parties' testimony)来固定。此术语亦可称为 usage of trade;course of trade。见 course of dealing;course of performance]
trade warehouse 商业货栈,商业仓库
trade-creation n. 贸易开辟
trade-diversion n. 贸易转向,贸易转移
trade-in n. 以物易物的交易;物物交易时卖方所认许的价值;(换取同类新物的)折价抵偿物
trade-off n. 折中方案,权衡,利益或让步的交换,条件的交换
trade-off decision 权衡决策
trade-off of the benefits and cost(s) 收入和成本间的比较
trade-off study 比较研究,折中研究
trade-off value 权衡值
Trade-Related Investment Measures (TRIMs) 与贸易有关的投资措施(指贸易与投资有密切关系,投资措施会影响贸易的发展;反之,贸易和贸易措施也会对外国直接投资交流的规模、方向和构成产生各种影响)
trade-state 贸易国家
trade-union bureaucrat 工会官僚(指资本主义国家黄色工会的领导人)
trademark n. 商标
Trademark Act 《商标法》
trademark counterfeiting 假冒商标
Trademark Dilution Revision Act (TARA) (2006年10月6日美国国会通过的)《商标淡化修正法案》
trademark dispute 商标争议,商标纠纷
trademark for future use 备用商标,将来使用的商标
(the) Trademark Law of the People's Republic of China 《中华人民共和国商标法》
trademark license contract (中)商标使用许可合同(契约)
trademark office 商标局

trademark register 商标登记簿
trademark registrant 商标注册人
trademark registration certificate 商标注册证
Trademark Registration Treaty (TRT) 商标注册条约
trader n. 1.交易者;商人 2.商船,贸易船 3.商品或股票投机者
trader ceasing payments 停止支付的商人
traders n. 贸易商,贸易经营者
tradesman n. 商人,店主,零售商,手工艺人
tradespeople n. (总称)商人,商界
tradeswoman n. 女商人,女店主,女零售商
trading n. 贸易,交易
trading account 贸易账户;交易账目
trading bank 贸易银行
trading book 交易账簿
trading commission 商业代理
trading contract 贸易合同
trading corporation (或 company) 贸易公司
trading market 交易市场
trading partners 商业合伙人
trading preference 特惠安排,贸易特惠
trading stamp (英)交易奖券(又译奖品兑换券,指零售商为招揽生意赠给顾客的一种有价奖券)
trading stamp company (英)赠(奖)品兑换券公司
Trading Standard Department (英)交易规范部
trading tax 交易税
trading venture 商业(贸易)企业
trading volume 交易额,贸易量
trading vote 交易投票
trading warranty 贸易保证(指遵守船舶装运货物种类规定的保证)
trading with enemy in wartime 战时与敌国贸易
traditio 引渡;让与;交付;转移(产权)
traditio brevi manu 简易交付(又译:短手交付,指收受人已以他人名义实际占有因而只变更名义的默示的交付)
traditio clavium 钥匙交付(象征交付的一种,指以交付海上货物的运送提单或交付

仓库、堆栈钥匙作为货物交付的一种间接交付办法)
traditio judicialis 审判上的交付
traditio longa manu 长手交付(指交付到手或交付到家,即送货上门的交付)
traditio rei 物的交付
traditio symbolica 象征交付(见 *traditio clavium*)
tradition n. 1.传统,惯例 2.移交;交付;引渡 3.口传,传说
tradition of efficient bureaucratic administration 有效的官僚传统
traditional a. 传统的
traditional air 民间文学,民风
traditional categories of jurisdiction 传统的管辖分类
traditional chiefdoms 传统的酋长制
traditional court 传统法院
traditional insider 传统内部人员(包括董事、监事、经理以及公司人员、有权的股东和公司的一般职工)
traditional institution 传统制度,传统体制,传统惯例
traditional law 传统法
traditional legal model 传统的法律模式
traditional mode 传统的模式
traditional morality 传统道德观念
traditional national law 传统自然法
traditional practice 传统习惯
traditional procedural rights 传统程序性(的)权利
traditional proposition 传统命题
(the) traditional rational relationship test 传统的合理关系检验准则
traditional respect for the bench 对法官的传统重视(或尊重)
traditional rule of law 传统的法治
traditional rules of African law 非洲法的传统准则
traditional self-defense doctrine 传统的正当防卫说(指包括具备必要的要件,即被告必须具有诚实和合理的信念使用合理的强力的必要性。见 honest and reasonable belief)
traditional state institution 传统的国家机构,传统的国家制度
traditional theory of transient jurisdiction 传统过境管辖理论
traditional tribal contract 传统的部落合同
traditional views 传统观点
traditionalism n. 传统主义,因循守旧
traditionary evidence 死者生前提供(有关家系、老415界等方面问题)的证据
traduce v. 1.诽谤,中伤,诋毁 2.违反,违背
traducement n. 诽谤;中伤;诋毁
traducer n. 诽谤者,中伤者
traffic n./v. 1.交通,运输;运输量;港口吞吐量 2.贸易,商业 3.买卖,交易 4.某一商品(尤指不合法的)交易/交易,买卖,做非法买卖;做肮脏交易
traffic accident 交通事故
traffic block 交通阻塞
Traffic Commissioners (英)交通专员署(1947年更名为公共车辆执照管理局)
traffic constable 交通警察
traffic control 交通管制
traffic cop (俗)交通警察
traffic court 交通法庭
traffic fatalities 交通祸害,交通灾难
traffic in persons 贩卖人口
traffic in transit 中转运输
traffic in women 贩卖妇女
traffic jam 交通拥挤,交通阻塞
traffic laws 交通法规
traffic light 交通指挥灯(即红绿灯)
traffic offence 违反交通规章罪
traffic orphan 交通事故造成的孤儿
traffic permit (车辆)通行证
traffic police 交通警察
traffic regulations 交通规则
traffic safety code 交通安全法规
traffic safety facilities 交通安全设施
traffic sign 交通标志
traffic signal 交通信号
traffic signs and marks 交通标志
traffic stop 路检
traffic ticket 对汽车驾驶员违反交通规则的传票
trafficker n. 贩卖者;买卖者;商人
trafficking in narcotics 私贩麻醉剂

trafficking in securities 非法买卖有价证券
tragedy n. 惨事,灾难,不幸;悲剧,悲惨的事
trail n. 1.踪迹;嗅迹;途径 2.跟踪,尾随 3.小径,小道
trailblazer (=trailbreaker) n. 开路先锋,创始人,先行者,领头人
train n. 火车,列车;连串,连续;随从人员
train safety regulation(s) 列车安全规则
trainbands n. (英)民团(古老的用语)
traineeship n. (澳大利亚)培训律师
training n. 训练,教育,培养
training centre 训练中心;教导所
traites-contrats 契约性条约
traites-lois 造法性条约
traitor n. 叛徒,叛逆;背信者;卖国贼
traitorism n. 卖国主义;叛卖行为
traitorous a. 叛逆的,背叛的;不忠的,阴险的
traitorous action 卖国行为,叛变行为
traitorous clique 卖国集团,叛徒集团
traitress n. 女叛徒,女卖国贼
trammel(s) n./v. (美)习惯,(礼节等的)束缚,妨碍/束缚,妨碍
trammels of authority 权力的束缚
tramp n. 1.流浪者,流浪乞丐,游民 2.航线不定的货船
tramp steamer (或 ship) 航线不定的船
trample n./v. 蔑视;踩蹦;虐待;践踏/蔑视;踩蹦,虐待;践踏
trample law and order 践踏(蔑视)法律与秩序
trance n./v 恍惚,出神,发呆,迷睡;入定;/使恍惚,使发呆,使迷睡
Trans-European Automated Real-Time Gross Settlement Express Transfer (TRAGET) 跨欧实时批量快捷传输自动结算体系
trans-shipment n. 转船,转载,转船运输
transact v. 办理,处理,执行;办事,处理事务,做交易
transactio 和解(指当事人之间互相让步,自行和解息讼)
transactio judicialis 审判上的和解

transaction n. 处理,办理,执行;(复)学报,会刊,议事录;和解,和解协议;交易;事务,事项
transaction as sale 销售交易,买卖法律行为
transaction control 贸易管制
transaction cost(s) 交易成本,交易费用
transaction for value 有偿交易
transaction in question 争论的处理(执行)
transaction information system 全面交易信息系统
transaction interactivity 交易交往
transaction involving the exchange of goods 易货贸易
transaction of business 经营业务,商业交易
transaction on exchange 场内交易
transaction or occurrence 交易或者事件
transaction price 成交价格
transaction set-off 同一交易内的抵销[指独立的抵销。即无关的两个交易中产生的两个相向债权的抵销。如买受人 A 对出卖人 B 负有支付货物价款的义务,可以与 B(作为借款人)对出借人 A 的借款返还义务相抵销。同一交易内的抵销,又称衡平抵销(set-off in equity)]
transaction underlying the instrument 票据背后的交易(指票据签发所根据的交易)
transaction-value 成交价格
transactional approach 交易性方法(追求最大司法效率与个案正义保持一致)
transactional IEL & regulatory IEL 交易性和管制性的国际经济法
transactional lawyer 见 office practioner
transactionalists n. 交易主义学派
transactor n. 执行(处理)人,经营人
transborderdata flow 跨境数据流通
transcend v. 超出,超越(理性、传统等范围),超越(宇宙、物质、世界等)
transcendent a. 出类拔萃的,卓越的,超常的
transcript n. 法院文本;(诉讼中审理或听审的)官方记录;记录的副本,抄本,誊本;整理的记录(指将速记下来的笔记经过整理的记录)
transcript of evidence 证供记录副本

transcript on appeal 上诉副本(=bill of exception)

transcription n. 1.抄写,誊写;抄本,誊本,打字复本 2.录音,录制

transfer n./v. 1.转移,传递,迁移 2.让与,转让(指把一个人的权利转让给另一个人) 3.调职;让渡证书;摹写;转印 4.汇兑;转账;(股票等的)过户,过户凭单 5.换乘;换车票,换车、船等的地点/l.转让;让渡;交付 2.换车,换船;转写;过户 3.调职

transfer agent 转让登记代理人;股票转让中间人;(股票)过户代理

transfer book (股票)过户登记簿

transfer by check 用支票转账

transfer capital 转让资本

transfer charge(s) 装卸区堆场操作费

transfer commission 转让手续费

transfer company 运输公司(尤指办理短程运输的公司)

transfer deed 转让文书

transfer entry 转账

transfer home the profits 将利润汇回本国

transfer inter vivos 生前转让

transfer of a case (1843年)案件的移送(指一个案件从一个管辖区移送到另一个管辖区法院审判。亦称 transfer of a cause。见 removal 2)

transfer of accounts 转账

transfer of actions 诉讼的转移(指可依命令或申请,由高等法院的一个庭转移到另一个庭或在高等法院和州郡法院之间转移)

transfer of cause 转移讼案(指法院将所属之讼案转移至另一法院)

transfer of claim 请求权的转让

transfer of debt 移转债务

transfer of development right(TDR)(美)土地发展权移转

transfer of funds 资金过户

transfer of knowledge 知识转让

transfer of names(或 title) 过户

transfer of obligation 债的转移

transfer of ownership 转让所有权,过户

transfer of patent 专利转让

transfer of payments 支付转让

transfer of portfolio 有价证券的转让;未满期业务转移

transfer of possession of movable (immovable) 动产(不动产)占有(权)的转移

transfer of power (民法意义上的)权利转让(见 power of attorney)

transfer of proprietary right 所有权的权利转移(让)

transfer of real rights 物权的转移

transfer of shares 股票过户,股份转让

transfer of sovereignty 政权过渡,政权移交

transfer of technology 技术转让

transfer of title 产权过户

transfer of titles on property 财产权转让

transfer paper 复写纸

transfer payment 转账性的支付,转付款项

transfer point 转运站

transfer price 内部调拨价格;转账价格

transfer pricing 转让定价(可以从价格分类角度做静态理解,也可以从转移利润角度做动态理解。税法上主要倾向于规制动态转让定价行为,从而控制静态的转让定价的形成,进而对有关商品和所得方面的税收加以控制)

transfer tax 遗产税,交易税,转让税,过户税[①指财产转让应课的税,尤指通过遗嘱、遗产或赠与而转让应课的税。②亦指无形财产如股票、债券等转让课征之税。③见 generation-skipping transfer tax]

transfer the power 让与代理权

Transfer to Minors Act 见 Uniform Transfers to Minors Act

transfer vouchers 转账传票,转账凭证

transferable a. (亦作 transferrable)可转让的;可转移的;可转印的

transferable credit 可转让信用证

transferable instrument 可转让证书

transferable securities 可转让的有价证券

transferable vote (比例代表选举制中)可转让的选票

transferee n. (财产等的)受让人,承买人;被调职者

transferee court 受移送法院

transferee liability (美)(税务)受让人的纳税义务[指受让人有义务支付转让人所

欠的税。这个义务仅限于受让财产的总价值。比如美国国内税务局(旧称国内税务署)可以强求受赠人在赠与人进行财产转让而未能交纳此项的情况下交纳此项税款]

transference n. 1.转移;转让;让与;让渡 2.调动,迁移

transferor n. 让与人,让股人,出让人,转让人;让渡人

transferred acquisition 转让取得

transferred officer 调任人员

transform v. 改变,转变,转化,转换

transform of society 社会转型

transform operation mechanism 转换经营机制,转换经营体制

transformable a. 可转化的,能改造的

transformation n. 1.变形;变性,变质 2.(女人的)假发

transformation of contradiction 矛盾的转化

transformation of money 币制变动

transformation of one's world outlook 世界观的改造

transformative a. 有改革能力的,起改造作用的

transformative use (版权法)转换性使用,改造使用[指对拥有版权的资料(copyrighted material)在一定程度上的使用,其目的和方式不同于原先的使用(original use),在表达、含义和信息上都是全新的方式。这个术语是由法官皮埃尔·N.利瓦尔(Judge Pierre N. Leval)于1990年在《趋于公正使用的标准》(Toward a Fair Use Standard)一文中创立的。该文发表在《哈佛法律评论》第103卷第1105、1111页(1990年)(103 Harv. L. Rev. 1105, 1111)(1990)。这一概念是在美国联邦最高法院审理的坎贝尔诉阿科夫-罗斯音乐股份有限公司案(Campbell v. Acuff-Rose Music Inc.)中首次适用。参见《美国联邦最高法院判例汇编》第510卷第569页、第114卷第1164页(1994年)。美国联邦最高法院认为在这一案件中,转换性使用是公正的,并不侵犯原告所拥有的版权]

transformed from another district 由其他地区移送

transfrontier a. 在国境外的,超越国界的

transfrontier element 跨国因素

transgress v. 1.超越(范围或限度)2.违反(法律、命令、条约等);违反法律,有罪

transgress a treaty 违反条约

transgress against the law 犯法,有罪

transgress one's competence 超越职权范围

transgressio (古英国法中的)违法;侵权行为,非法侵入他人住所或土地

transgression n. 侵越;违反;犯法,犯规,犯罪

transgression of authority 越权

transgressive a. 犯罪的,犯法的,违法的,有犯罪倾向的,易违犯的

transgressive trust 违法的信托

transgressor n. 违犯者;违法者;(宗教、道德上的)罪人

tranship (=transship) v. 转运;换车,换船

transhipment n. 转运

transhipment bill of lading 转运提单

transhipment cargo rule 中转(船上)货物规则

transhipment permit 转船准单

transient a. 短暂的,易逝的,过路的

transient causes 短暂的原因

transient jurisdiction 过境管辖

transindividualistic a. 超个人主义的

transire n. (海关发出的)货物准行单,(海关发给船主的)货物通行单,货物放行证,沿岸运输许可证

transit n. 1.通过,通行;过境 2.搬运,运送;改变 3.运输路线

transit agreement 过境协定

transit bill 货物免税通行证

transit cargo 过境货物

transit company 转运公司,中转公司

transit country 过境国

transit declaration 过境报关单

transit document 过境证件;过境单据

transit duty (货物的)通行税;过境税;中转税

transit godown 临时仓库

transit in rem judicatam 成为判决的事物;业已经过裁判(一事不再理之含义)

transit insurance 运送保险

transit interest 中转利息;邮程利息
transit letter of credit 转口信用证
transit of goods 货物的运送
transit shipment 中转,转运;过境转运
transit tax 通行税
transit visa 过境签证
transition n. 转移,变化,过渡,经过
transition period 过渡时期
transition phrase （专利）过渡词语[指在专利申请书(patent claim)中涉及正文中前言的短语。这种过渡通常是包含(comprising)、拥有(having)、包括(including)、由……组成(consisting of)或主要由……构成(consisting essentially of)。见preamble;body of a claim]
transition quarter (TQ) 预算年度变更时的衔接期
transitional a. 转移的,变化的,过渡的
Transitional Arrangement 过渡性安排[指与贸易有关的知识产权协定(TRIPS)第六部分第65条]
transitional credit 过渡性信贷
transitional government 过渡政府
transitional period 过渡时期
transitional provisions 暂行条文,过渡性条文,过渡的规定
transitional review mechanism 过渡性审议机制
transitional statute 过渡性法规
transitive a. 过渡的;有转移力的;中间的
transitive law 过渡性法律
transitive regime 过渡政权
transitory n./a. 临时性诉讼,可选择管辖区的诉讼(见 transitory action)/过渡的,有转移力的;中间的
transitory action 可选择管辖区的诉讼,（美）追身诉讼(指在美国随着被告到任何地方都能提起的诉讼,与只能在案件发生的某个特定地方才能提起的当地诉讼 local action 相对而言)
transitory provision 临时规定
translate an ideal into reality 把理想变为现实
translate an instruction (a policy) into action 使指示(政策)化为行动

translation n. 1.转移 2.调任 3.翻译,译本,译文
translative a. 权利让渡的;转移的;翻译的
translocation n. 迁移;移动;易位
transmigrant n. 移居者(人或动植物);移民(尤指自甲国移居至乙国,而在丙国暂时居留的人)
transmigrate v. 移居,移民
transmigration n. 移居,移民
transmigrator n. 移居者,移民
transmissible (=trasmissive;transmittible) a. 1.可传送的,可传达的 2.可遗传的,可传染的
transmission n. 1.(=transmittal) 传递,传达,传送 2.遗传,传染 3.(国际私法中的)转致
transmission belt theory 传送带理论(见 hypodermic needle theory;bullet theory)
transmission commission 传递手续费
transmission control protocal (TCP) 传输控制协议(网络体系结构传输层的一种协议)
transmit v. 传送,传给;留传,遗传;传播,传染;播送,(发送)信号,发报
transmitter n. 传送者,传达者
transmute v. 使变形;使变质(后均接 into)
transnational a. 超越国界的;超国家的;跨国的
transnational agreement 跨国协议
transnational company (或 corporation) 跨国公司
Transnational Corporation Center of the United Nations Organization 联合国跨国公司中心
transnational crime 跨国犯罪
transnational enterprises 跨国企业
transnational law 跨国法(又译:超国法,指制约跨国交易关系的各种法律)
transnational operation 跨国经营
transnationalism n. 跨国主义
transoceanic canal 通洋运河
transparency principle 透明原则
transplantation of organs/tissues 人体器官和组织的移植
Transparency International 透明国际(面

对全球化进程中的国际性大规模腐败活动出现的一种非政府组织。它们针对国际经济交易中的可疑现象进行研究,对证据确凿的腐败行为予以揭露,同时提出防范和解决国际腐败活动的建议,起到了国家与政府间组织难以发挥的作用)

transpersonal a. 超人格的

transpersonalism n. 超人格主义[赖特布鲁 Gustar Radbruch(1878—1949)的政治哲学中的一个很重要的组成部分]

transpire v. 泄漏,被人知道,发生;使排出,使发散

transplanation of organ 器官移植

transport n./v. 1.运输,运送;输送 2.流放犯 3.交通系统 4.运输船,运输舰;运输机/输,运送,流放,放逐,处以流刑

transport agent 货物过境或转口代理人

transport broker 运输经纪人,承运商

transport contractor 运输承包商,承运人

transport court 运输法院

transport document 运输单据

Transport International Routier 《国际公路车辆运输规则》

transport law 运输法

transport licensing 运输许可证颁发

transport operation 运输业务

transport service 运送服务,运输服务

transport tribunal 运输法庭

transportable a. 可运输的,可运送的,可移动的;应处以流放的

transportation n. 1.运输,输送,交通业 2.运输工具,运输费用 3.流刑,放逐 4.车票,船票

transportation for life 终身流放

transportation insurance 运输保险

transportation permit 转运许可证

transportation to a penal colony 移解至作为惩罚的殖民地,流放到服刑的殖民地

transportee n. 被放逐者

transporter n. 运输者,运送者;运输机,运送装置

Transports Aeriens Intercontinentaux (法)洲际航空运输公司

transports gratuitously 免费运送

transsexual n. 变性者,性转换者(心理渴望转变为异性者)(指出生时具有一种性别特征的人,经受或准备经受性改变的外科手术。见 sex reassignment)

transsexualism n. 异性模仿欲

transumpt n. (法律文件或著作的)抄本

transvestism n. 异装癖,异性模仿欲(指恋物症 fetishism 的一种特殊形式,表现对异性衣着的喜爱,反复出现穿戴异性服饰的强烈欲望并付诸行动。由此可引起性兴奋。这种行为受抑制时可引起明显的不安情绪。病人并不要求改变自身性别的解剖生理特征。一般无刑事责任能力。见 fetishism;sexual perversion)

trap n./v. 诡计,圈套,埋伏,捕获机,陷阱;(英)侦探,警察/诱捕;用计陷害,设陷阱;使受限制,使陷入困境

trapdoors n. 活动天窗(计算机犯罪手段之一,指一种由程序开发者有意安排的指令语句,利用人为设置窗口侵入系统,在程序差错、修改或再启动时通过这些窗口访问有关程序)

trash n. 废物,垃圾;糟粕,废话(小型无价值的杂物或作品)

trauma n. (因受外部打击)造成身体上的伤害;精神上的创伤;(过去事件造成)严重的精神损伤

travaux forcés 强制劳动,苦役

travaux préparatoires (法)(一项协议、立法或国际条约的)准备性文件

travel n. 游历,旅行;游行推销货物

travel accident 旅行事故

travel accident insurance 旅行平安保险,旅行意外事故险

travel agent 旅行业者,旅行社职员

travel bureau 旅行社

travel document 旅行证件

travel on home leave 探亲假

travel on official business 出差

traveling merchant 旅行商,巡回商

traveling psychosis 旅途性精神病(指在长途旅行中发生的急性应激反应,可能由于交通工具拥挤、饮食、睡眠不好、性格胆小、情绪紧张所致,应激源消除后一月内可自然缓解。如持续存在则要考虑为应激诱发了内因性精神障碍。一般为无刑

事责任能力)
traveling time 在途时间
traveller (=traveler) n. 旅行者,旅游者；旅客,旅行推销员
traveller's check (cheque) 旅行支票
traveller's circular credit 旅行信用证
travelling allowance 旅行津贴,出差津贴
traversable a. 可抗辩的；可否认的；可反驳的
traversable presentment 可抗辩的公诉
traverse n./v. 1.抗辩；否认,反驳 2.反对,阻止,妨碍 3.仔细检查,详细讨论/反驳,抗辩,否认
traverse jury 裁决陪审团；小陪审团
traverse of indictment 否认控诉(指对起诉书中主要事实与罪名的否认)
traverse upon a traverse 对反驳的再反驳
traverser n. 抗辩人,否认者,反驳者
traversing note 否认状,抗辩书
travesty of justice 枉法
trawl n. 海上捕鱼的大口拖网,排钩
trawler n. 拖网船；拖网捕鱼的船；拖网捕鱼的人
treacherous a. 奸诈的；背叛的；背信弃义的；危险的,叛逆的
treacherous acts 背叛行为
treachory n. 背叛；变节；背信弃义；叛国,叛逆
tread under foot 蹂躏；虐待；践踏
treadmill n. (古时用以惩罚囚犯的)踏车
treason n. 1.叛逆,通敌,叛国罪 2.不忠,背信,叛国
treason felony (英)叛国重罪,叛逆重刑罪
treasonable a. 犯叛国罪的,叛国的,叛逆的；不忠的,背信的
treasonable activities 叛国活动
treasonable misdemeanours 叛国轻罪
treasonable speech 叛国言论
treasonable treaty 卖国条约
treasr (=treasurer) n. 司库会计,财务,掌管金钱的人
treasure n. 埋藏物；金银财宝；财富；珍品
treasure house 宝库,宝藏室
treasure-trove 1.由地下或他处掘出的无主财宝 2.有价值的发现

treasurer n. 会计,司库,财务,掌管钱财者；总会计师；(大写)(苏格兰和英格兰的)财政部
treasury n. 国库,金库；宝库,仓库；资金,(国家或机关)所拥有的款项；(大写)(英)财政部
Treasury Bench (英)首席财政委员席位(指下议院议长右侧的第一个席位,坐该席位者为首席财政委员)
treasury bill 国库券；(美国短期)国库券；(见 treasury securities)；(英)财政部证券
treasury bond (美国长期)国库券(见 treasury securities)
treasury certificate (美国)国库券(指一年以下的短期公债,票面额自 1000 至 100000 美元)
treasury circular 库务通告
treasury counsel (英)财政部法律顾问(指财政部设的法律顾问处的成员,都是一些行业的高级律师)
Treasury Department (美)财政部
treasury note (美国中期)国库券(见 treasury securities)；(英国财政部发行的)证券
treasury securities 国库证券[指合法发行后由公司买回作为公司资产或作为公司资产存入国库以备将来用途。国库证券又称为政府证券(government securities 或 government stock),这是由财政部发行的计息政府债券,用以弥补政府预算赤字。一般上市国库证券有国库券(treasury bill)、国库中期券(treasury note)和国库长期券(treasury bond)三类。投资人可从银行或证券经销商处买到,其计息收入只需交纳联邦所得税。见 treasury stock]
treasury share 见 treasury stock
treasury solicitor (英)政府法务官
treasury stock 库存股票,回笼股票(指公司将它的股票,在发行后将其买回,作为库存财产,未被认购或未发行的股票不被视为库存股票。有些州取消这种分类,而把这类股票看作已经授权但未发行的股票。又称为 treasury security；treasury share；reacquired stock；retired stock)
treasury warrant 国库付款令状,国库支

付命令书

treat v. 1.看待,对待,视为 2.处理;探讨 3.交涉,谈判,商议,款待 4.论述 5.治疗

treater n. 谈判者

treaties and treaties power (美)条约与(缔结)条约权(条约是指由两国政府正式签订和批准的协议,以及由两个以上国家达成并受国际法约束的国际协议。联邦最高法院在确定条约的外延和解释条约方面所起作用甚微。联邦最高法院罕有认定任何条约违宪。联邦最高法院认为:政府部门制定国家外交政策应不受司法监督。美国联邦宪法第2条第2节规定赋予总统缔结条约的权力,但应接受参议院出席会议者2/3的同意或认可,并禁止各州缔结条约,并在第六条中宣布条约和联邦宪法、联邦政府法律一样都是全国最高法律,对各州均有约束力)

Treaties in Force (美)《有效条约》(1950年起发行的国务院的年度出版物)

treaties on the federal level (美)联邦级条约

treatise n. 论文;专题论著(指一个广泛、主要、缜密细致的专题论著,亦称 Learned treatise);大型综合性有关法律主题的书

Treatise of Human Nature 《人性契约论》[法理学家大卫·休谟(David Hume)1740年的专著]

treatment n. 处置,处理;待遇;治疗;论述

treatment for drug abuse 惩治毒品滥用

treatment of aliens 外国人待遇

treatment of disputes 争议处理,处理纠纷

treatment of offenders 罪犯的待遇

treatment tribunals 罪犯待遇裁判庭(一种设想中的机构)

treaty (15世纪)1.条约(指经过正式签署、批准和依附两国之间或两个主权政体之间的协议),国际协议(指两个或两个以上国家以书面形式签订的协议,并按国际法执行。亦称 accord; convention; covenant; declarations; pact。见 executive agreement) 2.合同,协议[指两个承保或保险单之间的合同或协议,根据保险法提供合约再保险(treaty ensurance)] 3.(经过协商的)协议,合约(指两个私人之间的合同,

合约或协议)

(the) treaty body 条约机构

treaty clause (宪法法)缔结条约权的条款(指美国联邦宪法第2条第2款赋予总统缔结条约的权力还需经参议院的咨询或参加缔结条约会议的参议员2/3的赞成或同意)

treaty concluded with a view to war 为进行战争缔结的条约

treaty contracts (= contractual treaty) 契约性条约

Treaty Documents (美)条约文件[以前又称参(议)院行政文件 Senate Executive Documents]

Treaty Establishing the Europe Economic Community (Treaty of Rome)1957 《建立欧洲经济共同体条约》(《罗马条约》)(1957年)

treaty in operation 现行条约,生效的条约

treaty in simplified form 简式条约

treaty intended to establish permanent condition 旨在建立一种永久状态的条约

treaty matching 条约搭配(指投资者将基础条约与第三方条约中的争端解决方式混合搭配,避开两个条约中对己不利的部分,仅留下有利于自己的部分)

treaty obligation 条约义务

treaty of alliance 同盟条约

treaty of amity and commerce 友好通商条约

treaty of cession 割让条约

Treaty of Commerce and Navigation 通商航海条约,商务及航海协定

treaty of equality 平等条约

treaty of extradition 引渡条约

treaty of friendship 友好条约

treaty of friendship, alliance and mutual assistance 友好同盟互助条约

treaty of friendship and commerce 友好通商条约

treaty of inequality 不平等条约

treaty of mutual defense 共同防御条约

treaty of mutual non-aggression 互不侵犯条约

treaty of peace 和平条约,和约

Treaty of Rome 《罗马条约》
Treaty of Versailles 《凡尔赛和约》(结束第一次世界大战时 1919 年 6 月 28 日在法国凡尔赛宫签订的对德和约)
Treaty on Antarctica 《南极条约》(1959 年 12 月 1 日在华盛顿签订的条约,规定南极专为和平目的而使用)
Treaty on Europe Union 1992 (Maestilicht Treaty) 《1992 年关于欧盟条约》(《马斯特里赫条约》)
Treaty on International Commercial Law (Montevideo, 1889) 1889 年关于国际商法的蒙得维的亚条约
Treaty on International Commercial Territorial Law (Montevideo, 1940) 1940 年关于国际陆地贸易法的蒙得维的亚条约
Treaty on International Procedural Law (Montevideo, 1940) 1940 年关于国际诉讼法的蒙得维的亚条约
treaty on legal assistance 司法协助条约
treaty on the non-proliferation of nuclear weapons 防止核扩散条约
treaty override 推翻协定
treaty participant 条约参加国
treaty particulars 合同摘要,合约要点
treaty port 按(不平等)条约开辟的商埠,通商口岸
treaty power 条约权,签订条约权,缔约权,缔结条约权(指总统在宪法上给予其缔结条约的权力,同时还需获得参议院的意见与同意)(见 treaty clause)
treaty ratification 条约批准
treaty reinsurance 合约分保;合约再保险
treaty right 条约上的权利
treaty series 条约汇编
treaty wording 合同文本,合约文本
treaty-making a. 缔约的,立约的
treaty-making incapacity 无权缔约
treaty-making power 缔约权
treble compensatory damages 三重应予以赔偿的损害
treble damages 三重损害赔偿(指在某些诉讼中对于严重使人沮丧的伤害行为将给予三倍的损害赔偿)
trebucket n. 见 cucking stool

tree n. (古时)绞架,绞首台
trench v. 侵犯,侵占;接近,近似
trench sb.'s right 侵犯某人的权利
trench upon plagiarism 接近剽窃
trespass n./v. 1.侵犯(行为)[普通法上的一种犯罪行为,(侵犯财产,侵犯人身,侵犯土地)受侵犯的一方可提起诉讼索取赔偿]2.侵害行为;侵害诉讼 3.非法侵入,侵犯,侵害/非法侵入(他人土地或住宅),侵犯(权利);犯罪,违犯(与 against 连用)
trespass *ab initio* 从开始便侵犯(指一个人经法律准许进入他人土地,但进入以后,滥用权利干了犯法的事,这样在他进入时的合法,也当成为不合法,犯了侵犯他人土地的罪行)
trespass by placing things on land 留置物件于他人土地上的侵犯行为
trespass by remaining on land 停留他人土地内的侵犯行为
trespass by wrongful entry 不法进入的侵犯行为
trespass *de bonis asportatis* 取走财物的侵权之诉
trespass for entering on land 侵入土地的侵犯行为
trespass for *mesne* profits (附加于收回非法侵占不动产之诉中的)追回非法占有期间所得收益之诉
trespass for personal harm 人身伤害侵犯行为
trespass for taking away chattel 取走动产的侵犯行为
trespass on the case 间接侵害诉讼[亦称 action on the case 或 action on case,其侵害因几种情况产生:①是间接和以后发生的,而不是直接和立即发生的;②并非来自暴力(或如果使用暴力,则所涉及之事不是有形财产);③来自不作为、疏忽或在履行合同中未使用正当技巧]
trespass *quare clausum fregit* 因非法侵占土地等造成损害赔偿的诉讼
trespass to chattel 侵害动产行为,侵物行为
trespass to goods 侵物行为,非法占物行为,对财物的侵犯行为

trespass to land 对土地的侵犯行为
trespass to person and property 对人身或财产权的侵犯行为
trespass to try title （美）请求因非法所造成的损害赔偿并收回所侵占不动产的诉讼
trespass upon the residence 侵入住宅罪
trespass vi et armis 使用暴力或武器的侵犯行为
trespasser n. 侵占他人土地者；侵入他人住宅者；侵害者；不法侵入者
trespasser *ab initio* 从开始便不法侵入者
tret n. 添头（指补偿损耗的添量）
tria capita （罗马法上的）公民权，自由权，家庭权
triable a. 可裁判的，可审讯（审理）的；可试验的
trial n. 1.审问，审判；审理，审讯 2.试用，试验，考验
trial a last resort 终审判决
trial argue 审判论点（论据）
trial at bar 会审（指英国高等法院的中央刑事法庭由三名法官会同陪审团一起审判较为重大的案件的审判）
trial at *nisi prius* 独审（指由一名法官主持有陪审员参加的审判）
trial attorney 诉讼代理人，专门出庭办理诉讼事件的律师（亦作 litigation lawyer）
trial balance 试算表，总账对照表
trial balancing 试算平衡
trial bar (=trial at bar) （高等法院合议庭的）会审
trial before a judge alone （英）（高等法院的）独任法官的审判
trial before a master （英）（高等法院的）司法主事官审判
trial before a master （或 **a judge**）**with assessors** （英）（高等法院的）一名司法主事官（或一名法官）会同几名技术法律顾问的审判
trial by battle 决斗裁判
trial by certificate 根据证书的审判
trial by compurgation 发誓的审判，根据保证的审判
trial by debt(s) 记录债务
trial by default 缺席审判

trial by fire 凭火决狱（一种古老的裁决方式）
trial by grand assize （英）大巡回法庭审判（指英国以前允许用权利状的特殊审判形式）
trial by inspection or examination 究问式审判
trial by jury （英美法）陪审审判，陪审团的审理［指由陪审员会同法官的审判。陪审团制度源于英国普通法，又从英国移植到美国并在美国生根发芽，茁壮成长。陪审团参加审判的权利由美国联邦宪法第三、第六、第七以及第十四修正案予以保障。因此，陪审团不受立法废止的影响。而英国则没有此种宪法保障，议会可以随时废止陪审参加审判，历史上曾经有过。案件的事实通常由陪审团而非由法官来裁决的审判。在美国，任何青少年的刑事诉讼只要可能判 6 个月以上的刑罚或在联邦民事案件中所涉争议在 20 美元以上（美国联邦宪法第七修正案），美国联邦宪法便确认由陪审团参加审判，各州的宪法规定提供同样保障］
trial by ordeal 问神裁判（古代一种迷信的审讯方法）
trial by pais 陪审团的审判
trial by production of chatter 出示特许状的审判
trial by record 依笔录审判（指以法庭记录作为裁判根据的审判）
trial by witness 依证人审判（指无陪审团参加而凭证人作证的审判）
trial counsel （美）1.代理当事人出庭的律师（此词与代理当事人提出上诉的律师相对而言）；2.（军事法）指代表政府提起刑事诉讼追究刑事责任人的律师。
trial court 审判法庭；初审法院
trial *de novo* 重审（指上级法院对下级法院所判决的案件全部推翻，重新审判）
trial division 审判庭，初审庭
trial docket (of the court) 法庭审判日程表，法院待审案件清单
trial execution 审判执行
trial for treason 因叛国罪受审
trial group 审判小组，审判组织

trial in camera 秘密审讯
trial judge 初审法官
trial jurisdiction 审判权,审判管辖权
trial jurisdiction under military law 军法审判权
trial jury 小陪审团,(由12人组成的)陪审团
trial justice 审判法官(指美国下级法院的法官)
trial lawyer 专门出庭辩护的律师
trial litigation 审理诉讼(其实际含义是初审案件一般由初审法院审理)
trial meeting 审判大会
trial of case 案件的审理
trial of fact 事实审
trial of final instance 终审
trial of first instance 初审,一审
trial of law 法律审
trial of second instance 二审
trial of war criminal 审判战犯
trial on appeal 上诉审
trial on indictment 刑事审判
trial on the merits 实体审
trial order 试购,试订购货单,试用订货,试用订单
trial *per pais* 由陪审团审理
trial period 试用期;受审期
trial practice courses 审判实践课程
trial procedure 审判程序
trial proceedings 审判程序
trial process 审理程序,审理进程
trial rate 试用率
trial rates 案件受审率
trial record 审判笔录
trial sale 试销
trial skills 审判技能
trial stage 审判阶段
trial supervision 审判监督
trial supervision procedure 审判监督程序
trial tactics 审理策略
trial without pleading 无辩护的审判
trial-setting memorandum 庭审安排备忘录
triarchy n. 实行三头政治的政府(或国家)
tribadia n. 女子同性恋爱;女子相奸
tribadism n. 女子同性恋爱;女子相奸

tribal area 部落地区
tribal contract 部落合同
Tribal Court （美)部落法院[指根据《印第安儿童福利法》(Indian Child Welfare Act)具有子女监护管辖权的一个法院。它是印第安人刑事法院(Court of Indian Offenses)设立并依部落习惯法运作的一个法院或授权子女监护权程序的一个部落行政机构。部落法院是由一些部落成员组成,通常设在部落居住地,并根据部落特点从一个部落转移到另一部落。它不属于任何州的司法体系的部分,或多或少地类似于异域民族的司法体制]
tribal land （美)部落土地(指印第安人居住地的一部分,它不是配置给印第安人个人的,也不是由印第安人个人占有的而是该部落的公有土地)
tribal law 部落法
tribun （古罗马的)保民官
tribunal n. 1.法庭,裁判所 2.裁判,批判 3.法官席,裁判席,审判员席
tribunal clerk 法庭书记员
tribunal *correctionel* 轻罪法庭
Tribunal *de Grande*, *Instance* 初审法院(相当于 first instance court),大审法庭(法国民事系统的法院,按1958年12月22日颁布的民事诉讼法典规定,各行政区设大审法庭,由审判长1人、法官2人和检察官1人组成)
tribunal *de première instance* (法)初级(审)法院
tribunal *des conflits* (法)确定管辖权法院;冲突法庭(指解决普通法院与行政法院两系统之间出现抵触问题的法庭)
tribunal for the protection of economic development 经济建设保护庭
tribunal of arbitration 仲裁法庭,公断法庭
tribunal of cassation (法国)最高(上诉)法院
tribunal of economic adjudication 经济审判庭
tribunal of inquiry 调查庭
Tribunal of International Composition in the Saar 萨尔国际和解法庭
Tribunal of Reform (埃及)改革裁判庭

tribunal without jurisdiction 无管辖权的法庭
tribunaux de commerce （法国）商业法庭
tribune n. 1.(古罗马的)护民官;支持公众要求的政治家 2.法官席,裁判所(=tribunal)
tribunus plebes 保民官(又译护民官)
tributary a./n. 进贡的,附庸的;从属的/进贡国,附庸国,属国,进贡者
tributary state 进贡国,附属国,从属国
tribute n. 贡金,贡物,贡税(指为交纳贡金而收的税);纳贡义务,纳贡地位,臣属地位,勒索款项,礼物;礼品,颂词,歌颂
tribute and tax 负税
tribute-state 贡税国家
trick n. 1.奸诈,欺诈手段 2.幻术,恶作剧 3.特别的习惯 4.(俗)少女,小孩 5.(俚)嫖客,妓女与嫖客的交易
tricker n. 诈欺者,恶作剧者
trickery n. 诡计,奸计,诈骗,欺骗
trickiness n. 诡计多端;(工作、问题等)棘手,复杂,微妙
trickish a. 狡猾的,诡诈的,惯用诈术的
trickster n. 骗子,欺骗者
tricky politician 奸诈的政客
tried a. 已经审讯的,已经查验的
triennial a. 每三年一次的,持续三年的
triennial election 每三年一次的选举
triennial variable premium 三年期保险费调整制
trier n. 1.试验者,检验者;检验用具 2.审问者;法官;(英)决定陪审员应否回避的裁定员(又称 trior);(判定陪审员所提出的异议能否成立的)裁定员;审判员
trier of fact 事实审理者,审理事实的司法官(指陪审团审理中的陪审团或法官审理中的法官评估案件中的证据并决定事实)
trier of the case 审理案件的司法官
Triffin Dilemma 特里芬难题(指美元在布雷顿森林体系中的清偿和信心之间的矛盾)
trifling expense 很少费用
trigamist n. 有三夫之妇;有三妻之夫;结婚三次者
trigamous a. 有三个丈夫的,有三个妻子的;结过三次婚的

trigamy n. 一夫三妻;一妻三夫;三次结婚
trigger v./n. 激起,引起(off);扣扳机开枪,发射/扳机,触发器
trigger man 开枪行凶的人
trilateral agreement 三边协定
trilogy n. (小说、音乐、戏曲)三部曲,(古希腊连续出演的)三部悲剧
trimester n. 每三个月;(一年分三学期制的)一学期
trimmer n. 整修者;(政治上)两面讨好的人,骑墙派,见风使舵者
trimoda neccessitas （前诺曼底英格兰的）土地三重负担(指附加在土地上的服兵役、捐税和修筑城堡、桥梁义务的三重负担)
TRIMs 《与贸易有关的投资措施协议》
Trinity House （海商法）(英)航务管理所,领航公司(1514年被允准培训,发领航证和正式管理领港工作。该领航公司还设有援助人员帮助领航,比如观察到英国海岸线的灯塔和浮标。见 Elden Brethern)
Trinity Master （英)海商促进公会的长辈会员(该公会有长辈会员和后辈会员之分,在海事法庭审理含有航运技术问题的案件时,会派两名长辈会员作法庭的技术顾问)
trinity sittings （英)(伦敦和米德尔萨克斯受理上诉的)高等法院的开庭期(自降灵节周后的星期四起至8月8日止)
trinity term （英普通法院的四个开庭期之一)三位一体节开庭期(起自5月22日,止于6月12日)
trinity theory of governmental powers 政府职权的三位一体论,统治权三位一体论
trinoda necessitas 三重负担(撒克逊法规定的拥有土地的人负有三种义务:修路;筑城堡;抗入侵之敌)
trip n./v. 1.摔倒,绊倒 2.失足,差错,过失 3.旅行 4.倒手买卖(指在交易所中同时买进和卖出同一商品或证券以达到获利的目的)/使犯错误,发觉(某人)错误,失误,差错
trip up witness 发现(觉)证人的差错
tripartite a./n. 一式三份(文件)中的一份;第二副本/一式三份的,三重的,三倍的,第

二副本的
tripartite agreement　三方协议
tripartite certificate　一式三份的证书
tripartite indenture　三方合同
tripartite trust receipt　三方的信托收据
triple derivative suit　三重代表诉讼（见double derivative suit）
TRIPs Action Network (TAN)　与贸易有关的知识产权行动网，TRIPs行动网（2001年成立）
triumph n./v.　（古罗马）凯旋仪式，凯旋，胜利，成功，成就/获胜，击败（over）；狂欢庆祝胜利
triumphalist scenario　赢家模式
triumvir n.　（古罗马）三执政官之一；三头政治中的执政者之一
triumvirate n.　1.(古罗马）三执政；三执政官的职位，the first triumvirate 即公元前60年的庞培（Pompey）、尤里乌斯·恺撒（Julius Caeasor）和克拉苏（Crassus）的三人执政。The second triumvirate 即公元前43年的马克·安洛尼（Mark Anlony）、屋大维（Octavius）和雷必达（Lepidus）的三人执政 2.三头政治，三党政治 3.三人一组，三位一体
trivia n.　琐事
trivial matters　无关紧要的事情
trivial offence　轻微过失，小过失
Trojan Horse　特洛伊木马（破坏计算机程序的一种形式，它提供任何隐蔽的、用户不希望或为用户所不知道的程序功能，其中包括一些用户不知的未经授予的代码，这些额外功能往往有害。特洛伊木马程序与病毒的区别是，前者不依附于任何载体而独立存在，后者则依附于其他载体且具有传染性。见 device bomb；logic bomb；rabbit；worm 等）
troll v./n.　网上招骂（Troll，作动词是钓鱼的意思，在网络中指发表某种侮辱性言论挑起骂战，等待别人的攻击性回复，从而获得快感。Troll 还有一个意思是斯堪的纳维亚神话中一种长相丑陋、爱恶作剧、令人讨厌的巨人，与那些找骂的人有相似之处，因此也被引申来形容那些人。在网上回 trolls 的帖则被称为"feed the trolls"，即给 trolls 喂食。Troll 的存在对网络公共空间是破坏性的。他们的留言会引起很多人回帖，甚至会有情绪激动者采用谩骂的方式回敬，这些人被称为"trollhunter"。这些行为正中 trolls 的下怀，使他们获得被骂的快乐，从而更加积极地 trolling)
troop withdrawal　撤军
trouble n.　困难，烦恼，烦扰；纷争，强扰
trouble clearing　排除故障
trouble maker　闹事者，惹是生非的人
trouble spot　纠纷地区，容易出故障处，事故多发（地）点
trouble-making activity　捣乱活动
trouble-shooting database　解答问题数据库
Troubled Asset Relief Program　（美）《问题资产解救方案》[指2008年美国的"紧急经济稳定法案"授权财政部通过《问题资产解救方案》来收购问题住房抵押贷款和其他资产，其救助对象限定为美国有"重要经营"（significant operation）的金融机构]
troubler n.　捣乱者，闹事者
troubleshooter n.　解决纠纷者，调解人；（政治、外交、商业等方面）解决麻烦问题的能手；(机器)等故障修理员
troublesome cases　令人烦恼的案子
troublous a.　（古）骚乱的，多事故的
troublous times　乱世
trove n.　发现物；收藏物
trover n.　追索非法占用；（对非法占用或使用动产者所提起的）损害赔偿诉讼；动产侵占之诉讼
trover and conversion　动产冒认与返还之诉，动产侵占与返还之诉
truancy n.　旷课；旷职，玩忽职守
truancy officer　（美）托管官员[指负责执行委托管理特定年龄（16岁以下）的少年入学上课的法律的官员。亦称 truant officer, attendance officer]
truant officer　同 truancy officer
truce n.　停战，休战；停止争执；休止，中止
truce agreement　休战条约
truce negotiation　停战谈判
truck　1.货车，卡车 2.(俗)垃圾，废物；胡说 3.交易，买卖 4.作为工资的实物

trucksystem 实物工资制,购货券工资制
true a. 真实的,确实的;准确的,可靠的,真正的,忠实的
true and first inventor 首先发明者
true bill (大陪审团签署的)正式起诉书(指大陪审团表示认为提出的犯罪指控有充分证据而签署的起诉书)
true claim 真正的索赔
true class action 真正的集团诉讼[美《联邦民事诉讼程序》第23条将集团诉讼分为三类,当集团成员之间具有"不可分割的"(joint)或者"共同的"(common)权利或享有诉讼第一位权利人拒绝行使其权利的第二位权利,则可运用真正的(true)集团诉讼;如集团成员之间权利是"单独的"(several),且诉讼目的是得到影响特定相关财产的判决,那么允许使用"混合"(hybrid)集团诉讼;第三种则为"虚假的"(spurious)集团诉讼,同样要求集团成员之间的权利关系寻求共同救济 common relief 时,则可用假托的集团诉讼]
true condition 真实条件
true conflict 真实冲突
true consent 真诚的同意,真实的同意
true copy 正式抄本,准确的副本
true discount 实在贴现,实在折扣
true heir 合法继承人,真正继承人
true lease 正式租赁
true owner 合法所有人,真正的所有人
true rate of interest 实际利率
true reserve 实际准备金
true reversion 未来所有权(又译:分剩权)(指英国普通法在土地上创设"将来利益"的一种制度)
true statement 真实供词;正确陈述
true to specimen 与样品一致,与样品质量相同
true verdict 公正的裁决
true-blue a. (对党派等)非常忠诚的,坚定的
true-born a. 嫡出的,十足的
truism n. 老生常谈,陈词滥调
trull n. 妓女,娼妓
Truman Declaration (美)《杜鲁门宣言》
Truman Democrats 杜鲁门民主党人(其观点即美国是一个"责无旁贷的国家"。他们既相信美国力量的榜样,也相信美国道义榜样的力量,同时也拥护美国军队是帮助实现这个国家目标的重要工具的观点)
trump n./v. 1.王牌,最后手段,最后良策 2.(俗)妇人,时时准备帮助别人的人/优于,胜于,击败
trump up 1.(以欺骗为目的的)捏造 2.鼓吹
trump up a charge against sb. 捏造某人的罪名
trumped-up a. 捏造的
trumped-up case 诬告案件
trumped-up charges 诬告
trumped-up excuse 捏造口实,捏造借口
trumpery n./a. 无价值物;垃圾,废物;废话/无聊的;虚假的,欺诈的,虚有其表的,浅薄的
truncated arbitration 缺员仲裁
truncation n. 裁决;切掉顶端;压缩、缩略
truncheon n./v. 警棒,警棍,权杖(用以作为权威标志的手杖)/用警棒打
truss v. 捆绑,扎住,捆住,束缚
truss up a criminal 捆绑一个罪犯
trusser n. 捆绑者,捆扎者
trust n. 1.托拉斯,操纵某一行业的组合 2.信托财产,信托物;业务信誉 3.相信,信任;委托;信托;照管 4.(受托付人可支配应用的)信托或托管财产 5.责任,职责
trust account 信托账单,信托账户,托管财产
Trust Act (美)《受托管理法》
trust *ad litem* 由法院指定的受托人
trust agent 信托代理商
trust and agency funds 信托与代理基金
trust and investment business 信托投资业务
trust assets 信托资产
trust bond 信用债券
trust business 信托业
trust buster 反托拉斯能手(指负责推行反托拉斯法以解散托拉斯的政府官员)
trust certificate 信托证书
trust company 信托公司

trust corporation (=public trust) (英)公益信托社(团)(指依据法院授权或公益受托人法例规定,接受慈善、教育等公益事业的信托的受托管理人或团体,它与为私人利益服务的信托 private trust 有别)
trust deed 信托契据;委托书
trust depositts 信托存证,信托存款
trust estate 受信托管理的房地
trust for relief of poverty 济贫信托
trust for sale 土地变卖委托,信托买卖
trust for the advancement of education 促进教育的信托
trust for the advancement of religion 促进宗教事业的信托
trust fund 信托基金,有价证券或财产信托资金(指受托人或受托组织按照信托之目的和要求为另一人或组织管理的财产和款项)
trust indenture 信托契据
trust instrument 信托证书;信托文件;信托文契,信托投资
Trust Law 《信托法》
trust legacy 信托遗产
trust money 信托款项,托管金,委托金
trust of housing loan bonds 住宅贷款信托债券
trust of imperfect obligation 不受法律拘束的信托
trust of perfect obligation 受法律拘束的信托
trust of the settlement 财产处分信托(英)财产授予信托
trust possession 信托占有
trust process (美)扣押债务人财产交给管财人的手续
trust property 信托财产,托管财产
trust receipt 信托收据
trust res 信托基金;信托财产[可以是动产或不动产,受托人对其拥有普通法上的所有权(legal title)]
trust service corporation 信托服务公司
trust state 信托状况(指被抵押的财产所有权在偿清债务之前已转让给受托人,亦称 trust theory jurisdiction)
trust stock company 信托股份公司
trust territory 托管地,托管领土
trust theory jurisdiction 信托理论管辖(见 trust state)
trust to the use 受益权信托
trust under will 依遗嘱设立的信托,遗嘱信托
trust-busting 推行反托拉斯以解散托拉斯
trust-like device 近似信托的方式
trustee n. (17世纪)受托人,受托管理人[指一个处于受托或有信托关系,特别是按照法律规定拥有信托财产、执行信托业务,并将所得利益交与受益人的人。总之,受托人的义务或职责是将全部债务和不能合法投资的证券转换为现金,再将这些现金投资到适当的有价证券之中,以保护并维持信托财产,并保证这些运作是唯一可以获得收益的,才符合信托文件(trust instrument)中所包含的指导精神]/(1818年)1.担任受托人 2.将人或财产交托给受托人 3.指定(一个人)作为受托人(通常为破产不动产的受托人,以便阻止债务人收集所欠钱财"moneys")4.扣押债务人在第三方手上的财产
Trustee Act 《受托人法》(指信托制度的母国英国并无直接的以"信托法"为名的法律,而是以《受托人法》作为信托的基本法,所以说受托人是信托制度的核心。信托法的完善很大程度上是受托人制度的完善,而受托人法律地位又是受托人制度的完善,受托人法律地位又是受托人制度的核心,它决定着信托财产的归属,决定着委托人的原始目的可否达到,决定着受益人利益是否可以实现等信托关系中最重要的问题)
trustee ad litem 由法院指定的受托人
trustee bank 信托银行
trustee council 理事会
trustee de son tort 无权受托人(指未经授权便干预他人信托事务者)
trustee ex maleficio 有不法或欺诈行为的受托人
trustee for debenture holder 债券持有者的受托人
trustee for sale 售卖受托人
trustee in bankruptcy (法院指定的)破产

财产管理人,破产财产受托人
trustee of company 公司受托人
trustee power 托管国
trustee process 附有扣押债权的出庭令
* *Trustee qua.* trustee (that is in his character as trustee) is not liable. 作为受托人,受托人是没有责任的(但作为个人则是有责任的)。
trusteeship n. 1.托管制度;托管人的职责、地位 2.(联合国的)托管;联合国托管的地区
trusteeship agreement 托管协定
Trusteeship Council (联合国)托管理事会
trusteeship system 托管制度
trustify v. 组成托拉斯;形成托拉斯
trustless a. 不可信任的,不可靠的;不信任的;怀疑的
trustor n. 财产授予者,信托人(常用 settlor),(交付财产)信托者
trustworthy a. 值得信赖的,可信任的,可靠的
trusty n. 1.可信任的人 2.模范囚犯(指因犯表现良好而被给予特别权益者)
truth n. 1.真实,真相;事实 2.真实性,确实 3.诚实,真理;(古)忠诚,誓言,订婚
truth claim 尚未被经验证实的假说
Truth in Lending 诚实贷款,贷款真实,借贷无虚言(见 Consumer Credit Protection Act)
Truth In-lending Act (= Consumer Credit Protection Act) (美)《诚实贷款法》;《诚实借出法》;《租借中诚实法》
(the) truth, the whole truth, and nothing but truth 所说全是事实,绝无谎言(证人在法庭上作誓言时的常用语)
truth-in-lending form 真实借贷表
truthful a. 真实的,说实话的,诚实的
truthless a. 不忠实的,不可靠的,不守信的,虚伪的,不说实话的
try v. 1.试,试行;试验,试用,试图 2.审问,审判,审理(案件)3 考验 4.解决(争执、问题)
try a case 审理案件,审判
try out for 竞争(位置、会员资格等)
trying n./a. 裁决,审判,审理/使人痛苦的,

难堪的,难处的
(a) trying person to deal with (一个)难以对付的人
(a) trying situation 难处境况,尴尬处境
tryst n./v. 通奸;约会;交媾;(苏格兰)市场,集市/和……约会;守约
tsar n. (俄史)(大)沙皇,皇帝;大权独揽人物,特权人物
tsarism n. (俄史)沙皇制;专制统治
Tsarist Russia 沙皇俄罗斯帝国
tsunami n.海啸
tu quoque "you also" (=a resort in kind) 同类方法,同样手段;指控一名同类罪行的原告(accusing an accuser of similar offense)
tub-man (英)享有特殊待遇的律师,享有特权的律师
tubman n. 塔卜曼(或译:财政律师)(指英国有权出席高等法院财政庭的大律师或在法院中有特殊地位的人),英国财政法院的首席律师
Tucker Act (美)《塔克法》(1887 年制定的涉及法院管辖的法律),《扩大权利诉讼法院管辖法》(美国国会为改变早期的权利申诉法院 court of claims 管辖权过窄而制定的法)
tug n. 拖船
tug hire 拖船租金
tuition program 讲授计划,教诲规划
tumble n. 见 cucking stool
tumbrel (tumbril) n. 1.肥料车 2.(1789 年法国大革命时)死刑犯押送车 3.见 cucking stool
tumult n. 1.骚乱,骚动,暴乱 2.喧嚣,激昂情绪
tumultuous a. 喧嚣的;骚乱的,凶猛的
tumultuous petitioning 请愿示威;闹事
tuna fisheries 金枪鱼渔业
tuning 调整,协调
turbary n. (在公地或私地上)挖掘泥炭权或割草作燃料权
turbationem n. 无秩,道德败坏;(指违反 "不公正的法"不会导致公愤或更大损害)
turf n. 赛马场,跑马场;都市中流氓地痞之势力范围
turkish law 土耳其法

turn v. 1.翻转,转动;改变 2.使回击;驱使,驱逐 3.使用,利用 4.使销售殆尽;得到,赚到;依赖 5.翻译;作成,形成 6.阻止
turn a deaf ear to 对……根本不听,对……置若罔闻
turn a quick profit 迅速获利
turn about 转身;反复思考;轮流,交替
turn down 拒绝,排斥
turn in 1.归还;移交;交出,上缴 2.告密
turn King's (Queen's 或 State's) evidence 供出对同犯不利的证据,共犯成为控告一方的证人
turn loose 1.释放;解放 2.使不受拘束 3.开枪,开火
turn on 取决于,视……而定,转视;拧开,开;反对,攻击;对……发怒
turn on a dispute 视争议而定;转向争议;放开争议
turn one's back on (upon) 别过脸去不理(以示轻视);背弃,违背,抛弃
turn out 逐出;驱逐;结果,判明为;罢工;培养,制造;出动;证明(是);生产出,产生出
turn out to be wrong 原来是错误的
(to) turn over 1.使打翻,使颠倒 2.营业额达到或做(一定数额的)买卖(turn over 5000 U.S.D a month) 3.周转(一定数额的商品) 4.移交,交给 5.把……逐渐翻查 6.翻阅(书籍) 7.反复考虑(turn a matter over in one's mind) 8.翻身,折腾(turn over in bed) 9.(胃)翻动;(心脏)惊怀 10.(机器等)转运 11.把(词,文章)接转到下一行(或栏,页)
turn over a new leaf 改过自新
turn screw at sb. 对某人施加压力
turn state's evidence 见 turn King's evidence
turn the tables 扭转局势,转变形势,转败为胜
turn thumbs down 表示反对,表示不赞成
turn to a right 诉讼收回占有物(指财产被霸占不能个人收回,必须凭借诉讼程序)
turn to advantage 使转化为有利
turn-key n. 监狱的看守;狱吏
turn-key contract 交钥匙合同(指公司通过与承包商签订固定价格的交钥匙合同,由后者承担工程延误的完工风险)
turn-key system 转匙系统,开机系统(电脑软件系统的又一称呼)
turn-or-pay contract 取否均付合同(项目公司与购买者之间订立的合同,约定购买者即使在货物或服务由于不可抗力或其他特殊原因不能提供的情况下也必须支付最少量的货款)
turn-pike (或 turnpike) n. 关卡;收通行税的路栅门;(旧时)收税栅,收税路;收税高速公路;(泛指)公路
turn-round n. 船只进港、卸货、装货、离岸全过程;回车场
turn-tail n. 逃跑者,懦夫
turncoat n. 脱党者,变节者,叛徒
turncoat witness 叛逆证人,知情人;反戈证人
turning point 转折点
turning state's evidence 见 state's evidence
turnkey contract 启钥契约(合同)(指订口成套特殊机器设备而签订的合同)
turnkey investment 启钥投资
turnkey job (由一个承包商)全部包办的工程
turnout n. (英)同盟罢工,同盟罢工者,集会的人群;出动,出动的人群
turnover (或 turn-over) n. 1.翻倒,翻转;倒转,周转 2.营业额,成交量;证券交易额 3.流动,流通,吞吐 4.人事变动
turnover of capital 资金周转
turnover rate 周转率,更换率
turnover tax 营业税,周转税
turnpike corporation (美)收税路公司
turnpike trust (英)收税路托管站
turpis causa (违背风俗习惯的或不能作为诉讼根据的)不道德的约因
turpis conditio 不法条件
turpis contractus 不道德合同(契约);非法合同(契约)
turpis personae 丧失名誉的人
turpitude n. 邪恶,可耻行为;卑鄙
turpitudo 污辱(又称事实上之破廉耻 infamia facti)
tussle n./v. 搏斗,剧烈的斗争,扭打;竞赛

或争论/搏斗,扭打;剧烈斗争
tussle with evil 与罪恶斗争
tutela 监护
tutela actio 监护的诉讼
tutela dativa 官选监护
tutela legitima 法定监护
tutela testamentaria 遗嘱指定的监护,遗嘱监护
tutelage n. 监护,保护;指导,教育;受保护期
tutelar (tutelary) a. 1.保护的;守护的 2.监护的,监护人的
tutelar authority 监护人的权力
* Tutius semper est errare acquitando quam in puniemdo; ex parte misericordiae quam ex parte justitiae. It is always safer to err in acquitting than in punishing; on the side of mercy than of strict justice. Thus arises the presumption of innocence, until conviction. 宁可错放,不可错惩,宁失公正,不失仁慈。
tutor n./v. 1.(英苏格兰和美路易斯安那州)监护人 2.家庭教师 3.保护人/教导,教授;保护;作……监护人
tutor *alienus* (英)外来监护人(指一外来人进占未满14岁未成年人的土地并获取收益时,该未成年人可对他提起诉讼,要求其报告账目,同时承担农役监护人之责)
tutor *impuberum* 未到结婚年龄的监护人
tutor *legitimus* 法定监护人
tutor *mulierum* 女子的监护人
tutor of law 法定监护人
tutor *proprius* (英古)正当监护人(与外来监护人不同,是合法管理未成年人之土地的监护人)
tutor-dative n. 法院指派的监护人
tutorage n. 监护的地位或职责
tutores *honorarii* 名誉监护人
tutoress n. 女家庭教师,女监护人
tutorial a. (未成年人的)监护人的
tutorial class 辅导小组
tutoris optio 监护选择
tutorship n. 保护(监护)人的职责或权力;保护(监护)权;(澳大利亚)助理律师

tutorship by nature 当然监护权(指父母一方死亡,则他方对其未成年子女有当然的监护权)
tutorship by will 依遗嘱而取得的监护权(只有最后死的父或母才能作此种遗嘱)
tutory n. (未成年人的)监护
Twelfth Amendment 美国联邦宪法第十二修正案[该修正案于1803年12月9日由国会提出,1804年6月15日批准生效。美国联邦宪法第十二修正案改变了选举总统的选举团制度(electoral college system)而规定分别投票选举总统和副总统,同时规定如果候选人中无人获得以州为单位的多数票时,由众议院选出总统,参议院选出副总统。该修正案就设立选举委员会达成妥协,但美国联邦最高法院却认为按照此修正案的票数计算条款,除参议院有权批准总统提名外,国会无权任命选举委员会成员]
Twelve Judges 全体法官会议(指英格兰刑事案件的共同讨论的合议制度,此种共同睿智得到不断巩固)
Twelve (Decemviral) Tables 《十二铜表法》(古罗马的初期法典,订于公元前451—450年)
Twentieth Amendment (1933年)美国联邦宪法第二十修正案[该修正案于1932年3月3日由国会提出,次年1月23日被批准。此时,人们称其为"诺利斯跛鸭修正案"(Norris Lame Duck Amendment)。它将总统、副总统以及国会议员任期从原来的3月4日分别提前至1月20和1月3日,避免政治交替期过长带来负面影响,同时该修正案规定,总统、议员任职日期及国会开会时期、当选总统的继任、参众两院复选时总统候选人死亡和继任等问题]
Twenty-fifth Amendment 美国联邦宪法第二十五修正案[指美国联邦宪法第2条规定在总统"死亡、辞职或丧失能力"时,副总统应该"履行总统职责"。它把总统和副总统均丧失履行职务能力的情况的处理交由国会以法律作出规定,但它没有解决如何认定丧失能力及如何将权力交还总统的问题。第20任美国总统詹姆

斯·伽菲尔德(James Garfield) 1881 年在车站遇刺后昏迷近两个月,伍德罗·威尔逊(Woodrow Wilson)总统(第 28 任总统) 1919—1921 年中风打击致残。不少总统都曾在短期内处于丧失能力状态,但尚未有出现援引丧失能力规定的例子。美国联邦宪法第二十五修正案设立了总统丧失履行职务能力时副总统"代理总统",以及总统可在丧失能力的情况终止时恢复权力的程序:通过总统或副总统以及大部高级行政官员发表的书面声明。丧失能力的认定可能遭到总统的反对,这时由国会进行审查,副总统若要继续代理总统职务则要在 21 天内获得两院 2/3 以上票数的支持。如果没有满足该规定,众议院便可向参议院提出弹劾(impeachment)。显然,副总统在解决此问题的 21 天内可以总统身份行事。遵循 1841 年由约翰·泰勒(John Tyler)所确立的先例,按美国联邦宪法第二十五修正案的规定,当总统死亡或辞职时由副总统继任,不仅是"履行"总统职责。该修正案还规定副总统职位空缺时的补充问题。该修正案于 1965 年 7 月 7 日由国会提出,1967 年 2 月 10 日批准公布。1973 年 10 月 10 日副总统斯皮罗·阿格纽(Spiro Agnew)因在位时的贿赂行为受到刑事指控,并因此辞职。杰拉尔德·R.福特(Gerald R. Ford)于 1973 年 12 月 6 日成为副总统。理查德·M.尼克松(Richard M. Nixon)因掩盖水门事件受到弹劾,并因此于 1974 年 8 月 9 日辞职,福特于 1974 年 12 月 19 日成为总统,纳尔逊·A.洛克菲勒(Nelson A. Rockefeller)成为副总统。当总统丧失履行职务能力时,美国联邦宪法第二十五修正案所提供的由副总统顶替总统职务的程序于 1985 年 7 月 13 日曾被使用过 7 小时。当时唐纳德·里根(Ronald Reagan)因肿瘤进行外科手术,副总统乔治·布什暂时承担了总统职务]

Twenty-first Amendment 美国联邦宪法第二十一修正案[指该修正案是唯一一个经选民而非立法委员批准的修正案,也是目前所有修正案中唯一一个废除了另外一个修正案,即美国联邦宪法第十八修正案(Eighteenth Amendment)的修正案。从 1919 年 1 月 16 日的全国禁酒修正案,到 1933 年 12 月 5 日联邦宪法第二十一修正案通过,将近过去 14 年。该修正案于 1933 年 12 月由州制宪会议(state convention)批准生效。不过,它仍保留州在其辖区内对酒类进行管制甚至禁止的权力,只是应受一定贸易权(commence power)限制而已。该修正案是美国宪法史上唯一一由州制宪会议批准的宪法修正案]

Twenty-fourth Amendment 美国联邦宪法第二十四修正案[该修正案于 1963 年 8 月 27 日由国会提出,1964 年 1 月 23 日批准公布。该修正案规定:"在总统或副总统、总统或副总统选举人以及国会参众两院议员的任何预选或其他选举中,合众国公民的投票权不得以未交人头税(poll tax)或其他税为理由,而被合众国或任何州加以否认或剥夺。"美国联邦宪法第二十四修正案遭到弗吉尼亚州的反对,该州要求没有在州选举中交纳人头税的选民进行特别的联邦登记。在"哈曼诉富森纽斯案" (Harman v. Forssenius) (1965) 中,联邦最高法院认为这种策略不合宪法,尽管新的修正案没有禁止州选举中的人头税,但在哈珀诉弗吉尼亚选举委员会案(Harper v. Virginia State Board of Elections) (1966) 中,联邦最高法院以这一实践违反了美国联邦宪法第十四修正案的平等保护条款(Equal Protection Clause of the Fourteenth Amendment)而裁定无效]

Twenty-second Amendment 美国联邦宪法第二十二修正案[指乔治·华盛顿(George Washington)以退休为借口拒绝成为第三任总统,托马斯·杰斐逊(Thomas Jefferson)以华盛顿总统为例也拒绝担当第三任总统,从而使两任期限成为了一个原则。在富兰克林·D.罗斯福(Franklin D. Roosevelt)之前,没有人担任总统超过两届。罗斯福在第二次世界大战的阴影下,请求继任总统,并于 1940 年和 1944 年均当选。他于 1945 年去世,由哈里·S.杜鲁门(Henry S. Truman)继任。联邦宪法第二十二修正案于 1947 年 3 月由国会提出,1951 年 2 月获得批准,从而将总统

的任期限制为两届。根据该修正案,此规不适用于本条开始生效时的时任总统哈里·杜鲁门,不过杜鲁门并没有竞选第三任期]

Twenty-seventh Amendment 美国联邦宪法第二十七修正案[该修正案有一段漫长而不同寻常的历史,也是美国联邦宪法上的一件奇事。它早在 1789 年就作为原《权利法案》十二条款中的第 2 条被提出,但却在 203 年之后的 1992 年才得到 3/4 州的批准。美国联邦宪法第二十七修正案规定:"新一届众议员选出之前,任何有关改变参议员和众议员任职报酬的法律,均不得生效。"实质上即国会议员不得自己投票决定提高自己的工资(pay raise),而只能决定增加后任国会众议员和参议员的工资]

Twenty-sixth Amendment 美国联邦宪法第二十六修正案[该修正案于 1971 年 3 月 23 日由国会提出,1971 年 7 月 1 日批准。该修正案规定:"已满 18 岁和 18 岁以上的合众国公民的选举权不得因年龄关系而被合众国或任何一州加以否定或剥夺。"尽管各州通常规定的选举年龄为 21 岁,但国会在 1970 年的选举法中规定联邦、州以及地区选举中的选举年龄是 18 岁。由于俄勒冈诉米切尔案(Oregon v. Mitchell)(1970)中的联邦最高法院四位法官支持国会意见,另四位法官反对国会意见,胡果·布莱克(Hugo Black)大法官掌握决定性一票。他认为,国会可以在联邦选举中将 18 岁作为选举年龄,但不能在州及地区选举中作如此规定,因为州选举资格只能由各州规定。这一判决决定使当时即将举行的 1972 年选举面临 XXX 局面。为了改变这种局势,该修正案得以出现。国会提出建议的 107 天内,该修正案必须得到 3/4 州的承认,从而成为联邦宪法的一部分。这是美国历史上最快通过的宪法修正案]

Twenty-third Amendment 美国联邦宪法第二十三修正案[该修正案由国会于 1960 年 6 月 17 日提出,1961 年 3 月 29 日获准。根据联邦宪法第 1 条规定,国会有权从各州接受领土并为政府资格对它管理。哥伦比亚特区就是根据这一权力从马里兰州和弗吉尼亚州分割出来的领土为基础形成的。国会以立法程序创立了该区,但联邦宪法对该特区的人民对总统和副总统的选举人均无任何规定。美国联邦宪法第二十三修正案规定哥伦比亚特区应按国会所指定的方式选派一定数目的总统和副总统选举人,其人数应如同一个州所享有的权利一样,等于其在国会的参议员和众议员人数的总和,但不得超过人口最少的州的选举人之数,与阿拉斯加州相同(3 票)。他们将参加各州任命的选举人行列,他们被认为是由一个州为选举总统、副总统的目的而任命的选举人,他们将在哥伦比亚集会、履行美国联邦宪法第十二修正案赋予他们的职责]

twice in jeopardy 见 jeopardy
twice-born a. 重获新生的,改过自新的
twicer n. 1.一事做两遍的人,做两件事的人。2.连败两次者 3.(英、澳)骗子,歹徒
twilight state 朦胧状态(指癫痫患者最常见的发作性精神障碍,也是司法精神医学鉴定中常遇的一类情况。主要表现为意识清晰度下降,范围缩小,幻想、妄想,易产生无缘无故的、盲目的暴力攻击行为,而事后又部分或全部遗忘。根据情况有部分或全部刑事责任能力)
twin n./a. 一对孪生子;孪生子之一/孪生子的;成双的
"twin aims" rationale of Erie (美)伊利案判决的"双重目标"理由(联邦最高法院大法官 Ginsburg 采用 Hanna 案的判决解释 Erie 案判决的"双重目标"理由,推论联邦标准的适用将会违反第一目标,因为联邦法院和纽约法院有关赔偿的实体法规定不同会鼓励当事人选择法院,同时也违反 Hanna 案判决的第二目标——在联邦法院和州法院间的法律实施的不合理)
"twin aims" test (美)"双重目标"标准(见"twin aims" rationale of Erie)
twin brother 孪生兄弟
twinge n. 刺痛,痛苦,苦恼
twinge of conscience 良心上的痛苦
twist v./n. 编造,歪曲;曲解/挖苦,嘲笑;谴责;责骂

twister n. 1.说谎的人;歪曲事实的人 2.令人难以相信的事
twisty a.歪曲事实的;不正直的
twitch v. 抽搐,抽动
two by two game 二对二博弈
two day's navigation 两日航程(旧时对领水带的标准)
two different kinds of contradictions 两类不同性质的矛盾
two hundred-mile limit 200海里范围(限度)
two laws in opposition 两法相反
two parliamentary assemblies 议会两院
two party draft 双名汇票
two robberies 两起抢劫案
two strawberries case (美)两个草莓案件(指1978年某陪审团受理一个女人因在一杂货店吃了两个草莓未付款而判处她18个月徒刑并罚款500美元,曾引起公众义愤因而不得不减刑)
two tier exchange rate 双重汇率
two tiered scheme of state court jurisdiction (美)州法院管辖的双重结构,州法院管辖的两层制度
two way trade 双轨贸易
two witness rule (美)双目击证人规则(指伪证罪的成立需有两名目击证人的直接证言或有一名目击证人的直接证言和一项旁证证明的规则)
two-by-two bimatrix 2×2 二元矩阵(指描述具有两个参与人,每个参与人具有数量不多战略的标准形式或博弈的标准方法)
two-chamber system 两院制
two-counsel rule 必须同时有两个诉讼代理人的原则
two-faced a. 两面派的;伪君子的;不可靠的
two-house legislative 两院制立法机关
two-level appellate system (美)两级上诉制,两级上诉法院制
two-level games 双层面博弈
two-partism 两党政治
two-party payment 向双方整付[指用一张支票整付(single payment)给两个人,通常以一个整数额应付给每人]
two-party system 两党制

two-round voting 两轮表决的制度[指一个在两轮中进行表决的制度,第一轮表决决定候选人的合格,然后进入第二轮表决。第二轮是从第一轮表决中的两个票数最高的候选人之间决定胜负的表决。由相对多数决定的选举(an election by plurality)是由其政党提名在第一轮表决决定赢得的候选人之间进行或是候选人在第一轮表决达到一定点(threshold)的相对多数决定的选举。见 run off election; election 3]
two-sided a. 两边的,两方面的;两面派的
two-step appeal (美)两级上诉(指采用两级上诉,州里的当事人先在中间上诉法院提出上诉,对其判决不服的可向更高一级的上诉法院提出上诉)
two-step due process 两步正当程序
two-step due process analyze (美)两步正当程序分析(指法院事先要决定被告在一个州里是否有最低程度联系;如果有,再决定行使管辖权是否与传统的公平对待和实体正义概念相一致)
two-step investigation 两步式侦查(指案件侦查过程明确地分为两个阶段,如初步侦查和后续侦查,或立案前侦查和立案后侦查。而且这两个阶段的侦查工作由不同部门的人员分别负责,又称为分段式侦查)
two-step "minimum contacts" analysis (美)(民事诉讼中)两步"最低联系"分析[第一,被告是否有目的地在该州建立最低联系;第二,合同纠纷中要考虑当事人以前的协商(prior negotiations)合同关系中预期发生的后果(contemplated future consequence)、合同的条款(terms of contract)以及当事人实际交易过程(parties actual course of dealing)等因素,如果有足够联系,管辖则合理,如果与公平对待和实体主义不符,管辖即被推翻。还要考虑被告的负担、诉讼地州在判决这一纠纷案中的利益、原告是否获得方便与有效救济以及州际司法系统在解决纠纷中的利益以及推进社会政策中的利益等与"公平对待和实体主义"是否相符]
two-thirds rule (美)三分之二多数制(指从前民主党规定总统候选人提名须经全

国代表大会三分之二代表投赞成票的制度)
two-tier a. 双重的
two-tiered systems 两(级)审(判)(体)制;双重体制
two-tiered tender offer 两级收购要约,双重收购要约(或称 front-end loaded tender offer。见 take over)
two-time loser 两次坐牢的人,两次离婚者,两次破产者,做某事两次失败者
two-tongued a. 说假话的,骗人的
tycoon n. 巨头,财阀;大企业家,实业界巨子
tyhelan v. (古英国法)控告,弹劾;指控(罪行)
tying a. 附有条件的,搭售的,搭配的
tying contract 附有条件的合同(契约);约束合同
tying down 束缚,约束(见 tie down)
tying in (sale) 必须有搭卖品的出售(指销售人拒绝售出货品,除非搭售另一种货物,如果销售人对此产品有垄断情况,则此搭售违反反托拉斯法)
typal a. 类型的,典型的
type n. 型,类型,式;典型,模范,样本,样版;标志,象征,符号
type face 字型
type line 指纹的线型,型线
type of Legislation 立法类型
types of evidence 证据的类型
types of law 法的类型,法律的类型
typical a. 典型性的,代表性的,象征性的
typical case 典型案件,典型判例
typical legal transaction 典型的法律行为
typicality n. 典型性,特征
tyrannic(al) a. 暴君的,专制的,专横的,暴虐的,残酷的
tyrannicide n. 诛杀暴君;诛杀暴君者
tyrannize v. 施暴政,实行极权统治,横行霸道
tyranny n. 苛政,暴政;专横;残暴,暴虐,暴行
tyrant n. 专制君主,暴君,压制他人者

U

uberrima fides 坦率诚实(用作一种合同分类名称,这类合同受约人应将自己所了解的一切有关事实和情况,告知订约人,各种保险合同即属此类)
uberrima fides contract 坦率诚实合同(契约)(见 uberrima fides)
* **Ubi cessat remedium ordinarium, ibi decurritur ad extraordinarium, et nunquam decuritur ad extraordinarium ubi valet ordinarium.** Where the ordinary remedy fails, that recourse must be had to an extraordinary one, but recourse is never had to the extraordinary where the ordinary is sufficient. 一般之救济失败时,求诸非常之救济,但只有在非正常者不能奏效时,才求助于正常者。
* **Ubi culpa est, ibi poena subesse debet.** Where the crime is committed, there ought the punishment to be undergone. 哪里有罪行,哪里就有处罚。
* **Ubi cunque est injuria, ibi damnum sequitur.** Where there is an injury, there a loss or damage follows. Wherever there is a legal wrong, there damage follows. 有不法行为,必随之产生损害。
* **Ubi factum nullum, ibi fortia nulla.** 1.Where there is no act, there can be no force. 无行为,无暴力。2.Where there is no fact there is no strong point. 无事实即无争点。3.Where there is no principle fact, there can be no accessory. 无主犯无从犯。
* **Ubi guis delinguit, ibi punietur.** Where a man offends, there he shall be punished. 罪犯在哪里犯罪,就应在哪里受罚。

ubi infra 下面提及之处,下面述及

* *Ubi jus, ibi remedium.* There is a right, there is a remedy. 有权利,就有法律救济。

* *Ubi jus incertum, ibi jus nullum.* Where the law is uncertain there is no law. 法无定法,则无法。

* *Ubi lex non distinguit, nec nos distigueredebemus.* Where the law does not distinguish, neither ought we to distinguish. 凡法律如不能识别者,即不予识别。

* *Ubi matrimonium, ibi dos.* Where there is marriage, there is dower. 有婚姻才有妆奁。

* *Ubi non est lex, ibi non est transgressio, quoad mundum.* Where there is no law, there is no transgression, so far as relates to the world. 在世界上要是没有法律,也就没有犯法。

* *Ubi non est principalis, non potest esse accessorius.* Where there is no principle, there can not be an accessory. 没有主犯,即无从犯。

ubi re vera 真实的地方;事实真相

Ubi remedium, ibi jus. Where there is a remedy, there is a right. (英美法)有法律救济就有权利。(古代和中世纪的法律原则)

ubi supra 上面提及之处,上面述及

* *Ubicunque est injuria, ibi damnum sequitur.* Wherever there is wrong, there damage follows. 有侵权必有损害。

ubiquity n. 到处存在,普遍存在

ubiquity of the king(或 **queen**) (设想的)君主正式在庭(指国王或女王存在于任何法庭);法官本身

ubiquity of the law 法律的普遍性,法律的一般性,法律之到处存在

ubiquity puzzle 普遍存在之谜

UCITA(**Uniform Computers Information Trade Act**) 《统一计算机信息交易法》

udal(或 **odal law**) (英史)土地自由保有法律制度(9世纪出现的一种制度)

ugly a. 1.丑陋的;邪恶的;险恶的;可憎的 2.脾气坏的,争吵的 3.令人困窘的,难处的

ugly customer 难以对付的家伙,可畏之人,难处之人

ugly fact of life 生活中的丑闻,阴暗面

ugly rumour 可怕的(险恶的)谣言,不堪入耳的谣言

ukase(或 **ukaas**) n. 官方的裁决,官方的法令;官方的宣告;俄国皇家法律

ullage n. 不足量;损耗量;漏损量

ULLCA(**Uniform Limited Liability Company Act**) (美)《统一有限责任公司法》(1996年由统一州委员会制定)

ulna n. 正箕形纹;尺骨

ulnar a. 尺骨的

ulnarloop n. 尺骨箕,正箕

Ulpianus Domitius 乌尔比安·多米梯厄斯(170—228)(古罗马最后的伟大法学家之一,其著作《乌尔比安选集》十分有名。他曾任许多职务,从222年起任地方执政官直至去世)

ulterior a. 1.进一步的,日后的,将来的;在彼方的,遥远的 2.隐蔽的,秘而不宣的

ulterior motive 隐秘不明的动机

ultima 最后的,最终的;最远的

ultima ratio 最后谈判;最后的论据;最后手段(尤指诉诸武力)

* *Ultima voluntas testatoris est perimplendasecundum veram intentionem suam.* The last will of a testator is to be fulfilled according to his true intention. 遗嘱应按本人真实意愿,以其最后者为有效。

ultimagenitary a. 幼子继承权的

ultimageniture n. 幼子继承制

ultimate n./a. 终极;根本;顶点;最后的

ultimate authority 最高权力,至高无上的权力

ultimate beneficiary 最终受益人,最后受遗赠人,最后获得信托财产者(指信托终止后获得信托财产的人)

ultimate cause 最终原因,终极原因

ultimate consumer 用户,最终消费者

ultimate estate 基本的地产权,最终的地产权

ultimate facts 基本事实,最后事实,关键事实;(与诉讼)有关事实,最终(受理)的

事实,最终事实
ultimate futility 基本无效
ultimate heir (英)最后继承人
ultimate issue 最后争点(指人身伤害疏忽的案件中必须回答的被告疏忽的问题)
ultimate liability 根本责任,主要责任
ultimate logical conclusion 最根本的逻辑结论,最高的逻辑结论,顶级的逻辑结论
ultimate power to lay down the law 最高立法权
ultimate principles 基本原理
ultimate purchaser 用户,最终购买者
ultimate recourse 最终追索权
ultimate reversion 最终归属权
ultimate rule of recognition 最终承认规则
ultimate solvency 最大偿债能力
ultimate venue 最终审判地
ultimately ad. 最后,终究,总之,终结
ultimatum n. 1.最后通牒,哀的美敦书 2.最后结论;基本原理,根本意义
ultimum supplicium 极刑,死刑
ultimus haeres 1.最后继承人;远亲继承人 2.君主,统治者
ultra a./n. 超乎寻常,极端的,过度的,额外的/过激派,走极端的人
ultra damages 额外损害赔偿
ultra vires (act) 越过(法定)权限,越权的,越权行为(与 *intra vires* 相对,指法人及其他超越普通法或成文法所承认的权利和能力范围所作的无效行为)
ultra vires doctrine (英国传统的)越权原则
ultra-contentious a. 过激争论的
ultra-democracy n. 极端民主化
ultra-individualist materials 超个人主义的材料,极端个人主义的材料
ultra-left a. 极"左"的
ultra-leftist a. 极"左"分子
ultra-reactionary a. 极端反动的
ultra-right a. 极"右"的
ultra-rightist n. 极"右"分子,极"右"派
ultraconservatism n. 极端保守主义
ultraconservative a. 极端保守(主义)的
ultraism n. 过激论,极端主义
ultraist n. 过激论者,极端主义者

ultramarine trade 海外贸易
ultramodern a. 极其现代化,超现代化的,最新的,极其时髦的
ultranationalism n. 极端民族主义
ultranationalist n. 极端民族主义分子
ultraprotective trade policy 超保护贸易政策
umbrella n./a. 雨伞,(政治等方面的)保护伞/包罗众多的;伞状的
umbrella articles 总括条款
umbrella solution 伞形解决办法(又译总解决方法)
umpirage n. 1.仲裁人(或公断人)的职权或地位;仲裁,公断 2.裁决,裁定
umpire n./v. 首席仲裁人;裁决者,公断人/仲裁,裁判;公断;作裁判员;作公断人
umpire in a dispute 在争论中担任公断人(或仲裁人)
umpireship n. 仲裁人(或公断人)的职权
UN Convention on the Recognition and Enforcement of Foreign Arbitral Awards 《联合国关于承认和执行外国仲裁裁决公约》
UN Emergency Force 联合国紧急救援部队
UN Office on Drugs and Crime 联合国反运毒和罪案办公室
UN form A 联合国格式 A(联合国文件标号)
* *Un ne doit prendre(or prise) avantagede son tort demesne.* One ought not to take advantage of his own wrong. 不能让人在其侵权行为中得利。
Un-American Activities Committee (美)(国会)非美活动调查委员会(美国国会众议院设立的所谓"防范外国间谍"的特务组织,1934 年建立,1938 年改组而扩大活动范围,1945 年成为常设的委员会)
Un-American Committee (美众议院设立的)非美洲调查委员会
una voce 一致意见,一致
unable a. 无能力的,无资格的,没有办法的,无能为力的
unable of controlling one's behavior 不能控制自己的行为
unable to act 不能履行职责
unabsovable a. 不能赦免的;不能免除的

unacceptable a. 不能接受的,不受欢迎的,难以承认的
unacceptable product 不合格产品
unaccepted a. 不被接纳的,被拒绝的;不由当局负责保护的
unaccompanied shipment 非随身载运的行李
unaccomplished a. 未完成的,未遂的
unaccomplished offense 未遂罪
unaccountable a. 难以申辩的,不可解释的;无关系的,无责任的
unaccredited a. 未经授权的;未被接受的;未呈递国书的
unaccustomed a. 不习惯的;非惯例的;反常的,奇怪的
unacknowledged a. 1.(身份资格等)不被人承认的;不被确认的 2.(错误等)未公开承认的;未答复的 3.不自白的,不忏悔的
unacknowledged succession 无人承认的继承
unacted a. 未演出的;未付诸行动的,未实行的
unaddressed envelope 无地址的信封
unadjudged a. 未仲裁的,未经审判的
unadjusted a. 1.未调整的,未调整好的 2.意见分歧的,不一致的
unadmitted a. 未被承认的;不让进入的
unadopted a. 未被采用的,未经采纳的
unadopted measures 未被采用的措施;有待解决的措施
unalienable a. 不可转让的;不可剥夺的;不可出卖的
unalienable or inalienable right 禁易权利(指不可转让或不可放弃的权利,特别是自然权利,即如拥有合法的财产权,亦称 inherent right。未经权利所有人的同意不得放弃或转让的权利,如自由权、财产所有权、宗教自由权、言论自由权、正当法律程序与法律平等保护权等。美国政治和宪法传统中的禁易权利是指受禁易规则保护的权利)
unalienable right 不容剥夺的权利
unaliened a. 未转让的,未让渡的
unaligned nations 不结盟国家
unallotted a. 未分配的
unallotted apportionment 未分配的预算,未分配额

unallotted shares 未分配的股份
unallowable a. 不许可的,禁止的
unallowed a. 不准许的,非法的,不许可的
unalterable a. 不变的,不能改变的
unalterable rules 不可更改的规则
Unam Sanctam 《唯至圣诏书》(教皇卜尼法斯八世于1302年宣布教会拥有至高无上权力的诏书)
unambiguous a. 清晰的,明白的,不模糊的
unambiguous evidence 确凿的证据
unamenable a. 不承担义务的,不承担责任的
unamendable a. 无法改(纠)正的,不可救药的;未能修改的,不可修正的
unamended bill 未修正的议案,未经修改的草案
unanimity n. 全体一致,一致同意;会意,协议
unanimity rule (全体)一致通过制(法则)
unanimous a. (全体)一致的,一致同意的;无异议的
unanimous ballot 一致投票
unanimous court 合议(意见一致的)法庭
unanimous tribunal 无异议法庭,一致的法庭,无异议的制裁
unanimous verdict 一致裁断,一致裁定
unanimous vote 一致的选票
unannounced a. 未经宣布的
unanswerable a. 1.不能回答的 2.无法争辩的;决定性的 3.无责任的
unanswerable argument 无法争辩的论据
(an) unanswerable question (一个)不能回答的问题
unanswered a. 未答复的,未驳斥的;无反应的
unappealable a. 不能上诉的
unapplied a. 未能应用的,未实施的,未能申请的
unapprehended a. 1.未被逮捕的;逍遥法外的 2.未被理解的
unapprehended theory 尚未被理解的理论
unapprehensive v. 反应迟钝的;无忧虑的,不理解的
unappropriated a. 非属于某人或机构的,

未派定特殊用场的;未占用的
unappropriated balance 未分配的余额
unappropriated profit 未分配利润
unappropriated territory 未占用的地区,无主地区
unapproved a. 未经认可的,未经承认的,未获准的
unapt a. 不适当的;笨拙的
unarguable a. 不容置疑的,无可争辩的,不可论证的
unascertainable a. 无法获知的,不能确定的
unascertained a. 未确定的,未确知的
unascertained goods 未经确定的货物
unashamed a. 厚颜无耻的,公然的;无羞耻的
unasked a. 未受请求的,未被要求的,未受请托的
unassailable a. 无可反驳的;无懈可击的
unasserted a. 不肯定的;不能断言的
unassessed a. 不可估价的,不可征税的
unassignable a. 不得转让的,不得让渡的;不能让与的
unassignable letter of credit 不可转户的信用证
unassigned personnel 未派职务的人员
unassured a. 未得到保证的,不安全的;缺乏自信的,不确定的;未保险的,无保险单的
unatonable a. 不能抵偿的,不能赎回的
unattached a. 1.未被逮捕的,未被扣押(财产)的 2.未订婚的;未结婚的 3.无所属的,中立的 4.不附着的;不束缚的
unattended a. 1.无(人)伴随的;无人注意的 2.无人出席的,无人参加的 3.被置之不理的,未执行的
unattending a. 不注意的
unattested a. 未经(证人或证词)证实的
unauthentic a. 无根据的,不可靠的,不确实的
unauthenticated a. 未经证实的
unauthorized a. 1.无权的,未经授权的;未经许可的;未经获准的 2.无根据的,未经公认的
unauthorized agency 无权代理
unauthorized departure from official duty 擅离职守
unauthorized killing 擅自杀人
unauthorized practice 擅自开业,(美)未授权的开业
unauthorized reduction or remission of taxes 自行决定减税免税
unauthorized representation 未经授权的代理
unauthorized withholding of possession 无权占有
unavailability (= unavailableness) n. 无法得到;不近便
unavailable a. 不能供人使用的,不能利用的,不能得到的,(美)不能采用的(原稿)
unavailing a. 无效的,无用的,无益的,无结果的
unavoidable a. 不可避免的;不得已的;不能废除的
unavoidable accident 不可避免的事故;未预料到的事故
unavoidable mistake 不可避免的错误
(an) unavoidably unsafe product (美)一种不可避免的不安全产品(指比如疫苗本身被视为一种不可避免的不安全产品,遭遇疫苗伤害的受害者要获得赔偿,必须证明疫苗生产商存在过错,这使得受害者几乎没有胜诉机会。美国正在进行疫苗伤害救济制度的变革,展示了疫苗伤害救济在过失侵权制度下遭遇的种种困难和救济制度的立法变革过程。法律规定生产商可以主张发展风险抗辩,对不能预知的、非生产过程的忽略或错误引起的伤害,生产商不承担责任。实践中,疫苗受害者根本无法通过证明疫苗存在不合理的危险而获得赔偿,为缓解该局面,20世纪六七十年代,有些法院在裁决中指出生产商必须对疫苗可能引起的副作用进行充分告诫,否则要对疫苗伤害承担责任)
unavowed a. 秘密的
unaware a. 不知道的,不察觉的,无意的
unawareness n. 不知觉,不留神;不觉察
unbailable a. 不能保释的
unbailable offense 不能保释的罪行
unbalanced a. 1.不均衡的,不平衡的 2.精神错乱的;不安定的,不稳定的 3.未决

算的
unbalanced books 未决算的账簿
unbalanced mind 精神错乱
unbecoming conduct 不适当的行为
unbias(s)ed a. 无偏见的;大公无私的;公平的
unbias(s)ed decision 不偏的判决,公正的判决
unbiassed estimation 公正的估价,公正的评价
unbiasedness hypothesis 无偏性假说(指未来某一时期的远期汇率是下一时间阶段后即期汇率的无偏估计,即无系统错误的值。这一假说又称无偶性说)
unbidden a. 未受命令的,未被指使的,自愿的,未被要求的,未受邀请的
unbigoted a. 无偏见的,不抱成见的;不一意孤行的
unbilical cord blood stem cells 脐带血干细胞(脐带血干细胞属人体组织,其与人体分离后成为"物",各国对于该物是否具有财产权之性质、是否可视为所有权之客体见解各异。现属于争论之焦点,至今尚无定论)
unbind v. 解开,松开;释放;解放
unbinding a. 无拘束作用的,无约束力的
unbinding contract 无约束力的合同(契约)
unborn a. 未诞生的;未来的;原来存在的
unborn child 未出生的胎儿;待生的婴儿
unbought a. 1.非买来的 2.未经贿赂的;未经雇用的
unbound a. 被释放的,被解放的,无约束的,解脱了束缚(或镣铐等)的
unbribable a. 无法贿赂的
unbroken a. 未被阻断的,未破损的,完好的;未开垦的;守信的;未驯服的
unbroken ground 未耕的土地,未开垦的土地
unbroken oath 被信守的誓言
unbroken possession 继续(连续)占有
unbroken promise 被信守的诺言
unburdened a. 不受累的;无牵累的
unbusinesslike a. 不认真的;无效能的;无次序的;无人组织的
unbusinesslike proceeding 不正确的程序

unbuttoned a. 无约束的,放纵的,肆意的,肆无忌惮的
uncalled a. 未经请求的;未叫到的;不必要的;未被召唤的
uncalled capital 未缴股本,未收资金
uncalled for 不适当的;不需要的;无理的
uncalled for insult 无理凌辱
uncalled subscription 不催缴的股款,未缴已认股款
uncatalogued a. 未列入(商品、图书等)目录的;目录上没有的
uncensored a. (出版物)未经审查的,(信件)未经检查的;无保留的,无拘束的
uncertain a. 1.不确定的,未定的 2.不确信的,不可靠的 3.模糊不清的
uncertain legal standard 不确定法律标准
uncertain witness 动摇不定的证人
uncertainty n. 无定性;不确定;无常;不明确(尤指一些有法律效力的字据、证明,因其字句不明确,将导致失效。又指对于诉状答辩固有不明确处将会被法院删去);有疑问
uncertainty of law 法律的不确定性
uncertificated a. 无证书证明的
uncertificated bankrupt 无证书证明的破产;无证明的破产
uncertified a. 未经证明的,无证书的
unchallengeable a. 无可置辩的;不必回避的;不可挑战的
unchallenged a. 未被要求回避的;未引起争论的;不成问题的
unchallenged jury 无人反对的陪审团,无要求回避的陪审团
unchangeable law 不能改变的法律,不变的法律
uncharge v. 1.从(船上)卸货 2.宣告……无罪
uncharged a. 未被指控的;没有负荷的;不付费用的
uncharted a. 1.无人探险过的,未知的 2.海图上未载明的
uncharted island 海图上未载明的岛屿
unchartered a. 1.不守法的,无法无天的,不合规则的 2.未得特许状的
unchaste a. 不守贞操的,淫荡的

unchaste conduct 淫荡的行为
unchaste woman 淫荡的女人
unchastity n. 不贞洁,淫荡,无节操
unchecked a. 未经检查的,未经核对的,未经检验的;未受制止的
UNCITRAL Arbitration Rules 《联合国国际贸易法委员会仲裁规则》
UNCITRAL Model Law on Cross-border Insolvency 《联合国国际贸易法委员会跨国界破产示范法》(1977年)
UNCITRAL Model Law on Electronic Commerce 1996 (with Guide to Enactment) 《联合国国际贸易法委员会电子商务示范法》(1996年)
UNCITRAL Model Law on International Commercial Arbitration 《联合国国际贸易法委员会国际商事仲裁模范法》
uncivil a. 不文明的,无礼的,不利于公民和睦(或福利)的
unclaimed a. 未经要求的,无请求者的,未要求索赔的,无人认领的
unclaimed balance 未提取的存款;余款;不动产余额
unclaimed corpse 无主尸体
unclaimed dividend 未取股利,未要求股利,未领股息
unclaimed fund 无人认领的资金
unclaimed goods 未领取货物,货主不明的货物
unclaimed letter (遭到严词拒绝的)拒绝书
unclaimed property 无请求权的财产,无人认领的财产,无主财产
unclaused credit 无条款限制的信用证
unclean bill of lading 不洁提单
unclean hands 不廉洁,不清白(指无资格取得衡平法上的救济)
unclear point 含糊不清之点
uncleared a. 1.不是无辜的 2.不能补偿的;未清偿的 3.未消除的(怀疑)
unclosed a. 未完成的,未终结的,未解决的;未封闭的,打开的
uncollected a. 1.不安的;狼狈的 2.未收集的,未收回的
uncollected debt 未收回的借款

uncollected mind 不安的思虑,思想动荡不定
uncollectible account(s) 坏账,呆账
uncollectible debt 无法收回的债
uncollectible tax 无法征收的税款
uncommitted a. 1.未被授权的,未受委托的 2.未遂的 3.不负义务的,不受诺言约束的 4.未被监禁的
uncommitted contract 不受约束的合同
uncommitted crime 未遂罪
uncommitted reserve 未决定用途的预备金
uncommon a. 难得的,罕见的,不平常的
uncommonsurate a. 不相称的,不相当的
uncompensated a. 无补偿的
uncompensated requisition 无偿征用
uncompensated use of fixed assets 固定资产无偿占用制
uncompleted contract 未完成的合同(契约)
uncomplicated matter 不麻烦的事项,不复杂的事项
uncompromising a. 坚定的,不妥协的,不能通融的
unconcerned a. 无关的;不相关的;不关心的,不介意的
unconcious negligence 无认识过失
uncondemned a. 未判有罪的,未受责难的
unconditional a. 无条件的;绝对的
unconditional acceptance 无条件承诺;无条件承兑
unconditional discharge 无条件(从监禁中)释放(无需经假释的时间要求);无条件免除债务(无进一步履行债务之责)
unconditional guaranty 不附条件的保证
unconditional heir 无条件继承人
unconditional legacy 无条件遗赠
unconditional most-favored-nation clause 无条件最惠国条款
unconditional non-prosecution 绝对的不起诉
unconditional order 绝对的命令
unconditional pardon 无条件赦免
unconditional promise in writing 无条件的书面允诺
unconditional state grants 不指定用途的

财政补贴(指美国各州州政府对地方政府的一种补贴)
unconditional surrender 无条件投降
unconfessed a. 未供认的,未承认的,未公认的;未评定的
unconfined a. 自由的,无拘束的,无限制的
unconfirmed a. 未经认可的,未经证实的,未确证的
unconfirmed (letter of) credit 未经保兑的信用证
unconformable a. 不符的,不一致的
unconnected a. 1.不关联的,不连贯的 2.无亲无戚的;无亲属关系的
unconnected phrases 语无伦次
unconscientious 不受良心引导约束的,不法的,不公平的,不合理的
unconscionability n. 不合常理,不公平;极不公正、肆无忌惮;昧良心性(这一概念贯穿于许多合同规则之中,每一情况法院最关注的是该合约或具体某一条款是否公平。如果违背良知,法院可拒绝执行该合约或条款)
unconscionable a. 1.不受良心引导或约束的;不法的,肆意的 2.不合理的,不公平的;过度的
unconscionable bargain 违背良心的合同(契约),不公平的合同(契约),不合理的交易(指因考虑欠妥,使另一方占便宜的交易)
unconscionable behavior 不合理的行为
unconscionable liar 恣肆的说谎者
unconscious a. 无意的,不知不觉的;未发觉的
unconscious destruction 无意识的毁损
unconscious neglect 无意的疏忽
unconsciousness n. 无意识
unconsensual claims 非合意的主张,非合意的债权
unconstitutional a. 违反宪法的;违宪的,不合宪法规定的
unconstitutional action 违宪行为
unconstitutional impairment of obligation of contract 对合同(契约)之债的违约责任
unconstitutional law 违宪的法律
unconstitutional ordinance 违宪的法令;违宪条例
unconstitutional statute 违宪制定法,违宪法律
unconstitutionality n. 违宪,违反宪法
unconstitutionality of course pursued 诉讼过程的违宪性
unconstrained a. 不拘束的,不勉强的,自由的;非强迫的
unconstraint n. 无拘无束,自由自在,无限制;自愿
unconsummated a. 未实现的,未完成的
uncontested a. 1.无争议的,无竞争的;无异议的 2.明白的,显然的,无争辩余地的
uncontested divorce 无争议的离婚(指夫妻双方都不表示反对的一种离婚。见 contested divorce)
uncontested election 无竞争的选举
uncontested owner 无争执的所有人
uncontested registration 无争议的注册
uncontinual real servitude 不能继续的地役权
uncontradictable a. 不能否认的,不能驳斥的
uncontradicted witness 未被否认的证人,不能否认的证人
uncontrollable a. 难控制的,无法管束的
uncontrollable fear 无法抑制的恐惧
uncontrollable impulse 难压制的刺激(又译:无法控制的冲动。这种冲动对刑事责任是没有影响的,但有用它作精神错乱的证据的可能,以求获得减轻罪责)
uncontrolled liberty 不受约束的自由,自由自在
uncontroverted a. 不容答辩的,无可置疑的
uncontrovertible proof 无可置疑的证据,不可驳倒的证据
unconventional a. 非常规的,不从惯例的
unconventional warfare 非常规战争
unconversant a. 不熟悉的,不太了解的
unconverted a. 1.未悔改的,未脱罪的 2.不改的,不变的
unconvertible a. 不能变换的,不能兑换的
unconvicted a. 未判罪的
unconvicted person 未经定罪的人

unconvinced a. 不相信的,怀疑的
uncooperative a. 不合作的,不配合的
uncooperative corporation 未注册的公司,不合作的公司
uncoordinated a. 不协调的;不对等的,不同等的;不并列的
uncore prist 迄今仍准备履行(指抗辩的一种,意思是如属合理,则依旧准备履行)
uncorrected a. 未修正的,未改正的;未调整的;未加管教的
uncorroborated a. 未经证实的
uncorroborated confession 无确证的证供,未确认的供认
uncovenanted a. 合同(契约)未规定的;无条件的;未参加公约的;不受公约约束的,公约中未规定的
uncover v. 揭露,暴露,揭开……盖子
uncovered a. 光头的;无担保的;无抵押品的;未经保险的;无掩护的
uncovered goods 未保险的货物
uncredited a. 无信用的;无债权的
uncrossed cheque(s) 非划线支票
uncustomed a. 未经海关检查的;走私的
undamaged a. 未损坏的,完好的
undated a. 未注明日期的,未限期的,不定期的
undated check 未注日期的支票
unde vi (罗马法)保护占有者令(罗马法上的禁令之一)
undealt a. 未处理的,未分发的
undebarred a. 不阻止的,不禁止的,自由的
undebarred from doing 自由地干(做),不受禁止地从事
undebatable a. 无争论余地的
undebatable facts 无争论余地的事实
undebatable motion 不可争论的动议
undecided a. 未决的,未定的,不果断的;不明确的
undeclared a. 未经宣布的;不公开的;(货物)未向海关申请的
undeclared war 不宣而战的战争
undefended a. 1.未防备的,未设防的;无论据证实的 2.无辩护人的(指在民事诉讼、刑事诉讼中无辩护人的被告)3.无辩护的(指民事诉讼中的被告的三种情况:没有呈递到案状;没有答辩陈述;未到庭受审);无抗辩的
undefended cause 无辩护的讼因
undefended city 不设防城市
undefended divorce cases 无抗辩的离婚案件
undefended localities 不设防地区
undefended prisoner 无辩护人的犯人
undefended suit 无抗辩的诉案,不作辩护的诉讼
undefined a. 未阐明的,未解释的;不确定的,不明确的
undefined legal (or statutory) concepts 不确定的法律概念
undelegated a. 未委付的;未授权的;未准许的
undeliberate promises 草率的允诺
undeliverable a. 无法投递的,无法送达的
undelivered a. 未被释放的;未送达的;未说出口的
undelivered prisoner 未被释放的犯人
undeniable a. 1.不可否认的,不可争辩的 2.不会错的,的确好的,明显的
undeniable ability 无可争辩的能力
undenominational a. 不受任何宗教教派约束的,非宗派的
under prep. 1.依据……的规定;在……规定下 2.受制于……,依据
under a charge of 根据……控告
under a pretence (或 under pretense) 借口,托词,借故
under an accusation of 被指控犯……罪
under arrest 被逮捕
under attack 受到攻击
under authority 经有关当局许可
under average 受损
under capitalization 资本不足,股本总额过小
under colo(u)r of law 根据法律的"权威",在法律的幌子下
under (或 on) compulsion 被迫地
under consideration 加以考虑,在考虑中
under contract 受合同的约束
under contract interest 依约定利息
under customs seal 经海关盖章
under detention 在拘押中

under duress 被迫,在胁迫下
under employment 就业不足
under escort 押送
under false colours 1.挂着假冒的旗帜航行 2.欺世盗名,冒充,欺骗 3.伪国籍的,伪身份的
under full age 未成年
under full guardianship 处于完全监护下
under fully competitive conditions 在充分竞争的条件下
under hot pursuit 正在追捕中
under house arrest 在软禁中
under inclusive 包括不足的
under insurance 部分保险;不足额保险(指保险金额总数低于被保险财产的价值者)
under license 领有执照
under limited guardianship 处于有限制的监护之下
under lock and key 锁起来
under martial law 在戒严中
under mild restriction 被软禁
under military rule 军事管制下
under my hand and seal 由本人签名盖章
under no consideration 绝不,不考虑
under orders 奉命
under pain of death 处死刑
under pledge of secrecy 誓不泄密
under probation 在缓刑中
under protest 有异议地,有保留地,不愿意,不服(比较 over protest)
under reserve 保留追偿权
under(或 with, in) safe-conduct 持有安全通行证
under seal contract 已加盖印鉴的合同(契约)
under sentence of death 被判处死刑
under suspicion 受嫌疑
under suspicion of smuggling 有走私嫌疑
under the aegis of 在……支(主)持下;在……庇护下;由……主办
under the control of 受……控制下;在……支配下
under the dotal system 在奁产制下,根据陪嫁制

under the guise of 以……为幌子,假借
under the hand of 由……处理
under the necessity of 根据需要
under the orders of 按照……旨意;受命于……
under the penalty of invalidity 为免无效之虞
under the pretense of 借口,以……为托辞
under the tutelage of law 受法律保护
under the umbrella 在……保护下
under the wardship of 在……监护下
under trust 委托保管;根据信托管理
under way 进行中,在行进中
under-age a. 未成年的,未达法定年龄的,未达规定年龄的
under-bid v. 愿以低价报酬做(某事);以低价售出,减价低于
under-bit n. (美)(表示对牛的所有权用的)牛耳下端作的记号
under-buy v. 低价购买
under-charge n./v. 索价低于常价;索要的低价/索低价
under-clerk n. 下(低)级职员
under-deck cargo 舱内货物,舱货
under-deterrence n. 威慑力量之下
under-developed a. 未充分发展的;落后的
under-developed bankrupt 无清偿能力的破产
under-developed country 不发达国家,自然资源开发国家
under-lease n. 转租,分租;转借
under-mentioned a. 下记的,下述的
under-payment n. 缴付不足
under-payment of a tax obligation 税款的缴付不足
under-represented a. 代表人数不足的;代表人数低于适当比例的
under-secretary n. 次长,副部长,助理秘书
under-Secretary for Foreign Affairs 外交次长
under-Secretary of State (美)副国务卿
under-Secretary of War 战争次长,战争副官
(the) under-signed n. 签署人,签名人
under-tenancy n. 转租,分租,重租

under-tenant n. 次承租人,分承租人,转租承租人
under-the-counter a. 偷偷摸摸出售的;非法的;未经授权的;开后门的
under-the-table a. 暗中进行的;秘密的,暗中的
under-world n. 1.下层社会,下流社会 2.地狱 3.以卖淫、盗窃为生的人们
underbidder n. 喊价过低者,喊价较低者
undercapitalization n. 投资不足
undercapitalize v. 对……投资不足
undercapitalized corporation 资本不足的公司
undercover a. 暗中从事的;秘密的
undercover agent 密探,特务,间谍
undercover men 秘密工作人员
undercover payments 私下塞给人的钱(指贿赂)
undercover traitor 暗藏的叛徒
undercut v./n. 削低,底切,掘/缺口,底切
undercutting the Federal Rule (美)削弱《联邦规则》(《联邦民事诉讼规则》)
underdog n. 受压迫者;在不健全的社会(或政治制度下)的受害者
underemployed a. 就业不充分的,只有部分时间被雇佣的;被雇佣做低于本人技术水平的工作的,才能和技术未充分被利用的
underemployment n. 未充分就业,许多工人失业的情况
underestimate v. 低估,轻视
undergo v. 经受,经历;忍受
undergo a prison sentence 受到监禁判处;被判徒刑
undergo the blood test 接受血(液)检(查)
underground n./a. 地下组织,秘密组织;秘密活动/地下的,秘密的,不公开反抗的
underground activities 地下活动
underground economy 地下经济(指非法逃税的一种交易)
underground illegal factory 地下(非法)工厂
underground press 地下刊物
underhand a. 卑鄙的;秘密的;欺诈的,不光明正大的
underhand activity 秘密活动

underinvestment n. 投资不足
underleasee n. 次承租人,分承租人,转租租人
underlessor n. 转租人,分租人,转借人
underlet v. 转租;廉价出租;分租
underlie v. 构成(理论、政策、制度)基础,支撑,位于……下面
underling v. 强调,突出,使突出(原动词:underline)
underlying a. 基本的,基础的,根本的;在下面的;暗示的,潜在的,隐晦的,不明显的,含糊的;(财政、商业上)优先的;附属的
underlying accounting data 会计基本数据
underlying action 主要诉讼
underlying bond 优先债券
underlying cause 深层原因
underlying claim 优先求偿权(指享有优先权的债权人优先于其他债权人受清偿的权利)
underlying company 附属公司,直属公司
underlying contract 主要合同,基本合同
underlying corporation claim 基础性公司请求
underlying cost(s) 基本成本
underlying debenture 优先债券
underlying document 原始凭证,主要文件字据
underlying law 基本的法律
underlying lien 优先留置权
underlying mortgage 第一担保,第一抵押,优先抵押(权)
underlying movement 潜在动向,基本动向
underlying obligation 基本债;主债
underlying personal rights 基本的个人权利,根据个人权利
underlying policies 潜在政策,基础政策
underlying price 基础价格
underlying retention 基本留置权;主要保留权,主要扣留权;分保自负额
underlying security 抵押担保
underlying substantive law 基本实体法
underlying syndicate 优先财团
underlying transaction 基本交易,优先交易

underlying trust 基本信托

underlying value 基础价值(指德国依据客观价值将人的尊严适用于普通法领域。人的尊严条款是第二次世界大战后德国宪法的重要特征,被作为第一章第一条规定在基本法中)

undermine v. 暗中破坏;以阴谋中伤,伤害;削弱

undermine the judicial rules 推翻这些司法裁决

underminer n. 暗中破坏者,阴谋伤害者

underpay v. 少付……工资,付给不足额的工资

underpin v. 加强……的基础;在……下面加基础,支撑,巩固

underpin a thesis with evidence 用证据支持这一论点

underprivileged a. 被剥夺基本社会权利的;穷的

underrepresentation n. 代表性偏低

underscore v. 画线;强调;在……画线

underscoring the right of political protection 强调政治保护权利

undersell v. 售价比……低,廉价出售

undersexed a. 缺乏性能力的,缺乏性功能的

undersheriff n. (州、县、地区)副警长;助理司法行政官,(英)副行政司法官

undersign v. 签名,签名于(文件或信等)末尾

undersigned a. 签名于文件或信件上的,签名于文件末尾的

undersigned all agree 签署人完全同意

undersirable person 不良分子

understanding n. 1.协商,协议;谅解 2.理解,理解力 3.意义,所了解的意义

Understanding on Rules and Procedures Governing the Settlement of Disputes 《关于争端解决规则与程序的谅解》(是GATT1947时代争端解决机制核心,也是WTO争端解决机制的核心)

(The) UN Global Compact(或 Contract) 联合国全球契约组织

understanding tests (美)理解力的测试 [指在内战重建(Reconstruction)时代由州法律或州宪法提出的一种要求,它要求可能的投票者在投票之前必须"理解"特定的法律,并向当地登记人员满意地"解释"法律。19世纪90年代至20世纪60年代,美国南部各州曾采取各种措施以规避宪法所禁止的投票时种族歧视的规定。但实际运作中,这种标准对白人执行得宽松,对黑人则很严格。许多黑人因不理解晦涩的法律语言而得不到投票权。虽然联邦最高法院在1949年维持了一个联邦地区法院所作的判决,并判定亚拉巴马州的理解力测试无效,但南方其他几个州到20世纪60年代仍继续使用这种策略。直到1965年 Louisiana v. United States 一案出现,联邦最高法院才发表废除理解力测试的意见。并且认为,这"不是一种测试,而是一种陷阱"。所以国会在《1965年投票权法》(Voting Right Act of 1965)和以后的修正案中都限制了使用识字能力、"理解力"和其他受教育程度的测试来确定投票者的选举资格]

understate v. 作较轻或较弱的陈述;避重就轻的陈述;掩饰地说;隐瞒地说

understeer n. (汽车)转向不灵;(对)驾驶盘反应迟钝

understock n. 存货不足

understood a. 被充分理解的,取得同意的,不讲自明的

understrapper n. 僚属,下属

undertake v. 1.从事,着手,承担 2.担保;许诺;答应

undertaker n. 承担者,担任者,许诺者,担保人;承办人,营业者,企业家

undertaking n. 1.保证,承担,许诺(尤指在诉讼程序进行时,当事人或他的律师所作的允诺或承担,法庭据此可用拘押、查封或禁令等方式来强制执行)2.企业,事业(单位)

undertaking an obligation to make payment 承诺履行支付义务

undertaking for profit 营利企业

undertaking independent resolution 承担(或许诺)独立解决

undertaking to appear (律师)允诺出庭(指律师在原始令状的空白处写下将为诉

讼当事人出庭的允诺）

undervote 少选[意指在选票上选定的人数少于规定的人数。vote 还有一些词组成短语动词，例如 vote off/out（投票使某人落选），vote in（投票选出），vote down（否决、投票击败）或 vote through（投票通过），最近又出现了 vote（something）up，通常指支持你在电视或互联网上喜欢的东西]

underweight n. 重量不足，不符合要求（标准）的重量

underworld gang 帮会

underworlding n. （俗）流氓；歹徒；作奸犯科者

underwrite v. 签名于下；负责保险；同意支付，同意负担；认购，认揭；承诺（支付赔偿等）

underwriter n. 1.承保人，保险人，（水上）保险商，保险业者；保险业务受理人 2.（股票、债券等的）承购人；证券包销人，承包人；承诺支付者

underwriter's contract 认购合同（契约）

underwriter's laboratories 美国保险业公司检验所

underwriter's option 认购人选择权

underwriting 1.包销；承保，分保 2.保险业；海上保险业

underwriting agreement 承包合约；包销合约，包销协议，认购协议

underwriting commission 包销佣金，保险佣金，认购人回扣

underwriting contract 股份保险承受契约，股份保险承保契约（合同）

underwriting limit 承保限额（制）

underwriting of shares 承保股份保险

underwriting pool 保险联营

underwriting portfolio of risk 承担风险组合

underwriting syndicate 承保辛迪加

underwriting year 保险业务年度

underwriting's guarantee 承保（人）保证书

undesirable n. 不受欢迎的人；不良分子，不法分子

undetealed act 未被察觉的行为

undetealed error 未发现（察觉）的错误

undetermined a. 1.未确定的，未解决的 2.不坚定的，不果断的

undetermined boundary 未定边界

undeveloped a. 1.未充分发展的，不发达的，生育不健全的 2.未开发的

undigested a. （证券）未出售的，尚未被市场吸收的；未充分理解的

undischarged a. 1.未引发的（弹药等）2.未清算的，未清理的；未清的 3.未实施的

undischarged bankrupt 未偿清债务的破产者

undischarged debt 未清理的债务

undisciplined a. 缺乏纪律的；任性的，无修养的

undisciplined behavior 无纪律的行为

undisclosed a. 身份不明的，隐名的；未透露的，保持秘密的

undisclosed agency （1871 年）隐名代理（指一种代理关系，代理人与第三人从事交易，但第三人并不知道该代理人系代表本人实施行为。代理关系被隐匿这一事实并不禁止该第三方向本人或代理人寻求补救）

undisclosed principal 隐名委托人（指在由代理人进行交易时，另一方并未得知这个代理人是代理委托人进行交易的，这个委托人即为"隐名委托人"）；隐名代理关系上的本人

undiscovered loss 未发觉的损失

undisputed a. 无需争论的，无疑问的，确然无疑的

undisputed facts 无可非议的事实

undissolved a. 未解除的（义务、契约等），未取消的（婚约）

undivested a. 未被剥夺的

undistributed-earning tax 见 accumulated earnings tax

undivided a. 不可分割的，完整的；未分割的

undivided estate 不可分的继承（财产），共有的继承财产

undivided responsibility 单独承担的责任

undivided right 不可分割的权利

undivided share 不可分割的股份；不可分割的份额（尤指共同租借房屋、土地的人们，对于所租的房、地产的部分是不可分割的）

undo v. 1.解开，打开 2.取消，消除 3.勾引；

诱奸 4.打消,废弃 5.解释,解决;反向交易(外汇)
undo a young girl 勾引少女
undoing n. 解开,打开;取消,复旧;破坏,毁灭,祸根
undoubted a. 无疑的,确实的
undue a. 不当的;过分的;非法的,不正当的;未到(支付)期的,不欠的
undue behavior 不适当的行为,不当行为
undue bill 未到期票据
undue bond(或 **debt**) 未到期的债券(或债务)
undue burden 非法负担
undue delay 不当延误,不应有的延误
undue delay of justice 审判的不当延迟
undue enrichment 不当得利
undue fluidity of law 法律的不当随意性
undue influence 不当威逼,不当压力,不适当影响(尤指对某人施加不适当的影响使其做不愿意做的事情,如违愿选举、立遗嘱等),不当影响,威胁手段
undue insistence upon public interests 对公共利益的不当主张,不当的公共利益主张,不当坚持对公共利益主张
undue interference 不当的干扰(涉)
undue loss 不当损失
undue means 不合法手段,非正当方法
undue paper 未到期票据
undue preference 不当特惠(指宣告破产者在破产前 3 个月内,完全还清了一个债权人的全部债款的行为)
undue prejudice 不当的偏见
undue punishment 不当的处罚
undue sentence 不当判决
unduly a. 过分的,过度的;不正当的,不适当的
unduly burdensome 过度负担,不公正负担
unduly clogging the calendar 不适当地阻碍审案日程表的进程
undum pactum 无法律约束的单纯合约
unearned a. 不劳而获的,不应得的,分外的
unearned income 非由劳力而获的收入(指利息、房租等收入)
unearned increment (土地的)自然增价;不劳增值
unearned premium (UP) 未到期保险费,未实现的保险金
uneconomic(al) a. 不经济的,浪费的
unemancipated children 未自立的子女
unemployable n./a. 不能受雇者(因年龄、体力、知识不足)/不能受雇用的;不使用的
unemployed a. 失业的;未用的,不被利用的;未受雇的
unemployed capital 游资
unemployment n. 失业;失业人数
unemployment benefit 失业救济,失业津贴
unemployment compensation (政府所发的)失业补助;(美)失业救济制度
Unemployment Compensation Amendments 失业救济修正法案
unemployment compensation taxes 失业补偿税
unemployment insurance 失业保险(指英国 1912 年实施过的失业保险)
unemployment tax 失业税
unenclosed a. 未用墙围起的,公共的
unenclosed land 公共土地
unencumbered a. 不受妨碍的,没有(抵押等)负担的,没有子女的
unencumbered estate 没有抵押负担的财产
unencumbered widow 无子女的寡妇
unendorsed a. 未背书的,未认可的,未准许的
unendorsed check 未背书的支票
unendowed a. 没有赋予的,没有赠与的;没有奁产的
unenforceable a. 不能强制的(指得不到法律上的帮助而不能强制执行);无强制执行力的;不能执行的;不能实行的
unenforceable contract 不能强制履行的合同(契约)
unenforceable reform 不能付诸实行的改革
unenforced a. 未执行的,未生效的
unenforced claims 未要求恢复的权利,放弃的权利要求
unenforced obedience 自愿听从,不受强制的服从
unenforced speed limit 未执行的速度限制
unenfranchised a. 不给予(公民)选举权

的;(英)不给予(城镇)选派议员的政治权力的
unengaged a. 未约定的,未定婚的;未占用的;无工作的
unentitled a. 无资格的,无权利的
unequal a. 不平等的;不公正的;不适合的;不相称的;不同的,不等的
unequal election 不公平选举
unequal share 不同等的份额
unequal treatment 不平等待遇,不公正的待遇
unequal treaty 不平等条约
unequity n. 不公平
unequivocal a. 1.不含混的,明白的,直率的 2.绝对的,无例外的;不容置疑的
unequivocal language of the laws 不含混的法律措辞
unequivocal legislation 无例外的立法
unerring a. 无过失的,无错误的,正确的
unescapable a. 必然的,不能避免的
unethical conduct 不道德行为,没有职业道德的行为(指违反职业道德标准的行为,如律师违反职业道德即违反律师的职业责任法)
uneven a. 不平坦,不规则,不一致;不稳定的,易变的
uneven economic development 经济发展不平衡
uneven market 不平静的市场,不稳定的市场,易变化的市场
unevenly ad. 不平坦地,不稳定地,不规则地,不稳妥地
unexaminable a. 无法审查的,不能检查的,无法勘验的
unexamined n./a. 未经(受)讯问的证人(等)/未经考查的,未经考验的,未经讯问的
unexceptionable a. 1.无缺点的,无可非难的 2.不能被拒绝的,不容置疑的,无懈可击的
unexecuted a. 未执行的,未根据条款履行的
unexecuted agreement 未履行的合同(契约)
unexpected a. 不能预料的,意外的
unexpected accident 不能预料的事故
unexpired a. 未满期的,未到期的

unexpired insurance 未到期保险
unexpired lease 未满的租期
unexplainable a. 不能说明的,无法解释的
unexplained a. 未经说明的,未经解释的
unexplained error 未经解释的错误
unexposed a. 未暴露的,未揭发的
unexposed case of official corruption 未揭发的官员贪污案
unextinguished debt 未消灭的债务
unfair a. 不正直的,不公平的,偏颇的,不正当的,不合理的
unfair advantage 不当得利
unfair bargain 不公平交易
unfair business 不正当经营
unfair commercial practice 不公平商业行为
unfair competition 不合理竞争,不公平竞争,不正当竞争
unfair competition prevention 防止不正当竞争法
Unfair Competition Prevention Act (中)《反不正当竞争法》(于1993年9月2日人大通过)
Unfair Contract Terms Act (英)《非公平合同条款法》
unfair dismissal 不公平的解雇
unfair judg(e)ment 不公平的判(断)决
unfair labo(u)r practice(s) 不公正的劳务惯例(指法律禁止的工会或雇主的行为;雇主企图强使雇员放弃工作的有组织活动);不公平劳动行为
unfair labor practice strike 不当劳动行为的罢工
unfair trade practice 不正当贸易行为
unfair verdict 不当裁决
unfairness n. 不公平,不公正,不正当
unfaithful a. 1.不正当的;不信实的;不正确的 2.有外遇的,犯通奸罪的
(an) unfaithful wife (一个)有外遇(或有奸情)的妻子
unfathered a. 1.无父亲的;私生的 2.找不到作者的;出处不明的
unfathered offspring 私生子
unfathered slanders 未知来源的谣言
unfathomed a. (刑事案件等)未解决的;

unfavo(u)rable a. 1.不利的,有害的;不吉祥的 2.相反的,不同意的
unfavo(u)rable answer 否定的回答
unfavo(u)rable balance of trade 贸易逆差,输入超过输出的贸易
unfavo(u)rable case 不利场合
unfavo(u)rable difference 逆差
unfavo(u)rable trade balance (对外)贸易逆差
unfeasible a. 不能实行的,难以实施的
unfetter v. 除去……脚镣;释放
unfetter a prisoner 除去囚犯的脚镣;释放囚犯
unfettered control 不受约束的支配权,不受约束的控制权
unfettered discretion 不受约束的自由裁量权
unfettered power 任意权
unfinished business 未完议程;余留事务
unfit a./v. (16世纪)不合适;不胜任;不可取,不够格[指①对专门使用或服务不合适,不适当,不适用〈the buyer returned the unfit goods to the seller and asked for a refund〉(买主退回一件不合适的物品给卖主,并要求退款)。②(家庭法)道义上不合格,无能力胜任〈the judge fund the mother unfit and so found that awording custody of the child to the father was in the child's best interests〉(法官判决母亲不适合,无能力胜任孩子的监护人,从孩子的利益考虑,故判定监护工作由父亲承担)]/使不适合中,使不能胜任,使无资格
unfit for trial 不宜接受审判(指一种精神状态,如被告处于精神失常状态进行审判将是不公平的,则不宜审判)
unfit to plead 无从辩护,不宜辩驳
unfitness to plead 不适宜辩护
unfold v. 展开,打开;开展(运动);逐步表明,阐明
unforbidden a. 不禁止的,准许的,认可的
unforced a. 自动的,自发的;非强迫的,不勉强的
unforensic a. 不适于法庭的
unforeseeable a. 不能预见的,预料不到的

unforeseeable act of a third party 不可预见的第三人行为
unforeseeable consequence 不能预见的后果
unforeseeable developments 不能预见的结果,不可预测的结果
unforeseeable loss 不可预见的损失
unforeseen circumstances 预料不到的情况
unforeseen developments 未预见的发展,未预料的情况,意外性,意外情况的发展
unforeseen events 不能预料的事件
unforeseen sudden and significant increase 未预见的、突然的重大增加
unforeseic rhetoric 不适于法庭的辞藻
unfounded a. 无根据的,无稽的;没有理的
unfounded charges 缺乏根据的指控
unfounded decision 无根据的判决
unfounded rumor 无稽的谣言
unfree a. 不自由的
unfree tenure (英史)不完全土地保有权
unfulfilled a. 未实现的,未履行的,未完成的
unfunded a. 未备基金的;(债务等)短期的,借款期在一年以内的
ungovernable a. 1.难控制的,难驾驭的,难统治的 2.放肆的,任性的
ungrounded a. 无事实根据的,无理由的
ungrudging a. 出自内心的;自愿的;情愿的;慷慨的
unheard a. 未予听审的;未予审讯的;未被给予申述机会的;不被倾听的
unheard-of speed 空前未有的速度
unhusbanded a. 1.无丈夫的;未嫁的 2.未耕耘的
uni-nominal majority voting into ballots 单记名多数两轮投票制
unicameral legislature 一院制的立法机关
unicameral system (议会)一院制
unicameralism n. (议会)一院制
unidentified a. 不能证明为同一人或物的;未确认的;来路不明的
unidentified plane 国籍不明的飞机
UNIDROIT 统一私法国际学社
unification n. 统一;一致;单元化
unification of law 法律的统一
unificationary activities (法律)统一化运动
unified a. 统一的,联合的

Unified Bar Association (美)统一律师协会(经政府批准建立的律师组织)

unified credit 见 unified estate-and-gift tax credit

unified estate-and-gift tax credit (1988年)统一遗产和赠与税减免[指针对联邦统一财产转让税适用税收减免,替代了遗产和赠与税豁免。参见美国《国内税收法》,《美国注释法典》第26标题卷第2001(c)(2)节,通常缩略为 unified credit。亦称 applicable exclusion credit]

unified identification 同一认定

unified judicial supervision 统一的司法监督

unified leadership 统一领导

unified purchase and sale (中)统购包销

unified tax-collection agency 统一的征税机构

unified transfer tax 统一转让税(指因赠与或死亡的联邦转让税,它可替代单独的联邦赠与税和不动产税)

uniform a. 相同的,一致的;统一的;一贯的,始终如一的

Uniform Act 1.统一法[指绝大多数或全部州均采用的法律草案(law drafted),特别是统一的法。见 Uniform Law; Model Act] 2.见 Uniform Statute

uniform administration 统一实施,统一管理

uniform administration of the law 实施法律的统一性

Uniform Adoption Act (UAA) (美)《统一收养法》[指1994年的规范法规,目的在于达到在收养法规领域的一致性或统一性目的。1994年美国统一州法委员会颁布的《统一收养法》(UAA)作了新近的释义,《统一收养法》关于州的收养始于1953年,1971年较早释义大部分不成功,虽经数次修订,但只有少数州正式立法颁布]

Uniform Anatomical Gift Act (美)《统一生理器官赠与法》,《统一器官捐献法》[指1968年的规范式法规,它制定管理(人体)结构赠与的赠与方与接受方的协议(protocols)。根据该法,一个人为了器官移植、治疗、研究或教育的目的可以捐赠自己身体的全部或部分器官。该法已由50个州以若干形式采用。同时,该法于1987年曾被修订,而且修订的释义亦被至少22个州以若干形式采用,缩略为UAGA]

Uniform Bills of Lading Act (美)《统一提单法》

uniform body of substantive federal maritime law 统一实体性质的联邦海事法体系,实体联邦海事法统一体系

Uniform Business Corporation Act (美)《统一公司法》

Uniform Child Custody Jurisdiction Act (UCCJA) (美)《统一儿童监护管辖法》[指1968年的规范制定法,该法宣布一项(基于儿童居所和某州关联的)标准。按此标准,该州法院可以决定对此特定儿童监护事宜是否具有管辖权,抑或它必须承认由另一州法院颁发的监护令(custody decree)。现《统一儿童监护管辖法》已由1997年的《统一儿童监护管辖与实施法》(the Uniform Child Custody Jurisdiction and Enforcement Act)所替代。见 home state; Parental Kidnapping Prevention Act; Uniform Child Custody Jurisdiction and Enforcement Act]

Uniform Child Custody Jurisdiction and Enforcement Act (UCCJEA) (美)《统一儿童监护管辖与实施法》[指1997年规范的制定法规,它提供统一的迅速处理州际监护和探访事宜的方法。该法规作为《统一儿童监护管辖法》(Uniform Child Custody Jurisdiction Act)的后继法而正式颁布。故此法规使得《预防双亲劫持儿童法》(Parental Kidnapping Prevention Act)和《强暴妇女法》(Violence Against Women Act)符合统一性或与该法规相一致。该法修改了儿童监护管辖,提出较明确的原管辖和连续管辖的标准。同时,该法还为实施州际儿童监护和探访事宜提供弥补程序。见 Uniform Child Custody Jurisdiction Act]

Uniform Class Action Rule (美)《统一集团诉讼规则》

Uniform Code of Military Justice (UCMJ)

(美)《统一军法典》[指①《军事法典》;②由治理国家军队的美国统一州法委员会正式颁布的规范法典。当时处于非联邦兵役(federal service)时期。参见《统一注释法规》第 11 卷第 335 页及以下(11U. L. A. 335 et seq.)(1974 年)]

Uniform Commercial Code (UCC, U. C. C.) (美)《统一商法典》[1957 年美国统一州法委员会通过了《统一商法典》,该商法典是由美国法学会(American Law Institute)和美国统一州法委员会联合起草的一部法律。美国各州都在不同程度上采用了该法典。该法典规定的内容有: 商品销售和租赁(sales and leasing of goods)、资金过户(transfer of funds)、商业文件(commercial paper)、银行押金和托收、银行存款和收款(bank deposits and collections)、信用证(letters of credit)、整体过户(bulk transfers)、仓库收据(warehouse receipt)、提货单(bills of lading)、投资证券(investment securities)和担保交易(secured transactions)等]

Uniform Computer Information Transaction (or Trade) Act (UCITA) (美)《统一计算机信息交易法》[指控制软件特许或计算机信息交易的示范法。该法依靠合同法和《统一商法典》为特许(licensing)创设制度规章的方案(regulatory scheme)而非进行买卖出租或交易。在其他方面,UCITA 适用于特许合同、购买软件合同、软件开发合同,以及通过互联网进入数据库的合同。在《统一商法典》范围内它并不包括动产或货物和服务合同]

Uniform Condition Sales Act (美)《统一附加条件销售法》

Uniform Consumer Credit Code (美)《统一分期付款销售法》,《统一消费者信贷法》[指旨在简化和使消费者适应现代化信贷和重利法的统一法规,使消费者易于理解贷款交易的期限(terms of credit transactions),保护消费者免受不公平行为和类似惯例之损害。此法已被个别州采用,缩略为 UCCC 或 U3C;亦称 Consumer Credit Code。见 Consumer Credit Protection Act]

Uniform Crime Reports (美)《统一犯罪报告》(指由联邦调查局准备的定题为"在美国的犯罪状况"的年度犯罪学系列研究丛刊。此报告或汇编包括有关 8 项罪行的索引、逮捕的统计、有关犯罪的资料、犯罪率以及类似项目。缩略为 UCR)

uniform customs 统一惯例

uniform customs and practice of commercial documentary credits 商业跟单信用证统一惯例

Uniform Determinate Sentencing Act (美)《统一确定量刑法》

Uniform Determination of Death Act (美)《统一死亡确定法》[指为确定死亡提供综合基准(comprehensive basis)的 1978 年示范法规。这是一项技术性法规,它只是对死亡作出临床的定义,而不涉及自杀、助杀(assisted suicide)或死亡权利(right to die)。该法于 1980 年修订,几乎为所有的州采用]

uniform discovery practice 统一披露实务,统一出示程序

Uniform Disposition of Community Property at Death Act (美)《统一处分共同财产消亡法》[指 1971 年对于非共同财产(non-community-property)的示范法规,该法规旨在说明在配偶双方将共同财产转到非共同财产州(non-community-property states)之前,保护一方配偶在财产(共同财产)方面的权利。如果他们已经切割或改变了他们的共同财产的权利则不属保护范畴。见 community property]

uniform distribution of materials 统一分配物资

Uniform Divorce Recognition Act (美)《统一离婚认可法》[指 1947 年由某些州对因有关充分诚信问题争议(full-faith-and-credit issues)所引起的离婚而采用的规范法规。缩略为 UDRA]

Uniform Enforcement of Foreign Money Judgment Act (美)《统一外国货币判决执行法》(指允许州法院之间执行适用类似的简化程序)

uniform expert evidence act 专家证据统一法;鉴定证据统一法

uniform federal law （美）统一联邦法
uniform federal practice 统一的联邦司法实务
Uniform Gifts to Minors Act 同 Uniform Transfer to Minors Act
uniform international law 统一国际法
Uniform Interstate and International Procedure Act （美）《统一州际与国际程序法》
Uniform Interstate Family Support Act （美）《统一州际家庭扶养法》[指1992年建立的"一令制"（one-order system）的示范法规。根据"一令制"，一个州颁发的离婚后一方承担另一方的扶养费（alimony）或子女扶养费令可以针对居住在另一个州的前夫（或妻）强制执行。该法已为美国各个州所采纳，并在子女扶养费的诉讼中作为审判的基础。该法的目的在于通过所有各州都能连续不断地承认并执行其他州颁布的扶养费令来使得州际子女扶养费和亲父认定的追求更能获得效果，长期稳定。在此法正式颁布之前，州际之间在处理州际子女扶养费问题上悬殊甚大。因为每个州对早期的统一法，即《统一扶养相互执行法》（Uniform Reciprocal Enforcement of Support Act）有各种不同的释意。此法已于1996年修订，缩略为UIFSA]
uniform invoice 统一发票
uniform judicial application of the law 法院适用法律的一致性
Uniform Jury Selection and Service Act （美）《统一陪审团选任和工作法》
Uniform Juvenile Court Act （美）《统一少年法庭法》[指1968年模范制定法规，旨在：①按此法规定，提供对少年的关照，保护以及在道德上、精神上和身体上健康发展；②规定对未成年的违法行为的处分、培训以及教育改造而不是进行刑事惩罚；③除非父母离异，尽可能维持其家庭团聚，让孩子具有必需的儿童幸福，并享有公共的利益；④为了公平审理并保护少年违法行为适用宪法上和其他法律上的权利而规定的司法程序；⑤规定简易州际程序（simple interstate procedure）以实施不同州之间的合作措施。缩略为 UJCA]

uniform law on cheques 统一支票法
Uniform Law （美）统一法，统一法规[指一种非官方（或非正式）的法律或法规，被建议作为全国各州的立法并严格采纳成为书面法规，旨在更大程度地提高法律、法规连贯性和一致性。所有的统一法规均由美国统一州法委员会正式颁布，其完整的汇集（complete collection）可参见《统一法规注释》（Uniform Laws Annotated）。见 Uniform Statute; Model Act]
Uniform Law Commissioners 见 National Conference of Commissioners on Uniform State Laws
uniform legislation 统一立法
uniform level of liability 统一责任标准
Uniform Limited Liability Company Act (ULLCA) （美）《统一有限责任公司法》（1996年由统一州法委员会制定）
Uniform Limited Partnership Act （美）《统一有限合伙法》[指由州立法机构采纳并于1916年正式颁布的示范法规，目的在于调整有限合伙的合伙人之间的关系。除路易斯安那州外，其他所有的州有一个时期都采用此法，美国统一州法委员会于1976年正式颁布了《修订统一有限合伙法》（Revised Uniform Limited Partnership Act）（RULPA），并于1985年又作了实质性的修订，大多数州业已采纳。缩略为 ULPA]
Uniform Mandatory Disposition of Detainers Act （美）《统一强制性处理羁押法》（指1958年的模范制定法规，它要求根据某州的罪犯的书面请求，要求该州及时处理任一被指控有罪的在押待审犯。该法已被一些州采用。见 Interstate Agreement on Detainers Act）
Uniform Marriage and Divorce Act （美）《统一结婚与离婚法》
Uniform Narcotic Drugs Act （美）《统一麻醉药剂法》
uniform national law 统一的国内法，统一的本国法
Uniform Negotiable Instruments Act （美）《统一票据法》

Uniform New Payment Code (美)《统一新支付法典》,《统一新支付法汇编》

Uniform Parentage Act (美)《统一家系法》,《统一父母双亲身份法》[指一部1973年的模范法规,该法规定了为子女或孩子的终生幸福和指明孩子的扶养而确定父母身份的一些方法。该法摒弃了婚生和非婚生子女身份之间的区别,而代之以法院在双亲与子女的关系存在的基础上确定孩子的权利和父母的责任。美国各州已采纳该法。2000年和2002年该法分别作了两次修订。修订的各项条款规定了建立包括婚生或非婚生父母的子女统一家系法规(特别是父系之源)以及确立遗传测试(genetic testing)的标准和规则,少数州已经颁布该修订法的阐释。该法已为全美各个州所采用]

Uniform Parental Act (美)《统一亲权法》

Uniform Partnership Act (美)《统一合伙法》[指一部1914年的模范制定法,旨在促进州治理无限责任和有限责任合伙关系(general and limited partnership)法规的一致性。该法几乎已为美国各州所采用,但在有些州,该法已由《统一合伙法》修订版(1994年)所替代。缩略为 UPA]

Uniform Premarital Agreement Act (UPAA) (美)《统一婚前协议法》[指一部1983年的模范法规,促使婚前契约草案(drafting)成为准则或先例,并规定一个更为可靠的框架以便此草案更为完善且便于执行的协议。根据《统一婚前协议法》(UPPA),婚前协议(premarital agreement)必须是书面的,而且经男女双方当事人签字,只要一结婚,即产生法律效力,在婚姻期间,或在配偶一方死亡或离婚情况时,按协议来解决资产、扶养和债务问题。美国约有1/3州以这种方式进行]

Uniform Principal and Income Act (美)《统一本金及收益法》[美国一些州已采纳这一统一法规,它对信托和遗产中本金和收益的分配(allocation)均予以规范]

Uniform Probate Code (美)《统一遗嘱检验法典》(指1969年的示范法规,该法为治理无遗嘱继承、遗嘱检验以及遗产管理等的规定原则现代化。1969年以来,该法已广泛地进行过多次修订,而且为绝大多数州所采用。缩略为 UPC)

uniform progressive tax 统一累进税

Uniform Putative and Unknown Fathers Act (美)《统一推定与不明父亲法》,《推定与不明父亲统一法》[指1988年的示范法规,旨在将联邦最高法院就未婚父亲与其子女关系的判决汇编成法。该法首先宣告未婚父亲权利(unwed father's right)终止,而后裁定为父亲身份(paternity)以收养程序去探视、监护。缩略为 UP-UFA 亦称为 Model Putative Fathers Act]

Uniform Reciprocal Enforcement of Divorce Act (美)《统一离婚相互执行法》

Uniform Reciprocal Enforcement of Support Act (美)《统一扶养相互执行法》[指1950年的示范法规(现已被替代),旨在追求以统一的方法使州际的扶养事宜得以办理,而且该方法中的一个管辖令(jurisdiction's orders)可以得到另一管辖区域的充分诚信与尊重(full faith and credit)。该法于1958年和1960年修订,并于1997年被《统一州际家庭扶养法》(Uniform Interstate Family Support Act)所替代。缩略 URESA。见 Uniform Interstate Family Support Act]

Uniform Rules for Contract Guarantees (美)《合同(契约)保证统一规则》

Uniform Rules of Conduct for the Interchange of Date Telecommunication 《数据电传交换统一行为守则》(1987年9月国际商会执行理事会第51届会议通过这一守则,旨在为用户提供一套国际公认的行为准则)

Uniform Sale Act (美)《统一销售法》

Uniform Simultaneous Death Act (美)《统一同时死亡法》,《同时死亡统一法》[指1940年的示范法规,该法确立一项规则,即某人必须比死者(decedent)多活至少120小时,以避免由于如共同灾难(common disaster)造成的同时死亡(simultaneous deaths)(谁先谁后死亡),或者由于很快相继死亡的两个人,他们之间是谁的财产或谁的人身保险金(death benefit)

给予幸存者或后死亡者的纠纷或争端(disputes)。在没有多活120小时规定的时间死亡,为了分配各自的遗产,每个人都被推定比另一个人后死亡或者是幸存者。该法于1993年修订,在某种程度上几乎为所有的州所采用。见 commorientes]

uniform standard for determining jurisdiction 决定管辖的统一标准

uniform standard of minimum contacts 统一的最低联系标准

uniform state law 统一州法律

uniform state property tax 统一国家财产税

Uniform status of Children of Assisted Conception Act (美)《协助怀孕子女的身份统一法》,《统一协助怀孕子女身份法》[指1988年的示范法规,旨在当运用帮助受孕时保证稳定的合法出身(legal parentage)。采用此法的州具有对代孕母亲(surrogate mother)规范订约或阻止订约的选择权]

Uniform Statute (美)统一法规,统一制定法[指旨在要全国全部或大部分州采纳起草的法规或法律草案(law drafted),特别是统一法规(Uniform Law)。亦称 model statute; uniform act。见 Model Act]

Uniform Stock Transfer Act (美)《统一股票过户法》,《统一股票转让法》

uniform substantive law 统一实体法

Uniform System of Citation (美)统一援引系统(指英美法国家援引判例和其他法规等的统一模式系统)

uniform system of weights and measures 统一的计量标准,统一的度量标准

uniform tax-collection agency 统一的征税机构

Uniform Trade Secret Act (美)《统一商业机(秘)密法》[指1979年的示范法规,已为大部分州正式颁布,并给予商业机密以定义,以区别普通法上因无继续使用要求的较广泛含意和以专门方法易于确定的信息(information readily ascertainable by proper means)不能证明合格的较狭窄含义。该法有三大要素:①此信息必须作为商业机密得以证实;②该信息通过不正当手段(wrongful means)或采用不履行保密义务(breaching duty of confidentiality)而必然被错误侵占;③机密拥有者必须采取合理预防以维护信息的机密,亦称 Uniform Trade Secrets Protection Act。缩略为 UTSA]

Uniform Trade Secrets Protection Act 同 Uniform Trade Secret Act

Uniform Transfers to Minors Act (美)《统一转让(财产)给未成年人法》,《统一给未成年人的转让法》[指1983年的模范法规,该法规定将财产转让给未成年人,并允准一个监护人以受托人的身份(fiduciary capacity)管理这笔投入的资本(investment),应用该资产的收入作为未成年人的扶养费用。该法已为大多数州所采用。1986年此法也作了修订。缩略为 UTMA, 亦称 Transfer to Minors Act, 以前称为 Uniform Gifts to Minors Act; Gifts to Minors Act]

uniform treatment of the jurisdiction question 统一处理管辖问题

Uniform Trust Receipts Act (美)《统一信托单据法》

Uniform Warehouse Receipts Act (美)《统一仓库单据法》

Uniform Written Obligations Act of 1925 《1925年统一债务文书法》

uniformity n. 一致(性),一式,一律,均匀(性)

Uniformity Clause (1881年)统一性条款[指美国联邦宪法的条款要求联邦税款统一征收(uniform collection)。美国联邦宪法第1条第8款第1节]

uniformity of application of law 适用法律的一致性

uniformity of law 法律的统一性

uniformity of law throughout the U. S. 全美的法律统一

uniformity of process 诉讼程序的一致性

unigeniture n. (古代)只有一个孩子的事实

unilateral a. 单方面的,片面的,单独的;一方的

unilateral act 单方行为,一方行为,单独

行为
unilateral act of the settler 信托人的单方面行为
unilateral act of will 自愿的单方行为
unilateral conflict rules 单边(方)冲突规范
unilateral contract 单务合同(契约),单方承担义务的契约
unilateral declaration of intent (will) 单方意思表示;单方宣告
unilateral denunciation 单方废除,片面废止
unilateral divorce (美)单方离婚(指一方向另一方支付赔偿就可以解除婚姻关系,有加利福尼亚等8个州根据《统一婚姻和离婚法》草案,建议如配偶一方决定单方离婚就有权自动取得在婚姻存在期间所积累的全部财产的1/2。这种办法成为对离婚的鼓励)
unilateral exportation (importation) 单边出口(进口)
unilateral instrument 单方证件,单方文件
unilateral juristic(al) acts 单方的法律行为
unilateral mistake 单方错误,一方错误
unilateral obligation 单方债务
unilateral preliminary agreement 片面预约,单方草约
unilateral procedure 单方诉讼程序
unilateral promise 单方允诺
unilateral record (提供证据的)单方记录
unilateral repudiation of a debt 单方否认债务,单方拒绝履行债务
unilateral repudiation of the wife 单方面遗弃妻子,休妻
unilateral requirement (婚姻实质要件中的)单方要件
unilateral statement 单方面声明
unilateral transaction 单方法律行为
unilateral transfer 单方面让与;国际收支中的单边资金转移;单边转移;片面转移
unilateral unanimity 单方的一致同意
unilateralis 一面亲(罗马法中指诸子女并不都是同一父母所生)
unimodal carrier 单一方式承运人
unimodal transport 单一方式运输
unimpaired a. 未受损害的,未减弱的;(价

位等)未减少的
unimpaired prestige 未受损害的威望(信)(或声誉)
unimpeachable a. 无可指责的;无过失的;无可怀疑的;无懈可击的,无缺陷的
unimpeachable parents 不可否认的父母
unimpeachable reputation 清白的名声
unimpeached a. 未受指责的,未受责问的
unimpeded a. 无阻的,不受阻碍的
unimpeded passage through 不受阻碍通过
unimplemented a. 未实施的,未实行的
unimplemented trade agreement 未实施的贸易协定
unimpugnable a. 无懈可击的,的确凿的,无可非议的;不可驳斥的
unincorporated a. 未组成公司(团体)的,未赋予组成法人资格的;未立案的,非法人的
unincorporated association 未取得法人资格的社团,非法人社团;非法人团体
unincorporated bank 未立案银行
unincorporated body 未取得法人资格的团体,非法人团体
unincorporated company 未取得法人资格的公司;未立案公司
unincorporated society 非法人团体,非法人社团,无法人资格的协会
unincumbered a. 未受牵累的;未负债的
uninfluenced a. 未受他人影响的;不偏心的;公正的;无偏见的
uninformed a. 1.未被告知的,未得通知的 2.无知的;未受教育的,蒙昧的
uninformed player 不拥有信息的参与人
uninhibited a. 不受禁令约束的,无拘束的
uninjured a. 未受损害的;未受伤害的
uninsured a. 未保险的,未经保险的
unintelligible a. 难于理解的,晦涩难懂的
unintended consequences 非故意结果
unintentional a. 非故意的,无意的,无心的
unintentional act 非故意的行为
unintentional crime 过失犯罪
unintentional defamation 非故意的毁损名誉
uninterested a. 无利害关系的(尤指财产方面的);不感兴趣的,不关心的,态度冷漠

的,无利害关系的
unintoxicating a. 不醉人的,不会使人醉的
unio n. 教会合并(指按教会法两个教会的合并)
union n. 1.联合,组合 2.工会,协会,联合会,公会,联盟 3.结婚,性交
union by laws 工会章程
union card 工会会员证
Union Congress of Soviets (原苏联)最高苏维埃
union contract 集体合同,劳动合同
Union House (英)公立贫民院
Union International Consultants 联合国际顾问公司
union Jack 英国国旗或国徽
union member(s) 工会会员
union mortgage clause 标准抵押权条款
union of concubinage 纳妾
Union of International Association (UIA) 国际协会联盟
union representative 工会代表
union security 工会安全
union shop 1.(全体从业人员的工资、工作时间、工作条件必须由资方和工会间的合同规定的)工商机构 2.(资方与工会订立合同允许雇用非工会会员,但受雇人员必须于规定期间加入工会,且在就业期间内永远为工会会员的)工商机构;工人限期加入工会的工厂或企业,(美)只雇用工会会员的商店或工厂 3.必须加入工会条款 4.(大写)消费合作社(布莱顿创办,又称共同商店。见 Brighton Co-operator Association)
union shop agreement (资方与企业约定的)雇用非工会会员的工人应限期加入工会协议
union trust (英)共同信托投资基金
union-security clause (美)工会安全条款[指旨在保护工会、抵制雇主、非工会组织的雇员以及竞争之联合会(competing unions)的劳动合同(union contract)中的规定条款]
unionism n. 工联主义,工会的制度(原则或理论);联合的原则
unionist n. 工会会员;工会主义者

unions outside of marriage 婚外结合(指巴巴多斯家庭立法所涵盖的一种婚外情况)
unipersonal trader 独资企业
unique a. 唯一的,独特的,无与伦比的
unique a./n. 独一无二的,无比的,唯一的,独特的,无可匹敌的,罕见的,不平凡的/独一无二的事物
uniqueness n. 独一无二的事物,唯一的事物
uniquity n. 独特性(此词为美国大法官霍尔姆斯为赞赏罗斯科·庞德的特点而创造的一个新词)
unissued capital 未发放的股本,未发行的股票
unissued mortgage bond 未发放抵押债券(指公司债券)
unissued stock (公司)未兑现的股票,已经授权但未发行的股本
unit n. 单位;单元;部队(单位);一部机器
unit cost 单位成本
unit investment quotas 单位投资额
unit limitation of liability (集装箱提单的)按单位的责任限制
unit load system 单位装运制
unit load transport system 成组货运制
unit of account 记账单位,计算单位
unit of measurement 计量单位
unit price 单价
unit rule (美)单元选票制,单位投票法
unit tax 单位税
unit trust 单位信托(指通过对大范围的股票交易证券进行投资后分散风险的一种方法);互惠投资公司,单元投资信托,单位信托公司,(英)共同信贷投资基金;联合托拉斯
unit value 单位价值
unital a. 两人间关系的[指只涉及两人之间法律关系(legal relations)的]
unitary a. 1.不可分割的;单一的 2.一元论的 3.中央集权论的
unitary business (税务)(美)关联企业,联合企业,连锁商业,综合商业[指在其他的州或在他国有附属部门或连锁商业部门的一个综合性商业或商店。在计算其

所得税时,则按附属部门或连锁部门所经营财产(或资本)在该州内经销活动的收入来决定,同时按那个州的百分比交付税款]

unitary circuit court (墨西哥)独任制巡回法庭

unitary constitution 单一宪法

unitary firm 单一性企业(指与 collective firm 相对而言)

unitary government 单一制政府,中央集权制的政府

unitary income tax 综合所得税

unitary multinational state 统一的多民族国家

unitary state 单一国(一个统一的主权国家,作为一个单一的国际法主体)

unitary system 单一制,单一税制,单一化制

unitary system of courts 单一的法院体制

unitary tax (美)单一所得税,单一税(指本州企业与本州或本国以外的分支机构之间进行交易所得收入的纳税。见 unitary business)

unitas personarum 人的结合(指夫妻、家系)

united a. 联合的,统一的;一致的,团结的

united family 和睦家庭

united front (中)统一战线;联合阵线

United Kingdom (英)联合王国(包括大不列颠和北爱尔兰,首都在伦敦)

United Kingdom for order 英国沿海指定港

United Kingdom Patent Office (UKPO) 英国专利局

(the) United Nations 联合国(根据1945年在旧金山会议签订的《联合国宪章》而成立的一个世界性国际组织)

(the) United Nations Assembly 联合国大会

United Nations Charter 《联合国宪章》(1945年6月26日在美国旧金山签订的,同年10月24日起生效)

United Nations Commission on Human Rights 联合国人权委员会

United Nations Convention against Corruption 联合国反腐败公约(2003年10月31日第58届联大通过,已有100多国家签署,我国于2003年12月10日签署)

United Nations Commission on International Trade Law (UNCITRAL) 联合国国际贸易法委员会

United Nations Convention on the Carriage of Goods by Sea, 1978 《1978年联合国海上货物运送公约》[简称汉堡规则(The Hamburg Rules),由联合国贸易暨发展会议起草,自1992年11月1日生效实施。全文共34条]

United Nations Convention on the Law of the Sea 《联合国海洋公约》(指1982年的海洋公约)

United Nations Declaration 《联合国家宣言》(亦称《联合国家共同宣言》,指第二次世界大战期间,正在参加对德、意、日轴心国家作战的中、苏、美、英等26个国家于1942年1月1日在华盛顿签署的共同反对法西斯的联合国家宣言)

United Nations Documents Index 《联合国文件和出版物书目索引》(1998年开始出版,其前身为 United Nations Documents Checklist)

United Nations Educational, Scientific and Cultural Organization 联合国教科文组织

United Nations Emergency Force 联合国紧急部队

United Nations Participation Act 《联合国参与法》(指1945年美国国会通过的《联合国参与法》,以一般授权的方式对《联合国宪章》第七章安理会制裁措施在美国国内执行作了规定。该法第5条规定:"无论其他法律规定如何,当安理会依据《联合国宪章》第七章的规定作出决定,要求美国采取措施以执行该决议时,美国总统应通过其任命或设立的机构以及其签发的命令、规章或条例,采取必要措施,以执行上述决议。")

United Nations Peace-keeping Force 联合国维持和平部队

United Nations Secretariat 联合国秘书处

United Nations Security Council 联合国安

全理事会

United Nations Treaty Series 《联合国条约丛书》(U. N. T. S.)（收入自1946年以来由会员国向联合国注册的所有条约和非会员国申请注册的一些条约的这套丛书,是1920年至1946年出版相似内容的《国际联盟条约丛书》的继续,有英、法文本）

United Nations War Crimes Commission 联合国战争罪行委员会

United Parcel Service, United States 美国联合包裹运送服务公司

United Republic 联合共和国

United States Arbitration Act 《美国仲裁法》

United States Army Criminal Investigation Laboratory 美军刑事调查试验室

United States attorney 美国检察官（指联邦的检察官）

United States Coast Guard 美国海岸警卫队[指兵役和武装部队的分支机构,强制执行按美国管辖适合海域的联邦法规和行政法规,并颁布管理条例以保护按美国管辖海域的生命和财产的安全,实施海上救助事宜(maritime rescue operation),进行海洋学研究(oceanographic research),同时充当一支特种海军分支。海岸警卫队建立于1915年,参见《美国注释法典》第14标题卷第1节。它已是美国财政部(U. S. Department of the Treasury)和美国交通部(U. S. Department of Transportation)的一部分。现今,和平时期它属美国国家安全部(U. S. Department of Homeland Security)。战争时期,它则属美国国防部(U. S. Department of Defense)。缩略为USCG]

United States Code(U. S. C.) 《美国法典》（指1926年出版的官方版的联邦法规汇典,共含50个标题。该法典每6年出版一次完整的修订本,并附有在此时期汇集的补充合订卷本。该法典1/3的题目所包含的法规均被重新宣布有效。因此,该法典已成为权威性的文本。但须注意对该法典的援引涉及的是标题和条款而不涉及卷本和页码。例如,18 U. S. C. § 1521,即为《美国法典》标题18第1621条）

United States Code Annotated (U. S. C. A.) 《美国注释法典》(指包括《美国法典》完整文本的多卷本出版物,它含有州的判例注释,附有解释和应用专门法规条款的联邦判决,以及有关条款的互参、历史说明和图书参考等。此注释法典由《美国法制会议和行政新闻》作进一步增补)

United States Copyright Office 美国版权局[指美国国会图书馆的分支机构,负责执行联邦版权法。除处理申请版权事宜之外,美国版权局存储已存在的版权资料,并根据要求发布有关版权保护问题的判决意见。在此机构储存的资料并非自动地增加到美国国会图书馆的藏书(collection)之中,而是根据要求单独直接提供给图书馆。该局还实施或执行制定法规中的各类特许条款,包括征收或分配版税(royalties)]

United States Court of Appeals 美国上诉法院（指1981年设立的中级上诉法院,目的是减轻最高法院处理联邦审理法院所有原判决的上诉案件的负担）

United States Court of Appeals for the Federal Circuit 美国联邦巡回上诉法院[指中级(mtermediate level)受理上诉法院,具有对专利案件,针对美国要求重新获得损害赔偿的各类诉讼案件,来自美国联邦权利申诉法院、美国国际贸易法院、美国退伍军人权利申诉上诉法院、功绩制度保护局(Merit System Protection Board)以及一些行政机构来的案件有管辖权或司法审判权。该法院是1982年合并海关和专利上诉法院(Court of Customs and Patent Appeals)与权利申诉法院(Court of Claims)（即使美国联邦权利申诉法院的审判管辖权已被给予一个新的美国权利法院）而创立的,根据其创立的目的,结束了专利诉讼中的竞择法院(forum-shopping)问题,解决了巡回裁判中专利法原则中的分歧,并允准单一管辖地(single forum)展开必要的专家鉴定去裁定引起专利诉讼的复杂的技术问题,此词条通常缩略为Federal Circuit; CAFC; Fed Cir.]

waiver of service 送达的放弃（指按美国《联邦民事规则》第4条规定的程序,原告

享有要求被告签署放弃送达传票的表格选择权。收到这一要求的被告有义务签署自愿放弃送达并避免传票所涉及的"不必要开支",该规则为被告设定两点好处:低费用和有较多时间答辩)

United States Court of Claims 美国索赔法院

United States Court of Customs and Patent Appeals 美国海关和专利上诉法院

United States Courts 美国法院(指美国最高法院、上诉法院、地区法院、权利请求法院等,相对于州法院而言)

United States Customs Bonded 美国海关保税

United States District Court 美国地区法院(指各州具有一般联邦管辖权的审理法院,现共有 90 个)

United States Government Life Insurance 美国政府人寿保险(指美国政府第一次世界大战时办的"人寿保险")

United States Maritime Commission (USMC) 美国海事委员会

United States Marshal (美)联邦行政执行官,联邦司法执行官[指执行联邦法院的各项指令(orders)的联邦官员。联邦司法执行官实际是政府行政部门的雇员]

United States Mint 美国造币厂[指美国财政部(Department of the Treasury)的一个部门,负责生产商贸经营活动中常常使用的硬币(coins)、古钱币(numismatic coins)、金币和银币以及国家级勋章等。它在诺克斯堡(Fort Knox)、肯塔基州具有经营金库的能力(gold-storage facility)。以前它曾名为 Bureau of the Mint]

United States of America Law 美利坚众国法;《美国法》

United States Patent Office (USPO) 美国专利局

United States Reports (U. S. Reports) 《美国判例汇编》(该汇编作为私人尝试始于 1790 年,但于 1817 年即成为官方的,并作为美国最高法院判决的官方出版物一直延续到今天)

United States Secret Service 美国特工作局,美国秘密工作局[指美国国家安全部(U. S. Department of Homeland Security)的法律强制执行机构,负责总统、副总统、某些其他政府官员以及来访的外国外交官的安全,并通过对于伪造仿制货币和信用卡诈骗强制执法以保护美国的通货。该局是 2003 年由财政部转过来的,通常缩略为 Secret Service]

United States Sentencing Commission 美国量刑委员会[指美国联邦政府司法部门中的一个独立委员会,负责制定和规范并调整(setting and regulating)在联邦法院中刑事判刑(或量刑)的准则(guidelines),同时发布政策说明以便适用。委员会的成员均由总统任命,经参议院同意。该委员会是依据《1984 年量刑改革法》(Sentencing Reform Act of 1984)而创立的。参见《美国注释法典》第 28 标题卷第 991 节]

United States Statutes at Large 见 Statutes at Large

United States Supreme Court Digest 《美国最高法院判决摘要汇编》[指由西方出版公司出版的美国最高法院判决摘要汇编,该汇编包括最高法院判例。但应注意:律师合作出版公司也为最高法院出版了一种判决摘要汇编,名称相同,即《美国最高法院判决摘要汇编,律师版》(United States Supreme Court Digest, Lawyers' Edition)]

United States sentencing guideline (美)美国量刑指南[指为法官对于联邦法规规定的犯罪(federal crime)作出适当判刑决定的系列详细指导说明。缩略为 USSG,亦称为 Federal sentencing guidenline]

United States Trade and Development Agency 美国贸易发展署(指一个独立的联邦机构,负责促进美国与发展中国家之间贸易的行政部门,并在美国创设一些职位,促进较贫困国家的经济发展。该机构作为贸易与发展项目创立于 1961 年,于 1992 年更名为现在的"美国贸易发展署"。缩略为 TDA;USTDA)

United States Treasury 美国财政部
uniting for peace 团结和平
unitized cargo 成组货载
unitized transport 成组货运

unitrust n. 统一信托(指每年支付给信托受益人的信托财产固定百分比的一种信托)
units of commodity 产品销量
units of product 产品数量
unity n. 统一(性),统一体,一致(性);协调(性);团结,联合;(目的、行动等的)一贯性,不变性;共同租地权
unity of an inheritance 继承财产的单一性(原则)
unity of command 统一指挥
unity of law 法律的统一(性)
unity of possession 共同占有
unity of private law 私法的单一性
unity of right 权利的共有
unity of seisin (1800年)混同占有[指在一个人已占有一块土地的情况下,而他(或她)在此土地上却已有了供役权,则此人造成混同占有,共同依法占有财产]
unity of seizin 共同依法占有的财产
unity of time (18世纪)同一时间[指全部共同保有人(joint tenants)的权益必须基于同一时间产生。亦称 time unity]
unity of title (18世纪)共同所有权,权利统一[指全部共同(地产)保有人必须基于同一文契获取他们的权益。亦称 title unity]
∗ *Unius omnino testis responsio non audiatur.* The answer of one witness shall not be heard at all. 绝不受理单独证人的辩论(作证)。
universal inheritance rule (遗嘱和遗产)普遍继承规则[指一项原则坚持认为一笔无遗嘱继承的财产,只有在死者没有存活的,哪怕是很远的亲属的情况下,该遗产则应归国家所有。即使在20世纪上半叶,这一规则在美国管辖地区仍广泛地受到遵循。《统一遗嘱检验法典》(Uniform Probate Code)摒弃了此项普遍继承规定,而且只要没有第三人或比死者活得更长时间的同一祖先的近亲属,则此无遗嘱继承的财产应归国家所有。亦称 rule of universal inheritance。见 laughing heir]
universal a. 普遍的;全体的;全世界的;通用的;一般的
universal adult franchise 成年人普选权
universal adult suffrage 成年人普选制
universal agency 总代理商,总代理公司(见 general agency)
universal agent 总代理人,全权代理人(指有权代委托人做一切合法之事的代理人)
universal banking system 多功能银行制度;综合性银行业务制
Universal Copyright Convention 《世界版权公约》[指对签署国有拘束力的1952年条约,它给其他成员国以与签署国本国公民所享有的相同的版权保护,参见《美国条约和其他国际协议》第25卷1341页(25 U. S. T. 1341),《美国条约和其他协议系列丛书》7868号(T. I. A. S. No. 7868)。由联合国教科文组织(UNESCO)主管的这个公约对于在那些也是《伯尔尼公约》(Berne Convention)的签署国并不适用。美国于1955年签署此条约。缩略为 UCC]
Universal Declaration of Human Rights 《世界人权宣言》[指由联合国于1948年12月正式宣告的国际权利宣言(international bill of rights),它是国际领域第一个对于人权和基本自由的全面明确规定。序言指出人类社会的每个人都具有与生俱来的尊严,所有的人都享有平等和不可剥夺的权利。对于这些的公认是世界上自由、公正和平的基础。"宣言的全文"见附录六]
universal election 大选,普选
universal good 普遍的善,广义的善行
universal jurisdiction 普遍管辖
universal law 一般规律,世界法,万国法
universal legacy (美)(路易斯安那法)遗嘱赠与分配全部财产(动产和不动产),给予一个或更多的受赠人。参见《路易斯安那州民法典》第1585条(La. Civ. Code art. 1585)(见 general legacy; legacy under a universal title; particular legacy)
universal legal order 普遍的法律秩序
universal legatee 全部遗产继承人
universal malice 无目的的恶意,一般的故意
Universal Postal Union (联合国)万国邮政联盟(1874年成立)

universal property 概括财产
universal recognition of the right of authors 确认作者的权利
universal rule 普遍法(或原)则(康德从其权利观念出发,详尽阐述关于权利的普遍法则;根据普遍法则,自由意志的外在行为能与其他所有人的自由相共存)
universal rule of law 法律普遍规则
universal sense of justice 普遍的正义感
universal succession 概括继承;全部财产的继承(权)
universal successor 概括继承人,全部财产继承人
universal successor on death 死亡时的普遍继承人
universal suffrage 普选;全民参政权
Universal Supremacy of Justice 普遍至上的正义原则,普遍的正义至上原则
universal theory of crime 犯罪世界性说(认为犯罪行为无论发生于何地,总是社会的祸害,任何文明国家都有权加以镇压)
* *Universalia sunt notiora singularibus.* Things universal are better known than things particular. 一般的事物比特殊的事物更易于了解。
universalism-internationalism school 普遍主义—国际主义学派
universality n. 普遍性;一般性;(知识、才能、兴趣等)多方面性;广泛性
(the) universality principle 普遍性原则
universalizing comparison 普遍化比较
universalization n. 世界化
universitas 法人团体
universitas facti 事实上的集合物(指特定有形物,如仓库中的货物)
universitas juris 法律上的集合物(指全部动产和不动产,如遗产)
universitas rerum 财产总体(指数件单独而无联系的物集合在一起视为一个整体)
universitates personarum 自然人的团体
university courts (英)大学法庭(指在牛津、剑桥等大学里设立的法庭,审理学校内民事和轻微刑事案件)
university of Bologna 波伦亚大学(欧洲最古老、最著名的大学,亦为欧洲最大的法律研究中心)
unjelled a. 未定案的
unjelled agreement 未定案的合约
unjudged a. 未经审判的
(the) unjust n. 不公正的人
unjust a. 不公正的
unjust acquittal 不当的释放,不公正的宣判无罪释放
unjust arrest 无故逮捕,不当的逮捕
unjust(或 unjustified)enrichment 不当得利(指依法扣他人的财物和利益。禁止不当得利是一项原则。也指一个人不公正地得到钱或财产时应退回的法定原则,只是这不包括极力讨价还价的交易或交易中的运气所得)
unjust, framed-up and wrong cases (中)冤假错案
unjust judge 不公正的法官
unjust judg(e)ment 误判,不当判决
unjust law 非正义的法律
unjust penalty 不适当的刑罚
unjust sentence 不当的判决,不公正的判决
unjust to condemn a prisoner unheard 犯人不经审讯而判罪是不公平的
unjustifiable a. 不合理的,无理的;辩护不了的
unjustifiable detention 不正当的拘留;无理羁押
unjustified a. 不正当的,不合理的
unjustified abuse 不正当的辱骂
unjustified benefit 不当得利
unjustified veto power 不合理的否决权
unknown n./a. 未知的事物(或人)/未知的,不明的,不详的,不确知的
unknown clause 不详条款(指提单上所注的货物内容不详的条款)
unknown persons 不能确定身份的人,身份不能查明的人
unknown quantity 未知量;尚待决定(或证实)的事,难以预测的人(或事)
unknown soldier 阵亡的无名英雄
unlaw n. 无法纪
unlawful a. 1.不法的,非法的,不合法的,不正当的,违法的 2.私生的(孩子)

unlawful act 不法行为,违法行为
unlawful activity 非法活动
unlawful allocation 非法开支,非法支用
unlawful arrest 非法逮捕
unlawful assembly 非法集会;非法聚众(罪)
unlawful association 非法结社;(英)非法联合
unlawful attack 不法侵害
unlawful business operation 非法经营
unlawful cause 不当诉因
unlawful children 非婚生子女,私生子女
unlawful cohabitation 非法同居
unlawful deprivation of personal liberty 非法剥夺人身自由
unlawful detainer 不法占有;非法留置他人的不动产的人,非法扣押他人财产者
unlawful detention 非法关押,不法拘留
unlawful disturbance of the possession of goods 非法妨害物的占有
unlawful entry 非法侵入(土地等)
unlawful fight 非法斗殴,非法打斗
unlawful homicide 非法杀人(罪)
unlawful infringement 不法侵害
unlawful interest 非法权益
unlawful interference with personal liberty 非法干涉人身自由
unlawful keeping 非法持有
unlawful means 非法手段,不法手段
unlawful meeting 非法集会
unlawful oath(s) (扰乱社会治安的)非法立誓;(英)违法立誓(罪)(指参加制造骚乱、煽动叛变或扰乱治安等行为)
unlawful outflow of foreign currency 外币的非法外流
unlawful personal violence 非法人身侵犯(害)
unlawful possession 非法占有
unlawful possession of drug 私藏毒品
unlawful possession of weapons 私藏武器
unlawful practice 非法执业,非法开业
unlawful profit-making 非法牟利
unlawful publication 非法出版物
unlawful punishment 非法处罚
unlawful regime 非法政权

unlawful search 非法搜查
unlawful sexual act 非法性行为
unlawful sexual conduct with a minor 见 impairing the morals of a minor
unlawful sexual intercourse 非法性交
unlawful society 非法社团,非法团体
unlawful trading 非法交易
unlawful violence 非法暴力侵犯(害)
unlawful wounding 不法伤害
unlawfully and maliciously 非法而且恶意地
unlawfully obtained property 非法所得财产
unlawfulness n. 不合法,非法;违反道德准则
unless conj. 除非,如果不
unless sooner berthed 除非较早靠泊
unlicensed a. 1.未经当局许可的,无执照的 2.无节制的
unlicensed driver 无执照的驾驶员
unlicensed hawker 无执照的小贩
unlicensed lawyer 无证律师
unlicensed meeting 未经许可而召开的会议
unlicensed peddler 无证商贩;(沿街叫卖的)无证小贩
unlicensed practice 无证开业
unlicensed prostitute 暗娼
unlimited a. 无限的;无边际的;不定的;不受约束的;无条件的;无例外的
unlimited company 无限公司
unlimited discretion 无限的裁量权
unlimited damages 未订定的(违约)损害赔偿金(指事先未限定用多少金钱来补偿损失的,如侵犯人身体所造成的损害等)
unlimited general average guarantee 共同海损保证书
unlimited jurisdiction 全权管辖
unlimited liability 无限责任
unlimited original jurisdiction 不受限制的初审管辖权
unlimited partner 无限责任合伙人
unlimited partnership 无限合伙
unlimited power of vote 不受限制的表决权
unlimited right of appeal 不受限制的上诉权
unliquidated a. 未清算的,未决算的,未偿

还的,未付的
事主

unliquidated claim 尚未最后决定的权利请求;有争执的索赔,未决争端
unliquidated damages 未确定的损害赔偿,等待法庭裁定的损害赔偿
unliquidated obligation 未清偿的债务
unlisted properties 账外财产
unlisted securities 非上市证券,不上市证券(指不在交易所挂牌的证券)
unlivery n. (从船上)卸货,卸下(此词常用于海事法中)
unload v. 1.卸货,卸下;摆脱……负担 2.退出(枪等)子弹 3.倾销,抛售,脱手
unloading costs 卸货费用
unlocked door 未锁的门
unmaintainable a. 1.难于维持的,难于供养的,不可保持的 2.不能容许的,不能容忍的
unmarred a. 未受损害的
unmarriageable a. 不适于结婚的;年纪太轻不能结婚的;未达结婚年龄的
unmarried a. 未婚的,独身的
unmarried couple 未(曾结)婚的夫妻;(一对)未婚男女
unmarried mother 未婚的母亲
unmarried status 独身,不婚
unmarry v. 离婚,和……离婚
unmeant a. 不是故意的,非存心的
unmentionable a. 不可提及的,不敢说出的,不堪出口的,不足挂齿的
unmerited a. (赏罚)不应得的,不当的,不配的
unmistakable a. 不会弄错的,不会被误解的,法理明的
unmitigated a. 1.全然的,绝对的 2.未减轻的,未缓和的
unmoral a. 1.不道德的 2.不属于道德范围的,无道德观念的
unmortgaged a. 未抵押的
unmortgaged assets 未抵押的资产
unmugged a. (美)(罪犯等)未拍照存档的
unnam(e)able a. 无名称的,无法说出其名称的
unnamed principal 隐名的委托人;隐名

unnatural a. 不自然的;违背人道的,邪恶的;反常的
unnatural act 鸡奸,兽奸;反常遗嘱(见 unnatural will)
unnatural crimes (或 offence; act) 违背自然罪(指鸡奸、兽奸等罪行)
unnatural death 非正常死亡
unnatural drop or rise (in stock's price) 反常的降落与上扬(股价)
unnatural offender 鸡奸犯,兽奸犯
unnatural sexual act 反常的性行为
unnatural will 反常遗嘱(指将合法继承人排除在外的遗嘱)
unnavigability n. 不可航行,不适航性,不适航状态
unnegotiable a. 1.不可转让的,不可流通的 2.不可谈判的,不可协商的 3.(道路、河流等)不可通行的
unneighbourly a. 不友善的,不善交际的,不似邻人的
unneutral a. 非中立的
unneutral service 非中立服务(指用中立国的运载工具,运载交战国乘客或驶往交战国的行为)
uno actu 单一行为;以一个或相同行为
uno animo 相同意图
uno flatu with the same breath and the same intent 同一时间同一目的
unnoticed 未被注意的,未被顾及的,不瞩目的
unobjectionable a. 无可反对的,无异议的;无阻碍的
unobjectionable alien 不予拒绝接受的外国人
unobservant a. 未注意到的;不遵守(规则、惯例等)的,不留心的
unobserved a. 未被遵守的;未被注意的,没有观察到的
unoffending a. 无罪的;无害的;不惹人厌恶的;不冒犯人的
unofficial a. 非正式的,非官方的
unofficial collections 非官方汇编
unofficial report (美)非官方的判例汇编(指由非官方出版的判例汇编)

unofficial statement 非正式声明,非官方声明
unofficial visit 非正式访问,非官方访问
unopposed a. 无反对的,无对手的
unopposed candidate 无对手(竞争)的候选人
unorganized a. (美)未参加工会组织的;没有组织的,未组织起来的
unorthodox a. 非正统的,异端的,异教的(unorthodoxly adv.)
unowned a. 无主的;未被承认的,未被准许的
unowned property 无主财产,无主物
unowned waste land 无主荒地
unpackaged transfer 分件转让
unpacked cargo 未包装的货
unpaid a. 未付的;未缴纳的;未还的(债务);无薪的;名誉职的
unpaid agent 免费代理人
unpaid case 免费案件
unpaid cheque 未兑付的支票
unpaid consul 名誉领事
unpaid debt 未清偿的债务
unpaid draft 未付汇票
unpaid paper 未付支票,未付期票
unpaid seller 未受清偿的出卖人
unpardonable a. 不可宽恕的,不可原谅的
unparliamentary a. 违反会议习惯或议会法的;不适于在议会使用的(如言语等)
unparliamentary language 辱骂性的言辞(尤指不适于在议会使用的)
unpatented a. 未获得专利权的;不受专利权保护的
unpatented inventions 未获专利权的发明
unpen v. 将……从拘禁中释放,释放
unplanned a. 无计划的,计划外的;未经筹划的,意外的
unpolitical a. 非政治性的,无政治意义的;与政治无关的;不关心政治的,不参与政治(活动)的
unpolled a. 1.(选民)尚未投票的;未登记的 2.未经民意调查访问的
unpopular a. 不得人心的,不受欢迎的
unportioned a. 无嫁妆的,无赠与的
unposted a. 1.没有悬挂"不得侵入"的告示的 2.(职位)无固定的 3.未付邮的;(俚)未接获通知的
unpractical a. 不实际的,不实用的
unpracticed a. 未实行的,未实施的;无经验的
unprecedented a. 无先例的;空前的,前所未有的
unpredictable behavior 不可预测的行为
unprejudiced a. 1.无偏见的,大公无私的,公正的 2.未受损害的(权利等)
unprejudiced judge 公正的法官
unpremeditated a. 1.非故意的;无预谋的;无准备的 2.临时的,即席的
unpremeditated crime 过失罪
unpremeditated homicide 非预谋杀人,过失杀人
unpresented cheque 未(作承兑)提示的支票
unpriced a. 无一定价格的,未标价的
unprincipled a. 无耻的;无原则的;不道德的
unprincipled disputes 无原则纠纷
unprison v. 自狱中释放
unprivileged a. 没有特权的;(美)贫穷的,社会最底层的
unprofessional 1.与专门职业无关的,不属于某一特殊职业的 2.专业以外的;违反职业道德、行规、习惯等的 3.外行的,非职业性的
unprofessional accident 违章事故
unprofessional conduct 违反职业道德的行为
unprofessional lawyer 非职业性律师;诉讼代理人;公证人
unprofessional operation 违章操作
unprofitable a. 无利可图的,无益的
unprotected a. 未设防的;没有保护人的;(工业等)不受关税保护的
unproved a. 未被证明的,未经证实的;未经检验的
unprovided a. 1.无供给的;无生活来源的 2.未做准备的;意料外的 3.无资格的 4.未规定的
unprovoked a. 无正当理由的;无缘无故的;未受刺激的

unprovoked assault 无缘无故的打人,无正当理由的攻击
unpunishable a. 不应处罚的,不能处罚的
unpunished a. 未受处罚的
unqualified a. 1.不合格的,不适宜的 2.无限制的,无条件的 3.绝对的,完全的
unqualified certificate 不合格证明
unqualified denial 绝对否认
unqualified job-seeker 不合格的就业者
unqualified right 无限制的权利
unquestionable a. 1.无可疑的,确定的,不成问题的 2.无可指责的,无可非议的
unquestionable evidence 确凿的证据
unquestioned a. 1.不成问题的,无疑的 2.未被调查的,未被讯问的 3.无争执的,未反对的
unquestioned authority 公认的权威
unquestioning a. 不问是非的;盲目的
unquestioning adherence 盲目追随
unquestioning adherence a political decision 盲目追随一项政治决议
unquotable a. 不能引用的,无引用价值的
unquoted securities 非挂牌证券
unquoted share 非挂牌股票
unratified a. 未批准的
unraveling result 告知后果
unrealistic prices 与现实不等的价格
unreasonable a. (14世纪) 1.无理性的,无道理的,愚蠢的;过度的,无节制的 2.对搜查令的要求得不到有效的支持〈unreasonable search and seizure〉(不合理的搜查和扣押或无搜查令的搜查和扣押)
unreasonable conduct 不正当行为,无理行为
unreasonable doubts 无理怀疑
unresolved dualism 未确定的二元论
unreasonable search and seizure 无理的搜查和扣押,非法搜查和扣押
unreasonably troublesome 无理取闹
unreasoning a. 无理性的;不合理的;不运用推理的
unrecognized a. 未被承认的;未被认出的
unreconciled a. 未和解的;未取得一致的
unrecorded a. 未登记的;无记录的;未录制的

unredeemed a. 1.未实现的,未履行的 2.未赎回的,未偿还的 3.未减轻的;未缓和的
unredeemed promises 未履行的诺言
unregistered a. 未登记的,未注册的
unregistered birth 未申报的出生,未登记的出生
unregistered immovable property 未登记的不动产
unregistered share 无记名股票
unregistered trademark 未注册的商标
unregulated a. 无规定的
unregulated market 无规则市场
unrelated a. 无关的
unrelated-business-income tax (1962年) 营业外收入税,与经营无关的收入税(指对非营利机构的应税收入,比如从出版社广告收入中征税)
unreliable a. 不可靠的,靠不住的
unrelieved a. 未受救济的,未经解除的,未免除的,未减轻的
unrepaired a. 未修缮的;破损的
unrepealable a. 不可撤销的,不得废止的
unrepealed a. 未被撤销的,未被废止的;有效的
unrepentant a. 毫不悔改的
unrepentant sinners 毫不悔改的罪人
unreported a. 1.未告发的,未揭发的 2.未引起(告发,或笔录)的;未汇编(判例)的
unrepresented a. 无代表权的,议会无代表的
unreprieved a. 未获得缓刑的
unrepudiated gift promise 未拒绝进行的赠与承诺,未被否认的赠与承诺
unrequited a. 1.无报酬的;得不到报答的 2.无报复的
unrescinded a. 有效的;未被废除的
unreserved a. 无决断力的,无决心的;未解决的,未议决的,(问题)未澄清的,意见尚未一致的
unresolved doubts 未解决的疑团
unresolved problem 悬而未决的问题
unresponsive evidence 不要求答复的证据问题
unrest n. 1.不安的状态;不安宁 2.动荡的局面;动乱,骚动

unrestrained a. 无拘束的;无限制的;自由的,过度的
unrestricted ballot 无限制的投票
unrevoked a. 未宣布为无效的,未收回的,未撤销的
unrighteous judgement 不公正的判决
unrightful a. 不公正的,不合法的,不义的
unripe girl 发育未成熟的女孩
unruly child 不守规矩的少年,难于管教的少年
unsalable a. 卖不掉的,无销路的
unsalaried a. 不拿薪水的,无薪俸的,只有名义而不取报酬的
unsanctioned a. 未批准的,未通过的,未认可的
unsanitary a. 不卫生的,有碍健康的
unsatisfied-judgment fund 不满意判决的基金,未满足判决的基金(指原为未经保险的或部分保险的机动车驾驶员造成车祸致使一些人员受到损伤,而由政府进行赔偿建立的基金)
unscheduled call 意外停靠,意外停泊
unsealed a. 1.未加封的,未封口的 2.未证实的,未确定的
unseaworthiness n. 不适航状态
unseaworthy a. 不适航的,不堪航海的,处于不适航状态的
unsecured a. 1.没有抵押的,没有担保的 2.没有系牢的,没有拴紧的
unsecured bill 无担保票据
unsecured creditor 无担保的债权人(贷款人)
unsecured liability 无担保债务
unsecured loan 没有抵押的贷款
unseemly squabble 不适当的争吵或争执
unsegregated a. 未实行种族隔离的,未分离的
unselfish a. 不谋私利的,无私的,慷慨的
unsentenced a. 未判决的,未判刑的;待判决的
unsentenced prisoner 待决犯,在押犯
unsettle land 荒无人烟的地方
unsettled a. 1.未决的,未定的;怀疑的 2.未偿付的;未偿清的;法律上未作处理的 3.无秩序的,繁乱的;动乱不定的

unsettled debts 未偿付的债务
unsettled law case 悬案,未决案
unsettled question 未(解)决的问题
unsettled transaction(s) 未结算的交易
unsettled writ for payment 未清偿的支付令
unsigned a. 未签名的,未签署的
unskilled a. 1.无特殊技能的;无专长的 2.不熟练的;拙劣的;不擅长的
unskilled labour 1.不需技术就能干的工作,粗活 2.做粗活的全体工人
unskilled worker 非熟练工人
unsociability n. 孤僻性,不善于交际性
unsolemn war 未经宣战的战争
unsolicited a. 多余的;未被恳求的;多事的;自愿的;主动的
unsolicited interference 多余的干涉
unsolicited offers 主动报价
unsound a. 1.不健康的;不健全的;有病的 2.不根据事实的,谬误的 3.有瑕疵的,有缺点的
unsound corporation 财产上有问题的公司
unsound mind 精神失常,神志不清
unsound theory 不健全的理论
unspeakable a. 1.说不出来的,不能说的;不能以言语表达的 2.苦不堪言的,极恶劣的
unspecified a. 未特别提到的,未特别指出的,未受限定的
unspoken requirement 默契
unstatutable a. 不法的,违背法规的;不符合法律的
unsteady a. 1.不稳的,不安定的 2.不规则的,不平均的 3.易变的
unsubdued legal reasoning 并不微妙的法律推理,不能说服的法律推理
unsubstantiated a. 未经证实的,不能肯定的
unsuccessful party 败诉的一方;败者
unsufficient weight 未充分考虑,未充分考量
unsuitable a. 不适合的,不适当的
unsupport hypothesis 未经证实的假设
unsupported a. 1.无赞助的,无支持的 2.未经证实的
unsuspected a. 未被怀疑的,无嫌疑的
unsuspecting a. 无怀疑的,信任的
unsustainable a. 未能证实的,不能成立的

unswear v. 毁弃前誓;毁弃誓言;发新誓以毁前誓
unswervingly a. 不歪的,不偏离的;不懈的,坚定的
unsworn a. 未宣誓的;未正式宣告的
unsworn statement 未经宣誓的陈述
unsworn witness 未宣誓的证人
untaxable a. 无税的,不需课税的
untenable a. 防守不住的,站不住脚的
untenanted a. 未有人租住的
untied loan 不附带条件的贷款
untimed prompt shipment 不限期即期装运
untimely recognition 不适时承认,过早地承认
untold a. 1.未说明的;未透露的;未说出的 2.未计数的
untold damage 极大的损害
untold wealth 大量财富
untraceable beneficiary 难于找到的(遗嘱、财产等)受益人
untrammeled a. 不受限制的,自由自在的
untrammeled jurisdiction of the federal courts 联邦法院畅通无阻的管辖权
untrammelled advocacy 自由辩护
untransferable a. 不能转移的,不能转让的
untried a. 未经审讯的,未审理的,未经考验的
untried offender (或 **prisoner**) 待审犯,未决犯,在押待审的犯人
untrue a. 1.虚伪的,不真实的,不正确的 2.不合原则的,不符标准的
untrustworthy a. 不能信赖的,不可靠的
* *Unumquodque est id quod est principaliusin ipso.* That which is the principal part of a thing is the thing itself. 物的主体部分就是物的本身。
* *Unus nullus.* The testimony of one witness is equivalent to the testimony of none. (大陆法证据原则)一人作证等于无人作证。
untruth n. 不真实,虚假,谎言;不忠实,不忠诚
unused a. 不习惯的;未用过的,空着的,不用的,新的,未耗用的,积累的
unused (或 **outstanding**) **balance** 未用余额

unused portion of letter of credit 信用证未用部分
* *Unusquisque debet esse gnarus conditionis ejus cum quo contrahit.* Everyone ought to be cognizant of the condition of the person with whom he makes contract. 人人应是与自己订立合同的人的情况的审视者。
unusual instance 非常情况
unusual need 非常必要
unusual power 独特的权力
unvalued a. 无价值的,不足轻重的;未曾估价的,未评价过的
unvalued policy 不定值保险单,开口保险单,保险金额未确定的保单
unvalued stock 未定价的股票
unverifiable a. 不能证实的,无法检验的,无法核实的
unviolability of the person 人身不可侵犯
unvouched (for) a. 1.未经……证实的,未经……证明的 2.无……担保的
unwaivable a. 不得弃权的
unwanted coherence event 意外(发生)事件
unwanted sexual attention 违反本意的性方面注意
unwarrantable a. 无正当理由的,难获许可的,不当的;难保证的
unwarrantable conduct 不当行为
unwarranted a. 1.无保险的;未经保证的;难保证的;难获许可的 2.不当的;无正当理由的
unwarranted accusation 无理控告;妄告
unwarranted arrest(s) 不当逮捕,擅自拘捕
unwarranted charge 莫须有的罪名
unwarranted demand 不适当的要求,不合理要求
unwarranted imprisonment 无理监禁,擅自监禁
unwarranted infringement 无端侵犯
unwarranted insult 无故侮辱
unwarranted intervention 不当干预,不当干涉
unwarranted killing 擅自杀人;无端杀人
unwarranted loss 不应有的损失
unwarranted proceedings 不合法律程序的议事录

unwarranted sentence 擅自判决
unwed mother 未婚的母亲
unwed parents 未婚父母
unwholesome a. 不卫生的;有害于健康的;不道德的
unwholesome demand 不健康需求
unwholesome food 非食用食品,有害食物
unwilling a. 不愿意的;勉强的;不服从的
unwillingness of juries 陪审团的不满
unwitnessed a. 无证人的;未被证明的;未见证人签名的;未注意到的
unwitnessed legal document 无见证人签名的法律文件
unwitting a. 不知情的,无意的,不是故意的,不知不觉的
unworkable a. 难以操作的,难以运用的,难以工作的,难以运转的
unworthy or deficient parents 鄙劣或不配为人父母
unwritten a. 习惯的;不成文的,未记诸文字的,口传的;空白的
unwritten code 不成文法(典)
unwritten constitution 不成文宪法
unwritten conventions 不成文惯例
unwritten custom 不成文的习惯
unwritten law 1.不成文法,习惯法 2.因杀死诱奸其妻或其女者的罪犯应减轻的原则(或公意)
unwritten political practice 不成文的政治惯例
up a tree 处于困境,进退维谷
up for (在选举等中)被提名供考虑;在法庭受(审)
up leg 发出的广播信号(多指广播组织为通过卫星传播节目而发向卫星的信号;如果信号从卫星发回地面,一般称 down leg "发回信号")
up the river (美俚)入狱,在狱中
up-to-date a. 直到最近的,现代的,新式的
upbraider n. 申斥者,责备者
upbraiding n. 谴责,申斥,责备
upbring v. 抚养,抚育,培育,培养,教育
update n./v. 现代化/跟上形势,使现代化,将最近之事记入,使依照最近之方法及思想等

updating process 更新过程
upgrade n./v. 增加,升级,上升/使提升,改良,提高(质量等)
uphold v. 确认,赞成,支持;保护,维护,保养;鼓励;拥护
uphold a verdict 确认(陪审团的)裁决
uphold national unity and territorial integrity 维护国家的统一和领土完整
uphold the decision 维持原判;赞成这项决定
upkeep n. 保养,维修;保养费;维修费
upkeep and improvements (不动产的)保养;修缮费
upon my word 1.=my word upon it(发誓) 2.的确,绝无虚言
upon reaching majority 已达到成年的人
upon sight 见票即付
upon the institution of an ordinary lawsuit 依通常诉讼程序
upon the table 尽人皆知的,已成为公开讨论的事
upon this 于是
upper and lower limit of official rate of exchange 官定汇率上下限
upper area court 高级区域法院
(the) Upper Bench (英)王座法庭(1649—1660年期间的称呼)
upper bound 上界,上限
Upper Exchequer (英史)上理财法院
Upper House (=Upper Chamber) (英)上议院
upper level administrator 高级行政官员
upper limit of exchange 外汇最高限额
upper space law 外层空间法
upper-class a. 上流社会的,上等阶层的
upright a. 1.正直的,合乎正道的,诚实的 2.直的,直立的
upright and incorruptible officials 清官,正直廉洁的官员
upright dealings 正常的交易
uprising n. 起义,暴动
uproaring conduct 骚乱行为
upset n. 翻倒,倾覆,打乱,推翻
upset a decision 推翻原判
upset price (拍卖时的)底价,开盘价格

urban a. 城市的,都市的,市区的
urban buildings 城市房产,城市建筑物
Urban Council Ordinance （英）《市政局条例》
urban crime rate 市区犯罪率
urban dust 城市尘埃
urban easement 城市地役权（指大多数街边房屋均应有采光、空气流通,以及从街边出入的权利）
urban household 城市户口
urban law 城市法
urban planning and redevelopment 城市规划和重建
urban pollutant 城市污染物
urban poor 城市贫民
urban population 城市人口
(the) Urban Real Estate Administrative Law （中）《城市房地产管理法》
urban renewal 城市更新（重建）
urban renewal statute 城市重建法规
urban servitude 城镇地役权
urbanite n. 城市居民
urbanization n. 城市化
urge v. 推进,极力主张,强烈要求;催促,力劝,激励
urgency n. 紧急,迫切,紧急之事
urgency of sale 急需售卖
urgency order （对于有危险的精神病人的）紧急拘禁令
urgency procedure 紧急程序
urgent a. 紧急的,急迫的;强求的
urgent cable 加急电
urgent motion 紧急动议
urgent notice 紧急通知,紧急公告
urgent order 紧急命令
urgent plea survey （海损）紧急起诉请求
urging commission of crime 纵容,唆使（他人）犯罪
Uruguay Round 乌拉圭回合
U. S. Arbitration and Mediation Service Lit. Co. 美国仲裁与调解服务有限公司（该公司为1987年创办的海外国际争端解决机构,现在加拿大、英、法、德、爱尔兰、挪威、日本、澳大利亚、俄罗斯均设有办事处）

U. S. attorney 美国联邦地区检察官(= district attorney)
U. S. Attorney-General 美国司法部长
USA Patriot Act 《美国爱国（者）法》[制定颁布此项法规旨在对2001年9·11恐怖分子袭击的回应,给予执法机构更广泛的权力去收集涉嫌的恐怖分子信息,分享国内外情报机构的信息,使国家的边境更为安全有保障,扣押新型刑事罪（criminal charges）的嫌疑犯,运用新的刑事诉讼程序。同时给予财政部（Treasury Department）更大的权力去调查并管控那些参与外国货币洗钱（foreign money laundering）的财政、金融机构。这个名称的头字语（acronym）由"团结和强势美国"（Uniting and Strengthening America）构成,由它提供所要求的适用"工具"（appropriate tools required）以阻止和堵塞恐怖主义（terrorism）。常缩略为Patriot]
U. S. Bureau of Census 美国人口调查局
U. S. Civil Service Commission 美国文官委员会
U. S. Code 《美国法典》（见 United States Code）
U. S. Code Congressional and Administrative News (U. S. C. C. A. N.) 《美国法制会议和行政新闻》（在国会会议期间,由西方出版公司每两周出版一次,在国会休会期间,则每月出版一次,刊登所有新的联邦公法完整文本的刊物。每届会议结束时,其合订卷本囊括经选择的有关重要法规的立法历史文件、国会新闻纪要、有选择的行政法规、行政文件以及有用的目录和索引）
U. S. Code Service 《美国法典服务》（指由美国律师合作出版公司出版的联邦法规另一主题汇编,并由每月先行本服务资料补充,即《美国法典服务先行本》。该法典服务提供公法文本及其立法历史概要、新法庭规则文本、执行令和总统公告）
U. S. Copyright Office 美国版权局
U. S. Court （美）联邦法院
U. S. Court of Customs and Patent Appeal 美国海关和专利上诉法院
U. S. Department of Justice （美）美国司

法部
U. S. General Accounting Office 美国会计总局
U. S. Merit System Protection Board 美国功绩制度保护局
U. S. Patriot Act (美)《爱国者法》(美国9·11事件后颁布)
U. S. plaintiff case 美国政府作为原告的案件
U. S. price 美国价格
U. S. Reports 《美国判例汇编》
U. S. Revised Statutes 《美国修订法规》[指1873年第一个官方联邦法规汇编及其1878年的第二版。这两版的一卷本的汇编将所有公共的、总的和长久的联邦法规纳入约七十五个标题或主题类别,并附有总索引。此汇编经重新颁布所包括的法规作为制定法(positive law),并明确废除原先在《法规大全》中的文本]
U. S. Statutes at large (Official) 美国法规大全(官方版)
U. S. tax laws 美国税务法规
U. S. registered mutual funds (美)注册的互助基金,注册的合股投资
usage n. 1.习惯,惯例,常例 2.处理,对待 3.习惯法
usage of trade 商业惯例,贸易惯例
usage of warfare 战争惯例
usance n. 1.习惯,惯例;使用 2.汇票支付期限(指对国外汇票习惯上所许可的支付期限,不包括days of grace在内。见days of grace) 3.财产的收益;利息
usance bill (依)习惯期限(付款)票据;远期汇票,有期限汇票
usance draft 见票后数天付款的期票,有期限汇票,远期汇票
usance letter of credit 远期信用证(指在习惯期限内的信用证)
use n./v. 1.用益权(制度)[指在一个信托中,受托人并不直接从信托财产中直接受益,而是应委托人要求为了受益人的利益作为法定的所有人(legal owner)而持有信托财产。信托缘起于英国13世纪前后出现的用益权制度,一种为了应对封建土地制度而创设的规避法律产权设计,与旧有制度相比,用益权制度在形式上最接近代理(agency),但用益权制度中的受让人(feoffee)从让与人(feoffor)处取得财产后,并不以让与人的名义也不为让与人的利益而行为,所以他不是让与人的代理人。受让人也不是受益人(或有用益物权的人)的代理人,只是为了受益人的利益(to the use of)行为而已。用益权制度与代理的根本区别在于代理关系中委托人不转移其财产给代理人,而用益权制度中,受托人因为委托人的行为取得受托财产所有权,在用益权制度产生初期,让与人将其财产转移给受让人,目的是由受让人负责管理该项财产,因此而产生的一切受益归让与人指定的受益人所有。受让人基于委托人的转让行为实际取得该项财产的所有权] 2.应用,使用,运用,享用(指对某物的应用或使用,特别是对一个事物的持续占有和使用以达到对其适用目的,这区别于对事物临时或短期占有上使用〈the neighbors complained to the city about the owner's use of the building as a dance club〉(邻居们都在就这幢房子所有人将它作为跳舞俱乐部使用而埋怨这个城市) 3.(专利)使用权(指专利权人使用其专利发明) 4.(罗马法)使用权[指日常收取某物孳息的权利,区别于用益权(usufruct),后者不仅有使用的含义,还有收取孳息的内容] 5.收益(用于地产转让中,与benefit含义相同) 6.(英)用益(指一种土地管理、保有的方式) 7.有目的的使用〈the tool had several uses〉(这一工具已有数项使用功能) 8.用益权,收益权[指从拥有的土地和他人占有的土地上所获取的利益,特别是收益权(right to take profits);相当于他人合法持有了土地拥有人的土地。见 *cestui que use*]/(12世纪前) 1.用应,使用,运用,享用,雇佣[指为了达到某一目的或完成某一任务雇佣人员帮助自己〈they use formbooks〉(他们使用格式文书)] 2.实行,实施,执行;专心于某事〈to use diligent research〉(专心、并勤奋于研究) 3.惯于做某件事〈I used to avoid public speaking, but no longer〉(我过去常常避开公开交谈,但现在不再如此) 4.处理,为人,

对待〈he uses me well〉(他待我很好) 5. 习惯于〈he is used to the pressure〉(他习惯于紧张繁忙工作) 6.提供,供应〈the firm uses 50 reams of paper each day〉(这个商行每日供应 50 令纸) 7.利用,自私地利用〈she uses her interns for personal errands〉(她利用她的实习医生为她跑腿) 8.运用不适当的优势(地位、职位和环境)〈she uses her board membership to threaten staffers〉(她运用其委员会委员身份来威胁她的员工) 9.参与,分享,有规律或常规吸取〈he dses heroin〉(他常吸海洛因)

(to) use a claim for set-off 以债权作抵消,抵消债权

use and occupation 使用和占有(的诉讼)(指由房地产的所有人和使用占据人因没有明确的租约或租金而引起的权利要求的诉讼;如租期已满,但仍占用,因此要求租金的诉讼)

use and wont 习惯,惯例
use drugs 吸毒
use in common 共同使用权
use of analogy 类推法的运用
use of evidence 证据的使用
use of force 使用武力
use of land 土地使用,土地用途
Use of Law 《法律的运用》[指弗朗西斯·培根(Francis Bacon,1561—1626)的著作]
use of public resources 公共资源使用权
use of reason 理性的运用
use of undue authority 滥用权力
use one's discretion 使用酌处权,相机行事,酌处
use permit 使用证
use tax 使用税[指在课税机构管辖区以外购买的货物或财产使用税,该税之目的在于劝阻(或阻止)购买不归属于营业税的产品]
use up 用尽
use value 实用价值
used fairly 合理使用
used for international navigation 用于国际航行
useful a. (专利法)实用的,有用的[((发明的专利)具有实际的应用性,"仅有发明的奇特,并未达到任何智慧目的,从可申请专利上讲,不是实用的"]
useful life 使用年度
usefulness n. 实用性,有用性
user (15 世纪) 1.对权利和财产等的实际使用和收益(它是财产权的主要特征)〈the neighbor argued that an easement arose by his continuous user over the last 15 years〉(该邻居根据他的超过 15 年的连续用户身份来主张地役权的争议)(见 non-user) 2.使用人,用户〈the staffer's last user did not put it away〉(该批发商的最后客户未放弃其批发产品) 3.占有人,受益人,有使用权益的人 4.不确定的占有
user department 业务部门
user name 用户名
user of a trademark 商标使用人
user of document 证书使用人
user terminal 用户终端
usher n. 1.法庭的庭警(指负责维持法庭的安宁和秩序的法警) 2.法院的门房,传达
usher of court 法庭传达员(旧译:庭丁)
using premises for prostitution 为卖淫提供场所
usual business hours 通常营业时间
usual name 常用名称,惯称
usual place of abode 常住地,常住所
usual practice 惯例,通常办法
usucapio n. (罗马法及大陆法)时效取得[指一种财产权取得的方式,即通过长期、连续不断而且一开始就是善意的占有人或所有人占有不明的财产。根据时效(prescription)取得所有权。按古典法(in classical law),最低时间要求:动产为 1 年,土地为 2 年。根据查士丁尼法(Justinian Laws),对于动产的最低占有时间为 3 年,土地则需占有 10 年。亦称 *usus*;见 prescription。*usucaption* n.; *usucapt* v.]
usucapt v. 使(财产权)取得时效(见 *usucaptio*)
usucaption(**usucapion**) n. (物权)取得时效,凭时效取得(财产权)
usufruct n./v. 受益权;使用权;使用收益权(指使用他人财产而不损害该财产之权)/

根据用益权占有
usufructuary n./a. 享有用益权的人,有用益权者/使用权的,受益权的;有用益权的
usufructus 使用收益权,用益权
usura maritima 海航重利[指根据押船贷款合同(bottomry)或货船抵押债券(respondentia bond)提取的利息或取得的权益,对于风险则按比例分成,而不受重利法(usury law)限制]
usurer n. 放高利贷者,重利盘剥者
usurious a. 1.放高利贷的,用高利盘剥的 2.取高利的,收高利的
usurious loan 高利贷,高利贷借款
usurp v. 1.篡夺,篡权 2.潜取,霸占,侵占
usurpation n. 篡夺,强夺;霸占,侵权,篡位;非法使用
usurper n. 篡位者,篡权者
usurping function 超越职权
usury n. 高利贷,高利剥削
Usury Law (美)《重利法》
usus n. (罗马法)1.使用权[指可使用他人财产的权利,但不得收取和保有该财产所产生的收益和孳息(fructus; fruits),使用权是一种人役权(personal servitude),它给予非财产所有人一种使用特定财产权利。见 usufruct]2.事实上的占有(财产)要求时效取得(usucapio)3.时效婚[指通过连续同居如同夫妻一样共同生活满一年以上,即获得对妻子的夫权(manus)而确立法律上的夫妻关系,谓之时效婚。见 manus 1; coemptio; confarreatio]
usus bellici (国际法)军事用途;军事目标
usus fructus 用益权
usus loquendi 习惯说法
usus modernus pandectarum 现代应用法学派[指欧洲大陆在 16 至 8 世纪间通过继受罗马法,尝试满足早期资本主义工商业日益发展的需要,形成重要的"现代应用法学派"),学说汇纂现代应用法学派
ut dictum 如所指示
ut infra 如下所述
* **Ut poena ad paucos**, **metus ad omnes perveniat.** Though few are punished, the fear of punishment affects all. 惩一儆百。
* **Ut res magis valeat quam pereat.** That the thing may rather have effect than be destroyed. 与其使之无效不如使之有效。It is better for a thing to have effect than to be made void. 使事情有效总比无效好。
ut supra 如上所述
Utah Digital Signature Act (美)(1995 年犹他州颁布的)《数字签名法》
uterine a. 同母异父的
uterine brothers 同母异父兄弟
uterine sisters 同母异父姐妹
uterini 同母异父血亲
utero-gestation 有孕,受胎
uti 使用;为特定目的而使用
uti frui 对物的用益权
uti possidetis (使交战国于战争结束时以)占领地为领土的原则,(国际法的)占领地保有原则
uti possidetis for immoveable 不动产占有令状
utilis annus (罗马法)有效诉期(指一年诉期,以原告起诉之日起,连续计算)
utilitarian school 功利主义学派
utilitarian theories of law 功利主义的法学
utilitarian theory of punishment 刑罚功利论
utilitarianism n. 功利主义
utiliter et equivalenter (古)及时并同等有效(duly and with equal effect)
utility n./a. (14 世纪)1.优质(指有益于社会的某些功能服务的质量),实用性;值得称赞(meritoriousness)2.(专利)资格(capacity)[指实现一种功能或达到专利申请的一种结果,或持有人有权请求作为知识产权保护。按专利法,实用性(utility)是专利权(patentability)的三个基本条件(base requirements)之一,另两个为非显而易见(nonboviousness)和新颖性(novelty)。对于专利侵权的损害赔偿的计算,实用性是专利产品或在产品诉讼进程上的特定权益(benefit)或优势,若有的话,在多次诉讼进程中被曾经使用过的特定权益或优势在过去会产生相同的结果]3.公益事业(指履行重大公共服务的工商企业并受政府管理)/多重用途的;实用的,经济实惠的;公用事业的;功利的
utility company 公用事业公司
utility function 效用函数

utility information 效用信息
utility model 实用新型,效用模式
utility model (专利)实用性模式[指有些国家提供专利相同权利(patent-like rights)的专利注册登记制度(system of patent registration),通常只要不怎么需要调查的较短期限。实用性模式的专利在美、两国并不适用,但日本和许多欧洲国家,包括德国和法国,均可提供这样的专利。它们的规定却有很大差异。这些国家只适用机械专利产品而不适用化学制品。亦称 petty patent; second-tier patent; small invention]
utility models register 实用新型登记簿
utility or other enterprise funds 公用事业或其他企业基金
utility service 公用事业
utility sinking fund 公用事业偿债基金
utilization n. 利用,应用
utitur jure auctoris (古)他在所有权(title)上行使先辈的权利
utitur jure communi (古)他依赖于普通法
utiture jure suo (古)他行使自己的权利
utlesse (=*utlepe*) 重罪犯人的越狱
utmost good faith 特别善意性,最大善意性
utmost good-faith contract 最大诚信合同(一般指保险合同,因从事保险活动须严格遵循诚实信用原则)
utopian socialism 空想社会主义
utrubi (罗马法)(动产)保持占有原则,(动产)保持占有令状
utrubi for moveable 动产保持占有令状
utter a./v. 完全的,绝对的;无条件的;无保留的/1.说出;发出 2.宣布;吐露,发表 3.使用(伪币等)
utter bar (英)外席(法)庭(指外席律师活动的法庭,又称 outer bar,见下条)
utter (或 **outer**) **barrister** (英)外席律师(指尚未取得王室律师资格 King's counsel 或 Queen's counsel 的青年律师,只能在外席庭 utter bar 活动,无资格出席高等法庭,不能被请入王室律师席位,即内席席位)
utter refusal 明确的拒绝
utter threats 大声恫吓
utterance n. 1.发表;发言,吐露;表达;说法;语调 2.使用货币(尤指伪币)3.死,终极
utterer n. 发表人,表达者
uttering n. 有意的使用(假货币、文件等)
uttering false coin 蓄意使用伪币
uttering (of) forged documents 故意使用伪造证券(罪)
uttering (of) forged instrument 故意使用伪造文件罪
uttermost a./n. 最大的,极度的,最远的/最大限度,极端
uxor (=**ux**) n. 女人;妻子
* ***Uxor non est sui juris, sed sub potestate viri.*** A wife is not sui juris, but is under the government of her husband. 妻子不是有自主权者,而是从属于其夫。
* ***Uxor sequitur domicilium viri.*** A wife follows the domicile of her husband. 妻子随丈夫居住(俗译:嫁鸡随鸡,嫁狗随狗)。
uxoricidal a. 杀妻的,犯杀妻罪的
uxoricide n. 杀妻;杀妻者;杀妻罪
uxorious a. 对妻子过分宠爱的;怕老婆的

V

vacancy n. 1.空的;空职;空缺 2.茫然若失,空间 3.出租的空房或空场所
vacancy by election 以选举方式填补空缺
vacancy of succession 无人继承,继承无人
vacant a. 1.空的,空虚的;闲暇的 2.无人利用的;无主的,遗弃的,无继承人的
vacant clause 空屋条款
vacant estate 无继承人的遗产
vacant land tax 土地闲置税
vacant possession 空的房屋(指房屋租借人实际已放弃使用租借的房子,法庭可以判定,要业主把它作空房处理);(广告用

语)空房出卖
vacant seat (议员的)空缺席位
vacant succession 无人继承(指还未知由谁来继承的继承物业)
vacantia bona 无主物(指无人主张权利而应归公之物)
vacate v. 1.取消;使无效;撤出;离开;辞去 2.使空出;搬出;空出(房屋、职位等)
vacate (或 reverse) **a judgement** 撤销判决
vacate a legal document 使一个法律文件无效
vacate office 提出辞职,提出辞呈
vacating a judgment 撤销判决
vacation n. 1.假期;(法院的)停审期,休庭期(尤指英国高等法院的法庭和议事室停止处理日常事务的假期。休庭期为:长假期;8月1日至9月10日;圣诞节假;12月22日至次年1月10日;复活节假;从本节前星期四至第二个星期一;圣灵降临节假;从本节前星期六至第二个星期一)2.退还租屋 3.辞职 4.休假
vacation judge 假日值班法官(指英国高等法院长期假中处理需要立刻处理的申请的法官)
vacation of judgment (因依据错误而)取消判决,宣布判决无效
vacation of the premises 房屋的腾让,退房
vacation ownership 分时度假
vacation sittings 休庭期的开庭(尤指英国高等法院在8月1日至9月10日的长假期中的开庭,有两名假日值班法官处理需立即处理的申请。亦指根据规定王座法庭的紧急案件在长假期中仍需审理的开庭)
vacation system 休假制度
vacillate v. 犹豫,踌躇;波动,振荡
vacillation n. 犹豫不决
vacua (vacuum 的复数)空的,无效的;未被占用的/真空,真空度
vacua possessio 无负担占有(见 vacant possession)
vades (大陆法)担保,保证;抵押,保释;(为被告出庭)担保
vadium (罗马法中的)抵押,以财产抵押作担保

vadium mortuum 死典权(指债务人以土地交与债权人占有,届期不赎时,则其土地归债权人所有)
vadium vivium 以收益抵债务之典权(指债权人占有债务人抵押之土地,而以收益拨付债务,至债务偿清时,应将土地交还给债务人,使债务人不致因无力偿还债务而丢失产权,亦称 living pledge)
vagabond n. 流浪,流浪汉的总称;流氓
vagabond group 流氓集团
vagrancy n. 1.流浪;流浪行乞,流浪者,流浪汉 2.流浪罪 3.(意见、思想的)犹豫不决
Vagrancy Act (英)《流浪法》(1824年)
vagrant n. 流氓,无赖,流浪汉
vague a. 含混的,模糊的,不明确的;无表情的
vague testimony 模糊的证言,未能说明事实真相之证言
vagueness doctrine (美)含糊原则,(刑法文本)不明确(指刑法如未明确说明所要求什么、禁止什么,那这也属违宪的原则)
valid a. 1.有效的,经过正当手续的 2.正当的,正确的,有根据的
valid act 有效行为
valid argument 正确的论点,有根据的争辩
valid ballot 有效选票
valid claims 有效的权利主张
valid contract 有效合同(契约)
valid encumbrance 有效的设定抵押权的债权
valid evidence 有效证据
valid guaranty 有效担保,有效保证
valid immunization card 有效免疫证明书
valid legal transaction 有效的法律行为
valid marriage 有效婚姻
valid notice 有效通知
valid period 有效期
valid reason 正当的理由(指有法律依据之理由)
valid transfer of ownership 所有权的有效转移(让)
valid verdict 有效裁决
valid will 有效的遗嘱
validate v. 1.使生效,使有法律效力 2.确认

validate a passport 使护照生效
validate an election 选举有效;使选举合法化
validation n. 生效,有效;批准,确认
validity n. 1.有效,效力;合法性 2.正当,正确,确实
validity in terms of the person 人的效力
validity in terms of time 时间的效力
validity of a declaration (合同的)意思表示的效力
validity (或 effect) of civil law 民法效力
validity of contract 合同(契约)的有效性,合同(契约)的效力
validity of criminal law 刑法效力
validity of law 法律效力
validity of marriage 婚姻的合法性,婚姻效力
validity of offer 报价的有效期
validity of treaties 条约的有效性,条约效力
valium n. 毒品,药品
valor (或 valour) n. 价值,价格;勇气,勇猛
valor beneficiorum 圣职评估[指所有圣职人员的圣奉和精神高职(spirit preferment)价值。即对圣职人员的估价收集和交纳圣奉什一税,并据此来确定圣职人员的级别。通常称为"国王之书"(King's Book)]
valor marilagii (英)拒婚金;征收拒婚金令
valorization n. (政府等)以各种补助形式维持(商品的)价格
valuable(s) a./n. 有价值的,有用的;可估价的/有价物,贵重物品
valuable consideration 有价约因,对价,有价格的报酬(包含为一方产生的权利、便利、利益或利润;或另一方所负担的责任、忍耐、损害或损失);与受益价值相等的报酬
valuable cultural relics 珍贵文物
valuable information 有价值的情报(或信息)
valuation n. 估值,计价,评价,估价;购买力;价格
valuation clause 估价条款
valuation for customs purposes 海关评估

valuational bindingness 价值拘束力(指某些观点或来源因符合客观或被共同接受的价值观念而对法院的司法裁判活动拥有拘束力。这要与规范拘束力区别开来。价值拘束力必须是客观、公认的,而不能是法官个人的主观判断。因为后者难谓"拘束力",它本身就属于法官个人的自由裁量的范畴)
valuator n. 估价者,评价者,价格核定者
value n. 价值,价格;重要性;意义,真义;评价
value added tax (VAT) 增值税
value added tax tribunals (英)增值税裁判所
value based on the weighed sum 加权定值
value compensation system 价值补偿制度
value date 起息日,结算日,存款生效日期
value in collection 托收价值
value in exchange 等价;等值
value in issue 争议标的价值
value in pledge 抵押品价值
value in use 使用价值
value investors 价值投资者
value judgment 价值评价[指讨论行为的标准。直接回答应该是什么(what ought to be)问题的思维逻辑。犯罪论中的价值评价当然指的是在犯罪论评价体系中直接回答针对行为主体有无价值、有什么价值以及有多大价值的评价,总的来说,价值评价是主观的,不是唯一的,但在法律中是经过选择规范了的。见 fact judgment]
value of assessment 估定价值,估值;课税价值
value of exports 出口额
value of fixed assets 固定资产值
value of foreign trade 对外贸易额
value of gross output 总产值
value of imports 进口额
value of labor power 劳工价值,劳力价值
value of life saving 挽救生命价值
value of shipment 工业交货值;装运值;工业销售值
value of the property 财产价值
value product 价值产品
value received 代价收讫(指票面价值已

支付。特别用于汇票上面表示已照该票面数额支付);已得代付
value stocks 价值股票
value-added tax (1935年)增值税[指在商品生产的每一阶段新课的税,即根据商品生产的成本价(cost)及其销售价(selling price)之间的总价在每一阶段的增值课税。欧洲一些国家也同样征收增值税。缩写为VAT]
value-based property tax 财产税定值
value-enhancing 价值提升
value-judgement 价值判断
valued a. 1.受尊重的;受重视的 2.贵重的;有价值的 3.被评价的;被估价的
valued policy 定值保险单
valueless a. 无价值的
valuer n. 评价者,(英)价格核定人
values n. 价值观(指可能对立法、政策适用和司法决策行为产生影响的超法律因素);社会准则
valuta n. 币值;货币兑换值;可使用的外汇总额
vamp n./v. (美俚)勾引男子勒索金钱的荡妇/勾引,诱惑
vampire n. 吸血鬼;放高利贷者;敲诈勒索者;勾引男子导致男子毁灭的女子
van n. 1.先头部队,(社会政治运动的)先驱,领导者 2.大篷车,运货车
van line (美)长途货运公司(尤指大型货车为人搬家者)
*** Vana est illa potentia quae nunquam venit in actum.** Vain is that power which never comes into play. 从未行使之权力无效。
vandalism n. 故意破坏文化、艺术的行动;故意损坏他人(或公共)财产的行为
vandalization n. 摧毁文化;破坏财产
vandalize v. 摧残(文化艺术等),破坏(他人或公共财产)
vanish v./n. 消失,消灭,成为零/(事物之)尽头
vanquish v. 征服,战胜;击败,克服;抑制(感情等)
vanquished country 战败国
Vape 电子烟[Vape可作为名词使用,意指电子烟或类似的装置,它还可作为动词使用,意思是吸入并呼出上述产品所产生的蒸气。而抽电子烟的人可称为Vaper。该词最早出现在20世纪80年代。当时一位名叫罗布·斯特普尼的作家为如今已经停刊的英国《新社会》杂志撰文时,描述了人们当时正在探究的一种假想用具:"一种吸入器或不可燃的香烟。它看起来与真的香烟很像,但只会释放出按规定量供给的尼古丁蒸气(这个新的习惯若能流行起来,将被称为抽电子烟)。"随着抽电子烟的做法成为主流,名人们都纷纷加入了这一行列,而有关电子烟给公众健康带来的危害以及是否需要对其实施监管的争议也变得愈发激烈,"电子烟及相关词汇的使用率因而在2014年有了显著提高"。据介绍,2014年被Vape打败的其他年度候选词包括indyref(苏格兰独立全民公投)、slacktivism(懒人行动主义)以及normcore(不赶时髦的日常穿搭潮流)等]
variable a. 易变的,常变的;可变的
variable annuity 可变更的年金(指根据投资策略的成功以变更的数额给予支付的年金。见variable annuity contract; straight annuity)
variable annuity contract (证券)可变更年金合同[指支付给某人的年金依据其背签的基金存款(通常为建立的普通股)是否有效来决定履行。证据交易委员会(SEC)规则O-1(e)(1),《美国联邦法规汇编》(CFR)第270节O-1(c)(1)。见variable annuity]
variable aspect 可变方面
variable capital 可变资本
variable cost 可变成本
variable costing 可变成本法,可变成本计算
variable dummy 虚构变量,虚假变量
variable import levy 进口差价税,进口差额税
variable lead time 变量前置时间
variable levies 差额税,可变税额,差价税
variable rate mortgage 可变利率的抵押(偿还)(指以一个标准指数为基础,每年或每5年以可变利率偿还债务)
variance n. 1.变化;变动;变异 2.分歧,争

论;不和 3.(诉状与供词之间)不一致 4.(对某种行为的)特殊许可
variant a. 差异的,不同的,改变的;改变了的
variation n. 改变,变更,变化;变量,变度
variation of order 更改令状
varied a. 不同的,种种的;变化的
varied life 多变化的生活
varied opinions 各种不同意见
variety n. 变化,多样性;种种;种类
variety of contexts 在多种前后关系中
variety of crimes 罪行的种类
variform a. 形形色色的;有多种形态的
variorum n. 集注本;集不同版本而成的版本
various a. 1.不同的,种种的,各式各样的 2.许多的;改变的,可改变的
various classes of heirs 各类继承人
various forms of socialist responsibility system for production 各种形式的社会主义生产责任制
various kinds of courts 各类法院
various level of courts 各级法院
varlet n. 无赖,流氓,恶棍,下贱人;仆人,侍从
varnish n./v. 油漆;粉饰,文饰/涂油漆;粉饰,文饰,虚饰
vary v. 1.改变,变换 2.交替,更换 3.违反,违背(from)
vary from a rule 违背规则
vas (大陆法)抵押,担保,(刑事或民事诉讼中的)保释或担保
vassal n. (封建时代的)诸侯,封臣;附庸,奴仆,奴隶
vassal state 附庸国
vassal troops 仆从军
vast majority of private house owner 大量的私有房产主
vasturm 荒地;共用(放牧家畜)地
Vatican n. 1.梵蒂冈(罗马教廷所在地) 2.(the Vatican)罗马教廷
vault-cash n. 库存现金
vectiga lia populi romani, 1734 《罗马人的税赋》[指荷兰学者 Pieter Burman(1713—1778)18世纪所写的关于对罗马税法的专著]
Vectigalia (罗马法)关税;(货物)进出口税
vector-sum n. 矢和
vectura (海事法中的)货运,装运;船货,运费
vehemence of this position 对此位置的热心
vehement a. 猛烈的,激烈的,热烈的
vehicle n. 车辆;媒介;传达工具
vehicle and ship use tax 车船使用牌照税
vehicle currency 周转货币,国际支付货币,媒介通货
vehicle exercise duty 车辆执照税
vehicle inspection centre 车辆检验中心
vehicle of civilization 传播文明工具
vehicle registration certificate 车辆执照,车辆登记牌照
vehicular homicide 车祸致死人命
vehicular safety devices 车辆的安全装置
veil of ignorance 无知之幕(指美国20世纪哲学家罗尔斯《正义论》对正义原则的观点)
vein n. 膨胀,血管,性情,气质,脉络
vejours n. (法院派出的)现场查验员;视察员
vel non 或者不是
velocity n. 速度,速率;迅速,快速
velocity of circulation 流通速度
velocity of money 资金周转率,货币流通速度,资金流通速度
venal a. 贪污的,可用金钱贿赂的,腐败的
venal officials 贪官污吏
venal practices 贿赂(受贿)行为
venality n. 贪污;唯利是图;甘受贿赂
vend v. 售卖;声明,发表
vendee n. 买主,买受人
* ***Vendens eandem rem duobus falsarius est.*** He is fraudulent who sells the same thing twice. 一物二卖乃属诈骗。
vendetta n. 1.血仇(指亲属为死者报仇,杀死凶手或其家属,因而演成血仇),近亲复仇 2.世仇;深仇;长年的斗争
vendettist n. 复仇者
vendibility n. 可卖,能卖,可售

vending-machine n. (出售小商品的)自动售货机

venditio 卖,销售行为

venditioni exponas 低价拍卖令(指法院一种执行令,用来命令执行官把得不到适当价格出售的查封货物,只要有人出得最高价格,即使不适当,亦可卖出以清偿判决债务)

venditor n. 卖主,出卖人

vendor n. 1.出卖人(尤指土地出卖人) 2.小贩 3.自动售货机

vendor's lien 卖主留置权(指买主在未交清购买物价款时,卖主对购买物有留置权)

vendue n. 公开拍卖,竞卖

vendue master 拍卖人

venenate v. 使中毒,把毒注入……

venenation n. 中毒

venereal a. 1.性欲的,性交的,因性交引起的 2.患性病的,花柳病的

venereal disease 性病(旧译:花柳病)

vengeance n. 报仇,复仇

* **Veniae facilitas incentivum est delinquendi.** Facility of pardon is an incentive to crime. 轻易赦免罪过实际上是鼓励犯罪。

venial a. 可宽恕的,可原谅的,轻微的(过失)

venial offense (或sin) 轻罪,微罪

veniality n. 可宽恕,可原宥

venire (被召集参加的)陪审团人员名单;到庭;出庭;(= venire facias)出庭陪审团召集令状

venire de novo 法院重审令(见 venire facias de novo)

venire facias 陪审团召集令

venire facias ad respondendum 传唤出庭受指控(或提审犯人出庭)令状

venire facias de novo (法院重新组织陪审团以代替原有不称职的陪审团进行)重审令

venire facias iuratores (英)陪审团召集令状

venire facias tot matronas (英)已婚妇女陪审团召集令状

venireman n. 受命到庭的陪审(团成)员,陪审团的陪审员

venit et defendit 前来辩护,出庭辩护

venter n. 1.腹;胃;子宫 2.母亲(指就其对子女的关系而言) 3.发表不正当或错误的言论者

ventilate v. 宣布

venture n./v. 1.冒险;投机,商业冒险,商业经营 2.敢说,敢为,敢于从事 3.企业;冒险,敢于从事

venture an opinion 大胆陈述一项意见

venture capital 投机资本,(股票)冒险资本,企业资本,风险投资

venture expansion fund 企业发展基金

venturer n. 冒险者;投机商人;企业经营者

venue n. 犯罪现场及其附近之地,诉讼原因发生地,审判地;初审法院的管辖区域,起诉书上指明的审判地点;法院的特定管辖地区;起诉状上关于审判地的指示;宣誓书上记载的宣誓地点;任何行为或事件发生现场;争论中某人采取的立场

venue defect 地域管辖缺陷

venue facts 诉讼听审中所成立的事实,确定审判地的事实

venue jurisdiction 特定法院的管辖权,法院的审判权或裁制权

venue of case 案件的审判地点

venue of the court 法院的管辖,法院的审判权

* **Vera lex, recta ratio, naturae congruens.** 礼法正义,合乎天道。

veracity n. 讲实话,诚实;真实(性),准确(性),精确(性)

verba 词,言词,言语

* **Verba accipienda sunt secundum subjectam materiam.** Words are to be understood with reference to the subject-matter. 对文字的理解应符合主题。

* **Verba artis ex arte.** Terms of art should be explained from art. 艺术的术语应从艺术角度来解释。

verba concepta 见 formulae

verba de futuro 根据许诺的结婚(相等于婚约或订婚)

verba de praesenti 根据现诺的结婚(具有婚姻效力)

* *Verba generalia generaliter sunt intelligenda.* General words are to be generally understood. 一般的词汇应按一般的意义来理解。

* *Verba ita sunt intelligenda, ut res magis valeat quam pereat.* The words(of an instrument) are to be so understood, that the subject-matter may rather be of force than perish(rather be preserved than destroyed; or, in other words, that the instrument may have effect, if possible). 如果合同既可以有效,也可以是无效时,应按有效方式而不是按无效方式来理解。

verbal a. 言辞的,口头的;字句的,非书面的
verbal accusation 口头控告
verbal agreement 口头协议
verbal confession 口供
verbal contract 口头合同(契约)
(a) verbal duel 争辩,舌战
verbal evidence 证言
verbal form 口头方式
verbal injury 口头伤害,诽谤
verbal message 口信,传言
verbal note (外交)不署名备忘录(述及非紧急但不容忽视的事情);口头通知
verbal obligation (罗马法)口头之债(指采用口头问答形式,即"要式口头合同"所产生的债务)
verbal promise 口头诺言;口头承诺
verbal sanction 口头制裁
verbal statement 言词陈述,口头陈述
verbal stipulations 口头约定
verbal threat 口头威胁,口头胁迫
verbal will (=oral will) 口头遗嘱
verbatim (照原文或原本)逐字地,照字面地/逐字的,照字面的
verbatim et lit(t)eratim 逐字逐句,完全照字面;直(译)
verbatim **record(s)** 逐字记录
verbatim transcript 证词副本
verbiage n. 空话,冗词,赘语;措辞,用语
verbiage of the Bill of Rights 《权利宣言》的解释
verbis 话语

verbis obligatio 口头合同(契约),口头之债
verbosity n. 唠叨,冗长,累赘
verbot des venire contra factum proprium 禁止国家自身矛盾原则(指国家不得自相矛盾,一方面去挑唆犯罪,另一方面却去追诉其自身所挑唆而引来的犯罪)
verderer n. (=verderor)(英史)王室护林官
verderers' Court in the Forest of Dean (英)迪安林区的护林官法院
verdict n. 定论;判断,意见;事实的认定,事实决定书;由陪审团一致通过而为法院接受的正式判决或裁决;裁决;陪审团或陪审调查后的认证书
verdict contrary to law 陪审团不顾法律之裁决
verdict for the defendant 有利于被告的裁决,被告胜诉的裁决
verdict for the plaintiff 有利于原告的裁决,原告胜诉的裁决
verdict of (not) guilty (陪审团的)有(无)罪的裁决
verge (=virge) n. 边缘,界限;临近;(英)王室司法官的管辖;司法管辖
verge of bankruptcy 破产边缘
verifiability n. 可证实(性),可检验(性),可核实(性)
verifiable a. 可检验的;可作证的,可证实的,可证明的;可核实的
verifiable certainty 可证实的确定性
verifiable information 可核实信息(如果拥有该信息,参与人能容易地向另一参与人及诸如法庭之类的第三当事人传递这一信息)
verifiableness n. 可证实,可核实,可检验
verification n. 核实,核查(真实性),鉴定;宣誓,证实,证明,宣誓证实;确定,确认;答辩书(或诉状)结尾的举证声明
verification by challenge 通过质疑进行鉴定
verification by consent 征得同意进行鉴定
verification certificate 检验证书
verificaton of death 死亡鉴定
verification of ducument(s) 文件检验,鉴定书
verification of fingerprint 指纹鉴定

verification of handprint 手纹鉴定
verification of handwriting 笔迹检验
verification of mental illness 精神病的鉴定
verification of seals and stamps 印章印文检验
verification of traces 痕迹检验
verification of voice print 声纹鉴定(见 voiceprint)
verified a. 经证明,经证实,作证的,鉴定的
verified by oath 宣誓证实
verified copy 作为独立证据的文件副本
verified names 经过验证签署
verified qualification 鉴定合格
verified written opinion 鉴定意见书
verifier n. 作证者,核实者,鉴定者,查对者
verify v. 1.证实;证明 2.宣誓后作证;把举证声明写入(诉状或答辩状的)末尾;鉴定,查对;认定
verisimilar a. 貌似真的,似乎是真的,可能的
verisimilitude n. 1.貌似真实,逼真 2.貌似真实的事物;逼真的事物
* **Verisimilitude is not proof.** 貌似真实不足为据。
verita convicii 定罪的真实性(指定罪的事实)
veritable a. 确实的,真正的,名副其实的
veritable blackguard 十足的无赖
veritas n. 1.诚实 2.(大写)国际船舶勘查和评估海事保险局(marine underwriters)机构(该机构于1828年建立在比利时,后于1832年迁移至巴黎。亦称 Bureau Veritas)
* **Veritas est justitae mater.** Truth is the mother of justice. 诚实为正义之母。
* **Veritas nihil veretur nisi abscondi.** Truth is afraid of nothing but concealment (or Truth fears nothing but to be hidden). 真相无所惧,唯恐被隐瞒。
* **Veritas nimium altercando amittitur.** Truth is lost by excessive altercation. 真理因过度争辩而消失。
veritatem dicere 证人之资格询问
verity n. 真实性,真理;事实;诚实可靠
vermin control 歹徒管制
vermo gemsnereicherung 财产得利

vernacular n. 本国语,本地话;日常语,方言;专门语;行话
versed a. 精通的(in),通晓的,熟练的
version n. 1.译文、译本;翻译 2.说法,看法(指个人对事件的看法)〈these are three different versions of what happened〉(对所发生的事情有了三种不同的看法) 3.(常作 V)基督教《圣经》的译本(the authorized version,基督教《圣经》的钦定译本) 4.改写本、改编的乐曲 5.版本、形式;变体 6.表演 7.(胎位)倒转(倒转位)
Verstehend Soziologic 理解的社会学[指马克斯·韦伯(Max Weber, 1864—1920)在研究近代法制合理化过程中曾提出的一个著名观点:法律的发展不仅受经济条件及权力结构的影响,而且,"法律名流"作为法律文化的维系者,其活动有及意识的创造也直接导致不同类型的法律传统模式的出现]
versus 1.诉;对(多用于诉讼、比赛中,如说某人诉某人,上海队对西安队:常缩写为 v.或 vs.) 2.相形,比较(两者中选一)
Versuslaw (美)沃尔舒斯网(指美国法律文献检索中的一种检索网址,免费给大学生使用,全称为 www.versuslaw.com。见 Loislaw)
vert (或 **verd**) n. 1.(英)砍伐森林中草木的特权 2.(英)改变宗教信仰(的人);背教
vertical a. 垂直的,竖立的,直立的;顶点的,绝顶的;(企业内)统管生产和销售全过程的;垂直系统的(指连锁销售中,从制造厂到批发商到零售商等);纵向结合的
vertical direct effect 垂直的直接效率,纵向的直接效率
vertical equity 垂直的公平,纵向的公平
vertical forum-shopping 纵向的法院选择
vertical integration 见 integration 5
vertical merger 纵向合并(指经营相同产品的不同层次企业之间的合并,比如一个制造厂家与一个批发商业之间合并成了买卖的合并企业。见 merger 8)
vertical occupational segregation 垂直系统职业分离
vertical price fixing 最高限价
vertical trust 反托拉斯法,纵向托拉斯(指

单一所有权的聚集联合体,亦即正连续生产或进入市场的许多企业或厂家的联合体。)
vertical uniformity 纵向的一致性
vertical union 同一工业内跨行业的工会
very ad./a. 很,甚,极其,非常/完全的,充分的,真正的;最大程度的;同一的
very close neighbour 近邻
very district judges 真正的地区法官
very lord and very tenant 直接的领主和租借人(指业主和借人之间没有中间业主的租借)
vessel n. 船;飞船;飞机(尤指水上飞机)
vessel flag nation 船旗国
vessel in distress 遇难船舶
vessel registry 船舶注册
vessel under a neutral flag 悬挂中立国旗的船舶
vessel-source pollution 船只造成的污染
vest v. 1.授给,赐给,赋予(财产、权利、权力等);(财产、权利等的)归属 2.置于……管理之下
vest X in B 授予 B 以 X(权利或义务)
vested 法律规定的,既得的;完全或永久享有的;无条件的;绝对的;确定的[用在涉及地产授予中,它与 contingent 一词含意相对。剩余地产权(remainder)分为确定的(vested)不确定的(contingent)。它也用于权利方面,则指权利或权益以及期待权的状态,而未给相应补偿,立法不可对之干预,如土地所有人的权利只能通过法律才能为公益目的而强行购买]
vested estate 既得财产
vested in interest 将来(可得)的权利(指现在确定而将来可以享有的权利,如租权回复等,这些权利回复不依靠确定的时间或事实)
vested in possession 现有的占有(权利)(指某地产是现在占有的地产)
vested interest (复)既得利益集团(指控制一国经济或财政的人或一群人);既得利益
vested legacy 既得遗产
vested remainder 既得(的指定)遗产继承权(见 remainder),既得剩余地产权

vested right(s) 既得权利,既得利益(指职工在未达退休年龄之前离职而仍应得退休福利的权利);既得权利说[美国学者比尔认为,跨国(州)民事纠纷实际上是当事人之间的权利(或义务)之争,当事人的民事权利并不是与生俱来的,而是法律赋予的]
vested right theory 既得权利说
vestige n. 形迹,行迹,痕迹,残余;证据
vestigial words 退化词语(指法定的一些词和短语经过连续修订已经成为无用或无意义的词语。法院不准许此类退化词语使成文法规的公正合理含义无效)
vestigium (古)(人或物体留下的)形迹,标记,或信号;轨迹,行迹,印痕,印记等
vesting n./a. 保留退休金的权利;授予/赋予的,授权的
vesting assent 授权认可
vesting day 授予日期
vesting declaration 信托财产授予声明(指任命人或指定人在把有关信托财产授予新受托人的证书中所作的声明,有了这种声明,就不再需用财产交付或让与的文据移交给新受托人)
vesting deed 授权契据,授产契据
vesting instrument 授权文件,授权证书
vesting notice 委托通知
vesting of right 授予权利
vesting order 1.财产交托命令(指高等法院衡平法组依据信托法例规定发出的命令,把合法财产交托给命令里所指定的人)2.许可占有的判决令
vesting period 归属期
vestita manus 法律规定的手,确定的手(指在就职仪式上使用右手)
vestitive facts 授予事实(引起权利授予或被剥夺的事实)
vestry n. 教堂法衣室(指教堂中放置法衣、圣物等的房间)
vesture n. 土地收益(指地面上树木之外的生长物,如草、谷类等)
vesture of land 地面上的一切生长物
vetera statuta (= *antiqua statuta*) (英)古制定法(指由 1215 年的大宪章起至爱德华二世未止的一段时间内所制定的法律);[爱德华三世时与"新制定法"(*nova*

statuta)相对所称的]旧制定法
veteran n. 老兵;(美)退伍军人
Veteran Administration (美)退伍军人管理局(指负责管理退伍军人福利事务的机构)
veteran judges 退伍军人法官
veterans' life insurance 军人保险,退伍军人人寿保险
veterans' preference (美)对退伍军人的优待(尤指文官考试录取时的优待)
veterans' property tax exemption 退伍军人财产税免税
veterinarian n. 兽医
veterinary a. 兽医的
veterinary certificate 兽医证书
veterinary code 兽医规范
veto n./v. 1.否决,禁止,拒绝;否决权;禁止权 2.行政机构反对立法机构所通过的法案时所申请的理由/不认可,否决,禁止
veto a bill 否决(一项)议案
veto message (美)否定咨文(指总统等对立法机构的议案予以否决并陈述理由的文件)
veto power 否决权[美国联邦宪法的制定者们一致认为总统的否决权能限制立法机关越权。联邦宪法第1条第9款赋予总统有权否决每一法案,或对此进行投票表决需要获得众参两院一致通过(或同意)。总统的否决权也并非绝对,但需国会两院2/3多数(出席会议的法定人数的2/3,而不是所有成员的2/3)造成,才能推翻它。在1883年这种否决权是指一个行政的有条件的权力以防止一个议案。经过立法机构变成法律]
veto-message (美)否决咨文(指总统等对立法机构的议案予以否决并陈述理由的文件)
vetoer n. 否决者
vetoing discrimination 表决(投票)的歧视
vetting n. 审查;修正
Vetus jus (罗马法与大陆法)1.十二铜表法 2.长期设立的或古代法 3.在后法通过之前的有效法律
vex v. 1.使烦恼;激怒 2.骚扰
vexata questio 久议不决的问题(见 vexed question)
vexation n. 1.招人烦恼的事物 2.烦恼,苦闷
vexations litigation (或 **proceedings**) 恶意诉讼
vexatious a. 1.缠诉的;诬告的;无理取闹的,困扰的 2.(诉讼)无根据的;旨在使对方为难的
vexatious action 滥用诉讼(指完全为了干扰或压制他人而提起的诉讼,其内容常含有丑闻,并无适当理由的。法院有权将这类诉讼搁置起来)
vexatious appeal 不能受理的上诉,无理的上诉
vexatious conduct 挑衅行为;滋扰行为
vexatious litigant 缠讼的诉讼当事人;诬告的诉讼当事人
vexatious litigation (= vexatious proceedings) 恶意诉讼,无合理理由的滥诉
vexed question 难解决的问题,争论不休的问题
vi et armis 用暴力(一般用于"侵犯"诉讼或检控书中,诉说被告用过"暴力"),用武力,诉诸武力(指在普通法诉状上用以表明某一非法侵害行为的用语)
vi statuti 通过强制执行法规,通过法规的强制执行
via 1.(大陆法)路,道路;经由,通过;通行权 2.(古英国法)道路;公路;马车路;一步,一英尺
* ***Via antiqua via est tuta.*** The old way is the safe way. 老路是安全的道路。
via publica 公共的道路,公路
via regia (英)皇家道路;大路,公路
via usucapiendi 以时效方式获得财产
viability n. 生存能力(亦称生活能力,指婴儿出生后有生存和养活的能力),生命力;生存性
viability-procedural observance test 遵守程序符合标准(指美国实行的一种原则,即公司在设立程序和形式上必须符合独立实体的特征)
viable a. (胎儿)能活的,能养活的
viable basis 有生命力的基础
viable basis for assertion 行使对人管辖的有生命力的基础,以强有力的基础行使对

人的管辖权
(a) viable business　可操作的商业,可维持的生意
viable child　能活的胎儿
viable *servitus* (= *viae sertitus*)　在他人土地上的通过权
viable suit　能存在的诉讼,能成立的诉讼
viable way　可行的办法,可行途径
vicar n.　1.代表,代理牧师;代理主教 2.代理人,受委托人
vicar-general n.　(英)代理监督(一种行政或司法雇员)
vicarial a.　代理的,受委托的;代理教区牧师职务的;教区牧师的
vicarious a.　代理的,代理人的,替代别人的
vicarious admission　代理的自认
vicarious agent　代理人
vicarious atonement　替代履行的赔偿
vicarious authority　代理的授权,受托有代的权力
vicarious liability　代理法律责任,替代责任
vicarious performance　替代履行,替代偿付
vicarious punishment　替代(他人)受的惩罚
vicarious responsibility (或 liability)　(英美法)转承责任;替代责任;代理责任
vice n.　1.恶;罪恶;邪恶;坏事;不道德 2.恶行;恶习,恶癖 3.缺点,毛病,瑕疵;(前缀)表示"副";"次";"代理"
vice crimes　不道德的罪行(指淫荡、下流的恶行)
vice inductive to crime　诱使犯罪的坏事
vice minister　副部长
vice of constitution　宪法的瑕疵
vice of intemperance　酗酒的恶习
vice prime minister　副总理,副首相
vice squad　(取缔卖淫、赌博等的)警察缉捕队
vice versa　反之亦然,反过来
vice-admiralty courts　附属海军法院(又译:附属海事法院,指英国以前设在海外属地的海事法院,现已由殖民地的海事法院代替),海岸事务法庭,域外海事法庭,副海事法院
vice-chairman n.　副主席;(中)(全国人民代表大会常务委员会)副委员长

vice-chancellor n.　(美)某些衡平法院主审法官代理;(英)御前大臣助理,副大法官(指以前具有衡平法审判权的司法官员,是大法官的副手,现已废);大学副校长,(英某些大学中的)主要行政官
vice-comes　执行
vice-consul n.　副领事
vice-governor n.　副总督,副地方长官
vice-king n.　见 viceroy
vice-premier n.　副首相,副总理
vice-presidency n.　副董事长职位
vice-president n.　(美国等的)副总统;(会议)副主席;(法院)副院长;(中)(国家)副主席
vice-president of the court　法院副院长,法庭副庭长
vice-principal n.　副校长
vice-regent n.　副摄政
vicegerency n.　代理职,代理权
vicegerent a./n.　代理的/1.代理人;代官 2.国家元首或最高当权者指定的代理人
viceregal a.　总督的,代表王权的
vicereine n.　女总督,总督夫人
viceroy (=vice-king) n.　(代表国王管辖行省或殖民地的)总督
viceroyship (或 viceroyalty) n.　总督的职权(任期、辖区)
vicinage　neighborhood(14 世纪)1.邻居,邻近地区,附近地区,近处;血缘关系,亲属关系;近邻 2.犯罪实施地;审判地(刑事被告人有权获得从犯罪实施地的邻近地区公民中遴选陪审团进行审判的权利,亦称 vicinetum)3.邻近佃户具有庄园或土地的共同权利
vicinetum　1.邻近地区,附近地区 2.犯罪实施地,审判地
vicinage n.　附近(地区);邻居(关系)
vicinity n.　附近,邻近;附近地区,近邻,近处
vicious a.　有恶意的;恶毒的;有恶习的;恶的;邪恶的
vicious circle (或 cycle; spiral)　恶性循环;循环论证
vicious habits　恶习
vicious language　讹语,讹诈的语言

vicious person 腐化堕落的人,恶人
vicious possession 恶意占有
vicious reasoning 谬误的推理
vicious words 恶言
vicontiel (=vicountiel) a. (英国早期法律上的)属于行政司法官(sheriff)或子爵(viscount)的
vicountiel jurisdiction 地方法官(行政司法官等)管辖权
vicissitude n. 变迁,盛衰,变化
vicissitudes of the supremacy of law 法律至上的沉浮,法律至上的沧桑变迁(或变化)
victim n. 受害人;被害人;遭难者,替罪羊
victim of a swindler 骗子所骗的人,受骗者
victim of aggression 被侵略者,侵略受害者
victim of crime 犯罪行为的受害人
victim of violence 暴力行为受害人
victim on legal decision making 法律判决的受害人
victim to an assassin 被暗杀者
victim's statement 被害人的陈述
victim-offender-reconciliation n. 加害人与被害人的和解,刑事和解(20世纪70年代,西方的法律改革者提出刑事和解理论,并在英美德国的司法实践中推广适用。简言之,即在犯罪嫌疑人犯罪之后,经由调停人使加害人与被害人直接协商解决纠纷冲突,目的是使罪犯能改过自新、复归社会,受害人得到公平补偿)
victimize v. 1.使受害;使作牺牲 2.欺骗;欺诈
victimless a. 没有受害者的
victimless crimes 没有被害人的犯罪
victimology n. 受害者心理学
victimologist n. 受害者心理学家
Victims of Child Abuse Laws (美)《虐待儿童受害人法》(缩略为 VOCAL)(见 False Memory Syndrome Foundation)
Victorian a./n. 维多利亚式的(指该时代陈腐伪善的道德标准和华丽辞藻修饰的文化等)/维多利亚女王(1837—1901)时代的人;维多利亚时代的代表作家
Victorian morals 维多利亚式的惯例(道德态度)

victorious powers 战胜国
victual v. 供应食物给……;(船只)装贮食物
victual(l)ing office 物资供应(或粮食供应)局
victualler n. 1.(英)客栈老板 2.(专为部队或船只)供应粮食者;补给船
victualling bill 装载船上用品的(海)关单
vide 见
vide ante 见上文
vide in fra 见下文
vide post 见后面
vide supra 见上文
videlicet 就是……,即是说(指叙述时间和事件所用的词);换句话说
video and audio recording 录音录像
video tape 录像带
videocast n. 电视广播
videogram n. 录像制品(见 moving pictures)
videotape 录像带;录像证据
vidimus n. 1.(账目的)检查,监察 2.(文件的)梗概,摘要,要略
viduage (=viduity) n. 守寡期间,孀居
vidual a. 守寡的,寡妇的
vie v. 竞争,冒……危险;使竞争
Vienna Convention of Consular Relations 《维也纳领事关系公约》(联合国于1964年4月在维也纳召开的国际会议上通过的)
Vienna Convention on Diplomatic Relation 《维也纳外交关系公约》(1961年维也纳国际会议通过的)
Vienna Convention on the Law of Treaties (1969) 《维也纳条约法公约》(1969年)
view n./v. (从屋内窗户的)眺望权;看,望;意见;见解;目的;意向,意图;视察(尤指在民事案件中涉及不动产如土地、房屋时,法官和陪审团亲自去物业所在地视察);(陪审团对有关财物、尸体、现场等)现场勘验;观察/(陪审团对有关财物、尸体、现场等)查验,观察;考虑,核查
view body 验尸
view of an inquest 陪审验尸团的查验
view of frankpledge 十户连保制的检查

view of *locus in quo* 现场视察
view of the scene 现场查验
view problem in its entirety 全面考虑问题
view the body 验尸
viewer n. 视察员,查验员,检查员
vif-gage (古英ី法)活典(权),活抵押(权)(见 *vivum vadium*)
vigil n. 警戒,监视;守夜
vigilance n. 警醒;警觉;注意;不眠
vigilance committee (美)治安委员会(指一种未经授权自行组织的民间团体,旨在维持治安,惩罚罪犯)
vigilant a. 警醒的,警戒的,注意的
vigilante n. (美)治安维持会成员;(美)逮捕和惩治罪犯的执法组成员
* *Vigilantibus et non dormientibus jura subveniunt.* The laws aid those who are vigilant, not those who sleep upon their rights. 法律帮助的是那些时刻警觉的人,而不是那些躺在权利上睡大觉的人。
vigilantism n. (美)治安维持会的政策(或制度);治安维持会会员的做法(指不按法律程序,立即裁决)
vigo(u)r n. (法律上的)效力;力量,魄力;活力,精力
vigorish n. (高利贷者等索取的)高额利息;(赌博中的)抽头
vigorous a. 强有力的,朝气蓬勃的;精力充沛的,健壮的
vigorous despot 强力的暴君,残酷的暴君
vigorous enforcement of laws 执法如山
vigorous good sense of judges 法官的强有力的理性
vigorous invective 有力抨击
vigorous lobby 有力的疏通、游说
vigorous pioneer race 强有力的拓荒者家族
vile a. 1.极坏的,恶劣的;卑鄙的,卑贱的 2.低廉的,价值极低的
vile actions 卑贱的行为
(a) vile character 卑贱(鄙)的人
(the) vile practice of bribery 卑鄙的贿赂行为
vilification n. 诋毁,诽谤;中伤
vilifier n. 诽谤者,中伤者,诬蔑者

vilify v. 诋毁;中伤;诽谤,损害名誉
vilipend v. 诽谤,蔑视
vill n. (英史)邑属镇(指百户邑的分区,亦即最小行政单位)
village a./n. 村的,乡下的/1.村,村庄 2.村民(总称)
village chief 村长
village community (史)(土地公有的)村社,农村公社
village fair 农村集市,集市贸易
village headman 村长
village industry 农村工业
village rules (日)村落法
villager n. 农民,乡下人
villagers' committee (中)村民委员会
villain n. 歹徒,恶棍,恶徒
villain of the piece 1.剧中的反面人物 2.首恶者,为害者
villainess n. 女恶棍,坏女人;女的反面人物
villainous a. 歹徒的,邪恶的,恶的
villainy n. 1.卑鄙;丑恶;邪恶 2.(复)邪恶的行为;犯罪行为
villein(s) n. (中世纪英格兰法)隶农(指包括奴隶,以及具有自由身份,但有一定人身依附性的耕作农民的一种混合型社会阶层),农奴,佃农
villein socage 停役(农役)租地土地保有权
villein tenure (英)役农土地保有权,佃农土地保有权;佃农保有地
ville(i)nage n. 佃农对土地的使用权;农奴(或佃农)身份
villenous judg(e)ment 剥夺公权的判决
vinculo matrimonii 离婚
vinculum juris (罗马法)法律约束(指当事人之间的法律关系,一经成立,即受其约束)
vinculum matrimonii 婚姻的约束
vindex (大陆法)保护人,辩护人
vindicability n. 可辩护性,可证明性
vindicable a. 可辩护的,可证明为正确的,可辩解的
vindicate v. (16世纪)1.澄清(人或事)嫌疑;批评,责难;怀疑〈DNA tests vindicated the suspect〉(DNA测试澄清了嫌疑)2.通

过诉讼维护、维持、确认个人利益〈claimants sought to vindicate their rights through a class-action suit〉(权利请求人想通过集体诉讼维护他们的权利) 3.为维护干预或侵犯个人的权利进行辩护〈the borrower vindicated its interest in court when the lender tried to foreclose〉[当出借人(lender)试图停止出借时,借用人在法庭上为维护其利益进行辩护] 4.(罗马法或大陆法)对(一项事物)主张合法权利;通过法律手段寻求收回物权〈Antony Honoratus attempted to vindicate the sword he had lent his cousin〉(安东尼·奥诺纳图斯意图索回借给他表弟的剑)(vindication n.; vindicator n.)

vindicatio (罗马法)主张物权之诉(指物的所有人,对占有该物的人可提出主张物上权利或所有权的诉讼请求)

vindicatio in libertatem (罗马法)释放奴隶之诉

vindicatio sevitutis (罗马法)地役权之诉,亦称 *actio confessoria*

vindicatio usufructus (罗马法)用益权之诉

vindication n. 1.辩明、辩白;辩护;证实 2.借口 3.证明有理的事

vindication of justice 维护公正权

vindication of right 辩护权,维护权利

vindication of right and justice 辩护和公平维护权,辩护权和维护公正权

vindicative a. 辩明的,辩护的,起辩护作用的

vindicator n. 辩护者;证明者;维护者

vindicatory a. 1.辩明的;辩护的,证明的 2.报复的,惩罚的

vindicatory part (1881年)制定法规宣布的因非法和失职而基处的部分

vindicatory parts of laws 法律条文中的有关制裁部分

vindicatory sanction 惩罚性的制裁

vindicta (罗马法) 1.棒,棍,剑把;(或)权杖和所有权 2.尤指持棒象征性地触及人和事以维护自由和所有权(见 festuca = fistuca)

vindictive a. 报复的,有报仇心的,复仇的;惩罚性的

vindictive action 报复行为

vindictive blow 报复性打击

vindictive damages 惩罚性损害赔偿(指民事诉讼中,为了惩罚被告,使其赔偿损害的金额比原告实际的损害为高的赔偿)

vindictive parts of laws 法律条文中规定的科刑部分;科刑的法律条文

vindictive punishment 报复性的惩罚

vintage n./a. 同年代的一批产品,同年代的一批人物;酒制造的时期/老式的,过时的

Vintage Brennan (美)布伦南代表作(指美国联邦最高法院大法官布伦南的判决意见书集)

viol n./v. 强奸,强奸罪/侵入,闯入

violable a. (条例等)可违反的,可侵犯的;易违反的,易受侵犯的

violate v. 1.违犯(法律、契约等),违反 2.妨害,妨碍,扰乱;干扰,骚扰 3.强奸,侮辱 4.侵犯

violate a frontier 侵犯边境

violate a law 违法,犯法

violate a nation's territory and sovereignty 侵犯国家的领土和主权

violate oath 背誓,违背誓言

violate rules and regulations 违章,违反规章制度

violation n. (15世纪) 1.违犯或违背法律;犯法,犯规,犯罪(见 infraction) 2.破坏法律,羞辱法律行为,违犯或破坏权利或义务 3.强奸,劫持妇女 4.《示范刑法典》规定的侵犯公共福利罪[就此意义上讲,violation 不是一种罪行(crime),参见《示范刑法典》第1.04(5)节。犯罪按刑罚轻重分为4等,分别是重罪、轻罪、微罪、违警罪;侵犯公共福利属违警违法行为。violate v.; violative a.; violator n.]

violation of a right 违犯权利;侵犯(他人的)权利

violation of constitution 违宪

violation of contract 违反合同(契约);违约

violation of international law 违反国际法

violation of law 违反法律,违法

violation of legal procedures 违反法定程序

violation of privacy 妨害私事;侵入或闯

入(某人)私室
violation of recognized rules of warfare 违反公认的战争规则
violation of the laws and breaches of disciplines 违法乱纪
violation of treaty 违反条约
violation of woman 强奸妇女
violative a. 违犯的,违反的;妨害的,侵犯的;强奸的;蹂躏的
violator n. 侵犯者;违犯者;妨碍者;强奸者
violator of the law 违章的人,违禁者,违法者
violence (14世纪)暴力[指对身体使用暴力,常常伴随着狂暴(furry)、激情(vehemence)或盛怒(outrage)、非法使用暴力、蓄意致人伤害(或财产损失)。有些法院认为劳资纠纷(labor disputes)中的暴力不受身体接触或伤害的限制,但包含有误导信号的纠察、虚假声明、违法宣传,以一些词语和行为暗藏着威胁]
violent a. 1.猛烈的,剧烈的,激烈的;极端的 2.由暴力引起的 3.曲解的,歪曲的
violent accident 由暴力引起的意外事故
violent conduct(或 **deeds**) 暴行
violent controversy 激烈的争论
violent crime 暴力犯罪
Violent Crime Control Act (美)(1994年)《暴力犯罪控制法》(该法案规定对触犯重罪的13岁以上未成年人依成年人犯罪起诉)
violent death 暴力死亡,横死
violent encounters 暴力冲突
violent interpretation 歪曲的解释
violent possession 暴力占有
violent presumption 足可作有力证据的推定(又译接近证据的推定,指推定的性质,几乎达到了可以证明事实的程度)
violent profits (苏格兰)由强占所引起的收益(类似英格兰的中间收益)
violent prosecution 由暴力引起的控告(诉)
* *Violenta praesumptio aliquando est plena probatio.* Very powerful presumption is sometimes full proof. 很有权威的推定有时是充分证据;有力的推断有时就是充分证据

vir 男人;丈夫
vir bonus 男人的红利,男人的额外津贴
vires 力;活力,生活力(*vis* 的复数形式)
virginal a. 1.处女的,有处女特性的 2.纯洁的,没有污染的
Virginia Declaration of Rights (美)《弗吉尼亚权利宣言》(指1776年6月12日由弗吉尼亚殖民地立宪会议通过的权利宣言,即1789年通过、1791年生效的美国宪法的权利法案,亦译权利宣言。见 Bill of Rights)
virginity n. 1.童贞,处女性;纯洁 2.未婚女子的独身生活
virility n. (男子的)成年;男子气概,精力充沛
virology n. 病毒学
virtu n. 古董癖,艺术品爱好;(总称)古董,艺术品
virtual a. 实际上的,实质上的
virtual acceptance 事实上的承兑,事实上接受,事实上承诺
virtual agreement 实际上的同意
virtual fraud 重大诈欺;实质性诈欺
virtual lie 谎言,撒谎
Virtual Mobbing 虚拟围攻[指利用互联网媒体和相关技术攻击或联合起来对付某个人的做法。这一表达方式最早出现在科技新闻网站 TechEYE.net 于2011年3月25日发表的一篇报道中。题为《德国把 cyber-mobbing(网络围攻)网站列入黑名单:虚拟围攻变成现实生活中的欺凌》的文章中提到了德国小学生间流行的 Isharegossi.com 网站。该网站列出了各地区学校的名单,学生们可匿名登录网站辱骂同学或老师,其中不乏种族主义的过激言论。多国青少年沦为网络暴力受害者,有人甚至在收到死亡威胁推文(death tweet)后自杀。据调研机构"欧盟儿童在线问题研究"统计,波兰、爱沙尼亚和意大利青少年网络欺凌受害率分别高达52%、31%和21%。上述情况已引起各国重视。《连线英国》月刊网站刊登题为《上议院得出结论认为英国现有法律涵盖社交媒体犯罪领域》的文章称,英国上议院通讯特别委员会"研究了网络欺凌、revenge porn

（色情报复）、trolling（为激怒他人而发送煽动性邮件或帖子）以及网络围攻等事例,以确定它们是否属于刑事犯罪;若答案肯定,又是否需要为处理它们制定新立法"。此外,新加坡国会日前通过"防止骚扰法案",纳入防止网络骚扰和网络欺凌。德国也要求谷歌公司、雅虎公司和必应公司删除搜索引擎中的不良网站]

virtual total loss 实际全损
virtual visitation 虚拟探视(指因离婚不得不与子女天各一方的家长与其子女通过宽带网络和视频聊天,即谓虚拟探视)
virtue n. 1.美德,贞操;优点,长处 2.效能,效力;英勇,刚毅
virtue of mortgage 抵押权的效力,质权的效力
virulence n. 1.毒力,毒性,致命性 2.恶毒,刻毒
virulent a. 剧毒的,致命的;刻毒的,恶毒的
virulent poison 致命的毒质
virus distribution robots and file servers 病毒分配"机器人"和文件"服务器"
virus distribution sites 病毒分配站点
virus exchange BBS 病毒交换电子广告
virus exchange network 病毒交换网(这些网络常被称为VX-Net/Nuk Enet)
virus for sale 销售病毒(指有些人专门出售计算机病毒,美国的某些杂志上刊登销售病毒的广告为合法)
virus instruction books 病毒介绍书籍(指如何编制计算机病毒的书籍,也是一种传播病毒方式)
vis 见 vires
vis absoluta 身体所受的威胁
vis armata 武力,武装力量
vis compulsiva 精神上所受威胁
vis divina (大陆法)超人能力,神力;不可抗力
vis fluminis (大陆法)水力
vis inermis (古英国法)非武装力量(与 vis armata 相对应)
vis injuriosa (古英国法)非法力量,不法力量
vis legibus est inimica 违法暴力,暴力是破坏法律的

vis legis 法律的力量
vis licita (古英国法)合法力量
vis major 不可抗力;不能抵抗的力量
vis perturbativa (古英国法)当事人之间互争占有权所使用的暴力
vis proxima 近似暴力
vis simplex 完全暴力,单纯暴力
vis-a-vis prep./ad./n. 和……面对面,和……相对,同……相比;关于,对……而言/面对面地;面对面/面对面的人或物,(职位上的)对等人物,对手;面对面的谈话
vis-a-vis third person 对抗第三人
visa n./v. (护照等上的)签证,检查核准/在(护照)上签证;审查核准
visa-granting office 签证机关
visaed passport 已签证的护照
Visby Rules 《维斯比规则》(全名为《修改统一提单若干法律规则的国际公约的议定书》,于1968年在布鲁塞尔签署,为《海牙规则》的修正文本。见 Hague Rules)
viscount n. (英)子爵;执行官的旧称号
vise 见 visa
visible a. 看得见的;有形的;明显的
visible act 表现行为
visible file 显露式文件夹
visible hand 看得见的手
visible means 有形财产
visible means of maintenance 有形抚养财产,有形生活财产
visible trade 有形贸易
visit n./v. 1.视察,调查 2.访问;参观;游览 3.(战时)海军人员对中立国船只的检查/1.访问,探望,参观,游览 2.视察;巡视 3.(疾病,灾害等的)侵袭 4.惩罚;惩治;施加
visit a prisoner 探监,看犯人
visit and search (国际法)(交战国双方)检查和搜查(中立国船只)权
visit to the scene 现场检查,现场视察,现场勘查
visitador n. (西班牙)巡视员(指由王室定期派往北部各城镇调查司法行政事宜的官员)
vitiated judgment 错误的判断

visitation n. 1.访问,探望;视察,巡视 2.(战时)海军人员对中立国船只的检查 3.(司法官对精神病患者的)巡视

visitation and search 临检;登船搜查(指在公海上交战国之军舰对任何商船如有怀疑得派员亲临检查)

visitation law (父母对子女的)探视法

visitation of providence 灾难;天灾;考验

visitation order (美)(家庭法)探视令,探视规定[指①确定非抚养的父(或母)探视孩子次数的规定;②确立对孩子和陪伴孩子的重要亲属(significant relationship)的探视次数的规定。这样的规定可允准祖孙之间、孩子和其他亲属之间、孩子和继父或继母之间、偶尔也包括孩子和心理父母(psychological parent)之间的探视。亦称 access order]

visitation rights 探视权利(指父母离婚,不管孩子由哪方抚养,另一方均有探视的权利)

visiting committees (英)视察监狱委员会(指1877年成立的一个非官方组织)

visiting day in prison 探监日

visiting forces 外国驻军

visiting lecturer 客座讲师

visiting (associate) professor 客座(副)教授

visiting scholar 访问学者

visitor n. 视察人,检视人;(海关等的)检查员,检验员

visitor's seat 旁听席

visitorial a. 有权视察的,有权检查的;视察的,巡视的

visits from the people (中)人民来访

visne n. 1.邻居 2.组成陪审团的(地)区;

VISTA 来美国服务的志愿者(全称为 Volunteers in Service to America)(指建立于1964年的联邦项目,旨在提供志愿者帮助改善美国及其属地,波多黎各的最贫困地区老百姓的生活条件)

visto 支票保付,凭证

Visual Artists Right Act of 1990 《1990年美国形象化艺术家权利法》

visual horizen 视线之距离(指国际法学家格劳秀斯所主张的领水带距离)

visual inspection 肉眼检查

vita 1.生命(复数为 vitae) 2.(博士论文等内所附的)个人简历;履历;传记

vital a. 1.生命的;维持生命所必需的 2.致命的;严重的 3.必需的,极重要的

vital areas of environmental law 环保法的严禁范围

vital aspects of the case 案件的关键方面

vital concern 重要关切,重大关注

vital decision 重大判决

vital effect 极为重要的影响

vital error 严重错误

vital interests 重大利益

vital justification 根本的正当性,根本的正当理由

vital problem 生死攸关的问题

vital statistics 人口动态统计(指关于出生、死亡、婚姻等统计)

vital wound 致命伤

vitally affect 重大影响

vitiate v. 1.败坏,污损;污染;使堕落,败坏(道德等) 2.使(契约、合同等)无效,使失效

vitiated a. 损坏的;败坏的;污损的;无效的

vitiated by a fundamental flaw (证据等的)根本无效的缺陷

vitiating defect 使(法律行为)失效的瑕疵

vitiation n. 1.败坏,污损;污染;破坏 2.无效,失效

vitiator n. 败坏者;污损者;使无效者(人或物)

vitious intromission (苏格兰)未经(法院)授权对死者动产的干预行为(指法院许可的遗嘱执行人以外的任何人对死者动产的占有、使用或处置的行为)

vitium reale 财产权的固有瑕疵

vitricus 后父;再嫁之夫

vitriol n. 1.尖刻的言辞;批评 2.硫酸盐

vitriol-throwing n. 浇硫酸(毁人容貌以报私仇)

vitriolize v. 以硫酸伤人(指毁人容貌)

vituperate v. 责骂,辱骂,漫骂

vituperation n. 辱骂,责骂;诽谤,漫骂

vituperator n. 责骂者,辱骂者,漫骂者

viva voce 口头,口头地

viva voce vote 口头表决

vivum vadium 活典质;活抵押
vixen n. 1.恶妇;刁妇;泼妇 2.雌狐
viz(或 *videlicet*) 即,就是说
vizier, vizir (伊斯兰教国家的)高级官员,大臣
vocabula artis 术语
vocal advocate 昌言无忌的律师
vocal print 声纹(见 voiceprint)
vocatio in jus 传呼出庭
vocation n. 行业,职业;职业上的才能;使命
vocational a. 职业上的,天职的
vocational discipline 职业纪律
vocational education 职业教育
vocational guidance 职业辅导
vogue n. 时尚,流行物;流行,风行
vogue among lawyers and laymen 在法律工作者和普通人之间流传
voice n. 1.声音;意愿;意见 2.发言能力,发音能力;发言权;参与决定权 3.发表,表示,吐露
voice identification 声纹鉴定,声音认定
voice mail 语音邮件
voice vote 呼声表决[根据"赞成"(ayes)与"反对"(noes)的声音大小来估计人数的表决,但不统计呼唤 ayes 和 noes 的实际人数]
voiceless a. 1.沉默的,无声的 2.未说出的 3.无发言权的;无权表示意见的
voiceprint n. 声纹(亦称声印、声模。指一个人声音的特有形态,以光谱形式所作成的记录来看,和指纹一样,每个人的声纹都不一样)
voiceprinter n. 声纹机,声印机,声模机
voiceprinting n. 声纹鉴别法
void a./v. 1.法律上无效的;无效的;无用的,作废的 2.无人担任的/使无效,使作废
void a check 使支票无效
void *ab initio* 自始无效
void act 无效行为
void after the fact 事后无效
void and voidable 无效的和可以撤销的
void and voidable marriage 无效且可撤销的婚姻
void ballot 无效票,废票
void before the fact 当初无效,自始无效,事前无效
void contract 无效合同(契约)
void deed 无效契据
void *ex post facto* 事后无效
void for uncertainty 因不明确而无效(见 uncertainty)
void for vagueness doctrine 因不明确而无效的理论
void from the beginning 自始无效
void in part 一部无效;部分无效
void *in toto* 全部无效
void in whole 全部无效
void *ipso jure* 于法当然无效
void judgment 无效判决(指自始不发生任何法律效力的判决)
void legacy 无效遗嘱(指此项遗赠从未合法)
void marriage 无效婚姻
void on its face 明显无效,表面无效
void process 无效的程序(指缺乏程序上的要件,如无权管辖)
void transaction 无效的法律行为;无效交易
voidable a. 可撤销的;可使无效的;可作废的
voidable contract 可撤销的合同(契约)
voidable juristic act 可撤销的法律行为
voidable marriage 可宣告无效的婚姻
voidable preference 可予撤销的优先权(如用不正当方法在破产程序中取得优先清偿之权等)
voidable transaction 可撤销的法律行为
voidance n. (契约、证书等的)取消;无效;放弃;废除
voidance(或 **voidness**)**of treaty** 条约的废除
voided a. (契约等)废弃的
voided check 作废支票
voiding 见 voidance
voidness n. (契约等的)无效,失效
voie de droit 法律途径,诉讼方法
voie du fait 事实手段
voir dire (= voire dire) 1.预备讯问(指从前英国星室法院所采用的一种讯问程序,法官在证人作证前向证人发问一些问题,看是否有作证能力。如证人精神不健全,

则会被拒绝作证)2.预先审核(在美国,这个词是指法院对前来充当证人或陪审员的人进行初步审查,看是否说真话,是否合格)

voir dire examination 预先审核的询问(见 voir dire),预备性询问

vola n. 掌心,脚底

volens 情愿的,欣然从事的,心甘情愿的;愿意,表示同意

* *Volenti non fit injuria.* That to which a man consents cannot be considered an injury. No injury is done to a willing persons. 对自愿者不构成侵害。自愿招致损害者不得主张所受的损害。

volition n. 意志,决断,意志力;自由意志的选择或决定

volition of the parties 当事人的主观意志,当事人的选择

volitional conduct 自愿的行为

volksgeist n. 民族精神

volksraad n. 人民议会(指1917年荷兰在东印度群岛建立的咨询机构)

Volstead Act (美)《禁酒法(案)》[指美国国会于1918年10月28日通过,并于1919年1月16日批准的一项法案,该法案由明尼苏达州议员沃尔斯泰德(Andrew Volstead)提出,故名];禁酒法(指现已废弃的联邦禁酒法规)

volsteadism n. (美)禁酒主义

* *Voluit, sed non dixit.* He may have intended so, but he did not say so. 意图如此,但未说出。(此习语常用于遗嘱的法律释义)

volume of trading 交易量

volumen (大陆法)卷、册(复数为volumina)

voluminous criminal code 多卷的刑法典,庞大的刑法典

volumus 我们愿意,(这是)我们的愿望(这是王室保护令状中第一个词句专用语,以我们作为第一人称,此为君主政体的传统口语)

voluntarii heredes 任意继承人

voluntarily relinquised nationality 自愿放弃国籍

voluntariness n. 自愿,志愿,自动,受主观意志控制

voluntarism n. 唯意志论;自愿捐助主义;实行志愿兵制主张

voluntarism in depth 深度的自愿论

voluntary n./a. 自愿做的事;自愿的行为/1.无偿的(在英国法中指无价格的报酬,如无偿的赠与文据等,如果正式签名盖印,可以有效,但无偿的财产交付文据,如在交付后二年内,财产所有人宣告破产,则这种交付是无效的)2.自愿的,自动的 3.故意的,为意志所控制的

voluntary abandonment 1.自愿遗弃者(作为法定离婚的依据)2.(收养上的)自动遗弃行为

voluntary acceptance of risk 自愿承担风险

voluntary acknowledgement 任意认领

voluntary acts 自觉的作为,自愿的行为

voluntary agency 任意代理

voluntary answer 自发答辩

voluntary appearance 自愿出庭(指被告在未收到传票传唤或其他正式通知情况下的自愿出庭)

voluntary arbitration 自行仲裁

voluntary assignment 自动转让,无偿转让

voluntary association 自愿组合的社团,民间社团,自愿(组成的)协会

voluntary assumption 无偿承担

voluntary attendance 自觉(自愿)出庭

voluntary auction 任意性拍卖

voluntary bankruptcy 自行申请的破产

voluntary benefit 自愿相助,主动相助(近似大陆法的无因管理)

voluntary bill of indictment 自行起诉书

voluntary compulsory license 自愿强制许可证,当然许可(指作者表示他人可不经专门许可而使用自己作品,但需付一定报酬,我国1990年《著作权法》第4章有此规定)

voluntary conduct 有意识行为

voluntary confession 自动认罪(指被检控人自认罪行,如果这种认罪不是被胁迫或利诱的,则法院可随时作为证据使用)

voluntary contribution 自愿捐助,自愿资助

voluntary conveyance 自愿让与,无偿让与

voluntary crime 有意犯罪,故意犯罪
voluntary dismissal （美）自愿撤诉(指依照《联邦民事诉讼规则》在被告提出答辩之前或答辩后,依双方共同协议不经法庭许可自行撤诉)
voluntary dissolution 自动解散
voluntary domicile 任意住所;意定住所
voluntary enlistment 志愿兵役制
voluntary escape 放纵罪犯逃escape (指公务员放纵或给予便利而使罪犯逃脱)
voluntary establishment 自愿设立的机构
voluntary foreign credit restraint (VFCR) 自愿限制对外信贷
voluntary gift 无偿赠与
voluntary grantee 无偿受让人
voluntary heir 任意继承人
voluntary ignorance 有意忽视;知而不理(指明知其然而不加理会的含义)
voluntary indictment （英）高等法院法官指示或同意的公诉
voluntary insurance 自愿保险,任意保险
voluntary juridical fact 有意的法律行为
voluntary jurisdiction 自愿管辖（又译:任意管辖,指古英国法中,一些宗教法庭行使的管辖范围)
voluntary labor 义务劳动
voluntary law 意志法(指国际法效力的根据,有人认为主要是自然法及为各国同意或公认的意志法)
voluntary law of nations 自愿的国际法;(国家间的)自然法
voluntary manslaughter 故意杀人
voluntary migration 自愿迁移
voluntary misstatement 故意误述
voluntary oath 自动宣誓
voluntary obligatory right 任意债权
voluntary office 义务职(务)
voluntary payment 自动支付
voluntary prosecution 自诉
voluntary prosecutor 自诉人
voluntary purchase and sale 任意买卖
voluntary redemption 自动赎回;自动(自愿)兑换
voluntary registration 自愿登记,任意登记
voluntary repatriation 自愿遣返

voluntary restraint of export 自动出口限制,自动限制出口
voluntary sale 自愿出售(指经出售者同意自由地出售。见 forced sale)
voluntary sanction 任意性制裁
voluntary service 志愿服役
voluntary settlement 自愿授产(见 settlement),抛弃权利之和解(指无对等条件之和解)
voluntary standing 故意坐礁;任意坐礁(指船舶为避免沉没,或被敌人、海盗捕获,故意搁坐于岩礁上)
voluntary surrender (to court) （向法院）投案自首,自首
voluntary transfer 无偿转让,自愿转让
voluntary trust 自愿信托,任意信托
voluntary union 自愿结合,自愿联合
voluntary waste （英）积极损毁（房屋或土地)(指租借人对其房屋的毁坏行为,例如拆毁房屋等,这在英国是一种罪行。见 waste)
voluntary winding up （公司等）自动停业清理
voluntary withdrawal 自动撤销
voluntary wrongdoing or culpable action 故意不当或犯罪行为
voluntary-registry law 自愿注册法(见 a-doption-registry statute)
voluntas 目的,动机,意图
voluntas civitatis maximae est servanda 遵守国际社会意志
* Voluntas est justa sententia de eo quod quis post mortem suam fieri velit. A will is an exact opinion or determination concerning that which each one wishes to be done after his death. 遗嘱是涉及每个人希望在其死后可实现的确切意见和决定。
* Voluntas in delictis, non exitus spectatur. In crimes, the will, and not the consequence, is looked to. 罪行成立,在于意图,而不在行为结果;犯罪看动机而不看后果。
voluntas moralis 道德意志
* Voluntas testatoris est ambulatoria usque ad extremum vitae exitum. The will of a

testator is ambulatory until the latest moment of life. 立遗嘱人的遗嘱直到生命的最后一刻仍可以变更。
* *Voluntas ultima testatoris est perimplenda secundum veram intentionem suam.* The last will of the testator is fulfilled according to his true intention. 必须完全按立遗嘱人的真实意志来执行其最后的遗嘱。
volunteer n./v. 志愿者,志愿从事者;志愿兵/自愿提供;自愿效劳;自动,自动献出
volunteer mediator (美)自愿调解人[指在美国的邻里调解法庭(neighborhood court)自愿调解纠纷的人]
volunteer the information 自动提供情报
voluptuary n./a. 耽于酒色的人;酒色之徒/贪恋酒色的
vonder (=vendor) n. 卖主;小贩;出卖人
votable a. 有选举权的,有投票权的;可付表决的
votable citizen 有选举权的公民
votaries of the social science 社会科学的信徒们
vote n./v. 1.投票,表决,选举;票;选票;选票数 2.投票权,表决权,选举权 3.选民,投票人 4.议决事项;投票方法,投票过程5.赞成或支持的表示/投票表决,投票选举
vote a measure through 通过一项议案
vote against 投票反对
vote article by article 逐条表决
vote by ballot 秘密投票选举,不记名投票表决,投票表决
vote by machine 用机器投票
vote by mail 邮寄方式投票
vote by open ballot 记名投票
vote by preponderance of voices 以表示同意的优势呼声方式的表决
vote by proxy 委任投票,代理投票
vote by registered ballot 记名投票表决
vote by roll 唱名投票
vote by secret ballot 秘密投票表决
vote by show of hands 举手表决
vote by sitting and standing 起立表决
vote cumulatively 累积投票
vote dilution 选票稀释(见 dilution ③)
vote down 否决

vote down a proposal 投票否决一项议案
vote for 赞成,投票赞成,选举(某人)
vote for one candidate only 单一候选人的选举
vote immediately 立付表决
vote in 选举,选出
vote in the affirmative 赞成票
vote in the negative 反对票
vote of assent 同意票
vote of censure 不信任投票
vote of censure on general government policy 对政府总政策的不信任投票
vote of confidence (国会对政府或其官员所投以表示支持其政策的)信任票;(任何)赞同和支持
vote of dissent 不同意票
vote of no confidence (或 of censure) 不信任投票;投不信任票
vote of 8 to 1 以 8:1 票表决
vote out (美)选举中击败(原任者)
vote the split ticket (美)兼投一个党以上的候选人的票
vote the straight ticket (美)只投某一政党全部候选人的票
vote through 表决通过,投票同意
vote without debate 不经辩论表决
vote-counting at election 选举计票
voteless a. 无投票权的
voter n. 选民,选举人,投票人,有投票权者
Votes and Proceedings (英)下议院会议详录
votes of persons entitled to vote 有选举权人的投票数
votes of persons present 出席者的投票数
voting n./a. 投票,表决/投票的,选举的,表决的
voting age 选民年龄,公民年龄
voting ballot paper 选票
voting booth 投票室
voting by class 见 class voting
voting by show of hands 举手表决
voting by voting group 见 class voting
voting discrimination 选举权歧视,对表决(投票)的歧视,对选民的歧视
voting district 选举区

voting machine 选票计算机;投票记录机
voting paper 选票
voting patterns 表决模式
voting procedure 表决程序,投票程序
voting public 选民
voting qualification 参加选举的(选民)资格,选民资格
voting register 选民名册
voting registration 选举(选民)登记,选民登记
voting result 表决结果,选举结果
voting right (或 right of election, suffrage) 选举权;表决权
Voting Rights Act of 1965 (美)《1965年投票权法》(指 1965 年国会通过的《投票权法》,用以提高非裔美国选民的登记率和参选率。根据该法,联邦治安官和其他联邦官员可以充当检查人员以确保非裔美国人和其他少数民族团体成员不受当地白人登记者的阻挠和侵犯,能够登记参加投票选举。他们被授权可直接登记成为合乎条件的投票人。见 right to vote; understanding tests)
voting rule 表决规则,表决准则
voting securities 股份
voting stock 有投票(表决)权的股票
voting structure 表决体制
voting trust 表决信托(指公司股东将股份拿出来合伙经营以表决控制)
voting witness 投票见证人
votum 1.宣誓,誓言 2.承诺,应允
vouch v. 1.担保(for),保证 2.证实;证明;引证,提出单据、凭证以证实 3.传唤某人出庭作证
vouchee n. 被担保者
voucher n. 1.证明人;担保人,保证人 2.证件,证书;凭票,凭证;收据
voucher check 凭单支票
voucher forms 凭单形式,单据形式
voucher register 凭单登记簿
voucher system 凭单制度,传票制度,应付凭单
vouching in 告知通知(指美国普通法中的一个程序,即已被他人提起诉讼的被告,应将诉讼起始情况告知有责任的第三人)

vouching to warranty 传唤不动产权担保人出庭
vouchsafe v. 准予,惠予,俯允,允诺
vow n./v. 誓;誓约;热诚的宣言,许愿/立誓,宣誓;许愿
vow and declare 郑重声明
vow obedience 立誓服从
vower n. 发誓者,立誓者
* *Vox emissa volat*; *litera scripta manet.* The spoken word flies; the written word remains. 口说无凭,立此为据。
vox populi 人民的呼声,舆论
voyage n. 海运航行;航海,航空,航程;旅行,航海记,航程
voyage charter 航次租船合同(契约),航次租赁(船);单程租船
voyage charter party 航程租赁合同,航次租赁合同
voyage clause 航程条款,航次条款
voyage policy 航程保险单,航次保险单
voyeur n. 偷看下流场合的人
voyeurism n. 观淫癖
vulgar a. 1.庸俗的,卑下的,粗俗的 2.平民的,不出色的 3.流行的,通行的
vulgar law 平民法(指对罗马法、地方习俗和惯例混杂而成的一种法律贬称)
vulgar style 庸俗作风
vulgar taste 低级趣味
vulgar vituperations 粗俗辱骂语言
vulgaria purgatio 洗冤,昭雪
vulgarian n. 庸俗的人;暴发户
vulgaris opinio 一般意见
vulgaris purgatio 神的裁判,神裁法
vulgarism n. 庸俗行为;粗俗语
vulgarity n. 粗鄙,粗野行为
vulgo concepti (或 *quaesiti*) (大陆法)非婚生子女,无父之子
vulgus 平民,庶民,公众,大众
vulnerability n. 弱点
vulnerability assessment 安全弱点评价
vulnerable a. 可伤害的;易受攻击的;难防守的,有弱点的
vulnerable adult 残废的成年人,残疾的成年人(指身体和精神上均有残疾,特别指依赖于社会慈善机构者)

vulnerable consumer　易受伤害消费者
vulnerable point　弱点,缺点;危险
vulnerable to fraud　易受骗
vulture n.　贪婪而残酷者;劫掠成性者

W

WA irrespective of percentage(WAIOP)　单独海损不计免赔率
wage(s) n.　1.工资;薪金 2.报酬;代价
wage and hour law　(美)工资和劳动工时法(指美国联邦和州的控制最大工时、付给最小报酬的法规的一般术语)
wage and price freeze　工资和物价冻结时期(指1943年美国政府禁止增加工资和物价上涨)
wage assignment　见 attachment of wages
wage differential　工资差别
wage discrimination　薪资歧视
wage earner (或 worker)　靠工资维持生活的人
wage earner's plan　靠工资维持生活的人的计划
wage for piecework　计件工资
wage freeze　工资冻结
wage garnishment　工资扣押(指扣押债务人之工资以执行对债权人之判决)
wage grade　工资级别
wage hike　提高工资;加薪
wage index　工资指数
wage labour　雇佣劳动
wage lever　工资水平
*(The) wage(s) of sin is death.　罪恶的报偿是死亡。
wage pattern　标准工资等级
wage rate　工资标准;工资率
wage scale　工资等级(表)
wage standard　工资标准
wage system　工资制度
wage-fund n.　工资基金
wage-price a.　工资和物价关系的
wage-price control　工资物价管制(指政府为限制工资和物价上涨所制定的方针,是收入政策中的一项重要手段)

wage-price-tax spiral　工资—物价—捐税螺旋
wage-withholding　见 attachment of wages
wager n./v.　1.赌注;赌博;赌物 2.(英)打赌(合同)(见 wagering contract)/打赌,赌博
wager of battle　(英)决斗断讼法,以决斗方式断决诉讼
wager of law　宣誓负责断讼法(见 compurgation)
wager policy　(美)(每日以数字打赌的)彩票
wagering n.　打赌(亦译:对赌,指两个人之间的赌博,与不限于两人的赌博 gaming 不同)
wagering contract　打赌合同(契约),射倖合同(契约)
Wages Board　工资局
Wages Council　工资委员会
Wagner Act　(美)《瓦格纳法》[指1935年通过的联邦法,规定可建立最基本的工会权利,它禁止雇主的一些行为,如强使一些雇工不得加入工会,并把这些行为称为"不公正劳务惯例"(unfair labor practices),同时还设立国家劳资关系委员会以帮助强制执行劳动法规]
wag(g)on n.　(美)(警察的)囚车;马车,运货车
wag(g)on boss　(美)(警察的)囚车指挥官
wagonage n.　运货(马)车运输(费);运货马车
waif n.　1.流浪者;无处可归者(尤指流浪儿童)2.偶尔发现的无主物;漂流物 3.(航海的)信号旗;以信号旗所作的信号 4.(复)(盗贼逃跑时丢弃的)赃物
wait and see statute　(美)情事等待原则,观望法规[这一原则是为了缓和"禁止永

久持有规则"所产生的严厉法律效果,为避免附有规定的某些问题与永久持有权(见 perpetuity)相抵触的州法规,如通过允许在一定时间内可以发现遗嘱或信托是否违背此项规则,在有些州又被称为重新考虑原则(second look doctrine)]

wait for dead men's shoes　等待别人死去以求继承遗产
wait-and-see attitude　观望态度
wait-and-see policy　观望政策
waiting clerk　(英)衡平法院的侍应官员
waiting game　伺机而动的策略
waiting insurance　有等待期的保险
waiting list　候补名单;等候批准的申请人名单
waiting period　1.(法定)等待期间(指取得结婚许可至结婚的一段规定时间) 2.(保险中要求赔偿与实际给付期间的一段)等待期间
waits and strays　流浪儿,被遗弃的儿童
waive v.　1.放弃(权力,要求等);丢弃(所偷赃物)2.撤回,停止,不继续,不起诉;延期进行
waive a benefit　放弃收益
waive one's right of appeal　放弃上诉权利
waiver n.　(自动)放弃,弃权,弃权声明书
waiver by election of remedies　补(救)偿选择的放弃,救济选择的放弃
waiver of exemption　豁免的放弃
waiver of immunity　放弃豁免权(指一个证人在开始提供证言以前,声明放弃宪法所给予的一项基本权利,即不得强迫一个人在刑事案件中充当反对自己的证人的权利)
waiver of obligation　债务免除
waiver of premium　免除保险费,放弃保险费;放弃酬金
waiver of private claim　放弃个人请求权
waiver of protest　放弃拒付证书(指放弃作出拒付或拒绝承兑汇票的证书的要求)
waiver of right of indemnity　放弃索赔权
waiver of sanction　免除处分
waiver of service　送达的放弃(指按美国《联邦民事诉讼规则》第4条规定的程序,原告享有书面要求被告签署放弃送达传票的选择权。收到这一要求的被告有义务签署表示自愿放弃以后所有的送达)
waiver of service of summons　(美)传票送达放弃书
waiver of succession　(= enunciation of succession)　抛弃继承
waiver of tort　放弃侵权行为的主张(指受损害的一方,只选择按违约取得的补偿损失来处理的主张,而放弃按侵权行为取得惩戒性赔偿来处理的主张)
waiver system　放弃承运权制度
waiving n.　放弃
waiving of age-limit　免除年龄限制
wake n.　通宵守灵(指在殡葬前夜在死者遗体旁守候,有时亦伴有悼念活动);(英格兰)守夜(指为了庆祝教区教堂落成,信徒通宵在教堂祈祷教义)
wakf　(阿拉伯文 waqf 的音译)互克夫[亦译"沃克夫""互格甫"或"卧各夫",意为"保留""扣留"或"留置",为伊斯兰教法用语。"保留"指安拉(阿拉伯语"AL"相当于上帝)对人世间一切财富的所有权;"留置"指部分土地、产业奉献于弘扬"主道事业",称为"义地""义产",在北非等地亦称哈伯斯 habis 或胡伯斯 hubus]
waldgrave n.　(神圣罗马帝国时代)王室管林官
walk n./v.　1.步行 2.行为;生活方式;行业;阶层 3.英仪仗队 4.放牧场;(英)森林管理员管辖的林区/1.步行 2.处† ,行事;徒步执行,徒步察看 3.使(人)走动;使(物)移动
walk guard　巡逻
walk into the trap　受骗上当,走入陷阱
walk off the job　罢工
walk on fine line　如履薄冰
walk out　(= walk-out)　罢工;退席抗议;抗议罢工
walk out on sb.　遗弃某人
walk sb. into jail　把某人押进监牢
walker n.　(英)山林巡视官
walking delegate　(代表工会到各工厂访问、调查工作环境、视察工会合同履行情况,并代表工会与雇主签订合同的)工会职员代表

walking papers （美）解雇令,解雇通知书
walking possession （英）(指司法行政官或执行官对判决债务人的财物进行巡视,亦指执达官每日步出管领扣押物的)巡视管领
walking ticket（或 **papers**） （美）解雇书,解雇通知书
wall n. 墙,围墙,城墙;(复)壁垒
＊**Wall have ears.** 隔墙有耳。(或译:墙有耳,壁有缝。)
(a) wall of tariff (= a tariff wall) 关税壁垒
Wall Street （美）华尔街(指美国纽约市的一条街,为大垄断组织和金融机构的集中地)
Wall Street lawyer 华尔街律师(指在纽约市金融区开业的律师,为大型商业和利益服务的成员之一)
Wall Streeter （美）华尔街人(指华尔街的大老板)
wallet n. 皮夹子,钱包;小工具袋,旅行袋
Walras's theory of capital 瓦尔拉斯的资本理论
Walrasian model 瓦尔拉斯模式
Walsh Act （美）《沃尔什法》[指原为1926 年颁布的制定法,该法授予联邦法院传票传唤和必要的(传票)返还的权力,和提供证言要求,以及(如果要求)出示文件或其他美国公民或在海外居民的证件的权力。这种传票传唤是适用于刑事诉讼程序,包括大陪审团程序(grand-jury proceedings)。参见《美国注释法典》第 28 卷第 1783 节 (28 USCA § 1783)]
wander n./v. 流浪汉/1.徘徊;漫步;流浪 2.精神错乱;神志昏迷;迷惘
wangle n./v. 哄骗;骗得物;假造;不正当手段;狡诈行为/伪造;(从困境中)设法脱身;使用诡计
wangle accounts 伪造账目
wangle business records 伪造业务记录
want n./v. 需要,需求;不足、缺少、缺乏/想,想要;需要,应该,必须;欠缺;(被动语态)征求,通缉
want of age 未足年龄,不够年龄
want of care 疏忽,懈怠,不细心

want of consideration 欠缺约因
want of jurisdiction 缺乏管辖权
want of necessary proof 缺乏必需的证明
want of prosecution 缺少控诉(指原告未出庭支持或积极支持其起诉,因此法庭可驳回此诉讼)
wanted list 通缉名单
wanted man 警察所通缉的人物
wanted poster 通缉告示
wanton a. 1.胡乱的;放纵的;任性的,放肆的 2.淫荡的,闲荡的,奢侈的
wanton act (不顾他人权利的)轻率行为,任性行为
wanton conduct 任性行为
wanton damage 任意损害
wanton destruction 任意破坏
wanton exercise of power 滥用权力
wanton injury 有意伤害(指有意或放任行为所致的伤害)
wanton mischief 恶意伤害,有意危害
wanton misconduct 轻率不法行为(指因粗心而造成的不法行为)
wanton negligence 任意过失(指因粗心所致的过失)
wanton woman 淫荡的女人
wantonness n. (对他人安全、财产、权利的)有意漠视;放肆;放纵
wapentake n. （英)小邑;百家村;(古时小邑的)法院;(古时小邑法院中的)监守员
war n. 战争;冲突;战争状态;军事
war aim 战争目标
war bond 战时公债
war bride 战时新娘(①战争时或军人服役国外时所娶的新娘;②战争中与即将派往国外服役的军人结婚的女人)
War Bride Act （美)《战时新娘法》
war cabinet 战时内阁
war communique 战报
war contribution (国际法)占领军税[指一个占领国(an occupying power)按照战争时期被占领领土的人口(居民)征收的一种特殊税金(an extraordinary payment),通常缩写为 contribution]
war council 战时委员会,军事会议
war crimes 战争罪行(包括四种特定的犯

罪行为:1.阴谋发动侵略战争 2.违反国际条约,发动侵略战争 3.违反战争法规和惯例,并出于军事需要,而杀害人命、掠夺财产 4.奴役,灭绝,违反人性的罪行)
war criminal 战犯,战争罪犯
war cry (政党在竞选时提出的)竞选口号(或标语)
war damages 战时损害赔偿,战争损失赔偿
war deviation clause 因战争绕航条款
war escalation 战争升级
war footing 备战状态;战时状态;战时编制
war game 军事演习
war hysteria 战争歇斯底里
war indemnity 战争赔款
war material 军事物资
war monger 战争贩子;好战者
war of aggressing 侵略战争
war of all against all 一切人对一切人的战争
war of intervention 干涉战争
war of self-defence 自卫战争
war on pornography 扫黄
war powers 军事大国
war preparation 战备
war proclamation 宣战书;战争宣言
war profiteer 发战争财者
war propaganda 战争宣传
war reparations 战争(损失)赔偿
war risk (agreement) 战争险(协定)
war risk clause 战争险条款
war risk insurance (美)(美国政府为军人举办的)战争保险
war shipvoy charter party 战时租船契约
war spoils 战利品
war supplies 军需品
war surplus 军用剩余物资
war tax 战争税(为筹集战费而征的税)
war treason 战争叛逆罪(指被占领区居民对交战一方作出怀有敌意的行为或违反这类居民应遵守占领国强行实施的法律义务)
war vessels 军用船只;军舰
war-mongering propaganda 煽动性战争宣传(指蓄谋引起民族拥护的战争并鼓励

政府宣布并参与战争而不顾法律之约束)
wartime seizure power (美)战时没收权(指战争期间美国政府没收敌侨民和公民的财产的权力。国会通过的有关没收立法的权力源于美国联邦宪法第1条第8款第11项赋予国会"宣战"和"制定关于陆上和水上捕获的条例"的权力)
warts and all 按照原样
war zone 战区,作战地带
war-baby n. 1.战时私生子(指士兵在战时同异国女人结合而生的子女)2.战时出生的婴儿 3.战时的工业股票
ward n. 1 守护,监护,保护,看护 2.被监护人,受监护人,被保护人,受政府保护者 3.区;大城市中选区 4.监狱的牢房 5.监禁,拘留;监督,监视
ward boss (美)选区的政客
ward in chancery 受衡平法庭监护的人
ward of court 1.受法院监护的未成年(人)2.(英)受衡平法庭保护的未成年人
ward-holding (苏格兰封建土地法)服役土地保有权(1747年废除)
warden n. 1.看守人;监护人;管理员,保管员 2.(美)看守长,监狱长 3.(英)校长;高级官员;同业公会会长;港务局长
warden of a prison (美)监狱长;看守长
warden of cinque ports (英)五港监察长官资格(指五港的总督或主持官员的头衔,这是高荣誉的官职,由政界元老担任)
wardenry n. warden 的职位、职权或辖区(见 warden)
warder n. 监狱看守人,门警;(英)管理人;狱吏
wardmote n. 区法庭(指从前英国伦敦市的区法庭)
wardress n. 女监视人;女看守,女狱吏;女警卫
wardrobe n. (英)(中世纪的)国王财库
wardrobe dealer 旧衣商
wards of the court 法院的受监护人
wardship n. 监护;保护;监督;(封建制度下对佃户的幼年子女及财产的)监督权
wardship and marriage (封建领主的)监护与主婚权
wardship proceeding 监护权的诉讼

warehouse n./v. 1.仓储,货栈,仓库 2.(英)大型零售商店/仓储
warehouse business 仓库业
warehouse certificate 仓库仓单
warehouse deposit contract 存仓合同(契约)
warehouse entry 入席证书;入仓,入栈(存货)
warehouse keeper's certificate 货仓管理人执照;管仓执照
warehouse receipt 仓单,提货单;仓库
warehouse system 公仓制度,仓库制度
warehouse warrant 货栈栈单,仓单
warehouse-to-warehouse clause 仓(库)至仓(库)条款
warehouse-to-warehouse cover 货栈到货栈的保险[指涵盖货物在运输过程中包括起讫时间、地点以及货物装卸的货物承保风险(单)。见 complete operation rule]
warehouseman n. 经营、管理货栈业者;管理仓库者
warehouseman's lien 管仓人留置权
warehousing n. 1.仓储;仓储费 2.(商业银行对需要长期资金者未觅得长期资金前所提供的)周转性短期贷款
warehousing contract 仓储合同(契约)
warehousing system 仓储(纳税)制度(指输入的货物,存入公共货仓,如果这些货物是转口的,则暂时可不纳税;如果是在国内销售的,则需在出仓时纳税)
warfare n. 战事,作战,交战,冲突
warfare at sea 海上战争;海战
warfare of poison gas 毒气战
warfare on land 陆上战争,陆战
warhawk n. (美)好战者;鹰派
warlike a. 好战的,军事的
warlord system (封建造就了西欧多中心的散沙式的)诸侯政治
warm bench (美)(上诉法院的)温庭(见 hot bench)
warm water port 不冻港
warmist n. 气候变暖主义者(指认为地球因变暖而面临危险的人。使用此词表示对全球变暖持怀疑态度)
warmonger n. 战争贩子
warmongering n. 煽动战争

warn v. 1.警告,警戒 2.预告,通知,命令;召唤
warn a person to appear in court 命令某人出庭
warner n. 警告者,告诫者,预告者
warning n./a. 1.警告,警戒 2.预告,通知;(雇主与被雇者之间)解除雇约通知/警告的,注意的
warning instrument 警告器,警报器(指车辆上用来警告人们知道它的行驶位置和驶进的声响器具)
warning network 警报网
warning of a *caveat* 预告的通知(指通知已在遗嘱检证组登记预告的人,来法庭说明他的利害关系。见 *caveat*);要求停止行动的警告
warning signal 警报信号
warning signs 警告标志
warning system 警报系统
warp v/n. 弄弯,弄歪,使(性格等)不正常;使有偏见;歪曲;引潮水入(低洼地带)/歪曲;偏见;偏差
warped account 歪曲真相的叙述
warped judg(e)ment 不公正的判断,不公正判决
warrandice n. (苏格兰法)保证(指转让物品或利益的一方当事人所负担的责任);担保
warrant n./v. 1.(正当)理由;根据;保证;证明;权利 2.授权,批准,许可证,逮捕状,搜查令,授权令(指有签名、盖印的命令,授权官员逮捕罪犯,依法审判;又指民事诉讼、刑事诉讼进程中,法院发出的各种执行令) 3.栈单,付款或收款清单;(公司发出的)认股证书/保证,担保,证明,授权,认为正当,成为……的根据,使……正当化
warrant for apprehension 逮捕令
warrant for attachment 扣押(财产)令;逮捕令;查封令
warrant for commitment to custody 收监执行令
warrant for delivery of goods 货物交付许可证
warrant of appearance 出庭令

warrant of arrest 逮捕令,逮捕证,拘捕令
warrant of attorney (给诉讼代理人或律师的)委托书
warrant of commitment 拘押令,收监令
warrant of committal 关押令,拘押令
warrant of deliverance 开释令
warrant of distress 财产扣押令
warrant of (或for) **payment** 支付或付款授权书
warrant of seizure 没收令,查封令
warrant officers (美国陆海空等多兵种中)授权任职的下级官员
warrant payable 应付支付令
warrant procedure 签发令状的手续
warrant to search a house 搜查房屋令
warrant to sue and defend 起诉和辩护的批准令(指由刑事法院发出的一项特别令,允许一方当事人指定一名律师为他起诉、作辩护)
warrantable a. 可保证的;可承认的,正当的;可证明的;可批准的
warranted a. 有权利的;有权威的,合法的
warrantee n. 被保证人
warranter (=warrantor) n. 保证人
warrantless search 无令(或证)搜查[无搜查令(或证)搜查是根据紧急情况特许的、或者是逮捕附带搜查]
warrantless arrest 无逮捕证的逮捕,无令状的逮捕
warranty n. 1.保证,担保;保单;担保合同(契约);令,状 2.正当理由;合理根据,依据 3.授权,批准
warranty against defects of right 权利的瑕疵担保
warranty against defects of thing 物的瑕疵担保
warranty clause 担保条款
warranty deed 担保契据(指担保不动产并未设定任何权利的契据)
warranty for quiet enjoyment 安静行使权利不受干扰的担保(一种权利的瑕疵担保)
warranty of fitness (商品的)适用性担保
warranty of goods safety 货物的安全保证
warranty of habitability 可居住性保证,适合居住保证(指对房屋购买人或房客的一种默示允诺,意思是此房适合居住)
warranty of legality 保证合法
warranty of merchantability (商品的)适销性担保
warranty of neutrality 中立保证
warranty of quality 质量保证
warranty of seaworthiness 船舶航海能力的保证,适航保证书
warranty of title 资格证明书;权利担保,产权担保
warranty period 保证期限,保证期间
warren (vivary) n. (英)有篱笆围起来的兽类繁殖场;在小猎物繁殖场的狩猎特权
Warren Commission Report (美)《沃伦委员会报告》[指由首席法官艾尔·沃伦(Earl Warren)为首的一个政府调查团,对1963年约翰·肯尼迪(John F. Kennedy)被杀事件进行调查,断定不是共谋而是被告单独进行谋杀的调查报告]
warring n. 战争;敌对行为
(the) Warring States (中国历史上的)战国(时期)
Warsaw Treaty 《华沙条约》(指1955年5月14日,苏联及7个东欧社会主义国家在华沙签订的八国友好互助条约)
Warsaw Treaty Organization (WTO) 华沙条约组织
Warsaw-Oxford Rules 华沙—牛津规则,运费的国际规则;成本保险费
wasband n. 前夫
warship n. 军舰
wash sale 虚买虚卖(指在一短时期内,同类财产的买进和卖出);(美)(为使股票市场呈现活跃而作的)虚抛,虚卖,诈欺交易
washout signal 铁路被冲坏的信号
wastage n. 1.废物,废料 2.消耗;消耗量;浪费
waste n./v. 1.浪费,消耗,滥用 2.废物,残物;损坏,损毁(尤指终身保有土地租借人或其他的特定租借人,在他们租借期间对所租借的房屋、土地、树木的损毁。如让房屋自行倾坏而不修理,这叫消极损毁,是允许的;但如拆坏房屋等,叫积极损毁,

是非法的) 3.荒地(尤指领地里未耕种的公用地),未开垦地/浪费,消耗;未充分利用;因使用不当而损坏
waste book (英)日记账,流水账
waste disposal business 废物处理企业
waste product (制造过程中产生的)废品
waster n. 1.浪费者;损毁者;挥霍者 2.废物,废品,次品
wasting a. 造成浪费的;毁坏性的;消耗性的
wasting asset(s) 损耗性资产,递耗资产(指因逐渐消耗而价值递减的任何资产,如油井、矿坑等)
wasting property 消耗性财产,递耗财产
watch n. 1.注意,警戒,监视;值班 2.观察,看护,守夜,照管 3.看守人,哨兵,警卫,值班人
watch and ward (英史)日夜守卫、日夜守勤(指一种封建义务,一些佃户必需守卫、日夜值勤,亦称 watching and warding)
watch committee (英)公安委员会(指由自治市市议会选出不超过 1/3 的议员组成的委员会,专门负责管理本市的警察队和委任警官等的机构)
watch dog (美)外部监督;监察人;看门狗
watch over 监视,保护,预防
watch system 值班制度
watch-dog n./v. 守卫,监察人;监督/为……看门;监察
watch-dog committee 监督委员会
watchhouse n. 哨房;哨所;看守所
watching brief 请求律师代为注意法院各种程序的委托状
watchmen n. 看守人;门警;哨兵;巡夜者
watchword n. 暗号,口号;命令;标语,格言
water n. 水;海道;海域
water bailiff (英)水上执达官(指负责搜索船只的海关检查员,又指执行鲑鱼渔业法例的检查员)
water carriage 水运;(由导管)送水
water carrier 水上运输货物或旅客的工具,运水夫;运水兽;输水管道或槽
water court 水上法院
water cure 灌水刑;水疗法
water damage 水渍

water damage insurance policy 水渍险保险单
water district 供水区域[指国家或地方政府按地理位置划分小区供应社会民众或公共场所(the public)用水]
water down 稀释,减弱
water dungeon 水牢
water law 水法
water line (船的)吃水线
water ordeal 浸水神判法(指古条顿族将嫌疑犯的手浸于沸水中,让神来裁决,如手无损则认为无罪,否则认为是有罪的一种裁决法)
water police station 水上警察派出所
water pollution 水污染
Water Pollution Control Act (中)《水污染防治法》
water pollution control law 水污染控制法,水污染管理法
Water Pollution Research International Association 国际水污染研究协会
water privilege 水利权、用水权;流水使用权
water quality standard 水质标准
Water Research Center (英)水研究中心
water right (= water privilege) 引水灌溉权(指使用河川、湖泊、运河等水流的灌溉权利);用水权
water source pollution 水源污染
water stain 水渍
water supply 供水;供水装置
water-borne 由水路运送的;(疾病等)由饮水传染的
water-borne agreement 战争险水面协定;水上范围协定
water-borne clause 战争险水面条款
water-borne only 只限水运
water-borne trade 海外贸易
water-gavel n. 捕鱼权,渔业权
water-heater n. 热水器
water-mark n. 水位标记
water-supply systems 城市供水系统
water-tight a. 1.不透水的 2.无懈可击的;十全十美的
water-tight *alibi* 无法驳倒的(犯罪时根本不在现场的)证据

water-tight argument　无懈可击的理由
water-tight regulations　十分完善的规定
water-transport court　水上交通法庭
waterage n.　(英)水运;水运费
watercourse n.　1.水流权(指一个人的土地,有从他人的土地引入或排出水流的权利) 2.河床;水路;运河
watered a.　票面额增加而实际价值未相应增加的
watered assets　实质低于账面的资产
watergate n.　(美)水门[水门是华盛顿特区的一座综合大厦。当年民主党的总统竞选总部就设在这里,后来在该总部发生窃听案,这件事导致美国总统尼克松(共和党)辞职]
watering stock　虚股、干股、掺水股票
waterlogged a.　(船等的)漏水或进水(以致不能操纵或行动缓慢)的,进水的
watershed n.　1.分水线;分水界;分水岭,(河床)分水界 2.流域 3.重要关头,转折点
waterside police　水上警察
waterway n.　水道,水路航道
wave v.　挥手示意;打信号示意
wave aside　对……置之不理,把……丢在一边
wave aside a proposal　将提议搁置一边
waver n./v.　犹豫,摇摆,踌躇/颤抖;摇摆,犹豫,踌躇,动摇
waver between two opinions　犹豫于两种意见之间
waver in determination　犹豫不决
waveson n.　(古英法律)(船沉后流失于海上的)漂流物
way n.　1.方向;方式;习惯,情形,状态 2.道路;路程,距离 3.行业,职业 4.规模,范围 5.通行权
way bill　(铁路或轮船的)托运单,乘客名单;货运单
way of necessity　(让与或出租土地时)保留必要通行权
way port trade　沿途货运
way-going n.　(苏格兰)动身,出发,离开
way-going crop　耕作地的收益或孳息(= emblements)
way-mark n.　路标

waybill of lading　提货单
waylay v.　拦路抢劫;拦路(询问);拦截;半路埋伏
waylayer n.　拦路抢劫者,埋伏者,拦截者
wayleave n.　(经过他人土地的)通行权
ways and means　方法和手段(有时指立法机构为应付政府开支的筹款办法)
ways and means business　(英)下议院的赋税职能
wayward a.　顽劣的,任性的;不规则的,不稳的
wayward minor　胡作非为的未成年人
weak a.　弱的,虚弱的,衰弱的;差的,薄弱的,淡薄的;无活力的,散漫的,不简练的
(a) weak candidate　(一个)无把握取胜的候选人
weak evidence　不充分的证据
weak law　无力(量)的法律;无权威的法律
weak parliamentarism　弱势内阁制
weal n.　鞭痕;条痕,伤痕
wealth n.　财富,财产;丰富,大量
wealth appropriation　财富的侵占,财富的拨款,财富挪用
wealth maximization　财富最大限度化
wealth maximizing function　财富最大化函数
wealth of contacts　大量联系
wealth of oceans　海洋资源
weapon n.　武器,凶器,兵器;斗争的工具,手段
Weapons of Mass Destruction (WMD)　大规模杀伤性武器
weapons of offence　进攻性武器;犯罪凶器,作案凶器
weapons rules　武器管理法规
wear and tear　磨损,损耗;使用或自然耗损
wear and tear of life　生活的折磨
wear stripes　坐牢(指美国囚犯穿横条衣因衣,因此美俚语称穿横条子衣为坐牢)
wear the gown　(穿上律师的长袍)当律师
weasel n./v.　1.狡猾的人,告密的人 2.(美)模棱两可的话,含糊的话/使用模棱两可的语言;影射,躲闪,(美)含糊其词;告密
weasel from an obligation　逃避责任

weather insurance 气象保险
weather permitting (WP) 雨天顺延
weather permitting clause (WPC) 雨天顺延条款
web n./v. 网,网状,网状组织;(阴谋等)圈套;一卷(筒)/落入圈套;用丝网绊住
Webb-Pomerene Act 《违布—波密伦出口贸易法》(该法于1918年制定,允许竞争者之间订立关于价格、数量以及划分市场的限制竞争协议)
webpage n. 网页
Webroom 在线调研后线下购物[为动词,意指先利用互联网研究相关产品,然后在线下实体店完成购买。亦可写作 web-room。Reverse-showroom(逆向的先逛店后网购)与它具有相反意思。信息技术服务企业埃森哲2013年4月15日发布调研结果时最早使用此一表达方式;"调查发现,随着在线购物继续受到消费者的偏爱,商店和在线销售渠道之间形成了一种互利的关系。举例而言,有73%的受访者表示,他们在参与本次调查之前的6个月里有过'先逛店后网购的行为'(show-room)。而更多的受访者——88%的人有过'在线调研后线下购物的行为'。究其原因,恶劣天气等因素会耽误网购商品的运输。北美地区去年的大雪让一些家庭渡过了没有礼物的圣诞节。此外,不少消费者认为,产品的材质和颜色必须眼见为实,而且省钱才是硬道理。调查发现,约36%的消费者在实体店购物时会要求商家按照网上的较低价格出售产品。他们还不用支付网购运费和退换商品产生的二次运费。"]
website n. 网址,网站(美国各州长臂法的行使管辖与在审判地州网站的互动性和商业性质有关,有的州法院还根据网址在该州的"商业招揽"达到最低联系要求而使管辖成立)
wed v. 1.嫁给;将……嫁给;娶 2.结合,结婚
wedded life 婚姻生活
wedded (或 lawful) wife (合法)妻子,正室,正妻
wedding n. 1.结婚;婚礼,结婚纪念日 2.融合,结合
wedding day 婚礼日,结婚纪念日
wedlock n. 婚姻,婚姻(生活)
weed v. 除去,剔除,淘汰
weed out 除去,清除〈weed out weeds〉(清除杂草),〈weed out dust pollution〉(清除污尘)
Weekly Compilation of Presidential Documents (美)《总统文件每周汇编》
Weekly Law Reports (英)《每周法律判例汇编》(由英格兰和威尔士法律判例联合委员会出版,包括1953年至今的最完整的现行英国法律判例汇编大全,并包括《法律判例汇编》中未发表过的许多判例)
Weekly Report (美)《每周报道》(指《国会季刊》附属的单行本,它包括一些重要文件的现行文本、年表、辩论和咨文概要,以及有关现行条约的一般资料)
weekly tenant 按周租赁的租户
weigh n./v. 称分量,过称;有分量;(有)重要(性),重压/1.估量……的轻重,过称 2.考虑;斟酌;权衡 3.起(锚)
weigh in 参加,介入
weigh in with (在讨论中)成功地提出(论点等)
weigh the advantages and disadvantages 权衡利弊
weighage n. (英)过磅税,过称费
weighing of the penalty 量刑
weight n. 1.重量,分量;衡量;衡量制 2.重压,压迫 3.重要性;影响力 4.权力,势力,权势
weight certificate 重量证明书
weight list 重量单
weight memo 重量单
weight of authority 权威力,重要权威;重要证据
weight of evidence 有分量的证据,证据的效力;衡量证据的分量
weight of proof 证据力,证据分量
weighted a. 加重的,衡量过的;(指一议员投票)有代表性的
weighted average 加权平均,加权平均数
weighted voting rule 加权表决制(法则)
weighted voting system 加权表决制

weighting and measuring apparatus 计量器具,度量衡器具
weights and measures 度量衡
weighty a. 有影响力的,重要的;重的,有力的
(a) weighty argument 有力的辩解
(a) weighty consideration 重要的考虑
Weimar Constitution 《德国魏玛宪法》(1919—1933)
welfare n. 幸福,福利,福利事业
welfare and security programs 福利和安全保障规划
welfare benefits （生活）福利费
welfare clause 福利条款(指美国宪法规定允许联邦政府为全体人民福利制定法规的第1条第8款)
welfare economics 福利经济学[1776年亚当·斯密(Adam Smith)出版《国富论》提出;追求利益是人类的主要动力;竞争这一看不见的手自发地将各种私利转变为一种共同利益;因此,对国民财富增长来说,政府的最好政策便是管得最少的政策]
welfare fund 福利基金
welfare law 福利法
welfare policy 福利政策
welfare rights 福利权
welfare services for juveniles 保护青少年的社会福利
welfare state 福利国家(指由国家通过其各个部门和机构提供福利和社会保障的社会)
welfare work 福利事业
welfare-state measures 福利国家的措施
well n./ad. 1.(法庭用栏杆围在法官席前面的)律师席 2.井;泉水;源泉/妥善地,令人满意地,好意地,优待地,有理由地,充分地,完全地
well balanced mind 精神正常的头脑
Well begun is half done. 开始得好,等于完成了一半。
well grounded (= well founded) 基础牢固的
well of court 法庭律师席
well off 富裕的,处于有利地位的,供应充足的
well seated prejudice 根深蒂固的偏见
well-being n. 福利,健康,幸福
Well-born a. 出自名门的,出自高贵的
well-connected a. 与权贵有关系的,出自名门的
well-earned punishment 罪有应得的惩罚
well-established evidence 确凿的证据
well-founded a. 基础牢固的,有充分根据的,理由充足的
well-founded argument 有充分根据的论点
well-grounded a. 有充分理由的,有充分根据的
well-informed a. 消息灵通的;博识的;得有确实消息的
well-judged a. 判断正确的,中肯的,适时的
well-known a. 众所周知的,出名的
well-known trademark （众所周知的）著名商标
well-meaner n. 善意的人
well-paid a. 高工资的,报酬优厚的
well-paying industry 赚钱的工业
well-pleaded complaint （1954年）（美）合理答辩的民事诉讼状[指原先或起始的足以提出要求救济的权利主张诉状,包括法院管辖的依据和判决要求。被告则可起草答辩状,回复对方提出的争点。在联邦法院合理答辩的民事诉讼状必须提出联邦法律可控制的争点（controlling issue）或法院对此诉讼不具有联邦问题管辖权（federal-question jurisdiction）]
well-pleaded complaint rules （美）合理答辩民事诉状
well-rounded a. 丰满的;经过周密计划的;各方面安排得很好的;有多方面能力的
well-secured advence 有确实担保的贷款
well-to-do a. 富有的,经济宽裕的
well-to-do peasants （中）富裕农民
well-work a. 1.用旧了的 2.老生常谈的,陈腐的,陈词滥调的 3.佩戴适当的
wellsettled a. 完全固定的,完全不变的,约定俗成的
welsh v. 1.赖赌债逃走,赖账 2.逃避义务,不履行义务（有时与on连用）

Welsh law 威尔士法
Welsh mortgage 威尔士式抵押(指一种以土地抵押担保债权的抵押,在还清债款时,可把抵押物赎回的抵押。这种抵押不定还款期限,抵押物收益由受抵押人获得,所以受抵押人不能强迫抵押人来赎回或向法院申请取消赎回抵押物权)
welsh on one's debt 赖账,赖债
welsh on one's promises 不履行诺言
welsher n. 不付赌金而逃走者,赖赌债而逃走者;骗子,赖账者
welt n. 1.(俗)重笞,重打 2.(俗)殴打;(鞭打或棒击所留的)伤痕
wench n./v. 少妇;乡妇;女佣;荡妇;妓女/嫖妓,私通
wencher n. 嫖妓者;私通者
wergild (=weregild, wergeld) n. 赎罪金,恤金;(中世纪日耳曼民族国家中为防止世代血仇而付给被谋杀者亲属的)被杀赔偿金
Weslayan (美)威斯莱(基督教卫理公会,又称美以美会,指信 John Weslayan 教义)
West Digest (美)《西方版判例摘要汇编》(见 American Digest System)
West-Saxon Law (英)西撒克逊法[指西撒克逊引入的一个法律体系,英格兰于 11 世纪初期即盛行的三大主要法律体系之一,另两大法律体系为丹麦法(Dane-Lage)和麦西亚法(Mercen-Lage),通用于肯特(Kent)和德文郡(Devonshire)两郡,现为英格兰西部和南部地区。亦称 West-Sexon Lage。见 Mercen-Lage; Dane-Law]
Western Powers 西方列强
western system of law 西方法律制度
WESTLAW (美)西方法律(出版公司)(中心设于明尼苏达州圣保罗市,在联邦和州判例的广泛范围内以各种不同数据库的形式提供计算机检索)
Westminster (英)威斯敏斯特(指靠近伦敦的城市,以前是王家高等法院所在地)
Westminster Assembly (英)威斯敏斯特会议(指 1643 年至 1652 年英格兰国会为在圣公会进行改革而召开的长期会议)
Westminster confession 威斯敏斯特信纲(指英语民族基督教长老派的信仰纲要)

Westphalia Treaty 《维斯特伐利亚条约》(1648 年德国和西班牙之间的条约)
Westphalian 威斯特伐利亚(此词来源于 1648 年建立了现代国家体系的《威斯特伐利亚和约》。西方国家通过推行残酷的殖民主义,将美洲、非洲和亚洲人民纳入威斯特伐利亚体系之中。只要其他地区的国家在社会制度上与欧美不同,就会被贴上"不开化"的标签)
wet state (美)不禁酒的州,允许制酒或卖酒的州
whaling n. 捕鲸业,炼鲸油业
Whaling Convention Act of 1949 《1949 年捕鲸公约法》
whammy n. 重击,可致命的重大打击(此词由 wham:"威猛乐队"——20 世纪八九十年代红极一时的流行乐队,现已解散——指中午碰撞的巨响,也指重击)
wharf n./v. 码头,停泊处/使靠码头;货物卸在码头上;设立码头
wharf due 码头税
wharf police officer 码头警官
wharfage n. 码头费,码头设备,码头,码头的使用(如装卸或贮存货物等)
wharfinger n. 码头所有者;码头管理人
wharfmaster (=wharfowner) n. 码头监督或管理人;码头所有者
∗ **What is not pleaded cannot be argued.** 如未申辩,则不能在法院争辩。
∗ **What's bred in the bone will come out in the flesh.** 本性总要表现出来。骨子里的东西总要在皮肤上显露出来。
wheedle v. 巧言哄骗
wheelage n. 车辆通过税
wheels of government 行政机关
when and where (案件发生的)时间和地点(系诉讼答辩中的术语)
∗ **Where the equity is equal, the first in time prevails.** 在衡平就是公平这一点上,前者要优先适用。
∗ **Where the king was, there was the law** "国王所至,法律必存"。(指在 12 世纪时的英格兰人们深信这一格言,认为国王是正义的泉源)
∗ **Where there is equal equity, the law shall**

prevails. 只要平等的衡平存在,普通法应优先适用。

* **Where there is on writ, there is no right.** (英)无令状即无权利。

whereabouts n. 下落,行踪,所在

whereabouts unknown 行止不明,下落不明

whereas conj. (公文用语)考虑到,鉴于,就……而论;既然

whereas clause 鉴于条款

whereas clause 鉴于条款(whereas 是个引语,表示既然如此……)

whereby ad. 因此,由是

wherefore ad. 因此,所以

wherewithal (=wherewith) n. 必要的方法(手段或所需的金钱),必要物,钱财

Whig n. 辉格党人(指英国自由党的前身);(美)现共和党(人)前身

Whig lawyer 辉格党人律师

whip n./v. 1.鞭;鞭挞 2.政党的国会副领袖;政党在议会中的首脑人物 3.(英)(常用大写)组织秘书发给本党议员要求出席辩论和投票的命令/鞭挞

whip hand 执鞭之手,右手;有利之势,优势,控制

whip-round n. 捐钱,募捐;(英)慈善募捐

whiplash injury 猛然将一个人的颈部抓住的)扭动伤害

whipping n. 笞刑,惩罚,用以捆缚的绳索

whipping post 鞭笞(犯人时用来绑缚犯人的)刑柱

whispering campaign 有计划的诽谤性造谣

whispering Charlie (美)善说的查理律师(查理是美国司法部前副部长,担任过巡回法官,此词用来比喻说话柔和中听、具有高度工作效率的辩护律师)

whistleblower (=whistle blower;whistle-blower) n. (1970年)举报人,告发人[由 whistle 和 blower 两个词组合而成。①指向公众或权威部门发告一个组织非法或不当行为的人,尤其指组织内部的告发者。Whistle 的本意是哨子,在一场比赛中,裁判员通过吹响哨子来指出犯规行为,whistleblower 这个"吹哨子的人"也就是我们所说的"举报人"或"告发者"。

1863年美国的《虚假申报法》是最早保护 whistleblowers 的法律之一,该法律通过承诺给举报者一定比例的物质奖励及保护他们免受不当解雇来鼓励这种告发行为(whistle blowing)。但事实上,举报人常常会面临报复(reprisal),有时这种报复来自他们所告发的组织或团体,有时来自法律的惩罚。②指调员举报雇主对政府和执法部门有违法或渎职行为,联邦和州法律均保护举报人免受雇主之报复]

white a. 1.白的,苍白的 2.清白的;公正的 3.(政治上)白色的,恐怖的,反革命的4.白人的

white blacklash (美国白人对黑人运动的)白人对抗

white bonnet 拍卖的同谋者

white book 白皮书(美国等政府发表的有关政治、外交的文件,英国称 white paper)

white cap (美国种族主义分子暴力组织)白帽队队员

white collar (美)白领阶层的(指一般不从事体力劳动的教师、企业机关职员等人的)

white collar crime 白领犯罪(指有上层社会经济身份的人在职务上的犯罪,如公务人员和企业公司人员的犯罪等)

white collar defense bar 白领阶层的辩护律师(指专门为高级的贸易职员和政府官员在刑事案件中辩护的律师)

white collar job 脑力工作,文职

white collar worker(s) 白领雇员,脑力劳动者,教师

white conspiracy 白色阴谋(城市内的中产阶级白人运动造成的种族歧视的紧张形势,迫使收入低的黑人家庭离开城市,黑人将此种情势看做白色阴谋)

white flag 白旗(指投降旗或休战旗)

White Hall 白厅(英)[指伦敦的一条厅道;从特拉法尔加广场(Trafalagr Square)到议会广场(Parliament Square)的一条厅道。此厅及其附近有许多英国政府机关、部门]

White House 白宫,美国政府

White horse case (1971年)(行话,隐语)白马案例,相同案例[指一个汇编过的案

例，其事实上与当前案件(instant case)的事实案情实质上完全相同，所以汇编过的案例的裁决(disposition)应该决定当前案件的后果。亦称 horse case；goose case；gray mule case；red-cow case。见 on all fours]
(the) White House Office (美)白宫办公室
white light 公正无私的裁判
white paper (英)白皮书(见 white book)
White Primary (美)白人预选[指美国联邦宪法第十五修正案明文禁止在投票方面的种族歧视，且 United States v. Reese (1876)一案判决"联邦宪法第十五修正案并未授权任何人在选举上的权利，运用各种方法如文化测试、人头税(Poll taxes)等剥夺黑人的选举投票权"，1923 年，得克萨斯州在民主党(那时该州只有一个党)预选中禁止黑人参加投票。这实际上阻止黑人参加地方和州的选举。后在 1932 年的尼克松诉康登(Nixon v. Condon)案中，联邦最高法院裁定民主党执委会实为该州立法机关的产物，因此对黑人投票的禁止相当于违宪的州行为。1944 年在史密斯诉奥尔赖特(Smith v. Allwright)中联邦最高法院以 8∶1 的表决结果作出新的裁决，认定白人预选违背了美国联邦宪法第十五修正案]
white slave 1.被卖为娼的妇女 2.被迫为奴隶的白种人
white slave traffic(trade) 贩卖妇女
white slavery (美俚)白奴，贩卖妇女为娼(指美国州与州之间运送妇女为娼的俚语，按 1910 年制定的曼诺法，对此种联合犯罪，应处以罚金 5000 美元或 5 年徒刑，或同时受到两种惩处)
white supremacy 白人优势；白人至上主义
white terror 白色恐怖
white war 不流血的战争；经济竞争
white-hall n. 白厅，(大写)英国政府；英国的政策
white-slaving n. 贩卖妇女为娼的非法行为
whitecapping (美)(刑法)指种族主义分子白帽暴力犯罪集团胁迫他人的犯行为，通常指未成年人的团伙以暴力掠夺或迫使停业；白帽法规(whitecapping statute)[旨在削弱或除去三 K 党(Ku Klux Klan)的活动]
whitley councils (英)惠特利协商会(指由经理和工人代表组成的一种机构，原来目的是促进劳资关系的改善，后来成为进行工资谈判的机构)
whole a. 总的,总体的；全部的,整个的；完全的,充分的,健康的
(a) whole arrest 大规模的逮捕
whole blood 1.全血亲(指同父母的血亲关系) 2.(从人身上抽出供输血用的)血
whole body of law 整个法律制度；整个法律体系
whole brother (sister) 嫡亲兄弟(姐妹)
whole course of the trial 整个审判过程
whole house (whole firm) 批发店(公司)
whole life insurance 终身人身保险
(the) whole man theory 完整人理论(指建立工伤保险制度的理论依据之一,该理论认为对遭受职业伤害的劳动者,除了应对其给予必要地医疗救治和经济补偿之外,还须向其提供康复保险服务,使受伤劳动者恢复劳动能力,重新成为"完整人"。另外的理论依据为：工伤保险费用计入成本；能够最大限度地降低社会成本)
whole parliament in joint session 议会两院联席会议
whole point of view 主要观点在于,关键在于,全部观点在于
whole-timer n. 按日(或周)计酬的工人
wholesale n./a. 批发,大批,大规模/大批的,大规模的,批发的
wholesale arrest 见 dragnet arrest
wholesale dealer 批发商
wholesale discharge of workers 大批解雇工人
wholesale merchant (或 wholesale dealer) 批发商人
wholesale price 批发价
wholesale price index 批发价格指数(指制造厂和批发商售价变动的指标)
wholesale slaughter 大屠杀
wholesale trade 批发贸易,批发业

wholesaler n. 批发商
wholesaling n. 批发
wholly ad. 完全地,统统地
wholly-owned subsidiary 附属公司,独家开设的分号或子公司
whop n. 毒打,鞭打,重击
whore n./v. 娼妓,淫妇/当娼妓;宿娼;卖淫
whore-house n. 妓院
whore-master (=whore-monger) n. 嫖客,淫媒
whoredom n. 卖淫;通奸
whoreson n. 私生子
whorish a. 淫秽的,妓女的,像妓女的
wicked a. 坏的,邪恶的;刻毒的,怀恶意的,恶劣的
wickedness n. 邪恶,不道德
 * **Wickedness does not go altogether unrequited.** 恶有恶报,只是时候未到。
wide area information server (WAIS) 广域信息服务系统(指一种易于检索并可获取远程数据文档的动态超文本系统)
wide interpretation 广义解释,扩大解释
wide-open a. 没有保护的,容易攻击的;(城市、地区对非法活动)开绿灯的;取缔不严的
widening of capital 扩大资本
widespread ownership 普遍拥有
widow n./v. 寡妇,遗孀/使成寡妇,使丧偶,成为……的寡妇;自……夺去(珍贵之物)
widow and widower benefit 鳏寡恤金
widow's allowance 寡妇可从亡夫的遗产中所获得的扶养费额
widow's benefit 寡妇恤金
widow's chamber 寡妇所得的亡夫留下的住房
widow's election (美)寡妇取得丈夫遗产的选择权
widow's gap (美)寡妇(享受社会保险金)资格欠缺期(指女人失去丈夫时,由于太年轻而未能取得享受社会保险金的资格期间)
widow's third 寡妇(所得亡夫遗产)的1/3
widow-bench n. 寡妇应得的亡夫不动产部分
widow-hood n. 寡居,寡居期
widow-maker n. 1.杀死有妻室的男人使其妻成为寡妇者 2.对男人(尤指工人)有危险者
widowed a. 寡居的,鳏居的
widower n. 鳏夫
widowered a. 成鳏夫的,鳏居的
wield v. 挥动,使用;行使权力;运用;处理;施加(影响)
wield influence 施加影响
wield power 行使权力
wield power, wield authority 行使权利
wieldy a. 有挥动能力的,有使用能力的
wife n. 妻子,已婚妇女
wife allowance 妻子扶养费
wife assaulter 殴妻者
wife's capacity to sue and be sued at common law 普通法上妻的起诉和应诉的能力
wife's equitable separate estate 妻在衡平法上的独立财产
wife's equitable to a settlement 妻在衡平法上的财产协约
wife's estates of inheritance 妻的继承财产
wife's interest in the matrimonial home 妻子在婚后家庭中的权益
wife's life estates 妻的终身财产
wife's personality in possession 妻所占有的动产
wife's power to charge equitable separate estate by contract 妻通过合同处分衡平法上的独立财产的权利
wife's power to contract under modern statutes in general 现代制定法中关于妻缔结合同的一般权利
wife's power to dispose of equitable separate estate 妻在衡平法上的独立财产的处分权
wifedom n. 妻子的身份(状态)
wifehood n. 妻子的身份
wifeless a. 无妻的,鳏夫的
wig n. (法官、律师戴的)假发
Wigmore on Evidence (美)《威格莫尔论证据》(一种多卷本专门领域的有一定深度的法学学术概论)
wild discretion 广泛的自由裁量权

wild idea 激进观点,轻率观点
wild land 荒地
wild life 野生生物
wild young man 放荡的青年
wild beast test (英)野兽条例[指1265年由英国首席法官布雷克顿(Bracton)制定的一项条例。其内容是:"因精神错乱的人的行为类同一头野兽,故应免于治罪"]
wildcat n./a. 未经工会同意的罢工/(企业等)不可靠的,不可信的,非法经营的,(列车等)未获批准行驶的;(罢工)未经工会批准的
wildcat strike 未经工会同意的罢工
wildcatter n. 冒险或欺骗性企业的发起人;冒险或欺骗性企业股票的出售者
wilderness area (政府划定的)保留自然环境面貌的地区
wildlife conservation 野生生物资源保护
Wildlife-Forestry Code (1948年)《野生生物林业法典》
wilful (=willful) a. 任性的,固执的;故意的,存心的,蓄意的
wilful act 故意行为
wilful and malicious injury 恶意伤害
wilful and wandon injury 故意和轻率的伤害
wilful damage 故意损害
wilful default 故意不出庭,故意拖延
wilful indifference to the safety of others 故意漠视他人安全
wilful misconduct 有意识的不当行为
wilful misrepresentation 故意歪曲(事实);故意虚假陈述
wilful murder 蓄意谋杀,故意杀人
wilful neglect 有意的玩忽(职守)
wilful negligence (=wanton and reckless negligence)(明知会发生结果的)有意的粗心过失
wilful obstruct 故意阻挠
wilful tort 故意的侵权行为
wilily ad. 狡猾地
wiliness n. 诡诈,狡猾
will n./v. 1.遗嘱 2.愿望,意志,意向/立遗嘱,遗嘱赠与;立志
will act 遗嘱法,遗嘱条例

will (one's property) away from sb. 立遗嘱剥夺某人财产继承权
will contest 求证遗嘱是否属实或是否有效的诉讼
will copy 遗嘱副本
will duplicate 遗嘱副本,遗嘱复本
will of leading officials 长官意志
will of the state 国家意志
will power 意志力
will-making n. 立遗嘱
willful blindness 故意之疏忽,有意之过失(与gross negligence同义)
William and Mary College of Law 威廉и玛丽法律学院(指美国最早的法律学院,1779年创办)
willing a. 情愿的,欣然从事的
willing covenant of conscious faith 理性诚实的自愿契约
willingness n. 意愿
willness a. 未留下遗嘱的;非出于本意的
wills act 遗嘱法令
wills and probate department 遗嘱及遗嘱检验认证部门
Wilmington ten (美)威尔明顿十人案(指北卡罗来纳州的一件案子,九名黑人和一名白人妇女被控纵火爆炸一白人的杂货店,后经查明,并非事实,以后成了美国20世纪70年代有名的"政治犯"案件)
Wilson Act (美)《威尔逊法》(至1890年实施的一项规范酒类交易的联邦法规和一部国会法,规定对烈性酒的控制)
Wilson Doctrine 威尔逊主义(美国总统威尔逊对墨西哥韦尔培将军以政变夺取政权拒绝承认的主张)
wily a. 狡猾的,诡计多端的
wily defender 诡计多端的辩护人
win v. 获胜,成功;获得,博得;赢得
win a bid 中标,得标
win one's case 胜诉
win out 最后会成功(克服困难)
win over 争取到;胜诉
Winchester measure (英)温切斯特标准测量
wind up 解散(公司),结束营业;了结,结(案)

windfall n. 意外;意外收获;横财;意外继承
windfall loss 意外损失
windfall profit tax (1973年)暴利税(指对工商业在短期突然增加巨额利润的课税,比如1980年石油公司由于阿拉伯石油自20世纪70年代禁运而获得暴利的征税)
winding up n. (1858年)停业清理[指在企业面临解散或破产之时,通过清理(清算)账目、资产,将净资产分给股东或合伙人的程序。见dissolution 4]
winding up an account 结账,清理账目
winding-up n. 清理,结束业务;结束
winding-up acts (英国法中的)(议会通常通过的)解散(公司)的法令
winding-up case 结案
winding-up of business 结束营业
winding-up of company 解散公司,公司清理
winding-up of partnership 结束合伙关系,拆伙
winding-up petition 申请结束营业,申请清盘
window industries 窗口行业(=representive industries 或 key industries)
window tax (=window duty) (英)窗户税(指从前房子上有6个以上的窗户每年应缴纳5镑以上的税)
wine n. 酒
wine and tobacco tax 烟酒税
wine duties 酒税
wing n./v. (政党等)派别,翼,翅;侧厅;飞行/飞行;空运;伤人,使加速,使飞
wing of court 法院的一派
wing of jurisdiction 管辖的观点,管辖的派别
winner n. 取胜者
winner of a lawsuit 胜诉人
*(The) **winner takes all** 胜者全得
winning a suit 胜诉
winter circuit 冬季开庭的巡回法院
wipe off 审核(账目),核对
wipe out 1.彻底消灭,彻底毁灭 2.(俗)谋杀;杀掉
WIPO Arbitration Center (或 Arbitration Board) 世界知识产权组织仲裁中心

wire-pull v. 从事幕后操纵
wire-puller n. 幕后操纵者
wire-pulling n. (以不正当方法)幕后操纵个人或政党等,幕后操纵
wire-tap n./v. 非法窃听(指偷接电话电报线以窃听秘密的行为)/非法窃听(指偷接电话电报线以窃听秘密)
wiretapper n. 窃听电话或电报者,以窃取的情报进行诈骗者
wiretapping n. 窃听电话电报秘密
wise Latina woman (美)聪明的拉丁女性[指法官索尼娅·索托马约尔(Sonia Sotomayor)在成为最高法院大法官之前在讲话中用到的一个词语]
wise men (美)明智之士,智囊团(指组成政府的官员的一批人,和为总统咨询研究有关外交政策危机的有经验的局外人士)
wish v./n. 命令,请求/希望,渴望;祝愿
witam (英)国王法律顾问,王国要人,熟悉法律的学者
witch n. 巫婆
witch craft 巫术,魔法
witch doctor 巫医
witch hunt 1.对政治可疑分子的调查;政治迫害 2.对行巫者搜捕
witch hunting 政治迫害
wite n. (古日耳曼法)重罪罚金(指因谋杀罪或类似重罪所科处的罚金,与赎罪金不同,因这种罚金要交给王室);惩罚,刑罚
witenagemot (英)(盎格鲁-撒克逊时期的)智者聚会(是该时期的全国最高议事机构,相当于现代的国会)
with a appropriate time 在相当期限内
with a string attached 附有条件
with a view to 为了要;拟
with a witness 千真万确,确确实实
with all faults (商)不保证商品没有瑕疵
with average 水渍险
with (particular) average or all risks 担保单独海损或一切险,分损担保
with consent 征得……同意或认可
with intent 蓄意
with particular average 基本险,水渍险(指国际海洋运输货物保险条款中的一种

险别。其责任范围不仅包括平安险的责任范围,而且还要负责由于海上自然灾害引起的货物的部分损失)

with prejudice 1.有偏见,有损 2.有偏袒的裁决(亦称不利于原告的裁决,用于撤销起诉。作出这种裁决,撤销起诉后,即排除原告以同一诉因重新起诉。见 without prejudice)

with *proviso* 附有条件

with recourse 有追索权

with recourse letter of credit 有追索权信用证

with reference to 关于,根据

with reference to the context 根据上下文

with reservation (让与或租赁财产时)附有权益保留

with respect to 涉及;关于

with strong hand 用强制手段

with suspended execution of sentence 缓期执行(判决)

with suspicion 有嫌疑,有怀疑

with the advice and consent 得……的指示及同意

with the approval of the authority 经当局批准

with the exception of 除……外

with the fixed period 指定期限内

with the good will of a business 具有商业信誉的

with the proper time 如期

with the view of 为了……目的

with this *proviso* that 以……为条件

withdraw v. 撤回,撤销;撤退;离开;收回,取回

with… to 关于

withdraw a bill 撤销议案

withdraw a charge 撤回一项控告

withdraw a claim 撤回诉讼;放弃要求

withdraw a confession 翻供

withdraw an action 撤回诉讼

withdraw an order 撤销命令

withdraw court 退庭

withdraw from business 歇业

withdraw one's bid 收回投标

withdrawal(s) n. 1.回避,忌避 2.撤销;撤 回;取回,收回 3.提取存款;提款 4.退股;退
出

withdrawal 28 USC 157 依据《美国法典》第 28 标题卷第 157 节要求的撤诉

withdrawal by notice 通知退约;通知退出,通知回避

withdrawal by petition 申请回避

withdrawal from treaty 退出条约

withdrawal of a juror (= withdrawing a juror) 撤回一名陪审员;要求一名陪审员回避

withdrawal of appearance 回避出庭

withdrawal of candidacy 撤销候选资格

withdrawal of candidate 撤销候选人

withdrawal of charges 撤回指控

withdrawal of claim 撤回要求

withdrawal of motion 撤回动议

withdrawal of proposal 撤回提案

withdrawing a juror 使一名陪审员回避

withdrawing partner 退伙人

withdrawing record (原告)撤回案件记录

withering away of the state 国家之消亡

withhold v. 1.不给;拒绝;扣留 2.制止;抑制;阻止 3.扣缴

withhold one's consent 不同意

withhold payment 拒绝付款

withhold promise 不作出承诺

withholding agent 扣缴义务人

withholding confidence (议会对政府的)撤回信任

withholding income tax return 扣缴所得税报告表

withholding of the truth 掩饰真相;隐瞒真情,不揭发(一项犯罪)真情

withholding or withdrawal of concessions 减让的停止或撤销

withholding tax (1927年)(美)预提税款,代扣税款[指扣得收入者(earner)在获得工薪之前,即由其雇主从其工资、报酬、红利或其他收入中扣除应纳的所得税。绝大多数的情况都是雇主从其雇员工资中扣除所得税和社会保险税(social-security tax)]

within prep./ad. 在……里面,在……内;不超过,在……范围内

within its four corners 1.包括在(法律文件的)全部范围内(指所要说的都包括在该文件内) 2.事实明显,昭然若揭
within legally defined limits 在法定的范围内
within living memory 自从记事以来,自有记忆时起
within sphere 在我的职权范围内
within the constitutional framework 在宪法框架内
within the four corners of the law 在法律(或法制)的范围内
within the law 在法律范围内
within the limits expressly stated by law 在法律规定的限度内
within the limits laid down by law 在法律所规定的范围内
within the limits of 在范围内
within the required time 在规定的期限内
within the statute 在法规范围之内;法规所禁止的;法规所允许的
without prep./ad. 1.无,没有,不 2.在……外面,在……外部
without a division 无分歧,(意见)一致
without acceptance of persons 无偏心,无不公正
without authority 未得准许
without authorization 擅自,私自
without benefit of clergy 无牧师恩典(指男女不经法律结婚手续而同居);(美国公开的)非法同居,姘居夫妻
without book 1.无权;无根据 2.凭记忆
without cause 无故
without compensation 毫无补偿
without cover 坦白地,开诚布公;无保险
without day 无限期的,不定期的
without debate 不经过辩论
without delay 毫无迟延地
without demur 无异议
without detriment to 无损于
without discrimination 一视同仁,无歧视
without engagement 无诺言,未承诺
without fail 必定,务必
without hindrance 无阻碍,无妨碍
without if and but 不含糊其词,不拖泥带水(指不说"如果"怎么,也不说"但是"如何,要干净利落之意)
without ignoring 并非无知;并非驳回
without impeachment of waste 不负毁坏祖产责任(常用于终身持有的文据或其他的特别租户的交付文据里,表示占有人或租户对所占有或所租用的土地或房屋不负任何损毁责任)
without issue 无后裔,无子孙
without jurisdiction 无管辖权
without need for implementing legislation 无需履行立法手续
without notice 没有事前通知,未经通知
without permission 未经许可
without possessing sufficient means 无足够的资力
without power to hold a hearing 无审讯之权
without prejudice 1.无偏见,无损 2.无偏袒的裁判(亦称没有不利于原告的裁决;这与 with prejudice 相对而言,用作撤销起诉裁决的一个术语。作出这种无偏袒的撤销起诉裁决后,仍允许原告以原案同样理由,重新提起诉讼)
without prejudice to 不妨害,没有损害,不使(合法权利)受损害;在不损害……的规定下;不影响将来的法律地位
without reason 无理由
without recourse 无追索权
without reference to 不论;与……无关
without reservation 无保留(权益)(见 with reservation)
without reserve 无保留(价格)(系在拍卖时应用的一个术语)
without resort to compulsion 不用强制手段
without respect to the results 不考虑后果
without suspending execution of the judg-(e)ment 不中止执行判决
without the good will of a business 不具有商业信誉的
without … to 1.不论 2.与……无关
without trial 未经审判
without unreasonable delay 无不合理推延(指英美法系逮捕程序中的"迅速带见法

官"要求,早已成世界各国通例。"迅速带见法官"的要求,通常以"无不合理推延"这一术语来表达)
withstand v. 抵挡,反抗;顶得住,经受住
witness n./v. 1.证人,连署者;目击者 2.证据,证明,证言/1.目击,目睹 2.(协议、遗嘱等的)连署 3.作证,证明;表示,表明
witness a document 在文件上连署
witness against the accused 证明被告有罪
witness an agreement 在协议上签署(作证),在协议上连署
witness box 证人席
witness chair (法庭中)证人席,给证人坐的椅子
witness for testament 遗嘱见证人
witness for the defence 为被告作证,为被告作辩白,被告证人
witness for the prisoner 有利于犯人的证言
witness for the prosecution 原告证人,公诉人方面的证人
witness in wedding 证婚人
witness my hand 证明是我的签名
witness order 传证人令(指英国法院对已作证的证人发出的命令,令其在刑事法院正式庭审时出庭作证)
witness stand 证人席
witness summons (传唤)证人(的)传票
witness testimony 证人证言
witness to a deed 契据的见证人
witness to a fact 为事实作证
witness to a will 遗嘱见证人
witness to the accident 事故见证人,车祸的目击者
witness to the wedding 证婚人
witness warrant 证人如期出庭令
witness with knowledge 知情证人
witness-fee n. 证人酬金
witnessed will 有人作证遗嘱
witnessing n. 作证;证明;确认(签名)
witting(ly) a./ad. 有意(地),故意(地),知晓的(地)
wolf n. 1.狼 2.残暴成性的人,阴险狡猾的人,追逐女性的人,贪婪的人
wolf call 色鬼狼嚎(指色鬼调戏或追逐女时的怪叫)
wolf pack (美俚)追逐妇女的流氓集团
Wolong Reservation (中)卧龙自然保护区
woman n. 成年女子,妇女;女性
woman about town 放荡的女人
woman of easy virtue 轻浮的女人
woman suffrage 妇女参政权,妇女选举权
woman's rights 妇女权利,女权运动
woman-hater n. 憎恨女人的人,厌恶女人者
womanize v. 宿娼;玩女人
womanpower n. 女权,妇女的力量
Women's Alliance for Job Equity (美)妇女就业平等联盟(简称 WAJE)
women's federation 妇女联合会
women's liberation movement 妇女解放运动
women's organization 妇女团体,妇女组织
wood leave 砍用树木权
woodwards n. (英)森林管理员,林务员
woolsack n. 英国上院大法官的座位;英国上院大法官的职位
word(s) n. 1.词句;言语;措辞,说话 2.诺言;保证 3.口角争论 4.命令;口令
word(s) and act(s) 言行
word(s) by mouth 口述,口头表达
word indexes 单词索引
word(s) of art 新词汇(或术语)(尤指其中的成语或特殊用语)
word(s) of honor 诺言
word(s) of limitation 限制性的(或约束性的)词句
word of mouse 网络口碑
word of mouth (通过)口头的
word(s) of procreation 创设性词句(指财产转让或遗嘱里用于创设限定权益的词句)
word(s) of purchase 指定性词句(指财产转让证书或遗嘱中用于指定将来接受地产人的词句);购买性文字(指契据或遗嘱中告知谁准可获得土地的用语)
work off the clock 无偿加班
word-of-mouth a. 口头的,口述的
word-splitter n. 咬文嚼字者;诡辩者
wordplay n. 双关语;文字的争论
Words and Phrases (美)《词语和习用语》(指西方公司出版的一部46卷本的百科全书,收有法学上重要的词语和习用语

的说明以及定义。此书将数以千计的词语和习用语按字母顺序排列,并附有说明、定义、解释的司法判例文摘,是一种很好的查找对口判例的工具)

words of actionable press 语言或文字本身可导致诉讼;可构成诉讼的语言文字(如侮辱性语言或文字等)

words of covenant 合同(契约)文字(指合同内双方互负义务之条款)

words of negotiability 指明流通之文字(如票据上的 to order 或 to tear 等)

* **Words pay no debts.** 空话还不了债。

work n./v. 工作,劳动;职业,业务;行为;(常用复)著作,作品;工程;工事;产品;成果/工作,劳动;运转,造成;形成;骗取

work a friend for a loan 骗取一个朋友的钱

work and pay 边营运,边付款(指加拿大的一种分期付款办法,可用购买商品获得收益来支付欠款,通常这类商品是车辆)

work at ground level 基层工作
work camp 囚犯劳动营,劳营营地
work capacity 工作能力
work category 工种
work contract 承揽合同(契约)
work council 工作理事会,(英)员工福利咨询委员会
work disturbance 制造动乱
work farm 少年感化农场,(轻刑罪犯的)劳改农场
work force 劳工,劳动力,劳动大军,工作人员,工作能力
work force level 工作力水准,工作能力水平
work force utilization 劳动力利用
work hours 工时
work house (美)劳改所;市监狱
Work House Act (英)《习艺所法案》(英国于1696年颁布,主要是对英国救济事业的补充和完善)

(a) work(或 **works**)**in private domain** 有版权的作品(或著作)

(a) work(或 **works**)**in public domain** 无版权的作品(或著作)

work injury compensation 工伤补偿金,工伤抚恤金

work load 工作量
(a) work of joint authorship 合著作品
(a) work of mind 智力作品
work on 1.继续工作,不断工作 2.做(某人)工作;说服,设法说服,影响
work one's way 通过努力取得,靠做工取得
work order 工作通知单
work out 作出;制定出;设计出;算出;消耗完(精力);做工抵偿
work over 研究,检查;重做;殴打
work permit (工会发给非会员的)工作许可证
work procedure 工序
work product (1947年)工作成果(指律师为案件所做的准备工作;会见记录、备忘录、通讯、案情摘要和辩护词等,均可免于披露)
work product rule (1954年)工作成果规则[指根据此规则,律师的工作成果有资格免于披露,其成果包括为诉讼进行准备的记录、备忘录、工作文件或其他类似文件等均免于披露,美国多数州均采用此项规定,参见《联邦民事诉讼规则》第26(b)(3)条。此项豁免的建立主要在于保护律师的诉讼策略(attorney's strategy)。希克曼诉泰勒案(Hickman v. Taylor),参见《美国联邦最高法院判例汇编》第329卷第495页、第67卷第385页(1947年)。亦称 work-product immunity; work-product privilege; work-product exemption; attorney work-product privilege]

Works Progress Administration (美)工程兴办署
work rule 工作规则
work schedule (美)工作时间表;工作议事日程;工作程序表
work status 就业状况
work style 工作作风
work to rule 1.一种迫使资方让步的变相怠工 2.用变相怠工方法迫使资方让步
work under public surveillance 管制劳动
work-caused disability 因工残废
work-caused injuries 因工负伤
work-day n. 一日的工作时间;工作日

work-girl n. 女工
work-house (=workhouse) n. （美）感化院，教养院；（英）贫民习艺所，济贫院
Work-Product Doctrine （美）"工作成果"原理（指律师为准备进行诉讼所作的记录、工作文件、备忘录或其他类似文件材料等都免予披露，多数州已将此规则纳入制定法或法院的规则之内，此原则亦称 work-product rule）
work-product rule 表白事实规则（指律师在办案中无必要向另一方表白为此案收集的任何事物的规则，除非另一方使法官相信如果这些事物隐瞒下来实属不公正，所以有必要表白）
work-related injury 因公（工）负伤
work-room n. 作业室，工作室
work-study school （中）（教育违法青少年的）工读学校
work-to-rule n./a. 死抠规章工作，教条地照章工作
workable competition 有效竞争
workable rules of justice 切实可行的正义原则
workable system 切实可行的制度
workaday a. 工作日的，日常的；普通的
workaholic n. 为免遭辞退而工作过分卖力的人
worker n. 工人，劳动者，无产者；工作者，人员
(the) worker-peasant alliance （中）工农联盟
workers'autonomy 工人自治
workers' compensation laws （美）职业灾害补偿法，劳工补偿法（规）（大部分州均通过此法规，工人因工受伤，不管是否有过失均应予以金钱补偿，企业捐资资金会支持此项支出）
workers' congress （中）职工代表大会
workers' management 工人自治
workers' organization 工人组织，劳动人民的组织
workers' party 劳动党
workers' supervision 工人监督
workfare n. （用物质刺激人们工作的）工作福利

working a. 工作的，劳动的；经营的，营业上的
working age 工龄
working agreement 劳动合同（契约）；临时解决有关劳动的办法
working assets 运用资产，劳动资产，流动资产
working attitude 工作态度
working capital 流动资本，流动资金；营业资本，运营资金
working capital funds 运用基本资金
working class 工人阶级
working condition 工作条件
working day （法定）工作日
working expense 工作费用，经营费用
working hours 工时，劳动时间，工作时间
working language 工作语言
working level 工作水平
working life 职业生活，在职期间
(a) working majority （议会票数等的）足够多数
working order （机器等的）正常运转状态
working out 制作，订出
working papers 工作文件，就业证件，（未成年人的）雇佣证书；工作报告，计划草案
Working Parliament （德）工作型的议会
working party （英）经营效率提高委员会；（政府指定的）专题调查委员会
Working Party on Domestic Regulations 国内监管工作组
working people 劳动人民
working rule 操作惯例，工作规则，操作规程
working years 工龄
workloads n. 工作量，工作负担
workmen's compensation 工人伤残赔偿，（英）工人抚恤金（指依据1925年劳工赔偿法规定工人工作时意外受伤，则雇主应就因而致死亡进行赔偿，应将总额一次交给死者家属。此法例经多次修改，现已由国家保险法例代替）
Workmen's Compensation Acts （英）《劳工赔偿法》
workmen's compensation court 劳工赔偿法院

workmen's compensation insurance 劳工（保）险

works council 劳资协议会，（英）员工福利咨询委员会

works of fact 事实作品（指地图、写生画、历史书等反映事实的作品，与之相对的为"学术作品"）

world n. 1.世界，地球；世人，人类 2.职业界 3.大量

World Association of Judge 世界法官协会（1966年在"世界和平法律中心"之下创立的，该协会有一万五千名以上法官，来自一百多个不同国家）

World Association of Law Professors 世界法学教授协会（见 World Peace Through Law Center）

World Association of Law Student 世界法科学者协会（见 World Peace Through Law Center）

World Association of Lawyers 世界律师协会（见 World Peace through Law Center）

World Bank 世界银行

world community 国际社会，世界社区

World Court （＝Permanent Court of International Justice; International Court of Justice） 国际法院

World Declaration Nutrition 《世界营养问题宣言》（1992年12月，在世界粮农组织召开的营养问题国际大会上通过）

world energy supplies 世界能源供应

world environment day 世界环（境）保（护）日（1972年联合国人类环境保护大会确定的日期，目的是引起人们对环保的重视，每年6月15日定为"世界环保日"）

World Environment Institute （WEI） （美）世界环境学会

World Food Council （联合国）世界粮食理事会

World Health Organization （WHO） （联合国）世界卫生组织

World Intellectual Property Organization （联合国）世界知识产权组织

world legal order 世界法律程序

world market 国际市场，世界市场

world market price 国际市场价格，世界价格

World Meteorological Organization （联合国）世界气象组织

World Peace Through Law Center 世界和平法律中心（1963年来自120个国家的律师在一次法官会议上成立的组织，下设10个部门，并在第九次世界和平法律中心的大会上接纳了一些分支组织，如世界法学教授协会、世界律师协会及世界法科学者协会等）

world power 列强，世界强国

World Refugee Year 世界难民年

World's Largest Law Firm 世界最大律师业公司（指美国私办的，在芝加哥，拥有450名律师；也指政府办的美国军事法务署，拥有1600名律师）

world-scale rate 世界运油价

world shipping powers 世界航运大国

World Society of Victimology 国际受害人学协会

World Trade Centers Association 世界贸易中心协会，世界贸易中心联合会

World Trade Law （＝International Trade Law） 国际贸易法

World Treaty Index 《世界条约索引》[由彼得·H.罗恩（Peter H.Rohn）编辑，1983年出版的5卷本索引，包括44,000个条约的援引，并把《联合国和国际联盟条约丛书》，以及1900年以来制定的许多其他条约丛书编入索引]

world war 世界大战

World Wide Fund for Nature 世界自然基金（非政府组织之一）

World Wide Web （WWW） 万维网（指一种超文本的信息服务系统，可使用户在因特网上搜索和浏览信息）

world-wide tax jurisdiction （对本国公民的）全球收入的税收管辖权

world-wide treaty 全球性分保合同

worldly goods 财产

(a) worldwide comparison of law 世界范畴的法律比较

worm n. 蠕虫（计算机蠕虫是一个程序或程序系列，它采取截取口令字并在系统中试图做非法动作的方式直接攻击计算机。）

writ of entry 收回被侵占的土地的令状（亦称进入令，指从直接不法占有人或其他不法占有人那里追索被占有土地而发出的令状）

writ of error （15世纪）1.纠正错误令状，错误审查令状[指在普通法里，错误审查令状是上诉法院给低级法院的，要求后者将案件记录材料发出以复查所称的法律错误（不包括事实）（见 assignment of error）。审查被限制在出现于记录材料中的明显错误，根据这种令状提起的诉讼只是一个新诉的开始，而非原诉的继续。当事人不能寻求上诉救济和纠错令救济，至少直至上诉请求被驳回后才能获得纠错令救济。20世纪以前，错误审查令状多出现于美国联邦最高法院的管辖权中，尽管1789年司法中就已经作审查涉及联邦问题的州法院判决的程序性手段而得以确立。此错误审查令状之功能被1916年和1928年美国联邦的立法分别转移调取案卷复审令（writ of certiorari）和进入上诉程序。故此种令状在美国联邦司法实践中已被废除] 2.(历史上)纠错复审令[指应在审理中失利的当事方之要求由大法官法庭(chancery)发出纠错复审令指示审理法院既审查案件本身记录材料，也要将此材料送至具有上诉管辖的法院进行审查。在此错误审查令状之功能分别于1916年和1928年被美国联邦立法以调取案卷复审令取代]

writ of error *coram nobis* 纠正有事实上错误的判决令状（指在同一法庭由于判决中有事实上的错误而用以纠正判决所发出的令状）

writ of error *coram vobis* 纠正有事实上错误的判决令状[在英国普通法上，不同于 writ of error *coram nobis*，前者是由高等法院（王座庭）对高等民事法院（court of common pleas）判决发出的令状，而后者则为高等法院发给王座庭的令状]

writ of evocation 移审令，提审令

writ of execution 强制执行法院判决的令状；执行令

writ of *exegi facias* (=exigent) 催促被告出庭令状

writ of extent 对债务人物业评价扣押令

writ of false judgment 误审修正令（指上级法院修正下级法院不保存记录因而在诉讼程序上有错误的命令）

writ of *fieri facias* 财务扣押令（指按判决金额扣押债务人的财产所发给司法行政官的执行令状）；扣押及拍卖债务人的动产以抵偿债务的执行令

writ of formedon （在限制财产继承争议中，有请求权的人和剩余财产取得人或已决定限定继承的未来继承人所发出的）追索财产的令状

writ of garnishment 扣押令（指强制执行判决的一种方法。依此被扣押的败诉当事人的财产是控制在第三人手中的，如银行账户、工资或其他对该当事人所欠的债务）

writ of *habeas corpus* （英国普通法中传统的法院令状之一的）人身保护状（见 *habeas corpus*）

writ of *habeas corpus ad subjiciendum* 解交被拘押者并说明其拘押的日期及原因令

writ of *habeas corpus ad testificandum* 传讯被扣押人出庭作证令

writ of injunction 禁止令，假处分令

writ of inquiry 评定损害赔偿数额调查令（指在损害赔偿未得到清偿的案件中，原告已得到缺席判决的情况下，发给司法行政官在陪审团协助下来评定损害赔偿的数额的令状）

writ of judg(e)ment by sale and distress 扣押与变卖财产判决令

writ of mainprize （或 **mainprise**）（英）保释候审令状（指要求司法行政官对可保释的在押犯取得出庭保证后，让其自由的令状）

writ of *mandamus* （上级法院给下级法院或官吏的）职务执行令状

writ of *mesne* 中间令状（指古英国法中诉讼中间阶段可发出的一切令状的总称。见 *mesne* process）

writ of possession 恢复土地占有判决的强制执行令状，归还土地于所有权人令

writ of prevention 防止令状（指在一些诉

讼可能提出之前,为防止因此损害权益而请求发出的令状。见 *quia timet*
writ of prohibition 禁止令状(指上级法院为阻止下级越越司法权限而发出的令状)
writ of protection 国王庇护令状(在英国,指国王可以给予他的仆从在民事诉讼中一整年内不受逮捕的特权所发出的令状)
writ of replevin 请求返还非法侵占的动产令状
writ of restitution (根据撤销判决所发出的)恢复被告因执行原判而丧失的财物令状,返还财物令状
writ of review 审查状,复审令状
writ of right 权利状(又译权利令,指依据人民权利发出的令状,即人民有权要求法院或大法官发出的令状,它和君主特权令相对,后者是依君主恩典和决定发出的,可参阅 writ)
writ of right of dower 寡妇产权令状(指因寡妇产权的一部分被人非法占去而发给的补救令状,今已废除)
writ of search (= search warrant) 搜查令状
writ of sequestration 查封令状,(法院裁决的)扣押令、临时拘押令
writ of subpoena 传审令,传讯令状,传票,传召出庭
writ of summons 传票,传唤令状(指按英国司法条例所有诉讼在开始时所发出的令状),传讯令
writ of summons to parliament 召入议会令
writ of summons under the Great Seal (英)盖有国玺的传唤令状
writ of supersedeas 中止一项法律手续的令状[指一种中止执行判决的令状,意思是中止审判庭根据上诉判决宣布执行的权力,如果执行令已发出,则由上诉法院发出一项禁止令来反对这项执行令的执行。现在,这种令状亦称中止诉讼程序(stay of proceedings),实际是中止诉讼程序中的一种程序]
writ of trial 审理案件令;审判令(指将原送上级法院审理的诉案交给下级法院或助理司法行政官审查的令状)
writ of waste 认定租户损毁房地产的令状

Writ System (英)令状制度
writ upon the case 本案令状(指法院根据具体案件颁布的令状)
writ-server n. 令状送达人,执达员
write v. 写,填写,开(票等);签字,承担(合同责任等)
write back 注销(保单);红字冲账
write down 1.记录,记下 2.以文字诋毁;诽谤 3.减记(资产账面价值)
write in 把……写入,填写后投入(选票等)
write off 勾销,冲销,注销;销账
write off an entry 抹去账上项目,抹去账项
write off bad debts 注销坏账
write out 誊写;全部写出(合同或协议条款等)
write up 1.记述,详细记载;补写 2.抬高(资产、货物)的账面价值 3.(美)写传票传唤
write-in n. 1.对非原定候选人所投的选票 2.在选票上被写入非原定候选人的名字
write-off (WO) n. 1.注销,冲销,勾销,销账,删除账面值 2.贬值,折旧 3.被勾销的项目
writer n. 作者,作家,撰稿人;文书;办事员;(苏格兰)律师
writer to the signet (苏格兰)公证人和诉讼代理人,律师
writing n. 1.书写;笔迹 2.写成的文件;(复)作品,著述;书写职业或写作工作 3.以视觉形式表达文字的做法(指手书、打印、照相等) 4.书面形式,书写,写作,文字,信件,书法,笔迹;作家职业
writing a line 承保部分责任
writing obligatory 诉状上所写明的债务
writs of assistance (英)(北美殖民地最高法院颁发的查缉走私物品的)协查令状
written a. 书面的,文字的,成文的
written accusation 书面控告
Written Affirmative Action Program (美)书面积极行为方案(见 Office of Federal Contract Compliance Programs)
written agreement 书面协议,书面合约
written agreement on arbitration 仲裁书面协议

written approval　书面许可,书面批准
written authorization　核准书,授权书
written bidding　书面投标
written code　成文法规;成文法典
written complaint　起诉状,书状起诉
written confirmation（或 document）　书面凭证
written consent　书面同意
written constitution　成文宪法
written contract　书面合同(契约)
written custom　成文习惯,成文惯例
written decision　书面裁决,判决书
written declaration　(合同的)书面意思表示,书面陈述,书面宣告;书面申请
written declaration of war　宣战书
written deposition　(经宣誓的)书面证言,书面询问,书面证词
written estimates of costs　费用计算书
written evidence　书面证据
written expert testimony　书面鉴定,鉴定书
written finding　书面事实认定(指美国1974年对1966年颁布的《信息自由法》修正案通过之前,司法审查不追究个人的行政责任。修改后,该法增加了这样的规定:"当法院命令机关对原告提交任何不适当地封锁的机关记录,并判决合众国负担合理的律师费和其他诉讼费用时,法院另外发出一个书面裁定,指出封锁记录的情况表明机关工作人员在拒绝提供该记录时存在主观武断行为,特别法律顾问就应迅速查明应否给予对该封锁行为负主要责任之工作人员或雇员以纪律处分。"依此规定,特别法律顾问" special counsel" 调查程序需要三项前提条件:①法院已判令机关应提供决定不公开的文件;②法院已判令由国家负担原告的律师费和诉讼费;③法院已发布一个存在主观武断行为的"书面事实认定")
written form　书面形式
written guarantee　书面保证,保证书
written instrument　书证,书面文据
written interrogatories　书面质询,质询书(见 interrogatories)
written judg(e)ments (proceedings)　书面判决,判决书,书面裁决(诉讼程序)

written justification　书面辩护,辩护书
written law　成文法
written laws and regulations　成文法规
written license contract　书面许可合同
written matter　书面文件,书面问题
written notice　书面通知
written objection　书面异议,书面反对
written obligation　书面之债
written off　冲销
written offer　书面要约
written opinion　意见书
written order　书面命令
written paper for loan　借据
written permission　书面许可
written petition　书面请愿,请愿书
written plea　书面申诉,答辩书
written pledge　保证书
written procedure　书面式诉讼程序
written proceeding(s)　书面诉讼,书面诉讼程序
written proof　书面证据,书面举证
written protest　书面抗议,抗议书;书面申诉
written receipt　受领证书
written record　书面记录
written request　书面要求书
written sources (of law)　成文法渊源(又译:成文的法律渊源);成文法源
written statement　书面声明,书面陈述,供述书,申请书
written summons　传票
written verdict　书面裁定,裁定书
written warning　书面警告
written will　书面遗嘱
wrong n./a./v.　1.过失,过错行为,错误 2.损害,不公正的待遇 3.邪恶;罪行/不正当的,不法的;邪恶的,不适当的;有毛病的,错误的/伤害;冤枉;屈待
wrong acquittal　错放(即有罪者被错误开释,即错放)
wrong claim　不当的索赔
wrong conduct　不道德行为;不法行为
wrong conviction　错判(指无辜者被定罪)
wrong detention and conviction　不法关押和判罪
wrong doing　不道德

W

wrong factual basis "错误事实根据"原则
wrong of strict liability 负有严格责任的不法行为
wrong verdict 错误裁决
wrong-doer n. 不法行为者;做坏事的人;犯罪的人,加害人,侵权人
wrong-doing n. 恶事,恶行,犯罪
wrongdoing state 不法行为国家
wronged individual 受害人,受加害的个人,被侵权人
wrongful a. 1.错误的,不正当的,伤害的,污辱的,不公正的 2.不法的,非法的
wrongful abuse of process 非法滥用诉讼
wrongful acts 不当行为,不法行为,非法行为
wrongful arrest 非法拘捕
wrongful civil proceedings 不合法的民事诉讼
wrongful criminal proceedings 不合法的刑事诉讼
wrongful conception 不当怀孕
wrongful dealing 不公平的交易
wrongful death 不法致死
wrongful death action 非正常死亡诉讼,意外致死诉讼
wrongful death statute(s) (美)非法致死法规(指美国各州对非法造成死亡的侵权行为作出的规定)
wrongful declared cargo 误报货物
wrongful delivery 非法交付;交货错误
wrongful dismissal 非法解雇
wrongful disposition 非法处分
wrongful imprisonment 非法监禁
wrongful intending 蓄意(伤害),含有恶意
wrongful interference 不正当干预
wrongful life action 指控医生对产妇造成医疗事故的诉讼
wrongful occupation of an estate 产业的非法占有
wrongful seizure 非法没收,错误充公
wrongful trading 不法交易
wronghead n. 坚持错误见解者;顽固者
wrongness n. 错误,过失;不正当,不正确
wrongous a. (苏格兰)非法的,不正当的
wrongous imprisonment 非法监禁(与false imprisonment 同义)
WS rate 世界运油价
wyte n. (古英国法)清了(或免除)罚款

X

X-film n. (英)限制性的影片(指16岁以下儿童不许观看的电影)
X-inefficiency X-非效率(理论)[指美国哈佛大学教授勒伯斯坦(Harvey Leibenstein)提出的反映大企业内部效率及水平状况的一个概念。他认为大企业,尤其是具有垄断地位的大企业,外部市场竞争压力小,内部层次多,关系复杂,机构庞大,加上企业制度安排方面的原因,使企业费用最小化和利润最大化的经营目标难以实现,导致企业内部资源配置效率降低]
X-rated a. (美)禁止(16岁以下)儿童观看的(指电影),限制性的
x-rated works (英)黄色作品(美国和许多国家认为黄色作品不应享有版权,我国著作权法中亦有类似规定)
X-ray X射线;X光;X光照片
xeniurn (古代希腊人或罗马人赠送客人的)礼物
xenodochium 旅店,招待所;医院(民法及古代英国法用语)
xenodochy 好客,款待
xenophile n. 亲外者,喜欢外国人及其文化者
xenophobe n. 仇视外国人;恐惧外国人者,害怕生人者
xenophobia n. 对外国人的仇视,对外国人的恐惧
xenophobic a. 仇外的,恐惧外国人的
xenophobic racism 仇外的种族主义

xerox v. 复制;影印
xeroxing n. 复印,静电复印

xylon n. 足枷(古希腊的一种刑具)

Y

ya and nay 承认与否认(指旧制,不经宣誓之答辩)
yacht n./a. 航船,船舶/航海的
yakuza (日)无赖(指暴力集团的歹徒)
Yale Law School (美)耶鲁(大学)法学院(位于美国康涅狄格州纽黑文市)
Yalta Agreement 《雅尔塔协定》(1945年2月11日,由苏、美、英三国首脑在苏联克里米亚半岛的雅尔塔举行的会议上背着中国秘密签订的协定,规定苏联参加对日作战的一些条件)
Yankee n. 美国的新英格兰人,扬基式美国人
yankee market (在英国交易所内的)美国证券交易市场
Yard (=the Scotland Yard) n. (英伦敦)苏格兰场(指英国刑警总署)
yard sale (美)庭院销售(指在美国家庭迁移时处理的物资、用品等以便宜价格卖出)
yardage n. (火车运家畜时的)站内栏舍的使用权;使用站内栏舍的费用
yardbird n. 未训练的新兵;(美俚)罪犯,囚犯
yardstick n. 尺度,衡量标准,任何评判或比较的标准
yea (=yes) n. 赞成票:投赞成票者,赞成者
yea(s) and nay(s) 赞成和反对,是与否(指立法机关中的口头表决通常是逐一呼叫每人姓名表决)
year n. 1.年;学年;年度;历年 2.(复)年岁,年龄 3.(复)年长,年老 4.(复)多年,长久
year, day and waste (指国王对犯重罪的土地领主没收的土地享有)一年零一日的特权
(a) year and a day 满一年(见 year-and-a-day-rule)
year book(s) 《年鉴》(英国的司法判例汇编的收集就是在年鉴中发现的,它包括1285—1537年的判例),年刊;年报;(英)法庭录事年报(指自1290—1535年间,由法庭录事们记录下来的案件录事报告)
year of account 结算年
year of assessment 评税年度
year(s) (或 age) of discretion 责任年龄
year of grace 1.宽限年限 2.公元年,西历年
year of mourning (罗马法)守寡年(指妻于夫死后应守寡一年,在此期内,不得再嫁,以免生育后发生谁为父亲的纠纷)
year-and-a-day rule 一年零一日原则(即满一年原则:1.某些事务所规定的法定年限,其目的在确认该段时间能满整一年 2.在美国,指一个人犯罪以后,如果受害者活了一年零一日,则罪犯不能构成谋杀罪)
year-end n./a. 年终,年底/年终的,年底的
year-end report 年终报告
year-end bonus 年终加薪
year-old precedent 年代久远的先例
Yearbook of Human Rights 《人权年鉴》(指联合国1946至今的《人权年鉴》)
yearly progress report 进展情况年度报告
years of discretion 自由裁量的年龄,负责任的年龄
yegg n. (美俚)罪犯(尤指抢金库者或盗贼)
yeggman n. (美俚,=yegg)
yell v./n. 呼喊,号叫/欢呼,呐喊
yellow book 黄皮书(指法国政府公布的正式文书)
yellow jack (或 **flag**) (正在检疫中的船上所悬挂的)黄色旗,检疫旗,黄色检疫旗
yellow journal 黄色报刊
yellow journalist 黄色新闻记者

yellow dog contracts （美）黄狗合同[指以不加入工会为条件的雇佣合同,这是19、20世纪防止雇工加入工会而使用的合同。根据这种合同,成为工会成员则为解雇理由。此合同迫使工人留在工会大门之外,找工作的人要么同意此条件签订合同,要么就失去就业机会,劳工们对此深恶痛绝,故将其称为"黄狗"(即卑鄙的)合同。国会和州立法机构明确宣布"黄狗合同"不受法律保护]

yellow-dog a. 卑鄙的,可耻的;反对工会的

yellow-dog contract 以不加入工会为条件的雇佣合同(契约)

yen n./v. 热望,渴望

yen pock 鸦片丸

yeoman n. （英）小地主,自耕农;（英史）自由民;（英）（由自由民组成的）志愿骑兵;（古）皇家贵族的仆从,卫士;公民,（罗马法）有恒产者(指有陪审员资格者)

yeoman usher of the black rod （英）黑杖侍卫助理(指上议院的一种议会侍卫官)

yeomanry n. （总称）自由民,自耕农;（英）义勇骑兵队

Yeomen of the Guard （英）王室警卫(指国王的警卫人员)

yes n. 赞成票;投赞成票者;赞成者;同意,赞成

yield n./v. 出产;出产量;收益/1.让与,给予 2.放弃,让渡;被迫放弃;投降 3.同意,承认 4.生产;出产,产生(效果,收益)

yield a point in a debate 在辩论中承认对方所说的一点是对的

yield consent 承诺

yield maintenance （美）交割债券、期货时高速价格的维持收益率

yield on long term government bonds 长期政府债券所得

yield oneself prisoner 投降当俘虏

yield possession 让出所有权,让与所有权;让渡占有权

yield rate 生利率(指股票债券所生利益率)

yield submission 服从

yield to crash 破产收益率

yield to muturity 期末收益,有效利率,到期收益率,全期获利率

yield to put （美）出售收益率

yielding a. 让步的,放弃的,屈服的

yoke n. 1.(史)架在俘虏脖子上的轭状枷锁;轭门(指状似牛轭的拱门,令俘虏通过以示服从) 2.(喻)束缚,压力,支配,管辖 3.(喻)(联结兄弟、夫妇等的)情义

yoke of brotherhood 手足之情(指不可分之兄弟关系)

York-Antwerp Rules (YAR) 约克·安特卫普规则(指一种共同海损理算规则,亦称统一提单原则),安特卫普共同海损规则

young a. 1.少年的,年轻的;年龄较小的 2.无经验的,未成熟的

young crops law 青苗法

Young Lawyers International Association 国际青年律师协会

young person （英）(14至17岁的)青少年

young prisoner n. 青少年犯

young state 年轻的国家,新兴的国家

young-offender 青少年犯

youngling n. 年轻人,没有经验的人,新手

youngster n. 儿童;少年;青年;(复)子女;后辈

your account 贵行账

Your Honor （英）法官阁下(通常指对法官或对某些高级官员的直接尊称,尤指对地方法院法官的尊称);法官大人

Your Lordship 法官阁下(对法官的尊称)

Your Worship （英）高等法院法官阁下(指对高等法院法官的尊称)

youth n. 青年;青年时期,青春时期;青少年时期

Youth Correct Act （美）《青少年教养法》(指专门为减少16岁至20岁青少年的犯罪行为而制定的一部联邦法规)

youth having been delinquent （中）失足青少年

youth organisation 青年组织

youth tribunal 青少年裁判庭

youthful a. 青年的,年轻的

youthful offenders 少年犯

yowl n./v. 嚎,厉声叫喊

Z

Zacchini case 扎尼奇判例(指美国1977年州法维护表演者权的著名判例)
zaibatsu (=*zaibatzu*) (日)财阀(指第二次世界大战前,同托拉斯或卡特尔相似的以一个家族为中心组成的日本大资本主义企业),大财团
zakonik *n.* 《系统大令简本》(指1349年塞尔维亚颁布的一部法典)
ZANGGER Committee 桑戈委员会(又称核出口国委员会)
zany *n./a.* 丑角,小丑;滑稽表演;追随者,笨人/荒唐的,愚蠢的
zeal *n.* 热心,热情,热忱
zealot *n.* 狂热分子,激烈分子
zealotry *n.* 狂热行为
zealous witness 偏袒一方的证人,有偏见的证人
zebra crossing (英)斑马线(指马路上涂有黑白相间颜色的人行横道线)
Zeitgeist 时代精神
zero *n.* 零;零号;最低点
zero access 立即存取
zero balance 零数余额
zero bracket amount 零等级额,免税额,(指从个人所得税方面的所得中统一扣减)起点额,最低等级额
zero defects 质量全部合格的要求,无缺陷,无瑕疵
zero economic growth 经济不发展
zero hour 关键性时刻,决定性时刻,紧急关头,开始时刻
zero hours contract 零工时雇佣合同(也可写作 zero hour contract,指的是一种雇员仅根据雇主需要随叫随到,工作量和工作时间均不固定的雇佣协议。美国《国际财经日报》2013年8月12日报道称,英国工会总会秘书长佛朗西斯·奥格雷迪指出:"为了在经济衰退和萧条期生存下去,已有数百万人接受了短时间的临时性工作和零工时雇佣合同。")
zero norm 最低定额
zero pollution policy 无缺点污染政策
zero rate of duty 免税
zero rated goods 免税货物,免税商品,零税率货物
zero tolerence policy 零容忍政策(指在破窗理论基础上衍生的对策,就是将问题消灭在萌芽状态)
zero transaction cost world 零交易成本世界
zero-duty bindings 免税待遇的冻结
zero-rated *a.* 零税率的
zero-sum *a.* 一方得益引起一方相应损失的,损人利己的
zero-sum games 零和博弈(指博弈中的一个战略组合,相对于另一个战略组合而形成的一个参与人收益的上升是相应的另一个参与人收益的下降,如果把每一战略组合中所有参与人的收益相加,可以发现其和为零)
zig-zag of politics 政治学的盘旋
zillah *n.* (印度的)一种行政区
zillionaire *n.* 亿万富翁
zionism *n.* 犹太复国主义
zionist *n./a.* 犹太复国主义者/犹太复国主义的
ZIP (或 zip) **code** 邮政编码,邮递区号,邮区代码
ZipCar Capitalism 同车资本主义(见 collaborative consumption)
zipper clause 不能重开谈判的条款;使协议合并的声明
Zollverein *n.* 关税同盟,商业同盟;(德)关税同盟(指1843年在普鲁士领导下成立的德国关税联盟)
zonal administration 地区行政管理
zonal commissioner 地区专员
zonal committee 地区委员会
zone *n.* 区,地区;区域;范围;界
zone court 地方法院

zone for revenue and sanitary laws 税收检疫法令施行地带
zone of competition 竞争地带
zone of employment 就业区,补偿范围[指一个实际区域或范围,只要雇员受到伤害,不管当时是否在职均有资格得到工人的补偿(worker's compensation)]
zone of influence 势力范围
zone of peace and security 和平安全区
zone of protective jurisdiction 保护管辖权地带
zone price 区域性价格
zone pricing system 分区定价制度
zone search 搜查地带,搜查范围(指犯罪现场的搜查。诸如失火或爆炸现场,分成几个特别的地段,亦可称作 sector search)
zone time 地方时间,区时
zoning n. 分区,分区制(指一种管理土地的立法措施,主要用于城市地区,即将土地划分为若干个区,如工厂区、住宅区等);城市区划
zoning commission 城市规划委员会

zoning law (美)城市区划法
zoning ordinance (美)市区划分法令
zoning regulation 分区法规(指美国最高法院认可的两类法规:一类对分区内建筑物高度、凸显结构等有特别的统一规范,二类对分区内建筑物的用途有特别的规定)
zoom v. 激增;调整摄影焦距,放大;(美)免费获得
zoophile n. 爱护动物者(尤指反对用动物作活体解剖试验者)
zoophobia n. 动物恐惧症
zygocephalum (大陆法)土地测量;土地数量
zygostates n. 过磅员;鉴定钱币含(金、银)量的官员
zygote 接合子,受精卵;合子
Zygote Intrafallopian Transfer 输卵管内输入精子,人工受孕(指在试管内使成熟的卵子受精,然后注入妇女的输卵管内。缩略 ZIFT, 亦称 Zygote Intrafallopian-tube Transfer。见 artificial insemination; gamete intrafallopian transfer; in vitro fertilization)

附录一：常用缩略语
Appendix I: Abbreviations Used in Common

A

A Adam's Justiciary Reports 亚当斯的司法判例汇编；affirmed 确实，(判决)确认，证实；Alabama (美)亚拉巴马州；American 美国的，美国人；Arabic 阿拉伯的；Arkansas (美)阿肯色州；association(s) 协会，结社，社团法人；Atlantic Reports (美)大西洋区判例汇编(全国判例汇编系统)

A. A. automatic approval(system) (进口许可证)自动核准制

A. A. A. American Arbitration Association 美国仲裁协会；Agricultural Adjustment Act 《农业调整法》

A. A. C. Anno ante Christum 公元前

AACC Afro-Asian Conciliation Commission 亚非调停委员会

AACR Association for the Advancement of Civil Right 民权促进协会

A. A. C. S. L. American Association for the Comparative Study of Law 美国法律比较研究协会

AAIC American Association for International Conciliation 美国国际和解协会

AAJC Afro-Asian Jurists Conference 亚非法律工作者会议

AAJE American Academy of Judicial Education 美国司法教育科学院

AAL American Airline 美国航空公司

AALC Afro-Asian Lawyer's Conference 亚非律师会议

AALCC Asian-African Law Consultative Committee 亚非法律协商委员会

A. A. L. L. American Association of Labor Legislation 美国劳动立法协会；American Association of Law Libraries 美国法律图书馆协会

A. A. L. S. Association of American Law Schools 美国法律学院联合会

AAPSO Afro-Asian People's Solidarity Organization 亚非人民团结组织

A. A. R. (a. a. r.) Against All Risks 承保一切的风险，负全险

AAS Automatic Approval System 自动核准制

AASO Association of American Steamship Owner 美国船东协会

AATA Anglo-American Treaty Association 英美条约协会

AAUP American Association of University Professor 美国大学教授联合会

Ab abridgment 节略，剥夺；abstracts 摘要；abridgments 法律年报摘要

A. B. Advisory Board 咨询委员会；Assembly Bill (美国州立法机关)议会法案；able-bodied seaman (英)一等水手

A/B Air Bill 空运提单

A. B. A. American Bar Association 美国律师协会；Annual Budget Authorization

年度预算批准权限

ABA Antitrust L. J. American Bar Association Antitrust Law Journal 《美国律师协会反托拉斯法律杂志》

ABACPD American Bar Association Center for Professional Discipline 美国律师协会职业纪律中心

A. B. A. D. R. American Bar Association Disciplinary Rule 美国律师协会纪律准则

A. B. A. J. American Bar Association Journal 《美国律师协会杂志》

ABAM Association Belgedes Assureurs Maritimes 比利时海事保险商协会

ABC Code ABC 密码

Ab. Eq. Cas. Equity Cases Abridged 衡平法上节略的判例

ABF (A. B. F.) American Bar Foundation 美国律师基金会

A. B. L. A. American Blind Lawyers Association 美国盲人律师协会

A. B. Rep. American Bankruptcy Reports 美国破产判例汇编

ABS (telex 用语) absent subscriber 对方用户无人

abs re absente reo(或 rec) 在被告缺席的情况下

A. C. (或 A/C) account current 往来账户;活期存款;Agent de Change(法)证券交易经纪人;American Conditions 美国条件;Appeal Cases 上诉案件;Appeal Court 上诉法院;Appellate Court 受理上诉法院;Ante Christum 公元前

1917, A. C. 1917, Appeal cases Can. (加拿大)1917 上诉判例

1918, A. C. Law Reports, 1918, Appeal cases, Eng. (英)法律判例汇编,1918 上诉判例

ACAS Advisory Conciliation and Arbitration Services 咨询、调解、仲裁服务局(1975 年英国政府设立的独立劳动争议调解机构)

ACC acceptance 接受,承兑;according to 根据,按照

ACDG according 根据,按照

ACHR American Council of Human Rights 美国人权理事会

ACI Agencia Central de Inteligencia (美)中央情报局;Agencia de Cooperation International (美)国际合作署

ACIEP Advisory Committee of International Economic Policy 国际经济政策咨询委员会

ACIR Advisory Commission on Intergovernmental Relations (美)政府间关系咨询委员会

ACLU American Civil Liberties Union 美国民权自由联盟

ACM Association of Computing Machinery 计算机协会

ACME Acme 爱支密码(美国 Acme code 公司编制出版电报密码书,全名为 Acme Commodity and Phrase Code)

A. C. O. administrative contracting officer (美国联邦政府的)承办合同的行政官员

ACOMR Advisory Committee on Marine Resources Research 海洋资源研究咨询委员会;Advisory Committee on Oceanic Meteorological Research 海洋气象研究咨询委员会

ACP 非加太集团[指 African,Caribbean and Pacific 若干国家(1983 年为 63 个国家)依照洛美会议(Lomé Convention),可享受欧洲经济共同体(EEC)优惠关税等利益]

ACPO Association of Chief Police Office (英)高级警察协会

ACPPD Asian Conference of Parliamentarians on Population and Development 亚洲议会关于人口和发展会议

ACTA Anti-Counterfeiting Trade Agreement 反假冒贸易协定

ACTL American College of Trial Lawyers 美国出庭律师协会

ACTN Advisory Committee on Trade Negotiation (美)贸易谈判咨询委员会

ACTU Arbitration Court of Trade Unions 工会仲裁法庭

A. 2d Atlantic Reporter, Second Series 大西洋地区判例汇编,第二套丛书

A. D. Anno Domini 公元;Appellate Divi-

sion (Supreme Court) （美最高法院）上诉法庭; application to deliver for export 出口交货申请
A/D after date 发票后定期付款
ADA Americans with Disabilities Act 《美国残疾法》;拥有残疾法的美国人
ADAMHA Alcohol, Drug Abuse, and Mental Health Administration 醉酒、吸毒和精神健康管理
A. D. B. African Development Bank 非洲开发银行; Asian Development Bank 亚洲开发银行
A. D. C. Appeal Cases, District of Columbia Reports 上诉案件,哥伦比亚特区判例汇编
ADCas. (BNA) Americans with Disabilities cases 丧失劳动能力的美国人判例,残疾美国人判例(国家事务局)
A. D. 2d Appellate Division Reports, Second Series, N. Y. 纽约受理上诉法庭判例汇编,第二套丛书
A. D. E. A. Age Discrimination in Employment Act 雇佣条例中的年(龄)差(异)
ADIRI Association de Droit Internationale et de Relations Internationales 国际法和国际关系协会
ADIZ Air Defense Identification Zone 防空识别区
ADJ adjacent 相邻的,相近的
Adj. Session adjourned session 延期开庭
Ad. L. Administrative Law 行政法
Ad. L. B. Administrative Law Bulletin 行政法公报
Admin. 1. Administration 行政,管理机关;局(署、处);(美)政府 2. Administrator 行政长官,管理人员,负责人员
Admin. Cd. Administrative Code 行政法典;行政规则
Admin. Dec. Administrative Decisions 行政决定(决议)
Admin. L. J. Am. U. Administrative Law Journal of American University 美国大学行政法期刊
Admin. L. Rev. Administrative Law Review 《行政法评论》

Admin. L. 3d Pike & Fisher Administrative Law, Third Series 派克和费希尔行政法,第三套系列丛书
Adol. & El. N. S. Adolphus and Ellis' English Queen's Bench Reports, New Series (英)阿道尔弗斯和艾利斯的英国后座法庭判例汇编,新丛书
ADR Accident Data Recording 事故数据记录; Alternative Dispute Resolution 任择解决争端方法; Asset Depreciation Range 资产折旧类
ADS (a. d. s.) autograph document signed 有签名的亲笔文件
ad valorem （拉）按照价值
ad valorem duty 从价税[指依货物价值比例课征之关税(customs duties)]
ad valorem fright 从价运费
Advoc. Q. Advocates' Quarterly 《律师季刊》
A. E. and P. Ambassador Extraordinary and Plenipotentiary 特命全权大使
A. E. C. Atomic Energy Commission Reports (1956–1975) （美）原子能委员会判例汇编(1956—1975)
A. & E. Cas. American & English Annotated Cases 美英注释判例
A. E. C. S. Australian-Europe Container Service 澳大利亚—欧洲集装箱联营集团
A. & E. Ency. Law American and English Encyclopedia of Law 美英法律百科全书
A. & E. R. Cas. American & English Railroad Cases 美英铁路判例(汇编)
AF as follows 如下,如次; Automatic Following 自动跟踪
AFA Automatic Foreign Exchange Allocation System 外汇自动分配制
AFAS Automatic Fund Allocation System 资金自动分配制
AFB Air Freight Bill 空运货单
AFDC Aid to Families with Dependent Children 帮助受抚养儿童家庭
AFEB Authorized Foreign Exchange Bank 指定的外汇银行
Affd. (Aff'd) Affirmed 确认,维持(原判),证实
A Fo Army Form （美）军用公文纸,军用

表格
A. F. Rep. Alaska Federal Reports （美）阿拉斯加联邦判例汇编
Afr. L. Stud. African Law Studies 非洲法律研究
AFSA American Foreign Service Association （美）外事人员协会
AFTR American Federal Tax Reports(P-H) 美国联邦税务判例汇编(P-H)
AG Attorney General 总检察长,（美）司法部长,（英）检察总长
Agio 差价
Agt agent 代理人,代理商；against 反对,对,凭；agreement 协定,协议
AGY agency 代理,代理商
AHD Ad hoc Division 临时仲裁机构
AHQ Allied Headquarters 盟军司令部
ahr acceptable hazard rate 容许公害率
AHRA Audio-Homo Recording Act 《版权》《音频图像记录法》
A. I. Amnesty International 国际大赦组织
A/I ad interim 暂时,临时
AIA Advance Informed Agreement 提前知情同意
A. I. Arb. Associate of the Institute of Arbitrators （英）仲裁人协会准会员
AIAT Association Internationale pour le Developement Economique et l'Aide Tech-nique 国际经济发展和技术援助联合会
AIB Anti-Inflation Board （美）反通货膨胀委员会；Association of Insurance Brokers 保险经纪人协会
AIBD Association of International Bond Dealer 国际债券交易人协会,国际证券商协会
A. I. C. A. Associate of the Institute of Chartered Accountants （英）特许会计师协会会员
AICD Association of International Cooperation and Disarmament 国际合作和裁军协会
AICPA American Institute of Certified Public Accountants 美国会计师协会
AID Agency of International Development （美）国际开发署
AIDA Association Internationale du Droit African 国际非洲法律协会；Association Internationale du Droit de l'Assurance 国际保险法协会
AIDS L. & Litig. Rep. AIDS Law and Litigation Reporter (Univ. Pub. Group) 艾滋病法和诉讼判例汇编
AIIL American Institute of International Law 美国国际法协会
AIJA Association Internationale des Jeunes Avocats 国际青年律师协会
AIJD Association Internationale des Juristes Democrates 国际民主法律工作者协会
AIPLA American Intellectual Property Law Association 美国知识产权法协会
AIPO American Institute of Public Opinion 美国民意测验研究所
AIPPI Association Internationale pour la Protection de la Propriete Industrielle 国际保护工业产权协会
Air & Space L. Air and Space Law 航空、航天法
A. J. American Jurist 美国法学家；Associate Judge 助理法官；Associate Justice 助理法官,副法官；British Guiana Supreme Court, Appellate Jurisdiction 英属圭亚那最高法院,受理上诉管辖区
A. J. (Am. Jm.) American Jurisprudence 《美国法理学》《美国法律百科全书》《美国法释义全书》
AJC Asian Judicial Conference 亚洲司法会议
A. J. C. L. American Journal of Comparative Law 《美国比较法杂志》
AJI Association Juridique Internationale 国际法律协会
A. J. I. L. American Journal of International Law 《美国国际法杂志》
AJS American Judicature Society 美国司法学会
AK acknowledge 电悉
Aka also known as 亦被认为是,以……著称
Ala Alabama （美）亚拉巴马州；Alabama Reports （美）亚拉巴马判例汇编；Alabama Supreme Court （美）亚拉巴马州最

高法院；Alabama Supreme Court Reports （美）亚拉巴马州最高法院判例汇编

A. L. A. A. American Labor Arbitration Awards (P-H) 美国劳资仲裁判定汇编(P-H)

Ala. App. Alabama Appellate Court （美）亚拉巴马州受理上诉法庭

Ala. Civ. App. Alabama Civil Appeals （美）亚拉巴马民事上诉

Ala. Cr. App. Alabama Criminal Appeals （美）亚拉巴马刑事上诉

Alaska stat. Alaska statute 阿拉斯加州成文法规

ALCC Asian Legal Consultative Committee 亚洲法律协商委员会

ALD at a later date 在以后的日期

A. L. I. American Law Institute 美国法律学会(1923年创立)

ALIABA American Law Institute American Bar Association Committee on Continuing Professional Education 美国法学会美国律师协会持续职(专)业教育委员会

A. L. J. Administrative Law Judge 行政法法官；Australian Law Journal 澳大利亚法律期刊

All. E. R. All England Law Reports 《全英判例汇编》

A. L. R. American Law Reports 《美国法律判例汇编》

A. L. R. 2d American Law Reports, Annotated Second Series 《美国法律判例汇编》，附注释第二套丛书；American Law Reports, Second Series 《美国法律判例汇编》，第二套丛书

A. L. R. 3d American Law Reports, Third Series 《美国法律判例汇编》，第三套丛书

A. L. Rec American Law Record Cincinati 美国法律记录(辛辛那提)

ALT Agricultural Land Tribunal （英）农业土地法庭

ALWD Association of Legal Writing Directors 法律文书指导者协会

Am. American Law Book Company 美国法律图书公司

Amb. Ambler's English Chancery Reports （英）安姆勃勒的英国大法官法庭判例汇编

Am. B. A. American Bar Association 美国律师协会

Am. B. R. American Bankruptcy Reports 美国破产案例汇编

A. M. C. American Maritime Cases 美国海事判例汇编

AMCOMAT American Commercial Attaché 美国商务参赞

AMCON American Consul 美国领事

AMCONGEN American Consul General 美国总领事

AMCONSUL American Consulate 美国领事馆

Am. Corp. Cas. American Corporation Cases 美国公司判例(汇编)

Am. Dec. American Decisions 美国的判决，美国判例(汇编)

Am E American English 美国英语

AMEMB American Embassy 美国大使馆

Am. & Eng. Corp. Cas. American & English Corporation Cases 美英公司判例(汇编)

Am. & Eng. Dec. Eq. American & English Decisions in Equity 美英衡平法判例汇编

Am. & Eng. Enc. Law. Sup. American and English Encyclopedia of Law, Supplement 《美英法律百科全书》(补编)

Am. & Eng. Ency. (Enc.) Law American and English Encyclopedia of Law 《美英法律百科全书》

Am. & Eng. Pat. Cas. American & English Patent Cases 美英专利判例(汇编)

Am. & Eng. Ry. Cas. American & English Railway Cases 美英铁路判例(汇编)

Am. & Eng. Ry. Cas. N. S. American & English Railway Cases New Series 美、英铁路判例(汇编)，新丛书

Amer. Jur. American Jurist 美国法学家

Amer. Law. American Lawyer, New York 美国律师(纽约)

Amer. Lawy. American Lawyer 美国律师

AMEX American Stock Exchange 美国证券交易所(纽约)

AMG　Allied Military Government　盟国军政府

Am. Ins. Rep.　American Insolvensy Reports　美国破产判例汇编

Am. Jur.　American Jurisprudence　《美国法律百科全书》，亦译作《美国法理学》

Am. Jur. 2d　American Jurisprudence Second Edition　《美国法理学》(第二版)

Am. Law J. N. S.　American Law Journal, New Series　美国法律杂志，新丛书

AM. Law Reg. O. S.　American Law Register, Old Series　美国法律记录册，旧丛书

Am. Law. Rev.　American Law Review　美国法律评论

AM. Lead. Cas.　American Leading Cases, Hire & Wallace's　海尔和华莱士的美国主要判例(汇编)

AMLEG　American Legation　美国公使馆,美国外交使团

Am. L. Ins.　American Law Institute　美国法学会

Am. L. S. Rev.　American Law School Review　美国法学院评论

Am. L. T. Bankr.　American Law Times, Bankruptcy Reports　美国法律时代,破产判例汇编

AMM　American Military Mission　美国军事代表团

Am. Negl. Cas.　American Negligence Cases　美国有关过失的判例(汇编)

Am. Negl. R.　American Negligence Reports　美国有关过失的判例汇编

Am. pr.　American practice　美国司法实践,美国审判实务;美国律师业务

Am. Prob.　American Probate　美国的遗嘱认证

Am. Property　American Law of Property　《美国财产法》

Am. Rail. Cas.　American Railway Cases　美国铁路判例(汇编)

AMREP　American Representative　美国代表,美方代表

Am. R. Rep.　American Railway Reports　美国铁路判例汇编

AMS　Aggregate Measurement of Support　综合支持量

A. M. S.　Administrative Management Service　行政管理处;Administrative Management Society　(美)行政管理学会

Am. St. R. D.　American Street Railway Decisions　美国市街铁路判例(汇编)

Am. St. Rep. (Am. st. R.)　American State Reports　美国州判例汇编

AMT (A. M. T.)　amount　数量,数额;airmail transfer　航空信汇;Alternative Minimum Tax　替代性最低税

Am. U. L.　American University Law Review　美国大学法律评论

AN　arrival notice　到达通知书

A/N　advice note　通知书,通知单

ANA　Air Navigation Act　(英)航行法,航空法

ANAF　Association Nationale des Avocates de France　法国全国律师协会

Angell on Lim.　A treatise on the Law of Limitation of Actions　关于诉讼时效法律的论文

Ann. Cas.　American & English Annotated Cases　美英注释判例(汇编);American Annotated Cases　美国注释判例(汇编)

Ann. Cas. 1913E 571　American Annotated Cases　美国注释判例卷1913E第571页

Ann. Code　Annotated Code　注释法典

Anno.　Annotated　注释的

Ann. St.　Annotated Statutes　注释法规

Ann. Tax. Cas.　Annotated Tax Cases (1922–date)　(英格兰和威尔士)注释的税务判例(汇编)(1922年至今)

a. o (ao)　and others　等等,和其他

A. O　administrative orders or directives　行政命令或指示

AOD　Action on Decision　有关判决的备忘录

AOL　American on line　美国在线公司

AP　airplane　飞机;airport　机场;American Patent　美国专利;Atlantic Pact　大西洋公约;Authority to Purchase　购买许可,委托购买证;account paid　账款已付,账单付讫,付讫

Ap. New York Supreme Court Appellate Division Reports 纽约最高法院上诉法庭判例汇编

A. P. authority to pay 授权付款

A/p authority to purchase 采购授权书，押汇票买入委托书

APA Administration Procedure Act （美国联邦）《行政诉讼法》; advance pricing agreement 预付价格协议

APC Arbitration Procedural Code 仲裁程序法典; Accounting Practice Committee 审计实务委员会; Alien Property Custodian (U. S.) （美）侨民财产保管人

APE Assemblée Parlementaire Européenne 欧洲议员会议

APEC Asia-Pacific Economic Co-operation 亚太经合组织

APLA American Patent Law Association 美国专利法协会

APP applicant 申请人，请求者; appellate 受理上诉的; appendix 附件,附录,补遗; appointed 指定的,任命的; apprehension 逮捕,拘押; appropriation 经费,拨款; approval 批准,许可

app. allowed appeal allowed 获准的上诉

App. Cas. Appeal cases (Eng. Rep) （英）上诉判例汇编（1875年至今）; Appeal Cases, English Law Reports 上诉判例,英国法律判例汇编

APP. Div Appellate Division 上诉庭

App. Div (N. Y.) New York Supreme Court Appellate Supreme Division Reports 纽约最高法院上诉庭判例汇编

Appx appendix 附件,附录,补遗;附属物

APR Annual percentage rate 年百分率

A. R. Administration Report 行政报告，(美) 政府报告,政府公报; all risks 综合险,一切险; annual report 年度报告; arrival 抵达,到达; anno regni 特定王国统治的时期或即位后的年次; American Reports 美国判例汇编; Anno Regni, in the year of the reign （国王的）执政年代; Army Regulation 军队法规; Argus Reports (Aus) 阿格斯判例汇编; Atlantic Reports 大西洋判例汇编; Industrial Arbitration Reports (New South Wales) 工业仲裁判例汇编（新南威尔士）; Ontario Appeal Reports （加）安大略上诉判例汇编

A/R acknowledgment of receipt 收据,账单的承认

arb. Arbiter, arbitrator 仲裁人,公断人; arbitration 仲裁,公断

Arbitr. Arbitration 公断,仲裁

A. R. C. American Railway Cases 美国铁路判例; American Red Cross 美国红十字会; American Ruling Cases 美国主导判例（汇编）

Ariz. Arizona Reports （美）亚利桑那州判例汇编

Ark. Arkansas Reports （美）阿肯色州判例汇编

ARP all risks policy 综合险保单

ARR arrangement 安排,协定; arrival 抵达,到达

A. R. S. Arizona Revised Statutes （美）亚利桑那州修订的法规

arts. articles 条款,项目,法条;文章,论文;商品,物品

A. S. American Standard 美国标准; amicable settlement 和解; Assistant Secretary 助理部长,(美)助理国务卿; as stated 如上所述; Alaska Statutes （美）阿拉斯加州法规

A/S at sight 见票即付; after sight 见票后即付; account sale 赊销

ASAP as soon as possible 尽快

ASC All Savers' Certificate 免税储蓄证书; Australia Securities Council 澳大利亚证券委员会

ASCAP American Society of Composer, Author and Publisher 美国作曲家、作家、出版商协会

ASE American Stock Exchange 美国证券交易所（与AMEX同）

ASEAN Association of South-East Asia Nations 东南亚国家联盟

ASFA Adoption and Safe Families Act （美）《收养和安全家庭法》（1997年联邦法）

ASIL American Society of International

Law 美国国际法学会
ASIPI Association Interamericaine de Propriété Industrielle 泛美工业产权协会
ASL Anti-Strike Law 反罢工法
ASP Anglo-Soviet Pact 英苏条约; Application Service Provider 应用服务提供商
ASPACTO Asian-Pacific Treaty Organization 亚洲太平洋条约组织
A. S. P. F. Association of Superannuation and Pension Funds （英）退职和养老基金会
Assem. Assembly, State Legislative （美）州议会,州立法机构
Assr. assignor 转让者
Asst assignment （财产、权利的）转让; 分配,委派
Asst JAG Assistant Judge Advocate General （英）军法署助理署长
AT air transport 空运; Antarctic Treaty 南极条约; Appeal Tribunal 上诉法庭
ATA actual time of arrival 实际抵（到）达时间; Atlantic Treaty Association 大西洋公约协会
ATD (A. T. D.) Australian Tax Decisions 澳大利亚税务判例（汇编）
ATL Anti-Trust Law （美）反托拉斯法
ATLA American Trial Lawyers Association 美国出庭律师协会
ATLB Air Transport Licensing Board

（英）空运特许局
ATM Act of Trade Marks 商标法
AT Pol army traffic police 军事交通警察
ATS (A. T. S.) at the suit of 根据……的请求,按诉讼程序
ATT attaché 随员,参赞; attachment 附件
Atty. Attorney 律师,代理人,检察官
Att'y. Gen. Attorney General （美）司法部长,（英）检察总长,（美）州检察长
Att'y Gen. Rep. United States Attorney General's Reports 美国司法部长报告集
AUS Ambassador of the United States 美国大使
Austr. Jur. Australian Jurist 澳大利亚法学家
Auth. Authorities; Authority 当局,官方
AV (a. v.) actual velocity 实际速度; ad-valorem 按价,从价
Av. L. Rep (CCH) Aviation Caw Reporter 航空判例汇编
awd. awarded 1.被判决的,被裁决的,被判给的 2.被授予的,荣获……的,受奖的
AWGS Annual Wage Guarantee System （美）年工资保证制
AWL absent with leave 准假离职,准假缺席
AWOL absent with out leave 擅离职守,未请假缺席

B

B bank 银行; bar 法庭,被告席,律师业; bay 海湾; board 委员会,局,署; British 英国（的）; budget 预算; buyer 买主; Baron （理财法院）法官,（英）贵族总称,男爵,（美）巨商
B and E （或 B&E） Breaing and Entering 破门而入（此两要素构成盗窃罪）
BA bank acceptance 银行承兑票据; British Ambassador 英国大使; budget authorization 预算权限

B. A. （或 B/A） bank acceptance 银行承兑汇票
BAC Blood alcohol content 血内酒精含量
BAFM British Association of Forensic Medicine 英国法医学学会
BAIU British Association for International Understanding 英国国际谅解协会
BAL balance 余额
Bal. Ballent Ballentine's Law Dictionary 《巴伦坦法律词典》

Bank. Ct. Rep. Bankrupt Court Reports 破产法庭判例汇编

BANKCY bankruptcy 破产

Bank. & Ins. R. Bankruptcy and Insolvency Reports (1853–1855), Eng. （英）破产和无力清偿判例汇编(1853—1855)

Bank. L. J. Banking Law Journal 银行法杂志,金融法杂志

Bankr. Act. Bankruptcy Act 破产法

Bankr. L. Rep. Bankruptcy Law Reporter (CCH) 《破产法判例汇编》(CCH)

Barb. Barbour's Supreme Court Report （美纽约）《巴布尔最高法院判例汇编》

Barb. Ch. Barbour's Chancery, N. Y. （纽约）巴布尔衡平法院

Barb. Ch. Pr. Barbour's Chancery Practice 巴布尔衡平法院诉讼程序

Barn. Barnardiston King's Bench, Eng. （英）巴尔纳尔迪斯顿高等法院(王座法庭); Barnes' English Common Pleas Reports 巴尔纳斯英国高等民事法院判例汇编; Barnfield's Reports (vols.19–20 Rhode Island) （美）巴尔菲尔判例汇编(19—20卷罗得岛)

Barn. & Adol. Barnewall and Adolphus's English King's Bench Reports 巴尔内沃尔和阿道尔富斯的英国高等法院(王座法庭)判例汇编

Barn. & Ald. Barnewall & Aldersons English King's Bench Reports 巴尔内沃尔和奥尔德逊英国高等法院(王座法院)判例汇编

Barn. Ch. Barnardiston Chancery, Eng. （英）巴尔纳尔迪斯顿大法官法院

Barnes Barnes' Practice Cases 巴尔纳斯诉讼实务判例(汇编)

BASF The Bar Association of San Francisco （美）旧金山律师协会

Bates Ch. Bates's Chancery Reports, Del. （美）巴特斯的特拉华州衡平法院判例汇编

Bate's Ann. St. Bate's Annotated Revised Statutes Ohio. （美）巴特斯的俄亥俄州注释修订法规(汇编)

Batt. Batty's Irish King's Bench Reports (1825–1826) 巴蒂的爱尔兰王座法院判例汇编(1825–1826)

Batts' Rev. St. Batts' Annotated Revised Civil Statutes, Tex. （美）巴特的得克萨斯州注释修订的民事法规

Bay Bay's Reports (1–3, 5–8 Missouri) （美）贝判例汇编(密苏里州1—3, 5—8); Bay's South Carolina Reports (1783–1804) （美）贝的南卡罗来纳州判例汇编(1783—1804)

B. B. bail bond 保释保证书; bank book 银行存折; bill book 发票簿,票据账簿,出纳簿,海关报告簿; blue book 蓝皮书,名人录; Bureau of the Budget （美）预算局; buy back 回购

BBB Better Business Bureau 良好商业局(指美国解决消费者争议仲裁的三种方式之一。其他两种为:法院仲裁和仲裁协会进行仲裁)

BBC British Broadcasting Corporation 英国广播公司

BBP Bavarian Border Police （联邦德国）巴伐利亚边界警察

BBS Bachelor of Business Science 管理科学学士; Bulletin Board System （电子）公告牌系统

BC Bankruptcy case 破产案件

BC before Christ 公元前; beneficial cost 受益成本; birth certificate 出生证; birth control 计划生育,节育; British Colony 英国殖民地; British Commonwealth 英联邦; Budget Committee 预算委员会; bulk cargo 散装货

B. C. Bail Court 保释法庭; Bankruptcy Cases 破产判例; British Columbia Law Reports (Canada) （加拿大）英国哥伦比亚法律判例汇编

B. C. (N. S. W.) New South Wales Bankruptcy Cases (1890–1899) 新南威尔士破产判例(汇编)(1890—1899)

B/C bill of collection 托收凭单,托收汇票

B. & C. Barnewall and Cresswell's English King's Bench Reports 巴尔尼沃尔和格雷斯韦尔的英国高等法院(王座法庭)判例

汇编

BCA border crossing agreement 过境协定

BCC border crossing card 过境证；British Commonwealth Conference 英联邦会议；British Copyright Council 英国版权委员会；British Crown Colony 英国直辖殖民地；Bureau Central de Compensation 赔偿总局

B. C. C. Bail Court Reports, Sanders & Cole (Eng.) （英）桑德尔斯和柯尔的保释法院判例汇编；Bail Court Cases Loundes & Maxwell (1852-1854) (Eng.) （英）保释法院判例，朗德斯和马克斯韦尔（1852—1854）；Brown's Chancery Cases (Eng.) （英）布朗的大法官法庭判例（汇编）；British Columbia Reports 英国哥伦比亚判例汇编

B. & C. Comp. Bellinger and Cotton's Annotated Codes and Statutes, Or. （美）贝林格和科顿的俄勒冈州注释法典和法规（汇编）

BCE Before the Christian Era 公元前

BCIA the Berne Convention Implementation Act （版权）美国1988年的《伯尔尼公约实施法》

B. C. L. Bachelor of Canon Law 教会法学士；Bachelor of Civil Law 民法学士

BCN British Commonwealth of Nations 英联邦

BCP British Civil Police 英国民事警察

BCPA British Copyright Protection Association 英国版权保护协会

BCPIT British Council for the Promotion of International Trade 英国国际贸易促进委员会

BCRA Bicameral Campaign Reform Act （美）《两院竞选活动改革法》（2002年制定）

BDFC Beijing Declaration Fighting Corruption 《北京反腐败宣言》（在APEC框架内加大合作执法力度，经中美两国首脑推动而完成）

B. D. I. L. British Digest of International Law 英国国际法判决摘要汇编

BE bill of exchange 汇票；British Embassy 英国大使馆；British Empire 大英帝国；Bureau of Economics （美）经济局

BEA Bureau of Economic Analysis （美）经济分析所(或署)

Beav. Beavan's English Rolls Court Reports (vols. 48-55 Eng. Reprint) （英）比万的英国主事案卷法官法院判例汇编（48—55卷英国再版）

Beavan Ch. Beavan's English Rolls Court Reports （英）比万的英国主事案卷法官法院判例汇编

Beav. R. & C. Beavan, Railway & Canal Cases (Eng.) （英）比万铁路和运河判例（汇编）

Bec. Cr. Beccaria on Crimes and Punishments 贝卡利亚论罪行与惩罚

Bee Bee's United States District Court Reports 比的美国联邦地区法院判例汇编

Bee Adm. Bee's Admiralty, An Appendix To Bee's District Court Reports （美）比的海事法，比的联邦地区法院判例汇编的附件

Beebe Cit. Beebe's Ohio Citations （美）毕比的俄亥俄（州）援引

Bee C. C. R. Bee's Crown Cases Reserved (Eng.) （英）比的巡回审判中留待刑事上诉法院解决的法律问题

Bel. Bellew's English King's Bench Reports (1378-1400) （英）贝柳的英国高等法院（王座法庭）判例汇编（1398—1400）；Belasis' Bombay Reports （印）贝拉西斯的孟买判例汇编；Beling's Ceylon Reports （锡）贝林的锡兰（现为斯里兰卡）判例汇编；Bellinger's Reports (vols. 4-8 Oregon) （美）贝林格的判例汇编（俄勒冈4—8卷本）

BEL below 在……下面

Bell. Bell, English Crown Cases Reserved 贝尔，英国巡回审判中留待刑事上诉法院解决的法律问题；Bell, Scotch Session Cases (1842-1850) 贝尔，苏格兰最高民事法院判例（1842—1850）；Bell, Calcutta Reports （印）贝尔，加尔各答判例汇编；Bellewe, English King's Bench Reports 贝尔维，英国高等法院（王座法庭）判例汇编；Brooke, New Cases, by Bellewe 布鲁

克,贝尔维的新判例; Bellinger, Reports (vols. 4-8 Oregon) （美）贝林格,判例汇编(俄勒冈 4—8 卷本); Bellasis Bombay Reports （英）贝拉西斯孟买判例汇编

Bell Cas. Bell's Cases, Scotch Court of Session 贝尔的判例,苏格兰最高民事法院

Bell C. C. Bell, English Crown Cases Reserved (vol.169 Eng.Reprint) 贝尔,英国巡回审判中留待刑事上诉法院解决法律问题(英国再版 169 卷本); Bellasis, Civil Cases (Bombay) （印）贝拉西斯民事判例(孟买); Bellasis, Criminal Cases (Bombay) （印）贝拉西斯刑事判例(孟买)

Bell Cr. C. Bell's English Crown Cases 贝尔的英国刑事案例判例; Beller's Criminal Cases (Bombay) （印）贝勒的刑事判例(孟买)

Bel. Prob. Belknap's Probate Law of California （美）贝尔纳普的加利福尼亚州遗嘱检验法

BEMA British Embassy Military Attache 英国大使馆武官

Ben. Adm. Benedict's American Admiralty Practice 本尼迪克特的美国海事法惯例

Benefit LLC Benefit limited Liablity Company （美）公益有限责任企业

Benth. Jud. Ev. Bentham's Judicial Evidence 本瑟姆的司法证据

BEP Bureau of Engraving and Printing （美）照相制版和印刷局

Berks Berks County Law Journal PA. （美）伯克县法律期刊(宾夕法尼亚州)

Best Ev. Best on Evidence 最佳证据

Best Pres. Best on Presumptions of Law and fact 贝斯特论法律与事实的推定

Best & S. Best and Smith's English Queen's Bench Reports 贝斯特和史密斯的英国高等法院(后座法庭)判例汇编

BF before 在……以前; bona fide 善意的,真实的

B. F. O. British Foreign Office （旧）英国外交部

b. f. p. (BFP) bona fide purchaser 善意购买人

BG Board of Governors 管理委员会,理事会

BGOVT British Government 英国政府

B. & H. Cr. Cas. Bennett & Heard Leading Criminal Cases, Eng. （英）贝内特和赫德的主要刑事判例(汇编)

BHC British High Commissioner 英国高级专员

BI Bulletin d'Information 新闻公报; Bureau of Investigation （美）调查局

BIA Bureau of Indian Affairs （美）印第安人事务局

BIDA Bureau International des Droits d'Auteurs 国际版权局

BIF Birth-Related Neurological Injury Compensation Fund 出生相关之神经系统损伤赔偿基金

Big. Cas. Torts Bigelow's Leading Cases in Torts 比奇洛的侵权中的主要判例(汇编)

BIICL British Institute of International and Comparative Law 英国国际比较法协会

BIITS (Fragile Five: Brazil, Indonesia, India, Turkey, South-Africa) 脆弱五国:巴西、印尼、印度、土耳其和南非

BIRPI Bureaux Internationaux Reunis pour la Protection de la Propriété Intellectuelle 国际知识产权保护局

BIS Bank of International Settlements 国际清算银行; Board of Inspection and Survey 检查和鉴定委员会; British Information Services 英国新闻处, British Intelligence Service 英国情报局; Bureau of Industry and Security （美）工业与安全局

BITD Bureau International des Tarifs Douaniers 国际关税局

BITs Bilateral Investment Treaties 双边投资条约

BJ Bar Journal 律师期刊

B. L. Bachelor of law 法学士; Barrister at law （英）律师; bill 票据,清单

B/L bill of lading 提货单

BLA bilateral agreement 双边协定; British Legal Association 英国法律协会

Black Black,U. S. Supreme Court Reports 布莱克,《美国联邦最高法院判例汇编》

Black, Const. Law Black on Constitutional Law （美）布莱克论宪法

Blackf. Blackford's Reports (Ind.) 布莱克福特判例汇编（印第安纳州）

Black, Judg. Black on Judgments （美）布莱克论审判

Black Law. Dict. Black's Law Dictionary 《布莱克法律词典》

Bla. H. Henry Blackstone's English Common Pleas Reports Eng. （英）亨利·布莱克斯通的英国高等民事法院判例汇编

BL. Comm. Blackstone, Commentaries on the Laws of England 布莱克斯通的英格兰法律评述

B. leader Bar Leader (ABA) 律师协会领导（美国律师协会）

BLM Bureau of Land Management 土地管理局

B. L. P. British Labour Party 英国工党

BLS Bureau of Labor Statistics （美）劳工统计局

BMLA British Maritime Law Association 英国海商法协会

BNA British North American Act (1867) 1867年的不列颠北美法案；Bureau of National Affairs （美）国家事务局（活页服务出版社）

BNU Bulletin des Nations Unies 联合国公报

BO blanket order 总括订货单；back order 暂时无法满足订货；Branch Office 分局,分理处,分公司,分店；Bulletin Officiel （法）《官方公报》；buyer's option 买主选择（权）

BOD biographic data 履历（书）；end of date 截止日期

B. of P. breach of promise suit 毁（婚）约诉讼

BOG Board of Governors 管理委员会,董事会

Bond L. Rev. Bond Law Review 《邦德法律评论》

BOOST build-own-operate-subsidize-transfer 建造—拥有—经营—补贴—转让（见 BOT）

BOOT build-own-operate-transfer 建造—拥有—经营—转让（见 BOT）

Booth, Real Act The Nature and Practice of Real Actions in their Writs and Process 物权诉讼在其令状及程序中的实务与性质

BOP Bureau of Prisons 监狱局

BOS brief of service 简历（表）

BOT build-operate-transfer 建造—经营—转让（指20世纪80年代以来全球兴起的一种投资方式,此处为狭义概念,广义概念还包括 BOOT,BOOST 和 ROO）

Bouv. L. Dict. Bouvier Law Dictionary 《布维尔法律词典》

BP balance of payments 国际收支；basic pay 基本工资,基薪；beacon point 海岸信标,信标点；birth place 出生地；blue print 蓝图,行动计划；boundary pillar 界桩；British Patent 英国专利；British preferential tariff 英国特惠关税

B/P balance of payments 国际收支；bill of parcels 包裹单,发票；bill payable 应付票据

B. & P. Bosanquet & Puller's English Common Pleas Reports 博赞克特和普勒的英国高等民事法院判例汇编

BPAI Board of Patent Appeal and Interference （美）专利上诉和调停委员（PTAB 的前身）

BPT(s) British preferential tariff (system) 英国特惠关税（制）

BR basic requirements 基本要求,基本要件；bills receivable 应收票据

B. R. (Bancus Regis) King's Bench 英国高等法院（王座法院）

B. R. Baltimore City Reports 巴尔的摩市判例汇编；Bancus Reginae, Queen's Bench 英国高等法院（后座法庭）；Bankruptcy Reports 破产判例汇编；Bankruptcy Register 破产事项登记；Board of Review, U. S. Army 1929-1949 评论委员会（美国军队）(1929—1949)；Brooklyn Law Review (N. Y.) 布鲁克莱因法律评论（纽约）

B/R Bill of Right （英）《权利法案》,（美）《人权法案》

B. R. C. British Ruling Cases 英国主导判例（汇编）

Br. C. C. British Crown Cases 英国刑事

案件汇编

Brev. Dig. Brevard's Digest of the Public Statute Law, S. C. 布雷瓦德的美国联邦最高法院公共法规法的判决摘要汇编

BRICs 巴俄印中四国（崛起）

Brit. y. B. Int'1 L. British Year Book of International Law 《大不列颠国际法年鉴》

Bro. C. C. Brown's English Chancery Cases or Reports 布朗的英国大法官法庭判例或判例汇编

Bro. Civ. Law Browne's Civil and Admiralty Law 布朗的民事和海事法

Brod. & Fr. Broderick & Fremantle's Ecclesiastical Cases 布罗德里克和弗里曼特尔的宗教判例（汇编）

Brodix, Am. & E. Pat. Cas. Brodix's American & English Patent Cases 布罗迪克斯的美、英专利判例（汇编）

Broom, Leg, Max. Broom's Legal Maxims 布鲁姆的法律格言

Bro. P. C. Brown's Parliament Cases, Eng. （英）布朗的议会判例（汇编）

Brown Brownlow (& Goldesborough's) English Common Pleas Reports 布朗路（和戈尔兹巴勒）的英国高等民事法院判例汇编; Brown's Reports (vols. 53-65 Mississippi) 布朗的判例汇编（53—65卷本，密西西比州）; Brown's English Parliamentary Reports 布朗的英国议会的判例汇编; Brown's English Chancery Reports 布朗的英国大法官法庭判例汇编; Brown's Law Dictionary 布朗法律词典; Brown's Scotch Reports 布朗的苏格兰判例汇编; Brown's United States District Court Reports 布朗的美国联邦地区法院判例汇编; Brown's Michigan Nisi Prius Reports 布朗的密歇根州巡回民事审判例汇编; Brown's Reports (vols. 4-25 Nebraska) 布朗的判例汇编（4—25卷本，内布拉斯加州）; Brown's Reports (vols. 80-137 Missouri) 布朗的判例汇编（80—137卷本，密苏里州）

Brown, Adm. Cases on the Law of Adminalty 海事法判例

Brown A. & R. Brown's United States District Court Reports (Admiralty and Revenue Cases) 布朗的美国联邦地区法院判例汇编（海事和税收判例）

Brown, C. C. Brown's English Chancery Cases or Reports 布朗的英国大法官法庭判例或判例汇编

Brown, Ch. Brown's English Chancery Reports 布朗的大法官法庭判例汇编

Browne, Civ. Law Browne's Civil and Admiralty Law 布朗的民事和海事法

Browne, Jud. Interp. Browne's Judicial Interpretation of Common Words and Phrases 布朗的对普通词语和引用语的司法解释

Browne, Div. G. Browne, A Treatise on the Principles and Practice of the Court for Divorce & Matrimonial Causes 吉·布朗,关于离婚和婚姻诉讼案件法庭的实务与原则的论文

Brown N. P. Brown's Michigan Nisi Prius 布朗的密歇根州巡回民事审判

Brown's Brown's Law Dictionary 《布朗法律词典》

Brown's Roman Law Brown's Epitome and Analysis of Savigny's Treatise on Obligations in Roman Law 布朗对萨维尼(Fniednich Carl Von Savigny) 有关罗马法中债的论文节录和分析

BRTA Bureau of Resources and Trade Assistance 资源和贸易协助局

Brunner, Col. Cas. Brunner's Collected Cases, U. S. （美）布鲁纳的判例全集

BS balance sheet 资产负债表; British standard 英国标准; buffer stock 缓冲库存,缓冲存货; Bureau of Standards （美）标准局

B. S. Bancus Superior, that is upper bench 南非高等法院, 即王座法庭（1649—1660年期间的称呼）; Brown's Suppt, to Morison's Dictionary of Decisions, Court of Sessions (1622-1780) (Sc.) 布朗对苏格兰高等民事法院莫里森判例词典的补篇

B/S bill of sale 卖契

B/ST bill at sight 见票即付票据

BT Board of Trade （英）贸易部; brain

trust 智囊团

BTA bilateral trade agreement 双边贸易协定;Board of Technical Assistance （联合国）技术援助局;border tax adjustment 边界税调整;border trade agreement 边境贸易协定;Board of Tax Appeals Reports 税务局上诉判例汇编

BTS Bureau of Transportation Statistic （美）交通运输统计局

bu bureau 局,司,处,办公署,社,所

Buff. Super. Ct Sheldon's Buffalo Superior Court Reports, N. Y. （美）谢尔顿的布法罗市高级法院判例汇编（纽约州）

BUL bulletin 公报,公告

Bull. Cr. Soc Bulletin of the Copyright Society of the USA 《美国版权协会公报》

Bull. N. P. Buller's Law of Nisi Prius 布勒的巡回民事审判法

Bulst. Bulstrode's English King's Bench Reports 布尔斯特罗德的英国高等法院（王座法庭）判例汇编

Bur. Bureau 局,司处;Burnett's Wisconsin Supreme Court Reports (1841-1843) 伯内特的威斯康星州最高法院判例汇编（1841—1843）;Burrow, English King's Bench Reports 伯罗,英国高等法院（王座法庭）判例汇编

Burdick, Roman Law Burdick's Principles of Roman Law 伯迪克的罗马法原理

Burn. Burnett's Reports (Wisconsin) （美）伯内特的判例汇编（威斯康星）

Burr. Burrow's English King's Bench Reports 伯罗的英国高等法院（王座法庭）判例汇编

Burr. S. Cas. Burrow's Settlement Cases, Eng. （英）伯罗的了结（财产授予等）判例

Bus. & Com. Business and Commerce 商务和商业

Bus. Corp Business Corporation 商业公司,贸易公司

Bush Dig. Bush's Digest of Florida Laws （美）布什的佛罗里达州法律判决摘要汇编

Bus. L. (或 **Law**) the Business Lawyer 商业律师

Bus. & Prof. C. Business and Professions Code 商业和职业服务法规

Buxton Buxton's Reports (vols. 123-129 North Carolina) （美）巴克斯顿的判例汇编（123—129卷本,北卡罗来纳州）

B/V book value 账面价值

B/W between 在……之间

BWC British War Cabinet 英国战时内阁

BWT bonded warehouse transaction 保税仓库交易

BXA Bureau of Export Administration （美）出口行政管理局

B. Y. I. L. British Yearbook of International Law 英国国际法年鉴

C

C. Command Paper(1836-1899, 1919-1956, 1956-date) （英）诏书;政府文件（1836—1899,1919—1956,1956年至今）

C (c) cargo 货物;cases 案件,判例,情况;Chancellor （英）大法官,（美）（某些州）衡平法院法官;Chancery （英）大法官法庭,（美）衡平法院;chapter 章,（大写）宪章;circuit 巡回审判,巡回区;civil 民法的,民事的,公民的;condemnation 定罪,罪的宣告,定罪理由,惩罚,谴责,宣告没收;congress 国会,大会;consul 领事;copy 抄本,副本;copyright 版权;council 委员会,院,理事会,协会;California Reports （美）加利福尼亚州判例汇编

ca. circa （用在年代前）大约

Ca. Cases 判例;California 加利福尼亚州

C. A. California Appellate Reports （美）

加州受理上诉法院判例汇编;capital allowances 资本限额;cash advance 预付现金;Charge d'Affaires 代办;City Attorney (美)市检察官;civil affairs 民政事务;Collective Agreement 集体协定;Commercial Attache 商务专员,商务参赞;Consular Agent 领事代理;court of appeal 上诉法院;current account 往来账户,活期存款账户;current assets 流动资产

C/A capital account 资本账;cash account 现金账;commercial agent 代理商,商业代理;credit account 赊购账

CAAP Conference of Afro-Asian Peoples 亚非人民会议;Conference of All African Peoples 全非人民会议;Council of Afro'Asian Peoples 亚非人民理事会

C. A. B. Civil Aeronautics Board Reports (1940-date) （美)民航委员会判例汇编(1940年至今)

CACA Chinese American Citizens Alliance 华裔美国公民联盟

CACI Cour d'Arbitrage Commercial International 国际商业仲裁法院

CAD Capital Adequacy Directive 资本充足率指令;cash against documents 凭单付款;Canadian Annual Digest 加拿大年度判决摘要汇编

CAEM Conseil d'Assistance Economique Mutuelle (苏联、东欧)经互会

CAF cost and freight 成本加运费价格

CAFC United States Court of Appeals for the Federal Circuit 美国联邦巡回上诉法院

Cal California Reports （美)加利福尼亚州判例汇编

Cal. Adm. Code California Administrative Code （美)加利福尼亚州行政法典

Cal. App. California Appellate Reports （美)加利福尼亚州受理上诉法院判例汇编

Cal. App. 2d California Appellate Reports, Second Series （美)加利福尼亚州受理上诉法院判例汇编,第二套丛书

Cal. App. Dec. California Appellate Decisions （美)加利福尼亚州受理上诉法院

判决(汇编)

Cal. App. Supp California Appellate Reports Supplement （美)加利福尼亚州受理上诉法院判例汇编补编

Cal. 2d California Reports, Second Series 加利福尼亚州判例汇编,第二套丛书

Cal. Jur. California Jurisprudence （美)加利福尼亚法理学(判例法)

Cal. L. Rev. California Law Review (美)加利福尼亚法律评论

Cal. P. Ch. Calendar of Proceedings in Chancery （美)衡平法院诉讼案件日程表

Cal. Rptr. California Reporter （美)加利福尼亚州判例汇编

CALT Center for Advanced Legal Training 高级法律训练中心

Cal. Unrep. California Unreported Cases （美)加利福尼亚州未汇编过的判例(汇编)

Calvin, Lex. Calvin's Lexicon Juridicum 卡尔文法律词典

Camp. Campbell's English Nisi Prius Reports 坎贝尔的英国(巡回)民事审判判例汇编

CAN cancel 删去,取消;customs assigned number 海关指定的号码

Canal Zone Canal Zone Supreme Court (巴拿马)运河区最高法院

Can. App. Cas. Canadian Appeal Cases 加拿大上诉判例(汇编)

Can. Cr. Cas. Canadian Criminal Cases 加拿大刑事判例(汇编)

CAND Candidate 候选人,候补者

Cane & L. Cane & Leigh Crown Cases Reserved, Eng. （英)凯恩和利的巡回审判中留待刑事上诉院解决的法律问题

Can. Exch. Canadian Exchequer 加拿大理财法院

CANM Committee on Admission of New Members （联合国)接纳新会员国委员会

Can. S. C. Canada Supreme Court 加拿大最高法院

Can. Stat. Statutes of Canada 加拿大法规

Cap (复Caps)1.capital letter 2.capitalize

(v) (大写)变成资本 3.capital (大写)资本;资本家;资源 4.capacity 能力 5.captain 陆军上将,首领

CAP capability 能力,性能;capacity 行为能力,容量;capital 资本,死刑的,(大写)首都;chapter 章节;Chief Administrative Patent judge (美国专利和商标局)行政专利法官的督察

CAPTA Child Abuse Prevention and Treatment Act (美)《预防虐待儿童与处置法》,(美)预防侵犯儿童和处理法

Car, Chas. 或 Cha Charles (英)查尔士(国王)

3 Car. 1, 1628 (英)查尔士一世,第3个执政年,1628年

C. A. R. Civil Air Regulations (Safety Regulation) (美)民航规则(安全规则);Commonwealth Arbitration Reports (Australia) (澳大利亚)联邦仲裁判例汇编;Criminal Appeal Reports (英)刑事上诉判例汇编

Car. & P. Carrington & Payne's English Nisi Prius Reports (英)卡林顿和佩恩的英国(巡回)民事审判判例汇编

Carp. P. C. Carpmael Patent Cases(1602-1842) Eng. (英)卡普米尔的专利判例(1602—1842)

Carr. & M. Carrington and Marshman's English Nisi Prius Reports 卡林顿和马什曼的英国(巡回)民事审判判例汇编

Carth. Carthew's English King's Bench Reports (英)卡肖的英国高等法院(王座法庭)判例汇编

Carv. Carr. Carver's Treatise on the Law Relating to the Carriage of Goods by Sea 卡弗的有关货物海运法律的论文

CAS Court of Arbitration for Sport 国际体育仲裁院

C. A. S. Collision Avoidance Systems (汽车用)防撞装置

Case & Com. Case and Comment 判例和评论

CAT catalog 目录,一览表

CAUS Color Association of the United States 美国黑人协会

C. A. V. curia advisari vult, the court deliberated before pronouncing judg(e)ment 法院延期判决,(英)法庭将考虑该事项(考虑后再判决)

CB cash book 现金账;Commercial Bank 商业银行;County Borough (英)郡府(或译:郡自治市);Cumulative Bulletin of Internal Revenue Service (美)国内(或地方)税务局加重税务公报

C. B. English Common Bench Reports, Manning, Granger & Scott 英国高等民事法庭判例汇编,曼宁,格兰杰和斯科特;Chief Baron (英)首席理财法院法官;English Common Bench Reports (1840-1856) 英国高等民事法庭判例汇编(1840—1856)

C/B clean bill 光票

CBA collective bargaining agreement 集体谈判协定

C. B. D. (CBD) Cash before delivery 交货前付政

C. B. Dig. U. S. Customs Bureau Digest of Customs and Related Law 美国海关署的关税和有关法规判决摘要汇编

C. B. N. S. English Common Bench Reports, New Series, by John Scott 约翰·斯科特的英国高等民事法庭判例汇编,新丛书

C. B. O. Congressional Budget Office 国会预算局

C. B. R. Canadian Bankruptcy Reports (Anno.) 加拿大破产判例汇编(注释本);Cour du Banc de la Reine (Quebec) 加拿大女王法庭(魁北克)

CC Connected Case, different case from case cited but arising out of same subject matter or intimately connected therewith (Used in Sheperd's Citations) 相关判例:与援引的判例不同,而是出于相同的标的或与此案密切相关的判例(谢泼德援引中使用)

C. C. carbon copy 复写副本;cash credit 银行现金透支;Circuit Court 巡回法庭;City Council 市议会;City Court 城市法院;City Councillor 市议员;Civil

Code 民法典; Civil Court 民事法庭; Code Civil Franqais (or Code Napoleon) 法国民法典(或拿破仑法典); Consular Clerk 领事馆职员,领事秘书; County Council （英）郡议会; County Court （英）郡法院,县法院; County Court Appeals （英）郡上诉法院; Court of Criminal Appeal （英）刑事上诉法院; Credentials Committee （联合国）全权证书审查委员会; Crown Colony （英）直辖殖民地

C. C. A. Centre for Commercial Arbitration 商业仲裁中心; Circuit Court of Appeal （美）巡回上诉法院; County Council Association （英）郡议会联合会; Court of Criminal Appeal （英）刑事上诉法院

CCAA Commonwealth Conciliation and Arbitration Act （澳）《联邦调解仲裁法》

CCAC Commonwealth Conciliation and Arbitration Commission （澳）联邦调解仲裁委员会

C. C. B. Code de Commerce Belge 比利时商法典

CCC Copyright Clearance Center （美）版权使用费结算中心(民间组织); Customs Cooperation Council （美）"海关合作理事会",WCO 前身

C. C. C. Canadian Criminal Cases 加拿大刑事判例; Central Criminal Court(Old Bailey) （英）中央刑事法庭(老贝利)

C. C. C. Bull Bulletin,Committee on Criminal Courts' Law & Procedure, Assn. of the Bar, City of New York 纽约市刑事法庭法律和程序委员会,律师协会公报

CC Comm Proc Code of Civil and Commercial Procedure 民事商事诉讼法典

C. C. F. Contract Case Federal (CCH) （美）联邦合同案件(CCH)

CCH （C. C. H.） Commerce Clearing House,Inc. （美）商业票据(或情报)交换所(公司)(活页服务的出版社)

CCI constabulary criminal investigation 保安人员刑事调查

C. C. J. Circuit Court Judge 巡回法庭法官; County Court Judge （英）郡法院法官

CCL Creative Common License （美）知识共享协议

C. C. N Chief Counsel Notice (IRS) 首席律师代表声明(或通知)

CCP (C. C. P.) Court of Common Pleas （英）高等民事法庭; Code of Civil Procedure, Calif. （美）加州民事诉讼法

C. C. P. A. Court of Customs and Patent Appeals （美）海关和专利上诉法院; Court of Customs and Patent Appeals Reports 海关和专利上诉法院判例汇编

CCPA Consumer Credit Protection Act （美）消费者信贷保护法

CCPIT China Council for Promotion of International Trade 中国国际贸易促进委员会

CC Proc Code of Civil Procedure 民事诉讼法典

C. C. R. Commission of Civil Rights （美）民权委员会; County Court Rules 郡（县）法院规程

CCRC Committee on Commercial Relation with China （美）对华贸易关系委员会

C. Cr. Pr. Code of Criminal Procedure 刑事诉讼法典

CCS Carbon Capture and Storage 碳捕捉与封存技术

Cd. command paper (1900-1918) （英）诏书;政府文件(1900—1918)

CD cash discount 现金贴现; certificate of delivery 交货单,交货证明书; certificate of deposit （可转让）存款证; civil defense 民防; Commerce Department （美）商业部; Committee on Disarmament 裁军委员会; complaint desk 申诉处,检举处; condemned 报废的,没收的,查封的; confidential document 密件,机密文件; contracting definition 合同确定(阶段); Corps Diplomatique （法）外交使团; creditor's damage 债权人损失; Chancery Division （英）大法官法庭

C/D certificate of delivery 交货证明书

CDA Camp David Agreement 戴维营协定; Chargé d'Affaires 代办; Communications Decency Act （美）《正当通讯法》

CDAAI Chargé d'Affaies ad Interim 临时

代办

CDC Center for Disease Control 疾病控制中心；Civil Defense Committee 民防委员会

C. D. C. Commissioners of the District of Columbia （美）哥伦比亚特区专员（市长或副市长）

C. D. Cal. Circuit Division, California （美）加利福尼亚州巡回庭

C. D. E. Cahiers de Droit Européen 欧洲法律手册

CDI Commission du Droit International 国际法委员会

CDM clean development mechanism 清洁发展机制

CDR cargo delivery receipt 交货收据

CD-ROM compact disk read only memory 高密度只读光盘（只读存储器）

CDS Credit Defraud Swap 信用违约互换

CEA Council of Economic Advisers 经济顾问委员会；Commodity Exchange Authority 货物交换局

CECC Committee of Expert Crime on Cyberspace 网络空间犯罪（研究）专家委员会

C. E. D. Canadian Encyclopedic Digest 加拿大综合性判决摘要汇编

C. E. Gr. C.E.Greene, New Jersey Equity Reports (vols.16-27) C. E. 格林，新泽西衡平法院判例汇编（16—27卷本）

Cent. Dig. Century Digest 百年判决摘要汇编（1658—1896）

CEO Chief Executive Officer 首席执行官，董事长，总裁

CEQ Council on Environmental Quality （美）国家环境质量委员会（总统咨询和协调机构，依《国家环境政策法》设立的）

CER carbon emission reduction (accords) 碳减排量

CERCLA Comprehensive Environmental Response Compensation and Liability Act （美）1980年《全面环境反应赔偿和责任法（案）》

Cert. certiorari 调卷令

Cert. den. Certiorari denied 调卷令被拒绝，调卷令被驳回

C. E. S. Court of Exchequer (Sc.) （苏格兰）理财法院

CETA Comprehensive Employment and Training Act 《综合性就业和培训法》

CETEX Committee on Contamination by Extra-terrestrial Exploration 陆外探测污染委员会；地球外探测造成污染问题委员会

Cf. confer 比较，参见

C. F. Code Forestier Francais 法国森林法典；common fund 共同基金；Consul de France 法国领事；counterpart fund 对等基金

C & F Cost and Freight 成本加货运价

CFA Consumer Federation of America 美洲消费者联盟

CFC Controlled Foreign Corporation 受控外国公司

C. F. & I. cost, freight and insurance 到岸价格，成本加运费及保险费价格

CFIUS Committee of Foreign Investment US （美）外国投资委员会

CFM Council of Foreign Ministers 外交部长会议，外长会议

CFN confirmation 证实

c. f. o. coast for orders 指命海岸（租船用语）

CFPA Consumer Financial Protection Agency （美）消费者金融保护局（2009年6月创立）

CFR Cumulative Failure Rate 累积平均故障率；Code of Federal Regulations 《美国联邦法规汇编》

C. F. R. Council on Foreign Relations （美）外交学会

C. F. S. Container Freight Station 集装箱货运站

CFTC Commodity Futures Trading Commission 货物期货交易委员会

CG Coast Guard （美）海岸警卫队；Commissioner General 高级专员；conference of Governors （美）州长会议；Consul General 总领事

CGA cargo's proportion of general average

共同海损货物分摊额
CGCMS Special Court-Martial, Coast Guard (U. S.) （美）（海岸警卫队）特别军事法庭
CGL Comprehensive General Liability （美）主要承认事故型责任保险
CGL policy Comprehensive General-liability Policy/commercial general-liability policy （美）商业综合责任保单
C. G. O. Committee of Good Offices 调停委员会
CGR Coast Guard Regulations (U. S.) （美）海岸警卫队法规
CGT capital gains tax 资本收益税
ch. chapter 章
Ch. Chancellor's Court (Eng.) （英）大法官法庭; Court of Chancery, New Jersey （美）衡平法院（新泽西州）; English Law Reports (1891 -) 英国判例汇编（1891—）; Chancery Appeals 大法官法庭上诉判例
CH (Ch.) Chairman 主席，委员长; chancellor （英）大臣，校长;（联邦德国的）总理; Chancellor's Court (Eng.) （英）衡平法院; Chancery Court or Division （美）衡平法院或法庭; chapter 章,（大写）宪章; Clearing House 票据交换所; Court of Chancery, New Jersey （美）新泽西衡平法院; Custom House 海关
Chan. Ct. Chancery Court （英）大法官法庭,（美）衡平法院
Chand. Chandler's Reports (vols. 20, 38 - 44, New Hampshire) （美）钱德勒的判例汇编（新罕布什尔州 20, 38—44 卷本）; Chandler's Reports (Wisconsin 1849 - 1852) （美）钱德勒的判例汇编（威斯康星州 1849—1852）
Chan. Rep. C. Reports in Chancery(1615- 1712) 大法官法庭的判例汇编（1615—1712）
Ch. App. (cas.) Chancery Appeal Cases 大法官法庭上诉判例; English Law Reports 英国判例汇编
31 Charles 2, 1679. （英）查尔士二世第 31 个执政年, 1679 年

Chase's St. Chase's Statutes at Large, Ohio （美）俄亥俄州蔡斯的法规大全
Chase, Steph, Dig. Ev. Chase on Stephens, Digest of Evidence 蔡斯论斯蒂芬的证据判决摘要汇编
Ch. Cas. English Cases in Chancery 英国大法官法庭判例
Ch. D. Chancery Division （英）（高等法院的）大法官法庭; Law Reports Chancery Division, Eng. （英）大法官法庭判例汇编
Chf J. Chief Justice 审判长，首席法官; 法院院长
Child. Ct. Children's Court 儿童法院
CHIPS Clearing House Interbank Payments System （美）银行间支付清算系统
Chit. Bl. Comm. Chitty's Edition of Blackstone's Commentaries 布莱克斯通评论的奇蒂版
Chit. Cont. Chitty on Contracts 奇蒂论合同
Chit. Cr. Law Chitty's Criminal Law 奇蒂的刑法
CHPG Constabulary Highway Patrol Group 警察公路巡逻队
chq. cheque 支票
CHR Commission on Human Rights （联合国）人权委员会
Ch. Repts. Reports in Chancery 大法官法庭判例汇编; Irish Chancery Reports 爱尔兰大法官法庭判例汇编
CHS crime on high seas 公海犯罪
Chy. Div. Chancery Division （英）（高等法院的）大法官法庭
C. J. Chief Justice 审判长，首席（大）法官; 法院院长; Chief Judge 主审法官, 审判长; Circuit Judge 巡回法官
CI Consumer International 国际消费者联盟 "International Organization of Consumer Unions" 的简称
CI channel islands （英）海峡群岛; Consular Invoice 领事签证发票; cost and insurance 成本加保险费价格
C/I certificate of insurance 保险证明书
CIA Central Intelligence Agency （美）中央情报局; Cooper's International Union of North America 库珀的北美国际联盟
C. I. A cash in advance 预付现金

CIAAC Commission Interamericaine d'Arbitrage Commercial 泛美商业仲裁委员会
CIC community interest Company （英）社区利益公司（以社区利益为目标）(2004年成立)
CID Committee on Interest and Dividends （美）利益和债息委员会；Criminal Investigation Department （警察局的）刑事调查部（处）
CIDA Comite Intergouvernemental du Droit d'Auteur 政府间版权委员
CIDC Comite International de Droit Compare 国际比较法委员会
Cie. Compagnie 公司
CIEP Council on International Economic Policy 国际经济政策委员会
CIETAC China International Economic and Trade Arbitration Commission 中国国际经济和贸易仲裁委员会
CIF (C. I. F., c. i. f.) cost, insurance and freight 到岸价格（成本、保险费加运费）
C. I. F. and C. Cost, Insurance, Freight and Commission 到岸价格加佣金价
C. I. F. and E. Cost, Insurance, Freight and Exchange 到岸价格加汇费价
C. I. F. and I. Cost, Insurance, Freight and Interest 到岸价格加利息价
C. I. F (CIF) and W Cost, Insurance, Freight and War Risks 到岸价格加战争险价
CIJ Commission Internationale de Juristes 国际法学家委员会；Cour International de Justice （联合国）国际法院
CILS Center for International Legal Studies 国际法学研究中心
CIME Committee on International Investment and Multination Enterprises 国际投资和多国企业委员会
Cin. R. Cincinnati Superior Court Reporter, Ohio （美）辛辛那提高等法院判例汇编（俄亥俄州）
CIO cash in order 订货时付款
CIP Carriage and Insurance Paid to 货运与保险支付
CIR (Cir.) Circuit Court of Appeals 巡回上诉法院；Commission on Intergovernmental Relations （美）政府间关系委员会
Circ. C. Circuit Court 巡回法庭（院）
circe. circumstance 事情，情况，详情
Circ. J. Circuit Judge 巡回审判法官
Cir. Ct. Circuit Court 巡回法院（庭）
Cir. Ct. App. Circuit Court of Appeal 巡回上诉法院
Cir. Ct. Dec. Circuit Court Decisions 巡回法院判决
Cir. Ct. Dec. Circuit Court Decision, Ohio （美）巡回法庭判决（俄亥俄州）
Cir. Ct. Rule Circuit Court Rule 巡回法庭规程
CIRDI Centre International pour le Réglement des Différends Relatifs aux Investissements 国际投资纠纷仲裁中心
Cir. Proc. R. Civil Procedure Reports, N. Y. （美）纽约民事诉讼判例汇编
Cis (CIS) Commonwealth of Independent State 独联体
Cis (CIS.) Congressional Information Service 国会信息服务部
CISG the Convention on Contracts for the International Sale of Goods 《联合国国际货物销售合同公约》
Cit. The Citator 援引集，引证集；citation 引证，引文，传讯，传票；cited 引证的
CIT The Court of International Trade （美）国际贸易法庭
CITEJA Comité International Technique d'Experts Juridiques Aériens 国际航空法专家技术委员会
CITO Charter of International Trade Organization 国际贸易组织宪章
City Crim. Ct. Act New York City Criminal Court Act 纽约城刑事法庭法
City Ct. City Court 城市法院
City. Ct. R. City Court Reports (New York) （美）城市法院判例汇编（纽约）
Civ Civil 民事的；Civile (for civil cases) 民事判例；Texas Civil Appeals Reports （美）得克萨斯州民事上诉判例汇编
CJ chief judge or justice 首席法官或首席大法官；circuit judge 巡回法庭法官；Cor-

pus Juris 法典,法令大全
C. J. Chief Justice 审判长,首席法官;法院院长;Circuit Judge 巡回法官;Corpus Juris 法典,《法令大全》;西方法律出版公司出版的《法律百科全书》第一版;Journal of the House of Commons （英）下议院公报,下议院议事录;Lord Chief Justice (Eng.) （英）首席法官,审判长,法院院长阁下
C. J. Ann. Corpus Juris Annotations 法律百科全书注释
C. J. Civ. Corpus Juris Civilis 《民法大全》《国法大全》
C. J. C. P. Chief Justice of Common Plea （英）高等民事法院首席法官
CJIA Comité Juridique International de l'Aviation 国际航空司法委员会
C. J. S. (CJS) Corpus Juris Secundum 《法律百科全书》,法律判例汇编大全
C. & K. Carrington and Kirwan's English Nisi Prius Reports 卡林顿和柯万的英国（巡回）民事审判判例汇编
CL Civil Law 民法,大陆法
C. L. Civil Law 民法;Compiled Laws 法律汇编;English Common Law Reports, American reprint 英国普通法判例汇编（美国再版）;Current Law Yearbook (1947) 现行法年鉴(1947);Irish Common Law Reports (17 vols.) 爱尔兰普通法判例汇编（卷17）
C/L circular letter 通报,传阅文件
Cl. clause 款,条款
CLA Computer Law Association 计算机法律协会;Copyright Licensing Agency 版权许可证贸易代理公司
C. L. A. I. T. Constitutions and Laws of American Indian Tribes 美国印第安部族的宪法与法规
CL. App. Clark's Appeal Cases, Eng. （英）克拉克的上诉判例（汇编）
Clark English House of Lords cases, by Clark 英国上议院判例汇集（克拉克编）
Clark & F. Clark and Finnelly's House of Lords Reports 克拉克和芬纳利的上议院判例汇编

Clark's Code Clark's Annotated Code of Civil Procedure, N. C. （美）北卡罗来纳,克拉克的民事诉讼注释法典
Clark's Reports (vol. 58 Alabama) 克拉克编判例汇编（亚拉巴马州,卷58）
Clay's Dig. Clay's Digest of Laws of Alabama （美）克莱的亚拉巴马法规的判决摘要汇编
CLC Civil Liability Convention (即International Convention of Civil Liability for Oil Pollution Damage 1969) 《国际油污损害民事责任公约》(1969年)
C. L. C. Current Law Consolidation (Eng.) （英）现行法律统一汇编
C. L. Ch. Common Law Chamber Reports (Ontario) （加）普通法法庭判例汇编(安大略)
C. L. D. Doctor of Civil Law 民法博士,罗马法博士
CLE Council of Legal Education 法律教育委员会,法制教育委员会;continuing legal education 继续法学教育
C. L. E. B. Continuing Legal Education of the Bar, University of California Extension. （美）加州大学附设律师法学进修教育部
CLEEC Committee on Legal Education Exchange with China 美中法学教育交流委员会
C. L. E. P. R. Council on Legal Education for Professional Responsibility 职业法律教育责任委员会
Clev. Law. Rep. Cleveland Law Reports 《克利夫兰判例汇编》
Clev. Insan. Clevenger, Medical Jurisprudence of Insanity of Forensic Psychiatry 克莱文杰,司法精神病学的精神病法医学
CLIRS （澳大利亚）全国计算机法学信息检索系统
CLK clerk 办事员,（法庭）书记员（官）
Clms. Claims 权利请求
CLO Chief Liaison Officer 首席联络官
CLODA closing date 结算日期,截止日期
CL of D Classification of Documents 文件

分类

C. L. P. Current Legal Problems 当今法律问题

CLPA Common Law Procedure Act （英）普通法诉讼条例

C. L. R. California Law Review 加利福尼亚法律评论; Canada Law Reports 加拿大判例汇编; Common Law Reports (1853-1855) (Eng.) （英）普通法判例汇编（1853—1855）; Commonwealth Law Reports (Aus.) 英联邦判例汇编（澳大利亚）; Crown Lands Reports, Queensland 英王室领地判例汇编，昆士兰（澳大利亚州名）; Current Law Reports (Palestine) 现行判例汇编（巴勒斯坦）; Cyprus Law Reports (1883) 塞浦路斯判例汇编（1883）

CLS Conference on the Law of the Sea 海洋法会议; Consular Law Society （美）领事法学会; Critical Legal Studies Movement （美）批判法律研究运动; Critical Legal Studies 批判法学派

CM (C. M.) Common Market （欧洲）共同市场; Court-Martial 军事法庭，军事法院

C/M chattel mortgage 动产抵押

C. M. A. Court of Military Appeals Reports (1951-1975) （美）军事上诉法庭判例汇编（1951—1975）

CMAAs Customs Manual Assistance Agreements 海关互助协定

CMC Cluster Munitions Coalition 集束弹药联盟

Cmd command 司令部，指挥部，部队，军区; Command Paper （英）诏书，政府文件（1919—1956）

CMI Convention Minitative Internationale 国际军事公约; Comité Maritime International 国际海事委员会

Cmm. (cmm.) communication 交通；通信，通讯

CMN Common Market Nations （欧洲）共同市场国家组织

cmnd command paper （英）诏书，政府文件（1956—）

CMO Court-Martial Order （美）军事法庭

命令

CMP Commissioner of Metropolitan Police （英）首都警察局长; Corps of Military Police （美）宪兵队

CMR Court-Martial Reports （美）军事法庭判例汇编

C. M. R. Court Martial Reports (1951-1977) （美）军事法庭判例汇编（1951—1977）

C., M. & R. Crompton, Meeson and Roscoe's English Exchequer Reports 克朗普顿、米森和罗斯科的英国理财法院判例汇编

C. N. Chinese Nationals 中国侨民; Code Napoléon(或 Civil Code) 《拿破仑法典》（或法国《民法典》）

CNC Conference of Non-aligned Countries 不结盟国家会议; councillor 参赞

CNCC China National Chartering Corporation 中国租船公司

CND condition 条件，情况

C. N. P. Cases at Nisi Prius （英）（巡回）民事审判判例（汇编）

CNU Charta des Nations Unies 联合国宪章

CNVA Committee for Nonviolent Action （美）非暴力行动委员会

cnvt convict 罪犯，囚徒

C. O. (co.) Coke's English King's Bench Reports 柯克的英国高等法院（王座法庭）判例汇编

C/O care of 由……转交; cash order 现金汇票

COAS Council of the Organization of American States 美洲国家组织理事会

COAU Charter of the Organization of African Unity 非洲统一组织宪章

c. o. b close of business 停止营业

Cobb. Dig. Cobb's Digest of Statute Laws (Ga.) （美）科布的法规判决摘要汇编（佐治亚州）

Cobbey' Ann. St. Cobbey's Annotated Statutes, Neb. （美）柯贝的注释法规，内布拉斯加州

COBRA Consolidated Omnibus Budget Re-

conciliation Act of 1985　《1985年综合预算调节法》(美国联邦法律,解决雇主为雇员的医保问题)
COCOM　Coordinating Committee (Controlling Eastwest Trade)　(巴黎)(联合国)(控制东西方贸易的)统筹委员会
Co. Ct.　County Court　郡(县)法院
C. O. D.　cash on delivery　货到付款; certificate of deposit　存款单, 储蓄存单
Code. Civ.　Code Civile Francais　《法国民法典》(或《拿破仑法典》)
Code Civ. Proc.　Code of Civil Procedure　民事诉讼法典
Code Com. B.　Code de Commerce, Belge　《比利时商法典》
Code Com. I.　Code de Commerce, Italien　《意大利商法典》
Code Cr. Pro. (或 **Proc.**)　Code of Criminal Procedure　《刑事诉讼法典》
Code d'Instr. Crim.　Code d'Instruction Criminelle　(法)《刑事诉讼法典》
Code For.　Code Forestier Francais　《法国森林法典》
Code Gen. Laws　Code of General Laws　普通法规汇编
Code I.　Coded' Instruction Criminelle　(法)《刑事诉讼法典》
Co DEL　Committee for Democratic Election Laws　(美)争取民主选举法委员会
CODEL　Congressional Delegation　(美)国会代表团
Code La.　Civil Code of Louisiana　(美)《路易斯安那州民法典》
Code M.　Code municipal, Quebec　(加)《魁北克城市法典》
Code N. (或 **Nap.**)　Code Napoleon　《拿破仑法典》
Code of Civ. Proc.　Code of Civil Procedure　《民事诉讼法典》
Code P.　Code Penal　《刑法典》
Code P. C.　Code de Procedure Civile　(法)《民事诉讼法典》
Code Prac.　Code of Practice　(律师、医生)开业法规, 业务守则
Code Pro.　Code of Procedure　程序法
Code R. N. S.　Code Reports, New Series, N. Y.　汇典判例汇编, 新丛书, 纽约
Code Supp.　Supplement to the Code　汇典的补编
Cod. St.　Codified Statutes　汇编法规
CoEnCo　Committee for Environmental Conservation　(英)环境保护委员会
COGSA　Carriage of Goods by Sea Act　根据海上法的货运, (美)海上货运法
coh.　coheir　共同继承人
Co. Inst.　Coke's Institutes (Eng.)　(英)柯克的法学概要
COINTELPRO　counterintelligence program　反情报计划
COJ　Court of Justice of the European Economic Community　欧洲经济共同体法院
Coke　Coke's English King's Bench Reports　柯克的英国高等法院(王座法庭)判例汇编
COL　control　管制, 控制, 管理; cost of living　生活费
C. O. L. A.　cost of living adjustment　调整生活费; cost of living allowance　生活费津贴
Col. C. C.　Collyer's Chancery Cases, Eng.　(英)科利尔的大法官法庭判例(汇编)
Coll. & E. Bank　Collyer and Eaton's American Bankruptcy Reports　科利尔和伊顿的美国破产判例汇编
Colles　Colles' Cases in Parliament, Eng.　(英)科尔斯的议会中的判例
Colly　Collyer's English Chancery Cases　科利尔的英国大法官法庭判例汇编
Colo.　Colorado Reports　科罗拉多判例汇编
Colo. App.　Colorado Court of Appeals Reports　科罗拉多上诉法院判例汇编
Colq. Rom. Civ. Law　Colquhoun's Roman Civil Law　科尔库汉的罗马法
Colum. L. Rev.　Columbia Law Review　哥伦比亚法律评论
COMAT　Commercial Attache　商务专员, 商务参赞
COMBICONBILL　combined transport bill of lading　联运提单

COMBIDOC combined transport document 联运单据

Com. B. N. S. English Common Bench Reports, New Series 英国高等民事法庭判例汇编,新丛书

Com. Cas. Commercial Cases (1895-1941) (英格兰和威尔士)商业判例汇编(1895—1941);Commercial Cases (Eng.) (英)商业判例汇编;Company Cases (India) (印度)公司判例汇编

Com. Dec. Commissioners' Decisions 地方长官的决定

Com. Dig. Comyns' Digest of the Laws of England 科明斯的英格兰法规判决摘要汇编

Com. L. Commercial Law (Canada) 加拿大商法

Com. Law Commercial Law 商法,商业法

Comment Period Notice-and Comment Period (行政法上用语)通知和评论时期

Comm'r Commissioner 长官,专员;司法行政长官;委员;特派员

comp complete 完整的,完备的,全套的

Comp. Dec. Decisions of the Comptroller of the Treasury (U. S.) (美)国库审计官的决定

Comp. Gen. Comptroller General 总会计师,总审计长;Decisions of Comptroller General 总会计师的决定

Comp. Laws Compiled Laws 编纂的法规,汇编的法规

Comp. St. Compiled Statutes 编纂的制定法,制定法汇编

COMSAT (C. O. M. S. A. T.) Communications Satellite Corporation (美)通信卫星公司(根据1952年通信卫星法规建立的,该公司包括代表许多国家的几百个通信公司)

COMTRAC computer aided traffic control 计算机交通管制系统

Comyn Comyns' Digest (Eng.) (英)科明斯的判决摘要汇编

Comyns' Comyns' English King's Bench Reports 科明斯英国高等法院(王座法庭)判例汇编

Comyns' Dig Comyris' Digest (Eng.) (英)科明斯判决摘要汇编

con. 1.confidence 信任 2.convict 囚犯,有罪,判罪 3.contra 相反,相对;反对 4.constitutional 宪法的

Con. Conover's Reports (Wisconsin) (美)康诺弗的判例汇编(威斯康星州);Continuation of Rolle's Reports (2 Rolle) 罗尔的判例汇编的续篇(罗尔 2);Connoly, New York Criminal 康诺利,纽约罪犯

CON consul 领事

COND condition 条件,情况

Cond. Ch. R. Condensed English Chancery Reports 英国大法官法庭判例汇编缩略本

Cond. H. C. Conders Highway Cases 康德利(高速)公路判例(汇编)

Condo. Condominium 共管,共有权,共同管辖权

Cong. Congress (美)国会

Cong. Rec. Congressional Record (U. S.) (美)国会议事录

Conn. Connecticut Reports 康涅狄格判例汇编

CONREP Forensic Conditional Release Program (美)司法假释程序(1985年)

Const. Amend. Amendment to Constitution 宪法修改

constl. constitutional 宪法的,立宪的

constn. constitution 宪法

Const. Rep. Constitutional Reports, S. C. (美)合宪案判例汇编(最高法院)

Cont Contracts 合同(契约);Control(s) 控制,管制,管理

Cont. Cas. Fed. Contract Cases, Federal (美)联邦合同判例(汇编)

CONTU Commission on New Technological Use of Copyright Works (美)版权作品的新科技使用委员会

Cooke Cooke, Act book of the Ecclesiaslical Court of Whalley 库克,惠利宗教法庭条例集;Cooke's Cases of Practice, English Common Pleas 库克的英国高等民事法院诉讼实践判例;Cases under Sugden's Act

(1838)(Eng.) （英）根据萨格登法（1838）的判例；Cooke's Reports (vol. 3 Tennessee)(1811-1814) 库克的判例汇编（卷本3，田纳西州）(1811—1814)

Cooke B. L. Cooke's Bankrupt Law 库克的破产法规

Coop. Eq. Pl. Cooper's Equity Pleading 库珀的衡平法上的辩护

COP (cop.) copyright 版权；copyrighted 版权所有；custom of the port 港口惯例，商港习惯

COPA Child Online Protection Act （美）《儿童在线保护法》(1988年联邦制定法规)

C. O. P. E. (COPE) Committee on Political Education （美）政治教育委员会

Copp, Pub. Land Laws Copp's United States Public Land Laws 科波的美国公共土地法规(汇编)

COPR copyright 版权

copter helicopter 直升飞机

Copy. Bull Copyright Bulletin 版权公报

Copy. Dec. Copyright Decisions (1909-date) （美）版权判决（例）(1909年至今)

Corb. & D. Corbett & Daniell's Election Cases, Eng. （英）科贝特和丹尼尔的选举判例(汇编)

CORC Central Office Review Committee （美）中央审查委员会

C. O. R. E. (CORE) Congress of Racial Equality （美）争取种族平等大会(1942年詹姆斯•法默和芝加哥大学的一批学生创立的民权组织)

Co. Rep. Coke's English King's Bench Reports 柯克的英国高等法院（王座法庭）判例汇编

corp. corporation 公司；企业实体

Corp. C. Corporations Code 公司法

Corp. Jur. Civ. Corpus Juris Civilis 《民法大全》《国法大全》

Corpus Juris 法典,《法令大全》；西方法律出版公司出版的《法律百科全书》第一版

COS cash on shipment 装货付款；Chief of Staff 参谋长

COSA China Ocean Shipping Agency 中国外轮代理总公司

County Ct. County Court （英）郡(县)法院

County J. Ct. County Judge's Court （英）郡(县)(法官)法院

Cow. Cr. R. Cowen's Criminal Reports, N. Y. （美）考恩的刑事判例汇编,纽约

Cowell. Cowell's Law Dictionary 考埃尔的法律词典

Cox Cox's English Chancery Cases 考克斯英国的大法官法庭判例(汇编)

Cox, C. C. Cox's English Criminal Cases 考克斯的英国刑事判例(汇编)

Cox, Ch. Cox's English Chancery Cases 考克斯的英国大法官法庭判例

C. P. cash price 现金付款的最低价格；付现价格；Chief of Police 警察,警察局局长；Code of Civil Procedure 《民事诉讼法典》；Command Post 指挥所；Common Pleas （美）（某些州的）中级法院；（英）（旧时的）高等民事法院,普通民事诉讼；commercial paper 商业票据；Commission Paritaire 对等委员会；Contracting Parties 缔约方,缔约国；Convict Prison 监狱；cost price 成本价格,原价；Court of Probate （美）遗嘱检验法庭

C/P Charter Party 租船公司；counter purchase 对等购买；custom of the port 港口惯例,商港习惯

C. & P. Carrington and Payne's English Nisi Prius Reports 卡林顿和佩恩的英国巡回民事审判法庭判例汇编

C. P. A. Certified Public Accountant （美）（特许）会计师；Chartered Patent Agent 特许专利代理人；Civil Practice Act, New York （纽约）民事惯例法；Contract Price Adjustment 合同价格调整；Control of Pollution Act （英）污染控制法；Cour Permanente d'Arbitrage 常设仲裁法庭

CPC Communist Party of China 中国共产党

C. P. C. C. P. Cooper's English Chancery Practice Cases (1837-1838) C. P. 库珀的英国大法官法庭审判判例实务（汇编）(1837—1838)；Code de Procedure Civile

民事诉讼法典; Code of Civil Procedure, Quebec （加）民事诉讼法典,魁北克
CPCPIT Chinese People's Committee for Promotion of International Trade 中国国际贸易促进委员会（正式英译名为 China Council for Promotion of International Trade）
CPF Counter Part Fund 对等基金
C. P. I. Consumer Price Index （美）消费者物价指数
CPIA Criminal Procedure and Investigation Act （英）《刑事诉讼与侦察法》
C. P. L. R. Civil Practice Law and Rules （纽约）民事判例法和规则
C. Pr. Code of Procedure 诉讼法典; Code de Procedure Civile （法）《民事诉讼法典》
CPR Canadian Patent Reports 加拿大专利判例集（或汇编）
CPS Crown Prosecution Service （苏格兰）检察署
CPSC Consumer Products Safety Commission 消费者产品安全委员会
CPU Central Processing Unit 中心处理机
CR (C. R.) California Reports 加利福尼亚州判例汇编; creditor 债权人; Canadian Reports, Appeal Cases 加拿大上诉判例汇编; Chancery Reports Tempore Car. I to Queen Anne （英）查尔斯一世至安娜女王时期大法官法院判例汇编; Criminal Reports(Canada) （加）刑事判例汇编
Cr. Act Criminal Act 刑事法案,刑法;犯罪行为
Craig & P. Craig and Phillips' English Chancery Reports 克雷格和菲利普的英国大法官法庭判例汇编
Cranch, C. C. Cranch's Circuit Court Reports, U. S. （美）克兰奇的巡回法庭判例汇编
Cranch, Pat. Dec. Cranch's Patent Decisions U. S. （美）克兰奇的专利判例（汇编）
CRC Chinese Red Cross 中国红十字会; Civil Right Commission （美）民权委员会
Cr. Code Criminal Code 刑法典
CREST International Committee on Reactor Safety Technology 国际反应堆安全技术委员会
CRI Croix-Rouge Internationale 国际红十字会; Critical Race Theory 批判种族理论
Crim. criminal 刑事的,罪犯
Crim. App. Court of Criminal Appeals 刑事上诉法院
Crim. Law Criminal Law 刑法
Crim. Pro. Criminal Procedure 刑事诉讼
C. Rob. Adm. Charles Robinson's English Admiralty Reports 查尔斯·鲁宾逊的英国海事判例汇编
Cromp. Just. Crompton's Office of Justice of the Peace 克朗普顿的治安法官办公室
Crompt. Star Chamber Cases by Cromptom 克朗普顿编的星室法院判例（汇编）
Crosul. Pat. Cas. Croswell's Collection of Patent Cases, U. S. （美）克罗斯威尔的专利判例集
CRP Committee to Reelect the President 改选总统委员会; Conference Room Paper 会议文件
Cr. Proc. Act. Criminal Procedure Act 刑事诉讼法
CRR Corporate Reorganization Reports, Inc. 公司重组判例汇编(社团公司)
CRS Congressional Research Service （美）国会研究所,其前身为国会参考所（congressional Reference Service）
Cr. St. Criminal Statutes 刑事法规
CRT Critic Race Theory （美）种族批判法学; Critical Race Theory 批判种族理论（法学界内部改革运动）
CRTN correction 更正
Cruise's Dig. Cruise's Digest of the Law of Real Property 克鲁斯的不动产法判决摘要汇编
C. S. (Cs.) capital stock 股本; civil services 文职人员,文官(制),公务人员,行政机构; Compiled Statutes 法规汇编; Consolidated Statutes 统一法规; Consul 领事; Consulate 领事馆; Court of Session, Scotland （苏格兰）高等法院
CSAAS Child-Sexual-Abuse Accommodation syndrome 儿童性侵犯融通综合征
C. S. B. C. Consolidated Statutes, British

Columbia （英）哥伦比亚统一法规
CSC Civil Service Commission （美）文官委员会
C. S. C. Canada Supreme Court 加拿大最高法院; Consolidated Statutes of Canada 加拿大统一法规
CSE agency Child-Support Enforcement agency 儿童抚养培育费强制执行机构
CSG council of state government （美）州政府委员会
CSI Council of the Securities Industry 证券业理事会; Container Security Initiative （美国海关的）"集装箱安全倡议"
CSJAGE Assistant Judge Advocate General for Procurement (Army) （军事法庭）助理军法官,助理军法检察官; Contract Division Office of Judge Advocate General of Army 军法官合同部办公室
C. S. Q. N. conditio sine qua non "如无前者即无后者"的关系,不可缺少的条件
CSR Corporate Social Responsibility 企业社会责任
CSRA of 1994 Child-Support Recovery Act of 1994 《1994年儿童抚养培育费追索法》
C. S. S. B. Civil Service Selection Board （英）文官选拔委员会
CSSDA Council for Social Science Data Archives （美）社会科学资料档案委员会
Ct. (ct.) Court 法院; circuit 巡回审判区; 巡回
CTA cum testamento annexo (with will annexed) 遗嘱附件; China Trade Association （美国）对华贸易协会; US Courts of Appeals Cases Database 美国上诉法院判例数据(库)
Ct. App. Court of Appeals 上诉法院
Ct. Cl. Court of Claims Reports 权利申诉法院判例汇编
Ct. Cl. (Cla.) Court of Claims, U. S. （美）索赔法院,权利申诉法院
Ct. Cl. Act Court of Claims Act 权利申诉法院法
Ct. Cls. R. Court of Claims Reports （美）权利申诉法院判例汇编

Ct. Com. Pl. (Pleas) Court of Common Pleas （美）普通法院,（英）民诉高等法院
Ct. Crim. App. Court of Criminal Appeal (Eng.) （英）刑事上诉法院
Ct. Cust. App. Court of Customs Appeals Reports (1919-1929) 海关法庭上诉判例汇编(1919—1929)
Ct. Cust. & Pat. App. Court of Customs & Patent Appeals 海关和专利上诉法院
Ct. Err. & App. Court of Errors and Appeals 上诉法院,对审判上错误的上诉法院
Ct. Errors and App. Court of Errors and Appeals (New Jersey) （美新泽西州）对审判上错误的上诉法院; 上诉法院
Ct. Gen. Sess. Court of General Sessions 按季开审法庭
Ct. Just. Court of Justiciary 司法法院
C. T. L. constructive total loss 推定全损
c. t. l. o. constructive total loss only 推定全损险
Ct/O. Court Order 法庭命令
CTO combined transport operator 联合运输营业人
Ct. of App. Court of Appeals 上诉法院
Ct. of Cls. U. S. Court of Claims （美）权利申诉法院
Ct. of Com. Pleas. Court of Common Pleas （美）普通法院,（英）民事高等法院
Ct. of Sp. App. Court of Special Appeals 特别上诉法院
C-TPAT Customs-Trade Partnership Against Terrorism 美国"海关商界反恐计划"
Ct. Rev. Court Review (American Judge Assoc.) 《法庭评论》(美国法官协会)
Cts. & Jud. Proc. Courts and Judicial Proceedings 法院和司法程序
Cty. Ct county court 郡（县）法院
CUN Charter of the United Nations 联合国宪章
Cust. A. (或 **App**) United States Customs Appeals 美国海关上诉(判例汇编)
Cust. App. United States Customs Appeals 美国海关上诉(判例汇编)

CVD countervailing duty 抵消关税
CVDW countervailing duty waiver 抵消关税豁免权
CVRA Crime Victims' Rights Act （美）《犯罪受害人权利法》(2004年)
C. W. O cash with order 现金订货
CXT common external tariff 共同对外关税率
CY copy 副本, 抄本
Cyc. Cyclopedia of Law & Procedure 法律和诉讼程序法百科全书
Cyc. Ann. Cyclopedia of Law & Procedure Annotations 法律和诉讼程序法注释百科全书
Cyc. Dict. Cyclopedic Law Dictionary 百科法律词典
C. Z. C.（或 **Code**） Canal Zone Code 运河区域法典
C. Z. M. A. Coastal Zone Management Act （美）沿海地区管理条例（指1972年由国会颁布的一个联邦规则, 鼓励各个州制定法律制度以保卫沿海土地和水产资源）

D

D datum 数据,资料; date 日期; decree 法令,政令; deed of arrangement （债务人与债权人之间缓付债务的）协议契约; defendant 被告; democrat 民主主义者,（美）民主党员; department 部,司,局,系; digest 判决摘要汇编; Dismissed, appeal from the same case dismissed 驳回, 因相同(同一)案情被驳回的上诉; district 地区; District Court (Federal) （美）（联邦）地区法院; Court of Divorce and Matrimorial Causes (Eng.) （英）离婚及婚姻法院; Democrat 民主党
D. A. day after acceptance 承兑后……日; delayed action (bomb) 定时炸弹; deposit account 存款账户; District Attorney （美）地区律师;（政府或国家的）地区检察官
D/A documents against acceptance 承兑交单
Daily Transc. Daily Transcript 每日官方（诉讼）记录
Dak Dakota Reports (Territorial) （美）达科他州（或地区的）判例汇编
Dal. Daly's Reports (New York) （美）戴利的判例汇编（纽约）; Benloe and Dalison's Common Pleas Reports (1486-1580) (Eng.)（英）本洛和达利森的高等民事法院判例汇编(1486—1580); Dalison's Common Pleas Reports (Eng.) （英）达利森的高等民事审判法院判例汇编
Dal. C. P. Dalison's Common Pleas, Eng. （英）达利森的高等民事审判法院
Dall. Dalls, U. S. Supreme Court Reports 达拉斯（宾夕法尼亚州）; Dalls (Pa.)
Dallam. Digest of laws of Texas 得克萨斯法规的案例摘要; Dallam's Opinions (Tex.) 达拉姆的判决意见书
Dall. Dig. Dallam's Digest and Opinions, Tex （美）达拉姆的判决摘要汇编和判决意见(得克萨斯州)
Dan. Dana's Reports (31-39, KY.) （美）达纳的判例汇编（肯塔基 31—39）; Daniels' Compendium Compensation Cases (Eng.) （英）丹尼尔斯的简要补偿判例(汇编); Danill's Excheq. in Equity Reports (Sc.)（苏格兰）丹尼尔的衡平法的理财判例汇编; Danner's Reports (42 Alabama) （美）丹纳的判例汇编（亚拉巴马州 42）
Dane's Abr. Dane's Abridgment of American Law 戴恩的美国法节略本
Daniell, Ch. Prac. Daniell's Chancery Pleading and Practice 丹尼尔的大法官法庭辩护和诉讼程序
D. A. P. Directorate of Accident Prevention （英）（飞机）驾驶安全管理局
DAP Application for Writ of Error Dis-

missed by Agreement of Parties　(英)根据当事人协议要求撤销纠正错误令状的申请

Dass. Ed.　Dassler's Edition, Kansas Reports　(美)堪萨斯州判例汇编,达斯勒版

DATA　Defense Air Transportation Administration　(美)(商务部)国防空运局

DATT　defense attaché　武官

Davis, Cr. Law　Davis Criminal Law　戴维斯刑法

Dawson's Code　Dawson's Code of Civil Procedure, (Colo.)　(美)道森的民事诉讼法(科罗拉多州)

Dayton　Dayton Ohio Reports　(美)戴登俄亥俄州判例汇编

D. B.　daily bulletin　每日公报,每日公告; day book　日记账,日志; depth bomb　深水炸弹; dock brief　(英)律师给无钱被告的免费辩护

d/b/a　doing business as　做生意如同(等同于一个商号名称,如 John James d/b/a James Productions)

DBS　Direct Broadcast Satellite　直接广播卫星

DC　District Court　(美)(联邦)地区法庭

D. C.　Death Certificate　死亡证书; Defense Council　国防委员会; Deputy Commissioner　副专员; Deputy Consul　副领事; detention clause　(租船)阻留条款,(装卸货)延迟条款; deviation clause　变更航线条款; Diplomatic Corps　外交使团; Disarmament Commission (UN)　(联合国)裁军委员会; District Commissioner　(英)区行政长官,区专员; District Court　(美)地方法院,(联邦)地区法院; District of Columbia　哥伦比亚特区; draft card　征兵卡,征兵证; Treasury Department Circular (U. S.)　(美)财政部通告

D. C.　District of Columbia Reports　(美)哥伦比亚特区判例汇编

D/C　discount　折扣,贴现

DCA　Defense Communication Agency　(美)国防通讯局; Department of Civil Aviation　(澳)民用航空部

D. & C.　Pennsylvania District & County Reports　宾夕法尼亚地区和县判例汇编

D. C. A.　Dorion's Queen's Bench Reports (Canada)　(加拿大)多里昂的后座法庭判例汇编

DCAA　Defense Contract Audit Agency　(美)国防合同审计局

D. C. App.　District of Columbia Appeals Reports　(美)哥伦比亚特区上诉判例汇编

D. CBA　the Bar Association of the District of Columbia　(美)哥伦比亚特区律师协会

DCC　digital control computer　数字控制计算机

D. C. C.　Diocesan Consistory Court　(英)主教管区宗教法庭

DCCA　District of Columbia Compensation Act　(美)哥伦比亚特区补偿法

D. C. C. E.　District of Columbia Code Encyclopedia　(美)哥伦比亚特区法规百科全书

D. C. Cir.　District of Columbia Court of Appeals Cases　(美)哥伦比亚特区上诉法院判例(汇编)

D. C. Code Encycl.　(West)District of Columbia Code Encyclopedia　(美)哥伦比亚特区法规百科全书(西方版)

D. C. 2d　Pennsylvania District and County Reports, Second Series　(美)宾夕法尼亚州地区和县判例汇编,第二套丛书

D. C. J.　District Court Judge　(美)地区法院法官

D. C. L.　Doctor of Canon Law　教会法学博士; Doctor of Civil Law　民法学博士; Doctor of Comparative Law　比较法学博士

DCM　Deputy Chief of Mission　(外交使团)副团长; District Court-Martial　地方军事法庭

D. C. Mun. App.　Municipal Court of Appeals, D. C.　(美)市上诉法院(哥伦比亚特区)

D & coh　daughter and coheiress　女儿及女性共同继承人

D. Ct.　District Court(usually U. S.)　(美)

地区法院

D. & C. 4th Pennsylvania District & County Reports Forth Series 宾夕法尼亚地区和县判例汇编第四套丛书

D. 2d Appellate Division, Second Series, N. Y. 纽约上诉庭判例汇编,第二套丛书

DD demand draft 即期汇票;Department of Defense (美)国防部;differential duties 差别关税;direct deal 直(接)销(售)

D/D (D/d) delivered at docks 码头交货;demand draft 即期汇票,汇票;documentary draft ary 押汇汇票,跟单汇票

D & D deaf and dumb (美)又聋又哑;drunk and disorderly (美)醉酒后扰乱治安的

DDA Doha Development Agenda 多哈发展议程

D. D. C. District Court, District of Columbia (美)哥伦比亚特区的地方法院

DDD deadline delivery date 交货最后截止日期

DEA Drug Enforcement Administration 毒品强制管理处

Deb. Debates (i. e. Parliamentary debates) 辩论(即议会的辩论)

Debt. & Cred. Debter and Creditor 债务人和债权人

Dec. decision 决议,判例,判决

Dec. Ch. Decisions from the Chair (Parliamentary) (Eng.) (英)议院议长的决定

Dec. Comm'r Pat. Decisions of the Commissioner of Patent 专利署署长的判决

Dec. Dig. Decennial Digest (美)十年判决摘要汇编

De Gex, J. & S. De Gex, Jones and Smith's English Chancery Reports 德·捷克斯,琼斯和史密斯的英国大法官法庭判例汇编

Del. Term R. Delaware Term Reports (美)特拉华州(高级法院)开庭期判例汇编

den. app. denying appeal 驳回上诉

Denver L. N. Denver Legal News (美)丹佛市法律新闻

Detroit L. Detroit Lawyer (美)底特律市律师

Dev. Ct. Cl. Devereux's Reports, Court of Claims, U. S. 美国德佛罗的权利申诉法院(索赔法院)判例汇编

Dev. Eq. Devereux's Equity (1826–1834) (N. C.) (美)德佛罗的衡平法(1826—1834)(北卡罗来纳州)

DF dead freight 空舱费

DFA Department of Foreign Affairs 外交部

D. F. M. Diploma in Forensic Medicine 法医学毕业文凭

DG director general 总干事;drafting group 起草小组

DGCL Delaware General Corporation Law (美)特拉华州一般公司法

DHS Department of Homeland Security (美)国家安全部

DI double insurance 双重保险

DIA Defense Intelligence Agency 国防情报局

Dickens Dickens' English Chancery Reports 迪肯斯的英国大法官法庭判例汇编

Dick. L. R. (Penn.) Dickinson Law Review (Pennsylvania) (美)《宾夕法尼亚迪金逊法律评论》

Dict. Droit Civil Dictionnaire Droit Civil 民法词典

di. et fi. dilecto et fideli 给他所爱的和忠实的

Dig. Digest 法规汇编,判决摘要汇编,(罗马法)学说汇纂;Digest of writ's 令状摘要汇编;Digesta of Justinian 查士丁尼法学家学说摘要汇编

Dig. Fla. Thompson's Digest of Laws, Fla. (美)汤普森的法规判决摘要汇编,佛罗里达州

Dig. St. English Digest of the Statutes, Ark. 英国的法规判决摘要汇编,阿肯色州

Dill. Laws Eng. & Am. Dillon's Laws and Jurisprudence of England and America 狄龙的英、美法规和法理学

Dirl. Dec. Dirleton's Decisions, Sc. (苏格兰)迪尔顿的判例(汇编)

Dist. Ct. District Court (State) (美)(州)地区法院

Dist. Ct. App. District Court of Appeal (美)地区上诉法院

Div. dividend 股息,红利,债息; division (英监狱中犯人待遇的)分级;(英)分庭区域;选区; divinity 神学,神学院; divorce proceedings 离婚手续

DJ District Judge (美)联邦地区法院或地方初审法院法官

DKt. Docket 判决记录;(美)法院的案件表;议事日程,备审案件目录表

D. L. R. Dominion Law Reports (Canada) (加)自治领判例汇编

DM diplomatic mail 外交邮件; Diplomatic Mission 外交使团; direct mail 直接邮寄,(广告)直接邮寄用户

DMCA Digital Millennium Copyright Act (美)《数字千年版权法》(1998年)(联邦法)

DN domain name 域名

DNA Deoxyronucleic acid 脱氧核糖核酸

DNS Domain Name System 域名系统

DO delivery order 交货单,栈单

DOA Directory of open access journals 开放资源共享

D. O. A. (DOA) date of arrival 到达日期; date of availability 有效期限; dead on arrival 送达医院时已经死去(警察或验尸报告常用语)

DOAJ Directory of open access journals 开放资料指南,开放资源共享

DOB date of birth 出生日期

DOC Department of Commerce (美)商业部; document 文件,单据

d. o. d. date of death 死亡日期; died of disease 病死,病故

DOD died of disease 因病死亡; Department of Defense (美)国防部

Dods. Dodson's Admiralty Reports (165 Eng.Reprint), Eng. (英)多德森的海事法判例汇编(英国再版165)

DOE Department of Energy 能源部

DOF delivery on field 当地交货

D of T Deed of Trust 信托书,委托书

DOI Department of Interior (美)内政部

DOJ Department of Justice (美)司法部

DOM domicile 住处,户籍

DOMA Defense of Marriage Act 婚姻法的辩护理由

Dom. Civ. Law Domat's Civil Law 多迈特的民法

Dom. L. R. Dominion Law Reports, Can. (加拿大)自治领判例汇编

Dom. Proc. Domus Procerum 贵族院,上院,上议院

DOS Department of State (美)国务院; disk operating system 磁盘操作系统

DOT Department of Oversea Trade (英)海外贸易部; Department of Transportation (美)运输部; Department of Treasury (美)财政部

Doug. Douglas' English King's Bench Reports 道格拉斯英国高等法院(王座法庭)判例汇编

Dougl. El. Cas. Douglas' Election Cases, Eng. (英)道格拉斯选举判例(汇编)

Dow & C. Dow and Clark's English House of Lord's Cases 道和克拉克的英国上院判例(汇编)

Dowl. & L. Dowling & Lowndes' English Bail Court Reports 道林和朗兹的英国保释法庭判例汇编

DP direct port 直达港口; displaced person 战时流民(指因战争无家可归的人); document against payment 付款交单,支付书; duty-paid (货物)已缴税的; Direct payments 直接支付

D. P. (Dom. Proc.) Domus Procerum 上议院

D/P deferred payment 迟付货款; delivery against payment 付款交货

DPA Data Protection Act 《数据保护法》

DPB date and place of birth 出生日期和地点; Dampier Paper Book 丹皮尔文件手册

DPM Deputy Prime Minister 副总理;副首相

D. P. P. deputy public prosecutor (英)副检察长; director of public prosecutions (英)检察长,公诉人

DPPA Deadbeat Parents Punishment Act 1998年美国制定的《拖欠的父母惩罚法》

Dpty deputy 代理人;副职(的)
DQ detention quarters 拘留所;禁闭室
DR Depository Receipts 存托凭证;Disciplinary Rule (美)惩戒性规则
DR (dr) debtor 债务人;debt relief 债务救济;degree 度,程度,等级;deposit receipt 存股证,存款收据;discount rate 贴现率;doctor 博士;drawing 草图;draft 汇票,吃水(船舶),制定;Democratic Republican 民主党和共和党的(杰弗逊派)
DRB Dispute Resolution Board 争议审查委员会,争议和解委员会
DRL Bureau of Democracy, Human Rights and Labor 民主、人权和劳动办公署
DRM direct-reduction mortgage 直接减少抵押
DRS debtor report system 债务人报告制度
DS Department of State (美)国务院;Deputy Sheriff (美)副地方行政司法官
D. S. Bureau of Diplomatic Security (美)外事安全局
DSB Dispute Settlement Body 世界贸易组织(WTO)的争端解决机构
DSM Dispute Settlement Mechanism (WTO) 争端解决机制
D. S. P. decessit sine prole 死后无子女
D. S. Sc. Doctor of Social Science 社会科学博士
DSU Understanding on Rule and Procedures Governing the Settlement of Dispute 《关于争端解决规则与程序的谅解》
DT delivery time 交货期
DTA Defense Transport Administration (U. S.) (美)国防运输管理局
Duer Duer's Superior Court, N.Y. or Duer's New York Superior Court Reports (美)杜尔的纽约高级法院判例汇编
DUI driving under influence 在酒精或药物强烈影响下驾车
DUIL 1.Driving Under the Influence (美)有影响下驾车 2.Driving Under the Influence of Liquor 酒类影响下驾车
Dup. Jur. Duponceau on Jurisdiction of United States Courts 杜邦索论美国法院的管辖
Durn. & E. Durnford and East's English King's Bench Reports, Term Reports 邓福和伊斯特的英国高等法院(王座法庭)判例汇编,开庭期判例汇编
D. V. Deo Volente 如果允许,如果(上帝)批准,若承天意
DVP delivery-versus-payment 款到交货
DWAI Driving While Ability Impaired 能力受伤害下驾车,能力已受伤害下驾驶
DWI driving while intoxicated 醉酒开车
DWOP Dismissal for Want of Prosecution 驳回提起公诉要求
dwr drawer 开票人,发票人
DWT (D. W. T., dwt) dead weight tons 总载重吨位(指船舶)
DWY driving while yakking 驾车时打电话穷聊
Dyer Dyer's English King's Bench Reports 戴尔的英国高等法院(王座法庭)判例汇编

E

E exchequer (英)财政部;(英)理财法院;equity 衡平法;east 东方;eastern 东方的;East's English King's Bench Reports (1801-1812) 伊斯特的英国王座法院判例汇编(1801—1812)
E. and O. E. errors and omissions excepted 错误或遗漏除外;错误遗漏不在此限
East. L. R. Eastern Law Reports (Canada) (加)东部法律判例汇编
East. P. C. East's Pleas of the Crown (1803) 伊斯特的刑事诉讼(1803)
EAT Employment Appeal Tribunal (英)

就业上诉法院

EB Bureau of Economic and Business Affairs （美）经济和商业事务局

E. & B. Ellis and Blackburn's English Queen's Bench Reports 埃利斯和布莱克本的英国高等法院（后座法庭）判例汇编

EBA European Banking Authority 欧洲银行业管理局

EBT examination before trial 审理前的询问

E. C. (EC) English Chancery 英国大法官法庭；European Community 欧洲共同体；executive commissioner 执行委员；Executive Committee 执行委员会；Electronic Commerce 电子商务；Ethical Consideration 道德对价

Eccles. law ecclesiastical law 教会法，宗教法

Eccl. R. English Ecclesiastical Reports 英国宗教判例汇编

Eccl. Stat. Ecclesiastical Statutes 宗教法规

ECCP European Committee on Crime Problems 欧洲犯罪问题委员会

ECGD Export Credits Guarantee Department （英）出口信用保证局

E. C. H. R. European Court of Human Right 欧洲人权法庭

ECJ European Court of Justice 欧洲法院

E. C. J. Court of Justice of the European Communities 欧洲共同体法院

E. C. L. (Eng.) English Common Law Reports 英国普通法判例汇编

ECLC Emergency Civil Liberties Committee （美）紧急公民自由权委员会

ECMS Electronic Copyright Management Systems 电子著作权管理系统

Eco. economy 经济，节约

ECOA Equal Credit Opportunity Act （美）《平等借贷机会法》

Econ. Cont. Economic Controls (CCH) 经济控制（CCH 版）

ECPA Electronic Communication Private Act （美）《电子交易隐私法案》

E. C. R. European Court Reports (European Community) 欧洲法庭判例汇编（欧洲共同体）

ECSC European Coal and Steel Community 欧洲煤（炭）钢（铁）联营

ECU European Currency Unit 欧洲货币单位

ed. edited; edition; editor 编辑，校订；版，版本，版次；编者，编辑

E. D. Eastern Dist 东部地区，东区，司法东区（美国司法地区）

EDA Economic Development Administration （美）经济开发署

EDC European Defense Community 欧洲防务集团

Ed. C. R. Edwards' New York Chancery Reports 爱德华兹的纽约大法官法庭判例汇编

Eden, Pen. Law Eden's Principals of Penal Law 艾登的刑法原理

EDI Electronic Data Interchange 电子数据交换

Edmonds' St at Large Edmonds' Statutes at Large (N. Y.) （美）埃德蒙的法规大全（纽约）

EDP electronic data processing 电子数据程序（处理）

EDR European depository receipts 欧洲存托凭证

Edw. Abr. Edwards' Abridgment of Prerogative Court Cases 爱德华兹的（审查遗嘱等）的大主教法庭判例节略本

EEC European Economic Community 欧洲经济共同体

EE (and) MP (E. E. M. P.) Envoy Extraordinary and Minister Plenipotentiary 特命全权公使

EEO Equal Employment Office 平等就业单位

EEOC Equal Employment Opportunity Commission （美）平等就业机会委员会

EEZ exclusive economic zone 专属经济区

E. F. Education(al) Foundation 教育基金会

EFOIA Electronic Freedom of Information Act （美）《电子情报自由法》

EFTA European Free Trade Association 欧洲自由贸易联盟

EG Expert Group 专家小组
e. g. for example 例如
EHS Environmental Health Services 环保健康服务部
EI Endorsement Irregular 背书不符
EIB European Investment Bank 欧洲投资银行
EIDs emerging infectious diseases 明显的传染性疾病
EIN Employer-identification number （美）雇主（纳税）识别号,雇主（纳税）认定号
EIOPA European Insurance and Occupational Pension Authorities 欧洲保险和职业养老金管理局
EIPR European Intellectual Property Review 《欧洲知识产权评论》
EIR Environmental Impact Report 环球影响报告（同 Environment Impact Statement）
EKC Environmental Kuznets Curve （经济学界曾提出）环境库兹涅茨曲线（理论）
E/L Export License 出口许可证
El., Bl. & El. Ellis, Blackburn and Ellis' English Queen's Bench Reports 埃利斯、布莱克本,以及埃利斯的英国高等法院（后座法院）判例汇编
Elec. C. Elections Code 选举法
E. L. & Eq. English Law and Equity, American Reprint 英国法和衡平法,美国再版
ELI Environmental Law Institute 环境保护法律学会
Elliot, Deb. Fed. Const. Elliot's Debates on the Federal Constitution 埃利奥特的关于联邦宪法的讨论
Ellis & Bl. Ellis and Blackburn's English Queen's Bench Reports 埃利斯和布莱克本的英国高等法院（后座法庭）判例汇编
Elm. Dig. Elmer's Digest of Laws. N. J. （美）埃尔默的法规判决摘要汇编,新泽西州
EM. App. (= Em. Ct. App.) Emergency Court of Appeal (U. S.) （美）紧急上诉法院
EMBA Executive Master of Business Administration 工商管理硕士

Em. Ct. App. Emergency Court of Appeals （美）紧急上诉法院
Emerig. Assur. Emerigon, Traité Des Assurances et des Contrats a la grosse 埃梅里贡,以大字书写的保险和合同协定
EMH Efficient Market Hypothesis 有效市场假说
EMS Environmental Management System 环境管理标准
Em. T. Employment Tax Ruling (U. S.) （美）就业税规定; Employment Tax, Social Security Act Rulings (U. S. Internal Revenue Service) （美）就业税社会保险法规定（美国内地税务局）
E/N Exchange of Note 互换照会,换文
Enc. Law (Ency. Law) American and English Encyclopedia of Law 美英法律百科全书
Ency. L. & P. American & English Encyclopedia of Law & Practice 英美法律和判例百科全书
Ency of EV Encyclopedia of Evidence 证据学百科全书
Ency. U. S. Sup. Ct. Encyclopedia of United State Supreme Court Reports 美国最高法院判例汇编百科全书
END endorsement 背书
End. Interp. St. Endlich's Commentaries on the Interpretation of Statutes 英德利希的有关制定法规解释的评述
Eng. Ad. English Admiralty 英国海事法; English Admiralty Reports 英国海事判例汇编
Eng. C. C. English Crown Cases 英国刑事案件（判例）
Eng. Ch. English Chancery （英）大法官法庭
Eng. C. L. English Common Law Reports, American Reprint 英国普通法判例汇编,美国再版
Eng. Cr. Cas. English Crown Cases 英国刑事判例汇编
Eng. Exch. English Exchequer Reports 英国理财法院判例汇编
Eng. Rep. English Reports (1220−1865)

英国判例汇编(1220—1865)

Eng. Rep. R.　English Reports-Full Reprint （英）英国判例汇编—正式再版(1094—1865)

Eng. Ry. & C. Cas.　English Railway and Canal Cases　英国铁路和运河判例(汇编)

ENTs　Economic needs tests　经济需求测试

Env. L.　Environmental Law　环境保护法

Env't Rep. Cas.　Environmental Reports of Cases　环境保护判例汇编

E. O.　Escorting Officer　陪同官员; Presidential Executive Order　（美）总统的行政命令; executive order　执行令

E. O. E.　errors and omissions excepted　错误、遗漏不在此限

EOHP　except otherwise herein provided　除非本法另有规定

EOL　end of life　死亡

E. O. M　End of month　月末(在一些销售合同中常用的支付术语)

E/P　export permit　出口许可证

E. P. A.　Employment Protection Act （英）《就业保护法》; Environmental Protection Agency　（美）环境保护局; Equal Pay Act　（英）《同工同酬法》

EPC　European Patent Convention　欧洲专利公约; European Patent Office　欧洲专利局

EPC　Environmental Protection Agency （美）环境保护署

E. P. C. A.　Energy Policy and Conservation Act　（美）《能源政策和能源保护法》

EPO　Emergency Protective Order　紧急保护令

EPR　Extended Producer Responsibility　生产者延伸责任,生产者责任延伸

EPROM　Erasable Programmable Read Only Memory　可涂抹、可编程序的只读存储器［它属于固件(firmware)的一种］

Eq.　Equity　衡平法; Equity Court（或Division）　衡平法院(或衡平分庭)

EEO　Equal Employment Opportunity　平等就业机会; Equal Employment Officials　平等就业官员

EEOC　Equal Employment Opportunity Commission　平等就业机会委员会

ERA　Equal Rights Amendment （美）宪法平等权利修正案; Emergency Relief Act （美）《紧急救济法》

E. R. C.　English Ruling Cases　英国主导判例(汇编)

ERISA　Employee Retirement Income Security Act　《受雇人员退休收入保障法》

ESA　Employment Standards Administration　就业标准管理局

ESC　Economic and Social Council　（联合国）经济及社会理事会

ESCB　European System of Central Banks　欧洲中央银行体系

ESGNCA　（美国联邦政府通过的）《全球及国家商务电子签名法》(2000年6月)

ESM　Emergency Safeguard Measure　紧急保障措施

ESMA　European Securities and Market Authority　欧洲证券市场管理局(2011年1月在金融监管框架下新设立三个监管局之一,另两个为:EBA、EIOPA)

Escriche, Dict　Escriche's Dictionary of Jurisprudence　埃斯克里奇的法理学词典

ESOP　Employee Stock Ownership Plan　雇员股份所有权计划

esp.　especial　特别的,特殊的; especially　特别,尤其,格外

Esp.　Espinasse's English Nisi Prius Reports　埃斯皮勒斯的英国巡回民事法庭判例汇编

ESRO　European Space Research Organization　欧洲空间研究组织

E. T.　Easter Term　（英）(法院)春季开庭期; except　除……之外

et al.　et alibi; and others　以及其他地方,以及其他

et seq.　et sequential = and those that follow　以及下列等等

etc.　et cetera, and so forth　等等

ETC　estimated time of completion　预定完成时间

ETD　estimated time of departure　预定离开时间

ETE estimated time of enroute 预定途中时间
ETF estimated time of flight 预定飞行时间
ETO estimated time over 预定飞越……时间
ETR estimated time of return 预定返回时间
ETS emissions trading scheme （美）(温室气体）排放交易体制
EU European Union 欧盟
Eur. Ass. Arb. European Assurance Arbitration (1872–1875) 欧洲保险仲裁局
EURIT European Investment Trust 欧洲投资信托证券
Eur. L. Rev. European Law Review 欧洲法律评论
EV (Ev.) Entry Visa 入境签证；evidence 证据
EW electronic warfare 电子战；electronic weapon 电子武器；environment warfare 环境战
EWS early warning system 预先通知制
EX exchange 汇兑
ex previous, from 前, 依据；从
Exch. Div. Exchequer Division, English Law Reports 英国高等法院理财法庭判例汇编
Ex. C. R. Canada Exchequer Court Reports 加拿大理财法院判例汇编；Canada Law Reports (Ex. Court) 加拿大法律判例汇编（理财法院）
Exec. executive 执行；executor 执行人
Exee. Order Presidential Executive Order (U. S.) （美国）总统行政令
Ex Exch. English Exchequer Reports, Welsby, Huristone & Gordon 韦尔斯帕伊、赫里斯通和戈顿的英国理财法院判例汇编
EXG Executive Group 执行小组
Ex. Or. Executive Orders 行政令, 执行令
exp. exit permit 出境许可证；expenditure 费用支出；expenses 开支, 费用；expire 满期
exr. executor 执行者
ex. rel. ex relation (on the relation of) 有关
exs. ads. & assns. executors, administrators and assignees 遗嘱执行人、遗产管理人及遗产受托人
EXSEC Executive Secretary 执行秘书
EXW ex works 工厂交货
EXTAFF Ministry for External Affairs （加）外交部
Eyre Eyre's Reports, Eng. （英）艾尔的判例汇编
EZ Economic Zone 经济区

F

F. felon 重罪犯；Federal reporter 联邦判例汇编
FA Financial Adviser 财政顾问；foreign exchange allocation system 外汇分配制；free alongside 船边交货价格
FAA Federal Arbitration Act （美）《联邦仲裁法》
F. A. A. (FAA) Foreign Assistance Act （美）《援外法》；free of all average 一切海损均不赔偿；Federal Aviation Administration （美）联邦航空管理局
FAB Foreign Affairs Bureau 外事局
Fac. Faculty of Advocate, Collection of Decisions 律师联合会(或苏格兰律师学院), 判例汇集
F. A. C. Foreign Affairs Committee （美）（国会众院）外交委员会
FACTA Fair and Accurate Credit Transaction Act （美）《公正、准确信用法》
F. A. D. Federal Anti-Trust Decisions （美）联邦反托拉斯决议
Falc. Falconer's Scotch Court of Sessions

Cases (1744–1751) Sc.福尔克纳的苏格兰最高民事法院判例(汇编)(1744—1751)

Fam. Ct. Act. Family Court Act 《家事法院法》

Family L. Q. Family Law Quarterly (美)《家庭法季刊》

Fannie Mae Federal National Mortgage Association (美)联邦抵押协会(Fannie Mae 为全国最大的抵押贷款提供者,故此协会以他的名字命名)

FAO Food and Agriculture Organization of the United Nations 联合国粮食和农业组织

FAQ fair average quality 平均中等品质,平均质量

F. A. S. (f. a. s.) fund allocation system 资金分配制; free alongside ship 起运地船边交货价格; free at quay 码头交货

FASB Financial Accounting Standards Board (美)财务会计标准委员会

FASIT Financial Asset Securitilization Investment Trust (美)金融资产证券化投资信托

FAST Federation Against Software Theft 反盗用软件协会(1984年由英国计算机协会发展成立的民间组织)

Faust Faust's Compiled Laws, S. C. (美)福斯特的汇编的法规(南卡罗来纳州)

FB freight bill 运货单

FBA Federal Bar Association (美)联邦律师协会

FBI Federal Bureau of Investigation (美)联邦调查局

F. C. Federal Cabinet (澳)联邦内阁; Federal Cases(31 Vols) (美)联邦判例(汇编)(31卷); Federal Constitution (美)联邦宪法; fire control 消防,射击(火力)控制; futures contract 期货贸易合同,期货合同

FCA Farm Credit Administration (美)农场信贷管理局

F. C. A. Federal Code Annotated (美)联邦注释法典; Federal Communications Act (美)《联邦电信法》

FCAC Financial Consumer Agency of Canada Act (加拿大)《金融消费者管理法》(2001年6月出台)

F. Cas Federal Cases (1789–1880) 联邦案件集(1789—1880年)

FCBP foreign currency bills payable 外币付款票据

FCC Federal Communications Commission (美)联邦电信委员会; first class certificate 一级品证明书

FCCA Federal Crime Control Act (美)《联邦犯罪控制(管理)法》

FCIA Foreign Credit Insurance Association (英)国外信贷保险协会; Fellow of Corporation of Insurance Agents (英)保险代理商公会会员

FCIC Federal Crop lnsurance Corporation (美)联邦农作物保险公司

FCIS foreign collective investment securities 外国集体投资证券

FCL Full Contain Load 整箱货

FCLI Fordham University School of Law, Corporate Law Institute (美)福德姆大学法学院,社团法学研究所

FCMA Fishery Conservation and Management Act (美)《渔业资源保护及管理法》; Magnuson Fishery Conservation and Management Act of 1976 (美)《1976年马格纳森渔业保护(区)和管理法》

FCN(T) Treaty of Friendship, Commerce and Navigation 友好通商航海条约

FCP Federal Rules of Civil Procedure (美)联邦民事诉讼法规

FCrP Federal Rules of Criminal Procedure (美)联邦刑事诉讼法规

FCRP Finance Committee to Re-elect the President (美)改选总统财政委员会

FCS fair cost system 合理运费制度; Farmer Cooperative Service 农民合作服务部

F. C. S. C. Foreign Claims Settlement Commission 外国索赔处理委员会(美国联邦政府的一个行政机构)

FCSE Federal Courts Study Committee (美)联邦法院研究委员会

FCSRCC　free of capture, seizure, riot and civil commotions　对捕获、劫持、骚扰和内乱不担保

FCU　Federal Credit Union　(美)联邦信贷联盟

F. 2d (F2d)　Federal Reporter, Second Series　(美)联邦判例汇编,第二套丛书; Second Series of the Federal Reporter　(美)联邦判例汇编第二套丛书

59 F3D 112 (9th cir, 1995)　《联邦判例汇编》第三套丛书第59卷第112页(第9巡回上诉法院1995年)

FD　Finance Department　财政部

F&D　freight and demurrage　运费及滞留费

FDA　Food and Drug Administration　(美)食品和药物管理局; Food Distribution Administration　(美)粮食分配管理局

FDAA　Federal Disaster Assistance Administration　(美)联邦灾难救助管理局

FDBK　feedback　反馈,回授

FDIC　Federal Deposit Insurance Corporation　(美)联邦存款保险公司(1933年成立)

FDL　Formal Deductive Logic　形式演绎逻辑

FDP (FODP)　Full Order of Protection　完整的保护令

FDPC　Federal Data Processing Centers　(美)联邦数据处理中心

FDPM　First Deputy Prime Minister　第一副总理,第一副首相

FDR　fixed deposit receipt　定期存款收据

F&E　Fair and Equitable Treatment　公正与公平待遇条款

FEA　free from alongside　船边交货价格; Federal Energy Administration　(美)联邦能源署

FEBs　Federal Executive Boards　(美)联邦执行委员会

F. E. C.　Federal Election Commission　(美)联邦选举委员会; Federal Exchange Commission　联邦交易委员会

FECA　Federal Employees' Compensation Act　(美)《联邦雇员补偿法》; Federal Election Campaign Act　《联邦选举运动法》

F. E. C. B.　Foreign Exchange Control Board　(英)外汇管理局

Fed.　Federal　联邦的,联合的,联邦政府的; Federal Reserve Bank System　联邦储备银行系统

Fed. B. News　Federal Bar News　(美)联邦律师新闻

Fed. Cas.　Federal Cases, U. S.　美国联邦判例(汇编)

Fed. Cir.　Federal Circuit Court of Appeals　联邦巡回上诉法庭; Federal Connecticut Circuit Court Reports　联邦康涅狄格州巡回法庭《判例汇编》; Federal Circuit　美国联邦巡回上诉法院(同CAFC)

Fed. R. App. P.　Federal Rules of Appellate Procedure　(美)联邦受理上诉程序规则

Fed. R. Civil. P.　Federal Rules of Civil Procedure　(美)联邦民事诉讼规则

FED. R. Civ. P.　Federal Rule of Civil Procedure　联邦民事诉讼规则

Fed. R. Crim. P.　Federal Rules of Criminal Procedure　(美)联邦刑事诉讼规则

Fed RD　Federal Rules Decisions　(美)联邦法律判决录

Fed. R. Evid.　Federal Rules of Evidence　(美)联邦证据规则

Fed. Reg.　Federal Register　(美)联邦每日公报;联邦注册;联邦公报

FEDSTD　Federal Standard　联邦标准

FEIN　Federal-employer-identification number　(美)联邦雇主(纳税)认定号,联邦雇主(纳税)鉴定号

FELA　Federal Employer's Liability Act　(美)《联邦雇主责任法》

F. E. M. A.　Federal Emergency Management Agency　(美)联邦紧急事务管理局

FEO　Formal Equal Opportunity　形式上的机会平等

FEPC　Fair Employment Practices Commission　(美)公正就业(雇佣)实施委员会

FERA　Federal Emergency Relief Administration　(美)联邦紧急救济署

Ferg. Cons. Reports　Feguson's (Sc.) Consistorial Reports　弗根森的(苏格兰)宗教法庭判例汇编

FET Federal Estate Tax 联邦房地产税
FF federal fund 联邦基金; frontier force 边防部队
F. Fa. fieri facias 财物扣押令
FFD free from damage 损失不担保; free from duty 免税
FG Federal Government 联邦政府
F. G. A. (f. g. a.) foreign general average 国外共同海损; foreign general agent 国外一般代理人,国外总代理人; free of general average 不担保共同海损
FGCM Field General Court-Martial 战地高等军事法庭
FGIS Federal Grain Inspection Service (美)联邦谷物检查部
FHA Federal Housing Administration (美)联邦住房管理局(1934年设立)
FHLB Federal Home Loan Bank (美)联邦住房贷款银行
FHLMC Federal Home Loan Mortgage Corporation (Freddie Mac) (美)联邦住房贷款抵押公司
FHWA Federal Highway Administration (美)联邦高速公路管理局
FI false information 假情报; finish 结束,完成; First International 第一国际; Free in 装货费在外(条件)
FIA Federal Insurance Administration (美)联邦保险管理局
FIB free into barge 驳船上交货价格; free into banker 舱内交货价格
FIBV Fédération Internationale des Bourses de Valeurs 国际证券交易所联合会
FIC Federal Information Centers (美)联邦情报中心(1965年约翰逊总统创立,分布全国,负责通过电话、邮件,回答公民的法律问题和其他有关联邦政府的问题); Foreign Investment Council 外国投资协会
F. I. C. A. Federal Insurance Contribution Administration (美)联邦保险捐献管理署; Federal Insurance Contributions Act (Social Security) (美)《联邦保险捐献法》(社会保险)
FICA Fellow of Commonwealth Institute of Accountants 英联邦会计学会会员; Fellow of the Institute of Chartered Accountants (英)特许会计师协会会员; Federal Income Contribution Act (美)《联邦收入捐助法》; Federal Insurance Contribution Act 《联邦保险捐助法》
FICB Federal Intermediate Credit Bank 联邦中介信贷银行; Fellow of Institute of Chartered Brokers (英)经纪人协会会员
F. I. C. J. F. Fédération Internationale des Conseils Juridques of Fiscaux 国际法律和财务顾问联合会
FIDA Federacion Internacional de Abogados 国际律师联合会
FIDE Fédération Internationale pour le Droit Européen 国际欧洲法律联合会
FIED Fédération Internationale des Etudiants en Droit 国际法科学生联合会
Fi. Fa fieri facias 财物扣押令
Fin. C. Financial Code 财政法典
FINSA the Foreign Investment and National Security Act of 2007 (美)《2007年外国投资与国家安全法》
FIO Free in & out 装卸货费在外(条件)
FIPS Federal Information Processing Standards (美)联邦信息处理标准
Fish. Dig. Fisher's English Common Law Digest 菲什的英国普通法判决摘要汇编
Fish. Pat. Cas. Fisher's Patent Cases, U. S. 菲什的美国专利判例(汇编)
Fish. Prize Cas. Fisher's Prize Cases, U. S. 菲什的美国捕获判例(汇编)
FIT (f. i. t.) Federal Income Tax (美)联邦所得税; free of income tax 免除所得税
f. i. t. w. federal income tax withholding (美)联邦所得税预扣
F. J. first judge 首席法官
F. J. C. Federal Judicial Center (美)联邦司法中心
F. L. falsa lectio 误读
Fla. Florida Reports (美)佛罗里达(州)判例汇编
Fla. stat. Florida statute 佛罗里达州制定法
Fla. St. U. L. Rev. Florida State University

Law Review （美）佛罗里达州立大学法学评论

FLB Federal Labor Board （美）联邦劳动委员会；Federal Land Bank （美）联邦土地银行

FLETC Federal Law Enforcement Training Center （美）联邦法律实施训练中心

FLIA Federation Life Insurance of America 美国人寿保险联合会

F. L. R. Federal Law Reports (India) （印）联邦法律判例汇编；Fiji Law Reports 斐济法律判例汇编；University of Florida Law Review （美）佛罗里达大学法律评论

F. L. R. A. Decisions of the Federal Labor Relations Authority 联邦劳资关系局判决

FLSA Fair Labor Standards Act, U. S. 《美国公平劳动标准法》

FM Field Marshal （英）陆军元帅；Foreign Minister 外交部长；Foreign Ministry 外交部；Foreign Mission 外国使团

FMA Federal Maritime Administration （美）联邦海事局

FMACC Foreign Military Assistance Coordinating Committee （美）对外军事援助协调委员会

F. M. C. Federal Maritime Commission （美）联邦海事委员会；Foreign Ministers' Conference （联合国）外长会议；Foreign Ministers' Council 外长理事会；Ford Motor Company （美）福特汽车公司

FMCS Federal Mediation and Conciliation Services （美）联邦调解斡旋署

FmHA Farmers Home Administration （美）农民住房管理局

FMSF False Memory Syndrome Foundation （美）虚假记忆综合基金

F. M. S. H. R. C. Federal Mine Safety & Health Review Commission Reports 联邦矿业安全与健康审查委员会判例汇编

FMV fair market value 公平市场价

FN footnote 脚注；foreign national 外国侨民

FNMA Federal National Morgage Association (Fannie Mac) （美）联邦国家抵押协会

FNMA Federal National Mortgage Association （美）联邦国民抵押贷款协会

F. O. firm offer 实盘，固定发价；firm order 确定的订货；Foreign Office （英）（旧）外交部；forwarding order 运输委托书；Free Out 卸货费在外（条件）；free overside 目的港船上交货（价格）

FOA (f. o. a.) Foreign Operations Administration （美）援外事务管理总局；free on aircraft 飞机上交货（价格）

FOB free on board 船上交货，离岸价格

FOB & C free on board and commission 离岸价格加佣金

FOBS free on board and stowed 包括理舱费在内的离岸价格

FOBST free on board stowed and trimmed 包括理舱费和平舱费在内的离岸价格

FOC flag of convenience 方便旗；free of charge 免费；free on car 车上交货价格

f. o. d. free of damage （保险上的）损坏除外条款

FOI for our information 供我方参考；free of interest 免交利息

FOIA Freedom of Information Act （美）《情报自由法》；（英）《新闻自由法》

Fonbl. Eq. Fonblanque's Equity, Eng. （英）方布兰克的衡平法

Fonbl. N. R. Fonblanque's Cases in Chancery (Eng.) （英）方布兰克的大法官法庭中的判例（汇编）；Fonblanque's Equity 方布兰克的衡平法；Fonblanque on Medical Jurisprudence 方布兰克论法医学；Fonblanque's English Cases (New Reports) in Bankruptcy (1849–1852) 方布兰克的英国新的破产判例（或判例汇编）(1849—1852)

Food Drug Cosm. L. Rep. (CCH) Food Drug Cosmetic Law Reports 食品、药品、化妆品判例汇编

FOP (FOOP) Full Order of Protection 完整

FOQ free on quay 码头交货价格

FOR foreign 外国的；forensic 法庭科学的；formula 方案；free on rail 火车上交货价格

For. Aff. foreign affairs 外交事务
forex foreign exchange 外汇
FOS free on steamer 驳船上交货价格；Financial Ombudsman Service Ltd. （英）金融督察服务公司（专门处理金融产品消费者投诉问题，采用 ADR 途径解决），金融申诉（或调查、巡视）专员机制
Fost. Crown Law Foster's English Crown Law or Crown Cases 福斯特的英国刑法或刑事判例（汇编）
Foster Legal Chronicle Reports By Foster, Pa. （美）福斯特的按年代记载的判例（汇编）（宾夕法尼亚州）
Fost. & F. Foster and Finlason's English Nisi Prius Reports 福斯特和芬莱森的英国巡回民事审判法庭判例汇编
FOT free of tax 免税；free on truck 卡车上交货价格
Fount. Dec. Fountainhall's Decisions, Sc. （苏格兰）方丹霍尔的判例
FOW free on wagon （铁路）货车上交货（价格）
Fox Fox Reports, Eng. （英）福克斯判例汇编
F. P. Federal Parliament 联邦会议；fixed price 固定价格；floating policy 流动保险单；floor price 最低价格；foreign policy 对外政策；French Patent 法国专利；fully paid 全部付讫
F/P fire policy 火险保险单
FPA free from particular average (free of particular average) 单独海损不赔，平安险；Foreign Policy Association 外交政策协会；Fire Protection Association 消防协会
F. P. A. A. C. free of particular average (American Conditions) （按美国条件）单独海损不担保，平安险
F. P. A. E. C. free of particular average (English Conditions) （按英国条件）单独海损不担保，平安险
FPC Federal Power Commission （美）联邦动力委员会；Flexible Purpose Corporation （美）弹性目标公司
FPMR Federal Property Management Regulation （美）联邦资产管理规则
FQS Federal Quarantine Service （美）联邦检疫局
FR final report 最后报告；Fishing Regulations 捕鱼条例
F. R. Federal Register （美）联邦每日公报；Federal Republic 联邦共和国
FRA Federal Railroad Administration （美）联邦铁路管理局；Federal Reports' Act （美）联邦判例汇编法
FRAP Federal Rules of Appellate Procedure （美）联邦受理上诉程序规则
FRB Federal Reserve Board （美）联邦储备委员会；Federal Reserve Bank （美）联邦储备银行
FRC Foreign Relations Committee （美参议院）外交委员会
FRCD floating rate certificates of deposit 浮动利率存款单
FRD Federal Rules Decisions （美）联邦诉讼规则判例
Free. Ch. Freeman's English Chancery Reports (1600-1702) 弗里曼英国衡平法院判例汇编(1600—1702)
Freem. Ch. Freeman's Chancery, Eng. (or Freeman's English Chancery Reports 22 Eng. Reprint) （英）弗里曼的英国大法官法庭判例汇编(22,英国再版)
FRN floating rate note 浮动汇率票据
FRP French Patent 法国专利
FRS flexible rate system 伸缩性汇率制；Federal Reserve System （美）联邦储备系统
FS feasibility study 可行性研究；federal specification （美）联邦规格；federal standards （美）联邦标准；Federal Supplement （美）联邦补篇（编）；final statement 最后声明
FSA Financial Services Authority （英）金融服务局
FSA Fiscal Services Authority （英）金融服务监管局
F. S. A. Florida Statutes Annotated （美）佛罗里达注释法规（汇编）
FSB Financial Stability Board 金融稳定理事会

FSC Forest Stewardship Council 森林高管委员会

FSF Financial Stability Forum 金融稳定论坛(指七国集团为维护金融稳定而创设的法律机制)

FSLIC Federal Savings and Loan Insurance Corporation (美)联邦储蓄与贷款保险公司

FSMA FDA Food Safety Modernization Act 《食品安全现代化法》(2011年通过)

F. S. O. Foreign Service Officer (美)外事官员,驻外使领馆官员

FSR Fleet Street Patent Law Reports (英)船队专利法判例汇编

FSS Foreign Service Staff 外事职员,驻外使领馆人员;Federal Supply Service (美)联邦供应署

F. Supp. Federal Supplement (美)联邦补篇(编)

FT free trade 自由贸易

FTA free trade area 自由贸易区;Free Trade Association 自由贸易协会

FTAC Foreign Trade Arbitration Commission 对外贸易仲裁委员会

FTAs Free Trade Areas 自由贸易区

FTAs Free Trade Agreements 自由贸易协定

F. T. C. (FIFC) Fair Trade Commission (美)公平贸易委员会;Federal Trade Commssion (美)联邦贸易委员会;Federal Trade Commission Decisions (美)联邦贸易委员会决议

FTCA Federal Tort Claims Act (美)联邦侵权赔偿法(1964年通过,以后又三次修改)

FTOF face to face 面对面

FTR Federal Travel Regulations (美)联邦旅行条例

FTS Federal Telecommunication System (美)联邦电信系统

FTZ free trade zone 自由贸易区

Fuller Fuller's Reports (59-105 Mich.) (美)富勒的判例汇编(密歇根州59—105)

Fulton Fulton, Supreme Court Reports Bengel(India) 富尔顿的印度孟加拉湾最高法院判例汇编

FURA Federal Utility Regulations Annotated (美)公用事业注释条例(汇编)

FUTA Federal Unemployment Tax Act (美)《联邦失业税法》

FV folio verso 见背面;foreign value 外国价格

FWPCA Federal Water Pollution Control Act (美)《联邦水流污染控制法》

FY fiscal year 财政年度,会计年度

FYG for your guidance 供遵照执行

FYI for your information 供参考

FYIG for your information and guidance 供参照执行

FYR for your reference 供参考

G

G (Geo) King George(as 15 Geo.Ⅱ) 乔治国王(如乔治二世第15个执政年)

G-5 五大工业发达国家(指美、日、德、英、法)

G/a general average 共同海损,平均值

Ga. Georgia Reports 佐治亚州判例汇编;Georgia Supreme Court Reports 佐治亚州最高法院判例汇编;General Appraisers' Decisions (U. S.) (美)总评估

GA (G. A.) general agent 总代理人;general agreement 总协定;General Assembly (UN) 联合国大会;general average 共同海损;give answer 请回答;government agent 政府官员,政府代理人;government affairs 政府事务

GAAP General Agreement on Antimonopoly Policies 反垄断政策总协定;Generally

Accepted Accounting Principles　（由财政会计标准委员会推出的)普遍接受的会计原则

Ga App.　Georgia Appeals (Reports) (1807-date)　（美）佐治亚上诉判例汇编（1807年至今）

G/A Con　general average contribution　共同海损分摊额

G/A Dep　general average deposit　共同海损保证金

GAAS　Generally Accepted Auditing Standards　（美国注册会计师协会推出的)普遍接受的审计标准

GAB　General Arrangements to Borrow　一般贷款协定

Ga. B. A.　Georgia Bar Association　（美）佐治亚律师协会

Ga. Code Ann　Code of Georgia Annotated　（美）佐治亚州注释法典

GACTI　General Arbitration Council of the Textile Industry　（美）纺织工业仲裁总会

Ga. L.　Georgia Law Review　佐治亚法律评论；Georgia Lawyer　佐治亚律师；Georgia Session Laws　佐治亚会期法

GAL　guardian ad litem　诉讼监护人

Gale　Gale's Exchequer Reports（1835-1836) (Eng.)　盖尔的英国理财法院判例汇编（1835—1836)；Galds New Decisions (Eng.) (1835-1836)　盖尔的英国新判例（汇编）(1835—1836)；Gale on Easements. 12 editions(1839-1950)　盖尔论地役权，12版（1839—1950)；Gale & Davison's Queen's Bench Reports (1841-1843) (Eng.)　盖尔和达维森的英国高等法院(后座法庭)判例汇编(1841—1843)

Gall.　Gallison's Reports, United States Circuit Courts　加利森的美国巡回法庭判例汇编

Gall Cr. Cas.　Gallick's Reports (French Criminal Cases)　加利克的法国刑事案件判例汇编

Ga. L. Rep.　Georgia Law Reporter　佐治亚法律判例汇编

GAMC　General Agreement on Multinational Companies　多国公司总协定

GAO　Government Accountability Office　（美）政府审计署

GAOR　General Assembly Official Record (UN)　联合国大会官方记录

GAP　General Average Price　一般平均价

Card. N. Y. Rep.　Gardenier's New York Reporter　加登尼尔的纽约判例汇编

GA & S.　general average and salvage　平安水险及救难

g. a. s. & s. c.　general average, salvage and special charge　共同海损,救助及特别费用

Ga. St. B. J.　Georgia State Bar Journal　（美）佐治亚州律师期刊

GATS　General Agreement of Trade in Service　服务贸易总协定

GATT　General Agreement on Tariffs and Trade　关税及贸易总协定

GAUN　General Assembly of the United Nations　联合国大会

GB　Governing Board　执行委员会,理事会

G. B. J.　Georgia Bar Journal　（美）佐治亚州律师期刊

GBL　Government bill of lading　政府海运提单

GBMI　Guilty but mentally ill　"有罪但有精神病"的规则(参见正文词条)

GC　general cargo　一般货物；general catalogue　总目录；General Committee (UN)　（联合国）总务委员会；Governing Committee　执行委员会；Grand Committee　（英下院）大委员会

G. C. A. (GCA)　General Claim Agent　一般索赔代理人；General Commercial Area　总商业面积,总生产面积

G. C. D. C.　Gold Coast Divisional Court Reports　黄金海岸分区法庭判例汇编

GCF　Green Climate Funds　绿色气候基金

G. C. M.　General Counsel Memorandum　总法律顾问备忘录

G. Coop.　G.Cooper's English Chancery (35 Eng. Reprint)　G.库珀的英国大法官法庭（35,英国再版）

GCP　Government Contract Program, George Washington University Law Center　（美）政府合同项目,乔治华盛顿大学法律中心

G. Dig. U. S.　General Digest of the United States　美国判决摘要总汇(美国判决摘要汇编系统的一部分)
gdn.　guardian　监护人,监管人
GDP　Gross Domestic Production　国内生产总值
GDR　Global Depository Receipts　全球存托凭证
GE　grant element　赠与部分
GEF　Good Earth Foundation　(美)美好地球基金会
Gen. Assem.　General Assembly　联合国大会;(美国某些州的)州议会
Gen. Conv.　Geneva Convention　日内瓦公约
Gen. Mtg.　general mortgage　一般抵押
Gen. Oblig.　general obligations　一般债务
Gen. R. R. Act　General Railroad Act　《普通铁路法》
Geo. Dec　Georgia Decisions　佐治亚州判例
Geo. L. J.　Georgetown Domestic Law Journal　乔治敦法律期刊
2 Geo 11c22　(英)乔治二世第二个执政年通过的第22个法
GI　government issue　(美)由政府发给军人的(装备、服装等),军用的;公家的
GIFT　gamete intrafallopian transfer　卵子体内输卵管转移
GII　Globe Information Infrastructure　全球信息基础设施
Gilb. C. P.　Gilbert's Common Pleas, Eng.　吉尔伯特的英国高等民事法庭
Gilb. K. B.　Gilbert's Cases in Law and Equity (Eng.)　(英)吉尔伯特普通法和衡平法上的判例
Gild　Gildersleeve's Reports (1–10 New Mexico)　(美)吉尔德斯利夫的新墨西哥州判例汇编(1—10 新墨西哥)
GL　general list　总目录,总表
GLC　Greater London Council　(英)大伦敦议会
GM　general manager　总经理; general mortgage　总括抵押
GMO　Genetically Modified Organisms　改变生物之特质
Gmb H.　German incorporated private company　德国私人有限责任公司
GMP　Garrison Military Police　警备宪兵,卫戍宪兵
GMT　Genetic-marker test　遗传标记(标本)测试
GNMA (Ginnie Mae)　Government National Mortgage Association　(美)全国抵押协会(住房和城市发展内的一个联邦机构)
GNP　gross national product　国民生产总值
Goeb.　Goebel's Probate Court Cases　(美)戈贝尔的遗嘱检验法院判例(汇编)
GOM　the Grand Old Man　英国的伟大人物
GOP　Government-Owned Property　政府财产; Grand Old Party　(美)共和党的别称
GOR　General Overruling Regulation (Office of Price Stabilization)　(美)(物价稳定局)总裁决规程
Gould. Pl.　Gould on the Principles of Pleading in Civil Actions　(美)克尔德论民事诉讼中辩护的原则
Gouids Dig.　Goulds Digest of Laws, Ark.　克尔德的阿肯色州法规判决摘要汇编
Gov.　government　政府; governor　地方长官;英(殖民地)总督;(美)州长
Govt.　government　政府
govtl.　governmental　政府的
Cow N. P.　Gow's English Nisi Prius Cases　高等英国民事巡回审判法庭判例(汇编)
GP　German Patent　德国专利; grace period　宽限期; Great Powers　各大国(又译:列强); guiding principle　指导原则
GPO　Government Printing Office　(美)政府出版局
GR　General Rules　总则
Grand Cout.　Grand Coutumier de Normandie　《诺曼底习惯法汇编》
GRASR　General Railroad and Airline Stabilization Regulations (U. S.)　(美)全美铁路、航线稳定法规
Gr. Brit.　Great Britain　大不列颠
GRC　Grievance Resolution on Committee

不满(不服)解决委员会(美国纽约州)
Green Cr. Green's Criminal law, Eng. 格林的英国刑法
Green Cr. Law R. Green's Criminal Law Reports, N.Y. (美)格林的纽约刑法判例汇编
G. R. O. B. D. M. General Register Office for Births, Deaths and Marriages 出生、死亡及结婚总登记处
Gross' St. Gross' Illinois Compiled laws, or Statutes (美)格罗斯的伊利诺伊州汇编法规
GRS Congressional Research Service (美)国会研究所,其前身为国会参考所(Congressional Reference Service)
GRUR Gewerblichr Rechts-Schutz und Urhebrrect 《工业产权与版权杂志》(德国马格思普朗格学会出版的知识产权刊物)
GS General Schedule (美)联邦政府职员级别表; General Secretary 秘书长
GSA General Service Administration (美)行政事务管理局
GSP Generalized System of Preference 普惠制
GSSR General Salary Stabilization Regulations (U. S.) (美)全面工薪稳定法规
GSW gunshot wound 枪伤
G. T. (GT) Gift Tax Ruling 赠礼税务规定; Gross Tonnage 总吨位; General terms (of delivery) (交货)一般条件
GTC good till canceled 解约前有效; Government's Telegram Code 政府电报密码; Government Trade Commissioner 政府贸易专员
GTOC government to government 政府间,政府对政府
GTT give and take trade 互通有无贸易,互让贸易
guar. guaranty 担保,保证(书); guaranteed 担保的,有保证的; guarantor 保证人,担保人

H

H harbour 港口,港; House Bill 议会法案; Handy's Reports 汉迪的判例汇编; Hare's Chancery Reports (Eng.) 黑尔的英国大法官法庭判例汇编; Hawaii Reports 夏威夷判例汇编; Hebew 希伯来人(语); Hertzogs High Court Reports (S. Af.) 赫佐格的高级法院判例汇编(南非); Hill New York Reports (1841–1844) 希尔纽约判例汇编(1841—1844); House Bill (State Legislatures) 议会法案(州立法机构); Howard Supreme Court Reports (42–65 U. S.) 霍华德最高法院判例汇编(42—65 美国)
h. a. heir apparent 有确定继承权的人
H. A. Hoc anno 今年,在这一年
habeas habeas corpus 人身保护令
Hab. Corp. habeas corpus 人身保护状; 人身保护权
Hab. fa. habere facias possessionem 收回土地占有令
HAC Hague Arbitration Convention 海牙仲裁公约
H. A. C. National Administrative Council (英)全国行政委员会; National Advising Commission (英)全国咨询委员会
Hagg. Adm. Haggard's English Admiralty Reports 哈格德的英国海事法庭判例汇编
Hagg. Cons Haggard's English Consistory Reports 哈格德的宗教法庭判例
Hailes Dec. Hailes' Decisions, Sc. 赫尔斯的苏格兰判例(汇编)
Hale Hale's Common Law, Eng. 黑尔的《英国普通法》
Hale, Com. Law Hale's History of the Common Law 黑尔的《普通法史》

Hale, Precedents and proceedings A series of Precedents and proceedings in Criminal Causes extending from the year 1475 to 1640 黑尔,先例与程序;刑事案件(1475至1640年)的先例与程序

Hale P. C. Hale's Pleas of the Crown (英)黑尔的《刑事诉讼》

Hall Hall's Superior Court, N. Y. (美)霍尔的纽约高级法院

Hall, Mex. Law Hall's Mexican Law. 霍尔的《墨西哥法》

Halst. Ch. Halsted's Chancery, N. J. 霍尔斯特德的新泽西衡平法院

h. app. heir apparent 有确定继承权的人

Hare Hare's English Vice Chancellors' Reports 哈尔的英国副大法官判例汇编

Hart. Dig. Hartley's Digest of Laws, Tex. (美)哈特利的得克萨斯法规判决摘要汇编

Harv. Int't. L. J Harvard International Law Journal 哈佛国际法杂志

Harv. L. Rev. Harvard Law Review 哈佛法律评论

Harv. L. S. Bull. Harvard Law School Bulletin 哈佛法学院学报

Hats. Hatsell's Parliamentary Precedents 哈特塞尔的议院判例(先例)(汇编)

Haw. Hawaii Reports 夏威夷判例汇编

Haw. Rev. Stat. Hawaii Revised Statutes 夏威夷修订法规

Hawes. Jur. Hawes On Jurisdiction of Courts 霍斯论法院管辖权

Hawk. Hawkings' Pleas of the Crown 霍金斯的《刑事诉讼》

Hawk. Wills Hawkins' Construction of Wills 霍金斯的《遗嘱解释》

Hayes Hayes' Irish Exchequer Reports 海斯的爱尔兰理财法院判例汇编

H. B. House Bill 议会议案; House Bill (State Legislatures) (州立法机构的)议会议案

H. Bl. H. Blackstonds Common Pleas Reports (1788-1796) H.布莱克斯通的(英国)高等民事法院判例汇编(1788—1796)

H. B. M. His Britannic Majesty 英王陛下

H. B. R. Hansell's Bankruptcy Reports (1915-1917) 汉赛尔的破产判例汇编(1915—1917)

H. C. habitual criminal 惯犯,累犯; Hague Convention 海牙公约; held covered (保险上的)暂予负责; High Commission (英)最高委员会; High Commissioner (英)联邦成员国与英国之间互派的高级专员; High Court of Justice (英)高等法院; House of Common (英)下(议)院; House of Correction 感化院,教养院,反省院

H. C. Habeas corpus (英)人身保护令状

H. C. A. High Court of Australia 澳大利亚高等法院

H. C. B. House of Commons Bill (英)下(议)院法案

H. C. J. High Court of Justiciary (Sc.) (苏格兰)高等司法法院

HCJJ National College of Juvenile Justice (美)国立审理青少年犯罪学院

H. C. Jour. House of Common Journals (United Kingdom) (英)下院公报

H. Cr. Houston's Criminal Reports (Del.) (美)豪斯顿的刑事判例汇编(特拉华州)

H. C. Res. House of Representatives Concurrent Resolution 众议院共同决议

H. D. heavy-duty 重税

H. D. C. holder in due course 合法权利人,正当执票人

HDI Human development index 人类发展指数(人均 GDP,人均教育水平和平均寿命三方面的评分)

Het. C. P. Hetley's Common Pleas, Eng. 赫特利的英国高等民事法院

HEW Department of Health, Education and Welfare (美)卫生、教育和福利部

HGB Handelsgesetzbuch (German Commercial Code) 德国商法典

H. Hal Halsbury's Law of England 霍尔斯伯里英国法

HHFA Housing & Home Finance Agency (U. S.) (美)住宅资产经理处,住房建筑及住房财政局

HHS Department of Health and Human

Service （美）健康与人类服务部

HICM High Commission （英）高级专员署

HICOMREF High Commissioner of Refugees (UN) （联合国）难民事务高级专员

H. I. Rep. Hawaiian Islands Reports 夏威夷岛判例汇编

H. J. Res. U. S. House of Representative Joint Resolution 美国众议院联合决议

H. K. L. R. Hong Kong Law Reports 香港判例汇编

HL House of Lords （英）上院，上议院；hard labo(u)r 强迫苦役

HLA test Human Leukocyte Antigen test 人体白细胞抗原测试

HLBB Home Loan Bank Board (U. S.) （美）住房贷款银行委员会

HLC High Level Committee 高级委员会

H. L. C. Clarks House of Lords Cases (Eng.) （英）克拉克的上议院判例

HLG High Level Group 高级小组

H. L. R. Harvard Law Review （美）哈佛法律评论

H. L. Rep. English House of Lords Reports （英）上议院判例汇编

H. L. S. Harvard Law School （美）哈佛法学院

H. L. Sc. App. Cas. English Law Reports, House of Lords, Scotch and Divorce Appeal Cases (1866-1875) 英国法律判例汇编，上议院，苏格兰以及离婚上诉判例（1866—1875）

HM Harbo(u)r Master 港务主任；His (Her) Majesty （英）英王（或女王）陛下

H. M. G. His (Her) Majesty's Government 英王（英女王）陛下政府，英国政府

H. M. I. His (Her) Majesty's Inspector 英国检察官

HMSO His (Her) Majesty's Stationery Office （英）皇家出版社

HO Head Office 总机构（如总公司、总店等）；Home Office （英）内政部

Hob. Hobart's English King's Bench Reports 霍巴特的英国高等法院（王座法庭）判例汇编

H. of C. House of Commons （英）下（议）院

Hoff. Land Cas. Hoffman's Land Cases, U. S. District Court 霍夫曼的美国（联邦）地区法院土地判例（汇编）

Hoff. Mast. Hoffman's Master in Chancery 霍夫曼的衡平法院主事官

H. of L. House of Lords （英）上（议）院

H. of R. House of Representative （美）众议院

HOLC Home Owners' Loan Corporation （美）房主贷款公司

Holl. Jur. Holland's Elements of Jurisprudence 荷兰的法理学基础

Holt Holt's English Kings Bench Reports 霍尔特的英国高等法院（王座法庭）判例汇编

Holt Adm. Cas. Holt's English Admiralty Cases 霍尔特的英国海事判例（汇编）

Holt K. B. Holt's King's Bench Reports (1688-1710) 霍尔特的英国高等法院（王座法庭）判例汇编（1688—1710）

Holt N. P. Holt's English Nisi Prius Reports (1815-1817) 霍尔特英国民事巡回审判法庭判例汇编（1815—1817）

Home Home's Manuscript Decisions, Scotch Court of Session 霍姆的苏格兰最高民事法庭判决手稿

Hope Dec. Hope's Manuscript Decisions, Scotch Court of Sessions 霍普的苏格兰最高民事法庭判决手稿

Hopk. Adm. Hopkinson's Pennsylvania Admiralty Judgments （美）霍普金森的宾夕法尼亚海事判决

Hopk. Ch. Hopkin's New York Chancery Reports (1823-1826) （美）霍普金的纽约衡平法院判例汇编（1823—1826）

Horner's Ann. St. Horner's Annotated Revised Statutes, Ind. （美）霍纳的印第安纳州注释修订法规（汇编）

Houst. Cr. Cas. Houston's Criminal Cases, Del. （美）豪斯顿的特拉华州刑事判例（汇编）

How. Howard's Reports (2-8 Mississippi) （美）霍华德的判例汇编（密西西比2—

8); Howard's New York Practice Reports (美)霍华德的纽约判例汇编; Howards Reports (42-65 U. S.) (美)霍华德的判例汇编(美国 42—65); Howell's Reports (23-26 Nevada) (美)豪厄尔判例汇编(内华达 23—26)

HOW Home Owners Warranty 住房所有权担保(单)

How. Ann. St. Howell's Annotated Statutes, Mich. (美)豪厄尔的密歇根州注释法规(汇编)

How. App. Cas. Howard's Appeal Cases, N. Y. (美)霍华德的纽约上诉判例(汇编)

Howell. St. Tr. Howell's English State Trials 豪厄尔的英国国家审判的案例

HP half-pay 半薪; Houses of Parliament (英)议会两院

HQ (HQs) Headquarters 司令部,总部

HR House of Representative (美)众议院

H. R. Conf. Rep. House of Representative Conference Report (美)众议院大会报告

H. R. Rep. House of Representatives Report (美)众议院报告(记录)

hrs heirs 继承人(复数)

HUD Department of Housing and Urban Development (美)住房和城市发展部

Humd's Hist. Eng. Humd's History of England 休姆的《英格兰史》

Hurl. & G. Hurlstone & Gordon's Reports, 10, 11, English Exchequer Reports 赫尔斯通和戈登的判例汇编,(第 10,11 集)英国理财法院判例汇编

Hurl. & N Hurlstone and Norman's English Exchequer Reports (156, 158, Eng. Reprint) 赫尔斯通和诺尔曼的英国理财法院判例汇编(第 156,158 集,英国再版)

I

I independent 独立的; inspection 检查,监察; inspector 检查员,监察员; Institutes of Justinian 查士丁尼法学纲要; intelligence 情报

1884. 63 Ia 558 1884 年《艾奥瓦州判例汇编》第 63 卷,558 页

I. A. (i. a.) in absentia 缺席; Incorporated Accountant (英)会计师协会会员; International arbitration 国际仲裁

IAA International Association of Art 国际艺术协会

IABA Inter-American Bar Association 泛美律师协会

IAC Industrial Accident Commission Decisions (美)工业事故委员会决议录

IACAC Inter-American Commercial Arbitration Commission 泛美商业仲裁委员会

IACJ Inter-American Council of Jurists 泛美法学家理事会

IACL International Academy of Comparative Law 国际比较法学会; International Association of Criminal Law 国际刑法协会

IACP International Association of Chiefs of Police 国际警长协会

IADL International Association of Democratic Lawyers 国际民主法律工作者协会

IAEA International Atomic Energy Agency 国际原子能机构

IAJC Inter-American Juridical Committee 泛美法律委员会

IAL International Arbitration League 国际仲裁同盟; International Association of Lawyers 国际律师协会

IALA International African Law Association 国际非洲法协会

IALL International Association for Labor Legislation 国际劳工立法协会; International Association of Law Libraries 国际法律图书馆协会

IALS Institute of Advanced Law Study 高级法律研究学会; International Association of Legal Science 国际法学协会

IAPL International Association for Penal Law 国际刑法协会

IAPS International Academy of Political Science and Constitutional History 国际政治学及宪法史学会

IA-ST-ANN Iowa Statutes-Annotated database 艾奥瓦州注释制定法数据库

IATL International Academy of Trial Lawyers 国际出庭律师协会

IATRIP International Association for the Advancement of Teaching and Research in Intellectual Property 国际知识产权教育学与研究促进协会

IAWL International Association for Water Law 国际领海法协会,国际水法协会

IBA Independent Broadcasting Authority (英)独立广播局(与BBC并列的一家广播组织); International Bar Association 国际律师协会

ibid. ibidam 出处同上

IBPO International Brotherhood of Police Officers (美)国际警官兄弟会

IBRD International Bank for Reconstruction and Development (UN) (联合国)国际复兴开发银行

i/c in charge of 负责,主管,掌管

IC Identity Card 身份证; Imperial Conference (英)帝国会议; in charge of 负责,主管,掌管; Industrial Court (英)产业法院,劳资法庭; Information Center 通报(新闻)中心; Information Circular 情况通报,资料通报

I. C. Idaho Code 爱达荷州法规; Indiana Code 印第安纳州法规; Iowa Code 艾奥瓦州法规; Indian Cases 印度判例(汇编); Industrial Arbitration Cases (West Australia) 劳资纠纷仲裁判例(西澳大利亚); Interstate Commerce Reports (美)州际商业判例(汇编)

ICA International Councilor Archives 国际档案协会; International Court of Arbitration 国际仲裁院

ICANN Internet Corporation Assigned Names and Numbers 国际管理域名体系的机构;互联网域名地址分配机构

I. C. A. O. International Civil Aviation Organization 国际民航组织

ICB International Competitive Bidding 国际竞争性投标

ICBL International Campaign to Ban Landmine 国际禁雷运动组织

ICC Intergovernmental Copyright Committee 政府间版权委员会; International Chamber of Commerce 国际商会; International Computer Center 国际计算中心; International Control Commission 国际监督委员会; Interstate Commerce Commission (U. S.) (美)州际商务委员会; Indian Claims Commission 印第安人权利请求委员会

ICCL International Committee of Comparative Law 国际比较法委员会

ICCLA International Center for the Coordination of Legal Assistance 国际法律援助协调中心

ICCS International Center of Criminological Studies 国际犯罪学研究中心

ICEL International Council of Environmental Law 国际环境法理事会

ICIC International Copyright Information Center 国际版权信息中心(联合国教科组织设立的一个资料中心)

ICJ International Commission of Jurists 国际法学家委员会; International Court of Justice 国际法院(联合国),国际法庭; International Court of Justice Reports (UN) (联合国)国际法庭判例汇编

I. C. J. Y. B. International Court of Justice Year Book 国际法庭年鉴

I. C. L. R. Irish Common Law Reports (1850-1866) 爱尔兰普通法判例汇编(1850—1866)

ICLS International Center of Legal Service 国际法律事务中心

ICM Institute for Court Management 法庭管理学会

ICNAF International Commission for the

Northwest Atlantic Fisheries 国际西北大西洋渔业委员会
ICNT International Composite Negotiating Text 国际非正式谈判综合条文
ICO in case of 如果发生……；若在……情况下
ICPC International Criminal Police Commission 国际刑事警察委员会
ICPO International Criminal Police Organization 国际刑事警察组织
ICRC The International Committee of the Red Cross 国际红十字会
ICS installment credit selling 分期付款赊销；International Chamber of Shipping 国际海运联盟
ICSID Convention on the Settlement of Investment Dispute Between States and Nationals of Other States 《解决国家与他国国民间投资争端公约》；International Center for Settlement of Investment Disputes 2000 年《国际投资争端解决中心》
ICTA 1970 Income and Corporation Tax Act 1970 （英）《1970 年所得税及公司法》
id. idem 同前，同上
ID identification 识别，鉴定，验明；Identification Card 身份证；immunite diplomatique 外交豁免权；income duty 所得税；intelligence detachment 侦察队，情报组；Investigation Department 调查局，侦讯局
I. D. Interior Department Decisions (U. S.)（美）内政部决议
IDA Import Duties Act 进口税法；Industrial Development Act 发展工业法；International Diplomatic Academy 国际外交学会；International Development Association 国际发展协会
IDC in due course 在适当时候，按时
Iddings D. R. D. Iddings Dayton Term Reports 伊丁斯·戴登开庭期判例汇编
IDEA Individuals with Disabilities Education Act （美）《残疾人教育法》（1990 年）
ident. identical 同一的，完全等同的，相等的

identfn. identification 识别，鉴定，验明，认定同一
i. e. id est 即，就是
IEA International Energy Agency 国际能源机构
IF insufficient funds 不足的资金
IFA International Federation of Accounts 国际会计师联合会
IFC International Finance Corporation 国际金融公司
IFLP Index of Foreign Legal Periodicals （美）《外国法学期刊索引》
i. f. p. in forma pauperis 贫民诉讼
I. F. S. P. O. International Federation of Senior Police Officers 国际高级警官联合会
i. g. d. illicit gold dealer 违法黄金商
IGD Inspector General's Department 总监署；interior guard duty 内部警察勤务，内部保卫勤务
IGP Inspector General of Police 警察总监
igr. igitur 因此，所以
IHL imprisonment with hard labour 监禁并服劳役
IHR International Health Regulations 国际卫生条例
I/I irregular indorsement 非正常背书，非正式签署
IIAL Institute of International Air Law 国际航空法学会
IIAS International Institute of Administrative Sciences 国际行政学会
IIDP Institut International de Droit Public 国际公法学会
IIL individual import license 个别进口许可证；Institute of International Law 国际公法学会
Ill. App 3d Illinois Appellate Court Reports, 3d Edition 伊利诺伊州上诉法院判例汇编第三版
IFP in forma paupers 贫民的方式
IIR Institute of International Relations 国际关系学会
IISL International Institute of Space Law 国际空间法学会

IIUPL International Institute of the Unification of Private Law　国际私法统一协会

IJI International Juridical Institute　国际司法学会

IJK International Juristen-Kommission　国际法学家委员会

IJO International Juridical Organization for Developing Countries　发展中国家国际司法组织

I/L import license　进口许可证

ILA International Law Association　国际法律协会

ILAA International Legal Aid Association　国际法律援助协会

ILC International Law Commission (UN)　(联合国)国际(公)法委员会; International Legal Center　国际法律中心

IL/C irrevocable letter of credit　不可撤销的信用证

ILCUN International Law Commission of the United Nations　联合国国际法委员会

ILL Illinois Reports　(美)伊利诺伊州判例汇编

ILL. App. 3d. Illinois Appellate Court Reports, third series　伊利诺伊州受理上诉法院判例汇编第三套丛书

ILL. 2d. Ininois Reports, Second Series　伊利诺伊州判例汇编第二套丛书

Illeg illegal　非法的,不合法的

ILL. Rev. Stat. Illinois Revised Statute, State Bar Association Edition　伊利诺伊州修订法规(汇编),州律师协会版

ILO International Labo(u)r Organization　(联合国)国际劳工组织

ILP Index of Legal Periodicals　《法学期刊索引》

ILRM International League for the Rights of Man　国际人权联盟

I. L. S. Incorporated Law Society　(英)法律联合会

ILU International Legal Union　国际法律联盟

IM immediately　立即,即刻

IMB International Maritime Bureau　国际海事局

IMC International Maritime Committee　国际海事委员会; International Monetary Conference　国际金融会议

IMCO (I. M. C. O.) Inter-governmental Maritime Consultative Organization (UN)　(联合国)政府间海事协商组织; Intergovernmental Maritime Consultative Organization　政府间海事协商组织

IMF International Monetary Fund　(联合国)国际货币基金组织

IMO International Maritime Organization　国际海洋组织

IMT International Military Tribunal　国际军事法庭

IMTIE International Military Tribunal for Europe　欧洲国际军事法庭

IMTFE International Military Tribunal for the Far East　远东国际军事法庭

INA Immigration and Nationality Act　《移民和国籍法》

inc. income　收入,收益,所得; incomplete　不完全的; incorporated　股份有限公司,组成法人组织的,法人的

INCADAT International Child Abduction Database　国际儿童诱拐公约数据库

INCB International Narcotics Control Board　国际麻醉品管理局

INCD included　包括

INCDG including　包括

INCMG incoming　外来的,输入的

INCOR Inter-governmental Conference on Oceanographic Research　政府间海洋调查会议

INCOTERMS International Rules for the Interpretation of Trade Terms　《国际贸易术语解释通则》

Ind. App. Indiana Appellate Court Reports　印第安纳州受理上诉法院判例汇编

I. & N. Dec. Administrative Decisions under Immigration and Nationality Laws (1940 – date)　(美)按移民法和国籍法的行政判决(例)(1940年至今)

Ind. Prop. industrial property　工业产权

Ind Super. Indiana Superior Court Reports (Wilson)　印第安纳州高级法院判例汇编

(威尔逊)

Incpt Acctt incorporated accountant （英）入会会计师

inf. inferior 下级的,下方的,下属的,下等的,劣等的; information 情报,资料,消息,信息

INHESJ L' Institut national des hautes etudes de la securite et de la justice （法国）国家安全和司法高级研究院

INL Bureau of International Narcotics and Law Enforcement （美）国际麻醉品和执法局

INPADOC International Patent Documentation Center 国际专利文献中心

INR Initial Negotiating Right 最初谈判权; Bureau of Intelligence and Research （美）情报与研究局

In re in reference 对于,关于

INS Immigration and Naturalization Service 移民和归化署

Ins. C Insurance Code 保险法规; insurance contract 保险合同(契约)

Ins. L. J. Insurance Law Journal 保险法杂志

Ins. L. Rep. Insurance Law Reports 保险法判例汇编

INSP (insp.) inspect 检查,监察; inspection 检查,监察; inspector 检查员,监察员

Insp-Gen. Inspector General 总检察官,总监

inspn inspection 检查,监察

Insp Off Inspecting Officer 检查军官

inst. instance 例子,事例; institute 学会,协会,学院,研究所; institution 学会,协会,(慈善事业等的)公共机构

Inst. I, 2, 31. Justinian's Institutes, Lib, 1. tit. 2, §31 (The Institutes of Justinian are divided into four books; each book is divided into titles, and each title into paragraphs, of which the first, described by the letters pr., or principle, is not numbered.) 《查士丁尼法学纲要》丛书1.篇名,2.第31节(《查士丁尼法学纲要》分为四部书,每本书又分出一些篇名,每篇名下分几个段落,其中第一段用字母Pr或Principle来表示,而不编号)

INT interior 国内的,内部的; international 国际的

INTA International Trademark Association 国际商标协会

Int. Com. Rep. Interstate Commerce (Commission) Reports （美）州际商务(委员会)判例汇编

INTEL intelligence 情报

inter. intermediate 中间的; interrogation 询问,审问

INTERGU International Gesellschaft Für Urtheberrecht 国际版权协会(该会设于德国,有70个会员国,英文名为International Copyright Society)

INTERPOL International Criminal Police Organization 国际刑事警察组织

Int. Law the International Lawyer 国际律师

Int. L. N. International Law Notes （英）国际(公)法注释

int. L. Q. International Law Quarterly （美）《国际法季刊》

INTLX International Telex 国际电报,国际用户电报

INTO International Navigation Transport Organization 国际航运组织

Int. Rev. Code (I. R. C.) Internal Revenue Code （美）国内税收法规

inv. invention 发明,创造; inventor 发明人,创造者

INVEST investigate 调查,研究

IO Bureau of International Organization Affairs （美）国际组织事务局

I. O. in order 状况良好,秩序井然,符合规程,适当

I/O instead of 代替

IOB Insurance Ombudsman Bureau 申诉(或巡视,调查)专员署

IOCU International Organization of Consumer Union 国际消费者联盟(简称CI)

IOS International Organization for Standardization （联合国）国际标准化组织

IOSCO International Organization of Secur-

ities Commission　国际证券会组织
I. O. T.　Institute of Transport　（英）运输学会
I. O. T. A.　Institute of Traffic Administration　（英）交通管理学会
I. O. U.　I owe you　借据；欠条
IP　Immunite Parlementaire　议员豁免权；Imperial Parliament　（英）帝国议会；imperial preference　（英）帝国特惠关税；import permit　进口许可证；industrial police　工业警察；initial point　出发点，起始点；integrated programme　综合方案；Internet Protocol　因特网协议
IP　intellectual property　知识产权
IPA　including particular average　包括单独海损；International Police Association　国际警察协会
IPAA　International Prisoners Aid Association　国际囚犯援助协会
IPI　Institute of Patentees and Inventors　（英）专利权人和发明人协会；International Patent Institute　国际专利学会
IPO　Installation Production Order　设备生产订货；Installation Planning Order　安装计划单；Initial Public Offering　首次公开发行
IPP　Integrated Product Policy　（1992年欧盟制定的）整合产品政策
I. P. P. C.　International Penal and Penitentiary Commission (UN)　（联合国）国际刑罚和感化问题委员会
IPPF　International Penal and Penitentiary Foundation　国际刑罚和感化基金会；International Planned Parenthood Federation　国际计划生育联合会
IPSA　International Police and Security Association　国际警察及治安协会；International Political Science Association　国际政治学学会
IPTA　International Patent and Trademark Association　国际专利权及商标协会
IPU　Inter-Parliamentary Union　各国议会联盟
i. q.　idem quod　与……相同
IQ　important question　重要问题；import quota system　进口配额制
IR　information retrieval　情报检索；inland revenue　（英）国内税收
IRA　Industrial Relations Act　（英）《劳资关系法》；individual retirement account　个人退休金账户
IRC　Internal Revenue Code　（美）《国内税收法》
Ir. Ch.　Irish Chancery　爱尔兰大法官法庭
Ir. C. L.　Irish Common Law　爱尔兰普通法
IRIS　Industrial Research and Information Service　（英）工业研究及情报服务处
Ir. Jur.　Irish Jurist Reports (1849-1866)　爱尔兰法官判例汇编(1849—1866)
IRL　Internal Revenue Law　（美）国内税务法
Ir. L. T. R.　Irish Law Times Reports (1874-date)　爱尔兰法律时代判例汇编(1874年至今)
IRO　International Refuge Organization　国际难民组织
Ir. R. C. L.　Irish Reports Common Law Series (1867-1878)　爱尔兰判例汇编(普通法系列)(1867—1878)
irred.　irredeemable　不能赎回的；（公债、纸币等）不能偿还的；不能兑成硬币的
I. R. S. (IRS)　Illinois Revised Statutes　（美）伊利诺伊州修订法规（汇编）；Internal Revenue Service　（美）国内税务署，内地税务局
IRTMS　Investment-Related Trade Measures　与投资有关的贸易措施
Irv. Just.　Irvine's Justiciary Cases Eng.　（英）欧文的司法判例（汇编）
IS　The Islamic State　伊拉克和黎凡特伊斯兰国（见 ISIS）
ISA　International Safety Agency　国际安全事务局；International Security Affairs　国际安全事务；International Sugar Act　《国际砂糖法》
ISC　International Scientific Committee for Tuna and Tuna like Species in the North Pacific Ocean　北太平洋鲔类国际科学委员会

I. S. C.　interstate commerce　州际间贸易
ISD　Investment Services Directive　投资服务指令
ISDA　International Swaps and Derivatives Association　国际互换和衍生商品(或工具)协会(1985年成立)
ISF　International Shipping Federation　国际海运联合会
ISFA　Institute of Shipping and Forwarding Agents　(英)货物运输商协会
ISIS　The Islamic State of Iraq and Greater Syria　伊拉克和黎凡特伊斯兰国是伊斯兰国(The Islamic State, IS)的全称(在伊拉克和叙利亚的极端恐怖组织)
ISL　Institute of Space Law　(美)空间法学会
ISLLSL　International Society for Labour Law and Social Legislation　国际劳动法和社会立法协会
ISLS　International Association of Legal Science　国际法律科学协会
ISN　internment serial number　战俘编号;拘留编号
ISNT　Informal Single Negotiating Text　非正式单一谈判条文
ISO　International Organization for Standards　国际标准
ISOs　incentive stock options　激励性股权期票
ISP　Internet Services Producer　网络服务提供商
I. T.　immunity test　免疫(性)试验; income tax　所得税; industrial tribunal　(英)劳资争议法庭; Inner Temple　(英)内殿法律学院; in transit　在运输中
ITA　International Investment Agreement　国际投资协定
ITC　International Telecommunication Convention　国际电信公约; International Trade Center　(联合国)国际贸易中心; International Trade Charter　国际贸易宪章; International Trade Committee　(美)国际贸易委员会; International Telecommunications Union　(联合国)国际电信联盟; Investment Tax Credit　投资税减免(或抵免)
ITDC　International Trade Development Committee　(美)国际贸易发展委员会
ITI　International Transit　国际过境运输
I. T. M.　Institute of Travel Managers　旅行经纪人协会; International Trade Mark　国际商标
I. T. M. A. 1964　Income Tax Management Act 1964　(英)《1964年所得税管理法》
ITO　International Trade Organization　国际贸易组织
ITR　International Telecommunication Regulation　国际电信规则
I. T. U.　International Telecommunication Union　国际电信联盟
IUC　Inter-Parliamentary Union Conference　各国议会联盟会议
IUPIP　International Union for the Protection of Industrial Property　国际保护工业产权联盟
IV-D agency　见 child-support-enforcement agency; Social Security Act. title IV (D)
IVF　in vitro fertilization　试管内授精
i. w.　indirect waste　间接损耗
IWCT　International War Crimes Tribunal　国际审判战争犯罪法庭
I. W. I.　Immigrant Welfare Incorporated　移民福利会

J

J Journal 杂志,记事录,期刊;Judge 法官,审判员;Justice （英）高等法院法官,（美）最高法院法官,司法,公正,审判;Judg(e)ment 审判,裁判,判决;Judiciary 司法的,法院的;Justiciary Cases (Scotland) （苏格兰）司法案例,司法案件;Institutes of Justinian 查士丁尼法学纲要;Scottish Jurist (1829-1873) 苏格兰法学家;Judge Johnson 法官约翰逊;Jurisprudence 法理学

JA joint account 共有账户;Joint Agency 联合代理处;Joint Agent 联合代理人;Judge Advocate 军法官,军法检察官;Justice of Appeal 上诉法院法官

JAC Jacobus (James) (Eng. Statutes) 雅各布（斯）（詹姆斯）（英国,制定法汇编）

Jac. L. Dict. Jacob's Law Dictionary 《雅各布法律词典》

Jae. Jacobus (King James) as 21 Jac. I 雅各布（斯）（国王詹姆斯）,如雅各布（斯）一世第21个执政年

J. A. F. Judge Advocate of the Fleet （英）海军军法官

J. A. G. Judge Advocate General （美）军法处长;高级军事法官

JAGC Judge Advocate Gener's Corps （美）军法组,军法处

JAGD Judge Advocate General's Department （美）军法署

JAG L. Rev. United States Air Force JAG Law Review 美国空军高级军事法官法律评论

JAGN Judge Advocate General of the Navy （美）海军军法处长

JAGO Judge Advocate General's Office （美）军法处

J. A. G. officer Judge Advocate General officer 高级军法官

JAMS Judicial Arbitration & Mediation Service Inc. （美）（设立在洛杉矶南部的）司法仲裁和调解服务公司

JATLA L. J. Journal of American Trial Lawyers Association 美国出庭辩护律师协会期刊

J. B. Jurun Baccalaureus 法学士;joint bonds 共同债券,合发债券

J. B. A. D. C. Journal of Bar Assn. of the District of Columbia （美）哥伦比亚特区律师协会期刊

J. B. K. Journal of the Bar Association of the State of Kansas （美）堪萨斯州律师协会期刊

J. Bridg. Sir John Bridgman's Reports, Common Pleas, English (123 Eng. Reprint) 约翰·布里奇曼爵士的英国高等民事法院判例汇编（英国再版123）

JC jurisconsult 法理学家,法官,律师

J. C. Juristice Clerk （英）（苏格兰）最高法院副院长;Juvenile Court 少年法庭

J. C. D. Juris Civilis Doctor 民法学博士

J. C. & U. L. Journal of College and University Law 大专院校法律期刊

J. D. Jurum（或 Juris) Doctor （或 Doctor of Jurisprudence） 法学博士;Justice Department （美）司法部;juvenile delinquent 少年犯

J. ENVTL. L. & LITIG Journal of Environmental Law and Litigation 环保法和诉讼期刊

Jeremy, Eq. Jeremy's Equity Jurisdiction 杰里米的衡平法管辖权

J. H. Journal, House of Representatives (U. S.) 美国众议院议事录（或公报、日志等）

JIC Joint Intelligence Center （美）联合情报中心;Joint Intelligence Committee （英）联合情报委员会

JIIC Japanese Information Industry Committee 日本信息产业委员会（指日本计

算机软件数据等产业的官方组织)

JJ. Judges or Justices （法官或州、联邦最高法院大法官）

J. J. judges 法官;Junior Judge 年轻法官(指资历浅的法官),低级法官;Justice (英)高等法院法官,(美)最高法院法官,公正,审判

J. J. Marsh. J. J. Marshall's Kentucky Supreme Court Reports (1829-1832) J. J. 马歇尔的肯塔基州最高法院判例汇编(1829—1832)

J. J. Marsh. (Ky.) Marshall's Reports (24-30 Kentucky) 马歇尔的判例汇编(肯塔基州24—30)

J. Jurn. Journal of Jurisprudence 法理学期刊

J. K. B. Justice of the King's Bench （英)高等法院(王座法庭)的法官

J. Kel. Sir John Kelyngs English Crown Cases (84 Eng.Reprint) 约翰·凯来因爵士的英国刑事判例(汇编)(英国再版 84)

J. L. R. Jamaica Law Reports (1953-1955) 贾马依卡法律判例汇编(1953—1955); Johore Law Reports (India) 乔荷尔判例汇编(印度)

J. M. jactitation of marriage 冒充配偶罪;juris magister 法学硕士;Master of Jurisprudence 法理学硕士

JNC Joint Negotiating Committee 联合谈判委员会

JNOV (jnov) judg(e)ment notwithstanding the verdict 否定裁决的判决,无视裁决的判决

Joar. Am. Jud. Soc. Journal of the American Judicature Society 美国司法学会杂志

JOBS Jumpstart Our Business Start-ups Act (美)《初创期企业推动法案》(简称JOBS 法案)(2013 年)

John. Eng. Ch. Johnson's English Vice-Chancellors' Reports 约翰逊的英国副大法官的判例汇编

John (s) Johnson's Report (Md.Chancery) 约翰逊判例汇编(马里兰州衡平法院)

Johnson's Report New York Supreme Court or Chancery 约翰逊判例汇编(纽约最高法院或衡平法院)

Jones T. Sir Thomas Jones' English King's Bench Reports (1667-1685) 托马斯·琼斯爵士的英国高等法院(王座法庭)判例汇编(1667—1685)

Jones W. Sir William Jones, English King's Bench Reports (1620-1644) 威廉·琼斯爵士的英国高等法院(王座法庭)判例汇编(1620—1644)

J. P. Justice of the Peace 兼理一般司法事务的行政官,治安法官;Justice of the Peace Reports(1837-date) （英格兰和威尔士)治安法官判例汇编(1837 年至今)

J. P. C. Judge of the Prize Court 捕获法庭法官;Justice of the Peace Clerk 副治安法官

J. P. Ct. Justice of the Peace's Court 治安法院法官

JPS Joint Parliamentary Secretary （英)联合政务次官

J. P. Smith J. P. Smith's English Kings Bench Reports J. P. 史密斯的英国高等法院(王座法庭)判例汇编

J. S. judicial separation 法院判决的夫妇分居;judg(e)ment summons （英)判决债务传票

JSA Joint Security Area 共同警备区

J. Scott, N. S. English Common Bench Reports, New Series, By John Scott. 约翰·斯科特的英国高等民事法庭判例汇编,新丛书

J. S. Ct. Hist. Journal of Supreme Court History 联邦最高法院历史期刊

J. S. D. Doctor of Juridical Science 法学博士;Doctor of Juristic Science 法学博士

J. S. M. Master of the Science of Law 法律学硕士

j. t. joint tenancy 合伙租赁,共同租赁,共有

Jt. Agt. joint agent 联合代理人

Jt. Corn. Joint Committee 联合委员会

Jud. judge 法官,审判员;judg(e)ment 审判,裁判;judicature 司法审判员的地位,司法权;judicial 司法的,审判的,法院的;judiciary 法官,法官的,裁决权,司

法上的
Ju. D. Doctor of Law 法学博士
J. U. D. Juris Utriusque Doctor; Doctor of Both (Canon and Civil) Laws 民法和教会法博士
Judgt judg(e)ment 审判,裁判
Jud. Pan. Mult. Lit. Judicial Penal on multidistrict Litigation 有关地方管辖区诉讼的司法惩罚
Jud. Repos. Judicial Repository, N. Y. (美)纽约司法陈列室
Jur Jurisdiction 司法,司法权,管辖权; Jurisprudence 法理学,法哲学,法学; Jurist 法学家
Jur. D Juris Doctor 法学博士
Juris. (Jurisp.) Jurisprudence 法理学,法哲学,法学
Jurispr. Jurisprudent 法理学家
Jur. N. S. The Jurist, New Series, London (英)《法学家》新丛书(伦敦)

Jus. justice (英)高等法院法官;(美)最高法院法官
Jus. P. Justice of the Peace 治安法官
Just. Justice (英)高等法院法官;(美)最高法院法官;审判;公正;合法;司法
Just. ct. Justice Court (美)审判法院
Just. Ct. Act Justice Court Act (美)《审判法院法》
Just. Inst. Institutes of Justinian 《查士丁尼法学纲要》
Just. L. R. Justices' Law Reporter (Pa. 1902-1918) (美)贾斯蒂斯的法律判例汇编(宾夕法尼亚州,1902—1918)
Juv. juvenile 青少年的;青少年
Juv. Ct. Juvenile Court 少年法庭
Juv. & Dom. Rel. Ct. Juvenile and Domestic Relations Court 少年和家(庭)事法院
JV joint venture 合营企业,合资经营企业,联合企业
JVC joint venture corporation 合营公司

K

K Students' abbreviation for Contract (美)学生对合同的缩写; Kenyon's Kings Bench Reports (England) 凯尼恩的英国高等法院(王座法庭)判例汇编; Keyes' Court of Appeals Reports (40-43 New York) 凯斯的上诉法院判例汇编(纽约40—43); Korean 朝鲜; Kotze's Reports, Transvaal High Court (South Africa) 科茨的德兰士瓦高级法院判例汇编(南非)
Kan. (Kan) Kansas Reports (美)堪萨斯州判例汇编; Kansas Supreme Courts Reports (美)堪萨斯最高法院判例汇编
Kan. C. L. Rep. Kansas City Law Reporter 堪萨斯城市法律判例汇编
Kan. Law. Kansas Lawyer 堪萨斯州律师
Kan. L. Rev. University of Kansas Law Review 堪萨斯大学法律评论
Kay & J. Kay and Johnson's English Vice Chancellors' Reports 凯和约翰逊的英国副大法官的判例汇编
K. B. Kings Bench (英)(高等法院)王座法庭; English Law Reports, King's Bench (1901-1952) 英国高等法院王座法庭法律判例汇编(1901—1952)
1917 K. B. Law Reports, 1917, King's Bench, Eng. 英国1917年(高等法院)王座法庭法律判例汇编
K. B. D. King's Bench Division (英)王座(法)庭
K. B. J. Kansas Bar Journal 堪萨斯律师杂志
K. C. King's Counsel (英)王室法律顾问
Keb. Keble's English Kings Bench Reports 基布尔的英国高等法院(王座法庭)判例汇编
Keen. Ch Keen's English Rolls Court Reports (48 Eng. Reprint) 基恩的案卷主事官法庭判例汇编(英再版48)

Kel. Sir John Kelyng's English Crown Cases 约翰·凯来因爵士的英国刑事判例(汇编)

Kent & R. St Kent and Radcliff's Law of New York, Revision of 1801 肯特和拉德克利夫的纽约法,1801年修订本

KGB Committee of State Security (前苏联)国家安全委员会,克格勃

KIA killed in action 战(斗)死(亡)

KID Key Industry Duty 基础工业保护关税

KP Key Point 要点

Kpr keeper 看守人,保管人,管理人

KRS Kentucky Revised Statutes (美)肯塔基州修订的法规(汇编)

K.S.A Kansas Statutes Annotated (美)堪萨斯州注释法规(汇编)

KWMS Killed, Wounded, Missing, Sick 死、伤、失踪、病号(人数)(用于表格中)

Ky. Kentucky Supreme Court Reports (1879–1951) (美)肯塔基州最高法院判例汇编(1879—1951)

Ky. Dec. Kentucky Decisions 肯塔基州的(最高法院)判决

Ky L. J Kentucky Law Journal (美)肯塔基法律期刊

Ky L. Rep Kentucky Law Reporter (美)肯塔基判例汇编

Ky. Op. Kentucky Court of Appeals Opinions (美)肯塔基州上诉法院的判决意见书

Ky. St. Law Morehead and Brown Digest of Statute Laws, Ky. (美)墨尔黑德和布朗的制定法判决摘要汇编,肯塔基

L

L. Law 法,法律,法令; leading 领导的,指导的,主要的; legal 法律上的,法定的,法制的; legitimate 合法的,合理的,正统的; lethal 致死的,致命的; Lansing, Supreme Court Reports (New York, 7vols) 兰辛的最高法院判例汇编(纽约,7卷本)

La. Lane, English Exchequer Reports (1605–1612) 莱恩的英国理财法院判例汇编(1605—1612); Louisiana Reports 路易斯安那州判例汇编; Louisiana Supreme Court Reports 路易斯安那州最高法院判例汇编

L. A. Labor Arbitration Reports 劳动仲裁判例汇编; law agent 法律代理人; Lawyers' Reports Annotated 律师注释判例汇编; legal adviser 法律顾问; loan agreement 贷款协定; local authority 地方当局; Los Angeles 洛杉矶

L/A landing account 起货上岸报告,栈单; letter of authority 委托书,授权书,使用许可证

La. Acts State of Louisiana, Acts of Legislature (路易斯安那州)立法机关的法规,立法机关的法案(汇编)

La. An Lawyers' Reports, Annotated 律师的判例汇编(注释本)

La. Ann. Louisiana Annual Reports 路易斯安那州年度判例汇编

La. App. Louisiana Court of Appeals Reports (美)路易斯安那州上诉法院判例汇编; Louisiana Court of Appeals 路易斯安那州上诉法院

Lab. Labatt's District Court Reports (Cal. 1857–1858) (美)拉拜特的地区法院判例汇编(加州 1857—1858); labor 劳动

La. B. A. Louisiana Bar Association 路易斯安那州律师协会

Lab. Arb. & Disp. Setti. Labor Arbitration and Dispute Settlements 劳资仲裁和争议处理

Lab. Cas. Labor Cases 劳动案例(汇编)

La. B. J. Louisiana Bar Journal 路易斯安那律师期刊

Lack. Leg. N. Lackawanna Legal News (Pa.) （美）拉卡瓦纳法律新闻（宾夕法尼亚）

L. Adv. Lord Advocate （苏格兰）检察（总）长

LAFTA Latin-American Free Trade Association 拉丁美洲自由贸易协会

LAGW Legal Action Group （英）合法行动集团

Lain. Ch. Lansing's Select Cases, Chancery (N. Y. 1824-1826) 兰辛的衡平法院判例选编（纽约 1824—1826）

Land Dec. Land Decisions U. S. 美国土地判例（汇编）

Land & Water L. R. Land & Water Law Review （美）《土地和水法律评论》

Lang. Ca Cont. Langdell's Cases on the Law of Contracts 兰代尔的关于合同法的判例

Lang. Cont. Langdell's Cases on Contracts 兰代尔的有关合同的判例; Langdell's Summary of the Law of Contracts 兰代尔的《合同法概要》

Lans. Lansing's Supreme Court Reports (N. Y. 1869-1873) （美）兰辛的最高法院判例汇编（纽约 1869—1873）

Law. Americas Lawyer of the Americas 美洲的律师

Law Bull. Law Bulletin, San Francisco （美）旧金山《法律公报》

Law Forum University of Ill. Law Forum （美）伊利诺伊大学《法律论坛》

Law J. Q. B. Law Journal, New Series. Queen's Bench, Eng. 英国高等法院（后座法庭）法律期刊,新丛书

Law Rep. Monthly Law Reporter, Boston, Mass.（美）每月法律判例汇编,马萨诸塞州,波士顿

Law Rep. Ex. English Law Reports, Exchequer 英国理财法院法律判例汇编

Law Rep. N. S. Law Reports, New Series, N.Y. （美）纽约法律判例汇编,新丛书

Law Stud. H. Law Students' Helper 法律学生的助手

Law T. English Law Times Reports 英国法律时代报道

Lawyers Co-op. (L. C.) Lawyers Cooperative Publishing Company （美）律师合作出版公司

L. b. long(-dated) bill （银行的）长期汇票,远期期票

LC Law Court 法院,法庭; Legal Committee 法律委员会,司法委员会; Legislative Council 1. （英）（议会的）上院 2.（英国殖民地或美国领地的）一院制议会 3.（美）州议会的常设委员会; Library of Congress （美）国会图书馆; Loco citato 在上述引文中; London cheque （英）伦敦（兑现的）支票; London clause （英）（准许船主到达伦敦后立即卸货的）伦敦条款; Lord Chamberliain （英）宫廷大臣; Lord Chancellor （英）大法官; Lower Chamber 下议院; leading case 主导判例

L. C. leading cases in a nutshell 主导判例概要

L3C Low-profit Limited Liability Company 低利润有限责任公司,2008 年美国佛蒙特州批准成立

L/C letter of credit 信用证

L/C A/S letter of credit at sight 见票即付信用证

L. C. B. Lord Chief Baron （英）首席法官阁下（指理财法院法官）

L. C. C. London County Council （英）伦敦郡议会

L. C. J. Lord Chief Justice （英）高等法院院长,首席法官阁下

L. C. Jut. Lower Canada Jurist 下加拿大法学家

L. C. L (LCL) less-than-car-load-lot 零星货运,零担货运

L. C. Rep. S. Qu Lower Canada Reports Seigniorial Questions 下加拿大领地问题判例汇编

LCSP Legislative Committee on Shipping and Ports （美）海运及港务立法委员会

L. D. law dictionary 法律词典; letter of deposit 押据,抵押证

LDCs Least Developed Countries 最不发

达国家
敦)法律年鉴

LDF Legal Defense Fund 法律辩护基金(指美国全国有色人种协进会下的机构)(1939 年成立)

Ldg loading 装载,负载;lodging 住房,寓所

Ldg & Dly (ldg. & dely.) landing and delivery 卸货和提货

Ld. Raym. Lord Raymond's English King's Bench Reports 雷蒙德法官的英国高等法院(王座法庭)判例汇编

LEAA Law Enforcement Assistance Administration (美)法律实施协助管理局;Law Enforcement Assistance Act 《法律实施协助法》

Leach, Cr Cas. Leach's English Crown Cases 利奇的英国刑事判例(汇编)

Learn. & Spic. Learning and Spicer's Laws, Grants, Concessions and Original Consititutions, N. J. (美)利明和斯派塞的法规、授予、租让和最初宪法,新泽西州

L. Ed. Lawyer's Edition Supreme Court Reports (United States) 美国律师(合作出版公司)版最高法院判例汇编

L. Ed. 2d. Lawyers' Edition Supreme Court Reports, Second Series (美)律师(合作出版公司)版最高法院判例汇编,第二套丛书

Lef. Dec. Lefeverd's Parliamentary Decisions, Eng. 英国利菲弗的议会决议

Leg Acts of Legislature 立法机关的法规,立法机关的法案

Legal adv. Legal Advertiser (美)法律广告刊登者;Legal Adviser (美)法律顾问

Leg. Gaz. R. Cammpbell's Legal Gazette Reports (Pennsylvania 1869–1871) 坎贝尔的法律公报判例汇编(宾夕法尼亚 1869—1871)

Legis. legislation 立法,法规;legislative 立法的

Leg. News Legal News, Chicago (美)芝加哥法律新闻

Leg. Per. Index to Legal Periodicals 法律期刊索引

Leg Y. B. Legal Year Book (London) (伦敦)法律年鉴

Leigh & C. Leigh and Cave's English Crown Cases 利和凯夫的英国刑事判例(汇编)

Leon. Leonard's English King's Bench Reports 伦纳德的英国高等法院(王座法庭)判例汇编

L. & E. Rep. Law & Equity Reporter, N. Y. (美)法律和衡平法判例汇编,纽约

Lev. Levinz's English King's Bench Reports 莱文的英国高等法院(王座法庭)判例汇编

LFQS License Fee Quota System 特许权使用费配额制

L. Fr. University of Illinois Law Forum (美)伊利诺伊大学法律论坛;Law French 法律(专业用)法语

L. G. law glossary 法律术语,法律词汇,法律小词典;liaison group 联络小组

L/G letter of guarantee 保证书

L. G. B. Local Government Board (英)地方(政府)自治委员会

LGBT Lesbian, Gay, Bisexual and Transgender 女同性恋者,男同性恋者,双性恋者,跨性恋者

L. G. C. Local Government Chronicle (1855) 地方政府编年史(1855 年)

L. G. R. Knight's local Government Reports (1903) 奈茨的地方政府判例汇编(1903 年);Local Government Reports (Eng.) (英)地方政府判例汇编;Local Government Reports, New South Wales (Australia) (澳大利亚)地方政府判例汇编,新南威尔士

L. G. R. A. Local Government Reports of Australia 澳大利亚地方政府判例汇编

L/I letter of intent 意向书

LIA Ligue Internationale d'Arbitrage 国际仲裁同盟

L. I. A. International Union of Life Insurance Agents 国际人寿保险代理联盟

Lib. liberty 自由;library 图书馆

LIBCON Library of Congress (美)国会图书馆

Lib. L. & Eq. Library of Law and Equity

法律和衡平法藏书(文库)
Lic. licence 许可,特许,特许证,执照
L. I. E. E. Law in Eastern Europe 东欧法律
L. I. F. O. last in, first out 后装货,先卸货;后进先出(办法)
LII London Insurance Institute 伦敦保险协会
L. I. L. O. last in, last out 后装货,后卸货;后进后出(办法)
lim. limited 有限的;股份有限公司
lit. literal 文字上的,本意的;little 小的;litre 升;literary 文学上的
L. I. T. Life Insurance Trust 人寿保险信托;London Insurance Institute 伦敦保险协会
L. i. w. loss in weight 重量损失,重量不足
L. J. Law Journal 法律杂志;law judge 法官;Lord Justice 大法官阁下;Ohio State Law Journal (美)俄亥俄州法律杂志;Lord Justice of Appeal (英)上诉法院常任法官
L. J. R. Law Journal Reports (1823–1949) 法律期刊判例汇编(1823—1949)
L. L. Law Latin 法律(专业用)拉丁语;Lend-Lease Act (美)《租借法》(1941年制定);lighterage limit 驳运费限额;limited liability 有限责任;live load 工作负载,实用负载,活载荷;Lord Lieutenant (英)旧爱尔兰总督,郡长(司法执行官)
LLA Lend-lease Act (美)《租借法》(1941年制定)
LL. B. Legun Baccalaureus 法学士;Bachelor of Law 法学学士
LLC Land-Locked Countries 内陆国;Limited Liability Company 有限责任公司
LL. C. M. Master of Comparative Laws 比较法学硕士
LL. D. Legum Doctor 法学博士;doctor of law 法学博士
L. Lieut. Lord Lieutenant (英)旧爱尔兰总督;郡长(司法执行长官)
LL. JJ. Lord justices (英)上诉法院法官(复数)
LL. M. Legum Magister 法学硕士;Master of Laws 法学硕士
Lloyd's Rep. Lloyd's Law Reports (formerly Lloyd's List Law Reports) (1949–date) (英格兰和威尔士)劳埃德的法律判例汇编(以前为:劳埃德标目法律判例汇编)(1949年至今)
L. L. T. London landed term 伦敦起卸货条件
LMAA London Maritime Arbitrators' Association 伦敦海事仲裁委员会
LMRA Labor-Management Relations Act (美)《劳资关系法》(1947年)
LMSA Labor Management Services Administration 劳动管理服务行政署
LN League of Nations 国际联盟;local national 当地国民;London (英国首都)伦敦
LNWT legal net weight 法定净重
LO liaison officer 联络官
L. O. A. leave of absence 准假,获准的假期,休假;letter of agreement 协议书;letter of offer and acceptance 要约与承诺书,交货验收单;Life Offices Association 人寿保险机构协会
loadg loading 装载,负载;装弹;装料
loadg & dischg loading and discharging 装货和卸货
loadg Pt loading port 装货港
LOC letter of credit 信用证
Loc. laws local laws 当地法律
LOF Lloyd's Standard for Salvage Agreement 劳埃德的海难救助合约标准格式
L. of A. letter of advice (发货、汇款等的)通知书,通知单
Lofft Lofft's English Kings Bench Reports 洛夫特的英国高等法院(王座法庭)判例汇编
Lom. C. H. Rep. Lomax's City Hall Reporter, N.Y. (美)洛马克斯的市政大厅判例汇编,纽约
Lom. Dig Lomax's Digest of Real Property 洛马克斯的不动产判决摘要汇编
L. O. S. Law of the Sea 海洋法

L. P. Labour Party （英）工党; listening post 窃听哨,监听哨; London Police （英）伦敦警察（队）; London Price 伦敦价格

L. P. R. Legal Personal Representative 法定代理人

L. P. R. A. Laws of Puerto Rico Annotated 波多黎各注释法规

LR law reports 法律判例汇编; law review 法律评论

L. R. A. Lawyer Report Annotated 律师注释判例汇编; Law Reports Annotated 注释的法律判例汇编

L. R. A. C. Law Reports, Appeal Cases （英）法律判例汇编——上诉判例汇编

LRAL Labour Relations Adjustment Law 劳工关系调整法

L. R. A. N. S. [L. R. A. (n. s)] Lawyer's Reports Annotated, New Series （美）律师的注释判例汇编,新丛书

L. R. APP. Cas. English Law Reports, Appeal Cases, House of Lord 英国上议院法律判例（上诉判例）汇编

L. R. C. C. Law Reports Crown Cases, Eng. 英国（刑事判例）法律判例汇编

L. R. Ch. Law Reports Chancery Appeal Cases, Eng. 英国大法官法庭（上诉判例）法律判例汇编; Law Reports, Chancery Division （英）大法官法庭法律判例汇编

L. R. Ch. Div. (Eng.) Law Reports, Chancery Division, English Supreme Court of Judicature （英）最高法院大法官法庭法律判例汇编

L. R. C. P. English Law Reports, Common Pleas 英国高等民事法院法律判例汇编

L. R-E. & I. APP Law Reports-English and Irish Appeals 《英格兰和爱尔兰上诉法院判例汇编》

L. R. Eq. English Law Reports, Equity 英国法律判例汇编,衡平法

L. R. H. L. Sc. English Law Reports, House of Lords, Scotch and Divorce Appeal Cases (1866-1875) 英国上议院,苏格兰法律判例汇编和离婚上诉判例（1866—1875）

LRI Legal Resources Index 法律渊源索引,法律资料索引

L. R. Ir. Law Reports Irish 爱尔兰法律判例汇编

LRM Labor Relations Reference Manual （美）劳资关系参考手册

L. R. P. C. Law Reports Privy Council (1865-1875) （英）枢密院法律判例汇编(1865—1875)

L. R. S. &D. App Law Reports, Scotch and Divorce Appeals (1866-1875) 《苏格兰和离婚上诉法院判例汇编》(1866—1875)

L. S. Locus sigilli (signed and sealed) 盖印之处,签署盖章处

L. S. A. Louisiana Statutes Annotated 路易斯安那州注释法规

LSAT Law School Admission Test 法学院入学考试[由美国宾夕法尼亚州法学院入学委员会（Law School Admission Council,简称 Law Services）负责主办的法学院入学资格考试]; Law School Aptitude（或admissions) Test 法学院入学考试

LSC. Legal Service Corporation （美）法律服务公司

L. Soc. Gaz Law Society's Gazettes 律师协会公报

LSSA Lloyd's Standard Salvage and Agreement Clause (LSSA Clause) 劳氏（劳埃德）标准海难救助及协议条款

LT letter telegram 书信电报; local time 当地时间

L/T letter of trust 信托单,信托书

LTA long-term arrangements （美）长期协定

Ltd (L'td; ltd) limited 有限的,股份有限（公司）

L. Teach law teacher 法律教师

Lt. Gov. lieutenant governor 代理总督,副总督;（美）副州长

L. T. R. Law Times Reports (1859-1947) （英格兰和威尔士）法律时代判例汇编(1859—1947)

L. T. R. O. S. Law Times Reports, Old Series (1843-1860) （英格兰和威尔士）法

律时代判例汇编,旧版丛书(1843—1860)
Lush. Lushington's English Admiralty Reports 勒欣顿的英国海事判例汇编
Lut. Lutwyche's English Common Pleas Reports 卢特韦奇的英国高等民事法院判例汇编
LWL low water line 低潮线
L. W. L. R. Land and Water Law Review (美)《水土法评论》,《土地和水法评论》
LWM low water mark 退潮标志
LWOP leave without pay 无薪休假

M

M. magistrate 地方行政官,文职官员,地方法官;maintenance 维修,保养;male 男(性)的,公的,雄的;manifest (飞机或货船的)货物清单,舱单,宣言,声明;New York Miscellaneous Reports 纽约各种判例汇编;Mortgage 抵押,抵押权,抵押物
MA mental age 智龄
MA Maritime Administration 海事管理局
M. A. Maritime Administration (美)海事管理局;Master of Arts 文科硕士;military attaché 武官;Missouri Appeals Reports (美)密苏里上诉判例汇编;Munitions Tribunals Appeals Great Britain High Court ot Justice (英)高等司法法院,军需上诉法庭
MAA Manufacturers Aircraft Association (MAA) 美国组建的飞机制造商协会
MAA Mutual Aid Agreement 相互援助协定
Macq. Macqneen's Scotch Appeal Cases (House of Lords) (苏格兰)麦奎因麦格兰上诉法院判例(汇编)(上议院)
MACRS Modified Accelerated Cost Recovery System 修正加速成本回收制
Madd. Maddock's Reports,English Chancery 马多克英国大法官法院判例汇编
Mag. The Magistrate,London (英)(伦敦)治安法官,地方法官
Mag. Magistrate (美)治安法官,基层司法官
Mag. Ct. Magistrates' Court 治安法院(庭)
MAI most advantageously involved (countries) 最受益(国家),最惠国;Multilateral Agreement on Investment (综合性)多边投资协定,多边投资协议
Maine Bar Maine State Bar Association Reports (美)缅因州律师协会判例汇编
M. A. L. Modern American Law 现代美国法律
M. A. L. D. Master of Arts in Law and Diplomacy 法律和外交文科硕士
Man. El. Cas. Manning's Election Cases, Eng. (英)曼宁的选举判例集
Man. Law Managerial Law 经营管理法
Man. & R. Manning & Ryland's English Magistrates Cases 曼宁和赖兰的英国治安法官的判例集
Mansf. Dig Mansfield's Digest of Statutes, Ark. (美)曼斯菲尔德阿肯色州制定法判决摘要汇编
MAP maximum average price 最高平均价格;Military Assistance Pact 军事援助条约
MARAD (Mar Ad) Maritime Administration (美)(运输部)海事管理局
MARP months after receipt of problem 收到问题后数月
MARPAC (Mar Pol) Pacific Headquarter of the United States Marine Corps 美国海军陆战队太平洋司令部
Mar. Prov. Maritime Province Reports, Can. (加)海事管辖判例汇编
MARs Market Access Rights 市场准入权利
Mars. adm. Marsden's Admiralty, Eng. (英)马尔斯登的《海事法》
mar. settl. marriage settlement 婚姻授产

协定,结婚财产赠与

Marsh. Marshall's English Common Pleas Reports 马歇尔的英国高等民事法院判例汇编

Mason's Code Mason's United States Code Annotated 梅森的美国注释法典

Maule & S. Maule and Selwyn's English King's Bench Reports 莫尔和塞尔温的英国高等法院(王座法庭)判例汇编

MAUSA military attaché of the United States of America 美国武官

MB memorandum book 备忘录

M. B. Miscellaneous Branch, Internal Revenue Bureau (U. S.) (美)内地税务局,各个分局; Morrell's Bankruptcy Reports (Eng.) (英)莫雷尔破产判例汇编; Munitions Board (U. S.) (美)军火(品)委员会

M. B. A. Master of Business Administration 工商业管理硕士

MBACLE Multnomah Bar Association Committee on Continuing Legal Education 莫尔特诺玛律师协会委员会法学进修教育部

MBCA Model Business Corporation Act 《标准商事公司法》(美国律师协会商法部公司法委员会1984年新修订的法)

MBF Medical Benefits Fund 医疗福利基金会

M. B. J. Michigan State Bar Journal 密歇根州律师杂志

MBS Mortgages-backed Securities 按揭证券

M. C. Member of Congress 国会议员; member of council 理事国;理事会成员; Ministerial Committee 部长级委员会

MCA Military Commissions Act (美)《军事委员会法》

MCABM manner common among businessmen 按商人惯例

MCAT Monthly Catalog of U. S. Government Publications 《美国政府出版物目录月报》

M. C. C. Member of the County Council (英)郡议会议员; Military Coordinating Committee 军事协调委员会

MCI marketing cost index 销售价格指数; multiple currency intervention system 复合货币干预制; Microware Communications Inc.微波通讯股份有限公司

M. C. L. Master of Civil Law 民法硕士; Master of Comparative Law 比较法硕士

M. C. L. A. Michigan Compiled Laws Annotated (美)密歇根州法规注释汇编

MCM Manual for Court Martials (美)军事法庭条例; Minister Consulting Meeting 部长协商会议

M. Com. (M. Comm.) Master of Commerce 商业硕士

M. Cord. L. (S. C.) M'cord, South Carolina Law Reports (美)麦科德的南卡罗来纳州法律判例汇编

MCPS Mechanical Copyright Protection Society (英)机器发明权保护协会

Md. Maryland Reports (美)马里兰州判例汇编

MD managing director 总裁; market disruption 市场混乱; maximum demand 最大需求量; Monroe Doctrine 门罗主义

M/D (m/d) memorandum of deposit 存款单,送款单; month's date (或 months after date) 发票后……月

Md. App. Maryland Appellate Reports (美)马里兰州受理上诉判例汇编

MDLEA Maritime Drug Law Enforcement Act (美)《海上毒品法(强制)执行法》

Md. L. Rep. Maryland Law Reporter, Baltimore (美)马里兰州法律判例汇编,巴的摩尔

Me. Maine Reports (美)缅因州判例汇编; Maine Supreme Judicial Court Reports 缅因州最高司法法院判例汇编

ME medical examiner 验尸官,体检医生; most excellent 最杰出的

M. Econ. Master of Economics 经济学硕士

M. Econ. S. Master of Economic Science 经济学硕士

Med. mediator 调停人,调解人

MEE Multistate Essay Examination (美)州际论文考试(美国律师考试的第二部分——专案分析)

Meigs. Dig. Meigs' Digest of Decisions of the Courts of Tennessee （美）梅格斯的田纳西州法院的判决摘要汇编

MEMO memorandum 备忘录；（事实和法律根据）摘要

Mer. Merivale's English Chancery Reports 梅里维尔的英国大法官法院判例汇编

Merl. Repert. Merlin, Repertoire de Jurisprudence 默林的判例汇编

MERM multilateral exchange rate model 多边汇率方式

Mess. & W. Meeson and Walsby's English Exchequer Reports 米森和沃尔斯巴依的英国理财法院判例汇编

MFA Minister of Foreign Affairs 外交部长；Ministry of Foreign Affairs 外交部

MFN most favoured nation 最惠国；Most Favored Nation Treatment 最惠国待遇

MFNC most favoured nation clause 最惠国条款

M. F. P. D. Modern Federal Practice Digest （美）现代联邦诉讼判决摘要汇编

MG military government 军政府；Major General 陆（空、陆战队）军少将

MGIC Mortgage Guaranty Insurance Corporation 抵押担保保险公司

M. G. L. A. Massachusetts General Laws Annotated （美）马萨诸塞州一般注释法规

MGO military government officer 军政府官员；Medical General Laboratory 医药总试验室

MHR member of the House of Representative （美）众议院议员

MI marine insurance 水险；medical inspection 检疫；military intelligence 军事情报，军事情报工作，军事情报部门

MIA Marine Insurance Act （英）《海上保险法》；Missing in Action 失踪，失踪人员

Mich. App. Michigan Court of Appeals (Reports) （美）密歇根州上诉法院判例汇编

Mich. Gen. Ct. Rule Michigan General Court Rule 美国密歇根州州议会规则

MICPEL The Maryland Institute for Continuing Professional Education of Lawyers 马里兰律师行业继续教育学院

MIGA Multilateral Investment Guarantee Agency 《多边投资担保机构公约》

Mill. Const. Mill's Constitutional Reports S. C. （美）米尔的宪法判例汇编，南卡罗来纳

Miller's Code Miller's Revised and Annotated Code, Iowa （美）米勒的修订和注释法规，艾奥瓦州

Mil. P. Off. Military Permit Office （美）军事（管制的）通行证发放处

Mil. Pris. Military Prison 军事监狱

MIN minimum 最小，最低限度；minister 部长

MINFA Ministry of Foreign Affairs 外交部

Minn. Minnesota (Supreme Court) Reports （美）明尼苏达州最高法院判例汇编

Minn. Ct. Rep. Minnesota Court Reporter （美）明尼苏达州法院判例汇编

MINS minor in need of supervision 需要监督的未成年人

MIP marine insurance policy 水险保险单

Misc Miscellaneous Reports (New York) 《混合判例汇编》（纽约）

Miss. Mississippi (Supreme Court) Reports （美）密西西比最高法院判例汇编

Mitf. Eq. Pl. Mitford's Equity Pleading 米尔福的衡平法诉讼程序

MJ (M. J.) Ministry of Justice 司法部；Military Justice Reporter (1975-date) （美）军事司法判例汇编（1975年至今）

M. J. S. Master of Juridical Science 法学硕士

Mkt. market 市场

ML Military Laws of the United States (Army) Annotated 美国注释军事法规

M. L. Magister Legum 法学硕士；Master of Laws 法学硕士

M. L. A. Member of the Legislative Assemble 立法议会议员；立宪（制宪）议会议员

MLATS Mutual Legal Assistance Treaties 司法互助协定

MLF multilateral force 多边力量,多国部队

MLR minimum lending rate （英）最低贷款利率

MLUS Military Laws of United States 美国军事法规

mm. matrimony 结婚;婚姻;婚姻生活

M. M. mercantile marine (merchant marine) 商船队; Mutatis Mutandis 在细节上已作必要的修正

M. M. A. Merchandise Marks Act （英）《商标法》

MMC Manual for Military Commissions （美）军事委员会手册

M. M. D. Merchantile Marine Department 海运局;商船局

MNC Multi National Company 多国公司

MNCs Multi National Corporations 多国公司,跨国公司

MNE multinational enterprises 跨国企业

mo month 月; monthly 一个月

Mo. Missouri Supreme Court Reports (1821-1956) （美）密苏里州最高法院判例汇编(1821—1956); Modern Reports (Eng.) (1669-1732) （英）现代判例汇编(1669—1732); Moor's Privy Council Reports (Eng.) (1836-1862) （英）穆尔的枢密院判例汇编(1836—1862); Moor's Common Pleas Reports (Eng.) (1817-1827) （英）穆尔的最高民事法院判例汇编(1817—1827); Moor's King's Bench Reports (Eng.) (1512-1621) （英）穆尔的英国高等法院(王座法庭)判例汇编(1512—1621)

M. O. mail order 函购,邮购; mass observation 民众考察,民意调查; military observer 军事观察员; military operations 军事行动; money order （邮政）汇票; movement order 调动命令,运输命令; municipal ownership 市所有权,市属产权,地方所有权; Military Order (issued by the President as Commander in Chief of the Armed Forces) （作为武装部队总司令的总统发布的）军事命令; Mineral Order (Defense Minerals Exploration Administration, Department of the Interior) U. S. 美国矿物令（内务部,国防矿物勘探管理局）

MOA memorandum of agreement 协议备忘录,协定要点; military occupation area 军事占领区

MOB Office of Management and Budget （美）管理和预算局

Mad. Am. Law Modern American Law 现代美国法

Mad. Rep. Modern Reports (1669-1732) (Eng.) （英）现代判例汇编(1669—1732)

Mon. Monaghan's Unreported Cases (Pennsylvania Superior Court) （美）莫纳汉的未汇编过的判例（汇编）（宾夕法尼亚州高级法院）; T. B. Monroe's Reports (17-23 Kentucky) （美）T. B. 门罗的判例汇编(17—23 肯塔基); Montana Reports （美）蒙大拿州判例汇编; Montana Territory 蒙大拿州领域

Mont. Montagu, English Bankruptcy Reports (1829-1832) 蒙塔古英国破产判例汇编(1829—1832); Montana Supreme Court Reports （美）蒙大拿州最高法院判例汇编

Montg. Montgomery County Law Reporter, Pa. 蒙哥马利县法律判例汇编,宾夕法尼亚州

Month. L. Rep. Monthly Law Reporter, Boston （美）每月法律判例汇编,波士顿

Mont. L. R. Montreal Law Reports, Can. （加）蒙特利尔法律判例汇编

Montr. Cond. Rep. Montreal Condensed Reports （加）蒙特利尔简明判例汇编

Montr. Leg. N. Montreal Legal News （加）蒙特利尔法律消息

Montr. Q. B. Montreal Law Reports, Queen's Bench （加）蒙特利尔（后座法庭）法律判例汇编

Montr. Super. Montreal Law Reports. Superior Court （加）蒙特利尔高级法院法律判例汇编

Moo Moody's English Crown Cases 穆迪的英国刑事判例; Francis Moore's English King's Bench Reports (1512-1621) 弗朗

西斯·穆尔的高等法院(王座法庭)判例汇编(1512—1621);J. M. Moore's English Common Pleas Reports. J. M. 穆尔的英国高等民事法院判例汇编

MOOC Massive Open Online Course 大型互联网公开课

Moo. C. C. Moody's English Crown Cases Reserved (1824-1844) 穆迪的英国(在巡回审判中发生而留待刑事上诉法院解决的)刑事判例(汇编)(1824—1844)

Moo. P. C. C. N. S. Moore's Privy Council Cases, New Series (Eng.) (英)穆尔的枢密院判例集(新丛书)

Moore P. C. Moore's Privy Council Reports 穆尔的枢密院判例汇编

Moo. Sep. Rep. Moore, Separate Report of Westerton v. Liddell 穆尔的韦斯特顿诉利德尔案的单独报告

MOP member of Parliament 议会议员

Mos. Mosely's English Chancery Reports 莫斯利的英国大法官法院判例汇编

Mo. St. Ann. Missouri Statutes Annotated (美)密苏里州注释法规

MOT Ministry of Transportation (英)交通部

MOU Memoranda of Understanding 双边谅解备忘录

MP maintenance prevention 安全措施,防护设施;market price 市场价格;member of Parliament 议会议员;(英)下院议员;Message of the President (美)总统咨文;Metropolitan Police (英)首都警察(队);Military Police 宪兵(队);Minister Plenipotentiary 全权公使;Mounted Police 骑警(队);Municipal Police 市警察队

M/P months after payment 支付后的几个月

M. P. B. Missing Persons' Bureau (美)失踪人员事务局

MPC Military Police Corps 宪兵总队

MP & DB military prison and detention bar racks 军事监狱和禁闭室

MPO Metropolitan Police Office (英)首都警察局

M. P. P. Member of Provincial Parliament 省议会议员

M. P. S. Ministry of Public Security 公安部

MPT Multistate Performance Test (美)州际履约检测(美国律师考试的第四部分——材料题,意在考察考生在执业实践的真实情形中运用基本律师技巧解决问题能力)

M. R. Master of the Rolls (英)(上诉法院的)录卷主任,保管案卷的法官;Mate's receipt 大副收据;maximum reserve 最高储备额;Minister Residentiary 常驻公使;Motorways Traffic Regulations 公路交通规则

MRPC Model Rules of Professional Conduct (美)《职业行为示范准则》,《律师职业行为示范准则》(1983年)

M. R. S. A. Maine Revised Statutes Annotated (美)缅因州修订的注释法规

M. S. maiden surname 未婚时娘家的姓;manuscript 抄本,原稿,手稿,手书;military standard 军事标准;Ministry of Supply (英)补给部;Military Science 军事科学;missile station 导弹站

MSA Maritime Safety Agency (日本)海上保安厅;Merchant, Shipping Act (英)商船海运条例;Military Service Act (美)兵役法;Mutual Security Act (美)共同安全法;Mutual Security Agency (美)(旧)共同安全署(局)

M. S. A. Minnesota Statutes Annotated (美)明尼苏达州注释法规(汇编)

m. s. l. mean sea level 平均海平面

MSE Mental State of the Offense Screening Evalution 精神状态筛选表

MSP minimum safeguard price 最低保护价格

MSPB Merit System Protection Board (美)择优录用制度保护委员会;Merit Systems Protection Board (美)功绩制度保护局

MT memorandum trade 备忘录贸易;multilateral trade 多边贸易;multimodal transport 多种方式联运

M/T mail transfer 信汇

mtg. meeting 会议; mortgage 抵押
mtgd mortgaged 抵押的
mtge mortgage 抵押; 抵押单, 典契
mtgee mortgagee 承受抵押者, 受押人
mtgor mortgagor 抵押人, 出押人
Mun. Municipal Law Reporter, Pa. （美）国内法判例汇编（宾夕法尼亚）
Mun. Corp. Cas. Municipal Corporation Cases （美）市政机构判例（汇编）
Mun. Ct. Municipal Court 市法院
Munic. municipal 市的, 市政的, 市立的
Mun. L. Ct. Dec. Municipal Law Court Decisions 市法院判决录
M. V. market value 市面价值; merchant vessel 商船
M. V. D. Motor Vehicle Department （美）机动车辆部
M. W. Most Worshipful （英）最尊敬的（用于对治安法官、市参议员等的称呼）
M. & W. Meeson and Welshy's English Exchequer Reports 米森和弗尔希的英国理财法院判例汇编
M. W. A. Married Women's Association （英）已婚妇女协会
MWPA Married Women's Property Act （英）《已婚妇女财产法》
My. Fed. Dec. Myer's Federal Decisions 麦耶的联邦判决（汇编）
Myl. & C. Mylne and Craig's English Chancery Reports 迈尔纳和克雷格的英国大法官法院判例汇编
Myr. Prob. Myrick's Probate Court Reports, Cal. （美）迈里克的遗嘱检验法庭判例汇编, 加利福尼亚州

N

n. footnote 脚注
N. normal 正常的; note 注, 说明; natus 生, 出生, 出生于 …… 的; Nebraska （美）内布拉斯加州; Nevada （美）内华达州; North 北方; Northeastern Reports （美）东北判例汇编; Northwestern Reporter （美）西北判例汇编
N. A. National Archives 国家档案馆; National Assembly 国民议会; Neutrality Act （美）中立法; not allowed 不允许; not applicable 不适用; non acquiescing 不默认
N/A next Assembly 下届大会, 下届议会; no advice 无通知; not available 陈列品, 非供应品
NAA National Academy of Arbitrators （美）全国仲裁学会; National Assistance Act （英）《国家济贫法》
NAACP National Association for the Advancement of Colored People （美）全国有色人种促进会
NAAEC North American Agreement on Environmental Cooperation 北美环境合作协定
NAB National Assistance Board （英）国家济贫局; National Aliance of Businessmen （美）全国商人联合会
NABE National Association of Bar Executives （美）全国律师理事协会
N. A. C. National Administrative Council （英）全国行政委员会; National Advising Commission （英）全国咨询委员会
NAFO Northwest Atlantic Fishes Organization 西北大西洋渔业组织
NAFTA North American Free Trade Agreement 1992年北美自由贸易协定
NALA National Association of Legal Assistants 全国法律助手协会
NALAO National Association of Legal Aid Organization （美）全国法律咨询援助机构联合会
NALS National Association of Legal Secretaries 全国（英以前殖民地的）司法官协会

NAM new approach method 新处理方法，新措施
NAP National Association of Publishers （美）全国出版商协会；Non-Agression Pact 互不侵犯条约
narr. narratio 原告陈述事实
NAS National Academy of Science 国家科学院
NASA National Aeronautics and Space Administration （美）国家航空和航天局
NASAA North American Securities Administrators Association 北美证券管理者协会
NASD National Association of Securities Dealers 美国证券业协会
NASDAQ National Association of Securities Dealers Automatic Quotation 纳斯达克（全美证券商协会自动报价系统）（前身为OTC 市场, 隶属于 NASD）
Nat. national 国家的，民族的；natural 自然的
N. A. T. National Arbitration Tribunal 全国仲裁法庭；no act taken 未采取行动；North Atlantic Treaty 北大西洋公约
NATB National Automobile Theft Bureau （美）全国汽车防盗管理局
Nat. Bankr. Law National Bankruptcy Law （美）《国家破产法》
Nat. Bankr. R. (N. B. R.) National Bankruptcy Register, U. S. （美）全国破产事项登记册
Nat. Corp. Rep. National Corporation Reporter （美）国家企业的判例汇编
NATO North Atlantic Treaty Organization 北大西洋公约组织
NAV Net Asset Value 净资产值, 净值
N. B. (n. b.) new bonds 新债券；newborn 新生的，新生儿；nota bene 注意，留心；New Brunswick Reports (Canada) （加）纽伯朗森威克判例汇编
NBA National Bankruptcy Act （美）《破产法》；National Bar Association （美）全国律师协会
N. B. N. Rep. National Bankruptcy News and Reports （美）全国破产消息和判例汇编
NBS National Bureau of Standards (U. S.) （美）国家标准局
NC net capital 纯资本；no change 无变化；noncommittal 不表明态度, 不承担义务
N. C. North Carolina Reports （美）北卡罗来纳州判例汇编；North Carolina Supreme Court Reports （美）北卡罗来纳州最高法院判例汇编；New Cases (Bingam's New Cases) in Common Pleas (1834 – 1840) 高等民事法院判例（宾厄姆的新判例）(1834—1840)（汇编）
N/C no charge 免费，不计价
N. C. A. North Carolina Court of Appeals Reports （美）北卡罗来纳州上诉法院判例汇编
NCAJ National Center for Administrative Justice （美）国家司法行政中心
NCB National Conservation Bureau （英）国家资源保护局；Nordic Copyright Bureau 北欧版权局
NCBF North Carolina Bar Foundation （美）北卡罗来纳州律师基金会
NCC Norfolk County Council （英）诺福克郡议会
N. C. C. A. 3d Negligence & Compensation Cases, Annotated, 3d Series 疏忽和补偿判例集, 注释本, 第三套丛书
NCCD National Council on Crime and Delinquency （美）全国（青少年）违法犯罪问题讨论会
NCCDL National College of Criminal Defense Lawyers and Public Defenders （美）国立刑事被告律师和公设辩护人学院
NCCUSL The National Conference of Commissioners on Uniform State Laws 美国统一州法委员会, 美国统一州法律委员全国会议
NCD negotiable certificate of deposit 不记名可转让定期存款证
NCD Nemine Contra dicente (No one dissenting) 一致同意, 无人异议
NCDA National College of District Attorneys （美）国立地区律师学院

NCDS National Center for Dispute Settlement 全面解决纠纷中心(指1968年接受福特基金会的援助,美国仲裁会设立此机构)
NCES the National Center for Education Statistics (美)国家教育权数据中心
N. C. H. National Clearing House (英)全国票据交换所
N. C. I. new capital issues 新发行的资本股票
NCIC National Crime Information Center (美)(联邦调查局)全国犯罪情报中心
N. C. L. Rev North Carolina Law Review (美)北卡罗来纳州法律评论
NCP National Contingency Plan 《美国国家应急计划》
NCPI New Commercial Policy Instrument (欧共体对抗1974年贸易法的)新商业政策文据
NCRMD not criminal responsibility due to mental disorder 因精神障碍无责任能力
NCSC National Center for State Courts (美)全国州法院中心
NCSL National Conference of State Legislatures (美)全国州立法会议
NCUA National Credit Union Administration (美)国家信贷联盟行政署
ND (n. d.) national debt 国债;New Deal (美国罗斯福总统实施的)新政;next day 次日,第二天;no date 无日期,日期不详;no delivery 未交付,未到货,无法投递;Norhtern district 北方区;North Dakota Supreme Court Reports (1890–1953) 北达科他州最高法院判例汇编(1890—1953)
N. D. North Dakota 北达科他;North Dakota Supreme Court Reports (1980–1953) 《北达科他州最高法院判例汇编》(1890—1953);Northern District 北部地区
N/D not dated 未注明日期
n. d. a. not dated at all 未注明(任何)日期
NDA National Defense Act (美)《国防法》;Naval Discipline Act (英)海军纪律条令,海军军纪惩处法
NDAA National District Attorneys Association (美)全国地区律师协会,全国地区检察官协会
NDCC North Dakota Century Code (美)北达科他州百年法规
NDEA National Defense Educations Act (美)《国防教育法》
Ne native 本地的,本国的,土著的
N. E. national emergency 全国紧急状态;National Executive 国家最高行政长官;no effects 无存款;noneffective 无效的;North, Eastern Reporter 东北判例汇编
N/E no effects 无存款(指空头支票);noneffective 无效的
Neb. Nebraska Reports (美)内布拉斯加州判例汇编
NEC necessary 必要的;Nuclear Energy Commission (美)核能委员会
N. E. C. Notes of Ecclesiastical Cases (Eng.) (英)宗教判例注释
N. E. 2d North Eastern Reporter, Second Series (美)东北区判例汇编,第二套丛书
NEET Not in Education, Employment or Training 不上学、不工作、不参加职业培训(指日本青年人越来越多的一种趋向)
n. e. i. Non est inventus 被告所在不明,未查获
NEPA Natioanl Environmental Policy Act (美)(1969年12月31日国会通过的)《国家环境政策法》
N. E. P. A. National Environmental Policy Act (美)《国家环保政策法》
N. E. R. New England Reporter 新英格兰判例汇编;North Eastern Reporter (Commonly Cited N. E.) (美)东北区判例汇编(通常用N. E. 作为援引)
NetGen Net Generation 网络一代
NEWPA new paragraph 另起一段
NF Normes Françaises 法国标准
NFA National Forward Association (美)全国期货协会(1976年成立)
NFFE National Federation of Federal Employees (美)联邦雇员全国联合会
NFLA National Farm Loan Association (U.

S.) （美）全国农场贷款协会
N. F. O. National Freight Organization （英）全国货运组织
NFPA National Fire Protection Association （美）全国消防协会
NFPCA National Fire Prevention and Control Administration （美）全国火警预防和控制管理局
NFS not for sale 不出售的；非卖品
NFU not the first to use (nuclear weapons) 不首先使用（核武器）
NFZ Nuclear Free Zone 无核区
NG National Guard （美）国民警卫队；negotiation group 谈判小组；no good（或 not good） 不行，无用，次品
NGOs Non-Governmental Organizations 非政府组织，非政府机构
NGRI not guilt by reason of insanity 无刑事责任能力者；因精神障碍而无罪
N. H. Act National Housing Act （美）《国家住房建筑法》
NHR National Hunt Rules （英）全国狩猎法规
N. H. R. S New Hampshire Revised Statutes （美）新罕布什尔州修订的法规
NHSB National Highway Safety Bureau （美）国家公路安全局
NHTSA National Highway Traffic Safety Administration （美）国家公路交通安全管理局
NI national income 国民收入；national insurance 国民保险
N. I. Northern Ireland Law Reports 北爱尔兰判例汇编
NIA National Intelligence Agency 国家情报局
NIC National Intelligence Committee 国家情报委员会；National Investors Council （美）全国投资者理事会
NIDA National Institute of Drug Abuse （美）全国吸毒问题研究会
NIDR National Institute for Dispute Resolution （美）争端解决全国协会（设于华盛顿）
NII National Information Infrastructure 全国信息基础机构（框架），（美）国家信息基础设施
N. I. L. Negotiable Instruments Law （流通）票据法
NIPLECC National Industrial and Intellectual Property Law Enforcement Coordinate Commission （美）1999年通过的"全国知识产权执法协调委员会"
N. Ir. Northern Ireland Law Reports (1924-date) 北爱尔兰法律判例汇编（1924年至今）
NIRC National Industrial Relations Court （英）全国劳资关系法院
nit. no filling time 未填时间；no fixed time 时间未定，不定期
N. J. S. A. New Jersey Statutes Annotated （美）新泽西州注释法规
N. J. Stat. Ann. (West) New Jersey Statutes Annotated （美）新泽西州注释法规（西方版）
N. J. Super. New Jersey Superior Court Reports （美）新泽西州高级法院判例汇编
N/K not known 不详，不明
NKKK Nippon Kaiji Kentei Kyokai 日本海事检定协会
n. l. new line 另起一行，提行；non licet 不允许；non liquet 不清楚
N. L. National Labour Party （英）工党；net loss 净损失，净亏；New Latin 新拉丁语
NLADA National Legal Aid and Defender Association 全国法律协助和辩护人协会
NLC National Legislative Council （美）全国立法委员会
N. L. F. (NLF) National Law Foundation （美）全国法律基金会；National Liberation Front （美）全国自由阵线，（南也门）民族解放阵线
NLG National Lawyers' Guild （美）全国律师公会
NLGOA National and Local Government Officers Association （英）国家和地方政府官员协会
NLRA National Labor Relations Act （美）

《全国劳资关系法》
NLRB National Labor Relation Board （美）国家劳工关系委员会
NLT not later than 不迟于……
N. M. New Mexico (Supreme Court) Reports （美）新墨西哥州（最高法院）判例汇编
NMAA New York Maritime Arbitrators Association 纽约海事仲裁委员会
N. M. Laws Laws of New Mexico 新墨西哥法
NMS national marine (service) ship （美）国家商船队船舶
N. M. S. New Mexico Statutes （美）新墨西哥州法规
NN names 名,姓名;名称（复数）
N. N. no name 无签名
NNC Non-Nuclear Countries 非核国家
NNI net national income 国民纯收入
NNSA National Nuclear Security Agency （美）国家核安全局
NNSC Neutral Nations Supervisory Commission 中立国监督委员会
NOAA (N. O. A. A.) National Oceanic and Atmospheric Administration （美）国家海洋和大气管理局
N. O. R. notice of readiness 准备（装货）通知书;not otherwise rated 不另估价,不另规定
N. O. V. Non Obstante Verdicto (the Judgment notwithstanding) 但是的裁定（指不顾陪审团的评断）
NOV. Sc. Nova Scotia Supreme Court Reports(Canada) （加）新斯科夏省最高法判例汇编
NOW negotiable order of withdrawal 可转让支提款单指令; National Organization of Women 全国妇女组织
NP National Police 国家警察; national price 国内价格; new paragraph 另起一段; Norwegian Patent 挪威专利; Notary Public 公证人
N. P. C. National Patent(s)Council （美）全国专利委员会; National People's Congress （中）全国人民代表大会; Nisi Prius Cases, English 英国民事审判法律判例; Non-Participating Countries 非参加国
NPF not provided for 不为……提供
NPL National Priorities List （美）国家优先名单
n. p. or d. no place or date （出版）地点或日期不详
NPQ negotiated price quota 谈判价格限额
NPR National Police Reserve 警察预备队; National Public Radio 国家公共广播电视台
NPSL National Public Service Law （日）《国家公务员法》
NPT Nine-Power Treaty 九国公约; Non Proliferation Treaty 不扩散核武器条约
NPV no par value 无票面价值
NR Bosanquet & Pullers New Reports (1804-1807) (Eng.) （英）博赞克特和普勒的新判例汇编(1804—1807); New Reports (1862-1865) (Eng.) （英）新判例汇编(1862—1865); Not Reported 未曾汇编（报道）过; nonresident 非居民,非居住本地的人
NRA 1.National Recovery Act （美）国家复兴法 2.National Rifle Association 全国来复（枪）协会
NRC National Research Council （美）全国科学研究委员会; Nuclear Research Council （美）核研究委员会; Nuclear Regulatory Commission （美）核管制委员会
NRWC National Right to Work Committee （美）全国劳动权利委员会
NS not sufficient 存款不足; new series 新丛书
NSA (N. S. A) National Service Act （美）《国民义务兵役法》; national Security Agency （美）国家安全局; National Security Act （美）《国家安全法》
N. S. C. National Security Council （美）国家安全委员会
N. S. C. A. National Society for Clean Air （英）全国空气净化学会
NSCO Naval Security Control Office （英）海军安全处

NSF　no sufficient funds　存款不足,资金不足
NT　National Treatment Principle　国民待遇原则;Narrower Term　狭义引语(术语)
NTB　Non-tariff Barriers　非关税壁垒
Nts.　Notes　注解,说明
N. T. S.　not to scale　不按比例
NU　name unknown　船名不详,名称不详;Nations Unies　联合国
NUSEC　National Union of Societies for Equal Citizenship　(英)全国公民身份平等协会联盟
N. V.　Nevada　(美)内华达州;nominal value　票面值;New Vension　基督教《圣经》新译本
NW　North Western Reporter　(美)西北区判例汇编
N/W　next week　下周
N. W. C.　National Water Council　(英)全国水质委员会
N. W. 2d.　North Western Reporter, Second Series　(美)西北区判例汇编,第二套丛书
N. W. L. Rev (N. W. U. L. R)　North Western University Law Review　(美)西北大学法律评论
NWRO　National Welfare Rights Organization　(美)全国福利权利组织
NWSA　National Women's Suffrage Association　(英)全国妇女选举权协会
N. Y.　New York Court of Appeals Reports　(美)纽约上诉法院判例汇编
N. Y. Ann. Cas.　New York Annotated Cases　(美)纽约注释判例集
N. Y. App. Dec.　New York Court of Appeals Decisions　纽约上诉法院判决录
N. Y. App. Div.　New York Supreme Court Appellate Division Reports　纽约最高法院

上诉庭判例汇编
N. Y. B.　New York Business Corporation Law　(美)《纽约贸易公司法》
N. Y. Ch. Sent.　New York Chancery Sentinel　纽约衡平法院守卫
N. Y. CITY Ct.　New York City Court　纽约城市法院
N. Y. L. F.　New York Law Forum　(美)纽约州法律论坛
NYLS　New York Law School　(美)纽约法学院
NYPOE　New York Port of Embarkation　(美)纽约起运港
NYS　New York Supplement　纽约补篇
N. Y. S.　New York State Reporter　纽约州判例汇编
N. Y. S. 2d.　New York Supplement Reporter, Second Series　纽约判例汇编补篇,第二套丛书
NYSB　New York State Bar Association　(美)纽约州律师协会
N. Y. S. B. A　New York State Bar Association　纽约州律师协会
NYSE (N. Y. S. E.)　New York Stock Exchange　纽约股票交易所
N. Y. St　New York State Reporter　纽约州判例汇编
N. Y. St. Rep.　New York State Reporter　(美)纽约州判例汇编
N. Y. Sup. Ct　New York Supreme Court Reporter (1873–1896)　纽约最高法院判例汇编(1873—1896)
N. Y. Wkly. Dig.　New York Weekly Digest　(美)纽约每周判决摘要汇编
N. Z. L. R.　New Zealand Law Reports (1883–date)　新西兰法律判例汇编(1883年至今)

O

o　occupation　占领,占据,职业;Ohio　俄亥俄州;Ohio Reports　俄亥俄州判例汇编;Otto' United States Supreme Court Reports (91–107 U. S. Reports)　奥托的美国

最高法院判例汇编(美国判例汇编 91—107);old 老的,旧的;operation 操作,运行;order 命令,勋位,勋章,订货,订单,次序,等级;owner 物主,所有人

O. A. official assignee 正式代理人,正式受托人,法定受让人;Ohio Appellate Reports (美)俄亥俄州上诉判例汇编;Oudh Appeals (印)奥德赫上诉案例(汇编)

O/A open account 往来账户,未结算账目

OAA Old-Age Assistance (美)老年补助

OAI Open access initiatives 开放获取

OAP Office of Alien Property 外侨财产办公室

OAPEC the Organization of Arab Petroleum Exporting Countries 阿拉伯石油输出国组织

OAS Organization of American States, (UN) (联合国)美洲国家组织

OASDB Old Age, Survivors and Disability Benefits 老年人、残存者和丧失能力者的福利

OASI Old Age and Survivors Insurance 老年人及残存者保险

OAU Organization of African Unity 非洲统一组织

Ob. observation 观察,观测;observe 观察,观测;observer 观察员,观测员

OB obsolete 已废的、陈旧的、过时的;official business 公务,公事;ordered back 被召回的;order book 订货单

O. B. Official Bulletin, International Commission for Air Navigation 官方公报(国际航空学委员会);Old Bailey (英)古代中央刑事法庭(老贝利)(现在中央刑事法院)

O. B. E. Office of Business Economics (美)(商务部)商业经济管理局;Officer of the British Empire 英国军官

obl. obligation 义务,职责,债,债务,证券;obligatory 必须履行,强制性的

Ob. S. P. Obit Sine Prole 死后无子女

OC occur 发生,出现;office copy 公文正本,正式抄本;Office of Censorship (美)(新闻、电影、书刊等的)检查局;Officer Commanding 司令官,指挥官;other countries 其他国家;overseas Chinese 华侨

O/C open charter 预约租船合同

O. C. A. Ohio Courts of Appeal Reports (1915-1922) (美)俄亥俄州上诉法院判例汇编(1915—1922)

Oc. B/L ocean bill of lading 海运提(货)单

O. C. C. Ohio Circuit (Court) Reports or Decisions (美)俄亥俄州巡回法院判例汇编或判例集

O. C. C. N. S. Ohio Circuit Court Reports, New Series (美)俄亥俄州巡回法院判例汇编,新丛书

O. C. D. (OCD) Ohio Circuit(Court)Decisions (1901-1918) (美)俄亥俄州巡回法院判例集(1901—1918);Office of Civilian Defense (美)民防署,民防局;Online Communication Driver 联机通信传动装置

OCP overland common point 共同卸货点

OCR Office for Civil Rights (美)民事权利局

OCS Outer Continental Shelf 大陆架以外

OD official documents 正式文件;overdraft 透支

O. D. Office Decision (U. S. International Revenue Bureau) 官方裁定(美国国际税收局);Overdose of narcotics 麻醉品过量;Ohio Decision (美)俄亥俄州判决

O/D on demand 见票即付

ODAP Office of Drug Abuse Policy (美)毒品滥用政策管理局

ODC Office of Domestic Commerce (U. S.) (美)国内商业局

ODECA Organization of Central American States 中美洲国家组织

ODR Online Dispute Resolution 在线解决纠纷机制,在线争端解决

OECD Organization for Economic Cooperation and Development 经济合作与发展组织;Organization for European Cooperation & Development 欧洲合作与发展组织

OECS Organization of Eastern Caribbean

States 东加勒比海国家组织(东哥伦比亚国家组织)
OES Bureau of Oceans and International Environment and Scientific Affairs (美)海洋,国际环保和科学事务局
OF ocean freight 远洋运费
OFCC (OFCCP) Office of Federal Contract Compliance (美)联邦契约(合同)遵循署
OFDI Office of Foreign Direct Investment (美)外国直接投资局
Off. Gaz. Pat. Office Official Gazette of the United States Patent Office (1872–date) 美国专利局的官方公报(1872年至今)
OFFJT off the job training 离职训练,离职培训
OFPC Office of Foreign Property Custodian (美)外国人财产管理局
OFR Office of the Federal Register (美)联邦注册登记局
OHIM Office for Harmonization of Internal Market 内部市场协调局
Ohio St. 3rd Ohio State Reports 3rd Series (美)俄亥俄州判例汇编,第三套丛书
OJ ordre du jour 议事日程
O. J. T. On-the-Job Training 不脱产训练;在职培训
O. K. (OK) all right, all correct 可以,行;approved 同意,予以认可
O. K.'d; Ok'd (Okayed) agree to 同意,在……上签上 OK;approve of 对……予以认可
OMB Office of Management and Budget (美)管理和预算局
OMBE Office of Minority Business Enterprise (美)少数民族商业企业局
OMC Open Method of Coordination 公开协商机制
OMP open market paper 公开市场票据
OMVUI Operating a Motor Vehicle Under the Influence 在有影响情况下驾驶机动车辆
OND *Observatoire national de la delinquance* (法国)全国犯罪观察所
ONDRP *Observatoire national de la delinquance et des reponses Penales* (法国)犯罪和刑事反应国家观察所
Ont. Ontario Reports 安大略判例汇编
Ont. El. Cas. Ontario Election Cases 安大略选举判例(集)
o/o on order 已订购而尚未交货的;order of 订货,订单,送交
O/o order of 订货,订单,送交;by the order of 奉……之命,根据……命令;to the order of 交付(某某)
Op. opinion 法院(或法官)判决意见书
OPA Office of Price Administration (美)物价管理局;Overall Payments Agreement 总括支付协定
Op. Att'y. Gen. Opinions of the Attorney General (美)司法部长的意见
Op. Attys. Gen. Opinions of the United States Attorneys General 美国州检察长的判决意见
OPCW the Organization for the Prohibition of Chemical Weapons 禁止化学武器组织
OPEC Organization of Petroleum Exporting Countries 石油出口国家组织
O. P. I. C. (OPIC) Overseas Private Investment Corporation (美)海外私人投资公司
OPM the U. S. Office of Personnel Management (美)人事管理局
O. P. O. One Price Only 不二价
Ops. operations 开业;操作
OPSR Office of Police (英)警察与公共办公室
opt. operate 操作,运转;optimal 最适宜的,最佳的;optimum 最适宜的,最佳的;option 选择,选择权;optional 随意的,任意的,非强制的
o. r. owner's risk (保险上的)货主负责
Or. order 命令,勋位,勋章,订货,订单,次序,等级;original 最初的,原始的;Oregon Reports (美)俄勒冈州判例汇编
OR official receiver (英)破产案产业管理官员,清算管理官员;Official Referee 官方调解人,正式仲裁人;owner's risk (保险上的)货主负责;" own recognizance"(或release without bail) "承认保

释"(或无保释放)

O/R outward remittance 汇出汇款

ORC Ohio Revised Code (美)俄亥俄州修订法规;Origin Receiving Charge 始发地收货费

Ord. ordain 任命,规定,制定;order 命令,勋位,勋章,订货,订单,次序,等级;ordinance 命令,条例

o. r. det. owner's risk of deterioration (保险上的)腐烂变质由货主负责

O. R. F. (o. r. f.) owner's risk of fire (保险上的)火灾由货主负责;owner's risk of freezing (保险上的)冻坏由货主负责

Orphan' Ct. Orphans' Court 孤儿法院

ORS Ohio Revised Statutes (美)俄亥俄州修订法规

O. S. offside 右侧,远侧,后面,反面;only son 独根,独生子;on spot 当场,立即,在现场;Operational Section (美)作战科;ordinary seaman (英)新水兵

OSA Official Secrets Act (英)《公务机密法》

OSHA The U. S. Occupational Safety and Health Administration (美)职业安全及健康管理署

OSK Osaka Shosen Kaisha 日本大阪商船会社

ot ought 应该,应当

o/t old terms 旧例,原条件

O/t on truck (美)卡车上交货

Ot. (Ott) Otto's United States Supreme Court Reports (91-107 U. S.) (美)奥托的美国最高法院判例汇编(91—107 U. S.)

OT ocean transportation 远洋运输;old terms 旧例,原条件;overtime 加班,加班费;on truck (美)卡车上交货;overseas trade 对外贸易;海外贸易,overseas transportation 远洋海运,海外运输

OT Office of Telecommunication 电信局

O. T. C. Overseas Trade Corporations 对外贸易公司,海外贸易公司

OTC Over the Counter 非处方药,买卖交易通过经纪人而不是交易所,电话交易

OTDS Overall Trade Distorting Support 总体性贸易扭曲支持

O. U. official use 公务使用

O. W. out of wedlock 非法婚姻的,私生的

OWI Operating Under Intoxicated 酗酒驾车

Owen Owen's English King's Bench Reports 欧文的英国高等法院(王座法庭)判例汇编

OWVI Operating a Motor Vehicle While Intoxicated 酗酒驾驶机动车

O. W. R. Ontario Weekly Reporter (加)安大略省判例汇编

OY (oy) optimum yield 最适度的产量,最适条件收益

P

P Pacific Reporter 太平洋区判例汇编;plaintiff 原告,检举人;page 页;park 停车场,公园;parts 部分,部位,成分;part 部分,成分;passable 可通行的,能通过的;patent 专利(权),专利品,专利的,有专利的;patrol 巡逻,巡查,巡逻队;pattern 模型,榜样,样品,样式,图样,图像;pondere 按重量;population 人口,全体居民;port 港口;position 位置,地位,形势,状态;power 力,能力,动力,权,权力,强国,国;powerful 强大的,效力大的;president 总统,(中)(国家)主席,议长,校长,会长,行长;pro 为了……,按照……;probate 遗嘱认证(检验)(的),认证的遗嘱;profession 职业

1891 P. Law Reports, 1891, Probate, Eng. (英)法律判例汇编,1891年,遗嘱检验

P. 2d Pacific Reporter, Second Series (美)太平洋地区判例汇编,第二套丛书

Pa. Pennsylvania Supreme Court Reports (1845-date) （美）宾夕法尼亚州最高法院判例汇编(1845年至今); Pennsylvania State Reports （美）宾夕法尼亚州判例汇编

P. A. particular average 单独海损; Payment Agreement 支付协定; paying agent 付款代理; personal accident 人身意外伤害,人身事故; Port Agency 港口代办处,港口经理处; Port Authority 港务局; Potsdam Agreement 波茨坦协定; press attaché 新闻专赞; professional association 专业协会,行业组织

P/A particular average 单独海损; power of attorney 代理权,委托书

Pa. Cas Pennsylvania Supreme Court Cases, Sadler （美）宾夕法尼亚州最高法院判例集,萨德勒编

Pa. Cmwith. Pennsylvania Commonwealth Court Reports （美）宾夕法尼亚州州法院判例汇编

Pa. Co. Ct. R. Pennsylvaria County Court Reporter （美）宾夕法尼亚州的县法院判例汇编

Pa. C. S. A. Pennsylvania Consolidated Statutes Annotated （美）宾夕法尼亚州合并的注释法规(汇编)

Pa. Dist. & Co. 2d Pennsylvania District and County Reports, Second Series （美）宾夕法尼亚地区和县判例汇编,第二套丛书

Pa. Dist, R. Pennsylvania District Reports （美）宾夕法尼亚地区判例汇编

Paine's Circuit Court Reports (U. S.) （美）佩纳斯巡回法庭判例汇编

Pa. Law Ser. Pennsylvania Law Series （美）宾夕法尼亚州法律丛书

Pa. Misc. Pennsylvania Miscellaneous Reports （美）宾夕法尼亚州综合判例汇编

Pamph. Laws Pamphlet Laws, Acts 法规、法案小册子

Par Paragraph 段落

Par. Dec. Parson's Decisions, Mass.（美）帕森的马萨诸塞州判例

Parker. Cr. R. Parker's Criminal Reports, N.Y. （美）帕克的纽约刑事判例汇编

Pall. parliament 国会,议会; parliamentary 国会的,议会的,议员的

Pari. Agt. Parliamentary Agent （英）议会财产代理人

parl. proc. parliamentary procedure 议会的议事程序

Parl. S. Parliamentary Secretary （英）政务次官

Parlt parliament 国会,议会

Parly parliamentary 国会的,议会的,议员的

Pars. Eq. Cas. Parsons' Select Equity Cases, Pa. 帕森斯的宾夕法尼亚州衡平法判例选

pas. passenger 乘客,旅客

Pas. Terminus Paschae （英）(法院)春季开庭期;(大学)春季学期

Paschal's Ann. Const. Paschal's United States Constitution, Annotated 帕斯卡尔的美国注释宪法

Pasch. Dig. Paschal's Texas Digest of Decisions （美）帕斯卡尔的得克萨斯州判决摘要汇编

pass. passage 通过,通行;飞越;航行;通路;航道;船费

Pa. Super. Pennsylvania Superior Court Reports （美）宾夕法尼亚州高级法院判例汇编

Pat. patent 专利(权),专利品,专利的,有专利权的; Patent Office （美）专利局; patrol 巡逻,巡查,巡逻队; pattern 模型,榜样,样品,样式,图样,图像; Paterson's Laws 佩特森的法规(汇编)

pat. pending A designation attached to a product while the Patent Office is considering the patent application 待决的产品名称(指专利局正考虑的专利申请)

patd (pat'd) patented 专利的,有专利权的

Pat. Law Rey. Patent Law Review, Washington, D.C. 美国首府华盛顿专利法律评论

Pat. Off. Patent Office （美）专利局

Pat. Off. Rep. Patent Office Reports （美）专利局判例汇编

PAYE　pay as you earn　（英）所得税预扣法（从工资中预扣）；pay as you enter　上船后即付
Paymt　payment　支付；偿还；报酬
Payt. (payt)　payment　支付,偿还,报酬
PB　Policy Board　政策委员会；Political Bureau　政治局；private brand　私人商标
PBA　Patrolmen's Brotherhood Association　（美）巡警兄弟会
PBGC　Pension Benefit Guaranty Corporation　养老福利担保公司
PBS　Public Build Service　公共建筑服务部（美国行政事务管理局内的一个单位）
PBS　Public Building Service　（美）公共建筑服务部
PBS　Public Broadcasting System　公共广播电视系统,公共广播系统
P/c　per cent　每百,百分之……；petty cash　小额现金；price catalogue　价目表,定价表；price(s) current　市价表,行情表
P. C.　Judicial Committee of the Privy Council　（英）枢密院司法委员会；paid cash　付现；Parliamentary Cases　议会判例；participation certificates　参加证书；Patent Cases　专利（案件）判例；Payments Committee　支付委员会；Penal Code　刑法典；Permanent Committee　常设委员会；personal computer　个人计算机；Pleas of the Crown　刑事诉讼；Police Constable　（英）普通警员；politically correct　政治上的惩罚；port of call　停靠港；Preparatory Commission　筹备委员会；prime cost　买进原价；Prison Commission　（英）监狱委员会；private contract　私人合同（契约）；Privy Council　（英）枢密院；Privy Councillor　（英）枢密院官员,枢密院顾问官；Prize Court　捕获法庭,处理战利品的（海军）军事法庭；Probate Court　遗嘱检验法院；Procedural Commission　程序委员会；procedure civile　民事诉讼（法）；Professional Corporation　行业法人,行业公司；Protective Custody　保护性监禁
PCA　Permanent Court of Arbitration　常设仲裁法庭
PCB　petty cash book　零用现金簿,private car benefits　私人车辆保险赔偿费
Pchar.　purchaser　买主,采购人
pchs.　purchase　购买,采购
pchsr　purchaser　买主,采购人
PCH (P. C. I. J.)　Permanent Court of International Justice　国际常设法庭；Permanent Court of International Justice Cases　国际常设法庭案件（案例）集；Permanent Court of International Justice Reports of Judg(e)ments　（国联）常设国际法庭判决汇编；Permanent Court of International Justice Reports of Judg(e)ments　（国联）常设国际法庭判决汇编
PCR　Stands for polymerase chain reaction, the newest method of DNA analysis.　聚合酶链反映（DNA 分析的最新方法）；post-conviction remedy　判罪后的补救
P. & C. R.　Property and Compensation Reports (Formerly Planning and Compensation Reports) (1949-date)　（英格兰和威尔士）财产和补偿判例汇编（以前为：计划与补偿判例汇编）(1949 年至今)
PCR actions　Post-conviciton relief (Remedies) proceeding　判罪后救济程序,判罪后补救程序
P. Ct.　Probate Court　遗嘱检验法庭
PCT　Patent Cooperation Treaty　专利合作条约
PCSD　President's Council on Sustainable Development　美国可持续发展总统委员会
P. D.　law reports, Probate Divorce and Admiralty Division (1875-1890) (Eng.)　（英）判例汇编,遗嘱检验,离婚和海事法庭（1875—1890）; Pension and Bounty (U. S. Department of Interior)　（美国内务部）养老金和补助费；paid　付讫；partial delivery　部分交付；per day　每日,按日；passport diplomatique　外交护照；per diem　每日,按日；Personnel Department　人事部门（局、处、科等）；Police Department　警察局；port dues　港口税；port of destination　目的港；preferential duties　特惠关税；President's Decision　总统决定；preventive detention　预防性拘留

PDA Personal Digital Assistant 个人数字助理
P. D. A. Probate, Divorce and Admiralty (Eng.) （英）遗嘱检验、离婚和海事法庭
P. D. A. D. Probate, Divorce and Admiralty Division （英）遗嘱检验、离婚与海事法庭
PDD past due date 过期；priority delivery date 优先交付日期
PDR Purchase of development right （美）土地发展权征购
PE preliminary enquiry 初步调查；Private Equity 私募股权投资；Private Equity Funds （美）私人股权基金
Peck. El. Cas. Peckwell's Election Cases, Eng.（英）皮克韦尔的选举判例（汇编）
Pennewill Pennewill Reports, Del. （美）彭尼韦尔判例汇编，特拉华州
Penn. L. J. R. Pennsylvania Law Journal Reports Edited by Clark （美）宾夕法尼亚法律期刊判例汇编（克拉克编）
Penol penologic(al) 刑罚学的, 监狱学的；penology 刑罚学, 监狱学
Pent Pentagon （美）五角大楼（国防部办公大楼）
PEP (P. E. P.) Public Employment Program 公众就业计划；Program Evaluation Procedure 计划评审程序；Patent Examining Procedure 专利审查程序
per. periodical 周期的, 定期的；person 人, 本人, 人身；personal 个人的, 本人的, 人身的；personnel 全体人员, 人事（部门）
Per. se 本身, 本来, 本质上
Pet. Adm. Peters' Admiralty, U. S. 美国彼得斯海事法院
PEU Pan-European Union 泛欧联盟
PF private flow 私人投资来源；private fund 私人资金
PFC Production Flexibility Contract Payments 生产灵活性合同支付
PFPA Pentagon Force Protection Agency （美）五角大楼武力保护局（2001 年 9 · 11 后成立）
PFS passengers and freight service 客运及货运业务
P. G. paying guest 搭伙房客；Persona Grata 受欢迎的人；postgraduate （大学的）研究生；Pressure Group 压力集团；Procurator General 检察总长；Provisional Government 临时政府
P-H Prentice-Hall （美）学徒厅堂（指印制法律活页服务机构）
P. H. A. Public Health Act （美）公共卫生法案；Public Housing Administration （美）公众房产管理局
Phil. Ch. Phillips' English Chancery Reports 菲利普斯英国大法官法庭判例汇编
Philippine Philippine Reports 菲利平判例汇编
PHS Public Health Service （美）公共卫生局
PHV Pro hac vice 只此一回, 仅限于这一特殊场合
PIC Prior informed consent 事先知情同意
PIK payment in kind 实物支付
PINS person in need of supervision 需要监管的人
pitiff plaintiff 原告
Pittsb. R. Pittsburgh Reports, Pa. （美）宾夕法尼亚州, 匹兹堡市判例汇编
PJ Presiding Judge 审判长, 主审法官
PKF Peace Keeping Force 维和部队
PKPA Parental Kidnapping Prevention Act 《防止父母劫持法》(1980 年)
P. L. partial loss 部分损失；Patent Licence 专利许可证；perfect liberty 完全自由；Public Law 公法；pamphlet laws 法规小册子
P/L partial loss 部分损失；payload 有效载荷, 净载荷
P&L profit and loss 损益
Plan employee benefit plan （美）雇员福利计划
PLI Practicing Law Institute 开业律师学会
P. & L. Laws Private and Local Laws 私法和地方法
Plow. Plowden's English King's Bench Reports 普洛登的英国高等法院（王座法

庭)判例汇编

P. L. & R. Postal Laws and Regulations (美)邮政法规

PLR Pacific Law Reporter (美)太平洋区法律判例汇编;Private Legislation Reports (Sc.) (苏格兰)私法立法判例汇编;Punjab Law Reporter (India) (印)旁遮普省法律判例汇编;Public Lending Right 公共借阅权

PLS professional legal secretary (通过法官协会考试的)专业司法官;profit and loss statement 损益计算书,损益表

P/m past month 上月

PM Bureau of Political Military Affairs (美)政治军事事务局;police militaire 宪兵;police mobile (法)机动警察;Prime minister 总理,首相;push money 佣金

PMRA Patent Misuse Reform Act (美)1998国会通过的《专利权滥用改革法》

PMSI Purchase Money Security Interests 购买价金担保权

PMT payment 支付

pnt patient 病人;患者

PNTBT Partial Nuclear Test Ban Treaty 部分禁止核试验条约

p. o. postal order (英)邮政汇票;previous orders 以前的命令,原令

PO par ordre 根据命令;Parcels Office 包裹房;Passport Office 护照局;Patent Office 专利局;Pay Office 收支处,付款处;postal order (英)邮政汇票;Public Officer 公职人员,公务员;purchase order 订购单

POA Police Officers' Association (美)警察协会

P. O. A. Prison Officers' Association (英)典狱官协会

POB place of birth 出生地

P. O. B. A. Patent Office Board of Appeals (美)专利申请委员会

POC port of call (沿途)停靠港

POD (P. O. D.) pay on delivery 货到付款;port of debarkation 卸载港,下船港;payable on death 死时支付

POE (P. O. E.) port of embarkation 装

载港,上船港;port of entry 进关港

P of W prisoner of war 战俘

Pol. police 警察,警察队;警察当局;policeman 警察

Pol. Code Political Code 政治准则

Pol. Cont. Pollock on Principles of Contract at Law and Equity 波洛克《论普通法和衡平法上的合同原理》

Pom. Eq. Jur. Pomeroy's Equity Jurisprudence 波默罗依的《衡平法原理》

P. O. M. O. post-office money order 邮政汇票

Pom. Rein Pomeroy on Civil Remedies 波默罗依《论民事法律补救》

Pom. Rein. & Rem. Rights Pomeroy on Civil Remedies & Remedial Rights 波默罗依《论民事法律补救和补救权利》

Poph Popham's English King's Bench Reports 波帕姆的英国高等法院(王座法庭)判例汇编

p. o. r. payable on receipt 收到后即付的,收货付款;pay on return 返回后付款;port of refuge 避难港

Pore. Code Rem. Pomeroy on Code Remedies 波默罗依《论法规补救》

Pore. Spee. Perf. Pomeroy on Specific Performance of Contracts 波默罗依《论合同(契约)的强制履行》

POS point of sale 销售点

Post-nup postnuptial Agreement 婚后协议

POW prisoner of war 战俘

Pow. App. Proc. Powell's Law of Appellate Proceedings 鲍威尔的《上诉程序法》

pp pages 页(复数);parliamentary papers (英)议会文件;per paragraph 根据某段(节);per procurationem 由……代表,由……代理;personal property 私人财产,动产;posted price 标价;producer's price 生产价格;public property 公共财产

P/p partial pay 部分付款,部分支付

P. P. (或 **per/pro**) per procurationem 由某某代表

p. pc. per procurationem 由……代表,由……代理

PPCC People's Political Consultative Conference （中）人民政治协商会议
P. P. I. policy proof of interest 保险单证明可保利益，凭保险单证明的保险利益
PPM Processing & Product Method 产品的加工过程和加工方法
PPP Public-Private-Partnership 公私合作制，亦称公私合作伙伴关系或公私伙伴关系（泛指公共行政部门与私人部门不同合作方式的综合）
P. Pro. （**P. Pro.** 或 **p. pro**） per procurationem 由……代表
pprs papers 文件；证件
P. Q. preceding question 优先考虑的问题，先决问题；previous question （议会中的）先决问题（或动议）
pr. per 每，经，由，靠，按照，根据；power 力，能力，权，权力，强国，国；practice 实践，实习；preferred 优先的；present 现在的，出席的；price 价格，价位；prove 证明，检验
P. R. parcel receipt 包裹收据；Parliamentary Reports （英）议会议事录；payroll 工资发放名册；People's Republic 人民共和国；press release 新闻稿，新闻公报；public relation （通过宣传手段建立的）与公众的联系，对外联络，对外宣传
Prac. Law practical lawyer 开业律师
PRC (P. R. C.) People's Republic of China 中华人民共和国；Postal Rate Commission （各种邮件）邮资委员会
Prec. Ch. Precedents in Chancery. Eng. （英）大法官法庭的先例（判例）
Prem. premier 总理，首相；premeditation 预想，预谋，计划；premium 奖金，保险费，贴水
prenup. prenuptial agreement 婚前协议，预备结婚协议
Prep. preparation 准备
PREPCON preparatory conference 筹备会议
Prer. Prerogative Court （英国历史上的）审查遗嘱的）大主教法庭
PRES president 总统，主席，议长，会长，校长，行长
Presdl presidential 总统（或校长等）的；

总统（或校长等）职务的；统辖的，支配的
Prest president 总统；主席，议长，会长；校长；行长
presv. preservation 保存，保管；保护；preserve 保存，保藏，保护
pri. primate 大主教；primitive 原始的，早期的，简单的，基本的；prison 监狱；private 个人的，私有的，列兵，士兵
pris prisoner 囚犯，拘留犯，俘虏
Priv (Priv.) private 个人的，私有的，列兵，士兵；privately 私下地，秘密地
Priv. Laws private laws 私法
PRM Bureau of Population, Refugees and Migration （美）人口，难民和移民局
pro probation 检验，鉴定，试用，见习，缓刑；probationer 试用人员，见习生，缓刑犯
prob. probation 检验，鉴定，试用，见习，缓刑；problem 问题；problematic 有问题的，未决定的
Prob. English Probate and Admiralty Reports for Year Cited 每年援引的英国遗嘱检验和海事法判例汇编
Prob. 1917 Law Reports, Probate Division. Eng. 遗嘱检验法庭，英国法律判例汇编（1917年）
Prob. Ct. Rep. Probate Court Reporter, Ohio （美）俄亥俄州遗嘱检验法庭判例汇编
Prob. Div. Probate Division, English Law Reports 遗嘱检验法庭，英国法律判例汇编
probn probation 检验，鉴定；试用，见习；缓刑
proc. procedure 过程，程序；process 过程，工序，方法，加工，处理；proclaim 宣告，声明；proclamation 宣告，声明
prof. profession 职业；professional 职业的，专业的，以……为职业的人，专业人员
promy promissory note 本票，期票
Pros. Atty (Pros. Atty.) Prosecuting Attorney （美）检察官
protec. protectorate 保护国；（强国对弱国的）保护关系
Pro tem pro tempore 当时，暂时，临时，及时

Prov. St. Statutes, Laws of the Province of Massachusetts （美）马萨诸塞州的制定法、法规（汇编）

PRP Potential Responsible Parties 潜在责任人

P. R. R Puerto Rico Supreme Court Reports （美）波多黎各最高法院判例汇编

ps. pseudo 假的,伪的,冒充的;pseudonym 笔名,假名;pseudonymous 用笔名（写）的,用假名（写）的

PS Public Statute 公共法规

P. S. Parliamentary Secretary （英）政务次官;penal servitude 劳役监禁;police sergeant 警官,巡官;police station 警察局,派出所;postscriptum （信末的）附言,再者,又及;press secretary 新闻秘书;private secretary 私人秘书;Privy Seal （英）御玺;production sharing 产品分享制;profit sharing 利润分享制;public sale 拍卖;Purdon's Pennsylvania Statutes Annotated 珀登的宾夕法尼亚州注释法规（汇编）

PSA Public Security Act 公共安全法;property settlement agreement 财产处理协议书

PSAAJC Permanent Secretariat Afro-Asian Jurists Conference 亚非法学家会议常设秘书处

PSB Preliminary Screening Board （美）预审委员会

P. S. D. pay supply depot （英）军需库;Petty Sessional Division （英）即决法庭

PSI presentence investigation 审判前调查

PSI Proliferation Security Initiative 防扩散安全倡议

PSP Principal supplier principle 主要供应者原则

PST Profit Sharing Trustee 利润分成受托人

PT Peace Treaty 和平条约;port 港口

PTA Preferential Trading Agreement 特惠贸易协定

PTAB Patent Trial and Appeal Board 专利审判与上诉委员会

PTCR Patent, Trademark and Copyright Research Institute （美）专利、商标和版权研究会

PTI previously taxed income 以前的税务收入

PTO the Patent and Trademark Office 专利商标局

P. Tr Private Trust (includes testamentary, investment, life insurance, holding title, etc.) 私人信托（包括遗嘱、投资、人寿保险、拥有产权等等）

pub (pub.) publication 出版,发行;出版物

Pub. Gen. Laws Public General Laws 一般性法规

publ. public 公共的,公开的,公立的,全国的;publication 出版,发行,出版物;publish 出版者,发行者

publr publisher 出版者,发行者

pubn publication 出版,发行;出版物

Pub. St. Public Statutes 公共法规

PUC Public Utilities Commission 公用事业委员会

Puffendorf Puffendorf's Law of Nature and Nations 普芬道尔夫的《自然法与民族》

PUFPB People United to Fight Police Brutality （美）国民反警察残暴联合会

pun. punish 处罚,惩罚;punishment 处罚,惩罚

PUNF Permanent United Nations Force 联合国永久部队

pur. purchase 购买,采购;purchaser 购买人,买主,采购人;purchasing 购买（的）,采购（的）;pursuit 追击,追踪

P. U. R. Public Utilities Reports （美）公用事业判例汇编

Purd. Dig. Laws Purdon's Digest of Laws, Pa. （美）珀登的法规判决摘要汇编,宾夕法尼亚州

Pv Par value （股票等的）票面价值;按价值

P. V. Proces Verbaux 逐字记录,会议记录

Pvt. private 个人的;私人的;列兵

PW per week 每周;per word 每字;prisoners of war 战俘

PWG the President's Working Group on Financial Markets 总统金融市场工作小组（美国金融危机全面爆发后成立的）

P. Wins. Peere Williams' English Chancery Reports 皮尔·威廉斯的大法官法庭判例汇编

Pwr. power 力,能力;权,权力;强国,国

Pymt. payment 支付,付款;偿还;报酬

Q

Q quantity 数量;quarantine （对港口船舶等的）检疫,留验,检疫处;quarterly 每季的;Queen 女王,王后;question 问题;Queensland （澳）昆士兰（州名）;Quebec （加）魁北克（省名）（港市）

Q 此缩略字母在审理的官方记录和证词中表示每一个所问的问题

QA qualification approval 资格认可;quality assurance 质量保证,质量担保;questions and answers 问与答

Q. B. Queen's Bench 英国高等法院（后座法庭）,英国议会的议员席;Queen's Bench Reports （英）后座法庭判例汇编;English Law Reports, Queen's Bench Division (1876–1890) （英）后座（法）庭英国判例汇编（1876—1890）; Law Reports, Queen's Bench Division, Eng. 英国高等法院（后座法庭）法律判例汇编

QC quality certificates 质量检查证,质量合格证;quality check 质量检查;quality control 质量管理;Queen's Counsel （英）（女王的）王室法律顾问;quit claim 放弃要求,（产权或其他权利的）转让合同（契约）

Q. C. F. quare clausum fregit 侵入私地

QDII Qualified Domestic Institutional Investor 合格的境内机构投资者

QDRO Qualified domestic relations order

有资格(合适)的家事(关系)法的安排

Q. E. (q. e.) quod est 即,这就是

Q. E. D. (q. e. d.) quod erat demonstrandum 已经得到证明,验讫

Q. E. F. (q. e. f.) Quod erat faciendum 这就是所要做的

Q. E. I. (q. e. i.) Quod erat inveniendum 这就是所要找的

QFII Qualified foreign institutional investors 合格境外投资者

Q. L. Quebec Law （加）魁北克法

Q. S. quarantine station 检疫站;quarter session （英）每季开审的地方法庭;（美）(某些州的)地方法庭

Queensl. J. P. Queensland Justice of the Peace （澳）昆士兰治安法官

Que. Q. B. Quebec Official Reports, Queen's Bench （加）魁北克后座法庭官方判例汇编

Que. Super (Que. S. C.) Quebec Official Reports, Surpourior Court （加）魁北克高级法院官方判例汇编

quor quorum （英）治安法官（总称）;法定人数

quot quotation 引用,引证;引语;行情报告;报价单

Q. V. (q. v.) Quod vide 见,参看;见该项;参照该条

R

r. rent 租金,租费,租;reply 回答,答复;residence 住处,住宅,公馆;resident

常驻的,驻外官员;road 路,公路
R. railway 铁路;recovery 恢复,复原,回收;register 登记簿,注册簿,商标注册中以 R 表示;registrar 档案管理员,登记员,注册员;regulating 调节,调整;regulations 规则,规章,法规(复数);Republican 共和国的,共和党的;report(s) 报告,公报,报道,(复)判决录,判(案)例汇编,议事录;rule 规定,规则,条例,准则;Rex 国王;the reports 判例汇编;rule 法则,规定;The Reports, Coke's King's Bench (Eng.) (英)科克的王座判例汇编;Regina 王后,女王
RA reinsurance agreement 再保险协定;Royal Academy (英)皇家学会;rule on appeal 上诉法规;Rules and Administration 法规与行政管理
RAM reports and memoranda 报告和备忘录
RAMS recently-acceded members (WTA 的)新成员
Raym. Lord Raymond's English King's Bench Reports 雷蒙德勋爵的英国高等法院(王座法庭)判例汇编
RBP restrictive business practice 限制性商业惯例
RC release clause 豁免条款;research center 研究中心
R. C. Ohio Revised Code 俄亥俄州修订法规;Revised Statutes 1855, Mo. 密苏里州修订法规(汇编)1885 年;Railway Cases 铁路判例集;Revue Critique de Legislation et de Jurisprudence de Canada 加拿大立法和评述杂志;Rolls of Court 法院的记录卷;Ruling Cases 主导的判例集
R. & Can. Cas. Railway & Canal Cases, Eng.(英)铁路和运河判例集
R. C. J. Royal Courts of Justice (英)皇家法院
R. C. L. Ruling Case Law (an Encyclopedia) 主导判例法(则)(一种百科全书)
R. C. M. Revised Code of Montana (美)蒙大拿州的修订法规
RCRA Resource Conservation and Recovery Act (美)1976 年国会通过的《资源保护和回收法》
RCRAS Rogers Criminal Responsibility Assessment Scales 罗杰斯刑事责任评定量表
RCWA Revised Code of Washington (美)华盛顿州的修订法规
RD refer to drawer 请询问出票人;registered 已注册,已登记
R/D record of discussions 讨论记录
R. D. C. Royal Defence Corp (英)皇家保卫团;running down clause (船舶)碰撞责任条款;Rural District Council (英)乡村区议会
r. d. d. required delivery date 要求交货日期
RDQ regimental detention quarters 团拘留所,团禁闭室
RE real estate 不动产,房地产;relative error 相对误差;Royal Exchange 伦敦交易所;with reference to 参照;rational expectation 理性预期
REA Rural Electrification Administration (美)农村电气化管理局
REAP Rural Environmental Assistance Program (美)农村环境协助规划署
rec. receipt 收条,收据;received 已收到,收讫;reciprocity 相互关系,交互作用,互易性,可逆性,倒易;reclamation (因商品质量低劣等)抗议,要求赔偿损失;record 记录,录音,录音带,唱片;recorder 录音机,记录器,记录员,收报机;recording 录音,记录,录音带
recap recapitulate 扼要重述,概括;recapitulation 扼要重述,概括
Recd. (**Rec'd** 或 **recd**) received 已收到,收讫;record 记录,录音,录音带
recog. recognition 认出,识别;recognize 认出,识别
recogns (rocogs) recognizances 保证书,具结;(交付法院的)保证金,保释金
Redf. & B. Redfield & Bigelow's Leading Cases, Eng. (英)雷德菲尔德和比奇洛的主导判例集
redise rediscount 再折扣,(期票)再贴现
Reeve Eng. L. Reeve's English Law 里夫

的英国法

ref. refer 参考,参看;referee 仲裁人,公断人;reference 查阅,参考;referred 已查阅,已参考;reform 改革,革新;reformer 改革者,革新者;refugee 避难者,流亡者,难民;refunding 归还,偿还;refuse 拒绝,拒受,拒给

refee reference 查阅,参考

refd. referred 已查阅,已参考;refund 归还,偿还

Reg. regent 摄政者;registered 已登记的,已注册的,(邮件)已挂号的;registrar 档案管理员,登记员,注册员,记录官员;regulation(s) 规则,规章,条例,办法,调节,调整

REGD registered 已注册,已登记

Reglts regulations 规章,规则,条例,办法

Reg-Neg Regulatory Negotiation (行政)立法协商(程序),制定规章协商

Reg. No. registered number 登记号,注册编号

Regs regions 地区,地带;行政区;regulations 规则,规章,条例,办法

Reg. T. M. registered trademark 注册商标

Reg. U. S. Pat. Off. registered in the United States Patent Office 美国专利局注册的

REIT Real Estate Investment Trust 不动产投资信托

REITA Real Estate Investment Trust Act (美)(1960年国会制定的)《不动产投资信托法》

REITS Real Estate Investment Treatment Trusts 不动产投资信托

REIO Regional Economic Integration Organization 区域经济一体化组织

rel. relate 有关,涉及,relating 与……有关(的),关于;relation 关系;relative 相对的;release 释放,放出;released 已释放的;relic 遗物,遗迹,遗俗

RELET refer to the letter 参照……信件,参照……书

relsd released 已释放的

relv relieve 替换;免除(职务)

Rem. remit 赦免,豁免,免除

Rembt reimbursement 偿还,付还(款项);赔偿

Rem'g remanding 押候

REMIC Real Estate Mortgage Investment Conduits (美)不动产抵押贷款投资代理

ren. reason 理由,原因

REOUR refer to our... 参照我方的(电报、信件……)

REOURLTR refer to our letter 参照我方……信件

REOURTEL refer to our telegram 参照我方……电报

rep. repair 修理,检修;reparation 补偿;(战败国的)赔款,赔偿;repeat 重复

Rep. representative 代表,代理人;(大写)(美)众议院议员

Rep. Coke's English King's Bench Reports 科克的英国高等法院(王座法庭)判例汇编;Knapp's Privy Council Reports (Eng.) (英)纳普的枢密院判例汇编;Wallace's "The Reporters" 华莱士的"判例汇编"

REP Request for Proposals 建议请求,为提案而请求

repr. representative 代表,代理人,(大写)(美)众议院议员;representing 代表,体现

Reps representatives 代表,代理人;(大写)(美)众议院议员

REPT repeat 重复

REQ request 请求,要求;申请

RES resolution 决议

resp. respondent 回答者,答辩人,被告人;responsibility 责任,职责,任务,责任心;responsible 有责任的,负责的,责任重大的

RESPA Real Estate Settlement Procedure Act (美)《不动产清理程序法》

RESTREP resident representative 常驻代表

REURAD referring to your advice 关于(或参照)你方……的通知

REURLET referring to your letter 关于(或参照)你方……的信件

REV revision 修正案,修正

Rev. Civ. Code Revised Civil Code 修订

的民法典

Rev. Civ. ST. Revised Civil Statutes 修订的民事法规(汇编)

Rev. Cr. Code Revised Criminal Code 修订的刑法典

Rev. de Jur. Revue de Jurisprudence, Can. (加)法学评论(期刊)

Rev. de Legis. Revue de Legislation, Can. (加)法律评论,立法评论

Rev. Leg. Revue Legale, Can. (加)法律评论

Rev. Proc. Revenue Procedure 税收程序

Rev. Rep. Revised Reports (1785-1866) (England and Wales) (英格兰和威尔士)修订的判例汇编(1785—1866)

Rev. Rul. Revenue Ruling 税务裁定

Rev. St Revised Statutes 修订的法规(汇编)

RFC Reconstruction Finance Corporation (U. S.) (美)重建金融公司

RFLP Restriction Fragment Length Polymorphism 限制片状长度多晶形(指的更能区别于 DNA 测试形式)

RFRA Religious Freedom Restoration Act (美)(1993 年国会通过的)《宗教自由恢复法》

R. G. D. I. P. Revue Générale de Droit Internationale Public 国际公法综合评论

RHC (R. H. C.) Road Haulage Cases (1950-1955) (Eng.) (英)公路拖运判例集(1950—1955)

R. I. (RI) Rhode Island Reports (美)罗得岛判例汇编;Rhode Island Supreme Court Reports (1828-date) (美)罗得岛最高法院判例汇编(1828 年至今);Rhode Islands (美)罗得岛(州)

Rich. C. P. Richardson's Practice Common Pleas, Eng. (英)理查森的普通高等民事法院

Rich. Eq. Cas. Richardson's Equity Cases, S. C. (美)理查森的衡平法判例集,南卡罗来纳州

Rich. Law Richardson's Law, S. C. (美)理查森的南卡罗来纳州法规

RICO Racketeer Influenced and Corrupt Organization Act (美)(1970 年)《反勒索及受贿组织法》

RIDA Revue International du Droit d'Auteur 国际作者权评论

Ridg. Ap. Ridgeway's Appeal Cases, Ir. 里奇韦的爱尔兰上诉法院判例集

Ridg. P. C. Ridgeway's Parliament Cases, Ir.里奇韦的爱尔兰议会判例集

RIF reduction in force 大批裁员,大规模解雇

RIL Res Ipsa Loquitur 事实不言自明

RJVs Research Joint Ventures (美)研发合营企业

R. L. Revised Laws 修订的法规(汇编);Revue legale (Canada) (加)法律评论;Roman Law 罗马法

rl. est. real estate 不动产,房地产

rlf relief 救济;救济金,救济品;免除(捐税);减轻(税款)

RLVI Revised Laws of Virgin Islands 英属维尔京群岛修订法律汇集

R. M. ready money 现金,现款; registered mail 挂号邮件;resident magistrate (爱尔兰)受薪治安官

RMA Revolution in Military Affairs 军事革命

RMA Risk Management Agency (美)风险管理局

R. O. Receiving Order 法院委派破产者产业管理人的委任书

Rob. Christopher Robinson's English Admiralty Reports 克里斯多弗·鲁宾森的英国海事判例汇编

Robb. Pat. Cas. Robb's Patent Cases, U. S. (美)罗布的专利判例集

ROD Record of Decision 判决记录

ROI return on investment 投资的回报

Rolle (Roll. Rep.) Rolle's English King's Bench Reports 罗尔的英国高等法院(王座法庭)判例汇编

Rom Textbook of Roman Law from Augustas to Justinian 从奥古斯塔至查士丁尼的罗马法课本

ROM read only memories 只读存储器

ROR release on own recognizance 被告提

供保证金释放,具结后释放

ROSCA Rotating Savings and Credit Association 转轮储蓄与信贷协会(又称标会、招会、摇会、义会、互助会等)

Ross Lead. Cas. Ross' Leading Cases, Eng. (英)罗斯的英国主导判例(汇编)

ROW risk of war 战争险

R. P. real property 不动产,房地产; reference price 参考价格; retail price 零售价格; return premium 退回保险费; Rule and Practice 规则和惯例; Rules of Procedure (诉讼)程序规则

R. P. C. Reports of Patent Cases (1884-date) (英格兰和威尔士)专利判例汇编(1884年至今)

R. P. D. & T. M. Reports of Patents, Design and Trade Mark Cases (1884-date) (英格兰和威尔士)专利、设计和商标判例汇编(1884年至今)

RPT repeat 重复; report 报告,判例汇编

RPTD reported 已报告

RQ reserved quota 保留份额

rqmt. requirement(s) 要求,必要条件,必需品

Rqn requisition 正式请求;申请;申请书,请领单;调拨单,征用书

rqr. require 需要,要求; requirement 要求,必要条件,必需品

rqst request 请求,要求;申请

R. & R. Russell & Ryan Crown Cases (Eng.) 拉塞尔和瑞安的英国刑事判例集

R. S. (Rs) Revised Statute(s) 修订的法规

R. S. A. Revised Statutes Annotated 注释的修订法规(汇编)

R. S. C. Revised Statutes of Canada 修订的加拿大法规(汇编); Rules of the Supreme Court (Eng.) (英)最高法院规程(或规则)

R. S. Comp. Statutes of Connecticut, Compilation of 1854 1854年康涅狄格州法规汇编

RSFSR Russian Soviet Federative Socialist Republic 俄罗斯苏维埃社会主义联邦共和国

rsn. reason 理由,原因

RSP Royal Service Police (英)皇家宪兵(队)

R. S. P. C. C. Royal Scottiish Society for Prevention of Cruelty to Children (英)皇家苏格兰防止虐待儿童协会

R. S. V. P. *répondez s'il vous plaît* 请答复(请帖用语); Retired Senior Volunteer Program 退休的高级志愿者规划

RT related terms 相关引语

RTA Regional Trade Agreements 美国在21世纪前签署的"区域贸易协议"

RTI Round Table International 国际圆桌会议

RTM registered trade mark 注册商标

R. T. R. Road Traffic Reports (1970-date) (英格兰和威尔士)公路交通判例汇编(1970年至今)

R. U. C. R. Royal Ulster Constabulary Reserve (英)皇家北爱尔兰警察后备队

RULLCA The Revised Uniform Limited Liability Company Act. 2006 《修改统一有限责任公司法》(2006年)

RULPA Revised Uniform Limited Partnership Act 《修订统一有限合伙法》,《统一有限合伙法》(修订版)(美)1976年

Russ. Ch. Russell's English Chancery Reports 拉塞尔的英国大法官法庭判例汇编

Russ. Eq. Cus. Russell's Equity Cases, N. S. (加)拉塞尔的新斯科夏半岛(Nova Scotia)衡平法判例集

Russ. & M. Russell and Mylne's English Chancery Reports 拉塞尔和迈尔纳的英国大法官法庭判例汇编

Russ. & R. Cr. Cus. Russell and Ryan's English Crown Cases Reserved 拉塞尔和瑞安的英国巡回审判中留待刑事上诉法庭解决的(法律问题)判例集

R. V. ratable value 可估价值; receipt voucher 收据,收条,收货凭证

Ry. & M. Ryan and Moody's English Nisi Prius Reports 瑞安和穆迪的英国巡回民事审判判例汇编

S

S New York Supplement 纽约补篇; scout 侦察员,侦察机; scribe 抄写员; seal 密封,封蜡,封铅,封印,印记,图章; seaman 海员,水兵; search 搜索,搜查,调查,探索; section 章节,款,项,科,室,分支; secret 秘密(的),机密(的); security 安全,保证,保障; Senate 上院,参议院; service 服务,服役,勤务军种,勤务部队,维修保养; sign 符号,记号; signal 信号; single 单(个)的,个别的,唯一的,单身的; socialist 社会主义的,社会主义者,(大写)社会党人,社会党; society 社团,学会,社; Southern Reports (美)南方区判例汇编; stock 存货,库存品,(美)(企业的)股份总额,股本,股票,(英)公债券,公债券; store 仓库,货栈,贮存; suit 起诉,诉讼; Supreme Court Reporter (美)最高法律判例汇编

S. Statute 制定法,法规

3S 指阿根廷"3S"一代,西班牙语中单身、分居和离异三词均以 S 开头

s. a. secundum artem 根据技术规定; sine anno 无年代,无日期; subject to approval (保险上的)有待批准,需经批准; subsistence allowance 生活津贴

S. A. safe arrival 平安到达; savings account 储蓄账户,存款账户; selective application 选择运用,选择适用; special action 特别行动; Shops Act (英)商店法; subsidiary arrangement 补充安排,补充协议; supplementary agreement 补充协定

SA subject to approval 以批准为条件

SACA Surplus Agricultural Commodities' Agreement 剩余农产品协会

SACB Subversive Activities Control Board 颠覆活动控制委员会

SACEM Society of Authors, Composers and Music Publishers 作者、作曲家与音乐出版商协会

SACU Society for Anglo-Chinese Understanding 英中了解协会

SAF Secretary of the Air Force (美)空军部长; Strategic Alert Forces (美)战略警戒部队

Salk Salkeld's English King's Bench Reports 索凯尔德的英国高等法院(王座法庭)判例汇编

S. A. L. T. Strategic Arms Limitation Talks 战略武器限制谈判; South African Law Times 南非法律时代

Sandf. ch. Sandford's Chancery Reports, N. Y. 桑德福的纽约衡平法院判例汇编

Sand. & H. Dig. Sandels and Hill's Digest of Statutes, Ark. (美)桑德尔斯和希尔的阿肯色州制定法判决摘要汇编

Sand. Inst. Just. Introd. Sandars' Edition of Justinian's Institutes 《查士丁尼法学纲要》桑达斯版

Sand. I. Rep. Sandwich Island Reports Hawaii (美)夏威夷岛判例汇编

SAR sea air rescue 海空救援; search and rescue 搜索救援

SARA Superfund Amendment and Reauthorization Act 美国国会 1986 年通过的《超级基金修正案与重新授权法案》

SAS Statement on Auditing Standard (美)审计准则公报

Saund. Pl. & Ev. Saunders' Pleading and Evidence 桑德斯的《诉讼程序和证据》

S. Austr. L. South Australia Law 南澳大利亚法

s. a. v. stock at valuation 估价存货

save savings 储蓄(金),存款

Sayer Sayer's English King's Bench Reports 塞耶的英国高等法院(王座法庭)判例汇编

Sayles'Ann. Civ. St. Sayles' Annotated

Civil Statutes, Tex. （美）塞尔斯的得克萨斯州注释民事法规（汇编）

Sayles' St. Sayles' Revised Civil Statutes, Tex. （美）塞尔斯的得克萨斯州修订的民事法规（汇编）

Sayles'Supp. Supplement to Sayles' Annotated Civil Statutes, Tex.（美）塞尔斯的得克萨斯州注释民事法规补篇

S. B. sales book 销货账簿; savings bank 储蓄银行; Senate Bill （美）州参议院议案; short bill 短期汇票; signal book 信号（密码）本; small business 小商业, 小企业; Special Branch (of Police) （警察局的）特别科; statute book 法令全书; Supreme Bench （美）最高法院

S. B. A. Small Business Administration （美）小企业管理局

S. Bar J. Journal of State Bar of California （美）加利福尼亚州律师杂志

SBC Soft Budget Constraint 软预算约束

SBIC Small Business Investment Companies 小企业投资公司

S. C. safe custody 妥善保管; salvage charges 救难费; Salvage Corps 救难队, 打捞队; Same Case 相同情况, 相同案件; Security Council （联合国）安全理事会; Sinatus Consultum （古罗马）元老院法令; Senior Controller 高级审调员, 审计长; Senior Counsel 法律顾问, 高级律师; South Carolina Reports （美）南卡罗来纳州判例汇编; special circular 特别通知, 特别通令; special constable （英）临时警察, 特种警察; Station Commander 卫戍司令, 警备司令; Statutory Committee （英）法定委员会; Superior Court 上级（或上一级）法院; Supreme Court （美）联邦最高法院,（州的）最高法院

S. C. senatus consulto （罗马法）元老院的决议（或法令）

1907 S. C. Court of Session Cases, Sc.苏格兰最高民事法院判例集（1907 年）

SCA Supreme and Excheque Courts Act (Canada) （加）《最高理财法院法》

S. C. A Supreme Court Appellate Division 联邦最高法院上诉庭

SCAA Southern California Arbitration Association （美）南加州仲裁协会

SCC State Commission of Correction （美）州教养委员会; Satellite Control Center （美）卫星控制中心

scd scheduled 预定的, 按计划的

Scd Surgeon's Certificate of Disability （美）（不宜服兵役的）病残证明书

S. C. Eq. South Carolina Equity Reports （美）南卡罗来纳州衡平法院判例汇编

Sch. schedule 一览表, 纲目表; 时间表; 计划表, 程序表

Schmidt. Civ. Law Schmidt on the Civil Law of Spain and Mexico 施米特论西班牙和墨西哥民法

scil scilicet 就是说, 即

1907 S. C. J. Court of Justiciary Cases, Sc. （苏格兰）最高刑事法庭判例（1907 年）

Sc. Jur. Scottish Jurist 苏格兰的法学家

S. C. L. South Carolina Law （美）南卡罗来纳州法

S. C. L. R. South Carolina Law Reports （美）南卡罗来纳州法律判例汇编

Sc. L. Rep. Scottish Law Reporter 苏格兰判例汇编

SCO Stock Control Office 仓库管理处, 股票管理处

SC of US Supreme Court of the United States 美国联邦最高法院

S Contr Senior Controller 高级审计员, 审计长

Scott. N. R. Scott's New Reports, Eng. （英）斯科特的新判例汇编

scp scrip （证券交易所用以换取正式股票的）临时凭证; script 手迹, 笔迹, 手稿, 原件, 正本

SCRAP Students Challenging Regulatory Agency Procedures 学生挑战规制机构程序

S. & C. Rev. St. Swan and Critchfield's Revised Statutes, Ohio （美）斯旺和克里奇菲尔德的俄亥俄州修订法规（汇编）

S. ct. Supreme Court （美）联邦最高法院,（州的）最高法院; Supreme Court Reporter （美国联邦或州的）最高法院判例

汇编

S. Ct. Supreme Court （美）联邦最高法院,（州的）最高法院；Supreme Court Reporter（美国联邦或州的）最高法院判例汇编

SCUS Supreme Court of the United States 美国最高法院

s. d. sine die 无限期,不定期,无日期

SD (S. D.) same date 同一日期,同一天；sea-damage 海损；sea damaged 海损的（货物）；secret document 秘密文件；Secretary of Defense （美）国防部长；shutdown （工厂、车间等）停工,关闭,（设备）停止运转；sight draft 即期汇票；South Dakota Reports 南达科他州判例汇编；Southern district （美）南方区；State Department （美）国务院

S/D security deposit 保证金,押金

S&D Special and different 特殊及差别待遇

S. 2d New York Supplement, Second Series 纽约补篇,第二套丛书

SDA share draft account 股金提款账户

S. D. C. Sea-Bed Disputes Chamber 海底（采矿）争端办公室

SDCL South Dakota Compiled Laws （美）南达科他州汇编的法规

SDDS special data dissemination standard 数据公布特殊标准；特殊数据公布标准

S. D. Fla Southern District Florida Reports （美）南方区佛罗里达州判例汇编

SDOs Standard Development Organizations （美）标准制定组织

SDR Special Drawing Rights 特别提款权（参见正文）

SDR Singapore depository receipts 新加坡存托凭证

S. D. R (SDRs) Special Drawing Rights 特别提款权

se select 选择,挑选；selected 选择的,精选的；selection 选择,挑选,精选物,选编

S. E. South-Eastern Reporter （美）《东南区判例汇编》(第一套丛书包括1887—1939年判例)

S/E Stock Exchange 证券交易所

SEA Single European Act of 1987 《1987年单一欧洲法》

SEC 1.secondary 第二的；次级的；次要的 2.section 部门；处,科,股,组；章,节款,项；地段,部分；截面 3.Securities and Exchange Commission （美）证券交易委员会

S. E. C. Securities and Exchange Commission Decisions and Reports （美）证券交易委员会的裁定和判例汇编

Secstate Secretary of State （美）国务卿；（英）(部的主管)大臣

SECURE Standard to be Employed by Customs for Uniforms Rights Enforcement 《海关统一知识产权执法的临时标准》

S. E. 2d South-Eastern Reporter, Second Series （美）东南区判例汇编,第二套丛书

Segm. segment 部分

SEH Speculative Efficiency Hypothesis 投资效率假说

Sel. Cas. Ch. Select Cases in Chancery, Eng. （英）大法官法庭判例选

Sel. Cas. N. Y. Yates' Select Cases, N.Y. （美）耶茨的纽约判例选

Selw. N. P. Selwyn Law of Nisi Prius, Eng. 塞尔温的英国（巡回）民事陪审判法

Sen. Senate （美）参议院,上议院；senator 参议员,上议员；senior 年长的,年纪较大的,老……,大……（加在姓名后）,地位（或级别）较高的,资历较深的

Sen. CLK Senior Clerk 高级文书,高级办事员

Sen Doc Senate Document （美）参议院文件

Sen. J. Senate Journal 参议院公报

Sens. Senators 参议员,上院议员

Sent. sentence 判决

SEP Simplified Employee Pension 单纯雇员退休金；employer payment to an IRA 雇主支付给雇员个人退休金额

Serl sterling 英国货币（的）；用英币支付（或计算）的

Sess. Cas. Court of Session Cases, Eng.

（英）最高民事法庭判例集

Sess. Laws Session Laws （美）定期汇编的法规

SF Shipping Federation （英）海运联盟；sinking fund 折旧基金，偿债基金；special flight 专机；special forces 特种部队；special fund 特别基金

SFCB San Francisco Community Board （美）旧金山社区委员会（调解机构）

S. F. L. R. San Francisco Law Review （美）旧金山法律评论

SFRC Senate Foreign Relations Committee （美）参议院外交委员会

sg. signal 信号；signature 署名，签名；signed （书信，文件等）已签署，已签名

SG safeguards 保证措施；Secretary General 秘书长；study group 研究小组；subgroup 下属小组，分组

SGA Sale of Goods Act （英）《货物买卖法》

sgl single 单（个）的；个别的；唯一的；单身的

S. H. A. Smith-Hund Illinois Annotated statutes （美）史密斯—赫德的伊利诺伊州的注释法规（汇编）

Shan, Cas. Shannon's Tennessee Cases （美）香农的田纳西州判例集

Shars. Bl. Comm. Sharswood's Edition of Blackstond's Commentaries 沙斯伍德版的布莱克斯通评述

Shars. & B. Lead. Cas Real Prop. Sharswood and Budd's Leading Cases of Real Property 沙斯伍德和巴德的不动产主导判例集

Shaw Dig. Shaw's Digest of Decisions, Sc. 肖的苏格兰判决摘要汇编

Shear. & R. Neg. Shearman and Redfield on Negligence 希尔曼和雷德菲尔德《论过失》

Shep. Touch. Sheppard's Touchstone of Common Assurances 谢泼德的《转移土地财产权的盖印证书(检验)准则》

Show. Shower's English King's Bench Reports, Eng. （英）肖沃的英国高等法院（王座法庭）判例汇编

Show. P. C. Shower's Parliament Cases, Eng. （英）肖沃的议会判例集

S. I. Statutory Instrument 制定法文件，成文法文件

Sid. Siderfin's English King's Bench Reports （英）西德尔芬的英国高等法院（王座法庭）判例汇编

SIEC significant impediments to effective competition 对有效竞争的重大阻碍

SIFIs Systemically Important Financial Institutions 重要系统性金融机构（指金融危机之后，人们称这类在危机中起着关键作用的大型复杂金融机构为重要系统性金融机构）

sig. unk. signature unknown 签名不详，签署不明

SIL special import license 特别进口许可证

Sim. N. S. Simon's English Vice Chancery Reports, New Series 西蒙的英国副大法官法庭判例汇编，新丛书

Sim. & S. Simons & Stuart's English Vice Chancery Reports 西蒙斯和斯图尔特的英国副大法官法庭判例汇编

SITREP situation report 情况报告

SJA Staff Judge Advocate （美）军法参谋；司令部军法处长

SJC supreme judicial court 最高法院

S. J. D. Scientiae Juridicae Doctor 法学博士

Skill. Pol. Rep. Skillman's Police Reports, N.Y. 斯基尔曼的治安官判例汇编（纽约）

Skin. Skinner's English King's Bench Reports 斯金纳的英国高等法院（王座法庭）判例汇编

sl. slang 俚语；行话，黑话

s. l. salvage loss 海难损失；seditious libel 煽动性的诽谤（罪）

S. L. Solicitor-at-Law （英）初级律师；session laws or statute law （美）定期汇编的法规

S/L special 特别的，专门的

S & L Savings and Loan Association （美）储蓄和借贷协会；Sea and Land 海陆

Slade Slade's Reports (15 Vermont) （美）斯莱德的判例汇编（佛蒙特州 15）

SLBM sea-launched ballistic missile 海上发射的弹道导弹

S. L. C. Statute Law Committee （英）制定法委员会

SLCM sea-launched cruise missile 海上发射的巡航导弹

sld sailed 已出海,已启航; sealed 密封的,封闭的; sold 已卖,已出售

Sld. sold 已卖,已出售

SLO Social License to Operate 社会许可证

s. I. p. sine legitima prole 无法定子女,无嫡出后代

SM special message （美）特别咨文; service mark 服务标记

SMA Society of Maritime Arbitration 海事仲裁员协会

Sm. C. C. M. Smith's Circuit Courts Martial Reports, Me. （美）史密斯的巡回法庭军事判例汇编（缅因州）

Smith Cond. Rep. Smith's Condensed Reports, Ala. （美）史密斯的简明判例汇编（亚拉巴马州）

Smith, **J. P.** J. P. Smith's English King's Bench Reports. J. P. 史密斯的英国高等法院（王座法庭）判例汇编

Smith Reg. Smith's Registration, Eng. （英）史密斯的《注册或登记》

Smith's Lead. Cas. Smith's Leading Cases. 史密斯的主导判例集

SMJ Society of Medical Jurisprudence （美）法医学学会

Sm. L. Cas. Com. L. Smith's Leading Cases on Commercial Law 史密斯的商业法上的主导判例

s. m. p. sine mascula prole 无男性后代

Sm. Re. Smith's Reports (61–84 Maine) （美）史密斯的判例汇编（缅因州 61—84）

s. n. shipping note 装货通知; sine nomine 姓名不译;无名译

So Southern Reporter （美）南方区判例汇编（见 National Reporter System）

S. O. Scottish Office （英）苏格兰事务部; seller's option 卖主选择权; Solicitor's Opinion 初级律师意见,状师意见; stand over 延缓,展期（再做考虑,决定等）; Stationery Office （英）文书局

S/O shipping order 装货单; switch off 关闭

So. Cal. L. R. Southern California Law Review （美）南加州法律评论

So. 2d. Southern Reporter, Second Series. （美）南方区的判例汇编,第二套丛书

SOEs state-owned enterprises 国营企业

SOF 或 **S/F** statute of Frauds （防止）诈骗法规

SOFA Statement of Financial Affairs 财物清册

S. of S. Secretary of State （美）国务卿

SOI sphere of influence 势力范围

Sol. solicitor （英）（初级）律师;（美）法务官

So. law. Southern Lawyer 南部（方）律师

Sol. Gen. Solicitor General （英）副检察长;（美）副司法部长;（美某些州的）首席司法官

Sol. J. Solicitor's Journal (1856–date) 律师期刊,律师记事录(1856 年至今)

Sol. L. J. Southern Law Journal & Reporter, Nashville, Tenn. （美）南方区法律杂志和判例汇编,田纳西州,纳什维尔

SOS save our ship （船舶）呼救,遇险求救信号

SP (S. P.) selling price 售价; shipping port 装货港; spare parts 备件; stop payment 止付

SP. seaport 海港,海市

S. P. same principle 相同原则; same point 相同要点; security police 保安警察; service passport 公务护照; special police 特种警察,军事警察,宪兵; shore patrol （美海军）岸上宪兵; special purpose 特种用途; stop payment 停止支付,止兑; Swiss Patent 瑞士专利; sine prole 无后代,无子女

Sp. Acts Special Acts 特别法令,特别法案

SPC South Pacific Commission (UN) （联合国）南太平洋委员会; suspendatur per-

collum　绞首；Social Purpose Corporation　（美）社会目标公司
Sp CM　Special Court-Martial　（美）（对士兵、士官的初级）军事专门法庭
Sp CMO　Special Court-Martial Order　（美）（初级）军事专门法庭命令
SPEC　specification　规格
Spence, Eq. Jur.　Spence's Equitable Jurisdiction of the Court of Chancery　（英）斯彭斯的大法官法院衡平法辖区
SPI　survey of personal income　（英）个人收入调查
Spinks　Spinks' Ecclesiastical and Admiralty Reports (164 Eng. Reprint)　（英）斯平克斯的英国宗教和海事判例汇编（英国再版164）
Spinks, P. C.　Spinks English Prize Cases　斯平克斯的捕获判例集
SPIW　special purpose individual weapon　个人专用随身武器
spl　special　特别的；专门的
Spl　supplement　增补，补充；补遗，附录；副刊，增刊
Sp. Laws　Special Laws　特别法规
SPLPP　special passport　特别护照
S. P. M. A.　Sewage Plant Manufacturers Association　污水处理设备制造商协会
S. P. O.　Senior Political Officer　高级（政府）官员
S. P. S (s. p. s.)　sine prole supersite　无后代,无子女；子女均已死亡,无后裔
SPV　Special-purpose Vehicle　特种工具（亦称"Special purpose Eutity"特种实体）
spvn　supervision　监督,管理
sq　sequence　连续,次序,顺序；sequens 以下；sequentes or sequentia 以下等等
S. R.　senate resolution　（美）参议院决议（案）；Special Regulation, U. S. Army　美军特别规定；strike risk　罢工险
SRA　Sentencing Reform Act of 1984　（美）《1984年科刑判决改革法》
S. R. C. C. risks　strikes, riots and civil commotion risks　罢工、暴动、民变险
SRD　statutory reserve of deposits　法定存款储备额

S. Rept　Senate Report　（美）参议院报告
S. Res.　Senate Resolution　（美）参议院决议（案）
S. R. I.　Sacrum Romanum Imperium　神圣罗马帝国
SRO　Statutory Rules and Orders　成文法令
SRO　Self-Regulatory Organization　自我规制组织
S. R. & O.　Statutory Rules and Orders　法规和法令
ss.　sworn statement　宣誓证词
S. S.　Secretary of State　（美）国务卿；social security　社会安全
S. S. A. (SSA)　Selective Service Act　（美）《选征兵役法》；Social Security Act　（美）《社会保障法》；Social Security Administration (U. S.)　（美）社会保障管理局,社会保险署
S. S. A. A.　Social Security Acts Amendments　（美）社会保障法修正案
SSAC　same sea and coast　同一海域和同一海岸；same sea and country　同一海域和同一国家
S. S. B.　Social Security Board　（美）社会保障委员会
SSBC　sinking, stranding, burning and collision　沉没、触礁、火灾及撞船（海上基本危险）
S. Sess. Cas.　Scotch Court of Session Cases　苏格兰最高民事法院判例（集）
S. S. R. C.　Social Science Research Council　（英）社会科学研究委员会
S. S. R. I.　Social Sciences Research Institute　（美）社会科学研究院
S. S. S.　Secretary of State for Scotland　（英）苏格兰事务大臣
st.　statement　声明,陈述,供述,财务报表；statute　法令,法规,制定法,成文法；statutory　法令的,法定的
St.　state　州,国家；statutes　法规,制定法；Story's Circuit Court Reports (U. S.)　（美）斯托里的巡回法庭判例汇编；United States Statutes at Large　美国法规大全；Stair's Decision, Court of Session (Sc.)　斯太尔的苏格兰最高民事法院判决

ST salvage tug 救助打捞拖船;sea trawler 海上拖网渔船;Secretariat 秘书处; shipping ticket 海运(货物)票; standard time 标准时间;Standing Committee 常务委员会; start time 开始时间; stock ticker 证券行情自动收录器;supply and transport 补给及运输

S/T search and track 搜索和跟踪

sta. mi. statute mile 法定英里

STANAG standardization agreement 标准化协定

Stan. L. R. Stanford Law Review (美)斯坦福法律评论

Stanton's Rev. St. Stanton's Revised Statutes, Ky. (美)斯坦顿的肯塔基州修订法规(汇编)

Starkie Starkie's English Nisi Prius Reports 斯塔基的英国(巡回)民事审判法庭判例汇编

stat. statute 法令,法规,制定法,成文法;statutory 法定的,法令的

Stat. at L. United States Statutes at Large 美国法规大全

Stat. R. & O. Statutory Rules and Orders (1890-1947) (Eng.) (英)(1890—1947)制定法法规和法令

Stat. R. & O. N. I. Statutory Rules and Orders of Northern Ireland 北爱尔兰制定法法规和法令

STAT. R. & O. N. IR. Statutory Rules and Orders of Northern Ireland (1922-date) (英)(根据国会授权)制定的北爱尔兰法规和法令(1922年至今)

St. Dft. sight draft 见票即付的汇票

sten. stenographer 速记员; stenographic(al) 速记的;stenography 速记(学)

steno. (stenog.) stenographer 速记员; stenographic(al) 速记的;stenography 速记(学)

Steph. Comm. Stephen's Commentaries on the Laws of England 斯蒂芬的《英格兰法规评述》

Steph. Cr. Law Stephen's General View of the Criminal Law 斯蒂芬的《刑法概观》

Steph. Ev. Stephen's Digest of the Law of Evidence 斯蒂芬的证据法判决摘要汇编

sterl. sterling 英国货币(的),用英币支付(计算的)

Stew. Dig Stewart's Digest of Decisions of the Courts of Law and Equity, N. J. (美)斯图尔特的新泽西州普通法院和衡平法院判决摘要汇编

St. Ex. Stock Exchange 证券交易所

STF special trust fund 特别信托基金

stip. stipulation (条约、契约等的)条款,项目

stk mkt stock market 证券市场;证券交易;证券行市

stkpr storekeeper 仓库管理员;军需品管理员

St. Law Longhborough's Digest of Statute Law, Ky. (美)拉夫巴勒的肯塔基州制定法判决摘要汇编

St. Lim. Statute of Limitations 诉讼时效法规

Stockton. Stockton's Vice-Admiralty Reports (New Brunswick) 斯托克顿附属海事法庭判例汇编(新布伦瑞克)

Story Story's United States Circuit Court Reports 斯托里的美国巡回法庭判例汇编

Story, Comm. Const. Story's Commentaries on the Constitution of the United States 斯托里的《关于美国宪法评述》

Story, Eq. Jut. Story on Equity Jurisprudence U. S. A. (1836-1926) 斯托里《论美国衡平法原理》(1836—1926)

Story, Eq, Pl. Story on Equity Pleading 斯托里《论衡平法诉讼程序》

Story, Sales Story on Sales of Personal Property 斯托里《论私人财产(或动产)买卖》

Story's Laws Story's United States Laws 斯托里的《美国法规》

STR special trade representative (美)贸易谈判特别代表

Strange Strange's English King's Bench Reports 斯特兰奇的英国高等法院(王座法庭)判例汇编

St. Rep. State Reporter (或 Reports)

(美)州判例汇编

Strob. Strobhart's Law, S. C. （美）斯特罗哈特的《南卡罗来纳州法律》

SUA Convention on the Suppression of Unlawful Act Against the Safety of Maritime Narigation 《制止危及海上航行安全非法行为公约》

Stuart, Vice-Adm. Stuart's Vice-Admiralty, (Reports) L. C. 斯图尔特的下加拿大附属海事法庭判例汇编

Student Law. student lawyer 学生律师

Studies Crim. L. Studies in Criminal Law and Procedure 刑法与刑事诉讼法研究

SUB supplemental unemployment benefits 补充的失业救济

subrogn subrogation 代替,取代;（债权人的）取代

subs. subscription 签署,赞同;subsidiary 辅助的,补充的,次要的

subv. subversion 颠覆,破坏;subversive 颠覆性的,起破坏作用的

SUCC. succeed 继……之后,继承,后裔

Succr（或 **suc**） successor 继承人,后继者,接班人

S. U. I. T. Scottish and Universal Investment Trust （英）苏格兰世界投资信托公司

Sum. summary 摘要,概要,一览;summons 传唤,传票;Sumner's Circuit Court Reports (U. S.) （美）萨姆纳的巡回法庭判例汇编

Sum. C. M. Summary Court-Martial （美）简易军事法庭

Sup. Superior 上级,长官,（职位,权力等）较高的,上级的;supersede 代替,取代,废弃,最高的

Sup. C. Supreme Court （美）联邦最高法院;州最高法院;最高法院

Sup. Ct Superior Court 上级法院,高级法院;Supreme Court （美）联邦最高法院;州最高法院

Sup. Ct. Pr. Supreme Court Practice 最高法院判例

Sup Dep supply depot 补给仓库

Sup Div Supply Division 供应处,补给处

Supdt superintendent 监督人;主管人;负责人;警察长

Super. Superior Court 上级法院,高级法院

Super. Ct. Superior Court 上级法院,高级法院;Superior Court Reports, Pa. （美）宾夕法尼亚州高级法院判例汇编

Super. Ct. App. Div. Superior Court Appellate Division (New Jersey) （美）（新泽西州）高级法院受理上诉法庭

Sup. Jnd. Ct. Supreme Judicial Court, Mass. （美）（马萨诸塞州）最高司法法院

Supp. Code Supplement to Code 法典的补篇

Supp. Gen. St. Supplement to the General Statutes 普通制定法规的补篇

Sup-Pro supplementary proceedings 补充程序

supra above(in the same article or treatise) 上文（同一条款、文章或论文）;超

Sup. Trib. Supreme Tribunal (Supreme Court of Appeal) 最高法庭（最高上诉法院）

surr. surrender 交出;投降,自首;逃犯的引渡

Sus. Per. Coll. (sus. per coll) Suspendatur per collum 绞首

Suth. Dam. Sutherland on the Law of Damages 萨瑟兰《论损害赔偿法》

Suth. St. Const. Sutherland on Statutes and Statutory Construction 萨瑟兰《论制定法规和依法规的解释》

sv severe 严重的,剧烈的（伤痛）

SV surveyor 测量员,(海关等的)检查人,鉴定人;salvage charges 救助费用,海难救助费用

SVD safe vertical distance （引信解脱危险的）垂直安全距离;Salvage Department 紧急救生处,海难救助局

S. W. South Western Reporter （美）西南区判例汇编（全国判例汇编系统）

Swab Swabey's English Admiralty Reports 斯韦比的英国海事法庭判例汇编

Swan & C. R. St. Swan and Critchfield's Revised Statutes, Ohio （美）斯万和克里

奇菲尔德的俄亥俄州修订法规(汇编) 要汇编
SWDA Solid Waste Disposal Act (美)(1965年)《固(或硬)物废物处理法》
Swift, Dig. Swift's Digest of Laws Conn. (美)斯威夫特的康涅狄格州法律判决摘
syi. syllabus 摘要,提纲;判词前的说明
sym see your message 参阅你的电文
Syn. Ser. Synopsis Series of Treasury Decisions, U. S. 美国财政判例纲要丛书

T

T. Term 开庭期,期限的;territorial 领土的,土地的,地区的;territory 领土,地区,领域;testamentum 遗嘱,遗言;title 头衔,题目,资格,所有权;transaction 处理,办理,交易;transport 运输工具

T. A. Board of Tax Appeals (美)税务上诉行政法庭;technical assistance 技术援助;time of arrival 抵达时间;trade agreement 贸易协定;trustee under agreement 按合同规定的受托人

TAA Trade Agreement Act (美)《贸易协定法》

TAB Technical Assistance Board (UN) (联合国)技术援助局;tax-anticipation bill (美)抵税国库券

TAC Technical Assistance Committee (联合国)技术援助委员会;Trade Agreement Committee (美)贸易协定委员会

T. Ad. tax advisor 税务顾问

TAN Trips Action Network 与贸易有关知识产权行动网,此行动网2001年成立

TANF Temporary Assistance to Needy Families 暂助贫困家庭,对贫困家庭的临时补助

TARA Trademark Dilution Revision Act 《商标淡化修正法案》(美 2006.10.6 国会通过)

Tariff Ind. , New New's Tariff Index 新的关税索引

Tate's Dig. Tate's Digest of Laws Va. (美)塔特的弗吉尼亚州法判决摘要汇编

Taun. (Taunt.) Taunton's English Common Pleas Reports 汤顿的英国高等民事法院判例汇编

tax i. d. tax-identification number 税务鉴定号,税务认定号

Tax Law. the tax lawyer 税务律师

Tax Law. Rev. Tax Law Review 税法评论

Tayl. St. Taylor's Revised Statutes, Wis. (美)泰勒的威斯康星州修订法规(汇编)

TB tariff barriers 关税壁垒;Tariff Bureau 关税局

T/B trial balance 试算表

t. b. a. to be announced 待宣布

TBA Tennessee Bar Association (美)田纳西州律师协会

TBC Trial before the Court 法官审判(无陪审团参加)

t. b. d. to be determined 待决定

T. B. M. Tax Board Memorandum(Internal Revenue Bulletin) U. S. (美)税务委员会备忘录(国内税收公报)

T. B. Moll. T. B. Monroe's Kentucky Supreme Court Reports (1824–1828) (17–23 Kentucky) (美)T.B.门罗的肯塔基州最高法院判例汇编(1824—1828)(肯塔基州 17—23)

TBR Trade Barrier Regulation (欧盟)贸易壁垒规则

TC target countries 对象国;Tariff Commission (美)关税委员会;Tax Court of the United States 美国税务法院;Town Council (英)镇议会;Town Councillor (英)镇议会议员;tracking camera 跟踪摄影机;trade corporation 贸易公司;traffic control 交通管制;trade mark 商标;tax court 税务法庭

T. C. Reports of the United States Tax

Court (1942-date) 美国税务法庭判例汇编(1942年至今)
T/C till countermanded 直至取消（或撤回）为止
T. & C. Thompson & Cook's New York Supreme Court Reports 汤普森和库克的纽约最高法院判例汇编
T. C. Gp Traffic Control Group 交通管制组
TCM =T. C. memo
T. C. memo A memorandum decision of U. S.Tax Court 美国税务法庭节略判决书，美国税务法院判决备忘录
TCP transmission control protocol 传输控制协议
T. Cv Tax Convention 税务惯例，税务协定
TD time and date 时间和日期；time delay 延期，时间延迟；time deposit 定期存款，定期保证金；time of departure 开航时间，出发时间
T. D. Treasury Decisions (U. S. Treasury Dept.) （美国财政部）财政决议
TDA 1.Trade Development Agency （美国）贸易发展局（同 USTDA）2. United States Trade and Development Agency 美国贸易与发展局
T. D. B. total disability benefit 全残废抚恤金
TDC temporary duty certificate 临时任职书，临时（关）税完税证书
TDI Trade Defence Instruments 贸易防御措施
TDR Transfer of development right （美）土地发展权转移
temp. temporary 临时的，暂时的；tempore 在……之时
tempo temporary 临时的，暂时的
tempy temporary 临时的，暂时的
ten. tenant 佃户，承租人
Tenn. Ch. A. Tennessee Chancery Appeals （美）田纳西州衡平法院上诉
Tenn. Civ. A. Tennessee Civil Appeals （美）田纳西州民事上诉
Tenn. Cri. App. Tennessee Criminal Appeals （美）田纳西州刑事上诉

Tenn. Leg. Rep. Tennessee Legal Reporter, Nashville Tenn. （美）田纳西州判例汇编（纳什维尔市）
Ter. territorial 领土的，地方的；territory 领土；地区，领域
Term R. (T. R.) Term Reports, English King's Bench, Durnford and East's Reports 开庭期判例汇编，英国高等法院（王座法庭），邓福德和伊斯特的判例汇编
terr. (territ) territorial 领土的，土地的，地区的；territory 领土，地区，领域
test. testator 立有（留有）遗嘱者；testimonial 证明书，介绍信；testimony 证据，证明
Tex Texas （美）得克萨斯州；Texas Supreme Court Reports （美）得克萨斯州最高法院判例汇编
Tex. App. Texas Civil Appeals Cases （美）得克萨斯州民事上诉判例；Texas Court of Appeals Reports (Criminals Cases) （美）得克萨斯州上诉判例汇编（刑事判例）
Tex. Civ. App Texas Civil Appeals Reports 得克萨斯州民事上诉判例汇编
Tex. Ct. App. R. Texas Court of Appeals Reports （美）得克萨斯州上诉法院判例汇编
Tex. S. Texas Supreme Court Reports, Supplement （美）得克萨斯州最高法院判例汇编，补篇
Tex. S. Ct. Texas Supreme Court Reporter （美）得克萨斯州最高法院判例汇编
Tex. Stat. Ann. Texas Statutes Annotated （美）得克萨斯州注释法规（汇编）
Tex. Unrep. Cas. Posey's Unreported Cases (Tex.) （美）波西的得克萨斯州未汇编过的判例（汇编）
T. & G. Tyrwhitt & Granger, English Exchequer Reports (1835-1836) 蒂里特和格兰杰的英国理财法院判例汇编（1835—1836）
THA Taft-Hartley Act （美）塔夫脱-哈特莱法（指1947年美国国会通过的《劳资关系法》）
THC Terminal Handing Change 集装箱码

头作业费

Thacher, Cr. Cas. Thacher's Criminal Cases, Mass. (美)撒切尔的马萨诸塞州刑事判例(汇编)

theor. theorem 定理;原理;theoretical 理论的;theory 理论,学说

Thomp. & C. Thompson & Cook's New York Supreme Court Reports (美)汤普森和库克的纽约最高法院判例汇编

Thomp. Corp. Thompson's Commentaries on Law of Private Corporations 汤普森《关于私有企业法的评述》

Thomp. Dig. Thompson's Digest Laws, Fla. (美)汤普森的佛罗里达州法规的判决摘要汇编

Thomp. Ternn. Cas Thompson's Unreported Tennessee Cases (美)汤普森的未汇编过的田纳西州判例(汇编)

TIAS United States Treaties and Other Agreements Series 《美国条约和其他协议系列丛书》

TIC Trust Investment Committee 信托投资委员会

TIF technical information file 技术情报档案;Tax-increment financing 税收增值信贷

TIG The Inspector General (美)监察主任;监察长

TIN Tax-identification number (美)税务认定号,纳税鉴定号

T. I. R (TIR) Technical Information Relies (或 Bureau) 技术情报局;Transport International Routier 国际公路运输规则;Transport International Routiers 国际公路运输服务

TIS Technical Information Service (美)技术情报服务处

tit. title 标题,题目,称号,头衔;titular 享有所有权的;挂名的,空衔的,有名无实的

T. L. (T/L) time loan 定期贷款;total loss 全(海)损

T. L. O. total loss only (保险上的)仅负完全损失的责任,全损险

TLRA Trademark Law Revison Act of 1988 美国《1988年商标法修正案》

T. Lwyr. tax lawyer 税务律师

T. M. (TM) trade mark 商标

T. & M. Temple & Mew's Criminal Appeal Cases (Eng.) (英)坦普尔和梅的刑事上诉判例集;Temple & Mew's Crown Cases (1848-1851) Eng. (英)坦普尔和梅的刑事判例集(1848—1851)

T. M. R. Trade Mark Reports 商标判例汇编

TNC transnational corporation 跨国公司

TNG Trade Negotiations Group 贸易谈判小组

TNRCC Texas Natural Resource Conservation Commission (美)得克萨斯州自然资源保护委员会

Toml. Law. Diet. Tomlins' Law Dictionary 汤姆林(的)法律词典

TOPSEC top secret 绝密

TOR terms of reference 职权范围,调查了解范围

tot. total 总的,全部的,总数

t. p. to pay 支付,付款

TP tax payer 纳税人;traffic police 交通警察;traffic post 交通(指挥)岗;treaty port (条约规定的)通商口岸;turning place 转弯处

T. P. N. D. risks theft, pilferage and non-delivery risks 盗窃和提货不着险

T. P. N. G. Trade Preference Negotiating Group 贸易特惠谈判组

TPPA Trans-Pacific Strategic Economic Partnership Agreement "跨太平洋战略经济伙伴关系协议"

TQ transition quarter 预算年度变更时的衔接期

T. R. terms of reference 职权范围,调查了解范围;trust receipt 信托收据;Taxation Reports (Eng.) (英)税务判例汇编;Term Reports (Durnford & East) (Eng.) (英)开庭期判例汇编(邓福德和伊斯特);Caine's Term Reports (N. Y.) (美)凯恩开庭期判例汇编(纽约)

trad. tradition 传统;traditional 传统的

trans transfer 转移,传递,变换,汇兑;

transport 运输（工具）；transportation 运输

Trans. App. Transcript Appeals (N. Y. 1867–1868) 法院文本的上诉案件（纽约1867—1868）；Transcript Appeals, New York (7 vols) 法院文本的上诉案件,纽约（7卷本）

transl. translate 翻译；translation 翻译，译文；translator 翻译者,译员

T. Raym. Sir Thomas Raymond's English King's Bench Reports 托马斯·雷蒙德爵士的英国高等法院（王座法庭）判例汇编

trbl. trouble 故障,事故

Trdg trading 贸易的

Trdg Co. trading company 贸易公司

Tre. treasurer 司库,会计；treasury 国库,金库

Tread. Const. Treadway's Constitutional Reports, S.C. （美）特雷德韦的宪法判例汇编（南卡罗来纳州）

Treas. (treasr) treasurer 司库,会计

Treas. Dec. Treasury Decisions, U. S. 美国财政决议

Treas. Reg. Treasury Regulation 财政法规

T. R. H. Their Royal Highnesses （英）殿下

Trib. tribunal 法庭,审判庭

Trib. admin. Tribunaux administratifs (France) （法国）行政法庭

TRIMs Trade Related Investment Measures (TRIMs agreement) 与贸易有关的投资措施协议

Trips (TRIPs) Trade Related Aspects of Intellectual Property Rights 与贸易有关的知识产权

TRO temporary restraining order 临时拘押令

T. R. R. Trade Regulation Reporter 贸易法规判例汇编

TRRs Trade Remedy Rights 贸易救济权利

trsd transferred 转账讫

trsp. transport 运输（工具）

trs (trs.) trustees 受托人；transfer 转移,传递,变换,汇兑

Trsy treasury 国库,金库

TRT Trademark Registration Treaty 商标注册条约

Trty territory 领土；地区,领域

Trus trustee 受托人

T. S. (TS) top secret 绝密；transit storage 过境运输保管,转运仓库；United States Treaty Series 美国条约丛书

T/T telegraphic transfer 电汇

TTAB the Trademark Trial and Appeal Board （美）商标审判和上诉委员会

TTBT Threshold Test Ban Treaty 有限禁止地下核试验条约

TTC&M tracking, telemetry, command and monitoring 跟踪、遥测、指挥和监控

TTD temporary travel document 临时传阅文件

TTPI Trust Territory of the Pacific Island 太平洋岛屿的托管地

T/U/Ag trustee under agreement 按合同规定的受托人

T. U. C. (TUC) Temporary Unemployment Compensation 临时失业救济；Trades Union Congress （英）职工大会,工会代表大会；Trades Union Council （英）工会理事会；Trade Union Congress 英国职工大会,（英）工会大会

T. U. C. G. C. Trades Union Congress General Council （英）工会大会最高委员会

Turn. & R. Turner and Russell's English Chancery Reports 特纳和拉塞尔的英国大法官法庭判例汇编

T. U. W. (T. W.) (TUW) trustee under will 按遗嘱规定的受托人

TV transit visa 过境签证

TW territorial water 领海,领水；transit warehouse 转口仓库

T. W. E. trading with enemy 对敌贸易,与敌国贸易

TWEA Trade with Enemy Act （英）《对敌贸易法》

tx. taxation 征税,纳税,税制

Tytler, Mil. Law Tytler on Military Law and Courts-Martial 泰特勒《论军事法和军事法庭》

U

U. uncle 伯父,叔父,舅父,姑丈,姨丈; union 联合,联盟,联邦,联合会,公会,工会; universal 宇宙的,万能的,通用的; universe 世界,宇宙; urgent 紧急的,急迫的; Utab Reports （美）犹他州判例汇编

UAA Uniform Adoption Act （美）1994年颁布的《统一收养法》

UAGA Uniform Anatomical Gift Act （美）《统一器官捐献法》(1968年),《统一生理器官赠与法》

U. B. Upper Bench （英）（高等法院）王座法庭

U. C. Upper Chamber 上议院；Urban Council （英）城镇（区）议会,上加拿大（1791—1840年间,英属加拿大之一省,今为安大略省之南部）

U/C unclassified 无类别的；不保密的

U. C. A. Utah Code Annotated （美）犹他州注释法规汇典

UCB Unemployment Compensation Board （美）失业救济理事会；Bureau of Unemployment Compensation （美）失业救济局；unemployment compensation Bureau （美）失业救济局；unless caused by 除由……所致外

UCC Unemployment Compensation Commission （美）失业救济委员会；Uniform Commercial Code （美）《统一商法典》；Universal Copyright Convention （世界）万国版权公约

UCCC (UC3, U3C) (U. C. C. C.) Uniform Consumer Credit Code （美）《统一消费者信贷法》,《统一分期付款法》

U. C Ch Upper Canada Chancery Reports 上加拿大大法官法庭判例汇编

U. C. Cham. Upper Canada Chamber Reports 上加拿大议院判例汇编

UCCJA Uniform Child Custody Jurisdiction Act （美）(1968年的)《统一儿童监护管辖法》

UCCJEA Uniform Child Custody Jurisdiction and Enforcement Act （美）(1997年的)《统一儿童监护管辖与实施法》

U. C. C. L. J. Uniform Commercial Code Law Journal （美）统一商法典期刊

U. C. C. P. (Can.) Upper Canada Common Pleas Reports （加）上加拿大高等民事法院判例汇编

U. C. D. L. Rev (U. C. Davis L. Rev.) University of California at Davis Law Review 加州大学达维斯分校法律评论

UCHILS The University of Chicago Law School 芝加哥大学法学院

UCITA Uniform Computers Information Trade Act （美）(1999年通过)《统一计算机信息交易法》

U. C. K. B. Upper Canada King's Bench Reports （加）上加拿大高等法院（王座法庭）判例汇编

U. C. L. A. Law R. Univ.of Cal.Los Angeles Law Review （美）加州大学洛杉矶法律评论

UCMJ Uniform Code of Military Justice （美）《军事法典》,《军法大全》

U. Com Uniform Commercial 统一商业的

UCR Uniform Crime Reports （美）统一犯罪报告,统一犯罪判例汇编

UCS uncompleted call signaling 未完成的电话讯号

U. C. T. United Commercial Travel(l)ers of America 美国商品旅行推销员联合会

U. 2d Utah Reports, Second Series （美）犹他州判例汇编,第二套丛书

UDC Undeveloped countries 不发达国家；Urban Development Corporation （美）城市开发公司

UDRA Uniform Divorce Recognition Act （美）（1947年的）《统一离婚认可法》
UEI Unemployment Insurance 失业保险
UETA Uniform Electronic Transaction Act （美）《统一电子交易法》(1999年7月美国统一洲法委员会通过)
UFCA Uniform Fraudulent Conveyance Act （美）(1918年通过)《统一反欺诈财产转让法》
UFN until further notice 在另行通知之前
UIA Unemployment Insurance Act 失业保险法
UIC Unemployment Insurance Commission 失业保险委员会; Union of International Conventions 国际公约联盟
UIFSA Uniform Interstate Family Support Act （美）(1992年的)《统一州际家庭扶养法》
UJCA Uniform Juvenile Court Act （美）《统一少年法庭法》
U. K. /C. United Kingdom or Continent 英联邦王国或欧洲大陆某一港口（租船用语）
U. K. F. O. United Kingdom for Order 英国沿岸的指定港口
UKHC United Kingdom High Commissioner （英）联合王国高级专员
UKPO United Kingdom Patent Office 英国专利局
U. K. T. S. United Kingdom Treaty Series 联合王国条约丛书
ul unload 卸载,卸货,卸料
U. L. A. Uniform Laws Annotated 统一注释法规(汇编)
ULLCA Uniform Limited Liability Company Act （美）《统一有限责任公司法》(1996年,由统一州委员会制定)
ULPA Uniform Limited Partnership Act （美）(1916年)《统一有限伙法》
UJ Universal Jurisdiction 普遍管辖
UMDA Uniform Marriage and Divorce Act （美）《统一结婚与离婚法》
Un underlying mortgage 优先抵押
Un. (un.) Union 联合,联盟,联邦,联合会,公会,工会; unified 统一的,一致的,

一元化的; united 联合的,统一的
U. N. United Nations 联合国
UNA United Nations Assembly 联合国大会
unarr unarrested 未拘留的,未制动的
unauth. unauthorized 未被授权的;未被批准的
UNB under bill 无日期汇票; under bond 保税货物
UNC United Nations Charter 联合国宪章; United Nations Command 联合国军司令部; United Nations Conference 联合国会议
UNCIO United Nations Conference on International Organizations 联合国国际组织会议
UNCIO Doc. United Nations Conference on International Organization Documents 联合国国际组织会议文件
UNCITRAL United Nations Commission on International Trade Law 联合国国际贸易法委员会
UNCLOS United Nations Conference on the Law of the Sea 联合国海洋法会议
UNCOPUOS United Nations Committee on the Peaceful Uses of Outer Space 联合国和平利用外层空间委员会
UNDoc. United Nations Documents 联合国文件
UNESCO United Nations Educational, Scientific and Cultural Organization 联合国教科文组织
UNFCCC United Nations Frame Convention of Climate Change 联合国气候变化框架公约
UNGA United Nations General Assembly 联合国大会
UNGCP United Nations Guideline for Consumer Production 联合国消费者保护准则
UNACC United Nations Anti-Corruption Conventions 《联合国反腐败公约》(2003年生效)
U. N. H. C. R United Nations High Commissioner for Refugees 联合国难民署高

级专员

Unif. unified 统一的；uniform 统一的，一样的，相同的

Uniform City Ct. Act. Uniform City Court Act （美）《统一城市法院法》

Uniform Dist. Ct. Act Uniform District Court Act （美）《统一地区法院法》

UNL United Nations Library 联合国图书馆

UNLL United Nations League of Lawyers 联合国律师联盟

unm unmarried 未婚的，独身的；under-mentioned 下述的

Unof. unofficial reports 非官方的判例汇编

UNPC Uniform New Payment Code （美）《统一新支付法典》

UNSC United Nations Security Council 联合国安全理事会

UNTC United Nations Treaty Collection 联合国条约集权数据库

UNTS United Nations Treaty Series 联合国条约丛书

UNWCC United Nations War Crimes Commission 联合国战争罪行调查委员会

UP unearned premium 未到期的保险费，未实现的保险金

UPA Uniform Partnership Act （美）《统一合伙法》(1914年)(1994年修订版)

UPAA Uniform Premarital Agreement Act （美）《统一婚前协议法》

U. Pa. L. Rev. University of Pennsylvania Law Review （美）宾夕法尼亚大学法律评论

UPC Uniform Probate Code （美）《统一遗嘱验证法典》(1969)

U. Pitt L. Rev University of Pittsburgh Law Review （美）《匹兹堡大学法律评论》

UPL International Institute for the Unification of Private Law 私法统一国际研究所

UPRONA Parti de l'Unité et du Progrèss National 民族统一进步党（布隆迪），乌普罗纳党

UPUFA Uniform Putative and Unknown Fathers Act （美）(1988年的)《统一推定与不明父亲法》

URESA Uniform Reciprocal Enforcement Support Act （美）《统一扶养相互执行法》(1950年)

U. S. Uncle Sam 山姆大叔(美国、美国政府或美国人的绰号)；unconditional selection 无条件选择；under secretary 副部长，次官；United Services （英）武装力量，(海陆空)三军；United States (of America) 美国, 美利坚合众国；United States Supreme Court Reports 美国最高法院判例汇编

USA United States Army 美军, 美国陆军；United States of America 美利坚合众国

USAA United States Arbitration Act 《美国仲裁法》

U. S. Ap United States Appeals Reports 美国上诉判例汇编

USASI United States Air Staff Intelligence 美国空军参谋部情报处

U. S. C. United States Code 《美国法典》；United States Congress 美国国会；United States Constabulary Forces 美国警察部队

28 U. S. C1441 《美国法典》第28标题卷本,第1441节

U. S. C. A. United States Code Annotated 《美国注释法典》；United States Court of Appeal 美国上诉法院

USCA. APP. Art. 1-9 United States Code Annotated 《美国注释法典》第18标题卷,附件第1—9条

USCC United States Circuit Court 美国巡回法庭；United States Court of Claims 美国权利请求法院,美国索赔法院；United States Customs Court 美国海关法院；United States Commercial Company 美国商业公司

USCCA United States Circuit Court of Appeals 美国巡回上诉法院

U. S. C. C. A. N. U. S. Code Congressional and Administrative News 《美国法制会议和行政新闻报道》

U. S. cert. den. Certiorari denied by U. S.

Supreme Court 美国最高法院拒绝（发出）诉讼文件移送书

U. S. cert. dis. Certiorari dismissed by U. S. Supreme Court 美国最高法院驳回诉讼文件移送书

USCG United States Consul General 美国总领事；United States Coast Guard 美国海岸警卫队（1915 年建立）

U. S. Const. United States Constitution 美国联邦宪法

USCPFA United States China People's Friendship Association 美中人民友好协会

USCRA United States Citizens Rights Association 美国公民权利协会

USCS United States Code Service 《美国法典服务》（一系列类似于 USCA 的法律丛书）

U. S. C. Supp United States Code Supplement 美国法典补编

U. S. Ct. Cls. (US Ct Cls) United States Court of Claims 美国权利请求法院，美国索赔法院

U. S. D. A. (USDA) United States Department of Agriculture 美国农业部

USDB United States Disciplinary Barracks 美国军人监狱（惩戒所）

U. S. D. C. United States District Court 美国地区法院，美国初审法院；United States District of Columbia 美国哥伦比亚特区（美国首都华盛顿所在的行政区域）

USES United States Employment Service 美国就业局

USGR United States Government Reports 美国政府报告

53 U. S. (12 How) 443 (1851) 《美国联邦最高法院判例汇编》（霍华德第 12 卷）第 53 卷第 443 页（1851 年）（参见附录六）

U. S. I. A. (USIA) United States Information Agency 美国新闻署

U. S. Jur. United States Jurist, Washington, D. C. 美国首府华盛顿法学界

U. S. L. Ed. Lawyers' Ed. Supreme Court Reports 美国律师（合作出版公司）版的最高法院判例汇编

U. S. L. W. (USLW) United States Law Week 美国法律周刊（由 Bloomberg BNA 出版）

US Line United States Line 美国直线通海运运输公司

U. S. M. P. U. S. Mint. Philadelphia 美国费城造币厂；U. S. Military Police 美国宪兵

USNG United States National Guard 美国国民警卫队

US of S Undersecretary of State （美）副国务卿

USP (U. S. Pat.) United States Patent 美国专利

U. S. P. H. S. United States Public Health Service 美国公共卫生署

USPL United States Public Law Database 美国公法数据库

USPO United States Patent Office 美国专利局；United States Post Office 美国邮政管理局

US Pol Ad United States Political Adviser 美国政府顾问

USS Under-Secretary of State （美）副国务卿；United States Senate 美国参议院；United States Standard 美国标准

U. S. S. C. (U. S. S. Ct) United States Supreme Court 美国联邦最高法院

USSG United States Sentencing Guideline 美国量刑指南

USSS United States Secretary of State 美国国务卿

USSt (U. S. St) United States Standard 美国标准

U. S. T. United States Treaties and other Agreements Series 《美国条约和其他协议系列丛书》

USTA The United States Trademark Association 美国商标协会

U. S. T. C. United States Tariff Commission 美国关税委员会

USTDA United States Trade and Development Agency 美国贸易发展署（见 TDA）

USTR United States Trade Representative

美国贸易谈判代表
U. S. Treas. Reg United States Treasury Regulations 美国财政条例
UTA Ulster Transport Authority （英）北爱尔兰运输管理局
Utah Utah Reports （美）犹他州判例汇编
Utah 2d Utah Reports, Second Series （美）犹他州判例汇编,第二套丛书
Utah S. B. A. Utah State Bar Association （美）犹他州律师学会
ut dict. ut dictum 依嘱

UTI undistributed taxable income 未分配的税务所得（或收入）
Util. L. Rep. Utilities Law Reporter (CCH) （美）公用事业公司股票法律判例汇编 (CCH)
UTMA Uniform Transforms to Minor Act （美）《统一转化未成年人法》
UTSA Uniform Trade Secrets Act （美）《统一商业机密法》(1979年)
u. w. underwriter 担保人；保险商；（证券,公债）认购者

V

V Vermont （美）佛蒙特州；Vermont Reports （美）佛蒙特州判例汇编；versus （诉讼中）…… 对 ……（案件）……诉……（案件）；volume 卷本；Virginia （美）弗吉尼亚州；Virginia Reports （美）弗吉尼亚判例汇编
Va. Virginia （美）弗吉尼亚州；Virginia Reports （美）弗吉尼亚州判例汇编；Virginia Supreme Court Reports （美）弗吉尼亚州最高法院判例汇编
VA Veterans Administration （美）退伍军人管理局
valid. validate 使生效,使合法化,批准；validation 使失效,使合法化,批准
V. A. M. S. Vernon's Annotated Missouri Statutes （美）弗农的注释密苏里州法规（汇编）
Vand. L. Rev. Vanderbilt Law Review 范德比尔特法律评论
VARS Visual Artists Rights Society 美术作者权利协会
VAT Value-added Tax 增值税
V. A. T. S. Vernon's Annotated Texas Statutes （美）弗农的得克萨斯州注释法规（汇编）
Vaux Rec. Dec. Vaux's Recorder's Decisions, Phila. （美）沃克斯的治安法官判例集（费城）

VAWA the Violence Against Women Act （美）1994年国会批准的《针对妇女的暴力法案》
VC venture capital 风险投资
V. C. Vice-Chairman 副主席,副议长,（中）副委员长；Vice-Chancellor （英）副大法官；Vice-Chancellor's Courts （英）副大法官法庭；Vice Consul 副领事；Visa Consulaire 领事签证
V. C. C. Vice-Chancellor's Court （英）副大法官法庭
V. C. G. Vice-Consul General 副总领事
VD violation of discipline 违反纪律
VDSC Uniform Determinate Sentence Act （美）《统一决定量刑法》
VDU Visual Display Unit （计算机）终端显示器
V. E. Venditioni exponas (q. v.) 出售扣押物令状
vel velocity 速度,速率
Vent. Ventris' English King's Bench Reports （英）文特雷斯英国王座法院判例汇编；Ventris' English Common Pleas Reports (86 Eng.Reprint) （英）文特雷斯英国高等法院判例汇编(英国再版：86页）
ver. verification 证实,证明,证据,核实；verify 证实,查证,核实；versus （诉讼中）……对……（案件）,……诉

（案件）
verdt. verdict （陪审团的）裁决，评决
Vern. Vernon's English Chancery Reports （英）弗农的英国大法官法庭判例汇编
Vernon's Ann. C. C. P. Vernon's Annotated Texas Code of Civil Procedure 弗农的得克萨斯州民事诉讼法典注释本
Vernon's Ann. P. C. Vernon's Annotated Texas Penal Code （美）弗农的注释得克萨斯州刑法典
vers. versus （诉讼中）……对……（案件）；……诉……（案件）
Ves. Vesey, Junior's English Chancery Reports (30–34 Eng. Reprint) （英）维齐, 朱尼奥的英国大法官法庭判例汇编（英国再版：30—34集）
V. I. C. Virgin Islands Code （美）维尔京群岛法规汇编
Vict Queen Victoria, as 5 & 6 Vict. （英）维多利亚女王（如维多利亚女王第5个和第6个执政年）
Vict. Victoria 维多利亚；Victoria Reports (Aus.) （澳）维多利亚判例汇编
Vict. L. T. Victorian Law Times （英）维多利亚法律时代
Vict. Rep. Victorian Reports （英）维多利亚的判例汇编
viz. videlicet 即，就是，就是说
V. L. R. Vanderbilt Law Review (Tenn.)

（美）范德比尔特法律评论（田纳西州）；Victorian Law Reports (Australia) （澳）维多利亚法律判例汇编
V. N. Van Ness' Prize Cases (U. S.) （美）范内斯的捕获判例集
VOCAL Victims of Child Abuse Laws （美）《虐待儿童受害人法》
VOM victim-offendent-mediation 受害人犯罪人协商
VOR victim-offender reconciliation 受害人加害人刑事和解
VP Vice-President 副总统；副主席
Vr voucher 证件，证书；收据；担保人；证人
VRM Variable Rate Mortgage 可变率抵押
Vs. versus （诉讼中）……对……（案件）；……诉……（案件）
V. S. Vermont Statutes （美）佛蒙特州法规（汇编）
Vt. Vermont Reports （美）佛蒙特州判例汇编
VTC voting trust certificate 投票委托证书
V. T. C. A. Vernon's Texas Code Annotated （美）弗农的得克萨斯州法典注释本
vtg. voting 投票，表决；投票的，表决的
Vt. Stat. Ann. Vermont Statutes Annoted 佛蒙特州注释法规

W

W warden （美）镇长，区长，监狱长，看守长；warehouse 仓库，货栈；warning 警告，警报；water 水；water compartments 水舱；week 星期，周；weekly 周报，周刊，每星期的；western 西方的；Wilson's Reports (Texas Civil Cases, Court of Appeals) （美）威尔逊的判例汇编（得克萨斯州上诉法院民事判例）
W. West Publishing Co. （美）（专出版法律书籍）西方法律出版公司；Whig （美）辉格党人
W. A. with average 海损担保，承保单独海损，水渍险
W. A. A War Assets Administration (U. S.) （美）战时资产管理局
W. A. A. R. Western Australia Arbitration Reports 西澳仲裁判例汇编
W. zd Washington State Reports.Second Series 《华盛顿州判例汇编》第二套丛书
WAF with all faults 不保证无瑕疵

Wag. St.　Wagner's Statute, Mo　瓦格纳的密苏里州法规

WAIS　wide area information service　广域信息服务系统

WAJ　World Association of Judges　世界法官协会

WAJE　Women's Alliance for Job Equity　(美)妇女就业平等联盟

WAL　World Association of Lawyers　世界律师协会

Wall. St. J.　Wall Street Journal　(美)华尔街日报

W. A. L. R.　Western Australia Law Reports　西澳法律判例汇编

WALS　World Association of Law Students　世界法科学生协会

WALT　West's Automatic Law Terminal　西方出版公司的自动法律(检索)终端

War Dept. B. C. A.　U. S. War Department, Decisions of Board of Contract Adjustment　美国作战部合同调整委员会决议

warrtd (wartd)　warranted　有理由的, 有根据的, 有保证的

warrty　warranty　根据, 担保; 证书; 保单

War Trade Reg.　War Trade Regulations (U. S.)　(美)军事贸易条例, 战时贸易规则

Wash.　Washington　华盛顿; Washington Territory or State Reports　(美)华盛顿领地或州判例汇编; Washington's Circuit Court Reports (U. S.)　(美)华盛顿巡回法庭判例汇编; Washington's Reports (16-23 Vt)　(美)华盛顿判例汇编(佛蒙特州16—23); Washington's Reports (1, 2 Virginia)　(美)华盛顿判例汇编(弗吉尼亚州1,2)

Wash. App.　Washington Appellate Reports　(美)华盛顿上诉判例汇编

Wash. C. C.　Washington's United States Circuit Court Reports　(美)华盛顿的美国巡回法庭判例汇编

Wash. Co.　Washington County Reports, Pennsylvania　(美)华盛顿的县判例汇编, 宾夕法尼亚州

Wash. Law. Rep.　Washington Law Reporter, D. C.　(美)华盛顿法律判例汇编, 哥伦比亚特区

WASP　White Anglo-Saxon Protestant　祖先是英国新教徒的美国人; 美国社会中享有特权的白人

Wayne L. Rev.　Wayne Law Review　韦恩法律评论

WB　Wage Board　(美)工资委员会; waybill　运货单; weekly benefits　(保险上的)每周赔偿金额; whistleblowing　内部揭发; World Bank　(联合国)世界银行

W. BL.　Sir William Blackstone's English King's Bench Reports　威廉·布莱克斯通伯爵的英国高等法院(王座法庭)判例汇编

WBO　water borne only　只限海上

WBS　without benefit of salvage　不包括援救利益

WC　War Cabinet　战时内阁; without charge　免费; working capital　流动资本

W. C. A.　Workmen's Compensation Act　(美)职工补偿法, 职工救济法

W. C. B.　Workmen's Compensation Bureau　职工补偿局, 职工救济局

WCC　War Claims Commission　(美)战争赔偿委员会; War Crimes Commission　战争罪行(调查)委员会; White Citizens Council　(美)白人公民协会; World Crafts Council　世界工艺协会

WCO　World Custom Organization　世界海关组织

wd.　ward　保护, 监护, 监房, 牢房, 病房, 病室; warranted　有理由的, 有根据的, 有保证的

W. zd　Washington State Reports. Second Series　《华盛顿州判例汇编》第二套丛书

W. D.　wife's divorce (suit)　女方离婚要求

WD　Western district　(美)西方区

WDC　World Disarmament Conference　世界裁军会议

WDEA　Montana's Wrongful Discharge from Employment Act of 1987　(美)1987年制定的《蒙大拿不当解雇保护法》(美国第一部在州的层面上制定的不当解雇保

护的专门立法）

WDNY　US District Court for Western District of New York　（美）纽约（市）西区法院

WE　War Establishment　战时体制

Webb. A'B. & W. I. P. & M.　Webb, A'Beckett & Williams' Insolvency, Probate and Matrimonial Reports, Victoria　韦布、艾贝克特和威廉的破产、遗嘱验证和婚姻的判例汇编（维多利亚）

Web. Pat. Cas.　Webstet's Patent Cases, Eng.　（英）韦伯斯特的专利判例

Webst. New Int. D.　Webster's New International Dictionary　韦伯斯特的新国际词典

Week. Trans. Rep.　Weekly Transcript Reports, N. Y.　（美）纽约每周法院文本判例汇编

WEF　World Economic Forum　世界经济论坛

W. E. I. A.　wife's earned income allowance　妻子挣得收入允许减免额

W. E. I. R.　wife's earned income relief　妻子挣得收入减免额

West. H. L.　West's Reports, English House of Lords　韦斯特的英国上议院判例汇编

West. L. R.　Western Law Reporter (Canada)　（加）西方法律判例汇编

Westm.　Statutes of Westminster　（英）威斯敏斯特的制定法规（汇编）

Weston　Weston's Reports (11–14, Vermont)　（美）韦斯顿的判例汇编（佛蒙特州 11—14）

West. R　Western Reporter　西方区判例汇编

Weth. U. C.　Wethey's Reports, Upper Canada Queen's Bench　（加）韦锡的上加拿大高等法院（后座法庭）判例汇编

W. E. U.　Western European Union　（北大西洋公约组织）西欧联盟

WFIJI　World Federation of International Juridical Institutions　国际司法机构世界联合会

WFS　World Fertility Survey　世界生育率调查

W. F. T. U.　World Federation of Trade Unions　世界工会联合会

Whart. Am. Cr. Law.　Wharton's American Criminal Law　（美）沃顿的《美国刑法》

Whart. Confl. Laws.　Wharton's Conflict of Laws　沃顿的《法律冲突》

Whart. Cr. EV.　Wharton on Criminal Evidence　沃顿《论刑事证据》

Whart. Cr. Pl. & Prac.（或 **Whart. Cr. Pl.**）Wharton's Criminal Pleading and Practice　沃顿的《刑事诉讼和实务》

Whart. Ev.　Wharton Evidence in Civil Issues　沃顿《论民事系争点上的证据》

Whart. Neg.　Wharton Negligence　沃顿论过失

Whart. & S. Med. Jur.　Wharton and Stille's Medical Jurisprudence　沃顿和斯蒂尔的《法医学》

Whart. St. Tr.　Wharton's State Trials, U. S.　沃顿的《美国州的审判》

Wheeler, Am. Cr. Law　Wheeler's Abridgment of American Common Law Cases　惠勒的美国普通法判例节本

Wheeler, Cr. Cas.　Wheeler's Criminal Cases, N. Y.　（美）惠勒的纽约刑事判例（汇编）

White & W. Civ. Cas. Ct. App.　White & Willson's Civil Cases Court of Appeals, Tex　（美）怀特和威尔森的得克萨斯州上诉法院民事判例（汇编）

Whitm. Pat. Cas.　Whitman's Patent Cases, U. S.　惠特曼的美国专利判例（汇编）

WHO　World Health Organization　世界卫生组织（联合国）

Will.　William, as I Will. Ⅳ　（英）威廉，如威廉四世, 第1个执政年

Willes　Willes' English Common Pleas Reports　威尔斯的英国高等民事法院判例汇编

Willson, Civ. Cas. Ct. App.　Willson's Civil Cases Court of Appeal, Tex.　（美）威尔森的得克萨斯州上诉法院民事判例（汇编）

Willson, Tex. Cr. Law　Willson's Revised Penal Code, Code of Criminal Procedure and Penal Law of Texas　（美）威尔森的刑法典、刑事诉讼法典和得克萨斯州的

刑法修订本

Wils. Wilson's English Common Pleas Reports 威尔逊的英国高等民事法院判例汇编

Wils. Ch. Wilson's English Chancery Reports (37 Eng. Reprint) 威尔逊的英国大法官法庭判例汇编(英国再版:37 集)

Wilson's Rev. & Ann. St. Wilson's Revised and Annotated Statutes, Okl. (美)威尔逊的制定法规修订和注释本,俄克拉何马州

Winch Winch's English Common Pleas Reports 温奇的英国高等民事法院判例汇编

WIPO World Industrial and Intellectual Property Organization 世界知识产权组织

Wis. 2d. Wisconsin Reports, Second Series (美)威斯康星州判例汇编,第二套丛书

WITS Worldwide Information and Trade System 全球咨询与贸易系统

Wkly, Dig. Weekly Digest, N. Y. 纽约每周判决摘要汇编

W. L. R. Weekly Law Reports (1953—date) (英格兰和威尔士)每周法律判例汇编(1953 年至今);Wisconsin Law Review (美)威斯康星法律评论

Wm. William, as 9 Wm.Ⅲ 威廉,如威廉三世,第 9 个执政年

Wm. BL. Sir William Blackstone's English King's Bench Reports 威廉·布来克斯通爵士的英国高等法院(王座法庭)判例汇编

Wm. Rob. Adm. William Robinson's English Admiralty Reports 威廉·鲁宾逊的英国海事判例汇编

Wolf. & B. Wolferstan & Bristow's Election Cases, Eng. (英)弗尔费斯坦和布里斯托的选举判例(汇编)

Wood's Civ. Law Wood's Institutes of the Civil Law of England (美)伍德英格兰民法研究所

Wood's Dig. Wood's Digest of Laws, Cal. (美)伍德的加利福尼亚州判决摘要汇编

Woolr. Waters Woolrych's Law of Waters 伍尔里奇的水法

W. O. P Want of Prosecution 缺少控诉

WP weather permitting 雨天顺延

W. P. (w/p) without prejudice 无偏见,不抱成见;working paper 工作文件;working party 专门工作小组

W. P. A. (W. p. a.) with particular average 基本险,水渍险,承保单独海损

WPC weather permitting clause 雨天顺延条款

W. P. C. World Peace Council 世界和平理事会

W. & Phr. Words and Phrases (美)词语和习用语(判例查找工具书)

W/R war risks 战争险

WRC weather permitting clause 雨天顺延条款;Water Research Center (英)水研究中心

WRO war risks only 仅保战争险

W. S. Writers to the Signet (苏格兰最古老最主要的律师组织)高级状师协会;公证人和诉讼代理人;律师

W. S. A. Wisconsin Statutes Annotated (美)威斯康星州注释法规

WSBA Washington State Bar Association (美)华盛顿州律师协会

wt. warrant 保证书,许可证;付(收)款凭单;(英)栈单;逮捕证:without 没有,不;在……外

W. T. (W. t.) war time 战时;withholding 预扣赋税

W. T. Washington Territory Reports (美)华盛顿领地判例汇编

WTH-LTG Westlaw Topical Highlights-Litigation Database Westlaw 专题重点诉讼—数据库

WTO World Trade Organization 世界贸易组织

W. V. West Virginia Reports (美)西弗吉尼亚州判例汇编

W. Va. West Virginia (美)西弗吉尼亚;West Virginia Supreme Court Reports (美)西弗吉尼亚州最高法院判例汇编

W. W. H. W. W. Harrington's Reports (31–39 Delaware) (美)W. W. 哈林顿的判例汇

编(特拉华州 31—39)
WWI　First World War　第一次世界大战(IWW)
WWII　Second World War　第二次世界大战(IIWW)
WWW　World Wide Web　万维网

X

X　extra　额外的,特别的
XB　extra-budgetary　预算外
XC　ex coupon　除息票,无利息票
xcpt.　except　除……以外,不计
XD　exdivident　无红利,除股息,不包括下期红利
xout　cross out　删除,勾销
xpr　ex privileges　无特权,无优惠,不予优待
XPT　express paid by telegraph　加快费已电汇付讫
xq　cross questioning　盘问,诘问,交叉询问,反诘
Xr　ex rights　无权认购新股
xtry　extraordinary　非常的,特别的;特命的,特派的
XW (X. W.)　ex warrants　无股息单,不附券;without warrants　无须担保
XX-LEGIS　State's Legislative Service Database　州立法服务数据库(XX 为州的两个字母邮政缩写)
XXX　international urgency signal　国际紧急信号

Y

Y A　Yalta Agreement　雅尔塔协定
Y. A. D.　Young's Admiralty Decision (Nova Scotia)　(加)扬的海事判例(新斯科夏半岛)
Yale L. J.　Yale Law Journal　《耶鲁法律杂志》
Y. A. R.　York-Antwerp Rules　约克-安特卫普共同海损规则
Yates Sel. Cas.　Yates Select Cases, N. Y.　(美)耶茨的纽约判例选
Y. B.　(英)《年鉴》
Y. B. 17　Edw. 4 fo. 2a. pl. 3　(1477)(英)《年鉴》爱德华四世第 17 个执政年对开页码 2a. pl. 3(1477 年)
Y. B. W. A.　Yearbook of World Affairs　世界事务年鉴
Y. & C.　Younge and Collyre's Chancery Reports, England (1841–1843)　(英)扬吉和科利尔的大法官法庭判例汇编,英格兰(1841—1843)
Y. C. A.　Youth Correct Act　(美)《青少年教养法》
YDY　yesterday　昨天
YE　Your Excellency　阁下
Yearbook E. C. H. R.　Yearbook of the European Convention on Human Rights　欧洲人权协定年鉴
Y. M.　your message　你方电报
Y. M. C. A.　Young Men's Christian Association　基督教青年会
Yo.　Younge's Exchequer Equity Reports (Eng.)　(英)扬吉的理财法院衡平法上的判例汇编
Younge　Younge Exchequer, Eng.　(英)扬吉理财法院
Younge & C. Ch.　Younge & C Collyer's

English Chancery Reports （英）扬吉和科利尔的英国大法官法庭判例汇编

Youth Ct. Youth Court 青少年法庭

Z

Z zone 区,地区,地带；zero 零
Zane Zane's Reports (4-9 Utah) （美）赞恩的判例汇编(犹他州 4—9)
ZD zero defects 无差错(运动),无缺陷
ZEG zero economic growth 经济无增长,经济零增长,零值经济增长
ZFR zollfrei 免税
ZG zero gravity 无重量,失重
ZI zone interdite 禁区
ZIFT Zygote Intrafallopian Transfer 输卵管内输入精子,人工受孕
ZL zero line 零位线,基准线
ZPG zero population growth 人口零增长,人口无增长
ZPO Zivilprozessordnung (German Code of Civil Procedure) 《德国民事诉讼法典》
ZT Zero Time 开始时间,零时

附录二: 西方主要国家的法院组织系统
Appendix II: Judicial System of Western Major Countries

ORGANIZATION OF THE FEDERAL COURTS IN THE UNITED STATES OF AMERICA

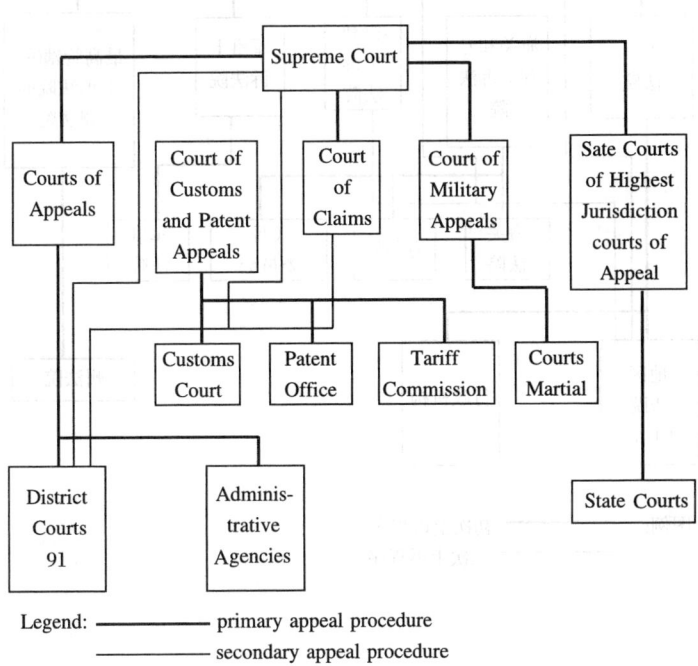

Legend: ──────── primary appeal procedure
────────── secondary appeal procedure

美国联邦法院组织系统

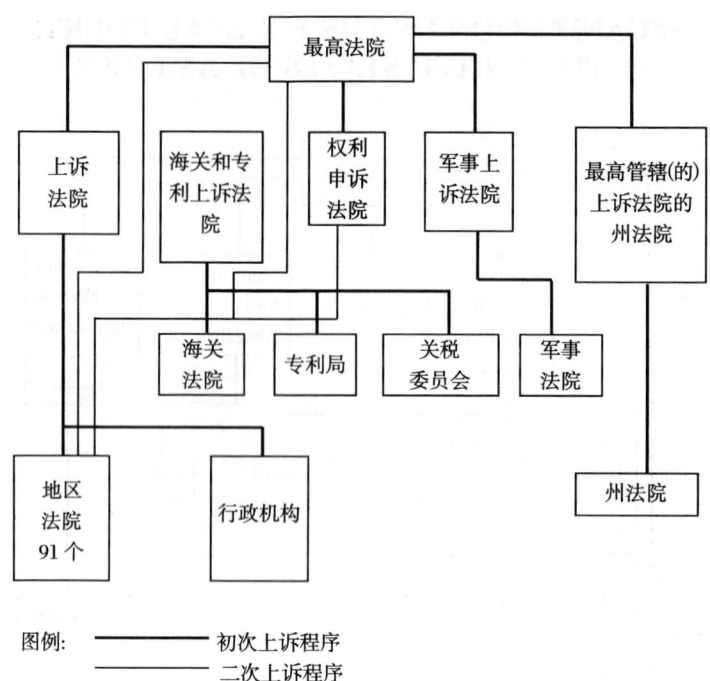

FEDERAL JUDICIAL SYSTEM IN THE UNITED STATES OF AMERICA

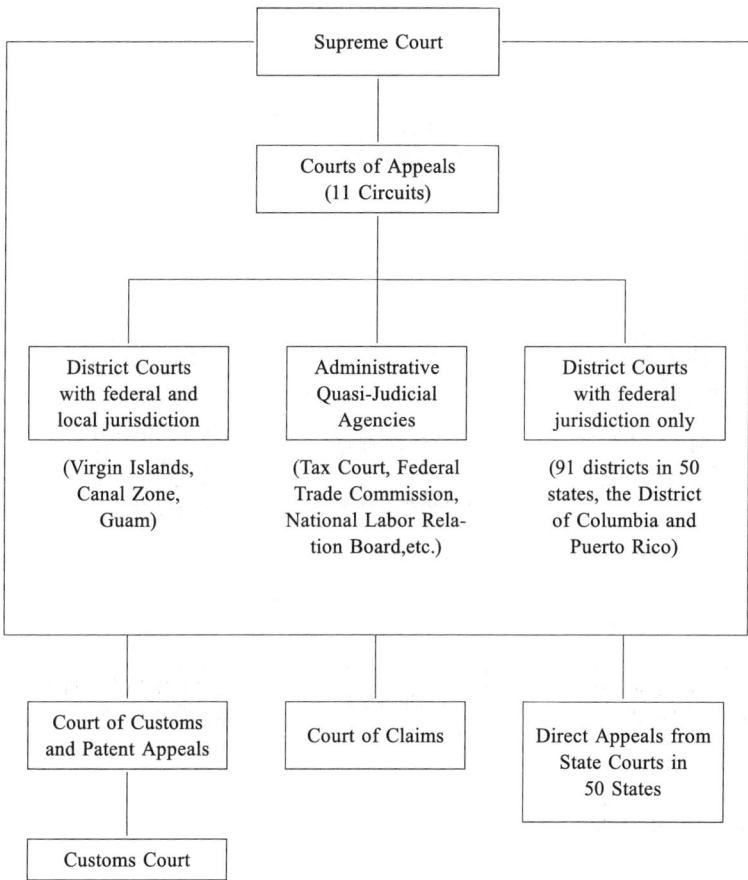

美国联邦司法系统

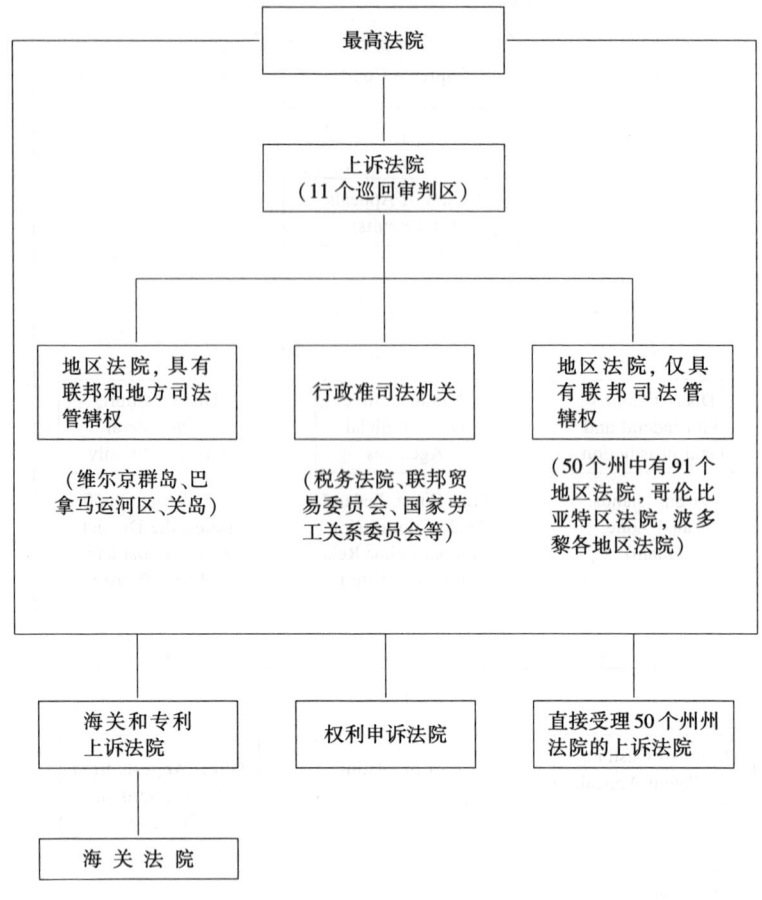

STATE JUDICIAL SYSTEM IN THE UNITED STATES OF AMERICA

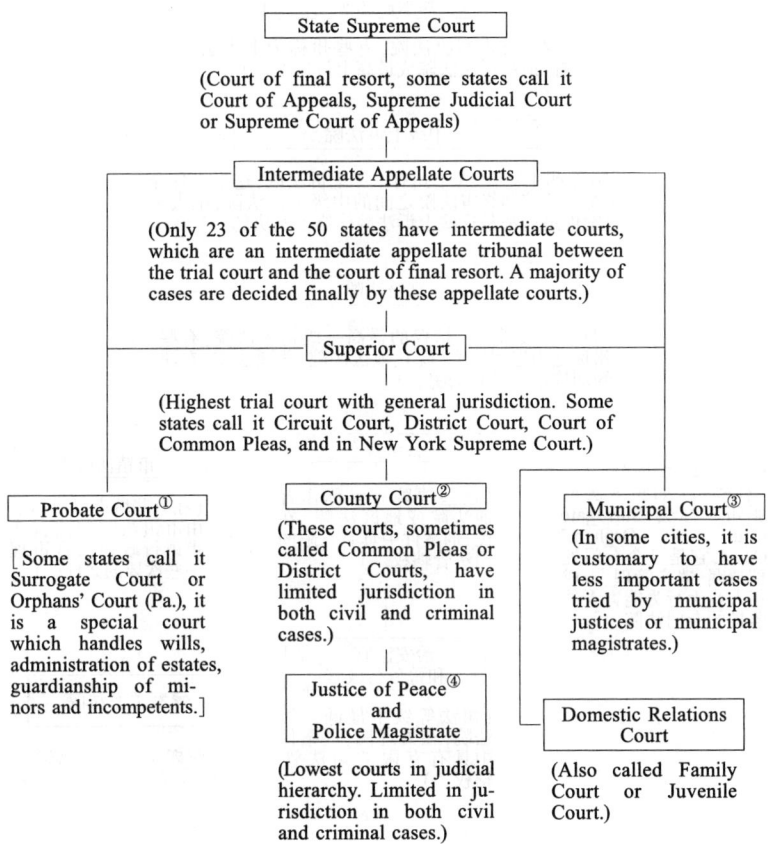

① ② ③ Court of special jurisdiction, such as Probate, Family or Juvenile and the so-called inferior courts, such as Common Pleas or Municipal courts, may be separate courts or may be part of the trial court of general jurisdiction.

④ Justices of the Peace do not exist in all states. Their jurisdiction vary greatly from state to state where they do exist.

美国州司法系统

州最高法院

(又称终审判决法院,有些州称为上诉法院、最高司法法院或最高上诉法院。)

中级上诉法院

(50个州中只有23个州有中级上诉法院,这是一种介于初审法院和终审法院之间的中级上诉法院,绝大多数案件最后都是这些上诉法院作终审判决的。)

高级法院

[具有一般司法管辖权的最高一级初审法院,有些州称之为巡回法庭(院)、地区法院、普通法院,在纽约却称之为最高法院。]

遗嘱检验法院①

[有些州(如宾夕法尼亚州)称为 Surrogate Court 或 Orphans' Court,它是一个专门处理遗嘱、遗产管理、未成年人或无行为能力人的监护的专门法院。]

县法院②

(这些法院有时称作普通法院或地区法院,在民、刑案件中具有有限的司法管辖权。)

市镇法院③

(在有些城市里习惯上由市镇法院的法官或市镇行政司法官审理一些次要的案件。)

治安法官④ 和警务行政官

(司法等级中最低一级法院,在处理民、刑案件中具有有限的司法管辖权。)

家庭关系法院

(亦称家庭法院或少年法院。)

①②③ 专门管辖的法院(或法庭),诸如遗嘱检验法院、家庭或少年法院,以及所称下级法院,诸如普通法院或者市镇法院等,可以是单独的法院,也可以是具有一般司法管辖权的初审法院的分庭。

④ 不是所有的州都有治安法官,他们的管辖权在各州之间区别很大。

STATE COURTS IN THE UNITED STATES OF AMERICA

Level		Courts	Functions
State	Court of appeal	1) Supreme Court	in all the States Court for civil proceedings only in the States in which there is a high court of criminal appeals
		2) High court of criminal appeals	for criminal proceedings in certain States
		Intermediary courts of appeal	in 13 States
	Courts judging in first instance	Circuit Court	original jurisdiction in civil matters or serious criminal offences
		District Court	
		Superior Court	——single judge
		Court of Chancery	——presided over by single judge
Municipal County	Court with limited competence	County Court	Original jurisdiction in civil matters or more serious offences
		Municipal Court	Jurisdiction of appeal for cases transferred by municipal courts and police courts
local		City Court	presided over by one magistrate, minor criminal cases
		Court of Justice or Police Court	presided over by the Justice of the Peace minor offences (road traffic, disputes among residents, police)

美国州法院系统

级别	法 院		职 能
州	上诉法院	1.最高法院	所有州法院均审理民事诉讼案件,只是在某些州才设有高级刑事上诉法院
		2.高级刑事上诉法院	在某些州可审理刑事诉讼案件
		中级上诉法院	在13个州设有此法院
	初审法院	巡回法院	具有一般管辖权,审理民事或严重刑事犯罪案件
		地区法院	
		高级法院	一个法院
		衡平法院	由一个法官主持
市县	有限权限的法院	县法院	有一般管辖权,审理民事或较严重的违法案件
		市法院	具有审理来自市镇法庭和警察法庭转来上诉案件的管辖权
当地		市镇法庭	由地方行政官主持,审理未成年刑事案件
		治安法庭或警察法庭	由治安法官主持,审理未成年违法案件(以及公路交通、居民间的纠纷或警务人员之间的纠纷)

UNITED STATES COURTS OF APPEALS

1st Cir.	U. S. Court of Appeals, First Judicial Circuit
2d Cir.	U. S. Court of Appeals, Second Judicial Circuit
3rd Cir.	U. S. Court of Appeals, Third Judicial Circuit
4th Cir.	U. S. Court of Appeals, Fourth Judicial Circuit
5th Cir.	U. S. Court of Appeals, Fifth Judicial Circuit
6th Cir.	U. S. Court of Appeals, Sixth Judicial Circuit
7th Cir.	U. S. Court of Appeals, Seventh Judicial Circuit
8th Cir.	U. S. Court of Appeals, Eighth Judicial Circuit
9th Cir.	U. S. Court of Appeals, Ninth Judicial Circuit
10th Cir.	U. S. Court of Appeals, Tenth Judicial Circuit
D. C. Cir.	U. S. Court of Appeals, District of Columbia Circuit

UNITED STATES DISTRICT COURTS

Alabama
    M. D. Ala.   U. S. District Court for the Middle District of Alabama
    N. D. Ala.   U. S. District Court for the Northern District of Alabama
    S. D. Ala.   U. S. District Court for the Southern District of Alabama
Alaska
    D. Alas.   U. S. District Court for the District of Alaska
Arizona
    D. Ariz.   U. S. District Court for the District of Arizona
Arkansas
    E. & W. D. Ark.   U. S. District Court for the Eastern and Western Districts of Arkansas
California
    C. D. Cal.   U. S. District Court for the Central District of California
    E. D. Cal.   U. S. District Court for the Eastern District of California
    N. D. Cal.   U. S. District Court for the Northern District of California
    S. D. Cal.   U. S. District Court for the Southern District of California
Colorado
    D. Colo.   U. S. District Court for the District of Colorado
Connecticut
    D. Conn.   U. S. District Court for the District of Connecticut
Delaware
    D. Del.   U. S. District Court for the District of Delaware Columbia
District of
    D. D. C.   U. S. District Court for the District of Columbia
Florida
    M. D. Fla.   U. S. District Court for the Middle District of Florida
    N. D. Fla.   U. S. District Court for the Northern District of Florida

S. D. Fla.	U. S. District Court for the Southern District of Georgia	
Georgia		
M. D. Ga.	U. S. District for the Middle District of Georgia	
N. D. Ga.	U. S. District for the Northern District of Georgia	
S. D. Ga.	U. S. District for the Southern District of Georgia	
Cuam		
D. Guam	U. S. District Court for the District of Guam	
Hawaii		
D. Hawaii	U. S. District Court for the District of Hawaii	
Idaho		
D. Idaho	U. S. District Court for the District of Idaho	
Illinois		
E. D. Ill.	U. S. District Court for the Eastern District of Illinois	
N. D. Ill.	U. S. District Court for the Northern District of Illinois	
S. D. Ill.	U. S. District Court for the Southern District of Illinois	
Indiana		
N. D. Ind.	U. S. District Court for the Northern District of Indiana	
S. D. Ind.	U. S. District Court for the Southern District of Indiana	
Iowa		
N. D. Iowa	U. S. District Court for the Northern District of Iowa	
S. D. Iowa	U. S. District Court for the Southern District of Iowa	
Kansas		
D. Kan.	U. S. District Court for the District of Kansas	
Kentucky		
E. D. Ky.	U. S. District Court for the Eastern District of Kentucky	
W. D. Ky.	U. S. District Court for the Western District of Kentucky	
Louisiana		
E. D. La.	U. S. District Court for the Eastern District of Louisiana	
M. D. La.	U. S. District Court for the Middle District of Louisiana	
W. D. La.	U. S. District Court for the Western District of Louisiana	
Maine		
D. Me.	U. S. District Court for the District of Maine	
Maryland		
D. Md.	U. S. District Court for the District of Maryland	
Massachusetts		
D. Mass.	U. S. District Court for the District of Massachusetts	
Michigan		
E. D. Mich.	U. S. District Court for the Eastern District of Michigan	
W. D. Mich.	U. S. District Court for the Western District of Michigan	
Minnesota		
D. Minn.	U. S. District Court for the District of Minnesota	
Mississippi		
N. D. Miss.	U. S. District Court for the Northern District of Mississippi	
S. D. Miss.	U. S. District Court for the Southern District of Mississippi	

Missouri
　　E. D. Mo.　　　　U. S. District Court for the Eastern District of Missouri
　　W. D. Mo.　　　　U. S. District Court for the Western District of Missouri
Montana
　　D. Mont.　　　　U. S. District Court for the District of Montana
Nebraska
　　D. Neb.　　　　U. S. District Court for the District of Nebraska
Nevada
　　D. Nev.　　　　U. S. District Court for the District of Nevada
New Hampshire
　　D. N. H.　　　　U. S. District Court for the District of New Hampshire
New Jersey
　　D. N. J.　　　　U. S. District Court for the District of New Jersey
New Mexico
　　D. N. M.　　　　U. S. District Court for the District of New Mexico
New York
　　E. D. N. Y.　　　U. S. District Court for the Eastern District of New York
　　N. D. N. Y.　　　U. S. District Court for the Northern District of New York
　　S. D. N. Y.　　　U. S. District Court for the Southern District of New York
　　W. D. N. Y.　　　U. S. District Court for the Western District of New York
North Carolina
　　E. D. N. C.　　　U. S. District Court for the Eastern District of North Carolina
　　M. D. N. C.　　　U. S. District Court for the Middle District of North Carolina
　　W. D. N. C.　　　U. S. District Court for the Western District of North Carolina
North Dakota
　　D. N. D.　　　　U. S. District Court for the District of North Dakota
Ohio
　　N. D. O.　　　　U. S. District Court for the Northern District of Ohio
　　S. D. O.　　　　U. S. District Court for the Southern District of Ohio
Oklahoma
　　E. D. Okl.　　　　U. S. District Court for the Eastern District of Oklahoma
　　N. D. Okl.　　　　U. S. District Court for the Northern District of Oklahoma
　　W. D. Okl.　　　　U. S. District Court for the Western District of Oklahoma
Oregon
　　D. Or.　　　　U. S. District Court for the District of Oregon
Pennsylvania
　　E. D. Pa.　　　　U. S. District Court for the Eastern District of Pennsylvania
　　M. D. Pa.　　　　U. S. District Court for the Middle District of Pennsylvania
　　W. D. Pa.　　　　U. S. District Court for the Western District of Pennsylvania
Puerto Rico
　　D. P. R.　　　　U. S. District Court for the District Court of Puerto Rico
Rhode Island
　　D. R. I.　　　　U. S. District Court for the District of Rhode Island
South Carolina
　　D. S. C.　　　　U. S. District Court for the District of South Carolina

South Dakota
    D. S. D.   U. S. District Court for the District of South Dakota
Tennessee
    E. D. Tenn.   U. S. District Court for the Eastern District of Tennessee
    M. D. Tenn.   U. S. District Court for the Middle District of Tennessee
    W. D. Tenn.   U. S. District Court for the Western District of Tennessee
Texas
    E. D. Tex.   U. S. District Court for the Eastern District of Texas
    N. D. Tex.   U. S. District Court for the Northern District of Texas
    S. D. Tex.   U. S. District Court for the Southern District of Texas
    W. D. Tex.   U. S. District Court for the Western District of Texas
Utah
    D. Ut.   U. S. District Court for the District of Utah
Vermont
    D. Vt.   U. S. District Court for the District of Vermont
Virgin Islands
    D. V. I.   U. S. District Court for the District of the Virgin Islands
Virginia
    E. D. Va.   U. S. District Court for the Eastern District of Virginia
    W. D. Va.   U. S. District Court for the Western District of Virginia
Washington
    E. D. Wash.   U. S. District Court for the Eastern District of Washington
    W. D. Wash.   U. S. District Court for the Western District of Washington
West Virginia
    N. D. W. Va.   U. S. District Court for the Northern District of West Virginia
    S. D. W. Va.   U. S. District Court for the Southern District of West Virginia
Wisconsin
    E. D. Wis.   U. S. District Court for the Eastern District of Wisconsin
    W. D. Wis.   U. S. District Court for the Western District of Wisconsin
Wyoming
    D. Wyo.   U. S. District Court for the District of Wyoming

美国联邦上诉法院

联邦上诉法院第一巡回审判庭(1st Cir.)
联邦上诉法院第二巡回审判庭(2d Cir.)
联邦上诉法院第三巡回审判庭(3rd Cir.)
联邦上诉法院第四巡回审判庭(4th Cir.)
联邦上诉法院第五巡回审判庭(5th Cir.)
联邦上诉法院第六巡回审判庭(6th Cir.)
联邦上诉法院第七巡回审判庭(7th Cir.)
联邦上诉法院第八巡回审判庭(8th Cir.)
联邦上诉法院第九巡回审判庭(9th Cir.)
联邦上诉法院第十巡回审判庭(10th Cir.)
联邦上诉法院哥伦比亚特区巡回法庭(D. C. Cir.)

美国联邦地区法院

亚拉巴马(Alabama)州
    亚拉巴马中部管区联邦地区法院　(M. D. Ala.)
    亚拉巴马北部管区联邦地区法院　(N. D. Ala.)
    亚拉巴马南部管区联邦地区法院　(S. D. Ala.)
阿拉斯加(Alaska)州
    阿拉斯加管区联邦地区法院　(D. Alas.)
亚利桑那(Arizona)州
    亚利桑那管区联邦地区法院　(D. Ariz.)
阿肯色(Arkansas)州
    阿肯色东部和西部管区联邦地区法院(E. & W. D. Ark.)
加利福尼亚(California)州
    加利福尼亚中部管区联邦地区法院　(C. D. Cal.)
    加利福尼亚东部管区联邦地区法院　(E. D. Cal.)
    加利福尼亚北部管区联邦地区法院　(N. D. Cal.)
    加利福尼亚南部管区联邦地区法院　(S. D. Cal.)
科罗拉多(Colorado)州
    科罗拉多管区联邦地区法院　　(D. Colo.)
康涅狄格(Connecticut)州
    康涅狄格管区联邦地区法院　　(D. Conn.)
特拉华(Delaware)州
    特拉华管区联邦地区法院　　(D. Del.)
哥伦比亚特区(District of Columbia)
    哥伦比亚特区联邦地区法院　　(D. D. C.)
佛罗里达(Florida)州
    佛罗里达中部管区联邦地区法院　(M. D. Fla.)
    佛罗里达北部管区联邦地区法院　(N. D. Fla.)

佛罗里达南部管区联邦地区法院　（S. D. Fla.）
佐治亚（Georgia）州
　　佐治亚中部管区联邦地区法院　（M. D. Ga.）
　　佐治亚北部管区联邦地区法院　（N. D. Ga.）
　　佐治亚南部管区联邦地区法院　（S. D. Ga.）
关岛（Guam）
　　关岛管区联邦地区法院　（D. Guam）
夏威夷（Hawaii）州
　　夏威夷管区联邦地区法院　（D. Hawaii）
爱达荷（Idaho）州
　　爱达荷管区联邦地区法院　（D. Idaho）
伊利诺伊（Illinois）州
　　伊利诺伊东部管区联邦地区法院　（E. D. Ill.）
　　伊利诺伊北部管区联邦地区法院　（N. D. Ill.）
　　伊利诺伊南部管区联邦地区法院　（S. D. Ill.）
印第安纳（Indiana）州
　　印第安纳北部管区联邦地区法院　（N. D. Ind.）
　　印第安纳南部管区联邦地区法院　（S. D. Ind.）
艾奥瓦（Iowa）州
　　艾奥瓦北部管区联邦地区法院　（N. D. Iowa）
　　艾奥瓦南部管区联邦地区法院　（S. D. Iowa）
堪萨斯（Kansas）州
　　堪萨斯管区联邦地区法院　（D. Kan.）
肯塔基（Kentucky）州
　　肯塔基东部管区联邦地区法院　（E. D. Ky.）
　　肯塔基西部管区联邦地区法院　（W. D. Ky.）
路易斯安那（Louisiana）州
　　路易斯安那东部管区联邦地区法院　（E. D. La.）
　　路易斯安那中部管区联邦地区法院　（M. D. La.）
　　路易斯安那西部管区联邦地区法院　（W. D. La.）
缅因（Maine）州
　　缅因管区联邦地区法院　（D. Me.）
马里兰（Maryland）州
　　马里兰管区联邦地区法院　（D. Md.）
马萨诸塞（Massachusetts）州
　　马萨诸塞管区联邦地区法院　（D. Mass.）
密歇根（Michigan）州
　　密歇根东部管区联邦地区法院　（E. D. Mich.）
　　密歇根西部管区联邦地区法院　（W. D. Mich.）
明尼苏达（Minnesota）州
　　明尼苏达管区联邦地区法院　（D. Minn.）
密西西比（Mississippi）州
　　密西西比北部管区联邦地区法院　（N. D. Miss.）
　　密西西比南部管区联邦地区法院　（S. D. Miss.）

密苏里(Missouri)州
　　密苏里东部管区联邦地区法院　(E. D. Mo.)
　　密苏里西部管区联邦地区法院　(W. D. Mo.)
蒙大拿(Montana)州
　　蒙大拿管区联邦地区法院　　(D. Mont.)
内布拉斯加(Nebraska)州
　　内布拉斯加管区联邦地区法院　(D. Neb.)
内华达(Nevada)州
　　内华达管区联邦地区法院　(D. Nev.)
新罕布什尔(New Hampshire)州
　　新罕布什尔管区联邦地区法院　(D. N. H.)
新泽西(New Jersey)州
　　新泽西管区联邦地区法院　(D. N. J.)
新墨西哥(New Mexico)州
　　新墨西哥管区联邦地区法院　(D. N. M.)
纽约(New York)州
　　纽约东部管区联邦地区法院　(E. D. N. Y.)
　　纽约北部管区联邦地区法院　(N. D. N. Y.)
　　纽约南部管区联邦地区法院　(S. D. N. Y.)
　　纽约西部管区联邦地区法院　(W. D. N. Y.)
北卡罗来纳(North Carolina)州
　　北卡罗来纳东部管区联邦地区法院　(E. D. N. C.)
　　北卡罗来纳中部管区联邦地区法院　(M. D. N. C.)
　　北卡罗来纳西部管区联邦地区法院　(W. D. N. C.)
北达科他(North Dakota)州
　　北达科他管区联邦地区法院　(D. N. D.)
俄亥俄(Ohio)州
　　俄亥俄北部管区联邦地区法院　(N. D. O.)
　　俄亥俄南部管区联邦地区法院　(S. D. O.)
俄克拉何马(Oklahoma)州
　　俄克拉何马东部管区联邦地区法院　(E. D. Okl.)
　　俄克拉何马北部管区联邦地区法院　(N. D. Okl.)
　　俄克拉何马西部管区联邦地区法院　(W. D. Okl.)
俄勒冈(Oregon)州
　　俄勒冈管区联邦地区法院　(D. Or.)
宾夕法尼亚(Pennsylvania)州
　　宾夕法尼亚东部管区联邦地区法院　(E. D. Pa.)
　　宾夕法尼亚中部管区联邦地区法院　(M. D. Pa.)
　　宾夕法尼亚西部管区联邦地区法院　(W. D. Pa.)
波多黎各(Puerto Rico)
　　波多黎各管区联邦地区法院　(D. P. R.)
罗得岛(Rhode Island)州
　　罗得岛管区联邦地区法院　(D. R. I.)
南卡罗来纳(South Carolina)州
　　南卡罗来纳管区联邦地区法院　(D. S. C.)

南达科他(South Dakota)州
　　南达科他管区联邦地区法院　(D. S. D.)
田纳西(Tennessee)州
　　田纳西东部管区联邦地区法院　(E. D. Tenn.)
　　田纳西中部管区联邦地区法院　(M. D. Tenn.)
　　田纳西西部管区联邦地区法院　(W. D. Tenn.)
得克萨斯(Texas)州
　　得克萨斯东部管区联邦地区法院　(E. D. Tex.)
　　得克萨斯北部管区联邦地区法院　(N. D. Tex.)
　　得克萨斯南部管区联邦地区法院　(S. D. Tex.)
　　得克萨斯西部管区联邦地区法院　(W. D. Tex.)
犹他(Utah)州
　　犹他管区联邦地区法院　(D. Ut.)
佛蒙特(Vermont)州
　　佛蒙特管区联邦地区法院　(D. Vt.)
维尔京群岛(Virgin Islands)
　　维尔京群岛管区联邦地区法院　(D. V. I.)
弗吉尼亚(Virginia)州
　　弗吉尼亚东部管区联邦地区法院　(E. D. Va.)
　　弗吉尼亚西部管区联邦地区法院　(W. D. Va.)
华盛顿(Washington)州
　　华盛顿东部管区联邦地区法院　(E. D. Wash.)
　　华盛顿西部管区联邦地区法院　(W. D. Wash.)
西弗吉尼亚(West Virginia)州
　　西弗吉尼亚北部管区联邦地区法院　(N. D. W. Va.)
　　西弗吉尼亚南部管区联邦地区法院　(S. D. W. Va.)
威斯康星(Wisconsin)州
　　威斯康星东部管区联邦地区法院　(E. D. Wis.)
　　威斯康星西部管区联邦地区法院　(W. D. Wis.)
怀俄明(Wyoming)州
　　怀俄明管区联邦地区法院　(D. Wyo.)

ORGANIZATION OF THE COURTS IN ENGLAND

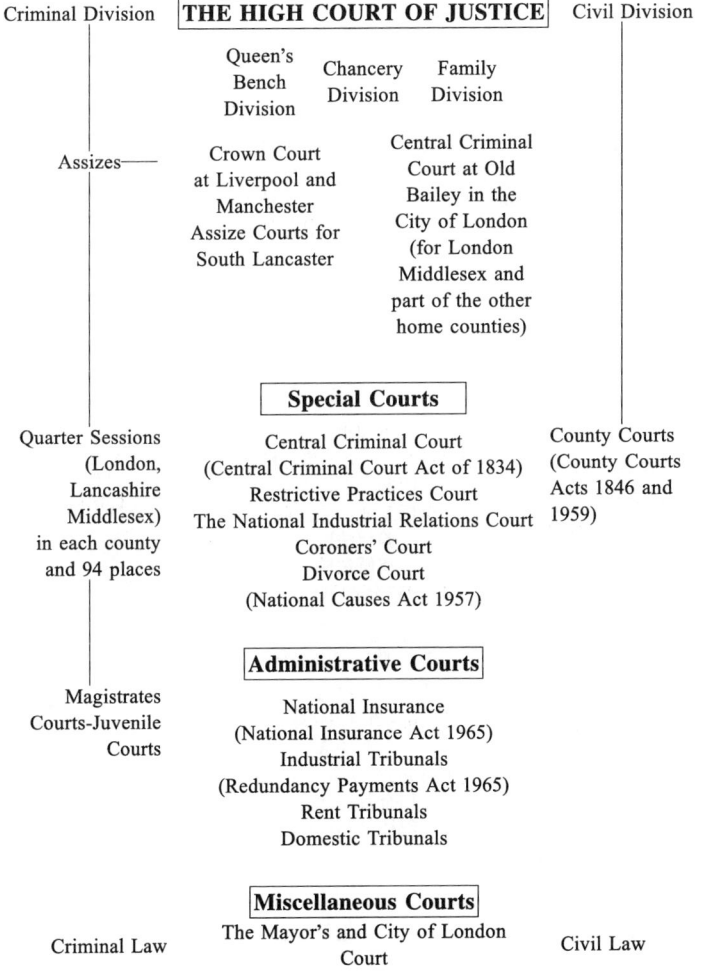

英国法院组织系统

```
                        上  议  院
                        上 诉 法 院
刑事上诉庭        ┌─高  等  法  院─┐        民事上诉庭

                 王座庭  大法官法庭  家事庭

巡回法庭──利物浦和曼彻斯特       伦敦老贝来中央刑
          刑事法庭,南兰开         事法庭(管辖伦敦、
          斯特巡回法庭            米德尔萨克斯和部
                                  分其他郡县)


                      ┌专  门  法  院┐

                        中央刑事法院
四季法庭              (按1834年中央刑事法院法)           郡法院
(伦敦、兰开夏、          限制开业法院              (按1846年和
米德尔萨克斯)           全国工业关系法院            1959年郡法院法)
(每郡设庭,有              验尸法院
   94处)                 离婚法院
                      (按1957年国家诉讼法)


                      ┌行  政  法  院┐

                         国家保险
治安法院──              (按1965年国家保险法)
 少年法院                  工业法庭
                      (按1965年超量支付法)
                         租金裁定法庭
                         纪律处罚法庭


                      ┌混  合  法  院┐

      刑  法           市长法庭和伦敦城法庭           民  法
```

ORGANIZATION JUDICIAIRE DE LA FRANCE

> La Haute Court de Justice
> Organisation administrative

> Conseil d'Etat
> (Constitution de l'an VIII)

> Tribunaux administratifs
> (décret du 30. 9. 1953)
> (25 en métropole)

> Tribunal des conflits
> (loi du 24 mai 1872)

ORGANIZATION PENALE
Cour de cassation (chambre criminelle)
Cours d'assises
Cours d'appel
Tribunaux correctionnels
Tribunaux de police

Juridictions pour enfants
Cour d'appel (chambre spéciale des mineurs)
Cour d'assises des mineurs
Tribunal pour enfants
Juge des enfants

Juridictions spécialisées
Juge de l'application des peines
Cour de Sureté de l'Etat
 (instituée en 1963)
Tribunaux militaires
Tribunaux maritimes commerciaux

ORGANIZATION CIVILE
A) **Tribunaux de droit commun**
Cour de cassation
Cours d'appel (29 en métropole)
Tribunaux de grande instance
 (175 en métropole)
Tribunaux d'instance (456 en métropole)

B) **Juridictions spécialies**
Tribunaux de commerce
Conscils de prud'hommers
Tribunaux paritaires des baux ruraux
Commissions de première instance du contentieux de la Sécurité sociale
Tribunaux départementaux des pensions
Juge des loyers
Juge des enfants
Juge des tutelles
Juge de l'expropriation

法 国 司 法 组 织 系 统

特别最高法庭
行政组织

行政法院
（八年宪法）

行政法庭
（1953年9月30日法令）
（在大城市共有25个此类法庭）

冲突法庭
（1872年5月24日法令）

刑法机构
最高法院(刑庭)
　重罪法庭
　上诉法庭
　轻罪法庭
　警察法庭
对儿童的管辖
　上诉法院(未成年人专门法庭)
　未成年人重罪法院
　儿童事务法庭
　儿童审判官
专门管辖
　刑罚实施法官
　国家安全法院(1963年设置)
　军事法庭
　海商法庭

民法机构
A. **普通法院**
　最高法院
　上诉法院(在大城市共有29个)
　民事法庭(在大城市共有175个)
　治安法庭(在大城市共有456个)
B. **专门管辖**
　商业法庭
　劳资调解委员会
　农村租赁仲裁法庭
　社会安全诉讼第一审特别法庭
　省(的)养老金法庭
　租金裁判法官
　儿童法官
　监护法官
　主管征用法官

DIE ORDENTLICHE GERICHTSBARKEIT IN DER BUNDESREPUBLIK DEUTSCHLAND

德意志联邦共和国正规审判机构

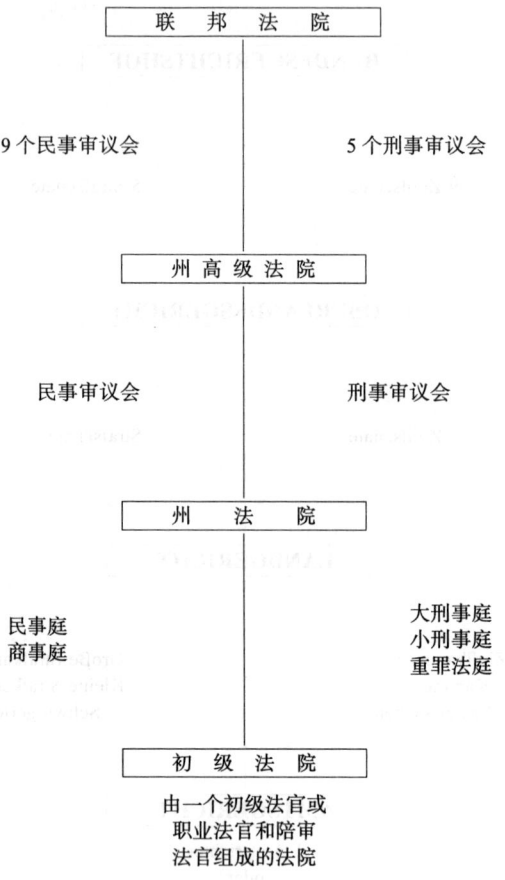

联 邦 法 院

9个民事审议会　　　5个刑事审议会

州 高 级 法 院

民事审议会　　　刑事审议会

州 法 院

民事庭
商事庭

大刑事庭
小刑事庭
重罪法庭

初 级 法 院

由一个初级法官或
职业法官和陪审
法官组成的法院

VERDELING VAN DE RECHTSMACHT IN HET KONINKRIJK BELGIË

HOF VAN VERBREKING (OF CASSATIE)
(Brussel)
(burgerlijk + strafrechtelijk)

BEROEPSHOVEN

Assisenhoven (in de provincie-hoofdplaatsen behalve te Tongeren voor Limburg)	Hoven Van Beroep (Brussel, Antwerpen, Gent, Liege. Mons) (burg. + strafrecht.)	Arbeidshoven (Brussel, Antwerpen, Gent, Liege. Mons) (burg + strafrecht.)	Militair Gerechtshof (Brussel)

ARRONDISSEMENISRECHTBANKEN

Rechtbanken Van Eerste Aanleg	Rechtbanken Van Koophandel	Jeugdrechtbanken	Arbeidsrechtbanken	Krijgsraden
		(in de hoofdplaats van elk rechterlijk arrondissement)		(Brussel. Gent. Antwerpen. te velde)
(burg. + strafrecht.)		(burg. + strafrecht.)	(burg. + strafrecht.)	

Vredegerechten (in clk rechterlijk kanton) eventueel bedienend politierechtbank (cf.: Diest-Landen)	Politierechtbanken (bij het Vredegerecht of elders) of bediend door griffie Vredcgerecht (cf.: Leuven Aarschot+Haacht+ Leuven I en Leuven II en Ticncn)

Vredegerechten en Politierechtbanken
van ecrste klasse: −in clke provincichoofdplaats
　　　　　　　　　−in ccn door de Koning bepaalde
　　　　　　　　　 agglomeratic waarm een provincie
　　　　　　　　　 hoofdplaats is geiegen
　　　　　　　　　−in kantons met ten minste 50,000 inwoners
van twecde klasse: −de andere vredegerechten en politicrechtbanken

比利时王国司法系统

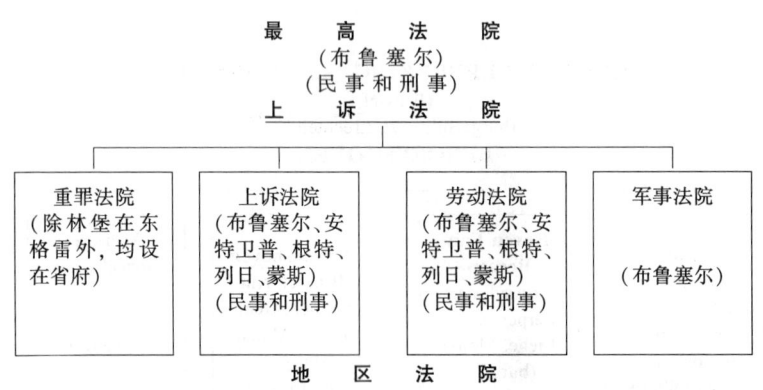

治 安 法 庭	警 察 法 庭
每司法区一个 一个警察法庭通常负责数个行政区 如艾斯特-朗登	设在治安法庭所在地或分别设立管辖几个行政区 各个行政区通常由治安法庭书记负责 （如勒文：阿斯索特+哈斯特+勒文Ⅰ和勒文Ⅱ以及第尔蒙特）

治安法庭和警察法庭

第一级：设在省府
　　　　设在国王指定的居民点、该居民点同时是省府的一部分
　　　　其所属行政区居民人口在50000人以上
第二级：另一些治安法庭和警察法庭

附录三：美国全国判例汇编系统
Appendix III: U. S. National Reporter System

1. Atlantic Reporter 大西洋区判例汇编
(1886 年至今)

Connecticut:	53 Connecticut;
Delaware:	12 Delaware (7 Houston);
	6 Delaware Chancery;
Maine:	77 Maine;
Maryland:	63 Maryland;
	1 Maryland Appellate;
New Hampshire:	63 New Hampshire;
New Jersey:	47 New Jersey Law;
	40 New Jersey Equity;
Pennsylvania:	108 Pennsylvania State;
	102 Pennsylvania Superior;
Rhode Island:	15 Rhode Island;
Vermont:	58 Vermont.

2. North Eastern Reporter 东北区判例汇编
(1885 年至今)

Illinois:	112 Illinois;
	284 Illinois Appellate;
Indiana:	102 Indiana;
	1 Indiana Appellate;
Massachusetts:	139 Massachusetts;
	1 Massachusetts Appeals;
New York:	99 New York;
Ohio:	43 Ohio State;
	20 Ohio Appellate.

3. North Western Reporter 西北区判例汇编
(1879 年至今)

Dakota:	1 Dakota;
Iowa:	51 Iowa;
Michigan:	41 Michigan;
	1 Michigan Appeals;

Minnesota:	26 Minnesota;
Nebraska:	8 Nebraska;
North Dakota:	1 North Dakota;
South Dakota:	1 South Dakota;
Wisconsin:	46 Wisconsin.

4. Pacific Reporter 太平洋区判例汇编
(1884 年至今)

Arizona:	1 Arizona;
	1 Arizona Appeals;
California:	64 California;
	1 California appellate;
Colorado:	7 Colorado;
	1 Colorado Appellate;
Hawaii:	43 Hawaii;
	1 Hawaii Appellate;
Idaho:	2 Idaho;
Kansas:	30 Kansas;
	1 Kansas Appellate;
Montana:	4 Montana;
Nevada:	17 Nevada;
New Mexico:	3 New Mexico;
Oklahoma:	1 Oklahoma;
	1 Oklahoma Criminal Appeals;
Oregon:	11 Oregon;
	1 Oregon Appeals;
Utah:	3 Utah;
Washington:	1 Washington;
	2 Washington Territory;
	1 Washington Appellate;
Wyoming:	3 Wyoming.

5. South Eastern Reporter 东南区判例汇编
(1887 年至今)

Georgia:	77 Georgia;
	1 Georgia Appellate;
North Carolina:	96 North Carolina;
	1 North Carolina Appeals;
Virginia:	82 Virginia;
West Virginia:	29 West Virginia.

6. South Western Reporter 西南区判例汇编
(1887 年至今)

Arkansas:	47 Arkansas;
	1 Arkansas Appellate;
Indiana:	1 Indiana Territory;
Kentucky:	84 Kentucky;
	8 Kentucky Law Reporter;
	1 Kentucky Decisions;
Missouri:	89 Missouri;
	93 Missouri Appellate;
Tennessee:	85 Tennessee;
	16 Tennessee Appellate;
Texas:	66 Texas;
	21 Texas Appellate;
	1 Texas Civil Appeals;
	31 Texas Criminal Reports.

7. Southern Reporter 南方区判例汇编
(1887 年至今)

Alabama:	80 Alabama;
	1 Alabama Appellate;
Florida:	22 Florida;
Louisiana:	104 Louisiana;
	39 Louisiana Annotated;
	9 Louisiana Appellate;
Mississippi:	64 Mississippi.

The National Reporter System also includes the Supreme Court Reporter, the Federal Reporter, the Federal Supplement, Federal Rules Decisions, West's Bankruptcy Reporter. The New York Supplement. West's California Reporter, West's Military Justice Reporter and West's United States Claims Court Reporter

1. The New York Supplement　纽约补篇(编)(1888—) 1 New York (1 Comstock); 1 Appellate Division; 1 Miscellaneous; and containing many other now discontinued lower court reporters, plus numerous decisions, not otherwise reported; Since February 1963, however, coverage is virtually the same as that of the three official reporters, New York, Appellate Decisions and Miscellaneous Reports.
2. California Reporter　加利福尼亚判例汇编(1960—) 53 California 2d; 176 California Appellate 2d.
3. The Supreme Court Reporter　(美国联邦)高等法院判例汇编(1882—)
4. The Federal Reporter　联邦法院判例汇编(1880—)
5. The Federal Supplement　联邦法院判例补篇(编)(1932—)
6. Federal Rules Decisions　联邦诉讼规则判例集汇编(1939—)
7. Military Justice Reporter　军事司法判例汇编
8. Bankruptcy Reporter　破产判例汇编
9. United States Claims Court Reporter　美国权利申诉法院判例汇编(1982—)

附录四:英国国王即位纪元表
Appendix IV: Table of British Regnal Years

Sovereign 国王	Names of Abbreviation 名字缩写	Accession 就任	Length of reign 执政时间
William I	(威廉一世)	Oct. 14, 1066	21 年
William II	(威廉二世)	Sept. 26, 1087	13 年
Henry I	(亨利一世)	Aug. 5, 1100	36 年
Stephen	(斯蒂芬)	Dec. 26, 1135	19 年
Henry II	(亨利二世)	Dec. 19, 1154	35 年
Richard I	(理查德一世)	Sep. 23, 1189	10 年
John	(约翰)	May 27, 1199	18 年
Henry III	(亨利三世)	Oct. 28, 1216	57 年
Edward I	(爱德华一世)	Nov. 20, 1272	35 年
Edward II	(爱德华二世)	July 8, 1307	20 年
Edward III	(爱德华三世)	Jan. 25, 1326	51 年
Richard II	(理查德二世)	June 22, 1377	23 年
Henry IV	(亨利四世)	Sept. 30, 1399	14 年
Henry V	(亨利五世)	March 21, 1413	10 年
Henry VI	(亨利六世)	Sept. 1, 1422	39 年
Edward IV	(爱德华四世)	March 4, 1461	23 年
Edward V	(爱德华五世)	April 9, 1483	1 年
Richard III	(理查德三世)	June 26, 1483	3 年
Henry VII	(亨利七世)	Aug. 22, 1485	24 年
Henry VIII	(亨利八世)	April 22, 1509	38 年
Edward VI	(爱德华六世)	Jan. 28, 1547	7 年
Mary	(玛丽)	July 6, 1553	6 年
Elizabeth	(伊丽莎白)	Nov. 17, 1558	45 年
James I	(詹姆斯一世)	March 24, 1603	23 年
Charles I	(查尔斯一世)	March 27, 1625	24 年
The Commonwealth	(共和政体)	Jan. 30, 1649	11 年
Charles II	(查尔斯二世)	May 29, 1660	37 年
James II	(詹姆斯二世)	Feb. 6, 1685	4 年
William and Mary	(威廉姆和玛丽)	Feb. 13, 1689	14 年
Anne	(安妮)	March 8, 1702	13 年
George I	(乔治一世)	Aug. 1, 1714	13 年
George II	(乔治二世)	June 11, 1727	34 年
George III	(乔治三世)	Oct. 25, 1760	60 年
George IV	(乔治四世)	Jan. 29, 1820	11 年
William IV	(威廉四世)	June 26, 1830	7 年
Victoria	(维多利亚)	June 20, 1837	64 年
Edward VII	(爱德华七世)	Jan. 22, 1901	9 年

George V	（乔治五世）	May 6, 1910	25 年
Edward VIII	（爱德华八世）	Jan. 20, 1936	1 年
George VI	（乔治六世）	Dec. 11, 1936	15 年
Elizabeth II	（伊丽莎白二世）	Feb. 6, 1952	

英国君主名称缩写

Anne	Ann.
Charles	Car., Chas 或 Cha.
Edward	Edw 或 Ed.
Elizabeth	Eliz.
George	Geo.
Henry	Hen.
James	Ja., Jac. 或 Jas
John	John
Mary	Mar.或 M.
Philip and Mary	Ph. & M.
Richard	Ric. 或 Rich.
Victoria	Vict.
William	Will., Wm. 或 Gul.
William and Mary	W. & M., Wm. & M. Will. & Mar. 或 Gul. & Mar.

附录五：美国联邦(司法)巡回区图
Appendix V: United States Federal Circuits Map

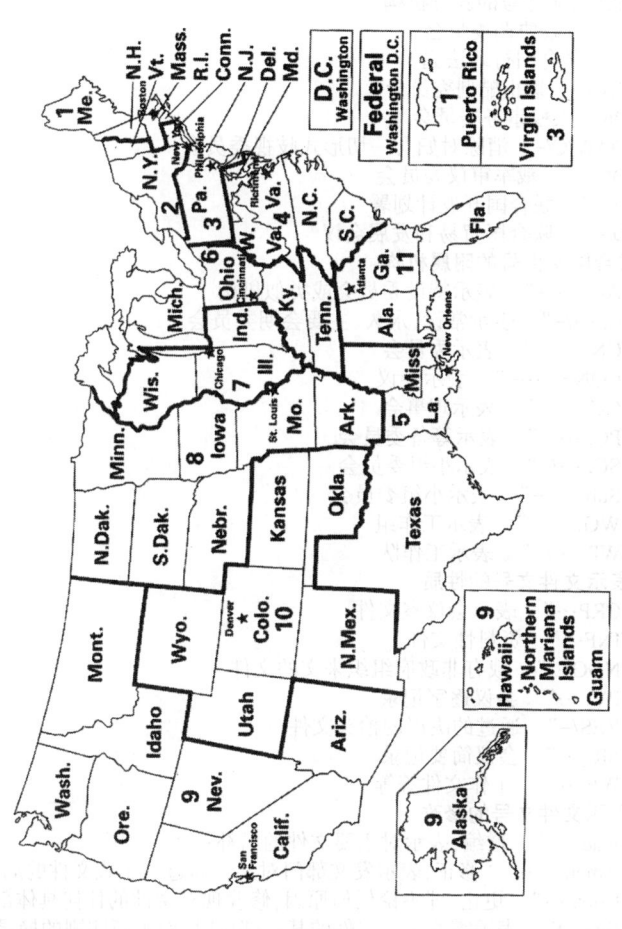

附录六
Appendix VI

1. 联合国文件号的发行机构
ACC　行政协调委员会
AT/-　联合国行政法庭
CAT/C/-　禁止酷刑委员会
CCPR　人权事务委员会
CEDAW/C/-　消除对妇女一切形式歧视委员会
"-DC/-"　裁军审议委员会
"DP/-"　联合国开发计划署
"TD/-"　联合国贸易和发展会议

2. 联合国文件号的附属机构
"-/AC. …/-"　表示特设委员会或类似机构
"-/C. …/-"　表示常设、永久、主要会期委员会
"-/CN. …/-"　表示委员会
"-/CONF. …/-"　表示会议
"-/GC. …/-"　表示理事会
"-/PC. …/-"　表示筹备委员会
"-/SC. …/-"　表示小组委员会
"-/Sub. …/-"　表示小组委员会
"-/WG. …/-"　表示工作组
"-/WP. …/-"　表示工作队

3. 表示文件文号的性质
"-/CRP…"　表示会议室文件
"-/INF…"　资料性文件
"-/NGO…"　载有非政府组织来文的文件
"-/PV. …"　会议逐字记录
"-/RES/-"　通过的决议的抬头文件
"-/SR. …"　会议简要记录
"-/WP. …"　工作文件等等

4. 表明文件文号的修改
"-/Add. …"　增编,表示对主要文件的增补;
"-/Amend. …"　修正,表示发文部门对某一通过的正式文件的局部更改;
"-/Corr. …"　更正,即不论任何原因,修改现有文件的任何具体部分;
"-/Except"　表示需要某一文件的某一部分时,而重新印刷的摘录;
"-/Rev. …"　订正,用新文件取代对应"-"部分相同的旧文件,如有具体规定,订正文本除了可以替代要件,还能取代其更正,修正和增编;
"-/Summary"　为便利机关审议而特别编写的报告摘要

5. 表明文件的分发等级

"–/L. …"　　表示限量分发,例如:E/1990/C.1/L.1;用于暂时性文件;

"–/R. …"　　表示限制分发;例如:E/1990/SR.I,用于其内容在印发时不得对外公开的文件和会议记录。

《联合国出版物目录》里,有反映出版物内容类别的清单,可作分类简表,每一项内容用罗马数字,有时再加上大写字母表明内容类别细目。例如:

"Ⅰ"类是一般资料和参政;

"Ⅱ.A"类是商业、经济、科学和技术;

"Ⅱ.B"类是经济发展;

"Ⅱ.C"类是世界经济…

"Ⅲ.A"类是联合国大学出版物;

"Ⅲ.B"类是开发计划署出版物;

"Ⅲ.H"类是人口基金出版社…

"Ⅳ"类是社会问题;

"Ⅴ"类是国际法;

"Ⅹ"类是国际行政;

"Ⅺ"类是麻醉品;

"ⅩⅣ"类是人权;

"ⅩⅦ"类是公共财政和会计问题;

"ⅩⅩ"类是儿童基金会出版物。

附录七:参考书目
Appendix VII: References

外文书目:
1. Black Laws Dictionary, Fifth Edition, West Publishing Co., 1979. Black Laws Dictionary, Eighth Edition, West, 2004, Black Laws Dictionary, Ninth Edition, West, 2009.
2. Henry Campbell Black, M. A., *Black's Law Dictionary*, Fifth Edition, St. Paul, Minn., West Publishing Co., 1979.
3. John Burke (two volumes), *Jowitt's Dictionary of English Law*, Second Edition, London, Sweet & Maxwell Limited, 1977.
4. William P. Statsky, *West's Legal Thesaurus Dictionary* (A Resource for the Writes and the Computer Researcher), St. Paul, New York, Los Angles, West Publishing Company, 1985.
5. Daniel Organ, *Law Dictionary for Nonlawyers*, Second Edition, West Publishing Company, 1985.
6. David M. Walker, *The Oxford Companion to Law*, Clarendon Press, Oxford, 1980.
7. Sir William Smith and Sir John Clckwood, *Chambers Murray Latin-English Dictionary*, Morrison & Gibb Ltd., London and Edinburgh, 1976.
8. Doris M. Bieber Compiled, *Dictionary of Legal Abbreviations Used in American Law Books*, William S. Hein & Co., Buffalo, N. Y., 1979.
9. Steven H., *Gifis Law Dictionary*, Berron's Educational Sevices Inc., Woodbury, New York, 1975.
10. A Uniform System of Citation, By The Columbia Law Review, The Harvard Law Review Association, The University of Pennsylvania Law Review and The Yale Law Journal. Fourteenth Edition, Lorell Press, Avon, Massachusetts, 1986.
11. Ralph Desola Expanded International, *Abbreviations Dictionary*, Sixth Edition, Elseviel North Holland Inc., New York, 1981.
12. Morris L. Cohen, Robert C.Berring, *How to Find the Law*, Eighth Edition, St. Paul, Minn., West Publishing Co., 1983.
13. Lawrence M. Friedman, *A History of American Law*, Second Edition, Published by Siman & Schusten Inc., New York, 1985.
14. Jean Dane and Philip A.Thomas, *How to use a law library*, London, Sweet & Maxwell, 1979.
15. Morris L.Cohen, *Legal Research (in a nut shell)*, 4th Edition, St.Paul, Minn., West Publishing Co., 1985.
16. He Jiahong, Jon R. Waltz, *Criminal Prosecution in the PRC and the USA., A Comparative Study*, China Procuratorial Press, Beijing, 1995.
17. Xianglan Zhang, *U. S. Admiralty Cases & Comments*, Wuhan University Press, 1995.
18. E. Allan Farnsworth, *An Introduction to the Legal System of the United States*, Second Edition, Oceana Publication Inc., New York, 1983.
19. John Flood, *The Legal Profession in the United States*, Third Edition, American Bar

Foundation, 1985.
20. Edward F. Willet, Jr., Esq., *How Our Laws Are Made*, United States Government Printing Office.
21. Victor Knapp, *International Encyclopedia of Comparative Law*, Vol. 1, National Reports, Washington: 1981; J. C. B. Mohr Türbingen Oceana Publications Inc., New York, 1972.
22. Jack H. Friedenthal Mary Kay Kane Authur R. *Civil Procedure Third Edition*, Miller Hornbook Series, West Group ST. Paul, Minn, 1999.
23. Webster's New world Law Dictionany Wiley Publishing Inc., 2006.
24. Dictionary of Law Sixth Edition L. B. Cwron 2003.(法律出版社影印版)
25. A Dictionary of Modern Logal Vsage 2nd Edition Bngrn A. Gavnal 2002.(法律出版社影印版)
26. Black's Law Dictionary Bryan A. Ganan Tenth Edition.
27. Legal Research 8th Edition.
Academic (2016) 12th Edition.
Morris L. Cohen.
Kent C. Olson.
28. The Bluebook A.uniform System of citation 20th Edition, 2016.
29. Webster's New World Law Dictionary Wiley P. Inc., 2006, Susan Ellis wild.
30. How our Laws are made? G. P. O. 2007.
31. The Wolters Kluwer Bouvier laws Dictionary Compact Edition Stephen Micheal sheppard Gen. Edi., 2011 年.

中文书目：
1. 彭金瑞等编译:《简明英汉法律词典》,商务印书馆 1990 年版。
2. 余文景编译:《汉译简明英国法律词典》,大块出版公司 1973 年版。
3. William S. H. Hung Y. D.:《英汉法律词典新编》,Michael Stevenson Limited Hong Kong 1979 年版。
4. 〔美〕科恩:《美国法律文献检索》,夏登峻译,商务印书馆 1994 年版。
5. 〔英〕戴维·M. 沃克:《牛津法律大辞典》,北京社会与科技发展研究所组织翻译,光明日报出版社 1988 年版。
6.《新英汉词典》编写组编:《新英汉词典》,上海人民出版社 1976 年版。
7. 梁实秋主编:《最新实用英汉词典》,远东图书公司 1984 年版。
8.《法汉词典》编写组编:《法汉词典》,上海译文出版社 1979 年版。
9. 广州外国语学院《简明德汉词典》组编:《简明德汉词典》,商务印书馆、广东人民出版社 1979 年版。
10. 清华大学《英汉技术词典》编写组编:《英汉技术词典》,国防工业出版社 1978 年版。
11. 陈允、应时:《罗马法》,商务印书馆 1931 年版。
12. 中国大百科全书总编辑委员会《法学》编辑委员会、中国大百科全书出版社编辑部编:《中国大百科全书:法学》,中国大百科全书出版社 1984 年版。

13. 四川外语学院《英汉缩略语词典》编写组编:《英汉缩略语辞典》,四川人民出版社 1979 年版。
14. 贝迪荣:《辣丁中华字典》,上海,土山湾 1924 年版。
15. 〔美〕布赖恩·H. 比克斯:《牛津法律理论词典》,邱昭继等译,法律出版社 2007 年版。
16. 〔美〕克米特·L. 雷尔主编:《牛津美国联邦最高法院指南》(第二版),许明月、夏登峻等译,北京大学出版社 2009 年版。
17. 中国社会科学院语言研究所词典编辑室编:《现代汉语词典》(第六版),商务印书馆 2012 年版。
18. 辞海编辑委员会主编:《辞海》(缩印本),上海辞书出版社 1980 年版。

20 世纪 90 年代美国法学期刊、评论:
1. Harvard Law Review.
2. Minnesota Law Review.
3. UCLA Law Review.
4. UCLA Journal of International Law and Foreign Affairs.
5. The Journal of International Law and Economics 1981, No. 1.
6. Index to Foreign Legal Periodicals.
7. Hawaii Law Review etc.